Baseball America®
2006 ALMANAC

BASEBALL AMERICA INC.
Durham, N.C.

Baseball America
2006 ALMANAC

A Comprehensive Review of the 2005 Season, Featuring Statistics and Commentary

PUBLISHED BY
Baseball America Inc.

EDITOR
Allan Simpson

ASSISTANT EDITORS
J.J. Cooper, Will Lingo

CONTRIBUTING EDITORS
Aaron Fitt, Will Kimmey, Chris Kline, John Manuel, Allan Matthews, Matt Meyers

CONTRIBUTING WRITERS
Jim Callis, Kevin Goldstein, John Perrotto

DESIGN & PRODUCTION
Phillip Daquila, Matthew Eddy, Linwood Webb

STATISTICAL CONSULTANTS
Major League Baseball
Advanced Media

Baseball America

PRESIDENT/CEO Catherine Silver
VICE PRESIDENT/PUBLISHER Lee Folger
EDITORS IN CHIEF Will Lingo, John Manuel
FOUNDING EDITOR Allan Simpson
DESIGN & PRODUCTION DIRECTOR Phillip Daquila

COVER PHOTOS Albert Pujols by Larry Goren; Delmon Young by Carl Kline; Lance Broadway by Andrew Woolley; Justin Upton by David Stoner

To order, call **800-845-2726** or send $18.95 (regular) or $21.95 (spiral) each plus $6 shipping and handling per order and $2 for each copy to:
Baseball America, P.O. Box 2089, Durham, NC 27702

Distributed by Simon & Schuster

EDITOR'S NOTE

- Major league statistics are based on final, unofficial 2005 averages.
- The organization statistics, which begin on page 55, include all players who participated in at least one game during the 2005 season. Pitchers' batting statistics are not included, nor are the pitching statistics of field players who pitched in less than two games. For players who played with more than one team in the same league, the player's cumulative statistics appear on the line immediately after the player's last-team statistics.
- Innings pitched have been rounded off to the nearest full inning.

TABLE OF CONTENTS

LARRY GOREN

MAJOR LEAGUES

2005 IN REVIEW

Palmeiro puts famous face on baseball's steroid issue

BY JOHN PERROTTO

On the night of July 15, with the clock already having struck midnight on the East Coast, Rafael Palmeiro made history when he stroked an opposite-field double into the left-field corner at Safeco Field in Seattle.

The Orioles first baseman recorded his 3,000th hit with the two-bagger off the Mariners' Joel Pineiro. Palmeiro also became only the fourth player in baseball history to have 500 home runs and 3,000 hits in his career, joining Hall of Famers Hank Aaron, Willie Mays and Eddie Murray.

Somehow, it seemed fitting that Palmeiro accomplished the feat when seemingly half of the nation was asleep. He had always been the quiet superstar, consistently racking up impressive statistics without ever gaining much notoriety.

CLIFF WELCH

Still waiting for his side of the story
Rafael Palmeiro's on-field accomplishments have been overshadowed

The postgame celebration in the Orioles clubhouse consisted of a simple champagne toast by manager Lee Mazzilli. Palmeiro was his usual low-key self when describing his historic hit.

"I was just trying to drive the runner in," Palmeiro said. "I was trying to do my thing and keep it simple. I did what I had to do and it was the 3,000th hit."

Palmeiro's days of anonymity came to an end barely more than two weeks later on Aug. 1. Suddenly, he went from underappreciated, surefire Hall of Fame candidate to national scourge as he became the new face of the steroids issue that had hovered over baseball for the last few years and exploded as the talk of the sport in 2005.

Palmeiro became the first big-name player suspended for steroids use under Major League Baseball's new performance-enhancing substance policy, agreed upon with the Major League Baseball Players Association a month before the start of spring training. A total of 12 players were punished with 10-day suspensions in 2005, the penalty for a first offense, but none of the others had the name recognition of Palmeiro.

Reports leaked to the media said Palmeiro tested positive for the steroid Stanozolol, which was even more shocking because he had testified under oath before Congress on March 17 that he had never used illegal performance-enhancing drugs. In fact, Palmeiro was one of the few players who came off looking good during the House Government Reform Committee's sometimes contentious hearings about steroids in baseball.

Just a month after he had been accused of being a steroid user in a tell-all book by former teammate Jose Canseco, Palmeiro stood before the committee and proclaimed, "I have never used steroids. Period," poking a finger in the air and raising his voice for emphasis.

Palmeiro appealed his suspension to an independent arbitrator, but it was upheld. He continued to insist through the end of the season that the only way steroids could have been found in his system was if he ingested them by accident, and he claimed during his appeal hearing that the positive test was a result of a vitamin B-12 shot administered by teammate Miguel Tejada.

"Ultimately, although I never intentionally put a banned substance into my body, the independent arbitrator ruled that I had to be suspended under the terms of the program," Palmeiro said.

Tejada, the Orioles' all-star shortstop, strongly denied he had given steroids to Palmeiro and was subsequently cleared by the committee.

The owners and players had agreed to a new testing policy and a stronger set of penalties in January, with a first-time offender receiving a 10-day suspension, a second-time offender getting 30 days, a third-time offender being suspended for 60 days and a fourth-time offender receiving a one-year suspension. Players would not be permanently expelled until a fifth offense.

Following the Palmeiro suspension, Selig proposed a tougher set of penalties in which players would be suspended 50 games for a first offense, 100 games for a second offense and banned for life after a third offense. The union, though, said those penalties were too harsh. It countered with a plan that could include up to a 30-game suspension for a first offense, a 100-game ban for a second offense and a lifetime ban for a third offense,

Cardinals find rare gem in Pujols

In the prehistoric period before cell phones became commonplace and e-mail went wireless, Jay Darnell would send his scouting reports to the Rockies as circumstances permitted.

"I remember pulling into a truck stop and leaving a voice mail," said Darnell, who is now a national cross-checker for the Padres. "I told them, 'Just in case something happens, I think this guy is going to hit for a lot of power.' "

PLAYER *OF THE* **YEAR**

The guy was Albert Pujols. The advice was ignored.

Pujols is the slugger who slipped beneath baseball's radar, the greatest player ever selected with the 402nd choice in the amateur draft. He signed his first contract in 1999 with the Cardinals for $60,000 and might have been a bargain at $60 million.

Long before he led the Cardinals into the World Series in 2005, before leading them to the best record in baseball—and before he became Baseball America's Major League Player of the Year—Pujols was recognized throughout the industry as the big one that got away.

More than any player in a generation, Pujols forced scouts to reevaluate their methods, their priorities and their eyeglass prescriptions.

His 2005 season provided yet another example of his excellence—.330-41-117, a league-best 129 runs, career highs in stolen bases (16 in 18 attempts), walks (97, with just 65 strikeouts) and intentional walks (a league-leading 27), a .430 on-base percentage and .609 slugging mark. He was the constant force in a Cardinals lineup riddled by injuries much of the season, playing through a painful case of plantar fasciitis in both feet.

The Cardinals first baseman is the first player to hit at least 30 home runs in each of his first five big league seasons, and he was just the third player to reach 500 RBIs in his first four seasons. The other two were Joe DiMaggio and Ted Williams.

Not that the nation's scouts need to be reminded of that.

"For a while, I just thought I was hexed," said Dan Jennings, who is now the vice president of player personnel for the Marlins. "I'd come in the room when he first got in the big leagues and it would be Pujols hitting a double, Pujols driving in a run. I'd say, 'God, I get the message.' You can make one bad decision and it will bite you forever."

Jennings was the scouting director for the Devil Rays in the spring of 1999 when area scout Fernando Arango started raving about this junior college shortstop in suburban Kansas City.

Albert Pujols was known as Jose Pujols then. He was playing out of position at Maple Woods Community College, and he was playing out of shape. Like many talented players with roots in the Dominican Republic, Pujols was suspected of being older than he claimed.

Nor did he meet the run-and-throw standards scouts have been trained to seek in amateur prospects. Darnell's May 14, 1999, scouting report, filed less than three weeks before the draft, described Pujols as "heavy legged," and observed that his throws "often tail and sink as fingers are not on top of the ball."

SPORTS ON FILM

Yet with a bat in his hands, Albert Pujols was precocious and powerful. If you were paying attention, he held it.

"Guys that can hit are going to play," said Brad Kullman, director of major league operations for the Reds. "Our reports were that he had power and he was undisciplined at the plate—a free swinger. That's one of his strengths now—he's so disciplined."

Arango was on record early that Pujols would ultimately hit 40 home runs in a season. In his first five years in the majors, Pujols hit 37, 34, 43, 46 and 41 homers.

"What I saw in him was tremendous athletic ability," said Arango, who is now the Latin American scouting coordinator for the Brewers. "He just hit the ball with an impact that you didn't see every day. I went to a game at Maple Woods, and he hit two home runs and the sound off the bat sounded like cannon shots."

Less than a month after Arango's lobbying led nowhere—and the Cardinals were still able to pluck Pujols in the 13th round—the scout tendered his resignation.

"I was a little frustrated," Arango said. "Dan Jennings asked me the question if I left because of Pujols. To me, it was very simple. If I can't get a guy like that, even in the 10th round, maybe I should take a sabbatical from amateur scouting."

—TIM SULLIVAN

PREVIOUS **WINNERS**

1998—Mark McGwire, 1b, Cardinals
1999—Pedro Martinez, rhp, Red Sox
2000—Alex Rodriguez, ss, Mariners
2001—Barry Bonds, of, Giants
2002—Alex Rodriguez, ss, Rangers
2003—Barry Bonds, of, Giants
2004—Barry Bonds, of, Giants

MAJOR LEAGUES

though all would be subject to an arbitrator's review.

Devil Rays outfielder Alex Sanchez made history when he became the first player suspended for performance-enhancing substances on April 3. Others suspended in 2005 were Rockies outfielder Jorge Piedra; Rangers pitchers Carlos Almanzar and Augustin Montero; pitcher Ryan Franklin, infielder/outfielder Michael Morse and outfielder Jamal Strong of the Mariners; Twins pitcher Juan Rincon; Indians pitcher Rafael Betancourt; Mets pitcher Felix Heredia; and Yankees outfielder Matt Lawton.

Talk of steroids hung over the game before spring training ever started.

The San Francisco Chronicle reported over the winter that Yankees first baseman Jason Giambi admitted he had used anabolic steroids and human growth hormone to federal investigators during the FBI's investigation of the Bay Area Laboratory Co-Operative in Burlingame, Calif. The Chronicle also reported that Giants slugger Barry Bonds admitted he had unwittingly used a steroid cream supplied to him by personal trainer Greg Anderson, who had ties to BALCO.

The issue came to a head during the 11-hour Congressional hearings in the middle of spring training. In addition to Palmeiro, Red Sox pitcher Curt Schilling and Orioles right fielder Sammy Sosa testified, along with retired sluggers Canseco and Mark McGwire.

The most memorable moments from the hearings came when McGwire continually refused to answer questions about steroid use during his playing days. McGwire responded repeatedly, "I'm not here to talk about the past," exasperating many members of the committee.

While most of the congressmen were deferential to the players, they were tough on commissioner Bud Selig and union leader Don Fehr about what they said was a soft drug policy.

"Why should we believe that the baseball commissioner and the baseball union will want to do something when we have a 30-year record of them not responding to the problem?" asked Rep. Henry Waxman of California, the committee's ranking Democrat.

Congress continued to turn up the heat throughout the season as a stronger policy was discussed but never implemented. On Sept. 28, the Senate Commerce, Science and Transportation Committee held hearings on legislation that would standardize steroid policies in professional sports.

While commissioners and union leaders from baseball, the NFL, the NBA and NHL all testified, the focus was on baseball.

"I particularly single out baseball," said Sen. Jay Rockefeller, a Democrat from West Virginia. "And in baseball, I particularly single out the players because they have negotiated reluctantly, if at all."

Said Arizona Republican Sen. John McCain, "We're at the end of the line. How many more Rafael Palmeiros is there going to be?

"Don't you get it that this is an issue that's greater than the issue of collective bargaining? Don't you understand that this is an issue of such transcendent importance that you should have acted months ago? The patience of this body is at an end."

Positive Baseball Story In Washington

While the sport took a beating on Capitol Hill, it thrived a few miles down the road as baseball returned to Washington in a big way and baseball saw its first franchise move in 33 years.

TOP 10 MAJOR LEAGUE STORIES OF 2005

1 White Sox are World Series champions. While their long streak without a title did not create the same folklore as the Red Sox, the White Sox followed Boston's success with a title of their own, holding onto to their playoff spot and then cruising through the postseason with timely hitting and strong pitching.

2 Baseball attendance continues to go up. Led by the Yankees breaking the four million fan barrier, major league attendance continued to set records, and minor league attendance broke the 40 million fan mark for the first time.

3 Steroid cloud won't blow away. Baseball's tougher performance-enhancing substance policy went into effect, resulting in several suspensions, but Rafael Palmeiro, congressional hearings and BALCO kept bringing negative attention to the game.

4 Don't bet against the Braves. The Braves cut their payroll further and then were hit by injuries at the beginning of the season, forcing them to rely on rookies more than ever before. And still they won their 14th straight division title.

5 Bonds' record pursuit hits a detour. Bonds' pursuit of Babe Ruth and Hank Aaron, as well as his role as a central figure in the steroids controversy, becomes muted as a knee injury keeps him out of action most of the year.

6 Expos find new home in Washington. Major League Baseball finally takes the Expos to Washington and renames them the Nationals. The team gets a warm reception and contends for much of the season. Next up: a new owner.

7 Baseball kicked out of Olympics, starts own tournament. In a surprise vote, baseball is removed from the Olympic schedule after 2008, but MLB's World Baseball Classic aims to bring the best players together in March 2006.

8 Houston finally reaches World Series. While they were swept once they got there, the Astros put years of postseason futility behind them when they made a stirring playoff run through the National League.

9 Angels aim to take over Southern California. With the Dodgers in decline and disarray, the Angels become the Los Angeles Angels (of Anaheim) and continue their run of success on the field and at the box office.

10 Futility continues in Pittsburgh and Kansas City. While the Brewers barely broke their run of losing seasons, going 81-81, the Pirates posted their 13th straight losing year and the Royals put together a 19-game losing streak for their third 100-loss season in the last four years.

3,000-HITS CLUB

No.	Player	Hits
1.	Pete Rose	4256
2.	Ty Cobb	4189
3.	Hank Aaron	3771
4.	Stan Musial	3630
5.	Tris Speaker	3514
6.	Honus Wagner	3420
7.	Carl Yastrzemski	3419
8.	Paul Molitor	3319
9.	Eddie Collins	3315
10.	Willie Mays	3283
11.	Eddie Murray	3255
12.	Nap Lajoie	3242
13.	Cal Ripken	3184
14.	George Brett	3154
15.	Paul Waner	3152
16.	Robin Yount	3142
17.	Tony Gwynn	3141
18.	Dave Winfield	3110
19.	Rickey Henderson	3055
20.	Rod Carew	3053
21.	Lou Brock	3023
22.	**Rafael Palmeiro**	**3020**
23.	Cap Anson	3012
24.	Wade Boggs	3010
25.	Al Kaline	3007
26.	Roberto Clemente	3000

Active players in bold type

AMERICAN LEAGUE STANDINGS

Page	EAST	W	L	PCT	GB	Manager(s)	General Manager(s)	Attend.	Avg.	Last Penn.
180	New York Yankees	95	67	.586	—	Joe Torre	Brian Cashman	4,090,440	50,449	2003
68	*Boston Red Sox	95	67	.586	—	Terry Francona	Theo Epstein	2,813,354	35,166	2004
253	Toronto Blue Jays	80	82	.494	15	John Gibbons	J.P. Ricciardi	1,977,949	24,724	1993
61	Baltimore Orioles	74	88	.457	21	Lee Mazzilli/Sam Perlozzo	Jim Beattie/Mike Flanagan	2,624,804	32,404	1983
239	Tampa Bay Devil Rays	67	95	.414	28	Lou Piniella	Chuck LaMar	1,124,189	14,052	None
Page	**CENTRAL**	**W**	**L**	**PCT**	**GB**	**Manager(s)**	**General Manager**	**Attend.**	**Avg.**	**Last Penn.**
84	Chicago White Sox	99	63	.611	—	Ozzie Guillen	Ken Williams	2,342,834	28,923	2005
99	Cleveland Indians	93	69	.574	6	Eric Wedge	Mark Shapiro	1,973,185	24,664	1997
164	Minnesota Twins	83	79	.512	16	Ron Gardenhire	Terry Ryan	2,013,453	25,168	1991
114	Detroit Tigers	71	91	.438	28	Alan Trammell	Dave Dombrowski	2,024,505	25,306	1984
136	Kansas City Royals	56	106	.346	43	Tony Pena/Buddy Bell	Allard Baird	1,371,181	17,356	1985
Page	**WEST**	**W**	**L**	**PCT**	**GB**	**Manager**	**General Manager**	**Attendance**	**Average**	**Last Penn.**
143	Los Angeles Angels	95	67	.586	—	Mike Scioscia	Bill Stoneman	3,404,686	42,033	2002
188	Oakland Athletics	88	74	.543	7	Ken Macha	Billy Beane	2,109,298	26,040	1990
246	Texas Rangers	79	83	.488	16	Buck Showalter	John Hart	2,486,925	31,480	None
231	Seattle Mariners	69	93	.426	26	Mike Hargrove	Bill Bavasi	2,689,529	33,619	None

*Won wild-card playoff berth

NOTE: Team's individual batting, pitching and fielding statistics can be found on page indicated in lefthand column.

After three years as a lame duck franchise in Montreal, including the previous two seasons when the team played part of its home schedule in San Juan, Puerto Rico, the Expos finally moved to Washington and became the Nationals. That came 33 years after the Washington Senators pulled up stakes and moved to Dallas-Fort Worth in 1972 to become the Texas Rangers. The team remained a ward of MLB, owned by the other 29 teams, but baseball leaders hoped to have the team in the hands of new ownership for the 2006 season.

The Nationals started off with an 8-4 loss to the Phillies in Philadelphia on April 4. Outfielder Brad Wilkerson had the first hit in franchise history when he led off the game with a single, while outfielder Terrmel Sledge had the first home run and RBI.

The first game back in Washington at a renovated Robert F. Kennedy Stadium was a smashing success as the Nationals beat the Arizona Diamondbacks 5-3 on April 14, the stands shaking during a three-run rally in the fourth inning. Livan Hernandez took a one-hitter into the ninth inning and third baseman Vinny Castilla had three hits and three RBIs in front of a crowd of 45,596.

President George W. Bush threw out the ceremonial first pitch, 95 years to the day after William Howard Taft became the first president to do the honors in a Washington home opener.

"Baseball is back and happy days are here again!" proclaimed 77-year-old former Senators public-address announcer Charlie Brotman, who returned to preside over one more home opener.

There were many happy days for the Nationals.

They had a 5½-game lead in the National League East on July 3, though they went 31-50 in the second half of the season after starting off 50-31 and were eventually overtaken by the Atlanta Braves. The team contended for the playoffs into September, however, and it was quite a turnaround for a team that went 67-95 in its last season in Montreal, where the Expos made just one postseason appearance in 36 seasons.

"It was a magical-type season, the first half. Things went right for us," Nationals manager Frank Robinson said. "And the second half was kind of like a nightmare."

The Nationals drew 2.7 million fans to antiquated RFK after Washington fans waited more than three decades for baseball to return. While the ownership issue still hadn't been resolved, a new ballpark was scheduled to open in 2008 along the Anacostia River that would include a view of the Capitol building.

"When we were in Montreal, we've always said that we were just missing a real small part, and that small part was moving to a new city and having a home. And we got that this year," Nationals catcher Brian Schneider said. "You could see in the first half how we responded to that. We were in this race."

Plenty Of Playoff Drama

The Nationals eventually faded from contention, but the pennant races in both leagues were tight until the final days of the season. In fact, seven of the eight playoff spots were not determined until the last week.

The St. Louis Cardinals were the only team that won their division going away, taking the National League Central by 11 games over the Houston Astros. The Cardinals won the division for a second straight year and posted consecutive 100-win seasons for just the second time in the franchise's storied history. The Cardinals won in triple digits for three consecutive seasons from 1942-44.

Tony La Russa

Despite cruising to the division title, the Cardinals had their share of adversity as third baseman Scott Rolen, left fielder Reggie Sanders, right fielder Larry Walker and catcher Yadier Molina all missed significant time with injuries.

"There is a mental and physical toughness to this team that has to be admired," Cardinals manager Tony La Russa said after clinching the 11th division title of his 27-year career. "It hasn't been easy."

The Astros wound up winning the wild-card playoff berth for a second straight season, and it certainly wasn't easy for them either. They became the second team in baseball history—joining the 1914 Boston Braves—to reach the playoffs in the same season when they fell as many as 15 games under .500.

NATIONAL LEAGUE STANDINGS

Page	EAST	W	L	PCT	GB	Manager	General Manager	Attendance	Average	Last Penn.
53	Atlanta Braves	90	72	.556	—	Bobby Cox	John Schuerholz	2,521,534	31,519	1999
195	Philadelphia Phillies	88	74	.543	2	Charlie Manuel	Ed Wade	2,665,301	33,316	1993
121	Florida Marlins	83	79	.512	7	Jack McKeon	Larry Beinfest	1,823,388	22,792	2003
171	New York Mets	83	79	.512	7	Willie Randolph	Omar Minaya	2,782,212	35,217	2000
260	Washington Nationals	81	81	.500	9	Frank Robinson	Jim Bowden	2,692,123	33,651	None
Page	**CENTRAL**	**W**	**L**	**PCT**	**GB**	**Manager(s)**	**General Manager**	**Attendance**	**Average**	**Last Penn.**
209	St. Louis Cardinals	100	62	.617	—	Tony La Russa	Walt Jocketty	3,491,837	44,489	2004
129	*Houston Astros	89	73	.549	11	Phil Garner	Tim Purpura	2,762,472	34,530	2005
157	Milwaukee Brewers	81	81	.500	19	Ned Yost	Doug Melvin	2,211,023	27,296	None
76	Chicago Cubs	79	83	.488	21	Dusty Baker	Jim Hendry	3,100,262	38,753	1945
91	Cincinnati Reds	73	89	.451	27	Dave Miley/Jerry Narron	Dan O'Brien	1,943,157	23,989	1990
202	Pittsburgh Pirates	67	95	.414	33	L. McClendon/P. Mackanin	Dave Littlefield	1,794,237	23,003	1979
Page	**WEST**	**W**	**L**	**PCT**	**GB**	**Manager**	**General Manager**	**Attendance**	**Average**	**Last Penn.**
217	San Diego Padres	82	80	.506	—	Bruce Bochy	Kevin Towers	2,832,039	35,400	1998
46	Arizona Diamondbacks	77	85	.475	5	Bob Melvin	J. Garagiola Jr./B. Gebhard	2,059,331	25,423	2001
224	San Francisco Giants	75	87	.463	7	Felipe Alou	Brian Sabean	3,140,781	39,259	2002
150	Los Angeles Dodgers	71	91	.438	11	Jim Tracy	Paul DePodesta	3,603,680	44,489	1988
107	Colorado Rockies	67	95	.414	15	Clint Hurdle	Dan O'Dowd	1,915,586	23,944	None

*Won wild-card playoff berth

NOTE: Team's individual batting, pitching and fielding statistics can be found on page indicated in lefthand column.

The Astros began the season 15-30 but rallied to go 74-43 from May 25 on, the best record in the major leagues during that span.

"We started out slow and everyone got down on us quick, but it says a lot about the character of our team that we never quit," said Astros pitcher Roy Oswalt, who beat the Chicago Cubs on the final day of the season to clinch the wild card and win his 20th game for a second consecutive season.

The Braves continued their incredible string of division titles, winning their 14th straight as they held off the Phillies by two games in the NL East. The Phillies finished one game behind the Astros in the wild-card chase. It might have been the most amazing in the Braves' record run of titles, as manager Bobby Cox used 18 rookies because of a string of injuries that hit his club.

"This is pretty special," Cox said after the clincher. "When the rookies came up, the veterans turned it up a notch. The young guys brought a lot of energy and made it fun."

While the Braves were adding to their record, the San Diego Padres set a dubious mark in winning the weak NL West. The Padres had to rally in the last weekend of the season just to get their record over .500 at 82-80 as they won the division by five games over the Diamondbacks.

The Padres' .506 winning percentage was the lowest ever by a playoff team. The previous worst was .509, when the Mets won the NL East in 1973 with an 82-79 mark.

After going 33-19 in the first two months of the season, the Padres went just 49-61 the rest of the way. They dealt with injuries as shortstop Khalil Greene, catcher Ramon Hernandez, center fielder Dave Roberts and second baseman Mark Loretta all spent time on the disabled list along with starting pitchers Adam Eaton, Woody Williams and Pedro Astacio.

"I think the one thing this team has shown is it had a lot of character," Padres right fielder Brian Giles said after the clincher. "You don't lose main pieces to your offense and still have a four-, five-, six-game lead pretty much the whole year unless you have character."

The schedule makers couldn't have done it any better in the American League, as they matched the New York Yankees and Boston Red Sox in a three-game series at Fenway Park to end the season after the archrivals had met in the AL Championship Series the previous two years.

As expected, the AL East wasn't decided until the final weekend. Neither was the wild-card berth. The Yankees clinched their eighth straight division title on the next-to-last day of the season with an 8-4 victory. The Red Sox then rolled to a 10-1 win in the finale to grab the wild card.

Joe Torre

Despite having the highest payroll in baseball history at $203 million, the Yankees needed a 35-13 finishing kick to overtake the Red Sox, who had a 5 ½-game lead Aug. 11. The Yankees won even though lefthander Randy Johnson, acquired from the Diamondbacks in a major offseason trade, was the only member of the Opening Day rotation not to miss time because of injuries.

"This was the best (division title) of them all," Yankees manager Joe Torre said. "The first is always memorable but this has to be the most special because of everything that went on this year."

The Red Sox blew the division lead but were still able to get into the playoffs for a third straight season after winning their first World Series in 86 years in 2004. The Yankees and Red Sox finished with identical 95-67 records, but New York won the division title based on winning the season series, 10-9.

"Co-division champs. That's what I'm calling it," Red Sox owner John Henry said. "I can understand why there isn't a playoff but, frankly, I would have liked to have had one. It would have been nice to settle the division championship."

The AL Central championship seemed to be clinched by midseason as the Chicago White Sox held a commanding 15-game lead over the Cleveland Indians at the beginning of August. The Indians came storming back to cut the White Sox' lead to 1½ games on Sept. 24, before

ANDREW WOOLLEY

Leading Astros into their first World Series
Roy Oswalt was MVP of the National League Championship Series

Chicago nailed down its first division title since 2000 by winning its final five games of the season, including a three-game sweep at Cleveland in the final weekend.

The White Sox wound up leading the AL in wins with a 99-63 record after coming close to one of the biggest collapses in baseball history.

"When you win that many games and people keep criticizing and second-guessing, it takes the fun away from the people," manager Ozzie Guillen said during the postgame celebration after the White Sox clinched the division. "This is a relief more than anything."

The Indians won 37 of 49 games to get close to the White Sox, but then lost six of their final seven games to miss out on the playoffs, finishing six games behind Chicago in the division and two games behind the Red Sox in the wild-card standings.

The AL West title went to the Angels for the third time in four years, but their first season with the longest official team name in baseball history. The Angels outdistanced the Oakland Athletics by seven games.

Owner Arte Moreno changed the team name from Anaheim Angels following the 2004 season, to Los Angeles Angels of Anaheim in order to increase the team's name recognition in Southern California and create new marketing opportunities.

The city of Anaheim engaged Moreno in a court fight, claiming the Angels violated the terms of their lease at Angel Stadium by changing their name.

On the field, the Angels won 14 of their last 16 games to pull away from the A's, who rebounded from a 17-32 start, including a 7-20 record in May, to eventually take over first place in the division before fading late.

"This team had to play very well to beat (the A's)," Angels manager Mike Scioscia said. "Our guys were in grind mode all year."

Another Drought Broken

The White Sox may have looked like they were faltering down the stretch, but they owned October as they won 11 of 12 games in the postseason and won their first World Series since 1917. The only longer championship drought among championship teams is 97 years by the Chicago Cubs, who last won the World Series in 1908.

The White Sox swept the Red Sox in three games in an AL Division Series, beat the Angels in five games in the AL Championship Series, then swept the Astros, who won their first National League pennant, in four games in the World Series.

White Sox right fielder Jermaine Dye was World Series MVP after going 7-for-16 (.438) with one homer and three RBIs. Dye's eighth-inning RBI single accounted for the lone run in the White Sox' clinching 1-0 victory in Game Four.

The Astros made it to the World Series by beating the Cardinals in six games in the NL Championship Series. The Game Six victory came in the last game at Busch Stadium, the Cardinals' home since 1966. St. Louis will open a new ballpark in April. The Cardinals had a 1,760-1,409 record in 40 seasons at Busch Stadium.

Astros righthander Roy Oswalt won MVP honors in the NLCS as he went 2-0 with a 1.29 ERA in two starts, while White Sox first baseman Paul Konerko was the ALCS MVP after going 6-for-21 (.286) with two homers and seven RBIs.

The Astros downed the Braves in four games in one NL Division Series, while the Cardinals swept the Padres in three games in the other. The Angels went the five-game limit to beat the Yankees in the other AL Division Series.

Umpires are fond of saying they know they have called a good game when no one notices them. Unfortunately, they were noticed quite a bit during the postseason.

A controversial call in Game Two of the ALCS helped turn the momentum in the White Sox' favor. With the Angels leading the series 1-0 and the score tied 1-1 with two outs in the bottom of the ninth inning, White Sox catcher A.J. Pierzynski swung and missed on a third strike that Angels catcher Josh Paul caught cleanly for an apparent inning-ending strikeout.

As Paul rolled the ball back to the mound and the Angels trotted off the field, Pierzynski took off for first base and home-plate umpire Doug Eddings ruled him safe although he had given a raised fist signal, which traditionally means strike three. The Angels argued that Paul caught the ball, to no avail.

Pablo Ozuna ran for Pierzynski , stole second and scored the game-winning run on Joe Crede's double. The White Sox went on to win four straight games and the series. They also took advantage of a bad call in Game Two of the World Series.

Trailing 4-2 with two outs and the bases loaded in the bottom of the seventh inning, an inside pitch by Astros reliever Dan Wheeler appeared to hit Dye's bat for a foul ball. Home-plate umpire Jeff Nelson, though, ruled Dye had been hit in the hand by the pitch.

That loaded the bases and Konerko followed with a grand slam off Chad Qualls that put Chicago ahead, 6-4. The White Sox eventually won 7-6 to take a 2-0 lead in the series.

Home-plate umpire Phil Cuzzi took heat in Game Four of the NLCS because he ejected La Russa and center fielder Jim Edmonds for calling balls and strikes. Many observers felt Cuzzi was too quick with the thumb, con-

2005 MAJOR LEAGUE ALL-STARS

TOM PRIDDY

Andruw Jones: Led NL in home runs and RBIs

DAVID SEELIG

Mariano Rivera: Still a dominant force in New York

Selected by Baseball America

FIRST TEAM

Pos.	Player, Team	B-T	HT	WT	Age	AVG	SLG	OBP	AB	R	H	2B	3B	HR	RBI	SB
C	Victor Martinez, Cleveland	B-R	6-2	170	26	.305	.475	.378	547	73	167	33	0	20	80	0
1B	Albert Pujols, St. Louis	R-R	6-3	225	25	.330	.609	.430	591	129	195	38	2	41	117	16
2B	Brian Roberts, Baltimore	B-R	5-9	172	27	.314	515	.387	561	92	176	45	7	18	73	27
3B	Alex Rodriguez, New York-A	R-R	6-3	210	29	.321	.610	.421	605	124	194	29	1	48	130	21
SS	Michael Young, Texas	R-R	6-1	190	28	.331	.513	.385	668	114	221	40	5	24	91	5
OF	Jason Bay, Pittsburgh	R-R	6-2	200	26	.306	.559	.402	599	110	183	44	6	32	101	21
OF	Miguel Cabrera, Florida	R-R	6-2	185	22	.323	.561	.385	613	106	198	43	2	33	116	1
OF	Andruw Jones, Atlanta	R-R	6-1	200	28	.263	.575	.347	586	95	154	24	3	51	128	5
DH	David Ortiz, Boston	L-L	6-4	230	29	.300	.604	.397	601	119	180	40	1	47	148	1

Pitcher						W-L	ERA	G	GS	CG	SV	IP	H	BB	SO	OBA
SP	Chris Carpenter, St. Louis	R-R	6-6	230	30	21-5	2.83	33	33	7	0	242	204	51	213	.231
SP	Roy Oswalt, Houston	R-R	6-0	175	27	20-12	2.94	35	35	4	0	242	243	48	184	.262
SP	Johan Santana, Minnesota	L-L	6-0	190	26	16-7	2.87	33	33	3	0	232	180	45	238	.210
SP	Dontrelle Willis, Florida	L-L	6-4	200	23	22-10	2.63	34	34	7	0	236	213	55	170	.243
RP	Mariano Rivera, New York-A	R-R	6-2	185	35	7-4	1.38	71	0	0	43	78	50	18	80	.177

SECOND TEAM

Pos.	Player, Team	B-T	HT	WT	Age	AVG	SLG	OBP	AB	R	H	2B	3B	HR	RBI	SB
C	Jason Varitek, Boston	B-R	6-2	230	33	.281	.489	.366	470	70	132	30	1	22	70	2
1B	Derrek Lee, Chicago-N	R-R	6-5	250	29	.335	.662	.418	594	120	199	50	3	46	107	15
2B	Chase Utley, Philadelphia	L-R	6-1	170	26	.291	.540	.376	543	93	158	39	6	28	105	16
3B	David Wright, New York-N	R-R	6-0	200	22	.306	.523	.388	575	99	176	42	1	27	102	17
SS	Miguel Tejada, Baltimore	R-R	5-9	200	29	.304	.515	.349	654	89	199	50	5	26	98	5
OF	Johnny Damon, Boston	L-L	6-2	190	31	.316	.439	.366	624	117	197	35	6	10	75	18
OF	Vladimir Guerrero, L.A.-A	R-R	6-3	220	29	.317	.565	.394	520	95	165	29	2	32	108	13
OF	Manny Ramirez, Boston	R-R	6-0	200	33	.292	.594	.388	554	112	162	30	1	45	144	1
DH	Mark Teixeira, Texas	B-R	6-3	220	25	.301	.575	.379	644	112	194	41	3	43	144	4

Pitcher						W-L	ERA	G	GS	CG	SV	IP	H	BB	SO	OBA
SP	Mark Buehrle, Chicago-A	L-L	6-2	200	26	16-8	3.12	33	33	3	0	237	240	40	149	.262
SP	Roger Clemens, Houston	R-R	6-4	235	42	13-8	1.87	32	32	1	0	211	151	62	185	.198
SP	Bartolo Colon, Anaheim	R-R	5-11	240	32	21-8	3.48	33	33	2	0	223	215	43	157	.254
SP	Jon Garland, Chicago-A	R-R	6-6	200	25	18-10	3.50	32	32	3	0	221	212	47	115	.255
RP	Brad Lidge, Houston	R-R	6-5	210	28	4-4	2.29	70	0	0	42	71	58	23	103	.223

Ages as of July 1, 2005

Organization of the Year: Atlanta. **Executive of the Year:** Mark Shapiro, Cleveland.

Player of the Year: Albert Pujols, St. Louis. **Pitcher of the Year:** Chris Carpenter, St. Louis. **Rookie of the Year:** Huston Street, Oakland. **Manager of the Year:** Ozzie Guillen, Chicago-A.

sidering the emotional setting of a playoff game.

The controversial calls also brought about cries for baseball to use instant replay in helping the umpires, following in the footsteps of the other professional sports. Commissioner Bud Selig remained strongly against replay, however.

Bud Selig

"There has never been support for it in the past and I don't believe support for the concept has grown," Selig said.

While the umpires had Selig's support, they also gained a measure of labor peace by agreeing to a five-year collective bargaining agreement with MLB.

The contract calls for 5 percent annual pay increases, with the 2005 salary scale ranging from $87,859-$357,530. The deal also resolved the grievance over MLB's use of the QuesTec computer system to evaluate umpires.

By The Numbers

While many of the pennant races went down to the wire, the National League ERA title was decided long before the final days of the season. However, that didn't mean that it wasn't a good story.

Ageless Astros ace Roger Clemens posted an outstanding 1.87 mark to capture his first NL title after winning it six times in the American League. The 43-year-old hadn't led the league in ERA since 1990, and his 15-year gap between first-place finishes was more than double the previous high, set by Warren Spahn when he won in 1947 and 1953.

Indians righthander Kevin Millwood went 9-11 with a 2.86 ERA and became the first AL ERA champion with a losing record since the Indians' Stan Coveleski in 1923. Millwood eked out his title over the Twins' Johan Santana, who finished with a 2.87 mark after allowing one run in seven innings against the Tigers on the final day of the season.

Yankees third baseman Alex Rodriguez won the AL home run crown for the fourth time in five seasons with 48, one more than Red Sox designated hitter David Ortiz. Braves center fielder Andruw Jones topped the NL with 51 homers as he had his long-awaited breakout season. Ortiz and Jones (128) also won their first RBI titles.

Each league had first-time batting champions, as Cubs first baseman Derrek Lee hit .335 to finish five points ahead of Cardinals first baseman Albert Pujols (.330) in the NL, while Rangers second baseman Michael Young batted .331 to outdistance Rodriguez (.321) in the AL.

"I never realized at the start of the year that I could win a batting title, but it's a great accomplishment for me," said Lee, who had a .266 career average in eight seasons going into 2005.

Said Young, "It's something I can carry with me the rest of my life."

Marlins lefthander Dontrelle Willis went 22-10 to lead the major leagues in wins. The Angels' Bartolo Colon was the AL leader as he finished 21-8.

Santana won his second straight AL strikeout title with 238 while the Padres' Jake Peavy paced the NL with 216. The Nationals' Chad Cordero led the majors with 47 saves while the Angels' Francisco Rodriguez and the Indians' Bob Wickman tied for the AL lead with 45.

Lee led the NL in slugging percentage at .662, and Rodriguez was first in the AL at .610. The Rockies' Todd Helton topped the major leagues with a .445 on-base percentage while the Yankees' Jason Giambi, bouncing back after a season plagued by injuries and illness, paced the AL with a .440 mark.

The Angels' Chone Figgins led the major leagues with 62 stolen bases and the Mets' Jose Reyes paced the NL with 60.

The Padres' Brian Giles led the majors with 119 walks, while Giambi's 108 topped the AL. Giles' walk total was nearly half of the record-setting 232 that Giants left fielder Barry Bonds drew in 2004.

Lost Season For Bonds

Bonds didn't have the chance to break his walk record in 2005 or make much of a dent in trying to overtake Henry Aaron as baseball's home run king.

Bonds missed the first 5½ months of the season after having three operations on his right knee between Jan. 31-May 2. He returned for the final two weeks of the season as the Giants unsuccessfully attempted to catch the Padres in the National League West.

Despite missing almost an entire season, Bonds was still able to hit .285 with five homers and 10 RBIs in 42 at-bats. He finished the season with 708 home runs, six behind Babe Ruth and 47 behind Aaron.

"There's just no doubt in my mind that I can play at a high level," Bonds said.

400-HOME RUN CLUB

No.	Player	Home Runs
1.	Hank Aaron	755
2.	Babe Ruth	714
3.	**Barry Bonds**	**708**
4.	Willie Mays	660
5.	**Sammy Sosa**	**588**
6.	Frank Robinson	586
7.	Mark McGwire	583
8.	Harmon Killebrew	573
9.	Reggie Jackson	563
10.	**Rafael Palmeiro**	**559**
11.	Mike Schmidt	548
12.	**Ken Griffey Jr.**	**536**
	Mickey Mantle	536
14.	Jimmie Foxx	534
15.	Ted Williams	521
	Willie McCovey	521
17.	Eddie Mathews	512
	Ernie Banks	512
19.	Mel Ott	511
20.	Eddie Murray	504
21.	Lou Gehrig	493
	Fred McGriff	493
23.	Stan Musial	475
	Willie Stargell	475
25.	Dave Winfield	465
26.	Jose Canseco	462
27.	Carl Yastrzemski	452
28.	**Jeff Bagwell**	**449**
	Gary Sheffield	**449**
30.	**Frank Thomas**	**448**
31.	Dave Kingman	442
32.	Andre Dawson	438
33.	**Manny Ramirez**	**435**
34.	**Juan Gonzalez**	**434**
35.	Cal Ripken	431
36.	**Jim Thome**	**430**
37.	**Alex Rodriguez**	**429**
38.	Billy Williams	426
39.	Darrell Evans	414
40.	Duke Snider	407

Bold indicates active player

DAVID SEELIG

Alex Rodriguez

Braves continue run with youngsters

DAVID STONER

Highlighting a steady stream of talent
Jeff Francoeur became a big contributor in Atlanta in 2005

ORGANIZATION OF THE **YEAR**

Chances are Bobby Cox gave little thought about the significance of the lineup he penned prior to facing the Rangers on June 15. The Braves manager was simply trying to win another regular season game, not concerning himself with any achievement that might give Baseball America readers goosebumps.

Yet with baseball on the verge of marking the 30th anniversary of the end of the reserve clause, Cox's lineup was a rarity in the free-agent era. Not only did the Braves field seven rookies—marking the first time since Oct. 1, 1978, the club had started that many at the same time—but Cox also went into battle with 10 players (including a DH) who were all homegrown.

The mix was nothing less than remarkable. Four players—left fielder Kelly Johnson (supplemental first-round pick), catcher Brian McCann (second), right fielder Ryan Langerhans (third) and pitcher Kyle Davies (fourth)—were drafted in the first four rounds. First baseman Adam LaRoche was a late-round (29th) pick, while second baseman Marcus Giles was a draft-and-follow selection. Three players—shortstop Wilson Betemit and third baseman Andy Marte (Dominican Republic) and center fielder Andruw Jones (Curacao)—were products of the organization's aggressive international scouting, and Canadian Peter Orr signed as a nondrafted free agent after attending an American junior college.

And the biggest contributor of all, outfielder Jeff Francoeur, was still to come, taking the National League by storm as the Braves won an unprecedented 14th straight division title and used 18 rookies along the way.

"I've always believed that a strong farm system is the cornerstone and foundation of a strong franchise," general manager John Schuerholz says. "If you look at most of the organizations that have been competitive over long periods of time, one of the common traits is a prosperous farm system that develops players that can help the major league team. It's a tried and true philosophy that has been a tremendous key to our success."

Homegrown players in Atlanta have become as common as a cold since Schuerholz arrived prior to the 1991 season. The list of Braves products has become a who's who of modern franchise history, featuring the likes of Tom Glavine, Ron Gant, David Justice, Chipper Jones, Andruw Jones and numerous others. Not surprisingly, the results are part of a plan in place from the major league level to the lowest rung of the organization.

"John stresses that every decision we make is one that is made for three to five years in the future," farm director Dayton Moore says. "We've stayed consistent with that approach. We're always moving forward and aggressively trying to stay ahead of the curve by evaluating our organization for both today and in the future."

To a man, everyone in the organization agrees Cox deserves much of the praise for making the most of what the farm system produces. Cox, who returned to the dugout in 1990 after rejoining Atlanta in 1985, heads an on-field staff that makes a 10-year veteran look like a beginner. High Class A Myrtle Beach manager Randy Ingle and Double-A Mississippi skipper Brian Snitker have been in the organization for more than two decades. The same holds true for coaches Rick Albert and Bruce Dal Canton.

And while most minor league instructors long to reach the big leagues, the Braves' coaches and managers take pride in knowing their efforts serve as significant building blocks for championship teams in Atlanta. Scouting also plays a key role, especially because few teams are more careful than Atlanta about filling minor league roster spots with players that have a realistic shot at contributing in the major leagues. With few exceptions, the Braves eschew roster fillers who are signed simply to play alongside prospects.

"We put a great emphasis on the fact that as long as a player has a Braves uniform on, he has a chance," Moore says. "We tell them over and over that they're here because someone thinks they could one day help our major league club. Once the day comes when we feel they will not be able to contribute, we move on and give someone else an opportunity. We preach that day in and day out."

PREVIOUS WINNERS

1982—Oakland Athletics
1983—New York Mets
1984—New York Mets
1985—Milwaukee Brewers
1986—Milwaukee Brewers
1987—Milwaukee Brewers
1988—Montreal Expos
1989—Texas Rangers
1990—Montreal Expos
1991—Atlanta Braves
1992—Cleveland Indians
1993—Toronto Blue Jays
1994—Kansas City Royals
1995—New York Mets
1996—Atlanta Braves
1997—Detroit Tigers
1998—New York Yankees
1999—Oakland Athletics
2000—Chicago White Sox
2001—Houston Astros
2002—Minnesota Twins
2003—Florida Marlins
2004—Minnesota Twins

Bonds also moved into ninth place on baseball's all-time RBI list with 1,853 and strengthened Giants general manager Brian Sabean's belief that Bonds can break Aaron's home run record.

"I think we all know he can still hit," Sabean said. "He never had spring training and he had no rehab assignment. So it's pretty impressive, not so much that the skills are still there, but for him to get back on the field to whatever degree, it spurs him to next year and more so how it translated to help the ballclub, I think it was good for everybody.

"I really believe especially a position player, no matter how great you are, it's very difficult to take a whole year off. He now knows, not that he wouldn't have if he had played, he knows firsthand that he's still the force he was before he missed all this time."

Bonds' strong finish allowed him to take something positive from a trying year. Besides missing nearly the whole season, he also was dogged by his admission during the FBI's BALCO probe that he unwittingly used a steroid cream. Bonds said he felt the entire steroids matter was overblown.

"You're talking about something that wasn't even illegal at the time," Bonds said. "All this stuff about supplements, protein shakes, whatever. Man, it's not like this is the Olympics. We don't train four years for, like, a 10-second event.

"We go 162 games. You've got to come back day after day after day. We're entertainers. If I can't go out there and somebody pays $60 for a ticket, and I'm not in the lineup, who's getting cheated? Not me. There are far worse things like cocaine, heroin and those types of things.

"So we all make mistakes. We need to turn the page. We need to forget about the past and let us play the game. We're entertainers. Let us entertain."

Jason Giambi also admitted during the BALCO investigation that he had used steroids and human growth hormone. That came after he had a miserable 2004 season in which he hit just .208 with 12 homers while being limited to 80 games by a variety of injuries and illnesses, including a benign tumor on his pituitary gland and an intestinal parasite.

Giambi held a strange press conference a week before spring training, when he tearfully apologized but would not say what he was sorry about. Giambi would have jeopardized having the remainder of the seven-year, $120 million contract he signed with the Yankees as a free agent following the 2001 season voided if he publicly admitted steroid use.

Following a slow start in which he refused the Yankees' request to go to Triple-A Columbus in order to regain his batting stroke, Giambi went on to have a big comeback season. He hit .271 with 32 homers and 87 RBIs in 139 games while leading the American League with a .440 on base percentage and 108 walks.

Giambi also reached three significant career milestones during the season with his 300th homer, 1,500th hit and 1,000th RBI.

"I wanted nothing more than to prove to the people of New York that I could face adversity and come back to be the player I once was," Giambi said.

300-SAVES CLUB

No.	Player	Saves
1.	Lee Smith	478
2.	**Trevor Hoffman**	**436**
3.	John Franco	424
4.	Dennis Eckersley	390
5.	**Mariano Rivera**	**379**
6.	Jeff Reardon	367
7.	Randy Myers	347
8.	Rollie Fingers	341
9.	John Wetteland	330
10.	**Roberto Hernandez**	**324**
	Troy Percival	**324**
12.	**Jose Mesa**	**319**
13.	Rick Aguilera	318
14.	Robb Nen	314
15.	Tom Henke	311
16.	Rich Gossage	310
17.	Jeff Montgomery	304
18.	Doug Jones	303
19.	Bruce Sutter	300

Active players in bold type

AMERICAN LEAGUE: BEST TOOLS

A Baseball America survey of American League managers, conducted at midseason 2005, ranked AL players with the best tools:

BEST HITTER
1. Vladimir Guerrero, Angels
2. Miguel Tejada, Orioles
3. Ichiro Suzuki, Mariners

BEST POWER
1. Alex Rodriguez, Yankees
2. Manny Ramirez, Red Sox
3. David Ortiz, Red Sox

BEST BUNTER
1. Scott Podsednik, White Sox
2. Ichiro Suzuki, Mariners
3. Chone Figgins, Angels

BEST STRIKE-ZONE JUDGMENT
1. David Dellucci, Rangers
2. Frank Thomas, White Sox
3. Gary Sheffield, Yankees

BEST HIT-AND-RUN ARTIST
1. Derek Jeter, Yankees
2. Jason Kendall, Athletics
3. Melvin Mora, Orioles

BEST BASERUNNER
1. Ichiro Suzuki, Mariners
2. Derek Jeter, Yankees
3. Scott Podsednik, White Sox

FASTEST BASERUNNER
1. Scott Podsednik, White Sox
2. Carl Crawford, Devil Rays
3. Nook Logan, Tigers

BEST PITCHER
1. Roy Halladay, Blue Jays
2. Mark Buehrle, White Sox
3. Jon Garland, White Sox

BEST FASTBALL
1. Daniel Cabrera, Orioles
2. Kyle Farnsworth, Tigers
3. Bartolo Colon, Angels

BEST CURVEBALL
1. Barry Zito, Athletics
2. Roy Halladay, Blue Jays
3. Mike Mussina, Yankees

BEST SLIDER
1. Frankie Rodriguez, Angels
2. Randy Johnson, Yankees
3. Matt Clement, Red Sox

BEST CHANGEUP
1. Johan Santana, Twins
2. Mark Buehrle, White Sox
3. Jamie Moyer, Mariners

BEST CONTROL
1. Brad Radke, Twins
2. Carlos Silva, Twins
3. Roy Halladay, Blue Jays

BEST PICKOFF MOVE
1. Kenny Rogers, Rangers
2. Mark Buehrle, White Sox
3. Brian Anderson, Royals

BEST RELIEVER
1. Mariano Rivera, Yankees
2. Frankie Rodriguez, Angels
3. B.J. Ryan, Orioles

BEST DEFENSIVE C
1. Jason Varitek, Red Sox
2. Ivan Rodriguez, Tigers
3. Bengie Molina, Angels

BEST DEFENSIVE 1B
1. Darin Erstad, Angels
2. Mark Teixeira, Rangers
3. Travis Lee, Devil Rays

BEST DEFENSIVE 2B
1. Brian Roberts, Orioles
2. Orlando Hudson, Blue Jays
3. Adam Kennedy, Angels

BEST DEFENSIVE 3B
1. Eric Chavez, Athletics
2. Hank Blalock, Rangers
3. Joe Crede, White Sox

BEST DEFENSIVE SS
1. Derek Jeter, Yankees
2. Miguel Tejada, Orioles
3. Michael Young, Rangers

BEST INFIELD ARM
1. Miguel Tejada, Orioles
2. Alex Rodriguez, Yankees
3. Michael Young, Rangers

BEST DEFENSIVE OF
1. Ichiro Suzuki, Mariners
2. Torii Hunter, Twins
3. Mark Kotsay, Athletics

BEST OUTFIELD ARM
1. Ichiro Suzuki, Mariners
2. Vladimir Guerrero, Angels
3. Torii Hunter, Twins

MOST EXCITING PLAYER
1. Vladimir Guerrero, Angels
2. Miguel Tejada, Orioles
3. Ichiro Suzuki, Mariners

BEST MANAGER
1. Mike Scioscia, Angels
2. Ron Gardenhire, Twins
3. Joe Torre, Yankees

Miles Of Milestones

While Palmeiro's legacy was tainted, he did reach the season's biggest statistical milestone July 15 when he recorded his 3,000th career hit with a fifth-inning double off the Mariners' Pineiro in Seattle. Palmeiro finished the season with 569 home runs, ranking ninth on the all-time list.

"Consistency. That's the only way you accomplish numbers like that," Yankees shortstop Derek Jeter said.

Street leads to success in Oakland

It was one of those spring-training moments so strange that the old hands around Oakland A's camp could not stop laughing.

Huston Street, a callow rookie just a few months of the campus of the University of Texas, stood on the mound shaking off Jason Kendall, the jut-jawed catcher who has spent more than a thousand major league games behind the plate. Just how brash can this kid be?

ROOKIE *OF THE* **YEAR**

Not brash at all, it turns out.

In a prolonged at-bat against Moises Alou of the Giants, Kendall wanted Street to throw a changeup, a pitch the youngster had barely begun tinkering with and had no confidence in his ability to execute. Street preferred a slider. Kendall demanded a changeup. Finally, Kendall got his way and Alou was retired.

"That was one of those profound moments when it really stuck with me," Street said. "He trusted my stuff. He told me to trust the catcher's call and to trust my stuff. 'Don't be afraid of your pitches.' It gave me the confidence that I can get people out with all my pitches, not just my go-to pitch."

At the age of 22, Street took over as the closer of the Oakland Athletics, a team in the middle of a pennant race. He still relies mostly on his fastball and go-to slider, but when Kendall puts down the sign for a change, Street follows orders. As a closer in a heated race, he owned one of the most high-pressure jobs in all of baseball. He did not flinch.

"He has no fear," said manager Ken Macha.

"His poise is as good as in any young player I've seen," said A's broadcaster and former all-star Ray Fosse, who has been catching or calling major league games since 1967.

"He gets better and better every time he goes out there. He wants to learn and find ways to keep improving," Kendall said.

Street finished the season with a 5-1 record, 23 saves and a 1.72 ERA a little more than a year after the A's drafted him out of the University of Texas, making him Baseball America's Major League Rookie of the Year in a season filled with significant rookie performances.

There is something special about this slender Texan from the suburbs of Austin. He has physical tools, but they were not dazzling enough for any major league team to call his name until the A's took him 40th overall. What makes Street so different is his refusal to be intimidated: not by situations, challenges, other players or the most intense forms of pressure. Street simply thrives on pressure.

Street has always treated every stop as a learning experience on the way to higher goals. At Texas, he worked with pitching coach Frank Anderson to perfect a three-quarters arm action that would bring more movement to his pitches. He was not afraid to change from the overhand style he used in high school because Anderson bred confidence that the new delivery would make him more effective. He was not afraid to move into the closer role when coach Augie Garrido needed someone to finish games back in '02, and now he loves the bullpen with passion.

What makes Street different from the hundreds of other 22-year-olds laboring through the minor leagues, slowly learning both the mental and physical demands of a professional, is the mindset to overcome challenges: the poise to perform. Street and the A's are a perfect match. There is an organization-wide philosophy that baseball aptitude is a tool, just as much as hitting or throwing; that knowing how to play the game is an underrated skill that makes for major league success. Street is aptitude in action.

LARRY GOREN

Sudden impact
Huston Street stepped in quickly as A's closer

PREVIOUS WINNERS

1989—Gregg Olson, rhp, Orioles
1990—Sandy Alomar, c, Indians
1991—Jeff Bagwell, 1b, Astros
1992—Pat Listach, ss, Brewers
1993—Mike Piazza, c, Dodgers
1994—Raul Mondesi, of, Dodgers
1995—Hideo Nomo, rhp, Dodgers
1996—Derek Jeter, ss, Yankees
1997—Nomar Garciaparra, ss, Red Sox
1998—Kerry Wood, rhp, Cubs
1999—Carlos Beltran, of, Royals
2000—Rafael Furcal, ss/2b, Braves
2001—Albert Pujols, of/3b/1b, Cardinals
2002—Eric Hinske, 3b, Blue Jays
2003—Brandon Webb, rhp, Diamondbacks
2004—Khalil Greene, ss, Padres

ALL-ROOKIE TEAM

Pos.	Player, Club	AVG	AB	H	HR	RBI	SB
C	Brian McCann, Braves	.278	180	50	5	23	1
1B	Ryan Howard, Phillies	.288	312	90	22	63	0
2B	Robinson Cano, Yankees	.297	522	155	14	62	1
3B	Garrett Atkins, Rockies	.287	519	149	13	89	0
SS	J.J. Hardy, Brewers	.247	372	92	9	50	0
OF	Jeff Francoeur, Braves	.300	257	77	14	45	3
OF	Jonny Gomes, Devil Rays	.282	348	98	21	54	9
OF	Willy Taveras, Astros	.291	592	172	3	29	34
DH	Dan Johnson, Athletics	.275	375	103	15	58	0
		W-L	ERA	IP	H	BB	SO
P	Joe Blanton, Athletics	12-12	3.53	201	178	67	116
P	Gustavo Chacin, Blue Jays	13-9	3.72	203	213	70	121
P	Scott Kazmir, Devil Rays	10-9	3.77	186	172	100	174
P	Chris Young, Rangers	12-7	4.26	165	162	45	137
P	Huston Street, Athletics	5-1	1.72	78	53	26	72

"You have to be very consistent for a long time and that's what he's done."

In an otherwise disappointing season with the Orioles after being acquired in an offseason trade with the Cubs, Sammy Sosa moved into fifth place on the career homer list when he hit his 587th on July 27 off the Rangers' Chris Young. Sosa finished the season with 588, as he hit just 14 in 102 games while batting .221.

Padres closer Trevor Hoffman became the third pitcher in major league history to reach 400 saves when he closed out a 6-5 victory over the Cardinals in St. Louis on May 6. That enabled Hoffman to join Lee Smith (478) and John Franco (424) in the 400-save club.

Hoffman eventually moved past Franco into second place and finished the season with 436, 42 away from Smith's record. Hoffman had 43 saves in 2005, giving him 10 seasons of 30 or more to tie the record set by Smith.

"Would I have thought in my wildest dreams I would be able to do something like this? Not necessarily," Hoffman said. "I felt confident I could do the job, but you can never perceive the consistency that it would take to reach this type of milestone.

"Hopefully it's not the last one we're talking about. Hopefully, we're talking about Lee Smith. It's something that's out there. But I try to keep it in perspective of what I do selfishly for myself can ultimately lead to a win out on the field for the ballclub."

The Pirates' Jose Mesa notched his 300th career save April 27 when he closed out a win over the Astros.

The Nationals' Chad Cordero tied a major league record for saves in a month with 15 in June, matching the mark set by Smith in 1993 and equaled by John Wettleland in 1996.

Randy Johnson notched his 250th win May 15 over the Athletics and Mariners lefty Jamie Moyer got win No. 200 on July 9 against the Angels.

A season after winning his 300th game, the Cubs' Greg Maddux recorded his 3,000th strikeout, getting Giants shortstop Omar Vizquel on July 26.

Roger Clemens notched his 4,500th strikeout on Oct. 1, fanning the Cubs' Jose Macias. Only Nolan Ryan stands ahead of Clemens on the all-time list with 5,714.

Red Sox left fielder Manny Ramirez and Yankees third baseman Alex Rodriguez both hit their 400th career home runs, becoming the 39th and 40th players to reach that level. Ramirez connected off the Mariners' Gil Meche on May 15 at Safeco Field. The eccentric Ramirez downplayed reaching the milestone.

"I'm going to put the ball on eBay and see how much I get," he said jokingly. "Maybe $200?"

Rodriguez became the first player in history to hit 400 homers before his 30th birthday when he connected off the Brewers' Jorge De la Rosa on June 8 in Milwaukee.

"It was very special for me," Rodriguez said. "Just to do it with this uniform, the New York Yankees uniform on, to me is something I'll never forget."

In addition to Yankees first baseman Jason Giambi, left fielder Luis Gonzalez and first baseman/outfielder Shawn Green of the Diamondbacks, Angels right fielder Vladimir Guerrero and Braves center fielder Andruw Jones hit their 300th career homers.

Ageless Braves first baseman Julio Franco notched his 2,500th hit on July 30 against the Pirates, less than a month before his 47th birthday. On the other end of the spectrum, 21-year-old Marlins outfielder Jeremy Hermida became the first player with a pinch-hit grand slam in his first major league plate appearance when he connected off the Cardinals' Al Reyes on Aug. 31.

Astros second baseman Craig Biggio set a painful major league record when he was by a pitch for the 268th time in his career June 29, getting plunked on the left elbow by the Rockies' Byung-Hyun Kim to break Don Baylor's mark. Biggio also stole his 400th career base May 2 against the Pirates.

Cardinals first baseman Albert Pujols and Mariners

3,000 STRIKEOUTS

No.	Player	Strikeouts
1.	Nolan Ryan	5,714
2.	**Roger Clemens**	**4,502**
3.	**Randy Johnson**	**4,372**
4.	Steve Carlton	4,136
5.	Bert Blyleven	3,701
6.	Tom Seaver	3,640
7.	Don Sutton	3,574
8.	Gaylord Perry	3,534
9.	Walter Johnson	3,508
10.	Phil Niekro	3,342
11.	Ferguson Jenkins	3,192
12.	Bob Gibson	3,117
13.	**Greg Maddux**	**3,052**

Active players in bold type

NATIONAL LEAGUE: BEST TOOLS

A Baseball America survey of National League managers, conducted at midseason 2005, ranked NL players with the best tools:

BEST HITTER
1. Albert Pujols, Cardinals
2. Derrek Lee, Cubs
3. Bobby Abreu, Phillies

BEST POWER
1. Albert Pujols, Cardinals
2. Derrek Lee, Cubs
3. Adam Dunn, Reds

BEST BUNTER
1. Juan Pierre, Marlins
2. Dave Roberts, Padres
3. Omar Vizquel, Giants

BEST STRIKE-ZONE JUDGMENT
1. Bobby Abreu, Phillies
2. Albert Pujols, Cardinals
3. Brian Giles, Padres

BEST HIT-AND-RUN ARTIST
1. Mark Loretta, Padres
2. David Eckstein, Cardinals
3. Jack Wilson, Pirates

BEST BASERUNNER
1. Juan Pierre, Marlins
2. Larry Walker, Cardinals
3. Bobby Abreu, Phillies

FASTEST BASERUNNER
1. Jose Reyes, Mets
2. Rafael Furcal, Braves
3. Juan Pierre, Marlins

BEST PITCHER
1. Roger Clemens, Astros
2. Pedro Martinez, Mets
3. Chris Carpenter, Cardinals

BEST FASTBALL
1. Billy Wagner, Phillies
2. A.J. Burnett, Marlins
3. Derrick Turnbow, Brewers

BEST CURVEBALL
1. Roy Oswalt, Astros
2. Ben Sheets, Brewers
3. Matt Morris, Cardinals

BEST SLIDER
1. Brad Lidge, Astros
2. John Smoltz, Braves
3. Pedro Martinez, Mets

BEST CHANGEUP
1. Pedro Martinez, Mets
2. Trevor Hoffman, Padres
3. Tom Glavine, Mets

BEST CONTROL
1. Greg Maddux, Cubs
2. Javier Vazquez, Diamondbacks
3. Livan Hernandez, Nationals

BEST PICKOFF MOVE
1. Andy Pettitte, Astros
2. Chris Capuano, Brewers
3. Livan Hernandez, Nationals

BEST RELIEVER
1. Chad Cordero, Nationals
2. Trevor Hoffman, Padres
3. Brad Lidge, Astros

BEST DEFENSIVE C
1. Mike Matheny, Giants
2. Yadier Molina, Cardinals
3. Brian Schneider, Nationals

BEST DEFENSIVE 1B
1. Derrek Lee, Cubs
2. J.T. Snow, Giants
3. Todd Helton, Rockies

BEST DEFENSIVE 2B
1. Luis Castillo, Marlins
2. Jose Castillo, Pirates
3. Jose Vidro, Nationals

BEST DEFENSIVE 3B
1. Scott Rolen, Cardinals
2. Vinny Castilla, Nationals
3. Aramis Ramirez, Cubs

BEST DEFENSIVE SS
1. Cesar Izturis, Dodgers
2. Omar Vizquel, Giants
3. Alex Gonzalez, Marlins

BEST INFIELD ARM
1. Rafael Furcal, Braves
2. Scott Rolen, Cardinals
3. Jose Reyes, Mets

BEST DEFENSIVE OF
1. Andruw Jones, Braves
2. Jim Edmonds, Cardinals
3. Carlos Beltran, Mets

BEST OUTFIELD ARM
1. Andruw Jones, Braves
2. Jose Guillen, Nationals
3. Carlos Beltran, Mets

MOST EXCITING PLAYER
1. Albert Pujols, Cardinals
2. Derrek Lee, Cubs
3. Jose Reyes, Mets

BEST MANAGER
1. Bobby Cox, Braves
2. Tony La Russa, Cardinals
3. Frank Robinson, Nationals

Shapiro's plan gets quick results

When Mark Shapiro took over as Indians general manager, he was charged with the unenviable task of tearing down a team that had been a playoff contender for the better part of a decade.

EXECUTIVE *OF THE* **YEAR**

Shapiro, 38, got rid of expensive, older players after the 2001 season and started bringing in the next generation of young Indians talent. Shapiro recognized the process would be painful, and it drew criticism locally as the club averaged 88 losses a year in his first three seasons. Attendance dwindled at Jacobs Field as Shapiro preached patience.

LARRY GOREN

Blueprint in place
Indians general manager Mark Shapiro

The team first showed signs of turning around in 2004, but in the second half of 2005 the team showed that Shapiro has reconstructed the Indians into one of the most exciting young teams in the American League.

By developing such players as Victor Martinez through the farm system and supplementing them with a series of shrewd trades and free-agent signings, the Indians posted double-digit win increases in each of the last two seasons, going from 68 wins in 2003 to 80 wins in 2004 to 93 wins in 2005. In fact, the Indians are only the fourth team since 1970 to accomplish consecutive double-digit win increases in full seasons. The 93 wins in 2005 tied for the eighth-highest win total in franchise history.

PREVIOUS WINNERS
1998—Doug Melvin, Rangers
1999—Jim Bowden, Reds
2000—Walt Jocketty, Cardinals
2001—Pat Gillick, Mariners
2002—Billy Beane, Athletics
2003—Brian Sabean, Giants
2004—Terry Ryan, Twins

The Indians were one of the best teams in baseball in the second half of 2005, even with the No. 25 payroll in the majors. The team was 15 games behind the White Sox as late as Aug. 1, but went on a 35-12 run over the next seven weeks and pulled to within a game and a half in September But the Indians lost five of their last six games to Tampa Bay and Chicago, falling short of both the division title and the wild card.

The team now has a core of players that should contend for the playoffs for years to come—exactly according to Shapiro's plan.

Shapiro completed his fourth season as GM after being named to the post in November 2001. A Princeton graduate, his tenure with the club began in 1992 as an assistant in baseball operations and he later served as assistant farm director, farm director and assistant GM prior to succeeding John Hart.

Guillen helps Sox break title drought

To many observers going into the 2005 season, the White Sox looked like an oddly built team with an oddball manager leading them into battle.

MANAGER *OF THE* **YEAR**

The unconventional combination of Ozzie Guillen and the White Sox worked to perfection, however. The team won 99 games to lead the American League Central wire-to-wire and put together the best record in the AL, then cruised through the playoffs to bring the White Sox their first World Series title since 1917. And with a team devoid of superstars, much of the credit fell to Guillen.

Guillen got attention from fans for his witty remarks and sometimes amusing actions, such as when he reached his arms high and wide as a signal to bring in Bobby Jenks during the World Series. But White Sox players knew he brought much more than that to the team.

LARRY GOREN

Driving his team to victory
White Sox manager Ozzie Guillen

"Early in the year, he told us there was going to be a rough spot," first baseman Paul Konerko said. "He knew it was coming, but during the rough spot he kept telling us, 'We're going to get out of this. I know how it's going to work. I've seen this so many times.' You know that, but it reinforces that, hey, we're still a good team."

PREVIOUS WINNERS
1998—Larry Dierker, Astros
1999—Jimy Williams, Red Sox
2000—Dusty Baker, Giants
2001—Lou Piniella, Mariners
2002—Mike Scioscia, Angels
2003—Jack McKeon, Marlins
2004—Bobby Cox, Braves

Guillen was in just his second season as a manager after 16 seasons as a major league player, most of them spent as the White Sox shortstop. He brought high expectations to the team, and the team fulfilled them all in 2005.

"Last year, it was, 'Rah, rah, good thing we have Ozzie,' " Guillen said before the season. "This year, forget all that rah-rah stuff. We are focused on winning from the first day."

right fielder Ichiro Suzuki reached significant hitting milestones.

Pujols became the first player to hit 30 homers and drive in 100 runs in each of his first five seasons. Suzuki became the third player to reach 1,000 hits before playing in his 700th game. He got to the milestone in career game No. 696. Only Chuck Klein (683 games) and Lloyd Waner (686) got there faster.

The Cardinals' Tony La Russa became the third-winningest manager in baseball history as he ran his career victory total to 2,214, trailing only Connie Mack (3,731) and John McGraw (2,763).

The Yankees became only the third franchise to reach 4 million fans in season attendance, joining the Blue Jays (1992, 1993) and Rockies (1993), as 4,090,696 tickets were sold to games at Yankee Stadium.

Boggs, Sandberg Join Hall

Rafael Palmeiro's possible inclusion in the Hall of Fame is a matter for future debates. The day before Palmeiro was suspended, Wade Boggs and Ryne Sandberg became the latest players to be enshrined in the Hall.

Boggs received the necessary 75 percent of the vote by 10-year members of the Baseball Writers' Association in his first year of eligibility, while Sandberg did not make it until his third year on the ballot.

Boggs had 3,010 hits and won five batting titles in his 18-year career as a third baseman with the Red Sox (1982-92), Yankees (1993-97) and Devil Rays (1998-99). He also had a .328 average and .415 on-base percentage in 2,440 career games to go with 118 homers and 1,014 RBIs.

Wade Boggs

Unlike most Hall of Fame-caliber players, Boggs spent nearly six full seasons in the Red Sox farm system before being promoted to the major leagues in 1981 after winning the International League batting title with Triple-A Pawtucket.

"Life is about obstacles," Boggs said. "Our lives are not determined by what happens to us, but how we react to what happens.

"I am living proof that dreams come true. In life, so many things are taken for granted, but one thing I can honestly say is that I took every day, enjoyed putting on that uniform and playing the great game of baseball."

Sandberg batted .285 with 282 homers and 1,061RBIs in 2,164 games over 16 seasons while playing primarily second base with the Phillies (1981) and Cubs (1982-94, 1996-97).

Sandberg, a nine-time Gold Glove winner who shunned the media spotlight during his playing days, repeatedly focused on his respect for the game during his induction speech.

"A lot of people say this honor validates my career," said Sandberg, the National League MVP in 1984. "But I didn't work hard to get validation. I didn't play the game right because I saw a reward at the end of the tunnel.

"I played it right because that's what you're supposed to do—play it right and with respect. Turning two is more important than knowing where to find the little

ALL-STAR GAME

LARRY GOREN

Stakes American League to big early lead
Mark Teixeira hit a two-run homer off Dontrelle Willis

AL stars hold on for All-Star win

Kenny Rogers' relief appearance in the All-Star Game in Detroit shortly after he assaulted a cameraman might have grabbed some headlines, but it could not completely overshadow an MVP performance by Orioles shortstop Miguel Tejada, who led the AL to its eighth straight win, 7-5. His leadoff home run off the Braves' John Smoltz in the second inning opened the scoring. Tejada also drove in a run with a ground out.

Playing at Detroit's Comerica Park, the AL again won home-field advantage for the World Series with its all-star victory.

The AL extended its lead to 7-0 in the sixth when Rangers first baseman Mark Teixeira hit a two-run homer off the Marlins' Dontrelle Willis.

The NL closed to 7-5 with two runs in the ninth, but Yankees closer Mariano Rivera struck out Astros third baseman Morgan Ensberg to end the game and notch the save.

White Sox lefthander Mark Buehrle was the starter and winner for the AL, striking out three in two scoreless innings. Fittingly, the White Sox benefited from his work, as the AL's victory in the All-Star Game once again gave his own team home-field advantage in the World Series—though it ended up being academic because of Chicago's sweep. Smoltz took the loss in relief of starter Chris Carpenter of the Cardinals.

"Tejada got us off to a great start and we were able to just go with it from there," said AL catcher Jason Varitek, one of four Red Sox in the starting lineup.

Rogers became a focal point at the All-Star Game, which came in the midst of his appeal of a 20-game suspension for shoving a cameraman and breaking camera equipment.

Rogers was selected in a vote of players, managers and coaches to be part of the American League pitching staff. Though he admitted he considered skipping the game to avoid potential negative publicity, Rogers wound up pitching in relief and earning a $50,000 performance bonus in his contract.

Bobby Abreu

Rogers was booed during pregame introductions, when he took the mound in the seventh inning, when he gave up a two-run home run to Andruw Jones and when he left the game.

"I would be lying if I said this was an easy thing to do," Rogers said. "It was difficult, a lot of stuff was going on, but I came to meet it head on, do things the right way and move on."

Earlier, Phillies right fielder Bobby Abreu won the Home Run Derby, setting a record by hitting 41 balls out in 71 swings. The old record was 27 by Tejada in 2004 in Houston, and Abreu nearly broke that in the first round when he belted 24 homers.

—JOHN PERROTTO

TOP VOTE-GETTERS

AMERICAN LEAGUE

CATCHER: 1. Jason Varitek, Red Sox, 2,939,648; 2. Ivan Rodriguez, Tigers, 1,841,385; 3. Jorge Posada, Yankees, 1,133,111.

FIRST BASE: 1. Mark Teixeira, Rangers, 2,187,115; 2. Tino Martinez, Yankees, 1,526,216; 3. Kevin Millar, Red Sox, 1,191,188.

SECOND BASE: 1. Brian Roberts, Orioles, 2,629,521; 2. Alfonso Soriano, Rangers, 2,434,840; 3. Mark Bellhorn, Red Sox, 1,035,293.

THIRD BASE: 1. Alex Rodriguez, Yankees, 3,553,235; 2. Bill Mueller, Red Sox, 1,295,233; 3. Melvin Mora, Orioles, 970,967.

SHORTSTOP: 1. Miguel Tejada, Orioles, 3,224,908; 2. Derek Jeter, Yankees, 2,012,448; 3. Edgar Renteria, Red Sox, 1,485,964.

OUTFIELD: 1. Manny Ramirez, Red Sox, 3,117,157; 2. Vladimir Guerrero, Angels, 3,006,512; 3. Johnny Damon, Red Sox, 2,800,610; 4. Ichiro Suzuki, Mariners, 2,743,784; 5. Gary Sheffield, Yankees, 1,737,779; 6. Hideki Matsui, Yankees, 1,475,969; 7. Torii Hunter, Twins, 1,185,290; 8. Trot Nixon, Red Sox, 1,134,892; 9. Sammy Sosa, Orioles, 1,072,110.

DESIGNATED HITTER: 1. David Ortiz, Red Sox, 4,138,141; 2. Rafael Palmeiro, Orioles, 1,081,805; 3. Jason Giambi, Yankees, 794,315.

NATIONAL LEAGUE

CATCHER: 1. Mike Piazza, Mets, 1,966,074; 2. Michael Barrett, Cubs, 1,659,800; 3. Yadier Molina, Cardinals, 1,659,577.

FIRST BASE: 1. Derrek Lee, Cubs, 3,560,316; 2. Albert Pujols, Cardinals, 3,455,017; 3. Doug Mientkiewicz, Mets, 567,964.

SECOND BASE: 1. Jeff Kent, Dodgers, 2,253,271; 2. Mark Grudzielanek, Cardinals, 1,985,128; 3. Todd Walker, Cubs, 1,376,827.

THIRD BASE: 1. Scott Rolen, Cardinals, 2,742,864; 2. Aramis Ramirez, Cubs, 2,373,677; 3. Troy Glaus, Diamondbacks, 1,142,358.

SHORTSTOP: 1. David Eckstein, Cardinals, 2,231,246; 2. Cesar Izturis, Dodgers, 1,659,010; 3. Nomar Garciaparra, Cubs, 1,307,973.

OUTFIELD: 1. Jim Edmonds, Cardinals, 2,826,306; 2. Bobby Abreu, Phillies, 2,532,742; 3. Carlos Beltran, Mets, 2,049,779; 4. Miguel Cabrera, Marlins, 1,650,369; 5. Larry Walker, Cardinals, 1,617,578; 6. Andruw Jones, Braves, 1,576,418; 7. Ken Griffey, Reds, 1,489,768; 8. Reggie Sanders, Cardinals, 1,340,401; 9. Jeromy Burnitz, Cubs, 1,195,019.

ROSTERS

AMERICAN LEAGUE

PITCHERS: Danys Baez, Devil Rays; **Mark Buehrle, White Sox**; Matt Clement, Red Sox; Bartolo Colon, Angels; Justin Duchscherer, Athletics; Jon Garland, White Sox; x-Roy Halladay, Blue Jays; Joe Nathan, Twins; Mariano Rivera, Yankees; Kenny Rogers, Rangers; B.J. Ryan, Orioles; Johan Santana, Twins; Bob Wickman, Indians.

CATCHERS: Ivan Rodriguez, Tigers; **Jason Varitek, Red Sox**.

INFIELDERS: Shea Hillenbrand, Blue Jays; Paul Konerko, White Sox; Melvin Mora, Orioles; **Brian Roberts, Orioles (2b)**; **Alex Rodriguez, Yankees (3b)**; Alfonso Soriano, Rangers; Mike Sweeney, Royals; **Mark Teixeira, Rangers (1b)**; **Miguel Tejada, Orioles (ss)**; Michael Young, Rangers.

OUTFIELDERS: Garret Anderson, Angels; **Johnny Damon, Red Sox**; **Vladimir Guerrero, Angels**; Scott Podsednik, White Sox; **Manny Ramirez, Red Sox**; Gary Sheffield, Yankees; Ichiro Suzuki, Mariners.

DESIGNATED HITTER: David Ortiz, Red Sox.

NATIONAL LEAGUE

PITCHERS: Chris Carpenter, Cardinals; Roger Clemens, Astros; Chad Cordero, Nationals; Brian Fuentes, Rockies; Livan Hernandez, Nationals; Jason Isringhausen, Cardinals; Brad Lidge, Astros; x-Pedro Martinez, Mets; Roy Oswalt, Astros; Jake Peavy, Padres; John Smoltz, Braves; Billy Wagner, Phillies; Dontrelle Willis, Marlins.

CATCHERS: Paul Lo Duca, Marlins; **Mike Piazza, Mets**.

INFIELDERS: Luis Castillo, Marlins; **David Eckstein, Cardinals (ss)**; Morgan Ensberg, Astros; x- Cesar Izturis, Dodgers; **Jeff Kent, Dodgers (2b)**; **Derrek Lee, Cubs (1b)**; Felipe Lopez, Reds; Albert Pujols, Cardinals; Aramis Ramirez, Cubs; x-**Scott Rolen, Cardinals (3b)**; Jimmy Rollins, Phillies.

OUTFIELDERS: Bobby Abreu, Phillies; Moises Alou, Giants; Jason Bay, Pirates; **Carlos Beltran, Mets**; Miguel Cabrera, Marlins; **Jim Edmonds, Cardinals**; Luis Gonzalez, Diamondbacks; Andruw Jones, Braves; Carlos Lee, Brewers.

Players voted to start in bold.
x-Injured, did not play.

July 12 in Detroit
American League 7, National League 5

NATIONAL	ab	r	h	bi	AMERICAN	ab	r	h	bi
Abreu, rf	2	0	1	0	Damon, cf	2	1	1	0
Rollins, ss	1	0	1	0	Suzuki, cf-rf	2	0	1	2
Gonzalez, L, ph	1	1	1	1	A.Rodriguez, 3b	2	1	1	0
Beltran, lf	3	0	1	0	Mora, 3b	1	0	0	0
Lo Duca, c	2	0	0	0	Hillenbrand, 3b	0	0	0	0
Pujols, dh	2	0	1	0	Ortiz, dh	3	0	2	1
C.Lee, ph-dh	3	0	0	1	Sweeney, ph-dh	1	0	0	0
D.Lee, 1b	3	0	1	0	M.Ramirez, lf	2	0	0	0
Ensberg, 1b	2	0	0	0	Anderson, lf	2	0	0	0
Edmonds, cf-rf	1	0	0	0	Tejada, ss	3	1	1	2
Alou, ph-rf	1	1	1	0	M.Young, ss	1	0	1	0
Ramirez, 3b	2	0	1	0	Guerrero, rf	3	0	1	0
F. Lopez, 3b	1	0	1	0	Soriano, pr-2b	1	1	0	0
Piazza, c	2	0	0	0	Teixeira, 1b	3	1	1	2
Cabrera, lf	2	0	0	1	Konerko, 1b	1	0	0	0
Kent, 2b	1	0	0	0	Varitek, c	1	1	1	0
Castillo, 2b	3	1	1	0	I. Rodriguez, c	1	0	0	0
Eckstein, ss	2	0	0	0	Roberts, 2b	2	1	1	0
A.Jones, cf	1	2	1	2	Sheffield, ph-rf	1	0	0	0
					Podsednik, cf	0	0	0	0
Totals	**32**	**7**	**11**	**7**	**Totals**	**35**	**5**	**11**	**5**

National	0	0	0	0	0	0	2	1	2—**5**
American	0	1	2	2	0	2	0	0	x—**7**

LOB—National 8, American 4. **2B**—D. Lee, Alou, L. Gonzalez, Roberts, M. Young. **HR**—A.Jones., Tejada, Teixeira.

NATIONAL	ip	h	r	er	bb	so	AMERICAN	ip	h	r	er	bb	so
Carpenter	1	2	0	0	0	0	Buehrle (W)	2	3	0	0	0	3
Smoltz (L)	1	2	1	1	0	0	Colon	1	1	0	0	0	0
Oswalt	1	2	2	2	1	1	Santana	1	1	0	0	1	0
Hernandez	1	2	2	2	1	0	Clement	1	0	0	0	1	1
Clemens	1	0	0	0	0	0	Garland	1	0	0	0	2	0
Willis	1	2	2	2	1	0	Rogers	1	3	2	2	0	1
Lidge	1	0	0	0	0	3	Nathan	1	2	1	1	0	0
Peavy	⅔	1	0	0	0	1	Wickman	0	0	1	1	1	0
Cordero, C	⅓	0	0	0	0	1	Ryan	⅔	1	1	1	0	0
							Rivera (S)	⅓	0	0	0	0	1

Wickman pitched to 1 batter in the 9th.

WP—Garland.

Umpires: **HP**—Joe West; **1B**—Tim Welke; **2B**—Eric Cooper; **3B**—Mike DiMuro; **LF**—C.B. Bucknor; **RF**—Andy Fletcher.

T—2:41. **A**—41,617.

MAJOR LEAGUE DEBUTS, 2005

ARIZONA DIAMONDBACKS

Bulger, Jason	Aug. 26
Jackson, Conor	July 28
Medders, Brandon	June 20
Nippert, Dustin	Sept. 8

ATLANTA BRAVES

Boyer, Blaine	June 12
Davies, Kyle	May 25
Devine, Joey	Aug. 20
Francoeur, Jeff	July 7
James, Chuck	Sept. 2
Johnson, Kelly	May 29
Lerew, Anthony	Sept. 4
Marte, Andy	June 7
McBride, Macay	July 22
McCann, Brian	June 1
Orr, Pete	April 5
Pena, Brayan	May 23

BALTIMORE ORIOLES

Calzado, Napoleon	May 29
Castro, Bernie	Sept. 1
Fiorentino, Jeff	May 12
Freire, Alejandro	Aug. 9
Penn, Hayden	June 7
Ray, Chris	June 25
Reed, Keith	May 11
Whiteside, Eli	July 5
Young, Walter	Sept. 6

BOSTON RED SOX

Delcarmen, Manny	July 26
Hansen, Craig	Sept. 19
Machado, Alejandro	Sept. 2
Meredith, Cla	May 8
Papelbon, Jonathan	July 31
Ramirez, Hanley	Sept. 20
Shoppach, Kelly	May 28
Stern, Adam	July 7

CHICAGO CUBS

Cedeno, Ronny	April 23
Fontenot, Mike	April 13
Greenberg, Adam	July 9
Hill, Rich	June 15
Koronka, John	June 1
Murton, Matt	July 8
Soto, Geovany	Sept. 23
Theriot, Ryan	Sept. 13
Van Buren, Jermaine	Aug. 31

CHICAGO WHITE SOX

Anderson, Brian	Aug. 16
Iguchi, Tadahito	April 4
Jenks, Bobby	July 6
Lopez, Pedro	May 1
McCarthy, Brandon	May 22

CINCINNATI REDS

Bergolla, William	May 9
Booker, Chris	Sept. 5
Coffey, Todd	April 19
Denorfia, Chris	Sept. 7
Encarnacion, Edwin	June 24
Perez, Miguel	Sept. 7
Shackelford, Brian	June 29

CLEVELAND INDIANS

Garko, Ryan	Sept. 18
Gutierrez, Franklin	Aug. 31

COLORADO ROCKIES

Baker, Jeff	April 4
Carvajal, Marcos	April 6
Esposito, Mike	Sept. 21
Garabito, Eddy	May 27
Quintanilla, Omar	July 31
Shealy, Ryan	June 14
Speier, Ryan	April 4
Spilborghs, Ryan	July 16
Sullivan, Cory	April 4

DETROIT TIGERS

Giarratano, Tony	June 1
Hooper, Kevin	July 9
Verlander, Justin	July 4
Woodyard, Mark	Sept. 17

FLORIDA MARLINS

Andino, Robert	Sept. 4
Bazardo, Yorman	May 26
Dillon, Joe	May 18
Hermida, Jeremy	Aug. 31
Johnson, Josh	Sept. 10
Jorgensen, Ryan	Aug. 8
Messenger, Randy	June 22
Olsen, Scott	June 30
Resop, Chris	June 28
Vargas, Jason	July 14
Wilson, Josh	Sept. 7

HOUSTON ASTROS

Astacio, Ezequiel	May 3
Burns, Mike	May 13
Jimerson, Charlton	Sept. 14
Rodriguez, Wandy	May 23
Scott, Luke	April 5
Self, Todd	May 12

KANSAS CITY ROYALS

Ambres, Chip	July 20
Bayliss, Jonah	June 26
Burgos, Ambiorix	June 9
Costa, Shane	June 2
Demaria, Chris	Sept. 9
Howell, J.P.	June 11
Huber, Justin	June 21
Nunez, Leo	June 9
Sisco, Andrew	June 11
Stemle, Steve	June 9
Teahen, Mark	April 4

LOS ANGELES ANGELS

Mathis, Jeff	Aug. 12
Peralta, Joel	June 7
Prieto, Chris	May 14
Santana, Ervin	May 17
Saunders, Joe	Aug. 16
Woods, Jake	April 26

LOS ANGELES DODGERS

Aybar, Willy	Aug. 31
Broxton, Jonathan	July 29
Houlton, D.J.	April 9
Kuo, Hong-Chih	Sept. 2
Myrow, Brian	Sept. 6
Nakamura, Norihiro	April 10
Osoria, Franquelis	June 7
Repko, Jason	April 6
Robles, Oscar	May 10
Schmoll, Steve	April 6
Thompson, Derek	May 28

MILWAUKEE BREWERS

Cruz, Nelson	Sept. 17
Eveland, Dana	July 16
Fielder, Prince	June 13
Hardy, J.J.	April 4

MINNESOTA TWINS

Baker, Scott	May 7
Bowyer, Travis	Sept. 10
Gassner, Dave	April 16
Heintz, Chris	Sept. 10
Liriano, Francisco	Sept. 5
Rodriguez, Luis	May 21
Williams, Glenn	June 7

NEW YORK METS

Hamulack, Tim	Sept. 2
Hernandez, Anderson	Sept. 18
Jacobs, Mike	Aug. 21
Koo, Dae-Sung	April 4
Ring, Royce	April 29

NEW YORK YANKEES

Bean, Colter	April 26
Cabrera, Melky	July 7
Cano, Robinson	May 3
Henn, Sean	May 4
Reese, Kevin	June 26
Vento, Mike	Sept. 13
Wang, Chien-Ming	June 10

OAKLAND ATHLETICS

Bynum, Freddie	Aug. 30
Flores, Ron	June 17
Johnson, Dan	May 27
Street, Huston	May 20
Yabu, Keiichi	May 20

PHILADELPHIA PHILLIES

Brito, Eude	Aug. 21
Sandoval, Danny	July 17
Tejeda, Rob	May 10

PITTSBURGH PIRATES

Bullington, Bryan	Sept. 18
Capps, Matt	Sept. 16
Doumit, Ryan	June 5
Duffy, Chris	April 7
Duke, Zach	July 2
Eldred, Brad	July 22
Furmaniak, J.J.	Sept. 13
Gorzelanny, Tom	Sept. 20
Maholm, Paul	Aug. 30
McLouth, Nate	June 29
Paulino, Ronny	Sept. 25
Sadler, Ray	May 8

SAN DIEGO PADRES

Breslow, Craig	July 23
Hensley, Clay	July 20
Johnson, Ben	June 26
McAnulty, Paul	June 22
Oxspring, Chris	Sept. 2
Stauffer, Tim	May 11

SAN FRANCISCO GIANTS

Accardo, Jeremy	May 4
Cain, Matt	Aug. 29
Chavez, Angel	Aug. 30
Clark, Doug	Sept. 14
Munter, Scott	May 11
Ortmeier, Dan	Sept. 5
Shabala, Adam	June 16
Taschner, Jack	June 11

SEATTLE MARINERS

Betancourt, Yuniesky	July 28
Bubela, Jaime	Sept. 15
Campillo, Jorge	May 20
Choo, Shin-Soo	April 21
Harris, Jeff	Aug. 2
Hernandez, Felix	Aug. 4
Morse, Mike	May 31

ST. LOUIS CARDINALS

Duncan, Chris	Sept. 10
Gall, John	July 26
Johnson, Tyler	Sept. 6
Reyes, Anthony	Aug. 9
Rodriguez, John	July 18
Schumaker, Skip	June 8
Thompson, Brad	May 8
Wainwright, Adam	Sept. 11

TAMPA BAY DEVIL RAYS

Corcoran, Tim	June 14
Cortez, Fernando	July 5
Orvella, Chad	June 8

TEXAS RANGERS

Botts, Jason	Sept. 14
Feldman, Scott	Aug. 31
McDougall, Marshall	June 7
Rupe, Josh	Sept. 16
Volquez, Edison	Aug. 30
Wilson, C.J.	June 10

TORONTO BLUE JAYS

Griffin, John-Ford	Sept. 6
Hill, Aaron	May 20
Marcum, Shaun	Sept. 6
McGowan, Dustin	July 30

WASHINGTON NATIONALS

Bergmann, Jason	Aug. 28
Blanco, Tony	April 4
Godwin, Tyrell	May 27
Rasner, Darrell	Sept. 6
Short, Rick	June 10
Watson, Brandon	Aug. 9
Zimmerman, Ryan	Sept. 1

red light on the dugout camera."

Also enshrined were longtime Padres announcer Jerry Coleman, winner of the Ford Frick Award presented annually for major contributions to baseball broadcasting; and veteran sportswriter and broadcaster Peter Gammons, recipient of the J.G. Taylor Spink Award, presented annually for meritorious contributions to baseball writing.

For the second time in as many elections since it was reconfigured in 2001, the veterans committee did not elect anyone to join the Hall of Fame.

Manager Job Security Remains Low

The 2005 season saw its usual share of managerial changes, with eight of 30 skippers leaving their jobs either during the season or soon after its conclusion.

The first to go was the Royals' Tony Pena, who resigned on May 10, less than two years after winning the American League manager of the year award. The Royals were off to an 8-25 start on their way to a 56-106 season, their third with at least 100 losses in the last four years

"I've been thinking about it for the last three weeks," said Pena, who went 198-285 in parts of four seasons. "It made me sick. I wasn't eating well or sleeping well because I thought so much about the way we played. I don't think we've played to the top of our ability."

Pena was replaced by Indians bench coach Buddy Bell, who had previously managed the Tigers and Rockies.

Reds manager Dave Miley, who had signed a two-year contract extension the previous winter, was fired June 21 with his team's record a dismal 27-43. Bench coach Jerry Narron, who had previously managed the Rangers, was promoted to take Miley's place. Miley guided the Reds to a 125-164 mark in parts of three seasons. Narron won the job on a permanent basis after the season.

The Orioles were one of the biggest surprises in baseball in the first half of the season, leading the AL East for 62 consecutive days from April 23-June 23 before falling from 14 games over .500 to five games under in the span of six weeks. That fade, which culminated in an eight-game losing streak that dropped the Orioles to 51-56, cost manager Lee Mazzilli his job on Aug. 4, as he was replaced by bench coach Sam Perlozzo. Mazzilli had a 129-140 record in his two seasons with the Orioles. Perlozzo also got the permanent job after season.

The Pirates' Lloyd McClendon was spared the dubious distinction of being the first man in major league history to have five straight losing seasons with the same team in his first manager's job, when he was fired Sept. 6. The Pirates were 55-81 at the time and on their way to a 13th consecutive losing season, three short of the major league record of 16 by the Phillies from 1933-48.

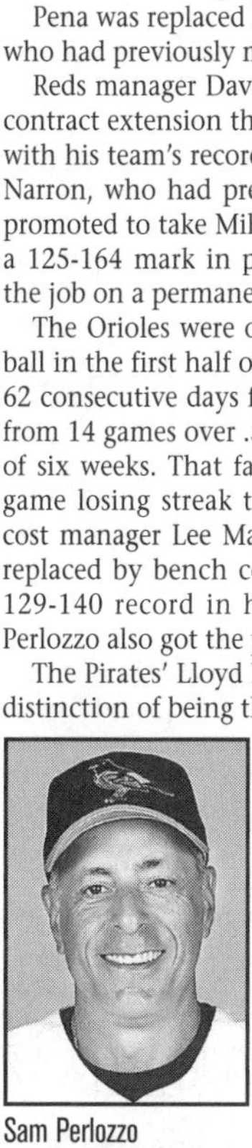

Sam Perlozzo

McClendon's final record was 336-446, and he was replaced by Jim Tracy, who left the Dodgers at the end of the season. Tracy, who exercised an escape clause on the final year of his contract with the Dodgers, was one of four managers who were either fired or left their jobs once the season ended.

GEORGE GOJKOVICH

Moving from Los Angeles to Pittsburgh
Jim Tracy says he looks forward to the challenge

Tracy compiled a 427-383 record in his five seasons with the Dodgers, but they slipped to 71-91 during an injury-plagued 2005 after winning the National League West the previous season. Tracy had no qualms about moving from a large-market club to one in a small market.

"Challenges are something that I like very, very much," Tracy said. "I like hearing people say or maybe think that this is a situation you don't have a chance to succeed in. I'm very challenged by that."

Lou Piniella reached a settlement with the Devil Rays to buy out the final year of his contract after going 200-285 in three seasons, including 67-95 in 2005, and becoming frustrated by the team's reluctance to spend money on players. The Devil Rays had the lowest payroll in the major leagues in 2005.

New York investor Stuart Sternberg took control of the Devil Rays from Vince Naimoli the day after the season ended and did not try to retain Piniella, who joined the Yankees' Joe Torre in 2005 as the two men to have 1,500 wins as a manager and 1,500 hits as a player.

"We've got a new ownership group taking over. They need to bring in their own manager that they can grow with," Piniella said.

Marlins manager Jack McKeon stepped down on the final day of the season, deciding to take on an adviser's role with the club. McKeon replaced Jeff Torborg early in the 2003 season and led the Marlins to the World Series title that year.

McKeon had a 241-197 record in his three seasons and notched his 1,000th career win on Sept. 3 over the Mets. However, the Marlins were 83-79 in '05, after many felt they could unseat the Braves as NL East champions.

"The last couple of years I haven't had as much fun as I'd like," McKeon said. "Since I'm the leader, I'll take full responsibility for the poor year we had."

Yankees bench coach Joe Girardi was hired as McKeon's successor.

The Tigers fired Alan Trammell the day after the season ended after going 71-91 and losing 29 of their final 39 games, making the team 186-300 in Trammell's three-year tenure.

"I'm a big boy," Trammell said. "I've been through enough that I understand how things are."

Former Pirates, Marlins and Rockies manager Jim Leyland was hired to replace Trammell. Leyland hadn't managed since he left the Rockies following the 1999 season, spending the past six years as a Cardinals scout.

The strangest managerial move was made by the Athletics' Ken Macha, whose contract expired at the end of the season.

Macha and the A's couldn't reach an agreement on a new contact three days after the season ended, and general manager Billy Beane began searching for a replacement. Nine days later, after interviewing for the Pirates job that wound up going to Tracy, Macha called Beane and they hammered out a three-year deal.

Executives On The Move

Changes weren't confined to the dugout as a number of front-office types decided to make moves in 2005.

The biggest in-season change came when Sandy Alderson left his post as Major League Baseball's executive vice president for baseball operations after nearly seven years to become president of the Padres.

Alderson had built the Athletics into a consistent winner as general manager then club president in the late 1980s and early 1990s and said he missed that challenge during his time in the MLB offices.

"I missed the rhythm of working for a franchise," Alderson said.

MLB made a pair of moves to fill Alderson's void. Jimmie Lee Solomon was promoted to executive VP of baseball operations from senior VP of baseball operations, and Diamondbacks GM Joe Garagiola Jr. was hired to take Solomon's old job.

"Major League Baseball is fortunate to have a man of Jimmie Lee's experience, intellect and dedication already on board to handle such a complex and important position," Bud Selig said. "Over the years, he has demonstrated considerable skill in working through the labyrinth of our minor league system. I have great confidence that he will be an enormous success in this key position."

Solomon is responsible for on-field discipline, security and facility management. Garagiola, who had been the Diamondbacks' GM since they joined the National League as an expansion franchise is 1998, has duties that include overseeing major league, minor league and international operations, the Arizona Fall League and the Major League Scouting Bureau.

"To have this opportunity, I hope to impact the game at a level that's beyond just the narrow focus of one of 30 teams is just such a wonderful opportunity for me," Garagiola said. "Having grown up in it, having seen it from a lot of different sides, I hope I can bring all of that experience to bear on this new job."

While Garagiola left his GM job on his own accord, the Orioles' Jim Beattie, the Phillies' Ed Wade, the Devil Rays' Chuck LaMar and the Dodgers' Paul DePodesta were all forced out at the end of the season.

Ed Wade

Beattie and Mike Flanagan had just concluded their third season as a GM tandem, when Orioles owner Peter Angelos decided to push Beattie out and have Flanagan handle the GM role in a more traditional manner.

Wade spent nine seasons as the Phillies' GM without seeing his team earn a playoff berth. He was replaced by former Blue Jays, Orioles and Mariners GM Pat Gillick.

LaMar had been the Devil Rays' GM since they joined the American League as an expansion franchise in 1998 and they never won more than 70 games in a season under his leadership. His firing was one of the first acts of new team president Stuart Sternberg when he took over the franchise from Vince Naimoli the day after the 2005 season ended.

DePodesta had been Dodgers GM for just 20 months when apparent disagreements with owner Frank McCourt over the direction of the team led to his dismissal—a month after the Dodgers parted ways with Tracy.

Texas GM John Hart decided to step down at the end of his fourth season on the job, during which the Rangers did not qualify for the playoffs, to become an adviser for the team.

Jon Daniels was promoted from assistant GM to replace Hart, becoming the youngest GM in baseball history at 28 years and 41 days, 10 months younger than when Theo Epstein became the Red Sox' GM on Nov. 25, 2002.

Epstein then pulled the biggest surprise of all, stepping down as Red Sox GM following a dispute that started with him asking for more money. It looked like the team and Epstein had reached an agreement on a new contract before he abruptly quit Oct. 31, prompting the usual media swirl in Boston and furor in Red Sox Nation about how it all came apart.

"I gave my entire heart and soul to the organization," Epstein said. "During the process leading up to today's decision, I came to the conclusion that I can no longer do so. In the end, my choice is the right one not only for me but for the Red Sox."

Three Teams Change Hands

Even with the Nationals ownership situation still unresolved, control of three other teams changed hands during the 2005 season.

Los Angeles developer Mark

MANAGERIAL CHANGES

Eight big league teams made managerial changes during or after the 2005 season—compared with six in 2004. Here are the changes and new managers for 2006:

Team	Original Manager	In-Season Change	Postseason Change
Baltimore	Lee Mazzilli	Sam Perlozzo	None
Cincinnati	Dave Miley	Jerry Narron	None
Detroit	Alan Trammell	—	Jim Leyland
Florida	Jack McKeon	—	Joe Girardi
Kansas City	Tony Pena	Buddy Bell	None
Los Angeles (NL)	Jim Tracy	—	
Pittsburgh	Lloyd McClendon	—	Jim Tracy
Tampa Bay	Lou Piniella	—	Joe Maddon

FRONT OFFICE CHANGES

Seven big league teams changed general managers after the 2005 season. Here are the changes and new GMs for 2006:

Team	Out	In
Arizona	Joe Garagiola Jr.	Josh Byrnes
Baltimore	Jim Beattie	Mike Flanagan
Boston	Theo Epstein	
Los Angeles (NL)	Paul DePodesta	Ned Colletti
Philadelphia	Ed Wade	Pat Gillick
Tampa Bay	Chuck LaMar	Gerry Hunsicker
Texas	John Hart	Jon Daniels

Attanasio bought the Brewers for $223 million from Selig's family.

The Brewers then broke their streak of 12 consecutive losing seasons by finishing 81-81. The Brewers had been tied with the Pirates, who went 67-95, for the longest active stretch of sub-.500 seasons in major American professional sports.

Another Los Angeles developer, Lewis Wolff, bought the Athletics from Steve Schott and Ken Hofmann for $180 million. Wolff had been working as the team's vice president for venue development.

Reggie Jackson, who began his Hall of Fame career with the A's, wanted to buy the club and was frustrated that his group's bid was not accepted despite being $25 million higher than Wolff's.

New York investor Stuart Sternberg took control of the Devil Rays from founding owner Vince Naimoli.

Naimoli led a determined campaign that wound up with Tampa Bay being awarded an expansion franchise in 1995, but his stewardship of the franchise went downhill from there. His stint as managing general partner was marred by numerous public-relations blunders and he became the man most associated with the Devil Rays' futility on and off the field.

Sternberg headed a group that acquired about 50 percent of the Devil Rays in May 2004. He originally had an agreement to take control from Naimoli in January 2007 but was willing to pay more to get Naimoli to step aside early.

Rogers Roasted

Hart had to deal with an ugly situation during his final season as GM as veteran Rangers pitcher Kenny Rogers got into an altercation with two television cameramen on June 29 before a game against the Angels at Ameriquest Field in Arlington.

Rogers had been upset by media reports that suggested he could have continued pitching after punching a water color in frustration following a bad start June 22 and breaking a bone in his right (non-pitching hand). He then became upset because he was being filmed while walking through the dugout and onto the field for a pregame stretch.

Rogers first shoved cameraman David Mammel, saying "I told you to get those cameras out of my face."

Rogers then approached another cameraman, Larry Rodriguez, and took the camera from him before throwing it to the ground and kicking it. Rodriguez was taken from the ballpark on a stretcher and went to a hospital, where he was treated and released.

Rogers yelled at two other cameramen, threatening to break their cameras as they captured footage of him being escorted off the field and back into the clubhouse by Rangers catcher Rod Barajas.

Rodriguez was bewildered by the incident.

"There's no question he was upset," Rodriguez said. "I don't know if we were the stem of the problem or what. I don't think we did anything wrong."

Rogers was suspended for 20 games, the equivalent of four starts, and fined $50,000. He appealed the suspension, which was trimmed from 20 games to 13 by an arbitrator Shyam Das. Das also ruled that Rogers' fine be converted into a charitable contribution.

Rodriguez sued Rogers and the Rangers at the end of the season, alleging that Rogers injured him in an unprovoked attack. The same day, the Rangers announced they would not attempt to re-sign Rogers as a free agent.

Rogers rarely talked to the media throughout the season. When he did, he never gave an explanation for his actions against the cameramen.

World's Best Will Finally Meet

Major League Baseball also used the all-star festivities to unveil plans for the World Baseball Classic, a World Cup-style tournament that will include 16 national teams in March 2006, with the semifinals and finals at Petco Park in San Diego.

"I don't think any of us truly understand how big this is going to be," Selig said. "I don't know what it's going to look like two decade from now but I really believe it is going to be something huge.

"We're going to take a great sport and put it on its biggest stage yet. It's going to be something that is fantastic for both the fans and the players. The possibilities are unlimited. It's really stunning. I can't wait for it."

The competition is scheduled to begin March 3 with pool play in the United States, Puerto Rico and Japan. Japan will be the host of a group that will include China, South Korea and Taiwan. Games in Puerto Rico will also feature Cuba, the Netherlands and Panama.

The U.S. will be one host team, playing against Canada, Mexico and South Africa, and a second group featuring Australia, the Dominican Republic, Italy and Venezuela will also play in the U.S.

The two top finishers in each pool will advance to the second round, which will consist of more pool play. The top four finishers from the second round will participate in a single-elimination tournament to determine the champion, with the semifinals set for March 18 and the final for March 20 in San Diego.

The plans were announced just days after baseball was dropped from the Olympics. The International Olympic Committee voted 54-50 against keeping baseball, with 53 votes in favor needed to remain. The move takes effect for the 2012 London Olympics.

IOC members cited Major League Baseball's unwillingness to let its players take part in the Olympics and the sport's doping problems as major reasons for the decision to remove it from the games. MLB was leading an effort to get baseball reinstated by 2016, however.

In the meantime, the March tournament seemed to have current major leaguers excited.

I would love to play for my country," said Cardinals first baseman Albert Pujols, who was born and raised in the Dominican Republic before attending high school and junior college in Kansas. "Why wouldn't you like to play? It helps the sport. It's going to be a great thing."

2005 AMERICAN LEAGUE STATISTICS

CLUB BATTING

	AVG	G	AB	R	H	2B	2B	HR	BB	SO	SB
Boston	.281	162	5626	910	1579	339	21	199	653	1044	45
New York	.276	162	5624	886	1552	259	16	229	637	989	84
Tampa Bay	.274	162	5552	750	1519	289	40	157	412	990	151
Detroit	.272	162	5602	723	1521	283	45	168	384	1038	66
Cleveland	.271	162	5609	790	1522	337	30	207	503	1093	62
Los Angeles	.270	162	5617	760	1517	278	30	147	446	847	161
Baltimore	.269	162	5551	729	1492	296	27	189	447	902	83
Texas	.267	162	5716	865	1528	311	29	260	495	1112	67
Toronto	.265	162	5581	775	1480	307	39	136	486	955	72
Kansas City	.263	162	5496	700	1443	289	34	126	424	1008	53
Oakland	.262	162	5627	772	1476	310	20	155	537	819	31
Chicago	.262	162	5529	741	1450	253	23	200	435	1002	137
Minnesota	.259	162	5564	688	1441	269	32	134	485	978	102
Seattle	.256	162	5507	699	1408	289	34	130	466	986	102

CLUB PITCHING

	ERA	G	CG	SHO	SV	IP	H	R	ER	BB	SO
Cleveland	3.606	162	6	10	51	1453	1363	642	582	413	1050
Chicago	3.611	162	9	10	54	1476	1392	645	592	459	1040
Los Angeles	3.68	162	7	11	54	1464	1419	643	598	443	1126
Oakland	3.69	162	9	12	38	1450	1315	658	594	504	1075
Minnesota	3.71	162	9	8	44	1464	1458	662	604	348	965
Toronto	4.06	162	9	8	35	1447	1475	705	653	444	958
Seattle	4.49	162	6	7	39	1428	1483	751	712	496	892
Detroit	4.51	162	7	2	37	1436	1504	787	719	461	907
New York	4.52	162	8	14	46	1431	1495	789	718	463	985
Baltimore	4.56	162	2	9	38	1428	1458	800	724	580	1052
Boston	4.74	162	6	8	38	1429	1550	805	752	440	959
Texas	4.96	162	2	6	46	1440	1589	858	794	522	932
Tampa Bay	5.39	162	1	4	43	1422	1570	936	851	615	949
Kansas City	5.49	162	4	4	25	1413	1640	935	862	580	924

CLUB FIELDING

	PCT	PO	A	E	DP
Oakland	.986	4351	1649	88	166
Seattle	.986	4283	1575	86	144
Los Angeles	.985	4381	1521	87	139
Toronto	.985	4341	1757	95	154
Chicago	.985	4427	1670	94	166
Minnesota	.984	4393	1764	102	171
New York	.984	4292	1688	95	151
Cleveland	.983	4358	1646	106	156
Baltimore	.982	4283	1679	107	154
Boston	.982	4287	1623	109	135
Detroit	.982	4307	1791	110	171
Texas	.982	4320	1678	108	149
Kansas City	.979	4237	1643	125	163
Tampa Bay	.979	4265	1446	124	139

INDIVIDUAL BATTING LEADERS

(Minimum 502 Plate Appearances)

	AVG	G	AB	R	H	2B	3B	HR	RBI	BB	SO	SB
Young, Michael, Texas	.331	159	668	114	221	40	5	24	91	58	91	5
Rodriguez, Alex, New York	.321	162	605	124	194	29	1	48	130	91	139	21
Guerrero, Vladimir, Los Angeles	.317	141	520	95	165	29	2	32	108	61	48	13
Damon, Johnny, Boston	.316	148	624	117	197	35	6	10	75	53	69	18
Roberts, Brian, Baltimore	.314	143	561	92	176	45	7	18	73	67	83	27
Jeter, Derek, New York	.309	159	654	122	202	25	5	19	70	77	117	14
Hafner, Travis, Cleveland	.305	137	486	94	148	42	0	33	108	79	123	0
Martinez, Victor, Cleveland	.305	147	547	73	167	33	0	20	80	63	78	0
Matsui, Hideki, New York	.305	162	629	108	192	45	3	23	116	63	78	2
Tejada, Miguel, Baltimore	.304	162	654	89	199	50	5	26	98	40	83	5

INDIVIDUAL PITCHING LEADERS

(Minimum 162 Innings)

	W	L	ERA	G	GS	CG	SV	IP	H	R	ER	BB	SO
Millwood, Kevin, Cleveland	9	11	2.86	30	30	1	0	192	182	72	61	52	146
Santana, Johan, Minnesota	16	7	2.87	33	33	3	0	232	180	77	74	45	238
Buehrle, Mark, Chicago	16	8	3.12	33	33	3	0	237	240	99	82	40	149
Washburn, Jarrod, Los Angeles	8	8	3.20	29	29	1	0	177	184	66	63	51	94
Lackey, John, Los Angeles	14	5	3.44	33	33	1	0	209	208	85	80	71	199
Silva, Carlos, Minnesota	9	8	3.44	27	27	2	0	188	212	83	72	9	71
Rogers, Kenny, Texas	14	8	3.46	30	30	1	0	195	205	86	75	53	87
Colon, Bartolo, Los Angeles	21	8	3.48	33	33	2	0	223	215	93	86	43	157
Garland, Jon, Chicago	18	10	3.50	32	32	3	0	221	212	93	86	47	115
Blanton, Joe, Oakland	12	12	3.53	33	33	2	0	201	178	86	79	67	116

AWARD WINNERS

Selected by Baseball Writers Association of America

MOST VALUABLE PLAYER

Player, Team	1st	2nd	3rd	Total
Alex Rodriguez, New York	16	11	1	331
David Ortiz, Boston	11	17	0	307
Vladimir Guerrero, L.A.	1	0	9	196
Manny Ramirez, Boston	0	0	9	156
Travis Hafner, Cleveland	0	0	5	151
Paul Konerko, Chicago	0	0	2	128
Mark Teixeira, Texas	0	0	1	106
Gary Sheffield, New York	0	0	0	84
Mariano Rivera, New York	0	0	1	59
Derek Jeter, New York	0	0	0	23
Michael Young, Texas	0	0	0	20
Scott Podsednik, Chicago	0	0	0	15
Johnny Damon, Boston	0	0	0	12
Hideki Matsui, New York	0	0	0	8
Richie Sexson, Seattle	0	0	0	7
Miguel Tejada, Baltimore	0	0	0	7
Chone Figgins, Los Angeles	0	0	0	6
Victor Martinez, Cleveland	0	0	0	5
Jason Giambi, New York	0	0	0	5
Brian Roberts, Baltimore	0	0	0	5
Jason Varitek, Boston	0	0	0	4
Eric Chavez, Oakland	0	0	0	4
Huston Street, Oakland	0	0	0	3

CY YOUNG AWARD

Player, Team	1st	2nd	3rd	Total
Bartolo Colon, Los Angeles	17	11	0	118
Mariano Rivera, New York	8	7	7	68
Johan Santana, Minnesota	3	8	12	51
Cliff Lee, Cleveland	0	2	2	8
Mark Buehrle, Chicago	0	0	5	5
Jon Garland, Chicago	0	0	1	1
Kevin Millwood, Cleveland	0	0	1	0

ROOKIE OF THE YEAR

Player, Team	1st	2nd	3rd	Total
Huston Street, Oakland	15	6	4	97
Robinson Cano, New York	4	10	7	57
Johnny Gomes, Tampa Bay	2	8	5	39
Tadahito Iguchi, Chicago	5	1	2	30
Gustavo Chacin, Toronto	2	0	4	14
Nick Swisher, Oakland	0	2	0	6
Joe Blanton, Oakland	0	1	3	6
Jesse Crain, Minnesota	0	0	2	2
Scott Kazmir, Tampa Bay	0	0	1	1

MANAGER OF THE YEAR

Manager, Team	1st	2nd	3rd	Total
Ozzie Guillen, Chicago	17	5	5	105
Eric Wedge, Cleveland	6	11	8	71
Joe Torre, New York	4	7	2	43
Ken Macha, Oakland	1	3	7	21
Mike Scioscia, Los Angeles	0	1	4	7
Terry Francona, Boston	0	1	1	4
John Gibbons, Toronto	0	0	1	1

NOTE: MVP balloting based on 14 points for first-place vote, nine for second, eight for third, etc. Cy Young Award, Rookie of the Year and Manager of the Year balloting based on five points for first-place votes, three for second and one for third.

GOLD GLOVE AWARDS

Selected by AL managers

C—Jason Varitek, Boston. **1B**—Mark Teixeira, Texas. **2B**—Orlando Hudson, Toronoto. **3B**—Eric Chavez, Oakland. **SS**—Derek Jeter, New York. **OF**—Torii Hunter, Minnesota; Ichiro Suzuki, Seattle; Vernon Wells, Toronto. **P**—Kenny Rogers, Texas.

SILVER SLUGGER AWARDS

Selected by AL managers, coaches

C—Jason Varitek, Boston. **1B**—Mark Teixeira, Texas. **2B**—Alfonso Soriano, Texas. **3B**—Alex Rodriguez, New York. **SS**—Miguel Tejada, Baltimore. **OF**—Vladimir Guerrero, Anaheim; Manny Ramirez, Boston; Gary Sheffield, New York. **DH**—David Ortiz, Boston.

AMERICAN LEAGUE
DEPARTMENT LEADERS

BATTING

GAMES

Raul Ibanez, Mariners	162
Hideki Matsui, Yankees	162
Alex Rodriguez, Yankees	162
Ichiro Suzuki, Mariners	162
Mark Teixeira, Rangers	162
Miguel Tejada, Orioles	162

AT-BATS

Ichiro Suzuki, Mariners	679
Michael Young, Rangers	668
Derek Jeter, Yankees	654
Miguel Tejada, Orioles	654
Hank Blalock, Rangers	647

RUNS

Alex Rodriguez, Yankees	124
Derek Jeter, Yankees	122
David Ortiz, Red Sox	119
Johnny Damon, Red Sox	117
Michael Young, Rangers	114

HITS

Michael Young, Rangers	221
Ichiro Suzuki, Mariners	206
Derek Jeter, Yankees	202
Miguel Tejada, Orioles	199
Johnny Damon, Red Sox	197

TOTAL BASES

Mark Teixeira, Rangers	370
Alex Rodriguez, Yankees	369
David Ortiz, Red Sox	363
Michael Young, Rangers	343
Miguel Tejada, Orioles	337

SINGLES

Ichiro Suzuki, Mariners	158
Derek Jeter, Yankees	153
Michael Young, Rangers	152
Johnny Damon, Red Sox	146
Chone Figgins, Angels	143

DOUBLES

Miguel Tejada, Orioles	50
Hideki Matsui, Yankees	45
Brian Roberts, Orioles	45
Alfonso Soriano, Rangers	43
Coco Crisp, Indians	42
Travis Hafner, Indians	42

TRIPLES

Carl Crawford, Devil Rays	15
Ichiro Suzuki, Mariners	12
Grady Sizemore, Indians	11
Chone Figgins, Angels	10
Brandon Inge, Tigers	9

HOME RUNS

Alex Rodriguez, Yankees	48
David Ortiz, Red Sox	47
Manny Ramirez, Red Sox	45
Mark Teixeira, Rangers	43
Paul Konerko, White Sox	40

HOME RUN RATIO
(At-bats per home run)

Manny Ramirez, Red Sox	12.31
Alex Rodriguez, Yankees	12.60
David Ortiz, Red Sox	12.79
Jason Giambi, Yankees	13.03
Richie Sexson, Mariners	14.31

RUNS BATTED IN

David Ortiz, Red Sox	148
Manny Ramirez, Red Sox	144
Mark Teixeira, Rangers	144
Alex Rodriguez, Yankees	130
Gary Sheffield, Yankees	123

LARRY GOREN

Michael Young: 221 hits

SACRIFICE BUNTS

Coco Crisp, Indians	13
Nook Logan, Tigers	12
Tadahito Iguchi, White Sox	11
Juan Uribe, White Sox	11
Angel Berroa, Royals	10
Nick Green, Devil Rays	10

SACRIFICE FLIES

Craig Monroe, Tigers	12
Carl Everett, White Sox	10
Juan Uribe, White Sox	10
Eric Chavez, Athletics	9
Johnny Damon, Red Sox	9
David Ortiz, Red Sox	9

HIT BY PITCHES

Shea Hillenbrand, Blue Jays	22
Aaron Rowand, White Sox	21
Jason Kendall, Athletics	20
Jason Giambi, Yankees	19
Lew Ford, Twins	16
Reed Johnson, Blue Jays	16
Alex Rodriguez, Yankees	16

WALKS

Jason Giambi, Yankees	108
David Ortiz, Red Sox	102
Paul Konerko, White Sox	81
Alex Rodriguez, Yankees	91
Richie Sexson, Mariners	89

INTENTIONAL WALKS

Vladimir Guerrero, Angels	26
Ichiro Suzuki, Mariners	23
Aubrey Huff, Devil Rays	13
Jacque Jones, Twins	12
Joe Mauer, Twins	12

STOLEN BASES

Chone Figgins, Angels	62
Scott Podsednik, White Sox	59
Carl Crawford, Devil Rays	46
Julio Lugo, Devil Rays	39
Ichiro Suzuki, Mariners	33

CAUGHT STEALING

Scott Podsednik, White Sox	23
Chone Figgins, Angels	17
Julio Lugo, Devil Rays	11
Jeremy Reed, Mariners	11
Brian Roberts, Orioles	10
Grady Sizemore, Indians	10

STRIKEOUTS

Richie Sexson, Mariners	167
Brandon Inge, Tigers	140
Alex Rodriguez, Yankees	139
Hank Blalock, Rangers	132
Grady Sizemore, Indians	132

TOUGHEST TO STRIKE OUT
(At-bats per strikeout)

Jason Kendall, Athletics	15.41
Mark Kotsay, Athletics	11.41
Orlando Cabrera, Angels	10.80
Vladimir Guerrero, Angels	10.77
Ichiro Suzuki, Mariners	10.29

GROUNDED INTO DOUBLE PLAYS

Jason Kendall, Athletics	26
Miguel Tejada, Orioles	26
Jorge Cantu, Devil Rays	24
Scott Hatteberg, Athletics	22
Bill Mueller, Red Sox	22

HITTING STREAKS

Johnny Damon, Red Sox	29
Michael Young, Rangers	25
Darin Erstad, Angels	21
Magglio Ordonez, Tigers	20
Brian Roberts, Orioles	20
Rondell White, Tigers	20

MULTIPLE-HIT GAMES

Michael Young, Rangers	66
Derek Jeter, Yankees	62
Ichiro Suzuki, Mariners	60
Mark Teixeira, Rangers	59
Carl Crawford, Devil Rays	57

ON-BASE PERCENTAGE

Jason Giambi, Yankees	.440
Alex Rodriguez, Yankees	.421
Travis Hafner, Indians	.408
David Ortiz, Red Sox	.397
Vladimir Guerrero, Angels	.393

SLUGGING PERCENTAGE

Alex Rodriguez, Yankees	.610
David Ortiz, Red Sox	.604
Travis Hafner, Indians	.595
Manny Ramirez, Red Sox	.594
Mark Teixeira, Rangers	.575

PITCHING

WINS

Bartolo Colon, Angels	21
Jon Garland, White Sox	18
Cliff Lee, Indians	18
Randy Johnson, Yankees	17
Mark Buehrle, White Sox	16
Johan Santana, Twins	16

ANDREW WOOLLEY

Chone Figgins: 62 stolen bases

Tim Wakefield, Red Sox ... 16

LOSSES
Zack Greinke, Royals ... 17
Jose Lima, Royals ... 16
Nate Robertson, Tigers ... 16
Ryan Franklin, Mariners ... 15
Jake Westbrook, Indians ... 15

WINNING PERCENTAGE
Cliff Lee, Indians ... .783
John Lackey, Angels ... .737
Bartolo Colon, Angels ... .724
Johan Santana, Twins ... .696
Matt Clement, Red Sox ... .684

GAMES
Mike Timlin, Red Sox ... 81
Scott Schoeneweis, Blue Jays ... 80
Tom Gordon, Yankees ... 79
Bob Howry, Indians ... 79
Scot Shields, Angels ... 78

GAMES STARTED
Rodrigo Lopez, Orioles ... 35
Barry Zito, Athletics ... 35
Gustavo Chacin, Blue Jays ... 34
Danny Haren, Athletics ... 34
Randy Johnson, Yankees ... 34
Mike Maroth, Tigers ... 34
Jake Westbrook, Indians ... 34

COMPLETE GAMES
Roy Halladay, Blue Jays ... 5
Jeremy Bonderman, Tigers ... 4
Randy Johnson, Yankees ... 4
Mark Buehrle, White Sox ... 3
Jon Garland, White Sox ... 3
Danny Haren, Athletics ... 3
Brad Radke, Twins ... 3
Johan Santana, Twins ... 3
Tim Wakefield, Red Sox ... 3

SHUTOUTS
Jon Garland, White Sox ... 3
Roy Halladay, Blue Jays ... 2
Mike Mussina, Yankees ... 2
Johan Santana, Twins ... 2
14 tied at ... 1

GAMES FINISHED
Mariano Rivera, Yankees ... 67
Danys Baez, Devil Rays ... 64
Miguel Batista, Blue Jays ... 62
B.J. Ryan, Orioles ... 61
Francisco Cordero, Rangers ... 60

SAVES
Francisco Rodriguez, Angels ... 45
Bob Wickman, Indians ... 45
Joe Nathan, Twins ... 43
Mariano Rivera, Yankees ... 43
Danys Baez, Devil Rays ... 41

INNINGS
Mark Buehrle, White Sox ... 237
Johan Santana, Twins ... 232
Barry Zito, Athletics ... 228
Freddy Garcia, White Sox ... 228
Randy Johnson, Yankees ... 226

HITS ALLOWED
Mark Buehrle, White Sox ... 240
Josh Towers, Blue Jays ... 237
Mike Maroth, Tigers ... 235
Zack Greinke, Royals ... 233
Jason Johnson, Tigers ... 233

RUNS ALLOWED
Jose Lima, Royals ... 140
Mark Hendrickson, Devil Rays ... 126
Rodrigo Lopez, Orioles ... 126
Zack Greinke, Royals ... 125
Mike Maroth, Tigers ... 123

HOME RUNS ALLOWED
Tim Wakefield, Red Sox ... 35
Bruce Chen, Orioles ... 33
Brad Radke, Twins ... 33
Scott Elarton, Indians ... 32
Randy Johnson, Yankees ... 32

WALKS
Scott Kazmir, Devil Rays ... 100
Barry Zito, Athletics ... 89
Daniel Cabrera, Orioles ... 87
Jose Contreras, White Sox ... 75
Gil Meche, Mariners ... 72

FEWEST WALKS PER NINE INNINGS
Carlos Silva, Twins ... 0.33
Brad Radke, Twins ... 0.99
David Wells, Red Sox ... 1.03
Josh Towers, Blue Jays ... 1.16
Paul Byrd, Angels ... 1.19

HIT BATSMEN
Casey Fossum, Devil Rays ... 18
Matt Clement, Red Sox ... 16
Bronson Arroyo, Red Sox ... 14
Dave Bush, Blue Jays ... 13
Zack Greinke, Royals ... 13
Barry Zito, Athletics ... 13

STRIKEOUTS
Johan Santana, Twins ... 238
Randy Johnson, Yankees ... 211
John Lackey, Angels ... 199
Scott Kazmir, Devil Rays ... 174
Barry Zito, Athletics ... 171

STRIKEOUTS PER NINE INNINGS
Johan Santana, Twins ... 9.25
John Lackey, Angels ... 8.57
Randy Johnson, Yankees ... 8.42
Scott Kazmir, Devil Rays ... 8.42
Chris Young, Rangers ... 7.49

PICKOFFS
Mike Maroth, Tigers ... 11
Mark Buehrle, White Sox ... 5
Gustavo Chacin, Blue Jays ... 5
Mark Hendrickson, Devil Rays ... 5
Bruce Chen, Orioles ... 4
Randy Johnson, Yankees ... 4
Jamie Moyer, Mariners ... 4
David Wells, Red Sox ... 4

WILD PITCHES
Jose Contreras, White Sox ... 20
Freddy Garcia, White Sox ... 20
John Lackey, Angels ... 18
Jason Johnson, Tigers ... 17
Matt Clement, Red Sox ... 13

BALKS
D.J. Carrasco, Royals ... 3
Steve Kline, Orioles ... 3
Nine tied at ... 2

OPPONENT BATTING AVERAGE
Johan Santana, Twins ... .210
Barry Zito, Athletics ... .221
Jose Contreras, White Sox ... .232
Joe Blanton, Athletics ... .236
Randy Johnson, Yankees ... .243

BILL NICHOLS

Jon Garland: 3 shutouts

MICHAEL WALBY

Mike Maroth: 11 pickoffs

FIELDING

PITCHER
PCT 12 tied at ... 1.000
PO Jake Westbrook, Indians ... 31
A Jake Westbrook, Indians ... 49
E Jeremy Bonderman, Tigers ... 5
TC Jake Westbrook, Indians ... 82
DP Kenny Rogers, Rangers ... 7

CATCHER
PCT A.J. Pierzynski, White Sox ... .999
PO Jason Kendall, Athletics ... 986
A Jorge Posada, Yankees ... 76
E Rod Barajas, Rangers ... 9
Toby Hall, Devil Rays ... 9
TC Jason Kendall, Athletics ... 1044
DP A.J. Pierzynski, White Sox ... 8
PB Bengie Molina, Angels ... 10

FIRST BASE
PCT Mark Teixeira, Rangers ... .998
PO Mark Teixeira, Rangers ... 1377
A Richie Sexson, Mariners ... 120
E Ben Broussard, Indians ... 9
TC Mark Teixeira, Rangers ... 1481
DP Paul Konerko, White Sox ... 135

SECOND BASE
PCT Orlando Hudson, Blue Jays ... .991
Adam Kennedy, Angels ... .991
PO Orlando Hudson, Blue Jays ... 302
A Alfonso Soriano, Rangers ... 448
E Alfonso Soriano, Rangers ... 21
TC Alfonso Soriano, Rangers ... 753
DP Alfonso Soriano, Rangers ... 101

THIRD BASE
PCT Hank Blalock, Rangers ... .973
PO Adrian Beltre, Mariners ... 140
A Brandon Inge, Tigers ... 378
E Brandon Inge, Tigers ... 23
TC Brandon Inge, Tigers ... 530
DP Brandon Inge, Tigers ... 42

SHORTSTOP
PCT Orlando Cabrera, Angels ... .988
PO Julio Lugo, Devil Rays ... 310
A Miguel Tejada, Orioles ... 479
E Edgar Renteria, Red Sox ... 30
TC Julio Lugo, Devil Rays ... 758
DP Angel Berroa, Royals ... 108

OUTFIELD
PCT Frank Catalanotto, Blue Jays ... 1.000
Jay Payton, Red Sox/Athletics ... 1.000
Vernon Wells, Blue Jays ... 1.000
PO Johnny Damon, Red Sox ... 394
A Manny Ramirez, Red Sox ... 17
E Emil Brown, Royals ... 12
TC Johnny Damon, Red Sox ... 405
DP Five tied at ... 4

2005 NATIONAL LEAGUE STATISTICS

CLUB BATTING

	AVG	G	AB	R	H	2B	2B	HR	BB	SO	SB
Florida	.272	162	5502	717	1499	306	32	128	512	918	96
Chicago	.270	162	5584	703	1506	323	23	194	419	920	65
St. Louis	.270	162	5538	805	1494	287	26	170	534	947	83
Philadelphia	.270	162	5542	807	1494	282	35	167	639	1083	116
Colorado	.267	162	5542	740	1477	280	34	150	509	1103	65
Atlanta	.265	162	5486	769	1453	308	37	184	534	1084	92
Cincinnati	.261	163	5565	820	1453	335	15	222	611	1303	72
San Francisco	.261	162	5462	649	1427	299	26	128	431	901	71
Pittsburgh	.259	162	5573	680	1445	292	38	139	471	1092	73
Milwaukee	.259	162	5448	726	1413	327	19	175	531	1162	79
New York	.258	162	5505	722	1421	279	32	175	486	1075	153
San Diego	.257	162	5502	684	1416	269	39	130	600	977	99
Arizona	.256	162	5550	696	1419	291	27	191	606	1094	67
Houston	.256	163	5462	693	1400	281	32	161	481	1037	115
Los Angeles	.253	162	5433	685	1374	284	21	149	541	1094	58
Washington	.252	162	5426	639	1367	311	32	117	491	1090	45

CLUB PITCHING

	ERA	G	CG	SHO	SV	IP	H	R	ER	BB	SO
St. Louis	3.49	162	15	14	48	1446	1399	634	560	443	974
Houston	3.51	163	6	11	45	1443	1336	609	563	440	1164
New York	3.76	162	8	11	38	1436	1390	648	599	491	1012
Washington	3.87	162	4	9	51	1458	1456	673	627	539	997
Milwaukee	3.97	162	7	6	46	1438	1382	697	635	569	1173
Atlanta	3.98	162	8	12	38	1444	1487	674	639	520	929
San Diego	4.13	162	4	8	45	1455	1452	726	668	503	1133
Florida	4.16	162	14	15	42	1442	1459	732	666	563	1125
Chicago	4.19	162	8	10	39	1440	1357	714	671	576	1256
Philadelphia	4.21	162	4	6	40	1435	1379	726	672	487	1159
San Francisco	4.33	162	4	8	46	1444	1456	745	695	592	972
Los Angeles	4.38	162	6	9	40	1427	1434	755	695	471	1004
Pittsburgh	4.42	162	4	14	35	1436	1456	769	706	612	958
Arizona	4.84	162	6	10	45	1456	1580	856	783	537	1038
Colorado	5.13	162	4	4	37	1419	1600	862	808	604	981
Cincinnati	5.15	163	2	1	31	1433	1657	889	820	492	955

CLUB FIELDING

	PCT	PO	A	E	DP
Atlanta	.986	4331	1802	86	170
Arizona	.985	4369	1794	94	159
Houston	.985	4329	1700	89	146
Washington	.985	4374	1548	92	156
San Francisco	.985	4333	1630	90	146
Philadelphia	.985	4305	1608	90	132
St. Louis	.984	4337	1951	100	196
Chicago	.983	4320	1658	101	136
Cincinnati	.983	4299	1587	104	133
Los Angeles	.983	4282	1727	106	141
New York	.983	4307	1657	106	146
Florida	.983	4327	1659	103	177
San Diego	.982	4366	1529	109	136
Colorado	.981	4256	1706	118	158
Pittsburgh	.981	4308	1803	117	193
Milwaukee	.980	4314	1482	119	139

INDIVIDUAL BATTING LEADERS

(Minimum 502 Plate Appearances)

	AVG	G	AB	R	H	2B	3B	HR	RBI	BB	SO	SB
Lee, Derrek, Chicago	.335	158	594	120	199	50	3	46	107	85	109	15
Pujols, Albert, St. Louis	.330	161	591	129	195	38	2	41	117	97	65	16
Cabrera, Miguel, Florida	.323	158	613	106	198	43	2	33	116	64	125	1
Helton, Todd, Colorado	.320	144	509	92	163	45	2	20	79	106	80	3
Casey, Sean, Cincinnati	.312	137	529	75	165	32	0	9	58	48	48	2
Tracy, Chad, Arizona	.308	145	503	73	155	34	4	27	72	35	78	3
Holliday, Matt, Colorado	.307	125	479	68	147	24	7	19	87	36	79	14
Clark, Brady, Milwaukee	.306	145	599	94	183	31	1	13	53	47	55	10
Wright, David, New York	.306	160	575	99	176	42	1	27	102	72	113	17
Bay, Jason, Pittsburgh	.306	162	599	110	183	44	6	32	101	95	142	21

INDIVIDUAL PITCHING LEADERS

(Minimum 162 Innings)

	W	L	ERA	G	GS	CG	SV	IP	H	R	ER	BB	SO
Clemens, Roger, Houston	13	8	1.87	32	32	1	0	211	151	51	44	62	185
Pettitte, Andy, Houston	17	9	2.39	33	33	0	0	222	188	66	59	41	171
Willis, Dontrelle, Florida	22	10	2.63	34	34	7	0	236	213	79	69	55	170
Martinez, Pedro, New York	15	8	2.82	31	31	4	0	217	159	69	68	47	208
Carpenter, Chris, St. Louis	21	5	2.83	33	33	7	0	242	204	82	76	51	213
Peavy, Jake, San Diego	13	7	2.88	30	30	3	0	203	162	70	65	50	216
Oswalt, Oswalt, Houston	20	12	2.94	35	35	4	0	242	243	85	79	48	184
Smoltz, John, Atlanta	14	7	3.06	33	33	3	0	230	210	83	78	53	169
Patterson, John, Washington	9	7	3.13	31	31	2	0	198	172	71	69	65	185
Zambrano, Carlos, Chicago	14	6	3.26	33	33	2	0	223	170	88	81	86	202

AWARD WINNERS

Selected by Baseball Writers Association of America

MOST VALUABLE PLAYER

Player, Team	1st	2nd	3rd	Total
Albert Pujols, St. Louis	18	14	0	378
Andruw Jones, Atlanta	13	17	2	351
Derrek Lee, Chicago	1	1	30	263
Morgan Ensberg, Houston	0	0	0	160
Miguel Cabrera, Florida	0	0	0	146
Carlos Delgado, Florida	0	0	0	84
Pat Burrell, Philadelphia	0	0	0	65
Chris Carpenter, St. Louis	0	0	0	52
Brian Giles, San Diego	0	0	0	48
Jimmy Rollins, Philadelphia	0	0	0	45
Dontrelle Willis, Florida	0	0	0	42
Jason Bay, Pittsburgh	0	0	0	41
Chase Utley, Philadelphia	0	0	0	22
Lance Berkman, Houston	0	0	0	21
Bobby Abreu, Philadelphia	0	0	0	21
Chad Cordero, Washington	0	0	0	21
Trevor Hoffman, San Diego	0	0	0	19
Carlos Lee, Milwaukee	0	0	0	19
Jeff Kent, Los Angeles	0	0	0	18
David Wright, New York	0	0	0	18
David Eckstein, St. Louis	0	0	0	15
Roger Clemens, Houston	0	0	0	8

CY YOUNG AWARD

Player, Team	1st	2nd	3rd	Total
Chris Carpenter, St. Louis	19	12	1	132
Dontrelle Willis, Florida	11	18	3	112
Roger Clemens, Houston	2	2	24	40
Roy Oswalt, Houston	0	0	2	2
Chad Cordero, Washington	0	0	1	1
Andy Pettitte, Houston	0	0	1	1

ROOKIE OF THE YEAR

Player, Team	1st	2nd	3rd	Total
Ryan Howard, Philadelphia	19	3	5	109
Willy Taveras, Houston	7	11	10	78
Jeff Francoeur, Atlanta	2	14	8	60
Garrett Atkins, Colorado	1	2	6	17
Zach Duke, Pittsburgh	3	0	1	16
Jeff Francis, Colorado	0	1	0	3
Rickie Weeks, Milwaukee	0	1	0	3
Clint Barmes, Colorado	0	0	1	1
Jason Vargas, Florida	0	0	1	1

MANAGER OF THE YEAR

Manager, Team	1st	2nd	3rd	Total
Bobby Cox, Atlanta	28	4	0	152
Tony La Russa, St. Louis	2	13	3	52
Phil Garner, Houston	0	9	11	38
Frank Robinson, Washington	2	4	7	29
Ned Yost, Milwaukee	0	0	7	7
Charlie Manuel, Philadelphia	0	1	2	5
Bruce Bochy, San Diego	0	1	1	4
Willie Randolph, New York	0	0	1	1

NOTE: MVP balloting based on 14 points for first-place vote, nine for second, eight for third, etc. Cy Young Award, Rookie of the Year and Manager of the Year balloting based on five points for first-place votes, three for second and one for third.

GOLD GLOVE AWARDS

Selected by AL managers

C—Mike Matheny, San Francisco. **1B**—Derrek Lee, Chicago. **2B**—Luis Castillo, Florida. **3B**—Mike Lowell, Florida. **SS**—Omar Vizquel, San Francisco. **OF**—Bobby Abreu, Philadelphia; Jim Edmonds, St. Louis; Andruw Jones, Atlanta. **P**—Greg Maddux, Chicago.

SILVER SLUGGER AWARDS

Selected by AL managers, coaches

C—Michael Barrett, Chicago. **1B**—Derrek Lee, Chicago. **2B**—Jeff Kent, Los Angeles. **3B**—Morgan Ensberg, Houston. **SS**—Felipe Lopez, Cincinnati. **OF**—Miguel Cabrera, Florida; Andruw Jones, Atlanta; Carlos Lee, Milwaukee. **P**—Jason Marquis, St. Louis.

NATIONAL LEAGUE DEPARTMENT LEADERS

BATTING

GAMES

Bobby Abreu, Phillies	162
Jason Bay, Pirates	162
Carlos Lee, Brewers	162
Juan Pierre, Marlins	162
Albert Pujols, Cardinals	161
Jose Reyes, Mets	161

AT-BATS

Jose Reyes, Mets	696
Jimmy Rollins, Phillies	677
Juan Pierre, Marlins	656
David Eckstein, Cardinals	630
Carlos Lee, Brewers	618

RUNS

Albert Pujols, Cardinals	129
Derrek Lee, Cubs	120
Jimmy Rollins, Phillies	115
Jason Bay, Pirates	110
Adam Dunn, Reds	107

HITS

Derrek Lee, Cubs	199
Miguel Cabrera, Marlins	198
Jimmy Rollins, Phillies	196
Albert Pujols, Cardinals	195
Jose Reyes, Mets	190

TOTAL BASES

Derrek Lee, Cubs	393
Albert Pujols, Cardinals	360
Miguel Cabrera, Marlins	344
Andruw Jones, Braves	337
Jason Bay, Pirates	335

SINGLES

Willy Taveras, Astros	152
Juan Pierre, Marlins	147
David Eckstein, Cardinals	144
Jose Reyes, Mets	142
Brady Clark, Brewers	138

DOUBLES

Derrek Lee, Cubs	50
Marcus Giles, Braves	45
Todd Helton, Rockies	45
Jason Bay, Pirates	44
Miguel Cabrera, Marlins	43
Joe Randa, Reds/Padres	43

TRIPLES

Jose Reyes, Mets	17
Juan Pierre, Marlins	13
Rafael Furcal, Braves	11
Jimmy Rollins, Phillies	11
Dave Roberts, Padres	10

GEORGE GOJKOVICH

Jose Reyes: 17 triples

MICHAEL WALBY

Brian Giles: 119 walks

HOME RUNS

Andruw Jones, Braves	51
Derrek Lee, Cubs	46
Albert Pujols, Cardinals	41
Adam Dunn, Reds	40
Troy Glaus, Diamondbacks	37

HOME RUN RATIO

(At-bats per home run)

Andruw Jones, Braves	11.49
Derrek Lee, Cubs	12.91
Adam Dunn, Reds	13.58
Ken Griffey, Reds	14.03
Albert Pujols, Cardinals	14.41

RUNS BATTED IN

Andruw Jones, Braves	128
Pat Burrell, Phillies	117
Albert Pujols, Cardinals	117
Miguel Cabrera, Marlins	116
Carlos Delgado, Marlins	115

SACRIFICE BUNTS

Omar Vizquel, Giants	20
Luis Castillo, Marlins	18
Andy Pettitte, Astros	15
Livan Hernandez, Nationals	14
Jamey Carroll, Nationals	13
Brandon Webb, Diamondbacks	13

SACRIFICE FLIES

Carlos Lee, Brewers	11
Jose Guillen, Nationals	9
Mike Lowell, Marlins	9
Five tied at	8

HIT BY PITCHES

Jose Guillen, Nationals	19
Geoff Jenkins, Brewers	19
Brady Clark, Brewers	18
Craig Biggio, Astros	17
Carlos Delgado, Marlins	17

WALKS

Brian Giles, Padres	119
Bobby Abreu, Phillies	117
Adam Dunn, Reds	114
Todd Helton, Rockies	106
Pat Burrell, Phillies	99

INTENTIONAL WALKS

Albert Pujols, Cardinals	27
Derrek Lee, Cubs	23
Todd Helton, Rockies	22
Carlos Delgado, Marlins	20
Bobby Abreu, Phillies	15

STOLEN BASES

Jose Reyes, Mets	60
Juan Pierre, Marlins	57
Rafael Furcal, Braves	46
Jimmy Rollins, Phillies	41
Ryan Freel, Reds	36

CAUGHT STEALING

Juan Pierre, Marlins	17
Jose Reyes, Mets	15
Brady Clark, Brewers	13
Dave Roberts, Padres	12
Willy Taveras, Astros	11

STRIKEOUTS

Adam Dunn, Reds	168
Pat Burrell, Phillies	160
Preston Wilson, Rockies/Nationals	148
Brad Wilkerson, Nationals	147
Troy Glaus, Diamondbacks	145

TOUGHEST TO STRIKE OUT

(At-bats per strikeout)

Juan Pierre, Marlins	14.58
David Eckstein, Cardinals	14.32
Luis Castillo, Marlins	13.72
Neifi Perez, Cubs	12.17
Sean Casey, Reds	11.02

GROUNDED INTO DOUBLE PLAYS

Sean Casey, Reds	27
David Bell, Phillies	24
Neifi Perez, Cubs	22
Miguel Cabrera, Marlins	20
Pedro Feliz, Giants	20

HITTING STREAKS

Jimmy Rollins, Phillies	36
Cliff Floyd, Mets	20
Jose Reyes, Mets	20
Derrek Lee, Cubs	18
Alex Gonzalez, Marlins	17
Albert Pujols, Cardinals	17
Freddy Sanchez, Pirates	17

MULTIPLE-HIT GAMES

Miguel Cabrera, Marlins	57
David Eckstein, Cardinals	57
Albert Pujols, Cardinals	57
Jimmy Rollins, Phillies	55
Jason Bay, Pirates	54
Derrek Lee, Cubs	54

ON-BASE PERCENTAGE

Todd Helton, Rockies	.445
Albert Pujols, Cardinals	.430
Brian Giles, Padres	.423
Derrek Lee, Cubs	.418
Lance Berkman, Astros	.411

SLUGGING PERCENTAGE

Derrek Lee, Cubs	.662
Albert Pujols, Cardinals	.609
Carlos Delgado, Marlins	.582
Ken Griffey, Reds	.576
Andruw Jones, Braves	.575

PITCHING

WINS

Dontrelle Willis, Marlins	22
Chris Carpenter, Cardinals	21
Roy Oswalt, Astros	20
Chris Capuano, Brewers	18
Jon Lieber, Phillies	17
Andy Pettitte, Astros	17

LOSSES

Kip Wells, Pirates	18
Jamey Wright, Rockies	16
Brian Lawrence, Padres	15
Derek Lowe, Dodgers	15
Greg Maddux, Cubs	15
Eric Milton, Reds	15
Mark Redman, Pirates	15

Brett Tomko, Giants 15
Javier Vazquez, Diamondbacks 15

WINNING PERCENTAGE

Chris Carpenter, Cardinals .... .808
Carlos Zambrano, Cubs .... .700
Dontrelle Willis, Marlins .... .688
Mark Mulder, Cardinals .... .667
John Smoltz, Braves .... .667

GAMES

Scott Eyre, Giants 86
Gary Majewski, Nationals 79
Duaner Sanchez, Dodgers 79
Brian Fuentes, Rockies 78
Ryan Madson, Phillies 78
Kent Mercker, Reds 78
Salomon Torres, Pirates 78

GAMES STARTED

Chris Capuano, Brewers 35
Doug Davis, Brewers 35
Livan Hernandez, Nationals 35
Jon Lieber, Phillies 35
Derek Lowe, Dodgers 35
Greg Maddux, Cubs 35
Roy Oswalt, Astros 35

COMPLETE GAMES

Chris Carpenter, Cardinals 7
Dontrelle Willis, Marlins 7
A.J. Burnett, Marlins 4
Pedro Martinez, Mets 4
Roy Oswalt, Astros 4

SHUTOUTS

Dontrelle Willis, Marlins 5
Chris Carpenter, Cardinals 4
Jake Peavy, Padres 3
A.J. Burnett, Marlins 2
Derek Lowe, Dodgers 2
Mark Mulder, Cardinals 2
Jeff Weaver, Dodgers 2

GAMES FINISHED

Billy Wagner, Phillies 70
Brad Lidge, Astros 65
Chad Cordero, Nationals 62
Derrick Turnbow, Brewers 62
Brian Fuentes, Rockies 55
Todd Jones, Marlins 55

SAVES

Chad Cordero, Nationals 47
Trevor Hoffman, Padres 43
Brad Lidge, Astros 42
Todd Jones, Marlins 40
Jason Isringhausen, Cardinals 39
Derrick Turnbow, Brewers 39

INNINGS

Livan Hernandez, Nationals 246
Chris Carpenter, Cardinals 242
Roy Oswalt, Astros 242
Dontrelle Willis, Marlins 236
John Smoltz, Braves 230

HITS ALLOWED

Livan Hernandez, Nationals 268
Roy Oswalt, Astros 243
Greg Maddux, Cubs 239
Eric Milton, Reds 237
Brandon Webb, Diamondbacks 229

RUNS ALLOWED

Eric Milton, Reds 141
Jeff Francis, Rockies 119
Jamey Wright, Rockies 119
Livan Hernandez, Nationals 116
Kip Wells, Pirates 116

HOME RUNS ALLOWED

Eric Milton, Reds 40
Javier Vazquez, Diamondbacks 35
Jeff Weaver, Dodgers 35
Ramon Ortiz, Reds 34
Jon Lieber, Phillies 33

WALKS

Kip Wells, Pirates 99
Doug Davis, Brewers 93
Chris Capuano, Brewers 91
Carlos Zambrano, Cubs 86
Jason Schmidt, Giants 85

FEWEST WALKS PER NINE INNINGS

Greg Maddux, Cubs 1.28
Jon Lieber, Phillies 1.44
Matt Morris, Cardinals 1.59
Andy Pettitte, Astros 1.66
Roy Oswalt, Astros 1.68

HIT BATSMEN

Jeff Weaver, Dodgers 18
Jamey Wright, Rockies 15
Victor Zambrano, Mets 15
Byung-Hyun Kim, Rockies 14
Livan Hernandez, Nationals 13

STRIKEOUTS

Jake Peavy, Padres 216
Chris Carpenter, Cardinals 213
Doug Davis, Brewers 208
Pedro Martinez, Mets 208
Brett Myers, Phillies 208

STRIKEOUTS PER NINE INNINGS

Mark Prior, Cubs 10.15
Jake Peavy, Padres 9.58
Brett Myers, Phillies 8.69
Pedro Martinez, Mets 8.63
Jason Schmidt, Giants 8.63

PICKOFFS

Chris Capuano, Brewers 12
Jamey Wright, Rockies 6
Doug Davis, Brewers 5
Jeff Fassero, Giants 5
Jeff Francis, Rockies 5
Mark Mulder, Cardinals 5

WILD PITCHES

Brandon Webb, Diamondbacks 14
A.J. Burnett, Marlins 12
Byung-Hyun Kim, Rockies 11
Jason Marquis, Cardinals 10
Mark Mulder, Cardinals 9
John Patterson, Nationals 9
Derrick Turnbow, Brewers 9

BALKS

Chris Capuano, Brewers 4
Brett Myers, Phillies 4
Jason Marquis, Cardinals 3
Mark Redman, Pirates 3
Wandy Rodriguez, Astros 3

OPPONENT BATTING AVERAGE

Roger Clemens, Astros .... .198
Pedro Martinez, Mets .... .204
Carlos Zambrano, Cubs .... .212
Jake Peavy, Padres .... .217
Mark Prior, Cubs .... .227

FIELDING

PITCHER

PCT 10 tied at 1.000

CARL KLINE

Jake Peavy: 216 strikeouts

ED WOLFSTEIN

Chad Cordero: 47 saves

PO Tim Hudson, Braves 27
A Mark Mulder, Cardinals 52
E Ramon Ortiz, Reds 7
TC Greg Maddux, Cubs 71
DP Horacio Ramirez, Braves 8

CATCHER

PCT Brad Ausmus, Astros .... .999
Mike Matheny, Giants .... .999
PO Brad Ausmus, Astros 884
A Mike Matheny, Giants 77
E J.D. Closser, Rockies 8
Ryan Doumit, Pirates 8
Ramon Hernandez, Padres 8
Paul Lo Duca, Marlins 8
TC Brad Ausmus, Astros 950
DP Mike Matheny, Giants 13
PB Humberto Cota, Pirates 8
Yadier Molina, Cardinals 8

FIRST BASE

PCT Sean Casey, Reds .... .998
PO Albert Pujols, Cardinals 1597
A Derrek Lee, Cubs 122
E Carlos Delgado, Marlins 14
Albert Pujols, Cardinals 14
TC Albert Pujols, Cardinals 1708
DP Albert Pujols, Cardinals 175

SECOND BASE

PCT Craig Counsell, Diamondbacks .... .990
PCT Mark Grudzielanek, Cardinals .... .990
PO Craig Counsell, Diamondbacks 305
A Marcus Giles, Braves 469
E Rickie Weeks, Brewers 21
TC Craig Counsell, Diamondbacks 772
DP Mark Grudzielanek, Cardinals 108

THIRD BASE

PCT Mike Lowell, Marlins .... .983
PO Vinny Castilla, Nationals 142
A David Wright, Mets 336
E Troy Glaus, Diamondbacks 24
David Wright, Mets 24
TC David Wright, Mets 461
DP Mike Lowell, Marlins 34

SHORTSTOP

PCT Omar Vizquel, Giants .... .988
PO Rafael Furcal, Braves 255
A Jack Wilson, Pirates 523
E Jose Reyes, Mets 18
TC Jack Wilson, Pirates 783
DP Jack Wilson, Pirates 126

OUTFIELD

PCT Shawn Green, Diamondbacks .... .100
PO Brady Clark, Brewers 399
A Cliff Floyd, Mets 15
E Moises Alou, Giants 8
E Jason Ellison, Giants 8
TC Brady Clark, Brewers 406
DP Geoff Jenkins, Brewers 7

Sox make dominant run to bring title to Chicago

BY JOHN PERROTTO

The finish to the 2005 postseason was eerily similar to the way 2004 ended. A team that had been waiting more than eight decades since its last championship wound up ending its drought in resounding fashion by sweeping the World Series.

The only difference was a change of socks. Uh, make that Sox.

The Chicago White Sox, following a script similar to that of the 2004 Boston Red Sox, captured their first championship since 1917 by sweeping the Houston Astros. The Red Sox had not won a World Series since 1918 until sweeping the St. Louis Cardinals in the 2004 series.

It had been so long since the White Sox claimed a championship that they had actually thrown a World Series since their last title. That came in 1919, when eight White Sox players including the great Shoeless Joe Jackson were banned for life by Commissioner Kennesaw Mountain Landis in the Black Sox scandal for conspiring with gamblers to lose to the Cincinnati Reds.

There was no question about the White Sox' motives this time around, as they stormed through the posteason with 11 wins in 12 games. They swept the Red Sox in three games in the American League Division Series, then downed the Los Angeles Angels in five games in the American League Championship Series.

LARRY GOREN

Celebrating at last
The White Sox won all three of their postseason series on the road

The White Sox became the second team to go 11-1 since the postseason was expanded to three rounds in 1995, joining the 1999 New York Yankees.

Throw in a five-game winning streak to end the regular season, and the White Sox wound up notching victories in 16 of their 17 final games of 2005. The hot streak came after they survived having their 15-game lead in the AL Central cut to 1 1/2 games on Sept. 24 by the Cleveland Indians, making them just the third team in baseball history to be in first place for every day of the regular season and then sweep the World Series. The others were the 1927 Yankees and 1990 Reds.

It was a quite a ride for a Chicago, a city starved for a baseball winner. The Windy City hadn't hosted a World Series since 1959, when the Go-Go White Sox lost to the Los Angeles Dodgers. Chicago hadn't had a champion since those '17 Sox beat the New York Giants in the World Series.

"The instant the Red Sox won last year, I thought maybe we're next," White Sox owner Jerry Reinsdorf said.

The only team with a longer championship drought is

WORLD SERIES YEAR-BY-YEAR

Year	Winner	Manager	Loser	Manager	Result	MVP
1903	Boston (AL)	Jimmy Collins	Pittsburgh (NL)	Fred Clarke	5-3	None Selected
1904	NO SERIES					
1905	New York (NL)	John McGraw	Philadelphia (AL)	Connie Mack	4-1	None Selected
1906	Chicago (AL)	Fielder Jones	Chicago (NL)	Frank Chance	4-2	None Selected
1907	Chicago (NL)	Frank Chance	Detroit (AL)	Hugh Jennings	4-0	None Selected
1908	Chicago (NL)	Frank Chance	Detroit (AL)	Hugh Jennings	4-1	None Selected
1909	Pittsburgh (NL)	Fred Clarke	Detroit (AL)	Hugh Jennings	4-3	None Selected
1910	Philadelphia (AL)	Connie Mack	Chicago (NL)	Frank Chance	4-1	None Selected
1911	Philadelphia (AL)	Connie Mack	New York (NL)	John McGraw	4-2	None Selected
1912	Boston (AL)	Jake Stahl	New York (NL)	John McGraw	4-3-1	None Selected
1913	Philadelphia (AL)	Connie Mack	New York (NL)	John McGraw	4-1	None Selected
1914	Boston (NL)	George Stallings	Philadelphia (AL)	Connie Mack	4-0	None Selected
1915	Boston (AL)	Bill Carrigan	Philadelphia (NL)	Pat Moran	4-1	None Selected
1916	Boston (AL)	Bill Carrigan	Brooklyn (NL)	Wilbert Robinson	4-1	None Selected
1917	Chicago (AL)	Pants Rowland	New York (NL)	John McGraw	4-2	None Selected
1918	Boston (AL)	Ed Barrow	Chicago (NL)	Fred Mitchell	4-2	None Selected
1919	Cincinnati (NL)	Pat Moran	Chicago (AL)	Kid Gleason	5-3	None Selected
1920	Cleveland (AL)	Tris Speaker	Brooklyn (NL)	Wilbert Robinson	5-2	None Selected
1921	New York (NL)	John McGraw	New York (AL)	Miller Huggins	5-3	None Selected
1922	New York (NL)	John McGraw	New York (AL)	Miller Huggins	4-0	None Selected
1923	New York (AL)	Miller Huggins	New York (NL)	John McGraw	4-2	None Selected
1924	Washington (AL)	Bucky Harris	New York (NL)	John McGraw	4-3	None Selected
1925	Pittsburgh (NL)	Bill McKechnie	Washington (AL)	Bucky Harris	4-3	None Selected
1926	St. Louis (NL)	Rogers Hornsby	New York (AL)	Miller Huggins	4-3	None Selected
1927	New York (AL)	Miller Huggins	Pittsburgh (NL)	Donie Bush	4-0	None Selected
1928	New York (AL)	Miller Huggins	St. Louis (NL)	Bill McKechnie	4-0	None Selected
1929	Philadelphia (AL)	Connie Mack	Chicago (NL)	Joe McCarthy	4-1	None Selected
1930	Philadelphia (AL)	Connie Mack	St. Louis (NL)	Gabby Street	4-2	None Selected
1931	St. Louis (NL)	Gabby Street	Philadelphia (AL)	Connie Mack	4-3	None Selected
1932	New York (AL)	Joe McCarthy	Chicago (NL)	Charlie Grimm	4-0	None Selected
1933	New York (NL)	Bill Terry	Washington (AL)	Joe Cronin	4-1	None Selected
1934	St. Louis (NL)	Frankie Frisch	Detroit (AL)	Mickey Cochrane	4-3	None Selected
1935	Detroit (AL)	Mickey Cochrane	Chicago (NL)	Charlie Grimm	4-2	None Selected
1936	New York (AL)	Joe McCarthy	New York (NL)	Bill Terry	4-2	None Selected
1937	New York (AL)	Joe McCarthy	New York (NL)	Bill Terry	4-1	None Selected
1938	New York (AL)	Joe McCarthy	Chicago (NL)	Gabby Hartnett	4-0	None Selected
1939	New York (AL)	Joe McCarthy	Cincinnati (NL)	Bill McKechnie	4-0	None Selected
1940	Cincinnati (NL)	Bill McKechnie	Detroit (AL)	Del Baker	4-3	None Selected
1941	New York (AL)	Joe McCarthy	Brooklyn (NL)	Leo Durocher	4-1	None Selected
1942	St. Louis (NL)	Billy Southworth	New York (AL)	Joe McCarthy	4-1	None Selected
1943	New York (AL)	Joe McCarthy	St. Louis (NL)	Billy Southworth	4-1	None Selected
1944	St. Louis (NL)	Billy Southworth	St. Louis (AL)	Luke Sewell	4-2	None Selected
1945	Detroit (AL)	Steve O'Neill	Chicago (NL)	Charlie Grimm	4-3	None Selected
1946	St. Louis (NL)	Eddie Dyer	Boston (AL)	Joe Cronin	4-3	None Selected
1947	New York (AL)	Bucky Harris	Brooklyn (NL)	Burt Shotton	4-3	None Selected
1948	Cleveland (AL)	Lou Boudreau	Boston (NL)	Billy Southworth	4-2	None Selected
1949	New York (AL)	Casey Stengel	Brooklyn (NL)	Burt Shotton	4-1	None Selected
1950	New York (AL)	Casey Stengel	Philadelphia (NL)	Eddie Sawyer	4-0	None Selected
1951	New York (AL)	Casey Stengel	New York (NL)	Leo Durocher	4-2	None Selected
1952	New York (AL)	Casey Stengel	Brooklyn (NL)	Chuck Dressen	4-3	None Selected
1953	New York (AL)	Casey Stengel	Brooklyn (NL)	Chuck Dressen	4-2	None Selected
1954	New York (NL)	Leo Durocher	Cleveland (AL)	Al Lopez	4-0	None Selected
1955	Brooklyn (NL)	Walter Alston	New York (AL)	Casey Stengel	4-3	Johnny Podres, p, Brooklyn
1956	New York (AL)	Casey Stengel	Brooklyn (NL)	Walter Alston	4-3	Don Larsen, p, New York
1957	Milwaukee (NL)	Fred Haney	New York (AL)	Casey Stengel	4-3	Lew Burdette, p, Milwaukee
1958	New York (AL)	Casey Stengel	Milwaukee (NL)	Fred Haney	4-3	Bob Turley, p, New York
1959	Los Angeles (NL)	Walter Alston	Chicago (AL)	Al Lopez	4-2	Larry Sherry, p, Los Angeles
1960	Pittsburgh (NL)	Danny Murtaugh	New York (AL)	Casey Stengel	4-3	Bobby Richardson, 2b, New York
1961	New York (AL)	Ralph Houk	Cincinnati (NL)	Fred Hutchinson	4-1	Whitey Ford, p, New York
1962	New York (AL)	Ralph Houk	San Francisco (NL)	Alvin Dark	4-3	Ralph Terry, p, New York
1963	Los Angeles (NL)	Walter Alston	New York (AL)	Ralph Houk	4-0	Sandy Koufax, p, Los Angeles
1964	St. Louis (NL)	Johnny Keene	New York (AL)	Yogi Berra	4-3	Bob Gibson, p, St. Louis
1965	Los Angeles (NL)	Walter Alston	Minnesota (AL)	Sam Mele	4-3	Sandy Koufax, p, Los Angeles
1966	Baltimore (AL)	Hank Bauer	Los Angeles (NL)	Walter Alston	4-0	Frank Robinson, of, Baltimore
1967	St. Louis (NL)	Red Schoendienst	Boston (AL)	Dick Williams	4-3	Bob Gibson, p, St. Louis
1968	Detroit (AL)	Mayo Smith	St. Louis (NL)	Red Schoendienst	4-3	Mickey Lolich, p, Detroit
1969	New York (NL)	Gil Hodges	Baltimore (AL)	Earl Weaver	4-1	Donn Clendenon, 1b, New York
1970	Baltimore (AL)	Earl Weaver	Cincinnati (NL)	Sparky Anderson	4-1	Brooks Robinson, 3b, Baltimore
1971	Pittsburgh (NL)	Danny Murtaugh	Baltimore (AL)	Earl Weaver	4-3	Roberto Clemente, of, Pittsburgh
1972	Oakland (AL)	Dick Williams	Cincinnati (NL)	Sparky Anderson	4-3	Gene Tenace, c, Oakland
1973	Oakland (AL)	Dick Williams	New York (NL)	Yogi Berra	4-3	Reggie Jackson, of, Oakland
1974	Oakland (AL)	Alvin Dark	Los Angeles (NL)	Walter Alston	4-1	Rollie Fingers, p, Oakland
1975	Cincinnati (NL)	Sparky Anderson	Boston (AL)	Darrell Johnson	4-3	Pete Rose, 3b, Cincinnati
1976	Cincinnati (NL)	Sparky Anderson	New York (AL)	Billy Martin	4-0	Johnny Bench, c, Cincinnati
1977	New York (AL)	Billy Martin	Los Angeles (NL)	Tom Lasorda	4-2	Reggie Jackson, of, New York
1978	New York (AL)	Bob Lemon	Los Angeles (NL)	Tom Lasorda	4-2	Bucky Dent, ss, New York
1979	Pittsburgh (NL)	Chuck Tanner	Baltimore (AL)	Earl Weaver	4-3	Willie Stargell, 1b, Pittsburgh
1980	Philadelphia (NL)	Dallas Green	Kansas City (AL)	Jim Frey	4-2	Mike Schmidt, 3b, Philadelphia
1981	Los Angeles (NL)	Tom Lasorda	New York (AL)	Bob Lemon	4-2	Cey/Guerrero/Yeager, L.A.
1982	St. Louis (NL)	Whitey Herzog	Milwaukee (AL)	Harvey Kuenn	4-3	Darrell Porter, c, St. Louis
1983	Baltimore (AL)	Joe Altobelli	Philadelphia (NL)	Paul Owens	4-1	Rick Dempsey, c, Baltimore
1984	Detroit (AL)	Sparky Anderson	San Diego (NL)	Dick Williams	4-1	Alan Trammell, ss, Detroit
1985	Kansas City (AL)	Dick Howser	St. Louis (NL)	Whitey Herzog	4-3	Bret Saberhagen, p, Kansas City
1986	New York (NL)	Dave Johnson	Boston (AL)	John McNamara	4-3	Ray Knight, 3b, New York
1987	Minnesota (AL)	Tom Kelly	St. Louis (NL)	Whitey Herzog	4-3	Frank Viola, p, Minnesota
1988	Los Angeles (NL)	Tom Lasorda	Oakland (AL)	Tony La Russa	4-1	Orel Hershiser, p, Los Angeles
1989	Oakland (AL)	Tony La Russa	San Francisco (NL)	Roger Craig	4-0	Dave Stewart, p, Oakland
1990	Cincinnati (NL)	Lou Piniella	Oakland (AL)	Tony La Russa	4-0	Jose Rijo, p, Cincinnati
1991	Minnesota (AL)	Tom Kelly	Atlanta (NL)	Bobby Cox	4-3	Jack Morris, p, Minnesota
1992	Toronto (AL)	Cito Gaston	Atlanta (NL)	Bobby Cox	4-2	Pat Borders, c, Toronto
1993	Toronto (AL)	Cito Gaston	Philadelphia (NL)	Jim Fregosi	4-2	Paul Molitor, dh, Toronto
1994	NO SERIES					
1995	Atlanta (NL)	Bobby Cox	Cleveland (AL)	Mike Hargrove	4-2	Tom Glavine, p, Atlanta
1996	New York (AL)	Joe Torre	Atlanta (NL)	Bobby Cox	4-2	John Wetteland, p, New York
1997	Florida (NL)	Jim Leyland	Cleveland (AL)	Mike Hargrove	4-3	Livan Hernandez, p, Florida
1998	New York (AL)	Joe Torre	San Diego (NL)	Bruce Bochy	4-0	Scott Brosius, 3b, New York
1999	New York (AL)	Joe Torre	Atlanta (NL)	Bobby Cox	4-0	Mariano Rivera, p, New York
2000	New York (AL)	Joe Torre	New York (NL)	Bobby Valentine	4-1	Derek Jeter, ss, New York
2001	Arizona (NL)	Bob Brenly	New York (AL)	Joe Torre	4-3	Johnson, p/Schilling, p, Arizona
2002	Anaheim (AL)	Mike Scioscia	San Francisco (NL)	Dusty Baker	4-3	Troy Glaus, 3b, Anaheim
2003	Florida (NL)	Jack McKeon	New York (AL)	Joe Torre	4-2	Josh Beckett, p, Florida
2004	Boston (AL)	Terry Francona	St. Louis (NL)	Tony La Russa	4-0	Manny Ramirez, of, Boston
2005	Chicago (AL)	Ozzie Guillen	Houston (NL)	Phil Garner	4-0	Jermaine Dye, of, Chicago

LARRY GOREN

Ending the suffering for White Sox fans
Paul Konerko helped lead the Chicago offense

the Chicago Cubs, who haven't won since 1908 or been in a World Series since 1945.

"I've been here for seven years, but compared with all the fans and all the people who put up with the frustrations of this team for all those years, that's nothing," White Sox first baseman Paul Konerko said. "Those are the people who have suffered for a long, long time.

"But when you win, people don't forget you. So now, we'll always be remembered as part of the team that finally jumped over that wall."

While the White Sox finished the sweep at Houston's Minute Maid Park—in fact, they won all three of their playoff series on the road—the celebration lasted long into the night on Chicago's South Side. Long considered the Second City's second franchise behind the Cubs, the White Sox and their long-suffering fans finally had reason to celebrate.

"I hope the people are partying like it's 1917," White Sox catcher A.J. Pierzynski said.

The Astros finally got their first invitation to baseball's big party, winning their first pennant since joining the National League as an expansion franchise in 1962. After beating the Atlanta Braves in four games in the National League Division Series and the Cardinals in six games in the National League Championship Series, the Astros' first World Series trip was short.

The Astros became the first team to be swept in their first World Series appearance, though their four losses were by a combined margin of six runs and no game was decided by more than two runs. The Astros hit just .208 with runners in scoring position and were shut out in the final 15 innings of the series, stranding 18 runners.

"It was more their destiny to win this Series than it was ours," said veteran Astros second baseman Criag Biggio, who had played more regular-season games, 2,564, than anyone in history before making his World Series debut.

All four games were nail biters, and the White Sox won a tense 1-0 thriller in Game Four to complete the sweep.

After starters Freddy Garcia of the White Sox and Brandon Backe of the Astros each pitched seven scoreless innings, Chicago pushed across the game's lone run in the eighth off Houston closer Brad Lidge.

Pinch-hitter Willie Harris lined a leadoff single to left, moved to second on Scott Podsednik's sacrifice bunt and took third on Carl Everett's ground out. Jermaine Dye then grounded a single up the middle to plate Harris with the winning run.

Dye was the series MVP after going 7-for-16 (.438) with one home runs and three RBIs.

"It feels unbelievable. This is an exciting moment," Dye said. "It's something I never will forget."

The White Sox' bullpen closed out the win for Garcia. Cliff Politte and Neal Cotts combined on a scoreless eighth inning and rookie closer Bobby Jenks, who began the season at Double-A Birmingham in the Southern League, pitched a scoreless ninth for his second save of the series.

Strong Pitching, Timely Hitting

Cotts and Jenks were the stars of Game One, getting out of a bases-loaded jam in the eighth inning with three straight strikeouts as the White Sox opened with a 5-3 win at U.S. Cellular Field in Chicago. Third baseman Joe Crede hit a go-ahead home run in the fourth inning off losing pitcher Wandy Rodriguz and saved two runs with a pair of diving stops later in the game.

At 43, the Astros' Roger Clemens hoped to become the oldest pitcher to win a World Series game, but he was forced to leave after just two innings because of a strained hamstring. Winning pitcher Jose Contreras allowed three runs in seven-plus innings and tied a World Series record by hitting three batters.

"Winning the game the way we did, it's amazing, truly amazing," White Sox center fielder Aaron Rowand said. "It just gives you chills, goosebumps."

Aaron Rowand

There were plenty of chills in Game Two, played on a cold and rainy night with temperatures dipping into the high 30s. That didn't lessen the thrills, though, as the White Sox won 7-6 on dramatic home runs by Konerko and Podsednik, the speedy left fielder who did not go deep in 568 plate appearances during the regular season.

Podsednik's solo homer with one out in the bottom of the ninth off Lidge snapped a 6-6 tie and gave the White Sox the win. Konerko's grand slam in the seventh off Chad Qualls had given the White Sox a 6-4 lead, but the Astros tied it on pinch-hitter Jose Vizcaino's two-run single off Jenks with two outs in the top of the ninth.

Podsednik led the AL with 62 stolen bases during the regular season, but he ended Game Two with his bat, not his legs.

"Wow! He hit a home run off Lidge!" Pierzynski said. "I'd like to take the odds in Vegas on that one. Put $100 on that and see what happens."

Pierzynski might have hit another long shot if he put money on Game Three lasting 14 innings and five hours and 41 minutes, the longest game by time in World Series history.

Reserve infielder Geoff Blum hit a tiebreaking home run in the top of the 14th inning off rookie Ezequiel Astacio, an inning after entering the game at second base as part of a double switch, and the White Sox added an insurance run for a 7-5 win and a 3-0 lead in the series.

The Astros took an early 4-0 lead, but the White Sox rallied with five runs in the fifth inning off Roy Oswalt, the only pitcher in the major leagues to win 20 games in each of the past two seasons. The Astros tied it at 5-5 in the eighth when Jason Lane's RBI double off Dustin Hermanson forced extra innings.

Mark Buehrle

After the White Sox went ahead in the top of the 14th, the Astros put runners at the corners in the bottom half against winner Damaso Marte. Mark Buehrle, who started and pitched seven innings in Game Two, came on as Chicago's ninth pitcher and the 17th of the game—both World Series records—and got Adam Everett to pop to shortstop for the final out at 1:20 a.m.

"It was just an unbelievable game," Blum said. "It's the stuff dreams are made of."

The White Sox' dream then came true in Game Four as they finished off the sweep.

Chisox March Through AL

The White Sox used exceptional starting pitching to dispatch the Angels in the ALCS.

After losing the first game, the White Sox came back to win the next four and got complete games in each from Buehrle, Jon Garland, Garcia and Contreras.

That was a stunning development in an age of deep bullpens and specialized relievers. In fact, four major league teams had fewer complete games in the regular season than the White Sox had in the ALCS.

"In the end, our pitching was amazing," Pierzynski said. "I don't know if you'll ever see it again."

That was the most complete games in succession in a postseason series since the 1956 Yankees beat the Brooklyn Dodgers in the World Series behind complete-game performances by Whitey Ford, Tom Sturdivant, Don Larsen, Bob Turley and Johnny Kucks. Larsen's start was the only perfect game in World Series history.

Buehrle started the string with a five-hitter in Game Two, and he was followed by Garland's four-hitter in Game Three, Garcia's six-hitter in Game Four and Contreras' five-hitter in Game Five. That left the White Sox' bullpen to get just two outs in the entire series.

The Angels hit just .175 in the series while scoring 11 runs. Their 27 hits were the fewest in any LCS going five games or longer. Right fielder Vladimir Guerrero had a particularly rough series as he went 1-for-20.

"I've never seen four horses like that come out of the gate," Angels manager Mike Scioscia said about the White Sox starters. "You might have to go back to Sandy Koufax, Don Drysdale, that group, or the group Baltimore had in, I guess, '66."

While the White Sox' starters were the talk of the ALCS, Konerko was the series MVP as he went 6-for-21 (.286) with two homers and seven RBIs, including first-inning home runs in Games Three and Four.

The Angels led 3-2 in the finale before Crede hit a tying homer in the seventh inning off losing pitcher Kelvim Escobar. An inning later, Crede drove home the winning run with an infield single as the White Sox went on to a 6-3 victory.

The Angels took the opener, 3-2, on the road as Paul Byrd pitched six innings for the win and left fielder Garret Anderson homered. It was all White Sox after that, as their starting pitchers dominated.

Crede's double in the bottom of the ninth inning gave the White Sox a controversial 2-1 win in Game Two, the hit coming after Pierzynski reached first with two outs on a wild pitch by Escobar after striking out. Pinch-runner Pablo Ozuna stole second and scored on Crede's hit into the left-field corner.

Pierzynski swung and missed at what appeared to be strike three, and catcher Josh Paul seemed to catch the ball cleanly before it hit the dirt. Home-plate umpire Doug Eddings raised his arm and closed his fist, signaling strike three.

However, Pierzynski took off for first while Paul rolled the ball back to the mound and the Angels trotted off the field. Eddings ruled that Paul had not caught the ball, allowing the winning run to reach base.

While Eddings' call remained the hot topic throughout the remainder of the series, the White Sox won three in a row at Anaheim to put the series away with Konerko playing a big role.

Konerko's two-run homer in the first capped a three-run first in Game Three, propelling the White Sox to a 5-2 victory. He then belted a three-run homer in the first inning of Game Four to get the White Sox started on an 8-2 win. Contreras then sealed the pennant for the White Sox in Game Five.

Astros Overtake Cardinals In NL

The Astros overcame a potentially devastating Game Five loss in the NLCS to beat the Cardinals in six games for the first pennant of their 44-year history.

"It was worth the wait," said Clemens, who scotched his retirement plans to join his hometown team prior to

Finally bringing a World Series to Houston
Roger Clemens took his hometown team to new heights

the 2004 season after spending the first 20 years of his career in the AL. "This is for the city. This was for our fans. They waited a long time."

The Astros seemed poised to wrap up the series at home in Minute Maid Park in Game Five as they led 4-2 in the ninth with Lidge on the mound, two outs, none on and two strikes on St. Louis shortstop David Eckstein. Eckstein battled, though, and grounded a single to left field. Jim Edmonds followed by drawing a walk.

The crowd was still at full roar when Albert Pujols came to the plate and hit a long, dramatic three-run home run to left field on the first pitch he saw from Lidge. The Astros couldn't score in the bottom of the ninth, giving the Cardinals a 5-4 win and making the Astros 0-5 all-time in NLCS-clinching games.

Though Houston still held a 3-2 lead in the series, the momentum seemed to be in the Cardinals' favor as they returned home to St. Louis for the final two games.

However, Oswalt stopped the Cardinals 5-1 in Game Six to win his second game of the series and capture series MVP honors. Oswalt gave up only one run and three hits in seven innings while striking out six and finished the series with a 1.29 ERA, allowing two runs in 14 innings.

The series started out well for the Cardinals as they posted a 5-3 win at home against ailing Astros starter Andy Pettitte, who was struck on the knee by a line drive in batting practice and gave up a 445-foot, two-run homer to left fielder Reggie Sanders in the first inning. Chris Carpenter gave allowed two runs in eight innings for the win.

The Astros evened the series with a 4-1 win in Game Two. Oswalt gave up one run in seven innings while rookie Chris Burke, making his first start of the postseason after being the hero in the Division Series win over the Braves, scored two runs and drove in another.

The Astros then took a 3-1 lead in the series with back-to-back wins once the series moved to Houston.

Clemens pitched six innings for the win, giving up three runs, and Mike Lamb homered in the Astros' 4-3 win in Game Three. In Game Four, Lidge got out of a first-and-third jam by getting John Mabry to hit into a double play as the Astros held on, 2-1.

Brad Lidge

Lidge couldn't close out Game Five, but the Astros took him off the hook by winning the decisive Game Six.

Burke, who hit .248 with five homers in the regular season, provided the most dramatic moment of the Division Series when his solo home run in the bottom of the 18th inning off fellow rookie Joey Devine gave the Astros a clinching 7-6 victory in Game Four. It was the longest playoff game in major league history, both in terms of innings and time (five hours, 50 minutes).

Clemens pitched three scoreless innings of relief for the victory in his first work out of the bullpen since his rookie season with the Red Sox in 1984.

The Astros used 23 of their 25 players—everyone but Oswalt and Pettitte—and Burke entered the game in the 10th inning as a pinch-runner.

The Braves were eliminated in the first round of the playoffs for a fourth straight season and continued to have just one World Series title to show for their record run of 14 consecutive division titles.

LARRY GOREN

Sending the Yankees packing
Ervin Santana stepped in when Bartolo Colon went down

The Cardinals swept the Padres in three games in the other NL Division Series. Sanders set Division Series record by driving in 10 runs.

The Padres had the worst winning percentage (.506) ever for a team that qualified for the playoffs and were overmatched against St. Louis, as their starting pitchers gave up 15 runs in just 10 innings.

The White Sox made sure the Red Sox would not defend their World Series championship by sweeping them in the first round of the AL Division Series.

Orlando Hernandez, a former October hero with the Yankees and the last man added to White Sox' postseason roster after struggling in the second half of the regular season, was hero of the decisive Game Three.

El Duque entered in the sixth with none out, the bases loaded and the White Sox clinging to a 4-3 lead, provided by Konerko's solo homer in the top of the sixth. Hernandez escaped the jam and the White Sox went on to a 5-3 victory.

The Angels outlasted the Yankees in five games in the other AL Division Series, extending the Yankees' championship drought to five straight seasons even though owner George Steinbrenner paid out a record $203 million in salaries and $30 million more in luxury tax.

Yankees third baseman Alex Rodriguez had a dismal series, going 2-for-15 (.133) with no RBIs. Another Yankees slugger, right fielder Gary Sheffield, failed to record an extra-base hit in the series.

Rookie Ervin Santana was the hero for the Angels in their 5-3 victory in Game Five. When Angels ace Bartolo Colon was forced to leave after one inning with a stiff shoulder, Santana stepped in and allowed three runs in 5⅓ relief innings.

WORLD SERIES
BOX SCORES

GAME ONE: October 22
Chicago White Sox 5, Houston Astros 3

Houston	ab	r	h	bi	bb	so	Chicago	ab	r	h	bi	bb	so
Biggio, 2b	4	1	1	0	0	0	Podsednik, lf	5	0	2	1	0	1
Taveras, cf	3	0	2	0	0	0	Iguchi, 2b	5	0	0	0	0	1
Berkman, lf	4	0	2	2	0	1	Dye, rf	2	1	1	1	2	0
1-Burke, pr-lf	0	0	0	0	0	0	Konerko, 1b	4	0	2	0	0	0
Ensberg, 3b	4	0	0	0	0	1	C. Everett, dh	3	1	1	0	0	1
Lamb, 1b	4	1	1	1	0	2	Rowand, cf	3	0	1	0	1	1
Bagwell, dh	2	0	0	0	0	1	Pierzynski, c	4	2	1	1	0	0
Lane, rf	4	0	0	0	0	1	Crede, 3b	4	1	1	1	0	0
Ausmus, c	3	0	1	0	0	0	Uribe, ss	2	0	1	1	2	0
A. Everett, ss	4	1	0	0	0	1							
Totals	**32**	**3**	**7**	**3**	**0**	**7**	**Totals**	**32**	**5**	**10**	**5**	**5**	**4**

Houston	**012 000 000—3**
Chicago	**120 100 01x—5**

E—A. Everett. **DP**—Houston 2, Chicago 1. **LOB**—Houston 6, Chicago 9. **2B**—Berkman (1), Taveras 2 (2), Uribe (1). **3B**—Podsednik (1). **HR**—Lamb (1), Dye (1), Crede (1). **SB**—Burke (1), Podsednik (1), Pierzynski (1). **SH**—C. Everett.

Houston	ip	h	r	er	bb	so	Chicago	ip	h	r	er	bb	so
Clemens	2	4	3	3	0	1	Contreras W	7	6	3	3	0	2
Rodriguez L	3⅓	4	1	1	5	1	Cotts	⅔	1	0	0	0	2
Qualls	1⅔	0	0	0	0	2	Jenks S	1⅓	0	0	0	0	3
Springer	1	2	1	1	0	0							

Contreras pitched to one batter in the 8th.

IBB—Rowand (by Rodriguez). **HBP**—Bagwell 2 (by Contreras 2), Ausmus (by Contreras).

Umpires: HP—Joe West. **1B**—Jeff Nelson. **2B**—Jerry Layne. **3B**—Derryl Cousins. **LF**—Gary Cederstrom. **RF**—Angel Hernandez.

T—3:13. **A**—41,206.

GAME TWO: October 23
Chicago White Sox 7, Houston Astros 6

Houston	ab	r	h	bi	bb	so	Chicago	ab	r	h	bi	bb	so
Biggio, 2b	4	0	0	0	0	1	Podsednik, lf	5	1	1	1	0	1
Bruntlett, 2b	0	0	0	0	0	0	Iguchi, 2b	3	1	1	0	1	1
Lamb, ph-1b	1	0	0	0	0	0	Dye, rf	3	1	1	1	0	0
Taveras, cf	4	2	2	0	0	0	Konerko, 1b	4	1	1	4	0	1
Berkman, 1b-lf	3	0	1	3	0	2	C. Everett, dh	4	0	2	0	0	1
Ensberg, 3b	4	1	1	1	0	1	Rowand, cf	4	1	2	0	0	0
Bagwell, dh	4	1	1	0	0	0	Pierzynski, c	4	1	1	0	0	1
Lane, rf	4	0	1	0	0	2	Crede, 3b	4	0	1	1	0	0
Burke, lf-2b	3	1	0	0	1	0	Uribe, ss	4	1	2	1	0	0
Ausmus, c	4	1	2	0	0	0							
A. Everett, ss	3	0	0	0	0	2							
Vizcaino, ph-ss	1	0	1	2	0	0							
Totals	**35**	**6**	**9**	**6**	**1**	**8**	**Totals**	**35**	**7**	**12**	**7**	**1**	**5**

LARRY GOREN

Game Two hero
Scott Podsednik showed rare power with his game-winning homer

Houston	**011 020 002—6**
Chicago	**020 000 401—7**

LOB—Houston 4, Chicago 5. **2B**—Ausmus (1), Berkman (2), Uribe (2), Rowand (1). **3B**—Taveras (1). **HR**—Ensberg (1), Konerko (1), Podsednik (1). **SB**—Lane (1), Uribe (1). **CS**—C. Everett. **SF**—Berkman.

Houston	ip	h	r	er	bb	so	Chicago	ip	h	r	er	bb	so
Pettitte	6	8	2	2	0	4	Buehrle	7	7	4	4	0	6
Wheeler	⅔	1	3	3	1	1	Politte	1	0	0	0	0	1
Qualls	⅔	2	1	1	0	0	Jenks	⅔	2	2	2	1	1
Gallo	⅔	0	0	0	0	0	Cotts W	⅓	0	0	0	0	0
Lidge L	⅓	1	1	1	0	0							

One out when winning run scored.

HBP—Dye (by Wheeler).

Umpires: HP—Jeff Nelson. **1B**—Jerry Layne. **2B**—Derryl Cousins. **3B**—Gary Cederstrom. **LF**—Angel Hernandez. **RF**—Joe West.

T—3:11 (:07 delay). **A**—41,432.

GAME THREE: October 25
Chicago White Sox 7, Houston Astros 5

Chicago	ab	r	h	bi	bb	so	Houston	ab	r	h	bi	bb	so
Podsednik, lf	8	1	2	0	0	2	Biggio, 2b	6	2	2	1	1	3
Iguchi, 2b	7	1	2	1	0	1	Astacio, p	0	0	0	0	0	0
Marte, p	0	0	0	0	0	0	Rodriguez, p	0	0	0	0	0	0
Buehrle, p	0	0	0	0	0	0	Taveras, cf	6	0	0	0	0	3
Dye, rf	7	1	2	1	0	1	Berkman, lf-1b	5	0	2	1	2	1
Konerko, 1b	4	0	1	0	2	0	Ensberg, 3b	6	1	1	1	1	3
Pierzynski, c	3	0	1	2	2	0	Lamb, 1b	3	0	0	0	1	1
Hernandez, p	0	0	0	0	0	0	Bruntlett, pr-lf	0	0	0	0	0	0
Vizcaino, p	0	0	0	0	0	0	Lidge, p	0	0	0	0	0	0
Perez, ph	1	0	0	0	0	0	Palmeiro, ph-lf	1	0	0	0	2	0
Jenks, p	0	0	0	0	0	0	Lane, rf	6	1	2	2	1	0
Blum, 2b	1	1	1	1	0	0	Ausmus, c	6	0	0	0	1	2
Rowand, cf	6	1	1	0	1	3	A. Everett, ss	5	1	1	0	1	1
Crede, 3b	5	1	2	1	1	0	Oswalt, p	1	0	0	0	0	0
Uribe, ss	6	1	1	0	1	1	Springer, p	0	0	0	0	0	0
Garland, p	3	0	0	0	0	2	Bagwell, ph	1	0	0	0	0	0
C. Everett, ph	1	0	1	0	0	0	Wheeler, p	0	0	0	0	0	0
Harris, pr	0	0	0	0	0	0	Gallo, p	0	0	0	0	0	0
Politte, p	0	0	0	0	0	0	Burke, lf	1	0	0	0	1	0
Cotts, p	0	0	0	0	0	0	Qualls, p	0	0	0	0	0	0
Hermanson, p	0	0	0	0	0	0	Vizcaino, ph-2b	0	0	0	0	1	0
Widger, c	1	0	0	1	2	1							
Totals	**53**	**7**	**14**	**7**	**9**	**11**	**Totals**	**47**	**5**	**8**	**5**	**12**	**14**

Chicago	**000 050 000 000 02—7**
Houston	**102 100 010 000 00—5**

E—Ensberg, Uribe 2, Hernandez. **DP**—Chicago 4, Houston 2. **LOB**—Chicago 15, Houston 15. **2B**—Konerko (1), Pierzynski (1), Biggio (1), Lane (1). **HR**—Crede (2), Lane (1), Blum (1). **SB**—Burke (2), Podsednik (2), Harris (1). **CS**—A. Everett. **SH**—Oswalt, A. Everett.

Chicago	ip	h	r	er	bb	so	Houston	ip	h	r	er	bb	so
Garland	7	7	4	2	2	4	Oswalt	6	8	5	5	5	3
Politte	⅔	0	1	1	1	1	Springer	1	0	0	0	0	1
Cotts	0	0	0	0	1	0	Wheeler	1⅓	1	0	0	0	0
Hermanson	⅓	1	0	0	0	1	Gallo	⅓	0	0	0	0	0
Hernandez	1	0	0	0	4	2	Lidge	1⅓	0	0	0	0	3
Vizcaino	1	0	0	0	1	0	Qualls	3	1	0	0	2	3
Jenks	2	0	0	0	1	3	Astacio L	⅔	4	2	2	2	0
Marte W	1⅔	0	0	0	2	3	Rodriguez	⅓	0	0	0	0	1
Buehrle S	⅓	0	0	0	0	0							

Cotts pitched to one batter in the 8th.

Hernandez pitched to one batter in the 10th.

Oswalt pitched to one batter in the 7th.

IBB—Berkman (by Hernandez), Konerko (by Qualls). **HBP**—Taveras (by Jenks), Crede (by Oswalt), Konerko (by Wheeler).

Umpires: HP—Jerry Layne. **1B**—Derryl Cousins. **2B**—Gary Cederstrom. **3B**—Angel Hernandez. **LF**—Joe West. **RF**—Jeff Nelson.

T—5:41. **A**—42,848.

GAME FOUR: October 26
Chicago White Sox 1, Houston Astros 0

Chicago	ab	r	h	bi	bb	so	Houston	ab	r	h	bi	bb	so
Podsednik, lf	3	0	1	0	0	0	Biggio, 2b	4	0	1	0	0	0
Iguchi, 2b	3	0	0	0	0	0	Taveras, cf	2	0	1	0	0	0
C. Everett, ph	1	0	0	0	0	0	Berkman, lf	1	0	0	0	3	1
Politte, p	0	0	0	0	0	0	Ensberg, 3b	4	0	0	0	0	2
Cotts, p	0	0	0	0	0	0	Lamb, 1b	2	0	1	0	1	0
Jenks, p	0	0	0	0	0	0	Vizcaino, ph-1b	1	0	0	0	0	0
Dye, rf	4	0	3	1	0	1	Lane, rf	4	0	1	0	0	2

Konerko, 1b	4	0	0	0	0	2	Ausmus, c	3	0	1	0	0	1
Pierzynski, c	4	0	1	0	0	1	A. Everett, ss	3	0	0	0	0	0
Rowand, cf	4	0	1	0	0	2	Burke, ph	1	0	0	0	0	0
Crede, 3b	4	0	1	0	0	2	Backe, p	2	0	0	0	0	1
Uribe, ss	4	0	0	0	0	2	Bagwell, ph	1	0	0	0	0	0
Garcia, p	2	0	0	0	0	0	Lidge, p	0	0	0	0	0	0
Harris, ph-2b	1	1	1	0	0	0	Palmeiro, ph	1	0	0	0	0	0
Totals	**34**	**1**	**8**	**1**	**0**	**10**	**Totals**	**29**	**0**	**5**	**0**	**4**	**7**

Chicago	**000 000 010—1**
Houston	**000 000 000—0**

DP—Chicago. **LOB**—Chicago 7, Houston 9. **2B**—Dye (1), Crede (1), Pierzynski (2), Lamb (1). **3B**—Podsednik (2). **SB**—Berkman (1), Taveras (1), Harris (1). **SH**—Podsednik.

Chicago	ip	h	r	er	bb	so	Houston	ip	h	r	er	bb	so
Garcia W	7	4	0	0	3	7	Backe	7	5	0	0	0	7
Politte	⅔	0	0	0	1	0	Lidge L	2	3	1	1	0	3
Cotts	⅓	0	0	0	0	0							
Jenks S	1	1	0	0	0	0							

WP—Politte. **IBB**—Lamb (by Garcia), Berkman (by Politte). **HBP**—Taveras (by Politte).

Umpires: HP—Derryl Cousins. **1B**—Gary Cederstrom. **2B**—Angel Hernandez. **3B**—Joe West. **LF**—Jeff Nelson. **RF**—Jerry Layne.

T—3:20. **A**—42,936.

First rookie to save a clincher
Bobby Jenks started the 2005 season in Double-A

COMPOSITE BOX

HOUSTON ASTROS

Player, Pos.	AVG	G	AB	R	H	2B	3B	HR	RBI	BB	SO	SB
Jose Vizcaino, ss	.500	3	2	0	1	0	0	0	2	1	0	0
Lance Berkman, of	.385	4	13	0	5	2	0	0	6	5	5	1
Willy Taveras, of	.333	4	15	2	5	2	1	0	0	0	3	1
Brad Ausmus, c	.250	4	16	1	4	1	0	0	0	1	3	0
Craig Biggio, 2b	.222	4	18	3	4	1	0	0	1	1	4	0
Jason Lane, of	.222	4	18	1	4	1	0	1	2	1	5	1
Mike Lamb, 1b	.200	4	10	1	2	1	0	1	1	2	3	0
Jeff Bagwell, dh	.125	4	8	1	1	0	0	0	0	0	1	0
Morgan Ensberg, 3b	.111	4	18	2	2	0	0	1	2	1	7	0
Adam Everett, ss	.067	4	15	2	1	0	0	0	0	1	4	0
Brandon Backe, p	.000	1	2	0	0	0	0	0	0	0	1	0
Chris Burke, of	.000	4	5	1	0	0	0	0	0	2	0	2
Orlando Palmeiro, of	.000	2	2	0	0	0	0	0	0	2	0	0
Totals	**.204**	**4**	**142**	**14**	**29**	**8**	**1**	**3**	**14**	**17**	**36**	**5**

Pitcher	W	L	ERA	G	GS	SV	IP	H	R	ER	BB	SO
Brandon Backe	0	0	0.00	1	1	0	7	5	0	0	0	7
Mike Gallo	0	0	0.00	2	0	0	1	0	0	0	0	0
Chad Qualls	0	0	1.69	3	0	0	5	3	1	1	2	5
Wandy Rodriguez	0	1	2.45	2	0	0	4	4	1	1	5	2
Andy Pettitte	0	0	3.00	1	1	0	6	8	2	2	0	4
Russ Springer	0	0	4.50	2	0	0	2	2	1	1	0	1
Brad Lidge	0	2	4.91	3	0	0	4	4	2	2	0	6
Roy Oswalt	0	0	7.50	1	1	0	6	8	5	5	5	3
Roger Clemens	0	0	13.50	1	1	0	2	4	3	3	0	1
Dan Wheeler	0	0	13.50	2	0	0	2	2	3	3	1	1
Ezequiel Astacio	0	1	27.00	1	0	0	1	4	2	2	2	0
Totals	**0**	**4**	**4.58**	**4**	**4**	**0**	**39**	**44**	**20**	**20**	**15**	**30**

CHICAGO WHITE SOX

Player, Pos.	AVG	G	AB	R	H	2B	3B	HR	RBI	BB	SO	SB
Geoff Blum, 2b	1.000	1	1	1	1	0	0	1	1	0	0	0
Carl Everett, dh	.444	4	9	1	4	0	0	0	0	0	2	0
Jermaine Dye, of	.438	4	16	3	7	1	0	1	3	2	2	0
Joe Crede, 3b	.294	4	17	2	5	1	0	2	3	1	2	0
Aaron Rowand, of	.294	4	17	2	5	1	0	0	0	2	6	0
Scott Podsednik, of	.286	4	21	2	6	0	2	1	2	0	4	2
A.J. Pierzynski, c	.267	4	15	3	4	2	0	0	3	2	2	1
Paul Konerko, 1b	.250	4	16	1	4	1	0	1	4	2	3	0
Juan Uribe, ss	.250	4	16	2	4	3	0	0	2	3	3	1
Tadahito Iguchi, 2b	.167	4	18	2	3	0	0	0	1	1	3	0
Freddy Garcia, p	.000	1	2	0	0	0	0	0	0	0	0	0
Jon Garland, p	.000	1	3	0	0	0	0	0	0	0	2	0
Totals	**.285**	**4**	**151**	**19**	**43**	**9**	**2**	**6**	**19**	**13**	**29**	**4**

Pitcher	W	L	ERA	G	GS	SV	IP	H	R	ER	BB	SO
Neil Cotts	1	0	0.00	4	0	0	1.1	1	0	0	1	2
Freddy Garcia	1	0	0.00	1	1	0	7.0	4	0	0	3	7
Dustin Hermanson	0	0	0.00	1	0	0	0.1	1	0	0	0	1
Orlando Hernandez	0	0	0.00	1	0	0	1.0	0	0	0	4	2
Damaso Marte	1	0	0.00	1	0	0	1.2	0	0	0	2	3
Luis Vizcaino	0	0	0.00	1	0	0	1.0	0	0	0	1	0
Jon Garland	0	0	2.57	1	1	0	7.0	7	4	2	2	4
Bobby Jenks	0	0	3.60	4	0	2	5.0	3	2	2	2	7
Jose Contreras	1	0	3.86	1	1	0	7.0	6	3	3	0	2
Cliff Politte	0	0	3.86	3	0	0	2.1	0	1	1	2	2
Mark Buehrle	0	0	4.91	2	1	1	7.1	7	4	4	0	6
Totals	4	0	2.63	4	4	3	41.0	29	14	12	17	36

SCORE BY INNING

Houston	**125 120 012 000 00—14**
Chicago	**140 150 421 000 02—20**

E—Ensberg, A. Everett, Uribe 2, O. Hernandez. **DP**—Houston 6, Chicago 4. **LOB**—Houston 34, Chicago 36. **CS**—A. Everett, C. Everett. **SH**—Ausmus, Oswalt, Taveras 2, C. Everett, Podsednik. **SF**—Berkman. **HBP**—Bagwell 2 (by Contreras 2), Ausmus (by Contreras), Taveras (by Jenks), Taveras (by Politte), Crede (by Oswalt), Dye (by Wheeler), Konerko (by Wheeler). **IBB**—Berkman (by O. Hernandez), Berkman (by Politte), Lamb (by Garcia), Konerko (by Qualls), Rowand (by W. Rodriguez). **WP**—Politte.

AMERICAN LEAGUE CHAMPIONS, 1901-2005

	PENNANT	PCT	GA
1901	Chicago	.610	4
1902	Philadelphia	.610	5
1903	Boston	.659	14½
1904	Boston	.617	1½
1905	Philadelphia	.622	2
1906	Chicago	.616	3
1907	Detroit	.613	1½
1908	Detroit	.588	½
1909	Detroit	.645	3½
1910	Philadelphia	.680	14½
1911	Philadelphia	.669	13½
1912	Boston	.691	14
1913	Philadelphia	.627	6½
1914	Philadelphia	.651	8½
1915	Boston	.669	2½
1916	Boston	.591	2
1917	Chicago	.649	9
1918	Boston	.595	2½
1919	Chicago	.629	3½
1920	Cleveland	.636	2
1921	New York	.641	4½
1922	New York	.610	1
1923	New York	.645	16
1924	Washington	.597	2
1925	Washington	.636	8½
1926	New York	.591	3
1927	New York	.714	19
1928	New York	.656	2½
1929	Philadelphia	.693	18
1930	Philadelphia	.662	8
1931	Philadelphia	.704	13½
1932	New York	.695	13
1933	Washington	.651	7
1934	Detroit	.656	7
1935	Detroit	.616	3
1936	New York	.667	19½
1937	New York	.662	13
1938	New York	.651	9½
1939	New York	.702	17
1940	Detroit	.584	1
1941	New York	.656	17
1942	New York	.669	9
1943	New York	.636	13½
1944	St. Louis	.578	1
1945	Detroit	.575	1½
1946	Boston	.675	12
1947	New York	.630	12
1948	Cleveland	.626	1
1949	New York	.630	1
1950	New York	.636	3
1951	New York	.636	5
1952	New York	.617	2
1953	New York	.656	8½
1954	Cleveland	.721	8
1955	New York	.623	3
1956	New York	.630	9
1957	New York	.636	8
1958	New York	.597	10
1959	Chicago	.610	5
1960	New York	.630	8
1961	New York	.673	8
1962	New York	.593	5
1963	New York	.646	10½
1964	New York	.611	1
1965	Minnesota	.630	7
1966	Baltimore	.606	9
1967	Boston	.568	1
1968	Detroit	.636	12

TWO-DIVISION FORMAT * Won first half; defeated Milwaukee 3-2 in best-of-5 playoff. ** Won first half, defeated Kansas City 3-0 in best-of-5 playoff.

	EAST	PCT	GA	WEST	PCT	GA	PENNANT		MVP
1969	Baltimore	.673	19	Minnesota	.599	9	Baltimore	3-0	Harmon Killebrew, 1b-3b, Minnesota
1970	Baltimore	.667	15	Minnesota	.605	9	Baltimore	3-0	Boog Powell, 1b, Baltimore
1971	Baltimore	.639	12	Oakland	.627	16	Baltimore	3-0	Vida Blue, lhp, Oakland
1972	Detroit	.551	½	Oakland	.600	5½	Oakland	3-2	Dick Allen, 1b, Chicago
1973	Baltimore	.599	8	Oakland	.580	6	Oakland	3-2	Reggie Jackson, of, Oakland
1974	Baltimore	.562	2	Oakland	.556	5	Oakland	3-1	Jeff Burroughs, of, Texas
1975	Boston	.594	4½	Oakland	.605	7	Boston	3-0	Fred Lynn, of, Boston
1976	New York	.610	10½	Kansas City	.556	2½	New York	3-2	Thurman Munson, c, New York
1977	New York	.617	2½	Kansas City	.630	8	New York	3-2	Rod Carew, 1b, Minnesota
1978	New York	.613	1	Kansas City	.568	5	New York	3-1	Jim Rice, of, Boston
1979	Baltimore	.642	8	California	.543	3	Baltimore	3-1	Don Baylor, dh, California
1980	New York	.636	3	Kansas City	.599	14	Kansas City	3-0	George Brett, 3b, Kansas City
1981	New York*	.607	2	Oakland**	.587	—	New York	3-0	Rollie Fingers, rhp, Milwaukee
	Milwaukee	.585	1½	Kansas City	.566	1			
1982	Milwaukee	.586	1	California	.574	3	Milwaukee	3-2	Robin Yount, ss, Milwaukee
1983	Baltimore	.605	6	Chicago	.611	20	Baltimore	3-1	Cal Ripken, ss, Baltimore
1984	Detroit	.642	15	Kansas City	.519	3	Detroit	3-0	Willie Hernandez, lhp, Detroit
1985	Toronto	.615	2	Kansas City	.562	1	Kansas City	4-3	Don Mattingly, 1b, New York
1986	Boston	.590	5½	California	.568	5	Boston	4-3	Roger Clemens, rhp, Boston
1987	Detroit	.605	2	Minnesota	.525	2	Minnesota	4-1	George Bell, of, Toronto
1988	Boston	.549	1	Oakland	.642	13	Oakland	4-0	Jose Canseco, of, Oakland
1989	Toronto	.549	2	Oakland	.611	7	Oakland	4-1	Robin Yount, of, Milwaukee
1990	Boston	.543	2	Oakland	.636	9	Oakland	4-0	Rickey Henderson, of, Oakland
1991	Toronto	.562	7	Minnesota	.586	8	Minnesota	4-1	Cal Ripken, ss, Baltimore
1992	Toronto	.593	4	Oakland	.593	6	Toronto	4-2	Dennis Eckersley, rhp, Oakland
1993	Toronto	.586	7	Chicago	.580	8	Toronto	4-2	Frank Thomas, 1b, Chicago

THREE-DIVISION FORMAT/WILD CARD

	EAST	PCT	GA	CENTRAL	PCT	GA	WEST	PCT	GA	WILD CARD	PCT
1994	New York	.619	6½	Chicago	.593	1	Texas	.456	1	None	
	PENNANT: None (season incomplete)						**MVP:** Frank Thomas, 1b, Chicago				
1995	Boston	.597	7	Cleveland	.694	30	Seattle	.545	1	New York (East)	.549
	PENNANT: Cleveland def. Seattle 4-2						**MVP:** Mo Vaughn, 1b, Boston				
1996	New York	.568	4	Cleveland	.615	14½	Texas	.556	4	Baltimore (East)	.543
	PENNANT: New York def. Baltimore 4-1						**MVP:** Juan Gonzalez, of, Texas				
1997	Baltimore	.605	2	Cleveland	.534	6	Seattle	.556	6	New York (East)	.593
	PENNANT: Cleveland def. Baltimore 4-2						**MVP:** Ken Griffey, of, Seattle				
1998	New York	.704	22	Cleveland	.549	9	Texas	.543	3	Boston (East)	.568
	PENNANT: New York def. Cleveland 4-2						**MVP:** Juan Gonzalez, of, Texas				
1999	New York	.605	4	Cleveland	.599	21½	Texas	.586	8	Boston (East)	.580
	PENNANT: New York def. Boston 4-1						**MVP:** Ivan Rodriguez, c, Texas				
2000	New York	.540	2½	Chicago	.586	5	Oakland	.565	½	Seattle (West)	.562
	PENNANT: New York def. Seattle 4-2						**MVP:** Jason Giambi, 1b, Oakland				
2001	New York	.594	13½	Cleveland	.562	6	Seattle	.716	14	Oakland (West)	.630
	PENNANT: New York def. Seattle 4-1						**MVP:** Ichiro Suzuki, of, Seattle				
2002	New York	.640	10½	Minnesota	.584	13½	Oakland	.636	4	Anaheim (West)	.611
	PENNANT: Anaheim def. Minnesota 4-1						**MVP:** Miguel Tejada, ss, Oakland				
2003	New York	.623	6	Minnesota	.556	4	Oakland	.593	3	Boston (East)	.586
	PENNANT: New York def. Boston 4-3						**MVP:** Alex Rodriguez, ss, Texas				
2004	New York	.623	3	Minnesota	.568	9	Anaheim	.568	1	Boston (East)	.605
	PENNANT: Boston def. New York 4-3						**MVP:** Vladimir Guerrero, of, Anaheim				
2005	New York	.586	—	Chicago	.611	6	Los Angeles	.586	7	Boston (East)	.586
	PENNANT: Chicago def. Los Angeles 4-1						**MVP:** Alex Rodriguez, 3b, New York				

NATIONAL LEAGUE CHAMPIONS, 1901-2005

	PENNANT	PCT	GA		PENNANT	PCT	GA		PENNANT	PCT	GA
1901	Pittsburgh	.647	1½	1924	New York	.608	1½	1947	Brooklyn	.610	5
1902	Pittsburgh	.741	27½	1925	Pittsburgh	.621	8½	1948	Boston	.595	6½
1903	Pittsburgh	.650	6½	1926	St. Louis	.578	2	1949	Brooklyn	.630	1
1904	New York	.693	13	1927	Pittsburgh	.610	1½	1950	Philadelphia	.591	2
1905	New York	.686	9	1928	St. Louis	.617	2	1951	New York	.624	1
1906	Chicago	.763	20	1929	Chicago	.645	10½	1952	Brooklyn	.627	4½
1907	Chicago	.704	17	1930	St. Louis	.597	2	1953	Brooklyn	.682	13
1908	Chicago	.643	1	1931	St. Louis	.656	13	1954	New York	.630	5
1909	Pittsburgh	.724	6½	1932	Chicago	.584	4	1955	Brooklyn	.641	13½
1910	Chicago	.675	13	1933	New York	.599	5	1956	Brooklyn	.604	1
1911	New York	.647	7½	1934	St. Louis	.621	2	1957	Milwaukee	.617	8
1912	New York	.682	10	1935	Chicago	.649	4	1958	Milwaukee	.597	8
1913	New York	.664	12½	1936	New York	.597	5	1959	Los Angeles	.564	2
1914	Boston	.614	10½	1937	New York	.625	3	1960	Pittsburgh	.617	7
1915	Philadelphia	.592	7	1938	Chicago	.586	2	1961	Cincinnati	.604	4
1916	Brooklyn	.610	2½	1939	Cincinnati	.630	4½	1962	San Francisco	.624	1
1917	New York	.636	10	1940	Cincinnati	.654	12	1963	Los Angeles	.611	6
1918	Chicago	.651	10½	1941	Brooklyn	.649	2½	1964	St. Louis	.574	1
1919	Cincinnati	.686	9	1942	St. Louis	.688	2	1965	Los Angeles	.599	2
1920	Brooklyn	.604	7	1943	St. Louis	.682	18	1966	Los Angeles	.586	1½
1921	New York	.614	4	1944	St. Louis	.682	14½	1967	St. Louis	.627	10½
1922	New York	.604	7	1945	Chicago	.636	3	1968	St. Louis	.599	9
1923	New York	.621	4½	1946	St. Louis	.628	2				

TWO-DIVISION FORMAT *Won second half; defeated Philadelphia 3-2 in best-of-5 playoff. **Won first half; defeated Houston 3-2 in best-of-5 playoff.

	EAST	PCT	GA	WEST	PCT	GA	PENNANT		MVP
1969	New York	.617	8	Atlanta	.574	3	New York	3-0	Willie McCovey, 1b, San Francisco
1970	Pittsburgh	.549	5	Cincinnati	.630	14½	Cincinnati	3-0	Johnny Bench, c, Cincinnati
1971	Pittsburgh	.599	7	San Francisco	.556	1	Pittsburgh	3-1	Joe Torre, 3b, St. Louis
1972	Pittsburgh	.619	11	Cincinnati	.617	10½	Cincinnati	3-2	Johnny Bench, c, Cincinnati
1973	New York	.509	1½	Cincinnati	.611	3½	New York	3-2	Pete Rose, of, Cincinnati
1974	Pittsburgh	.543	1½	Los Angeles	.630	4	Los Angeles	3-1	Steve Garvey, 1b, Los Angeles
1975	Pittsburgh	.571	6½	Cincinnati	.667	20	Cincinnati	3-0	Joe Morgan, 2b, Cincinnati
1976	Philadelphia	.623	9	Cincinnati	.630	10	Cincinnati	3-0	Joe Morgan, 2b, Cincinnati
1977	Philadelphia	.623	5	Los Angeles	.605	10	Los Angeles	3-1	George Foster, of, Cincinnati
1978	Philadelphia	.556	1½	Los Angeles	.586	2½	Los Angeles	3-1	Dave Parker, of, Pittsburgh
1979	Pittsburgh	.605	2	Cincinnati	.559	1½	Pittsburgh	3-0	Hernandez, St. Louis; Stargell, Pittsburgh
1980	Philadelphia	.562	1	Houston	.571	1	Philadelphia	3-2	Mike Schmidt, 3b, Philadelphia
1981	Montreal*	.566	½	Los Angeles**	.632	½	Los Angeles	3-2	Mike Schmidt, 3b, Philadelphia
	Philadelphia	.618	1½	Houston	.623	1			
1982	St. Louis	.568	3	Atlanta	.549	1	St. Louis	3-0	Dale Murphy, of, Atlanta
1983	Philadelphia	.556	6	Los Angeles	.562	3	Philadelphia	3-1	Dale Murphy, of, Atlanta
1984	Chicago	.596	6½	San Diego	.568	12	San Diego	3-2	Ryne Sandberg, 2b, Chicago
1985	St. Louis	.623	3	Los Angeles	.586	5½	St. Louis	4-2	Willie McGee, of, St. Louis
1986	New York	.667	21½	Houston	.593	10	New York	4-2	Mike Schmidt, 3b, Philadelphia
1987	St. Louis	.586	3	San Francisco	.556	6	St. Louis	4-3	Andre Dawson, of, Chicago
1988	New York	.625	15	Los Angeles	.584	7	Los Angeles	4-3	Kirk Gibson, of, Los Angeles
1989	Chicago	.571	6	San Francisco	.568	3	San Francisco	4-1	Kevin Mitchell, of, San Francisco
1990	Pittsburgh	.586	4	Cincinnati	.562	5	Cincinnati	4-2	Barry Bonds, of, Pittsburgh
1991	Pittsburgh	.605	14	Atlanta	.580	1	Atlanta	4-3	Terry Pendleton, 3b, Atlanta
1992	Pittsburgh	.593	9	Atlanta	.605	8	Atlanta	4-3	Barry Bonds, of, Pittsburgh
1993	Philadelphia	.599	3	Atlanta	.642	1	Philadelphia	4-2	Barry Bonds, of, San Francisco

THREE-DIVISION FORMAT/WILD CARD

	EAST	PCT	GA	CENTRAL	PCT	GA	WEST	PCT	GA	WILD CARD	PCT
1994	Montreal	.649	6	Cincinnati	.593	½	Los Angeles	.509	3½	None	
		PENNANT: None (season incomplete)				**MVP:** Jeff Bagwell, 1b, Houston					
1995	Atlanta	.625	21	Cincinnati	.590	9	Los Angeles	.542	1	Colorado (West)	.535
		PENNANT: Atlanta def. Cincinnati, 4-2				**MVP:** Barry Larkin, ss, Cincinnati					
1996	Atlanta	.593	8	St. Louis	.543	6	San Diego	.562	1	Los Angeles (West)	.556
		PENNANT: Atlanta def. St. Louis 4-3				**MVP:** Ken Caminiti, 3b, Houston					
1997	Atlanta	.623	9	Houston	.519	5	San Francisco	.556	2	Florida (East)	.568
		PENNANT: Florida def. Atlanta 4-2				**MVP:** Larry Walker, of, Colorado					
1998	Atlanta	.654	18	Houston	.630	12½	San Diego	.605	9½	Chicago (Central)	.552
		PENNANT: San Diego def. Atlanta 4-2				**MVP:** Sammy Sosa, of, Chicago					
1999	Atlanta	.636	6½	Houston	.599	1½	Arizona	.617	14	New York (East)	.595
		PENNANT: Atlanta def. New York 4-2				**MVP:** Chipper Jones, 3b, Atlanta					
2000	Atlanta	.586	½	St. Louis	.586	10	San Francisco	.599	11	New York (East)	.580
		PENNANT: New York def. St. Louis 4-1				**MVP:** Jeff Kent, 2b, San Francisco					
2001	Atlanta	543	2	Houston	574	—	Arizona	.568	2	St. Louis (Central)	.574
		PENNANT: Arizona def. Atlanta 4-1				**MVP:** Barry Bonds, of, San Francisco					
2002	Atlanta	.631	19	St. Louis	.599	13	Arizona	.605	2½	San Francisco (West)	.590
		PENNANT: San Francisco def. St. Louis 4-1				**MVP:** Barry Bonds, of, San Francisco					
2003	Atlanta	.623	10	Chicago	.543	1	San Francisco	.621	15½	Florida (East)	.562
		PENNANT: Florida def. Chicago 4-3				**MVP:** Barry Bonds, of, San Francisco					
2004	Atlanta	.593	10	St. Louis	.648	13	Los Angeles	.574	2	Houston (Central)	.568
		PENNANT: St. Louis def. Houston 4-3				**MVP:** Barry Bonds, of, San Francisco					
2005	Atlanta	.556	2	St. Louis	.617	11	San Diego	.506	5	Houston (Central)	.549
		PENNANT: Houston def. St. Louis 4-2				**MVP:** Albert Pujols, 1b, St. Louis					

AMERICAN LEAGUE DIVISION SERIES

CHICAGO vs. BOSTON

COMPOSITE BOX

BOSTON

Player, Pos.	AVG	G	AB	R	H	2B	3B	HR	RBI	BB	SO	SB
Kevin Millar, 1b	.333	2	3	0	1	1	0	0	1	0	1	0
David Ortiz, dh	.333	3	12	2	4	2	0	1	1	0	3	0
Manny Ramirez, of	.300	3	10	2	3	0	0	2	4	2	0	0
Jason Varitek, c	.300	3	10	1	3	0	0	0	1	0	2	0
John Olerud, 1b	.286	3	7	0	2	1	0	0	0	2	0	0
Trot Nixon, of	.273	3	11	1	3	0	0	0	1	1	1	0
Tony Graffanino, 2b	.250	3	12	0	3	2	0	0	0	0	0	0
Johnny Damon, of	.231	3	13	2	3	1	0	0	0	1	4	0
Edgar Renteria, ss	.231	3	13	1	3	2	0	0	0	1	1	0
Alex Cora, ss	.000	1	0	0	0	0	0	0	0	0	0	0
Adam Hyzdu, of	.000	1	0	0	0	0	0	0	0	0	0	0
Alejandro Machado, pr	.000	1	0	0	0	0	0	0	0	0	0	0
Doug Mirabelli, c	.000	1	2	0	0	0	0	0	0	0	0	0
Bill Mueller, 3b	.000	3	11	0	0	0	0	0	0	1	2	0
Totals	**.240**	**3**	**104**	**9**	**25**	**9**	**0**	**3**	**8**	**8**	**14**	**0**

Pitcher	W	L	ERA	G	GS	SV	IP	H	R	ER	BB	SO
Chad Bradford	0	0	0.00	2	0	0	1	1	0	0	0	1
Jon Papelbon	0	0	0.00	2	0	0	4	2	0	0	0	2
David Wells	0	1	2.70	1	1	0	7	7	5	2	0	2
Tim Wakefield	0	1	6.75	1	1	0	5	6	4	4	1	4
Mike Timlin	0	0	9.00	1	0	0	1	1	1	1	0	1
Jeremi Gonzalez	0	0	15.43	1	0	0	2	2	4	4	1	0
Bronson Arroyo	0	0	18.00	1	0	0	1	2	2	2	2	1
Matt Clement	0	1	21.60	1	1	0	3	7	8	8	0	0
Mike Myers	0	0	inf	1	0	0	0	0	0	0	1	0
Totals	**0**	**3**	**7.56**	**3**	**3**	**0**	**25**	**28**	**24**	**21**	**5**	**11**

CHICAGO

Player, Pos.	AVG	G	AB	R	H	2B	3B	HR	RBI	BB	SO	SB
Willie Harris, 2b	1.000	1	1	0	1	0	0	0	1	0	0	0
A.J. Pierzynski, c	.444	3	9	5	4	2	0	2	4	1	0	1
Aaron Rowand, of	.400	3	10	3	4	2	0	0	2	1	1	1
Juan Uribe, ss	.400	3	10	4	4	1	0	1	4	0	2	0
Carl Everett, dh	.273	3	11	2	3	0	0	0	0	0	0	0
Scott Podsednik, of	.273	3	11	3	3	1	0	1	4	1	1	1
Tadahito Iguchi, 2b	.250	3	12	1	3	0	0	1	4	0	3	0
Paul Konerko, 1b	.250	3	12	3	3	0	0	2	4	0	1	0
Jermaine Dye, of	.200	3	10	1	2	0	0	0	0	1	2	0
Joe Crede, 3b	.111	3	9	2	1	0	0	0	1	1	1	0
Geoff Blum, 1b	.000	1	1	0	0	0	0	0	0	0	0	0
Timo Perez, of	.000	1	1	0	0	0	0	0	0	0	0	0
Totals	**.289**	**3**	**97**	**24**	**28**	**6**	**0**	**7**	**24**	**5**	**11**	**3**

Pitcher	W	L	ERA	G	GS	SV	IP	H	R	ER	BB	SO
Neal Cotts	0	0	0.00	1	0	0	0	0	0	0	0	0
Orlando Hernandez	0	0	0.00	1	0	0	3	1	0	0	0	4
Bobby Jenks	0	0	0.00	2	0	2	3	1	0	0	1	1
Cliff Politte	0	0	0.00	1	0	0	1	1	0	0	0	0
Jose Contreras	1	0	2.35	1	1	0	8	8	2	2	0	6
Mark Buehrle	1	0	5.14	1	1	0	7	8	4	4	1	2
Freddy Garcia	1	0	5.40	1	1	0	5	5	3	3	4	1
Damaso Marte	0	0	inf	1	0	0	0	1	0	0	2	0
Totals	**3**	**0**	**3.00**	**3**	**3**	**2**	**27**	**25**	**9**	**9**	**8**	**14**

SCORE BY INNINGS	
Boston	202 401 000— 9
Chicago	503 256 021—24

E—Graffanino, Timlin, Crede. **DP**—Boston 3, Chicago 2. **LOB**—Boston 22, Chicago 11. **CS**—Podsednik 2. **SH**—Crede, Iguchi, Uribe. **HBP**—Dye (by Clement), Everett (by Wakefield), Pierzynski (by Gonzalez), Podsednik (by Gonzalez), Podsednik (by Wakefield). **IBB**—M Ramirez (by Buehrle). **WP**—Contreras. **PB**—None.

LOS ANGELES vs. NEW YORK

COMPOSITE BOX

NEW YORK

Player, Pos.	AVG	G	AB	R	H	2B	3B	HR	RBI	BB	SO	SB
Jason Giambi, 1b	.421	5	19	1	8	3	0	0	2	3	4	0
Derek Jeter, ss	.333	5	21	4	7	0	0	2	5	1	5	1
Ruben Sierra, of	.333	3	3	0	1	0	0	0	1	0	1	0
Gary Sheffield, of	.286	5	21	1	6	0	0	0	2	1	2	0
Robinson Cano, 2b	.263	5	19	3	5	3	0	0	5	2	4	0
Bubba Crosby, of	.250	3	8	0	2	0	0	0	1	0	1	1
Jorge Posada, c	.231	5	13	3	3	1	0	1	2	6	2	0
Bernie Williams, of	.211	5	19	2	4	2	0	0	1	1	3	0
Hideki Matsui, of	.200	5	20	4	4	1	0	1	1	2	3	0
Alex Rodriguez, 3b	.133	5	15	2	2	1	0	0	0	6	5	1
Mark Bellhorn, pr	.000	1	0	0	0	0	0	0	0	0	0	0
John Flaherty, c	.000	1	0	0	0	0	0	0	0	1	0	0
Tino Martinez, 1b	.000	4	8	0	0	0	0	0	0	1	2	0
Tony Womack, pr	.000	2	0	0	0	0	0	0	0	0	0	0
Totals	**.253**	**5**	**166**	**20**	**42**	**11**	**0**	**4**	**20**	**24**	**32**	**3**

Pitcher	W	L	ERA	G	GS	SV	IP	H	R	ER	BB	SO
Scott Proctor	0	0	0.00	2	0	0	2	3	0	0	0	1
Chien-Ming Wang	0	1	1.35	1	1	0	7	6	4	1	0	1
Shawn Chacon	0	0	2.84	1	1	0	6	4	2	2	1	5
Mariano Rivera	0	0	3.00	2	0	2	3	1	1	1	1	2
Tom Gordon	0	0	3.86	3	0	0	2	2	2	1	0	2
Mike Mussina	1	1	5.40	2	2	0	8	11	5	5	1	7
Russ Johnson	0	0	6.14	2	1	0	7	12	5	5	1	4
Aaron Small	0	1	6.75	1	0	0	3	4	2	2	0	2
Al Leiter	1	0	7.36	4	0	0	4	2	3	3	1	2
Tanyan Sturtze	0	0	13.50	2	0	0	1	1	1	1	0	0
Totals	**2**	**3**	**4.40**	**5**	**5**	**2**	**43**	**46**	**25**	**21**	**5**	**26**

Unlikely offensive hero
Bengie Molina hit three home runs against the Yankees

LOS ANGELES

Player, Pos.	AVG	G	AB	R	H	2B	3B	HR	RBI	BB	SO	SB
Jose Molina, c	1.000	1	1	1	1	0	0	0	1	0	0	0
Robb Quinlan, 3b	.500	2	2	0	1	0	0	0	0	0	0	0
Bengie Molina, c	.444	5	18	5	8	0	0	3	5	0	0	0
Juan Rivera, dh	.353	5	17	3	6	1	0	1	1	1	2	0
Vladimir Guerrero, of	.333	5	18	5	6	0	0	0	0	2	2	1
Darin Erstad, 1b	.300	5	20	1	6	2	0	0	3	0	6	0
Garret Anderson, of	.263	5	19	2	5	0	1	2	7	0	0	0
Orlando Cabrera, ss	.238	5	21	3	5	2	0	0	3	0	1	0
Adam Kennedy, 2b	.235	5	17	0	4	0	1	0	2	0	3	0
Chone Figgins, 3b	.143	5	21	2	3	1	1	0	2	1	8	0
Steve Finley, of	.091	5	11	2	1	1	0	0	1	1	4	0
Jeff DaVanon, ph	.000	1	0	1	0	0	0	0	0	0	0	0
Casey Kotchman, ph	.000	2	2	0	0	0	0	0	0	0	0	0
Josh Paul, pr	.000	1	0	0	0	0	0	0	0	0	0	0
Totals	**.275**	**5**	**167**	**25**	**46**	**7**	**3**	**6**	**25**	**5**	**26**	**1**

Pitcher	W	L	ERA	G	GS	SV	IP	H	R	ER	BB	SO
Kelvim Escobar	1	0	1.29	4	0	0	7	2	1	1	5	5
John Lackey	0	0	2.38	2	2	0	11	7	3	3	9	9
Francisco Rodriguez	0	0	2.70	3	0	2	3	5	1	1	0	2

Scot Shields	1	1	3.60	4	0	0	5	4	2	2	3	5
Bartolo Colon	0	1	4.50	2	2	0	8	10	4	4	2	7
Ervin Santana	1	0	5.06	1	0	0	5	5	3	3	2	2
Paul Byrd	0	0	9.82	1	1	0	4	7	4	4	2	2
Brendan Donnelly	0	0	27.00	1	0	0	0	2	2	1	1	0
Totals	**3**	**2**	**3.89**	**5**	**5**	**2**	**44**	**42**	**20**	**19**	**24**	**32**

SCORE BY INNINGS

New York	**340 431 311—20**
Los Angeles	**334 015 531—25**

E—Cano 2, Matsui, A. Rodriguez, Sheffield, Wang, Cabrera. **DP**—New York 3, Los Angeles 4. **LOB**—New York 43 Los Angeles 26. **CS**—Cano, A Rodriguez, Kennedy 2, Figgins, Guerrero. **SH**—Crosby, Finley 3, Kennedy. **SF**—Jeter, Williams, Anderson . **HBP**—A. Rodriguez 2 (by Colon, by Santana), Guerrero (by Wang), B. Molina (by Gordon). **IBB**—Guerrero (by Leiter). WP—Proctor, Escobar 2, Lackey 2. **PB**—None.

AMERICAN LEAGUE CHAMPIONSHIP SERIES

CHICAGO vs. LOS ANGELES

COMPOSITE BOX

LOS ANGELES

Player, Pos.	AVG	G	AB	R	H	2B	3B	HR	RBI	BB	SO	SB
Jose Molina, c	.333	1	3	0	1	0	0	0	0	0	0	0
Robb Quinlan, 3b	.333	1	3	1	1	0	0	1	1	0	2	0
Adam Kennedy, 2b	.286	5	14	3	4	0	0	0	1	0	1	0
Casey Kotchman, dh	.286	2	7	0	2	1	0	0	1	1	1	0
Darin Erstad, 1b	.235	5	17	1	4	1	0	0	0	1	2	1
Steve Finley, of	.222	3	9	1	2	0	0	0	0	0	2	0
Orlando Cabrera, ss	.200	5	20	1	4	1	0	1	3	0	2	0
Garret Anderson, of	.176	5	17	2	3	0	0	1	2	1	5	0
Chone Figgins, 3b	.118	5	17	1	2	1	0	0	1	1	3	1
Bengie Molina, c	.118	5	17	0	2	0	0	0	1	0	2	0
Juan Rivera, of	.111	3	9	1	1	1	0	0	0	0	1	0
Vladimir Guerrero, of	.050	5	20	0	1	0	0	0	1	0	1	0
Jeff DaVanon, ph	.000	3	1	0	0	0	0	0	0	0	0	0
Maicer Izturis, ss	.000	1	0	0	0	0	0	0	0	0	0	0
Josh Paul, c	.000	1	0	0	0	0	0	0	0	0	0	0
Totals	**.175**	**5**	**154**	**11**	**27**	**5**	**0**	**3**	**11**	**4**	**22**	**2**

Pitcher	W	L	ERA	G	GS	SV	IP	H	R	ER	BB	SO
Brendan Donnelly	0	0	0.00	3	0	0	3	2	0	0	1	5
Kevin Gregg	0	0	0.00	1	0	0	2	1	0	0	1	3
Francisco Rodriguez	0	0	0.00	2	0	1	2	2	2	0	3	3
Scot Shields	0	0	0.00	4	0	0	6	4	0	0	1	5
Jarrod Washburn	0	0	0.00	1	1	0	5	4	1	0	1	1
Kelvim Escobar	0	2	2.08	2	0	0	4	4	3	1	2	10
Paul Byrd	1	0	3.38	2	2	0	11	10	4	4	2	2
John Lackey	0	1	9.00	1	1	0	5	8	5	5	1	3
Esteban Yan	0	0	9.00	1	0	0	2	3	2	2	1	2
Ervin Santana	0	1	10.38	1	1	0	4	3	6	5	3	2
Totals	**1**	**4**	**3.43**	**5**	**5**	**1**	**45**	**41**	**23**	**17**	**16**	**36**

CHICAGO

Player, Pos.	AVG	G	AB	R	H	2B	3B	HR	RBI	BB	SO	SB
Joe Crede, 3b	.368	5	19	2	7	2	0	2	7	0	3	0
Scott Podsednik, of	.294	5	17	4	5	0	1	0	0	6	5	3
Paul Konerko, 1b	.286	5	21	2	6	1	0	2	7	1	4	0
Jermaine Dye, of	.263	5	19	3	5	2	0	0	3	3	3	1
Carl Everett, dh	.250	5	20	2	5	0	0	0	3	1	4	0
Juan Uribe, ss	.250	5	16	1	4	1	0	0	0	2	3	0
Tadahito Iguchi, 2b	.176	5	17	4	3	1	0	0	0	1	6	0
A.J. Pierzynski, c	.167	5	18	1	3	0	0	1	2	1	6	0
Aaron Rowand, of	.167	5	18	3	3	3	0	0	1	1	2	0
Pablo Ozuna, pr	.000	2	0	1	0	0	0	0	0	0	0	1
Totals	**.248**	**5**	**165**	**23**	**41**	**10**	**1**	**5**	**23**	**16**	**36**	**5**

LARRY GOREN

Little need for a White Sox reliever
Jose Contreras threw one of four ALCS complete games

Pitcher	W	L	ERA	G	GS	SV	IP	H	R	ER	BB	SO
Neal Cotts	0	0	0.00	1	0	0	1	0	0	0	0	0
Mark Buehrle	1	0	1.00	1	1	0	9	5	1	1	0	4
Freddy Garcia	1	0	2.00	1	1	0	9	6	2	2	1	5
Jon Garland	1	0	2.00	1	1	0	9	4	2	2	1	7
Jose Contreras	1	1	3.12	2	2	0	17	12	6	6	2	6
Totals	**4**	**1**	**2.20**	**5**	**5**	**0**	**45**	**27**	**11**	**11**	**4**	**22**

SCORE BY INNINGS

Los Angeles	**023 132 000—11**
Chicago	**713 230 133—23**

E—Cabrera, Escobar, Guerrero, Kennedy, Paul, Washburn, Contreras, Garcia, Uribe. **DP**—Los Angeles 5, Chicago 4. **LOB**—Los Angeles 17 Chicago 33. **CS**—Crede, Iguchi, Pieryznski Podsednik. **SH**—Figgins 2 , Kennedy, Iguchi 2, Pierzynski. **SF**—Anderson, Crede, Rowand. **HBP**—B. Molina (by Buehrle), Iguchi (by Washburn), Iguchi (by Santana) Iguchi (by Byrd), Rowand (by Byrd). **IBB**—Konerko (by Shields). **PB**—Pierzynski 2.

NATIONAL LEAGUE DIVISION SERIES

ATLANTA vs. HOUSTON

COMPOSITE BOX

HOUSTON

Player, Pos.	AVG	G	AB	R	H	2B	3B	HR	RBI	BB	SO	SB
Chris Burke, of	.667	3	3	1	2	1	0	1	1	1	0	0
Jeff Bagwell, ph	.500	2	2	1	1	0	0	0	1	0	0	0
Mike Lamb, 1b	.500	2	6	1	3	0	0	1	1	2	0	0
Andy Pettitte, p	.500	1	2	1	1	1	0	0	0	0	1	0
Lance Berkman, 1b	.357	4	14	4	5	1	0	1	5	3	4	0
Willy Taveras, of	.357	4	14	2	5	1	0	0	0	1	1	0
Craig Biggio, 2b	.316	4	19	6	6	4	0	0	1	2	5	1
Morgan Ensberg, 3b	.278	4	18	2	5	2	0	0	7	2	3	0
Jason Lane, of	.235	4	17	1	4	1	0	0	3	1	3	0
Brad Ausmus, c	.222	4	18	3	4	1	0	1	1	2	4	0
Adam Everett, ss	.214	4	14	1	3	0	0	0	1	1	1	0
Eric Bruntlett, of	.167	3	6	1	1	0	0	0	0	0	4	1
Orlando Palmeiro, of	.143	4	7	0	1	0	0	0	3	2	0	0
Brandon Backe, p	.000	2	1	0	0	0	0	0	0	0	0	0
Raul Chavez, 1b	.000	1	1	0	0	0	0	0	0	1	0	0
Roger Clemens, p	.000	2	3	0	0	0	0	0	0	0	2	0
Mike Gallo, p	.000	3	0	0	0	0	0	0	0	0	0	0
Brad Lidge, p	.000	3	0	0	0	0	0	0	0	0	0	0
Roy Oswalt, p	.000	1	3	0	0	0	0	0	0	0	0	0
Chad Qualls, p	.000	2	0	0	0	0	0	0	0	0	0	0
Wandy Rodriguez, p	.000	1	0	0	0	0	0	0	0	0	0	0
Luke Scott, of	.000	2	2	1	0	0	0	0	0	1	1	0
Russ Springer, p	.000	2	0	0	0	0	0	0	0	0	0	0
Jose Vizcaino, ss	.000	2	5	0	0	0	0	0	0	0	1	0
Dan Wheeler, p	.000	3	0	0	0	0	0	0	0	0	0	0
Totals	**.265**	**4**	**155**	**25**	**41**	**12**	**0**	**4**	**24**	**19**	**30**	**2**

Pitcher	W	L	ERA	G	GS	SV	IP	H	R	ER	BB	SO
Mike Gallo	0	0	0.00	3	0	0	2	1	0	0	1	0
Brad Lidge	0	0	0.00	3	0	0	4	2	0	0	4	5
Dan Wheeler	0	0	2.08	3	0	0	4	4	1	1	3	5
Roy Oswalt	1	0	3.68	1	1	0	7	6	3	3	2	7
Andy Pettitte	1	0	3.86	1	1	0	7	4	3	3	2	6
Russ Springer	0	0	3.86	2	0	0	2	5	1	1	1	1
Roger Clemens	1	1	5.63	2	1	0	8	7	5	5	3	6
Chad Qualls	0	0	6.00	2	0	0	3	5	2	2	2	1
Brandon Backe	0	0	8.44	2	1	0	5	6	5	5	3	3
Wandy Rodriguez	0	0	9.00	1	0	0	1	1	1	1	0	2
Totals	**3**	**1**	**4.30**	**4**	**4**	**0**	**44**	**41**	**21**	**21**	**21**	**36**

ATLANTA

Player, Pos.	AVG	G	AB	R	H	2B	3B	HR	RBI	BB	SO	SB
Wilson Betemit, ph	.500	2	2	0	1	0	0	0	0	0	1	0
Adam LaRoche, 1b	.500	3	8	2	4	1	0	1	6	3	1	0
Jorge Sosa, p	.500	1	2	0	1	0	0	0	1	0	1	0
Andruw Jones, of	.471	4	17	5	8	3	0	1	5	2	3	0
Tim Hudson, p	.333	2	6	0	2	1	0	0	0	0	1	0
Ryan Langerhans, of	.333	4	12	1	4	1	0	0	0	3	3	1
Johnny Estrada, c	.250	1	4	0	1	0	0	0	1	0	2	0
Jeff Francoeur, of	.235	4	17	2	4	1	1	0	1	2	4	0
John Franco, 1b	.222	3	9	0	2	0	0	0	0	1	3	0
Marcus Giles, 2b	.200	4	20	5	4	1	0	0	0	2	5	0
Brian Jordan, of	.200	3	5	0	1	1	0	0	0	0	0	0
Brian McCann, c	.188	3	16	2	3	0	0	2	5	0	6	0
Chipper Jones, 3b	.176	4	17	3	3	2	0	1	2	4	4	0
Rafael Furcal, ss	.150	4	20	1	3	0	0	0	0	3	2	3
Joe Borchard, p	.000	3	0	0	0	0	0	0	0	0	0	0
Joey Devine, p	.000	3	0	0	0	0	0	0	0	0	0	0
Kyle Farnsworth, p	.000	2	0	0	0	0	0	0	0	0	0	0
John Flaherty, p	.000	2	0	0	0	0	0	0	0	0	0	0
Kelly Johnson, ph	.000	4	2	0	0	0	0	0	0	1	0	0
Macay McBride, p	.000	1	0	0	0	0	0	0	0	0	0	0
Pete Orr, ph	.000	3	2	0	0	0	0	0	0	0	0	0
Chris Reitsma, p	.000	4	0	0	0	0	0	0	0	0	0	0
John Smoltz, p	.000	1	2	0	0	0	0	0	0	0	0	0
John Thomson, p	.000	1	0	0	0	0	0	0	0	0	0	0
Totals	**.255**	**4**	**161**	**21**	**41**	**11**	**1**	**5**	**21**	**21**	**36**	**4**

Pitcher	W	L	ERA	G	GS	SV	IP	H	R	ER	BB	SO
Jim Brower	0	0	0.00	3	0	0	5	0	0	0	3	2
Macay McBride	0	0	0.00	1	0	0	1	0	0	0	0	1
John Thomson	0	0	0.00	1	0	0	2	0	0	0	1	3
John Smoltz	1	0	1.29	1	1	0	7	7	1	1	1	5
Jorge Sosa	0	1	4.50	1	1	0	6	7	3	3	2	3
Tim Hudson	0	1	5.27	2	2	0	14	13	8	8	6	8
Kyle Farnsworth	0	0	9.00	2	0	0	3	2	3	3	1	4
Joey Devine	0	1	10.80	3	0	0	2	3	2	2	1	3
Chris Reitsma	0	0	16.20	4	0	0	3	7	6	6	2	0
John Foster	0	0	54.00	2	0	0	0	2	2	2	2	1
Totals	**1**	**3**	**5.19**	**4**	**4**	**0**	**43**	**41**	**25**	**25**	**19**	**30**

SCORE BY INNINGS	
Houston	403 110 591 000 000 001—25
Atlanta	156 210 240 000 000 000—21

E—Ensberg, Everett, Qualls, Vizcaino. **DP**—Houston 4, Atlanta 7. **LOB**—Houston 31, Atlanta 38. **SH**—Biggio, Clemens, Taveras, Pettitte 2, Francoeur, Furcal, LaRoche, Smoltz. **SF**—Biggio, Palmeiro, Lane, Everett, A. Jones. **HBP**—Palmeiro (by Hudson), Lane (by Devine), Berkman (by Sosa), Francoeur (by Oswalt), Giles (by Wheeler), A. Jones (by Backe), Langerhans (by Gallo). **IBB**—Ensberg (by Reitsma), Lamb (by Devine), Lamb (by Sosa), Ausmus (by Sosa), Berkman (by Hudson), Lane (by Foster), Biggio (by Reitsma), Palmeiro (by Smoltz), Langerhans (by Wheeler), Francoeur (by Gallo), LaRoche (by Qualls). **WP**—Foster, Backe.

ST. LOUIS vs. SAN DIEGO

COMPOSITE BOX

SAN DIEGO

Player, Pos.	AVG	G	AB	R	H	2B	3B	HR	RBI	BB	SO	SB
Damian Jackson, of	.667	3	3	1	2	0	0	0	0	0	1	1
Mark Sweeney, 1b	.667	3	3	1	2	1	0	0	0	2	1	0
Ramon Hernandez, c	.455	3	11	2	5	0	0	1	1	2	1	0
Khalil Greene, ss	.400	3	10	2	4	2	0	0	1	1	2	0
Joe Randa, 3b	.364	3	11	1	4	1	0	0	0	1	0	0
Xavier Nady, 1b	.333	2	3	0	1	0	0	0	2	0	1	0
Eric Young, of	.333	3	6	2	2	0	0	1	3	0	0	0
Mark Loretta, 2b	.267	3	15	0	4	0	0	0	2	0	0	0
Brian Giles, of	.231	3	13	0	3	0	0	0	1	1	2	1
Dave Roberts, of	.222	3	9	1	2	0	0	1	1	0	1	0
Robert Fick, 1b	.200	2	5	0	1	0	0	0	0	1	0	0
Ryan Klesko, of	.200	3	10	1	2	0	0	0	0	2	4	0
Pedro Astacio, p	.000	1	1	0	0	0	0	0	0	0	0	0
Sean Burroughs, ph	.000	2	1	0	0	0	0	0	0	0	0	0
Clay Hensley, p	.000	3	0	0	0	0	0	0	0	0	0	0
Trevor Hoffman, p	.000	1	0	0	0	0	0	0	0	0	0	0
Ben Johnson, of	.000	2	2	0	0	0	0	0	0	0	2	0
Brian Lawrence, p	.000	2	0	0	0	0	0	0	0	0	0	0
Scott Linebrink, p	.000	1	0	0	0	0	0	0	0	0	0	0
Miguel Olivo, ph	.000	1	1	0	0	0	0	0	0	0	0	0
Akinori Otsuka, p	.000	3	0	0	0	0	0	0	0	0	0	0
Jake Peavy, p	.000	1	2	0	0	0	0	0	0	0	2	0
Rudy Seanez, p	.000	2	0	0	0	0	0	0	0	0	0	0
Woody Williams, p	.000	1	0	0	0	0	0	0	0	0	0	0
Totals	**.302**	**3**	**106**	**11**	**32**	**4**	**0**	**3**	**11**	**10**	**17**	**2**

Pitcher	W	L	ERA	G	GS	SV	IP	H	R	ER	BB	SO
Trevor Hoffman	0	0	0.00	1	0	0	1	1	0	0	0	0
Brian Lawrence	0	0	0.00	2	0	0	2	1	0	0	0	2
Scott Linebrink	0	0	0.00	1	0	0	1	2	0	0	0	1
Akinori Otsuka	0	0	0.00	3	0	0	3	1	0	0	1	0
Clay Hensley	0	0	3.86	3	0	0	5	4	2	2	3	1
Pedro Astacio	0	1	4.50	1	1	0	4	3	4	2	3	4
Rudy Seanez	0	0	6.00	2	0	0	3	3	2	2	1	4
Jake Peavy	0	1	16.62	1	1	0	4	8	8	8	3	3
Woody Williams	0	1	27.00	1	1	0	2	6	5	5	2	2
Totals	**0**	**3**	**6.84**	**3**	**3**	**0**	**25**	**29**	**21**	**19**	**13**	**17**

ST. LOUIS

Player, Pos.	AVG	G	AB	R	H	2B	3B	HR	RBI	BB	SO	SB
Albert Pujols, 1b	.556	3	9	4	5	2	0	0	2	4	0	0
John Mabry, of	.500	2	2	0	1	0	0	0	0	0	0	0
Matt Morris, p	.500	1	2	1	1	0	0	0	0	0	0	0
David Eckstein, ss	.385	3	13	3	5	0	0	1	4	1	1	0
Jim Edmonds, of	.364	3	11	5	4	2	0	1	1	2	2	0
Abraham Nunez, 3b	.364	3	11	3	4	1	0	0	0	2	3	1
Reggie Sanders, of	.333	3	12	1	4	2	0	1	10	1	2	0
Yadier Molina, c	.231	3	13	1	3	0	0	0	3	0	1	0
Mark Grudzielanek, 2b	.154	3	13	2	2	0	0	0	0	0	1	0
Chris Carpenter, p	.000	1	3	0	0	0	0	0	0	0	1	0
Cal Eldred, p	.000	1	0	0	0	0	0	0	0	0	0	0
Randy Flores, p	.000	3	0	0	0	0	0	0	0	0	0	0
John Gall, ph	.000	1	1	0	0	0	0	0	0	0	0	0
Jason Isringhausen, p	.000	3	0	0	0	0	0	0	0	0	0	0
Mark Mulder, p	.000	1	1	0	0	0	0	0	0	1	1	0
John Rodriguez, ph	.000	1	1	0	0	0	0	0	0	0	0	0
So Taguchi, of	.000	3	1	0	0	0	0	0	0	0	0	0

Julian Tavarez, p	.000	2	0	0	0	0	0	0	0	0	0	0
Brad Thompson, p	.000	2	0	0	0	0	0	0	0	0	0	0
Larry Walker, of	.000	3	9	1	0	0	0	0	0	2	5	0
Totals	**.284**	**3**	**102**	**21**	**29**	**7**	**0**	**3**	**20**	**13**	**17**	**1**

Pitcher	W	L	ERA	G	GS	SV	IP	H	R	ER	BB	SO
Chris Carpenter	1	0	0.00	1	1	0	6	3	0	0	3	3
Mark Mulder	1	0	1.35	1	1	0	7	8	1	1	1	2
Jason Isringhausen	0	0	3.00	3	0	1	3	5	1	1	1	4
Matt Morris	1	0	3.00	1	1	0	6	5	2	2	3	4
Randy Flores	0	0	4.50	3	0	0	2	2	1	1	0	3
Julian Tavarez	0	0	13.50	2	0	0	1	4	2	2	1	0
Brad Thompson	0	0	13.50	2	0	0	1	3	2	2	0	1
Cal Eldred	0	0	27.00	1	0	0	1	2	2	2	1	0
Totals	**3**	**0**	**3.67**	**3**	**3**	**1**	**27**	**32**	**11**	**11**	**10**	**17**

SCORE BY INNINGS	
San Diego	**000 020 333—11**
St. Louis	**245 260 020—21**

E—Greene 2, Eckstein 2. **DP**—San Diego 3, St. Louis 7. **LOB**—San Diego 28 St. Louis 23. **SH**—Eckstein, Morris, Mulder. **SF**—Greene. **HBP**—Nady 2 (by Mulder, by Tavarez), Jackson (by Mulder), Walker (by Williams). **IBB**—Pujols 3 (by Otsuka, by Peavy, by Williams), Walker (by Peavy). **WP**—Peavy.

NATIONAL LEAGUE CHAMPIONSHIP SERIES

ST. LOUIS vs. HOUSTON

COMPOSITE BOX

HOUSTON

Player, Pos.	AVG	G	AB	R	H	2B	3B	HR	RBI	BB	SO	SB
Roger Clemens, p	.500	1	2	0	1	0	0	0	0	0	1	0
Willy Taveras, of	.357	6	14	1	5	0	0	0	0	1	1	0
Craig Biggio, 2b	.333	6	24	2	8	0	0	0	3	2	3	0
Roy Oswalt, p	.333	2	3	0	1	0	0	0	0	1	1	0
Orlando Palmeiro, ph	.333	4	3	0	1	0	0	0	0	1	0	0
Brad Ausmus, c	.318	6	22	3	7	2	0	0	1	1	6	1
Adam Everett, ss	.304	6	23	2	7	1	1	0	2	0	4	0
Chris Burke, of	.300	6	20	5	6	0	1	1	3	1	3	0
Lance Berkman, 1b	.286	6	21	2	6	2	0	1	3	4	3	0
Morgan Ensberg, 3b	.238	6	21	1	5	1	0	0	2	2	2	0
Jason Lane, of	.238	6	21	3	5	0	0	2	3	2	4	0
Mike Lamb, 1b	.188	4	16	3	3	1	0	1	2	0	3	0
Ezequiel Astacio, p	.000	1	0	0	0	0	0	0	0	0	0	0
Brandon Backe, p	.000	1	2	0	0	0	0	0	0	0	1	0
Jeff Bagwell, ph	.000	1	1	0	0	0	0	0	0	0	0	0
Eric Bruntlett, 2b	.000	5	1	0	0	0	0	0	0	0	1	0
Mike Gallo, p	.000	2	0	0	0	0	0	0	0	0	0	0
Brad Lidge, p	.000	4	0	0	0	0	0	0	0	0	0	0
Andy Pettitte, p	.000	2	2	0	0	0	0	0	0	0	0	0
Chad Qualls, p	.000	4	0	0	0	0	0	0	0	0	0	0
Russ Springer, p	.000	1	0	0	0	0	0	0	0	0	0	0
Jose Vizcaino, ph	.000	2	2	0	0	0	0	0	0	0	0	0
Dan Wheeler, p	.000	3	0	0	0	0	0	0	0	0	0	0
Totals	**.278**	**6**	**198**	**22**	**55**	**7**	**2**	**5**	**19**	**15**	**33**	**1**

Pitcher	W	L	ERA	G	GS	SV	IP	H	R	ER	BB	SO
Ezequiel Astacio	0	0	0.00	1	0	0	1	0	0	0	0	2
Mike Gallo	0	0	0.00	2	0	0	1	0	0	0	0	0
Chad Qualls	1	0	0.00	4	0	0	5	0	0	0	0	4
Russ Springer	0	0	0.00	1	0	0	1	0	0	0	1	1
Dan Wheeler	0	0	0.00	3	0	0	3	2	0	0	0	2
Roy Oswalt	2	0	1.29	2	2	0	14	8	2	2	4	12
Brandon Backe	0	0	1.59	1	1	0	6	2	1	1	3	7
Roger Clemens	1	0	3.00	1	1	0	6	6	2	2	2	1
Andy Pettitte	0	1	5.11	2	2	0	12	15	7	7	4	6
Brad Lidge	0	1	7.20	4	0	3	5	6	4	4	2	7
Totals	**4**	**2**	**2.72**	**6**	**6**	**3**	**53**	**39**	**16**	**16**	**16**	**42**

ST. LOUIS

PLAYER, POS	AVG	G	AB	R	H	2B	3B	HR	RBI	BB	SO	SB
Abraham Nunez, 3b	.385	4	13	1	5	0	0	0	0	0	1	0
Yadier Molina, c	.318	6	22	1	7	3	0	0	0	0	2	0
Albert Pujols, 1b	.304	6	23	3	7	0	0	2	6	1	3	0
Mark Grudzielanek, 2b	.227	6	22	2	5	0	0	0	2	0	3	0
Jim Edmonds, of	.211	6	19	2	4	1	0	0	0	5	5	1
David Eckstein, ss	.200	6	20	5	4	0	0	0	2	3	2	1
Reggie Sanders, of	.167	5	18	1	3	0	0	1	2	1	8	1
Larry Walker, of	.158	6	19	0	3	1	0	0	1	4	4	0
John Mabry, of	.125	5	8	0	1	1	0	0	1	0	3	0
Chris Carpenter, p	.000	2	4	0	0	0	0	0	1	0	1	0
Randy Flores, p	.000	2	0	0	0	0	0	0	0	0	0	0
Jason Isringhausen, p	.000	3	0	0	0	0	0	0	0	0	0	0
Hector Luna, 3b	.000	2	4	0	0	0	0	0	0	0	2	0
Jason Marquis, p	.000	3	1	0	0	0	0	0	0	0	0	0
Matt Morris, p	.000	1	1	0	0	0	0	0	0	0	0	0
Mark Mulder, p	.000	2	3	0	0	0	0	0	0	0	3	0
John Rodriguez, ph	.000	5	2	1	0	0	0	0	1	2	1	0
Jeff Suppan, p	.000	1	2	0	0	0	0	0	0	0	1	0
So Taguchi, of	.000	6	6	0	0	0	0	0	0	0	3	0
Julian Tavarez, p	.000	3	0	0	0	0	0	0	0	0	0	0
Brad Thompson, p	.000	2	0	0	0	0	0	0	0	0	0	0
Totals	**.209**	**6**	**187**	**16**	**39**	**6**	**0**	**3**	**16**	**16**	**42**	**3**

Pitcher	W	L	ERA	G	GS	SV	IP	H	R	ER	BB	SO
Randy Flores	0	0	0.00	2	0	0	1	0	0	0	1	0
Jason Isringhausen	1	0	0.00	3	0	1	4	3	1	0	0	2
Brad Thompson	0	0	0.00	2	0	0	1	2	0	0	0	0
Jeff Suppan	0	0	1.80	1	1	0	5	3	1	1	3	5
Chris Carpenter	1	0	3.00	2	2	0	15	14	6	5	4	9
Mark Mulder	0	2	3.09	2	2	0	12	14	5	4	3	8
Jason Marquis	0	1	3.38	3	0	0	5	6	3	2	3	4
Matt Morris	0	1	5.06	1	1	0	5	8	4	3	1	3
Julian Tavarez	0	0	5.40	3	0	0	3	5	2	2	0	2
Totals	**2**	**4**	**2.94**	**6**	**6**	**1**	**52**	**55**	**22**	**17**	**15**	**33**

SCORE BY INNINGS	
Houston	**022 413 721—22**
St. Louis	**212 143 004—17**

E—Ensberg Everett, Lamb, Luna 2, Eckstein Edmonds, Marquis. **DP**—Houston 4, St. Louis 3. **LOB**—Houston 46, St. Louis 38. **CS**—Taveras, Eckstein. **SH**—Pettitte 2, Oswalt 2, Biggio, Burke, Everett, Taveras, Carpenter 2, Morris. **SF**—Ausmus, Ensberg, Eckstein, Pujols, J Rodriguez, Walker. **HBP**—Lane (by Carpenter), Eckstein 2 (by Oswalt, by Pettitte). Grudzielanek (by Oswalt). **IBB**—Ausmus (by Mulder). **WP**—Mulder 2, Tavarez, 2. **PB**—Molina.

ORGANIZATION
STATISTICS

ARIZONA DIAMONDBACKS

BY JACK MAGRUDER

The remade Diamondbacks made major league history with their recovery in 2005, although they consider it only a step in the right direction.

One of only 12 teams in the modern era (since 1900) to lose as many as 111 games after going 51-111 in a disastrous 2004, the Diamondbacks made a 26-game improvement. They spent lavishly in the offseason and by finishing 77-85, they set records for the most victories and the best winning percentage after a 111-loss season.

"There's a lot of work to do," said general partner Jeff Moorad, whose first order of offseason business was to hire a permanent replacement for Joe Garagiola Jr., who left for a position in the commissioner's office Aug. 1 after 10 years (and a 2001 World Series ring) with the Diamondbacks.

"I think the nucleus of the players that we have on the field today gives me hope for a bright future," Moorad said. "Having taken a step forward, we're anxious to take that next step. Our ownerhship group will not be content until we are back on top in the NL West."

The Diamondbacks were not eliminated from the National League West race until the final Wednesday of the season, although that had more to do with the scuffling NL West than anything else. After leading the division by percentage points the day Garagiola's move was announced, the D-Backs lost 22 of their next 31, finally betrayed by a bullpen that had an NL-high 5.50 ERA and an offense that hit an NL-low .237 with runners in scoring position, .225 with runners in scoring position and two outs.

Arizona committed $88 million to acquire free agents Troy Glaus, Russ Ortiz, Craig Counsell, Royce Clayton and Tony Clark as part of the retooling, and also acquired Shawn Green, Javier Vazquez and Brad Halsey in a de facto three-team trade that fulfilled Randy Johnson's wish to be dealt to the Yankees while enabling the D-Backs to net three starters and $19 million.

ORGANIZATION LEADERS

BATTING		
*AVG	Jackson, Conor, Tucson	.354
R	Green, Andy, Tucson	125
H	Green, Andy, Tucson	182
TB	Green, Andy, Tucson	311
2B	Green, Andy, Tucson	46
3B	Green, Andy, Tucson	13
HR	Carter, Chris, Lancaster/Tennessee	31
RBI	Carter, Chris, Lancaster/Tennessee	115
BB	Schindewolf, Erik, Lancaster	87
SO	Garthwaite, Jay, Lancaster	131
SB	Bonifacio, Emilio, South Bend	55
*OBP	Jackson, Conor, Tucson	.457
*SLG	Drew, Stephen, Lancaster/Tennessee	.596
PITCHING		
W	Shappi, A.J., Lancaster/South Bend	16
L	Kinsey, Chris, Lancaster/South Bend	15
#ERA	Perrault, Josh, South Bend	1.74
G	Stockman, Phil, Tennessee/Tucson	64
CG	Michalak, Chris, Tucson	3
CG	Nippert, Dustin, Tennessee	3
SV	Elliott, Matt, South Bend	32
IP	Shappi, A.J., Lancaster/South Bend	181
BB	Rocha, Angel, South Bend/Yakima	89
SO	Mock, Garrett, Lancaster	160

*Minimum 250 at-bats. #Minimum 75 innings.

PLAYERS OF THE YEAR

MAJOR LEAGUE: Tony Clark, 1b

When the Diamondbacks brought in Clark as a free agent to start 2004, they expected him to be a platoon player to help break in Chad Tracy at first base. What they didn't expect was production, but Clark wound up hitting .304-30-87 in 2005, while leading the club in slugging (.636).

MINOR LEAGUE: Conor Jackson, 1b

BILL MITCHELL

One of the most patient hitters in the minor leagues, Jackson finished fifth overall in on-base percentage (.457) with a 69-32 walk-strikeout ratio in 333 at-bats at Triple-A Tucson. The only thing lacking was power, but scouts feel he'll provide enough offensive punch at the next level.

Vazquez won 11 games in his sixth consecutive season of double-digit victories although Brandon Webb pitched himself to the front of the rotation by going 14-12 while setting career bests in victories, ERA and innings. He tied his career high in strikeouts.

While starters Ortiz and Shawn Estes missed two months apiece because of injuries, the greatest losses were felt in the bullpen. Nominal closer Greg Aquino was set back by a spring elbow injury, although Brandon Lyon picked up the slack and had a major league-leading 13 saves until an elbow injury May 12 cost him three months. The D-Backs never recovered, and pitching coach Mark Davis took the fall when he lost his job.

Chad Tracy took a step toward becoming a franchise cornerstone by hitting .308 with a career-high 27 home runs. He drove in 72 runs despite a spring position change to first base and an August switch to right field in his first full season in the majors.

Clark, whose offense caused Tracy's shift to the outfield, was born again while playing at home. He hit 30 homers and drove in 87 runs in 349 at-bats, ratios that would have ranked in the top three in the NL had he had sufficient plate appearances to qualify.

The D-Backs promoted first baseman Conor Jackson, their top prospect, in late July after he hit .353 at Triple-A Tucson. He is one of a talented group of position players in the system that also included fellow former No. 1 draft choices Carlos Quentin, Sergio Santos and Stephen Drew.

The D-Backs signed Drew, their top draft pick in 2004, to a major league contract worth $5.5 million (including a $4 million signing bonus) less than 15 minutes before their window expired May 31. A week later, they selected Justin Upton with the No. 1 selection in the 2005 draft.

Some scouts believed Drew and Upton were the two best players available in both drafts, though the D-Backs hadn't reached an agreement with Upton before the 2005 season ended.

ARIZONA DIAMONDBACKS

Manager: Bob Melvin.

2005 Record: 77-85, .465 (2nd, NL West).

BATTING	B-T	HT	WT	DOB	AVG	vLH	vRH	G	AB	R	H	2B	3B	HR	RBI	BB	HBP	SH	SF	SO	SB	CS	SLG	OBP
Cintron, Alex	B-R	6-1	205	12-17-78	.273	.301	.263	122	330	36	90	19	2	8	48	12	1	2	3	33	1	2	.415	.298
Clark, Tony	B-R	6-7	245	6-15-72	.304	.313	.299	130	349	47	106	22	2	30	87	37	1	0	6	88	0	0	.636	.366
Clayton, Royce	R-R	6-0	200	1-2-70	.270	.296	.259	143	522	59	141	28	4	2	44	38	1	10	2	105	13	3	.351	.320
Counsell, Craig	L-R	6-0	185	8-21-70	.256	.269	.253	150	578	85	148	34	4	9	42	78	8	2	4	69	26	7	.375	.350
Cruz Jr., Jose	B-R	6-0	210	4-19-74	.213	.182	.222	64	202	23	43	9	0	12	28	42	0	0	1	54	0	1	.436	.347
Glaus, Troy	R-R	6-5	240	8-3-76	.258	.244	.263	149	538	78	139	29	1	37	97	84	7	0	5	145	4	2	.522	.363
Gonzalez, Luis	L-R	6-2	200	9-3-67	.271	.269	.272	155	579	90	157	37	0	24	79	78	11	0	4	90	4	1	.459	.366
Green, Shawn	L-L	6-4	210	11-10-72	.286	.226	.306	158	581	87	166	37	4	22	73	62	5	0	8	95	8	4	.477	.355
Green, Andy	R-R	5-9	180	7-7-77	.226	.385	.111	17	31	5	7	1	0	0	2	7	0	0	1	3	0	0	.258	.359
Hairston, Scott	R-R	6-0	200	5-25-80	.100	.182	.000	15	20	0	2	1	0	0	0	0	0	0	0	6	0	0	.150	.100
Hill, Koyie	B-R	6-0	220	3-9-79	.218	.261	.200	34	78	6	17	5	0	0	6	11	0	0	2	27	0	1	.282	.308
Jackson, Conor	R-R	6-2	225	5-7-82	.200	.258	.167	40	85	8	17	3	0	2	8	12	1	0	1	11	0	0	.306	.303
Kata, Matt	B-R	6-1	195	3-14-78	.194	.250	.158	30	31	6	6	2	1	0	0	5	0	2	0	4	0	1	.323	.306
McCracken, Quinton	B-R	5-8	185	8-16-70	.237	.261	.231	134	215	23	51	4	3	1	13	23	1	6	1	35	4	0	.298	.313
Snyder, Chris	R-R	6-3	230	2-12-81	.202	.260	.185	115	326	24	66	14	0	6	28	40	4	3	0	87	0	1	.301	.297
Stinnett, Kelly	R-R	5-11	235	2-4-70	.248	.214	.257	59	129	15	32	4	0	6	12	12	1	1	0	32	0	0	.419	.317
Terrero, Luis	R-R	6-3	225	5-18-80	.230	.247	.211	88	161	23	37	6	1	4	20	14	6	2	1	40	3	2	.354	.313
Tracy, Chad	L-R	6-2	200	5-22-80	.308	.236	.324	145	503	73	155	34	4	27	72	35	8	1	6	78	3	1	.553	.359

PITCHING	B-T	HT	WT	DOB	W	L	ERA	G	GS	CG	SV	IP	H	R	ER	HR	BB	SO	AVG	vLH	vRH	K/9	BB/9
Almanza, Armando	L-L	6-3	230	10-26-72	0	0	2.25	6	0	0	0	4	5	1	1	1	3	2	.313	.286	.333	4.50	6.75
Aquino, Greg	R-R	6-1	190	1-11-78	0	1	7.76	35	0	0	1	31	42	29	27	7	17	34	.318	.304	.329	9.77	4.88
Bruney, Brian	R-R	6-2	245	2-17-82	1	3	7.43	47	0	0	12	46	56	39	38	6	35	51	.299	.280	.314	9.98	6.85
Bulger, Jason	R-R	6-4	215	12-6-78	1	0	5.40	9	0	0	0	10	14	6	6	1	5	9	.333	.294	.360	8.10	4.50
Choate, Randy	L-L	6-1	195	9-5-75	0	0	9.00	8	0	0	0	7	8	7	7	0	5	4	.276	.294	.250	5.14	6.43
Cormier, Lance	R-R	5-11	200	8-19-80	7	3	5.11	67	0	0	0	79	86	50	45	7	43	63	.285	.300	.273	7.15	4.88
Estes, Shawn	R-L	6-2	220	2-18-73	7	8	4.80	21	21	2	0	124	132	70	66	15	45	63	.280	.259	.284	4.58	3.27
Gonzalez, Edgar	R-R	6-0	225	2-23-83	0	0	108.00	1	0	0	0	0	2	4	4	1	2	1	.667	.667	.000	27.00	54.00
Gosling, Mike	L-L	6-2	210	9-23-80	0	3	4.45	13	5	0	0	32	40	20	16	2	19	14	.301	.231	.330	3.90	5.29
Groom, Buddy	L-L	6-2	205	7-10-65	0	1	4.70	23	0	0	1	15	19	8	8	2	5	7	.302	.207	.382	4.11	2.93
Halsey, Brad	L-L	6-1	185	2-14-81	8	12	4.61	28	26	0	0	160	191	101	82	20	39	82	.300	.267	.309	4.61	2.19
Herges, Matt	L-R	6-0	210	4-1-70	0	0	13.50	7	0	0	0	8	12	12	12	4	5	3	.343	.250	.421	3.38	5.63
2-team (21 San Francisco)					1	1	7.14	28	0	0	0	29	35	23	23	6	12	9	.304	.256	.333	2.79	3.72
Koplove, Mike	R-R	5-11	175	8-30-76	2	1	5.07	44	0	0	0	50	48	31	28	6	20	28	.257	.256	.257	5.07	3.62
Ligtenberg, Kerry	R-R	6-2	220	5-11-71	0	0	13.97	7	0	0	0	10	16	15	15	4	4	5	.364	.250	.429	4.66	3.72
Lopez, Javier	L-L	6-4	200	7-11-77	1	1	9.42	29	0	0	2	14	19	15	15	2	11	11	.311	.258	.367	6.91	6.91
2-team (3 Colorado)					1	1	11.02	32	0	0	2	16	26	20	20	2	11	12	.351	.286	.410	6.61	6.06
Lyon, Brandon	R-R	6-1	190	8-10-79	0	2	6.44	32	0	0	14	29	44	25	21	6	10	17	.341	.317	.364	5.22	3.07
Medders, Brandon	R-R	6-1	190	1-26-80	4	1	1.78	27	0	0	0	30	21	6	6	2	11	31	.194	.239	.161	9.20	3.26
Nippert, Dustin	R-R	6-7	215	5-6-81	1	0	5.52	3	3	0	0	15	10	9	9	1	13	11	.185	.182	.188	6.75	7.98
Ortiz, Russ	R-R	6-1	220	6-5-74	5	11	6.89	22	22	0	0	115	147	92	88	18	65	46	.313	.329	.296	3.60	5.09
Valverde, Jose	R-R	6-4	255	7-24-79	3	4	2.44	61	0	0	15	66	51	19	18	5	20	75	.211	.168	.241	10.18	2.71
Vargas, Claudio	R-R	6-3	230	6-19-78	9	6	4.81	21	19	0	0	120	124	66	64	21	40	90	.266	.269	.263	6.77	3.01
2-team (4 Washington)					9	9	5.24	25	23	0	0	132	146	81	77	25	47	95	.278	.269	.287	6.46	3.20
Vazquez, Javier	R-R	6-2	215	7-25-76	11	15	4.42	33	33	3	0	216	223	112	106	35	46	192	.266	.244	.285	8.01	1.92
Villarreal, Oscar	L-R	6-0	215	11-22-81	2	0	5.27	11	0	0	0	14	11	8	8	2	6	5	.234	.207	.278	3.29	3.95
Webb, Brandon	R-R	6-2	230	5-9-79	14	12	3.54	33	33	1	0	229	229	98	90	21	59	172	.265	.298	.228	6.76	2.32
Worrell, Tim	R-R	6-4	240	7-5-67	1	1	2.27	32	0	0	0	32	30	13	8	4	9	22	.250	.259	.242	6.25	2.56
2-team (19 Philadelphia)					1	2	4.07	51	0	0	1	49	59	30	22	8	12	39	.299	.295	.303	7.21	2.22

FIELDING

Catcher	PCT	G	PO	A	E	DP	PB
Hill	1.000	32	144	13	0	1	3
Snyder	.997	113	679	44	2	0	7
Stinnett	.977	56	237	15	6	2	1

First Base	PCT	G	PO	A	E	DP
Clark	.997	83	663	44	2	59
Jackson	.973	20	171	12	5	19
Tracy	.996	80	705	47	3	75

Second Base	PCT	G	PO	A	E	DP
Cintron	.986	23	31	39	1	12
Counsell	.990	143	305	459	8	97
A. Green	1.000	5	10	12	0	4
Kata	1.000	7	8	12	0	6

Third Base	PCT	G	PO	A	E	DP
Cintron	.966	32	15	41	2	9
Glaus	.946	145	113	310	24	26

Shortstop	PCT	G	PO	A	E	DP
Cintron	.966	39	43	99	5	19
Clayton	.982	141	180	404	11	91
Counsell	.000	1	0	0	0	0
A. Green	1.000	2	1	4	0	0

Outfield	PCT	G	PO	A	E	DP
Cruz Jr.	.980	58	98	2	2	0
Gonzalez	.989	152	270	7	3	1
S. Green	1.000	155	313	4	0	1
A. Green	1.000	2	3	0	0	0
Hairston	1.000	4	3	0	0	0
Jackson	.000	1	0	0	0	0
McCracken	.975	59	75	2	2	0
Terrero	.984	77	124	1	2	0
Tracy	.979	51	93	2	2	0

FARM SYSTEM

General Manager: Joe Garagiola Jr. **Director, Minor Leagues:** Bob Miller. **Scouting Director:** Mike Rizzo.

Class	Farm Team	League	W	L	Pct.	Finish*	Manager	Affiliate Since
AAA	Tucson (Ariz.) Sidewinders	Pacific Coast	68	76	.472	t-11th (16)	Chip Hale	1998
AA	Tennessee Smokies (Kodiak)	Southern	64	76	.457	7th (10)	Tony Perezchica	2005
High A	Lancaster (Calif.) Jethawks	California	75	65	.536	**3rd (10)**	Bill Plummer	2001
Low A	South Bend (Ind.) Silver Hawks	Midwest	84	56	.600	**+1st (14)**	Mark Haley	1997
SS A	Yakima (Wash.) Bears	Northwest	30	46	.395	8th (8)	Jay Gainer	1999
Rookie	Missoula (Mont.) Osprey	Pioneer	34	42	.447	t-6th (8)	Hector De la Cruz	1999

*Finish in overall standings (No. of teams in league)/playoff teams in **boldface** +League champion

TUCSON SIDEWINDERS — Class AAA

PACIFIC COAST LEAGUE

BATTING	B-T	HT	WT	DOB	AVG	vLH	vRH	G	AB	R	H	2B	3B	HR	RBI	BB	HBP	SH	SF	SO	SB	CS	SLG	OBP
Ansman, Craig	R-R	6-3	250	3-10-78	.167	.100	.192	11	36	4	6	0	0	1	3	3	2	0	0	9	0	0	.250	.268
Barden, Brian	R-R	5-11	195	4-2-81	.307	.319	.302	135	518	78	159	36	5	15	85	38	11	3	6	111	14	5	.483	.363
Brito, Juan	R-R	5-11	220	11-7-79	.260	.257	.261	72	235	30	61	10	0	6	31	21	1	3	1	58	0	0	.379	.322
Brown, Neb	L-R	6-0	190	11-7-79	.346	.400	.333	14	26	2	9	1	1	0	4	2	1	1	0	4	0	0	.462	.414
Camilo, Juan	L-R	6-0	200	6-24-76	.200	.667	.118	8	20	3	4	1	0	1	3	2	0	0	1	6	0	0	.400	.261
Cota, Jesus	L-R	6-3	220	11-7-81	.214	.194	.221	37	126	16	27	4	1	3	17	6	0	0	1	22	0	0	.333	.248
Cruz Jr., Jose	B-R	6-0	210	4-19-74	.333	.000	.333	1	3	1	1	1	0	0	1	0	0	0	0	1	0	0	.667	.333
De Renne, Keoni	B-R	5-7	170	4-30-79	.293	.316	.286	72	232	43	68	11	2	3	26	22	2	6	3	23	5	0	.397	.355
DeVore, Doug	L-L	6-4	225	12-14-77	.289	.200	.311	44	149	25	43	9	1	7	32	13	0	0	1	34	3	1	.503	.344
Doster, David	R-R	6-4	220	10-8-70	.338	.370	.319	24	74	12	25	4	0	0	10	7	2	2	1	10	0	0	.392	.405
Green, Andy	R-R	5-9	180	7-7-77	.343	.319	.352	135	530	125	182	46	13	19	80	68	6	2	3	82	9	6	.587	.422
Hairston, Scott	R-R	6-0	200	5-25-80	.311	.382	.277	58	209	45	65	8	3	16	40	21	5	0	2	40	3	0	.608	.384
Hammock, Robby	R-R	5-10	185	5-13-77	.364	.333	.400	3	11	0	4	0	0	0	3	0	0	0	1	1	0	0	.364	.333
Hill, Koyie	B-R	6-0	220	3-9-79	.244	.293	.228	50	168	22	41	9	1	5	26	23	1	0	1	37	3	0	.399	.337
Jackson, Conor	R-R	6-2	225	5-7-82	.354	.356	.354	93	333	66	118	38	2	8	73	69	0	0	7	32	3	2	.553	.457
Kata, Matt	B-R	6-1	195	3-14-78	.310	.250	.336	46	200	25	62	10	3	3	28	6	1	4	3	25	5	1	.435	.329
Kroeger, Josh	L-L	6-3	220	8-31-82	.261	.234	.269	129	472	73	123	28	3	14	62	36	4	0	4	108	17	4	.422	.316
Myers, Corey	R-R	6-1	225	6-5-80	.238	.231	.244	82	260	30	62	10	2	4	36	25	0	0	2	55	0	1	.338	.303
Porter, Colin	L-L	6-2	210	11-23-75	.177	.067	.213	25	62	7	11	2	0	0	1	4	1	1	0	24	0	0	.210	.239
Quentin, Carlos	R-R	6-1	225	8-28-82	.301	.317	.294	136	452	98	136	28	4	21	89	72	29	0	8	71	9	1	.520	.422
Santos, Sergio	R-R	6-2	240	7-4-83	.239	.148	.279	132	490	55	117	21	3	12	68	34	2	0	6	108	2	2	.367	.288
Stinnett, Kelly	R-R	5-11	235	2-4-70	.229	.250	.222	11	35	4	8	2	0	1	2	3	2	0	0	12	0	0	.371	.325
Terrero, Luis	R-R	6-3	225	5-18-80	.267	.364	.211	7	30	4	8	1	0	0	1	1	1	1	0	9	1	0	.300	.313
Zinter, Alan	B-R	6-1	195	5-19-68	.216	.222	.213	47	111	9	24	4	1	2	14	12	0	0	0	30	0	0	.324	.293

PITCHING	B-T	HT	WT	DOB	W	L	ERA	G	GS	CG	SV	IP	H	R	ER	HR	BB	SO	AVG	vLH	vRH	K/9	BB/9
Abreu, Winston	R-R	6-2	155	2-5-78	2	3	6.48	27	0	0	2	33	37	24	24	6	15	42	.274	.254	.289	11.34	4.05
Almanza, Armando	L-L	6-3	230	10-26-72	1	0	1.80	15	0	0	1	15	12	6	3	2	7	19	.218	.158	.250	11.40	4.20
Aquino, Greg	R-R	6-1	190	1-11-78	1	0	1.04	6	0	0	0	9	4	1	1	0	0	7	.129	.143	.118	7.27	0.00
Bruney, Brian	R-R	6-2	245	2-17-82	1	0	1.93	4	0	0	0	5	3	3	1	0	5	3	.188	.222	.143	5.79	9.64
Bulger, Jason	R-R	6-4	215	12-6-78	3	6	3.54	56	0	0	4	56	50	28	22	3	27	55	.244	.275	.224	8.84	4.34
Cannon, Jon	R-L	6-3	215	1-1-75	3	5	4.17	15	13	0	0	73	72	46	34	11	43	44	.262	.239	.270	5.40	5.28
Choate, Randy	L-L	6-1	195	9-5-75	1	1	3.38	47	0	0	3	40	44	22	15	4	22	20	.278	.228	.307	4.50	4.95
Cormier, Lance	R-R	5-11	200	8-19-80	0	1	14.73	1	1	0	0	4	6	6	6	1	5	5	.429	.250	.667	12.27	12.27
Duran, Enmanuel	R-R	6-1	178	11-7-84	0	0	0.00	1	0	0	0	1	1	0	0	0	0	1	.250	.000	.500	9.00	0.00
Estes, Shawn	R-L	6-2	220	2-18-73	0	0	1.64	2	2	0	0	11	5	2	2	1	4	9	.132	.375	.067	7.36	3.27
Freed, Mark	L-L	6-4	226	8-10-78	8	6	4.86	34	13	0	0	130	149	75	70	14	39	83	.292	.266	.304	5.76	2.71
Gonzalez, Edgar	R-R	6-0	225	2-23-83	11	6	4.37	28	24	0	0	167	185	94	81	20	38	116	.283	.322	.240	6.25	2.05
Gosling, Mike	L-L	6-2	210	9-23-80	4	6	5.95	18	17	0	0	92	129	70	61	11	30	76	.328	.260	.352	7.41	2.92
Herges, Matt	L-R	6-0	210	4-1-70	1	2	3.14	26	0	0	0	29	39	13	10	3	8	29	.339	.377	.306	9.10	2.51
Koplove, Mike	R-R	5-11	175	8-30-76	0	2	13.00	9	0	0	0	9	12	13	13	1	7	6	.316	.357	.292	6.00	7.00
Ligtenberg, Kerry	R-R	6-2	220	5-11-71	4	3	3.24	38	3	0	1	50	51	18	18	4	7	50	.266	.283	.250	9.00	1.26
Lizarraga, Sergio	R-R	6-4	195	7-23-81	0	1	7.94	5	2	0	0	11	18	10	10	2	7	10	.353	.500	.174	7.94	5.56
Lopez, Javier	L-L	6-4	200	7-11-77	0	1	2.22	27	0	0	2	24	17	7	6	0	12	16	.213	.152	.294	5.92	4.44
Lyon, Brandon	R-R	6-1	190	8-10-79	0	1	5.40	5	4	0	0	5	5	3	3	0	0	4	.250	.429	.154	7.20	0.00
Medders, Brandon	R-R	6-1	190	1-26-80	3	2	2.48	36	0	0	8	36	31	11	10	3	18	44	.230	.339	.152	10.90	4.46
Michalak, Chris	L-L	6-2	195	1-4-71	9	13	4.47	26	25	3	0	165	174	88	82	27	42	74	.274	.236	.290	4.04	2.29
Murphy, Bill	L-L	5-11	215	5-9-81	6	8	5.65	23	21	0	0	121	135	81	76	14	78	87	.284	.278	.286	6.47	5.80
Nance, Shane	L-L	5-8	190	9-7-77	0	2	3.63	22	0	0	2	22	16	9	9	2	11	25	.205	.115	.250	10.07	4.43
Nina, Elvin	R-R	6-0	180	11-25-75	1	0	5.91	12	1	0	0	21	30	15	14	5	12	17	.337	.316	.353	7.17	5.06
Nunez, Vladimir	R-R	6-4	240	3-15-75	1	2	5.02	15	0	0	1	14	14	8	8	4	6	13	.259	.333	.212	8.16	3.77
3-team (17 Oklahoma, 17 Memphis)					3	4	3.92	49	0	0	12	57	55	27	25	6	23	56	.256	.279	.240	8.79	3.61
Oliver, Darren	R-L	6-2	220	10-6-70	1	0	6.38	4	4	0	0	18	33	14	13	3	3	8	.393	.586	.291	3.93	1.47
Ortiz, Russ	R-R	6-1	220	6-5-74	0	1	13.00	2	2	0	0	9	14	14	13	4	5	5	.341	.286	.370	5.00	5.00
Peterson, Adam	R-R	6-2	225	5-18-79	0	0	12.00	3	0	0	0	3	5	6	4	1	6	4	.357	.250	.500	12.00	18.00
Silva, Jesus	R-R	6-0	199	12-24-82	0	0	13.50	2	0	0	0	3	5	4	4	0	3	2	.417	.375	.500	6.75	10.13
Stockman, Phil	R-R	6-8	250	1-25-80	1	1	6.25	17	4	0	0	32	35	29	22	4	27	16	.285	.283	.286	4.55	7.67
Thompson, Chris	R-R	6-3	195	1-2-82	0	0	0.00	1	0	0	0	1	1	0	0	0	0	1	.250	.000	.500	9.00	0.00
Tolar, Kevin	R-L	6-2	255	1-28-71	6	0	3.86	27	0	0	2	33	29	21	14	3	15	26	.240	.081	.310	7.16	4.13
Valverde, Jose	R-R	6-4	255	7-24-79	0	0	0.00	2	0	0	0	2	1	0	0	0	1	3	.143	.250	.000	13.50	4.50
Villarreal, Oscar	L-R	6-0	215	11-22-81	0	3	5.19	12	8	0	0	17	19	12	10	1	4	8	.292	.344	.242	4.15	2.08

FIELDING

Catcher	PCT	G	PO	A	E	DP	PB
Ansman	.984	10	59	4	1	0	1
Brito	.998	70	452	35	1	1	2
Hill	.993	43	247	19	2	4	3
Myers	.986	22	127	9	2	4	5
Stinnett	.973	10	69	4	2	1	0

First Base	PCT	G	PO	A	E	DP
Cota	1.000	28	249	11	0	23
Doster	1.000	2	11	2	0	1
Jackson	.990	73	625	53	7	65
Myers	.995	41	357	29	2	34
Zinter	1.000	9	60	2	0	10

Second Base	PCT	G	PO	A	E	DP
Barden	.971	20	39	60	3	14
Brown	.750	1	1	2	1	0
De Renne	.974	51	87	138	6	30
Doster	1.000	11	21	24	0	7
Green	.981	64	139	166	6	45
Hairston	1.000	1	1	0	0	0
Kata	.945	14	30	39	4	13

Third Base	PCT	G	PO	A	E	DP
Barden	.963	115	87	253	13	27
De Renne	1.000	3	1	6	0	0
Doster	.750	2	0	3	1	0
Green	.946	14	10	25	2	3
Kata	.900	6	3	15	2	2
Myers	.957	10	6	16	1	2
Zinter	1.000	1	1	1	0	1

Shortstop	PCT	G	PO	A	E	DP
Barden	1.000	2	1	4	0	1
De Renne	1.000	10	7	11	0	5
Green	.966	6	11	17	1	4
Kata	.941	11	16	32	3	6
Santos	.953	128	152	371	26	76

Outfield	PCT	G	PO	A	E	DP
Brown	1.000	2	1	0	0	0
Camilo	1.000	5	4	0	0	0
Cota	1.000	4	7	0	0	0
Cruz Jr.	1.000	1	2	0	0	0
DeVore	.952	38	59	1	3	0
Doster	1.000	2	6	1	0	0
Green	.977	47	82	3	2	0
Hairston	.979	50	88	4	2	0
Hammock	1.000	3	11	0	0	0
Jackson	.929	17	26	0	2	0
Kata	1.000	14	29	0	0	0
Kroeger	.968	124	234	8	8	2
Porter	1.000	19	30	1	0	0
Quentin	.996	125	256	11	1	4
Terrero	1.000	7	9	0	0	0

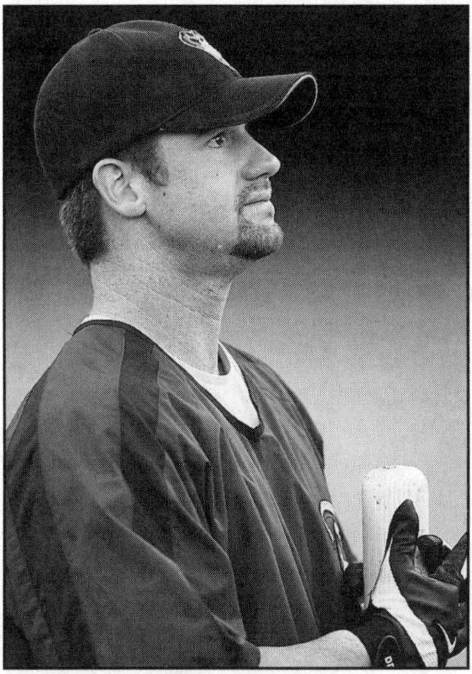

LARRY GOREN

Chad Tracy: A career-high 27 home runs

LARRY GOREN

Stephen Drew: A year off had no effect on his game

TENNESSEE SMOKIES — Class AA

SOUTHERN LEAGUE

BATTING	B-T	HT	WT	DOB	AVG	vLH	vRH	G	AB	R	H	2B	3B	HR	RBI	BB	HBP	SH	SF	SO	SB	CS	SLG	OBP
Avlas, Phil	R-R	5-11	183	12-17-82	.239	.175	.274	41	113	15	27	5	0	2	18	18	1	0	2	21	5	2	.336	.343
Ball, Jarred	B-R	6-0	195	4-18-83	.253	.216	.273	128	399	69	101	19	2	7	34	74	6	8	1	115	39	18	.363	.377
Brown, Neb	L-R	6-0	190	11-7-79	.260	.275	.255	49	146	18	38	8	0	1	17	14	1	3	0	26	9	3	.336	.329
Carter, Chris	L-L	5-10	210	9-16-82	.297	.300	.295	36	128	21	38	4	0	10	30	19	3	0	1	11	0	3	.563	.397
Cota, Jesus	L-R	6-3	220	11-7-81	.266	.276	.261	95	349	40	93	14	0	14	68	28	5	0	6	46	2	2	.427	.325
D'Antona, Jamie	R-R	6-2	210	5-12-82	.249	.235	.258	125	410	58	102	25	2	9	49	44	1	2	1	67	5	6	.385	.322
DiRosa, Mike	R-R	5-11	190	1-17-80	.239	.333	.160	39	92	9	22	2	0	3	8	14	0	0	0	33	1	1	.359	.340
Drew, Stephen	L-R	6-1	195	3-16-83	.218	.257	.197	27	101	11	22	5	0	4	13	12	0	0	0	24	2	3	.386	.301
Gil, Jerry	R-R	6-3	195	10-14-82	.256	.268	.248	55	199	28	51	7	3	10	29	8	1	4	0	52	10	7	.472	.288
Haley, Adam	L-R	6-0	171	9-4-80	.286	.248	.301	124	377	56	108	16	2	4	28	31	5	6	0	72	13	8	.371	.349
Montero, Miguel	L-R	5-11	190	7-9-83	.250	.364	.221	30	108	13	27	1	2	2	13	7	3	1	1	26	1	0	.352	.311
Morgan, Matt	R-R	6-3	220	8-10-81	.274	.278	.272	90	270	19	74	13	1	3	35	17	2	5	1	39	0	4	.363	.321
Uggla, Dan	R-R	5-10	200	3-11-80	.297	.299	.296	135	498	88	148	33	3	21	87	52	14	3	2	103	15	8	.502	.378
Varner, Noochie	R-R	6-0	204	12-7-80	.278	.253	.293	128	421	64	117	30	2	3	41	52	3	0	2	80	19	7	.380	.360
Williams, Marland	R-R	5-9	185	6-22-81	.234	.281	.209	121	381	55	89	13	7	7	46	37	0	2	6	108	38	7	.360	.297
Zeringue, Jon	R-R	6-2	215	3-29-83	.241	.244	.239	126	436	46	105	18	4	6	51	19	8	4	4	86	11	8	.342	.283

PITCHING	B-T	HT	WT	DOB	W	L	ERA	G	GS	CG	SV	IP	H	R	ER	HR	BB	SO	AVG	vLH	vRH	K/9	BB/9
Almanza, Armando	L-L	6-3	230	10-26-72	1	0	4.91	6	0	0	1	7	9	5	4	1	4	7	.290	.444	.227	8.59	4.91
Bass, Adam	R-R	6-6	220	7-31-81	5	10	3.99	27	27	1	0	158	158	75	70	14	40	120	.260	.271	.250	6.84	2.28
Biggs, Billy	R-R	6-0	198	9-9-79	0	1	3.97	9	0	0	0	11	13	7	5	3	6	6	.277	.294	.267	4.76	4.76

PITCHING	B-T	HT	WT	DOB	W	L	ERA	G	GS	CG	SV	IP	H	R	ER	HR	BB	SO	AVG	vLH	vRH	K/9	BB/9
Chico, Matt	L-L	5-11	190	6-10-83	1	7	5.98	10	10	0	0	53	75	44	35	8	15	35	.341	.354	.337	5.98	2.56
Daigle, Casey	R-R	6-5	250	4-4-81	9	3	2.67	58	2	0	19	64	75	24	19	3	18	50	.290	.305	.280	7.03	2.53
Gonzalez, Enrique	R-R	5-10	210	8-6-82	11	8	3.46	27	27	2	0	161	160	76	62	8	52	146	.264	.286	.246	8.14	2.90
Goocher, Clint	L-L	6-2	195	6-15-82	9	11	5.37	27	25	2	0	141	185	105	84	20	37	77	.323	.278	.337	4.93	2.37
Lizarraga, Sergio	R-R	6-4	195	7-23-81	0	1	6.63	12	2	0	0	19	31	17	14	3	3	16	.356	.387	.339	7.58	1.42
Nina, Elvin	R-R	6-0	180	11-25-75	0	1	6.43	4	1	0	0	7	10	5	5	0	4	4	.370	.462	.286	5.14	5.14
Nippert, Dustin	R-R	6-7	215	5-6-81	8	3	2.38	18	18	3	0	117	95	33	31	4	42	97	.226	.186	.255	7.44	3.22
Pena, Tony	R-R	6-1	220	1-9-82	7	13	4.43	25	25	2	0	148	165	86	73	17	40	95	.283	.319	.252	5.76	2.43
Schultz, Mike	R-R	6-7	220	11-28-79	4	6	3.58	63	0	0	6	65	70	31	26	3	41	68	.288	.326	.266	9.37	5.65
Sikaras, Pete	R-R	6-2	205	5-5-79	2	3	6.12	44	1	0	2	65	77	47	44	7	32	38	.297	.358	.253	5.29	4.45
Silva, Jesus	R-R	6-0	199	12-24-82	1	0	6.35	2	1	0	0	6	9	4	4	0	1	5	.375	.333	.417	7.94	1.59
Slaten, Doug	L-L	6-5	198	2-4-80	2	2	4.26	58	0	0	1	61	61	45	29	2	26	72	.262	.230	.281	10.57	3.82
Stockman, Phil	R-R	6-8	250	1-25-80	1	3	3.25	47	1	0	1	36	31	16	13	2	24	30	.237	.233	.239	7.50	6.00
Thompson, Chris	R-R	6-3	195	1-2-82	0	0	2.45	3	0	0	0	4	1	1	1	0	1	2	.083	.125	.000	4.91	2.45
Wechsler, Justin	R-R	6-0	255	4-6-80	3	2	6.14	42	0	0	0	56	62	41	38	7	26	43	.291	.304	.284	6.95	4.20
White, Bill	L-L	6-4	215	11-20-78	0	2	4.50	60	0	0	0	42	40	28	21	1	26	33	.253	.169	.312	7.07	5.57

FIELDING

Catcher	PCT	G	PO	A	E	DP	PB
Avlas	.976	35	218	23	6	3	5
Dirosa	.990	27	175	19	2	1	3
Montero	.983	29	211	18	4	3	3
Morgan	.990	59	371	43	4	6	10

First Base	PCT	G	PO	A	E	DP
Carter	.979	22	170	17	4	21
Cota	.989	89	737	69	9	73
D'Antona	.991	14	109	4	1	11
Haley	1.000	1	2	0	0	0
Montero	.000	1	0	0	0	0
Morgan	.984	9	56	6	1	7
Uggla	.988	10	81	3	1	9

Varner	1.000	1	3	0	0	0
Williams	1.000	1	3	0	0	0

Second Base	PCT	G	PO	A	E	DP
Brown	.950	35	60	92	8	20
Haley	.983	12	23	36	1	12
Morgan	1.000	5	10	11	0	5
Uggla	.959	97	192	232	18	62

Third Base	PCT	G	PO	A	E	DP
D'Antona	.933	100	65	172	17	17
Gil	1.000	2	0	3	0	0
Haley	.951	31	28	49	4	8
Morgan	.955	12	8	13	1	3
Uggla	.971	11	10	23	1	1

Shortstop	PCT	G	PO	A	E	DP
Drew	.935	27	36	80	8	16
Gil	.963	52	76	160	9	28
Haley	.946	56	94	153	14	35
Uggla	.896	10	15	28	5	5

Outfield	PCT	G	PO	A	E	DP
Avlas	.000	1	0	0	0	0
Ball	.979	119	225	10	5	1
Carter	1.000	5	3	1	0	0
Haley	1.000	4	1	0	0	0
Varner	1.000	93	137	9	0	1
Williams	.979	104	221	10	5	5
Zeringue	.955	119	239	18	12	4

LANCASTER JETHAWKS — High Class A

CALIFORNIA LEAGUE

BATTING	B-T	HT	WT	DOB	AVG	vLH	vRH	G	AB	R	H	2B	3B	HR	RBI	BB	HBP	SH	SF	SO	SB	CS	SLG	OBP
Avlas, Phil	R-R	5-11	183	12-17-82	.367	.372	.365	37	147	29	54	12	1	5	24	10	0	3	1	25	1	1	.565	.405
Brito, Javier	R-R	6-3	210	3-25-83	.292	.265	.309	25	89	17	26	6	0	2	11	10	2	0	0	17	0	0	.427	.376
Brown, Neb	L-R	6-0	190	11-7-79	.274	.292	.267	45	168	33	46	7	1	2	24	28	1	2	3	32	5	4	.363	.375
Bruce, Derek	R-R	6-2	190	8-3-82	.341	.362	.317	30	88	19	30	10	0	3	13	4	1	4	1	21	0	0	.557	.372
Carter, Chris	L-L	5-10	210	9-16-82	.296	.294	.298	103	412	71	122	26	2	21	85	46	6	0	6	66	0	0	.522	.370
Cook, Jeff	L-R	5-10	190	10-4-80	.314	.244	.338	129	526	96	165	43	7	19	89	46	1	13	6	75	2	4	.530	.366
De Renne, Keoni	B-R	5-7	170	4-30-79	.293	.500	.257	10	41	10	12	1	0	0	4	9	0	0	0	3	1	0	.317	.420
Downing, Ramon	B-R	5-10	187	9-1-83	.200	.000	.200	2	5	0	1	0	0	0	0	0	0	0	0	1	0	0	.200	.200
Drew, Stephen	L-R	6-1	195	3-16-83	.389	.389	.393	38	149	33	58	16	3	10	39	26	2	0	0	25	1	1	.738	.486
Frazier, Alex	R-R	6-4	225	12-21-80	.265	.271	.263	98	388	72	103	19	4	19	69	49	15	0	3	96	5	4	.482	.367
Garcia, Lino	R-R	6-3	192	10-12-83	.159	.167	.154	18	63	3	10	0	0	0	6	4	1	3	0	12	2	2	.159	.221
Garrabrants, Steve	R-R	5-10	170	11-18-81	.318	.350	.303	95	358	79	114	28	5	7	58	39	12	7	4	45	8	4	.483	.400
Garthwaite, Jay	R-R	6-2	220	11-26-80	.300	.302	.300	124	487	81	146	36	4	21	102	33	8	5	7	131	1	3	.520	.350
Kaplan, Jonny	R-R	6-9	180	1-11-80	.152	.200	.095	21	46	11	7	3	0	0	3	7	2	3	0	11	2	0	.217	.291
Montero, Miguel	L-R	5-11	190	7-9-83	.349	.252	.393	85	355	73	124	24	1	24	82	26	10	2	6	52	1	2	.625	.403
Nunez, Argelis	R-R	6-1	170	10-25-81	.091	.000	.125	4	11	0	1	1	0	0	0	0	0	0	0	7	0	0	.182	.091
Perez, Kenny	B-R	6-2	190	9-28-81	.320	.269	.338	22	97	25	31	7	1	1	10	9	0	1	0	15	0	0	.443	.377
Richar, Danny	L-R	6-0	170	6-9-83	.300	.250	.314	121	454	78	136	32	8	20	79	32	3	10	4	64	9	3	.537	.347
Rose, Brian	R-R	6-2	230	9-17-80	.289	.304	.278	72	253	37	73	22	0	6	37	22	12	7	3	44	0	1	.447	.369
Schindewolf, Erik	L-R	5-11	180	10-1-81	.274	.307	.265	109	391	76	107	19	5	4	33	87	3	9	2	67	7	3	.379	.408
Simon, Brandon	L-L	5-11	190	9-9-80	.256	.083	.288	23	78	12	20	3	1	0	6	4	4	3	0	20	2	2	.321	.326
Stinnett, Kelly	R-R	5-11	235	2-4-70	.273	.333	.250	3	11	4	3	1	0	1	5	2	0	0	0	1	0	0	.636	.385
Varela, Edgar	L-R	6-1	213	8-9-80	.309	.250	.320	106	395	58	122	30	2	9	60	18	6	4	9	74	1	2	.463	.341

PITCHING	B-T	HT	WT	DOB	W	L	ERA	G	GS	CG	SV	IP	H	R	ER	HR	BB	SO	AVG	vLH	vRH	K/9	BB/9
Biggs, Billy	R-R	6-0	198	9-9-79	3	6	6.04	39	0	0	1	45	66	34	30	5	16	26	.349	.354	.345	5.24	3.22
Bono, Kyle	R-R	6-3	205	6-29-83	1	0	7.04	6	0	0	0	8	7	7	6	2	5	9	.226	.333	.125	10.57	5.87
Castellanos, Jon	R-R	6-0	214	9-17-81	10	3	4.65	28	28	0	0	161	186	96	83	24	41	116	.284	.298	.272	6.50	2.30
Chico, Matt	L-L	5-11	190	6-10-83	7	2	3.76	18	18	0	0	110	101	50	46	13	39	102	.243	.280	.229	8.35	3.19
Coffin, Ryan	R-R	6-5	205	8-5-81	4	2	6.28	33	0	0	2	43	51	34	30	7	13	45	.285	.351	.254	9.42	2.72
Cremidan, Alex	L-R	6-3	210	1-15-81	1	5	4.58	44	0	0	0	57	55	35	29	5	34	49	.247	.258	.238	7.74	5.37
Glant, Dustin	R-R	6-2	200	7-20-81	0	1	7.19	50	0	0	16	46	74	41	37	10	12	49	.351	.387	.322	9.52	2.33
Holsten, Ryan	R-R	6-4	215	5-5-79	0	0	18.00	3	0	0	0	3	10	6	6	1	1	1	.556	.429	.636	3.00	3.00
Kerbs, Reuben	L-L	6-2	185	10-19-80	2	1	4.74	57	0	0	0	38	37	26	20	8	19	28	.253	.135	.439	6.63	4.50
Kinsey, Chris	R-R	6-3	230	10-18-82	3	11	6.56	15	15	0	0	73	112	72	53	10	29	60	.351	.402	.316	7.43	3.59
Liebeck, Jered	R-R	6-1	200	1-27-81	1	1	5.81	18	0	0	1	26	34	18	17	1	14	24	.304	.318	.294	8.20	4.78
Mock, Garrett	R-R	6-4	215	4-25-83	14	7	4.18	28	28	0	0	174	202	95	81	19	33	160	.284	.256	.311	8.26	1.70
Ortiz, Russ	R-R	6-1	220	6-5-74	0	1	42.43	1	1	0	0	2	12	11	11	2	1	1	.706	.600	.857	3.86	3.86
Owings, Micah	R-R	6-5	220	9-28-82	1	1	2.45	16	0	0	0	22	17	6	6	0	4	30	.221	.179	.245	12.27	1.64
Ramsey, Keith	B-L	6-1	175	3-5-80	0	1	4.50	4	0	0	0	4	3	2	2	0	5	4	.231	.250	.222	9.00	11.25
Scarbery, Chad	R-R	6-1	200	9-23-80	5	6	6.11	25	24	1	0	131	174	103	89	17	53	77	.323	.342	.308	5.29	3.64
Shappi, A.J.	R-R	6-2	195	10-16-82	5	6	5.10	12	12	0	0	78	94	51	44	13	20	56	.297	.289	.305	6.49	2.32
Silva, Jesus	R-R	6-0	199	12-24-82	5	2	6.91	29	3	0	1	42	64	40	32	11	16	38	.344	.294	.386	8.21	3.46
Smith, Samuel	R-R	6-4	227	8-23-79	7	6	5.44	41	11	0	0	101	132	73	61	21	33	66	.310	.333	.293	5.88	2.94
Thompson, Chris	R-R	6-3	195	1-2-82	3	1	5.13	27	0	0	0	33	32	20	19	3	16	24	.252	.222	.274	6.48	4.32
Watson, Mike	R-R	6-1	180	9-28-80	0	1	6.98	16	0	0	0	19	25	16	15	2	11	14	.313	.323	.306	6.52	5.12

PITCHING	B-T	HT	WT	DOB	W	L	ERA	G	GS	CG	SV	IP	H	R	ER	HR	BB	SO	AVG	vLH	vRH	K/9	BB/9
Wells, Carlton	L-L	6-2	205	3-25-80	3	1	2.70	14	0	0	0	17	16	6	5	0	5	3	.239	.286	.188	1.62	2.70
Wilkinson, Matt	L-R	6-3	205	10-25-77	0	0	3.06	20	0	0	15	18	19	7	6	2	8	20	.279	.419	.162	10.19	4.08

FIELDING

Catcher	PCT	G	PO	A	E	DP	PB
Avlas	.986	36	281	11	4	2	2
Montero	.983	59	439	33	8	4	8
Rose	.994	45	291	21	2	3	5
Stinnett	1.000	2	9	2	0	0	0

First Base	PCT	G	PO	A	E	DP
Brito	.987	18	144	12	2	12
Carter	.982	69	553	44	11	55
Garthwaite	1.000	4	39	5	0	2
Montero	1.000	1	2	0	0	0
Rose	1.000	1	1	0	0	0
Varela	.990	53	444	35	5	52

Second Base	PCT	G	PO	A	E	DP
Brown	.987	17	31	47	1	11
Bruce	.929	5	12	14	2	4
De Renne	1.000	1	3	2	0	2
Garrabrants	.917	3	4	7	1	0
Richar	.972	49	95	150	7	38
Schindewolf	.965	72	143	215	13	39

Third Base	PCT	G	PO	A	E	DP
Brown	.925	21	17	45	5	5
Bruce	1.000	6	2	6	0	0
De Renne	.889	4	0	8	1	0
Downing	.000	1	0	0	0	0
Garrabrants	.875	6	7	14	3	1
Garthwaite	.870	28	10	57	10	4
Richar	.905	6	4	15	2	4
Schindewolf	.947	36	20	51	4	5
Varela	.942	49	27	87	7	4

Shortstop	PCT	G	PO	A	E	DP
Bruce	.986	19	22	48	1	11
De Renne	1.000	4	4	13	0	2
Drew	.950	36	52	101	8	21
Garrabrants	.833	3	1	4	1	0
Perez	.953	22	34	68	5	19
Richar	.920	65	102	163	23	39

Outfield	PCT	G	PO	A	E	DP
Brito	1.000	3	2	0	0	0
Brown	.867	9	12	1	2	0
Carter	.974	25	37	0	1	0
Cook	.981	129	256	8	5	1
Frazier	.930	61	92	1	7	0
Garcia	.977	18	41	1	1	0
Garrabrants	.991	80	225	7	2	1
Garthwaite	.960	81	110	9	5	2
Kaplan	1.000	18	38	1	0	0
Nunez	1.000	3	5	0	0	0
Richar	.000	2	0	0	0	0
Simon	.965	23	54	1	2	0

SOUTH BEND SILVER HAWKS — Low Class A

MIDWEST LEAGUE

BATTING	B-T	HT	WT	DOB	AVG	vLH	vRH	G	AB	R	H	2B	3B	HR	RBI	BB	HBP	SH	SF	SO	SB	CS	SLG	OBP
Bonifacio, Emilio	B-R	5-11	178	4-23-85	.270	.229	.281	127	522	81	141	14	7	1	44	56	2	7	4	90	55	17	.330	.341
Brito, Javier	R-R	6-3	210	3-25-83	.296	.320	.291	78	284	43	84	18	1	5	52	41	6	1	6	37	1	2	.419	.389
Buhagiar, Josh	L-L	6-0	186	2-23-81	.098	.000	.102	17	51	0	5	1	0	0	1	4	0	2	1	8	0	0	.118	.161
Castillo, Wilkin	B-R	6-0	170	6-1-84	.302	.298	.303	113	411	65	124	21	3	6	53	26	4	16	4	38	9	9	.411	.346
Gonzales, Alberto	R-R	5-11	167	4-18-83	.318	.269	.332	95	352	60	112	21	7	1	42	20	5	5	5	42	12	5	.426	.359
Gonzales, Carlos	L-L	6-1	180	10-17-85	.307	.277	.314	129	515	91	158	28	6	18	92	48	5	0	1	86	7	3	.489	.371
Gulick, Travis	R-R	6-3	215	5-17-83	.217	.299	.186	69	244	28	53	13	3	3	30	20	1	2	0	56	2	5	.332	.279
Lockin, Billy	R-R	5-8	155	11-27-82	.286	.294	.284	28	91	18	26	5	0	0	11	8	3	1	1	9	1	2	.341	.359
Mercado, Orlando	R-R	5-10	195	3-13-85	.249	.267	.244	67	225	31	56	10	0	6	35	34	2	6	5	34	1	2	.373	.346
Milons, Jereme	R-R	6-2	205	2-5-83	.265	.292	.256	123	491	81	130	28	8	10	66	32	3	3	7	114	11	6	.415	.310
Mottram, Allen	R-R	6-1	210	6-24-81	.309	.462	.261	59	217	51	67	20	1	15	39	23	2	0	3	32	1	3	.618	.376
Murillo, Agustin	R-R	6-2	193	5-5-82	.296	.227	.312	126	494	94	146	34	3	17	82	53	8	1	8	80	5	1	.480	.368
Nicolas, Cesar	R-R	6-4	230	4-17-82	.302	.215	.323	91	325	70	98	30	1	21	70	58	15	0	2	60	1	0	.594	.428
Reynolds, Mark	R-R	6-1	200	8-3-83	.253	.276	.249	118	434	65	110	26	2	19	76	37	6	5	2	107	4	1	.454	.319
Simon, Brandon	L-L	5-11	190	9-9-80	.268	.238	.272	58	168	22	45	5	3	0	22	13	8	6	2	34	11	6	.333	.346

PITCHING	B-T	HT	WT	DOB	W	L	ERA	G	GS	CG	SV	IP	H	R	ER	HR	BB	SO	AVG	vLH	vRH	K/9	BB/9
Coffin, Ryan	R-R	6-5	205	8-5-81	1	0	3.32	14	0	0	0	19	12	7	7	3	10	21	.176	.174	.178	9.95	4.74
Duran, Enmanuel	R-R	6-1	178	11-7-84	0	3	8.06	10	4	0	0	22	32	21	20	0	11	14	.344	.314	.362	5.64	4.43
Elliott, Matt	R-R	6-0	190	4-6-84	3	4	2.14	53	0	0	32	55	35	18	13	1	22	71	.183	.186	.182	11.69	3.62
Guerrero, Hipolito	L-L	6-0	149	6-13-83	4	3	2.67	46	0	0	1	64	51	20	19	3	31	45	.218	.197	.225	6.33	4.36
Howard, Adam	R-R	6-4	200	8-16-83	2	2	2.56	20	1	0	0	32	29	11	9	2	11	16	.254	.310	.222	4.55	3.13
Jackson, Steven	R-R	6-5	215	3-15-82	10	5	5.33	28	28	0	0	159	205	109	94	14	57	89	.321	.346	.303	5.05	3.23
Kinsey, Chris	R-R	6-3	230	10-18-82	4	4	5.31	13	13	0	0	78	88	55	46	5	27	48	.288	.290	.286	5.54	3.12
Kolberg, Koley	R-R	6-1	176	11-26-82	6	7	3.90	20	20	0	0	115	111	58	50	13	36	110	.251	.253	.250	8.58	2.81
Medlin, Corbey	R-R	6-2	200	8-4-81	1	1	7.88	9	0	0	0	8	12	7	7	1	7	6	.375	.500	.318	6.75	7.88
Ohlendorf, Ross	R-R	6-4	235	8-8-82	11	10	4.53	27	26	1	0	157	181	97	79	10	48	144	.286	.279	.292	8.25	2.75
Perrault, Josh	R-R	6-3	205	6-11-82	7	2	2.07	45	2	0	0	78	61	24	18	4	19	63	.218	.223	.214	7.24	2.18
Raab, Kellen	L-L	6-6	225	2-16-82	7	6	4.44	27	22	1	0	150	170	83	74	10	36	133	.288	.273	.291	7.98	2.16
Rocha, Angel	L-L	6-3	205	11-15-84	2	1	6.98	13	9	0	0	40	41	33	31	3	36	43	.270	.300	.262	9.68	8.10
Rosen, Mark	L-L	5-11	210	6-30-84	6	1	4.87	46	0	0	2	44	39	25	24	2	41	42	.231	.236	.228	8.53	8.32
Shappi, A.J.	R-R	6-2	195	10-16-82	11	1	2.86	15	15	2	0	104	98	38	33	7	15	59	.250	.303	.206	5.12	1.30
Stein, Todd	L-L	6-0	190	6-9-81	3	2	3.83	45	0	0	1	49	55	28	21	3	17	48	.270	.246	.280	8.76	3.10
Vasquez, Esmerling	R-R	6-1	154	11-7-83	6	4	3.64	53	0	0	3	72	63	33	29	2	47	79	.238	.289	.208	9.92	5.90

FIELDING

Catcher	PCT	G	PO	A	E	DP	PB
Castillo	.983	60	417	42	8	4	8
Mercado	.984	59	440	47	8	1	13
Mottram	.995	26	160	22	1	2	1

First Base	PCT	G	PO	A	E	DP
Brito	.989	42	342	23	4	36
Mottram	1.000	4	29	3	0	1
Murillo	1.000	13	110	9	0	8
Nicolas	.985	85	807	66	13	73

Second Base	PCT	G	PO	A	E	DP
Bonifacio	.964	119	222	386	23	74
A. Gonzales	1.000	6	9	15	0	3
Lockin	.974	16	31	45	2	14

Third Base	PCT	G	PO	A	E	DP
Castillo	.750	3	2	1	1	1
A. Gonzales	1.000	1	0	1	0	0
Lockin	1.000	2	0	2	0	0
Murillo	.928	105	68	190	20	18
Reynolds	.872	34	15	53	10	3

Shortstop	PCT	G	PO	A	E	DP
A. Gonzales	.975	84	126	307	11	62
Lockin	1.000	3	0	9	0	1
Reynolds	.922	56	75	163	20	29

Outfield	PCT	G	PO	A	E	DP
Brito	.951	28	37	2	2	0
Buhagiar	.973	17	35	1	1	0
Castillo	.981	28	50	3	1	0
C. Gonzales	.973	127	239	13	7	3
Gulick	.991	60	108	3	1	0
Milons	.972	116	234	6	7	1
Simon	.951	54	94	3	5	2

YAKIMA BEARS — Short-Season Class A

NORTHWEST LEAGUE

BATTING	B-T	HT	WT	DOB	AVG	vLH	vRH	G	AB	R	H	2B	3B	HR	RBI	BB	HBP	SH	SF	SO	SB	CS	SLG	OBP
Batten, Jo Jo	R-R	5-10	175	12-14-84	.300	.286	.313	9	30	5	9	2	0	0	1	6	1	0	0	9	4	2	.367	.432
Biguenet, Michael	R-R	5-11	185	11-20-81	.200	.087	.230	41	110	14	22	3	0	3	7	9	1	0	0	51	0	1	.309	.267
Bruce, Derek	R-R	6-2	190	8-3-82	.278	.364	.248	75	299	40	83	28	0	3	27	15	7	3	4	57	2	5	.401	.323
Burgess, Brandon	B-R	6-3	220	2-24-83	.336	.286	.364	33	119	21	40	10	2	3	18	14	6	0	0	34	1	0	.529	.432

BATTING	B-T	HT	WT	DOB	AVG	vLH	vRH	G	AB	R	H	2B	3B	HR	RBI	BB	HBP	SH	SF	SO	SB	CS	SLG	OBP
Centeno, Jaen	R-R	6-3	181	1-1-84	.198	.298	.161	66	212	21	42	12	0	9	32	22	3	5	3	67	2	4	.382	.279
Contreras, Lester	R-R	5-11	190	7-30-84	.223	.227	.221	46	148	18	33	8	1	4	14	13	2	1	1	37	1	1	.372	.293
Del Campo, Manny	R-R	5-10	200	5-11-83	.160	.167	.157	38	119	9	19	6	0	1	9	5	4	0	0	29	0	0	.235	.219
Downing, Ramon	B-R	5-10	187	9-1-83	.277	.197	.311	68	256	35	71	15	3	7	34	20	4	7	5	40	7	4	.441	.333
Ford, Josh	R-R	6-2	235	1-17-83	.282	.238	.298	43	163	12	46	7	0	0	25	15	3	0	4	30	0	1	.325	.346
Hendricks, Trey	B-R	6-4	210	8-8-82	.296	.282	.301	76	301	33	89	16	2	8	42	25	0	0	3	46	2	1	.442	.347
Mercado, Richard	R-R	6-0	220	5-23-83	.233	.500	.214	10	30	3	7	2	1	0	3	5	1	0	1	5	0	0	.367	.351
Olivares, Juan	R-R	6-2	178	8-2-84	.225	.292	.203	53	191	21	43	3	3	1	18	13	3	2	1	47	6	2	.288	.284
Rahl, Chris	R-R	6-0	185	12-5-83	.269	.295	.261	47	182	29	49	12	5	1	10	12	1	3	0	44	10	5	.407	.318
Septimo, Leyson	L-L	6-0	150	7-7-85	.241	.136	.275	67	237	20	57	11	2	2	21	10	1	4	2	51	2	3	.329	.272
Sosa, Ricardo	R-R	6-1	200	5-24-84	.254	.280	.247	32	118	17	30	9	1	4	18	10	2	1	2	22	2	0	.449	.318
Williams, Kevin	R-R	6-0	175	10-30-81	.202	.160	.215	33	104	17	21	5	0	0	4	10	8	2	0	45	11	4	.250	.320

PITCHING	B-T	HT	WT	DOB	W	L	ERA	G	GS	CG	SV	IP	H	R	ER	HR	BB	SO	AVG	vLH	vRH	K/9	BB/9
Bauer, Garrett	R-L	6-1	175	9-4-81	1	0	5.06	18	0	0	1	27	25	15	15	2	27	42	.248	.212	.265	14.18	9.11
Cahill, John	R-R	6-2	195	3-30-83	0	0	8.25	8	0	0	0	12	20	11	11	1	7	8	.392	.421	.375	6.00	5.25
Doherty, Ryan	R-R	7-1	225	2-2-84	3	3	3.27	22	0	0	1	33	26	16	12	3	9	38	.213	.265	.178	10.36	2.45
Dove, Shane	L-L	6-1	170	7-22-84	2	4	5.49	9	7	0	0	39	51	33	24	3	18	30	.321	.300	.328	6.86	4.12
Duran, Enmanuel	R-R	6-1	178	11-7-84	0	1	2.72	24	1	0	2	36	34	14	11	0	14	25	.246	.220	.266	6.19	3.47
Fowles, Matt	B-R	6-3	220	6-3-83	2	2	4.15	23	0	0	2	26	26	18	12	2	19	30	.260	.292	.231	10.38	6.58
Howard, Adam	R-R	6-4	200	8-16-83	4	5	4.29	13	13	0	0	71	88	36	34	8	12	59	.304	.294	.314	7.44	1.51
Kemlo, Chris	R-R	6-5	205	9-23-83	5	7	5.08	16	16	1	0	89	116	65	50	6	28	47	.312	.326	.297	4.77	2.84
Krohe, Matt	L-L	6-3	200	1-9-84	0	2	3.14	20	0	0	0	29	30	14	10	2	9	18	.268	.241	.277	5.65	2.83
Newby, Kyler	R-R	6-4	225	2-22-85	1	0	2.18	24	0	0	2	41	25	12	10	1	14	66	.172	.200	.150	14.37	3.05
Pfautz, Craig	R-L	6-3	190	9-13-84	1	6	5.46	20	0	0	0	28	39	29	17	2	16	16	.339	.351	.333	5.14	5.14
Rocha, Angel	L-L	6-3	205	11-15-84	3	8	5.43	15	15	0	0	71	62	50	43	4	53	93	.233	.324	.198	11.73	6.69
Schreppel, Ryan	L-L	6-2	195	6-2-84	2	2	3.35	14	7	0	0	46	41	23	17	2	17	50	.238	.304	.207	9.85	3.35
Thompson, Chris	R-R	6-3	195	1-2-82	3	0	1.89	16	0	0	5	19	10	5	4	4	5	26	.149	.083	.226	12.32	2.37
Torra, Matt	R-R	6-3	225	6-29-84	0	1	1.80	5	2	0	0	10	11	3	2	1	4	10	.297	.188	.381	9.00	3.60
Urquidez, Jason	R-R	6-2	175	9-12-82	1	1	1.80	11	1	0	0	15	14	7	3	0	7	19	.246	.303	.167	11.40	4.20
Wilkinson, Matt	L-R	6-3	205	10-25-77	1	0	0.90	9	0	0	2	10	6	1	1	0	6	11	.176	.154	.190	9.90	5.40
Wright, Kyle	R-R	6-3	170	4-27-83	1	4	4.22	15	14	0	0	79	88	47	37	4	22	65	.275	.253	.295	7.41	2.51

GAMES BY POSITION: C—Biguenet 12, Contreras 1, Del Campo 34, Ford 33, Mercado 8. **1B**—Contreras 8, Hendricks 73. **2B**—Batten 8, Bruce 23, Biguenet 8, Downing 39. **3B**—Biguenet 9, Contreras 34, Olivares 6, Sosa 29. **SS**—Bruce 50, Olivares 26. **OF**—Batten 1, Biguenet 6, Burgess 27, Centeno 64, Olivares 13, Rahl 41, Septimo 63, Williams 30.

MISSOULA OSPREY — Rookie

PIONEER LEAGUE

BATTING	B-T	HT	WT	DOB	AVG	vLH	vRH	G	AB	R	H	2B	3B	HR	RBI	BB	HBP	SH	SF	SO	SB	CS	SLG	OBP
Batten, Jo Jo	R-R	5-10	175	12-14-84	.173	.133	.189	23	52	11	9	2	0	1	10	8	1	1	0	11	1	2	.269	.295
Bustamante, Gerardo	R-R	5-8	184	6-10-86	.067	.000	.067	11	15	0	1	0	0	0	0	1	0	0	0	5	0	0	.067	.125
Byrne, Bryan	L-R	6-3	200	4-30-84	.267	.292	.256	64	221	39	59	15	1	4	36	42	3	0	0	50	3	4	.398	.391
Ciriaco, Pedro	R-R	6-0	150	9-27-85	.240	.153	.284	69	254	28	61	9	4	2	31	7	2	3	2	50	7	2	.331	.264
Crouch, Will	R-R	6-3	220	8-13-82	.282	.294	.276	58	202	43	57	19	0	8	37	39	10	0	0	54	6	5	.495	.422
Cruz, Ricardo	R-R	5-11	175	8-11-83	.256	.272	.248	62	238	33	61	16	0	10	40	16	6	0	0	83	3	7	.450	.319
DeCarlo, Mike	R-R	6-1	215	3-13-82	.235	.214	.244	42	132	22	31	9	0	3	19	12	5	1	1	32	1	2	.371	.320
Diaz, Osvaldo	R-R	6-2	210	12-31-82	.270	.280	.265	63	252	35	68	18	1	6	38	14	3	1	3	63	1	4	.421	.313
Elder, Jake	R-R	6-1	205	3-21-83	.288	.306	.280	40	111	22	32	7	0	2	10	16	8	1	0	14	2	3	.405	.415
Lajara, Luis	L-L	6-1	180	12-12-84	.182	.000	.190	11	22	2	4	0	0	1	4	3	0	0	0	6	0	1	.318	.280
Melendez, Norman	R-R	5-11	170	9-18-85	.103	.091	.111	24	29	3	3	1	0	0	1	1	0	1	0	10	0	0	.138	.133
Mena, Steve	R-R	6-4	200	1-24-85	.274	.278	.272	66	248	40	68	18	3	5	46	19	2	0	1	69	9	4	.431	.330
Roman, Edwin	B-R	5-10	215	4-18-85	.238	.250	.233	21	63	13	15	1	1	2	5	2	11	1	1	22	5	5	.381	.364
Ryal, Rusty	R-R	6-2	195	3-16-83	.333	.340	.330	72	294	59	98	22	4	6	46	14	15	1	2	47	11	3	.497	.391
Santiago, Jayson	L-L	6-1	175	10-9-85	.254	.289	.238	35	122	20	31	3	2	2	11	6	1	1	0	29	8	0	.361	.295
Summers, Houston	R-R	5-10	180	8-20-87	.182	.000	.222	12	11	1	2	1	0	0	0	2	0	0	0	3	0	0	.273	.308
Terrell, Josh	R-R	6-5	240	9-3-83	.294	.333	.250	6	17	0	5	1	0	0	1	3	0	0	0	7	1	0	.353	.400
Thomson, Greg	L-L	6-1	205	6-13-84	.270	.417	.207	49	200	29	54	10	3	1	20	12	6	0	3	43	5	8	.365	.326
Tully, Travis	L-L	5-8	170	1-31-84	.281	.175	.328	53	185	35	52	9	1	0	22	27	2	1	2	35	11	7	.341	.375

PITCHING	B-T	HT	WT	DOB	W	L	ERA	G	GS	CG	SV	IP	H	R	ER	HR	BB	SO	AVG	vLH	vRH	K/9	BB/9
Baeza, Eddie	R-R	6-0	180	10-19-84	1	2	2.25	25	0	0	3	40	31	12	10	1	13	50	.212	.192	.233	11.25	2.93
Bongiovanni, Vince	R-R	6-5	215	1-11-83	0	2	5.29	23	0	0	1	34	31	23	20	2	28	36	.240	.315	.187	9.53	7.41
Church, Lorenzo	R-R	5-11	180	8-16-86	1	2	5.58	20	0	0	0	40	53	31	25	3	26	48	.317	.356	.287	10.71	5.80
Cupps, Anthony	R-R	6-3	198	5-31-83	4	6	5.05	15	12	0	0	68	76	48	38	6	29	54	.292	.341	.240	7.18	3.86
Davis, Vince	R-L	6-6	245	8-22-82	2	2	3.16	16	0	0	1	26	24	12	9	2	15	28	.250	.172	.284	9.82	5.26
Duda, Peter	R-R	6-4	215	9-10-83	1	2	10.80	19	1	0	0	32	49	44	38	9	31	29	.358	.339	.372	8.24	8.81
Evans, Cody	R-R	6-5	190	9-3-83	0	2	9.23	20	3	0	0	40	68	44	41	4	25	27	.378	.363	.390	6.08	5.63
Green, Matt	R-R	6-5	195	1-5-82	4	3	5.55	15	12	0	0	60	77	41	37	6	26	59	.316	.343	.294	8.85	3.90
Julio, Donald	R-R	6-1	164	8-12-83	3	2	5.32	21	2	0	2	46	50	34	27	6	22	43	.270	.267	.273	8.47	4.34
Neighborgall, Jason	R-R	6-5	205	12-19-83	1	2	11.12	15	7	0	0	23	21	40	28	1	45	29	.236	.229	.244	11.51	17.87
Nippert, Derik	R-R	6-7	220	5-6-81	1	1	6.56	15	3	0	0	36	44	27	26	4	12	35	.291	.297	.287	8.83	3.03
Pohlman, Dan	R-R	6-1	215	1-1-82	2	4	3.63	27	3	0	13	45	41	24	18	2	21	48	.243	.256	.231	9.67	4.23
Romanczuk, Mark	L-L	6-1	195	9-24-83	4	5	4.55	13	13	0	0	61	70	37	31	6	17	59	.282	.232	.302	8.66	2.49
Sanchez, Ramon	R-R	6-3	180	6-6-84	2	2	5.71	9	6	0	0	35	39	26	22	4	14	37	.285	.333	.235	9.61	3.63
Smith, Greg	L-L	6-2	190	12-22-83	8	5	4.15	16	14	0	0	82	69	40	38	8	18	100	.231	.221	.234	10.93	1.97
Venas, Miliade	R-R	6-1	170	2-23-83	0	0	10.64	8	0	0	0	11	18	16	13	0	8	6	.353	.375	.333	4.91	6.55

GAMES BY POSITION: C—Bustamante 7, DeCarlo 41, Elder 39, Summers 6. **1B**—Byrne 57, Crouch 1, Diaz 3, Mena 16, Terrell 1. **2B**—Batten 20, Cruz 54, Ryal 12. **3B**—Cruz 2, Mena 17, Ryal 61. **SS**—Ciriaco 69, Cruz 12. **OF**—Crouch 19, Diaz 42, Melendez 20, Mena 22, Roman 19, Lajara 11, Santiago 33, Thomson 42, Tully 50.

ATLANTA BRAVES

BY BILL BALLEW

From afar it would be easy to lump the Braves' continuing consistency of 2005 with the more recent campaigns that resulted in ultimate disappointment. Granted, Atlanta departed the playoffs by dropping the National League Division Series for the fourth straight season, bowing out in an 18-inning epic at Houston in Game 4.

But unlike so many of the heartbreaking days during the team's run of 14 consecutive division championships—the longest such streak in the history of professional sports—the Braves' efforts of 2005 leave the front office and fans with more hope and enthusiasm than at any point since winning the World Series in 1995.

The Braves entered 2005 believing its rotation ranked among the best they had fielded since the Cy Young award-winning trio of Tom Glavine, Greg Maddux and John Smoltz. Tim Hudson, acquired from Oakland during the offseason, and the return of Smoltz to the starting staff after three-plus seasons as a closer, gave Atlanta as formidable a one-two punch as any team in the National League.

While both pitchers won 14 games, the extended losses of Mike Hampton and John Thomson made the unheralded spring training pickup of Jorge Sosa the most important move of the slate. Sosa started 20 times in his 44 appearances and finished 13-3, 2.55.

Atlanta also received assistance from many of its mainstays, beginning with MVP candidate Andruw Jones, who clubbed a franchise-record 51 home runs while continuing to display his Gold Glove defense in center field. Chipper Jones overcame an extended stint on the disabled list to rake with abandon down the stretch. The double-play duo of Marcus Giles and Rafael Furcal also had strong second halves at the plate and in the field.

Yet the story of the Braves' season centered on the new blood that arrived in Atlanta out of need. With the extended injuries of Chipper Jones, catcher Johnny Estrada and outfielder Brian Jordan and the failure to catch lightning in a bottle with Raul Mondesi, the Braves went from having four rookies on their Opening Day roster to employing 18 green peas over the course of the campaign. Eight made the playoff roster and saw action against the Astros, which set a record for the most rookies ever used by one team in the postseason.

Headlining the excitement was outfielder Jeff Francoeur, who made the jump from Double-A Mississippi in July and proceeded to hit .300-14-45 in 70 games. Similar moves were made by such fellow Atlanta-area products as pitcher Blaine Boyer and catcher Brian McCann, who became the first Brave to hit a home run in his first postseason plate appearance when he took Roger Clemens deep in Game 2 of the Division Series.

Manager Bobby Cox, once known for his preference for playing veterans, did his usual masterful job while mixing and matching the new additions to the roster. "We could have finished dead last with everything that happened," Cox said. "But these guys hung together and played hard and stayed after it. I couldn't be prouder of them."

The needs of the major league club contributed to a 324-348 record in the minors, good for 24th among the 30 organizations. Triple-A Richmond suffered most and fell to a disappointing 56-88 mark after winning the International League South Division title in 2004. Class A Rome (72-65) was the lone full-season team to finish with a winning record.

The Braves also maintained their depth of talent in the farm system, which should lead to even more days of starting lineups in Atlanta consisting completely of homegrown players. Switch-hitting catcher Jarrod Saltalamacchia was a year-end all-star in the Carolina League, while righthander Joey Devine and shortstop Yunel Escobar topped yet another impressive draft headed by scouting director Roy Clark.

PLAYERS OF THE YEAR

MAJOR LEAGUE: Andruw Jones, of

Even though he didn't finish strong, batting .208 in September, Jones set career highs in homers (51) and RBIs (129) in an MVP-caliber season in 2005. Along with Rafael Furcal and Marcus Giles, he was one of the most consistent hitters on the club, leading the Braves in OPS (.922).

MINOR LEAGUE: Chuck James, lhp

TOM PRIDDY

James skipped through three levels in 2005, beginning at high Class A Myrtle Beach and ending at Triple-A Richmond. He tied with righthander James Parr for the organization lead in wins with 13, and led the system in strikeouts with 193. He finished 1-3, 3.48 in 34 innings at Richmond.

ORGANIZATION LEADERS

BATTING

*AVG	Pena, Brayan, Richmond	.326
R	Young, Matt, Rome	85
H	Thorman, Scott, Mississippi/Richmond	164
TB	Thorman, Scott, Mississippi/Richmond	268
2B	Saltalamacchia, Jarrod, Myrtle Beach	35
3B	Blanco, Gregor, Mississippi	12
HR	Jurries, J.J., Richmond	21
	Thorman, Scott, Mississippi/Richmond	21
RBI	Thorman, Scott, Mississippi/Richmond	92
BB	Blanco, Gregor, Mississippi	73
SO	Esquivel, Matt, Myrtle Beach	140
SB	Snead, Esix, Richmond	46
	Suero, Ovandy, Danville	46
*OBP	Young, Matt, Rome	.412
*SLG	Campbell, Eric, Danville	.634

PITCHING

W	James, Chuck, Mississippi/Myrtle Beach/Richmond	13
	Parr, James, Rome	13
L	Villa, Kelvin, Myrtle Beach/Rome	11
#ERA	James, Chuck, Mississippi/Myrtle Beach/Richmond	1.79
G	Brooks, Frank, Las Vegas/Richmond	54
CG	Harrison, Matt, Rome	2
SV	Childers, Jason, Richmond	16
IP	Harrison, Matt, Rome	167
BB	O'Connor, Brian, Mississippi/Richmond	65
SO	James, Chuck, Mississippi/Myrtle Beach/Richmond	193

*Minimum 250 at-bats. #Minimum 75 innings.

ATLANTA BRAVES

Manager: Bobby Cox.

2005 Record: 90-72, .556 (1st, NL East).

BATTING	B-T	HT	WT	DOB	AVG	vLH	vRH	G	AB	R	H	2B	3B	HR	RBI	BB	HBP	SH	SF	SO	SB	CS	SLG	OBP
Betemit, Wilson	B-R	6-3	200	7-28-80	.305	.256	.327	115	246	36	75	12	4	4	20	22	0	4	2	55	1	3	.435	.359
Estrada, Johnny	B-R	5-11	215	6-27-76	.261	.214	.280	105	357	31	93	26	0	4	39	20	3	0	3	38	0	0	.367	.303
Franco, Julio	R-R	6-1	210	8-23-58	.275	.271	.278	108	233	30	64	12	1	9	42	27	1	1	3	57	4	0	.451	.348
Francoeur, Jeff	R-R	6-4	220	1-8-84	.300	.379	.272	70	257	41	77	20	1	14	45	11	4	0	2	58	3	2	.549	.336
Furcal, Rafael	B-R	5-10	175	10-24-77	.284	.294	.280	154	616	100	175	31	11	12	58	62	1	5	5	78	46	10	.429	.348
Giles, Marcus	R-R	5-8	175	5-18-78	.291	.298	.289	152	577	104	168	45	4	15	63	64	5	4	4	108	16	3	.461	.365
Hollandsworth, Todd	L-L	6-2	215	4-20-73	.171	.500	.129	24	35	3	6	0	0	1	1	5	0	0	0	13	0	1	.257	.275
2-team (107 Chicago)					.244	.293	.237	131	303	26	74	17	2	6	36	23	1	1	2	66	4	5	.373	.298
Johnson, Kelly	L-R	6-1	205	2-22-82	.241	.257	.236	87	290	46	70	12	3	9	40	40	1	2	1	75	2	1	.397	.334
Jones, Andruw	R-R	6-1	210	4-23-77	.263	.256	.265	160	586	95	154	24	3	51	128	64	15	0	7	112	5	3	.575	.347
Jones, Chipper	B-R	6-4	210	4-24-72	.296	.270	.303	109	358	66	106	30	0	21	72	72	0	0	2	56	5	1	.556	.412
Jordan, Brian	R-R	6-1	225	3-29-67	.247	.263	.239	76	231	25	57	8	2	3	24	14	3	0	3	46	2	0	.338	.295
Langerhans, Ryan	L-L	6-3	205	2-20-80	.267	.293	.261	128	326	48	87	22	3	8	42	37	5	2	3	75	0	2	.426	.348
LaRoche, Adam	L-L	6-3	185	11-6-79	.259	.188	.268	141	451	53	117	28	0	20	78	39	4	2	6	87	0	2	.455	.320
Marte, Andy	R-R	6-1	185	10-21-83	.140	.174	.118	24	57	3	8	2	1	0	4	7	0	0	2	13	0	1	.211	.227
McCann, Brian	L-R	6-3	210	2-20-84	.278	.333	.264	59	180	20	50	7	0	5	23	18	1	4	1	26	1	1	.400	.345
Mondesi, Raul	R-R	5-11	225	3-12-71	.211	.269	.198	41	142	17	30	7	1	4	17	12	0	0	1	35	0	1	.359	.271
Orr, Pete	L-R	6-1	185	6-8-79	.300	.391	.283	112	150	32	45	8	1	1	8	6	1	5	0	23	7	1	.387	.331
Pena, Brayan	B-R	5-11	220	1-7-82	.179	.273	.143	18	39	2	7	2	0	0	4	1	0	0	0	7	0	0	.231	.200
Perez, Eddie	R-R	6-1	220	5-4-68	.211	.333	.154	16	38	3	8	2	0	2	6	1	0	0	0	5	0	0	.421	.231

PITCHING	B-T	HT	WT	DOB	W	L	ERA	G	GS	CG	SV	IP	H	R	ER	HR	BB	SO	AVG	vLH	vRH	K/9	BB/9
Bernero, Adam	R-R	6-4	220	11-28-76	4	3	6.51	36	0	0	0	47	61	35	34	5	12	37	.313	.263	.365	7.09	2.30
Boyer, Blaine	R-R	6-3	215	7-11-81	4	2	3.11	43	0	0	0	38	32	13	13	1	17	33	.234	.298	.200	7.88	4.06
Brooks, Frank	L-L	6-1	190	9-6-78	0	0	0.00	1	0	0	0	0	1	0	0	0	0	0	1.000	1.000	.000	0.00	0.00
Brower, Jim	R-R	6-3	215	12-29-72	1	2	4.20	37	0	0	0	30	33	14	14	6	17	28	.282	.277	.286	8.40	5.10
2-team (32 San Francisco)					3	3	5.37	69	0	0	1	60	73	36	36	11	32	53	.302	.303	.301	7.91	4.77
Childers, Matt	R-R	6-5	215	12-3-78	0	0	4.50	3	0	0	0	4	5	2	2	1	3	2	.294	.125	.444	4.50	6.75
Colon, Roman	R-R	6-6	225	8-13-79	1	5	5.28	23	4	0	0	44	47	28	26	10	14	30	.272	.253	.287	6.09	2.84
Davies, Kyle	R-R	6-2	205	9-9-83	7	6	4.93	21	14	0	0	88	98	51	48	8	49	62	.280	.264	.295	6.37	5.03
Devine, Joey	R-R	6-0	210	9-19-83	0	1	12.60	5	0	0	0	5	6	7	7	2	5	3	.286	.429	.214	5.40	9.00
Farnsworth, Kyle	R-R	6-4	240	4-14-76	0	0	1.98	26	0	0	10	27	15	6	6	4	7	32	.161	.179	.135	10.54	2.30
Foster, John	L-L	6-0	200	5-17-78	4	2	4.15	62	0	0	1	35	27	17	16	3	19	32	.213	.219	.204	8.31	4.93
Greisinger, Seth	R-R	6-3	200	7-29-75	0	0	3.60	1	1	0	0	5	7	2	2	1	1	2	.350	.556	.182	3.60	1.80
Gryboski, Kevin	R-R	6-5	255	11-15-73	0	0	2.95	31	0	0	0	21	24	10	7	0	12	8	.300	.250	.327	3.38	5.06
Hampton, Mike	R-L	5-10	195	9-9-72	5	3	3.50	12	12	1	0	69	74	28	27	5	18	27	.281	.338	.263	3.50	2.34
Hudson, Tim	R-R	6-1	170	7-14-75	14	9	3.52	29	29	2	0	192	194	79	75	20	65	115	.265	.285	.240	5.39	3.05
James, Chuck	L-L	6-0	170	11-9-81	0	0	1.59	2	0	0	0	6	4	1	1	0	3	5	.200	.250	.188	7.94	4.76
Kolb, Dan	R-R	6-4	230	3-29-75	3	8	5.93	65	0	0	11	58	78	39	38	5	29	39	.329	.336	.323	6.09	4.53
Lerew, Anthony	L-R	6-3	220	10-28-82	0	0	5.63	7	0	0	0	8	9	5	5	1	5	5	.290	.267	.313	5.63	5.63
Martin, Tom	L-L	6-1	205	5-21-70	0	0	19.29	4	0	0	0	2	6	5	5	1	2	0	.500	.800	.286	0.00	7.71
McBride, Macay	L-L	5-11	210	10-24-82	1	0	5.79	23	0	0	1	14	18	11	9	0	7	22	.305	.172	.433	14.14	4.50
Powell, Jay	R-R	6-4	230	1-9-72	0	0	0.00	5	0	0	0	3	1	0	0	0	4	1	.091	.000	.143	2.70	10.80
Ramirez, Horacio	L-L	6-1	210	11-24-79	11	9	4.63	33	32	1	0	202	214	108	104	31	67	80	.282	.267	.286	3.56	2.98
Reitsma, Chris	R-R	6-5	235	12-31-77	3	6	3.93	76	0	0	15	73	79	32	32	3	14	42	.272	.252	.298	5.15	1.72
Smoltz, John	R-R	6-3	220	5-15-67	14	7	3.06	33	33	3	0	230	210	83	78	18	53	169	.243	.252	.233	6.62	2.08
Sosa, Jorge	R-R	6-2	175	4-28-77	13	3	2.55	44	20	0	0	134	122	42	38	12	64	85	.241	.247	.235	5.71	4.30
Thomson, John	R-R	6-3	220	10-1-73	4	6	4.47	17	17	1	0	99	111	52	49	6	28	61	.284	.276	.292	5.56	2.55
Vasquez, Jorge	R-R	6-1	165	7-16-78	1	0	3.00	7	0	0	0	9	11	4	3	2	5	9	.297	.333	.273	9.00	5.00

FIELDING

Catcher	PCT	G	PO	A	E	DP	PB
Estrada	.997	104	574	51	2	6	2
McCann	.991	57	310	21	3	1	5
Pena	1.000	15	46	5	0	0	0
Perez	1.000	13	38	4	0	1	1

First Base	PCT	G	PO	A	E	DP
Franco	.990	62	450	37	5	47
Hollandsworth	.000	1	0	0	0	0
LaRoche	.994	125	1070	77	7	105

Second Base	PCT	G	PO	A	E	DP
Betemit	1.000	1	1	3	0	0
Giles	.984	149	266	469	12	97
Orr	.948	25	35	57	5	11

Third Base	PCT	G	PO	A	E	DP
Betemit	.952	63	26	94	6	6
C. Jones	.980	101	80	169	5	18
Giles	1.000	1	0	6	0	0
Marte	.857	17	4	14	3	1
Orr	.941	12	2	14	1	3

Shortstop	PCT	G	PO	A	E	DP
Betemit	.985	25	24	40	1	10
Furcal	.981	152	255	504	15	119
Orr	.000	1	0	0	0	0

Outfield	PCT	G	PO	A	E	DP
A. Jones	.995	159	365	11	2	1
Francoeur	.966	67	131	13	5	3
Hollandsworth	1.000	9	10	0	0	0
Johnson	1.000	79	166	6	0	1
Jordan	1.000	62	112	6	0	1
Langerhans	.995	114	194	3	1	1
Mondesi	.986	40	67	2	1	0
Orr	1.000	3	5	0	0	0

FARM SYSTEM

General Manager: John Schuerholz. **Director, Player Personnel:** Dayton Moore. **Scouting Director:** Roy Clark.

Class	Farm Team	League	W	L	Pct.	Finish*	Manager	Affiliate Since
AAA	Richmond (Va.) Braves	International	56	88	.389	14th (14)	Pat Kelly	1966
AA	Mississippi Braves (Pearl)	Southern	64	68	.485	6th (10)	Brian Snitker	2005
High A	Myrtle Beach (S.C.) Pelicans	Carolina	61	79	.436	7th (8)	Randy Ingle	1999
Low A	Rome (Ga.) Braves	South Atlantic	72	65	.526	5th (16)	Rocket Wheeler	2003
Rookie	Danville (Va.) Braves	Appalachian	47	20	.701	**2nd (10)**	Paul Runge	1993
Rookie	Orlando (Fla.) Braves	Gulf Coast	24	28	.462	8th (12)	Luis Ortiz	1998

*Finish in overall standings (No. of teams in league)/playoff teams in **boldface**

DAVID STONER

Rafael Furcal: Double figures in doubles, triples and homers

TOM PRIDDY

Jarrod Saltalamacchia: The best catcher in the minors?

RICHMOND BRAVES — Class AAA

INTERNATIONAL LEAGUE

BATTING	B-T	HT	WT	DOB	AVG	vLH	vRH	G	AB	R	H	2B	3B	HR	RBI	BB	HBP	SH	SF	SO	SB	CS	SLG	OBP
Arteaga, Josh	R-R	5-9	170	3-14-80	.256	.200	.286	13	43	3	11	3	0	0	4	0	0	0	0	13	0	0	.326	.256
Barkett, Andy	L-L	6-1	205	9-5-74	.203	.381	.165	37	118	9	24	7	0	1	12	18	1	0	1	25	0	0	.288	.312
Barnes, John	R-R	6-2	210	4-24-76	.277	.203	.297	90	318	30	88	18	0	3	29	21	6	1	2	25	1	1	.362	.331
Bernard, Miguel	R-R	5-11	220	1-1-81	.143	.000	.200	2	7	0	1	1	0	0	1	0	0	0	0	1	0	0	.286	.143
Boscan, Jean	R-R	6-2	215	12-26-79	.222	.281	.196	72	212	17	47	6	0	3	20	25	4	5	2	59	1	2	.292	.313
Bourgeois, Jason	R-R	5-9	185	1-4-82	.240	.261	.231	119	388	33	93	20	2	2	16	31	4	3	2	57	8	5	.317	.301
Burrus, Josh	R-R	6-1	195	8-20-83	.316	.125	.455	5	19	1	6	2	0	0	0	2	1	0	0	5	2	0	.421	.409
Duran, Carlos	L-L	6-1	165	12-27-82	.273	.300	.250	6	22	3	6	1	0	2	4	0	0	2	0	4	0	0	.591	.273
Franco, Iker	R-R	6-1	212	5-5-81	.250	.000	.276	9	32	0	8	1	0	0	1	2	0	0	0	9	0	0	.281	.294
Gibson, Derrick	R-R	6-2	244	2-5-75	.200	.267	.182	27	70	7	14	2	0	2	7	2	3	0	0	13	0	0	.314	.253
Johnson, Kelly	L-R	6-1	205	2-22-82	.310	.306	.311	44	155	35	48	12	3	8	22	34	2	0	1	22	7	1	.581	.438
Jurries, J.J.	R-R	6-0	205	4-13-79	.284	.261	.292	106	363	53	103	23	3	21	72	41	5	0	8	107	1	1	.537	.357
Marte, Andy	R-R	6-1	185	10-21-83	.275	.305	.265	109	389	51	107	26	2	20	74	64	0	0	7	83	0	3	.506	.372
McCarthy, Bill	R-R	6-2	205	12-2-79	.226	.258	.215	66	239	26	54	10	1	5	23	17	7	1	1	58	1	4	.339	.295
Mendez, Carlos	R-R	6-0	225	6-18-74	.246	.262	.241	47	179	13	44	8	0	3	18	10	1	1	3	22	0	0	.341	.285
O'Keefe, Mike	L-L	5-10	200	6-28-78	.154	.000	.167	5	13	1	2	0	0	1	1	3	0	0	0	3	0	0	.385	.313
Pena, Tony	R-R	6-1	180	3-23-81	.249	.233	.254	138	490	49	122	25	4	5	40	21	5	6	4	113	17	15	.347	.285
Pena, Brayan	B-R	5-11	220	1-7-82	.326	.507	.265	81	282	27	92	21	2	0	25	28	0	6	3	19	3	1	.415	.383
Pratt, Scott	L-R	5-10	185	2-4-77	.257	.219	.265	106	343	38	88	23	5	9	38	37	2	4	0	94	4	5	.431	.332
Pyzik, Steve	R-R	5-10	185	5-18-81	.067	.000	.067	6	15	1	1	0	0	0	1	0	0	0	0	1	0	0	.067	.067
Robinson, Kerry	L-L	6-0	175	10-3-73	.328	.433	.285	58	204	29	67	9	1	1	12	13	1	8	1	23	13	6	.397	.370
Rosamond, Michael	R-R	6-4	220	4-18-78	.224	.133	.256	26	58	5	13	3	0	1	7	2	1	1	0	20	1	0	.328	.262
Schuerholz, Jonathan	R-R	5-11	188	6-25-80	.175	.195	.167	44	143	10	25	2	1	0	12	16	0	1	2	29	1	2	.203	.255
Snead, Esix	B-R	5-11	170	6-7-76	.242	.194	.260	95	347	49	84	11	5	1	10	48	10	11	0	62	46	14	.311	.351
Thorman, Scott	L-R	6-3	235	1-6-82	.276	.262	.283	52	210	23	58	10	3	6	27	9	3	0	2	42	0	0	.438	.313
Timmons, Wes	R-R	6-0	190	7-12-79	.222	.286	.182	5	18	1	4	1	0	0	3	2	0	0	2	0	0	0	.278	.273

PITCHING	B-T	HT	WT	DOB	W	L	ERA	G	GS	CG	SV	IP	H	R	ER	HR	BB	SO	AVG	vLH	vRH	K/9	BB/9
Almonte, Hector	R-R	6-1	220	10-17-75	1	1	2.70	18	0	0	0	27	30	12	8	2	16	25	.283	.170	.373	8.44	5.40
Barry, Kevin	R-R	6-2	235	8-18-78	5	3	2.85	32	8	0	1	79	60	28	25	8	44	73	.209	.189	.225	8.32	5.01
Basner, Ryan	R-R	6-3	230	7-15-81	0	0	0.00	2	0	0	0	2	1	0	0	0	3	0	.167	.000	.333	0.00	16.20
Bernero, Adam	R-R	6-4	220	11-28-76	5	5	3.40	10	9	0	0	53	57	27	20	6	15	41	.274	.295	.258	6.96	2.55
Brooks, Frank	L-L	6-1	190	9-6-78	3	4	2.73	54	0	0	0	56	46	27	17	4	24	49	.222	.188	.244	7.88	3.86
Brower, Jim	R-R	6-3	215	12-29-72	0	1	2.25	4	0	0	1	4	1	1	1	0	2	1	.091	.000	.125	2.25	4.50
Childers, Matt	R-R	6-5	215	12-3-78	4	2	3.93	51	1	0	2	73	69	37	32	4	21	62	.247	.261	.238	7.61	2.58
Childers, Jason	R-R	6-0	160	1-13-75	1	2	2.09	38	0	0	16	39	32	14	9	2	20	31	.232	.288	.181	7.22	4.66
Colon, Roman	R-R	6-6	225	8-13-79	1	1	1.93	3	3	0	0	14	12	3	3	0	5	9	.235	.143	.300	5.79	3.21
Curtis, Dan	R-R	6-4	215	11-3-79	3	8	5.20	18	17	0	0	88	102	61	51	5	38	40	.293	.308	.276	4.08	3.87
Davies, Kyle	R-R	6-2	205	9-10-83	5	2	3.44	13	13	0	0	73	66	28	28	6	34	62	.245	.218	.267	7.61	4.17
DeHart, Casey	L-L	6-1	190	11-1-77	0	1	13.50	2	0	0	0	2	5	5	3	1	1	2	.417	.500	.375	9.00	4.50
Devine, Joey	R-R	6-0	210	9-19-83	0	0	18.00	1	0	0	0	1	3	2	2	0	1	1	.600	1.000	.333	9.00	9.00
Foster, John	L-L	6-0	200	5-17-78	0	0	1.59	3	0	0	1	6	2	1	1	0	1	5	.105	.100	.111	7.94	1.59
Greisinger, Seth	R-R	6-3	200	7-29-75	4	7	3.01	16	16	1	0	99	75	36	33	4	28	56	.212	.220	.205	5.11	2.55
Hampton, Mike	R-L	5-10	195	9-9-72	0	0	2.25	1	1	0	0	4	4	1	1	0	0	3	.250	.333	.200	6.75	0.00
Hernandez, Buddy	R-R	5-9	180	3-3-79	0	2	6.75	7	0	0	0	12	15	9	9	3	8	11	.300	.300	.300	8.25	6.00
Herrera, Alex	L-L	5-11	190	11-5-76	0	1	7.27	13	0	0	0	17	15	15	14	3	18	14	.246	.333	.209	7.27	9.35
Hodges, Trey	R-R	6-3	195	6-29-78	0	3	8.10	6	4	0	0	17	26	22	15	4	9	9	.342	.354	.321	4.86	4.86
2-team (9 Rochester)					0	3	6.89	15	4	0	0	33	43	32	25	4	19	21	.312	.307	.317	5.79	5.23
James, Chuck	L-L	6-0	170	11-9-81	1	3	3.48	6	6	0	0	34	21	13	13	4	10	30	.176	.154	.183	8.02	2.67
Lerew, Anthony	L-R	6-3	220	10-28-82	4	4	3.48	13	13	0	0	72	63	34	28	9	23	53	.232	.255	.217	6.59	2.86
McBride, Macay	L-L	5-11	210	10-24-82	1	5	4.33	25	1	0	2	44	49	27	21	5	22	47	.290	.300	.284	9.69	4.53
McConnell, Sam	L-L	6-5	230	12-31-75	4	9	5.48	20	17	0	0	92	130	63	56	18	22	44	.332	.385	.315	4.30	2.15
Mears, Chris	R-R	6-4	200	1-20-78	3	3	5.20	31	1	0	3	45	46	27	26	4	23	12	.282	.292	.276	2.40	4.60
Miner, Zach	R-R	6-3	200	3-12-82	2	7	4.23	17	17	0	0	89	97	47	42	6	45	63	.275	.283	.268	6.35	4.53
O'Connor, Brian	R-L	6-2	210	6-21-77	1	0	1.59	2	1	0	0	6	4	1	1	0	2	2	.200	.250	.188	3.18	3.18
Paronto, Chad	R-R	6-5	250	7-28-75	3	1	3.95	26	0	0	0	41	43	18	18	4	17	28	.281	.266	.292	6.15	3.73
Porzio, Mike	L-L	6-3	215	8-20-72	0	1	6.75	2	1	0	0	5	5	4	4	1	4	2	.263	.000	.385	3.38	6.75
Ray, Ken	R-R	6-2	200	11-27-74	2	4	3.90	17	10	0	0	67	68	34	29	6	35	40	.274	.216	.315	5.37	4.70
Thomson, John	R-R	6-3	220	10-1-73	0	0	4.91	1	1	0	0	4	5	2	2	0	1	2	.357	.222	.600	4.91	2.45
Tucker, Glenn	B-R	6-3	205	4-9-81	0	0	0.00	2	0	0	0	1	1	0	0	0	1	1	.250	.000	.333	6.75	6.75
Van Hekken, Andy	R-L	6-3	185	7-31-79	0	3	9.16	4	4	0	0	19	25	20	19	4	8	11	.329	.250	.350	5.30	3.86
Vasquez, Jorge	R-R	6-1	165	7-16-78	0	1	10.93	14	0	0	2	14	16	17	17	1	9	20	.286	.333	.257	12.86	5.79
Ward, Jeremy	R-R	6-3	235	2-24-78	3	4	3.74	31	0	0	0	55	51	36	23	8	19	30	.248	.279	.225	4.88	3.09

FIELDING

Catcher	PCT	G	PO	A	E	DP	PB
Bernard	1.000	2	11	1	0	0	0
Boscan	.986	68	400	32	6	5	5
Franco	1.000	9	55	7	0	1	0
Mendez	1.000	4	12	0	0	1	0
B. Pena	.991	63	402	22	4	6	3
Pyzik	1.000	6	35	3	0	1	1

First Base	PCT	G	PO	A	E	DP
Barkett	.989	34	245	21	3	33
Jurries	.991	29	204	9	2	19
Mendez	1.000	29	247	17	0	23
O'Keefe	1.000	2	16	0	0	1
B. Pena	1.000	1	3	0	0	0
Pratt	1.000	2	9	0	0	2
Rosamond	.982	7	55	1	1	3
Thorman	.991	52	435	27	4	41

Second Base	PCT	G	PO	A	E	DP
Arteaga	.857	2	1	5	1	1
Bourgeois	.964	92	160	246	15	60
Pratt	.955	18	27	37	3	8
Schuerholz	.972	43	71	101	5	19

Third Base	PCT	G	PO	A	E	DP
Johnson	1.000	4	6	4	0	0
Marte	.950	109	68	220	15	21
Mendez	.875	8	6	8	2	2
Pratt	1.000	22	14	32	0	0
Timmons	1.000	5	5	11	0	2

Shortstop	PCT	G	PO	A	E	DP
Arteaga	1.000	3	2	7	0	0
Bourgeois	.857	1	2	4	1	1
Johnson	.833	1	3	2	1	2
T. Pena	.953	136	222	420	32	94
Pratt	1.000	7	9	6	0	1

Outfield	PCT	G	PO	A	E	DP
Arteaga	1.000	1	3	0	0	0
Barnes	.976	52	118	5	3	1
Bourgeois	.976	21	38	3	1	0
Burrus	.909	5	10	0	1	0
Duran	.944	6	16	1	1	0
Gibson	.960	17	23	1	1	0
Johnson	.978	40	87	1	2	0
Jurries	1.000	43	62	1	0	0
McCarthy	1.000	58	113	5	0	2
O'Keefe	1.000	2	2	0	0	0
Pratt	.973	53	105	2	3	0
Robinson	.990	55	103	1	1	0
Rosamond	1.000	15	26	0	0	0
Snead	.986	95	271	8	4	2

MISSISSIPPI BRAVES — Class AA

SOUTHERN LEAGUE

BATTING	B-T	HT	WT	DOB	AVG	vLH	vRH	G	AB	R	H	2B	3B	HR	RBI	BB	HBP	SH	SF	SO	SB	CS	SLG	OBP
Arteaga, Josh	R-R	5-9	170	3-14-80	.248	.294	.224	42	101	7	25	6	0	0	11	9	0	1	1	26	0	2	.307	.306
Barnes, John	R-R	6-2	210	4-24-76	.400	.000	.444	3	10	2	4	0	0	0	0	0	0	0	0	0	0	0	.400	.400
Bernard, Miguel	R-R	5-11	220	1-1-81	.237	.240	.235	20	76	7	18	2	1	0	13	5	0	0	0	15	1	0	.289	.284
Blanco, Gregor	L-L	5-11	170	12-24-83	.252	.231	.262	123	401	64	101	11	12	6	37	73	2	7	3	124	28	12	.384	.367
Burrus, Josh	R-R	6-1	195	8-20-83	.221	.229	.218	46	172	21	38	6	2	5	21	22	1	0	1	53	9	4	.366	.311
Duran, Carlos	L-L	6-1	165	12-27-82	.266	.189	.289	63	158	12	42	8	5	1	11	4	0	1	2	31	0	2	.399	.280
Franco, Iker	R-R	6-1	212	5-5-81	.296	.323	.281	48	179	14	53	7	0	3	23	8	0	2	2	31	0	3	.385	.323
Francoeur, Jeff	R-R	6-4	220	1-8-84	.275	.281	.271	84	335	40	92	28	2	13	62	21	5	0	6	76	13	4	.487	.322
Gibson, Derrick	R-R	6-2	244	2-5-75	.133	.111	.167	6	15	1	2	1	0	0	2	0	0	0	0	4	1	0	.200	.133
Hernandez, Luis	B-R	5-10	165	6-26-84	.243	.228	.251	122	415	47	101	12	5	2	32	41	4	6	3	56	5	5	.311	.315
Joseph, Onil	R-R	6-2	165	2-12-82	.249	.204	.278	121	426	45	106	21	5	3	53	29	4	9	2	121	18	8	.343	.302
McCann, Brian	L-R	6-3	210	2-20-84	.265	.305	.243	48	166	27	44	13	2	6	26	25	2	0	5	26	2	3	.476	.359
O'Keefe, Mike	L-L	5-10	200	6-28-78	.200	.125	.286	6	15	3	3	1	0	0	1	3	0	0	0	2	0	0	.267	.333
Prado, Martin	R-R	5-11	188	10-27-83	.280	.242	.291	39	143	17	40	7	1	1	11	17	0	1	1	17	3	3	.364	.354
Pyzik, Steve	R-R	5-10	185	5-18-81	.500	.000	.500	2	8	1	4	1	0	0	1	0	0	0	0	1	0	0	.625	.500
Rosamond, Michael	R-R	6-4	220	4-18-78	.225	.218	.229	74	244	37	55	10	1	9	26	26	2	2	2	66	5	2	.385	.303
Schuerholz, Jonathan	R-R	5-11	188	6-25-80	.278	.289	.271	86	302	38	84	12	2	4	21	27	5	1	0	51	8	1	.371	.347
Serrano, Ray	R-R	5-8	221	1-19-81	.284	.269	.290	33	88	7	25	6	2	0	11	7	1	0	1	10	1	0	.398	.340
Thorman, Scott	L-R	6-3	235	1-6-82	.305	.226	.355	90	348	49	106	21	2	15	65	28	4	0	3	76	2	2	.506	.360
Timmons, Wes	R-R	6-0	190	7-12-79	.272	.265	.275	119	427	73	116	31	2	7	34	62	21	6	3	46	4	7	.403	.388
Velazquez, Juan	B-R	5-11	175	8-22-78	.253	.279	.243	52	154	19	39	8	0	0	13	20	1	4	0	29	3	2	.305	.343

PITCHING	B-T	HT	WT	DOB	W	L	ERA	G	GS	CG	SV	IP	H	R	ER	HR	BB	SO	AVG	vLH	vRH	K/9	BB/9
Barry, Kevin	R-R	6-2	235	8-18-78	0	0	1.23	3	0	0	0	7	3	1	1	0	6	7	.120	.250	.000	8.59	7.36
Basner, Ryan	R-R	6-3	230	7-15-81	2	10	5.34	35	11	1	1	96	114	61	57	8	23	64	.298	.289	.307	6.00	2.16
Bobbitt, Seth	R-R	6-1	180	3-24-79	0	0	1.80	2	0	0	0	5	1	1	1	0	2	3	.067	.125	.000	5.40	3.60
Boyer, Blaine	R-R	6-3	215	7-11-81	2	4	5.03	14	8	0	0	48	62	28	27	4	18	40	.321	.324	.319	7.45	3.35
Bush, Paul	R-R	6-1	175	10-5-79	2	0	2.39	19	5	0	1	53	29	17	14	2	22	52	.161	.221	.117	8.89	3.76
Coenen, Matt	L-L	6-6	230	3-13-80	3	9	5.27	19	18	0	0	96	112	64	56	8	43	52	.305	.247	.321	4.89	4.05
Colon, Roman	R-R	6-6	225	8-13-79	0	0	1.17	2	2	0	0	8	6	1	1	0	2	7	.222	.083	.333	8.22	2.35
Curtis, Dan	R-R	6-4	215	11-3-79	2	2	2.67	9	3	0	0	30	30	9	9	0	8	25	.273	.300	.250	7.42	2.37
DeHart, Casey	L-L	6-1	190	11-1-77	4	2	5.87	38	1	0	0	61	67	41	40	10	31	38	.286	.258	.298	5.58	4.55
Devine, Joey	R-R	6-0	210	9-19-83	1	1	2.70	18	0	0	5	20	19	13	6	2	12	28	.250	.342	.158	12.60	5.40
James, Chuck	L-L	6-0	170	11-9-81	9	1	2.09	16	16	0	0	86	62	25	20	4	18	104	.199	.175	.208	10.88	1.88
Kent, Steve	B-L	5-11	170	10-3-78	2	5	4.28	33	0	0	3	40	43	21	19	1	18	29	.279	.214	.304	6.53	4.05
Lerew, Anthony	L-R	6-3	220	10-28-82	6	2	3.93	14	14	1	0	76	70	34	33	6	32	64	.246	.223	.269	7.61	3.81
McBride, Macay	L-L	5-11	210	10-24-82	3	1	3.65	6	3	0	0	25	21	11	10	2	12	16	.233	.233	.233	5.84	4.38
Miner, Zach	R-R	6-3	200	3-12-82	0	1	4.32	4	2	0	1	17	21	10	8	0	5	18	.313	.344	.286	9.72	2.70
O'Connor, Brian	R-L	6-2	210	6-21-77	9	7	3.65	30	19	0	0	133	127	66	54	7	63	98	.256	.274	.249	6.62	4.25
Porzio, Mike	L-L	6-3	215	8-20-72	2	3	4.26	14	4	0	0	32	36	15	15	3	12	20	.295	.306	.291	5.68	3.41
Powell, Jay	R-R	6-4	230	1-9-72	2	0	0.64	11	0	0	0	14	6	1	1	0	3	8	.136	.100	.167	5.14	1.93
Richardson, Jason	R-R	6-4	225	6-11-80	0	2	4.11	17	0	0	0	31	34	17	14	3	11	29	.279	.193	.354	8.51	3.23
Roberts, Ralph	R-R	6-2	215	3-28-80	0	0	0.00	1	0	0	0	2	0	0	0	0	1	0	.000	.000	.000	0.00	5.40
Thomson, John	R-R	6-3	220	10-1-73	1	0	1.50	1	1	0	0	6	4	1	1	0	0	4	.190	.100	.273	6.00	0.00
Tucker, Glenn	B-R	6-3	205	4-9-81	4	2	3.09	49	0	0	5	64	64	24	22	4	22	42	.272	.312	.246	5.91	3.09
Van Hekken, Andy	R-L	6-3	185	7-31-79	0	0	5.63	3	3	0	0	16	22	10	10	1	12	8	.361	.333	.378	4.50	6.75
Vasquez, Jorge	R-R	6-1	165	7-16-78	2	1	1.12	29	0	0	10	40	22	7	5	1	11	45	.163	.155	.169	10.04	2.45
Ward, Jeremy	R-R	6-3	235	2-24-78	0	2	2.63	12	0	0	2	14	16	4	4	0	1	18	.286	.350	.250	11.85	0.66
White, Sean	R-R	6-4	210	4-25-81	2	5	4.11	8	8	0	0	50	43	25	23	2	18	33	.231	.301	.175	5.90	3.22
Wright, Matt	R-R	6-4	230	3-13-82	6	8	6.11	17	14	0	1	84	101	60	57	7	37	63	.299	.301	.297	6.75	3.96

FIELDING

Catcher	PCT	G	PO	A	E	DP	PB
Bernard	.965	20	150	15	6	1	1
Franco	.980	43	318	29	7	1	1
McCann	.997	45	300	31	1	3	2
Pyzik	1.000	2	11	1	0	0	1
Serrano	.983	26	159	11	3	0	1

First Base	PCT	G	PO	A	E	DP
Arteaga	1.000	1	4	0	0	0
Franco	.000	1	0	0	0	0
Rosamond	.984	42	336	26	6	36
Thorman	.990	90	830	47	9	82
Timmons	1.000	1	1	0	0	0

Second Base	PCT	G	PO	A	E	DP
Arteaga	.960	8	12	12	1	0
Prado	.989	39	80	105	2	30
Schuerholz	.974	81	146	259	11	60
Velazquez	1.000	14	19	38	0	9

Third Base	PCT	G	PO	A	E	DP
Arteaga	.909	11	6	14	2	2
Timmons	.949	113	88	228	17	19
Velazquez	.889	17	7	25	4	2

Shortstop	PCT	G	PO	A	E	DP
Arteaga	1.000	9	5	19	0	3
Hernandez	.961	117	176	337	21	77
Velazquez	.946	14	17	36	3	8

Outfield	PCT	G	PO	A	E	DP
Barnes	1.000	2	5	1	0	0
Blanco	.969	112	234	14	8	5
Burrus	1.000	43	78	0	0	1
Duran	.985	41	64	2	1	0
Francoeur	.981	83	144	10	3	0
Joseph	.974	109	174	10	5	1
O'Keefe	.857	3	6	0	1	0
Rosamond	.927	20	36	2	3	0
Velazquez	1.000	1	5	0	0	0

MYRTLE BEACH PELICANS — High Class A

CAROLINA LEAGUE

BATTING	B-T	HT	WT	DOB	AVG	vLH	vRH	G	AB	R	H	2B	3B	HR	RBI	BB	HBP	SH	SF	SO	SB	CS	SLG	OBP
Barksdale, James	R-R	5-10	215	12-7-81	.192	.111	.235	8	26	3	5	1	0	0	2	3	0	0	0	3	0	0	.231	.276
Bernard, Miguel	R-R	5-11	220	1-1-81	.323	.368	.304	18	65	9	21	10	0	4	14	1	3	0	0	8	0	1	.662	.362
Burrus, Josh	R-R	6-1	195	8-20-83	.284	.250	.304	76	299	54	85	20	0	11	53	28	4	0	4	75	25	8	.462	.349
Creek, Greg	L-R	6-3	225	8-29-82	.375	.800	.182	4	16	2	6	2	0	0	2	3	0	0	0	5	0	1	.500	.474
Doetsch, Steve	R-R	6-2	195	12-2-83	.258	.254	.260	118	461	60	119	23	2	4	32	43	3	6	2	105	14	15	.343	.324
Duran, Carlos	L-L	6-1	165	12-27-82	.255	.267	.250	12	47	6	12	2	0	0	2	3	0	0	0	12	2	0	.298	.300
Esquivel, Matt	R-R	6-2	225	12-17-82	.265	.290	.251	127	468	58	124	31	0	17	81	49	8	0	2	140	9	6	.440	.343
Guzman, Carlos	R-R	6-3	180	7-5-83	.158	.241	.129	34	114	8	18	10	0	1	12	12	2	2	1	57	0	1	.272	.248
Hernandez, Diory	R-R	5-11	170	4-8-84	.253	.247	.255	73	265	30	67	15	1	5	30	18	8	4	5	53	5	5	.374	.314
James, Willie	B-R	5-8	165	4-30-81	.158	.203	.127	77	184	25	29	3	0	1	9	20	4	5	1	27	12	9	.190	.254
Jansen, Ardley	R-R	6-2	160	2-16-83	.216	.227	.210	52	185	18	40	6	1	5	20	12	2	1	2	57	6	3	.341	.269
Jones, Brandon	L-R	6-2	195	12-10-83	.350	.421	.317	17	60	7	21	4	0	0	5	9	1	0	1	9	0	1	.417	.437
Jurich, Mark	L-L	5-10	195	12-29-80	.197	.139	.219	37	132	13	26	8	1	2	13	17	2	0	1	39	1	0	.318	.296
Loadenthal, Carl	L-L	5-11	185	12-27-81	.283	.259	.297	60	230	47	65	13	4	5	20	20	3	7	0	46	17	6	.439	.348
Pope, Van	R-R	6-0	200	2-26-84	.167	.167	.167	25	84	7	14	1	0	1	5	9	1	0	1	21	0	0	.214	.253
Prado, Martin	R-R	5-11	188	10-27-83	.306	.267	.327	75	297	44	91	13	3	4	34	24	0	0	5	48	9	6	.411	.353
Pyzik, Steve	R-R	5-10	185	5-18-81	.245	.267	.235	17	49	8	12	2	0	1	3	4	1	0	0	10	0	0	.347	.315
Rozema, Mike	L-R	6-2	180	9-16-81	.227	.205	.241	59	211	34	48	10	1	1	20	27	2	3	1	33	8	3	.299	.320
Ruelas, Alonzo	R-R	6-0	195	4-2-81	.140	.191	.100	38	107	7	15	5	0	0	7	9	2	1	0	26	1	1	.187	.220
Saltalamacchia, Jarrod	B-R	6-4	220	5-2-85	.314	.305	.319	129	459	70	144	35	1	19	81	57	7	1	5	99	4	2	.519	.394
Schade, Scott	R-R	6-1	220	2-22-82	.226	.248	.213	95	332	46	75	17	0	10	48	43	1	1	5	130	1	2	.367	.312
Serrano, Ray	R-R	5-8	221	1-19-81	.000	.000	.000	1	5	0	0	0	0	0	0	0	0	0	0	1	0	0	.000	.000
Thomas, Ben	L-R	6-0	200	6-30-82	.231	.154	.254	72	229	16	53	7	2	0	19	34	1	2	0	53	4	4	.279	.333
Trejo, Jaime	R-R	6-3	187	9-7-83	.206	.206	.206	92	320	23	66	9	0	3	25	13	1	4	2	73	3	2	.263	.238
Velazquez, Juan	B-R	5-11	175	8-22-78	.214	.167	.250	4	14	0	3	1	0	0	1	1	0	0	0	4	0	0	.286	.267

PITCHING	B-T	HT	WT	DOB	W	L	ERA	G	GS	CG	SV	IP	H	R	ER	HR	BB	SO	AVG	vLH	vRH	K/9	BB/9
Acosta, Manny	R-R	6-4	170	5-1-81	2	2	4.43	18	0	0	7	22	22	12	11	1	9	18	.253	.178	.333	7.25	3.63
Alvarez, Juan	L-L	6-0	170	5-6-82	0	1	4.80	12	6	0	0	45	47	25	24	4	29	33	.281	.230	.311	6.60	5.80
Ascanio, Jose	R-R	5-10	170	5-2-85	3	1	6.10	5	3	0	0	21	26	17	14	5	9	12	.310	.382	.260	5.23	3.92
Blakeney, Jacob	R-R	6-1	200	7-26-80	2	0	3.27	24	0	0	3	41	41	16	15	2	22	36	.263	.277	.253	7.84	4.79
Bobbitt, Seth	R-R	6-1	180	3-24-79	3	0	4.58	9	0	0	0	18	19	10	9	0	8	7	.284	.313	.257	3.57	4.08
Bullock, Tyler	R-R	6-3	225	1-22-84	0	0	0.00	1	0	0	0	3	2	0	0	0	1	2	.182	.000	.286	6.00	3.00
Burrows, Angelo	L-R	6-1	195	7-2-80	1	2	3.15	14	0	0	0	20	14	11	7	1	10	22	.192	.139	.243	9.90	4.50
Bush, Paul	R-R	6-1	175	10-5-79	1	3	2.32	18	3	0	4	43	36	16	11	3	13	40	.231	.305	.186	8.44	2.74
Devine, Joey	R-R	6-0	210	9-19-83	0	0	0.00	4	0	0	1	5	0	0	0	0	3	7	.000	.000	.000	12.60	5.40

PITCHING	B-T	HT	WT	DOB	W	L	ERA	G	GS	CG	SV	IP	H	R	ER	HR	BB	SO	AVG	vLH	vRH	K/9	BB/9
Digby, Bryan	R-R	6-2	220	12-31-81	1	4	8.89	25	0	0	3	28	40	29	28	3	30	28	.333	.400	.286	8.89	9.53
Endl, Brady	R-L	6-5	230	4-14-82	6	7	3.39	20	20	0	0	109	87	55	41	8	61	101	.219	.197	.229	8.34	5.04
James, Chuck	L-L	6-0	170	11-9-81	3	3	1.08	7	7	0	0	42	20	6	5	1	8	59	.139	.042	.188	12.74	1.73
Letson, Wes	L-L	6-0	200	9-13-82	2	4	3.92	41	0	0	1	64	75	34	28	4	22	37	.296	.243	.341	5.18	3.08
Lorenzo, Matt	L-R	6-3	205	6-21-82	1	4	3.72	9	5	0	0	36	41	20	15	6	13	17	.293	.371	.214	4.21	3.22
Pudewell, Nate	R-R	6-7	215	7-28-81	0	0	1.04	5	0	0	0	9	8	1	1	0	1	9	.250	.231	.263	9.35	1.04
Rayo, Pedro	R-R	6-0	145	5-6-84	1	0	3.86	3	1	0	0	9	8	4	4	3	3	16	.222	.238	.200	15.43	2.89
Richards, Glen	R-L	5-11	175	10-27-84	0	0	18.69	4	0	0	0	4	11	10	9	1	9	2	.478	.333	.571	4.15	18.69
Richardson, Jason	R-R	6-4	225	6-11-80	1	2	4.04	19	0	0	0	36	33	23	16	2	11	34	.244	.379	.143	8.58	2.78
Roberts, Ralph	R-R	6-2	215	3-28-80	4	5	2.93	38	4	0	1	77	74	37	25	7	37	64	.261	.303	.234	7.51	4.34
Rodriguez, Ricardo	R-R	6-0	170	4-28-81	3	9	5.34	33	9	0	1	86	82	56	51	12	47	80	.254	.243	.262	8.37	4.92
Schreiber, Zach	R-R	6-1	200	6-24-82	0	2	2.84	15	0	0	0	25	15	10	8	4	11	25	.169	.214	.148	8.88	3.91
Smith, Dan	L-L	6-5	250	9-9-83	2	2	2.61	25	0	0	6	38	33	11	11	1	17	32	.232	.283	.202	7.58	4.03
Stevens, Jake	L-L	6-2	215	3-15-85	10	9	4.93	28	28	0	0	148	167	90	81	13	62	102	.288	.308	.280	6.20	3.77
Tucker, Glenn	B-R	6-3	205	4-9-81	0	1	16.20	1	0	0	0	2	3	3	3	1	1	0	.429	1.000	.333	0.00	5.40
Villa, Kelvin	L-L	5-10	160	12-14-85	2	10	5.13	22	19	0	0	100	112	65	57	10	48	78	.280	.324	.265	7.02	4.32
Waters, Chris	L-L	6-0	170	8-17-80	4	5	4.27	17	17	1	0	103	106	54	49	10	31	67	.270	.211	.303	5.84	2.70
White, Sean	R-R	6-4	210	4-25-81	9	3	3.71	18	18	0	0	97	112	46	40	5	29	65	.296	.297	.294	6.03	2.69

FIELDING

Catcher	PCT	G	PO	A	E	DP	PB
Barksdale	1.000	1	9	0	0	0	1
Bernard	.986	9	63	6	1	0	2
Pyzik	1.000	12	69	5	0	0	1
Ruelas	.996	35	227	31	1	3	2
Saltalamacchia	.986	93	639	49	10	7	9

First Base	PCT	G	PO	A	E	DP
Guzman	.975	23	189	10	5	19
Jurich	.973	29	240	9	7	31
Rozema	1.000	3	8	1	0	0
Schade	.993	80	649	45	5	74
Thomas	.976	15	78	5	2	7

Second Base	PCT	G	PO	A	E	DP
W. James	.966	34	65	78	5	17
Prado	.974	72	141	201	9	59
Rozema	.982	35	70	93	3	23
Trejo	1.000	1	3	2	0	1
Velazquez	1.000	3	5	9	0	2

Third Base	PCT	G	PO	A	E	DP
Creek	.917	4	2	9	1	0
W. James	1.000	3	0	1	0	0
Pope	.921	25	26	56	7	6
Rozema	.857	8	5	7	2	0
Schade	.917	6	2	9	1	0
Thomas	.933	57	32	94	9	17
Trejo	.929	47	39	78	9	13
Velazquez	1.000	1	1	0	0	0

Shortstop	PCT	G	PO	A	E	DP
Hernandez	.983	71	118	179	5	45
W. James	.975	17	25	53	2	11
Rozema	.962	13	10	40	2	6
Trejo	.952	47	65	153	11	36

Outfield	PCT	G	PO	A	E	DP
Burrus	.960	67	115	6	5	3
Doetsch	.970	107	249	8	8	4
Duran	.963	11	24	2	1	0
Esquivel	.951	114	222	12	12	2
W. James	.833	8	14	1	3	0
Jansen	.971	47	96	6	3	1
Jones	1.000	15	42	0	0	0
Loadenthal	.960	57	114	7	5	1

ROME BRAVES — Low Class A

SOUTH ATLANTIC LEAGUE

BATTING	B-T	HT	WT	DOB	AVG	vLH	vRH	G	AB	R	H	2B	3B	HR	RBI	BB	HBP	SH	SF	SO	SB	CS	SLG	OBP
Armstrong, Cole	L-R	6-3	220	8-24-83	.228	.250	.221	105	378	33	86	26	1	7	42	32	0	1	7	71	0	2	.357	.283
Barksdale, James	R-R	5-10	215	12-7-81	.170	.167	.174	16	47	2	8	0	0	1	6	1	1	0	1	24	0	2	.234	.200
Brown, Bo	R-R	6-0	178	4-3-83	.101	.100	.103	29	69	6	7	2	0	0	3	7	0	0	0	35	0	0	.130	.184
Creek, Greg	L-R	6-3	225	8-29-82	.333	.333	.333	7	24	3	8	1	0	1	1	4	0	0	0	4	1	0	.500	.429
Doetsch, Steve	R-R	6-2	195	12-2-83	.364	.278	.405	13	55	13	20	1	2	1	9	8	0	0	0	12	5	0	.509	.444
Eichas, Keith	R-R	6-2	200	6-29-83	.212	.192	.222	61	231	19	49	10	1	2	25	8	2	1	0	56	1	0	.290	.245
Escobar, Yunel	R-R	6-2	200	11-2-82	.313	.268	.325	48	198	30	62	13	3	4	19	14	0	2	0	30	0	2	.470	.358
Guzman, Carlos	R-R	6-3	180	7-5-83	.195	.185	.198	30	113	15	22	5	0	7	15	6	1	0	3	54	3	2	.425	.236
Holt, J.C.	L-R	5-10	172	12-8-82	.268	.252	.272	123	441	60	118	23	3	5	50	37	2	12	4	89	12	8	.367	.324
Jansen, Ardley	R-R	6-2	160	2-16-83	.271	.156	.305	58	199	31	54	11	1	10	38	15	3	2	3	60	3	1	.487	.327
Jones, Chipper	B-R	6-4	210	4-24-72	.500	.000	.600	3	6	1	3	0	0	0	2	3	0	0	0	1	0	0	.500	.667
Jones, Brandon	L-R	6-2	195	12-10-83	.308	.294	.311	43	156	37	48	12	3	8	27	29	3	0	1	29	4	1	.577	.423
Jordan, Brian	R-R	6-1	225	3-29-67	.500	.667	.462	5	16	5	8	1	0	1	7	2	0	0	2	2	1	0	.750	.500
Jurich, Mark	L-L	5-10	195	12-29-80	.290	.317	.278	52	193	33	56	8	2	11	37	18	1	0	2	39	2	1	.523	.350
Loadenthal, Carl	L-L	5-11	185	12-27-81	.262	.173	.291	63	210	35	55	13	1	1	23	28	4	1	2	28	17	4	.348	.357
Marcial, Robert	R-R	5-10	170	4-21-84	.263	.182	.375	6	19	1	5	0	1	0	1	1	0	0	0	1	1	0	.368	.300
Owings, Jon Mark	R-R	6-4	192	4-4-85	.286	.000	.400	2	7	2	2	1	0	0	1	1	0	0	0	0	0	0	.429	.375
Pope, Van	R-R	6-0	200	2-26-84	.277	.320	.262	100	386	48	107	24	7	6	60	42	2	1	5	70	0	1	.422	.347
Pyzik, Steve	R-R	5-10	185	5-18-81	.283	.304	.267	19	53	2	15	2	0	0	6	2	0	1	2	11	0	0	.321	.298
Rozema, Mike	L-R	6-2	180	9-16-81	.272	.275	.271	51	195	27	53	19	3	0	30	18	5	3	3	44	13	4	.400	.344
Sammons, Clint	R-R	6-0	210	5-15-83	.286	.265	.293	121	427	60	122	29	0	4	62	55	5	0	7	66	4	1	.382	.368
Silva, Johan	L-R	5-11	192	6-21-84	.225	.125	.258	38	129	14	29	3	3	0	18	10	1	3	2	35	0	2	.295	.282
Terrazas, Ivan	B-R	5-11	168	11-11-83	.277	.263	.282	87	321	42	89	17	1	3	41	10	1	4	2	48	1	3	.364	.299
Thomas, Ben	L-R	6-0	200	6-30-82	.353	.000	.400	11	34	6	12	2	0	2	8	1	0	0	1	4	0	0	.588	.361
Trejo, Jaime	R-R	6-3	187	9-7-83	.160	.240	.120	24	75	7	12	0	0	1	2	6	1	0	0	31	0	0	.200	.232
White, Dean	R-R	6-4	190	2-12-83	.238	.279	.224	72	235	34	56	9	1	1	14	20	3	3	0	67	3	3	.298	.306
Young, Matt	L-R	5-8	175	10-3-82	.312	.292	.319	114	423	85	132	15	4	6	52	66	7	7	2	65	10	11	.409	.412

PITCHING	B-T	HT	WT	DOB	W	L	ERA	G	GS	CG	SV	IP	H	R	ER	HR	BB	SO	AVG	vLH	vRH	K/9	BB/9
Alvarez, Juan	L-L	6-0	170	5-6-82	0	0	0.00	1	0	0	0	1	1	0	0	0	1	1	.250	.000	1.000	9.00	9.00
Anderson, Devin	L-L	6-5	220	1-24-84	0	2	4.32	16	0	0	0	25	25	13	12	0	15	14	.258	.259	.257	5.04	5.40
Atilano, Luis	R-R	6-3	200	5-10-85	8	9	4.17	24	24	1	0	136	138	77	63	17	32	66	.261	.297	.233	4.37	2.12
Bacot, Paul	R-R	6-5	220	8-16-84	1	2	5.53	9	5	0	1	41	58	27	25	3	12	12	.347	.338	.355	2.66	2.66
Bobbitt, Seth	R-R	6-1	180	3-24-79	0	0	0.00	2	0	0	0	3	1	0	0	0	1	1	.100	.250	.000	3.00	3.00
Burrows, Angelo	L-R	6-1	195	7-2-80	3	1	3.48	16	0	0	3	21	23	8	8	0	9	18	.271	.282	.261	7.84	3.92
Covington, Marcus	R-R	6-0	185	5-17-85	0	0	5.87	5	0	0	0	8	7	5	5	1	8	4	.250	.154	.333	4.70	9.39
Digby, Bryan	R-R	6-2	220	12-31-81	0	0	10.80	2	0	0	0	2	0	2	2	0	6	1	.000	.000	.000	5.40	32.40
Gryboski, Kevin	R-R	6-5	255	11-15-73	0	0	0.00	1	1	0	0	1	1	0	0	0	0	0	.250	.500	.000	0.00	0.00
Harrison, Matt	L-L	6-4	221	8-16-85	12	7	3.23	27	27	2	0	167	151	65	60	17	30	118	.239	.286	.227	6.36	1.62
Jimenez, Rodny	R-R	6-2	192	3-16-82	0	0	4.63	7	0	0	0	12	9	6	6	1	14	16	.225	.222	.227	12.34	10.80
Morton, Charlie	R-R	6-5	218	11-12-83	5	9	5.20	26	22	0	1	125	124	84	72	7	62	86	.261	.272	.249	6.21	4.48
Nix, Michael	R-R	6-5	235	5-21-83	1	3	7.17	18	0	0	5	21	24	18	17	1	15	22	.273	.265	.278	9.28	6.33
Oakes, Jerry	L-R	6-5	191	4-29-82	0	0	108.00	1	0	0	0	0	0	4	4	0	3	0	.000	.000	.000	0.00	81.00

PITCHING	B-T	HT	WT	DOB	W	L	ERA	G	GS	CG	SV	IP	H	R	ER	HR	BB	SO	AVG	vLH	vRH	K/9	BB/9
Parr, James	R-R	6-1	185	2-27-86	13	4	3.41	26	18	0	3	127	134	54	48	13	24	98	.269	.279	.260	6.96	1.71
Paul, Jason	R-R	6-3	200	10-10-81	1	2	5.45	28	0	0	0	35	48	23	21	8	15	30	.329	.338	.321	7.79	3.89
Payano, Nelson	L-L	6-2	180	11-13-82	0	0	0.00	1	0	0	0	4	3	1	0	0	3	2	.250	.500	.125	4.50	6.75
Russell, Stephen	R-R	6-6	185	12-20-83	0	2	3.80	10	2	0	0	24	24	14	10	2	12	28	.258	.333	.178	10.65	4.56
Santos, Arthur	R-R	6-0	180	2-20-82	4	2	3.35	27	3	0	4	51	62	24	19	1	13	35	.295	.281	.306	6.18	2.29
Schreiber, Zach	R-R	6-1	200	6-24-82	1	3	2.94	27	0	0	2	34	24	14	11	0	22	31	.207	.217	.200	8.29	5.88
Smith, Dan	L-L	6-5	250	9-9-83	3	2	1.89	19	0	0	5	33	24	8	7	1	18	45	.205	.111	.233	12.15	4.86
Startup, Will	L-L	6-0	195	8-4-84	3	2	2.37	25	0	0	5	38	31	13	10	3	6	30	.221	.108	.262	7.11	1.42
Thomson, John	R-R	6-3	220	10-1-73	0	0	0.00	1	1	0	0	4	2	0	0	0	1	1	.143	.143	.143	2.25	2.25
Venters, Jonny	L-L	6-3	188	3-20-85	8	6	3.93	23	12	0	3	103	100	51	45	4	52	66	.258	.289	.249	5.77	4.54
Villa, Kelvin	L-L	5-10	160	12-14-85	2	1	1.33	7	3	1	0	27	19	7	4	1	7	25	.196	.269	.169	8.33	2.33
Vines, Chris	R-R	6-5	215	2-26-85	6	7	4.80	23	19	1	0	129	156	77	69	17	31	104	.301	.270	.326	7.24	2.16
Ward, Josh	R-R	6-3	190	4-1-86	0	0	5.40	3	0	0	0	5	6	3	3	0	1	7	.300	.091	.556	12.60	1.80
Wiggins, Trae	L-L	6-3	195	10-15-82	0	1	10.50	12	0	0	0	18	32	23	21	1	12	9	.381	.211	.431	4.50	6.00
Williams, David	R-R	6-4	190	5-6-85	1	0	3.86	7	0	0	1	12	11	5	5	2	0	12	.239	.269	.200	9.26	0.00

FIELDING

Catcher	PCT	G	PO	A	E	DP	PB
Armstrong	.988	42	237	18	3	0	5
Barksdale	1.000	8	36	6	0	0	5
Pyzik	.990	17	91	4	1	1	2
Sammons	.988	83	531	62	7	4	12

First Base	PCT	G	PO	A	E	DP
Armstrong	.967	11	85	4	3	8
Creek	.967	3	27	2	1	2
Eichas	.994	56	460	33	3	46
Guzman	.988	26	236	21	3	17
Jurich	.990	25	193	11	2	20
Terrazas	.988	10	73	6	1	8
Thomas	1.000	7	41	4	0	2
White	.981	6	42	9	1	5

Second Base	PCT	G	PO	A	E	DP
Brown	1.000	5	6	18	0	4
Holt	.972	119	204	311	15	62
Marcial	1.000	1	1	3	0	0
White	.962	18	21	30	2	3

Third Base	PCT	G	PO	A	E	DP
Brown	.909	6	4	6	1	1
Creek	.778	4	1	6	2	0
C. Jones	.833	2	1	4	1	0
Marcial	1.000	3	0	5	0	0
Pope	.944	96	75	179	15	17
Thomas	1.000	2	0	3	0	0
Trejo	.944	10	5	12	1	2
White	.922	22	13	34	4	3

Shortstop	PCT	G	PO	A	E	DP
Brown	.938	4	6	9	1	1
Escobar	.977	48	96	159	6	25
Rozema	.951	50	97	175	14	36
Trejo	.986	14	24	44	1	10
White	.935	24	40	60	7	14

Outfield	PCT	G	PO	A	E	DP
Brown	1.000	10	18	0	0	0
Doetsch	1.000	12	21	0	0	0
Eichas	1.000	1	4	0	0	0
Jansen	.995	57	173	8	1	4
B. Jones	.960	40	71	1	3	0
Jordan	1.000	1	2	0	0	0
Jurich	.953	22	41	0	2	0
Loadenthal	.968	58	115	5	4	0
Marcial	.667	1	2	0	1	0
Owings	.750	2	3	0	1	0
Silva	.980	36	94	5	2	1
Terrazas	.936	73	127	4	9	0
White	1.000	1	2	0	0	0
Young	.992	112	229	8	2	2

DANVILLE BRAVES — Rookie

APPALACHIAN LEAGUE

BATTING	B-T	HT	WT	DOB	AVG	vLH	vRH	G	AB	R	H	2B	3B	HR	RBI	BB	HBP	SH	SF	SO	SB	CS	SLG	OBP
Andrus, Elvis	R-R	6-0	185	8-26-88	.278	.000	.417	6	18	3	5	1	0	0	1	4	0	0	0	4	1	0	.333	.409
Arnold, Derrick	B-R	5-10	165	8-3-83	.269	.291	.259	51	171	20	46	9	0	2	16	14	0	8	2	38	7	2	.357	.321
Barksdale, James	R-R	5-10	215	12-7-81	.171	.167	.174	10	35	4	6	0	0	0	2	1	0	0	0	15	0	0	.171	.194
Campbell, Eric	R-R	6-0	195	8-6-85	.313	.333	.304	66	262	77	82	26	2	18	64	28	4	0	4	64	15	4	.634	.383
Davis, Quentin	L-R	5-10	170	3-7-83	.323	.267	.348	49	201	44	65	9	2	3	36	14	4	0	1	26	8	4	.433	.377
Escobar, Yunel	R-R	6-2	200	11-2-82	.400	.250	.500	8	30	9	12	2	1	2	8	5	0	0	1	4	0	0	.733	.472
Guerra, Junior	R-R	5-11	213	1-16-85	.261	.241	.267	37	115	6	30	10	0	3	18	3	2	0	1	22	0	0	.426	.289
Jones, Brandon	L-R	6-2	195	12-10-83	.286	1.000	.000	2	7	0	2	0	0	0	1	1	0	0	0	0	0	0	.286	.375
Kaaihue, Kala	R-R	6-2	230	3-29-85	.438	.750	.333	5	16	4	7	3	0	2	3	0	0	0	0	5	0	0	1.000	.438
Owings, Jon Mark	R-R	6-4	192	4-4-85	.293	.342	.269	33	116	27	34	8	2	12	31	6	5	1	0	31	1	2	.707	.354
Picornell, Carlos	B-R	5-9	175	8-21-82	.211	.125	.224	22	57	16	12	2	0	0	4	11	1	4	1	10	5	1	.246	.343
Ramirez, Max	R-R	5-11	175	10-11-84	.347	.329	.355	63	239	45	83	19	0	8	47	31	4	0	4	41	1	2	.527	.424
Rodriguez, Manuel	L-L	6-3	190	1-6-85	.300	.270	.313	65	250	34	75	19	2	8	47	12	0	0	5	69	1	1	.488	.326
Romak, Jamie	R-R	6-2	220	9-30-85	.274	.220	.301	34	124	25	34	10	1	7	27	14	5	1	1	38	2	1	.540	.368
Santos, Jose	R-R	6-0	165	10-7-84	.228	.203	.240	51	180	31	41	9	3	2	25	26	3	2	0	39	5	5	.344	.335
Shehan, Jonathan	R-R	5-9	205	5-13-82	.158	.071	.208	15	38	2	6	2	0	0	2	6	3	1	0	9	0	0	.211	.319
Silva, Yohan	B-R	5-11	175	1-30-85	.208	.194	.215	64	216	27	45	15	1	1	22	27	1	1	4	51	3	5	.301	.294
Suero, Ovandy	B-R	5-10	160	6-20-82	.300	.324	.290	60	247	53	74	5	8	4	17	14	3	6	2	54	46	11	.433	.342

PITCHING	B-T	HT	WT	DOB	W	L	ERA	G	GS	CG	SV	IP	H	R	ER	HR	BB	SO	AVG	vLH	vRH	K/9	BB/9
Acosta, Manny	R-R	6-4	170	5-1-81	0	0	3.00	3	2	0	0	6	3	2	2	0	1	8	.167	.500	.071	12.00	1.50
Anderson, Devin	L-L	6-5	220	1-24-84	4	1	2.49	13	6	0	0	51	36	15	14	5	15	38	.198	.258	.185	6.75	2.66
Blackford, Todd	L-R	6-4	215	6-10-85	5	3	3.17	12	12	0	0	60	48	24	21	2	22	30	.219	.241	.206	4.53	3.32
Bullock, Tyler	R-R	6-3	225	1-22-84	1	0	3.60	14	0	0	3	20	13	8	8	1	10	14	.183	.188	.182	6.30	4.50
Cho, Jung Ji	R-R	6-1	210	7-11-83	4	2	0.94	7	3	0	0	29	22	4	3	0	6	35	.214	.300	.159	10.99	1.88
Cuevas, Jairo	R-R	6-2	217	1-24-84	6	1	1.95	12	10	0	0	55	35	20	12	3	22	69	.179	.089	.216	11.22	3.58
Demme, Asher	R-R	6-3	205	11-1-84	1	0	3.76	12	8	0	2	53	48	30	22	3	18	35	.251	.280	.233	5.98	3.08
Hendricks, Donavon	L-L	6-0	175	3-9-86	1	2	6.99	17	0	0	0	28	41	27	22	3	13	25	.350	.200	.373	7.94	4.13
Jackson, Drew	L-L	6-0	210	10-12-83	3	1	4.02	12	0	0	0	16	16	7	7	0	9	13	.276	.286	.273	7.47	5.17
Johnson, Bryan	L-L	6-2	200	11-9-82	3	4	2.20	20	0	0	4	33	26	15	8	1	17	27	.210	.179	.219	7.44	4.68
Nix, Michael	R-R	6-5	235	5-21-83	1	0	0.00	5	0	0	0	6	1	0	0	0	2	11	.053	.000	.077	16.50	3.00
Oakes, Jerry	L-R	6-5	191	4-29-82	0	0	18.00	2	0	0	0	2	3	4	4	0	3	3	.375	1.000	.286	13.50	13.50
Pudewell, Nate	R-R	6-7	215	7-28-81	1	1	12.15	3	1	0	0	7	13	10	9	2	0	3	.406	.200	.444	4.05	0.00
Quinonez, Rudy	R-R	6-2	200	6-17-84	1	0	2.60	24	0	0	10	28	17	11	8	5	8	40	.170	.188	.162	13.01	2.60
Reyes, Jo Jo	L-L	6-2	230	11-20-84	3	0	3.53	9	8	0	0	43	37	18	17	3	6	27	.228	.238	.227	5.61	1.25
Richards, Glen	R-L	5-11	175	10-27-84	1	0	1.93	10	0	0	0	14	7	4	3	0	5	15	.143	.083	.162	9.64	3.21
Rivas, Carlos	L-L	6-3	160	1-3-85	4	1	4.24	13	10	0	1	51	49	28	24	7	25	33	.254	.219	.261	5.82	4.41
Rosario, Eduardo	L-L	6-0	177	6-7-84	1	1	3.38	11	2	0	0	29	33	13	11	1	20	26	.295	.211	.312	7.98	6.14
Russell, Stephen	R-R	6-6	185	12-20-83	1	1	4.05	2	1	0	0	7	7	3	3	1	2	5	.269	.250	.278	6.75	2.70
Santiago, Jose	R-R	6-4	180	8-1-81	0	0	8.22	8	0	0	0	8	11	7	7	1	8	13	.324	.429	.296	15.26	9.39
Stanley, Adam	L-L	6-0	201	11-20-84	1	0	5.79	4	0	0	0	9	12	7	6	0	3	8	.308	.143	.344	7.71	2.89
Tisone, Nick	R-R	6-2	185	8-2-83	4	1	3.05	17	3	0	2	38	38	17	13	1	7	30	.255	.289	.243	7.04	1.64
Wiggins, Trae	L-L	6-3	195	10-15-82	1	1	10.00	5	1	0	0	9	10	10	10	1	8	6	.278	.500	.233	6.00	8.00

GAMES BY POSITION: C—Barksdale 2, Guerra 33, Ramirez 29, Shehan 14. **1B**—Guerra 2, Kaaihue 5, Rodriguez 65, Santos 1. **2B**—Arnold 5, Picornell 5, Santos 36, Suero 26. **3B**—Arnold 4, Campbell 65. **SS**—Arnold 43, Andrus 5, Barksdale 1, Escobar 8, Santos 14. **OF**—Davis 47, Jones 2, Owings 31, Picornell 8, Romak 34, Silva 64, Suero 24.

GCL BRAVES — Rookie

GULF COAST LEAGUE

BATTING	B-T	HT	WT	DOB	AVG	vLH	vRH	G	AB	R	H	2B	3B	HR	RBI	BB	HBP	SH	SF	SO	SB	CS	SLG	OBP
Andrus, Elvis	R-R	6-0	185	8-26-88	.295	.400	.277	46	166	26	49	6	1	3	20	19	4	0	2	28	7	4	.398	.377
Bernard, Miguel	R-R	5-11	220	1-1-81	.321	.000	.391	10	28	3	9	1	0	1	6	3	0	0	1	2	1	1	.464	.375
Brezeale, Danny	R-R	5-11	200	5-13-86	.278	.667	.200	5	18	2	5	2	0	0	2	0	1	0	0	5	0	0	.389	.316
Britton, Phillip	R-R	6-0	180	9-25-84	.231	.250	.229	18	39	3	9	1	0	1	2	2	3	0	0	7	0	0	.333	.318
Camarena, Jose	B-R	5-10	176	5-29-84	.279	.200	.293	22	68	6	19	4	1	1	8	7	1	0	0	14	1	1	.412	.355
Carmona, Eliazar	R-R	6-1	170	12-12-85	.208	.000	.229	34	77	10	16	1	0	0	4	4	1	2	0	12	4	1	.221	.256
Creek, Greg	L-R	6-3	225	8-29-82	.322	.222	.336	41	143	21	46	10	1	2	14	11	0	0	0	22	0	0	.448	.370
Disla, Bienvenido	B-R	5-9	165	7-13-83	.146	.083	.167	22	48	3	7	1	1	0	2	10	0	0	0	19	1	0	.208	.293
Garcia, Steven	R-R	5-11	190	9-7-86	.231	.167	.239	23	52	7	12	2	0	1	4	6	2	0	0	7	0	0	.327	.333
Griffin, Trevion	R-R	5-11	175	11-8-84	.162	.111	.173	31	99	14	16	3	1	0	5	7	3	0	2	11	6	2	.212	.234
Hernandez, Luis	B-R	5-10	165	6-26-84	.250	.000	.250	1	4	1	1	0	0	1	1	0	0	0	0	2	0	0	1.000	.250
Hernandez, Diory	R-R	5-11	170	4-8-84	.357	.000	.370	7	28	5	10	1	0	1	4	0	0	0	0	2	0	2	.500	.357
Jones, Brandon	L-R	6-2	195	12-10-83	.125	.000	.167	2	8	0	1	0	0	0	2	0	0	0	0	2	0	1	.125	.125
Kaaihue, Kala	R-R	6-2	230	3-29-85	.283	.118	.309	40	127	18	36	8	2	6	22	15	2	0	4	38	0	0	.520	.358
Marcial, Robert	R-R	5-10	170	4-21-84	.192	.200	.188	24	26	4	5	2	0	0	1	0	0	0	1	5	0	1	.269	.185
Mejia, Ernesto	R-R	6-6	190	12-2-85	.223	.160	.235	44	157	21	35	4	0	7	22	3	5	0	1	42	0	1	.382	.259
Monk, Brandon	R-R	5-11	180	2-22-87	.269	.318	.261	46	156	19	42	10	0	3	18	9	4	1	1	16	0	1	.391	.324
Mota, Juan	R-R	6-0	180	5-8-84	.214	.167	.227	18	28	2	6	1	1	0	2	4	1	0	0	9	1	0	.321	.333
Parliament, Adam	R-R	6-4	220	12-16-85	.236	.318	.222	46	157	15	37	6	0	4	16	10	2	0	1	44	0	1	.350	.288
Rivadeneira, Deivis	B-R	5-11	160	11-28-85	.193	.250	.187	33	83	6	16	3	1	0	7	4	2	1	2	13	1	4	.253	.242
Schafer, Jordan	L-L	6-1	190	9-4-86	.203	.172	.209	49	182	18	37	12	3	3	19	13	1	1	3	49	13	6	.352	.256

PITCHING	B-T	HT	WT	DOB	W	L	ERA	G	GS	CG	SV	IP	H	R	ER	HR	BB	SO	AVG	vLH	vRH	K/9	BB/9
Acosta, Jorge	L-L	5-11	185	9-18-83	0	1	5.11	9	0	0	0	12	12	7	7	4	5	16	.250	.182	.270	11.68	3.65
Broadway, Michael	R-R	6-5	190	3-30-87	1	2	5.40	7	3	0	0	22	30	18	13	3	8	12	.337	.318	.343	4.98	3.32
Castro, Yeliar	R-R	6-3	180	12-3-87	0	2	9.82	5	2	0	0	11	13	12	12	3	12	6	.317	.417	.276	4.91	9.82
Cofield, Kyle	R-R	6-5	190	1-23-87	0	0	7.31	10	0	0	2	16	16	15	13	0	6	15	.254	.300	.212	8.44	3.38
Covington, Marcus	R-R	6-0	185	5-17-85	1	1	8.18	10	0	0	1	11	14	10	10	0	9	12	.298	.263	.321	9.82	7.36
Gonzalez, Raul	R-R	6-2	155	7-12-85	0	2	3.06	6	4	0	0	18	16	8	6	2	3	14	.250	.231	.255	7.13	1.53
Hampton, Mike	R-L	5-10	195	9-10-72	0	0	0.00	1	1	0	0	5	6	0	0	0	0	4	.300	.333	.294	7.20	0.00
Jones, Beau	L-L	6-1	195	8-25-86	3	2	3.86	8	7	0	0	35	25	15	15	0	16	41	.212	.115	.239	10.54	4.11
Katz, Jeff	R-R	6-4	217	4-18-86	2	0	9.64	9	0	0	0	14	21	16	15	0	14	14	.339	.258	.419	9.00	9.00
Lyman, Jeff	R-R	6-3	215	1-14-87	0	3	4.24	8	7	0	0	34	41	27	16	2	7	28	.295	.276	.309	7.41	1.85
Nelson, Brad	R-R	6-1	220	1-5-82	0	0	0.00	1	0	0	1	1	0	0	0	0	1	1	.000	.000	.000	9.00	9.00
Oakes, Jerry	L-R	6-5	191	4-29-82	0	0	0.00	3	0	0	0	5	6	4	0	0	5	1	.286	.222	.333	1.80	9.00
Powell, Jay	R-R	6-4	230	1-9-72	0	0	4.50	2	2	0	0	2	4	2	1	0	1	1	.444	.333	.500	4.50	4.50
Rayo, Pedro	R-R	6-0	145	5-6-84	1	1	1.50	11	2	0	1	30	18	6	5	2	8	28	.173	.148	.182	8.40	2.40
Reyes, Jo Jo	L-L	6-2	230	11-20-84	0	1	1.69	3	2	0	0	5	6	2	1	0	1	6	.273	.400	.235	10.13	1.69
Richmond, Jamie	R-R	6-3	185	3-23-86	2	0	3.09	8	0	0	0	12	7	4	4	0	2	12	.179	.143	.200	9.26	1.54
Russell, Stephen	R-R	6-6	185	12-20-83	0	0	2.89	3	0	0	0	9	8	8	3	0	5	9	.222	.200	.231	8.68	4.82
Santiago, Jose	R-R	6-4	180	8-1-81	0	0	6.48	6	0	0	0	8	6	8	6	1	10	9	.188	.200	.182	9.72	10.80
Shaffer, Jared	R-R	6-2	170	3-27-86	3	5	5.40	9	5	0	0	37	41	30	22	2	15	31	.273	.333	.250	7.61	3.68
Stanley, Adam	L-L	6-0	201	11-20-84	1	0	0.00	4	0	0	0	8	6	1	0	0	0	9	.194	.200	.190	10.57	0.00
Tejada, Jonathan	R-R	6-0	160	6-4-84	2	2	4.37	8	6	0	0	35	34	19	17	4	11	35	.252	.204	.279	9.00	2.83
Thompson, Michael	B-R	5-10	170	5-3-85	1	0	0.64	12	1	0	1	14	8	1	1	0	5	11	.167	.263	.103	7.07	3.21
Valenzuela, Sergio	R-R	6-0	175	9-15-84	1	4	3.60	8	7	0	0	35	35	16	14	1	4	16	.259	.242	.274	4.11	1.03
Ward, Josh	R-R	6-3	190	4-1-86	1	0	2.25	12	0	0	0	16	17	6	4	0	5	9	.274	.227	.300	5.06	2.81
Warren, Jesse	L-L	6-3	180	3-21-86	2	0	7.62	10	0	0	0	13	13	11	11	1	9	11	.265	.300	.256	7.62	6.23
Williams, David	R-R	6-4	190	5-6-85	0	1	0.47	13	0	0	7	19	8	1	1	0	4	25	.129	.158	.116	11.84	1.89
Wilson, Tyler	L-L	6-1	190	7-11-86	2	0	0.79	9	0	0	0	11	5	3	1	0	5	11	.128	.125	.129	8.74	3.97
Wright, Matt	R-R	6-4	230	3-13-82	1	1	3.12	3	3	0	0	9	11	8	3	0	2	9	.297	.438	.190	9.35	2.08

GAMES BY POSITION: C—Bernard 9, Britton 16, Camarena 10, Garcia 22, Marcial 1, Mota 18. **1B**—Brezeale 1, Camarena 10, Creek 4, Kaaihue 39, Rivadeneira 1. **2B**—Andrus 1, Disla 3, Marcial 13, Monk 41, Rivadeneira 14. **3B**—Brezeale 4, Creek 37, Disla 12, Rivadeneira 7. **SS**—Andrus 40, Creek 1, L. Hernandez 1, J. Hernandez 4, Marcial 3, Rivadeneira 10. **OF**—Camarena 2, Carmona 32, Griffin 30, Jones 2, Marcial 1, Mejia 18, Parliament 45, Rivadeneira 1, Schafer 47.

BALTIMORE ORIOLES

BY ROCH KUBATKO

A season that began with such promise for the Orioles ended in tatters, with players and management unable to piece it back together. The fall was swift, the impact grotesque.

The Orioles spent 62 consecutive days in first place in the American League East in 2005, giving fans false hope that the club would end a streak of seven consecutive losing seasons. But they went 32-60 in their last 92 games, posting the worst winning percentage (.348) for any team since 1900 that played .600 ball over its first 70 games.

Fourth place awaited a club that made more news for what happened off the field than on it. Each day seemed to bring more embarrassment and controversy, and the weight of it brought down the Orioles with a thunderous crash.

The Orioles were a season-high 14 games above .500 on June 21, but they ended up 74-88, with four fewer victories than in 2004. They changed managers on Aug. 4, with bench coach Sam Perlozzo replacing Lee Mazzilli. But they couldn't change their luck.

Rafael Palmeiro became the fourth member of the 3,000-hit, 500-home run club on July 15, but he was suspended on Aug. 1 after testing positive for steroids. The Orioles canceled a planned ceremony for him at Camden Yards.

Sammy Sosa, acquired in a trade with the Cubs, missed a month with a staph infection beneath his left foot and proved to be a bust. Palmeiro and Sosa didn't finish the season with the Orioles, rehabbing injuries at their respective homes after the team showed no interest in having them in uniform down the stretch.

Righthander Sidney Ponson was arrested in August for the third time in nine months, his second alcohol-related offense, and the Orioles terminated his contract—an action that brought a grievance from the players association on his behalf. Lefthander Eric DuBose also was arrested on a DUI charge in spring training. And key players went down with injuries, including lefthander Erik Bedard, who was 5-1, 2.08 in the first half before being forced out of the rotation, and catcher Javy Lopez.

"People can say the distractions didn't affect us, but I think it did," backup catcher Sal Fasano said. "A lot of focus moved away from playing the game. It was like, 'What's going to happen today? Is the manager going to get fired? Is somebody going to get a DUI? Is someone going to get accused of steroids? Is there going to be another injury? There was always something."

Some of it was good.

Second baseman Brian Roberts, in his first full season as a starter, batted .314-18-72 and was chosen the team's MVP by members of the media. But typical of the Orioles' misfortune, he suffered a detached tendon and torn ligament in his left elbow during an Aug. 20 collision with the Yankees' Bubba Crosby and might not be ready for Opening Day.

"You lose Brian Roberts, it's like you lose half the team," third baseman Melvin Mora said.

The Orioles made some immediate changes in the front office, promoting Mike Flanagan to executive vice president of baseball operations and offering former executive Jim Beattie a consultant job. They retained Perlozzo as manager and hired his best friend, Leo Mazzone, as pitching coach.

The Orioles' six minor league affiliates posted a combined 352-355 record. In 2004, they were 57 games below .500.

Class A Frederick and low Class A Delmarva qualified for the playoffs, with the Keys winning their first Carolina League championship since 1990. None of the affiliates made the playoffs in 2004.

Outfielder Nick Markakis spent the first four months with Frederick before being promoted to Double-A Bowie on Aug. 1. He batted .300-12-62 in 91 games at Frederick and .339-3-30 in 39 games at Bowie.

PLAYERS OF THE YEAR

MAJOR LEAGUE: Brian Roberts, 2b

Roberts came out of the gate like gangbusters in 2005, hitting safely in 47 of his first 51 games and posting a .365 average and 1.052 OPS after three months. He cooled off in the second half and had his season cut short when he dislocated his left elbow in mid-September.

MINOR LEAGUE: Nick Markakis, of

RODGER WOOD

The Orioles' No. 1 prospect lived up to lofty preseason expectations in stops at high Class A Frederick and Double-A Bowie in 2005. He showed extra-base power (15 homers and 41 doubles between the two levels) and an improved ability to hit for average (.310 in 474 combined at-bats).

ORGANIZATION LEADERS

BATTING		
*AVG	Florence, Branden, Aberdeen/Frederick	.325
R	Castro, Bernie, Ottawa	81
H	Castro, Bernie, Ottawa	158
TB	Delgado, Mario, Frederick	240
2B	Markakis, Nick, Bowie/Frederick	41
3B	Rivas, Arturo, Delmarva	8
HR	Delgado, Mario, Frederick	26
RBI	Fransz, Jason, Delmarva	111
BB	Markakis, Nick, Bowie/Frederick	61
	Rivas, Arturo, Delmarva	61
SO	Bass, Bryan, Frederick	135
SB	Castro, Bernie, Ottawa	41
*OBP	Markakis, Nick, Bowie/Frederick	.390
*SLG	Florence, Branden, Aberdeen/Frederick	.572
PITCHING		
W	Johnson, J.J., Bowie/Frederick	12
L	Four tied at	11
#ERA	Britton, Chris, Frederick	1.38
G	Rakers, Aaron, Ottawa	57
	Rice, Scott, Bowie	57
CG	J.J. Johnson, Bowie/Frederick	2
SV	Haehnel, David, Delmarva/Frederick	18
	Ray, Chris, Bowie	18
IP	Borkowski, Dave, Ottawa	183
BB	Loewen, Adam, Frederick	86
SO	Johnson, J.J., Bowie/Frederick	174

*Minimum 250 at-bats. #Minimum 75 innings.

BALTIMORE ORIOLES

Managers: Lee Mazzilli, Sam Perlozzo.

2005 Record: 74-88, .457 (4th, AL East).

BATTING	B-T	HT	WT	DOB	AVG	vLH	vRH	G	AB	R	H	2B	3B	HR	RBI	BB	HBP	SH	SF	SO	SB	CS	SLG	OBP
Bigbie, Larry	L-R	6-4	210	11-4-77	.248	.271	.238	67	206	22	51	9	1	5	21	21	0	5	2	49	3	3	.374	.314
Byrnes, Eric	R-R	6-2	210	2-16-76	.192	.220	.176	52	167	17	32	7	1	3	11	11	1	2	0	33	3	0	.299	.246
2-team (59 Oakland)					.231	.284	.197	111	359	47	83	22	3	10	35	25	8	3	1	60	5	2	.393	.295
Calzado, Napoleon	R-R	6-3	200	2-9-77	.200	.200	.000	4	5	0	1	0	0	0	0	0	0	0	0	1	0	0	.200	.200
Castro, Bernie	B-R	5-10	165	7-14-79	.288	.200	.308	24	80	14	23	3	1	0	7	9	0	0	0	10	6	2	.350	.360
Cummings, Midre	L-R	6-0	225	10-14-71	.000	.000	.000	2	2	0	0	0	0	0	0	0	0	0	0	1	0	0	.000	.000
Fasano, Sal	R-R	6-2	245	8-10-71	.250	.310	.229	64	160	25	40	3	0	11	20	9	5	0	0	41	0	0	.475	.310
Fiorentino, Jeff	L-R	6-1	190	4-14-83	.250	.176	.296	13	44	7	11	2	0	1	5	2	0	0	1	10	1	0	.364	.277
Freire, Alejandro	R-R	6-2	225	8-23-74	.246	.200	.350	25	65	7	16	3	0	1	4	6	1	0	0	17	0	0	.338	.319
Gibbons, Jay	L-L	6-0	205	3-2-77	.277	.250	.287	139	488	72	135	33	3	26	79	28	1	0	1	56	0	0	.516	.317
Gil, Geronimo	R-R	6-2	230	8-7-75	.192	.200	.187	64	125	7	24	3	0	4	17	5	0	2	2	23	0	0	.312	.220
Gomez, Chris	R-R	6-1	185	6-16-71	.279	.317	.243	89	219	27	61	11	0	1	18	27	1	6	1	17	2	1	.342	.359
Lopez, Javy	R-R	6-3	230	11-5-70	.278	.284	.276	103	395	47	110	24	1	15	49	19	7	0	2	68	0	1	.458	.322
Marrero, Eli	R-R	6-1	180	11-17-73	.220	.306	.000	22	50	8	11	3	2	3	10	4	0	0	2	20	0	0	.540	.268
2-team (32 Kansas City)					.181	.247	.061	54	138	19	25	7	2	7	19	11	1	1	5	38	1	0	.413	.239
Matos, Luis	R-R	6-0	210	10-30-78	.280	.297	.273	121	389	53	109	20	2	4	32	27	10	3	4	58	17	9	.373	.340
Mora, Melvin	R-R	5-11	200	2-2-72	.283	.232	.304	149	593	86	168	30	1	27	88	50	10	8	3	112	7	4	.474	.348
Newhan, David	L-R	5-10	180	9-7-73	.202	.250	.195	96	218	31	44	9	0	5	21	22	2	5	2	45	9	2	.312	.279
Nivar, Ramon	R-R	5-10	185	2-22-80	.308	.364	.000	7	13	1	4	0	0	0	1	0	1	1	0	2	0	1	.308	.357
Palmeiro, Rafael	L-L	6-0	215	9-24-64	.266	.221	.281	110	369	47	98	13	0	18	60	43	2	0	8	43	2	0	.447	.339
Reed, Keith	R-R	6-4	205	10-8-78	.200	.000	.500	6	5	1	1	0	0	0	1	1	0	0	0	2	0	0	.200	.333
Roberts, Brian	B-R	5-9	180	10-9-77	.314	.273	.332	143	561	92	176	45	7	18	73	67	3	5	4	83	27	10	.515	.387
Rogers, Ed	R-R	6-1	190	8-29-78	1.000	1.000	.000	8	1	4	1	0	0	1	2	0	0	0	0	0	0	2	4.000	1.000
Sosa, Sammy	R-R	6-0	230	11-12-68	.221	.288	.196	102	380	39	84	15	1	14	45	39	2	0	3	84	1	1	.376	.295
Surhoff, B.J.	L-R	6-1	215	8-4-64	.257	.255	.259	91	303	30	78	11	2	5	34	11	1	2	4	32	0	0	.356	.282
Tejada, Miguel	R-R	5-9	215	5-25-76	.304	.293	.308	162	654	89	199	50	5	26	98	40	7	0	3	83	5	1	.515	.349
Whiteside, Eli	R-R	6-2	210	10-22-79	.250	.400	.143	9	12	1	3	0	0	0	1	0	0	0	0	2	0	0	.250	.250
Young, Walter	L-R	6-5	320	2-18-80	.303	.667	.267	14	33	2	10	1	0	1	3	4	0	0	0	7	0	0	.424	.378

PITCHING	B-T	HT	WT	DOB	W	L	ERA	G	GS	CG	SV	IP	H	R	ER	HR	BB	SO	AVG	vLH	vRH	K/9	BB/9
Baldwin, James	R-R	6-3	265	7-15-71	0	0	3.20	20	0	0	0	39	36	18	14	5	9	20	.245	.220	.277	4.58	2.06
2-team (8 Texas)					0	2	3.81	28	0	0	1	57	54	28	24	8	16	29	.254	.209	.301	4.61	2.54
Bauer, Rick	R-R	6-6	225	1-10-74	0	0	9.72	5	0	0	0	8	13	9	9	2	4	5	.361	.412	.316	5.40	4.32
Bedard, Erik	L-L	6-1	195	3-6-79	6	8	4.00	24	24	0	0	142	139	66	63	10	57	125	.260	.252	.263	7.94	3.62
Byrdak, Tim	L-L	5-11	190	10-31-73	0	1	4.05	41	0	0	1	27	27	14	12	1	21	31	.255	.214	.300	10.46	7.09
Cabrera, Daniel	R-R	6-7	250	5-28-81	10	13	4.52	29	29	0	0	161	144	92	81	14	87	157	.235	.285	.174	8.76	4.85
Chen, Bruce	L-L	6-1	210	6-19-77	13	10	3.83	34	32	1	0	197	187	94	84	33	63	133	.248	.324	.224	6.07	2.87
DuBose, Eric	L-L	6-3	235	5-15-76	2	3	5.52	15	3	0	0	29	28	21	18	4	19	17	.243	.146	.313	5.22	5.83
Grimsley, Jason	R-R	6-3	205	8-7-67	1	2	5.73	22	0	0	0	22	24	15	14	5	9	10	.289	.324	.265	4.09	3.68
Julio, Jorge	R-R	6-1	235	3-3-79	3	5	5.90	67	0	0	0	72	76	50	47	14	24	58	.269	.281	.257	7.28	3.01
Kline, Steve	R-L	6-1	240	8-22-72	2	4	4.28	67	0	0	0	61	59	34	29	11	30	36	.257	.317	.209	5.31	4.43
Lopez, Rodrigo	R-R	6-1	190	12-14-75	15	12	4.90	35	35	0	0	209	232	126	114	28	63	118	.276	.288	.262	5.07	2.71
Maine, John	R-R	6-4	205	5-8-81	2	3	6.30	10	8	0	0	40	39	30	28	8	24	24	.248	.227	.275	5.40	5.40
Parrish, John	L-L	5-11	200	11-26-77	1	0	3.12	14	0	0	0	17	19	6	6	1	17	25	.279	.200	.342	12.98	8.83
Penn, Hayden	R-R	6-3	195	10-13-84	3	2	6.34	8	8	0	0	38	46	30	27	6	21	18	.295	.289	.301	4.23	4.93
Ponson, Sidney	R-R	6-1	255	11-2-76	7	11	6.21	23	23	1	0	130	177	97	90	16	48	68	.331	.360	.299	4.70	3.31
Rakers, Aaron	R-R	6-3	220	1-22-77	1	0	3.29	10	0	0	0	14	11	5	5	3	3	11	.220	.227	.214	7.24	1.98
Ray, Chris	R-R	6-3	200	1-12-82	1	3	2.66	41	0	0	0	41	34	15	12	5	18	43	.222	.284	.174	9.52	3.98
Reed, Steve	R-R	6-2	210	3-11-65	1	2	6.61	30	0	0	0	33	41	24	24	5	11	15	.308	.349	.271	4.13	3.03
Ryan, B.J.	L-L	6-6	260	12-28-75	1	4	2.43	69	0	0	36	70	54	20	19	4	26	100	.208	.211	.206	12.80	3.33
Williams, Todd	R-R	6-3	220	2-13-71	5	5	3.30	72	0	0	1	76	72	34	28	5	26	38	.252	.263	.244	4.48	3.07

FIELDING

Catcher	PCT	G	PO	A	E	DP	PB
Fasano	.987	60	284	26	4	1	6
Gil	.993	62	265	25	2	5	3
Lopez	.994	75	500	26	3	4	4
Whiteside	.926	9	21	4	2	1	0

First Base	PCT	G	PO	A	E	DP
Fasano	.000	1	0	0	0	0
Freire	.991	16	101	5	1	10
Gibbons	.994	22	171	8	1	10
Gomez	.993	42	252	15	2	29
Lopez	1.000	1	1	0	0	1
Palmeiro	.995	93	747	58	4	68
Surhoff	.992	18	116	8	1	14
Young	1.000	10	55	6	0	9

Second Base	PCT	G	PO	A	E	DP
Castro	.941	11	17	31	3	7
Gomez	.986	18	31	40	1	12
Roberts	.988	141	238	413	8	93

Third Base	PCT	G	PO	A	E	DP
Gomez	.971	17	11	23	1	1
Mora	.957	148	96	302	18	23
Newhan	1.000	8	1	3	0	1

Shortstop	PCT	G	PO	A	E	DP
Gomez	.929	10	5	8	1	3
Rogers	.000	1	0	0	0	0
Tejada	.971	160	252	479	22	105

Outfield	PCT	G	PO	A	E	DP
Bigbie	1.000	62	108	3	0	0
Byrnes	.969	51	91	2	3	0
Calzado	1.000	2	2	0	0	0
Castro	.500	1	1	0	1	0
Cummings	.000	1	0	0	0	0
Fiorentino	1.000	12	29	0	0	0
Freire	.000	1	0	0	0	0
Gibbons	.986	71	133	6	2	1
Marrero	.966	16	28	0	1	0
Matos	.984	120	298	7	5	2
Newhan	.990	73	99	1	1	0
Nivar	1.000	4	10	0	0	0
Reed	1.000	6	3	0	0	0
Sosa	.976	66	121	3	3	1
Surhoff	.991	60	109	3	1	0

FARM SYSTEM

General Managers: Jim Beattie, Mike Flanagan. **Director, Minor League Operations:** David Stockstill. **Scouting Director:** Joe Jordan.

Class	Farm Team	League	W	L	Pct.	Finish*	Manager	Affiliate Since
AAA	Ottawa (Ontario) Lynx	International	69	75	.479	t-9th (14)	Dave Trembley	2003
AA	Bowie (Md.) Baysox	Eastern	74	68	.521	4th (12)	Don Werner	1993
High A	Frederick (Md.) Keys	Carolina	79	61	.564	**+1st (8)**	Bien Figueroa	1989
Low A	Delmarva (Md.) Shorebirds	South Atlantic	72	67	.518	**9th (16)**	Gary Kendall	1997
SS A	Aberdeen (Md.) IronBirds	New York-Penn	27	48	.360	14th (14)	Andy Etchebarren	2002
Rookie	Bluefield (W.Va.) Orioles	Appalachian	31	36	.463	5th (10)	Jesus Alfaro	1958

*Finish in overall standings (No. of teams in league)/playoff teams in **boldface** +League Champion

OTTAWA LYNX — Class AAA

INTERNATIONAL LEAGUE

BATTING	B-T	HT	WT	DOB	AVG	vLH	vRH	G	AB	R	H	2B	3B	HR	RBI	BB	HBP	SH	SF	SO	SB	CS	SLG	OBP
Bigbie, Larry	L-R	6-4	210	11-4-77	.294	.250	.308	4	17	3	5	2	0	1	2	0	0	0	0	6	0	0	.588	.294
Calzado, Napoleon	R-R	6-3	200	2-9-77	.306	.296	.310	120	447	54	137	22	1	11	61	21	6	1	3	46	10	6	.434	.344
Castro, Bernie	B-R	5-10	165	7-14-79	.315	.282	.326	126	502	81	158	21	5	1	36	42	0	9	6	50	41	6	.382	.364
Cliffords, Woody	L-R	6-2	194	12-2-80	.190	.143	.214	9	21	3	4	1	1	0	2	6	0	1	0	5	0	0	.333	.370
Cummings, Midre	L-R	6-0	225	10-14-71	.284	.250	.301	74	264	39	75	14	0	12	40	36	4	0	5	69	0	1	.473	.372
Darula, Bobby	L-R	5-10	190	10-29-74	.311	.359	.294	109	402	66	125	25	6	2	40	28	11	2	0	36	17	5	.418	.372
Fasano, Sal	R-R	6-2	245	8-10-71	.267	.200	.286	14	45	6	12	3	0	4	12	2	2	0	0	15	0	0	.600	.327
Freire, Alejandro	R-R	6-2	225	8-23-74	.299	.267	.310	106	391	57	117	24	1	19	69	40	9	0	2	57	1	0	.512	.376
Grimm, Eric	B-R	6-0	185	4-30-81	.200	.333	.000	2	5	0	1	0	0	0	0	1	0	0	0	3	0	0	.200	.333
Hubele, Ryan	R-R	5-11	193	9-9-80	.175	.188	.167	13	40	4	7	1	1	1	8	2	0	1	2	10	0	0	.325	.205
Kingsale, Gene	B-R	6-3	190	8-20-76	.344	.353	.340	20	64	10	22	6	0	0	3	6	2	1	0	7	1	2	.438	.417
Martinez, Octavio	R-R	6-0	190	7-30-79	.233	.267	.221	39	116	8	27	1	2	0	12	5	1	3	0	16	0	1	.276	.270
McCurdy, Josh	R-R	6-6	220	12-28-79	.421	.500	.364	5	19	1	8	0	0	0	7	1	0	0	0	5	1	0	.421	.450
Moriarty, Mike	R-R	6-0	190	3-8-74	.215	.231	.207	69	200	24	43	17	0	4	18	23	6	1	1	51	5	1	.360	.313
2-team (6 Pawtucket)					.210	.227	.201	75	210	25	44	18	0	4	18	23	6	1	1	54	5	1	.352	.304
Newhan, David	L-R	5-10	180	9-7-73	.366	.353	.375	11	41	11	15	4	0	1	8	2	1	0	1	6	2	0	.537	.400
Nivar, Ramon	R-R	5-10	185	2-22-80	.198	.200	.198	33	111	13	22	4	0	1	5	3	2	4	1	10	9	4	.261	.231
Raines, Tim	B-R	5-10	195	8-31-79	.254	.264	.250	122	457	69	116	28	5	6	42	30	2	20	1	116	27	13	.376	.302
Reed, Keith	R-R	6-4	205	10-8-78	.292	.229	.313	80	271	39	79	19	1	8	37	10	1	1	3	55	1	3	.458	.316
Rogers, Ed	R-R	6-1	190	8-29-78	.262	.293	.253	125	431	52	113	21	3	7	48	17	1	5	1	66	14	6	.374	.291
Whiteside, Eli	R-R	6-2	210	10-22-79	.233	.265	.225	95	317	28	74	22	1	4	27	21	2	1	3	65	1	3	.347	.283
Wilken, Kris	B-R	5-11	188	4-11-79	.229	.263	.221	86	192	15	44	8	0	2	18	15	0	1	1	45	0	0	.302	.284
Wilson, Enrique	B-R	5-11	190	7-27-73	.279	.125	.302	20	61	7	17	4	0	3	8	8	0	2	0	5	1	0	.492	.362
Young, Walter	L-R	6-5	320	2-18-80	.288	.225	.307	123	466	48	134	29	1	13	81	30	5	0	5	91	1	1	.438	.334

PITCHING	B-T	HT	WT	DOB	W	L	ERA	G	GS	CG	SV	IP	H	R	ER	HR	BB	SO	AVG	vLH	vRH	K/9	BB/9
Baldwin, James	R-R	6-3	265	7-15-71	3	2	4.60	8	8	0	0	47	52	25	24	6	4	25	.272	.267	.278	4.79	0.77
Bauer, Rick	R-R	6-6	225	1-10-77	3	8	4.00	30	10	0	1	74	84	38	33	12	35	43	.294	.267	.313	5.21	4.24
Borkowski, Dave	R-R	6-1	235	2-7-77	10	10	4.34	29	28	1	0	183	217	99	88	18	38	104	.297	.345	.262	5.12	1.87
Bruback, Matt	R-R	6-5	205	1-12-79	0	6	5.37	9	9	0	0	52	64	36	31	7	14	28	.303	.309	.298	4.85	2.42
Byrdak, Tim	L-L	5-11	190	10-31-73	3	2	2.09	37	0	0	11	39	23	12	9	4	15	44	.170	.163	.174	10.24	3.49
Cahill, Casey	R-R	6-3	197	3-15-82	0	0	18.00	1	0	0	0	2	4	4	4	2	2	1	.400	.000	.667	4.50	9.00
DuBose, Eric	L-L	6-3	235	5-15-76	0	1	11.42	2	2	0	0	9	17	13	11	5	1	7	.395	.429	.389	7.27	1.04
Estrada, Horacio	L-L	6-0	160	10-19-75	2	2	7.56	5	4	0	0	17	23	14	14	2	4	5	.343	.316	.354	2.70	2.16
Fiore, Tony	R-R	6-4	230	10-12-71	9	5	3.63	30	28	0	0	166	168	79	67	14	49	97	.264	.246	.276	5.25	2.65
Maine, John	R-R	6-4	205	5-8-81	6	11	4.56	23	23	1	0	128	128	72	65	13	42	111	.257	.247	.266	7.78	2.95
McNichol, Brian	L-L	6-5	225	5-20-74	6	7	4.32	36	9	0	0	83	90	41	40	9	28	49	.279	.315	.264	5.29	3.02
Mitchell, Andy	R-R	6-3	206	9-10-78	8	0	4.87	47	0	0	0	78	83	47	42	6	31	38	.272	.315	.249	4.40	3.59
Ormond, Rodney	R-R	6-4	213	6-17-77	4	1	3.63	40	1	0	0	69	56	31	28	7	32	53	.229	.277	.194	6.88	4.15
Oropesa, Eddie	L-L	6-0	205	11-23-71	0	0	0.00	5	0	0	0	6	3	0	0	0	2	5	.150	.125	.167	7.50	3.00
Piersoll, Chris	R-R	6-4	215	9-25-77	1	0	3.46	9	0	0	1	13	8	6	5	2	3	11	.182	.111	.231	7.62	2.08
Rakers, Aaron	R-R	6-3	220	1-22-77	6	5	2.57	57	0	0	7	77	69	26	22	9	21	92	.235	.202	.257	10.75	2.45
Rodriguez, Eddy	R-R	6-1	215	8-8-81	2	3	3.77	50	0	0	3	62	57	30	26	2	36	51	.248	.233	.257	7.40	5.23
Sedlacek, Shawn	R-R	6-4	210	6-29-77	0	2	11.00	2	2	0	0	9	13	11	11	1	4	8	.325	.350	.300	8.00	4.00
Sequea, Jacobo	R-R	6-1	220	8-31-81	0	1	7.58	18	0	0	5	19	27	18	16	1	10	7	.338	.289	.381	3.32	4.74
Smith, Chuck	R-R	6-1	180	10-21-69	2	7	5.37	11	11	1	0	67	72	41	40	6	27	46	.279	.299	.262	6.18	3.63
Stephens, John	R-R	6-1	215	11-15-79	4	2	4.41	12	9	0	0	51	52	25	25	6	8	41	.268	.244	.288	7.24	1.41
3-team (1 Pawtucket, 10 Charlotte)					4	5	4.48	23	13	0	0	84	92	45	42	9	17	59	.281	.248	.309	6.30	1.81

FIELDING

Catcher	PCT	G	PO	A	E	DP	PB
Calzado	1.000	1	7	0	0	0	0
Fasano	.984	12	54	9	1	3	0
Hubele	.986	13	66	6	1	2	2
Martinez	1.000	38	226	23	0	1	2
Whiteside	.993	91	544	40	4	4	9

First Base	PCT	G	PO	A	E	DP
Calzado	1.000	2	0	1	0	0
Fasano	1.000	1	8	0	0	2
Freire	.988	63	543	50	7	48
Martinez	1.000	1	1	1	0	0
Wilken	.986	49	207	10	3	27
Young	.981	63	478	43	10	48

Second Base	PCT	G	PO	A	E	DP
Castro	.972	120	238	357	17	72
Moriarty	1.000	2	1	1	0	1
Nivar	.750	1	1	2	1	0
Rogers	.979	25	63	74	3	26
Wilson	1.000	1	1	1	0	1

Third Base	PCT	G	PO	A	E	DP
Calzado	.953	91	66	178	12	22
Grimm	1.000	2	0	3	0	1
Rogers	.929	31	13	52	5	6
Whiteside	.000	1	0	0	0	0
Wilken	.961	31	13	60	3	5

Shortstop	PCT	G	PO	A	E	DP
Moriarty	.964	65	95	174	10	35
Rogers	.970	67	98	195	9	39
Wilson	.959	18	15	56	3	12

Outfield	PCT	G	PO	A	E	DP
Bigbie	.000	2	0	0	0	0
Calzado	.953	34	60	1	3	1
Cliffords	1.000	9	16	0	0	0
Cummings	.981	51	101	3	2	0
Darula	.994	97	154	4	1	0
Kingsale	.926	19	24	1	2	0
McCurdy	1.000	5	6	0	0	0
Newhan	1.000	11	21	0	0	0

Catcher	PCT	G	PO	A	E	DP
Nivar	.968	31	83	8	3	2
Raines	.990	119	277	6	3	1

	PCT	G	PO	A	E	DP
Reed	.983	76	164	5	3	0
Rogers	.000	1	0	0	0	0

	PCT	G	PO	A	E	DP
Wilken	1.000	6	8	1	0	0

BOWIE BAYSOX — Class AA

EASTERN LEAGUE

BATTING	B-T	HT	WT	DOB	AVG	vLH	vRH	G	AB	R	H	2B	3B	HR	RBI	BB	HBP	SH	SF	SO	SB	CS	SLG	OBP
Alvarez, Gerardo	R-R	5-10	185	10-31-79	.261	.333	.235	7	23	4	6	2	0	0	1	1	1	0	0	5	0	1	.348	.320
Bergeron, Peter	L-R	6-0	205	11-9-77	.296	.216	.323	91	348	54	103	14	2	5	33	34	1	14	4	82	13	6	.391	.357
Cates, Gary	R-R	5-7	155	7-3-81	.226	.276	.203	30	93	13	21	5	0	0	9	10	0	0	2	11	5	2	.280	.295
Clendenin, Morgan	L-R	6-0	187	10-2-81	.247	.000	.276	44	150	19	37	8	0	7	16	2	2	0	0	49	0	0	.440	.266
Cliffords, Woody	L-R	6-2	194	12-2-80	.241	.250	.239	93	315	36	76	19	1	1	31	51	1	8	4	68	8	7	.317	.345
Fahey, Brandon	L-R	6-2	160	1-18-81	.291	.268	.299	139	502	63	146	21	4	3	47	44	4	22	6	71	17	8	.367	.349
Freire, Alejandro	R-R	6-2	225	8-23-74	.385	.333	.429	3	13	0	5	0	0	0	2	0	0	0	1	1	0	0	.385	.357
Gil, Geronimo	R-R	6-2	230	8-7-75	.429	.667	.250	3	7	2	3	0	0	0	1	1	1	0	0	1	0	0	.429	.556
Hammond, Joey	R-R	6-1	186	10-27-77	.278	.274	.280	115	424	53	118	18	3	9	49	37	1	1	5	78	5	2	.399	.334
Herrera, Jose	L-L	6-0	165	8-30-72	.250	.000	.267	5	16	0	4	1	0	0	1	0	0	0	1	3	0	0	.313	.235
Hubele, Ryan	R-R	5-11	193	9-9-80	.304	.395	.220	24	79	13	24	2	0	5	8	8	4	1	0	19	2	1	.519	.396
Huggins, Michael	R-R	6-3	219	8-29-80	.212	.230	.204	118	397	34	84	15	2	4	35	43	3	0	4	101	0	1	.290	.291
Inglin, Jeff	R-R	5-11	180	10-8-75	.195	.286	.167	43	149	18	29	7	0	2	19	24	3	0	4	25	1	2	.282	.311
Johnson, Tripper	R-R	6-1	199	4-28-82	.249	.286	.235	134	507	62	126	29	4	11	59	41	5	1	4	108	7	5	.387	.309
Keylor, Cory	L-R	6-3	216	8-25-79	.213	.150	.221	48	160	17	34	6	0	4	17	17	1	0	0	38	0	0	.325	.292
Kingsale, Gene	B-R	6-3	190	8-20-76	.229	.327	.190	51	175	21	40	7	3	1	15	20	3	3	1	31	4	2	.320	.317
Lopez, Javy	R-R	6-3	230	11-5-70	.400	.286	.500	4	15	1	6	1	0	0	3	0	0	0	1	3	0	0	.467	.375
Markakis, Nick	L-L	6-1	175	11-17-83	.339	.295	.363	33	124	19	42	16	2	3	30	18	0	0	1	30	0	1	.573	.420
Marsters, Brandon	R-R	5-11	220	3-14-75	.214	.291	.184	111	364	43	78	18	0	5	22	21	6	1	1	73	3	1	.305	.268
Martinez, Octavio	R-R	6-0	190	7-30-79	.354	.636	.270	14	48	8	17	5	1	1	9	2	3	0	0	4	0	2	.563	.415
Matos, Luis	R-R	6-0	210	10-30-78	.250	.250	.250	5	20	4	5	0	0	1	2	1	1	0	0	4	1	1	.400	.318
Nivar, Ramon	R-R	5-10	185	2-22-80	.247	.270	.230	41	150	22	37	7	0	1	12	12	2	2	0	21	11	6	.313	.311
Pond, Simon	L-R	6-1	190	10-27-76	.266	.239	.276	110	406	50	108	25	1	19	75	43	4	0	1	114	8	3	.473	.341
Rogers, Omar	R-R	6-1	186	10-12-79	.205	.188	.214	67	239	23	49	14	0	3	31	20	3	7	0	28	1	1	.301	.275

PITCHING	B-T	HT	WT	DOB	W	L	ERA	G	GS	CG	SV	IP	H	R	ER	HR	BB	SO	AVG	vLH	vRH	K/9	BB/9
Bailie, Matthew	R-R	5-10	195	10-1-75	2	3	5.40	6	5	1	0	28	26	17	17	5	10	18	.239	.123	.409	5.72	3.18
Bedard, Erik	L-L	6-1	195	3-5-75	0	1	9.00	1	1	0	0	2	2	2	2	0	1	4	.250	.500	.167	18.00	4.50
Birkins, Kurt	L-L	6-2	185	8-10-76	7	11	3.91	26	24	0	0	129	134	69	56	8	42	114	.270	.267	.270	7.95	2.93
Bruback, Matt	R-R	6-5	205	1-12-79	5	2	4.14	22	10	0	0	83	79	44	38	9	20	71	.253	.235	.267	7.73	2.18
Cabrera, Daniel	R-R	6-7	250	5-28-81	1	0	3.00	1	1	0	0	6	8	3	2	1	2	7	.320	.313	.333	10.50	3.00
DuBose, Eric	L-L	6-3	235	5-15-76	8	10	3.25	21	20	0	0	122	113	52	44	10	29	114	.247	.189	.265	8.41	2.14
Forystek, Brian	L-L	6-1	180	10-30-78	2	5	4.22	14	14	0	0	70	81	42	33	9	23	66	.297	.309	.294	8.45	2.94
Grimsley, Jason	R-R	6-3	205	8-7-67	2	0	1.13	8	2	0	0	8	4	1	1	0	4	4	.143	.250	.063	4.50	4.50
Hammond, Joey	R-R	6-1	186	10-27-77	0	0	11.57	3	0	0	0	2	6	3	3	1	0	1	.462	.600	.375	3.86	0.00
Hundley, Jeff	L-L	6-1	205	2-19-77	0	0	7.85	11	0	0	0	18	29	19	16	3	9	15	.363	.217	.421	7.36	4.42
Johnson, J.J.	R-R	6-5	232	6-27-83	0	0	0.00	1	1	0	0	7	3	0	0	0	2	6	.136	.143	.133	7.71	2.57
Keefer, Ryan	L-R	6-3	197	8-10-81	7	3	3.20	54	1	0	1	84	64	33	30	7	32	92	.211	.234	.194	9.82	3.42
Manning, David	R-R	6-3	227	8-14-72	1	1	12.71	8	0	0	0	6	8	8	8	0	6	4	.333	.250	.375	6.35	9.53
McCurdy, Nick	R-R	6-3	185	1-24-80	5	5	4.22	30	2	0	2	64	70	37	30	10	15	48	.277	.243	.303	6.75	2.11
Morris, Cory	R-R	6-2	189	12-7-79	8	5	3.03	29	25	0	0	143	116	50	48	11	78	159	.226	.221	.230	10.03	4.92
Parrish, John	L-L	5-11	200	11-26-77	0	0	2.89	5	0	0	0	9	7	3	3	0	6	13	.212	.143	.231	12.54	5.79
Pearson, Jason	L-L	6-0	190	12-29-75	0	0	1.59	5	0	0	0	6	3	1	1	1	1	7	.167	.333	.083	11.12	1.59
2-team (14 Portland)					1	1	4.15	19	0	0	0	22	24	11	10	3	9	24	.286	.300	.273	9.97	3.74
Penn, Hayden	R-R	6-3	195	10-13-84	7	6	3.83	20	19	1	0	110	101	51	47	11	37	120	.248	.211	.286	9.79	3.02
Piersoll, Chris	R-R	6-4	215	9-25-77	5	1	1.61	27	0	0	1	50	29	12	9	3	13	63	.163	.209	.135	11.26	2.32
Ray, Chris	R-R	6-3	200	1-12-82	1	2	0.96	31	0	0	18	37	17	5	4	3	7	40	.140	.121	.159	9.64	1.69
Rice, Scott	L-L	6-6	220	9-21-81	4	1	3.27	57	0	0	1	74	68	29	27	4	32	42	.253	.219	.263	5.09	3.87
Rleal, Sendy	R-R	5-10	172	6-21-80	4	4	2.04	56	0	0	16	71	46	19	16	4	18	75	.187	.209	.168	9.55	2.29
Stahl, Richard	R-L	6-7	220	4-11-81	3	6	4.04	18	17	0	0	89	83	46	40	5	58	52	.250	.228	.257	5.26	5.87
Torres, Melqui	R-R	6-2	205	5-27-77	2	2	5.28	25	0	0	0	29	31	18	17	7	18	33	.284	.288	.281	10.24	5.59

FIELDING

Catcher	PCT	G	PO	A	E	DP	PB
Clendenin	.992	20	119	5	1	1	2
Gil	1.000	3	18	2	0	1	1
Hubele	1.000	14	107	9	0	1	2
Lopez	1.000	2	14	0	0	0	0
Marsters	.991	107	865	83	9	5	7
Martinez	.988	10	68	12	1	1	1

First Base	PCT	G	PO	A	E	DP
Freire	1.000	1	7	1	0	0
Hammond	.875	2	13	1	2	0
Huggins	.992	115	950	77	8	82
Martinez	1.000	1	7	0	0	1
Pond	.996	30	236	16	1	22

Second Base	PCT	G	PO	A	E	DP
Alvarez	.947	4	6	12	1	2
Cates	.957	20	29	38	3	7
Hammond	.987	76	113	202	4	53
Rogers	.979	49	78	105	4	26

Third Base	PCT	G	PO	A	E	DP
Alvarez	.800	3	3	5	2	0
Hammond	.950	17	7	31	2	2
Johnson	.952	124	89	231	16	17

Shortstop	PCT	G	PO	A	E	DP
Fahey	.962	139	221	413	25	84
Hammond	1.000	4	5	9	0	2

Outfield	PCT	G	PO	A	E	DP
Bergeron	.982	89	158	9	3	0
Cliffords	.962	86	121	6	5	0
Hammond	1.000	7	8	0	0	0
Herrera	1.000	3	7	0	0	0
Inglin	.950	36	52	5	3	0
Keylor	.935	30	43	0	3	0
Kingsale	.944	50	97	4	6	0
Markakis	1.000	33	66	0	0	0
Matos	1.000	3	9	1	0	1
Nivar	.941	40	74	6	5	1
Pond	.976	62	78	5	2	0

FREDERICK KEYS — High Class A

CAROLINA LEAGUE

BATTING	B-T	HT	WT	DOB	AVG	vLH	vRH	G	AB	R	H	2B	3B	HR	RBI	BB	HBP	SH	SF	SO	SB	CS	SLG	OBP
Alvarez, Gera	R-R	5-10	185	10-31-79	.256	.250	.261	70	227	39	58	16	0	6	34	26	6	11	1	45	2	6	.405	.346
Arko, Tommy	R-R	6-2	207	7-28-82	.143	.120	.158	19	63	5	9	4	0	3	5	5	0	0	0	25	1	0	.349	.206
Bass, Bryan	B-R	6-1	190	4-12-82	.241	.273	.226	117	352	59	85	22	0	12	51	41	6	8	2	135	11	4	.406	.329
Bock, Brian	R-R	6-1	210	8-24-81	.254	.283	.230	37	134	16	34	5	0	3	26	5	1	2	0	19	1	0	.358	.286
Brown, Travis	R-R	5-11	180	8-1-80	.253	.272	.237	118	392	41	99	11	1	3	40	29	7	13	5	63	3	5	.309	.312
Delgado, Mario	L-L	6-0	220	8-5-79	.306	.303	.308	119	435	53	133	27	1	26	86	31	7	0	0	80	1	0	.552	.362

BATTING	B-T	HT	WT	DOB	AVG	vLH	vRH	G	AB	R	H	2B	3B	HR	RBI	BB	HBP	SH	SF	SO	SB	CS	SLG	OBP
Fiorentino, Jeff	L-R	6-1	190	4-14-83	.286	.256	.314	103	413	70	118	18	4	22	66	34	4	4	0	90	12	6	.508	.346
Florence, Branden	R-R	6-2	230	10-29-80	.325	.318	.331	78	283	50	92	18	2	16	51	16	11	0	3	29	0	0	.572	.380
Grimm, Eric	B-R	6-0	185	4-30-81	.216	.125	.241	11	37	3	8	2	0	1	2	3	1	1	0	10	0	0	.351	.293
Hubele, Ryan	R-R	5-11	193	9-9-80	.282	.222	.312	53	195	25	55	16	0	4	29	7	5	4	2	37	1	0	.426	.321
Markakis, Nick	L-L	6-1	175	11-17-83	.300	.372	.264	91	350	59	105	25	1	12	62	43	4	0	4	65	2	1	.480	.379
McCurdy, Josh	R-R	6-6	220	12-28-79	.238	.207	.258	63	210	27	50	9	2	2	23	18	4	1	2	41	10	4	.329	.308
Reimold, Nolan	R-R	6-4	207	10-12-83	.265	.323	.231	23	83	17	22	6	0	6	11	12	2	0	0	27	3	0	.554	.371
Rine, Jarod	L-R	6-1	190	11-14-81	.209	.199	.211	115	369	53	77	11	3	3	23	36	6	6	1	89	21	7	.279	.289
Russell, Michael	R-R	6-0	197	8-14-81	.236	.238	.235	75	229	38	54	14	0	10	37	31	6	2	0	82	1	0	.428	.342
Scalabrini, Pat	R-R	6-1	215	3-7-77	.245	.229	.259	45	151	25	37	8	0	3	19	12	2	2	1	33	1	0	.358	.307
Spears, Nate	L-R	5-11	165	5-3-85	.294	.281	.304	112	445	63	131	30	6	6	41	36	2	14	1	82	8	4	.429	.349
Wargo, Cody	R-R	6-3	210	12-13-81	.000	.000	.000	4	4	0	0	0	0	0	0	0	0	0	0	2	0	0	.000	.000
Yount, Dustin	L-R	6-1	198	10-27-82	.258	.268	.258	110	368	57	95	16	1	12	52	60	8	4	2	102	4	2	.405	.372

PITCHING	B-T	HT	WT	DOB	W	L	ERA	G	GS	CG	SV	IP	H	R	ER	HR	BB	SO	AVG	vLH	vRH	K/9	BB/9
Baysinger, Trent	L-L	6-0	185	9-1-81	0	1	18.00	5	0	0	0	5	13	10	10	1	2	6	.464	.400	.500	10.80	3.60
Britton, Chris	R-R	6-3	250	12-16-82	6	0	1.60	46	0	0	6	79	47	15	14	5	23	110	.172	.175	.171	12.58	2.63
Caughey, Trevor	L-L	6-1	172	11-23-82	5	1	6.31	33	1	0	1	51	61	39	36	6	16	47	.290	.308	.281	8.24	2.81
Deza, Fredy	R-R	6-2	170	12-11-82	5	8	6.12	28	18	0	0	104	134	75	71	13	36	64	.311	.366	.274	5.52	3.11
Dixon, Zach	L-L	6-2	195	11-2-80	1	7	6.13	14	9	0	0	54	61	43	37	8	27	38	.280	.295	.298	6.29	4.47
Finch, Brian	R-R	6-4	195	9-27-81	10	10	3.38	27	27	1	0	154	157	72	58	13	60	124	.265	.243	.286	7.23	3.50
Haehnel, David	L-L	6-4	200	7-21-82	3	1	3.41	23	0	0	2	34	27	15	13	1	10	37	.218	.261	.192	9.70	2.62
Hale, Beau	R-R	6-2	202	12-1-78	1	2	5.23	22	5	0	0	53	51	34	31	7	23	48	.256	.291	.230	8.10	3.88
Jan, Carlos	L-L	5-11	165	11-3-79	5	2	3.78	16	11	0	0	67	53	33	28	8	45	61	.224	.235	.223	8.24	6.08
Johnson, J.J.	R-R	6-5	232	6-27-83	12	9	3.49	28	27	2	1	160	139	77	62	11	64	168	.231	.253	.214	9.47	3.61
Loewen, Adam	L-L	6-5	215	4-9-84	10	8	4.12	28	27	1	0	142	130	77	65	8	86	146	.245	.203	.257	9.25	5.45
McCurdy, Nick	R-R	6-3	185	1-24-80	2	0	6.91	12	1	0	1	29	36	23	22	5	8	26	.305	.333	.289	8.16	2.51
Montani, Jeff	R-R	5-11	174	11-22-80	1	2	7.59	31	1	0	0	51	70	49	43	10	27	40	.329	.345	.317	7.06	4.76
Neal, Tony	R-R	6-2	210	9-12-80	3	6	4.85	20	0	0	8	26	29	17	14	5	10	29	.271	.323	.250	10.04	3.46
Olson, Garrett	R-L	6-1	200	10-18-83	0	0	3.14	3	3	0	0	14	10	5	5	0	7	19	.192	.235	.171	11.93	4.40
Piersoll, Chris	R-R	6-4	215	9-25-77	5	0	3.41	17	0	0	1	29	22	12	11	3	10	34	.210	.281	.178	10.55	3.10
Salas, Marino	R-R	6-0	175	2-2-81	4	2	3.63	50	0	0	16	62	54	32	25	7	28	63	.233	.299	.185	9.15	4.06
Salazar, Richard	L-L	5-11	191	10-6-81	2	1	4.47	23	1	0	0	44	44	22	22	5	27	40	.268	.260	.272	8.12	5.48
Stahl, Richard	R-L	6-7	220	4-11-81	4	1	2.77	9	9	0	0	52	48	19	16	3	26	43	.249	.200	.258	7.44	4.50
Tiller, James	R-R	6-5	210	4-13-83	0	0	12.91	5	0	0	0	8	8	11	11	1	7	2	.267	.167	.292	2.35	8.22
Torres, Melqui	R-R	6-2	205	5-27-77	0	0	2.25	3	0	0	1	4	4	1	1	1	2	8	.250	.000	.250	18.00	4.50

FIELDING

Catcher	PCT	G	PO	A	E	DP	PB
Arko	.986	16	129	7	2	1	5
Bock	.988	37	307	25	4	5	5
Delgado	1.000	1	1	0	0	0	0
Hubele	.996	30	245	16	1	4	4
Russell	.992	64	491	33	4	2	14
Wargo	1.000	1	3	0	0	0	0

First Base	PCT	G	PO	A	E	DP
Alvarez	.000	1	0	0	0	0
Delgado	.979	45	346	26	8	31
Hubele	1.000	1	1	0	0	0
Scalabrini	1.000	4	30	3	0	3
Yount	.991	95	784	29	7	80

Second Base	PCT	G	PO	A	E	DP
Alvarez	.990	25	40	61	1	16
Grimm	.933	7	12	16	2	4
Scalabrini	.920	7	6	17	2	2
Spears	.981	105	195	308	10	79

Third Base	PCT	G	PO	A	E	DP
Alvarez	.963	17	6	20	1	1
Bass	.906	106	70	171	25	14
Grimm	1.000	1	0	2	0	0
Hubele	.889	3	4	4	1	0
Scalabrini	.925	18	14	35	4	5

Shortstop	PCT	G	PO	A	E	DP
Alvarez	.963	25	30	75	4	19
Brown	.966	115	189	348	19	78
Spears	.842	6	3	13	3	1

Outfield	PCT	G	PO	A	E	DP
Delgado	.917	14	10	1	1	0
Fiorentino	.968	102	174	8	6	1
Florence	.963	21	26	0	1	0
Hubele	.941	13	15	1	1	0
Markakis	.971	88	165	2	5	0
McCurdy	.979	58	91	3	2	0
Reimold	.955	23	41	1	2	0
Rine	.985	108	191	7	3	0
Scalabrini	1.000	10	13	2	0	0

DELMARVA SHOREBIRDS — Low Class A

SOUTH ATLANTIC LEAGUE

BATTING	B-T	HT	WT	DOB	AVG	vLH	vRH	G	AB	R	H	2B	3B	HR	RBI	BB	HBP	SH	SF	SO	SB	CS	SLG	OBP
Ascencion, Quincy	R-R	6-0	212	11-1-82	.254	.266	.250	126	441	59	112	21	4	3	44	31	13	15	1	75	16	12	.340	.321
Bock, Brian	R-R	6-1	210	8-24-81	.258	.229	.270	33	124	4	32	7	0	0	15	8	1	1	3	23	2	0	.315	.301
Cates, Gary	R-R	5-7	155	7-3-81	.280	.289	.276	75	300	51	84	16	1	2	30	25	4	7	2	37	12	5	.360	.341
Delacruz, Miguel	R-R	6-2	180	10-18-79	.267	.158	.304	23	75	10	20	1	2	2	7	9	2	0	0	17	0	0	.413	.360
Diaz, Rafael	R-R	6-0	202	6-13-81	.185	.189	.183	55	173	8	32	7	0	0	13	5	1	3	0	30	1	0	.225	.212
Duncan, Jacob	L-L	5-11	190	11-20-81	.296	.211	.314	110	402	73	119	20	6	5	39	49	3	8	0	66	11	6	.413	.377
Figueroa, Francisco	R-R	5-11	182	2-19-83	.307	.375	.282	40	150	30	46	7	2	0	12	24	5	2	0	25	6	3	.380	.419
Finan, Ryan	L-R	6-5	220	1-5-82	.195	.300	.161	10	41	3	8	2	0	1	9	1	0	0	1	17	0	0	.317	.209
Fransz, Jason	R-R	6-3	212	2-5-81	.308	.279	.316	103	396	70	122	33	1	22	111	31	13	0	6	77	4	1	.563	.372
Grimm, Eric	B-R	6-0	185	4-30-81	.190	.179	.195	38	116	18	22	4	0	1	11	19	0	2	1	27	2	3	.250	.301
Guerrero, Francisco	R-R	6-0	177	5-5-83	.190	.306	.154	48	153	14	29	6	1	0	12	11	2	3	0	19	2	2	.242	.253
Gutierrez, Juan	B-R	6-0	195	8-1-81	.264	.192	.272	84	254	36	67	13	2	4	35	46	1	2	2	49	1	1	.378	.376
Houston, Matt	R-R	5-11	195	2-1-82	.290	.254	.303	77	252	29	73	10	0	3	26	27	7	6	0	31	0	0	.365	.374
Kitch, Denver	R-R	6-2	185	11-25-80	.189	.321	.154	35	132	13	25	3	0	2	17	5	0	2	0	45	2	3	.258	.219
Maestrales, Pete	B-R	5-11	190	7-4-79	.303	.372	.283	52	195	48	59	14	3	8	16	39	3	1	0	35	6	4	.528	.426
Marconi, Rob	R-R	6-1	200	9-14-82	.181	.100	.206	38	127	15	23	5	0	2	9	9	1	4	2	34	2	0	.268	.237
McCurdy, Josh	R-R	6-6	220	12-28-79	.298	.276	.307	29	104	13	31	5	0	2	15	8	0	1	0	16	6	1	.404	.348
Moffitt, Drew	R-R	6-1	215	8-19-81	.216	.316	.188	31	88	13	19	5	0	3	14	27	2	0	0	28	4	1	.375	.410
Puente, Dan	R-R	6-3	200	12-3-81	.091	.000	.125	9	22	1	2	0	0	0	2	2	0	2	0	10	0	0	.091	.167
Rivas, Arturo	R-R	6-0	205	2-2-84	.251	.206	.265	125	434	78	109	29	8	9	62	61	12	5	6	94	11	5	.417	.355
Scalabrini, Pat	R-R	6-1	215	3-7-77	.260	.241	.266	62	235	29	61	13	0	7	37	15	6	1	3	52	5	2	.404	.317
Shier, Peter	R-R	6-2	176	3-16-81	.260	.242	.265	37	150	18	39	5	1	2	13	14	2	0	1	28	6	3	.347	.329
Smith, C.J.	R-R	6-3	210	2-22-82	.227	.250	.219	83	295	34	67	18	1	6	45	37	2	0	3	65	0	0	.356	.315
Zapata, Jose	R-R	6-3	184	4-4-84	.171	.100	.194	14	41	4	7	1	1	1	9	1	1	3	1	11	1	1	.317	.205

PITCHING	B-T	HT	WT	DOB	W	L	ERA	G	GS	CG	SV	IP	H	R	ER	HR	BB	SO	AVG	vLH	vRH	K/9	BB/9
Baysinger, Trent	L-L	6-0	185	9-1-81	2	0	3.25	29	0	0	3	36	41	16	13	1	5	25	.283	.357	.265	6.25	1.25
Bedard, Erik	L-L	6-1	195	3-6-79	1	0	0.00	1	1	0	0	5	3	0	0	0	1	9	.176	1.000	.125	16.20	1.80
Cahill, Casey	R-R	6-3	197	3-15-82	6	7	3.42	53	0	0	5	84	78	39	32	7	30	75	.242	.292	.218	8.00	3.20
Coppinger, Joe	R-R	6-3	230	7-23-82	2	3	5.47	14	9	0	1	51	64	37	31	7	18	25	.305	.344	.289	4.41	3.18
Forbes, Derek	B-R	6-1	185	9-11-78	0	0	2.41	16	0	0	1	19	13	5	5	3	13	18	.194	.115	.244	8.68	6.27
Gutierrez, Juan	B-R	6-0	195	8-1-81	0	0	.000	0	0	0	0	0	0	1	1	0	1	0	.000	.000	.000	.000	.000
Haehnel, David	L-L	6-4	200	7-21-82	1	1	0.79	28	0	0	16	34	20	3	3	1	10	34	.171	.222	.156	9.00	2.65
Hart, Kevin	R-R	6-4	215	11-29-82	9	8	4.55	28	28	0	0	152	170	101	77	9	54	164	.278	.331	.242	9.69	3.19
Henington, Justin	R-R	6-3	210	2-24-82	3	2	2.31	33	0	0	16	35	34	15	9	1	7	31	.248	.256	.245	7.97	1.80
Henry, Paul	R-R	6-3	190	6-27-81	4	1	3.34	28	0	0	0	35	30	14	13	1	18	28	.236	.283	.210	7.20	4.63
Jan, Carlos	L-L	5-11	165	11-3-79	1	2	4.37	28	0	0	1	47	36	27	23	2	30	55	.203	.191	.208	10.46	5.70
Liz, Radhames	R-R	6-2	170	6-10-79	2	3	4.46	10	10	0	0	38	33	23	19	2	23	55	.231	.220	.238	12.91	5.40
Maestrales, Pete	B-R	5-11	190	7-4-79	0	0	0.00	1	0	0	0	1	0	0	0	0	0	1	.000	.000	.000	9.00	0.00
Owen, Blake	R-R	6-3	215	10-29-83	1	1	8.44	5	0	0	0	5	4	5	5	0	3	6	.200	.000	.308	10.13	5.06
Perez, Carlos	L-L	6-1	189	5-20-82	11	8	4.28	27	27	0	0	151	168	84	72	10	61	146	.281	.257	.285	8.68	3.63
Petrick, Russ	L-L	6-1	185	2-12-83	6	3	3.98	47	2	0	1	75	89	41	33	1	30	58	.294	.217	.316	6.99	3.62
Potter, Josh	R-R	6-4	175	4-8-83	4	3	4.63	42	5	0	1	84	102	54	43	5	25	67	.297	.325	.282	7.21	2.69
Ramirez, Luis	R-R	6-4	202	6-9-82	9	7	2.55	28	27	1	0	162	131	53	46	7	54	155	.220	.246	.204	8.59	2.99
Robinson, Dennis	R-R	6-3	205	7-29-82	5	10	6.04	25	22	0	0	110	161	95	74	11	30	56	.335	.376	.306	4.57	2.45
Salazar, Richard	L-L	5-11	191	10-6-81	1	0	9.00	3	0	0	0	4	2	6	4	1	5	5	.143	.333	.091	11.25	11.25
Schmidt, Kyle	R-R	6-3	220	8-25-83	0	1	4.50	1	0	0	0	2	2	1	1	0	0	1	.286	.250	.333	4.50	0.00
Schwabe, Ryan	L-L	6-3	210	2-24-82	0	1	5.40	3	0	0	0	8	14	9	5	0	3	7	.359	.222	.400	7.56	3.24
Smith, Chris	L-L	5-11	222	12-10-79	1	1	8.54	13	0	0	0	26	46	26	25	3	15	23	.380	.344	.393	7.86	5.13
Spillers, Larry	R-R	6-3	216	3-12-82	1	0	4.76	12	0	0	0	17	23	12	9	0	9	6	.311	.281	.333	3.18	4.76
Tiller, James	R-R	6-5	210	4-13-83	2	5	6.02	11	8	0	1	49	58	44	33	3	23	36	.291	.283	.299	6.57	4.20

FIELDING

Catcher	PCT	G	PO	A	E	DP	PB
Bock	.993	32	269	26	2	3	5
Gutierrez	.988	30	216	23	3	1	7
Houston	.970	76	554	37	18	7	13
Puente	.984	7	54	7	1	0	0

First Base	PCT	G	PO	A	E	DP
Delacruz	1.000	1	6	0	0	1
Finan	1.000	7	50	1	0	7
Fransz	.971	14	95	6	3	8
Gutierrez	.966	15	111	4	4	11
Scalabrini	.992	31	240	16	2	25
Smith	.980	76	605	45	13	48

Second Base	PCT	G	PO	A	E	DP
Cates	.961	30	63	85	6	23
Diaz	.955	4	4	17	1	2
Figueroa	.972	30	52	88	4	12
Grimm	.949	24	27	48	4	8
Guerrero	.958	27	53	60	5	8
Maestrales	.889	19	31	41	9	7
Marconi	.970	7	17	15	1	6
Zapata	1.000	7	11	17	0	5

Third Base	PCT	G	PO	A	E	DP
Cates	.921	18	13	22	3	2
Delacruz	.690	10	3	17	9	0
Diaz	.836	28	15	31	9	7
Grimm	.789	8	3	12	4	3
Gutierrez	.837	17	4	32	7	2
Maestrales	.952	9	5	15	1	1
Marconi	.904	29	23	62	9	6
Scalabrini	.938	32	20	70	6	3
Zapata	1.000	2	1	0	0	0

Shortstop	PCT	G	PO	A	E	DP
Cates	.991	27	39	69	1	12
Kitch	.913	35	66	92	15	21
Shier	.937	37	67	110	12	24
Guerrero	.925	20	15	34	4	6
Diaz	.895	22	28	74	12	12
Zapata	.688	4	5	6	5	1

Outfield	PCT	G	PO	A	E	DP
Ascencion	.989	121	252	9	3	0
Cates	.000	1	0	0	0	0
Delacruz	.500	3	1	0	1	0
Duncan	.983	100	158	11	3	0
Figueroa	1.000	12	19	0	0	0
Fransz	.920	11	22	1	2	0
Maestrales	1.000	14	23	3	0	1
McCurdy	.979	26	45	1	1	0
Moffitt	.980	22	47	2	1	1
Rivas	.966	124	297	17	11	7

ABERDEEN IRONBIRDS — Short-Season Class A

NEW YORK-PENN LEAGUE

BATTING	B-T	HT	WT	DOB	AVG	vLH	vRH	G	AB	R	H	2B	3B	HR	RBI	BB	HBP	SH	SF	SO	SB	CS	SLG	OBP
Andrews, Bobby	R-R	6-0	200	12-23-83	.227	.241	.223	35	141	18	32	7	1	0	12	19	2	2	0	39	8	2	.291	.327
Avila, Angel	R-R	6-1	170	6-26-84	.159	.125	.170	19	63	4	10	1	0	0	1	0	2	1	0	22	1	2	.175	.185
Dahlberg, Kyle	R-R	6-3	211	4-9-83	.174	.222	.164	54	149	11	26	6	0	3	9	15	2	3	1	62	1	1	.275	.257
Davis, Zachary	L-L	6-0	173	2-20-84	.258	.250	.261	47	178	21	46	11	2	1	25	22	0	1	3	53	3	5	.360	.335
Finan, Ryan	L-R	6-5	220	1-5-82	.258	.243	.261	60	213	21	55	15	0	2	33	25	1	0	5	41	0	1	.357	.332
Fleisher, Mark	R-R	6-4	235	9-18-83	.277	.292	.273	61	231	34	64	12	0	7	32	25	6	0	5	55	0	2	.420	.356
Guerrero, Francisco	R-R	6-0	177	5-5-83	.277	.269	.279	35	112	8	31	5	0	0	11	4	1	4	1	22	6	1	.321	.305
Marconi, Rob	R-R	6-1	200	9-14-82	.302	.324	.298	60	205	34	62	14	4	3	17	22	3	3	1	38	5	1	.454	.377
Maxey, Jason	L-R	5-11	215	3-31-83	.256	.125	.268	36	90	9	23	8	0	1	16	11	0	0	2	22	0	0	.378	.330
Michalski, Joe	R-R	6-4	225	10-26-83	.163	.250	.135	23	49	1	8	1	0	0	6	6	0	1	0	18	1	0	.184	.255
Pulley, Matt	L-R	6-3	200	5-15-85	.146	.091	.151	40	130	10	19	5	0	0	7	10	1	0	1	32	1	0	.185	.211
Reed, Keith	R-R	6-4	205	10-8-78	.258	.133	.298	16	62	10	16	2	0	4	11	7	0	0	0	18	2	0	.484	.333
Reimold, Nolan	R-R	6-4	207	10-12-83	.294	.333	.286	50	180	33	53	15	2	9	30	29	1	0	2	44	2	0	.550	.392
Scott, Lorenzo	L-L	6-3	210	3-1-82	.218	.045	.252	34	133	18	29	6	0	3	12	14	0	0	0	58	7	4	.331	.293
Shafer, Corey	L-L	6-3	221	12-17-82	.215	.273	.204	39	130	13	28	5	2	2	19	11	1	0	0	29	0	0	.331	.282
Snyder, Brandon	R-R	6-2	205	11-23-86	.393	.200	.500	8	28	4	11	2	0	0	6	2	0	0	1	7	0	0	.464	.419
Steinbach, Ryan	B-R	6-0	180	10-30-82	.272	.321	.259	65	250	32	68	5	0	0	9	36	6	2	2	65	1	4	.292	.374
Wargo, Cody	R-R	6-3	210	12-13-81	.000	.000	.000	2	5	1	0	0	0	0	0	2	0	1	0	1	0	0	.000	.286
Wiggins, Brad	L-L	6-0	185	7-9-83	.109	.143	.098	23	55	3	6	1	0	1	2	2	0	0	0	26	0	1	.182	.140
Zapata, Jose	R-R	6-3	184	4-4-84	.145	.034	.185	37	110	11	16	5	0	1	8	14	3	0	0	36	0	0	.218	.260

PITCHING	B-T	HT	WT	DOB	W	L	ERA	G	GS	CG	SV	IP	H	R	ER	HR	BB	SO	AVG	vLH	vRH	K/9	BB/9
Bergesen, Brad	L-R	6-2	205	9-25-85	1	3	4.82	15	15	0	0	71	89	45	38	5	14	54	.308	.242	.342	6.85	1.77
Boehm, Kyle	R-R	6-1	190	4-20-83	0	1	5.73	19	1	0	0	33	41	22	21	7	8	24	.306	.333	.293	6.55	2.18
Brocato, Russ	R-R	6-6	200	11-9-82	1	3	5.88	21	0	0	0	34	41	24	22	1	15	23	.301	.226	.349	6.15	4.01
Chamberlin, Bryce	R-R	6-2	195	12-22-82	1	2	5.64	18	0	0	1	30	35	21	19	2	20	37	.292	.260	.314	10.98	5.93
Dumesnil, Bryan	R-L	6-3	210	9-19-83	1	3	5.06	18	0	0	1	27	38	21	15	4	15	18	.333	.189	.403	6.08	5.06
Erbe, Brandon	R-R	6-4	180	12-25-87	1	1	7.71	3	1	0	0	7	6	6	6	0	4	9	.261	.250	.273	11.57	5.14
Gallaway, Bruce	R-L	6-4	190	9-17-82	0	1	1.59	3	2	0	0	6	5	1	1	1	4	6	.238	.000	.250	9.53	6.35
Hamblet, Reid	R-R	6-1	205	9-11-83	4	4	3.93	22	4	0	0	53	51	27	23	3	21	40	.246	.301	.210	6.84	3.59
Hernandez, David	R-R	6-2	180	5-13-85	1	2	3.89	12	8	0	0	42	41	21	18	2	17	47	.255	.310	.195	10.15	3.67
Hernandez, Moises	R-R	6-1	168	3-18-84	0	4	3.08	11	7	1	0	53	43	21	18	2	24	56	.217	.241	.207	9.57	4.10
Hoey, James	R-R	6-6	200	12-30-82	1	1	4.80	9	0	0	0	15	11	10	8	1	10	15	.216	.214	.217	9.00	6.00

PITCHING	B-T	HT	WT	DOB	W	L	ERA	G	GS	CG	SV	IP	H	R	ER	HR	BB	SO	AVG	vLH	vRH	K/9	BB/9
Levinski, Don	R-R	6-4	200	10-20-82	0	3	19.29	6	0	0	0	5	11	14	10	0	6	4	.423	.273	.533	7.71	11.57
Liz, Radhames	R-R	6-2	170	6-10-83	5	4	1.77	11	11	0	0	56	36	14	11	1	19	82	.188	.193	.184	13.18	3.05
Lozado, Henry	R-R	6-3	178	1-19-84	2	1	3.90	15	0	0	1	30	27	18	13	0	14	28	.237	.227	.243	8.40	4.20
McCrory, Rob	R-R	6-1	205	5-3-82	2	1	3.28	5	5	0	0	25	21	9	9	2	8	21	.233	.212	.246	7.66	2.92
Mendez, Winer	R-R	6-2	171	1-5-84	0	0	0.00	4	0	0	0	6	4	0	0	0	5	4	.200	.000	.308	6.00	7.50
Montani, Jeff	R-R	5-11	174	11-22-80	0	0	1.00	6	0	0	2	9	8	2	1	0	3	7	.250	.313	.188	7.00	3.00
Olson, Garrett	R-L	6-1	200	10-18-83	2	1	1.58	11	6	0	1	40	22	7	7	1	13	40	.164	.194	.153	9.00	2.93
Owen, Blake	R-R	6-3	215	10-29-83	1	2	1.57	23	0	0	8	23	18	8	4	0	13	27	.212	.250	.189	10.57	5.09
Robinson, Dennis	R-R	6-3	205	7-29-82	1	1	5.06	5	5	0	0	21	22	16	12	1	7	15	.265	.255	.278	6.33	2.95
Schmidt, Kyle	R-R	6-3	220	8-25-83	0	1	5.40	1	1	0	0	5	7	4	3	0	1	7	.304	.333	.286	12.60	1.80
Schwabe, Ryan	L-L	6-3	210	2-24-82	2	6	4.09	18	7	0	0	55	57	32	25	2	20	41	.265	.200	.288	6.71	3.27
Soriano, Julio	R-R	6-2	160	9-24-83	1	2	0.66	6	2	0	0	14	10	5	1	2	8	18	.189	.143	.219	11.85	5.27
Stadanlick, Ryan	R-R	6-3	210	8-3-84	0	1	11.37	4	0	0	0	6	7	8	8	0	5	7	.269	.375	.100	9.95	7.11

GAMES BY POSITION: C—Dahlberg 54, Guerrero 1, Maxey 7, Michalski 23, Snyder 5, Wargo 2. **1B**—Finan 38, Fleisher 39, Maxey 1, Pulley 1, Reimold 1. **2B**—Guerrero 31, Marconi 22, Zapata 24. **3B**—Marconi 38, Pulley 39, Snyder 1, Zapata 2. **SS**—Guerrero 1, Wiggins 1, Steinbach 65, Zapata 10. **OF**—Andrews 35, Avila 18, Davis 47, Reed 4, Reimold 46, Scott 32, Shafer 35, Wiggins 13.

BLUEFIELD ORIOLES — Rookie

APPALACHIAN LEAGUE

BATTING	B-T	HT	WT	DOB	AVG	vLH	vRH	G	AB	R	H	2B	3B	HR	RBI	BB	HBP	SH	SF	SO	SB	CS	SLG	OBP
Abreu, Miguel	R-R	6-0	190	11-14-84	.226	.179	.250	43	115	24	26	5	3	4	15	8	1	2	2	24	9	0	.426	.278
Andrews, Bobby	R-R	6-0	200	12-23-83	.276	.313	.258	27	98	19	27	4	3	3	15	9	1	0	1	23	9	0	.469	.339
Aqueron, Rene	L-R	5-10	180	10-14-81	.405	.297	.437	56	163	35	66	15	1	4	32	17	4	0	2	24	9	3	.583	.468
Avila, Angel	R-R	6-1	170	6-26-84	.268	.385	.225	30	97	12	26	5	0	3	14	6	0	2	0	31	2	1	.412	.311
Chmiel, Paul	L-R	6-5	200	5-17-87	.200	.167	.203	24	75	13	15	4	0	2	10	8	1	0	1	19	1	1	.333	.282
Howell, Joey	R-R	6-1	205	9-22-85	.194	.077	.278	10	31	5	6	1	0	1	1	2	0	0	0	9	0	0	.323	.242
Huches, Leonardo	R-R	6-2	195	11-9-85	.171	.269	.120	30	76	5	13	3	0	0	5	4	0	1	0	26	0	0	.211	.213
Kitch, Denver	R-R	6-2	185	11-25-80	.261	.302	.236	37	115	17	30	8	2	2	16	6	1	4	0	32	1	1	.417	.303
Kotch, Kevin	L-R	6-4	235	8-31-84	.157	.235	.143	37	108	15	17	4	0	2	11	10	2	1	0	35	1	1	.250	.242
Martinez, Gilberto	B-R	6-0	174	4-4-82	.235	.270	.218	43	115	13	27	3	0	0	12	7	1	6	1	40	3	1	.261	.282
Moffitt, Drew	R-R	6-1	215	8-19-81	.333	.417	.300	24	84	17	28	6	1	7	18	11	2	0	0	21	4	1	.679	.423
Musslewhite, Stuart	R-R	5-11	195	8-28-82	.300	.282	.309	57	223	36	67	18	0	8	36	11	0	0	2	33	4	1	.489	.331
Pacheco, Joel	R-R	6-2	190	3-2-82	.271	.298	.258	35	140	16	38	4	0	5	16	4	1	0	0	31	4	0	.407	.297
Pope, Kieron	R-R	6-1	195	10-3-86	.228	.186	.245	41	149	23	34	3	1	5	22	8	7	0	1	62	5	0	.362	.297
Puente, Dan	R-R	6-3	200	12-3-81	.308	.313	.304	14	39	5	12	3	0	0	6	5	1	0	0	12	0	0	.385	.400
Snyder, Brandon	R-R	6-2	205	11-23-86	.271	.238	.284	44	144	26	39	8	0	8	35	28	1	1	6	36	7	2	.493	.380
Thiel, Emile	R-R	6-2	155	2-15-87	.238	.143	.286	9	21	2	5	0	0	0	1	3	1	0	0	10	0	0	.238	.360
Tucker, Jonathan	R-R	5-7	170	7-2-83	.291	.353	.262	59	213	39	62	13	3	1	24	19	2	0	4	22	13	1	.394	.349
Turner, Alex	R-R	6-2	198	9-25-83	.308	.375	.278	7	26	6	8	2	0	1	1	1	0	0	0	10	2	0	.500	.333
Wargo, Cody	R-R	6-3	210	12-13-81	.167	.286	.000	5	12	1	2	0	0	0	3	3	0	0	1	4	0	0	.167	.313
Winterling, Paul	R-R	6-3	220	7-31-83	.280	.298	.271	47	132	30	37	9	1	6	23	18	2	0	1	37	7	0	.500	.373
Yeme, Leonel	L-L	6-4	198	9-25-85	.205	.143	.210	36	88	9	18	4	0	2	10	1	1	3	0	25	0	1	.318	.222

PITCHING	B-T	HT	WT	DOB	W	L	ERA	G	GS	CG	SV	IP	H	R	ER	HR	BB	SO	AVG	vLH	vRH	K/9	BB/9
Bastardo, Alberto	L-L	6-0	160	4-6-84	4	1	4.04	14	7	0	3	42	40	23	19	4	13	58	.244	.421	.221	12.33	2.76
Camacho, Gustavo	R-R	6-3	218	10-17-84	0	2	4.78	16	0	0	1	32	36	27	17	6	13	17	.259	.280	.247	4.78	3.66
Chamberlin, Bryce	R-R	6-2	195	12-25-82	0	0	5.40	2	2	0	0	5	4	3	3	0	3	6	.235	.375	.111	10.80	5.40
DeNaball, Fernando	R-R	6-3	180	6-16-84	2	3	6.41	14	12	0	0	53	56	42	38	9	38	59	.265	.211	.296	9.96	6.41
Erbe, Brandon	R-R	6-4	180	12-25-87	1	1	3.09	11	3	0	1	23	8	10	8	1	10	48	.103	.067	.125	18.51	3.86
Furrow, Jason	R-L	6-4	184	12-31-84	0	1	8.56	15	0	0	0	27	51	29	26	6	5	21	.408	.417	.406	6.91	1.65
Gustavo, Luis	R-R	6-1	172	3-15-85	2	4	11.16	14	7	0	0	25	34	37	31	2	22	45	.318	.327	.310	16.20	7.92
Horner, Mark	L-L	6-3	220	11-12-82	5	6	3.34	18	1	0	2	35	35	17	13	3	10	30	.254	.200	.265	7.71	2.57
Lonsberry, Daniel	R-R	6-4	200	7-6-83	0	1	2.25	20	1	0	7	32	28	11	8	2	11	40	.231	.275	.210	11.25	3.09
Minor, Zach	L-L	6-3	185	4-24-84	0	0	9.72	8	0	0	0	8	13	9	9	3	11	8	.342	.429	.323	8.64	11.88
Moore, Jeff	R-R	6-1	195	3-26-83	1	2	2.08	17	2	0	1	43	39	14	10	2	8	52	.235	.196	.250	10.80	1.66
Perez, Wilfrido	L-L	6-0	145	8-12-84	3	4	3.26	12	12	0	0	58	54	30	21	4	27	75	.242	.158	.259	11.64	4.19
Schindling, Andrew	R-R	6-2	165	8-15-86	1	0	5.06	15	0	0	1	27	26	21	15	2	23	16	.268	.265	.270	5.40	7.76
Schmidt, Kyle	R-R	6-3	220	8-25-83	5	3	4.50	13	13	0	0	70	77	37	35	6	26	76	.273	.248	.289	9.77	3.34
Soriano, Julio	R-R	6-2	160	9-24-83	2	3	4.46	12	3	0	0	34	31	23	17	0	23	44	.240	.200	.262	11.53	6.03
Spoone, Chorye	R-R	6-1	215	9-16-85	2	5	8.03	15	3	0	0	25	27	25	22	3	13	27	.273	.353	.231	9.85	4.74
Stadanlick, Ryan	R-R	6-3	210	8-3-84	3	0	2.25	12	1	0	1	24	14	9	6	1	18	19	.161	.179	.153	7.13	6.75

GAMES BY POSITION: C—Huches 29, Kotch 18, Puente 9, Snyder 22, Wargo 4. **1B**—Chmiel 20, Kotch 7, Pacheco 32, Puente 3, Winterling 13. **2B**—Abreu 23, Aqueron 9, Kitch 1, Musslewhite 3, Tucker 48, Winterling 1. **3B**—Aqueron 30, Kitch 20, Martinez 1, Musslewhite 1, Snyder 9, Thiel 7, Tucker 11. **SS**—Abreu 3, Kitch 14, Musslewhite 50, Tucker 4. **OF**—Abreu 19, Andrews 23, Aqueron 1, Avila 29, Howell 9, Martinez 42, Moffitt 20, Pope 36, Tucker 1, Turner 4, Winterling 28, Yeme 30.

BOSTON RED SOX

BY JOHN TOMASE

A season that started with the Red Sox flaunting their championship rings for the Yankees ended with Boston being swept from the playoffs and the sudden resignation of general manager Theo Epstein.

The oft-trying 2005 season was filled with highs and lows that yielded 95 victories and gave the Red Sox a chance to defend their World Series title. But beset by injuries to an aging nucleus and troubled by a shaky pitching staff, they bowed meekly to the White Sox in a first-round sweep.

Epstein, 31, elected to leave the organization a month later, passing on a three-year contract extension that would have quadrupled his salary.

For a team with the second-highest payroll in baseball, the Red Sox endured their share of hardship. Significant injuries to ace Curt Schilling and closer Keith Foulke. A woeful bullpen. Inconsistent starting pitching. An offense that never quite cracked under the pressure of needing to deliver.

An MVP-caliber season from DH David Ortiz kept the Sox in contention, but not even Big Papi could carry the team past its issues.

The first signs of trouble came during spring training. Schilling arrived intent on opening the season against former teammate Randy Johnson in New York. But he made just one spring start and shut it down so he could continue recovering from offseason ankle surgery.

He spoke bravely of returning in early April, but lasted just three starts. He came back after the all-star break as a closer, stayed there until Aug. 25, then didn't even pitch in the playoffs.

Meanwhile, Foulke imploded. The rock of 2004's postseason run battled a knee injury and flagging confidence. He didn't pitch in a meaningful situation after July 4 and finished with a 5.91 ERA.

ORGANIZATION LEADERS

BATTING

*AVG	Otness, John, Greenville	.331
R	Pinckney, Andrew, Greenville	91
H	Pinckney, Andrew, Greenville	158
TB	Pinckney, Andrew, Greenville	272
2B	Pinckney, Andrew, Greenville	33
3B	Youngbauer, Scott, Portland/Wilmington	10
HR	Shoppach, Kelly, Pawtucket	26
RBI	Pinckney, Andrew, Greenville	98
BB	Lombard, George, Pawtucket	67
SO	Lombard, George, Pawtucket	159
SB	Ramirez, Hanley, Portland	26
*OBP	Petagine, Roberto, Pawtucket	.452
*SLG	Petagine, Roberto, Pawtucket	.635

PITCHING

W	Three tied at	11
L	Hottovy, Tommy, Wilmington	12
#ERA	Lester, Jon, Portland	2.19
G	Beam, Randy, Portland/Wilmington	53
	Meredith, Cla, Pawtucket/Portland/Wilmington	53
CG	Lester, Jon, Portland	3
SV	Meredith, Cla, Pawtucket/Portland/Wilmington	19
IP	Kester, Tim, Pawtucket	165
BB	Gabbard, Kason, Portland	65
SO	Lester, Jon, Portland	163

*Minimum 250 at-bats. #Minimum 75 innings.

PLAYERS OF THE YEAR

MAJOR LEAGUE: David Ortiz, dh

Ortiz increased his home run and RBI totals for the fourth straight year, leading the majors with 148 RBIs and finishing third with 47 homers. He launched a strong bid for the AL MVP award with his repeated heroics in clutch spots, batting .346-11-33 in "close and late" situations.

MINOR LEAGUE: Jon Lester, lhp

JOHN SPEAR

In his first Double-A campaign, Lester led Red Sox minor leaguers with 163 strikeouts, tied for the organization lead with 11 wins and led all Sox starters with a 2.61 ERA. The powerful lefty, Boston' top draft pick (second round) in 2002, should vie for a big league rotation spot sometime in 2006.

In his place, veteran Mike Timlin was solid. The 39-year-old headed into free agency with a 7-3, 2.24 record with 13 saves in one of the best seasons of his career.

Despite their flaws, the Red Sox occupied first place for 64 days from July until September. For that, they could thank the heart of their order, particularly Ortiz, whose popularity rivaled that of two-time Super Bowl MVP Tom Brady in Boston.

Ortiz batted .300-47-148 and recorded an inordinate number of clutch hits. His performance improved with pressure—he batted .315 with runners on base, .352 with runners in scoring position, .368 with runners in scoring position and two outs, and .400 with the bases loaded.

Not far behind was outfielder Manny Ramirez, whose torrid final two weeks (9 homers, 19 RBIs) carried the Sox into the postseason. Ramirez finished at .292-45-144, despite almost being traded at the July 31 deadline after bemoaning his lack of privacy in Boston. At the end of the season, Ramirez reiterated his desire to be traded.

Ortiz and Ramirez teamed for the most productive duo in the majors, combining for 92 home runs and 292 RBIs.

Now if only the pitchers had kept pace. The Red Sox ranked fourth to last in the AL in ERA at 4.76. Boston's bullpen ERA of 5.19 ranked dead last in the AL.

The offense tired down the stretch and New York pounced to claim its eighth straight division title. It's not as if Boston played horribly over the final month; its .563 winning percentage projects to 91 victories. The Yankees heated up at the right time, winning 15 of 20, including two of three during a pivotal series against the Sox in the Bronx.

The farm system contributed something useful for the first time in almost a decade in the form of righthander Jonathan Papelbon, who finished the season as Boston's principal setup man. He will fight for a 2006 rotation slot in the spring.

No. 1 draft pick Craig Hansen shot from St. John's to the majors, though a dead arm limited his effectiveness. And top prospect Hanley Ramirez received a taste of the big leagues in late September, giving the Sox hope for the future.

BOSTON RED SOX

Manager: Terry Francona.

2005 Record: 95-67, .586 (Tied-1st, AL East).

BATTING	B-T	HT	WT	DOB	AVG	vLH	vRH	G	AB	R	H	2B	3B	HR	RBI	BB	HBP	SH	SF	SO	SB	CS	SLG	OBP
Bellhorn, Mark	B-R	6-1	205	8-23-74	.216	.234	.206	85	283	41	61	20	0	7	28	49	0	0	3	109	3	0	.360	.328
Cora, Alex	L-R	6-0	200	10-18-75	.269	.182	.293	47	104	14	28	3	2	2	16	6	1	3	2	12	1	2	.394	.310
2-team (49 Cleveland)					.232	.273	.226	96	250	25	58	8	4	3	24	11	5	4	3	30	7	2	.332	.275
Cruz Jr., Jose	B-R	6-0	210	4-19-74	.250	.000	.300	4	12	0	3	1	0	0	0	1	0	0	0	4	0	0	.333	.308
Damon, Johnny	L-L	6-2	205	11-5-73	.316	.327	.310	148	624	117	197	35	6	10	75	53	2	0	9	69	18	1	.439	.366
Graffanino, Tony	R-R	6-1	190	6-6-72	.319	.321	.319	51	188	39	60	12	1	4	20	9	2	0	1	23	4	1	.457	.355
2-team (59 Kansas City)					.309	.297	.316	110	379	68	117	17	3	7	38	31	4	2	1	51	7	2	.425	.366
Hyzdu, Adam	R-R	6-2	220	12-6-71	.250	.333	.200	12	16	1	4	1	0	0	0	2	0	0	0	3	0	0	.313	.333
Kapler, Gabe	R-R	6-2	200	7-31-75	.247	.314	.210	36	97	15	24	7	0	1	9	3	2	1	1	15	1	0	.351	.282
Machado, Alejandro	B-R	6-0	185	4-26-82	.200	.000	.200	10	5	4	1	1	0	0	0	1	0	0	0	1	0	0	.400	.333
McCarty, David	R-L	6-5	210	11-23-69	.500	.000	.500	13	4	2	2	0	0	0	2	2	0	0	0	0	0	0	.500	.667
Millar, Kevin	R-R	6-0	210	9-24-71	.272	.246	.283	134	449	57	122	28	1	9	50	54	8	0	8	74	0	1	.399	.355
Mirabelli, Doug	R-R	6-1	220	10-18-70	.228	.240	.221	50	136	16	31	7	0	6	18	14	2	0	0	48	2	0	.412	.309
Mueller, Bill	B-R	5-10	180	3-17-71	.295	.275	.302	150	519	69	153	34	3	10	62	59	6	0	6	74	0	0	.430	.369
Nixon, Trot	L-L	6-2	210	4-11-74	.275	.224	.288	124	408	64	112	29	1	13	67	53	3	0	6	59	2	1	.446	.357
Olerud, John	L-L	6-5	225	8-5-68	.289	.300	.286	87	173	18	50	7	0	7	37	16	0	0	3	20	0	0	.451	.344
Ortiz, David	L-L	6-4	230	11-18-75	.300	.302	.298	159	601	119	180	40	1	47	148	102	1	0	9	124	1	0	.604	.397
Payton, Jay	R-R	5-10	185	11-22-72	.263	.292	.230	55	133	24	35	7	0	5	21	10	0	0	1	14	0	0	.429	.313
Petagine, Roberto	L-L	6-1	170	6-7-71	.281	.333	.276	18	32	4	9	2	0	1	9	4	0	0	0	5	0	0	.438	.361
Ramirez, Manny	R-R	6-0	200	5-30-72	.292	.236	.316	152	554	112	162	30	1	45	144	80	10	0	6	119	1	0	.594	.388
Ramirez, Hanley	R-R	6-3	195	12-23-83	.000	.000	.000	2	2	0	0	0	0	0	0	0	0	0	0	2	0	0	.000	.000
Renteria, Edgar	R-R	6-1	200	8-7-75	.276	.326	.253	153	623	100	172	36	4	8	70	55	3	6	5	100	9	4	.385	.335
Shoppach, Kelly	R-R	6-1	210	4-29-80	.000	.000	.000	9	15	1	0	0	0	0	0	0	1	0	0	7	0	0	.000	.063
Stern, Adam	L-R	5-11	180	2-12-80	.133	.000	.222	36	15	4	2	0	0	1	2	0	1	0	0	4	1	1	.333	.188
Varitek, Jason	B-R	6-2	230	4-11-72	.281	.320	.267	133	470	70	132	30	1	22	70	62	3	1	3	117	2	0	.489	.366
Vazquez, Ramon	L-R	5-11	170	8-21-76	.197	.267	.174	27	61	6	12	2	0	0	4	3	0	2	0	14	0	0	.230	.234
Wooten, Shawn	R-R	5-10	230	7-24-72	.000	.000	.000	1	1	0	0	0	0	0	0	0	0	0	0	0	0	0	.000	.000
Youkilis, Kevin	R-R	6-1	220	3-15-79	.278	.300	.265	44	79	11	22	7	0	1	9	14	2	0	0	19	0	1	.405	.400

PITCHING	B-T	HT	WT	DOB	W	L	ERA	G	GS	CG	SV	IP	H	R	ER	HR	BB	SO	AVG	vLH	vRH	K/9	BB/9
Alvarez, Abe	L-L	6-2	190	10-17-82	0	0	15.43	2	0	0	0	2	6	4	4	1	0	1	.462	.750	.333	3.86	0.00
Arroyo, Bronson	R-R	6-5	190	2-24-77	14	10	4.51	35	32	0	0	205	213	116	103	22	54	100	.266	.288	.234	4.38	2.37
Bradford, Chad	R-R	6-5	205	9-14-74	2	1	3.86	31	0	0	0	23	29	10	10	1	4	10	.312	.409	.282	3.86	1.54
Cassidy, Scott	R-R	6-2	180	10-3-75	0	0	40.50	1	0	0	0	1	4	3	3	0	0	0	.667	.500	.750	0.00	0.00
Clement, Matt	R-R	6-3	210	8-12-74	13	6	4.57	32	32	1	0	191	192	102	97	18	68	146	.260	.275	.244	6.88	3.20
Delcarmen, Manny	R-R	6-2	190	2-16-82	0	0	3.00	10	0	0	0	9	8	3	3	0	7	9	.242	.267	.222	9.00	7.00
DiNardo, Lenny	L-L	6-4	195	9-19-79	0	1	1.84	8	1	0	0	15	13	6	3	1	5	15	.236	.263	.222	9.20	3.07
Embree, Alan	L-L	6-2	190	1-23-70	1	4	7.65	43	0	0	1	38	42	33	32	8	11	30	.284	.304	.266	7.17	2.63
Foulke, Keith	R-R	6-0	210	10-19-72	5	5	5.91	43	0	0	15	46	53	30	30	8	18	34	.288	.255	.333	6.70	3.55
Gonzalez, Jeremi	R-R	6-0	220	1-8-75	2	1	6.11	28	3	0	0	56	64	39	38	7	16	28	.288	.340	.246	4.50	2.57
Halama, John	L-L	6-5	210	2-23-72	1	1	6.18	30	1	0	0	44	56	33	30	5	9	26	.299	.328	.286	5.36	1.85
Hansen, Craig	R-R	6-6	210	11-15-83	0	0	6.00	4	0	0	0	3	6	2	2	1	1	3	.429	.600	.333	9.00	3.00
Harville, Chad	R-R	5-9	185	9-16-76	0	1	6.43	8	0	0	0	7	7	5	5	1	3	3	.269	.231	.308	3.86	3.86
Mantei, Matt	R-R	6-1	205	7-7-73	1	0	6.49	34	0	0	0	26	23	20	19	1	24	22	.240	.293	.200	7.52	8.20
Meredith, Cla	R-R	6-0	180	6-4-83	0	0	27.00	3	0	0	0	2	6	7	7	1	4	0	.462	.500	.400	0.00	15.43
Miller, Wade	R-R	6-2	220	9-13-76	4	4	4.95	16	16	0	0	91	96	53	50	8	47	64	.267	.255	.282	6.33	4.65
Myers, Mike	L-L	6-3	220	6-26-69	3	1	3.13	65	0	0	0	37	30	14	13	3	13	21	.224	.158	.385	5.06	3.13
Neal, Blaine	L-R	6-5	250	4-6-78	0	1	9.00	8	0	0	0	8	15	9	8	2	3	3	.429	.467	.400	3.38	3.38
Papelbon, Jonathan	R-R	6-4	230	11-23-80	3	1	2.65	17	3	0	0	34	33	11	10	4	17	34	.260	.190	.319	9.00	4.50
Perisho, Matt	L-L	6-0	200	6-8-75	0	0	.000	1	0	0	0	0	1	1	1	0	0	0	1.000	.000	1.000	.000	.000
Remlinger, Mike	L-L	6-1	215	3-23-66	0	0	14.85	8	0	0	0	7	15	14	11	2	5	5	.417	.182	.520	6.75	6.75
Schilling, Curt	R-R	6-5	235	11-14-66	8	8	5.69	32	11	0	9	93	121	59	59	12	22	87	.314	.290	.343	8.39	2.12
Stanton, Mike	L-L	6-1	215	6-4-67	0	0	0.00	1	0	0	0	1	1	0	0	0	0	1	.333	.333	.000	9.00	0.00
2-team (28 New York)					1	2	6.60	29	0	0	0	15	18	11	11	1	6	13	.300	.189	.478	7.80	3.60
Timlin, Mike	R-R	6-4	210	3-10-66	7	3	2.24	81	0	0	13	80	86	23	20	2	20	59	.277	.299	.257	6.61	2.24
Wakefield, Tim	R-R	6-2	210	8-2-66	16	12	4.15	33	33	3	0	225	210	113	104	35	68	151	.245	.202	.278	6.03	2.72
Wells, David	L-L	6-3	250	5-20-63	15	7	4.45	30	30	2	0	184	220	95	91	21	21	107	.296	.343	.282	5.23	1.03

FIELDING

Catcher	PCT	G	PO	A	E	DP	PB
Mirabelli	.988	43	224	17	3	0	6
Shoppach	1.000	7	14	0	0	0	0
Varitek	.990	130	784	32	8	4	7
Wooten	.000	1	0	0	0	0	0

First Base	PCT	G	PO	A	E	DP
McCarty	1.000	12	19	3	0	3
Millar	.992	110	798	85	7	67
Olerud	.998	80	416	40	1	41
Ortiz	.976	10	69	11	2	8
Petagine	.983	10	51	6	1	4
Youkilis	1.000	9	48	0	0	4

Second Base	PCT	G	PO	A	E	DP
Bellhorn	.985	83	148	253	6	54
Cora	.983	35	52	63	2	18
Graffanino	.987	51	90	140	3	29
Machado	.000	3	0	0	0	0
Mueller	.958	5	10	13	1	1
Vazquez	.818	4	3	6	2	1
Youkilis	1.000	2	0	2	0	0

Third Base	PCT	G	PO	A	E	DP
Cora	.750	5	2	7	3	0
Mueller	.972	142	87	265	10	20
Vazquez	1.000	8	6	11	0	3
Youkilis	1.000	24	10	29	0	3

Shortstop	PCT	G	PO	A	E	DP
Bellhorn	.800	1	1	3	1	0
Cora	1.000	11	9	24	0	5
Machado	1.000	1	1	1	0	0
H. Ramirez	1.000	2	0	1	0	0
Renteria	.954	153	227	398	30	90
Vazquez	.969	12	16	15	1	3

Outfield	PCT	G	PO	A	E	DP
Cruz	1.000	4	2	0	0	0
Damon	.985	147	394	5	6	0
Hyzdu	.909	12	10	0	1	0
Kapler	1.000	36	65	0	0	0
Machado	1.000	6	3	0	0	0

McCarty	.000	1	0	0	0	0
Millar	1.000	34	41	1	0	0
Nixon	.996	118	240	8	1	3
Payton	1.000	53	82	3	0	0
Petagine	.000	2	0	0	0	0
M. Ramirez	.974	149	243	17	7	0
Stern	1.000	21	10	0	0	0

FARM SYSTEM

General Manager: Theo Epstein. **Director, Player Development:** Ben Cherington. **Director, Amateur Scouting:** Jason McLeod.

Class	Farm Team	League	W	L	Pct.	Finish*	Manager	Affiliate Since
AAA	Pawtucket (R.I.) Red Sox	International	75	69	.521	t-6th (14)	Ron Johnson	1973
AA	Portland (Maine) Sea Dogs	Eastern	76	66	.535	**t-2nd (12)**	Todd Claus	2003
High A	Wilmington (Del.) Blue Rocks	Carolina	60	80	.429	8th (8)	Dann Bilardello	2005
Low A	Greenville (S.C.) Bombers	South Atlantic	72	66	.522	t-6th (16)	Chad Epperson	2005
SS A	Lowell (Mass.) Spinners	New York-Penn	42	33	.560	5th (14)	Luis Alicea	1996
Rookie	Fort Myers (Fla.) Red Sox	Gulf Coast	30	24	.556	**3rd (12)**	Ralph Treuel	1993

*Finish in overall standings (No. of teams in league)/playoff teams in **boldface**

LARRY GOREN

Manny Ramirez: Another monster campaign, .292-45-144

KEN BABBITT

Dustin Pedroia: Seamless transition from short to second base

PAWTUCKET RED SOX — Class AAA

INTERNATIONAL LEAGUE

BATTING	B-T	HT	WT	DOB	AVG	vLH	vRH	G	AB	R	H	2B	3B	HR	RBI	BB	HBP	SH	SF	SO	SB	CS	SLG	OBP
Ambres, Chip	R-R	6-1	190	12-19-79	.294	.299	.292	84	279	47	82	20	3	10	50	47	4	0	2	64	19	5	.495	.401
Bailey, Jeff	R-R	6-2	200	11-19-78	.253	.192	.275	31	95	15	24	5	0	6	12	8	1	0	0	26	1	0	.495	.317
Bellhorn, Mark	B-R	6-1	205	8-23-74	.176	.235	.157	16	68	9	12	4	0	2	9	4	2	0	0	24	0	0	.324	.243
Berg, Dave	R-R	5-11	205	9-3-70	.306	.322	.300	112	425	73	130	28	1	3	60	63	4	0	9	67	1	0	.398	.393
Buckley, Jim	R-R	6-1	223	9-14-79	.158	.214	.125	15	38	7	6	1	0	0	5	7	0	1	0	18	0	0	.184	.289
Figueroa, Luis	R-R	5-9	145	2-16-74	.289	.303	.283	109	402	58	116	22	1	7	48	29	1	2	5	28	2	6	.400	.334
Hummel, Tim	R-R	6-2	190	11-18-78	.250	.327	.227	64	224	35	56	18	1	4	27	26	6	2	2	35	1	1	.393	.341
Hyzdu, Adam	R-R	6-2	220	12-6-71	.254	.261	.253	31	118	17	30	7	0	4	25	16	0	0	0	32	0	1	.415	.343
Jeroloman, Chuck	R-R	6-1	190	9-14-82	.000	.000	.000	2	4	0	0	0	0	0	0	1	0	0	0	2	0	0	.000	.200
Kapler, Gabe	R-R	6-2	200	7-31-75	.636	.333	.684	6	22	7	14	3	1	2	6	0	0	0	0	3	0	0	1.136	.636
Lockwood, Mike	L-L	6-0	196	12-27-76	.229	.250	.226	97	327	40	75	13	4	10	50	25	1	0	4	43	5	1	.385	.283
Lombard, George	L-R	6-0	210	9-14-75	.262	.252	.265	131	496	90	130	28	8	20	65	67	9	2	5	159	23	5	.472	.357
Machado, Alejandro	B-R	6-0	185	4-26-82	.300	.289	.303	117	383	60	115	17	2	3	43	32	5	4	3	47	21	4	.379	.359
Moriarty, Mike	R-R	6-0	190	3-8-74	.100	.000	.111	6	10	1	1	1	0	0	0	0	0	0	0	3	0	0	.200	.100
Nieves, Raul	B-R	6-1	190	1-1-79	.125	.250	.000	2	8	0	1	0	0	0	0	0	0	0	0	1	0	0	.125	.125
Nixon, Trot	L-L	6-2	210	4-11-74	.500	.000	.750	2	6	3	3	0	0	1	2	2	0	0	1	2	0	0	1.000	.556
Olerud, John	L-L	6-5	225	8-5-68	.300	.333	.286	3	10	2	3	0	0	1	2	2	0	0	0	1	0	0	.600	.417
Pedroia, Dustin	R-R	5-9	180	8-17-83	.255	.326	.236	51	204	39	52	9	1	5	24	24	9	1	2	17	1	0	.382	.356

BATTING	B-T	HT	WT	DOB	AVG	vLH	vRH	G	AB	R	H	2B	3B	HR	RBI	BB	HBP	SH	SF	SO	SB	CS	SLG	OBP
Perez, Kenny	B-R	6-2	190	9-28-81	.167	.111	.182	14	42	10	7	2	0	1	5	7	1	1	0	7	0	0	.286	.300
Petagine, Roberto	L-L	6-1	170	6-7-71	.327	.290	.340	74	266	54	87	18	2	20	69	63	2	0	5	46	0	1	.635	.452
Pond, Simon	L-R	6-1	190	10-27-76	.500	.000	.500	1	4	1	2	0	0	0	1	1	0	0	0	2	0	0	.500	.600
Schrager, Tony	R-R	6-1	170	6-14-77	.216	.364	.175	15	51	4	11	1	1	0	0	6	0	0	0	13	0	0	.275	.298
Sherrod, Justin	R-R	6-2	210	1-11-78	.259	.217	.272	120	433	65	112	29	1	16	65	45	5	0	7	141	2	2	.441	.331
Shoppach, Kelly	R-R	6-1	210	4-29-80	.253	.194	.268	102	371	60	94	16	0	26	75	46	12	0	3	116	0	0	.507	.352
Stachowsky, Mitch	R-R	6-3	230	10-2-84	.000	.000	.000	4	4	0	0	0	0	0	0	0	1	0	0	3	0	0	.000	.200
Stern, Adam	L-R	5-11	180	2-12-80	.321	.345	.308	20	81	16	26	8	0	2	14	8	1	1	1	10	3	1	.494	.385
Wooten, Shawn	R-R	5-10	230	7-24-72	.267	.343	.243	114	427	45	114	20	0	17	60	35	9	0	9	72	0	0	.433	.329
Youkilis, Kevin	R-R	6-1	220	3-15-79	.322	.379	.309	43	152	30	49	15	1	8	27	35	5	0	2	29	1	2	.592	.459

PITCHING	B-T	HT	WT	DOB	W	L	ERA	G	GS	CG	SV	IP	H	R	ER	HR	BB	SO	AVG	vLH	vRH	K/9	BB/9
Alvarez, Abe	L-L	6-2	190	10-17-82	11	6	4.85	26	26	0	0	145	143	84	78	17	31	109	.255	.238	.261	6.78	1.93
Bausher, Tim	R-R	6-4	200	4-23-79	3	2	3.41	44	0	0	5	71	66	36	27	9	36	65	.247	.277	.223	8.20	4.54
Bottalico, Ricky	L-R	6-1	215	8-26-69	0	0	4.32	6	0	0	0	8	5	4	4	1	4	6	.200	.000	.278	6.48	4.32
Cassidy, Scott	R-R	6-2	180	10-3-75	6	3	4.05	26	3	0	0	60	54	31	27	5	23	66	.243	.284	.208	9.90	3.45
Cressend, Jack	R-R	6-1	190	5-13-75	5	5	5.06	40	3	0	0	69	79	42	39	15	23	68	.287	.303	.277	8.83	2.99
Delcarmen, Manny	R-R	6-2	190	2-16-82	3	1	1.29	15	0	0	2	21	17	3	3	0	13	23	.218	.214	.220	9.86	5.57
Deschenes, Marc	R-R	6-2	175	1-6-73	2	2	2.94	11	4	0	0	34	22	12	11	5	5	28	.179	.255	.125	7.49	1.34
DiNardo, Lenny	L-L	6-4	195	9-19-79	6	3	3.15	23	22	0	0	109	109	51	38	7	35	93	.265	.288	.256	7.70	2.90
Gonzalez, Jeremi	R-R	6-0	220	1-8-75	5	2	2.61	11	11	0	0	69	63	20	20	8	14	62	.245	.254	.236	8.09	1.83
Kershner, Jason	L-L	6-2	185	12-19-76	0	2	5.68	15	0	0	2	19	24	12	12	3	6	10	.312	.500	.204	4.74	2.84
Kester, Tim	R-R	6-4	202	12-1-71	11	9	4.95	30	28	1	0	165	199	101	91	17	29	105	.301	.316	.287	5.72	1.58
Malaska, Mark	L-L	6-3	210	1-17-78	5	3	4.14	39	5	0	1	87	74	44	40	2	39	86	.234	.240	.232	8.90	4.03
Martinez, Anastacio	R-R	6-2	180	11-3-78	3	4	5.98	35	6	0	1	59	74	43	39	4	27	46	.302	.381	.250	7.06	4.14
Meredith, Cla	R-R	6-0	180	6-4-83	2	5	5.59	40	0	0	10	48	63	30	30	6	12	42	.312	.359	.282	7.82	2.23
Miller, Wade	R-R	6-2	220	9-13-76	0	0	2.53	2	2	0	0	11	10	4	3	1	6	10	.250	.259	.231	8.44	5.06
Narveson, Chris	L-L	6-3	205	12-20-81	4	5	4.77	21	20	0	0	111	109	62	59	15	46	66	.262	.260	.263	5.34	3.72
Papelbon, Jonathan	R-R	6-4	230	11-23-80	1	2	2.93	7	4	0	1	28	21	9	9	2	3	27	.208	.255	.167	8.78	0.98
Perez, Juan	R-L	6-0	170	9-3-78	4	5	4.50	40	1	0	1	62	61	31	31	7	29	74	.261	.298	.240	10.74	4.21
Perisho, Matt	L-L	6-0	200	6-8-75	2	0	2.08	13	0	0	0	13	6	3	3	0	6	7	.140	.100	.174	4.85	4.15
Schilling, Curt	R-R	6-5	235	11-14-66	0	2	6.63	6	3	0	0	19	27	15	14	3	3	21	.321	.288	.375	9.95	1.42
Shoemaker, Scott	R-R	6-4	210	9-21-81	0	1	5.56	2	2	0	0	11	11	7	7	2	4	7	.256	.381	.136	5.56	3.18
Stephens, John	R-R	6-1	215	11-15-79	0	1	9.00	1	1	0	0	4	6	4	4	1	1	4	.333	.400	.308	9.00	2.25
Tomori, Denney	R-R	6-4	200	9-21-67	0	5	5.03	15	2	0	1	34	37	21	19	6	8	27	.280	.300	.264	7.15	2.12
Zink, Charlie	R-R	6-1	190	8-26-79	2	1	10.45	4	1	0	0	10	17	12	12	1	8	5	.386	.476	.304	4.35	6.97

FIELDING

Catcher	PCT	G	PO	A	E	DP	PB
Bailey	1.000	4	8	0	0	0	0
Buckley	.991	15	103	5	1	0	1
Shoppach	.993	87	644	42	5	4	7
Stachowsky	1.000	3	5	1	0	0	1
Wooten	.986	50	326	15	5	4	3

First Base	PCT	G	PO	A	E	DP
Bailey	1.000	13	85	3	0	8
Berg	1.000	25	158	9	0	15
Hummel	1.000	6	44	2	0	5
Lockwood	1.000	2	1	0	0	1
Olerud	1.000	2	11	4	0	2
Petagine	.994	60	447	38	3	46
Wooten	.996	34	240	19	1	24
Youkilis	.993	16	126	10	1	16

Second Base	PCT	G	PO	A	E	DP
Bellhorn	.914	9	16	16	3	3
Berg	.945	11	24	28	3	8
Figueroa	.982	22	52	56	2	15
Hummel	1.000	1	3	2	0	3
Machado	.989	69	121	156	3	37
Moriarty	.800	1	2	2	1	1
Pedroia	.990	39	83	110	2	27
Youkilis	.900	2	5	4	1	2

Third Base	PCT	G	PO	A	E	DP
Bailey	.000	1	0	0	0	0
Berg	.949	42	17	57	4	5
Figueroa	.980	44	26	73	2	7
Hummel	.902	22	11	35	5	4
Jeroloman	1.000	1	0	1	0	0
Moriarty	1.000	2	2	1	0	0
Perez	1.000	3	0	5	0	1
Schrager	.833	6	1	9	2	2
Wooten	.912	17	9	22	3	4
Youkilis	.946	24	15	38	3	4

Shortstop	PCT	G	PO	A	E	DP
Berg	1.000	1	1	6	0	1
Figueroa	.930	45	67	120	14	30
Hummel	.977	33	44	81	3	17
Jeroloman	.750	1	1	2	1	0
Machado	.977	39	60	109	4	25
Moriarty	1.000	1	1	2	0	0
Nieves	1.000	2	2	9	0	0
Pedroia	1.000	10	12	27	0	3
Perez	1.000	10	19	35	0	11
Schrager	.971	7	9	24	1	3

Outfield	PCT	G	PO	A	E	DP
Ambres	.973	73	137	5	4	2
Bailey	1.000	8	16	0	0	0
Berg	1.000	16	13	1	0	0
Hyzdu	1.000	29	61	0	0	0
Kapler	1.000	6	15	0	0	0
Lockwood	.982	75	160	4	3	0
Lombard	.996	124	249	3	1	1
Machado	1.000	7	16	0	0	0
Nixon	1.000	1	3	0	0	0
Sherrod	.974	99	218	8	6	3
Stern	.980	20	47	1	1	0

PORTLAND SEA DOGS — Class AA

EASTERN LEAGUE

BATTING	B-T	HT	WT	DOB	AVG	vLH	vRH	G	AB	R	H	2B	3B	HR	RBI	BB	HBP	SH	SF	SO	SB	CS	SLG	OBP
Bailey, Jeff	R-R	6-2	200	11-19-78	.250	.343	.216	43	132	21	33	7	0	7	26	20	8	1	0	36	3	1	.462	.381
Bailie, Stefan	R-R	6-0	212	5-16-80	.147	.103	.160	35	129	9	19	5	0	5	11	7	1	0	0	47	1	0	.302	.197
Borowiak, Zach	R-R	6-1	185	5-18-81	.150	.250	.083	6	20	1	3	1	0	0	0	0	0	0	0	3	1	0	.200	.150
Buckley, Jim	R-R	6-1	223	9-14-79	.194	.158	.209	50	129	13	25	8	0	3	11	18	1	0	1	55	1	0	.326	.295
Chavez, Dirimo	R-R	6-0	170	8-10-83	.000	.000	.000	2	5	0	0	0	0	0	0	0	0	0	0	1	0	0	.000	.000
Concepcion, Alberto	R-R	6-1	220	4-18-81	.249	.187	.268	101	329	42	82	19	1	6	45	33	3	2	8	86	3	3	.368	.316
Durbin, Chris	R-R	6-0	180	9-8-81	.282	.264	.288	103	394	55	111	31	1	12	57	35	5	1	5	67	3	4	.457	.344
Fulse, Sheldon	B-R	6-1	200	11-10-81	.175	.241	.161	60	166	21	29	9	2	2	15	17	1	2	2	50	14	7	.289	.253
LeVier, Bret	R-R	6-3	195	4-26-83	.216	.182	.231	13	37	3	8	2	0	0	2	1	0	1	0	8	0	0	.270	.237
Moss, Brandon	L-R	6-0	181	9-16-83	.268	.268	.269	135	503	87	135	31	4	16	61	53	3	1	8	129	6	3	.441	.337
Murphy, David	L-L	6-4	192	10-18-81	.275	.285	.271	135	484	71	133	25	4	14	75	46	1	1	3	83	13	6	.430	.337
Nieves, Raul	B-R	6-1	190	1-1-79	.209	.210	.208	90	235	29	49	9	2	1	11	27	1	2	2	41	6	1	.277	.291
O'Keefe, Mike	L-L	5-10	200	6-28-78	.175	.100	.200	11	40	6	7	0	0	1	8	4	0	0	1	7	0	0	.250	.244
Pedroia, Dustin	R-R	5-9	180	8-17-83	.324	.391	.302	66	256	39	83	19	2	8	40	34	4	2	2	26	7	3	.508	.409
Perez, Kenny	B-R	6-2	190	9-28-81	.285	.250	.298	66	253	35	72	9	1	4	28	18	0	2	3	35	7	3	.375	.328
Ramirez, Hanley	R-R	6-3	195	12-23-83	.271	.254	.276	122	465	66	126	21	7	6	52	39	7	5	3	62	26	13	.385	.335
Sandberg, Jared	R-R	6-3	225	3-2-78	.233	.264	.224	130	463	64	108	29	0	18	71	62	10	1	2	131	3	3	.413	.335
Spann, Chad	R-R	6-1	195	10-25-83	.207	.500	.095	9	29	1	6	2	0	0	1	3	0	2	0	8	1	1	.276	.281
Vanderbosch, Matt	L-L	5-8	190	4-12-82	.239	.308	.212	11	46	3	11	1	1	0	3	2	1	0	0	14	1	0	.304	.286
West, Jeremy	R-R	6-0	200	11-8-81	.267	.300	.258	127	472	48	126	32	3	10	50	41	14	0	6	76	1	0	.411	.340
Youngbauer, Scott	B-R	6-1	175	1-14-79	.311	.345	.304	45	164	29	51	14	5	5	20	11	2	2	1	39	5	2	.549	.360

PITCHING	B-T	HT	WT	DOB	W	L	ERA	G	GS	CG	SV	IP	H	R	ER	HR	BB	SO	AVG	vLH	vRH	K/9	BB/9
Beam, Randy	L-L	6-3	205	5-21-82	2	3	2.53	34	0	0	2	46	35	18	13	3	20	49	.211	.197	.219	9.52	3.88
Brooks, Conor	L-R	6-1	190	6-11-78	4	2	4.85	52	0	0	2	69	76	40	37	4	18	42	.290	.319	.274	5.50	2.36
Delcarmen, Manny	R-R	6-2	190	2-6-82	4	4	3.23	31	0	0	3	39	31	23	14	3	20	49	.212	.234	.202	11.31	4.62
Deschenes, Marc	R-R	6-2	175	1-6-73	4	3	3.74	39	0	0	8	43	42	24	18	4	24	54	.247	.172	.286	11.22	4.98
Devey, Phil	L-L	5-11	178	5-31-77	1	6	3.79	30	1	0	0	38	34	20	16	3	16	38	.239	.180	.284	9.00	3.79
Fisher, Peter	R-R	6-4	220	7-7-77	0	0	9.82	7	0	0	0	7	14	8	8	2	5	4	.400	.357	.429	4.91	6.14
Gabbard, Kason	L-L	6-3	200	4-8-82	9	11	4.61	27	25	0	0	133	128	80	68	10	65	96	.255	.225	.263	6.51	4.41
Gonzalez, Alex	R-R	5-10	185	3-8-83	0	0	5.40	1	0	0	0	3	2	2	2	1	2	3	.167	.143	.200	8.10	5.40
Haines, Talley	R-R	6-5	205	11-16-76	0	1	0.87	6	0	0	0	10	6	1	1	1	3	8	.176	.125	.222	6.97	2.61
Hansen, Craig	R-R	6-6	210	11-15-83	0	0	0.00	8	0	0	1	10	9	0	0	0	1	10	.243	.455	.154	9.31	0.93
Hertzler, Barry	R-R	6-2	215	2-15-81	0	0	5.14	3	0	0	0	7	11	5	4	0	3	6	.367	.600	.133	7.71	3.86
Jackson, Kyle	R-R	6-3	192	4-9-83	0	0	6.43	3	0	0	1	7	10	5	5	4	0	7	.323	.375	.267	9.00	0.00
Jordan, Brantley	L-L	6-0	190	4-24-81	0	0	0.00	1	0	0	0	0	1	1	0	0	1	1	.333	.500	.000	27.00	27.00
Lester, Jon	L-L	6-4	200	1-7-84	11	6	2.61	26	26	3	0	148	114	52	43	10	57	163	.215	.255	.199	9.89	3.46
Mann, Jim	R-R	6-3	225	11-17-74	3	1	1.80	23	0	0	12	25	12	6	5	0	13	34	.143	.098	.186	12.24	4.68
Martinez, Edgar	R-R	6-0	222	10-23-81	0	0	1.50	15	0	0	1	18	12	3	3	0	8	13	.190	.192	.189	6.50	4.00
Meredith, Cla	R-R	6-0	180	6-4-83	1	0	0.00	12	0	0	9	15	5	0	0	0	3	12	.106	.095	.115	7.20	1.80
Pahucki, David	R-R	6-2	210	10-17-80	3	1	7.31	13	1	0	0	16	16	16	13	2	20	15	.258	.148	.343	8.44	11.25
Papelbon, Jonathan	R-R	6-4	230	11-23-80	5	2	2.48	14	14	0	0	87	59	28	24	9	23	83	.193	.201	.184	8.59	2.38
Pauley, David	R-R	6-2	185	6-17-83	9	7	3.81	27	27	1	0	156	169	86	66	18	34	104	.274	.294	.257	6.00	1.96
Pearson, Jason	L-L	6-0	190	12-29-75	1	1	5.06	14	0	0	0	16	21	10	9	2	8	17	.318	.294	.344	9.56	4.50
Sanchez, Anibal	R-R	6-0	180	2-27-84	3	5	3.45	11	11	0	0	57	53	28	22	5	16	63	.244	.250	.239	9.89	2.51
Shoemaker, Scott	R-R	6-4	210	9-21-81	0	0	12.27	1	1	0	0	4	6	5	5	1	2	5	.375	.143	.556	12.27	4.91
Smith, Chris	R-R	6-2	200	4-9-81	4	4	5.23	15	15	0	0	76	95	46	44	13	15	49	.315	.321	.309	5.83	1.78
Sturge, Justin	R-L	6-4	200	5-4-81	2	1	4.88	33	0	0	0	48	52	30	26	3	16	33	.281	.356	.246	6.19	3.00
Tomori, Denney	R-R	6-4	200	9-21-67	2	3	3.42	19	6	1	0	53	65	31	20	3	12	35	.314	.350	.280	5.98	2.05
Zink, Charlie	R-R	6-1	190	8-26-79	8	5	4.87	29	15	1	0	105	102	65	57	12	53	70	.261	.247	.271	5.98	4.53

FIELDING

Catcher	PCT	G	PO	A	E	DP	PB
Bailey	.982	13	101	8	2	0	0
Buckley	.982	45	312	20	6	2	6
Concepcion	.988	92	700	55	9	4	10

First Base	PCT	G	PO	A	E	DP
Bailey	.977	11	78	8	2	6
Bailie	.985	9	62	2	1	7
Concepcion	1.000	1	1	0	0	0
O'Keefe	1.000	6	67	1	0	4
Sandberg	.986	46	318	32	5	33
West	.990	79	632	43	7	64

Second Base	PCT	G	PO	A	E	DP
Borowiak	1.000	2	4	10	0	0
Chavez	1.000	2	1	3	0	0
LeVier	.000	1	0	0	0	0
Nieves	.988	17	44	41	1	14
Pedroia	.980	58	91	160	5	41
Perez	.959	22	41	30	3	9
Ramirez	.875	5	9	12	3	4
Youngbauer	.962	43	82	120	8	32

Third Base	PCT	G	PO	A	E	DP
Borowiak	.500	2	1	0	1	0
Concepcion	.875	3	1	6	1	0
LeVier	.947	11	3	15	1	3
Nieves	.925	44	22	89	9	7
Perez	.936	20	12	32	3	2
Ramirez	1.000	1	0	2	0	0
Sandberg	.902	67	48	126	19	14
Spann	.903	9	10	18	3	8
Youngbauer	.000	1	0	0	0	0

Shortstop	PCT	G	PO	A	E	DP
Borowiak	1.000	3	1	4	0	2
Nieves	.923	7	9	15	2	6
Pedroia	1.000	6	7	17	0	1
Perez	.924	21	35	50	7	12
Ramirez	.960	115	156	305	19	57
Spann	1.000	1	1	0	0	0

Outfield	PCT	G	PO	A	E	DP
Sandberg	.923	12	12	0	1	0
O'Keefe	1.000	3	6	0	0	0
Bailey	1.000	5	8	0	0	0
Durbin	.957	95	170	10	8	1
Fulse	.976	46	81	0	2	0
LeVier	.667	1	2	0	1	0
Vanderbosch	1.000	9	14	3	0	1
Moss	.968	126	226	13	8	3
Nieves	1.000	18	27	0	0	0
Murphy	.985	131	254	4	4	2

WILMINGTON BLUE ROCKS — High Class A

CAROLINA LEAGUE

BATTING	B-T	HT	WT	DOB	AVG	vLH	vRH	G	AB	R	H	2B	3B	HR	RBI	BB	HBP	SH	SF	SO	SB	CS	SLG	OBP
Arias, Claudio	R-R	6-2	218	5-9-82	.245	.167	.310	14	53	5	13	2	0	4	9	2	0	0	1	11	0	1	.509	.268
Bladergroen, Ian	L-L	6-5	210	2-23-83	.240	.193	.263	75	263	25	63	6	3	4	31	30	10	1	3	77	0	1	.331	.337
Boran, Patrick	B-R	6-2	200	8-8-80	.250	.286	.200	5	12	1	3	1	0	0	1	2	0	0	0	1	1	0	.333	.357
Borowiak, Zach	R-R	6-1	185	5-18-81	.254	.274	.240	114	406	72	103	27	3	11	59	33	15	11	4	72	6	4	.416	.330
Brown, Dustin	R-R	6-0	195	6-19-82	.256	.301	.222	62	219	32	56	12	0	8	36	31	1	0	2	52	1	1	.420	.348
Chauncey, Clinton	R-R	6-1	192	1-1-81	.144	.138	.147	36	97	6	14	2	1	1	6	7	1	3	1	35	1	1	.216	.208
Chavez, Dirimo	R-R	6-0	170	8-10-83	.205	.226	.189	41	127	19	26	7	2	1	12	16	0	1	2	25	1	2	.315	.290
Cronkhite, Ian	L-L	6-1	189	8-11-83	.250	.000	.333	6	16	0	4	2	0	0	0	2	0	0	0	2	0	0	.375	.333
Devries, Jon	R-R	6-3	235	8-22-82	.283	.282	.284	34	113	16	32	10	0	4	13	14	8	0	0	40	0	0	.478	.400
Goelz, Bryan	L-L	6-0	171	4-10-80	.208	.167	.220	75	207	30	43	9	2	2	19	28	2	2	6	45	4	5	.300	.300
Hall, Mickey	L-L	6-1	195	5-20-85	.216	.115	.270	71	250	31	54	16	4	6	25	32	0	1	1	98	5	3	.384	.304
Kelly, Dustin	R-R	6-0	185	5-23-83	.229	.231	.227	11	35	5	8	1	0	0	3	1	2	0	0	5	1	1	.257	.289
LeVier, Bret	R-R	6-3	195	4-26-83	.238	.250	.200	7	21	2	5	1	0	0	3	5	0	0	0	3	0	0	.286	.385
Mota, Willy	R-R	6-1	165	10-25-85	.056	.000	.091	6	18	2	1	0	0	1	4	3	0	0	0	6	0	0	.222	.190
Ontiveros, Jeff	R-R	6-0	220	4-26-79	.251	.237	.259	87	303	48	76	20	0	13	48	47	9	0	2	96	0	1	.446	.366
Pritz, Bryan	R-R	5-10	180	5-5-82	.299	.303	.296	97	328	51	98	15	1	2	25	53	3	7	5	53	18	4	.369	.396
Segovia, Luis	B-R	5-10	150	7-19-86	.083	.000	.118	8	24	2	2	0	0	0	0	1	0	0	0	9	0	0	.083	.120
Spann, Chad	R-R	6-1	195	10-25-83	.248	.308	.213	111	400	55	99	23	4	13	48	39	8	1	7	106	1	4	.423	.322
Stone, Greg	L-R	5-0	180	2-19-81	.129	.000	.160	15	31	5	4	0	0	0	1	7	1	3	0	12	1	0	.129	.308
Suarez, Ignacio	R-R	5-11	165	5-3-81	.233	.235	.232	116	403	38	94	20	1	0	38	29	2	5	2	73	9	6	.288	.287
Ust, Brant	R-R	6-2	200	7-17-78	.262	.295	.244	115	443	54	116	20	0	13	71	27	8	1	6	107	1	1	.395	.312
Vanderbosch, Matt	L-L	5-8	190	4-12-82	.283	.283	.283	69	265	45	75	11	3	5	28	27	0	5	2	69	16	5	.404	.347
White, Scott	R-L	6-3	196	10-18-83	.238	.176	.279	123	445	57	106	22	2	13	60	43	9	2	3	96	0	4	.384	.316
Youngbauer, Scott	B-R	6-1	175	1-14-79	.321	.262	.358	27	109	18	35	5	5	2	18	9	2	2	1	21	3	1	.514	.380

PITCHING	B-T	HT	WT	DOB	W	L	ERA	G	GS	CG	SV	IP	H	R	ER	HR	BB	SO	AVG	vLH	vRH	K/9	BB/9
Beam, Randy	L-L	6-3	205	5-21-82	2	3	2.25	19	0	0	5	28	19	7	7	2	11	28	.181	.278	.130	9.00	3.54
Bono, Kyle	R-R	6-3	205	6-29-83	2	2	4.07	24	0	0	0	49	39	29	22	5	32	56	.222	.282	.165	10.36	5.92
Cedeno, Juan	L-L	6-1	160	8-19-83	2	6	5.49	22	12	0	0	80	85	52	49	11	37	71	.267	.333	.235	7.95	4.15
Dobies, Andrew	L-L	6-1	180	4-20-83	4	6	4.40	16	16	0	0	86	89	54	42	7	18	50	.273	.351	.249	5.23	1.88
Fisher, Peter	R-R	6-4	220	7-7-77	1	4	3.89	26	1	0	8	42	42	25	18	3	14	26	.264	.266	.263	5.62	3.02
Flores, Eugenio	R-R	5-10	160	4-8-82	0	0	9.00	2	0	0	0	2	4	2	2	0	0	1	.400	.333	.429	4.50	0.00

PITCHING	B-T	HT	WT	DOB	W	L	ERA	G	GS	CG	SV	IP	H	R	ER	HR	BB	SO	AVG	vLH	vRH	K/9	BB/9
Gardner, Jarrett	R-R	6-1	175	3-26-81	1	2	6.00	10	7	0	0	42	54	28	28	13	7	35	.305	.395	.229	7.50	1.50
Goodson, Matt	R-R	6-3	195	9-26-82	1	1	4.38	9	4	0	0	25	26	14	12	3	13	24	.268	.308	.188	8.76	4.74
Hertzler, Barry	R-R	6-2	215	2-15-81	5	3	4.21	33	1	0	1	83	80	47	39	4	24	58	.249	.282	.223	6.26	2.59
Hottovy, Tommy	L-L	6-1	195	7-9-81	3	12	5.45	25	23	0	0	104	116	74	63	18	37	82	.282	.298	.276	7.10	3.20
James, Michael	R-R	6-1	185	6-2-81	0	1	3.06	14	0	0	3	18	9	7	6	2	7	12	.153	.115	.182	6.11	3.57
Langone, Steve	R-R	6-2	193	1-12-78	3	4	3.92	18	5	1	0	44	44	21	19	4	5	34	.272	.291	.253	7.01	1.03
Martinez, Edgar	R-R	6-0	222	10-23-81	1	1	2.10	28	0	0	7	34	20	10	8	3	12	46	.167	.114	.197	12.06	3.15
Mendoza, Luis	R-R	6-3	180	10-31-83	4	9	6.34	23	22	1	0	119	145	91	84	17	36	60	.297	.265	.326	4.53	2.72
Meredith, Cla	R-R	6-0	180	6-4-83	0	0	0.00	1	0	0	0	1	1	0	0	0	0	2	.250	.000	.500	18.00	0.00
Miller, Wade	R-R	6-2	220	9-13-76	0	0	1.80	1	1	0	0	5	6	1	1	1	0	6	.316	.222	.400	10.80	0.00
Newsom, Randy	R-R	6-2	200	5-6-82	0	1	0.00	2	0	0	1	3	0	1	0	0	2	2	.000	.000	.000	6.75	6.75
Pahucki, David	R-R	6-2	210	10-17-80	2	1	1.23	4	0	0	0	7	7	3	1	0	3	6	.292	.167	.417	7.36	3.68
Rios, Travis	R-R	6-2	205	10-3-81	2	1	8.49	16	0	0	2	23	31	23	22	2	14	15	.333	.471	.254	5.79	5.40
Rogers, Joe	L-L	6-2	193	7-19-81	1	1	2.57	6	1	0	0	14	17	7	4	2	6	8	.309	.154	.357	5.14	3.86
Romero, Felix	R-R	6-1	192	6-18-80	5	7	2.93	34	3	0	1	74	72	28	24	3	11	87	.259	.270	.248	10.63	1.34
Rudrude, Brett	R-R	6-3	195	1-23-79	2	1	0.46	14	0	0	0	20	13	3	1	1	14	18	.186	.235	.139	8.24	6.41
Sanchez, Anibal	R-R	6-0	180	2-27-84	6	1	2.40	14	14	0	0	79	53	25	21	7	24	95	.187	.213	.150	10.87	2.75
Schroyer, Ryan	R-R	6-1	215	9-28-81	1	1	4.50	13	0	0	1	26	30	20	13	3	14	22	.286	.327	.245	7.62	4.85
Shoemaker, Scott	R-R	6-4	210	9-21-81	1	3	7.94	5	5	0	0	23	34	22	20	5	9	13	.354	.409	.308	5.16	3.57
Sturge, Justin	R-L	6-4	200	5-4-81	3	1	3.58	13	2	0	1	33	33	15	13	2	6	18	.275	.360	.214	4.96	1.65
Tabeek, Kyle	R-R	5-11	190	8-2-83	0	1	19.64	4	0	0	1	4	9	8	8	0	6	3	.500	.200	.615	7.36	14.73
Vaquedano, Jose	R-R	6-4	167	7-9-81	8	7	3.75	28	23	0	1	146	120	66	61	12	50	117	.224	.203	.241	7.20	3.08

FIELDING

Catcher	PCT	G	PO	A	E	DP	PB
Brown	.971	29	182	21	6	2	6
Chauncey	.992	34	228	20	2	3	3
Devries	.978	33	203	21	5	3	4
Ontiveros	.988	53	390	25	5	3	15

First Base	PCT	G	PO	A	E	DP
Bladergroen	.984	64	519	28	9	40
Chavez	1.000	7	51	5	0	5
Ontiveros	.994	18	152	13	1	16
Ust	1.000	12	95	10	0	11
White	.992	44	362	29	3	31

Second Base	PCT	G	PO	A	E	DP
Borowiak	.974	71	104	198	8	36
Chavez	.978	23	42	46	2	10
Kelly	.956	11	18	25	2	6
LeVier	1.000	4	12	7	0	2
Segovia	1.000	6	13	11	0	1
Ust	.983	13	23	36	1	7
Youngbauer	.962	22	34	67	4	17

Third Base	PCT	G	PO	A	E	DP
Borowiak	.915	16	7	36	4	0
LeVier	1.000	3	3	5	0	1
Spann	.909	72	48	152	20	17
White	.929	53	38	93	10	3

Shortstop	PCT	G	PO	A	E	DP
Borowiak	.952	30	45	74	6	13
Segovia	.909	3	1	9	1	1
Suarez	.932	115	147	289	32	65

Outfield	PCT	G	PO	A	E	DP
Arias	.941	7	16	0	1	0
Boran	1.000	4	4	0	0	0
Borowiak	1.000	2	4	0	0	0
Brown	.986	34	68	3	1	0
Chavez	1.000	3	0	1	0	0
Cronkhite	1.000	3	6	0	0	0
Goelz	.993	73	129	4	1	1
Hall	.969	67	121	6	4	2
Mota	1.000	6	13	0	0	0
Ontiveros	1.000	1	1	0	0	0
Pritz	.971	89	189	9	6	3
Stone	1.000	14	21	2	0	0
Ust	.984	79	115	5	2	4
Vanderbosch	.977	67	165	4	4	0

GREENVILLE BOMBERS — Low Class A

SOUTH ATLANTIC LEAGUE

BATTING	B-T	HT	WT	DOB	AVG	vLH	vRH	G	AB	R	H	2B	3B	HR	RBI	BB	HBP	SH	SF	SO	SB	CS	SLG	OBP
Arias, Claudio	R-R	6-2	218	5-9-82	.312	.260	.329	50	199	33	62	15	2	13	38	11	5	0	2	55	2	0	.603	.359
Chavez, Dirimo	R-R	6-0	170	8-10-83	.259	.143	.277	13	54	6	14	4	0	0	7	5	1	0	0	10	0	0	.333	.333
Ciaramella, Matt	B-L	6-1	190	10-25-82	.302	.333	.288	60	225	27	68	13	1	4	30	21	0	0	1	39	2	1	.422	.360
Corsaletti, Jeff	L-R	6-0	190	2-22-83	.357	.346	.360	59	249	49	89	17	2	4	26	32	0	0	1	38	9	4	.490	.429
Cronkhite, Ian	L-L	6-1	189	8-11-83	.258	.171	.281	42	163	20	42	7	5	2	16	11	0	0	0	34	2	2	.399	.305
Devries, Jon	R-R	6-3	235	8-22-82	.214	.000	.231	4	14	1	3	0	0	0	1	1	1	0	0	4	0	0	.214	.313
Easley, Austin	R-R	6-2	215	1-15-82	.233	.213	.241	62	219	32	51	11	2	7	26	25	3	0	0	64	4	2	.397	.320
Granadillo, Tony	B-R	5-10	165	8-10-84	.291	.254	.304	67	234	43	68	11	3	5	31	27	9	0	1	52	2	0	.427	.384
Jeroloman, Chuck	R-R	6-1	190	9-14-82	.236	.206	.246	80	259	44	61	21	1	4	29	60	4	0	1	93	5	1	.371	.386
Kelly, Dustin	R-R	6-0	185	5-23-83	.160	.000	.211	7	25	3	4	0	0	1	4	3	1	0	0	7	0	1	.280	.276
Lara, Christian	B-R	5-11	150	4-11-85	.232	.247	.227	112	384	64	89	14	3	2	31	37	3	3	0	90	6	2	.299	.304
LeVier, Bret	R-R	6-3	195	4-26-83	.245	.216	.253	59	229	25	56	16	0	2	31	10	4	0	2	27	2	1	.341	.286
Moreno, Junior	R-R	6-1	185	2-27-85	.000	.000	.000	3	7	0	0	0	0	0	0	0	0	0	0	2	0	0	.000	.000
Natale, Jeff	R-R	5-9	180	8-24-82	.338	.256	.364	47	160	35	54	19	4	2	35	28	11	1	2	14	1	0	.544	.463
Otness, John	R-R	5-11	200	9-15-81	.331	.340	.328	117	441	59	146	25	0	12	67	35	21	0	11	42	1	1	.469	.398
Paniagua, Salvador	R-R	6-1	240	5-21-83	.243	.190	.260	72	267	34	65	12	1	8	37	12	1	0	3	91	0	0	.386	.276
Perry, Patrick	L-R	6-1	190	10-3-82	.241	.000	.265	16	54	5	13	4	0	0	8	6	0	0	2	15	0	0	.315	.306
Pinckney, Andrew	B-R	6-1	195	4-7-82	.311	.262	.326	128	508	91	158	33	9	21	98	36	7	0	5	78	6	0	.535	.362
Pritz, Bryan	R-R	5-10	180	5-5-82	.297	.000	.333	10	37	6	11	5	0	0	7	4	0	0	0	4	0	0	.432	.366
Sorensen, Logan	L-L	6-1	195	8-12-81	.225	.267	.213	95	315	44	71	16	0	4	32	39	5	0	2	61	2	2	.314	.319
Soto, Luis	B-R	6-1	179	12-7-85	.212	.263	.197	23	85	6	18	4	0	0	10	4	0	0	0	19	1	0	.259	.247
Stachowsky, Mitch	R-R	6-3	230	10-2-84	.165	.147	.173	37	115	18	19	8	0	5	16	16	7	0	1	49	1	0	.365	.302
Turner, Chris	R-R	5-11	195	12-2-83	.289	.250	.300	79	301	53	87	29	3	11	66	28	7	0	2	85	9	1	.515	.361
Vanderbosch, Matt	L-L	5-8	190	4-12-82	.290	.167	.330	35	124	22	36	8	3	1	13	28	3	2	2	32	8	3	.427	.427

PITCHING	B-T	HT	WT	DOB	W	L	ERA	G	GS	CG	SV	IP	H	R	ER	HR	BB	SO	AVG	vLH	vRH	K/9	BB/9
Blackley, Adam	L-L	6-1	218	2-22-85	2	7	6.15	14	13	0	0	60	75	49	41	11	26	42	.302	.364	.280	6.30	3.90
Cabrera, Henry	R-R	6-4	190	12-17-83	0	4	6.45	6	4	0	0	22	23	18	16	3	15	27	.267	.243	.286	10.88	6.04
Delgado, Jesus	R-R	6-1	198	4-19-84	7	3	3.50	33	0	0	2	72	57	30	28	3	39	69	.215	.177	.243	8.63	4.88
Dobies, Andrew	L-L	6-1	180	4-20-83	5	3	3.59	10	10	0	0	58	69	25	23	5	12	52	.300	.241	.320	8.12	1.87
Fernandes, Kyle	L-L	6-0	190	9-12-85	1	0	5.40	1	0	0	0	3	2	2	2	2	0	2	.167	.167	.167	5.40	0.00
Galvez, Gary	R-R	6-2	200	3-24-84	10	4	3.35	31	18	0	0	126	118	64	47	12	40	87	.242	.229	.254	6.20	2.85
Garcia, Harvey	R-R	6-2	170	3-16-84	3	5	2.01	32	0	0	6	45	49	18	10	3	18	54	.275	.333	.236	10.88	3.63
Gardner, Jarrett	R-R	6-1	175	3-26-81	2	9	5.06	17	17	1	0	105	136	63	59	12	14	67	.316	.312	.320	5.74	1.20
Goodson, Matt	R-R	6-3	195	9-26-82	6	4	2.76	17	12	0	2	78	60	33	24	4	20	60	.209	.206	.212	6.89	2.30
Guanchez, Argimiro	L-L	6-0	192	12-30-82	0	0	8.10	3	0	0	0	3	6	8	3	0	7	1	.353	.333	.364	2.70	18.90
Guyette, Kevin	R-R	6-4	215	12-3-82	4	0	3.26	12	3	0	1	30	30	13	11	2	6	28	.254	.255	.254	8.31	1.78
Jackson, Kyle	R-R	6-3	192	4-9-83	3	5	4.78	26	5	0	2	85	96	51	45	5	25	92	.282	.368	.211	9.78	2.66
James, Michael	R-R	6-1	185	6-2-81	1	1	3.77	30	0	0	11	43	41	22	18	1	16	38	.244	.222	.257	7.95	3.35

PITCHING	B-T	HT	WT	DOB	W	L	ERA	G	GS	CG	SV	IP	H	R	ER	HR	BB	SO	AVG	vLH	vRH	K/9	BB/9
Jordan, Brantley	L-L	6-0	190	4-24-81	4	3	1.95	17	0	0	2	32	31	9	7	0	11	28	.261	.244	.269	7.79	3.06
Lincoln, Roger	L-L	5-10	175	7-19-80	4	2	4.21	9	9	0	0	51	63	24	24	5	14	51	.301	.284	.310	8.94	2.45
Marshall, Brian	L-L	6-5	190	8-20-82	1	0	2.08	9	0	0	1	13	5	3	3	1	9	12	.116	.333	.032	8.31	6.23
Miller, Wade	R-R	6-2	220	9-13-76	0	0	3.86	1	1	0	0	5	4	2	2	1	1	4	.222	.125	.300	7.71	1.93
Newsom, Randy	R-R	6-2	200	5-6-82	1	0	5.06	15	0	0	1	37	39	26	21	2	15	20	.262	.221	.296	4.82	3.62
Ozuna, Modesto	R-R	6-1	184	1-14-82	1	0	6.35	15	0	0	1	23	29	23	16	3	11	7	.315	.362	.267	2.78	4.37
Peralta, Yader	R-R	6-1	170	2-22-86	0	0	10.38	4	0	0	0	4	7	7	5	0	3	2	.350	.444	.273	4.15	6.23
Rozier, Michael	L-L	6-5	210	7-4-85	6	5	3.90	21	20	0	0	92	94	50	40	8	49	52	.268	.284	.263	5.07	4.78
Schroyer, Ryan	R-R	6-1	215	9-28-81	3	3	2.91	26	1	0	4	59	52	23	19	1	18	45	.239	.188	.279	6.90	2.76
Shoemaker, Scott	R-R	6-4	210	9-21-81	6	3	3.50	16	15	1	0	80	76	35	31	6	36	69	.256	.252	.259	7.79	4.07
Vaughan, Beau	B-R	6-4	230	6-4-81	2	5	5.81	11	10	1	0	53	72	41	34	4	22	39	.320	.371	.287	6.66	3.76

FIELDING

Catcher	PCT	G	PO	A	E	DP	PB
Devries	1.000	3	23	2	0	0	0
Moreno	1.000	2	6	1	0	0	0
Otness	.987	29	218	18	3	1	1
Paniagua	.975	58	351	35	10	3	18
Perry	1.000	14	89	7	0	1	4
Stachowsky	.970	36	242	20	8	1	17

First Base	PCT	G	PO	A	E	DP
Chavez	1.000	1	12	1	0	1
Easley	1.000	5	39	2	0	5
LeVier	.889	1	6	2	1	0
Otness	.991	49	406	26	4	38
Paniagua	1.000	1	3	0	0	0
Pinckney	1.000	3	33	2	0	0
Sorensen	.997	85	684	58	2	68

Second Base	PCT	G	PO	A	E	DP
Chavez	.971	12	24	42	2	9
Lara	1.000	1	2	4	0	1
Jeroloman	.984	27	46	81	2	20
Granadillo	.978	55	106	158	6	32
Kelly	.960	5	8	16	1	3
LeVier	1.000	1	1	2	0	0
Natale	.972	38	74	99	5	21

Third Base	PCT	G	PO	A	E	DP
Granadillo	.946	10	10	25	2	1
Jeroloman	.930	24	15	38	4	5
LeVier	.870	10	6	14	3	1
Otness	1.000	4	4	9	0	0
Pinckney	.903	93	53	181	25	19

Shortstop	PCT	G	PO	A	E	DP
Jeroloman	.946	25	40	66	6	12
Kelly	1.000	2	5	4	0	0
Lara	.951	106	165	284	23	64
LeVier	.950	7	7	12	1	4
Natale	1.000	1	0	1	0	0

Outfield	PCT	G	PO	A	E	DP
Arias	.932	40	64	4	5	0
Ciaramella	.961	56	95	4	4	2
Corsaletti	.992	58	131	0	1	0
Cronkhite	.975	40	78	1	2	0
Easley	.988	46	76	6	1	1
LeVier	.971	39	94	5	3	1
Otness	1.000	10	12	1	0	0
Pritz	1.000	10	13	0	0	0
Soto	.923	15	24	0	2	0
Turner	.967	75	140	6	5	1
Vanderbosch	.973	33	68	3	2	1

LOWELL SPINNERS — Short-Season Class A

NEW YORK-PENN LEAGUE

BATTING	B-T	HT	WT	DOB	AVG	vLH	vRH	G	AB	R	H	2B	3B	HR	RBI	BB	HBP	SH	SF	SO	SB	CS	SLG	OBP
Burgess, Tim	L-L	6-2	205	11-3-81	.231	.167	.242	10	39	5	9	4	0	1	7	3	0	0	0	15	1	0	.410	.286
Ellsbury, Jacoby	L-L	6-1	185	9-11-83	.317	.345	.309	35	139	28	44	3	5	1	19	24	1	0	1	20	23	3	.432	.418
Farkes, Zak	R-R	5-11	190	5-30-83	.174	.190	.171	40	132	12	23	7	0	2	13	8	2	1	0	36	2	1	.273	.232
Johnson, Jay	R-R	6-2	185	12-19-82	.273	.250	.277	60	220	35	60	12	2	3	38	23	2	0	7	40	3	2	.386	.337
Kapler, Gabe	R-R	6-2	200	7-31-75	.125	.250	.000	2	8	1	1	0	0	0	0	1	0	0	0	3	0	0	.125	.222
Kelly, Dustin	R-R	6-0	185	5-23-83	.222	.115	.244	44	153	21	34	6	0	1	15	24	1	0	1	27	2	0	.281	.330
Leonard, Mike	R-R	6-0	210	5-4-82	.300	.462	.263	22	70	8	21	1	1	1	7	9	0	0	1	9	0	0	.386	.375
Lipsey, Carl	R-R	5-10	175	6-5-83	.200	.000	.250	4	5	2	1	0	0	0	0	3	0	0	0	2	0	0	.200	.500
Lowrie, Jed	B-R	6-0	180	4-17-84	.328	.256	.348	53	201	36	66	12	0	4	32	34	2	2	1	30	7	5	.448	.429
Mercurio, Matt	R-R	6-2	180	11-26-82	.225	.324	.208	66	231	33	52	9	2	2	28	33	9	3	3	48	2	4	.307	.341
Mota, Willy	R-R	6-1	165	10-25-85	.205	.143	.217	37	127	26	26	6	1	1	9	23	2	0	1	47	3	2	.291	.333
Natale, Jeff	R-R	5-9	180	8-24-82	.488	.400	.500	12	41	9	20	5	0	0	9	3	1	0	1	3	2	0	.610	.522
Perry, Patrick	L-R	6-1	190	10-3-82	.159	.000	.189	14	44	7	7	2	1	0	5	6	2	0	0	9	0	0	.250	.288
Ramos, Dominic	R-R	5-10	180	3-10-83	.260	.239	.265	65	265	42	69	8	3	5	29	26	2	2	2	56	10	3	.370	.329
Sanchez, Ricardo	R-R	5-11	215	9-6-82	.000	.000	.000	4	5	1	0	0	0	0	0	1	1	0	0	4	0	0	.000	.286
Soto, Luis	B-R	6-1	179	12-7-85	.293	.345	.277	65	246	39	72	11	1	7	48	27	7	0	1	46	2	3	.431	.377
Stachowsky, Mitch	R-R	6-3	230	10-2-84	.226	.286	.218	36	115	17	26	3	0	7	15	4	8	0	0	55	0	0	.435	.299
Twomley, Jason	L-L	6-0	215	9-20-82	.252	.128	.276	66	242	28	61	16	3	7	36	24	13	2	0	79	2	0	.430	.351
Wagner, Mark	R-R	6-1	205	6-11-84	.203	.143	.218	24	69	10	14	2	1	0	6	9	2	0	1	7	1	1	.261	.309
Yema, Yahmed	L-L	6-0	195	9-3-84	.301	.267	.307	55	219	35	66	17	2	1	29	17	0	0	1	21	8	1	.411	.350

PITCHING	B-T	HT	WT	DOB	W	L	ERA	G	GS	CG	SV	IP	H	R	ER	HR	BB	SO	AVG	vLH	vRH	K/9	BB/9
Baxter, Jim	L-L	6-0	195	8-8-83	0	0	3.27	10	0	0	0	11	8	4	4	1	5	4	.211	.143	.250	3.27	4.09
Blackley, Adam	L-L	6-1	218	2-22-85	6	3	4.01	15	15	0	0	74	82	41	33	11	23	86	.273	.362	.252	10.46	2.80
Buchholz, Clay	L-R	6-3	190	8-14-84	0	1	2.61	15	15	0	0	41	34	15	12	2	9	45	.219	.222	.217	9.80	1.96
Casillas, Ismael	R-R	6-3	215	12-8-82	2	1	3.09	18	0	0	0	32	31	12	11	0	8	40	.248	.156	.280	11.25	2.25
Cox, Tim	R-L	5-10	165	7-8-86	1	1	3.86	2	0	0	0	7	10	3	3	1	3	10	.313	.267	.353	12.86	3.86
Fernandes, Kyle	L-L	6-0	190	9-12-85	0	0	13.50	1	0	0	0	2	5	3	3	0	1	3	.500	.750	.333	13.50	4.50
Flores, Eugenio	R-R	5-10	160	4-8-82	2	1	5.06	14	0	0	0	21	23	15	12	0	7	14	.277	.269	.281	5.91	2.95
Foulke, Keith	R-R	6-0	210	10-19-72	0	0	7.36	3	0	0	0	4	8	4	3	0	1	5	.421	.400	.429	12.27	2.45
Frias, Junior	R-R	6-3	211	8-26-84	0	0	9.00	1	0	0	0	2	3	2	2	0	0	2	.333	.600	.000	9.00	0.00
Guanchez, Argimiro	L-L	6-0	192	12-30-82	1	4	4.25	26	0	0	8	36	47	28	17	1	13	41	.294	.270	.301	10.25	3.25
Guyette, Kevin	R-R	6-4	215	12-3-82	2	1	0.00	6	0	0	1	12	3	2	0	0	1	10	.081	.111	.071	7.71	0.77
Hancock, Matt	L-L	6-3	195	10-1-82	3	2	5.59	22	0	0	0	37	45	25	23	6	11	34	.290	.375	.252	8.27	2.68
Jones, Chris	R-R	6-3	205	6-9-84	3	1	2.59	11	0	0	0	24	23	10	7	1	5	26	.256	.206	.286	9.62	1.85
Jones, Hunter	L-L	6-4	235	1-10-84	1	1	3.21	12	1	0	1	28	29	12	10	2	5	30	.257	.250	.258	9.64	1.61
Large, T.J.	R-R	6-4	185	5-28-83	0	1	6.23	12	0	0	5	13	20	13	9	1	6	10	.345	.421	.308	6.92	4.15
Marshall, Brian	L-L	6-5	190	8-20-82	3	0	2.35	11	0	0	0	23	19	8	6	1	9	31	.224	.294	.206	12.13	3.52
Maxwell, Blake	R-R	6-5	255	8-1-84	3	3	2.76	26	0	0	7	46	31	16	14	1	11	29	.188	.275	.149	5.72	2.17
Newsom, Randy	R-R	6-2	200	5-6-82	0	0	0.00	1	0	0	0	3	1	0	0	0	2	4	.111	.000	.125	13.50	6.75
Ozuna, Modesto	R-R	6-1	184	1-14-82	2	0	6.35	13	0	0	0	23	25	16	16	1	12	15	.272	.167	.323	5.96	4.76
Pena, Mario	L-L	6-4	170	12-7-84	6	8	4.50	16	16	0	0	82	97	56	41	6	10	31	.286	.261	.295	3.40	1.10
Peralta, Yader	R-R	6-1	170	2-22-86	0	0	3.97	6	0	0	0	11	7	5	5	0	6	11	.184	.111	.207	8.74	4.76
Phillips, Ryan	L-L	6-4	210	5-29-84	7	2	2.28	14	14	0	0	67	45	19	17	2	31	61	.188	.214	.180	8.19	4.16
Tabeek, Kyle	R-R	5-11	190	8-2-83	0	0	9.75	7	0	0	0	12	19	15	13	1	10	6	.358	.375	.345	4.50	7.50
Zink, J.T.	R-R	6-2	195	5-6-85	0	3	2.63	14	14	0	0	48	46	19	14	2	18	26	.253	.289	.226	4.88	3.38

GAMES BY POSITION: C—Leonard 8, Perry 14, Sanchez 4, Stachowsky 36, Wagner 24. **1B**—Burgess 9, Farkes 2, Kelly 6, Leonard 7, Mercurio 20, Twomley 36. **2B**—Farkes 6, Kelly 14, Lipsey 2, Lowrie 11, Mercurio 11, Natale 10, Ramos 28. **3B**—Farkes 22, Kelly 19, Leonard 1, Mercurio 33, Ramos 3. **SS**—Kelly 3, Lowrie 40, Mercurio 1, Ramos 33. **OF**—Ellsbury 27, Johnson 48, Mota 34, Soto 62, Twomley 19, Yema 45.

GCL RED SOX — Rookie

GULF COAST LEAGUE

BATTING	B-T	HT	WT	DOB	AVG	vLH	vRH	G	AB	R	H	2B	3B	HR	RBI	BB	HBP	SH	SF	SO	SB	CS	SLG	OBP
Arambarris, Manuel	R-R	6-0	178	8-25-85	.247	.211	.258	26	85	11	21	7	0	0	3	7	2	0	0	11	1	1	.329	.319
Arias, Claudio	R-R	6-2	218	5-9-82	.368	.333	.375	4	19	5	7	0	0	3	6	0	0	0	0	3	1	0	.842	.368
Bell, Bubba	L-R	6-0	195	10-9-82	.317	.351	.307	43	164	18	52	13	2	2	27	10	3	0	2	14	2	4	.457	.363
Bladergroen, Ian	L-L	6-5	210	2-23-83	.444	.333	.467	5	18	4	8	1	1	1	6	3	0	0	0	3	0	0	.778	.524
Brown, Dustin	R-R	6-0	195	6-19-82	.222	.500	.188	6	18	3	4	1	0	0	3	4	0	0	0	2	0	0	.278	.364
Ciaramella, Matt	B-L	6-1	190	10-25-82	.205	.250	.194	11	44	3	9	1	0	0	5	3	0	0	1	8	0	1	.227	.250
Cronkhite, Ian	L-L	6-1	189	8-11-83	.435	.500	.412	6	23	6	10	3	2	1	6	1	0	0	0	2	1	0	.870	.458
Egan, Jon	R-R	6-4	210	10-12-86	.222	.200	.229	35	126	19	28	6	0	1	15	21	2	0	1	29	0	1	.294	.340
Engel, Reid	L-R	6-2	175	5-7-87	.233	.300	.217	27	103	9	24	2	1	2	8	11	1	2	0	36	2	2	.330	.313
Fulse, Sheldon	B-R	6-1	200	11-10-81	.091	.167	.000	4	11	3	1	1	0	0	1	3	1	0	0	2	0	0	.182	.333
Garcia, Jesus	R-R	5-9	150	10-10-85	.264	.320	.247	32	106	12	28	5	0	2	12	10	1	0	4	19	1	0	.368	.322
Gilbert, Archie	R-R	5-8	180	7-8-83	.219	.143	.250	24	73	9	16	3	0	0	7	2	6	1	1	10	0	0	.260	.293
Granadillo, Tony	B-R	5-10	165	8-10-84	.269	.273	.268	14	52	9	14	3	0	1	9	11	1	0	0	10	0	1	.385	.406
Hall, Mickey	L-L	6-1	195	5-20-85	.259	.250	.261	9	27	4	7	1	0	0	1	5	1	0	0	10	0	0	.296	.394
Hurst, Jason	R-R	6-0	205	3-16-81	.233	.185	.250	32	103	18	24	4	0	3	20	14	4	0	2	19	2	0	.359	.341
Jones, Michael	L-R	6-3	220	6-14-85	.306	.217	.329	31	108	13	33	9	0	2	15	10	4	0	0	18	0	1	.444	.385
Linares, Emilio	B-R	5-11	170	5-1-86	.231	.182	.253	36	108	16	25	7	0	1	8	9	0	2	1	35	1	2	.324	.288
Lipsey, Carl	R-R	5-10	175	6-5-83	.154	.000	.174	7	26	5	4	0	0	0	4	4	0	0	0	7	0	1	.154	.267
Moreno, Junior	R-R	6-1	185	2-27-85	.083	.000	.083	4	12	2	1	0	0	1	1	0	1	0	0	2	0	0	.333	.154
Rafael, Manuel	B-R	6-0	175	5-11-84	.217	.217	.217	35	129	13	28	6	0	0	12	13	1	0	1	21	2	2	.264	.292
Sanchez, Ricardo	R-R	5-11	215	9-6-82	.213	.188	.226	18	47	4	10	5	1	0	5	8	2	0	0	17	0	2	.362	.351
Santa, Moises	R-R	6-0	180	12-13-85	.309	.304	.310	30	110	15	34	4	0	2	9	4	1	0	0	16	5	2	.400	.339
Santana, Richard	R-R	5-11	160	4-20-86	.255	.086	.309	40	145	23	37	9	1	1	15	11	4	3	0	28	7	5	.352	.325
Segovia, Luis	B-R	5-10	150	7-19-86	.267	.235	.276	45	161	20	43	5	2	1	15	19	2	3	2	35	12	2	.342	.348

PITCHING	B-T	HT	WT	DOB	W	L	ERA	G	GS	CG	SV	IP	H	R	ER	HR	BB	SO	AVG	vLH	vRH	K/9	BB/9
Albury, James	L-R	6-3	185	4-1-86	2	2	4.83	10	7	0	0	32	29	21	17	4	13	22	.236	.200	.253	6.25	3.69
Blue, Scott	R-R	6-2	215	4-5-87	0	0	21.00	4	1	0	0	3	3	8	7	1	9	2	.250	.500	.125	6.00	27.00
Bowden, Michael	R-R	6-3	215	9-9-86	1	0	0.00	4	2	0	0	6	4	0	0	0	4	10	.190	.250	.176	15.00	6.00
Cabrera, Henry	R-R	6-4	190	12-17-83	2	2	3.67	7	2	0	0	27	18	13	11	5	8	27	.184	.125	.203	9.00	2.67
Cox, Tim	R-L	5-10	165	7-8-86	3	1	2.19	11	5	0	1	49	36	17	12	3	7	56	.195	.344	.163	10.22	1.28
Fernandes, Kyle	L-L	6-0	190	9-12-85	2	3	3.59	11	7	0	0	43	35	19	17	1	10	47	.224	.350	.206	9.91	2.11
Frias, Junior	R-R	6-3	211	8-26-84	0	0	0.00	1	1	0	0	1	0	0	0	0	0	2	.000	.000	.000	18.00	0.00
Garces, Rich	R-R	6-0	250	5-18-71	0	0	3.00	3	3	0	0	3	1	1	1	1	0	4	.100	.000	.167	12.00	0.00
German, Yulkin	L-L	6-2	180	8-27-83	2	1	2.57	11	8	0	0	49	33	19	14	1	29	56	.192	.278	.182	10.29	5.33
Gonzalez, Alex	R-R	5-10	185	3-8-83	2	2	3.04	18	0	0	7	27	15	12	9	2	12	21	.167	.348	.104	7.09	4.05
Hansen, Craig	R-R	6-6	210	11-15-83	1	0	0.00	2	1	0	0	3	2	0	0	0	0	4	.182	.000	.250	12.00	0.00
James, Jimmy	R-R	6-2	175	10-16-84	2	1	2.54	7	5	0	0	28	23	12	8	3	6	13	.215	.216	.214	4.13	1.91
Jefferson, John	R-R	6-1	210	7-4-83	0	1	9.53	4	0	0	0	6	8	6	6	0	2	2	.364	.000	.471	3.18	3.18
Jones, Chris	R-R	6-3	205	6-9-84	0	1	0.00	1	1	0	0	2	3	4	0	0	0	1	.333	.750	.000	5.40	0.00
Linares, Remos	R-R	6-3	180	4-23-85	1	1	2.31	13	0	0	3	23	19	7	6	1	9	20	.221	.261	.206	7.71	3.47
Ortiz, Jose	L-L	6-0	166	7-19-85	3	1	3.82	14	0	0	1	35	24	18	15	1	17	39	.195	.250	.187	9.93	4.33
Pahucki, David	R-R	6-2	210	10-17-80	0	0	27.00	1	1	0	0	1	1	2	2	0	2	1	.333	1.000	.000	13.50	27.00
Peralta, Yader	R-R	6-1	170	2-22-86	2	3	3.94	17	0	0	4	30	33	16	13	0	5	21	.289	.125	.354	6.37	1.52
Phillips, Ryan	L-L	6-4	210	5-29-84	0	0	0.00	1	0	0	0	1	0	0	0	0	0	0	.000	.000	.000	0.00	0.00
Phillips, William	R-R	6-3	177	8-23-82	0	1	4.15	9	0	0	0	17	16	10	8	0	7	14	.267	.250	.271	7.27	3.63
Prieto, Victor	R-R	6-2	175	4-24-83	0	1	27.00	1	0	0	0	0	0	1	1	0	0	1	.000	.000	.000	27.00	0.00
Rios, Travis	R-R	6-2	205	10-3-81	1	0	0.00	4	0	0	1	6	2	0	0	0	0	10	.105	.167	.077	15.88	0.00
Rudrude, Brett	R-R	6-3	195	1-23-79	0	1	2.70	4	4	0	0	7	4	3	2	0	2	8	.167	.000	.182	10.80	2.70
Smith, Chris	R-R	6-2	200	4-9-81	0	0	0.00	1	1	0	0	3	0	0	0	0	0	4	.000	.000	.000	12.00	0.00
Tabeek, Kyle	R-R	5-11	190	8-2-83	1	0	1.56	8	0	0	1	17	12	3	3	0	1	17	.197	.176	.205	8.83	0.52
Taylor, Rhys	R-R	6-3	154	10-9-85	2	2	1.49	11	5	0	0	36	28	13	6	1	7	15	.209	.239	.193	3.72	1.73
Towery, Dane	R-R	6-4	205	5-31-83	3	0	1.48	12	0	0	1	24	24	8	4	1	5	16	.253	.250	.253	5.92	1.85

GAMES BY POSITION: C—Brown 2, Egan 23, Garcia 22, Moreno 1, Sanchez 11. **1B**—Arambarris 23, Bladergroen 5, Garcia 6, M. Jones 20, Linares 2, Moreno 2. **2B**—Granadillo 12, Linares 17, Lipsey 1, Rafael 1, Santana 21, Segovia 6. **3B**—Arambarris 2, Garcia 2, Granadillo 1, Linares 16, Rafael 34, Santana 1. **SS**—Santana 17, Segovia 39. **OF**—Arias 3, Bell 37, Brown 2, Ciaramella 9, Cronkhite 5, Engel 24, Fulse 3, Gilbert 22, Hall 7, Hurst 29, Jones 7, Sanchez 1, Santa 29.

CHICAGO CUBS

BY JEFF VORVA

There was plenty of champagne flowing after games involving the Cubs in 2005. Unfortunately for the Cubs, it wasn't flowing in their clubhouse.

On Sept. 17, the Cardinals celebrated in the Wrigley Field visitor's locker room after clinching the National League Central title.

On Oct. 2, the last day of the regular season, the Cubs were at Minute Maid Park and lost a 6-4 contest to Houston and the Astros claimed the National League wild card title and enjoyed a champagne celebration of their own.

The Cubs, meanwhile, were on the outside looking in as they failed to make the playoffs for the second straight season after a magical 2003 season in which they were five outs away from a World Series. Despite high expectations, they suffered through a sub-.500 season at 79-83, a year after fading from the playoff picture in the final week.

"It's almost like one year ran into another year," Cubs manager Dusty Baker said. "There were injuries (nine players went on the DL in 2005) and different things that just spilled over. From the very beginning it was like putting your finger in the dike. There was always a leak or a hole. As soon as you get one guy back something else would happen and another guy would get hurt and it makes you wonder what the heck is going on."

In a dismal season there were two players who had high-quality campaigns.

First baseman Derrek Lee, 30, had a breakout season. He entered 2005 with a lifetime .266 average yet heading into August was a Triple Crown threat. At the end of the season, he led the National League—as well as all of the major leagues—in hitting with a .335 mark. He was second in home runs with 46 and seventh in RBIs with 107.

PLAYERS OF THE YEAR

MAJOR LEAGUE: Derrek Lee, 1b

Lee won the National League batting title in 2005, hitting .335. His 50 doubles were a career high, and he tied with Orioles' shortstop Miguel Tejada for the major league lead. His 46 homers, also a career high, ranked fourth overall. Lee was actually better on the road, hitting .342/.421/.654 away from Wrigley Field.

MINOR LEAGUE: Rich Hill, lhp

STEVE MOORE

Hill racked up 194 strikeouts in 2005, highlighted by 11 double-digit strikeout performances, including an eight-inning, 12-strikeout cameo in low Class A Peoria. Hill had 90 strikeouts at Double-A West Tenn and added another 92 at Triple-A Iowa, where Pacific Coast League hitters batted just .212 against him.

"I really didn't expect to win a batting title because you have these guys winning by hitting .340 and .350," Lee said. "But it's a great accomplishment and I'm proud of myself. It's nice to have one under my belt. Nomar (Garciaparra) told me I got my first credential by winning a batting title. It feels pretty good."

Righthander Ryan Dempster, who opened the 2005 season in the starting rotation, became the team's closer in early May and converted 33 out of 35 save opportunities. He could have been a red-hot commodity on the free agent market, but the Cubs locked him up for the next three years with a $15.5 million extension that Dempster signed at the end of the season.

Despite plenty of expected changes to the roster in 2006, the Cubs have an outstanding group of players returning including Lee, third baseman Aramis Ramirez (.302-31-92 despite missing a month with a quadriceps injury), catchers Michael Barrett (.276-16-61) and Henry Blanco and pitchers Dempster, Mark Prior (11-7, 3.67), Kerry Wood (who will be returning from arthoscopic shoulder surgery), Carlos Zambrano (14-6, 3.26 and a team-high 202 strikeouts) and Greg Maddux (13-15, 4.24).

Meanwhile, there was an interesting dynamic developing with brothers Corey and Eric Patterson.

Corey, a starting center fielder since the middle of the 2001 campaign, struggled with a .215 average and had a team-high 118 strikeouts even though he missed a month because he was sent to Triple-A Iowa to work on his swing.

But his younger brother, Eric, had a monster year in his first campaign as a professional. He was named the club's minor league position player of the year after hitting .333-13-71 for Class A Peoria. The 22-year-old Georgia Tech product stole 40 bases and hit 26 doubles and 11 triples.

The organization named Sean Gallagher, 19, as its minor league pitcher of the year after he posted a 14-5, 2.71 record with 139 strikeouts in 146 innings.

In other minor league accomplishments, first baseman Brandon Sing set a Dounle-A West Tenn franchise record with 26 home runs and Jermaine Van Buren notched a franchise best 25 saves for Triple-A Iowa.

ORGANIZATION LEADERS

BATTING

*AVG	Murton, Matt, Iowa/West Tenn	.343
R	Walker, Chris, Daytona	97
H	Walker, Chris, Daytona	152
TB	McClain, Scott, Iowa	244
2B	Montanez, Luis, Peoria/West Tenn	37
3B	Walker, Chris, Daytona	14
HR	McClain, Scott, Iowa	30
RBI	Harvey, Ryan, Peoria	100
BB	Sing, Brandon, West Tenn	91
SO	Harvey, Ryan, Peoria	137
SB	Walker, Chris, Daytona	60
*OBP	Murton, Matt, Iowa/West Tenn	.405
*SLG	McClain, Scott, Iowa	.577

PITCHING

W	Gallagher, Sean, Daytona/Peoria	14
	Nolasco, Ricky, West Tenn	14
L	Estrada, Jesse, Peoria	12
	Tavares, Anderson, Daytona/Iowa/West Tenn	12
#ERA	Gwaltney, Lee, Daytona/Peoria/West Tenn	2.07
G	Searles, Jonathan, West Tenn	59
	Shipman, Andy, West Tenn	59
CG	12 tied at	1
SV	Van Buren, Jermaine, Iowa	25
IP	Ryu, Jae-kuk, West Tenn	170
BB	Pinto, Renyel, Iowa/West Tenn	82
SO	Hill, Rich, Iowa/Peoria/West Tenn	194

*Minimum 250 at-bats. #Minimum 75 innings.

CHICAGO CUBS

Manager: Dusty Baker.

2005 Record: 79-83, .488 (4th, NL Central).

BATTING	B-T	HT	WT	DOB	AVG	vLH	vRH	G	AB	R	H	2B	3B	HR	RBI	BB	HBP	SH	SF	SO	SB	CS	SLG	OBP
Barrett, Michael	R-R	6-3	210	10-22-76	.276	.320	.258	133	424	48	117	32	3	16	61	40	7	2	4	61	0	3	.479	.345
Blanco, Henry	R-R	5-11	220	8-29-71	.242	.194	.254	54	161	16	39	6	0	6	25	11	0	4	2	24	0	0	.391	.287
Burnitz, Jeromy	L-R	6-0	210	4-15-69	.258	.236	.267	160	605	84	156	31	2	24	87	57	3	1	5	109	5	4	.435	.322
Cedeno, Ronny	R-R	6-0	180	2-2-83	.300	.256	.341	41	80	13	24	3	0	1	6	5	2	2	0	11	1	0	.375	.356
Dubois, Jason	R-R	6-5	220	3-26-79	.239	.232	.244	52	142	15	34	12	0	7	22	7	3	0	0	49	0	1	.472	.289
Fontenot, Mike	L-R	5-8	160	6-9-80	.000	.000	.000	7	2	4	0	0	0	0	0	2	1	0	0	0	0	0	.000	.600
Garciaparra, Nomar	R-R	6-0	190	7-23-73	.283	.281	.284	62	230	28	65	12	0	9	30	12	2	0	3	24	0	0	.452	.320
Gerut, Jody	L-L	6-0	190	9-18-77	.071	1.000	.000	11	14	1	1	1	0	0	0	2	0	0	0	3	0	0	.143	.188
Greenberg, Adam	L-L	5-9	180	2-21-81	.000	.000	.000	1	0	0	0	0	0	0	0	0	1	0	0	0	0	0	.000	1.000
Grieve, Ben	L-R	6-4	215	5-4-76	.250	.000	.278	23	20	1	5	0	0	0	1	5	0	0	0	7	0	0	.250	.400
Hairston, Jerry	R-R	5-10	185	5-29-76	.261	.255	.263	114	380	51	99	25	2	4	30	31	12	7	0	46	8	9	.368	.336
Hollandsworth, Todd	L-L	6-2	215	4-20-73	.254	.270	.251	107	268	23	68	17	2	5	35	18	1	1	2	53	4	4	.388	.301
Lawton, Matt	L-R	5-10	190	11-3-71	.244	.136	.286	19	78	8	19	2	0	1	5	4	1	0	0	8	1	0	.308	.289
2-team (101 Pittsburgh)					.268	.219	.287	120	452	61	121	30	1	11	49	62	10	0	4	69	17	9	.412	.366
Lee, Derrek	R-R	6-5	245	9-6-75	.335	.333	.336	158	594	120	199	50	3	46	107	85	5	0	7	109	15	3	.662	.418
Macias, Jose	B-R	5-8	190	1-25-72	.254	.277	.246	112	177	15	45	8	0	1	13	6	0	4	3	24	4	3	.316	.274
McClain, Scott	R-R	6-4	220	5-19-72	.143	.000	.182	13	14	1	2	1	0	0	1	2	0	0	0	2	0	0	.214	.250
Murton, Matt	R-R	6-1	215	10-3-81	.321	.380	.261	51	140	19	45	3	2	7	14	16	0	2	2	22	2	1	.521	.386
Patterson, Corey	L-R	5-9	180	8-13-79	.215	.169	.231	126	451	47	97	15	3	13	34	23	1	5	1	118	15	5	.348	.254
Perez, Neifi	B-R	6-0	195	6-2-73	.274	.267	.277	154	572	59	157	33	1	9	54	18	3	12	4	47	8	4	.383	.298
Ramirez, Aramis	R-R	6-1	215	6-25-78	.302	.355	.284	123	463	72	140	30	0	31	92	35	6	0	2	60	0	1	.568	.358
Soto, Geovany	R-R	6-1	230	1-20-83	.000	.000	.000	1	1	0	0	0	0	0	0	0	0	0	0	0	0	0	.000	.000
Theriot, Ryan	R-R	5-11	175	12-7-79	.154	.250	.000	9	13	3	2	1	0	0	0	1	0	0	0	2	0	0	.231	.214
Walker, Todd	L-R	6-0	185	5-25-73	.305	.352	.291	110	397	50	121	25	3	12	40	31	1	2	2	40	1	1	.474	.355
Wilson, Enrique	B-R	5-11	190	7-27-73	.136	.333	.105	15	22	1	3	2	0	0	0	3	0	0	0	1	0	0	.227	.240

PITCHING	B-T	HT	WT	DOB	W	L	ERA	G	GS	CG	SV	IP	H	R	ER	HR	BB	SO	AVG	vLH	vRH	K/9	BB/9
Bartosh, Cliff	L-L	6-2	190	9-5-79	0	2	5.49	19	0	0	0	20	23	13	12	7	11	15	.307	.269	.327	6.86	5.03
Borowski, Joe	R-R	6-2	225	5-4-71	0	0	6.55	11	0	0	0	11	12	8	8	5	1	11	.261	.067	.355	9.00	0.82
Dempster, Ryan	R-R	6-2	215	5-3-77	5	3	3.13	63	6	0	33	92	83	35	32	4	49	89	.242	.278	.216	8.71	4.79
Fox, Chad	R-R	6-3	210	9-3-70	0	0	6.75	11	0	0	1	8	8	6	6	2	8	11	.276	.308	.250	12.38	9.00
Hawkins, LaTroy	R-R	6-5	215	12-21-72	1	4	3.32	21	0	0	4	19	18	9	7	4	7	13	.250	.200	.286	6.16	3.32
Hill, Rich	L-L	6-5	205	3-11-80	0	2	9.13	10	4	0	0	24	25	24	24	3	17	21	.260	.227	.270	7.99	6.46
Koronka, John	L-L	6-1	180	7-3-80	1	2	7.47	4	3	0	0	16	19	13	13	2	8	10	.284	.385	.259	5.74	4.60
Leicester, Jon	R-R	6-3	230	2-7-79	0	2	9.00	6	1	0	0	9	11	10	9	2	9	7	.324	.462	.238	7.00	9.00
Maddux, Greg	R-R	6-0	180	4-14-66	13	15	4.24	35	35	3	0	225	239	112	106	29	36	136	.275	.283	.270	5.44	1.44
Mitre, Sergio	R-R	6-4	210	2-16-81	2	5	5.37	21	7	1	0	60	62	37	36	11	23	37	.261	.294	.235	5.52	3.43
Novoa, Roberto	R-R	6-5	200	8-15-79	4	5	4.43	49	0	0	0	45	47	22	22	4	25	47	.264	.221	.291	9.47	5.04
Ohman, Will	L-L	6-2	195	8-13-77	2	2	2.91	69	0	0	0	43	32	14	14	6	24	45	.201	.173	.231	9.35	4.98
Prior, Mark	R-R	6-5	230	9-7-80	11	7	3.67	27	27	1	0	167	143	73	68	25	59	188	.227	.216	.236	10.15	3.19
Remlinger, Mike	L-L	6-1	215	3-23-66	0	3	4.91	35	0	0	0	33	31	19	18	5	12	30	.250	.326	.210	8.18	3.27
Rusch, Glendon	L-L	6-1	225	11-7-74	9	8	4.52	46	19	1	0	145	175	79	73	14	53	111	.302	.333	.294	6.87	3.28
Van Buren, Jermaine	R-R	6-1	220	7-2-80	0	2	3.00	6	0	0	0	6	2	2	2	0	9	3	.118	.000	.125	4.50	13.50
Wellemeyer, Todd	R-R	6-3	205	8-30-78	2	1	6.12	22	0	0	1	32	32	23	22	7	22	32	.264	.234	.284	8.91	6.12
Williams, Jerome	R-R	6-3	245	12-4-81	6	8	3.91	18	17	0	0	106	98	50	46	12	45	59	.253	.286	.230	5.01	3.82
2-team (4 San Francisco)					6	10	4.26	22	20	0	0	123	119	62	58	14	49	70	.262	.299	.236	5.14	3.60
Williamson, Scott	R-R	6-0	185	2-17-76	0	0	5.65	17	0	0	0	14	15	9	9	3	6	23	.273	.333	.250	14.44	3.77
Wood, Kerry	R-R	6-5	225	6-16-77	3	4	4.23	21	10	0	0	66	52	32	31	14	26	77	.215	.220	.211	10.50	3.55
Wuertz, Michael	R-R	6-3	205	12-15-78	6	2	3.81	75	0	0	0	76	60	36	32	6	40	89	.219	.260	.197	10.59	4.76
Zambrano, Carlos	B-R	6-5	255	6-1-81	14	6	3.26	33	33	2	0	223	170	88	81	21	86	202	.212	.212	.212	8.14	3.47

FIELDING

Catcher	PCT	G	PO	A	E	DP	PB
Barrett	.994	122	870	51	6	8	4
Blanco	.998	54	407	31	1	2	2

First Base	PCT	G	PO	A	E	DP
Hollandsworth	1.000	1	3	0	0	0
Lee	.996	158	1322	122	6	118
McClain	1.000	4	16	0	0	1
Walker	1.000	4	26	4	0	4
Wilson	1.000	3	7	0	0	1

Second Base	PCT	G	PO	A	E	DP
Cedeno	1.000	1	0	1	0	0
Hairston	.973	44	69	111	5	23
Macias	1.000	20	27	34	0	8
Perez	.975	26	32	47	2	10
Theriot	1.000	3	3	9	0	0
Walker	.985	97	164	243	6	44
Wilson	.929	5	4	9	1	5

Third Base	PCT	G	PO	A	E	DP
Garciaparra	.934	34	20	65	6	1
Macias	.913	23	6	15	2	1
McClain	1.000	3	1	1	0	0
Perez	1.000	4	0	1	0	0
Ramirez	.947	119	70	218	16	14
Wilson	.000	1	0	0	0	0

Shortstop	PCT	G	PO	A	E	DP
Cedeno	.986	29	30	39	1	8
Garciaparra	.939	26	41	51	6	16
Hairston	1.000	1	1	1	0	1
Perez	.982	130	175	385	10	81
Wilson	1.000	3	2	6	0	1

Outfield	PCT	G	PO	A	E	DP
Burnitz	.984	160	311	6	5	1
Dubois	.980	38	47	2	1	0
Gerut	1.000	5	9	0	0	0
Grieve	.000	1	0	0	0	0
Hairston	.983	62	114	3	2	0
Hollandsworth	.980	95	96	2	2	0
Lawton	.971	19	33	0	1	0
Macias	.933	20	26	2	2	0
Murton	.969	43	62	1	2	1
Patterson	.980	122	239	6	5	2

FARM SYSTEM

General Manager: Jim Hendry. **Director, Player Development:** Oneri Fleita. **Scouting Director:** John Stockstill.

Class	Farm Team	League	W	L	Pct.	Finish*	Manager	Affiliate Since
AAA	Iowa Cubs (Des Moines)	Pacific Coast	64	75	.460	13th (16)	Mike Quade	1981
AA	West Tenn Diamond Jaxx (Jackson)	Southern	83	56	.597	**1st (10)**	Bobby Dickerson	1998
High A	Daytona (Fla.) Cubs	Florida State	69	66	.511	5th (12)	Richie Zisk	1993
Low A	Peoria (Ill.) Chiefs	Midwest	68	72	.486	9th (14)	Julio Garcia	2005
SS A	Boise (Idaho) Hawks	Northwest	34	42	.447	t-6th (8)	Trey Forkerway	2001
Rookie	Mesa (Ariz.) Cubs	Arizona	19	37	.339	9th (9)	Steve McFarland	1997

*Finish in overall standings (No. of teams in league)/playoff teams in **boldface**

ED WOLFSTEIN

Ryan Dempster: Now a successful closer

TONY FARLOW

Matt Murton: Highest batting average in the system

IOWA CUBS — Triple-A

PACIFIC COAST LEAGUE

BATTING	B-T	HT	WT	DOB	AVG	vLH	vRH	G	AB	R	H	2B	3B	HR	RBI	BB	HBP	SH	SF	SO	SB	CS	SLG	OBP
Arteaga, Josh	R-R	5-9	170	3-14-80	.250	.000	.333	4	4	1	1	0	0	0	0	1	0	1	0	0	0	0	.250	.400
Bacon, Dwaine	B-R	5-11	190	4-11-79	.173	.000	.205	18	52	8	9	1	1	0	3	7	1	1	0	15	7	0	.231	.283
Bell, Rick	R-R	6-2	195	4-5-79	.200	.333	.077	16	25	6	5	1	0	0	2	4	0	0	1	5	0	0	.240	.300
Cedeno, Ronny	R-R	6-0	180	2-2-83	.355	.397	.342	65	245	42	87	14	1	8	36	20	1	7	2	31	11	3	.518	.403
Dubois, Jason	R-R	6-5	220	3-26-79	.529	.800	.417	4	17	4	9	1	0	1	6	1	0	0	0	3	0	0	.765	.556
Echevarria, Angel	R-R	6-4	235	5-25-71	.137	.133	.139	18	51	4	7	0	0	1	7	2	1	0	0	13	0	0	.196	.185
Fontenot, Mike	L-R	5-8	160	6-9-80	.272	.257	.275	111	379	60	103	22	10	6	39	59	6	3	2	77	3	2	.430	.377
Frese, Nate	R-R	6-3	205	7-10-77	.245	.217	.257	67	204	25	50	10	0	5	27	15	1	3	1	44	0	0	.368	.299
Grieve, Ben	L-R	6-4	215	5-4-76	.266	.219	.282	86	293	44	78	19	1	14	51	48	1	0	0	59	0	0	.481	.371
Hairston, Jerry	R-R	5-10	185	5-29-76	.318	.250	.333	5	22	3	7	0	1	0	2	0	2	0	1	3	3	0	.409	.360
Halter, Shane	R-R	6-0	195	11-8-69	.229	.556	.154	16	48	10	11	4	0	1	8	7	0	0	0	8	1	0	.375	.327
Hoffpauir, Micah	L-L	6-3	190	3-1-80	.268	.237	.278	119	392	48	105	14	3	3	47	38	3	1	4	59	2	0	.342	.334
Hubbard, Trenidad	R-R	5-9	200	5-11-66	.320	.340	.314	62	244	34	78	17	0	4	29	25	4	1	0	26	15	8	.439	.392
2-team (12 Round Rock)					.301	.333	.293	79	302	42	91	19	1	4	32	33	5	2	1	36	19	10	.411	.378
Johnson, Mark	L-R	6-0	200	9-12-75	.266	.216	.279	60	177	19	47	10	1	3	26	34	2	2	1	25	0	1	.384	.388
Kelton, David	R-R	6-3	195	12-17-79	.283	.297	.278	122	460	59	130	28	1	11	67	30	3	0	2	78	14	5	.420	.329
Lewis, Richard	R-R	6-1	195	6-29-80	.217	.290	.191	87	263	28	57	10	3	2	23	18	4	2	0	64	4	2	.300	.277
McClain, Scott	R-R	6-4	220	5-19-72	.291	.339	.272	121	423	75	123	27	2	30	93	45	4	0	9	84	1	1	.577	.358
Moriarty, Mike	R-R	6-0	190	3-8-74	.217	.231	.212	18	46	3	10	2	1	2	7	5	1	0	0	15	0	1	.435	.308
Murray, Calvin	R-R	5-11	190	7-30-71	.297	.321	.288	135	499	77	148	26	7	5	50	58	12	5	5	72	18	7	.407	.380
Murton, Matt	R-R	6-1	215	10-3-81	.353	.556	.280	9	34	4	12	2	0	1	3	4	0	0	0	8	0	0	.500	.421
Patterson, Corey	L-R	5-9	180	8-13-79	.297	.324	.281	24	91	16	27	4	0	5	12	8	2	1	0	19	6	1	.505	.366
Ransom, Cody	R-R	6-2	210	2-17-76	.234	.235	.233	65	171	22	40	5	1	2	16	14	1	0	2	56	6	0	.310	.293
2-team (24 Oklahoma)					.243	.250	.241	89	263	35	64	10	1	7	33	22	1	0	2	88	6	1	.369	.302

BATTING	B-T	HT	WT	DOB	AVG	vLH	vRH	G	AB	R	H	2B	3B	HR	RBI	BB	HBP	SH	SF	SO	SB	CS	SLG	OBP
Soto, Geovany	R-R	6-1	230	1-20-83	.253	.280	.243	91	292	30	74	14	0	4	39	48	0	3	2	77	0	1	.342	.357
Walker, Todd	L-R	6-0	185	5-25-73	.216	.125	.241	9	37	3	8	3	0	0	3	1	0	0	0	4	0	0	.297	.237

PITCHING	B-T	HT	WT	DOB	W	L	ERA	G	GS	CG	SV	IP	H	R	ER	HR	BB	SO	AVG	vLH	vRH	K/9	BB/9
Anderson, Jimmy	L-L	6-1	210	1-22-76	0	0	3.38	1	1	0	0	5	6	2	2	1	2	2	.300	1.000	.222	3.38	3.38
Baez, Federico	R-R	6-2	185	8-4-81	0	0	8.31	4	0	0	0	4	5	4	4	0	3	6	.278	.200	.308	12.46	6.23
Bartosh, Cliff	L-L	6-2	190	9-5-79	1	2	5.08	22	0	0	1	28	40	18	16	3	16	26	.342	.343	.341	8.26	5.08
Borowski, Joe	R-R	6-2	225	5-4-71	0	0	2.25	7	0	0	0	8	3	4	2	2	3	4	.107	.143	.095	4.50	3.38
Brownlie, Bobby	R-R	6-0	210	10-5-80	6	7	4.74	27	14	0	0	104	98	56	55	11	42	73	.253	.277	.236	6.30	3.62
Cunnane, Will	R-R	6-1	200	4-24-74	1	1	6.32	24	0	0	0	37	49	29	26	8	17	33	.320	.294	.333	8.03	4.14
Dawley, Joe	R-R	6-4	230	9-19-71	1	1	11.81	4	0	0	0	5	10	7	7	0	7	5	.400	.400	.400	8.44	11.81
2-team (13 Portland)					2	1	8.44	17	0	0	0	21	26	21	20	1	23	22	.299	.324	.280	9.28	9.70
Haines, Talley	R-R	6-5	205	11-16-76	2	1	2.36	21	0	0	0	27	26	9	7	2	5	29	.260	.250	.268	9.79	1.69
Hill, Rich	L-L	6-5	205	3-11-80	6	1	3.60	11	10	1	0	65	53	28	26	11	14	92	.218	.203	.223	12.74	1.94
Koronka, John	L-L	6-1	180	7-3-80	9	11	4.24	23	21	0	0	136	135	65	64	12	48	96	.265	.231	.274	6.35	3.18
Leicester, Jon	R-R	6-3	230	2-7-79	3	8	5.51	24	16	0	1	98	115	65	60	17	42	73	.294	.360	.247	6.70	3.86
McGlinchy, Kevin	R-R	6-5	250	6-28-77	0	1	5.52	18	1	0	0	29	32	21	18	5	11	18	.286	.382	.244	5.52	3.38
Mendez, Adalberto	R-R	6-2	160	3-22-82	0	0	0.00	3	0	0	0	3	1	0	0	0	1	3	.100	.000	.167	9.00	3.00
Mercedes, Jose	R-R	6-1	180	3-5-71	1	1	6.75	10	0	0	0	13	19	13	10	4	7	14	.333	.429	.302	9.45	4.73
Mitre, Sergio	R-R	6-4	210	2-16-81	5	6	4.33	13	13	1	0	71	72	34	34	5	22	55	.263	.307	.237	7.00	2.80
Nolen, Walt	R-R	6-1	180	10-11-81	0	0	6.23	3	0	0	0	4	5	3	3	1	0	4	.313	.200	.364	8.31	0.00
Norton, Phil	R-L	6-0	215	2-1-76	3	4	5.49	25	7	0	0	57	55	36	35	11	24	43	.259	.290	.247	6.75	3.77
2-team (8 Round Rock)					3	5	5.97	33	7	0	0	63	62	46	42	11	34	46	.264	.288	.253	6.54	4.83
Novoa, Roberto	R-R	6-5	200	8-15-79	2	2	3.29	19	0	0	4	27	20	11	10	1	11	18	.217	.243	.200	5.93	3.62
Ohman, Will	L-L	6-2	195	8-13-77	1	0	4.15	8	0	0	1	9	4	4	4	2	2	12	.138	.100	.158	12.46	2.08
Oliver, Darren	R-L	6-2	220	10-6-70	0	3	13.50	3	3	0	0	13	28	20	20	3	5	10	.444	.722	.333	6.75	3.38
2-team (4 Tucson)					1	3	9.38	7	7	0	0	32	61	34	33	6	8	18	.415	.638	.310	5.12	2.27
O'Malley, Ryan	R-L	6-1	190	4-9-80	3	2	6.33	7	4	0	0	27	40	19	19	6	11	26	.351	.385	.341	8.67	3.67
Oropesa, Eddie	L-L	6-0	205	11-23-71	0	1	7.36	7	0	0	0	7	12	8	6	1	7	10	.375	.000	.462	12.27	8.59
Phelps, Travis	R-R	6-2	170	7-25-77	2	0	5.28	18	0	0	0	29	29	18	17	7	17	28	.261	.189	.297	8.69	5.28
2-team (7 Colorado Springs)					3	1	7.68	25	0	0	0	41	55	36	35	13	26	36	.329	.274	.362	7.90	5.71
Pignatiello, Carmen	L-L	6-1	180	9-12-82	1	5	5.51	22	5	0	0	47	52	34	29	6	20	43	.274	.370	.235	8.18	3.80
Pinto, Renyel	L-L	6-4	195	7-8-82	1	2	9.53	6	6	0	0	23	31	30	24	3	24	24	.348	.368	.343	9.53	9.53
Prior, Mark	R-R	6-5	230	9-7-80	0	1	10.50	1	1	0	0	6	9	7	7	0	1	7	.360	.429	.333	10.50	1.50
Rohlicek, Russ	R-L	6-6	230	12-26-79	3	1	4.33	55	0	0	3	62	48	35	30	5	45	54	.213	.243	.199	7.80	6.50
Tavares, Anderson	R-R	6-1	165	2-14-82	0	1	10.80	2	1	0	0	3	7	4	4	0	1	4	.438	.200	.545	10.80	2.70
Teut, Nate	R-L	6-7	220	3-11-76	0	0	0.00	2	0	0	0	3	2	0	0	0	0	1	.250	.000	.286	3.38	0.00
Valdes, Raul	L-L	5-11	190	11-27-77	6	7	5.93	25	17	0	1	99	135	71	65	7	39	73	.330	.327	.331	6.66	3.56
Van Buren, Jermaine	R-R	6-1	220	7-2-80	2	3	1.98	52	0	0	25	55	33	13	12	5	22	65	.181	.221	.158	10.70	3.62
Wellemeyer, Todd	R-R	6-3	205	8-30-78	3	2	3.02	12	12	0	0	54	47	21	18	2	25	48	.235	.247	.223	8.05	4.19
Williams, Jerome	R-R	6-3	245	12-4-81	1	1	2.22	4	4	0	0	24	27	10	6	2	6	17	.265	.171	.328	6.29	2.22
2-team (6 Fresno)					2	5	6.22	10	10	0	0	55	74	44	38	5	23	32	.320	.220	.386	5.24	3.76
Williamson, Scott	R-R	6-0	185	2-17-76	1	0	3.86	6	0	0	0	7	4	3	3	1	3	10	.154	.143	.167	12.86	3.86
Wood, Kerry	R-R	6-5	225	6-16-77	0	0	2.84	3	3	0	0	13	11	4	4	1	6	18	.239	.190	.280	12.79	4.26

FIELDING

Catcher	PCT	G	PO	A	E	DP	PB
Halter	.000	1	0	0	0	0	0
Johnson	.988	53	378	24	5	2	3
Soto	.995	87	672	62	4	8	11

First Base	PCT	G	PO	A	E	DP
Bell	.962	6	25	0	1	3
Halter	1.000	1	6	0	0	1
Hoffpauir	.999	98	752	52	1	84
Johnson	1.000	2	0	1	0	0
Kelton	1.000	10	60	3	0	5
McClain	.989	45	328	23	4	44
Ransom	1.000	1	1	0	0	0

Second Base	PCT	G	PO	A	E	DP
Fontenot	.984	63	145	162	5	48
Frese	.800	3	3	1	1	1
Hairston	1.000	2	5	5	0	1
Lewis	.991	75	140	179	3	50
Ransom	1.000	5	5	8	0	3
Walker	1.000	6	8	17	0	4

Third Base	PCT	G	PO	A	E	DP
Arteaga	.000	1	0	0	0	0
Bell	.889	3	0	8	1	1
Fontenot	.918	41	22	68	8	8
Frese	.944	30	11	57	4	5
Halter	.750	4	0	3	1	0
Johnson	1.000	1	1	1	0	0
Lewis	1.000	2	1	4	0	0
McClain	.951	69	42	113	8	15
Ransom	1.000	14	6	22	0	0

Shortstop	PCT	G	PO	A	E	DP
Arteaga	1.000	2	1	0	0	0
Cedeno	.961	65	100	198	12	50
Fontenot	1.000	3	3	2	0	0
Frese	.965	27	39	70	4	14
Halter	.977	12	13	30	1	5
McClain	1.000	3	4	2	0	1
Moriarty	.955	16	21	43	3	9
Ransom	.971	30	47	89	4	23

Outfield	PCT	G	PO	A	E	DP
Bacon	.941	14	15	1	1	0
Dubois	1.000	4	11	0	0	0
Echevarria	.950	14	18	1	1	1
Fontenot	.000	1	0	0	0	0
Grieve	.980	65	94	2	2	0
Hairston	1.000	2	3	0	0	0
Halter	1.000	1	2	0	0	0
Hoffpauir	.929	15	13	0	1	0
Hubbard	.981	58	99	5	2	0
Kelton	.983	107	163	7	3	1
Murray	.983	131	229	6	4	1
Murton	.923	9	12	0	1	0
Patterson	1.000	23	60	3	0	1

WEST TENN DIAMOND JAXX — Double-A

SOUTHERN LEAGUE

BATTING	B-T	HT	WT	DOB	AVG	vLH	vRH	G	AB	R	H	2B	3B	HR	RBI	BB	HBP	SH	SF	SO	SB	CS	SLG	OBP
Bacon, Dwaine	B-R	5-11	190	4-11-79	.267	.228	.285	98	292	57	78	10	7	2	15	46	5	4	0	90	37	14	.370	.376
Coats, Buck	L-R	6-3	195	6-9-82	.282	.299	.276	127	439	47	124	32	6	1	49	38	2	1	4	80	17	5	.390	.340
Craig, Matt	B-R	6-2	200	4-16-81	.275	.299	.260	99	327	51	90	24	0	12	57	32	4	0	8	62	7	4	.459	.340
Creighton, Matt	R-R	6-1	205	2-22-79	.245	.342	.188	42	102	11	25	7	0	2	11	6	1	0	0	18	0	1	.373	.294
Frese, Nate	R-R	6-3	205	7-10-77	.375	.471	.267	14	32	3	12	2	0	2	7	4	0	0	0	5	0	0	.625	.444
Garciaparra, Nomar	R-R	6-0	190	7-23-73	.231	.286	.167	4	13	2	3	0	0	0	0	1	1	0	0	1	0	0	.231	.333
Greenberg, Adam	L-L	5-9	180	2-21-81	.269	.283	.263	95	305	51	82	12	9	4	33	56	4	14	3	68	15	4	.407	.386
Hoffpauir, Micah	L-L	6-3	190	3-1-80	.160	.300	.067	7	25	1	4	0	0	1	2	0	0	0	0	6	0	0	.280	.160
Kopitzke, Casey	R-R	6-1	205	5-31-78	.220	.225	.216	55	177	12	39	3	1	0	10	13	1	2	1	28	1	1	.249	.276
Lewis, Richard	R-R	6-1	195	6-29-80	.246	.160	.295	28	69	8	17	1	1	1	7	13	1	0	0	18	2	1	.333	.373
McGehee, Casey	R-R	6-1	195	10-12-82	.297	.308	.291	124	455	67	135	31	1	8	72	43	1	0	6	64	2	2	.422	.354
Montanez, Luis	R-R	6-2	185	12-15-81	.268	.385	.228	45	153	20	41	9	1	2	14	12	2	2	2	21	0	2	.379	.325
Murton, Matt	R-R	6-1	215	10-3-81	.342	.359	.332	78	313	46	107	17	4	8	46	29	4	3	1	42	18	5	.498	.403
O'Toole, Paul	L-R	6-1	220	2-24-80	.083	.000	.120	12	36	4	3	1	0	0	4	4	2	0	1	11	1	1	.111	.209

BATTING	B-T	HT	WT	DOB	AVG	vLH	vRH	G	AB	R	H	2B	3B	HR	RBI	BB	HBP	SH	SF	SO	SB	CS	SLG	OBP
Patterson, Eric	L-R	5-11	170	4-8-83	.200	.333	.067	9	30	5	6	2	0	0	2	6	0	0	1	7	3	2	.267	.324
Pie, Felix	L-L	6-2	175	2-8-85	.304	.289	.313	59	240	41	73	17	5	11	25	16	2	1	3	53	13	9	.554	.349
Reyes, Jose	B-R	5-11	180	2-26-84	.257	.272	.251	97	319	27	82	10	0	3	50	27	1	5	3	48	6	3	.317	.314
Sing, Brandon	R-R	6-3	200	3-13-81	.276	.272	.279	127	409	74	113	29	0	26	71	91	1	0	7	110	2	5	.538	.404
Sisk, Aaron	R-R	6-0	190	9-17-78	.241	.239	.242	48	137	18	33	6	1	6	19	19	0	1	1	32	1	1	.431	.331
Spearman, Jemel	R-R	6-0	190	12-27-80	.348	.471	.276	14	46	6	16	3	2	0	6	0	1	0	0	6	2	1	.500	.362
Theriot, Ryan	R-R	5-11	175	12-7-79	.304	.326	.290	120	448	52	136	28	4	1	53	45	1	4	5	38	24	10	.391	.365
Weston, Aaron	L-L	6-5	173	11-5-80	.316	.375	.273	11	19	4	6	3	0	0	2	1	0	0	0	3	0	0	.474	.350

PITCHING	B-T	HT	WT	DOB	W	L	ERA	G	GS	CG	SV	IP	H	R	ER	HR	BB	SO	AVG	vLH	vRH	K/9	BB/9
Aardsma, David	R-R	6-5	200	12-27-81	4	1	3.91	33	3	0	2	51	48	22	22	3	32	43	.259	.265	.255	7.64	5.68
Atlee, Thomas	R-R	5-10	200	8-6-79	3	1	3.63	29	0	0	3	35	39	21	14	3	10	20	.273	.227	.312	5.19	2.60
Baez, Federico	R-R	6-2	185	8-4-81	4	3	4.58	41	2	0	2	55	68	29	28	4	30	35	.315	.321	.311	5.73	4.91
Cherry, Rocky	R-R	6-5	215	8-19-79	0	0	2.89	3	3	0	0	9	8	5	3	0	4	9	.229	.167	.241	8.68	3.86
Connolly, Jon	R-L	6-0	205	8-24-83	3	2	4.44	9	4	0	0	26	29	17	13	3	9	20	.282	.200	.308	6.84	3.08
Ferreras, Yorkin	L-L	6-1	155	1-28-81	2	4	5.52	30	0	0	2	29	43	26	18	5	6	31	.333	.321	.342	9.51	1.84
Gwaltney, Lee	R-R	6-6	210	5-6-80	0	0	0.00	1	0	0	0	1	1	0	0	0	0	0	.333	.000	.333	0.00	0.00
Haines, Talley	R-R	6-5	205	11-16-76	4	2	1.78	23	0	0	13	25	24	7	5	0	2	20	.250	.167	.315	7.11	0.71
Hill, Rich	L-L	6-5	205	3-11-80	4	3	3.28	10	10	0	0	58	42	22	21	9	21	90	.200	.185	.207	14.05	3.28
Hoerman, Jared	R-R	6-4	230	4-25-77	0	0	0.00	2	0	0	0	1	0	0	0	0	2	0	.000	.000	.000	0.00	13.50
Marmol, Carlos	R-R	6-2	170	10-14-82	3	4	3.65	14	14	0	0	81	70	33	33	10	40	70	.239	.223	.252	7.75	4.43
Marshall, Sean	L-L	6-5	185	8-30-82	0	1	2.52	4	4	0	0	25	16	7	7	1	5	24	.180	.182	.179	8.64	1.80
McGlinchy, Kevin	R-R	6-5	250	6-28-77	0	1	4.32	9	0	0	3	8	12	6	4	0	4	7	.316	.231	.360	7.56	4.32
Nolasco, Ricky	R-R	6-1	205	12-13-82	14	3	2.89	27	27	1	0	162	151	57	52	13	46	173	.245	.259	.234	9.63	2.56
O'Malley, Ryan	R-L	6-1	190	4-9-80	3	3	3.91	31	9	0	0	78	78	41	34	7	25	55	.257	.347	.227	6.32	2.87
Pignatiello, Carmen	L-L	6-1	180	9-12-82	5	4	2.68	16	10	0	0	81	67	26	24	3	28	77	.228	.193	.242	8.59	3.12
Pinto, Renyel	L-L	6-4	195	7-8-82	10	3	2.71	22	21	1	0	130	101	43	39	3	58	123	.223	.273	.207	8.54	4.03
Ramos, Victor	L-R	6-3	220	10-4-81	2	3	3.24	19	0	0	0	25	21	9	9	1	12	18	.239	.279	.200	6.48	4.32
Ryu, Jae-kuk	R-R	6-3	175	5-30-83	11	8	3.34	27	27	1	0	170	154	67	63	12	49	133	.246	.223	.264	7.06	2.60
Searles, Jonathan	R-R	6-3	200	1-18-81	6	3	3.35	59	0	0	1	81	74	30	30	5	29	72	.245	.237	.250	8.03	3.24
Shipman, Andy	R-R	6-3	185	10-18-81	3	6	3.17	59	0	0	15	65	60	32	23	1	27	68	.241	.221	.255	9.37	3.72
Tavares, Anderson	R-R	6-1	165	2-14-82	0	0	0.00	1	0	0	0	2	1	0	0	0	1	0	.167	.000	.167	0.00	4.50
Valdes, Raul	L-L	5-11	190	11-27-77	2	0	5.09	5	5	0	0	23	28	13	13	1	3	18	.322	.400	.290	7.04	1.17
Wells, Randy	R-R	6-3	200	8-28-82	0	1	3.86	6	0	0	1	9	13	4	4	0	7	4	.371	.200	.440	3.86	6.75

FIELDING

Catcher	PCT	G	PO	A	E	DP	PB
Kopitzke	.998	52	379	29	1	6	1
O'Toole	.975	4	35	4	1	1	0
Reyes	.994	91	712	75	5	13	1

First Base	PCT	G	PO	A	E	DP
Craig	.986	49	393	33	6	41
Hoffpauir	1.000	3	28	0	0	3
McGehee	1.000	9	66	7	0	6
O'Toole	.980	6	46	2	1	9
Reyes	1.000	2	17	1	0	1
Sing	.989	84	606	34	7	46

Second Base	PCT	G	PO	A	E	DP
Creighton	.938	3	8	7	1	3
Frese	1.000	2	4	7	0	2
Lewis	.988	20	36	45	1	15
McGehee	1.000	2	1	5	0	0
Patterson	.977	9	19	23	1	3
Sisk	.989	20	34	57	1	11
Spearman	1.000	11	15	15	0	2
Theriot	.982	86	178	202	7	47

Third Base	PCT	G	PO	A	E	DP
Craig	.950	24	17	40	3	3
Lewis	.800	2	0	4	1	0
McGehee	.953	110	67	199	13	27
Sisk	.957	8	6	16	1	2
Spearman	1.000	1	0	5	0	0
Theriot	1.000	5	0	7	0	0

Shortstop	PCT	G	PO	A	E	DP
Coats	.913	94	112	236	33	40
Frese	.909	6	7	13	2	2
Garciaparra	.933	4	7	7	1	4
Sisk	.978	13	13	31	1	6
Theriot	.953	36	38	83	6	21

Outfield	PCT	G	PO	A	E	DP
Bacon	.993	79	147	3	1	0
Coats	.984	24	60	3	1	1
Creighton	.939	23	30	1	2	0
Greenberg	.988	90	164	3	2	0
Hoffpauir	.750	3	3	0	1	0
Montanez	.988	45	75	7	1	1
Murton	.971	77	130	5	4	2
O'Toole	1.000	1	2	0	0	0
Pie	.965	58	105	5	4	1
Sing	.932	45	63	5	5	3
Sisk	1.000	1	2	0	0	0
Weston	1.000	4	11	0	0	0

DAYTONA CUBS — High Class A

FLORIDA STATE LEAGUE

BATTING	B-T	HT	WT	DOB	AVG	vLH	vRH	G	AB	R	H	2B	3B	HR	RBI	BB	HBP	SH	SF	SO	SB	CS	SLG	OBP
Arteaga, Josh	R-R	5-9	170	3-14-80	.190	.000	.333	5	21	3	4	0	0	0	1	0	0	0	0	2	0	0	.190	.190
Boyer, Kyle	R-R	6-1	210	11-23-81	.189	.257	.158	39	111	15	21	4	0	3	13	6	3	0	0	35	2	0	.306	.250
Chirinos, Robinson	R-R	6-1	175	6-5-84	.273	.323	.254	74	231	30	63	6	0	7	27	16	3	1	2	42	3	4	.390	.325
Collins, Kevin	L-L	6-2	200	5-6-81	.265	.211	.284	85	294	42	78	15	1	18	52	36	3	0	5	114	0	3	.507	.346
Creighton, Matt	R-R	6-1	205	2-22-79	.258	.188	.295	27	93	10	24	5	0	3	10	5	4	0	0	14	0	1	.409	.324
Cruz, Enrique	R-R	5-10	185	7-13-81	.197	.133	.230	47	132	16	26	5	0	4	18	14	2	2	1	30	6	0	.326	.282
2-team (9 Tampa)					.185	.131	.218	56	162	21	30	5	0	4	19	18	3	2	2	40	6	0	.290	.276
Culpepper, Jeff	L-R	6-1	190	12-30-81	.343	.286	.356	38	108	14	37	7	0	1	10	9	5	2	0	15	1	5	.435	.418
Dopirak, Brian	R-R	6-4	225	12-20-83	.235	.255	.226	132	507	53	119	26	0	16	76	37	4	0	5	107	1	4	.381	.289
Fox, Jacob	R-R	5-11	210	7-20-82	.281	.329	.261	83	270	37	76	20	0	9	40	26	8	1	4	48	5	2	.456	.357
Granato, Anthony	B-R	6-0	200	3-18-81	.226	.160	.250	34	93	14	21	4	0	0	4	20	0	1	0	22	9	3	.269	.363
Johnson, J.J.	R-R	6-2	195	11-3-81	.261	.259	.263	121	417	52	109	29	5	10	50	24	3	2	2	77	12	5	.427	.305
Larsen, Drew	R-R	6-0	190	3-9-83	.333	.333	.333	4	12	1	4	1	2	0	3	1	0	0	0	4	3	1	.750	.385
Lewis, Richard	R-R	6-1	195	6-29-80	.182	.000	.222	3	11	1	2	1	1	0	0	2	0	0	0	6	0	0	.455	.308
Moore, Scott	L-R	6-2	180	11-17-83	.281	.329	.260	128	466	77	131	31	2	20	82	55	6	0	9	134	22	7	.485	.358
O'Toole, Paul	L-R	6-1	220	2-24-80	.274	.333	.264	55	164	23	45	7	1	3	19	14	4	1	5	40	1	3	.384	.337
Richie, Tony	R-R	6-1	215	2-9-82	.280	.250	.297	78	257	29	72	18	0	4	27	15	1	1	5	45	1	1	.397	.317
Rojas, Carlos	R-R	6-1	175	1-11-84	.244	.336	.209	111	398	47	97	6	0	0	29	35	6	6	2	68	4	7	.259	.313
Salas, Issmael	R-R	5-10	175	7-25-82	.264	.206	.285	78	254	32	67	17	2	10	36	14	6	4	3	42	1	0	.465	.314
Walker, Chris	R-R	5-8	180	7-3-80	.284	.267	.291	133	536	97	152	21	14	6	57	41	9	0	1	111	60	21	.409	.344
Weston, Aaron	L-L	6-5	173	11-5-80	.421	.500	.385	7	19	5	8	2	1	1	6	1	1	0	0	2	0	0	.789	.476
Westphal, J.D.	R-R	6-1	185	2-10-83	.105	.136	.063	17	38	4	4	0	0	0	1	3	0	0	0	15	0	0	.105	.171

PITCHING	B-T	HT	WT	DOB	W	L	ERA	G	GS	CG	SV	IP	H	R	ER	HR	BB	SO	AVG	vLH	vRH	K/9	BB/9
Atlee, Thomas	R-R	5-10	200	8-6-79	1	3	2.61	20	0	0	8	21	18	11	6	1	8	15	.234	.286	.204	6.53	3.48
Baez, Federico	R-R	6-2	185	8-4-81	0	0	3.86	3	0	0	0	9	8	4	4	1	3	14	.235	.500	.154	13.50	2.89
Burrows, Angelo	L-R	6-1	195	7-2-80	0	0	0.00	3	0	0	0	4	2	0	0	0	1	6	.143	.000	.182	13.50	2.25

PITCHING	B-T	HT	WT	DOB	W	L	ERA	G	GS	CG	SV	IP	H	R	ER	HR	BB	SO	AVG	vLH	vRH	K/9	BB/9
Crews, Jordan	R-R	6-5	220	9-21-82	0	0	6.23	10	0	0	0	13	19	10	9	2	3	9	.322	.357	.311	6.23	2.08
Ferreras, Yorkin	L-L	6-1	155	1-28-81	3	5	5.21	14	13	1	0	66	58	39	38	3	26	75	.238	.370	.207	10.28	3.56
Gallagher, Sean	R-R	6-1	210	12-30-85	0	0	1.80	1	1	0	0	5	6	1	1	1	0	7	.286	.222	.333	12.60	0.00
Gerk, Jordan	L-L	6-1	180	7-6-79	4	4	3.72	52	0	0	0	65	66	36	27	4	26	53	.266	.174	.302	7.30	3.58
Gross, Kris	R-R	6-2	185	12-28-80	0	1	6.75	6	0	0	0	8	14	7	6	3	5	6	.378	.462	.333	6.75	5.63
Gwaltney, Lee	R-R	6-6	210	5-6-80	2	3	2.63	22	5	0	3	51	39	22	15	4	16	55	.209	.117	.252	9.64	2.81
Layden, Tim	L-L	6-2	180	12-22-82	1	0	1.35	3	0	0	0	7	5	1	1	1	1	4	.227	.250	.222	5.40	1.35
Marmol, Carlos	R-R	6-2	170	10-14-82	6	2	2.99	13	13	0	0	72	60	30	24	7	37	71	.227	.167	.262	8.83	4.60
Marshall, Sean	L-L	6-5	185	8-30-82	4	4	2.74	12	12	1	0	69	63	24	21	7	26	61	.246	.295	.231	7.96	3.39
Mateo, Juan	R-R	6-2	180	12-17-82	10	5	3.21	32	16	1	2	109	99	47	39	9	27	123	.240	.274	.222	10.13	2.22
Mathes, J.R.	L-L	6-3	205	11-9-81	11	8	4.49	24	24	1	0	132	161	77	66	9	37	97	.300	.313	.296	6.60	2.52
Mendez, Adalberto	R-R	6-2	160	3-22-82	1	1	6.67	23	0	0	3	28	37	24	21	2	25	32	.311	.263	.333	10.16	7.94
O'Brien, Weston	R-R	6-6	220	10-4-82	2	2	5.64	21	0	0	0	30	34	21	19	3	20	29	.281	.302	.269	8.60	5.93
Petrick, Billy	R-R	6-6	220	4-29-84	1	4	5.59	9	9	0	0	37	39	23	23	0	19	25	.275	.286	.266	6.08	4.62
Phelps, Michael	R-R	6-4	195	5-26-84	1	0	4.76	4	0	0	1	6	2	3	3	0	4	8	.100	.000	.133	12.71	6.35
Polanco, Alfredo	R-R	6-1	160	3-16-82	2	2	11.49	13	1	0	0	16	20	21	20	2	23	11	.328	.231	.400	6.32	13.21
Rapada, Clay	R-L	6-5	180	3-9-81	1	3	3.83	27	0	0	5	42	40	21	18	2	16	61	.245	.240	.248	12.97	3.40
Schappert, Paul	L-L	6-5	215	12-21-81	0	0	0.82	21	0	0	4	44	36	5	4	2	8	29	.224	.233	.221	5.98	1.65
Sevier, Nathan	R-R	6-0	200	9-14-79	3	0	3.88	31	3	0	5	51	50	24	22	4	10	48	.256	.293	.230	8.47	1.76
Shaver, Chris	L-L	6-7	235	8-21-81	2	3	2.12	6	6	0	0	34	33	15	8	2	7	19	.258	.118	.279	5.03	1.85
Stiles, Brad	L-L	6-6	233	2-9-81	0	0	3.86	5	0	0	0	9	9	4	4	0	10	5	.281	.500	.231	4.82	9.64
Tavares, Anderson	R-R	6-1	165	2-14-82	4	11	5.40	27	20	0	0	113	145	81	68	14	35	92	.322	.316	.326	7.31	2.78
Weber, Matt	R-R	6-3	200	5-5-85	0	2	12.71	2	2	0	0	6	16	10	8	1	3	4	.471	.250	.538	6.35	4.76
Wells, Randy	R-R	6-3	200	8-28-82	10	2	2.74	41	10	0	2	99	93	33	30	5	22	106	.245	.319	.203	9.67	2.01
Wylie, Jason	R-R	6-5	220	5-27-81	0	1	4.26	10	0	0	0	13	8	8	6	0	5	15	.174	.375	.132	10.66	3.55

FIELDING

Catcher	PCT	G	PO	A	E	DP	PB
Fox	.992	63	470	47	4	3	11
Granato	1.000	1	2	0	0	0	0
O'Toole	.981	9	49	3	1	1	0
Richie	.995	71	568	44	3	6	5

First Base	PCT	G	PO	A	E	DP
Boyer	1.000	1	8	0	0	1
Collins	.984	13	120	7	2	15
Creighton	1.000	5	35	5	0	6
Dopirak	.984	117	963	58	17	84
Salas	1.000	3	4	0	0	0

Second Base	PCT	G	PO	A	E	DP
Arteaga	1.000	3	4	10	0	3
Chirinos	.962	69	135	191	13	42
Creighton	.800	1	1	3	1	0
Cruz	.979	36	61	82	3	25
Granato	.978	12	20	24	1	6
Lewis	1.000	1	0	2	0	0
Salas	1.000	23	54	61	0	21

Third Base	PCT	G	PO	A	E	DP
Arteaga	1.000	1	1	2	0	0
Cruz	.778	3	2	5	2	0
Larsen	1.000	1	0	1	0	0
Moore	.904	120	79	205	30	13
Salas	.972	17	8	27	1	3

Shortstop	PCT	G	PO	A	E	DP
Arteaga	1.000	2	2	4	0	1
Chirinos	1.000	1	0	1	0	0
Cruz	.750	1	0	3	1	0
Granato	.938	4	7	8	1	1
Rojas	.968	111	151	360	17	72
Salas	.964	30	18	62	3	11

Outfield	PCT	G	PO	A	E	DP
Boyer	1.000	34	43	0	0	0
Collins	.968	51	58	2	2	0
Creighton	.947	15	17	1	1	1
Cruz	.000	1	0	0	0	0
Culpepper	.980	37	48	1	1	0
Fox	.000	1	0	0	1	0
Granato	.667	4	2	0	1	0
Johnson	.971	114	220	11	7	5
Larsen	1.000	3	1	1	0	0
O'Toole	1.000	28	29	1	0	0
Walker	.996	130	232	8	1	0
Weston	1.000	3	4	0	0	0
Westphal	1.000	16	16	0	0	0

PEORIA CHIEFS — Low Class A

MIDWEST LEAGUE

BATTING	B-T	HT	WT	DOB	AVG	vLH	vRH	G	AB	R	H	2B	3B	HR	RBI	BB	HBP	SH	SF	SO	SB	CS	SLG	OBP
Arteaga, Josh	R-R	5-9	170	3-14-80	.256	.351	.217	32	129	15	33	9	1	2	23	4	2	1	1	17	2	2	.388	.287
Balcom, Jasha	L-R	5-11	180	7-7-82	.231	.333	.200	6	13	1	3	1	0	0	0	2	0	0	0	4	0	1	.308	.333
Bernard, Oscar	R-R	6-2	170	6-27-83	.236	.254	.228	66	225	29	53	11	0	2	23	13	7	1	2	40	2	4	.311	.296
Corbeil, Al	L-R	6-0	210	12-16-78	.000	.000	.000	2	4	0	0	0	0	0	0	0	0	0	0	1	0	0	.000	.000
Douillard, Jonathan	L-R	6-0	190	1-24-82	.200	.500	.154	9	30	2	6	1	0	1	3	2	0	0	0	4	0	0	.333	.250
Flowers, Bo	R-R	6-0	185	11-12-83	.238	.286	.224	105	365	44	87	10	4	8	49	19	7	0	4	121	10	1	.353	.286
Fuld, Sam	L-L	5-10	180	11-20-81	.300	.294	.302	125	443	82	133	32	6	5	37	50	7	4	4	44	18	11	.433	.377
Garcia, Alberto	R-R	6-0	160	6-5-83	.316	.366	.304	58	209	19	66	8	1	1	25	15	2	1	1	29	1	1	.378	.366
Garciaparra, Nomar	R-R	6-0	190	7-23-73	.200	.000	.200	2	5	1	1	0	0	0	2	2	0	0	0	0	0	0	.200	.429
Granato, Anthony	B-R	6-0	200	3-18-81	.283	.313	.277	75	254	46	72	10	4	4	35	41	3	1	3	55	15	4	.402	.385
Harris, Steve	R-R	6-3	205	9-24-84	.206	.375	.154	8	34	2	7	3	0	1	5	0	0	0	1	6	3	0	.382	.200
Harvey, Ryan	R-R	6-5	220	8-30-84	.257	.250	.259	117	467	71	120	30	2	24	100	24	9	1	6	137	8	4	.484	.302
Joseph, Alfred	R-R	5-11	185	7-25-86	.296	.200	.318	7	27	2	8	1	0	0	2	2	1	0	0	4	0	1	.333	.367
Larsen, Drew	R-R	6-0	190	3-9-83	.245	.310	.229	120	424	52	104	25	4	5	48	42	19	1	4	108	9	6	.358	.337
Mallory, Mike	R-R	6-3	190	12-8-80	.293	.308	.288	29	99	17	29	4	0	3	14	18	2	0	2	25	2	1	.424	.405
Montanez, Luis	R-R	6-2	185	12-15-81	.305	.358	.290	82	315	54	96	28	2	12	48	32	10	2	2	46	10	4	.521	.384
Patterson, Eric	L-R	5-11	170	4-8-83	.333	.312	.339	110	432	90	144	26	11	13	71	53	4	4	7	94	40	11	.535	.405
Puello, Elvin	R-R	6-2	175	12-18-84	.238	.400	.188	6	21	0	5	2	0	0	2	1	1	0	0	6	0	0	.333	.304
Reed, Mark	L-R	5-11	175	4-13-86	.135	.143	.133	14	52	2	7	1	1	0	6	1	1	0	0	12	0	0	.192	.167
Rick, Alan	L-R	6-3	205	9-8-83	.197	.212	.194	77	249	32	49	11	3	3	32	28	1	0	0	67	0	1	.301	.281
Rios, Jose	R-R	6-1	160	4-6-84	.242	.105	.276	28	95	9	23	2	0	0	6	6	3	1	1	9	0	2	.263	.305
Rivera, Luis	R-R	6-1	165	1-25-84	.348	.429	.339	25	69	7	24	0	0	0	12	2	0	1	0	7	3	1	.348	.366
Schmidt, Jesse	B-R	6-1	200	10-27-81	.246	.282	.235	50	175	27	43	13	2	3	22	30	2	1	2	40	5	1	.394	.359
Simokaitis, Joe	R-R	6-1	200	12-27-82	.190	.357	.157	51	168	20	32	2	2	0	13	24	0	0	2	34	2	0	.226	.289
Sisk, Aaron	R-R	6-0	190	9-17-78	.316	.389	.293	39	152	36	48	13	2	7	29	20	2	1	1	42	5	5	.566	.400
Smith, Aaron	R-R	6-1	185	4-9-82	.247	.275	.240	78	259	35	64	15	1	3	22	16	1	3	2	61	2	1	.347	.291

PITCHING	B-T	HT	WT	DOB	W	L	ERA	G	GS	CG	SV	IP	H	R	ER	HR	BB	SO	AVG	vLH	vRH	K/9	BB/9
Baez, Edgar	R-R	6-2	170	2-16-83	0	0	0.00	4	0	0	0	6	3	1	0	0	7	2	.150	.222	.091	3.00	10.50
Berg, Justin	R-R	6-3	195	6-7-84	0	0	9.45	2	1	0	0	7	9	7	7	0	6	3	.360	.375	.353	4.05	8.10
Billek, Mike	R-R	6-4	235	3-4-84	2	0	4.06	8	8	0	0	38	33	18	17	6	10	25	.234	.238	.231	5.97	2.39
Blackford, Todd	L-R	6-4	215	6-10-85	1	0	0.00	1	1	0	0	5	3	0	0	0	2	1	.188	.000	.333	1.80	3.60
Blevins, Jerry	L-L	6-6	185	9-6-83	3	7	5.54	48	2	0	14	76	75	51	47	6	38	96	.260	.246	.263	11.32	4.48
Brito, Luis	R-R	6-3	185	10-19-83	1	0	11.74	6	0	0	0	8	14	11	10	1	3	6	.378	.308	.417	7.04	3.52
Campusano, Edward	L-L	6-4	175	7-14-82	2	2	2.63	19	0	0	1	27	25	11	8	0	14	23	.240	.333	.208	7.57	4.61

PITCHING	B-T	HT	WT	DOB	W	L	ERA	G	GS	CG	SV	IP	H	R	ER	HR	BB	SO	AVG	vLH	vRH	K/9	BB/9
Dickson, Drew	R-R	6-1	230	3-3-84	0	2	4.45	25	0	0	4	32	28	17	16	2	24	26	.237	.341	.176	7.24	6.68
Downs, Darin	R-L	6-3	176	12-26-84	0	2	18.47	2	2	0	0	6	12	14	13	1	4	3	.387	.000	.444	4.26	5.68
Estrada, Jesse	R-R	6-8	260	10-27-83	6	12	5.35	27	27	1	0	151	193	104	90	15	41	65	.308	.260	.340	3.87	2.44
Fenton, Will	R-R	6-2	205	4-7-83	0	0	11.37	6	0	0	0	6	12	8	8	1	5	7	.375	.357	.389	9.95	7.11
Francisco, Alfredo	R-R	6-3	235	8-27-84	1	0	3.07	6	0	0	0	15	14	5	5	0	7	14	.255	.455	.121	8.59	4.30
Gallagher, Sean	R-R	6-1	210	12-30-85	14	5	2.71	26	26	0	0	146	107	53	44	10	55	139	.206	.217	.198	8.57	3.39
Guzman, Angel	R-R	6-3	190	12-14-81	0	1	4.26	2	2	0	0	6	10	5	3	1	0	7	.345	.364	.333	9.95	0.00
Gwaltney, Lee	R-R	6-6	210	5-6-80	4	1	2.56	10	10	0	0	56	45	17	16	1	17	50	.210	.271	.181	7.99	2.72
Hill, Rich	L-L	6-5	205	3-11-80	1	0	1.13	1	1	0	0	8	5	2	1	0	0	12	.179	.000	.200	13.50	0.00
Hunton, Jon	R-R	6-9	230	11-30-82	0	2	7.42	25	0	0	3	30	38	28	25	3	17	30	.302	.295	.305	8.90	5.04
Hyle, Michael	R-R	6-2	190	2-20-82	1	0	15.63	4	0	0	0	6	14	11	11	5	3	0	.438	.333	.478	0.00	4.26
Johnson, Grant	R-R	6-6	220	5-26-83	3	8	3.82	14	14	1	0	73	65	45	31	7	26	52	.242	.218	.262	6.41	3.21
Jones, Michael	R-R	6-0	190	3-12-82	2	3	9.11	18	0	0	1	27	48	29	27	1	10	19	.400	.429	.380	6.41	3.38
Layden, Tim	L-L	6-2	180	12-22-82	4	4	4.62	38	0	0	4	51	43	30	26	2	22	53	.223	.188	.234	9.41	3.91
Mendez, Adalberto	R-R	6-2	160	3-22-82	2	1	3.10	22	0	0	6	29	26	10	10	1	10	24	.236	.267	.215	7.45	3.10
Nolen, Walt	R-R	6-1	180	10-11-81	7	4	4.61	37	2	0	0	66	61	47	34	2	48	60	.234	.208	.250	8.14	6.51
Phelps, Michael	R-R	6-4	195	5-26-83	0	1	1.59	12	0	0	1	17	12	5	3	0	3	17	.197	.300	.146	9.00	1.59
Polanco, Alfredo	R-R	6-1	160	3-16-82	3	0	5.59	22	1	0	0	37	34	24	23	2	23	44	.243	.333	.181	10.70	5.59
Ramos, Victor	L-R	6-3	220	10-4-81	0	1	2.70	5	0	0	0	7	5	3	2	1	3	5	.208	.125	.250	6.75	4.05
Schappert, Paul	L-L	6-5	215	12-21-81	1	0	4.50	20	0	0	0	24	26	15	12	1	8	18	.283	.200	.333	6.75	3.00
Shaver, Chris	L-L	6-7	235	8-21-81	3	7	4.31	19	19	0	0	102	92	59	49	9	45	76	.244	.301	.230	6.68	3.96
Teasley, Jeff	R-R	6-6	220	5-9-83	0	0	3.86	4	0	0	3	5	4	2	2	1	3	7	.211	.100	.333	13.50	5.79
Thompson, Nick	R-R	6-0	180	8-12-81	0	0	27.00	3	0	0	0	2	4	5	5	1	5	2	.500	.000	.667	10.80	27.00
Weber, Matt	R-R	6-3	200	5-5-85	7	9	3.91	25	24	1	0	143	173	71	62	12	27	85	.299	.305	.296	5.36	1.70
Wood, Kerry	R-R	6-5	225	6-16-77	0	0	0.00	2	0	0	0	2	1	0	0	0	0	5	.125	.000	.250	19.29	0.00

FIELDING

Catcher	PCT	G	PO	A	E	DP	PB
Bernard	.972	62	405	39	13	4	11
Douillard	1.000	8	47	5	0	0	3
Reed	.991	14	104	10	1	0	5
Rick	.994	63	432	43	3	5	5

First Base	PCT	G	PO	A	E	DP
Bernard	1.000	3	12	1	0	0
Douillard	1.000	1	10	0	0	0
Francisco	1.000	1	11	0	0	0
Garcia	.989	55	441	23	5	36
Granato	.989	20	170	11	2	19
Larsen	.978	62	512	32	12	44
Rick	.971	10	64	3	2	6
Smith	1.000	3	14	0	0	3

Second Base	PCT	G	PO	A	E	DP
Arteaga	.938	4	6	9	1	1
Granato	1.000	12	27	26	0	9
Patterson	.982	106	183	315	9	61
Rios	1.000	4	6	5	0	1
Rivera	1.000	3	1	4	0	0
Smith	.978	20	46	41	2	11

Third Base	PCT	G	PO	A	E	DP
Arteaga	.895	17	8	26	4	2
Bernard	1.000	1	0	2	0	0
Francisco	.667	1	2	2	2	1
Garcia	1.000	3	1	10	0	1
Granato	.851	14	9	31	7	3
Larsen	.932	45	25	84	8	6
Puello	.727	6	5	3	3	0
Rios	1.000	1	0	4	0	0
Rivera	.956	19	9	34	2	2
Sisk	.929	12	7	19	2	2
Smith	.904	39	19	56	8	6

Shortstop	PCT	G	PO	A	E	DP
Arteaga	.937	13	21	38	4	9
Garciaparra	1.000	2	1	3	0	2
Granato	.975	26	32	86	3	12
Rios	.893	23	33	67	12	9
Rivera	1.000	4	3	7	0	1
Simokaitis	.945	51	59	163	13	33
Sisk	.946	21	24	63	5	10
Smith	.950	7	3	16	1	0

Outfield	PCT	G	PO	A	E	DP
Balcom	.875	4	7	0	1	0
Flowers	.936	74	126	6	9	0
Fuld	.981	123	308	7	6	4
Harris	1.000	5	8	0	0	0
Harvey	.988	94	148	10	2	3
Joseph	1.000	7	16	0	0	0
Larsen	.938	19	27	3	2	1
Mallory	1.000	3	5	0	0	0
Montanez	1.000	76	115	7	0	2
Schmidt	1.000	38	80	2	0	1

BOISE HAWKS — Short-Season Class A

NORTHWEST LEAGUE

BATTING	B-T	HT	WT	DOB	AVG	vLH	vRH	G	AB	R	H	2B	3B	HR	RBI	BB	HBP	SH	SF	SO	SB	CS	SLG	OBP
Culpepper, Jeff	L-R	6-1	190	12-30-81	.304	.467	.259	20	69	10	21	3	0	1	7	10	4	1	0	9	5	0	.391	.422
Defendis, John	L-R	6-1	195	3-12-84	.327	.293	.338	44	171	23	56	8	0	2	20	17	0	2	0	21	3	4	.409	.388
Douillard, Jonathan	L-R	6-0	190	1-24-82	.111	.500	.000	5	9	1	1	0	0	0	1	1	0	0	1	4	0	0	.111	.182
Farina, Peter	R-R	6-1	205	9-7-83	.226	.000	.250	13	31	0	7	1	0	0	1	2	0	0	0	8	0	0	.258	.273
Gaskin, Chris	R-R	6-4	228	6-30-83	.256	.185	.282	65	246	30	63	15	0	6	39	23	9	1	1	50	4	0	.390	.341
Gregg, Davy	L-R	6-2	170	5-31-83	.280	.337	.256	74	300	53	84	9	0	1	19	23	2	11	0	50	36	12	.320	.335
Hode, Scott	R-R	6-0	180	3-11-83	.280	.409	.233	22	82	6	23	3	0	1	9	3	3	0	0	9	1	1	.354	.330
Joseph, Alfred	R-R	5-11	185	7-25-86	.271	.286	.263	16	59	7	16	5	0	0	9	4	1	2	0	15	2	1	.356	.328
Mota, Jonathan	R-R	6-0	165	6-1-87	.236	.208	.244	63	212	18	50	7	1	0	22	16	2	5	0	49	4	5	.278	.296
Muyco, Jake	R-R	6-1	170	9-16-84	.215	.176	.230	37	121	10	26	1	0	1	8	8	0	5	0	31	0	2	.248	.264
Puello, Elvin	R-R	6-2	175	12-18-84	.238	.271	.226	61	227	32	54	15	2	3	20	15	6	0	1	54	3	0	.361	.301
Quinones, Carlos	B-R	6-2	170	3-12-83	.236	.306	.216	43	161	11	38	4	0	0	15	7	0	0	1	29	0	3	.261	.266
Reed, Mark	L-R	5-11	175	4-13-86	.250	.227	.257	55	184	32	46	10	0	4	18	15	1	2	0	53	7	5	.370	.310
Reynolds, Kyle	L-R	6-2	190	9-1-83	.256	.232	.266	52	199	28	51	6	3	5	24	12	3	0	1	52	4	2	.392	.307
Rios, Jose	R-R	6-1	160	4-6-84	.323	.303	.333	35	99	11	32	7	0	0	8	0	1	1	0	11	1	3	.394	.330
Taylor, Brandon	R-R	6-1	195	7-26-82	.262	.345	.229	57	202	28	53	16	1	7	30	14	2	1	2	53	2	5	.455	.314
Valdez, Jesus	R-R	6-2	170	11-2-84	.244	.200	.259	61	234	30	57	13	1	5	38	9	1	0	2	49	4	3	.372	.272

PITCHING	B-T	HT	WT	DOB	W	L	ERA	G	GS	CG	SV	IP	H	R	ER	HR	BB	SO	AVG	vLH	vRH	K/9	BB/9
Atkins, Mitch	R-R	6-3	215	10-1-85	3	6	5.03	15	15	0	0	73	85	45	41	8	30	59	.291	.291	.291	7.24	3.68
Avery, Matt	R-R	6-5	230	9-7-83	1	3	4.62	11	11	0	0	49	53	27	25	7	15	25	.288	.250	.320	4.62	2.77
Baez, Edgar	R-R	6-2	170	2-16-83	0	0	8.86	20	0	0	0	21	30	21	21	2	11	16	.337	.444	.264	6.75	4.64
Billek, Mike	R-R	6-4	235	3-4-84	0	1	2.65	5	5	0	0	17	16	10	5	0	6	20	.239	.303	.176	10.59	3.18
Chambers, Ryan	L-L	6-0	165	12-31-82	1	2	4.91	18	0	0	1	26	25	14	14	3	9	31	.248	.250	.247	10.87	3.16
Downs, Darin	R-L	6-3	176	12-26-84	5	4	3.50	14	13	0	0	62	61	30	24	5	22	63	.260	.163	.281	9.19	3.21
Evenson, Roger	R-R	6-4	235	8-18-83	4	4	5.58	24	1	0	4	40	41	26	25	3	14	39	.266	.313	.233	8.70	3.12
Hagerty, Luke	R-L	6-7	230	4-1-81	0	1	31.05	14	1	0	0	7	14	26	23	0	30	4	.438	.333	.478	5.40	40.50
Holden, Kyle	R-R	6-6	205	12-13-83	2	2	7.45	20	1	0	0	29	48	30	24	2	9	19	.361	.345	.373	5.90	2.79
Hunton, Jon	R-R	6-9	230	11-30-82	1	3	3.20	19	0	0	4	25	22	16	9	2	15	28	.220	.324	.159	9.95	5.33
Hyle, Michael	R-R	6-2	190	2-20-82	3	5	3.18	15	6	0	0	45	37	24	16	0	20	37	.219	.200	.232	7.35	3.97
Jones, Michael	R-R	6-0	190	3-12-82	0	1	0.00	1	0	0	0	2	3	2	0	0	1	2	.300	.333	.250	9.00	4.50
Koerber, Scott	L-L	6-4	215	9-30-82	1	1	3.67	23	0	0	1	34	35	15	14	2	20	23	.267	.368	.226	6.03	5.24

PITCHING	B-T	HT	WT	DOB	W	L	ERA	G	GS	CG	SV	IP	H	R	ER	HR	BB	SO	AVG	vLH	vRH	K/9	BB/9
Lopez, Aleurys	R-L	6-3	195	8-20-83	0	0	9.90	7	0	0	1	10	20	11	11	1	6	10	.426	.538	.382	9.00	5.40
Ortiz, Jose	R-R	6-2	165	11-17-83	0	2	4.43	15	0	0	0	22	28	16	11	0	13	12	.298	.286	.305	4.84	5.24
Pawelek, Mark	L-L	6-3	190	8-18-86	0	0	0.00	1	1	0	0	3	6	1	0	0	1	4	.462	.000	.462	12.00	3.00
Ramos, Victor	L-R	6-3	220	10-4-81	1	1	3.68	5	0	0	0	7	6	3	3	0	3	11	.222	.250	.200	13.50	3.68
Santana, Andy	L-L	6-3	160	8-17-83	4	1	2.47	19	1	0	0	44	44	18	12	3	23	45	.256	.289	.244	9.27	4.74
Taylor, Scott	R-R	6-3	240	12-28-86	0	0	5.63	2	2	0	0	8	7	5	5	0	2	7	.233	.294	.154	7.88	2.25
Teasley, Jeff	R-R	6-6	220	5-9-83	1	0	5.19	20	0	0	4	26	24	15	15	4	12	28	.247	.286	.226	9.69	4.15
Thompson, Nick	R-R	6-0	180	8-12-81	2	1	3.51	25	0	0	2	33	27	19	13	5	19	34	.221	.267	.195	9.18	5.13
Veal, Donald	L-L	6-3	215	9-18-84	1	2	2.48	7	6	0	0	29	18	11	8	2	15	34	.180	.318	.141	10.55	4.66
Yepez, Jesus	L-L	6-1	175	4-15-84	4	2	3.92	14	13	0	0	62	57	31	27	3	28	46	.245	.275	.238	6.68	4.06

GAMES BY POSITION: C—Douillard 4, Farina 9, Muyco 33, Reed 40. **1B**—Gaskin 60, Puello 14, Taylor 2, Valdez 1. **2B**—Hode 20, Mota 20, Reynolds 17, Rios 22. **3B**—Puello 41, Rios 2, Taylor 37. **SS**—Hode 1, Mota 43, Reynolds 26, Rios 9. **OF**—Culpepper 19, Defendis 42, Gregg 73, Joseph 14, Quinones 27, Valdez 59.

AZL CUBS — Rookie

ARIZONA LEAGUE

BATTING	B-T	HT	WT	DOB	AVG	vLH	vRH	G	AB	R	H	2B	3B	HR	RBI	BB	HBP	SH	SF	SO	SB	CS	SLG	OBP
Baez, Sammy	R-R	6-2	175	12-10-84	.213	.324	.177	41	150	13	32	4	1	0	10	5	1	0	1	26	3	2	.253	.242
Brown, Randy	R-R	6-0	172	11-12-85	.275	.263	.278	52	189	27	52	8	5	0	26	11	7	1	1	34	8	7	.370	.337
Canzler, Russ	R-R	6-2	190	4-11-86	.299	.355	.286	49	157	22	47	11	3	1	20	24	1	2	4	41	1	5	.427	.387
Carter, Yusuf	B-R	6-2	205	2-6-85	.263	.400	.214	11	38	6	10	2	0	1	8	1	0	0	1	14	1	0	.395	.275
Crouch, Nick	R-R	6-4	215	1-26-83	.286	.171	.316	46	168	20	48	13	0	2	25	19	8	1	3	51	0	0	.399	.379
Defendis, John	L-R	6-1	195	3-12-84	.316	.273	.333	18	76	13	24	4	1	0	13	4	0	0	1	5	2	1	.395	.346
Episcopo, Ryan	L-R	6-2	180	7-20-85	.298	.361	.280	46	168	30	50	7	1	2	26	25	0	1	3	48	7	3	.387	.383
Farina, Peter	R-R	6-1	205	9-7-83	.333	.000	.462	9	18	1	6	0	0	0	3	2	0	0	0	2	0	0	.333	.400
Garciaparra, Nomar	R-R	6-0	190	7-23-73	.200	.000	.200	2	5	0	1	0	0	0	0	0	0	0	0	1	0	0	.200	.200
Harris, Steve	R-R	6-3	205	9-24-84	.330	.385	.309	22	94	12	31	4	1	0	14	3	0	3	0	16	1	1	.394	.351
Heredia, Valerio	B-R	5-10	150	3-14-86	.230	.500	.149	18	61	7	14	2	1	0	5	3	1	3	0	18	7	3	.295	.277
Johnston, Dylan	L-R	6-0	180	3-25-87	.182	.231	.161	13	44	4	8	2	0	0	5	6	0	0	0	24	0	3	.227	.280
Lewis, D.J.	R-R	6-0	210	8-25-85	.322	.341	.316	45	174	37	56	14	5	0	27	17	2	1	4	23	3	3	.460	.381
Liriano, Victor	L-L	6-0	200	5-19-84	.417	.750	.250	3	12	2	5	1	1	0	1	1	0	0	0	4	0	0	.667	.462
Mercedes, Mario	R-R	5-10	160	11-22-86	.298	.316	.292	34	84	12	25	3	0	1	11	5	1	1	1	5	1	2	.369	.341
Morgan, Justin	R-R	6-1	193	2-1-82	.221	.188	.231	30	68	6	15	4	0	0	7	4	1	0	0	20	0	0	.279	.274
Muyco, Jake	R-R	6-1	170	9-16-84	.500	.000	.500	1	2	0	1	1	0	0	0	0	0	0	0	0	0	0	1.000	.500
Reynolds, Kyle	L-R	6-2	190	9-1-83	.000	.000	.000	1	5	0	0	0	0	0	0	0	0	0	0	1	0	0	.000	.000
Rivera, Anthony	R-R	6-1	180	7-19-84	.333	.500	.300	3	12	2	4	0	0	0	1	0	0	0	0	2	0	0	.333	.333
Rivera, Luis	R-R	6-1	165	1-25-84	.282	.200	.301	27	103	15	29	5	0	0	9	6	3	2	0	15	9	2	.330	.339
Seara, Dave	R-R	5-10	174	6-16-83	.226	.240	.222	34	106	10	24	9	1	1	7	9	0	3	1	16	6	1	.358	.284
Serrano, Eduard	B-R	5-10	150	6-2-85	.250	.235	.253	47	180	30	45	4	4	1	13	16	0	5	3	43	19	5	.333	.307
Westphal, J.D.	R-R	6-1	185	2-10-83	.368	.000	.389	5	19	4	7	0	1	0	3	1	0	0	0	6	1	1	.474	.400
Wick, Olin	B-R	6-0	180	5-6-82	.225	.300	.200	26	40	7	9	3	0	0	4	6	0	1	0	14	0	0	.300	.326

PITCHING	B-T	HT	WT	DOB	W	L	ERA	G	GS	CG	SV	IP	H	R	ER	HR	BB	SO	AVG	vLH	vRH	K/9	BB/9
Avery, Matt	R-R	6-5	230	9-7-83	0	0	10.80	1	1	0	0	2	2	2	2	0	2	1	.333	1.000	.200	5.40	10.80
Bronder, Stephen	R-R	6-1	180	6-5-84	1	1	3.80	6	0	0	0	21	26	9	9	0	9	9	.313	.421	.281	3.80	3.80
Campusano, Edward	L-L	6-4	175	7-14-82	0	0	0.00	1	1	0	0	2	1	0	0	0	0	2	.125	.000	.125	9.00	0.00
Castillo, Julio	R-R	6-3	180	7-10-87	1	1	5.57	7	2	0	0	21	29	16	13	0	12	8	.341	.516	.241	3.43	5.14
Chambers, Ryan	L-L	6-0	165	12-31-82	0	1	2.08	5	0	0	0	9	4	2	2	0	1	9	.133	.000	.160	9.35	1.04
Crews, Jordan	R-R	6-5	220	9-21-82	1	2	3.21	11	0	0	3	14	9	9	5	1	3	15	.176	.111	.190	9.64	1.93
Fernandez, Armando	R-R	6-2	225	2-2-82	1	2	8.03	17	2	0	1	25	36	23	22	1	11	23	.350	.424	.314	8.39	4.01
Foor, Erik	R-R	6-4	210	2-5-82	0	4	4.95	16	0	0	1	20	17	15	11	1	18	20	.243	.182	.271	9.00	8.10
Francisco, Alfredo	R-R	6-3	235	8-27-84	2	3	3.89	12	5	0	0	42	40	23	18	1	16	37	.252	.234	.263	7.99	3.46
Greenhouse, Michael	L-L	5-11	200	4-18-83	0	3	3.31	19	0	0	1	33	32	16	12	3	11	32	.258	.471	.224	8.82	3.03
Guerrero, Carlos	L-L	6-2	150	3-8-87	0	0	21.60	4	1	0	0	3	10	8	8	1	6	3	.588	1.000	.462	8.10	16.20
Guzman, Angel	R-R	6-3	190	12-14-81	0	0	1.50	4	4	0	0	12	10	3	2	0	1	17	.217	.267	.194	12.75	0.75
Jackson, Brett	R-R	6-3	200	9-28-84	1	0	5.91	4	1	0	0	11	11	7	7	0	6	9	.268	.111	.313	7.59	5.06
Joseph, Alfred	R-R	5-11	185	7-25-86	0	0	0.00	1	0	0	0	0	0	2	0	0	2	0	.000	.000	.000	0.00	54.00
Krawiec, Aaron	L-L	6-6	215	3-17-79	0	0	8.10	2	0	0	0	3	5	3	3	0	1	1	.333	.250	.364	2.70	2.70
Lefort, Michael	R-R	6-1	195	8-23-83	0	1	15.19	6	0	0	0	5	7	10	9	0	6	1	.333	.429	.286	1.69	10.13
Lopez, Aleurys	R-L	6-3	195	8-20-83	2	1	2.95	10	0	0	0	21	23	10	7	0	9	29	.264	.174	.297	12.23	3.80
Moore, Tyrell	L-L	6-0	180	8-31-81	0	0	27.00	3	0	0	0	3	13	9	9	1	2	4	.619	.500	.632	12.00	6.00
Paganetti, Billy	R-R	6-3	195	7-23-83	2	0	1.08	5	0	0	0	8	4	1	1	0	3	7	.138	.143	.136	7.56	3.24
Pawelek, Mark	L-L	6-3	190	8-18-86	0	3	2.72	14	13	0	0	43	25	18	13	0	21	56	.170	.267	.159	11.72	4.40
Phelps, Michael	R-R	6-4	195	5-26-84	0	0	0.00	1	0	0	0	1	0	0	0	0	0	2	.000	.000	.000	27.00	0.00
Pina, Jose	R-R	6-2	150	11-2-85	3	5	4.78	14	11	0	0	53	59	34	28	4	14	37	.285	.387	.227	6.32	2.39
Rayborn, Justin	R-R	6-5	210	11-29-82	2	1	2.08	13	0	0	1	26	17	8	6	0	4	37	.189	.136	.206	12.81	1.38
Santana, Felin	R-R	6-4	185	3-26-84	1	1	4.50	6	3	0	0	24	36	15	12	1	4	13	.343	.231	.380	4.88	1.50
Taylor, Trey	R-L	6-2	200	11-12-85	0	0	0.00	2	2	0	0	4	2	0	0	0	2	5	.143	.500	.083	11.25	4.50
Taylor, Scott	R-R	6-3	240	12-28-86	0	3	6.89	6	6	0	0	16	21	14	12	0	7	13	.313	.286	.326	7.47	4.02
Terry, Jason	L-L	6-3	200	9-26-82	0	1	6.41	14	0	0	0	20	24	16	14	3	12	17	.320	.222	.351	7.78	5.49
Thomley, Morrow	R-R	6-2	206	4-5-83	0	0	12.15	7	0	0	0	7	13	17	9	0	11	4	.371	.333	.391	5.40	14.85
Underwood, Chad	R-R	6-4	215	5-18-82	2	1	2.10	15	0	0	0	34	29	13	8	0	6	30	.223	.268	.202	7.86	1.57
Veal, Donald	L-L	6-3	215	9-18-84	0	1	5.06	4	3	0	0	11	8	6	6	2	5	14	.205	.375	.161	11.81	4.22
Williamson, Scott	R-R	6-0	185	2-17-76	0	2	2.45	4	1	0	0	7	7	8	2	0	2	9	.226	.100	.286	11.05	2.45

GAMES BY POSITION: C—Carter 4, Farina 9, Mercedes 32, Morgan 29, Muyco 1, Wick 23. **1B**—Canzler 41, Crouch 17, Seara 1, Wick 1. **2B**—Baez 1, L. Rivera 1, Seara 19, Serrano 40. **3B**—Baez 5, Crouch 18, Heredia 16, A. Rivera 1, L. Rivera 18, Seara 2. **SS**—Baez 35, Garciaparra 2, Johnston 11, A. Rivera 2, L. Rivera 9, Seara 1. **OF**—Brown 48, Defendis 13, Episcopo 40, Harris 22, Lewis 38, Liriano 3, Seara 5, Westphal 5.

CHICAGO WHITE SOX

BY PHIL ROGERS

With less expected from them than in many recent seasons, the White Sox delivered more in 2005 than they had in 88 seasons—a World Series title.

After losing Magglio Ordonez to free agency and trading Carlos Lee to Milwaukee, the Sox were forecast to finish behind Minnesota and possibly Cleveland in the improving American League Central.

But with leadoff man Scott Podsednik and fellow newcomers Tadahito Iguchi, A.J. Pierzynski and Jermaine Dye helping set the tone, they used an old approach that was new to them—building on speed and defense—to lead the Central wire to wire, then made like the 2004 Boston Red Sox in the playoffs.

Or White, the new Red, as some called it.

A 57-29 first half put the White Sox in control of the Central, and their lead grew to 15 games on Aug. 1. No team had ever had such a large lead without going to the playoffs, but Cleveland made a strong run at the Sox, closing within 1½ games on Sept. 22, which could have forced Ozzie Guillen's team to battle the AL East runner up for a wild-card spot.

Then, behind a deep starting rotation featuring second-half sensation Jose Contreras (11-2, 2.96 in 15 starts after the break) along with Mark Buehrle, Jon Garland, Freddy Garcia and rookie Brandon McCarthy, the White Sox caught fire. They won eight of their last 10 regular season games, clinching the Central title Sept. 29 in Detroit, to finish an AL-best 99-63.

It turned out the Sox were only warming up. They won their last five regular season games, including a season-ending sweep in Cleveland that knocked the Indians out of the playoffs, and then won 11 of 12 playoff games against the Red Sox, Angels and Astros.

"At times I've felt all 88 of years of losing, and some nights, some of the Cubs years too," said White Sox owner Jerry Reinsdorf, who bought the team from Bill Veeck in 1981. "Tony La Russa taught me years ago, you like to leave spring training thinking you can win your division. We thought that. I never thought we'd ever have a 15-game lead and I never thought we'd blow 13 games of it. So once we got into the postseason it was kind of a relief."

Reinsdorf's players felt the same. After undergoing in an intense trial in September, when they were in danger of suffering one of the greatest collapses in history, they seemed to relax and enjoy the ride in October.

The White Sox swept the Red Sox, beat the Angels in five and then swept the Astros, winning their last eight games overall. The 11-1 run through October matched the record of the 1999 Yankees, the best mark of any champion since the 1976 Cincinnati Reds went 7-0.

Paul Konerko, a free agent at the end of the season, was the team's steadiest player. He hit .283-40-100 during the regular season and then delivered five more homers and 15 RBIs in the 12 playoff games.

The farm system helped plug the few holes that arose, with righthanders Bobby Jenks and McCarthy playing roles in winning the division title after spending the first half in the minors.

Jenks, who was claimed on waivers from the Angels after 2004, was a standout closer at Double-A Birmingham before replacing Dustin Hermanson as Chicago's closer down the stretch. He wound up with four saves in the postseason, including one for Garcia in the combined shutout that wrapped up the World Series.

The strength of the organization was outfield depth, with Triple-A Charlotte's Brian Anderson pushing for big league consideration and Birmingham's outfield of Chris Young, Jerry Owens and Ryan Sweeney standing out.

Three of the top four farm teams earned spots in the playoffs, with low Class A Kannapolis winning the South Atlantic League title. Birmingham and high Class A Winston-Salem also qualified for playoffs in their leagues. Leo Daigle won a triple crown and was named MVP in the Carolina League.

PLAYERS OF THE YEAR

MAJOR LEAGUE: Paul Konerko, 1b

On a team that relied heavily upon the longball in 2005, Konerko led the way with 40 homers and was the only White Sox player to register 100 RBIs. It was the second year in a row Konerko eclipsed the 40-homer, 100-RBI marks, establishing him as a legitimate power hitter as he entered free agency.

MINOR LEAGUE: Chris Young, of

STEVE MOORE

The 21-year-old Young had no problem skipping a level in 2005, leading the Double-A Southern League in runs, doubles and home runs despite missing two weeks with a minor oblique strain. He also stole 32 bases and played stellar defense in center field for a Birmingham team that reached the SL playoffs.

ORGANIZATION LEADERS

BATTING		
*AVG	Hall, Noah, Winston-Salem	.332
R	Hall, Noah, Winston-Salem	112
H	Owens, Jerry, Birmingham	173
TB	Daigle, Leo, Charlotte/Winston-Salem	293
2B	Young, Chris, Birmingham	41
3B	Valido, Robert, Winston-Salem	7
HR	Daigle, Leo, Charlotte/Winston-Salem	31
RBI	Daigle, Leo, Charlotte/Winston-Salem	120
BB	Hall, Noah, Winston-Salem	86
SO	Collaro, Tom, Winston-Salem	153
SB	Valido, Robert, Winston-Salem	52
*OBP	Hall, Noah, Winston-Salem	.459
*SLG	Hall, Noah, Winston-Salem	.633
PITCHING		
W	Four tied at	14
L	Munoz, Arnie, Charlotte	14
#ERA	Liotta, Ray, Kannapolis/Winston-Salem	1.64
G	Smith, Matt, Charlotte	66
CG	Egbert, Jack, Kannapolis	4
SV	Zaleski, Matt, Kannapolis	22
IP	Haeger, Charles, Birmingham/Winston-Salem	167
	Rodriguez, Ryan, Winston-Salem	167
BB	Haeger, Charles, Birmingham/Winston-Salem	85
SO	Gonzalez, Gio, Kannapolis/Winston-Salem	163

*Minimum 250 at-bats. #Minimum 75 innings.

CHICAGO WHITE SOX

Manager: Ozzie Guillen.

2005 Record: 99-63, .611 (1st, AL Central).

BATTING	B-T	HT	WT	DOB	AVG	vLH	vRH	G	AB	R	H	2B	3B	HR	RBI	BB	HBP	SH	SF	SO	SB	CS	SLG	OBP
Anderson, Brian	R-R	6-2	205	3-11-82	.176	.083	.227	13	34	3	6	1	0	2	3	0	0	1	0	12	1	0	.382	.176
Blum, Geoff	B-R	6-3	200	4-26-73	.200	.158	.211	31	95	6	19	2	1	1	3	4	0	0	0	15	0	1	.274	.232
Borchard, Joe	B-R	6-5	220	11-25-78	.417	1.000	.364	7	12	0	5	2	0	0	0	0	0	0	0	4	0	1	.583	.417
Burke, Jamie	R-R	6-0	225	9-24-71	.000	.000	.000	1	1	0	0	0	0	0	0	0	0	0	0	0	0	0	.000	.000
Casanova, Raul	B-R	6-0	230	8-23-72	.200	.000	.333	6	5	0	1	0	0	0	0	0	0	0	0	1	0	0	.200	.200
Crede, Joe	R-R	6-1	195	4-26-78	.252	.277	.246	132	432	54	109	21	0	22	62	25	8	2	4	66	1	1	.454	.303
Dye, Jermaine	R-R	6-5	220	1-28-74	.274	.252	.281	145	529	74	145	29	2	31	86	39	9	0	2	99	11	4	.512	.333
Everett, Carl	B-R	6-0	215	6-3-71	.251	.265	.246	135	490	58	123	17	2	23	87	42	5	0	10	99	4	5	.435	.311
Gload, Ross	L-L	6-0	200	4-5-76	.167	.000	.189	28	42	2	7	2	0	0	5	2	0	0	0	9	0	0	.214	.205
Harris, Willie	L-R	5-9	170	6-22-78	.256	.286	.252	56	121	17	31	2	1	1	8	13	1	4	0	25	10	3	.314	.333
Iguchi, Tadahito	R-R	5-10	185	12-4-74	.278	.274	.279	135	511	74	142	25	6	15	71	47	6	11	6	114	15	5	.438	.342
Konerko, Paul	R-R	6-2	215	3-5-76	.283	.261	.290	158	575	98	163	24	0	40	100	81	5	0	3	109	0	0	.534	.375
Lopez, Pedro	R-R	6-1	160	4-28-84	.286	.333	.000	2	7	1	2	0	0	0	2	0	0	1	0	1	0	0	.286	.286
Ozuna, Pablo	R-R	5-10	185	8-25-74	.276	.306	.248	70	203	27	56	7	2	0	11	7	4	3	0	26	14	7	.330	.313
Perez, Timo	L-L	5-9	180	4-8-75	.218	.105	.231	76	179	13	39	8	0	2	15	12	0	4	1	25	2	2	.296	.266
Pierzynski, A.J.	L-R	6-3	240	12-30-76	.257	.230	.263	128	460	61	118	21	0	18	56	23	12	1	1	68	0	2	.420	.308
Podsednik, Scott	L-L	6-0	190	3-18-76	.290	.330	.280	129	507	80	147	28	1	0	25	47	3	6	5	75	59	23	.349	.351
Rowand, Aaron	R-R	6-0	200	8-29-77	.270	.303	.258	157	578	77	156	30	5	13	69	32	21	5	4	116	16	5	.407	.329
Thomas, Frank	R-R	6-5	275	5-27-68	.219	.281	.192	34	105	19	23	3	0	12	26	16	0	0	3	31	0	0	.590	.315
Uribe, Juan	R-R	5-11	215	7-22-79	.252	.311	.231	146	481	58	121	23	3	16	71	34	4	11	10	77	4	6	.412	.301
Widger, Chris	R-R	6-2	215	5-21-71	.241	.237	.246	45	141	18	34	8	0	4	11	10	1	2	0	22	0	2	.383	.296

PITCHING	B-T	HT	WT	DOB	W	L	ERA	G	GS	CG	SV	IP	H	R	ER	HR	BB	SO	AVG	vLH	vRH	K/9	BB/9
Adkins, Jon	L-R	5-11	215	8-23-77	0	1	8.64	5	0	0	0	8	13	8	8	0	4	1	.351	.389	.316	1.08	4.32
Bajenaru, Jeff	R-R	6-1	200	3-21-78	0	0	6.23	4	0	0	0	4	4	3	3	2	0	3	.222	.300	.125	6.23	0.00
Buehrle, Mark	L-L	6-2	220	3-23-79	16	8	3.12	33	33	3	0	237	240	99	82	20	40	149	.262	.271	.260	5.67	1.52
Contreras, Jose	R-R	6-4	245	12-6-71	15	7	3.61	32	32	1	0	205	177	91	82	23	75	154	.232	.231	.233	6.77	3.30
Cotts, Neal	L-L	6-2	205	3-25-80	4	0	1.94	69	0	0	0	60	38	15	13	1	29	58	.179	.206	.155	8.65	4.33
Garcia, Freddy	R-R	6-4	250	6-10-76	14	8	3.87	33	33	2	0	228	225	102	98	26	60	146	.259	.268	.249	5.76	2.37
Garland, Jon	R-R	6-6	215	9-27-79	18	10	3.50	32	32	3	0	221	212	93	86	26	47	115	.255	.267	.242	4.68	1.91
Hermanson, Dustin	R-R	6-2	200	12-21-72	2	4	2.04	57	0	0	34	57	46	17	13	4	17	33	.222	.240	.206	5.18	2.67
Hernandez, Orlando	R-R	6-2	220	10-11-69	9	9	5.12	24	22	0	1	128	137	77	73	18	50	91	.275	.291	.257	6.38	3.51
Jenks, Bobby	R-R	6-3	270	3-14-81	1	1	2.75	32	0	0	6	39	34	15	12	3	15	50	.225	.105	.298	11.44	3.43
Marte, Damaso	L-L	6-2	205	2-14-75	3	4	3.77	66	0	0	4	45	45	21	19	5	33	54	.256	.267	.244	10.72	6.55
McCarthy, Brandon	R-R	6-7	190	7-7-83	3	2	4.03	12	10	0	0	67	62	30	30	13	17	48	.242	.205	.276	6.45	2.28
Politte, Cliff	R-R	5-10	200	2-27-74	7	1	2.00	68	0	0	1	67	42	15	15	7	21	57	.181	.182	.181	7.62	2.81
Sanders, David	L-L	6-0	200	8-29-79	0	0	13.50	2	0	0	0	2	3	3	3	1	1	1	.375	.500	.250	4.50	4.50
Takatsu, Shingo	R-R	6-0	180	11-25-68	1	2	5.97	31	0	0	8	29	30	19	19	9	16	32	.270	.239	.292	10.05	5.02
Vizcaino, Luis	R-R	5-11	185	8-6-74	6	5	3.73	65	0	0	0	70	74	30	29	8	29	43	.275	.321	.242	5.53	3.73
Walker, Kevin	L-L	6-3	215	9-20-76	0	1	9.00	9	0	0	0	7	10	7	7	1	5	5	.333	.421	.182	6.43	6.43

FIELDING

Catcher	PCT	G	PO	A	E	DP	PB
Casanova	1.000	6	9	0	0	0	0
Pierzynski	.999	128	803	48	1	8	7
Widger	.981	42	252	12	5	1	2

First Base	PCT	G	PO	A	E	DP
Blum	1.000	12	91	6	0	7
Burke	.000	1	0	0	0	0
Dye	1.000	1	7	1	0	0
Gload	.987	24	72	4	1	9
Konerko	.996	146	1321	82	5	135
Ozuna	1.000	2	2	1	0	0
Perez	.933	2	13	1	1	1
Widger	.000	1	0	0	0	0

Second Base	PCT	G	PO	A	E	DP
Blum	1.000	2	3	4	0	2
Harris	.986	32	58	78	2	20
Iguchi	.978	133	235	375	14	85
Lopez	1.000	1	3	5	0	2
Ozuna	.923	6	6	6	1	0

Third Base	PCT	G	PO	A	E	DP
Blum	.917	12	4	29	3	2
Crede	.971	130	95	243	10	28
Ozuna	.941	32	29	67	6	4
Widger	1.000	1	1	1	0	0

Shortstop	PCT	G	PO	A	E	DP
Blum	1.000	6	6	10	0	2
Crede	1.000	1	1	3	0	2
Dye	.000	1	0	0	0	0
Harris	1.000	5	1	9	0	1
Lopez	1.000	1	0	2	0	0
Ozuna	.964	15	19	35	2	12
Uribe	.977	146	249	422	16	98

Outfield	PCT	G	PO	A	E	DP
Anderson	1.000	12	19	1	0	1
Borchard	1.000	2	3	0	0	0
Dye	.971	140	259	9	8	2
Everett	1.000	22	34	1	0	1
Gload	1.000	3	5	0	0	0
Ozuna	1.000	10	10	0	0	0
Perez	.964	50	75	5	3	1
Podsednik	.989	127	274	3	3	1
Rowand	.992	157	388	3	3	1

FARM SYSTEM

General Manager: Kenny Williams. **Director, Player Development:** David Wilder. **Scouting Director:** Duane Shaffer.

Class	Farm Team	League	W	L	Pct.	Finish*	Manager(s)	Affiliate Since
AAA	Charlotte (N.C.) Knights	International	57	87	.396	13th (14)	Nick Leyva/Manny Trillo	1999
AA	Birmingham (Ala.) Barons	Southern	82	57	.590	**2nd (10)**	Razor Shines	1986
High A	Winston-Salem (N.C.) Warthogs	Carolina	77	64	.546	**3rd (8)**	Chris Cron	1997
Low A	Kannapolis (N.C.) Intimidators	South Atlantic	74	59	.556	**+4th (16)**	Nick Capra	2001
Rookie	Great Falls (Mont.) White Sox	Pioneer	32	44	.421	8th (8)	John Orton	2003
Rookie	Bristol (Va.) White Sox	Appalachian	30	36	.455	6th (10)	Jerry Hairston	1995

*Finish in overall standings (No. of teams in league)/playoff teams in **boldface** +League champion

CARL KLINE

Tadahito Iguchi: One of the American League's top rookies

SPORTS ON FILM

Brian Anderson: Hit .295-16-57 in Triple-A

CHARLOTTE KNIGHTS — Class AAA

INTERNATIONAL LEAGUE

BATTING	B-T	HT	WT	DOB	AVG	vLH	vRH	G	AB	R	H	2B	3B	HR	RBI	BB	HBP	SH	SF	SO	SB	CS	SLG	OBP
Aceves, Jonathan	R-R	6-2	220	3-7-78	.204	.176	.216	16	54	8	11	4	1	1	2	5	0	1	0	18	0	0	.370	.271
Alvarez, Tony	R-R	6-1	200	5-10-79	.211	1.000	.167	5	19	1	4	1	0	0	2	0	0	0	0	2	0	1	.263	.211
Anderson, Brian	R-R	6-2	205	3-11-82	.295	.290	.296	118	448	71	132	24	3	16	57	44	4	1	4	115	4	2	.469	.360
Becker, Brian	R-R	6-7	247	5-26-75	.158	.143	.167	7	19	3	3	0	1	2	2	0	0	0	0	8	0	0	.579	.158
Bikowski, Scott	L-L	6-0	194	2-12-77	.236	.176	.244	94	296	36	70	18	2	2	26	30	2	4	1	67	3	5	.331	.310
Borchard, Joe	B-R	6-5	220	11-25-78	.263	.192	.282	134	494	69	130	20	0	29	67	50	4	1	1	143	6	4	.480	.335
Brown, Roosevelt	L-R	5-10	205	8-3-75	.306	.281	.313	103	389	62	119	31	2	12	53	42	5	2	7	59	3	2	.488	.375
Burke, Jamie	R-R	6-0	225	9-24-71	.265	.233	.272	102	358	50	95	22	1	10	53	36	13	3	4	53	1	3	.416	.350
Casanova, Raul	B-R	6-0	230	8-23-72	.266	.220	.276	70	233	25	62	13	0	13	42	20	1	0	1	29	0	0	.489	.325
Coquillette, Trace	R-R	5-11	180	6-4-74	.272	.182	.296	36	103	10	28	5	0	4	18	7	1	6	2	29	0	1	.437	.319
Daigle, Leo	R-R	6-4	225	9-18-79	.220	.103	.274	25	91	8	20	5	0	2	8	2	0	1	0	27	0	0	.341	.237
Davis, Ben	B-R	6-4	215	3-10-77	.242	.200	.250	10	33	1	8	0	0	1	3	1	0	0	1	4	0	0	.333	.257
Giambi, Jeremy	L-L	5-11	215	9-30-74	.000	.000	.000	4	8	0	0	0	0	0	0	2	0	0	0	4	0	0	.000	.200
Gload, Ross	L-L	6-0	200	4-5-76	.364	.277	.398	60	236	45	86	22	1	15	45	22	1	1	3	37	0	1	.657	.416
Guerrero, Wilton	B-R	6-0	175	10-24-74	.241	.219	.255	21	83	11	20	5	0	2	12	6	0	3	0	9	1	2	.373	.292
Gutierrez, Ricky	R-R	6-1	195	5-23-70	.186	.208	.181	36	118	15	22	3	0	0	8	15	3	7	1	22	1	0	.212	.292
Harris, Willie	L-R	5-9	170	6-22-78	.266	.250	.269	28	109	21	29	11	1	1	10	16	0	4	0	27	10	2	.413	.360
Leon, Donny	B-R	6-2	180	5-7-77	.143	.000	.182	4	14	1	2	0	0	0	1	4	0	0	0	0	0	0	.143	.333
Lopez, Pedro	R-R	6-1	160	4-28-84	.202	.132	.220	55	188	14	38	6	0	3	17	7	2	9	2	24	1	1	.282	.236
Martinez, Felix	B-R	6-0	200	5-18-74	.251	.288	.241	97	346	36	87	22	0	3	27	23	3	3	4	57	3	3	.341	.301
Norton, Greg	B-R	6-1	200	7-6-72	.285	.257	.293	90	330	57	94	19	1	17	56	47	1	1	2	67	0	2	.503	.374
Podsednik, Scott	L-L	6-0	190	3-18-76	.222	.000	.222	2	9	2	2	2	0	0	1	0	0	0	0	2	0	0	.444	.222
Reyes, Guillermo	B-R	5-9	177	12-29-81	.249	.286	.237	59	205	24	51	8	2	1	12	12	1	4	3	32	2	2	.322	.290
Rosa, Wally	R-R	6-1	182	11-28-81	.185	.167	.190	18	54	3	10	1	0	0	3	1	0	3	2	10	0	0	.204	.193

BATTING	B-T	HT	WT	DOB	AVG	vLH	vRH	G	AB	R	H	2B	3B	HR	RBI	BB	HBP	SH	SF	SO	SB	CS	SLG	OBP
Spidale, Mike	R-R	6-1	190	3-12-82	.230	.224	.232	46	161	17	37	4	0	1	7	10	3	3	0	22	5	3	.273	.287
Thomas, Frank	R-R	6-5	275	5-27-68	.190	.167	.200	11	42	3	8	1	0	1	4	4	0	0	0	9	0	0	.286	.261
Toca, Jorge	R-R	6-3	220	1-7-75	.302	.337	.292	115	454	56	137	24	1	24	77	24	6	0	3	87	0	1	.518	.343

PITCHING	B-T	HT	WT	DOB	W	L	ERA	G	GS	CG	SV	IP	H	R	ER	HR	BB	SO	AVG	vLH	vRH	K/9	BB/9
Adkins, Jon	L-R	5-11	215	8-30-77	4	9	5.37	23	21	0	0	127	148	81	76	20	43	92	.295	.323	.267	6.50	3.04
Bajenaru, Jeff	R-R	6-1	200	3-21-78	4	6	1.41	61	0	0	19	70	45	14	11	4	29	83	.185	.301	.125	10.62	3.71
Bullard, Jim	L-L	6-7	212	12-29-79	3	2	5.67	15	9	0	0	54	57	34	34	12	31	39	.268	.225	.289	6.50	5.17
Bullinger, Jim	R-R	6-2	185	8-21-65	1	0	9.53	10	0	0	0	17	23	20	18	3	9	13	.329	.409	.292	6.88	4.76
Diaz, Felix	R-R	6-1	190	7-27-80	6	8	5.00	21	21	1	0	122	149	72	68	15	33	108	.308	.310	.306	7.95	2.43
Fields, Josh	R-R	6-1	180	1-20-80	4	5	2.75	55	0	0	0	69	61	23	21	6	21	51	.241	.210	.256	6.68	2.75
Hernandez, Orlando	R-R	6-2	220	10-11-69	0	1	2.25	1	1	0	0	4	4	1	1	0	0	2	.267	.200	.300	4.50	0.00
Jones, Bobby M.	R-L	6-0	170	4-11-72	0	2	8.39	16	2	0	0	25	37	25	23	3	14	25	.343	.412	.311	9.12	5.11
Little, Jeff	R-R	6-3	200	4-30-80	2	1	4.91	9	3	0	0	26	20	15	14	5	8	17	.215	.229	.207	5.96	2.81
Marte, Damaso	L-L	6-2	205	2-14-75	0	0	5.40	1	0	0	0	2	4	1	1	0	1	2	.400	.333	.429	10.80	5.40
McCarthy, Brandon	R-R	6-7	190	7-7-83	7	7	3.92	20	19	1	0	119	104	53	52	16	32	130	.233	.210	.251	9.80	2.41
Munoz, Arnie	L-L	5-9	175	6-21-82	8	14	4.27	40	18	0	1	133	150	79	63	16	60	109	.287	.298	.283	7.39	4.07
Ortiz, Javier	R-R	6-0	155	11-28-79	1	1	7.84	10	2	0	0	21	37	19	18	2	4	10	.416	.447	.392	4.35	1.74
Person, Robert	R-R	6-0	195	10-6-69	2	3	7.00	7	7	0	0	36	34	28	28	11	25	24	.250	.356	.169	6.00	6.25
Phillips, Heath	L-L	6-3	242	3-24-82	0	3	8.31	5	5	0	0	22	29	22	20	10	13	16	.333	.240	.371	6.65	5.40
Sanders, David	L-L	6-0	200	8-29-79	4	2	3.02	57	0	0	1	66	68	28	22	10	32	47	.268	.220	.303	6.44	4.39
Smith, Matt	R-R	6-5	240	8-14-78	1	6	3.86	66	0	0	4	84	95	41	36	12	32	56	.285	.345	.256	6.00	3.43
Stephens, John	R-R	6-1	215	11-15-79	0	2	3.99	10	3	0	0	29	34	16	13	2	8	14	.296	.241	.344	4.30	2.45
Stewart, Josh	L-L	6-3	205	12-5-78	4	4	4.25	14	11	0	0	66	65	34	31	6	16	41	.257	.253	.259	5.62	2.19
Ulacia, Dennis	L-L	6-1	185	4-2-81	4	7	6.54	21	17	1	0	96	116	73	70	21	40	58	.302	.286	.307	5.42	3.74
Villacis, Eduardo	R-R	6-2	215	8-29-79	1	2	9.47	9	5	0	0	26	37	28	27	9	13	24	.343	.432	.281	8.42	4.56
Walker, Kevin	L-L	6-3	215	9-20-76	1	2	5.28	51	0	0	5	46	49	35	27	7	21	52	.269	.208	.314	10.17	4.11
Winkelsas, Joe	R-R	6-3	188	9-14-73	0	0	6.48	4	0	0	0	8	11	6	6	2	4	3	.333	.222	.375	3.24	4.32

FIELDING

Catcher	PCT	G	PO	A	E	DP	PB
Aceves	.992	16	118	8	1	1	2
Burke	.991	48	319	26	3	7	2
Casanova	.990	62	460	27	5	2	6
Davis	.989	10	80	6	1	0	1
Rosa	.989	15	86	7	1	0	1

First Base	PCT	G	PO	A	E	DP
Becker	1.000	3	24	1	0	2
Burke	1.000	3	21	2	0	2
Casanova	1.000	1	3	0	0	0
Daigle	1.000	3	20	3	0	0
Gload	1.000	36	314	12	0	41
Norton	.989	10	78	9	1	9
Toca	.991	91	690	52	7	76

Second Base	PCT	G	PO	A	E	DP
Burke	1.000	5	7	11	0	0
Coquillette	.963	25	43	60	4	20
Guerrero	.957	21	39	50	4	14
Harris	.977	28	71	59	3	19
Lopez	.956	10	15	28	2	5
Martinez	.985	52	117	153	4	40
Reyes	1.000	5	7	12	0	6
Rosa	.778	2	2	5	2	1

Third Base	PCT	G	PO	A	E	DP
Burke	.971	47	30	72	3	4
Coquillette	.857	8	4	14	3	1
Daigle	.875	19	12	30	6	2
Gutierrez	.887	18	13	34	6	5
Leon	.800	4	2	2	1	0
Martinez	.958	16	7	16	1	0
Norton	.929	45	35	70	8	11
Toca	1.000	1	0	2	0	0

Shortstop	PCT	G	PO	A	E	DP
Gutierrez	1.000	17	24	46	0	10
Lopez	.943	45	59	122	11	35
Martinez	.961	34	57	92	6	28
Reyes	.936	53	70	136	14	27

Outfield	PCT	G	PO	A	E	DP
Alvarez	1.000	3	2	0	0	0
Anderson	.986	115	278	14	4	4
Bikowski	1.000	80	132	10	0	2
Borchard	.989	123	261	1	3	1
Brown	.983	88	164	13	3	3
Coquillette	.000	1	0	0	0	0
Giambi	1.000	2	1	0	0	0
Gload	.952	11	20	0	1	0
Podsednik	1.000	2	6	1	0	0
Rosa	1.000	1	1	0	0	0
Spidale	1.000	27	56	0	0	0

BIRMINGHAM BARONS — Class AA

SOUTHERN LEAGUE

BATTING	B-T	HT	WT	DOB	AVG	vLH	vRH	G	AB	R	H	2B	3B	HR	RBI	BB	HBP	SH	SF	SO	SB	CS	SLG	OBP
Aceves, Jonathan	R-R	6-2	220	3-7-78	.267	.232	.284	70	217	32	58	14	1	7	34	26	7	3	1	47	0	1	.438	.363
Acosta, Christian	R-R	5-11	178	7-14-83	.000	.000	.000	2	7	1	0	0	0	0	0	1	0	0	0	1	0	0	.000	.125
Blakely, Darren	B-R	6-1	190	3-14-77	.283	.333	.258	128	460	71	130	29	3	18	89	45	4	3	8	122	5	5	.476	.346
Fields, Josh	R-R	6-1	215	12-14-82	.252	.254	.251	134	477	76	120	27	0	16	79	55	13	9	6	142	7	6	.409	.341
Garcia, Cipriano	R-R	5-11	215	10-23-78	.364	.000	.500	4	11	2	4	0	0	0	0	0	1	0	0	6	0	0	.364	.417
Giambi, Jeremy	L-L	5-11	215	9-30-74	.273	.333	.250	5	11	1	3	1	0	0	2	2	0	0	0	3	0	0	.364	.385
Gonzalez, Angel	R-R	6-2	192	12-15-81	.274	.305	.261	123	434	50	119	19	2	4	63	61	4	5	7	91	6	6	.355	.364
Gray, Antoin	R-R	5-9	195	5-19-81	.239	.234	.242	76	230	37	55	14	1	7	30	27	4	6	2	65	1	1	.400	.327
Haggerty, Cory	L-R	6-0	180	8-25-81	.216	.125	.223	46	111	12	24	3	1	2	14	17	0	3	1	26	2	1	.315	.318
Lopez, Pedro	R-R	6-1	160	4-28-84	.238	.250	.235	68	239	26	57	7	1	3	24	13	4	13	2	29	0	2	.314	.287
Nicholson, Tommy	L-R	5-9	160	8-23-79	.267	1.000	.214	4	15	2	4	2	0	0	3	1	0	0	1	2	0	0	.400	.294
Owens, Jerry	L-L	6-3	195	2-16-81	.331	.305	.342	130	522	99	173	21	6	2	52	52	2	9	2	72	38	20	.406	.393
Reyes, Guillermo	B-R	5-9	177	12-29-81	.280	.245	.297	48	150	28	42	7	3	1	18	15	1	5	4	18	7	3	.387	.341
Rogowski, Casey	L-L	6-3	230	5-1-81	.293	.241	.317	134	505	83	148	37	6	9	78	58	11	3	6	111	20	12	.444	.374
Rosa, Wally	R-R	6-1	182	11-28-81	.273	.250	.286	16	44	7	12	2	0	0	3	3	2	1	0	8	0	1	.318	.347
Stewart, Chris	R-R	6-4	215	2-19-82	.286	.279	.289	95	311	39	89	21	0	11	51	24	3	10	2	37	3	3	.460	.341
Sweeney, Ryan	L-L	6-4	200	2-20-85	.298	.319	.289	113	429	64	128	22	3	1	47	35	7	7	5	53	6	6	.371	.357
Young, Chris	R-R	6-2	182	9-5-83	.277	.295	.269	126	466	100	129	41	3	26	77	70	7	7	3	129	32	6	.545	.377

PITCHING	B-T	HT	WT	DOB	W	L	ERA	G	GS	CG	SV	IP	H	R	ER	HR	BB	SO	AVG	vLH	vRH	K/9	BB/9
Bullard, Jim	L-L	6-7	212	12-29-79	2	3	6.85	8	6	0	0	24	30	18	18	2	10	19	.319	.310	.323	7.23	3.80
Dizard, Fraser	L-L	6-0	195	8-6-81	0	0	3.38	5	0	0	0	8	9	5	3	1	5	11	.281	.125	.333	12.38	5.63
Glen, Willie	R-R	6-1	185	10-30-77	1	0	8.84	11	0	0	0	19	29	20	19	3	11	16	.349	.290	.385	7.45	5.12
Haeger, Charles	R-R	6-1	202	9-19-83	6	3	3.78	13	13	3	0	86	84	43	36	1	45	48	.263	.255	.270	5.04	4.73
Haigwood, Daniel	R-L	6-2	197	11-19-83	6	1	1.74	11	11	0	0	67	39	14	13	0	31	76	.170	.250	.141	10.16	4.14
Honel, Kris	R-R	6-5	190	11-7-82	5	7	5.88	21	18	0	0	93	101	68	61	10	64	70	.278	.314	.246	6.75	6.17
Jenks, Bobby	R-R	6-3	270	3-14-81	1	2	2.85	35	0	0	19	41	34	17	13	1	20	48	.224	.225	.222	10.54	4.39
LaMura, B.J.	R-R	6-1	189	1-1-81	5	2	4.79	55	0	0	1	71	73	46	38	5	57	79	.265	.268	.264	9.97	7.19
Lubisich, Nik	L-L	6-2	195	4-19-79	9	4	3.00	21	18	0	1	105	111	43	35	8	22	49	.280	.248	.291	4.20	1.89
Malone, Corwin	R-L	6-3	200	7-3-80	5	5	4.53	33	13	0	1	97	100	55	49	6	55	81	.272	.202	.295	7.49	5.09
Meaux, Ryan	L-L	5-11	170	10-5-78	5	2	2.96	38	0	0	3	67	77	27	22	2	18	64	.291	.221	.324	8.60	2.42
Ortiz, Javier	R-R	6-0	155	11-28-79	2	1	3.52	5	0	0	0	8	8	4	3	1	4	7	.267	.455	.158	8.22	4.70

PITCHING	B-T	HT	WT	DOB	W	L	ERA	G	GS	CG	SV	IP	H	R	ER	HR	BB	SO	AVG	vLH	vRH	K/9	BB/9
Pacheco, Enemencio	R-R	6-1	170	8-31-78	0	1	6.97	3	3	0	0	10	16	8	8	0	5	9	.372	.600	.250	7.84	4.35
Phillips, Heath	L-L	6-3	242	3-24-82	9	5	4.07	22	21	2	0	135	161	64	61	12	30	78	.308	.306	.309	5.20	2.00
Pollok, Dwayne	R-R	6-3	195	11-12-80	4	5	3.08	56	0	0	11	88	88	42	30	7	19	58	.257	.275	.245	5.95	1.95
Reynoso, Paulino	L-L	6-3	215	8-10-80	4	4	3.92	54	0	0	8	57	63	37	25	6	41	46	.285	.309	.277	7.22	6.44
Tracey, Sean	L-R	6-3	210	11-14-80	14	6	4.07	28	28	2	0	164	154	80	74	13	76	106	.257	.269	.248	5.83	4.18
Ulacia, Dennis	L-L	6-1	185	4-2-81	0	0	0.00	2	0	0	0	4	3	0	0	0	0	3	.188	.333	.154	6.75	0.00
Villacis, Eduardo	R-R	6-2	215	8-29-79	2	5	7.06	9	8	0	1	43	64	40	34	10	18	37	.339	.313	.358	7.68	3.74
Wassermann, Ehren	B-R	6-0	185	12-6-80	2	0	2.14	14	0	0	0	21	23	6	5	0	7	18	.291	.351	.238	7.71	3.00
Yofu, Tetsu	R-R	6-0	182	6-26-73	0	1	7.11	2	0	0	0	6	6	5	5	0	6	7	.273	.333	.250	9.95	8.53

FIELDING

Catcher	PCT	G	PO	A	E	DP	PB
Aceves	.994	51	302	25	2	2	3
Garcia	1.000	3	7	0	0	0	0
Rosa	.965	10	51	4	2	0	4
Stewart	.988	90	601	55	8	8	23

First Base	PCT	G	PO	A	E	DP
Aceves	.984	11	57	4	1	7
Fields	.875	2	6	1	1	1
Rogowski	.991	133	1126	87	11	133

Second Base	PCT	G	PO	A	E	DP
Acosta	1.000	1	0	1	0	0
Gonzalez	.988	48	118	122	3	48
Gray	.936	55	82	137	15	33
Haggerty	.949	20	29	45	4	12
Nicholson	1.000	4	5	15	0	4
Reyes	.990	24	36	61	1	14

Third Base	PCT	G	PO	A	E	DP
Fields	.933	133	95	239	24	22
Gonzalez	1.000	5	3	5	0	1
Reyes	1.000	11	6	18	0	2

Shortstop	PCT	G	PO	A	E	DP
Gonzalez	.926	61	91	170	21	40
Lopez	.970	68	106	216	10	59
Reyes	.948	13	16	39	3	3

Outfield	PCT	G	PO	A	E	DP
Blakely	.992	71	123	6	1	1
Haggerty	1.000	1	2	0	0	0
Owens	.987	120	209	11	3	0
Rogowski	1.000	1	1	0	0	0
Sweeney	.987	107	212	12	3	1
Young	.990	123	289	6	3	2

WINSTON-SALEM WARTHOGS — High Class A

CAROLINA LEAGUE

BATTING	B-T	HT	WT	DOB	AVG	vLH	vRH	G	AB	R	H	2B	3B	HR	RBI	BB	HBP	SH	SF	SO	SB	CS	SLG	OBP
Amador, Chris	R-R	5-10	167	12-14-82	.267	.241	.282	64	210	34	56	13	1	11	35	10	3	2	0	52	19	5	.495	.309
Collaro, Tom	R-R	6-4	216	4-4-83	.264	.277	.254	133	531	68	140	27	3	29	100	25	2	0	1	153	5	3	.490	.299
Daigle, Leo	R-R	6-4	225	9-18-79	.341	.323	.352	108	411	85	140	33	1	29	112	50	6	0	6	72	10	4	.637	.414
Garcia, Cipriano	R-R	5-11	215	10-23-78	.316	.250	.346	24	38	7	12	2	0	3	9	2	2	0	0	12	0	0	.605	.381
Haggerty, Cory	L-R	6-0	180	8-25-81	.247	.136	.284	34	89	16	22	4	1	0	3	6	0	2	1	21	2	1	.315	.292
Hall, Noah	R-R	5-11	200	6-9-77	.332	.351	.319	120	425	112	141	38	6	26	92	86	19	1	6	76	24	5	.633	.459
Hinton, Travis	L-L	6-1	206	11-21-80	.257	.233	.268	112	381	55	98	34	2	14	67	44	5	0	5	80	1	0	.467	.338
Lee, Carlos	R-R	6-1	228	9-29-81	.289	.289	.289	84	294	35	85	9	1	14	48	14	4	0	2	33	2	1	.469	.328
Martel, Norm	L-R	6-0	195	8-4-78	.138	.100	.158	11	29	3	4	0	0	0	0	4	0	0	0	6	0	0	.138	.242
Molina, Gustavo	R-R	6-2	210	2-24-82	.261	.295	.238	109	345	38	90	20	1	11	41	30	6	8	3	47	1	2	.420	.328
Myers, Michael	R-R	6-1	194	12-11-79	.255	.254	.256	120	419	81	107	27	2	9	42	69	7	6	4	74	37	8	.394	.367
Nanita, Ricardo	L-L	6-1	180	6-12-81	.292	.290	.293	120	415	73	121	36	2	9	54	61	10	8	4	53	14	11	.453	.392
Schnurstein, Micah	R-R	6-1	207	7-18-84	.268	.279	.261	132	488	78	131	21	3	15	68	40	7	0	2	98	12	8	.416	.331
Shaffer, Josh	L-R	6-1	165	6-26-80	.200	.160	.211	51	115	19	23	3	0	0	6	16	0	1	1	33	3	2	.226	.295
Spidale, Mike	R-R	6-1	190	3-12-82	.250	.306	.207	39	144	19	36	2	0	0	8	11	4	2	0	15	6	2	.264	.321
Valido, Robert	R-R	6-2	180	5-16-85	.288	.288	.289	119	513	86	148	28	7	8	59	21	4	9	3	64	52	5	.417	.320

PITCHING	B-T	HT	WT	DOB	W	L	ERA	G	GS	CG	SV	IP	H	R	ER	HR	BB	SO	AVG	vLH	vRH	K/9	BB/9
Bakker, Garry	R-R	6-2	208	3-28-83	1	2	9.09	16	3	0	0	33	54	34	33	7	11	16	.378	.362	.392	4.41	3.03
Broadway, Lance	R-R	6-4	190	8-20-83	1	3	4.58	11	11	0	0	55	68	31	28	4	20	58	.306	.277	.336	9.49	3.27
Castro, Fabio	L-L	5-8	157	1-20-85	5	5	2.28	53	0	0	6	79	58	23	20	7	37	75	.209	.214	.207	8.54	4.22
Dizard, Fraser	L-L	6-0	195	8-6-81	4	7	6.72	31	10	0	1	86	103	66	64	11	38	87	.298	.328	.282	9.14	3.99
Flores, Rafael	R-R	6-7	246	4-26-84	3	4	4.77	28	9	0	2	89	93	52	47	12	27	65	.274	.288	.264	6.60	2.74
Gonzalez, Gio	R-L	5-11	185	9-19-85	8	3	3.56	13	13	0	0	73	61	33	29	5	25	79	.228	.298	.190	9.70	3.07
Haeger, Charles	R-R	6-1	202	9-19-83	8	2	3.20	14	13	0	0	82	82	33	29	3	40	64	.267	.227	.296	7.05	4.41
Haigwood, Daniel	R-L	6-2	197	11-19-83	8	2	3.77	15	15	0	0	76	79	39	32	8	33	84	.265	.243	.272	9.90	3.89
Hernandez, Fernando	R-R	5-11	190	7-31-84	4	1	5.14	45	0	0	1	70	83	44	40	6	30	59	.303	.286	.315	7.59	3.86
Liotta, Ray	L-L	6-3	220	4-3-83	6	2	1.45	8	8	0	0	50	46	11	8	1	16	37	.254	.286	.237	6.70	2.90
Logan, Boone	R-L	6-5	200	8-13-84	0	0	5.06	4	0	0	0	5	7	3	3	2	4	5	.318	.300	.333	8.44	6.75
Lopez, Orionny	R-R	6-2	170	4-1-84	2	2	5.14	36	1	0	2	61	56	36	35	5	25	45	.237	.250	.229	6.60	3.67
Miller, Brian	R-R	6-3	212	10-18-82	0	0	6.19	11	0	0	0	16	15	14	11	2	8	18	.231	.154	.282	10.13	4.50
Moat, Mike	R-R	6-1	190	10-25-81	1	2	5.56	12	3	0	1	23	25	15	14	5	12	15	.272	.282	.264	5.96	4.76
Ortiz, Javier	R-R	6-0	155	11-28-79	0	1	4.50	3	0	0	0	4	7	2	2	1	3	3	.389	.444	.333	6.75	6.75
Ovalles, Juan	R-R	6-0	165	5-15-82	5	6	4.15	52	0	0	3	87	86	46	40	7	51	89	.263	.306	.238	9.24	5.30
Rodriguez, Ryan	L-L	6-4	233	7-10-84	13	7	4.09	29	29	2	0	167	180	87	76	17	49	108	.281	.259	.291	5.81	2.64
Sabo, Tim	R-R	6-3	215	2-6-84	0	0	4.91	7	0	0	0	11	9	6	6	1	9	4	.225	.167	.250	3.27	7.36
Wassermann, Ehren	B-R	6-0	185	12-6-80	4	2	1.37	42	0	0	20	46	41	10	7	0	9	37	.247	.250	.245	7.24	1.76
Whisler, Wes	L-L	6-5	235	4-7-83	4	9	6.73	26	21	1	1	112	153	93	84	10	42	79	.325	.277	.351	6.33	3.36
Wing, Ryan	L-L	6-2	170	2-1-82	0	4	8.69	5	5	0	0	20	25	20	19	4	13	19	.321	.217	.364	8.69	5.95

FIELDING

Catcher	PCT	G	PO	A	E	DP	PB
Garcia	.975	20	70	8	2	1	3
Lee	.996	36	229	26	1	4	11
Molina	.993	107	744	107	6	9	23

First Base	PCT	G	PO	A	E	DP
Daigle	.992	87	681	44	6	62
Hinton	.996	62	472	37	2	44
Lee	.875	2	6	1	1	0
Molina	.923	2	12	0	1	0
Myers	1.000	3	15	0	0	0
Shaffer	.000	1	0	0	0	0

Second Base	PCT	G	PO	A	E	DP
Amador	.966	24	53	60	4	13
Haggerty	.974	29	47	66	3	12
Myers	.992	58	95	147	2	33
Schnurstein	.961	13	26	23	2	5
Shaffer	.970	39	55	73	4	15

Third Base	PCT	G	PO	A	E	DP
Daigle	.794	16	5	22	7	1
Molina	1.000	3	0	4	0	0
Myers	1.000	5	4	11	0	1
Schnurstein	.929	122	83	192	21	16
Shaffer	1.000	7	1	6	0	0

Shortstop	PCT	G	PO	A	E	DP
Haggerty	.000	1	0	0	0	0
Myers	.929	25	36	56	7	13
Shaffer	.818	2	4	5	2	2
Valido	.978	118	166	362	12	84

Outfield	PCT	G	PO	A	E	DP
Amador	.963	35	77	0	3	0
Collaro	.972	120	228	13	7	3
Daigle	1.000	1	0	1	0	0
Hall	.987	88	145	5	2	1
Martel	1.000	8	12	1	0	1
Myers	.977	36	83	2	2	1
Nanita	.977	115	250	7	6	1
Spidale	.986	36	71	0	1	0

KANNAPOLIS INTIMIDATORS — Low Class A

SOUTH ATLANTIC LEAGUE

BATTING	B-T	HT	WT	DOB	AVG	vLH	vRH	G	AB	R	H	2B	3B	HR	RBI	BB	HBP	SH	SF	SO	SB	CS	SLG	OBP
Berry, Layne	L-R	5-11	180	12-5-80	.266	.196	.280	101	342	56	91	13	2	4	32	52	11	4	3	70	15	3	.351	.377
Brice, Tom	L-L	6-5	211	8-24-81	.286	.400	.278	20	77	13	22	5	0	1	7	4	1	0	1	11	2	0	.390	.325
Castillo, Javier	R-R	6-2	185	8-29-83	.226	.281	.203	50	190	16	43	11	1	3	20	13	1	2	0	49	2	1	.342	.279
Cook, David	R-R	5-11	195	7-21-81	.283	.264	.289	109	368	75	104	21	3	24	65	72	4	0	3	105	8	6	.552	.403
Cunningham, Aaron	R-R	5-11	195	4-24-86	.115	.000	.136	10	26	7	3	0	0	0	2	3	0	0	0	7	1	0	.115	.207
De los Santos, Jose	R-R	5-11	160	8-10-84	.294	.315	.286	103	391	45	115	18	3	0	34	18	4	10	3	42	1	2	.355	.329
Getz, Chris	L-R	6-0	175	8-30-83	.304	.313	.301	55	214	38	65	13	2	1	28	35	3	0	1	10	11	4	.397	.407
Gonzalez, Bernard	R-R	6-2	208	5-10-80	.263	.264	.263	83	315	38	83	19	2	5	35	24	9	0	1	53	2	1	.384	.332
Hansen, Josh	R-R	5-10	215	9-16-81	.276	.307	.264	126	490	69	135	28	1	24	90	48	6	0	6	130	2	1	.484	.344
Hernandez, Francisco	B-R	5-9	160	2-4-86	.222	.227	.220	44	153	15	34	5	0	3	18	13	3	0	2	29	0	0	.314	.292
Kelly, Chris	R-R	6-1	195	2-23-82	.220	.286	.200	28	91	10	20	5	0	4	13	6	0	1	1	30	1	1	.407	.265
King, Clint	L-R	5-11	205	8-6-82	.228	.232	.227	92	333	40	76	18	2	5	41	40	6	1	3	83	7	5	.339	.319
Lisk, Charles	R-R	6-3	206	1-3-83	.160	.100	.200	9	25	4	4	1	0	0	1	3	1	2	0	11	0	0	.200	.276
Lucy, Donny	R-R	6-3	210	8-8-82	.264	.255	.268	54	178	25	47	5	0	1	22	21	5	4	3	41	6	3	.309	.353
Martel, Norm	L-R	6-0	195	8-4-78	.182	.375	.120	9	33	3	6	1	0	0	2	4	0	0	0	6	1	0	.212	.270
McCarthy, Ryan	R-R	6-3	195	9-4-82	.234	.234	.235	98	354	46	83	20	3	7	45	34	1	5	2	79	6	2	.367	.302
Ricks, Adam	B-R	5-10	195	9-24-82	.260	.235	.267	87	285	41	74	9	3	1	23	62	5	11	1	46	1	1	.323	.399
Roberts, Daron	R-R	6-0	215	2-25-83	.241	.167	.262	22	79	5	19	1	0	0	5	4	1	1	1	23	3	2	.253	.282
Rosa, Wally	R-R	6-1	182	11-28-81	.182	.000	.222	12	33	1	6	0	0	0	1	2	0	2	0	10	0	0	.182	.229
Smith, Sean	R-R	6-0	194	8-24-82	.281	.325	.266	110	437	63	123	25	1	14	62	26	9	8	1	71	35	7	.439	.334

PITCHING	B-T	HT	WT	DOB	W	L	ERA	G	GS	CG	SV	IP	H	R	ER	HR	BB	SO	AVG	vLH	vRH	K/9	BB/9
Bakker, Garry	R-R	6-2	208	3-28-83	5	4	3.69	18	5	0	3	54	47	27	22	5	19	38	.233	.240	.228	6.37	3.19
Banks, Demetrius	L-L	6-1	158	5-23-83	0	0	1.93	9	0	0	0	9	6	2	2	0	5	11	.194	.143	.208	10.61	4.82
Brice, Tom	L-L	6-5	211	8-24-81	0	0	4.50	7	0	0	0	4	2	2	2	0	5	4	.143	.250	.100	9.00	11.25
Brooks, Ricky	R-R	6-3	180	7-18-84	1	2	9.13	6	5	1	0	24	30	26	24	3	10	19	.316	.250	.333	7.23	3.80
Egbert, Jack	L-R	6-3	205	5-12-83	10	5	3.12	30	24	4	0	147	127	66	51	5	48	107	.236	.198	.264	6.55	2.94
Gonzalez, Gio	R-L	5-11	185	9-19-85	5	3	1.87	11	10	0	0	58	36	16	12	3	22	84	.175	.147	.180	13.11	3.43
Hansen, Grant	R-R	6-6	225	2-25-83	1	5	6.11	10	7	0	0	35	33	29	24	2	29	26	.254	.262	.246	6.62	7.39
Harrell, Lucas	B-R	6-2	200	6-3-85	7	11	3.65	26	26	0	0	133	128	86	54	8	71	85	.248	.247	.248	5.74	4.79
Hurd, John	R-R	5-11	185	1-29-83	7	3	3.54	44	0	0	4	69	56	34	27	3	33	41	.217	.263	.197	5.37	4.33
Liotta, Ray	L-L	6-3	220	4-3-83	8	3	2.26	20	20	1	0	115	108	39	29	5	35	107	.252	.237	.257	8.35	2.73
Little, Jeff	R-R	6-3	200	4-30-80	5	3	3.70	34	0	0	0	58	60	28	24	5	18	49	.269	.275	.265	7.56	2.78
Mayi, Leonardo	L-L	6-0	160	12-20-79	1	1	5.12	41	0	0	1	32	32	20	18	5	16	29	.271	.263	.279	8.24	4.55
Moat, Mike	R-R	6-1	190	10-25-81	6	1	2.35	38	0	0	1	69	61	26	18	5	9	66	.233	.309	.190	8.61	1.17
Perez, Oneli	R-R	6-2	163	5-26-83	4	2	3.71	36	2	0	2	80	84	41	33	7	32	62	.265	.292	.249	6.98	3.60
Richard, Clayton	L-L	6-5	225	9-12-83	0	1	5.23	3	2	0	0	10	14	7	6	1	1	8	.326	.000	.341	6.97	0.87
Rodriguez, Noe	L-L	6-0	165	8-12-84	0	0	2.63	16	0	0	0	14	12	4	4	0	13	13	.226	.250	.216	8.56	8.56
Rote, Ryan	R-R	6-4	225	8-8-82	0	1	14.63	9	0	0	0	8	12	16	13	3	7	13	.316	.500	.267	14.63	7.88
Russell, Adam	R-R	6-8	250	4-14-83	9	7	3.78	24	24	0	0	126	116	61	53	10	55	82	.246	.225	.263	5.84	3.92
Torres, Carlos	R-R	6-2	180	10-22-82	1	3	3.53	8	8	0	0	43	28	20	17	4	23	54	.179	.204	.168	11.22	4.78
Zaleski, Matt	R-R	6-0	205	12-2-81	4	4	3.38	48	0	0	22	61	73	29	23	2	16	42	.292	.276	.303	6.16	2.35

FIELDING

Catcher	PCT	G	PO	A	E	DP	PB
Hernandez	.981	39	279	26	6	1	3
Lisk	1.000	3	13	3	0	0	0
Lucy	.991	48	309	26	3	2	9
Ricks	.987	35	274	26	4	1	14
Rosa	.977	12	72	13	2	1	3

First Base	PCT	G	PO	A	E	DP
Brice	1.000	3	28	0	0	1
De los Santos	.909	2	19	1	2	3
Gonzalez	.857	1	6	0	1	0
Hansen	.989	78	710	26	8	69
Kelly	.987	27	286	9	4	15
Ricks	.991	23	202	22	2	15

Second Base	PCT	G	PO	A	E	DP
Berry	.977	72	125	208	8	39
De los Santos	1.000	8	10	18	0	5
Getz	.969	36	68	118	6	23
Kelly	.833	1	3	2	1	0
McCarthy	.941	16	36	59	6	10
Ricks	.963	5	8	18	1	4

Third Base	PCT	G	PO	A	E	DP
Berry	.868	26	18	41	9	0
Castillo	.848	10	7	21	5	0
De los Santos	.892	83	39	127	20	7
Gonzalez	1.000	1	0	1	0	0
McCarthy	.800	2	1	3	1	0
Ricks	.925	13	3	34	3	2

Shortstop	PCT	G	PO	A	E	DP
Berry	1.000	1	0	1	0	0
Castillo	.934	37	58	126	13	17
De los Santos	.889	1	3	5	1	1
Getz	.946	19	21	49	4	11
McCarthy	.957	76	119	256	17	53

Outfield	PCT	G	PO	A	E	DP
Brice	1.000	3	3	0	0	0
Cook	.976	100	154	7	4	1
Cunningham	1.000	4	5	0	0	0
Gonzalez	.990	56	91	7	1	0
Hansen	1.000	15	20	0	0	0
King	.949	84	126	3	7	0
Martel	1.000	8	12	0	0	0
McCarthy	1.000	3	6	0	0	0
Roberts	.972	22	35	0	1	0
Smith	.992	110	229	5	2	0

GREAT FALLS WHITE SOX — Rookie

PIONEER LEAGUE

BATTING	B-T	HT	WT	DOB	AVG	vLH	vRH	G	AB	R	H	2B	3B	HR	RBI	BB	HBP	SH	SF	SO	SB	CS	SLG	OBP
Acosta, Rolando	R-R	5-11	170	4-13-83	.277	.182	.304	45	148	25	41	5	2	4	24	18	4	3	0	25	5	0	.419	.371
Allen, Brandon	L-R	6-2	235	2-12-86	.264	.250	.268	66	231	41	61	11	2	11	42	32	7	0	3	69	7	5	.472	.366
Castillo, Javier	R-R	6-2	185	8-29-83	.219	.163	.237	52	178	24	39	7	1	1	20	16	6	3	1	43	5	2	.287	.303
Getz, Chris	L-R	6-0	175	8-30-83	.333	.250	.375	6	24	3	8	1	0	0	4	1	0	1	1	2	2	1	.375	.346
Guest, Garrett	R-R	5-11	170	7-3-82	.230	.200	.242	67	230	21	53	11	0	0	21	27	1	5	5	33	5	2	.278	.308
Hernandez, Francisco	B-R	5-9	160	2-4-86	.349	.280	.370	58	212	37	74	19	0	6	34	19	3	0	3	25	0	1	.524	.405
Hollis, Eric	R-R	6-2	225	9-26-82	.265	.323	.239	34	102	12	27	6	0	0	8	12	6	0	1	21	1	1	.324	.372
Johnson, Brandon	L-R	6-0	190	7-23-84	.278	.244	.287	61	212	30	59	13	2	2	20	16	3	3	0	45	19	5	.387	.338
Landry, Mike	L-L	5-8	195	8-17-79	.231	.000	.261	20	52	10	12	3	0	2	8	8	4	0	0	20	1	1	.404	.375
Roberts, Daron	R-R	6-0	215	2-25-83	.269	.230	.283	64	234	40	63	13	6	7	29	16	6	4	4	55	19	9	.466	.327
Rodriguez, Manuel	R-R	6-2	185	5-24-83	.272	.286	.268	64	246	43	67	18	4	9	43	10	8	0	2	103	2	1	.488	.320
Schmidt, J.J.	R-R	6-3	210	8-15-85	.259	.229	.274	42	143	13	37	13	0	1	15	7	2	2	0	43	4	3	.371	.303
Sharp, Matt	L-R	6-0	205	8-3-82	.214	.125	.235	25	84	9	18	6	1	0	8	12	0	0	0	22	1	1	.310	.313
Tartaglia, Evan	L-L	5-11	165	5-21-82	.305	.286	.310	69	266	41	81	9	5	1	26	34	0	6	2	51	38	13	.387	.381
Tribble, Matt	L-L	6-2	200	11-27-81	.276	.255	.282	65	246	38	68	16	3	1	31	28	3	5	5	45	8	7	.378	.351

PITCHING	B-T	HT	WT	DOB	W	L	ERA	G	GS	CG	SV	IP	H	R	ER	HR	BB	SO	AVG	vLH	vRH	K/9	BB/9
Brennan, Chris	L-L	6-0	185	12-5-82	0	0	5.68	8	0	0	0	13	12	8	8	2	8	14	.267	.190	.333	9.95	5.68
Casey, James	R-R	6-4	215	9-22-84	1	4	5.71	22	0	0	0	35	32	24	22	3	32	39	.254	.306	.233	10.13	8.31
Chirino, Israel	L-L	6-1	200	11-8-83	0	2	11.25	10	0	0	0	12	18	20	15	0	16	14	.327	.500	.268	10.50	12.00
Doyle, Travis	L-L	6-6	225	8-15-83	3	2	4.68	13	4	0	0	33	40	23	17	2	11	33	.294	.279	.301	9.09	3.03
Everly, Eric	L-L	6-3	215	12-8-83	1	2	3.12	8	8	0	0	43	41	26	15	1	17	35	.255	.182	.273	7.27	3.53
Lemon, Nick	R-R	6-3	195	10-4-81	3	4	2.63	30	0	0	3	41	30	17	12	1	18	46	.204	.234	.190	10.10	3.95
Logan, Boone	R-L	6-5	200	8-13-84	1	1	3.31	21	0	0	2	35	34	15	13	1	4	29	.258	.345	.233	7.39	1.02
Marshall, Jay	L-L	6-5	185	2-25-83	2	0	2.70	29	0	0	6	43	35	20	13	3	7	43	.215	.188	.226	8.93	1.45
Moviel, Paul	R-R	6-6	220	9-28-82	4	1	4.04	15	15	0	0	78	89	40	35	3	20	72	.290	.320	.263	8.31	2.31
Nachreiner, Matt	L-R	6-2	190	11-17-84	4	3	6.55	22	0	0	1	33	39	31	24	1	23	31	.287	.275	.292	8.45	6.27
Novoa, Yunior	L-L	6-3	159	9-11-84	1	7	7.32	15	13	0	0	63	83	58	51	11	28	44	.324	.259	.343	6.32	4.02
Pena, Luis	R-R	6-0	170	1-21-81	0	1	6.75	18	0	0	0	33	44	32	25	5	22	25	.319	.343	.311	6.75	5.94
Perez, Carlos	L-L	6-2	175	2-19-84	4	6	4.38	16	10	0	0	62	67	39	30	7	22	40	.278	.208	.295	5.84	3.21
Rice, Jason	R-R	6-0	190	5-13-86	0	0	10.38	2	0	0	0	4	6	6	5	0	5	4	.375	.500	.333	8.31	10.38
Richard, Clayton	L-L	6-5	225	9-12-83	2	1	2.85	10	9	0	0	41	37	19	13	2	12	39	.240	.190	.248	8.56	2.63
Rodriguez, Noe	L-L	6-0	165	8-12-84	2	5	4.50	13	12	0	0	58	60	38	29	4	20	71	.261	.216	.274	11.02	3.10
Rote, Ryan	R-R	6-4	225	8-8-82	3	3	3.52	12	0	0	2	15	13	10	6	0	6	19	.232	.400	.139	11.15	3.52
Stumm, Jason	R-R	6-2	240	4-13-81	0	1	5.06	3	0	0	0	5	10	7	3	1	0	4	.385	.800	.286	6.75	0.00
Torres, Carlos	R-R	6-2	180	10-22-82	1	1	2.88	5	5	0	0	25	18	8	8	1	8	26	.205	.257	.170	9.36	2.88

GAMES BY POSITION: C—Hernandez 39, Hollis 29, Landry 3, Sharp 13. **1B**—Allen 51, Rodriguez 20, Schmidt 7, Sharp 4. **2B**—Acosta 13, Castillo 1, Getz 1, Guest 62, Johnson 4. **3B**—Castillo 1, Guest 1, Hollis 1, Johnson 54, Rodriguez 1, Schmidt 25. **SS**—Acosta 31, Castillo 43, Getz 5, Guest 2. **OF**—Johnson 3, Roberts 62, Rodriguez 40, Schmidt 8, Tartaglia 66, Tribble 63.

BRISTOL WHITE SOX — Rookie

APPALACHIAN LEAGUE

BATTING	B-T	HT	WT	DOB	AVG	vLH	vRH	G	AB	R	H	2B	3B	HR	RBI	BB	HBP	SH	SF	SO	SB	CS	SLG	OBP
Acosta, Christian	R-R	5-11	178	7-14-83	.314	.250	.331	65	220	40	69	20	0	5	41	29	7	1	2	48	0	2	.473	.407
Acosta, Leonardo	R-R	6-2	165	4-29-86	.189	.200	.185	56	159	15	30	8	1	0	15	8	2	6	3	41	4	0	.252	.233
Batista, Franklin	R-R	5-11	155	10-17-84	.206	.250	.171	41	63	7	13	3	1	0	3	9	2	0	1	24	3	3	.286	.320
Carter, Chris	R-R	6-4	210	12-18-86	.283	.222	.302	65	233	33	66	17	0	10	37	17	8	2	2	64	2	1	.485	.350
Causey, Marcos	R-R	5-10	195	7-4-84	.218	.091	.267	43	119	10	26	1	0	0	6	4	3	1	0	32	1	1	.227	.262
Combs, Trey	R-R	6-2	200	3-14-81	.235	.227	.239	30	68	3	16	5	0	0	10	0	0	1	0	21	0	0	.309	.235
Cunningham, Aaron	R-R	5-11	195	4-24-86	.315	.344	.304	56	222	41	70	10	2	5	25	16	14	0	3	45	6	5	.446	.392
Garcia, Santo	B-L	6-0	168	8-6-84	.153	.067	.171	34	85	7	13	4	1	2	8	4	3	1	0	35	1	2	.294	.217
Lachapel, Alex	B-R	6-0	173	11-25-84	.148	.353	.054	33	54	6	8	2	0	0	2	14	0	1	0	29	1	1	.185	.324
Morgan, Josh	R-R	6-2	215	7-20-84	.240	.207	.251	62	229	36	55	18	2	1	19	26	3	1	1	60	7	0	.349	.324
Sanchez, Salvador	R-R	6-6	195	9-13-85	.260	.209	.279	64	246	38	64	17	1	4	30	17	2	3	0	62	14	2	.386	.313
Shafer, Dustin	R-R	6-3	190	3-31-85	.180	.158	.190	24	61	5	11	1	0	0	12	2	0	0	1	8	1	0	.197	.203
Swain, Michael	L-R	6-0	190	4-30-84	.259	.167	.266	55	166	29	43	11	4	4	28	24	3	1	1	53	0	0	.446	.361
Tavares, Reymundo	R-R	5-10	165	2-7-83	.227	.105	.277	45	132	17	30	4	0	2	16	12	3	5	1	21	7	2	.303	.304
Welker, Kris	R-R	6-0	205	9-8-82	.303	.302	.303	54	198	31	60	16	0	3	29	17	6	4	1	34	2	1	.429	.374

PITCHING	B-T	HT	WT	DOB	W	L	ERA	G	GS	CG	SV	IP	H	R	ER	HR	BB	SO	AVG	vLH	vRH	K/9	BB/9
Banks, Demetrius	L-L	6-1	158	5-3-83	0	0	0.00	2	1	0	0	4	2	0	0	0	3	4	.154	.000	.200	9.82	7.36
Brooks, Ricky	R-R	6-3	180	7-18-84	0	2	2.89	5	5	0	0	19	15	7	6	2	4	25	.217	.133	.282	12.05	1.93
Cortes, Daniel	R-R	6-5	205	3-4-87	1	4	5.17	15	7	0	0	38	44	23	22	2	13	38	.289	.250	.321	8.92	3.05
Cortez, Martin	L-L	6-0	175	12-27-82	1	1	6.35	17	1	0	0	28	36	24	20	5	10	26	.300	.233	.322	8.26	3.18
Day, Tim	L-R	6-4	210	9-22-82	4	0	3.16	17	0	0	3	31	27	14	11	3	6	33	.227	.243	.220	9.48	1.72
Evans, Raleigh	L-L	6-0	185	2-15-85	0	1	3.38	13	0	0	1	21	25	10	8	3	3	17	.287	.167	.319	7.17	1.27
Gutierrez, Santiago	L-L	6-3	160	2-26-86	1	0	4.50	13	0	0	0	12	10	8	6	1	6	3	.200	.273	.179	2.25	4.50
Jean, Jacob	L-L	6-1	175	5-24-83	3	4	6.56	16	8	0	1	48	63	46	35	5	20	40	.317	.188	.358	7.50	3.75
Rice, Jason	R-R	6-0	190	5-13-86	3	2	4.70	18	7	0	0	44	40	23	23	2	25	40	.241	.235	.243	8.18	5.11
Rodriguez, Derek	R-R	6-1	190	5-17-83	1	3	3.82	11	6	0	0	35	35	19	15	2	7	36	.255	.305	.218	9.17	1.78
Sabo, Tim	R-R	6-3	215	2-6-84	3	2	3.38	16	0	0	2	29	24	14	11	0	18	33	.220	.167	.254	10.13	5.52
Sanchez, Ramon	R-R	5-11	175	11-3-83	0	0	3.00	2	2	0	0	9	10	5	3	1	2	9	.270	.250	.280	9.00	2.00
Squires, Steven	R-R	6-1	175	6-17-83	0	1	9.95	17	0	0	0	19	29	21	21	5	8	14	.333	.464	.271	6.63	3.79
Viola, Frank	R-R	6-4	188	6-19-84	5	2	3.84	13	12	0	0	70	74	35	30	2	20	59	.268	.265	.270	7.55	2.56
Walters, Nichols	L-L	6-2	170	9-30-85	2	5	3.44	20	0	0	1	34	34	23	13	6	8	26	.256	.231	.262	6.88	2.12
Williamson, Logan	L-L	6-0	190	3-31-85	3	7	5.03	13	12	0	1	59	64	41	33	6	21	60	.263	.194	.274	9.15	3.20
Winn, Joe	R-R	6-0	195	9-1-84	2	2	4.50	18	5	0	1	48	55	29	24	5	11	32	.291	.259	.315	6.00	2.06
Woodson, Alex	L-L	6-1	195	10-10-85	1	0	2.55	16	0	0	3	25	23	8	7	1	5	21	.258	.471	.208	7.66	1.82

GAMES BY POSITION: C—Combs 10, Tavares 30, Welker 36. **1B**—Carter 20, Combs 2, Morgan 45, Shafer 4. **2B**—C. Acosta 11, Batista 25, Shafer 3, Swain 47, Tavares 3. **3B**—C. Acosta 29, L. Acosta 2, Batista 2, Carter 38, Swain 2. **SS**—C. Acosta 17, L. Acosta 54, Batista 11, Carter 1, Shafer 1, Swain 2. **OF**—Batista 1, Causey 36, Cunningham 52, Garcia 32, Lachapel 23, Morgan 13, Sanchez 63, Shafer 12.

CINCINNATI REDS

BY JOHN FAY

You don't need to be a baseball genius to figure out what went wrong for the Reds in 2005. Even if you don't know OPS from UPS, you can look at the stats and figure it out: The Reds couldn't overcome another year of awful pitching.

Cincinnati finished first in the National League in runs, doubles, home runs and slugging percentage. Ken Griffey returned to form, earning the National League comeback player of the year award.

Adam Dunn showed for the second year in a row that he is one of the game's top power hitters. Felipe Lopez went from an afterthought to an all-star in the course of a season. The Reds set club records with 222 home runs and 335 doubles.

But all that good stuff was negated by the fact the Reds finished second to last in pitching—ahead of only the altitude-challenged Rockies.

This is not a new problem. The Reds finished under .500 for the fifth straight year. That streak has been marked by a whole lot of bad pitching.

The bad pitching cost manager Dave Miley and pitching coach Don Gullett their jobs. They were fired June 21 after the club started 27-43. The team finished 46-46 under interim manager Jerry Narron.

This was not supposed to be that kind of year for the Reds. The club boosted the payroll by $14 million and tried to solve the pitching problem by adding veteran free agents.

They signed lefthander Eric Milton, along with righthander Paul Wilson and traded for righthander Ramon Ortiz to bolster the staff.

Wilson and Milton, the top two starters, combined to begin the season 3-10. Wilson was 1-5 when he shut it down for the season with a bad shoulder. Milton went 8-15, 6.47 and Ortiz finished 9-11, 5.36.

ORGANIZATION LEADERS

BATTING

*AVG	Rosales, Adam, Billings/Dayton	.325
R	Denorfia, Chris, Chattanooga/Louisville	90
H	Denorfia, Chris, Chattanooga/Louisville	162
TB	Denorfia, Chris, Chattanooga/Louisville	269
2B	Smitherman, Stephen, Chattanooga/Louisville	39
3B	Anderson, Drew, Dayton/Louisville	10
HR	Piepkorn, Jeremiah, Dayton/Sarasota	25
RBI	Piepkorn, Jeremiah, Dayton/Sarasota	90
BB	Jimenez, D'Angelo, Chattanooga	69
SO	Schramek, Mark, Sarasota	143
SB	Roberts, Brandon, Billings	32
*OBP	Hanigan, Ryan, Chattanooga	.418
*SLG	Rosales, Adam, Billings/Dayton	.558

PITCHING

W	Basham, Bobby, Chattanooga/Sarasota	10
	Lohse, Erik, Sarasota	10
L	Dumatrait, Phil, Chattanooga/Sarasota	12
#ERA	Edens, Kyle, Sarasota	2.10
G	Booker, Chris, Louisville	59
CG	Five tied at	1
SV	Booker, Chris, Louisville	20
IP	Kozlowski, Ben, Chattanooga/Louisville	156
BB	Dumatrait, Phil, Chattanooga/Sarasota	73
SO	Bailey, Homer, Dayton	125

*Minimum 250 at-bats. #Minimum 75 innings.

PLAYERS OF THE YEAR

MAJOR LEAGUE: Ken Griffey, of

New York's Jason Giambi was the American League 2005 comeback player of the year, but his overall numbers paled in comparison to Griffey, the National League winner. Junior hit .301, adding 30 doubles and 35 homers—the first time he was over 30 in each of those categories since 1998.

MINOR LEAGUE: Chris Denorfia, of

BILL MITCHELL

Denorfia became the first player ever drafted out of Wheaton (Mass.) College, when the Reds took him in the 19th round in 2002. He also became the first player from the school to make it to the big leagues. Denorfia was second in the organization in RBIs and led Triple-A Louisville with a .391 on-base percentage.

The bullpen was just as much of a mess. Closer Danny Graves was designated for assignment after going 1-1, 7.36 in 20 appearances. The Reds patched things together in the closer role from there. Ryan Wagner, who started the season as the top set-up man, spent most of the year on the DL with a sore shoulder.

As far as position players, things went considerably better for the Reds.

Rich Aurilia, a late free agent signee, had a very solid season at second base (.282-14-68). Aurilia was at second base because Lopez won the shortstop job while Aurilia was hurt in May. Lopez (.290-23-85) had one of the best years ever by a Reds' shortstop.

General manager Dan O'Brien is convinced that Edwin Encarnacion is the answer at third, though he was horribly inconsistent in 2005. Encarnacion (.232-9-31) took over at third after the Reds traded Joe Randa at the July 31 trade deadline.

"We're fairly secure with Edwin (Encarnacion) and Felipe (Lopez)," O'Brien said.

Dunn had his second straight 100-RBI season. That's something no Red had done since Dave Parker in 1985-86. Catching was a bright spot, with Jason LaRue (.260-14-60) and Javier Valentin (.281-14-50) making an impact offensively.

Most of that offense will be back in 2006. But, if the Reds can't fix the pitching, none of that will matter.

And fixing it won't be easy. There are only three ways to fix a big league club, but only one looks like a viable option for the Reds:

■ The farm system: The Reds don't have immediate help there. The one impact pitcher they have, righthander Homer Bailey, is at least two years away.

■ Free agency: The Reds won't have an abundance of money to spend on free agents. O'Brien said the 2006 payroll will be in the same range as 2005.

■ Trades: O'Brien's softening of his stance on trading an outfielder indicates the Reds will likely go this route. He said the Reds are "more open-minded" about trading an outfielder—most likely Austin Kearns or Wily MoPena—than they were after the 2004 season.

CINCINNATI REDS

Managers: Dave Miley, Jerry Narron. **2005 Record:** 73-89, .451 (5th, NL Central).

BATTING	B-T	HT	WT	DOB	AVG	vLH	vRH	G	AB	R	H	2B	3B	HR	RBI	BB	HBP	SH	SF	SO	SB	CS	SLG	OBP
Aurilia, Rich	R-R	6-1	190	9-2-71	.282	.272	.286	114	426	61	120	23	2	14	68	37	1	1	3	67	2	0	.444	.338
Bergolla, William	R-R	6-0	175	2-4-83	.132	.214	.083	17	38	3	5	0	0	0	1	0	0	0	0	10	0	0	.132	.132
Casey, Sean	L-R	6-4	235	7-2-74	.312	.335	.298	137	529	75	165	32	0	9	58	48	5	0	5	48	2	0	.423	.371
Cruz, Jacob	L-L	6-0	215	1-28-73	.236	.400	.222	110	127	12	30	10	0	4	18	16	1	0	1	46	0	0	.409	.324
Denorfia, Chris	R-R	6-0	195	7-15-80	.263	.273	.259	18	38	8	10	3	0	1	2	6	0	0	0	9	1	0	.421	.364
Dunn, Adam	L-R	6-6	275	11-9-79	.247	.197	.273	160	543	107	134	35	2	40	101	114	12	0	2	168	4	2	.540	.387
Encarnacion, Edwin	R-R	6-1	195	1-7-83	.232	.246	.226	69	211	25	49	16	0	9	31	20	3	0	0	60	3	0	.436	.308
Freel, Ryan	R-R	5-10	180	3-8-76	.271	.299	.260	103	369	69	100	19	3	4	21	51	8	3	0	59	36	10	.371	.371
Griffey, Ken	L-L	6-3	220	11-21-69	.301	.278	.314	128	491	85	148	30	0	35	92	54	3	0	7	93	0	1	.576	.369
Holbert, Aaron	R-R	6-1	180	1-9-73	.222	.273	.188	22	27	3	6	3	0	0	2	3	0	1	1	8	1	0	.333	.290
Jimenez, D'Angelo	B-R	6-0	215	12-21-77	.229	.355	.176	35	105	14	24	7	0	0	5	14	0	0	0	23	2	1	.295	.319
Kearns, Austin	R-R	6-3	245	5-20-80	.240	.233	.243	112	387	62	93	26	1	18	67	48	8	0	5	107	0	0	.452	.333
Kelly, Kenny	R-R	6-2	190	1-26-79	.333	.333	.333	7	9	2	3	0	0	0	2	0	0	0	0	3	0	1	.333	.333
LaRue, Jason	R-R	5-11	205	3-19-74	.260	.257	.262	110	361	38	94	27	0	14	60	41	13	5	2	101	0	0	.452	.355
Lopez, Luis	B-R	5-11	190	9-4-70	.222	.000	.261	17	27	0	6	3	0	0	2	1	0	0	0	6	0	0	.333	.250
Lopez, Felipe	B-R	6-1	185	5-12-80	.291	.243	.312	148	580	97	169	34	5	23	85	57	1	3	7	111	15	7	.486	.352
Machado, Anderson	L-R	5-11	160	1-25-81	.000	.000	.000	2	2	0	0	0	0	0	0	0	0	0	0	1	0	0	.000	.000
Olmedo, Ray	B-R	5-11	155	5-31-81	.221	.111	.235	54	77	10	17	4	1	1	4	6	1	3	1	22	4	0	.338	.282
Pena, Wily Mo	R-R	6-3	245	1-23-82	.254	.291	.234	99	311	42	79	17	0	19	51	20	3	0	1	116	2	1	.492	.304
Perez, Miguel	R-R	6-3	190	9-25-83	.000	.000	.000	2	3	0	0	0	0	0	0	0	0	0	0	1	0	0	.000	.000
Randa, Joe	R-R	5-11	190	12-18-69	.289	.270	.297	92	332	44	96	26	1	13	48	33	2	0	1	52	0	0	.491	.356
Romano, Jason	R-R	6-0	185	6-24-79	.267	.294	.231	19	30	3	8	2	0	1	3	3	1	0	0	9	0	0	.433	.353
Sardinha, Dane	R-R	6-0	215	4-8-79	.000	.000	.000	1	3	0	0	0	0	0	0	0	0	0	0	1	0	0	.000	.000
Valentin, Javier	B-R	5-10	210	9-19-75	.281	.184	.301	76	221	36	62	11	0	14	50	30	0	0	3	37	0	0	.520	.362

PITCHING	B-T	HT	WT	DOB	W	L	ERA	G	GS	CG	SV	IP	H	R	ER	HR	BB	SO	AVG	vLH	vRH	K/9	BB/9
Belisle, Matt	R-R	6-3	195	6-6-80	4	8	4.41	60	5	0	1	86	101	49	42	11	26	59	.294	.331	.273	6.20	2.73
Booker, Chris	R-R	6-3	235	12-9-76	0	0	31.50	3	0	0	0	2	6	8	7	2	4	2	.545	.667	.500	9.00	18.00
Claussen, Brandon	R-L	6-1	200	5-1-79	10	11	4.21	29	29	0	0	167	178	89	78	24	57	121	.273	.242	.280	6.53	3.08
Coffey, Todd	R-R	6-5	230	9-9-80	4	1	4.50	57	0	0	1	58	84	33	29	5	11	26	.344	.337	.348	4.03	1.71
Graves, Danny	R-R	6-0	200	8-7-73	1	1	7.36	20	0	0	10	18	30	18	15	4	12	8	.357	.441	.300	3.93	5.89
Hancock, Josh	R-R	6-3	205	4-11-78	1	0	1.93	11	0	0	0	14	11	4	3	1	1	5	.208	.111	.257	3.21	0.64
Harang, Aaron	R-R	6-7	270	5-9-78	11	13	3.83	32	32	1	0	212	217	93	90	22	51	163	.267	.253	.279	6.93	2.17
Hudson, Luke	R-R	6-3	195	5-2-77	6	9	6.38	19	16	0	0	85	83	62	60	14	50	53	.268	.255	.278	5.63	5.31
Keisler, Randy	L-L	6-3	190	2-24-76	2	1	6.27	24	4	0	0	56	64	45	39	10	28	43	.277	.304	.265	6.91	4.50
Mercker, Kent	L-L	6-2	205	2-1-68	3	1	3.65	78	0	0	4	62	64	27	25	8	19	45	.270	.225	.304	6.57	2.77
Milton, Eric	L-L	6-3	205	8-4-75	8	15	6.47	34	34	0	0	186	237	141	134	40	52	123	.302	.284	.307	5.94	2.51
Ortiz, Ramon	R-R	6-0	175	5-23-73	9	11	5.36	30	30	1	0	171	206	110	102	34	51	96	.302	.288	.315	5.04	2.68
Ramirez, Elizardo	L-R	6-0	180	1-28-83	0	3	8.46	6	4	0	0	22	33	22	21	5	10	9	.344	.386	.282	3.63	4.03
Shackelford, Brian	L-L	6-1	195	8-30-76	1	0	2.43	37	0	0	0	30	21	9	8	2	9	17	.204	.205	.203	5.16	2.73
Simpson, Allan	R-R	6-4	200	8-26-77	0	1	6.75	9	0	0	0	7	3	5	5	1	5	6	.136	.143	.133	8.10	6.75
2-team (2 Colorado)					0	1	12.27	11	0	0	0	7	6	10	10	1	8	6	.231	.143	.263	7.36	9.82
Standridge, Jason	R-R	6-4	230	11-9-78	2	2	4.06	32	0	0	0	31	38	14	14	3	16	17	.314	.343	.302	4.94	4.65
Stone, Ricky	R-R	6-1	195	2-28-75	0	0	6.75	23	0	0	0	31	48	24	23	8	7	15	.364	.333	.387	4.40	2.05
Valentine, Joe	R-R	6-2	210	12-24-79	0	1	8.16	16	0	0	0	14	18	15	13	4	11	9	.295	.350	.268	5.65	6.91
Wagner, Ryan	R-R	6-4	225	7-15-82	3	2	6.11	42	0	0	0	46	56	33	31	4	17	39	.303	.311	.297	7.69	3.35
Weathers, David	R-R	6-3	230	9-25-69	7	4	3.94	73	0	0	15	78	71	36	34	7	29	61	.241	.265	.226	7.07	3.36
Weber, Ben	R-R	6-4	205	11-17-69	0	0	8.03	10	0	0	0	12	20	11	11	0	9	8	.364	.375	.359	5.84	6.57
Wilson, Paul	R-R	6-5	210	3-28-73	1	5	7.77	9	9	0	0	46	68	41	40	10	17	30	.343	.417	.289	5.83	3.30

FIELDING

Catcher	PCT	G	PO	A	E	DP	PB
LaRue	.993	109	646	52	5	2	6
Perez	1.000	1	2	0	0	0	0
Sardinha	1.000	1	7	0	0	0	0
Valentin	.992	62	341	28	3	2	3

First Base	PCT	G	PO	A	E	DP
Casey	.998	134	1153	55	2	91
Cruz	1.000	5	15	1	0	2
Dunn	.985	33	244	11	4	31
Holbert	1.000	2	4	0	0	0
Valentin	1.000	2	21	0	0	2

Second Base	PCT	G	PO	A	E	DP
Aurilia	.981	68	128	175	6	38
Bergolla	1.000	9	11	29	0	6
Freel	.973	48	91	127	6	24
Holbert	.950	4	11	8	1	3
Jimenez	.983	27	56	63	2	17
L. Lopez	1.000	4	3	5	0	0
F. Lopez	1.000	7	15	11	0	4
Olmedo	.975	31	38	40	2	9

Third Base	PCT	G	PO	A	E	DP
Aurilia	.978	18	12	33	1	4
Encarnacion	.944	56	54	116	10	10
Freel	.938	10	5	25	2	1
Holbert	1.000	2	0	5	0	0
L. Lopez	.900	6	5	4	1	0
F. Lopez	1.000	1	0	1	0	0
Randa	.974	84	76	148	6	13

Shortstop	PCT	G	PO	A	E	DP
Aurilia	.975	30	29	86	3	14
Bergolla	1.000	1	0	1	0	0
F. Lopez	.970	140	186	358	17	71
Olmedo	1.000	5	4	6	0	2

Outfield	PCT	G	PO	A	E	DP
Cruz	1.000	20	12	1	0	1
Denorfia	.962	12	25	0	1	0
Dunn	.981	133	246	6	5	0
Freel	1.000	51	109	7	0	0
Griffey	.990	124	285	6	3	1
Kearns	.988	107	238	8	3	3
Kelly	1.000	4	4	0	0	0
LaRue	1.000	1	1	0	0	0
Pena	.976	83	161	2	4	0
Romano	.941	14	15	1	1	0

FARM SYSTEM

General Manager: Dan O'Brien. **Director, Player Development:** Tim Naehring. **Director, Amateur Scouting:** Terry Reynolds.

Class	Farm Team	League	W	L	Pct.	Finish*	Manager	Affiliate Since
AAA	Louisville (Ky.) RiverBats	International	66	78	.458	11th (14)	Rick Sweet	2000
AA	Chattanooga (Tenn.) Lookouts	Southern	53	83	.390	10th (10)	Jayhawk Owens	1988
High A	Sarasota (Fla.) Reds	Florida State	65	67	.492	8th (12)	Edgar Caceres	2005
Low A	Dayton (Ohio) Dragons	Midwest	60	79	.432	14th (14)	Alonzo Powell	2000
Rookie	Billings (Mont.) Mustangs	Pioneer	43	33	.566	**2nd (8)**	Rick Burleson	1974
Rookie	Sarasota (Fla.) Reds	Gulf Coast	22	32	.407	11th (12)	Luis Aguayo	1999

*Finish in overall standings (No. of teams in league)/playoff teams in **boldface**

LARRY GOREN

Adam Dunn: Another 40-home run season

CLIFF WELCH

Jay Bruce: Impressive pro debut

LOUISVILLE BATS — Class AAA

INTERNATIONAL LEAGUE

BATTING	B-T	HT	WT	DOB	AVG	vLH	vRH	G	AB	R	H	2B	3B	HR	RBI	BB	HBP	SH	SF	SO	SB	CS	SLG	OBP
Anderson, Drew	B-R	5-9	170	2-2-83	.154	.200	.138	13	39	4	6	2	1	0	1	0	0	1	0	13	0	0	.256	.154
Asadoorian, Rick	R-R	6-2	180	7-23-80	.211	.194	.218	33	109	10	23	5	2	1	7	4	1	2	0	29	6	0	.321	.246
Aurilia, Rich	R-R	6-1	190	9-2-71	.333	.000	.333	1	3	2	1	1	0	0	1	2	0	0	0	1	0	0	.667	.600
Bannon, Jeff	R-R	6-4	185	8-21-79	.282	.342	.265	41	174	20	49	14	1	4	18	2	2	1	1	41	2	0	.443	.296
Bell, Rick	R-R	6-2	195	4-5-79	.178	.333	.042	17	45	3	8	1	0	0	5	2	1	1	2	7	0	0	.200	.220
Bergolla, William	R-R	6-0	175	2-4-83	.293	.361	.274	98	400	59	117	23	5	2	38	19	1	6	2	39	16	3	.390	.325
Crozier, Eric	L-L	6-4	200	8-11-78	.227	.276	.206	27	97	5	22	10	1	1	10	15	0	0	1	38	3	2	.381	.327
2-team (37 Syracuse)					.226	.220	.228	64	221	25	50	22	2	6	24	24	1	0	2	77	4	2	.425	.302
Denorfia, Chris	R-R	6-0	195	7-15-80	.310	.368	.291	91	323	50	100	12	6	13	61	41	4	3	3	54	8	3	.505	.391
Encarnacion, Edwin	R-R	6-1	195	1-7-83	.314	.343	.305	78	290	44	91	23	0	15	54	33	4	0	3	53	7	2	.548	.388
Fernandez, Alex	L-L	6-1	200	5-15-81	.267	.258	.270	44	120	14	32	6	0	4	17	3	0	1	0	16	1	1	.417	.285
Holbert, Aaron	R-R	6-1	180	1-9-73	.304	.292	.308	68	230	33	70	14	2	6	23	11	6	4	1	31	12	5	.461	.351
Kearns, Austin	R-R	6-3	245	5-20-80	.342	.379	.329	28	111	24	38	15	1	7	21	11	1	0	0	30	0	0	.685	.407
Kelly, Kenny	R-R	6-2	190	1-26-79	.326	.340	.322	61	233	43	76	9	4	3	17	20	1	6	0	49	18	4	.438	.382
Kroski, Chris	L-R	6-1	231	5-17-82	.000	.000	.000	1	0	0	0	0	0	0	0	0	1	0	0	0	0	0	.000	1.000
Leon, Jose	R-R	6-1	225	12-8-76	.216	.133	.237	20	74	6	16	4	0	0	7	4	0	0	0	18	0	0	.270	.256
2-team (71 Indianapolis)					.256	.236	.264	91	305	31	78	15	2	10	52	24	1	0	3	83	0	0	.416	.309
Lomasney, Steve	R-R	6-0	205	8-29-77	.160	.182	.153	50	144	11	23	4	0	1	9	11	1	1	1	62	0	0	.208	.223
Lopez, Luis	B-R	5-11	190	9-4-70	.264	.238	.273	29	87	10	23	8	0	1	9	8	3	0	0	18	0	2	.391	.347
Machado, Anderson	L-R	5-11	160	1-25-81	.138	.148	.132	21	80	9	11	2	1	0	6	12	0	0	1	23	1	2	.188	.247
Olmedo, Ray	B-R	5-11	155	5-31-81	.276	.400	.182	14	58	8	16	3	0	1	5	1	1	0	0	11	2	2	.379	.300
Patchett, Gary	R-R	6-2	180	9-25-78	.227	.250	.222	9	22	3	5	1	0	0	1	3	1	0	1	7	0	0	.273	.333
Pelaez, Alex	R-R	5-9	190	4-6-76	.241	.244	.239	89	316	23	76	18	1	3	26	13	0	1	2	32	0	0	.332	.269
Pena, Wily Mo	R-R	6-3	245	1-23-82	.292	.000	.318	7	24	1	7	1	0	1	4	1	0	0	0	10	0	0	.458	.320
Perez, Santiago	B-R	6-2	160	12-30-75	.309	.291	.315	64	233	40	72	22	3	2	17	22	2	4	3	58	10	2	.455	.369

BATTING	B-T	HT	WT	DOB	AVG	vLH	vRH	G	AB	R	H	2B	3B	HR	RBI	BB	HBP	SH	SF	SO	SB	CS	SLG	OBP
Perez, Miguel	R-R	6-3	190	9-25-83	.208	.235	.200	21	72	5	15	3	0	1	5	5	2	0	1	19	0	0	.292	.275
Romano, Jason	R-R	6-0	185	6-24-79	.308	.404	.279	56	224	34	69	17	2	4	32	14	1	2	2	36	5	1	.455	.349
Sardinha, Dane	R-R	6-0	215	4-8-79	.224	.261	.213	86	299	36	67	10	0	10	36	22	4	3	2	72	1	0	.358	.284
Smitherman, Stephen	R-R	6-4	235	9-1-78	.248	.225	.257	40	141	12	35	9	0	1	11	5	0	0	1	34	1	0	.333	.272
Stratton, Robert	R-R	6-4	250	10-7-77	.308	.333	.300	8	26	5	8	0	0	4	5	2	1	0	0	5	0	0	.769	.379
Swann, Pedro	L-R	6-0	205	10-27-70	.285	.253	.293	127	456	67	130	29	5	18	85	36	15	0	4	101	5	0	.489	.354
Zapp, A.J.	L-R	6-3	190	4-24-78	.243	.224	.248	125	399	31	97	28	0	6	40	38	6	2	1	113	0	0	.358	.318

PITCHING	B-T	HT	WT	DOB	W	L	ERA	G	GS	CG	SV	IP	H	R	ER	HR	BB	SO	AVG	vLH	vRH	K/9	BB/9
Acevedo, Jose	R-R	6-0	220	12-18-77	0	0	0.00	1	1	0	0	4	2	0	0	0	0	3	.167	.000	.286	6.75	0.00
Booker, Chris	R-R	6-3	235	12-9-76	8	4	2.49	59	0	0	20	65	45	20	18	2	28	91	.195	.178	.206	12.60	3.88
Bruksch, Jeffrey	R-R	6-4	212	4-29-80	1	0	1.80	1	1	0	0	5	4	1	1	1	2	1	.250	.375	.125	1.80	3.60
Childress, Daylan	R-R	6-1	200	7-31-78	0	0	6.75	11	0	0	0	15	18	11	11	1	7	7	.305	.214	.333	4.30	4.30
Coffey, Todd	R-R	6-5	230	9-9-80	0	0	5.19	8	0	0	3	9	8	5	5	1	2	5	.242	.333	.222	5.19	2.08
Fernandez, Jared	R-R	6-1	235	2-2-72	5	5	4.38	13	13	0	0	84	86	45	41	8	26	51	.270	.296	.250	5.44	2.77
Germano, Justin	R-R	6-1	190	8-6-82	3	2	4.01	8	8	0	0	49	62	27	22	7	5	38	.313	.288	.331	6.93	0.91
Graman, Alex	L-L	6-4	210	11-17-77	2	1	3.09	5	4	0	0	23	23	9	8	2	12	19	.258	.222	.268	7.33	4.63
2-team (23 Columbus)					7	7	3.16	28	20	0	1	120	118	49	42	14	48	115	.257	.314	.241	8.65	3.61
Hancock, Josh	R-R	6-3	205	4-11-78	1	2	5.93	11	8	0	0	44	59	33	29	5	17	38	.328	.333	.323	7.77	3.48
Keisler, Randy	L-L	6-3	190	2-24-76	5	2	2.88	12	7	0	2	56	54	19	18	6	13	46	.250	.308	.232	7.35	2.08
Kelly, Steven	R-R	6-1	195	9-30-79	5	5	4.82	19	19	0	0	105	108	62	56	10	41	67	.272	.298	.246	5.76	3.53
Kozlowski, Ben	L-L	6-6	230	8-16-80	2	3	4.63	8	8	0	0	45	52	29	23	3	18	30	.294	.500	.245	6.04	3.63
Phelps, Travis	R-R	6-2	170	7-25-77	1	0	6.50	16	0	0	1	18	17	14	13	3	12	16	.246	.185	.286	8.00	6.00
Ramirez, Elizardo	L-R	6-0	180	1-28-83	7	7	3.77	21	21	0	0	131	150	63	55	14	18	82	.287	.306	.272	5.62	1.23
Robertson, Jeriome	L-L	6-2	215	3-30-77	5	11	5.46	28	18	0	0	120	162	77	73	18	29	82	.325	.315	.328	6.13	2.17
Rose, Brian	R-R	6-3	215	2-13-76	5	6	6.82	18	13	0	0	69	90	60	52	11	23	34	.317	.327	.306	4.46	3.01
Saladin, Miguel	R-R	5-11	200	5-22-75	0	2	7.79	22	1	0	0	32	47	34	28	2	11	29	.341	.333	.346	8.07	3.06
Salmon, Brad	L-R	6-4	220	1-3-80	0	0	3.31	9	0	0	0	16	14	6	6	2	5	8	.226	.179	.265	4.41	2.76
Serrano, Jimmy	R-R	5-10	170	5-9-76	4	4	3.75	12	12	0	0	70	69	34	29	10	29	70	.256	.269	.245	9.04	3.75
Shackelford, Brian	L-L	6-1	195	8-30-76	1	6	5.23	31	0	0	1	33	35	19	19	1	10	21	.282	.286	.279	5.79	2.76
Shearn, Tom	R-R	6-4	200	8-28-77	4	5	4.26	44	9	0	1	93	83	50	44	11	44	93	.236	.272	.209	9.00	4.26
Simpson, Allan	R-R	6-4	200	8-26-77	4	4	4.06	50	0	0	1	64	51	30	29	5	38	89	.213	.279	.162	12.45	5.32
Standridge, Jason	R-R	6-4	230	11-9-78	0	0	16.20	2	0	0	0	2	3	3	3	0	1	4	.375	.667	.200	21.60	5.40
Stone, Ricky	R-R	6-1	195	2-28-75	2	1	2.57	9	0	0	3	14	10	4	4	0	3	15	.192	.227	.167	9.64	1.93
Valentine, Joe	R-R	6-2	210	12-24-79	0	7	5.70	49	0	0	3	54	56	36	34	4	39	44	.272	.263	.279	7.38	6.54
Van Hekken, Andy	R-L	6-3	185	7-31-79	1	0	3.89	27	1	0	0	37	36	16	16	4	11	24	.263	.267	.260	5.84	2.68
2-team (4 Richmond)					1	3	5.66	31	5	0	0	56	61	36	35	8	19	35	.286	.263	.299	5.66	3.07
Weber, Ben	R-R	6-4	205	11-17-69	0	1	6.43	7	0	0	0	7	8	5	5	0	6	5	.296	.111	.389	6.43	7.71

FIELDING

Catcher	PCT	G	PO	A	E	DP	PB
Kroski	1.000	1	3	0	0	0	0
Lomasney	.987	43	275	32	4	2	16
M. Perez	1.000	21	166	16	0	1	4
Sardinha	.991	84	603	46	6	7	6

First Base	PCT	G	PO	A	E	DP
Bell	.987	10	69	5	1	5
Crozier	1.000	1	7	1	0	0
Holbert	1.000	8	36	2	0	1
Lomasney	.833	5	4	1	1	0
Pelaez	1.000	25	172	5	0	27
S. Perez	1.000	1	5	1	0	2
Zapp	.993	113	868	72	7	88

Second Base	PCT	G	PO	A	E	DP
Anderson	1.000	5	5	4	0	0
Bergolla	.979	80	162	204	8	62
Holbert	.948	23	40	70	6	15
Lopez	1.000	2	4	2	0	0
Machado	1.000	1	1	4	0	0
Olmedo	1.000	14	28	39	0	10
Patchett	1.000	2	1	3	0	1
Pelaez	.991	26	41	68	1	19
S. Perez	.960	4	9	15	1	2

Third Base	PCT	G	PO	A	E	DP
Bannon	1.000	5	3	8	0	2
Bell	1.000	5	0	8	0	0
Encarnacion	.917	77	51	158	19	20
Holbert	.933	9	5	23	2	4
Leon	.911	20	13	28	4	2
Pelaez	.977	41	23	62	2	7
S. Perez	.923	5	5	7	1	1

Shortstop	PCT	G	PO	A	E	DP
Aurilia	1.000	1	1	6	0	1
Bannon	.989	38	56	120	2	30
Bergolla	.912	20	11	41	5	4
Holbert	.965	23	35	47	3	13
Lopez	.956	23	33	53	4	11
Machado	.946	20	27	43	4	8
Olmedo	1.000	1	1	3	0	1
Patchett	.952	7	4	16	1	4
S. Perez	.921	25	24	46	6	7

Outfield	PCT	G	PO	A	E	DP
Anderson	.800	5	4	0	1	0
Asadoorian	1.000	31	63	4	0	1
Crozier	.983	26	54	5	1	0
Denorfia	1.000	89	205	6	0	0
Fernandez	.954	34	60	2	3	1
Kearns	1.000	26	50	2	0	0
Kelly	1.000	59	155	3	0	2
Pena	.889	5	8	0	1	0
S. Perez	1.000	30	64	3	0	0
Romano	.985	53	122	6	2	0
Smitherman	1.000	29	45	3	0	0
Swann	.959	60	89	5	4	1
Zapp	1.000	5	5	0	0	0

CHATTANOOGA LOOKOUTS — Class AA

SOUTHERN LEAGUE

BATTING	B-T	HT	WT	DOB	AVG	vLH	vRH	G	AB	R	H	2B	3B	HR	RBI	BB	HBP	SH	SF	SO	SB	CS	SLG	OBP
Anderson, Bryan	R-R	6-2	170	7-10-78	.184	.231	.164	113	261	27	48	18	0	4	22	26	5	6	2	69	1	2	.299	.269
Asadoorian, Rick	R-R	6-2	180	7-23-80	.271	.256	.278	93	295	44	80	20	3	6	39	14	5	6	2	79	11	4	.420	.313
Bannon, Jeff	R-R	6-4	185	8-21-79	.266	.316	.242	93	365	51	97	23	1	14	60	26	4	3	6	72	14	1	.449	.317
Bell, Rick	R-R	6-2	195	4-5-79	.215	.250	.203	29	93	10	20	7	0	2	16	3	0	2	4	19	0	0	.355	.230
Denorfia, Chris	R-R	6-0	195	7-15-80	.330	.362	.311	46	188	40	62	17	3	7	26	17	2	2	0	38	4	3	.564	.391
Fernandez, Alex	L-L	6-1	200	5-15-81	.327	.386	.302	42	150	18	49	6	0	2	23	12	0	1	2	25	4	1	.407	.372
Freel, Ryan	R-R	5-10	180	3-8-76	.176	.143	.200	5	17	3	3	0	0	0	1	3	0	0	1	5	0	1	.176	.286
Gutierrez, Jesse	R-R	6-2	195	6-16-78	.310	.306	.313	26	100	11	31	8	1	4	25	8	2	0	4	20	0	0	.530	.360
Hanigan, Ryan	R-R	6-1	185	8-16-80	.321	.351	.309	100	333	45	107	14	1	4	29	50	5	2	0	41	4	1	.405	.418
Hopper, Norris	R-R	5-10	198	3-24-79	.310	.315	.306	116	451	70	140	15	4	1	37	27	4	4	1	38	25	7	.368	.354
Howard, Kevin	L-R	6-2	185	6-25-81	.296	.271	.306	129	479	63	142	23	2	12	70	33	5	2	3	64	13	8	.428	.346
Jimenez, D'Angelo	B-R	6-0	215	12-21-77	.278	.306	.266	90	327	55	91	20	0	9	45	69	0	0	3	34	16	4	.422	.401
Moran, Javon	R-R	5-11	175	9-30-82	.301	.174	.350	23	83	14	25	5	1	0	2	5	0	0	0	21	7	4	.386	.341
Nichols, Kyle	R-R	6-2	225	3-29-78	.191	.184	.195	38	115	12	22	4	0	4	18	11	0	0	3	37	0	0	.330	.256
Patchett, Gary	R-R	6-2	180	9-25-78	.215	.205	.221	48	107	7	23	6	0	0	8	4	6	2	2	26	0	0	.271	.277
Perez, Santiago	B-R	6-2	160	12-30-75	.272	.358	.217	40	136	20	37	9	1	4	12	23	2	0	0	40	9	3	.441	.385
Peterson, Brian	R-R	6-2	225	10-22-78	.270	.239	.286	100	348	37	94	25	3	6	40	24	4	5	2	56	0	0	.411	.323
Purdom, John	R-R	6-2	230	5-28-81	.222	.333	.167	4	9	0	2	0	0	0	2	0	0	0	0	3	0	0	.222	.222
Renick, Josh	R-R	5-11	175	12-28-78	.118	.167	.107	25	34	1	4	0	0	0	2	2	0	1	0	10	0	0	.118	.167

BATTING	B-T	HT	WT	DOB	AVG	vLH	vRH	G	AB	R	H	2B	3B	HR	RBI	BB	HBP	SH	SF	SO	SB	CS	SLG	OBP
Ruiz, Junior	L-R	5-10	195	6-7-80	.287	.227	.310	74	272	37	78	10	1	1	19	29	3	2	2	28	14	6	.342	.359
Smitherman, Stephen	R-R	6-4	235	9-1-78	.278	.315	.262	86	313	45	87	30	1	11	62	48	6	0	5	78	3	1	.486	.379

PITCHING	B-T	HT	WT	DOB	W	L	ERA	G	GS	CG	SV	IP	H	R	ER	HR	BB	SO	AVG	vLH	vRH	K/9	BB/9
Andrew, Jason	R-R	6-1	185	1-29-80	3	4	3.59	48	2	0	0	80	78	39	32	4	28	63	.258	.278	.246	7.06	3.14
Barreto, Joel	R-R	5-11	152	10-14-80	3	0	3.60	3	0	0	0	5	5	2	2	0	4	3	.278	.375	.200	5.40	7.20
Basham, Bobby	R-R	6-3	205	3-7-80	5	3	2.98	10	10	0	0	51	52	20	17	5	9	46	.275	.282	.270	8.06	1.58
Bruksch, Jeffrey	R-R	6-4	212	4-29-80	3	9	4.81	28	14	0	0	92	86	56	49	10	67	84	.256	.264	.251	8.25	6.58
Caraccioli, Lance	L-L	6-4	200	12-14-77	5	5	3.97	15	10	0	0	68	65	35	30	6	31	61	.258	.254	.259	8.07	4.10
Cherry, Brad	R-R	6-4	200	2-12-81	0	2	7.71	7	0	0	0	9	15	10	8	3	3	8	.326	.227	.417	7.71	2.89
Chick, Travis	R-R	6-3	225	6-10-84	2	2	4.86	8	8	0	0	46	47	25	25	5	27	21	.270	.282	.260	4.08	5.24
2-team (19 Mobile)					4	11	5.14	27	27	1	0	144	154	90	82	17	67	113	.276	.322	.237	7.08	4.20
Cruz, Arian	L-L	5-10	170	5-30-78	3	1	3.26	13	0	0	0	19	23	9	7	1	6	16	.303	.238	.327	7.45	2.79
Dumatrait, Phil	R-L	6-2	170	7-12-81	4	12	3.17	24	24	0	0	128	115	58	45	4	70	101	.245	.167	.270	7.12	4.93
Eckenstahler, Eric	L-L	6-7	220	12-17-76	0	0	9.24	35	0	0	0	37	53	42	38	4	41	29	.349	.347	.350	7.05	9.97
Gardner, Richie	R-R	6-3	185	2-1-82	3	6	5.73	13	13	0	0	66	80	46	42	6	24	47	.309	.311	.307	6.41	3.27
Hall, Josh	R-R	6-3	195	12-16-80	5	6	3.53	18	18	0	0	112	115	49	44	7	35	92	.269	.329	.230	7.37	2.80
Hudson, Luke	R-R	6-3	195	5-2-77	0	1	5.40	1	1	0	0	7	6	4	4	2	1	7	.231	.111	.294	9.45	1.35
Kozlowski, Ben	L-L	6-6	230	8-16-80	4	4	4.04	20	20	0	0	111	129	58	50	10	31	82	.290	.255	.301	6.63	2.51
Mallett, Justin	R-R	6-7	215	11-11-81	0	0	5.91	3	2	0	0	11	12	7	7	3	5	9	.293	.214	.333	7.59	4.22
Nelson, Bubba	R-R	6-1	195	8-26-81	2	4	4.61	42	0	0	12	68	67	38	35	5	27	70	.256	.243	.265	9.22	3.56
Phelps, Travis	R-R	6-2	170	7-25-77	0	1	5.40	7	0	0	0	10	14	6	6	1	1	10	.350	.300	.400	9.00	0.90
Saladin, Miguel	R-R	5-11	200	5-22-75	0	0	3.45	10	0	0	1	16	19	6	6	2	5	15	.306	.400	.219	8.62	2.87
Salmon, Brad	L-R	6-4	220	1-3-80	3	8	3.34	38	0	0	4	73	66	31	27	3	31	71	.247	.262	.238	8.79	3.84
Schmidt, Jeremy	R-R	6-2	203	11-15-79	3	5	4.36	46	0	0	0	64	64	35	31	6	23	56	.264	.306	.236	7.88	3.23
Shafer, David	R-R	6-3	185	3-7-82	1	6	4.08	34	0	0	6	40	31	21	18	3	24	41	.217	.231	.209	9.30	5.45
Valdez, Edward	R-R	6-2	165	2-8-80	1	3	6.94	12	11	0	0	58	85	48	45	10	24	47	.356	.367	.345	7.25	3.70
Van Hekken, Andy	R-L	6-3	185	7-31-79	2	0	3.24	3	3	0	0	17	19	6	6	2	3	10	.271	.333	.266	5.40	1.62
2-team (3 Mississippi)					2	0	4.41	6	6	0	0	33	41	16	16	3	15	18	.313	.333	.307	4.96	4.13
Weber, Ben	R-R	6-4	205	11-17-69	1	1	2.31	9	0	0	0	12	9	3	3	2	3	5	.209	.313	.148	3.86	2.31

FIELDING

Catcher	PCT	G	PO	A	E	DP	PB
Hanigan	.986	46	314	32	5	4	3
Peterson	.991	92	682	82	7	10	6
Purdom	1.000	3	7	1	0	0	0

First Base	PCT	G	PO	A	E	DP
Anderson	.986	30	200	14	3	17
Bell	1.000	3	16	0	0	6
Gutierrez	.986	26	197	22	3	26
Hanigan	.998	47	410	25	1	33
Nichols	.990	23	193	9	2	16
Peterson	1.000	2	9	0	0	0
Smitherman	.966	20	163	7	6	16

Second Base	PCT	G	PO	A	E	DP
Anderson	.970	12	11	21	1	5
Freel	1.000	2	2	4	0	2
Hopper	1.000	1	0	1	0	0
Howard	.960	119	239	332	24	84
Jimenez	1.000	9	19	23	0	8
Renick	.917	6	4	7	1	0

Third Base	PCT	G	PO	A	E	DP
Anderson	.950	16	7	31	2	3
Bannon	.907	55	29	118	15	9
Bell	1.000	25	14	39	0	3
Freel	1.000	1	0	3	0	0
Howard	.000	1	0	0	0	0
Patchett	.933	11	8	20	2	1
Perez	.899	34	19	52	8	2
Renick	1.000	3	0	3	0	0

Shortstop	PCT	G	PO	A	E	DP
Anderson	1.000	13	18	20	0	6
Bannon	.976	38	57	105	4	25
Jimenez	.976	73	107	215	8	43
Patchett	.982	17	16	39	1	6
Perez	.857	6	7	5	2	2

Outfield	PCT	G	PO	A	E	DP
Anderson	1.000	9	7	0	0	0
Asadoorian	.985	78	187	7	3	5
Denorfia	.979	44	92	3	2	1
Fernandez	.983	36	53	5	1	0
Freel	1.000	2	6	0	0	0
Hopper	.973	102	199	15	6	3
Moran	1.000	20	49	5	0	3
Perez	.000	1	0	0	0	0
Ruiz	.984	69	115	6	2	1
Smitherman	.956	65	82	5	4	0

SARASOTA REDS — High Class A

FLORIDA STATE LEAGUE

BATTING	B-T	HT	WT	DOB	AVG	vLH	vRH	G	AB	R	H	2B	3B	HR	RBI	BB	HBP	SH	SF	SO	SB	CS	SLG	OBP
Bolivar, Luis	B-R	6-1	150	2-15-81	.243	.176	.269	103	366	45	89	19	4	2	27	18	11	6	2	62	17	4	.333	.297
Chapman, Travis	R-R	6-2	180	6-5-78	.271	.333	.233	13	48	4	13	1	0	1	6	4	0	0	0	5	0	3	.354	.327
Conley, Evan	R-R	6-1	200	2-25-81	.333	.333	.333	2	6	0	2	0	0	0	0	0	0	0	0	1	0	0	.333	.333
Dickerson, Chris	L-L	6-4	212	4-10-82	.236	.211	.248	119	436	68	103	17	7	11	43	53	6	7	3	124	19	3	.383	.325
Gentry, Philip	L-R	5-11	195	9-2-80	.227	.171	.247	31	128	14	29	7	0	2	13	3	0	1	1	22	1	2	.328	.242
Himes, Ben	L-R	6-4	210	3-9-81	.320	.233	.348	71	244	44	78	19	3	9	53	20	2	2	3	71	6	1	.533	.372
Hudson, Will	B-R	6-1	190	1-26-81	.176	.205	.165	52	136	11	24	3	0	1	4	14	2	1	0	49	3	3	.221	.263
Kelly, Kenny	R-R	6-2	190	1-26-79	.167	.333	.111	3	12	1	2	1	0	0	0	1	0	0	0	2	0	0	.250	.231
Mejia, Jorge	R-R	5-11	175	8-15-82	.256	.348	.224	29	90	13	23	3	1	0	5	11	1	2	0	25	7	2	.311	.343
Moran, Javon	R-R	5-11	175	9-30-82	.329	.310	.336	53	210	35	69	4	2	2	23	14	4	1	2	32	13	7	.395	.378
Motooka, Rafael	R-R	6-0	200	4-18-82	.200	.333	.143	10	30	2	6	0	0	1	2	2	0	0	0	5	0	0	.300	.250
Olmstead, Walter	B-R	6-6	240	12-5-80	.244	.270	.233	36	123	8	30	4	1	4	16	5	0	0	2	37	1	0	.390	.269
Perez, Miguel	R-R	6-3	190	9-25-83	.268	.304	.255	80	291	36	78	11	0	4	33	16	1	1	3	63	7	1	.347	.305
Piepkorn, Jeremiah	R-R	6-3	215	2-18-81	.225	.200	.234	27	89	12	20	2	3	3	13	8	1	0	2	13	1	2	.416	.290
Rojo, Billy	R-R	5-10	144	4-23-83	.167	.000	.333	2	6	0	1	0	0	0	0	0	0	0	0	3	0	0	.167	.167
Ruiz, Junior	L-R	5-10	195	6-7-80	.312	.328	.305	54	186	40	58	10	2	3	24	33	2	0	1	20	17	2	.435	.419
Schramek, Mark	L-R	6-3	230	6-2-80	.214	.216	.213	118	416	52	89	23	1	11	51	37	3	0	3	143	5	0	.353	.281
Smith, Kyle	R-R	6-2	205	5-17-81	.219	.191	.232	72	219	20	48	8	1	5	20	27	5	1	2	92	2	3	.333	.316
Sulbaran, Orlando	R-R	6-2	160	11-16-81	.091	.000	.167	4	11	0	1	1	0	0	0	2	0	0	0	2	0	0	.182	.231
Tiburcio, Hector	B-R	6-0	155	6-11-81	.259	.317	.235	116	401	56	104	13	4	8	42	23	1	3	2	89	12	9	.372	.300
Urgelles, Jeff	R-R	6-1	200	6-19-82	.223	.321	.185	63	202	19	45	14	0	2	23	17	6	1	3	40	0	1	.322	.298
Vavao, Jason	R-R	6-4	205	5-5-81	.236	.240	.235	67	237	26	56	16	1	6	26	24	4	1	1	82	4	4	.388	.316
Votto, Joey	L-R	6-3	200	9-10-83	.256	.196	.283	124	464	64	119	23	2	17	83	52	3	1	9	122	4	5	.425	.330

PITCHING	B-T	HT	WT	DOB	W	L	ERA	G	GS	CG	SV	IP	H	R	ER	HR	BB	SO	AVG	vLH	vRH	K/9	BB/9
Adames, Geovanny	R-R	6-2	184	1-15-83	0	0	38.57	2	0	0	0	2	7	11	10	1	4	3	.467	.667	.333	11.57	15.43
Barreto, Joel	R-R	5-11	152	10-14-80	3	1	2.45	18	0	0	5	26	16	8	7	3	17	31	.182	.189	.176	10.87	5.96
Basham, Bobby	R-R	6-3	205	3-7-80	5	2	3.75	10	10	0	0	50	60	22	21	3	6	42	.309	.314	.306	7.51	1.07
Bong, Jung	L-L	6-3	215	7-15-80	0	0	4.50	1	1	0	0	4	4	3	2	0	1	1	.250	.500	.214	2.25	2.25
Cherry, Brad	R-R	6-4	200	2-12-81	1	0	1.96	13	0	0	1	18	14	6	4	1	10	19	.197	.172	.214	9.33	4.91
Cueto, Johnny	R-R	5-11	174	2-15-86	0	1	3.00	2	1	0	0	6	5	2	2	0	2	6	.217	.300	.154	9.00	3.00

PITCHING	B-T	HT	WT	DOB	W	L	ERA	G	GS	CG	SV	IP	H	R	ER	HR	BB	SO	AVG	vLH	vRH	K/9	BB/9
Dumatrait, Phil	R-L	6-2	170	7-12-81	0	0	2.70	3	2	0	0	10	8	4	3	0	3	13	.211	.200	.214	11.70	2.70
Edens, Kyle	R-R	5-10	190	1-25-80	8	3	2.62	37	3	0	3	82	79	33	24	4	27	64	.256	.218	.281	7.00	2.95
Garmon, Ryan	L-L	6-1	208	5-9-82	0	0	3.09	8	0	0	0	12	14	8	4	0	10	2	.292	.474	.172	1.54	7.71
Griffin, David	L-L	6-0	180	8-16-81	0	0	18.00	2	0	0	0	3	7	6	6	1	3	1	.438	.000	.438	3.00	9.00
Guevara, Carlos	R-R	6-0	175	3-18-82	4	3	2.45	44	0	0	14	51	39	17	14	2	14	65	.203	.164	.224	11.40	2.45
Hall, Josh	R-R	6-3	195	12-16-80	0	3	6.83	7	7	0	0	29	46	30	22	5	14	21	.354	.311	.391	6.52	4.34
Hendley, Blake	R-R	6-3	195	9-1-81	0	1	4.24	10	0	0	1	17	15	8	8	1	5	18	.227	.273	.182	9.53	2.65
Lanier, Bo	R-R	6-0	160	11-20-82	0	0	0.00	2	1	0	0	5	2	0	0	0	4	2	.118	.000	.222	3.60	7.20
Lohse, Erik	R-R	6-2	193	6-6-80	10	5	4.69	39	2	0	0	81	90	49	42	10	25	66	.283	.233	.319	7.36	2.79
Mallett, Justin	R-R	6-7	215	11-11-81	2	3	2.87	16	5	0	1	53	44	23	17	3	18	60	.226	.293	.197	10.13	3.04
Mattox, D.J.	R-R	6-2	195	5-24-80	4	8	5.94	16	16	0	0	73	76	57	48	6	37	62	.271	.279	.266	7.68	4.58
Medlock, Calvin	R-R	5-10	175	11-8-82	6	3	3.06	25	17	0	0	109	95	42	37	6	22	98	.234	.195	.258	8.12	1.82
Morenko, Brad	R-R	6-4	215	8-15-81	2	2	4.98	9	1	0	2	22	29	14	12	4	3	6	.312	.231	.370	2.49	1.25
O'Neal, Charles	R-L	6-4	165	9-12-83	0	0	5.87	10	0	0	0	15	14	12	10	1	9	13	.246	.412	.175	7.63	5.28
Ortiz, Ramon	R-R	6-0	175	5-23-73	0	1	9.00	1	1	0	0	3	7	4	3	1	0	3	.412	.250	.556	9.00	0.00
Paduch, Jim	R-R	6-3	185	11-2-82	4	9	3.81	23	17	1	1	104	104	51	44	6	25	66	.262	.270	.256	5.71	2.16
Pelland, Tyler	R-L	6-0	198	10-9-83	5	8	4.05	30	15	0	0	102	103	52	46	5	63	103	.270	.323	.253	9.06	5.54
Powers, Joe	R-R	6-3	215	8-5-78	0	1	8.25	4	1	0	0	12	14	15	11	1	8	8	.286	.273	.296	6.00	6.00
Rincon, Daniel	R-R	6-3	165	10-11-82	3	2	5.17	16	3	0	0	47	55	30	27	6	16	46	.284	.321	.255	8.81	3.06
Schmidt, Jeremy	R-R	6-2	203	11-15-79	0	3	2.61	7	0	0	0	10	10	5	3	0	5	9	.250	.280	.200	7.84	4.35
Shafer, David	R-R	6-3	185	3-7-82	1	0	0.00	10	0	0	5	14	9	0	0	0	2	18	.188	.231	.171	11.85	1.32
Till, Brock	R-R	5-10	195	7-1-80	4	6	4.09	29	16	0	0	106	116	64	48	7	42	77	.279	.263	.289	6.56	3.58
Valdez, Edward	R-R	6-2	165	2-8-80	3	2	1.95	14	13	1	0	69	58	21	15	2	21	62	.229	.203	.252	8.05	2.73

FIELDING

Catcher	PCT	G	PO	A	E	DP	PB
Motooka	.985	9	61	3	1	0	1
Perez	.987	77	588	70	9	7	14
Urgelles	.985	51	375	30	6	1	5

First Base	PCT	G	PO	A	E	DP
Mejia	1.000	2	7	1	0	0
Olmstead	1.000	5	37	2	0	2
Piepkorn	.929	2	13	0	1	1
Sulbaran	1.000	1	13	1	0	0
Urgelles	.969	4	29	2	1	2
Vavao	.980	15	134	10	3	18
Votto	.991	107	851	75	8	84

Second Base	PCT	G	PO	A	E	DP
Bolivar	.977	100	164	262	10	53
Chapman	1.000	1	3	5	0	2
Conley	1.000	2	1	12	0	0
Hudson	.973	9	12	24	1	7
Mejia	.957	19	26	40	3	9
Rojo	1.000	2	2	4	0	1
Tiburcio	.864	4	10	9	3	4

Third Base	PCT	G	PO	A	E	DP
Chapman	1.000	2	0	4	0	1
Hudson	.880	14	4	18	3	1
Mejia	1.000	2	1	4	0	0
Olmstead	.714	3	2	3	2	0
Piepkorn	.667	1	1	1	1	1
Schramek	.908	116	65	213	28	20

Shortstop	PCT	G	PO	A	E	DP
Bolivar	1.000	2	1	10	0	2
Hudson	.899	19	20	51	8	10
Mejia	1.000	6	5	16	0	1
Tiburcio	.943	111	198	313	31	67

Outfield	PCT	G	PO	A	E	DP
Dickerson	.963	112	231	5	9	1
Gentry	1.000	30	62	2	0	0
Himes	.946	68	98	7	6	3
Hudson	1.000	8	5	0	0	0
Kelly	1.000	3	4	1	0	0
Moran	.961	51	93	5	4	3
Olmstead	.923	9	12	0	1	0
Piepkorn	1.000	21	22	3	0	0
Ruiz	.980	50	95	4	2	1
Smith	.975	55	77	1	2	0
Vavao	.917	10	11	0	1	0

DAYTON DRAGONS — Low Class A

MIDWEST LEAGUE

BATTING	B-T	HT	WT	DOB	AVG	vLH	vRH	G	AB	R	H	2B	3B	HR	RBI	BB	HBP	SH	SF	SO	SB	CS	SLG	OBP
Anderson, Drew	B-R	5-9	170	2-2-83	.246	.298	.230	105	407	59	100	15	9	6	37	31	0	3	2	96	15	9	.371	.298
Belcher, Jordan	R-R	6-2	185	2-17-84	.292	.286	.294	25	89	14	26	7	0	1	8	11	0	0	1	12	2	2	.404	.366
Conley, Evan	R-R	6-1	200	2-25-81	.180	.167	.184	22	61	7	11	2	0	1	8	10	2	0	1	17	0	0	.262	.311
Gentry, Philip	L-R	5-11	195	9-2-80	.271	.233	.279	88	365	51	99	23	7	5	47	23	7	5	4	79	13	5	.414	.323
Gonzalez, Reinaldo	R-R	6-0	185	8-16-84	.091	.000	.200	4	11	0	1	0	0	0	0	0	0	0	0	5	0	0	.091	.091
Gutierrez, Tonys	L-L	6-2	180	8-18-83	.324	.299	.331	109	410	65	133	21	5	7	48	40	11	0	4	71	6	0	.451	.396
Hernandez, Habelito	R-R	6-0	180	1-11-81	.282	.293	.279	47	181	18	51	14	1	3	23	3	2	5	0	31	3	0	.420	.301
Himes, Ben	L-R	6-4	210	3-9-81	.255	.304	.241	27	106	18	27	11	0	2	18	16	2	0	0	33	1	2	.415	.363
Janish, Paul	R-R	6-2	180	10-12-82	.245	.235	.248	55	208	30	51	10	2	5	29	29	5	8	4	38	5	2	.385	.346
Key, Bradley	R-R	6-0	185	3-14-83	.242	.263	.236	68	256	25	62	4	0	6	31	16	0	0	2	76	0	0	.328	.285
Kroski, Chris	L-R	6-1	231	5-17-82	.270	.118	.284	59	211	29	57	11	3	6	32	24	2	0	1	48	3	1	.436	.349
Lawhorn, Trevor	R-R	6-2	182	12-18-82	.261	.344	.238	84	303	39	79	19	4	6	45	13	4	6	7	63	11	6	.409	.294
Lewis, Kenny	L-L	5-9	195	10-13-84	.211	.217	.209	26	90	9	19	2	2	1	6	8	2	1	0	25	11	6	.311	.290
Mejia, Jorge	R-R	5-11	175	8-15-82	.197	.190	.200	49	157	22	31	5	1	1	14	22	0	1	2	35	4	3	.261	.293
Mosby, Robert	R-R	6-3	240	4-9-82	.245	.245	.244	52	188	25	46	8	0	9	28	14	3	0	3	60	0	0	.431	.303
Piepkorn, Jeremiah	R-R	6-3	215	2-18-81	.266	.330	.246	107	421	68	112	24	3	22	77	30	11	1	4	94	4	3	.494	.328
Purdom, John	R-R	6-2	230	5-28-81	.277	.269	.279	89	318	36	88	19	0	2	39	33	13	1	2	52	1	0	.355	.366
Rosales, Adam	R-R	6-2	195	5-20-83	.328	.389	.306	32	134	24	44	8	0	9	21	10	2	0	2	24	3	1	.590	.378
Sandoval, Mayker	R-R	5-10	170	2-9-84	.165	.083	.197	26	85	11	14	4	2	0	4	9	4	1	0	39	2	1	.259	.276
Strait, Cody	R-R	6-1	185	5-28-83	.266	.298	.256	116	413	63	110	16	4	14	60	38	15	7	1	102	25	7	.426	.349
Szymanski, B.J.	B-R	6-5	210	10-1-82	.262	.200	.281	50	191	32	50	8	1	10	26	21	0	0	2	57	7	1	.471	.332
Tatum, Craig	R-R	6-1	215	3-18-83	.188	.097	.216	37	128	16	24	7	1	1	12	21	2	0	0	30	0	2	.281	.311
Ziemendorf, Chad	R-R	5-11	195	4-9-81	.172	.250	.160	9	29	4	5	1	0	0	4	4	1	0	0	10	0	0	.207	.294

PITCHING	B-T	HT	WT	DOB	W	L	ERA	G	GS	CG	SV	IP	H	R	ER	HR	BB	SO	AVG	vLH	vRH	K/9	BB/9
Avery, James	R-R	6-1	210	6-10-84	1	1	3.94	5	2	0	0	16	17	8	7	1	6	8	.274	.227	.300	4.50	3.38
Bailey, Homer	R-R	6-4	185	5-3-86	8	4	4.43	28	21	0	0	104	89	64	51	5	62	125	.232	.227	.236	10.85	5.38
Bohorquez, Carlos	R-R	5-11	165	10-6-81	2	5	4.52	37	5	0	1	76	73	44	38	8	35	65	.244	.230	.254	7.73	4.16
Cherry, Brad	R-R	6-4	200	2-12-81	1	0	1.95	17	0	0	0	28	13	8	6	3	9	24	.140	.170	.109	7.81	2.93
Farfan, Alex	R-R	6-3	175	1-6-83	2	7	7.69	44	0	0	0	57	68	57	49	4	58	29	.304	.313	.298	4.55	9.10
Frias, Juan	L-L	5-11	170	8-7-79	1	5	4.19	14	8	0	1	54	49	31	25	4	20	30	.243	.137	.278	5.03	3.35
Garrison, Aaron	R-R	6-1	205	10-25-81	1	1	7.04	8	2	0	1	15	19	14	12	0	12	12	.288	.258	.314	7.04	7.04
George, Jonathan	R-R	6-4	220	7-6-84	5	8	5.33	35	12	0	0	98	129	66	58	9	17	52	.321	.313	.326	4.78	1.56
Gonzalez, Rafael	R-R	6-3	225	3-21-86	3	5	9.35	10	5	0	0	26	24	29	27	5	24	22	.250	.250	.250	7.62	8.31
Hendley, Blake	R-R	6-3	195	9-1-81	7	0	2.12	38	0	0	14	51	31	12	12	2	12	45	.172	.132	.196	7.94	2.12
Morenko, Brad	R-R	6-4	215	8-15-81	6	1	2.49	16	5	0	1	61	62	25	17	7	9	34	.250	.293	.224	4.99	1.32
Morrison, James	R-R	6-1	190	2-21-81	0	5	5.46	31	3	1	6	63	76	52	38	7	20	44	.295	.311	.284	6.32	2.87

PITCHING	B-T	HT	WT	DOB	W	L	ERA	G	GS	CG	SV	IP	H	R	ER	HR	BB	SO	AVG	vLH	vRH	K/9	BB/9
Powers, Joe	R-R	6-3	215	8-5-78	2	0	6.43	5	2	0	0	14	10	11	10	3	8	8	.200	.217	.185	5.14	5.14
Ramirez, Ramon	R-R	6-0	160	9-16-82	5	7	4.50	30	19	0	0	114	114	69	57	8	50	90	.265	.229	.288	7.11	3.95
Sanders, Jared	R-R	6-2	210	11-19-81	1	6	4.28	42	0	0	6	61	77	42	29	7	31	31	.306	.353	.273	4.57	4.57
Segovia, Omar	L-L	6-2	210	5-28-83	1	2	5.10	10	4	0	2	30	27	17	17	7	21	29	.248	.269	.241	8.70	6.30
Stott, Zac	R-R	6-5	200	7-26-83	2	2	4.16	40	2	0	0	71	89	37	33	8	29	48	.309	.423	.251	6.06	3.66
Thigpen, Josh	R-R	6-4	205	6-27-82	4	4	4.99	13	5	0	0	40	34	24	22	2	30	40	.231	.246	.222	9.08	6.81
Ursin, Damian	R-R	6-0	197	11-27-82	0	4	5.16	9	4	0	0	30	33	21	17	1	20	19	.284	.289	.282	5.76	6.07
Valiquette, Philippe-Alexandre	L-L	6-0	175	2-14-87	2	5	6.30	19	16	0	0	64	81	54	45	3	44	42	.315	.271	.328	5.88	6.16
Vazquez, Camilo	L-L	6-0	180	10-3-83	4	4	5.18	29	18	0	0	99	91	63	57	10	62	88	.243	.307	.227	8.00	5.64
Weber, Ben	R-R	6-4	205	11-17-69	0	0	0.00	2	0	0	0	3	1	0	0	0	0	4	.100	.000	.100	12.00	0.00
Wilson, Joseph	L-L	6-3	195	8-2-82	2	3	8.20	12	6	0	0	37	45	35	34	14	18	31	.302	.343	.289	7.47	4.34

FIELDING

Catcher	PCT	G	PO	A	E	DP	PB
Gonzalez	.929	4	22	4	2	0	3
Kroski	1.000	26	185	20	0	1	1
Purdom	.988	69	429	51	6	5	5
Tatum	.968	36	243	31	9	2	7
Ziemendorf	.985	9	56	11	1	0	2

First Base	PCT	G	PO	A	E	DP
Anderson	1.000	1	8	1	0	1
Conley	.926	3	24	1	2	0
Gutierrez	.987	98	855	58	12	81
Kroski	.925	6	47	2	4	5
Mosby	.980	22	183	10	4	20
Piepkorn	.975	7	38	1	1	5
Purdom	1.000	8	73	3	0	5

Second Base	PCT	G	PO	A	E	DP
Anderson	.970	39	69	93	5	16
Conley	1.000	5	11	10	0	2
Gutierrez	1.000	1	2	2	0	2
Lawhorn	.962	69	151	176	13	42
Mejia	.956	10	19	24	2	6
Sandoval	.945	21	43	61	6	13

Third Base	PCT	G	PO	A	E	DP
Anderson	.875	7	4	10	2	0
Conley	.862	12	5	20	4	0
Hernandez	.930	16	9	31	3	2
Key	.879	68	39	121	22	13
Lawhorn	.727	3	2	6	3	2
Mejia	1.000	3	0	11	0	0
Piepkorn	.879	27	18	69	12	1
Purdom	.800	7	5	7	3	0
Sandoval	1.000	2	0	5	0	0

Shortstop	PCT	G	PO	A	E	DP
Anderson	.942	27	42	89	8	21
Janish	.963	55	96	188	11	34
Lawhorn	.667	1	3	1	2	1
Mejia	.973	27	40	69	3	15
Rosales	.957	32	48	87	6	16

Outfield	PCT	G	PO	A	E	DP
Anderson	1.000	33	61	3	0	1
Belcher	.954	25	59	3	3	0
Gentry	1.000	83	131	6	0	2
Gutierrez	.750	2	3	0	1	0
Himes	.944	27	34	0	2	0
Kroski	.000	1	0	0	0	0
Lewis	1.000	26	47	1	0	0
Piepkorn	.955	73	122	6	6	0
Purdom	.000	1	0	0	0	0
Strait	.978	112	257	13	6	2
Szymanski	.969	44	91	3	3	2

BILLINGS MUSTANGS — Rookie

PIONEER LEAGUE

BATTING	B-T	HT	WT	DOB	AVG	vLH	vRH	G	AB	R	H	2B	3B	HR	RBI	BB	HBP	SH	SF	SO	SB	CS	SLG	OBP
Belcher, Jordan	R-R	6-2	185	2-17-84	.266	.318	.231	30	109	16	29	13	1	3	28	8	1	0	2	23	2	2	.486	.317
Blumenthal, Ben	R-R	6-2	210	4-24-83	.196	.222	.185	29	92	13	18	3	0	2	11	8	1	1	0	39	0	1	.293	.267
Bruce, Jay	L-L	6-3	195	4-3-87	.257	.179	.310	17	70	16	18	2	0	4	13	11	0	0	0	22	2	2	.457	.358
De Jesus, Michael	L-R	5-8	180	7-16-83	.234	.074	.268	53	154	25	36	8	0	1	20	40	1	3	0	40	10	2	.305	.395
Delgado, Ronny	R-R	6-0	155	5-4-84	.286	.273	.300	6	21	4	6	1	0	1	1	3	2	0	0	6	1	0	.476	.423
Denove, Chris	R-R	6-1	200	12-9-82	.261	.279	.253	49	138	28	36	8	0	3	23	23	6	2	0	29	2	1	.384	.389
Eymann, Eric	R-R	6-3	185	2-9-84	.239	.382	.177	34	113	16	27	4	2	3	12	11	2	0	0	33	2	0	.389	.317
Feiner, Kevyn	R-R	6-1	170	6-11-87	.100	.000	.200	3	10	2	1	0	0	0	1	0	0	0	0	3	0	0	.100	.100
Griffin, Michael	R-R	5-9	200	10-1-83	.263	.250	.273	13	38	12	10	0	0	2	4	5	4	0	0	6	1	0	.421	.404
Holden, Josh	L-L	6-2	220	12-10-80	.251	.328	.213	59	203	26	51	6	5	0	30	27	3	4	1	60	13	6	.330	.346
Langham, James	R-R	6-2	190	9-3-82	.188	.164	.205	44	138	20	26	10	0	4	19	14	6	0	0	53	0	2	.348	.291
Lasso, Yoni	R-R	5-11	170	11-22-84	.095	.154	.000	9	21	1	2	0	0	0	1	6	0	0	1	8	0	0	.095	.286
Lewis, Kenny	L-L	5-9	195	10-13-84	.238	.259	.229	59	172	23	41	6	2	1	15	29	1	4	1	60	14	5	.314	.350
Mummy, Ben	R-R	6-3	220	8-14-84	.209	.241	.191	44	148	25	31	10	2	1	14	20	7	0	0	47	4	2	.324	.331
Reininger, J.D.	R-R	5-10	190	12-3-82	.305	.338	.284	48	177	24	54	12	1	5	35	23	0	0	1	41	4	3	.469	.383
Roberts, J.D.	L-R	6-4	225	8-8-81	.284	.278	.287	63	204	40	58	14	0	9	39	28	2	1	3	64	3	0	.485	.371
Roberts, Brandon	L-R	6-0	185	11-9-84	.318	.329	.313	68	274	50	87	9	6	4	36	24	8	3	2	44	32	7	.438	.386
Rodriguez, Mark	R-R	6-0	200	6-1-83	.162	.150	.176	17	37	6	6	2	0	0	3	6	0	0	0	15	0	0	.216	.279
Ronda, Jose	B-R	6-2	175	6-8-85	.253	.280	.241	29	83	18	21	3	3	1	15	18	0	1	1	25	0	1	.398	.382
Rosales, Adam	R-R	6-2	195	5-20-83	.321	.366	.303	34	140	29	45	14	0	5	25	13	5	0	1	37	2	2	.529	.396
Sandoval, Mayker	R-R	5-10	170	2-9-84	.266	.269	.264	59	218	33	58	11	6	3	28	13	6	3	5	65	15	2	.413	.318

PITCHING	B-T	HT	WT	DOB	W	L	ERA	G	GS	CG	SV	IP	H	R	ER	HR	BB	SO	AVG	vLH	vRH	K/9	BB/9
Camardese, Brandon	R-L	6-2	205	7-2-83	1	1	4.42	15	4	0	0	39	46	21	19	1	11	36	.301	.263	.313	8.38	2.56
Feliz, Rainer	R-R	6-5	170	3-22-83	2	2	7.12	16	2	0	1	30	43	30	24	2	12	17	.352	.327	.371	5.04	3.56
Fisher, Carlos	R-R	6-4	220	2-22-83	4	4	4.19	15	8	0	1	54	56	30	25	3	19	45	.268	.264	.270	7.55	3.19
Garrison, Aaron	R-R	6-1	205	10-25-81	4	1	3.41	8	4	0	0	29	23	12	11	1	6	24	.211	.233	.197	7.45	1.86
Geiersbach, Ken	R-R	6-1	190	5-20-82	3	4	4.34	23	1	0	2	37	36	24	18	2	15	33	.261	.269	.256	7.96	3.62
Gonzalez, Rafael	R-R	6-3	225	3-21-86	3	0	3.43	11	6	0	1	42	36	18	16	7	23	37	.234	.226	.239	7.93	4.93
Haltiwanger, Kevin	R-R	6-2	180	4-21-84	0	0	6.43	3	2	0	0	7	10	8	5	0	4	7	.323	.375	.267	9.00	5.14
Lanier, Bo	R-R	6-0	160	11-20-82	0	0	6.23	5	0	0	0	4	8	4	3	1	4	3	.381	.333	.400	6.23	8.31
Lecure, Samuel	R-R	6-1	190	5-4-84	5	1	3.27	13	6	0	0	41	43	18	15	2	15	44	.272	.218	.301	9.58	3.27
Morris, James	L-L	6-8	255	6-3-83	1	1	6.88	17	0	0	0	17	20	14	13	3	13	14	.303	.235	.327	7.41	6.88
Ondrusek, Logan	R-R	6-8	195	2-13-85	1	6	6.02	15	9	0	0	55	72	49	37	9	19	46	.314	.327	.303	7.48	3.09
O'Neal, Charles	R-L	6-4	165	9-12-83	0	1	6.20	17	2	0	0	25	31	17	17	1	17	17	.316	.333	.308	6.20	6.20
Rojas, Jose	R-R	6-0	165	3-2-83	2	4	5.90	22	4	0	4	40	41	27	26	7	22	34	.283	.241	.310	7.71	4.99
Stevens, Jeff	R-R	6-1	200	9-5-83	4	4	2.98	13	8	0	0	54	44	20	18	4	15	58	.220	.210	.227	9.61	2.48
Ursin, Damian	R-R	6-0	197	11-27-82	1	0	2.00	3	1	0	0	9	9	2	2	1	5	7	.273	.333	.167	7.00	5.00
Valiquette, Philippe	L-L	6-0	175	2-14-87	2	1	6.43	7	3	0	0	21	23	16	15	1	10	18	.291	.263	.300	7.71	4.29
Vecchio, Jason	R-R	5-11	195	4-7-84	0	2	5.06	5	0	0	1	5	5	4	3	1	2	8	.238	.222	.250	13.50	3.38
Wachman, Cory	R-R	6-5	216	4-10-82	3	1	4.58	16	5	0	0	53	60	33	27	3	19	54	.286	.276	.293	9.17	3.23
Wilson, David	R-L	5-11	160	2-28-83	2	0	4.41	13	7	0	1	49	48	25	24	5	14	35	.261	.263	.260	6.43	2.57
Wood, Travis	R-L	6-0	165	2-6-87	2	0	1.82	6	4	0	0	25	15	6	5	0	13	22	.174	.200	.164	8.03	4.74
Woody, Abe	R-R	5-11	215	11-9-82	3	0	2.03	25	0	0	14	27	28	9	6	1	5	38	.255	.231	.276	12.83	1.69

GAMES BY POSITION: C—Blumenthal 28, Denove 47, Rodriguez 15. **1B**—Langham 9, Mummy 44, J.D. Roberts 28, Rodriguez 1, Ronda 2. **2B**—De Jesus 40, Lasso 1, Sandoval 45. **3B**—De Jesus 1, Delgado 4, Griffin 3, Reininger 45, Ronda 20, Sandoval 9. **SS**—De Jesus 7, Eymann 30, Feiner 3, Lasso 8, Rosales 33. **OF**—Belcher 29, Bruce 14, Holden 53, Langham 26, Lewis 53, B. Roberts 63.

GULF COAST LEAGUE

BATTING	B-T	HT	WT	DOB	AVG	vLH	vRH	G	AB	R	H	2B	3B	HR	RBI	BB	HBP	SH	SF	SO	SB	CS	SLG	OBP
Aguilar, Jose	R-R	6-3	185	11-23-85	.241	.303	.215	33	112	20	27	6	2	1	14	10	1	1	2	31	3	0	.357	.304
Bruce, Jay	L-L	6-3	195	4-3-87	.270	.290	.264	37	122	29	33	9	2	5	25	11	1	0	2	31	4	6	.500	.331
Buck, Juan	R-R	6-3	214	1-26-85	.103	.083	.111	14	39	2	4	0	0	0	0	1	0	0	0	23	0	0	.103	.125
Cabrera, Gerardo	R-R	6-2	185	12-23-83	.284	.222	.313	32	95	10	27	7	2	3	13	14	1	1	1	24	2	4	.495	.378
Colon, Angel	R-R	6-4	210	9-27-83	.255	.270	.250	47	145	21	37	12	0	1	24	15	10	0	3	41	0	2	.359	.358
Delgado, Ronny	R-R	6-0	155	5-4-84	.310	.206	.358	38	116	13	36	8	1	3	16	22	3	1	2	41	0	1	.474	.427
Eymann, Eric	R-R	6-3	185	2-9-84	.333	.500	.000	1	3	1	1	1	0	0	0	0	1	0	0	1	0	0	.667	.500
Feiner, Kevyn	R-R	6-1	170	6-11-87	.250	.238	.253	25	96	15	24	3	0	0	7	4	2	0	0	12	2	0	.281	.294
Garrett, Matt	R-R	6-4	195	12-22-84	.167	.176	.163	23	66	3	11	1	0	0	1	7	2	2	0	31	0	1	.182	.267
Gonzalez, Reinaldo	R-R	6-0	185	8-16-84	.212	.143	.234	30	85	12	18	6	0	1	8	12	2	3	0	22	3	3	.318	.323
Hernandez, Habelito	R-R	6-0	180	1-11-81	.316	.333	.313	5	19	2	6	0	0	1	3	1	0	0	0	2	1	0	.474	.350
Honey, Blake	R-R	6-1	175	12-24-85	.202	.222	.197	25	84	15	17	5	1	2	9	3	2	2	0	26	1	3	.357	.247
Johnson, Taylor	L-L	6-0	195	7-25-83	.222	.130	.245	39	117	10	26	10	0	1	17	18	1	2	1	26	3	1	.333	.328
Jones, Michael	R-R	6-3	180	11-19-86	.202	.216	.194	27	99	9	20	4	0	1	5	4	2	0	0	37	1	0	.273	.248
Lasso, Yoni	R-R	5-11	170	11-22-84	.233	.176	.250	23	73	8	17	5	0	0	13	10	2	0	1	22	0	0	.301	.337
Lewis, Kenny	L-L	5-9	195	10-13-84	.286	.500	.200	2	7	2	2	0	0	0	0	1	0	0	0	0	1	0	.286	.375
Mesa, Maikol	R-R	6-3	180	9-24-85	.250	.267	.245	20	68	9	17	2	1	0	6	1	1	2	0	12	1	3	.309	.271
Mosby, Robert	R-R	6-3	240	4-9-82	.182	.000	.182	3	11	2	2	0	0	0	1	1	0	0	0	3	0	0	.182	.250
Nunez, Runi	R-R	5-11	170	7-14-84	.000	.000	.000	3	4	1	0	0	0	0	0	0	0	0	0	0	0	0	.000	.000
Pena, Hannsel	R-R	5-11	181	1-30-84	.109	.154	.098	24	55	7	6	1	0	0	2	5	4	0	1	30	1	1	.127	.231
Quintana, Estevan	R-R	5-9	195	8-11-83	.213	.188	.222	20	61	6	13	2	1	0	7	9	2	0	1	18	1	0	.279	.329
Roa, Lonny	R-R	6-3	215	11-28-85	.211	.077	.292	15	38	3	8	2	0	0	4	5	0	0	1	16	0	1	.263	.295
Rodriguez, Mark	R-R	6-0	200	6-1-83	.077	.000	.143	5	13	1	1	0	0	0	1	4	0	1	0	6	2	0	.077	.294
Rogers, Jose	R-R	6-3	170	9-10-83	.200	.174	.216	19	60	8	12	0	0	0	3	5	1	2	0	15	2	1	.200	.273
Rojo, Billy	R-R	5-10	144	4-23-83	.274	.250	.281	24	73	11	20	6	0	2	11	5	3	3	0	14	1	3	.438	.346
Rumbos, Javier	R-R	5-10	170	7-5-85	.280	.368	.226	20	50	3	14	4	0	0	7	9	1	0	0	6	0	0	.360	.400

PITCHING	B-T	HT	WT	DOB	W	L	ERA	G	GS	CG	SV	IP	H	R	ER	HR	BB	SO	AVG	vLH	vRH	K/9	BB/9
Adames, Geovanny	R-R	6-2	184	1-15-83	0	0	0.96	9	0	0	3	9	5	1	1	0	3	9	.156	.182	.143	8.68	2.89
Avery, James	R-R	6-1	210	6-10-84	0	1	2.12	6	5	0	0	17	16	7	4	0	3	18	.239	.393	.128	9.53	1.59
Brito, Jose	L-L	6-5	210	6-17-84	1	0	10.13	11	0	0	0	13	15	16	15	1	12	15	.273	.364	.250	10.13	8.10
Cueto, Johnny	R-R	5-11	174	2-15-86	2	2	5.02	13	6	0	1	43	49	31	24	2	8	38	.285	.292	.280	7.95	1.67
Dillard, Johnny	R-R	6-1	160	1-14-81	1	1	4.32	13	0	0	4	17	21	12	8	0	9	15	.313	.464	.205	8.10	4.86
Frias, Juan	L-L	5-11	170	8-7-79	0	0	3.75	3	2	0	0	12	13	6	5	1	3	8	.295	.200	.308	6.00	2.25
Garmon, Ryan	L-L	6-1	208	5-9-82	0	3	4.97	9	1	0	0	13	14	13	7	0	6	5	.269	.182	.293	3.55	4.26
Gray, Matt	L-L	6-2	205	4-18-84	0	1	11.45	10	0	0	0	11	9	17	14	0	21	4	.209	.125	.229	3.27	17.18
Haltiwanger, Kevin	R-R	6-2	180	4-21-84	2	4	1.83	13	3	0	2	39	28	10	8	2	17	30	.204	.157	.233	6.86	3.89
Howington, Ty	B-L	6-4	225	11-4-80	0	0	3.60	3	3	0	0	5	4	2	2	0	1	4	.211	.000	.267	7.20	1.80
Huddy, Kyle	R-R	6-2	220	6-13-83	3	5	4.38	13	4	0	0	37	34	28	18	1	25	39	.250	.302	.217	9.49	6.08
Jimenez, Santos	R-R	6-1	181	9-2-83	0	0	0.00	5	0	0	0	5	5	3	0	0	2	6	.250	.300	.200	11.57	3.86
Johnson, Tod	L-L	6-3	210	11-29-80	1	0	1.42	9	0	0	1	13	8	4	2	1	4	8	.178	.167	.179	5.68	2.84
Lanier, Bo	R-R	6-0	160	11-20-82	1	2	3.33	10	3	0	0	27	19	14	10	1	13	18	.194	.167	.220	6.00	4.33
Mateo, Marcos	R-R	6-1	160	4-18-84	2	3	4.30	13	4	0	0	44	54	26	21	2	10	23	.309	.313	.306	4.70	2.05
Moya, Luis	R-R	6-0	170	1-4-84	0	1	1.23	3	1	0	0	7	10	6	1	0	0	5	.303	.273	.318	6.14	0.00
Newman, Brandon	L-L	6-2	220	3-12-82	2	6	4.89	13	8	0	0	46	62	38	25	1	13	26	.320	.351	.312	5.09	2.54
Powers, Joe	R-R	6-3	215	8-5-78	0	0	0.00	1	1	0	0	2	1	0	0	0	1	3	.167	.000	.250	16.20	5.40
Rios, Cristian	L-L	6-4	215	7-1-84	0	1	9.58	8	0	0	0	10	14	13	11	1	11	8	.311	.571	.263	6.97	9.58
Segovia, Omar	L-L	6-2	210	5-28-83	0	1	3.07	6	4	0	0	15	13	5	5	0	8	23	.228	.250	.224	14.11	4.91
Smiley, Wesley	R-R	6-1	217	7-21-81	2	0	5.47	14	2	0	2	26	30	18	16	2	13	28	.291	.282	.297	9.57	4.44
Sparks, Terrance	L-L	6-0	170	2-16-83	3	1	4.50	12	0	0	0	18	12	13	9	1	17	13	.188	.111	.200	6.50	8.50
Wood, Travis	R-L	6-0	165	2-6-87	0	0	0.75	8	7	0	0	24	13	3	2	0	7	45	.157	.250	.134	16.88	2.63
Young, Terrell	R-R	6-3	175	8-7-85	2	0	6.75	3	0	0	0	4	4	3	3	0	2	6	.267	.333	.250	13.50	4.50

GAMES BY POSITION: C—Gonzalez 30, Roa 15, Rodriguez 5, Rumbos 11. **1B**—Colon 20, Taylor Johnson 35, Tod Johnson 1, Mosby 1. **2B**—Feiner 8, Lasso 14, Mesa 1, Rogers 16, Rojo 23. **3B**—Colon 18, Delgado 36, Hernandez 1, Taylor Johnson 1, Lasso 4. **SS**—Eymann 1, Feiner 7, Honey 23, Jones 22, Lasso 3. **OF**—Aguilar 32, Bruce 27, Buck 7, Cabrera 31, Garrett 23, Taylor Johnson 1, Lewis 2, Mesa 17, Nunez 3, Pena 21, Quintana 14.

CLEVELAND INDIANS

BY JIM INGRAHAM

The Indians went farther than anyone expected in 2005, but it turned out to be one game short of far enough. In a season in which they had sensational pitching and remarkable offensive balance, the Indians nearly completed a comeback of historic proportions in the American League Central.

Their attempt to run down the division champion White Sox in the last week of the regular season ultimately ran out of gas. In the wild-card race, the Indians led by 1½ games with seven games to play. That race went right down to the last day of the regular season, when a Cleveland loss coupled with a Boston win sent the Red Sox to the playoffs and the Indians home.

Nevertheless, the Indians' record of 93-69 marked a 13-game improvement from 2004.

"It was a season of mixed emotions for us," general manager Mark Shapiro said. "It was bitterly disappointing to miss an opportunity to reach the playoffs, and given the fragility of our market, we can't take missed opportunities lightly. At the same time, though, there was an enormous sense of pride in what this team accomplished."

What the Indians accomplished in 2005 was essentially making Shapiro's rebuilding blueprint a reality. In the middle of the 2002 season, when Shapiro and his staff began dismantling a roster that had won six of the previous seven AL Central titles, Shapiro declared that he hoped to have the rebuilding of the franchise completed in time to be a contender by 2005. That's exactly what happened, and a big reason Shapiro was able to hit the bulls-eye on his rebuilding projection was the first trade he made at the beginning of the process.

The rebuilding of the Indians officially began in the middle of the 2002 season, when Shapiro traded Bartolo Colon to Montreal for three top-rated prospects, two of whom were cornerstones of the Indians' success story in 2005.

ORGANIZATION LEADERS

BATTING

***AVG**	Kouzmanoff, Kevin, Akron/Kinston/Mahoning Valley	.333
R	Snyder, Brad, Akron/Kinston	92
H	Reyes, Argenis, Kinston/Lake County	154
TB	Mulhern, Ryan, Akron/Kinston	258
2B	Kinkade, Mike, Buffalo	35
3B	Inglett, Joe, Buffalo	9
HR	Mulhern, Ryan, Akron/Kinston	32
RBI	Cooper, Jason, Akron/Buffalo	100
BB	Panther, Nathan, Akron/Kinston	67
SO	Snyder, Brad, Akron/Kinston	158
SB	Torres, Eider, Akron	33
***OBP**	Barton, Brian, Kinston/Lake County	.442
***SLG**	Mulhern, Ryan, Akron/Kinston	.640

PITCHING

W	Sowers, Jeremy, Akron/Buffalo/Kinston	14
L	Traber, Billy, Akron/Buffalo/Kinston	11
#ERA	Roehl, Scott, Akron/Kinston/Lake County	1.39
G	Collins, Kyle, Kinston/Lake County	57
CG	12 tied at	1
SV	Mattison, Kieran, Buffalo/Kinston/Lake County	25
IP	Carmona, Fausto, Akron/Buffalo	174
BB	Smith, Sean, Kinston	71
SO	Sowers, Jeremy, Akron/Buffalo/Kinston	149

*Minimum 250 at-bats. #Minimum 75 innings.

PLAYERS OF THE YEAR

MAJOR LEAGUE: Travis Hafner, dh

Hafner was hitting just .269-5-20 after the first two months of the 2005 season, but then he caught fire and nearly led the Indians to the American League playoffs. Hafner led the Indians in the triple crown categories and clubbed 11 homers in September to keep Cleveland in postseason contention.

MINOR LEAGUE: Jeremy Sowers, lhp

MIKE JANES

The Indians' first-round pick in 2004 was outstanding at three levels in his first professional season, going a combined 14-4, 2.37. Command continued to be his calling card, as Sowers posted an impressive 149-29 strikeout-walk ratio in 159 innings. He positioned himself to be a big league starter in '06.

Lefthander Cliff Lee went 18-5, leading the AL with a .783 winning percentage. Center fielder Grady Sizemore was a catalyst for the Indians' offense from his leadoff spot in the batting order. In his first full season in the majors, Sizemore hit .289-22-81 with 22 stolen bases, and he ranked third in the league with 11 triples and 10th in the league with 111 runs.

Sizemore was the first spoke in a wheel of consistency that was the Indians' lineup. All nine hitters in the everyday lineup hit 15 or more home runs, led by DH Travis Hafner, who hit .305, tying him with catcher Victor Martinez for the team lead, while leading the team with 33 home runs and 108 RBIs.

The Indians hit 207 home runs, the sixth-highest single-season total in club history, and perhaps the most surprising home run total was the 24 hit by Jhonny Peralta, who was more than equal to the daunting challenge of replacing fan favorite and perennial Gold Glover Omar Vizquel at shortstop.

The Indians' offense struggled early and late in the season, but for the bulk of the year it provided more than enough offense for what was the best pitching staff in the league. The Indians led the league in ERA (3.61) for the first time since 1996.

Virtually every pitcher on the staff had a career year, or a near-career year. Lee and C.C. Sabathia, who went 15-10, gave the Indians two lefthanders with 15 or more wins for the first time in 65 years.

The Indians also seemed to buy into manager Eric Wedge's one-game-at-a-time philosophy, and were able to rebound from a 9-14 start in April. After falling 15 games behind the division-leading White Sox in late July, the Indians were 39-18 after the break, the best record in the majors in that span.

The organization's success was not confined to the big league level, as the Indians' top four affiliates all posted winning records. Double-A Akron was the most successful, winning the Eastern League title under the leadership of up-and-coming manager Torey Luvullo and the rock-steady pitching of ace lefthander Jeremy Sowers, the Indians' first-round pick in 2004.

CLEVELAND INDIANS

Manager: Eric Wedge.

2005 Record: 93-69, .574 (2nd, AL Central).

BATTING	B-T	HT	WT	DOB	AVG	vLH	vRH	G	AB	R	H	2B	3B	HR	RBI	BB	HBP	SH	SF	SO	SB	CS	SLG	OBP
Bard, Josh	B-R	6-3	215	3-30-78	.193	.148	.214	34	83	6	16	4	0	1	9	9	0	1	2	11	0	0	.277	.266
Belliard, Ronnie	R-R	5-8	195	4-7-75	.284	.287	.282	145	536	71	152	36	1	17	78	35	1	8	7	72	2	2	.450	.325
Blake, Casey	R-R	6-2	210	8-23-73	.241	.241	.241	147	523	72	126	32	1	23	58	43	10	2	5	116	4	5	.438	.308
Boone, Aaron	R-R	6-2	200	3-9-73	.243	.229	.247	143	511	61	124	19	1	16	60	35	9	4	6	92	9	3	.378	.299
Broussard, Ben	L-L	6-2	220	9-24-76	.255	.225	.262	142	466	59	119	30	5	19	68	32	4	0	3	98	2	2	.464	.307
Cora, Alex	L-R	6-0	200	10-18-75	.205	.455	.185	49	146	11	30	5	2	1	8	5	4	1	1	18	6	0	.288	.250
Crisp, Coco	B-R	6-0	180	11-1-79	.300	.252	.324	145	594	86	178	42	4	16	69	44	0	13	5	81	15	6	.465	.345
Dubois, Jason	R-R	6-5	220	3-26-79	.222	.200	.233	14	45	6	10	0	0	2	2	5	0	0	0	25	0	0	.356	.300
Garko, Ryan	R-R	6-2	225	1-2-81	.000	.000	.000	1	1	0	0	0	0	0	0	0	0	0	0	1	0	0	.000	.000
Gerut, Jody	L-L	6-0	190	9-18-77	.275	.080	.319	44	138	12	38	9	1	1	12	18	0	0	1	14	1	1	.377	.357
Gonzalez, Juan	R-R	6-3	220	10-16-69	.000	.000	.000	1	1	0	0	0	0	0	0	0	0	0	0	0	0	0	.000	.000
Gutierrez, Franklin	R-R	6-2	180	2-21-83	.000	.000	.000	7	1	2	0	0	0	0	0	1	0	0	0	0	0	0	.000	.500
Hafner, Travis	L-R	6-3	240	6-3-77	.305	.269	.321	137	486	94	148	42	0	33	108	79	9	0	4	123	0	0	.595	.408
Hernandez, Jose	R-R	6-1	190	7-14-69	.231	.269	.169	84	234	28	54	7	0	6	31	14	2	3	3	60	1	3	.338	.277
Liefer, Jeff	L-R	6-3	210	8-17-74	.196	.000	.220	19	56	5	11	2	0	1	8	1	0	0	0	15	0	0	.286	.211
Ludwick, Ryan	R-L	6-3	210	7-13-78	.220	.200	.250	19	41	8	9	0	0	4	5	7	0	0	0	13	0	1	.512	.333
Martinez, Victor	B-R	6-2	195	12-23-78	.305	.274	.319	147	547	73	167	33	0	20	80	63	5	0	7	78	0	1	.475	.378
Peralta, Jhonny	R-R	6-1	210	5-28-82	.292	.305	.286	141	504	82	147	35	4	24	78	58	3	1	4	128	0	2	.520	.366
Phillips, Brandon	R-R	5-11	190	6-28-81	.000	.000	.000	6	9	1	0	0	0	0	0	0	0	0	0	4	0	0	.000	.000
Sizemore, Grady	L-L	6-2	210	8-2-82	.289	.245	.307	158	640	111	185	37	11	22	81	52	7	5	2	132	22	10	.484	.348
Vazquez, Ramon	L-R	5-11	170	8-21-76	.250	.000	.261	12	24	1	6	3	0	0	1	2	0	0	0	3	0	0	.375	.308
2-team (27 Boston)					.212	.250	.203	39	85	7	18	5	0	0	5	5	0	2	0	17	0	0	.271	.256

PITCHING	B-T	HT	WT	DOB	W	L	ERA	G	GS	CG	SV	IP	H	R	ER	HR	BB	SO	AVG	vLH	vRH	K/9	BB/9
Betancourt, Rafael	R-R	6-2	200	4-29-75	4	3	2.79	54	0	0	1	68	57	23	21	5	17	73	.224	.264	.204	9.71	2.26
Cabrera, Fernando	R-R	6-4	225	11-16-81	2	1	1.47	15	0	0	0	31	24	7	5	1	11	29	.212	.196	.224	8.51	3.23
Davis, Jason	R-R	6-6	225	5-8-80	4	2	4.69	11	4	0	0	40	44	22	21	4	20	32	.282	.193	.333	7.14	4.46
Elarton, Scott	R-R	6-8	240	2-23-76	11	9	4.61	31	31	1	0	182	189	100	93	32	48	103	.267	.275	.261	5.10	2.38
Guthrie, Jeremy	R-R	6-1	200	4-8-79	0	0	6.00	1	0	0	0	6	9	4	4	2	2	3	.360	.375	.333	4.50	3.00
Howry, Bob	L-R	6-5	220	8-4-73	7	4	2.47	79	0	0	3	73	49	23	20	4	16	48	.191	.180	.198	5.92	1.97
Lee, Cliff	L-L	6-3	190	8-30-78	18	5	3.79	32	32	1	0	202	194	91	85	22	52	143	.251	.293	.237	6.37	2.32
Miller, Matt	R-R	6-3	215	11-23-71	1	0	1.82	23	0	0	1	30	22	6	6	1	10	23	.212	.194	.221	6.98	3.03
Millwood, Kevin	R-R	6-4	230	12-24-74	9	11	2.86	30	30	1	0	192	182	72	61	20	52	146	.248	.269	.227	6.84	2.44
Rhodes, Arthur	L-L	6-2	210	10-24-69	3	1	2.08	47	0	0	0	43	33	13	10	2	12	43	.206	.286	.155	8.93	2.49
Riske, David	R-R	6-2	180	10-23-76	3	4	3.10	58	0	0	1	73	55	28	25	11	15	48	.208	.213	.204	5.94	1.86
Sabathia, C.C.	L-L	6-7	290	7-21-80	15	10	4.03	31	31	1	0	197	185	92	88	19	62	161	.248	.248	.248	7.37	2.84
Sauerbeck, Scott	R-L	6-3	200	11-9-71	1	0	4.04	58	0	0	0	36	35	18	16	4	16	35	.259	.162	.377	8.83	4.04
Tadano, Kazuhito	R-R	6-0	180	4-25-80	0	0	2.25	1	0	0	0	4	4	1	1	0	0	1	.250	.250	.250	2.25	0.00
Tallet, Brian	L-L	6-7	220	9-21-77	0	0	7.71	2	0	0	0	5	6	4	4	2	3	2	.300	.400	.267	3.86	5.79
Westbrook, Jake	R-R	6-3	200	9-29-77	15	15	4.49	34	34	2	0	211	218	121	105	19	56	119	.265	.275	.255	5.08	2.39
Wickman, Bob	R-R	6-1	240	2-6-69	0	4	2.47	64	0	0	45	62	57	17	17	9	21	41	.247	.243	.250	5.95	3.05

FIELDING

Catcher	PCT	G	PO	A	E	DP	PB
Bard	.983	31	164	10	3	2	3
Martinez	.995	142	904	58	5	6	3

First Base	PCT	G	PO	A	E	DP
Blake	.971	4	28	5	1	4
Broussard	.992	138	1082	60	9	112
Hafner	1.000	1	6	2	0	0
Hernandez	.995	45	339	27	2	28
Liefer	.950	5	17	2	1	2

Second Base	PCT	G	PO	A	E	DP
Belliard	.981	141	257	413	13	95
Cora	1.000	15	24	47	0	11
Hernandez	1.000	4	6	9	0	6
Phillips	1.000	2	5	4	0	2
Vazquez	1.000	8	17	10	0	5

Third Base	PCT	G	PO	A	E	DP
Blake	.929	6	4	9	1	1
Boone	.955	142	81	299	18	20
Hernandez	1.000	21	15	36	0	2

Shortstop	PCT	G	PO	A	E	DP
Cora	.974	24	29	83	3	11
Hernandez	1.000	1	1	1	0	0
Peralta	.970	141	207	413	19	104
Phillips	.750	1	1	2	1	1
Vazquez	1.000	2	2	5	0	1

Outfield	PCT	G	PO	A	E	DP
Blake	.973	138	287	3	8	0
Cora	.000	1	0	0	0	0
Crisp	.985	145	315	3	5	0
Dubois	1.000	7	14	0	0	0
Gerut	1.000	38	58	1	0	0
Gutierrez	1.000	2	1	0	0	0
Hernandez	1.000	6	4	0	0	0
Liefer	1.000	3	4	0	0	0
Ludwick	.957	15	22	0	1	0
Sizemore	.992	155	373	3	3	1

FARM SYSTEM

General Manager: Mark Shapiro. **Director, Player Development:** John Farrell. **Scouting Director:** John Mirabelli.

Class	Farm Team	League	W	L	Pct.	Finish*	Manager(s)	Affiliate Since
AAA	Buffalo (N.Y.) Bisons	International	82	62	.569	**2nd (14)**	Marty Brown	1995
AA	Akron (Ohio) Aeros	Eastern	84	58	.592	**+1st (12)**	Torey Lovullo	1997
High A	Kinston (N.C.) Indians	Carolina	76	64	.543	**4th (8)**	Luis Rivera	1987
Low A	Lake County (Ohio) Captains	South Atlantic	72	66	.522	t-6th (16)	Mike Sarbaugh	2003
SS A	Mahoning Valley (Ohio) Indians	New York-Penn	33	43	.434	10th (14)	Rouglas Odor	1999
Rookie	Burlington (N.C.) Indians	Appalachian	25	43	.368	10th (10)	Sean McNally/Lee May Jr.	1986

*Finish in overall standings (No. of teams in league)/playoff teams in **boldface** +League champion

LARRY GOREN

Grady Sizemore: A breakout season, hitting .289-22-81

RICH ABEL

Stephen Head: A second-round pick, he came out swinging

BUFFALO BISONS

Class AAA

INTERNATIONAL LEAGUE

BATTING	B-T	HT	WT	DOB	AVG	vLH	vRH	G	AB	R	H	2B	3B	HR	RBI	BB	HBP	SH	SF	SO	SB	CS	SLG	OBP
Abad, Andy	L-L	6-1	190	8-25-72	.293	.214	.327	121	423	68	124	29	1	20	85	44	3	0	4	60	3	4	.508	.361
Cardona, Javier	R-R	6-1	210	9-15-75	.340	.333	.341	16	50	5	17	4	0	1	7	3	0	4	0	10	0	0	.480	.377
Cooper, Jason	L-L	6-2	215	12-6-80	.257	.137	.287	73	253	43	65	12	3	14	58	23	2	1	6	76	1	4	.494	.317
Dubois, Jason	R-R	6-5	220	3-26-79	.283	.385	.250	13	53	7	15	3	0	4	10	3	1	0	0	14	1	1	.566	.333
Finegan, Brian	R-R	6-0	190	12-15-81	.333	.000	.364	4	12	1	4	0	0	0	0	0	0	1	0	2	0	0	.333	.333
Francisco, Ben	R-R	6-1	185	10-23-81	.500	.000	.500	4	16	4	8	1	0	0	3	1	0	0	1	3	1	0	.563	.500
Garcia, Danny	R-R	6-1	180	4-12-80	.167	.000	.250	2	6	0	1	0	0	0	0	0	0	0	0	2	0	0	.167	.167
Garko, Ryan	R-R	6-2	225	1-2-81	.303	.236	.329	127	452	75	137	25	3	19	77	44	18	2	4	92	1	3	.498	.384
Gautreau, Jake	L-R	6-0	195	11-14-79	.253	.250	.254	113	427	75	108	30	1	18	57	38	7	2	3	87	2	2	.454	.322
Gerut, Jody	L-L	6-0	190	9-18-77	.438	.273	.486	12	48	12	21	5	0	3	8	6	2	0	0	7	0	0	.729	.518
Gonzalez, Juan	R-R	6-3	220	10-16-69	.286	.429	.214	5	21	1	6	0	0	0	1	0	0	0	0	3	0	0	.286	.286
Gutierrez, Franklin	R-R	6-2	180	2-21-83	.254	.176	.280	19	67	10	17	6	2	0	7	6	1	0	1	13	2	2	.403	.320
Inglett, Joe	L-R	5-9	177	6-29-78	.330	.266	.351	95	327	57	108	20	9	2	40	17	9	10	3	41	13	6	.465	.376
Kinkade, Mike	R-R	6-1	215	5-6-73	.283	.288	.282	128	473	84	134	35	3	16	74	38	30	0	7	82	8	5	.471	.369
Liefer, Jeff	L-R	6-3	210	8-17-74	.321	.291	.332	89	321	59	103	27	2	19	68	35	2	0	3	62	2	1	.595	.388
Ludwick, Ryan	R-L	6-3	210	7-13-78	.191	.232	.174	54	188	27	36	10	2	4	16	17	5	0	3	48	0	1	.330	.272
McCullough, Clayton	L-R	5-10	180	12-27-79	.333	.000	.333	1	3	0	1	1	0	0	1	0	0	0	0	0	0	0	.667	.333
McDonald, Darnell	R-R	5-11	210	11-17-78	.270	.233	.295	26	74	11	20	7	0	1	4	7	2	0	0	19	0	1	.405	.349
Morban, Jose	R-R	6-1	170	10-2-79	.269	.257	.273	43	134	20	36	6	0	4	19	10	0	0	0	39	6	0	.403	.319
Ortega, Jose	R-R	5-11	180	12-29-80	.000	.000	.000	2	1	0	0	0	0	0	0	2	0	0	0	0	0	1	.000	.667
Phillips, Brandon	R-R	5-11	190	6-28-81	.256	.202	.276	112	465	79	119	24	1	15	46	39	10	2	2	90	7	5	.409	.326
Pinckney, Brandon	R-R	5-10	165	4-12-82	.000	.000	.000	3	9	0	0	0	0	0	0	0	0	0	0	0	0	0	.000	.000
Rodriguez, John	L-L	6-0	205	1-20-78	.247	.279	.236	46	170	25	42	13	3	5	23	15	6	1	4	40	5	0	.447	.323
Thrower, Jake	B-R	5-11	180	11-19-75	.261	.238	.273	35	119	12	31	9	0	0	9	3	1	1	2	16	2	2	.336	.280

BATTING	B-T	HT	WT	DOB	AVG	vLH	vRH	G	AB	R	H	2B	3B	HR	RBI	BB	HBP	SH	SF	SO	SB	CS	SLG	OBP
Vazquez, Ramon	L-R	5-11	170	8-21-76	.214	.231	.207	21	84	13	18	3	1	0	4	7	0	1	0	16	1	1	.274	.275
Wathan, Dusty	R-R	6-4	215	8-22-73	.262	.278	.254	83	256	41	67	9	0	14	51	24	14	4	2	51	2	2	.461	.355
Young, Ernie	R-R	6-1	230	7-8-69	.277	.254	.288	114	393	76	109	14	0	20	78	64	12	0	3	115	6	3	.466	.392

PITCHING	B-T	HT	WT	DOB	W	L	ERA	G	GS	CG	SV	IP	H	R	ER	HR	BB	SO	AVG	vLH	vRH	K/9	BB/9
Amaya, Jose	R-R	6-2	205	9-7-81	0	1	14.73	1	1	0	0	4	8	6	6	1	4	1	.421	.429	.417	2.45	9.82
Bere, Jason	R-R	6-3	230	5-26-71	1	1	13.15	3	3	0	0	13	26	20	19	5	5	5	.419	.364	.450	3.46	3.46
Brown, Andrew	R-R	6-6	230	2-17-81	4	2	3.36	49	0	0	4	70	52	28	26	7	19	81	.204	.186	.218	10.46	2.45
Cabrera, Fernando	R-R	6-4	225	11-16-81	6	1	1.23	30	0	0	3	51	36	8	7	3	11	68	.196	.219	.180	11.92	1.93
Carmona, Fausto	R-R	6-4	220	12-7-83	7	4	3.25	13	12	1	0	83	76	32	30	10	15	49	.244	.299	.205	5.31	1.63
Cevette, Dan	L-L	6-4	205	10-19-83	0	1	14.40	1	1	0	0	5	9	8	8	5	2	2	.429	.500	.385	3.60	3.60
Cooper, Chris	L-L	5-11	195	10-31-78	0	0	5.74	12	0	0	0	16	20	11	10	5	3	15	.317	.250	.333	8.62	1.72
Cruceta, Francisco	R-R	6-2	215	7-4-81	6	4	5.19	30	13	1	0	102	123	65	59	16	32	92	.297	.312	.285	8.09	2.81
Davis, Jason	R-R	6-6	225	5-8-80	8	5	4.61	16	16	1	0	96	106	65	49	9	27	77	.283	.270	.296	7.24	2.54
Denham, Dan	R-R	6-0	195	12-24-82	0	2	10.80	3	3	0	0	10	16	13	12	3	8	6	.381	.400	.364	5.40	7.20
Denney, Kyle	R-R	6-2	210	7-27-77	1	1	5.12	9	9	0	0	39	52	22	22	9	10	22	.317	.360	.267	5.12	2.33
Diaz, Jose	R-R	6-0	225	4-13-80	1	2	3.89	20	0	0	2	35	27	19	15	4	26	44	.221	.146	.270	11.42	6.75
Evans, Kyle	R-R	6-3	190	10-10-78	0	1	3.00	1	0	0	0	3	2	3	1	0	2	3	.200	.333	.143	9.00	6.00
Guthrie, Jeremy	R-R	6-1	200	4-8-79	12	10	5.08	25	25	1	0	136	152	88	77	15	49	100	.286	.282	.289	6.60	3.23
Kleine, Victor	L-L	6-4	185	9-12-79	0	0	2.45	6	0	0	0	11	9	3	3	2	7	5	.237	.143	.292	4.09	5.73
Mattison, Kieran	L-R	6-0	205	6-21-80	0	0	27.00	1	0	0	0	1	2	3	3	0	2	2	.400	1.000	.000	18.00	18.00
Miller, Matt	R-R	6-3	215	11-23-71	0	0	0.87	9	0	0	3	10	3	1	1	0	2	15	.088	.067	.105	13.06	1.74
Rayborn, Kenny	R-R	6-4	210	11-22-74	2	0	4.89	17	0	0	2	39	46	25	21	3	12	32	.289	.295	.286	7.45	2.79
Robbins, Jake	R-R	6-4	220	5-23-76	3	5	3.08	49	0	0	23	53	51	19	18	2	25	28	.251	.244	.257	4.78	4.27
Sowers, Jeremy	L-L	6-2	175	5-17-83	1	0	1.59	1	1	0	0	6	7	1	1	0	1	4	.292	.333	.278	6.35	1.59
Stanford, Jason	L-L	6-2	200	1-23-77	0	0	1.29	4	1	0	0	7	7	2	1	0	1	7	.241	.500	.174	9.00	1.29
Stark, Denny	R-R	6-2	210	10-27-74	0	1	9.45	3	1	0	0	7	12	9	7	1	6	7	.400	.385	.412	9.45	8.10
Tadano, Kazuhito	R-R	6-0	180	4-25-80	5	5	4.39	32	8	0	5	96	105	54	47	16	22	86	.277	.265	.286	8.03	2.06
Tallet, Brian	L-L	6-7	220	9-21-77	6	5	4.05	22	17	0	0	98	98	51	44	17	25	61	.260	.287	.252	5.62	2.30
Traber, Billy	L-L	6-5	205	9-18-79	3	7	5.75	19	12	0	0	77	96	59	49	7	30	55	.301	.200	.338	6.46	3.52
Watkins, Steve	R-R	6-4	215	7-19-78	9	2	4.16	31	17	0	0	130	142	72	60	13	34	86	.281	.298	.268	5.97	2.36
Young, Jason	R-R	6-5	215	9-28-79	2	0	5.87	4	4	0	0	23	26	17	15	4	9	21	.283	.333	.227	8.22	3.52
Zerbe, Chad	L-L	6-0	210	4-27-72	5	2	3.62	16	0	0	0	27	33	12	11	3	6	11	.297	.206	.338	3.62	1.98

FIELDING

Catcher	PCT	G	PO	A	E	DP	PB
Cardona	.992	16	114	9	1	1	0
Garko	.993	59	401	20	3	7	7
Kinkade	1.000	2	10	2	0	0	0
McCullough	.000	1	0	0	0	0	0
Wathan	.990	76	460	52	5	9	3

First Base	PCT	G	PO	A	E	DP
Abad	.992	30	237	11	2	21
Garko	.991	66	503	43	5	53
Kinkade	.991	15	109	7	1	6
Liefer	.994	35	299	11	2	18
Wathan	1.000	8	53	9	0	7
Young	.857	2	6	0	1	0

Second Base	PCT	G	PO	A	E	DP
Finegan	1.000	1	4	3	0	0
Gautreau	.968	56	114	162	9	40
Inglett	.970	56	103	155	8	26
Morban	.929	3	7	6	1	4
Ortega	1.000	2	1	6	0	1
Pinckney	1.000	3	7	6	0	3
Thrower	1.000	24	41	67	0	13
Vazquez	.929	3	4	9	1	3

Third Base	PCT	G	PO	A	E	DP
Gautreau	.967	53	43	103	5	10
Kinkade	.912	82	64	142	20	21
Liefer	1.000	2	2	3	0	1
Morban	.913	11	3	18	2	1
Thrower	1.000	3	0	5	0	1
Vazquez	1.000	1	1	2	0	0

Shortstop	PCT	G	PO	A	E	DP
Finegan	1.000	2	5	1	0	1
Inglett	1.000	3	6	8	0	1
Morban	.971	9	12	21	1	5
Phillips	.958	111	151	331	21	55
Thrower	.938	7	11	19	2	1
Vazquez	.963	17	24	54	3	14

Outfield	PCT	G	PO	A	E	DP
Abad	.984	68	120	3	2	0
Cooper	.992	70	118	4	1	0
Dubois	1.000	12	16	1	0	0
Francisco	1.000	4	9	0	0	0
Gerut	.947	8	17	1	1	0
Gonzalez	1.000	4	7	0	0	0
Gutierrez	1.000	19	57	2	0	2
Inglett	.987	33	73	1	1	1
Kinkade	.947	19	36	0	2	0
Liefer	1.000	16	26	0	0	0
Ludwick	.983	54	115	2	2	2
McDonald	1.000	25	48	2	0	2
Morban	.971	20	29	4	1	1
Rodriguez	.989	45	90	2	1	0
Young	.992	52	115	5	1	2

AKRON AEROS — Class AA

EASTERN LEAGUE

BATTING	B-T	HT	WT	DOB	AVG	vLH	vRH	G	AB	R	H	2B	3B	HR	RBI	BB	HBP	SH	SF	SO	SB	CS	SLG	OBP
Aubrey, Michael	L-L	6-0	195	4-15-82	.283	.290	.280	28	106	17	30	5	1	4	20	7	3	0	3	18	1	0	.462	.336
Camacaro, Armando	R-R	5-11	170	4-6-79	.257	.433	.187	34	105	12	27	3	0	3	13	6	4	2	1	25	3	2	.371	.319
Cardona, Javier	R-R	6-1	210	9-15-75	.288	.222	.302	15	52	7	15	3	0	3	13	5	0	1	1	9	0	0	.519	.345
Cooper, Jason	L-L	6-2	215	12-6-80	.254	.131	.306	57	205	41	52	9	2	11	42	30	6	0	4	67	3	2	.478	.359
Crowe, Trevor	B-R	6-0	190	11-17-83	.100	.000	.143	3	10	1	1	0	0	0	0	0	0	0	0	3	0	0	.100	.100
Francisco, Ben	R-R	6-1	185	10-23-81	.307	.299	.310	83	323	45	99	19	7	7	46	24	2	2	1	59	15	4	.474	.357
Gutierrez, Franklin	R-R	6-2	180	2-21-83	.261	.268	.258	95	383	70	100	25	2	11	42	30	7	1	5	77	14	4	.423	.322
Hafner, Travis	L-R	6-3	240	6-3-77	.000	.000	.000	3	9	0	0	0	0	0	0	1	1	0	0	0	0	0	.000	.182
Herrera, Javier	R-R	6-1	200	1-8-81	.226	.202	.235	98	328	45	74	20	0	6	36	18	14	7	0	78	3	3	.341	.294
Larkin, Shaun	L-R	5-9	175	9-7-79	.257	.244	.261	90	331	48	85	24	4	13	55	38	2	3	3	48	0	2	.471	.334
Lunetta, Anthony	R-R	5-9	185	10-9-80	.223	.258	.208	34	103	18	23	3	0	1	10	6	3	0	1	25	1	1	.282	.283
McCullough, Clayton	L-R	5-10	180	12-27-79	.091	.125	.000	4	11	0	1	0	0	0	1	1	0	0	0	5	1	0	.091	.167
Morban, Jose	R-R	6-1	170	10-2-79	.248	.279	.232	65	254	35	63	11	2	9	33	24	1	5	2	79	10	8	.413	.313
Morris, Warren	L-R	5-11	190	1-11-74	.091	.000	.133	5	22	1	2	1	0	0	2	1	0	0	0	4	1	0	.136	.130
Mulhern, Ryan	R-R	6-2	195	11-29-80	.311	.354	.291	67	244	40	76	18	3	15	46	28	3	0	2	64	4	2	.594	.386
Ochoa, Ivan	B-R	5-10	175	12-16-82	.265	.213	.288	126	422	46	112	13	6	2	30	30	12	8	3	81	16	12	.339	.330
Osborn, Pat	R-R	6-4	210	2-27-81	.287	.255	.300	129	478	66	137	18	1	10	63	37	7	2	1	66	14	4	.391	.346
Panther, Nathan	L-L	6-1	180	7-12-81	.275	.273	.277	22	80	13	22	3	1	1	6	10	1	0	0	15	1	1	.375	.363
Sherrill, J.J.	B-R	5-7	190	8-11-80	.250	.105	.317	21	60	8	15	3	2	1	5	6	1	1	2	16	0	2	.417	.319
Snyder, Brad	L-L	6-3	200	5-25-82	.280	.252	.294	75	304	56	85	21	5	16	54	25	6	1	1	94	5	3	.539	.345
Torres, Eider	B-R	5-9	175	1-16-83	.285	.233	.310	108	452	73	129	27	5	6	57	16	11	19	5	66	33	9	.407	.322
Van Every, Jonathan	L-L	6-1	195	11-27-79	.244	.248	.243	118	389	71	95	14	2	27	64	66	7	3	1	155	16	6	.499	.363
Youngbauer, Scott	B-R	6-1	175	1-14-79	.216	.286	.183	41	153	13	33	4	1	5	19	11	2	4	1	40	3	1	.353	.275

PITCHING	B-T	HT	WT	DOB	W	L	ERA	G	GS	CG	SV	IP	H	R	ER	HR	BB	SO	AVG	vLH	vRH	K/9	BB/9
Bay, Bear	R-R	6-3	155	8-7-83	3	3	4.76	8	8	0	0	45	45	24	24	5	13	40	.265	.227	.295	7.94	2.58
Brooks, Jacob	R-R	6-1	175	3-23-78	0	0	5.06	6	0	0	0	5	4	3	3	0	1	2	.211	.286	.167	3.38	1.69
Carmona, Fausto	R-R	6-4	220	12-7-83	6	5	4.07	14	14	0	0	91	100	46	41	7	20	57	.276	.273	.279	5.66	1.99
Cooper, Chris	L-L	5-11	195	10-31-78	4	1	2.08	43	0	0	8	56	50	19	13	3	18	60	.237	.291	.218	9.59	2.88
Denham, Dan	R-R	6-0	195	12-24-82	9	7	3.15	21	21	1	0	140	115	55	49	6	30	108	.222	.223	.222	6.94	1.93
Diaz, Jose	R-R	6-0	225	4-13-80	0	0	0.00	8	0	0	1	16	5	0	0	0	3	19	.100	.087	.111	10.91	1.72
Dittler, Jake	R-R	6-4	220	11-24-82	10	9	3.64	28	27	0	0	173	187	94	70	12	61	107	.270	.261	.278	5.57	3.17
Eisentrager, Dan	R-R	6-3	180	12-30-80	0	0	6.00	1	1	0	0	3	4	3	2	1	1	1	.333	.333	.333	3.00	3.00
Evans, Kyle	R-R	6-3	190	10-10-78	1	1	5.73	7	0	0	0	11	13	7	7	2	6	7	.310	.353	.280	5.73	4.91
Foley, Travis	R-R	6-0	205	3-11-83	6	2	3.86	36	0	0	1	54	53	30	23	5	26	40	.260	.292	.231	6.71	4.36
Gomez, Mariano	L-L	6-6	190	9-12-82	4	3	6.30	18	4	1	0	40	45	35	28	4	20	27	.274	.174	.314	6.08	4.50
Green, Steve	R-R	6-2	200	1-26-78	2	2	3.45	26	0	0	1	44	36	22	17	4	23	45	.221	.257	.191	9.14	4.67
Hanson, Adam	R-R	6-2	195	8-6-81	1	0	8.00	2	0	0	0	9	7	9	8	1	8	2	.200	.286	.143	2.00	8.00
Hernandez, Mike	L-L	6-4	215	4-8-81	0	0	6.23	4	0	0	0	4	4	3	3	1	1	3	.250	.000	.333	6.23	2.08
Kleine, Victor	L-L	6-4	185	9-12-79	1	6	4.40	27	5	0	0	61	63	33	30	6	24	38	.267	.270	.266	5.58	3.52
Knippschild, Ryan	L-L	6-1	195	9-24-82	0	0	0.00	2	0	0	0	3	1	0	0	0	2	1	.111	.000	.200	3.00	6.00
Laffey, Aaron	L-L	6-0	170	4-15-85	1	0	3.60	1	1	0	0	5	8	2	2	0	2	6	.364	.125	.500	10.80	3.60
Lara, Juan	R-L	6-1	200	1-26-81	1	2	4.56	18	0	0	5	24	27	15	12	1	14	16	.290	.350	.274	6.08	5.32
Martin, J.D.	R-R	6-4	170	1-2-83	3	1	2.38	10	10	0	0	57	42	17	15	3	8	63	.201	.216	.190	10.01	1.27
Mastny, Tom	R-R	6-6	220	2-4-81	1	1	2.18	5	3	0	0	21	18	7	5	0	5	18	.225	.190	.263	7.84	2.18
Miller, Matt	R-R	6-3	215	11-23-71	0	0	0.00	1	0	0	0	1	0	0	0	0	0	0	.000	.000	.000	0.00	0.00
Mujica, Edward	R-R	6-4	211	5-10-84	2	1	2.88	27	0	0	10	34	36	11	11	2	5	33	.273	.309	.247	8.65	1.31
Pekarek, Justin	R-L	6-4	195	12-4-80	1	0	0.00	1	1	0	0	5	6	0	0	0	2	2	.333	.000	.400	3.60	3.60
Pennington, Todd	R-R	6-2	220	4-6-80	2	1	4.19	19	0	0	9	19	18	10	9	2	15	21	.243	.262	.219	9.78	6.98
Perez, Rafael	L-L	6-3	184	5-15-82	4	3	1.76	15	8	0	1	67	53	22	13	5	12	46	.215	.133	.241	6.21	1.62
Rhodes, Arthur	L-L	6-2	210	10-24-69	0	0	0.00	1	1	0	0	1	0	0	0	0	0	0	.000	.000	.000	0.00	0.00
Roehl, Scott	R-R	6-1	195	8-19-81	0	1	7.71	2	0	0	0	2	4	2	2	2	1	3	.364	.200	.500	11.57	3.86
Sabathia, C.C.	L-L	6-7	290	7-21-80	0	1	1.00	2	2	0	0	9	4	3	1	0	2	9	.121	.125	.120	9.00	2.00
Shuey, Paul	R-R	6-2	235	9-16-70	0	0	4.50	1	0	0	0	2	2	1	1	0	2	2	.286	.333	.250	9.00	9.00
Slocum, Brian	R-R	6-4	190	3-27-81	7	5	4.40	21	18	1	0	102	98	52	50	9	36	95	.255	.288	.231	8.36	3.17
Sowers, Jeremy	L-L	6-2	175	5-17-83	5	1	2.08	13	13	0	0	82	74	25	19	8	9	70	.241	.186	.254	7.65	0.98
Stanford, Jason	L-L	6-2	200	1-23-77	2	0	2.45	8	0	0	0	15	15	5	4	1	4	13	.273	.333	.261	7.98	2.45
Thompson, Travis	R-R	6-5	225	7-3-77	4	0	1.80	15	0	0	0	25	15	7	5	1	8	16	.174	.143	.205	5.76	2.88
Traber, Billy	L-L	6-5	205	9-18-79	3	2	2.65	5	5	0	0	34	25	11	10	2	5	27	.197	.185	.200	7.15	1.32
Van Dusen, Derrick	L-L	6-2	170	6-6-81	1	0	1.69	4	0	0	0	5	6	1	1	1	2	4	.286	.400	.250	6.75	3.38

FIELDING

Catcher	PCT	G	PO	A	E	DP	PB
Camacaro	.996	34	223	30	1	4	5
Cardona	.972	15	94	12	3	2	3
Herrera	.987	96	653	48	9	4	13
McCullough	1.000	4	32	1	0	1	0

First Base	PCT	G	PO	A	E	DP
Aubrey	.996	25	218	12	1	21
Herrera	.000	1	0	0	0	0
Larkin	.995	59	554	37	3	41
Mulhern	.988	47	395	29	5	28
Youngbauer	.986	16	136	10	2	6

Second Base	PCT	G	PO	A	E	DP
Larkin	.957	6	11	11	1	2
Lunetta	.971	17	25	41	2	10
Morban	.971	20	43	57	3	12
Morris	1.000	3	4	13	0	2
Torres	.973	102	184	313	14	46
Youngbauer	.000	1	0	0	0	0

Third Base	PCT	G	PO	A	E	DP
Larkin	.909	11	2	18	2	0
Lunetta	.000	1	0	0	0	0
Morban	.921	12	8	27	3	2
Osborn	.928	119	75	248	25	16
Youngbauer	.909	6	4	6	1	0

Shortstop	PCT	G	PO	A	E	DP
Lunetta	.896	13	13	30	5	2
Morban	.917	8	10	12	2	4
Ochoa	.970	126	203	375	18	69

Outfield	PCT	G	PO	A	E	DP
Cooper	.990	50	104	0	1	0
Crowe	1.000	3	2	0	0	0
Francisco	.991	70	105	1	1	0
Gutierrez	.995	83	183	2	1	2
Morban	1.000	15	18	0	0	0
Panther	1.000	20	38	1	0	1
Sherrill	.972	18	35	0	1	0
Snyder	.961	68	143	6	6	2
Van Every	.982	106	214	8	4	3

KINSTON INDIANS — High Class A

CAROLINA LEAGUE

BATTING	B-T	HT	WT	DOB	AVG	vLH	vRH	G	AB	R	H	2B	3B	HR	RBI	BB	HBP	SH	SF	SO	SB	CS	SLG	OBP
Barton, Brian	R-R	6-3	187	4-25-82	.274	.288	.257	64	223	42	61	15	6	3	32	34	15	1	0	57	13	8	.435	.404
Brock, Caleb	R-R	5-11	200	3-30-80	.236	.221	.249	87	318	39	75	17	2	6	48	25	7	2	3	55	3	2	.358	.303
Butia, Mike	L-R	6-2	215	11-29-82	.198	.173	.215	35	131	12	26	4	0	2	13	10	2	0	1	33	0	0	.275	.264
Choy Foo, Rodney	B-R	6-1	190	12-12-81	.286	.333	.229	65	238	38	68	15	5	5	31	34	3	2	6	56	7	3	.454	.374
Conroy, Mike	L-L	6-3	210	10-3-82	.241	.246	.237	61	232	33	56	16	2	9	38	24	5	3	1	76	3	2	.444	.324
Cotto, Luis	R-R	6-0	175	7-9-81	.217	.229	.209	64	198	20	43	10	1	1	14	11	2	2	0	39	2	3	.293	.265
De la Cruz, Chris	B-R	6-0	165	5-3-82	.230	.234	.228	77	274	30	63	5	2	0	20	14	1	5	2	42	7	5	.263	.268
Goleski, Ryan	R-R	6-3	225	3-19-82	.212	.218	.207	122	458	59	97	27	0	17	67	39	4	0	6	134	6	4	.382	.276
Head, Stephen	L-L	6-3	220	1-13-84	.286	.276	.296	47	203	31	58	15	0	4	36	8	0	0	2	33	4	0	.419	.310
Kouzmanoff, Kevin	R-R	6-1	200	7-25-81	.339	.351	.329	68	254	47	86	20	4	12	58	24	5	0	4	51	3	1	.591	.401
Larkin, Shaun	L-R	5-9	175	9-7-79	.284	.282	.286	31	116	16	33	5	3	2	17	21	2	0	1	21	3	0	.431	.400
Lunetta, Anthony	R-R	5-9	185	10-9-80	.301	.420	.189	32	103	20	31	9	0	3	14	15	4	4	3	13	2	3	.476	.400
Matulich, Mario	R-R	6-3	225	9-22-82	.138	.059	.250	8	29	3	4	2	0	1	5	1	0	0	0	10	0	1	.310	.167
McCullough, Clayton	L-R	5-10	180	12-27-79	.000	.000	.000	2	5	1	0	0	0	0	0	3	0	0	0	4	0	0	.000	.375
Mulhern, Ryan	R-R	6-2	195	11-29-80	.321	.320	.321	45	159	32	51	11	0	17	48	19	3	0	4	50	2	2	.711	.395
Panther, Nathan	L-L	6-1	180	7-12-81	.246	.230	.257	102	370	60	91	14	3	12	41	57	4	1	4	73	11	5	.397	.349
Pinckney, Brandon	R-R	5-10	165	4-12-82	.260	.286	.236	87	319	39	83	19	2	2	26	23	1	3	4	31	4	2	.351	.308
Reyes, Argenis	B-R	5-10	165	9-25-82	.257	.200	.326	52	202	23	52	4	1	1	13	8	1	5	1	38	8	3	.302	.288
Rojas, Ricardo	R-R	6-0	178	2-3-83	.217	.214	.220	35	92	10	20	5	1	1	6	3	0	3	0	28	5	1	.326	.242
Schilling, Micah	L-R	5-11	185	12-27-82	.241	.213	.252	67	220	27	53	9	0	4	24	30	1	0	0	62	1	2	.336	.335
Sherrill, J.J.	B-R	5-7	190	8-11-80	.143	.000	.200	2	7	0	1	0	0	0	0	2	0	0	0	3	0	1	.143	.333
Snyder, Brad	L-L	6-3	200	5-25-82	.278	.235	.305	58	209	36	58	10	2	6	28	24	6	0	2	64	12	1	.431	.365
Wallace, David	R-R	6-4	230	10-17-79	.193	.193	.193	96	311	38	60	18	0	10	29	47	13	2	2	102	3	2	.347	.322

PITCHING	B-T	HT	WT	DOB	W	L	ERA	G	GS	CG	SV	IP	H	R	ER	HR	BB	SO	AVG	vLH	vRH	K/9	BB/9
Bay, Bear	R-R	6-3	155	8-7-83	6	5	3.38	15	15	1	0	85	82	35	32	14	15	85	.254	.226	.271	8.96	1.58
Collins, Kyle	R-R	6-1	165	8-17-81	3	4	4.03	21	0	0	2	29	23	15	13	1	20	24	.213	.255	.175	7.45	6.21

PITCHING	B-T	HT	WT	DOB	W	L	ERA	G	GS	CG	SV	IP	H	R	ER	HR	BB	SO	AVG	vLH	vRH	K/9	BB/9
Davis, Matt	R-R	6-2	205	11-19-81	5	6	5.55	44	0	0	1	73	91	55	45	13	33	61	.304	.319	.294	7.52	4.07
Douglas, Shea	L-L	6-1	200	2-3-81	1	2	9.56	12	0	0	0	16	24	19	17	2	7	16	.338	.406	.282	9.00	3.94
Eisentrager, Dan	R-R	6-3	180	12-30-80	2	2	5.75	25	0	0	0	52	63	33	33	6	17	32	.300	.250	.336	5.57	2.96
Gomez, Mariano	L-L	6-6	190	9-12-82	2	1	2.83	17	1	0	1	35	28	13	11	1	17	30	.220	.233	.214	7.71	4.37
Lara, Juan	R-L	6-1	200	1-26-81	0	1	4.04	26	0	0	0	42	40	22	19	4	15	46	.244	.291	.220	9.78	3.19
Lubrano, Paul	L-L	6-1	170	12-19-81	2	0	0.00	3	0	0	0	3	4	0	0	0	0	0	.364	.250	.429	0.00	0.00
Mastny, Tom	R-R	6-6	220	2-4-81	7	3	2.35	29	11	0	2	88	78	28	23	4	26	94	.237	.250	.228	9.61	2.66
Mattison, Kieran	L-R	6-0	205	6-21-80	1	0	2.25	5	0	0	1	8	8	2	2	0	5	6	.276	.333	.235	6.75	5.63
Miller, Adam	R-R	6-4	175	11-26-84	2	4	4.83	12	12	0	0	60	76	43	32	5	17	45	.318	.327	.310	6.79	2.56
Mujica, Edward	R-R	6-4	211	5-10-84	1	0	2.08	25	0	0	14	26	17	6	6	3	2	32	.183	.176	.186	11.08	0.69
Niesel, Chris	R-R	5-11	195	11-18-82	1	1	4.57	10	2	0	1	22	23	14	11	2	11	18	.264	.244	.283	7.48	4.57
Pekarek, Justin	R-L	6-4	195	12-4-80	2	0	4.84	5	4	0	0	22	25	13	12	2	5	21	.281	.259	.290	8.46	2.01
Pennington, Todd	R-R	6-2	220	4-6-80	0	0	3.20	25	0	0	5	25	22	12	9	3	21	28	.229	.190	.259	9.95	7.46
Perez, Rafael	L-L	6-3	184	5-15-82	8	5	3.36	14	14	0	0	78	54	33	29	6	32	48	.194	.216	.185	5.56	3.71
Pesco, Nick	R-R	6-6	195	9-17-83	11	10	3.82	27	26	0	0	153	168	77	65	15	39	101	.281	.285	.277	5.93	2.29
Roehl, Scott	R-R	6-1	195	8-19-81	2	0	1.04	15	10	0	0	61	41	9	7	1	16	57	.190	.187	.193	8.46	2.37
Sipp, Tony	L-L	6-0	185	7-12-83	2	2	2.66	22	5	0	2	47	34	19	14	4	23	59	.205	.140	.239	11.22	4.37
Smith, Sean	R-R	6-4	195	10-13-83	5	8	3.60	29	23	0	2	142	123	63	57	15	71	120	.237	.251	.224	7.59	4.49
Soto, Jesus	R-R	5-11	170	8-26-80	0	0	0.00	1	0	0	0	2	1	0	0	0	0	4	.125	.000	.200	15.43	0.00
Sowers, Jeremy	L-L	6-2	175	5-17-83	8	3	2.78	13	13	0	0	71	60	25	22	5	19	75	.223	.173	.242	9.46	2.40
Traber, Billy	L-L	6-5	205	9-18-79	2	2	4.98	4	4	0	0	22	19	12	12	2	6	13	.241	.238	.241	5.40	2.49
Warden, Jim Ed	R-R	6-7	195	5-7-79	3	5	3.72	46	0	0	4	68	68	38	28	8	32	72	.266	.296	.247	9.58	4.26

FIELDING

Catcher	PCT	G	PO	A	E	DP	PB
Brock	1.000	43	333	29	0	3	7
McCullough	1.000	2	14	1	0	0	0
Wallace	.988	95	737	76	10	8	14

First Base	PCT	G	PO	A	E	DP
Brock	.991	23	191	18	2	14
Choy Foo	.993	18	138	8	1	14
Head	.994	43	329	27	2	42
Larkin	.969	13	111	13	4	12
Lunetta	.980	6	47	2	1	4
Matulich	1.000	6	46	1	0	4
Mulhern	.987	34	292	21	4	27

Second Base	PCT	G	PO	A	E	DP
Choy Foo	1.000	2	3	5	0	2
Cotto	.957	10	14	31	2	7
De la Cruz	.923	14	21	39	5	13
Lunetta	.983	12	29	28	1	10
Pinckney	1.000	13	29	36	0	8
Reyes	.989	39	72	109	2	25
Schilling	.965	59	116	156	10	32

Third Base	PCT	G	PO	A	E	DP
Choy Foo	.963	31	17	61	3	3
Cotto	.949	36	23	71	5	9
Kouzmanoff	.925	56	40	108	12	14
Larkin	.964	7	6	21	1	3
Lunetta	.846	12	5	17	4	1
Reyes	.895	8	7	10	2	1

Shortstop	PCT	G	PO	A	E	DP
Cotto	.954	18	24	38	3	6
De la Cruz	.957	61	76	166	11	34
Pinckney	.954	68	85	162	12	43

Outfield	PCT	G	PO	A	E	DP
Barton	.992	55	120	4	1	1
Brock	1.000	6	13	0	0	0
Butia	.976	26	39	2	1	0
Conroy	.953	44	74	7	4	1
Cotto	1.000	1	4	0	0	0
Goleski	.972	111	197	12	6	3
Panther	.983	98	167	8	3	1
Reyes	1.000	6	17	0	0	0
Rojas	.985	34	63	2	1	0
Sherrill	1.000	1	3	0	0	0
Snyder	.990	50	99	3	1	1

LAKE COUNTY CAPTAINS — Low Class A

SOUTH ATLANTIC LEAGUE

BATTING	B-T	HT	WT	DOB	AVG	vLH	vRH	G	AB	R	H	2B	3B	HR	RBI	BB	HBP	SH	SF	SO	SB	CS	SLG	OBP
Barton, Brian	R-R	6-3	187	4-25-82	.414	.526	.395	35	133	31	55	14	1	4	32	18	8	0	1	21	7	2	.624	.506
Butia, Mike	L-R	6-2	215	11-29-82	.252	.235	.255	74	298	45	75	18	1	6	48	27	2	0	3	71	1	1	.379	.315
Clem, Chris	R-R	6-0	195	2-3-84	.211	.333	.154	6	19	3	4	0	0	0	0	4	1	0	0	5	0	0	.211	.375
Conroy, Mike	L-L	6-3	210	10-3-82	.333	.500	.267	5	21	2	7	1	0	0	1	2	0	0	0	4	0	0	.381	.391
Constanza, Jose	B-L	5-9	150	9-1-83	.236	.400	.224	23	72	9	17	0	0	0	4	15	0	1	0	13	2	1	.236	.368
Crowe, Trevor	B-R	6-0	190	11-17-83	.258	.258	.259	44	178	18	46	8	2	0	23	18	1	0	2	25	7	5	.326	.327
De la Cruz, Chris	B-R	6-0	165	5-3-82	.262	.100	.294	17	61	5	16	2	0	0	6	5	0	2	1	9	1	2	.295	.313
Finegan, Brian	R-R	6-0	190	12-15-81	.292	.341	.280	115	435	77	127	30	1	9	60	44	16	5	5	76	16	5	.428	.374
Gimenez, Chris	R-R	6-2	190	12-27-82	.234	.230	.235	112	384	54	90	24	1	13	66	48	25	2	4	90	4	3	.404	.354
Holmes, Justin	R-R	5-11	185	11-28-81	.222	.500	.143	3	9	0	2	0	0	0	0	0	0	0	0	3	0	0	.222	.222
Longworth, Chad	R-R	6-3	205	6-11-83	.250	.346	.215	57	196	22	49	8	1	4	25	12	3	0	3	48	3	1	.362	.299
Lunetta, Anthony	R-R	5-9	185	10-9-80	.158	.000	.200	6	19	1	3	1	0	0	2	3	1	0	1	9	0	0	.211	.292
Montgomery, Tim	R-R	6-3	210	6-2-82	.239	.250	.236	53	201	28	48	10	0	7	28	17	2	0	4	77	3	1	.393	.299
Noviskey, Josh	L-R	6-4	230	3-15-83	.247	.161	.261	63	215	37	53	8	3	6	38	35	2	0	2	46	0	2	.395	.354
Obradovich, Mark	B-R	6-2	190	10-26-80	.188	.375	.125	9	32	3	6	1	0	0	1	2	0	1	0	8	0	0	.219	.235
Ortega, Jose	R-R	5-11	180	12-29-80	.220	.240	.215	43	118	15	26	3	0	0	7	17	2	0	1	17	1	2	.246	.326
Pacheco, Fernando	L-L	6-1	205	10-1-84	.235	.242	.234	119	456	47	107	21	4	11	68	36	5	1	4	113	0	0	.371	.295
Reyes, Argenis	B-R	5-10	165	9-25-82	.322	.235	.345	71	317	51	102	14	5	2	36	16	1	3	2	36	16	6	.416	.354
Rojas, Ricardo	R-R	6-0	178	2-3-83	.228	.250	.224	40	145	14	33	7	1	3	17	4	2	5	2	27	6	2	.352	.255
Szabo, Marshall	B-R	5-11	180	2-13-83	.249	.143	.268	105	377	60	94	15	0	6	35	40	11	1	1	54	5	0	.337	.338
Toregas, Wyatt	R-R	5-11	200	12-2-82	.231	.162	.245	104	411	57	95	22	0	5	42	37	6	2	3	76	0	1	.321	.302
Valdes, Juan	B-R	6-0	150	6-22-85	.220	.191	.226	107	373	50	82	13	2	8	47	41	3	6	2	109	12	9	.330	.301
Whitney, Matt	R-R	6-3	200	2-13-84	.242	.096	.276	74	277	38	67	7	0	6	27	34	5	0	3	64	0	3	.332	.332

PITCHING	B-T	HT	WT	DOB	W	L	ERA	G	GS	CG	SV	IP	H	R	ER	HR	BB	SO	AVG	vLH	vRH	K/9	BB/9
Ashabraner, Bo	R-R	6-7	230	2-19-81	0	1	7.04	7	0	0	2	8	8	6	6	1	5	3	.267	.308	.235	3.52	5.87
Bunkelman, Cody	R-R	6-3	200	2-6-85	5	5	4.08	16	16	0	0	79	75	43	36	5	39	61	.251	.293	.230	6.92	4.42
Burton, T.J.	L-R	6-3	185	7-30-83	4	8	3.80	49	1	0	2	71	78	39	30	5	20	42	.278	.301	.268	5.32	2.54
Cevette, Dan	L-L	6-4	205	10-19-83	5	4	2.73	17	17	0	0	82	74	35	25	7	30	85	.239	.245	.238	9.29	3.28
Collins, Kyle	R-R	6-1	165	8-17-81	4	5	2.80	36	0	0	0	45	41	18	14	5	17	39	.243	.220	.252	7.80	3.40
Hanson, Adam	R-R	6-2	195	8-6-81	0	2	7.71	10	0	0	1	23	34	24	20	3	17	18	.358	.385	.348	6.94	6.56
Harris, Josh	R-R	6-0	205	11-23-80	1	0	13.03	9	0	0	4	10	16	14	14	0	15	7	.390	.353	.417	6.52	13.97
Hernandez, Mike	L-L	6-4	215	4-8-81	3	2	1.82	18	0	0	0	35	30	14	7	2	12	35	.233	.206	.242	9.09	3.12
Hoyman, Justin	R-R	6-3	195	4-17-82	2	0	3.00	9	9	0	0	48	44	23	16	3	18	36	.242	.235	.247	6.75	3.38
Knippschild, Ryan	L-L	6-1	195	9-24-82	2	1	4.00	19	1	0	0	36	37	16	16	4	7	36	.262	.241	.268	9.00	1.75
Knox, Matt	R-R	6-4	220	12-29-79	0	0	0.00	2	0	0	1	2	1	0	0	0	0	2	.143	.167	.000	9.00	0.00
Laffey, Aaron	L-L	6-0	170	4-15-85	7	7	3.22	25	23	1	1	142	123	62	51	5	52	69	.239	.258	.236	4.36	3.29
Lofgren, Chuck	L-L	6-3	190	1-29-86	5	5	2.81	18	18	0	0	93	73	31	29	6	43	89	.218	.267	.207	8.61	4.16

PITCHING	B-T	HT	WT	DOB	W	L	ERA	G	GS	CG	SV	IP	H	R	ER	HR	BB	SO	AVG	vLH	vRH	K/9	BB/9
Mattison, Kieran	L-R	6-0	205	6-21-80	1	2	3.52	45	0	0	24	46	45	20	18	5	23	52	.256	.271	.250	10.17	4.50
Niesel, Chris	R-R	5-11	195	11-18-82	5	3	4.48	19	11	0	0	74	82	46	37	8	20	69	.279	.254	.294	8.35	2.42
Pinto, Julio	R-R	6-0	170	10-23-84	0	1	3.86	1	0	0	0	2	4	1	1	0	3	1	.400	.000	.571	3.86	11.57
Rickert, Brandon	R-R	6-3	203	1-23-81	7	1	3.81	35	0	0	2	54	53	30	23	8	20	43	.256	.222	.268	7.12	3.31
Riera, Jorge	R-R	6-0	170	6-17-83	0	1	5.14	2	1	0	0	7	4	4	4	1	5	2	.174	.200	.154	2.57	6.43
Roehl, Scott	R-R	6-1	195	8-19-81	4	3	2.34	24	0	0	0	42	41	15	11	2	7	35	.253	.242	.260	7.44	1.49
Santos, Reid	L-L	6-1	170	8-24-82	5	8	4.94	27	27	0	0	148	168	93	81	17	46	127	.288	.213	.302	7.74	2.80
Schau, Adrian	R-R	6-2	200	1-8-82	4	4	4.89	38	2	1	1	77	84	50	42	6	16	53	.275	.324	.250	6.17	1.86
Sipp, Tony	L-L	6-0	185	7-12-83	4	1	2.22	13	12	0	0	69	47	19	17	5	19	71	.196	.189	.197	9.26	2.48
Soto, Jesus	R-R	5-11	170	8-26-80	4	1	1.98	21	0	0	2	27	23	8	6	2	6	17	.240	.174	.260	5.60	1.98
Stanford, Jason	L-L	6-2	200	1-23-77	0	1	18.00	1	0	0	0	1	3	3	2	0	1	0	.600	1.000	.500	0.00	9.00
Valdez, Luis	R-R	6-4	175	3-11-84	0	0	4.50	1	0	0	0	4	3	2	2	2	0	2	.188	.100	.333	4.50	0.00

FIELDING

Catcher	PCT	G	PO	A	E	DP	PB
Toregas	.989	98	728	103	9	10	28
Noviskey	.967	34	193	12	7	2	3
Obradovich	.989	9	79	9	1	1	2

First Base	PCT	G	PO	A	E	DP
Gimenez	1.000	20	169	5	0	13
Pacheco	.986	119	1162	62	18	123

Second Base	PCT	G	PO	A	E	DP
Clem	.833	3	5	5	2	2
De la Cruz	.944	7	17	17	2	6
Holmes	1.000	1	0	1	0	0
Lunetta	1.000	2	3	6	0	1
Ortega	.988	18	38	46	1	10
Reyes	.966	16	43	43	3	17
Szabo	.984	96	175	268	7	74

Third Base	PCT	G	PO	A	E	DP
Clem	1.000	3	1	2	0	1
De la Cruz	.000	1	0	0	0	0
Gimenez	.923	47	29	103	11	7
Holmes	1.000	2	3	4	0	0
Ortega	.875	10	2	19	3	1
Reyes	.976	29	16	67	2	11
Whitney	.901	55	32	141	19	15

Shortstop	PCT	G	PO	A	E	DP
De la Cruz	1.000	7	11	20	0	7
Finegan	.945	111	196	351	32	72
Lunetta	.818	3	4	5	2	1
Ortega	.935	13	15	43	4	12
Reyes	1.000	8	15	26	0	7
Szabo	1.000	1	0	1	0	0

Outfield	PCT	G	PO	A	E	DP
Barton	.983	31	55	2	1	0
Butia	1.000	57	85	1	0	0
Conroy	.889	4	6	2	1	0
Constanza	.971	23	30	3	1	0
Crowe	1.000	43	92	2	0	0
Gimenez	.981	40	46	6	1	1
Longworth	.976	52	81	2	2	0
Montgomery	.962	22	25	0	1	0
Reyes	1.000	11	18	0	0	0
Rojas	.931	39	65	2	5	0
Valdes	.980	103	190	7	4	1

MAHONING VALLEY SCRAPPERS — Short-Season Class A

NEW YORK-PENN LEAGUE

BATTING	B-T	HT	WT	DOB	AVG	vLH	vRH	G	AB	R	H	2B	3B	HR	RBI	BB	HBP	SH	SF	SO	SB	CS	SLG	OBP
Brown, Jordan	L-L	6-0	210	12-18-83	.253	.231	.258	19	75	15	19	1	0	3	7	3	1	0	0	7	2	1	.387	.291
Casillas, Omar	R-R	6-1	194	9-17-83	.286	.314	.278	43	161	31	46	10	4	1	16	16	1	1	2	40	3	1	.416	.350
Chavez, Jose	B-R	5-9	170	1-2-85	.216	.282	.193	43	148	18	32	2	0	1	8	16	2	3	0	27	4	4	.250	.301
Clark, Boodle	R-R	6-0	200	12-28-83	.206	.238	.200	38	131	20	27	5	1	1	9	16	3	0	0	41	0	1	.282	.307
Clem, Chris	R-R	6-0	195	2-3-84	.224	.240	.221	46	161	23	36	9	0	3	17	24	4	1	1	26	2	0	.335	.337
Constanza, Jose	B-L	5-9	150	9-1-83	.263	.211	.277	64	270	30	71	5	5	0	20	28	4	1	1	39	24	6	.319	.340
Crowe, Trevor	B-R	6-0	190	11-17-83	.255	.300	.244	12	51	9	13	2	1	1	6	6	1	0	0	8	4	3	.392	.345
Cumberbatch, Cirilo	B-R	6-2	176	7-11-86	.260	.231	.267	45	146	21	38	2	0	3	21	13	3	0	2	41	5	2	.336	.329
De Leon, Evandy	R-R	6-0	175	6-29-83	.260	.258	.261	45	146	28	38	4	1	7	30	28	5	3	2	37	13	4	.445	.392
Fornasiere, Matt	L-R	6-1	190	11-19-83	.256	.200	.273	67	238	37	61	15	1	1	28	48	6	2	3	50	5	0	.340	.390
Garcia, Julio	B-R	5-11	170	10-18-84	.250	.250	.250	6	20	5	5	1	0	0	4	3	0	0	0	6	0	1	.300	.348
Head, Stephen	L-L	6-3	220	1-13-84	.432	.500	.424	10	37	11	16	4	0	6	14	8	0	0	0	5	0	0	1.027	.533
Hiser, P.J.	R-R	6-1	195	8-18-81	.263	.269	.260	25	99	14	26	5	3	6	18	6	1	0	0	33	1	0	.556	.311
Kouzmanoff, Kevin	R-R	6-1	200	7-25-81	.143	.000	.200	3	7	0	1	0	0	0	0	1	0	0	0	2	0	0	.143	.250
Longworth, Chad	R-R	6-3	205	6-11-83	.234	.185	.254	25	94	8	22	4	1	0	14	6	2	1	2	19	5	3	.298	.288
Lytle, Andy	R-R	6-1	165	9-15-82	.257	.311	.242	56	210	20	54	6	2	0	18	16	0	3	1	33	6	6	.305	.308
Mortensen, Trevor	R-R	5-10	190	2-12-83	.262	.250	.265	50	172	22	45	5	0	2	19	16	2	4	1	36	8	1	.326	.330
Peterson, Derrick	R-R	6-3	190	5-23-82	.204	.222	.199	60	201	19	41	12	1	2	31	33	1	2	0	36	7	2	.303	.319
Reifenberger, David	R-R	6-1	205	8-4-83	.206	.222	.200	12	34	4	7	1	0	0	1	3	0	0	0	11	0	1	.235	.270
Spilman, Ryan	R-R	6-2	180	8-25-84	.000	.000	.000	6	18	0	0	0	0	0	0	2	0	0	0	8	0	0	.000	.100
Thomas, Brent	R-R	6-0	165	2-12-83	.222	.200	.228	20	72	8	16	5	1	0	4	3	2	0	1	25	0	2	.319	.269
Woodson, Mike	R-R	5-10	195	12-11-84	.183	.267	.161	22	71	6	13	0	0	1	7	4	2	4	0	16	1	0	.225	.247

PITCHING	B-T	HT	WT	DOB	W	L	ERA	G	GS	CG	SV	IP	H	R	ER	HR	BB	SO	AVG	vLH	vRH	K/9	BB/9
Amaya, Jose	R-R	6-2	205	9-7-81	2	2	4.19	8	1	0	0	19	22	14	9	2	5	8	.282	.350	.259	3.72	2.33
Cowley, Thomas	L-L	6-3	190	12-30-83	3	3	3.43	21	0	0	2	42	30	19	16	4	20	47	.205	.333	.154	10.07	4.29
Denney, Kyle	R-R	6-2	210	7-27-77	0	0	18.00	1	1	0	0	1	2	2	2	1	1	2	.400	.667	.000	18.00	9.00
Deters, James	R-R	6-3	185	6-4-83	3	4	2.97	14	14	0	0	70	73	37	23	1	17	49	.264	.205	.291	6.33	2.20
Dixon, Kevin	R-R	6-3	225	12-16-83	3	6	4.53	14	14	0	0	58	66	34	29	6	11	31	.287	.319	.273	4.84	1.72
Douglas, Shea	L-L	6-1	200	2-3-81	1	2	6.94	6	0	0	0	12	10	11	9	2	3	14	.213	.231	.206	10.80	2.31
Edell, Ryan	L-L	6-1	195	7-6-83	3	4	2.95	14	11	0	0	64	65	26	21	5	18	62	.265	.255	.268	8.72	2.53
Haynes, Matt	L-R	6-4	200	4-18-83	1	2	5.77	18	0	0	2	39	39	27	25	7	21	47	.253	.333	.223	10.85	4.85
Hiraldo, Nelson	R-R	5-11	175	9-17-83	1	1	12.88	18	0	0	0	22	28	32	31	8	16	15	.308	.400	.273	6.23	6.65
Jecmen, Mark	R-R	6-8	235	2-16-83	1	2	3.35	23	0	0	1	48	36	27	18	1	28	40	.207	.250	.184	7.45	5.21
Kite, Josh	L-L	6-2	190	3-2-82	1	1	7.59	9	0	0	1	11	18	17	9	0	9	14	.360	.308	.378	11.81	7.59
Knippschild, Ryan	L-L	6-1	195	9-24-82	0	0	4.50	1	0	0	0	4	3	2	2	0	0	5	.214	.000	.333	11.25	0.00
Knox, Matt	R-R	6-4	220	12-29-79	0	0	3.00	5	0	0	0	6	6	2	2	0	0	4	.261	.500	.176	6.00	0.00
Lewis, Jensen	R-R	6-3	185	5-16-84	4	2	3.20	13	11	0	0	59	58	24	21	6	11	59	.253	.247	.256	9.00	1.68
Lewis, Scott	B-L	6-0	185	9-26-83	0	1	4.60	7	6	0	0	16	13	8	8	2	6	24	.224	.083	.261	13.79	3.45
Loberg, Matt	R-R	6-3	220	8-31-82	0	4	2.29	22	0	0	7	35	32	16	9	2	8	16	.244	.265	.232	4.08	2.04
Miller, Adam	R-R	6-4	175	11-26-84	0	0	5.06	3	3	0	0	11	17	6	6	0	4	6	.405	.421	.391	5.06	3.38
Miller, Matt	R-R	6-3	215	11-23-71	0	0	54.00	1	1	0	0	1	5	4	4	0	0	1	.714	.667	.750	13.50	0.00
Ness, Joe	R-R	6-5	230	11-4-83	4	2	1.67	14	10	0	0	59	52	15	11	0	19	68	.234	.198	.255	10.31	2.88
Pekarek, Justin	R-L	6-4	195	12-4-80	2	1	1.50	9	2	0	0	30	26	8	5	0	10	43	.232	.148	.259	12.90	3.00
Roddy, Dustin	R-R	6-2	195	11-10-82	3	3	2.70	25	0	0	6	37	35	22	11	4	9	43	.250	.204	.275	10.55	2.21
Stanford, Jason	L-L	6-2	200	1-23-77	0	0	0.00	2	2	0	0	2	1	0	0	0	2	1	.143	1.000	.000	5.40	10.80
Vargas, Albert	R-R	6-0	175	10-19-84	1	3	4.43	10	0	0	0	20	26	11	10	3	6	13	.317	.136	.383	5.75	2.66
Woodson, Mike	R-R	5-10	195	12-11-84	0	0	9.00	2	0	0	0	2	2	4	2	0	1	1	.250	.500	.167	4.50	4.50
Zerbe, Chad	L-L	6-0	210	4-27-72	0	0	0.00	1	0	0	0	1	1	0	0	0	0	0	.250	.000	.333	0.00	0.00

GAMES BY POSITION: C—Casillas 41, Reifenberger 12, Spilman 6, Woodson 22. **1B**—Brown 3, Clark 30, Clem 1, Head 7, Hiser 19, Lytle 11, Peterson 7. **2B**—Clem 18, Fornasiere 40, Garcia 6, Lytle 13. **3B**—Chavez 1, Clem 20, Kouzmanoff 3, Lytle 5, Peterson 51. **SS**—Chavez 42, Clem 1, Fornasiere 18, Lytle 17. **OF**—Brown 15, Clark 1, Clem 1, Constanza 64, Crowe 12, Cumberbatch 21, De Leon 45, Longworth 24, Mortensen 40, Thomas 20.

BURLINGTON INDIANS — Rookie

APPALACHIAN LEAGUE

BATTING	B-T	HT	WT	DOB	AVG	vLH	vRH	G	AB	R	H	2B	3B	HR	RBI	BB	HBP	SH	SF	SO	SB	CS	SLG	OBP
Ard, Alfred	R-R	6-0	185	8-3-82	.228	.250	.218	50	162	25	37	4	4	1	17	15	5	0	0	38	10	2	.321	.313
Arnal, Cristo	R-R	6-0	177	9-17-85	.223	.320	.178	43	157	21	35	2	1	0	13	14	1	1	3	30	7	0	.248	.286
Chavez, Jose	B-R	5-9	170	1-2-85	.137	.133	.139	13	51	4	7	2	0	0	6	3	0	0	1	13	0	0	.176	.182
Clark, Boodle	R-R	6-0	200	12-28-83	.250	.233	.258	25	92	14	23	4	0	2	14	10	1	1	0	24	0	0	.359	.330
De Leon, Evandy	R-R	6-0	175	6-29-83	.194	.235	.180	18	67	14	13	3	0	4	9	9	2	0	0	18	4	0	.418	.308
Denham, Jason	L-L	6-0	170	5-1-86	.197	.245	.173	46	147	13	29	4	1	0	13	22	0	1	2	43	5	0	.238	.298
Drennen, John	L-L	5-11	185	8-26-86	.238	.218	.248	51	168	24	40	7	1	8	29	18	5	1	3	37	6	3	.435	.325
Garcia, Julio	B-R	5-11	170	10-18-84	.190	.176	.200	18	42	5	8	1	0	0	2	4	1	0	1	12	1	0	.214	.271
Hiser, P.J.	R-R	6-1	195	8-18-81	.326	.354	.310	38	135	29	44	15	2	11	36	18	1	0	1	43	1	2	.711	.406
Holmes, Justin	R-R	5-11	185	11-28-81	.159	.200	.147	17	44	4	7	1	0	0	5	7	2	0	0	11	0	0	.182	.302
Infante, Jansy	B-R	6-1	170	2-27-86	.187	.160	.202	37	139	19	26	2	1	0	8	11	0	0	0	27	6	2	.216	.247
Petrucci, Nicholas	R-R	6-2	195	7-16-85	.246	.258	.241	58	211	28	52	8	1	8	29	17	3	1	2	69	3	2	.408	.309
Roberts, Josh	L-R	6-1	176	7-17-86	.212	.214	.211	50	156	18	33	7	2	2	15	20	5	0	1	44	3	1	.321	.319
Romero, Niuman	B-R	6-0	160	1-24-85	.275	.302	.265	63	218	33	60	12	2	2	29	31	4	3	1	45	6	6	.376	.374
Spilman, Ryan	R-R	6-2	180	8-25-84	.195	.176	.203	37	113	7	22	4	0	1	10	14	0	2	0	27	0	0	.257	.283
Tavarez, Aregenis	B-R	5-11	165	2-19-84	.200	.267	.180	21	65	10	13	3	0	0	2	7	0	1	0	13	4	0	.246	.278
Vasquez, Enrique	R-R	6-0	195	3-14-84	.204	.167	.228	31	93	7	19	3	0	2	10	7	1	0	0	23	0	0	.301	.267
Weglarz, Nick	L-L	6-3	215	12-16-87	.231	.185	.258	41	147	22	34	11	0	2	13	17	1	0	1	42	2	1	.347	.313

PITCHING	B-T	HT	WT	DOB	W	L	ERA	G	GS	CG	SV	IP	H	R	ER	HR	BB	SO	AVG	vLH	vRH	K/9	BB/9
Cruz, Wilander	R-R	6-3	185	12-15-84	2	1	4.88	15	0	0	0	24	24	17	13	3	11	22	.253	.211	.281	8.25	4.13
Finocchi, Michael	R-R	6-0	195	4-28-85	0	2	3.14	18	0	0	1	29	32	15	10	0	5	22	.274	.243	.288	6.91	1.57
Hanson, Adam	R-R	6-2	195	8-6-81	1	2	4.94	5	2	0	0	24	32	16	13	2	3	16	.327	.281	.348	6.08	1.14
Harris, Josh	R-R	6-3	220	10-23-77	1	4	10.80	16	0	0	0	20	36	32	24	5	13	15	.367	.417	.351	6.75	5.85
Hicks, Chris	L-L	5-11	165	11-28-85	2	4	4.02	13	13	0	0	54	46	31	24	3	21	61	.234	.182	.244	10.23	3.52
Kite, Josh	L-L	6-2	190	3-2-82	0	0	0.82	9	0	0	0	11	8	2	1	0	7	11	.205	.182	.214	9.00	5.73
Lubrano, Paul	L-L	6-1	170	12-19-81	2	1	1.91	16	1	0	1	33	19	8	7	2	6	31	.171	.294	.149	8.45	1.64
Mercedes, Gerson	R-R	6-1	170	7-8-81	2	2	3.13	16	0	0	2	37	35	14	13	2	4	38	.243	.176	.280	9.16	0.96
Montero, Joanniel	R-R	6-5	191	2-2-86	0	3	12.86	4	4	0	0	14	26	22	20	5	8	5	.419	.440	.405	3.21	5.14
Morffe, Edgar	R-R	5-11	176	7-5-83	0	0	19.80	4	0	0	0	5	10	11	11	3	4	6	.385	.125	.500	10.80	7.20
Pinto, Julio	R-R	6-0	170	10-23-84	3	0	2.52	16	0	0	0	39	27	12	11	2	7	38	.193	.256	.165	8.69	1.60
Pry, Jeff	R-R	6-4	205	11-12-84	1	1	5.87	15	0	0	0	23	28	15	15	4	14	24	.295	.379	.258	9.39	5.48
Riera, Jorge	R-R	6-0	170	6-17-83	3	2	3.10	13	6	0	0	52	45	21	18	2	19	38	.237	.259	.227	6.54	3.27
Schutt, Jason	R-R	6-3	225	12-11-83	2	7	6.53	12	11	1	0	51	73	45	37	11	9	27	.335	.326	.341	4.76	1.59
Smith, Carlton	L-R	6-1	200	1-23-86	0	2	4.76	9	9	0	0	28	30	16	15	3	5	25	.261	.256	.263	7.94	1.59
Soto, Jesus	R-R	5-11	170	8-26-80	0	2	3.00	6	0	0	0	6	6	4	2	2	2	8	.261	.400	.222	12.00	3.00
Storey, Mike	B-L	6-3	189	9-4-85	1	4	6.41	13	9	0	1	39	47	36	28	2	18	30	.296	.200	.309	6.86	4.12
Valdez, Luis	R-R	6-4	175	3-11-84	3	6	3.54	13	13	1	0	61	64	31	24	8	12	59	.271	.342	.239	8.70	1.77
Vargas, Albert	R-R	6-0	175	10-19-84	2	0	1.42	10	0	0	0	19	15	5	3	0	4	16	.217	.300	.184	7.58	1.89

GAMES BY POSITION: C—Roberts 7, Spilman 36, Tavarez 12, Vasquez 24. **1B**—Clark 21, Hiser 34, Holmes 1, Roberts 15. **2B**—Arnal 41, Garcia 8, Holmes 6, Romero 16. **3B**—Holmes 7, Petrucci 49, Romero 15. **SS**—Chavez 8, Garcia 8, Holmes 1, Infante 33, Romero 22. **OF**—Ard 46, De Leon 15, Denham 43, Drennen 50, Roberts 15, Tavarez 1, Weglarz 40.

COLORADO ROCKIES

BY TRACY RINGOLSBY

Todd Helton has yet to play a truly meaningful September game in his big-league career. But he sees hope in Colorado. He feels that the struggles the Rockies dealt with in 2005 were a down payment on the reward of eventual success.

"Better be," Helton said. "That's the reason we put up with this year."

The 2005 season was a struggle, but showed promise. It ended with the Rockies battling on the final weekend to avoid the worst record in franchise history, but then a couple of months earlier there were those who suggested they were destined to compile the worst record in baseball history.

From a nightmarish beginning—they were 36-67 on the morning of July 31 and had lost 40 of 50 games on the road—the Rockies found respect in the final two months of 2005. They also found hope because they stood by the commitment of a year earlier, broke in the bulk of a new lineup and never wavered in allowing the players to grow together in anticipation of a long-term payoff.

"Nothing bodes confidence like success," manager Clint Hurdle said. "Once you get a feel for it, it reaffirms how much you like it."

The payoff should begin in 2006.

"We are moving forward with a large group of players rather than having five or six guys we brought in to bridge a gap for a year," Hurdle said. "We had our first taste of the process. The first two months it was a very bitter taste. We took a lot of ridicule. But we hung together. We are not out of the woods yet, but we've taken steps forward."

Ten rookies were given legitimate chances to make an impact in 2005, and only one, catcher J.D. Closser, struggled to meet the challenge.

Meanwhile, the Rockies look at 2006 with every reason to feel they will be better because of the return of shortstop Clint Barmes, third baseman Garrett Atkins, center fielder Cory Sullivan and right fielder Brad Hawpe having shown they can step into the lineup with Helton, and left fielder Matt Holliday and second baseman Luis Gonzalez, who both finished just their second seasons.

"They are not kids, and they are not inexperienced anymore," said Helton. "They have to go into the off-season knowing they can compete here."

The pitching staff benefited from a solid effort by rookie starter Jeff Francis along with the mid-season emergence of David Cortes. And then there was the return of Aaron Cook for the final two months, recovered from blood clots in his lungs that knocked him out for a year, and showing that he is ready to be a dominant top-of-the-rotation starter, along with Jason Jennings.

While Francis led major-league rookies with 14 wins, and Atkins drove in more runs than any other rookie in 2005, the only player on the team who could be credited with having a career-type year would be reliever Brian Fuentes, who assumed the closer role in mid-May and was among the most consistent late-inning men in baseball from that point on.

For the first time in franchise history, the Rockies had neither a 25-home run nor a 100-RBI season. Holliday and Atkins, however, both surpassed the former club record for RBI in September of 28 that was set by Dante Bichette, and Helton did rebound from the worst first half in his career to finish third in the NL batting race.

"I only see us getting better," Jennings said. "We've been the best team in our division for almost four months. And nobody had one of those career years, where you don't know if they can match it next year. We had a lot of guys have solid years, years they can build off."

And the Rockies can see more help on the way. There is another wave of talent coming, though the core of that group was at Class A Modesto in 2005. They did help the Nuts into the California League playoffs. Double-A Tulsa, meanwhile, advanced to the Texas League playoffs for the second year in a row.

Triple-A Colorado Springs (65-78) was the only full-season team to have a losing record.

PLAYERS OF THE YEAR

MAJOR LEAGUE: Brian Fuentes, lhp

Fuentes missed 62 games in 2004 with a strained back muscle, which was a major cause for the implosion of the Rockies bullpen. Primarily a setup man prior to 2005, Fuentes blossomed into the closer role and finished with 31 saves and a 2.91 ERA. He allowed just 59 hits in 74 innings.

MINOR LEAGUE: Joe Koshansky, 1b

TONY FARLOW

Koshansky has excellent raw power and led the Rockies organization in homers (38) and RBIs (115) in 2005. While Koshansky spent the majority of the season at low Class A Asheville, the Virginia college product held his own at Double-A Tulsa, hitting .267 in 45 at-bats in August.

ORGANIZATION LEADERS

BATTING		
***AVG**	Wimberly, Corey, Casper	.381
R	Miller, Tony, Tulsa	102
H	Miller, Matt, Asheville/Modesto	170
TB	Koshansky, Joe, Asheville/Tulsa	294
	Miller, Matt, Asheville/Modesto	294
2B	Spilborghs, Ryan, Colorado Springs/Tulsa	46
3B	Three tied at	8
HR	Koshansky, Joe, Asheville/Tulsa	38
RBI	Koshansky, Joe, Asheville/Tulsa	115
BB	Miller, Tony, Tulsa	87
SO	Davies, Michael, Modesto	145
SB	Wimberly, Corey, Casper	36
***OBP**	Wimberly, Corey, Casper	.427
***SLG**	Gaetti, Joe, Modesto	.605
PITCHING		
W	Nin, Sandy, Modesto/Tulsa	14
L	Hampson, Justin, Colorado Springs	13
#ERA	Ulloa, Enmanuel, Tulsa	2.38
G	Miller, Jim, Modesto/Tulsa	64
CG	Asahina, Jon, Tulsa	4
	Nin, Sandy, Modesto/Tulsa	4
SV	Miller, Jim, Modesto/Tulsa	34
IP	Asahina, Jon, Tulsa	170
BB	Morillo, Juan, Asheville/Modesto	78
SO	Morillo, Juan, Asheville/Modesto	144

*Minimum 250 at-bats. #Minimum 75 innings.

COLORADO ROCKIES

Manager: Clint Hurdle.

2005 Record: 67-95, .414 (5th, NL West).

BATTING	B-T	HT	WT	DOB	AVG	vLH	vRH	G	AB	R	H	2B	3B	HR	RBI	BB	HBP	SH	SF	SO	SB	CS	SLG	OBP
Amezaga, Alfredo	B-R	5-10	165	1-6-78	.333	.000	1.000	2	3	1	1	0	0	0	0	0	0	0	0	0	0	0	.333	.333
Ardoin, Danny	R-R	6-0	220	7-8-74	.229	.277	.215	80	210	28	48	10	0	6	22	20	9	7	2	69	1	1	.362	.320
Atkins, Garrett	R-R	6-3	210	12-12-79	.287	.291	.286	138	519	62	149	31	1	13	89	45	5	0	4	72	0	2	.426	.347
Baker, Jeff	R-R	6-2	210	6-21-81	.211	.278	.150	12	38	6	8	4	0	1	4	5	0	0	0	12	0	0	.395	.302
Barmes, Clint	R-R	6-0	190	3-6-79	.289	.289	.288	81	350	55	101	19	1	10	46	16	6	4	1	36	6	4	.434	.330
Bigbie, Larry	L-R	6-4	210	11-4-77	.212	.143	.231	23	66	5	14	1	1	0	2	3	1	0	0	18	2	0	.258	.257
Byrnes, Eric	R-R	6-2	210	2-16-76	.189	.067	.237	15	53	2	10	2	0	0	5	7	0	0	0	11	2	0	.226	.283
Closser, J.D.	B-R	5-10	195	1-15-80	.219	.270	.210	92	237	31	52	12	2	7	27	32	1	1	1	48	1	0	.376	.314
Freeman, Choo	R-R	6-2	200	10-20-79	.273	.231	.333	18	22	6	6	1	1	0	0	0	0	0	0	5	0	0	.409	.273
Garabito, Eddy	B-R	5-8	190	12-2-76	.307	.192	.355	42	88	15	27	5	0	1	8	8	3	3	0	12	3	2	.398	.384
Gonzalez, Luis	R-R	5-11	200	6-26-79	.292	.380	.244	128	404	51	118	25	0	9	44	20	6	8	3	63	3	4	.421	.333
Greene, Todd	R-R	5-10	210	5-8-71	.254	.294	.227	38	126	10	32	4	0	7	23	7	1	0	0	21	0	0	.452	.299
Hawpe, Brad	L-L	6-3	205	6-22-79	.262	.250	.264	101	305	38	80	10	3	9	47	43	0	0	3	70	2	2	.403	.350
Helton, Todd	L-L	6-2	210	8-20-73	.320	.245	.353	144	509	92	163	45	2	20	79	106	9	1	1	80	3	0	.534	.445
Holliday, Matt	R-R	6-4	235	1-15-80	.307	.324	.302	125	479	68	147	24	7	19	87	36	7	0	4	79	14	3	.505	.361
Machado, Anderson	L-R	5-11	160	1-25-81	.000	.000	.000	4	10	1	0	0	0	0	2	2	0	0	1	5	0	0	.000	.154
2-team (2 Cincinnati)					.000	.000	.000	6	12	1	0	0	0	0	2	2	0	0	1	6	0	0	.000	.133
Miles, Aaron	B-R	5-7	180	12-15-76	.281	.234	.292	99	324	37	91	12	3	2	28	8	4	10	1	38	4	2	.355	.306
Mohr, Dustan	R-R	6-1	215	6-19-76	.214	.274	.170	98	266	34	57	10	3	17	38	23	2	0	2	94	1	2	.466	.280
Olson, Tim	R-R	6-2	200	8-1-78	.000	.000	.000	3	2	0	0	0	0	0	0	1	0	0	0	2	0	0	.000	.333
Piedra, Jorge	L-L	6-0	200	4-17-79	.313	.500	.309	61	112	19	35	8	1	6	16	10	1	0	1	15	2	1	.563	.371
Quintanilla, Omar	L-R	5-9	190	10-24-81	.219	.067	.239	39	128	16	28	1	1	0	7	9	0	6	0	15	2	1	.242	.270
Relaford, Desi	B-R	5-9	180	9-16-73	.224	.240	.219	73	210	24	47	13	2	1	16	22	4	1	1	42	3	3	.319	.308
Restovich, Michael	R-R	6-4	250	1-3-79	.290	.304	.250	14	31	5	9	2	0	1	3	3	0	0	0	5	0	0	.452	.353
Shealy, Ryan	R-R	6-5	240	8-29-79	.330	.125	.373	36	91	14	30	7	0	2	16	13	0	0	0	22	1	0	.473	.413
Spilborghs, Ryan	R-R	6-1	190	9-5-79	.500	.000	1.000	1	4	0	2	0	0	0	1	0	0	0	0	1	0	0	.500	.500
Sullivan, Cory	L-L	6-0	180	8-20-79	.294	.250	.299	139	378	64	111	15	4	4	30	28	3	10	5	83	12	3	.386	.343
Wilson, Preston	R-R	6-2	215	7-19-74	.258	.280	.249	71	267	39	69	15	1	15	47	25	1	1	2	77	3	2	.491	.322

PITCHING	B-T	HT	WT	DOB	W	L	ERA	G	GS	CG	SV	IP	H	R	ER	HR	BB	SO	AVG	vLH	vRH	K/9	BB/9
Acevedo, Jose	R-R	6-0	220	12-18-77	2	4	6.47	36	5	0	1	64	86	48	46	13	16	31	.321	.346	.295	4.36	2.25
Anderson, Matt	R-R	6-4	200	8-17-76	0	0	12.60	12	0	0	0	10	19	17	14	3	11	4	.404	.611	.276	3.60	9.90
Carvajal, Marcos	R-R	6-4	175	8-19-84	0	2	5.09	39	0	0	0	53	52	30	30	8	21	47	.259	.233	.278	7.98	3.57
Chacon, Shawn	R-R	6-3	220	12-23-77	1	7	4.09	13	12	0	0	73	69	33	33	7	36	39	.260	.241	.280	4.83	4.46
Cook, Aaron	R-R	6-3	205	2-8-79	7	2	3.67	13	13	2	0	83	101	38	34	8	16	24	.301	.317	.281	2.59	1.73
Cortes, David	R-R	5-11	220	10-15-73	2	0	4.10	50	0	0	2	53	50	24	24	9	10	36	.251	.278	.229	6.15	1.71
Day, Zach	R-R	6-4	215	6-15-78	0	1	7.15	5	3	0	0	11	20	11	9	2	7	7	.385	.368	.394	5.56	5.56
2-team (12 Washington)					1	3	6.85	17	8	0	0	47	61	40	36	6	32	23	.314	.330	.300	4.37	6.08
DeJean, Mike	R-R	6-2	220	9-28-70	2	3	3.19	38	0	0	0	37	26	14	13	0	12	35	.195	.246	.153	8.59	2.95
2-team (28 New York)					5	4	4.48	66	0	0	0	62	62	33	31	3	30	52	.255	.252	.257	7.51	4.33
Dohmann, Scott	R-R	6-1	190	2-13-78	2	1	6.10	32	0	0	0	31	33	21	21	6	19	35	.266	.328	.212	10.16	5.52
Esposito, Mike	R-R	6-0	190	9-27-81	0	2	6.75	3	3	0	0	15	21	11	11	3	9	5	.333	.432	.192	3.07	5.52
Francis, Jeff	L-L	6-5	200	1-8-81	14	12	5.68	33	33	0	0	184	228	119	116	26	70	128	.311	.285	.317	6.27	3.43
Fuentes, Brian	L-L	6-4	220	8-9-75	2	5	2.91	78	0	0	31	74	59	25	24	6	34	91	.218	.167	.236	11.02	4.12
Jennings, Jason	L-R	6-2	245	7-17-78	6	9	5.02	20	20	1	0	122	130	73	68	11	62	75	.274	.269	.279	5.53	4.57
Kennedy, Joe	R-L	6-4	245	5-24-79	4	8	7.04	16	16	0	0	92	128	81	72	12	44	52	.334	.294	.343	5.09	4.30
Kim, Byung-Hyun	R-R	5-9	180	1-19-79	5	12	4.86	40	22	0	0	148	156	82	80	17	71	115	.275	.308	.244	6.99	4.32
Kim, Sunny	R-R	6-1	185	9-4-77	5	1	4.22	12	8	1	0	53	56	26	25	7	13	38	.268	.263	.272	6.41	2.19
2-team (12 Washington)					6	3	4.90	24	10	1	0	83	97	46	45	10	21	55	.293	.279	.304	5.99	2.29
Lopez, Aquilino	R-R	6-3	165	4-21-75	0	0	2.25	1	0	0	0	4	3	1	1	0	0	6	.200	.222	.167	13.50	0.00
Lopez, Javier	L-L	6-4	200	7-11-77	0	0	22.50	3	0	0	0	2	7	5	5	0	0	1	.538	.500	.556	4.50	0.00
Miceli, Dan	R-R	6-0	215	9-9-70	1	2	5.89	19	0	0	0	18	19	12	12	1	13	19	.271	.303	.243	9.33	6.38
Neal, Blaine	L-R	6-5	250	4-6-78	1	2	6.14	11	0	0	0	15	20	10	10	2	9	8	.339	.435	.278	4.91	5.52
Seay, Bobby	L-L	6-2	235	6-20-78	0	0	8.49	17	0	0	0	12	18	11	11	3	8	11	.367	.421	.333	8.49	6.17
Simpson, Allan	R-R	6-4	200	8-26-77	0	0	67.50	2	0	0	0	1	3	5	5	0	3	0	.750	.000	.750	0.00	40.50
Speier, Ryan	R-R	6-7	200	7-24-79	2	1	3.65	22	0	0	0	25	26	12	10	0	13	10	.277	.289	.268	3.65	4.74
Tsao, Chin-hui	R-R	6-2	190	6-2-81	1	0	6.55	10	0	0	3	11	16	8	8	3	5	4	.333	.462	.182	3.27	4.09
Williams, Randy	L-L	6-3	195	9-18-75	2	1	5.73	30	0	0	0	22	26	15	14	4	9	19	.289	.234	.349	7.77	3.68
2-team (2 San Diego)					3	1	6.84	32	0	0	0	26	33	21	20	5	13	21	.300	.283	.316	7.18	4.44
Witasick, Jay	R-R	6-4	240	8-28-72	0	4	2.52	32	0	0	0	36	27	11	10	2	12	40	.209	.214	.205	10.09	3.03
Wright, Jamey	R-R	6-6	235	12-24-74	8	16	5.46	34	27	0	0	171	201	119	104	22	81	101	.296	.314	.279	5.31	4.25

FIELDING

Catcher	PCT	G	PO	A	E	DP	PB
Ardoin	.988	80	452	48	6	5	6
Closser	.982	80	410	25	8	1	5
Greene	.975	33	151	7	4	0	3

First Base	PCT	G	PO	A	E	DP
Gonzalez	1.000	10	37	3	0	4
Helton	.996	144	1237	120	5	136
Shealy	1.000	19	155	8	0	8

Second Base	PCT	G	PO	A	E	DP
Garabito	.986	18	33	37	1	12
Gonzalez	1.000	83	121	196	0	40
Miles	.984	79	154	208	6	48
Quintanilla	1.000	6	10	10	0	5
Relaford	.953	11	10	31	2	4

Third Base	PCT	G	PO	A	E	DP
Amezaga	.000	1	0	0	0	0
Atkins	.950	136	78	262	18	23
Baker	.958	10	3	20	1	1
Gonzalez	1.000	12	6	7	0	1
Relaford	.939	21	9	22	2	2

Shortstop	PCT	G	PO	A	E	DP
Barmes	.958	80	138	247	17	62
Garabito	1.000	2	3	5	0	0
Gonzalez	.939	17	28	34	4	13
Machado	.929	4	7	6	1	1
Miles	.000	1	0	0	1	0

Quintanilla	.992	31	41	89	1	16
Relaford	.960	37	45	100	6	16

Outfield	PCT	G	PO	A	E	DP
Bigbie	1.000	15	36	1	0	1
Byrnes	.976	14	39	1	1	1
Freeman	1.000	6	12	2	0	1
Gonzalez	1.000	8	16	0	0	0
Hawpe	.981	89	148	10	3	2
Holliday	.972	123	236	5	7	2
Mohr	.987	76	147	4	2	1
Piedra	1.000	26	27	1	0	0
Relaford	1.000	4	0	1	0	0
Restovich	1.000	8	18	0	0	0
Spilborghs	1.000	1	6	1	0	1
Sullivan	.986	114	211	7	3	2
Wilson	.979	69	140	2	3	0

FARM SYSTEM

General Manager: Dan O'Dowd. **Director, Player Development:** Bill Geivett. **Scouting Director:** Bill Schmidt.

Class	Farm Team	League	W	L	Pct.	Finish*	Manager	Affiliate Since
AAA	Colorado Springs (Colo.) Sky Sox	Pacific Coast	65	78	.455	15th (16)	Marv Foley	1993
AA	Tulsa (Okla.) Drillers	Texas	75	65	.536	**3rd (8)**	Tom Runnells	2003
High A	Modesto (Calif.) Nuts	California	72	67	.518	**5th (10)**	Stu Cole	2005
Low A	Asheville (N.C.) Tourists	South Atlantic	71	67	.514	10th (16)	Joe Mikulik	1994
SS A	Tri-City (Wash.) Dust Devils	Northwest	36	40	.474	5th (8)	Ron Gideon	2001
Rookie	Casper (Wyo.) Rockies	Pioneer	38	38	.500	t-4th (8)	P.J. Carey	2001

*Finish in overall standings (No. of teams in league)/playoff teams in **boldface**

COLORADO SPRINGS SKY SOX — Class AAA

PACIFIC COAST LEAGUE

BATTING	B-T	HT	WT	DOB	AVG	vLH	vRH	G	AB	R	H	2B	3B	HR	RBI	BB	HBP	SH	SF	SO	SB	CS	SLG	OBP
Ardoin, Danny	R-R	6-0	220	7-8-74	.338	.258	.360	44	142	27	48	12	2	6	24	20	6	1	1	38	3	1	.577	.438
Atkins, Garrett	R-R	6-3	210	12-12-79	.333	.444	.250	5	21	4	7	1	0	1	3	2	0	0	0	4	0	0	.524	.391
Baker, Jeff	R-R	6-2	210	6-21-81	.303	.303	.302	61	228	40	69	16	1	10	41	16	1	1	2	44	3	1	.513	.348
Bigbie, Larry	L-R	6-4	210	11-4-77	.375	.000	.600	3	8	4	3	2	1	0	2	2	0	0	0	3	0	0	.875	.500
Buchanan, Brian	R-R	6-4	230	7-21-73	.297	.294	.298	72	259	50	77	17	2	10	41	27	7	0	1	55	4	1	.494	.378
Conway, Dan	R-R	6-2	190	10-13-79	.216	.267	.202	46	134	14	29	6	2	1	18	11	7	1	0	39	1	0	.313	.309
Davis, J.J.	R-R	6-5	250	10-25-78	.224	.286	.208	21	67	12	15	3	0	3	15	7	1	0	3	20	1	1	.403	.295
2-team (51 New Orleans)					.266	.283	.261	72	241	46	64	13	0	15	46	25	4	0	3	73	4	5	.506	.341
Delarosa, Tomas	R-R	5-10	185	1-28-78	.293	.320	.284	89	311	44	91	18	1	6	48	29	1	9	5	39	9	4	.415	.350
Freeman, Choo	R-R	6-2	200	10-20-79	.280	.333	.265	97	354	46	99	10	6	10	59	29	2	1	4	78	4	3	.427	.334
Garabito, Eddy	B-R	5-8	190	12-2-76	.306	.288	.314	67	258	56	79	16	3	8	39	29	2	6	1	34	8	4	.484	.379
Greene, Todd	R-R	5-10	210	5-8-71	.394	.444	.375	11	33	4	13	0	0	3	8	1	0	0	0	3	0	0	.667	.412
Hawpe, Brad	L-L	6-3	205	6-22-79	.464	.385	.533	7	28	7	13	3	0	3	11	6	0	0	0	7	0	0	.893	.559
Helton, Todd	L-L	6-2	210	8-20-73	.600	.600	.000	2	5	1	3	2	0	0	1	1	1	0	0	0	0	0	1.000	.714
Kirby, Brian	L-R	6-1	200	8-3-79	.000	.000	.000	2	2	0	0	0	0	0	0	0	0	0	0	2	0	0	.000	.000
Machado, Anderson	L-R	5-11	160	1-25-81	.159	.333	.118	25	63	6	10	3	1	0	8	16	0	1	1	17	0	1	.238	.325
Matos, Pascual	R-R	6-2	180	12-23-74	.275	.390	.241	56	178	24	49	13	0	4	24	6	1	2	1	43	1	1	.416	.301
Miles, Aaron	B-R	5-7	180	12-15-76	.219	.250	.214	8	32	6	7	0	1	0	1	0	1	1	0	3	1	0	.281	.242
Mohr, Dustan	R-R	6-1	215	6-19-76	.250	.000	.375	3	12	2	3	2	0	1	4	0	0	0	0	4	0	0	.667	.250
Nicholson, Tommy	L-R	5-9	160	8-23-79	.294	.308	.292	32	85	9	25	3	0	0	6	6	0	2	0	18	1	0	.329	.341
Olson, Tim	R-R	6-2	200	8-1-78	.298	.286	.302	89	322	53	96	26	2	12	51	28	5	5	4	70	9	7	.503	.359
Pena, Elvis	B-R	5-11	160	8-15-74	.290	.306	.284	92	255	34	74	16	2	0	27	32	2	5	0	44	4	5	.369	.374
Pickler, Jeff	L-R	5-10	180	1-6-76	.331	.274	.345	128	423	72	140	26	6	5	50	41	1	6	4	46	16	6	.456	.388
Piedra, Jorge	L-L	6-0	200	4-17-79	.312	.283	.321	47	186	35	58	20	1	6	45	18	1	0	2	23	4	2	.527	.372
Quintanilla, Omar	L-R	5-9	190	10-24-81	.346	.182	.390	13	52	14	18	3	2	1	7	3	0	1	1	8	0	0	.538	.375
Relaford, Desi	B-R	5-9	180	9-16-73	.333	.000	.364	3	12	4	4	1	0	0	0	3	1	0	0	3	1	0	.417	.500
Salazar, Jeff	L-L	6-0	190	11-24-80	.263	.222	.280	59	236	42	62	17	3	6	26	32	0	3	1	58	5	2	.436	.349
Sardinha, Duke	R-R	6-0	200	12-9-80	.000	.000	.000	1	0	0	0	0	0	0	0	1	0	0	0	0	0	0	.000	1.000
Shealy, Ryan	R-R	6-5	240	8-29-79	.328	.330	.328	108	411	85	135	30	2	26	88	41	7	2	7	81	4	0	.601	.393
Spilborghs, Ryan	R-R	6-1	190	9-5-79	.339	.389	.324	60	227	49	77	23	5	5	30	22	3	1	0	53	7	3	.551	.405
Taylor, Reggie	L-R	6-1	180	1-12-77	.250	.000	.250	1	4	0	1	1	0	0	1	0	0	0	0	0	0	0	.500	.250
Tena, Hector	R-R	6-0	160	6-20-82	.176	.111	.200	12	34	1	6	2	0	0	2	0	0	1	1	11	1	0	.235	.171
Thigpen, Jud	R-R	6-0	180	10-3-80	.317	.556	.250	12	41	4	13	5	1	0	2	2	0	1	0	10	0	0	.488	.349
Tracy, Andy	L-R	6-3	220	12-11-73	.325	.231	.370	12	40	14	13	1	1	4	13	15	0	0	0	12	2	1	.700	.509
Wilson, Tom	R-R	6-3	220	12-19-70	.333	.279	.356	64	210	39	70	18	2	11	49	33	1	0	2	43	0	0	.595	.423

PITCHING	B-T	HT	WT	DOB	W	L	ERA	G	GS	CG	SV	IP	H	R	ER	HR	BB	SO	AVG	vLH	vRH	K/9	BB/9
Acevedo, Jose	R-R	6-0	220	12-18-77	1	2	3.29	4	4	0	0	14	17	5	5	3	2	11	.309	.244	.500	7.24	1.32
Anderson, Matt	R-R	6-4	200	8-17-76	3	3	4.21	46	0	0	9	47	36	23	22	5	21	46	.212	.247	.183	8.81	4.02
Bevis, P.J.	R-R	6-3	175	7-28-80	2	1	11.57	13	0	0	0	21	34	29	27	5	15	14	.374	.436	.327	6.00	6.43
Chacon, Shawn	R-R	6-3	220	12-23-77	0	2	9.95	3	3	0	0	13	19	14	14	3	4	11	.339	.286	.393	7.82	2.84
Chavez, Wilton	R-R	6-2	165	6-13-78	5	7	5.02	28	15	0	0	113	137	73	63	7	44	79	.299	.303	.295	6.29	3.50
Chiasson, Scott	R-R	6-3	205	8-14-77	0	2	9.00	11	0	0	0	16	25	17	16	6	6	18	.342	.192	.426	10.13	3.38
Cook, Aaron	R-R	6-3	205	2-8-79	1	0	5.51	3	3	0	0	16	18	10	10	0	7	11	.295	.297	.292	6.06	3.86
Cortes, David	R-R	5-11	220	10-15-73	1	0	4.02	12	0	0	1	16	15	9	7	3	7	15	.250	.261	.243	8.62	4.02
Crockett, Ben	R-R	6-3	200	12-19-79	0	0	7.36	1	1	0	0	4	6	3	3	0	1	2	.400	.333	.444	4.91	2.45
Day, Zach	R-R	6-4	215	6-15-78	2	3	5.89	7	7	0	0	37	46	29	24	4	15	17	.305	.343	.274	4.17	3.68
Dohmann, Scott	R-R	6-1	190	2-13-78	2	1	4.38	34	0	0	1	39	41	19	19	5	16	53	.266	.333	.197	12.23	3.69
Drew, Tim	R-R	6-1	190	8-31-78	4	3	7.55	11	11	1	0	56	71	48	47	11	22	56	.310	.275	.342	9.00	3.54
Esposito, Mike	R-R	6-0	190	9-27-81	8	9	5.49	27	27	0	0	156	197	110	95	20	41	94	.308	.305	.310	5.43	2.37
Hampson, Justin	L-L	6-1	200	5-24-80	5	13	5.99	27	26	1	0	144	167	109	96	18	71	93	.287	.281	.290	5.80	4.43
Kent, Steve	B-L	5-11	170	10-3-78	1	0	19.44	6	0	0	0	8	18	19	18	2	9	3	.439	.556	.406	3.24	9.72
Lopez, Aquilino	R-R	6-3	165	4-21-75	2	0	2.75	14	0	0	0	20	14	10	6	2	4	25	.194	.176	.211	11.44	1.83
2-team (27 Las Vegas)					5	4	4.79	41	0	0	5	56	54	34	30	11	10	57	.249	.244	.252	9.11	1.60
McClellan, Zach	R-R	6-5	210	11-25-78	3	3	5.96	44	2	0	0	71	91	48	47	10	26	67	.313	.280	.340	8.49	3.30
Miceli, Dan	R-R	6-0	215	9-9-70	0	0	5.40	5	0	0	0	5	4	3	3	1	2	8	.200	.182	.222	14.40	3.60
Molina, Gabe	R-R	6-2	187	5-3-75	1	2	3.86	12	0	0	0	16	16	11	7	1	8	11	.262	.360	.194	6.06	4.41
Neal, Blaine	L-R	6-5	250	4-6-78	0	0	0.00	1	0	0	0	1	1	0	0	0	0	0	.250	.500	.000	0.00	0.00

PITCHING	B-T	HT	WT	DOB	W	L	ERA	G	GS	CG	SV	IP	H	R	ER	HR	BB	SO	AVG	vLH	vRH	K/9	BB/9
Parker, Christian	R-R	6-1	200	7-3-75	2	5	6.47	12	11	1	0	65	92	52	47	7	27	24	.343	.340	.346	3.31	3.72
Phelps, Travis	R-R	6-2	170	7-25-77	1	1	13.50	7	0	0	0	12	26	18	18	6	9	8	.464	.400	.516	6.00	6.75
Randall, Scott	R-R	6-3	225	10-29-75	1	1	6.75	10	0	0	0	19	20	14	14	3	12	15	.274	.333	.216	7.23	5.79
Seay, Bobby	L-L	6-2	235	6-20-78	1	0	2.38	17	0	0	3	23	23	8	6	2	10	24	.271	.393	.211	9.53	3.97
Sedlacek, Shawn	R-R	6-4	210	6-29-77	0	0	3.60	1	1	0	0	5	3	2	2	1	1	5	.167	.143	.182	9.00	1.80
Serrano, Alex	R-R	6-1	180	2-18-81	4	3	5.85	21	0	0	0	32	33	25	21	6	11	24	.256	.259	.254	6.68	3.06
Songster, Judd	R-R	6-3	195	12-26-79	0	0	3.86	1	0	0	0	2	2	1	1	0	1	0	.250	.333	.200	0.00	3.86
Speier, Ryan	R-R	6-7	200	7-24-79	2	2	4.99	45	0	0	6	52	70	30	29	2	18	45	.327	.367	.286	7.74	3.10
Stark, Denny	R-R	6-2	210	10-27-74	2	5	6.58	11	11	0	0	52	54	41	38	4	33	38	.271	.291	.257	6.58	5.71
Tsao, Chin-hui	R-R	6-2	190	6-2-81	0	0	0.00	1	1	0	0	1	1	0	0	0	0	1	.250	.000	.333	9.00	0.00
Williams, Randy	L-L	6-3	195	9-18-75	2	2	3.49	26	0	0	4	28	18	14	11	1	10	36	.180	.214	.155	11.44	3.18
2-team (12 Portland)					3	3	4.39	38	0	0	4	41	31	24	20	2	19	43	.209	.188	.226	9.44	4.17
Witasick, Jay	R-R	6-4	240	8-28-72	0	0	3.60	8	0	0	0	10	10	5	4	0	5	14	.270	.368	.167	12.60	4.50
Young, Jason	R-R	6-5	215	9-28-79	9	8	6.39	21	20	0	0	106	127	76	75	16	44	92	.306	.286	.324	7.84	3.75

FIELDING

Catcher	PCT	G	PO	A	E	DP	PB
Ardoin	.997	40	286	23	1	3	3
Conway	.989	41	258	19	3	3	2
Greene	.980	10	46	2	1	0	0
Matos	.984	46	275	25	5	1	7
Wilson	.992	22	119	12	1	2	1

First Base	PCT	G	PO	A	E	DP
Ardoin	.000	1	0	0	1	0
Buchanan	.992	16	118	11	1	7
Conway	1.000	2	18	0	0	2
Helton	1.000	2	16	0	0	1
Olson	1.000	3	22	1	0	1
Pickler	.957	6	41	4	2	10
Shealy	.987	101	885	90	13	79
Tracy	1.000	2	18	0	0	2
Wilson	1.000	16	128	9	0	14

Second Base	PCT	G	PO	A	E	DP
Delarosa	1.000	4	15	5	0	3
Garabito	.966	31	61	111	6	19
Miles	.978	8	14	30	1	4
Nicholson	1.000	7	4	21	0	3
Olson	.973	20	47	60	3	12
Pena	.965	56	108	167	10	30
Pickler	.967	24	51	67	4	13
Relaford	1.000	1	1	3	0	1
Tena	1.000	1	3	2	0	0

Third Base	PCT	G	PO	A	E	DP
Atkins	.917	5	1	10	1	1
Baker	.917	59	32	112	13	8
Delarosa	.979	16	13	33	1	4
Nicholson	.844	13	5	22	5	2
Olson	.970	33	26	39	2	6
Pena	.714	2	1	4	2	0
Relaford	1.000	1	0	2	0	0
Tena	1.000	9	2	4	0	0
Tracy	.972	10	9	26	1	2
Wilson	.800	3	1	3	1	0

Shortstop	PCT	G	PO	A	E	DP
Delarosa	.965	63	100	177	10	37
Garabito	.952	36	50	108	8	22
Machado	.919	22	28	40	6	10
Olson	.966	15	23	34	2	9
Pickler	1.000	1	0	1	0	0
Quintanilla	1.000	13	17	46	0	8
Relaford	.875	1	4	3	1	1

Outfield	PCT	G	PO	A	E	DP
Bigbie	1.000	3	5	0	0	0
Buchanan	.967	36	55	3	2	0
Davis	1.000	17	20	2	0	0
Freeman	.989	95	181	3	2	0
Hawpe	1.000	5	6	0	0	0
Kirby	1.000	1	1	0	0	0
Matos	1.000	2	5	0	0	0
Mohr	1.000	3	7	0	0	0
Olson	.960	20	24	0	1	0
Pena	1.000	14	12	0	0	0
Pickler	.970	74	116	12	4	2
Piedra	.960	46	67	5	3	2
Salazar	1.000	57	130	4	0	1
Shealy	1.000	1	1	0	0	0
Spilborghs	.979	60	88	6	2	2
Taylor	1.000	1	2	0	0	0
Thigpen	1.000	12	11	0	0	0
Tracy	.000	1	0	0	0	0
Wilson	1.000	2	1	0	0	0

TULSA DRILLERS — Class AA

TEXAS LEAGUE

BATTING	B-T	HT	WT	DOB	AVG	vLH	vRH	G	AB	R	H	2B	3B	HR	RBI	BB	HBP	SH	SF	SO	SB	CS	SLG	OBP
Barker, Sean	R-R	6-3	220	5-26-80	.261	.280	.251	125	468	72	122	24	8	14	76	37	4	2	2	133	15	7	.436	.319
Barmes, Clint	R-R	6-0	190	3-6-79	.324	.571	.259	8	34	6	11	1	0	0	0	1	0	0	0	3	1	0	.353	.343
Bernier, Douglas	B-R	5-11	175	6-24-80	.203	.220	.195	117	369	33	75	14	2	3	39	46	8	11	7	103	1	4	.276	.300
Cardona, Javier	R-R	6-1	210	9-15-75	.182	.200	.167	13	44	1	8	2	0	0	4	3	0	1	0	9	0	0	.227	.234
Colina, Alvin	R-R	6-1	184	12-26-81	.256	.268	.248	59	207	23	53	5	0	9	35	20	4	1	2	42	0	2	.411	.330
Conway, Dan	R-R	6-2	190	10-13-79	.247	.250	.245	51	170	22	42	11	1	5	28	25	4	1	2	42	0	0	.412	.353
Czarniecki, Jordan	R-R	6-1	175	10-4-80	.255	.250	.257	46	145	17	37	7	0	4	14	14	3	1	0	29	4	3	.386	.333
Escobar, Gustavo	R-R	5-10	170	1-30-80	.224	.283	.181	43	125	17	28	3	0	0	9	5	1	0	2	31	10	2	.248	.256
Guance, Luis	R-R	5-9	160	3-6-82	.222	.321	.188	65	216	27	48	16	0	5	23	31	1	4	4	59	4	3	.366	.317
Holliday, Matt	R-R	6-4	235	1-15-80	.538	.444	.588	7	26	6	14	3	0	1	6	1	0	0	1	3	1	0	.769	.536
Iannetta, Chris	R-R	5-11	195	4-8-83	.233	.211	.244	19	60	7	14	3	1	2	11	8	1	0	1	15	0	0	.417	.329
Koshansky, Joe	L-L	6-4	225	5-26-82	.267	.133	.333	12	45	5	12	3	0	2	12	2	0	0	1	15	0	0	.467	.292
Macri, Matt	R-R	6-2	200	5-29-82	.000	.000	.000	1	3	1	0	0	0	0	0	1	0	0	0	0	0	0	.000	.250
McNeal, Aaron	R-R	6-3	230	4-28-78	.151	.111	.175	28	93	8	14	2	0	2	6	8	1	0	1	28	0	0	.237	.223
Miller, Tony	R-R	5-9	195	8-18-80	.280	.273	.284	129	460	102	129	17	6	18	58	87	5	9	1	116	26	14	.461	.400
Nicholson, Tommy	L-R	5-9	160	8-23-79	.286	.000	.333	17	49	7	14	4	0	0	5	8	0	1	0	6	0	0	.367	.386
Nix, Jayson	R-R	5-11	185	8-26-82	.236	.217	.244	131	501	68	118	27	0	11	47	29	11	4	6	92	10	6	.355	.289
Perez, Nestor	R-R	5-10	172	11-24-76	.143	.000	.174	10	28	1	4	0	0	0	0	2	0	1	0	2	0	0	.143	.200
Salazar, Jeff	L-L	6-0	190	11-24-80	.278	.248	.299	69	266	47	74	13	2	6	35	44	2	4	3	49	12	8	.410	.381
Sanchez, Tino	B-R	6-0	175	2-2-79	.235	.255	.228	62	200	22	47	14	1	2	24	24	1	1	2	37	0	3	.345	.317
Slavik, Corey	L-R	6-0	190	3-24-80	.236	.181	.267	131	458	59	108	21	5	10	70	61	6	3	7	92	4	2	.369	.329
Spilborghs, Ryan	R-R	6-1	190	9-5-79	.341	.324	.353	71	255	52	87	23	3	6	54	42	2	0	2	49	10	3	.525	.435
Tena, Hector	R-R	6-0	160	6-20-82	.250	.136	.290	31	84	8	21	2	0	3	5	5	1	1	0	24	0	1	.381	.300
Thigpen, Jud	R-R	6-0	180	10-3-80	.266	.333	.244	61	207	32	55	8	2	11	33	18	5	2	3	40	3	2	.483	.335

PITCHING	B-T	HT	WT	DOB	W	L	ERA	G	GS	CG	SV	IP	H	R	ER	HR	BB	SO	AVG	vLH	vRH	K/9	BB/9
Arakawa, Yusuke	R-R	6-0	165	3-26-78	4	4	5.09	41	0	0	0	53	57	33	30	9	21	40	.278	.311	.242	6.79	3.57
Asahina, Jon	B-R	6-1	190	12-31-80	12	10	4.19	26	26	4	0	170	189	88	79	16	34	94	.290	.321	.255	4.99	1.80
Beckstead, Jentry	R-R	6-0	175	6-9-80	5	3	4.10	51	0	0	3	68	79	34	31	4	15	45	.296	.350	.252	5.96	1.99
Bevis, P.J.	R-R	6-3	175	7-28-80	0	5	4.26	41	0	0	21	38	38	19	18	4	14	17	.264	.273	.254	4.03	3.32
Cook, Aaron	R-R	6-3	205	2-8-79	0	1	17.18	1	1	0	0	4	10	9	7	2	1	1	.476	.333	.583	2.45	2.45
Crockett, Ben	R-R	6-3	200	12-19-79	0	0	4.00	18	2	0	0	36	44	19	16	1	11	20	.319	.295	.338	5.00	2.75
Jimenez, Ubaldo	R-R	6-4	200	1-22-84	2	5	5.43	12	11	0	0	63	58	40	38	12	31	53	.243	.277	.194	7.57	4.43
Mendoza, Marcos	L-L	5-9	180	10-31-80	0	0	7.15	10	0	0	0	11	16	9	9	3	4	12	.333	.444	.267	9.53	3.18
Miller, Jim	R-R	6-1	200	4-28-82	1	1	0.60	16	0	0	9	15	6	5	1	2	8	19	.118	.154	.080	11.40	4.80
Neal, Blaine	L-R	6-5	250	4-6-78	0	1	9.00	4	1	0	0	3	4	4	3	1	1	2	.308	.375	.200	6.00	3.00
Nin, Sandy	R-R	6-0	186	8-13-80	10	6	3.19	20	20	4	0	130	109	50	46	15	16	80	.226	.211	.242	5.55	1.11
Parker, Christian	R-R	6-1	200	7-3-75	4	1	2.06	12	12	0	0	70	57	18	16	1	17	50	.223	.207	.236	6.43	2.19
Parker, Zach	R-L	6-2	205	8-19-81	12	10	3.79	27	27	0	0	162	171	83	68	15	35	87	.275	.312	.265	4.84	1.95
Ramirez, Ramon	R-R	5-11	190	8-31-81	2	1	5.33	9	3	0	0	25	27	17	15	6	8	23	.273	.327	.220	8.17	2.84

PITCHING	B-T	HT	WT	DOB	W	L	ERA	G	GS	CG	SV	IP	H	R	ER	HR	BB	SO	AVG	vLH	vRH	K/9	BB/9
Ramsey, Keith	B-L	6-1	175	3-5-80	1	3	7.68	10	10	0	0	41	58	37	35	8	19	23	.343	.357	.336	5.05	4.17
Randall, Scott	R-R	6-3	225	10-29-75	3	4	4.84	9	9	0	0	45	49	31	24	1	22	36	.290	.320	.246	7.25	4.43
Seay, Bobby	L-L	6-2	235	6-20-78	1	0	1.80	4	0	0	1	5	3	1	1	0	0	3	.188	.000	.200	5.40	0.00
Serrano, Alex	R-R	6-1	180	2-18-81	1	0	0.63	11	0	0	4	14	10	1	1	1	1	5	.208	.125	.292	3.14	0.63
Sierra, Edwardo	R-R	6-3	185	4-15-82	0	3	10.20	13	0	0	0	15	23	17	17	3	13	7	.377	.433	.323	4.20	7.80
Simpson, Gerrit	R-R	6-3	200	12-18-79	3	0	3.83	27	1	0	0	42	48	23	18	3	19	32	.282	.273	.290	6.80	4.04
Songster, Judd	R-R	6-3	195	12-26-79	3	2	2.10	50	0	0	0	69	54	18	16	5	21	67	.217	.211	.222	8.78	2.75
Ulloa, Enmanuel	R-R	6-2	190	11-26-78	8	3	2.96	18	17	0	0	103	88	37	34	9	24	101	.228	.230	.226	8.80	2.09
Young, Chris	R-R	6-4	218	4-19-81	3	2	4.75	35	0	0	1	53	53	29	28	6	17	35	.255	.225	.283	5.94	2.89

FIELDING

Catcher	PCT	G	PO	A	E	DP	PB
Cardona	1.000	6	36	2	0	1	0
Colina	.982	42	249	27	5	2	2
Conway	.967	48	296	29	11	2	3
Iannetta	.980	16	86	10	2	1	0
Sanchez	.992	35	217	17	2	2	1

First Base	PCT	G	PO	A	E	DP
Bernier	.000	1	0	0	0	0
Cardona	.981	6	48	4	1	5
Colina	.974	16	143	8	4	12
Koshansky	1.000	12	98	10	0	11
McNeal	.992	22	229	30	2	21
Sanchez	.994	19	159	14	1	17
Slavik	.993	72	612	57	5	61

Second Base	PCT	G	PO	A	E	DP
Bernier	1.000	2	2	5	0	1
Guance	.905	6	10	9	2	1
Nicholson	1.000	1	4	2	0	1
Nix	.975	131	274	433	18	85
Tena	1.000	4	6	11	0	3

Third Base	PCT	G	PO	A	E	DP
Bernier	1.000	1	2	0	0	0
Escobar	.939	26	10	36	3	3
Guance	.904	50	24	79	11	7
Nicholson	.880	8	4	18	3	4
Slavik	.946	63	47	112	9	8
Tena	1.000	5	2	12	0	2

Shortstop	PCT	G	PO	A	E	DP
Barmes	.957	6	4	18	1	3
Bernier	.974	114	178	356	14	77
Escobar	.900	2	4	5	1	0
Guance	.889	3	0	8	1	1
Macri	1.000	1	1	2	0	0
Nicholson	.952	4	7	13	1	3
Perez	.946	8	14	21	2	6
Slavik	.000	2	0	0	1	0
Tena	.969	10	12	19	1	5

Outfield	PCT	G	PO	A	E	DP
Barker	.980	112	189	11	4	1
Czarniecki	1.000	42	95	5	0	1
Guance	1.000	4	8	0	0	0
Holliday	1.000	7	12	0	0	0
Miller	.958	115	238	12	11	2
Salazar	.994	66	155	6	1	1
Spilborghs	.991	50	97	12	1	3
Tena	.875	3	6	1	1	0
Thigpen	.973	28	35	1	1	0

MODESTO NUTS — High Class A

CALIFORNIA LEAGUE

BATTING	B-T	HT	WT	DOB	AVG	vLH	vRH	G	AB	R	H	2B	3B	HR	RBI	BB	HBP	SH	SF	SO	SB	CS	SLG	OBP
Blood, Randy	L-R	5-10	180	1-7-81	.251	.280	.240	101	367	53	92	25	4	5	54	35	3	4	3	76	0	4	.381	.319
Colina, Alvin	R-R	6-1	184	12-26-81	.265	.200	.292	9	34	2	9	3	0	0	3	3	0	0	0	14	0	1	.353	.324
Colonel, Christian	R-R	6-2	210	12-25-81	.310	.292	.318	96	364	73	113	32	3	7	60	47	8	1	5	66	1	3	.473	.396
Czarniecki, Jordan	R-R	6-1	175	10-4-80	.318	.250	.351	46	170	38	54	15	1	6	23	31	2	3	1	33	1	5	.524	.426
Davies, Michael	L-L	6-3	195	3-29-81	.278	.211	.302	108	407	53	113	23	5	14	62	22	0	3	0	145	2	4	.462	.315
Dean, Erik	L-R	6-0	198	2-7-82	.271	.233	.289	79	288	48	78	15	3	6	43	23	8	2	0	67	3	5	.406	.342
Ferrer, Simon	B-R	5-10	175	6-24-80	.209	.259	.190	58	191	20	40	8	2	0	21	16	1	7	2	59	0	1	.272	.271
Gaetti, Joe	R-R	5-11	205	10-16-81	.332	.303	.344	113	395	90	131	29	8	21	87	52	9	4	3	114	5	7	.605	.418
Gonzalez, Bernard	R-R	6-2	208	5-10-80	.236	.160	.277	20	72	3	17	4	2	1	9	6	1	0	0	15	0	1	.389	.304
Guance, Luis	R-R	5-9	160	3-6-82	.272	.259	.278	47	180	26	49	11	3	0	16	20	3	3	0	44	6	6	.367	.355
Guarno, Rick	R-R	6-0	185	8-16-82	.255	.260	.255	57	188	26	48	10	0	1	23	17	7	5	1	41	0	1	.324	.338
Herrera, Jonathan	B-R	5-9	155	11-3-84	.258	.268	.256	73	310	48	80	9	4	2	30	23	3	8	1	52	9	4	.332	.315
Iannetta, Chris	R-R	5-11	195	4-8-83	.276	.319	.259	74	261	51	72	17	3	11	58	45	2	0	4	61	1	2	.490	.381
Macri, Matt	R-R	6-2	200	5-29-82	.283	.241	.303	64	244	40	69	16	1	7	34	33	7	6	2	67	6	1	.443	.381
Miller, Matt	R-R	6-2	210	12-26-82	.400	1.000	.250	1	5	0	2	0	0	0	1	0	0	0	0	0	0	0	.400	.400
Smith, Seth	L-L	6-3	215	9-30-82	.300	.256	.317	129	533	87	160	45	6	9	72	44	1	4	3	115	5	3	.458	.353
Stewart, Ian	L-R	6-3	205	4-5-85	.274	.246	.283	112	435	83	119	32	7	17	86	52	5	0	7	113	2	2	.497	.353
Thigpen, Jud	R-R	6-0	180	10-3-80	.304	.420	.256	45	171	23	52	9	2	4	27	21	1	1	2	35	0	0	.450	.379
Tulowitzki, Troy	R-R	6-3	205	10-10-84	.266	.276	.262	22	94	17	25	6	0	4	14	9	2	0	0	18	1	0	.457	.343
Wilson, Neil	R-R	6-1	190	12-7-83	.400	1.000	.250	1	5	0	2	0	1	0	1	0	0	0	0	0	0	0	.800	.400
Wilson, Kyle	R-R	6-1	215	8-23-82	.282	.217	.309	21	78	12	22	3	1	5	15	5	1	1	0	22	0	0	.538	.333

PITCHING	B-T	HT	WT	DOB	W	L	ERA	G	GS	CG	SV	IP	H	R	ER	HR	BB	SO	AVG	vLH	vRH	K/9	BB/9
Arias, Alberto	R-R	5-11	155	10-14-83	4	4	4.37	37	7	0	2	91	99	48	44	4	25	53	.277	.268	.282	5.26	2.48
Balbuena, Caleb	R-R	6-7	240	3-23-77	2	0	2.65	12	0	0	0	17	21	6	5	0	4	15	.296	.217	.333	7.94	2.12
Beerer, Scott	R-R	6-1	200	7-4-82	1	0	17.18	5	0	0	0	4	6	7	7	1	3	3	.375	.286	.444	7.36	7.36
Burch, Jason	R-R	6-5	215	10-15-82	7	3	2.85	49	0	0	4	60	49	22	19	1	25	73	.222	.216	.226	10.95	3.75
Clarke, Darren	R-R	6-8	235	3-19-81	0	0	9.00	5	0	0	0	6	13	8	6	2	3	4	.433	.444	.429	6.00	4.50
Cook, Aaron	R-R	6-3	205	2-8-79	1	0	1.80	1	1	0	0	5	5	1	1	0	0	5	.263	.286	.250	9.00	0.00
Corpas, Manuel	R-R	6-3	170	12-3-82	3	2	3.78	47	0	0	2	69	83	33	29	2	14	52	.299	.364	.256	6.78	1.83
Jimenez, Ubaldo	R-R	6-4	200	1-22-84	5	3	3.98	14	14	0	0	72	61	35	32	5	40	78	.232	.195	.267	9.71	4.98
Kaiser, Marc	R-R	6-2	205	5-7-82	7	6	4.45	22	20	0	0	127	160	81	63	12	26	82	.312	.336	.287	5.80	1.84
Marsden, Aaron	L-L	6-5	225	11-18-81	6	12	6.62	27	24	0	0	125	172	110	92	19	53	73	.330	.307	.341	5.26	3.82
Merricks, Matt	L-L	6-0	200	8-6-82	0	0	7.71	2	0	0	0	2	4	3	2	0	2	2	.364	.200	.500	7.71	7.71
Miller, Jim	R-R	6-1	200	4-28-82	1	3	3.78	48	0	0	25	48	39	22	20	3	17	68	.213	.210	.216	12.84	3.21
Morel, Eudy	R-R	5-10	175	8-31-79	1	2	6.29	45	0	0	1	69	81	54	48	11	25	46	.293	.326	.264	6.03	3.28
Morillo, Juan	R-R	6-3	190	11-5-83	6	5	4.41	20	20	0	0	112	107	69	55	10	65	101	.258	.256	.259	8.09	5.21
Newman, Josh	L-L	6-1	200	6-11-82	5	2	3.13	41	0	0	0	63	45	22	22	5	40	99	.198	.178	.212	14.07	5.68
Nin, Sandy	R-R	6-0	186	8-13-80	4	1	2.55	7	7	0	0	35	30	11	10	3	7	34	.233	.244	.226	8.66	1.78
Register, Steven	R-R	6-1	170	5-16-83	9	11	4.44	27	27	1	0	156	184	98	77	16	35	108	.291	.219	.361	6.23	2.02
Robles, Larry	R-R	6-2	205	10-29-80	4	4	8.07	12	11	0	0	61	90	58	55	3	21	32	.345	.390	.304	4.70	3.08
Santiago, Tomas	R-R	6-4	210	10-30-81	3	9	5.02	38	8	0	4	84	94	55	47	7	42	69	.287	.303	.273	7.36	4.48
Steinborn, Chris	L-L	6-4	215	3-23-82	3	0	7.90	11	0	0	0	14	22	14	12	1	6	8	.344	.400	.327	5.27	3.95
Tsao, Chin-hui	R-R	6-2	190	6-2-81	0	0	0.00	1	0	0	0	1	0	0	0	0	0	1	.000	.000	.000	9.00	0.00

FIELDING

Catcher	PCT	G	PO	A	E	DP	PB
Colina	.984	7	58	5	1	2	0
Dean	.962	8	48	3	2	0	3
Guarno	.982	56	384	46	8	5	9
Iannetta	.989	70	522	40	6	3	14
K. Wilson	1.000	1	6	0	0	0	0
N. Wilson	1.000	1	3	0	0	0	1

First Base	PCT	G	PO	A	E	DP
Colonel	.992	13	112	10	1	17
Davies	.991	102	848	82	8	106
Dean	.993	14	133	8	1	19
Ferrer	1.000	12	69	15	0	7

Second Base	PCT	G	PO	A	E	DP
Blood	.975	79	160	232	10	67
Dean	.966	28	70	74	5	26
Ferrer	.857	2	2	10	2	1
Guance	.945	14	33	36	4	13
Herrera	.977	19	26	60	2	11

Third Base	PCT	G	PO	A	E	DP
Blood	1.000	2	2	1	0	0
Colonel	1.000	3	2	0	0	0
Ferrer	.882	7	3	12	2	1
Guance	.915	21	15	50	6	5
Stewart	.923	107	87	190	23	24

Shortstop	PCT	G	PO	A	E	DP
Ferrer	.938	5	13	17	2	5
Guance	.967	6	11	18	1	5
Herrera	.964	51	90	180	10	46
Macri	.965	58	92	158	9	50
Tulowitzki	.948	19	36	56	5	13

Outfield	PCT	G	PO	A	E	DP
Colonel	.963	76	124	5	5	0
Czarniecki	.968	43	90	2	3	1
Ferrer	.953	23	41	0	2	0
Gaetti	.966	108	214	10	8	3
Gonzalez	.975	16	37	2	1	0
Miller	1.000	1	4	0	0	0
Smith	.958	124	191	15	9	2
Thigpen	1.000	30	37	0	0	0

ASHEVILLE TOURISTS — Low Class A

SOUTH ATLANTIC LEAGUE

BATTING	B-T	HT	WT	DOB	AVG	vLH	vRH	G	AB	R	H	2B	3B	HR	RBI	BB	HBP	SH	SF	SO	SB	CS	SLG	OBP
Allen, Trevor	R-R	6-2	215	12-26-79	.250	.100	.273	21	76	9	19	2	0	4	11	11	1	0	0	31	1	1	.434	.352
Almonte, Sandy	B-R	5-11	150	11-19-82	.208	.042	.250	28	120	21	25	2	4	2	9	8	1	0	0	30	5	0	.342	.264
Dragicevich, Jeff	R-R	6-2	200	8-1-82	.281	.263	.287	104	374	57	105	29	2	4	44	47	7	3	3	86	5	4	.401	.369
Guarno, Rick	R-R	6-0	185	8-16-82	.261	.368	.220	19	69	7	18	7	0	0	2	6	3	1	1	6	1	0	.362	.342
Hahn, Dustin	L-R	6-1	200	10-21-82	.281	.290	.278	130	488	70	137	32	2	11	59	55	5	1	2	96	6	4	.422	.358
Herrera, Jonathan	B-R	5-9	155	11-3-84	.310	.389	.290	19	87	17	27	2	0	0	5	8	3	0	1	11	6	6	.333	.384
Hosgood, Robert	L-L	6-2	210	12-5-81	.234	.263	.228	34	111	18	26	6	2	3	14	17	2	0	0	42	4	2	.405	.346
Koshansky, Joe	L-L	6-4	225	5-26-82	.291	.309	.286	120	453	92	132	31	1	36	103	53	11	0	8	122	6	6	.603	.373
Miller, Matt	R-R	6-2	210	12-26-82	.331	.310	.337	127	508	79	168	34	0	30	100	26	12	0	3	71	9	8	.575	.375
Nelson, Chris	R-R	5-11	176	9-3-85	.241	.183	.258	79	315	51	76	13	3	3	38	25	5	0	4	88	7	4	.330	.304
Nelson, Justin	L-L	6-3	205	4-23-83	.278	.260	.284	113	413	77	115	36	1	21	64	61	6	2	3	102	14	6	.523	.377
Nunez, Florentino	B-R	6-0	164	3-23-84	.256	.233	.263	76	250	43	64	10	0	10	36	28	1	3	1	54	9	4	.416	.332
Restrepo, John	L-L	6-1	185	7-27-82	.213	.269	.202	44	155	15	33	4	0	0	10	20	0	1	0	48	4	7	.239	.303
Reynolds, Tila	R-R	5-11	180	2-7-81	.182	.000	.250	3	11	0	2	1	0	0	0	2	0	1	0	3	0	0	.273	.308
Robledo, Nelson	R-R	6-1	180	6-13-84	.239	.243	.238	93	322	46	77	22	0	2	34	37	6	5	1	71	1	1	.326	.328
Sardinha, Duke	R-R	6-0	200	12-9-80	.129	.200	.115	9	31	3	4	1	0	0	1	4	0	0	0	5	0	1	.161	.229
Strop, Pedro	B-R	6-0	160	6-13-85	.167	.000	.200	4	12	2	2	0	0	0	0	0	0	1	0	6	0	0	.167	.167
Valdez, Jose	L-R	6-1	152	9-6-83	.292	.220	.308	115	439	75	128	19	2	21	56	45	1	8	0	64	8	8	.487	.359
Wilson, Neil	R-R	6-1	190	12-7-83	.271	.281	.268	81	299	33	81	25	0	10	51	23	8	2	1	48	3	0	.455	.338
Wilson, Kyle	R-R	6-1	215	8-23-82	.301	.267	.310	40	143	19	43	10	0	10	36	11	4	0	0	34	0	4	.580	.367

PITCHING	B-T	HT	WT	DOB	W	L	ERA	G	GS	CG	SV	IP	H	R	ER	HR	BB	SO	AVG	vLH	vRH	K/9	BB/9
Beerer, Scott	R-R	6-1	200	7-4-82	2	3	3.69	45	0	0	23	46	52	23	19	3	15	44	.280	.271	.284	8.55	2.91
Bright, Adam	L-L	5-11	175	8-11-84	4	2	3.38	51	0	0	6	64	56	26	24	6	28	51	.243	.170	.266	7.17	3.94
Buechner, Chris	R-R	6-3	235	8-23-83	4	3	5.07	53	0	0	3	66	68	40	37	8	26	68	.259	.263	.257	9.32	3.56
Daley, Matt	R-R	6-2	175	6-23-82	8	2	3.99	45	0	0	1	79	90	46	35	10	16	49	.285	.287	.284	5.58	1.82
Deduno, Samuel	R-R	6-1	156	7-2-83	8	8	5.62	20	20	1	0	90	82	67	56	9	65	110	.248	.269	.235	11.04	6.52
Delgado, George	R-R	6-2	175	3-22-84	0	1	10.32	10	0	0	1	11	22	17	13	2	3	13	.386	.400	.378	10.32	2.38
Diangelo, Jason	R-R	6-1	200	9-9-80	4	4	5.52	46	0	0	0	73	93	59	45	11	29	74	.299	.289	.303	9.08	3.56
Grube, Jarrett	R-R	6-4	220	11-5-81	5	5	6.02	32	11	0	0	105	119	76	70	17	30	98	.286	.324	.267	8.43	2.58
Lira, Efren	R-R	6-3	240	8-5-81	0	0	0.00	1	0	0	0	0	0	0	0	0	0	0	.000	.000	.000	0.00	0.00
Lo, Ching	R-R	6-4	165	8-20-85	7	9	5.65	24	24	1	0	121	148	90	76	23	38	91	.303	.287	.312	6.77	2.83
Mattheus, Ryan	R-R	6-3	215	11-10-83	7	6	5.82	23	23	0	0	128	142	90	83	16	52	102	.278	.259	.287	7.15	3.65
Merrell, Darric	R-R	6-4	210	1-22-82	3	4	3.76	52	0	0	6	84	78	37	35	7	15	68	.249	.215	.267	7.31	1.61
Morales, Franklin	L-L	6-0	175	1-24-86	8	4	3.08	21	15	0	1	96	73	40	33	6	48	108	.214	.180	.220	10.09	4.48
Morillo, Juan	R-R	6-3	190	11-5-83	1	3	4.54	7	7	0	0	34	40	24	17	2	13	43	.290	.299	.282	11.50	3.48
Patton, David	R-R	6-3	175	5-18-84	0	3	10.93	4	4	0	0	14	26	23	17	4	8	9	.377	.360	.386	5.79	5.14
Postlewait, Jacob	B-L	6-0	195	11-3-81	7	8	5.99	26	26	0	0	137	177	96	91	21	49	91	.312	.289	.315	5.99	3.23
Robles, Larry	R-R	6-2	205	10-29-80	3	2	3.00	8	8	0	0	42	31	15	14	6	20	33	.209	.212	.208	7.07	4.29

FIELDING

Catcher	PCT	G	PO	A	E	DP	PB
Guarno	.991	12	101	13	1	0	0
Robledo	.991	67	514	54	5	7	19
K. Wilson	.995	52	371	26	2	4	9
N. Wilson	1.000	12	73	2	0	1	6

First Base	PCT	G	PO	A	E	DP
Dragicevich	1.000	13	97	11	0	5
Koshansky	.989	116	1059	84	13	86
Robledo	1.000	12	112	6	0	11
Sardinha	1.000	1	11	0	0	1

Second Base	PCT	G	PO	A	E	DP
Almonte	.985	27	40	90	2	15
Dragicevich	.966	28	37	77	4	14
Herrera	1.000	3	6	8	0	0
Reynolds	.947	3	5	13	1	2
Sardinha	1.000	3	7	10	0	2
Valdez	.964	76	119	202	12	43

Third Base	PCT	G	PO	A	E	DP
Dragicevich	.978	41	31	100	3	11
Hahn	.921	92	54	192	21	10
Sardinha	1.000	1	4	1	0	0
Strop	1.000	2	0	3	0	2
Valdez	.833	4	1	4	1	0

Shortstop	PCT	G	PO	A	E	DP
C. Nelson	.930	69	116	202	24	37
Dragicevich	.929	19	29	49	6	7
Herrera	.938	15	18	43	4	7
Strop	.818	2	2	7	2	0
Valdez	.949	36	59	109	9	21

Outfield	PCT	G	PO	A	E	DP
Allen	.912	17	28	3	3	3
Dragicevich	.000	1	0	0	0	0
Hahn	.980	36	48	2	1	0
Hosgood	.955	20	21	0	1	0
Miller	.988	121	163	8	2	1
J. Nelson	.960	102	153	13	7	2
Nunez	1.000	66	118	10	0	2
Restrepo	.966	44	81	4	3	0
Sardinha	1.000	3	7	1	0	0
Wilson	1.000	8	14	0	0	0

TRI-CITY DUST DEVILS — Short-Season Class A

NORTHWEST LEAGUE

BATTING	B-T	HT	WT	DOB	AVG	vLH	vRH	G	AB	R	H	2B	3B	HR	RBI	BB	HBP	SH	SF	SO	SB	CS	SLG	OBP
Almonte, Sandy	B-R	5-11	150	11-19-82	.290	.288	.291	50	193	37	56	10	3	2	19	23	1	4	1	46	7	3	.404	.367
Becktel, Travis	R-R	6-1	195	4-3-83	.314	.316	.313	68	255	50	80	17	4	4	27	37	7	1	2	57	5	2	.459	.412
Boggs, Steve	B-R	5-10	164	2-29-84	.261	.250	.266	33	115	13	30	6	0	0	8	15	2	2	0	24	0	6	.313	.356
Carte, Daniel	R-R	6-0	190	5-18-84	.225	.214	.230	62	218	30	49	11	2	6	25	19	6	6	2	66	4	3	.376	.302
Cuadrado, Phil	B-R	6-1	210	11-4-83	.264	.244	.273	72	265	37	70	21	1	5	45	35	20	3	4	61	2	3	.408	.386
Frey, Chris	L-L	6-1	180	8-11-83	.206	.145	.226	64	252	30	52	6	0	0	17	29	3	9	3	38	8	4	.230	.293
Hosgood, Robert	L-L	6-2	210	12-5-81	.061	.000	.067	9	33	1	2	0	0	0	0	4	0	1	0	13	1	1	.061	.162
Kirby, Brian	L-R	6-1	200	8-3-79	.234	.234	.234	53	201	27	47	11	1	7	35	24	2	0	3	69	0	1	.403	.317
Materano, Oscar	R-R	6-1	170	11-18-81	.174	.000	.211	17	69	7	12	2	1	0	6	1	0	2	0	13	2	1	.232	.186
Milliron, Mike	R-R	6-0	175	8-3-82	.111	.083	.128	23	63	6	7	2	0	1	6	6	0	3	0	23	1	0	.190	.188

BATTING	B-T	HT	WT	DOB	AVG	vLH	vRH	G	AB	R	H	2B	3B	HR	RBI	BB	HBP	SH	SF	SO	SB	CS	SLG	OBP
Paulk, Mike	L-L	6-2	195	4-23-84	.312	.260	.335	68	253	32	79	17	2	4	45	37	3	2	4	45	1	0	.443	.401
Rodriguez, Ramon	R-R	5-11		9-3-84	.071	.000	.080	9	28	3	2	0	0	0	0	5	0	1	0	9	1	0	.071	.212
Sargent, Luke	R-R	5-9	190	7-14-82	.208	.100	.286	14	48	4	10	2	0	0	1	5	1	0	0	19	0	0	.250	.296
Strop, Pedro	B-R	6-0	160	6-13-85	.236	.205	.253	62	229	26	54	11	2	3	25	6	2	9	1	86	7	2	.341	.261
Sweeney, James	R-R	6-1	197	6-13-83	.210	.194	.217	28	100	12	21	4	0	2	15	18	2	0	1	32	3	1	.310	.339
Valdez, Angel	R-R	6-0	145	8-2-84	.143	.000	.200	2	7	0	1	0	0	0	0	1	0	1	0	3	0	0	.143	.250
Van Kooten, Jason	R-R	6-0	170	9-1-84	.299	.390	.254	64	251	34	75	14	2	5	36	14	7	7	2	57	2	2	.430	.350

PITCHING	B-T	HT	WT	DOB	W	L	ERA	G	GS	CG	SV	IP	H	R	ER	HR	BB	SO	AVG	vLH	vRH	K/9	BB/9
Bechtold, David	L-L	6-2	200	2-11-83	0	1	11.17	8	0	0	0	10	17	12	12	3	5	6	.386	.308	.419	5.59	4.66
Burok, James	R-R	6-3	212	11-16-82	2	3	5.08	24	0	0	2	34	36	22	19	2	12	26	.279	.327	.247	6.95	3.21
Clarke, Darren	R-R	6-8	235	3-19-81	0	0	0.64	12	0	0	3	14	9	1	1	0	2	18	.184	.176	.188	11.57	1.29
Cook, Aaron	R-R	6-3	205	2-8-79	0	0	0.00	2	2	0	0	7	1	0	0	0	0	0	.043	.000	.059	0.00	0.00
Delgado, George	R-R	6-2	175	3-22-84	1	3	2.43	32	0	0	15	33	26	14	9	0	11	37	.215	.157	.257	9.99	2.97
Edsall, Stephen	R-R	6-4	205	10-19-81	0	1	2.54	15	0	0	0	28	34	11	8	0	7	13	.298	.400	.232	4.13	2.22
Fox, Ryan	R-R	6-3	220	10-13-80	1	2	3.86	22	0	0	0	33	33	15	14	1	13	34	.277	.306	.257	9.37	3.58
Freeman, Jimmy	L-L	5-11	205	3-27-82	3	5	4.56	16	10	0	0	49	43	35	25	4	46	46	.236	.295	.217	8.39	8.39
Katz, Ethan	R-R	6-5	210	7-4-83	4	1	2.35	21	7	0	0	61	55	18	16	2	11	49	.248	.217	.266	7.19	1.61
Kreidermacher, Andy	B-R	6-2	195	1-27-83	1	4	3.93	14	7	0	0	53	61	28	23	4	16	32	.285	.366	.223	5.47	2.73
Lindsay, Shane	R-R	6-1	205	1-25-85	6	1	1.89	13	13	0	0	67	37	21	14	1	34	107	.163	.179	.152	14.45	4.59
Lira, Efren	R-R	6-3	240	8-5-81	0	0	0.00	6	0	0	2	7	3	0	0	0	1	3	.136	.125	.143	3.86	1.29
Patton, David	R-R	6-3	175	5-18-84	3	5	6.00	8	7	0	0	42	49	29	28	7	13	39	.293	.378	.226	8.36	2.79
Prendergast, Matt	R-R	6-4	210	3-26-82	0	0	6.00	2	0	0	0	3	8	2	2	0	0	1	.500	.750	.417	3.00	0.00
Ruthven, Sean	R-R	6-4	195	9-13-82	0	2	2.13	5	1	0	1	13	8	3	3	0	5	16	.182	.105	.240	11.37	3.55
Sanchez, Rafael	R-R	6-2	174	9-20-82	1	0	4.11	7	0	0	0	15	14	7	7	2	3	15	.246	.391	.147	8.80	1.76
Simons, Zach	L-R	6-3	200	5-23-85	6	5	3.81	15	15	0	0	83	75	39	35	8	23	40	.240	.223	.254	4.35	2.50
Stanley, Patrick	R-R	6-7	200	1-4-83	2	2	5.24	18	0	0	0	34	43	28	20	1	14	32	.307	.368	.265	8.39	3.67
Sullivan, Josh	R-R	6-4	205	7-5-84	0	1	27.00	1	0	0	0	1	3	3	3	0	1	1	.500	.500	.500	9.00	9.00
Vargas, Buzz	R-R	6-6	220	10-21-83	4	4	4.14	16	14	0	0	83	75	44	38	11	21	55	.242	.276	.212	5.99	2.29
White, Jeremey	R-L	6-2	205	1-15-82	2	0	0.00	3	0	0	0	5	3	0	0	0	1	2	.176	.333	.143	3.86	1.93

GAMES BY POSITION: C—Kirby 29, Rodriguez 8, Sargent 14, Sweeney 26. **1B**—Cuadrado 15, Kirby 17, Paulk 45. **2B**—Almonte 25, Milliron 19, Strop 24, Van Kooten 14. **3B**—Cuadrado 52, Materano 4, Strop 22. **SS**—Almonte 10, Materano 12, Milliron 1, Strop 15, Van Kooten 43. **OF**—Becktel 64, Boggs 28, Carte 62, Frey 64, Hosgood 5, Kirby 1, Paulk 5, Valdez 2.

CASPER ROCKIES — Rookie

PIONEER LEAGUE

BATTING	B-T	HT	WT	DOB	AVG	vLH	vRH	G	AB	R	H	2B	3B	HR	RBI	BB	HBP	SH	SF	SO	SB	CS	SLG	OBP
Allen, Trevor	R-R	6-2	215	12-26-79	.385	.367	.391	31	122	23	47	12	0	5	33	9	3	0	3	34	5	3	.607	.431
Berglund, Bret	R-R	6-4	210	12-9-82	.218	.197	.228	53	188	26	41	11	1	4	27	25	9	0	1	66	10	4	.351	.336
Blumenthal, Kyle	L-R	5-10	195	1-11-83	.276	.327	.258	60	214	32	59	14	1	6	42	37	0	1	0	45	4	3	.435	.382
Brownell, Jesse	R-R	6-1	195	3-15-82	.215	.162	.250	31	93	14	20	4	0	3	9	11	3	2	0	39	3	3	.355	.318
Cook, Chris	R-R	6-4	222	7-3-83	.283	.269	.289	50	187	29	53	10	0	15	46	19	4	0	9	59	0	2	.578	.347
Dombek, Greg	R-R	6-2	205	3-17-82	.400	.000	.667	3	10	1	4	1	0	0	2	1	1	0	0	3	0	0	.500	.500
Fowler, Dexter	R-R	6-4	173	3-22-86	.273	.304	.258	62	220	43	60	10	4	4	23	27	2	3	0	73	18	6	.409	.357
Garner, Cole	B-R	6-2	210	12-15-84	.260	.279	.254	66	265	34	69	21	1	10	48	9	8	0	2	105	2	8	.460	.303
Loupadiere, Maruis	R-R	6-1	150	4-28-85	.262	.240	.271	25	84	12	22	4	0	0	5	5	3	2	0	11	3	4	.310	.326
Mayora, Daniel	R-R	5-11	145	7-27-85	.265	.220	.282	47	151	20	40	12	1	1	14	9	5	2	1	36	4	3	.377	.325
Nazario, Radames	R-R	6-0	166	6-14-87	.225	.358	.171	56	182	24	41	5	1	0	12	19	4	4	0	40	7	4	.264	.312
Polanco, Armando	R-R	5-9	165	3-2-84	.250	.333	.207	17	44	4	11	3	0	0	5	1	2	0	0	7	0	0	.318	.298
Rodriguez, Ramon	R-R	5-11	170	9-3-84	.250	.194	.279	29	92	8	23	4	0	1	9	9	3	1	2	16	1	1	.326	.330
Sargent, Luke	R-R	5-9	190	7-14-82	.276	.250	.286	9	29	4	8	0	0	1	4	3	0	0	1	9	0	0	.379	.333
Strickland, Geoff	B-R	5-10	180	7-1-84	.228	.281	.209	36	123	13	28	5	3	0	7	11	0	0	0	34	6	7	.317	.291
Suarez, Steven	L-R	6-0	210	2-24-82	.276	.458	.228	35	116	13	32	3	0	3	19	8	0	1	0	24	0	3	.379	.323
Wimberly, Corey	B-R	5-8	180	10-26-83	.381	.349	.395	67	281	58	107	10	0	1	22	18	6	2	2	27	36	13	.427	.427
Young, Eric	B-R	5-10	180	5-25-85	.301	.297	.303	63	219	48	66	7	7	3	25	35	4	4	2	52	25	10	.438	.404

PITCHING	B-T	HT	WT	DOB	W	L	ERA	G	GS	CG	SV	IP	H	R	ER	HR	BB	SO	AVG	vLH	vRH	K/9	BB/9
Binda, Byron	R-R	6-0	185	6-30-83	4	1	4.60	21	0	0	0	31	39	24	16	5	12	38	.305	.323	.288	10.91	3.45
Cedeno, Xavier	L-L	6-1	165	8-26-86	1	3	5.43	12	12	0	0	53	62	36	32	4	17	47	.300	.300	.299	7.98	2.89
De los Santos, Riquy	R-R	6-2	162	6-17-85	2	3	6.48	21	0	0	0	25	27	20	18	2	24	21	.287	.270	.298	7.56	8.64
Durden, Brandon	R-L	6-3	215	7-20-84	1	4	6.02	12	11	0	0	49	72	42	33	7	23	49	.344	.345	.344	8.94	4.20
Espinosa, Sandy	R-R	6-1	145	12-28-84	1	2	4.64	21	0	0	0	33	32	23	17	3	22	30	.258	.235	.274	8.18	6.00
Fabian, Robinson	R-R	6-3	152	2-10-86	1	3	11.79	12	3	0	0	24	43	33	31	8	8	20	.394	.368	.423	7.61	3.04
Hipke, Ross	R-R	5-10	180	8-11-86	1	1	6.75	19	0	0	0	32	41	33	24	11	9	26	.311	.300	.317	7.31	2.53
Johnson, Alan	R-R	6-1	180	8-24-83	3	2	3.97	15	15	0	0	79	90	44	35	1	24	78	.281	.275	.287	8.85	2.72
Johnston, Andy	R-R	6-5	205	4-20-84	1	2	1.06	30	0	0	18	34	22	10	4	0	7	24	.171	.097	.239	6.35	1.85
Manzueta, Radhames	R-R	6-2	160	4-13-83	0	4	8.78	4	4	0	0	13	25	22	13	1	8	13	.385	.292	.439	8.78	5.40
Metzger, Jason	L-L	6-4	205	12-12-81	6	1	5.13	22	4	0	0	47	50	29	27	7	13	40	.273	.362	.243	7.61	2.47
Pichardo, Manuel	R-R	6-1	154	2-18-84	1	0	5.34	23	0	0	0	32	37	29	19	5	18	29	.289	.283	.293	8.16	5.06
Rodriguez, Aneury	R-R	6-3	180	12-13-87	3	4	7.55	15	15	0	0	62	77	54	52	7	26	47	.309	.298	.322	6.82	3.77
Roe, Chaz	R-R	6-5	180	10-9-86	5	2	4.17	12	12	0	0	50	31	25	23	2	36	55	.175	.205	.152	9.97	6.52
Ruthven, Sean	R-R	6-4	195	9-13-82	2	1	3.58	18	0	0	1	28	25	20	11	5	11	35	.231	.209	.246	11.39	3.58
Sanchez, Rafael	R-R	6-2	174	9-20-82	2	1	3.24	13	0	0	0	17	15	7	6	0	7	18	.234	.263	.192	9.72	3.78
Strickland, Brett	R-R	6-0	170	2-15-83	4	3	1.43	30	0	0	3	44	34	11	7	0	16	45	.207	.258	.173	9.20	3.27
Webb, Lindsay	R-R	6-1	180	7-1-86	0	1	5.40	15	0	0	0	18	20	13	11	2	10	9	.274	.379	.205	4.42	4.91

GAMES BY POSITION: C—Blumenthal 16, Dombek 2, R. Rodriguez 29, Sargent 9, Suarez 24. **1B**—Berglund 6, Blumenthal 29, Cook 38, Suarez 5. **2B**—Polanco 4, Wimberly 22, Young 56. **3B**—Berglund 3, Cook 1, Mayora 32, Polanco 13, Strickland 5, Wimberly 33. **SS**—Mayora 15, Nazario 56, Wimberly 12. **OF**—Allen 31, Berglund 44, Brownell 30, Fowler 59, Garner 49, Loupadiere 24,

DETROIT TIGERS

BY DANNY KNOBLER

You didn't have to watch the whole season. You only had to see two weeks of it, in late August and early September, to know the whole story of the Tigers' 2005 season.

First, the Tigers went through a six-game span where they gave up eight or more runs in each game. It was the first time in 105 years of club history that had happened.

Then, just after that, the Tigers had a nine-game losing streak in which they scored 12 runs total. It was the first time that had happened to a Tiger team in 100 years—since 1905.

Mixed in, just for good measure, there was a key injury, as ace righthander Jeremy Bonderman was hit on the right wrist by a line drive off the bat of Oakland's Marco Scutaro. And there were issues in the clubhouse, with right fielder Magglio Ordonez summing up the Tigers by saying, "I think we stink."

And there you have it, in a nutshell, the story of the 2005 Tigers. When they hit, they didn't pitch. When they pitched, they didn't hit. They got hurt. They complained.

They finished 71-91, one game worse than in 2004. They lost more games than they won for the 12th consecutive year. They lost as many games in September as any team in club history. They cost manager Alan Trammell his job, and convinced owner Mike Ilitch and general manager Dave Dombrowski to replace him with Jim Leyland just two days after the end of the season.

It was quite a year, but it wasn't all bad. Placido Polanco hit .338, the second-best average by a Tiger in 44 years. Polanco, acquired in a June trade with Philadelphia, found a home and signed a four-year contract extension.

Chris Shelton, who barely played in 2004 as a Rule 5 draft pick, emerged as an everyday player at first base. He just missed hitting .300 and led the Tigers in on-base-plus-slugging percentage in what was in reality—if not officially—his rookie season.

Justin Verlander, the 2004 first-round draft pick, zoomed through the minor leagues and even made two big league starts in his first season as a pro. Joel Zumaya, a 20-year-old fireballer, didn't make it to the big leagues but did advance as far as Triple-A Toledo to give himself a chance at a big league job in 2006, when he'll be just 21.

Toledo won the International League's Governor's Cup championship, the first for the Mud Hens since 1967 and the first for a Tigers Triple-A affiliate since Evansville won the American Association in 1979. The entire minor league system had a good year, with Class A Lakeland posting the best record in the minors and the Tigers six affiliates producing the best overall record in the minors.

It wasn't enough to keep Dombrowski from saying on the final day of the big league season: "It was disappointing. It was a disappointing season."

It began with great hope, with the Tigers signing free agents Troy Percival and Ordonez and with Ilitch proclaiming in spring training, "I'm going to keep spending until we win."

But it also began with great concern, with Ordonez bothered by a mysterious stomach ailment that would eventually be diagnosed as a sports hernia and cost him the first three months of the season.

Percival tore a muscle in the elbow and went on the disabled list in early May, then tore it even worse and didn't pitch after the all-star break.

The Polanco trade was a positive, but even that came out of a negative. The Tigers were forced to make a move, after reliever Ugueth Urbina fought with teammates on a team flight to California. The Tigers felt fortunate to land Polanco in a deal they had to make.

The Tigers rallied in mid August, winning eight of nine games for their best stretch of the season, but the very next day, Bonderman was hit on the wrist and that awful two-week stretch began.

It was typical Tigers, 2005. Anything good was immediately followed by something bad.

PLAYERS OF THE YEAR

MAJOR LEAGUE: Placido Polanco, 2b

Acquired in a midseason 2005 deal with the Phillies in exchange for reliever Ugueth Urbina, Polanco might have won the American League batting title if he'd had enough at-bats to qualify. He established himself as more than just a versatile utilityman, posting an .846 OPS that ranked second on the Tigers.

MINOR LEAGUE: Justin Verlander, rhp

In his first season, Verlander dominated at two levels and even made a pair of spot starts in the majors. His upper-90s fastball overwhelmed hitters in the Florida State and Eastern leagues. He went 11-2, 1.29 with 136 strikeouts in 119 innings before a tired arm ended his season in early August.

ORGANIZATION LEADERS

BATTING		
***AVG**	Thames, Marcus, Toledo	.340
R	Frazier, Jeff, West Michigan	79
	Granderson, Curtis, Toledo	79
H	Francia, Juan, Erie/Lakeland	170
TB	Frazier, Jeff, West Michigan	243
2B	Frazier, Jeff, West Michigan	45
3B	Granderson, Curtis, Toledo	13
HR	Hessman, Mike, Toledo	28
RBI	Clevlen, Brent, Lakeland	102
BB	Espinosa, David, Erie/Toledo	74
SO	Hessman, Mike, Toledo	154
SB	Francia, Juan, Erie/Lakeland	41
***OBP**	Thames, Marcus, Toledo	.427
***SLG**	Thames, Marcus, Toledo	.679
PITCHING		
W	Tata, Jordan, Lakeland	13
L	Cornejo, Nate, Erie	12
#ERA	Verlander, Justin, Erie/Lakeland	1.11
G	Karnuth, Jason, Toledo	63
CG	Grilli, Jason, Toledo	3
	Kauten, Josh, Lakeland/West Michigan	3
SV	Almonte, Edwin, Erie	33
IP	Grilli, Jason, Toledo	167
BB	Zumaya, Joel, Erie/Toledo	76
SO	Zumaya, Joel, Erie/Toledo	199

*Minimum 250 at-bats. #Minimum 75 innings.

DETROIT TIGERS

Manager: Alan Trammell.

2005 Record: 71-91, .438 (4th, AL Central).

BATTING	B-T	HT	WT	DOB	AVG	vLH	vRH	G	AB	R	H	2B	3B	HR	RBI	BB	HBP	SH	SF	SO	SB	CS	SLG	OBP
Giarratano, Tony	B-R	6-0	180	11-29-82	.143	.000	.162	15	42	4	6	0	0	1	4	5	0	0	0	7	1	0	.214	.234
Gomez, Alexis	L-L	6-2	180	8-8-78	.188	.000	.214	9	16	2	3	0	0	0	1	2	0	0	0	2	0	0	.188	.278
Granderson, Curtis	L-R	6-1	185	3-16-81	.272	.320	.263	47	162	18	44	6	3	8	20	10	0	2	0	43	1	1	.494	.314
Guillen, Carlos	B-R	6-1	215	9-30-75	.320	.368	.306	87	334	48	107	15	4	5	23	24	2	0	1	45	2	3	.434	.368
Higginson, Bobby	L-R	5-11	195	8-18-70	.077	.000	.083	10	26	1	2	0	0	0	1	1	0	0	0	5	0	0	.077	.111
Hooper, Kevin	R-R	5-10	160	12-7-76	.200	.333	.000	6	5	0	1	0	0	0	0	0	0	2	0	1	0	0	.200	.200
Infante, Omar	R-R	6-0	180	12-26-81	.222	.174	.236	121	406	36	90	28	2	9	43	16	2	8	2	73	8	0	.367	.254
Inge, Brandon	R-R	5-11	190	5-19-77	.261	.281	.256	160	616	75	161	31	9	16	72	63	3	6	6	140	7	6	.419	.330
Logan, Nook	B-R	6-3	180	11-28-79	.258	.281	.249	129	322	47	83	12	5	1	17	21	1	12	0	52	23	6	.335	.305
Martinez, Ramon	R-R	6-1	190	10-10-72	.268	.200	.293	19	56	4	15	1	0	0	5	3	0	2	1	4	0	0	.286	.300
McDonald, John	R-R	5-11	175	9-24-74	.260	.167	.306	31	73	10	19	3	1	0	4	5	0	0	0	12	1	1	.329	.308
2-team (37 Toronto)					.277	.291	.263	68	166	18	46	6	1	0	16	11	2	3	2	24	6	1	.325	.326
Monroe, Craig	R-R	6-1	215	2-27-77	.277	.303	.270	157	567	69	157	30	3	20	89	40	3	1	12	95	8	3	.446	.322
Ordonez, Magglio	R-R	6-0	215	1-28-74	.302	.308	.300	82	305	38	92	17	0	8	46	30	1	0	7	35	0	0	.436	.359
Pena, Carlos	L-L	6-2	210	5-17-78	.235	.157	.254	79	260	37	61	9	0	18	44	31	4	0	0	95	0	1	.477	.325
Polanco, Placido	R-R	5-10	190	10-10-75	.338	.385	.320	86	343	58	116	20	2	6	36	21	8	2	4	16	4	3	.461	.386
Rodriguez, Ivan	R-R	5-9	195	11-30-71	.276	.294	.271	129	504	71	139	33	5	14	50	11	2	1	7	93	7	3	.444	.290
Shelton, Chris	R-R	6-0	215	6-26-80	.299	.278	.306	107	388	61	116	22	3	18	59	34	5	0	4	87	0	0	.510	.360
Smith, Jason	L-R	6-3	200	7-24-77	.190	.143	.196	27	58	4	11	1	2	0	2	0	1	4	0	16	2	1	.276	.203
Thames, Marcus	R-R	6-2	205	3-6-77	.196	.222	.183	38	107	11	21	2	0	7	16	9	1	0	1	38	0	0	.411	.263
White, Rondell	R-R	6-1	225	2-23-72	.313	.325	.309	97	374	49	117	24	3	12	53	17	5	0	4	48	1	0	.489	.348
Wilson, Vance	R-R	5-11	190	3-17-73	.197	.214	.191	61	152	18	30	4	0	3	19	11	6	2	2	26	0	0	.283	.275
Young, Dmitri	B-R	6-2	245	10-11-73	.271	.277	.269	126	469	61	127	25	3	21	72	29	9	0	1	100	1	0	.471	.325

PITCHING	B-T	HT	WT	DOB	W	L	ERA	G	GS	CG	SV	IP	H	R	ER	HR	BB	SO	AVG	vLH	vRH	K/9	BB/9
Bonderman, Jeremy	R-R	6-2	220	10-28-82	14	13	4.57	29	29	4	0	189	199	101	96	21	57	145	.271	.287	.249	6.90	2.71
Colon, Roman	R-R	6-6	225	8-13-79	1	1	6.12	12	3	0	0	25	35	17	17	7	7	17	.327	.373	.271	6.12	2.52
Creek, Doug	L-L	6-0	225	3-1-69	0	0	6.85	20	0	0	0	22	27	18	17	7	7	18	.293	.282	.302	7.25	2.82
Darensbourg, Vic	L-L	5-10	180	11-13-70	1	1	2.82	22	0	0	0	22	24	7	7	2	7	9	.282	.231	.326	3.63	2.82
Dingman, Craig	R-R	6-4	230	3-12-74	2	3	3.66	34	0	0	4	32	30	14	13	5	9	24	.259	.208	.294	6.75	2.53
Douglass, Sean	R-R	6-6	220	4-28-79	5	5	5.56	18	16	0	0	87	92	57	54	13	33	55	.276	.315	.232	5.67	3.40
Farnsworth, Kyle	R-R	6-4	240	4-14-76	1	1	2.32	46	0	0	6	43	29	12	11	1	20	55	.192	.213	.178	11.60	4.22
German, Franklyn	R-R	6-7	260	1-20-80	4	0	3.66	58	0	0	1	59	63	26	24	7	34	38	.284	.267	.294	5.80	5.19
Ginter, Matt	R-R	6-1	220	12-24-77	0	1	6.17	14	1	0	0	35	49	25	24	6	9	15	.340	.349	.333	3.86	2.31
Good, Andrew	R-R	6-1	210	9-19-79	0	0	5.40	2	0	0	0	5	4	3	3	1	1	7	.211	.167	.231	12.60	1.80
Grilli, Jason	R-R	6-5	210	11-11-76	1	1	3.38	3	2	0	0	16	14	6	6	1	6	5	.255	.222	.286	2.81	3.38
Johnson, Jason	R-R	6-6	220	10-27-73	8	13	4.54	33	33	1	0	210	233	117	106	23	49	93	.285	.310	.258	3.99	2.10
Karnuth, Jason	R-R	6-2	190	5-15-76	0	0	5.40	3	0	0	0	2	2	1	1	0	0	0	.286	.000	.667	0.00	0.00
Ledezma, Wilfredo	L-L	6-4	210	1-21-81	2	4	7.07	10	10	0	0	50	61	46	39	10	24	30	.303	.352	.286	5.44	4.35
Maroth, Mike	L-L	6-0	190	8-17-77	14	14	4.74	34	34	0	0	209	235	123	110	30	51	115	.288	.275	.293	4.95	2.20
Percival, Troy	R-R	6-3	235	8-9-69	1	3	5.76	26	0	0	8	25	19	16	16	7	11	20	.207	.173	.250	7.20	3.96
Robertson, Nate	R-L	6-2	220	9-3-77	7	16	4.48	32	32	2	0	197	202	113	98	28	65	122	.266	.244	.272	5.58	2.97
Rodney, Fernando	R-R	5-11	210	3-18-77	2	3	2.86	39	0	0	9	44	39	14	14	5	17	42	.238	.265	.219	8.59	3.48
Spurling, Chris	R-R	6-5	230	6-28-77	3	4	3.44	56	0	0	0	71	58	30	27	8	22	26	.230	.223	.234	3.31	2.80
Urbina, Ugueth	R-R	6-0	205	2-15-74	1	3	2.63	25	0	0	9	27	21	9	8	4	14	31	.208	.289	.143	10.21	4.61
Verlander, Justin	R-R	6-5	200	2-20-83	0	2	7.15	2	2	0	0	11	15	9	9	1	5	7	.313	.333	.278	5.56	3.97
Walker, Jamie	L-L	6-2	185	7-1-71	4	3	3.70	66	0	0	0	49	49	22	20	5	13	30	.257	.245	.271	5.55	2.40
Woodyard, Mark	R-R	6-2	195	12-29-78	0	0	1.50	3	0	0	0	6	4	1	1	1	0	3	.182	.222	.154	4.50	0.00

FIELDING

Catcher	PCT	G	PO	A	E	DP	PB
Rodriguez	.995	123	702	60	4	4	4
Wilson	.989	60	234	29	3	4	0

First Base	PCT	G	PO	A	E	DP
Martinez	1.000	2	3	0	0	0
Pena	.993	51	418	35	3	46
Shelton	.993	84	778	60	6	87
Smith	1.000	1	10	1	0	0
Young	.990	30	265	22	3	25

Second Base	PCT	G	PO	A	E	DP
Hooper	1.000	1	2	1	0	0
Infante	.988	69	153	186	4	52
Martinez	.917	4	10	12	2	3
McDonald	1.000	8	5	9	0	3
Polanco	.993	84	187	248	3	69
Smith	.960	6	8	16	1	4

Third Base	PCT	G	PO	A	E	DP
Inge	.957	160	129	378	23	42
Martinez	.000	1	0	0	0	0
McDonald	1.000	1	2	0	0	0
Polanco	1.000	1	1	3	0	0
Smith	1.000	3	5	6	0	2

Shortstop	PCT	G	PO	A	E	DP
Giarratano	.949	13	16	40	3	5
Guillen	.978	75	85	228	7	44
Hooper	.833	2	2	3	1	0
Infante	.975	50	82	149	6	35
Martinez	.955	12	13	29	2	4
McDonald	.951	22	29	69	5	16
Smith	1.000	15	14	27	0	6

Outfield	PCT	G	PO	A	E	DP
Gomez	1.000	9	9	0	0	0
Granderson	1.000	45	129	2	0	0
Higginson	1.000	7	8	1	0	0
Hooper	1.000	3	1	0	0	0
Inge	1.000	2	2	0	0	0
Logan	.979	123	282	3	6	2
Monroe	.981	156	294	10	6	4
Ordonez	.993	81	139	5	1	0
Shelton	.000	1	0	0	0	0
Thames	.978	31	45	0	1	0
White	1.000	65	119	0	0	0
Young	1.000	20	35	1	0	0

FARM SYSTEM

General Manager: Dave Dombrowski. **Director, Minor League Operations:** Dan Lunetta. **Scouting Director:** David Chadd.

Class	Farm Team	League	W	L	Pct.	Finish*	Manager	Affiliate Since
AAA	Toledo (Ohio) Mud Hens	International	89	55	.618	**+1st (14)**	Larry Parrish	1987
AA	Erie (Pa.) Sea Wolves	Eastern	63	79	.444	t-11 (12)	Duffy Dyer	2001
High A	Lakeland (Fla.) Tigers	Florida State	85	48	.639	**1st (12)**	Mike Rojas	1967
Low A	West Michigan Whitecaps (Grand Rapids)	Midwest	73	67	.521	**3rd (14)**	Matt Walbeck	1997
SS A	Oneonta (N.Y.) Tigers	New York-Penn	48	27	.640	**2nd (14)**	Tom Brookens	1999
Rookie	Lakeland (Fla.) Tigers	Gulf Coast	24	30	.444	t-9th (12)	Kevin Bradshaw	1995

*Finish in overall standings (No. of teams in league)/playoff teams in **boldface** +League champion

LARRY GOREN

Carlos Guillen: A fine season shortened by injury

RICK BATTLE

Brent Clevlen: 101 RBIs in the Florida State League

TOLEDO MUD HENS — Class AAA

INTERNATIONAL LEAGUE

BATTING	B-T	HT	WT	DOB	AVG	vLH	vRH	G	AB	R	H	2B	3B	HR	RBI	BB	HBP	SH	SF	SO	SB	CS	SLG	OBP
Dawkins, Gookie	R-R	6-1	180	5-12-79	.242	.257	.236	103	355	56	86	21	5	10	38	31	7	3	3	75	10	7	.414	.313
Espinosa, David	B-R	6-2	190	12-16-81	.244	.286	.235	17	41	8	10	0	1	0	2	8	0	1	0	10	5	2	.293	.367
Gettis, Byron	R-R	6-0	240	3-13-80	.189	.250	.157	35	106	13	20	2	0	3	12	10	1	0	0	33	1	1	.292	.265
Gomez, Alexis	L-L	6-2	180	8-8-78	.307	.288	.314	114	424	51	130	28	6	7	55	27	2	3	4	91	21	7	.450	.348
Granderson, Curtis	L-R	6-1	185	3-16-81	.290	.295	.288	111	445	79	129	29	13	15	65	48	3	2	5	129	22	6	.515	.359
Hannahan, Jack	L-R	6-2	205	3-4-80	.269	.329	.241	68	238	31	64	15	0	4	28	25	3	0	3	58	6	3	.382	.342
Harper, Brandon	R-R	6-4	200	4-29-76	.246	.228	.258	81	252	33	62	14	1	6	34	28	7	0	3	36	4	0	.381	.334
Hessman, Mike	R-R	6-5	215	3-5-78	.214	.258	.197	134	473	69	101	19	1	28	74	58	11	3	2	154	5	4	.436	.313
Hooper, Kevin	R-R	5-10	160	12-7-76	.240	.255	.233	85	313	41	75	13	2	1	27	22	2	10	3	37	16	4	.304	.291
Kelly, Don	L-R	6-4	190	2-15-80	.250	.289	.238	43	160	22	40	8	0	1	13	13	0	3	0	15	8	2	.319	.306
Martinez, Sandy	L-R	6-2	215	10-8-70	.265	.190	.278	81	272	29	72	17	0	5	35	20	2	0	4	58	2	2	.382	.315
Martinez, Ramon	R-R	6-1	190	10-10-72	.733	.714	.750	3	15	4	11	0	0	0	1	1	0	0	0	1	0	0	.733	.750
Ordonez, Magglio	R-R	6-0	215	1-28-74	.214	.000	.250	4	14	3	3	1	0	1	2	2	0	0	0	3	0	0	.500	.313
Pena, Carlos	L-L	6-2	210	5-17-78	.311	.247	.339	71	257	43	80	17	1	12	45	45	6	0	1	65	3	4	.525	.424
Raburn, Ryan	R-R	6-0	185	4-17-81	.253	.288	.241	130	471	62	119	22	4	19	64	45	5	1	2	109	8	3	.437	.323
Shelton, Chris	R-R	6-0	215	6-26-80	.331	.328	.333	48	181	34	60	19	0	8	39	25	3	0	2	33	0	2	.569	.417
Smith, Jason	L-R	6-3	200	7-24-77	.230	.286	.217	55	187	24	43	11	2	6	25	11	0	6	3	53	8	4	.406	.269
Thames, Marcus	R-R	6-2	205	3-6-77	.340	.242	.369	73	265	53	90	18	3	22	56	41	3	0	5	59	4	1	.679	.427
Wise, Dewayne	L-L	6-1	180	2-24-78	.234	.248	.230	108	384	42	90	12	5	8	45	23	5	3	2	76	22	7	.354	.285

PITCHING	B-T	HT	WT	DOB	W	L	ERA	G	GS	CG	SV	IP	H	R	ER	HR	BB	SO	AVG	vLH	vRH	K/9	BB/9
Baugh, Kenny	R-R	6-4	195	2-5-79	12	8	3.38	28	28	1	0	165	159	72	62	13	60	107	.253	.256	.251	5.82	3.27
Bumatay, Mike	L-L	6-0	170	10-9-79	0	0	0.00	3	0	0	0	4	4	0	0	0	2	5	.250	.250	.250	10.38	4.15
Bynum, Mike	L-L	6-4	200	3-20-78	2	1	6.97	8	2	0	0	21	26	21	16	5	13	12	.313	.391	.283	5.23	5.66
Creek, Doug	L-L	6-0	225	3-1-69	2	2	4.61	28	1	0	0	27	28	14	14	2	14	32	.267	.293	.250	10.54	4.61

PITCHING	B-T	HT	WT	DOB	W	L	ERA	G	GS	CG	SV	IP	H	R	ER	HR	BB	SO	AVG	vLH	vRH	K/9	BB/9
Cruz, Nelson	R-R	6-1	185	9-13-72	5	4	4.20	14	11	0	0	64	69	31	30	8	17	55	.278	.234	.312	7.69	2.38
Darensbourg, Vic	L-L	5-10	180	11-13-70	2	0	0.29	44	0	0	7	31	17	3	1	0	11	30	.172	.120	.224	8.80	3.23
Dingman, Craig	R-R	6-4	230	3-12-74	2	1	2.81	35	0	0	4	48	42	18	15	3	13	67	.230	.282	.196	12.56	2.44
Douglass, Sean	R-R	6-6	220	4-28-79	9	1	2.87	14	14	0	0	82	61	26	26	5	27	76	.205	.214	.198	8.38	2.98
Ennis, John	R-R	6-5	240	10-17-79	3	5	4.85	50	1	0	1	72	77	41	39	7	30	65	.276	.237	.303	8.09	3.73
Ginter, Matt	R-R	6-1	220	12-24-77	4	3	4.33	17	10	0	0	69	72	35	33	9	10	49	.269	.280	.261	6.42	1.31
Good, Andrew	R-R	6-1	210	9-19-79	9	5	3.68	23	23	0	0	134	129	61	55	18	42	89	.253	.241	.265	5.96	2.81
Green, Steve	R-R	6-2	200	1-26-78	2	2	5.29	24	0	0	2	32	42	20	19	2	20	41	.316	.326	.311	11.41	5.57
Grilli, Jason	R-R	6-5	210	11-11-76	12	9	4.09	28	28	3	0	167	170	89	76	21	58	120	.263	.277	.252	6.45	3.12
Henkel, Rob	R-L	6-3	210	8-3-78	1	1	7.82	10	0	0	0	13	14	12	11	2	11	9	.280	.263	.290	6.39	7.82
Johnson, Mark	R-R	6-3	225	5-2-75	0	1	8.05	7	2	0	0	19	24	19	17	2	8	14	.316	.273	.375	6.63	3.79
Karnuth, Jason	R-R	6-2	190	5-15-76	7	2	2.13	63	0	0	23	68	65	19	16	1	17	36	.261	.287	.245	4.79	2.26
Ledezma, Wilfredo	L-L	6-4	210	1-21-81	5	3	5.29	11	10	0	0	51	52	30	30	3	27	44	.260	.282	.255	7.76	4.76
Miner, Zach	R-R	6-3	200	3-12-82	3	1	2.36	6	6	0	0	34	28	10	9	4	20	20	.230	.232	.227	5.24	5.24
2-team (17 Richmond)					5	8	3.71	23	23	0	0	124	125	57	51	10	65	83	.263	.270	.258	6.04	4.73
Rodney, Fernando	R-R	5-11	210	3-18-77	0	0	3.00	3	0	0	0	3	2	1	1	0	1	4	.182	.000	.333	12.00	3.00
Rodney, Lee	R-R	6-2	187	11-6-77	0	0	2.25	1	0	0	0	4	4	1	1	0	3	0	.308	.333	.300	0.00	6.75
Roney, Matt	R-R	6-3	245	1-10-80	1	1	0.95	14	0	0	3	28	23	3	3	0	11	27	.225	.267	.193	8.58	3.49
Spurling, Chris	R-R	6-5	230	6-28-77	2	1	4.12	12	0	0	1	20	18	10	9	2	3	15	.243	.185	.277	6.86	1.37
Woodyard, Mark	R-R	6-2	195	12-19-84	5	2	3.84	45	0	0	1	70	67	34	30	7	32	62	.251	.257	.247	7.93	4.09
Zumaya, Joel	R-R	6-3	215	11-9-84	1	2	2.66	8	8	1	0	44	30	13	13	2	24	56	.194	.197	.190	11.45	4.91

FIELDING

Catcher	PCT	G	PO	A	E	DP	PB
Harper	.997	74	536	34	2	2	7
Hooper	1.000	1	1	0	0	0	0
S. Martinez	.982	76	515	46	10	5	4
Shelton	.958	3	21	2	1	1	0

First Base	PCT	G	PO	A	E	DP
Hannahan	.974	5	36	2	1	4
Harper	1.000	1	11	1	0	2
Hessman	1.000	31	278	21	0	26
Hooper	.000	1	0	0	0	0
S. Martinez	.000	1	0	0	1	0
Pena	.986	62	519	33	8	49
Shelton	.989	31	252	22	3	34
Smith	.986	17	134	8	2	15

Second Base	PCT	G	PO	A	E	DP
Hannahan	1.000	2	5	5	0	3
Hooper	.974	36	80	105	5	28
R. Martinez	1.000	1	1	2	0	0
Raburn	.959	99	214	277	21	63
Smith	.965	14	20	35	2	10

Third Base	PCT	G	PO	A	E	DP
Hannahan	.946	52	39	102	8	7
Hessman	.987	75	52	169	3	16
Hooper	1.000	4	0	6	0	2
Kelly	.917	7	1	10	1	0
Smith	.962	14	7	18	1	4

Shortstop	PCT	G	PO	A	E	DP
Dawkins	.946	79	122	213	19	52
Hooper	.963	25	32	73	4	20
Kelly	.951	34	38	98	7	25
R. Martinez	1.000	2	3	2	0	0
Smith	.968	8	16	14	1	3

Outfield	PCT	G	PO	A	E	DP
Dawkins	1.000	9	9	1	0	0
Espinosa	1.000	7	5	0	0	0
Gettis	.980	30	45	5	1	0
Gomez	.968	113	177	7	6	1
Granderson	.985	107	256	15	4	3
Harper	1.000	3	1	0	0	0
Hessman	1.000	16	17	1	0	0
Hooper	1.000	21	29	3	0	1
Kelly	.000	1	0	0	0	0
Ordonez	1.000	3	3	0	0	0
Raburn	.000	1	0	0	0	0
Smith	1.000	5	3	0	0	0
Thames	.975	56	75	4	2	0
Wise	.980	92	190	3	4	0

ERIE SEAWOLVES — Class AA

EASTERN LEAGUE

BATTING	B-T	HT	WT	DOB	AVG	vLH	vRH	G	AB	R	H	2B	3B	HR	RBI	BB	HBP	SH	SF	SO	SB	CS	SLG	OBP
Airoso, Kurt	R-R	6-2	190	2-12-75	.281	.292	.276	99	381	67	107	29	1	22	71	38	10	0	4	105	2	2	.535	.358
Espinosa, David	B-R	6-2	190	12-16-81	.262	.255	.266	112	431	66	113	21	8	9	40	66	4	1	4	109	11	6	.411	.362
Francia, Juan	B-R	5-9	145	1-4-82	.290	.273	.300	72	300	38	87	9	6	3	27	17	5	7	2	43	15	7	.390	.336
Gettis, Byron	R-R	6-0	240	3-13-80	.274	.293	.263	69	252	44	69	12	1	9	40	23	8	1	0	81	3	3	.437	.353
Giarratano, Tony	B-R	6-0	180	11-29-82	.266	.237	.280	89	346	40	92	22	3	3	32	32	5	3	3	75	12	5	.373	.334
Hannahan, Jack	L-R	6-2	205	3-4-80	.136	.125	.143	7	22	1	3	0	0	0	1	4	0	0	0	8	0	0	.136	.269
Kelly, Don	L-R	6-4	190	2-15-80	.340	.324	.348	82	329	54	112	22	3	9	54	36	1	0	5	43	10	2	.508	.402
Knoedler, Jason	B-R	6-0	185	7-17-80	.228	.233	.224	32	79	10	18	6	0	1	8	10	1	1	0	26	1	0	.342	.322
Maples, Chris	R-R	5-10	180	10-31-79	.225	.219	.228	93	333	41	75	24	0	12	54	20	8	4	4	98	2	1	.405	.282
Mejia, Gilberto	B-R	5-9	160	9-1-82	.190	.185	.192	60	211	31	40	2	2	3	18	19	3	6	0	56	2	1	.261	.266
Melian, Jackson	R-R	6-2	205	1-7-80	.261	.333	.214	7	23	2	6	2	0	0	1	1	0	0	1	5	0	0	.348	.280
Mendez, Victor	B-R	5-11	160	6-28-80	.231	.297	.205	96	325	46	75	14	2	10	39	32	1	5	0	82	7	5	.378	.302
Patino, Jorge	R-R	5-10	150	1-25-86	.059	.000	.083	6	17	1	1	0	0	0	0	0	2	0	0	5	0	1	.059	.158
Rabelo, Mike	B-R	6-1	200	1-17-80	.273	.271	.274	77	282	33	77	18	1	2	26	18	9	3	2	42	0	1	.365	.334
Roughton, Jody	L-R	6-1	190	5-6-81	.429	.500	.400	2	7	0	3	1	0	0	0	1	0	0	0	2	0	0	.571	.500
St. Pierre, Max	R-R	6-0	175	4-17-80	.278	.256	.289	95	360	46	100	18	0	5	46	23	1	1	3	55	1	1	.369	.320
Tejeda, Juan	R-R	6-2	195	1-26-82	.291	.319	.277	122	470	64	137	27	2	14	82	41	7	0	5	86	2	4	.447	.354
Tousa, Scott	L-R	5-11	180	8-3-79	.245	.236	.250	60	212	30	52	4	2	4	31	24	9	2	3	34	0	3	.340	.343
Woods, Michael	R-R	6-1	200	9-11-80	.231	.229	.231	130	451	52	104	18	6	8	47	50	3	4	7	119	5	5	.350	.307

PITCHING	B-T	HT	WT	DOB	W	L	ERA	G	GS	CG	SV	IP	H	R	ER	HR	BB	SO	AVG	vLH	vRH	K/9	BB/9
Almonte, Edwin	R-R	6-3	220	12-17-76	1	5	4.97	52	0	0	33	51	57	31	28	10	14	50	.279	.282	.277	8.88	2.49
Beech, Matt	L-L	6-2	195	1-20-72	2	3	4.68	6	5	1	0	33	34	19	17	4	18	23	.272	.280	.267	6.34	4.96
Bierd, Randor	R-R	6-4	190	3-14-84	1	3	5.40	4	4	0	0	22	28	19	13	2	8	10	.315	.184	.412	4.15	3.32
Birtwell, John	R-R	6-2	225	9-4-79	0	2	4.46	29	0	0	0	40	40	23	20	6	16	23	.258	.250	.263	5.13	3.57
Bumatay, Mike	L-L	6-0	170	10-9-79	2	4	4.08	50	0	0	2	64	56	33	29	8	36	72	.232	.226	.236	10.13	5.06
Bynum, Mike	L-L	6-4	200	3-20-78	3	0	2.40	5	5	0	0	30	21	8	8	2	9	34	.194	.048	.230	10.20	2.70
Cornejo, Nate	R-R	6-5	245	9-24-79	4	12	4.59	19	19	0	0	102	126	57	52	15	17	48	.307	.321	.296	4.24	1.50
De la Cruz, Eulogio	R-R	5-11	160	3-12-84	0	1	16.20	1	0	0	0	2	2	3	3	0	4	0	.286	.250	.333	0.00	21.60
Hamman, Corey	L-L	6-2	198	4-12-80	3	5	4.29	45	5	0	3	92	109	56	44	8	17	60	.291	.264	.305	5.85	1.66
Henkel, Rob	R-L	6-3	210	8-3-78	6	7	5.70	18	14	0	0	79	104	60	50	14	30	53	.320	.286	.332	6.04	3.42
Hensen, Brian	L-L	6-4	170	8-12-82	0	0	0.00	2	0	0	0	2	2	0	0	0	1	0	.286	.000	.333	0.00	4.50
Johnson, Jeremy	R-R	6-3	170	7-19-82	9	8	4.91	24	24	0	0	132	161	91	72	23	42	82	.300	.359	.263	5.59	2.86
Johnson, Mark	R-R	6-3	225	5-2-75	4	3	5.06	32	7	0	0	80	89	50	45	11	15	50	.276	.295	.261	5.63	1.69
Kobow, Michael	R-R	6-4	190	4-9-79	0	0	10.13	3	0	0	0	3	4	3	3	0	4	0	.333	.500	.167	0.00	13.50
Larrison, Preston	R-R	6-4	235	11-19-80	4	3	5.23	7	7	0	0	33	38	21	19	3	9	11	.290	.350	.239	3.03	2.48
Peterson, Adam	R-R	6-2	225	5-18-79	4	3	6.58	47	0	0	0	64	78	51	47	8	35	54	.299	.280	.311	7.55	4.90
Rodney, Lee	R-R	6-2	187	11-6-77	5	3	3.99	45	1	0	3	79	91	42	35	5	29	53	.292	.311	.278	6.04	3.30
Roney, Matt	R-R	6-3	245	1-10-80	0	1	1.25	11	0	0	1	22	13	3	3	1	6	23	.173	.250	.116	9.55	2.49

PITCHING	B-T	HT	WT	DOB	W	L	ERA	G	GS	CG	SV	IP	H	R	ER	HR	BB	SO	AVG	vLH	vRH	K/9	BB/9
Sanchez, Humberto	R-R	6-6	230	5-28-83	3	5	5.57	15	11	0	0	65	72	42	40	10	27	65	.283	.306	.269	9.05	3.76
Vasquez, Virgil	R-R	6-3	205	6-7-82	2	8	5.27	15	15	0	0	84	93	59	49	10	14	53	.281	.275	.287	5.70	1.51
Verlander, Justin	R-R	6-5	200	2-20-83	2	0	0.28	7	7	0	0	33	11	1	1	1	7	32	.103	.130	.082	8.82	1.93
Weis, Brad	L-L	6-1	187	11-29-77	0	0	4.60	10	0	0	0	16	19	8	8	2	8	12	.317	.227	.368	6.89	4.60
Zumaya, Joel	R-R	6-3	215	11-9-84	8	3	2.77	18	18	0	0	107	71	40	33	8	52	143	.187	.205	.174	11.99	4.36

FIELDING

Catcher	PCT	G	PO	A	E	DP	PB
Rabelo	.986	55	376	38	6	2	3
St. Pierre	.990	89	591	72	7	9	12

First Base	PCT	G	PO	A	E	DP
Gettis	1.000	1	5	0	0	2
Knoedler	1.000	4	24	1	0	3
Maples	1.000	23	150	11	0	16
Rabelo	.992	16	115	9	1	6
Roughton	1.000	2	16	1	0	2
Tejeda	.987	104	860	49	12	82

Second Base	PCT	G	PO	A	E	DP
Francia	.965	66	145	162	11	33
Maples	.949	8	17	20	2	7
Mejia	.974	55	133	170	8	42
Tousa	1.000	1	4	3	0	0
Woods	1.000	18	28	40	0	8

Third Base	PCT	G	PO	A	E	DP
Hannahan	.967	6	15	14	1	1
Kelly	.875	57	34	92	18	7
Maples	.925	37	31	80	9	7
Mendez	1.000	1	2	3	0	0
Rabelo	1.000	2	0	1	0	0
Tousa	.950	45	35	99	7	8

Shortstop	PCT	G	PO	A	E	DP
Francia	.806	6	6	19	6	3
Giarratano	.954	89	120	255	18	47
Kelly	.939	24	36	56	6	15
Maples	1.000	2	4	6	0	2
Mejia	.926	7	10	15	2	2
Patino	.960	5	8	16	1	2
Tousa	.958	14	25	44	3	10

Outfield	PCT	G	PO	A	E	DP
Airoso	1.000	10	21	1	0	0
Espinosa	.977	106	160	11	4	4
Gettis	.941	62	118	9	8	2
Knoedler	1.000	24	43	3	0	0
Maples	.955	30	39	3	2	0
Melian	1.000	5	9	0	0	0
Mendez	.978	94	256	9	6	1
Woods	.972	111	198	7	6	1

LAKELAND TIGERS — High Class A

FLORIDA STATE LEAGUE

BATTING	B-T	HT	WT	DOB	AVG	vLH	vRH	G	AB	R	H	2B	3B	HR	RBI	BB	HBP	SH	SF	SO	SB	CS	SLG	OBP
Blue, Vince	L-R	6-2	180	2-8-83	.297	.232	.319	124	498	67	148	17	3	0	50	47	1	6	4	84	40	29	.343	.356
Cleveland, Russ	R-R	6-3	215	12-26-79	.274	.364	.238	44	113	14	31	3	2	2	10	8	0	3	0	22	3	1	.389	.322
Clevlen, Brent	R-R	6-2	190	10-27-83	.302	.275	.310	130	494	77	149	28	4	18	102	65	5	2	2	118	14	5	.484	.387
Cotto, Pedro	L-L	5-11	175	5-26-82	.235	.167	.273	9	17	3	4	0	0	0	1	1	0	1	0	0	1	0	.235	.278
Francia, Juan	B-R	5-9	145	1-4-82	.325	.338	.320	60	255	39	83	5	0	3	29	27	5	2	1	34	26	10	.380	.399
Gonzalez, Juan	B-R	6-0	165	2-23-82	.274	.321	.259	64	219	30	60	6	4	1	12	17	1	5	1	33	5	5	.352	.328
Graham, Andrew	R-R	6-4	215	4-22-82	.286	.500	.250	7	14	1	4	0	0	0	2	0	0	0	0	2	0	0	.286	.286
Hunt, Kelly	R-R	6-5	240	4-15-81	.216	.221	.214	128	501	59	108	26	0	18	86	29	3	0	8	122	6	10	.375	.259
Kirkland, Kody	R-R	6-4	205	6-9-83	.266	.162	.299	125	443	78	118	24	9	16	65	36	16	0	2	102	12	3	.470	.342
Knoedler, Jason	B-R	6-0	185	7-17-80	.281	.269	.286	40	89	18	25	6	0	0	9	16	0	1	1	21	3	1	.348	.387
McKinney, Garth	R-R	6-3	210	5-7-82	.242	.204	.254	115	401	70	97	17	3	23	71	26	9	0	3	151	16	5	.471	.301
Mejia, Gilberto	B-R	5-9	160	9-1-82	.265	.222	.279	64	260	32	69	8	2	2	21	19	3	2	0	64	10	8	.335	.323
Nicholson, Derek	L-R	5-11	205	6-17-76	.297	.302	.296	119	427	78	127	24	4	18	66	59	4	0	7	77	13	0	.499	.382
Reynolds, Wilton	R-R	6-4	195	3-5-80	.206	.143	.250	15	34	3	7	5	0	0	4	0	0	0	0	13	1	1	.353	.206
Rodland, Eric	L-R	6-1	180	2-23-80	.278	.231	.288	72	230	33	64	12	2	5	28	22	3	1	2	42	8	5	.413	.346
Sanchez, Danilo	R-R	5-11	185	10-25-80	.284	.294	.280	103	349	58	99	18	0	22	68	38	7	0	5	52	0	1	.524	.361
Skelton, James	L-R	5-11	165	10-28-85	.000	.000	.000	1	1	0	0	0	0	0	0	0	0	0	0	1	0	0	.000	.000
Tousa, Scott	L-R	5-11	180	8-3-79	.310	.396	.280	59	203	40	63	6	2	1	20	25	9	2	1	39	8	4	.374	.408

PITCHING	B-T	HT	WT	DOB	W	L	ERA	G	GS	CG	SV	IP	H	R	ER	HR	BB	SO	AVG	vLH	vRH	K/9	BB/9
Baldwin, Andy	R-R	6-2	190	2-28-82	1	1	5.30	12	0	0	0	19	17	14	11	0	10	13	.250	.350	.208	6.27	4.82
Bierd, Randor	R-R	6-4	190	3-14-84	1	3	5.66	4	4	0	0	21	22	14	13	4	4	18	.268	.288	.233	7.84	1.74
Bumstead, Nate	R-R	6-2	215	5-5-82	12	4	2.58	25	25	2	0	161	136	61	46	11	58	111	.227	.249	.209	6.22	3.25
De la Cruz, Eulogio	R-R	5-11	160	3-12-84	4	3	3.39	40	10	0	5	96	66	46	36	5	36	97	.191	.175	.200	9.13	3.39
French, Lucas	L-L	6-4	220	9-13-85	3	1	4.43	4	4	0	0	22	29	14	11	3	9	17	.309	.263	.320	6.85	3.63
Hensen, Brian	L-L	6-4	170	8-12-82	2	1	3.77	43	0	0	0	62	69	28	26	7	17	36	.289	.213	.315	5.23	2.47
Homer, Chris	R-R	6-1	190	3-6-81	7	4	3.09	54	0	0	29	64	55	25	22	4	25	50	.240	.235	.243	7.03	3.52
Kauten, Josh	R-R	6-3	200	4-5-82	4	2	2.84	6	6	1	0	38	31	13	12	1	17	18	.226	.212	.235	4.26	4.03
Kobow, Michael	R-R	6-4	190	4-9-79	1	1	4.80	14	0	0	0	15	14	9	8	1	11	12	.259	.235	.270	7.20	6.60
Larrison, Preston	R-R	6-4	235	11-19-80	1	2	4.70	9	9	0	0	38	48	22	20	0	12	25	.318	.275	.354	5.87	2.82
Martinez, Cristhian	R-R	6-1	160	3-6-82	2	0	4.91	3	2	0	0	11	11	6	6	0	4	9	.256	.250	.263	7.36	3.27
McDowell, Kevin	L-L	6-2	200	11-20-78	2	6	6.06	35	12	0	0	85	97	64	57	8	42	63	.294	.290	.296	6.70	4.46
Ostlund, Ian	R-L	6-1	200	10-17-78	4	3	2.93	19	0	0	0	28	29	11	9	4	3	18	.284	.167	.348	5.86	0.98
Rodriguez, Jermy	R-R	5-10	160	1-10-80	4	5	4.73	21	11	0	0	65	60	40	34	7	24	50	.247	.270	.231	6.96	3.34
Rogers, Brian	R-R	6-4	190	7-17-82	4	1	2.06	52	1	0	2	66	50	16	15	2	21	65	.212	.214	.211	8.91	2.88
Sanchez, Felix	R-L	6-3	195	8-3-81	2	1	2.93	22	0	0	2	28	28	11	9	2	12	13	.264	.240	.272	4.23	3.90
Tata, Jordan	R-R	6-6	220	9-20-81	13	2	2.79	25	25	2	0	155	138	55	48	12	41	134	.239	.245	.233	7.78	2.38
Vasquez, Virgil	R-R	6-3	205	6-7-82	4	1	4.21	8	8	1	0	47	52	23	22	6	7	31	.289	.304	.279	5.94	1.34
Verlander, Justin	R-R	6-5	200	2-20-83	9	2	1.67	13	13	2	0	86	70	19	16	3	19	104	.230	.192	.256	10.88	1.99
Zell, Danny	L-L	6-5	210	11-27-81	5	5	2.15	49	3	0	0	75	71	20	18	3	26	50	.248	.229	.258	5.97	3.11

FIELDING

Catcher	PCT	G	PO	A	E	DP	PB
Cleveland	.996	41	210	16	1	0	3
Graham	1.000	7	25	3	0	0	1
Roa	1.000	1	2	0	0	0	0
Sanchez	.996	103	711	56	3	10	13
Skelton	.000	1	0	0	0	0	0

First Base	PCT	G	PO	A	E	DP
Hunt	.992	125	1092	117	10	129
Knoedler	.000	1	0	0	0	0
Nicholson	1.000	9	83	7	0	10
Rodland	1.000	2	1	2	0	1

Second Base	PCT	G	PO	A	E	DP
Francia	.976	60	125	206	8	51
Gonzalez	1.000	2	1	6	0	0
Mejia	.969	48	89	158	8	31
Rodland	.992	30	47	73	1	23

Third Base	PCT	G	PO	A	E	DP
Cleveland	1.000	1	0	3	0	1
Gonzalez	1.000	1	0	4	0	1
Kirkland	.924	122	77	237	26	32
Rodland	.931	13	2	25	2	2

Shortstop	PCT	G	PO	A	E	DP
Gonzalez	.971	56	95	141	7	38
Kirkland	1.000	1	2	2	0	1
Mejia	.905	18	21	46	7	12
Rodland	.833	2	1	4	1	0
Tousa	.980	58	76	173	5	44

Outfield	PCT	G	PO	A	E	DP
Blue	.983	123	293	5	5	2
Clevlen	.979	129	259	16	6	5
Cotto	.889	7	7	1	1	0
Knoedler	.915	28	41	2	4	0
McKinney	.972	115	162	14	5	1
Nicholson	1.000	10	16	1	0	0
Reynolds	1.000	4	2	0	0	0

WEST MICHIGAN WHITECAPS — Low Class A

MIDWEST LEAGUE

BATTING	B-T	HT	WT	DOB	AVG	vLH	vRH	G	AB	R	H	2B	3B	HR	RBI	BB	HBP	SH	SF	SO	SB	CS	SLG	OBP
Colvin, Brooks	R-R	5-10	175	12-11-81	.230	.340	.197	111	417	50	96	20	1	3	33	53	3	6	3	79	9	8	.305	.319
Dlugach, Brent	R-R	6-4	200	3-3-83	.283	.256	.292	124	488	54	138	26	5	5	61	19	7	4	4	121	13	5	.387	.317
Frazier, Jeff	R-R	6-3	195	8-10-82	.287	.297	.284	137	537	79	154	45	4	12	81	46	10	1	8	86	16	3	.453	.349
Graham, Andrew	R-R	6-4	215	4-22-82	.190	.229	.169	32	100	6	19	4	0	0	10	3	3	3	1	21	2	1	.230	.234
Justice, Justin	L-L	6-0	185	2-19-85	.230	.185	.240	78	287	37	66	10	5	2	24	15	3	1	1	63	5	1	.321	.275
Lee, Josh	L-R	6-4	220	9-13-82	.239	.263	.229	104	397	35	95	14	1	7	63	24	4	0	4	116	0	3	.332	.287
McIntyre, Nick	B-R	5-10	185	3-11-81	.303	.257	.317	118	442	61	134	30	2	7	45	42	4	7	6	85	11	9	.428	.364
Parrish, Matt	R-R	5-11	205	8-25-82	.228	.279	.213	76	263	30	60	15	0	2	28	26	8	1	2	87	4	6	.308	.314
Ramirez, Wilkin	R-R	6-2	190	10-25-85	.262	.306	.247	131	493	69	129	21	2	16	65	35	7	1	5	143	21	8	.410	.317
Robinson, Chris	R-R	6-0	200	5-12-84	.257	.250	.259	41	148	16	38	8	1	2	18	15	1	1	0	39	0	0	.365	.329
Roughton, Jody	L-R	6-1	190	5-6-81	.183	.095	.196	46	164	5	30	5	2	0	8	10	0	1	0	27	0	1	.238	.230
Ryan, Dusty	R-R	6-4	220	9-2-84	.183	.241	.166	75	241	21	44	11	0	4	21	22	2	4	2	70	3	3	.278	.255
Sabino, Luis	B-R	6-2	190	5-24-83	.238	.314	.211	118	399	77	95	18	4	5	49	70	8	4	4	111	11	5	.341	.360
Thomas, Clete	L-R	5-11	195	11-14-83	.284	.273	.288	51	194	39	55	8	5	0	11	21	2	2	2	37	11	3	.376	.356
Young, Stephen	B-R	5-9	165	4-9-82	.233	.308	.215	63	202	21	47	5	0	0	10	18	10	13	0	23	5	3	.257	.326

PITCHING	B-T	HT	WT	DOB	W	L	ERA	G	GS	CG	SV	IP	H	R	ER	HR	BB	SO	AVG	vLH	vRH	K/9	BB/9
Ardoin, Kevin	R-R	6-1	167	8-6-82	5	1	2.84	22	0	0	0	44	33	19	14	3	16	47	.202	.273	.155	9.54	3.25
Bierd, Randor	R-R	6-4	190	3-14-84	4	1	2.64	7	7	0	0	44	30	14	13	2	10	42	.194	.196	.192	8.53	2.03
Clelland, Ed	L-L	6-0	165	6-27-82	7	2	3.40	37	0	0	1	42	39	16	16	3	8	37	.250	.172	.304	7.87	1.70
Dolsi, Freddy	R-R	6-0	160	1-9-83	1	0	2.43	23	0	0	0	37	36	16	10	5	14	27	.247	.196	.278	6.57	3.41
Finigan, P.J.	R-R	6-0	185	9-30-82	2	2	2.39	25	0	0	4	38	35	11	10	0	7	32	.243	.276	.221	7.65	1.67
French, Lucas	L-L	6-4	220	9-13-85	1	2	5.45	6	6	0	0	35	42	23	21	4	14	24	.298	.345	.286	6.23	3.63
Hahn, Jeff	R-R	6-4	210	9-28-81	4	2	3.25	6	6	0	0	36	36	14	13	0	9	14	.265	.364	.198	3.50	2.25
Jurrjens, Jair	R-R	6-1	160	1-29-86	12	6	3.41	26	26	0	0	143	132	62	54	5	36	108	.246	.233	.255	6.81	2.27
Kauten, Josh	R-R	6-3	200	4-5-82	4	3	3.32	14	14	2	0	79	76	33	29	7	12	49	.259	.250	.265	5.61	1.37
Konecny, Daniel	R-R	6-4	210	9-4-77	2	6	3.28	22	2	0	0	49	49	31	18	0	22	16	.258	.241	.270	2.92	4.01
Kown, Andrew	L-R	6-7	210	10-7-82	8	11	4.36	26	26	1	0	151	152	83	73	13	52	98	.259	.236	.275	5.85	3.11
Lewis, Lavon	R-R	6-4	205	12-17-83	2	0	2.38	24	1	0	1	45	33	13	12	2	17	31	.206	.231	.189	6.15	3.38
Mahoney, Collin	R-R	6-4	245	12-26-82	0	2	5.24	25	0	0	10	22	20	16	13	0	21	23	.241	.176	.286	9.27	8.46
Ostlund, Ian	R-L	6-1	200	10-17-78	2	3	2.40	32	0	0	2	49	32	15	13	3	5	54	.186	.163	.194	9.99	0.92
Peralta, Tony	L-L	6-2	187	9-13-83	1	2	7.71	22	0	0	0	30	34	28	26	3	7	28	.268	.343	.239	8.31	2.08
Rainwater, Josh	R-R	6-1	220	4-9-85	3	7	4.24	16	16	0	0	81	84	45	38	8	20	75	.266	.291	.246	8.37	2.23
Righter, Matt	R-R	6-5	190	8-7-81	4	1	3.14	27	10	0	0	77	79	33	27	5	24	48	.261	.219	.286	5.59	2.79
Sborz, Jay	R-R	6-4	210	1-24-85	1	1	7.90	21	0	0	0	27	36	27	24	2	23	31	.321	.273	.353	10.21	7.57
Tomey, Anthony	R-R	6-4	245	8-17-81	3	4	2.98	59	0	0	8	60	42	26	20	2	45	70	.194	.135	.224	10.44	6.71
Trahern, Dallas	R-R	6-3	190	11-29-85	7	11	3.58	26	26	2	0	156	158	78	62	9	50	66	.265	.263	.266	3.81	2.88
Whelan, Kevin	R-R	6-0	200	1-8-84	0	0	0.73	14	0	0	11	12	4	1	1	0	2	22	.098	.133	.077	16.05	1.46

FIELDING

Catcher	PCT	G	PO	A	E	DP	PB
Graham	.987	32	205	17	3	2	1
Robinson	.987	41	286	21	4	1	5
Ryan	.990	75	459	58	5	1	13

First Base	PCT	G	PO	A	E	DP
Frazier	1.000	1	0	1	0	0
Lee	.990	103	993	61	11	87
McIntyre	1.000	1	7	2	0	0
Roughton	.994	37	324	21	2	39

Second Base	PCT	G	PO	A	E	DP
Colvin	.971	85	170	260	13	57
McIntyre	.900	2	5	4	1	0
Young	.980	56	113	184	6	41

Third Base	PCT	G	PO	A	E	DP
Colvin	.915	15	12	31	4	1
McIntyre	.933	74	51	145	14	15
Ramirez	.843	57	34	106	26	8

Shortstop	PCT	G	PO	A	E	DP
Colvin	.977	8	17	25	1	3
Dlugach	.955	121	176	457	30	81
McIntyre	.946	13	20	33	3	10

Outfield	PCT	G	PO	A	E	DP
Frazier	.977	127	205	8	5	0
Justice	.989	77	185	3	2	1
McIntyre	1.000	2	3	0	0	0
Parrish	.967	58	84	3	3	3
Sabino	.968	113	233	6	8	3
Thomas	.991	50	110	4	1	0

ONEONTA TIGERS — Short-Season Class A

NEW YORK-PENN LEAGUE

BATTING	B-T	HT	WT	DOB	AVG	vLH	vRH	G	AB	R	H	2B	3B	HR	RBI	BB	HBP	SH	SF	SO	SB	CS	SLG	OBP
Cotto, Pedro	L-L	5-11	175	5-26-82	.276	.000	.308	9	29	2	8	1	1	0	5	1	0	1	1	4	0	1	.379	.290
Grullon, Leonardo	R-R	6-3	210	5-8-82	.245	.275	.224	30	98	17	24	6	0	4	19	2	4	2	0	39	0	2	.429	.288
Haske, Mark	L-R	5-10	165	5-28-83	.270	.200	.290	45	159	29	43	6	2	1	27	15	3	0	4	25	2	2	.352	.337
Hollimon, Michael	B-R	6-1	185	6-14-82	.277	.337	.249	72	256	66	71	13	10	13	53	48	2	2	5	76	8	3	.559	.389
Joyce, Matt	L-R	6-2	185	8-3-84	.331	.254	.362	65	245	51	81	10	4	4	45	30	1	1	6	29	9	5	.453	.397
Justice, Justin	L-L	6-0	185	2-19-85	.275	.372	.239	46	160	23	44	12	4	2	35	24	5	0	1	51	3	1	.438	.384
Larish, Jeff	L-R	6-2	200	10-11-82	.297	.250	.318	18	64	16	19	3	0	6	13	13	2	0	0	6	0	0	.625	.430
Laster, Jeramy	R-R	6-1	185	4-5-85	.208	.217	.203	43	120	19	25	3	2	2	14	13	1	1	2	53	6	2	.317	.287
Mendez, Rafael	R-R	6-0	190	4-24-84	.186	.122	.222	39	113	19	21	7	1	1	13	21	0	0	2	34	0	3	.292	.309
Middleton, Cory	R-R	6-1	185	10-3-85	.247	.239	.251	68	259	39	64	22	0	7	52	19	9	2	3	60	3	1	.413	.317
Patino, Jorge	R-R	5-10	150	1-25-86	.259	.268	.250	27	81	14	21	2	1	0	4	4	4	0	1	10	1	1	.309	.322
Rhymes, Will	L-R	5-9	155	4-1-83	.328	.310	.333	61	250	48	82	11	3	2	27	25	1	3	0	15	14	3	.420	.391
Roa, Joel	R-R	6-0	175	1-2-84	.239	.257	.233	42	138	20	33	4	1	4	14	9	3	0	1	57	0	0	.370	.298
Roberson, Ryan	R-R	6-5	240	8-1-83	.284	.244	.311	52	197	26	56	13	2	7	47	14	1	0	2	60	0	0	.477	.332
Robinson, Chris	R-R	6-0	200	5-12-84	.154	.222	.000	4	13	2	2	0	0	0	1	1	0	0	1	3	0	0	.154	.200
Thomas, Clete	L-R	5-11	195	11-14-83	.386	.379	.390	18	70	19	27	5	1	1	14	12	2	0	0	11	9	0	.529	.488
Timm, Brandon	R-R	6-2	200	12-4-84	.260	.273	.252	50	169	28	44	5	2	0	14	25	2	2	2	50	9	3	.314	.359
Torres, Chris	R-R	6-0	195	1-27-83	.270	.370	.194	23	63	9	17	2	0	1	8	3	0	0	0	24	0	0	.349	.303
Williamson, Schuyler	R-R	6-1	225	10-27-82	.203	.190	.209	25	64	11	13	3	0	0	6	5	3	0	1	11	1	0	.250	.288

PITCHING	B-T	HT	WT	DOB	W	L	ERA	G	GS	CG	SV	IP	H	R	ER	HR	BB	SO	AVG	vLH	vRH	K/9	BB/9
Badenhop, Burke	R-R	6-5	220	2-8-83	6	4	2.92	14	14	1	0	77	69	32	25	0	26	55	.238	.243	.235	6.43	3.04
Baxter, Jake	R-R	6-5	210	11-9-83	2	2	4.45	16	0	0	2	30	30	18	15	3	12	31	.261	.326	.222	9.20	3.56
Claggett, Anthony	B-R	6-2	185	7-15-84	0	1	4.03	21	0	0	7	22	23	10	10	1	12	25	.271	.464	.175	10.07	4.84

PITCHING	B-T	HT	WT	DOB	W	L	ERA	G	GS	CG	SV	IP	H	R	ER	HR	BB	SO	AVG	vLH	vRH	K/9	BB/9
Fragoso, Jose	R-R	6-0	175	11-12-84	6	2	2.25	13	4	0	0	44	33	17	11	0	22	50	.210	.196	.217	10.23	4.50
Fraser, Loren	R-R	6-6	235	8-20-82	2	2	3.45	19	0	0	4	29	33	12	11	0	12	30	.303	.444	.233	9.42	3.77
Hahn, Jeff	R-R	6-4	210	9-28-81	4	0	0.00	10	1	0	0	23	20	2	0	0	3	17	.238	.200	.250	6.75	1.19
Konecny, Daniel	R-R	6-4	210	9-5-81	4	3	6.26	15	11	0	0	55	73	43	38	2	18	30	.323	.319	.326	4.94	2.96
Lyons, Thomas	R-R	6-2	195	3-22-83	0	1	11.85	6	1	0	0	14	19	20	18	1	14	14	.317	.304	.324	9.22	9.22
Mahoney, Collin	R-R	6-4	245	12-26-82	0	1	7.82	18	0	0	0	25	22	23	22	5	26	26	.242	.409	.188	9.24	9.24
Moscoso, Guillermo	R-R	6-1	165	11-14-83	2	2	4.37	11	10	0	0	47	49	27	23	4	11	44	.261	.300	.246	8.37	2.09
Norfleet, Matt	R-R	6-1	225	3-29-83	3	1	2.29	18	1	0	0	39	32	15	10	1	17	32	.219	.192	.234	7.32	3.89
O'Brien, Matt	R-R	6-3	215	8-10-82	6	3	3.34	15	15	0	0	89	79	42	33	6	24	57	.232	.182	.271	5.76	2.43
Robertson, Tim	R-R	6-2	215	12-27-82	1	1	2.65	16	0	0	1	37	38	13	11	3	12	27	.262	.229	.278	6.51	2.89
Rusch, Matt	R-R	5-11	180	5-20-83	1	0	1.80	2	0	0	0	5	6	1	1	0	0	5	.300	.167	.357	9.00	0.00
Sborz, Jay	R-R	6-4	210	1-24-85	1	3	4.34	9	7	0	0	29	24	15	14	1	27	25	.224	.229	.220	7.76	8.38
Vasquez, Sendy	B-R	6-1	160	8-10-82	7	0	3.63	15	11	0	0	67	53	30	27	4	34	60	.218	.169	.238	8.06	4.57
Whelan, Kevin	R-R	6-0	200	1-8-84	1	1	2.25	11	0	0	4	12	2	4	3	1	6	19	.051	.077	.038	14.25	4.50
Wilson, Gibbs	R-R	6-2	170	6-9-85	2	0	2.61	9	0	0	3	10	4	3	3	1	6	17	.125	.167	.100	14.81	5.23

GAMES BY POSITION: C—Roa 42, Robinson 4, Torres 20, Williamson 25. **1B**—Haske 2, Larish 16, Mendez 34, Roberson 30. **2B**—Haske 10, Mendez 2, Patino 22, Rhymes 51. **3B**—Haske 12, Middleton 65, Patino 4. **SS**—Haske 9, Hollimon 68. **OF**—Cotto 6, Grullon 21, Joyce 63, Justice 45, Laster 38, Thomas 18, Timm 43, Torres 1.

GCL TIGERS — Rookie

GULF COAST LEAGUE

BATTING	B-T	HT	WT	DOB	AVG	vLH	vRH	G	AB	R	H	2B	3B	HR	RBI	BB	HBP	SH	SF	SO	SB	CS	SLG	OBP
Bautista, Pedruin	R-R	5-11	162	5-12-84	.230	.207	.237	36	122	15	28	7	2	1	21	3	1	1	2	30	6	2	.344	.250
Berry, Vince	R-R	5-9	170	9-1-83	.248	.250	.247	37	101	14	25	3	1	0	5	1	4	0	0	20	5	2	.297	.283
Brea, Manuel	R-R	5-11	157	4-6-84	.173	.182	.171	40	104	6	18	1	2	0	5	6	0	0	1	39	5	1	.221	.216
Ciriaco, Audy	R-R	6-3	195	6-16-87	.250	.214	.258	40	152	20	38	3	4	5	23	10	1	0	1	46	5	1	.421	.299
Cotto, Pedro	L-L	5-11	175	5-26-82	.196	.333	.175	13	46	5	9	0	1	0	1	2	0	0	0	2	0	1	.239	.229
De la Cruz, Jason	R-R	6-3	205	11-21-84	.173	.375	.116	33	110	11	19	2	0	2	15	7	3	0	0	40	0	0	.245	.242
De Leon, Santo	R-R	6-2	175	11-1-83	.239	.050	.278	33	117	15	28	6	1	4	19	1	1	0	2	22	0	0	.410	.248
Flores, Angel	R-R	6-0	195	8-16-86	.111	.167	.095	15	27	3	3	1	0	0	1	7	0	1	1	7	0	0	.148	.286
Guzman, Agustin	R-R	6-0	185	10-10-87	.198	.222	.195	28	86	10	17	6	0	2	12	9	1	2	2	24	5	2	.337	.276
Larish, Jeff	L-R	6-2	200	10-11-82	.222	.250	.214	6	18	1	4	1	0	0	4	4	1	0	1	5	0	1	.278	.375
Linares, Miguel	R-R	6-2	180	12-16-83	.279	.167	.311	37	136	18	38	7	1	3	12	7	1	1	0	34	5	0	.412	.319
Miller, Cole	R-R	5-11	200	10-20-84	.182	.000	.200	24	55	3	10	3	0	0	2	1	0	0	1	22	1	0	.236	.193
Ott, Louis	B-R	6-0	185	2-22-85	.231	.133	.247	32	108	16	25	2	2	0	8	11	3	0	0	27	6	1	.287	.320
Reyes, Angel	R-R	6-3	180	1-9-84	.225	.370	.194	44	151	23	34	8	0	9	25	14	1	0	0	48	2	0	.457	.295
Rodriguez, Wilkin	L-L	5-10	150	9-5-82	.311	.303	.313	44	164	23	51	7	0	2	17	14	2	4	0	25	14	5	.390	.372
Sandoval, Daniel	R-R	5-11	170	5-7-85	.314	.278	.322	30	105	14	33	4	0	4	14	5	1	0	0	16	0	0	.467	.351
Skelton, James	L-R	5-11	165	10-28-85	.182	.125	.200	17	33	6	6	1	0	0	1	13	0	1	0	9	0	0	.212	.413
Wells, Casper	R-R	6-2	210	11-23-84	.220	.192	.226	45	141	25	31	9	5	5	20	18	8	0	0	59	6	0	.461	.341

PITCHING	B-T	HT	WT	DOB	W	L	ERA	G	GS	CG	SV	IP	H	R	ER	HR	BB	SO	AVG	vLH	vRH	K/9	BB/9
Averill, Erik	L-L	6-2	190	2-9-84	1	2	1.59	6	3	0	0	23	12	6	4	0	7	18	.156	.200	.140	7.15	2.78
Beattie, Eric	R-R	6-3	190	4-2-83	0	1	20.25	10	1	0	0	11	10	25	24	0	30	6	.278	.182	.320	5.06	25.31
Berger, Garrett	R-R	6-3	240	5-11-83	0	0	11.32	7	0	0	0	10	9	18	13	0	27	11	.225	.222	.227	9.58	23.52
Caraballo, Jesse	R-R	6-1	190	7-17-86	1	3	5.23	12	5	0	0	43	49	26	25	7	13	26	.288	.290	.287	5.44	2.72
Cruz, Rhiner	R-R	6-2	165	11-1-86	1	0	4.50	14	0	0	1	28	35	15	14	5	12	23	.299	.225	.338	7.39	3.86
French, Lucas	L-L	6-4	220	9-13-85	1	0	7.59	2	2	0	0	11	16	10	9	3	0	9	.340	.364	.333	7.59	0.00
Garcia, Ramon	L-L	6-2	165	10-30-84	5	3	3.65	10	10	0	0	57	53	27	23	4	14	25	.248	.191	.263	3.97	2.22
Gil, Luis	R-R	6-1	170	2-12-84	3	3	3.04	9	8	0	0	53	42	24	18	1	12	47	.214	.299	.171	7.93	2.03
Lyons, Thomas	R-R	6-2	195	3-22-84	1	2	3.45	7	3	0	0	16	13	17	6	2	11	13	.213	.192	.229	7.47	6.32
Napolitan, Phil	R-R	6-1	185	1-29-82	0	0	0.00	1	0	0	0	1	0	0	0	0	1	2	.000	.000	.000	18.00	9.00
Perdomo, Orlando	R-R	6-0	160	5-3-84	3	2	2.65	17	5	0	7	37	25	14	11	0	19	39	.185	.106	.227	9.40	4.58
Rusch, Matthew	R-R	5-11	180	5-20-83	1	3	3.06	7	6	0	1	35	35	18	12	2	2	16	.252	.286	.233	4.08	0.51
Santos, Adriano	R-R	6-2	170	9-8-84	1	3	4.13	20	0	0	5	28	31	15	13	1	15	30	.279	.294	.267	9.53	4.76
Sierra, Waldy	R-R	6-2	190	8-23-86	2	2	9.27	12	1	0	0	22	25	27	23	1	22	13	.278	.333	.241	5.24	8.87
Trejo, Miguel	R-R	6-3	190	4-14-85	2	1	2.08	19	0	0	3	26	20	7	6	1	10	24	.217	.237	.204	8.31	3.46
Watts, Joey	L-L	5-11	170	2-22-82	0	1	1.69	5	0	0	0	5	7	4	1	0	1	3	.333	.000	.412	5.06	1.69
Wise, Brendan	L-R	6-2	190	1-9-86	2	4	4.87	10	10	0	0	57	60	39	31	6	9	35	.268	.292	.252	5.49	1.41

GAMES BY POSITION: C—Flores 14, Miller 15, Sandoval 26, Skelton 16. **1B**—De Leon 14, Larish 3, Miller 9, Reyes 35. **2B**—Bautista 35, Guzman 21. **3B**—Ciriaco 1, De Leon 16, Linares 27, Ott 13. **SS**—Ciriaco 38, Linares 8, Ott 10. **OF**—Berry 33, Brea 37, Cotto 11, De la Cruz 28, Rodriguez 39, Wells 39.

FLORIDA MARLINS

BY MIKE BERARDINO

A 2005 Marlins season that began with more optimism than perhaps any other in franchise history ended only with disappointment.

Despite authorizing a club-record $66 million payroll and bolstering the lineup with the $52 million addition of free-agent slugger Carlos Delgado, Marlins owner Jeffrey Loria saw his team fall short of the playoffs for the third time in his four seasons in South Florida.

They did this by plummeting to an injury-marred 83-79 finish that saw them lose 12 of 14 games during a crucial late September stretch. The late fade contributed to the season-ending departure of manager Jack McKeon, who resigned at age 74 shortly after reaching his 1,000th win in the major leagues. He was replaced by former Yankees bench coach Joe Girardi, 34 years his junior.

The Marlins wasted four of the best individual seasons in club history in 2005.

Delgado did his part, bashing 33 homers and driving in 115 runs. So did righthanded-hitting counterpart Miguel Cabrera, who hit .323-33-116, made his second straight All-Star Game and cemented his place as one of the game's top under-25 stars.

On the mound, energetic lefty Dontrelle Willis went 22-10 in a Cy Young-quality season. Willis, in his third season, became the first Marlins pitcher to reach the 20-win plateau.

Closer Todd Jones, signed for $1.1 million in the offseason, stepped in for injured Guillermo Mota in April and posted a 40-save comeback.

While many predicted the Marlins would end the Braves' run of National League East titles, too many off seasons by key players kept that from happening.

Third baseman Mike Lowell, coming off three straight all-star seasons, started slowly and never got going. He finished the year splitting time between the bench and second base, where he hadn't played since the minor leagues.

Center fielder Juan Pierre, so vital to the team's success in the World Series run of 2003, stumbled early due to a lingering calf injury and saw his hit total fall from 221 to 181. He was dropped from leadoff to seventh in the batting order as his on-base percentage fell by 48 points.

Former World Series hero Josh Beckett landed on the disabled list with another blister, but he still enjoyed his best year overall. Beckett won 15 games and exceeded 178 innings, both career bests.

The Marlins nearly traded righthander A.J. Burnett in July, but opted to hold on to the prospective free agent—one of 13 on their roster—after a deal with the Orioles fell through. Burnett rewarded their confidence with a run of seven straight victories in July and August, but he slowed to a crawl in a September fade that ended with his dismissal from the team with a week left in the season.

Among the bright spots were a few imports from the minors, including rookie lefties Jason Vargas and Scott Olsen. Vargas, who began the year at low Class A Greensboro, was in the majors by mid-July despite being picked in the second round of the 2004 draft.

Top prospect Jeremy Hermida appeared in the Futures Game and was MVP of the Southern League All-Star Game. Hermida, a 21-year-old right fielder, was called up on Aug. 31 and, despite missing the previous 10 days with a wrist injury, hit a grand slam in his first big-league plate appearance.

Hermida, who should inherit a starting job in 2006, joined "Frosty" Bill Duggleby (1898) as the only players in big league history with a career-opening slam.

Just two minor league affiliates produced winning records, but they were Triple-A Albuquerque (78-66) and Double-A Carolina (77-57). Overall, the Marlins system posted a 341-339 (.501) record and funneled half a dozen relievers to the big league staff.

The Marlins also made the most of their bounty of high draft picks. They took five pitchers in the top 44 selections and signed them all.

PLAYERS OF THE YEAR

MAJOR LEAGUE: Dontrelle Willis, lhp

Willis was a workhorse for the Marlins in 2005, finishing fifth in the majors with 236 innings pitched. He led the National League in wins with 22, and was third in ERA. Willis would have been an easy pick for the NL Cy Young Award if not for Houston's Roger Clemens and St. Louis' Chris Carpenter.

MINOR LEAGUE: Jeremy Hermida, of

STEVE MOORE

Hermida made history in his 2005 major league debut, rocking a grand slam in his first major league at-bat. Hermida exhibited patience to go along with his power, as he drew 111 walks at Double-A Carolina. He also has above-average speed, and was efficient on the basepaths with 23 steals in 25 attempts.

ORGANIZATION LEADERS

BATTING		
***AVG**	Dillon, Joe, Albuquerque	.360
R	Wilson, Josh, Albuquerque	88
H	McCann, Brad, Carolina/Greensboro	141
TB	McCann, Brad, Carolina/Greensboro	264
2B	McCann, Brad, Carolina/Greensboro	35
3B	De Aza, Alejandro, Jupiter	9
	Shanks, James, Albuquerque/Carolina	9
HR	McCann, Brad, Carolina/Greensboro	28
RBI	McCann, Brad, Carolina/Greensboro	106
BB	Hermida, Jeremy, Carolina	111
SO	Mitchell, Lee, Jupiter	142
SB	Reed, Eric, Albuquerque/Carolina	40
***OBP**	Dillon, Joe, Albuquerque	.459
***SLG**	Dillon, Joe, Albuquerque	.631
PITCHING		
W	Johnson, Josh, Carolina/Jupiter	12
	Russ, James, Carolina/Jupiter	12
L	Castillo, Frank, Albuquerque	11
#ERA	Vargas, Jason, Carolina/Greensboro/Jupiter	2.08
G	Nestor, Scott, Greensboro	58
CG	Walrond, Les, Albuquerque	2
SV	Mobley, Chris, Greensboro	34
IP	Russ, James, Carolina/Jupiter	167
BB	Fulchino, Jeff, Albuquerque	67
SO	Russ, James, Carolina/Jupiter	148

*Minimum 250 at-bats. #Minimum 75 innings.

FLORIDA MARLINS

Manager: Jack McKeon.

2005 Record: 83-79, .512 (3rd, NL East).

BATTING	B-T	HT	WT	DOB	AVG	vLH	vRH	G	AB	R	H	2B	3B	HR	RBI	BB	HBP	SH	SF	SO	SB	CS	SLG	OBP
Aguila, Chris	R-R	5-11	180	2-23-79	.244	.240	.245	65	78	11	19	3	0	0	4	3	0	0	0	19	0	1	.282	.272
Andino, Robert	R-R	6-0	170	4-25-84	.159	.111	.171	17	44	4	7	4	0	0	1	5	0	1	0	8	1	0	.250	.245
Cabrera, Miguel	R-R	6-2	210	4-18-83	.323	.299	.329	158	613	106	198	43	2	33	116	64	2	0	6	125	1	0	.561	.385
Castillo, Luis	B-R	5-11	190	9-12-75	.301	.423	.259	122	439	72	132	12	4	4	30	65	1	18	1	32	10	7	.374	.391
Conine, Jeff	R-R	6-1	220	6-26-66	.304	.280	.312	131	335	42	102	20	2	3	33	38	3	2	6	58	2	0	.403	.374
Delgado, Carlos	L-R	6-3	240	6-25-72	.301	.234	.326	144	521	81	157	41	3	33	115	72	17	0	6	121	0	0	.582	.399
Dillon, Joe	R-R	6-2	215	8-2-75	.167	.222	.148	27	36	6	6	1	0	1	1	1	1	1	0	8	0	0	.278	.211
Easley, Damion	R-R	5-11	190	11-11-69	.240	.333	.218	102	267	37	64	19	1	9	30	26	4	3	4	47	4	1	.419	.312
Encarnacion, Juan	R-R	6-3	215	3-8-76	.287	.309	.282	141	506	59	145	27	3	16	76	41	9	4	3	104	6	5	.447	.349
Gonzalez, Alex	R-R	6-0	200	2-15-77	.264	.216	.277	130	435	45	115	30	0	5	45	31	5	4	3	81	5	3	.368	.319
Harris, Lenny	L-R	5-10	235	10-28-64	.314	.333	.313	83	70	5	22	4	0	1	13	7	1	0	0	11	0	1	.414	.385
Hermida, Jeremy	L-R	6-4	200	1-30-84	.293	.200	.306	23	41	9	12	2	0	4	11	6	0	0	0	12	2	0	.634	.383
Jorgensen, Ryan	R-R	6-2	220	5-4-79	.000	.000	.000	4	4	0	0	0	0	0	0	0	0	0	0	3	0	0	.000	.000
Lo Duca, Paul	R-R	5-10	185	4-12-72	.283	.314	.276	132	445	45	126	23	1	6	57	34	4	5	8	31	4	3	.380	.334
Lowell, Mike	R-R	6-3	210	2-24-74	.236	.304	.221	150	500	56	118	36	1	8	58	46	2	1	9	58	4	0	.360	.298
Mordecai, Mike	R-R	5-10	180	12-13-67	.000	.000	.000	2	2	0	0	0	0	0	0	0	0	0	0	1	0	0	.000	.000
Pierre, Juan	L-L	6-0	180	8-14-77	.276	.299	.270	162	656	96	181	19	13	2	47	41	9	10	2	45	57	17	.354	.326
Treanor, Matt	R-R	6-0	205	3-3-76	.201	.148	.215	58	134	10	27	8	0	0	13	16	3	1	0	28	0	0	.261	.301
Willingham, Josh	R-R	6-1	200	2-17-79	.304	.429	.250	16	23	3	7	1	0	0	4	2	2	1	0	5	0	0	.348	.407
Wilson, Josh	R-R	6-1	180	3-26-81	.100	.000	.100	11	10	2	1	1	0	0	0	0	1	0	0	4	0	0	.200	.182

PITCHING	B-T	HT	WT	DOB	W	L	ERA	G	GS	CG	SV	IP	H	R	ER	HR	BB	SO	AVG	vLH	vRH	K/9	BB/9
Alfonseca, Antonio	R-R	6-5	250	4-16-72	1	1	4.94	33	0	0	0	27	29	15	15	2	14	16	.299	.244	.346	5.27	4.61
Bazardo, Yorman	R-R	6-2	200	7-11-84	0	0	21.60	1	0	0	0	2	5	5	4	0	2	2	.500	.250	.667	10.80	10.80
Beckett, Josh	R-R	6-5	220	5-15-80	15	8	3.38	29	29	2	0	179	153	75	67	14	58	166	.234	.217	.252	8.36	2.92
Bentz, Chad	R-L	6-2	210	5-5-80	0	0	31.50	4	0	0	0	2	8	7	7	2	0	0	.571	.333	.750	0.00	0.00
Bump, Nate	L-R	6-2	195	7-24-76	0	3	4.03	31	0	0	0	38	43	18	17	5	12	18	.289	.265	.309	4.26	2.84
Burnett, A.J.	R-R	6-4	230	1-3-77	12	12	3.44	32	32	4	0	209	184	97	80	12	79	198	.237	.226	.249	8.53	3.40
Castillo, Frank	R-R	6-1	200	4-1-69	0	1	10.38	1	1	0	0	4	4	5	5	0	5	4	.235	.125	.333	8.31	10.38
Crowell, Jim	R-L	6-4	225	5-14-74	0	0	21.60	4	0	0	0	3	10	8	8	1	0	2	.526	.500	.533	5.40	0.00
De los Santos, Valerio	L-L	6-2	210	10-6-72	1	2	6.14	27	0	0	0	22	25	15	15	4	12	16	.281	.324	.250	6.55	4.91
Johnson, Josh	L-R	6-7	240	1-31-84	0	0	3.65	4	1	0	0	12	11	5	5	0	10	10	.256	.407	.000	7.30	7.30
Jones, Todd	L-R	6-3	230	4-24-68	1	5	2.10	68	0	0	40	73	61	19	17	2	14	62	.230	.231	.229	7.64	1.73
Kensing, Logan	R-R	6-1	185	7-3-82	0	0	11.12	3	0	0	0	6	11	7	7	2	3	4	.407	.636	.250	6.35	4.76
Leiter, Al	L-L	6-3	220	10-23-65	3	7	6.64	17	16	0	0	80	88	61	59	9	60	52	.292	.278	.297	5.85	6.75
Mecir, Jim	B-R	6-1	230	5-16-70	1	4	3.12	52	0	0	0	43	39	17	15	2	17	34	.248	.226	.263	7.06	3.53
Messenger, Randy	R-R	6-6	245	8-13-81	0	0	5.35	29	0	0	0	37	39	22	22	5	30	29	.273	.271	.274	7.05	7.30
Moehler, Brian	R-R	6-3	235	12-31-71	6	12	4.55	37	25	0	0	158	198	82	80	16	42	95	.313	.320	.305	5.40	2.39
Mota, Guillermo	R-R	6-4	210	7-25-73	2	2	4.70	56	0	0	2	67	65	38	35	5	32	60	.254	.243	.262	8.06	4.30
Olsen, Scott	L-L	6-4	200	1-12-84	1	1	3.98	5	4	0	0	20	21	13	9	5	10	21	.259	.333	.238	9.30	4.43
Perisho, Matt	L-L	6-0	200	6-8-75	2	0	1.93	24	0	0	0	14	12	4	3	1	11	10	.245	.346	.130	6.43	7.07
Quantrill, Paul	L-R	6-1	200	11-3-68	0	1	8.44	6	0	0	0	5	8	7	5	1	5	1	.348	.400	.308	1.69	8.44
Resop, Chris	R-R	6-3	220	11-4-82	2	0	8.47	15	0	0	0	17	22	16	16	1	9	15	.324	.316	.333	7.94	4.76
Riedling, John	R-R	5-11	190	8-29-75	4	1	7.16	29	0	0	0	28	34	23	22	3	13	16	.298	.306	.288	5.20	4.23
Smith, Travis	R-R	5-10	170	11-7-72	0	0	6.75	12	0	0	0	11	17	8	8	1	5	9	.370	.500	.227	7.59	4.22
Valdez, Ismael	R-R	6-4	230	8-21-73	2	2	5.33	14	7	0	0	51	64	32	30	6	22	27	.314	.341	.292	4.80	3.91
Vargas, Jason	L-L	6-0	215	2-2-83	5	5	4.03	17	13	1	0	74	71	34	33	4	31	59	.249	.192	.269	7.21	3.79
Villone, Ron	L-L	6-3	245	1-16-70	3	2	6.85	27	0	0	0	24	24	20	18	2	12	29	.264	.243	.278	11.03	4.56
Willis, Dontrelle	L-L	6-4	240	1-12-82	22	10	2.63	34	34	7	0	236	213	79	69	11	55	170	.243	.222	.247	6.47	2.09

FIELDING

Catcher	PCT	G	PO	A	E	DP	PB
Jorgensen	1.000	3	7	0	0	0	0
Lo Duca	.991	128	817	61	8	8	4
Treanor	.985	55	309	14	5	4	4
Willingham	1.000	8	22	0	0	0	1

First Base	PCT	G	PO	A	E	DP
Conine	.985	45	247	17	4	27
Delgado	.989	141	1147	83	14	133
Dillon	1.000	1	2	0	0	0
Harris	1.000	1	3	0	0	2

Second Base	PCT	G	PO	A	E	DP
Castillo	.988	120	245	352	7	87
Dillon	.923	4	5	7	1	2
Easley	.978	46	80	98	4	26
Lowell	.969	8	18	13	1	3
Mordecai	1.000	1	2	2	0	0
Wilson	1.000	4	1	1	0	0

Third Base	PCT	G	PO	A	E	DP
Cabrera	.971	29	22	46	2	5
Dillon	1.000	2	2	1	0	0
Easley	.962	10	9	16	1	1
Harris	.000	2	0	0	0	0
Lowell	.983	135	107	243	6	34

Shortstop	PCT	G	PO	A	E	DP
Andino	.956	17	18	25	2	7
Easley	.968	30	43	77	4	14
Gonzalez	.974	124	221	367	16	102
Mordecai	.000	1	0	0	0	0
Wilson	1.000	6	3	6	0	2

Outfield	PCT	G	PO	A	E	DP
Aguila	1.000	42	40	1	0	0
Cabrera	.976	134	188	12	5	3
Conine	.973	61	105	2	3	0
Dillon	1.000	3	2	0	0	0
Encarnacion	.983	139	226	4	4	0
Harris	.000	2	0	0	0	0
Hermida	1.000	14	20	0	0	0
Pierre	.988	160	332	7	4	3
Willingham	.000	1	0	0	0	0

FARM SYSTEM

General Manager: Larry Beinfest. **Director, Player Development:** Brian Chattin. **Scouting Director:** Stan Meek.

Class	Farm Team	League	W	L	Pct.	Finish*	Manager	Affiliate Since
AAA	Albuquerque (N.M.) Isotopes	Pacific Coast	78	66	.542	5th (16)	Dean Treanor	2003
AA	Carolina (Zebulon, N.C.) Mudcats	Southern	77	57	.575	**3rd (10)**	Gary Allenson	2003
High A	Jupiter (Fla.) Hammerheads	Florida State	64	71	.474	9th (12)	Tim Cossins	2002
Low A	Greensboro (N.C.) Grasshoppers	South Atlantic	67	71	.486	11th (16)	Brandon Hyde	2003
SS A	Jamestown (N.Y.) Jammers	New York-Penn	31	44	.413	12th (14)	Mike Mordecai	2002
Rookie	Jupiter (Fla.) Marlins	Gulf Coast	24	30	.444	t-9th (12)	Edwin Rodriguez	1992

*Finish in overall standings (No. of teams in league)/Playoffs teams in **boldface**

TONY DeFALCO

Miguel Cabrera: Just 22 and already a star

ED WOLFSTEIN

Jason Vargas: From low Class A to the big leagues

ALBUQUERQUE ISOTOPES — Class AAA

PACIFIC COAST LEAGUE

BATTING	B-T	HT	WT	DOB	AVG	vLH	vRH	G	AB	R	H	2B	3B	HR	RBI	BB	HBP	SH	SF	SO	SB	CS	SLG	OBP
Aguila, Chris	R-R	5-11	180	2-23-79	.355	.412	.337	35	138	27	49	13	2	7	25	14	0	0	1	21	8	2	.630	.412
Ashby, Chris	R-R	6-3	213	12-15-74	.247	.324	.194	67	174	20	43	6	0	0	14	18	2	2	1	26	0	2	.282	.323
Barnes, Larry	L-L	6-1	195	7-23-74	.251	.234	.256	71	219	30	55	9	1	8	26	11	1	1	2	45	2	2	.411	.288
Colangelo, Mike	R-R	6-1	200	10-22-76	.293	.340	.274	98	334	58	98	18	2	16	55	31	10	2	6	73	2	2	.503	.365
Delgado, Wilson	B-R	5-11	160	7-15-72	.285	.255	.299	98	351	52	100	22	5	6	37	29	1	3	3	55	3	4	.427	.339
Dillon, Joe	R-R	6-2	215	8-2-75	.360	.374	.354	98	350	80	126	21	1	24	72	57	12	0	6	59	11	1	.631	.459
Erickson, Matt	L-R	5-11	190	7-30-75	.286	.462	.222	18	49	6	14	1	0	0	4	3	2	2	0	8	0	0	.306	.352
2-team (16 Nashville)					.313	.375	.294	34	67	8	21	2	0	0	6	6	4	3	0	10	0	0	.343	.403
Hill, Jason	R-R	6-3	210	3-17-77	.333	.000	.333	2	3	0	1	0	0	0	1	0	0	0	1	2	0	0	.333	.250
Jorgensen, Ryan	R-R	6-2	220	5-4-79	.197	.208	.191	53	137	20	27	5	0	2	11	21	1	2	0	46	1	0	.277	.308
Little, Mark	R-R	6-0	190	7-11-72	.276	.352	.253	83	312	62	86	13	5	18	52	32	14	1	3	84	16	7	.522	.366
Niles, Drew	B-R	6-1	185	3-17-77	.295	.273	.300	25	61	11	18	3	0	2	13	6	0	1	1	13	1	0	.443	.353
Pachot, John	R-R	6-2	210	11-11-74	.198	.250	.172	35	96	6	19	5	0	1	8	4	0	2	1	11	0	1	.281	.228
Padgett, Matt	L-L	6-2	215	7-22-77	.296	.328	.282	123	460	71	136	28	3	17	72	47	3	0	5	131	3	1	.480	.361
Reed, Eric	L-L	5-11	170	12-2-80	.310	.345	.292	39	171	19	53	5	4	1	20	3	4	2	1	31	17	7	.404	.335
Romano, Jason	R-R	6-0	185	6-24-79	.000	.000	.000	1	1	0	0	0	0	0	0	1	0	0	0	0	0	0	.000	.500
Sears, Todd	L-R	6-5	210	10-23-75	.323	.313	.326	92	316	46	102	14	2	13	63	38	4	0	3	75	0	1	.503	.399
Shanks, James	R-R	6-0	190	1-26-79	.268	.136	.327	19	71	11	19	3	3	0	5	7	0	0	0	15	1	1	.394	.333
Stokes, Jason	R-R	6-4	225	1-23-82	.283	.250	.294	13	46	12	13	1	1	5	15	3	1	0	0	16	2	0	.674	.340
Wathan, Derek	B-R	6-3	190	12-13-76	.232	.286	.211	83	250	34	58	14	2	5	36	19	2	4	2	40	10	3	.364	.289
Willingham, Josh	R-R	6-1	200	2-17-79	.324	.240	.349	66	219	56	71	14	3	19	54	47	9	0	4	54	5	1	.676	.455
Wilson, Josh	R-R	6-1	180	3-26-81	.257	.238	.264	143	526	88	135	31	6	17	82	48	9	3	12	114	17	7	.435	.323
Wood, Jason	R-R	6-1	200	12-16-69	.301	.322	.290	129	452	75	136	18	3	21	77	48	8	2	6	81	5	3	.493	.374

PITCHING	B-T	HT	WT	DOB	W	L	ERA	G	GS	CG	SV	IP	H	R	ER	HR	BB	SO	AVG	vLH	vRH	K/9	BB/9
Bauer, Peter	L-R	6-7	243	11-6-78	3	5	6.91	15	14	0	0	72	88	63	55	14	33	43	.304	.305	.304	5.40	4.14
Bentz, Chad	R-L	6-2	210	5-5-80	0	1	4.01	31	0	0	1	34	36	20	15	4	14	32	.273	.200	.304	8.55	3.74
Blank, Matt	L-L	6-2	195	4-5-76	3	0	2.91	13	3	0	0	34	35	12	11	1	10	19	.282	.353	.256	5.03	2.65
Bump, Nate	L-R	6-2	195	7-24-76	1	0	1.80	1	1	0	0	5	4	1	1	0	0	6	.211	.286	.167	10.80	0.00
Castillo, Frank	R-R	6-1	200	4-1-69	9	11	5.53	27	24	0	0	143	161	102	88	20	58	80	.288	.272	.299	5.02	3.64
Clontz, Brad	R-R	6-1	195	4-25-71	1	0	0.69	11	0	0	3	13	9	1	1	0	0	11	.196	.200	.194	7.62	0.00
Corey, Bryan	R-R	6-0	180	10-21-73	3	6	7.65	44	1	0	0	60	78	52	51	11	20	44	.312	.330	.302	6.60	3.00
Crowell, Jim	R-L	6-4	225	5-14-74	2	4	2.67	55	0	0	12	61	54	19	18	6	14	44	.241	.193	.270	6.53	2.08
De los Santos, Valerio	L-L	6-2	210	10-6-72	0	0	1.69	6	0	0	1	5	7	1	1	0	1	6	.304	.167	.353	10.13	1.69
Flannery, Mike	R-R	6-2	225	9-20-79	1	0	5.40	14	0	0	0	17	16	10	10	3	12	11	.250	.292	.225	5.94	6.48
Flury, Pat	R-R	6-1	220	3-14-73	1	1	5.53	22	0	0	0	28	27	24	17	4	19	21	.267	.290	.257	6.83	6.18
Fuell, Jerrod	R-R	6-4	210	10-3-80	0	1	5.68	8	0	0	0	6	8	4	4	2	4	4	.333	.400	.286	5.68	5.68
Fulchino, Jeff	R-R	6-5	252	11-26-79	11	7	5.06	29	29	0	0	153	179	102	86	21	67	101	.297	.285	.306	5.94	3.94
Gracesqui, Franklyn	B-L	6-5	210	8-20-79	0	0	5.56	16	0	0	1	11	11	8	7	2	10	12	.256	.167	.320	9.53	7.94
Howard, Ben	R-R	6-2	225	1-15-79	6	3	4.63	54	3	0	2	84	85	49	43	13	29	87	.257	.281	.244	9.36	3.12
Martinez, Carlos	R-R	6-2	170	5-26-82	0	0	9.00	2	0	0	0	2	4	2	2	1	0	0	.400	.333	.429	0.00	0.00
Messenger, Randy	R-R	6-6	245	8-13-81	4	2	3.88	39	0	0	7	49	46	25	21	5	17	35	.251	.258	.248	6.47	3.14
Miadich, J.B.	R-R	6-4	225	2-3-76	3	2	2.20	29	0	0	11	33	23	10	8	2	20	59	.190	.143	.222	16.26	5.51
Osborne, Donovan	L-L	6-2	215	6-21-69	5	3	4.87	14	14	0	0	81	91	49	44	12	27	53	.286	.312	.276	5.86	2.99
Perisho, Matt	L-L	6-0	200	6-8-75	0	2	11.93	17	1	0	1	14	25	20	19	4	7	10	.391	.414	.371	6.28	4.40
Prieto, Ariel	R-R	6-3	245	10-22-69	9	5	3.78	25	21	1	0	133	144	65	56	13	37	98	.283	.293	.276	6.62	2.50
Riedling, John	R-R	5-11	190	8-29-75	4	0	3.00	14	0	0	3	21	19	9	7	0	9	15	.250	.080	.333	6.43	3.86
Rodriguez, Joe	L-L	6-1	200	12-18-74	0	0	6.23	14	0	0	0	13	16	10	9	1	8	10	.302	.333	.281	6.92	5.54
Smith, Travis	R-R	5-10	170	11-7-72	7	8	4.08	18	17	0	0	104	107	54	47	12	31	73	.268	.280	.261	6.34	2.69
Sodowsky, Clint	L-R	6-4	200	7-13-72	0	0	9.00	6	0	0	0	5	10	6	5	1	3	1	.417	.444	.400	1.80	5.40
Valdez, Ismael	R-R	6-4	230	8-21-73	1	0	0.00	1	1	0	0	6	3	0	0	0	4	4	.158	.000	.231	6.00	6.00
Walrond, Les	L-L	6-0	210	11-7-72	4	5	4.57	15	15	2	0	87	97	50	44	13	37	61	.291	.216	.313	6.33	3.84

FIELDING

Catcher	PCT	G	PO	A	E	DP	PB
Ashby	.972	27	162	14	5	0	5
Jorgensen	.990	45	263	28	3	1	3
Pachot	.995	28	169	25	1	3	4
Willingham	.988	60	387	26	5	4	8

First Base	PCT	G	PO	A	E	DP
Ashby	.994	17	143	10	1	16
Barnes	.977	16	155	12	4	20
Sears	.991	74	635	56	6	67
Stokes	.981	11	95	7	2	12
Wathan	1.000	1	5	0	0	1
Wood	.994	36	285	23	2	46

Second Base	PCT	G	PO	A	E	DP
Delgado	.980	81	160	242	8	63
Dillon	1.000	3	4	7	0	0
Erickson	.981	13	16	36	1	5
Niles	.986	14	24	47	1	20
Wathan	.972	33	71	101	5	30
Wilson	1.000	2	6	3	0	1
Wood	1.000	14	29	25	0	10

Third Base	PCT	G	PO	A	E	DP
Delgado	1.000	1	0	1	0	0
Dillon	.941	81	56	168	14	25
Erickson	1.000	1	2	0	0	0
Niles	.000	1	0	0	1	0
Willingham	1.000	5	2	7	0	1
Wood	.963	67	39	141	7	11

Shortstop	PCT	G	PO	A	E	DP
Delgado	1.000	7	8	19	0	5
Wathan	1.000	4	8	10	0	6
Wilson	.973	136	226	452	19	112
Wood	1.000	3	3	6	0	1

Outfield	PCT	G	PO	A	E	DP
Aguila	1.000	33	72	0	0	0
Ashby	.500	3	1	0	1	0
Barnes	.969	42	58	4	2	1
Colangelo	.969	84	90	5	3	0
Dillon	1.000	19	27	1	0	0
Little	.983	74	166	12	3	5
Padgett	.976	120	193	11	5	2
Reed	.989	39	91	1	1	1
Romano	1.000	1	1	0	0	0
Shanks	.943	18	32	1	2	1
Wathan	1.000	23	43	0	0	0

CAROLINA MUDCATS — Class AA

SOUTHERN LEAGUE

BATTING	B-T	HT	WT	DOB	AVG	vLH	vRH	G	AB	R	H	2B	3B	HR	RBI	BB	HBP	SH	SF	SO	SB	CS	SLG	OBP
Abercrombie, Reggie	R-R	6-3	225	7-15-80	.253	.237	.257	49	178	28	45	7	2	10	23	11	6	0	2	40	7	5	.483	.315
Anderson, Dennis	B-R	6-0	200	2-1-78	.333	.212	.361	67	177	22	59	12	0	1	26	22	3	5	1	22	1	2	.418	.414
Andino, Robert	R-R	6-0	170	4-25-84	.269	.333	.237	127	516	63	139	30	0	5	48	37	6	8	3	111	22	7	.357	.324
Ashby, Chris	R-R	6-3	213	12-15-74	.247	.237	.256	23	81	7	20	3	0	3	9	2	1	0	0	8	0	0	.395	.274
Bass, Chris	R-R	6-2	180	10-18-81	.252	.163	.297	116	313	36	79	25	0	5	36	34	0	2	2	74	1	4	.380	.324
DeMarco, Matt	L-R	6-0	172	1-24-80	.208	.400	.158	14	24	1	5	1	0	0	0	2	3	0	0	4	0	0	.250	.345
Hermida, Jeremy	L-R	6-4	200	1-30-84	.293	.275	.304	118	386	77	113	29	2	18	63	111	7	1	2	89	23	2	.518	.457
Hill, Jason	R-R	6-3	210	3-17-77	.296	.328	.280	116	416	50	123	33	1	18	74	31	3	1	3	63	2	1	.510	.347
Molina, Angel	R-R	6-2	226	11-4-81	.333	.000	.382	11	39	3	13	3	0	1	3	4	0	0	0	8	0	0	.487	.395
Moore, Frank	L-R	6-2	213	7-2-78	.269	.281	.268	82	245	39	66	11	5	4	24	22	2	2	0	64	6	2	.404	.335
Muniz, Juan Carlos	R-R	6-1	175	1-28-76	.280	.355	.246	106	304	35	85	19	1	9	43	23	5	1	4	77	4	6	.438	.336
Niles, Drew	B-R	6-1	185	3-17-77	.267	.235	.278	93	273	34	73	15	1	2	25	49	3	5	3	68	4	3	.352	.381
Reed, Eric	L-L	5-11	170	12-2-80	.255	.260	.251	71	271	35	69	9	0	1	15	17	4	3	3	62	23	8	.299	.305
Rogers, Tanner	R-R	6-0	180	1-11-85	.000	.000	.000	3	3	0	0	0	0	0	0	0	0	0	0	0	0	0	.000	.000
Rohleder, Andy	R-R	6-0	195	2-27-80	.000	.000	.000	3	3	0	0	0	0	0	0	0	0	0	0	2	0	0	.000	.000
Rundgren, Rex	R-R	6-1	170	11-20-80	.231	.270	.214	111	363	26	84	6	3	1	21	28	4	7	1	75	1	1	.273	.293
Sears, Todd	L-R	6-5	210	10-23-75	.317	.356	.286	31	101	16	32	8	0	3	19	10	0	0	0	22	0	0	.485	.378
Shanks, James	R-R	6-0	190	1-26-79	.296	.333	.277	98	371	55	110	19	6	9	51	35	6	2	4	103	16	10	.453	.363
Tucker, Michael	R-R	6-3	225	11-7-79	.233	.269	.206	64	180	19	42	11	0	2	19	21	1	2	3	61	1	0	.328	.312

PITCHING	B-T	HT	WT	DOB	W	L	ERA	G	GS	CG	SV	IP	H	R	ER	HR	BB	SO	AVG	vLH	vRH	K/9	BB/9
Aguilar, Ray	B-L	5-11	210	1-18-80	5	2	3.20	13	13	1	0	84	70	32	30	6	17	49	.224	.274	.208	5.23	1.81
Baker, Ryan	R-R	6-0	200	3-20-78	3	2	4.31	25	0	0	0	40	42	21	19	4	24	29	.286	.379	.225	6.58	5.45
Bauer, Peter	L-R	6-7	243	11-6-78	0	1	7.20	1	1	0	0	5	10	4	4	1	1	2	.455	.750	.286	3.60	1.80
Bazardo, Yorman	R-R	6-2	200	7-11-84	8	7	3.99	19	19	0	0	108	108	60	48	12	36	73	.263	.277	.254	6.06	2.99
Bentz, Chad	R-L	6-2	210	5-5-80	1	0	1.29	7	0	0	0	7	6	3	1	0	4	5	.222	.167	.238	6.43	5.14
Bostick, Adam	L-L	6-2	220	3-17-83	4	3	4.67	9	9	0	0	44	42	26	23	3	25	39	.250	.379	.223	7.92	5.08
Cave, Kevin	R-R	6-2	220	5-25-80	5	3	4.04	37	0	0	1	42	32	19	19	1	24	35	.206	.250	.182	7.44	5.10
Demontel, Jimmy	R-R	6-4	245	6-7-80	0	0	9.00	2	0	0	0	2	1	2	2	0	5	1	.167	.000	.250	4.50	22.50
Flannery, Mike	R-R	6-2	225	9-20-79	1	3	2.21	31	0	0	13	37	30	9	9	2	6	39	.222	.250	.207	9.57	1.47
Flury, Pat	R-R	6-1	220	3-14-73	1	0	0.00	3	0	0	0	3	1	0	0	0	2	3	.125	.000	.250	10.13	6.75
Fuell, Jerrod	R-R	6-4	210	10-3-80	4	2	3.31	39	0	0	4	54	50	21	20	3	20	43	.244	.247	.242	7.12	3.31
Johnson, Josh	L-R	6-7	240	1-31-84	12	4	3.87	26	26	1	0	140	139	67	60	4	50	113	.261	.284	.244	7.28	3.22

PITCHING	B-T	HT	WT	DOB	W	L	ERA	G	GS	CG	SV	IP	H	R	ER	HR	BB	SO	AVG	vLH	vRH	K/9	BB/9
Kensing, Logan	R-R	6-1	185	7-3-82	4	1	3.18	7	7	0	0	40	35	16	14	4	14	33	.229	.281	.191	7.49	3.18
Lockwood, Luke	L-L	6-3	170	7-21-81	2	8	3.24	34	15	1	1	114	110	45	41	6	23	79	.263	.187	.288	6.24	1.82
Martinez, Carlos	R-R	6-2	170	5-26-82	0	0	9.00	1	0	0	1	1	1	1	1	0	1	1	.250	.500	.000	9.00	9.00
McNutt, Michael	R-R	6-2	190	10-18-79	3	2	3.83	31	0	0	1	54	46	23	23	9	24	37	.234	.216	.244	6.17	4.00
Molldrem, Craig	R-R	6-6	205	9-17-81	0	1	7.71	1	1	0	0	5	5	4	4	1	5	4	.263	.500	.091	7.71	9.64
Olsen, Scott	L-L	6-4	200	1-12-84	6	4	3.92	14	14	1	0	80	75	38	35	7	27	94	.251	.194	.267	10.53	3.02
Overman, Matt	R-R	6-0	185	9-10-80	1	0	0.00	6	0	0	0	7	8	0	0	0	0	8	.333	.300	.357	10.80	0.00
Resop, Chris	R-R	6-3	220	11-4-82	3	2	2.57	43	0	0	24	49	47	15	14	2	16	56	.242	.234	.246	10.29	2.94
Rodriguez, Joe	L-L	6-1	200	12-18-74	0	0	7.71	6	0	0	1	5	6	4	4	2	2	4	.300	.286	.308	7.71	3.86
Russ, James	R-R	6-4	210	10-24-80	1	0	0.00	1	1	0	0	5	4	0	0	0	0	5	.200	.333	.091	9.00	0.00
Sodowsky, Clint	L-R	6-4	200	7-13-72	0	1	5.03	12	1	0	0	20	20	12	11	0	4	24	.263	.250	.271	10.98	1.83
Torres, Andy	R-R	5-9	160	4-12-78	0	0	3.86	1	1	0	0	5	4	4	2	1	2	2	.222	.125	.300	3.86	3.86
Tucker, Michael	R-R	6-3	225	11-7-79	0	0	4.50	2	0	0	0	2	3	1	1	0	0	0	.375	.250	.500	0.00	0.00
Ungs, Nick	R-R	6-1	220	9-3-79	7	5	3.68	22	22	1	0	120	123	57	49	8	34	79	.268	.276	.262	5.93	2.55
Vargas, Jason	L-L	6-0	215	2-2-3	1	0	2.84	3	3	0	0	19	13	6	6	3	7	25	.194	.200	.193	11.84	3.32
Wolf, Ross	R-R	6-0	185	10-18-82	5	4	4.96	54	1	0	1	78	106	54	43	6	31	59	.321	.292	.340	6.81	3.58
Yourkin, Matt	R-L	6-3	225	7-4-81	0	2	4.05	11	0	0	0	7	7	4	3	0	4	4	.259	.200	.333	5.40	5.40

FIELDING

Catcher	PCT	G	PO	A	E	DP	PB
Anderson	.984	53	345	23	6	3	2
Ashby	1.000	22	176	9	0	1	5
Hill	.990	71	440	36	5	3	4

First Base	PCT	G	PO	A	E	DP
Ashby	1.000	1	1	0	0	0
Bass	.997	38	332	13	1	24
Hill	.986	34	258	17	4	20
Moore	1.000	22	164	10	0	6
Niles	1.000	4	26	1	0	0
Sears	.996	25	218	19	1	23
Tucker	.992	32	235	22	2	28

Second Base	PCT	G	PO	A	E	DP
Andino	1.000	1	3	3	0	0
Moore	.952	27	52	67	6	15
Niles	.984	19	26	37	1	7
Rundgren	.974	102	185	265	12	62
Tucker	1.000	3	0	2	0	0

Third Base	PCT	G	PO	A	E	DP
Bass	.908	47	29	80	11	8
DeMarco	.938	7	6	9	1	0
Hill	1.000	2	0	2	0	0
Moore	.833	14	2	18	4	0
Niles	.984	63	40	143	3	16
Tucker	.948	22	11	44	3	1

Shortstop	PCT	G	PO	A	E	DP
Andino	.951	126	150	378	27	70
Niles	.900	2	5	4	1	1
Rundgren	.972	10	9	26	1	7

Outfield	PCT	G	PO	A	E	DP
Abercrombie	.966	46	112	2	4	0
Hermida	.982	114	212	6	4	3
Molina	1.000	10	16	0	0	0
Moore	1.000	10	10	1	0	0
Muniz	.965	75	106	5	4	1
Reed	.994	67	150	4	1	1
Shanks	.978	95	128	4	3	1

JUPITER HAMMERHEADS — High Class A

FLORIDA STATE LEAGUE

BATTING	B-T	HT	WT	DOB	AVG	vLH	vRH	G	AB	R	H	2B	3B	HR	RBI	BB	HBP	SH	SF	SO	SB	CS	SLG	OBP
Abercrombie, Reggie	R-R	6-3	225	7-15-80	.274	.270	.276	76	299	51	82	12	3	15	45	14	5	2	1	87	19	6	.485	.317
Arlis, Patrick	R-R	6-0	215	12-18-80	.243	.284	.228	91	305	38	74	9	2	6	35	25	0	8	4	72	9	1	.344	.296
Arnerich, Tony	R-R	6-0	200	12-14-79	.212	.222	.210	29	99	8	21	3	0	0	14	9	3	1	0	29	1	0	.242	.297
Batista, Norberto	R-R	6-1	155	8-5-83	.333	.333	.333	7	9	2	3	1	0	0	3	1	0	0	0	2	1	0	.444	.400
Bear, Ryan	R-R	6-2	220	1-26-81	.294	.325	.284	129	472	76	139	25	3	3	46	45	7	2	5	72	23	4	.379	.361
Blake, Ryan	R-R	6-1	206	1-2-80	.125	.000	.125	3	8	0	1	0	0	0	0	1	0	0	0	2	0	0	.125	.222
Brock, Todd	R-R	6-0	190	4-7-78	.195	.167	.205	83	231	23	45	9	1	4	17	15	5	0	2	70	4	6	.294	.257
Brown, Gregory	R-R	5-11	195	5-4-80	.196	.267	.171	27	56	5	11	2	0	0	9	11	0	1	1	17	0	0	.232	.324
Campusano, Jose	B-R	5-11	165	12-19-83	.277	.256	.286	89	300	37	83	9	3	0	32	9	4	5	2	67	13	5	.327	.305
De Aza, Alejandro	L-L	6-0	174	4-11-84	.286	.305	.279	123	472	75	135	24	9	3	37	58	8	11	5	87	34	17	.394	.370
DeMarco, Matt	L-R	6-0	172	1-24-80	.243	.200	.250	29	107	13	26	1	0	0	6	4	1	1	0	13	2	0	.252	.277
2-team (30 Palm Beach)					.225	.093	.261	59	204	29	46	6	0	0	11	13	4	1	0	25	3	0	.255	.285
Figueroa, Juan	L-L	6-0	200	12-9-81	.259	.218	.274	80	293	30	76	15	1	0	33	26	2	0	3	72	3	1	.317	.321
Lindsey, John	R-R	6-3	240	1-30-77	.219	.195	.236	30	96	13	21	8	0	1	16	11	4	0	0	22	0	0	.333	.324
Messner, Nathan	R-R	6-3	210	11-21-85	.000	.000	.000	4	4	1	0	0	0	0	0	2	0	0	0	2	1	0	.000	.333
Mitchell, Lee	R-R	6-1	198	4-21-82	.226	.214	.231	126	468	65	106	27	1	14	60	51	8	2	3	142	4	1	.378	.311
Molina, Angel	R-R	6-2	226	11-4-81	.261	.289	.251	120	456	59	119	23	3	9	84	48	3	0	7	89	7	7	.384	.331
Moore, Frank	L-R	6-2	213	7-2-78	.288	.269	.292	37	146	15	42	8	1	0	21	16	2	1	0	30	6	3	.356	.366
Ochoa, Blake	R-R	6-0	180	9-5-85	.000	.000	.000	1	1	0	0	0	0	0	0	0	0	0	0	0	0	0	.000	.000
Randel, Kevin	L-R	6-1	180	6-11-81	.285	.314	.275	114	393	59	112	19	1	9	50	58	6	7	1	95	15	3	.407	.384
Rohleder, Andy	R-R	6-0	195	2-27-80	.214	.190	.224	87	271	25	58	13	0	4	27	17	4	0	5	70	5	2	.306	.266
Schade, Ryan	R-R	5-9	175	11-21-78	.222	.294	.179	28	45	3	10	1	0	0	1	6	0	1	0	11	1	0	.244	.314
Smolarski, Freddy	R-R	6-1	180	9-24-84	.250	.000	.500	1	4	0	1	0	0	0	0	0	0	0	0	0	0	0	.250	.250
Tucker, Michael	R-R	6-3	225	11-7-79	.229	.000	.258	12	35	7	8	2	0	2	5	8	0	0	0	7	0	0	.457	.372
Willingham, Josh	R-R	6-1	200	2-17-79	.222	.000	.222	2	9	1	2	1	0	0	1	0	1	0	0	2	0	0	.333	.300

PITCHING	B-T	HT	WT	DOB	W	L	ERA	G	GS	CG	SV	IP	H	R	ER	HR	BB	SO	AVG	vLH	vRH	K/9	BB/9
Aguilar, Ray	B-L	5-11	210	1-18-80	1	0	5.40	1	1	0	0	5	6	3	3	0	1	2	.273	.000	.273	3.60	1.80
Alfonseca, Antonio	R-R	6-5	250	4-16-72	0	0	3.00	3	1	0	0	3	3	1	1	1	0	4	.300	.000	.333	12.00	0.00
Baker, Ryan	R-R	6-0	200	3-20-78	0	0	1.08	6	0	0	2	8	7	1	1	0	1	4	.233	.375	.182	4.32	1.08
Baxter, Allen	R-R	6-4	215	7-6-83	0	5	7.15	12	5	0	0	34	52	27	27	4	28	38	.356	.367	.351	10.06	7.41
Bostick, Adam	L-L	6-2	220	3-17-83	4	5	3.84	17	17	0	0	91	95	47	39	7	36	94	.270	.338	.252	9.26	3.55
Brandenburg, Adam	L-L	6-5	225	8-17-81	0	1	2.66	7	2	0	0	20	20	11	6	0	10	16	.260	.250	.261	7.08	4.43
Cave, Kevin	R-R	6-2	220	5-25-80	0	0	4.35	11	0	0	7	10	9	6	5	3	5	9	.220	.375	.182	7.84	4.35
De la Cruz, Jose	R-R	6-0	165	7-26-84	0	0	15.00	2	0	0	0	3	5	5	5	0	4	2	.385	.667	.300	6.00	12.00
De los Santos, Valerio	L-L	6-2	210	10-6-72	0	0	0.00	3	0	0	0	4	4	0	0	0	2	4	.250	.000	.250	9.00	4.50
Demontel, Jimmy	R-R	6-4	245	6-7-80	1	4	5.36	32	0	0	0	47	63	32	28	4	17	39	.328	.333	.326	7.47	3.26
Flury, Pat	R-R	6-1	220	3-14-73	0	0	1.23	8	0	0	0	7	4	2	1	0	5	5	.160	.200	.133	6.14	6.14
Galbizo, Rafael	R-R	6-1	185	2-18-85	0	0	2.25	3	0	0	0	4	2	2	1	0	4	6	.143	.333	.091	13.50	9.00
Garcia, Jose	R-R	5-11	165	1-7-85	0	0	18.00	1	1	0	0	2	2	4	4	0	2	0	.286	.500	.200	0.00	9.00
Gogal, Jeff	R-L	6-2	195	6-10-82	2	4	5.69	13	10	0	0	62	83	40	39	4	11	49	.322	.244	.338	7.15	1.61
Hoff, Brian	R-R	6-4	225	1-28-82	2	4	4.72	28	0	0	0	34	49	22	18	2	9	33	.325	.250	.355	8.65	2.36
Holdzkom, Lincoln	R-R	6-4	240	3-23-82	0	1	5.79	9	0	0	1	9	7	6	6	0	5	9	.206	.250	.192	8.68	4.82
Iehl, Jason	R-R	6-2	185	4-23-84	1	5	5.67	23	7	0	0	54	75	41	34	6	23	45	.326	.267	.364	7.50	3.83

PITCHING	B-T	HT	WT	DOB	W	L	ERA	G	GS	CG	SV	IP	H	R	ER	HR	BB	SO	AVG	vLH	vRH	K/9	BB/9
Jones, Blake	R-R	6-5	220	4-15-81	1	2	6.43	16	0	0	0	21	30	16	15	3	7	14	.323	.296	.333	6.00	3.00
Koehler, Kurt	R-R	6-1	190	9-5-84	1	0	1.50	3	0	0	1	6	2	2	1	0	3	9	.111	.000	.118	13.50	4.50
Lerch, Zach	R-R	6-4	188	11-23-82	2	1	8.66	7	2	0	1	18	20	18	17	2	4	15	.274	.267	.279	7.64	2.04
Martinez, Carlos	R-R	6-2	170	5-26-82	4	5	3.12	47	0	0	22	61	52	25	21	5	22	65	.226	.262	.205	9.64	3.26
McCormack, Zach	L-L	6-3	210	1-18-82	1	1	6.23	4	0	0	0	4	2	3	3	1	2	3	.133	.400	.000	6.23	4.15
McNutt, Michael	R-R	6-2	190	10-18-79	1	2	4.13	13	0	0	0	24	22	11	11	4	11	24	.239	.231	.242	9.00	4.13
Mildren, Paul	R-L	6-1	195	5-3-84	10	3	3.08	29	20	0	0	140	115	55	48	13	42	111	.225	.170	.237	7.12	2.69
Molldrem, Craig	R-R	6-6	205	9-17-81	0	2	6.26	5	4	0	0	23	40	20	16	0	12	10	.388	.270	.455	3.91	4.70
Mota, Guillermo	R-R	6-4	210	7-25-73	0	0	0.00	2	2	0	0	3	3	1	0	0	0	4	.300	.333	.286	13.50	0.00
Olivera, Manuel	R-L	5-11	205	12-8-77	3	4	3.94	35	8	1	0	75	68	43	33	4	34	56	.245	.264	.240	6.69	4.06
Overman, Matt	R-R	6-0	185	9-10-80	5	1	5.35	27	0	0	1	39	42	27	23	5	19	20	.278	.250	.293	4.66	4.42
Rasowky, Avi	L-L	6-1	195	5-17-83	0	0	0.00	1	0	0	0	1	0	0	0	0	0	0	.000	.000	.000	0.00	0.00
Russ, James	R-R	6-4	210	10-24-80	11	8	3.51	27	26	0	0	162	133	72	63	7	48	143	.227	.252	.213	7.96	2.67
Schade, Ryan	R-R	5-9	175	11-21-78	0	0	12.00	3	0	0	0	3	5	4	4	3	5	1	.417	.333	.444	3.00	15.00
Spooneybarger, Tim	R-R	6-3	205	10-21-79	0	0	3.00	4	1	0	0	3	1	1	1	0	4	2	.100	.000	.125	6.00	12.00
Strelitz, Brian	R-R	6-1	208	1-8-80	1	1	11.37	5	0	0	0	6	10	9	8	1	3	2	.345	.333	.348	2.84	4.26
Tankersley, Taylor	L-L	6-1	220	3-7-83	1	0	3.38	4	4	1	0	24	21	10	9	1	9	19	.247	.167	.260	7.13	3.38
Teekel, Josh	R-R	6-5	210	9-18-80	1	3	8.06	5	5	0	0	22	31	24	20	2	15	11	.330	.355	.317	4.43	6.04
Tillman, Derek	R-R	6-2	185	7-12-80	2	1	5.23	23	0	0	3	31	26	21	18	1	12	22	.230	.235	.228	6.39	3.48
Torres, Andy	R-R	5-9	160	4-12-78	4	1	3.53	6	6	0	0	36	36	15	14	4	12	27	.269	.333	.225	6.81	3.03
Treanor, Bryan	R-R	5-11	185	2-11-80	0	0	0.00	1	0	0	0	1	0	0	0	0	0	1	.000	.000	.000	9.00	0.00
Valdez, Ismael	R-R	6-4	230	8-21-73	1	1	7.88	2	2	0	0	8	7	7	7	1	2	5	.226	.077	.333	5.63	2.25
Vanden Hurk, Rick	R-R	6-5	195	5-22-85	0	1	4.05	2	2	0	0	7	7	4	3	0	0	6	.259	.500	.190	8.10	0.00
Vargas, Jason	L-L	6-0	215	2-2-83	2	3	3.42	9	9	0	0	55	47	24	21	6	14	60	.225	.306	.200	9.76	2.28
Yourkin, Matt	R-L	6-3	225	7-4-81	2	2	4.30	22	0	0	0	29	25	15	14	2	11	30	.225	.257	.211	9.20	3.38

FIELDING

Catcher	PCT	G	PO	A	E	DP	PB
Arlis	.982	90	632	68	13	7	12
Arnerich	.984	29	224	24	4	4	4
Blake	1.000	1	4	0	0	0	0
Brown	.987	25	143	11	2	0	2
Ochoa	.000	1	0	0	0	0	0
Willingham	1.000	2	14	0	0	0	0

First Base	PCT	G	PO	A	E	DP
Bear	.990	74	582	18	6	47
DeMarco	1.000	1	3	0	0	0
Figueroa	.973	57	448	17	13	41
Lindsey	.985	9	62	4	1	5
Messner	.889	3	8	0	1	0
Moore	1.000	3	21	1	0	3
Tucker	1.000	1	6	1	0	2

Second Base	PCT	G	PO	A	E	DP
Batista	1.000	4	2	1	0	0
Brock	.951	13	26	13	2	5
DeMarco	1.000	10	18	24	0	4
Moore	1.000	8	24	30	0	5
Randel	.956	102	211	224	20	51
Schade	.960	22	24	24	2	3

Third Base	PCT	G	PO	A	E	DP
Batista	.000	1	0	0	0	0
Brock	.905	13	3	16	2	0
DeMarco	1.000	4	1	5	0	0
Mitchell	.938	124	86	245	22	24
Moore	1.000	1	2	3	0	0
Tucker	.929	4	2	11	1	2

Shortstop	PCT	G	PO	A	E	DP
Brock	.971	59	70	163	7	25
Campusano	.906	86	117	238	37	43
DeMarco	.909	2	4	6	1	2
Schade	1.000	1	0	3	0	0

Outfield	PCT	G	PO	A	E	DP
Abercrombie	.977	75	202	6	5	2
Batista	1.000	1	1	0	0	0
Bear	.983	31	56	1	1	0
De Aza	.976	111	234	9	6	3
Figueroa	1.000	4	7	0	0	0
Molina	.995	103	183	9	1	1
Moore	.942	25	45	4	3	1
Rohleder	.982	76	105	3	2	0
Schade	1.000	1	0	1	0	0

GREENSBORO BATS — Low Class A

SOUTH ATLANTIC LEAGUE

BATTING	B-T	HT	WT	DOB	AVG	vLH	vRH	G	AB	R	H	2B	3B	HR	RBI	BB	HBP	SH	SF	SO	SB	CS	SLG	OBP
Alen, Luis	R-R	6-1	175	4-16-85	.181	.273	.165	39	116	9	21	4	0	0	8	3	0	2	0	11	0	0	.216	.202
Arroyo, Xavier	R-R	6-1	175	8-9-84	.200	.192	.202	40	115	17	23	3	1	0	9	25	3	1	0	38	4	3	.243	.357
Batista, Norberto	R-R	6-1	155	8-5-83	.333	.125	.438	11	24	8	8	1	0	0	0	5	0	0	0	4	0	1	.375	.448
Brown, Greg	R-R	5-11	195	5-4-80	.186	.125	.200	30	86	9	16	4	0	2	12	6	4	0	0	22	2	0	.302	.271
Carroll, Brett	R-R	6-0	190	10-3-82	.243	.276	.232	118	412	57	100	28	1	18	54	17	15	3	2	108	10	10	.447	.296
Cleveland, Brian	R-R	6-1	185	1-7-82	.277	.253	.286	109	444	66	123	21	2	8	50	24	10	1	2	71	20	7	.387	.327
D'Antonio, Trent	B-R	5-9	180	8-14-85	.282	.000	.282	24	71	11	20	6	0	3	15	8	0	0	1	9	1	1	.493	.350
Davis, Brad	R-R	6-2	185	12-29-82	.228	.267	.214	64	228	26	52	13	1	5	24	17	2	3	2	62	0	2	.360	.285
Figueroa, Juan	L-L	6-0	200	12-9-81	.326	.250	.338	24	86	13	28	4	0	1	15	19	1	0	0	23	0	1	.407	.453
Fulton, Jon	R-R	6-4	200	12-1-83	.232	.315	.205	76	267	34	62	10	3	11	39	20	5	0	1	72	1	1	.416	.297
Gaston, Jared	R-R	6-2	195	4-15-84	.265	.339	.247	75	253	41	67	11	1	4	17	29	7	0	1	46	5	5	.364	.355
Gendron, Steve	R-R	6-3	195	11-25-81	.252	.261	.247	128	485	65	122	22	1	9	56	40	4	1	4	95	14	5	.357	.311
Jenkins, Andy	R-R	6-0	205	7-23-83	.220	.216	.221	48	168	22	37	9	0	3	20	14	2	1	1	33	1	3	.327	.286
McCann, Brad	R-R	6-3	190	12-9-82	.295	.245	.309	123	478	67	141	35	2	28	106	37	9	0	3	97	1	1	.552	.355
McMillan, Beau	R-R	5-11	185	9-15-81	.214	.200	.216	47	117	19	25	3	1	2	12	20	5	1	2	41	7	1	.308	.347
Miller, Jai	R-R	6-4	195	1-17-85	.207	.333	.172	115	415	69	86	14	2	13	34	57	3	1	3	139	16	11	.345	.305
Pietro, Joe	L-R	6-0	190	12-13-82	.167	.000	.222	11	36	6	6	0	0	0	5	8	0	0	1	15	5	1	.167	.311
Restko, J.T.	R-R	6-5	190	12-15-84	.313	.367	.295	115	403	69	126	22	3	15	70	53	18	0	2	91	3	0	.494	.414
Schade, Ryan	R-R	5-9	175	11-21-78	.357	.286	.381	13	28	5	10	2	0	0	3	3	0	1	0	5	1	1	.429	.419
Seifrig, Cole	R-R	6-3	190	9-10-84	.219	.228	.213	69	237	32	52	10	0	10	34	17	4	0	3	73	7	2	.388	.280
Sewell, Kevin	L-R	5-11	205	1-28-81	.238	.250	.235	49	143	23	34	10	0	4	24	16	2	0	3	35	1	0	.392	.317
Smolarski, Freddy	R-R	6-1	180	9-24-84	.182	.000	.200	3	11	0	2	0	0	0	0	0	0	0	0	2	0	0	.182	.182
Webb, Justin	R-R	6-1	175	11-5-82	.167	.000	.167	2	6	1	1	1	0	0	1	1	0	0	0	2	1	0	.333	.286
Witt, Paul	R-R	5-11	180	12-8-82	.231	.500	.182	4	13	1	3	0	0	0	0	2	0	0	0	2	0	1	.231	.333

PITCHING	B-T	HT	WT	DOB	W	L	ERA	G	GS	CG	SV	IP	H	R	ER	HR	BB	SO	AVG	vLH	vRH	K/9	BB/9
Barone, Daniel	R-R	6-2	185	4-24-83	2	2	4.12	12	6	0	1	39	35	19	18	4	10	29	.238	.282	.222	6.64	2.29
Baxter, Allen	R-R	6-4	215	7-6-83	1	3	4.15	11	11	0	0	56	57	34	26	8	37	53	.264	.256	.273	8.47	5.91
Bille, Mike	R-R	6-2	220	11-2-81	0	0	81.00	2	0	0	0	1	4	6	6	1	3	1	.800	1.000	.750	13.50	40.50
Brandenburg, Adam	L-L	6-5	225	8-17-81	5	6	4.70	27	19	0	1	100	128	72	52	8	42	65	.319	.302	.322	5.87	3.79
Brazell, Landon	R-R	5-11	210	5-5-82	1	0	10.24	2	2	0	0	10	15	11	11	3	8	5	.349	.417	.323	4.66	7.45
Castor, Parrish	L-L	6-2	180	9-18-83	1	1	18.00	3	0	0	0	3	9	6	6	2	5	5	.500	.500	.500	15.00	15.00
Garcia, Jose	R-R	5-11	165	1-7-85	3	0	1.27	5	4	0	0	28	11	5	4	1	4	39	.115	.103	.123	12.39	1.27
Gogal, Jeff	R-L	6-2	195	6-10-82	2	1	3.10	9	0	0	0	20	15	7	7	3	6	19	.205	.263	.185	8.41	2.66
Hoff, Brian	R-R	6-4	225	1-28-82	0	0	9.53	4	0	0	0	6	13	6	6	1	2	4	.448	.357	.533	6.35	3.18
Hogan, Patrick	R-R	6-4	235	4-10-81	1	1	7.66	24	0	0	1	25	39	26	21	5	9	17	.348	.294	.372	6.20	3.28

PITCHING	B-T	HT	WT	DOB	W	L	ERA	G	GS	CG	SV	IP	H	R	ER	HR	BB	SO	AVG	vLH	vRH	K/9	BB/9
Humen, David	R-R	6-2	210	6-11-81	3	2	3.90	18	9	0	1	65	57	30	28	7	33	79	.228	.292	.188	10.99	4.59
James, Rhett	R-R	6-1	215	10-17-82	0	0	.000	1	0	0	0	0	0	0	0	0	1	0	.000	.000	.000	.000	.000
Koehler, Kurt	R-R	6-1	190	9-5-84	2	9	5.23	29	18	0	0	117	152	81	68	7	48	90	.321	.353	.292	6.92	3.69
Lerch, Zach	R-R	6-4	188	11-23-82	4	4	4.91	14	11	0	0	70	78	53	38	9	24	37	.277	.253	.290	4.78	3.10
Marceaux, Jacob	R-R	6-1	195	2-14-84	0	3	12.36	5	5	0	0	20	40	32	27	4	9	12	.426	.314	.492	5.49	4.12
McCormack, Zach	L-L	6-3	210	1-18-82	4	2	4.61	26	0	0	2	41	41	24	21	2	17	33	.263	.321	.233	7.24	3.73
Mobley, Chris	R-R	5-11	171	8-16-83	3	5	2.23	54	0	0	34	61	32	16	15	7	33	74	.155	.176	.143	10.98	4.90
Molldrem, Craig	R-R	6-6	205	9-17-81	6	1	2.83	16	10	1	0	64	47	26	20	5	27	47	.202	.179	.220	6.64	3.82
Nestor, Scott	R-R	6-4	225	8-20-84	4	6	3.96	58	0	0	2	73	59	40	32	7	46	80	.227	.264	.208	9.91	5.70
Nowicki, Nathan	R-R	6-4	190	4-25-82	4	3	5.20	29	0	0	0	45	54	36	26	6	19	24	.298	.329	.279	4.80	3.80
Santos, Jarrett	R-R	6-4	215	8-18-81	7	4	3.70	52	0	0	2	83	94	43	34	4	23	52	.281	.244	.302	5.66	2.50
Talbott, Travis	L-L	5-11	175	5-23-82	0	1	3.00	18	0	0	0	21	13	8	7	1	10	13	.183	.182	.184	5.57	4.29
Tankersley, Taylor	L-L	6-1	220	3-7-83	2	7	5.18	12	12	0	0	66	74	45	38	12	25	63	.279	.188	.300	8.59	3.41
Vanden Hurk, Rick	R-R	6-5	195	5-22-85	1	2	2.45	4	4	1	0	22	17	7	6	1	11	26	.218	.250	.190	10.64	4.50
Vargas, Jason	L-L	6-0	215	2-2-83	4	1	0.80	5	5	0	0	34	16	4	3	1	10	33	.140	.083	.156	8.82	2.67
Wood, Adam	L-L	6-0	190	7-12-82	0	0	4.50	2	0	0	0	2	2	1	1	0	1	3	.250	.000	.286	13.50	4.50
Wood, Tim	R-R	6-1	185	11-16-82	1	2	9.28	5	5	0	0	21	29	23	22	2	15	10	.312	.283	.340	4.22	6.33
Yourkin, Matt	R-L	6-3	225	7-4-81	1	1	2.67	21	0	0	2	30	25	11	9	5	7	33	.216	.200	.224	9.79	2.08

FIELDING

Catcher	PCT	G	PO	A	E	DP	PB
Alen	.989	39	240	41	3	2	18
Brown	.987	30	200	20	3	0	9
D'Antonio	1.000	15	100	8	0	0	4
Davis	.982	59	435	48	9	5	15
Jenkins	1.000	4	20	0	0	0	1
Smolarski	1.000	3	29	1	0	0	0

First Base	PCT	G	PO	A	E	DP
Figueroa	.975	21	186	9	5	17
Gendron	.986	8	68	4	1	4
Jenkins	1.000	9	46	3	0	7
McCann	.989	103	967	67	11	85
Restko	1.000	1	4	0	0	0

Second Base	PCT	G	PO	A	E	DP
Cleveland	.988	51	88	161	3	26
Gendron	.000	1	0	0	0	0
McMillan	.915	23	25	40	6	11
Schade	.968	7	9	21	1	5
Seifrig	.983	66	106	180	5	37
Webb	.800	1	1	3	1	2
Witt	1.000	1	1	2	0	0

Third Base	PCT	G	PO	A	E	DP
Batista	.600	1	1	2	2	0
Fulton	.832	73	26	118	29	4
Gendron	.949	25	16	58	4	3
Jenkins	.939	38	23	69	6	4
McMillan	.625	6	0	10	6	0
Schade	1.000	1	0	1	0	0
Seifrig	.600	5	2	4	4	0
Webb	.000	1	0	0	0	0

Shortstop	PCT	G	PO	A	E	DP
Batista	1.000	9	13	21	0	9
Cleveland	.948	42	70	129	11	32
Gendron	.944	88	160	295	27	61
McMillan	.846	3	5	6	2	2
Seifrig	1.000	1	0	2	0	0
Webb	1.000	1	3	3	0	2
Witt	.667	1	2	0	1	0

Outfield	PCT	G	PO	A	E	DP
Arroyo	.947	37	54	0	3	0
Carroll	.964	114	199	18	8	5
Figueroa	1.000	2	2	0	0	0
Gaston	1.000	69	95	7	0	1
Miller	.983	114	232	6	4	2
Pietro	1.000	11	14	1	0	0
Restko	.910	64	78	3	8	1
Sewell	.982	32	53	1	1	0

JAMESTOWN JAMMERS — Short-Season Class A

NEW YORK-PENN LEAGUE

BATTING	B-T	HT	WT	DOB	AVG	vLH	vRH	G	AB	R	H	2B	3B	HR	RBI	BB	HBP	SH	SF	SO	SB	CS	SLG	OBP
Aranda, Mark	L-L	5-11	215	5-12-83	.201	.175	.209	51	179	27	36	7	2	9	24	15	3	0	1	62	2	1	.413	.273
Burns, Greg	L-L	6-2	185	11-7-86	.257	.255	.258	65	241	43	62	5	2	1	11	39	3	4	1	84	17	11	.307	.366
Cabral, Marcos	R-R	6-0	180	4-4-84	.224	.269	.203	24	85	9	19	1	0	2	6	3	1	2	0	16	3	1	.306	.258
D'Antonio, Trent	B-R	5-9	180	8-14-85	.214	.333	.182	7	14	5	3	1	0	0	2	3	0	0	1	2	0	0	.286	.333
Ellington, Matt	L-L	6-1	294	1-15-84	.355	.143	.417	9	31	3	11	1	1	0	1	2	2	0	0	6	1	0	.452	.429
Guerrero, James	R-R	5-7	175	6-8-84	.243	.222	.249	62	235	35	57	12	3	3	26	20	9	0	1	56	7	2	.357	.325
Harvey, Kris	R-R	6-2	195	1-5-84	.300	.333	.289	65	263	34	79	14	3	9	38	9	0	0	3	60	4	0	.479	.320
Hayes, Brett	R-R	6-1	200	2-13-84	.239	.118	.289	36	117	11	28	6	1	1	12	12	1	0	1	21	3	3	.333	.313
Jenkins, Andy	R-R	6-0	205	7-23-83	.500	.750	.400	4	14	2	7	2	0	0	1	2	0	0	1	0	1	0	.643	.529
Kutler, Matt	L-L	6-0	185	2-25-82	.448	.333	.478	8	29	8	13	4	1	1	9	0	0	0	0	2	0	0	.759	.448
Messner, Nathan	R-R	6-3	210	11-21-85	.203	.250	.194	36	128	11	26	4	0	2	14	8	1	0	0	35	1	1	.281	.255
Padgett, Kyle	R-R	6-1	185	1-16-83	.208	.000	.227	6	24	1	5	0	0	0	1	0	0	0	0	8	0	0	.208	.208
Roche, Gary	R-R	5-11	180	12-28-83	.310	.270	.320	49	187	20	58	5	1	1	20	8	1	7	1	24	3	1	.364	.340
Rogers, Tanner	R-R	6-0	180	1-11-85	.227	.250	.220	50	150	22	34	3	2	3	15	16	7	2	1	33	5	9	.333	.328
Sanchez, Gaby	R-R	6-2	225	9-2-83	.355	.340	.358	62	234	34	83	16	0	5	42	16	4	0	3	24	11	5	.487	.401
Van Houten, Jeff	R-R	5-10	175	11-14-82	.283	.260	.290	62	226	35	64	18	2	7	36	24	5	3	1	41	2	5	.473	.363
Walton, Jamar	L-R	6-4	195	1-5-86	.225	.098	.261	64	227	19	51	2	5	2	22	17	5	1	0	84	1	3	.304	.293
Witt, Paul	R-R	5-11	180	12-8-82	.205	.192	.208	35	132	14	27	4	1	0	9	4	0	0	0	38	1	2	.250	.228

PITCHING	B-T	HT	WT	DOB	W	L	ERA	G	GS	CG	SV	IP	H	R	ER	HR	BB	SO	AVG	vLH	vRH	K/9	BB/9
Barone, Daniel	R-R	6-2	185	4-24-83	2	0	0.46	9	0	0	2	20	14	2	1	1	4	17	.197	.286	.140	7.78	1.83
Berkenbosch, Kenny	R-R	6-2	204	3-17-85	1	0	4.81	17	0	0	1	34	29	18	18	7	15	30	.240	.289	.217	8.02	4.01
Bille, Mike	R-R	6-2	220	11-2-81	3	2	3.45	18	0	0	2	31	27	17	12	0	12	25	.225	.216	.232	7.18	3.45
Brauer, Jim	R-R	6-4	210	7-16-82	3	2	4.22	10	10	1	0	43	38	32	20	1	14	31	.225	.167	.268	6.54	2.95
Brazell, Landon	R-R	5-11	210	5-5-82	2	3	5.09	14	9	0	0	53	56	37	30	3	25	38	.273	.344	.241	6.45	4.25
Camilo, Juan	R-R	6-3	168	4-22-83	1	2	7.94	10	0	0	3	11	20	12	10	3	3	9	.377	.389	.371	7.15	2.38
Castor, Parrish	L-L	6-2	180	9-18-83	0	0	2.25	3	0	0	0	4	4	1	1	0	4	6	.250	.000	.267	13.50	9.00
Doolittle, Michael	R-R	5-10	175	11-1-82	4	5	4.03	22	3	0	2	58	61	36	26	4	20	71	.263	.256	.266	11.02	3.10
Easton, Aaron	L-R	6-10	240	9-8-81	0	0	5.16	17	0	0	0	30	27	22	17	2	13	25	.239	.196	.269	7.58	3.94
Galbizo, Rafael	R-R	6-1	185	2-18-85	1	0	2.77	8	0	0	0	13	15	4	4	0	5	18	.288	.412	.229	12.46	3.46
Goyen, Matt	R-L	6-5	220	1-19-83	1	5	4.03	10	10	0	0	45	44	25	20	8	21	44	.253	.290	.245	8.87	4.23
Lerch, Zach	R-R	6-4	188	11-23-82	0	0	0.00	1	0	0	0	1	0	0	0	0	0	0	.000	.000	.000	0.00	0.00
Lewis, Jon	R-R	6-1	190	5-16-83	1	2	5.85	19	0	0	0	32	43	29	21	5	17	25	.314	.302	.321	6.96	4.73
Marceaux, Jacob	R-R	6-1	195	2-14-84	3	5	5.55	10	10	0	0	47	56	33	29	5	13	32	.287	.337	.250	6.13	2.49
McCamie, Zac	R-R	6-3	205	9-28-82	0	0	11.05	5	0	0	0	7	16	9	9	3	1	8	.457	.286	.500	9.82	1.23
Nickerson, Jon-Michael	L-L	6-5	180	12-4-84	2	5	5.93	17	14	0	0	58	59	44	38	9	37	62	.266	.275	.261	9.68	5.77
Rasowky, Avi	L-L	6-1	195	5-17-83	0	0	7.36	2	0	0	0	7	10	6	6	1	5	8	.333	.167	.375	9.82	6.14
Talbott, Travis	L-L	5-11	175	5-23-82	0	2	5.11	7	0	0	0	12	16	9	7	0	8	8	.333	.182	.378	5.84	5.84
Thompson, Aaron	L-L	6-3	195	2-28-87	1	2	3.10	5	5	0	0	20	25	13	7	1	10	17	.301	.375	.293	7.52	4.43
Tucker, Ryan	R-R	6-2	190	12-6-86	1	1	8.36	4	4	0	0	14	21	14	13	3	8	18	.323	.136	.419	11.57	5.14
Volstad, Chris	R-R	6-7	190	9-23-86	3	2	2.13	7	7	0	0	38	43	19	9	0	11	29	.279	.343	.226	6.87	2.61

PITCHING	B-T	HT	WT	DOB	W	L	ERA	G	GS	CG	SV	IP	H	R	ER	HR	BB	SO	AVG	vLH	vRH	K/9	BB/9
West, Sean	L-L	6-8	200	6-15-86	0	2	5.73	3	3	0	0	11	17	7	7	1	5	14	.362	.286	.375	11.45	4.09
Wood, Adam	L-L	6-0	190	7-12-82	1	1	3.97	25	0	0	0	34	36	19	15	0	16	30	.279	.217	.292	7.94	4.24
Zarate, Mauro	R-R	6-1	180	2-8-83	1	3	4.28	24	0	0	7	27	24	13	13	3	8	35	.233	.174	.281	11.52	2.63

GAMES BY POSITION: C—D'Antonio 7, Hayes 34, Rogers 31, Sanchez 11. **1B**—Aranda 24, Ellington 9, Jenkins 3, Messner 2, Messner 32, Sanchez 12. **2B**—Guerrero 48, Roche 31. **3B**—Cabral 2, Harvey 25, Jenkins 1, Padgett 1, Roche 11, Rogers 9, Sanchez 30. **SS**—Cabral 22, Guerrero 15, Hayes 1, Padgett 5, Witt 35. **OF**—Aranda 22, Berkenbosch 7, Burns 60, Harvey 24, Hayes 1, Kutler 6, Rogers 9, Van Houten 49, Walton 58.

GCL MARLINS — Rookie

GULF COAST LEAGUE

BATTING	B-T	HT	WT	DOB	AVG	vLH	vRH	G	AB	R	H	2B	3B	HR	RBI	BB	HBP	SH	SF	SO	SB	CS	SLG	OBP
Adduci, James	L-L	6-2	185	5-15-85	.378	.429	.367	11	37	3	14	3	1	0	7	3	0	0	0	5	1	0	.514	.425
Agustin, Juan	R-R	5-11	160	10-30-84	.269	.304	.259	31	104	15	28	6	1	1	9	7	2	3	0	24	2	1	.375	.327
Allen, Cody	R-R	6-2	190	9-19-86	.223	.257	.212	45	139	16	31	8	1	1	10	19	3	0	0	48	1	2	.317	.329
Barnes, Larry	L-L	6-1	195	7-23-74	.333	.500	.286	3	9	1	3	1	0	0	3	1	1	0	0	0	0	1	.444	.455
Batista, Norberto	R-R	6-1	155	8-5-83	.183	.235	.167	24	71	12	13	3	0	0	5	18	3	7	2	10	0	0	.225	.362
de Vrieze, Jeff	R-R	6-0	180	1-20-86	.179	.105	.208	30	67	8	12	3	0	1	8	5	1	0	1	30	0	0	.269	.243
Ellington, Matt	L-L	6-1	294	1-15-84	.316	.381	.293	21	79	12	25	8	1	3	13	5	3	0	1	12	0	0	.557	.375
Haupt, Chris	R-R	6-0	200	5-18-87	.050	.000	.067	21	40	2	2	0	0	0	1	6	2	0	0	18	0	0	.050	.208
Hayes, Brett	R-R	6-1	200	2-13-84	.417	.250	.500	3	12	2	5	1	0	0	2	0	0	0	0	2	0	1	.500	.417
Kutler, Matt	L-L	6-0	185	2-25-82	.337	.380	.319	44	169	27	57	14	0	1	25	13	2	2	1	24	8	3	.438	.389
Little, Mark	R-R	6-0	190	7-11-72	.500	1.000	.333	2	4	2	2	0	0	2	6	0	0	0	0	1	0	0	2.000	.500
Messner, Nathan	R-R	6-3	210	11-21-85	.300	.250	.313	5	20	6	6	1	0	0	5	2	1	0	0	5	0	0	.350	.391
Ochoa, Blake	R-R	6-0	180	9-5-85	.278	.241	.291	37	115	10	32	9	0	2	17	12	6	0	0	20	0	1	.409	.376
Padgett, Kyle	R-R	6-1	185	1-16-83	.227	.190	.236	35	110	13	25	6	1	1	11	7	2	4	1	20	2	1	.327	.283
Ramos, Luis	L-R	6-2	180	3-10-87	.267	.188	.295	23	60	9	16	3	1	0	6	5	0	1	0	18	0	3	.350	.323
Roberson, Colin	R-R	6-5	205	7-15-83	.222	.174	.239	48	180	15	40	8	1	2	16	10	0	0	1	56	5	3	.311	.262
Rodriguez, Jesus	R-R	5-11	175	10-30-84	.286	.368	.262	45	168	16	48	10	0	2	17	5	3	0	0	17	2	2	.381	.318
Silverio, Rigoberto	B-R	6-1	156	7-2-86	.302	.364	.283	34	139	24	42	5	2	1	9	15	1	1	0	21	5	5	.388	.374
Smolarski, Freddy	R-R	6-1	180	9-24-84	.280	.148	.333	28	93	10	26	5	0	1	11	3	2	0	2	14	1	1	.366	.310
Tejada, Abraham	R-R	6-1	175	3-1-87	.100	.077	.105	25	70	7	7	2	0	0	4	5	1	2	0	30	2	1	.129	.171
Verley, Brandon	L-L	6-2	202	6-25-85	.200	.182	.222	8	20	2	4	0	1	0	2	3	1	0	1	6	0	0	.300	.320
Webb, Justin	R-R	6-1	175	11-5-82	.292	.250	.304	24	72	11	21	5	0	0	5	14	6	0	2	14	0	1	.361	.436

PITCHING	B-T	HT	WT	DOB	W	L	ERA	G	GS	CG	SV	IP	H	R	ER	HR	BB	SO	AVG	vLH	vRH	K/9	BB/9
Castor, Parrish	L-L	6-2	180	9-18-83	4	2	2.93	15	2	0	0	40	36	14	13	4	15	40	.240	.294	.233	9.00	3.38
De la Cruz, Jose	R-R	6-0	165	7-26-84	1	0	1.56	17	0	0	6	17	14	4	3	0	9	24	.219	.316	.178	12.46	4.67
Flores, Adalberto	R-R	6-7	227	11-4-86	2	2	2.59	13	1	0	0	31	33	17	9	1	6	21	.260	.373	.184	6.03	1.72
Galbizo, Rafael	R-R	6-1	185	2-18-85	3	0	2.45	12	0	0	3	26	27	7	7	0	8	23	.287	.400	.234	8.06	2.81
Garcia, Jose	R-R	5-11	165	1-7-85	0	0	0.00	1	1	0	0	2	1	0	0	0	1	3	.167	1.000	.000	13.50	4.50
Gracesqui, Franklyn	B-L	6-5	210	8-20-79	0	0	0.00	3	1	0	1	3	1	1	0	0	2	5	.100	1.000	.000	15.00	6.00
Holdzkom, Lincoln	R-R	6-4	240	3-23-82	0	0	2.25	3	0	0	0	4	5	3	1	0	1	6	.313	.167	.400	13.50	2.25
Jarrett, Jason	R-R	6-5	195	5-29-82	0	0	3.12	9	0	0	2	9	10	8	3	0	3	7	.263	.214	.292	7.27	3.12
Jones, Blake	R-R	6-5	220	4-15-81	0	0	1.13	6	0	0	0	8	6	2	1	0	2	11	.214	.111	.263	12.38	2.25
Lewis, Jon	R-R	6-1	190	5-16-83	1	0	2.25	3	0	0	0	4	2	1	1	1	2	8	.154	.000	.222	18.00	4.50
Lindeen, Scott	R-R	6-3	205	12-26-81	0	1	3.64	15	1	0	3	30	34	14	12	1	8	25	.298	.410	.240	7.58	2.43
Olivo, Haydersman	R-R	6-2	185	6-7-85	0	0	3.77	14	0	0	0	14	10	9	6	1	15	6	.192	.130	.241	3.77	9.42
Pello, Brandon	R-R	6-1	210	7-8-83	0	1	2.31	7	0	0	0	12	9	5	3	1	2	6	.214	.250	.200	4.63	1.54
Pie, Esequier	R-R	6-2	165	3-6-84	1	5	5.13	12	8	0	0	40	44	27	23	3	27	36	.273	.228	.298	8.03	6.02
Rasowky, Avi	L-L	6-1	195	5-17-83	1	2	2.66	6	1	0	0	20	22	8	6	1	2	18	.286	.308	.281	7.97	0.89
Ruzic, Dushan	R-R	6-8	277	1-5-82	2	2	6.41	17	0	0	0	27	31	21	19	1	12	24	.287	.325	.265	8.10	4.05
Thompson, Aaron	L-L	6-3	195	2-28-87	2	4	4.50	8	8	0	0	32	42	20	16	1	10	41	.316	.500	.304	11.53	2.81
Treanor, Bryan	R-R	5-11	185	2-11-80	1	0	7.20	5	0	0	0	5	6	6	4	0	2	1	.300	.400	.200	1.80	3.60
Tucker, Ryan	R-R	6-2	190	12-6-86	3	3	3.69	8	7	0	0	32	35	13	13	0	16	23	.315	.444	.253	6.54	4.55
Volstad, Chris	R-R	6-7	190	9-23-86	1	1	2.33	6	6	0	0	27	25	14	7	1	4	26	.243	.185	.263	8.67	1.33
West, Sean	L-L	6-8	200	6-15-86	2	3	2.35	9	8	0	0	38	33	12	10	2	7	40	.229	.150	.242	9.39	1.64
Winters, Kyle	R-R	6-4	190	4-22-87	0	4	3.64	11	10	0	0	42	37	26	17	4	12	33	.237	.204	.252	7.07	2.57

GAMES BY POSITION: C—de Vrieze 15, Haupt 12, Hayes 2, Ochoa 16, Smolarski 22, Webb 7. **1B**—Adduci 5, Barnes 1, de Vrieze 6, Ellington 20, Messner 3, Ochoa 19, Padgett 2, Ramos 1, Rodriguez 2. **2B**—Batista 3, Padgett 6, Rodriguez 9, Silverio 30, Webb 9. **3B**—Allen 15, de Vrieze 1, Haupt 1, Padgett 8, Ramos 1, Rodriguez 33, Tejada 1, Webb 1. **SS**—Batista 21, Padgett 15, Silverio 1, Tejada 15, Webb 6. **OF**—Adduci 5, Agustin 30, Allen 21, Batista 1, Haupt 1, Kutler 41, Little 2, Ramos 18, Roberson 47, Verley 8, Webb 1.

HOUSTON ASTROS

BY BRIAN McTAGGART

The Astros would like to remember 2005 more for what they accomplished in the six months leading up to the World Series than what happened over those four tight games against the White Sox.

They would like to remember how they rebounded from a miserable 15-30 start to become the first team since the 1914 Boston Braves to reach the playoffs after being 15 games under .500.

They would like to remember how they had perhaps the best starting rotation in baseball, led by a rejuvenated Andy Pettitte, underrated Roy Oswalt and the ageless Roger Clemens.

And they would like to remember how they overcame the loss of sluggers Carlos Beltran and Jeff Kent to free agency and stars Jeff Bagwell and Lance Berkman to injuries to take the franchise to new heights.

"I'm real proud of the season we had," closer Brad Lidge said. "Our guys did unbelievable this year. We came from just a bad spot to get to where we are. We didn't quite finish it off but we have nothing to hang our heads about. We accomplished so much this year and we got to the World Series. That's pretty amazing."

While the Astros were swept in the World Series by the White Sox—getting outscored by only six runs—the franchise's finest season in its 44-year history was one to remember.

"I never thought we'd ever be in the World Series," relief pitcher Dan Wheeler said. "Some people play their whole careers and never get the opportunity to play in the postseason, and this has just been a tremendous honor."

Houston reached .500 on July 9 and 20 days later took the lead in the NL wild-card race and stayed near the top the rest of the way, winning 13 of its final 18 games to again clinch the wild card on the final day.

Along the way, the pitching was dominant.

Pettitte, coming off season-ending elbow surgery, went 17-9, 2.39, which ranked second in the majors. He was unbelievably consistent in the second half, going 14-2 with a 1.56 ERA in his final 20 starts.

Oswalt became the first pitcher to win 20 games in consecutive seasons since 2001-02 by beating Greg Maddux on the final day of the season to finish 20-12, 2.94.

Clemens, who turned 43 in August, posted a career-best 1.89 ERA, going 13-8. He would have pushed for 20 wins had the Astros not been shut out in a whopping nine of his 32 starts.

Meanwhile, the bullpen flourished behind Lidge's 42 saves, rookie Chad Qualls coming into his own and Wheeler growing into an effective set-up man.

"Everybody in our clubhouse had something to do with us getting here and it's a pretty good story," Astros manager Phil Garner said. "I'm proud of these guys. We played hard, we came together as a team and we never did fracture apart for a team that was playing as poorly as we did the first part of the year."

After beating the Braves in the National League Division Series for the second year in a row, the Astros beat the Cardinals in six games in an NLCS rematch of a year earlier to earn their first World Series berth.

"We battled out there and the stuff that plagued us all season plagued us in the World Series," first baseman Mike Lamb said. "You've got to tip your hat to the White Sox because they're a good team. These guys that we have in this clubhouse, they became men this year. This organization has a very bright future."

Round Rock finished its inaugural season in Triple-A with a 74-70 record, losing seven of its final eight games.

Double-A Corpus Christi finished 64-76 in its inaugural season, but went 37-33 in the second half and wound up two games out of first place in the West Division of the Texas League. Righthander Jason Hirsh was named Texas League pitcher of the year after leading the league in strikeouts (185) and ERA (2.87).

PLAYERS OF THE YEAR

MAJOR LEAGUE: Roger Clemens, rhp

Not even age could slow The Rocket down in 2005. The 43-year-old won the National League ERA title with a 1.87 mark in 211 innings—over a point lower than what it was in 2004. Clemens has been remarkably consistent in his 40s, making 30 or more starts annually since 2003.

MINOR LEAGUE: Hunter Pence, of

SPORTS ON FILM

Pence's power was on full display during high Class A Salem's playoff quest. He batted .500 (11-for-22), with three homers and eight RBIs. A second-round pick in 2004 out of Texas-Arlington, Pence's best run came at low Class A Lexington, where he batted .338-25-60 in 302 at-bats.

ORGANIZATION LEADERS

BATTING

*AVG	Sellers, Neil, Tri-City	.344
R	Conrad, Brooks, Corpus Christi/Round Rock	97
H	Ash, Jonny, Lexington/Salem	154
TB	Pence, Hunter, Lexington/Salem	271
2B	Saccomanno, Mark, Corpus Christi	36
3B	Anderson, Josh, Corpus Christi	9
	Rodriguez, Mike, Corpus Christi	9
HR	Pence, Hunter, Lexington/Salem	31
	Scott, Luke, Round Rock	31
RBI	Coolbaugh, Mike, Round Rock	101
BB	Zobrist, Ben, Lexington/Salem	84
SO	Jimerson, Charlton, Corpus Christi/Round Rock	152
SB	Anderson, Josh, Corpus Christi	50
*OBP	Zobrist, Ben, Lexington/Salem	.437
*SLG	Scott, Luke, Round Rock	.603

PITCHING

W	Hirsh, Jason, Corpus Christi	13
	Martinez, Ronnie, Lexington	13
L	Four tied at	12
#ERA	Escobar, Rodrigo, Salem	1.75
G	Wigdahl, Jeff, Lexington/Salem	52
CG	Three tied at	2
SV	Wigdahl, Jeff, Lexington/Salem	17
	Williams, Aaron, Corpus Christi/Salem	17
IP	Hirsh, Jason, Corpus Christi	172
BB	Englebrook, Evan, Lexington	65
SO	Nieve, Fernando, Corpus Christi/Round Rock	171

*Minimum 250 at-bats. #Minimum 75 innings.

HOUSTON ASTROS

Manager: Phil Garner.

2005 Record: 89-73, .549 (2nd, NL Central).

BATTING	B-T	HT	WT	DOB	AVG	vLH	vRH	G	AB	R	H	2B	3B	HR	RBI	BB	HBP	SH	SF	SO	SB	CS	SLG	OBP
Ausmus, Brad	R-R	5-11	190	4-14-69	.258	.293	.247	134	387	35	100	19	0	3	47	51	5	7	1	48	5	3	.331	.351
Bagwell, Jeff	R-R	6-0	215	5-27-68	.250	.300	.238	39	100	11	25	4	0	3	19	18	1	0	4	21	0	0	.380	.358
Berkman, Lance	B-L	6-1	220	2-10-76	.293	.294	.292	132	468	76	137	34	1	24	82	91	4	0	2	72	4	1	.524	.411
Biggio, Craig	R-R	5-11	185	12-14-65	.264	.243	.271	155	590	94	156	40	1	26	69	37	17	4	3	90	11	1	.468	.325
Bruntlett, Eric	R-R	6-0	190	3-29-78	.220	.295	.125	91	109	19	24	5	2	4	14	10	1	1	0	25	7	2	.413	.292
Burke, Chris	R-R	5-11	180	3-11-80	.248	.265	.239	108	318	49	79	19	2	5	26	23	6	9	3	62	11	6	.368	.309
Chavez, Raul	R-R	5-11	215	3-18-73	.172	.133	.188	37	99	6	17	3	0	2	6	4	1	0	1	18	1	0	.263	.210
Ensberg, Morgan	R-R	6-2	210	8-26-75	.283	.299	.278	150	526	86	149	30	3	36	101	85	8	0	5	119	6	7	.557	.388
Everett, Adam	R-R	6-0	170	2-5-77	.248	.227	.256	152	549	58	136	27	2	11	54	26	8	8	4	103	21	7	.364	.290
Gipson, Charles	R-R	6-0	190	12-16-72	.182	.000	.500	19	11	2	2	1	0	0	1	1	0	2	0	3	1	1	.273	.250
Lamb, Mike	L-R	6-1	190	8-9-75	.236	.179	.248	125	322	41	76	13	5	12	53	22	1	0	4	65	1	1	.419	.284
Lane, Jason	R-L	6-2	220	12-22-76	.267	.237	.280	145	517	65	138	34	4	26	78	32	7	0	5	105	6	2	.499	.316
Palmeiro, Orlando	L-L	5-11	180	1-19-69	.284	.136	.302	114	204	22	58	17	2	3	20	15	4	5	3	23	3	1	.431	.341
Quintero, Humberto	R-R	5-9	215	8-2-79	.185	.200	.179	18	54	6	10	1	0	1	8	1	0	2	0	10	0	0	.259	.200
Scott, Luke	L-R	6-0	210	6-25-78	.188	.286	.178	34	80	6	15	4	2	0	4	9	0	0	0	23	1	1	.288	.270
Self, Todd	L-R	6-5	215	11-9-78	.200	.167	.205	21	45	7	9	2	0	1	4	3	0	1	0	9	0	0	.311	.250
Taveras, Willy	R-R	6-0	160	12-25-81	.291	.233	.312	152	592	82	172	13	4	3	29	25	7	7	4	103	34	11	.341	.325
Vizcaino, Jose	B-R	6-1	190	3-26-68	.246	.295	.222	98	187	15	46	10	2	1	23	15	0	1	2	40	2	0	.337	.299

PITCHING	B-T	HT	WT	DOB	W	L	ERA	G	GS	CG	SV	IP	H	R	ER	HR	BB	SO	AVG	vLH	vRH	K/9	BB/9
Astacio, Ezequiel	R-R	6-3	150	11-4-79	3	6	5.67	22	14	0	0	81	100	56	51	23	25	66	.301	.313	.290	7.33	2.78
Backe, Brandon	R-R	6-0	180	4-5-78	10	8	4.76	26	25	1	0	149	151	82	79	19	67	97	.263	.258	.267	5.85	4.04
Burns, Mike	R-R	6-0	205	7-14-78	0	0	4.94	27	0	0	0	31	29	18	17	6	8	20	.238	.328	.156	5.81	2.32
Clemens, Roger	R-R	6-4	235	8-4-62	13	8	1.87	32	32	1	0	211	151	51	44	11	62	185	.198	.195	.202	7.88	2.64
Driskill, Travis	R-R	6-0	215	8-1-71	0	0	0.00	1	0	0	0	1	1	0	0	0	0	2	.250	.000	.333	18.00	0.00
Duckworth, Brandon	R-R	6-2	190	1-23-76	0	1	11.02	7	2	0	0	16	24	20	20	4	7	10	.348	.258	.421	5.51	3.86
Franco, John	L-L	5-10	185	9-17-60	0	1	7.20	31	0	0	0	15	23	13	12	0	9	16	.343	.310	.400	9.60	5.40
Gallo, Mike	L-L	6-0	175	4-2-77	0	1	2.66	36	0	0	0	20	18	6	6	1	10	12	.250	.268	.226	5.31	4.43
Harville, Chad	R-R	5-9	185	9-16-76	0	2	4.46	37	0	0	0	38	36	21	19	7	24	33	.254	.246	.260	7.75	5.63
Lidge, Brad	R-R	6-5	210	12-23-76	4	4	2.29	70	0	0	42	71	58	21	18	5	23	103	.223	.244	.202	13.12	2.93
Oswalt, Roy	R-R	6-0	185	8-29-77	20	12	2.94	35	35	4	0	242	243	85	79	18	48	184	.262	.279	.247	6.85	1.79
Pettitte, Andy	L-L	6-5	225	6-15-72	17	9	2.39	33	33	0	0	222	188	66	59	17	41	171	.230	.200	.239	6.92	1.66
Qualls, Chad	R-R	6-5	220	8-17-78	6	4	3.28	77	0	0	0	80	73	33	29	7	23	60	.249	.218	.275	6.78	2.60
Rodriguez, Wandy	B-L	5-11	160	1-18-79	10	10	5.53	25	22	0	0	129	135	82	79	19	53	80	.274	.275	.273	5.60	3.71
Springer, Russ	R-R	6-4	215	11-7-68	4	4	4.73	62	0	0	0	59	49	34	31	9	21	54	.222	.209	.231	8.24	3.20
Strickland, Scott	R-R	5-11	195	4-26-76	0	0	6.75	5	0	0	0	4	4	3	3	2	0	2	.250	.400	.182	4.50	0.00
Wheeler, Dan	R-R	6-3	220	12-10-77	2	3	2.21	71	0	0	3	73	53	18	18	7	19	69	.204	.204	.204	8.47	2.33

FIELDING

Catcher	PCT	G	PO	A	E	DP	PB
Ausmus	.999	134	884	65	1	6	5
Chavez	.991	36	213	19	2	2	1
Quintero	.989	16	86	5	1	0	0

First Base	PCT	G	PO	A	E	DP
Bagwell	1.000	24	211	14	0	13
Berkman	.994	96	772	49	5	77
Bruntlett	1.000	1	1	0	0	0
Lamb	.989	68	428	28	5	38
Quintero	1.000	1	0	1	0	0
Vizcaino	.971	13	63	4	2	7

Second Base	PCT	G	PO	A	E	DP
Ausmus	.000	1	0	0	0	0
Biggio	.976	141	250	396	16	82
Bruntlett	.929	28	10	16	2	3
Burke	1.000	18	15	24	0	5
Vizcaino	1.000	23	30	39	0	14

Third Base	PCT	G	PO	A	E	DP
Bruntlett	1.000	8	1	1	0	0
Ensberg	.964	148	100	296	15	31
Lamb	.980	15	16	34	1	0
Vizcaino	.786	8	2	9	3	2

Shortstop	PCT	G	PO	A	E	DP
Ausmus	1.000	1	1	1	0	1
Bruntlett	1.000	10	9	21	0	4
Everett	.978	150	209	421	14	96
Vizcaino	1.000	17	9	34	0	1

Outfield	PCT	G	PO	A	E	DP
Berkman	.958	49	66	2	3	1
Bruntlett	1.000	26	46	3	0	2
Burke	.992	84	121	3	1	1
Gipson	1.000	13	6	0	0	0
Jimerson	.000	1	0	0	0	0
Lamb	1.000	13	12	0	0	0
Lane	.976	141	239	4	6	0
Palmeiro	.986	71	68	2	1	2
Scott	.963	24	24	2	1	0
Self	1.000	15	23	0	0	0
Taveras	.991	148	332	10	3	2

FARM SYSTEM

General Manager: Tim Purpura. **Director, Player Development:** Ricky Bennett. **Scouting Director:** Paul Ricciarini.

Class	Farm Team	League	W	L	Pct.	Finish*	Manager	Affiliate Since
AAA	Round Rock (Texas) Express	Pacific Coast	74	70	.514	7th (16)	Jackie Moore	2000
AA	Corpus Christi (Texas) Hooks	Texas	64	76	.457	7th (8)	Dave Clark	2005
High A	Salem (Va.) Avalanche	Carolina	67	74	.475	5th (8)	Ivan DeJesus	2003
Low A	Lexington (Ky.) Legends	South Atlantic	81	58	.583	1st (16)	Tim Bogar	2001
SS A	Tri-City ValleyCats (Troy, N.Y.)	New York-Penn	34	42	.447	9th (14)	Gregg Langbehn	2001
Rookie	Greeneville (Tenn.) Astros	Appalachian	29	37	.439	7th (10)	Russ Nixon	2004

*Finish in overall standings (No. of teams in league)/Playoff teams in **boldface**

ROUND ROCK EXPRESS — Class AAA

PACIFIC COAST LEAGUE

BATTING	B-T	HT	WT	DOB	AVG	vLH	vRH	G	AB	R	H	2B	3B	HR	RBI	BB	HBP	SH	SF	SO	SB	CS	SLG	OBP
Berkman, Lance	B-L	6-1	220	2-10-76	.286	.000	.364	4	14	2	4	1	0	0	1	3	0	0	0	4	0	0	.357	.412
Burke, Chris	R-R	5-11	180	3-11-80	.311	.353	.286	22	90	15	28	6	2	2	11	8	2	1	0	13	9	0	.489	.380
Chavez, Raul	R-R	5-11	215	3-18-73	.252	.194	.273	34	119	9	30	8	0	0	14	5	3	1	0	24	0	0	.319	.299
Conrad, Brooks	B-R	5-11	185	1-16-80	.263	.291	.252	113	418	84	110	22	3	21	57	52	4	5	4	104	12	3	.481	.347
Coolbaugh, Mike	R-R	6-1	190	6-5-72	.281	.326	.263	123	488	88	137	30	1	27	101	47	5	1	9	111	10	0	.512	.344
Eckelman, Alex	R-R	5-11	187	7-16-74	.250	.231	.259	61	168	16	42	7	0	2	15	7	4	0	1	21	3	2	.327	.294
Gipson, Charles	R-R	6-0	190	12-16-72	.303	.364	.280	110	393	58	119	24	3	2	25	25	8	4	1	75	19	9	.394	.356
Hubbard, Trenidad	R-R	5-9	200	5-11-66	.224	.300	.208	17	58	8	13	2	1	0	3	8	1	1	1	10	4	2	.293	.324
Huffman, Royce	R-R	6-0	205	1-11-77	.284	.371	.243	124	391	57	111	32	2	7	45	55	4	0	5	54	8	3	.430	.374
Jimerson, Charlton	R-R	6-3	210	9-22-79	.304	.333	.294	7	23	1	7	1	0	0	1	0	0	1	1	7	3	0	.348	.292
Klassen, Danny	R-R	6-0	190	9-22-75	.319	.394	.290	88	342	61	109	23	3	15	53	27	5	2	2	80	7	1	.535	.375
Phillips, J.R.	L-L	6-1	185	4-29-70	.235	.333	.182	9	17	3	4	1	0	0	0	3	0	0	0	4	0	0	.294	.350
Quintero, Humberto	R-R	5-9	215	8-2-79	.288	.316	.276	52	191	23	55	13	0	8	31	10	2	0	2	30	2	1	.482	.327
Reynolds, Wilton	R-R	6-4	195	3-5-80	.200	.500	.125	5	10	1	2	0	0	1	2	1	0	0	0	3	0	0	.500	.273
Rivera, Carlos	L-L	5-11	230	6-10-78	.312	.268	.324	129	455	64	142	35	1	17	68	30	8	0	3	65	0	0	.505	.363
Scott, Luke	L-R	6-0	210	6-25-78	.286	.322	.272	103	398	69	114	25	4	31	87	43	6	0	2	96	2	2	.603	.363
Self, Todd	L-R	6-5	215	11-9-78	.298	.176	.340	100	326	42	97	25	2	8	47	58	4	0	3	91	4	1	.460	.407
Tremie, Chris	R-R	6-0	210	10-17-69	.205	.184	.211	63	190	17	39	5	0	3	23	14	2	0	3	37	0	0	.279	.263
Wesson, Barry	R-R	6-2	210	4-6-77	.271	.280	.267	126	402	39	109	19	3	9	43	19	2	4	3	84	6	2	.400	.305
Whiteman, Tommy	R-R	6-3	180	7-14-79	.203	.255	.188	80	237	23	48	5	0	5	27	27	1	2	3	69	0	0	.287	.284

PITCHING	B-T	HT	WT	DOB	W	L	ERA	G	GS	CG	SV	IP	H	R	ER	HR	BB	SO	AVG	vLH	vRH	K/9	BB/9
Anderson, Jimmy	L-L	6-1	210	1-22-76	2	2	3.24	4	4	1	0	25	30	14	9	1	10	12	.300	.364	.282	4.32	3.60
2-team (1 Iowa)					2	2	3.26	5	5	1	0	30	36	16	11	2	12	14	.300	.417	.271	4.15	3.56
Astacio, Ezequiel	R-R	6-3	150	11-4-79	4	4	3.02	13	12	0	1	66	53	25	22	6	12	57	.220	.196	.237	7.81	1.64
Barzilla, Philip	L-L	5-11	180	1-25-79	0	0	.000	1	0	0	0	0	0	1	0	0	0	0	.000	.000	.000	.000	.000
Bauer, Peter	L-R	6-7	243	11-6-78	1	0	0.00	1	1	0	0	7	6	0	0	0	1	3	.250	.222	.267	3.86	1.29
2-team (15 Albuquerque)					4	5	6.29	16	15	0	0	79	94	63	55	14	34	46	.300	.300	.301	5.26	3.89
Buchholz, Taylor	R-R	6-4	220	10-13-81	6	0	4.81	20	14	0	0	77	79	41	41	14	27	45	.275	.279	.273	5.28	3.17
Burba, Dave	R-R	6-4	255	7-7-66	4	3	4.58	18	1	0	0	35	46	19	18	1	10	22	.315	.365	.287	5.60	2.55
Burns, Mike	R-R	6-0	205	7-14-78	2	1	2.10	25	0	0	13	30	22	7	7	4	4	34	.200	.179	.211	10.20	1.20
Cunnane, Will	R-R	6-1	200	4-24-74	0	4	3.45	27	0	0	8	29	30	11	11	2	10	21	.273	.319	.238	6.59	3.14
2-team (24 Iowa)					1	5	5.07	51	0	0	8	66	79	40	37	10	27	54	.300	.306	.297	7.40	3.70
Driskill, Travis	R-R	6-0	215	8-1-71	9	5	4.37	47	3	0	4	101	99	52	49	16	32	84	.261	.247	.270	7.49	2.85
Duckworth, Brandon	R-R	6-2	190	1-23-76	8	6	4.62	20	19	0	0	115	138	68	59	17	37	89	.301	.345	.266	6.97	2.90
Fussell, Chris	R-R	6-2	210	5-19-76	1	6	6.83	20	8	0	0	54	57	42	41	9	50	30	.288	.321	.263	5.00	8.33
Gallo, Mike	L-L	6-0	175	4-2-77	4	2	3.64	37	1	0	0	54	56	29	22	2	20	33	.271	.258	.277	5.47	3.31
Giron, Roberto	R-R	6-2	195	3-24-76	4	3	3.95	22	10	0	1	66	64	31	29	5	25	56	.257	.226	.280	7.64	3.41
Gothreaux, Jared	R-R	6-0	200	1-27-80	3	8	4.29	15	15	0	0	86	87	45	41	8	29	47	.269	.304	.246	4.92	3.03
Griffiths, Jeremy	R-R	6-6	235	3-22-78	0	1	11.79	9	1	0	0	24	30	34	31	2	26	8	.316	.326	.308	3.04	9.89
Hernandez, Carlos	B-L	5-10	200	4-22-80	5	8	5.56	21	21	0	0	89	99	57	55	17	54	66	.289	.318	.279	6.67	5.46
Hodge, Kevin	R-R	5-11	185	10-28-76	0	0	3.68	6	0	0	0	7	7	3	3	1	1	3	.259	.286	.250	3.68	1.23
Kieschnick, Brooks	L-R	6-4	250	6-6-72	2	4	5.72	45	0	0	1	57	77	45	36	13	26	34	.329	.390	.284	5.40	4.13
MacRae, Scott	R-R	6-3	205	8-13-74	3	0	3.21	16	1	0	0	42	38	16	15	4	15	20	.244	.300	.198	4.29	3.21
Martin, Tom	L-L	6-1	205	5-21-70	0	0	3.62	20	0	0	5	27	33	11	11	4	13	13	.308	.333	.299	4.28	4.28
Mathews, T.J.	R-R	6-1	225	1-19-70	1	1	4.03	22	0	0	0	29	33	13	13	4	6	22	.287	.328	.241	6.83	1.86
McClaskey, Tim	B-R	6-1	175	1-11-76	0	2	9.28	2	2	0	0	11	14	11	11	2	6	8	.304	.231	.333	6.75	5.06
McDaniel, Denton	L-L	6-3	220	8-12-76	1	0	6.00	18	0	0	1	27	34	19	18	7	8	10	.324	.308	.333	3.33	2.67
Nieve, Fernando	R-R	6-0	195	7-15-82	4	4	4.83	13	13	2	0	82	92	45	44	10	33	75	.281	.319	.242	8.23	3.62
Norton, Phil	R-L	6-0	215	2-1-76	0	1	10.50	8	0	0	0	6	7	10	7	0	10	3	.304	.273	.333	4.50	15.00
Rodriguez, Wandy	B-L	5-11	160	1-18-79	4	2	3.69	8	8	0	0	46	43	20	19	7	16	48	.246	.182	.267	9.32	3.11
Strickland, Scott	R-R	5-11	195	4-26-76	2	0	2.37	15	0	0	5	19	11	5	5	2	4	20	.167	.226	.114	9.47	1.89
Tollberg, Brian	R-R	6-3	195	9-16-72	4	3	4.66	10	10	0	0	64	71	34	33	11	12	41	.295	.277	.311	5.80	1.70

FIELDING

Catcher	PCT	G	PO	A	E	DP	PB
Chavez	.992	34	223	19	2	4	3
Eckelman	.984	11	58	5	1	0	2
Huffman	.895	3	17	0	2	0	0
Quintero	.994	51	280	33	2	4	2
Tremie	.993	58	363	40	3	6	7

First Base	PCT	G	PO	A	E	DP
Huffman	.996	63	473	31	2	54
Rivera	.993	98	713	49	5	92
Self	1.000	2	4	0	0	1
Tremie	1.000	1	2	0	0	0

Second Base	PCT	G	PO	A	E	DP
Burke	.989	19	45	48	1	15
Conrad	.987	108	217	335	7	80
Eckelman	1.000	1	2	3	0	2
Huffman	.985	13	29	37	1	11
Klassen	1.000	9	17	24	0	5

Third Base	PCT	G	PO	A	E	DP
Coolbaugh	.968	114	98	240	11	24
Eckelman	.964	14	7	20	1	1
Huffman	.818	15	7	20	6	4
Klassen	.950	7	6	13	1	1

Shortstop	PCT	G	PO	A	E	DP
Eckelman	.907	21	33	45	8	17
Klassen	.973	63	101	184	8	47
Whiteman	.954	69	106	183	14	53

Outfield	PCT	G	PO	A	E	DP
Berkman	1.000	4	3	1	0	0
Burke	1.000	6	10	0	0	0
Gipson	.980	101	235	11	5	6
Hubbard	1.000	16	39	1	0	0
Jimerson	.950	6	19	0	1	0
Klassen	1.000	3	5	0	0	0
Reynolds	1.000	3	4	0	0	0
Rivera	1.000	22	21	2	0	0
Scott	.996	100	222	3	1	0
Self	.977	95	161	9	4	1
Wesson	.978	119	246	17	6	5

CORPUS CHRISTI HOOKS — Class AA

TEXAS LEAGUE

BATTING	B-T	HT	WT	DOB	AVG	vLH	vRH	G	AB	R	H	2B	3B	HR	RBI	BB	HBP	SH	SF	SO	SB	CS	SLG	OBP
Anderson, Josh	L-R	6-2	195	8-10-82	.282	.210	.331	127	524	67	148	16	9	1	26	29	8	10	2	80	50	19	.353	.329
Bagwell, Jeff	R-R	6-0	215	5-27-68	.222	.000	.400	3	9	1	2	0	0	0	1	3	0	0	0	3	0	0	.222	.417
Clements, Jason	B-R	5-10	180	3-1-78	.302	.333	.286	15	43	5	13	3	1	0	7	1	0	0	0	7	0	0	.419	.318
Conrad, Brooks	B-R	5-11	185	1-16-80	.234	.194	.268	22	77	13	18	6	1	2	11	16	1	0	0	15	8	0	.416	.372
Eckelman, Alex	R-R	5-11	187	7-16-74	.274	.389	.188	26	84	6	23	3	0	1	6	4	3	0	1	9	0	1	.345	.326
Fagan, John	R-R	6-5	217	8-8-79	.254	.253	.255	68	173	18	44	4	1	3	15	22	7	0	0	50	4	0	.341	.361
Fatheree, Danny	R-R	5-11	245	8-25-78	.000	.000	.000	1	0	0	0	0	0	0	0	0	1	1	0	0	0	0	.000	1.000
Gimenez, Hector	B-R	5-10	180	9-28-82	.273	.290	.262	121	454	47	124	19	1	12	58	32	2	7	3	88	2	3	.399	.322
Jimerson, Charlton	R-R	6-3	210	9-22-79	.259	.283	.244	115	425	67	110	24	3	16	44	29	8	3	2	145	27	10	.442	.317
Navarrete, Ray	R-R	6-0	202	5-20-78	.232	.291	.191	52	194	23	45	12	0	5	16	7	5	1	1	30	1	3	.371	.275
Norris, Dax	R-R	5-10	190	1-14-72	.223	.227	.220	106	355	28	79	16	0	13	50	27	0	0	5	42	0	1	.377	.274
Peavey, Pat	R-R	6-1	205	5-5-80	.065	.000	.105	12	31	0	2	0	0	0	1	3	2	2	0	8	0	0	.065	.194
Phillips, J.R.	L-L	6-1	185	4-29-70	.295	.318	.286	43	156	20	46	5	0	8	20	21	0	0	3	42	2	2	.481	.372
Quintero, Humberto	R-R	5-9	215	8-2-79	.182	.000	.250	4	11	0	2	1	0	0	1	1	0	0	0	2	0	0	.273	.250
Riggs, Eric	B-R	6-2	190	8-19-76	.261	.294	.241	130	452	40	118	27	3	7	57	52	4	8	8	77	5	7	.381	.337
Robinson, Wade	L-R	6-2	165	1-12-81	.242	.153	.286	69	219	19	53	4	0	1	16	20	0	10	3	51	8	10	.274	.302
Rodriguez, Carlos	R-R	6-1	227	6-12-77	.245	.304	.202	88	318	30	78	12	1	9	42	8	2	0	1	71	3	4	.374	.267
Rodriguez, Mike	L-L	5-10	180	10-15-80	.281	.281	.281	116	392	51	110	16	9	5	50	47	4	7	6	50	25	7	.406	.359
Saccomanno, Mark	R-R	6-3	210	4-30-80	.278	.313	.258	134	514	66	143	36	1	12	51	27	4	0	1	108	5	3	.422	.319
Whiteman, Tommy	R-R	6-3	180	7-14-79	.250	.279	.231	41	152	13	38	9	0	1	15	18	1	2	0	40	3	4	.329	.333
Wright, Gavin	R-R	6-1	200	5-6-79	.200	.250	.000	4	10	1	2	1	0	0	0	1	0	1	0	1	0	0	.300	.273
Zamora, Junior	R-R	6-2	198	5-3-76	.198	.232	.158	45	126	10	25	7	0	0	4	5	3	0	0	31	0	0	.254	.246

PITCHING	B-T	HT	WT	DOB	W	L	ERA	G	GS	CG	SV	IP	H	R	ER	HR	BB	SO	AVG	vLH	vRH	K/9	BB/9
Allen, Blake	R-L	6-2	205	7-17-81	1	3	5.36	16	6	0	0	42	44	28	25	4	18	31	.263	.244	.270	6.64	3.86
Backe, Brandon	R-R	6-0	180	4-5-78	0	1	2.25	2	2	0	0	8	4	2	2	1	1	11	.143	.231	.067	12.38	1.13
Barzilla, Philip	L-L	5-11	180	1-25-79	7	7	3.03	41	14	0	0	113	126	49	38	6	30	87	.281	.358	.257	6.93	2.39
Bauer, Peter	L-R	6-7	243	11-6-78	3	4	3.31	11	8	0	1	52	46	25	19	5	9	39	.231	.227	.234	6.79	1.57
Giron, Roberto	R-R	6-2	195	3-24-76	2	3	3.07	21	0	0	0	29	27	11	10	3	6	28	.248	.245	.250	8.59	1.84
Hirsh, Jason	R-R	6-8	250	2-20-82	13	8	2.87	29	29	1	0	172	137	63	55	12	42	165	.218	.230	.208	8.62	2.19
Hodge, Kevin	R-R	5-11	185	10-28-76	1	4	5.48	14	0	0	2	23	23	15	14	3	8	25	.256	.286	.236	9.78	3.13
Kieschnick, Brooks	L-R	6-4	250	6-6-72	0	0	1.08	5	0	0	0	8	10	2	1	0	2	5	.303	.375	.235	5.40	2.16
MacRae, Scott	R-R	6-3	205	8-13-74	3	3	2.70	16	4	0	1	47	51	19	14	2	9	29	.277	.274	.280	5.59	1.74
Mansfield, Monte	R-R	6-4	215	3-22-81	3	2	3.82	43	0	0	0	75	65	35	32	7	33	78	.234	.262	.216	9.32	3.94
McClaskey, Tim	B-R	6-1	175	1-11-76	8	10	3.33	27	26	2	0	160	141	67	59	16	21	105	.233	.196	.265	5.92	1.18
McLemore, Mark	L-L	6-2	220	10-9-80	5	6	2.81	15	15	1	0	74	59	34	23	5	34	65	.220	.224	.219	7.94	4.15
Merchant, Jamie	R-R	6-4	270	3-19-81	3	3	4.26	24	1	0	2	51	43	25	24	7	21	46	.228	.194	.264	8.17	3.73
Miller, Josh	R-R	6-1	200	2-7-79	0	1	7.04	3	0	0	0	8	9	6	6	1	1	5	.281	.267	.294	5.87	1.17
Nieve, Fernando	R-R	6-0	195	7-15-82	4	3	2.65	14	14	0	0	85	62	27	25	7	29	96	.205	.218	.194	10.16	3.07
Peguero, Jailen	R-R	5-11	180	1-4-81	2	2	2.94	50	0	0	12	64	62	25	21	3	25	63	.254	.271	.243	8.81	3.50
Rijo, Fernando	R-R	5-11	175	11-15-77	3	2	4.40	34	2	0	1	61	58	35	30	11	34	44	.254	.247	.259	6.46	4.99
Rodriguez, Wandy	B-L	5-11	160	1-18-79	0	0	2.70	1	1	0	0	3	3	1	1	0	2	3	.273	.000	.273	8.10	5.40
Sampson, Chris	R-R	6-1	180	5-23-78	4	12	3.12	32	19	2	4	150	147	67	52	11	19	92	.256	.308	.210	5.52	1.14
Williams, Aaron	R-R	6-2	180	10-7-80	2	1	2.64	22	0	0	0	31	27	10	9	2	15	19	.241	.333	.179	5.58	4.40

FIELDING

Catcher	PCT	G	PO	A	E	DP	PB
Eckelman	.000	1	0	0	0	0	0
Gimenez	.990	87	640	75	7	3	8
Norris	.995	55	402	29	2	3	2
Quintero	1.000	3	24	4	0	1	0

First Base	PCT	G	PO	A	E	DP
Fagan	1.000	9	43	4	0	3
Gimenez	.992	15	126	5	1	16
Norris	.985	25	191	8	3	19
Peavey	1.000	1	5	2	0	1
Phillips	.989	36	347	20	4	26
Saccomanno	.996	48	444	22	2	30
Zamora	.986	20	128	10	2	13

Second Base	PCT	G	PO	A	E	DP
Clements	.930	12	24	29	4	4
Conrad	.972	22	39	64	3	14
Navarrete	.971	29	45	88	4	11
Riggs	.975	72	126	226	9	48
Robinson	.922	13	38	33	6	12

Third Base	PCT	G	PO	A	E	DP
Eckelman	.917	8	5	6	1	1
Navarrete	.903	15	8	20	3	1
Peavey	.889	5	1	7	1	0
Riggs	1.000	3	0	3	0	1
Saccomanno	.901	79	39	134	19	13
Whiteman	.946	20	11	42	3	2
Zamora	.860	22	9	40	8	2

Shortstop	PCT	G	PO	A	E	DP
Clements	.667	2	1	1	1	0
Eckelman	1.000	16	13	23	0	5
Riggs	.978	52	71	147	5	24
Robinson	.917	53	80	174	23	36
Whiteman	.969	24	32	62	3	14
Zamora	.000	1	0	0	0	0

Outfield	PCT	G	PO	A	E	DP
Anderson	.973	126	287	6	8	0
Eckelman	1.000	1	3	0	0	0
Fagan	.962	33	48	2	2	1
Jimerson	.971	112	227	10	7	2
Navarrete	1.000	7	9	0	0	0
C. Rodriguez	.949	48	70	4	4	0
M. Rodriguez	.994	109	169	7	1	1
Wright	1.000	2	4	0	0	0

SALEM AVALANCHE — High Class A

CAROLINA LEAGUE

BATTING	B-T	HT	WT	DOB	AVG	vLH	vRH	G	AB	R	H	2B	3B	HR	RBI	BB	HBP	SH	SF	SO	SB	CS	SLG	OBP
Alcantara, Ervin	R-R	5-11	180	10-3-80	.245	.253	.240	130	417	47	102	27	2	5	44	57	1	5	2	109	17	9	.355	.335
Ash, Jonny	L-R	5-9	185	9-11-82	.320	.308	.331	59	225	32	72	19	2	1	25	14	3	4	2	15	3	5	.436	.365
Caraballo, Francisco	R-R	6-1	200	10-21-83	.244	.167	.333	14	45	8	11	2	0	2	12	1	2	1	2	9	1	0	.422	.280
Davidson, Kevin	R-R	5-7	180	7-21-80	.283	.297	.272	86	269	25	76	16	1	5	41	31	3	7	2	45	1	1	.405	.361
Fagan, John	R-R	6-5	217	8-8-79	.261	.205	.288	37	119	14	31	11	0	3	13	19	6	1	0	36	4	2	.429	.389
Fernando, Osvaldo	R-R	6-0	175	10-15-80	.207	.171	.230	67	208	27	43	4	1	2	14	16	5	8	2	39	12	7	.264	.277
Floyd, Mike	R-R	6-3	185	1-15-80	.273	.254	.286	119	433	63	118	24	4	12	62	51	6	2	7	112	14	7	.430	.352
Garza, Mario	L-R	6-0	202	5-26-81	.292	.269	.308	80	260	41	76	25	0	9	43	47	3	2	3	74	5	2	.492	.403

BATTING	B-T	HT	WT	DOB	AVG	vLH	vRH	G	AB	R	H	2B	3B	HR	RBI	BB	HBP	SH	SF	SO	SB	CS	SLG	OBP
Humphries, Justin	R-R	6-4	225	2-24-83	.179	.200	.171	35	112	12	20	2	0	4	10	12	2	2	0	30	0	0	.304	.270
Kochen, Ryan	R-R	6-2	195	6-13-79	.143	.091	.171	20	63	6	9	0	0	1	6	8	0	0	0	16	0	0	.190	.239
Mackor, Jeff	R-R	6-0	210	6-17-80	.178	.196	.170	52	146	9	26	9	1	0	8	11	2	3	1	33	0	2	.253	.244
Maysonet, Edwin	R-R	6-1	180	10-17-81	.195	.200	.191	66	236	29	46	9	2	1	16	26	3	12	4	69	4	2	.263	.279
Peavey, Pat	R-R	6-1	205	5-5-80	.227	.224	.230	97	343	32	78	13	0	4	36	33	1	1	0	39	1	0	.300	.297
Pence, Hunter	R-R	6-4	210	4-13-83	.305	.318	.294	41	151	24	46	8	1	6	30	18	0	0	2	37	1	2	.490	.374
Reynolds, Wilton	R-R	6-4	195	3-5-80	.262	.348	.198	62	210	29	55	18	3	7	31	25	7	1	1	70	4	5	.476	.358
Robinson, Scott	L-L	6-1	195	10-14-83	.278	.283	.273	74	288	31	80	13	1	3	40	31	0	2	4	29	2	2	.361	.344
Robinson, Wade	L-R	6-2	165	1-12-81	.256	.140	.315	46	168	13	43	5	2	1	11	10	1	4	1	27	4	5	.327	.300
Ruiz, Reinaldo	R-R	6-0	200	2-4-80	.222	.184	.256	29	81	11	18	3	0	1	5	4	0	0	0	15	0	0	.296	.259
Seuss, Adam	L-R	6-0	195	8-31-80	.148	.109	.171	39	128	10	19	3	0	2	8	13	7	0	0	30	0	1	.219	.264
Sutton, Drew	B-R	6-3	185	6-30-83	.257	.271	.250	43	148	22	38	5	1	3	12	29	1	0	0	34	4	3	.365	.382
Torres, Saul	R-R	6-3	220	2-18-82	.255	.225	.275	86	322	47	82	11	1	6	26	31	0	5	3	77	3	4	.351	.317
Triplett, Bryan	R-R	6-0	185	4-16-82	.186	.182	.189	22	59	5	11	4	1	0	4	2	0	2	0	18	0	1	.288	.213
Zobrist, Ben	B-R	6-3	200	5-26-81	.333	.324	.343	42	141	25	47	12	1	3	13	37	1	1	0	17	2	1	.496	.475

PITCHING	B-T	HT	WT	DOB	W	L	ERA	G	GS	CG	SV	IP	H	R	ER	HR	BB	SO	AVG	vLH	vRH	K/9	BB/9
Albers, Matt	L-R	6-0	208	1-20-83	8	12	4.66	28	27	0	0	149	161	86	77	15	62	146	.278	.307	.250	8.84	3.75
Allen, Blake	R-L	6-2	205	7-17-81	1	2	3.08	21	0	0	1	38	35	15	13	1	16	43	.236	.281	.209	10.18	3.79
Barthmaier, Jimmy	R-R	6-5	220	1-6-84	1	0	1.50	1	0	0	0	6	4	4	1	1	1	6	.167	.083	.250	9.00	1.50
Beltre, Jonathan	L-L	5-10	175	7-1-80	5	1	6.12	36	0	0	1	60	52	41	41	10	34	55	.231	.194	.248	8.20	5.07
Dewitt, Anthony	R-R	6-0	225	5-30-82	6	2	4.15	31	0	0	2	52	55	27	24	4	19	29	.274	.300	.256	5.02	3.29
Douglass, Chance	R-R	6-1	200	2-24-84	12	9	2.90	27	27	1	0	168	157	59	54	7	44	128	.249	.243	.253	6.87	2.36
Escobar, Rodrigo	R-R	5-11	170	2-11-83	3	4	2.14	47	0	0	14	76	63	26	18	6	36	76	.227	.243	.216	9.04	4.28
Freeman, Daniel	R-R	6-2	215	8-3-82	3	5	3.57	39	0	0	4	53	51	24	21	4	29	37	.255	.261	.250	6.28	4.92
Gutierrez, Juan	R-R	6-3	200	7-14-83	1	1	3.00	3	2	0	0	12	10	4	4	1	8	9	.233	.250	.200	6.75	6.00
Merchant, Jamie	R-R	6-4	270	3-19-81	0	2	4.50	21	2	0	0	52	54	27	26	3	22	56	.260	.261	.259	9.69	3.81
Muecke, Josh	L-L	6-3	195	1-9-82	10	12	3.67	28	28	1	0	159	164	81	65	10	47	98	.268	.301	.257	5.54	2.65
Patton, Troy	B-L	6-1	185	9-3-85	1	4	2.63	10	9	0	0	41	34	12	12	2	8	38	.227	.119	.269	8.34	1.76
Shortell, Rory	R-R	6-2	205	6-3-81	7	7	3.87	22	18	0	0	109	94	51	47	8	53	60	.237	.281	.204	4.94	4.36
Stiehl, Robert	R-R	6-3	215	12-9-80	1	0	5.11	22	1	0	1	37	36	24	21	5	26	40	.254	.278	.239	9.73	6.32
Talbot, Mitch	R-R	6-1	180	10-17-83	8	11	4.34	27	27	1	0	151	169	90	73	15	46	100	.280	.264	.292	5.95	2.74
Wigdahl, Jeff	L-L	6-0	190	6-4-82	0	1	3.98	22	0	0	4	32	30	16	14	2	18	30	.248	.250	.247	8.53	5.12
Williams, Aaron	R-R	6-2	180	10-7-80	0	1	2.34	27	0	0	17	35	19	9	9	2	10	35	.158	.140	.171	9.09	2.60

FIELDING

Catcher	PCT	G	PO	A	E	DP	PB
Davidson	.982	78	484	62	10	6	9
Mackor	.995	49	342	27	2	3	8
Ruiz	1.000	28	173	12	0	4	1

First Base	PCT	G	PO	A	E	DP
Fagan	1.000	1	2	0	0	0
Garza	.988	8	77	5	1	3
Humphries	.994	33	304	12	2	18
Peavey	1.000	31	249	18	0	33
S. Robinson	.997	74	660	58	2	58

Second Base	PCT	G	PO	A	E	DP
Ash	.981	58	96	160	5	41
Fernando	.976	23	52	70	3	18
Peavey	1.000	4	4	9	0	0
W. Robinson	.949	37	72	96	9	15
Sutton	.973	25	44	65	3	15
Triplett	1.000	3	2	7	0	1

Third Base	PCT	G	PO	A	E	DP
Peavey	.934	48	30	97	9	4
Torres	.903	86	46	188	25	19
Triplett	.919	15	5	29	3	1

Shortstop	PCT	G	PO	A	E	DP
Fernando	.943	42	52	97	9	17
Maysonet	.950	66	83	203	15	38
Peavey	.000	1	0	0	0	0
W. Robinson	.955	6	6	15	1	2
Triplett	.833	1	2	3	1	0
Zobrist	.983	39	55	121	3	25

Outfield	PCT	G	PO	A	E	DP
Alcantara	.996	126	233	14	1	3
Caraballo	1.000	14	19	1	0	0
Davidson	1.000	3	2	0	0	0
Fagan	.984	36	62	1	1	0
Floyd	.986	115	201	8	3	1
Garza	.000	1	0	0	0	0
Kochen	1.000	16	18	0	0	0
Pence	1.000	37	66	6	0	1
Reynolds	.990	53	92	5	1	0
Seuss	.985	36	62	4	1	1
Triplett	1.000	1	3	0	0	0

LEXINGTON LEGENDS — Low Class A

SOUTH ATLANTIC LEAGUE

BATTING	B-T	HT	WT	DOB	AVG	vLH	vRH	G	AB	R	H	2B	3B	HR	RBI	BB	HBP	SH	SF	SO	SB	CS	SLG	OBP
Ash, Jonny	L-R	5-9	185	9-11-82	.320	.250	.332	67	256	44	82	11	2	8	38	25	10	3	5	20	3	7	.473	.395
Babilonia, Edgar	R-R	5-10	190	8-5-83	.198	.179	.205	39	106	11	21	4	0	0	7	5	0	4	0	12	10	1	.236	.234
Barganier, Brandon	L-R	6-1	175	5-5-83	.297	.192	.320	40	148	21	44	12	1	1	18	9	2	4	2	21	4	1	.412	.342
Caraballo, Francisco	R-R	6-1	200	10-21-83	.279	.240	.290	112	409	63	114	23	2	23	69	30	8	3	2	119	8	7	.513	.339
Clark, Robert	R-R	6-3	180	8-10-82	.238	.271	.225	51	168	20	40	8	0	4	23	16	6	0	0	45	3	0	.357	.326
Einertson, Mitch	R-R	5-10	178	4-4-86	.234	.304	.212	101	355	52	83	19	1	7	45	52	14	0	1	99	5	4	.352	.353
Flores, Josh	R-R	6-0	195	11-18-85	.278	.000	.313	5	18	1	5	2	0	0	1	1	0	1	0	4	4	0	.389	.316
Garza, Mario	L-R	6-0	202	5-26-81	.216	.167	.224	29	88	18	19	4	0	6	19	10	4	0	3	32	0	1	.466	.314
Humphries, Justin	R-R	6-4	225	2-24-83	.270	.240	.274	36	122	20	33	10	0	5	16	22	3	0	2	27	0	0	.475	.389
Maysonet, Edwin	R-R	6-1	180	10-17-81	.260	.250	.263	45	173	29	45	11	1	4	17	15	10	2	1	29	11	4	.405	.352
McGill, Clint	R-R	5-10	175	9-13-81	.201	.203	.198	75	239	27	48	6	3	3	16	9	3	5	0	69	10	11	.289	.239
Pence, Hunter	R-R	6-4	210	4-13-83	.338	.299	.349	80	302	59	102	14	3	25	60	38	1	0	0	53	8	3	.652	.413
Reed, Ryan	L-L	6-4	210	12-19-83	.265	.500	.245	29	102	12	27	5	0	2	14	10	0	2	1	41	6	3	.373	.327
Robinson, Scott	L-L	6-1	195	10-14-83	.291	.222	.319	34	127	20	37	10	1	3	34	19	1	0	1	15	3	2	.457	.385
Santangelo, Lou	R-R	6-1	200	3-16-83	.268	.231	.278	70	239	43	64	14	2	14	39	24	1	3	1	86	4	3	.519	.336
Sheldon, Ole	R-R	6-4	210	11-25-82	.259	.232	.267	68	247	34	64	12	0	5	35	29	3	0	5	36	2	5	.368	.338
Sutil, Wladimir	R-R	5-10	135	10-31-84	.261	.333	.235	6	23	2	6	1	0	0	3	0	0	0	0	5	2	0	.304	.261
Sutton, Drew	B-R	6-3	185	6-30-83	.286	.302	.281	62	231	46	66	19	2	13	42	36	6	1	1	51	4	2	.554	.394
Torbert, Wallace	R-R	6-4	205	5-1-83	.301	.220	.320	71	256	40	77	20	4	8	47	16	6	0	2	63	13	3	.504	.354
Torres, Saul	R-R	6-3	220	2-18-82	.277	.389	.234	36	130	29	36	12	0	7	24	12	4	0	1	29	1	1	.531	.354
Towles, Justin	R-R	6-2	175	2-11-84	.346	.343	.346	45	162	35	56	14	2	5	23	16	10	5	0	29	11	7	.549	.436
Triplett, Bryan	R-R	6-0	185	4-16-82	.214	.133	.234	90	336	42	72	15	2	4	36	29	3	6	3	81	21	4	.307	.280
Vital, Kevin	L-R	6-0	230	2-9-80	.178	.200	.172	61	197	20	35	8	0	6	27	30	1	4	1	58	3	0	.310	.288
Zobrist, Ben	B-R	6-3	200	5-26-81	.304	.259	.316	68	247	45	75	17	2	2	32	47	5	4	7	35	16	5	.413	.415

PITCHING	B-T	HT	WT	DOB	W	L	ERA	G	GS	CG	SV	IP	H	R	ER	HR	BB	SO	AVG	vLH	vRH	K/9	BB/9
Alvarado, Andy	R-R	6-1	200	12-3-82	2	0	3.38	9	0	0	0	11	13	4	4	1	6	5	.310	.313	.308	4.22	5.06
Barthmaier, Jimmy	R-R	6-5	220	1-6-84	11	6	2.27	25	25	0	0	135	108	41	34	3	55	142	.220	.205	.229	9.49	3.68
Blazek, Chris	L-L	6-0	195	3-2-84	1	0	6.18	18	0	0	0	28	27	20	19	7	16	20	.252	.276	.244	6.51	5.20

PITCHING	B-T	HT	WT	DOB	W	L	ERA	G	GS	CG	SV	IP	H	R	ER	HR	BB	SO	AVG	vLH	vRH	K/9	BB/9
Diaz, Raymar	R-R	6-7	190	11-13-83	1	3	4.48	43	3	0	1	82	77	50	41	15	38	87	.245	.267	.232	9.51	4.15
Englebrook, Evan	R-R	6-8	225	4-28-82	8	6	4.32	30	17	0	0	115	103	69	55	10	65	101	.238	.222	.249	7.93	5.10
Estrada, Paul	R-R	6-2	215	9-10-82	6	7	2.69	46	3	0	3	90	65	31	27	6	34	94	.202	.226	.188	9.37	3.39
Gant, Jamie	R-R	6-2	190	9-14-82	0	0	2.63	17	0	0	0	27	25	8	8	1	12	26	.253	.200	.281	8.56	3.95
Gervacio, Sam	R-R	5-11	160	1-10-85	1	0	0.96	5	0	0	0	9	4	1	1	0	1	11	.125	.154	.105	10.61	0.96
Gutierrez, Juan	R-R	6-3	200	7-14-83	9	5	3.21	22	21	1	0	121	106	55	43	10	43	100	.239	.203	.262	7.46	3.21
Martinez, Ronnie	R-R	5-11	205	7-6-83	13	3	3.67	27	26	0	0	152	142	73	62	14	50	113	.249	.234	.258	6.69	2.96
McGill, Clint	R-R	5-10	175	9-13-81	0	0	0.00	1	0	0	0	1	0	0	0	0	0	0	.000	.000	.000	0.00	0.00
McKeller, Ryan	R-R	6-5	220	7-8-83	4	4	4.99	12	11	1	0	58	68	36	32	6	23	42	.292	.352	.242	6.55	3.59
Melendez, German	R-R	6-0	185	9-13-81	0	0	5.40	2	0	0	0	2	3	3	1	0	3	0	.333	.333	.333	0.00	16.20
Murdy, Garrett	R-R	6-4	215	3-15-83	3	2	7.82	25	2	0	1	51	70	49	44	10	19	45	.323	.304	.331	7.99	3.38
Patton, Troy	B-L	6-1	185	9-3-85	5	2	1.94	15	15	0	0	79	59	24	17	3	20	94	.211	.146	.224	10.75	2.29
Paulino Del Guidice, Felipe	R-R	6-2	180	10-5-83	1	1	1.85	7	5	0	0	24	21	8	5	2	6	30	.233	.304	.209		
Reineke, Chad	R-R	6-6	210	4-9-82	10	8	3.52	42	11	0	4	102	84	46	40	5	49	108	.230	.206	.243	9.50	4.31
Romero, Levi	R-R	6-5	185	4-12-84	0	0	0.00	2	0	0	0	4	3	1	0	0	3	6	.231	.500	.182	14.73	7.36
Soto, Enyelbert	L-L	6-1	200	8-20-82	2	1	4.44	16	0	0	2	26	36	14	13	5	2	16	.327	.314	.333	5.47	0.68
Thompson, Ryan	R-R	6-4	220	8-6-82	3	9	3.89	50	0	0	11	72	78	31	31	5	15	76	.282	.259	.292	9.54	1.88
Triplett, Bryan	R-R	6-0	185	4-16-82	0	0	9.00	1	0	0	0	1	2	1	1	0	0	0	.400	.000	.500	0.00	0.00
Wigdahl, Jeff	L-L	6-0	190	6-4-82	1	1	1.83	30	0	0	13	39	21	9	8	1	17	58	.156	.114	.170	13.27	3.89

FIELDING

Catcher	PCT	G	PO	A	E	DP	PB
Clark	.973	46	357	36	11	7	17
Santangelo	.980	64	544	49	12	4	9
Towles	.993	36	280	19	2	3	2
Vital	1.000	2	3	0	0	0	0

First Base	PCT	G	PO	A	E	DP
Einertson	.000	1	0	0	0	0
Garza	1.000	1	4	0	0	0
Humphries	.979	28	220	10	5	13
Robinson	.982	32	250	21	5	24
Sheldon	.993	66	565	44	4	57
Sutton	1.000	1	6	0	0	0
Vital	.965	15	130	9	5	12

Second Base	PCT	G	PO	A	E	DP
Ash	.979	54	100	134	5	31
Babilonia	.938	9	13	17	2	1
McGill	.961	38	50	73	5	19
Sutton	.958	46	82	101	8	32
Triplett	1.000	1	4	2	0	1

Third Base	PCT	G	PO	A	E	DP
Ash	.944	8	5	12	1	1
Babilonia	1.000	4	2	5	0	0
Caraballo	.000	1	0	0	0	0
McGill	.929	9	2	11	1	0
Sutton	1.000	1	1	1	0	1
Torres	.906	36	23	64	9	2
Triplett	.955	88	62	190	12	15

Shortstop	PCT	G	PO	A	E	DP
Maysonet	.987	45	78	142	3	26
McGill	.938	21	32	59	6	9
Sutil	1.000	6	5	15	0	3
Sutton	.960	9	15	33	2	5
Zobrist	.962	63	100	204	12	41

Outfield	PCT	G	PO	A	E	DP
Babilonia	1.000	11	6	0	0	0
Barganier	.970	34	61	3	2	0
Caraballo	.980	109	191	7	4	1
Einertson	.953	99	137	6	7	3
Flores	.857	4	6	0	1	0
Garza	1.000	12	6	0	0	0
McGill	1.000	1	2	0	0	0
Pence	.992	72	117	5	1	2
Reed	.900	27	48	6	6	3
Torbert	.973	61	100	7	3	1
Vital	1.000	1	5	0	0	0

TRI-CITY VALLEYCATS — Short-Season Class A

NEW-YORK PENN LEAGUE

BATTING	B-T	HT	WT	DOB	AVG	vLH	vRH	G	AB	R	H	2B	3B	HR	RBI	BB	HBP	SH	SF	SO	SB	CS	SLG	OBP
Barganier, Brandon	L-R	6-1	175	5-5-83	.270	.167	.320	10	37	5	10	5	1	0	6	1	0	0	0	4	0	0	.459	.289
Bueno, Manuel	B-R	5-11	165	9-22-83	.500	.000	.500	3	2	2	1	0	0	0	0	0	0	0	0	0	2	0	.500	.500
Bulkley, Aaron	R-R	6-4	195	5-6-83	.258	.317	.229	37	124	20	32	5	0	0	9	14	3	3	0	30	6	3	.298	.348
Cavers, Eric	R-R	6-1	205	11-9-82	.228	.263	.217	27	79	9	18	3	0	0	11	12	1	0	0	24	1	0	.266	.337
Clemens, Koby	R-R	5-11	193	12-4-86	.281	.125	.333	9	32	3	9	1	2	0	6	4	0	0	0	5	1	0	.438	.361
Cooper, James	R-R	6-3	185	2-12-82	.260	.280	.254	58	192	30	50	9	3	2	29	25	2	5	2	50	5	4	.370	.348
Cruceta, Jose	B-R	6-0	185	5-17-84	.333	.000	.333	2	3	0	1	0	0	0	1	0	0	0	0	0	0	0	.333	.333
Cunningham, Matt	R-R	6-2	205	9-24-81	.295	.317	.288	66	217	46	64	11	0	8	46	30	21	0	4	35	10	3	.456	.423
Garcia, Antonio	B-R	6-5	260	8-21-82	.267	.250	.286	4	15	1	4	1	0	0	1	1	0	0	1	2	0	0	.333	.294
Goethals, James	R-R	5-11	200	7-12-82	.200	.087	.300	21	55	11	11	4	0	2	4	11	1	2	0	23	0	0	.382	.343
Hart, Billy	R-R	6-2	215	11-2-82	.282	.235	.318	10	39	4	11	0	0	0	4	5	0	0	0	7	0	0	.282	.364
King, Eric	R-R	5-9	175	7-2-82	.305	.344	.289	55	210	31	64	10	3	0	24	19	2	5	4	23	5	1	.381	.362
Kroeker, Andy	L-R	6-1	205	6-1-83	.125	.000	.125	3	8	0	1	0	0	0	0	0	0	0	0	3	0	0	.125	.125
Lopez, Jose	R-R	5-11	195	3-8-85	.268	.240	.276	33	112	17	30	4	2	3	13	4	0	1	1	20	1	0	.420	.291
Manzella, Tommy	R-R	6-2	190	4-16-83	.232	.185	.252	53	220	24	51	6	4	0	18	9	0	2	2	40	5	3	.295	.260
Mulhern, Bryan	R-R	6-3	210	5-24-82	.385	.750	.222	5	13	2	5	1	0	1	3	1	0	0	0	3	0	0	.692	.429
Ori, Mark	L-R	6-4	225	12-16-83	.280	.333	.255	62	225	35	63	3	1	4	26	21	5	0	2	40	7	4	.356	.352
Parraz, Jordan	R-R	6-3	220	10-8-84	.259	.280	.248	71	282	31	73	11	2	5	35	12	8	0	1	46	17	3	.365	.307
Sellers, Neil	R-R	6-0	195	4-3-82	.344	.375	.333	74	279	46	96	18	1	11	50	35	4	0	6	27	7	6	.534	.417
Sutil, Wladimir	R-R	5-10	135	10-31-84	.329	.385	.307	59	231	42	76	13	0	0	21	22	4	3	1	12	13	6	.385	.395
Thompson, Michael	R-R	6-4	210	2-9-84	.262	.256	.261	53	202	23	53	7	1	3	28	10	2	1	1	35	4	0	.351	.302

PITCHING	B-T	HT	WT	DOB	W	L	ERA	G	GS	CG	SV	IP	H	R	ER	HR	BB	SO	AVG	vLH	vRH	K/9	BB/9
Alvarado, Andy	R-R	6-1	200	12-3-82	0	0	9.00	1	0	0	0	2	2	2	2	1	0	2	.250	.000	.333	9.00	0.00
Arguello, Douglas	L-L	6-3	190	11-21-84	2	6	5.62	14	14	0	0	66	66	44	41	7	31	46	.264	.164	.296	6.30	4.25
Blazek, Chris	L-L	6-0	195	3-2-84	0	0	0.00	3	0	0	1	6	1	0	0	0	2	9	.059	.000	.100	14.29	3.18
Bogusevic, Brian	L-L	6-3	215	2-18-84	0	2	7.59	13	0	0	3	21	30	20	18	2	9	17	.316	.412	.262	7.17	3.80
Davis, Cliff	R-R	6-5	215	12-31-84	1	6	6.50	15	15	0	0	64	63	49	46	10	50	68	.264	.310	.220	9.61	7.07
Fairchild, Tip	R-R	6-2	200	12-5-83	3	6	4.88	20	6	0	0	59	70	38	32	7	14	62	.295	.301	.291	9.46	2.14
Gant, Jamie	R-R	6-2	190	9-14-82	0	0	3.09	5	0	0	0	12	7	4	4	0	9	11	.175	.200	.160	8.49	6.94
Himes, Drew	R-R	6-6	215	10-21-83	3	0	6.37	17	0	0	0	35	35	28	25	5	19	19	.259	.333	.188	4.84	4.84
Knobel, Adam	R-R	6-0	175	4-24-83	2	0	5.40	13	0	0	1	30	28	18	18	4	18	29	.252	.220	.279	8.70	5.40
Lapinski, Cory	R-L	6-0	210	3-8-84	1	1	6.27	18	0	0	0	33	21	26	23	3	38	42	.178	.211	.163	11.45	10.36
McKeller, Ryan	R-R	6-5	220	7-8-83	6	5	4.50	15	14	0	0	82	69	47	41	5	33	76	.232	.267	.205	8.34	3.62
Melendez, German	R-R	6-0	185	9-13-80	7	0	2.86	15	0	0	2	28	20	10	9	5	13	32	.196	.150	.226	10.16	4.13
Paulino Del Guidice, Felipe	R-R	6-2	180	10-5-83	2	2	3.82	13	2	0	1	31	21	15	13	2	11	34	.189	.140	.230	9.98	
Pluta, Anthony	R-R	6-2	225	10-28-82	2	4	11.45	14	10	0	0	42	49	55	53	6	51	32	.304	.309	.300	6.91	11.02
Romero, Levi	R-R	6-5	185	4-12-84	0	0	3.60	1	1	0	0	5	2	2	2	0	2	6	.125	.167	.100	10.80	3.60
Sarver, Scott	L-L	6-2	205	11-4-82	1	1	2.57	7	3	0	0	14	13	8	4	0	6	12	.241	.188	.263	7.71	3.86
Sheridan, Eric	R-R	6-1	175	9-22-83	1	3	5.61	15	6	0	0	43	45	31	27	4	28	28	.265	.279	.250	5.82	5.82
Soto, Enyelbert	L-L	6-1	200	8-20-82	0	1	3.60	9	0	0	0	10	9	5	4	0	4	12	.225	.267	.200	10.80	3.60

PITCHING	B-T	HT	WT	DOB	W	L	ERA	G	GS	CG	SV	IP	H	R	ER	HR	BB	SO	AVG	vLH	vRH	K/9	BB/9
Stricklen, Brandon	R-R	6-1	200	2-20-84	3	2	6.32	17	0	0	1	31	36	22	22	4	11	29	.298	.321	.279	8.33	3.16
Walker, Sean	R-R	6-1	175	10-31-82	0	3	4.93	13	5	0	2	35	45	25	19	3	14	33	.315	.319	.311	8.57	3.63

GAMES BY POSITION: C—Cavers 25, Goethals 21, Kroeker 2, Lopez 33, Mulhern 4. **1B**—Garcia 1, Mulhern 1, Ori 58, Sellers 20. **2B**—King 39, Sellers 13, Sutil 24. **3B**—Clemens 4, Cruceta 2, Hart 4, Sellers 22, Thompson 47. **SS**—King 3, Manzella 45, Sutil 28. **OF**—Barganier 10, Bulkley 37, Cooper 55, Cunningham 61, Ori 2, Parraz 68.

GREENEVILLE ASTROS — Rookie

APPALACHIAN LEAGUE

BATTING	B-T	HT	WT	DOB	AVG	vLH	vRH	G	AB	R	H	2B	3B	HR	RBI	BB	HBP	SH	SF	SO	SB	CS	SLG	OBP
Barnes, Brandon	R-R	6-2	210	5-15-86	.200	.263	.178	39	145	21	29	5	2	2	13	10	5	0	1	36	3	2	.303	.273
Clemens, Koby	R-R	5-11	193	12-4-86	.297	.407	.262	33	111	14	33	8	0	4	17	18	2	0	2	26	4	0	.477	.398
Espinoza, Pedro	R-R	6-1	170	5-6-85	.271	.222	.286	32	118	15	32	6	1	0	8	7	2	1	1	8	1	2	.339	.320
Florentino, Jhon	R-R	6-0	155	8-22-83	.246	.132	.289	50	195	31	48	8	3	4	28	11	2	2	0	32	5	2	.379	.293
Flores, Josh	R-R	6-0	195	11-18-85	.335	.275	.358	59	248	49	83	12	5	8	25	16	4	1	0	57	20	6	.520	.384
Garcia, Antonio	B-R	6-5	260	8-21-82	.257	.250	.260	41	140	15	36	10	0	6	32	6	1	0	0	51	0	0	.457	.293
Gonzalez, Esteban	L-R	5-10	185	1-19-84	.183	.304	.143	26	93	9	17	1	1	0	7	9	2	0	1	31	1	1	.215	.267
Graham, Cole	R-R	6-2	220	3-14-84	.209	.242	.200	42	153	19	32	4	0	3	16	20	1	1	1	43	0	0	.294	.303
Henriquez, Ralph	B-R	6-1	190	4-7-87	.215	.211	.217	46	158	15	34	11	3	1	26	6	1	0	2	46	1	0	.342	.246
Iorg, Eli	R-R	6-3	200	3-14-83	.333	.300	.347	35	138	36	46	7	2	7	34	9	4	0	0	27	12	3	.565	.391
Johnson, Tim	R-R	6-1	180	10-15-86	.192	.243	.175	43	151	20	29	4	3	2	23	8	4	1	1	46	3	2	.298	.250
Kady, David	L-R	5-11	205	7-29-80	.103	.100	.105	11	29	4	3	0	0	0	0	6	1	0	0	6	0	0	.103	.278
Langdon, Allen	L-R	5-11	220	9-7-86	.162	.000	.171	11	37	1	6	2	1	0	4	1	1	1	0	17	0	0	.270	.205
Lopez, Jose	R-R	5-11	195	3-8-85	.250	.000	.333	6	24	4	6	2	0	0	1	2	0	1	0	4	0	0	.333	.308
Mulhern, Bryan	R-R	6-3	210	5-24-82	.190	.286	.143	12	21	3	4	2	0	0	2	6	0	0	0	6	0	0	.286	.370
Ramirez, Reinaldo	R-R	6-1	160	9-16-85	.253	.167	.284	29	91	8	23	1	3	0	7	4	3	0	0	28	4	4	.330	.306
Reed, Ryan	L-L	6-4	210	12-19-83	.366	.333	.372	24	93	20	34	2	2	7	25	3	1	0	2	21	1	3	.656	.384
Rodriguez, Yamber	R-R	6-1	180	2-3-85	.262	.281	.255	37	130	19	34	8	1	1	17	16	4	0	1	25	5	1	.362	.358
Warrick, Nathan	L-L	6-0	170	9-10-83	.291	.255	.305	52	196	39	57	5	1	0	15	28	4	0	1	36	21	3	.327	.389

PITCHING	B-T	HT	WT	DOB	W	L	ERA	G	GS	CG	SV	IP	H	R	ER	HR	BB	SO	AVG	vLH	vRH	K/9	BB/9
Babilonia, Edgar	R-R	5-10	190	8-5-83	0	2	11.77	11	0	0	0	13	25	22	17	0	18	10	.410	.435	.395	6.92	12.46
Bass, Corey	R-R	6-3	210	2-8-85	3	3	2.93	20	1	0	0	40	50	24	13	3	10	41	.289	.358	.245	9.23	2.25
Campos, Christian	L-L	6-1	193	8-28-83	0	2	5.84	11	0	0	1	12	15	11	8	1	6	22	.294	.333	.286	16.05	4.38
Garate, Victor	L-L	6-1	160	9-25-84	4	1	5.57	19	0	0	0	32	21	20	20	2	26	53	.189	.190	.189	14.75	7.24
Gervacio, Sam	R-R	5-11	160	1-10-85	3	2	2.67	21	0	0	8	34	24	10	10	1	6	53	.190	.233	.169	14.17	1.60
Hirsh, Matt	R-R	6-5	235	8-29-84	1	2	5.61	16	7	0	1	51	61	33	32	8	19	30	.293	.364	.261	5.26	3.33
Hurry, Jacob	L-L	6-3	220	8-12-82	2	3	5.73	12	12	0	0	55	51	36	35	5	23	34	.244	.129	.264	5.56	3.76
James, Brad	R-R	6-2	200	6-19-84	3	3	4.97	13	13	0	0	63	65	42	35	2	24	48	.265	.298	.248	6.82	3.41
Mayora, Cesar	R-R	6-2	185	1-1-84	2	3	4.54	19	0	0	1	34	36	21	17	5	8	43	.269	.346	.220	11.50	2.14
Mitchell, Ryan	R-R	6-5	235	8-13-87	3	1	3.34	11	8	0	0	35	30	15	13	0	14	33	.219	.143	.253	8.49	3.60
Noel, Wilton	R-R	6-5	180	1-1-83	2	3	5.30	18	4	0	1	36	35	27	21	1	22	30	.248	.255	.245	7.57	5.55
Polanco, Celson	R-R	6-5	200	8-28-84	1	2	5.65	18	0	0	0	37	46	23	23	4	9	24	.317	.310	.320	5.89	2.21
Severino, Sergio	L-L	5-11	150	9-1-84	3	5	4.67	13	13	0	0	62	47	35	32	3	36	69	.210	.241	.205	10.07	5.25
Sheridan, Eric	R-R	6-1	175	9-22-83	0	0	3.86	3	0	0	0	5	2	2	2	0	1	6	.143	.200	.111	11.57	1.93
Stricklen, Brandon	R-R	6-1	200	2-20-84	1	3	1.69	5	0	0	0	11	10	9	2	2	3	10	.233	.214	.241	8.44	2.53
Trinidad, Polin	L-L	6-2	170	11-19-84	1	2	4.89	14	8	0	2	50	65	34	27	5	11	47	.308	.250	.320	8.52	1.99

GAMES BY POSITION: C—Henriquez 46, Kady 11, Lopez 6, Mulhern 12. **1B**—Espinoza 1, Garcia 41, Graham 34. **2B**—Espinoza 30, Florentino 12, Gonzalez 5, Ramirez 21. **3B**—Clemens 28, Espinoza 1, Florentino 14, Gonzalez 21, Ramirez 4. **SS**—Florentino 22, Johnson 42, Ramirez 2. **OF**—Barnes 26, Flores 57, Iorg 31, Langdon 5, Reed 22, Rodriguez 19, Warrick 42.

KANSAS CITY ROYALS

BY ALAN ESKEW

There is a proud past, a bleak present and a bleary future.

In a look back, the Royals, once a thriving franchise that advanced to the playoffs seven times between 1976-85, celebrated the 20-year anniversary of their 1985 World Series victory over the Cardinals. The pregame ceremonies to honor the stars of that team, including George Brett, Bret Saberhagen, Frank White, Jim Sundberg, Danny Jackson and Steve Balboni, occurred during a downpour and the game was rained out.

While the '85 team may have been the Royals' best, the 2005 team was the worst. The Royals lost a franchise-record 106 games and had the worst record in the majors. The season included more lowlights than highlights, including a 19-game losing streak, which was the longest in the majors since the Orioles' American League-record 21-game skid in 1988.

The Royals have lost 100 or more games in three of the past four years and have lost 97 or more games five times since 1999. They've had only one winning year since the strike-shortened 1994 season. They have not sniffed the playoffs since 1985.

The Royals went through three managers in 2005. Tony Pena, the 2003 AL manager of the year, abruptly resigned on May 10 with the club losing 25 of its first 33 games. Interim manager Bob Schaefer, the bench coach, had a 5-12 record before the Royals hired Buddy Bell on May 31.

The galaxy of 2005 embarrassments began in spring training when Calvin Pickering hit an apparent grand slam, but passed Justin Huber, who had returned to first base to tag up. During their 19-game losing streak, the Royals led the Indians 7-2 after eight innings, before allowing 11 runs and committing two errors in the ninth.

Then there was the game the Royals batted out of order to start the game, depriving David DeJesus a single. The Royals turned in a lineup card with Angel Berroa leading off, not DeJesus. And the Royals' final Fireworks Friday was abbreviated when thieves stole the flatbed truck outside Kauffman Stadium.

It was that kind of year for the Royals.

The Royals' rotation won a major league-low 33 games, had the highest ERA (6.00) and worked the fewest innings (861). Zack Greinke's sophomore season was a step back as he went 5-17, 5.80. Jose Lima (5-16, 6.99) had the highest ERA in big league history with a minimum of 30 starts. Runelvys Hernandez, who sat out the 2004 season after having Tommy John surgery, led the staff with eight victories, but had none after July 22.

The offense was not much better than the pitching. The Royals' .320 on-base percentage and .396 slugging percentage ranked next-to-last in the AL. Mike Sweeney hit .300 and was the Royals' lone representative in the All-Star Game but was limited to 122 games because of injuries.

The strength of the Royals was their bullpen, led by hard throwers Mike MacDougal (24 saves), lefthanders Jeremy Affeldt and Andrew Sisco (a Rule 5 pick from the Cubs), and righthander Ambiorix Burgos, who like Sisco pitched in Class A in 2004.

Help may soon be on the way, at least offensively. Billy Butler, a 2004 first-round pick, hit .348-25-94 in 92 games at High Desert in the California League. He was promoted to Double-A Wichita, where he hit .313-5-19 in 29 games. Chris Lubanski, a 2003 first-round pick, hit .301-28-116 with High Desert, leading the Cal League in RBIs. First baseman Justin Huber, a 23-year-old Australian, won the Texas League batting crown with a .343 average and also topped the league with a .570 slugging percentage and a .432 on-base percentage. He was also named the MVP of the Futures Game.

The Royals also signed third baseman Alex Gordon, the second overall pick in the draft, for a club record $4 million. Gordon, who led Nebraska to the College World Series and was considered the best collegiate position player available in the draft, could move rapidly.

PLAYERS OF THE YEAR

MAJOR LEAGUE: Mike Sweeney, 1b

In a very rough year for the Royals, Sweeney was his usual reliable self, leading the team in the triple crown categories (.300-21-83), doubles (39) and OPS (.864). In the last seven years, Sweeney has eclipsed the 20-homer mark six times and the 80-RBI mark six times.

MINOR LEAGUE: Billy Butler, of

STEVE MOORE

The Royals' top prospect continued to be a hitting machine in his first full pro season in 2005, going .340-30-110 between high Class A High Desert and Double-A Wichita. Butler kept raking as a 19-year-old against advanced competition despite making the transition from third base to left field at midseason.

ORGANIZATION LEADERS

BATTING

*AVG	Diaz, Matt, Omaha/Wichita	.366
R	Brown, Adrian, Omaha	104
H	Sanchez, Angel, High Desert	183
TB	Butler, Billy, High Desert/Wichita	300
2B	Maier, Mitch, High Desert/Wichita	47
3B	Stocker, Mel, High Desert/Wichita	11
HR	Four tied at	30
RBI	Lubanski, Chris, High Desert	116
BB	Kaaihue, Kila, High Desert	97
SO	Moye, Alan, Burlington/High Desert	154
SB	Falu, Irving, Burlington/Wichita	34
*OBP	Maestrales, Pete, Burlington/High Desert	.445
*SLG	Diaz, Matt, Omaha/Wichita	.624

PITCHING

W	Gragg, John, High Desert	13
L	Buckner, Billy, Burlington/High Desert	13
#ERA	Demaria, Chris, High Desert/Wichita	1.70
G	Demaria, Chris, High Desert/Wichita	58
CG	Baerlocher, Ryan, Omaha/Wichita	2
SV	Demaria, Chris, High Desert/Wichita	20
IP	Middleton, Kyle, Wichita	171
BB	Buckner, Billy, Burlington/High Desert	63
	Cota, Luis, Burlington	63
SO	Buckner, Billy, Burlington/High Desert	152

*Minimum 250 at-bats. #Minimum 75 innings.

KANSAS CITY ROYALS

Managers: Tony Pena, Bob Schaefer, Buddy Bell. **2005 Record:** 56-106, .346 (5th, AL Central).

BATTING	B-T	HT	WT	DOB	AVG	vLH	vRH	G	AB	R	H	2B	3B	HR	RBI	BB	HBP	SH	SF	SO	SB	CS	SLG	OBP
Ambres, Chip	R-R	6-1	190	12-19-79	.241	.239	.246	53	145	25	35	8	0	4	9	16	2	3	1	32	3	2	.379	.323
Berroa, Angel	R-R	6-0	180	1-27-78	.270	.278	.266	159	608	68	164	21	5	11	55	18	14	10	2	108	7	5	.375	.305
Blanco, Andres	B-R	5-10	180	4-11-84	.215	.111	.269	26	79	6	17	0	1	0	5	0	1	4	2	5	0	1	.241	.220
Brown, Emil	R-R	6-2	200	12-29-74	.286	.313	.273	150	545	75	156	31	5	17	86	48	8	1	7	108	10	1	.455	.349
Buck, John	R-R	6-3	220	7-7-80	.242	.310	.214	118	401	40	97	21	1	12	47	23	3	1	2	94	2	2	.389	.287
Castillo, Alberto	R-R	6-0	215	2-10-70	.210	.143	.246	34	100	13	21	5	1	1	14	12	0	1	1	21	1	0	.310	.292
Costa, Shane	L-R	6-0	220	12-12-81	.235	.000	.268	27	81	13	19	2	0	2	7	5	1	1	0	11	0	0	.333	.287
DeJesus, David	L-L	6-0	185	12-20-79	.293	.270	.303	122	461	69	135	31	6	9	56	42	9	5	6	76	5	5	.445	.359
Diaz, Matt	R-R	6-1	205	3-3-78	.281	.370	.143	34	89	7	25	4	2	1	9	4	2	1	1	15	0	1	.404	.323
Gotay, Ruben	B-R	5-11	175	12-25-82	.227	.212	.230	86	282	32	64	14	2	5	29	22	4	4	5	51	2	2	.344	.288
Graffanino, Tony	R-R	6-1	190	6-6-72	.298	.284	.313	59	191	29	57	5	2	3	18	22	2	2	0	28	3	1	.393	.377
Guiel, Aaron	L-R	5-10	200	10-5-72	.294	.200	.315	33	109	18	32	5	0	4	7	6	5	0	1	21	1	0	.450	.355
Harvey, Ken	R-R	6-2	250	3-1-78	.222	.263	.192	12	45	4	10	3	0	1	5	3	0	0	0	13	0	0	.356	.271
Hocking, Denny	B-R	5-10	185	4-2-70	.267	.375	.250	23	60	14	16	1	0	0	7	10	0	1	0	10	0	1	.283	.371
Huber, Justin	R-R	6-2	200	7-1-82	.218	.179	.256	25	78	6	17	3	0	0	6	5	1	0	1	20	0	0	.256	.271
Long, Terrence	L-L	6-1	200	2-29-76	.279	.291	.276	137	455	62	127	21	3	6	53	30	0	0	4	56	3	3	.378	.321
Marrero, Eli	R-R	6-1	180	11-17-73	.159	.208	.086	32	88	11	14	4	0	4	9	7	1	1	3	18	1	0	.341	.222
McEwing, Joe	R-R	5-11	170	10-19-72	.239	.237	.241	83	180	16	43	7	0	1	6	6	0	5	0	35	4	4	.294	.263
Murphy, Donnie	R-R	5-10	200	3-10-83	.156	.146	.167	32	77	4	12	5	0	1	8	9	0	1	1	23	0	1	.260	.241
Phillips, Paul	R-R	5-11	200	4-15-77	.269	.227	.289	23	67	6	18	4	1	1	9	0	0	0	0	5	0	0	.403	.269
Pickering, Calvin	L-L	6-5	295	9-29-76	.148	.000	.200	7	27	4	4	0	0	1	3	3	0	0	1	14	0	0	.259	.226
Stairs, Matt	L-R	5-9	215	2-27-68	.275	.259	.278	127	396	55	109	26	1	13	66	60	5	0	5	69	1	2	.444	.373
Sweeney, Mike	R-R	6-3	235	7-22-73	.300	.279	.309	122	470	63	141	39	0	21	83	33	4	1	6	61	3	0	.517	.347
Teahen, Mark	L-R	6-3	210	9-6-81	.246	.200	.263	130	447	60	110	29	4	7	55	40	1	2	1	107	7	2	.376	.309

PITCHING	B-T	HT	WT	DOB	W	L	ERA	G	GS	CG	SV	IP	H	R	ER	HR	BB	SO	AVG	vLH	vRH	K/9	BB/9
Affeldt, Jeremy	L-L	6-4	220	6-6-79	0	2	5.26	49	0	0	0	50	56	35	29	3	29	39	.277	.263	.283	7.07	5.26
Anderson, Brian	R-L	6-1	190	4-26-72	1	2	6.75	6	6	0	0	31	39	24	23	7	4	17	.305	.080	.359	4.99	1.17
Bautista, Denny	R-R	6-5	180	8-23-80	2	2	5.80	7	7	0	0	36	36	23	23	2	17	23	.259	.288	.220	5.80	4.29
Bayliss, Jonah	R-R	6-2	210	8-13-80	0	0	4.63	11	0	0	0	12	7	6	6	2	4	10	.167	.200	.136	7.71	3.09
Burgos, Ambiorix	R-R	6-3	235	4-19-84	3	5	3.98	59	0	0	2	63	60	29	28	6	31	65	.251	.300	.216	9.24	4.41
Camp, Shawn	R-R	6-1	200	11-18-75	1	4	6.43	29	0	0	0	49	69	40	35	4	13	28	.332	.407	.274	5.14	2.39
Carrasco, D.J.	R-R	6-1	215	4-12-77	6	8	4.79	21	20	1	0	115	129	67	61	11	51	49	.289	.286	.292	3.85	4.00
Cerda, Jaime	L-L	6-0	200	10-26-78	1	4	6.63	20	0	0	0	19	21	14	14	3	11	18	.284	.231	.343	8.53	5.21
Demaria, Chris	B-R	6-3	210	9-28-80	1	0	9.00	8	0	0	0	9	14	10	9	3	5	11	.359	.588	.182	11.00	5.00
Field, Nate	R-R	6-2	205	12-11-75	0	0	9.45	7	0	0	0	7	13	7	7	1	5	4	.433	.250	.500	5.40	6.75
Gobble, Jimmy	L-L	6-3	200	7-19-81	1	1	5.70	28	4	0	0	54	64	34	34	9	30	38	.299	.310	.294	6.37	5.03
Greinke, Zack	R-R	6-2	175	10-21-83	5	17	5.80	33	33	2	0	183	233	125	118	23	53	114	.309	.340	.279	5.61	2.61
Hernandez, Runelvys	R-R	6-1	250	4-27-78	8	14	5.52	29	29	0	0	160	172	101	98	18	70	88	.277	.261	.290	4.96	3.95
Howell, J.P.	L-L	6-0	175	4-25-83	3	5	6.19	15	15	0	0	73	73	55	50	9	39	54	.264	.229	.271	6.69	4.83
Jensen, Ryan	R-R	6-0	250	9-17-75	3	2	7.11	9	3	0	0	25	31	20	20	4	7	18	.298	.269	.327	6.39	2.49
Lima, Jose	R-R	6-2	210	9-30-72	5	16	6.99	32	32	1	0	169	219	140	131	31	61	80	.314	.302	.324	4.27	3.25
MacDougal, Mike	B-R	6-4	185	3-5-77	5	6	3.33	68	0	0	21	70	69	32	26	6	24	72	.257	.240	.270	9.21	3.07
Nunez, Leo	R-R	6-1	160	8-14-83	3	2	7.55	41	0	0	0	54	73	45	45	9	18	32	.329	.374	.298	5.37	3.02
Sisco, Andrew	L-L	6-10	270	1-13-83	2	5	3.11	67	0	0	0	75	68	27	26	6	42	76	.243	.216	.255	9.08	5.02
Snyder, Kyle	B-R	6-8	220	9-9-77	1	3	6.75	13	3	0	0	36	55	29	27	3	10	19	.353	.333	.366	4.75	2.50
Stemle, Steve	R-R	6-4	200	5-20-77	0	0	5.06	6	0	0	0	11	10	6	6	0	4	9	.256	.211	.300	7.59	3.38
Wood, Mike	R-R	6-3	210	4-26-80	5	8	4.46	47	10	0	2	115	129	66	57	18	52	60	.287	.295	.279	4.70	4.07

FIELDING

Catcher	PCT	G	PO	A	E	DP	PB
Buck	.996	117	640	56	3	5	3
Phillips	.990	20	91	10	1	2	2

First Base	PCT	G	PO	A	E	DP
Graffanino	.993	22	137	8	1	19
Harvey	1.000	5	41	0	0	2
Huber	.978	19	123	8	3	16
Marrero	.987	9	72	3	1	7
McEwing	1.000	20	101	11	0	16
Stairs	.993	64	499	37	4	60
Sweeney	.998	49	441	29	1	29

Second Base	PCT	G	PO	A	E	DP
Blanco	.977	24	57	68	3	23
Gotay	.980	81	155	232	8	50
Graffanino	.987	22	31	46	1	8
Hocking	.976	13	33	48	2	13
McEwing	1.000	11	15	25	0	6
Murphy	.972	29	42	61	3	14

Third Base	PCT	G	PO	A	E	DP
Graffanino	.884	17	7	31	5	3
Hocking	.000	1	0	0	0	0
McEwing	.962	29	18	57	3	2
Teahen	.947	128	113	245	20	24

Shortstop	PCT	G	PO	A	E	DP
Berroa	.965	159	254	441	25	108
Blanco	1.000	7	7	7	0	2
Graffanino	1.000	1	1	0	0	0
Hocking	1.000	1	1	3	0	2
McEwing	.944	6	7	10	1	4
Murphy	.000	2	0	0	1	0

Outfield	PCT	G	PO	A	E	DP
Ambres	.988	47	83	2	1	0
Brown	.958	139	264	9	12	0
Costa	1.000	20	30	1	0	0
DeJesus	.987	119	306	7	4	3
Diaz	.950	21	38	0	2	0
Guiel	.985	30	64	1	1	0
Long	.986	121	203	12	3	0
Marrero	.967	20	27	2	1	0
McEwing	1.000	5	1	0	0	0
Stairs	1.000	15	18	0	0	0

FARM SYSTEM

General Manager: Allard Baird. **Director, Player Development:** Shaun McGinn. **Scouting Director:** Deric Ladnier.

Class	Farm Team	League	W	L	Pct.	Finish*	Manager	Affiliate Since
AAA	Omaha (Neb.) Royals	Pacific Coast	72	72	.500	8th (16)	Mike Jirschele	1969
AA	Wichita (Kan.) Wranglers	Texas	68	72	.486	6th (8)	Frank White	1995
High A	High Desert (Calif.) Mavericks	California	75	65	.536	**t-3rd (10)**	Billy Gardner	2005
Low A	Burlington (Iowa) Bees	Midwest	65	75	.464	t-11th (14)	Jim Gabella	2001
Rookie	Idaho Falls (Idaho) Chukars	Pioneer	34	42	.447	t-6th (8)	Brian Rupp	2004
Rookie	Surprise (Ariz.) Royals	Arizona	34	22	.607	2nd (9)	Lloyd Simmons	2003

*Finish in overall standings (No. of teams in league)/Playoff teams in **boldface**

OMAHA ROYALS — Class AAA

PACIFIC COAST LEAGUE

BATTING	B-T	HT	WT	DOB	AVG	vLH	vRH	G	AB	R	H	2B	3B	HR	RBI	BB	HBP	SH	SF	SO	SB	CS	SLG	OBP
Aldridge, Cory	L-R	6-1	225	6-13-79	.195	.222	.174	24	82	8	16	4	0	3	7	6	0	0	0	28	4	0	.354	.250
Blanco, Andres	B-R	5-10	180	4-11-84	.254	.273	.247	35	114	13	29	4	2	1	9	10	3	2	0	23	2	0	.351	.331
Brown, Adrian	B-R	6-0	190	2-7-74	.273	.266	.277	140	553	104	151	28	8	9	49	74	4	6	3	73	33	7	.401	.361
Costa, Shane	L-R	6-0	220	12-12-81	.188	.000	.231	4	16	1	3	1	0	0	1	0	0	0	0	1	0	0	.250	.188
Diaz, Matt	R-R	6-1	205	3-3-78	.371	.403	.358	65	259	48	96	22	4	14	56	12	5	0	1	49	10	3	.649	.408
Duenas, Tomas	R-R	5-11	205	7-16-81	.250	.500	.200	4	12	1	3	0	0	0	0	1	0	0	0	6	0	0	.250	.308
Gemoll, Justin	R-R	6-2	218	11-19-77	.261	.202	.285	121	448	58	117	21	1	8	50	38	5	4	1	101	7	1	.366	.325
Gomez, Rudy	R-R	5-11	187	9-14-74	.224	.278	.194	13	49	5	11	0	0	0	2	3	0	1	0	7	0	0	.224	.269
Guiel, Aaron	L-R	5-10	200	10-5-72	.276	.260	.284	128	496	94	137	32	4	30	95	64	15	0	7	103	6	3	.538	.371
Harvey, Ken	R-R	6-2	250	3-1-78	.346	.241	.387	25	104	10	36	4	1	3	18	5	0	0	1	18	0	0	.490	.373
Hocking, Denny	B-R	5-10	185	4-2-70	.287	.305	.277	68	230	37	66	14	2	0	24	25	0	5	3	44	1	0	.365	.353
Huber, Justin	R-R	6-2	200	7-1-82	.274	.387	.232	32	113	19	31	6	1	7	23	16	2	0	0	33	3	0	.531	.374
Jones, Jaime	L-L	6-4	229	8-2-76	.267	.184	.295	58	195	37	52	8	1	5	21	17	2	0	2	48	0	2	.395	.329
McEwing, Joe	R-R	5-11	170	10-19-72	.167	.000	.250	5	18	4	3	1	0	0	1	4	0	0	0	2	0	0	.222	.318
Phillips, Paul	R-R	5-11	200	4-15-77	.268	.351	.244	87	332	45	89	21	1	7	42	21	4	2	3	44	1	4	.401	.317
Pickering, Calvin	L-L	6-5	295	9-29-76	.275	.259	.283	92	335	56	92	16	0	23	67	56	4	0	1	130	1	0	.528	.384
Price, Jared	R-R	6-1	220	3-18-82	.239	.143	.283	24	88	8	21	4	0	5	11	2	1	1	0	23	0	1	.455	.264
Prieto, Alejandro	R-R	5-11	205	6-19-76	.281	.222	.298	46	160	17	45	11	1	2	23	12	0	3	1	34	4	2	.400	.329
Santos, Chad	L-L	6-0	229	4-28-81	.259	.225	.272	120	433	50	112	26	0	16	64	38	5	1	1	133	2	1	.430	.325
Teahen, Mark	L-R	6-3	210	9-6-81	.259	.250	.261	8	27	4	7	2	0	0	4	7	0	0	0	9	0	0	.333	.412
Truby, Chris	R-R	6-2	220	12-9-73	.242	.283	.228	106	396	56	96	19	3	20	66	36	0	0	3	82	1	3	.457	.303
Ugueto, Luis	R-R	6-0	195	2-15-79	.208	.253	.188	80	265	39	55	8	6	7	29	32	3	2	3	73	11	2	.362	.297
Walter, Scott	R-R	6-2	210	12-28-78	.269	.302	.250	38	145	20	39	9	0	8	30	4	3	1	0	33	0	0	.497	.303

PITCHING	B-T	HT	WT	DOB	W	L	ERA	G	GS	CG	SV	IP	H	R	ER	HR	BB	SO	AVG	vLH	vRH	K/9	BB/9
Affeldt, Jeremy	L-L	6-4	220	6-6-79	0	1	6.48	9	0	0	0	8	9	7	6	1	6	9	.290	.333	.273	9.72	6.48
Anderson, Brian	R-L	6-1	190	4-26-72	0	0	6.23	1	1	0	0	4	3	3	3	1	1	2	.188	.167	.200	4.15	2.08
Baerlocher, Ryan	R-R	6-5	220	8-6-77	0	1	6.00	3	3	0	0	9	10	6	6	1	9	9	.303	.400	.222	9.00	9.00
Bautista, Denny	R-R	6-5	180	8-23-80	0	1	2.77	6	6	0	0	13	8	4	4	0	6	12	.174	.095	.240	8.31	4.15
Bray, Steve	R-R	6-1	193	12-22-80	0	0	4.50	1	0	0	0	2	2	1	1	0	1	4	.286	.333	.250	18.00	4.50
Camp, Shawn	R-R	6-1	200	11-18-75	3	6	3.86	21	7	0	1	68	71	36	29	9	22	42	.275	.317	.248	5.59	2.93
Carrasco, D.J.	R-R	6-1	215	4-12-77	3	2	2.28	11	3	0	0	28	24	9	7	1	11	21	.245	.118	.313	6.83	3.58
Cerda, Jaime	L-L	6-0	200	10-26-78	4	1	5.26	35	0	0	2	50	48	33	29	6	21	47	.249	.190	.277	8.52	3.81
DeHoyos, Gabe	R-R	5-11	226	4-14-80	0	0	23.14	2	0	0	0	2	3	7	6	1	5	0	.273	.000	.375	0.00	19.29
Ebert, Derrin	R-L	6-3	200	8-21-76	0	0	12.27	2	0	0	0	4	5	5	5	0	4	1	.313	.000	.357	2.45	9.82
Elder, Dave	R-R	6-0	180	9-23-75	2	0	0.00	11	0	0	0	16	8	2	0	0	7	16	.140	.037	.233	9.00	3.94
Embry, Byron	R-R	6-2	240	9-5-76	1	0	5.02	16	0	0	8	14	19	9	8	3	5	12	.333	.286	.361	7.53	3.14
Field, Nate	R-R	6-2	205	12-11-75	1	0	4.91	16	0	0	0	22	26	12	12	1	14	24	.295	.355	.263	9.82	5.73
Ford, Matt	B-L	6-1	190	4-8-81	0	1	2.61	9	0	0	0	10	9	3	3	1	6	5	.250	.154	.304	4.35	5.23
George, Chris	L-L	6-2	195	9-16-79	8	8	5.63	32	20	0	0	147	175	97	92	27	51	103	.296	.222	.321	6.31	3.12
Gobble, Jimmy	L-L	6-3	200	7-19-81	2	7	6.63	12	12	0	0	58	76	48	43	8	21	45	.314	.232	.339	6.94	3.24
Gomez, Rudy	R-R	5-11	187	9-14-74	0	0	0.00	1	0	0	0	2	1	0	0	0	0	1	.143	.000	.167	4.50	0.00
Howell, J.P.	L-L	6-0	175	4-25-83	3	1	4.06	7	7	0	0	38	40	19	17	1	19	29	.286	.300	.280	6.93	4.54
Huisman, Justin	R-R	6-1	200	4-16-79	8	2	3.92	42	1	0	1	78	89	41	34	12	40	57	.280	.381	.214	6.58	4.62
Jensen, Ryan	R-R	6-0	250	9-17-75	2	11	7.20	18	18	0	0	90	123	80	72	12	38	55	.325	.348	.308	5.50	3.80
Nance, Shane	L-L	5-8	190	9-7-77	3	2	6.08	23	0	0	0	37	40	25	25	7	17	31	.278	.277	.278	7.54	4.14
2-team (22 Tucson)					3	4	5.16	45	0	0	2	59	56	34	34	9	28	56	.252	.219	.268	8.49	4.25
Ramirez, Santiago	R-R	5-11	210	8-15-78	5	5	5.21	50	1	0	17	67	81	43	39	11	21	53	.299	.302	.297	7.08	2.81
Snyder, Kyle	B-R	6-8	220	9-9-77	2	3	3.55	15	12	0	0	66	61	32	26	3	22	48	.244	.240	.247	6.55	3.00
Sonnier, Shawn	R-R	6-5	210	7-5-76	3	0	4.81	19	0	0	1	34	34	18	18	7	13	37	.264	.240	.278	9.89	3.48
Stemle, Steve	R-R	6-4	200	5-20-77	1	1	0.45	14	0	0	3	20	13	3	1	0	3	12	.191	.207	.179	5.40	1.35
Sullivan, Scott	R-R	6-3	200	3-13-71	1	0	9.00	2	0	0	0	2	3	2	2	0	0	1	.333	.000	.429	4.50	0.00
Tamayo, Danny	R-R	6-1	219	6-3-79	9	8	5.28	30	27	0	0	160	192	99	94	27	50	103	.300	.279	.315	5.78	2.81
Tankersley, Dennis	R-R	6-2	215	2-24-79	9	8	4.24	32	23	1	0	136	148	72	64	15	59	104	.276	.295	.263	6.88	3.90
Wilkerson, Wes	R-R	6-4	216	9-11-76	2	3	4.99	36	1	0	3	58	66	35	32	8	11	31	.283	.293	.278	4.84	1.72
Wood, Mike	R-R	6-3	210	4-26-80	0	0	2.00	2	2	0	0	9	10	2	2	0	2	8	.286	.381	.143	8.00	2.00

FIELDING

Catcher	PCT	G	PO	A	E	DP	PB
Duenas	.963	4	21	5	1	0	0
Phillips	.990	83	550	53	6	4	6
Price	.978	24	169	9	4	0	3
Walter	.991	33	221	7	2	0	4

First Base	PCT	G	PO	A	E	DP
Harvey	.989	18	169	7	2	14
Hocking	1.000	3	20	0	0	4
Huber	.990	31	260	23	3	25
Pickering	.975	9	74	3	2	7
Santos	.991	83	701	46	7	75

Second Base	PCT	G	PO	A	E	DP
Gemoll	.980	83	168	232	8	48
Gomez	.974	8	14	23	1	9
Hocking	.972	29	55	85	4	20
McEwing	1.000	1	4	4	0	1
Ugueto	1.000	29	54	70	0	17

Third Base	PCT	G	PO	A	E	DP
Gemoll	.963	30	18	60	3	5
Gomez	.500	1	0	1	1	0
Hocking	.500	1	2	0	2	0
McEwing	.875	5	1	6	1	1
Teahen	.923	5	4	8	1	0
Truby	.958	104	63	185	11	19
Walter	.000	2	0	0	2	0

Shortstop	PCT	G	PO	A	E	DP
Blanco	.944	35	46	123	10	27
Gomez	.941	5	5	11	1	1
Hocking	.961	12	23	26	2	3
Prieto	.973	46	60	158	6	35
Ugueto	.954	52	95	131	11	28

Outfield	PCT	G	PO	A	E	DP
Aldridge	1.000	24	41	0	0	0
Brown	.986	139	336	6	5	1
Costa	1.000	4	9	0	0	0
Diaz	.969	65	119	6	4	2
Guiel	.993	127	255	18	2	3
Hocking	1.000	11	18	2	0	0
Jones	.966	51	82	4	3	2
Santos	.947	16	36	0	2	0
Ugueto	.667	1	2	0	1	0

WICHITA WRANGLERS — Class AA

TEXAS LEAGUE

BATTING	B-T	HT	WT	DOB	AVG	vLH	vRH	G	AB	R	H	2B	3B	HR	RBI	BB	HBP	SH	SF	SO	SB	CS	SLG	OBP
Aldridge, Cory	L-R	6-1	225	6-13-79	.271	.273	.270	98	388	66	105	20	4	27	77	29	2	1	3	94	9	4	.552	.322
Aviles, Mike	R-R	5-11	198	3-13-81	.280	.283	.279	133	521	79	146	33	6	14	80	30	1	2	5	64	11	6	.447	.318
Blanco, Andres	B-R	5-10	180	4-11-84	.189	.200	.185	9	37	5	7	0	0	1	5	3	0	1	0	7	0	0	.270	.250
Butler, Billy	R-R	6-2	225	4-18-86	.313	.385	.291	29	112	14	35	9	0	5	19	7	0	0	0	18	0	0	.527	.353
Costa, Shane	L-R	6-0	220	12-12-81	.282	.253	.296	75	277	37	78	18	2	8	43	24	8	1	6	23	5	1	.448	.349
Diaz, Matt	R-R	6-1	205	3-3-78	.269	.333	.235	7	26	6	7	0	0	1	6	3	0	0	1	5	1	0	.385	.333
Draper, John	R-R	6-2	191	8-11-80	.247	.266	.233	62	182	30	45	10	1	1	14	29	2	0	0	38	10	3	.330	.357
Falu, Irving	B-R	6-0	173	6-6-83	.235	.667	.143	6	17	1	4	1	0	0	2	1	0	0	0	0	0	0	.294	.278
Gomez, Rudy	R-R	5-11	187	9-14-74	.262	.269	.256	39	130	16	34	7	0	1	14	13	2	1	2	15	2	1	.338	.333
Gotay, Ruben	B-R	5-11	175	12-25-82	.245	.143	.280	28	110	22	27	8	0	3	15	12	0	0	0	13	0	2	.400	.320
Groves, Brett	B-R	5-11	180	10-1-78	.234	.292	.207	86	273	43	64	9	0	2	25	29	4	7	3	50	2	2	.289	.314
Huber, Justin	R-R	6-2	200	7-1-82	.343	.382	.324	88	335	68	115	22	3	16	74	51	5	0	5	70	7	3	.570	.432
Keim, Adam	R-R	5-11	196	1-5-81	.333	.313	.340	17	69	11	23	1	0	4	18	3	0	1	2	12	1	1	.522	.351
King, Brennan	R-R	6-3	218	1-20-81	.285	.308	.272	118	435	58	124	28	2	9	56	29	5	6	3	68	5	1	.421	.335
Maduro, Jorge	R-R	6-2	220	3-11-81	.143	.000	.200	2	7	0	1	0	0	0	0	1	0	0	0	1	0	0	.143	.250
Maier, Mitch	L-R	6-2	200	6-30-82	.255	.293	.239	80	322	55	82	21	5	7	49	15	2	0	3	47	10	3	.416	.289
Murphy, Donnie	R-R	5-10	200	3-10-83	.313	.304	.319	50	214	33	67	13	1	10	32	13	4	3	1	32	1	1	.523	.362
Pressley, Josh	L-R	6-6	225	4-2-80	.311	.268	.336	119	440	74	137	25	0	22	88	60	7	0	3	71	0	2	.518	.400
Price, Jared	R-R	6-1	220	3-18-82	.300	.200	.400	4	10	1	3	1	0	1	2	0	0	0	0	4	0	0	.700	.300
Ruan, Wilkin	R-R	6-0	180	9-18-78	.254	.220	.281	76	244	31	62	4	3	0	20	14	2	4	2	19	18	7	.295	.298
Stocker, Mel	B-R	5-9	156	8-15-80	.245	.242	.247	80	277	35	68	6	10	2	27	27	3	7	3	42	16	6	.361	.316
Tupman, Mat	L-R	5-11	180	11-25-79	.263	.287	.255	109	365	59	96	16	2	2	32	46	8	3	3	62	1	2	.334	.355

PITCHING	B-T	HT	WT	DOB	W	L	ERA	G	GS	CG	SV	IP	H	R	ER	HR	BB	SO	AVG	vLH	vRH	K/9	BB/9
Anderson, Brian	R-L	6-1	190	4-26-72	0	0	13.50	1	1	0	0	1	5	3	2	1	0	2	.500	.000	.714	13.50	0.00
Armitage, Barry	R-R	6-5	277	5-11-79	4	3	3.87	41	2	0	7	79	69	35	34	5	40	62	.235	.269	.211	7.06	4.56
Baerlocher, Ryan	R-R	6-5	220	8-6-77	7	5	3.44	15	15	2	0	89	76	37	34	5	27	63	.230	.209	.249	6.37	2.73
Bass, Brian	R-R	6-0	200	1-6-82	12	8	5.24	27	27	0	0	165	185	106	96	14	53	102	.286	.301	.272	5.56	2.89
Bayliss, Jonah	R-R	6-2	210	8-13-80	1	2	2.84	30	0	0	8	57	43	19	18	5	26	63	.208	.216	.200	9.95	4.11
Braun, Ryan	R-R	6-1	215	7-29-80	0	1	17.36	6	0	0	0	5	15	10	9	0	7	1	.536	.467	.615	1.93	13.50
Bray, Steve	R-R	6-1	193	12-22-80	1	1	4.40	20	0	0	0	31	38	22	15	3	11	40	.299	.429	.218	11.74	3.23
Burgos, Ambiorix	R-R	6-3	235	4-19-84	1	1	4.97	12	0	0	1	13	8	7	7	1	8	19	.170	.227	.120	13.50	5.68
Cedeno, Juan	L-L	6-1	160	8-19-83	0	2	7.20	11	1	0	0	20	21	17	16	4	11	16	.266	.286	.259	7.20	4.95
Damico, Yovany	R-R	5-11	223	8-18-84	0	1	17.18	1	1	0	0	4	7	7	7	1	3	3	.412	.750	.308	7.36	7.36
Demaria, Chris	B-R	6-3	210	9-28-80	0	1	1.76	10	0	0	1	15	12	3	3	3	2	19	.218	.150	.257	11.15	1.17
Ebert, Derrin	R-L	6-3	200	8-21-76	7	3	4.89	27	16	0	1	105	123	69	57	10	35	54	.289	.343	.273	4.63	3.00
Endicott, Drew	R-R	6-2	181	3-30-81	1	0	1.50	2	0	0	0	6	1	1	1	0	6	1	.056	.000	.091	1.50	9.00
Gomez, Rudy	R-R	5-11	187	9-14-74	1	0	0.00	3	0	0	0	4	3	0	0	0	1	3	.188	.286	.111	6.23	2.08
Griffin, Colt	R-R	6-3	229	9-29-82	1	1	4.02	37	0	0	1	56	45	30	25	4	43	36	.225	.242	.210	5.79	6.91
Hicklen, Patrick	R-R	6-4	210	12-30-81	0	1	14.73	1	1	0	0	4	5	6	6	1	5	4	.357	.333	.364	9.82	12.27
Hoelscher, Nate	L-L	6-2	183	11-11-79	3	2	5.63	51	1	0	4	54	62	38	34	4	25	40	.282	.154	.352	6.63	4.14
Howell, J.P.	L-L	6-0	175	4-25-83	2	0	2.50	3	3	0	0	18	12	5	5	2	5	23	.188	.250	.167	11.50	2.50
Lowery, Devon	L-R	6-1	195	3-24-83	0	4	24.84	4	4	0	0	8	21	24	23	1	14	5	.525	.619	.421	5.40	15.12
Markray, Thad	R-R	6-2	236	9-20-79	4	7	5.26	22	11	0	1	65	62	43	38	10	20	44	.255	.307	.209	6.09	2.77
McGill, Trae	R-R	6-0	195	8-7-77	3	4	5.01	29	1	0	2	47	51	30	26	4	27	40	.279	.329	.235	7.71	5.21
Middleton, Kyle	R-R	6-4	232	6-13-80	10	9	5.31	28	28	1	0	171	218	118	101	22	37	109	.310	.303	.314	5.73	1.94
Nunez, Leo	R-R	6-1	160	8-14-83	1	0	0.69	12	0	0	4	13	8	3	1	1	2	14	.170	.143	.192	9.69	1.38
Perry, Brandon	L-L	5-11	204	9-27-84	0	1	5.40	1	0	0	0	2	3	2	1	0	2	0	.429	1.000	.333	0.00	10.80
Snyder, Kyle	B-R	6-8	220	9-9-77	1	0	5.40	1	1	0	0	5	5	3	3	1	1	1	.263	.214	.400	1.80	1.80
Sonnier, Shawn	R-R	6-5	210	7-5-76	3	0	2.18	18	0	0	5	33	26	9	8	0	12	46	.220	.324	.173	12.55	3.27
Stodolka, Mike	L-L	6-2	210	9-24-81	4	11	5.92	25	24	0	0	125	153	93	82	12	36	66	.301	.259	.314	4.76	2.60
Wilkerson, Wes	R-R	6-4	216	9-11-76	1	4	6.53	14	3	0	0	21	34	26	15	0	7	14	.351	.444	.295	6.10	3.05

FIELDING

Catcher	PCT	G	PO	A	E	DP	PB
Draper	.996	40	230	20	1	2	6
Maduro	.923	2	10	2	1	0	0
Price	.944	4	15	2	1	0	1
Tupman	.986	102	648	82	10	12	7

First Base	PCT	G	PO	A	E	DP
Gomez	1.000	3	21	1	0	3
Groves	1.000	4	23	1	0	0
Huber	.981	66	591	36	12	49
King	.988	9	80	5	1	6
Pressley	.976	63	527	40	14	49

Second Base	PCT	G	PO	A	E	DP
Aviles	.943	12	19	31	3	6
Gomez	.950	22	40	56	5	12
Gotay	1.000	27	50	72	0	14
Groves	.981	45	86	120	4	18
Keim	.980	11	20	28	1	8
Murphy	.988	30	48	110	2	18

Third Base	PCT	G	PO	A	E	DP
Aviles	.922	20	17	42	5	7
Gomez	.889	5	0	8	1	1
Groves	.846	10	3	8	2	1
Keim	.867	4	6	7	2	0
King	.951	107	60	195	13	14
Maier	1.000	1	0	3	0	0

Shortstop	PCT	G	PO	A	E	DP
Aviles	.934	102	171	295	33	62
Blanco	1.000	9	9	29	0	2
Falu	.923	6	7	17	2	4
Groves	.972	7	13	22	1	2
Murphy	.964	20	34	72	4	13

Outfield	PCT	G	PO	A	E	DP
Aldridge	.980	77	148	1	3	0
Butler	.914	26	31	1	3	0
Costa	.975	72	117	2	3	1
Diaz	1.000	5	11	1	0	0
Draper	.957	17	20	2	1	2
Groves	1.000	13	22	1	0	0
Maier	.984	79	176	4	3	1
Ruan	1.000	67	141	8	0	2
Stocker	.988	75	166	3	2	0

HIGH DESERT MAVERICKS — High Class A

CALIFORNIA LEAGUE

BATTING	B-T	HT	WT	DOB	AVG	vLH	vRH	G	AB	R	H	2B	3B	HR	RBI	BB	HBP	SH	SF	SO	SB	CS	SLG	OBP
Batista, Alexander	R-R	5-11	196	8-11-83	.202	.212	.196	25	89	9	18	5	0	1	10	4	2	0	0	28	1	0	.292	.253
Blanco, Andres	B-R	5-10	180	4-11-84	.500	.000	.556	3	10	0	5	1	0	0	3	0	0	0	0	1	1	2	.600	.500
Butler, Billy	R-R	6-2	225	4-18-86	.348	.429	.312	92	379	70	132	30	2	25	91	42	6	0	3	80	0	0	.636	.419
Donachie, Adam	R-R	6-1	200	3-3-84	.294	.449	.237	95	347	64	102	24	0	12	48	43	2	2	0	78	1	0	.467	.375
Draper, John	R-R	6-2	191	8-11-80	.333	.429	.250	5	15	3	5	2	2	0	0	3	0	0	0	2	0	0	.733	.444
Espino, Damaso	R-R	6-0	165	5-8-83	.231	.290	.200	25	91	10	21	1	0	1	12	9	1	1	1	8	1	0	.275	.304
Everett, Brady	R-R	6-0	205	7-8-83	.278	.667	.200	6	18	3	5	1	0	0	2	2	0	0	2	2	0	0	.333	.318
Gaffney, Michael	R-R	6-1	190	11-11-81	.299	.387	.265	44	134	14	40	6	1	0	8	8	2	4	0	17	1	3	.358	.347
Gonzalez, Luis	R-R	6-2	208	11-8-82	.286	.333	.273	6	14	5	4	1	0	0	1	5	0	0	0	5	0	0	.357	.474
Kaaihue, Kila	L-R	6-3	233	3-29-84	.304	.366	.281	132	493	84	150	31	2	20	90	97	12	0	3	97	2	1	.497	.428
Keim, Adam	R-R	5-11	196	1-5-81	.282	.238	.296	85	351	59	99	19	1	26	68	20	1	1	1	73	0	0	.564	.322
Lubanski, Chris	L-L	6-3	206	3-24-85	.301	.277	.311	126	531	91	160	38	6	28	116	38	5	0	7	131	14	1	.554	.349
Maestrales, Pete	B-R	5-11	190	7-4-79	.333	.326	.335	54	225	55	75	18	3	7	33	47	1	0	2	41	6	3	.533	.447
Maier, Mitch	L-R	6-2	200	6-30-82	.336	.455	.283	50	211	42	71	26	1	8	32	12	1	0	3	43	6	1	.583	.370
Moye, Alan	R-R	6-2	200	10-8-82	.309	.243	.329	76	320	68	99	15	4	20	64	20	2	0	1	97	10	6	.569	.353
Powell, Brandon	L-R	6-0	191	8-15-80	.287	.277	.290	106	397	74	114	29	3	18	69	28	4	0	2	97	6	4	.511	.339
Price, Jared	R-R	6-1	220	3-18-82	.318	.286	.326	30	107	21	34	10	0	11	32	4	1	0	0	31	1	0	.720	.348
Salazar, Darwinson	R-R	6-3	208	12-12-82	.182	.286	.162	14	44	5	8	2	0	1	3	11	0	0	0	18	0	0	.295	.345
Sanchez, Angel	R-R	6-2	180	9-20-83	.313	.340	.304	133	585	102	183	33	4	5	70	39	3	7	5	54	10	5	.409	.356
Sevilla, Walter	R-R	5-8	180	8-24-81	.248	.361	.185	68	234	40	58	15	0	6	27	32	1	1	2	42	3	4	.389	.338
Stephens, Bernard	L-R	6-0	208	11-11-79	.303	.276	.314	120	485	96	147	33	6	14	67	43	3	2	2	102	12	3	.482	.362
Stocker, Mel	B-R	5-9	156	8-15-80	.231	.200	.250	7	26	3	6	0	1	0	4	1	0	0	0	3	2	1	.308	.259

PITCHING	B-T	HT	WT	DOB	W	L	ERA	G	GS	CG	SV	IP	H	R	ER	HR	BB	SO	AVG	vLH	vRH	K/9	BB/9
Ackerman, Eric	L-L	6-0	199	10-19-79	3	2	5.54	31	0	0	1	50	61	36	31	7	13	30	.296	.271	.318	5.36	2.32
Atencio, Greg	R-R	6-2	191	7-15-81	3	1	5.65	19	1	0	0	37	43	28	23	4	24	36	.287	.355	.239	8.84	5.89
Blackwell, Chad	R-R	5-9	159	1-7-83	0	0	13.50	1	0	0	0	2	4	3	3	1	0	5	.400	.500	.333	22.50	0.00
Braun, Ryan	R-R	6-1	215	7-29-80	1	0	4.50	2	0	0	0	4	3	2	2	0	2	6	.214	.143	.286	13.50	4.50
Bray, Steve	R-R	6-1	193	12-22-80	3	1	4.93	26	0	0	9	35	37	21	19	9	8	39	.268	.169	.342	10.13	2.08
Buckner, Billy	R-R	6-2	210	8-27-83	5	6	5.36	17	17	0	0	94	105	65	56	10	46	92	.285	.302	.270	8.81	4.40
Chamberlain, Stephen	L-R	6-2	216	7-20-80	3	0	7.61	44	0	0	0	76	102	71	64	15	36	41	.323	.277	.360	4.88	4.28
Coughlin, Chris	R-R	5-11	180	9-30-80	5	11	7.31	29	11	0	0	85	133	88	69	21	29	52	.358	.458	.266	5.51	3.07
DeHoyos, Gabe	R-R	5-11	226	4-14-80	2	0	0.93	7	0	0	2	10	10	1	1	0	2	7	.286	.222	.353	6.52	1.86
Demaria, Chris	B-R	6-3	210	9-28-80	4	2	2.23	48	0	0	19	61	57	19	15	8	10	73	.247	.185	.301	10.83	1.48
Endicott, Drew	R-R	6-2	181	3-30-81	2	3	6.40	42	1	0	1	83	117	71	59	12	30	37	.334	.352	.319	4.01	3.25
Gragg, John	L-L	5-8	170	5-9-81	13	5	4.36	27	27	1	0	149	178	92	72	18	47	95	.296	.332	.278	5.75	2.85
Green, Patrick	L-R	6-2	193	2-13-82	3	4	4.33	7	7	0	0	44	43	27	21	4	8	40	.254	.276	.237	8.24	1.65
Herrera, Cesar	R-R	6-1	193	10-5-81	7	7	7.27	31	23	0	0	125	177	118	101	21	45	81	.329	.361	.301	5.83	3.24
Howell, J.P.	L-L	6-0	175	4-25-83	3	1	1.96	8	8	0	0	46	33	16	10	2	24	48	.202	.220	.192	9.39	4.70
Hughes, Dusty	L-L	5-10	187	6-29-82	5	7	5.67	19	19	0	0	92	119	74	58	13	45	87	.319	.362	.286	8.51	4.40
Kaanoi, Kahi	L-R	5-11	215	8-19-82	4	8	5.91	18	15	0	0	85	120	71	56	10	42	37	.340	.358	.325	3.90	4.43
Lowery, Devon	L-R	6-1	195	3-24-83	6	3	3.84	14	11	0	0	70	70	34	30	8	25	50	.266	.308	.226	6.40	3.20
Moore, Nate	R-R	6-3	225	6-14-83	2	4	4.99	40	0	0	0	58	76	36	32	5	29	33	.322	.292	.350	5.15	4.53
Nunez, Leo	R-R	6-1	160	8-14-83	0	0	9.00	8	0	0	0	13	23	15	13	2	3	15	.377	.458	.324	10.38	2.08
Steffek, Brian	R-R	6-2	199	3-2-78	1	0	5.60	15	0	0	3	18	20	11	11	3	9	18	.274	.273	.275	9.17	4.58

FIELDING

Catcher	PCT	G	PO	A	E	DP	PB
Donachie	.986	92	620	67	10	6	6
Draper	.923	1	12	0	1	0	0
Espino	.979	25	170	15	4	2	10
Everett	1.000	5	29	3	0	0	1
Gonzalez	.960	6	23	1	1	0	0
Price	1.000	17	77	12	0	0	3

First Base	PCT	G	PO	A	E	DP
Gaffney	1.000	10	79	8	0	16
Kaaihue	.986	126	1220	95	19	136
Keim	1.000	1	19	0	0	0
Price	.983	5	46	11	1	8

Second Base	PCT	G	PO	A	E	DP
Blanco	1.000	3	3	7	0	2
Gaffney	.969	5	12	19	1	3
Keim	.978	46	75	150	5	25
Maestrales	.970	37	75	119	6	29
Powell	.930	11	15	25	3	5
Sevilla	.967	45	79	159	8	41

Third Base	PCT	G	PO	A	E	DP
Butler	.842	41	13	83	18	5
Gaffney	.902	22	10	45	6	4
Keim	.971	30	16	51	2	8
Maestrales	.857	2	3	3	1	2
Powell	.922	39	16	79	8	11
Sevilla	.953	14	10	31	2	2

Shortstop	PCT	G	PO	A	E	DP
Gaffney	1.000	5	6	10	0	4
Keim	.889	2	5	3	1	2
Sanchez	.964	133	253	451	26	110
Sevilla	.929	3	4	9	1	0

Outfield	PCT	G	PO	A	E	DP
Batista	.960	18	22	2	1	0
Butler	.932	34	38	3	3	0
Lubanski	.967	121	222	12	8	6
Maestrales	1.000	8	7	0	0	0
Maier	.971	48	93	6	3	2
Moye	.934	68	110	3	8	1
Powell	1.000	2	4	1	0	0
Salazar	.909	11	9	1	1	1
Stephens	.952	108	186	14	10	1
Stocker	1.000	7	11	0	0	0

BURLINGTON BEES — Low Class A

MIDWEST LEAGUE

BATTING	B-T	HT	WT	DOB	AVG	vLH	vRH	G	AB	R	H	2B	3B	HR	RBI	BB	HBP	SH	SF	SO	SB	CS	SLG	OBP
Brown, Rusty	R-R	6-3	210	8-19-81	.267	.235	.277	124	445	54	119	29	0	16	70	39	3	0	7	95	1	2	.440	.326
Cure, Cody	R-R	5-9	180	8-3-82	.241	.200	.252	55	191	15	46	9	2	1	17	16	1	1	0	38	11	2	.325	.303
Del Rosario, Felipe	R-R	6-0	204	9-8-82	.256	.200	.270	26	78	9	20	6	0	2	9	10	0	0	0	19	1	2	.410	.341
Ellis, Jared	R-R	6-2	215	3-27-82	.158	.154	.160	14	38	4	6	2	0	0	3	5	0	1	0	21	2	0	.211	.256
Espino, Damaso	R-R	6-0	165	5-8-83	.263	.250	.267	74	278	26	73	6	0	0	41	27	3	0	5	27	3	1	.284	.329
Falu, Irving	B-R	6-0	173	6-6-83	.254	.252	.254	119	445	71	113	20	5	1	28	61	3	9	7	39	34	15	.328	.343
Grana, Robert	R-R	6-3	208	8-4-83	.168	.188	.165	42	113	11	19	1	0	0	8	11	0	4	1	29	1	2	.177	.240
Lisson, Mario	R-R	6-2	193	5-31-84	.250	.222	.256	78	260	57	65	15	4	6	36	53	6	3	2	68	23	4	.408	.386
Lucas, Ed	R-R	6-4	205	5-21-82	.292	.348	.277	113	425	52	124	12	4	1	36	40	2	7	0	67	29	10	.346	.355
Maduro, Jorge	R-R	6-2	220	3-11-81	.118	.000	.154	7	17	2	2	1	0	0	1	1	0	0	0	2	0	0	.176	.167
Maestrales, Pete	B-R	5-11	190	7-4-79	.316	.455	.283	16	57	11	18	3	1	0	6	10	2	0	0	9	3	1	.404	.435
Mc Fall, Brian	R-R	6-3	215	3-17-84	.234	.198	.244	103	364	53	85	17	1	14	58	31	18	1	7	113	17	3	.401	.319

BATTING	B-T	HT	WT	DOB	AVG	vLH	vRH	G	AB	R	H	2B	3B	HR	RBI	BB	HBP	SH	SF	SO	SB	CS	SLG	OBP
Moye, Alan	R-R	6-2	200	10-8-82	.259	.222	.267	46	162	26	42	8	1	4	32	11	3	2	3	57	10	5	.395	.313
Norman, Derek	R-R	5-11	195	2-21-82	.271	.235	.278	30	96	13	26	4	0	0	9	13	0	0	0	12	1	5	.313	.358
Perez, Gary	R-R	5-11	165	8-28-83	.252	.231	.258	29	115	10	29	6	0	4	16	7	1	0	0	25	4	1	.409	.301
Salazar, Darwinson	R-R	6-3	208	12-12-82	.167	.079	.188	66	198	23	33	6	0	2	16	22	6	5	0	71	5	5	.227	.270
Solis, Eddie	R-R	5-11	200	9-19-84	.204	.121	.224	107	343	39	70	19	0	9	47	52	11	3	2	89	1	1	.338	.326
Springer, Kenard	R-R	5-11	209	9-18-83	.233	.244	.230	115	387	44	90	12	0	3	30	25	17	3	2	53	20	8	.287	.306
Valentin, Geraldo	R-R	6-0	184	9-8-82	.235	.207	.243	121	477	58	112	19	5	3	43	38	10	3	0	55	10	14	.314	.305
Vega, Miguel	R-R	6-3	224	7-31-85	.276	.292	.273	38	134	13	37	8	2	3	14	6	1	0	1	42	2	1	.433	.310

PITCHING	B-T	HT	WT	DOB	W	L	ERA	G	GS	CG	SV	IP	H	R	ER	HR	BB	SO	AVG	vLH	vRH	K/9	BB/9
Atencio, Greg	R-R	6-2	191	7-15-81	5	2	4.15	17	2	0	0	43	33	22	20	0	18	40	.209	.174	.236	8.31	3.74
Begnaud, Rusty	R-R	6-2	194	12-19-80	0	1	4.28	15	1	0	1	27	33	14	13	4	12	10	.297	.362	.250	3.29	3.95
Blackwell, Chad	R-R	5-9	159	1-7-83	7	4	2.23	48	0	0	14	69	62	21	17	4	27	74	.241	.247	.238	9.70	3.54
Buckner, Billy	R-R	6-2	210	8-27-83	3	7	3.88	11	11	0	0	60	66	36	26	9	17	60	.268	.280	.259	8.95	2.54
Campbell, Matt	L-L	6-2	170	12-27-82	1	5	4.66	13	12	0	0	64	74	41	33	3	37	48	.291	.333	.282	6.79	5.23
Carlson, Zane	R-R	5-10	180	8-11-80	2	1	5.82	13	0	0	0	22	28	18	14	0	15	12	.315	.306	.321	4.98	6.23
Christensen, Daniel	L-L	6-1	205	8-10-83	3	7	3.54	26	21	0	1	109	100	54	43	9	53	110	.238	.250	.235	9.05	4.36
Cota, Luis	R-R	6-0	193	8-19-85	5	8	4.01	26	26	0	0	148	143	75	66	10	63	137	.253	.255	.251	8.33	3.83
Crist, Kyle	R-R	6-3	194	6-27-83	9	3	4.73	16	10	1	0	70	73	39	37	3	22	44	.267	.310	.243	5.63	2.82
Damico, Yovany	R-R	5-11	223	8-18-84	2	3	4.66	35	0	0	3	75	77	47	39	5	25	72	.259	.291	.239	8.60	2.99
DeHoyos, Gabe	R-R	5-11	226	4-14-80	4	1	1.56	28	3	0	3	69	51	24	12	2	27	81	.202	.220	.193	10.51	3.50
Dossett, Dustin	R-R	6-1	168	4-11-80	1	1	4.07	4	4	0	0	24	27	11	11	0	5	13	.287	.283	.292	4.81	1.85
Green, Patrick	L-R	6-2	193	2-13-82	6	7	4.09	19	18	0	0	103	124	60	47	4	22	60	.303	.308	.300	5.23	1.92
Hicklen, Patrick	R-R	6-4	210	12-30-81	6	8	4.19	25	20	0	0	135	156	82	63	15	52	79	.287	.277	.295	5.25	3.46
Moore, Nate	R-R	6-3	225	6-14-83	0	1	3.94	7	0	0	1	16	20	9	7	1	5	21	.317	.333	.308	11.81	2.81
Oliveros, Rayner	R-R	6-2	180	9-23-85	0	0	6.43	2	1	0	0	7	12	5	5	0	3	2	.414	.333	.500	2.57	3.86
Rowe, Adam	L-L	6-0	192	1-24-82	6	6	4.78	45	0	0	7	75	87	46	40	5	21	62	.292	.269	.302	7.41	2.51
Schambough, Kraig	R-R	6-0	185	1-21-82	2	2	4.32	14	0	0	0	33	28	20	16	1	18	29	.224	.271	.195	7.83	4.86
Sherman, Justin	R-R	6-3	216	12-6-80	3	8	4.90	21	11	0	0	86	96	54	47	6	21	51	.278	.325	.238	5.32	2.19

FIELDING

Catcher	PCT	G	PO	A	E	DP	PB
Del Rosario	.953	16	113	9	6	0	3
Espino	.983	64	422	41	8	3	10
Grana	.990	41	277	24	3	2	3
Maduro	.968	7	53	7	2	0	2
Norman	.990	24	170	21	2	2	8

First Base	PCT	G	PO	A	E	DP
Brown	.981	63	540	37	11	36
Espino	1.000	6	49	3	0	3
Lucas	1.000	14	84	11	0	12
Solis	.990	32	279	16	3	21
Vega	.984	34	286	16	5	33

Second Base	PCT	G	PO	A	E	DP
Falu	.968	56	113	159	9	36
Maestrales	1.000	8	10	18	0	1
Perez	.955	21	37	68	5	12
Solis	1.000	25	66	74	0	25
Valentin	.986	35	53	90	2	10

Third Base	PCT	G	PO	A	E	DP
Espino	.750	2	1	2	1	0
Lisson	.910	62	51	130	18	12
Lucas	.899	53	34	99	15	3
Maestrales	.000	1	0	0	0	0
Solis	.917	26	25	52	7	2
Valentin	.933	4	3	11	1	0

Shortstop	PCT	G	PO	A	E	DP
Falu	.958	62	90	186	12	27
Lisson	.977	7	17	25	1	4
Lucas	.929	38	46	111	12	22
Perez	.805	7	13	20	8	4
Valentin	.923	28	35	73	9	22

Outfield	PCT	G	PO	A	E	DP
Cure	.967	52	114	3	4	1
Ellis	1.000	13	15	0	0	0
Lucas	.846	7	10	1	2	0
Maestrales	1.000	5	7	0	0	0
Mc Fall	.963	97	173	7	7	1
Moye	.975	45	76	2	2	1
Norman	1.000	4	6	2	0	0
Salazar	.962	57	97	3	4	1
Springer	.955	101	171	22	9	4
Valentin	.974	51	106	8	3	1

IDAHO FALLS CHUKARS — Rookie

PIONEER LEAGUE

BATTING	B-T	HT	WT	DOB	AVG	vLH	vRH	G	AB	R	H	2B	3B	HR	RBI	BB	HBP	SH	SF	SO	SB	CS	SLG	OBP
Adkison, Blake	R-R	6-2	225	12-3-80	.274	.412	.197	27	95	15	26	3	0	6	22	8	2	0	2	31	0	0	.495	.336
Barber, Byron	B-R	5-9	185	12-10-82	.304	.381	.282	31	92	20	28	4	0	0	10	12	4	3	0	6	3	2	.348	.407
Colafemina, Josh	R-R	5-8	150	8-25-82	.238	.216	.250	49	151	30	36	8	1	1	17	17	2	5	1	20	12	1	.325	.322
Everett, Brady	R-R	6-0	205	7-8-83	.361	.308	.391	29	108	24	39	8	1	5	21	13	6	0	0	16	0	2	.593	.457
Hayes, Shawn	L-R	6-4	220	11-5-84	.214	.353	.154	17	56	6	12	4	0	0	8	8	0	0	1	21	3	1	.286	.308
Herrera, Brenan	R-R	6-1	180	6-16-82	.254	.342	.214	29	122	25	31	8	1	2	17	14	4	1	0	27	0	0	.385	.350
Howell, Jeff	R-R	6-0	200	4-1-83	.346	.317	.358	39	136	29	47	9	1	1	17	29	0	0	2	36	1	2	.449	.455
Jirschele, Jeremy	R-R	5-9	195	11-14-82	.189	.167	.200	16	53	8	10	0	0	0	4	5	3	0	1	16	0	0	.189	.290
Johnson, Josh	B-R	5-11	170	1-11-86	.240	.114	.287	37	129	20	31	5	4	2	26	25	2	3	1	25	3	6	.388	.369
Larsen, Andrew	R-R	6-0	200	12-14-82	.271	.262	.276	64	229	41	62	6	2	7	31	26	7	2	1	43	10	3	.406	.361
McConnell, Chris	R-R	5-11	170	12-18-85	.331	.372	.312	70	275	56	91	17	8	6	39	31	7	7	7	34	7	6	.516	.403
Peguero, Felix	L-R	6-1	190	7-1-82	.267	.253	.273	64	251	38	67	18	1	6	46	28	7	0	2	79	0	1	.418	.354
Perez, Gary	R-R	5-11	165	8-28-83	.362	.409	.337	36	127	29	46	11	4	2	23	24	3	1	3	33	3	6	.559	.465
Sabatini, Antonio	R-L	6-0	195	4-1-83	.238	.147	.288	51	193	27	46	7	2	2	30	21	3	0	1	72	3	4	.326	.321
Santana, Ethien	L-L	5-11	153	1-25-84	.300	.303	.299	63	240	51	72	8	5	3	29	33	7	5	0	54	20	17	.413	.400
Thibault, Kiel	R-R	6-0	200	3-2-84	.310	.295	.317	41	145	27	45	12	1	9	34	10	9	2	1	26	3	2	.593	.388
Turner, Jase	L-R	6-3	215	2-22-83	.282	.235	.297	56	209	36	59	9	0	12	44	30	5	0	0	73	2	1	.498	.385

PITCHING	B-T	HT	WT	DOB	W	L	ERA	G	GS	CG	SV	IP	H	R	ER	HR	BB	SO	AVG	vLH	vRH	K/9	BB/9
Begnaud, Rusty	R-R	6-2	194	12-19-80	2	4	5.63	12	11	0	1	54	77	46	34	5	17	37	.329	.400	.266	6.13	2.82
Brantley, Brandon	R-R	6-4	225	8-13-82	0	2	7.11	18	7	0	0	51	70	44	40	8	24	47	.333	.352	.320	8.35	4.26
Bulger, Kevin	R-R	6-4	195	2-16-83	0	1	9.53	10	0	0	0	11	15	13	12	0	8	9	.319	.286	.333	7.15	6.35
Carlson, Zane	R-R	5-10	180	8-11-80	0	0	1.00	8	0	0	5	9	6	1	1	0	2	6	.207	.308	.125	6.00	2.00
Cromer, Bennett	R-R	6-3	192	3-26-82	7	3	5.07	16	10	0	0	60	74	45	34	9	13	55	.298	.302	.296	8.20	1.94
Davidson, Phil	R-R	6-4	175	1-3-83	4	2	6.75	9	5	0	0	35	46	27	26	3	14	29	.317	.316	.318	7.53	3.63
DiPietro, Ryan	L-L	6-0	175	7-21-84	1	6	5.63	15	15	0	0	64	72	45	40	8	17	56	.274	.290	.272	7.88	2.39
Eckley, Jacob	L-L	6-2	220	6-27-83	3	2	7.18	21	0	0	3	31	49	31	25	3	8	25	.345	.290	.360	7.18	2.30
Garcia, Eliszer	L-L	6-1	185	6-7-84	2	2	3.45	20	0	0	1	44	41	20	17	1	22	45	.247	.250	.246	9.14	4.47
Goins, Mitch	R-R	6-3	232	1-18-83	0	0	8.72	8	0	0	0	22	35	22	21	4	4	12	.361	.366	.357	4.98	1.66
Harkcom, Cody	R-R	6-1	180	12-15-83	3	5	8.16	16	8	0	2	46	71	46	42	12	16	47	.357	.393	.327	9.13	3.11
Henninger, David	R-R	6-7	210	8-23-83	5	1	3.60	21	0	0	1	60	58	33	24	2	23	64	.258	.178	.311	9.60	3.45
Kalkhof, Adam	L-L	6-6	230	9-4-83	3	2	4.31	19	0	0	1	40	44	21	19	4	12	52	.273	.260	.279	11.80	2.72
Kniginyzky, Matt	L-R	6-3	185	10-5-82	2	5	4.66	21	0	0	5	29	35	22	15	0	13	40	.287	.300	.278	12.41	4.03

PITCHING	B-T	HT	WT	DOB	W	L	ERA	G	GS	CG	SV	IP	H	R	ER	HR	BB	SO	AVG	vLH	vRH	K/9	BB/9
McCleland, Bruce	R-R	6-5	215	12-16-84	0	0	17.18	3	0	0	0	4	7	7	7	1	0	3	.412	.429	.400	7.36	0.00
Nicoll, Chris	R-R	6-2	190	10-30-83	0	3	3.62	7	7	0	0	27	26	14	11	4	9	34	.250	.255	.245	11.20	2.96
Penn, Michael	R-R	6-4	205	4-21-82	0	1	5.06	5	5	0	0	21	23	13	12	2	4	20	.280	.256	.302	8.44	1.69
Santiago, Mario	R-R	6-2	210	12-16-85	0	3	6.61	10	8	0	0	33	39	34	24	3	20	20	.289	.296	.284	5.51	5.51
Schambough, Kraig	R-R	6-0	185	1-21-82	0	0	2.70	7	0	0	0	7	7	2	2	1	3	9	.269	.273	.267	12.15	4.05
Trammell, Travis	R-R	6-5	240	8-19-81	2	0	7.31	15	0	0	0	16	27	16	13	3	3	16	.370	.400	.354	9.00	1.69

GAMES BY POSITION: C—Everett 9, Howell 33, Thibault 35. **1B**—Adkison 20, Everett 8, Herrera 2, Howell 2, Turner 48. **2B**—Colafemina 16, Jirschele 4, Johnson 37, Perez 22. **3B**—Colafemina 20, Hayes 10, Herrera 22, Jirschele 13, Perez 14. **SS**—Colafemina 10, Hayes 3, McConnell 66. **OF**—Barber 30, Larsen 59, Peguero 46, Sabatini 43, Santana 60.

AZL ROYALS — Rookie

ARIZONA LEAGUE

BATTING	B-T	HT	WT	DOB	AVG	vLH	vRH	G	AB	R	H	2B	3B	HR	RBI	BB	HBP	SH	SF	SO	SB	CS	SLG	OBP
Arce, Valentino	R-R	5-11	167	6-7-85	.335	.282	.351	47	170	37	57	10	0	1	21	7	13	1	0	17	7	5	.412	.405
Aughey, Jon	R-R	5-11	190	3-31-83	.133	.000	.160	13	30	8	4	1	0	2	3	7	2	0	0	14	1	0	.367	.333
Avila, Carlos	R-R	5-9	146	5-8-85	.246	.214	.256	17	57	5	14	2	0	1	7	2	1	4	0	16	3	0	.333	.283
Bianchi, Jeff	R-R	6-0	175	10-5-86	.408	.435	.400	28	98	29	40	7	4	6	30	16	3	0	5	22	5	2	.745	.484
Blanco, Andres	B-R	5-10	180	4-11-84	.320	.250	.353	7	25	6	8	1	0	2	9	1	1	1	0	7	1	2	.600	.370
Boudreaux, Ross	R-R	5-11	197	4-30-82	.259	.500	.209	27	81	24	21	7	0	2	13	14	6	0	0	25	1	0	.420	.406
Diaz, Matt	R-R	6-1	205	3-3-78	.462	.667	.400	3	13	2	6	2	0	0	2	0	0	0	0	2	0	1	.615	.462
Dickerson, Joe	L-L	6-1	190	10-3-86	.294	.216	.319	56	214	27	63	12	9	4	40	27	1	0	3	46	9	12	.491	.371
Doscher, Nick	R-R	6-2	205	5-20-87	.146	.100	.158	17	48	13	7	1	0	0	4	15	0	0	0	10	2	0	.167	.349
Duarte, Jose	R-R	5-10	165	3-7-85	.309	.405	.284	47	178	33	55	7	6	3	36	25	0	0	3	32	11	7	.466	.388
Gonzalez, O.D.	R-R	6-1	180	9-12-84	.284	.250	.294	55	197	40	56	5	5	4	31	22	4	0	2	68	17	5	.421	.364
Infante, Jefferson	R-R	5-11	205	10-5-82	.286	.500	.250	16	28	6	8	3	0	2	7	5	2	0	0	12	0	1	.607	.429
Johnson, Josh	B-R	5-11	170	1-11-86	.259	.167	.284	28	112	24	29	8	2	1	16	23	1	2	1	24	7	1	.393	.387
Lopez, Pedro	B-R	5-10	165	10-31-86	.277	.270	.279	46	166	28	46	6	3	0	27	12	3	2	1	39	4	6	.349	.335
Lowen, J.P.	L-R	6-3	215	3-27-84	.152	.000	.194	18	46	4	7	2	0	0	3	3	1	0	0	18	0	2	.196	.220
Marrero, Oscar	B-R	6-0	177	1-26-87	.246	.500	.204	21	57	6	14	0	0	0	5	6	0	0	0	11	0	0	.246	.317
Matos, Willie	R-R	6-2	202	4-23-84	.243	.200	.257	45	148	18	36	7	1	2	18	14	0	2	2	54	0	3	.345	.305
Morel, Alvi	L-L	6-0	153	8-28-84	.313	.179	.350	46	131	23	41	6	6	2	23	15	1	0	1	32	15	4	.496	.385
Peralta, Felix	R-R	6-0	175	9-30-85	.281	.242	.295	35	128	21	36	6	2	3	25	8	5	0	2	33	1	2	.430	.343
Saavedra, Jonathan	L-L	5-9	180	10-1-86	.167	.000	.167	5	6	2	1	0	1	0	0	4	0	0	0	1	0	1	.500	.500

PITCHING	B-T	HT	WT	DOB	W	L	ERA	G	GS	CG	SV	IP	H	R	ER	HR	BB	SO	AVG	vLH	vRH	K/9	BB/9
Abreu, Juan	R-R	6-0	167	4-8-85	2	5	6.88	14	13	0	0	52	72	49	40	4	27	52	.327	.294	.342	8.94	4.64
Barrera, Henry	R-R	6-0	205	11-25-85	1	1	4.73	19	0	0	6	27	33	15	14	1	9	23	.289	.286	.291	7.76	3.04
Coffey, Drew	L-L	6-0	205	11-2-85	0	0	8.82	12	0	0	0	16	28	17	16	0	16	16	.400	.429	.397	8.82	8.82
Davidson, Phil	R-R	6-4	175	1-3-83	3	1	2.40	9	3	0	1	30	22	10	8	0	11	29	.206	.200	.208	8.70	3.30
De la Vara, Gilbert	L-L	5-11	160	10-4-84	4	1	2.33	16	1	0	3	39	31	10	10	2	13	43	.226	.171	.245	10.01	3.03
Fisher, Brent	L-L	6-2	190	8-6-87	5	2	3.04	13	8	0	1	50	48	20	17	2	13	69	.249	.171	.266	12.34	2.32
Garrett, Troy	R-R	6-5	220	8-18-81	2	2	5.01	13	0	0	1	23	25	14	13	2	7	21	.284	.222	.311	8.10	2.70
Morales, Angelo	R-R	6-1	192	5-2-86	3	2	4.26	10	10	0	0	44	53	29	21	1	6	32	.294	.351	.255	6.50	1.22
Oliveros, Rayner	R-R	6-2	180	9-23-85	7	1	2.39	14	14	0	0	75	73	26	20	1	5	48	.253	.290	.242	5.73	0.60
Pena, Matt	L-L	5-11	155	7-30-82	1	1	4.55	13	0	0	4	32	39	19	16	0	10	20	.298	.176	.316	5.68	2.84
Raglione, Paul	R-R	6-5	195	1-15-87	3	4	5.94	13	7	0	1	47	66	40	31	4	18	37	.332	.292	.351	7.09	3.45
Rice, Tim	L-L	6-1	185	8-5-83	0	0	5.25	7	0	0	0	12	11	8	7	0	7	14	.250	.833	.158	10.50	5.25
Santiago, Mario	R-R	6-2	210	12-16-85	0	1	18.00	2	0	0	0	2	6	4	4	0	0	1	.545	.500	.600	4.50	0.00
Sokoll, John	L-L	6-6	220	11-9-84	1	0	4.63	13	0	0	1	23	24	15	12	1	8	23	.253	.304	.236	8.87	3.09
Trifolio, Nelson	R-R	6-0	160	1-30-85	2	1	3.32	12	0	0	0	22	19	8	8	1	12	17	.247	.208	.264	7.06	4.98

GAMES BY POSITION: C—Boudreaux 25, Doscher 17, Infante 16, Lowen 14. **1B**—Marrero 20, Matos 44. **2B**—Arce 23, Avila 13, Johnson 24, Lopez 3, Lowen 1. **3B**—Arce 26, Aughey 13, Lopez 25. **SS**—Arce 2, Avila 5, Bianchi 26, Blanco 6, Johnson 6, Lopez 20, Morel 1. **OF**—Diaz 2, Dickerson 51, Duarte 45, Gonzalez 51, Morel 27, Peralta 6.

LOS ANGELES ANGELS

BY BILL SHAIKIN

If ever owner Arte Moreno's vision for the Angels could be distilled into one evening, this was the one. The Angels playing the Yankees, another packed house in Anaheim, winner advances to the American League Championship Series, loser goes home for the winter.

The Angels started Bartolo Colon, the ace upon whom Moreno lavished $51 million. Colon won 21 games in 2005, the Angels' first 20-game winner since Nolan Ryan in 1974.

In the second inning, pain shot through Colon's pitching shoulder. He was done for the evening, but the Angels were not. From the bullpen emerged 22-year-old rookie Ervin Santana, who pitched into the seventh inning for the victory that extended the season.

By blending premium free agents such as Colon with minor league products such as Santana, Moreno believes he can field a perennial contender on a $100 million payroll and continue to attract sellout crowds; the Angels sold a record 3.4 million tickets in 2005. If rookies making small salaries can fill a few positions, that clears millions to fill other positions via free agency.

On that score, the results were mixed in 2005. The Angels did not bid to retain closer Troy Percival and third baseman Troy Glaus, replacing them with youngsters Francisco Rodriguez and Dallas McPherson. In his first season as closer, Rodriguez recorded 45 saves, one shy of Bryan Harvey's club record. McPherson hit eight home runs and missed 101 games because of injury.

A year that started in controversy—with Moreno adding "Los Angeles" to the team name and the city of Anaheim filing suit in response—ended in the first back-to-back division championships in club history. The Angels spent all but 12 days in first place and won 95 games, same as the Yankees and Red Sox. They held off another furious second-half charge by the Athletics to end up winning the AL West by seven games.

The Angels' quest for their second World Series victory was derailed in a strange ALCS by the White Sox. Things started auspiciously enough for the Angels, who took Game One of the series behind six strong innings from righthander Paul Byrd on short rest. They were poised to take a 2-0 lead heading to Anaheim, but Game Two took a bizarre twist in the ninth inning, tied 1-1. White Sox catcher A.J. Pierzynski ran to first base after swinging at a pitch near the dirt for strike three, and Angels catcher Josh Paul did not make a throw to first base, thinking he had caught the third strike and the inning was over. Two batters later, Joe Crede drove him home to give Chicago the game and the momentum. The White Sox won the next three games rather handily thanks to their rock-solid starting pitching and the Angels' struggling bats.

But there were plenty of reasons for the Angels to feel good about 2005. Right fielder Vladimir Guerrero might be remembered for his 1-for-20 horror show in the ALCS, but he hit .317-32-108 during the regular season, ranking in the league's top 10 in all three triple crown categories. Chone Figgins played six positions, hit .290-8-57 as the leadoff man and led the majors with 62 stolen bases. Washburn (3.20), John Lackey (3.40) and Colon (3.48) all ranked in the top 10 in ERA, and Lackey ranked third in strikeouts, behind Johan Santana and Randy Johnson.

The prospects in the pipeline include shortstop Brandon Wood, who led the minor leagues in home runs and hit .321-43-115 at Class A Rancho Cucamonga; and second baseman Howie Kendrick, who hit .384-12-47 at Rancho Cucamonga and .342-7-42 at Double-A Arkansas.

The organization did celebrate one minor league championship, in the Rookie-level Pioneer League, for the second consecutive season. Tom Kotchman—Casey's father—managed the Orem Owlz to victory, in the first summer after moving from Provo. No other Angels affiliate made the postseason.

PLAYERS OF THE YEAR

MAJOR LEAGUE: Vladimir Guerrero, of

While many Angels struggled with injuries and prolonged offensive slumps in 2005, Guerrero did what he always does, providing the punch in the middle of the American League West champs' lineup. He followed up his 2004 MVP performance by leading his team in the triple crown categories.

MINOR LEAGUE: Brandon Wood, ss

STEVE MOORE

Wood, a first-round pick in 2003, had a season for the ages at high Class A Rancho Cucamonga in 2005. After collecting a pair of doubles and a triple in a four-game stint at Triple-A Salt Lake at the end of the year, Wood became the first minor leaguer in a half century to exceed 100 extra-base hits in a season.

ORGANIZATION LEADERS

BATTING

*AVG	Kendrick, Howie, Arkansas/Rancho Cucamonga	.367
R	Wood, Brandon, Rancho Cucamonga/Salt Lake	110
H	Wood, Brandon, Rancho Cucamonga/Salt Lake	178
TB	Wood, Brandon, Rancho Cucamonga/Salt Lake	370
2B	Wood, Brandon, Rancho Cucamonga/Salt Lake	53
3B	Prieto, Chris, Salt Lake	12
HR	Wood, Brandon, Rancho Cucamonga/Salt Lake	43
RBI	Wood, Brandon, Rancho Cucamonga/Salt Lake	116
BB	Napoli, Mike, Arkansas	88
SO	Napoli, Mike, Arkansas	140
SB	Aybar, Erick, Arkansas	49
	Casilla, Alexi, Arkansas/Cedar Rapids/Salt Lake	49
*OBP	Prieto, Chris, Salt Lake	.418
*SLG	Wood, Brandon, Rancho Cucamonga/Salt Lake	.667

PITCHING

W	Davidson, Daniel, Arkansas	13
L	Hunter, Chris, Rancho Cucamonga/Salt Lake	10
	Rodriguez, Fernando, Cedar Rapids	10
	Torres, Joe, Cedar Rapids/Rancho Cucamonga	10
#ERA	Lee, Corey, Salt Lake	2.27
G	Austen, David, Arkansas/Rancho Cucamonga	56
	Wilhite, Matt, Arkansas	56
CG	Rodriguez, Fernando, Cedar Rapids	4
SV	Zimmermann, Bob, Rancho Cucamonga	17
IP	Saunders, Joe, Arkansas/Salt Lake	161
BB	Torres, Joe, Cedar Rapids/Rancho Cucamonga	92
SO	Holcomb, James, Rancho Cucamonga	128
	Rodriguez, Fernando, Cedar Rapids	128

*Minimum 250 at-bats. #Minimum 75 innings.

LOS ANGELES ANGELS

Manager: Mike Scioscia.

2005 Record: 95-67, .586 (1st, AL West).

BATTING	B-T	HT	WT	DOB	AVG	vLH	vRH	G	AB	R	H	2B	3B	HR	RBI	BB	HBP	SH	SF	SO	SB	CS	SLG	OBP
Anderson, Garret	L-L	6-3	225	6-30-72	.283	.330	.261	142	575	68	163	34	1	17	96	23	0	0	5	84	1	1	.435	.308
Cabrera, Orlando	R-R	5-9	180	11-2-74	.257	.242	.264	141	540	70	139	28	3	8	57	38	3	4	2	50	21	2	.365	.309
DaVanon, Jeff	B-R	6-0	200	12-8-73	.231	.393	.208	108	225	42	52	10	1	2	15	39	2	3	2	44	11	6	.311	.347
Erstad, Darin	L-L	6-2	215	6-4-74	.273	.232	.289	153	609	86	166	33	3	7	66	47	1	4	2	109	10	3	.371	.325
Figgins, Chone	B-R	5-7	180	1-22-78	.290	.244	.313	158	642	113	186	25	10	8	57	64	0	9	5	101	62	17	.397	.352
Finley, Steve	L-L	6-2	195	3-12-65	.222	.271	.201	112	406	41	90	20	3	12	54	26	3	1	4	71	8	4	.374	.271
Guerrero, Vladimir	R-R	6-3	225	2-9-76	.317	.313	.319	141	520	95	165	29	2	32	108	61	8	0	5	48	13	1	.565	.394
Izturis, Maicer	B-R	5-8	150	9-12-80	.246	.191	.264	77	191	18	47	8	4	1	15	17	0	1	1	21	9	3	.346	.306
Kennedy, Adam	L-R	6-1	185	1-10-76	.300	.296	.302	129	416	49	125	23	0	2	37	29	7	5	3	64	19	4	.370	.354
Kotchman, Casey	L-L	6-3	215	2-22-83	.278	.250	.286	47	126	16	35	5	0	7	22	15	0	1	1	18	1	1	.484	.352
Mathis, Jeff	R-R	6-0	180	3-31-83	.333	.000	.333	5	3	1	1	0	0	0	0	0	0	0	0	1	0	0	.333	.333
Matranga, Dave	R-R	6-0	185	1-8-77	.000	.000	.000	1	1	0	0	0	0	0	0	0	0	0	0	0	0	0	.000	.000
McPherson, Dallas	L-R	6-4	230	7-23-80	.244	.196	.258	61	205	29	50	14	2	8	26	14	1	0	0	64	3	3	.449	.295
Merloni, Lou	R-R	5-10	200	4-6-71	.000	.000	.000	5	5	1	0	0	0	0	1	1	0	0	1	2	0	0	.000	.143
Molina, Bengie	R-R	5-11	225	7-20-74	.295	.393	.253	119	410	45	121	17	0	15	69	27	1	5	6	41	0	2	.446	.336
Molina, Jose	R-R	6-2	220	6-3-75	.228	.306	.189	75	184	14	42	4	0	6	25	13	2	4	0	41	2	0	.348	.286
Paul, Josh	R-R	6-1	220	5-19-75	.189	.143	.200	34	37	4	7	1	0	2	4	2	0	1	0	9	0	0	.378	.231
Pride, Curtis	L-R	6-0	210	12-17-68	.091	.000	.100	11	11	2	1	1	0	0	0	0	0	0	0	4	0	0	.182	.091
Prieto, Chris	L-L	5-11	185	8-24-72	.000	.000	.000	2	2	0	0	0	0	0	0	0	0	1	0	0	0	0	.000	.000
Quinlan, Robb	R-R	6-1	200	3-17-77	.231	.289	.137	54	134	17	31	8	0	5	14	7	1	0	1	26	0	1	.403	.273
Rivera, Juan	R-R	6-2	205	7-3-78	.271	.252	.284	106	350	46	95	17	1	15	59	23	0	2	1	44	1	9	.454	.316
Sorensen, Zach	B-R	6-0	190	1-3-77	.167	.167	.167	12	12	3	2	1	0	0	0	0	0	1	0	2	0	0	.250	.167

PITCHING	B-T	HT	WT	DOB	W	L	ERA	G	GS	CG	SV	IP	H	R	ER	HR	BB	SO	AVG	vLH	vRH	K/9	BB/9
Bootcheck, Chris	R-R	6-5	200	10-24-78	0	1	3.38	5	2	0	1	19	19	7	7	1	4	8	.257	.273	.244	3.86	1.93
Byrd, Paul	R-R	6-1	190	12-3-70	12	11	3.74	31	31	2	0	204	216	95	85	22	28	102	.272	.306	.234	4.49	1.23
Christiansen, Jason	R-L	6-5	230	9-21-69	0	0	2.45	12	0	0	0	4	7	1	1	0	2	4	.389	.462	.200	9.82	4.91
Colon, Bartolo	R-R	5-11	250	5-24-73	21	8	3.48	33	33	2	0	223	215	93	86	26	43	157	.254	.250	.258	6.35	1.74
Donnelly, Brendan	R-R	6-3	240	7-4-71	9	3	3.72	65	0	0	0	65	60	30	27	9	19	53	.244	.213	.274	7.30	2.62
Escobar, Kelvim	R-R	6-1	230	4-11-76	3	2	3.02	16	7	0	1	60	45	21	20	4	21	63	.207	.278	.138	9.50	3.17
Gregg, Kevin	R-R	6-6	235	6-20-78	1	2	5.04	33	2	0	0	64	70	37	36	8	29	52	.273	.267	.279	7.27	4.06
Jones, Greg	R-R	6-2	195	11-15-76	0	0	6.75	6	0	0	0	5	7	4	4	2	2	6	.318	.444	.231	10.13	3.38
Lackey, John	R-R	6-6	235	10-23-78	14	5	3.44	33	33	1	0	209	208	85	80	13	71	199	.258	.274	.241	8.57	3.06
Peralta, Joel	R-R	5-11	170	3-23-76	1	0	3.89	28	0	0	0	35	28	15	15	6	14	30	.219	.273	.178	7.79	3.63
Prinz, Bret	R-R	6-2	215	6-15-77	0	1	3.00	3	0	0	0	3	4	1	1	1	1	1	.308	.500	.143	3.00	3.00
Rodriguez, Francisco	R-R	6-0	180	1-7-82	2	5	2.67	66	0	0	45	67	45	20	20	7	32	91	.184	.213	.153	12.16	4.28
Santana, Ervin	R-R	6-2	160	1-10-83	12	8	4.65	23	23	1	0	134	139	73	69	17	47	99	.266	.261	.271	6.67	3.16
Saunders, Joe	L-L	6-3	210	6-16-81	0	0	7.71	2	2	0	0	9	10	8	8	3	4	4	.270	.417	.200	3.86	3.86
Shields, Scot	R-R	6-1	170	7-22-75	10	11	2.75	78	0	0	7	92	66	33	28	5	37	98	.201	.199	.203	9.62	3.63
Washburn, Jarrod	L-L	6-1	195	8-13-74	8	8	3.20	29	29	1	0	177	184	66	63	19	51	94	.274	.266	.276	4.77	2.59
Woods, Jake	L-L	6-1	190	9-3-81	1	1	4.55	28	0	0	0	28	30	18	14	7	8	20	.270	.229	.302	6.51	2.60
Yan, Esteban	R-R	6-4	255	6-22-75	1	1	4.59	49	0	0	0	67	66	36	34	8	30	45	.258	.252	.264	6.08	4.05

FIELDING

Catcher	PCT	G	PO	A	E	DP	PB
B. Molina	.996	105	641	47	3	5	10
J. Molina	.993	65	408	41	3	6	3
Mathis	1.000	3	4	0	0	0	0
Paul	.989	29	84	4	1	0	0

First Base	PCT	G	PO	A	E	DP
Erstad	.997	147	1218	79	4	109
Kotchman	1.000	20	112	7	0	10
Merloni	.000	1	0	0	0	0
Molina	1.000	4	10	0	0	2
Quinlan	1.000	9	38	1	0	5

Second Base	PCT	G	PO	A	E	DP
Figgins	.971	42	67	101	5	20
Izturis	1.000	1	4	4	0	0
Kennedy	.991	127	212	352	5	71
Matranga	1.000	1	2	1	0	1
Sorensen	1.000	5	3	5	0	1

Third Base	PCT	G	PO	A	E	DP
Figgins	.977	56	34	95	3	8
Izturis	.911	45	20	62	8	5
McPherson	.944	60	32	86	7	14
Merloni	1.000	4	1	8	0	0
Quinlan	.913	33	22	51	7	4
Sorensen	.833	1	2	3	1	0

Shortstop	PCT	G	PO	A	E	DP
Cabrera	.988	140	229	347	7	81
Figgins	1.000	4	2	4	0	1
Izturis	.980	29	44	55	2	8

Outfield	PCT	G	PO	A	E	DP
Anderson	.976	106	201	4	5	1
DaVanon	.991	63	105	1	1	0
Figgins	.989	72	170	3	2	1
Finley	.985	104	266	5	4	2
Guerrero	.988	120	242	8	3	2
Izturis	1.000	1	1	1	0	1
Paul	.000	2	0	0	0	0
Pride	1.000	4	2	0	0	0
Prieto	1.000	2	5	0	0	0
Quinlan	1.000	6	3	0	0	0
Rivera	.992	74	127	5	1	1

FARM SYSTEM

General Manager: Bill Stoneman. **Director, Player Development:** Tony Reagins. **Scouting Director:** Eddie Bane.

Class	Farm Team	League	W	L	Pct.	Finish*	Manager	Affiliate Since
AAA	Salt Lake (Utah) Stingers	Pacific Coast	79	65	.549	4th (16)	Dino Ebel	2001
AA	Arkansas Travelers (Little Rock)	Texas	71	69	.507	**+4th (8)**	Tom Gamboa	2001
High A	Rancho Cucamonga (Calif.) Quakes	California	62	77	.446	8th (10)	Tyrone Boykin	2001
Low A	Cedar Rapids (Iowa) Kernels	Midwest	65	75	.464	t-11th (14)	Bobby Magallanes	1993
Rookie	Orem (Utah) Owlz	Pioneer	38	38	.500	**+t-4th (8)**	Tom Kotchman	2001
Rookie	Mesa (Ariz.) Angels	Arizona	25	31	.446	7th (9)	Brian Harper	2001

*Finish in overall standings (No. of teams in league)/playoff teams in **boldface** +League champion

SALT LAKE STINGERS — Class AAA

PACIFIC COAST LEAGUE

BATTING	B-T	HT	WT	DOB	AVG	vLH	vRH	G	AB	R	H	2B	3B	HR	RBI	BB	HBP	SH	SF	SO	SB	CS	SLG	OBP
Allen, Luke	L-R	6-2	220	8-4-78	.287	.262	.296	128	460	85	132	20	7	23	92	54	1	0	4	87	13	3	.511	.360
Budde, Ryan	R-R	5-11	205	8-15-79	.230	.277	.215	58	196	26	45	9	3	6	25	9	1	2	0	41	3	1	.398	.267
Caldera, Jose	R-R	5-10	160	12-18-85	.231	.000	.231	6	13	3	3	0	0	0	1	1	0	0	0	2	0	0	.231	.286
Callaspo, Alberto	B-R	5-10	175	4-19-83	.316	.250	.331	50	212	28	67	21	2	1	31	10	1	2	3	13	2	5	.448	.345
Casilla, Alexi	B-R	5-9	168	7-20-84	.256	.429	.219	13	39	3	10	0	0	0	1	3	0	4	0	6	1	1	.256	.310
Del Chiaro, Brent	R-R	6-3	240	6-26-79	.333	.500	.000	2	3	1	1	0	0	1	1	0	0	0	0	2	0	0	1.333	.333
Fox, Andy	L-R	6-4	200	1-12-71	.208	.167	.214	15	48	8	10	2	1	1	7	10	1	0	0	10	1	1	.354	.356
Gordon, Brian	L-R	6-0	190	8-16-78	.274	.244	.284	101	343	50	94	25	4	17	55	26	1	3	5	103	7	5	.519	.323
Gorneault, Nick	R-R	6-3	220	4-19-79	.293	.303	.290	130	488	106	143	25	11	26	108	58	2	1	6	119	7	6	.549	.366
Infante, Larry	B-R	5-10	160	4-4-85	.286	.500	.200	7	7	0	2	0	0	0	2	0	0	0	0	2	0	0	.286	.286
Izturis, Maicer	B-R	5-8	150	9-12-80	.452	.438	.467	10	31	10	14	4	0	0	2	7	0	1	0	4	4	2	.581	.553
Kennedy, Adam	L-R	6-1	185	1-10-76	.412	1.000	.375	4	17	4	7	1	0	0	4	2	0	0	1	2	2	0	.471	.450
Kotchman, Casey	L-L	6-3	215	2-22-83	.289	.325	.272	94	363	62	105	23	1	10	58	43	7	0	4	40	0	2	.441	.372
Martinez, Brett	R-R	6-0	200	10-14-83	.200	.500	.125	4	10	2	2	2	0	0	0	0	0	0	0	5	0	0	.400	.200
Mathis, Jeff	R-R	6-0	180	3-31-83	.276	.277	.276	112	427	78	118	26	3	21	73	42	1	5	4	85	4	3	.499	.340
Matranga, Dave	R-R	6-0	185	1-8-77	.239	.200	.254	56	176	31	42	12	2	3	19	31	3	6	2	39	6	3	.381	.358
McPherson, Dallas	L-R	6-4	230	7-23-80	.278	.300	.265	14	54	8	15	1	2	6	19	7	0	0	2	20	1	2	.704	.349
Merloni, Lou	R-R	5-10	200	4-6-71	.320	.333	.316	6	25	6	8	3	0	0	6	2	1	0	0	5	0	0	.440	.393
Paul, Josh	R-R	6-1	220	5-19-75	.273	.333	.259	9	33	6	9	4	0	0	6	6	0	0	0	7	1	0	.394	.385
Pavkovich, Adam	R-R	6-2	190	12-31-81	.269	.246	.275	106	342	50	92	19	4	8	51	27	3	7	5	65	5	6	.418	.324
Pride, Curtis	L-R	6-0	210	12-17-68	.289	.276	.294	82	280	44	81	17	6	9	56	49	1	0	0	65	10	5	.489	.397
Prieto, Chris	L-L	5-11	185	8-24-72	.317	.298	.323	97	363	71	115	18	12	3	45	60	5	12	3	41	26	10	.457	.418
Quinlan, Robb	R-R	6-1	200	3-17-77	.383	.350	.400	15	60	13	23	6	0	1	4	2	0	0	0	8	0	0	.533	.403
Smith, Casey	R-R	6-3	200	5-7-77	.221	.213	.223	83	272	37	60	6	2	0	18	24	3	2	2	40	6	3	.257	.289
Sorensen, Zach	B-R	6-0	190	1-3-77	.303	.320	.297	78	287	47	87	11	3	2	41	34	1	10	6	55	21	9	.383	.372
Specht, Brian	B-R	5-11	185	10-19-80	.308	.304	.309	73	263	40	81	18	5	8	36	25	2	1	0	47	12	7	.506	.372
Wood, Brandon	R-R	6-3	200	3-2-85	.316	.500	.267	4	19	1	6	2	1	0	1	0	0	0	0	6	0	0	.526	.316

PITCHING	B-T	HT	WT	DOB	W	L	ERA	G	GS	CG	SV	IP	H	R	ER	HR	BB	SO	AVG	vLH	vRH	K/9	BB/9
Andrews, Clayton	R-L	6-0	180	5-15-78	8	8	6.31	28	20	0	0	123	165	97	86	16	45	58	.330	.283	.341	4.26	3.30
Beck, Bradley	L-L	5-11	185	1-10-85	0	0	0.00	1	0	0	0	1	1	0	0	0	0	1	.333	.000	.500	9.00	0.00
Bergman, Dusty	L-L	6-5	200	2-1-78	8	5	3.17	44	0	0	8	71	77	25	25	10	18	55	.275	.330	.249	6.97	2.28
Bootcheck, Chris	R-R	6-5	200	10-24-78	7	4	5.42	21	21	0	0	116	144	75	70	13	50	90	.312	.277	.352	6.96	3.87
Borbon, Pedro	R-L	6-1	230	11-15-67	0	0	6.75	8	0	0	0	5	7	4	4	1	3	4	.292	.300	.286	6.75	5.06
Brunet, Michael	R-R	6-2	195	3-5-77	5	3	7.53	19	0	0	0	29	37	25	24	4	12	25	.325	.265	.369	7.85	3.77
Collazo, Willie	L-L	5-9	175	11-7-79	0	1	7.71	11	1	0	0	23	29	20	20	7	9	12	.337	.321	.345	4.63	3.47
Cyr, Eric	R-L	6-4	210	2-11-79	5	5	5.64	38	9	0	1	99	130	71	62	14	28	61	.317	.351	.307	5.55	2.55
Dunn, Scott	R-R	6-3	200	5-23-78	5	7	3.82	47	6	0	9	92	83	44	39	7	41	98	.242	.264	.226	9.59	4.01
Escobar, Kelvim	R-R	6-1	230	4-11-76	1	0	2.51	4	4	0	0	14	14	4	4	2	8	22	.250	.229	.286	13.81	5.02
Gelinas, Karl	R-R	6-4	202	8-6-83	1	0	1.80	3	0	0	0	5	5	1	1	0	0	3	.263	.333	.200	5.40	0.00
Gregg, Kevin	R-R	6-6	235	6-20-78	3	1	3.89	7	6	0	0	35	36	15	15	2	10	36	.273	.260	.291	9.35	2.60
Hunter, Chris	R-R	6-4	200	12-12-80	1	2	5.86	8	4	0	0	28	40	19	18	1	18	12	.345	.321	.367	3.90	5.86
Jones, Greg	R-R	6-2	195	11-15-76	1	2	3.20	23	0	0	10	25	20	9	9	3	6	25	.215	.240	.186	8.88	2.13
Lee, Corey	B-L	6-1	190	12-26-74	6	2	2.72	14	13	0	0	79	62	25	24	5	40	77	.217	.180	.225	8.74	4.54
Lynch, Kevin	R-R	6-2	200	1-2-83	0	0	0.00	2	0	0	0	3	6	0	0	0	1	3	.500	.200	.714	10.13	3.38
Moseley, Dustin	R-R	6-4	190	12-26-81	4	6	5.03	17	17	0	0	82	102	51	46	11	30	38	.312	.267	.358	4.15	3.28
Olson, Jason	R-R	6-2	180	6-12-78	0	0	9.00	3	0	0	0	3	4	3	3	1	2	2	.333	.500	.000	6.00	6.00
Peralta, Joel	R-R	5-11	170	3-23-76	4	1	2.70	19	0	0	10	20	11	6	6	0	6	18	.159	.133	.179	8.10	2.70
Prinz, Bret	R-R	6-2	215	6-15-77	0	0	5.59	5	0	0	1	10	12	7	6	1	6	8	.293	.241	.417	7.45	5.59
Ramirez, Edwar	R-R	6-3	155	3-28-81	0	0	0.00	1	0	0	0	2	0	0	0	0	0	2	.000	.000	.000	9.00	0.00
Rouwenhorst, Jonathon	L-L	6-1	180	9-25-79	4	3	5.27	25	0	0	1	43	60	25	25	3	17	31	.339	.232	.388	6.54	3.59
Santana, Ervin	R-R	6-2	160	1-10-83	1	0	4.19	3	3	0	0	19	19	11	9	2	2	17	.260	.273	.250	7.91	0.93
Saunders, Joe	L-L	6-3	210	6-16-81	3	3	4.58	9	9	1	0	55	65	38	28	3	21	29	.304	.301	.305	4.75	3.44
Schneider, Scott	R-R	6-4	210	5-4-78	2	2	8.59	36	4	0	0	73	102	74	70	12	39	47	.330	.338	.323	5.77	4.79
Sessions, Doug	R-R	6-1	210	9-28-76	0	4	7.30	8	8	0	0	41	53	36	33	10	16	17	.323	.308	.342	3.76	3.54
Thomas, Evan	R-R	5-10	170	6-14-74	7	5	6.73	20	14	0	0	92	131	75	69	16	30	48	.338	.371	.304	4.68	2.92
Watson, Mark	R-L	6-3	220	1-23-74	0	0	5.06	6	0	0	0	11	14	10	6	1	6	9	.298	.250	.308	7.59	5.06
Woods, Jake	L-L	6-1	190	9-3-81	3	1	5.89	15	5	0	0	37	50	27	24	7	17	36	.314	.279	.337	8.84	4.17

FIELDING

Catcher	PCT	G	PO	A	E	DP	PB
Budde	.993	46	275	20	2	3	0
Del Chiaro	1.000	2	3	0	0	0	0
Martinez	.929	4	12	1	1	0	0
Mathis	.986	94	598	47	9	5	6
Paul	1.000	4	28	1	0	0	1

First Base	PCT	G	PO	A	E	DP
Budde	.978	9	85	4	2	15
Kotchman	.995	89	790	59	4	103
Matranga	1.000	1	3	1	0	1
Quinlan	.983	6	54	3	1	10
Smith	.994	19	144	14	1	19
Sorensen	1.000	24	158	14	0	19

Second Base	PCT	G	PO	A	E	DP
Callaspo	.978	48	91	127	5	41
Casilla	.982	11	23	33	1	11
Fox	.984	14	20	41	1	8
Infante	1.000	5	0	2	0	0
Izturis	1.000	1	1	0	0	0
Kennedy	1.000	3	5	11	0	5
Matranga	1.000	9	13	32	0	5
Merloni	1.000	1	1	4	0	2
Pavkovich	1.000	1	1	1	0	1
Smith	1.000	14	21	35	0	11
Sorensen	1.000	5	6	9	0	1
Specht	.963	44	89	119	8	45

Third Base	PCT	G	PO	A	E	DP
Allen	.000	1	0	0	1	0
Budde	1.000	1	0	1	0	0
Caldera	.000	3	0	0	0	0
Fox	1.000	1	0	1	0	0
Izturis	1.000	2	0	2	0	0
Matranga	.957	11	5	17	1	4
McPherson	.931	11	5	22	2	0
Merloni	1.000	3	0	3	0	0
Pavkovich	.947	103	81	207	16	24
Quinlan	1.000	5	4	8	0	1
Smith	.929	10	4	22	2	4
Sorensen	1.000	3	1	8	0	2
Specht	.875	6	4	10	2	0

Shortstop	PCT	G	PO	A	E	DP
Caldera	.600	3	2	4	4	0
Casilla	.833	2	0	5	1	0
Infante	1.000	2	1	3	0	1
Izturis	1.000	6	3	8	0	2
Matranga	.958	37	57	102	7	26
Pavkovich	.667	1	1	1	1	0
Smith	.941	34	44	115	10	32
Sorensen	.985	47	73	125	3	37
Specht	.959	22	37	57	4	15
Wood	.909	4	6	14	2	6

Outfield	PCT	G	PO	A	E	DP
Allen	.981	94	189	13	4	3
Gordon	.959	80	136	5	6	1
Gorneault	.980	120	228	12	5	1
Pride	.978	45	87	0	2	0
Prieto	1.000	94	241	7	0	3
Sorensen	1.000	5	9	0	0	0

ARKANSAS TRAVELERS — Class AA

TEXAS LEAGUE

BATTING	B-T	HT	WT	DOB	AVG	vLH	vRH	G	AB	R	H	2B	3B	HR	RBI	BB	HBP	SH	SF	SO	SB	CS	SLG	OBP
Aspito, Jason	L-R	6-0	210	1-3-79	.268	.267	.268	52	157	25	42	8	0	8	32	12	4	0	3	28	1	2	.471	.330
Aybar, Erick	B-R	5-10	170	1-14-84	.303	.352	.282	134	535	101	162	29	10	9	54	29	14	4	8	51	49	23	.445	.350
Caldera, Jose	R-R	5-10	160	12-18-85	1.000	1.000	.000	4	1	3	1	0	0	0	0	0	0	0	0	0	1	0	1.000	1.000
Callaspo, Alberto	B-R	5-10	175	4-19-83	.297	.238	.322	89	350	53	104	8	0	10	49	28	1	1	5	17	9	8	.406	.346
Casilla, Alexi	B-R	5-9	168	7-20-84	.211	.286	.167	7	19	4	4	0	0	0	4	2	0	0	0	3	1	1	.211	.286
Del Chiaro, Brent	R-R	6-3	240	6-26-79	.162	.195	.145	49	117	13	19	7	1	4	16	10	2	4	3	50	0	0	.342	.235
Duff, Tim	R-R	6-2	210	6-26-81	.222	.143	.273	7	18	1	4	1	0	0	1	0	0	0	0	4	0	0	.278	.222
Eylward, Mike	R-R	6-2	215	9-28-79	.287	.289	.286	123	418	62	120	26	2	14	72	37	6	3	5	58	3	5	.459	.350
Gates, David	R-R	6-1	215	9-23-80	.247	.244	.248	115	381	59	94	22	3	16	58	35	10	2	4	97	1	0	.446	.323
Kendrick, Howie	R-R	5-10	195	7-12-83	.342	.293	.356	46	190	35	65	20	2	7	42	6	7	0	1	20	12	4	.579	.382
Leahy, Ryan	R-R	5-10	180	7-8-81	.231	.304	.187	43	121	12	28	4	1	1	10	6	4	6	0	17	0	2	.306	.290
Matranga, Dave	R-R	6-0	185	1-8-77	.192	.200	.188	9	26	4	5	2	0	1	2	1	0	0	1	6	0	1	.385	.214
Morales, Kendry	B-R	6-1	220	6-20-83	.306	.264	.321	74	281	47	86	12	0	17	54	17	2	0	1	43	2	0	.530	.349
Morris, Chris	B-R	5-8	185	7-1-79	.273	.167	.291	52	128	13	35	3	3	0	12	17	0	4	0	28	10	6	.344	.359
Murphy, Tommy	B-R	6-0	185	8-27-79	.288	.323	.275	135	500	85	144	24	11	17	76	43	5	2	7	97	26	12	.482	.346
Napoli, Mike	R-R	6-0	205	10-31-81	.237	.308	.211	131	439	96	104	22	2	31	99	88	9	0	5	140	12	4	.508	.372
Pavkovich, Adam	R-R	6-2	190	12-31-81	.407	.455	.375	8	27	2	11	3	1	1	3	0	0	0	0	3	1	1	.704	.407
Porter, Greg	L-R	6-5	240	8-15-80	.286	.336	.269	129	448	63	128	24	4	11	56	22	4	0	6	84	2	6	.431	.321
Ramos, Jason	B-R	5-11	185	8-9-82	.000	.000	.000	1	0	0	0	0	0	0	0	1	0	0	0	0	0	0	.000	1.000
Reyes, Ivan	R-R	6-2	185	6-6-81	.364	.375	.357	8	22	5	8	2	0	3	10	2	0	0	1	8	0	0	.864	.400
Santana, Emmanuel	L-R	5-11	210	8-4-80	.143	.000	.167	5	14	2	2	0	0	0	4	0	0	0	1	3	1	0	.143	.133
Willits, Reggie	B-R	5-11	185	5-30-81	.304	.371	.276	123	487	75	148	23	6	2	46	54	8	4	8	78	40	14	.388	.377

PITCHING	B-T	HT	WT	DOB	W	L	ERA	G	GS	CG	SV	IP	H	R	ER	HR	BB	SO	AVG	vLH	vRH	K/9	BB/9
Andrews, Clayton	R-L	6-0	180	5-15-78	1	0	0.00	2	1	0	1	10	4	0	0	0	7	6	.133	.125	.136	5.59	6.52
Arredondo, Jose	R-R	6-0	175	3-30-84	0	0	3.38	5	0	0	0	5	5	2	2	0	4	4	.278	.333	.250	6.75	6.75
Austen, David	R-R	6-1	185	5-21-81	4	3	4.05	27	0	0	0	47	43	24	21	4	12	30	.256	.280	.237	5.79	2.31
Bittner, Tim	L-L	6-2	200	6-9-80	1	7	6.33	14	14	0	0	58	76	43	41	5	33	41	.333	.338	.331	6.33	5.09
Borbon, Pedro	R-L	6-1	230	11-15-67	0	0	0.00	6	0	0	0	4	1	0	0	0	0	3	.083	.000	.143	6.23	0.00
Collazo, Willie	L-L	5-9	175	11-7-79	1	5	6.78	26	10	0	0	72	85	60	54	16	29	58	.293	.295	.292	7.28	3.64
Davidson, Daniel	L-L	6-4	195	1-8-81	13	5	4.72	28	26	1	0	154	179	94	81	22	45	110	.289	.299	.285	6.41	2.62
James, Delvin	R-R	6-4	230	1-3-78	3	4	5.58	17	8	0	0	60	77	40	37	6	25	30	.321	.330	.314	4.53	3.77
Jones, Greg	R-R	6-2	195	11-15-76	0	1	2.70	3	0	0	0	3	2	1	1	0	1	2	.167	.200	.143	5.40	2.70
Lynch, Kevin	R-R	6-2	200	1-2-83	0	0	11.25	2	0	0	0	4	7	5	5	2	2	0	.368	.556	.200	0.00	4.50
Olenberger, Kasey	R-R	6-4	235	3-18-78	9	7	3.71	32	17	0	0	124	135	64	51	14	37	69	.278	.259	.294	5.02	2.69
Olson, Jason	R-R	6-2	180	6-12-78	0	0	4.50	4	0	0	1	6	9	3	3	1	1	0	.360	.222	.438	0.00	1.50
O'Sullivan, Mark	R-R	6-1	215	10-24-78	1	4	6.16	45	4	0	0	76	92	59	52	10	38	45	.307	.322	.296	5.33	4.50
Pullin, Aaron	R-R	6-3	200	2-17-81	5	6	5.03	51	0	0	5	77	80	45	43	13	34	53	.262	.306	.232	6.19	3.97
Rouwenhorst, Jonathon	L-L	6-1	180	9-25-79	3	1	1.59	22	0	0	2	23	13	4	4	2	10	19	.169	.125	.200	7.54	3.97
Santana, Ervin	R-R	6-2	160	1-10-83	5	1	2.31	7	7	0	0	39	34	12	10	2	15	32	.234	.295	.190	7.38	3.46
Saunders, Joe	L-L	6-3	210	6-16-81	7	4	3.49	18	18	2	0	106	107	52	41	9	32	80	.263	.209	.278	6.81	2.73
Serrano, Alex	R-R	6-1	180	2-18-81	1	3	1.73	24	0	0	11	26	24	9	5	1	6	18	.245	.200	.283	6.23	2.08
2-team (11 Tulsa)					2	3	1.34	35	0	0	15	40	34	10	6	2	7	23	.233	.174	.286	5.13	1.56
Shell, Steven	R-R	6-5	190	1-1-83	10	8	4.57	27	27	1	0	160	175	90	81	18	58	126	.283	.251	.305	7.10	3.27
Stertzbach, Von	R-R	6-2	190	5-15-81	3	5	5.23	44	0	0	10	52	60	36	30	8	25	42	.294	.400	.239	7.32	4.35
Weaver, Jered	R-R	6-7	205	10-4-82	3	3	3.98	8	8	0	0	43	43	22	19	5	19	46	.250	.278	.226	9.63	3.98
Wilhite, Matt	R-R	6-1	185	7-3-81	1	2	4.07	56	0	0	2	60	67	31	27	5	15	32	.300	.302	.300	4.83	2.26

FIELDING

Catcher	PCT	G	PO	A	E	DP	PB
Del Chiaro	.995	39	179	10	1	4	4
Duff	1.000	7	34	6	0	0	0
Napoli	.981	109	638	76	14	7	13
Santana	1.000	3	18	2	0	0	1

First Base	PCT	G	PO	A	E	DP
Eylward	.992	72	583	50	5	83
Morales	.987	60	504	41	7	64
Napoli	1.000	3	16	1	0	4
Porter	.966	11	81	5	3	8

Second Base	PCT	G	PO	A	E	DP
Caldera	1.000	1	1	2	0	1
Callaspo	.983	89	172	245	7	73
Casilla	1.000	1	0	1	0	0
Eylward	1.000	1	2	2	0	1
Kendrick	.974	46	77	146	6	38
Leahy	1.000	6	7	11	0	2
Matranga	1.000	2	1	5	0	1
Reyes	1.000	1	2	1	0	1

Third Base	PCT	G	PO	A	E	DP
Eylward	.850	10	5	12	3	1
Leahy	.985	28	21	44	1	12
Matranga	.952	7	7	13	1	1
Pavkovich	1.000	8	5	20	0	1
Porter	.904	96	85	169	27	25
Reyes	.882	4	4	11	2	1

Shortstop	PCT	G	PO	A	E	DP
Aybar	.953	134	243	403	32	108
Casilla	.833	3	5	10	3	4
Leahy	1.000	1	0	4	0	0
Matranga	.800	1	1	3	1	0
Pavkovich	1.000	1	0	1	0	0
Reyes	.875	3	1	6	1	1

Outfield	PCT	G	PO	A	E	DP
Aspito	.978	49	86	4	2	0
Eylward	1.000	7	10	0	0	0
Gates	.972	92	135	3	4	0
Leahy	1.000	5	5	1	0	0
Morales	1.000	1	3	1	0	1
Morris	.972	33	64	5	2	0
Murphy	.990	130	283	18	3	7
Porter	1.000	1	1	0	0	0
Willits	.986	120	269	8	4	1

RANCHO CUCAMONGA QUAKES — High Class A

CALIFORNIA LEAGUE

BATTING	B-T	HT	WT	DOB	AVG	vLH	vRH	G	AB	R	H	2B	3B	HR	RBI	BB	HBP	SH	SF	SO	SB	CS	SLG	OBP
Balkcom, Brandon	R-R	6-2	225	8-25-82	.244	.210	.255	87	320	37	78	19	2	6	35	22	3	5	2	102	0	2	.372	.297
Brown, Matt	R-R	6-0	200	8-8-82	.262	.271	.259	125	488	68	128	39	4	12	65	40	11	3	5	125	4	5	.432	.329
Day, Devin	R-R	6-2	200	9-3-80	.284	.286	.283	60	215	34	61	13	1	5	22	13	0	0	2	55	3	3	.423	.322
Duff, Tim	R-R	6-2	210	6-26-81	.190	.250	.182	22	63	10	12	3	0	2	4	10	2	1	0	14	0	2	.333	.320
Finley, Steve	L-L	6-2	195	3-12-65	.500	.000	.500	1	4	2	2	1	0	0	0	1	0	0	0	0	0	0	.750	.600
Fuller, Cody	R-R	6-0	190	9-19-82	.270	.357	.257	32	115	19	31	13	1	3	11	10	7	2	0	44	4	1	.478	.364
Hughes, Michael	R-R	6-3	230	9-8-81	.136	.143	.133	12	44	3	6	0	1	0	4	2	1	0	0	13	1	0	.182	.191
Johnson, Ben	B-R	6-0	196	10-17-81	.271	.226	.281	78	277	38	75	19	2	11	36	22	10	0	3	58	1	1	.473	.343
Kendrick, Howie	R-R	5-10	195	7-12-83	.384	.333	.399	63	279	69	107	23	6	12	47	14	7	0	4	42	13	4	.638	.421
Kennedy, Adam	L-R	6-1	185	1-10-76	.400	.000	.667	2	5	1	2	0	0	0	1	1	0	0	0	1	1	1	.400	.500
Leahy, Ryan	R-R	5-10	180	7-8-81	.253	.313	.237	39	150	27	38	5	1	1	18	22	4	2	4	20	4	4	.320	.356
Lopez, Baltazar	L-L	6-1	185	11-22-83	.258	.167	.283	52	194	15	50	12	0	0	25	17	0	1	3	57	3	2	.320	.313
McPherson, Dallas	L-R	6-4	230	7-23-80	.438	1.000	.400	5	16	3	7	2	0	2	5	3	1	0	0	4	1	1	.938	.550
Melgarejo, Ransel	R-R	6-0	199	8-28-81	.178	.235	.143	13	45	2	8	2	0	0	3	4	2	0	0	10	2	1	.222	.275
Morales, Kendry	B-R	6-1	220	6-20-83	.344	.333	.348	22	90	18	31	3	0	5	17	6	3	0	1	11	0	0	.544	.400
Pali, Matt	L-L	6-1	220	12-10-80	.257	.205	.273	135	513	81	132	18	1	12	77	55	9	5	7	86	15	5	.366	.336
Peel, Aaron	R-R	6-0	195	2-8-83	.311	.258	.319	51	222	46	69	12	4	11	35	15	9	0	2	57	1	2	.550	.375
Remole, Clifton	L-L	6-1	205	10-24-82	.300	.333	.293	49	200	27	60	11	2	3	24	12	0	1	3	19	3	1	.420	.335
Reyes, Ivan	R-R	6-2	185	6-6-81	.186	.100	.217	33	113	14	21	2	1	4	15	11	1	1	1	41	1	1	.327	.262
Rosario, Anderson	R-R	6-0	170	3-2-85	.122	.250	.081	14	49	3	6	1	0	0	1	1	1	1	0	20	0	0	.143	.157
Santana, Emmanuel	L-R	5-11	210	8-4-80	.000	.000	.000	2	4	0	0	0	0	0	0	2	0	0	0	1	0	0	.000	.333
Shankle, Brooks	R-R	6-4	217	2-4-83	.250	.286	.222	5	16	1	4	1	0	0	1	5	0	0	0	7	0	0	.313	.429
Statia, Hainley	B-R	5-11	162	1-19-86	.245	.333	.211	23	106	12	26	2	0	1	8	5	1	0	0	13	6	3	.292	.286
Sugden, Jason	B-R	6-3	205	10-11-81	.247	.292	.234	83	316	35	78	13	7	3	35	15	4	6	6	81	4	7	.361	.284
Weed, B.J.	B-R	5-11	185	11-11-79	.186	.150	.200	19	70	10	13	0	2	0	2	6	0	0	0	16	1	0	.243	.250
Wilson, Bobby	R-R	6-0	205	4-8-83	.290	.286	.291	115	466	66	135	32	1	14	77	30	2	0	3	61	2	1	.453	.333
Wood, Brandon	R-R	6-3	200	3-2-85	.321	.368	.308	130	536	109	172	51	4	43	115	48	7	2	2	128	7	3	.672	.383

PITCHING	B-T	HT	WT	DOB	W	L	ERA	G	GS	CG	SV	IP	H	R	ER	HR	BB	SO	AVG	vLH	vRH	K/9	BB/9
Austen, David	R-R	6-1	185	5-21-81	3	2	1.80	29	0	0	4	45	33	12	9	1	14	38	.205	.250	.165	7.60	2.80
Buckley, Allen	R-R	6-6	240	9-18-79	4	4	4.20	54	0	0	3	79	76	43	37	7	52	96	.253	.238	.268	10.89	5.90
Carney, Frederic	R-R	6-3	220	8-21-82	1	1	8.91	23	0	0	1	33	48	33	33	9	22	29	.350	.333	.371	7.83	5.94
Cruz, Rafael	R-R	6-2	175	8-20-85	0	0	3.75	5	0	0	0	12	13	5	5	2	1	4	.265	.241	.300	3.00	0.75
Dowdy, Justin	L-L	6-1	175	8-13-83	3	4	4.98	46	3	0	0	78	87	47	43	13	36	64	.280	.301	.257	7.42	4.17
Edwards, Bill	R-R	6-3	185	3-26-81	1	7	5.91	17	17	0	0	91	115	73	60	12	48	66	.310	.339	.267	6.50	4.73
Escobar, Kelvim	R-R	6-1	230	4-11-76	0	0	0.00	1	1	0	0	3	1	0	0	0	2	7	.100	.000	.200	21.00	6.00
Gonzalez, Miguel	R-R	6-1	165	5-27-84	0	0	0.00	2	0	0	0	5	0	0	0	0	2	3	.000	.000	.000	5.79	3.86
Holcomb, James	R-R	6-4	205	11-28-80	10	7	5.02	27	26	0	0	142	153	93	79	16	50	128	.279	.268	.289	8.13	3.18
Hunter, Chris	R-R	6-4	200	12-12-80	6	8	5.11	21	20	0	0	118	130	77	67	10	60	72	.278	.321	.230	5.49	4.58
Jepsen, Kevin	R-R	6-3	215	7-26-84	0	1	10.66	4	4	0	0	13	19	18	15	2	10	11	.333	.407	.267	7.82	7.11
MacKenzie, Aaron	R-R	6-4	225	4-14-81	0	3	5.58	49	0	0	0	79	93	51	49	8	49	62	.293	.296	.291	7.06	5.58
Mendoza, Tommy	R-R	6-2	185	8-18-87	1	0	0.00	2	1	0	1	10	4	0	0	0	0	12	.121	.154	.100	10.80	0.00
Posey, Micah	L-L	6-5	220	10-18-82	0	2	12.00	6	6	0	0	18	29	24	24	1	17	14	.387	.357	.404	7.00	8.50
Prinz, Bret	R-R	6-2	215	6-15-77	0	0	1.80	2	0	0	0	5	2	1	1	0	3	6	.143	.000	.182	10.80	5.40
Ray, Ronnie	R-R	6-3	195	5-11-84	1	2	5.79	20	0	0	0	33	43	25	21	5	20	24	.321	.227	.412	6.61	5.51
Rodriguez, Rafael	R-R	6-1	175	9-24-84	4	4	6.75	14	14	0	0	72	84	58	54	11	33	44	.292	.292	.291	5.50	4.13
Simard, Michel	R-R	6-4	200	9-4-81	3	5	7.32	13	13	0	0	68	82	62	55	13	32	48	.309	.385	.231	6.38	4.26
Smith, Jesse	R-R	6-2	214	7-11-80	3	2	4.70	13	2	0	0	31	36	18	16	4	9	30	.286	.296	.273	8.80	2.64
Thompson, Richard	R-R	6-1	188	7-1-84	6	8	5.27	42	15	0	3	121	132	76	71	20	53	92	.277	.262	.290	6.82	3.93
Toledo, Jean	R-R	6-2	195	3-6-83	2	2	3.28	8	4	0	0	36	41	14	13	1	13	21	.308	.210	.394	5.30	3.28
Torres, Joseph	L-L	6-2	193	9-3-82	0	4	18.00	10	6	0	0	20	39	43	40	4	31	15	.424	.326	.510	6.75	13.95
Touchstone, Nic	L-L	6-4	220	11-19-81	4	2	10.94	23	0	0	0	26	41	37	32	5	29	23	.360	.306	.400	7.86	9.91
Weaver, Jered	R-R	6-7	205	10-4-82	4	1	3.82	7	7	0	0	33	25	18	14	3	7	49	.205	.233	.177	13.36	1.91
West, James	R-R	6-2	175	12-21-84	0	0	5.40	2	0	0	0	2	2	1	1	0	3	2	.333	.250	.500	10.80	16.20
Zimmermann, Bob	R-R	6-5	245	11-17-81	6	8	3.32	52	0	0	17	60	50	25	22	3	27	62	.229	.276	.192	9.35	4.07

FIELDING

Catcher	PCT	G	PO	A	E	DP	PB
Duff	.981	22	134	18	3	0	2
Johnson	.987	16	140	9	2	2	3
Santana	1.000	2	7	1	0	0	0
Wilson	.984	103	745	104	14	9	14

First Base	PCT	G	PO	A	E	DP
Lopez	.988	36	299	25	4	31
Morales	.973	15	136	7	4	14
Pali	.991	49	401	38	4	41
Remole	.974	41	346	29	10	30

Second Base	PCT	G	PO	A	E	DP
Day	.978	9	13	31	1	10
Kendrick	.973	59	98	195	8	32
Kennedy	1.000	1	2	2	0	1
Leahy	.972	39	66	110	5	21
Reyes	.930	9	15	25	3	7
Statia	.983	22	44	72	2	14

Third Base	PCT	G	PO	A	E	DP
Brown	.948	119	92	202	16	18
Day	.800	3	0	4	1	0
McPherson	.857	4	1	5	1	0
Morales	.900	3	5	4	1	1
Reyes	.933	11	9	19	2	0

Shortstop	PCT	G	PO	A	E	DP
Day	.950	6	10	9	1	2
Reyes	.894	9	21	21	5	7
Statia	1.000	1	1	3	0	1
Wood	.966	124	208	352	20	76

Outfield	PCT	G	PO	A	E	DP
Balkcom	.989	63	91	3	1	2
Day	.986	35	68	4	1	0
Fuller	.986	32	67	1	1	0
Hughes	.917	11	18	4	2	0
Johnson	.981	28	48	3	1	0
Melgarejo	.950	12	19	0	1	0
Morales	1.000	2	2	0	0	0
Pali	.971	77	128	4	4	0
Peel	.972	47	98	5	3	2
Remole	1.000	2	3	0	0	0
Rosario	.974	14	35	2	1	1
Sugden	.979	82	184	3	4	1
Weed	.957	19	42	2	2	0

CEDAR RAPIDS KERNELS — Low Class A

MIDWEST LEAGUE

BATTING	B-T	HT	WT	DOB	AVG	vLH	vRH	G	AB	R	H	2B	3B	HR	RBI	BB	HBP	SH	SF	SO	SB	CS	SLG	OBP
Boyer, Billy	B-R	6-1	195	3-8-84	.183	.385	.138	21	71	8	13	5	1	2	11	2	1	0	0	31	3	2	.366	.216
Caldera, Jose	R-R	5-10	160	12-18-85	.083	.000	.111	5	12	0	1	0	0	0	1	0	0	0	0	2	0	0	.083	.083

BATTING	B-T	HT	WT	DOB	AVG	vLH	vRH	G	AB	R	H	2B	3B	HR	RBI	BB	HBP	SH	SF	SO	SB	CS	SLG	OBP
Casilla, Alexi	B-R	5-9	168	7-20-84	.325	.359	.313	78	308	62	100	11	3	3	17	29	6	3	1	31	47	12	.409	.392
Collins, Michael	R-R	6-3	215	7-18-84	.320	.299	.325	100	363	64	116	32	3	7	64	34	25	1	3	44	16	8	.482	.412
Dini, Greg	R-R	6-2	200	1-18-83	.172	.333	.100	9	29	1	5	2	0	0	1	2	2	1	0	6	0	0	.241	.273
Duenas, Tomas	R-R	5-11	205	7-16-81	.209	.222	.206	55	191	20	40	6	1	6	19	15	5	2	0	56	4	0	.346	.284
Duff, Tim	R-R	6-2	210	6-26-81	.170	.167	.171	13	47	3	8	0	0	0	0	5	0	0	0	15	1	0	.170	.250
Giannotti, Richard	B-R	6-3	210	8-9-83	.235	.231	.236	104	353	42	83	18	2	3	28	23	5	6	2	107	17	11	.323	.290
Johnson, Ben	B-R	6-0	196	10-17-81	.250	.250	.250	22	72	9	18	5	1	2	14	10	1	0	3	14	2	0	.431	.337
Leblanc, Josh	L-R	6-1	190	9-15-81	.274	.204	.295	63	230	30	63	12	5	0	27	27	1	3	3	66	18	5	.370	.349
Madrigal, Warner	R-R	6-0	200	3-21-84	.247	.283	.236	111	405	43	100	21	2	15	53	22	2	1	2	90	6	7	.420	.288
Martinez, Brett	R-R	6-0	200	10-14-83	.125	1.000	.000	3	8	1	1	0	0	0	0	1	0	0	0	2	1	0	.125	.222
Peel, Aaron	R-R	6-0	195	2-8-83	.308	.238	.329	52	182	31	56	13	0	8	34	21	11	0	2	46	6	4	.511	.407
Ramos, Jason	B-R	5-11	185	8-9-82	.165	.063	.188	26	85	5	14	3	0	1	6	8	0	0	0	21	2	1	.235	.237
Remole, Clifton	L-L	6-1	205	10-24-82	.308	.667	.200	5	13	1	4	1	0	0	0	1	0	0	0	0	1	0	.385	.357
Renz, Jordan	B-R	6-3	225	7-21-83	.198	.247	.183	103	353	29	70	10	0	9	55	35	1	1	8	126	7	5	.303	.267
Rodriguez, Sean	R-R	6-1	198	4-26-85	.250	.206	.262	124	448	86	112	29	3	14	45	78	9	9	2	85	27	11	.422	.371
Sandoval, Freddy	B-R	6-2	205	8-16-82	.281	.248	.292	117	427	54	120	34	4	4	63	53	4	6	7	58	17	12	.407	.360
Sutton, Nate	L-R	6-0	190	9-1-82	.242	.255	.240	91	314	41	76	12	5	1	25	40	4	7	3	60	15	6	.322	.332
Toussaint, Drew	R-R	6-2	175	10-24-82	.261	.220	.273	109	391	68	102	25	3	21	68	45	7	2	3	125	11	5	.501	.345
Walston, Chris	R-R	6-6	225	10-1-84	.164	.115	.178	79	280	22	46	2	0	11	26	12	3	0	2	113	1	2	.289	.205

PITCHING	B-T	HT	WT	DOB	W	L	ERA	G	GS	CG	SV	IP	H	R	ER	HR	BB	SO	AVG	vLH	vRH	K/9	BB/9
Abreu, Francis	R-R	6-2	185	6-2-83	0	1	6.52	10	1	0	0	19	32	19	14	1	7	8	.390	.371	.404	3.72	3.26
Arnold, Mitchell	R-R	6-8	235	1-31-82	0	2	6.94	12	0	0	4	12	14	9	9	0	10	11	.298	.333	.276	8.49	7.71
Carney, Frederic	R-R	6-3	220	8-21-82	0	0	3.57	21	0	0	7	23	24	10	9	1	6	20	.279	.290	.273	7.94	2.38
Cordova, Francisco	R-R	6-3	231	8-26-83	4	5	4.35	29	9	0	4	89	80	48	43	8	36	67	.233	.247	.222	6.78	3.64
Douglas, Jaime	L-L	6-4	205	3-19-83	1	2	7.88	24	0	0	0	32	37	41	28	7	27	21	.289	.233	.306	5.91	7.59
Edwards, Bill	R-R	6-3	185	3-26-81	5	1	3.20	10	9	0	0	56	46	25	20	4	20	43	.231	.297	.200	6.87	3.20
Espinoza, Gustavo	L-L	6-0	170	9-9-86	1	0	1.69	1	1	0	0	5	5	2	1	1	1	3	.238	.000	.263	5.06	1.69
Gelinas, Karl	R-R	6-4	202	8-6-83	11	8	3.81	26	25	1	0	151	180	77	64	14	20	78	.294	.288	.298	4.65	1.19
Gonzalez, Miguel	R-R	6-1	165	5-27-84	2	5	4.70	28	0	0	8	44	47	30	23	4	8	42	.266	.225	.299	8.59	1.64
Green, Nick	R-R	6-4	180	8-20-84	3	3	3.58	26	8	1	2	101	95	47	40	11	14	74	.249	.235	.259	6.62	1.25
Layman, Bill	R-R	6-4	202	11-25-82	0	2	7.31	7	3	0	0	16	11	15	13	0	22	17	.193	.087	.265	9.56	12.38
Morillo, Lennyn	R-R	6-3	166	7-19-83	0	1	8.68	3	1	0	0	9	10	11	9	0	10	6	.270	.100	.333	5.79	9.64
Mutter, Casey	R-R	6-4	220	2-23-82	2	1	2.63	19	0	0	0	27	19	11	8	3	19	20	.196	.135	.233	6.59	6.26
Ray, Ronnie	R-R	6-3	195	5-11-84	6	3	3.42	19	9	0	1	71	69	29	27	2	30	43	.266	.220	.296	5.45	3.80
Rodriguez, Rafael	R-R	6-1	175	9-24-84	5	2	2.78	13	13	0	0	74	61	24	23	5	27	74	.220	.212	.226	8.96	3.27
Rodriguez, Fernando	R-R	6-3	210	6-18-84	8	10	4.18	28	28	4	0	157	161	87	73	8	49	128	.265	.293	.244	7.32	2.80
Simard, Michel	R-R	6-4	200	9-4-81	6	4	3.80	20	5	1	2	64	55	27	27	7	23	60	.231	.278	.199	8.44	3.23
Smith, Jesse	R-R	6-2	214	7-11-80	4	6	4.97	23	15	1	1	100	112	68	55	6	32	75	.286	.345	.252	6.77	2.89
Stanton, T.J.	L-R	6-4	230	5-4-81	4	4	4.62	35	0	0	4	51	67	33	26	5	20	43	.322	.325	.320	7.64	3.55
Torres, Joe	L-L	6-2	193	9-3-82	1	6	8.50	20	9	0	0	36	32	38	34	2	61	25	.258	.182	.286	6.25	15.25
Touchstone, Nic	L-L	6-4	220	11-19-81	1	4	7.83	11	4	0	0	23	27	23	20	3	29	18	.310	.278	.319	7.04	11.35
Waters, Chris	R-R	6-2	210	4-23-82	1	5	5.05	49	0	0	4	57	63	37	32	7	30	46	.279	.330	.246	7.26	4.74

FIELDING

Catcher	PCT	G	PO	A	E	DP	PB
Collins	.974	59	387	31	11	3	6
Dini	.986	9	65	5	1	1	1
Duenas	.964	55	397	61	17	4	4
Duff	.975	12	68	11	2	0	1
Johnson	.955	3	20	1	1	0	0
Martinez	1.000	2	9	0	0	0	0

First Base	PCT	G	PO	A	E	DP
Collins	.989	40	352	15	4	41
Johnson	.969	19	140	16	5	19
Martinez	.000	1	0	0	0	0
Remole	1.000	4	19	2	0	6
Sandoval	1.000	6	25	1	0	2
Sutton	1.000	1	7	0	0	1
Walston	.979	75	701	43	16	69

Second Base	PCT	G	PO	A	E	DP
Boyer	1.000	7	9	17	0	5
Casilla	.953	37	70	112	9	27
Leblanc	.872	8	14	20	5	6
Ramos	.969	12	24	38	2	9
Rodriguez	.974	12	29	45	2	16
Sutton	.975	70	110	197	8	43

Third Base	PCT	G	PO	A	E	DP
Boyer	.929	4	4	9	1	1
Ramos	.889	11	5	19	3	1
Rodriguez	.852	14	9	14	4	3
Sandoval	.947	113	75	245	18	21
Sutton	1.000	5	4	10	0	1

Shorstop	PCT	G	PO	A	E	DP
Boyer	.892	8	14	19	4	4
Caldera	.952	5	8	12	1	3
Casilla	.969	41	74	113	6	33
Ramos	.880	4	7	15	3	3
Rodriguez	.964	85	169	238	15	63

Outfield	PCT	G	PO	A	E	DP
Giannotti	.954	99	200	7	10	4
Leblanc	.976	50	118	2	3	1
Madrigal	.955	82	140	8	7	3
Peel	.943	30	32	1	2	0
Remole	1.000	1	4	0	0	0
Renz	.973	68	103	5	3	1
Rodriguez	.980	14	46	4	1	0
Toussaint	.963	79	122	8	5	0

OREM OWLZ — Rookie

PIONEER LEAGUE

BATTING	B-T	HT	WT	DOB	AVG	vLH	vRH	G	AB	R	H	2B	3B	HR	RBI	BB	HBP	SH	SF	SO	SB	CS	SLG	OBP
Albano, Marco	R-R	5-11	215	8-26-83	.190	.268	.136	34	100	14	19	3	0	3	10	14	1	0	0	40	0	0	.310	.296
Boyer, Billy	B-R	6-1	195	3-8-84	.249	.256	.245	67	241	37	60	15	1	8	30	23	6	1	4	87	8	5	.419	.325
Caldera, Jose	R-R	5-10	160	12-18-85	.238	.222	.250	7	21	3	5	0	1	0	3	0	0	1	0	2	0	0	.333	.238
Coon, Brad	L-L	6-0	175	12-11-82	.300	.244	.313	61	223	42	67	7	3	0	18	28	1	2	0	47	19	7	.359	.381
Cowles, Josh	R-R	6-2	210	6-7-84	.203	.244	.179	44	123	25	25	3	0	6	23	16	7	1	2	46	3	1	.374	.324
Dini, Greg	R-R	6-2	200	1-18-83	.351	.182	.423	12	37	6	13	4	0	0	4	1	0	1	0	6	0	0	.459	.368
Hughes, Michael	R-R	6-3	230	9-8-81	.205	.204	.205	49	127	20	26	5	2	2	13	12	4	1	0	48	3	1	.323	.294
Lepage, Patrice	L-R	6-1	210	7-10-84	.000	.000	.000	1	2	0	0	0	0	0	1	0	0	0	0	1	0	0	.000	.000
Maldonado, Martin	R-R	6-1	190	8-16-86	.250	.250	.250	9	32	4	8	0	0	1	2	2	0	0	0	6	0	0	.344	.294
Martinez, Brett	R-R	6-0	200	10-14-83	.277	.143	.321	53	173	30	48	8	3	4	25	27	6	1	2	40	7	0	.428	.389
Morris, Dallas	R-R	6-2	210	7-13-82	.302	.230	.323	70	295	47	89	23	3	9	52	16	5	0	1	52	4	3	.492	.347
Overstreet, Colby	L-R	6-4	220	10-15-83	.240	.182	.246	45	125	9	30	4	0	1	17	17	2	1	1	43	1	3	.296	.338
Reilly, Patrick	L-L	6-1	205	12-2-81	.308	.100	.327	41	120	14	37	9	0	3	14	4	1	2	2	35	3	1	.458	.331
Rosario, Anderson	R-R	6-0	170	3-2-85	.254	.289	.235	47	130	25	33	6	3	2	14	9	4	1	0	57	9	4	.392	.322
Silva, Johan	L-R	5-11	192	6-21-84	.214	.000	.250	17	42	4	9	3	0	1	7	5	0	1	0	15	0	0	.357	.298
Smith, Stan	R-R	6-4	211	10-21-83	.256	.276	.250	64	227	25	58	11	3	3	28	6	0	3	2	68	8	4	.370	.272
Statia, Hainley	B-R	5-11	162	1-19-86	.300	.303	.300	68	277	44	83	17	6	2	41	23	3	5	0	40	12	10	.426	.360
Trumbo, Mark	R-R	6-4	220	1-16-86	.274	.341	.249	71	299	45	82	23	1	10	45	21	1	0	2	67	2	2	.458	.322
Wipke, Flint	R-R	6-0	195	1-22-83	.295	.241	.327	28	78	17	23	5	1	5	19	14	3	4	1	25	1	1	.577	.417

PITCHING	B-T	HT	WT	DOB	W	L	ERA	G	GS	CG	SV	IP	H	R	ER	HR	BB	SO	AVG	vLH	vRH	K/9	BB/9
Abreu, Francis	R-R	6-2	185	6-2-83	0	2	4.15	8	0	0	0	17	23	10	8	1	5	12	.311	.208	.360	6.23	2.60
Adenhart, Nick	R-R	6-4	190	8-24-86	1	0	0.00	1	1	0	0	6	3	1	0	0	0	7	.143	.143	.143	10.50	0.00
Aldridge, Ryan	R-R	6-2	210	9-10-83	0	0	0.00	2	0	0	0	4	1	0	0	0	2	4	.083	.000	.167	9.00	4.50
Arredondo, Jose	R-R	6-0	175	3-30-84	5	0	4.19	15	13	0	0	69	76	34	32	4	20	60	.285	.235	.336	7.86	2.62
Cruz, Rafael	R-R	6-2	175	8-20-85	3	2	3.76	19	0	0	1	38	46	21	16	5	3	26	.301	.370	.238	6.10	0.70
Didjurgis, Tim	R-R	6-5	230	12-16-82	3	1	2.89	25	0	0	0	47	41	20	15	2	18	55	.232	.234	.230	10.61	3.47
Espinoza, Gustavo	L-L	6-0	170	9-9-86	0	0	9.00	1	0	0	0	2	3	2	2	0	0	1	.333	.000	.500	4.50	0.00
Hawkins, Daniel	R-R	6-3	200	8-11-82	6	2	3.32	16	10	0	0	60	53	25	22	2	23	58	.240	.226	.252	8.75	3.47
Hill, Andrew	R-R	6-3	195	10-31-84	3	4	4.64	13	4	0	0	33	35	22	17	1	14	32	.267	.294	.238	8.73	3.82
Lynch, Kevin	R-R	6-2	200	1-2-83	1	1	1.71	24	0	0	9	32	22	8	6	1	9	34	.198	.200	.197	9.66	2.56
Marek, Stephen	R-R	6-2	200	9-3-83	1	3	4.50	15	14	0	0	66	74	37	33	7	25	55	.292	.288	.297	7.50	3.41
Mattison, Tim	R-R	6-1	225	6-22-82	1	2	8.66	20	0	0	1	18	27	22	17	3	5	14	.329	.375	.300	7.13	2.55
Morillo, Lennyn	R-R	6-3	166	7-19-83	0	3	6.93	13	2	0	0	25	31	21	19	5	16	24	.304	.250	.352	8.76	5.84
Mosebach, Bobby	R-R	6-4	195	9-14-84	3	3	4.57	15	13	0	0	65	69	36	33	6	18	52	.280	.243	.313	7.20	2.49
Mutter, Casey	R-R	6-4	220	2-23-82	0	0	12.00	2	0	0	0	3	4	4	4	1	2	0	.333	.286	.400	0.00	6.00
Pete, Mike	L-L	6-0	170	1-29-83	2	1	0.99	20	0	0	2	27	27	5	3	0	9	24	.276	.296	.268	7.90	2.96
Romero, Robert	R-R	5-10	190	3-28-85	0	2	4.50	10	0	0	0	12	9	7	6	1	11	8	.214	.167	.250	6.00	8.25
Shearer, Kelly	L-L	6-3	200	4-8-85	2	4	3.62	15	13	0	0	65	60	34	26	3	23	45	.243	.313	.226	6.26	3.20
Sullivan, Anthony	R-R	5-11	185	7-2-84	5	2	6.03	19	1	0	0	37	48	26	25	5	16	30	.314	.328	.304	7.23	3.86
Whittington, Anthony	R-L	6-5	225	10-9-84	1	1	3.82	15	4	0	0	33	30	29	14	2	31	41	.234	.293	.207	11.18	8.45
Wilson, Brendan	R-R	6-1	183	10-7-85	1	5	7.71	11	1	0	0	21	24	18	18	3	15	17	.293	.302	.282	7.29	6.43

GAMES BY POSITION: C—Dini 10, Lepage 1, Maldonado 9, Martinez 49, Wipke 17. **1B**—Overstreet 7, Trumbo 70. **2B**—Albano 2, Boyer 66, Caldera 7, Silva 10. **3B**—Albano 9, Cowles 1, Morris 70, Silva 1. **SS**—Albano 10, Caldera 1, Silva 5, Statia 68. **OF**—Coon 57, Cowles 34, Hughes 42, Overstreet 19, Reilly 6, Rosario 44, Smith 64.

AZL ANGELS — Rookie

ARIZONA LEAGUE

BATTING	B-T	HT	WT	DOB	AVG	vLH	vRH	G	AB	R	H	2B	3B	HR	RBI	BB	HBP	SH	SF	SO	SB	CS	SLG	OBP
Bambino, Ricky	R-R	6-4	210	4-16-84	.179	.214	.160	16	39	5	7	2	0	0	6	0	1	1	1	9	0	0	.231	.195
Davies, Josh	R-R	6-4	200	9-12-85	.293	.306	.287	44	157	19	46	11	0	2	23	6	1	0	1	30	5	6	.401	.321
Edwards, Madison	L-R	5-11	175	9-1-83	.284	.278	.286	27	81	13	23	4	2	3	17	12	2	0	2	26	2	4	.494	.381
Fuller, Cody	R-R	6-0	190	9-19-82	.210	.217	.205	19	62	14	13	3	3	0	6	12	5	0	1	12	5	3	.355	.375
Gregorio, Tom	R-R	6-2	215	5-5-77	.167	.400	.000	4	12	1	2	0	0	0	1	0	1	0	0	3	0	0	.167	.231
Harper, Grant	R-R	6-1	185	10-3-85	.239	.222	.247	32	113	8	27	5	1	1	6	5	3	0	0	31	0	1	.327	.289
Infante, Larry	B-R	5-10	160	4-4-85	.227	.160	.245	36	119	17	27	4	1	3	13	16	1	2	0	22	5	3	.353	.324
Johnson, Tyler	R-R	6-2	220	11-2-85	.265	.200	.289	47	166	23	44	10	1	3	23	13	3	0	2	64	9	3	.392	.326
Leblanc, Josh	L-R	6-1	190	9-15-81	.111	.500	.000	2	9	1	1	1	0	0	2	0	0	0	0	4	1	0	.222	.111
Maldonado, Martin	R-R	6-1	190	8-16-86	.256	.238	.262	27	86	6	22	2	0	0	10	2	1	1	1	9	0	0	.279	.278
Matranga, Dave	R-R	6-0	185	1-8-77	.000	.000	.000	3	10	0	0	0	0	0	0	0	0	0	0	6	0	0	.000	.000
McPherson, Dallas	L-R	6-4	230	7-23-80	.222	.500	.143	3	9	1	2	1	1	0	2	0	0	0	0	5	0	0	.556	.222
Merloni, Lou	R-R	5-10	200	4-6-71	.333	.167	.444	6	15	3	5	1	0	0	2	2	0	0	0	2	0	0	.400	.412
Moore, Jeremy	L-R	6-1	190	6-29-87	.227	.296	.205	34	110	15	25	3	1	0	11	11	1	2	0	46	12	6	.273	.303
Mount, Ryan	L-R	6-1	180	8-17-86	.216	.040	.273	29	102	15	22	7	1	1	17	17	1	0	3	31	4	1	.333	.325
Nieves, Abel	R-R	5-11	175	8-14-85	.273	.333	.259	23	66	17	18	3	0	0	7	13	2	0	0	19	3	0	.318	.407
Phillips, P.J.	R-R	6-3	170	9-23-86	.291	.269	.300	49	182	25	53	6	6	1	24	9	2	0	2	53	13	5	.407	.328
Pressley, Ryan	B-R	6-6	255	9-29-86	.133	.063	.159	23	60	5	8	0	0	1	6	6	0	0	0	28	1	0	.183	.212
Pruitt, Dave	R-R	6-3	220	2-17-82	.000	.000	.000	1	1	0	0	0	0	0	0	0	0	0	0	0	0	0	.000	.000
Quinlan, Robb	R-R	6-1	200	3-17-77	.250	.000	.333	4	12	3	3	2	0	0	3	2	0	0	1	3	1	0	.417	.333
Rivera, Luis	R-R	6-1	190	10-12-86	.280	.233	.294	42	132	25	37	9	4	0	15	16	1	0	0	43	8	2	.409	.362
Ryan, Matt	L-L	6-4	205	4-4-86	.261	.286	.250	45	165	26	43	12	2	3	22	17	0	0	0	46	3	0	.412	.330
Sales, Darrell	R-R	6-1	210	9-12-85	.282	.267	.288	31	103	15	29	9	2	1	11	14	2	0	1	31	2	1	.437	.375
Silva, Johan	L-R	5-11	192	6-21-84	.222	.125	.250	10	36	2	8	3	1	0	2	1	1	0	0	8	1	0	.361	.263

PITCHING	B-T	HT	WT	DOB	W	L	ERA	G	GS	CG	SV	IP	H	R	ER	HR	BB	SO	AVG	vLH	vRH	K/9	BB/9
Adenhart, Nick	R-R	6-4	190	8-24-86	2	3	3.68	13	12	1	0	44	39	26	18	0	24	52	.245	.325	.218	10.64	4.91
Aldridge, Ryan	R-R	6-2	210	9-10-83	0	0	1.00	7	0	0	0	9	6	1	1	0	7	19	.194	.167	.200	19.00	7.00
Arnold, Mitch	R-R	6-8	235	1-31-82	0	0	1.59	6	0	0	1	6	3	1	1	0	1	10	.143	.000	.188	15.88	1.59
Arredondo, Felipe	R-R	6-4	225	10-4-86	2	5	5.03	14	7	0	0	59	63	38	33	3	13	62	.268	.310	.250	9.46	1.98
Beck, Bradley	L-L	5-11	185	1-10-85	2	3	1.91	20	0	0	0	28	23	9	6	1	4	32	.225	.261	.215	10.16	1.27
Bell, Trevor	L-R	6-2	180	10-12-86	0	0	4.50	4	4	0	0	8	10	4	4	0	3	7	.313	.200	.364	7.88	3.38
Cassevah, Bobby	R-R	6-3	195	9-11-85	2	5	5.40	15	4	0	0	45	57	28	27	2	14	27	.318	.381	.284	5.40	2.80
Diaz, Amalio	R-R	6-2	170	9-10-86	4	2	4.31	19	0	0	4	31	34	21	15	2	9	28	.272	.256	.279	8.04	2.59
Espinoza, Gustavo	L-L	6-0	170	9-9-86	5	3	3.84	13	12	0	0	70	72	36	30	3	12	78	.257	.333	.246	9.98	1.54
Gamboa, Felix	R-R	6-4	191	7-18-85	1	0	7.04	4	0	0	1	8	8	7	6	1	5	10	.242	.125	.280	11.74	5.87
Gonzalez, Miguel	R-R	6-1	165	5-27-84	1	0	0.00	3	0	0	0	4	0	0	0	0	0	7	.000	.000	.000	15.75	0.00
Herrera, Pedro	R-R	6-0	155	2-14-86	2	0	6.00	16	0	0	5	24	29	17	16	1	15	17	.299	.308	.296	6.38	5.63
Howell, Chris	R-R	6-0	210	5-11-83	0	1	6.30	9	0	0	0	10	10	7	7	0	5	8	.256	.000	.333	7.20	4.50
Jepsen, Kevin	R-R	6-3	215	7-26-84	0	1	5.52	7	7	0	0	15	8	10	9	1	11	17	.151	.188	.135	10.43	6.75
Mendoza, Tommy	R-R	6-2	185	8-18-87	3	3	1.55	13	4	0	0	52	42	14	9	1	13	56	.221	.182	.242	9.63	2.24
Peacock, Dylan	R-R	6-3	190	4-29-86	1	1	7.71	15	0	0	0	19	30	20	16	0	8	24	.357	.273	.387	11.57	3.86
Petke, Tim	R-R	6-3	220	4-17-80	0	1	11.81	5	0	0	0	5	9	7	7	1	2	4	.375	.667	.278	6.75	3.38
Posey, Micah	L-L	6-5	220	10-18-82	0	0	6.14	4	4	0	0	7	13	7	5	1	2	9	.342	.125	.400	11.05	2.45
Prinz, Bret	R-R	6-2	215	6-15-77	0	1	12.00	2	2	0	0	3	5	5	4	1	2	6	.333	.333	.333	18.00	6.00
Romero, Robert	R-R	5-10	190	3-28-85	0	0	2.70	7	0	0	3	7	7	3	2	1	0	8	.280	.375	.235	10.80	0.00
Stanton, T.J.	L-R	6-4	230	5-4-81	0	0	0.00	2	0	0	0	2	3	0	0	0	0	2	.375	.500	.333	10.80	0.00
West, Jim	R-R	6-2	175	12-21-84	0	2	3.71	14	0	0	0	27	25	15	11	1	12	30	.248	.182	.279	10.13	4.05

GAMES BY POSITION: C—Bambino 16, Edwards 19, Gregorio 4, Maldonado 26, Pruitt 1. **1B**—Davies 2, Harper 1, Johnson 1, Pressley 12, Quinlan 1, Ryan 42, Sales 6. **2B**—Davies 9, Infante 19, Matranga 1, Mount 8, Nieves 15, Phillips 5, Silva 5. **3B**—Davies 27, Infante 9, Matranga 1, McPherson 3, Merloni 4, Nieves 2, Phillips 9, Quinlan 1, Sales 9, Silva 4. **SS**—Davies 5, Infante 6, Matranga 1, Mount 17, Nieves 5, Phillips 27. **OF**—Davies 3, Edwards 8, Fuller 19, Harper 15, Johnson 43, Leblanc 2, Moore 33, Rivera 38, Ryan 1, Sales 12.

LOS ANGELES DODGERS

BY TONY JACKSON

A lot of heads turned and a lot of eyebrows went up during the offseason of 2004-05 when Dodgers general manager Paul DePodesta effectively blew up a division-winning team. But while many questioned what DePodesta was doing during his first offseason as a major league GM, no one ever imagined the Dodgers would fall this far and this hard in 2005.

Especially not manager Jim Tracy, who left the club the day after the season ended by what officially was termed "a mutual agreement." Less than a month later, DePodesta himself was fired.

Following an eight-game winning streak in early April that gave the Dodgers a 12-2 record, they suddenly and inexplicably hit a wall, never winning more than three in a row the rest of the season. They finished a catastrophic 71-91, fourth in the National League West, with their season drowned in a sea of injuries, offensive ineptitude and clubhouse acrimony.

The Dodgers lost Paul Bako, J.D. Drew, Eric Gagne, Cesar Izturis and Jose Valentin for at least three months each, and they lost several others for shorter periods.

Jayson Werth, one of the unsung heroes of the 2004 run to the division title, suffered a broken bone in his left wrist when he was hit by a pitch in the Grapefruit League opener in spring training. He missed the first two months of the season and never really recovered, finishing with a .234 average and a staggering 114 strikeouts in 337 at-bats.

Milton Bradley also was lost for the season in late August with an injury that conveniently led to season-ending surgery, preventing the club from having to suspend him for the season after he publicly ripped teammate Jeff Kent, implying Kent was a racist. Although no decision had been made on the future of Bradley, who was eligible for arbitration, it was clear the troubled center fielder would be either traded or non-tendered.

ORGANIZATION LEADERS

BATTING

*AVG	Flores, Jose, Las Vegas	.336
R	Donovan, Todd, Jacksonville/Las Vegas	96
H	Young, Delwyn, Jacksonville/Las Vegas	162
TB	LaRoche, Andy, Jacksonville/Vero Beach	263
2B	Young, Delwyn, Jacksonville/Las Vegas	37
3B	Donovan, Todd, Jacksonville/Las Vegas	11
	Hoffmann, Jamie, Columbus/Vero Beach	11
HR	LaRoche, Andy, Jacksonville/Vero Beach	30
RBI	LaRoche, Andy, Jacksonville/Vero Beach	94
BB	Denker, Travis, Columbus/Vero Beach	82
SO	Guzman, Joel, Jacksonville	128
SB	Donovan, Todd, Jacksonville/Las Vegas	65
*OBP	Flores, Jose, Las Vegas	.435
*SLG	Kemp, Matt, Vero Beach	.569

PITCHING

W	Billingsley, Chad, Jacksonville	13
L	Jackson, Edwin, Jacksonville/Las Vegas	11
#ERA	Alvarez, Carlos, Columbus/Jacksonville	2.03
G	Dannemiller, Beau, Jacksonville/Las Vegas	56
CG	Billingsley, Chad, Jacksonville	2
	Malone, Chris, Columbus	2
SV	Alexander, Mark, Vero Beach	23
IP	Billingsley, Chad, Jacksonville	146
	Stults, Eric, Jacksonville/Las Vegas	146
BB	Weeden, Brandon, Columbus	69
SO	Billingsley, Chad, Jacksonville	162

*Minimum 250 at-bats. #Minimum 75 innings.

PLAYERS OF THE YEAR

MAJOR LEAGUE: Jeff Kent, 2b

Kent has parlayed his short, compact swing into a 13-year career as a hitting machine. The 37-year-old did it all for the Dodgers in 2005, leading the club in hits, doubles, homers, RBIs and total bases. He also showed off excellent knowledge of the strike zone, with an 85-72 strikeout-walk ratio.

MINOR LEAGUE: Andy LaRoche, 3b

STEVE MOORE

LaRoche started 2005 at high Class A Vero Beach, where he kept pace with Angels' shortstop Brandon Wood for the minor league home run lead until he was promoted to Double-A Jacksonville in mid-June. LaRoche struggled making adjustments at the higher level but finished with 30 bombs overall.

Kent, meanwhile, became one of the few bright spots in an otherwise-lost season for the Dodgers. After signing a two-year, $17 million free-agent deal after the 2004 season to come home and play for the team he grew up rooting for, Kent, at age 37, put up some of the best numbers of his career. He batted .289-29-105 with very little protection in an otherwise-punchless lineup.

The Dodgers committed $60 million to free-agent pitchers Derek Lowe and Odalis Perez, in addition to the $9.35 million they already were committed to paying Jeff Weaver. Although Lowe and Weaver combined to win 26 games and each pitched more than 220 innings, they also combined to give up a disastrous 63 home runs.

As for Gagne, just two years removed from the greatest season any reliever ever had, he began the season on the disabled list with an injury he suffered when he stepped awkwardly during a spring-training drill. He then went down for the season in early June with what originally was thought to be Tommy John surgery, which would have kept him out until midway through 2006.

Once doctors cut him open, though, they found that Gagne needed a less serious procedure. He was throwing on flat ground by season's end and should be fully recovered by spring training.

Whoever replaces DePodesta and Tracy should benefit from a stockpile of talent in the minor leagues.

The Dodgers' Double-A Jacksonville affiliate, one of the most stacked minor league clubs in recent memory, cruised to the Southern League title behind its "big five" prospects, righthanders Chad Billingsley and Jonathan Broxton and infielders Joel Guzman, Andy LaRoche and James Loney.

Thanks largely to the draft success in recent years of scouting director Logan White and his staff, the Dodgers' farm system has become the envy of all of baseball. But on the down side, ballyhooed pitching prospect Edwin Jackson continued to take his lumps, both at Triple-A Las Vegas and in the big leagues. In between, though, Jackson was demoted to Jacksonville and went a respectable 6-4, 3.48 in 11 starts.

LOS ANGELES DODGERS

Manager: Jim Tracy.

2005 Record: 71-91, .438. (4th, NL West).

BATTING	B-T	HT	WT	DOB	AVG	vLH	vRH	G	AB	R	H	2B	3B	HR	RBI	BB	HBP	SH	SF	SO	SB	CS	SLG	OBP
Aybar, Willy	B-R	6-0	175	3-9-83	.326	.241	.368	26	86	12	28	8	0	1	10	18	1	0	0	11	3	1	.453	.448
Bako, Paul	L-R	6-2	215	6-20-72	.250	.250	.250	13	40	1	10	2	0	0	4	7	0	0	0	12	0	0	.300	.362
Bradley, Milton	B-R	6-0	190	4-15-78	.290	.278	.294	75	283	49	82	14	1	13	38	25	2	4	1	47	6	1	.484	.350
Chen, Chin-Feng	R-R	6-1	190	10-27-77	.250	.400	.000	7	8	1	2	0	0	0	2	0	0	0	0	4	0	0	.250	.250
Choi, Hee-Seop	L-L	6-5	240	3-16-79	.253	.207	.258	133	320	40	81	15	2	15	42	34	8	2	4	80	1	3	.453	.336
Cruz Jr., Jose	B-R	6-0	210	4-19-74	.301	.529	.238	47	156	23	47	14	2	6	22	23	0	0	0	43	0	1	.532	.391
2-team (64 Arizona)					.251	.333	.229	111	358	46	90	23	2	18	50	65	0	0	1	97	0	2	.478	.366
Drew, J.D.	L-R	6-1	200	11-20-75	.286	.235	.304	72	252	48	72	12	1	15	36	51	5	0	3	50	1	1	.520	.412
Edwards, Mike	R-R	6-1	185	11-24-76	.247	.253	.244	88	239	23	59	9	2	3	15	16	2	1	0	34	1	1	.339	.300
Grabowski, Jason	L-R	6-3	200	5-24-76	.161	.111	.165	65	112	14	18	0	0	4	12	10	0	0	1	29	1	0	.268	.228
Izturis, Cesar	B-R	5-9	180	2-10-80	.257	.303	.242	106	444	48	114	19	2	2	31	25	4	4	1	51	8	8	.322	.302
Kent, Jeff	R-R	6-1	210	3-7-68	.289	.306	.285	149	553	100	160	36	0	29	105	72	8	0	4	85	6	2	.512	.377
Ledee, Ricky	L-L	6-1	215	11-22-73	.278	.200	.286	102	237	31	66	16	1	7	39	20	3	0	6	55	0	0	.443	.335
Myrow, Brian	L-R	5-11	190	9-4-76	.200	.000	.200	19	20	2	4	1	0	0	0	5	0	0	0	8	0	0	.250	.360
Nakamura, Norihiro	R-R	5-10	205	7-24-73	.128	.118	.136	17	39	1	5	2	0	0	3	2	0	0	0	7	0	0	.179	.171
Navarro, Dioner	B-R	5-10	190	2-9-84	.273	.435	.248	50	176	21	48	9	0	3	14	20	2	1	0	21	0	0	.375	.354
Perez, Antonio	R-R	5-11	175	1-26-80	.297	.312	.291	98	259	28	77	13	2	3	23	21	5	1	1	61	11	4	.398	.360
Phillips, Jason	R-R	6-1	220	9-27-76	.238	.270	.229	121	399	38	95	20	0	10	55	25	4	2	4	50	0	1	.363	.287
Repko, Jason	R-R	5-11	175	12-27-80	.221	.235	.213	129	276	43	61	15	3	8	30	16	7	2	0	80	5	0	.384	.281
Robles, Oscar	L-R	5-11	155	4-9-76	.272	.267	.273	110	364	44	99	18	1	5	34	31	2	1	1	33	0	8	.368	.332
Rose, Mike	B-R	6-1	225	8-25-76	.209	.125	.259	15	43	2	9	2	0	1	1	3	0	0	0	6	0	0	.326	.261
Ross, Cody	R-L	5-11	180	12-23-80	.160	.333	.063	14	25	1	4	1	0	0	1	1	0	0	0	10	0	0	.200	.192
Saenz, Olmedo	R-R	5-11	220	10-8-70	.263	.261	.265	109	319	39	84	24	0	15	63	27	3	0	2	63	0	1	.480	.325
Valentin, Jose	L-R	5-10	190	10-12-69	.170	.316	.148	56	147	17	25	4	2	2	14	31	4	0	2	38	3	1	.265	.326
Werth, Jayson	R-R	6-5	210	5-20-79	.234	.239	.233	102	337	46	79	22	2	7	43	48	6	1	3	114	11	2	.374	.338

PITCHING	B-T	HT	WT	DOB	W	L	ERA	G	GS	CG	SV	IP	H	R	ER	HR	BB	SO	AVG	vLH	vRH	K/9	BB/9
Alvarez, Wilson	L-L	6-1	255	3-24-70	1	4	5.63	21	2	0	0	24	31	15	15	7	7	16	.316	.387	.284	6.00	2.63
Brazoban, Yhency	R-R	6-1	170	6-11-80	4	10	5.33	74	0	0	21	73	70	46	43	11	32	61	.258	.267	.250	7.56	3.96
Broxton, Jonathan	R-R	6-4	275	6-16-84	1	0	5.93	14	0	0	0	14	13	11	9	0	12	22	.245	.304	.200	14.49	7.90
Carlyle, Buddy	L-R	6-3	175	12-21-77	0	0	8.36	10	0	0	0	14	16	13	13	4	4	13	.291	.296	.286	8.36	2.57
Carrara, Giovanni	R-R	6-2	230	3-4-68	7	4	3.93	72	0	0	0	76	65	35	33	6	38	56	.243	.234	.248	6.66	4.52
Dessens, Elmer	R-R	5-10	200	1-13-71	1	2	3.56	28	7	0	0	66	63	30	26	6	19	37	.249	.243	.254	5.07	2.60
Erickson, Scott	R-R	6-4	230	2-2-68	1	4	6.02	19	8	0	0	55	62	37	37	12	25	15	.288	.295	.282	2.44	4.07
Gagne, Eric	R-R	6-2	235	1-7-76	1	0	2.70	14	0	0	8	13	10	4	4	2	3	22	.200	.217	.185	14.85	2.03
Houlton, D.J.	R-R	6-4	220	8-12-79	6	9	5.16	35	19	0	0	129	145	79	74	21	52	90	.289	.314	.271	6.28	3.63
Jackson, Edwin	R-R	6-3	190	9-9-83	2	2	6.28	7	6	0	0	29	31	22	20	2	17	13	.272	.333	.236	4.08	5.34
Kuo, Hong-Chih	L-L	6-0	200	7-23-81	0	1	6.75	9	0	0	0	5	5	4	4	1	5	10	.238	.385	.000	16.88	8.44
Lowe, Derek	R-R	6-6	210	6-1-73	12	15	3.61	35	35	2	0	222	223	113	89	28	55	146	.260	.296	.219	5.92	2.23
Osoria, Franquelis	R-R	6-0	165	9-12-81	0	2	3.94	24	0	0	0	30	28	14	13	3	8	15	.259	.392	.140	4.55	2.43
Penny, Brad	R-R	6-4	250	5-24-78	7	9	3.90	29	29	1	0	175	185	78	76	17	41	122	.270	.263	.276	6.26	2.10
Perez, Odalis	L-L	6-0	220	6-7-77	7	8	4.56	19	19	0	0	109	109	59	55	13	28	74	.262	.256	.264	6.13	2.32
Sanchez, Duaner	R-R	6-0	190	10-14-79	4	7	3.73	79	0	0	8	82	75	36	34	8	36	71	.248	.310	.182	7.79	3.95
Schmoll, Steve	R-R	6-2	200	2-4-80	2	2	5.01	48	0	0	3	47	47	29	26	4	22	29	.275	.303	.244	5.59	4.24
Thompson, Derek	L-L	6-2	180	1-8-81	0	0	3.50	4	3	0	0	18	16	7	7	0	10	13	.258	.231	.265	6.50	5.00
Weaver, Jeff	R-R	6-5	200	8-22-76	14	11	4.22	34	34	3	0	224	220	111	105	35	43	157	.256	.297	.208	6.31	1.73
Wunsch, Kelly	L-L	6-5	225	7-12-72	1	1	4.56	45	0	0	0	24	20	12	12	2	14	22	.227	.194	.308	8.37	5.32

FIELDING

Catcher	PCT	G	PO	A	E	DP	PB
Bako	.985	13	61	6	1	0	1
Navarro	.995	50	336	29	2	1	3
Phillips	.992	93	564	34	5	6	4
Rose	.978	13	83	5	2	2	1

First Base	PCT	G	PO	A	E	DP
Choi	.997	83	698	62	2	59
Grabowski	1.000	3	11	0	0	1
Kent	.980	14	92	6	2	9
Myrow	1.000	5	20	0	0	2
Nakamura	.947	4	18	0	1	2
Phillips	1.000	21	143	12	0	16
Saenz	.998	66	460	19	1	36

Second Base	PCT	G	PO	A	E	DP
Aybar	1.000	6	2	6	0	1
Kent	.978	140	284	424	16	87
Nakamura	1.000	1	1	0	0	0
Perez	.970	29	40	58	3	10
Robles	.500	1	0	1	1	1

Third Base	PCT	G	PO	A	E	DP
Aybar	.962	20	16	35	2	3
Edwards	.918	39	22	56	7	5
Nakamura	1.000	10	3	16	0	2
Perez	.946	35	18	70	5	5
Robles	.979	40	24	70	2	5
Saenz	.951	17	17	22	2	3
Valentin	.913	29	19	54	7	4

Shortstop	PCT	G	PO	A	E	DP
Edwards	1.000	1	0	2	0	0
Izturis	.977	106	145	327	11	61
Nakamura	1.000	2	0	1	0	1
Perez	.972	9	10	25	1	6
Robles	.981	54	75	132	4	28
Valentin	1.000	1	0	2	0	1

Outfield	PCT	G	PO	A	E	DP
Bradley	.989	72	181	6	2	0
Chen	1.000	3	2	0	0	0
Cruz	.954	45	100	3	5	0
Drew	.987	72	147	3	2	0
Edwards	1.000	34	53	0	0	0
Grabowski	.974	32	36	1	1	0
Ledee	.975	69	76	2	2	1
Perez	.000	1	0	0	0	0
Repko	.968	118	173	7	6	3
Ross	.933	9	12	2	1	1
Valentin	.972	22	35	0	1	0
Werth	.987	101	218	6	3	2

FARM SYSTEM

General Manager: Paul DePodesta. **Director, Player Development:** Terry Collins. **Scouting Director:** Logan White.

Class	Farm Team	League	W	L	Pct.	Finish*	Manager	Affiliate Since
AAA	Las Vegas (Nev.) 51s	Pacific Coast	57	86	.399	16th (16)	Jerry Royster	2001
AA	Jacksonville (Fla.) Suns	Southern	79	61	.564	**+4th (10)**	John Shoemaker	2002
Hi A	Vero Beach (Fla.) Dodgers	Florida State	77	56	.579	**3rd (12)**	Scott Little	1980
Lo A	Columbus (Ga.) Catfish	South Atlantic	57	79	.419	14th (16)	Travis Barbary	2002
Rookie	Ogden (Utah) Raptors	Pioneer	39	37	.513	**3rd (8)**	Juan Bustabad	2003
Rookie	Vero Beach (Fla.) Dodgers	Gulf Coast	25	29	.463	7th (12)	Luis Salazar	2001

*Finish in overall standings (No. of teams in league)/Playoff teams in **boldpace** +League champion

LAS VEGAS 51s — Class AAA

PACIFIC COAST LEAGUE

BATTING	B-T	HT	WT	DOB	AVG	vLH	vRH	G	AB	R	H	2B	3B	HR	RBI	BB	HBP	SH	SF	SO	SB	CS	SLG	OBP
Apodaca, Juan	R-R	5-11	188	7-15-86	.143	.000	.250	2	7	0	1	0	0	0	0	0	0	0	0	1	0	0	.143	.143
Aybar, Willy	B-R	6-0	175	3-9-83	.297	.254	.320	108	401	47	119	26	4	5	60	40	1	1	7	56	1	6	.419	.356
Bradley, Milton	B-R	6-0	190	4-15-78	.308	.167	.429	5	13	2	4	0	0	0	1	1	0	0	0	2	1	1	.308	.357
Cabrera, Mayke	L-R	6-1	204	2-10-81	.250	.000	.333	3	8	0	2	0	0	0	0	0	0	0	0	1	0	0	.250	.250
Chen, Chin-Feng	R-R	6-1	190	10-27-77	.278	.269	.281	87	317	59	88	20	2	15	63	38	2	1	5	82	3	3	.495	.354
Donovan, Todd	R-R	6-1	180	8-12-78	.378	.471	.321	13	45	7	17	1	1	0	6	5	1	0	1	8	3	3	.444	.442
Edwards, Mike	R-R	6-1	185	11-24-76	.280	.293	.273	32	118	18	33	6	0	4	21	11	3	0	1	21	3	1	.432	.353
Flores, Jose	R-R	5-11	180	6-28-73	.336	.330	.339	96	327	64	110	11	6	4	42	54	6	6	4	33	1	6	.443	.435
Gil, Rotsen	B-R	5-10	207	3-2-84	.333	.167	.444	7	15	3	5	1	0	1	3	0	0	0	0	4	0	0	.600	.333
Grabowski, Jason	L-R	6-3	200	5-24-76	.309	.283	.320	52	181	37	56	16	1	6	33	30	0	0	0	26	0	0	.508	.408
Gutierrez, Gabriel	R-R	5-11	175	11-24-83	.462	.200	.625	4	13	1	6	0	0	0	3	0	2	0	0	2	0	0	.462	.533
Jackson, D.J.	R-R	6-1	190	6-13-84	.259	.250	.263	9	27	4	7	0	1	1	6	0	0	1	0	10	1	0	.444	.259
Michaelis, Derek	L-L	6-7	240	12-2-78	.156	.000	.172	16	32	2	5	0	0	1	4	4	0	0	0	9	1	0	.250	.250
Myrow, Brian	L-R	5-11	190	9-4-76	.282	.250	.293	121	393	83	111	28	5	22	73	74	9	0	5	83	4	2	.547	.403
Nakamura, Norihiro	R-R	5-10	205	7-24-73	.249	.262	.244	101	357	54	89	17	1	22	67	45	1	0	5	70	0	0	.487	.331
Navarro, Dioner	B-R	5-10	190	2-9-84	.266	.267	.265	75	241	31	64	12	0	6	29	38	2	2	3	24	2	2	.390	.366
Nixon, Mike	R-R	6-3	210	8-17-83	.226	.208	.239	46	124	12	28	6	0	2	17	5	1	1	3	28	0	0	.323	.256
Perez, Antonio	R-R	5-11	175	1-26-80	.232	.222	.234	16	56	8	13	3	0	2	6	3	1	1	1	20	2	1	.393	.279
Repko, Jason	R-R	5-11	175	12-27-80	.387	.467	.313	8	31	6	12	0	0	3	6	0	0	1	0	4	1	0	.677	.387
Rohan, Jimmy	R-R	6-1	190	5-13-84	.250	.250	.250	10	20	1	5	0	0	0	1	2	0	0	0	4	0	1	.250	.318
Rose, Mike	B-R	6-1	225	8-25-76	.259	.212	.281	69	205	31	53	20	1	5	36	25	3	0	3	51	2	0	.439	.343
Ross, Cody	R-L	5-11	180	12-23-80	.267	.262	.269	115	393	79	105	21	4	22	63	49	2	0	4	103	4	2	.509	.348
Schrager, Tony	R-R	6-1	170	6-14-77	.233	.193	.255	86	249	47	58	15	0	10	34	43	3	3	6	53	3	3	.414	.346
Stanley, Henri	L-L	5-10	185	12-15-77	.255	.243	.258	99	337	52	86	15	5	15	46	35	1	5	2	72	7	7	.463	.325
Theodorou, Nick	B-R	5-11	180	6-7-75	.252	.299	.224	97	262	40	66	10	3	1	23	30	3	3	0	43	6	1	.324	.336
Thurston, Joe	L-R	5-11	190	9-29-79	.288	.260	.295	84	257	32	74	10	2	6	35	13	3	10	3	36	4	5	.412	.326
Valentin, Jose	L-R	5-10	190	10-12-69	.400	.381	.429	12	35	8	14	3	0	2	5	7	1	0	0	6	1	0	.657	.512
Werth, Jayson	R-R	6-5	210	5-20-79	.367	.500	.333	15	49	9	18	0	0	3	10	13	2	0	0	17	6	1	.551	.516
Young, Delwyn	B-R	5-10	180	6-30-82	.325	.269	.352	36	160	23	52	12	0	4	14	8	1	1	0	35	0	0	.475	.361

PITCHING	B-T	HT	WT	DOB	W	L	ERA	G	GS	CG	SV	IP	H	R	ER	HR	BB	SO	AVG	vLH	vRH	K/9	BB/9
Alvarez, Wilson	L-L	6-1	255	3-24-70	0	1	2.35	4	4	0	0	8	4	2	2	1	2	9	.154	.167	.150	10.57	2.35
Brooks, Frank	L-L	6-1	190	9-6-78	0	0	0.00	1	0	0	0	2	2	2	0	0	1	0	.250	.000	.250	0.00	5.40
Carlyle, Buddy	L-R	6-3	175	12-21-77	1	2	4.88	20	6	0	2	48	51	28	26	7	21	53	.280	.282	.279	9.94	3.94
Dannemiller, Beau	R-R	6-0	210	12-26-79	0	0	6.81	29	0	0	1	37	42	28	28	7	25	32	.294	.328	.263	7.78	6.08
Dessens, Elmer	R-R	5-10	200	1-13-71	0	0	3.38	3	3	0	0	8	6	3	3	1	2	6	.214	.308	.133	6.75	2.25
Eckert, Harold	R-R	6-3	218	7-18-77	5	10	6.38	33	20	1	1	135	159	105	96	23	63	121	.293	.332	.258	8.05	4.19
Erickson, Scott	R-R	6-4	230	2-2-68	2	4	7.20	7	7	0	0	40	47	34	32	6	21	26	.294	.313	.280	5.85	4.73
Farmer, Tom	R-R	6-2	195	7-27-79	1	2	15.19	20	0	0	0	21	45	41	36	4	21	16	.409	.450	.360	6.75	8.86
Gagne, Eric	R-R	6-2	235	1-7-76	0	0	0.00	3	0	0	0	4	0	0	0	0	0	7	.000	.000	.000	15.75	0.00
Gonzalez, Alfredo	B-R	5-11	165	9-17-79	2	2	4.91	46	0	0	3	66	72	39	36	10	34	43	.279	.330	.242	5.86	4.64
Gonzalez, Luis	L-L	6-0	205	2-27-83	0	1	9.31	10	0	0	0	10	13	10	10	3	11	10	.342	.455	.296	9.31	10.24
Hull, Eric	R-R	5-11	190	12-3-79	0	1	7.88	2	2	0	0	8	9	11	7	0	8	7	.281	.267	.294	7.88	9.00
Jackson, Edwin	R-R	6-3	190	9-9-83	3	7	8.62	12	11	1	0	55	76	61	53	13	37	33	.328	.319	.336	5.37	6.02
Lopez, Aquilino	R-R	6-3	165	4-21-75	3	4	5.89	27	0	0	5	37	40	24	24	9	6	32	.276	.286	.270	7.85	1.47
Mahomes, Pat	R-R	6-4	200	8-9-70	9	9	5.35	40	15	0	1	133	158	87	79	23	67	94	.301	.336	.270	6.36	4.53
Nall, T.J.	R-R	6-1	207	11-4-80	6	7	7.17	29	15	0	0	108	154	95	86	20	47	96	.338	.371	.311	8.00	3.92
Neu, Mike	B-R	5-10	175	3-9-78	2	3	5.56	35	9	0	1	89	101	62	55	11	62	54	.294	.313	.276	5.46	6.27
Osoria, Franquelis	R-R	6-0	165	9-12-81	6	4	2.62	40	0	0	9	55	63	18	16	3	13	35	.299	.271	.317	5.73	2.13
Penny, Brad	R-R	6-4	250	5-24-78	1	0	3.00	1	1	0	0	6	5	2	2	1	2	9	.217	.250	.200	13.50	3.00
Perez, Odalis	L-L	6-0	220	6-7-77	1	0	4.30	4	4	0	0	15	14	7	7	1	4	11	.255	.222	.261	6.75	2.45
Rodriguez, Orlando	L-L	5-10	155	11-28-80	0	0	6.23	5	0	0	0	4	1	3	3	0	9	3	.083	.250	.000	6.23	18.69
Rupe, Ryan	R-R	6-5	250	3-31-75	4	6	6.42	23	11	1	0	76	94	60	54	13	24	74	.303	.324	.287	8.80	2.85
Schmoll, Steve	R-R	6-2	200	2-4-80	0	3	4.78	22	0	0	5	26	24	15	14	1	13	31	.253	.289	.228	10.59	4.44
Stults, Eric	L-L	6-2	225	12-9-79	3	7	6.58	15	14	0	0	78	107	60	57	15	24	60	.322	.347	.315	6.92	2.77
Thompson, Derek	L-L	6-2	180	1-8-81	1	2	3.43	4	3	0	0	21	21	11	8	1	11	17	.273	.250	.277	7.29	4.71
Totten, Heath	R-R	6-2	235	9-30-78	7	9	7.12	20	18	0	0	104	149	98	82	18	28	71	.339	.322	.355	6.16	2.43
Venafro, Mike	L-L	5-10	180	8-2-73	0	1	6.85	53	0	0	1	45	60	38	34	4	35	24	.335	.275	.384	4.84	7.05
Wayne, Justin	R-R	6-3	205	4-16-79	0	1	14.40	4	0	0	0	5	5	8	8	1	10	3	.263	.200	.500	5.40	18.00

FIELDING

Catcher	PCT	G	PO	A	E	DP	PB
Apodaca	1.000	2	14	0	0	1	0
Gil	.960	4	22	2	1	0	1
Gutierrez	.926	4	23	2	2	0	0
Navarro	.998	66	452	39	1	10	2
Nixon	.995	32	180	17	1	0	3
Rose	.997	46	314	19	1	4	2
Theodorou	1.000	1	3	0	0	0	1

First Base	PCT	G	PO	A	E	DP
Edwards	.991	14	97	10	1	2
Grabowski	1.000	1	2	0	0	0
Myrow	.991	104	798	102	8	105
Nakamura	.967	35	265	25	10	35
Rose	.800	1	3	1	1	2

Second Base	PCT	G	PO	A	E	DP
Aybar	.974	28	45	68	3	17

	PCT	G	PO	A	E	DP
Flores	.897	7	10	16	3	5
Schrager	.920	11	18	28	4	6
Theodorou	1.000	8	7	18	0	4
Thurston	.981	75	151	202	7	46
Young	.980	36	85	115	4	38

Third Base	PCT	G	PO	A	E	DP
Aybar	.963	78	42	141	7	17
Cabrera	1.000	2	2	3	0	0
Edwards	1.000	5	2	4	0	1
Myrow	1.000	1	1	1	0	0
Nakamura	.932	51	29	95	9	20
Perez	.926	14	9	16	2	3
Rohan	.000	2	0	0	0	0
Schrager	.750	4	0	3	1	0
Theodorou	.824	7	4	10	3	2
Valentin	1.000	4	0	6	0	0

Shortstop	PCT	G	PO	A	E	DP
Flores	.949	74	114	167	15	39
Nakamura	.979	14	22	25	1	8
Perez	1.000	2	2	5	0	1
Schrager	.972	53	70	137	6	36
Theodorou	.923	11	21	27	4	10

Outfield	PCT	G	PO	A	E	DP
Bradley	1.000	5	2	0	0	0
Chen	.950	82	122	11	7	4
Donovan	1.000	13	25	1	0	0
Edwards	1.000	15	22	0	0	0
Grabowski	.938	32	41	4	3	0
Jackson	1.000	9	18	0	0	0
Michaelis	1.000	6	6	0	0	0
Myrow	.900	11	9	0	1	0
Nixon	1.000	10	10	1	0	0
Repko	1.000	7	15	0	0	0
Rohan	1.000	4	5	1	0	0
Rose	1.000	7	18	0	0	0
Ross	.995	110	209	7	1	2
Schrager	1.000	8	10	0	0	0
Stanley	.963	87	181	1	7	0
Theodorou	.976	52	76	6	2	1
Valentin	1.000	4	7	2	0	0
Werth	.957	15	20	2	1	0

JACKSONVILLE SUNS — Class AA

SOUTHERN LEAGUE

BATTING	B-T	HT	WT	DOB	AVG	vLH	vRH	G	AB	R	H	2B	3B	HR	RBI	BB	HBP	SH	SF	SO	SB	CS	SLG	OBP
Abreu, Tony	R-R	5-11	160	11-13-84	.250	.241	.254	24	96	10	24	3	2	0	9	4	1	0	1	21	0	2	.323	.284
Alvarez, Nick	R-R	6-3	207	2-8-77	.295	.291	.298	98	237	27	70	11	0	2	35	26	2	0	4	32	2	0	.367	.364
Donovan, Todd	R-R	6-1	180	8-12-78	.275	.279	.272	119	459	89	126	16	10	8	36	43	14	6	0	89	62	13	.405	.355
Garcia, Sergio	R-R	5-10	170	3-29-80	.248	.268	.239	80	234	30	58	8	0	4	38	26	7	5	1	44	1	1	.333	.340
Gonzalez, Adolfo	B-R	5-11	160	6-13-85	.268	.429	.185	14	41	3	11	3	0	1	3	2	0	1	1	11	0	0	.415	.295
Guzman, Joel	R-R	6-6	225	11-24-84	.287	.300	.283	122	442	63	127	31	2	16	75	42	5	0	7	128	7	3	.475	.351
Langill, Eric	R-R	5-9	190	4-4-79	.266	.182	.311	35	94	5	25	0	0	0	5	7	0	3	0	23	0	1	.266	.317
LaRoche, Andy	R-R	5-11	185	9-13-83	.273	.296	.266	64	227	41	62	12	0	9	43	32	3	0	2	54	2	2	.445	.367
Loney, James	L-L	6-3	200	5-7-84	.284	.258	.296	138	504	74	143	31	2	11	65	59	2	1	6	87	1	4	.419	.357
Martin, Russell	R-R	5-11	200	2-15-83	.311	.275	.325	129	409	83	127	17	1	9	61	78	10	5	3	69	15	7	.423	.430
Meadows, Tydus	R-R	6-2	220	9-5-77	.274	.355	.241	108	325	59	89	27	0	15	65	79	3	0	2	96	3	1	.495	.418
Medero-Stullz, Carlos	R-R	5-8	190	5-30-86	.500	.000	1.000	2	2	0	1	1	0	0	0	0	0	0	0	0	0	0	1.000	.500
Michaelis, Derek	L-L	6-7	240	12-2-78	.237	.250	.233	45	114	13	27	7	0	1	11	14	0	0	0	42	1	2	.325	.320
Mitchell, Russ	R-R	6-1	182	2-15-85	.200	.500	.000	3	5	1	1	1	0	0	3	0	0	0	0	4	0	0	.400	.200
Nicholson, David	R-R	6-0	175	10-22-82	.118	.125	.115	17	34	4	4	1	0	0	1	2	0	0	0	13	0	0	.147	.167
Nixon, Mike	R-R	6-3	210	8-17-83	.150	.000	.300	6	20	0	3	0	0	0	0	2	0	0	0	4	0	0	.150	.227
Perez, Eduardo	B-R	6-1	175	8-30-84	.000	.000	.000	2	4	0	0	0	0	0	0	0	0	0	0	2	0	0	.000	.000
Rohan, Jimmy	R-R	6-1	190	5-13-84	.296	.286	.303	22	54	8	16	2	0	0	4	2	0	1	0	8	1	0	.333	.321
Ruggiano, Justin	R-R	6-2	205	4-12-82	.342	.383	.325	53	161	23	55	10	1	6	29	17	6	0	1	56	8	3	.528	.422
Soto, Jesus	B-R	5-11	178	9-7-86	.000	.000	.000	3	5	0	0	0	0	0	0	0	0	0	0	5	0	0	.000	.000
Sprout, Brian	R-R	6-0	205	6-28-80	.254	.227	.269	57	205	30	52	11	1	5	23	17	3	0	1	32	2	0	.390	.319
Weber, Jon	L-L	5-10	190	1-20-78	.300	.198	.340	117	450	81	135	27	5	11	68	45	5	2	1	78	10	6	.456	.369
Young, Delwyn	B-R	5-10	180	6-30-82	.296	.359	.263	95	371	52	110	25	1	16	62	27	3	1	4	86	1	3	.499	.346

PITCHING	B-T	HT	WT	DOB	W	L	ERA	G	GS	CG	SV	IP	H	R	ER	HR	BB	SO	AVG	vLH	vRH	K/9	BB/9
Alvarez, Carlos	L-L	5-9	160	3-31-85	4	0	3.99	25	0	0	0	38	38	18	17	4	16	31	.264	.364	.234	7.28	3.76
Bartlett, Richard	R-R	6-3	221	10-6-81	3	3	4.88	35	1	0	3	59	63	39	32	3	43	30	.276	.289	.269	4.58	6.56
Billingsley, Chad	R-R	6-2	215	7-29-84	13	6	3.51	28	26	2	0	146	116	60	57	12	50	162	.215	.217	.213	9.99	3.08
Bott, Glenn	L-L	6-0	190	9-17-81	2	4	5.12	25	1	0	1	39	34	24	22	6	25	42	.231	.185	.258	9.78	5.82
Broxton, Jonathan	R-R	6-4	275	6-16-84	5	3	3.17	33	13	0	5	97	79	36	34	4	31	107	.223	.275	.179	9.96	2.89
Dannemiller, Beau	R-R	6-0	210	12-26-79	1	3	4.81	27	0	0	4	43	32	24	23	4	28	37	.208	.250	.167	7.74	5.86
Gonzalez, Alfredo	B-R	5-11	165	9-17-79	2	1	3.86	5	0	0	0	7	4	4	3	0	4	8	.167	.167	.167	10.29	5.14
Gonzalez, Luis	L-L	6-0	205	2-27-83	7	2	2.21	41	0	0	7	61	35	17	15	1	34	46	.165	.183	.158	6.79	5.02
Hanrahan, Joel	R-R	6-3	215	10-6-81	9	8	4.92	23	21	0	0	112	118	71	61	17	55	102	.273	.316	.233	8.22	4.43
Hull, Eric	R-R	5-11	190	12-3-79	7	7	3.38	27	18	1	3	117	105	50	44	9	44	117	.237	.258	.218	9.00	3.38
Jackson, Edwin	R-R	6-3	190	9-9-83	6	4	3.48	11	11	0	0	62	52	31	24	7	18	44	.224	.235	.215	6.39	2.61
Juarez, William	R-R	6-2	203	4-22-81	6	5	4.59	38	14	0	0	104	116	60	53	11	48	75	.289	.333	.251	6.49	4.15
Kuo, Hong-Chih	L-L	6-0	200	7-23-81	1	1	1.91	17	0	0	3	28	22	7	6	1	11	44	.210	.250	.198	13.98	3.49
Miller, Greg	L-L	6-5	220	11-3-84	0	0	2.77	12	0	0	2	13	14	6	4	1	15	17	.275	.250	.286	11.77	10.38
Ojeda, Alvis	R-R	6-0	170	9-23-83	1	0	2.38	7	1	0	0	11	10	3	3	0	2	9	.244	.385	.179	7.15	1.59
Olson, Jason	R-R	6-2	180	6-12-78	1	3	5.86	36	0	0	5	66	67	44	43	8	39	62	.260	.264	.255	8.45	5.32
Orenduff, Justin	R-R	6-4	205	5-27-83	5	2	4.07	14	13	0	0	66	59	33	30	6	24	65	.241	.267	.221	8.82	3.26
Perez, Beltran	R-R	6-2	180	10-24-81	2	3	2.90	17	1	0	3	31	22	11	10	1	16	32	.200	.213	.190	9.29	4.65
Rodriguez, Orlando	L-L	5-10	155	11-28-80	0	0	5.54	8	0	0	0	13	14	11	8	1	11	13	.280	.231	.297	9.00	7.62
Stults, Eric	L-L	6-2	225	12-9-79	4	3	3.31	12	12	0	0	68	73	33	25	6	14	58	.266	.277	.262	7.68	1.85
Thompson, Derek	L-L	6-2	180	1-8-81	0	2	3.89	8	8	0	0	42	45	20	18	3	19	43	.283	.140	.336	9.29	4.10

FIELDING

Catcher	PCT	G	PO	A	E	DP	PB
Langill	.985	27	187	7	3	1	3
Martin	.989	117	960	90	12	4	14
Medero-Stullz	.000	1	0	0	0	0	0
Nixon	.906	4	25	4	3	0	1

First Base	PCT	G	PO	A	E	DP
Alvarez	1.000	7	36	1	0	5
Langill	1.000	4	11	0	0	1
LaRoche	.000	1	0	0	0	0
Loney	.993	136	948	92	7	61
Michaelis	1.000	4	29	3	0	4
Nixon	1.000	1	2	0	0	0

Second Base	PCT	G	PO	A	E	DP
Abreu	.954	21	47	36	4	7
Donovan	1.000	1	0	1	0	0
Garcia	.947	16	21	33	3	6
Gonzalez	.952	10	21	19	2	2
Mitchell	.000	1	0	0	0	0
Nicholson	1.000	7	6	8	0	2
Rohan	.941	5	10	6	1	3
Soto	.750	1	3	3	2	2
Young	.965	90	139	189	12	26

Third Base	PCT	G	PO	A	E	DP
Alvarez	.714	8	4	6	4	0
Garcia	.833	10	1	4	1	0
Guzman	.889	21	10	22	4	3
LaRoche	.941	63	43	85	8	11
Mitchell	1.000	2	0	1	0	1
Perez	1.000	2	1	4	0	0
Rohan	.833	6	2	3	1	1
Sprout	.942	52	22	75	6	6
Young	1.000	1	0	1	0	0

Shortstop	PCT	G	PO	A	E	DP
Abreu	1.000	4	5	4	0	2
Garcia	.985	38	40	90	2	8
Gonzalez	.667	1	1	1	1	0
Guzman	.934	99	116	238	25	35
Nicholson	.933	6	3	11	1	1
Rohan	.974	8	14	23	1	5

Outfield	PCT	G	PO	A	E	DP
Alvarez	1.000	36	61	4	0	0
Donovan	.990	117	287	4	3	1
Garcia	.972	16	30	5	1	2
Gonzalez	1.000	1	3	0	0	0
Loney	1.000	3	1	0	0	0
Martin	.000	1	0	0	0	0
Meadows	.993	95	139	3	1	0
Michaelis	1.000	21	21	2	0	0
Nicholson	1.000	2	1	0	0	0
Nixon	1.000	1	1	0	0	0
Ruggiano	.978	49	84	3	2	1
Sprout	1.000	10	10	0	0	0
Weber	.972	115	226	19	7	7
Young	1.000	1	1	0	0	0

VERO BEACH DODGERS — High Class A

FLORIDA STATE LEAGUE

BATTING	B-T	HT	WT	DOB	AVG	vLH	vRH	G	AB	R	H	2B	3B	HR	RBI	BB	HBP	SH	SF	SO	SB	CS	SLG	OBP
Abreu, Tony	R-R	5-11	160	11-13-84	.327	.327	.327	96	394	54	129	23	7	4	43	15	5	3	4	56	14	10	.452	.356
Bellorin, Edwin	R-R	5-11	170	2-21-82	.273	.347	.249	87	308	36	84	18	2	3	33	14	4	1	2	44	1	1	.373	.311
Bruce, Cole	R-R	6-3	195	1-20-82	.247	.357	.197	56	178	26	44	6	1	6	21	14	1	2	4	56	6	0	.393	.299
Cabrera, Mayke	L-R	6-1	204	2-10-81	.274	.063	.303	48	135	12	37	2	0	0	16	19	1	0	0	33	0	2	.289	.368
Denker, Travis	R-R	5-9	170	8-5-85	.185	.143	.200	31	108	14	20	3	0	2	9	15	2	0	0	26	1	2	.269	.296
Dewitt, Blake	L-R	5-11	175	8-20-85	.419	.500	.400	8	31	4	13	3	0	1	7	1	0	0	0	3	0	0	.613	.438
Dunlap, Cory	L-L	6-1	205	4-13-84	.291	.331	.276	121	430	61	125	25	0	7	77	65	3	0	7	64	5	2	.398	.382
Dyson, Trey	L-L	6-4	215	3-11-80	.161	.000	.185	10	31	6	5	1	0	0	5	3	0	0	1	6	0	0	.194	.229
Ellis, A.J.	R-R	6-3	240	4-9-81	.256	.224	.271	57	176	27	45	8	0	3	22	22	6	1	1	26	1	3	.352	.356
Hoffmann, Jamie	R-R	6-3	205	8-20-84	.241	.239	.242	46	166	26	40	6	2	1	10	10	1	0	1	45	3	1	.319	.287
Hu, Chin-lung	R-R	5-9	152	2-2-84	.313	.300	.318	116	470	80	147	29	1	8	56	19	7	7	2	40	23	6	.430	.347
Kemp, Matt	R-R	6-4	210	9-23-84	.306	.304	.307	109	418	76	128	21	4	27	90	25	5	1	5	92	23	6	.569	.349
LaRoche, Andy	R-R	5-11	185	9-13-83	.333	.269	.357	63	249	54	83	14	1	21	51	19	1	0	2	38	6	1	.651	.380
Laurin, Dominique	R-R	6-0	185	10-7-82	.118	.111	.125	16	34	3	4	2	0	0	0	3	0	3	0	18	0	0	.176	.189
Mitchell, Russ	R-R	6-1	182	2-15-85	.303	.167	.333	13	33	5	10	1	0	1	4	2	0	1	1	6	0	0	.424	.333
Nixon, Mike	R-R	6-3	210	8-17-83	.231	.200	.250	23	65	13	15	5	0	2	11	11	1	1	0	21	1	2	.400	.351
Paul, Matt	R-R	5-10	190	9-3-82	.000	.000	.000	4	8	0	0	0	0	0	0	0	0	0	0	3	0	0	.000	.000
Paul, Xavier	L-R	6-0	200	2-25-85	.247	.134	.281	85	288	42	71	15	3	7	41	32	4	4	2	81	1	5	.392	.328
Raglani, Anthony	L-L	6-2	215	4-6-83	.289	.287	.289	124	419	82	121	20	5	19	77	60	7	0	5	98	9	2	.496	.383
Rohan, Jimmy	R-R	6-1	190	5-13-84	.274	.290	.267	70	223	33	61	12	0	3	33	20	4	1	3	20	6	3	.368	.340
Ruggiano, Justin	R-R	6-2	205	4-12-82	.310	.276	.325	71	242	47	75	15	4	9	37	28	9	0	1	65	16	5	.517	.400
Russ, Ryan	B-R	6-2	200	3-7-81	.264	.278	.257	16	53	7	14	4	0	0	4	2	0	1	0	11	0	1	.340	.291

PITCHING	B-T	HT	WT	DOB	W	L	ERA	G	GS	CG	SV	IP	H	R	ER	HR	BB	SO	AVG	vLH	vRH	K/9	BB/9
Alexander, Mark	R-R	5-10	190	12-6-80	5	4	3.03	52	0	0	23	65	64	25	22	6	23	91	.256	.346	.215	12.54	3.17
Bailey, Chad	L-L	6-4	190	6-24-83	0	0	13.06	7	0	0	0	10	19	17	15	4	6	9	.373	.364	.375	7.84	5.23
Bott, Glenn	L-L	6-0	190	9-17-81	0	2	5.08	14	3	0	0	28	24	17	16	3	24	36	.220	.222	.220	11.44	7.62
Diaz, Jose	R-R	6-4	247	2-27-84	0	1	0.00	14	0	0	0	16	6	3	0	0	12	18	.122	.200	.103	10.34	6.89
Figueroa, Jonathan	L-L	6-5	205	9-15-83	4	3	6.00	22	16	0	0	81	81	54	54	14	53	52	.266	.153	.294	5.78	5.89
Hanrahan, Joel	R-R	6-3	215	10-6-81	1	0	5.91	5	5	0	0	21	25	15	14	5	11	25	.291	.296	.288	10.55	4.64
Hoorelbeke, Casey	R-R	6-8	245	4-4-80	9	3	2.40	42	1	0	4	83	74	25	22	0	35	58	.253	.280	.240	6.31	3.81
Kuo, Hong-Chih	L-L	6-0	200	7-23-81	1	1	2.08	11	3	0	0	26	19	7	6	2	10	42	.202	.240	.188	14.54	3.46
Megrew, Mike	L-L	6-6	210	1-29-84	0	2	20.25	2	2	0	0	4	9	9	9	1	2	2	.429	.333	.444	4.50	4.50
Merricks, Matt	L-L	6-0	200	8-6-82	2	1	4.88	10	4	0	0	28	23	18	15	6	10	27	.219	.158	.233	8.78	3.25
Miller, Greg	L-L	6-5	220	11-3-84	1	0	0.93	5	3	0	0	10	4	1	1	0	7	10	.138	.000	.190	9.31	6.52
Muegge, Danny	L-R	6-5	180	3-6-81	8	2	3.38	31	18	0	0	128	124	53	48	11	34	91	.255	.254	.255	6.42	2.40
Ojeda, Alvis	R-R	6-0	170	9-23-83	5	1	3.36	28	2	0	1	62	47	27	23	1	20	36	.216	.197	.224	5.25	2.92
Orenduff, Justin	R-R	6-4	205	5-27-83	5	3	2.24	12	12	1	0	60	35	21	15	3	26	81	.167	.130	.189	12.08	3.88
Penny, Brad	R-R	6-4	250	5-24-78	1	0	1.80	1	1	0	0	5	2	1	1	1	1	3	.125	.167	.100	5.40	1.80
Perez, Beltran	R-R	6-2	180	10-24-81	3	2	3.78	19	0	0	0	33	31	15	14	3	15	33	.256	.350	.210	8.91	4.05
Pilkington, Brian	R-R	6-5	248	9-17-82	7	9	3.71	19	17	1	0	107	112	54	44	10	24	70	.267	.295	.252	5.91	2.03
Pimentel, Julio	R-R	6-1	190	12-14-85	8	10	5.08	26	24	1	0	124	149	79	70	9	43	105	.305	.308	.304	7.62	3.12
Plummer, Jarod	R-R	6-5	200	1-27-84	1	1	3.20	9	1	0	0	25	22	9	9	1	7	23	.239	.294	.207	8.17	2.49
Rodriguez, Orlando	L-L	5-10	155	8-31-82	1	0	4.15	12	0	0	1	17	14	9	8	2	9	25	.212	.308	.189	12.98	4.67
Rodriguez, Mike	R-R	6-1	180	11-28-80	0	0	9.95	10	0	0	0	13	18	17	14	3	10	13	.327	.267	.350	9.24	7.11
Simmons, Justin	L-L	6-3	225	10-5-81	4	2	4.42	44	0	0	1	57	63	29	28	4	30	51	.281	.278	.282	8.05	4.74
Tiffany, Chuck	L-L	6-1	195	1-25-85	11	7	3.93	22	21	0	0	110	91	52	48	17	43	134	.226	.188	.233	10.96	3.52
Wilson, Kyle	R-R	6-2	200	4-21-83	0	2	8.05	18	0	0	4	19	30	20	17	3	7	18	.349	.400	.328	8.53	3.32
Wright, Wesley	R-L	5-11	160	1-28-85	0	0	9.45	6	0	0	0	7	8	7	7	0	10	8	.296	.400	.273	10.80	13.50

FIELDING

Catcher	PCT	G	PO	A	E	DP	PB
Bellorin	.997	82	635	52	2	3	5
Ellis	.990	54	443	44	5	2	4
Nixon	1.000	3	20	1	0	0	0

First Base	PCT	G	PO	A	E	DP
Bruce	.990	14	90	13	1	11
Cabrera	.967	10	54	4	2	5
Dunlap	.985	98	748	46	12	89
Dyson	1.000	2	10	0	0	2
Laurin	1.000	5	24	2	0	0
Mitchell	.943	4	32	1	2	0
Nixon	1.000	4	23	2	0	2
Rohan	.976	8	37	4	1	5

Second Base	PCT	G	PO	A	E	DP
Abreu	.977	88	181	206	9	49
Bruce	1.000	3	2	4	0	0
Cabrera	.000	1	0	0	0	0
Denker	.964	28	45	88	5	17
Laurin	1.000	6	13	6	0	1
Mitchell	1.000	1	0	3	0	0
Rohan	.989	19	34	54	1	17

Third Base	PCT	G	PO	A	E	DP
Bruce	.895	32	6	45	6	3
Cabrera	.905	13	7	12	2	1
Dewitt	1.000	8	5	7	0	0
LaRoche	.920	55	45	105	13	8
Laurin	.000	1	0	0	0	0
Mitchell	.800	5	2	6	2	0
Rohan	.943	28	17	49	4	5

Shortstop	PCT	G	PO	A	E	DP
Abreu	1.000	9	15	19	0	6
Bruce	1.000	3	4	2	0	0
Hu	.958	116	157	340	22	70
Laurin	1.000	1	1	6	0	1
Rohan	.857	11	15	15	5	5

Outfield	PCT	G	PO	A	E	DP
Dunlap	1.000	1	1	0	0	0
Dyson	1.000	4	6	1	0	0
Hoffmann	1.000	42	84	0	0	0
Kemp	.976	103	198	4	5	0
Laurin	1.000	3	4	0	0	0
Nixon	1.000	12	10	0	0	0
M. Paul	1.000	1	4	0	0	0
X. Paul	.923	56	76	8	7	0
Raglani	.983	103	169	5	3	1
Rohan	1.000	12	8	0	0	0
Ruggiano	.955	66	101	4	5	0
Russ	1.000	15	27	2	0	0

COLUMBUS CATFISH — Low Class A

SOUTH ATLANTIC LEAGUE

BATTING	B-T	HT	WT	DOB	AVG	vLH	vRH	G	AB	R	H	2B	3B	HR	RBI	BB	HBP	SH	SF	SO	SB	CS	SLG	OBP
Apodaca, Juan	R-R	5-11	188	7-15-86	.244	.313	.220	35	123	10	30	3	1	4	20	7	0	1	2	21	0	1	.382	.280
Batz, Daniel	R-R	6-2	210	3-19-82	.280	.262	.281	120	429	59	120	27	2	4	46	38	9	0	5	45	5	2	.380	.347
Brown, Jeremy	R-R	6-1	195	4-2-84	.200	.000	.333	5	20	2	4	0	0	0	4	0	2	0	0	4	0	0	.200	.273
Bruce, Cole	R-R	6-3	195	1-20-82	.304	.286	.309	22	69	10	21	4	1	5	11	2	0	0	2	20	1	1	.609	.315
Carter, Brandon	L-R	5-7	170	11-12-82	.221	.190	.225	75	276	38	61	6	0	1	33	30	4	1	2	33	0	4	.254	.304
Carter, Ryan	R-R	6-2	175	1-4-83	.281	.346	.262	60	224	35	63	13	1	14	44	8	3	0	0	68	4	0	.536	.315
Crist, Justin	R-R	5-10	175	8-6-82	.176	.375	.115	12	34	3	6	1	0	0	4	2	0	0	1	8	0	0	.206	.216

BATTING	B-T	HT	WT	DOB	AVG	vLH	vRH	G	AB	R	H	2B	3B	HR	RBI	BB	HBP	SH	SF	SO	SB	CS	SLG	OBP
Denker, Travis	R-R	5-9	170	8-5-85	.310	.299	.318	101	358	65	111	23	1	21	68	67	3	0	6	78	2	5	.556	.417
Dewitt, Blake	L-R	5-11	175	8-20-85	.283	.218	.301	120	481	61	136	31	3	11	65	34	4	0	3	79	0	1	.428	.333
Gutierrez, Gabriel	R-R	5-11	175	11-24-83	.259	.304	.244	71	232	25	60	9	1	3	18	18	6	2	1	40	0	1	.345	.327
Hoffmann, Jamie	R-R	6-3	205	8-20-84	.308	.295	.313	79	321	53	99	13	9	1	24	39	1	5	2	73	10	4	.414	.383
Laurin, Dominique	R-R	6-0	185	10-7-82	.161	.154	.159	54	168	20	27	4	0	5	18	17	3	3	4	62	2	1	.274	.245
May, Lucas	R-R	6-0	190	10-24-84	.229	.175	.251	99	385	46	88	14	2	9	53	16	7	1	7	92	5	2	.345	.267
Medero-Stullz, Carlos	R-R	5-8	190	5-30-86	.333	.000	.500	1	3	0	1	0	0	0	0	2	0	0	0	2	0	0	.333	.600
Nicholson, David	R-R	6-0	175	10-22-82	.246	.247	.246	92	345	49	85	14	2	2	28	28	4	0	1	67	7	5	.316	.310
Pedroza, Sergio	L-R	5-11	180	2-23-84	.207	.184	.213	49	179	31	37	11	1	12	30	16	6	0	0	58	0	0	.480	.294
Perez, Eduardo	B-R	6-1	175	8-30-84	.212	.429	.154	10	33	0	7	2	0	0	4	1	1	0	0	10	0	0	.273	.257
Peterson, James	L-L	6-0	210	10-14-83	.243	.087	.288	30	103	8	25	4	0	2	10	15	0	1	1	29	2	0	.340	.336
Richmond, B.J.	L-L	6-3	185	2-3-84	.103	.091	.107	12	39	2	4	1	0	0	2	4	0	0	0	14	1	0	.128	.186
Russ, Ryan	B-R	6-2	200	3-7-81	.279	.308	.271	98	351	48	98	20	5	8	49	24	8	2	2	66	4	6	.433	.338
Sapp, Steven	R-R	6-3	190	11-17-85	.130	.000	.158	10	23	2	3	1	0	0	1	2	0	0	0	9	0	0	.174	.200
Steidl, Sam	L-L	5-10	185	5-9-81	.244	.235	.246	55	193	25	47	7	0	0	12	29	3	6	1	24	2	0	.280	.350
Westervelt, Chris	R-R	5-11	205	11-20-81	.263	.280	.246	53	179	31	47	15	0	5	29	33	4	0	0	35	0	0	.430	.389

PITCHING	B-T	HT	WT	DOB	W	L	ERA	G	GS	CG	SV	IP	H	R	ER	HR	BB	SO	AVG	vLH	vRH	K/9	BB/9
Akin, Brian	R-R	6-3	185	10-13-81	1	4	4.35	35	1	0	2	72	77	38	35	8	31	54	.277	.243	.299	6.72	3.86
Alvarez, Carlos	L-L	5-9	160	3-31-85	2	2	0.93	20	0	0	3	39	24	9	4	0	12	63	.176	.205	.165	14.66	2.79
Bailey, Chad	L-L	6-4	190	6-24-83	2	4	4.93	19	1	0	0	42	57	34	23	3	15	29	.322	.244	.348	6.21	3.21
Castillo, Albenis	R-R	6-4	178	12-24-83	1	5	3.99	38	0	0	10	56	61	33	25	4	26	48	.271	.292	.256	7.67	4.15
Castillo, Arismendy	R-R	6-3	190	12-10-84	0	2	6.43	3	1	0	0	7	14	12	5	0	2	6	.389	.250	.500	7.71	2.57
Castillo, Jesus	R-R	6-1	178	5-31-84	1	2	2.96	6	5	0	0	24	18	8	8	0	7	28	.205	.238	.174	10.36	2.59
Elbert, Scott	L-L	6-2	190	8-13-85	8	5	2.66	25	24	1	0	115	83	37	34	8	57	128	.200	.144	.215	10.02	4.46
Guerra, Javy	R-R	6-1	185	10-31-85	2	5	4.96	11	11	0	0	53	51	35	29	3	23	40	.249	.177	.312	6.84	3.93
Hammes, Zach	R-R	6-7	246	5-15-84	3	4	4.81	22	8	0	1	64	69	43	34	7	52	46	.273	.257	.286	6.50	7.35
Hochgesang, Nathan	R-R	6-4	220	12-18-81	1	0	6.62	6	2	0	0	18	25	14	13	1	7	26	.321	.333	.303	13.25	3.57
Johnson, Blake	R-R	6-3	185	6-14-85	9	4	3.33	24	17	1	0	100	83	47	37	4	36	88	.226	.234	.219	7.92	3.24
Malone, Chris	R-R	6-4	230	6-28-83	9	7	3.88	31	21	2	0	142	133	77	61	10	41	127	.248	.247	.248	8.07	2.60
Nelson, Steve	L-R	6-3	224	11-10-82	4	4	4.53	19	4	1	1	50	53	32	25	9	11	26	.270	.244	.289	4.71	1.99
O'Flaherty, Liam	R-L	6-0	165	1-18-85	3	2	5.96	16	0	0	0	26	30	17	17	2	16	19	.309	.250	.338	6.66	5.61
Plummer, Jarod	R-R	6-5	200	1-27-84	3	2	4.14	9	8	0	0	54	52	27	25	5	6	49	.244	.175	.302	8.12	0.99
Pratt, Jordan	R-R	6-3	195	5-17-85	0	1	6.06	6	1	0	0	16	13	13	11	1	11	14	.213	.214	.212	7.71	6.06
Reina, Dimas	R-R	5-10	231	2-23-82	0	3	5.06	11	6	0	0	32	27	21	18	2	34	20	.235	.224	.246	5.63	9.56
Sobkow, Philip	R-R	6-5	210	6-17-81	2	2	8.39	11	2	0	0	25	40	24	23	4	17	19	.370	.387	.348	6.93	6.20
Troncoso, Ramon	R-R	6-2	187	2-16-83	2	3	6.69	13	6	0	1	38	58	33	28	2	13	27	.360	.349	.372	6.45	3.11
Wade, Cory	R-R	6-2	180	5-28-83	0	2	4.05	12	0	0	2	20	29	19	9	2	10	14	.341	.289	.383	6.30	4.50
Weeden, Brandon	R-R	6-4	195	10-14-83	2	9	5.70	26	18	0	1	95	101	67	60	13	69	96	.277	.247	.300	9.13	6.56
Wilson, Kyle	R-R	6-2	200	4-21-83	1	2	2.16	20	0	0	2	25	16	6	6	1	9	31	.184	.211	.163	11.16	3.24
Wright, Wesley	R-L	5-11	160	1-28-85	1	5	1.93	30	0	0	1	61	38	21	13	2	33	68	.178	.136	.195	10.09	4.90

FIELDING

Catcher	PCT	G	PO	A	E	DP	PB
Apodaca	.989	35	263	18	3	2	6
Gutierrez	.993	71	552	53	4	4	9
Medero-Stullz	1.000	1	10	1	0	0	0
Westervelt	.985	34	254	15	4	2	5

First Base	PCT	G	PO	A	E	DP
Batz	.993	111	909	76	7	96
Bruce	1.000	9	72	4	0	9
Nicholson	.993	18	123	10	1	17

Second Base	PCT	G	PO	A	E	DP
Bruce	1.000	2	2	8	0	2
Carter	.960	44	63	127	8	29
Crist	.875	8	9	12	3	2
Denker	.972	67	120	226	10	54
Nicholson	.987	19	22	54	1	9

Third Base	PCT	G	PO	A	E	DP
Dewitt	.918	109	73	172	22	16
Nicholson	.954	20	18	44	3	7
Perez	.750	7	3	9	4	1

Shortstop	PCT	G	PO	A	E	DP
Bruce	.909	8	11	19	3	6
Carter	.833	3	4	6	2	3
Crist	1.000	1	0	1	0	0
Laurin	.937	54	81	126	14	35
May	.893	46	87	131	26	35
Nicholson	.966	28	38	77	4	20

Outfield	PCT	G	PO	A	E	DP
Batz	1.000	3	3	0	0	0
Brown	1.000	5	8	1	0	1
Carter	.982	55	103	5	2	1
Carter	1.000	13	14	2	0	0
Hoffmann	.967	79	144	3	5	1
May	.935	26	25	4	2	0
Pedroza	.967	45	86	1	3	1
Peterson	.879	22	27	2	4	1
Richmond	1.000	12	17	1	0	0
Russ	.982	96	214	5	4	2
Sapp	1.000	6	8	1	0	0
Steidl	.976	54	76	7	2	1

OGDEN RAPTORS

Rookie

PIONEER LEAGUE

BATTING	B-T	HT	WT	DOB	AVG	vLH	vRH	G	AB	R	H	2B	3B	HR	RBI	BB	HBP	SH	SF	SO	SB	CS	SLG	OBP
Apodaca, Juan	R-R	5-11	188	7-15-86	.278	.128	.328	42	158	24	44	7	0	10	31	14	2	0	0	33	2	0	.513	.345
Arias, Hector	R-R	6-3	205	9-5-84	.000	.000	.000	1	4	0	0	0	0	0	0	0	0	0	0	2	0	0	.000	.000
Brooks, Parker	B-R	5-10	175	8-1-81	.226	.444	.136	10	31	4	7	3	0	0	2	2	0	0	0	7	0	0	.323	.273
Crist, Justin	R-R	5-10	175	8-6-82	.232	.286	.214	16	56	9	13	1	0	1	7	3	0	0	0	5	2	1	.304	.271
DeJesus, Ivan	R-R	5-11	182	5-1-87	.208	.205	.212	20	72	4	15	1	0	0	3	6	3	0	0	18	3	3	.222	.296
Gil, Rotsen	B-R	5-10	207	3-2-84	.163	.071	.207	12	43	5	7	3	0	2	4	2	0	0	0	10	0	0	.372	.200
Godwin, Adam	R-R	5-11	170	12-13-82	.310	.357	.291	55	197	38	61	12	1	1	21	12	5	4	4	32	12	7	.396	.358
Jackson, D.J.	R-R	6-1	190	6-13-84	.200	.194	.203	35	100	17	20	4	1	1	13	6	3	2	0	40	2	0	.290	.266
Jansen, Kenley	B-R	6-2	178	9-30-87	.182	.333	.125	3	11	2	2	1	0	0	1	1	0	0	0	5	0	0	.273	.250
Justis, Shane	R-R	5-10	175	3-11-83	.273	.200	.307	36	110	20	30	7	2	2	15	9	5	1	1	17	3	3	.427	.352
Locke, Drew	R-R	6-1	205	2-28-83	.272	.203	.314	50	169	34	46	9	0	13	31	19	2	2	0	37	1	1	.556	.353
McDonald, James	L-R	6-5	195	10-19-84	.229	.143	.246	28	83	12	19	3	1	0	8	9	1	1	0	25	3	0	.289	.312
Mitchell, Russ	R-R	6-1	182	2-15-85	.289	.271	.295	69	270	54	78	19	1	13	54	26	4	1	2	52	3	3	.511	.358
Mooneyham, Jason	L-L	5-11	210	4-19-82	.280	.200	.303	56	182	27	51	11	0	6	27	29	10	0	1	32	1	0	.440	.405
Pedroza, Sergio	L-R	5-11	180	2-23-84	.500	.250	.553	12	46	13	23	1	0	4	18	6	2	0	0	8	4	0	.783	.574
Pujols, Kengshill	R-R	6-0	187	3-3-85	.195	.179	.203	32	87	7	17	2	0	2	11	8	2	0	1	25	0	1	.287	.276
Richmond, B.J.	L-L	6-3	185	2-3-84	.284	.226	.306	66	232	29	66	14	0	5	30	31	1	0	4	55	12	4	.409	.366
Rivera, Juan	B-R	6-0	148	3-17-87	.251	.135	.284	41	171	27	43	5	0	1	16	14	2	2	2	32	9	7	.298	.312
Robinson, Trayvon	R-R	5-10	175	9-1-87	.217	.300	.154	8	23	2	5	0	0	1	2	0	0	0	0	9	0	0	.348	.217
Soto, Jesus	B-R	5-11	178	9-7-86	.280	.300	.272	63	254	57	71	16	0	6	28	21	2	5	4	44	13	1	.413	.335
Steidl, Sam	L-L	5-10	185	5-9-81	.192	.000	.208	8	26	4	5	1	0	0	3	7	0	0	0	3	1	1	.231	.364
Sutherland, David	L-L	6-6	175	5-2-85	.336	.309	.346	66	247	44	83	13	2	4	47	34	4	0	2	27	4	1	.453	.422
Taloa, Rick	R-R	6-4	250	12-14-84	.267	.233	.289	22	75	7	20	6	0	2	9	0	3	0	1	26	0	1	.427	.291

PITCHING	B-T	HT	WT	DOB	W	L	ERA	G	GS	CG	SV	IP	H	R	ER	HR	BB	SO	AVG	vLH	vRH	K/9	BB/9
Alvarez, Mario	R-R	6-0	150	3-26-84	3	3	6.14	12	12	0	0	56	63	39	38	8	22	53	.290	.351	.226	8.57	3.56
Arias, Marlon	L-L	6-3	155	9-1-84	4	4	5.48	14	14	0	0	71	81	53	43	11	27	73	.282	.262	.286	9.30	3.44
Gomez de Segura, Matt	R-R	6-5	230	5-9-83	1	2	6.57	17	0	0	1	25	31	22	18	2	24	19	.310	.436	.230	6.93	8.76
Hayes, Alvin	R-R	6-6	195	8-19-83	2	1	7.26	19	2	0	0	31	28	26	25	4	27	38	.241	.227	.250	11.03	7.84
Hochgesang, Nathan	R-R	6-4	220	12-18-81	1	2	4.25	14	0	0	0	30	36	22	14	2	12	28	.295	.279	.304	8.49	3.64
Horlacher, David	R-R	6-4	175	6-22-82	0	0	1.69	11	0	0	0	16	10	5	3	1	9	25	.179	.227	.147	14.06	5.06
Klusman, Aaron	R-R	6-4	225	9-9-80	4	2	3.09	20	0	0	0	32	35	16	11	1	10	24	.278	.295	.268	6.75	2.81
Krise, Kris	R-R	6-6	215	2-1-84	0	4	7.90	15	4	0	0	35	51	40	31	8	14	28	.331	.338	.326	7.13	3.57
Leach, Brent	L-L	6-5	205	11-18-82	5	3	2.43	14	13	1	0	67	53	21	18	4	29	77	.227	.262	.215	10.40	3.92
McDonald, James	L-R	6-5	195	10-19-84	0	0	1.50	4	0	0	0	6	4	3	1	0	2	9	.174	.333	.000	13.50	3.00
Meloan, Jon	R-R	6-3	225	7-11-84	0	2	3.69	16	6	0	1	39	30	16	16	4	18	54	.210	.213	.207	12.46	4.15
Obispo, Jose	R-R	6-1	160	5-11-84	0	0	8.53	6	0	0	0	6	6	6	6	0	15	6	.261	.500	.176	8.53	21.32
Paredes, Ramon	L-L	6-3	192	11-28-84	1	1	7.59	3	1	0	0	11	12	10	9	2	7	6	.300	.417	.250	5.06	5.91
Pfeiffer, David	L-L	6-3	190	8-17-85	7	3	5.63	15	7	0	1	56	62	42	35	4	14	47	.281	.300	.273	7.55	2.25
Pratt, Jordan	R-R	6-3	195	5-17-85	2	2	3.25	14	0	0	0	28	24	12	10	0	14	35	.235	.233	.237	11.39	4.55
Ramirez, Miguel	R-R	5-11	180	7-15-83	0	0	2.31	7	0	0	0	12	9	3	3	2	3	21	.209	.211	.208	16.20	2.31
Troncoso, Ramon	R-R	6-2	187	2-16-83	6	2	3.68	29	0	0	13	37	40	19	15	0	12	30	.278	.290	.268	7.36	2.95
Wade, Cory	R-R	6-2	180	5-28-83	2	3	4.35	16	11	1	0	72	81	42	35	12	19	60	.291	.264	.312	7.47	2.36
White, Cody	L-L	6-3	185	2-27-85	1	3	6.92	17	6	0	0	40	59	35	31	2	27	36	.351	.414	.338	8.03	6.02

GAMES BY POSITION: C—Apodaca 38, Gil 12, Jansen 3, Pujols 30. **1B**—Mooneyham 22, Sutherland 45, Taloa 11. **2B**—Brooks 8, Crist 4, Justis 10, Soto 61. **3B**—Crist 2, Justis 10, Mitchell 66. **SS**—Crist 9, DeJesus 17, Justis 13, Rivera 41. **OF**—Godwin 51, Jackson 30, Locke 48, McDonald 26, Pedroza 12, Pujols 1, Richmond 61, Robinson 6, Steidl 8.

GCL DODGERS — Rookie

GULF COAST LEAGUE

BATTING	B-T	HT	WT	DOB	AVG	vLH	vRH	G	AB	R	H	2B	3B	HR	RBI	BB	HBP	SH	SF	SO	SB	CS	SLG	OBP
Ayres, Mitchell	L-R	6-0	210	4-9-86	.250	.500	.185	16	32	6	8	0	0	0	4	5	0	0	0	7	1	0	.250	.351
Bell, Josh	B-R	6-3	205	11-13-86	.318	.542	.278	45	157	26	50	7	1	1	21	20	1	0	0	33	5	2	.395	.399
Brooks, Parker	B-R	5-10	175	8-1-81	.222	.000	.231	15	27	7	6	0	0	0	2	5	1	1	0	3	2	0	.222	.364
Brown, Jeremy	R-R	6-1	195	4-2-84	.248	.143	.264	29	101	17	25	1	2	2	12	11	5	0	2	23	2	5	.356	.345
DeJesus, Ivan	R-R	5-11	182	5-1-87	.339	.348	.337	33	121	18	41	5	0	0	11	10	0	1	0	22	8	2	.380	.389
Dyson, Trey	L-L	6-4	215	3-11-80	.000	.000	.000	2	7	0	0	0	0	0	0	1	0	0	0	2	0	0	.000	.125
Garcia, Yosanddy	R-R	6-0	170	10-20-87	.175	.083	.179	41	120	12	21	4	1	2	10	16	2	2	3	47	1	0	.275	.277
Gonzalez, Adolfo	B-R	5-11	160	6-13-85	.286	.250	.293	37	119	18	34	7	2	0	15	7	6	3	1	9	2	2	.378	.353
Gutierrez, Eloy	B-R	6-1	178	11-25-84	.269	.263	.278	41	119	19	32	4	1	1	19	15	5	1	1	26	2	6	.345	.371
Guzman, Amauri	R-R	6-3	200	10-12-86	.125	.000	.167	2	8	1	1	0	0	0	2	1	0	0	0	5	0	0	.125	.222
Jansen, Kenley	B-R	6-2	178	9-30-87	.304	.222	.321	34	102	16	31	9	1	1	18	6	0	1	1	19	1	0	.441	.339
Medero-Stullz, Carlos	R-R	5-8	190	5-30-86	.313	.462	.286	31	99	11	31	5	0	2	18	8	1	1	2	10	0	0	.424	.364
Mora, Jesus	R-R	6-2	185	12-25-83	.264	.176	.279	31	106	20	28	4	3	1	10	5	5	1	2	14	0	2	.387	.322
Nunez, Jose	R-R	6-2	200	12-1-83	.222	.333	.198	36	99	13	22	5	0	1	16	17	0	0	3	15	1	0	.303	.328
Paul, Matt	R-R	5-10	190	9-3-82	.246	.143	.263	24	65	5	16	3	0	0	8	1	1	3	0	9	0	1	.292	.269
Perez, Eduardo	B-R	6-1	175	8-30-84	.352	.324	.352	48	179	35	63	16	1	6	37	12	4	2	0	26	4	0	.553	.405
Robinson, Trayvon	R-R	5-10	175	9-1-87	.296	.286	.297	40	115	19	34	7	2	3	15	8	3	0	0	25	6	4	.470	.357
Santana, Carlos	B-R	5-11	170	4-8-86	.295	.357	.281	32	78	14	23	4	1	1	14	16	1	0	2	8	0	2	.410	.412
Sapp, Steven	R-R	6-3	190	11-17-85	.313	.364	.302	21	64	12	20	3	0	0	8	3	2	1	1	16	0	2	.359	.357
Van Slyke, Scott	R-R	6-5	195	7-24-86	.282	.250	.300	24	85	15	24	4	1	2	15	4	3	1	2	19	4	3	.424	.330

PITCHING	B-T	HT	WT	DOB	W	L	ERA	G	GS	CG	SV	IP	H	R	ER	HR	BB	SO	AVG	vLH	vRH	K/9	BB/9
Carlyle, Buddy	L-R	6-3	175	12-21-77	0	0	3.00	1	1	0	0	3	3	1	1	0	0	1	.273	.200	.333	3.00	0.00
Castillo, Arismendy	R-R	6-3	190	12-10-84	3	2	4.19	12	4	0	0	39	37	26	18	0	24	41	.250	.152	.294	9.54	5.59
Dasni, Chales	R-R	6-3	168	7-21-85	1	5	7.35	12	6	0	0	45	52	38	37	5	23	41	.283	.333	.263	8.14	4.57
Diaz, Jose	R-R	6-4	247	2-27-84	0	0	4.50	2	1	0	0	2	1	1	1	1	0	2	.143	.000	.250	9.00	0.00
Diaz, Wilfredo	L-L	5-11	180	1-22-87	1	2	3.67	13	1	0	0	27	27	15	11	2	11	22	.250	.440	.193	7.33	3.67
Dominguez, Kelvin	L-L	6-2	180	4-4-85	0	0	0.00	2	0	0	0	2	1	0	0	0	1	2	.143	.250	.000	10.80	5.40
Flores, Juan	L-L	6-0	175	5-3-85	1	1	5.24	15	0	0	0	22	26	15	13	2	16	19	.299	.294	.300	7.66	6.45
Garrison, Kale	L-L	6-1	175	3-1-82	0	0	7.59	5	4	0	0	11	19	9	9	1	1	13	.396	.333	.405	10.97	0.84
Gearhart, Kalen	R-R	6-2	210	8-12-85	1	2	3.09	14	1	0	0	23	19	8	8	3	8	19	.221	.333	.177	7.33	3.09
Haldis, Jon	R-R	6-1	170	3-9-87	0	1	1.96	12	0	0	3	18	11	5	4	0	4	5	.169	.286	.137	2.45	1.96
Hobdy, Chris	R-R	6-4	210	12-16-86	0	1	20.25	5	1	0	0	5	14	12	12	1	6	4	.483	.545	.444	6.75	10.13
Johnson, Steve	R-R	6-1	185	8-31-87	0	2	9.53	6	3	0	0	11	18	12	12	1	4	14	.360	.412	.333	11.12	3.18
Looney, Marshal	L-L	6-4	251	3-23-84	0	1	5.79	3	2	0	0	5	8	6	3	1	0	4	.348	.250	.368	7.71	0.00
Lorenzo, Pedro	R-R	6-4	189	2-4-86	0	1	10.13	1	0	0	0	3	3	3	3	0	3	0	.300	.000	.375	0.00	10.13
Megrew, Michael	L-L	6-6	210	1-29-84	0	0	5.40	3	3	0	0	5	4	3	3	0	4	8	.250	.000	.286	14.40	7.20
Miller, Greg	L-L	6-5	220	11-3-84	0	0	2.25	4	3	0	0	12	7	5	3	0	4	14	.159	.100	.176	10.50	3.00
Norrito, Giuseppe	R-R	5-10	180	8-4-82	2	1	2.48	11	1	0	3	29	30	12	8	2	9	21	.268	.087	.315	6.52	2.79
Obispo, Jose	R-R	6-1	160	5-11-84	0	0	14.73	2	1	0	0	4	7	7	6	0	2	3	.438	.400	.455	7.36	4.91
Paredes, Ramon	L-L	6-3	192	11-28-84	6	0	2.34	9	6	0	0	42	36	12	11	2	10	39	.222	.219	.223	8.29	2.13
Paris, Gary	L-L	6-1	160	11-6-86	2	2	5.03	14	3	0	0	34	36	21	19	0	20	40	.283	.333	.275	10.59	5.29
Plummer, Jarod	R-R	6-5	200	1-27-84	0	0	4.50	1	1	0	0	4	4	2	2	0	0	2	.267	.400	.200	4.50	0.00
Quintana, Eduardo	R-R	6-2	175	6-30-85	1	1	6.29	15	3	0	1	34	51	25	24	4	18	24	.362	.366	.360	6.29	4.72
Ramirez, Miguel	R-R	5-11	180	7-15-83	0	1	1.64	15	0	0	5	22	20	4	4	0	4	22	.247	.190	.267	9.00	1.64
Reina, Dimas	R-R	5-10	231	2-23-82	0	0	0.00	1	1	0	0	2	0	0	0	0	0	2	.000	.000	.000	9.00	0.00
Rodriguez, Orlando	L-L	5-10	155	11-28-80	0	0	0.00	1	1	0	0	1	1	0	0	0	0	2	.250	.000	.250	18.00	0.00
Sanfler, Miguel	L-L	5-11	165	10-5-84	5	3	3.79	13	3	0	0	40	40	23	17	4	25	41	.250	.344	.227	9.15	5.58
Wall, Josh	R-R	6-6	190	1-21-87	1	3	3.86	5	4	0	0	14	13	8	6	2	8	5	.245	.211	.265	3.21	5.14
Zuleta, Howar	R-R	6-0	180	1-8-86	1	0	0.00	2	0	0	0	4	3	0	0	0	3	1	.200	.167	.222	2.08	6.23

GAMES BY POSITION: C—Ayres 14, Jansen 28, Medero-Stullz 28, Santana 3. **1B**—Ayres 1, Dasni 1, Dyson 1, Gonzalez 10, Gutierrez 1, Jansen 6, Nunez 36, Perez 11. **2B**—Brooks 8, Garcia 15, Gonzalez 27, Paul 13, Robinson 1, Santana 2. **3B**—Bell 26, Perez 21, Santana 14. **SS**—Bell 1, Brooks 4, DeJesus 33, Garcia 24, Gonzalez 2. **OF**—Brown 28, Gutierrez 36, Guzman 2, Jansen 1, Mora 30, Robinson 35, Santana 7, Sapp 21, Van Slyke 22.

MILWAUKEE BREWERS

BY TOM HAUDRICOURT

Never has a .500 record been such a cause for celebration within an organization.

After 12 consecutive losing seasons, the Brewers finally ended the madness in 2005, finishing 81-81 to provide tangible evidence that the franchise is moving forward. Coming off a 67-94 season and four consecutive last-place finishes, the players and staff had reason to be optimistic about the future.

"We were all tired of being called losers," manager Ned Yost said. "Now, we don't have to focus on that anymore. We can put that behind us."

The Brewers were able to take a big leap toward respectability thanks to breakthrough performances by several previously unheralded players as well as an influx of youth from a highly regarded farm system. It was the plan the organizational brain trust had had from the beginning—try to win while also developing young players.

It is a fine line that isn't easy to negotiate without slippage. By the end of the season, rookies J.J. Hardy and Rickie Weeks formed the double play combination, first baseman Prince Fielder was used as a bat off the bench and several young pitchers, including Dana Eveland, Jose Capellan and Justin Lehr, were making regular contributions out of the bullpen.

"It's just nice to turn that corner and learn how to win," said veteran lefthander Doug Davis, whose 11-11 record was deceiving (he had 24 quality starts). "The young guys are coming around. They're only going to get better."

While the youth movement was entertaining for Brewer fans to watch, much of the team's success could be traced to watershed seasons by a trio of players who took advantage of opportunities—center fielder Brady Clark, infielder Bill Hall and closer Derrick Turnbow.

ORGANIZATION LEADERS

BATTING

*AVG	Salome, Angel, Helena/West Virginia	.347
R	Hart, Corey, Nashville	85
H	Anderson, Drew, Brevard County	158
TB	Cruz, Nelson, Huntsville/Nashville	245
2B	Cruz, Enrique, Huntsville	34
	Richardson, Grant, West Virginia	34
3B	Ezi, Travis, Brevard County/Huntsville	12
HR	Fielder, Prince, Nashville	28
RBI	Fielder, Prince, Nashville	86
BB	Gwynn, Anthony, Huntsville	76
SO	Eure, Jeff, Brevard County	140
SB	Iribarren, Hernan, West Virginia	38
*OBP	Salome, Angel, Helena/West Virginia	.399
*SLG	Salome, Angel, Helena/West Virginia	.570

PITCHING

W	Dillard, Tim, Brevard County	12
	Taubenheim, Ty, Brevard County/Huntsville	12
L	Kloosterman, Gregory, West Virginia	19
#ERA	Dillard, Tim, Brevard County	2.01
G	Stetter, Mitch, Huntsville/Nashville	59
CG	Dillard, Tim, Brevard County	5
SV	Hinton, Robert, West Virginia	14
IP	Dillard, Tim, Brevard County	185
BB	Housman, Jeff, Nashville	72
SO	Villanueva, Carlos, Brevard County/Huntsville	138

*Minimum 250 at-bats. #Minimum 75 innings.

PLAYERS OF THE YEAR

MAJOR LEAGUE: Carlos Lee, of

A dangerous hitter over the past two years, Lee became an even more formidable threat in 2005 after being traded from the White Sox. Lee accomplished something he hadn't done in his entire career—play in all 162 games—and set personal bests in homers (32), doubles (41) and RBIs (114).

MINOR LEAGUE: Prince Fielder, 1b

A dangerous hitter for both average and power, Fielder had about as loud a year as it gets in 2005 for a 21-year-old. He hit .291-28-86 in 387 at-bats for Triple-A Nashville and was equally impressive after getting called up to the big leagues, He batted .288 with a pair of homers in 59 at-bats in Milwaukee.

Clark had never been considered an everyday player in the past, Hall was labeled a bench player because of inconsistent play and Turnbow had a reputation for wildness that threatened his career.

Getting his chance after the Brewers traded Scott Podsednik to the White Sox for Carlos Lee, Clark led the club with a .306 batting average, 94 runs scored and 53 multi-hit games. Assigned the difficult task of shuttling between three infield positions, Hall emerged as an everyday player by hitting .291-17-62.

There were other feel-good stories. Lefthander Chris Capuano became one of the top winners in the league, finishing with an 18-12 record. In the second half, Hardy showed why he was considered a top prospect, batting .308 to finish at .247 with 50 RBIs for the season. Right fielder Geoff Jenkins got sizzling hot over the final three months, batting .339 after July 1.

And, despite tapering off after the break (10 homers), Lee, who earned his first All-Star Game selection, finished with a career-high 114 RBIs. Lee was acquired to provide more oomph to an offense that foundered the previous season, and he did exactly that.

Considering how many times the Brewers raided Triple-A Nashville for talent, it was amazing that the Sounds went on to win the Pacific Coast League championship. A major factor in that title run was outfielder Nelson Cruz, who was promoted from Double-A Huntsville at midseason and went on to hit four homers and drive in 11 runs during the postseason for Nashville.

Cruz, who hit 27 homers with 81 RBIs at his two stops, was selected as the Brewers' minor league player of the year. Earning the pitching honors was righthander Tim Dillard, a converted catcher who went 12-10, 2.48 at high Class A Brevard County.

While the starting pitching thinned out at the top rungs of the farm system because of injuries, inconsistent performances and changes in assignment, there obviously was plenty of young talent near the bottom. Rookie-level Helena won both halves of its season, and first-round draft pick Ryan Braun made a big splash, hitting .352-10-45 at Helena and low Class A West Virginia.

MILWAUKEE BREWERS

Manager: Ned Yost.

2005 Record: 81-81, .500 (3rd, NL Central).

BATTING	B-T	HT	WT	DOB	AVG	vLH	vRH	G	AB	R	H	2B	3B	HR	RBI	BB	HBP	SH	SF	SO	SB	CS	SLG	OBP
Branyan, Russell	L-R	6-3	195	12-19-75	.257	.050	.280	85	202	23	52	11	0	12	31	39	0	1	0	80	1	0	.490	.378
Cirillo, Jeff	R-R	6-1	200	9-23-69	.281	.400	.231	77	185	29	52	15	0	4	23	23	4	7	0	22	4	2	.427	.373
Clark, Brady	R-R	6-2	200	4-18-73	.306	.308	.305	145	599	94	183	31	1	13	53	47	18	8	2	55	10	13	.426	.372
Cruz, Nelson	R-R	6-3	175	7-1-80	.200	.000	.333	8	5	1	1	1	0	0	0	2	0	0	0	0	0	0	.400	.429
Durrington, Trent	R-R	5-10	190	8-27-75	.214	.333	.125	28	14	3	3	1	0	0	2	1	0	3	0	3	5	2	.286	.267
Fielder, Prince	L-R	6-0	260	5-9-84	.288	.500	.281	39	59	2	17	4	0	2	10	2	0	0	1	17	0	0	.458	.306
Hall, Bill	R-R	6-0	195	12-28-79	.291	.336	.277	146	501	69	146	39	6	17	62	39	1	2	3	103	18	6	.495	.342
Hardy, J.J.	R-R	6-2	180	8-19-82	.247	.268	.240	124	372	46	92	22	1	9	50	44	1	8	2	48	0	0	.384	.327
Hart, J. Corey	R-R	6-6	200	3-24-82	.193	.211	.184	21	57	9	11	2	1	2	7	6	0	0	0	11	2	0	.368	.270
Helms, Wes	R-R	6-4	225	5-12-76	.298	.301	.294	95	168	18	50	13	1	4	24	14	3	0	3	30	0	1	.458	.356
Jenkins, Geoff	L-R	6-1	210	7-21-74	.292	.255	.307	148	538	87	157	42	1	25	86	56	19	0	5	138	0	0	.513	.375
Krynzel, Dave	L-L	6-1	180	11-7-81	.000	.000	.000	5	7	0	0	0	0	0	0	0	0	0	0	3	0	0	.000	.000
Lee, Carlos	R-R	6-2	240	6-20-76	.265	.261	.267	162	618	85	164	41	0	32	114	57	2	0	11	87	13	4	.487	.324
Magruder, Chris	B-R	5-11	200	4-26-77	.203	.256	.182	101	138	16	28	9	0	2	13	7	5	4	1	33	3	0	.312	.265
Miller, Damian	R-R	6-3	220	10-13-69	.273	.231	.286	114	385	50	105	25	1	9	43	37	4	2	3	94	0	1	.413	.340
Moeller, Chad	R-R	6-3	210	2-18-75	.206	.180	.215	66	199	23	41	9	1	7	23	13	1	2	1	48	0	0	.367	.257
Mosquera, Julio	R-R	6-0	190	1-29-72	.000	.000	.000	1	1	0	0	0	0	0	0	0	0	0	0	0	0	0	.000	.000
Overbay, Lyle	L-L	6-2	225	1-28-77	.276	.269	.278	158	537	80	148	34	1	19	72	78	2	1	4	98	1	0	.449	.367
Spivey, Junior	R-R	6-0	200	1-28-75	.236	.306	.211	49	182	22	43	8	1	5	17	18	1	1	0	57	7	3	.374	.308
Weeks, Rickie	R-R	6-0	195	9-13-82	.239	.222	.243	96	360	56	86	13	2	13	42	40	11	2	1	96	15	2	.394	.333

PITCHING	B-T	HT	WT	DOB	W	L	ERA	G	GS	CG	SV	IP	H	R	ER	HR	BB	SO	AVG	vLH	vRH	K/9	BB/9
Adams, Mike	R-R	6-5	190	7-29-78	0	1	2.70	13	0	0	1	13	12	4	4	2	10	14	.235	.200	.258	9.45	6.75
Bottalico, Ricky	L-R	6-1	215	8-26-69	2	2	4.54	40	0	0	2	42	43	24	21	7	19	29	.265	.260	.271	6.26	4.10
Capellan, Jose	R-R	6-4	235	1-13-81	1	1	2.87	17	0	0	0	16	17	6	5	1	5	14	.293	.235	.317	8.04	2.87
Capuano, Chris	L-L	6-2	220	8-19-78	18	12	3.99	35	35	0	0	219	212	105	97	31	91	176	.256	.202	.270	7.23	3.74
Davis, Doug	R-L	6-4	215	9-21-75	11	11	3.84	35	35	2	0	223	196	103	95	26	93	208	.235	.259	.228	8.41	3.76
Davis, Kane	R-R	6-3	190	6-25-75	1	1	2.70	15	0	0	0	17	10	6	5	2	10	11	.167	.158	.171	5.94	5.40
De la Rosa, Jorge	L-L	6-1	190	4-5-81	2	2	4.46	38	0	0	0	42	48	23	21	1	38	42	.289	.321	.273	8.93	8.08
Eveland, Dana	L-L	6-1	219	10-29-83	1	1	5.97	27	0	0	1	32	40	21	21	2	18	23	.317	.324	.315	6.54	5.12
Glover, Gary	R-R	6-5	220	12-3-76	5	4	5.57	15	11	0	0	65	74	41	40	10	20	58	.288	.256	.318	8.07	2.78
Helling, Rick	R-R	6-3	240	12-15-70	3	1	2.39	15	7	0	0	49	39	13	13	2	18	42	.219	.219	.219	7.71	3.31
Lehr, Justin	R-R	6-2	200	8-3-77	1	1	3.89	23	0	0	0	35	32	19	15	4	18	23	.242	.207	.270	5.97	4.67
Obermueller, Wes	R-R	6-2	210	12-22-76	1	4	5.26	23	8	0	0	65	74	41	38	7	36	33	.289	.262	.307	4.57	4.98
Ohka, Tomo	R-R	6-1	200	3-18-76	7	6	4.35	22	20	1	0	126	145	65	61	16	28	81	.285	.296	.275	5.77	1.99
2-team (10 Washington)					11	9	4.04	32	29	1	0	180	189	88	81	22	55	98	.268	.258	.277	4.89	2.74
Phelps, Tommy	L-L	6-3	215	3-4-74	0	2	4.63	29	0	0	1	23	25	12	12	2	12	14	.272	.308	.245	5.40	4.63
Santana, Julio	R-R	6-0	210	1-20-74	3	5	4.50	41	0	0	1	42	34	21	21	6	19	49	.221	.247	.198	10.50	4.07
Santos, Victor	R-R	6-3	190	10-2-76	4	13	4.57	29	24	1	0	142	153	87	72	20	60	89	.269	.259	.277	5.65	3.81
Sheets, Ben	R-R	6-1	220	7-18-78	10	9	3.33	22	22	3	0	157	142	66	58	19	25	141	.237	.234	.241	8.10	1.44
Turnbow, Derrick	R-R	6-3	210	1-25-78	7	1	1.74	69	0	0	39	67	49	15	13	5	24	64	.199	.233	.167	8.55	3.21
Wise, Matt	R-R	6-4	195	11-18-75	4	4	3.36	49	0	0	1	64	37	25	24	6	25	62	.160	.130	.187	8.67	3.50

FIELDING

Catcher	PCT	G	PO	A	E	DP	PB
Miller	.996	111	723	50	3	10	4
Moeller	.994	65	454	32	3	6	4

First Base	PCT	G	PO	A	E	DP
Branyan	1.000	5	28	2	0	0
Cirillo	.000	1	0	0	0	0
Fielder	1.000	7	26	4	0	2
Helms	.991	16	103	9	1	9
Overbay	.992	154	1134	96	10	104

Second Base	PCT	G	PO	A	E	DP
Cirillo	1.000	3	4	2	0	1
Hall	.960	23	44	53	4	5
Spivey	.968	48	93	117	7	27
Weeks	.951	95	178	233	21	60

Third Base	PCT	G	PO	A	E	DP
Branyan	.946	59	40	82	7	10
Cirillo	.951	53	28	70	5	8
Durrington	.000	1	0	0	3	0
Hall	.953	59	39	84	6	11
Helms	.964	35	12	41	2	4

Shortstop	PCT	G	PO	A	E	DP
Hall	.976	66	87	158	6	31
Hardy	.975	119	133	259	10	52

Outfield	PCT	G	PO	A	E	DP
Branyan	1.000	3	1	0	0	0
Clark	.995	145	399	5	2	4
Cruz	1.000	8	4	0	0	0
J. Corey Hart	.966	16	27	1	1	0
Jenkins	.984	144	307	10	5	7
Krynzel	1.000	1	2	0	0	0
Lee	.981	162	308	8	6	3
Magruder	.964	45	54	0	2	0

FARM SYSTEM

General Manager: Doug Melvin. **Director, Player Development:** Reid Nichols. **Scouting Director:** Jack Zduriencik.

Class	Farm Team	League	W	L	Pct.	Finish*	Manager	Affiliate Since
AAA	Nashville (Tenn.) Sounds	Pacific Coast	75	69	.521	**+6th (16)**	Frank Kremblas	2005
AA	Huntsville (Ala.) Stars	Southern	60	79	.432	8th (10)	Don Money	1999
High A	Brevard County Manatees (Melbourne, Fla.)	Florida State	63	73	.463	10th (12)	Johnny Narron	2005
Low A	West Virginia Power (Charleston)	South Atlantic	60	78	.435	13th (16)	Ramon Aviles	2005
Rookie	Helena (Mont.) Brewers	Pioneer	46	30	.605	**1st (8)**	Ed Sedar	2003
Rookie	Phoenix (Ariz.) Brewers	Arizona	22	34	.393	7th (9)	Mike Guerrero	2001

*Finish in overall standings (No. of teams in league)/Playoff teams in **boldface** +League champion

NASHVILLE SOUNDS — Class AAA

PACIFIC COAST LEAGUE

BATTING	B-T	HT	WT	DOB	AVG	vLH	vRH	G	AB	R	H	2B	3B	HR	RBI	BB	HBP	SH	SF	SO	SB	CS	SLG	OBP
Barnwell, Chris	R-R	5-10	176	3-1-79	.245	.306	.222	100	261	30	64	14	1	3	20	18	3	4	2	46	5	3	.341	.299
Borders, Pat	R-R	6-2	200	5-14-63	.245	.286	.238	26	98	8	24	2	0	3	14	3	0	0	1	18	1	2	.357	.265
Branyan, Russell	L-R	6-3	195	12-19-75	.294	.250	.333	6	17	4	5	4	0	1	3	3	0	0	0	8	0	0	.706	.400
Cirillo, Jeff	R-R	6-1	200	9-23-69	.241	.222	.250	9	29	2	7	1	0	0	6	0	1	1	2	5	0	1	.276	.250
Cruz, Nelson	R-R	6-3	175	7-1-80	.269	.240	.278	60	208	33	56	13	0	11	27	30	8	0	0	62	9	4	.490	.382
Durrington, Trent	R-R	5-10	190	8-27-75	.300	.286	.305	92	313	61	94	15	2	5	31	41	5	11	1	63	30	12	.409	.389
Erickson, Matt	L-R	5-11	190	7-30-75	.389	.000	.467	16	18	2	7	1	0	0	2	3	2	1	0	2	0	0	.444	.522
Fielder, Prince	L-R	6-0	260	5-9-84	.291	.317	.281	103	378	68	110	21	0	28	86	54	7	0	2	93	8	5	.569	.388
Hart, J. Corey	R-R	6-6	200	3-24-82	.308	.283	.316	113	429	85	132	29	9	17	69	48	3	3	6	88	31	7	.536	.377
Hart, Corey D.	B-R	6-0	198	9-5-75	.179	.240	.157	54	95	9	17	5	0	1	5	17	0	1	0	20	1	1	.263	.304
Knox, Ryan	R-R	6-1	184	6-28-77	.233	.261	.221	99	301	31	70	12	0	5	26	23	7	8	5	70	20	8	.322	.298
Krynzel, Dave	L-L	6-1	180	11-7-81	.256	.231	.264	115	450	71	115	25	7	11	51	43	5	8	5	138	24	8	.416	.324
Morris, Warren	L-R	5-11	190	1-11-74	.265	.213	.279	64	230	39	61	7	2	7	27	22	0	2	2	32	9	2	.404	.327
Mosquera, Julio	R-R	6-0	190	1-29-72	.258	.257	.259	64	240	32	62	18	0	4	30	10	1	1	1	34	4	1	.383	.290
Nelson, Brad	L-R	6-2	220	12-23-82	.253	.265	.249	81	281	50	71	16	2	7	39	45	2	2	1	74	4	5	.399	.359
Orie, Kevin	R-R	6-5	220	9-1-72	.344	.333	.349	61	180	32	62	18	0	12	49	31	3	0	3	20	4	1	.644	.442
Rivera, Mike	R-R	6-0	215	9-8-76	.285	.246	.299	60	214	34	61	12	1	16	43	9	3	0	2	37	3	1	.575	.320
Rottino, Vinny	R-R	6-0	199	4-7-80	.345	.286	.364	9	29	4	10	1	0	1	2	3	0	0	0	6	0	1	.483	.406
Scarborough, Steve	R-R	6-0	160	3-10-78	.255	.310	.241	130	404	50	103	27	2	11	58	39	4	7	5	93	6	5	.413	.323
Weeks, Rickie	R-R	6-0	195	9-13-82	.320	.340	.314	55	203	43	65	14	9	12	48	28	14	3	1	51	10	1	.655	.435
Zuniga, Tony	R-R	6-0	205	1-13-75	.323	.290	.335	65	235	35	76	14	0	7	43	18	2	0	0	28	5	0	.472	.376

PITCHING	B-T	HT	WT	DOB	W	L	ERA	G	GS	CG	SV	IP	H	R	ER	HR	BB	SO	AVG	vLH	vRH	K/9	BB/9
Adams, Mike	R-R	6-5	190	7-29-78	3	4	5.75	26	0	0	2	36	35	23	23	3	12	45	.263	.277	.256	11.25	3.00
Barnwell, Chris	R-R	5-10	176	3-1-79	1	0	0.00	4	0	0	0	5	3	0	0	0	2	3	.158	.143	.167	5.79	3.86
Bennett, Jeff	R-R	6-3	200	6-10-80	2	3	3.03	49	0	0	13	62	44	24	21	6	25	56	.197	.178	.213	8.09	3.61
Capellan, Jose	R-R	6-4	235	1-13-81	5	3	3.87	36	12	0	6	91	88	42	39	4	42	76	.257	.263	.251	7.54	4.17
Davis, Kane	R-R	6-3	190	6-25-75	4	2	2.44	45	0	0	1	63	49	18	17	5	23	81	.216	.213	.217	11.63	3.30
Evert, Brett	L-R	6-6	200	10-23-80	2	2	4.78	13	2	0	0	32	31	19	17	3	15	41	.250	.309	.203	11.53	4.22
2-team (8 Tacoma)					2	2	5.36	21	3	0	0	45	50	30	27	4	20	49	.278	.341	.224	9.73	3.97
Glover, Gary	R-R	6-5	220	12-3-76	6	4	3.03	17	16	1	1	92	91	39	31	9	29	75	.258	.307	.216	7.34	2.84
Helling, Rick	R-R	6-3	240	12-15-70	9	3	4.13	21	21	0	0	131	128	74	60	12	50	105	.256	.284	.236	7.23	3.44
Hendrickson, Ben	R-R	6-4	190	2-4-81	6	12	4.97	28	27	1	0	156	176	100	86	17	58	122	.292	.287	.296	7.05	3.35
Housman, Jeff	L-L	6-3	180	8-4-81	5	12	6.54	28	24	0	0	131	155	99	95	27	72	110	.305	.268	.315	7.58	4.96
Lehr, Justin	R-R	6-2	200	8-3-77	7	7	3.99	27	11	0	1	88	102	49	39	8	32	68	.290	.287	.292	6.95	3.27
Meyers, Mike	R-R	6-2	210	10-18-77	7	4	5.31	33	7	0	0	80	87	51	47	16	40	75	.276	.283	.270	8.47	4.52
Obermueller, Wes	R-R	6-2	210	12-22-76	3	1	2.55	9	8	0	1	42	39	14	12	1	14	39	.255	.296	.220	8.29	2.98
Paronto, Chad	R-R	6-5	250	7-28-75	3	1	2.75	27	0	0	4	39	40	17	12	1	19	38	.263	.193	.305	8.69	4.35
Phelps, Tommy	L-L	6-3	215	3-4-74	1	0	1.13	5	4	0	0	16	13	3	2	0	2	14	.224	.059	.293	7.88	1.13
Pratt, Andy	L-L	6-0	180	8-27-79	4	4	8.35	23	8	0	0	51	66	54	47	11	40	51	.311	.245	.331	9.06	7.11
Santana, Julio	R-R	6-0	210	1-20-74	2	0	1.50	8	0	0	1	12	8	2	2	0	4	15	.190	.294	.120	11.25	3.00
Sarfate, Dennis	R-R	6-4	210	4-9-81	0	1	2.25	2	1	0	0	12	6	3	3	1	4	10	.150	.091	.172	7.50	3.00
Scarborough, Steve	R-R	6-0	160	3-10-78	1	0	9.00	4	0	0	0	5	13	5	5	0	1	3	.500	.417	.571	5.40	1.80
Stetter, Mitch	L-L	6-5	187	1-16-81	1	1	4.26	27	0	0	0	25	23	16	12	5	11	23	.237	.196	.275	8.17	3.91
Weibl, Clint	R-R	6-3	180	3-17-75	2	5	5.15	39	3	0	2	73	81	49	42	8	45	55	.281	.231	.317	6.75	5.52
Zumwalt, Alec	R-R	6-2	205	1-20-81	1	0	4.61	9	0	0	1	14	11	7	7	1	8	11	.234	.308	.206	7.24	5.27

FIELDING

Catcher	PCT	G	PO	A	E	DP	PB
Borders	.976	25	192	10	5	2	2
Mosquera	.983	62	483	49	9	8	11
Rivera	.988	55	450	31	6	5	6
Rottino	1.000	2	21	1	0	1	0

First Base	PCT	G	PO	A	E	DP
Durrington	1.000	12	94	5	0	11
Orie	1.000	10	60	9	0	5
Rivera	1.000	3	11	0	0	0
Zuniga	.990	25	170	28	2	20
Fielder	.985	94	745	60	12	82
Barnwell	1.000	2	19	1	0	2
J. Corey Hart	1.000	4	20	5	0	1
Nelson	.968	5	26	4	1	2
Rottino	1.000	1	3	0	0	1

Second Base	PCT	G	PO	A	E	DP
Barnwell	.981	11	27	24	1	6
Durrington	1.000	13	25	30	0	5
Corey D. Hart	.988	20	26	57	1	13
Morris	.981	53	81	128	4	29
Weeks	.961	55	108	136	10	32

Third Base	PCT	G	PO	A	E	DP
Barnwell	.941	49	22	89	7	11
Branyan	.000	2	0	0	0	0
Cirillo	.875	8	2	5	1	2
Durrington	.913	39	26	68	9	7
Erickson	1.000	6	0	5	0	0
Corey D. Hart	1.000	4	1	2	0	0
Morris	1.000	4	4	5	0	1
Orie	.974	22	9	29	1	4
Rottino	1.000	5	3	11	0	1
Scarborough	.000	1	0	0	0	0
Zuniga	.904	38	19	56	8	6

Shortstop	PCT	G	PO	A	E	DP
Barnwell	.935	28	41	75	8	18
Durrington	.917	8	12	21	3	4
Corey D. Hart	1.000	1	1	1	0	1
Scarborough	.959	121	155	340	21	66

Outfield	PCT	G	PO	A	E	DP
Branyan	1.000	4	5	0	0	0
Cruz	.983	58	107	9	2	3
Durrington	.960	17	21	3	1	1
J. Corey Hart	.985	104	189	8	3	2
Housman	.000	1	0	0	0	0
Knox	.988	79	159	6	2	0
Krynzel	.959	109	231	5	10	3
Nelson	.972	68	99	6	3	2
Rottino	1.000	1	2	0	0	0
Scarborough	1.000	1	2	0	0	0
Zumwalt	.000	1	0	0	0	0

HUNTSVILLE STARS — Class AA

SOUTHERN LEAGUE

BATTING	B-T	HT	WT	DOB	AVG	vLH	vRH	G	AB	R	H	2B	3B	HR	RBI	BB	HBP	SH	SF	SO	SB	CS	SLG	OBP
Barnwell, Chris	R-R	5-10	176	3-1-79	.257	.417	.174	15	35	6	9	2	1	1	4	1	1	0	1	7	0	0	.457	.289
Bibbs, Kennard	L-L	5-9	143	3-5-80	.279	.281	.278	105	359	45	100	18	6	1	25	34	2	12	4	47	23	9	.370	.341
Castro, Nelson	B-R	5-10	200	6-4-76	.225	.234	.219	45	120	18	27	6	0	0	14	8	1	3	3	32	1	0	.275	.273
Crabbe, Callix	B-R	5-7	171	2-14-83	.243	.262	.234	119	387	42	94	15	4	1	33	65	2	20	1	65	18	6	.310	.354
Cruz, Enrique	R-R	6-1	205	11-21-81	.300	.367	.269	137	496	68	149	34	3	14	60	37	5	2	1	107	4	4	.466	.354
Cruz, Nelson	R-R	6-3	175	7-1-80	.306	.416	.257	68	248	45	76	19	0	16	54	31	4	0	3	71	10	3	.577	.388
Ezi, Travis	B-L	6-0	175	9-5-81	.226	.500	.130	17	31	7	7	1	1	0	3	4	1	0	1	10	1	2	.323	.324
Gemoll, Brandon	L-L	6-1	212	9-15-80	.303	.252	.320	120	432	53	131	27	5	7	59	30	4	3	4	104	3	3	.438	.351
Gwynn, Anthony	L-R	6-0	180	10-4-82	.271	.234	.287	133	509	83	138	21	5	1	41	76	5	9	2	75	34	15	.338	.370
Heether, Adam	R-R	6-0	190	1-14-82	.314	.143	.378	14	51	11	16	5	0	0	9	2	1	0	2	8	2	1	.412	.339
Nelson, Brad	L-R	6-2	220	12-23-82	.293	.290	.295	55	208	27	61	8	1	6	38	26	1	0	3	42	1	2	.428	.370
Rodriguez, Guilder	B-R	6-0	151	7-24-83	.301	.302	.300	65	133	17	40	3	1	0	7	19	0	8	0	28	3	0	.338	.388
Rottino, Vinny	R-R	6-0	199	4-7-80	.296	.270	.309	120	469	63	139	20	6	6	52	40	2	0	5	68	2	1	.403	.351
Stanfield, Jimmy	R-R	6-0	215	8-20-82	.000	.000	.000	3	4	0	0	0	0	0	1	0	0	0	1	3	0	0	.000	.000
Van Iderstine, Ben	R-L	6-2	200	1-20-78	.262	.299	.223	84	229	24	60	7	3	2	35	15	2	2	2	35	2	2	.345	.310
Vanden Berg, John	R-R	6-2	210	2-5-80	.252	.111	.300	81	214	22	54	16	1	2	26	35	1	4	0	62	1	0	.364	.360
Winchester, Jeff	R-R	6-0	205	1-21-80	.264	.228	.287	78	265	27	70	15	0	0	29	20	9	3	0	40	0	2	.321	.337
Zuniga, Tony	R-R	6-0	205	1-13-75	.258	.264	.254	57	190	17	49	7	0	3	28	17	2	0	3	27	0	1	.342	.321

PITCHING	B-T	HT	WT	DOB	W	L	ERA	G	GS	CG	SV	IP	H	R	ER	HR	BB	SO	AVG	vLH	vRH	K/9	BB/9
Ballouli, Khalid	R-R	6-2	188	3-20-80	4	7	4.82	24	9	0	2	75	94	49	40	5	23	61	.302	.272	.326	7.35	2.77
Bradley, David	R-R	6-1	175	8-28-77	6	5	3.35	35	14	1	0	105	99	48	39	9	32	83	.252	.304	.206	7.14	2.75
Costello, Ryan	L-L	6-6	225	7-13-79	0	5	10.13	9	7	0	0	32	54	39	36	5	14	20	.365	.326	.382	5.63	3.94
DeWitt, Matt	R-R	6-3	225	9-4-77	1	3	4.65	26	0	0	5	31	46	25	16	2	11	31	.338	.375	.313	9.00	3.19
Eveland, Dana	L-L	6-1	219	10-29-83	10	4	2.72	18	18	0	0	109	96	42	33	4	38	98	.237	.250	.233	8.09	3.14
Evert, Brett	L-R	6-6	200	10-23-80	0	0	2.97	16	0	0	1	30	31	13	10	6	7	32	.254	.204	.288	9.49	2.08
Ford, Matt	B-L	6-1	190	4-8-81	1	3	5.40	17	0	0	0	22	34	20	13	2	14	19	.343	.478	.303	7.89	5.82
Gamble, Jerome	R-R	6-2	200	4-5-80	4	1	6.33	31	0	0	5	43	51	30	30	2	12	48	.287	.222	.330	10.13	2.53
Habel, Josh	L-L	6-1	210	9-10-80	3	7	5.65	21	9	0	0	65	85	54	41	12	28	47	.316	.375	.298	6.47	3.86
Meyers, Mike	R-R	6-2	210	10-18-77	0	0	1.71	11	0	0	1	21	21	9	4	0	4	16	.247	.324	.196	6.86	1.71
Miller, Ryan	R-R	6-1	208	2-12-78	0	0	5.40	4	0	0	1	5	3	3	3	2	1	4	.167	.000	.333	7.20	1.80
Parra, Manuel	L-L	6-3	200	10-30-82	5	6	3.96	16	16	0	0	91	111	47	40	4	21	86	.295	.277	.301	8.51	2.08
Pratt, Andy	L-L	6-0	180	8-27-79	0	1	2.96	21	0	0	2	27	22	11	9	3	24	33	.212	.286	.184	10.87	7.90
Sarfate, Dennis	R-R	6-4	210	4-9-81	9	9	3.88	24	24	1	0	130	120	65	56	13	59	110	.245	.250	.241	7.62	4.08
Simpson, Gerrit	R-R	6-3	200	12-18-79	1	0	2.29	13	0	0	5	20	17	5	5	0	7	15	.230	.250	.217	6.86	3.20
Stamler, Keith	L-R	6-2	195	8-20-79	0	1	3.73	23	1	0	1	51	55	29	21	3	19	27	.276	.207	.325	4.80	3.38
Stetter, Mitch	L-L	6-5	187	1-16-81	2	3	2.61	32	0	0	8	52	46	15	15	3	11	47	.241	.154	.273	8.19	1.92
Taubenheim, Ty	R-R	6-6	229	11-17-82	2	6	4.36	11	11	0	0	64	64	36	31	7	24	44	.269	.316	.236	6.19	3.38
Villanueva, Carlos	B-R	6-3	201	11-28-83	1	3	7.40	4	4	0	0	21	21	18	17	3	9	14	.256	.143	.340	6.10	3.92
Wolfe, Brian	R-R	6-2	215	11-29-80	3	1	3.38	16	0	0	0	24	32	12	9	1	8	19	.311	.256	.344	7.13	3.00
Woolard, Glenn	R-R	6-1	199	4-18-81	7	11	4.91	29	26	0	0	147	160	87	80	15	64	113	.278	.309	.259	6.93	3.93
Zumwalt, Alec	R-R	6-2	205	1-20-81	1	2	4.15	28	0	0	3	52	49	28	24	5	22	37	.245	.235	.252	6.40	3.81

FIELDING

Catcher	PCT	G	PO	A	E	DP	PB
Rottino	.995	22	176	10	1	2	6
Stanfield	1.000	1	7	1	0	0	1
Vanden Berg	.992	48	336	27	3	3	10
Winchester	.993	72	497	52	4	3	14

First Base	PCT	G	PO	A	E	DP
Gemoll	.983	109	873	62	16	76
Rottino	.995	21	170	11	1	12
Vanden Berg	.991	12	110	6	1	7

Second Base	PCT	G	PO	A	E	DP
Barnwell	.952	5	11	9	1	3
Castro	1.000	4	7	12	0	1
Crabbe	.974	107	227	288	14	56
Rodriguez	.963	30	67	91	6	17

Third Base	PCT	G	PO	A	E	DP
Barnwell	1.000	3	2	3	0	0
Castro	.857	13	12	30	7	2
Heether	.840	13	17	25	8	5
Rottino	.947	63	42	119	9	5
Zuniga	.924	51	25	121	12	10

Shortstop	PCT	G	PO	A	E	DP
Castro	.857	1	0	6	1	1
E. Cruz	.939	135	188	386	37	63
Rodriguez	.938	5	7	8	1	1

Outfield	PCT	G	PO	A	E	DP
Bibbs	.983	101	171	6	3	4
Castro	1.000	6	16	0	0	0
N. Cruz	.967	66	109	8	4	1
Ezi	1.000	11	17	0	0	0
Gemoll	1.000	1	1	0	0	0
Gwynn	.984	133	294	8	5	3
Habel	.000	1	0	0	0	0
Nelson	.971	53	99	3	3	0
Pratt	.000	1	0	0	0	0
Rottino	.900	9	17	1	2	0
Van Iderstine	.978	60	84	3	2	1

BREVARD COUNTY MANATEES — High Class A

FLORIDA STATE LEAGUE

BATTING	B-T	HT	WT	DOB	AVG	vLH	vRH	G	AB	R	H	2B	3B	HR	RBI	BB	HBP	SH	SF	SO	SB	CS	SLG	OBP
Anderson, Drew	L-R	6-2	190	6-9-81	.311	.277	.326	129	508	69	158	17	7	6	62	39	3	2	6	95	19	8	.407	.360
Blevins, Clay	L-R	6-1	190	5-1-83	.333	.000	.333	1	3	0	1	0	0	0	0	0	0	0	0	1	0	0	.333	.333
Brady, Josh	R-R	5-10	185	10-24-80	.146	.050	.171	27	96	7	14	1	0	2	8	2	3	0	0	22	1	1	.219	.188
Campana, Wandel	R-R	6-0	175	6-6-78	.270	.241	.281	86	318	31	86	18	2	4	37	7	2	4	3	31	0	5	.377	.288
Chavez, Ozzie	B-R	6-1	159	7-31-83	.233	.218	.238	125	451	39	105	17	6	4	35	32	3	5	1	73	8	9	.324	.287
Corredor, Nestor	R-R	6-1	185	5-25-84	.277	.300	.270	15	47	5	13	2	0	0	4	3	1	0	1	7	0	0	.319	.327
De la Cruz, Carlos	R-R	6-3	175	3-1-82	.206	.207	.205	36	107	4	22	3	0	1	12	4	3	3	1	34	1	1	.262	.252
Deevers, Robby	R-R	6-0	200	6-23-80	.169	.160	.173	60	177	11	30	7	2	0	10	3	2	5	0	57	4	2	.232	.192
Eure, Jeff	R-R	6-1	215	8-17-80	.229	.150	.254	130	467	64	107	31	2	17	66	31	13	0	3	140	2	3	.413	.294
Ezi, Travis	B-L	6-0	175	9-5-81	.272	.257	.278	102	389	62	106	12	11	3	27	27	4	10	3	120	22	11	.383	.324
Festa, Tony	L-R	6-2	200	12-1-80	.257	.143	.286	12	35	3	9	0	0	1	4	5	2	0	0	3	1	0	.343	.381
Heether, Adam	R-R	6-0	190	1-14-82	.305	.286	.313	93	338	48	103	27	2	6	54	34	13	0	4	48	3	1	.450	.386
Medlin, C.J.	R-R	6-2	210	3-3-82	.253	.333	.213	48	162	24	41	9	0	6	27	18	4	1	2	52	0	1	.420	.339
Moss, Steve	R-R	6-2	185	1-12-84	.281	.241	.293	118	442	62	124	19	7	9	51	36	1	3	6	113	18	12	.416	.332
Murray, Josh	R-R	6-1	193	8-12-84	.444	.400	.462	5	18	6	8	0	0	0	0	2	0	0	0	4	0	0	.444	.500
Palmisano, Lou	R-R	6-1	185	9-16-82	.255	.308	.237	118	432	47	110	16	7	5	49	34	5	1	3	65	3	1	.359	.314
Serfass, Jake	L-R	6-2	190	12-15-81	.129	.000	.133	10	31	3	4	1	0	0	1	3	0	0	0	16	0	0	.161	.206

BATTING	B-T	HT	WT	DOB	AVG	vLH	vRH	G	AB	R	H	2B	3B	HR	RBI	BB	HBP	SH	SF	SO	SB	CS	SLG	OBP
Sollmann, Steve	R-R	5-11	195	4-1-82	.272	.301	.262	127	430	61	117	12	1	0	34	44	26	11	6	60	21	15	.305	.370
Van Iderstine, Ben	R-L	6-2	200	1-20-78	.160	.154	.162	13	50	1	8	0	0	0	4	1	0	0	1	10	0	0	.160	.173

PITCHING	B-T	HT	WT	DOB	W	L	ERA	G	GS	CG	SV	IP	H	R	ER	HR	BB	SO	AVG	vLH	vRH	K/9	BB/9
Anderson, Ryan	L-L	6-10	215	7-12-79	0	1	6.30	6	6	0	0	10	10	9	7	1	3	17	.222	.000	.263	15.30	2.70
Costello, Ryan	L-L	6-6	225	7-13-79	6	6	3.21	24	14	1	2	101	79	43	36	8	34	99	.212	.238	.205	8.82	3.03
Diggins, Ben	R-R	6-7	230	6-13-79	0	1	5.27	12	2	0	0	14	11	8	8	0	17	13	.229	.133	.273	8.56	11.20
Dillard, Tim	B-R	6-4	228	7-19-83	12	10	2.48	28	28	5	0	185	150	64	51	9	31	128	.219	.245	.204	6.22	1.51
Durost, Kenny	R-R	6-3	191	10-10-81	1	9	5.57	29	11	0	0	84	91	62	52	14	41	90	.278	.313	.259	9.64	4.39
Evert, Brett	L-R	6-6	200	10-23-80	0	2	5.06	7	0	0	2	11	9	6	6	1	4	7	.225	.263	.190	5.91	3.38
Grybash, Daniel	R-R	6-0	198	12-26-80	0	1	8.24	17	0	0	1	20	32	21	18	2	11	25	.364	.480	.317	11.44	5.03
Habel, Josh	L-L	6-1	210	9-10-80	5	4	2.56	11	10	0	0	63	45	23	18	7	17	60	.195	.208	.191	8.53	2.42
Hall, Bo	R-R	6-0	187	9-5-80	2	3	4.04	45	3	0	0	89	87	46	40	12	40	83	.256	.279	.245	8.39	4.04
Hammond, Steve	R-L	6-2	205	4-30-82	1	3	2.78	8	7	0	0	36	33	17	11	2	9	30	.244	.125	.282	7.57	2.27
Lewis, Jeremy	R-L	6-4	180	9-12-80	6	7	2.95	55	0	0	10	79	69	31	26	5	23	73	.234	.190	.250	8.28	2.61
Martin, Forrest	R-R	6-1	201	1-8-80	3	3	6.15	12	4	0	0	34	46	27	23	5	18	30	.336	.328	.343	8.02	4.81
Miller, Ryan	R-R	6-1	208	2-12-78	0	0	0.00	2	0	0	1	2	0	0	0	0	1	1	.000	.000	.000	4.50	4.50
Pena, Luis	R-R	6-5	190	1-10-83	2	6	4.26	15	12	0	0	76	72	39	36	6	28	51	.258	.253	.260	6.04	3.32
Rival, Kevin	R-R	6-2	210	11-27-79	0	1	6.43	6	0	0	0	7	9	5	5	0	5	9	.321	.167	.364	11.57	6.43
Slack, Nick	R-R	5-11	215	1-5-83	3	4	6.54	39	0	0	5	52	60	43	38	6	14	46	.294	.267	.310	7.91	2.41
Soto, Darwin	R-R	6-2	195	1-15-82	0	2	6.26	17	0	0	0	23	33	18	16	0	10	22	.330	.429	.292	8.61	3.91
Stockman, Landon	R-R	6-2	190	8-28-79	3	4	3.60	31	0	0	1	40	43	20	16	4	15	36	.285	.222	.330	8.10	3.38
Taubenheim, Ty	R-R	6-6	229	11-17-82	10	2	2.63	16	16	2	0	106	86	34	31	7	26	75	.224	.258	.201	6.37	2.21
Thatcher, Joe	L-L	6-2	203	4-10-81	0	0	0.00	7	0	0	2	9	6	0	0	0	0	14	.188	.300	.136	14.00	0.00
Thomas, Eric	R-R	6-7	246	3-24-81	0	2	17.55	4	2	0	0	7	12	13	13	1	6	1	.414	.333	.471	1.35	8.10
Villanueva, Carlos	B-R	6-3	201	11-28-83	8	1	2.32	21	21	0	0	112	78	31	29	11	32	124	.195	.200	.191	9.93	2.56
Wolfe, Brian	R-R	6-2	215	11-29-80	1	1	0.79	18	0	0	8	23	19	3	2	0	8	22	.229	.290	.192	8.74	3.18

FIELDING

Catcher	PCT	G	PO	A	E	DP	PB
Blevins	1.000	1	9	0	0	0	0
Corredor	.993	15	117	18	1	1	2
Medlin	.985	35	254	11	4	2	3
Palmisano	.995	89	674	71	4	9	6

First Base	PCT	G	PO	A	E	DP
Brady	.983	21	169	9	3	19
De la Cruz	1.000	12	83	8	0	8
Diggins	.833	1	5	0	1	0
Eure	.990	109	896	39	9	90

Second Base	PCT	G	PO	A	E	DP
Campana	.967	13	28	31	2	7
Sollmann	.969	124	233	359	19	94

Third Base	PCT	G	PO	A	E	DP
Campana	.854	23	10	25	6	4
De la Cruz	.889	7	1	7	1	0
Eure	.786	10	8	14	6	1
Festa	.842	7	2	14	3	1
Heether	.943	90	51	166	13	15
Murray	1.000	4	2	5	0	0

Shortstop	PCT	G	PO	A	E	DP
Campana	.944	15	20	47	4	7
Chavez	.960	121	160	370	22	91
Murray	1.000	1	3	1	0	0

Outfield	PCT	G	PO	A	E	DP
Anderson	.986	127	201	10	3	3
Brady	1.000	2	2	0	0	0
De la Cruz	1.000	10	15	0	0	0
Deevers	.989	52	83	7	1	5
Eure	1.000	1	1	0	0	0
Ezi	.990	97	195	7	2	3
Moss	.996	115	250	9	1	2
Serfass	1.000	6	6	0	0	0
Van Iderstine	1.000	7	17	0	0	0

WEST VIRGINIA POWER — Low Class A

SOUTH ATLANTIC LEAGUE

BATTING	B-T	HT	WT	DOB	AVG	vLH	vRH	G	AB	R	H	2B	3B	HR	RBI	BB	HBP	SH	SF	SO	SB	CS	SLG	OBP
Bates, Dallas	L-L	5-7	177	7-20-84	.237	.154	.257	40	131	15	31	3	1	3	13	13	2	2	2	26	2	1	.344	.311
Blevins, Clay	L-R	6-1	190	5-1-83	.200	.091	.211	42	120	16	24	6	1	1	10	20	2	3	0	19	0	0	.292	.324
Brady, Josh	R-R	5-10	185	10-24-80	.246	.286	.234	80	272	37	67	15	2	6	48	29	5	1	9	64	6	6	.382	.321
Braun, Ryan	R-R	6-2	200	11-17-83	.355	.389	.351	37	152	21	54	16	2	8	35	9	2	2	1	34	2	4	.645	.396
Cormier, Richard	B-R	5-10	190	3-17-83	.000	.000	.000	3	4	0	0	0	0	0	0	2	0	0	0	1	0	0	.000	.333
Corporan, Carlos	B-R	6-2	209	1-7-84	.239	.183	.251	99	343	46	82	15	2	9	38	28	7	9	3	97	0	0	.373	.307
Corredor, Nestor	R-R	6-1	185	5-25-84	.203	.231	.192	45	138	7	28	10	0	0	16	6	0	2	0	32	2	1	.275	.236
Escobar, Alcides	R-R	6-1	155	12-16-86	.271	.321	.257	127	520	80	141	25	8	2	36	20	7	11	4	90	30	13	.362	.305
Fermaint, Charlie	R-R	5-9	180	10-11-85	.248	.240	.250	27	113	18	28	7	0	5	17	8	1	1	1	39	4	2	.442	.301
Festa, Tony	L-R	6-2	200	12-1-80	.129	.000	.140	18	62	6	8	1	0	0	5	5	0	0	0	10	1	0	.145	.194
Gamel, Mat	L-R	6-0	205	7-26-85	.174	.000	.235	8	23	2	4	0	0	1	1	5	0	0	0	9	0	0	.304	.321
Iribarren, Hernan	L-R	6-1	162	6-29-84	.290	.250	.301	126	486	72	141	15	8	4	48	51	5	13	5	99	38	15	.379	.360
Katin, Brendan	R-R	6-1	235	1-28-83	.202	.160	.220	23	84	7	17	1	0	1	5	8	2	0	0	29	0	0	.250	.287
Lewis, William	R-R	5-9	170	8-18-81	.279	.274	.281	98	340	42	95	17	5	3	56	20	23	4	3	49	8	10	.385	.358
Lozada, Charlie	R-R	5-9	194	6-28-83	.149	.172	.111	15	47	1	7	2	0	0	7	0	2	1	0	7	0	0	.191	.184
Mannon, Adam	R-R	6-2	216	12-12-83	.151	.057	.190	42	119	13	18	1	0	4	14	24	0	3	1	44	0	1	.261	.292
Murray, Josh	R-R	6-1	193	8-12-84	.206	.125	.235	89	301	33	62	8	1	8	32	25	7	1	1	98	4	4	.319	.281
Parejo, Freddy	R-R	6-2	175	10-16-84	.231	.206	.240	82	268	26	62	9	3	2	21	12	4	4	1	44	16	7	.310	.274
Rasheed, Hasan	L-L	5-8	170	1-26-84	.305	.294	.307	79	259	41	79	11	0	2	21	39	2	0	3	66	14	5	.371	.396
Richardson, Grant	R-R	6-1	210	2-26-83	.285	.260	.290	112	411	54	117	34	0	12	55	52	6	0	3	86	7	5	.455	.371
Rodriguez, Guilder	B-R	6-0	151	7-24-83	.174	.000	.216	20	46	3	8	1	0	0	3	4	1	2	1	6	2	0	.196	.250
Salome, Angel	R-R	5-7	190	6-8-86	.254	.346	.228	29	118	15	30	7	1	4	21	8	0	0	0	17	1	0	.432	.302
Savas, Garry	R-R	6-0	200	2-24-83	.000	.000	.000	4	12	0	0	0	0	0	0	0	0	0	0	3	0	0	.000	.000
Septimo, Agustin	L-R	5-11	170	5-27-84	.264	.216	.282	44	140	18	37	10	1	2	13	9	1	1	1	33	3	0	.393	.311
Serfass, Jake	L-R	6-2	190	12-15-81	.242	.333	.222	14	33	6	8	1	0	1	5	13	1	0	0	18	1	1	.364	.468
Tuttle, Jason	L-L	5-8	165	11-27-79	.000	.000	.000	7	24	0	0	0	0	0	0	0	0	0	0	5	0	1	.000	.000
Yoho, Nathan	L-R	5-11	190	12-21-82	.200	.167	.222	4	15	1	3	1	0	0	0	2	0	0	0	4	0	1	.267	.294

PITCHING	B-T	HT	WT	DOB	W	L	ERA	G	GS	CG	SV	IP	H	R	ER	HR	BB	SO	AVG	vLH	vRH	K/9	BB/9
Baker, Josh	R-R	6-5	220	4-2-82	1	4	6.12	19	10	0	0	65	76	47	44	14	27	51	.290	.252	.314	7.10	3.76
Barnes, Justin	R-R	6-4	200	8-21-82	9	2	3.18	29	3	0	1	79	63	33	28	5	25	76	.220	.280	.192	8.62	2.84
Beresford, Simon	R-R	6-5	222	1-2-83	1	1	7.18	19	0	0	1	26	36	26	21	8	11	26	.327	.289	.347	8.89	3.76
Brady, Josh	R-R	5-10	185	10-24-80	0	0	0.00	3	0	0	0	2	2	0	0	0	2	4	.222	.250	.200	15.43	7.71
Decarlo, Derek	R-R	6-3	170	3-24-83	6	4	4.94	32	5	0	0	95	101	59	52	11	37	60	.275	.250	.289	5.70	3.52
Gallardo, Yovani	R-R	6-2	190	2-27-86	8	3	2.74	26	18	0	1	121	100	46	37	5	51	110	.230	.197	.247	8.16	3.78
Hammond, Steve	R-L	6-2	205	4-30-82	3	0	2.45	4	1	0	0	15	12	4	4	0	5	11	.235	.200	.244	6.75	3.07
Hinton, Robert	R-R	6-2	190	8-13-84	3	4	2.53	46	0	0	14	75	54	24	21	7	27	77	.199	.205	.197	9.28	3.25

PITCHING	B-T	HT	WT	DOB	W	L	ERA	G	GS	CG	SV	IP	H	R	ER	HR	BB	SO	AVG	vLH	vRH	K/9	BB/9
Johnson, Dave	R-R	6-5	205	8-25-82	4	2	3.90	30	1	0	1	60	65	35	26	6	25	57	.275	.253	.287	8.55	3.75
Kloosterman, Greg	L-L	6-2	198	6-21-82	4	19	5.24	28	27	0	0	143	166	105	83	17	58	113	.287	.247	.294	7.13	3.66
Mannon, Adam	R-R	6-2	216	12-12-83	0	0	0.00	2	0	0	0	2	2	0	0	0	1	0	.222	.000	.500	0.00	4.50
Martin, Forrest	R-R	6-1	201	1-8-80	1	5	4.87	10	8	0	0	41	45	25	22	6	14	37	.287	.288	.286	8.19	3.10
Miller, Derek	L-L	6-0	195	11-8-81	2	1	3.50	8	7	0	0	36	35	14	14	3	10	27	.263	.333	.254	6.75	2.50
Montalbo, Brian	B-R	6-5	225	11-22-81	1	6	6.22	27	7	0	1	72	92	62	50	9	38	46	.317	.320	.316	5.72	4.73
Renkert, Dane	R-R	6-1	210	10-17-81	2	0	0.00	8	0	0	0	14	3	1	0	0	7	14	.071	.077	.069	8.79	4.40
Roberts, Kevin	R-R	6-0	190	5-15-84	2	2	4.94	9	3	0	0	27	31	21	15	4	12	20	.272	.212	.296	6.59	3.95
Rogers, Mark	R-R	6-2	205	1-30-86	2	9	5.11	25	20	0	1	99	87	65	56	11	70	109	.238	.219	.248	9.94	6.39
Stanczyk, Ben	R-R	6-2	210	9-26-82	5	4	2.44	47	0	0	11	63	47	20	17	4	22	58	.200	.200	.200	8.33	3.16
Thomas, Eric	R-R	6-7	246	3-24-81	0	1	3.44	7	3	0	1	18	20	8	7	2	6	15	.294	.208	.341	7.36	2.95
Wahpepah, Josh	R-R	6-4	185	7-17-84	5	6	3.95	27	19	0	0	116	126	63	51	12	25	79	.275	.255	.286	6.11	1.93
Wooley, Robert	R-R	6-1	190	12-7-84	1	5	6.53	13	6	0	0	41	63	37	30	0	18	24	.341	.378	.311	5.23	3.92

FIELDING

Catcher	PCT	G	PO	A	E	DP	PB
Blevins	.983	32	212	24	4	1	7
Cormier	1.000	2	4	0	0	0	0
Corporan	.977	59	446	64	12	6	10
Corredor	.986	32	180	32	3	1	8
Lozada	1.000	9	36	11	0	2	0
Salome	.984	15	112	12	2	2	6
Savas	1.000	2	14	0	0	0	0

First Base	PCT	G	PO	A	E	DP
Brady	.979	24	219	9	5	16
Corporan	.984	8	54	6	1	3
Lozada	1.000	1	8	0	0	0
Richardson	.991	108	923	90	9	94

Second Base	PCT	G	PO	A	E	DP
Iribarren	.967	122	255	367	21	71
Lewis	1.000	8	14	21	0	3
Murray	1.000	1	4	4	0	1
Rodriguez	1.000	5	10	12	0	3
Septimo	1.000	3	10	9	0	4

Third Base	PCT	G	PO	A	E	DP
Brady	.800	5	2	6	2	0
Braun	.885	33	22	70	12	5
Festa	.972	12	7	28	1	1
Gamel	.800	7	5	11	4	2
Murray	.882	72	29	135	22	12
Rodriguez	1.000	3	1	4	0	0
Septimo	.964	10	7	20	1	3

Shortstop	PCT	G	PO	A	E	DP
Escobar	.936	122	204	395	41	90
Festa	1.000	1	5	3	0	1
Murray	.906	8	9	20	3	2
Rodriguez	.929	4	3	10	1	2
Septimo	.962	8	6	19	1	2

Outfield	PCT	G	PO	A	E	DP
Bates	.982	36	53	1	1	0
Brady	.970	45	63	1	2	0
Fermaint	.987	27	76	2	1	1
Katin	1.000	21	34	0	0	0
Lewis	.990	62	95	9	1	2
Mannon	.938	37	57	3	4	1
Parejo	.987	79	152	4	2	0
Rasheed	.987	78	151	3	2	1
Rodriguez	1.000	6	6	0	0	0
Rogers	.000	1	0	0	0	0
Septimo	.865	21	29	3	5	1
Serfass	1.000	12	13	1	0	0
Tuttle	1.000	7	12	1	0	0
Yoho	1.000	4	3	0	0	0

HELENA BREWERS — Rookie

PIONEER LEAGUE

BATTING	B-T	HT	WT	DOB	AVG	vLH	vRH	G	AB	R	H	2B	3B	HR	RBI	BB	HBP	SH	SF	SO	SB	CS	SLG	OBP
Alonso, John	R-R	6-0	215	2-19-86	.323	.200	.381	9	31	6	10	2	0	2	5	3	0	0	0	10	1	0	.581	.382
Bell, Michael	R-R	6-0	185	3-30-85	.300	.361	.270	58	213	38	64	17	1	3	42	23	3	3	1	39	9	6	.432	.375
Blevins, Clay	L-R	6-1	190	5-1-83	.333	.625	.258	12	39	6	13	2	0	0	5	6	0	0	1	3	1	0	.385	.413
Brantley, Michael	L-L	6-2	180	5-15-87	.324	.125	.385	10	34	8	11	2	0	0	3	6	0	0	0	4	2	0	.382	.425
Braun, Ryan	R-R	6-2	200	11-17-83	.341	.417	.310	10	41	6	14	2	1	2	10	2	2	0	2	6	2	1	.585	.383
Cain, Lorenzo	R-R	6-2	165	4-13-86	.208	.200	.214	6	24	4	5	0	0	0	1	1	3	0	0	6	0	0	.208	.321
Chapman, Stephen	L-L	6-0	180	10-12-85	.269	.174	.285	54	167	25	45	9	1	6	25	20	3	3	3	38	10	3	.443	.352
Crew, Ryan	R-R	6-0	175	8-31-83	.346	.293	.373	58	217	45	75	19	1	4	29	22	1	2	4	21	5	5	.498	.402
Emeterio, Oscar	B-R	6-1	165	11-14-85	.000	.000	.000	1	2	0	0	0	0	0	1	0	0	0	0	0	0	0	.000	.000
Fermaint, Charlie	R-R	5-9	180	10-11-85	.364	.419	.347	31	129	46	47	9	2	12	32	15	0	1	4	28	11	2	.744	.419
Ford, Darren	R-R	6-1	195	10-1-85	.271	.267	.274	61	236	57	64	4	3	1	24	33	3	3	2	70	18	4	.326	.365
Gallardo, Carlos	L-L	6-0	200	3-31-83	.221	.250	.214	28	68	10	15	6	0	1	7	5	2	1	0	15	0	0	.353	.293
Gamel, Mat	L-R	6-0	205	7-26-85	.327	.316	.331	50	199	34	65	15	2	5	37	12	4	0	1	49	7	4	.497	.375
Holmberg, Kenny	R-R	5-9	175	2-21-83	.372	.372	.372	59	207	40	77	16	0	12	51	29	3	6	3	34	2	2	.623	.450
Jimenez, Jose	R-R	6-2	185	5-9-87	.158	.200	.111	7	19	4	3	3	0	0	0	1	1	0	0	6	0	0	.316	.238
Katin, Brendan	R-R	6-1	235	1-28-83	.386	.472	.346	33	114	30	44	6	0	8	26	17	3	0	2	25	3	1	.649	.471
Mannon, Adam	R-R	6-2	216	12-12-83	.237	.222	.261	22	59	10	14	2	0	4	9	9	0	0	0	23	3	0	.475	.338
McKnight, Scott	L-R	6-1	155	12-22-84	.242	.324	.213	40	128	16	31	8	1	0	14	9	2	3	4	25	3	0	.320	.294
Opdyke, Bryan	L-R	6-1	197	8-7-84	.171	.200	.161	22	41	7	7	2	1	0	3	14	1	0	0	22	1	0	.268	.393
Parejo, Freddy	R-R	6-2	175	10-16-84	.339	.407	.286	33	124	20	42	3	0	1	19	9	9	2	1	21	12	3	.387	.420
Salome, Angel	R-R	5-7	190	6-8-86	.415	.413	.416	37	159	34	66	17	0	8	50	15	1	0	0	16	6	2	.673	.469
Septimo, Agustin	L-R	5-11	170	5-27-84	.314	.176	.337	36	121	27	38	3	1	5	16	9	1	1	2	22	10	2	.479	.361
Willcutt, Brad	R-R	6-1	220	2-18-82	.225	.227	.223	48	178	24	40	10	0	5	20	14	2	1	2	38	0	1	.365	.286
Yost, Ned	R-R	6-2	195	7-8-82	.302	.324	.289	57	202	34	61	10	4	4	32	26	6	0	0	46	6	1	.450	.397

PITCHING	B-T	HT	WT	DOB	W	L	ERA	G	GS	CG	SV	IP	H	R	ER	HR	BB	SO	AVG	vLH	vRH	K/9	BB/9
Beresford, Simon	R-R	6-5	222	1-2-83	1	1	2.55	7	4	0	0	25	24	10	7	1	8	25	.264	.229	.286	9.12	2.92
Bernal, Luis	R-R	6-1	195	1-24-83	1	1	10.91	9	0	0	0	16	22	21	19	3	6	8	.314	.320	.311	4.60	3.45
Breshears, Richard	R-R	6-3	194	8-12-83	1	2	4.50	12	0	0	3	16	15	8	8	1	11	21	.234	.292	.200	11.81	6.19
Hammond, Steve	R-L	6-2	205	4-30-82	1	0	1.06	4	2	0	0	17	13	5	2	1	0	23	.206	.286	.143	12.18	0.00
Inman, Will	R-R	6-0	200	2-6-87	6	0	2.00	13	5	0	1	45	29	11	10	5	11	58	.182	.095	.240	11.60	2.20
Jean, Chris	R-R	6-4	175	10-31-82	0	0	5.91	15	3	0	0	32	46	26	21	4	8	16	.333	.323	.342	4.50	2.25
Kretzschmar, Mat	R-R	6-3	215	8-2-86	0	0	5.55	8	4	0	0	24	28	15	15	3	11	23	.289	.262	.309	8.51	4.07
Laureano, Wilfrido	R-R	6-6	175	3-4-84	0	0	3.29	14	1	0	0	27	24	10	10	2	13	36	.231	.238	.226	11.85	4.28
Lluberes, Rafael	L-L	6-4	155	9-21-84	4	4	6.00	16	8	0	2	48	55	39	32	4	19	27	.289	.328	.273	5.06	3.56
Louis, Joshua	R-R	6-2	220	3-9-85	1	2	5.64	17	0	0	5	30	38	23	19	3	8	28	.297	.293	.300	8.31	2.37
Malave, Ronny	R-R	6-1	181	1-1-86	4	0	1.91	14	0	0	1	28	25	11	6	0	11	16	.253	.293	.224	5.08	3.49
Mannon, Adam	R-R	6-2	216	12-12-83	0	0	36.00	1	0	0	0	1	3	4	4	1	1	1	.500	1.000	.400	9.00	9.00
Marion, Ryan	R-R	6-1	215	9-23-84	4	3	5.90	17	10	0	1	58	57	47	38	9	36	49	.247	.252	.242	7.60	5.59
Miller, Derek	L-L	6-0	195	11-8-81	1	1	2.75	9	6	0	1	36	31	16	11	4	4	35	.226	.241	.222	8.75	1.00
Morrison, Tyler	R-R	5-10	210	5-1-85	5	3	5.78	17	12	0	0	67	91	51	43	7	14	63	.320	.343	.299	8.46	1.88
Parillo, Brandon	L-L	5-10	185	9-22-85	2	1	2.14	12	0	0	1	21	18	10	5	0	9	19	.231	.250	.222	8.14	3.86
Renkert, Dane	R-R	6-1	210	10-17-81	2	1	2.70	15	0	0	2	27	22	11	8	0	12	34	.212	.196	.224	11.48	4.05
Roberts, Kevin	R-R	6-0	190	5-15-84	1	2	2.82	8	3	0	0	22	19	8	7	0	8	34	.221	.186	.256	13.70	3.22
Ryan, Patrick	R-R	6-0	200	5-31-83	0	0	3.15	17	0	0	1	20	19	9	7	1	6	20	.247	.211	.282	9.00	2.70
Thatcher, Joe	L-L	6-2	203	4-10-81	2	0	3.52	6	0	0	2	8	8	3	3	1	1	10	.258	.250	.261	11.74	1.17

PITCHING	B-T	HT	WT	DOB	W	L	ERA	G	GS	CG	SV	IP	H	R	ER	HR	BB	SO	AVG	vLH	vRH	K/9	BB/9
Thomas, Eric	R-R	6-7	246	3-24-81	0	1	2.53	3	2	0	0	11	6	5	3	0	2	7	.167	.190	.133	5.91	1.69
Welch, David	R-L	6-4	215	6-2-83	4	1	2.77	12	3	0	3	26	21	10	8	2	12	29	.216	.267	.194	10.04	4.15
Wooley, Robert	R-R	6-1	190	12-7-84	6	7	4.70	18	13	0	1	75	86	48	39	7	20	69	.284	.270	.296	8.32	2.41

GAMES BY POSITION: C—Blevins 11, Opdyke 22, Salome 20, Willcutt 38. **1B**—Alonso 5, Gallardo 26, Gamel 3, Willcutt 9, Yost 48. **2B**—Crew 3, Holmberg 49, McKnight 22, Septimo 12. **3B**—Bell 22, Braun 6, Crew 6, Gamel 41, Holmberg 1, Jimenez 7, Septimo 3. **SS**—Bell 32, Crew 35, McKnight 20. **OF**—Brantley 9, Cain 3, Chapman 51, Crew 19, Fermaint 30, Ford 60, Katin 28, Mannon 10, Parejo 33, Septimo 12, Yost 4.

AZL BREWERS — Rookie

ARIZONA LEAGUE

BATTING	B-T	HT	WT	DOB	AVG	vLH	vRH	G	AB	R	H	2B	3B	HR	RBI	BB	HBP	SH	SF	SO	SB	CS	SLG	OBP
Alonso, John	R-R	6-0	215	2-19-86	.292	.267	.303	15	48	5	14	4	0	1	6	7	0	0	1	17	0	0	.438	.375
Angoma, Ruben	R-R	6-1	167	8-17-86	.273	.286	.267	8	22	5	6	2	0	0	3	1	0	0	0	5	1	0	.364	.304
Ayala, Angel	L-R	6-2	208	7-24-86	.147	.000	.179	12	34	1	5	2	0	0	4	7	0	0	0	9	1	1	.206	.293
Blanc, Jhonathan	R-R	6-3	180	3-22-85	.217	.375	.153	29	83	8	18	2	1	0	5	2	1	2	0	21	1	3	.265	.244
Brantley, Michael	L-L	6-2	180	5-15-87	.347	.300	.361	44	173	34	60	3	1	0	19	22	2	4	0	13	14	5	.376	.426
Cain, Lorenzo	R-R	6-2	165	4-13-86	.356	.386	.345	50	205	45	73	18	5	5	37	20	4	0	3	32	12	3	.566	.418
De la Cruz, Fredy	R-R	6-2	180	10-17-85	.264	.250	.271	28	106	15	28	2	0	5	20	4	2	1	1	26	0	1	.425	.301
Delarosa, Anderson	R-R	6-0	166	8-1-84	.248	.194	.267	37	137	21	34	7	0	1	11	12	0	0	2	34	4	1	.321	.305
Dennis, Bernie	R-R	6-0	200	7-5-83	.296	.357	.281	25	71	8	21	6	0	0	6	7	1	2	0	16	1	2	.380	.367
Emeterio, Oscar	B-R	6-1	165	11-14-85	.188	.208	.180	30	85	17	16	4	3	0	6	4	0	2	0	28	2	1	.306	.225
Festa, Tony	L-R	6-2	200	12-1-80	.442	.444	.441	12	43	11	19	5	3	1	10	3	3	1	0	4	1	0	.767	.510
Jimenez, Herman	R-R	6-3	203	1-20-85	.216	.143	.243	16	51	6	11	1	0	0	8	2	0	1	0	11	0	1	.235	.245
Jimenez, Jose	R-R	6-2	185	5-9-87	.299	.365	.274	47	187	26	56	14	3	2	33	16	2	0	0	38	2	0	.439	.361
Leclercq, Lenny	R-R	6-2	180	9-7-85	.268	.286	.261	38	97	21	26	2	3	1	11	9	0	2	1	41	6	1	.381	.327
McKnight, Scott	L-R	6-1	155	12-22-84	.275	.250	.286	11	40	7	11	0	0	0	4	4	1	1	0	8	1	1	.275	.356
Mejia, Harold	R-R	6-1	155	8-28-87	.233	.175	.252	44	163	19	38	11	3	0	12	2	1	3	0	54	2	2	.337	.247
Palencia, Isaac	R-R	6-4	202	8-14-85	.400	.300	.440	22	70	10	28	4	0	0	11	6	3	0	0	13	2	3	.457	.468
Stanfield, Jimmy	R-R	6-0	215	8-20-82	.241	.333	.203	30	83	4	20	1	0	1	13	9	2	0	2	18	1	1	.289	.323
Vicioso, Osvaldo	B-R	6-2	171	11-12-86	.237	.150	.267	43	156	17	37	5	3	0	17	5	0	1	0	44	2	5	.308	.261
Yoho, Nathan	L-R	5-11	190	12-21-82	.298	.173	.353	40	168	31	50	5	5	2	29	11	3	0	3	25	6	1	.423	.346

PITCHING	B-T	HT	WT	DOB	W	L	ERA	G	GS	CG	SV	IP	H	R	ER	HR	BB	SO	AVG	vLH	vRH	K/9	BB/9
Alliston, Josh	R-R	6-5	232	2-29-80	0	1	2.25	4	2	0	0	4	3	1	1	0	0	3	.200	.167	.222	6.75	0.00
Anderson, Ryan	L-L	6-10	215	7-12-79	0	0	7.36	3	3	0	0	4	4	4	3	0	1	6	.286	.000	.333	14.73	2.45
Beltre, Jose	R-R	6-3	170	11-27-84	0	1	7.20	13	6	0	0	35	49	33	28	0	21	50	.327	.385	.296	12.86	5.40
Blanc, Jhonathan	R-R	6-3	180	3-22-85	0	0	0.00	2	0	0	0	2	0	0	0	0	2	2	.000	.000	.000	10.80	10.80
Cespedes, Carlos	R-R	6-6	257	3-26-86	0	0	8.49	10	0	0	0	12	18	21	11	1	13	15	.321	.250	.350	11.57	10.03
Chourio, Jesus	R-R	6-2	180	10-31-86	1	3	6.82	14	0	0	0	30	33	25	23	1	23	24	.282	.225	.312	7.12	6.82
Emeterio, Oscar	B-R	6-1	165	11-14-85	0	0	3.38	3	0	0	0	3	3	1	1	1	2	1	.273	.000	.333	3.38	6.75
Fermin, Jorge	R-R	6-3	175	9-23-85	0	0	9.82	2	0	0	0	4	8	6	4	2	2	2	.364	.300	.417	4.91	4.91
Garcia, Jose	R-R	6-3	170	5-25-88	1	2	6.00	12	5	0	0	30	27	28	20	3	16	23	.233	.184	.256	6.90	4.80
Garrison, Steve	B-L	6-1	185	9-12-86	2	2	2.86	11	4	0	2	35	39	13	11	0	5	28	.300	.200	.324	7.27	1.30
Guzman, Julio	L-L	6-1	170	12-10-87	1	1	9.33	8	3	0	0	18	22	19	19	3	15	18	.301	.211	.333	8.84	7.36
Inman, Will	R-R	6-0	200	2-6-87	0	0	0.00	1	0	0	0	2	0	0	0	0	1	1	.000	.000	.000	4.50	4.50
James, Mark	R-R	6-1	185	7-24-87	1	3	10.50	9	4	0	0	18	26	23	21	2	18	14	.338	.267	.383	7.00	9.00
Kretzschmar, Mat	R-R	6-3	215	8-2-86	1	0	2.45	7	0	0	2	18	20	6	5	1	5	19	.278	.333	.255	9.33	2.45
Labasta, William	R-R	6-3	175	9-7-85	2	2	5.09	14	0	0	0	23	21	19	13	3	21	14	.239	.324	.185	5.48	8.22
Langille, Craig	R-R	6-2	190	11-12-85	2	3	6.84	14	5	0	0	50	80	46	38	2	14	20	.374	.360	.381	3.60	2.52
Ledezma, Alirio	R-R	6-3	211	4-1-87	3	3	3.89	20	1	0	4	42	41	23	18	2	19	37	.258	.218	.279	7.99	4.10
Mercedes, Roque	B-R	6-3	186	10-28-86	2	3	6.60	14	8	0	0	44	53	42	32	5	34	45	.294	.217	.333	9.27	7.01
Miller, Ryan	R-R	6-1	208	2-12-78	0	0	4.50	2	2	0	0	2	3	1	1	0	0	0	.333	.333	.333	0.00	0.00
Parejo, Miguel	R-R	6-1	176	6-7-86	3	4	4.33	19	0	0	2	35	41	22	17	1	17	24	.293	.204	.341	6.11	4.33
Parillo, Brandon	L-L	5-10	185	9-22-85	1	2	2.00	6	3	0	0	18	5	6	4	0	10	22	.082	.111	.077	11.00	5.00
Periard, Alexandre	L-R	6-1	180	6-15-87	0	1	5.08	11	4	0	1	28	43	23	16	1	10	22	.358	.432	.316	6.99	3.18
Rivas, Amaury	R-R	6-2	185	12-20-85	2	3	6.91	14	6	0	0	42	56	36	32	1	16	34	.326	.333	.322	7.34	3.46
Villar, Nathanael	R-R	6-4	170	10-18-85	0	0	13.50	1	0	0	0	1	4	2	2	0	1	1	.571	.667	.500	6.75	6.75

GAMES BY POSITION: C—Angoma 8, Delarosa 3, Dennis 25, Palencia 11, Stanfield 29. **1B**—Alonso 14, Ayala 10, De la Cruz 5, Festa 11, H. Jimenez 7, J. Jimenez 1, Leclercq 18, Palencia 1. **2B**—De la Cruz 1, Emeterio 11, J. Jimenez 1, Leclercq 9, McKnight 6, Vicioso 35. **3B**—Alonso 1, De la Cruz 15, Festa 1, H. Jimenez 2, J. Jimenez 35, Mejia 2, Vicioso 3. **SS**—De la Cruz 1, H. Jimenez 3, J. Jimenez 8, Leclercq 1, McKnight 5, Mejia 41, Vicioso 4. **OF**—Blanc 21, Brantley 42, Cain 41, Delarosa 31, Emeterio 4, J. Jimenez 1, Leclercq 2, Yoho 37.

MINNESOTA TWINS

BY JOHN MILLEA

After winning three consecutive American League Central championships, the Twins are now going back to the drawing board. The 2005 season was forgettable in almost all measures, but the bottom line was that the Twins failed to meet their own expectations, much less those of the prognosticators who had marked Minnesota as a possible World Series threat.

An 83-79 record and third-place division finish fell, most of all, at the hands of the offense, or lack thereof. The Twins ranked dead last in the league with 688 runs scored, and their .259 team batting average ranked ahead of only Seattle's .256. There were high hopes before the season, especially with youngsters Joe Mauer and Justin Morneau appearing to be on the brink of solid production.

Mauer was not a disappointment. The catcher remained healthy and hit .294, although his power numbers (nine homers, 55 RBIs) were lower than the organization would have liked. Morneau, meanwhile, came into the season as the cleanup hitter but never came around. He was hit in the head by a pitch in the third game of the year, which proved to be an omen. Morneau hit .239-22-79, but he hit just .209 with runners in scoring position and .204 after the all-star break. Another disappointment was third baseman Michael Cuddyer, who hit .263 overall and just .200 with runners in scoring position.

Pitching was the strength of the club in 2004, but it wasn't enough to overcome the anemic offense. That shortfall at the plate, coupled with injuries and almost constant lineup shifts, were major culprits in the disappointing season.

How fractured was the starting lineup? Seven different players started games at second base, five shortstops were used and six third basemen. Injuries? Four-time Gold Glove winner Torii Hunter suffered a broken ankle in late July and missed the rest of the season. Left fielder Shannon Stewart, a career .300 hitter, battled injuries and hit just .274, his lowest average in seven years as a big leaguer.

Starter Johan Santana was again solid, coming off a Cy Young season and finishing 16-7, 2.87. Starters Brad Radke and Carlos Silva were solid in combining for an 18-20 record. And the bullpen was another strength of the Twins behind setup man Juan Rincon and two-time all-star closer Joe Nathan. The pitching staff, in fact, was among the league leaders in ERA for much of the season. But the task is doubly hard when the team's offense is so weak.

The Twins' ultimately disappointing season can be traced in part to their heavy reliance on young players who might not have been quite ready. Mauer, Morneau, Cuddyer and shortstop Jason Bartlett had never before been full-time starters in the big leagues. In retrospect, putting so much of the team's fortunes in the hands of so many untested players was probably the biggest reason for what took place during the season.

One of the major organizational goals during the offseason was to bring in at least one reputable power hitter. The Twins learned their lesson the hard way in 2005: small ball won't always cut it. This club needs some bang at the plate, and everyone knows it.

The pitching will almost certainly be the team's strength again in the season ahead. Santana, Radke, Silva, Nathan and young reliever Jesse Crain will be back as the strong pitching nucleus. Scott Baker and Francisco Liriano, who made their major league debuts in 2005, also should contend for spots in the 2006 rotation. Liriano enjoyed a dominant minor league season, split between Triple-A Rochester and Double-A New Britain.

Outfielder Jason Kubel also could figure into the Twins' plans. The minor league slugging star missed the 2005 season after a knee injury in the 2004 Arizona Fall League, but he has the pedigree of an outstanding hitter from the left side.

PLAYERS OF THE YEAR

MAJOR LEAGUE: Johan Santana, lhp

Santana's encore to his 2004 Cy Young Award season was another dandy, if not as spectacular as the year before. The 26-year-old Venezuelan waged another Cy Young run by leading the AL with 238 strikeouts, finishing second with a 2.87 ERA and tying for fifth with 16 wins.

MINOR LEAGUE: Francisco Liriano, lhp

Liriano used his Santana-like repertoire to pull off a Santana-like feat: he led the minor leagues with 204 strikeouts. He was solid at Double-A New Britain in the first half of the 2005 season, but he was downright dominant after a promotion to Triple-A Rochester, going 9-2, 1.78 in 91 innings.

ORGANIZATION LEADERS

BATTING

*AVG	Span, Denard, Fort Myers/New Britain	.307
R	Burns, Deacon, Beloit	90
H	Winfree, David, Beloit	165
TB	Matienzo, Danny, New Britain	259
2B	Burns, Deacon, Beloit	36
	Matienzo, Danny, New Britain	36
3B	Burns, Deacon, Beloit	13
HR	Jones, Garrett, Rochester	24
RBI	Winfree, David, Beloit	101
BB	Deeds, Doug, New Britain	56
SO	Whitrock, Scott, Fort Myers	158
SB	Whitrock, Scott, Fort Myers	25
*OBP	Deeds, Doug, New Britain	.382
*SLG	Matienzo, Danny, New Britain	.488

PITCHING

W	Simonitsch, Errol, Fort Myers/New Britain	14
L	Speigner, Levale, New Britain/Rochester	11
	Waldrop, Kyle, Beloit	11
#ERA	Martinez, J.P., Beloit	1.50
G	Kemp, Beau, Rochester	62
CG	Blackburn, Nick, Fort Myers/New Britain/Rochester	3
SV	Neshek, Pat, New Britain	24
IP	Liriano, Francisco, New Britain/Rochester	168
BB	Harben, Adam, Fort Myers	62
SO	Liriano, Francisco, New Britain/Rochester	204

*Minimum 250 at-bats. #Minimum 75 innings.

MINNESOTA TWINS

Manager: Ron Gardenhire.

2005 Record: 83-79, .512 (3rd, AL Central).

BATTING	B-T	HT	WT	DOB	AVG	vLH	vRH	G	AB	R	H	2B	3B	HR	RBI	BB	HBP	SH	SF	SO	SB	CS	SLG	OBP
Abernathy, Brent	R-R	6-0	185	9-23-77	.239	.227	.244	24	67	5	16	1	0	1	6	7	1	3	1	9	2	0	.299	.316
Bartlett, Jason	R-R	6-0	190	10-30-79	.241	.277	.226	74	224	33	54	10	1	3	16	21	4	2	1	37	4	0	.335	.316
Boone, Bret	R-R	5-10	190	4-6-69	.170	.176	.167	14	53	3	9	0	0	0	3	4	1	0	0	13	0	0	.170	.241
2-team (74 Seattle)					.221	.203	.227	88	326	33	72	15	3	7	37	28	4	1	1	65	4	2	.350	.290
Castro, Juan	R-R	5-11	195	6-20-72	.257	.247	.262	97	272	27	70	18	1	5	33	9	0	9	2	39	0	1	.386	.279
Cuddyer, Michael	R-R	6-2	220	3-27-79	.263	.273	.259	126	422	55	111	25	3	12	42	41	3	1	3	93	3	4	.422	.330
Ford, Lew	R-R	6-0	200	8-12-76	.264	.233	.277	147	522	70	138	30	4	7	53	45	16	2	5	85	13	6	.377	.338
Heintz, Chris	R-R	6-1	210	8-6-74	.200	.231	.167	8	25	1	5	3	0	0	2	1	0	0	0	6	0	0	.320	.231
Hunter, Torii	R-R	6-2	220	7-18-75	.269	.283	.263	98	372	63	100	24	1	14	56	34	6	0	4	65	23	7	.452	.337
Jones, Jacque	L-L	5-10	205	4-25-75	.249	.201	.268	142	523	74	130	22	4	23	73	51	5	2	4	120	13	4	.438	.319
LeCroy, Matt	R-R	6-2	230	12-13-75	.260	.306	.228	101	304	33	79	5	0	17	50	41	4	0	1	85	0	0	.444	.354
Mauer, Joe	L-R	6-4	225	4-19-83	.294	.225	.323	131	489	61	144	26	2	9	55	61	1	0	3	64	13	1	.411	.372
Miller, Corky	R-R	6-1	245	3-18-76	.000	.000	.000	5	12	0	0	0	0	0	0	0	0	0	0	2	0	0	.000	.000
Morneau, Justin	L-R	6-4	225	5-15-81	.239	.201	.256	141	490	62	117	23	4	22	79	44	4	0	5	94	0	2	.437	.304
Punto, Nick	B-R	5-9	190	11-8-77	.239	.210	.246	112	394	45	94	18	4	4	26	36	0	7	2	86	13	8	.335	.301
Redmond, Mike	R-R	5-11	200	5-5-71	.311	.345	.289	45	148	17	46	9	0	1	26	6	3	2	0	14	0	0	.392	.350
Rivas, Luis	R-R	5-11	190	8-30-79	.257	.283	.241	59	136	21	35	3	1	1	12	9	2	0	1	17	4	0	.316	.311
Rodriguez, Luis	B-R	5-9	180	6-27-80	.269	.233	.276	79	175	21	47	10	2	2	20	18	1	6	3	23	2	2	.383	.335
Ryan, Michael	L-R	6-0	215	7-6-77	.231	.167	.234	57	117	7	27	5	0	2	13	9	0	4	1	22	1	2	.325	.283
Stewart, Shannon	R-R	5-11	210	2-25-74	.274	.244	.283	132	551	69	151	27	3	10	56	34	8	1	5	73	7	5	.388	.323
Tiffee, Terry	B-R	6-3	210	4-21-79	.207	.194	.211	54	150	9	31	8	1	1	15	8	0	0	1	15	1	0	.293	.245
Tyner, Jason	L-L	6-1	185	4-23-77	.321	.333	.318	18	56	8	18	1	1	0	5	4	0	0	0	4	2	0	.375	.367
Williams, Glenn	B-R	6-2	195	7-18-77	.425	.533	.360	13	40	3	17	1	0	0	3	2	0	1	0	7	1	2	.450	.452

PITCHING	B-T	HT	WT	DOB	W	L	ERA	G	GS	CG	SV	IP	H	R	ER	HR	BB	SO	AVG	vLH	vRH	K/9	BB/9
Baker, Scott	R-R	6-4	220	9-19-81	3	3	3.35	10	9	0	0	54	48	21	20	5	14	32	.241	.221	.257	5.37	2.35
Bowyer, Travis	R-R	6-3	210	8-3-81	0	1	5.59	8	0	0	0	10	10	6	6	3	3	12	.270	.286	.250	11.17	2.79
Crain, Jesse	R-R	6-1	205	7-5-81	12	5	2.71	75	0	0	1	80	61	28	24	6	29	25	.219	.209	.225	2.82	3.28
Gassner, Dave	R-L	6-2	190	12-14-78	1	0	5.87	2	2	0	0	8	9	7	5	1	1	2	.281	.250	.292	2.35	1.17
Guerrier, Matt	R-R	6-3	190	8-2-78	0	3	3.39	43	0	0	0	72	71	29	27	6	24	46	.259	.279	.247	5.78	3.01
Liriano, Francisco	L-L	6-2	185	10-26-83	1	2	5.70	6	4	0	0	24	19	15	15	4	7	33	.221	.222	.221	12.55	2.66
Lohse, Kyle	R-R	6-2	200	10-4-78	9	13	4.18	31	30	0	0	179	211	85	83	22	44	86	.299	.291	.305	4.33	2.22
Mays, Joe	B-R	6-1	200	12-10-75	6	10	5.65	31	26	1	0	156	203	109	98	23	41	59	.318	.273	.364	3.40	2.37
Mulholland, Terry	R-L	6-3	225	3-9-63	0	2	4.27	49	0	0	0	59	61	30	28	6	17	18	.276	.202	.321	2.75	2.59
Nathan, Joe	R-R	6-4	220	11-22-74	7	4	2.70	69	0	0	43	70	46	22	21	5	22	94	.183	.158	.206	12.09	2.83
Radke, Brad	R-R	6-2	185	10-27-72	9	12	4.04	31	31	3	0	201	214	98	90	33	23	117	.272	.291	.252	5.25	1.03
Rincon, Juan	R-R	5-11	215	1-23-79	6	6	2.45	75	0	0	0	77	63	26	21	2	30	84	.224	.218	.228	9.82	3.51
Romero, J.C.	B-L	5-11	205	6-4-76	4	3	3.47	68	0	0	0	57	50	26	22	6	39	48	.235	.198	.268	7.58	6.16
Santana, Johan	L-L	6-0	205	3-13-79	16	7	2.87	33	33	3	0	232	180	77	74	22	45	238	.210	.256	.200	9.25	1.75
Silva, Carlos	R-R	6-4	250	4-23-79	9	8	3.44	27	27	2	0	188	212	83	72	25	9	71	.290	.302	.277	3.39	0.43

FIELDING

Catcher	PCT	G	PO	A	E	DP	PB
Heintz	1.000	8	48	1	0	0	0
LeCroy	.000	1	0	0	0	0	0
Mauer	.993	116	693	44	5	6	6
Miller	1.000	4	24	2	0	0	2
Redmond	1.000	45	230	12	0	2	1

First Base	PCT	G	PO	A	E	DP
Cuddyer	1.000	8	37	1	0	8
LeCroy	.986	23	204	8	3	18
Morneau	.994	138	1191	91	8	123
Tiffee	.990	13	92	7	1	6

Second Base	PCT	G	PO	A	E	DP
Abernathy	.968	17	24	37	2	9
Boone	.974	14	38	37	2	11
Castro	1.000	5	4	9	0	3
Cuddyer	1.000	11	12	18	0	7
Punto	.979	73	131	193	7	44
Rivas	.995	53	77	112	1	26
Rodriguez	1.000	40	53	73	0	22

Third Base	PCT	G	PO	A	E	DP
Castro	.900	22	14	22	4	1
Cuddyer	.942	95	56	189	15	14
Punto	1.000	12	6	22	0	4
Rodriguez	.950	27	14	43	3	4
Ryan	.000	1	0	0	0	0
Tiffee	.912	24	18	34	5	6
Williams	.929	12	7	19	2	2

Shortstop	PCT	G	PO	A	E	DP
Bartlett	.979	68	95	227	7	45
Castro	.985	73	97	232	5	50
Punto	.984	34	47	76	2	16
Rivas	.889	6	3	5	1	1
Rodriguez	1.000	10	8	14	0	4

Outfield	PCT	G	PO	A	E	DP
Abernathy	1.000	5	5	0	0	0
Cuddyer	1.000	20	35	0	0	0
Ford	.972	95	198	9	6	1
Hunter	.987	93	218	9	3	4
Jones	.986	132	278	10	4	2
Punto	1.000	3	1	0	0	0
Ryan	1.000	25	30	2	0	1
Stewart	.985	125	249	7	4	2
Tyner	1.000	15	30	0	0	0

FARM SYSTEM

General Manager: Terry Ryan. **Director, Minor Leagues**: Jim Rantz. **Scouting Director:** Mike Radcliff.

Class	Farm Team	League	W	L	Pct.	Finish*	Manager(s)	Affiliate Since
AAA	Rochester (N.Y.) Red Wings	International	75	69	.521	t-6th (14)	Phil Roof/Rich Miller	2003
AA	New Britain (Conn.) Rock Cats	Eastern	70	72	.493	7th (12)	Stan Cliburn	1995
High A	Fort Myers (Fla.) Miracle	Florida State	74	59	.556	4th (12)	Riccardo Ingram	1993
Low A	Beloit (Wisc.) Snappers	Midwest	69	71	.493	**8th (14)**	Kevin Boles	2005
Rookie	Elizabethton (Tenn.) Twins	Appalachian	48	19	.716	**+1st (10)**	Ray Smith	1974
Rookie	Fort Myers (Fla.) Twins	Gulf Coast	28	26	.519	t-4th (12)	Nelson Prada	1989

*Finish in overall standings (No. of teams in league)/Playoff teams in **boldface** +League champion

LARRY GOREN

Joe Mauer: Posted a .372 on-base percentage in first full season

ROBERT GURGANUS

Denard Span: Had the highest average in the Twins system

ROCHESTER RED WINGS — Class AAA

INTERNATIONAL LEAGUE

BATTING	B-T	HT	WT	DOB	AVG	vLH	vRH	G	AB	R	H	2B	3B	HR	RBI	BB	HBP	SH	SF	SO	SB	CS	SLG	OBP
Abernathy, Brent	R-R	6-0	185	9-23-77	.326	.382	.299	57	215	35	70	13	0	6	25	21	3	7	3	20	7	3	.470	.388
Bartlett, Jason	R-R	6-0	190	10-30-79	.332	.345	.327	61	229	41	76	10	2	5	33	29	4	0	7	34	2	2	.459	.405
Bowen, Rob	B-R	6-3	225	2-24-81	.267	.266	.268	87	262	38	70	13	2	6	25	37	4	0	0	68	0	2	.401	.366
Buchanan, Brian	R-R	6-4	230	7-21-73	.316	.458	.278	29	114	17	36	7	0	4	16	7	0	0	0	31	0	1	.482	.355
Cuddyer, Michael	R-R	6-2	220	3-27-79	.111	.000	.200	3	9	1	1	0	0	0	0	3	0	0	0	1	2	0	.111	.333
Dunwoody, Todd	L-L	6-1	215	4-11-75	.247	.231	.249	96	300	30	74	18	2	5	40	17	2	2	2	69	6	6	.370	.290
Heintz, Chris	R-R	6-1	210	8-6-74	.304	.330	.295	89	329	38	100	18	2	8	58	22	0	4	5	61	0	0	.444	.343
Jones, Garrett	L-L	6-4	245	6-21-81	.244	.211	.253	134	488	71	119	22	2	24	72	36	1	1	1	109	5	1	.445	.297
Maza, Luis	R-R	5-9	180	6-22-80	.291	.264	.300	76	275	43	80	14	2	11	43	11	2	1	4	34	2	1	.476	.318
Miller, Corky	R-R	6-1	245	3-18-76	.229	.279	.213	59	170	35	39	7	0	11	25	27	14	8	0	30	0	2	.465	.379
Ojeda, Augie	B-R	5-8	180	12-20-74	.224	.247	.216	105	313	42	70	16	0	3	33	33	14	7	3	33	3	2	.304	.322
Punto, Nick	B-R	5-9	190	11-8-77	.200	.000	.231	4	15	2	3	1	0	0	1	2	0	0	0	2	0	0	.267	.294
Rabe, Josh	R-R	6-3	215	10-15-78	.239	.264	.230	90	285	50	68	17	0	11	49	29	3	2	2	57	5	2	.414	.313
Rivas, Luis	R-R	5-11	190	8-30-79	.248	.302	.225	43	145	17	36	14	0	2	22	8	0	2	4	18	3	2	.386	.280
Rodriguez, Luis	B-R	5-9	180	6-27-80	.304	.206	.337	40	138	19	42	10	0	1	17	16	1	2	0	14	0	1	.399	.381
Ryan, Michael	L-R	6-0	215	7-6-77	.283	.452	.240	46	152	16	43	7	1	6	26	15	0	1	2	34	0	3	.461	.343
Tiffee, Terry	B-R	6-3	210	4-21-79	.266	.159	.307	58	229	33	61	11	1	10	39	15	3	0	5	24	0	1	.454	.313
Tyner, Jason	L-L	6-1	185	4-23-77	.286	.285	.287	133	524	81	150	18	2	1	36	48	5	13	1	57	18	6	.334	.351
Velazquez, Gilbert	R-R	6-2	170	10-17-79	.265	.231	.286	17	34	3	9	1	1	0	3	0	0	0	0	8	0	0	.353	.265
West, Kevin	R-R	6-2	208	1-1-80	.271	.257	.276	125	425	60	115	26	1	20	64	45	12	0	3	94	2	2	.478	.355
Williams, Glenn	B-R	6-2	195	7-18-77	.303	.262	.316	48	175	21	53	12	1	5	22	7	3	2	0	35	2	0	.469	.341

PITCHING	B-T	HT	WT	DOB	W	L	ERA	G	GS	CG	SV	IP	H	R	ER	HR	BB	SO	AVG	vLH	vRH	K/9	BB/9
Abbott, Jim	B-R	6-3	192	10-12-79	0	3	9.00	6	0	0	0	13	14	15	13	5	8	10	.264	.208	.310	6.92	5.54
Anderson, Jimmy	L-L	6-1	210	1-22-76	4	4	2.90	12	11	0	0	62	62	24	20	5	32	41	.258	.233	.267	5.95	4.65

PITCHING	B-T	HT	WT	DOB	W	L	ERA	G	GS	CG	SV	IP	H	R	ER	HR	BB	SO	AVG	vLH	vRH	K/9	BB/9
Baker, Scott	R-R	6-4	220	9-19-81	5	8	3.01	22	22	1	0	135	123	50	45	15	26	107	.242	.198	.286	7.15	1.74
Barrett, Ricky	L-L	5-11	190	3-9-81	4	4	6.71	40	5	0	0	63	70	48	47	10	48	64	.287	.254	.301	9.14	6.86
Blackburn, Nick	R-R	6-4	230	2-24-82	0	0	5.14	3	3	0	0	14	20	11	8	2	3	7	.328	.333	.324	4.50	1.93
Bonilla, Henry	R-R	6-0	195	8-16-78	6	7	5.11	35	16	0	2	118	138	75	67	14	44	63	.299	.333	.273	4.81	3.36
Bonser, Boof	R-R	6-4	260	10-14-81	11	9	3.99	28	28	0	0	160	153	80	71	22	57	168	.251	.240	.260	9.43	3.20
Bowyer, Travis	R-R	6-3	210	8-3-81	4	2	2.78	59	0	0	23	74	51	23	23	4	40	96	.195	.175	.209	11.62	4.84
Childress, Daylan	R-R	6-1	200	7-31-78	0	1	10.38	5	0	0	0	9	10	11	10	2	5	9	.286	.200	.320	9.35	5.19
2-team (11 Louisville)					0	1	8.10	16	0	0	0	23	28	22	21	3	12	16	.298	.208	.329	6.17	4.63
Durbin, J.D.	R-R	6-0	210	2-24-82	5	5	4.33	22	19	0	0	104	97	52	50	8	51	90	.251	.268	.239	7.79	4.41
Eyre, Willie	R-R	6-2	205	7-21-78	10	3	2.72	56	0	0	7	83	79	30	25	3	28	74	.252	.211	.281	8.06	3.05
Gassner, Dave	R-L	6-2	190	12-14-78	8	8	4.95	22	20	2	0	116	138	65	64	18	33	64	.302	.288	.306	4.95	2.55
Hodges, Trey	R-R	6-3	195	6-29-78	0	0	5.63	9	0	0	0	16	17	10	10	0	10	12	.274	.222	.314	6.75	5.63
Kemp, Beau	R-R	6-0	195	10-31-80	4	5	3.38	62	0	0	5	80	74	35	30	1	32	68	.239	.257	.230	7.65	3.60
Liriano, Francisco	L-L	6-2	185	10-26-83	9	2	1.78	14	14	0	0	91	56	25	18	4	24	112	.177	.177	.176	11.08	2.37
Miller, Jason	R-L	6-1	202	7-20-82	2	0	3.81	13	0	0	0	26	28	14	11	4	17	27	.272	.273	.272	9.35	5.88
Schoening, Brent	R-R	6-1	184	4-7-78	2	4	6.05	35	4	0	0	64	78	45	43	9	29	50	.304	.248	.342	7.03	4.08
Smith, Bud	L-L	6-0	170	10-23-79	1	0	4.76	3	0	0	0	6	5	4	3	0	3	4	.217	.400	.167	6.35	4.76
Speigner, Levale	R-R	5-11	170	9-24-80	0	1	7.36	2	1	0	0	7	14	7	6	0	1	5	.412	.450	.357	6.14	1.23
Thomas, John	L-L	6-2	207	7-24-81	0	1	15.00	1	1	0	0	3	11	5	5	0	1	1	.579	.500	.588	3.00	3.00
Wolfe, Brian	R-R	6-2	215	11-29-80	0	2	8.53	3	0	0	0	6	10	8	6	1	2	5	.345	.286	.400	7.11	2.84

FIELDING

Catcher	PCT	G	PO	A	E	DP	PB
Bowen	.992	69	467	38	4	4	5
Heintz	.996	31	208	15	1	0	3
Miller	.993	53	425	22	3	4	4

First Base	PCT	G	PO	A	E	DP
Buchanan	.983	8	56	3	1	10
Cuddyer	1.000	1	8	1	0	2
Dunwoody	1.000	7	44	3	0	8
Jones	.990	124	979	81	11	100
Miller	1.000	2	11	0	0	1
Tiffee	1.000	10	76	5	0	9
Williams	1.000	1	14	0	0	2

Second Base	PCT	G	PO	A	E	DP
Abernathy	.960	25	35	61	4	18
Maza	.991	30	43	64	1	17
Ojeda	1.000	27	42	66	0	15
Punto	.900	4	8	10	2	6
Rivas	.973	38	49	96	4	25
Rodriguez	.992	27	45	78	1	16
Velazquez	1.000	6	9	15	0	5
Williams	1.000	3	2	6	0	0

Third Base	PCT	G	PO	A	E	DP
Abernathy	.800	3	4	4	2	0
Cuddyer	1.000	2	0	3	0	0
Heintz	.879	21	7	22	4	1
Maza	.914	32	22	42	6	2
Ojeda	.955	10	4	17	1	1
Rodriguez	1.000	7	1	9	0	0
Tiffee	.940	46	41	69	7	13
Velazquez	1.000	3	0	2	0	1
Williams	.927	38	24	77	8	6

Shortstop	PCT	G	PO	A	E	DP
Bartlett	.956	59	86	176	12	45
Ojeda	.974	70	92	173	7	51
Rivas	.955	5	8	13	1	5
Rodriguez	1.000	11	21	26	0	9
Velazquez	.905	6	6	13	2	2
Williams	.875	4	3	4	1	1

Outfield	PCT	G	PO	A	E	DP
Abernathy	1.000	19	24	0	0	0
Buchanan	1.000	6	7	1	0	0
Dunwoody	.989	86	183	2	2	0
Jones	.750	7	3	0	1	0
Maza	.950	22	18	1	1	0
Rabe	.972	75	103	3	3	0
Ryan	1.000	39	69	0	0	0
Tyner	.996	126	247	9	1	2
West	.968	89	174	7	6	4

NEW BRITAIN ROCK CATS — Class AA

EASTERN LEAGUE

BATTING	B-T	HT	WT	DOB	AVG	vLH	vRH	G	AB	R	H	2B	3B	HR	RBI	BB	HBP	SH	SF	SO	SB	CS	SLG	OBP
Bell, Rick	R-R	6-2	195	4-5-79	.242	.270	.232	44	149	14	36	6	1	2	13	12	1	1	1	36	0	0	.336	.301
Deeds, Doug	L-L	6-2	195	6-2-81	.304	.295	.307	133	493	77	150	34	2	16	82	56	8	1	3	119	2	4	.479	.382
Jimenez, Luis	L-L	6-4	242	5-7-82	.278	.207	.306	116	431	61	120	29	1	16	69	45	2	0	0	104	3	2	.462	.349
Kennedy, Bryan	L-R	6-2	215	10-4-78	.239	.147	.255	72	230	23	55	9	0	1	26	19	10	3	3	43	0	0	.291	.321
Langaigne, Selwyn	L-L	6-0	190	3-22-76	.255	.105	.286	34	110	9	28	6	0	3	12	7	1	1	3	31	2	0	.391	.298
Matienzo, Danny	R-R	5-11	200	9-3-80	.282	.288	.281	138	531	81	150	36	2	23	87	40	8	0	7	112	1	1	.488	.338
Mauer, Jake	R-R	6-2	180	12-20-78	.250	.333	.217	25	32	4	8	2	0	0	0	0	3	1	0	5	1	0	.313	.314
Maza, Luis	R-R	5-9	180	6-22-80	.249	.154	.272	49	197	28	49	9	0	6	23	12	3	1	2	34	0	1	.386	.299
Molina, Felix	B-R	5-9	175	5-5-83	.287	.179	.319	36	122	17	35	10	0	2	18	8	2	6	3	27	0	2	.418	.333
Morales, Jose	B-R	6-0	195	2-20-83	.250	.000	.357	7	20	1	5	1	0	0	0	1	0	0	0	3	0	0	.300	.286
Moses, Matt	L-R	6-0	210	2-20-85	.210	.255	.191	48	186	25	39	9	1	6	30	14	3	0	1	51	3	2	.366	.275
Pattee, Ben	R-R	6-0	184	9-24-81	.205	.174	.220	42	146	22	30	12	0	0	12	15	4	3	1	20	0	1	.288	.295
Phillips, Kyle	L-R	6-2	210	4-3-84	.209	.250	.203	22	67	6	14	1	0	2	8	6	0	1	3	17	0	0	.313	.263
Romero, Alex	L-R	6-1	183	9-9-83	.301	.282	.308	139	509	65	153	31	2	15	77	36	8	4	3	69	12	11	.458	.354
Scanlon, Matt	L-R	5-11	182	6-19-78	.158	.000	.158	7	19	2	3	0	0	0	1	3	0	0	0	4	0	0	.158	.273
Span, Denard	L-L	6-0	185	2-27-84	.285	.264	.292	68	267	47	76	6	5	0	26	22	8	5	2	41	10	8	.345	.355
Taylor, J.R.	B-R	5-8	170	11-6-82	.276	.333	.256	32	105	14	29	4	0	1	9	11	1	3	1	14	1	5	.343	.347
Tomlin, James	R-R	6-0	183	8-12-82	.274	.264	.278	119	343	50	94	21	1	5	34	26	1	17	0	50	10	5	.385	.327
Torres, Gabby	R-R	5-10	205	3-22-78	.242	.213	.270	66	178	15	43	8	0	2	20	16	8	3	1	23	1	1	.320	.330
Velazquez, Gilbert	R-R	6-2	170	10-17-79	.231	.239	.228	81	286	36	66	13	0	1	28	22	6	6	3	52	3	3	.287	.297
Watkins, Thomas	R-R	5-10	205	6-18-80	.229	.239	.225	116	319	50	73	19	0	4	24	31	5	13	0	65	12	7	.326	.307

PITCHING	B-T	HT	WT	DOB	W	L	ERA	G	GS	CG	SV	IP	H	R	ER	HR	BB	SO	AVG	vLH	vRH	K/9	BB/9
Abbott, Jim	B-R	6-3	192	10-12-79	7	3	5.31	24	12	1	0	97	104	59	57	7	26	71	.277	.237	.312	6.61	2.42
Barrett, Ricky	L-L	5-11	190	3-9-81	1	0	0.51	10	0	0	0	18	11	4	1	0	7	25	.180	.091	.231	12.74	3.57
Blackburn, Nick	R-R	6-4	230	2-24-82	2	4	1.84	7	7	2	0	49	35	16	10	1	10	27	.206	.254	.172	4.96	1.84
Cameron, Kevin	R-R	6-1	192	12-15-79	6	2	2.72	43	0	0	6	79	76	38	24	8	27	60	.244	.225	.257	6.81	3.06
Childress, Daylan	R-R	6-1	200	7-31-78	3	4	5.19	29	6	0	2	68	60	40	39	7	29	59	.242	.167	.285	7.85	3.86
Granado, Jan	L-L	6-0	190	9-26-82	2	2	5.61	12	2	0	0	26	28	17	16	3	9	19	.286	.227	.303	6.66	3.16
Gutierrez, Jannio	R-R	5-11	187	5-3-82	1	0	2.70	9	0	0	0	13	11	4	4	3	6	12	.220	.176	.242	8.10	4.05
Korecky, Bobby	R-R	5-11	180	9-16-79	0	0	6.75	2	0	0	0	1	2	1	1	0	1	1	.333	.000	.500	6.75	6.75
Liriano, Francisco	L-L	6-2	185	10-26-83	3	5	3.64	13	13	0	0	77	70	36	31	6	26	92	.242	.196	.253	10.80	3.05
Miller, Colby	R-R	6-2	190	3-19-82	2	7	3.60	12	12	1	0	70	70	33	28	7	19	41	.265	.295	.243	5.27	2.44
Miller, Jason	R-L	6-1	202	7-20-82	1	2	2.72	26	0	0	4	50	34	17	15	5	22	56	.188	.212	.178	10.15	3.99
Neshek, Pat	B-R	6-3	207	9-4-80	6	4	2.19	55	0	0	24	82	69	25	20	9	21	95	.225	.288	.190	10.38	2.30
Olson, Justin	R-R	6-3	215	4-5-80	9	8	4.79	31	15	0	0	109	94	67	58	17	49	103	.232	.222	.238	8.50	4.05
Perkins, Glen	L-L	6-0	200	3-2-83	4	4	4.90	14	14	0	0	79	80	45	43	4	35	67	.263	.275	.259	7.63	3.99
Randazzo, Jeff	R-L	6-7	210	8-12-81	0	1	4.91	2	0	0	0	4	4	2	2	0	2	1	.333	.600	.143	2.45	4.91
Simonitsch, Errol	L-L	6-4	225	8-24-82	6	5	4.12	14	14	0	0	79	92	51	36	6	28	52	.288	.264	.296	5.95	3.20

PITCHING	B-T	HT	WT	DOB	W	L	ERA	G	GS	CG	SV	IP	H	R	ER	HR	BB	SO	AVG	vLH	vRH	K/9	BB/9
Speigner, Levale	R-R	5-11	170	9-24-80	6	10	4.13	23	23	2	0	144	149	75	66	14	28	94	.268	.248	.281	5.89	1.75
Thomas, John	L-L	6-2	207	7-24-81	5	4	6.92	39	8	0	0	79	114	71	61	14	37	52	.337	.354	.331	5.90	4.20
Wolfe, Brian	R-R	6-2	215	11-29-80	1	0	7.04	5	0	0	0	8	10	6	6	0	7	4	.333	.167	.375	4.70	8.22
Yeatman, Matt	R-R	6-4	230	8-2-82	5	7	4.08	28	16	1	0	104	99	55	47	5	39	74	.256	.243	.267	6.42	3.39

FIELDING

Catcher	PCT	G	PO	A	E	DP	PB
Kennedy	.988	70	463	33	6	2	10
Morales	.970	4	31	1	1	0	0
Phillips	.994	22	141	15	1	2	1
Torres	.988	61	381	42	5	5	7

First Base	PCT	G	PO	A	E	DP
Bell	1.000	5	13	1	0	4
Deeds	1.000	1	2	1	0	1
Jimenez	.980	64	462	39	10	45
Matienzo	.990	81	640	48	7	63
Moses	1.000	1	2	0	0	0

Second Base	PCT	G	PO	A	E	DP
Mauer	1.000	4	3	7	0	3
Maza	.987	49	90	145	3	40
Molina	1.000	13	14	23	0	6
Moses	1.000	1	0	1	0	0
Pattee	.961	42	74	100	7	19
Velazquez	.964	19	46	35	3	12
Watkins	.975	25	58	58	3	17

Third Base	PCT	G	PO	A	E	DP
Bell	.932	41	25	84	8	6
Matienzo	.810	9	5	12	4	2
Mauer	.889	9	5	11	2	0
Molina	.938	23	9	36	3	3
Morales	.800	1	0	4	1	0
Moses	.931	48	29	92	9	9
Watkins	.925	26	14	35	4	10

Shortstop	PCT	G	PO	A	E	DP
Mauer	1.000	1	1	0	0	0
Molina	.750	1	1	2	1	0
Taylor	.935	32	59	85	10	17
Velazquez	.952	62	92	165	13	40
Watkins	.951	55	78	118	10	22

Outfield	PCT	G	PO	A	E	DP
Deeds	.988	125	235	2	3	0
Langaigne	1.000	11	18	1	0	0
Romero	.975	134	258	13	7	1
Scanlon	1.000	2	3	0	0	0
Span	.976	66	160	5	4	1
Tomlin	.981	102	199	6	4	1
Watkins	1.000	2	3	0	0	0

FORT MYERS MIRACLE — High Class A

FLORIDA STATE LEAGUE

BATTING	B-T	HT	WT	DOB	AVG	vLH	vRH	G	AB	R	H	2B	3B	HR	RBI	BB	HBP	SH	SF	SO	SB	CS	SLG	OBP
Arneson, Justin	B-R	5-11	175	12-17-81	.199	.237	.188	56	171	23	34	4	1	3	22	19	5	0	3	62	6	1	.287	.293
Burgos, Omar	R-R	6-2	216	11-11-82	.168	.071	.205	34	101	8	17	1	0	1	8	11	2	0	0	24	2	0	.208	.263
de San Miguel, Allan	R-R	5-9	182	2-1-88	.242	.286	.231	11	33	3	8	2	0	0	4	4	1	0	1	11	0	0	.303	.333
Fermin, Angelo	B-R	5-8	169	11-6-83	.250	.200	.264	35	112	14	28	5	2	0	10	7	4	0	2	25	0	1	.330	.312
Geiger, Kyle	R-R	6-3	215	5-8-82	.257	.286	.247	81	292	34	75	8	0	6	33	24	7	0	1	55	1	3	.346	.327
Hughes, Luke	R-R	5-11	186	8-2-84	.202	.273	.177	23	84	9	17	3	1	0	7	2	1	2	3	15	0	0	.262	.222
Leger, Jose	R-R	5-10	175	5-19-82	.279	.341	.259	51	179	18	50	10	0	1	24	13	2	1	5	39	3	3	.352	.327
Mauer, Jake	R-R	6-2	180	12-20-78	.319	.286	.327	19	69	11	22	3	0	0	8	3	2	2	0	8	0	0	.362	.365
Merchan, Jesus	R-R	6-0	184	3-26-81	.179	.100	.207	12	39	3	7	1	0	0	7	4	1	1	0	2	0	2	.205	.273
Molina, Felix	B-R	5-9	175	5-5-83	.258	.190	.269	46	155	23	40	9	2	0	9	16	1	0	0	16	1	2	.342	.331
Moses, Matt	L-R	6-0	210	2-20-85	.306	.320	.300	73	265	37	81	16	1	7	42	28	3	0	2	59	13	4	.453	.376
Oeltjen, Trent	L-L	6-1	190	2-28-83	.287	.268	.293	98	341	44	98	17	4	4	43	26	20	5	3	77	21	9	.396	.369
Pattee, Ben	R-R	6-0	184	9-24-81	.333	.367	.314	22	81	17	27	1	2	0	9	10	1	0	0	9	0	1	.395	.413
Perodin, Ronald	L-L	5-11	181	10-13-80	.226	.206	.231	103	318	41	72	9	0	0	21	32	5	8	2	56	13	6	.255	.305
Peterson, Brock	R-R	6-3	215	11-20-83	.250	.262	.246	119	424	49	106	22	3	12	60	46	9	0	6	102	1	2	.401	.332
Phillips, Kyle	L-R	6-2	210	4-3-84	.230	.242	.227	83	278	20	64	12	1	2	32	31	2	1	3	47	2	0	.302	.309
Span, Denard	L-L	6-0	185	2-27-84	.339	.400	.313	49	186	38	63	3	3	1	19	22	1	2	1	25	13	4	.403	.410
Taylor, J.R.	B-R	5-8	170	11-6-82	.256	.200	.278	72	262	37	67	10	2	0	23	28	1	6	2	34	10	9	.309	.328
Thompson, Drew	L-R	6-1	160	11-7-86	.308	.000	.333	4	13	2	4	1	0	0	1	1	0	0	0	4	0	0	.385	.357
Tolbert, Matt	B-R	6-0	180	5-4-82	.266	.269	.265	111	417	55	111	20	6	3	46	35	3	15	2	80	11	4	.365	.326
Whitrock, Scott	R-R	6-2	190	12-18-80	.222	.280	.201	111	379	56	84	22	0	15	50	25	5	3	1	158	25	5	.398	.278
Zamojc, Mark	L-R	6-2	200	12-21-81	.222	.000	.256	30	99	12	22	4	0	1	8	8	0	0	1	19	1	1	.293	.278

PITCHING	B-T	HT	WT	DOB	W	L	ERA	G	GS	CG	SV	IP	H	R	ER	HR	BB	SO	AVG	vLH	vRH	K/9	BB/9
Blackburn, Nick	R-R	6-4	230	2-24-82	7	5	3.36	15	15	1	0	94	95	43	35	5	16	55	.265	.336	.223	5.28	1.54
Crawford, Tristan	R-R	6-3	193	7-22-82	6	5	4.15	32	7	0	2	80	89	44	37	11	23	88	.276	.268	.282	9.86	2.58
DePaula, Julio	R-R	6-0	176	12-31-82	4	3	2.24	36	0	0	4	64	52	18	16	0	25	51	.226	.305	.170	7.13	3.50
Edlich, Kyle	R-L	6-2	180	3-9-86	0	1	6.75	2	0	0	0	3	3	2	2	0	3	3	.273	.000	.429	10.13	10.13
Granado, Jan	L-L	6-0	190	9-26-82	6	6	2.92	25	2	0	2	49	52	25	16	5	13	31	.272	.255	.279	5.66	2.37
Gray, Josh	L-L	6-4	195	11-20-80	1	3	3.34	32	3	0	1	62	59	27	23	5	28	49	.254	.170	.279	7.11	4.06
Gutierrez, Jannio	R-R	5-11	187	5-3-82	1	1	1.78	15	0	0	6	25	22	7	5	2	10	39	.232	.286	.200	13.86	3.55
Harben, Adam	R-R	6-5	205	8-19-83	10	5	2.66	25	25	2	0	135	102	52	40	6	62	119	.207	.217	.200	7.91	4.12
Henkenjohann, Tim	L-R	6-5	218	9-3-80	0	0	5.06	7	0	0	0	11	10	6	6	1	9	9	.256	.364	.214	7.59	7.59
Hill, Josh	R-R	6-3	216	3-27-83	0	0	6.97	7	0	0	0	10	9	9	8	1	9	12	.231	.188	.261	10.45	7.84
Jones, Justin	L-L	6-4	185	9-25-84	7	3	3.01	13	13	2	0	78	78	28	26	5	28	54	.268	.250	.274	6.26	3.24
Mijares, Jose	L-L	6-0	180	10-29-84	0	0	1.50	5	1	0	0	12	5	4	2	1	5	17	.116	.158	.083	12.75	3.75
Perkins, Glen	L-L	6-0	200	3-2-83	3	2	2.13	10	9	2	0	55	41	14	13	2	13	66	.205	.217	.201	10.80	2.13
Rainville, Jay	R-R	6-3	230	10-16-85	4	3	2.67	9	9	1	0	54	54	22	16	7	6	35	.256	.207	.287	5.83	1.00
Sawatski, Jay	L-L	6-2	195	5-7-82	3	3	3.94	43	0	0	13	62	71	35	27	5	21	50	.287	.273	.294	7.30	3.06
Schutt, Chris	R-R	6-1	200	2-8-82	4	4	3.24	38	3	0	5	67	60	30	24	1	30	70	.240	.323	.191	9.45	4.05
Simonitsch, Errol	L-L	6-4	225	8-24-82	8	3	2.69	14	13	2	0	80	70	27	24	5	12	72	.236	.274	.223	8.07	1.34
Swarzak, Anthony	R-R	6-3	195	9-10-85	3	4	3.66	10	10	0	0	59	72	25	24	3	11	55	.300	.299	.301	8.39	1.68
Tautor, Peter	L-R	6-4	220	6-26-81	0	0	14.77	16	0	0	1	18	25	30	29	2	22	16	.329	.353	.310	8.15	11.21
Tyler, Scott	R-R	6-5	265	8-20-82	7	8	3.95	23	23	0	0	118	106	61	52	18	48	109	.245	.214	.263	8.29	3.65
Williams, Matt	R-R	6-1	170	2-18-87	0	0	0.00	1	0	0	0	2	2	0	0	0	1	2	.250	.333	.000	9.00	4.50

FIELDING

Catcher	PCT	G	PO	A	E	DP	PB
de San Miguel	.973	11	63	8	2	0	1
Geiger	.985	59	425	26	7	2	10
Phillips	.995	70	514	55	3	3	10

First Base	PCT	G	PO	A	E	DP
Burgos	1.000	17	150	8	0	16
Mauer	1.000	9	73	5	0	5
Peterson	.988	96	772	53	10	89
Phillips	1.000	1	2	0	0	0
Zamojc	.973	14	104	3	3	10

Second Base	PCT	G	PO	A	E	DP
Fermin	.980	12	19	30	1	5
Hughes	.948	21	33	58	5	17
Leger	1.000	4	10	11	0	4
Molina	.961	33	55	94	6	27
Pattee	1.000	4	7	9	0	5
Thompson	.955	4	3	18	1	1
Tolbert	.973	58	95	155	7	43

Third Base	PCT	G	PO	A	E	DP
Burgos	.941	15	5	27	2	3
Fermin	.909	8	5	15	2	2
Leger	.933	46	26	86	8	9
Mauer	1.000	2	1	2	0	0
Merchan	1.000	1	0	4	0	0
Molina	1.000	3	2	8	0	1
Moses	.945	59	24	97	7	11
Pattee	1.000	4	3	9	0	1

Shortstop	PCT	G	PO	A	E	DP
Fermin	.954	14	22	40	3	5
Merchan	.943	10	17	33	3	9
Taylor	.959	64	89	169	11	48
Tolbert	.931	47	64	137	15	31

Outfield	PCT	G	PO	A	E	DP
Arneson	.989	47	90	3	1	1
Burgos	.750	2	3	0	1	0
Oeltjen	.987	86	148	3	2	1

Pattee	1.000	9	19	0	0	0
Perodin	.967	100	202	4	7	2
Span	.976	48	75	5	2	1

Taylor	1.000	1	1	0	0	0
Whitrock	.976	109	223	17	6	4
Zamojc	1.000	10	12	0	0	0

BELOIT SNAPPERS — Low Class A

MIDWEST LEAGUE

BATTING	B-T	HT	WT	DOB	AVG	vLH	vRH	G	AB	R	H	2B	3B	HR	RBI	BB	HBP	SH	SF	SO	SB	CS	SLG	OBP
Brown, Chris	R-R	6-2	215	12-28-82	.265	.297	.256	87	332	46	88	19	5	11	39	30	1	1	2	104	4	2	.452	.326
Burns, Deacon	L-L	5-8	185	10-28-82	.271	.202	.287	132	527	90	143	36	13	12	78	50	12	1	5	92	13	3	.457	.345
Burt, Landon	L-L	5-10	180	8-16-82	.241	.275	.234	62	241	37	58	10	2	0	24	22	1	5	1	22	3	2	.299	.306
Feiner, Korey	R-R	5-10	210	9-25-81	.188	.213	.181	63	202	25	38	4	1	1	18	37	7	2	2	36	0	0	.233	.331
Fermin, Angelo	B-R	5-8	169	11-6-83	.224	.258	.214	42	143	23	32	5	1	0	11	33	2	0	0	40	9	3	.273	.376
Hughes, Luke	R-R	5-11	186	8-2-84	.257	.255	.257	72	292	42	75	14	2	7	42	21	7	2	3	63	4	2	.390	.319
Kelly, Paul	R-R	6-0	185	10-19-86	.313	.250	.333	5	16	2	5	2	0	1	4	2	0	1	1	3	0	0	.625	.368
Patterson, Tarrence	R-R	5-7	168	6-12-84	.254	.263	.251	91	307	55	78	14	1	4	38	32	7	1	7	69	18	4	.345	.331
Pickrel, Jeremy	L-R	6-4	225	4-3-83	.277	.282	.276	108	393	52	109	18	7	12	65	50	11	0	5	121	15	5	.450	.370
Plouffe, Trevor	R-R	6-1	175	6-15-86	.223	.194	.231	127	466	58	104	18	0	13	60	50	4	5	7	78	8	4	.345	.300
Rutgers, Paul	R-R	5-10	193	1-17-84	.230	.239	.227	70	230	22	53	6	1	2	30	22	4	2	4	38	4	2	.291	.304
Sanchez, Javier	R-R	6-2	205	11-8-81	.251	.100	.277	84	271	45	68	12	0	1	27	34	6	0	2	33	8	0	.306	.345
Tolleson, Steven	R-R	5-10	180	11-1-83	.176	.125	.186	31	102	16	18	2	0	3	10	17	3	3	0	23	3	0	.284	.311
White, Dwayne	L-L	6-1	195	4-7-83	.261	.297	.255	78	268	35	70	11	1	2	30	25	2	1	3	44	2	4	.332	.326
Winfree, David	R-R	6-3	215	8-5-85	.294	.272	.299	135	562	80	165	31	5	16	101	22	11	0	6	93	3	2	.452	.329
Woodard, Johnny	L-R	6-4	208	9-15-84	.235	.233	.236	60	217	36	51	9	1	8	27	24	2	1	1	65	0	0	.396	.316
Zamojc, Mark	L-R	6-2	200	12-21-81	.237	.143	.258	62	236	31	56	8	3	5	30	22	2	0	1	57	8	2	.360	.307

PITCHING	B-T	HT	WT	DOB	W	L	ERA	G	GS	CG	SV	IP	H	R	ER	HR	BB	SO	AVG	vLH	vRH	K/9	BB/9
Aselton, Kyle	R-L	6-5	215	2-28-83	6	2	2.49	41	10	0	2	112	80	38	31	9	61	113	.199	.227	.192	9.08	4.90
Cordero, Jose	R-R	6-2	230	8-7-83	0	1	4.70	7	0	0	1	8	9	4	4	0	5	8	.290	.100	.381	9.39	5.87
Culpepper, Kevin	R-L	6-5	185	6-28-82	7	6	4.45	49	0	0	1	85	92	47	42	9	31	74	.276	.203	.297	7.84	3.28
Duguay, Steven	R-R	6-1	200	10-29-82	1	2	1.91	17	0	0	4	28	12	6	6	1	15	35	.130	.079	.167	11.12	4.76
Garcia, Angel	R-R	6-7	220	10-28-83	2	0	4.26	17	3	0	0	25	14	13	12	2	20	33	.161	.156	.164	11.72	7.11
Garza, Matt	R-R	6-4	190	11-11-83	3	3	3.54	10	10	0	0	56	53	24	22	5	15	64	.251	.245	.256	10.29	2.41
Hill, Josh	R-R	6-3	216	3-27-83	4	7	3.66	35	10	0	4	106	89	45	43	4	46	82	.228	.245	.218	6.98	3.92
Martinez, J.P.	R-R	6-2	205	6-8-82	5	2	1.83	53	0	0	20	88	63	26	18	5	31	92	.194	.248	.163	9.37	3.16
Mauer, Bill	R-R	6-4	200	5-6-80	0	0	20.25	1	0	0	0	1	2	3	3	0	3	3	.333	.500	.250	20.25	20.25
Meek, Evan	R-R	6-0	215	5-12-83	0	1	10.00	13	0	0	0	18	15	26	20	0	36	11	.231	.321	.162	5.50	18.00
Mijares, Jose	L-L	6-0	180	10-29-84	6	3	4.31	20	6	0	2	54	43	28	26	6	40	78	.219	.042	.244	12.92	6.63
Morlan, Eduardo	R-R	6-2	210	3-1-86	4	4	4.38	10	10	0	0	51	39	25	25	5	31	55	.207	.182	.225	9.64	5.44
Pettit, Bo	R-R	6-1	205	6-18-80	0	0	4.22	6	0	0	0	11	11	5	5	2	8	9	.289	.300	.278	7.59	6.75
Rainville, Jay	R-R	6-3	230	10-16-85	8	2	3.77	16	16	0	0	88	83	39	37	14	27	77	.243	.223	.256	7.85	2.75
Shinskie, David	R-R	6-4	205	5-4-84	2	8	7.22	29	10	0	1	77	111	72	62	11	24	51	.333	.388	.299	5.94	2.79
Silva, Carlos	R-R	6-4	250	4-23-79	0	0	1.80	1	1	0	0	5	5	1	1	1	0	3	.263	.308	.167	5.40	0.00
Slowey, Kevin	R-R	6-3	190	5-4-84	3	2	2.24	13	9	1	0	64	42	18	16	4	8	69	.183	.161	.197	9.65	1.12
Smit, Alexander	L-L	6-4	205	10-2-85	1	9	5.98	14	10	0	0	50	58	41	33	9	28	54	.283	.348	.264	9.79	5.07
Swarzak, Anthony	R-R	6-3	195	9-10-85	9	5	4.04	18	18	0	0	91	81	48	41	7	32	101	.238	.250	.230	9.95	3.15
Waldrop, Kyle	R-R	6-4	190	10-27-85	6	11	4.98	27	27	2	0	152	182	93	84	17	23	108	.291	.276	.299	6.41	1.36
Williams, John	R-L	6-4	190	12-19-81	2	3	4.54	38	0	0	1	75	83	43	38	7	30	66	.277	.194	.300	7.88	3.58

FIELDING

Catcher	PCT	G	PO	A	E	DP	PB
Feiner	.991	63	524	55	5	7	7
Sanchez	.985	84	691	56	11	3	8

First Base	PCT	G	PO	A	E	DP
Brown	.982	38	258	16	5	26
Winfree	.000	1	0	0	0	0
Woodard	.985	51	427	19	7	41
Zamojc	.986	54	460	29	7	32

Second Base	PCT	G	PO	A	E	DP
Fermin	.964	26	36	72	4	14
Hughes	.966	67	116	167	10	42
Kelly	.964	5	12	15	1	4
Rutgers	.978	24	39	48	2	12
Tolleson	.981	27	38	67	2	14

Third Base	PCT	G	PO	A	E	DP
Brown	1.000	3	1	8	0	0
Fermin	1.000	2	0	1	0	0
Kelly	.000	1	0	0	0	0
Rutgers	1.000	3	2	2	0	0
Winfree	.895	133	80	211	34	18

Shortstop	PCT	G	PO	A	E	DP
Fermin	.975	14	29	48	2	10
Plouffe	.933	125	168	319	35	67
Rutgers	.750	1	1	2	1	0
Tolleson	.941	5	3	13	1	3

Outfield	PCT	G	PO	A	E	DP
Burns	.981	111	199	6	4	0
Burt	.972	60	102	3	3	2
Patterson	.988	83	159	6	2	2
Pickrel	.986	94	207	2	3	0
Rutgers	1.000	36	56	0	0	0
White	1.000	48	70	1	0	0
Zamojc	1.000	1	2	0	0	0

ELIZABETHTON TWINS — Rookie

APPALACHIAN LEAGUE

BATTING	B-T	HT	WT	DOB	AVG	vLH	vRH	G	AB	R	H	2B	3B	HR	RBI	BB	HBP	SH	SF	SO	SB	CS	SLG	OBP
Arratia, Jilmer	R-R	5-11	170	6-28-84	.270	.353	.227	28	100	9	27	1	1	1	12	1	0	2	1	21	0	0	.330	.275
Bensko, Dustin	R-R	6-4	200	3-6-83	.270	.245	.290	38	122	21	33	7	0	6	18	11	3	0	2	33	0	0	.475	.341
Betsill, Matt	B-R	6-5	190	8-16-84	.277	.159	.327	45	148	24	41	5	1	2	19	18	1	0	0	34	4	2	.365	.359
Gardenhire, Toby	R-R	6-0	170	9-11-82	.200	.206	.197	30	100	10	20	3	0	0	5	8	4	1	0	21	2	1	.230	.286
Jones, Larry	R-R	6-1	210	9-19-84	.287	.357	.242	36	108	20	31	9	1	1	12	14	4	0	0	30	4	2	.417	.389
Kalin, Travis	R-R	6-3	180	7-30-84	.265	.194	.299	30	98	14	26	2	2	3	13	10	1	0	0	34	3	1	.418	.339
Land, Josh	L-L	6-1	185	2-6-85	.306	.308	.305	24	72	9	22	7	1	0	10	3	2	0	1	18	0	2	.431	.346
Lis, Erik	L-L	6-1	220	3-8-84	.315	.278	.326	49	168	29	53	12	1	10	41	9	2	0	1	35	0	0	.577	.356
Moore, Caleb	R-R	5-11	205	5-17-83	.309	.244	.341	36	123	20	38	6	0	3	13	9	1	1	0	19	2	2	.431	.361
Ortiz, Yancarlos	B-R	5-9	145	9-15-84	.289	.304	.282	49	187	30	54	4	0	0	17	19	3	1	1	38	10	5	.310	.362
Ovalle, Edward	R-R	5-11	178	6-15-85	.285	.232	.312	65	239	44	68	13	1	7	27	25	9	0	0	49	6	3	.435	.374
Portes, Juan	R-R	5-11	170	11-26-85	.286	.277	.290	64	245	40	70	13	1	12	39	22	4	0	4	43	6	3	.494	.349
Richardson, Sean	R-R	6-1	185	10-2-83	.298	.292	.300	28	94	14	28	4	0	7	21	8	1	0	1	20	0	2	.564	.356
Robinson, Mark	B-R	6-1	180	4-7-86	.245	.203	.263	61	229	31	56	7	3	4	29	18	5	0	2	35	7	4	.354	.311
Tintor, Eli	R-R	6-2	190	12-24-84	.281	.259	.294	40	139	20	39	6	0	4	18	6	4	0	1	26	0	1	.410	.327
Tolleson, Steven	R-R	5-10	180	11-1-83	.321	.200	.389	16	56	18	18	6	1	2	8	11	3	3	0	4	2	1	.571	.457

PITCHING	B-T	HT	WT	DOB	W	L	ERA	G	GS	CG	SV	IP	H	R	ER	HR	BB	SO	AVG	vLH	vRH	K/9	BB/9
Duensing, Brian	L-L	5-11	195	2-22-83	4	3	2.32	12	9	0	0	50	49	19	13	4	16	55	.249	.250	.249	9.83	2.86
Gabino, Armando	R-R	6-3	200	8-31-83	1	2	8.10	17	3	0	0	30	45	28	27	7	12	23	.338	.333	.341	6.90	3.60
Garza, Matt	R-R	6-4	190	11-11-83	1	1	3.66	4	4	0	0	20	14	10	8	3	6	25	.200	.207	.195	11.44	2.75
Gault, Joe	R-R	6-5	193	12-28-84	2	0	5.94	15	0	0	0	17	17	11	11	2	6	8	.270	.174	.325	4.32	3.24
Gehring, Ryan	L-L	6-4	205	5-17-82	1	0	3.00	17	0	0	0	30	23	11	10	3	16	31	.213	.250	.197	9.30	4.80
Hawes, Adam	L-R	6-4	190	4-25-83	4	0	1.53	14	9	1	1	59	38	13	10	2	16	68	.183	.217	.165	10.37	2.44
Lahey, Tim	R-R	5-10	235	2-7-82	0	1	3.55	26	0	0	15	25	21	13	10	0	8	30	.212	.278	.175	10.66	2.84
Morlan, Eduardo	R-R	6-2	210	3-1-86	2	0	0.82	4	4	0	0	22	6	2	2	0	6	30	.085	.143	.047	12.27	2.45
Mullins, Ryan	L-L	6-6	180	11-13-83	3	0	2.18	11	11	0	0	54	34	16	13	4	13	60	.182	.156	.187	10.06	2.18
Pino, Yohan	R-R	6-3	158	12-26-83	9	2	3.72	12	12	1	0	68	68	31	28	3	13	64	.255	.221	.273	8.51	1.73
Powers, Danny	R-R	6-1	195	7-24-82	3	3	2.53	22	0	0	4	43	30	18	12	1	20	47	.197	.212	.190	9.91	4.22
Slowey, Kevin	R-R	6-3	190	5-4-84	0	0	1.17	4	0	0	1	8	2	1	1	1	0	15	.080	.111	.063	17.61	0.00
Smit, Alexander	L-L	6-4	205	10-2-85	6	1	1.97	21	0	0	3	46	25	12	10	3	12	86	.157	.324	.112	16.95	2.36
Sosa, Oswaldo	R-R	6-2	187	9-19-85	6	5	4.95	12	11	0	0	56	59	37	31	4	21	40	.265	.221	.292	6.39	3.36
Vais, Danny	R-R	6-1	210	11-21-84	6	1	4.95	13	4	0	0	40	42	24	22	5	5	30	.264	.207	.297	6.75	1.13

GAMES BY POSITION: C—Moore 30, Richardson 24, Tintor 17. **1B**—Bensko 32, Lis 41. **2B**—Gardenhire 12, Kalin 11, Portes 43, Tolleson 1. **3B**—Betsill 44, Gardenhire 7, Kalin 17. **SS**—Gardenhire 9, Ortiz 47, Tolleson 11. **OF**—Arratia 24, Jones 35, Land 14, Lis 1, Ovalle 65, Portes 13, Robinson 57.

GCL TWINS — Rookie

GULF COAST LEAGUE

BATTING	B-T	HT	WT	DOB	AVG	vLH	vRH	G	AB	R	H	2B	3B	HR	RBI	BB	HBP	SH	SF	SO	SB	CS	SLG	OBP
Abellera, Joe	R-R	6-4	200	8-2-85	.179	.167	.184	22	56	3	10	1	0	0	5	0	1	1	0	9	0	0	.196	.193
Barrientos, Miguel	L-R	5-10	185	9-26-86	.159	.200	.138	18	44	3	7	1	0	0	7	5	0	1	1	4	1	1	.182	.240
Berg, Daniel	R-R	6-0	190	11-21-84	.159	.217	.138	28	88	13	14	1	0	1	8	8	5	2	1	20	4	4	.205	.265
Connor, Wesley	B-R	6-2	195	4-11-85	.246	.188	.265	27	65	13	16	2	2	1	8	4	0	3	1	13	5	1	.385	.286
de San Miguel, Allan	R-R	5-9	182	2-1-88	.204	.211	.200	23	54	9	11	3	0	1	11	3	4	1	0	14	1	2	.315	.295
Dean, Josh	L-R	6-1	205	12-24-86	.340	.333	.341	34	106	21	36	4	0	1	20	15	1	0	0	9	5	1	.406	.426
Delgado, Juan	B-R	6-3	170	7-18-86	.097	.043	.122	27	72	8	7	2	1	2	5	2	0	1	1	28	3	1	.236	.120
Fletcher, Simon	R-R	6-1	200	6-16-85	.200	.136	.237	21	60	8	12	2	0	1	4	10	1	3	0	22	6	1	.283	.324
Kelly, Paul	R-R	6-0	185	10-19-86	.277	.325	.258	40	137	16	38	6	0	2	20	14	5	6	3	36	3	5	.365	.358
Knowles, Marion	R-R	6-1	215	3-8-83	.248	.211	.265	36	121	16	30	4	1	1	17	17	0	0	0	30	3	1	.322	.341
Kuhaulua, Kaulana	R-R	6-0	170	1-30-80	.000	.000	.000	3	5	0	0	0	0	0	0	2	0	0	0	3	0	0	.000	.286
Luque, William	R-R	5-9	165	4-24-84	.322	.370	.302	33	90	21	29	1	2	0	11	10	4	3	2	16	13	4	.378	.406
Lysaught, Michael	R-R	5-11	175	9-30-85	.250	.391	.184	23	72	17	18	5	1	1	10	8	0	2	0	26	3	1	.389	.325
Mauer, Jake	R-R	6-2	180	12-20-78	.333	.000	.400	2	6	0	2	0	0	0	0	2	0	0	0	0	1	0	.333	.500
Palacios, Rodolfo	R-R	5-10	176	6-26-85	.000	.000	.000	2	3	0	0	0	0	0	0	1	0	0	0	0	0	0	.000	.250
Prady, Ricky	L-R	6-4	195	3-5-85	.206	.308	.143	10	34	4	7	2	1	1	5	1	4	0	0	11	1	1	.412	.308
Sanchez, Henri	R-R	6-3	235	11-29-86	.229	.174	.255	21	70	8	16	2	0	2	11	7	1	0	2	28	0	0	.343	.300
Santiesteban, Danny	R-R	6-2	170	2-17-85	.307	.269	.327	21	75	16	23	5	1	6	24	7	1	0	2	19	1	0	.640	.365
Sojo, Richard	R-R	6-2	194	9-24-84	.318	.362	.297	43	148	36	47	11	5	0	15	13	4	0	0	32	11	7	.459	.388
Thompson, Drew	L-R	6-1	160	11-7-86	.257	.371	.203	35	109	22	28	4	1	2	20	22	2	1	2	22	6	4	.367	.385
Valdez, Odannys	B-R	5-10	154	5-9-85	.219	.233	.214	39	114	22	25	2	0	1	14	21	1	7	3	19	15	2	.263	.338
Wilson, John	R-R	6-2	195	8-19-86	.229	.240	.224	26	83	18	19	3	0	1	13	14	0	1	2	22	3	3	.301	.333
Woodard, Johnny	L-R	6-4	208	9-15-84	.235	.250	.222	6	17	3	4	0	1	0	2	2	0	0	0	3	0	0	.353	.316
Yersich, Greg	R-R	6-0	205	10-7-86	.238	.192	.259	31	84	13	20	4	0	1	11	10	4	2	2	15	1	2	.321	.340

PITCHING	B-T	HT	WT	DOB	W	L	ERA	G	GS	CG	SV	IP	H	R	ER	HR	BB	SO	AVG	vLH	vRH	K/9	BB/9
Bryant, Patrick	R-R	6-4	190	10-26-85	1	3	6.44	13	6	0	1	36	38	31	26	1	22	25	.273	.286	.267	6.19	5.45
Burgos, Omar	R-R	6-2	216	11-11-82	0	0	6.64	15	0	0	2	20	29	17	15	0	7	5	.333	.429	.288	2.21	3.10
Burnett, Alex	R-R	6-0	190	7-26-87	4	2	4.10	13	8	0	0	48	50	25	22	6	14	33	.267	.282	.259	6.14	2.61
Castillo, Jose	R-R	6-1	175	12-23-84	4	4	3.00	11	9	0	0	48	50	27	16	0	19	27	.270	.328	.240	5.06	3.56
Cordero, Jose	R-R	6-2	230	8-7-83	0	2	2.25	12	0	0	1	24	24	9	6	0	10	20	.270	.250	.279	7.50	3.75
Craig, Aaron	R-R	6-1	205	3-22-86	1	3	3.97	21	0	0	10	23	20	12	10	2	7	23	.225	.185	.242	9.13	2.78
Crawford, Nathan	R-R	6-6	200	11-5-86	0	0	5.09	14	0	0	1	23	25	15	13	0	15	16	.278	.212	.316	6.26	5.87
Edlich, Kyle	R-L	6-2	180	3-9-86	4	2	1.70	10	9	0	0	48	42	13	9	1	15	53	.243	.286	.237	10.01	2.83
Hernandez, Danny	R-R	6-1	158	11-19-85	1	1	5.48	13	2	0	0	21	18	16	13	0	17	19	.231	.174	.255	8.02	7.17
McConnell, Brandon	R-R	6-4	205	2-8-85	5	4	4.14	11	11	1	0	63	76	33	29	4	12	39	.298	.291	.303	5.57	1.71
Patton, Walter	R-R	6-1	190	3-13-85	3	1	7.43	17	1	0	0	23	25	20	19	0	24	20	.294	.258	.315	7.83	9.39
Schoenbachler, Jeff	L-L	6-1	185	9-13-85	2	2	3.97	9	8	0	0	45	50	28	20	3	15	45	.272	.333	.258	8.93	2.98
Williams, Matt	R-R	6-1	170	2-18-87	3	2	1.93	20	0	0	3	37	33	11	8	2	13	42	.241	.220	.253	10.13	3.13

GAMES BY POSITION: C—Barrientos 11, de San Miguel 23, Palacios 2, Yersich 31. **1B**—Abellera 11, Dean 19, Knowles 14, Sanchez 15, Wilson 1, Woodard 6. **2B**—Berg 11, Luque 3, Lysaught 14, Mauer 2, Thompson 19, Valdez 10. **3B**—Abellera 8, Berg 12, Delgado 14, Kelly 9, Kuhaulua 1, Luque 11, Lysaught 5, Santiesteban 1. **SS**—Delgado 5, Kelly 29, Kuhaulua 2, Luque 13, Thompson 10. **OF**—Berg 1, Connor 23, Delgado 1, Fletcher 21, Knowles 15, Lysaught 1, Prady 7, Santiesteban 19, Sojo 41, Valdez 26, Wilson 22.

NEW YORK METS

BY MARTY NOBLE

Cliff Floyd plopped into the chair in front of his locker, acting older than his 32 years, and acknowledged fatigue. It had been a long 2005 season already, and three games remained. It had been a particularly grueling push for the Mets because they had run four races in the sixth months since they left behind spring training.

They chased the Braves from the beginning. Later, when the Braves appeared out of reach, they chased the other National League East teams for the wild card. For most of five months, they tried to stay over .500, and, having failed to escape its gravity, they spent the final two weeks chasing the very mark of mediocrity. So with 159 games gone, their uniforms had become fatigues.

In the hours before Floyd tried to recline in a chair not made for horizontal living, the Mets had secured their 81st victory and made certain their renaissance season would end at sea level or better. At that point, their reaction was a mixture of half empty and half full. "One part of you is proud because you know we have a good shot at finishing with a winning record," Floyd said. "But at the same time, you're disappointed because we didn't get what we wanted.

The Mets' performance had been mostly uneven, and their record so often was exactly even. Twenty-seven times in the course of 162 games, they were a .500 team. For months, they were convinced they weren't half bad. But beating the Rockies three times in their final four games wasn't sufficient confirmation. Or was it?

A record three games better than break-even wasn't such a bad place to be for a team that had had lost 91 times the previous season.

"I'm very proud of what we did," Willie Randolph said in the minutes following his first season as a manager.

ORGANIZATION LEADERS

BATTING

*AVG	Keppinger, Jeff, Norfolk	.337
R	Brinkley, Dante, Hagerstown/St. Lucie	84
R	Ragsdale, Corey, Binghamton/St. Lucie	84
H	Hernandez, Anderson, Binghamton/Norfolk	168
TB	Harper, Brett, Binghamton/St. Lucie	261
2B	Jacobs, Mike, Binghamton	37
	Psomas, Grant, Hagerstown/St. Lucie	37
	Redman, Prentice, Binghamton/Norfolk	37
3B	Lydon, Wayne, Binghamton/Norfolk	13
HR	Harper, Brett, Binghamton/St. Lucie	36
RBI	Harper, Brett, Binghamton/St. Lucie	102
BB	Psomas, Grant, Hagerstown/St. Lucie	77
SO	Ragsdale, Corey, Binghamton/St. Lucie	169
SB	Gomez, Carlos, Hagerstown	64
*OBP	Brinkley, Dante, Hagerstown/St. Lucie	.427
*SLG	Jacobs, Mike, Binghamton	.589

PITCHING

W	Scobie, Jason, Norfolk	15
L	Portobanco, Luz, Binghamton	12
#ERA	Worthington, Tim, Hagerstown/St. Lucie	1.91
G	Lavigne, Tim, Binghamton/Norfolk	53
CG	Five tied at	2
SV	Muniz, Carlos, GCL Mets/Hagerstown/St. Lucie	14
IP	MacLane, Evan, Binghamton/St. Lucie	171
BB	Landing, Jeff, Brooklyn/Hagerstown	61
SO	Petit, Yusmeiro, Binghamton/Norfolk	144

*Minimum 250 at-bats. #Minimum 75 innings.

PLAYERS OF THE YEAR

MAJOR LEAGUE: David Wright, 3b

While Wright's coming-out party as a rising major league star began in 2004, the 22-year-old third baseman burst on the scene in a big way in 2005. Wright led the Mets in average (.306), doubles (42), RBIs (102), total bases (301) and OPS (.912). His best month came in August, when he batted .378/.470/.633.

MINOR LEAGUE: Brian Bannister, rhp

STEVE MOORE

Bannister was dominant from the start of 2005, going 4-0, 0.33 at Double-A Binghamton in April before jumping to Triple-A Norfolk after 18 starts for the B-Mets. He held his own in the International League, going 4-1, 3.18 in 45 innings. Bannister finished second in the organization in wins (13) and strikeouts (142).

"But I don't want anyone being satisfied with 83 wins and [a tie for] a third-place finish."

With the arrival of Pedro Martinez and Carlos Beltran, the Mets had obviously hoped for more. But the mid-August loss of Mike Cameron, Beltran's unremarkable season, a second year of shortfall by Kaz Matsui, the lack of production at first base, the failure of Braden Looper in high-profile situations and the loss of Mike Piazza for almost four weeks undermined their hopes.

At the same time, though, the performances of Floyd, Martinez, David Wright, Jose Reyes, Tom Glavine (in the second half) and Roberto Hernandez were uplifting. And as the Mets packed away 2005 on Oct. 2, those performances already were fueling the hopes of 2006.

Although Wright and Reyes and Glavine's stunning, second-half reversal provide promise, there is little that suggests an improvement even approaching the 12-game upgrade the 2005 team accomplished is likely. The Mets entered the offseason without a designated closer, a catcher, a semblance of a right side of the infield and much of an offense. Moreover, they knew they probably shouldn't rely too much on Martinez, Floyd and their core of pinch-hitters to match the production provided in 2005.

Martinez gave the Mets what he had, and that was a lot and some of it spectacular. He won 15 games and could have won 18 with even average support. But seven of his last 11 starts were losses. Late summer fatigue became as much an issue for him as the inflamed large toe on his right foot as he approached his 34th birthday.

Floyd, so motivated by Randolph, had played in 150 games, the second highest total in his 12-year career, and produced a season—34 home runs, 98 RBI and 15 assists—that would have warranted bottom-of-the-MVP ballot consideration had the Mets won the wild card. But a feeling existed within the organization that his trade value was at its peak.

The Mets are likely to add more free agents heading into 2006, but where they fit in and how Randolph guides them in his sophomore season remains to be seen. But the club's best record since 2000 is certainly something to build on.

NEW YORK METS

Manager: Willie Randolph.

2005 Record: 83-79, .512 (Tied 3rd, NL East).

BATTING	B-T	HT	WT	DOB	AVG	vLH	vRH	G	AB	R	H	2B	3B	HR	RBI	BB	HBP	SH	SF	SO	SB	CS	SLG	OBP
Anderson, Marlon	L-R	5-11	200	1-6-74	.264	.267	.264	123	235	31	62	9	0	7	19	18	1	4	2	45	6	1	.391	.316
Beltran, Carlos	B-R	6-1	190	4-24-77	.266	.308	.254	151	582	83	155	34	2	16	78	56	2	4	6	96	17	6	.414	.330
Cairo, Miguel	R-R	6-1	210	5-4-74	.251	.191	.273	100	327	31	82	18	0	2	19	19	4	12	5	31	13	3	.324	.296
Cameron, Mike	R-R	6-2	200	1-8-73	.273	.311	.261	76	308	47	84	23	2	12	39	29	4	1	1	85	13	1	.477	.342
Castro, Ramon	R-R	6-3	235	3-1-76	.244	.290	.236	99	209	26	51	16	0	8	41	25	0	3	3	58	1	0	.435	.321
Daubach, Brian	L-R	6-1	230	2-11-72	.120	.250	.095	15	25	4	3	2	0	1	3	7	1	0	1	5	0	0	.320	.324
Diaz, Victor	R-R	6-0	200	12-10-81	.257	.259	.257	89	280	41	72	17	3	12	38	30	1	0	2	82	6	2	.468	.329
DiFelice, Mike	R-R	6-2	200	5-28-69	.118	.000	.143	11	17	0	2	0	0	0	0	2	0	0	0	5	0	0	.118	.211
Floyd, Cliff	L-R	6-4	230	12-5-72	.273	.224	.290	150	550	85	150	22	2	34	98	63	11	0	2	98	12	2	.505	.358
Hernandez, Anderson	B-R	5-9	170	10-30-82	.056	.000	.056	6	18	1	1	0	0	0	0	1	0	0	0	4	0	1	.056	.105
Jacobs, Mike	L-R	6-2	200	10-30-80	.310	.400	.305	30	100	19	31	7	0	11	23	10	1	0	1	22	0	0	.710	.375
Matsui, Kazuo	B-R	5-10	185	10-23-75	.255	.279	.246	87	267	31	68	9	4	3	24	14	5	5	4	43	6	1	.352	.300
Mientkiewicz, Doug	L-R	6-2	205	6-19-74	.240	.214	.245	87	275	36	66	13	0	11	29	32	2	2	2	39	0	1	.407	.322
Offerman, Jose	B-R	6-1	200	11-8-68	.250	.167	.278	53	72	5	18	2	0	1	10	6	1	1	0	11	0	0	.319	.316
2-team (33 Philadelphia)					.229	.111	.269	86	105	11	24	3	1	2	13	11	1	1	0	17	0	0	.333	.308
Piazza, Mike	R-R	6-3	215	9-4-68	.251	.269	.246	113	398	41	100	23	0	19	62	41	3	0	0	67	0	0	.452	.326
Reyes, Jose	B-R	6-0	175	6-11-83	.273	.288	.269	161	696	99	190	24	17	7	58	27	2	4	4	78	60	15	.386	.300
Valent, Eric	L-L	5-11	195	4-4-77	.186	.000	.200	28	43	4	8	3	0	0	1	7	0	0	0	17	0	0	.256	.300
Williams, Gerald	R-R	6-2	185	8-10-66	.233	.222	.238	39	30	9	7	2	0	1	3	1	0	1	0	7	2	0	.400	.258
Woodward, Chris	R-R	6-0	190	6-27-76	.283	.260	.312	81	173	16	49	10	0	3	18	13	2	2	2	46	0	0	.393	.337
Wright, David	R-R	6-0	200	12-20-82	.306	.336	.298	160	575	99	176	42	1	27	102	72	7	0	3	113	17	7	.523	.388

PITCHING	B-T	HT	WT	DOB	W	L	ERA	G	GS	CG	SV	IP	H	R	ER	HR	BB	SO	AVG	vLH	vRH	K/9	BB/9
Aybar, Manny	R-R	6-1	175	5-4-72	0	0	6.04	22	0	0	0	25	31	17	17	4	7	27	.301	.270	.318	9.59	2.49
Bell, Heath	R-R	6-3	225	9-29-77	1	3	5.59	42	0	0	0	47	56	30	29	3	13	43	.298	.312	.288	8.29	2.51
Benson, Kris	R-R	6-4	205	11-7-74	10	8	4.13	28	28	0	0	174	171	86	80	24	49	95	.253	.268	.240	4.90	2.53
DeJean, Mike	R-R	6-2	220	9-28-70	3	1	6.31	28	0	0	0	26	36	19	18	3	18	17	.327	.261	.375	5.96	6.31
Glavine, Tom	L-L	6-0	185	3-25-66	13	13	3.53	33	33	2	0	211	227	88	83	12	61	105	.279	.323	.267	4.47	2.60
Graves, Danny	R-R	6-0	200	8-7-73	0	0	5.75	20	0	0	0	20	29	17	13	5	8	12	.337	.378	.306	5.31	3.54
2-team (20 Cincinnati)					1	1	6.52	40	0	0	10	39	59	35	28	9	20	20	.347	.408	.303	4.66	4.66
Hamulack, Tim	L-L	6-4	220	11-14-76	0	0	23.14	6	0	0	0	2	7	6	6	3	1	2	.583	.429	.800	7.71	3.86
Heilman, Aaron	R-R	6-5	220	11-12-78	5	3	3.17	53	7	1	5	108	87	40	38	6	37	106	.223	.208	.236	8.83	3.08
Heredia, Felix	L-L	6-0	180	6-20-75	0	0	0.00	3	0	0	0	3	1	0	0	0	1	2	.125	.000	.167	6.75	3.38
Hernandez, Roberto	R-R	6-4	250	11-11-64	8	6	2.58	67	0	0	4	70	57	20	20	5	28	61	.228	.244	.213	7.88	3.62
Ishii, Kaz	L-L	6-0	215	9-9-73	3	9	5.14	19	16	0	0	91	87	59	52	13	49	53	.257	.208	.271	5.24	4.85
Koo, Dae-Sung	L-L	6-1	185	8-2-69	0	0	3.91	33	0	0	0	23	22	12	10	2	13	23	.250	.239	.262	9.00	5.09
Looper, Braden	R-R	6-3	220	10-28-74	4	7	3.94	60	0	0	28	59	65	31	26	7	22	27	.271	.336	.210	4.10	3.34
Martinez, Pedro	R-R	5-11	180	10-25-71	15	8	2.82	31	31	4	0	217	159	69	68	19	47	208	.204	.215	.192	8.63	1.95
Matthews, Mike	L-L	6-2	205	10-24-73	1	0	10.80	6	0	0	0	5	9	6	6	0	4	2	.429	.400	.455	3.60	7.20
Padilla, Juan	R-R	6-0	200	2-17-77	3	1	1.49	24	0	0	1	36	24	7	6	0	13	17	.180	.153	.203	4.21	3.22
Ring, Royce	L-L	6-0	220	12-21-80	0	2	5.06	15	0	0	0	11	10	6	6	0	10	8	.250	.250	.250	6.75	8.44
Santiago, Jose	R-R	6-3	225	11-5-74	0	0	3.18	4	0	0	0	6	10	2	2	0	2	3	.417	.500	.375	4.76	3.18
Seo, Jae	R-R	6-1	215	5-24-77	8	2	2.59	14	14	1	0	90	84	26	26	9	16	59	.251	.233	.272	5.88	1.59
Takatsu, Shingo	R-R	6-0	180	11-25-68	1	0	2.35	9	0	0	0	8	11	2	2	2	3	6	.314	.308	.318	7.04	3.52
Trachsel, Steve	R-R	6-4	205	10-31-70	1	4	4.14	6	6	0	0	37	37	20	17	6	12	24	.264	.288	.243	5.84	2.92
Zambrano, Victor	B-R	6-0	205	8-6-75	7	12	4.17	31	27	0	0	166	170	85	77	12	77	112	.264	.260	.268	6.06	4.17

FIELDING

Catcher	PCT	G	PO	A	E	DP	PB
Castro	.993	99	402	22	3	3	2
DiFelice	.976	11	39	2	1	1	0
Piazza	.997	101	618	39	2	5	3

First Base	PCT	G	PO	A	E	DP
Anderson	.990	23	173	16	2	18
Cairo	.980	8	48	2	1	6
Daubach	.977	6	39	3	1	3
Jacobs	.984	28	237	10	4	24
Mientkiewicz	.995	83	691	42	4	59
Offerman	.988	11	81	4	1	9
Woodward	.991	34	206	10	2	16

Second Base	PCT	G	PO	A	E	DP
Anderson	.988	20	35	47	1	9
Cairo	.984	82	150	212	6	58
Hernandez	1.000	5	9	18	0	1
Matsui	.970	71	107	187	9	32
Offerman	.000	1	0	0	0	0
Woodward	.846	5	4	7	2	1

Third Base	PCT	G	PO	A	E	DP
Cairo	1.000	3	0	2	0	0
Woodward	1.000	6	1	11	0	0
Wright	.948	160	101	336	24	23

Shortstop	PCT	G	PO	A	E	DP
Hernandez	.000	2	0	0	1	0
Reyes	.974	161	236	428	18	105
Woodward	.923	7	5	7	1	1

Outfield	PCT	G	PO	A	E	DP
Anderson	1.000	23	22	2	0	1
Beltran	.990	150	378	5	4	1
Cairo	1.000	3	1	0	0	0
Cameron	.963	76	151	3	6	1
Diaz	.981	81	156	3	3	1
Floyd	.993	150	283	15	2	0
Valent	.955	12	21	0	1	0
Williams	1.000	27	16	1	0	0
Woodward	.969	23	28	3	1	1

FARM SYSTEM

General Manager: Omar Minaya. **Director, Minor League Operations:** Kevin Morgan. **Director, Amateur Scouting:** Russ Bove.

Class	Farm Team	League	W	L	Pct.	Finish*	Manager	Affiliate Since
AAA	Norfolk (Va.) Tides	International	79	65	.549	**3rd (14)**	Ken Oberkfell	1969
AA	Binghamton (N.Y.) Mets	Eastern	63	79	.444	t-11th (12)	Jack Lind	1992
High A	St. Lucie (Fla.) Mets	Florida State	66	68	.493	7th (12)	Tim Teufel	1988
Low A	Hagerstown (Md.) Suns	South Atlantic	71	66	.518	**8th (16)**	Gene Richards	2005
SS A	Brooklyn (N.Y.) Cyclones	New York-Penn	40	36	.526	6th (14)	Mookie Wilson	2001
Rookie	Kingsport (Tenn.) Mets	Appalachian	28	40	.412	9th (10)	Jesse Levis	1980
Rookie	St. Lucie (Fla.) Mets	Gulf Coast	37	16	.698	**1st (12)**	Gary Carter	2004

*Finish in overall standings (No. of teams in league)/Playoff teams in **boldface**

DAVID SEELIG

Pedro Martinez: Dominated from day one for the Mets

MIKE JANES

Brett Harper: Was third in the minors with 36 home runs

NORFOLK TIDES — Class AAA

INTERNATIONAL LEAGUE

BATTING	B-T	HT	WT	DOB	AVG	vLH	vRH	G	AB	R	H	2B	3B	HR	RBI	BB	HBP	SH	SF	SO	SB	CS	SLG	OBP
Bacani, David	R-R	5-7	170	7-30-79	.125	.000	.167	9	24	1	3	1	0	0	5	2	2	0	0	2	1	1	.167	.250
Basak, Chris	R-R	6-2	190	12-6-78	.272	.250	.279	93	279	52	76	17	4	8	41	30	3	9	5	54	17	3	.448	.344
Brazell, Craig	L-R	6-3	210	5-10-80	.249	.275	.241	52	173	22	43	11	2	6	28	13	0	1	0	32	2	0	.439	.301
Calloway, Ron	L-L	6-1	200	9-4-76	.263	.242	.269	110	392	56	103	25	0	10	44	42	2	5	2	81	14	6	.403	.336
Cameron, Mike	R-R	6-2	200	1-8-73	.286	.000	.286	2	7	2	2	0	1	0	2	3	0	0	0	3	0	0	.571	.500
Cordero, Wil	R-R	6-2	230	10-3-71	.129	.000	.154	8	31	3	4	2	0	0	2	5	0	0	0	11	0	0	.194	.250
Daubach, Brian	L-R	6-1	230	2-11-72	.325	.309	.332	99	345	63	112	29	1	16	62	62	1	1	3	68	1	2	.554	.426
Diaz, Victor	R-R	6-0	200	12-10-81	.300	.286	.304	42	170	30	51	11	0	10	34	14	0	0	0	47	6	2	.541	.353
DiFelice, Mike	R-R	6-2	200	5-28-69	.247	.211	.259	81	300	31	74	17	0	14	52	36	5	2	0	72	1	2	.443	.337
Duncan, Jeff	L-L	6-2	190	12-9-78	1.000	.000	1.000	3	1	2	1	0	0	0	0	0	0	0	0	0	0	0	1.000	1.000
Garcia, Luis	R-R	6-4	180	11-5-78	.219	.227	.215	41	151	23	33	6	0	9	24	14	0	0	0	37	2	0	.437	.285
Gil, Benji	R-R	6-2	210	10-6-72	.258	.339	.231	68	229	27	59	9	0	7	28	14	4	1	1	64	4	6	.389	.310
Hansen, Jed	R-R	6-1	190	8-19-72	.185	.200	.182	17	54	8	10	5	0	0	3	6	3	0	0	19	1	0	.278	.302
Hernandez, Anderson	B-R	5-9	170	10-30-82	.303	.321	.298	66	261	34	79	6	4	2	30	22	1	5	4	46	24	9	.379	.354
Hietpas, Joe	R-R	6-3	220	5-1-79	.194	.000	.246	26	72	5	14	2	0	0	6	8	3	3	1	15	0	0	.222	.298
Keppinger, Jeff	R-R	6-0	180	4-21-80	.337	.329	.341	64	255	40	86	15	3	3	29	16	1	5	1	13	5	1	.455	.377
Lambin, Chase	B-R	6-2	195	7-7-79	.289	.378	.270	61	211	35	61	16	2	10	34	20	1	2	2	47	2	3	.526	.350
Lunar, Fernando	R-R	6-1	225	5-25-77	.170	.240	.143	28	88	5	15	2	0	1	8	2	0	1	0	15	0	0	.227	.189
Nye, Rodney	R-R	6-4	212	12-2-76	.288	.303	.283	108	375	47	108	19	4	8	54	36	3	5	3	63	5	5	.424	.353
Offerman, Jose	B-R	6-1	200	11-8-68	.167	.231	.130	9	36	1	6	0	0	0	1	1	0	0	0	4	1	0	.167	.189
Pachot, John	R-R	6-2	210	11-11-74	.203	.143	.233	21	64	6	13	7	0	1	9	1	0	1	2	9	0	1	.359	.209
Pagan, Angel	B-R	6-1	180	7-2-81	.271	.282	.267	129	516	69	140	20	10	8	40	49	1	9	4	111	27	15	.395	.333
Piazza, Tony	R-R	6-2	215	6-22-80	.000	.000	.000	2	6	0	0	0	0	0	0	1	0	0	0	2	0	0	.000	.143

BATTING	B-T	HT	WT	DOB	AVG	vLH	vRH	G	AB	R	H	2B	3B	HR	RBI	BB	HBP	SH	SF	SO	SB	CS	SLG	OBP
Redman, Prentice	R-R	6-3	185	8-23-79	.297	.316	.291	76	256	34	76	25	1	5	32	23	1	3	4	49	9	1	.461	.352
Santiago, Benito	R-R	6-1	190	3-9-65	.242	.000	.267	9	33	5	8	1	0	0	4	4	1	0	1	8	0	0	.273	.333
Valent, Eric	L-L	5-11	195	4-4-77	.255	.218	.264	79	275	44	70	13	1	9	38	55	1	1	1	58	1	1	.407	.380
Williams, Gerald	R-R	6-2	185	8-10-66	.230	.250	.220	47	139	24	32	10	2	4	16	9	1	1	1	21	1	2	.417	.280
Wilson, Andy	R-R	6-2	210	11-20-80	.000	.000	.000	3	7	0	0	0	0	0	0	1	0	0	0	0	0	0	.000	.125

PITCHING	B-T	HT	WT	DOB	W	L	ERA	G	GS	CG	SV	IP	H	R	ER	HR	BB	SO	AVG	vLH	vRH	K/9	BB/9
Aybar, Manny	R-R	6-1	175	5-4-72	3	0	1.41	24	0	0	4	32	26	7	5	1	8	27	.224	.200	.237	7.59	2.25
Bannister, Brian	R-R	6-1	205	2-28-81	4	1	3.18	8	8	0	0	45	48	19	16	0	13	48	.270	.271	.269	9.53	2.58
Bell, Heath	R-R	6-3	225	9-29-77	1	0	1.69	13	2	0	6	27	15	5	5	1	5	29	.167	.171	.163	9.79	1.69
Chenard, Ken	R-R	6-3	175	8-30-78	1	0	1.35	1	1	0	0	7	3	1	1	0	4	4	.130	.125	.133	5.40	5.40
Colyer, Steve	L-L	6-4	235	2-22-79	4	2	5.67	28	0	0	1	27	25	17	17	2	19	31	.250	.195	.288	10.33	6.33
Graves, Danny	R-R	6-0	200	8-7-73	0	1	18.00	5	0	0	0	6	15	12	12	2	7	4	.484	.583	.421	6.00	10.50
Hamulack, Tim	L-L	6-4	220	11-14-76	3	1	1.02	28	0	0	6	35	20	5	4	1	9	34	.167	.195	.152	8.66	2.29
Hill, Jeremy	R-R	5-11	200	8-8-77	0	0	0.00	2	0	0	0	2	1	0	0	0	0	1	.200	.500	.000	5.40	0.00
Ishii, Kaz	L-L	6-0	215	9-9-73	2	2	1.76	5	2	0	0	15	16	4	3	3	8	18	.267	.111	.294	10.57	4.70
Junge, Eric	R-R	6-5	215	1-5-77	10	7	3.80	26	22	0	2	135	125	61	57	18	52	114	.247	.236	.254	7.60	3.47
Keppel, Bob	R-R	6-5	205	6-11-82	2	1	3.29	5	5	0	0	27	24	11	10	0	6	19	.238	.220	.250	6.26	1.98
Koo, Dae-Sung	L-L	6-1	185	8-2-69	0	0	0.00	2	1	0	0	4	4	0	0	0	0	0	.267	.000	.364	0.00	0.00
Lavigne, Tim	R-R	5-11	180	7-4-78	1	3	3.65	45	0	0	1	69	66	29	28	5	35	41	.257	.283	.241	5.35	4.57
Lee, David	R-R	6-1	200	3-12-73	2	2	3.09	28	0	0	5	35	32	13	12	4	13	25	.248	.245	.250	6.43	3.34
Matthews, Mike	L-L	6-2	205	10-24-73	0	1	12.10	5	3	0	0	10	14	13	13	1	8	6	.341	.273	.367	5.59	7.45
McGinley, Blake	R-L	6-1	175	8-2-78	4	4	3.43	44	5	0	2	84	77	39	32	16	21	69	.244	.310	.218	7.39	2.25
Musser, Neal	L-L	6-2	185	8-25-80	6	11	5.02	24	24	0	0	124	140	75	69	12	52	89	.287	.234	.302	6.48	3.78
Padilla, Juan	R-R	6-0	200	2-17-77	3	2	1.42	37	2	0	11	63	45	13	10	4	9	59	.197	.188	.205	8.38	1.28
Petit, Yusmeiro	R-R	6-0	230	11-22-84	0	3	9.20	3	3	0	0	15	24	16	15	5	6	14	.375	.333	.412	8.59	3.68
Ring, Royce	L-L	6-0	220	12-21-80	3	0	3.26	33	0	0	2	39	34	16	14	2	13	26	.239	.145	.299	6.05	3.03
Santiago, Jose	R-R	6-3	225	11-5-74	7	6	4.26	29	17	0	0	123	138	62	58	10	40	61	.288	.282	.293	4.48	2.93
Scobie, Jason	R-R	6-1	195	9-1-78	15	7	3.34	27	26	0	0	167	163	71	62	13	55	96	.260	.258	.262	5.17	2.96
Seo, Jae	R-R	6-1	215	5-24-77	7	4	4.29	19	19	0	0	122	126	64	58	13	30	111	.268	.291	.246	8.21	2.22
Stewart, Scott	R-L	6-2	225	8-14-75	1	2	5.25	20	1	0	0	24	29	16	14	2	5	16	.299	.314	.290	6.00	1.88
Strickland, Scott	R-R	5-11	195	4-26-76	0	3	5.40	13	0	0	5	12	14	9	7	1	5	9	.298	.278	.310	6.94	3.86
Takatsu, Shingo	R-R	6-0	180	11-25-68	0	1	3.38	7	1	0	0	8	6	3	3	3	1	10	.200	.167	.222	11.25	1.13
Trachsel, Steve	R-R	6-4	205	10-31-70	0	1	2.57	2	2	0	0	14	10	4	4	2	2	12	.192	.150	.219	7.71	1.29

FIELDING

Catcher	PCT	G	PO	A	E	DP	PB
DiFelice	.993	71	498	49	4	2	3
Hietpas	.984	25	170	14	3	0	4
Lunar	.982	24	148	19	3	1	0
Pachot	.992	21	110	14	1	2	1
Piazza	.800	1	4	0	1	0	0
Santiago	1.000	8	51	3	0	1	0
Wilson	1.000	1	1	0	0	0	0

First Base	PCT	G	PO	A	E	DP
Brazell	.987	8	67	9	1	9
Cordero	1.000	7	57	4	0	3
Daubach	.997	71	617	47	2	61
Diaz	.992	26	225	16	2	20
Garcia	.974	14	141	7	4	14
Nye	1.000	3	11	3	0	1
Offerman	1.000	9	75	3	0	4
Valent	.991	13	101	6	1	8

Second Base	PCT	G	PO	A	E	DP
Basak	.990	38	77	119	2	29
Gil	1.000	2	2	6	0	1
Hernandez	.973	37	76	101	5	23
Keppinger	.989	54	111	159	3	39
Lambin	.958	21	33	58	4	7
Nye	1.000	1	1	2	0	1

Third Base	PCT	G	PO	A	E	DP
Bacani	1.000	6	4	5	0	1
Basak	1.000	2	1	2	0	0
Gil	.889	7	5	11	2	0
Hansen	.895	17	11	40	6	6
Keppinger	.938	5	2	13	1	2
Lambin	.828	11	8	16	5	1
Nye	.953	101	62	223	14	19

Shortstop	PCT	G	PO	A	E	DP
Basak	.960	47	59	110	7	29
Gil	.969	53	71	146	7	34
Hernandez	.969	30	45	80	4	17
Keppinger	1.000	3	4	5	0	3
Lambin	.902	21	21	62	9	7

Outfield	PCT	G	PO	A	E	DP
Brazell	.818	22	18	0	4	0
Calloway	.961	101	168	6	7	1
Cameron	1.000	2	3	0	0	0
Daubach	.875	9	7	0	1	0
Diaz	1.000	17	36	1	0	1
Duncan	1.000	1	1	0	0	0
Garcia	1.000	23	33	2	0	2
Lambin	1.000	2	4	1	0	0
Pagan	.972	110	306	8	9	3
Redman	.973	67	104	4	3	1
Valent	.983	58	109	6	2	0
Williams	1.000	35	67	4	0	0

BINGHAMTON METS — Class AA

EASTERN LEAGUE

BATTING	B-T	HT	WT	DOB	AVG	vLH	vRH	G	AB	R	H	2B	3B	HR	RBI	BB	HBP	SH	SF	SO	SB	CS	SLG	OBP
Arroyo, Rafael	R-R	5-9	170	10-26-82	.167	.200	.143	4	12	2	2	0	0	0	1	1	1	0	0	5	0	0	.167	.286
Bacani, David	R-R	5-7	170	7-30-79	.294	.234	.319	90	262	35	77	18	2	5	42	30	6	8	3	56	3	6	.435	.375
Baldiris, Aarom	R-R	6-2	195	1-5-83	.275	.321	.257	131	495	69	136	35	1	11	63	45	6	9	2	81	7	1	.416	.341
Caligiuri, Jay	R-R	6-0	190	3-29-80	.236	.202	.251	109	373	50	88	20	3	15	50	38	7	1	5	92	1	1	.426	.314
Clements, Zac	R-R	6-2	215	4-17-80	.225	.296	.194	57	178	12	40	8	0	0	10	6	0	3	0	48	0	2	.270	.250
Duncan, Jeff	L-L	6-2	190	12-9-78	.245	.253	.241	87	278	33	68	9	4	5	26	37	1	1	2	63	11	4	.360	.333
Garcia, Yunir	R-R	6-0	170	8-3-82	.250	.333	.222	4	12	1	3	1	0	0	2	1	0	0	0	4	0	0	.333	.308
Hall, Victor	L-L	5-10	160	9-16-80	.207	.179	.214	64	179	20	37	6	2	5	21	8	2	3	2	51	7	1	.346	.246
Harper, Brett	L-R	6-4	185	7-31-81	.273	.286	.268	67	227	37	62	11	0	16	42	26	2	0	1	85	0	0	.533	.352
Hernandez, Anderson	B-R	5-9	170	10-30-82	.326	.378	.307	66	273	46	89	14	1	7	24	14	1	7	1	58	11	9	.462	.360
Hietpas, Joe	R-R	6-3	220	5-1-79	.216	.175	.234	65	204	18	44	8	0	5	24	26	9	6	0	56	1	1	.328	.331
Jacobs, Mike	L-R	6-2	200	10-30-80	.321	.311	.324	117	433	66	139	37	2	25	93	35	7	1	6	94	1	2	.589	.376
Lambin, Chase	B-R	6-2	195	7-7-79	.331	.262	.353	53	181	26	60	17	0	14	29	20	0	2	1	38	2	0	.657	.396
Lydon, Wayne	B-R	6-2	190	4-17-81	.244	.255	.240	129	491	70	120	15	13	2	43	46	4	19	2	101	42	14	.340	.313
Malek, Bobby	L-R	6-1	205	7-6-81	.277	.274	.278	116	394	47	109	23	4	4	37	32	4	6	3	80	1	5	.386	.335
Matsui, Kazuo	B-R	5-10	185	10-23-75	.444	.500	.429	3	9	4	4	1	0	0	0	1	0	0	0	1	2	0	.556	.500
Milledge, Lastings	R-R	6-1	185	4-5-85	.337	.377	.318	48	193	33	65	17	0	4	24	14	4	2	1	47	11	5	.487	.392
Ragsdale, Corey	R-R	6-4	175	11-10-82	.226	.203	.235	64	217	33	49	5	3	9	31	21	4	5	1	75	4	3	.401	.305
Redman, Prentice	R-R	6-3	185	8-23-79	.311	.419	.271	45	161	30	50	12	1	4	29	17	2	1	6	37	2	3	.472	.371
Slack, Jon	L-L	5-11	180	12-4-81	.224	.211	.229	23	67	7	15	2	0	0	7	6	0	6	1	16	1	0	.254	.284
Triplett, Russ	R-R	5-11	180	1-18-81	.333	.250	.362	18	63	11	21	6	0	1	7	6	0	0	1	9	0	0	.476	.386
Watts, Derran	R-R	6-2	180	6-28-80	.400	.500	.333	2	5	1	2	0	0	1	1	1	0	0	0	1	0	0	1.000	.500

PITCHING	B-T	HT	WT	DOB	W	L	ERA	G	GS	CG	SV	IP	H	R	ER	HR	BB	SO	AVG	vLH	vRH	K/9	BB/9
Bacani, David	R-R	5-7	170	7-30-79	0	0	0.00	4	0	0	0	4	1	0	0	0	1	2	.083	.000	.143	4.50	2.25
Bannister, Brian	R-R	6-1	205	2-28-81	9	4	2.56	18	18	1	0	109	91	36	31	11	27	94	.232	.243	.223	7.76	2.23
Byard, David	R-R	6-3	235	6-1-78	0	0	0.00	1	0	0	0	2	1	0	0	0	2	0	.143	.333	.000	0.00	9.00
Chenard, Ken	R-R	6-3	175	8-30-78	7	8	5.12	22	22	1	0	104	107	69	59	15	45	95	.263	.247	.275	8.25	3.91
Cordova, Vince	R-R	6-3	210	4-16-82	0	1	2.57	1	1	0	0	7	4	2	2	0	2	7	.148	.182	.000	9.00	2.57
Cullen, Ryan	L-L	6-2	204	1-20-80	0	0	9.00	1	0	0	0	2	3	2	2	1	1	3	.333	.429	.000	13.50	4.50
Deaton, Kevin	R-R	6-4	265	8-7-81	3	4	4.19	11	10	0	0	54	56	31	25	7	13	55	.262	.227	.291	9.22	2.18
Edwards, Bryan	R-R	6-0	195	8-21-79	6	6	3.65	35	13	0	1	118	124	53	48	8	46	85	.271	.259	.280	6.46	3.50
Garcia, Anderson	R-R	6-2	178	3-23-81	4	2	4.97	30	1	0	5	51	59	32	28	8	20	41	.299	.349	.263	7.28	3.55
Hamulack, Tim	L-L	6-4	220	11-14-76	2	2	1.26	21	0	0	6	29	20	7	4	0	6	27	.187	.138	.205	8.48	1.88
Hill, Jeremy	R-R	5-11	200	8-8-77	1	3	4.29	19	0	0	4	21	29	13	10	1	10	20	.309	.378	.263	8.57	4.29
Humber, Philip	R-R	6-4	210	12-21-82	0	1	6.75	1	1	0	0	4	4	3	3	0	2	2	.250	.167	.300	4.50	4.50
Junge, Eric	R-R	6-5	215	1-5-77	1	1	4.15	3	0	0	0	13	14	7	6	0	2	14	.269	.118	.343	9.69	1.38
Lavigne, Tim	R-R	5-11	180	7-4-78	0	0	1.04	8	0	0	5	9	8	1	1	0	3	7	.235	.182	.261	7.27	3.12
Lindstrom, Matt	R-R	6-4	210	2-11-80	2	5	5.40	35	10	0	0	73	90	61	44	11	55	58	.302	.286	.314	7.12	6.75
Lopez, Rafael	R-R	6-4	170	10-24-78	2	10	5.98	32	6	0	0	84	109	64	56	9	35	59	.315	.340	.294	6.30	3.74
MacLane, Evan	L-L	6-2	185	11-4-82	3	2	4.14	9	9	1	0	59	63	31	27	7	9	48	.266	.217	.282	7.36	1.38
Maldonado, Ivan	R-R	6-3	210	6-7-80	1	1	4.26	5	1	0	0	13	12	6	6	3	3	13	.250	.333	.185	9.24	2.13
McGinley, Blake	R-L	6-1	175	8-2-78	1	0	2.25	2	0	0	0	4	4	1	1	0	0	4	.250	.250	.250	9.00	0.00
McNab, Tim	R-R	6-0	175	6-4-80	2	4	5.61	42	2	0	1	85	105	63	53	6	21	64	.297	.297	.298	6.78	2.22
Petit, Yusmeiro	R-R	6-0	230	11-22-84	9	3	2.91	21	21	2	0	118	90	41	38	15	18	130	.209	.236	.191	9.94	1.38
Portobanco, Luz	R-R	6-3	205	9-15-79	2	12	7.56	40	7	0	2	75	101	73	63	9	48	49	.325	.339	.315	5.88	5.76
Riggan, Jerrod	R-R	6-3	195	5-16-74	0	1	5.79	4	0	0	0	5	7	4	3	0	3	3	.333	.143	.429	5.79	5.79
Rodriguez, Jose	R-R	6-0	175	1-15-82	3	5	3.96	33	0	0	2	61	63	37	27	3	30	59	.266	.196	.314	8.66	4.40
Roman, Orlando	R-R	6-2	185	11-28-78	4	4	4.95	31	18	0	0	120	123	75	66	18	58	136	.269	.253	.280	10.20	4.35
Strayhorn, Kole	R-R	6-0	196	10-1-82	0	0	0.00	1	0	0	0	2	0	0	0	0	0	1	.000	.000	.000	4.50	0.00
Trachsel, Steve	R-R	6-4	205	10-31-70	1	0	3.00	2	2	1	0	12	8	4	4	2	4	7	.190	.304	.053	5.25	3.00
Urdaneta, Lino	R-R	6-1	170	11-20-79	0	0	5.40	1	0	0	0	2	2	1	1	0	1	0	.286	.500	.200	0.00	5.40

FIELDING

Catcher	PCT	G	PO	A	E	DP	PB
Arroyo	1.000	3	27	4	0	1	1
Clements	.986	50	324	24	5	5	3
Garcia	1.000	3	22	0	0	0	0
Hietpas	.989	54	398	32	5	6	5
Jacobs	.981	43	341	12	7	1	9

First Base	PCT	G	PO	A	E	DP
Caligiuri	.991	37	200	28	2	18
Garcia	1.000	1	6	0	0	1
Harper	.983	53	377	34	7	35
Hietpas	.978	13	86	4	2	3
Jacobs	.985	54	439	22	7	37

Second Base	PCT	G	PO	A	E	DP
Bacani	.960	20	34	38	3	8
Baldiris	.964	117	219	296	19	57
Hernandez	.979	8	21	26	1	7
Lambin	.778	2	3	4	2	2
Matsui	1.000	3	2	12	0	2

Third Base	PCT	G	PO	A	E	DP
Bacani	.884	36	22	39	8	1
Caligiuri	.936	78	49	113	11	8
Lambin	.922	31	17	54	6	5
Triplett	.936	17	9	35	3	1

Shortstop	PCT	G	PO	A	E	DP
Bacani	.960	23	37	60	4	16
Hernandez	.938	57	72	125	13	27
Lambin	.897	8	15	20	4	6
Ragsdale	.947	63	105	165	15	28

Outfield	PCT	G	PO	A	E	DP
Baldiris	.000	1	0	0	0	0
Duncan	.986	77	135	1	2	1
Hall	.965	47	80	3	3	0
Jacobs	.000	1	0	0	0	0
Lambin	1.000	4	3	0	0	0
Lydon	.959	121	253	4	11	1
Malek	.962	108	189	12	8	0
Milledge	.979	44	90	3	2	0
Redman	.909	29	39	1	4	1
Slack	1.000	21	28	4	0	1
Watts	.667	2	2	0	1	0

ST. LUCIE METS — High Class A

FLORIDA STATE LEAGUE

BATTING	B-T	HT	WT	DOB	AVG	vLH	vRH	G	AB	R	H	2B	3B	HR	RBI	BB	HBP	SH	SF	SO	SB	CS	SLG	OBP
Batista, Wilson	B-R	6-0	170	2-7-81	.274	.216	.311	61	248	33	68	7	4	5	22	20	2	2	5	37	12	13	.395	.327
Bowman, Shawn	R-R	6-2	190	12-9-84	.221	.310	.188	87	326	44	72	15	1	17	53	22	6	1	0	110	4	1	.429	.282
Brinkley, Dante	R-R	5-10	180	8-21-81	.266	.229	.287	54	192	36	51	5	2	5	24	24	8	2	2	64	9	6	.391	.367
Cairo, Miguel	R-R	6-1	210	5-4-74	.250	.000	.250	1	4	0	1	0	0	0	0	0	0	0	0	1	0	0	.250	.250
Cameron, Mike	R-R	6-2	200	1-8-73	.300	.000	.300	4	10	3	3	2	0	0	0	3	2	0	0	3	0	0	.500	.533
Clements, Zac	R-R	6-2	215	4-17-80	.174	.143	.188	7	23	4	4	1	0	0	5	1	0	0	0	8	0	0	.217	.208
Davidson, Tyler	R-R	6-4	240	9-23-80	.161	.192	.139	39	124	14	20	3	0	2	8	12	5	1	1	46	1	1	.234	.261
Garcia, Emmanuel	L-R	6-2	180	3-4-86	.222	.000	.333	2	9	1	2	1	0	0	0	0	0	0	0	2	0	0	.333	.222
Garcia, Yunir	R-R	6-0	170	8-3-82	.171	.122	.190	59	170	27	29	5	2	4	18	29	9	2	1	70	5	0	.294	.321
Harper, Brett	L-R	6-4	185	7-31-81	.280	.141	.348	62	239	35	67	11	1	20	60	21	1	0	3	64	0	1	.586	.337
Harvey, Ryan	R-R	6-0	190	12-17-79	.309	.333	.297	16	55	4	17	3	0	0	10	3	2	0	0	8	2	1	.364	.367
Hathaway, Aaron	R-R	6-0	190	12-2-82	.311	.345	.286	38	135	22	42	8	0	0	15	16	0	3	2	33	3	2	.370	.379
Hill, Jamar	R-R	6-3	200	9-20-82	.252	.279	.239	125	456	64	115	23	3	15	64	47	4	5	2	151	13	9	.414	.326
Maldonado, Brahiam	R-R	6-0	185	9-18-85	.313	.375	.250	6	16	4	5	1	0	0	3	2	1	2	0	6	0	0	.375	.421
Malo, Jonathan	R-R	6-1	175	9-29-83	.143	.000	.182	5	14	1	2	1	0	0	2	2	0	0	0	4	1	0	.214	.250
Martinez, Joan	B-R	5-11	175	5-7-84	.250	1.000	.000	2	4	1	1	0	0	0	1	1	0	0	0	2	0	0	.250	.400
McCraw, Sean	L-R	6-0	185	3-11-86	.500	.000	.500	1	2	1	1	0	0	0	0	1	0	0	0	1	0	0	.500	.667
Mientkiewicz, Doug	L-R	6-2	205	6-19-74	.259	.316	.125	8	27	3	7	4	0	0	2	7	0	0	0	7	0	0	.407	.412
Milledge, Lastings	R-R	6-1	185	4-5-85	.302	.410	.263	62	232	48	70	15	0	4	22	19	13	4	1	41	18	13	.418	.385
Piazza, Tony	R-R	6-2	215	6-22-80	.226	.179	.246	33	93	12	21	4	0	1	4	8	0	1	0	24	2	0	.301	.287
Psomas, Grant	R-R	6-3	195	9-2-82	.305	.306	.304	34	118	15	36	10	0	1	15	15	0	2	0	29	1	1	.415	.383
Ragsdale, Corey	R-R	6-4	175	11-10-82	.260	.267	.258	68	273	51	71	16	8	10	38	33	4	1	1	94	8	7	.487	.347
Rios, Kevin	R-R	6-2	180	7-21-81	.253	.236	.263	94	332	33	84	18	1	5	35	11	4	1	3	82	2	4	.358	.283
Santiago, Benito	R-R	6-1	190	3-9-65	.333	.400	.250	3	9	1	3	1	0	0	1	1	0	0	0	0	0	0	.444	.400
Slack, Jon	L-L	5-11	180	12-4-81	.258	.243	.263	77	275	33	71	15	1	3	24	24	0	3	1	52	14	5	.353	.317
Stewart, Caleb	R-R	6-2	230	6-11-82	.286	.381	.229	17	56	12	16	6	0	3	7	7	3	3	1	13	3	1	.554	.388
Turay, Alhaji	R-R	6-0	205	9-22-82	.193	.212	.188	42	145	15	28	7	0	4	13	7	4	5	0	54	4	6	.324	.250
Watts, Derran	R-R	6-2	180	6-28-80	.268	.194	.311	28	97	14	26	4	2	0	14	11	4	3	0	19	3	4	.351	.366
Whealy, Blake	R-R	5-11	175	5-27-80	.212	.138	.241	88	292	29	62	13	0	10	36	28	7	3	3	96	3	4	.360	.294
Wilson, Andy	R-R	6-2	210	11-20-80	.284	.308	.272	127	464	81	132	25	3	28	89	68	0	0	8	88	8	4	.532	.370
Wilson, Brandon	R-R	6-4	195	9-1-82	.667	.000	.667	2	3	0	2	0	0	0	0	0	0	0	0	0	0	0	.667	.667

PITCHING	B-T	HT	WT	DOB	W	L	ERA	G	GS	CG	SV	IP	H	R	ER	HR	BB	SO	AVG	vLH	vRH	K/9	BB/9
Almenar, Aristides	R-R	6-0	175	12-27-83	0	0	.000	1	0	0	0	0	2	0	0	0	0	0	1.000	1.000	1.000	.000	.000
Belson, Greg	R-R	5-10	170	8-16-78	3	2	5.09	25	2	0	0	53	69	31	30	7	17	28	.309	.278	.326	4.75	2.89
Benson, Kris	R-R	6-4	205	11-7-74	0	0	0.00	1	1	0	0	3	0	0	0	0	0	4	.000	.000	.000	12.00	0.00
Camacho, Eddie	L-L	6-1	180	9-17-82	2	4	2.74	45	0	0	10	49	49	17	15	2	21	40	.261	.242	.270	7.30	3.83
Castillo, Jonathan	R-R	5-11	195	12-27-83	0	1	20.25	1	0	0	0	3	3	6	6	1	4	0	.333	.333	.333	0.00	13.50
Cordova, Vince	R-R	6-3	210	4-16-82	8	9	4.01	25	25	2	0	141	150	78	63	14	26	110	.270	.240	.291	7.00	1.66
Cox, Michael	L-L	5-11	195	11-3-78	0	0	.000	1	0	0	0	0	0	0	0	0	1	0	.000	.000	.000	.000	.000
Cullen, Ryan	L-L	6-2	204	1-20-80	0	1	8.76	13	0	0	0	12	27	13	12	1	1	7	.450	.316	.512	5.11	0.73
Foli, Daniel	R-R	6-2	180	3-30-81	5	2	3.74	37	0	0	6	67	68	29	28	5	21	53	.269	.286	.259	7.08	2.81
Garcia, Anderson	R-R	6-2	178	3-23-81	2	2	2.70	16	0	0	3	27	21	9	8	2	9	20	.212	.364	.136	6.75	3.04
Heredia, Felix	L-L	6-0	180	6-20-75	0	1	13.50	5	0	0	0	4	6	6	6	0	2	3	.375	.333	.400	6.75	4.50
Hernandez, Gaby	R-R	6-3	215	5-21-86	2	5	5.74	10	10	0	0	42	48	28	27	1	10	32	.298	.288	.304	6.80	2.13
Hill, Jeremy	R-R	5-11	200	8-8-77	0	0	2.35	7	0	0	1	8	8	4	2	1	3	5	.267	.182	.316	5.87	3.52
Humber, Philip	R-R	6-4	210	12-21-82	2	6	4.99	14	14	0	0	70	74	41	39	6	18	65	.273	.189	.327	8.32	2.30
Ishii, Kaz	L-L	6-0	215	9-9-73	0	0	0.00	1	1	0	0	4	0	0	0	0	1	3	.000	.000	.000	6.75	2.25
King, Bryan	R-R	6-1	185	5-20-81	0	0	11.70	6	0	0	0	10	14	14	13	2	9	11	.326	.444	.294	9.90	8.10
Lopez, Rafael	R-R	6-4	170	10-24-78	1	0	4.00	5	0	0	0	9	10	4	4	1	1	4	.278	.333	.250	4.00	1.00
MacLane, Evan	L-L	6-2	185	11-4-82	8	5	3.20	19	19	1	0	112	96	51	40	14	15	92	.224	.284	.208	7.37	1.20
Maldonado, Ivan	R-R	6-3	210	6-7-80	4	5	5.46	27	3	0	1	59	62	43	36	6	23	43	.264	.329	.235	6.52	3.49
Mannix, Kevin	R-R	6-2	207	12-20-80	0	0	.000	1	0	0	0	0	3	3	3	0	0	0	1.000	1.000	1.000	.000	.000
Muniz, Carlos	R-R	6-1	180	3-12-81	3	0	5.82	14	0	0	0	17	13	11	11	3	9	19	.210	.176	.222	10.06	4.76
Nall, Brandon	R-R	6-4	190	3-18-82	0	0	11.57	2	0	0	0	2	3	3	3	0	3	1	.300	.200	.400	3.86	11.57
Owens, Henry	R-R	6-3	230	4-23-79	2	5	3.15	38	1	0	4	54	49	29	19	2	24	74	.233	.229	.236	12.26	3.98
Pinango, Miguel	R-R	6-1	160	1-20-83	3	2	4.13	12	11	0	0	61	75	30	28	5	11	26	.301	.314	.293	3.84	1.62
Ramirez, Greg	R-R	6-4	205	9-12-80	4	5	4.17	18	12	0	0	69	66	38	32	6	21	64	.245	.236	.252	8.35	2.74
Riggan, Jerrod	R-R	6-3	195	5-16-74	1	0	3.86	4	0	0	0	5	3	2	2	1	0	4	.176	.200	.167	7.71	0.00
Rodriguez, Jose	R-R	6-0	175	1-15-82	0	0	2.70	3	0	0	2	3	2	1	1	0	1	3	.182	.200	.167	8.10	2.70
Smith, Chuck	R-R	6-3	205	12-13-81	4	4	4.94	24	20	0	0	117	129	70	64	12	40	59	.284	.289	.281	4.55	3.09
Strayhorn, Kole	R-R	6-0	196	10-1-82	5	3	4.46	33	0	0	2	38	44	25	19	4	22	31	.288	.389	.232	7.28	5.17
Strickland, Scott	R-R	5-11	195	4-26-76	0	0	10.80	1	0	0	0	2	4	2	2	1	0	2	.444	.667	.333	10.80	0.00
Swindell, Mike	R-R	6-1	190	9-26-81	0	2	2.90	6	5	0	0	31	28	12	10	1	8	15	.231	.229	.233	4.35	2.32
Trachsel, Steve	R-R	6-4	205	10-31-70	0	1	1.35	2	2	0	0	7	5	2	1	0	1	5	.208	.000	.294	6.75	1.35
Urdaneta, Lino	R-R	6-1	170	11-20-79	0	0	1.93	3	0	0	0	5	2	1	1	0	1	4	.118	.000	.154	7.71	1.93
Walker, Brian	L-L	6-3	210	2-20-80	3	1	4.80	17	1	0	0	30	33	17	16	4	15	25	.280	.324	.262	7.50	4.50
Worthington, Tim	R-R	6-2	200	7-29-80	4	2	2.98	13	7	2	0	51	39	21	17	3	13	49	.209	.279	.168	8.59	2.28

FIELDING

Catcher	PCT	G	PO	A	E	DP	PB
Clements	.974	6	30	8	1	1	1
Garcia	.991	59	421	41	4	3	5
Hathaway	.985	27	171	26	3	0	5
Martinez	1.000	2	8	0	0	0	0
McCraw	1.000	1	3	0	0	0	0
Piazza	.970	29	156	8	5	1	2
Santiago	1.000	2	9	2	0	0	1
A. Wilson	.985	20	116	18	2	2	5
B. Wilson	1.000	2	11	1	0	0	0

First Base	PCT	G	PO	A	E	DP
Cummins	1.000	1	1	1	0	0
Davidson	1.000	15	124	3	0	16
Harper	.988	48	375	26	5	36
Mientkiewicz	.985	6	63	4	1	3
Rios	1.000	3	11	0	0	0
Whealy	1.000	9	53	3	0	7
A. Wilson	.986	59	537	30	8	48

Second Base	PCT	G	PO	A	E	DP
Rios	.974	84	150	218	10	50
Whealy	.934	54	90	135	16	26

Third Base	PCT	G	PO	A	E	DP
Bowman	.928	87	59	186	19	19
Garcia	1.000	1	2	0	0	0
Hathaway	1.000	7	7	14	0	3
Malo	1.000	1	0	3	0	0
Psomas	.926	34	20	68	7	6
Rios	1.000	5	1	9	0	0
A. Wilson	1.000	3	1	1	0	0

Shortstop	PCT	G	PO	A	E	DP
Batista	.944	61	96	157	15	35
Garcia	.750	1	1	2	1	0
Malo	.944	4	5	12	1	1
Ragsdale	.949	68	111	225	18	42
Rios	.833	1	1	4	1	1

Outfield	PCT	G	PO	A	E	DP
Brinkley	.978	52	86	3	2	0
Cameron	1.000	4	2	0	0	0
Davidson	1.000	2	1	0	0	0
Harvey	1.000	10	12	0	0	0
Hill	.979	122	277	7	6	3
Maldonado	.857	5	6	0	1	0
Milledge	.968	61	146	3	5	1
Slack	1.000	69	119	3	0	1
Stewart	1.000	15	28	1	0	0
Turay	.960	36	47	1	2	0
Watts	.967	28	55	3	2	0
A. Wilson	.966	13	27	1	1	0

HAGERSTOWN SUNS — Low Class A

SOUTH ATLANTIC LEAGUE

BATTING	B-T	HT	WT	DOB	AVG	vLH	vRH	G	AB	R	H	2B	3B	HR	RBI	BB	HBP	SH	SF	SO	SB	CS	SLG	OBP
Arroyo, Rafael	R-R	5-9	170	10-26-82	.220	.300	.197	28	91	15	20	3	0	5	11	14	6	2	0	25	0	2	.418	.360
Bacon, Matt	L-R	6-2	203	2-18-81	.200	.000	.207	15	30	4	6	2	0	0	5	3	1	0	1	8	0	0	.267	.286
Batista, Wilson	B-R	6-0	170	2-7-81	.238	.281	.224	68	265	41	63	11	3	7	28	24	1	6	2	46	13	14	.381	.301
Brinkley, Dante	R-R	5-10	180	8-21-81	.364	.267	.391	61	214	48	78	17	4	10	41	38	10	1	2	57	20	13	.621	.477
Brown, Kyle	R-R	6-0	187	10-4-81	.220	.211	.222	27	91	17	20	3	1	2	16	8	4	3	4	29	6	2	.341	.299
Burt, James	R-L	5-11	230	4-23-81	.255	.265	.252	63	192	35	49	13	1	4	16	26	7	3	2	47	4	5	.396	.361
Carp, Mike	L-R	6-2	205	6-30-86	.249	.221	.258	89	313	49	78	12	1	19	63	35	21	1	5	96	2	2	.476	.358
Coles, Corey	L-L	6-1	170	1-30-82	.307	.276	.311	69	264	27	81	16	0	4	33	12	2	3	0	40	11	5	.413	.342
Concepcion, Ambiorix	R-R	6-2	180	3-19-82	.251	.291	.239	130	521	68	131	29	5	15	61	22	9	3	8	136	35	15	.413	.289
Coronado, Jose	B-R	6-1	175	4-13-86	.225	.125	.255	18	71	4	16	2	1	0	4	7	0	3	0	17	1	4	.282	.295
Coultas, Ryan	R-R	6-3	180	4-24-82	.289	.315	.279	89	304	43	88	22	4	6	36	20	4	4	3	57	11	6	.447	.338
Davidson, Tyler	R-R	6-4	240	9-23-80	.205	.300	.172	23	78	12	16	4	0	2	13	5	1	0	0	27	1	0	.333	.262
Fisher, Matt	R-R	5-9	180	9-3-81	.248	.139	.286	45	141	24	35	6	2	2	14	17	0	5	2	26	2	3	.362	.325
Flores, Jesus	R-R	6-1	180	10-26-84	.216	.263	.201	82	319	34	69	18	0	7	42	12	3	1	2	90	2	2	.339	.250
Gaerlan, Armand	R-R	5-10	180	8-22-82	.259	.303	.248	50	170	28	44	7	2	1	14	21	3	5	2	39	13	3	.341	.347
Gamero, Jesus	R-R	6-1	170	1-24-84	.164	.167	.162	16	55	8	9	2	0	0	2	4	2	0	0	9	0	1	.200	.246
Gomez, Carlos	R-R	6-2	175	12-4-85	.275	.271	.277	120	487	75	134	13	6	8	48	32	9	10	1	88	64	24	.376	.331
Hathaway, Aaron	R-R	6-0	190	12-2-82	.259	.182	.274	39	139	18	36	8	0	1	13	8	1	1	1	32	0	2	.338	.302
Mihalics, Joe	R-R	5-9	170	4-7-83	.267	.200	.275	17	45	3	12	3	0	0	8	4	1	4	1	5	0	1	.333	.333
Piazza, Tony	R-R	6-2	215	6-22-80	.150	.000	.200	5	20	1	3	1	0	0	1	1	0	0	0	9	1	0	.200	.190
Psomas, Grant	R-R	6-3	195	9-2-82	.300	.293	.302	99	350	66	105	27	2	19	54	62	2	2	5	79	6	4	.551	.403
Santana, Yury	R-R	6-1	170	8-15-82	.182	.273	.091	8	22	4	4	1	0	0	0	1	0	0	0	10	0	0	.227	.217
Triplett, Russ	R-R	5-11	180	1-18-81	.265	.394	.223	43	136	20	36	9	2	3	18	18	5	4	2	26	2	4	.426	.366
Watts, Derran	R-R	6-2	180	6-28-80	.285	.205	.324	65	221	31	63	17	1	4	40	24	4	1	1	55	6	5	.425	.364

BATTING	B-T	HT	WT	DOB	AVG	vLH	vRH	G	AB	R	H	2B	3B	HR	RBI	BB	HBP	SH	SF	SO	SB	CS	SLG	OBP
Wyrick, Josh	L-L	6-3	190	3-11-82	.296	.429	.269	23	81	17	24	6	0	1	7	6	1	2	1	16	3	2	.407	.348

PITCHING	B-T	HT	WT	DOB	W	L	ERA	G	GS	CG	SV	IP	H	R	ER	HR	BB	SO	AVG	vLH	vRH	K/9	BB/9
Alfonzo, Edgar	L-L	5-10	170	12-14-84	2	2	0.92	13	0	0	0	20	13	3	2	1	5	13	.181	.211	.170	5.95	2.29
Almenar, Aristides	R-R	6-0	175	12-27-83	0	0	9.82	2	0	0	0	4	1	4	4	0	5	2	.091	.000	.167	4.91	12.27
Bowman, Charles	R-R	6-6	220	8-16-80	2	2	2.98	26	0	0	0	54	58	22	18	4	18	30	.279	.321	.265	4.97	2.98
Castillo, Jonathan	R-R	5-11	195	12-27-83	1	0	2.57	2	1	0	0	7	4	3	2	1	3	4	.182	.000	.250	5.14	3.86
Cova, Rafael	R-R	6-2	174	3-5-82	5	6	4.60	24	5	0	1	63	62	45	32	5	33	61	.261	.329	.224	8.76	4.74
Devaney, Michael	R-R	6-4	220	7-31-82	10	4	3.88	32	15	2	0	137	107	73	59	9	51	121	.214	.204	.220	7.95	3.35
Durkin, Matt	R-R	6-4	220	2-22-83	4	5	3.77	19	14	0	0	76	54	42	32	9	54	79	.205	.210	.203	9.31	6.37
Eager, Blake	R-R	6-3	205	5-19-82	6	3	3.76	21	20	0	0	105	109	50	44	13	16	83	.261	.230	.281	7.09	1.37
Gomez, Jose	R-R	6-2	165	12-16-80	1	4	6.75	17	0	0	0	31	29	30	23	6	23	24	.240	.179	.268	7.04	6.75
Hernandez, Gaby	R-R	6-3	215	5-21-86	6	1	2.43	18	18	1	0	93	59	29	25	4	30	99	.179	.197	.166	9.62	2.91
Landing, Jeff	R-R	6-3	190	7-31-83	5	5	4.40	14	14	0	0	76	74	41	37	7	34	45	.265	.250	.275	5.35	4.04
Mannix, Kevin	R-R	6-2	207	12-20-80	3	6	5.36	29	9	0	2	86	98	63	51	10	40	48	.287	.261	.301	5.04	4.20
Miramontes, Mateo	R-R	6-4	200	12-24-81	3	2	6.48	25	1	0	1	42	38	34	30	3	35	34	.252	.239	.263	7.34	7.56
Muniz, Carlos	R-R	6-1	180	3-12-81	3	4	4.78	30	0	0	14	38	37	22	20	6	19	43	.257	.309	.225	10.27	4.54
Nall, Brandon	R-R	6-4	190	3-18-82	1	2	7.06	12	2	0	0	22	21	20	17	1	19	30	.266	.381	.224	12.46	7.89
Perez, Marcelo	R-R	6-1	166	10-10-80	2	6	3.79	43	0	0	13	59	63	37	25	7	32	53	.258	.247	.265	8.04	4.85
Rengel, Orlando	R-R	6-1	172	5-11-83	2	5	4.97	14	9	0	0	54	64	40	30	5	25	46	.298	.286	.303	7.62	4.14
Sanchez, Jose	R-R	6-0	170	5-12-84	11	5	4.20	26	24	0	0	133	147	73	62	18	37	87	.282	.310	.266	5.89	2.50
Serfass, Joey	R-R	6-3	215	5-6-81	1	1	1.23	16	0	0	4	44	32	6	6	1	9	35	.209	.178	.222	7.16	1.84
Smith, Chuck	R-R	6-3	205	12-13-81	0	0	0.00	6	0	0	0	14	3	0	0	0	2	17	.065	.111	.036	10.93	1.29
Weintraub, Jason	R-R	6-3	165	8-13-82	1	1	3.04	10	0	0	0	24	24	12	8	2	5	15	.258	.233	.270	5.70	1.90
Williams, Joe	L-L	6-2	220	4-8-81	0	0	5.06	3	1	0	0	5	7	5	3	1	6	3	.333	.000	.389	5.06	10.13
Worthington, Tim	R-R	6-2	200	7-29-80	2	2	1.52	15	4	0	1	41	35	10	7	1	23	46	.230	.224	.234	10.02	5.01

FIELDING

Catcher	PCT	G	PO	A	E	DP	PB
Arroyo	.991	26	201	21	2	0	5
Bacon	1.000	8	44	5	0	0	2
Flores	.987	71	501	50	7	10	12
Hathaway	.983	32	242	49	5	3	2
Piazza	.961	5	41	8	2	1	1

First Base	PCT	G	PO	A	E	DP
Bacon	1.000	2	3	0	0	0
Burt	.991	41	314	26	3	25
Carp	.984	80	646	48	11	71
Coles	1.000	2	7	0	0	0
Davidson	.985	17	121	14	2	13
Fisher	.800	1	4	0	1	2
Hathaway	1.000	1	6	0	0	0
Psomas	.966	4	26	2	1	2
Wyrick	1.000	2	15	1	0	3

Second Base	PCT	G	PO	A	E	DP
Batista	.966	22	47	67	4	21
Coultas	.949	36	75	93	9	19
Fisher	.980	34	76	74	3	24
Gaerlan	.940	34	64	76	9	15
Mihalics	1.000	7	12	13	0	2
Psomas	1.000	2	2	5	0	1
Triplett	.979	13	16	30	1	6

Third Base	PCT	G	PO	A	E	DP
Carp	1.000	1	0	1	0	0
Fisher	.818	4	2	7	2	2
Gaerlan	.897	14	5	30	4	1
Hathaway	1.000	4	1	8	0	1
Mihalics	.667	1	0	2	1	0
Psomas	.911	93	72	173	24	16
Santana	.750	1	2	1	1	0
Triplett	.958	25	14	55	3	7

Shortstop	PCT	G	PO	A	E	DP
Batista	.940	46	92	144	15	34
Coronado	.939	18	28	65	6	10
Coultas	.925	54	108	175	23	44
Gaerlan	.833	1	2	3	1	0
Mihalics	.973	8	13	23	1	5
Santana	.923	7	8	16	2	3
Triplett	.900	8	4	23	3	1

Outfield	PCT	G	PO	A	E	DP
Brinkley	.986	37	68	3	1	1
Brown	.957	21	42	3	2	1
Burt	.950	14	18	1	1	0
Coles	.913	35	41	1	4	0
Concepcion	.980	123	287	14	6	1
Gamero	.923	13	12	0	1	0
Gomez	.959	116	227	8	10	2
Watts	.951	52	73	4	4	0
Wyrick	.885	15	22	1	3	0

BROOKLYN CYCLONES — Short-Season Class A

NEW YORK-PENN LEAGUE

BATTING	B-T	HT	WT	DOB	AVG	vLH	vRH	G	AB	R	H	2B	3B	HR	RBI	BB	HBP	SH	SF	SO	SB	CS	SLG	OBP
Anderson, Matt	L-R	6-2	205	12-9-82	.278	.235	.288	23	90	10	25	4	0	3	10	8	1	0	1	13	0	0	.422	.340
Arroyo, Rafael	R-R	5-9	170	10-26-82	.189	.400	.140	19	53	8	10	5	1	0	4	7	1	1	0	17	1	1	.321	.295
Bergeron, Jabe	R-R	6-3	230	12-19-81	.154	.167	.143	4	13	1	2	0	0	0	4	2	0	0	0	4	0	0	.154	.267
Brown, Kyle	R-R	6-0	187	10-4-81	.264	.294	.250	17	53	5	14	4	0	0	3	8	1	1	0	16	4	3	.340	.371
Butera, Drew	R-R	6-1	190	8-9-83	.217	.231	.213	55	175	13	38	9	1	1	23	22	2	1	4	33	1	0	.297	.305
Chavez, Dirimo	R-R	6-0	170	8-10-83	.187	.167	.193	23	75	4	14	3	0	1	6	6	0	5	1	18	3	1	.267	.244
Cummins, Daniel	R-R	5-9	190	12-11-82	.429	.333	.500	2	7	1	3	1	0	0	0	0	0	0	0	0	0	0	.571	.429
Evans, Nick	R-R	6-2	180	1-30-86	.252	.255	.251	57	226	30	57	11	3	6	33	17	0	0	2	34	0	1	.407	.302
Fisher, Matt	R-R	5-9	180	9-3-81	.125	.250	.000	2	8	2	1	0	0	0	0	1	0	0	0	2	1	0	.125	.222
Gaerlan, Armand	R-R	5-10	180	8-22-82	.218	.000	.237	28	101	14	22	4	1	2	15	7	0	1	3	19	8	1	.337	.261
Gamero, Jesus	R-R	6-1	170	1-24-84	.237	.279	.224	53	190	21	45	3	2	1	20	10	3	2	4	26	5	2	.289	.280
Gonzalez, Greg	L-L	5-11	165	10-1-82	.290	.294	.290	33	124	20	36	4	1	0	11	10	0	2	0	17	18	3	.339	.343
Grogan, Tim	L-R	6-0	195	3-30-84	.163	.286	.143	17	49	7	8	2	0	1	2	13	1	1	0	12	1	0	.265	.349
Holden, Joe	L-R	5-11	175	4-10-84	.291	.263	.297	64	223	33	65	7	5	0	15	22	3	2	1	30	22	8	.368	.361
Malo, Jonathan	R-R	6-1	175	9-29-83	.231	.286	.220	46	130	25	30	4	4	2	15	33	2	2	1	31	7	3	.369	.392
Matsui, Kazuo	B-R	5-10	185	10-23-75	.000	.000	.000	1	3	0	0	0	0	0	1	2	0	0	0	0	0	0	.000	.400
Mihalics, Joe	R-R	5-9	170	4-7-83	.125	.000	.158	12	24	4	3	0	0	0	2	6	0	1	0	6	2	0	.125	.300
Naccarata, Ivan	L-R	6-0	190	2-26-82	.234	.242	.232	55	158	18	37	7	1	5	20	33	1	0	1	30	4	3	.386	.368
Pacheco, Jonel	R-R	5-9	170	10-3-82	.274	.280	.272	54	201	34	55	10	0	6	30	17	5	1	1	35	20	6	.413	.344
Petersen, Josh	R-R	6-3	215	4-15-83	.286	.256	.295	46	182	27	52	13	1	3	22	6	4	1	0	34	1	3	.418	.323
Santana, Yury	R-R	6-1	170	8-15-82	.181	.111	.214	25	83	8	15	2	0	0	6	3	3	5	0	25	2	0	.205	.236
Santana, Luis	R-R	5-11	185	2-26-85	.111	.000	.118	8	18	0	2	0	0	0	1	2	0	0	0	6	0	0	.111	.200
Sharpe, Michael	L-R	6-0	190	3-10-83	.146	.222	.125	21	41	4	6	0	0	0	1	5	1	1	0	14	1	0	.146	.255
Stewart, Caleb	R-R	6-2	230	6-11-82	.272	.203	.291	74	265	39	72	23	2	10	45	47	3	0	2	64	6	3	.487	.385
Timmons, Jeff	R-R	6-1	195	10-2-82	.045	.250	.000	10	22	2	1	0	0	1	1	1	0	0	0	13	0	0	.182	.087
Ventura, Leivi	R-R	6-1	185	7-19-83	.286	.500	.200	2	7	0	2	0	0	0	2	0	1	0	0	4	0	0	.286	.375
Wabick, D.J.	L-R	6-2	185	5-30-84	.162	.250	.152	10	37	2	6	2	0	0	3	2	0	0	1	9	0	0	.216	.200

PITCHING	B-T	HT	WT	DOB	W	L	ERA	G	GS	CG	SV	IP	H	R	ER	HR	BB	SO	AVG	vLH	vRH	K/9	BB/9
Aguilar, Salvador	R-R	6-0	190	1-9-82	5	0	2.24	15	2	0	1	52	49	16	13	4	9	45	.253	.258	.250	7.74	1.55
Alfonzo, Edgar	L-L	5-10	170	12-14-84	0	1	5.40	2	0	0	0	5	6	3	3	0	1	4	.300	.375	.250	7.20	1.80
Almenar, Aristides	R-R	6-0	175	12-27-83	0	2	1.76	17	0	0	4	31	19	8	6	3	17	24	.174	.178	.172	7.04	4.99
Brown, Eric	R-R	6-6	225	2-23-84	3	2	3.97	16	0	0	4	34	33	16	15	3	7	31	.254	.355	.162	8.21	1.85

PITCHING	B-T	HT	WT	DOB	W	L	ERA	G	GS	CG	SV	IP	H	R	ER	HR	BB	SO	AVG	vLH	vRH	K/9	BB/9
D'Alessandro, Joe	R-R	5-11	195	2-20-84	1	2	5.14	17	0	0	2	21	20	16	12	1	10	22	.247	.063	.367	9.43	4.29
Domangue, Eric	L-L	6-5	200	8-16-84	1	0	6.97	15	0	0	0	21	25	16	16	0	17	12	.301	.409	.262	5.23	7.40
Eichelberger, Jared	R-R	6-7	210	8-4-83	0	0	0.00	1	0	0	0	2	2	0	0	0	1	0	.286	.333	.250	0.00	5.40
Hinchman, Grady	L-L	5-9	170	9-10-81	0	0	3.38	3	0	0	0	5	7	2	2	0	4	7	.350	.429	.308	11.81	6.75
Hope, Travis	R-R	6-3	200	1-29-81	5	1	3.95	22	0	0	2	41	41	21	18	2	16	26	.253	.284	.227	5.71	3.51
Joseph, Jake	R-R	6-1	205	1-24-78	0	1	1.80	6	0	0	0	10	7	2	2	0	6	5	.206	.308	.143	4.50	5.40
Landing, Jeff	R-R	6-3	190	7-31-83	6	6	2.87	16	16	0	0	85	78	35	27	3	27	59	.247	.234	.255	6.27	2.87
Manuel, Robert	R-R	6-3	190	7-9-83	0	0	1.80	2	0	0	0	5	5	1	1	1	0	5	.250	.100	.400	9.00	0.00
Marte, German	R-R	6-1	180	4-29-85	0	0	0.00	1	0	0	0	1	2	0	0	0	1	0	.500	.000	.667	0.00	9.00
Mateo, Waner	R-R	6-5	175	2-5-85	4	2	2.56	14	12	0	0	63	59	28	18	4	30	53	.240	.196	.266	7.53	4.26
Meyers, Ryan	L-R	6-5	195	7-17-85	1	5	4.08	9	8	0	0	35	40	25	16	1	14	18	.276	.278	.274	4.58	3.57
Parnell, Bobby	R-R	6-3	180	9-8-84	2	3	1.73	15	14	0	0	73	48	20	14	1	29	67	.185	.191	.181	8.26	3.58
Paulk, Robert	R-R	5-11	175	3-14-81	4	0	0.95	14	0	0	4	19	16	4	2	0	10	21	.222	.120	.277	9.95	4.74
Rengel, Orlando	R-R	6-1	172	5-11-83	0	0	3.51	6	6	0	0	26	24	12	10	1	9	22	.255	.234	.277	7.71	3.16
Reyes, Jorge	R-R	6-4	170	5-15-84	4	5	5.20	13	13	1	0	62	80	40	36	5	19	35	.313	.306	.317	5.05	2.74
Risinger, Kyle	R-R	6-4	200	8-15-84	1	3	4.04	15	0	0	0	36	47	23	16	1	15	23	.324	.362	.299	5.80	3.79
Ruckle, Jacob	R-R	6-1	180	5-27-86	0	0	0.00	2	0	0	0	2	1	0	0	0	0	2	.125	.250	.000	7.71	0.00
Tomasiewicz, Kevin	L-L	6-2	225	9-17-83	3	3	5.62	20	5	0	3	42	56	32	26	5	18	37	.324	.294	.331	7.99	3.89
Weintraub, Jason	R-R	6-3	165	8-13-82	0	0	4.70	4	0	0	0	8	7	4	4	0	5	9	.241	.308	.188	10.57	5.87

GAMES BY POSITION: C—Arroyo 18, Butera 54, Cummins 1, L. Santana 3, Timmons 8. **1B**—Anderson 1, Bergeron 2, Evans 56, Petersen 14, Wabick 5. **2B**—Chavez 5, Gaerlan 27, Malo 15, Matsui 1, Mihalics 4, Naccarata 33. **3B**—Anderson 22, Grogan 16, Naccarata 11, Petersen 28, Ventura 2. **SS**—Chavez 18, Gaerlan 1, Malo 30, Mihalics 6, L. Santana 2, Y. Santana 25. **OF**—Brown 15, Gamero 50, Gonzalez 32, Holden 58, Pacheco 53, Sharpe 19, Stewart 22.

KINGSPORT METS — Rookie

APPALACHIAN LEAGUE

BATTING	B-T	HT	WT	DOB	AVG	vLH	vRH	G	AB	R	H	2B	3B	HR	RBI	BB	HBP	SH	SF	SO	SB	CS	SLG	OBP
Anderson, Matt	L-R	6-2	205	12-9-82	.314	.364	.289	47	169	27	53	8	0	5	30	15	4	0	2	22	0	3	.450	.379
Austin, Parris	R-R	6-2	185	12-13-85	.367	.357	.371	13	49	7	18	5	1	1	9	3	1	1	1	12	4	1	.571	.407
Brown, Kyle	R-R	6-0	187	10-4-81	.279	.154	.333	15	43	16	12	4	0	0	4	11	3	0	0	10	12	0	.372	.456
Castro, Jose	B-R	5-8	160	11-5-86	.286	.500	.125	8	14	1	4	0	0	0	1	2	1	0	0	1	0	1	.286	.412
Coronado, Jose	B-R	6-1	175	4-13-86	.266	.324	.245	39	139	24	37	5	1	1	8	22	4	7	0	27	6	4	.338	.382
Cruz, Elvis	R-R	6-2	195	11-23-83	.148	.196	.113	38	108	14	16	4	0	4	16	10	0	0	0	29	0	1	.296	.220
Cummins, Daniel	R-R	5-9	190	12-11-82	.222	.000	.222	2	9	3	2	1	0	1	3	0	0	0	0	0	0	0	.667	.222
Evans, Nick	R-R	6-2	180	1-30-86	.344	.294	.362	15	64	11	22	7	0	6	22	4	0	0	0	17	1	0	.734	.382
Gonzalez, Greg	L-L	5-11	165	10-1-82	.357	.289	.386	33	126	26	45	8	2	0	7	8	2	2	0	13	15	6	.452	.404
Henry, Sean	R-R	5-10	154	8-18-85	.255	.342	.225	42	149	24	38	7	1	5	31	22	2	2	4	43	15	1	.416	.350
Lietz, Todd	R-R	6-0	175	12-21-82	.175	.211	.143	11	40	6	7	0	0	0	2	0	1	0	0	6	0	1	.175	.195
Manuel, Anthony	R-R	6-0	175	8-17-82	.246	.306	.218	36	114	18	28	3	0	1	11	12	4	3	1	17	1	2	.298	.336
Martinez, Joan	B-R	5-11	175	5-7-84	.233	.283	.205	37	129	15	30	3	1	5	20	3	2	1	1	36	0	1	.388	.259
Mateo, Jose	R-R	6-1	175	6-18-83	.270	.250	.279	37	126	20	34	7	0	4	19	18	1	1	1	31	5	4	.421	.363
McCraw, Sean	L-R	6-0	185	3-11-86	.218	.120	.250	32	101	8	22	1	0	1	7	10	4	0	0	27	0	0	.257	.313
Montero, Juan	R-R	6-2	165	10-5-85	.157	.182	.146	19	70	8	11	1	0	2	6	3	2	1	0	30	1	1	.257	.213
Oliveros, Riky	R-R	6-2	175	9-23-83	.286	.333	.262	56	210	22	60	12	0	4	31	12	3	0	2	38	4	1	.400	.330
Piazza, Thomas	L-R	6-0	200	10-9-81	.150	.200	.133	19	60	3	9	2	0	0	2	2	0	0	0	25	0	0	.183	.177
Santana, Luis	R-R	5-11	185	2-26-85	.205	.133	.250	14	39	4	8	1	1	1	4	1	0	0	0	6	1	0	.359	.225
Santana, Yury	R-R	6-1	170	8-15-82	.243	.182	.269	12	37	7	9	6	0	0	5	2	1	1	0	11	0	0	.405	.300
Wabick, D.J.	L-R	6-2	185	5-30-84	.303	.190	.341	45	165	27	50	9	0	0	20	14	3	0	0	25	0	0	.358	.368
Wells, Cory	R-R	6-0	185	11-18-84	.226	.167	.256	51	177	26	40	13	0	4	18	9	2	0	1	51	5	4	.367	.270
Werman, Kyle	B-R	5-8	150	4-15-82	.118	.071	.150	11	34	5	4	1	0	0	1	3	2	0	0	6	1	0	.147	.231
Wyrick, Josh	L-L	6-3	190	3-11-82	.203	.222	.198	39	123	17	25	6	2	2	14	7	1	0	1	29	6	0	.333	.250

PITCHING	B-T	HT	WT	DOB	W	L	ERA	G	GS	CG	SV	IP	H	R	ER	HR	BB	SO	AVG	vLH	vRH	K/9	BB/9
Arizmendi, Daniel	L-L	5-11	200	6-13-84	4	4	4.63	17	7	1	1	45	62	26	23	4	17	35	.333	.346	.331	7.05	3.43
Beras, Alexis	R-R	6-5	215	9-24-83	1	2	5.73	19	0	0	0	33	30	22	21	3	17	32	.246	.182	.282	8.73	4.64
Castillo, Jonathan	R-R	5-11	195	12-27-83	2	3	2.04	11	11	1	0	53	42	17	12	3	16	41	.213	.149	.246	6.96	2.72
Childress, Dustin	L-L	6-0	182	5-19-83	1	5	6.98	16	6	0	0	40	50	34	31	3	17	34	.314	.435	.294	7.65	3.83
Eichelberger, Jared	R-R	6-7	210	8-4-83	0	1	5.96	17	1	0	0	26	30	24	17	5	17	18	.278	.308	.261	6.31	5.96
Frias, Jusef	R-R	6-2	180	12-31-84	1	5	6.99	13	13	0	0	55	70	44	43	3	24	43	.310	.376	.270	6.99	3.90
Gonzalez, Jose	R-R	6-2	170	7-18-85	2	4	7.13	13	12	0	0	53	62	49	42	6	29	35	.295	.338	.269	5.94	4.92
Harrington, Jake	R-R	6-6	210	2-18-85	1	0	7.20	6	0	0	0	10	18	12	8	0	5	6	.400	.316	.462	5.40	4.50
Heil, Ryan	R-R	6-4	215	11-7-81	4	4	4.44	19	0	0	3	26	35	21	13	1	7	17	.310	.319	.303	5.81	2.39
Koons, David	R-R	6-1	180	3-13-84	4	2	3.46	24	0	0	2	39	38	15	15	2	9	25	.250	.176	.287	5.77	2.08
Marte, German	R-R	6-1	180	4-29-85	3	2	2.91	21	3	0	4	43	29	16	14	1	12	53	.190	.204	.182	11.01	2.49
Perdomo, Javier	R-R	6-0	170	9-24-84	1	1	6.69	22	0	0	0	39	56	34	29	5	15	19	.331	.350	.321	4.38	3.46
Quaglieri, Will	R-R	6-3	210	3-14-81	0	0	0.00	1	0	0	0	2	1	1	0	0	0	1	.111	.200	.000	4.50	0.00
Serfass, Joey	R-R	6-3	215	5-6-81	1	0	0.00	7	0	0	3	13	6	2	0	0	1	10	.140	.125	.148	7.11	0.71
Simmons, Jeramy	R-R	6-0	200	9-30-82	1	5	4.26	13	12	0	0	57	58	39	27	5	15	47	.253	.289	.227	7.42	2.37
Wladyka, Jim	R-R	6-1	190	5-15-83	2	2	1.98	18	3	0	0	50	47	22	11	5	18	40	.249	.215	.266	7.20	3.24

GAMES BY POSITION: C—Cummins 2, Martinez 25, McCraw 25, Piazza 9, L. Santana 14. **1B**—Evans 11, Oliveros 28, Wabick 33. **2B**—Castro 6, Henry 23, Manuel 30, Y. Santana 1, Werman 11. **3B**—Anderson 46, Lietz 4, Manuel 7, Oliveros 10, Y. Santana 6. **SS**—Coronado 39, Henry 19, Lietz 7, Y. Santana 7. **OF**—Austin 13, Brown 12, Cruz 27, Gonzalez 32, Mateo 34, Montero 19, Wells 47, Wyrick 33.

GCL METS — Rookie

GULF COAST LEAGUE

BATTING	B-T	HT	WT	DOB	AVG	vLH	vRH	G	AB	R	H	2B	3B	HR	RBI	BB	HBP	SH	SF	SO	SB	CS	SLG	OBP
Austin, Parris	R-R	6-2	185	12-13-85	.287	.250	.306	29	87	20	25	3	0	1	8	4	1	1	1	18	8	1	.356	.323
Billingslea, Courtney	R-R	6-6	200	2-16-86	.233	.152	.265	33	116	16	27	5	1	5	17	10	5	4	1	48	2	1	.422	.318
Blaquiere, Jean Luc	R-R	6-0	196	2-27-86	.212	.200	.219	21	52	6	11	1	0	1	7	6	1	0	0	17	0	0	.288	.305
Bucce, Yasmil	R-R	6-1	180	8-29-84	.337	.150	.390	34	98	14	33	6	0	1	17	19	5	0	1	21	1	0	.429	.463
Cain, Greg	R-R	6-1	205	5-1-87	.202	.222	.200	30	94	13	19	5	1	1	11	20	4	2	2	39	7	3	.309	.358

BATTING	B-T	HT	WT	DOB	AVG	vLH	vRH	G	AB	R	H	2B	3B	HR	RBI	BB	HBP	SH	SF	SO	SB	CS	SLG	OBP
Cairo, Miguel	R-R	6-1	210	5-4-74	.308	.200	.375	3	13	3	4	1	0	0	0	0	0	0	0	0	0	0	.385	.308
Castro, Jose	B-R	5-10	153	5-13-83	.293	.368	.247	31	116	15	34	3	2	1	10	6	6	5	0	9	2	0	.379	.359
Contreras, Junior	R-R	6-5	220	1-12-86	.291	.190	.330	46	148	28	43	7	0	8	31	26	2	0	1	49	1	1	.500	.401
Coronado, Jose	B-R	6-1	175	4-13-86	.404	.429	.394	11	47	9	19	1	1	0	4	1	1	1	0	9	1	1	.468	.429
Cummins, Daniel	R-R	5-9	190	12-11-82	.327	.406	.293	32	107	21	35	8	1	1	19	5	1	3	0	24	0	1	.449	.363
Garcia, Emmanuel	L-R	6-2	180	3-4-86	.339	.358	.331	45	186	43	63	7	0	2	30	21	3	1	1	36	17	1	.409	.412
Maldonado, Brahiam	R-R	6-0	185	9-18-85	.256	.207	.273	33	117	23	30	7	1	1	21	17	2	1	2	36	8	1	.359	.355
Mateo, Jose	R-R	6-1	175	6-18-83	.271	.273	.271	21	59	13	16	3	0	2	10	11	1	2	2	9	5	1	.424	.384
Matsui, Kazuo	B-R	5-10	185	10-23-75	.444	.400	.500	3	9	3	4	0	0	1	3	1	1	0	0	3	0	0	.778	.545
Mientkiewicz, Doug	L-R	6-2	205	6-19-74	.500	.000	.556	4	10	2	5	1	0	1	5	4	0	0	0	1	0	0	.900	.643
Montero, Juan	R-R	6-2	165	10-5-85	.260	.150	.302	20	73	9	19	5	1	0	12	2	1	4	1	27	2	1	.356	.286
Schemmel, Jonathan	R-R	5-11	190	1-27-83	.347	.269	.378	34	101	22	35	5	2	0	20	30	4	4	2	16	2	0	.436	.504
Spath, Matt	R-R	6-2	185	10-21-86	.233	.233	.232	29	86	18	20	2	7	0	11	13	1	1	0	28	3	2	.419	.340
Thole, Josh	L-R	6-1	190	10-28-86	.269	.310	.243	35	104	14	28	2	1	1	12	20	4	2	0	11	1	1	.337	.406
Ventura, Leivi	R-R	6-1	185	7-19-83	.263	.238	.273	46	175	34	46	6	1	7	33	10	7	1	1	35	4	2	.429	.326
Wallace, James	R-R	6-3	220	3-27-81	.333	.000	.000	1	3	0	1	0	0	0	0	0	0	0	0	1	0	0	.333	.333

PITCHING	B-T	HT	WT	DOB	W	L	ERA	G	GS	CG	SV	IP	H	R	ER	HR	BB	SO	AVG	vLH	vRH	K/9	BB/9
Appell, Josh	L-L	6-1	195	6-23-83	3	0	4.91	11	0	0	1	18	7	10	10	1	14	24	.117	.143	.113	11.78	6.87
Battista, Michael	R-R	6-2	210	1-16-83	1	0	6.16	10	0	0	0	19	26	15	13	3	3	15	.317	.429	.259	7.11	1.42
Durkin, Matt	R-R	6-4	220	2-22-83	0	0	0.00	1	1	0	0	3	2	0	0	0	0	4	.200	.250	.167	12.00	0.00
Eager, Blake	R-R	6-3	205	5-19-82	0	0	5.79	2	2	0	0	5	6	3	3	0	0	4	.300	.429	.231	7.71	0.00
Figueroa, Jorge	R-R	6-1	194	2-24-85	0	1	4.13	15	0	0	3	24	26	12	11	0	11	24	.286	.289	.283	9.00	4.13
Hakey, Patrick	L-R	6-7	210	1-21-82	1	2	14.63	6	0	0	0	8	12	14	13	0	14	6	.353	.389	.313	6.75	15.75
Harrington, Jake	R-R	6-6	210	2-18-85	1	2	4.85	9	3	0	0	26	27	19	14	1	12	14	.267	.220	.314	4.85	4.15
Hinchman, Grady	L-L	5-9	170	9-10-81	2	1	1.85	14	0	0	5	24	18	6	5	1	12	38	.209	.111	.221	14.05	4.44
Hirota, Rodrigo	R-R	6-2	190	4-29-84	3	3	5.34	8	4	0	0	32	35	19	19	2	6	21	.280	.318	.259	5.91	1.69
Holquin, Steven	R-R	6-3	215	6-30-85	2	1	6.85	11	2	0	1	22	28	23	17	2	6	11	.295	.306	.288	4.43	2.42
Joseph, Jake	R-R	6-1	205	1-24-78	0	0	1.80	4	2	0	0	5	4	1	1	1	0	4	.211	.111	.300	7.20	0.00
Jostock, Will	R-R	6-6	190	9-10-86	1	0	4.87	9	0	0	0	20	22	13	11	1	7	18	.289	.294	.286	7.97	3.10
Lawrence, Horace	L-L	6-4	215	1-6-81	0	0	7.94	5	0	0	1	6	8	6	5	2	4	5	.308	.000	.320	7.94	6.35
Manuel, Robert	R-R	6-3	190	7-9-83	8	1	2.06	12	5	0	0	57	55	19	13	2	4	49	.250	.214	.267	7.78	0.64
McIntyre, Robert	R-R	5-10	170	12-8-80	4	2	4.54	11	6	0	0	42	44	21	21	1	18	38	.273	.259	.280	8.21	3.89
Medina, Josvic	R-R	6-3	190	5-19-84	1	0	2.70	8	0	0	0	17	12	7	5	2	8	9	.203	.250	.171	4.86	4.32
Meyers, Ryan	L-R	6-5	195	7-17-85	0	0	5.84	5	4	0	0	12	13	9	8	2	6	12	.271	.250	.281	8.76	4.38
Muniz, Carlos	R-R	6-1	180	3-12-81	0	1	16.20	2	0	0	0	2	6	4	3	0	0	0	.545	.667	.400	0.00	0.00
Niese, Jon	L-L	6-3	190	10-27-86	1	0	3.65	7	5	0	0	25	23	10	10	1	10	24	.245	.143	.263	8.76	3.65
Paulk, Robert	R-R	5-11	175	3-14-81	0	0	0.00	1	1	0	0	3	4	2	0	0	0	1	.333	.286	.400	3.00	0.00
Pinango, Miguel	R-R	6-1	160	1-20-83	0	0	0.00	1	1	0	0	4	3	0	0	0	0	4	.214	.400	.111	9.00	0.00
Quaglieri, Will	R-R	6-3	210	3-14-81	0	0	9.00	1	0	0	0	1	2	1	1	0	0	2	.500	.000	.500	18.00	0.00
Riggan, Jerrod	R-R	6-3	195	5-16-74	1	0	0.00	6	3	0	0	7	3	1	0	0	3	11	.125	.100	.143	14.14	3.86
Ruckle, Jacob	R-R	6-1	180	5-27-86	8	1	2.10	11	8	0	0	56	49	20	13	2	10	33	.231	.348	.175	5.34	1.62
Williams, Joe	L-L	6-2	220	4-8-81	0	0	0.00	3	3	0	0	8	8	0	0	0	3	7	.267	.250	.273	7.88	3.38
Wilson, Brandon	R-R	6-4	195	9-1-82	0	1	5.71	4	3	0	1	17	17	13	11	2	2	17	.243	.229	.257	8.83	1.04

GAMES BY POSITION: C—Blaquiere 20, Bucce 29, Cummins 12, Thole 7. **1B**—Bucce 1, Cain 1, Contreras 33, Cummins 4, Maldonado 1, Mientkiewicz 3, Thole 21. **2B**—Cairo 2, Castro 19, Cummins 1, Garcia 6, Matsui 2, Schemmel 27. **3B**—Cummins 10, Schemmel 2, Ventura 44. **SS**—Castro 12, Coronado 8, Cummins 1, Garcia 36. **OF**—Austin 26, Billingslea 30, Cain 23, Cummins 1, Maldonado 28, Mateo 19, Montero 16, Spath 27.

NEW YORK YANKEES

BY GEORGE KING

Can a season that produced 95 wins and an eighth straight American League East title be called a disappointment?

When that season belongs to the Yankees, the answer is a resounding yes. Every February when the Yankees convene in Tampa, their only goal is to win the World Series. So 2005, the fifth straight season the Yankees didn't add their 27th World Series title, couldn't be viewed as a success. Certainly not by the high standards set by owner George Steinbrenner.

Predictably, the Yankees were devastated after being eliminated in Game Five of the Division Series by the Angels.

"I am terribly disappointed," manager Joe Torre said afterward. "I am proud of the way the ballclub came together. They were very unselfish. I feel deep disappointment. I wanted this badly—it's tough."

Was it worse than flushing a 3-0 lead to the Red Sox in the 2004 ALCS?

"Yes, (2004) was a gradual thing," Torre said. "Deep down I thought we would find a way to get it done."

Torre was so down he barely left his Westchester, N.Y., home for a week. Inside, he didn't sleep, contemplating his future even though he is owed $13.1 million for 2006 and 2007.

Finally, seven days after the final out, Torre flew to Tampa and met one-on-one with Steinbrenner. Steinbrenner told Torre he trusted him with the Yankees, and the first big step toward 2006 was taken.

Beyond the gloom and doom that always smothers the Yankees when they don't win the World Series—let alone when they get eliminated in the first round—there were positives.

On Aug. 18 they trailed the Red Sox by 4½ games and went 30-13 the rest of the way to tie Boston with a 95-76 mark. Since the Yankees took the head-to-head season series, 10-9, the Yankees were crowned AL East champs.

The strong final six weeks convinced Torre and many of his players that with the hot bats and Randy Johnson pitching like the future Hall of Famer he had been the year before in Arizona and throughout his career, they had a serious shot at reaching the World Series. That's why the loss to the Angels ripped their stomachs up.

Much of the blame fell on Alex Rodriguez' shoulders. The MVP candidate, who batted .321 with an AL-leading 48 homers and 130 RBIs in the regular season, hit .133 (2-for-15) and didn't drive in a run against the Angels.

Rodriguez wasn't alone in the blame game. Johnson, who finished the season 17-8 and on a six-game winning streak, was spanked in Game Three, lasting three innings and giving the Yankees no chance of taking a 2-1 lead in the best-of-five series.

Hideki Matsui, a free agent in waiting, batted .200 (4-for-20) and Bernie Williams likely ended his Yankees career with a .211 (4-for-19) series.

As bad as it was at the end, there were bright spots. And two of the biggest were supplied from an unexpected source: the beleaguered Yankees farm system.

In early May, general manager Brian Cashman looked at the Yankees' 10-15 record and decided Tony Womack, who was signed to a two-year, $4 million contract in the offseason, wasn't helping at second base and recalled Robinson Cano from Triple-A Columbus.

The player Arizona didn't want in the Johnson trade looked like a veteran, not like the raw rookie he was. When the season ended, Cano's .297 average, 14 homers and flashy defense turned him into a rookie of the year candidate.

There was more good news in the farm system, as every Yankees affiliate except high Class A Tampa finished with a winning record. Two affiliates even won league titles, as the short-season Staten Island Yankees took home their third New York-Penn League title in six years, and the Rookie-level Gulf Coast League Yankees beat the Red Sox and Mets on their way to the league championship.

PLAYERS OF THE YEAR

MAJOR LEAGUE: Mariano Rivera, rhp

Several Yankees had big seasons offensively in 2005, but Rivera almost single-handedly stabilized New York's beleaguered pitching staff. He led all big league closers with a 1.38 ERA and finished third with 43 saves, carrying the Yankees to another American League East title.

MINOR LEAGUE: Philip Hughes, rhp

STEVE MOORE

Hughes battled through shoulder tendinitis and a tired arm in his first full pro season to go 9-1, 2.19 with 93 strikeouts in 86 innings between low Class A Charleston and high A Tampa. The 2004 first-round pick held opponents to a paltry .182 average and secured his place as the Yankees' top prospect.

ORGANIZATION LEADERS

BATTING		
***AVG**	Nunez, Eduardo, Staten Island	.313
R	Battle, Tim, Charleston	97
H	Thompson, Kevin, Columbus/Trenton	155
TB	Duncan, Shelley, Trenton	263
2B	Thompson, Kevin, Columbus/Trenton	45
3B	Battle, Tim, Charleston	11
HR	Duncan, Shelley, Trenton	34
RBI	Duncan, Shelley, Trenton	92
BB	Thompson, Kevin, Columbus/Trenton	76
SO	Battle, Tim, Charleston	195
SB	Christian, Justin, Charleston/Columbus/Tampa	55
***OBP**	Thompson, Kevin, Columbus/Trenton	.394
***SLG**	Phillips, Andy, Columbus	.573
PITCHING		
W	Karstens, Jeff, Trenton	12
L	Jones, Jason, Tampa	13
	Marquez, Jeff, Charleston	13
#ERA	Beam, T.J., Charleston/Tampa	1.62
G	Bean, Colter, Columbus	65
CG	Five tied at	1
SV	Martinez, Mike, Charleston	30
IP	Karstens, Jeff, Trenton	169
BB	Gomez, Abel, Charleston/GCL/Tampa	75
SO	Clippard, Tyler, Charleston/Columbus/Tampa	181

*Minimum 250 at-bats. #Minimum 75 innings.

NEW YORK YANKEES

Manager: Joe Torre.

2005 Record: 95-67, .586 (Tied-1st, AL East).

BATTING	B-T	HT	WT	DOB	AVG	vLH	vRH	G	AB	R	H	2B	3B	HR	RBI	BB	HBP	SH	SF	SO	SB	CS	SLG	OBP
Bellhorn, Mark	B-R	6-1	205	8-23-74	.118	.143	.100	9	17	2	2	0	0	1	2	3	0	0	0	3	0	0	.294	.250
2-team (85 Boston)					.210	.228	.201	94	300	43	63	20	0	8	30	52	0	0	3	112	3	0	.357	.324
Cabrera, Melky	B-L	5-11	170	8-11-84	.211	.333	.154	6	19	1	4	0	0	0	0	0	0	0	0	2	0	0	.211	.211
Cano, Robinson	L-R	6-0	170	10-22-82	.297	.270	.307	132	522	78	155	34	4	14	62	16	3	7	3	68	1	3	.458	.320
Crosby, Bubba	L-L	5-11	185	8-11-76	.276	.273	.276	76	98	15	27	0	1	1	6	4	0	1	0	14	4	1	.327	.304
Escalona, Felix	R-R	6-0	190	3-12-79	.286	.222	.400	10	14	0	4	1	0	0	2	1	1	1	0	4	0	0	.357	.375
Flaherty, John	R-R	6-1	200	10-21-67	.165	.161	.167	47	127	10	21	5	0	2	11	6	1	2	2	26	0	0	.252	.206
Giambi, Jason	L-R	6-3	230	1-8-71	.271	.261	.276	139	417	74	113	14	0	32	87	108	19	0	1	109	0	0	.535	.440
Jeter, Derek	R-R	6-3	195	6-26-74	.309	.317	.306	159	654	122	202	25	5	19	70	77	11	7	3	117	14	5	.450	.389
Johnson, Russ	R-R	5-10	185	2-22-73	.222	.182	.286	22	18	5	4	2	0	0	0	1	1	0	0	4	0	0	.333	.300
Lawton, Matt	L-R	5-10	190	11-3-71	.125	.118	.129	21	48	6	6	0	0	2	4	7	2	0	0	8	1	0	.250	.263
Martinez, Tino	L-R	6-2	230	12-7-67	.241	.217	.250	131	303	43	73	9	0	17	49	38	3	0	4	54	2	0	.439	.328
Matsui, Hideki	L-R	6-2	230	6-12-74	.305	.354	.281	162	629	108	192	45	3	23	116	63	3	0	8	78	2	2	.496	.367
Nieves, Wil	R-R	5-11	190	9-25-77	.000	.000	.000	3	4	0	0	0	0	0	0	0	0	0	0	1	0	0	.000	.000
Phillips, Andy	R-R	6-0	205	4-6-77	.150	.150	.150	27	40	7	6	4	0	1	4	1	0	0	0	13	0	0	.325	.171
Posada, Jorge	B-R	6-2	205	8-17-71	.262	.281	.251	142	474	67	124	23	0	19	71	66	2	0	4	94	1	0	.430	.352
Reese, Kevin	L-L	5-11	195	3-11-78	.000	.000	.000	2	1	0	0	0	0	0	0	1	0	0	0	1	0	0	.000	.500
Rodriguez, Alex	R-R	6-3	225	7-27-75	.321	.300	.327	162	605	124	194	29	1	48	130	91	16	0	3	139	21	6	.610	.421
Sanchez, Rey	R-R	5-9	170	10-5-67	.279	.364	.190	23	43	7	12	1	0	0	2	2	1	2	0	3	0	1	.302	.326
Sheffield, Gary	R-R	6-0	215	11-18-68	.291	.359	.266	154	584	104	170	27	0	34	123	78	8	0	5	76	10	2	.512	.379
Sierra, Ruben	B-R	6-1	215	10-6-65	.229	.221	.237	61	170	14	39	12	0	4	29	9	0	0	2	41	0	0	.371	.265
Vento, Mike	R-R	6-0	195	5-25-78	.000	.000	.000	2	2	0	0	0	0	0	0	0	0	0	0	1	0	0	.000	.000
Williams, Bernie	B-R	6-2	205	9-13-68	.249	.231	.261	141	485	53	121	19	1	12	64	53	1	1	6	75	1	2	.367	.321
Womack, Tony	L-R	5-9	170	9-25-69	.249	.254	.248	108	329	46	82	8	1	0	15	12	1	7	2	49	27	5	.280	.276

PITCHING	B-T	HT	WT	DOB	W	L	ERA	G	GS	CG	SV	IP	H	R	ER	HR	BB	SO	AVG	vLH	vRH	K/9	BB/9
Anderson, Jason	L-R	6-0	170	6-9-79	1	0	7.94	3	0	0	0	6	4	5	5	0	7	2	.200	.125	.250	3.18	11.12
Bean, Colter	L-R	6-6	255	1-16-77	0	0	4.50	1	0	0	0	2	1	1	1	0	2	2	.143	.500	.000	9.00	9.00
Brown, Kevin	R-R	6-4	220	3-14-65	4	7	6.50	13	13	0	0	73	107	57	53	5	19	50	.341	.335	.347	6.14	2.33
Chacon, Shawn	R-R	6-3	220	12-23-77	7	3	2.85	14	12	0	0	79	66	26	25	7	30	40	.225	.225	.225	4.56	3.42
De Paula, Jorge	R-R	6-1	160	11-10-78	0	0	8.10	3	0	0	0	7	8	6	6	2	3	3	.296	.313	.273	4.05	4.05
Embree, Alan	L-L	6-2	190	1-23-70	1	1	7.53	24	0	0	0	14	20	14	12	2	3	8	.328	.344	.310	5.02	1.88
2-team (43 Boston)					2	5	7.62	67	0	0	1	52	62	47	44	10	14	38	.297	.317	.278	6.58	2.42
Franklin, Wayne	L-L	6-2	200	3-9-74	0	1	6.39	13	0	0	0	13	11	12	9	1	8	10	.239	.286	.200	7.11	5.68
Gordon, Tom	R-R	5-10	190	11-18-67	5	4	2.57	79	0	0	2	81	59	25	23	8	29	69	.203	.187	.217	7.70	3.24
Graman, Alex	L-L	6-4	210	11-17-77	0	0	13.50	2	0	0	0	1	3	2	2	1	2	0	.429	.750	.000	0.00	13.50
Groom, Buddy	L-L	6-2	205	7-10-65	1	0	4.91	24	0	0	0	26	32	14	14	3	7	13	.305	.265	.339	4.56	2.45
Henn, Sean	R-L	6-5	200	4-23-81	0	3	11.12	3	3	0	0	11	18	16	14	3	11	3	.360	.429	.333	2.38	8.74
Johnson, Randy	R-L	6-10	230	9-10-63	17	8	3.79	34	34	4	0	226	207	102	95	32	47	211	.243	.185	.257	8.42	1.87
Karsay, Steve	R-R	6-3	215	3-24-72	0	0	6.00	6	0	0	0	6	10	5	4	0	2	5	.385	.357	.417	7.50	3.00
Leiter, Al	L-L	6-3	220	10-23-65	4	5	5.49	16	10	0	0	62	66	42	38	4	38	45	.268	.221	.290	6.50	5.49
May, Darrell	L-L	6-2	185	6-13-72	0	1	16.71	2	1	0	0	7	14	13	13	4	3	3	.400	.333	.435	3.86	3.86
Mendoza, Ramiro	R-R	6-2	190	6-15-72	0	0	18.00	1	0	0	0	1	2	2	2	1	0	1	.400	.000	.500	9.00	0.00
Mussina, Mike	L-R	6-2	190	12-8-68	13	8	4.41	30	30	2	0	180	199	93	88	23	47	142	.284	.282	.286	7.11	2.35
Pavano, Carl	R-R	6-5	240	1-8-76	4	6	4.77	17	17	1	0	100	129	66	53	17	18	56	.315	.335	.294	5.04	1.62
Proctor, Scott	R-R	6-1	200	1-2-77	1	0	6.04	29	1	0	0	45	46	32	30	10	17	36	.257	.315	.217	7.25	3.43
Quantrill, Paul	L-R	6-1	200	11-3-68	1	0	6.75	22	0	0	0	32	48	24	24	5	7	11	.361	.382	.346	3.09	1.97
Redding, Tim	R-R	6-0	195	2-12-78	0	1	54.00	1	1	0	0	1	4	6	6	0	4	2	.571	.600	.500	18.00	36.00
Rivera, Mariano	R-R	6-2	185	11-29-69	7	4	1.38	71	0	0	43	78	50	18	12	2	18	80	.177	.177	.176	9.19	2.07
Rodriguez, Felix	R-R	6-1	210	9-9-72	0	0	5.01	34	0	0	0	32	33	18	18	2	20	18	.264	.239	.278	5.01	5.57
Small, Aaron	R-R	6-5	220	11-23-71	10	0	3.20	15	9	1	0	76	71	27	27	4	24	37	.250	.252	.248	4.38	2.84
Stanton, Mike	L-L	6-1	215	6-2-67	1	2	7.07	28	0	0	0	14	17	11	11	1	6	12	.298	.176	.478	7.71	3.86
Sturtze, Tanyon	R-R	6-5	225	10-12-70	5	3	4.73	64	1	0	1	78	76	43	41	10	27	45	.257	.233	.273	5.19	3.12
Wang, Chien-Ming	R-R	6-3	200	3-31-80	8	5	4.02	18	17	0	0	116	113	58	52	9	32	47	.256	.258	.254	3.64	2.48
Wright, Jaret	R-R	6-2	230	12-29-75	5	5	6.08	13	13	0	0	64	81	51	43	8	32	34	.313	.273	.358	4.81	4.52

FIELDING

Catcher	PCT	G	PO	A	E	DP	PB
Flaherty	.994	45	291	19	2	3	3
Nieves	1.000	3	11	0	0	0	0
Posada	.996	133	718	76	3	6	8

First Base	PCT	G	PO	A	E	DP
Escalona	1.000	1	2	0	0	0
Flaherty	1.000	1	1	0	0	0
Giambi	.988	78	581	19	7	50
R. Johnson	1.000	7	30	0	0	5
Martinez	.991	122	797	49	8	73
Phillips	.987	19	75	2	1	7

Second Base	PCT	G	PO	A	E	DP
Bellhorn	.938	2	4	11	1	2
Cano	.974	131	258	391	17	77
Escalona	1.000	1	1	4	0	1
R. Johnson	.000	1	0	0	0	0
Sanchez	.977	9	18	24	1	5
Womack	.992	24	42	89	1	22

Third Base	PCT	G	PO	A	E	DP
Bellhorn	1.000	4	1	3	0	0
Escalona	1.000	3	0	1	0	0
R. Johnson	1.000	8	1	2	0	0
Phillips	.000	1	0	0	0	0
Rodriguez	.971	161	115	288	12	26
Sanchez	.000	1	0	0	0	0

Shortstop	PCT	G	PO	A	E	DP
Bellhorn	1.000	2	2	2	0	0
Escalona	1.000	5	8	8	0	3
Jeter	.979	157	262	454	15	96
Rodriguez	1.000	3	1	2	0	0
Sanchez	.955	10	7	14	1	4

Outfield	PCT	G	PO	A	E	DP
Cabrera	1.000	6	9	0	0	0
Crosby	1.000	67	83	2	0	1
R. Johnson	1.000	3	1	0	0	0
Lawton	.969	19	31	0	1	0
Matsui	.990	142	279	7	3	1
Phillips	.000	1	0	0	0	0
Reese	1.000	2	2	0	0	0
Sheffield	.988	131	239	5	3	0
Sierra	.958	18	23	0	1	0
Vento	1.000	2	2	1	0	1
Williams	.991	112	226	6	2	1
Womack	.983	66	113	2	2	0

FARM SYSTEM

General Manager: Brian Cashman. **Director, Player Development:** Pat Roessler. **Scouting Director:** Damon Oppenheimer.

Class	Farm Team	League	W	L	Pct.	Finish*	Manager(s)	Affiliate Since
AAA	Columbus (Ohio) Clippers	International	77	67	.535	5th (14)	Bucky Dent	1979
AA	Trenton (N.J.) Thunder	Eastern	74	68	.521	**t-4th (12)**	Bill Masse	2003
High A	Tampa (Fla.) Yankees	Florida State	56	79	.415	11th (12)	Joe Breeden	1994
Low A	Charleston (S.C.) Riverdogs	South Atlantic	80	58	.580	**2nd (14)**	Bill Mosiello	2005
SS A	Staten Island (N.Y.) Yankees	New York-Penn	52	24	.684	**+1st (14)**	Andy Stankiewicz	1999
Rookie	Tampa (Fla.) Yankees	Gulf Coast	33	20	.623	**+2nd (12)**	Oscar Acosta	1980

*Finish in overall standings (No. of teams in league)/Playoff teams in **boldface** +League champion

DAVID SEELIG

Alex Rodriguez: Set team record for most homers by righthander

MICKEY WEINSTEIN

Eduardo Nunez: A New York-Penn League all-star at 18

COLUMBUS CLIPPERS — Class AAA

INTERNATIONAL LEAGUE

BATTING	B-T	HT	WT	DOB	AVG	vLH	vRH	G	AB	R	H	2B	3B	HR	RBI	BB	HBP	SH	SF	SO	SB	CS	SLG	OBP
Cabrera, Melky	B-L	5-11	170	8-11-84	.248	.409	.203	26	101	15	25	3	0	3	17	9	0	2	0	15	2	0	.366	.309
Cannizaro, Andy	R-R	5-10	170	12-19-78	.253	.268	.246	56	170	22	43	10	2	1	18	17	9	6	0	11	1	1	.353	.352
Cano, Robinson	L-R	6-0	170	10-22-82	.333	.250	.363	24	108	19	36	8	3	4	24	6	0	0	0	13	0	0	.574	.368
Cosme, Caonabo	R-R	6-2	160	3-18-79	.265	.375	.226	62	211	26	56	13	1	6	24	23	3	2	1	41	5	1	.422	.345
Crosby, Bubba	L-L	5-11	185	8-11-76	.231	.205	.240	42	160	18	37	7	1	4	22	12	6	3	2	28	2	1	.363	.306
Duenas, Yobal	R-R	6-1	215	5-4-72	.000	.000	.000	2	6	0	0	0	0	0	0	0	0	1	0	2	0	0	.000	.000
Escalona, Felix	R-R	6-0	190	3-12-79	.274	.368	.242	91	307	42	84	14	1	7	45	28	18	10	5	58	5	0	.394	.363
Hankins, Ryan	R-R	5-11	200	6-30-76	.258	.234	.268	79	275	31	71	18	2	5	27	27	5	3	1	56	1	0	.393	.334
Johnson, Russ	R-R	5-10	185	2-22-73	.292	.382	.259	73	281	43	82	26	0	9	40	39	1	1	3	50	5	5	.480	.377
Jones, Mitch	R-R	6-2	215	10-15-77	.268	.331	.248	128	489	82	131	30	3	27	79	52	8	0	2	174	2	5	.507	.347
Lopez, Gabe	R-R	5-8	170	3-11-80	.227	.238	.223	44	163	24	37	4	0	3	15	16	5	7	3	20	2	2	.307	.310
Mendez, Deivi	R-R	6-1	165	5-24-83	.273	.000	.310	12	33	5	9	1	0	0	1	2	0	0	0	6	0	0	.303	.314
Nieves, Wil	R-R	5-11	190	9-25-77	.289	.305	.284	102	380	45	110	22	3	4	37	13	2	4	5	38	1	1	.395	.313
Parrish, David	R-R	6-3	220	6-13-79	.247	.318	.217	79	283	35	70	10	0	8	35	24	4	5	1	79	0	0	.367	.314
Phillips, Andy	R-R	6-0	205	4-6-77	.300	.365	.279	75	300	60	90	14	1	22	54	36	3	0	1	61	2	0	.573	.379
Porter, Colin	L-L	6-2	210	11-23-75	.177	.128	.192	57	198	26	35	9	1	2	14	25	1	1	2	62	1	3	.263	.270
Reese, Kevin	L-L	5-11	195	3-11-78	.276	.275	.276	133	540	92	149	38	7	14	69	63	10	2	5	86	16	5	.450	.359
Rojas, Tom	R-R	6-2	185	3-31-82	.000	.000	.000	1	1	0	0	0	0	0	0	0	0	0	0	1	0	0	.000	.000
Rolls, Damian	R-R	6-2	215	9-15-77	.261	.222	.271	25	88	10	23	5	0	1	9	11	1	1	2	24	4	2	.352	.343
Sierra, Ruben	B-R	6-1	215	10-6-65	.182	.333	.000	3	11	2	2	0	0	1	1	2	0	0	0	3	0	0	.455	.308
Thompson, Kevin	R-R	5-10	185	9-18-79	.249	.294	.234	58	209	28	52	17	0	2	28	23	6	4	4	45	18	5	.359	.335
Thurston, Joe	L-R	5-11	190	9-29-79	.234	.318	.212	29	107	13	25	3	3	2	7	7	1	3	0	19	2	2	.374	.287
Urick, John	L-L	6-2	210	2-22-82	.000	.000	.000	1	2	0	0	0	0	0	0	0	1	0	0	0	0	0	.000	.333
Vento, Mike	R-R	6-0	195	5-25-78	.291	.371	.263	130	501	62	146	37	2	12	84	49	13	1	7	96	1	4	.445	.365

PITCHING	B-T	HT	WT	DOB	W	L	ERA	G	GS	CG	SV	IP	H	R	ER	HR	BB	SO	AVG	vLH	vRH	K/9	BB/9
Anderson, Jason	L-R	6-0	170	6-9-79	4	1	2.66	55	0	0	10	68	44	21	20	4	18	60	.190	.191	.189	7.98	2.39
Artiles, Carlos	L-L	5-11	165	1-21-81	0	0	4.50	2	0	0	1	2	4	1	1	0	1	0	.444	.600	.250	0.00	4.50
Bean, Colter	L-R	6-6	255	1-16-77	4	7	3.01	65	0	0	0	72	60	33	24	5	39	82	.226	.314	.172	10.30	4.90
Boehringer, Brian	B-R	6-2	195	1-8-70	0	1	21.32	6	0	0	0	6	12	15	15	3	6	2	.414	.300	.474	2.84	8.53
Clippard, Tyler	R-R	6-4	170	2-14-85	0	0	0.00	1	0	0	0	1	0	0	0	0	0	2	.000	.000	.000	18.00	0.00
De Paula, Jorge	R-R	6-1	160	11-10-78	4	2	4.58	21	20	0	0	116	109	63	59	22	41	90	.248	.264	.233	6.98	3.18
Franklin, Wayne	L-L	6-2	200	3-9-74	2	3	3.61	46	0	0	1	42	36	18	17	4	11	50	.231	.271	.198	10.63	2.34
Graman, Alex	L-L	6-4	210	11-17-77	5	6	3.18	23	16	0	1	96	95	40	34	12	36	96	.257	.333	.234	8.97	3.36
Groom, Buddy	L-L	6-2	205	7-10-65	0	0	5.79	6	0	0	0	5	6	4	3	2	0	5	.333	.000	.400	9.64	0.00
Hankins, Ryan	R-R	5-11	200	6-30-76	0	1	9.00	1	0	0	0	1	2	2	1	0	0	0	.400	.000	.500	0.00	0.00
Henn, Sean	R-L	6-5	200	4-23-81	5	5	3.23	16	16	1	0	86	79	37	31	5	27	64	.254	.250	.256	6.67	2.81
Isaacson, Charlie	R-R	6-2	190	5-5-80	0	0	6.75	7	0	0	0	11	19	8	8	1	7	7	.373	.400	.346	5.91	5.91
King, Jeremy	R-R	6-2	210	11-12-81	0	0	0.00	1	1	0	0	6	3	1	0	0	0	3	.136	.111	.154	4.50	0.00
Maduro, Calvin	R-R	6-0	200	9-5-74	0	0	4.97	6	2	0	0	13	20	8	7	0	4	6	.364	.318	.394	4.26	2.84
Manning, Charlie	L-L	6-2	180	3-31-79	1	1	5.59	7	0	0	0	10	8	6	6	0	9	6	.216	.154	.250	5.59	8.38
Marsonek, Sam	R-R	6-6	225	7-10-78	3	7	6.61	49	3	0	7	78	93	63	57	8	35	61	.302	.261	.328	7.07	4.06
May, Darrell	L-L	6-2	185	6-13-72	6	2	4.17	10	7	0	0	58	67	29	27	6	5	39	.288	.250	.299	6.02	0.77
Mendoza, Ramiro	R-R	6-2	190	6-15-72	1	0	0.75	8	0	0	1	12	4	2	1	0	1	15	.100	.095	.105	11.25	0.75
Munro, Pete	R-R	6-3	210	6-14-75	10	7	4.56	43	13	0	0	116	132	68	59	14	37	80	.281	.267	.294	6.19	2.86
Nomo, Hideo	R-R	6-2	235	8-31-68	2	3	3.62	7	7	0	0	37	30	19	15	1	22	41	.221	.236	.203	9.88	5.30
Proctor, Scott	R-R	6-1	200	1-2-77	6	1	4.22	35	1	0	14	43	47	20	20	8	11	54	.280	.316	.247	11.39	2.32
Ramirez, Ramon	R-R	5-11	190	8-31-81	1	3	5.33	6	6	0	0	27	32	16	16	3	9	26	.305	.206	.352	8.67	3.00
Redding, Tim	R-R	6-0	195	2-12-78	3	4	5.08	10	10	0	0	51	62	29	29	5	13	47	.295	.297	.294	8.24	2.28
Schmitt, Eric	R-R	6-4	210	7-23-78	4	2	4.61	23	5	0	0	55	58	30	28	10	17	31	.272	.267	.278	5.10	2.80
Small, Aaron	R-R	6-5	220	11-23-71	1	4	4.96	11	10	0	0	49	62	30	27	5	8	21	.310	.357	.265	3.86	1.47
Smith, Josh	R-R	6-4	225	11-15-81	1	0	0.00	2	0	0	0	1	1	0	0	0	0	2	.167	.000	.333	13.50	0.00
Smith, Matt	L-L	6-5	225	6-15-79	2	0	2.60	25	0	0	1	28	24	9	8	3	13	33	.226	.150	.273	10.73	4.23
Valdes, Marc	R-R	6-0	188	12-20-71	0	0	9.82	8	0	0	0	7	15	8	8	0	1	4	.441	.316	.600	4.91	1.23
Voyles, Brad	R-R	6-0	195	12-30-76	6	5	4.97	19	14	0	1	89	88	55	49	15	31	73	.263	.265	.262	7.41	3.15
Wang, Chien-Ming	R-R	6-3	200	3-31-80	2	1	4.24	6	6	0	0	34	40	16	16	4	6	21	.301	.362	.253	5.56	1.59
Wilson, Kris	R-R	6-4	220	8-6-76	4	1	4.28	29	7	0	0	67	78	39	32	8	17	52	.288	.341	.241	6.95	2.27

FIELDING

Catcher	PCT	G	PO	A	E	DP	PB
Hankins	1.000	4	29	1	0	0	2
Nieves	.991	87	695	52	7	5	4
Parrish	.979	56	361	20	8	0	9
Rojas	1.000	1	2	0	0	0	0

First Base	PCT	G	PO	A	E	DP
Hankins	1.000	2	16	1	0	4
Johnson	1.000	6	42	3	0	6
Jones	.986	110	905	79	14	94
Phillips	.984	27	224	16	4	24
Rolls	1.000	1	13	0	0	0
Urick	1.000	1	9	0	0	0

Second Base	PCT	G	PO	A	E	DP
Cannizaro	1.000	1	4	2	0	2
Cano	.966	22	48	65	4	18
Christian	1.000	1	0	1	0	0
Cosme	.986	33	53	91	2	24
Escalona	1.000	14	22	37	0	8
Johnson	1.000	3	7	3	0	1
Lopez	.972	44	92	116	6	29
Phillips	1.000	4	4	7	0	0
Rolls	1.000	1	0	2	0	0
Thurston	.969	28	61	65	4	12

Third Base	PCT	G	PO	A	E	DP
Cano	1.000	1	2	2	0	0
Cosme	1.000	4	2	3	0	0
Duenas	1.000	2	0	6	0	1
Escalona	.886	12	9	22	4	2
Hankins	.956	37	27	59	4	2
Johnson	.980	53	24	125	3	13
Mendez	1.000	2	1	0	0	0
Phillips	.960	29	14	58	3	8
Rolls	.857	11	7	11	3	2

Shortstop	PCT	G	PO	A	E	DP
Cannizaro	.970	54	65	132	6	24
Cosme	.958	23	37	55	4	8
Escalona	.965	65	96	207	11	52
Mendez	.973	10	10	26	1	3

Outfield	PCT	G	PO	A	E	DP
Cabrera	1.000	23	63	2	0	0
Cosme	1.000	4	5	1	0	0
Crosby	.989	38	84	2	1	0
Hankins	1.000	6	8	0	0	0
Johnson	1.000	11	20	0	0	0
Jones	.933	7	14	0	1	0
Porter	.991	56	110	2	1	0
Reese	.984	122	235	7	4	3
Rolls	.957	12	21	1	1	1
Thompson	.967	54	113	3	4	1
Vento	.982	109	216	8	4	1

TRENTON THUNDER — Class AA

EASTERN LEAGUE

BATTING	B-T	HT	WT	DOB	AVG	vLH	vRH	G	AB	R	H	2B	3B	HR	RBI	BB	HBP	SH	SF	SO	SB	CS	SLG	OBP
Brown, Dee	L-R	6-0	225	3-27-78	.118	.100	.122	13	51	4	6	1	0	2	6	5	1	0	0	17	0	0	.255	.211
Brown, Jason	R-R	6-2	200	5-22-74	.248	.233	.252	51	153	20	38	6	1	4	19	17	2	2	1	46	0	1	.379	.329
Cabrera, Melky	B-L	5-11	170	8-11-84	.275	.306	.262	106	426	57	117	22	3	10	60	28	4	1	5	72	11	2	.411	.322
Cannizaro, Andy	R-R	5-10	170	12-19-78	.248	.241	.250	54	202	28	50	12	0	0	20	11	4	1	1	19	5	0	.307	.298
Carson, Matt	R-R	6-2	195	7-1-81	.192	.280	.162	28	99	10	19	5	0	1	5	0	2	2	0	25	2	3	.273	.208
Coleman, Michael	R-R	5-11	215	8-16-75	.265	.250	.271	42	151	20	40	8	1	9	34	18	2	0	3	41	0	0	.510	.345
Crozier, Eric	L-L	6-4	200	8-11-78	.174	.172	.174	34	121	13	21	6	0	3	18	9	1	2	1	52	1	2	.298	.235
Cruz, Enrique	R-R	5-10	185	7-13-81	.400	.333	.500	3	5	1	2	1	0	0	0	1	0	1	0	1	0	0	.600	.500
Duenas, Yobal	R-R	6-1	215	5-4-72	.271	.329	.243	76	258	28	70	16	3	3	28	11	1	0	1	47	0	5	.391	.303
Duncan, Eric	L-R	6-3	195	12-7-84	.235	.230	.237	126	451	60	106	15	3	19	61	59	4	2	4	136	9	3	.408	.326
Duncan, Shelley	R-R	6-5	215	9-29-79	.240	.213	.250	142	537	86	129	28	2	34	92	56	11	0	2	140	3	2	.490	.323
Guillen, Rudy	R-R	6-3	186	11-23-83	.257	.152	.303	28	109	12	28	2	0	2	8	5	0	0	0	20	0	1	.330	.289
Koutnik, Jared	R-R	6-3	190	11-9-79	.145	.167	.135	15	55	7	8	2	0	0	2	3	1	0	1	15	0	0	.182	.200
Lopez, Gabe	R-R	5-8	170	3-11-80	.291	.315	.280	82	296	50	86	14	1	5	42	48	3	6	6	30	6	3	.395	.388
Mendez, Deivi	R-R	6-1	165	5-24-83	.000	.000	.000	3	8	0	0	0	0	0	0	0	0	0	0	0	0	0	.000	.000
Pena, Ramiro	B-R	5-11	165	7-18-85	.250	.246	.251	68	236	28	59	5	2	0	12	10	0	8	1	48	4	1	.288	.279
Porter, Colin	L-L	6-2	210	11-23-75	.200	.143	.235	15	55	5	11	2	0	1	5	7	0	0	0	23	0	1	.291	.290
Santos, Omir	R-R	6-0	200	4-29-81	.252	.234	.260	111	401	44	101	17	0	10	48	11	9	1	3	75	0	1	.369	.285
Sardinha, Bronson	L-R	6-1	195	4-6-83	.258	.239	.266	133	503	63	130	30	2	12	68	55	7	1	3	115	11	5	.398	.338
Stotts, J.T.	R-R	5-11	190	1-21-80	.221	.231	.217	103	349	51	77	10	1	2	30	33	4	4	3	52	9	2	.272	.293
Thompson, Kevin	R-R	5-10	185	9-18-79	.329	.256	.355	81	313	59	103	28	5	12	43	53	6	2	3	68	25	6	.565	.432
Verbryke, Eric	L-L	6-2	220	8-6-81	.143	.000	.200	5	14	3	2	0	0	0	2	4	0	1	0	3	2	0	.143	.333
Walsh, Nick	L-R	5-9	180	5-6-80	.450	.333	.471	8	20	4	9	1	0	0	2	2	0	0	0	2	0	0	.500	.500

PITCHING	B-T	HT	WT	DOB	W	L	ERA	G	GS	CG	SV	IP	H	R	ER	HR	BB	SO	AVG	vLH	vRH	K/9	BB/9
Artiles, Carlos	L-L	5-11	165	1-21-81	3	2	3.55	32	0	0	0	46	49	27	18	4	29	37	.274	.208	.302	7.29	5.72
Borrell, Danny	L-L	6-3	200	1-24-79	1	1	6.34	10	7	0	0	38	49	30	27	8	16	32	.310	.300	.314	7.51	3.76
Brunet, Michael	R-R	6-2	195	3-5-77	2	1	3.43	15	0	0	0	21	23	10	8	0	6	21	.271	.257	.280	9.00	2.57

PITCHING	B-T	HT	WT	DOB	W	L	ERA	G	GS	CG	SV	IP	H	R	ER	HR	BB	SO	AVG	vLH	vRH	K/9	BB/9
Desalvo, Matt	R-R	6-0	170	9-11-80	9	5	3.02	25	24	0	0	149	106	55	50	8	67	151	.202	.178	.221	9.12	4.05
Henn, Sean	R-L	6-5	200	4-23-81	2	1	0.71	4	4	0	0	25	16	2	2	1	9	21	.188	.143	.203	7.46	3.20
Isaacson, Charlie	R-R	6-2	190	5-5-80	6	4	3.26	22	13	0	0	91	102	42	33	7	36	87	.279	.277	.281	8.60	3.56
Julianel, Ben	B-L	6-2	184	9-4-79	5	3	3.90	46	2	0	1	88	88	43	38	7	50	106	.260	.257	.262	10.88	5.13
Karstens, Jeff	R-R	6-3	175	9-24-82	12	11	4.15	28	27	0	0	169	192	91	78	16	42	147	.285	.256	.307	7.83	2.24
Kennard, Jeff	R-R	6-2	195	7-26-81	0	1	0.00	5	0	0	0	7	6	1	0	0	5	4	.250	.400	.211	5.40	6.75
King, Jeremy	R-R	6-2	210	11-12-81	0	0	2.31	5	0	0	0	12	7	3	3	1	7	9	.171	.091	.200	6.94	5.40
Maduro, Calvin	R-R	6-0	200	9-5-74	4	2	3.18	7	7	0	0	34	33	17	12	2	9	21	.264	.167	.338	5.56	2.38
Manning, Charlie	L-L	6-2	180	3-31-79	4	3	3.33	45	0	0	2	73	64	33	27	6	37	67	.234	.151	.273	8.26	4.56
Pope, Justin	B-R	6-0	190	11-8-79	6	4	2.81	57	0	0	29	77	65	29	24	2	20	55	.235	.250	.225	6.43	2.34
Ramirez, Ramon	R-R	5-11	190	8-31-81	6	5	3.84	15	15	0	0	89	79	44	38	10	35	82	.236	.281	.204	8.29	3.54
Roberts, Grant	R-R	6-3	205	9-13-77	1	1	5.25	9	3	0	0	24	25	14	14	2	17	20	.269	.333	.228	7.50	6.38
Rodriguez, Felix	R-R	6-1	210	9-9-72	0	0	0.00	2	2	0	0	3	1	0	0	0	3	3	.125	.167	.000	9.00	9.00
Schmitt, Eric	R-R	6-4	210	7-23-78	1	2	5.17	16	6	0	0	47	51	27	27	6	7	34	.283	.231	.313	6.51	1.34
Sierra, Edwardo	R-R	6-3	185	4-15-82	3	1	3.28	33	0	0	2	58	37	26	21	4	38	50	.187	.257	.148	7.80	5.93
Skaggs, Jon	R-R	6-5	225	3-27-78	2	7	6.16	22	15	0	1	80	99	67	55	14	38	48	.301	.321	.288	5.38	4.26
Small, Aaron	R-R	6-5	220	11-23-71	1	0	3.60	1	1	0	0	5	7	3	2	1	1	3	.333	.250	.385	5.40	1.80
Smith, Matt	L-L	6-5	225	6-15-79	3	4	2.80	22	4	0	2	55	46	24	17	2	23	59	.230	.173	.250	9.71	3.79
Thorp, Paul	R-R	6-1	200	9-23-80	0	0	0.00	2	0	0	1	3	1	0	0	0	0	1	.091	.200	.000	3.00	0.00
Valdes, Marc	R-R	6-0	188	12-20-71	1	3	5.28	10	1	0	0	15	18	11	9	0	5	14	.300	.280	.314	8.22	2.93
White, Steven	R-R	6-5	205	6-15-81	2	7	6.44	11	11	0	0	50	61	41	36	9	26	54	.296	.354	.260	9.66	4.65

FIELDING

Catcher	PCT	G	PO	A	E	DP	PB
Brown	.988	44	307	30	4	7	3
Santos	.989	104	842	77	10	10	9

First Base	PCT	G	PO	A	E	DP
Crozier	.933	5	26	2	2	4
Duenas	1.000	3	12	1	0	0
S. Duncan	.987	138	1178	78	16	123
Verbryke	1.000	1	10	0	0	1

Second Base	PCT	G	PO	A	E	DP
Cruz	1.000	1	0	1	0	0
Duenas	.977	14	20	22	1	7
Koutnik	1.000	1	1	1	0	0
Lopez	.982	80	162	230	7	56
Stotts	.983	56	115	168	5	49
Walsh	.000	1	0	0	0	0

Third Base	PCT	G	PO	A	E	DP
Duenas	.875	21	8	34	6	2
E. Duncan	.908	116	61	204	27	18
Stotts	.962	13	9	16	1	1

Shortstop	PCT	G	PO	A	E	DP
Cannizaro	.969	54	69	147	7	42
Cruz	.000	1	0	0	0	0
Koutnik	.750	1	0	3	1	1
Mendez	.667	1	2	0	1	0
Pena	.951	68	86	204	15	47
Stotts	.948	23	31	61	5	15

Outfield	PCT	G	PO	A	E	DP
Cabrera	.985	105	256	7	4	1
Carson	1.000	26	43	1	0	1
Coleman	1.000	11	19	1	0	0
Crozier	.966	21	25	3	1	0
Duenas	.875	7	6	1	1	0
Guillen	.962	28	50	0	2	0
Koutnik	1.000	5	8	0	0	0
Porter	.941	15	30	2	2	0
Sardinha	.969	123	180	9	6	3
Stotts	.875	14	7	0	1	0
Thompson	.977	75	125	4	3	0
Verbryke	1.000	4	5	1	0	1
Walsh	1.000	4	6	1	0	0

TAMPA YANKEES — High Class A

FLORIDA STATE LEAGUE

BATTING	B-T	HT	WT	DOB	AVG	vLH	vRH	G	AB	R	H	2B	3B	HR	RBI	BB	HBP	SH	SF	SO	SB	CS	SLG	OBP
Allen, Rod	R-R	6-2	210	9-21-82	.282	.250	.304	14	39	4	11	1	0	1	4	2	0	0	1	9	1	1	.385	.310
Almario-Cabrera, Yosvany	R-R	5-11	190	6-21-80	.286	.237	.308	50	192	25	55	7	1	1	18	12	2	0	1	31	5	0	.349	.333
Andrus, Erold	B-L	6-2	170	7-16-84	.241	.281	.224	125	461	53	111	24	2	5	49	42	6	1	3	88	5	3	.334	.311
Carroll, Mark	R-R	6-2	170	10-14-81	.346	.286	.368	9	26	3	9	1	0	1	2	2	0	2	0	3	0	0	.500	.393
Carson, Matt	R-R	6-2	195	7-1-81	.252	.211	.268	84	321	43	81	14	3	8	39	31	8	0	4	68	10	2	.389	.330
Christian, Justin	R-R	6-1	188	4-3-80	.306	.272	.318	95	372	52	114	27	6	8	37	33	6	4	1	47	38	5	.476	.371
Corona, Reegie	B-R	5-11	160	11-7-86	.000	.000	.000	3	12	1	0	0	0	0	0	2	0	0	0	3	0	0	.000	.143
Cruz, Enrique	R-R	5-10	185	7-13-81	.133	.125	.143	9	30	5	4	0	0	0	1	4	1	0	1	10	0	0	.133	.250
Dunn, Michael	L-L	6-1	185	5-23-85	.167	.171	.164	28	90	8	15	5	0	0	6	11	1	0	0	28	2	2	.222	.265
Ehlers, Cody	L-L	5-11	190	4-16-82	.240	.275	.225	35	129	14	31	10	0	3	11	10	0	0	0	20	1	1	.388	.295
Ellison, Josh	R-R	5-9	199	7-24-83	.208	.286	.167	27	101	16	21	4	0	0	9	7	1	1	1	17	3	2	.248	.264
Faison, Vince	L-R	6-0	180	1-22-81	.383	.417	.375	14	60	4	23	5	4	1	14	4	0	0	1	10	5	1	.650	.415
Greenwood, Jared	L-R	5-10	210	2-28-83	.105	.000	.138	11	38	0	4	1	0	0	2	4	0	0	0	14	0	0	.132	.190
Guillen, Rudy	R-R	6-3	186	11-23-83	.260	.360	.219	100	389	51	101	14	4	6	39	19	7	0	2	70	10	5	.362	.305
Haag, Ryan	L-R	5-9	180	11-20-81	.232	.167	.250	18	56	5	13	1	1	0	6	12	0	0	0	9	2	2	.286	.368
Hollingsworth, Josh	R-R	6-3	210	6-28-80	.233	.316	.195	18	60	8	14	0	0	4	12	1	0	1	0	13	0	0	.433	.246
Kartler, Bryce	L-L	6-2	215	6-9-80	.189	.125	.204	43	122	13	23	2	0	1	9	23	2	1	1	30	4	4	.230	.324
Koutnik, Jared	R-R	6-3	190	11-9-79	.241	.320	.182	33	116	7	28	2	0	3	19	3	1	1	1	26	1	2	.336	.264
Made, Hector	R-R	6-1	154	12-18-84	.218	.167	.250	43	170	17	37	5	1	0	22	12	0	0	2	27	1	1	.259	.266
Mendez, Deivi	R-R	6-1	165	5-24-83	.232	.250	.220	27	82	6	19	3	0	0	8	7	0	1	1	16	0	1	.268	.289
Nunez, Luis	R-R	5-11	160	11-21-86	.400	1.000	.250	1	5	0	2	1	0	0	0	0	0	0	0	2	1	0	.600	.400
Pena, Ramiro	B-R	5-11	165	7-18-85	.247	.250	.245	23	73	11	18	4	1	1	6	9	0	2	2	12	1	0	.370	.321
Plumley, Grant	R-R	6-0	185	12-21-81	.250	.324	.223	43	140	18	35	3	1	0	15	10	3	0	4	22	0	0	.286	.306
Rivera, Ruben	R-R	6-0	196	11-14-73	.118	1.000	.063	6	17	2	2	0	0	0	1	2	0	0	0	6	0	0	.118	.211
Robles, Luis	R-R	6-4	185	3-2-82	.174	.077	.300	9	23	2	4	0	0	0	1	0	0	0	0	6	0	0	.174	.174
Rojas, Tom	R-R	6-2	185	3-31-82	.276	.257	.287	81	272	34	75	13	1	5	35	26	6	0	3	60	0	1	.386	.349
Sprowl, Jon-Mark	L-R	6-1	200	8-1-80	.228	.208	.235	63	184	19	42	7	2	2	22	27	4	0	1	29	1	2	.321	.338
Tejeda, Ferdin	R-R	5-11	170	9-15-82	.207	.300	.158	9	29	5	6	3	0	0	4	3	0	0	2	8	0	0	.310	.265
Tierce, Evan	L-L	5-11	190	7-19-82	.206	.059	.255	20	68	9	14	3	1	1	7	12	1	1	0	13	1	0	.324	.333
Urick, John	L-L	6-2	210	2-22-82	.238	.211	.249	94	340	38	81	23	1	11	46	32	7	0	1	56	0	0	.409	.316
Verbryke, Eric	L-L	6-2	220	8-6-81	.190	.200	.188	12	42	5	8	1	0	1	2	4	1	0	1	9	0	2	.286	.271
Walsh, Nick	L-R	5-9	180	5-6-80	.227	.292	.203	26	88	9	20	0	0	1	5	16	1	0	1	13	4	2	.261	.349
Zamora, Hector	L-R	6-1	215	10-19-81	.241	.305	.215	87	282	39	68	19	1	3	28	33	6	1	2	66	0	0	.348	.331

PITCHING	B-T	HT	WT	DOB	W	L	ERA	G	GS	CG	SV	IP	H	R	ER	HR	BB	SO	AVG	vLH	vRH	K/9	BB/9
Artiles, Carlos	L-L	5-11	165	1-21-81	0	1	7.71	9	0	0	0	9	12	8	8	1	4	6	.293	.231	.321	5.79	3.86
Beam, T.J.	R-R	6-7	215	8-28-80	1	1	3.12	12	0	0	1	17	14	7	6	2	7	27	.215	.292	.171	14.02	3.63
Boehringer, Brian	B-R	6-2	195	1-8-70	0	0	1.80	2	2	0	0	5	1	1	1	0	2	2	.071	.250	.000	3.60	3.60
Borrell, Danny	L-L	6-3	200	1-24-79	0	4	4.25	6	6	0	0	30	24	14	14	1	7	21	.222	.250	.214	6.37	2.12
Brumit, Mathew	R-R	6-4	220	10-28-79	1	2	5.59	20	1	0	0	39	51	29	24	3	11	29	.305	.266	.330	6.75	2.56
Castle, Heath	L-L	6-0	200	1-6-82	3	2	2.55	36	0	0	1	35	42	21	10	1	15	25	.292	.277	.299	6.37	3.82

PITCHING	B-T	HT	WT	DOB	W	L	ERA	G	GS	CG	SV	IP	H	R	ER	HR	BB	SO	AVG	vLH	vRH	K/9	BB/9
Clippard, Tyler	R-R	6-4	170	2-14-85	10	9	3.18	26	25	0	0	147	118	56	52	12	34	169	.219	.196	.236	10.32	2.08
Cox, J. Brent	L-R	6-3	205	5-13-84	1	2	2.60	16	0	0	0	28	20	9	8	1	5	27	.206	.233	.185	8.78	1.63
De Paula, Jorge	R-R	6-1	160	11-10-78	0	2	4.58	4	4	0	0	18	14	9	9	2	4	14	.215	.192	.231	7.13	2.04
Gardner, Michael	R-R	6-0	190	5-23-81	3	1	3.38	21	0	0	1	35	35	16	13	1	10	31	.254	.273	.241	8.05	2.60
Gomez, Abel	L-L	6-0	170	11-29-84	2	5	3.79	15	13	0	0	81	70	43	34	2	51	69	.233	.203	.242	7.70	5.69
Harmsen, Brandon	R-R	6-3	205	12-13-81	1	8	6.26	19	6	0	0	46	63	39	32	8	14	28	.333	.370	.310	5.48	2.74
Hughes, Philip	R-R	6-5	220	6-24-86	2	0	3.06	5	4	0	0	18	8	6	6	0	4	21	.140	.158	.132	10.70	2.04
Japa, Rolando	R-R	6-1	165	1-24-85	0	0	0.00	1	0	0	0	4	1	0	0	0	0	2	.083	.143	.000	4.50	0.00
Jones, Jason	R-R	6-5	225	11-20-82	5	13	5.68	26	24	1	0	128	171	89	81	11	20	76	.323	.341	.309	5.33	1.40
Kennard, Jeff	R-R	6-2	195	7-26-81	7	3	3.40	42	0	0	0	53	40	23	20	3	25	49	.209	.263	.171	8.32	4.25
King, Jeremy	R-R	6-2	210	11-12-81	5	5	3.61	24	16	0	0	100	93	49	40	8	30	83	.242	.226	.256	7.49	2.71
Knox, Michael	R-R	6-4	195	9-19-83	1	0	11.50	14	0	0	0	18	31	23	23	2	9	14	.378	.393	.370	7.00	4.50
Maduro, Calvin	R-R	6-0	200	9-5-74	0	1	4.50	3	1	0	0	8	11	4	4	1	2	7	.314	.368	.250	7.88	2.25
Mendez, Jesus	R-R	6-2	163	2-14-86	0	0	0.00	1	0	0	0	2	2	0	0	0	0	0	.250	.000	.400	0.00	0.00
Morales, Jorge	R-R	6-0	170	5-16-83	0	1	3.38	11	0	0	0	19	15	7	7	1	4	23	.214	.250	.184	11.09	1.93
Moscat, Marvin	R-R	6-0	170	5-15-82	3	1	3.29	31	0	0	1	55	59	26	20	4	20	35	.280	.316	.248	5.76	3.29
Pavano, Carl	R-R	6-5	240	1-8-76	0	1	4.50	1	1	0	0	6	6	3	3	1	0	3	.250	.429	.176	4.50	0.00
Quezada, Elvys	R-R	6-1	210	12-15-81	4	1	5.94	19	4	0	1	47	50	33	31	5	26	49	.270	.284	.258	9.38	4.98
Rosario, Carlos	R-R	5-10	180	2-23-84	0	0	18.41	5	0	0	0	7	12	16	15	2	13	1	.375	.294	.467	1.23	15.95
Skaggs, Jon	R-R	6-5	225	3-27-78	0	3	6.00	6	6	0	0	27	32	19	18	1	22	13	.302	.250	.360	4.33	7.33
Smith, Brett	R-R	6-5	220	11-15-81	4	7	5.21	14	13	0	0	74	71	44	43	9	17	34	.254	.215	.277	4.12	2.06
Smith, Josh	R-R	6-4	225	8-12-83	0	0	7.30	9	1	0	0	12	23	14	10	1	8	7	.377	.259	.471	5.11	5.84
Solis, Hairo	R-R	6-1	190	3-3-84	0	0	2.25	2	0	0	0	4	4	1	1	1	0	1	.235	.200	.286	2.25	0.00
Soto, Edgar	L-L	5-11	175	12-28-84	0	1	9.39	2	2	0	0	8	13	8	8	1	1	8	.371	.125	.444	9.39	1.17
Sturtze, Tanyon	R-R	6-5	225	10-12-70	0	1	6.00	2	2	0	0	3	4	2	2	0	0	4	.286	.143	.429	12.00	0.00
Thorp, Paul	R-R	6-1	200	9-23-80	2	4	4.10	50	0	0	25	48	43	25	22	5	12	38	.231	.176	.268	7.08	2.23
White, Steven	R-R	6-5	205	6-15-81	0	0	3.09	3	2	0	0	12	8	4	4	1	2	8	.195	.333	.156	6.17	1.54
Wright, Jaret	R-R	6-2	230	12-29-75	1	0	1.50	2	2	0	0	12	9	2	2	0	3	12	.220	.333	.100	9.00	2.25

FIELDING

Catcher	PCT	G	PO	A	E	DP	PB
Greenwood	1.000	8	73	3	0	0	1
Kartler	.000	1	0	0	1	0	0
Robles	.958	8	42	4	2	0	0
Rojas	.991	74	510	36	5	4	12
Sprowl	.989	54	341	25	4	1	10

First Base	PCT	G	PO	A	E	DP
Andrus	.982	15	105	7	2	3
Ehlers	.989	32	243	24	3	20
Greenwood	1.000	1	6	0	0	0
Urick	.988	85	724	39	9	46
Verbryke	1.000	4	38	1	0	2

Second Base	PCT	G	PO	A	E	DP
Christian	.962	94	145	238	15	33
Corona	1.000	3	9	11	0	1
Cruz	.933	3	2	12	1	0
Koutnik	1.000	8	12	17	0	3
Mendez	.857	2	3	3	1	0
Tejeda	.886	8	14	17	4	2
Walsh	.988	20	29	54	1	11

Third Base	PCT	G	PO	A	E	DP
Carroll	.889	7	3	5	1	0
Hollingsworth	.885	16	5	18	3	0
Koutnik	.886	15	10	29	5	1
Mendez	1.000	11	3	19	0	1
Nunez	1.000	1	1	0	0	0
Plumley	1.000	10	3	16	0	1
Sprowl	.000	1	0	0	0	0
Zamora	.947	82	57	158	12	6

Shortstop	PCT	G	PO	A	E	DP
Carroll	1.000	1	1	0	0	0
Haag	1.000	18	23	55	0	8
Hollingsworth	.875	3	1	6	1	0
Koutnik	.960	7	6	18	1	2
Made	.922	43	75	126	17	17
Mendez	.952	10	15	25	2	8
Pena	.965	23	32	78	4	11
Plumley	.943	35	51	98	9	11

Outfield	PCT	G	PO	A	E	DP
Allen	1.000	12	13	0	0	0
Almario-Cabrera	.879	21	29	0	4	0
Andrus	.990	108	195	4	2	0
Carroll	1.000	1	4	0	0	0
Carson	.988	69	156	10	2	2
Dunn	.982	26	53	2	1	0
Ellison	1.000	9	14	0	0	0
Faison	1.000	14	42	2	0	0
Guillen	.969	98	214	6	7	2
Kartler	1.000	28	51	1	0	0
Koutnik	.000	1	0	0	0	0
Rivera	1.000	6	9	0	0	0
Tierce	1.000	20	42	3	0	1
Walsh	1.000	1	1	0	0	0

CHARLESTON RIVERDOGS — Low Class A

SOUTH ATLANTIC LEAGUE

BATTING	B-T	HT	WT	DOB	AVG	vLH	vRH	G	AB	R	H	2B	3B	HR	RBI	BB	HBP	SH	SF	SO	SB	CS	SLG	OBP
Allen, Rod	R-R	6-2	210	9-21-82	.185	.300	.159	17	54	5	10	3	0	0	2	3	2	1	0	13	1	1	.241	.254
Almario-Cabrera, Yosvany	R-R	5-11	190	6-21-80	.316	.429	.274	45	155	25	49	10	3	5	20	6	2	0	1	26	2	0	.516	.348
Battle, Tim	R-R	6-2	185	9-10-85	.259	.267	.257	134	525	97	136	33	11	16	60	50	11	4	2	195	40	16	.455	.335
Christian, Justin	R-R	6-1	188	4-3-80	.290	.292	.289	29	100	31	29	5	0	3	10	14	3	1	0	12	17	2	.430	.393
Devoir, Jordan	R-R	6-2	210	8-13-82	.175	.200	.163	27	63	6	11	2	0	2	4	9	2	1	2	27	0	1	.302	.289
Ehlers, Cody	L-L	5-11	190	4-16-82	.278	.270	.280	92	324	46	90	17	2	9	59	59	1	1	4	60	4	4	.426	.387
Gonzalez, Edwar	R-R	5-10	200	1-1-83	.286	.315	.276	89	294	36	84	12	4	10	52	11	5	0	3	54	6	4	.456	.319
Haag, Ryan	L-R	5-9	180	11-20-81	.175	.091	.188	58	160	19	28	5	0	1	12	8	1	1	1	19	2	1	.225	.218
Harris, Estee	L-R	5-11	170	1-8-85	.216	.156	.228	113	375	48	81	23	2	10	42	33	2	1	3	106	20	7	.368	.281
Holmann, Mario	B-R	6-0	165	5-21-84	.271	.214	.285	78	277	45	75	7	1	0	20	38	4	6	0	54	40	8	.303	.367
Jones, Ben	R-R	6-3	196	7-3-81	.288	.271	.293	128	475	64	137	33	2	14	77	42	18	0	6	103	6	0	.455	.364
Made, Hector	R-R	6-1	154	12-18-84	.310	.214	.337	37	129	16	40	4	0	1	10	9	1	1	0	20	4	2	.364	.360
Nelson, Kevin	R-R	6-3	215	4-8-81	.000	.000	.000	4	7	1	0	0	0	0	0	0	0	0	0	1	0	0	.000	.000
Plaza, William	R-R	6-0	186	10-6-82	.192	.122	.226	62	125	13	24	2	1	0	13	18	3	1	1	26	3	1	.224	.306
Plumley, Grant	R-R	6-0	185	12-21-81	.267	.200	.288	87	303	29	81	16	1	2	31	16	2	5	3	44	8	4	.347	.306
Poterson, Jon	B-R	6-1	215	2-10-86	.173	.135	.189	36	127	7	22	6	0	2	13	7	0	0	1	37	1	0	.268	.215
Robles, Luis	R-R	6-4	185	3-2-82	.250	.500	.214	6	16	1	4	1	0	0	1	2	0	1	0	3	0	1	.313	.333
Rojas, Irwil	L-R	6-1	175	8-11-84	.281	.267	.283	103	345	37	97	16	0	1	44	33	2	2	3	31	2	1	.336	.345
Tierce, Evan	L-L	5-11	190	7-19-82	.288	.167	.317	42	156	24	45	6	1	6	28	20	2	0	3	20	10	4	.455	.370
Vechionacci, Marcos	B-R	6-2	170	8-7-86	.252	.327	.233	128	503	83	127	26	8	2	62	43	4	3	5	83	16	2	.348	.314
Walsh, Nick	L-R	5-9	180	5-6-80	.211	.167	.218	35	128	16	27	3	0	1	12	19	4	3	2	16	5	1	.258	.327

PITCHING	B-T	HT	WT	DOB	W	L	ERA	G	GS	CG	SV	IP	H	R	ER	HR	BB	SO	AVG	vLH	vRH	K/9	BB/9
Beam, T.J.	R-R	6-7	215	8-28-80	3	3	1.66	35	2	0	2	60	45	15	11	2	18	78	.206	.206	.207	11.77	2.72
Beltran, Saydel	L-L	5-11	175	1-23-83	3	0	4.45	24	0	0	1	30	27	15	15	3	12	40	.243	.122	.314	11.87	3.56
Blackwell, Brad	R-R	6-2	215	5-8-82	3	0	4.71	12	0	0	0	21	28	14	11	0	15	17	.329	.375	.289	7.29	6.43
Castle, Heath	L-L	6-0	200	1-6-82	1	0	0.00	7	0	0	0	9	4	0	0	0	4	7	.129	.000	.154	6.75	3.86
Clippard, Tyler	R-R	6-4	170	2-14-85	0	1	7.50	1	1	0	0	6	9	5	5	1	0	10	.333	.400	.294	15.00	0.00
Coke, Phil	L-L	6-1	210	7-19-82	8	11	5.42	24	18	0	0	103	122	67	62	11	34	68	.293	.245	.308	5.94	2.97

PITCHING	B-T	HT	WT	DOB	W	L	ERA	G	GS	CG	SV	IP	H	R	ER	HR	BB	SO	AVG	vLH	vRH	K/9	BB/9
Garcia, Christian	R-R	6-4	175	8-24-85	5	6	3.91	21	20	0	0	106	102	57	46	3	53	103	.249	.246	.251	8.75	4.50
Gardner, Michael	R-R	6-0	190	5-23-81	1	0	0.90	9	0	0	1	10	8	3	1	1	2	10	.211	.182	.222	9.00	1.80
Gomez, Abel	L-L	6-0	170	11-29-84	1	2	12.79	5	4	0	0	19	28	27	27	0	19	17	.341	.280	.368	8.05	9.00
Hacker, Eric	B-R	6-1	215	3-26-83	5	2	1.60	10	10	1	0	62	49	14	11	0	14	40	.219	.218	.219	5.81	2.03
Harmsen, Brandon	R-R	6-3	205	12-13-81	5	2	2.87	20	2	0	0	47	47	19	15	1	11	37	.266	.235	.292	7.09	2.11
Hughes, Philip	R-R	6-5	220	6-24-86	7	1	1.97	12	12	1	0	69	46	19	15	1	16	72	.192	.214	.176	9.44	2.10
Knox, Michael	R-R	6-4	195	9-19-83	1	2	4.30	6	4	0	0	23	20	15	11	2	12	17	.233	.250	.222	6.65	4.70
Marquez, Jeff	L-R	6-0	200	11-5-81	9	13	3.42	27	27	1	0	140	138	64	53	4	61	107	.257	.252	.261	6.89	3.93
Martinez, Mike	R-R	6-2	190	4-12-81	3	1	4.02	50	0	0	30	54	63	30	24	4	15	32	.290	.303	.280	5.37	2.52
Moscat, Marvin	R-R	6-0	170	5-15-82	0	1	5.00	11	0	0	0	18	18	11	10	3	7	8	.261	.344	.189	4.00	3.50
Parker, Shaun	L-L	6-3	205	7-30-81	3	1	5.13	41	0	0	0	54	57	39	31	2	40	41	.268	.295	.257	6.79	6.63
Quezada, Elvys	R-R	6-1	210	12-15-81	1	1	1.95	16	1	0	1	32	28	13	7	1	11	38	.228	.245	.216	10.58	3.06
Rival, Kevin	R-R	6-2	210	11-27-79	2	2	3.07	38	0	0	0	56	47	25	19	4	27	58	.224	.176	.261	9.38	4.37
Rosario, Carlos	R-R	5-10	180	2-23-84	2	1	7.04	12	0	0	0	15	20	13	12	3	9	3	.328	.306	.360	1.76	5.28
Smith, Brett	R-R	6-5	220	8-12-83	3	2	4.07	12	11	0	0	66	67	33	30	5	14	61	.262	.260	.264	8.28	1.90
Smith, Josh	R-R	6-4	225	11-15-81	1	1	2.88	34	0	0	1	50	39	16	16	3	19	56	.213	.178	.236	10.08	3.42
Tejeda, Ferdin	R-R	5-11	170	9-15-82	0	0	6.00	1	1	0	0	3	5	2	2	1	0	1	.417	.667	.167	3.00	0.00
Vanderplow, Randy	R-R	6-3	210	7-21-80	3	1	4.24	14	1	0	0	23	26	16	11	2	9	18	.265	.244	.283	6.94	3.47
Wright, Chase	L-L	6-2	190	2-8-83	10	4	3.75	25	24	0	0	144	128	71	60	10	69	110	.242	.206	.255	6.88	4.31

FIELDING

Catcher	PCT	G	PO	A	E	DP	PB
Nelson	1.000	4	22	3	0	1	1
Plaza	.988	62	304	21	4	2	7
Robles	1.000	5	29	6	0	0	0
Rojas	.988	100	677	76	9	11	23

First Base	PCT	G	PO	A	E	DP
Devoir	1.000	2	8	0	0	1
Ehlers	.992	50	463	33	4	49
Gonzalez	1.000	14	117	2	0	7
Jones	.988	75	662	53	9	62
Robles	1.000	1	4	0	0	1

Second Base	PCT	G	PO	A	E	DP
Christian	.940	27	54	87	9	19
Holmann	.974	78	144	236	10	51
Walsh	.984	14	27	36	1	8
Haag	.967	26	35	84	4	18
Plumley	.667	1	0	2	1	0

Third Base	PCT	G	PO	A	E	DP
Devoir	.882	19	7	23	4	4
Haag	.950	8	4	15	1	0
Plumley	.960	53	25	94	5	10
Vechionacci	.956	66	44	130	8	17
Walsh	1.000	1	0	1	0	0

Shortstop	PCT	G	PO	A	E	DP
Haag	.971	10	13	21	1	2
Made	.951	36	63	111	9	22
Plumley	.981	35	44	111	3	21
Vechionacci	.956	61	99	204	14	44
Walsh	.500	1	0	1	1	0

Outfield	PCT	G	PO	A	E	DP
Allen	1.000	11	14	1	0	0
Almario-Cabrera	.957	38	67	0	3	0
Battle	.958	134	311	10	14	3
Gonzalez	.966	72	102	10	4	1
Harris	.950	97	131	3	7	0
Poterson	.982	36	54	2	1	1
Tierce	.969	41	59	3	2	0
Walsh	1.000	6	9	0	0	0

STATEN ISLAND YANKEES — Short-Season Class A

NEW YORK-PENN LEAGUE

BATTING	B-T	HT	WT	DOB	AVG	vLH	vRH	G	AB	R	H	2B	3B	HR	RBI	BB	HBP	SH	SF	SO	SB	CS	SLG	OBP
Allen, Rod	R-R	6-2	210	9-21-82	.235	.200	.250	6	17	2	4	0	1	0	1	0	0	0	0	4	1	0	.353	.235
Anson, Kyle	B-R	6-0	200	4-21-83	.252	.222	.260	37	131	24	33	7	0	0	10	27	3	3	1	26	7	2	.305	.389
Burke, Joe	L-R	6-0	195	12-16-83	.220	.227	.219	37	118	14	26	4	0	1	13	8	0	2	2	12	3	1	.280	.266
Canada, Brad	R-R	6-1	210	8-12-82	.130	.111	.143	10	23	0	3	0	0	0	1	1	0	0	0	8	0	0	.130	.167
Carroll, Mark	R-R	6-2	170	10-14-81	.206	.222	.200	20	68	10	14	1	0	0	4	11	2	0	0	15	2	1	.221	.333
Cooper, James	L-R	5-10	190	2-18-84	.247	.207	.259	64	243	30	60	7	3	1	34	27	10	3	2	27	5	9	.313	.344
Corona, Reegie	B-R	5-11	160	11-7-86	.227	.196	.234	72	255	32	58	11	0	0	20	27	1	4	2	32	9	3	.271	.302
Devoir, Jordan	R-R	6-2	210	8-13-82	.235	.350	.161	16	51	4	12	3	0	0	3	4	0	0	0	17	1	0	.294	.291
Garcia, Felipe	R-R	6-3	225	5-15-83	.253	.295	.237	50	162	30	41	7	1	3	17	16	10	0	2	38	1	2	.364	.353
Gardner, Brett	L-L	5-10	180	8-24-83	.284	.318	.273	73	282	62	80	9	1	5	32	39	6	3	5	49	19	3	.376	.377
Gonzalez, Hector	B-R	6-2	180	2-23-85	.167	.000	.200	23	66	13	11	1	3	1	7	11	1	3	1	16	2	0	.318	.291
Lafountain, J.T.	B-R	6-0	190	10-26-81	.333	.000	.500	3	9	1	3	0	1	0	0	0	0	0	0	3	0	0	.556	.333
Larsen, Kyle	L-L	6-5	240	6-30-83	.308	.286	.315	67	240	32	74	19	0	6	49	18	13	3	3	35	3	2	.463	.383
Nunez, Eduardo	B-R	6-0	155	6-15-87	.313	.310	.314	73	281	37	88	11	6	3	46	20	3	6	0	43	6	3	.427	.365
Perez, Jose	R-R	6-1	160	3-16-85	.256	.333	.233	28	78	15	20	4	1	0	13	11	0	0	0	17	5	1	.333	.348
Pilittere, P.J.	R-R	6-0	215	11-23-81	.250	.231	.255	53	176	18	44	11	0	4	25	12	8	3	4	17	0	0	.381	.320
Poterson, Jon	B-R	6-1	215	2-10-86	.247	.324	.225	75	295	33	73	19	0	6	52	22	2	1	2	72	2	1	.373	.302
Roth, Tony	R-R	6-0	175	10-20-82	.270	.265	.275	26	74	16	20	3	0	1	6	11	3	1	1	21	1	2	.351	.382

PITCHING	B-T	HT	WT	DOB	W	L	ERA	G	GS	CG	SV	IP	H	R	ER	HR	BB	SO	AVG	vLH	vRH	K/9	BB/9
Bahr, Jesse	L-L	6-2	200	1-30-83	0	0	0.00	3	0	0	0	2	2	0	0	0	1	3	.200	.333	.143	11.57	3.86
Berg, Justin	R-R	6-3	195	6-7-84	6	2	3.53	15	9	0	0	59	48	26	23	3	20	52	.226	.275	.203	7.98	3.07
Conroy, Jim	R-R	6-4	195	11-4-82	5	1	2.04	18	9	0	1	66	52	20	15	2	20	67	.210	.237	.192	9.09	2.71
Everitt, Keaton	R-R	6-7	220	2-4-83	1	0	6.00	5	2	0	0	12	10	9	8	0	11	8	.227	.333	.172	6.00	8.25
Japa, Rolando	R-R	6-1	165	1-24-85	0	0	16.20	1	0	0	0	2	5	4	3	1	1	2	.455	.200	.667	10.80	5.40
Kroenke, Zach	R-L	6-3	210	4-21-84	1	1	2.54	11	5	0	2	39	30	14	11	2	15	28	.219	.188	.229	6.46	3.46
Lara, Toni	L-L	6-0	155	1-31-84	2	5	7.00	17	5	0	0	45	51	41	35	6	29	42	.287	.149	.336	8.40	5.80
Morrison, Erik	R-R	6-0	180	10-23-85	3	1	2.67	21	0	0	0	27	23	11	8	2	11	22	.232	.226	.235	7.33	3.67
Patterson, Garrett	L-L	6-2	220	5-11-82	1	2	3.71	17	11	0	0	51	37	22	21	1	38	71	.204	.162	.215	12.53	6.71
Pendleton, Lance	L-R	6-3	195	9-10-83	1	0	2.33	9	6	0	0	27	27	11	7	1	13	23	.248	.273	.237	7.67	4.33
Rodriguez, Felix	R-R	6-1	210	9-9-72	0	0	3.00	2	2	0	0	3	4	1	1	1	0	5	.308	.333	.300	15.00	0.00
Rosario, Carlos	R-R	5-10	180	2-23-84	0	0	3.12	9	0	0	0	9	11	3	3	1	7	5	.324	.250	.346	5.19	7.27
Rueger, Bryan	L-L	6-3	185	2-22-83	1	0	6.00	4	0	0	0	6	8	5	4	0	2	5	.320	.167	.368	7.50	3.00
Schmidt, Josh	R-R	6-4	175	11-14-82	5	1	0.27	26	0	0	13	33	14	1	1	0	8	47	.128	.233	.089	12.82	2.18
Schroer, Steve	R-R	6-2	195	12-28-82	3	3	1.60	23	0	0	0	39	24	10	7	2	12	39	.176	.167	.182	8.92	2.75
Seccombe, David	R-R	6-1	200	1-9-82	8	2	2.15	17	9	0	1	71	45	18	17	4	26	53	.178	.235	.151	6.72	3.30
Solis, Hairo	R-R	6-1	190	3-3-84	7	1	3.23	21	0	0	1	31	23	12	11	3	8	24	.215	.345	.167	7.04	2.35
Stephens, Jason	R-R	6-4	190	10-10-84	4	1	2.82	18	10	0	1	67	55	25	21	3	19	52	.229	.287	.196	6.99	2.55
Stuart, Cory	R-R	6-2	185	3-15-82	3	1	0.83	22	0	0	7	33	17	8	3	1	13	50	.153	.256	.097	13.78	3.58
Villalona, Guillermo	R-R	6-2	170	9-15-82	1	0	2.30	8	6	0	0	31	29	8	8	0	7	25	.252	.245	.258	7.18	2.01
Wagner, Michael	L-L	6-4	225	3-28-85	0	1	1.59	19	0	0	0	17	18	4	3	1	7	19	.257	.115	.341	10.06	3.71
Wordekemper, Eric	R-R	6-1	200	8-8-83	0	2	4.50	2	2	0	0	10	15	5	5	1	2	3	.417	.294	.526	2.70	1.80

GAMES BY POSITION: C—Burke 33, Canada 4, Pilittere 49. **1B**—Garcia 22, Larsen 58, Pilittere 3, Poterson 1. **2B**—Corona 67, Lafountain 2, Roth 10. **3B**—Anson 36, Canada 2, Carroll 18, Devoir 8, Gardner 1, Gonzalez 1, Roth 16. **SS**—Corona 4, Nunez 72. **OF**—Allen 2, Burke 1, Carroll 2, Cooper 60, Devoir 6, Garcia 3, Gardner 67, Perez 22, Poterson 70.

GCL YANKEES — Rookie

GULF COAST LEAGUE

BATTING	B-T	HT	WT	DOB	AVG	vLH	vRH	G	AB	R	H	2B	3B	HR	RBI	BB	HBP	SH	SF	SO	SB	CS	SLG	OBP
Carroll, Mark	R-R	6-2	170	10-14-81	.250	.000	.250	4	8	0	2	0	0	0	0	2	1	1	0	2	1	0	.250	.455
Cervelli, Francisco	B-R	6-1	175	3-6-86	.190	.000	.196	24	58	10	11	2	0	1	9	8	2	0	2	13	1	0	.276	.300
De la Rossa, Wilkins	L-L	6-0	156	2-21-85	.270	.200	.274	49	185	32	50	12	2	0	30	21	3	0	2	25	7	2	.357	.351
Dunn, Michael	L-L	6-1	185	5-23-85	.194	.000	.200	24	62	4	12	2	2	0	9	8	1	0	3	16	0	1	.290	.284
Fermin, Angel	R-R	6-2	190	10-30-85	.305	.400	.299	44	154	35	47	17	1	5	32	7	8	0	3	27	2	1	.526	.360
Gil, Jose	B-R	6-0	170	9-4-86	.279	.400	.274	41	140	21	39	11	0	1	20	19	1	0	2	18	1	1	.379	.364
Greenwood, Jared	L-R	5-10	210	2-28-83	.278	.000	.278	12	36	3	10	1	1	0	6	6	1	0	0	12	0	0	.361	.395
Henry, C.J.	R-R	6-3	205	5-31-86	.249	.333	.244	48	181	32	45	9	3	3	17	17	6	0	0	39	17	4	.381	.333
Jackson, Austin	R-R	6-1	185	2-1-87	.304	.250	.307	40	148	32	45	11	2	0	14	18	1	0	4	26	11	2	.405	.374
Lafountain, J.T.	B-R	6-0	190	10-26-81	.184	.000	.200	19	49	9	9	1	0	0	5	12	0	0	0	5	0	0	.204	.344
Malec, Chris	B-R	5-11	195	8-28-82	.384	.250	.391	21	73	16	28	4	0	1	14	7	1	0	1	4	1	1	.479	.439
Mann, Schuyler	R-R	6-1	215	12-19-83	.333	.500	.286	5	9	1	3	0	0	0	0	1	1	0	0	0	0	0	.333	.455
Nunez, Luis	R-R	5-11	160	11-21-86	.230	.300	.224	42	126	16	29	3	2	0	23	6	0	4	3	15	2	3	.286	.259
Perez, Joel	R-R	5-10	190	3-28-82	.242	.083	.259	42	124	17	30	4	2	5	25	17	4	0	2	40	3	2	.427	.347
Phillips, Nathan	B-R	6-2	190	1-24-86	.263	.222	.267	33	114	16	30	5	0	1	11	10	1	0	1	38	2	2	.333	.325
Pino, Wilmer	R-R	5-11	165	1-23-86	.223	.444	.202	35	103	20	23	3	1	1	7	11	10	0	0	21	12	3	.301	.355
Tabata, Jose	R-R	5-11	160	8-12-88	.314	.300	.315	44	156	30	49	5	1	3	25	15	2	0	0	14	22	6	.417	.382

PITCHING	B-T	HT	WT	DOB	W	L	ERA	G	GS	CG	SV	IP	H	R	ER	HR	BB	SO	AVG	vLH	vRH	K/9	BB/9
Amador, Anderson	R-R	6-2	180	11-4-84	2	0	3.00	7	1	0	0	12	11	4	4	2	5	9	.262	.273	.258	6.75	3.75
Bahr, Jesse	L-L	6-2	200	1-30-83	1	1	4.32	14	0	0	5	17	17	9	8	0	5	13	.266	.214	.280	7.02	2.70
Boehringer, Brian	B-R	6-2	195	1-8-70	0	0	0.00	1	1	0	0	1	0	0	0	0	0	1	.000	.000	.000	9.00	0.00
Borrell, Danny	L-L	6-3	200	1-24-79	0	0	1.50	3	3	0	0	12	12	3	2	0	2	12	.267	.400	.229	9.00	1.50
Cabrera, Domingo	L-L	6-1	150	2-23-86	4	1	2.30	11	2	0	1	31	23	12	8	2	9	37	.193	.194	.193	10.63	2.59
Carter, Andy	R-R	6-4	215	3-9-83	2	1	3.92	11	1	0	0	21	19	12	9	1	5	19	.232	.310	.189	8.27	2.18
Castillo, Francisco	R-R	6-2	195	10-3-86	3	1	1.76	12	5	0	0	41	25	13	8	1	14	34	.170	.215	.134	7.46	3.07
Duff, Grant	R-R	6-6	210	12-19-82	0	1	6.48	4	2	0	0	8	7	12	6	1	8	9	.219	.200	.227	9.72	8.64
Everitt, Keaton	R-R	6-7	220	2-4-83	3	0	3.19	8	3	0	0	31	30	15	11	2	7	28	.259	.256	.260	8.13	2.03
Garcia, Christian	R-R	6-4	175	8-24-85	0	0	4.50	2	1	0	0	6	4	4	3	0	5	7	.200	.167	.214	10.50	7.50
Gomez, Abel	L-L	6-0	170	11-29-84	1	0	6.28	4	3	0	0	14	15	13	10	3	5	20	.263	.385	.227	12.56	3.14
Japa, Rolando	R-R	6-1	165	1-24-85	2	3	3.50	12	5	0	0	36	33	21	14	3	19	41	.241	.235	.244	10.25	4.75
Kroenke, Zach	R-L	6-3	210	4-21-84	0	1	4.50	1	1	0	0	2	4	2	1	0	0	2	.400	.667	.286	9.00	0.00
Mendez, Deivi	R-R	6-1	165	5-24-83	0	0	9.00	1	0	0	0	1	2	1	1	0	0	2	.400	.000	.400	18.00	0.00
Mendez, Jesus	R-R	6-2	163	2-14-86	3	2	4.50	12	0	0	0	16	19	9	8	1	4	12	.302	.278	.311	6.75	2.25
Mendoza, Ramiro	R-R	6-2	190	6-15-72	0	0	0.00	2	2	0	0	5	3	1	0	0	1	3	.167	.286	.091	5.40	1.80
Mlotkowski, Mike	R-R	6-5	245	11-14-81	0	0	6.00	1	1	0	0	3	4	2	2	0	1	0	.333	.375	.250	0.00	3.00
Montan, Miguel	R-R	6-0	160	11-4-85	1	2	3.52	12	0	0	3	15	18	6	6	3	4	13	.305	.188	.349	7.63	2.35
Morales, Jorge	R-R	6-0	170	5-16-83	1	1	2.30	11	0	0	3	16	11	4	4	1	1	17	.190	.167	.200	9.77	0.57
Omana, Edgar	L-L	6-3	175	9-12-83	1	0	1.59	9	0	0	0	11	8	2	2	0	8	17	.205	.143	.219	13.50	6.35
Pavano, Carl	R-R	6-5	240	1-8-76	0	0	1.80	1	1	0	0	5	2	2	1	1	0	5	.118	.000	.182	9.00	0.00
Rueger, Bryan	L-L	6-3	185	2-22-83	1	0	0.00	4	0	0	0	6	3	0	0	0	0	6	.136	.250	.111	9.00	0.00
Selenes, Josue	R-R	6-0	180	10-8-85	3	2	5.19	12	3	0	1	26	26	16	15	1	10	22	.263	.281	.254	7.62	3.46
Soto, Edgar	L-L	5-11	175	12-28-84	0	2	4.24	8	6	0	0	23	21	12	11	1	9	26	.236	.182	.254	10.03	3.47
Tejeda, Ferdin	R-R	5-11	170	9-15-82	2	0	1.80	7	1	0	0	15	12	3	3	1	3	15	.218	.222	.216	9.00	1.80
Velazquez, Juan	R-R	6-4	190	10-11-83	1	0	1.96	10	0	0	0	18	10	5	4	0	7	12	.156	.130	.171	5.89	3.44
Villalona, Guillermo	R-R	6-2	170	9-15-82	0	1	3.32	7	5	0	0	22	21	9	8	3	5	19	.263	.323	.224	7.89	2.08
Wordekemper, Eric	R-R	6-1	200	8-8-83	2	0	2.12	9	5	0	0	30	28	7	7	2	1	24	.250	.289	.230	7.28	0.30
Wright, Jaret	R-R	6-2	230	12-29-75	0	1	7.71	1	1	0	0	2	4	2	2	0	2	3	.364	.333	.375	11.57	7.71

GAMES BY POSITION: C—Cervelli 21, Gil 35, Greenwood 4, Lafountain 2, Mann 1. **1B**—Dunn 5, Fermin 43, Gil 2, Greenwood 6, Phillips 2. **2B**—Carroll 1, Lafountain 1, Malec 19, Nunez 7, Pino 30. **3B**—Dunn 1, Lafountain 12, Malec 1, Nunez 15, Phillips 29, Pino 1. **SS**—Henry 39, Lafountain 1, Nunez 17. **OF**—Carroll 3, Cervelli 1, De la Rossa 48, Dunn 12, Fermin 2, Jackson 35, Nunez 2, Perez 30, Tabata 41.

OAKLAND ATHLETICS

BY CASEY TEFERTILLER

This was never supposed to be the season when the A's contended for the postseason. After trading away star pitchers Tim Hudson and Mark Mulder during the offseason, general manager Billy Beane preached patience in 2005 and talked of reloading for future pennant races in the improving American League West.

The Athletics began the year young, with rookies Nick Swisher in right field, Joe Blanton in the rotation and Huston Street winning the final job in the bullpen. The bumps came quickly, as the A's began the season 17-32, seemingly buried so deep in the standings that they would never again see .500, let alone find their way into the playoff race.

Then strange things started happening. Injuries began to both help and hurt the A's. Shortstop Bobby Crosby, the 2004 Rookie of the Year, returned to the lineup. Erratic closer Octavio Dotel went down to arm problems and consistent dominator Street took over. Slumping DH Erubiel Durazo went down and Dan Johnson came up from Triple-A. Oakland emerged from its stupor to become one of the dominant teams in baseball during the final 113 games, going 71-42 to challenge the Angels up to the final week of the season. On Aug. 30, the A's had put together a run of 58-24 after the dreadful start to take a two-game lead in the division, only to have the Angels overtake them in September.

"They're one of the best stories of the year," Yankees manager Joe Torre said in early September. "No matter what they do the rest of the way, they've certainly surprised the heck out of everyone."

What most impressed manager Ken Macha was the heart of the team—never giving up despite the early foibles. "Even coming out of spring training, I thought our makeup was going to be an important part of how we did," Macha said. "It turned out to be our strength. When it was all told, we came out with flying colors."

The makeup of the young players proved to be critical in midseason, when the A's built win after win to climb back into the race. Johnson proved a key force in the lineup, finishing at .275-15-59 in 375 at-bats. Street, just a year out of the University of Texas, collected 23 saves along with a 5-1, 1.72 record to solidify the bullpen. He converted all 18 of his save opportunities after the all-star break. Blanton finished 12-12 and allowed three or fewer runs in 11 of his final 14 starts as he improved through the season. The switch-hitting Swisher hit 21 homers and drove in 74 in what the A's hope will be the emergence of a power hitter for the middle of the lineup.

All four members of the starting infield were 27 or younger, with Johnson at first, Mark Ellis at second, Eric Chavez at third and Crosby at short. After missing all of '04 with a shoulder injury, Ellis found his stride in the second half of the season and finished the year with a .316 average and a .384 on-base percentage, moving into the leadoff job late in the year.

The A's finished the year enthused for the future, since there were no major free agencies pending. However, a pair of shocks came within days as popular hitting coach Dave Hudgens was let go, then Beane could not reach agreement with Macha on a new contract. Days later, Macha called Beane and said he'd made a mistake turning down the three-year, $2.6 million offer, and Beane welcomed the well-respected manager back into the fold.

Success also followed throughout the system, as four of the A's affiliates made the playoffs and Midland won the Double-A Texas League title. Sacramento came within one victory of winning its third straight Pacific Coast League championship under manager Tony DeFrancesco. The emerging star of the farm system was outfielder Andre Ethier, who hit .319-18-80 for Midland to be named the Texas League player of the year.

The A's again managed to combine youth with success in the major leagues while developing prospects on the farm.

PLAYERS OF THE YEAR

MAJOR LEAGUE: Huston Street, rhp

The rookie closer was a sensation in his first full professional season after being drafted in the supplemental first round out of Texas in 2004. He finished second among major league closers with a 1.72 ERA while saving 23 games through his uncanny feel for pitching and competitiveness.

MINOR LEAGUE: Andre Ethier, of

BILL MITCHELL

Ethier busted out in a big way in 2005 in his Double-A debut, winning Texas League player of the year honors after leading the league in runs and finishing third in batting. He showed enough power to hit 18 homers while maintaining his mature approach at the plate and playing solid defense.

ORGANIZATION LEADERS

BATTING		
*AVG	Barton, Daric, Midland/Stockton	.317
R	Ethier, Andre, Midland/Sacramento	104
H	Ethier, Andre, Midland/Sacramento	165
TB	Melillo, Kevin, Kane County/Midland/Stockton	268
2B	Majewski, Dustin, Stockton	43
3B	Bynum, Freddie, Sacramento	9
HR	Melillo, Kevin, Kane County/Midland/Stockton	24
RBI	Putnam, Danny, Midland/Stockton	100
BB	Cust, Jack, Sacramento	115
SO	Cust, Jack, Sacramento	153
SB	Herrera, Javier, Kane County/Sacramento	27
*OBP	Barton, Daric, Midland/Stockton	.426
*SLG	Morris, Jed, Midland/Sacramento/Stockton	.538
PITCHING		
W	Braden, Dallas, Midland/Stockton	15
L	Webb, Ryan, Kane County	11
#ERA	Madsen, Mike, Vancouver	1.39
G	Kohn, Shawn, Midland	55
	Robertson, Connor, Kane Co./Sacramento/Stockton	55
CG	Three tied at	1
SV	Garcia, Jairo, Midland/Sacramento	26
	Santos, Alex, Midland/Sacramento/Stockton	26
IP	Bondurant, Steven, Midland	165
BB	Sharpe, Steven, AZL Athletics/Kane County/Stockton	61
SO	Ziegler, Brad, Midland/Stockton	164

*Minimum 250 at-bats. #Minimum 75 innings.

OAKLAND ATHLETICS

Manager: Ken Macha. **2005 Record:** 88-74, .543 (2nd, AL West).

BATTING	B-T	HT	WT	DOB	AVG	vLH	vRH	G	AB	R	H	2B	3B	HR	RBI	BB	HBP	SH	SF	SO	SB	CS	SLG	OBP
Bocachica, Hiram	R-R	5-11	180	3-4-76	.105	.286	.000	9	19	2	2	0	0	0	0	0	0	0	0	7	0	0	.105	.105
Bynum, Freddie	L-R	6-1	180	3-15-80	.286	.000	.333	7	7	0	2	1	0	0	1	0	0	0	0	3	0	0	.429	.286
Byrnes, Eric	R-R	6-2	210	2-16-76	.266	.329	.218	59	192	30	51	15	2	7	24	14	7	1	1	27	2	2	.474	.336
Castillo, Alberto	R-R	6-0	215	2-10-70	.000	.000	.000	1	1	0	0	0	0	0	0	0	0	0	0	1	0	0	.000	.000
2-team (34 Kansas City)					.208	.139	.246	35	101	13	21	5	1	1	14	12	0	1	1	22	1	0	.307	.289
Chavez, Eric	L-R	6-1	205	12-7-77	.269	.264	.271	160	625	92	168	40	1	27	101	58	2	0	9	129	6	0	.466	.329
Clark, Jermaine	L-R	5-10	170	9-29-76	.000	.000	.000	4	0	2	0	0	0	0	0	1	0	0	0	0	0	0	.000	1.000
Crosby, Bobby	R-R	6-3	195	1-12-80	.276	.314	.260	84	333	66	92	25	4	9	38	35	1	1	1	54	0	0	.456	.346
Durazo, Erubiel	L-L	6-3	240	1-23-75	.237	.350	.196	41	152	15	36	6	1	4	16	14	1	0	0	24	1	0	.368	.305
Ellis, Mark	R-R	5-11	180	6-6-77	.316	.313	.317	122	434	76	137	21	5	13	52	44	4	4	0	51	1	3	.477	.384
Ginter, Keith	R-R	5-10	195	5-5-76	.161	.164	.158	51	137	12	22	5	0	3	25	13	1	2	3	25	0	0	.263	.234
Hatteberg, Scott	L-R	6-1	210	12-14-69	.256	.214	.271	134	464	52	119	19	0	7	59	51	4	2	2	54	0	1	.343	.334
Johnson, Dan	L-R	6-2	220	8-10-79	.275	.283	.272	109	375	54	103	21	0	15	58	50	1	0	8	52	0	1	.451	.355
Kendall, Jason	R-R	6-0	195	6-26-74	.271	.293	.263	150	601	70	163	28	1	0	53	50	20	0	5	39	8	3	.321	.345
Kielty, Bobby	B-R	6-1	225	8-5-76	.263	.322	.226	116	377	55	99	20	0	10	57	50	2	2	2	67	3	2	.395	.350
Kotsay, Mark	L-L	6-0	200	12-2-75	.280	.324	.261	139	582	75	163	35	1	15	82	40	1	2	4	51	5	5	.421	.325
Melhuse, Adam	B-R	6-2	200	3-27-72	.247	.077	.274	39	97	11	24	7	0	2	12	5	0	0	0	28	0	0	.381	.284
Payton, Jay	R-R	5-10	185	11-22-72	.269	.275	.267	69	275	38	74	9	1	13	42	14	0	0	2	33	0	1	.451	.302
2-team (55 Boston)					.267	.283	.258	124	408	62	109	16	1	18	63	24	0	0	3	47	0	1	.444	.306
Scutaro, Marco	R-R	5-10	170	10-30-75	.247	.171	.266	118	381	48	94	22	3	9	37	36	0	4	2	48	5	2	.391	.310
Swisher, Nick	B-L	6-0	195	1-25-80	.236	.203	.248	131	462	66	109	32	1	21	74	55	4	0	1	110	0	1	.446	.322
Thomas, Charles	L-L	6-0	190	12-26-78	.109	.143	.103	30	46	4	5	0	0	0	1	5	4	0	0	8	0	1	.109	.255
Watson, Matt	L-R	5-11	200	9-5-78	.188	.000	.220	19	48	4	9	3	0	0	5	2	0	0	0	4	0	0	.250	.220

PITCHING	B-T	HT	WT	DOB	W	L	ERA	G	GS	CG	SV	IP	H	R	ER	HR	BB	SO	AVG	vLH	vRH	K/9	BB/9
Blanton, Joe	R-R	6-3	225	12-11-80	12	12	3.53	33	33	2	0	201	178	86	79	23	67	116	.236	.228	.246	5.19	3.00
Calero, Kiko	R-R	6-1	185	1-9-75	4	1	3.23	58	0	0	1	56	45	20	20	6	18	52	.216	.319	.162	8.41	2.91
Cruz, Juan	R-R	6-2	165	10-15-78	0	3	7.44	28	0	0	0	33	38	33	27	5	22	34	.290	.283	.296	9.37	6.06
Dotel, Octavio	R-R	6-0	210	11-25-73	1	2	3.52	15	0	0	7	15	10	6	6	2	11	16	.185	.269	.107	9.39	6.46
Duchscherer, Justin	R-R	6-3	190	11-19-77	7	4	2.21	65	0	0	5	86	67	25	21	7	19	85	.215	.225	.208	8.93	2.00
Etherton, Seth	R-R	6-1	200	10-17-76	1	1	6.62	3	3	0	0	18	16	13	13	4	5	10	.235	.289	.167	5.09	2.55
Flores, Ron	L-L	5-11	190	8-9-79	0	0	1.04	11	0	0	0	9	8	1	1	1	0	6	.235	.154	.286	6.23	0.00
Garcia, Jairo	R-R	6-0	165	3-7-83	0	0	3.00	3	0	0	0	3	2	1	1	0	1	1	.182	.222	.000	3.00	3.00
Glynn, Ryan	R-R	6-3	200	11-1-74	0	4	6.88	5	3	0	0	17	24	16	13	5	7	15	.320	.385	.250	7.94	3.71
Harden, Rich	L-R	6-1	180	11-30-81	10	5	2.53	22	19	2	0	128	93	42	36	7	43	121	.201	.179	.221	8.51	3.02
Haren, Danny	R-R	6-5	220	9-17-80	14	12	3.73	34	34	3	0	217	212	101	90	26	53	163	.255	.252	.258	6.76	2.20
Harikkala, Tim	R-R	6-2	185	7-15-71	0	0	6.39	8	0	0	0	13	16	9	9	3	4	7	.308	.370	.240	4.97	2.84
Kennedy, Joe	R-L	6-4	245	5-24-79	4	5	4.45	19	8	0	0	61	64	33	30	8	20	45	.267	.234	.278	6.68	2.97
Reames, Britt	R-R	5-10	180	8-19-73	0	0	9.53	2	0	0	0	6	10	6	6	2	2	4	.400	.250	.471	6.35	3.18
Rincon, Ricardo	L-L	5-9	190	4-13-70	1	1	4.34	67	0	0	0	37	34	19	18	7	20	27	.246	.250	.240	6.51	4.82
Saarloos, Kirk	R-R	6-0	180	5-23-79	10	9	4.17	29	27	2	0	160	170	75	74	11	54	53	.278	.304	.249	2.99	3.04
Street, Huston	R-R	6-0	185	8-2-83	5	1	1.72	67	0	0	23	78	53	17	15	3	26	72	.194	.224	.172	8.27	2.99
Witasick, Jay	R-R	6-4	240	8-28-72	1	1	3.25	28	0	0	1	28	26	15	10	2	17	33	.239	.212	.263	10.73	5.53
Yabu, Keiichi	R-R	6-1	200	9-28-68	4	0	4.50	40	0	0	1	58	64	34	29	6	26	44	.287	.291	.283	6.83	4.03
Zito, Barry	L-L	6-4	215	5-13-78	14	13	3.86	35	35	0	0	228	185	106	98	26	89	171	.221	.215	.223	6.74	3.51

FIELDING

Catcher	PCT	G	PO	A	E	DP	PB
Castillo	1.000	1	2	0	0	0	0
Kendall	.993	147	986	51	7	6	4
Melhuse	1.000	24	115	7	0	0	1

First Base	PCT	G	PO	A	E	DP
Durazo	1.000	1	8	0	0	2
Ellis	1.000	2	3	0	0	0
Hatteberg	.985	53	423	38	7	47
Johnson	.994	101	897	57	6	94
Swisher	1.000	21	109	10	0	10

Second Base	PCT	G	PO	A	E	DP
Bynum	.000	3	0	0	0	0
Clark	.000	2	0	0	0	0
Ellis	.989	115	203	333	6	82
Ginter	.975	25	49	69	3	17
Scutaro	.993	30	56	92	1	19

Third Base	PCT	G	PO	A	E	DP
Bocachica	1.000	2	2	3	0	1
Chavez	.966	153	121	302	15	28
Ginter	.885	12	12	11	3	0
Scutaro	1.000	5	4	6	0	1

Shortstop	PCT	G	PO	A	E	DP
Crosby	.981	84	117	251	7	60
Ellis	1.000	7	6	15	0	4
Scutaro	.976	81	115	213	8	50

Outfield	PCT	G	PO	A	E	DP
Bocachica	1.000	6	6	0	0	0
Bynum	1.000	2	5	0	0	0
Byrnes	.984	54	117	4	2	2
Clark	.000	1	0	0	0	0
Ginter	.000	2	0	0	0	0
Kielty	.983	96	166	5	3	1
Kotsay	.987	137	299	7	4	3
Payton	1.000	69	153	2	0	0
Scutaro	1.000	2	5	0	0	0
Swisher	.990	121	196	6	2	2
Thomas	.951	27	38	1	2	0
Watson	1.000	17	30	0	0	0

FARM SYSTEM

General Manager: Billy Beane. **Director, Player Development:** Keith Lieppman. **Scouting Director:** Eric Kubota.

Class	Farm Team	League	W	L	Pct.	Finish*	Manager	Affiliate Since
AAA	Sacramento (Calif.) RiverCats	Pacific Coast	80	64	.556	**t-2nd (16)**	Tony DeFrancesco	2000
AA	Midland (Texas) RockHounds	Texas	78	62	.557	**+1st (8)**	Von Hayes	1999
High A	Stockton (Calif.) Ports	California	78	62	.557	**2nd (10)**	Todd Stevenson	2005
Low A	Kane County Cougars (Geneva, Ill.)	Midwest	67	72	.482	10th (14)	Dave Joppie	2003
SS A	Vancouver (B.C.) Canadians	Northwest	46	30	.605	**1st (8)**	Juan Navarrette	2000
Rookie	Phoenix (Ariz.) Athletics	Arizona	30	26	.536	3rd (9)	Ruben Escalera	1988

*Finish in overall standings (No. of teams in league)/Playoff teams in **boldface** +League champion

SACRAMENTO RIVERCATS — Class AAA

PACIFIC COAST LEAGUE

BATTING	B-T	HT	WT	DOB	AVG	vLH	vRH	G	AB	R	H	2B	3B	HR	RBI	BB	HBP	SH	SF	SO	SB	CS	SLG	OBP
Appert, Luke	L-R	6-0	185	7-14-80	.000	.000	.000	1	1	0	0	0	0	0	0	0	0	0	0	0	0	0	.000	.000
Baker, John	L-R	6-1	215	1-20-81	.234	.229	.236	103	346	43	81	24	3	5	41	30	4	7	0	90	1	0	.364	.303
Beattie, Andrew	B-R	5-10	165	2-28-78	.296	.348	.278	113	442	80	131	36	4	8	55	57	3	5	10	100	10	6	.450	.373
Bocachica, Hiram	R-R	5-11	180	3-4-76	.412	.000	.500	4	17	2	7	2	0	2	6	1	0	0	0	4	0	0	.882	.444
Bynum, Freddie	L-R	6-1	180	3-15-80	.278	.329	.263	102	378	56	105	16	9	2	40	38	3	7	2	83	23	7	.384	.347
Castillo, Alberto	R-R	6-0	215	2-10-70	.077	.000	.077	4	13	2	1	0	0	0	0	1	0	0	0	4	0	0	.077	.143
Clark, Jermaine	L-R	5-10	170	9-29-76	.250	.274	.242	70	256	32	64	13	4	5	28	41	2	2	4	33	14	8	.391	.353
Colamarino, Brant	L-L	5-10	221	12-4-80	.243	.221	.251	74	280	37	68	15	3	11	47	19	4	1	3	76	0	0	.436	.297
Crosby, Bobby	R-R	6-3	195	1-12-80	.083	.333	.000	3	12	0	1	0	0	0	1	0	0	0	0	0	0	0	.083	.083
Cust, Jack	L-R	6-1	230	1-16-79	.257	.305	.241	134	479	95	123	28	1	19	75	115	3	0	3	153	2	4	.438	.402
Ethier, Andre	L-L	6-3	195	4-10-82	.267	.000	.308	4	15	0	4	1	0	0	2	2	0	0	0	3	0	0	.333	.353
Garrett, Shawn	B-R	6-3	220	11-2-78	.295	.238	.313	131	508	69	150	27	1	17	82	29	5	6	10	111	13	4	.453	.333
Ginter, Keith	R-R	5-10	195	5-5-76	.333	.412	.300	14	57	9	19	8	0	3	12	4	1	1	0	11	0	0	.632	.387
Gomez, Francis	R-R	5-11	184	9-2-81	.500	.000	.667	3	12	5	6	2	0	0	1	1	0	1	0	4	0	1	.667	.538
Gregorio, Tom	R-R	6-2	215	5-5-77	.281	.314	.259	29	89	4	25	6	0	0	16	5	1	0	0	20	0	0	.348	.326
Herrera, Javier	R-R	5-11	191	4-9-85	.417	1.000	.364	5	12	5	5	1	0	1	3	1	2	0	0	1	1	0	.750	.533
Jackson, Steve	R-R	6-5	235	12-13-77	.181	.318	.145	33	105	11	19	5	1	3	12	4	0	0	1	31	0	0	.333	.209
Johnson, Dan	L-R	6-2	220	8-10-79	.324	.200	.371	47	182	36	59	17	0	8	41	32	1	0	2	24	0	1	.549	.424
Morris, Jed	L-R	5-11	200	3-4-80	.500	.000	.500	1	2	2	1	0	0	0	0	1	0	1	0	1	0	0	.500	.667
Morrissey, Adam	R-R	5-11	170	6-8-81	.250	.239	.254	55	188	30	47	7	0	4	21	27	1	3	1	74	3	1	.351	.346
Rouse, Mike	L-R	5-11	185	4-25-80	.269	.239	.278	130	469	69	126	30	3	7	72	59	7	17	2	115	2	4	.390	.358
Smith, Bobby	R-R	6-3	210	5-10-74	.286	.293	.284	102	409	64	117	19	2	13	64	37	4	1	2	74	9	0	.438	.350
Swisher, Nick	B-L	6-0	195	1-25-80	.391	.636	.167	6	23	4	9	3	0	0	1	2	1	0	0	7	0	1	.522	.462
Thomas, Charles	L-L	6-0	190	12-26-78	.227	.274	.214	75	277	43	63	16	3	5	33	35	3	3	2	56	16	4	.361	.319
Watson, Matt	L-R	5-11	200	9-5-78	.315	.349	.304	113	419	82	132	27	3	17	81	67	2	2	10	57	12	1	.516	.404

PITCHING	B-T	HT	WT	DOB	W	L	ERA	G	GS	CG	SV	IP	H	R	ER	HR	BB	SO	AVG	vLH	vRH	K/9	BB/9
Bradford, Chad	R-R	6-5	205	9-14-74	0	0	6.00	3	1	0	0	3	4	2	2	1	0	1	.333	.286	.400	3.00	0.00
Calero, Kiko	R-R	6-1	185	1-9-75	0	0	9.00	2	2	0	0	2	4	2	2	0	0	2	.400	.400	.400	9.00	0.00
Cruz, Juan	R-R	6-2	165	10-15-78	5	1	2.40	13	13	0	0	75	51	23	20	4	28	90	.192	.179	.203	10.80	3.36
Etherton, Seth	R-R	6-1	200	10-17-76	7	7	2.72	20	19	0	0	112	93	44	34	11	30	99	.220	.207	.230	7.93	2.40
Flores, Ron	L-L	5-11	190	8-9-79	5	3	2.39	52	0	0	3	60	46	18	16	5	30	66	.213	.207	.216	9.85	4.48
Garcia, Jairo	R-R	6-0	165	3-7-83	3	6	4.47	44	0	0	20	48	45	30	24	6	20	73	.239	.253	.230	13.59	3.72
Glynn, Ryan	R-R	6-3	200	11-1-74	3	1	2.78	11	11	0	0	55	46	20	17	4	23	54	.225	.253	.204	8.84	3.76
Gwyn, Marcus	R-R	6-3	219	11-4-77	2	2	5.66	34	0	0	3	41	41	28	26	1	37	37	.261	.258	.263	8.06	8.06
Harden, Rich	L-R	6-1	180	11-30-81	0	0	0.00	1	1	0	0	3	1	0	0	0	0	7	.100	.000	.167	21.00	0.00
Harikkala, Tim	R-R	6-2	185	7-15-71	1	2	1.27	11	0	0	3	21	13	5	3	1	7	14	.181	.148	.200	5.91	2.95
Johnson, Adam	R-R	6-2	210	7-12-79	1	0	6.23	4	4	0	0	22	29	17	15	1	4	17	.315	.271	.364	7.06	1.66
Mabeus, Chris	R-R	6-3	210	2-11-79	9	2	4.21	42	0	0	1	62	61	31	29	4	24	72	.256	.238	.266	10.45	3.48
Mattioni, Nick	R-R	6-3	195	3-14-79	0	1	11.42	7	0	0	0	9	13	12	11	4	7	3	.361	.400	.333	3.12	7.27
Meyer, Dan	R-L	6-3	210	7-3-81	2	8	5.36	19	17	0	0	89	101	64	53	15	43	63	.286	.277	.289	6.37	4.35
Moreno, Victor	R-R	6-0	212	6-10-79	4	2	4.50	49	0	0	2	74	72	37	37	4	46	71	.258	.259	.257	8.64	5.59
Muessig, Jeff	R-R	6-2	208	2-27-82	0	0	9.00	1	0	0	0	1	2	1	1	0	0	0	.400	.000	.500	0.00	0.00
Ramos, Mario	L-L	5-11	180	10-19-77	4	6	5.21	49	7	0	0	86	107	59	50	13	37	78	.301	.280	.311	8.13	3.86
Reames, Britt	R-R	5-10	180	8-19-73	6	6	3.31	42	7	0	8	92	91	46	34	3	35	85	.253	.206	.283	8.29	3.41
Rheinecker, John	L-L	6-2	215	5-29-79	4	0	1.77	7	7	0	0	46	29	15	9	0	14	24	.181	.250	.158	4.73	2.76
Robertson, Connor	R-R	6-2	215	9-10-81	0	0	1.80	3	0	0	0	5	2	1	1	0	3	5	.118	.143	.100	9.00	5.40
Saipe, Mike	R-R	6-1	190	9-10-73	4	2	2.80	27	4	0	0	61	58	26	19	4	17	51	.244	.240	.246	7.52	2.51
Santos, Alex	R-R	6-1	215	8-9-77	0	0	0.00	3	0	0	0	4	0	0	0	0	0	0	.000	.000	.000	0.00	0.00
Serrano, Jimmy	R-R	5-10	170	5-9-76	8	3	3.91	16	16	0	0	92	85	42	40	7	41	89	.247	.225	.266	8.71	4.01
Shibilo, Andy	R-R	6-7	220	9-16-76	0	0	3.00	3	0	0	0	3	3	1	1	0	0	4	.250	.500	.000	12.00	0.00
Smyth, Steve	L-L	6-1	205	6-3-78	1	1	10.07	10	4	0	0	22	36	27	25	2	17	20	.371	.286	.395	8.06	6.85
Sparks, Steve	R-R	6-0	190	7-2-65	5	5	6.95	12	11	0	0	66	87	52	51	10	26	31	.323	.284	.350	4.23	3.55
2-team (3 Portland)					7	5	5.92	15	14	0	0	84	102	58	55	11	32	40	.304	.269	.333	4.30	3.44
Stamler, Keith	L-R	6-2	195	8-20-79	0	0	8.44	6	0	0	0	5	13	7	5	0	3	4	.433	.455	.421	6.75	5.06
2-team (16 Oklahoma)					3	1	7.56	22	0	0	5	25	40	23	21	4	14	20	.354	.356	.353	7.20	5.04
Sylvester, Billy	R-R	6-5	210	10-1-76	0	0	11.57	12	0	0	0	14	17	19	18	1	20	13	.304	.429	.229	8.36	12.86
Ziegler, Mike	R-R	6-3	229	7-25-79	6	6	5.01	22	20	0	0	115	159	78	64	11	33	65	.335	.326	.340	5.09	2.58

FIELDING

Catcher	PCT	G	PO	A	E	DP	PB
Baker	.995	102	743	56	4	4	8
Castillo	.964	4	26	1	1	0	0
Gregorio	.991	29	210	11	2	2	7
Jackson	.984	25	177	10	3	1	3

First Base	PCT	G	PO	A	E	DP
Colamarino	.990	71	562	33	6	41
Garrett	1.000	19	123	12	0	16
Jackson	.980	8	44	6	1	3
Johnson	.990	45	361	23	4	25
Smith	1.000	8	61	3	0	8
Swisher	1.000	1	9	0	0	1

Second Base	PCT	G	PO	A	E	DP
Appert	1.000	1	0	1	0	0
Beattie	.971	66	132	165	9	36
Bynum	1.000	1	1	1	0	0
Clark	.996	54	87	143	1	27
Ginter	1.000	4	4	11	0	1
Gomez	.889	3	7	9	2	1
Morrissey	1.000	8	15	20	0	4
Rouse	.981	11	28	23	1	6

Third Base	PCT	G	PO	A	E	DP
Beattie	.973	19	9	27	1	0
Bocachica	1.000	3	2	5	0	0
Clark	.963	9	7	19	1	0
Ginter	.958	9	6	17	1	3
Morrissey	.953	18	11	30	2	2
Smith	.915	91	56	193	23	17

Shortstop	PCT	G	PO	A	E	DP
Beattie	1.000	7	5	14	0	3
Bynum	.904	22	28	47	8	8
Crosby	1.000	2	3	4	0	2
Rouse	.962	118	200	261	18	54

Outfield	PCT	G	PO	A	E	DP
Beattie	.944	16	33	1	2	1
Bynum	.983	77	170	4	3	1
Clark	1.000	4	7	1	0	0
Cust	.971	77	129	4	4	0
Ethier	.800	4	3	1	1	0
Garrett	.983	88	162	8	3	3
Herrera	1.000	5	9	0	0	0
Johnson	1.000	2	4	0	0	0
Swisher	1.000	2	1	0	0	0
Thomas	.984	72	184	1	3	0
Watson	.978	99	181	0	4	0

MIDLAND ROCKHOUNDS

Class AA

TEXAS LEAGUE

BATTING	B-T	HT	WT	DOB	AVG	vLH	vRH	G	AB	R	H	2B	3B	HR	RBI	BB	HBP	SH	SF	SO	SB	CS	SLG	OBP
Allegra, Matt	R-R	6-3	214	7-10-81	.187	.200	.180	56	203	19	38	8	0	6	23	10	2	1	3	75	0	0	.315	.229
Barton, Daric	L-R	6-0	205	8-16-85	.316	.250	.340	56	212	38	67	20	1	5	37	35	0	0	2	30	1	1	.491	.410
Beattie, Andrew	B-R	5-10	165	2-28-78	.293	.375	.259	22	82	13	24	6	0	3	17	17	0	1	0	22	1	0	.476	.414
Brown, Jeremy	R-R	5-10	210	10-25-79	.261	.250	.266	115	394	65	103	27	1	20	72	52	11	0	5	88	0	0	.487	.359
Colamarino, Brant	L-L	5-10	221	12-4-80	.321	.391	.280	46	187	31	60	13	4	10	45	18	0	0	2	34	0	0	.594	.377
Ethier, Andre	L-L	6-3	195	4-10-82	.319	.291	.332	131	505	104	161	30	3	18	80	48	11	0	8	93	1	4	.497	.385
Gomez, Francis	R-R	5-11	184	9-2-81	.223	.236	.219	68	224	27	50	12	2	4	20	8	3	3	4	62	2	3	.348	.255
Jackson, Steve	R-R	6-5	235	12-13-77	.303	.308	.300	11	33	7	10	2	2	2	6	6	0	1	0	8	0	0	.667	.410
Kiger, Mark	R-R	5-10	180	5-30-80	.267	.293	.256	131	460	68	123	31	0	5	45	68	2	6	6	94	9	4	.367	.360
Melillo, Kevin	L-R	5-11	185	5-14-82	.282	.316	.277	35	131	33	37	10	0	7	34	14	0	0	2	23	9	2	.519	.347
Morris, Jed	L-R	5-11	200	3-4-80	.111	.182	.000	4	18	1	2	1	0	0	0	1	0	0	0	2	0	0	.167	.158
Morrissey, Adam	R-R	5-11	170	6-8-81	.240	.265	.230	34	121	16	29	3	1	2	15	5	0	1	0	38	0	1	.331	.270
Myers, Casey	R-R	5-10	209	10-23-78	.340	.323	.348	57	203	31	69	11	0	7	42	14	5	0	4	11	0	0	.498	.389
Perry, Jason	L-R	6-0	200	8-18-80	.257	.212	.273	124	435	68	112	21	4	22	77	45	13	0	4	126	1	4	.476	.342
Quintanilla, Omar	L-R	5-9	190	10-24-81	.293	.241	.313	78	294	46	86	14	2	4	25	23	2	1	1	40	2	3	.395	.347
Spanos, Vasili	R-R	6-1	225	2-25-81	.235	.267	.221	43	149	20	35	6	0	6	27	12	9	0	4	40	1	0	.396	.322
Stanley, Steve	L-L	5-8	161	12-23-79	.290	.296	.288	128	514	87	149	26	4	6	46	61	2	6	5	62	8	8	.391	.364
Stavisky, Brian	L-R	6-2	210	7-6-80	.316	.310	.318	135	510	84	161	36	6	11	88	69	3	0	4	84	0	5	.475	.398
Turner, Lloyd	R-R	6-1	175	4-11-80	.250	.261	.241	48	148	15	37	6	0	2	18	18	0	3	0	25	6	3	.331	.331

PITCHING	B-T	HT	WT	DOB	W	L	ERA	G	GS	CG	SV	IP	H	R	ER	HR	BB	SO	AVG	vLH	vRH	K/9	BB/9
Bondurant, Steven	L-L	6-0	185	3-3-80	12	9	4.58	28	28	0	0	165	171	94	84	20	59	128	.271	.220	.284	6.98	3.22
Braden, Dallas	L-L	6-1	180	8-13-83	9	5	3.90	16	16	0	0	97	104	43	42	5	32	71	.281	.282	.281	6.59	2.97
Brannon, Nick	L-L	6-5	190	4-23-78	1	1	4.21	26	1	0	0	36	32	23	17	3	33	31	.239	.333	.221	7.68	8.17
Crowell, Kyle	R-R	5-11	190	6-16-79	3	1	3.44	39	1	0	0	65	64	26	25	7	21	49	.255	.275	.244	6.75	2.89
Dickinson, Drew	L-L	6-2	174	12-13-79	6	10	5.91	27	26	0	0	120	167	91	79	11	54	53	.332	.202	.370	3.96	4.04
Fahrner, Evan	R-R	6-2	200	3-4-78	7	2	2.48	45	0	0	3	76	71	27	21	4	28	68	.245	.255	.235	8.02	3.30
Garcia, Jairo	R-R	6-0	165	3-7-83	0	0	1.08	10	0	0	6	17	9	3	2	1	9	30	.153	.211	.125	16.20	4.86
Gwyn, Marcus	R-R	6-3	219	11-4-77	0	1	2.86	19	0	0	0	28	24	9	9	1	17	21	.240	.195	.271	6.67	5.40
Kohn, Shawn	R-R	6-2	208	1-28-80	4	3	2.89	55	0	0	8	84	64	28	27	5	20	92	.215	.235	.205	9.86	2.14
Komine, Shane	R-R	5-8	186	10-18-80	2	1	3.16	5	5	0	0	31	27	12	11	5	7	33	.235	.212	.254	9.48	2.01
Landeros, Leonard	L-L	6-3	177	12-12-80	2	2	5.68	18	3	0	0	32	44	21	20	3	11	20	.328	.414	.305	5.68	3.13
Lynch, Matt	L-L	6-1	195	1-14-81	7	7	4.40	35	15	0	1	110	126	71	54	7	38	65	.284	.316	.275	5.30	3.10
Mattioni, Nick	R-R	6-3	195	3-14-79	2	4	2.58	42	0	0	4	70	56	24	20	6	21	71	.216	.289	.173	9.17	2.71
Nannini, Mike	R-R	5-11	190	8-9-80	8	1	5.79	13	13	0	0	75	80	51	48	10	13	44	.274	.268	.279	5.30	1.57
Obenchain, Stephen	R-R	6-5	220	7-29-81	4	3	5.92	11	11	0	0	52	67	40	34	4	29	37	.312	.315	.310	6.45	5.05
Santos, Alex	R-R	6-1	215	8-9-77	2	3	2.95	37	0	0	19	43	33	14	14	2	15	46	.210	.161	.238	9.70	3.16
Weis, Brad	L-L	6-1	187	11-29-77	1	1	3.27	29	0	0	1	33	32	18	12	2	22	25	.244	.086	.302	6.82	6.00
Windsor, Jason	R-R	6-2	209	7-16-82	3	6	5.72	11	11	0	0	57	69	40	36	5	23	39	.303	.301	.304	6.19	3.65
Ziegler, Brad	R-R	6-4	190	10-10-79	2	1	6.86	4	4	0	0	21	27	16	16	1	4	20	.310	.250	.372	8.57	1.71
Ziegler, Mike	R-R	6-3	229	7-25-79	3	1	6.54	6	6	0	0	32	51	27	23	3	8	21	.357	.380	.344	5.97	2.27

FIELDING

Catcher	PCT	G	PO	A	E	DP	PB
Brown	.984	106	691	58	12	6	9
Jackson	.962	8	48	3	2	0	2
Morris	1.000	4	31	4	0	0	0
Myers	.991	31	197	16	2	1	1

First Base	PCT	G	PO	A	E	DP
Allegra	.990	18	191	10	2	10
Barton	.990	55	448	26	5	35
Brown	.975	4	39	0	1	3
Colamarino	.998	46	416	18	1	33
Jackson	1.000	2	18	2	0	3
Myers	1.000	3	25	0	0	3
Spanos	.982	11	108	4	2	11
Stavisky	.909	1	10	0	1	0
Turner	1.000	1	9	1	0	3

Second Base	PCT	G	PO	A	E	DP
Beattie	1.000	1	2	0	0	0
Gomez	1.000	9	25	20	0	6
Kiger	.988	74	141	192	4	41
Melillo	.986	34	59	87	2	25
Morrissey	.939	14	19	27	3	5
Quintanilla	.923	5	14	10	2	3
Turner	.957	15	35	31	3	7

Third Base	PCT	G	PO	A	E	DP
Allegra	.864	9	5	14	3	1
Beattie	.915	18	10	44	5	3
Gomez	.957	54	24	109	6	15
Morrissey	.900	19	4	32	4	2
Perry	1.000	1	0	1	0	0
Spanos	.932	31	18	50	5	2
Turner	.881	24	15	44	8	2

Shortstop	PCT	G	PO	A	E	DP
Beattie	.800	2	2	6	2	3
Gomez	.918	12	15	30	4	7
Kiger	.969	61	79	175	8	32
Quintanilla	.963	74	81	229	12	33

Outfield	PCT	G	PO	A	E	DP
Allegra	1.000	24	42	1	0	0
Barton	.000	1	0	0	0	0
Beattie	1.000	1	2	0	0	0
Ethier	.990	127	275	16	3	2
Perry	.984	93	183	6	3	2
Stanley	.997	125	297	9	1	2
Stavisky	.989	55	92	1	1	0
Turner	.000	2	0	0	0	0

STOCKTON PORTS — High Class A

CALIFORNIA LEAGUE

BATTING	B-T	HT	WT	DOB	AVG	vLH	vRH	G	AB	R	H	2B	3B	HR	RBI	BB	HBP	SH	SF	SO	SB	CS	SLG	OBP
Allegra, Matt	R-R	6-3	214	7-10-81	.258	.209	.273	50	182	29	47	11	1	9	36	27	4	0	0	62	1	1	.478	.366
Appert, Luke	L-R	6-0	185	7-14-80	.251	.248	.252	113	410	72	103	27	7	12	72	69	5	7	3	65	1	3	.439	.363
Arias, Roberto	R-R	6-1	190	1-2-83	.273	.000	.375	3	11	4	3	0	0	0	2	4	0	1	0	2	0	0	.273	.467
Barton, Daric	L-R	6-0	205	8-16-85	.318	.313	.321	79	292	60	93	16	2	8	52	62	3	0	4	49	0	1	.469	.438
Cornejo, Eddie	L-R	5-10	175	11-19-81	.304	.294	.306	89	316	45	96	14	0	2	38	31	3	6	2	34	2	3	.367	.369
Crosby, Bobby	R-R	6-3	195	1-12-80	.333	.250	.400	3	9	1	3	1	0	0	1	2	0	0	0	1	0	0	.444	.455
Gomez, Francis	R-R	5-11	184	9-2-81	.269	.222	.284	51	186	22	50	13	0	6	27	16	2	2	2	42	7	1	.435	.330
Majewski, Dustin	L-L	5-11	190	8-16-81	.272	.230	.287	136	533	91	145	43	3	20	73	60	4	4	4	130	13	7	.477	.348
McCurdy, John	R-R	6-1	200	4-17-81	.252	.245	.255	94	341	47	86	16	3	8	44	34	2	2	3	85	3	4	.387	.321
Melillo, Kevin	L-R	5-11	185	5-14-82	.400	.423	.391	22	90	21	36	7	1	9	23	12	1	0	1	18	2	0	.800	.471
Morris, Jed	L-R	5-11	200	3-4-80	.302	.212	.332	75	268	49	81	26	1	14	55	31	3	0	4	59	1	3	.563	.376
Perez, Luis	R-R	5-10	193	8-17-83	.302	.436	.234	31	116	16	35	9	2	2	18	8	0	0	2	20	0	2	.466	.341
Putnam, Danny	L-L	5-11	195	9-17-82	.307	.299	.311	131	514	97	158	37	3	15	100	66	6	1	7	92	1	3	.479	.388
Robnett, Richie	L-L	5-10	200	9-17-83	.243	.222	.251	115	457	77	111	30	0	20	74	56	1	1	4	151	8	4	.440	.324
Spanos, Vasili	R-R	6-1	225	2-25-81	.310	.286	.319	77	281	51	87	21	4	9	57	46	14	0	2	73	5	2	.509	.429
Suzuki, Kurt	R-R	6-0	200	10-4-83	.277	.317	.262	114	441	85	122	26	5	12	65	63	12	2	5	61	5	3	.440	.378
Turner, Lloyd	R-R	6-1	175	4-11-80	.282	.313	.270	63	252	49	71	13	5	6	23	26	8	2	2	54	11	5	.444	.365
Wayment, Kory	R-R	6-1	173	2-18-81	.185	.211	.163	25	81	10	15	4	0	0	6	10	0	1	1	21	0	0	.235	.272
Winslow, Ben	R-R	6-2	192	10-16-79	.236	.278	.216	23	55	9	13	4	1	1	6	6	2	0	0	23	0	0	.400	.333

PITCHING	B-T	HT	WT	DOB	W	L	ERA	G	GS	CG	SV	IP	H	R	ER	HR	BB	SO	AVG	vLH	vRH	K/9	BB/9
Acevedo, Danielin	R-R	6-3	195	4-2-83	1	3	8.00	8	6	0	0	36	56	43	32	4	16	24	.346	.333	.357	6.00	4.00
Avendano, Elvis	R-R	6-1	196	2-8-83	2	4	5.49	39	0	0	0	57	71	37	35	7	18	51	.305	.340	.281	8.01	2.83
Braden, Dallas	L-L	6-1	180	8-13-83	6	0	2.68	7	7	1	0	44	31	14	13	4	11	64	.201	.145	.232	13.19	2.27
Bradford, Chad	R-R	6-5	205	9-14-74	0	0	3.86	3	0	0	0	2	3	1	1	0	1	1	.300	.000	.600	3.86	3.86
Burton, Jared	R-R	6-5	224	6-2-81	4	4	2.60	52	0	0	24	55	44	21	16	2	20	67	.212	.250	.189	10.90	3.25
Cabaniel, Tomas	R-R	6-0	196	2-10-83	1	0	12.60	4	0	0	0	5	7	7	7	1	5	2	.318	.167	.375	3.60	9.00
Corchado, Jose	R-R	6-0	196	4-5-84	0	1	11.81	4	0	0	0	5	5	7	7	1	7	4	.250	.000	.385	6.75	11.81
Crowder, Justin	L-L	6-0	208	9-24-79	3	2	2.47	50	1	0	1	55	53	21	15	4	23	60	.248	.250	.245	9.88	3.79
Dickinson, Drew	L-L	6-2	174	12-13-79	0	0	0.00	1	0	0	0	1	0	0	0	0	2	1	.000	.000	.000	13.50	27.00
Drucker, Scot	R-R	6-2	192	5-30-82	7	1	5.51	29	9	0	1	83	107	54	51	11	26	61	.318	.346	.300	6.59	2.81
Dunn, Keith	R-R	6-2	180	4-18-78	11	4	4.56	18	18	0	0	101	112	64	51	18	28	77	.277	.265	.284	6.88	2.50
Dunwell, Chris	R-R	6-1	193	1-29-80	9	5	5.63	30	12	0	1	88	115	61	55	15	31	89	.320	.331	.312	9.10	3.17
Fritz, Ben	R-R	6-4	238	3-29-81	0	0	8.10	2	2	0	0	7	10	6	6	0	2	3	.345	.600	.211	4.05	2.70
Knox, Brad	R-R	6-2	230	5-27-82	8	7	4.27	20	20	0	0	112	109	59	53	13	34	93	.258	.285	.242	7.50	2.74
Komine, Shane	R-R	5-8	186	10-18-80	0	0	4.15	2	2	0	0	9	10	4	4	0	3	11	.294	.313	.278	11.42	3.12
Landeros, Leonard	L-L	6-3	177	12-12-80	0	0	1.93	1	1	0	0	5	4	1	1	0	4	7	.250	.000	.286	13.50	7.71
Leon, Brigmer	R-R	6-3	213	4-7-81	0	4	5.83	27	1	0	1	46	65	40	30	7	20	39	.328	.325	.331	7.58	3.88
McBeth, Marcus	R-R	6-2	183	8-23-80	0	0	0.00	2	0	0	0	3	1	0	0	0	2	3	.125	.000	.333	10.13	6.75
Muessig, Jeff	R-R	6-2	208	2-27-82	1	5	4.80	49	0	0	15	60	56	43	32	6	35	80	.245	.214	.267	12.00	5.25
Peterson, Trent	R-L	6-1	180	11-16-81	4	6	6.04	15	15	0	0	79	107	64	53	10	25	59	.317	.324	.313	6.72	2.85
Pickens, Joseph	L-R	6-0	227	6-22-80	1	1	7.59	16	0	0	0	21	28	19	18	1	10	21	.311	.313	.310	8.86	4.22
Reynolds, Grant	R-R	5-10	185	2-2-80	0	0	14.40	4	0	0	0	5	9	8	8	3	4	3	.375	.125	.500	5.40	7.20
Robertson, Connor	R-R	6-2	215	9-10-81	5	2	2.76	32	0	0	1	42	37	17	13	1	23	68	.228	.294	.198	14.46	4.89
Rodriguez, Manuel	R-R	6-3	183	5-2-81	0	0	8.10	6	0	0	0	10	16	9	9	4	2	3	.364	.438	.321	2.70	1.80
Santos, Alex	R-R	6-1	215	8-9-77	0	0	0.56	12	0	0	7	16	8	2	1	1	2	20	.143	.130	.152	11.25	1.13
Shank, Chris	R-R	6-1	200	1-31-81	0	2	4.82	8	0	0	0	9	11	8	5	1	4	10	.297	.545	.192	9.64	3.86
Sharpe, Steven	R-R	6-1	195	7-20-81	1	0	5.40	3	1	0	0	7	4	4	4	0	6	9	.182	.167	.200	12.15	8.10
Smyth, Steve	L-L	6-1	205	6-3-78	3	1	6.02	9	9	0	0	43	53	36	29	5	24	32	.293	.333	.279	6.65	4.98
Sullivan, Brad	R-R	6-0	195	9-12-81	0	1	7.30	13	2	0	0	25	36	26	20	4	21	11	.356	.381	.339	4.01	7.66
Windsor, Jason	R-R	6-2	209	7-16-82	2	2	3.58	10	10	0	0	55	52	28	22	5	8	64	.244	.293	.202	10.41	1.30
Ziegler, Brad	R-R	6-4	190	10-10-79	9	7	4.66	24	24	0	0	141	166	84	73	13	20	144	.288	.294	.284	9.19	1.28

FIELDING

Catcher	PCT	G	PO	A	E	DP	PB
Arias	1.000	3	21	2	0	0	0
Barton	1.000	1	1	0	0	0	0
Morris	.993	36	287	16	2	0	2
Suzuki	.984	104	882	50	15	7	19

First Base	PCT	G	PO	A	E	DP
Allegra	.972	40	294	20	9	32
Appert	1.000	4	25	5	0	4
Barton	.980	58	421	31	9	40
Morris	.955	8	56	7	3	6
Spanos	.996	29	208	14	1	27
Turner	1.000	2	21	0	0	3
Winslow	.967	7	27	2	1	2

Second Base	PCT	G	PO	A	E	DP
Appert	.933	65	110	127	17	32
Cornejo	.988	17	34	47	1	10
Melillo	.959	21	35	58	4	13
Turner	.945	37	69	87	9	30
Wayment	.500	1	2	0	2	0

Third Base	PCT	G	PO	A	E	DP
Appert	.929	14	5	21	2	3
Barton	1.000	1	1	0	0	0
Cornejo	.971	28	21	46	2	3
McCurdy	.952	54	31	89	6	7
Morris	1.000	1	0	2	0	0
Spanos	.953	32	21	60	4	5
Turner	.818	13	6	12	4	1
Winslow	.889	3	4	4	1	0

Shortstop	PCT	G	PO	A	E	DP
Cornejo	.960	36	53	117	7	21
Crosby	1.000	2	1	2	0	1
Gomez	.926	50	74	152	18	35
McCurdy	.961	36	51	96	6	17
Wayment	.966	19	30	56	3	14
Winslow	1.000	1	2	4	0	2

Outfield	PCT	G	PO	A	E	DP
Allegra	1.000	9	13	1	0	0
Appert	.000	1	0	0	0	0
Barton	1.000	1	2	0	0	0
Majewski	.981	133	295	9	6	2
Morris	1.000	4	5	2	0	2
Perez	.938	17	30	0	2	0
Putnam	.971	129	222	10	7	0
Robnett	.970	113	218	10	7	3
Turner	1.000	9	20	0	0	0
Wayment	1.000	2	1	0	0	0
Winslow	1.000	12	19	1	0	1

KANE COUNTY COUGARS — Low Class A

MIDWEST LEAGUE

BATTING	B-T	HT	WT	DOB	AVG	vLH	vRH	G	AB	R	H	2B	3B	HR	RBI	BB	HBP	SH	SF	SO	SB	CS	SLG	OBP
Arias, Roberto	R-R	6-1	190	1-2-83	.095	.167	.000	8	21	1	2	1	0	0	1	4	0	0	0	6	0	0	.143	.240
Blasi, Nick	R-R	5-10	200	9-23-81	.263	.248	.268	116	411	57	108	25	0	4	52	47	3	3	4	81	19	1	.353	.340
Buck, Travis	L-R	6-3	210	11-18-83	.341	.258	.370	32	123	17	42	13	0	1	22	19	0	1	1	19	3	1	.472	.427

BATTING	B-T	HT	WT	DOB	AVG	vLH	vRH	G	AB	R	H	2B	3B	HR	RBI	BB	HBP	SH	SF	SO	SB	CS	SLG	OBP
Castillo, David	R-R	5-9	185	9-15-81	.204	.107	.246	32	93	17	19	5	0	1	9	11	3	0	1	22	0	0	.290	.306
Chapman, Travis	R-R	6-1	215	9-6-80	.111	.160	.096	45	108	8	12	5	0	0	10	16	1	1	2	24	0	1	.157	.228
Everidge, Tommy	R-R	6-1	215	4-20-83	.279	.365	.240	114	365	59	102	26	3	14	66	56	1	0	8	73	1	0	.482	.370
Herrera, Javier	R-R	5-11	191	4-9-85	.275	.250	.283	94	360	70	99	18	2	13	62	47	12	0	3	110	26	5	.444	.374
Kim, Eddie	L-R	6-3	260	4-16-81	.248	.205	.257	77	246	39	61	14	0	12	54	20	3	0	6	50	1	0	.451	.305
Leslie, Myron	B-R	6-3	220	5-2-82	.275	.255	.281	131	472	77	130	32	2	15	68	78	2	0	5	89	2	1	.447	.377
Long, Wes	R-R	5-11	195	6-12-82	.193	.133	.226	29	83	10	16	1	1	1	6	10	0	0	1	16	1	0	.265	.277
Melillo, Kevin	L-R	5-11	185	5-14-82	.286	.261	.294	78	280	47	80	18	3	8	36	53	3	1	5	40	10	4	.457	.399
Padron, Raul	L-R	6-0	195	9-17-84	.259	.212	.268	113	394	40	102	17	2	6	57	27	3	0	7	78	0	0	.358	.306
Pennington, Cliff	B-R	5-11	180	6-15-84	.276	.253	.284	69	290	49	80	15	0	3	29	39	2	2	1	47	25	6	.359	.364
Perez, Luis	R-R	5-10	193	8-17-83	.286	.379	.257	56	245	38	70	13	2	8	39	11	0	0	2	30	4	1	.453	.314
Petit, Gregorio	R-R	5-10	160	12-10-84	.289	.238	.304	87	287	55	83	10	4	9	33	26	1	3	1	44	8	2	.446	.349
Pineda, Jose	R-R	6-2	175	2-25-82	.255	.229	.264	76	278	43	71	15	2	6	43	37	6	0	1	72	5	2	.388	.354
Ruiz, Ryan	R-R	5-9	185	10-18-81	.247	.205	.263	93	283	60	70	16	1	11	45	53	5	5	4	68	8	5	.428	.371
Tietje, Chalon	R-R	6-0	198	6-11-82	.231	.357	.178	42	143	20	33	7	1	1	18	11	5	3	0	30	2	1	.315	.308
Tritle, Chris	R-R	6-3	210	6-22-82	.216	.260	.205	34	102	16	22	5	0	3	11	21	0	0	0	52	5	3	.353	.350
Wayment, Kory	R-R	6-1	173	2-18-81	.228	.205	.235	58	193	27	44	10	1	3	20	16	1	3	1	49	0	1	.337	.289

PITCHING	B-T	HT	WT	DOB	W	L	ERA	G	GS	CG	SV	IP	H	R	ER	HR	BB	SO	AVG	vLH	vRH	K/9	BB/9
Cabaniel, Tomas	R-R	6-0	196	2-10-83	1	3	4.43	31	0	0	2	41	38	24	20	4	30	32	.252	.271	.243	7.08	6.64
Corchado, Jose	R-R	6-0	196	4-5-84	0	2	7.30	12	0	0	1	12	10	11	10	0	21	13	.238	.167	.267	9.49	15.32
Drucker, Scot	R-R	6-2	192	5-30-82	2	3	2.86	21	0	0	11	22	22	13	7	1	9	24	.256	.333	.214	9.82	3.68
Evans, Tony	R-R	6-4	198	11-27-79	6	6	4.24	15	15	1	0	91	85	50	43	15	35	70	.240	.233	.245	6.90	3.45
Ford, Ryan	L-L	6-3	180	7-10-82	14	7	4.26	26	26	0	0	144	141	83	68	10	58	85	.265	.289	.261	5.32	3.63
Fyvie, Dan	R-R	6-0	207	8-12-82	2	0	2.01	13	0	0	1	22	18	8	5	0	6	22	.217	.194	.231	8.87	2.42
Heuser, James	L-L	6-5	200	3-30-84	0	2	4.30	18	0	0	0	15	11	8	7	0	16	10	.212	.261	.172	6.14	9.82
Martinez, Shawn	R-R	6-3	240	3-7-82	0	0	4.70	14	0	0	0	23	26	13	12	2	11	15	.274	.167	.339	5.87	4.30
McBeth, Marcus	R-R	6-2	183	8-23-80	1	2	5.03	16	0	0	1	20	20	11	11	2	13	21	.263	.269	.260	9.61	5.95
Mitchell, Mike	R-R	6-2	185	10-27-81	0	0	3.24	19	0	0	3	25	24	11	9	2	11	19	.258	.256	.259	6.84	3.96
Perez, Keith	R-R	6-2	200	1-18-80	2	0	6.39	26	0	0	1	31	37	24	22	1	20	26	.296	.176	.378	7.55	5.81
Peterson, Trent	R-L	6-1	180	11-16-81	3	3	3.13	16	8	0	0	63	65	25	22	4	11	54	.271	.372	.249	7.67	1.56
Pickens, Joe	L-R	6-0	227	6-22-80	5	2	4.92	33	0	0	2	57	59	37	31	3	27	37	.271	.253	.281	5.88	4.29
Robertson, Connor	R-R	6-2	215	9-10-81	2	2	2.93	20	0	0	1	28	23	10	9	0	14	47	.232	.200	.243	15.29	4.55
Rogers, Michael	R-R	6-1	205	10-24-82	6	8	4.90	26	26	0	0	138	147	83	75	15	51	111	.274	.264	.280	7.26	3.33
Scott, Joseph	R-R	6-0	185	7-30-80	5	2	4.66	14	9	0	1	58	61	37	30	5	30	35	.271	.290	.258	5.43	4.66
Semerano, Rob	R-R	6-1	185	7-18-81	4	2	3.28	39	0	0	10	47	38	17	17	3	18	48	.221	.180	.243	9.26	3.47
Sharpe, Steven	R-R	6-1	195	7-20-81	3	4	5.85	18	10	0	0	60	68	50	39	5	39	33	.287	.315	.269	4.95	5.85
Tharpe, Derek	L-L	5-11	188	10-30-81	2	7	4.67	36	12	0	0	91	96	56	47	9	26	67	.270	.240	.279	6.65	2.58
Tichota, Clay	R-R	6-4	210	11-26-81	0	1	7.76	18	0	0	0	27	34	27	23	2	16	23	.306	.265	.325	7.76	5.40
Trout, Jared	R-R	6-0	175	1-15-82	4	5	4.78	38	10	0	2	92	99	60	49	6	29	58	.267	.283	.256	5.65	2.83
Webb, Ryan	R-R	6-6	195	2-5-86	5	11	4.76	24	23	0	0	129	139	82	68	16	41	84	.280	.311	.258	5.88	2.87

FIELDING

Catcher	PCT	G	PO	A	E	DP	PB
Arias	.967	6	29	0	1	0	2
Castillo	.981	29	190	21	4	2	5
Chapman	.989	45	255	23	3	0	4
Padron	.980	87	486	40	11	3	15

First Base	PCT	G	PO	A	E	DP
Everidge	.988	95	693	55	9	60
Kim	.987	57	410	33	6	33
Melillo	1.000	1	6	2	0	1
Padron	.981	7	48	4	1	3

Second Base	PCT	G	PO	A	E	DP
Long	1.000	1	1	1	0	1
Melillo	.968	68	135	167	10	37
Petit	.980	43	94	102	4	26
Ruiz	.936	37	89	71	11	22

Third Base	PCT	G	PO	A	E	DP
Leslie	.915	118	89	234	30	12
Long	.816	14	5	26	7	2
Petit	.935	10	5	24	2	2
Wayment	1.000	2	0	6	0	0

Shortstop	PCT	G	PO	A	E	DP
Melillo	1.000	1	0	2	0	0
Pennington	.958	65	99	194	13	31
Petit	.951	29	50	87	7	21
Ruiz	.987	23	21	57	1	11
Wayment	.951	29	35	100	7	21

Outfield	PCT	G	PO	A	E	DP
Blasi	.991	111	204	7	2	1
Buck	.985	30	64	0	1	0
Herrera	.967	88	222	10	8	0
Perez	.990	48	95	5	1	1
Pineda	.971	59	128	4	4	1
Ruiz	.000	1	0	0	0	0
Tietje	1.000	36	54	3	0	1
Tritle	1.000	33	71	0	0	0
Wayment	1.000	28	44	3	0	1

VANCOUVER CANADIANS — Short-Season Class A

NORTHWEST LEAGUE

BATTING	B-T	HT	WT	DOB	AVG	vLH	vRH	G	AB	R	H	2B	3B	HR	RBI	BB	HBP	SH	SF	SO	SB	CS	SLG	OBP
Acosta, Jesse	R-R	5-9	185	11-19-80	.182	.000	.222	3	11	2	2	0	0	0	0	1	0	1	0	5	0	0	.182	.250
Baisley, Jeff	R-R	6-3	215	12-19-82	.252	.237	.258	61	218	28	55	15	1	6	38	27	12	2	3	27	3	5	.413	.362
Bieker, Jeff	R-R	6-4	185	6-3-83	.239	.276	.227	34	117	9	28	5	0	1	10	9	8	2	0	31	1	0	.308	.336
Boyd, Chad	L-L	5-10	190	3-21-85	.283	.295	.278	56	212	28	60	15	0	1	27	22	1	1	2	24	9	5	.368	.350
Bubalo, Ty	R-R	6-3	214	8-8-83	.205	.132	.234	42	132	13	27	8	0	5	23	9	1	0	2	60	0	0	.379	.257
Buck, Travis	L-R	6-3	210	11-18-83	.361	.250	.417	9	36	7	13	1	0	2	9	5	0	0	0	8	1	1	.556	.439
Callahan, Shawn	R-R	6-2	215	9-14-82	.216	.216	.215	31	102	10	22	6	1	1	9	15	3	1	2	29	2	1	.324	.328
Garcia, Jose	R-R	6-3	210	9-23-82	.257	.224	.276	51	183	23	47	8	3	2	20	14	3	3	2	40	3	2	.366	.317
Kleen, Steve	R-R	6-4	205	5-21-83	.273	.267	.275	58	209	30	57	11	0	1	14	17	5	3	0	35	6	1	.340	.342
Long, Wes	R-R	5-11	195	6-12-82	.346	.263	.394	13	52	8	18	6	0	0	5	5	1	0	0	8	3	0	.462	.414
Martinez, Frank	B-R	6-0	164	7-19-85	.167	.056	.233	14	48	6	8	1	0	0	3	12	0	0	1	18	3	1	.188	.328
Massaro, Mike	L-L	5-11	155	4-15-84	.251	.250	.252	58	191	35	48	5	2	1	15	26	0	1	1	51	5	2	.314	.339
Omura, Isaac	L-R	5-9	170	1-21-84	.198	.441	.113	40	131	11	26	5	0	1	11	18	0	2	0	36	2	1	.260	.295
Parraz, Zeke	R-R	6-0	180	9-29-82	.250	.300	.232	26	76	10	19	3	0	0	6	10	3	0	0	20	2	0	.289	.360
Perez, Wilber	B-R	6-1	183	5-15-84	.273	.205	.307	39	132	19	36	6	1	2	20	9	1	2	1	20	10	4	.379	.322
Piper-Jordan, Andre	R-R	6-0	195	12-5-83	.200	.250	.167	6	10	0	2	1	0	0	1	2	0	0	0	4	1	0	.300	.333
Pratt, Haas	R-R	6-3	215	9-17-81	.269	.297	.258	59	223	30	60	16	0	6	29	17	5	0	2	51	2	1	.422	.332
Recker, Anthony	R-R	6-3	230	8-29-83	.233	.273	.217	43	150	16	35	8	0	5	18	16	2	1	0	40	0	0	.387	.315
Sellers, Justin	R-R	5-10	155	2-1-86	.274	.226	.295	47	175	31	48	8	1	0	13	19	8	4	1	24	8	3	.331	.369
Tietje, Chalon	R-R	6-0	198	6-11-82	.225	.179	.239	32	120	17	27	3	0	0	12	13	3	1	1	30	4	3	.250	.314
Tritle, Chris	R-R	6-3	210	6-22-82	.254	.333	.220	18	59	11	15	3	1	1	8	10	0	0	1	20	7	1	.390	.357

PITCHING	B-T	HT	WT	DOB	W	L	ERA	G	GS	CG	SV	IP	H	R	ER	HR	BB	SO	AVG	vLH	vRH	K/9	BB/9
Acevedo, Danielin	R-R	6-3	195	4-2-83	4	3	4.81	17	0	0	1	24	28	15	13	4	5	18	.298	.318	.280	6.66	1.85
Bryant, Stephen	R-R	5-10	190	9-10-82	3	3	3.03	21	0	0	3	30	24	10	10	1	7	34	.220	.255	.194	10.31	2.12
Carter, Steven	R-R	6-2	215	6-9-80	1	1	2.08	6	0	0	1	13	9	4	3	0	3	11	.176	.167	.179	7.62	2.08
Corchado, Jose	R-R	6-0	196	4-5-84	3	2	5.40	17	0	0	0	25	24	18	15	2	16	34	.253	.214	.283	12.24	5.76
Davis, Brad	R-L	6-1	185	12-20-82	4	1	0.52	23	0	0	4	35	26	6	2	1	9	44	.202	.243	.185	11.42	2.34
Fairbanks, Scott	R-R	6-3	200	4-26-81	0	0	36.00	2	0	0	0	1	0	4	4	0	4	1	.000	.000	.000	9.00	36.00
Gray, Jeff	R-R	6-3	205	11-19-81	4	2	2.51	12	11	0	0	47	33	16	13	0	5	24	.191	.214	.175	4.63	0.96
Herrera, John	R-R	6-6	195	3-8-83	1	1	6.08	16	0	0	0	24	24	16	16	1	14	16	.276	.344	.236	6.08	5.32
Kilby, Brad	L-L	6-2	225	2-19-83	2	0	1.95	23	0	0	14	28	20	7	6	2	11	38	.194	.303	.143	12.36	3.58
Madej, Ron	L-L	6-2	195	5-21-83	0	0	2.81	17	0	0	0	26	27	9	8	0	15	28	.284	.214	.313	9.82	5.26
Madsen, Mike	R-R	6-0	160	11-29-82	6	1	1.69	15	12	0	0	80	56	21	15	2	14	68	.192	.206	.180	7.65	1.58
Martinez, Shawn	R-R	6-3	240	3-7-82	1	1	4.70	4	0	0	0	8	6	5	4	1	5	8	.214	.167	.227	9.39	5.87
Mitchell, Mike	R-R	6-2	185	10-27-81	0	0	0.00	7	0	0	5	9	4	1	0	0	4	6	.118	.188	.056	5.79	3.86
Newby, Joey	R-R	6-2	205	3-8-82	5	5	4.29	15	15	0	0	78	71	39	37	2	24	50	.242	.237	.247	5.79	2.78
Piekarz, Joe	R-L	6-2	175	1-1-82	3	3	3.38	15	12	0	0	77	67	32	29	2	24	59	.232	.169	.252	6.87	2.79
Ray, Jason	R-R	6-0	208	7-14-84	0	1	2.12	20	0	0	0	30	17	8	7	1	23	56	.163	.182	.150	16.99	6.98
Scott, Joseph	R-R	6-0	185	7-30-80	2	0	2.45	4	4	0	0	22	20	6	6	2	6	12	.256	.139	.357	4.91	2.45
Shields, Trey	R-R	6-6	210	5-27-84	3	3	3.34	12	9	0	0	59	47	26	22	2	25	54	.220	.226	.212	8.19	3.79
Shull, Jimmy	R-R	6-2	175	8-21-83	4	3	2.47	14	13	0	0	73	65	25	20	3	10	81	.233	.273	.197	9.99	1.23

GAMES BY POSITION: C—Bubalo 19, Callahan 24, Recker 39. **1B**—Boyd 2, Garcia 1, Kleen 46, Pratt 31. **2B**—Acosta 3, Martinez 2, Omura 36, Parraz 2, Perez 33. **3B**—Baisley 60, Callahan 3, Long 10, Parraz 2, Perez 5. **SS**—Martinez 12, Parraz 17, Sellers 47. **OF**—Bieker 32, Boyd 46, Bubalo 9, Buck 9, Garcia 44, Kleen 1, Massaro 55, Piper-Jordan 6, Tietje 29, Tritle 17.

AZL ATHLETICS — Rookie

ARIZONA LEAGUE

BATTING	B-T	HT	WT	DOB	AVG	vLH	vRH	G	AB	R	H	2B	3B	HR	RBI	BB	HBP	SH	SF	SO	SB	CS	SLG	OBP
Alvarado, Ramon	R-R	6-1	185	6-3-85	.296	.250	.319	48	169	37	50	10	3	6	32	23	11	0	1	36	9	4	.497	.412
Bocachica, Hiram	R-R	5-11	180	3-4-76	.083	.000	.100	4	12	1	1	1	0	0	1	0	0	0	0	3	0	0	.167	.083
Hernandez, Samuel	R-R	5-10	162	9-9-84	.219	.286	.190	39	114	19	25	2	1	0	14	17	4	1	1	29	4	5	.254	.338
Ingold, Ben	R-R	6-2	205	8-18-82	.271	.254	.278	54	207	31	56	9	3	1	31	31	3	1	4	44	4	4	.357	.367
Klug, Michael	R-R	5-9	190	10-7-82	.182	.167	.190	29	88	19	16	4	1	1	13	29	5	1	1	29	14	5	.284	.407
Long, Wes	R-R	5-11	195	6-12-82	.276	.318	.250	16	58	13	16	1	0	1	7	9	2	0	2	12	3	0	.345	.380
Maldonado, Pedro	R-R	6-0	195	11-2-84	.253	.259	.250	30	87	18	22	7	2	0	7	17	3	0	0	30	2	1	.379	.393
Martinez, Frank	B-R	6-0	164	7-19-85	.205	.171	.220	35	117	28	24	6	0	1	7	24	3	2	0	39	3	2	.282	.354
Medina, Fernando	R-R	6-2	183	12-18-84	.151	.125	.163	38	126	12	19	2	4	1	12	8	2	2	0	52	4	2	.254	.213
Mendez, Ramiro	R-R	6-2	175	4-14-85	.275	.368	.219	13	51	7	14	3	1	0	6	3	0	0	0	12	1	0	.373	.315
Morales, Carlos	R-R	6-3	170	7-20-85	.255	.193	.281	52	192	22	49	8	2	1	28	23	8	0	1	52	4	4	.333	.357
Parraz, Zeke	R-R	6-0	180	9-29-82	.283	.231	.303	12	46	7	13	1	1	2	10	5	2	0	2	6	3	2	.478	.364
Piper-Jordan, Andre	R-R	6-0	195	12-5-83	.244	.233	.248	52	201	44	49	10	7	1	24	21	5	6	5	55	19	10	.378	.323
Rivera, Julio	R-R	5-11	178	7-20-87	.167	.100	.192	12	36	2	6	2	0	0	5	3	0	0	1	15	0	0	.222	.225
Rosendo, Gustavo	R-R	6-2	205	3-1-86	.246	.194	.268	34	118	13	29	3	0	0	9	9	3	1	0	18	1	1	.271	.315
Snyder, Brian	R-R	6-0	195	3-17-82	.000	.000	.000	1	1	1	0	0	0	0	0	1	0	0	0	1	0	0	.000	.500
Sutton, Don	R-R	6-1	220	11-21-83	.320	.222	.375	8	25	2	8	2	0	0	4	2	0	0	1	10	0	0	.400	.357
Valdez, Alexander	R-R	6-1	160	9-2-84	.222	.105	.273	51	189	24	42	5	5	4	39	21	4	5	3	44	8	4	.365	.309

PITCHING	B-T	HT	WT	DOB	W	L	ERA	G	GS	CG	SV	IP	H	R	ER	HR	BB	SO	AVG	vLH	vRH	K/9	BB/9
Acevedo, Danielin	R-R	6-3	195	4-2-83	0	0	6.00	2	1	0	0	3	3	2	2	0	0	1	.250	.250	.250	3.00	0.00
Bradford, Chad	R-R	6-5	205	9-14-74	0	0	0.00	3	3	0	0	3	3	0	0	0	0	2	.273	.250	.286	6.00	0.00
Bunch, Kevin	R-R	6-5	215	11-4-86	2	0	2.70	5	0	0	1	10	6	3	3	1	3	11	.176	.091	.217	9.90	2.70
Deal, Scott	R-R	6-4	180	12-11-86	1	2	4.97	9	7	0	0	25	34	17	14	2	12	19	.340	.235	.394	6.75	4.26
Eusebio, Keith	B-R	5-10	173	1-31-83	1	2	5.40	14	2	0	1	30	36	24	18	3	12	17	.303	.306	.301	5.10	3.60
Franco,T.J.	R-R	6-2	190	6-28-83	5	6	3.66	14	8	1	0	64	76	34	26	1	15	51	.299	.314	.289	7.17	2.11
Fritz, Ben	R-R	6-4	238	3-29-81	0	0	0.00	4	4	0	0	11	3	1	0	0	3	9	.088	.071	.100	7.36	2.45
Fyvie, Dan	R-R	6-0	207	8-12-82	0	0	1.80	3	3	0	0	5	4	1	1	0	2	3	.211	.000	.286	5.40	3.60
Granados, Ivan	L-L	6-2	185	9-30-85	1	0	0.00	1	0	0	0	4	2	1	0	0	1	7	.133	.000	.182	14.54	2.08
Italiano, Craig	R-R	6-3	190	7-22-86	1	2	6.75	8	3	0	0	19	20	17	14	0	8	27	.267	.345	.217	13.02	3.86
Kay, Josh	R-R	6-0	185	10-3-82	0	1	3.38	16	0	0	5	19	17	7	7	0	3	24	.246	.429	.167	11.57	1.45
Komine, Shane	R-R	5-8	186	10-18-80	0	1	9.72	4	4	0	0	8	10	10	9	0	7	11	.294	.250	.333	11.88	7.56
Lansford, Jared	R-R	6-2	190	10-22-86	0	1	1.27	7	6	0	0	21	16	4	3	0	5	20	.216	.290	.163	8.44	2.11
Luces, Victor	R-R	6-3	191	10-10-84	3	1	3.86	9	0	0	0	21	21	10	9	0	10	20	.269	.167	.315	8.57	4.29
Lugo, Jose	L-L	6-1	159	4-10-84	2	3	5.23	15	5	0	0	53	57	42	31	0	18	44	.273	.271	.273	7.43	3.04
Martinez, Jesus	R-R	6-2	171	5-27-84	0	0	0.00	1	0	0	0	1	2	0	0	0	0	0	.500	1.000	.000	0.00	0.00
McBeth, Marcus	R-R	6-2	183	8-23-80	1	0	0.90	8	0	0	4	10	5	2	1	1	5	13	.147	.154	.143	11.70	4.50
Noboa, Leandro	R-R	6-0	175	11-10-85	0	0	8.78	12	0	0	0	13	24	23	13	2	7	4	.375	.261	.439	2.70	4.73
Pena, Francisco	R-R	6-0	171	1-22-85	4	0	3.00	14	0	0	0	27	26	12	9	0	8	29	.250	.351	.194	9.67	2.67
Piekarz, Joe	R-L	6-2	175	1-1-82	0	0	0.00	1	0	0	0	1	0	0	0	0	1	0	.000	.000	.000	0.00	9.00
Rea, Anthony	R-R	5-11	180	8-3-82	1	2	7.36	11	0	0	1	26	40	26	21	1	8	21	.354	.324	.368	7.36	2.81
Sharpe, Steven	R-R	6-1	195	7-20-81	4	0	2.66	9	4	0	0	44	31	18	13	1	16	40	.200	.292	.159	8.18	3.27
Sullivan, Brad	R-R	6-0	195	9-12-81	0	1	9.26	3	3	0	0	12	17	13	12	1	6	10	.321	.429	.282	7.71	4.63
Tichota, Clay	R-R	6-4	210	11-26-81	2	0	8.10	9	0	0	0	17	20	15	15	2	9	14	.303	.400	.244	7.56	4.86
Torres, Luis	R-R	6-1	173	10-23-84	2	4	5.50	14	3	0	0	52	63	35	32	1	12	29	.301	.356	.272	4.99	2.06

GAMES BY POSITION: C—Maldonado 27, Rivera 10, Rosendo 25. **1B**—Hernandez 2, Ingold 19, Maldonado 1, Morales 24, Rivera 1, Rosendo 10, Sutton III 8. **2B**—Hernandez 29, Klug 23, Valdez 5. **3B**—Ingold 18, Valdez 38. **SS**—Hernandez 3, Ingold 6, Martinez 35, Parraz 12. **OF**—Alvarado 45, Bocachica 2, Hernandez 1, Klug 1, Medina 36, Mendez 10, Morales 31, Piper-Jordan 51.

PHILADELPHIA PHILLIES

BY JIM SALISBURY

The 2005 Phillies had their highest win total in a dozen years and stayed in the National League wild card race until the final day of the season.

It sounds nice, but it really wasn't. With a veteran nucleus, several exciting youngsters, and a $95-million payroll, anything short of a postseason berth was going to be a failure. Ultimately, that's what the season was.

"It's all about how deep you go into the postseason," general manager Ed Wade said after Houston edged the Phillies for the wild card on the last day of the year. "We know we haven't been there, and that's the primary measuring stick."

Days later, Wade was fired after eight seasons and no postseason berths. Twenty-two different teams have been to the postseason since the Phils last went in 1993, and fans are fed up. Their frustration hit the club in the pocketbook as attendance at two-year-old Citizens Bank Park dropped by nearly 600,000 from 3.25 million in 2004. With an average ticket price of $26.60, that's a hit of almost $16 million, and that's not counting lost concession and parking revenues.

To the customer, Wade had become the face of the team's failure. Ownership, with a high payroll to maintain and stadium debt to pay, couldn't ignore that.

"If the decision was made based on the performance of the club, obviously, not getting to the postseason plays a big role in that," Wade said. "But I also believe that I became a lightning rod for criticism for the organization. With me being out of the picture, it may make things easier in that respect."

Ironically, Wade had one of his better seasons. Jon Lieber won 17 games, more than any other pitcher from the previous winter's free-agent class. Veteran Kenny Lofton, acquired in an offseason trade, hit .335 with a .392 on-base percentage in 110 games. June acquisition Ugueth Urbina teamed with closer Billy Wagner and setup man Ryan Madson to give the Phils strength at the back of the bullpen. Young players Chase Utley and Ryan Howard both emerged as game-breakers, not long after Wade resisted trading them because they were blocked by veterans.

Utley became the regular second baseman when Placido Polanco was traded to Detroit for Urbina. He hit .291-28-105.

Howard may have been the team's most pleasing addition. He took over first base on July 1, when Jim Thome went down with an elbow injury. Howard led all rookies with 22 homers and a .567 slugging percentage en route to 63 RBIs in 88 games.

Shortstop Jimmy Rollins continued to emerge. He played stellar defense and ended the season with a 36-game hitting streak, the longest ever by a Phillie.

Veterans Pat Burrell and Bobby Abreu both drove in 100-plus runs. Abreu won the home run contest at the All-Star Game, but hit just six after that.

First-year manager Charlie Manuel was criticized by fans and media for some unorthodox moves, but he succeeded at galvanizing a clubhouse that had been beaten down by previous manager Larry Bowa.

"Charlie did a hell of a job," catcher Todd Pratt said. "He takes care of things behind closed doors and doesn't show you up. He generally cares about everyone on the squad, where, in the past, that wasn't always the case. "

The starting rotation suffered a setback when Randy Wolf went down in May. The Phils had hoped prized prospects Gavin Floyd and Cole Hamels would be ready to contribute in 2005, but neither were. Floyd had a difficult season in Triple-A, and Hamels was limited to just six starts between high Class A and Double-A due to a broken hand suffered in an offseason fight and a back injury.

Howard and righthander Robinson Tejeda both came up and made strong contributions. On the whole, though, it was a weak season in the farm system, which had been thinned by trades and forfeited draft picks.

PLAYERS OF THE YEAR

MAJOR LEAGUE: Chase Utley, 2b

On a club filled with high-priced stars, the Phillies best player made $345,000 in 2005. Utley was the most consistent everyday player on the club, leading the team in doubles and total bases. A line-drive gap hitter, Utley also showed off some pop, hitting 28 home runs—second on the team behind Pat Burrell's 32.

MINOR LEAGUE: Shane Victorino, of

A Rule 5 pick from the Padres in December 2004, Victorino blossomed in 2005 at Triple-A Scranton/Wilkes-Barre. The 25-year-old set career highs in nearly every offensive category en route to winning the International League MVP award. He led the league in triples (16), and was second in runs with 93.

ORGANIZATION LEADERS

BATTING		
*AVG	Ruiz, Randy, Reading	.349
R	Victorino, Shane, Scranton	93
H	Roberson, Chris, Reading	172
TB	Victorino, Shane, Scranton	264
2B	Dzurilla, Michael, Lakewood	33
3B	Victorino, Shane, Scranton	16
HR	Ruiz, Randy, Reading	27
RBI	Coste, Chris, Scranton	89
	Ruiz, Randy, Reading	89
BB	Orr, Sam, Lakewood	72
SO	Moss, Tim, Clearwater	129
SB	Bourn, Michael, Reading	38
*OBP	Gredvig, Doug, Clearwater/Lakewood	.413
*SLG	Ruiz, Randy, Reading	.669
PITCHING		
W	Davis, Allen, Reading/Scranton	14
L	Segovia, Zach, Clearwater	14
	Smith, Mike, Reading/Scranton	14
#ERA	Minix, Travis, Reading/Scranton	1.48
G	Three tied at	58
CG	De la Cruz, Maximino, Lakewood	5
SV	Perez, Franklin, Scranton	23
IP	Davis, Allen, Reading/Scranton	196
BB	Smith, Mike, Reading/Scranton	85
SO	Griffith, Derek, Lakewood	131

*Minimum 250 at-bats. #Minimum 75 innings.

PHILADELPHIA PHILLIES

Manager: Charlie Manuel.

2005 Record: 88-74, .543 (2nd, NL East).

BATTING	B-T	HT	WT	DOB	AVG	vLH	vRH	G	AB	R	H	2B	3B	HR	RBI	BB	HBP	SH	SF	SO	SB	CS	SLG	OBP
Abreu, Bobby	L-R	6-0	210	3-11-74	.286	.275	.291	162	588	104	168	37	1	24	102	117	6	0	8	134	31	9	.474	.405
Bell, David	R-R	5-10	190	9-14-72	.248	.400	.199	150	557	53	138	31	1	10	61	47	5	4	4	69	0	1	.361	.310
Burrell, Pat	R-R	6-4	230	10-10-76	.281	.318	.267	154	562	78	158	27	1	32	117	99	3	0	5	160	0	0	.504	.389
Byrd, Marlon	R-R	6-0	235	8-30-77	.308	.000	.400	5	13	0	4	0	0	0	0	1	1	0	0	3	0	0	.308	.400
Chavez, Endy	L-L	5-10	155	2-7-78	.215	.400	.185	91	107	17	23	3	3	0	10	4	0	7	0	13	2	1	.299	.243
2-team (7 Washington)					.216	.381	.179	98	116	19	25	4	3	0	11	7	0	7	0	14	2	2	.302	.260
Howard, Ryan	L-L	6-4	260	11-19-79	.288	.148	.323	88	312	52	90	17	2	22	63	33	1	0	2	100	0	1	.567	.356
Kata, Matt	B-R	6-1	195	3-14-78	.167	.000	.250	10	6	1	1	0	0	0	0	0	0	0	0	2	0	0	.167	.167
2-team (30 Arizona)					.189	.214	.174	40	37	7	7	2	1	0	0	5	0	2	0	6	0	1	.297	.286
Lieberthal, Mike	R-R	6-0	185	1-18-72	.263	.276	.259	118	392	48	103	25	0	12	47	35	11	0	5	35	0	0	.418	.336
Lofton, Kenny	L-L	6-0	190	5-31-67	.335	.348	.333	110	367	67	123	15	5	2	36	32	2	5	0	41	22	3	.420	.392
Martinez, Ramon	R-R	6-1	190	10-10-72	.286	.281	.292	33	56	7	16	2	0	1	9	3	1	2	3	7	0	0	.375	.317
Michaels, Jason	R-R	6-0	205	5-4-76	.304	.323	.289	105	289	54	88	16	2	4	31	44	4	2	4	45	3	3	.415	.399
Offerman, Jose	B-R	6-1	200	11-8-68	.182	.000	.250	33	33	6	6	1	1	1	3	5	0	0	0	6	0	0	.364	.289
Perez, Tomas	B-R	5-11	190	12-29-73	.233	.283	.212	94	159	17	37	7	0	0	22	11	2	3	1	27	1	0	.277	.289
Polanco, Placido	R-R	5-10	190	10-10-75	.316	.292	.333	43	158	26	50	7	0	3	20	12	3	0	0	9	0	0	.418	.376
Pratt, Todd	R-R	6-3	235	2-9-67	.251	.300	.237	60	175	17	44	4	0	7	23	19	2	0	0	50	0	0	.394	.332
Rollins, Jimmy	B-R	5-8	175	11-27-78	.290	.278	.294	158	677	115	196	38	11	12	54	47	4	2	2	71	41	6	.431	.338
Sandoval, Danny	B-R	5-11	190	4-7-79	.000	.000	.000	3	2	1	0	0	0	0	0	0	0	0	0	1	0	0	.000	.000
Thome, Jim	L-R	6-4	245	8-27-70	.207	.164	.233	59	193	26	40	7	0	7	30	45	2	0	2	59	0	0	.352	.360
Tucker, Michael	L-R	6-2	210	6-25-71	.222	1.000	.176	22	18	3	4	0	0	0	3	3	0	0	0	4	0	0	.222	.333
2-team (104 San Francisco)					.239	.152	.251	126	268	35	64	16	1	5	36	31	2	2	4	52	4	0	.362	.318
Utley, Chase	L-R	6-1	185	12-17-78	.291	.219	.313	147	543	93	158	39	6	28	105	69	9	0	7	109	16	3	.540	.376
Victorino, Shane	B-R	5-9	160	11-30-80	.294	1.000	.250	21	17	5	5	0	0	2	8	0	0	0	2	3	0	0	.647	.263

PITCHING	B-T	HT	WT	DOB	W	L	ERA	G	GS	CG	SV	IP	H	R	ER	HR	BB	SO	AVG	vLH	vRH	K-9	BB-9
Adams, Terry	R-R	6-3	225	3-6-73	0	2	12.83	16	0	0	0	13	25	19	19	3	10	4	.403	.385	.417	2.70	6.75
Brito, Eude	L-L	5-11	160	8-19-78	1	2	3.68	6	5	0	0	22	20	9	9	2	11	15	.250	.231	.254	6.14	4.50
Cormier, Rheal	L-L	5-10	200	4-23-67	4	2	5.89	57	0	0	0	47	56	33	31	9	16	34	.296	.256	.324	6.46	3.04
Floyd, Gavin	R-R	6-4	225	1-27-83	1	2	10.04	7	4	0	0	26	30	31	29	5	16	17	.283	.283	.283	5.88	5.54
Fultz, Aaron	L-L	6-0	210	9-4-73	4	0	2.24	62	0	0	0	72	47	21	18	6	23	54	.186	.220	.170	6.72	2.86
Geary, Geoff	R-R	6-0	180	8-26-76	2	1	3.72	40	0	0	0	58	54	29	24	5	21	42	.248	.192	.294	6.52	3.26
Lidle, Cory	R-R	5-11	190	3-22-72	13	11	4.53	31	31	1	0	185	210	105	93	18	40	121	.289	.289	.289	5.90	1.95
Lieber, Jon	L-R	6-2	230	4-2-70	17	13	4.20	35	35	1	0	218	223	107	102	33	41	149	.263	.302	.223	6.14	1.69
Liriano, Pedro	R-R	6-2	170	10-23-80	0	0	10.57	5	0	0	0	8	10	11	9	3	6	6	.313	.400	.235	7.04	7.04
Lopez, Aquilino	R-R	6-3	165	4-21-75	0	1	2.13	10	0	0	0	13	13	4	3	2	7	16	.265	.412	.188	11.37	4.97
2-team (1 Colorado)					0	1	2.16	11	0	0	0	17	16	5	4	2	7	22	.250	.346	.184	11.88	3.78
Madson, Ryan	L-R	6-6	195	8-28-80	6	5	4.14	78	0	0	0	87	84	44	40	11	25	79	.259	.292	.233	8.17	2.59
Myers, Brett	R-R	6-4	225	8-17-80	13	8	3.72	34	34	2	0	215	193	94	89	31	68	208	.237	.241	.233	8.69	2.84
Padilla, Vicente	R-R	6-2	220	9-27-77	9	12	4.71	27	27	0	0	147	146	79	77	22	74	103	.260	.297	.222	6.31	4.53
Tejeda, Rob	R-R	6-3	190	3-24-82	4	3	3.57	26	13	0	0	86	67	36	34	5	51	72	.218	.210	.226	7.56	5.36
Telemaco, Amaury	R-R	6-3	230	1-19-74	0	1	4.22	7	0	0	0	11	5	5	5	2	4	8	.139	.150	.125	6.75	3.38
Urbina, Ugueth	R-R	6-0	205	2-15-74	4	3	4.13	56	0	0	1	52	35	25	24	8	25	66	.186	.191	.181	11.35	4.30
Wagner, Billy	L-L	5-11	200	7-25-71	4	3	1.51	75	0	0	38	78	45	17	13	6	20	87	.165	.128	.173	10.08	2.32
Wolf, Randy	L-L	6-0	200	8-22-76	6	4	4.39	13	13	0	0	80	87	40	39	14	26	61	.282	.238	.293	6.86	2.93
Worrell, Tim	R-R	6-4	240	7-5-67	0	1	7.41	19	0	0	1	17	29	17	14	4	3	17	.377	.353	.395	9.00	1.59

FIELDING

Catcher	PCT	G	PO	A	E	DP	PB
Lieberthal	.993	117	808	44	6	5	7
Pratt	.997	57	377	18	1	4	5

First Base	PCT	G	PO	A	E	DP
Howard	.993	84	707	40	5	53
Martinez	1.000	10	75	6	0	8
Offerman	.938	4	15	0	1	1
Perez	1.000	24	148	10	0	17
Thome	1.000	52	405	30	0	36
Utley	.982	8	45	9	1	7

Second Base	PCT	G	PO	A	E	DP
Kata	.000	3	0	0	0	0
Martinez	.750	1	1	2	1	0
Polanco	1.000	29	57	74	0	26
Utley	.978	135	296	376	15	72

Third Base	PCT	G	PO	A	E	DP
Bell	.951	150	105	304	21	22
Martinez	1.000	3	1	3	0	0
Perez	1.000	15	11	17	0	2
Polanco	1.000	8	6	17	0	2

Shortstop	PCT	G	PO	A	E	DP
Kata	.000	1	0	0	0	0
Martinez	1.000	3	2	0	0	0
Perez	1.000	14	8	12	0	2
Polanco	1.000	1	3	2	0	1
Rollins	.981	157	207	411	12	80
Sandoval	1.000	1	0	1	0	0

Outfield	PCT	G	PO	A	E	DP
Abreu	.986	158	266	7	4	0
Burrell	.972	153	236	10	7	2
Byrd	1.000	5	6	0	0	0
Chavez	.980	51	45	4	1	1
Kata	.000	1	0	0	0	0
Lofton	.981	97	201	7	4	1
Michaels	.990	91	185	8	2	2
Polanco	1.000	5	10	0	0	0
Tucker	.000	1	0	0	0	0
Victorino	.000	12	0	0	0	0

FARM SYSTEM

General Manager: Ed Wade. **Director, Minor Leagues:** Steve Noworyta. **Scouting Director:** Marti Wolever.

Class	Farm Team	League	W	L	Pct.	Finish*	Manager	Affiliate Since
AAA	Scranton/W-B (Pa.) Red Barons	International	69	75	.479	t-9th (14)	Gene Lamont	1989
AA	Reading (Pa.) Phillies	Eastern	69	73	.486	8th (12)	Steve Swisher	1967
High A	Clearwater (Fla.) Threshers	Florida State	41	95	.301	12th (12)	Greg Legg	1985
Low A	Lakewood (N.J.) Blue Claws	South Atlantic	56	83	.403	16th (16)	P.J. Forbes	2001
SS A	Batavia (N.Y.) Muckdogs	New York-Penn	36	39	.480	8th (14)	Manny Amador	1988
Rookie	Clearwater (Fla.) Phillies	Gulf Coast	24	27	.471	6th (12)	Jim Morrison	1999

*Finish in overall standings (No. of teams in league)/Playoff teams in **boldface**

SCRANTON/WILKES-BARRE RED BARONS — Class AAA

ORGANIZATION STATISTICS

INTERNATIONAL LEAGUE

BATTING	B-T	HT	WT	DOB	AVG	vLH	vRH	G	AB	R	H	2B	3B	HR	RBI	BB	HBP	SH	SF	SO	SB	CS	SLG	OBP
Budzinski, Mark	L-L	6-2	180	8-26-73	.270	.214	.280	124	467	72	126	26	8	5	42	42	3	6	1	108	9	4	.392	.333
Byrd, Marlon	R-R	6-0	235	8-30-77	.368	.300	.444	5	19	4	7	1	0	3	5	0	0	0	0	3	0	0	.895	.368
Castellano, John	R-R	5-11	180	9-8-77	.271	.293	.261	90	299	44	81	16	0	6	45	27	3	0	6	41	3	2	.385	.331
Coste, Chris	R-R	6-1	200	2-4-73	.292	.316	.284	134	506	73	148	26	1	20	89	40	9	0	7	85	3	4	.466	.351
Fleming, Ryan	L-L	5-9	177	2-11-76	.200	.000	.200	3	10	0	2	0	0	0	0	0	0	0	0	1	0	1	.200	.200
Gradoville, Tim	R-R	6-3	195	1-30-80	.263	.500	.235	9	19	0	5	0	0	0	4	1	0	1	0	6	0	1	.263	.300
Grindell, Nate	R-R	6-1	180	4-9-77	.238	.297	.212	60	210	17	50	11	0	1	23	10	2	1	3	29	1	3	.305	.276
Hannahan, Buzz	R-R	6-2	182	6-29-76	.241	.288	.223	95	295	38	71	12	4	1	22	28	9	9	3	81	4	4	.319	.322
Hinch, A.J.	R-R	6-1	210	5-15-74	.279	.282	.278	85	269	30	75	15	2	3	44	22	9	2	4	45	0	0	.383	.349
Howard, Ryan	L-L	6-4	260	11-19-79	.371	.338	.387	61	210	38	78	19	0	16	54	39	3	0	5	66	0	0	.690	.467
Kata, Matt	B-R	6-1	195	3-14-78	.313	.333	.304	24	96	10	30	5	1	0	4	4	0	2	0	14	2	1	.385	.340
Leon, Carlos	R-R	5-10	181	8-31-79	.211	.667	.125	6	19	2	4	2	0	0	3	3	1	0	0	2	0	1	.316	.348
Medrano, Anthony	R-R	5-10	170	12-8-74	.221	.173	.234	111	367	45	81	15	0	3	45	27	6	16	6	46	6	1	.286	.281
Padilla, Jorge	R-R	6-2	205	8-11-79	.270	.324	.257	59	204	25	55	6	1	1	17	15	2	5	1	41	4	5	.324	.324
Ruiz, Carlos	R-R	5-10	180	1-22-79	.300	.315	.295	100	347	50	104	25	9	4	40	30	3	1	7	48	4	5	.458	.354
Rushford, Jim	L-L	6-1	220	3-24-74	.312	.212	.337	117	414	61	129	29	1	10	63	34	11	2	6	40	5	1	.459	.374
Sandoval, Danny	B-R	5-11	190	4-7-79	.331	.353	.323	104	390	53	129	20	0	7	48	31	2	11	4	49	11	11	.436	.379
Sosa, Juan	R-R	6-1	175	8-19-75	.244	.279	.233	56	172	18	42	10	2	1	15	4	0	6	2	23	1	0	.343	.258
Victorino, Shane	B-R	5-9	160	11-30-80	.310	.403	.278	126	494	93	153	25	16	18	70	51	5	5	4	74	17	9	.534	.377

PITCHING	B-T	HT	WT	DOB	W	L	ERA	G	GS	CG	SV	IP	H	R	ER	HR	BB	SO	AVG	vLH	vRH	K-9	BB-9
Adams, Terry	R-R	6-3	225	3-6-73	1	2	4.41	14	0	0	0	16	22	14	8	1	8	14	.306	.371	.243	7.71	4.41
Bacsik, Mike	L-L	6-3	190	11-11-77	7	10	4.55	30	27	0	0	160	184	90	81	23	41	112	.288	.232	.309	6.29	2.30
Brito, Eude	L-L	5-11	160	8-19-78	6	2	4.85	28	15	0	0	98	97	59	53	13	39	76	.266	.255	.270	6.96	3.57
Burke, Erick	L-L	6-4	230	8-14-77	3	0	2.97	32	0	0	1	33	29	12	11	2	22	33	.242	.296	.197	8.91	5.94
Chantres, Carlos	R-R	6-3	190	4-1-76	0	0	3.00	1	1	0	0	6	4	4	2	1	3	3	.182	.000	.267	4.50	4.50
Condrey, Clay	R-R	6-3	195	11-19-75	7	8	4.15	25	24	2	0	132	159	66	61	13	29	74	.300	.298	.302	5.03	1.97
Davis, Allen	L-L	6-4	220	10-1-75	1	1	2.03	3	3	0	0	13	11	3	3	0	1	6	.234	.143	.250	4.05	0.68
Ellis, Robert	R-R	6-5	220	12-15-70	0	1	6.38	4	4	0	0	18	24	14	13	2	7	13	.320	.281	.349	6.38	3.44
Fernandez, Jared	R-R	6-1	235	2-2-72	4	2	2.66	7	7	0	0	41	40	18	12	4	14	30	.255	.263	.250	6.64	3.10
2-team (13 Louisville)					9	7	3.82	20	20	0	0	125	126	63	53	12	40	81	.265	.286	.250	5.83	2.88
Fesh, Sean	L-L	6-2	185	11-3-72	2	0	5.89	27	0	0	0	18	21	13	12	3	15	11	.300	.297	.303	5.40	7.36
Floyd, Gavin	R-R	6-4	225	1-27-83	6	9	6.16	24	23	0	0	137	155	103	94	11	66	97	.290	.303	.278	6.36	4.33
Franco, Martire	R-R	6-0	170	2-25-78	5	6	4.86	44	10	0	2	100	122	59	54	7	39	71	.301	.340	.267	6.39	3.51
Geary, Geoff	R-R	6-0	180	8-26-76	1	2	2.70	10	0	0	1	17	15	5	5	0	2	14	.238	.278	.222	7.56	1.08
Giese, Dan	R-R	6-3	200	5-19-77	3	4	5.68	26	0	0	2	38	51	28	24	9	1	28	.317	.324	.311	6.63	0.24
Hernandez, Yoel	R-R	6-2	170	4-15-80	6	4	3.40	40	0	0	3	56	53	21	21	5	24	52	.256	.256	.256	8.41	3.88
Hodge, Kevin	R-R	5-11	185	10-28-76	3	2	5.40	20	0	0	3	28	27	17	17	5	8	28	.260	.150	.328	8.89	2.54
Lee, Seung Hak	R-R	6-4	225	6-2-79	0	1	23.63	1	0	0	0	3	5	7	7	2	3	1	.385	.667	.143	3.38	10.13
Liriano, Pedro	R-R	6-2	170	10-23-80	4	9	3.90	22	17	1	0	99	90	49	43	11	48	79	.245	.247	.242	7.16	4.35
Lopez, Aquilino	R-R	6-3	165	4-21-75	0	0	1.00	4	0	0	0	9	5	1	1	0	1	11	.156	.267	.059	11.00	1.00
Minix, Travis	R-R	6-1	199	8-8-77	1	0	1.53	14	0	0	1	18	9	3	3	2	3	13	.153	.188	.140	6.62	1.53
Padilla, Vicente	R-R	6-2	220	9-27-77	1	0	3.60	1	1	0	0	5	6	2	2	0	2	4	.316	.333	.300	7.20	3.60
Perez, Franklin	R-R	6-2	230	6-10-78	1	7	4.96	58	0	0	23	65	60	40	36	11	35	42	.248	.194	.285	5.79	4.82
Rojas, Chris	R-R	6-1	205	3-20-77	0	1	3.86	1	1	0	0	7	6	4	3	1	2	4	.240	.222	.286	5.14	2.57
Sanches, Brian	R-R	6-0	190	8-8-78	5	3	3.69	51	2	0	1	83	81	36	34	9	27	75	.260	.212	.296	8.13	2.93
Smith, Mike	R-R	5-11	205	9-19-77	0	0	9.82	1	1	0	0	4	5	4	4	1	3	2	.313	.250	.333	4.91	7.36
Tejeda, Rob	R-R	6-3	190	3-24-82	2	0	2.22	5	5	0	0	28	21	8	7	0	13	28	.214	.213	.216	8.89	4.13
Telemaco, Amaury	R-R	6-3	230	1-19-74	0	1	4.09	9	3	0	0	22	24	11	10	1	8	14	.279	.250	.310	5.73	3.27

FIELDING

Catcher	PCT	G	PO	A	E	DP	PB
Castellano	.000	1	0	0	0	0	0
Coste	.980	9	43	7	1	1	1
Gradoville	.929	6	24	2	2	1	0
Hinch	.985	80	499	33	8	7	9
Ruiz	.991	56	402	30	4	6	3

First Base	PCT	G	PO	A	E	DP
Castellano	.000	1	0	0	0	0
Coste	1.000	29	225	27	0	25
Howard	.986	58	533	40	8	64
Ruiz	1.000	2	14	0	0	0
Rushford	.986	65	506	49	8	68

Second Base	PCT	G	PO	A	E	DP
Hannahan	.990	20	43	59	1	16
Kata	1.000	11	23	39	0	11
Leon	1.000	1	3	5	0	2
Medrano	.978	108	179	315	11	82
Sandoval	1.000	1	1	4	0	0
Sosa	.980	12	21	27	1	7

Third Base	PCT	G	PO	A	E	DP
Coste	.956	93	47	192	11	22
Grindell	1.000	7	2	15	0	2
Hannahan	.910	26	16	55	7	9
Kata	.800	4	1	3	1	0
Sosa	.947	23	15	57	4	12

Shortstop	PCT	G	PO	A	E	DP
Hannahan	.947	21	23	66	5	18
Kata	.895	6	4	13	2	1
Leon	.923	5	6	18	2	3
Medrano	1.000	1	2	2	0	0
Sandoval	.976	102	162	321	12	79
Sosa	.984	18	25	37	1	11

Outfield	PCT	G	PO	A	E	DP
Budzinski	.990	120	192	8	2	2
Byrd	.824	5	14	0	3	0
Castellano	.966	17	27	1	1	0
Fleming	.800	2	3	1	1	0
Grindell	.973	52	69	4	2	2

Hannahan	.976	25	39	2	1	0
Kata	.923	6	11	1	1	0
Padilla	.983	59	113	5	2	1
Rushford	.970	49	61	4	2	3
Victorino	.991	126	307	14	3	4

READING PHILLIES — Class AA

EASTERN LEAGUE

BATTING	B-T	HT	WT	DOB	AVG	vLH	vRH	G	AB	R	H	2B	3B	HR	RBI	BB	HBP	SH	SF	SO	SB	CS	SLG	OBP
Barthelemy, Ryan	L-R	6-3	225	5-19-80	.237	.242	.236	117	358	39	85	25	2	12	35	16	3	0	3	90	1	1	.419	.274
Bourn, Michael	L-R	5-11	180	12-27-82	.268	.297	.253	135	544	80	146	18	8	6	44	63	3	4	0	123	38	12	.364	.348
Bramasco, Omar	R-R	6-0	180	10-28-81	.000	.000	.000	3	1	1	0	0	0	0	0	1	1	0	0	0	0	0	.000	.667
Castellano, John	R-R	5-11	180	9-8-77	.350	.364	.333	6	20	2	7	1	0	0	3	3	0	1	0	4	0	0	.400	.435
Cortez, Jose	B-R	6-1	215	12-15-80	.100	.000	.143	4	10	0	1	0	0	0	0	1	0	1	0	3	0	0	.100	.182
Deschaine, Jim	R-R	6-0	220	9-18-77	.242	.255	.233	125	389	47	94	22	1	16	62	36	9	0	3	67	2	2	.427	.318
Fleming, Ryan	L-L	5-9	177	2-11-76	.281	.180	.316	126	431	55	121	19	3	12	58	48	2	6	3	62	13	10	.422	.353
Gonzalez, Daniel	B-R	6-0	185	11-20-81	.218	.319	.150	56	179	13	39	5	1	2	16	18	3	2	1	41	0	0	.291	.299
Gradoville, Tim	R-R	6-3	195	1-30-80	.205	.191	.214	72	229	19	47	6	1	2	14	14	2	2	3	73	1	0	.266	.254
Grindell, Nate	R-R	6-1	180	4-9-77	.247	.340	.200	49	158	16	39	10	0	3	16	20	1	0	3	35	1	2	.367	.330
Hitchcox, Brian	L-R	5-11	180	7-21-78	.234	.218	.239	120	372	38	87	16	1	6	41	33	3	5	3	82	3	4	.331	.299
Leon, Carlos	R-R	5-10	181	8-31-79	.280	.259	.292	75	225	32	63	11	1	1	9	20	6	5	1	37	4	9	.351	.353
Lombardi, Michael	B-R	6-1	210	12-14-81	.000	.000	.000	1	1	0	0	0	0	0	0	0	0	0	0	1	0	0	.000	.000
Merchan, Jesus	R-R	6-0	184	3-26-81	.265	.333	.223	48	151	18	40	7	1	0	12	6	4	5	0	16	2	2	.325	.311
Pratt, Trent	R-R	6-2	210	8-25-79	.196	.234	.181	74	219	27	43	8	1	2	18	26	5	4	1	43	0	1	.269	.295
Prieto, Alejandro	R-R	5-11	205	6-19-76	.213	.100	.243	16	47	5	10	2	0	2	7	10	0	0	1	8	1	0	.383	.345
Richardson, Juan	R-R	6-1	215	1-27-79	.249	.243	.253	122	385	51	96	15	1	15	51	34	4	0	2	108	0	4	.410	.315
Roberson, Chris	R-R	6-2	175	8-23-79	.311	.291	.321	139	553	90	172	24	8	15	70	40	9	5	4	112	34	14	.465	.365
Ruiz, Randy	R-R	6-3	235	10-19-77	.349	.357	.345	89	344	59	120	29	0	27	89	30	6	0	5	87	0	2	.669	.405
Sosa, Juan	R-R	6-1	175	8-19-75	.284	.300	.276	40	155	18	44	4	0	4	19	10	1	1	0	25	1	0	.387	.331

PITCHING	B-T	HT	WT	DOB	W	L	ERA	G	GS	CG	SV	IP	H	R	ER	HR	BB	SO	AVG	vLH	vRH	K-9	BB-9
Bauer, Greg	R-R	6-2	206	11-30-77	0	1	1.29	5	0	0	0	7	6	2	1	0	4	4	.240	.267	.200	5.14	5.14
Bucktrot, Keith	L-R	6-2	220	11-27-80	3	4	5.52	11	11	0	0	62	76	40	38	10	26	34	.305	.270	.336	4.94	3.77
Burke, Erick	L-L	6-4	230	8-14-77	3	2	3.15	26	0	0	2	40	32	14	14	1	12	47	.218	.357	.162	10.58	2.70
Butto, Francisco	R-R	6-1	200	5-11-80	2	5	3.65	36	1	0	3	57	57	35	23	9	21	55	.254	.267	.246	8.74	3.34
Cameron, Ryan	R-R	6-1	175	9-13-77	6	5	2.55	58	0	0	19	88	70	27	25	11	31	99	.216	.182	.244	10.09	3.16
Chantres, Carlos	R-R	6-3	190	4-1-76	5	12	4.64	26	24	0	0	142	160	90	73	18	55	76	.290	.282	.297	4.83	3.49
Davis, Allen	L-L	6-4	220	10-1-75	13	9	3.64	27	25	3	0	183	208	79	74	20	22	97	.291	.297	.289	4.77	1.08
Devey, Philip	L-L	5-11	178	5-31-77	1	1	7.90	8	1	0	0	14	21	12	12	2	5	11	.356	.353	.357	7.24	3.29
2-team (30 Portland)					2	7	4.88	38	2	0	0	52	55	32	28	5	21	49	.274	.218	.309	8.54	3.66
Fesh, Sean	L-L	6-2	185	11-3-72	2	0	1.48	20	0	0	0	24	23	7	4	0	5	15	.253	.286	.238	5.55	1.85
Geary, Geoff	R-R	6-0	180	8-26-76	0	0	0.00	1	0	0	0	2	0	0	0	0	0	2	.000	.000	.000	9.00	0.00
Hamels, Cole	L-L	6-3	175	12-27-83	2	0	2.37	3	3	0	0	19	10	6	5	2	12	19	.159	.118	.174	9.00	5.68
Happ, J.A.	L-L	6-5	205	10-19-82	1	0	1.50	1	1	0	0	6	3	1	1	0	2	8	.150	.000	.176	12.00	3.00
Hernandez, Yoel	R-R	6-2	170	4-15-80	2	0	1.32	9	0	0	0	14	12	2	2	0	6	15	.231	.211	.242	9.88	3.95
Hutchison, Ryan	R-R	6-0	205	8-9-78	0	1	9.00	3	0	0	0	3	3	3	3	1	1	2	.250	.250	.250	6.00	3.00
Lee, Seung Hak	R-R	6-4	225	6-2-79	3	1	1.97	14	11	0	0	64	58	17	14	2	24	50	.242	.200	.274	7.03	3.38
Matos, Josue	R-R	6-4	190	3-15-78	3	0	1.23	7	4	0	0	29	18	4	4	2	2	21	.170	.170	.170	6.44	0.61
2-team (9 New Hampshire)					3	1	1.31	16	4	0	0	48	32	7	7	2	5	48	.184	.202	.167	9.00	0.94
Minix, Travis	R-R	6-1	199	8-8-77	1	1	1.84	39	0	0	7	59	44	13	12	3	15	55	.206	.226	.192	8.44	2.30
Moreno, Edwin	R-R	6-1	170	7-30-80	1	3	4.35	4	4	0	0	21	20	10	10	4	2	17	.244	.158	.318	7.40	0.87
Parcus, Kyle	L-L	6-2	190	10-7-81	0	0	9.64	4	0	0	0	5	6	5	5	1	3	1	.300	.500	.250	1.93	5.79
Raggio, Brady	R-R	6-4	210	9-17-72	1	2	5.34	8	4	0	0	30	38	18	18	2	6	19	.319	.306	.329	5.64	1.78
Rojas, Chris	R-R	6-1	205	3-20-77	12	6	3.92	22	22	1	0	131	126	62	57	17	36	107	.253	.239	.265	7.35	2.47
Shafer, Adam	L-R	6-5	250	2-1-79	0	1	2.65	11	0	0	1	17	13	8	5	2	5	19	.206	.300	.121	10.06	2.65
Smith, Mike	R-R	5-11	205	9-19-77	5	14	4.48	28	28	1	0	171	162	97	85	18	82	113	.254	.248	.259	5.96	4.32
Sweeney, Matt	R-R	6-2	195	2-25-83	1	0	3.00	1	1	0	0	6	4	2	2	0	3	5	.182	.250	.100	7.50	4.50
Thompson, Travis	R-R	6-5	225	7-3-77	0	1	3.00	11	0	0	1	18	20	6	6	0	3	10	.290	.323	.263	5.00	1.50
2-team (15 Akron)					4	1	2.30	26	0	0	1	43	35	13	11	1	11	26	.226	.219	.232	5.44	2.30
Villegas, Felix	R-R	6-2	220	8-8-78	2	2	5.67	26	0	0	0	33	40	21	21	3	15	25	.308	.304	.310	6.75	4.05
Wilson, Jeff	R-L	6-2	206	5-30-76	0	2	7.76	22	1	0	0	29	40	28	25	6	12	28	.325	.351	.314	8.69	3.72
Worrell, Tim	R-R	6-4	240	7-5-67	0	0	0.00	2	1	0	0	3	0	0	0	0	0	3	.000	.000	.000	9.00	0.00

FIELDING

Catcher	PCT	G	PO	A	E	DP	PB
Castellano	1.000	4	32	0	0	0	0
Cortez	.962	3	23	2	1	0	0
Gradoville	.984	69	441	54	8	4	5
Hitchcox	1.000	1	5	0	0	0	1
Leon	1.000	1	1	0	0	0	0
Lombardi	.000	1	0	0	0	0	0
Pratt	.987	72	507	33	7	7	15

First Base	PCT	G	PO	A	E	DP
Barthelemy	.997	84	618	48	2	51
Fleming	1.000	1	6	0	0	0
Gradoville	1.000	1	1	0	0	0
Grindell	1.000	3	11	2	0	2
Richardson	1.000	16	103	11	0	11
Ruiz	.976	55	435	19	11	51

Second Base	PCT	G	PO	A	E	DP
Hitchcox	.989	111	215	312	6	74
Leon	.974	28	46	68	3	12
Merchan	1.000	3	4	8	0	3
Prieto	1.000	7	16	12	0	4
Smith	.500	1	1	0	1	0
Sosa	1.000	9	17	25	0	2

Third Base	PCT	G	PO	A	E	DP
Barthelemy	.000	2	0	0	0	0
Bramasco	.000	2	0	0	0	0
Deschaine	.944	25	9	42	3	4
Grindell	.887	31	23	63	11	9
Hitchcox	1.000	2	0	2	0	0
Leon	.895	20	0	17	2	3
Prieto	.875	2	0	7	1	0
Richardson	.911	82	58	136	19	12
Sosa	.778	5	4	3	2	1

Shortstop	PCT	G	PO	A	E	DP
Bramasco	.000	1	0	0	0	0
Gonzalez	.942	47	75	121	12	29
Leon	.942	29	64	66	8	19
Merchan	.948	43	51	112	9	26
Prieto	1.000	6	9	11	0	2
Sosa	1.000	27	38	78	0	10

Outfield	PCT	G	PO	A	E	DP
Barthelemy	1.000	2	3	0	0	0
Bourn	.997	133	310	21	1	9
Castellano	1.000	2	3	0	0	0
Deschaine	.977	52	79	5	2	1
Fleming	.986	116	211	5	3	0
Grindell	1.000	4	8	0	0	0
Roberson	.982	134	320	16	6	4
Ruiz	.882	10	15	0	2	0

FLORIDA STATE LEAGUE

BATTING	B-T	HT	WT	DOB	AVG	vLH	vRH	G	AB	R	H	2B	3B	HR	RBI	BB	HBP	SH	SF	SO	SB	CS	SLG	OBP
Blalock, Jake	R-R	6-4	205	8-6-83	.279	.301	.271	134	502	50	140	22	0	11	65	60	5	0	4	100	10	1	.388	.359
Bramasco, Omar	R-R	6-0	180	10-28-81	.223	.231	.220	108	323	45	72	19	2	3	40	32	7	7	4	88	6	3	.322	.303
Carter, Josh	R-R	6-2	214	11-5-80	.218	.120	.247	27	110	11	24	2	0	3	18	2	1	0	1	11	1	1	.318	.237
Correll, Brad	R-R	6-2	205	6-17-81	.282	.325	.265	117	415	41	117	21	2	12	54	37	2	2	3	68	3	7	.429	.341
Cortez, Jose	B-R	6-1	215	12-15-80	.137	.086	.154	46	139	9	19	2	0	1	8	13	2	1	1	30	1	1	.173	.219
Davidson, Seth	B-R	6-0	184	2-26-79	.250	.083	.306	14	48	5	12	2	1	0	7	2	4	1	2	5	3	1	.333	.321
Floyd, Mike	R-R	6-3	185	1-15-80	.136	.250	.111	7	22	3	3	1	0	0	2	4	2	0	0	3	0	1	.182	.321
Gredvig, Doug	R-R	6-3	245	8-25-79	.246	.143	.295	20	65	11	16	1	0	2	9	14	1	0	1	20	0	1	.354	.383
Guevara, Orlando	B-R	6-1	175	9-13-83	.000	.000	.000	1	1	0	0	0	0	0	0	0	0	0	0	1	0	0	.000	.000
Hansen, Bryan	L-L	6-2	200	5-8-83	.266	.318	.247	90	331	44	88	12	1	8	38	37	5	0	3	44	0	0	.381	.346
Isaacson, Greg	L-R	6-1	200	2-18-82	.259	.154	.272	53	116	20	30	6	1	0	13	18	0	4	0	31	2	2	.328	.358
Klemm, Chris	L-L	6-2	185	4-25-81	.191	.000	.237	14	47	5	9	1	0	0	1	1	2	0	0	8	1	1	.213	.240
Leon, Carlos	R-R	5-10	181	8-31-79	.273	.150	.316	24	77	11	21	1	0	0	3	5	3	3	0	13	6	3	.286	.341
Littleton, B.J.	B-L	5-10	173	10-3-79	.257	.161	.283	80	268	32	69	8	4	1	24	31	1	9	0	50	20	9	.328	.337
Lombardi, Michael	B-R	6-1	210	12-14-81	.000	.000	.000	4	7	0	0	0	0	0	0	1	0	0	0	3	0	0	.000	.125
Moni-Erigbali, Timi	R-R	6-1	205	6-11-82	.200	.286	.147	16	55	7	11	0	0	2	7	5	1	0	0	14	0	1	.309	.279
Moss, Tim	R-R	5-9	150	1-26-82	.269	.300	.257	123	469	87	126	30	5	17	61	45	14	4	4	129	28	10	.463	.348
Nichols, Kyle	R-R	6-2	225	3-29-78	.186	.186	.186	35	113	8	21	3	0	0	7	16	0	0	1	24	0	0	.212	.285
Norman, Zachary	R-R	6-0	210	1-20-82	.224	.266	.209	72	241	28	54	16	0	5	28	16	3	4	1	61	1	3	.353	.280
Padilla, Jorge	R-R	6-2	205	8-11-79	.305	.333	.295	14	59	9	18	4	0	0	6	3	2	0	0	7	1	0	.373	.359
Plumsky, R.T.	R-R	6-0	200	1-19-84	.231	.333	.200	6	13	1	3	2	0	0	0	1	0	1	0	6	0	0	.385	.286
Rodriguez, Carlos	B-R	6-0	180	10-4-83	.235	.259	.226	88	293	39	69	14	0	2	21	29	5	5	2	46	14	7	.304	.313
Sellier, Brian	L-R	6-0	200	1-12-78	.266	.303	.254	99	379	46	101	28	3	12	50	29	0	1	8	51	11	2	.451	.313
Sosa, Juan	R-R	6-1	175	8-19-75	.000	.000	.000	1	2	0	0	0	0	0	0	0	0	0	0	1	0	0	.000	.000
Thome, Jim	L-R	6-4	245	8-27-70	.333	.000	.400	5	12	2	4	0	0	1	3	6	0	0	0	1	0	0	.583	.556
Tugwell, Marc	R-R	6-0	190	4-16-81	.295	.274	.303	110	383	52	113	21	0	7	43	29	10	5	2	57	2	7	.405	.358

PITCHING	B-T	HT	WT	DOB	W	L	ERA	G	GS	CG	SV	IP	H	R	ER	HR	BB	SO	AVG	vLH	vRH	K-9	BB-9
Alvarez, Juan	R-R	6-3	162	10-17-84	0	0	6.75	3	0	0	0	4	5	3	3	0	5	3	.294	.000	.385	6.75	11.25
Arteaga, Erick	R-R	6-7	170	4-2-81	2	4	5.91	32	7	0	2	78	108	62	51	6	21	28	.321	.321	.322	3.24	2.43
Barrack, Jacob	R-R	5-11	165	5-19-82	1	1	3.72	7	0	0	0	10	10	4	4	1	4	11	.270	.211	.333	10.24	3.72
Bauer, Greg	R-R	6-2	206	11-30-77	2	6	5.32	24	4	0	2	46	63	34	27	3	18	32	.320	.313	.325	6.31	3.55
Blasdell, Jared	R-R	6-3	185	5-14-79	0	1	7.94	8	0	0	0	11	16	14	10	3	9	9	.348	.476	.240	7.15	7.15
Bramasco, Omar	R-R	6-0	180	10-28-81	0	0	6.75	2	0	0	0	1	2	1	1	0	1	3	.333	.333	.333	20.25	6.75
Bucktrot, Keith	L-R	6-2	220	11-27-80	1	1	4.60	3	3	0	0	16	12	8	8	3	7	9	.218	.286	.195	5.17	4.02
Butto, Francisco	R-R	6-1	200	5-11-80	1	2	3.49	17	0	0	3	28	28	12	11	1	7	33	.246	.267	.232	10.48	2.22
Carlsen, Clary	R-R	6-1	200	5-17-82	4	7	4.59	32	15	0	0	116	132	77	59	7	46	56	.285	.302	.271	4.36	3.58
Currier, Rik	R-R	5-10	180	5-26-78	1	1	6.05	16	0	0	1	19	22	13	13	2	22	17	.282	.276	.286	7.91	10.24
Evangelista, Nick	R-R	6-4	215	3-17-82	7	6	3.03	37	0	0	2	68	54	26	23	5	20	68	.220	.250	.201	8.96	2.63
Glaser, Eric	R-R	6-6	217	1-23-78	0	7	7.44	9	8	0	0	42	62	35	35	9	8	29	.337	.373	.307	6.17	1.70
Hamels, Cole	L-L	6-3	175	12-27-83	2	0	2.25	3	3	0	0	16	7	5	4	0	7	18	.137	.105	.156	10.13	3.94
Hernandez, Yoel	R-R	6-2	170	4-15-80	1	1	11.81	4	0	0	0	5	8	10	7	1	3	7	.320	.250	.444	11.81	5.06
Honsa, Chris	R-R	6-3	185	8-13-83	4	5	4.71	25	5	1	0	63	64	37	33	2	20	39	.263	.202	.302	5.57	2.86
Kendrick, Kyle	R-R	6-3	185	8-26-84	0	1	0.00	1	1	0	0	4	5	1	0	0	2	1	.333	.364	.250	2.25	4.50
Lee, Seung Hak	R-R	6-4	225	6-2-79	0	1	1.80	2	1	0	0	5	5	2	1	1	1	5	.250	.500	.083	9.00	1.80
Mathieson, Scott	R-R	6-4	195	2-27-84	3	8	4.14	23	23	1	0	122	111	62	56	17	34	118	.241	.195	.277	8.73	2.52
Mejias, Jose	R-R	6-0	150	8-18-85	0	0	9.00	1	0	0	0	2	3	2	2	0	2	2	.333	.400	.250	9.00	9.00
Padilla, Vicente	R-R	6-2	220	9-27-77	0	1	1.80	1	1	0	0	5	4	1	1	0	1	3	.200	.286	.154	5.40	1.80
Parcus, Kyle	L-L	6-2	190	10-7-81	1	2	4.17	38	0	0	1	54	59	29	25	6	22	53	.285	.316	.267	8.83	3.67
Perez, Jose	R-R	6-3	190	8-8-83	0	0	6.75	3	0	0	0	5	10	6	4	0	4	1	.385	.600	.250	1.69	6.75
Ramsey, Keith	S-L	6-1	175	3-5-80	2	4	5.07	12	10	0	0	60	59	42	34	11	31	32	.259	.277	.252	4.77	4.62
Ribas, Gabe	R-R	6-4	220	2-3-80	3	1	4.53	11	7	0	0	44	51	25	22	7	13	27	.291	.250	.342	5.56	2.68
Richardson, Beau	L-L	6-2	205	11-23-79	0	1	7.65	15	0	0	1	20	17	18	17	1	12	13	.230	.206	.250	5.85	5.40
Schultz, Cory	R-R	6-1	205	9-26-80	0	0	4.05	3	0	0	0	7	9	5	3	0	5	7	.346	.385	.308	9.45	6.75
Segovia, Zach	R-R	6-2	220	4-11-83	4	14	5.54	27	27	0	0	145	168	98	89	18	48	83	.291	.297	.287	5.16	2.99
Shafer, Adam	L-R	6-5	250	2-1-79	0	5	5.09	20	0	0	8	23	25	16	13	1	9	31	.260	.462	.123	12.13	3.52
Squires, Matt	L-L	5-10	200	1-24-79	0	2	4.88	22	0	0	0	31	32	19	17	1	19	26	.271	.311	.247	7.47	5.46
Sweeney, Matt	R-R	6-2	195	2-25-83	1	8	6.62	14	12	1	0	68	99	55	50	13	19	31	.352	.321	.381	4.10	2.51
Tompkins, Jacob	R-R	6-0	190	3-10-80	0	0	9.53	5	0	0	0	6	10	7	6	0	7	4	.370	.538	.214	6.35	11.12
Waldie, Andrew	L-R	6-5	195	7-18-84	0	0	0.00	2	0	0	0	4	5	2	0	0	3	3	.250	.182	.333	6.23	6.23
Webb, Alan	L-L	6-0	185	11-26-79	1	2	11.66	13	6	0	0	29	47	39	38	6	17	19	.367	.354	.375	5.83	5.22
Woodrow, C.J.	R-R	6-3	200	8-21-81	0	3	14.34	3	3	0	0	11	23	18	17	4	5	7	.426	.300	.500	5.91	4.22

FIELDING

Catcher	PCT	G	PO	A	E	DP	PB
Cortez	.968	45	223	21	8	1	3
Guevara	.000	1	0	0	0	0	0
Lombardi	1.000	3	7	0	0	0	0
Norman	.986	59	371	48	6	5	22
Tugwell	.989	43	242	34	3	6	12

First Base	PCT	G	PO	A	E	DP
Bramasco	1.000	1	3	0	0	0
Gredvig	.966	19	182	16	7	15
Hansen	.990	90	754	60	8	65
Isaacson	.980	9	47	2	1	4
Klemm	.957	3	18	4	1	3
Nichols	.980	13	97	3	2	11
Norman	1.000	2	13	2	0	2
Tugwell	1.000	9	59	7	0	4

Second Base	PCT	G	PO	A	E	DP
Bramasco	1.000	3	2	6	0	2
Davidson	1.000	2	3	7	0	0
Isaacson	.970	12	15	17	1	3
Leon	1.000	1	1	0	0	0
Moss	.967	120	220	329	19	74
Rodriguez	.975	9	19	20	1	4

Third Base	PCT	G	PO	A	E	DP
Bramasco	.959	17	14	33	2	6
Correll	.667	1	0	2	1	1
Davidson	.926	7	11	14	2	2
Isaacson	.778	16	9	12	6	0
Leon	.931	13	5	22	2	2
Norman	.833	10	4	16	4	0
Rodriguez	.896	29	16	44	7	5
Sosa	1.000	1	0	3	0	0
Tugwell	.940	54	30	96	8	11

Shortstop	PCT	G	PO	A	E	DP
Bramasco	.952	85	131	265	20	45
Davidson	.938	3	3	12	1	2
Leon	1.000	3	7	4	0	1
Rodriguez	.939	53	75	124	13	26

Outfield	PCT	G	PO	A	E	DP
Blalock	.987	125	215	10	3	4
Carter	.959	27	68	3	3	0
Correll	.974	78	141	11	4	6
Floyd	.917	5	9	2	1	0
Isaacson	1.000	2	1	0	0	0
Klemm	1.000	10	18	1	0	0
Leon	1.000	4	9	0	0	0
Littleton	.984	77	184	1	3	0
Moni-Erigbali	.980	16	50	0	1	0
Padilla	1.000	14	25	2	0	2
Plumsky	.923	6	11	1	1	0
Sellier	.992	56	123	5	1	2

LAKEWOOD BLUECLAWS — Low Class A

SOUTH ATLANTIC LEAGUE

BATTING	B-T	HT	WT	DOB	AVG	vLH	vRH	G	AB	R	H	2B	3B	HR	RBI	BB	HBP	SH	SF	SO	SB	CS	SLG	OBP
Brant, Derek	R-R	6-4	205	1-29-82	.206	.206	.205	35	107	11	22	6	0	0	8	9	3	1	0	24	0	0	.262	.286
Crosland, Jason	R-R	6-2	215	8-30-82	.174	.000	.211	6	23	2	4	1	0	1	2	1	1	0	0	7	0	0	.348	.240
Drobiak, Jayson	L-R	6-2	190	3-3-79	.189	.130	.208	26	95	9	18	8	1	1	11	7	2	0	1	29	1	1	.326	.257
Dzurilla, Mike	R-R	6-0	192	5-4-78	.320	.394	.300	110	434	73	139	33	4	12	60	48	5	5	3	71	2	4	.498	.392
Fisher, Kiel	L-R	6-4	190	9-29-83	.173	.158	.177	29	98	9	17	2	1	0	6	7	0	0	0	30	0	3	.214	.229
Frith, Ryan	R-R	6-2	185	8-17-82	.268	.333	.247	110	399	54	107	24	2	15	54	29	10	5	1	112	8	6	.451	.333
Galloway, Carl	R-R	6-0	215	8-5-83	.237	.167	.269	20	76	4	18	4	0	0	7	1	4	0	0	17	0	0	.289	.284
Gamble, Sean	L-L	6-0	195	6-23-83	.251	.309	.234	117	427	55	107	16	6	2	33	36	6	12	2	56	7	6	.330	.316
Golson, Greg	R-R	6-0	190	9-17-85	.264	.346	.241	89	375	51	99	19	8	4	27	26	6	2	0	106	25	9	.389	.322
Gredvig, Doug	R-R	6-3	245	8-25-79	.304	.314	.302	79	273	44	83	16	0	10	50	51	6	1	3	49	1	2	.473	.420
Hardy, John	R-R	6-1	180	9-28-82	.107	.034	.127	39	131	12	14	4	1	0	6	12	1	3	0	28	2	0	.153	.188
Harman, Brad	R-R	6-1	175	11-19-85	.303	.213	.329	105	419	63	127	23	1	11	58	45	7	1	0	89	5	11	.442	.380
Isaacson, Greg	L-R	6-1	200	2-18-82	.238	.083	.275	21	63	8	15	4	0	0	13	10	0	1	0	16	0	0	.302	.342
Jaramillo, Jason	B-R	6-0	200	10-9-82	.304	.360	.287	119	448	46	136	28	4	8	63	44	2	1	1	72	2	3	.438	.368
Klemm, Chris	L-L	6-2	185	4-25-81	.214	.226	.211	87	295	43	63	12	3	3	32	29	5	6	5	73	2	2	.305	.290
Lombardi, Michael	B-R	6-1	210	12-14-81	.205	.111	.229	14	44	6	9	3	0	0	9	7	0	0	1	13	0	0	.273	.308
Mader, Josh	R-R	6-0	180	8-23-83	.193	.188	.195	62	207	24	40	6	1	0	16	14	3	4	0	51	7	1	.232	.254
Merchan, Jesus	R-R	6-0	184	3-26-81	.277	.407	.235	28	112	10	31	7	0	0	12	5	3	0	1	4	1	2	.339	.322
Moni-Erigbali, Timi	R-R	6-1	205	6-11-82	.246	.339	.209	68	195	35	48	5	1	4	20	38	11	5	1	50	9	7	.344	.396
Orr, Sam	L-R	6-2	190	6-1-83	.222	.238	.218	129	464	64	103	21	4	12	64	72	4	3	4	122	0	2	.362	.329
Plumsky, R.T.	R-R	6-0	200	1-19-84	.250	.200	.286	4	12	0	3	0	0	0	1	1	0	1	0	6	0	0	.250	.308
Szabo, Jordan	R-R	6-3	195	8-24-83	.444	.400	.500	3	9	2	4	0	0	0	0	0	0	0	0	2	0	0	.444	.444

PITCHING	B-T	HT	WT	DOB	W	L	ERA	G	GS	CG	SV	IP	H	R	ER	HR	BB	SO	AVG	vLH	vRH	K-9	BB-9
Allen, Kyle	R-L	6-0	190	7-27-83	0	4	4.55	21	0	0	0	28	28	17	14	3	18	27	.262	.261	.262	8.78	5.86
Baldwin, Andy	R-R	6-5	215	10-20-82	5	12	4.77	27	27	1	0	168	183	106	89	16	43	100	.278	.301	.263	5.36	2.30
Barrack, Jacob	R-R	5-11	165	5-19-82	4	4	2.33	39	0	0	12	54	42	19	14	2	10	66	.212	.203	.216	11.00	1.67
Bisenius, Joe	R-R	6-5	210	9-18-82	6	4	5.88	40	4	1	4	64	66	45	42	5	37	56	.264	.269	.261	7.83	5.18
Carrasco, Carlos	R-R	6-3	178	3-21-87	1	7	7.04	13	13	1	0	63	78	50	49	11	28	46	.302	.269	.321	6.61	4.02
Cerrato, Justin	R-R	6-2	205	6-14-82	0	1	3.24	4	0	0	0	8	8	6	3	1	3	7	.250	.308	.211	7.56	3.24
Correa, Jose	R-R	6-3	185	9-20-81	0	1	5.63	4	0	0	0	8	11	6	5	1	5	5	.333	.188	.471	5.63	5.63
De la Cruz, Maximino	R-R	6-1	163	5-29-85	8	12	5.10	27	27	5	0	162	186	109	92	15	48	105	.290	.301	.284	5.82	2.66
Dueitt, Cory	R-R	6-0	212	8-16-82	2	6	3.21	49	0	0	7	73	62	33	26	8	23	48	.226	.289	.196	5.92	2.84
Griffith, Derek	L-L	6-6	205	10-28-82	7	11	3.95	26	26	1	0	162	152	79	71	11	59	131	.252	.231	.256	7.29	3.28
Happ, J.A.	L-L	6-5	205	10-19-82	4	4	2.36	14	12	0	0	72	57	26	19	3	26	70	.213	.250	.209	8.71	3.24
Honsa, Chris	R-R	6-3	185	8-13-83	0	0	3.38	4	0	0	0	8	9	5	3	1	7	4	.290	.368	.167	4.50	7.88
Johnson, Nathan	R-R	6-1	210	1-13-82	12	8	5.04	40	11	0	0	104	129	67	58	7	16	84	.308	.269	.325	7.29	1.39
Kendrick, Kyle	R-R	6-3	185	8-26-84	0	3	9.13	5	5	0	0	23	38	24	23	2	10	11	.369	.455	.305	4.37	3.97
Martinez, Jason	L-L	5-11	170	12-29-81	0	0	8.18	7	0	0	0	11	22	14	10	2	1	9	.400	.400	.400	7.36	0.82
Paddock, Josh	R-R	6-2	200	10-15-80	1	0	5.47	19	0	0	0	26	28	16	16	1	9	24	.283	.444	.190	8.20	3.08
Rawl, Aaron	R-R	6-0	190	7-21-83	1	0	3.68	16	0	0	0	22	26	9	9	2	6	10	.310	.308	.310	4.09	2.45
Rose, Kevin	R-R	6-2	180	1-25-82	1	0	4.60	13	0	0	0	16	14	8	8	1	12	14	.264	.375	.244	8.04	6.89
Schultz, Cory	R-R	6-1	205	9-26-80	0	0	3.86	2	0	0	0	2	3	1	1	0	0	1	.300	1.000	.222	3.86	0.00
Shafer, Adam	L-R	6-5	250	2-1-79	1	0	2.51	10	0	0	0	14	13	5	4	1	2	11	.245	.063	.324	6.91	1.26
Sweeney, Matt	R-R	6-2	195	2-25-83	3	4	2.43	13	7	1	1	56	41	21	15	2	13	25	.207	.192	.212	4.04	2.10
Tompkins, Jacob	R-R	6-0	190	3-10-80	0	2	3.86	15	0	0	1	23	20	17	10	4	16	17	.233	.265	.212	6.56	6.17
Woodrow, C.J.	R-R	6-3	200	8-21-81	0	0	3.34	10	4	0	0	35	39	16	13	4	4	28	.285	.333	.265	7.20	1.03
Worrell, Tim	R-R	6-4	240	7-5-67	0	0	2.08	3	3	0	0	4	7	3	1	0	0	6	.350	.250	.375	12.46	0.00

FIELDING

Catcher	PCT	G	PO	A	E	DP	PB
Brant	.963	35	235	25	10	2	3
Jaramillo	.974	106	656	86	20	8	17
Lombardi	1.000	6	25	3	0	1	0

First Base	PCT	G	PO	A	E	DP
Drobiak	.973	26	209	11	6	16
Dzurilla	.990	41	352	33	4	24
Galloway	.980	6	43	6	1	3
Gredvig	.992	57	483	25	4	52
Isaacson	.952	6	38	2	2	1
Klemm	1.000	5	32	3	0	2

Second Base	PCT	G	PO	A	E	DP
Dzurilla	.972	50	95	114	6	28
Hardy	.935	8	13	16	2	2
Harman	.940	26	65	61	8	15
Isaacson	.000	1	0	0	0	0
Mader	.976	47	92	109	5	25
Merchan	.985	11	24	40	1	10

Third Base	PCT	G	PO	A	E	DP
Dzurilla	1.000	6	8	11	0	3
Harman	1.000	1	0	2	0	0
Isaacson	.913	8	5	16	2	0
Mader	.905	7	4	15	2	0
Orr	.913	120	113	253	35	39

Shortstop	PCT	G	PO	A	E	DP
Hardy	.960	31	31	89	5	9
Harman	.936	78	128	225	24	43
Mader	.913	7	8	13	2	1
Merchan	.957	17	28	61	4	13
Orr	.964	6	10	17	1	1

Outfield	PCT	G	PO	A	E	DP
Crosland	1.000	3	13	0	0	0
Frith	.985	105	245	12	4	2
Gamble	.978	102	170	8	4	1
Golson	.991	89	209	7	2	2
Klemm	.967	68	108	9	4	5
Moni-Erigbali	.945	56	98	5	6	1
Plumsky	1.000	4	6	0	0	0
Szabo	1.000	3	6	1	0	0

BATAVIA MUCKDOGS — Short-Season Class A

NEW YORK-PENN LEAGUE

BATTING	B-T	HT	WT	DOB	AVG	vLH	vRH	G	AB	R	H	2B	3B	HR	RBI	BB	HBP	SH	SF	SO	SB	CS	SLG	OBP
Antoniato, P.J.	R-R	5-9	185	7-2-83	.198	.190	.200	34	121	12	24	2	1	0	13	5	2	1	2	10	1	1	.231	.238
Baez, Welinson	R-R	6-3	190	7-7-84	.324	.357	.309	45	170	34	55	14	1	6	37	22	3	0	1	45	2	1	.524	.408
Blanton, Ben	R-R	6-2	185	6-26-82	.133	.000	.143	6	15	0	2	1	0	0	2	2	0	1	1	3	0	0	.200	.222
Costanzo, Mike	L-R	6-3	215	9-9-83	.274	.170	.304	73	281	47	77	17	3	11	50	35	3	0	4	89	0	1	.473	.356
Dalton, Brett	R-R	5-10	180	11-26-82	.229	.259	.226	36	144	18	33	6	1	0	13	20	4	0	0	29	1	3	.285	.339
Diaz, Dennis	R-R	5-9	185	2-7-83	.297	.421	.271	37	118	22	35	3	0	0	10	14	1	1	0	22	12	7	.322	.376
Edwards, Matt	R-R	6-2	205	3-6-83	.187	.222	.180	42	155	23	29	3	0	3	17	15	3	0	2	35	0	1	.265	.269
Galloway, Carl	R-R	6-0	215	8-5-83	.242	.222	.258	34	120	7	29	10	1	1	15	2	5	0	1	29	0	0	.367	.281
Gosewisch, Tuffy	R-R	5-11	190	8-17-83	.237	.400	.179	10	38	2	9	1	0	0	5	2	0	0	0	6	0	0	.263	.275
Guevara, Orlando	B-R	6-1	175	9-13-83	.255	.333	.237	14	47	6	12	1	1	0	5	1	0	1	0	12	0	3	.319	.271

BATTING	B-T	HT	WT	DOB	AVG	vLH	vRH	G	AB	R	H	2B	3B	HR	RBI	BB	HBP	SH	SF	SO	SB	CS	SLG	OBP
Hardy, John	R-R	6-1	180	9-28-82	.295	.176	.311	36	139	11	41	10	2	0	17	8	1	2	1	21	3	2	.396	.336
Harris, Clay	R-R	6-4	220	8-25-82	.311	.333	.298	71	280	44	87	22	2	2	40	30	6	0	3	48	1	1	.425	.386
Lombardi, Michael	B-R	6-1	210	12-14-81	.111	.000	.125	3	9	1	1	0	0	0	0	1	0	0	0	3	0	0	.111	.200
MacFarlane, Andy	R-L	6-0	195	8-18-83	.204	.212	.201	48	167	20	34	8	2	2	19	7	1	0	2	64	6	3	.311	.237
Marson, Lou	R-R	6-1	195	6-26-86	.245	.351	.228	60	220	25	54	11	3	5	25	27	1	3	1	52	0	1	.391	.329
Slayden, Jeremy	L-R	6-0	185	7-28-82	.268	.303	.258	54	194	35	52	11	0	9	36	28	5	1	1	45	1	0	.464	.373
Szabo, Jordan	R-R	6-3	195	8-24-83	.254	.300	.239	37	138	21	35	8	3	1	14	11	2	1	1	30	8	1	.377	.316
Williams, Julian	R-R	5-11	175	7-27-83	.272	.354	.250	70	272	55	74	10	3	2	25	30	8	5	0	33	13	6	.353	.361

PITCHING	B-T	HT	WT	DOB	W	L	ERA	G	GS	CG	SV	IP	H	R	ER	HR	BB	SO	AVG	vLH	vRH	K-9	BB-9
Barb, Andrew	R-R	6-3	190	10-6-84	3	2	3.23	11	11	0	0	64	59	27	23	7	27	57	.249	.241	.253	8.02	3.80
Blaine, Justin	L-L	6-4	188	3-12-84	2	1	3.26	11	4	0	1	30	27	13	11	0	23	23	.235	.083	.275	6.82	6.82
Carrasco, Carlos	R-R	6-3	178	3-21-87	0	3	13.50	4	4	0	0	15	29	25	23	8	5	12	.392	.417	.368	7.04	2.93
Correa, Jose	R-R	6-3	185	9-20-81	1	0	4.73	18	0	0	0	27	29	16	14	2	12	21	.274	.333	.247	7.09	4.05
Diaz, Dennis	R-R	5-9	185	2-7-83	0	0	18.00	1	0	0	0	1	0	2	2	0	3	0	.000	.000	.000	0.00	27.00
Guevara, Orlando	S-R	6-1	175	9-13-83	0	0	0.00	1	0	0	0	1	1	0	0	0	1	0	.333	.500	.000	0.00	9.00
Harker, Brett	R-R	6-3	185	7-9-84	1	2	5.06	9	7	0	0	37	38	23	21	5	12	15	.257	.240	.265	3.62	2.89
Henyan, Pete	R-R	6-0	195	4-25-82	2	0	4.46	19	1	0	0	38	48	19	19	1	18	24	.312	.350	.287	5.63	4.23
Hill, Ronald	R-R	6-3	225	11-29-82	2	3	2.96	20	0	0	4	49	50	17	16	0	23	48	.265	.257	.270	8.88	4.25
Kendrick, Kyle	R-R	6-3	185	8-26-84	5	4	3.74	14	14	1	0	91	94	49	38	7	22	70	.262	.212	.298	6.90	2.17
Maloney, Matt	L-L	6-4	220	1-16-84	2	1	3.89	8	8	0	0	37	38	20	16	2	15	36	.277	.333	.265	8.76	3.65
Mitchinson, Scott	R-R	6-3	185	12-28-84	5	6	5.35	13	13	1	0	71	88	49	42	1	16	57	.311	.318	.306	7.26	2.04
Outman, Josh	L-L	6-1	180	9-14-84	2	1	2.76	11	4	0	0	29	23	14	9	1	14	31	.207	.148	.226	9.51	4.30
Overholt, Pat	R-R	6-0	190	2-8-84	2	3	2.65	21	0	0	5	34	28	12	10	1	13	51	.224	.277	.192	13.50	3.44
Quijada, Fernando	R-R	6-3	165	10-9-84	2	3	4.13	23	0	0	8	33	34	19	15	0	14	39	.266	.233	.282	10.74	3.86
Rawl, Aaron	R-R	6-0	190	7-21-83	0	2	3.38	8	0	0	2	16	22	7	6	0	0	8	.338	.292	.366	4.50	0.00
Shepard, Kevin	L-L	6-0	185	6-13-83	2	1	4.76	18	1	0	0	34	43	21	18	1	14	28	.312	.214	.336	7.41	3.71
Stewart, Clayton	R-R	6-5	220	10-15-82	2	3	2.74	14	0	0	0	23	23	8	7	0	7	17	.258	.276	.250	6.65	2.74
Zagurski, Michael	L-L	6-0	225	1-27-83	3	4	4.60	15	8	0	0	45	47	29	23	2	15	43	.266	.342	.245	8.60	3.00

GAMES BY POSITION: C—Gosewisch 5, Guevara 13, Lombardi 3, MacFarlane 1, Marson 56. **1B—**Edwards 28, Galloway 16, Harris 35. **2B—**Antoniato 3, Dalton 34, Hardy 21, Harris 23. **3B—**Baez 4, Blanton 1, Costanzo 69, Hardy 1, Harris 5. **SS—**Antoniato 32, Baez 25, Blanton 5, Hardy 16. **OF—**Diaz 32, Edwards 1, MacFarlane 45, Slayden 51, Szabo 36, Williams 69.

GCL PHILLIES — Rookie

GULF COAST LEAGUE

BATTING	B-T	HT	WT	DOB	AVG	vLH	vRH	G	AB	R	H	2B	3B	HR	RBI	BB	HBP	SH	SF	SO	SB	CS	SLG	OBP
Baez, Welinson	R-R	6-3	190	7-7-84	.267	.273	.265	15	45	6	12	4	1	2	6	8	2	0	0	14	1	0	.533	.400
Blanton, Ben	R-R	6-2	185	6-26-82	.217	.200	.222	7	23	4	5	1	0	0	5	3	0	0	0	5	2	0	.261	.308
Cambero, Alberto	B-R	5-9	152	4-23-86	.191	.182	.194	28	89	13	17	3	0	0	8	9	1	0	0	31	9	1	.225	.273
Cheesman, Aaron	R-R	5-10	195	9-25-81	.348	.417	.323	31	89	17	31	9	1	1	16	14	2	2	1	9	3	2	.506	.443
Cortez, Jose	B-R	6-1	215	12-15-80	.000	.000	.000	1	2	0	0	0	0	0	0	0	0	0	0	1	0	0	.000	.000
Creswell, Reese	L-R	6-3	205	7-5-85	.176	.308	.145	23	68	5	12	3	0	1	1	4	0	0	0	25	2	2	.265	.222
Cuevas, Phillip	R-R	5-11	168	6-30-85	.167	.167	.167	22	60	9	10	1	0	0	3	5	0	1	0	22	2	2	.183	.231
Durant, Michael	R-R	6-5	230	1-2-87	.190	.220	.176	39	126	21	24	4	0	6	22	16	4	0	0	56	3	0	.365	.301
Frazee, Joe	L-R	5-11	190	6-16-83	.261	.174	.290	30	92	13	24	7	1	0	9	16	1	1	0	16	5	4	.359	.376
Hernandez, Fidel	R-R	5-11	160	1-18-86	.260	.237	.271	35	123	16	32	3	0	0	14	3	1	1	2	12	10	8	.285	.279
Kennelly, Tim	R-R	6-0	180	12-5-86	.295	.147	.359	38	112	15	33	11	0	1	15	21	2	0	0	16	3	1	.420	.415
Miaso, Curt	R-R	6-3	205	9-28-85	.243	.250	.240	42	140	28	34	6	0	4	24	18	0	0	1	34	13	2	.371	.327
Mitchell, Derrick	R-R	6-2	170	1-5-87	.213	.200	.218	21	75	14	16	4	0	1	9	5	2	1	2	27	1	1	.307	.274
Morales, Douglas	L-L	6-0	180	6-22-86	.301	.300	.301	37	113	21	34	6	1	1	10	14	4	0	0	21	12	4	.398	.397
Naughton, Joel	L-R	6-1	178	8-27-86	.275	.233	.295	29	91	12	25	3	0	1	11	5	0	0	0	7	1	1	.341	.313
Osteen, Cooper	B-R	5-10	170	11-10-82	.362	.379	.355	35	105	17	38	7	2	1	15	14	2	6	0	9	11	5	.495	.446
Paterson, Tommy	L-L	6-2	195	9-18-82	.214	.226	.210	34	112	10	24	2	2	0	11	8	0	1	2	18	12	2	.268	.262
Shaw, Buck	L-R	6-4	210	11-18-83	.216	.080	.260	29	102	9	22	4	2	2	16	7	0	0	4	15	0	2	.353	.257
Williams, Jermaine	R-R	6-3	210	3-25-87	.250	.345	.209	30	96	14	24	4	0	1	8	3	1	0	0	29	2	2	.323	.280

PITCHING	B-T	HT	WT	DOB	W	L	ERA	G	GS	CG	SV	IP	H	R	ER	HR	BB	SO	AVG	vLH	vRH	K-9	BB-9
Alvarez, Juan	R-R	6-3	162	10-17-84	1	2	5.23	11	0	0	0	21	23	13	12	1	4	18	.277	.323	.250	7.84	1.74
Barb, Andrew	R-R	6-3	190	10-6-84	0	2	3.27	2	2	0	0	11	11	6	4	0	0	16	.250	.238	.261	13.09	0.00
Blasdell, Jared	R-R	6-3	185	5-14-79	0	0	6.00	2	0	0	0	3	2	2	2	2	1	4	.200	.000	.286	12.00	3.00
Byrd, Darren	R-R	6-3	170	10-24-86	3	1	2.66	9	8	0	0	44	36	14	13	1	10	24	.220	.289	.193	4.91	2.05
Carrasco, Carlos	R-R	6-3	178	3-21-87	0	0	1.80	2	2	0	0	5	3	1	1	0	1	2	.176	.200	.167	3.60	1.80
Concepcion, Alexander	R-R	6-1	180	9-27-84	0	0	4.91	7	0	0	0	11	9	7	6	0	7	20	.225	.300	.200	16.36	5.73
Cruz, Reymond	R-R	6-2	170	10-23-83	3	4	4.00	9	8	0	0	45	49	26	20	3	7	43	.280	.310	.265	8.60	1.40
Garcia, Edgar	R-R	6-2	190	9-20-87	4	4	3.56	10	10	0	0	56	63	26	22	4	13	42	.284	.250	.303	6.79	2.10
Gazo, Lenin	R-R	6-1	145	7-25-84	2	3	2.81	11	2	0	2	32	23	14	10	1	9	16	.198	.216	.190	4.50	2.53
Gooch, Tyler	R-R	5-11	185	4-12-82	0	0	3.00	5	1	0	0	9	8	3	3	1	3	8	.242	.200	.261	8.00	3.00
Kelly, Mark	R-R	6-4	200	4-18-84	2	1	3.27	13	0	0	1	22	22	10	8	0	6	28	.244	.222	.254	11.45	2.45
Linder, Matt	R-R	6-5	195	9-15-84	2	1	8.16	12	0	0	1	14	19	14	13	2	4	10	.317	.350	.300	6.28	2.51
McEnaney, Alex	R-R	6-4	175	1-8-86	0	0	5.56	10	0	0	1	11	16	8	7	2	1	6	.320	.400	.286	4.76	0.79
Mejias, Jose	R-R	6-0	150	8-18-85	0	3	3.32	15	0	0	3	19	22	12	7	1	5	12	.289	.464	.188	5.68	2.37
Mitchinson, Scott	R-R	6-3	185	12-28-84	0	0	0.00	1	1	0	0	3	1	0	0	0	0	4	.100	.250	.000	12.00	0.00
Naatjes, Darin	L-R	6-9	245	7-27-80	0	0	0.00	1	0	0	0	2	1	0	0	0	1	2	.143	.250	.000	9.00	4.50
Olson, Matt	R-R	6-4	200	11-27-86	3	3	3.07	9	8	0	0	41	43	15	14	2	12	27	.281	.289	.278	5.93	2.63
Pichardo, Kelvin	R-R	6-0	160	10-13-85	3	2	4.17	10	9	0	0	54	59	28	25	4	3	37	.273	.237	.293	6.17	0.50
Raulinaitis, Chris	R-R	6-3	235	11-25-83	0	1	5.57	12	0	0	0	21	29	17	13	2	4	15	.330	.222	.377	6.43	1.71
Stewart, Clayton	R-R	6-5	220	10-15-82	0	0	0.00	2	0	0	0	2	1	0	0	0	0	1	.125	.000	.167	4.50	0.00
Waldie, Andrew	L-R	6-5	195	7-18-84	1	0	2.19	8	0	0	1	12	9	3	3	1	9	8	.205	.200	.206	5.84	6.57

GAMES BY POSITION: C—Cheesman 18, Cortez 1, Creswell 17, Kennelly 1, Naughton 27. **1B—**Durant 36, Morales 3, Shaw 17. **2B—**Cambero 20, Cuevas 20, Hernandez 6, Osteen 17. **3B—**Baez 9, Blanton 6, Cambero 1, Hernandez 4, Kennelly 34, Osteen 8. **SS—**Baez 2, Cambero 5, Hernandez 27, Mitchell 21, Osteen 6. **OF—**Frazee 30, Miaso 42, Morales 34, Paterson 34, Williams 29.

PITTSBURGH PIRATES

BY JOHN PERROTTO

The Pirates endured yet another losing season in 2005. However, this time, there was reason for optimism.

The Pirates were last in the National League Central at 67-95, tying the Colorado Rockies for the worst record in the NL and finishing below .500 for the 13th consecutive season. But the Pirates gained a dubious distinction when they lost to the Brewers 6-5 with two days remaining in the season. The Pirates took over sole possession of the longest streak of losing seasons in major American professional sports as the Brewers snapped theirs at 12 by finishing 81-81.

The Pirates also closed in on history with their 13th consecutive losing season. The major-league record is 16, set by the Phillies from 1933-48.

The losing led to the Pirates making their first in-season managerial change in 32 years when they fired Lloyd McClendon on Sept. 6. That move came when the Pirates went 25-51 after reaching the .500 mark on June 11 at 30-30 with 12 wins in 15 games.

However, the Pirates also had hope that the losing might finally end someday soon. After beginning the season with no rookies on the roster, the Pirates wound up having 12 players make their major-league debuts in 2005.

Many of the rookies looked like they could be long-term fixtures for the Pirates, particularly lefthanders Zach Duke and Paul Maholm. Duke went 8-2, 1.81 in 14 starts and Maholm was 3-1, 2.18 in six starts.

Duke was also the International Pitcher of the Year after going 12-3, 2.92 in 16 starts for Indianapolis. Maholm was picked by the Pirates as their Minor League Pitcher of the Year as he went a combined 7-3, 3.30 in 22 starts for Indianapolis and Altoona, a year after being hit in the eye by a line drive while pitching for high Class A Lynchburg.

ORGANIZATION LEADERS

BATTING

*AVG	Carlin, Michael, Hickory	.318
R	Magness, Pat, Lynchburg	98
H	Walker, Neil, Hickory/Lynchburg	157
TB	Stansberry, Craig, Altoona/Indianapolis/Lynchburg	251
2B	Magness, Pat, Lynchburg	39
3B	Stansberry, Craig, Altoona/Indianapolis/Lynchburg	13
HR	Eldred, Brad, Altoona/Indianapolis	28
RBI	Bautista, Jose, Altoona/Indianapolis	94
BB	Magness, Pat, Lynchburg	141
SO	Bixler, Brian, Hickory	134
SB	Thompson, Rich, Altoona/Indianapolis	58
*OBP	Magness, Pat, Lynchburg	.481
*SLG	Eldred, Brad, Altoona/Indianapolis	.674

PITCHING

W	Duke, Zach, Indianapolis	12
L	Five tied at	10
#ERA	Brady Borner, Altoona	2.08
G	Corey, Mark, Indianapolis	61
CG	O'Brien, Patrick, Lynchburg	2
	Snell, Ian, Indianapolis	2
SV	Corey, Mark, Indianapolis	28
IP	Hankins, Derek, Hickory	156
BB	Bloom, Kyle, Hickory/Lynchburg	76
SO	Gorzelanny, Tom, Altoona/Indianapolis	124

*Minimum 250 at-bats. #Minimum 75 innings.

PLAYERS OF THE YEAR

MAJOR LEAGUE: Jason Bay, of

Bay led a youth movement by leading the Pirates in nearly every offensive category. His 32 homers and .306 average set career marks, as well as his 44 doubles. He paced the Pirates with 183 hits and scored 110 runs. His 335 total bases were over a hundred more than anyone else in the lineup.

MINOR LEAGUE: Zach Duke, lhp

Duke caused a frenzy in Pittsburgh in 2005 as the club saw an attendance spike on his scheduled days to pitch at PNC Park. The 22-year-old lefthander started the season at Triple-A Indianapolis, where he dominated hitters with slightly above-average stuff but went 12-3, 2.92.

Center fielder Chris Duffy was one of many rookie position players who showed promise as he hit .341 in 39 games, while playing outstanding defense.

Switch-hitting catcher Ryan Doumit hit .255-6-35 in 75 games, first baseman Brad Eldred batted only .221 but hit 12 homers in 55 games, and outfielder Nate McLouth hit .257 with five homers in 41 games.

Eldred wound up hitting a combined 40 home runs at three levels as he also hit 13 in 21 games for Altoona then 15 in 54 games for Indianapolis. He became only the third player to hit 10 homers at the major league, Triple-A and Double-A levels in the same season.

Left fielder Jason Bay built on his NL Rookie of the Year season in 2004 with a fabulous 2005 as he hit .306 with 110 runs scored, 44 doubles, 32 home runs, 101 RBIs and 21 stolen bases while becoming the first Pirates player to start all 162 games in a season since Johnny Ray in 1982. Bay was the first player in club history to hit .300 with 100 runs, 40 doubles, 30 homers, 100 RBIs and 20 steals in a season.

Second baseman Jose Castillo also showed signs of blossoming into a star as he hit .268-11-53 in 101 games while turning a number of acrobatic double plays.

Castillo's emergence offset disappointing seasons by lefthander Oliver Perez, shortstop Jack Wilson and right fielder Craig Wilson, considered franchise cornerstones in 2004 when Perez had a 2.98 ERA, Wilson hit .308 with 201 hits and Wilson belted 29 homers. In 2005, Perez had a 5.85 ERA, Jack Wilson's batting average slipped to .257 and Craig Wilson managed just five homers in 59 games as he was sidelined twice by left hand injuries.

The Pirates had a winning season in the minor leagues for the fourth time in as many seasons since Brian Graham took over as player development director and four of the six affiliates qualified for the playoffs. Prior to Graham's arrival, Pirates' farm clubs had one winning season in 33 years.

Third baseman Jose Bautista was chosen by the Pirates as their minor league player of the year as he hit a combined .280-24-94 RBIs in 130 games for Indianapolis and Altoona.

PITTSBURGH PIRATES

Managers: Lloyd McClendon, Pete Mackanin. **2005 Record:** 67-95, .414 (6th, NL Central).

BATTING	B-T	HT	WT	DOB	AVG	vLH	vRH	G	AB	R	H	2B	3B	HR	RBI	BB	HBP	SH	SF	SO	SB	CS	SLG	OBP
Amezaga, Alfredo	B-R	5-10	165	1-6-78	.000	.000	.000	3	3	1	0	0	0	0	0	1	0	0	0	0	1	0	.000	.250
2-team (2 Colorado)					.167	.000	.500	5	6	2	1	0	0	0	0	1	0	0	0	0	1	0	.167	.286
Bautista, Jose	R-R	6-0	190	10-19-80	.143	.273	.059	11	28	3	4	1	0	0	1	3	0	0	0	7	1	0	.179	.226
Bay, Jason	R-R	6-2	200	9-20-78	.306	.347	.292	162	599	110	183	44	6	32	101	95	6	0	7	142	21	1	.559	.402
Castillo, Jose	R-R	6-1	200	3-19-81	.268	.258	.271	101	370	49	99	16	3	11	53	23	0	1	4	59	2	3	.416	.307
Cota, Humberto	R-R	6-0	195	2-7-79	.242	.294	.222	93	297	29	72	20	1	7	43	17	2	1	3	80	0	0	.387	.285
Doumit, Ryan	B-R	6-0	200	4-3-81	.255	.296	.243	75	231	25	59	13	1	6	35	11	13	1	1	48	2	1	.398	.324
Duffy, Chris	L-L	5-10	180	4-20-80	.341	.355	.337	39	126	22	43	4	2	1	9	7	2	1	0	22	2	2	.429	.385
Eldred, Brad	R-R	6-5	270	7-12-80	.221	.260	.207	55	190	23	42	9	0	12	27	13	3	0	2	77	1	1	.458	.279
Furmaniak, J.J.	R-R	6-3	190	7-31-79	.192	.000	.192	13	26	3	5	1	1	0	1	4	0	0	0	4	0	0	.308	.300
Gerut, Jody	L-L	6-0	190	9-18-77	.222	.000	.267	4	18	2	4	1	0	0	2	0	0	0	0	3	0	0	.278	.222
2-team (9 Chicago)					.156	.250	.143	15	32	3	5	2	0	0	2	2	0	0	0	6	0	0	.219	.206
Hill, Bobby	B-R	5-9	175	4-3-78	.269	.357	.253	58	93	12	25	6	0	0	11	9	2	0	1	17	0	0	.333	.343
Lawton, Matt	L-R	5-10	190	11-3-71	.273	.236	.287	101	374	53	102	28	1	10	44	58	9	0	4	61	16	9	.433	.380
Mackowiak, Rob	L-R	5-10	190	6-20-76	.272	.275	.272	142	463	57	126	21	3	9	58	43	3	2	1	100	8	4	.389	.337
McLouth, Nate	L-R	5-11	185	10-28-81	.257	.100	.292	41	109	20	28	6	0	5	12	3	5	2	1	20	2	0	.450	.305
Paulino, Ronny	R-R	6-3	235	4-21-81	.500	.500	.500	2	4	1	2	0	0	0	0	1	0	0	0	0	0	0	.500	.600
Redman, Tike	L-L	5-11	175	3-10-77	.251	.260	.248	135	319	33	80	12	4	2	26	19	1	2	3	27	4	1	.332	.292
Restovich, Michael	R-R	6-4	250	1-3-79	.214	.231	.158	52	84	10	18	3	1	2	5	8	0	0	0	24	0	0	.345	.283
2-team (14 Colorado)					.235	.250	.185	66	115	15	27	5	1	3	8	11	0	0	0	29	0	0	.374	.302
Ross, David	R-R	6-2	215	3-19-77	.222	.200	.229	40	108	9	24	8	0	3	15	6	1	1	3	24	0	0	.380	.263
Sadler, Ray	R-R	6-1	200	9-19-80	.250	.167	.500	3	8	1	2	0	0	1	1	0	0	0	0	1	0	0	.625	.250
Sanchez, Freddy	R-R	5-10	190	12-21-77	.291	.326	.277	132	453	54	132	26	4	5	35	27	5	4	3	36	2	2	.400	.336
Santiago, Benito	R-R	6-1	190	3-9-65	.261	.125	.333	6	23	1	6	1	1	0	0	0	0	0	0	3	0	0	.391	.261
Ward, Daryle	L-L	6-1	240	6-27-75	.260	.200	.281	133	407	46	106	21	1	12	63	37	1	0	8	60	0	2	.405	.318
Wigginton, Ty	R-R	6-0	225	10-11-77	.258	.247	.268	57	155	20	40	9	1	7	25	14	1	1	0	30	0	1	.465	.324
Wilson, Craig	R-R	6-2	220	11-30-76	.264	.283	.257	59	197	23	52	14	1	5	22	30	10	0	1	69	3	0	.421	.387
Wilson, Jack	R-R	6-0	180	12-29-77	.257	.257	.257	158	587	60	151	24	7	8	52	31	6	11	4	58	7	3	.363	.299

PITCHING	B-T	HT	WT	DOB	W	L	ERA	G	GS	CG	SV	IP	H	R	ER	HR	BB	SO	AVG	vLH	vRH	K/9	BB/9
Bullington, Bryan	R-R	6-4	220	9-30-80	0	0	13.50	1	0	0	0	1	1	2	2	0	1	1	.250	1.000	.000	6.75	6.75
Capps, Matt	R-R	6-3	240	9-3-83	0	0	4.50	4	0	0	0	4	5	2	2	0	0	3	.333	.250	.364	6.75	0.00
Duke, Zach	L-L	6-2	210	4-19-83	8	2	1.81	14	14	0	0	85	79	20	17	3	23	58	.253	.146	.273	6.17	2.44
Fogg, Josh	R-R	6-0	205	12-13-76	6	11	5.05	34	28	0	0	169	196	106	95	27	53	85	.291	.340	.249	4.52	2.82
Gonzalez, Mike	R-L	6-1	205	5-23-78	1	3	2.70	51	0	0	3	50	35	15	15	2	31	58	.197	.152	.223	10.44	5.58
Gorzelanny, Tom	L-L	6-2	205	7-12-82	0	1	12.00	3	1	0	0	6	10	8	8	1	3	3	.357	.000	.455	4.50	4.50
Grabow, John	L-L	6-1	210	11-4-78	2	3	4.85	63	0	0	0	52	46	31	28	6	25	42	.238	.219	.250	7.27	4.33
Johnston, Mike	L-L	6-2	225	3-30-79	0	0	36.00	1	0	0	0	1	4	4	4	2	0	2	.571	.500	.600	18.00	0.00
Maholm, Paul	L-L	6-2	225	6-25-82	3	1	2.18	6	6	0	0	41	31	10	10	2	17	26	.209	.087	.232	5.66	3.70
Meadows, Brian	R-R	6-4	220	11-21-75	3	1	4.58	65	0	0	0	75	84	42	38	8	21	44	.287	.301	.279	5.30	2.53
Mesa, Jose	R-R	6-3	235	5-22-66	2	8	4.76	55	0	0	27	57	61	30	30	7	26	37	.285	.309	.265	5.88	4.13
Perez, Oliver	L-L	6-2	200	8-15-81	7	5	5.85	20	20	0	0	103	102	68	67	23	70	97	.264	.313	.255	8.48	6.12
Redman, Mark	L-L	6-5	245	1-5-74	5	15	4.90	30	30	2	0	178	188	100	97	18	56	101	.278	.256	.283	5.10	2.83
Snell, Ian	R-R	5-11	180	10-30-81	1	2	5.14	15	5	0	0	42	43	25	24	5	24	34	.267	.304	.239	7.29	5.14
Torres, Salomon	R-R	5-11	210	3-11-72	5	5	2.76	78	0	0	3	95	76	34	29	7	36	55	.222	.272	.189	5.23	3.42
Vogelsong, Ryan	R-R	6-3	210	7-22-77	2	2	4.43	44	0	0	0	81	82	43	40	5	40	52	.259	.275	.250	5.75	4.43
Wells, Kip	R-R	6-3	205	4-21-77	8	18	5.09	33	33	1	0	182	186	116	103	23	99	132	.266	.288	.249	6.53	4.90
White, Rick	R-R	6-4	230	12-23-68	4	7	3.72	71	0	0	2	75	90	39	31	3	29	40	.308	.314	.305	4.80	3.48
Williams, Dave	L-L	6-3	230	3-12-79	10	11	4.41	25	25	1	0	139	137	74	68	20	58	88	.261	.281	.256	5.71	3.76

FIELDING

Catcher	PCT	G	PO	A	E	DP	PB
Cota	.992	87	475	38	4	4	8
Doumit	.975	50	286	30	8	1	4
Paulino	1.000	2	10	0	0	0	0
Ross	.986	35	183	23	3	4	4
Santiago	1.000	6	43	0	0	0	0

First Base	PCT	G	PO	A	E	DP
Eldred	.985	50	435	15	7	46
Mackowiak	1.000	3	18	1	0	4
Ward	.994	109	863	77	6	114
Wigginton	1.000	3	22	2	0	1
C. Wilson	.989	15	86	7	1	10

Second Base	PCT	G	PO	A	E	DP
Castillo	.977	100	237	279	12	93
Furmaniak	.960	9	14	10	1	1
Hill	.000	1	0	0	1	0
Mackowiak	.976	20	37	43	2	10
Sanchez	.991	58	108	115	2	40
Wigginton	1.000	1	3	2	0	0

Third Base	PCT	G	PO	A	E	DP
Bautista	.952	8	6	14	1	2
Hill	.977	24	10	32	1	4
Mackowiak	.952	65	38	122	8	15
Sanchez	.977	65	39	130	4	19
Wigginton	.894	40	19	57	9	5

Shortstop	PCT	G	PO	A	E	DP
Amezaga	1.000	1	1	2	0	1
Furmaniak	1.000	2	1	4	0	0
Sanchez	1.000	11	11	25	0	3
J. Wilson	.982	157	246	523	14	126

Outfield	PCT	G	PO	A	E	DP
Bay	.988	162	322	4	4	1
Doumit	.000	3	0	0	0	0
Duffy	.988	34	80	1	1	0
Gerut	1.000	4	3	0	0	0
Lawton	.995	98	206	4	1	2
Mackowiak	.981	63	102	4	2	2
McLouth	.958	29	46	0	2	0
Redman	.962	85	170	5	7	0
Restovich	.976	31	39	1	1	0
Sadler	1.000	3	4	0	0	0
C. Wilson	.988	47	77	4	1	1

General Manager: David Littlefield. **Director, Player Development:** Brian Graham. **Scouting Director:** Ed Creech.

Class	Farm Team	League	W	L	Pct.	Finish*	Manager	Affiliate Since
AAA	Indianapolis (Ind.) Indians	International	78	66	.542	**4th (14)**	Trent Jewett	2005
AA	Altoona (Pa.) Curve	Eastern	76	66	.535	**t-2nd (12)**	Tony Beasley	1999
High A	Lynchburg (Va.) Hillcats	Carolina	78	62	.557	**2nd (8)**	Tim Leiper	1995
Low A	Hickory (N.C.) Crawdads	South Atlantic	54	80	.403	15th (16)	Jeff Branson	1999
SS A	Williamsport (Pa.) Crosscutters	New York-Penn	44	32	.579	**4th (14)**	Tom Prince	1999
Rookie	Bradenton (Fla.) Pirates	Gulf Coast	28	26	.519	t-4th (12)	Jeff Livesey	1967

*Finish in overall standings (No. of teams in league)/Playoff teams in **boldface**

INDIANAPOLIS INDIANS — Class AAA

INTERNATIONAL LEAGUE

BATTING	B-T	HT	WT	DOB	AVG	vLH	vRH	G	AB	R	H	2B	3B	HR	RBI	BB	HBP	SH	SF	SO	SB	CS	SLG	OBP
Amezaga, Alfredo	B-R	5-10	165	1-6-78	.341	.489	.293	64	185	28	63	12	2	1	12	17	2	5	2	27	14	7	.443	.398
Bautista, Jose	R-R	6-0	190	10-19-80	.255	.143	.273	13	51	6	13	3	0	1	4	4	0	0	0	10	1	1	.373	.309
Castillo, Jose	R-R	6-1	200	3-19-81	.385	.000	.385	4	13	2	5	1	0	2	2	2	0	0	0	1	0	0	.923	.467
Chiaffredo, Paul	R-R	6-2	210	5-30-76	.207	.200	.211	56	135	18	28	8	0	7	21	4	0	5	0	45	2	0	.422	.230
Cota, Humberto	R-R	6-0	195	2-7-79	.273	.500	.000	3	11	0	3	0	0	0	1	0	0	0	0	3	0	0	.273	.273
Crespo, Cesar	B-R	5-11	190	5-23-79	.266	.257	.269	112	399	73	106	22	4	9	51	50	2	4	2	68	31	9	.409	.349
De Caster, Yurendell	R-R	6-1	206	9-26-79	.280	.314	.268	122	415	60	116	31	4	11	61	37	6	2	2	103	7	5	.453	.346
Doumit, Ryan	B-R	6-0	200	4-3-81	.345	.293	.363	51	165	41	57	11	0	12	35	16	5	0	2	36	1	3	.630	.415
Duffy, Chris	L-L	5-10	180	4-20-80	.308	.309	.308	78	308	55	95	13	7	7	31	16	10	2	4	57	17	9	.464	.358
Eldred, Brad	R-R	6-5	270	7-12-80	.282	.291	.279	54	195	31	55	13	1	15	48	14	3	0	2	57	4	0	.590	.336
Furmaniak, J.J.	R-R	6-3	190	7-31-79	.288	.233	.303	36	139	12	40	5	3	2	21	4	2	1	1	32	5	3	.410	.315
Guzman, Edwards	L-R	5-11	205	9-11-76	.262	.294	.250	21	65	2	17	3	0	1	5	2	1	1	0	4	0	1	.354	.294
Hill, Bobby	B-R	5-9	175	4-3-78	.241	.200	.248	35	116	15	28	4	0	0	5	14	3	3	1	29	2	0	.276	.336
Koonce, Graham	L-L	6-4	230	5-15-75	.268	.176	.293	120	422	60	113	22	1	23	77	57	7	0	8	109	0	1	.488	.358
Leon, Jose	R-R	6-1	225	12-8-76	.268	.257	.274	71	231	25	62	11	2	10	45	20	1	0	3	65	0	0	.463	.325
McLouth, Nate	L-R	5-11	185	10-28-81	.297	.315	.290	110	397	64	118	20	3	5	39	39	7	5	7	58	34	8	.401	.364
Nunnally, Jon	L-R	5-10	205	11-9-71	.225	.200	.230	80	213	30	48	6	3	7	30	27	1	0	0	55	6	1	.380	.315
Olszta, Eddie	R-R	5-10	190	3-8-79	.000	.000	.000	8	5	2	0	0	0	0	0	0	0	0	0	4	2	0	.000	.000
Paulino, Ronny	R-R	6-3	235	4-21-81	.315	.329	.310	77	273	49	86	18	2	13	42	26	0	1	2	48	3	0	.538	.372
Raymundo, G.J.	R-R	5-11	185	3-3-77	.167	.250	.000	6	6	1	1	0	0	0	0	2	0	0	0	1	0	0	.167	.375
Ross, David	R-R	6-2	215	3-19-77	.211	.250	.200	6	19	1	4	1	0	0	1	3	0	0	1	7	0	0	.263	.304
Sadler, Ray	R-R	6-1	200	9-19-80	.259	.345	.235	69	251	28	65	9	1	10	30	15	5	1	3	57	8	6	.422	.310
Skrehot, Shaun	R-R	5-10	180	12-5-75	.231	.100	.313	34	78	5	18	2	0	0	8	1	0	4	1	14	2	1	.256	.238
Thompson, Rich	L-R	6-1	185	4-23-79	.209	.261	.191	29	91	9	19	1	2	1	3	9	4	3	0	12	13	2	.297	.308
Velandia, Jorge	R-R	5-9	180	1-12-75	.277	.207	.301	105	328	47	91	22	2	3	39	33	4	5	6	48	2	3	.384	.345
Wigginton, Ty	R-R	6-0	225	10-11-77	.293	.265	.302	72	280	53	82	18	0	14	52	45	1	0	2	56	8	5	.507	.390
Wilson, Craig	R-R	6-2	220	11-30-76	.381	.200	.438	7	21	4	8	1	0	3	11	3	1	0	0	6	1	0	.857	.480

PITCHING	B-T	HT	WT	DOB	W	L	ERA	G	GS	CG	SV	IP	H	R	ER	HR	BB	SO	AVG	vLH	vRH	K/9	BB/9
Bradley, Bobby	R-R	6-1	190	12-15-80	0	1	13.14	11	2	0	0	12	10	23	18	0	30	8	.217	.278	.179	5.84	21.89
Bullinger, Kirk	R-R	6-0	170	10-28-69	2	7	3.39	55	0	0	4	69	72	29	26	7	15	40	.273	.274	.272	5.22	1.96
Bullington, Bryan	R-R	6-4	220	9-30-80	9	5	3.38	18	18	1	0	109	104	48	41	11	26	82	.251	.266	.239	6.75	2.14
Chiavacci, Ron	R-R	6-1	245	9-5-77	0	1	1.50	10	0	0	0	12	6	2	2	1	0	14	.143	.160	.118	10.50	0.00
Connolly, Mike	L-L	6-0	197	6-2-82	2	4	4.42	13	13	0	0	71	74	37	35	9	29	44	.268	.250	.275	5.55	3.66
Corey, Mark	R-R	6-3	230	11-16-74	5	5	4.02	61	0	0	28	65	62	30	29	6	23	60	.243	.265	.229	8.31	3.18
Duke, Zach	L-L	6-2	210	4-19-83	12	3	2.92	16	16	1	0	108	108	39	35	8	23	66	.267	.222	.278	5.50	1.92
Enochs, Chris	R-R	6-2	210	10-11-75	4	4	5.17	33	14	0	0	103	116	62	59	8	42	58	.293	.293	.293	5.08	3.68
Gonzalez, Mike	R-L	6-1	205	5-23-78	0	0	0.00	2	0	0	0	3	0	0	0	0	0	5	.000	.000	.000	13.50	0.00
Izquierdo, Hansel	R-R	6-1	200	1-2-77	1	1	6.14	7	5	0	0	29	45	27	20	3	10	23	.344	.319	.371	7.06	3.07
Johnston, Mike	L-L	6-2	225	3-30-79	2	1	2.97	52	0	0	0	58	43	21	19	5	30	52	.208	.190	.219	8.12	4.68
Maholm, Paul	L-L	6-2	225	6-25-82	1	1	3.53	6	6	0	0	36	40	19	14	2	12	21	.286	.259	.292	5.30	3.03
Mallette, Brian	R-R	5-11	205	1-19-75	2	1	4.46	25	0	0	0	38	38	22	19	6	21	30	.266	.250	.276	7.04	4.93
McDade, Neal	R-R	6-3	190	6-16-76	0	2	6.33	14	2	0	0	27	37	23	19	3	8	27	.336	.341	.333	9.00	2.67
Miller, Jeff	R-R	6-3	235	2-1-80	5	7	3.53	58	0	0	0	82	79	37	32	13	27	62	.256	.307	.226	6.83	2.98
Nitkowski, C.J.	L-L	6-3	210	3-9-73	2	0	0.83	18	0	0	2	22	6	5	2	0	9	18	.091	.042	.119	7.48	3.74
Nunez, Vladimir	R-R	6-4	240	3-15-75	1	0	0.90	7	0	0	0	10	5	1	1	0	3	11	.152	.176	.125	9.90	2.70
Perez, Oliver	L-L	6-2	200	8-15-81	0	1	9.90	3	3	0	0	10	14	11	11	3	12	4	.326	.143	.361	3.60	10.80
Reid, Justin	R-R	6-5	225	6-30-77	7	5	5.82	25	18	0	0	99	122	74	64	20	44	61	.307	.349	.276	5.55	4.00
Reith, Brian	R-R	6-4	220	2-28-78	2	2	4.94	24	1	0	1	31	35	22	17	4	12	19	.287	.293	.284	5.52	3.48
Roa, Joe	R-R	6-2	210	10-11-71	1	1	6.05	6	4	0	1	19	27	13	13	4	7	13	.342	.304	.357	6.05	3.26
Snell, Ian	R-R	5-11	180	10-30-81	11	3	3.70	18	18	2	0	112	90	49	46	14	23	104	.216	.269	.178	8.36	1.85
Stewart, Cory	L-L	6-4	215	11-14-79	7	10	5.52	24	23	1	0	132	144	91	81	18	67	77	.286	.364	.261	5.25	4.57
Stewart, Paul	R-R	6-5	200	10-21-78	2	0	0.87	3	1	0	0	10	6	1	1	0	1	10	.167	.100	.192	8.71	0.87

FIELDING

Catcher	PCT	G	PO	A	E	DP	PB
Chiaffredo	.997	54	264	21	1	2	3
Cota	1.000	3	21	2	0	0	2
Doumit	.983	39	221	12	4	1	2
Paulino	.989	69	410	33	5	3	5
Ross	.971	6	31	3	1	1	1

First Base	PCT	G	PO	A	E	DP
Chiaffredo	1.000	1	1	0	0	0
De Caster	.994	25	150	12	1	18
Eldred	.989	41	325	22	4	38
Guzman	1.000	8	54	6	0	4
Koonce	.990	75	632	45	7	59
Leon	1.000	2	10	0	0	1
Olszta	1.000	1	1	0	0	0
Wigginton	1.000	11	76	10	0	11
Wilson	1.000	2	13	2	0	2

Second Base	PCT	G	PO	A	E	DP
Amezaga	.961	18	26	47	3	15
Castillo	1.000	4	5	5	0	2
Crespo	.976	68	114	165	7	43
De Caster	.948	13	28	27	3	9
Furmaniak	1.000	2	3	4	0	0
Guzman	.933	5	5	9	1	1
Hill	1.000	19	25	35	0	9
Olszta	1.000	1	1	0	0	1
Raymundo	.818	2	5	4	2	1
Skrehot	.965	15	22	33	2	5
Velandia	1.000	22	40	50	0	9

	PCT	G	PO	A	E	DP
Wigginton	.968	5	12	18	1	7

Third Base	PCT	G	PO	A	E	DP
Amezaga	1.000	3	0	4	0	0
Bautista	1.000	13	6	26	0	2
Crespo	.667	2	2	4	3	0
De Caster	.915	28	15	39	5	6
Furmaniak	1.000	4	2	4	0	0
Guzman	.947	6	6	12	1	2
Hill	.739	13	4	13	6	3
Leon	.974	40	14	62	2	5
Olszta	1.000	1	1	0	0	0
Raymundo	1.000	1	0	1	0	0
Skrehot	.750	1	1	2	1	0
Wigginton	.963	55	32	125	6	11

Shortstop	PCT	G	PO	A	E	DP
Amezaga	.957	26	29	59	4	16
Crespo	1.000	9	8	18	0	5
Furmaniak	.965	29	48	90	5	15
Hill	1.000	1	0	1	0	0
Olszta	.000	1	0	0	0	0
Skrehot	1.000	13	18	33	0	7
Velandia	.977	82	110	223	8	53

Outfield	PCT	G	PO	A	E	DP
Amezaga	.958	14	23	0	1	0
Crespo	.988	37	78	1	1	0
De Caster	.983	58	114	4	2	1
Doumit	1.000	4	6	0	0	0
Duffy	.989	76	172	3	2	1
Furmaniak	1.000	1	1	0	0	0
Koonce	1.000	15	20	1	0	1
McLouth	.986	105	214	3	3	0
Nunnally	.942	61	109	4	7	1
Olszta	.667	3	2	0	1	0
Sadler	.980	68	137	9	3	0
Thompson	.985	26	65	2	1	1
Velandia	1.000	1	1	1	0	1
Wilson	.800	4	4	0	1	0

ALTOONA CURVE — Class AA

EASTERN LEAGUE

BATTING	B-T	HT	WT	DOB	AVG	vLH	vRH	G	AB	R	H	2B	3B	HR	RBI	BB	HBP	SH	SF	SO	SB	CS	SLG	OBP
Bautista, Jose	R-R	6-0	190	10-19-80	.283	.301	.276	117	445	63	126	27	1	23	90	48	10	2	2	101	7	3	.503	.364
Boeve, Adam	R-R	6-2	216	6-20-80	.288	.303	.277	47	160	24	46	9	1	5	23	22	1	1	1	54	5	2	.450	.375
Bonifay, Josh	R-R	6-0	185	7-30-78	.282	.324	.265	103	376	53	106	22	3	25	77	33	2	0	5	110	0	1	.556	.339
Buttler, Vic	L-L	6-0	174	8-12-80	.313	.278	.323	25	83	15	26	3	1	0	7	10	1	1	0	10	6	2	.373	.394
Chaves, Brandon	B-R	6-3	181	8-5-79	.215	.244	.205	52	172	20	37	6	2	0	8	16	2	3	1	38	2	2	.273	.288
Chiaffredo, Paul	R-R	6-2	210	5-30-76	.267	.000	.296	8	30	4	8	4	0	1	7	1	0	1	0	11	0	0	.500	.290
Clark, Howie	L-R	5-10	190	2-13-74	.373	.406	.359	31	110	15	41	3	0	2	13	19	0	0	1	5	2	1	.455	.462
Cortes, Jorge	L-L	5-10	195	10-17-80	.259	.202	.276	110	363	50	94	18	1	6	49	49	4	4	5	81	2	1	.364	.349
Davis, Rajai	R-R	5-11	190	10-19-80	.281	.269	.286	123	499	82	140	22	5	4	34	43	12	6	1	76	45	9	.369	.351
Eldred, Brad	R-R	6-5	270	7-12-80	.333	.280	.356	21	84	22	28	6	0	13	27	8	0	0	1	25	1	1	.869	.387
Evans, Tom	R-R	6-1	200	7-9-74	.278	.289	.274	100	338	62	94	24	3	15	55	51	8	1	7	91	8	3	.500	.379
Guzman, Javier	B-R	5-11	140	5-4-84	.236	.271	.219	68	263	27	62	9	1	3	24	10	0	4	2	46	8	5	.312	.262
Lee, Taber	B-R	6-1	185	10-18-80	.203	.160	.222	24	79	8	16	2	1	2	10	7	1	1	1	13	1	0	.329	.273
Lytle, Chaz	L-L	6-1	190	10-27-80	.217	.125	.267	6	23	3	5	1	0	0	1	1	2	0	0	5	2	0	.261	.308
Maldonado, Carlos	R-R	6-1	235	1-3-79	.252	.272	.242	82	278	27	70	14	0	7	34	35	2	5	1	63	0	1	.378	.339
Meath, Matt	B-R	6-0	175	10-6-79	.333	.500	.000	2	3	2	1	1	0	0	1	1	1	0	0	0	0	0	.667	.600
Mercedes, Victor	B-R	5-11	184	4-15-79	.326	.286	.333	12	43	7	14	2	1	2	6	2	0	0	0	5	0	0	.558	.356
Neuberger, Scott	R-R	6-3	227	8-14-77	.263	.200	.304	10	38	1	10	0	0	0	4	1	0	1	0	7	0	0	.263	.282
Paulino, Ronny	R-R	6-3	235	4-21-81	.292	.310	.286	43	168	24	49	6	0	6	20	15	0	1	0	30	3	0	.435	.350
Raymundo, G.J.	R-R	5-11	185	3-3-77	.232	.190	.257	23	56	5	13	3	0	0	2	3	1	1	0	12	0	0	.286	.283
Sadler, Ray	R-R	6-1	200	9-19-80	.244	.217	.255	62	209	23	51	17	2	5	23	17	0	1	0	54	4	4	.416	.301
Snusz, Chris	R-R	6-0	210	11-8-72	.258	.350	.217	22	66	5	17	3	0	1	1	4	0	2	0	13	0	0	.348	.300
Stansberry, Craig	R-R	6-0	185	3-8-82	.238	.273	.222	116	421	62	100	22	11	18	67	44	6	5	7	114	14	5	.470	.314
Thompson, Rich	L-R	6-1	185	4-23-79	.257	.275	.250	94	346	58	89	11	5	3	30	30	8	10	1	60	45	6	.344	.330
Wilson, Andy	L-R	5-6	165	8-12-75	.235	.000	.308	7	17	1	4	0	0	0	1	3	0	1	0	4	0	0	.235	.350

PITCHING	B-T	HT	WT	DOB	W	L	ERA	G	GS	CG	SV	IP	H	R	ER	HR	BB	SO	AVG	vLH	vRH	K/9	BB/9
Borner, Brady	L-L	5-10	182	4-12-79	6	1	2.08	48	0	0	0	91	77	22	21	8	13	90	.231	.226	.234	8.93	1.29
Candelario, Eddie	R-R	6-0	173	11-3-77	3	4	3.12	13	13	0	0	75	76	33	26	5	15	59	.262	.320	.218	7.08	1.80
Capps, Matt	R-R	6-3	240	9-3-83	0	2	2.70	17	0	0	7	20	21	8	6	2	1	26	.250	.237	.261	11.70	0.45
Connolly, Mike	L-L	6-0	197	6-2-82	5	6	3.32	15	15	1	0	84	90	35	31	4	24	60	.271	.270	.271	6.43	2.57
Gorzelanny, Tom	L-L	6-2	205	7-12-82	8	5	3.26	23	23	1	0	130	114	50	47	6	46	124	.236	.258	.228	8.61	3.19
Harts, Jeremy	B-L	6-0	225	6-6-80	1	2	8.08	29	0	0	0	39	33	42	35	4	53	46	.237	.119	.289	10.62	12.23
Izquierdo, Hansel	R-R	6-1	200	1-2-77	7	5	4.51	24	17	0	0	104	104	61	52	6	41	84	.261	.302	.222	7.29	3.56
Jacobsen, Landon	R-R	6-3	220	5-4-79	2	0	3.86	11	0	0	1	23	21	14	10	1	11	23	.233	.244	.224	8.87	4.24
Johnson, James	B-L	6-0	175	8-7-76	5	4	3.33	31	1	0	1	51	50	25	19	4	16	54	.248	.293	.229	9.47	2.81
Kaye, Justin	R-R	6-4	195	6-9-76	3	3	4.09	53	0	0	22	62	63	29	28	4	29	54	.259	.283	.238	7.88	4.23
Maholm, Paul	L-L	6-2	225	6-25-82	6	2	3.20	16	16	0	0	82	73	32	29	5	26	75	.243	.169	.271	8.27	2.87
Martin, Greg	L-L	6-1	190	4-10-80	0	1	16.88	3	0	0	0	3	5	5	5	0	1	0	.385	.250	.444	0.00	3.38
Peterson, Matt	R-R	6-5	205	2-11-82	11	9	5.51	27	26	0	0	144	156	102	88	19	74	87	.281	.237	.322	5.45	4.64
Roach, Jason	R-R	6-4	205	4-20-76	1	3	4.42	10	4	0	2	37	45	21	18	7	11	19	.308	.394	.227	4.66	2.70
Sanchez, Romulo	R-R	6-6	208	4-28-84	1	0	3.60	2	2	0	0	10	11	4	4	2	4	5	.282	.375	.217	4.50	3.60
Shaffar, Ben	B-R	6-3	195	9-28-77	2	3	3.44	44	0	0	9	73	73	33	28	6	26	69	.257	.263	.253	8.47	3.19
Sharpless, Josh	R-R	6-5	243	1-26-81	1	0	2.89	7	0	0	0	9	6	3	3	0	3	13	.171	.077	.227	12.54	2.89
Stewart, Paul	R-R	6-5	200	10-21-78	6	10	4.92	26	20	0	0	121	143	78	66	19	44	76	.297	.263	.326	5.67	3.28
Youman, Shane	L-L	6-4	205	10-11-79	8	6	3.92	44	5	0	2	101	102	54	44	10	48	77	.258	.221	.273	6.86	4.28

FIELDING

Catcher	PCT	G	PO	A	E	DP	PB
Chiaffredo	1.000	8	62	3	0	0	0
Maldonado	.982	79	571	42	11	10	5
Paulino	.991	40	314	27	3	5	5
Snusz	.993	21	120	13	1	0	5

First Base	PCT	G	PO	A	E	DP
Bonifay	.995	88	698	66	4	54
Eldred	.989	19	177	3	2	15
Evans	.983	39	319	25	6	33

Second Base	PCT	G	PO	A	E	DP
Evans	.931	6	11	16	2	7
Lee	1.000	8	15	15	0	0
Mercedes	.940	12	13	34	3	6
Raymundo	1.000	5	4	10	0	1
Stansberry	.974	115	255	308	15	68
Wilson	1.000	1	1	2	0	1

Third Base	PCT	G	PO	A	E	DP
Bautista	.924	116	72	221	24	15
Evans	.839	26	10	42	10	1
Raymundo	.000	2	0	0	1	0
Wilson	.700	3	4	3	3	1

Shortstop	PCT	G	PO	A	E	DP
Chaves	.914	52	68	133	19	24
Evans	1.000	2	3	6	0	0
Guzman	.972	68	94	221	9	48
Lee	1.000	15	20	39	0	8
Raymundo	1.000	9	20	14	0	7

Outfield	PCT	G	PO	A	E	DP
Boeve	.947	43	71	1	4	0
Bonifay	1.000	4	1	0	0	0
Buttler	.969	20	28	3	1	0
Clark	.917	10	11	0	1	0
Cortes	.972	93	168	8	5	1
Davis	.966	118	276	10	10	3
Lytle	1.000	4	9	0	0	0
Meath	.000	1	0	0	0	0
Neuberger	1.000	9	20	1	0	0
Sadler	.970	53	91	7	3	3
Thompson	.989	86	171	7	2	1

LYNCHBURG HILLCATS — High Class A

CAROLINA LEAGUE

BATTING	B-T	HT	WT	DOB	AVG	vLH	vRH	G	AB	R	H	2B	3B	HR	RBI	BB	HBP	SH	SF	SO	SB	CS	SLG	OBP
Asprilla, Avelino	R-R	6-0	194	1-1-81	.269	.285	.259	112	375	51	101	20	1	12	56	26	5	0	3	78	4	4	.424	.323
Benick, Jon	B-R	6-2	217	9-26-79	.160	.104	.192	50	187	16	30	7	0	4	30	16	2	0	4	44	0	0	.262	.230
Bocchino, Anthony	L-L	5-10	193	5-15-80	.269	.346	.231	41	78	16	21	4	0	1	11	11	0	1	2	14	0	2	.359	.352
Boeve, Adam	R-R	6-2	216	6-20-80	.313	.348	.294	71	249	60	78	15	1	13	47	39	9	0	4	66	12	0	.538	.419
Buttler, Vic	L-L	6-0	174	8-12-80	.333	.366	.308	57	231	40	77	13	3	5	38	4	7	0	1	34	8	2	.481	.362
Chaves, Brandon	B-R	6-3	181	8-5-79	.300	.250	.339	61	210	34	63	8	4	1	25	28	1	0	0	46	2	3	.390	.385
Cockrell, Michael	R-R	5-10	173	7-25-81	.167	.077	.207	11	42	3	7	1	0	1	1	2	0	0	0	7	0	1	.262	.205
Guzman, Javier	B-R	5-11	140	5-4-84	.324	.351	.309	69	256	40	83	13	7	5	35	20	1	1	1	41	13	5	.488	.374
Harris, Justin	R-R	6-0	169	5-25-81	.300	.206	.368	46	150	25	45	4	2	1	17	6	1	2	2	21	1	0	.373	.327
Hernandez, Jose	R-R	6-1	214	11-3-80	.268	.278	.260	43	149	14	40	4	1	1	20	9	2	2	0	34	2	1	.329	.319
Kingsbury, Bobby	L-L	6-1	184	8-30-80	.246	.261	.236	86	289	42	71	18	4	9	55	41	5	1	7	69	5	3	.429	.342
Lee, Taber	B-R	6-1	185	10-18-80	.241	.245	.238	84	311	44	75	15	1	4	34	60	5	3	0	70	5	4	.334	.372
Lytle, Chaz	L-L	6-1	190	10-27-80	.296	.289	.299	76	247	43	73	7	1	0	19	20	6	5	1	45	12	5	.332	.361
Magness, Pat	L-R	6-3	245	1-19-78	.308	.276	.331	133	425	98	131	39	1	24	92	141	2	0	2	114	0	1	.574	.481
McCuistion, Mike	L-R	6-2	213	5-14-82	.293	.275	.302	98	335	43	98	19	2	8	59	39	3	0	5	64	5	1	.433	.366
Meath, Matt	B-R	6-0	175	10-6-79	.267	.188	.357	13	30	5	8	0	0	0	1	5	3	2	0	8	0	0	.267	.421
Mercedes, Victor	B-R	5-11	184	4-15-79	.264	.300	.242	13	53	10	14	2	1	1	6	5	1	1	0	15	3	1	.396	.339
Morgan, Nyjer	L-L	6-0	170	7-2-80	.286	.287	.285	60	252	36	72	12	3	0	24	11	7	3	4	40	24	10	.357	.328
Pena, Rudy	R-R	6-0	215	3-7-79	.308	.364	.267	9	26	2	8	1	0	1	1	0	0	1	0	6	0	0	.462	.308
Powell, Pedro	B-R	5-7	143	5-20-84	.294	.500	.182	8	34	9	10	1	1	0	1	3	0	0	0	2	2	0	.382	.351
Raymundo, G.J.	R-R	5-11	185	3-3-77	.167	.250	.125	3	12	1	2	1	0	0	3	0	0	0	1	1	0	0	.250	.154
Rea, Brad	R-R	6-4	220	7-29-79	.269	.306	.238	118	435	58	117	37	2	8	58	61	6	0	2	78	0	0	.418	.365
Stansberry, Craig	R-R	6-0	185	3-8-82	.351	.263	.411	24	94	17	33	7	2	3	19	11	2	0	0	13	7	1	.564	.430
Walker, Neil	B-R	6-2	215	9-10-85	.262	.294	.240	9	42	4	11	2	1	0	12	0	0	0	3	12	0	0	.357	.244
Wilson, Andy	L-R	5-6	165	8-12-75	.297	.346	.262	58	185	30	55	11	2	0	18	32	1	0	1	22	1	1	.378	.402

PITCHING	B-T	HT	WT	DOB	W	L	ERA	G	GS	CG	SV	IP	H	R	ER	HR	BB	SO	AVG	vLH	vRH	K/9	BB/9
Albaladejo, Jon	R-R	6-5	251	10-30-82	4	3	3.91	28	6	0	2	78	74	40	34	9	21	76	.246	.262	.237	8.73	2.41
Allen, Wyatt	R-R	6-4	205	4-12-80	0	0	8.38	3	2	0	0	10	17	10	9	2	4	8	.395	.267	.464	7.45	3.72
Bishop, Matt	R-R	6-2	215	6-5-82	0	2	11.08	8	0	0	0	13	26	18	16	5	9	10	.400	.364	.419	6.92	6.23
Bloom, Kyle	R-L	6-3	185	2-21-83	3	5	5.86	12	12	0	0	63	61	45	41	12	43	34	.255	.188	.280	4.86	6.14
Craig, Dustin	R-R	6-4	240	4-9-82	0	0	0.00	1	0	0	0	2	0	0	0	0	2	2	.000	.000	.000	9.00	9.00
Davila, Marcus	R-R	6-1	200	8-14-81	4	3	5.82	46	0	0	1	73	84	50	47	8	24	45	.294	.314	.283	5.57	2.97
Guerrero, Julio	R-R	6-4	200	1-4-81	4	2	5.35	14	1	0	0	34	44	25	20	0	9	17	.303	.295	.307	4.54	2.41
Hernandez, Chris	R-R	6-0	204	8-3-80	6	3	3.82	45	0	0	16	61	62	32	26	7	25	69	.259	.253	.263	10.13	3.67
Hernandez, Jose	R-R	6-1	214	11-3-80	0	0	13.50	2	0	0	0	3	6	4	4	2	0	0	.429	.200	.556	0.00	0.00
Holliday, Brian	L-L	6-2	202	6-1-84	5	4	5.40	19	19	0	0	93	106	66	56	5	54	39	.286	.264	.293	3.76	5.21
Jacobsen, Landon	R-R	6-3	220	5-4-79	3	1	2.10	5	5	0	0	30	29	12	7	0	13	25	.261	.256	.265	7.50	3.90
Linares, Ramon	R-R	6-1	215	4-28-79	0	1	2.33	12	0	0	1	19	14	7	5	0	11	16	.203	.194	.211	7.45	5.12
Martin, Greg	L-L	6-1	190	4-10-80	5	2	7.30	23	1	0	0	41	51	38	33	5	25	43	.311	.236	.349	9.52	5.53
Mazurek, Dave	R-R	6-5	235	7-23-80	0	2	6.00	30	1	0	2	51	52	39	34	9	19	40	.259	.233	.273	7.06	3.35
Michael, Mark	R-R	6-3	177	1-20-81	1	2	10.29	4	3	0	0	14	24	17	16	4	4	14	.375	.304	.415	9.00	2.57
O'Brien, Patrick	R-R	6-5	220	11-20-80	4	8	5.01	17	16	2	0	83	94	51	46	7	26	49	.290	.311	.277	5.33	2.83
Ozias, Todd	R-R	6-0	195	8-19-76	1	1	3.38	25	0	0	13	29	20	11	11	4	8	29	.190	.219	.178	8.90	2.45
Shafer, Kurt	R-R	6-4	195	12-4-81	1	0	5.40	9	1	0	0	23	29	17	14	4	9	19	.293	.350	.254	7.33	3.47
Sharpless, Josh	R-R	6-5	243	1-26-81	3	0	0.00	17	0	0	5	27	7	1	0	0	11	46	.081	.125	.065	15.33	3.67
Shortslef, Josh	R-L	6-4	230	2-1-82	10	5	4.58	22	22	1	0	120	132	69	61	8	44	84	.284	.282	.285	6.30	3.30
Starling, Wardell	R-R	6-4	205	3-14-83	10	10	5.22	28	28	1	0	153	168	98	89	18	55	102	.279	.286	.274	5.99	3.23
Torrealba, Yoann	R-R	5-11	187	6-24-82	3	1	4.07	16	1	0	2	49	54	24	22	4	14	24	.280	.338	.246	4.44	2.59
Van Dusen, Derrick	L-L	6-2	170	6-6-81	11	6	4.24	22	22	1	0	123	123	73	58	16	36	92	.255	.234	.262	6.73	2.63
Young, Chris	R-R	6-4	218	4-19-81	0	1	3.00	10	0	0	2	15	9	5	5	1	5	14	.188	.273	.115	8.40	3.00

FIELDING

Catcher	PCT	G	PO	A	E	DP	PB
Hernandez	.993	42	248	26	2	4	4
McCuistion	.984	88	565	67	10	2	23
Pena	.966	8	51	5	2	1	0
Walker	1.000	4	32	2	0	0	1

First Base	PCT	G	PO	A	E	DP
Benick	.989	46	407	28	5	39
Harris	1.000	2	6	0	0	0
Magness	.992	39	359	21	3	29
Rea	.991	57	512	30	5	43

Second Base	PCT	G	PO	A	E	DP
Harris	.991	24	51	54	1	17
Lee	.977	73	119	215	8	42
Mercedes	.934	13	28	29	4	11
Raymundo	.833	2	6	4	2	1
Stansberry	.952	24	38	62	5	11
Wilson	1.000	9	30	18	0	5

Third Base	PCT	G	PO	A	E	DP
Asprilla	.938	110	72	243	21	20
Cockrell	.903	11	14	14	3	1
Harris	.939	12	5	26	2	3
Raymundo	.000	1	0	0	2	0
Wilson	.950	18	10	28	2	0

Shortstop	PCT	G	PO	A	E	DP
Asprilla	1.000	1	0	1	0	0
Chaves	.956	61	82	198	13	36
Guzman	.927	69	92	213	24	39
Lee	.949	13	15	41	3	9

Outfield	PCT	G	PO	A	E	DP
Bocchino	.961	38	47	2	2	1
Boeve	.986	66	131	5	2	1
Buttler	.991	56	97	8	1	2
Harris	1.000	7	10	0	0	0
Kingsbury	.983	82	173	5	3	3
Lytle	.959	68	111	6	5	3
Magness	.958	37	44	2	2	1
Meath	1.000	11	14	0	0	0
Morgan	.965	58	138	1	5	0
Powell	1.000	8	9	1	0	0
Wilson	1.000	25	42	1	0	1

HICKORY CRAWDADS — Low Class A

SOUTH ATLANTIC LEAGUE

BATTING	B-T	HT	WT	DOB	AVG	vLH	vRH	G	AB	R	H	2B	3B	HR	RBI	BB	HBP	SH	SF	SO	SB	CS	SLG	OBP
Bixler, Brian	R-R	6-1	190	10-22-82	.281	.234	.294	126	502	74	141	23	2	9	50	38	11	3	3	134	21	10	.388	.343
Bocchino, Anthony	L-L	5-10	193	5-15-80	.258	.173	.282	65	233	44	60	13	4	10	45	37	10	0	3	45	1	2	.476	.378
Buttler, Vic	L-L	6-0	174	8-12-80	.207	.250	.194	25	92	7	19	2	0	0	5	4	1	3	0	11	3	1	.228	.247
Carlin, Michael	R-R	6-0	205	7-6-81	.318	.364	.300	89	308	53	98	21	4	16	65	29	14	0	3	70	6	1	.568	.398
Cho, Hyung	R-R	5-9	190	8-20-82	.157	.161	.156	31	108	13	17	2	0	0	11	8	0	1	3	10	1	0	.176	.210
Cockrell, Michael	R-R	5-10	173	7-25-81	.267	.321	.253	99	371	47	99	14	6	7	44	25	5	3	6	29	7	5	.394	.317
Delgado, Dario	R-R	6-1	186	3-30-80	.278	.231	.400	6	18	0	5	0	0	0	1	3	0	1	0	4	0	1	.278	.381

BATTING	B-T	HT	WT	DOB	AVG	vLH	vRH	G	AB	R	H	2B	3B	HR	RBI	BB	HBP	SH	SF	SO	SB	CS	SLG	OBP
Elliott, Justin	R-R	5-11	195	4-27-82	.600	.000	.600	1	5	2	3	0	0	0	1	0	0	0	0	1	0	0	.600	.600
Hofius, Mike	L-L	6-2	210	5-3-82	.222	.111	.234	82	266	27	59	8	0	4	30	29	6	0	4	58	2	1	.297	.308
Holmes, Brett	R-R	6-1	183	3-13-81	.343	.200	.400	9	35	8	12	1	0	2	3	6	0	0	0	18	1	1	.543	.439
Johnson, A.J.	R-R	6-1	190	9-26-83	.227	.278	.209	97	348	38	79	12	2	9	44	24	6	0	1	88	3	10	.351	.288
Lerud, Steven	L-R	6-1	196	10-13-84	.088	.000	.115	25	80	6	7	2	2	2	13	4	2	0	1	27	0	1	.238	.149
Lomack, Jermel	B-R	5-8	160	5-13-83	.243	.100	.284	59	181	18	44	4	1	0	12	21	1	4	0	33	12	10	.276	.325
Macia, Wanell	L-L	5-11	180	7-20-82	.266	.050	.306	40	128	12	34	4	1	0	15	2	1	0	2	28	3	4	.313	.278
Mansolino, Tony	R-R	6-0	190	9-28-82	.207	.167	.217	8	29	4	6	2	0	1	5	3	0	0	2	4	0	0	.379	.265
Mercedes, Victor	B-R	5-11	184	4-15-79	.500	.333	.600	2	8	1	4	0	0	0	0	0	0	0	0	1	0	1	.500	.500
Nino, Denny	R-R	6-1	211	6-4-83	.000	.000	.000	3	6	0	0	0	0	0	0	0	0	0	0	1	0	0	.000	.000
Powell, Pedro	B-R	5-7	143	5-20-84	.272	.342	.249	112	445	75	121	6	4	1	24	41	4	6	1	83	44	16	.310	.338
Reyes, Milver	R-R	5-11	200	9-3-82	.188	.206	.182	43	133	10	25	2	2	1	13	12	1	0	1	18	0	0	.256	.259
Santiago, John	R-R	6-1	157	12-26-84	.185	.111	.222	9	27	3	5	3	0	0	0	2	0	0	0	2	0	0	.296	.241
Schwartzbauer, Daniel	R-R	5-11	175	11-2-81	.269	.247	.275	97	324	38	87	17	1	5	34	25	6	4	3	70	3	5	.373	.330
Solano, Euvi	R-R	6-0	167	4-28-82	.000	.000	.000	1	3	0	0	0	0	0	0	0	1	0	0	0	0	0	.000	.250
Sucre, Antonio	R-R	6-2	180	8-13-83	.265	.248	.271	107	393	38	104	12	0	10	54	22	10	0	3	109	3	3	.372	.318
Walker, Neil	B-R	6-2	215	9-10-85	.301	.270	.310	120	485	78	146	33	2	12	68	20	6	0	7	71	7	4	.452	.332

PITCHING	B-T	HT	WT	DOB	W	L	ERA	G	GS	CG	SV	IP	H	R	ER	HR	BB	SO	AVG	vLH	vRH	K/9	BB/9
Bishop, Matt	R-R	6-2	215	6-5-82	3	7	4.58	24	1	0	0	53	63	34	27	5	22	34	.296	.238	.333	5.77	3.74
Bloom, Kyle	R-L	6-3	185	2-21-83	4	1	1.87	12	12	0	0	63	38	15	13	3	33	58	.176	.158	.180	8.33	4.74
Capps, Matt	R-R	6-3	240	9-3-83	3	4	2.52	35	0	0	14	54	47	15	15	0	5	39	.239	.270	.220	6.54	0.84
Craig, Dustin	R-R	6-4	240	4-9-82	4	5	5.14	34	0	0	2	56	56	35	32	7	37	61	.260	.311	.234	9.80	5.95
Davidson, David	L-L	6-1	187	4-23-84	1	2	9.78	10	2	0	0	19	16	22	21	4	21	23	.225	.455	.183	10.71	9.78
Drage, Derek	R-R	6-3	215	12-10-81	3	5	4.46	37	1	0	6	75	73	42	37	13	30	58	.260	.295	.239	6.99	3.62
Garavito, Jean	R-R	5-11	186	1-11-85	2	4	5.20	33	0	0	0	62	81	39	36	5	27	35	.314	.310	.316	5.05	3.90
Garcia, Felipe	R-R	5-11	165	9-20-82	4	5	4.37	36	0	0	4	58	59	39	28	7	29	53	.263	.295	.240	8.27	4.53
Guerrero, Julio	R-R	6-4	200	1-4-81	7	3	4.41	17	16	0	0	96	97	50	47	14	14	61	.259	.240	.269	5.72	1.31
Guillory, Matt	R-R	6-4	175	3-13-83	4	7	2.64	22	22	0	0	109	106	44	32	11	31	82	.251	.281	.233	6.77	2.56
Hankins, Derek	R-R	6-4	190	7-1-83	6	6	4.49	27	27	1	0	156	176	90	78	17	43	118	.277	.291	.267	6.79	2.48
Herman, Jason	R-R	6-3	210	12-9-81	1	0	4.50	1	1	0	0	6	5	3	3	2	2	2	.227	.000	.227	3.00	3.00
Johnson, Blair	R-R	6-4	218	3-25-84	1	0	4.02	3	3	0	0	16	17	7	7	0	7	6	.293	.357	.273	3.45	4.02
Lissir, Alexander	R-R	6-0	207	12-29-82	0	1	36.00	1	0	0	0	1	3	4	4	1	1	0	.500	.400	1.000	0.00	9.00
Martin, Greg	L-L	6-1	190	4-10-80	0	0	3.00	2	0	0	0	3	3	2	1	0	0	3	.250	.333	.222	9.00	0.00
Michael, Mark	R-R	6-3	177	1-20-81	0	2	7.07	3	3	0	0	14	19	11	11	2	5	13	.328	.324	.333	8.36	3.21
Munoz, Luis	R-R	6-2	150	1-10-82	0	0	0.00	1	0	0	0	3	2	1	0	0	1	4	.182	.000	.222	13.50	3.38
Pearson, Kyle	R-R	6-1	200	10-8-84	2	10	6.17	24	15	0	1	101	141	79	69	13	34	55	.338	.383	.303	4.92	3.04
Quarles, Jason	R-R	6-0	195	4-20-83	0	3	2.61	19	1	0	0	38	31	15	11	2	26	45	.226	.293	.198	10.66	6.16
Sanchez, Romulo	R-R	6-6	208	4-28-84	3	3	4.70	10	10	0	0	54	59	34	28	5	19	24	.292	.274	.300	4.02	3.19
Shafer, Kurt	R-R	6-4	195	12-4-81	0	5	5.55	5	4	1	0	24	35	25	15	3	9	11	.337	.370	.310	4.07	3.33
Smith, H. Clifford	R-R	6-5	215	10-13-79	0	0	8.68	7	0	0	0	9	16	9	9	2	2	6	.364	.333	.379	5.79	1.93
Torrealba, Yoann	R-R	5-11	187	6-24-82	6	5	3.52	14	14	0	0	87	94	38	34	5	14	42	.276	.295	.263	4.34	1.45
Valdez, Luis	R-R	6-2	180	5-5-84	0	2	7.50	7	2	0	0	18	24	19	15	1	9	9	.320	.320	.320	4.50	4.50

FIELDING

Catcher	PCT	G	PO	A	E	DP	PB
Elliott	1.000	1	7	0	0	0	0
Lerud	.975	14	66	11	2	0	3
Nino	1.000	3	16	0	0	0	1
Reyes	.985	43	233	28	4	4	3
Walker	.982	79	521	86	11	3	22

First Base	PCT	G	PO	A	E	DP
Carlin	.997	76	712	44	2	60
Delgado	1.000	2	11	1	0	3
Hofius	.985	62	493	38	8	43

Second Base	PCT	G	PO	A	E	DP
Cockrell	.975	14	34	45	2	11
Lomack	.947	51	114	135	14	24
Mercedes	1.000	1	3	5	0	2
Schwartzbauer	.980	76	155	244	8	51

Third Base	PCT	G	PO	A	E	DP
Cho	.913	30	23	50	7	6
Cockrell	.940	76	64	172	15	16
Mansolino	.778	8	6	15	6	3
Santiago	.840	9	3	18	4	1
Schwartzbauer	.900	13	11	25	4	3

Third Base	PCT	G	PO	A	E	DP
Solano	1.000	1	0	2	0	0
Bixler	.948	126	195	407	33	67
Schwartzbauer	.976	11	13	27	1	9

Outfield	PCT	G	PO	A	E	DP
Bocchino	.989	54	88	3	1	0
Buttler	1.000	22	38	2	0	0
Cockrell	.889	4	8	0	1	0
Holmes	1.000	9	19	1	0	0
Johnson	.960	75	136	9	6	4
Lomack	1.000	8	12	2	0	1
Macia	.966	30	54	3	2	1
Powell	.966	111	244	10	9	4
Sucre	.979	96	178	5	4	0

WILLIAMSPORT CROSSCUTTERS — Short-Season Class A

NEW YORK-PENN LEAGUE

BATTING	B-T	HT	WT	DOB	AVG	vLH	vRH	G	AB	R	H	2B	3B	HR	RBI	BB	HBP	SH	SF	SO	SB	CS	SLG	OBP
Blair, Cameron	R-R	5-11	175	10-27-82	.212	.300	.192	64	222	38	47	11	1	2	26	43	10	3	6	46	9	4	.297	.356
Boone, James	B-R	6-2	175	3-16-83	.291	.322	.283	68	278	44	81	12	4	8	42	16	7	0	2	85	8	4	.450	.343
Corley, Brad	R-R	6-2	198	12-28-83	.279	.333	.266	68	265	29	74	10	6	4	35	16	5	0	1	56	3	7	.408	.331
Delaney, Jason	R-R	6-3	215	11-9-82	.213	.225	.210	55	197	19	42	8	0	0	13	19	0	4	1	33	2	2	.254	.281
Grandstrand, Brett	R-R	6-0	175	11-13-82	.228	.154	.242	24	79	8	18	6	1	0	7	11	0	1	2	15	3	1	.329	.315
Hicks, Joseph	R-R	5-11	187	4-22-84	.234	.250	.225	17	64	9	15	3	0	0	5	6	0	0	0	15	1	0	.281	.300
Jones, Chris	R-R	6-0	205	2-27-83	.228	.211	.232	32	114	6	26	4	0	0	13	7	3	1	1	20	2	1	.263	.288
Lerud, Steven	L-R	6-1	196	10-13-84	.125	.000	.133	10	32	3	4	0	0	1	2	2	0	0	0	14	0	0	.219	.176
Lillibridge, Brent	R-R	5-11	185	9-18-83	.243	.306	.226	42	169	19	41	12	4	4	18	14	2	4	2	35	10	3	.432	.305
Lomack, Jermel	B-R	5-8	160	5-13-83	.257	.263	.256	27	101	17	26	2	0	0	8	11	1	5	1	13	19	2	.277	.333
McCutchen, Andrew	R-R	5-11	175	10-10-86	.346	.600	.319	13	52	12	18	3	1	0	5	8	1	1	0	6	4	1	.442	.443
Nino, Denny	R-R	6-1	211	6-4-83	.231	.400	.190	12	26	4	6	1	0	0	2	2	0	0	1	2	0	0	.269	.276
Pearce, Steve	R-R	5-11	200	4-13-83	.301	.340	.292	72	272	48	82	26	0	7	52	35	2	0	3	43	2	4	.474	.381
Poni, Francis	R-R	6-0	223	8-1-83	.147	.167	.143	12	34	2	5	1	0	0	2	0	2	1	1	11	1	0	.176	.189
Prasch, Eddie	L-R	6-0	180	1-25-86	.217	.333	.195	26	92	11	20	2	0	0	7	12	3	1	2	17	3	2	.239	.321
Reddinger, Brandon	R-R	6-2	210	8-16-82	.163	.120	.179	30	92	18	15	1	0	0	5	9	6	0	1	23	1	1	.174	.278
Santiago, John	R-R	6-1	157	12-26-84	.241	.364	.212	49	170	22	41	6	1	3	15	13	6	0	0	32	1	2	.341	.317
Searage, Ryan	R-R	5-11	200	11-23-82	.134	.091	.143	22	67	8	9	3	0	1	10	8	0	3	0	26	0	0	.224	.227
Solano, Euvi	R-R	6-0	167	4-28-82	.269	.323	.257	50	175	24	47	5	0	3	27	19	4	2	1	34	1	4	.349	.352
Stevens, Anthony	R-R	6-0	171	8-27-84	.195	.250	.189	16	41	7	8	1	1	0	1	2	2	1	0	16	3	2	.268	.267

BATTING	B-T	HT	WT	DOB	AVG	vLH	vRH	G	AB	R	H	2B	3B	HR	RBI	BB	HBP	SH	SF	SO	SB	CS	SLG	OBP
Wulf, Kent	B-R	5-11	175	4-26-85	.158	.250	.147	16	38	1	6	0	0	0	2	5	0	1	0	14	1	1	.158	.256

PITCHING	B-T	HT	WT	DOB	W	L	ERA	G	GS	CG	SV	IP	H	R	ER	HR	BB	SO	AVG	vLH	vRH	K/9	BB/9
Antelo, Derek	R-R	6-1	205	11-30-82	6	3	3.48	13	13	0	0	67	52	32	26	3	21	52	.217	.256	.176	6.95	2.81
Bauserman, Joe	R-R	6-2	220	10-4-85	6	2	2.84	14	14	0	0	70	64	30	22	3	26	45	.253	.291	.214	5.81	3.36
Cuffman, Jacob	R-R	6-4	200	3-3-85	1	1	3.86	21	0	0	2	35	19	17	15	2	25	32	.162	.143	.180	8.23	6.43
Davidson, David	L-L	6-1	187	4-23-84	1	1	3.18	5	4	0	0	17	14	7	6	0	8	23	.226	.333	.182	12.18	4.24
Heisel, Ian	R-R	6-3	225	10-19-81	2	3	3.86	28	0	0	0	44	43	20	19	1	16	44	.249	.259	.239	8.93	3.25
Krebs, Eric	R-R	6-3	185	5-16-85	1	1	4.68	7	7	0	0	33	34	18	17	1	17	14	.266	.297	.234	3.86	4.68
Michael, Mark	R-R	6-3	177	1-20-81	1	0	2.70	2	2	0	0	10	7	3	3	1	1	7	.194	.250	.167	6.30	0.90
Miller, Kevin	R-R	6-3	220	3-17-82	5	1	2.08	29	0	0	3	39	30	9	9	2	10	24	.222	.281	.179	5.54	2.31
Moeves, Derrik	R-R	6-3	190	8-5-83	3	4	4.12	24	0	0	0	39	39	21	18	1	22	32	.258	.304	.220	7.32	5.03
Munoz, Luis	R-R	6-2	150	1-10-82	6	3	3.81	16	13	0	0	78	69	41	33	8	22	46	.240	.286	.200	5.31	2.54
Newlin, Darren	R-R	6-1	200	11-20-82	3	1	3.53	20	1	0	1	43	49	24	17	3	17	31	.293	.324	.271	6.44	3.53
Redmond, Todd	R-R	6-3	185	5-17-85	1	2	1.98	15	14	0	0	73	62	22	16	2	21	63	.232	.231	.233	7.80	2.60
Salas, Joe	L-L	5-10	200	11-24-81	0	0	3.86	5	0	0	0	7	6	3	3	0	1	6	.222	.571	.100	7.71	1.29
Suero, Nicolas	R-R	6-2	160	12-10-84	0	2	4.50	3	1	0	0	12	14	8	6	1	2	7	.280	.212	.412	5.25	1.50
Swanson, Matt	R-R	6-8	240	10-17-82	4	2	1.61	19	0	0	6	28	16	6	5	2	7	30	.163	.125	.190	9.64	2.25
Vaclavik, Justin	R-R	6-1	185	5-27-84	0	1	4.38	20	0	0	9	25	24	12	12	0	10	28	.261	.390	.157	10.22	3.65
Valdez, Luis	R-R	6-2	180	5-5-84	4	5	4.53	16	7	0	0	60	67	39	30	4	17	30	.284	.337	.244	4.53	2.56

GAMES BY POSITION: C—Jones 32, Lerud 10, Nino 12, Reddinger 30. **1B**—Pearce 71, Poni 9. **2B**—Blair 32, Grandstrand 4, Lomack 3, Santiago 28, Solano 11. **3B**—Grandstrand 9, Prasch 25, Santiago 10, Solano 34. **SS**—Blair 30, Grandstrand 5, Lillibridge 42, Solano 1. **OF**—Boone 13, Corley 65, Delaney 53, Hicks 15, Lomack 24, McCutchen 13, Searage 22, Solano 2, Stevens 13, Wulf 16.

GCL PIRATES — Rookie

GULF COAST LEAGUE

BATTING	B-T	HT	WT	DOB	AVG	vLH	vRH	G	AB	R	H	2B	3B	HR	RBI	BB	HBP	SH	SF	SO	SB	CS	SLG	OBP
Cedron, Jhon	R-R	5-11	160	6-28-85	.204	.000	.306	21	54	10	11	0	0	1	7	7	1	0	1	9	3	0	.259	.302
Clark, Howie	L-R	5-10	190	2-13-74	.481	.385	.571	8	27	7	13	3	1	0	4	3	0	0	0	2	0	0	.667	.533
Gonzalez, Angel	B-R	5-11	165	12-28-85	.274	.200	.305	19	84	9	23	4	2	1	8	2	2	0	0	23	4	5	.405	.307
Igsema, Victor	R-R	6-2	172	11-16-85	.237	.146	.278	38	131	21	31	10	0	1	15	16	4	0	0	40	3	0	.336	.338
Laboy, Albert	R-R	6-0	175	12-1-86	.189	.167	.200	30	111	15	21	3	0	1	13	5	3	1	1	14	5	0	.243	.242
Lerud, Steven	L-R	6-1	196	10-13-84	.267	.158	.317	18	60	13	16	3	1	2	15	7	3	0	4	13	0	0	.450	.351
Loyola, Maiko	R-R	5-11	174	7-19-85	.274	.261	.284	41	164	32	45	4	3	2	14	13	0	2	0	32	10	2	.372	.328
Made, Kelington	R-R	5-11	204	6-25-83	.146	.000	.207	14	41	3	6	0	1	1	2	1	0	0	0	5	0	0	.268	.167
Mansolino, Tony	R-R	6-0	190	9-28-82	.242	.196	.263	42	165	21	40	10	2	3	21	11	1	0	2	20	0	3	.382	.291
McCutchen, Andrew	R-R	5-11	175	10-10-86	.297	.420	.241	45	158	36	47	9	3	2	30	29	3	0	2	24	13	1	.430	.411
Mesa, Juan	R-R	6-1	190	4-8-85	.156	.167	.150	12	32	3	5	1	0	1	2	2	0	0	0	13	0	0	.281	.206
Munoz, David	B-R	6-2	177	12-28-84	.231	.273	.209	23	65	10	15	4	0	1	5	9	0	1	0	13	0	2	.338	.324
Peabody, John	R-R	6-4	215	8-24-85	.226	.243	.213	25	84	9	19	4	2	1	7	12	1	0	0	24	1	1	.357	.330
Peralta, Alex	R-R	5-11	170	12-27-84	.336	.250	.378	29	110	16	37	8	0	2	18	6	1	1	1	14	0	2	.464	.373
Perez, Smelin	B-R	5-10	150	8-26-85	.280	.186	.326	34	132	22	37	7	0	2	13	12	0	1	2	19	8	3	.379	.336
Picart, Greg	B-R	5-11	175	9-25-85	.301	.366	.258	26	103	17	31	10	2	1	8	9	1	2	0	14	6	2	.466	.363
Prasch, Eddie	L-R	6-0	180	1-25-86	.302	.167	.341	15	53	9	16	2	0	0	6	9	0	0	0	12	0	0	.340	.403
Rios, Daniel	L-L	6-1	200	7-10-85	.183	.240	.165	32	104	11	19	4	0	0	15	12	3	0	1	19	0	0	.221	.283
Roman, Willman	R-R	6-1	160	9-7-84	.273	.275	.271	31	110	12	30	7	0	3	23	5	4	0	5	15	1	0	.418	.315
Walk, John	R-R	6-2	220	9-12-82	.222	.222	.222	6	18	2	4	0	0	0	3	1	1	0	1	3	1	0	.222	.286
Westfield, Antonio	R-R	6-1	205	10-10-84	.289	.313	.273	12	38	1	11	1	0	0	3	1	0	1	0	6	0	0	.316	.308

PITCHING	B-T	HT	WT	DOB	W	L	ERA	G	GS	CG	SV	IP	H	R	ER	HR	BB	SO	AVG	vLH	vRH	K/9	BB/9
Acors, Matt	R-R	6-2	190	7-27-82	2	0	1.98	7	0	0	0	14	8	7	3	1	7	8	.163	.167	.162	5.27	4.61
Alvarez, Basilio	R-R	6-3	160	1-2-84	1	1	8.10	2	1	0	0	7	8	6	6	0	1	5	.286	.214	.357	6.75	1.35
Arias, Keily	L-L	6-0	180	7-23-85	3	2	4.23	16	1	0	1	28	28	15	13	3	8	22	.269	.214	.278	7.16	2.60
Brown, Jared	L-L	6-4	220	5-24-82	1	0	6.75	7	0	0	0	12	15	9	9	1	8	12	.306	.714	.238	9.00	6.00
Candelario, Eddie	R-R	6-0	173	11-3-77	0	0	3.00	1	1	0	0	3	6	1	1	0	1	1	.500	.250	.625	3.00	3.00
Castro, Julio	R-R	6-2	210	1-4-85	4	3	3.38	13	7	1	3	53	45	23	20	4	11	47	.231	.212	.240	7.93	1.86
Clapp, Brad	R-R	6-4	215	5-19-86	1	2	4.28	9	9	0	0	34	25	20	16	0	25	35	.208	.154	.235	9.36	6.68
Colina, Ederson	L-L	6-1	160	1-16-84	2	1	8.25	9	0	0	0	12	13	17	11	1	13	13	.271	.083	.333	9.75	9.75
Cramer, Terrence	R-R	6-5	250	6-8-83	1	0	2.96	18	0	0	1	24	23	11	8	0	10	21	.264	.348	.234	7.77	3.70
Herbort, Ryan	R-R	6-2	200	3-13-86	0	1	1.98	4	2	0	0	14	9	6	3	1	5	7	.191	.222	.184	4.61	3.29
Herman, Jason	R-R	6-3	210	12-9-81	3	3	1.93	11	9	0	1	51	43	13	11	3	7	37	.224	.231	.220	6.49	1.23
Hernandez, Bladimil	R-R	6-1	170	2-4-84	0	1	6.20	8	5	0	0	25	31	23	17	3	13	19	.307	.277	.333	6.93	4.74
Jacobsen, Landon	R-R	6-3	220	5-4-79	3	1	3.72	5	5	1	0	19	13	9	8	0	9	26	.183	.185	.182	12.10	4.19
Marte, Enmanuel	L-L	6-2	165	8-15-85	1	0	1.86	10	0	0	0	19	16	4	4	1	4	18	.216	.000	.258	8.38	1.86
Martinez, Yoffri	R-R	6-3	170	12-3-85	0	1	5.23	14	0	0	0	21	22	16	12	3	13	14	.268	.300	.250	6.10	5.66
McDade, Neal	R-R	6-3	190	6-16-76	0	0	0.00	1	0	0	0	1	0	2	0	0	0	1	.000	.000	.000	9.00	0.00
Molleken, Dustin	L-R	6-4	228	8-21-84	0	4	7.20	9	5	0	0	30	34	29	24	5	16	22	.283	.386	.224	6.60	4.80
Ramirez, Emmanuel	R-R	6-3	165	11-2-79	0	1	5.56	8	0	0	0	11	13	7	7	1	2	14	.277	.278	.276	11.12	1.59
Robertson, Nash	R-R	6-2	225	8-24-82	0	0	5.00	6	0	0	0	9	10	7	5	1	3	9	.270	.353	.200	9.00	3.00
Salas, Joe	L-L	5-10	200	11-24-81	0	0	0.75	9	0	0	3	12	10	4	1	0	3	13	.217	.333	.200	9.75	2.25
Sanchez, Romulo	R-R	6-6	208	4-28-84	1	0	1.80	2	1	0	0	10	7	2	2	1	4	7	.206	.100	.250	6.30	3.60
Suero, Nicolas	R-R	6-2	160	12-10-84	5	5	3.28	11	8	0	0	58	72	37	21	4	10	35	.303	.270	.322	5.46	1.56
Walk, John	R-R	6-2	220	9-12-82	0	0	36.00	1	0	0	0	2	6	9	8	2	3	0	.462	.375	.600	0.00	13.50

GAMES BY POSITION: C—Lerud 15, Made 13, Roman 26, Walk 6. **1B**—Clark 1, Peabody 24, Rios 32. **2B**—Peralta 21, Perez 22, Picart 14. **3B**—Clark 1, Mansolino 39, Peralta 3, Picart 4, Prasch 9. **SS**—Gonzalez 19, Munoz 19, Perez 11, Picart 8. **OF**—Cedron 21, Clark 3, Igsema 38, Laboy 7, Loyola 41, McCutchen 43, Mesa 12, Westfield 10.

ST. LOUIS CARDINALS

BY DERRICK GOOLD

Their quest complicated by injuries at every step, the Cardinals, powered by pitching, finished the 2005 regular season with baseball's best record for the second consecutive season yet didn't have enough health or oomph to reach a World Series return.

In the final season of the final cookie-cutter stadium, the Cardinals brought down Busch Stadium with a second consecutive 100-win season. Eighty of those wins came from the starting rotation, led by Chris Carpenter's sheer dominance and two 16-game winners in Mark Mulder and Jeff Suppan. Carpenter went 21-5, 2.83, at one point winning 13 consecutive decisions and stringing 22 consecutive quality starts, the longest such streak in the National League since 1968.

The pitching staff with the lowest ERA in the league stabilized a club rocked repeatedly by injuries. There were stretches when the Cardinals were delighted they had four Opening Day starters available.

Gold Glove third baseman Scott Rolen missed all but 56 games because of two shoulder surgeries. Former MVP Larry Walker, on the cusp of retirement, received four cortisone shots through the season to tame a herniated disc in his neck. Reggie Sanders had his career season halted by a broken leg.

Replacements such as Abraham Nunez at third and So Taguchi in the outfield kept the Cardinals cruising to a fifth division title in the past six seasons. But the lineup was too tattered to outlast Houston—which finished 11 games behind the Cardinals in the division—in the N.L. Championship Series.

"We all know if this team was at full strength, what this team could have been," Sanders said.

Sanders returned from the fracture and set a league record with 10 RBIs in the Division Series sweep of San Diego. But, in Game 2 of the NLCS, Sanders sustained whiplash in a warning-track tumble that limited him for the rest of the series. Albert Pujols' six RBIs in the NLCS were more than the combined total of Sanders, Walker, Mark Grudzielanek and Jim Edmonds.

The Cardinals did, however, produce a last burst of drama.

Down to their final strike of the season, the Cardinals rallied in Game 5 of the NLCS. Leadoff hitter David Eckstein struck a two-strike single to bring the tying run to the plate and Edmonds walked to bring up Pujols. The Cardinals' slugger had his standard historic year—doing for a fifth consecutive season what no hitter has ever done in his five first seasons.

The bedrock of the injury-riddled lineup and the cornerstone of the franchise as it opens new Busch Stadium in 2006, Pujols hit .330-41-117. In his third consecutive season with 40 homers, Pujols became the second fastest player in baseball history to hit his 200th home run.

At the end of the NLCS, three-time batting champ Walker retired after 17 seasons—ending a career that included seven Gold Gloves, the 1997 NL MVP award, three seasons with a .360-plus average and 1,311 RBIs.

Only one of the Cardinals' minor league teams finished the season better than .500, but another, high Class A Palm Beach, won the Florida State League championship. Closer Mark Worrell anchored the champs by leading the minors with 35 saves.

In Triple-A Memphis, Chris Duncan blossomed with a team-high 73 RBIs. Cody Haerther hit .307-18-67 over 112 games at two levels. And, in his first year as an outfielder, Rick Ankiel—who retired from pitching during spring training—hit 21 homers and drove in 75 runs in 85 total games, including 30 RBIs and 10 home runs in his final 28 games with Double-A Springfield.

The Cardinals were further emboldened by the quantity of draft picks they had in 2005 and their chances at quality. They signed 21 of the first 22 players they drafted, and the half-season performances were highlighted by outfielder Nick Stavinoha (.344-14-53) and both first-round picks, outfielder Colby Rasmus (.296-7-27) and shortstop Tyler Greene (.265-3-23).

PLAYERS OF THE YEAR

MAJOR LEAGUE: Albert Pujols, 1b

Prior to hitting the most dramatic home run of 2005 in Game 5 of the NLCS, Pujols put up another MVP-caliber season in St. Louis. The 25-year-old first baseman led the National League in runs (129), and was second in average (.330), RBIs (117), slugging percentage (.609) and on-base percentage (.430).

MINOR LEAGUE: Travis Hanson, 3b

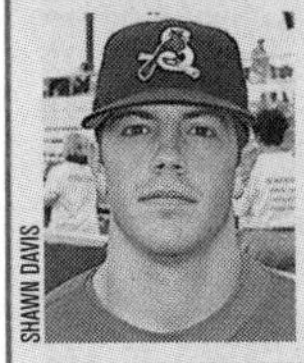

SHAWN DAVIS

Hanson, a ninth-round pick out of Portland in 2002, had a breakout season in 2005. A broken ankle curtailed his development in 2004, but Hanson came back strong, ranking among Texas League leaders in RBIs and hits. Primarily a shortstop in college, Hanson moved to third base as a pro.

ORGANIZATION LEADERS

BATTING

*AVG	Stavinoha, Nick, Quad Cities	.344
R	Minges, Tyler, New Jersey/Springfield	98
H	Hanson, Travis, Springfield	155
TB	Hanson, Travis, Springfield	250
2B	Minges, Tyler, New Jersey/Springfield	34
3B	Haerther, Cody, Palm Beach/Springfield	8
HR	Four tied at	21
RBI	Hanson, Travis, Springfield	97
BB	Shepherd, Matt, Quad Cities	87
SO	Nelson, John, Memphis	141
SB	Lemanczyk, Matt, Quad Cities	48
*OBP	Shepherd, Matt, Quad Cities	.402
*SLG	Minges, Tyler, New Jersey/Springfield	.564

PITCHING

W	Leek, Randy, Memphis/Springfield	15
L	Three tied at	11
#ERA	Webber, Nick, New Jersey/Quad Cities	1.93
G	Torres, Jaymie, Palm Beach/Quad Cities	59
CG	Leek, Randy, Memphis/Springfield	3
SV	Worrell, Mark, Palm Beach	35
IP	Leek, Randy, Memphis/Springfield	192
BB	Lambert, Chris, Palm Beach/Springfield	63
SO	Wainwright, Adam, Memphis	147

*Minimum 250 at-bats. #Minimum 75 innings.

ST. LOUIS CARDINALS

Manager: Tony La Russa.

2005 Record: 100-62, .617 (1st, NL Central).

BATTING	B-T	HT	WT	DOB	AVG	vLH	vRH	G	AB	R	H	2B	3B	HR	RBI	BB	HBP	SH	SF	SO	SB	CS	SLG	OBP
Cedeno, Roger	B-R	6-1	205	8-16-74	.158	.333	.111	37	57	4	9	1	0	0	8	2	1	0	1	6	0	2	.175	.197
Diaz, Einar	R-R	5-10	200	12-28-72	.208	.229	.200	58	130	14	27	6	0	1	17	5	2	2	0	12	0	0	.277	.248
Duncan, Chris	L-R	6-5	210	5-5-81	.200	1.000	.000	9	10	2	2	1	0	1	3	0	0	0	0	5	0	0	.600	.200
Eckstein, David	R-R	5-7	165	1-20-75	.294	.257	.307	158	630	90	185	26	7	8	61	58	13	8	4	44	11	8	.395	.363
Edmonds, Jim	L-L	6-1	210	6-27-70	.263	.296	.251	142	467	88	123	37	1	29	89	91	4	1	4	139	5	5	.533	.385
Gall, John	R-R	6-0	195	4-2-78	.270	.313	.238	22	37	5	10	3	0	2	10	1	0	0	1	8	0	0	.514	.282
Grudzielanek, Mark	R-R	6-1	190	6-30-70	.294	.303	.290	137	528	64	155	30	3	8	59	26	7	0	2	81	8	6	.407	.334
Luna, Hector	R-R	6-1	170	2-1-80	.285	.310	.266	64	137	26	39	10	2	1	18	9	4	2	1	25	10	2	.409	.344
Mabry, John	L-R	6-4	210	10-17-70	.240	.226	.242	112	246	26	59	15	1	8	32	20	0	6	2	63	0	0	.407	.295
Mahoney, Mike	R-R	6-1	200	12-5-72	.156	.100	.167	26	64	5	10	1	0	1	6	4	1	6	0	10	0	0	.219	.217
Molina, Yadier	R-R	5-11	225	7-13-82	.252	.309	.229	114	385	36	97	15	1	8	49	23	2	8	3	30	2	3	.358	.295
Nunez, Abraham	B-R	5-11	190	3-16-76	.285	.324	.277	139	421	64	120	13	2	5	44	37	0	9	0	63	0	1	.361	.343
Pujols, Albert	R-R	6-3	225	1-16-80	.330	.300	.340	161	591	129	195	38	2	41	117	97	9	0	3	65	16	2	.609	.430
Rodriguez, John	L-L	6-0	205	1-20-78	.295	.296	.295	56	149	15	44	6	0	5	24	19	3	3	2	45	2	0	.436	.382
Rolen, Scott	R-R	6-4	240	4-4-75	.235	.237	.234	56	196	28	46	12	1	5	28	25	1	0	1	28	1	2	.383	.323
Sanders, Reggie	R-R	6-1	205	12-1-67	.271	.257	.280	93	295	49	80	14	2	21	54	28	4	0	2	75	14	1	.546	.340
Schumaker, Skip	L-R	5-10	175	2-3-80	.250	.500	.227	27	24	9	6	1	0	0	1	2	0	0	0	2	1	0	.292	.308
Seabol, Scott	R-R	6-4	200	5-17-75	.219	.224	.214	59	105	11	23	5	0	1	10	8	0	0	1	23	0	0	.295	.272
Taguchi, So	R-R	5-10	165	7-2-69	.288	.276	.296	143	396	45	114	21	2	8	53	20	2	2	4	62	11	2	.412	.322
Walker, Larry	L-R	6-3	235	12-1-66	.289	.214	.305	100	315	66	91	20	1	15	52	41	9	0	2	64	2	1	.502	.384

PITCHING	B-T	HT	WT	DOB	W	L	ERA	G	GS	CG	SV	IP	H	R	ER	HR	BB	SO	AVG	vLH	vRH	K/9	BB/9
Cali, Carmen	L-L	5-10	185	11-4-78	0	0	10.50	6	0	0	0	6	10	8	7	3	6	5	.385	.333	.412	7.50	9.00
Carpenter, Chris	R-R	6-6	230	4-27-75	21	5	2.83	33	33	7	0	242	204	82	76	18	51	213	.231	.264	.199	7.93	1.90
Eldred, Cal	R-R	6-4	240	11-24-67	1	0	2.19	31	1	0	0	37	35	9	9	3	18	29	.259	.230	.284	7.05	4.38
Flores, Randy	L-L	6-0	180	7-31-75	3	1	3.46	50	0	0	1	42	37	22	16	5	13	43	.240	.173	.304	9.29	2.81
Isringhausen, Jason	R-R	6-3	230	9-7-72	1	2	2.14	63	0	0	39	59	43	14	14	4	27	51	.202	.168	.229	7.78	4.12
Jarvis, Kevin	L-R	6-2	200	8-1-69	0	1	13.50	4	0	0	0	3	3	5	5	1	3	2	.250	.333	.167	5.40	8.10
Johnson, Tyler	B-L	6-2	180	6-7-81	0	0	0.00	5	0	0	0	3	3	0	0	0	3	4	.300	.400	.200	13.50	10.13
Journell, Jimmy	R-R	6-4	210	12-29-77	0	1	10.38	5	0	0	0	4	6	6	5	1	5	5	.333	1.000	.200	10.38	10.38
King, Ray	L-L	6-1	240	1-15-74	4	4	3.38	77	0	0	0	40	46	17	15	4	16	23	.293	.244	.352	5.18	3.60
Marquis, Jason	L-R	6-1	210	8-21-78	13	14	4.13	33	32	3	0	207	206	110	95	29	69	100	.262	.238	.280	4.35	3.00
Morris, Matt	R-R	6-5	220	8-9-74	14	10	4.11	31	31	2	0	193	209	101	88	22	37	117	.276	.279	.273	5.47	1.73
Mulder, Mark	L-L	6-6	215	8-5-77	16	8	3.64	32	32	3	0	205	212	90	83	19	70	111	.273	.201	.289	4.87	3.07
Pulsipher, Bill	R-L	6-3	230	10-9-73	0	0	6.75	5	0	0	0	4	5	3	3	0	2	1	.357	.167	.500	2.25	4.50
Reyes, Al	R-R	6-1	210	4-10-70	4	2	2.15	65	0	0	3	63	38	15	15	5	20	67	.177	.184	.172	9.62	2.87
Reyes, Anthony	R-R	6-2	215	10-16-81	1	1	2.70	4	1	0	0	13	6	4	4	2	4	12	.133	.111	.148	8.10	2.70
Suppan, Jeff	R-R	6-2	220	1-2-75	16	10	3.57	32	32	0	0	194	206	93	77	24	63	114	.275	.271	.279	5.28	2.92
Tavarez, Julian	L-R	6-2	195	5-22-73	2	3	3.43	74	0	0	4	66	68	28	25	6	19	47	.278	.294	.271	6.44	2.60
Thompson, Brad	R-R	6-1	190	1-31-82	4	0	2.95	40	0	0	1	55	46	22	18	5	15	29	.227	.224	.228	4.75	2.45
Wainwright, Adam	R-R	6-7	205	8-30-81	0	0	13.50	2	0	0	0	2	2	3	3	1	1	0	.250	.500	.167	0.00	4.50
White, Gabe	L-L	6-2	215	11-20-71	0	0	2.16	6	0	0	0	8	14	2	2	1	1	1	.378	.250	.440	1.08	1.08

FIELDING

Catcher	PCT	G	PO	A	E	DP	PB
Diaz	.995	50	189	21	1	1	4
Mahoney	.984	25	110	11	2	2	0
Molina	.991	114	684	66	7	4	8

First Base	PCT	G	PO	A	E	DP
Diaz	1.000	3	9	0	0	2
Duncan	1.000	2	1	0	0	0
Mabry	1.000	14	55	8	0	8
Molina	.000	1	0	0	0	0
Pujols	.992	157	1597	97	14	175
Seabol	1.000	5	33	3	0	4

Second Base	PCT	G	PO	A	E	DP
Grudzielanek	.990	137	245	442	7	108
Luna	.979	22	41	52	2	15
Nunez	.970	22	26	38	2	15
Seabol	1.000	8	1	5	0	0

Third Base	PCT	G	PO	A	E	DP
Luna	1.000	7	4	7	0	2
Mabry	.969	18	12	19	1	2
Nunez	.963	98	54	203	10	19
Rolen	.966	56	22	150	6	17
Seabol	.929	20	9	30	3	5

Shortstop	PCT	G	PO	A	E	DP
Eckstein	.981	156	243	517	15	123
Luna	.857	6	3	3	1	0
Nunez	.957	21	14	30	2	9

Outfield	PCT	G	PO	A	E	DP
Cedeno	.818	16	9	0	2	0
Duncan	.000	1	0	0	0	0
Edmonds	.994	139	318	6	2	1
Gall	1.000	10	7	1	0	0
Luna	.947	25	33	3	2	0
Mabry	.965	70	54	1	2	0
Rodriguez	.973	45	69	3	2	0
Sanders	.983	81	108	6	2	0
Schumaker	1.000	21	13	0	0	0
Seabol	1.000	4	6	0	0	0
Taguchi	.989	131	183	5	2	1
Walker	.983	83	108	5	2	0

FARM SYSTEM

General Manager: Walt Jocketty. **Director, Player Development:** Bruce Manno. **Scouting Director:** Jeff Luhnow.

Class	Farm Team	League	W	L	Pct.	Finish*	Manager	Affiliate Since
AAA	Memphis (Tenn.) Redbirds	Pacific Coast	71	72	.497	9th (16)	Danny Sheaffer	1998
AA	Springfield (Mo.) Cardinals	Texas	70	70	.500	5th (8)	Chris Maloney	2005
High A	Palm Beach (Fla.) Cardinals	Florida State	69	71	.493	**+6th (12)**	Ron Warner	2003
Low A	Swing of the Quad Cities (Davenport, Iowa)	Midwest	72	67	.518	**t-4th (14)**	Joe Cunningham	2005
SS A	New Jersey Cardinals (Augusta)	New York-Penn	37	39	.487	7th (14)	Mark DeJohn	1994
Rookie	Johnson City (Tenn.) Cardinals	Appalachian	28	39	.418	8th (10)	Tommy Kidwell	1974

*Finish in overall standings (No. of teams in league)/Playoff teams in **boldface** +League champion

LARRY GOREN

Chris Carpenter: Second-most wins in the NL

MIKE JANES

Nick Webber: A 1.87 ERA in his pro debut

MEMPHIS REDBIRDS — Class AAA

PACIFIC COAST LEAGUE

BATTING	B-T	HT	WT	DOB	AVG	vLH	vRH	G	AB	R	H	2B	3B	HR	RBI	BB	HBP	SH	SF	SO	SB	CS	SLG	OBP
Allen, Chad	R-R	6-1	200	2-6-75	.291	.320	.279	25	86	11	25	6	0	3	13	7	0	0	2	14	1	2	.465	.337
2-team (45 Oklahoma)					.329	.287	.349	70	286	45	94	18	0	11	46	17	0	0	3	45	10	4	.507	.363
Bell, Mike	R-R	6-2	210	12-7-74	.071	.000	.091	8	14	0	1	0	0	0	1	0	0	1	0	1	0	1	.071	.071
Berger, Brandon	R-R	5-11	205	2-21-75	.233	.276	.203	109	300	48	70	13	0	19	57	30	4	1	3	58	3	2	.467	.309
Cancel, Robinson	R-R	6-0	195	5-4-76	.253	.226	.266	29	95	12	24	3	1	3	13	8	1	0	1	18	0	0	.400	.314
Cardona, Javier	R-R	6-1	210	9-15-75	.211	.250	.200	7	19	3	4	0	0	2	6	3	0	0	0	1	0	0	.526	.318
Cedeno, Roger	B-R	6-1	205	8-16-74	.174	.000	.211	8	23	3	4	1	0	0	2	3	0	0	0	5	0	0	.217	.269
Cresse, Brad	R-R	6-2	230	7-31-78	.209	.111	.239	41	115	10	24	10	0	3	16	12	3	2	2	26	0	0	.374	.295
Duncan, Chris	L-R	6-5	210	5-5-81	.265	.233	.273	128	431	57	114	21	2	21	73	63	2	0	4	104	1	3	.469	.358
Gall, John	R-R	6-0	195	4-2-78	.270	.269	.271	114	374	61	101	22	0	13	64	45	1	0	6	42	9	2	.433	.345
Gonzalez, Raul	R-R	5-9	190	12-27-73	.308	.346	.292	93	347	62	107	21	3	14	50	38	0	1	2	47	3	5	.507	.375
Guerrero, Wilton	B-R	6-0	175	10-24-74	.309	.235	.333	36	68	7	21	6	1	1	6	5	1	0	0	8	1	1	.471	.365
Hart, Bo	R-R	5-11	175	9-27-76	.269	.278	.266	133	468	78	126	33	1	9	47	46	3	8	7	74	11	3	.402	.334
Haynes, Dee	R-R	6-0	205	2-22-78	.200	.000	.200	2	5	1	1	0	0	0	0	0	0	0	0	2	0	0	.200	.200
Hummel, Tim	R-R	6-2	190	11-18-78	.275	.328	.252	56	189	20	52	12	0	6	23	13	1	1	1	22	0	1	.434	.324
Jaramillo, Milko	B-R	5-10	182	1-21-80	.395	.222	.448	20	38	5	15	1	0	0	2	3	1	0	0	6	0	1	.421	.452
Luna, Hector	R-R	6-1	170	2-1-80	.224	.216	.228	57	223	24	50	13	1	3	21	20	2	2	0	38	11	4	.332	.294
Mahoney, Mike	R-R	6-1	200	12-5-72	.265	.278	.259	71	230	30	61	19	1	5	27	14	7	2	2	40	2	0	.422	.324
McKay, Cody	L-R	6-0	210	1-11-74	.213	.500	.186	19	47	4	10	2	0	1	5	8	3	0	0	10	0	0	.319	.362
Moylan, Dan	L-R	6-0	190	4-24-79	.059	.000	.063	7	17	0	1	0	0	0	0	1	0	0	0	1	0	0	.059	.111
Nelson, John	R-R	6-1	195	3-3-79	.241	.316	.213	128	427	56	103	27	1	14	49	51	4	1	2	141	2	3	.407	.326
Rodriguez, John	L-L	6-0	205	1-20-78	.342	.205	.407	34	120	24	41	5	0	17	47	13	3	1	0	28	1	1	.808	.419
Schumaker, Skip	L-R	5-10	175	2-3-80	.287	.255	.296	115	443	66	127	24	3	7	34	29	2	8	5	54	14	3	.402	.330
Seabol, Scott	R-R	6-4	200	5-17-75	.266	.362	.237	54	203	34	54	18	2	9	33	20	0	0	1	40	0	0	.507	.330
Taylor, Reggie	L-R	6-1	180	1-12-77	.234	.250	.227	34	107	18	25	5	2	1	11	5	1	2	1	21	1	5	.346	.272
2-team (1 Colorado Springs)					.234	.250	.228	35	111	18	26	6	2	1	12	5	1	2	1	21	1	5	.351	.271
Zoccolillo, Peter	L-R	6-2	200	2-2-77	.261	.138	.280	79	222	27	58	9	0	9	34	25	1	0	4	30	0	2	.423	.333

PITCHING	B-T	HT	WT	DOB	W	L	ERA	G	GS	CG	SV	IP	H	R	ER	HR	BB	SO	AVG	vLH	vRH	K/9	BB/9
Almanza, Armando	L-L	6-3	230	10-26-72	0	0	6.30	10	0	0	0	10	13	7	7	2	2	9	.317	.333	.308	8.10	1.80
3-team (2 Fresno, 15 Tucson)					1	1	4.76	27	0	0	1	28	30	18	15	5	11	31	.275	.263	.282	9.85	3.49
Borland, Toby	R-R	6-6	215	5-29-69	1	2	7.71	19	0	0	6	19	35	16	16	2	7	16	.417	.577	.345	7.71	3.38
Cali, Carmen	L-L	5-10	185	11-4-78	4	5	5.40	50	0	0	2	58	74	47	35	6	28	45	.306	.256	.336	6.94	4.32
Cummings, Jeremy	R-R	6-2	215	11-7-76	7	1	2.77	14	6	0	0	52	38	16	16	6	20	41	.207	.174	.235	7.10	3.46
Falkenborg, Brian	R-R	6-6	225	1-18-78	1	0	1.69	13	0	0	5	16	10	3	3	1	5	14	.182	.130	.219	7.88	2.81
2-team (28 Portland)					4	4	4.15	41	0	0	6	52	45	28	24	3	26	40	.236	.182	.293	6.92	4.50
Flores, Randy	L-L	6-0	180	7-31-75	1	0	6.43	6	0	0	0	7	8	6	5	1	0	6	.296	.400	.235	7.71	0.00
Gissell, Chris	R-R	6-5	210	1-4-78	8	8	3.54	23	23	2	0	137	134	63	54	16	36	123	.256	.277	.239	8.06	2.36
Jarvis, Kevin	L-R	6-2	200	8-1-69	11	6	3.38	26	25	1	0	157	164	63	59	19	39	112	.272	.274	.271	6.42	2.24
Johnson, Tyler	B-L	6-2	180	6-7-81	2	1	4.27	57	0	0	7	59	51	31	28	6	26	77	.232	.250	.220	11.75	3.97
Journell, Jimmy	R-R	6-4	210	12-29-77	1	4	4.68	34	0	0	1	42	39	25	22	5	38	49	.245	.274	.227	10.42	8.08
Kinney, Josh	R-R	6-1	195	3-31-79	1	2	7.36	26	0	0	0	26	40	21	21	4	19	25	.354	.457	.308	8.77	6.66
Lee, David	R-R	6-1	200	3-12-73	0	1	23.14	4	0	0	0	2	7	6	6	0	3	1	.538	.600	.500	3.86	11.57
2-team (8 Fresno)					0	3	12.08	12	0	0	0	13	23	20	17	3	7	8	.390	.346	.424	5.68	4.97
Leek, Randy	L-L	6-0	175	4-18-77	0	1	1.50	1	1	0	0	6	6	1	1	0	0	2	.261	.111	.357	3.00	0.00
Narveson, Chris	L-L	6-3	205	12-20-81	0	1	12.15	2	2	0	0	7	11	9	9	2	7	8	.379	.231	.500	10.80	9.45
Nunez, Vladimir	R-R	6-4	240	3-15-75	1	1	2.14	17	0	0	7	21	14	7	5	1	10	26	.189	.133	.227	11.14	4.29
Nussbeck, Mark	L-R	6-4	205	5-25-74	3	6	3.42	19	8	0	2	68	66	27	26	6	11	59	.254	.220	.286	7.77	1.45
Pearce, Josh	R-R	6-3	220	8-20-77	2	3	4.31	24	1	0	0	40	48	24	19	9	7	31	.312	.221	.384	7.03	1.59
Pulsipher, Bill	R-L	6-3	230	10-9-73	6	7	4.49	25	18	0	0	124	152	72	62	17	29	96	.301	.345	.284	6.95	2.10
Reyes, Anthony	R-R	6-2	215	10-16-81	7	6	3.64	23	23	2	0	129	105	55	52	13	34	136	.222	.282	.174	9.51	2.38
Rodriguez, Nerio	R-R	6-1	220	3-4-71	0	3	6.95	4	4	0	0	22	33	18	17	6	3	11	.344	.429	.255	4.50	1.23
Rust, Evan	R-R	6-1	210	5-4-78	1	0	5.40	13	0	0	0	17	16	12	10	1	11	10	.258	.167	.316	5.40	5.94
Sedlacek, Shawn	R-R	6-4	210	6-29-77	1	2	10.80	5	3	0	0	15	23	20	18	2	11	11	.354	.333	.368	6.60	6.60
2-team (1 Colorado Springs)					1	2	9.00	6	4	0	0	20	26	22	20	3	12	16	.313	.294	.327	7.20	5.40
Stone, Ricky	R-R	6-1	195	2-28-75	1	1	1.65	14	0	0	6	16	12	5	3	0	2	16	.203	.138	.267	8.82	1.10
Thompson, Brad	R-R	6-1	190	1-31-82	2	1	3.29	9	0	0	0	14	12	5	5	1	7	11	.240	.294	.212	7.24	4.61
Wainwright, Adam	R-R	6-7	205	8-30-81	10	10	4.40	29	29	0	0	182	204	98	89	18	51	147	.282	.285	.280	7.27	2.52
White, Gabe	L-L	6-2	215	11-20-71	0	0	0.00	8	0	0	1	7	4	0	0	0	1	8	.154	.125	.167	9.82	1.23

FIELDING

Catcher	PCT	G	PO	A	E	DP	PB
Cancel	.988	26	222	17	3	1	4
Cardona	.978	7	41	3	1	0	0
Cresse	.989	39	260	19	3	1	4
Mahoney	.996	71	487	50	2	3	4
McKay	.967	10	58	1	2	0	0
Moylan	.979	5	42	4	1	0	1

First Base	PCT	G	PO	A	E	DP
Cancel	1.000	2	2	0	0	0
Cresse	1.000	1	2	0	0	1
Duncan	.980	104	771	66	17	77
Gall	.983	46	279	18	5	34
Zoccolillo	.988	10	70	9	1	6

Second Base	PCT	G	PO	A	E	DP
Bell	1.000	2	4	6	0	2
Guerrero	1.000	14	13	23	0	4
Hart	.992	86	155	213	3	53
Hummel	.972	7	16	19	1	5
Jaramillo	1.000	2	1	1	0	0
Luna	.981	47	94	112	4	35

Third Base	PCT	G	PO	A	E	DP
Bell	.333	1	0	1	2	0
Gall	1.000	2	1	1	0	0
Guerrero	1.000	9	5	11	0	0
Hart	.951	30	20	57	4	7
Hummel	.968	45	30	62	3	7
Jaramillo	1.000	3	2	1	0	0
McKay	.909	4	2	8	1	0
Seabol	.951	52	44	91	7	9
Zoccolillo	.909	7	6	14	2	3

Shortstop	PCT	G	PO	A	E	DP
Guerrero	.000	1	0	0	0	0
Hart	1.000	9	6	15	0	1
Jaramillo	.935	14	9	20	2	4
Luna	.977	12	17	25	1	5
Nelson	.971	126	178	326	15	79

Outfield	PCT	G	PO	A	E	DP
Allen	1.000	25	40	3	0	0
Bell	1.000	2	1	0	0	0
Berger	.990	62	98	1	1	0
Cedeno	1.000	6	7	1	0	0
Duncan	.929	19	25	1	2	1
Gall	.978	62	86	1	2	1
Gonzalez	.987	84	141	8	2	0
Guerrero	.000	1	0	0	0	0
Haynes	.000	1	0	0	0	0
Nelson	.000	1	0	0	0	0
Rodriguez	.983	31	56	1	1	0
Schumaker	.996	111	274	6	1	0
Taylor	.985	30	63	2	1	0
Zoccolillo	.953	46	60	1	3	0

SPRINGFIELD CARDINALS — Class AA

TEXAS LEAGUE

BATTING	B-T	HT	WT	DOB	AVG	vLH	vRH	G	AB	R	H	2B	3B	HR	RBI	BB	HBP	SH	SF	SO	SB	CS	SLG	OBP
Ankiel, Rick	L-L	6-1	215	7-19-79	.243	.286	.231	34	136	18	33	7	0	10	30	10	0	0	0	29	0	0	.515	.295
Bolivar, Papo	R-R	5-11	214	10-18-78	.271	.359	.225	121	425	60	115	22	3	10	62	34	4	1	2	81	17	8	.407	.329
Boyd, Shaun	R-R	5-11	188	8-15-81	.275	.288	.268	127	502	82	138	22	2	7	60	45	3	9	3	97	14	8	.369	.336
Cancel, Robinson	R-R	6-0	195	5-4-76	.287	.333	.262	65	230	31	66	13	0	8	26	29	1	1	4	36	4	2	.448	.364
Cresse, Brad	R-R	6-2	230	7-31-78	.205	.182	.214	11	39	3	8	4	0	0	6	5	1	0	0	11	0	0	.308	.311
DeMarco, Matt	L-R	6-0	172	1-24-80	.180	.143	.194	17	50	4	9	1	0	0	1	6	1	2	0	6	0	1	.200	.281
Diaz, Juan	R-R	6-2	270	2-19-74	.308	.328	.299	57	198	27	61	13	0	13	38	17	4	0	0	43	0	0	.571	.374
Estrada, Kevin	B-R	6-2	185	10-1-80	.295	.279	.301	90	292	39	86	19	2	5	19	27	0	8	0	51	18	7	.425	.354
Gorecki, Reid	R-R	6-1	180	12-22-80	.182	.167	.188	46	159	12	29	6	0	3	16	18	0	4	1	38	1	3	.277	.264
Haerther, Cody	L-R	6-1	198	7-14-83	.298	.361	.285	65	208	30	62	10	1	10	37	9	2	0	0	44	0	1	.500	.333
Hanson, Travis	L-R	6-2	197	1-24-81	.284	.301	.277	137	546	82	155	29	3	20	97	54	2	1	6	99	2	2	.458	.347
Herr, Aaron	R-R	6-0	202	3-7-81	.298	.343	.277	112	426	56	127	20	1	21	81	15	10	4	1	108	2	3	.498	.336
Jaramillo, Milko	B-R	5-10	182	1-21-80	.234	.185	.256	59	175	16	41	13	0	1	7	8	1	2	0	37	1	1	.326	.272
Johnson, Gabe	R-R	6-1	195	9-21-79	.251	.235	.258	51	183	15	46	6	0	7	31	19	5	2	2	53	0	0	.399	.335
Laya, Rayner	R-R	5-10	150	9-30-80	.393	.333	.421	12	28	5	11	1	1	0	4	1	0	0	0	1	0	1	.500	.414
McCoy, Mike	R-R	5-9	171	4-2-81	.143	.000	.182	5	14	1	2	0	0	0	1	0	1	0	1	5	0	0	.143	.188
Minges, Tyler	R-R	6-0	185	11-15-79	.324	.409	.288	116	429	98	139	34	6	19	60	47	4	1	5	61	5	4	.564	.392
Motte, Jason	R-R	6-0	200	6-22-82	.333	.333	.000	1	3	1	1	0	0	0	1	1	0	0	0	1	0	0	.333	.500
Moylan, Dan	L-R	6-0	190	4-24-79	.210	.270	.196	65	195	29	41	8	1	2	18	35	0	1	0	34	1	3	.292	.330
Pagnozzi, Matt	R-R	6-2	195	11-10-82	.139	.091	.160	15	36	3	5	1	0	0	1	3	1	0	0	8	0	0	.167	.225
Parker, Tyler	R-R	6-2	200	5-13-81	.263	.267	.261	13	38	5	10	3	0	1	5	3	1	1	0	10	0	1	.421	.333
Robinson, Bo	R-R	6-2	195	8-21-75	.222	.273	.188	12	27	1	6	0	0	0	3	1	0	1	0	3	0	0	.222	.250
Ryan, Brendan	R-R	6-2	195	3-26-82	.273	.242	.281	43	154	28	42	8	1	2	9	15	2	2	1	19	6	0	.377	.343
Schutzenhofer, Andy	L-L	6-0	195	1-24-81	.269	.171	.296	63	193	25	52	9	0	2	17	15	8	2	2	28	2	1	.347	.344
Zoccolillo, Peter	L-R	6-2	200	2-2-77	.270	.333	.246	23	89	12	24	3	0	4	9	3	2	0	0	17	0	0	.438	.309

PITCHING	B-T	HT	WT	DOB	W	L	ERA	G	GS	CG	SV	IP	H	R	ER	HR	BB	SO	AVG	vLH	vRH	K/9	BB/9
Alvarez, Oscar	L-L	6-0	204	9-17-80	6	2	3.40	29	14	0	0	106	112	47	40	11	40	59	.277	.274	.278	5.01	3.40
Axelson, Josh	R-R	6-1	202	12-4-78	1	2	8.45	28	2	0	0	49	62	50	46	8	30	46	.321	.313	.327	8.45	5.51
Benes, Alan	R-R	6-5	240	1-21-72	1	0	5.49	15	0	0	0	20	20	13	12	5	7	16	.253	.244	.265	7.32	3.20
Blair, Buddy	L-L	6-1	205	7-2-81	1	6	8.50	8	8	0	0	36	55	35	34	7	20	21	.364	.407	.355	5.25	5.00
Cavazos, Andy	R-R	6-3	224	1-5-81	1	2	4.03	23	0	0	1	29	27	15	13	4	7	24	.248	.222	.273	7.45	2.17
Cook, Jeremy	R-R	6-6	235	5-11-78	3	8	5.57	37	11	0	0	103	140	78	64	12	26	54	.321	.333	.310	4.70	2.26
Cotton, Nate	L-R	6-2	195	7-19-79	1	1	6.97	8	0	0	0	10	13	10	8	1	6	4	.333	.278	.381	3.48	5.23
Cummings, Jeremy	R-R	6-2	215	11-7-76	5	3	4.50	12	12	0	0	70	67	39	35	9	19	56	.248	.203	.286	7.20	2.44
Doyne, Cory	R-R	6-0	210	8-13-81	2	1	1.95	48	0	0	19	55	37	14	12	5	36	53	.188	.182	.192	8.62	5.86
Eldred, Cal	R-R	6-4	240	11-24-67	1	0	0.00	3	0	0	0	6	5	0	0	0	0	1	.238	.111	.333	1.50	0.00
Ferrari, Anthony	L-L	5-9	165	6-22-78	2	3	4.50	29	0	0	0	24	22	18	12	2	24	24	.237	.250	.228	9.00	9.00
Kinney, Josh	R-R	6-1	195	3-31-79	5	2	1.29	32	0	0	11	42	28	9	6	2	12	42	.185	.213	.167	9.00	2.57
Lambert, Chris	R-R	6-1	205	3-8-83	3	8	6.35	18	18	0	0	85	97	69	60	10	48	69	.291	.335	.250	7.31	5.08
Leek, Randy	L-L	6-0	175	4-18-77	15	7	3.83	28	27	3	0	186	190	85	79	29	29	102	.266	.233	.275	4.94	1.41
Mears, Chris	R-R	6-4	200	1-20-78	0	2	5.25	13	0	0	0	12	13	7	7	0	5	6	.289	.077	.375	4.50	3.75
Nelson, Joe	R-R	6-2	205	10-25-74	0	0	2.03	9	0	0	1	13	4	3	3	1	7	22	.093	.143	.045	14.85	4.73
Nussbeck, Mark	L-R	6-4	205	5-25-74	3	0	3.12	6	2	0	0	17	17	6	6	3	3	14	.270	.267	.273	7.27	1.56
Ool, Kevin	L-L	5-11	185	1-4-81	1	0	6.63	14	0	0	0	19	26	16	14	1	8	13	.310	.250	.339	6.16	3.79
Pals, Jordan	R-R	6-8	205	10-18-80	7	11	3.83	27	27	0	0	160	162	87	68	16	41	102	.261	.280	.244	5.75	2.31
Pearce, Josh	R-R	6-3	220	8-20-77	0	0	2.50	7	0	0	0	18	12	6	5	3	2	14	.190	.300	.091	7.00	1.00
Pomeranz, Stuart	R-R	6-7	220	12-17-84	5	6	5.29	18	18	0	0	99	110	65	58	12	40	66	.278	.303	.258	6.02	3.65
Pulsipher, Bill	R-L	6-3	230	10-9-73	1	0	2.70	1	1	0	0	7	8	2	2	2	1	7	.296	.000	.296	9.45	1.35
Rawson, Anthony	L-L	5-11	180	7-31-80	4	3	4.35	38	0	0	1	41	45	21	20	7	21	37	.281	.271	.286	8.06	4.57
Rust, Evan	R-R	6-1	210	5-4-78	2	1	4.50	17	0	0	4	18	21	11	9	1	7	17	.280	.250	.298	8.50	3.50
Scalamandre, Rich	R-R	6-0	189	8-20-80	0	0	4.05	7	0	0	0	7	9	3	3	0	7	5	.346	.500	.300	6.75	9.45
Stocks, Nick	R-R	6-0	185	8-27-78	0	1	12.71	8	0	0	0	6	9	11	8	1	4	6	.360	1.000	.273	9.53	6.35
Wallace, Shane	L-L	6-2	225	12-29-80	0	1	9.82	7	0	0	0	7	13	9	8	0	4	2	.406	.417	.400	2.45	4.91

FIELDING

Catcher	PCT	G	PO	A	E	DP	PB
Cancel	.989	60	402	48	5	2	8
Cresse	.983	11	54	5	1	0	0
Johnson	.982	10	48	8	1	1	4
Motte	1.000	1	8	5	0	1	2
Moylan	.981	56	330	28	7	4	7
Pagnozzi	.971	11	61	5	2	0	1

First Base	PCT	G	PO	A	E	DP
Diaz	.978	31	247	21	6	21
Estrada	1.000	5	33	3	0	5
Hanson	1.000	1	1	0	0	0
Johnson	.981	40	343	23	7	29
Minges	1.000	3	17	1	0	2
Robinson	1.000	5	54	2	0	3
Schutzenhofer	.996	57	476	25	2	42
Zoccolillo	.992	14	115	4	1	15

Second Base	PCT	G	PO	A	E	DP
DeMarco	.969	13	22	41	2	6
Estrada	.971	14	25	41	2	6
Hanson	1.000	1	0	3	0	0
Herr	.959	112	202	308	22	74
Laya	1.000	5	10	18	0	1
McCoy	1.000	1	2	1	0	1

Third Base	PCT	G	PO	A	E	DP
Estrada	.889	5	1	7	1	1
Hanson	.909	136	95	264	36	20
Laya	.000	1	0	0	0	0

Shortstop	PCT	G	PO	A	E	DP
Bolivar	.000	1	0	0	0	0
Estrada	.943	50	76	124	12	18
Jaramillo	.973	55	79	172	7	34
Laya	1.000	4	6	5	0	1
McCoy	1.000	2	4	4	0	1
Ryan	.942	43	69	125	12	20

Outfield	PCT	G	PO	A	E	DP
Ankiel	.981	25	48	3	1	1
Bolivar	.980	97	141	8	3	1
Boyd	.968	121	295	10	10	4
Estrada	1.000	14	26	2	0	0
Gorecki	.981	44	100	3	2	0
Haerther	.926	36	48	2	4	0
Minges	.971	94	195	7	6	0
Parker	.958	10	23	0	1	0
Zoccolillo	1.000	8	19	0	0	0

PALM BEACH CARDINALS — High Class A

FLORIDA STATE LEAGUE

BATTING	B-T	HT	WT	DOB	AVG	vLH	vRH	G	AB	R	H	2B	3B	HR	RBI	BB	HBP	SH	SF	SO	SB	CS	SLG	OBP
DeMarco, Matt	L-R	6-0	172	1-24-80	.206	.036	.275	30	97	16	20	5	0	0	5	9	3	0	0	12	1	0	.258	.294
Dryer, Matt	R-R	6-2	195	11-12-79	.219	.148	.245	121	433	58	95	20	1	21	76	45	4	0	5	130	3	1	.416	.296
Evans, Terry	R-R	6-4	211	1-19-82	.221	.204	.227	114	385	34	85	16	1	8	47	29	7	1	3	110	12	6	.330	.285
Gorecki, Reid	R-R	6-1	180	12-22-80	.286	.328	.269	64	234	38	67	18	2	6	41	32	3	2	4	55	24	7	.457	.374
Greene, Tyler	R-R	6-2	185	8-17-83	.271	.385	.220	20	85	17	23	4	0	2	5	5	2	0	0	28	6	0	.388	.326
Haerther, Cody	L-R	6-1	198	7-14-83	.318	.182	.364	47	173	29	55	8	7	8	30	17	1	0	1	31	8	3	.584	.380
Hayes, Calvin	R-R	5-9	187	3-21-84	.215	.159	.234	51	181	23	39	7	3	1	16	13	5	2	1	44	6	3	.304	.285
Hoffpauir, Jarrett	R-R	5-9	165	6-18-83	.257	.189	.277	63	226	23	58	10	1	0	19	32	0	5	2	26	11	5	.310	.346
Kaplan, Jonny	R-R	6-9	180	1-11-80	.189	.143	.205	15	53	8	10	2	0	1	3	4	2	0	0	12	3	2	.283	.271
Laya, Rayner	R-R	5-10	150	9-30-80	.255	.270	.249	75	267	29	68	9	1	1	26	13	1	5	1	21	10	4	.307	.291
Marcelli, Brandon	R-R	6-2	205	1-2-81	.172	.167	.174	18	58	4	10	2	0	0	4	3	2	1	0	13	0	1	.207	.238
Martin, Brian	R-R	6-2	224	6-14-80	.297	.371	.269	60	222	36	66	16	0	5	38	22	2	2	2	67	6	1	.437	.363
Mather, Joe	R-R	6-5	210	7-23-82	.275	.241	.289	57	200	37	55	12	2	8	27	12	9	3	1	39	4	0	.475	.342
McCoy, Mike	R-R	5-9	171	4-2-81	.270	.260	.273	86	282	47	76	13	2	1	27	36	3	8	3	56	18	3	.340	.355
McQuade, Tony	B-R	6-2	205	12-24-81	.250	.214	.264	32	100	17	25	4	2	2	13	9	3	1	2	21	4	0	.390	.325
Mendez, Jose	R-R	5-8	184	7-17-83	.000	.000	.000	1	3	0	0	0	0	0	0	0	0	0	0	1	0	0	.000	.000
Monegan, Anthony	L-R	6-1	165	5-11-79	.189	.125	.211	24	95	8	18	4	1	0	5	4	0	1	0	21	4	0	.253	.222
Motte, Jason	R-R	6-0	200	6-22-82	.172	.156	.178	40	122	7	21	4	0	3	10	4	0	2	0	41	1	0	.279	.198
Pagnozzi, Matt	R-R	6-2	195	11-10-82	.193	.186	.195	61	187	14	36	11	0	1	18	20	2	2	0	49	3	2	.267	.278
Parker, Tyler	R-R	6-2	200	5-13-81	.268	.263	.270	93	325	46	87	20	3	9	54	36	5	2	0	102	15	3	.431	.350
Rich, Dominic	L-R	5-10	195	8-22-79	.125	.000	.125	3	8	0	1	0	0	0	0	1	0	0	0	1	0	0	.125	.222
Rosenthal, Ben	L-R	6-0	210	7-25-79	.158	.333	.125	8	19	3	3	0	0	0	0	2	0	0	0	1	1	0	.158	.238
Ryan, Brendan	R-R	6-2	195	3-26-82	.303	.405	.274	49	188	29	57	17	0	1	16	15	0	4	0	20	8	1	.410	.355
Santor, John	B-R	6-1	224	11-16-81	.218	.241	.206	98	321	30	70	18	1	7	35	27	6	1	0	92	1	3	.346	.291
Schutzenhofer, Andy	L-L	6-0	195	1-24-81	.257	.105	.294	57	191	29	49	6	0	0	13	29	13	3	2	32	2	1	.288	.387
Toops, Brady	L-R	6-2	200	7-31-81	.158	.214	.145	25	76	6	12	2	0	0	8	11	1	1	0	18	3	1	.184	.273
Williams, Simon	R-L	6-2	220	6-30-82	.261	.190	.292	20	69	6	18	2	0	2	8	5	1	0	0	18	1	2	.377	.320

PITCHING	B-T	HT	WT	DOB	W	L	ERA	G	GS	CG	SV	IP	H	R	ER	HR	BB	SO	AVG	vLH	vRH	K/9	BB/9
Adamczyk, Tyler	R-R	6-6	202	11-9-82	3	7	6.68	14	13	0	0	67	83	57	50	10	32	33	.302	.330	.284	4.41	4.28
Alvarez, Oscar	L-L	6-0	204	9-17-80	3	2	1.80	7	4	0	0	35	30	9	7	0	10	21	.244	.240	.245	5.40	2.57
Axelson, Josh	R-R	6-1	202	12-4-78	5	2	4.10	9	9	1	0	53	47	27	24	5	19	32	.237	.243	.234	5.47	3.25
Batista, Roberto	R-R	6-1	195	3-10-82	4	2	3.29	43	8	0	1	101	96	50	37	3	31	36	.253	.290	.234	3.20	2.75

PITCHING	B-T	HT	WT	DOB	W	L	ERA	G	GS	CG	SV	IP	H	R	ER	HR	BB	SO	AVG	vLH	vRH	K/9	BB/9
Bechtel, Chuck	R-R	6-4	215	11-12-79	1	2	7.71	5	4	0	0	16	24	20	14	1	13	11	.338	.429	.300	6.06	7.16
Blair, Buddy	L-L	6-1	205	7-2-81	2	3	6.10	6	6	0	0	31	34	21	21	6	12	24	.276	.207	.298	6.97	3.48
Cavazos, Andy	R-R	6-3	224	1-5-81	1	5	3.41	28	0	0	1	32	36	20	12	1	7	43	.279	.360	.228	12.22	1.99
Cotton, Nate	L-R	6-2	195	7-19-79	0	0	10.80	2	0	0	0	2	3	2	2	0	1	1	.375	.667	.200	5.40	5.40
Dove, Dennis	R-R	6-4	205	8-31-81	2	4	4.85	8	8	0	0	43	48	24	23	1	15	23	.286	.349	.248	4.85	3.16
Doyne, Cory	R-R	6-0	210	8-13-81	1	0	0.00	6	0	0	0	9	3	0	0	0	2	11	.100	.111	.095	11.00	2.00
Garcia, Jose	R-R	6-1	160	6-2-81	7	5	4.35	30	20	0	0	134	147	74	65	11	41	122	.281	.286	.277	8.17	2.75
Garza, Justin	R-R	6-1	190	7-13-82	0	0	3.57	29	0	0	0	40	41	17	16	1	13	26	.266	.200	.303	5.80	2.90
Haberer, Eric	L-L	6-2	205	9-14-82	8	6	3.71	17	17	1	0	95	96	42	39	2	35	58	.270	.177	.297	5.51	3.33
Knoff, Justin	R-R	6-4	195	6-22-81	0	0	7.36	2	1	0	0	7	10	6	6	1	1	3	.333	.400	.320	3.68	1.23
Lambert, Chris	R-R	6-1	205	3-8-83	7	1	2.63	10	10	0	0	55	53	20	16	4	15	46	.255	.247	.259	7.57	2.47
Lundgren, Wayne	R-R	6-7	218	4-21-82	3	3	4.15	25	0	0	0	43	53	22	20	3	8	19	.319	.422	.255	3.95	1.66
Michael, Mark	R-R	6-4	215	8-25-82	4	5	4.04	18	17	0	0	82	68	47	37	7	35	57	.224	.170	.254	6.23	3.83
Morris, Matt	R-R	6-5	220	8-9-74	0	1	6.52	2	2	0	0	10	12	7	7	0	2	15	.300	.375	.250	13.97	1.86
Ool, Kevin	L-L	5-11	185	1-4-81	1	0	1.37	12	0	0	0	20	16	5	3	0	3	17	.222	.227	.220	7.78	1.37
Parisi, Michael	R-R	5-11	185	4-18-83	5	6	3.23	13	13	1	0	78	79	31	28	6	22	63	.264	.313	.224	7.27	2.54
Pomeranz, Stuart	R-R	6-7	220	12-17-84	2	5	3.35	8	8	0	0	48	56	26	18	1	10	29	.296	.273	.317	5.40	1.86
Randazzo, Jeff	R-L	6-7	210	8-12-81	0	1	9.31	8	0	0	1	10	14	11	10	1	5	8	.333	.235	.400	7.45	4.66
Rawson, Anthony	L-L	5-11	180	7-31-80	2	1	2.78	18	0	0	0	23	24	8	7	2	4	19	.282	.429	.234	7.54	1.59
Russ, Chris	R-R	5-11	175	3-27-79	2	3	5.35	29	0	0	0	37	44	29	22	1	11	19	.295	.314	.286	4.62	2.68
Scalamandre, Rich	R-R	6-0	189	8-20-80	3	2	3.15	47	0	0	2	54	51	23	19	3	22	45	.255	.232	.267	7.45	3.64
Schweitzer, Scott	L-L	6-2	235	5-4-80	0	2	4.07	22	0	0	0	24	23	14	11	1	12	23	.253	.258	.250	8.51	4.44
Torres, Jaymie	R-R	5-11	195	1-12-82	1	0	0.00	3	0	0	0	6	0	0	0	0	1	6	.000	.000	.000	9.00	1.50
Wallace, Shane	L-L	6-2	225	12-29-80	0	0	18.00	1	0	0	0	1	3	2	2	0	0	1	.500	1.000	.400	9.00	0.00
Worrell, Mark	R-R	6-1	190	3-8-83	2	3	2.25	53	0	0	35	56	38	20	14	6	19	53	.191	.159	.208	8.52	3.05

FIELDING

Catcher	PCT	G	PO	A	E	DP	PB
Marcelli	.981	18	99	5	2	1	0
Mendez	1.000	1	6	2	0	0	0
Motte	.988	40	230	25	3	0	4
Pagnozzi	.990	60	368	32	4	5	8
Parker	1.000	4	10	0	0	0	1
Rosenthal	1.000	4	18	1	0	1	0
Toops	.988	25	154	15	2	2	3

First Base	PCT	G	PO	A	E	DP
DeMarco	.992	13	117	4	1	11
Dryer	.900	1	9	0	1	0
Rosenthal	1.000	1	3	0	0	0
Santor	.987	79	704	59	10	76
Schutzenhofer	.996	53	490	44	2	58

Second Base	PCT	G	PO	A	E	DP
DeMarco	1.000	1	1	0	0	0
Hayes	.942	47	101	128	14	33
Hoffpauir	.970	62	117	203	10	55
Laya	1.000	7	13	16	0	7
McCoy	.944	25	43	59	6	19
Rich	1.000	2	2	6	0	0

Third Base	PCT	G	PO	A	E	DP
DeMarco	.917	14	6	16	2	2
Dryer	.931	102	60	195	19	21
Mather	.667	2	0	2	1	0
McCoy	.951	25	14	44	3	2
Santor	.867	5	2	11	2	3

Shortstop	PCT	G	PO	A	E	DP
DeMarco	1.000	1	3	6	0	1
Greene	.913	20	32	62	9	19
Laya	.975	64	107	210	8	41
McCoy	.944	11	17	34	3	4
Ryan	.938	49	77	179	17	41

Outfield	PCT	G	PO	A	E	DP
Evans	.958	110	171	13	8	3
Gorecki	1.000	63	131	7	0	1
Haerther	.967	16	28	1	1	0
Kaplan	.938	14	29	1	2	0
Laya	1.000	2	3	0	0	0
Martin	1.000	7	12	0	0	0
Mather	.969	55	85	9	3	3
McCoy	.978	23	38	7	1	1
McQuade	.974	20	37	1	1	0
Monegan	.978	24	44	0	1	0
Pagnozzi	.000	2	0	0	0	0
Parker	.978	79	128	7	3	2
Schutzenhofer	1.000	1	2	0	0	0
Williams	.956	20	43	0	2	0

SWING OF THE QUAD CITIES — Low Class A

MIDWEST LEAGUE

BATTING	B-T	HT	WT	DOB	AVG	vLH	vRH	G	AB	R	H	2B	3B	HR	RBI	BB	HBP	SH	SF	SO	SB	CS	SLG	OBP
Ankiel, Rick	L-L	6-1	215	7-19-79	.270	.196	.295	51	185	33	50	10	1	11	45	27	5	0	6	37	0	0	.514	.368
Brown, Andy	L-L	6-6	195	4-14-80	.176	.000	.214	7	17	1	3	0	1	0	0	1	0	0	0	9	0	0	.294	.222
Danielson, Sean	B-R	5-8	165	8-6-82	.333	.125	.438	6	24	5	8	0	2	0	1	3	0	0	0	3	1	1	.500	.407
Delgado, Jose	B-R	5-9	180	9-10-83	.143	.333	.000	4	7	1	1	0	0	0	1	1	0	0	0	3	0	0	.143	.250
Ferris, Michael	L-L	6-2	220	12-31-82	.230	.188	.240	127	439	65	101	26	0	16	69	69	2	3	5	88	2	3	.399	.334
Hammond, Derry	R-R	6-2	205	10-19-79	.224	.267	.214	43	156	23	35	7	1	7	27	12	3	0	1	43	2	1	.417	.291
Hayes, Calvin	R-R	5-9	187	3-21-84	.242	.200	.253	28	95	11	23	1	0	0	12	3	1	2	1	21	1	0	.253	.270
Herbert, Samuel	R-R	5-10	185	10-12-81	.176	.000	.214	5	17	1	3	1	0	0	2	2	0	1	0	2	1	0	.235	.263
Hoffpauir, Jarrett	R-R	5-9	165	6-18-83	.313	.262	.324	61	227	27	71	15	1	2	28	21	4	1	3	14	5	1	.414	.376
Lemanczyk, Matt	R-R	6-2	201	10-5-80	.266	.279	.263	115	413	92	110	20	5	9	47	45	10	12	3	62	48	6	.404	.350
Lucena, Juan	R-R	5-10	155	1-20-84	.301	.360	.284	99	332	39	100	10	0	2	43	12	4	7	5	11	9	5	.349	.329
Mather, Joe	R-R	6-5	210	7-23-82	.220	.294	.196	54	209	30	46	15	2	9	33	20	3	0	2	49	0	0	.440	.295
Mendez, Jose	R-R	5-8	184	7-17-83	1.000	.000	1.000	1	1	0	1	1	0	0	0	0	0	0	0	0	0	0	2.000	1.000
Mullinax, Jacob	R-R	6-1	200	6-13-82	.283	.282	.283	99	357	56	101	21	4	3	49	27	10	1	3	61	9	5	.389	.348
Palmer, Cody	R-R	6-1	190	8-25-81	.163	.250	.135	31	98	8	16	5	0	2	5	8	1	2	1	44	0	1	.276	.231
Patrick, Chris	R-R	5-9	180	2-20-82	.307	.296	.311	79	251	43	77	18	0	7	50	28	6	2	5	34	2	0	.462	.383
Rowlett, Casey	R-R	5-8	175	2-8-83	.213	.118	.250	21	61	5	13	3	0	1	10	6	0	0	0	10	0	0	.311	.284
Shepherd, Matt	B-R	5-10	175	5-5-83	.292	.283	.295	130	479	78	140	26	4	1	57	87	2	16	1	72	21	9	.370	.402
Stavinoha, Nick	R-R	6-2	225	5-3-82	.344	.265	.363	65	250	54	86	9	2	14	53	23	2	0	4	25	4	0	.564	.398
Swackhamer, Wes	L-L	6-2	210	1-21-83	.239	.164	.258	91	284	43	68	15	2	6	30	18	0	2	3	45	5	3	.370	.282
Toops, Brady	L-R	6-2	200	7-31-81	.203	.286	.188	49	138	21	28	7	1	3	8	16	4	3	0	28	3	3	.333	.304
Verbryke, Eric	L-L	6-2	220	8-6-81	.275	.222	.287	63	233	31	64	14	0	9	39	29	3	0	2	49	4	3	.451	.360
Williams, Simon	R-L	6-2	220	6-30-82	.287	.297	.285	64	181	38	52	13	1	6	27	32	6	1	0	55	8	5	.470	.411
Wyman, Spencer	L-R	6-0	205	5-10-82	.197	.143	.208	35	117	16	23	6	0	1	10	21	1	2	0	22	0	0	.274	.324
Yarbrough, Brandon	L-R	6-2	180	11-9-84	.203	.243	.188	38	133	17	27	5	1	4	17	12	1	1	1	40	1	0	.346	.272

PITCHING	B-T	HT	WT	DOB	W	L	ERA	G	GS	CG	SV	IP	H	R	ER	HR	BB	SO	AVG	vLH	vRH	K/9	BB/9
Adamczyk, Tyler	R-R	6-6	202	11-9-82	4	3	7.83	15	9	0	0	54	68	51	47	8	26	25	.308	.298	.315	4.17	4.33
Aguero, Miguel	R-R	6-0	210	5-19-82	0	1	19.29	2	0	0	0	2	6	5	5	2	1	0	.500	.400	.571	0.00	3.86
Andersen, Phillip	R-R	6-3	175	10-28-83	5	1	2.96	17	17	0	0	100	79	41	33	9	37	86	.216	.209	.222	7.71	3.32
Blair, Buddy	L-L	6-1	205	7-2-81	0	0	9.00	4	0	0	0	3	4	3	3	0	2	3	.308	.500	.222	9.00	6.00
Brown, Justin	R-R	5-11	190	10-6-80	0	1	94.50	3	2	0	0	1	6	14	14	0	11	2	.667	.500	.800	13.50	74.25
Cairns, Jason	R-R	6-4	205	11-13-82	0	3	2.65	22	1	0	8	34	31	14	10	3	19	17	.238	.286	.216	4.50	5.03
Cooper, Michael	R-R	6-2	205	2-2-84	1	4	6.70	10	10	0	0	48	58	40	36	6	19	32	.293	.325	.271	5.96	3.54

PITCHING	B-T	HT	WT	DOB	W	L	ERA	G	GS	CG	SV	IP	H	R	ER	HR	BB	SO	AVG	vLH	vRH	K/9	BB/9
Dickerson, Bo	R-L	6-3	200	5-11-82	2	2	4.91	22	0	0	0	22	19	20	12	1	21	15	.213	.111	.258	6.14	8.59
Dove, Dennis	R-R	6-4	205	8-31-81	7	5	3.88	18	18	2	0	102	93	47	44	6	30	72	.242	.234	.248	6.35	2.65
Doyne, Cory	R-R	6-0	210	8-13-81	0	0	0.00	2	0	0	0	2	0	0	0	0	0	5	.000	.000	.000	19.29	0.00
Gross, Michael	R-R	6-4	235	10-4-81	2	6	4.53	36	0	0	0	50	50	35	25	3	25	29	.251	.333	.198	5.26	4.53
Haberer, Eric	L-L	6-2	205	9-14-82	4	2	2.11	9	9	0	0	55	52	20	13	0	17	33	.248	.205	.259	5.37	2.77
Knoff, Justin	R-R	6-4	195	6-22-81	2	0	4.18	22	0	0	0	28	23	17	13	4	18	31	.215	.205	.222	9.96	5.79
Lundgren, Wayne	R-R	6-7	218	4-21-82	1	0	8.76	10	0	0	0	12	16	12	12	0	6	7	.314	.421	.250	5.11	4.38
McClellan, Kyle	R-R	6-4	205	6-12-84	1	4	4.83	17	8	0	1	54	59	33	29	4	26	36	.286	.289	.284	6.00	4.33
McCormick, Mark	R-R	6-2	195	10-15-83	1	2	5.48	9	9	0	0	43	41	27	26	4	28	45	.253	.185	.299	9.49	5.91
Meacham, Cory	R-R	6-1	185	7-31-84	2	2	5.47	18	0	0	0	25	24	17	15	1	13	19	.250	.222	.267	6.93	4.74
Medina, Dennis	R-R	6-3	199	1-17-83	1	2	1.95	20	1	0	0	32	20	9	7	1	9	39	.174	.255	.118	10.86	2.51
Miller, Brian	R-R	6-3	212	10-18-82	0	1	6.00	14	0	0	0	24	23	19	16	7	7	23	.242	.235	.246	8.63	2.63
Ool, Kevin	L-L	5-11	185	1-4-81	9	2	2.15	30	0	0	3	38	25	10	9	1	8	22	.194	.143	.218	5.26	1.91
Parisi, Michael	R-R	5-11	185	4-18-83	5	5	4.08	14	14	0	0	86	98	42	39	5	25	66	.286	.286	.286	6.91	2.62
Paz, Jackson	R-L	6-1	160	7-10-82	1	0	2.45	6	0	0	0	7	5	4	2	1	3	12	.179	.200	.167	14.73	3.68
Randazzo, Jeff	R-L	6-7	210	8-12-81	0	0	6.17	7	0	0	0	12	12	8	8	3	8	12	.250	.125	.313	9.26	6.17
Robertson, Quinton	L-R	6-5	210	12-18-81	1	2	6.07	22	7	0	0	46	63	36	31	4	11	34	.323	.337	.311	6.65	2.15
Scherer, Matt	R-R	6-5	230	1-20-83	9	8	3.96	24	24	0	0	134	146	74	59	15	43	96	.268	.301	.243	6.45	2.89
Sillman, Mike	R-R	6-1	190	12-3-81	8	2	2.74	56	0	0	22	66	39	23	20	3	49	77	.171	.186	.162	10.55	6.72
Smith, Donnie	R-R	6-2	210	1-14-83	1	2	6.00	5	5	0	0	24	24	20	16	2	11	15	.253	.350	.182	5.63	4.13
Torres, Jaymie	R-R	5-11	195	1-12-82	4	3	3.31	56	0	0	5	71	67	33	26	5	27	56	.242	.250	.236	7.13	3.44
Trent, Matthew	R-R	6-2	220	8-7-82	1	0	4.11	11	0	0	0	15	13	8	7	2	9	9	.236	.273	.212	5.28	5.28
Webber, Nick	R-R	6-7	210	5-9-84	0	4	3.41	5	5	1	0	29	28	15	11	1	9	11	.250	.233	.261	3.41	2.79
Zick, Jeremy	R-R	6-1	210	8-25-82	0	0	6.23	2	0	0	0	4	7	3	3	2	2	3	.389	.364	.429	6.23	4.15

FIELDING

Catcher	PCT	G	PO	A	E	DP	PB
Mendez	1.000	1	4	0	0	0	1
Palmer	.985	31	181	16	3	1	5
Toops	.985	47	304	25	5	4	2
Wyman	.983	35	223	14	4	0	6
Yarbrough	.964	37	246	20	10	2	3

First Base	PCT	G	PO	A	E	DP
Ferris	.991	123	1046	86	10	96
Mather	.963	14	100	3	4	15
Mullinax	1.000	6	32	3	0	1
Stavinoha	1.000	7	50	2	0	5
Williams	1.000	1	1	0	0	0

Second Base	PCT	G	PO	A	E	DP
Delgado	1.000	1	1	2	0	0
Hayes	.942	21	47	50	6	10
Hoffpauir	.981	61	118	185	6	46
Lucena	1.000	2	0	3	0	0
Patrick	.953	16	20	41	3	8
Rowlett	1.000	1	0	1	0	0
Shepherd	.956	49	99	142	11	28

Third Base	PCT	G	PO	A	E	DP
Mullinax	.869	79	55	164	33	18
Patrick	.963	30	20	58	3	4
Rowlett	.800	8	4	8	3	0
Shepherd	.917	32	19	58	7	4

Shortstop	PCT	G	PO	A	E	DP
Lucena	.942	93	98	244	21	47
Shepherd	.935	61	91	153	17	37

Outfield	PCT	G	PO	A	E	DP
Ankiel	.949	30	54	2	3	0
Danielson	1.000	6	15	0	0	0
Hammond	1.000	6	5	0	0	0
Hayes	1.000	1	1	0	0	0
Herbert	1.000	5	4	0	0	0
Hoffpauir	.000	2	0	0	0	0
Lemanczyk	.987	105	227	4	3	1
Mather	1.000	42	82	4	0	1
Rowlett	1.000	12	21	1	0	0
Stavinoha	.991	55	103	5	1	1
Swackhamer	.980	68	96	4	2	0
Verbryke	.961	55	98	1	4	0
Williams	.992	62	129	0	1	0

NEW JERSEY CARDINALS — Short-Season Class A

NEW YORK-PENN LEAGUE

BATTING	B-T	HT	WT	DOB	AVG	vLH	vRH	G	AB	R	H	2B	3B	HR	RBI	BB	HBP	SH	SF	SO	SB	CS	SLG	OBP
Cormier, Richard	B-R	5-10	190	3-17-83	.133	.000	.182	4	15	1	2	0	0	0	2	0	0	0	1	2	0	0	.133	.125
Danielson, Sean	B-R	5-8	165	8-6-82	.344	.250	.374	40	131	20	45	1	2	0	9	13	1	2	0	33	19	1	.382	.407
De la Cruz, Carlos	L-L	6-0	181	1-8-84	.281	.297	.276	44	160	17	45	5	3	1	12	9	1	2	1	44	13	6	.369	.322
Delgado, Jose	B-R	5-9	180	9-10-83	.179	.222	.167	47	123	13	22	1	1	1	5	19	5	0	0	39	5	4	.228	.313
Dobson, Sean	R-L	5-9	180	7-24-82	.273	.276	.273	44	161	17	44	2	2	0	13	14	3	1	0	30	2	2	.311	.343
Gabriel, Chad	R-R	6-2	195	5-19-84	.309	.340	.300	56	207	30	64	13	1	2	29	12	3	4	2	44	6	1	.411	.353
Greene, Tyler	R-R	6-2	185	8-17-83	.261	.208	.272	35	138	28	36	12	0	1	18	15	5	0	1	37	13	1	.370	.352
Hayes, Calvin	R-R	5-9	187	3-21-84	.189	.091	.231	9	37	5	7	0	0	0	1	3	0	0	0	4	3	0	.189	.250
Madden, Scott	R-R	6-1	205	1-6-82	.167	.250	.000	3	6	0	1	0	0	0	1	0	0	0	0	2	0	0	.167	.167
Marcelli, Brandon	R-R	6-2	205	1-2-81	.167	.000	.167	2	6	1	1	0	0	0	2	0	0	0	0	2	0	0	.167	.167
Mendez, Jose	R-R	5-8	184	7-17-83	.207	.100	.229	20	58	7	12	3	0	0	5	4	0	2	1	10	0	0	.259	.254
Morris, Adam	R-R	6-3	190	12-1-82	.242	.143	.254	21	66	10	16	0	0	1	11	9	2	0	2	23	0	0	.288	.342
Nelson, Dan	B-R	5-11	180	2-12-84	.283	.212	.299	52	187	24	53	10	3	0	22	17	3	0	4	31	2	5	.369	.346
Newton, Craig	L-R	5-11	175	10-1-81	.260	.400	.250	24	73	13	19	6	1	2	10	8	1	0	0	18	1	1	.452	.341
Richmond, Kevin	B-R	5-11	165	4-1-83	.268	.063	.350	20	56	6	15	2	1	1	7	2	2	0	2	13	2	1	.393	.306
Rodgers, Adam	R-R	6-1	200	12-1-82	.287	.277	.290	60	202	29	58	16	0	5	38	26	4	1	3	40	2	1	.441	.374
Roth, Randy	R-R	6-1	205	3-5-82	.244	.278	.229	32	119	8	29	6	1	3	14	6	1	1	1	21	0	2	.387	.283
Rowlett, Casey	R-R	5-8	175	2-8-83	.252	.250	.252	36	139	18	35	8	1	0	9	18	1	1	0	24	4	4	.324	.342
Sivira, Yonathan	R-R	6-1	165	1-25-84	.253	.178	.272	61	225	27	57	12	1	2	17	17	2	2	1	42	8	7	.342	.310
Skorupski, John	R-R	6-0	200	7-13-83	.194	.500	.148	10	31	3	6	2	0	0	2	1	3	0	0	14	0	0	.258	.286
Solano, Donovan	R-R	5-10	165	12-17-87	.247	.250	.246	22	77	7	19	5	0	0	11	7	4	1	0	12	1	0	.312	.341
Van Slyke, A.J.	L-R	6-2	210	11-19-83	.343	.000	.364	9	35	6	12	2	0	2	5	3	1	0	0	5	0	0	.571	.410
Wilkerson, Matt	R-R	6-4	215	12-18-82	.239	.200	.248	45	163	17	39	6	1	8	25	20	0	0	1	59	2	0	.436	.321
Yarbrough, Brandon	L-R	6-2	180	11-9-84	.255	.209	.269	51	188	27	48	17	2	2	25	24	1	0	3	58	3	3	.399	.338

PITCHING	B-T	HT	WT	DOB	W	L	ERA	G	GS	CG	SV	IP	H	R	ER	HR	BB	SO	AVG	vLH	vRH	K/9	BB/9
Blair, Buddy	L-L	6-1	205	7-2-81	0	0	0.96	6	0	0	0	9	5	1	1	0	6	12	.161	.111	.182	11.57	5.79
Boggs, Mitchell	R-R	6-3	195	2-15-84	4	4	3.89	15	14	0	0	72	77	38	31	5	24	61	.271	.268	.273	7.66	3.01
Brown, Justin	R-R	5-11	190	10-6-80	1	0	9.00	2	1	0	0	5	7	6	5	0	3	4	.350	.667	.294	7.20	5.40
Cairns, Jason	R-R	6-4	205	11-13-82	0	0	0.00	2	0	0	0	3	2	0	0	0	0	1	.154	.286	.000	3.00	0.00
Clem, Chris	R-R	6-1	210	5-27-83	1	2	5.57	12	4	0	0	32	45	23	20	2	9	22	.349	.255	.402	6.12	2.51
Cooper, Michael	R-R	6-2	205	2-2-84	1	2	1.71	4	3	0	0	21	11	4	4	1	6	18	.155	.114	.194	7.71	2.57
Daniels, Adam	L-L	6-2	190	8-16-82	2	1	4.50	10	5	0	0	26	18	14	13	0	18	25	.189	.120	.214	8.65	6.23
Dickerson, Bo	R-L	6-3	200	5-11-82	0	0	4.50	1	0	0	0	2	3	1	1	0	3	3	.375	.000	.375	13.50	13.50
Farley, Chris	R-R	6-2	178	2-24-83	0	1	7.23	5	3	0	0	19	23	16	15	1	10	18	.303	.283	.333	8.68	4.82
Grant, Jessen	R-R	6-7	200	6-25-82	1	0	3.34	24	0	0	1	32	29	13	12	2	22	26	.232	.244	.225	7.24	6.12
Gross, Michael	R-R	6-4	235	10-4-81	0	0	2.70	11	1	0	0	17	13	6	5	1	1	17	.206	.107	.286	9.18	0.54

PITCHING	B-T	HT	WT	DOB	W	L	ERA	G	GS	CG	SV	IP	H	R	ER	HR	BB	SO	AVG	vLH	vRH	K/9	BB/9
Hawksworth, Blake	R-R	6-3	199	3-1-83	0	3	7.98	7	6	0	0	15	18	18	13	0	10	12	.321	.321	.321	7.36	6.14
Hearne, Trey	R-R	6-1	190	8-19-83	4	2	2.56	24	1	0	0	39	25	15	11	2	12	42	.181	.222	.155	9.78	2.79
Hooks, Ashley	R-R	6-3	190	5-18-83	0	1	7.59	9	0	0	1	11	14	11	9	0	7	12	.311	.292	.333	10.13	5.91
McCormick, Mark	R-R	6-2	195	10-15-83	0	0	0.00	2	2	0	0	6	1	0	0	0	3	10	.053	.000	.100	15.00	4.50
Meacham, Cory	R-R	6-1	185	7-31-84	0	2	1.98	11	0	0	1	14	6	4	3	1	8	11	.136	.167	.100	7.24	5.27
Meagher, Michael	L-L	6-3	230	9-24-84	0	0	0.00	2	0	0	0	2	1	0	0	0	2	4	.167	.000	.333	21.60	10.80
Repole, Michael	R-R	6-5	225	7-12-83	7	2	5.30	25	0	0	1	37	49	25	22	3	17	34	.310	.294	.322	8.20	4.10
Robertson, Quinton	L-R	6-5	210	12-18-81	2	3	3.02	12	7	0	0	48	55	19	16	5	7	30	.284	.253	.308	5.66	1.32
Sadlowski, Kyle	R-R	6-3	190	6-19-84	0	4	7.91	11	6	0	0	33	54	34	29	3	11	25	.360	.511	.295	6.82	3.00
Schellinger, Michael	R-R	6-2	190	12-2-82	0	0	5.23	4	0	0	1	10	9	6	6	1	3	13	.237	.200	.250	11.32	2.61
Stevens, Daniel	L-L	6-0	170	6-8-85	0	0	2.70	5	0	0	1	3	6	2	1	0	3	3	.375	.400	.364	8.10	8.10
Trent, Matthew	R-R	6-2	220	8-7-82	1	1	0.68	14	0	0	9	13	8	1	1	0	6	13	.186	.154	.200	8.78	4.05
Vander Weg, Scott	R-R	6-3	210	12-14-82	2	2	2.45	24	0	0	4	26	21	8	7	0	14	29	.223	.324	.167	10.17	4.91
Webber, Nick	R-R	6-7	210	5-9-84	5	2	1.87	10	9	0	0	53	35	18	11	2	15	43	.179	.217	.159	7.30	2.55
Zick, Jeremy	R-R	6-1	210	8-25-82	1	0	2.79	25	0	0	0	42	42	26	13	4	14	37	.246	.222	.263	7.93	3.00
Zuercher, Zach	L-L	6-2	215	4-10-84	5	7	3.73	16	14	0	0	82	66	36	34	9	25	63	.223	.193	.230	6.91	2.74

GAMES BY POSITION: C—Cormier 2, Madden 3, Marcelli 2, Mendez 12, Newton 21, Rodgers 1, Yarbrough 44. **1B**—Delgado 1, Mendez 5, Rodgers 55, Roth 4, Skorupski 9, Van Slyke 5, Wilkerson 4. **2B**—Delgado 43, Hayes 4, Nelson 5, Richmond 10, Rowlett 20, Solano 3. **3B**—Mendez 3, Morris 17, Nelson 22, Richmond 4, Roth 24, Rowlett 8, Solano 8. **SS**—Greene 35, Nelson 27, Richmond 3, Rowlett 5, Solano 11. **OF**—Danielson 36, De la Cruz 37, Dobson 35, Gabriel 37, Richmond 1, Rowlett 6, Sivira 60, Wilkerson 27.

JOHNSON CITY CARDINALS — Rookie

APPALACHIAN LEAGUE

BATTING	B-T	HT	WT	DOB	AVG	vLH	vRH	G	AB	R	H	2B	3B	HR	RBI	BB	HBP	SH	SF	SO	SB	CS	SLG	OBP
Anderson, Bryan	L-R	6-0	190	12-16-86	.331	.303	.339	51	154	28	51	8	1	6	36	15	1	1	5	29	6	1	.513	.383
Carter, Chuck	R-R	6-2	215	9-27-82	.294	.283	.300	59	180	33	53	9	4	5	32	33	1	0	7	29	12	2	.472	.394
Chacin, Steward	R-R	6-0	170	12-31-85	.301	.414	.241	37	83	13	25	6	1	0	9	2	0	0	0	16	2	0	.398	.318
Desmond, Geoff	R-R	6-3	215	7-9-83	.211	.317	.147	41	109	15	23	9	1	3	15	11	1	0	2	29	3	1	.394	.285
Garner, Brandon	R-R	6-0	165	8-27-86	.181	.135	.211	35	94	13	17	2	0	1	5	5	0	1	0	30	0	1	.234	.222
Gonzalez, Steve	R-R	5-10	190	5-31-87	.190	.167	.207	37	100	8	19	3	0	1	6	12	1	0	2	31	2	0	.250	.278
Jones, Daryl	L-L	5-11	180	6-25-87	.209	.204	.211	61	182	36	38	6	1	2	10	15	13	0	2	41	10	4	.286	.311
Lopez, Christian	R-R	6-0	162	1-23-87	.203	.158	.218	36	74	7	15	1	0	0	7	10	1	0	1	31	2	1	.216	.302
Martinez, Jose	R-R	5-11	175	1-24-86	.300	.294	.303	55	150	28	45	8	2	6	31	20	2	1	1	15	9	2	.500	.387
Mikrut, Jon	R-R	6-4	195	11-22-82	.215	.188	.230	33	93	10	20	7	0	5	11	4	1	1	0	16	1	1	.452	.255
Morris, Adam	R-R	6-3	190	12-1-82	.212	.100	.288	30	99	15	21	7	0	2	14	15	1	0	0	25	3	2	.343	.322
Owens, Malcolm	R-R	6-3	210	3-23-84	.215	.259	.197	38	93	12	20	2	0	1	8	10	6	0	0	21	7	5	.269	.330
Palmer, Cody	R-R	6-1	190	8-25-81	.333	.273	.375	9	27	3	9	2	0	2	9	3	1	0	0	5	2	1	.630	.419
Preston, Tim	R-R	6-0	195	11-30-81	.206	.167	.259	29	63	7	13	2	1	2	10	2	1	0	0	17	2	1	.365	.242
Pujols, Wilfrido	R-R	6-1	185	9-11-87	.143	.105	.159	27	63	5	9	2	0	0	4	2	2	0	0	31	0	0	.175	.194
Rasmus, Colby	L-L	6-1	175	8-11-86	.296	.305	.293	62	216	47	64	16	5	7	27	21	3	1	3	73	13	3	.514	.362
Roth, Randy	R-R	6-1	205	3-5-82	.328	.467	.281	35	119	27	39	13	1	7	27	6	4	0	4	24	3	1	.630	.368
Skorupski, John	R-R	6-0	200	7-13-83	.260	.250	.267	22	73	6	19	7	1	1	11	2	0	0	1	22	2	0	.425	.276
Solano, Donovan	R-R	5-10	165	12-17-87	.262	.441	.207	45	145	27	38	4	0	0	11	14	3	1	1	22	3	2	.290	.337
Van Slyke, A.J.	L-R	6-2	210	11-19-83	.380	.500	.364	13	50	11	19	3	2	2	14	1	1	0	2	7	0	0	.640	.389

PITCHING	B-T	HT	WT	DOB	W	L	ERA	G	GS	CG	SV	IP	H	R	ER	HR	BB	SO	AVG	vLH	vRH	K/9	BB/9
Barone, Daniel	R-R	6-2	185	4-24-83	0	0	9.00	1	0	0	0	1	1	1	1	1	0	1	.250	.000	.500	9.00	0.00
Borne, James	L-L	6-3	185	5-5-83	1	0	2.74	15	0	0	0	23	20	10	7	1	8	18	.230	.235	.229	7.04	3.13
Campbell, Ryan	R-R	6-1	175	8-2-83	4	2	6.33	20	0	0	1	27	20	19	19	2	24	43	.208	.133	.242	14.33	8.00
Chacin, Steward	R-R	6-0	170	12-31-85	0	0	6.75	4	0	0	0	3	5	3	2	1	1	3	.417	.500	.375	10.13	3.38
De la Rosa, Jose	R-R	5-11	175	2-23-86	0	1	8.20	15	0	0	0	19	26	21	17	4	8	10	.310	.222	.351	4.82	3.86
Dixon, Ryan	R-R	6-0	190	7-8-83	1	2	2.81	15	2	0	0	26	21	10	8	3	16	23	.219	.273	.190	8.06	5.61
Fitzgerald, Kevin	R-R	6-3	225	11-27-83	2	4	8.04	26	0	0	12	28	37	26	25	5	7	21	.311	.389	.277	6.75	2.25
Garceau, Shaun	B-R	6-1	185	8-28-87	2	7	7.66	12	12	1	0	45	55	47	38	7	23	42	.296	.312	.284	8.46	4.63
Guerrero, Alberto	R-R	6-2	170	10-7-85	2	0	9.22	17	0	0	0	27	49	32	28	1	12	26	.377	.395	.368	8.56	3.95
Herron, Tyler	R-R	6-3	190	8-5-86	0	3	5.62	13	13	0	0	50	47	35	31	11	27	49	.245	.200	.280	8.88	4.89
Hooks, Ashley	R-R	6-3	190	5-18-83	1	1	5.68	16	0	0	0	25	34	21	16	4	8	24	.306	.300	.309	8.53	2.84
Lane, Matt	R-R	6-8	225	8-17-84	2	6	5.37	13	13	0	0	55	68	40	33	7	22	51	.293	.239	.317	8.30	3.58
Leach, Tyler	R-R	6-3	200	9-8-86	3	3	6.31	10	8	0	0	36	47	32	25	5	13	29	.311	.250	.343	7.32	3.28
Meacham, Cory	R-R	6-1	185	7-31-84	0	0	9.00	2	0	0	0	2	4	2	2	1	1	2	.400	.333	.429	9.00	4.50
Mikrut, Jon	R-R	6-4	195	11-22-82	0	0	0.00	2	0	0	0	3	1	0	0	0	0	5	.091	.167	.000	15.00	0.00
Parish, Brian	R-R	5-11	185	1-20-82	0	1	23.63	4	0	0	0	3	8	10	7	1	2	1	.500	.250	.583	3.38	6.75
Phillips, David	L-R	6-3	200	5-21-85	1	0	5.02	12	0	0	1	14	17	12	8	0	8	19	.283	.320	.257	11.93	5.02
Powell, John	R-R	6-5	205	7-30-84	3	3	6.87	12	3	0	0	38	40	40	29	5	24	27	.261	.259	.263	6.39	5.68
Sadlowski, Kyle	R-R	6-3	190	6-19-84	1	1	2.35	3	0	0	1	8	4	4	2	0	3	6	.143	.000	.182	7.04	3.52
Schwartz, Josh	L-L	5-11	175	2-11-82	2	0	4.24	24	0	0	0	34	30	16	16	2	11	28	.229	.208	.234	7.41	2.91
Soriano, Alex	L-L	6-0	165	7-15-82	0	0	9.64	5	0	0	0	5	8	7	5	2	3	7	.364	.250	.389	13.50	5.79
Weagle, Matt	R-R	6-4	210	7-11-82	1	3	7.00	18	4	0	3	36	52	34	28	3	12	34	.338	.362	.327	8.50	3.00
Wilson, Josh	R-R	5-11	180	9-6-86	2	2	4.22	12	12	0	0	53	49	37	25	7	23	32	.250	.291	.222	5.40	3.88

GAMES BY POSITION: C—Anderson 40, Chacin 1, Gonzalez 31, Palmer 4. **1B**—Carter 15, Chacin 13, Desmond 35, Skorupski 13, Van Slyke 10. **2B**—Chacin 17, Garner 18, Lopez 20, Martinez 34, Solano 3. **3B**—Chacin 4, Lopez 10, Mikrut 18, Morris 27, Roth 21. **SS**—Chacin 3, Garner 15, Lopez 1, Martinez 23, Solano 44. **OF**—Anderson 1, Carter 48, Chacin 2, Desmond 1, Jones 58, Owens 32, Preston 23, Pujols 12, Rasmus 62, Roth 2.

SAN DIEGO PADRES

BY JOHN MAFFEI

With a National League West championship and a berth in the playoffs for the first time since 1998, there was cause for celebration in San Diego in 2005.

But realistically speaking, the team's 82-80 record was five games worse than 2004 when the Padres finished third in the NL West.

General manager Kevin Towers knows his team took advantage of being in baseball's weakest division. And he knows he has some work to do if the Padres want to make it back-to-back playoff appearances for the first time in the organization's history.

First base was a merry-go-round all season. Xavier Nady, Mark Sweeney and Robert Fick all had at least 20 starts there. Nady (.261-13-43) is the most-talented player of the group, but he lacks instincts at first and his arm strength was wasted there.

Fick (.265-3-30) was the team's best defender at first, but he's a valued utilityman, starting 20 games behind the plate, six in right and two in left. And Sweeney (.294-8-40) is among the best pinch-hitters in the game.

The middle of the infield is among the best in baseball.

At second, Mark Loretta (.280-3-38) is the anchor, but he played only 105 games in 2005 because of a thumb injury. Shortstop Khalil Greene (.250-15-70) is an acrobat and showed great power for his position. Greene, however, must stay healthy. He missed 40 games with a variety of injuries.

Joe Randa (.256-4-20 in 58 games) plugged a major hole at third after he was acquired from Kansas City. He pushed 1998 first-round draft pick Sean Burroughs (.250-1-17) to the minors and maybe out of the team picture.

Catcher Ramon Hernandez (.290-12-58) was solid when he was healthy, but twice during the season he went down with injuries, playing in just 99 games.

ORGANIZATION LEADERS

BATTING

*AVG	Baker, Steve, Lake Elsinore/Mobile	.314
R	Bonvechio, Brett, Lake Elsinore	85
H	Barfield, Josh, Portland	160
TB	Knott, Jon, Portland	243
2B	Kottaras, George, Lake Elsinore/Mobile	36
3B	Dowdy, Brett, Fort Wayne/Lake Elsinore	9
HR	Johnson, Ben, Portland	25
	Knott, Jon, Portland	25
RBI	Johnson, Ben, Portland	83
	Valenzuela, Fernando, Lake Elsinore	83
BB	Bonvechio, Brett, Lake Elsinore	86
SO	Bonvechio, Brett, Lake Elsinore	163
SB	Robinson, Kerry, Portland/Richmond	26
*OBP	Delucchi, Dustin, Mobile/Portland/Tacoma	.424
*SLG	Johnson, Michael, Lake Elsinore	.618

PITCHING

W	Ekstrom, Michael, Fort Wayne	13
	Wells, Jared, Lake Elsinore/Mobile	13
L	Jimenez, Fabian, Eugene/Fort Wayne	14
#ERA	Carter, Brent, Eugene/Fort Wayne	1.42
G	Abraham, Paul, Lake Elsinore/Mobile	65
CG	Oxspring, Chris, Portland	3
SV	Varner, Matt, Fort Wayne/Lake Elsinore	34
IP	Thompson, Mike, Mobile/Portland	175
BB	Oyervidez, Jose, Mobile	82
SO	Thompson, Sean, Lake Elsinore/Mobile	139

*Minimum 250 at-bats. #Minimum 75 innings.

PLAYERS OF THE YEAR

MAJOR LEAGUE: Jake Peavy, rhp

Peavy made headlines during the National League Division Series as he pitched with a broken rib he sustained during the Padres' on-field celebration when they locked up the NL West title. But Peavy was San Diego's ace during the regular season, topping the league with 216 strikeouts in 203 innings.

MINOR LEAGUE: Ben Johnson, of

Johnson put up career numbers at Triple-A Portland in 2005, earning a September callup to the big leagues. He set a career mark in homers (25), but the biggest improvement came with controlling the strike zone more. Johnson hit .312 and lowered his strikeouts from 136 in 2004 to 88 in 2005.

In the outfield, Brian Giles (.301-15-83) led the team in RBIs, runs scored and doubles and was No. 1 in the NL with 119 walks, but he became a free agent at the end of the season. Dave Roberts (.275-8-38) did a nice job in center field and in the leadoff spot, stealing 23 bases and finishing with 11 triples. But injuries limited him to 101 starts. Klesko started 120 games in left field, but he's considered a defensive liability in the outfield. Ben Johnson (.213-3-13) had moments of brilliance after he was recalled from Portland, where he hit .312-25-83.

Without question, pitching was the strength of the team in 2005.

Righthander Jake Peavy (13-7, 2.88) is a front-of-the-rotation guy, leading the NL with 216 strikeouts after winning the league ERA title in 2004. Adam Eaton (11-5, 4.27) was 9-1 when he injured a finger in June. Veteran Woody Williams (9-12, 4.85) was a disappointment, but he was a major influence on the young pitchers.

Closer Trevor Hoffman was successful on 43 of 46 save opportunities and now ranks second on baseball's all-time saves list with 436. Scott Linebrink (8-1, 1.83) might have been the best seventh-inning setup man in the game and Akinori Otsuka (2-8, 3.59) was solid, though erratic, in an eighth inning setup role.

Most of San Diego's best young position talent—second baseman Josh Barfield, catchers Nick Trzesniak, George Kottaras and Colt Morton, outfielder Kennard Jones, third baseman Corey Smith and first baseman Michael Johnson—is a year or two away from making any kind of impact at the big league level.

But there are plenty of good arms on the rise. Clay Hensley (1-1, 1.70) was impressive in 24 appearances after he was called up from Portland. Righthanders Chris Oxspring, Tim Stauffer, Mike Thompson, Jared Wells, Leo Rosales, Mike Ekstrom and lefties Craig Breslow and Rusty Tucker all have a chance to earn a spot with the big-league club. And 2005 twin first-round picks Cesar Carrillo and Cesar Ramos were every bit as good as advertised.

Still, for the Padres to make it two in a row in the NL West, the stars will have to align properly and the rest of the division must continue to struggle.

SAN DIEGO PADRES

Manager: Bruce Bochy.

2005 Record: 82-80, .506 (1st, NL West).

BATTING	B-T	HT	WT	DOB	AVG	vLH	vRH	G	AB	R	H	2B	3B	HR	RBI	BB	HBP	SH	SF	SO	SB	CS	SLG	OBP
Alexander, Manny	R-R	5-10	180	3-20-71	.111	.250	.071	10	18	0	2	1	0	0	0	2	1	0	0	5	0	0	.167	.238
Blum, Geoff	B-R	6-3	200	4-26-73	.241	.227	.248	78	224	26	54	13	1	5	22	24	3	0	1	28	3	2	.375	.321
Burroughs, Sean	L-R	6-2	180	9-12-80	.250	.172	.270	93	284	20	71	7	2	1	17	24	5	3	1	41	4	0	.299	.318
Fick, Robert	L-R	6-1	205	3-15-74	.265	.297	.259	93	230	25	61	10	2	3	30	26	1	1	2	33	0	2	.365	.340
Garcia, Jesse	R-R	5-10	170	9-24-73	.167	.357	.045	16	36	4	6	0	0	2	4	3	0	0	0	11	0	0	.333	.231
Giles, Brian	L-L	5-10	205	1-20-71	.301	.289	.306	158	545	92	164	38	8	15	83	119	2	0	8	64	13	5	.483	.423
Greene, Khalil	R-R	5-11	210	10-21-79	.250	.200	.266	121	436	51	109	30	2	15	70	25	6	3	6	93	5	0	.431	.296
Hernandez, Ramon	R-R	6-0	210	5-20-76	.290	.238	.304	99	369	36	107	19	2	12	58	18	1	1	3	40	1	0	.450	.322
Hyzdu, Adam	R-R	6-2	220	12-6-71	.150	.083	.250	17	20	1	3	1	0	0	4	3	0	1	1	4	1	0	.200	.250
Jackson, Damian	R-R	5-11	185	8-16-73	.255	.289	.240	118	275	44	70	9	0	5	23	30	4	3	1	45	15	2	.342	.335
Johnson, Ben	R-R	6-1	200	6-18-81	.213	.185	.229	31	75	10	16	8	1	3	13	11	0	1	1	23	0	2	.467	.310
Klesko, Ryan	L-L	6-3	220	6-12-71	.248	.200	.262	137	443	61	110	19	1	18	58	75	1	0	1	80	3	4	.418	.358
Loretta, Mark	R-R	6-0	185	8-14-71	.280	.309	.271	105	404	54	113	16	1	3	38	45	8	2	4	34	8	4	.347	.360
McAnulty, Paul	L-R	5-10	220	2-24-81	.208	.500	.182	22	24	4	5	0	0	0	0	3	1	1	0	7	1	0	.208	.321
Nady, Xavier	R-R	6-2	205	11-14-78	.261	.323	.223	124	326	40	85	15	2	13	43	22	7	1	0	67	2	1	.439	.321
Nevin, Phil	R-R	6-2	230	1-19-71	.256	.228	.267	73	281	31	72	11	1	9	47	19	1	0	5	67	1	0	.399	.301
Ojeda, Miguel	R-R	6-1	230	1-29-75	.137	.148	.130	43	73	6	10	3	1	0	6	9	0	1	0	21	1	1	.205	.232
Olivo, Miguel	R-R	6-0	220	7-15-78	.304	.400	.263	37	115	16	35	7	1	4	16	4	3	1	1	31	6	1	.487	.341
Randa, Joe	R-R	5-11	190	12-18-69	.256	.368	.217	58	223	27	57	17	1	4	20	14	2	0	2	29	0	1	.395	.303
2-team (92 Cincinnati)					.276	.306	.264	150	555	71	153	43	2	17	68	47	4	0	3	81	0	1	.452	.335
Roberts, Dave	L-L	5-10	180	5-31-72	.275	.258	.278	115	411	65	113	19	10	8	38	53	1	11	4	59	23	12	.428	.356
Ross, David	R-R	6-2	215	3-19-77	.353	.200	.417	11	17	2	6	0	1	0	0	0	1	1	0	4	0	0	.471	.389
2-team (40 Pittsburgh)					.240	.200	.253	51	125	11	30	8	1	3	15	6	2	2	3	28	0	0	.392	.279
Sweeney, Mark	L-L	6-1	215	10-26-69	.294	.200	.303	135	221	31	65	12	1	8	40	40	0	1	5	58	4	0	.466	.395
Valdez, Wilson	R-R	5-11	170	5-20-78	.231	.125	.400	9	13	0	3	2	0	0	1	2	0	0	0	1	0	0	.385	.333
Young, Eric	R-R	5-9	185	5-18-67	.275	.318	.237	56	142	22	39	9	0	2	12	18	0	3	0	12	7	6	.380	.356

PITCHING	B-T	HT	WT	DOB	W	L	ERA	G	GS	CG	SV	IP	H	R	ER	HR	BB	SO	AVG	vLH	vRH	K/9	BB/9
Astacio, Pedro	R-R	6-2	210	11-28-69	4	2	3.17	12	10	0	0	60	54	21	21	4	26	33	.247	.220	.283	4.98	3.92
Breslow, Craig	L-L	6-1	180	8-8-80	0	0	2.20	14	0	0	0	16	15	6	4	1	13	14	.238	.063	.298	7.71	7.16
Cassidy, Scott	R-R	6-2	180	10-3-75	1	1	6.57	10	0	0	0	12	15	10	9	3	3	12	.306	.350	.276	8.76	2.19
Eaton, Adam	R-R	6-2	190	11-23-77	11	5	4.27	24	22	0	0	129	140	70	61	14	44	100	.275	.297	.255	6.99	3.08
Falkenborg, Brian	R-R	6-6	225	1-18-78	0	0	8.18	10	0	0	0	11	17	11	10	2	5	10	.347	.316	.367	8.18	4.09
Hammond, Chris	L-L	6-1	210	1-21-66	5	1	3.84	55	0	0	0	59	51	25	25	9	14	34	.229	.164	.260	5.22	2.15
Hensley, Clay	R-R	5-11	190	8-31-79	1	1	1.70	24	1	0	0	48	33	12	9	0	17	28	.195	.275	.103	5.29	3.21
Hoffman, Trevor	R-R	6-0	215	10-13-67	1	6	2.97	60	0	0	43	58	52	23	19	3	12	54	.235	.298	.179	8.43	1.87
Lawrence, Brian	R-R	6-0	195	5-14-76	7	15	4.83	33	33	1	0	196	211	106	105	18	57	109	.273	.300	.249	5.01	2.62
Linebrink, Scott	R-R	6-2	200	8-4-76	8	1	1.83	73	0	0	1	74	55	17	15	4	23	70	.209	.195	.223	8.55	2.81
May, Darrell	L-L	6-2	185	6-13-72	1	3	5.61	22	8	0	0	59	73	38	37	10	20	32	.303	.200	.330	4.85	3.03
Otsuka, Akinori	R-R	6-0	200	1-13-72	2	8	3.59	66	0	0	1	63	55	28	25	3	34	60	.234	.207	.263	8.62	4.88
Oxspring, Chris	L-R	6-0	185	5-13-77	0	0	3.75	5	0	0	0	12	9	8	5	2	6	11	.225	.222	.227	8.25	4.50
Park, Chan Ho	R-R	6-2	210	6-30-73	4	3	5.91	10	9	0	0	46	50	33	30	3	26	33	.278	.295	.261	6.50	5.12
Peavy, Jake	R-R	6-0	180	5-31-81	13	7	2.88	30	30	3	0	203	162	70	65	18	50	216	.217	.223	.212	9.58	2.22
Quantrill, Paul	L-R	6-1	200	11-3-68	1	1	3.41	22	0	0	0	32	37	13	12	2	2	24	.294	.283	.303	6.82	0.57
2-team (6 Florida)					1	2	4.14	28	0	0	0	37	45	20	17	3	7	25	.302	.300	.304	6.08	1.70
Redding, Tim	R-R	6-0	195	2-12-78	0	5	9.10	9	6	0	0	30	40	35	30	7	13	17	.328	.274	.383	5.16	3.94
Reyes, Dennys	R-L	6-3	245	4-19-77	3	2	5.15	36	1	0	0	44	57	30	25	3	32	35	.315	.208	.359	7.21	6.60
Seanez, Rudy	R-R	5-11	200	10-20-68	7	1	2.69	57	0	0	0	60	49	19	18	4	22	84	.222	.231	.212	12.53	3.28
Stauffer, Tim	R-R	6-1	215	6-2-82	3	6	5.33	15	14	0	0	81	92	50	48	10	29	49	.286	.289	.283	5.44	3.22
Williams, Randy	L-L	6-3	195	9-18-75	1	0	12.46	2	0	0	0	4	7	6	6	1	4	2	.350	.667	.214	4.15	8.31
Williams, Woody	R-R	6-0	200	8-19-66	9	12	4.85	28	28	0	0	160	174	92	86	24	51	106	.275	.259	.288	5.97	2.87

FIELDING

Catcher	PCT	G	PO	A	E	DP	PB
Fick	.978	28	167	10	4	0	2
Hernandez	.988	97	640	36	8	4	6
Nevin	1.000	2	11	1	0	0	0
Ojeda	1.000	25	100	7	0	1	2
Olivo	.979	37	224	14	5	2	2
Ross	1.000	7	28	0	0	1	0

First Base	PCT	G	PO	A	E	DP
Blum	1.000	2	1	0	0	0
Fick	.992	29	224	12	2	23
Klesko	1.000	1	2	0	0	0
McAnulty	1.000	1	4	0	0	1
Nady	.986	44	261	27	4	26
Nevin	.994	71	579	38	4	51
Sweeney	.988	53	314	21	4	26

Second Base	PCT	G	PO	A	E	DP
Alexander	1.000	5	1	4	0	0
Blum	1.000	19	28	48	0	9
Garcia	1.000	2	2	3	0	1
Jackson	.993	35	53	93	1	21
Loretta	.987	105	201	262	6	61
Young	.944	14	25	26	3	8

Third Base	PCT	G	PO	A	E	DP
Alexander	.000	1	0	0	0	0
Blum	.965	34	20	62	3	7
Burroughs	.962	78	59	145	8	16
Fick	.000	1	0	0	0	0
Jackson	.889	8	2	6	1	1
Loretta	.000	1	0	0	0	0
Nady	1.000	3	0	6	0	0
Randa	.955	58	50	77	6	8

Shortstop	PCT	G	PO	A	E	DP
Alexander	.933	4	4	10	1	1
Blum	1.000	14	12	25	0	6
Burroughs	.000	1	0	0	0	0
Garcia	1.000	13	15	19	0	4
Greene	.971	121	161	312	14	64
Jackson	.926	26	34	54	7	14
Valdez	.944	8	9	8	1	2

Outfield	PCT	G	PO	A	E	DP
Fick	1.000	13	17	1	0	0
Giles	.988	155	329	6	4	1
Hyzdu	1.000	12	14	1	0	1
Jackson	1.000	52	48	2	0	0
Johnson	.962	29	51	0	2	0
Klesko	.981	121	204	7	4	1
McAnulty	1.000	6	5	0	0	0
Nady	.976	68	83	0	2	0
Ojeda	1.000	5	10	0	0	0
Roberts	.992	109	235	4	2	0
Sweeney	.833	6	5	0	1	0
Young	1.000	25	53	0	0	0

FARM SYSTEM

General Manager: Kevin Towers. **Director, Player Development:** Tye Waller. **Scouting Director:** Bill Gayton.

Class	Farm Team	League	W	L	Pct.	Finish*	Manager	Affiliate Since
AAA	Portland (Ore.) Beavers	Pacific Coast	70	73	.490	10th (16)	Craig Colbert	2001
AA	Mobile (Ala.) BayBears	Southern	58	80	.420	9th (10)	Gary Jones	1997
High A	Lake Elsinore (Calif.) Storm	California	70	68	.507	**6th (10)**	Rick Renteria	2001
Low A	Fort Wayne (Ind.) Wizards	Midwest	65	75	.464	**t-11th (14)**	Randy Ready	1999
SS A	Eugene (Ore.) Emeralds	Northwest	34	42	.447	t-6th (8)	Roy Howell	2001
Rookie	Peoria (Ariz.) Padres	Arizona	29	27	.518	4th (9)	Carlos Lezcano	2004

*Finish in overall standings (No. of teams in league)/Playoff teams in **boldface**

PORTLAND BEAVERS — Class AAA

PACIFIC COAST LEAGUE

BATTING	B-T	HT	WT	DOB	AVG	vLH	vRH	G	AB	R	H	2B	3B	HR	RBI	BB	HBP	SH	SF	SO	SB	CS	SLG	OBP
Alexander, Manny	R-R	5-10	180	3-20-71	.250	.167	.500	4	16	0	4	2	0	0	1	1	0	0	0	4	0	1	.375	.294
2-team (108 Oklahoma)					.307	.326	.299	112	433	64	133	25	6	12	68	39	4	2	6	70	27	10	.476	.365
Barfield, Josh	R-R	6-0	185	12-17-82	.310	.323	.303	137	516	74	160	25	1	15	72	52	1	2	7	108	20	5	.450	.370
Bozied, Tagg	R-R	6-3	210	7-24-79	.259	.300	.208	14	54	6	14	4	0	2	10	3	3	0	2	6	0	0	.444	.323
Burroughs, Sean	L-R	6-2	180	9-12-80	.290	.238	.317	32	124	21	36	8	0	3	14	9	5	0	0	15	0	0	.427	.362
Cameron, Troy	B-R	5-11	180	8-31-78	.071	.000	.143	10	14	1	1	0	0	0	0	1	0	0	0	7	0	0	.071	.133
Delucchi, Dustin	L-L	6-0	190	12-23-77	.305	.290	.311	64	197	49	60	17	2	2	15	48	1	3	2	29	9	3	.442	.440
2-team (23 Tacoma)					.287	.314	.275	87	279	61	80	18	2	3	20	57	1	8	3	43	12	3	.398	.406
Evans, Lee	B-R	6-1	190	7-20-77	.027	.000	.040	12	37	1	1	1	0	0	0	5	0	0	0	14	0	0	.054	.143
Fick, Robert	L-R	6-1	205	3-15-74	.375	.417	.350	10	32	5	12	1	0	3	11	10	1	0	1	3	1	0	.688	.523
Furmaniak, J.J.	R-R	6-3	190	7-31-79	.266	.266	.266	99	387	54	103	16	4	14	47	28	6	5	2	86	9	5	.437	.324
Garcia, Jesse	R-R	5-10	170	9-24-73	.200	.205	.197	63	210	18	42	7	2	3	26	6	0	3	2	34	6	1	.295	.220
Gerber, Joe	L-L	6-2	220	8-27-78	.109	.154	.091	28	46	2	5	1	0	0	4	4	0	0	1	16	0	0	.130	.176
Hernandez, Michel	R-R	6-0	210	8-12-78	.288	.380	.238	82	264	19	76	9	1	3	31	37	0	2	6	34	0	0	.364	.368
Hyzdu, Adam	R-R	6-2	220	12-6-71	.275	.304	.258	62	207	38	57	9	1	11	32	47	1	1	1	61	2	5	.488	.410
Jackson, Damian	R-R	5-11	185	8-16-73	.353	.400	.323	14	51	14	18	4	1	3	10	13	0	0	1	9	1	1	.647	.477
Johnson, Ben	R-R	6-1	200	6-18-81	.312	.304	.315	107	414	79	129	27	0	25	83	51	6	0	1	88	6	1	.558	.394
Jones, Kennard	L-L	5-11	185	9-8-81	.212	.222	.200	8	33	3	7	1	0	0	3	1	1	0	0	11	0	1	.242	.257
Knott, Jon	R-R	6-3	220	8-4-78	.250	.251	.250	134	503	81	126	34	4	25	78	55	11	0	8	112	1	0	.483	.333
Loretta, Mark	R-R	6-0	185	8-14-71	.100	.500	.000	3	10	0	1	0	0	0	0	2	0	0	0	1	0	0	.100	.250
McAnulty, Paul	L-R	5-10	220	2-24-81	.344	.302	.367	38	151	27	52	15	0	6	27	16	0	0	1	29	0	0	.563	.405
McCauley, Seth	B-R	6-2	190	6-19-81	.000	.000	.000	3	3	0	0	0	0	0	0	0	0	0	0	2	0	0	.000	.000
Merrill, Ronnie	B-R	6-1	185	11-13-78	.240	.364	.205	14	50	7	12	2	0	0	2	7	0	0	0	10	0	0	.280	.333
Nevin, Phil	R-R	6-2	230	1-19-71	.143	.333	.000	2	7	0	1	0	0	0	1	0	0	0	0	2	0	0	.143	.143
Ojeda, Miguel	R-R	6-1	230	1-29-75	.193	.105	.237	17	57	8	11	1	0	3	5	7	1	0	0	16	0	0	.368	.292
Risinger, Benjamin	R-R	6-0	206	11-25-77	.211	.263	.189	41	128	17	27	7	0	3	14	19	13	0	0	28	0	1	.336	.369
Robinson, Kerry	L-L	6-0	175	10-3-73	.289	.275	.296	61	253	40	73	5	2	2	17	10	1	3	2	26	26	7	.348	.316
Ross, David	R-R	6-2	215	3-19-77	.143	.125	.154	6	21	3	3	1	0	0	1	2	0	0	0	4	0	0	.190	.217
Sain, Greg	R-R	6-2	218	12-26-79	.273	.190	.314	56	176	22	48	13	0	8	38	14	1	0	3	29	1	0	.483	.325
Scales, Bobby	B-R	6-0	185	10-4-77	.274	.333	.238	120	376	50	103	19	2	14	61	53	6	0	1	98	9	4	.447	.372
Trzesniak, Nick	R-R	6-0	210	11-19-80	.380	.250	.436	24	79	13	30	8	0	1	12	5	2	0	0	16	1	1	.519	.430
Valdez, Wilson	R-R	5-11	170	5-20-78	.245	.214	.263	50	155	14	38	5	3	1	15	15	0	4	1	27	8	0	.335	.310
2-team (1 Tacoma)					.239	.214	.252	51	159	14	38	5	3	1	16	15	0	4	1	28	8	0	.327	.303
Young, Eric	R-R	5-9	185	5-18-67	.000	.000	.000	5	16	3	0	0	0	0	0	6	0	0	0	2	0	0	.000	.273

PITCHING	B-T	HT	WT	DOB	W	L	ERA	G	GS	CG	SV	IP	H	R	ER	HR	BB	SO	AVG	vLH	vRH	K/9	BB/9
Asencio, Miguel	R-R	6-2	190	9-29-80	0	3	9.42	3	3	0	0	14	27	17	15	1	6	7	.409	.360	.439	4.40	3.77
Ashby, Andy	R-R	6-1	195	7-11-67	0	0	3.00	1	1	0	0	3	2	1	1	1	0	3	.182	.000	.286	9.00	0.00
Astacio, Pedro	R-R	6-2	210	11-28-69	0	1	15.75	1	1	0	0	4	10	7	7	0	0	1	.500	.455	.556	2.25	0.00
Baker, Brad	R-R	6-2	180	11-6-80	4	5	4.75	59	0	0	27	66	69	36	35	9	32	75	.272	.288	.257	10.18	4.34
Bonine, Eddie	R-R	6-5	220	6-6-81	1	0	0.00	1	0	0	0	2	0	0	0	0	0	5	.000	.000	.000	22.50	0.00
Breslow, Craig	L-L	6-1	180	8-8-80	0	1	4.00	7	0	0	0	9	11	4	4	1	1	9	.314	.222	.346	9.00	1.00
Bumstead, Michael	R-R	6-4	210	7-8-77	2	2	5.26	12	4	0	0	26	32	16	15	3	10	14	.299	.319	.283	4.91	3.51
Cassel, Jack	R-R	6-2	215	8-8-80	3	2	4.62	23	3	0	0	39	54	25	20	2	17	21	.335	.337	.333	4.85	3.92
Cassidy, Scott	R-R	6-2	180	10-3-75	0	1	1.89	17	0	0	11	19	10	5	4	2	7	19	.156	.083	.250	9.00	3.32
Dawley, Joe	R-R	6-4	230	9-19-71	1	0	7.31	13	0	0	0	16	16	14	13	1	16	17	.258	.296	.229	9.56	9.00
Deago, Roger	R-L	5-10	184	6-21-69	0	2	11.42	2	2	0	0	9	18	11	11	2	5	5	.429	.600	.405	5.19	5.19
Eaton, Adam	R-R	6-2	190	11-23-77	0	0	5.63	2	2	0	0	8	11	5	5	3	1	4	.344	.278	.429	4.50	1.13
Emanuel, Brandon	R-R	6-3	215	4-9-76	2	3	5.29	37	6	0	0	65	64	49	38	12	25	65	.253	.273	.231	9.05	3.48
Falkenborg, Brian	R-R	6-6	225	1-18-78	3	4	5.25	28	0	0	1	36	35	25	21	2	21	26	.257	.197	.333	6.50	5.25
Germano, Justin	R-R	6-1	190	8-6-82	7	6	3.70	19	19	1	0	112	111	56	46	13	32	100	.259	.233	.286	8.04	2.57
Hensley, Clay	R-R	5-11	190	8-31-79	2	2	2.99	15	14	0	0	90	63	31	30	8	22	71	.197	.191	.201	7.07	2.19
Kershner, Jason	L-L	6-2	185	12-19-76	5	2	3.15	46	0	0	1	60	50	22	21	4	11	44	.227	.274	.204	6.60	1.65
McLeary, Marty	R-R	6-5	230	10-26-74	5	8	4.75	41	12	1	0	110	122	68	58	10	51	104	.280	.288	.273	8.51	4.17
Oxspring, Chris	L-R	6-0	185	5-13-77	12	6	4.03	26	26	3	0	161	148	81	72	15	42	125	.243	.229	.257	7.00	2.35
Patterson, Danny	R-R	6-0	190	2-17-71	1	1	9.82	9	0	0	0	11	17	13	12	1	5	4	.347	.324	.400	3.27	4.09
Polanco, Phil	R-R	6-0	200	11-10-81	0	0	9.00	1	0	0	0	1	2	1	1	0	0	0	.500	.667	.000	0.00	0.00
Redding, Tim	R-R	6-0	195	2-12-78	0	0	0.90	2	2	0	0	10	7	1	1	0	2	5	.200	.176	.222	4.50	1.80
Snare, Ryan	L-L	6-0	200	2-8-79	4	2	5.93	6	6	0	0	30	37	20	20	6	11	23	.306	.400	.275	6.82	3.26
2-team (17 Oklahoma)					5	7	6.23	23	13	0	2	91	117	69	63	14	39	58	.317	.356	.299	5.74	3.86
Sparks, Steve	R-R	6-0	190	7-2-65	2	0	2.04	3	3	0	0	18	15	6	4	1	6	9	.224	.234	.200	4.58	3.06
Spiehs, R.D.	R-R	6-3	224	10-18-79	1	1	4.70	12	0	0	1	15	15	9	8	4	9	11	.259	.143	.324	6.46	5.28
Stauffer, Tim	R-R	6-1	215	6-2-82	3	5	5.14	13	13	1	0	75	90	48	43	5	17	64	.296	.283	.310	7.65	2.03
Stewart, Scott	R-L	6-2	225	8-14-75	1	5	6.65	17	0	0	0	22	22	17	16	2	10	16	.262	.214	.286	6.65	4.15
Sweeney, Brian	R-R	6-2	200	6-13-74	4	5	3.98	20	16	0	0	111	121	51	49	15	16	72	.281	.262	.301	5.86	1.30
Thompson, Mike	R-R	6-4	205	11-6-80	4	2	3.15	9	9	0	0	60	58	22	21	6	13	25	.258	.290	.229	3.75	1.95

PITCHING	B-T	HT	WT	DOB	W	L	ERA	G	GS	CG	SV	IP	H	R	ER	HR	BB	SO	AVG	vLH	vRH	K/9	BB/9
Tovar, Angel	R-R	6-4	195	4-25-78	2	3	6.65	16	0	0	0	22	31	20	16	5	14	11	.352	.455	.250	4.57	5.82
Whitaker, Brian	R-R	6-4	205	11-5-79	0	0	9.00	2	1	0	0	6	12	6	6	1	1	4	.429	.583	.313	6.00	1.50
Williams, Randy	L-L	6-3	195	9-18-75	1	1	6.39	12	0	0	0	13	13	10	9	1	9	7	.271	.136	.385	4.97	6.39

FIELDING

Catcher	PCT	G	PO	A	E	DP	PB
Evans	.986	11	68	5	1	1	1
Fick	1.000	2	14	1	0	0	3
Hernandez	.992	79	541	56	5	6	2
Ojeda	.991	14	94	11	1	0	1
Risinger	1.000	14	98	10	0	0	1
Ross	1.000	6	48	2	0	0	1
Trzesniak	.986	20	134	8	2	0	1

First Base	PCT	G	PO	A	E	DP
Bozied	.988	9	74	5	1	10
Fick	.986	8	65	8	1	6
Gerber	.988	12	71	8	1	6
Knott	.984	40	287	22	5	33
McAnulty	.989	21	163	11	2	17
Nevin	1.000	2	3	0	0	1
Risinger	1.000	13	101	10	0	10
Sain	.990	46	365	28	4	36

Second Base	PCT	G	PO	A	E	DP
Barfield	.980	137	264	365	13	83
Furmaniak	1.000	3	7	10	0	3
Jackson	.833	1	2	3	1	1
Loretta	1.000	2	4	5	0	1
Merrill Jr.	1.000	1	0	1	0	0
Scales	1.000	2	5	7	0	1
Young	1.000	2	2	7	0	1

Third Base	PCT	G	PO	A	E	DP
Burroughs	.949	32	23	51	4	7
Cameron	1.000	2	3	3	0	1
Furmaniak	.942	55	41	105	9	8
Garcia	.933	10	4	10	1	0
Jackson	.909	4	5	5	1	1
Merrill Jr.	.917	4	3	8	1	0
Risinger	.975	16	16	23	1	4
Scales	.905	28	21	46	7	7

Shortstop	PCT	G	PO	A	E	DP
Alexander	.933	4	3	11	1	1
Furmaniak	.954	38	47	78	6	15
Garcia	.967	49	59	117	6	33
Jackson	.944	5	7	10	1	2
Merrill Jr.	.931	10	11	16	2	5
Valdez	.981	46	87	116	4	28

Outfield	PCT	G	PO	A	E	DP
Delucchi	1.000	56	128	6	0	1
Gerber	.000	1	0	0	0	0
Hyzdu	.993	62	141	7	1	3
Jackson	1.000	4	7	0	0	0
Johnson	.981	107	205	6	4	0
Jones	1.000	8	14	0	0	0
Knott	.976	85	149	11	4	0
McAnulty	1.000	15	36	1	0	0
Ojeda	1.000	1	1	0	0	0
Robinson	.992	58	125	5	1	1
Scales	.989	46	90	2	1	1

MOBILE BAYBEARS — Class AA

SOUTHERN LEAGUE

BATTING	B-T	HT	WT	DOB	AVG	vLH	vRH	G	AB	R	H	2B	3B	HR	RBI	BB	HBP	SH	SF	SO	SB	CS	SLG	OBP
Baker, Casey	R-R	5-10	180	8-7-80	.218	.327	.153	101	271	39	59	9	1	1	14	30	3	7	1	64	9	2	.269	.302
Baker, Steve	R-R	6-3	200	4-20-80	.288	.329	.270	66	260	26	75	13	2	6	33	10	3	0	1	70	4	2	.423	.321
Bozied, Tagg	R-R	6-3	210	7-24-79	.333	.286	.355	12	45	9	15	0	0	3	12	3	1	0	0	9	0	0	.533	.388
Burgamy, Brian	B-R	5-10	190	6-27-81	.199	.222	.191	56	176	15	35	6	2	2	15	27	0	2	0	45	2	0	.290	.305
Cameron, Troy	B-R	5-11	180	8-31-78	.138	.200	.071	14	29	2	4	1	0	0	5	3	0	0	0	9	0	0	.172	.219
Carlin, Luke	B-R	5-11	185	12-20-80	.257	.275	.248	88	230	24	59	8	1	2	25	35	1	1	1	46	3	3	.326	.356
Clements, Jason	B-R	5-10	180	3-1-78	.225	.221	.228	70	182	25	41	5	2	3	18	17	2	5	1	48	2	1	.324	.297
Cruz, Luis	R-R	6-1	200	2-10-84	.159	.088	.202	44	151	14	24	2	1	3	6	9	2	1	1	31	0	1	.245	.215
Delucchi, Dustin	L-L	6-0	190	12-23-77	.280	.290	.276	34	107	11	30	5	0	0	8	16	4	3	0	24	4	2	.327	.394
Duncan, Jeff	L-L	6-2	190	12-9-78	.300	.333	.283	22	70	12	21	3	2	2	7	9	2	2	1	20	1	1	.486	.390
Garcia, Jesse	R-R	5-10	170	9-24-73	.194	.250	.185	7	31	4	6	2	0	1	3	0	1	1	1	4	1	1	.355	.212
Gerber, Joe	L-L	6-2	220	8-27-78	.277	.295	.268	83	271	41	75	15	0	16	41	38	6	4	1	88	0	1	.509	.377
Jones, Kennard	L-L	5-11	185	9-8-81	.281	.292	.275	124	487	62	137	23	4	1	60	71	3	5	1	112	23	14	.351	.375
Kottaras, George	L-R	6-0	190	5-16-83	.287	.292	.286	29	101	16	29	7	0	2	15	19	0	0	1	23	0	0	.416	.397
McAnulty, Paul	L-R	5-10	220	2-24-81	.282	.247	.299	79	298	39	84	17	2	10	42	34	6	0	3	66	5	2	.453	.364
Merrill, Ronnie	B-R	6-1	185	11-13-78	.246	.258	.240	120	455	65	112	24	5	8	58	52	4	6	7	81	8	4	.374	.324
Ramos, Peeter	R-R	5-11	180	3-18-82	.173	.172	.173	31	104	8	18	1	0	1	8	6	3	0	0	20	2	0	.212	.239
Richardson, Mike	R-R	5-9	205	7-11-79	.162	.229	.128	68	142	19	23	3	0	2	12	26	1	2	0	53	0	1	.225	.296
Sain, Greg	R-R	6-2	218	12-26-79	.260	.235	.282	64	223	27	58	11	0	5	25	21	0	1	6	48	0	3	.377	.316
Smith, Corey	R-R	6-1	200	4-15-82	.254	.263	.249	135	516	64	131	30	2	18	73	46	4	0	5	144	4	3	.424	.317
Trzesniak, Nick	R-R	6-0	210	11-19-80	.249	.243	.252	67	233	37	58	13	1	5	25	22	2	1	1	61	7	0	.378	.318

PITCHING	B-T	HT	WT	DOB	W	L	ERA	G	GS	CG	SV	IP	H	R	ER	HR	BB	SO	AVG	vLH	vRH	K/9	BB/9
Abraham, Paul	R-R	6-2	220	1-10-80	2	1	3.98	30	0	0	0	41	46	21	18	3	13	24	.288	.276	.294	5.31	2.88
Breslow, Craig	L-L	6-1	180	8-8-80	2	1	2.75	40	0	0	0	52	38	16	16	3	17	47	.212	.220	.209	8.08	2.92
Bumstead, Michael	R-R	6-4	210	7-8-77	0	1	3.94	3	3	0	0	16	14	8	7	0	5	10	.237	.440	.088	5.63	2.81
Carrillo, Cesar	R-R	6-3	177	4-29-84	4	0	3.23	5	5	0	0	31	23	11	11	2	7	35	.204	.180	.222	10.27	2.05
Cassel, Jack	R-R	6-2	215	8-8-80	3	3	3.35	24	3	0	1	43	45	18	16	1	16	29	.273	.254	.284	6.07	3.35
Chick, Travis	R-R	6-3	225	6-10-84	2	9	5.27	19	19	1	0	97	107	65	57	12	40	92	.279	.339	.225	8.51	3.70
Deago, Roger	R-L	5-10	184	6-21-69	1	0	1.38	3	3	0	0	13	10	3	2	0	8	15	.208	.273	.189	10.38	5.54
Hayhurst, Dirk	L-R	6-3	200	3-24-81	1	0	2.57	1	1	1	0	7	5	2	2	1	4	4	.227	.250	.214	5.14	5.14
Jones, Geoff	L-L	6-5	230	8-10-79	3	5	4.37	55	0	0	0	70	76	43	34	2	32	60	.281	.207	.320	7.71	4.11
Mateo, Nathanel	R-R	6-1	160	12-24-80	3	4	3.08	48	0	0	1	53	57	22	18	2	15	39	.275	.212	.320	6.66	2.56
Meaux, Ryan	L-L	5-11	170	10-5-78	2	0	3.18	15	0	0	0	17	16	7	6	2	2	12	.239	.200	.255	6.35	1.06
2-team (38 Birmingham)					7	2	3.00	53	0	0	3	84	93	34	28	4	20	76	.280	.217	.310	8.14	2.14
Oyervidez, Jose	R-R	5-11	195	2-18-82	7	9	3.81	27	27	0	0	154	129	77	65	16	82	130	.232	.231	.232	7.61	4.80
Richardson, Mike	R-R	5-9	205	7-11-79	0	0	3.00	3	0	0	0	3	0	1	1	0	4	3	.000	.000	.000	9.00	12.00
Snare, Ryan	L-L	6-0	200	2-8-79	0	2	6.23	2	2	1	0	13	16	9	9	3	3	8	.320	.500	.263	5.54	2.08
Spiehs, R.D.	R-R	6-3	224	10-18-79	0	1	7.98	10	0	0	0	15	19	18	13	4	3	9	.306	.250	.333	5.52	1.84
Steidlmayer, Luke	R-R	6-5	205	8-13-80	0	3	6.32	3	3	0	0	16	23	14	11	2	7	13	.333	.360	.318	7.47	4.02
Steinborn, Chris	L-L	6-4	215	3-23-82	0	1	8.31	3	0	0	0	4	4	4	4	1	4	4	.250	.333	.231	8.31	8.31
Thayer, Dale	R-R	6-0	195	12-17-80	3	5	2.34	56	0	0	27	58	60	16	15	5	26	59	.279	.256	.295	9.21	4.06
Thompson, Mike	R-R	6-4	205	11-6-80	6	6	3.22	18	18	2	0	115	116	50	41	6	27	68	.269	.259	.278	5.34	2.12
Thompson, Sean	L-L	6-0	210	10-13-82	4	5	4.67	20	20	0	0	114	127	67	59	10	55	94	.294	.346	.277	7.44	4.35
Tovar, Angel	R-R	6-4	195	4-25-78	2	1	6.57	8	1	0	0	12	19	12	9	1	8	10	.339	.296	.379	7.30	5.84
Tucker, Rusty	L-L	6-0	190	7-15-80	3	2	5.31	52	0	0	0	63	66	42	37	4	49	69	.280	.262	.287	9.91	7.04
Villatoro, Wilmer	R-R	6-1	160	11-2-81	0	3	15.55	10	1	0	0	11	22	19	19	4	12	8	.431	.409	.448	6.55	9.82
Wells, Jared	R-R	6-4	200	10-31-81	2	5	4.40	7	7	0	0	43	51	25	21	3	16	22	.307	.293	.315	4.60	3.35
Whitaker, Brian	R-R	6-4	205	11-5-79	8	13	4.33	25	25	0	0	148	180	85	71	4	53	101	.308	.323	.293	6.16	3.23

FIELDING

Catcher	PCT	G	PO	A	E	DP	PB
Carlin	.984	58	396	46	7	8	3
Kottaras	.995	25	161	21	1	0	1
Richardson	1.000	3	7	0	0	0	1
Trzesniak	.990	60	437	46	5	5	3

First Base	PCT	G	PO	A	E	DP
Bozied	.988	9	75	10	1	4
Gerber	.988	69	591	66	8	73
McAnulty	1.000	9	60	6	0	6
Richardson	1.000	1	2	0	0	0
Sain	.992	52	436	39	4	58
Trzesniak	1.000	4	21	4	0	2

Second Base	PCT	G	PO	A	E	DP
C. Baker	.967	51	102	135	8	38
Burgamy	.889	2	2	6	1	2

	PCT	G	PO	A	E	DP
Cameron	.900	3	2	7	1	0
Clements	.945	40	63	91	9	15
Merrill	.978	32	56	126	4	23
Ramos	.976	27	49	74	3	21
Richardson	1.000	1	1	3	0	0

Third Base	PCT	G	PO	A	E	DP
Cameron	1.000	1	0	1	0	0
Clements	.929	3	4	9	1	2
Cruz	1.000	1	2	5	0	2
Smith	.903	134	106	221	35	26

Shortstop	PCT	G	PO	A	E	DP
C. Baker	1.000	3	3	6	0	1
Clements	.875	3	4	3	1	0
Cruz	.960	42	59	110	7	32
Garcia	.923	6	12	24	3	4
Merrill Jr.	.976	93	122	249	9	60
Ramos	1.000	3	7	7	0	2

Outfield	PCT	G	PO	A	E	DP
C. Baker	.981	35	49	2	1	1
S. Baker	.976	65	119	2	3	0
Burgamy	.985	47	65	1	1	1
Cameron	1.000	3	4	0	0	0
Clements	.833	8	4	1	1	0
Delucchi	1.000	32	61	2	0	0
Duncan	1.000	20	29	0	0	0
Gerber	1.000	2	1	1	0	0
Jones	.971	123	257	8	8	3
McAnulty	.962	71	117	8	5	1
Richardson	1.000	36	43	3	0	1

LAKE ELSINORE STORM — HIGH CLASS A

CALIFORNIA LEAGUE

BATTING	B-T	HT	WT	DOB	AVG	vLH	vRH	G	AB	R	H	2B	3B	HR	RBI	BB	HBP	SH	SF	SO	SB	CS	SLG	OBP
Adams, Skip	R-R	6-0	200	10-18-79	.269	.316	.249	82	245	30	66	19	1	5	38	17	3	6	2	65	6	4	.416	.322
Baker, Steve	R-R	6-3	200	4-20-80	.344	.339	.346	54	221	33	76	17	1	4	37	13	2	1	0	46	6	2	.484	.386
Blum, Geoff	B-R	6-3	200	4-26-73	.250	.200	.333	2	8	3	2	0	0	2	5	1	0	0	0	2	0	0	1.000	.333
Bonvechio, Brett	L-R	6-1	200	11-13-82	.267	.231	.278	131	480	85	128	24	6	19	73	86	8	3	2	163	1	2	.460	.385
Bourassa, Adam	L-L	5-8	165	3-31-81	.356	.275	.377	48	194	36	69	11	2	2	15	25	1	4	2	13	8	5	.464	.428
2-team (30 Bakersfield)					.303	.230	.322	78	297	42	90	13	2	2	21	36	1	5	2	31	11	6	.380	.378
Burgamy, Brian	B-R	5-10	190	6-27-81	.295	.314	.287	59	234	43	69	12	4	7	40	25	1	3	2	47	4	3	.470	.363
Chang, Ray	R-R	6-1	195	8-24-83	.500	.500	.500	3	4	2	2	0	0	0	0	0	0	0	0	0	0	0	.500	.500
Ciriaco, Juan	R-R	6-0	159	8-15-83	.281	.277	.282	120	466	73	131	29	6	9	77	33	3	7	2	84	17	10	.427	.331
Dowdy, Brett	R-R	6-0	190	2-22-82	.265	.545	.222	21	83	7	22	5	0	1	5	7	1	1	1	13	0	0	.361	.326
Fryer, Brian	R-R	6-1	185	8-16-82	.120	.143	.111	11	25	7	3	1	1	0	1	1	0	0	0	5	0	0	.240	.154
Greene, Khalil	R-R	5-11	210	10-21-79	.500	.500	.500	4	12	4	6	1	0	0	3	2	1	0	0	1	0	0	.583	.600
Howard, Joshua	L-L	5-11	180	4-6-83	.263	.200	.286	6	19	3	5	0	1	0	4	2	1	1	0	4	2	0	.368	.364
Johnson, Craig	L-L	6-1	185	4-11-82	.221	.194	.227	55	172	25	38	7	1	2	17	23	4	1	1	37	2	0	.308	.325
Johnson, Michael	L-L	6-3	225	6-25-80	.295	.275	.303	73	288	59	85	20	5	21	76	37	0	0	8	89	0	3	.618	.366
Kolkhorst, Chris	L-R	5-9	180	3-7-82	.327	.429	.302	26	107	18	35	6	4	0	6	15	2	2	0	21	2	0	.458	.419
Kottaras, George	L-R	6-0	190	5-16-83	.303	.323	.295	91	337	54	102	29	0	9	50	50	1	2	4	60	2	1	.469	.390
Macias, Drew	L-L	6-3	175	3-7-83	.289	.252	.303	128	492	79	142	23	6	6	66	46	6	5	2	78	15	15	.396	.355
Morton, Colt	R-R	6-5	230	4-10-82	.323	.368	.312	26	96	19	31	4	0	9	19	14	1	0	2	30	0	1	.646	.407
Pagan, Andres	R-R	6-4	200	3-18-81	.230	.227	.232	47	139	16	32	6	1	4	23	6	1	1	1	30	3	0	.374	.265
Pickens, Jordan	R-R	6-2	220	6-10-81	.245	.291	.227	77	277	42	68	19	1	10	46	32	16	2	1	75	2	2	.430	.356
Ramos, Peeter	R-R	5-11	180	3-18-82	.278	.261	.285	100	424	69	118	14	2	2	46	36	5	10	2	58	18	3	.335	.340
Roberts, Dave	L-L	5-10	180	5-31-72	.200	.000	.333	3	10	2	2	1	0	0	0	3	0	0	0	1	0	1	.300	.385
Thayer, Matt	R-L	5-10	173	2-21-82	.293	.333	.270	23	58	10	17	1	1	1	6	10	2	1	0	11	2	0	.397	.414
Turner, Tim	R-L	6-2	190	6-12-82	.250	.000	.500	4	4	1	1	0	0	0	0	1	0	0	0	1	0	0	.250	.400
Valenzuela, Fernando	L-L	5-10	210	9-30-82	.296	.299	.295	133	530	78	157	28	4	12	83	56	12	0	5	84	5	0	.432	.373

PITCHING	B-T	HT	WT	DOB	W	L	ERA	G	GS	CG	SV	IP	H	R	ER	HR	BB	SO	AVG	vLH	vRH	K/9	BB/9
Abraham, Paul	R-R	6-2	220	1-10-80	2	1	1.07	35	0	0	4	42	29	8	5	1	10	36	.200	.219	.185	7.71	2.14
Asencio, Miguel	R-R	6-2	190	9-29-80	1	0	1.80	1	1	0	0	5	2	1	1	0	4	2	.125	.200	.000	3.60	7.20
Ashby, Andy	R-R	6-1	195	7-11-67	0	0	0.00	1	1	0	0	3	3	1	0	0	0	1	.231	.250	.200	3.00	0.00
Baca, Daniel	R-R	5-10	175	10-17-85	0	0	10.97	6	0	0	0	11	23	13	13	1	7	5	.460	.455	.464	4.22	5.91
Blackwell, Brad	R-R	6-2	215	5-8-82	0	0	4.22	15	0	0	0	21	22	11	10	0	9	14	.265	.216	.304	5.91	3.80
Bonine, Eddie	R-R	6-5	220	6-6-81	5	6	6.47	36	10	0	0	104	142	88	75	14	42	77	.323	.315	.329	6.64	3.62
Carrillo, Cesar	R-R	6-3	177	4-29-84	1	2	7.01	7	7	0	0	26	30	21	20	3	9	29	.280	.340	.233	10.17	3.16
Eaton, Adam	R-R	6-2	190	11-23-77	0	0	0.00	1	1	0	0	3	1	0	0	0	2	2	.111	.200	.000	6.00	6.00
Fernandez, Alfredo	R-R	6-4	224	9-15-84	0	0	0.00	3	0	0	0	3	1	0	0	0	3	1	.100	.000	.125	3.00	9.00
Frieri, Ernesto	R-R	6-2	168	7-19-85	0	0	2.70	2	0	0	0	3	3	1	1	1	1	3	.231	.222	.250	8.10	2.70
Girardeau, Clark	R-R	6-5	210	4-12-82	3	9	7.13	20	17	0	0	88	125	85	70	18	30	50	.326	.333	.320	5.09	3.06
Hamilton, Clayton	R-R	6-5	200	6-15-82	2	2	5.14	7	6	0	0	28	39	19	16	2	9	18	.339	.364	.324	5.79	2.89
Hayhurst, Dirk	L-R	6-3	200	3-24-81	5	5	5.38	38	7	0	1	94	106	66	56	9	27	69	.283	.281	.284	6.63	2.59
Huerta, Edgar	L-L	5-11	200	10-21-79	1	0	10.95	8	0	0	0	12	21	15	15	0	4	14	.375	.360	.387	10.22	2.92
Klatt, Ryan	R-R	6-0	185	9-30-81	2	0	7.71	17	0	0	0	23	27	21	20	6	7	17	.284	.273	.294	6.56	2.70
Lopez, Arturo	L-L	5-10	165	2-22-83	5	11	5.85	27	27	0	0	140	174	108	91	13	49	94	.302	.328	.287	6.04	3.15
Martinez, Javier	B-R	6-3	193	12-9-82	4	2	4.77	17	17	0	0	100	100	59	53	16	29	76	.256	.272	.243	6.84	2.61
Mendoza, Luis	R-R	6-3	180	10-31-83	0	1	9.28	2	2	0	0	11	18	14	11	1	4	3	.391	.368	.407	2.53	3.38
Pence, Howard	R-R	6-5	210	10-1-79	4	5	4.56	41	0	0	1	49	56	33	25	3	27	34	.283	.275	.287	6.20	4.93
Rosales, Leonel	R-R	6-1	185	5-28-81	8	7	3.18	61	0	0	27	65	53	26	23	5	24	77	.219	.200	.236	10.66	3.32
Seanez, Rudy	R-R	5-11	200	10-20-68	0	1	36.00	1	0	0	0	1	3	4	4	2	1	0	.500	.333	.667	0.00	9.00
Steidlmayer, Luke	R-R	6-5	205	8-13-80	0	3	4.33	9	8	0	0	52	59	37	25	7	10	34	.278	.278	.279	5.88	1.73
Thompson, Sean	L-L	6-0	210	10-13-82	4	1	2.16	6	6	0	0	33	26	15	8	4	13	45	.210	.167	.232	12.15	3.51
Tierney, Chris	L-L	6-6	230	9-1-83	4	6	6.35	41	9	0	0	89	114	81	63	9	61	50	.308	.390	.270	5.04	6.15
Trytten, Ryan	R-R	6-3	216	5-10-81	6	2	3.73	50	0	0	0	51	59	28	21	7	23	52	.284	.341	.239	9.24	4.09
Villatoro, Wilmer	R-R	6-1	160	11-2-81	2	1	3.88	52	0	0	1	60	61	36	26	4	34	44	.265	.284	.252	6.56	5.07
Wells, Jared	R-R	6-4	200	10-31-81	11	3	3.44	19	19	2	0	120	116	51	46	6	26	80	.257	.246	.263	5.98	1.94

FIELDING

Catcher	PCT	G	PO	A	E	DP	PB
Kottaras	.986	84	520	48	8	4	12
Morton	.989	25	168	14	2	0	5
Pagan	.982	46	255	18	5	5	4

First Base	PCT	G	PO	A	E	DP
Adams	1.000	7	19	2	0	0
M. Johnson	.988	57	481	23	6	47
C. Johnson	1.000	1	8	1	0	0
Pickens	.964	3	26	1	1	2
Valenzuela	.986	77	722	52	11	67

Second Base	PCT	G	PO	A	E	DP
Adams	.945	22	34	70	6	10
Blum	1.000	1	4	2	0	1
Chang	1.000	1	1	3	0	1
Ciriaco	1.000	1	2	4	0	2
Dowdy	.974	20	42	34	2	8
Ramos	.975	99	211	335	14	71

Third Base	PCT	G	PO	A	E	DP
Adams	.762	9	5	11	5	1
Bonvechio	.905	130	97	235	35	25
Dowdy	.000	1	0	0	1	0

Shortstop	PCT	G	PO	A	E	DP
Adams	.933	23	35	63	7	15
Blum	.917	1	5	6	1	2
Ciriaco	.924	119	182	363	45	63
Greene	1.000	4	5	9	0	0

Outfield	PCT	G	PO	A	E	DP
Adams	.905	16	17	2	2	1
Baker	.966	54	105	8	4	1
Bourassa	.957	46	79	10	4	2
Burgamy	.970	52	96	2	3	0
Fryer	.923	8	12	0	1	0
Howard	1.000	6	11	1	0	0
C. Johnson	.986	38	68	4	1	1
Kolkhorst	.960	26	44	4	2	0
Macias	.968	126	322	15	11	4
Pickens	.964	34	51	2	2	0
Roberts	1.000	3	4	0	0	0
Thayer	.893	19	24	1	3	0
Turner	.000	4	0	0	0	0

FORT WAYNE WIZARDS — Low Class A

MIDWEST LEAGUE

BATTING	B-T	HT	WT	DOB	AVG	vLH	vRH	G	AB	R	H	2B	3B	HR	RBI	BB	HBP	SH	SF	SO	SB	CS	SLG	OBP
Alley, Josh	L-L	5-9	180	9-6-83	.263	.263	.264	45	167	26	44	3	0	2	11	40	2	0	0	26	5	4	.317	.411
Baxter, Michael	L-R	6-0	190	12-7-84	.219	.227	.216	45	183	11	40	12	1	1	17	12	0	0	0	29	4	1	.311	.267
Bush, Matt	R-R	5-11	170	2-8-86	.221	.226	.219	126	453	56	100	13	3	2	32	33	5	1	3	76	8	4	.276	.279
Cavanaugh, Brian	L-R	6-1	190	8-21-83	.150	.000	.214	7	20	1	3	1	0	0	2	5	0	0	0	11	0	0	.200	.320
Ciofrone, Peter	R-R	5-10	201	9-28-83	.301	.267	.313	104	395	56	119	20	2	5	59	50	10	0	3	53	7	1	.400	.391
Dale, Lachlan	R-R	6-3	190	6-22-83	.189	.141	.208	89	328	41	62	18	0	12	37	22	2	0	8	108	0	0	.354	.239
Davidson, Drew	R-R	6-0	190	5-7-82	.262	.346	.224	21	84	9	22	2	0	5	15	1	4	1	2	21	0	0	.464	.297
Dowdy, Brett	R-R	6-0	190	2-22-82	.272	.271	.273	77	301	47	82	10	9	2	41	32	1	1	2	44	7	0	.385	.342
Figueroa, Baudilio	R-R	6-2	175	6-28-83	.234	.238	.233	51	171	21	40	4	0	1	12	8	1	1	3	39	0	3	.275	.268
Fryer, Brian	R-R	6-1	185	8-16-82	.279	.295	.267	31	104	12	29	2	1	2	11	7	1	1	1	19	6	3	.375	.327
Headley, Chase	B-R	6-2	195	5-9-84	.200	.200	.200	4	15	2	3	0	0	0	1	1	0	0	0	4	0	0	.200	.250
Hundley, Nick	R-R	6-1	210	9-8-83	.222	.111	.259	10	36	2	8	2	0	0	5	4	1	0	1	9	0	0	.278	.310
Johnson, Craig	L-L	6-1	185	4-11-82	.156	.250	.100	10	32	4	5	2	1	0	1	6	1	1	0	6	0	0	.281	.308
Johnston, Trey	R-R	5-11	190	7-4-85	.000	.000	.000	1	3	1	0	0	0	0	0	1	0	0	0	1	0	0	.000	.250
Kazmar, Sean	R-R	5-9	160	8-5-84	.267	.211	.286	125	469	47	125	26	0	10	48	44	1	2	3	69	7	4	.386	.329
Kolkhorst, Chris	L-R	5-9	180	3-7-82	.282	.300	.277	100	393	65	111	21	1	1	30	65	7	4	2	57	19	6	.349	.392
Lauderdale, Matt	R-R	5-10	200	4-14-81	.282	.227	.303	75	273	35	77	25	2	10	54	38	3	0	5	52	2	1	.498	.370
Lobaton, Jose	B-R	6-0	175	10-21-84	.176	.222	.160	9	34	2	6	1	0	0	1	2	0	1	0	5	0	0	.206	.222
Mora, Ruben	B-R	6-0	190	10-1-82	.198	.265	.169	32	111	11	22	3	1	1	7	12	0	2	0	19	3	1	.270	.276
Morton, Colt	R-R	6-5	230	4-10-82	.261	.308	.247	63	222	27	58	15	0	10	46	35	3	0	5	57	0	0	.464	.362
Ramirez, Yordany	R-R	6-2	180	7-31-84	.222	.218	.223	104	369	50	82	19	3	8	46	18	4	1	4	71	15	5	.355	.263
Thayer, Matt	R-L	5-10	173	2-21-82	.353	.267	.377	37	136	21	48	10	0	2	19	21	3	3	0	25	6	2	.471	.450
Vazquez, Kelvin	B-R	6-1	170	9-30-83	.320	.333	.317	14	50	9	16	5	0	0	7	4	0	0	0	12	0	0	.420	.370
Vincent, Tom	L-R	6-3	215	3-3-82	.242	.265	.236	98	392	43	95	20	2	1	32	21	3	0	2	84	18	5	.311	.285

PITCHING	B-T	HT	WT	DOB	W	L	ERA	G	GS	CG	SV	IP	H	R	ER	HR	BB	SO	AVG	vLH	vRH	K/9	BB/9
Carter, Brenton	R-L	6-3	200	10-10-82	2	0	0.75	2	2	0	0	12	7	1	1	1	1	13	.171	.400	.139	9.75	0.75
Ekstrom, Michael	R-R	6-0	185	8-30-83	13	6	3.70	28	28	1	0	168	167	76	69	11	36	112	.257	.273	.247	6.01	1.93
Ellis, Jonathan	R-R	6-0	190	10-3-82	5	3	3.89	43	5	0	0	79	82	41	34	8	24	69	.268	.304	.243	7.89	2.75
Garcia, Geivy	R-R	6-2	175	7-8-82	2	2	5.01	41	0	0	0	56	57	43	31	5	27	44	.257	.244	.265	7.11	4.37
Geer, Josh	R-R	6-3	190	6-2-83	1	1	4.25	5	5	0	0	30	29	16	14	3	9	23	.259	.255	.262	6.98	2.73
Girardeau, Clark	R-R	6-5	210	4-12-82	1	1	4.15	6	6	0	0	30	34	17	14	3	6	22	.281	.320	.254	6.53	1.78
Hamilton, Clayton	R-R	6-5	200	6-15-82	9	6	2.88	20	20	0	0	122	101	44	39	9	36	86	.226	.235	.221	6.34	2.66
Jamison, Neil	R-R	6-3	185	8-4-83	1	1	2.70	7	0	0	0	10	11	3	3	0	5	12	.282	.375	.217	10.80	4.50
Jimenez, Fabian	L-L	6-2	187	8-27-86	4	11	7.03	20	20	0	0	90	120	80	70	8	59	38	.331	.274	.345	3.81	5.92
Kintzler, Brandon	R-R	6-1	180	8-1-84	1	2	3.09	19	0	0	0	23	20	12	8	2	7	19	.230	.176	.264	7.33	2.70
Klatt, Ryan	R-R	6-0	185	9-30-81	0	2	2.87	16	0	0	1	16	18	7	5	1	5	14	.277	.300	.257	8.04	2.87
Perez, Henry	R-R	6-4	238	10-27-82	0	2	8.18	11	0	0	0	11	17	11	10	2	5	11	.354	.222	.433	9.00	4.09
Polanco, Phil	R-R	6-0	200	11-10-81	1	3	6.20	26	1	0	0	45	51	33	31	5	23	33	.298	.286	.309	6.60	4.60
Ramos, Cesar	L-L	6-2	190	6-22-84	3	2	4.19	7	7	1	0	39	42	19	18	0	7	32	.282	.300	.277	7.45	1.63
Santo, Joel	R-R	6-3	194	6-4-84	4	11	4.75	27	27	0	0	140	156	90	74	14	51	86	.280	.252	.299	5.52	3.27
Steidlmayer, Luke	R-R	6-5	205	8-13-80	7	2	2.28	16	8	0	0	59	46	17	15	3	21	53	.212	.174	.240	8.04	3.19
Steik, Ricky	L-R	6-3	210	1-24-84	0	6	2.40	54	0	0	3	60	54	17	16	5	24	53	.247	.241	.250	7.95	3.60
Steinborn, Chris	L-L	6-4	215	3-23-82	1	4	4.18	19	7	0	0	56	65	34	26	4	16	24	.289	.325	.281	3.86	2.57
Sterry, Vern	R-R	6-2	210	2-7-82	4	3	4.58	20	4	0	0	55	58	33	28	5	13	50	.265	.239	.282	8.18	2.13
Stutes, Kyle	L-L	5-10	185	1-22-82	1	2	2.42	45	0	0	1	52	52	22	14	3	16	61	.254	.283	.243	10.56	2.77
Trytten, Ryan	R-R	6-3	216	5-10-81	1	0	1.20	10	0	0	0	15	13	2	2	0	3	17	.255	.450	.129	10.20	1.80
Varner, Matt	R-R	5-11	200	1-16-82	4	5	4.00	54	0	0	34	54	47	24	24	5	18	62	.229	.318	.167	10.33	3.00

FIELDING

Catcher	PCT	G	PO	A	E	DP	PB
Hundley	.973	8	66	7	2	0	1
Killian	1.000	1	1	0	0	0	0
Lauderdale	.977	65	430	36	11	2	6
Lobaton	.985	9	64	3	1	0	2
Morton	.984	59	415	27	7	3	12

First Base	PCT	G	PO	A	E	DP
Baxter	.993	45	365	34	3	38
Ciofrone	.971	8	62	6	2	9
Dale	.988	87	773	43	10	78
Figueroa	1.000	1	10	0	0	0
Morton	1.000	1	6	0	0	0

Second Base	PCT	G	PO	A	E	DP
Figueroa	.959	11	20	27	2	3
Kazmar	.973	125	243	375	17	92
Vazquez	.900	5	6	12	2	3

Third Base	PCT	G	PO	A	E	DP
Ciofrone	.895	40	25	60	10	5
Dowdy	.933	75	60	120	13	18
Figueroa	.922	20	13	46	5	5
Headley	.800	4	3	5	2	0
Vazquez	.714	3	2	3	2	0

Shortstop	PCT	G	PO	A	E	DP
Bush	.941	125	185	422	38	83
Figueroa	.903	17	21	44	7	8

Outfield	PCT	G	PO	A	E	DP
Alley	.964	41	80	0	3	0
Cavanaugh	.909	6	10	0	1	0
Davidson	1.000	10	16	0	0	0
Fryer	.966	18	28	0	1	0
Johnson	.875	5	7	0	1	0
Kolkhorst	.985	95	129	5	2	1
Mora	.986	32	70	1	1	0
Ramirez	.963	104	294	20	12	1
Thayer	1.000	25	42	1	0	0
Vazquez	1.000	1	1	0	0	0
Vincent	.975	87	149	6	4	1

EUGENE EMERALDS — Short-Season Class A

NORTHWEST LEAGUE

BATTING	B-T	HT	WT	DOB	AVG	vLH	vRH	G	AB	R	H	2B	3B	HR	RBI	BB	HBP	SH	SF	SO	SB	CS	SLG	OBP
Alley, Josh	L-L	5-9	180	9-6-83	.365	.125	.409	14	52	11	19	5	1	0	6	15	0	0	1	9	3	3	.500	.500
Cavanaugh, Brian	L-R	6-1	190	8-21-83	.232	.294	.218	53	190	25	44	6	0	1	18	17	3	0	2	68	2	4	.279	.302
Cleland, Clint	R-R	6-1	195	9-16-82	.235	.133	.257	24	85	11	20	6	1	1	7	8	0	2	0	32	3	0	.365	.301
Davidson, Drew	R-R	6-0	190	5-7-82	.297	.333	.288	34	138	18	41	7	1	4	19	10	3	1	1	26	2	3	.449	.355
Diaz, Javis	L-L	5-10	165	6-25-84	.211	.167	.231	5	19	3	4	0	0	0	0	4	0	0	0	4	2	0	.211	.348
Gottier, Brandon	R-R	5-11	195	1-5-82	.231	.318	.196	25	78	2	18	4	0	1	9	3	4	2	1	11	0	0	.321	.291
Guerrero, Santiago	R-R	6-0	176	11-28-83	.253	.200	.271	55	194	22	49	5	7	2	31	15	10	1	4	43	9	6	.381	.332
Headley, Chase	B-R	6-2	195	5-9-84	.268	.241	.277	57	220	29	59	14	3	6	33	34	4	0	1	48	1	1	.441	.375
Hundley, Nick	R-R	6-1	210	9-8-83	.250	.200	.265	43	148	30	37	7	1	7	22	33	2	0	1	35	1	0	.453	.391
Johnston, Seth	R-R	6-3	200	3-12-83	.253	.256	.252	47	170	15	43	8	1	2	23	13	0	4	3	41	2	4	.347	.301
Jones, Daryl	R-R	6-3	200	9-1-86	.188	.130	.204	73	255	28	48	8	0	4	16	21	5	1	0	81	0	2	.267	.263
Killian, Billy	L-R	6-1	190	6-12-86	.189	.286	.167	14	37	0	7	0	1	0	4	4	1	0	0	13	0	0	.243	.286

BATTING	B-T	HT	WT	DOB	AVG	vLH	vRH	G	AB	R	H	2B	3B	HR	RBI	BB	HBP	SH	SF	SO	SB	CS	SLG	OBP
Lobaton, Jose	B-R	6-0	175	10-21-84	.281	.167	.308	11	32	4	9	2	0	0	3	6	1	3	0	8	0	0	.344	.410
Richardson, Billy	R-R	5-8	170	7-23-82	.174	.208	.162	55	178	19	31	8	1	1	7	17	4	4	1	46	4	1	.247	.260
Rivera, Jodam	B-R	5-10	180	2-4-86	.241	.214	.246	24	83	10	20	2	0	0	6	10	1	4	1	20	0	1	.265	.326
Sansoe, Mike	R-R	6-0	185	11-6-82	.290	.267	.297	49	193	32	56	8	1	0	20	20	6	3	1	48	13	3	.342	.373
Smith, Casey	R-R	6-4	230	2-24-84	.101	.045	.123	25	79	4	8	0	0	1	5	8	0	0	2	27	0	0	.139	.180
Steiner, Chad	R-R	5-11	190	12-25-83	.250	.154	.279	14	56	8	14	1	1	1	8	4	0	0	0	9	0	0	.357	.300
Turner, Tim	R-L	6-2	190	6-12-82	.238	.139	.270	36	151	19	36	1	2	6	14	9	0	0	0	52	9	1	.391	.281
Vazquez, Kelvin	B-R	6-1	170	9-30-83	.254	.214	.265	23	63	13	16	5	0	1	4	14	2	6	1	17	4	2	.381	.400
Venable, Will	L-L	6-2	205	10-29-82	.216	.216	.216	42	139	17	30	5	2	2	14	14	2	0	1	38	2	1	.324	.295

PITCHING	B-T	HT	WT	DOB	W	L	ERA	G	GS	CG	SV	IP	H	R	ER	HR	BB	SO	AVG	vLH	vRH	K/9	BB/9
Baca, Daniel	R-R	5-10	175	10-17-85	0	1	9.53	7	0	0	0	11	17	13	12	2	4	11	.333	.263	.375	8.74	3.18
Carter, Brent	R-L	6-3	200	10-10-82	4	2	1.88	13	13	0	0	72	58	24	15	3	7	66	.221	.258	.208	8.25	0.88
De La O, Danny	L-L	6-0	185	8-25-83	0	0	16.20	4	0	0	0	3	7	6	6	2	1	4	.438	.500	.417	10.80	2.70
Delabar, Steve	R-R	6-5	220	7-17-83	4	6	4.76	16	16	0	0	76	84	45	40	7	18	59	.279	.241	.313	7.02	2.14
Fernandez, Alfredo	R-R	6-4	224	9-15-84	3	2	2.63	33	0	0	7	38	36	20	11	1	13	35	.243	.200	.273	8.36	3.11
Geer, Josh	R-R	6-3	190	6-2-83	3	1	3.69	7	6	0	0	32	35	13	13	5	4	13	.285	.304	.269	3.69	1.14
Gold, Adam	R-R	6-4	200	10-7-83	3	3	4.91	28	0	0	0	37	35	23	20	3	22	33	.259	.321	.220	8.10	5.40
Higelin, Brandon	L-L	6-0	195	4-8-83	0	2	5.00	22	0	0	0	27	40	18	15	2	11	21	.342	.343	.341	7.00	3.67
Hughey, Arnold	L-L	6-2	215	11-19-82	5	1	3.06	26	3	0	1	47	43	17	16	4	12	58	.240	.271	.225	11.11	2.30
Jamison, Neil	R-R	6-3	185	8-4-83	1	2	1.32	25	0	0	8	27	23	5	4	0	8	31	.225	.256	.203	10.21	2.63
Jimenez, Juan	R-R	6-2	180	5-18-86	0	0	0.00	1	0	0	0	1	1	0	0	0	0	0	.333	.000	.500	0.00	0.00
Jimenez, Fabian	L-L	6-2	187	8-27-86	1	3	2.22	7	6	0	0	28	31	19	7	0	12	18	.261	.074	.315	5.72	3.81
Kintzler, Brandon	R-R	6-1	180	8-1-84	0	0	0.00	3	0	0	0	3	3	0	0	0	0	1	.273	.000	.429	2.70	0.00
Krosschell, Ben	R-R	6-1	165	10-2-85	2	7	4.70	16	15	0	0	77	83	50	40	4	18	59	.272	.316	.238	6.93	2.11
Link, Jon	R-R	6-1	175	3-23-84	3	3	4.42	25	7	0	0	59	67	33	29	5	8	44	.285	.333	.248	6.71	1.22
Madden, John	R-R	6-4	225	12-2-82	2	5	3.48	38	0	0	5	41	49	27	16	1	17	55	.285	.372	.213	11.98	3.70
Polanco, Phil	R-R	6-0	200	11-10-81	1	0	2.00	6	0	0	0	9	6	3	2	0	2	5	.188	.200	.176	5.00	2.00
Ponce, William	R-R	6-2	210	2-9-84	2	1	4.15	21	0	0	0	26	30	13	12	1	15	16	.297	.213	.370	5.54	5.19
Ramos, Cesar	L-L	6-2	190	6-22-84	0	1	6.53	6	4	0	0	21	27	21	15	3	7	13	.303	.176	.333	5.66	3.05
Vandel, Geoff	L-L	6-1	190	6-9-87	0	0	0.90	2	2	0	0	10	8	1	1	0	1	11	.229	.182	.250	9.90	0.90
Varnell, Grant	R-R	6-2	215	9-27-82	0	2	3.21	8	4	0	0	28	28	10	10	3	2	24	.264	.233	.286	7.71	0.64

GAMES BY POSITION: C—Gottier 22, Hundley 40, Killian 7, Lobaton 11. **1B**—Cleland 2, Jones 71, Smith 4. **2B**—Cleland 18, Johnston 8, Richardson 10, Rivera 24, Vazquez 17. **3B**—Headley 57, Johnston 1, Steiner 14, Vazquez 6. **SS**—Johnston 35, Richardson 43. **OF**—Alley 11, Cavanaugh 36, Cleland 2, Davidson 24, Diaz 3, Guerrero 50, Sansoe 44, Smith 3, Turner 36, Venable 27.

AZL PADRES — Rookie

ARIZONA LEAGUE

BATTING	B-T	HT	WT	DOB	AVG	vLH	vRH	G	AB	R	H	2B	3B	HR	RBI	BB	HBP	SH	SF	SO	SB	CS	SLG	OBP
Aguilar, Abraham	R-R	6-2	155	9-18-84	.298	.308	.294	22	94	15	28	5	1	1	12	7	0	3	0	15	5	3	.404	.347
Blanks, Kyle	R-R	6-6	270	9-11-86	.299	.324	.291	48	164	33	49	10	1	7	30	25	10	0	1	49	3	1	.500	.420
Chang, Ray	R-R	6-1	195	8-24-83	.167	.143	.171	15	48	9	8	2	0	0	4	5	1	0	1	12	0	0	.208	.255
Cleland, Clinton	R-R	6-1	195	9-16-82	.323	.263	.338	25	93	14	30	10	0	0	8	5	2	2	2	18	0	2	.430	.363
Crafort, Willy	R-R	6-3	165	2-9-85	.248	.160	.267	38	145	19	36	10	2	2	19	8	0	2	4	52	2	0	.386	.280
Diaz, Javis	L-L	5-10	165	6-25-84	.352	.391	.344	39	145	22	51	5	6	2	24	17	3	1	2	30	19	5	.510	.425
Gill, Ray	R-R	6-3	235	11-24-82	.234	.208	.240	37	124	17	29	8	0	4	16	14	5	1	0	44	0	0	.395	.336
Gonzalez, Jarol	R-R	6-0	171	12-28-84	.233	.259	.228	42	150	19	35	5	1	0	14	4	3	4	2	33	5	2	.280	.264
Howard, Josh	L-L	5-11	180	4-6-83	.354	.333	.358	23	96	21	34	6	2	0	14	10	1	1	2	15	12	2	.458	.413
Johnston, Trey	R-R	5-11	190	7-4-85	.302	.100	.349	20	53	11	16	5	0	2	10	11	5	0	0	18	0	3	.509	.464
Killian, Billy	L-R	6-1	190	6-12-86	.287	.167	.313	32	115	6	33	8	2	0	10	3	0	0	2	28	4	1	.391	.300
Lobaton, Jose	B-R	6-0	175	10-21-84	.357	.250	.400	5	14	2	5	2	0	0	2	6	0	0	0	4	1	0	.500	.550
Parker, David	R-R	6-0	180	12-5-82	.219	.241	.214	44	160	24	35	2	1	0	15	16	6	3	0	31	5	3	.244	.313
Sanchez, Luany	R-R	6-1	180	6-18-85	.302	.325	.295	43	169	27	51	15	1	1	26	7	0	1	2	23	1	3	.420	.326
Smith, Casey	R-R	6-4	230	2-24-84	.357	.429	.343	21	84	13	30	7	0	3	18	8	0	0	1	23	1	2	.548	.409
Steiner, Chad	R-R	5-11	190	12-25-83	.277	.250	.283	35	137	21	38	7	0	0	13	5	0	1	1	23	3	0	.328	.301
Thayer, Matt	R-L	5-10	173	2-21-82	.375	.600	.000	3	8	1	3	0	0	0	1	2	1	0	0	0	1	1	.375	.545
Thomas-Dotson, Josh	L-R	6-3	230	9-30-84	.189	.231	.171	19	53	4	10	0	0	1	5	3	1	0	1	30	1	0	.245	.241
Turner, Tim	R-L	6-2	190	6-12-82	.230	.182	.247	28	126	20	29	4	3	1	11	7	1	2	0	33	5	3	.333	.276
Venable, Will	L-L	6-2	205	10-29-82	.322	.267	.341	15	59	13	19	4	2	1	12	2	4	0	0	9	4	0	.508	.385

PITCHING	B-T	HT	WT	DOB	W	L	ERA	G	GS	CG	SV	IP	H	R	ER	HR	BB	SO	AVG	vLH	vRH	K/9	BB/9
Baca, Daniel	R-R	5-10	175	10-17-85	1	2	3.54	12	0	0	0	20	21	8	8	1	3	23	.266	.269	.264	10.18	1.33
Baena, Orlando	R-R	6-1	175	12-21-85	1	0	5.56	6	0	0	0	11	11	7	7	0	8	10	.250	.313	.214	7.94	6.35
Clayton, Patrick	R-R	6-5	220	8-13-84	5	3	8.03	16	0	0	0	25	20	22	22	1	31	33	.241	.250	.236	12.04	11.31
Daigle, Richie	R-R	6-0	185	9-9-82	0	0	3.60	6	5	0	0	25	27	12	10	0	10	12	.290	.353	.254	4.32	3.60
De Montigny, Mat	R-R	6-1	170	9-22-84	0	0	0.00	1	0	0	0	1	0	0	0	0	1	0	.000	.000	.000	0.00	9.00
Decker, Chad	L-L	6-1	185	5-14-84	1	0	6.75	13	0	0	0	15	16	12	11	1	12	15	.281	.250	.293	9.20	7.36
Fogelson, Scott	L-L	6-0	220	7-1-81	1	0	3.08	5	3	1	0	26	17	12	9	2	9	21	.195	.200	.194	7.18	3.08
Frieri, Ernesto	R-R	6-2	168	7-19-85	7	1	1.17	17	5	0	0	46	21	7	6	0	29	59	.137	.143	.135	11.46	5.63
Hussey, John	R-R	6-3	172	11-22-86	1	3	6.44	9	9	0	0	36	38	30	26	2	13	31	.275	.254	.293	7.68	3.22
Javier, Alfredo	R-R	6-3	190	11-19-86	0	1	9.00	11	0	0	0	16	25	20	16	1	13	10	.362	.240	.432	5.63	7.31
Jimenez, Juan	R-R	6-2	180	5-18-86	4	4	3.86	13	13	0	0	79	95	45	34	5	18	67	.297	.248	.324	7.60	2.04
Jolliff, Dave	R-R	6-1	173	9-22-82	0	2	6.21	10	4	0	0	29	42	26	20	6	11	23	.331	.350	.322	7.14	3.41
Kintzler, Brandon	R-R	6-1	180	8-1-84	2	0	4.09	8	0	0	1	11	15	5	5	2	4	17	.306	.308	.306	13.91	3.27
Paewai, Riki	R-R	6-2	180	3-28-86	1	2	3.77	7	6	0	0	29	25	15	12	3	25	15	.258	.256	.259	4.71	7.85
Rojas, Cesar	R-R	6-3	205	7-15-86	2	4	6.75	13	11	0	0	49	48	41	37	1	32	33	.261	.333	.237	6.02	5.84
Sanchez, Julio	R-R	6-1	158	7-11-85	2	3	4.28	24	0	0	4	40	33	22	19	0	27	32	.223	.245	.212	7.20	6.08
Upwood, Jacob	L-L	5-11	175	9-19-80	0	0	2.45	4	0	0	0	4	2	1	1	0	1	1	.154	.000	.200	2.45	2.45
Vandel, Geoff	L-L	6-1	190	6-9-87	1	1	0.43	11	0	0	1	21	12	2	1	0	5	32	.164	.118	.179	13.71	2.14
Varnell, Grant	R-R	6-2	215	9-27-82	0	1	3.12	14	0	0	3	26	31	13	9	2	2	26	.295	.361	.261	9.00	0.69

GAMES BY POSITION: C—Johnston 8, Killian 24, Lobaton 3, Sanchez 32. **1B**—Blanks 40, Gill 18, Sanchez 3, Smith 2, Steiner 1. **2B**—Aguilar 10, Chang 3, Cleland 3, Parker 42. **3B**—Aguilar 1, Cleland 17, Johnston 7, Steiner 33. **SS**—Aguilar 11, Chang 11, Cleland 2, Gonzalez 36. **OF**—Blanks 2, Crafort 38, Diaz 38, Gill 14, Howard 23, Smith 11, Steiner 1, Thayer 3, Thomas-Dotson 5, Turner 28, Venable 15.

SAN FRANCISCO GIANTS

BY ANDY BAGGARLY

The Giants began the 2005 season with high expectations after adding free agents Mike Matheny, Omar Vizquel, Armando Benitez and Moises Alou to an already seasoned and experienced roster that narrowly missed the playoffs the previous season.

But Barry Bonds wasn't healthy enough to play until Sept. 12, and his supporting cast couldn't contend despite competing in one of the weakest divisions in baseball history.

Bonds had three surgeries on his right knee from Jan. 31 to May 2, the final one to flush out a post-operative bacterial infection. When he was medically cleared to return in mid-September, he did so without a rehab assignment and nearly a year had elapsed since he saw his last competitive pitch.

Bonds, who turned 41 in July, hit five home runs in 42 at-bats to give him 708 in his career, six away from tying Babe Ruth for second place on the all-time list. The Giants were 6-3 in the nine games that Bonds and Moises Alou appeared in the lineup together, helping the club make a late if improbable push for the division title despite a record not fit for a contender.

But injuries to Alou and Benitez, coupled with a vastly overrated rotation, put the Giants in too deep of a midsummer hole. They finished with a 75-87 record, their first sub-.500 season since 1996—the year before Brian Sabean took over as general manager.

The Giants had one of the oldest opening-day lineups in history, but by the end, they had used 16 rookies—the most since '96. The overhaul was predictably rough on the clubhouse, as veterans Kirk Rueter, Marquis Grissom, Jim Brower and Matt Herges were designated for assignment or released. Of the 25 players on the opening day roster, 10 did not survive the season. Among those, only Tony Torcato remained in the organization.

"I'm embarrassed we had to do it," Sabean said. "The blame starts with me. We made choices and they obviously didn't turn out."

The four free-agent signings weren't among them.

Sabean's folly was relying too heavily on incumbent starting pitchers. Jason Schmidt struggled to pitch with reduced velocity the first two months and the rest of the staff crumbled around him.

"I think we all over-evaluated our starting staff," Sabean said. "Having said that, I've got to be realistic, they were under a tremendous amount of pressure when they lost (Armando) Benitez and Barry. We just weren't able to be strong enough when Barry went down. We were challenged against righthanded pitching because we were so deficient."

Yet there were some emerging positives, some of which gave the Giants hope for 2006.

Sabean thought he added a nice, complementary player July 30 when he acquired Randy Winn from Seattle for Yorvit Torrealba and Jesse Foppert. But Winn turned out to be far more than that. The switch-hitting center fielder hit .359 with 23 doubles, five triples, 14 home runs and 26 RBIs over 58 games as a Giant.

The Giants also found a few more talents within their system, none brighter than Matt Cain. The righthander made his big league debut as a 20-year-old on Aug. 28 and went 2-1, 2.33 ERA in seven starts.

The youth movement wasn't by design. Sabean is well known for eschewing young players in favor of veterans. Yet the GM said he might have learned a lesson after watching the club improve in the second half.

"We did get better with the turnover and our play improved in a lot of ways," Sabean said. "All other things being equal, sometimes you have to lean on a kid."

The kids played well on nearly all levels. Despite lacking a draft pick until the fourth round, the Giants' Rookie-level Arizona League club won its second straight title. San Jose also won the high Class A California League title, and the Giants' aggregate minor league record of 385-309 (.554) was the second best among the 30 franchises.

PLAYERS OF THE YEAR

MAJOR LEAGUE: Randy Winn, of

Winn was one of the catalysts of the Giants' late-season run at the National League West title, as he batted .359-14-26 over the last 58 games after coming over from the Mariners in trade for Yorvit Torrealba and Jesse Foppert. Winn was brilliant in September, batting .447 with 11 homers.

MINOR LEAGUE: Kevin Frandsen, 2b/ss

BILL MITCHELL

Frandsen, a 12th-round pick out of San Jose State in 2004, had a breakout season in 2005. He started the year at high Class A San Jose, represented the organization at the Futures Game, and then earned promotions to Double-A Norwich and Triple-A Fresno. Overall, he hit .335-6-76.

ORGANIZATION LEADERS

BATTING		
***AVG**	Horwitz, Brian, Augusta/San Jose	.349
R	Frandsen, Kevin, Fresno/Norwich/San Jose	97
H	Frandsen, Kevin, Fresno/Norwich/San Jose	172
TB	Schierholtz, Nate, San Jose	258
2B	Martinez-Esteve, Eddy, San Jose	44
3B	Timpner, Clay, San Jose	12
HR	Linden, Todd, Fresno	30
RBI	Cervenak, Mike, Fresno	103
BB	Martinez-Esteve, Eddy, San Jose	89
SO	Schierholtz, Nate, San Jose	132
SB	Sanders, Marcus, Augusta	57
***OBP**	Linden, Todd, Fresno	.437
***SLG**	Linden, Todd, Fresno	.682
PITCHING		
W	Three tied at	12
L	Misch, Pat, Fresno/Norwich	11
#ERA	Bateman, Joe, Fresno/San Jose	1.57
G	Villafuerte, Brandon, Fresno	57
CG	Misch, Pat, Fresno/Norwich	2
	Sack, Darren, Augusta	2
SV	Bateman, Joe, Fresno/San Jose	21
	Wilson, Brian, Augusta/Fresno/Norwich	21
IP	Broshuis, Garrett, Fresno/San Jose	163
	Misch, Pat, Fresno/Norwich	163
BB	Cain, Matt, Fresno	73
SO	Cain, Matt, Fresno	176

*Minimum 250 at-bats. #Minimum 75 innings.

SAN FRANCISCO GIANTS

Manager: Felipe Alou.

2005 Record: 75-87, .463 (3rd, NL West).

BATTING	B-T	HT	WT	DOB	AVG	vLH	vRH	G	AB	R	H	2B	3B	HR	RBI	BB	HBP	SH	SF	SO	SB	CS	SLG	OBP
Alfonzo, Edgardo	R-R	5-11	210	11-8-73	.277	.267	.281	109	368	36	102	17	1	2	43	27	2	1	4	34	2	0	.345	.327
Alou, Moises	R-R	6-3	220	7-3-66	.321	.372	.306	123	427	67	137	21	3	19	63	56	3	0	4	43	5	1	.518	.400
Bonds, Barry	L-L	6-2	230	7-24-64	.286	.600	.243	14	42	8	12	1	0	5	10	9	0	0	1	6	0	0	.667	.404
Chavez, Angel	R-R	6-1	195	7-22-81	.263	.000	.294	10	19	1	5	1	0	0	1	0	0	1	0	3	0	0	.316	.263
Clark, Doug	L-R	6-2	205	3-5-76	.000	.000	.000	8	5	2	0	0	0	0	0	1	0	0	0	2	0	0	.000	.167
Cruz, Deivi	R-R	6-0	200	11-6-72	.268	.314	.236	81	209	26	56	10	1	5	19	10	0	2	0	31	0	1	.397	.301
Dallimore, Brian	R-R	6-1	205	11-15-73	.143	.167	.000	7	7	1	1	1	0	0	0	0	0	0	0	0	0	0	.286	.143
Durham, Ray	B-R	5-8	195	11-30-71	.290	.290	.290	142	497	67	144	33	0	12	62	48	7	1	7	59	6	3	.429	.356
Ellison, Jason	R-R	5-10	180	4-4-78	.264	.328	.232	131	352	49	93	18	2	4	24	24	3	6	1	44	14	6	.361	.316
Feliz, Pedro	R-R	6-1	210	4-27-75	.250	.271	.243	156	569	69	142	30	4	20	81	38	1	1	6	102	0	2	.422	.295
Grissom, Marquis	R-R	5-11	210	4-17-67	.212	.217	.209	44	137	8	29	4	0	2	15	7	0	2	1	18	1	1	.285	.248
Haad, Yamid	R-R	6-2	215	9-2-77	.071	.000	.074	17	28	0	2	1	0	0	1	3	0	0	1	7	0	0	.107	.156
Knoedler, Justin	R-R	6-2	215	7-17-80	.100	.000	.111	8	10	0	1	0	0	0	0	0	1	0	0	1	0	0	.100	.182
Linden, Todd	B-R	6-3	230	6-30-80	.216	.300	.199	60	171	20	37	8	0	4	13	10	5	1	0	54	3	0	.333	.280
Matheny, Mike	R-R	6-3	220	9-22-70	.242	.269	.233	134	443	42	107	34	0	13	59	29	6	3	4	91	0	2	.406	.295
Niekro, Lance	R-R	6-3	215	1-29-79	.252	.324	.206	113	278	32	70	16	3	12	46	17	2	0	5	53	0	2	.460	.295
Ortmeier, Dan	B-R	6-4	220	5-11-81	.136	.000	.136	15	22	1	3	0	0	0	1	3	1	0	0	5	1	0	.136	.269
Ramirez, Julio	R-R	5-11	195	8-10-77	.250	1.000	.000	12	4	3	1	0	0	0	1	0	0	0	0	1	0	0	.250	.250
Sanchez, Alex	L-L	5-10	180	8-26-76	.256	.333	.235	19	43	4	11	3	0	0	3	1	1	2	0	9	2	2	.326	.289
Shabala, Adam	L-R	6-1	190	2-6-78	.200	.333	.167	6	15	1	3	0	0	0	4	1	0	1	1	5	0	0	.200	.235
Snow, J.T.	L-L	6-2	210	2-26-68	.275	.243	.279	117	367	40	101	17	2	4	40	32	7	2	2	61	1	0	.365	.343
Torcato, Tony	L-R	6-1	220	10-25-79	.273	.000	.300	11	11	1	3	0	0	0	0	1	0	0	0	2	0	0	.273	.333
Torrealba, Yorvit	R-R	5-11	200	7-19-78	.226	.480	.132	34	93	18	21	8	0	1	7	9	1	2	0	25	1	0	.344	.301
Tucker, Michael	L-R	6-2	210	6-25-71	.240	.125	.257	104	250	32	60	16	1	5	33	28	2	2	4	48	4	0	.372	.317
Vizquel, Omar	B-R	5-9	185	4-24-67	.271	.253	.277	152	568	66	154	28	4	3	45	56	5	20	2	58	24	10	.350	.341
Winn, Randy	B-R	6-2	195	6-9-74	.359	.367	.358	58	231	39	83	22	5	14	26	11	1	4	0	38	7	5	.680	.391

PITCHING	B-T	HT	WT	DOB	W	L	ERA	G	GS	CG	SV	IP	H	R	ER	HR	BB	SO	AVG	vLH	vRH	K/9	BB/9
Accardo, Jeremy	R-R	6-2	190	12-18-81	1	5	3.94	28	0	0	0	30	26	13	13	2	9	16	.232	.182	.265	4.85	2.73
Benitez, Armando	R-R	6-4	245	11-3-72	2	3	4.50	30	0	0	19	30	25	17	15	5	16	23	.229	.212	.246	6.90	4.80
Brower, Jim	R-R	6-3	215	12-29-72	2	1	6.53	32	0	0	1	30	40	22	22	5	15	25	.320	.327	.315	7.42	4.45
Cain, Matt	R-R	6-3	230	10-1-84	2	1	2.33	7	7	1	0	46	24	12	12	4	19	30	.151	.160	.143	5.83	3.69
Christiansen, Jason	R-L	6-5	230	9-21-69	6	1	5.36	56	0	0	0	42	48	27	25	4	15	17	.286	.253	.315	3.64	3.21
Cooper, Brian	R-R	6-1	195	8-19-74	0	1	3.06	8	1	0	0	18	15	6	6	0	8	7	.234	.190	.256	3.57	4.08
Correia, Kevin	R-R	6-3	210	8-24-80	2	5	4.63	16	11	0	0	58	61	31	30	12	31	44	.274	.311	.242	6.79	4.78
Eyre, Scott	L-L	6-1	215	5-30-72	2	2	2.63	86	0	0	0	68	48	21	20	3	26	65	.200	.182	.213	8.56	3.42
Fassero, Jeff	L-L	6-1	200	1-5-63	4	7	4.05	48	6	0	0	91	92	48	41	7	31	60	.268	.194	.296	5.93	3.07
Foppert, Jesse	R-R	6-6	220	7-10-80	0	0	5.23	3	2	0	0	10	11	7	6	2	13	6	.297	.200	.364	5.23	11.32
Hawkins, LaTroy	R-R	6-5	215	12-21-72	1	4	4.10	45	0	0	2	37	40	18	17	3	17	30	.272	.239	.303	7.23	4.10
2-team (21 Chicago)					2	8	3.83	66	0	0	6	56	58	27	24	7	24	43	.265	.228	.297	6.87	3.83
Hennessey, Brad	R-R	6-2	195	2-7-80	5	8	4.64	21	21	0	0	118	127	63	61	15	52	64	.276	.320	.244	4.87	3.95
Herges, Matt	L-R	6-0	210	4-1-70	1	1	4.71	21	0	0	0	21	23	11	11	2	7	6	.288	.259	.302	2.57	3.00
Kinney, Matt	R-R	6-5	215	12-16-76	2	0	6.00	5	1	0	0	12	18	8	8	2	6	3	.383	.471	.333	2.25	4.50
Levine, Al	L-R	6-3	190	5-22-68	0	0	9.58	9	0	0	0	10	16	11	11	2	4	4	.340	.417	.261	3.48	3.48
Lowry, Noah	R-L	6-2	210	10-10-80	13	13	3.78	33	33	0	0	205	193	92	86	21	76	172	.249	.213	.259	7.56	3.34
Munter, Scott	R-R	6-6	240	3-7-80	2	0	2.56	45	0	0	0	39	40	15	11	1	12	11	.280	.353	.239	2.56	2.79
Puffer, Brandon	R-R	6-3	190	10-5-75	0	0	10.29	3	0	0	0	7	9	8	8	2	2	1	.310	.250	.353	1.29	2.57
Rueter, Kirk	L-L	6-2	210	12-1-70	2	7	5.95	20	18	0	0	107	131	78	71	12	47	25	.305	.286	.311	2.10	3.94
Schmidt, Jason	R-R	6-5	215	1-29-73	12	7	4.40	29	29	0	0	172	160	90	84	16	85	165	.246	.264	.223	8.63	4.45
Taschner, Jack	L-L	6-3	205	4-21-78	2	0	1.59	24	0	0	0	23	15	5	4	0	13	19	.185	.265	.128	7.54	5.16
Tomko, Brett	R-R	6-4	225	4-7-73	8	15	4.48	33	30	3	1	191	205	99	95	20	57	114	.274	.282	.264	5.38	2.69
Walker, Tyler	R-R	6-3	240	5-15-76	6	4	4.23	67	0	0	23	62	68	31	29	9	27	54	.281	.284	.278	7.88	3.94
Williams, Jerome	R-R	6-3	245	12-4-81	0	2	6.48	4	3	0	0	17	21	12	12	2	4	11	.313	.385	.268	5.94	2.16

FIELDING

Catcher	PCT	G	PO	A	E	DP	PB
Haad	.957	16	61	6	3	1	0
Knoedler	1.000	4	8	1	0	0	0
Matheny	.999	132	784	77	1	13	4
Torrealba	1.000	27	147	16	0	1	1

First Base	PCT	G	PO	A	E	DP
Feliz	.988	15	76	7	1	7
Niekro	.991	74	544	38	5	56
Snow	.997	108	814	57	3	62

Second Base	PCT	G	PO	A	E	DP
Alfonzo	1.000	2	4	4	0	2
Chavez	1.000	5	3	4	0	0
Cruz	.985	33	54	76	2	22
Dallimore	1.000	2	0	6	0	3
Durham	.982	133	249	341	11	82

Third Base	PCT	G	PO	A	E	DP
Alfonzo	.967	97	76	158	8	10
Chavez	.000	1	0	0	0	0
Cruz	1.000	5	1	11	0	0
Feliz	.969	79	47	143	6	17

Shortstop	PCT	G	PO	A	E	DP
Chavez	.917	4	6	5	1	2
Cruz	.986	16	22	48	1	13
Dallimore	.000	1	0	0	0	0
Vizquel	.988	150	234	426	8	81

Outfield	PCT	G	PO	A	E	DP
Alou	.966	117	222	5	8	3
Bonds	1.000	13	18	0	0	0
Durham	.000	1	0	0	0	0
Ellison	.968	122	235	5	8	1
Feliz	.979	75	138	0	3	0
Grissom	.986	36	69	0	1	0
Linden	.983	52	114	0	2	0
Ortmeier	1.000	7	13	0	0	0
Ramirez	1.000	6	3	0	0	0
Sanchez	.870	10	19	1	3	0
Shabala	.875	5	7	0	1	0
Torcato	1.000	1	1	0	0	0
Tucker	.983	72	109	6	2	1
Winn	.994	55	165	1	1	1

FARM SYSTEM

General Manager: Brian Sabean. **Director, Player Development:** Jack Hiatt. **Scouting Director:** Dick Tidrow.

Class	Farm Team	League	W	L	Pct.	Finish*	Manager	Affiliate Since
AAA	Fresno (Calif.) Grizzlies	Pacific Coast	68	76	.472	t-11th (16)	Shane Turner	1998
AA	Norwich (Conn.) Navigators	Eastern	71	71	.500	6th (12)	Dave Machemer	2003
High A	San Jose (Calif.) Giants	California	85	55	.607	**+1st (10)**	Lenn Sakata	1988
Low A	Augusta (Ga.) GreenJackets	South Atlantic	77	59	.566	3rd (16)	Roberto Kelly	2005
SS A	Salem-Keizer (Ore.) Volcanoes	Northwest	45	31	.592	2nd (8)	Steve Decker	1997
Rookie	Scottsdale (Ariz.) Giants	Arizona	39	17	.696	**+1st (9)**	Bert Hunter	2000

*Finish in overall standings (No. of teams in league)/Playoff teams in **boldface** +League champion

FRESNO GRIZZLIES — Class AAA

PACIFIC COAST LEAGUE

BATTING	B-T	HT	WT	DOB	AVG	vLH	vRH	G	AB	R	H	2B	3B	HR	RBI	BB	HBP	SH	SF	SO	SB	CS	SLG	OBP
Alfonzo, Edgardo	R-R	5-11	210	11-8-73	.467	.625	.286	4	15	2	7	2	0	0	1	0	0	0	0	0	0	0	.600	.467
Alfonzo, Eliezer	R-R	6-0	225	2-7-79	.286	.000	.364	4	14	3	4	1	0	1	3	1	1	0	0	2	0	0	.571	.375
Athas, Jamie	L-R	6-2	190	10-14-79	.211	.000	.216	35	76	7	16	1	0	3	10	6	0	1	1	18	0	2	.342	.265
Cervenak, Mike	R-R	5-11	200	8-17-76	.312	.339	.303	127	494	68	154	29	3	19	103	38	10	0	5	61	5	0	.498	.369
Chavez, Angel	R-R	6-1	195	7-22-81	.281	.299	.275	89	334	46	94	17	3	11	64	17	3	5	2	59	5	1	.449	.320
Clark, Doug	L-R	6-2	205	3-5-76	.316	.217	.339	127	472	81	149	30	5	13	59	35	5	3	3	87	29	12	.483	.367
Dallimore, Brian	R-R	6-1	205	11-15-73	.302	.299	.302	100	398	67	120	26	2	8	45	32	12	1	2	43	7	2	.437	.369
DeVore, Doug	L-L	6-4	225	12-14-77	.299	.244	.314	65	201	34	60	13	1	11	35	20	2	0	4	51	1	1	.537	.361
2-team (44 Tucson)					.294	.227	.313	109	350	59	103	22	2	18	67	33	2	0	5	85	4	2	.523	.354
Ellison, Jason	R-R	5-10	180	4-4-78	.237	.571	.161	8	38	5	9	2	0	0	3	2	1	0	0	9	0	0	.289	.293
Frandsen, Kevin	R-R	6-0	175	5-24-82	.351	.200	.392	20	94	18	33	10	1	2	16	2	2	0	0	5	1	1	.543	.378
Grissom, Marquis	R-R	5-11	210	4-17-67	.200	.000	.273	4	15	4	3	0	0	1	2	0	0	0	0	3	0	0	.400	.200
Haad, Yamid	R-R	6-2	215	9-2-77	.282	.327	.268	63	216	23	61	13	1	10	34	8	2	2	3	32	2	0	.491	.310
Hansen, Jed	R-R	6-1	190	8-19-72	.250	.301	.228	71	240	49	60	16	2	8	30	22	6	1	3	62	8	2	.433	.325
Knoedler, Justin	R-R	6-2	215	7-17-80	.272	.302	.263	85	287	35	78	19	1	4	32	26	7	5	2	61	5	5	.387	.345
Linden, Todd	B-R	6-3	230	6-30-80	.321	.398	.294	95	340	81	109	25	4	30	80	62	10	1	2	97	6	2	.682	.437
Lopez, Mickey	B-R	5-9	170	11-17-73	.286	.344	.262	113	423	65	121	24	9	6	42	32	12	4	7	65	18	9	.428	.348
Mendez, Donaldo	R-R	6-1	190	6-7-78	.257	.333	.241	18	70	7	18	3	0	1	4	2	1	0	0	23	0	0	.343	.288
Munhall, Brian	R-R	6-0	192	6-17-80	.264	.125	.289	19	53	8	14	4	0	1	6	4	1	3	0	12	0	0	.396	.328
Niekro, Lance	R-R	6-3	215	1-29-79	.250	.000	.333	1	4	0	1	0	0	0	0	0	0	0	0	1	0	0	.250	.250
Ramirez, Julio	R-R	5-11	195	8-10-77	.241	.301	.216	113	386	57	93	13	1	23	60	22	3	3	2	113	22	8	.459	.286
Sanchez, Alex	L-L	5-10	180	8-26-76	.111	.000	.111	2	9	0	1	0	0	0	1	0	0	0	0	0	0	1	.111	.111
Shabala, Adam	L-R	6-1	190	2-6-78	.273	.281	.271	95	373	58	102	24	1	14	42	35	4	3	1	73	10	2	.456	.341
Swanson, Brent	L-R	5-11	190	9-11-80	.000	.000	.000	6	3	1	0	0	0	0	0	2	1	0	0	1	0	0	.000	.500
Torcato, Tony	L-R	6-1	220	10-25-79	.269	.250	.274	105	376	41	101	15	5	10	57	21	4	1	5	43	3	4	.415	.310

PITCHING	B-T	HT	WT	DOB	W	L	ERA	G	GS	CG	SV	IP	H	R	ER	HR	BB	SO	AVG	vLH	vRH	K/9	BB/9
Accardo, Jeremy	R-R	6-2	190	12-18-81	2	0	1.95	25	0	0	3	32	25	7	7	0	10	30	.214	.204	.221	8.35	2.78
Almanza, Armando	L-L	6-3	230	10-26-72	0	1	13.50	2	0	0	0	3	5	5	5	1	2	3	.385	.500	.333	8.10	5.40
Anderson, Luke	R-R	6-5	210	4-9-78	0	0	10.29	6	0	0	0	7	11	8	8	2	4	7	.355	.273	.400	9.00	5.14
Bergman, Dusty	L-L	6-5	200	2-1-78	0	0	18.00	3	0	0	0	3	8	6	6	0	3	4	.500	.375	.625	12.00	9.00
2-team (44 Salt Lake)					8	5	3.77	47	0	0	8	74	85	31	31	10	21	59	.287	.333	.264	7.18	2.55
Broshuis, Garrett	R-R	6-2	185	12-18-81	0	1	5.25	2	2	0	0	12	17	9	7	1	2	2	.347	.375	.294	1.50	1.50
Cain, Matt	R-R	6-3	230	10-1-84	10	5	4.39	26	26	1	0	146	118	77	71	22	73	176	.218	.210	.225	10.87	4.51
Cooper, Brian	R-R	6-1	195	8-19-74	7	8	4.53	29	21	0	0	137	139	72	69	23	54	82	.270	.267	.272	5.39	3.55
Correia, Kevin	R-R	6-3	210	8-24-80	3	2	6.07	31	3	0	7	46	50	38	31	6	23	35	.273	.301	.250	6.85	4.50
Espineli, Eugene	L-L	6-4	195	9-8-82	1	1	6.38	12	0	0	0	18	22	13	13	3	8	12	.306	.258	.341	5.89	3.93
Fikac, Jeremy	R-R	6-2	200	4-8-75	4	10	4.42	50	6	0	1	100	112	57	49	17	35	86	.279	.250	.305	7.77	3.16
Foppert, Jesse	R-R	6-6	220	7-10-80	3	1	4.50	10	9	0	0	44	43	25	22	5	27	41	.250	.190	.301	8.39	5.52
Hawkins, LaTroy	R-R	6-5	215	12-21-72	0	0	0.00	2	0	0	0	2	2	0	0	0	0	1	.250	.500	.000	4.50	0.00
Hennessey, Brad	R-R	6-2	195	2-7-80	4	2	5.19	11	11	0	0	68	75	40	39	7	22	46	.279	.290	.272	6.12	2.93
Kinney, Matt	R-R	6-5	215	12-16-76	7	8	5.21	19	19	1	0	114	117	68	66	18	45	110	.271	.299	.244	8.68	3.55
Lee, David	R-R	6-1	200	3-12-73	0	2	9.58	8	0	0	0	10	16	14	11	3	4	7	.348	.286	.400	6.10	3.48
Levine, Al	L-R	6-3	190	5-22-68	0	0	2.84	9	0	0	1	13	12	5	4	0	7	6	.267	.500	.161	4.26	4.97
Misch, Pat	R-L	6-2	195	8-18-81	3	9	6.35	19	19	1	0	102	135	80	72	18	40	69	.325	.333	.323	6.09	3.53
Munter, Scott	R-R	6-6	240	3-7-80	1	3	5.11	12	0	0	0	12	17	8	7	0	4	5	.362	.333	.379	3.65	2.92
Petersen, Jeff	R-R	6-4	225	10-16-81	0	0	0.00	2	0	0	0	3	0	0	0	0	0	1	.000	.000	.000	3.00	0.00
Puffer, Brandon	R-R	6-3	190	10-5-75	6	5	5.52	54	0	0	0	73	85	54	45	9	23	48	.296	.282	.308	5.89	2.82
Randolph, Stephen	L-L	6-3	200	5-1-74	1	1	3.40	22	2	0	0	40	23	18	15	4	35	50	.169	.164	.173	11.34	7.94
Reina, Jesus	L-L	6-2	175	4-20-84	0	0	6.23	1	1	0	0	4	3	3	3	0	6	3	.200	.286	.125	6.23	12.46
Song, Seung	R-R	6-1	190	6-29-80	2	4	4.42	10	10	0	0	55	50	32	27	6	36	37	.244	.221	.267	6.05	5.89
Spiehs, R.D.	R-R	6-3	224	10-18-79	0	0	5.87	10	0	0	1	15	17	10	10	0	10	11	.274	.297	.240	6.46	5.87
2-team (12 Portland)					1	1	5.28	22	0	0	2	31	32	19	18	4	19	22	.267	.241	.290	6.46	5.58
Taschner, Jack	L-L	6-3	205	4-21-78	3	0	1.64	44	0	0	10	49	30	9	9	3	24	62	.173	.230	.143	11.31	4.38
Villafuerte, Brandon	R-R	5-11	195	12-17-75	6	3	3.91	57	0	0	3	76	83	38	33	5	32	57	.284	.304	.264	6.75	3.79
Williams, Jerome	R-R	6-3	245	12-4-81	1	4	9.39	6	6	0	0	31	47	34	32	3	17	15	.364	.260	.430	4.40	4.99
Wilson, Brian	R-R	6-1	205	3-16-82	1	1	3.97	9	0	0	0	11	8	7	5	0	8	13	.190	.182	.200	10.32	6.35
Wylie, Mitch	R-R	6-3	190	1-14-77	3	5	4.50	22	9	0	2	66	68	36	33	6	15	58	.261	.209	.320	7.91	2.05

FIELDING

Catcher	PCT	G	PO	A	E	DP	PB
Alfonzo	1.000	4	26	1	0	0	0
Haad	.991	57	429	22	4	3	5
Knoedler	.994	80	568	50	4	6	7
Munhall	1.000	12	91	6	0	1	1

First Base	PCT	G	PO	A	E	DP
Cervenak	.993	75	533	39	4	64
Dallimore	1.000	1	1	0	0	0
Haad	1.000	1	2	0	0	0
Hansen	1.000	1	1	0	0	0
Munhall	.500	1	0	1	1	0
Niekro	1.000	1	5	0	0	2
Torcato	.994	76	554	62	4	53

Second Base	PCT	G	PO	A	E	DP
Athas	1.000	5	7	9	0	3
Chavez	1.000	11	21	40	0	9
Dallimore	1.000	43	99	104	0	26
Frandsen	.940	20	36	58	6	13
Hansen	.667	1	1	1	1	1
Lopez	.970	75	155	198	11	51

Third Base	PCT	G	PO	A	E	DP
Alfonzo	1.000	2	2	2	0	0
Cervenak	.925	50	37	74	9	7
Chavez	.000	1	0	0	1	0
Dallimore	.929	49	35	83	9	7
Hansen	.962	39	20	56	3	4
Lopez	.893	16	7	18	3	1

Shortstop	PCT	G	PO	A	E	DP
Athas	.923	22	19	53	6	15
Chavez	.967	77	115	177	10	51
Dallimore	.915	10	20	23	4	6
Hansen	.925	10	16	21	3	6
Lopez	.919	19	21	47	6	10
Mendez	.882	17	21	39	8	9

Outfield	PCT	G	PO	A	E	DP
Clark	.992	103	241	8	2	2
DeVore	.985	41	64	3	1	0
Ellison	1.000	8	27	1	0	1
Grissom	1.000	3	8	0	0	0
Hansen	1.000	9	16	0	0	0
Linden	.977	87	168	5	4	1
Ramirez	.987	103	220	8	3	2
Sanchez	1.000	2	3	0	0	0
Shabala	.989	84	182	5	2	2
Torcato	.923	15	24	0	2	0

NORWICH NAVIGATORS — Class AA

EASTERN LEAGUE

BATTING	B-T	HT	WT	DOB	AVG	vLH	vRH	G	AB	R	H	2B	3B	HR	RBI	BB	HBP	SH	SF	SO	SB	CS	SLG	OBP
Alfonzo, Eliezer	R-R	6-0	225	2-7-79	.313	.377	.278	49	176	30	55	9	0	9	31	8	4	0	1	39	1	0	.517	.354
Athas, Jamie	L-R	6-2	190	10-14-79	.262	.343	.236	45	141	19	37	6	2	2	8	10	1	4	1	34	7	0	.376	.314
Benavidez, Julian	R-R	6-2	218	4-14-82	.146	.080	.167	38	103	8	15	3	0	5	13	4	1	0	0	35	0	1	.320	.185
Buscher, Brian	L-R	6-0	200	4-18-81	.228	.282	.216	64	215	19	49	8	1	1	23	20	6	0	6	36	5	3	.288	.304
Cordido, Julio	R-R	6-1	220	7-30-80	.210	.204	.213	101	272	35	57	9	0	6	29	17	4	6	3	53	3	2	.309	.264
Curry, Chris	R-R	6-1	203	11-17-77	.219	.236	.212	72	228	31	50	12	0	9	26	10	4	6	0	57	1	1	.390	.264
Frandsen, Kevin	R-R	6-0	175	5-24-82	.287	.350	.258	33	129	22	37	8	0	2	20	4	6	2	1	14	7	3	.395	.336
Holm, Stephen	R-R	6-0	206	10-21-79	.217	.375	.133	11	23	4	5	1	0	0	2	4	2	2	0	7	1	0	.261	.379
Hutting, Tim	R-R	6-0	190	10-29-81	.259	.165	.297	111	320	54	83	17	2	2	27	41	10	14	1	68	9	3	.344	.360
Knoedler, Justin	R-R	6-2	215	7-17-80	.300	.000	.429	4	10	2	3	0	0	0	0	2	0	1	0	0	2	1	.300	.417
LaBarbera, Anthony	R-R	5-10	190	3-17-80	.265	.222	.280	135	472	47	125	20	0	4	61	47	7	4	3	65	14	10	.333	.338
Lewis, Fred	L-R	6-2	190	12-9-80	.273	.234	.288	137	512	79	140	28	7	7	47	69	3	6	4	124	30	13	.396	.361
Lunsford, Trey	R-R	6-1	210	5-25-79	.171	.188	.165	36	111	8	19	1	0	1	11	10	0	2	1	20	0	1	.207	.238
Ortmeier, Dan	B-R	6-4	220	5-11-81	.274	.322	.255	135	503	85	138	23	6	20	79	48	21	0	3	115	35	12	.463	.360
Rodriguez, Guillermo	R-R	5-11	195	5-15-78	.267	.000	.286	6	15	1	4	1	0	0	1	3	1	0	1	4	0	0	.333	.400
Trumble, Dan	R-R	6-2	219	9-29-79	.216	.333	.179	21	37	6	8	3	0	1	3	9	0	1	0	11	1	0	.378	.370
Valderrama, Carlos	R-R	5-11	195	11-30-77	.294	.336	.278	130	493	61	145	33	3	8	58	34	6	2	4	84	29	7	.422	.345
Vericker, Brad	L-L	6-2	210	5-8-81	.270	.273	.270	30	74	7	20	2	0	0	8	6	1	0	0	19	0	0	.297	.333
Von Schell, Tyler	R-R	6-3	229	7-7-79	.240	.263	.231	134	512	52	123	24	1	14	75	29	6	2	6	131	5	4	.373	.286
Walter, Randy	R-R	6-1	212	4-14-81	.281	.253	.295	83	228	38	64	13	2	5	31	19	1	1	1	58	10	6	.421	.337

PITCHING	B-T	HT	WT	DOB	W	L	ERA	G	GS	CG	SV	IP	H	R	ER	HR	BB	SO	AVG	vLH	vRH	K/9	BB/9
Aardsma, David	R-R	6-5	200	12-27-81	6	2	2.93	9	8	0	0	46	44	17	15	2	13	30	.256	.273	.245	5.87	2.54
Accardo, Jeremy	R-R	6-2	190	12-18-81	1	0	0.93	8	0	0	4	10	8	3	1	0	1	15	.211	.200	.217	13.97	0.93
Anderson, Luke	R-R	6-5	210	4-9-78	0	2	7.24	8	0	0	0	14	18	11	11	4	2	14	.321	.286	.343	9.22	1.32
Begg, Chris	R-R	6-4	195	9-12-79	8	7	3.07	23	21	0	0	138	142	57	47	9	23	86	.265	.332	.214	5.61	1.50
Burres, Brian	L-L	6-1	180	4-8-81	9	6	4.20	26	24	0	0	129	130	66	60	13	57	105	.264	.294	.253	7.34	3.99
Chiasson, Scott	R-R	6-3	205	8-14-77	0	0	5.68	15	0	0	0	19	15	12	12	1	13	25	.217	.194	.237	11.84	6.16
Garcia, James	R-R	6-2	210	2-3-80	6	7	4.93	32	15	0	0	95	112	56	52	20	35	74	.292	.295	.289	7.01	3.32
Mazone, Brian	L-L	6-4	205	7-26-76	11	8	3.10	30	20	0	1	128	122	52	44	9	34	89	.258	.250	.262	6.27	2.40
Mercado, Arnoldo	R-R	6-1	168	12-28-81	0	0	7.20	4	0	0	0	5	9	4	4	1	1	5	.429	.500	.385	9.00	1.80
Misch, Pat	R-L	6-2	195	8-18-81	4	2	3.52	9	9	1	0	61	63	25	24	7	7	43	.270	.296	.259	6.31	1.03
Montero, Oscar	R-R	6-2	175	5-9-78	5	4	3.88	36	0	0	0	51	45	23	22	7	28	62	.241	.299	.200	10.94	4.94
Montes, Alberto	R-R	6-2	198	12-11-79	0	2	7.36	23	0	0	0	37	54	30	30	6	9	26	.355	.392	.337	6.38	2.21
Moreno, Anthony	R-R	5-11	198	5-4-83	2	4	5.01	18	7	0	0	50	59	37	28	4	22	33	.291	.219	.355	5.90	3.93
Palmer, Matt	R-R	6-2	224	3-21-79	0	1	2.67	11	2	0	1	27	22	14	8	2	9	20	.212	.240	.185	6.67	3.00
Pannone, Anthony	R-R	6-3	212	7-7-81	1	2	5.70	24	1	0	1	36	41	28	23	2	23	17	.287	.308	.275	4.21	5.70
Sadler, Billy	R-R	6-0	190	9-21-81	6	5	3.31	47	0	0	5	84	64	34	31	4	33	81	.208	.146	.257	8.64	3.52
Simon, Alfredo	R-R	6-4	230	5-8-81	3	8	5.03	43	9	0	19	91	104	54	51	6	24	60	.293	.340	.259	5.91	2.36
Song, Seung	R-R	6-1	190	6-29-80	3	2	2.48	6	6	0	0	36	34	10	10	4	7	29	.246	.250	.241	7.18	1.73
Threets, Erick	L-L	6-5	240	11-4-81	1	2	5.06	30	0	0	2	43	43	28	24	2	31	35	.259	.185	.295	7.38	6.54
Valdez, Merkin	R-R	6-3	220	11-10-81	5	6	3.53	24	19	1	0	107	99	48	42	7	45	96	.252	.259	.247	8.07	3.79
Walk, Mitch	L-L	6-2	199	4-7-78	0	1	4.50	1	1	0	0	6	5	3	3	1	2	3	.227	.111	.308	4.50	3.00
Wilson, Brian	R-R	6-1	205	3-16-82	0	0	0.57	15	0	0	8	16	6	1	1	0	5	22	.115	.136	.100	12.64	2.87

FIELDING

Catcher	PCT	G	PO	A	E	DP	PB
Alfonzo	.990	38	268	26	3	3	6
Curry	.982	68	411	36	8	4	9
Holm	1.000	4	27	3	0	0	0
Knoedler	1.000	3	15	3	0	0	1
Lunsford	.988	36	228	12	3	0	6
Rodriguez	1.000	5	30	2	0	0	0

First Base	PCT	G	PO	A	E	DP
Benavidez	1.000	5	50	3	0	3
Cordido	1.000	4	10	2	0	2
Vericker	1.000	9	49	5	0	6
Von Schell	.991	131	1115	109	11	111

Second Base	PCT	G	PO	A	E	DP
Athas	1.000	2	2	3	0	0
Cordido	.958	5	11	12	1	5
Frandsen	.993	26	55	78	1	19
Hutting	1.000	4	10	9	0	3
Labarbera	.977	110	206	335	13	77

Third Base	PCT	G	PO	A	E	DP
Athas	1.000	4	4	2	0	0
Benavidez	.939	13	9	22	2	7
Buscher	.939	42	18	74	6	8
Cordido	.942	67	30	100	8	14
Frandsen	1.000	1	0	1	0	0
Holm	1.000	6	4	7	0	1
Hutting	.870	12	10	10	3	0
Labarbera	.960	21	11	37	2	8

Shortstop	PCT	G	PO	A	E	DP
Athas	.929	38	41	89	10	20
Benavidez	.000	1	0	0	0	0
Cordido	.981	14	19	32	1	3
Frandsen	1.000	5	11	10	0	3
Hutting	.953	93	143	262	20	55

Outfield	PCT	G	PO	A	E	DP
Cordido	1.000	12	22	0	0	0
Lewis	.948	127	252	3	14	0
Ortmeier	.983	127	223	13	4	2
Trumble	1.000	5	8	0	0	0
Valderrama	.983	120	219	6	4	1
Walter	.989	48	90	1	1	0

SAN JOSE GIANTS — High Class A

CALIFORNIA LEAGUE

BATTING	B-T	HT	WT	DOB	AVG	vLH	vRH	G	AB	R	H	2B	3B	HR	RBI	BB	HBP	SH	SF	SO	SB	CS	SLG	OBP
Alfonzo, Eliezer	R-R	6-0	225	2-7-79	.357	.302	.378	53	196	35	70	16	0	13	45	11	8	0	2	49	1	3	.638	.410
Bowker, John	L-L	6-2	190	7-8-83	.267	.250	.273	121	464	66	124	27	1	13	67	36	3	2	8	108	3	7	.414	.319
Buscher, Brian	L-R	6-0	200	4-18-81	.282	.303	.277	55	206	37	58	12	1	5	29	27	2	0	2	47	0	2	.422	.367
Chavez, Angel	R-R	6-1	195	7-22-81	.283	.242	.299	30	120	22	34	2	1	5	19	5	0	0	1	21	4	0	.442	.310
Contreras, Anthony	L-R	5-11	185	9-26-83	.214	.200	.217	17	56	5	12	3	0	0	3	3	0	0	1	11	1	0	.268	.250
Dobson, Pat	R-R	6-3	210	12-8-80	.280	.250	.297	87	232	41	65	13	3	4	27	30	3	4	0	60	2	4	.414	.370
Felix, Maximo	R-R	5-11	218	8-9-82	.000	.000	.000	4	4	2	0	0	0	0	1	2	0	0	0	3	0	0	.000	.333
Frandsen, Kevin	R-R	6-0	175	5-24-82	.351	.405	.324	75	291	57	102	22	3	2	40	26	15	2	1	22	13	11	.467	.429
Haines, Kyle	L-R	6-1	170	7-28-82	.176	.067	.229	17	51	6	9	2	0	0	5	4	2	0	0	7	2	0	.216	.263
Hornostaj, Aaron	L-R	6-1	178	5-19-83	.121	.000	.133	9	33	0	4	2	0	0	2	0	0	2	0	9	0	0	.182	.121
Ishikawa, Travis	L-L	6-3	200	9-24-83	.282	.317	.273	127	432	87	122	28	7	22	79	70	7	2	5	129	1	4	.532	.387
Jennings, Todd	R-R	6-0	190	12-10-81	.288	.258	.298	128	504	64	145	22	1	10	67	23	6	6	9	77	7	5	.395	.321
Martinez-Esteve, Eddy	R-R	6-2	215	7-14-83	.313	.310	.315	132	479	89	150	44	3	17	94	89	8	0	3	82	4	2	.524	.427
McMains, Derin	B-R	6-0	180	11-3-79	.325	.160	.397	22	83	17	27	3	0	2	10	7	1	0	2	12	2	3	.434	.376
Munhall, Brian	R-R	6-0	192	6-17-80	.314	.286	.329	31	105	21	33	6	0	6	25	8	7	1	1	28	1	1	.543	.397
Rodriguez, Guillermo	R-R	5-11	195	5-15-78	.273	.207	.298	67	209	36	57	14	3	9	43	12	10	3	7	50	5	1	.498	.332
Schierholtz, Nate	L-R	6-2	215	2-15-84	.319	.271	.330	128	502	83	160	37	8	15	86	32	6	3	5	132	5	7	.514	.363
Timpner, Clay	L-L	6-2	195	5-13-83	.291	.269	.299	126	549	85	160	22	12	4	39	34	3	2	3	93	34	13	.397	.334
Wagner, Michael	R-R	6-3	210	9-13-81	.321	.286	.357	8	28	4	9	3	0	1	4	2	1	0	0	8	0	0	.536	.387
Wald, Jake	R-R	6-2	180	2-8-81	.293	.299	.292	86	304	56	89	14	1	15	62	29	4	6	5	87	11	2	.493	.357

PITCHING	B-T	HT	WT	DOB	W	L	ERA	G	GS	CG	SV	IP	H	R	ER	HR	BB	SO	AVG	vLH	vRH	K/9	BB/9
Accardo, Jeremy	R-R	6-2	190	12-18-81	0	0	0.00	2	0	0	1	2	1	0	0	0	1	3	.143	.333	.000	13.50	4.50
Anderson, Luke	R-R	6-5	210	4-9-78	0	1	31.50	1	1	0	0	2	7	7	7	3	2	1	.538	.750	.200	4.50	9.00
Bateman, Joe	R-R	6-1	182	5-6-80	3	4	1.91	56	0	0	21	75	54	20	16	1	22	80	.196	.208	.189	9.56	2.63
Benitez, Armando	R-R	6-4	245	11-3-72	0	0	0.00	2	2	0	0	2	0	0	0	0	1	0	.000	.000	.000	0.00	4.50
Broshuis, Garrett	R-R	6-2	185	12-18-81	12	9	4.40	26	26	0	0	151	173	80	74	16	35	124	.285	.268	.297	7.37	2.08
Correia, Kevin	R-R	6-3	210	8-24-80	0	1	2.57	1	1	0	0	7	5	2	2	0	5	7	.208	.231	.182	9.00	6.43
Coutlangus, Jon	L-L	6-1	180	10-21-80	4	0	3.04	50	0	0	3	77	64	27	26	3	29	79	.234	.197	.261	9.23	3.39
Cox, Ben	R-R	6-2	220	9-20-81	0	0	4.91	2	0	0	0	4	3	3	2	1	1	6	.214	.125	.333	14.73	2.45
Espineli, Eugene	L-L	6-4	195	9-8-82	4	0	2.66	40	0	0	1	64	57	22	19	2	24	55	.242	.204	.266	7.69	3.36
Floyd, Jesse	R-R	6-5	185	1-2-81	12	6	5.18	27	26	0	0	141	155	93	81	20	59	121	.277	.288	.268	7.74	3.77
Foppert, Jesse	R-R	6-6	220	7-10-80	1	0	2.08	3	3	0	0	9	5	2	2	0	6	9	.172	.176	.167	9.35	6.23
Hedrick, Justin	R-R	6-3	225	6-8-82	3	4	3.55	51	0	0	12	58	42	24	23	7	23	75	.195	.219	.176	11.57	3.55
Kinney, Matt	R-R	6-5	215	12-16-76	3	0	2.10	5	5	0	0	30	23	8	7	3	14	34	.215	.184	.232	10.20	4.20
Martinez, Gregorio	R-R	6-1	160	7-2-82	1	0	10.66	4	2	0	0	13	25	16	15	5	4	7	.410	.345	.469	4.97	2.84
McNiven, Brooks	R-R	6-5	180	6-19-81	7	2	4.24	39	6	0	0	93	109	49	44	8	30	51	.299	.252	.335	4.92	2.89
Pendley, Nathan	L-L	6-4	220	9-5-81	1	1	1.86	14	0	0	1	19	7	4	4	0	15	17	.111	.094	.129	7.91	6.98
Petersen, Jeff	R-R	6-4	225	10-16-81	4	4	4.97	40	2	0	0	67	80	45	37	5	34	61	.299	.342	.264	8.19	4.57
Reina, Jesus	L-L	6-2	175	4-20-84	2	4	5.16	18	13	0	0	68	58	48	39	8	42	72	.227	.205	.238	9.53	5.56
Sadowski, Ryan	R-R	6-4	185	10-4-82	9	6	4.64	24	23	0	0	126	120	70	65	12	42	118	.247	.275	.224	8.43	3.00
Sanchez, Jose	R-R	6-1	202	10-11-81	0	0	13.50	7	1	0	0	9	15	14	14	2	11	10	.375	.438	.333	9.64	10.61
Serrato, Juan	R-R	6-3	205	11-4-81	5	6	6.10	27	15	0	0	87	97	67	59	12	48	88	.280	.317	.246	9.10	4.97
Song, Seung	R-R	6-1	190	6-29-80	5	2	1.95	9	6	0	0	37	27	11	8	3	17	47	.199	.176	.212	11.43	4.14
Thurmond, Ben	R-R	6-0	190	10-2-81	2	3	6.64	5	4	0	0	20	29	18	15	5	11	10	.322	.302	.340	4.43	4.87
Waddell, Jason	R-L	6-2	206	6-11-81	5	1	3.40	26	2	0	0	48	42	20	18	4	15	44	.240	.169	.288	8.31	2.83
Walk, Mitch	L-L	6-2	199	4-7-78	2	1	3.04	12	2	0	1	27	33	16	9	2	15	17	.314	.343	.300	5.74	5.06

FIELDING

Catcher	PCT	G	PO	A	E	DP	PB
Alfonzo	.983	47	411	39	8	6	5
Felix	1.000	4	8	0	0	0	1
Jennings	1.000	9	51	0	0	0	0
Munhall	.994	22	151	10	1	0	2
Rodriguez	.990	67	540	51	6	2	3

First Base	PCT	G	PO	A	E	DP
Dobson	.992	15	118	4	1	13
Ishikawa	.993	127	999	98	8	96

Second Base	PCT	G	PO	A	E	DP
Contreras	.975	10	16	23	1	8
Dobson	.955	4	8	13	1	1
Frandsen	.978	62	107	163	6	31
Haines	.962	7	9	16	1	5
Hornostaj	1.000	2	2	5	0	3
Jennings	.974	43	73	114	5	28
McMains	.963	20	39	38	3	6
Wald	1.000	2	3	2	0	0

Third Base	PCT	G	PO	A	E	DP
Buscher	.879	54	23	79	14	9
Haines	.900	4	4	5	1	0
Hornostaj	.909	3	2	8	1	0
Jennings	.927	79	40	125	13	6
Wald	.900	3	4	5	1	0

Shortstop	PCT	G	PO	A	E	DP
Chavez	.974	30	50	100	4	24
Contreras	.917	7	10	23	3	7
Frandsen	.967	15	29	30	2	6
Haines	.958	5	14	9	1	3
Hornostaj	1.000	4	14	12	0	4
Wald	.943	81	124	238	22	49

Outfield	PCT	G	PO	A	E	DP
Bowker	.971	104	134	2	4	2
Dobson	1.000	61	88	5	0	0
Martinez-Esteve	1.000	34	55	3	0	0
Schierholtz	.986	113	191	15	3	3
Timpner	.990	125	308	4	3	1
Wagner	.941	8	15	1	1	0

AUGUSTA GREENJACKETS — Low Class A

SOUTH ATLANTIC LEAGUE

BATTING	B-T	HT	WT	DOB	AVG	vLH	vRH	G	AB	R	H	2B	3B	HR	RBI	BB	HBP	SH	SF	SO	SB	CS	SLG	OBP
Abreu, Johany	B-R	6-0	165	4-3-84	.308	.750	.227	10	26	3	8	2	1	0	0	2	0	1	0	5	1	0	.462	.357
Armitage, Jon	B-R	6-5	210	10-29-80	.244	.250	.242	120	406	63	99	23	1	10	54	62	6	0	2	89	6	6	.379	.351
Benavidez, Julian	R-R	6-2	218	4-14-82	.221	.195	.229	48	172	23	38	12	0	6	25	17	2	0	1	49	0	0	.395	.297
Buller, Dayton	R-R	6-0	213	6-22-81	.231	.368	.174	20	65	7	15	3	0	0	4	7	1	0	0	26	1	0	.277	.315
Columbus, Jason	R-R	6-6	224	9-27-79	.258	.243	.265	71	240	27	62	15	1	1	29	25	7	0	3	59	2	2	.342	.342
Conte, Nick	R-R	5-10	175	1-25-82	.233	.259	.223	64	202	20	47	9	0	2	24	17	3	1	0	40	2	4	.307	.302
Disla, Lisandro	R-R	5-11	177	4-6-84	.197	.264	.168	68	233	24	46	3	1	1	19	17	1	2	3	61	3	2	.232	.252
Haines, Kyle	L-R	6-1	170	7-28-82	.371	.350	.380	35	132	19	49	7	0	1	15	15	0	1	1	15	7	4	.447	.432
Holm, Stephen	R-R	6-0	206	10-21-79	.233	.286	.220	56	176	16	41	7	0	5	31	17	3	2	3	36	1	1	.358	.307
Hornostaj, Aaron	L-R	6-1	178	5-19-83	.253	.308	.246	74	237	27	60	13	4	3	29	19	5	1	1	41	13	7	.380	.321
Horwitz, Brian	R-R	6-1	180	11-7-82	.349	.340	.351	123	470	77	164	38	4	2	88	50	8	0	7	39	6	6	.460	.415

BATTING	B-T	HT	WT	DOB	AVG	vLH	vRH	G	AB	R	H	2B	3B	HR	RBI	BB	HBP	SH	SF	SO	SB	CS	SLG	OBP
Klink, Simon	B-R	6-1	215	12-21-81	.253	.244	.256	131	474	70	120	30	0	8	83	59	15	0	3	128	1	4	.367	.352
McCarthy, Greg	R-R	6-4	215	5-10-83	.239	.417	.176	13	46	1	11	2	0	0	3	0	0	0	0	13	0	0	.283	.239
Requena, Alex	B-R	5-11	155	8-13-80	.252	.183	.270	109	449	78	113	23	7	1	23	47	4	3	1	84	56	14	.341	.327
Sanders, Marcus	R-R	6-0	160	8-25-85	.300	.327	.292	111	420	86	126	19	4	5	40	69	9	3	3	90	57	9	.400	.407
Sosa, Carlos	L-L	6-1	195	10-20-81	.290	.269	.295	108	379	61	110	25	3	9	71	62	1	0	2	96	4	2	.443	.390
Trumble, Dan	R-R	6-2	219	9-29-79	.200	.292	.157	24	75	16	15	4	1	2	6	11	0	0	0	18	4	0	.360	.302
Vericker, Brad	L-L	6-2	210	5-8-81	.264	.308	.255	51	163	14	43	7	0	4	20	18	0	0	2	22	1	0	.380	.333
Wagner, Michael	R-R	6-3	210	9-13-81	.298	.321	.288	54	171	31	51	9	5	4	26	20	11	1	4	42	2	1	.480	.398
Wald, Jake	R-R	6-2	180	2-8-81	.237	.250	.222	14	38	10	9	4	1	0	6	3	1	1	2	11	1	1	.395	.295

PITCHING	B-T	HT	WT	DOB	W	L	ERA	G	GS	CG	SV	IP	H	R	ER	HR	BB	SO	AVG	vLH	vRH	K/9	BB/9
Acosta, Kelyn	R-R	6-2	195	4-24-85	0	1	1.42	11	0	0	5	13	10	2	2	0	3	6	.222	.278	.185	4.26	2.13
Alvarez, Tim	L-L	6-4	235	1-5-81	1	1	5.08	25	0	0	1	34	40	25	19	2	15	34	.282	.260	.293	9.09	4.01
Gardner, Adam	L-L	6-0	185	2-14-82	3	1	3.44	39	1	0	1	68	59	32	26	2	25	80	.229	.212	.237	10.59	3.31
MacKay, Doug	R-R	6-1	205	3-29-83	1	0	1.96	10	0	0	0	18	19	6	4	0	12	13	.264	.313	.225	6.38	5.89
Martin, Sean	R-R	6-1	190	3-27-80	6	1	3.74	46	0	0	7	87	96	39	36	6	19	70	.280	.273	.284	7.27	1.97
Matos, Osiris	R-R	6-1	189	8-6-84	8	8	4.99	29	22	0	0	135	162	83	75	12	31	79	.297	.280	.316	5.25	2.06
Mercado, Arnoldo	R-R	6-1	168	12-28-81	0	2	3.94	16	1	0	0	32	22	14	14	3	14	27	.193	.234	.164	7.59	3.94
Minor, Matt	R-R	6-0	180	9-20-82	0	1	7.00	8	0	0	1	9	14	7	7	2	8	4	.368	.263	.474	4.00	8.00
Montero, Oscar	R-R	6-2	175	5-9-78	1	0	0.00	2	0	0	0	4	1	0	0	0	1	10	.071	.000	.167	20.77	2.08
Moreno, Anthony	R-R	5-11	198	5-4-83	6	0	3.81	16	0	0	1	26	20	13	11	3	12	31	.215	.300	.151	10.73	4.15
Musgrave, Mike	R-R	6-2	185	4-10-84	3	3	4.93	21	17	0	0	88	96	59	48	7	43	48	.272	.263	.282	4.93	4.41
Odom, John	R-R	6-2	185	1-6-82	1	1	4.91	3	1	0	0	7	9	4	4	0	1	7	.290	.364	.250	8.59	1.23
Pannone, Anthony	R-R	6-3	212	7-7-81	2	1	2.90	10	7	0	1	40	37	16	13	4	14	30	.237	.263	.213	6.69	3.12
Ray, Ronnie	R-R	6-3	195	5-11-84	0	1	3.38	1	1	0	0	5	6	4	2	0	3	6	.250	.600	.158	10.13	5.06
Sack, Darren	R-R	6-4	190	7-19-82	8	7	5.08	26	25	2	0	126	144	90	71	10	38	114	.286	.285	.287	8.16	2.72
Salankey, Caleb	R-R	6-1	180	5-10-82	12	8	4.20	28	17	0	0	111	93	58	52	6	38	116	.230	.270	.195	9.38	3.07
Sanchez, Jonathan	L-L	6-2	165	11-19-82	5	7	4.08	25	25	0	0	126	122	59	57	8	39	166	.254	.211	.269	11.89	2.79
Stirm, Brian	R-R	6-6	220	3-13-82	7	7	3.89	41	4	0	4	83	82	41	36	4	46	72	.253	.257	.250	7.78	4.97
Thurmond, Ben	R-R	6-0	190	10-2-81	5	4	3.72	19	9	1	0	65	72	38	27	6	15	59	.276	.233	.310	8.13	2.07
Whitaker, Craig	R-R	6-4	170	11-19-84	3	4	4.66	29	6	0	5	58	54	36	30	3	39	72	.245	.280	.212	11.17	6.05
Wilson, Brian	R-R	6-1	205	3-16-82	5	1	0.82	26	0	0	13	33	23	7	3	0	7	30	.190	.216	.171	8.18	1.91

FIELDING

Catcher	PCT	G	PO	A	E	DP	PB
Buller	.982	20	151	10	3	3	4
Conte	.982	63	457	47	9	3	3
Holm	.995	47	373	31	2	2	5
McCarthy	.973	13	104	3	3	0	2

First Base	PCT	G	PO	A	E	DP
Benavidez	.989	48	337	26	4	33
Columbus	.988	47	369	35	5	27
Holm	1.000	1	5	0	0	0
Hornostaj	1.000	2	7	0	0	0
Sosa	.963	31	224	13	9	20
Vericker	.983	21	159	16	3	14

Second Base	PCT	G	PO	A	E	DP
Abreu	1.000	1	0	1	0	0
Disla	.947	65	89	178	15	30
Haines	.984	33	44	80	2	18
Holm	.889	2	6	2	1	1
Hornostaj	.970	42	48	112	5	23
Wald	1.000	3	7	8	0	1

Third Base	PCT	G	PO	A	E	DP
Abreu	.000	1	0	0	0	0
Disla	1.000	2	1	1	0	0
Holm	.000	1	0	0	1	0
Hornostaj	.000	4	0	0	0	0
Klink	.904	131	66	198	28	16

Shortstop	PCT	G	PO	A	E	DP
Abreu	.947	5	7	11	1	2
Haines	.889	3	1	7	1	1
Hornostaj	.938	22	47	58	7	18
Sanders	.940	109	163	291	29	59
Wald	1.000	1	3	2	0	0

Outfield	PCT	G	PO	A	E	DP
Abreu	1.000	3	8	0	0	0
Armitage	.974	111	175	9	5	1
Horwitz	.956	116	210	8	10	0
Requena	.968	108	231	8	8	1
Sosa	.966	36	56	1	2	0
Trumble	1.000	6	9	0	0	0
Wagner	.986	39	69	1	1	0

SALEM-KEIZER VOLCANOES — Short-Season Class A

NORTHWEST LEAGUE

BATTING	B-T	HT	WT	DOB	AVG	vLH	vRH	G	AB	R	H	2B	3B	HR	RBI	BB	HBP	SH	SF	SO	SB	CS	SLG	OBP
Abreu, Johany	B-R	6-0	165	4-3-84	.189	.158	.206	22	53	5	10	2	1	0	8	1	0	0	0	12	3	2	.264	.204
Babineaux, Charlie	R-R	6-4	215	5-16-81	.204	.255	.172	47	142	13	29	7	0	4	18	14	6	1	1	44	0	2	.338	.301
Busch, Andy	R-R	6-2	205	10-28-81	.210	.234	.190	36	105	10	22	5	0	2	9	7	1	6	0	44	0	0	.314	.265
Contreras, Anthony	L-R	5-11	185	9-26-83	.250	.143	.262	22	72	10	18	3	0	0	4	7	1	3	1	8	4	1	.292	.321
Copeland, Ben	L-L	6-1	195	12-17-83	.306	.257	.326	29	121	25	37	5	4	4	23	11	0	1	0	25	2	1	.512	.364
Dixon, D.J.	L-R	5-10	180	12-11-82	.297	.286	.298	42	101	13	30	6	0	1	9	11	1	2	0	14	1	0	.386	.372
Dyche, Joey	R-R	6-1	185	10-27-82	.289	.354	.254	70	284	43	82	6	2	3	26	25	6	2	0	44	17	10	.356	.359
Gunther, Barry	B-R	6-0	190	3-18-82	.337	.231	.383	31	86	15	29	6	1	1	15	13	1	1	0	13	1	0	.465	.430
Gutierrez, Henry	R-R	5-11	195	5-7-83	.222	.350	.180	23	81	12	18	4	0	1	8	10	1	0	0	14	0	0	.309	.315
Maroul, David	R-R	6-2	210	2-15-83	.263	.304	.236	44	175	20	46	8	1	5	27	4	3	4	2	61	0	1	.406	.288
Minicozzi, Mark	R-R	6-1	210	2-11-83	.321	.365	.297	70	243	42	78	14	3	2	36	35	4	3	3	41	4	7	.428	.411
Mooney, Michael	R-R	6-1	205	6-8-83	.342	.418	.306	73	304	57	104	20	9	5	29	20	5	2	3	64	13	4	.516	.389
Paulino, Adalberto	R-R	5-11	179	9-6-82	.255	.200	.296	29	47	6	12	0	0	1	6	2	3	1	0	15	0	3	.319	.327
Sandoval, Pablo	B-R	5-11	180	8-11-86	.330	.343	.323	75	294	46	97	15	2	3	50	21	6	3	3	33	2	3	.425	.383
Santoro, Michael	R-R	6-3	225	8-20-82	.148	.250	.067	10	27	4	4	1	0	0	2	4	0	1	0	10	1	0	.185	.258
Stanton, Chris	R-R	6-2	175	4-4-83	.247	.250	.246	26	93	11	23	3	0	0	7	8	2	1	0	18	3	0	.280	.320
Thompson, Will	L-L	6-1	180	11-20-82	.384	.420	.362	48	185	25	71	12	1	2	35	23	1	1	1	22	0	1	.492	.452
Todd, Chris	B-R	5-10	170	9-20-82	.206	.235	.196	34	63	7	13	0	0	0	8	14	4	0	0	9	3	0	.206	.383
Yens, Jose	R-R	6-1	190	10-16-82	.280	.242	.306	61	225	34	63	13	2	9	42	8	2	2	1	46	3	4	.476	.309

PITCHING	B-T	HT	WT	DOB	W	L	ERA	G	GS	CG	SV	IP	H	R	ER	HR	BB	SO	AVG	vLH	vRH	K/9	BB/9
Anderson, Brian	R-R	6-3	210	5-25-83	3	1	1.95	27	0	0	19	28	16	6	6	2	3	42	.162	.300	.068	13.66	0.98
Cepeda, Benny	R-R	6-2	175	5-2-83	0	1	6.43	6	2	0	0	14	13	10	10	2	13	5	.250	.286	.226	3.21	8.36
Cody, Buck	R-L	6-2	200	6-22-82	0	2	3.78	15	0	0	0	17	19	10	7	3	6	22	.279	.268	.296	11.88	3.24
Foltin, Wayne	R-R	6-1	195	12-11-82	2	1	3.38	17	0	0	1	21	24	14	8	1	7	20	.282	.259	.293	8.44	2.95
Griffin, Daniel	R-R	6-7	231	9-29-84	3	2	2.39	8	8	0	0	38	33	11	10	1	12	49	.241	.227	.254	11.71	2.87
Hinshaw, Alex	L-L	6-3	180	10-31-82	0	1	3.68	25	0	0	0	22	17	9	9	1	18	33	.227	.308	.184	13.50	7.36
Ludwig, Kellen	R-R	6-5	225	11-19-82	1	3	5.19	18	8	0	0	52	63	32	30	2	21	46	.297	.337	.270	7.96	3.63
Martinez, Joe	L-R	6-2	170	2-26-83	4	3	4.30	15	13	0	0	69	69	33	33	9	15	59	.264	.271	.258	7.70	1.96
McKae, Dave	R-R	6-2	190	11-24-81	3	2	2.42	19	4	0	3	67	55	27	18	5	17	83	.219	.225	.215	11.15	2.28
Millikan, Bryan	R-R	6-5	202	8-13-83	1	3	4.84	20	2	0	1	35	39	23	19	2	15	27	.281	.368	.220	6.88	3.82

PITCHING	B-T	HT	WT	DOB	W	L	ERA	G	GS	CG	SV	IP	H	R	ER	HR	BB	SO	AVG	vLH	vRH	K/9	BB/9
Minor, Matt	R-R	6-0	180	9-20-82	3	1	2.72	23	0	0	3	36	21	11	11	3	18	33	.171	.140	.192	8.17	4.46
Nieto, Ben	L-L	5-11	225	4-4-84	3	0	1.05	5	5	0	0	26	21	4	3	1	7	23	.223	.226	.222	8.06	2.45
Pereira, Nick	R-R	6-0	190	9-22-82	5	3	3.04	14	9	0	0	50	54	21	17	0	14	41	.277	.267	.286	7.33	2.50
Putman, Rickey	R-R	6-3	225	10-1-82	1	1	5.14	17	0	0	0	28	27	20	16	3	14	18	.257	.273	.246	5.79	4.50
Quinowski, David	L-L	5-10	170	4-23-86	2	1	3.21	19	0	0	0	14	12	7	5	1	14	19	.235	.259	.208	12.21	9.00
Raguse, Matt	R-R	6-2	195	9-28-82	4	3	4.91	11	6	0	0	37	33	22	20	2	12	38	.234	.228	.238	9.33	2.95
Romo, Sergio	R-R	5-11	185	3-4-83	7	1	2.75	15	14	0	0	69	70	24	21	7	9	65	.261	.246	.274	8.52	1.18
Sanchez, Jose	R-R	6-1	202	10-11-81	1	1	2.08	8	0	0	0	17	9	5	4	2	4	13	.150	.115	.176	6.75	2.08
Wilding, Taylor	R-R	6-1	190	10-22-84	2	1	6.44	15	5	0	0	43	46	35	31	12	16	42	.271	.260	.280	8.72	3.32

GAMES BY POSITION: C—Busch 36, Dixon 3, Gunther 29, Gutierrez 23, Sandoval 1. **1B**—Babineaux 2, Gunther 1, Sandoval 1, Stanton 26, Thompson 48, Todd 2. **2B**—Abreu 1, Contreras 2, Minicozzi 69, Paulino 5, Todd 8. **3B**—Abreu 2, Minicozzi 1, Paulino 2, Sandoval 70, Todd 6. **SS**—Abreu 9, Contreras 20, Maroul 43, Paulino 1, Todd 15. **OF**—Abreu 5, Babineaux 21, Copeland 28, Dyche 68, Mooney 72, Paulino 9, Santoro 6, Yens 37.

AZL GIANTS — Rookie

ARIZONA LEAGUE

BATTING	B-T	HT	WT	DOB	AVG	vLH	vRH	G	AB	R	H	2B	3B	HR	RBI	BB	HBP	SH	SF	SO	SB	CS	SLG	OBP
Acha, John	R-R	6-0	200	6-3-81	.282	.143	.323	40	124	20	35	6	2	0	21	14	5	1	4	32	4	1	.363	.367
Bone, Kyle	R-R	6-1	200	6-30-80	.000	.000	.000	2	2	0	0	0	0	0	0	1	0	0	0	2	0	0	.000	.333
Borg, Hector	B-R	5-10	160	5-26-85	.254	.238	.260	46	169	28	43	4	2	0	24	20	5	10	2	23	8	3	.302	.347
Buller, Dayton	R-R	6-0	213	6-22-81	.351	.200	.375	14	37	8	13	2	0	1	10	5	4	0	2	8	0	1	.486	.458
Cividanes, Manny	L-L	6-1	175	10-31-84	.346	.400	.338	31	81	12	28	8	1	0	17	7	0	1	0	20	6	0	.469	.398
Copeland, Ben	L-L	6-1	195	12-17-83	.333	.214	.370	18	60	16	20	4	2	1	14	5	1	0	1	14	2	0	.517	.388
Desouza, Dan	L-L	6-1	175	11-27-84	.227	.333	.211	16	44	8	10	2	0	0	2	8	0	1	0	10	1	1	.273	.346
Disla, Lisandro	R-R	5-11	177	4-6-84	.424	.286	.462	8	33	6	14	3	1	1	12	1	0	1	0	4	0	0	.667	.441
Groth, Brad	R-R	6-0	185	7-14-82	.226	.091	.255	22	62	10	14	0	1	0	5	13	2	0	2	15	5	1	.258	.367
Gunther, Barry	B-R	6-0	190	3-18-82	.267	.143	.304	11	30	3	8	1	0	0	4	3	1	0	0	5	0	0	.300	.353
Gutierrez, Henry	R-R	5-11	195	5-7-83	.262	.200	.280	20	65	8	17	1	0	2	10	8	3	0	1	6	3	0	.369	.364
Haynes, Nathan	L-L	5-9	190	9-7-79	.250	.250	.250	7	16	4	4	1	2	0	1	3	0	0	0	3	3	0	.563	.368
Janeway, Rich	L-R	6-2	190	7-22-81	.231	.188	.242	48	160	29	37	6	2	2	28	24	4	2	5	30	5	2	.331	.337
King, Lisandro	R-R	6-1	175	5-27-86	.326	.111	.382	16	43	2	14	1	0	0	6	4	2	2	1	12	2	0	.349	.400
Luster, Jeremiah	R-R	5-10	175	8-31-86	.056	.000	.065	12	36	1	2	0	0	0	0	4	0	1	0	14	1	0	.056	.150
Maroul, David	R-R	6-2	210	2-15-83	.345	.000	.385	8	29	6	10	5	0	1	5	1	0	0	1	7	0	0	.621	.355
McCarthy, Greg	R-R	6-4	215	5-10-83	.333	.333	.333	18	51	7	17	4	0	2	11	1	1	0	2	8	1	1	.529	.345
Nunez, Ariel	R-R	6-3	190	8-3-85	.367	.364	.368	46	150	30	55	4	4	0	21	18	7	4	0	43	28	6	.447	.457
Perez, Hector	R-R	6-2	186	3-3-86	.263	.250	.268	22	57	11	15	2	0	0	7	7	1	1	0	22	2	1	.298	.354
Richardson, Antoan	B-R	5-8	165	10-8-83	.321	.250	.342	53	193	45	62	4	2	1	10	44	8	7	0	43	40	6	.378	.465
Rojas, Nestor	R-R	6-0	200	11-18-83	.233	.077	.267	29	73	11	17	1	1	0	10	5	1	4	1	15	3	1	.274	.288
Sanchez, Alex	L-L	5-10	180	8-26-76	.600	.600	.600	4	10	5	6	1	0	0	2	3	1	0	0	1	1	0	.700	.714
Santoro, Michael	R-R	6-3	225	8-20-82	.237	.111	.276	14	38	5	9	4	1	1	8	3	1	0	0	11	0	1	.474	.310
Schoop, Sharlon	R-R	6-0	160	4-15-87	.254	.314	.239	48	169	29	43	4	0	1	19	14	5	7	1	18	10	4	.296	.328
Stanton, Chris	R-R	6-2	175	4-4-83	.286	.433	.243	33	133	24	38	12	1	2	23	7	8	2	2	23	12	4	.436	.353

PITCHING	B-T	HT	WT	DOB	W	L	ERA	G	GS	CG	SV	IP	H	R	ER	HR	BB	SO	AVG	vLH	vRH	K/9	BB/9
Acosta, Kelyn	R-R	6-2	195	4-24-85	0	0	9.00	2	0	0	0	3	5	3	3	0	0	1	.417	.333	.444	3.00	0.00
Bauer, Ricky	R-R	6-2	170	3-1-83	1	0	0.00	6	0	0	0	8	3	0	0	0	0	12	.115	.111	.118	12.96	0.00
Brinson, Morgan	R-R	-		12-11-86	0	0	21.21	8	0	0	0	5	7	15	11	1	14	5	.350	.000	.467	9.64	27.00
Cabeza, Manuel	R-R	6-2	180	2-6-85	2	1	3.24	11	5	0	1	33	29	15	12	3	14	33	.227	.263	.211	8.91	3.78
Callahan, Ryan	L-L	6-0	165	11-19-80	0	1	2.03	11	0	0	0	13	14	4	3	0	6	16	.286	.214	.314	10.80	4.05
Cepeda, Benny	R-R	6-2	175	5-2-83	0	0	8.10	5	0	0	0	7	10	7	6	0	3	10	.313	.250	.333	13.50	4.05
Cody, Buck	R-L	6-2	200	6-22-82	0	0	5.40	2	0	0	0	2	3	2	1	0	0	0	.333	.000	.333	0.00	0.00
De la Rosa, Carlos	L-L	6-2	190	7-15-84	1	1	2.57	11	5	0	3	35	32	11	10	2	11	32	.252	.231	.254	8.23	2.83
Farrach, Juan	L-L	5-11	155	7-7-85	0	0	6.43	8	0	0	0	7	9	6	5	1	2	5	.321	.250	.350	6.43	2.57
Gomez, Josue	L-L	6-3	200	3-14-85	2	0	2.65	11	6	0	2	34	27	16	10	2	19	37	.223	.172	.239	9.79	5.03
Gornati, Tom	R-R	6-1	205	3-16-81	6	0	1.30	11	5	0	0	42	32	6	6	1	8	44	.212	.196	.220	9.50	1.73
Grace, Robert	R-R	6-1	165	2-2-83	6	1	2.85	11	6	0	0	41	37	17	13	2	9	33	.247	.267	.242	7.24	1.98
Griffin, Daniel	R-R	6-7	231	9-29-84	0	0	0.75	4	4	0	0	12	9	2	1	0	6	20	.214	.182	.226	15.00	4.50
Grogan, John	L-L	6-4	215	10-10-82	2	0	1.65	12	0	0	0	16	12	4	3	0	5	13	.226	.250	.222	7.16	2.76
Joaquin, Waldis	R-R	6-2	190	12-25-86	1	1	3.64	10	5	0	1	30	28	17	12	1	10	37	.241	.260	.227	11.22	3.03
Lussier, Paul	R-R	6-2	220	11-7-85	1	1	3.05	11	5	0	0	38	40	14	13	4	6	32	.272	.238	.286	7.51	1.41
Martinez, Gregorio	R-R	6-1	160	7-2-82	4	2	1.99	11	5	0	2	41	25	11	9	2	9	46	.174	.196	.163	10.18	1.99
Martis, Shairon	R-R	6-1	175	3-30-87	2	1	1.85	11	5	0	1	34	28	10	7	1	9	50	.226	.261	.205	13.24	2.38
McGovern, Ryan	L-L	6-1	185	6-23-84	1	1	5.73	11	0	0	0	11	14	9	7	0	6	10	.304	.444	.270	8.18	4.91
Nesmith, Travis	L-L	6-3	225	4-26-82	0	0	3.60	4	0	0	0	5	6	2	2	0	2	3	.286	.500	.200	5.40	3.60
Nieto, Ben	L-L	5-11	225	4-4-84	2	2	1.26	8	3	0	0	29	22	8	4	1	6	38	.200	.115	.226	11.93	1.88
Ramirez, Froilan	R-R	6-3	195	5-31-84	2	2	13.50	8	0	0	0	7	9	12	11	1	9	9	.310	.429	.273	11.05	11.05
Shaver, Ryan	R-R	6-5	175	12-17-84	3	2	3.18	9	2	0	0	23	24	12	8	0	4	24	.279	.310	.263	9.53	1.59
Thomson, Jordan	R-R	6-2	205	12-3-81	2	0	2.77	13	0	0	7	13	13	7	4	0	2	9	.255	.188	.286	6.23	1.38
Ventura, Robert	R-R	6-2	160	8-26-81	0	0	0.00	1	0	0	0	0	1	0	0	0	1	0	.500	.000	.500	0.00	27.00
Walk, Mitch	L-L	6-2	199	4-7-78	1	1	2.70	3	0	0	0	3	2	2	1	0	0	3	.154	.000	.154	8.10	0.00

GAMES BY POSITION: C—Bone 2, Buller 9, Gunther 10, Gutierrez 15, McCarthy 17, Rojas 25. **1B**—Acha 4, Borg 1, Janeway 30, Santoro 1, Stanton 26. **2B**—Acha 7, Borg 36, Groth 17, King 3, Schoop 1, Stanton 1. **3B**—Acha 27, Borg 1, Disla 8, King 10, Luster 8, Maroul 7. **SS**—Borg 9, King 1, Luster 1, Maroul 1, Schoop 46. **OF**—Cividanes 25, Copeland 14, Desouza 16, Gutierrez 1, Haynes 7, Janeway 9, Luster 1, Nunez 45, Perez 8, Richardson 53, Sanchez 4, Santoro 7, Stanton 4.

SEATTLE MARINERS

BY COREY BROCK

You can say this much about the 2005 Mariners—they weren't nearly as bad as when they lost 99 games in 2004.

But even with a new manager (Mike Hargrove) and a handful of fresh faces, the Mariners still struggled, going 69-93.

The Mariners got good returns on their $114 million free agent signings in Adrian Beltre and Richie Sexson, though it wasn't enough to overcome inconsistent starting pitching and nearly anemic results from the remainder of the offense.

"We thought we were going to be better than this coming out of spring training," Sexson said. "We didn't reach our goals, we went through a lot of changes. The kids that came up, they showed up and played."

One of those kids—19-year-old righthander Felix Hernandez—proved to be as good as or better than advertised after his late-summer promotion from Triple-A Tacoma. Hernandez went 4-4, 2.67 in 12 starts and showed he's capable of becoming the Mariners' ace in 2006.

Hernandez was just one of several young players to play prominent roles with the Mariners in 2005. After the club released second baseman Bret Boone, and with injured shortstop Pokey Reese never playing, Seattle turned over its middle infield to Cuban shortstop Yuniesky Betancourt and second baseman Jose Lopez.

The second half of the season was spent developing these young players—along with shortstop/outfielder Mike Morse, catcher Rene Rivera and infielder Greg Dobbs. The young players have Hargrove encouraged about the future.

"We've got some good things going," Hargrove said. "You hope that during the offseason the kids keep up the lines of development we have going. It's always interesting in training camp to see how close they have followed the regimen."

ORGANIZATION LEADERS

BATTING

*AVG	Boucher, Sebastien, Inland Empire/Wisconsin	.340
R	Wilson, Michael, Wisconsin	93
H	Bohn, T.J., San Antonio/Tacoma	161
TB	Balentien, Wladimir, Inland Empire	272
2B	Balentien, Wladimir, Inland Empire	38
3B	Cabrera, Asdrubal, Inland Empire/Tacoma/Wisconsin	10
HR	Balentien, Wladimir, Inland Empire	25
RBI	Lahair, Bryan, Inland Empire	113
BB	Nunez, Abraham, Tacoma	71
SO	Balentien, Wladimir, Inland Empire	160
SB	Bubela, Jaime, San Antonio	40
*OBP	Boucher, Sebastien, Inland Empire/Wisconsin	.434
*SLG	Balentien, Wladimir, Inland Empire	.553

PITCHING

W	Livingston, Bobby, Everett/San Antonio/Tacoma	14
L	Jensen, Aaron, Wisconsin	13
#ERA	Key, Chris, Inland Empire/San Antonio/Tacoma	1.78
G	Green, Sean, San Antonio/Tacoma	54
CG	Lorraine, Andrew, Tacoma	2
SV	Kida, Masao, Tacoma	22
IP	Mackintosh, Jason, Inland Empire	180
BB	Rivera, Mumba, Inland Empire/Wisconsin	76
SO	Mackintosh, Jason, Inland Empire	141

*Minimum 250 at-bats. #Minimum 75 innings.

PLAYERS OF THE YEAR

MAJOR LEAGUE: Richie Sexson, 1b

Sexson proved the better of Seattle's two big-ticket free-agent corner infielders, providing excellent power (39 homers, 121 RBIs) despite having to adjust to spacious Safeco Field. Just as importantly, he stayed healthy and played in 156 games after appearing in just 23 for the Diamondbacks in 2004.

MINOR LEAGUE: Felix Hernandez, rhp

Before receiving his long-awaited big league callup and becoming the most exciting teenage pitcher in the majors since Dwight Gooden, Hernandez won the Triple-A Pacific Coast League's pitcher of the year honors by going 9-4, 2.25. He did that despite missing a month with shoulder bursitis.

By most counts, the young players stole most of the thunder from the veterans in 2005—Sexson excluded.

After appearing in just 23 games with Arizona in 2004 when shoulder surgery ended his season, Sexson rebounded big in 2005, hitting 39 home runs to go with 121 RBIs. That was a good first return on the four-year, $50 million contract the Mariners gave him.

The Mariners had hoped for bigger things from Beltre, the third baseman who hit 48 home runs with the Dodgers in 2004. He hit .255-19-87 in 2005, not a good return on his five-year, $64 million contract.

"Normally you want to put it behind you," Beltre said. "But I don't know how I'm not going to be thinking about this season every day. I never thought it would be like this."

Despite the signings of Sexson and Beltre, the Mariners scored only one more run (699) than they did in 2004. Worse, Seattle's .256 team batting average was the lowest in the American League.

Right fielder Ichiro Suzuki extended his string of consecutive 200-hit, .300-plus seasons to five, but just barely. Ichiro needed eight hits in the final weekend of the regular season to reach those marks, as he finished well below the monster numbers he compiled in 2004 (.372 average and a major league-record 262 hits).

The pitching wasn't much better. Despite pitching with a torn rotator cuff in his left shoulder, 35-year-old closer Eddie Guardado had the best season among the Mariners' pitchers with 36 saves.

Mariners minor league affiliates got a taste of success, particularly Tacoma, which overcame a 2-0 deficit in the best-of-five Pacific Coast League semifinals to knock off defending champion Sacramento. The Rainiers were swept by Nashville in the championship series, but the season was a success, especially in light of the players that graduated from Tacoma to Seattle. Hernandez earned PCL pitcher of the year honors before his big league callup, and Betancourt, Lopez and Morse also made the successful jump.

Double-A San Antonio and low Class A Wisconsin also reached the playoffs in their respective leagues.

SEATTLE MARINERS

Manager: Mike Hargrove.

2005 Record: 69-93, .426 (4th, AL West).

BATTING	B-T	HT	WT	DOB	AVG	vLH	vRH	G	AB	R	H	2B	3B	HR	RBI	BB	HBP	SH	SF	SO	SB	CS	SLG	OBP
Beltre, Adrian	R-R	5-11	220	4-7-79	.255	.275	.249	156	603	69	154	36	1	19	87	38	5	0	4	108	3	1	.413	.303
Betancourt, Yuniesky	R-R	5-10	190	1-31-82	.256	.286	.247	60	211	24	54	11	5	1	15	11	2	2	2	24	1	3	.370	.296
Bloomquist, Willie	R-R	5-11	185	11-27-77	.257	.247	.262	82	249	27	64	15	2	0	22	11	1	4	2	38	14	1	.333	.289
Boone, Bret	R-R	5-10	190	4-6-69	.231	.210	.237	74	273	30	63	15	3	7	34	24	3	1	1	52	4	2	.385	.299
Borders, Pat	R-R	6-2	200	5-14-63	.197	.324	.138	39	117	12	23	5	0	1	7	4	1	2	1	22	0	0	.265	.228
Bubela, Jaime	L-R	6-1	200	6-6-78	.105	.167	.077	11	19	3	2	0	0	0	0	1	0	0	0	4	1	0	.105	.150
Choo, Shin-Soo	L-L	5-11	180	7-13-82	.056	.000	.091	10	18	1	1	0	0	0	1	3	0	0	0	4	0	0	.056	.190
Dobbs, Greg	L-R	6-1	205	7-2-78	.246	.300	.242	59	142	8	35	7	1	1	20	9	0	1	2	25	1	0	.331	.288
Gonzalez, Wiki	R-R	5-11	205	5-17-74	.267	.444	.222	14	45	7	12	5	0	0	2	2	0	0	0	3	0	0	.378	.298
Hansen, Dave	L-R	6-0	195	11-24-68	.173	.000	.178	60	75	5	13	0	0	2	11	9	0	2	2	19	1	0	.253	.256
Ibanez, Raul	L-R	6-2	220	6-2-72	.280	.275	.282	162	614	92	172	32	2	20	89	71	2	0	3	99	9	4	.436	.355
Lopez, Jose	R-R	6-2	200	11-24-83	.247	.276	.235	54	190	18	47	19	0	2	25	6	4	1	2	25	4	2	.379	.282
Morse, Mike	R-R	6-4	220	3-22-82	.278	.272	.282	72	230	27	64	10	1	3	23	18	8	0	2	50	3	1	.370	.349
Ojeda, Miguel	R-R	6-1	230	1-29-75	.172	.000	.263	16	29	2	5	0	0	1	3	6	0	2	0	3	0	1	.276	.314
Olivo, Miguel	R-R	6-0	220	7-15-78	.151	.179	.142	54	152	14	23	4	0	5	18	4	0	0	1	49	1	1	.276	.172
Reed, Jeremy	L-L	6-0	195	6-15-81	.254	.200	.269	141	488	61	124	33	3	3	45	48	2	4	2	74	12	11	.352	.322
Rivera, Rene	R-R	5-10	190	7-31-83	.396	.364	.405	16	48	3	19	3	0	1	6	1	0	1	0	11	0	0	.521	.408
Santiago, Ramon	B-R	5-11	175	8-31-79	.125	.000	.143	8	8	2	1	0	0	0	0	1	3	1	0	2	0	0	.125	.417
Sexson, Richie	R-R	6-8	235	12-29-74	.263	.333	.244	156	558	99	147	36	1	39	121	89	6	0	3	167	1	1	.541	.369
Snelling, Chris	L-L	5-10	205	12-3-81	.276	.333	.269	15	29	4	8	2	0	1	1	5	0	1	0	2	0	2	.448	.382
Spiezio, Scott	B-R	6-2	220	9-21-72	.064	.000	.100	29	47	2	3	1	0	1	1	4	0	0	0	18	0	0	.149	.137
Strong, Jamal	R-R	5-10	185	8-5-78	.250	.273	.222	16	20	6	5	0	1	0	2	2	1	0	1	6	0	0	.350	.333
Suzuki, Ichiro	L-R	5-9	170	10-22-73	.303	.352	.284	162	679	111	206	21	12	15	68	48	4	2	6	66	33	8	.436	.350
Torrealba, Yorvit	R-R	5-11	200	7-19-78	.241	.143	.275	42	108	14	26	4	0	2	8	7	1	3	0	25	0	0	.333	.293
Valdez, Wilson	R-R	5-11	170	5-20-78	.198	.147	.217	42	126	9	25	5	1	0	8	6	0	1	0	25	2	2	.254	.235
Wilson, Dan	R-R	6-3	215	3-25-69	.185	.000	.278	11	27	2	5	0	0	0	2	0	1	0	0	10	0	1	.185	.214
Winn, Randy	B-R	6-2	195	6-9-74	.275	.246	.288	102	386	46	106	25	1	6	37	37	4	6	3	53	12	6	.391	.342

PITCHING	B-T	HT	WT	DOB	W	L	ERA	G	GS	CG	SV	IP	H	R	ER	HR	BB	SO	AVG	vLH	vRH	K/9	BB/9
Atchison, Scott	R-R	6-2	195	3-29-76	0	0	6.75	6	0	0	0	7	7	5	5	1	1	9	.269	.091	.400	12.15	1.35
Campillo, Jorge	R-R	6-1	190	8-10-78	0	0	0.00	2	1	0	0	2	1	0	0	0	1	1	.125	.000	.250	4.50	4.50
Franklin, Ryan	R-R	6-3	190	3-5-73	8	15	5.10	32	30	2	0	191	212	110	108	28	62	93	.280	.266	.295	4.39	2.93
Guardado, Eddie	R-L	6-0	205	10-2-70	2	3	2.72	58	0	0	36	56	52	23	17	7	15	48	.239	.231	.242	7.67	2.40
Harris, Jeff	R-R	6-1	190	7-4-74	2	5	4.19	11	8	0	0	54	48	27	25	9	20	25	.238	.180	.294	4.19	3.35
Hasegawa, Shigetoshi	R-R	5-11	175	8-1-68	1	3	4.19	46	0	0	0	67	66	31	31	4	16	30	.259	.281	.239	4.05	2.16
Hernandez, Felix	R-R	6-3	170	4-8-86	4	4	2.67	12	12	0	0	84	61	26	25	5	23	77	.203	.182	.224	8.22	2.45
Kida, Masao	R-R	6-3	210	9-12-68	0	0	4.50	1	0	0	0	2	2	1	1	1	0	0	.250	.500	.167	0.00	0.00
Madritsch, Bobby	L-L	6-2	220	2-28-76	0	1	6.23	1	1	0	0	4	4	3	3	1	1	1	.235	.250	.231	2.08	2.08
Mateo, Julio	R-R	6-0	220	8-2-77	3	6	3.06	55	1	0	0	88	79	32	30	12	17	52	.237	.209	.261	5.30	1.73
Meche, Gil	R-R	6-3	215	9-8-78	10	8	5.09	29	26	0	0	143	153	92	81	18	72	83	.275	.266	.285	5.21	4.52
Moyer, Jamie	L-L	6-0	180	11-18-62	13	7	4.28	32	32	1	0	200	225	99	95	23	52	102	.283	.294	.278	4.59	2.34
Nageotte, Clint	R-R	6-3	225	10-25-80	0	0	6.75	3	0	0	0	4	6	3	3	0	1	1	.353	.500	.273	2.25	2.25
Nelson, Jeff	R-R	6-8	225	11-17-66	1	3	3.93	49	0	0	1	37	32	17	16	3	22	34	.237	.342	.196	8.35	5.40
Pineiro, Joel	R-R	6-1	200	9-25-78	7	11	5.62	30	30	2	0	189	224	118	118	23	56	107	.300	.295	.305	5.10	2.67
Putz, J.J.	R-R	6-5	245	2-22-77	6	5	3.60	64	0	0	1	60	58	27	24	8	23	45	.254	.321	.197	6.75	3.45
Sele, Aaron	R-R	6-5	230	6-25-70	6	12	5.66	21	21	1	0	116	147	76	73	18	41	53	.315	.325	.302	4.11	3.18
Sherrill, George	L-L	6-0	220	4-19-77	4	3	5.21	29	0	0	0	19	13	12	11	3	7	24	.194	.156	.273	11.37	3.32
Soriano, Rafael	R-R	6-1	220	12-19-79	0	0	2.45	7	0	0	0	7	6	2	2	0	1	9	.222	.571	.100	11.05	1.23
Thornton, Matt	L-L	6-6	230	9-15-76	0	4	5.21	55	0	0	0	57	54	33	33	13	42	57	.248	.262	.235	9.00	6.63
Villone, Ron	L-L	6-3	245	1-16-70	2	3	2.45	52	0	0	1	40	33	14	11	2	23	41	.226	.213	.242	9.15	5.13

FIELDING

Catcher	PCT	G	PO	A	E	DP	PB
Borders	.990	39	174	16	2	2	3
Gonzalez	1.000	14	78	8	0	2	1
Ojeda	.986	16	69	3	1	2	2
Olivo	.987	54	281	15	4	1	5
Rivera	.961	15	69	4	3	2	3
Torrealba	1.000	41	225	18	0	2	0
Wilson	.975	11	36	3	1	1	0

First Base	PCT	G	PO	A	E	DP
Bloomquist	1.000	1	0	1	0	0
Dobbs	1.000	5	32	8	0	0
Hansen	1.000	9	18	2	0	3
Ibanez	1.000	4	26	3	0	0
Sexson	.995	151	1148	120	7	121
Spiezio	1.000	4	31	0	0	1

Second Base	PCT	G	PO	A	E	DP
Betancourt	1.000	9	23	21	0	5
Bloomquist	.986	32	58	81	2	22
Boone	.979	74	131	192	7	43
Lopez	.979	51	123	159	6	32
Santiago	1.000	2	0	4	0	1
Spiezio	1.000	1	1	1	0	0

Third Base	PCT	G	PO	A	E	DP
Beltre	.967	155	140	271	14	27
Bloomquist	1.000	6	1	4	0	0
Dobbs	1.000	2	4	5	0	1
Hansen	1.000	7	5	7	0	0
Lopez	.800	1	2	2	1	0
Spiezio	1.000	6	1	1	0	1

Shortstop	PCT	G	PO	A	E	DP
Betancourt	.978	53	83	138	5	34
Bloomquist	.965	24	34	49	3	6
Morse	.946	55	91	120	12	34
Santiago	.500	2	0	1	1	0
Valdez	.973	42	66	111	5	22

Outfield	PCT	G	PO	A	E	DP
Bloomquist	.963	15	25	1	1	1
Bubela	1.000	7	17	0	0	0
Choo	1.000	5	16	0	0	0
Dobbs	1.000	4	4	0	0	0
Ibanez	.982	58	106	6	2	3
Morse	1.000	8	10	1	0	1
Reed	.992	137	383	7	3	1
Snelling	1.000	10	20	2	0	1
Strong	1.000	11	12	1	0	0
Suzuki	.995	158	381	10	2	2
Winn	1.000	96	245	3	0	0

FARM SYSTEM

General Manager: Bill Bavasi. **Director, Player Development:** Benny Looper. **Scouting Director:** Bob Fontaine.

Class	Farm Team	League	W	L	Pct.	Finish*	Manager	Affiliate Since
AAA	Tacoma (Wash.) Rainiers	Pacific Coast	80	64	.556	**t-2nd (16)**	Dan Rohn	1995
AA	San Antonio (Texas) Missions	Texas	76	64	.543	**2nd (8)**	Dave Brundage	2001
High A	Inland Empire (Calif.) 66ers	California	58	82	.414	9th (10)	Daren Brown	2001
Low A	Wisconsin Timber Rattlers (Appleton)	Midwest	76	63	.547	**2nd (14)**	Scott Steinmann	1993
SS A	Everett (Wash.) AquaSox	Northwest	42	34	.553	3rd (8)	Pedro Grifol	1995
Rookie	Peoria (Ariz.) Mariners	Arizona	27	29	.482	t-5th (9)	Dana Williams	2001

*Finish in overall standings (No. of teams in league)/Playoff teams in **boldface**

LARRY GOREN

Eddie Guardado: Seventh in the AL with 36 saves

LARRY GOREN

Wladimir Balentien: Led organization in doubles and homers

TACOMA RAINIERS — Class AAA

PACIFIC COAST LEAGUE

BATTING	B-T	HT	WT	DOB	AVG	vLH	vRH	G	AB	R	H	2B	3B	HR	RBI	BB	HBP	SH	SF	SO	SB	CS	SLG	OBP
Auty, Tim	R-R	6-0	180	12-21-85	.100	.000	.167	3	10	1	1	0	0	0	0	1	0	0	0	1	0	0	.100	.182
Betancourt, Yuniesky	R-R	5-10	190	1-31-82	.295	.231	.321	49	183	13	54	9	6	2	30	6	2	2	1	14	7	5	.443	.323
Blakeley, Eric	R-R	6-1	188	9-8-79	.273	.000	.429	4	11	3	3	0	0	0	2	3	0	0	0	2	0	0	.273	.429
Bohn, T.J.	R-R	6-4	215	1-17-80	.321	.294	.328	22	81	15	26	3	0	1	7	2	3	0	0	23	4	0	.395	.360
Bradford, Sam	B-R	6-1	185	10-15-81	.125	.200	.000	3	8	1	1	0	0	0	2	1	0	0	2	1	0	0	.125	.182
Brown, Hunter	R-R	6-2	210	10-24-79	.291	.315	.282	100	337	53	98	30	1	7	53	33	8	0	2	71	8	4	.448	.366
Cabrera, Asdrubal	B-R	6-0	170	11-13-85	.217	.500	.190	6	23	4	5	0	1	0	3	1	0	1	0	4	0	0	.304	.250
Cho, Hyung	R-R	5-9	190	8-20-82	.000	.000	.000	2	5	0	0	0	0	0	0	0	0	0	0	1	0	0	.000	.000
Choo, Shin-Soo	L-L	5-11	180	7-13-82	.282	.236	.301	115	429	73	121	21	5	11	54	69	1	2	1	97	20	10	.431	.382
Christianson, Ryan	R-R	6-2	210	4-21-81	.245	.257	.241	79	286	36	70	13	0	9	40	35	2	1	0	96	2	1	.385	.331
Delucchi, Dustin	L-L	6-0	190	12-23-77	.244	.375	.190	23	82	12	20	1	0	1	5	9	0	5	1	14	3	0	.293	.315
Dobbs, Greg	L-R	6-1	205	7-2-78	.321	.389	.294	50	190	27	61	9	0	3	22	14	1	1	2	22	5	2	.416	.367
Dominguez, Jeff	B-R	6-2	153	7-31-86	.000	.000	.000	2	1	0	0	0	0	0	0	0	0	0	0	0	0	0	.000	.000
Gonzalez, Wiki	R-R	5-11	205	5-17-74	.313	.327	.306	47	176	25	55	10	1	5	28	16	2	1	1	13	0	0	.466	.374
Hansen, Dave	L-R	6-0	195	11-24-68	.300	.333	.286	6	20	2	6	0	0	0	3	2	0	0	1	4	0	0	.300	.348
Jacobs, Greg	L-L	5-9	195	10-9-76	.203	.333	.180	16	59	6	12	1	0	3	8	3	0	0	1	11	0	0	.373	.238
Jacobsen, Bucky	R-R	6-4	255	8-30-75	.136	.067	.157	18	66	7	9	3	0	0	8	7	2	0	0	18	0	0	.182	.240
Leone, Justin	R-R	6-1	200	3-9-77	.243	.258	.236	87	313	51	76	19	2	7	38	51	2	2	2	93	5	2	.383	.351
Lopez, Jose	R-R	6-2	200	11-24-83	.319	.175	.359	44	182	29	58	19	0	5	31	8	2	2	0	25	2	3	.505	.354
Morse, Mike	R-R	6-4	220	3-22-82	.253	.212	.269	49	182	20	46	12	2	4	23	16	2	1	2	36	1	0	.407	.317
Nunez, Abraham	B-R	6-3	210	2-5-77	.274	.309	.260	127	481	82	132	26	3	17	86	71	1	2	8	109	12	10	.447	.364
Ojeda, Miguel	R-R	6-1	230	1-29-75	.333	.385	.300	9	33	7	11	1	0	3	11	1	1	0	0	5	0	0	.636	.371
2-team (17 Portland)					.244	.219	.259	26	90	15	22	2	0	6	16	8	2	0	0	21	0	0	.467	.320
Olivo, Miguel	R-R	6-0	220	7-15-78	.233	.333	.197	24	90	13	21	4	1	3	21	7	1	0	1	19	8	1	.400	.293

BATTING	B-T	HT	WT	DOB	AVG	vLH	vRH	G	AB	R	H	2B	3B	HR	RBI	BB	HBP	SH	SF	SO	SB	CS	SLG	OBP
Pellow, Kit	R-R	6-1	205	8-28-73	.417	.400	.429	4	12	3	5	1	0	1	3	3	1	0	1	4	0	0	.750	.529
Rifkin, Aaron	L-L	6-3	220	3-12-79	.258	.263	.256	105	384	55	99	30	3	14	54	47	4	1	2	87	4	2	.461	.343
Rivera, Rene	R-R	5-10	190	7-31-83	.204	.125	.220	14	49	3	10	3	0	1	6	2	0	0	0	12	0	1	.327	.235
Santiago, Ramon	B-R	5-11	175	8-31-79	.252	.250	.253	129	441	68	111	22	3	10	50	38	15	17	6	62	18	7	.383	.328
Snelling, Chris	L-L	5-10	205	12-3-81	.370	.397	.358	65	246	50	91	17	2	8	46	36	4	1	4	43	2	3	.553	.452
Spiezio, Scott	B-R	6-2	220	9-21-72	.328	.444	.275	14	58	11	19	3	1	2	9	1	1	0	3	9	0	0	.517	.333
Strong, Jamal	R-R	5-10	185	8-5-78	.293	.260	.309	93	382	57	112	16	5	4	36	43	5	6	1	67	25	6	.393	.371
Terveen, Bryce	L-R	6-1	200	3-1-78	.246	.368	.190	19	61	5	15	4	0	1	8	3	3	0	1	15	0	1	.361	.309
Valbuena, Luis	L-R	5-10	160	11-30-85	.000	.000	.000	3	4	0	0	0	0	0	0	1	0	0	0	2	0	0	.000	.200
Valdez, Wilson	R-R	5-11	170	5-20-78	.000	.000	.000	1	4	0	0	0	0	0	1	0	0	0	0	1	0	0	.000	.000

PITCHING	B-T	HT	WT	DOB	W	L	ERA	G	GS	CG	SV	IP	H	R	ER	HR	BB	SO	AVG	vLH	vRH	K/9	BB/9
Arias, Oliver	R-R	6-5	210	8-17-81	0	0	18.00	1	0	0	0	1	2	2	2	2	0	0	.400	.000	1.000	0.00	0.00
Atchison, Scott	R-R	6-2	195	3-29-76	0	0	4.15	10	0	0	0	13	13	6	6	0	5	17	.255	.280	.231	11.77	3.46
Baek, Cha Seung	R-R	6-4	220	5-29-80	8	8	6.41	25	21	0	0	114	147	87	81	19	36	73	.313	.303	.322	5.78	2.85
Brandt, Adam	R-L	6-2	230	5-18-82	0	0	0.00	1	0	0	0	1	0	0	0	0	0	0	.000	.000	.000	0.00	0.00
Buglovsky, Chris	L-R	6-1	170	11-22-79	4	5	4.24	35	13	0	0	110	120	55	52	7	40	72	.284	.247	.312	5.87	3.26
Bumstead, Michael	R-R	6-4	210	7-8-77	0	1	4.15	13	0	0	0	22	22	10	10	1	8	9	.275	.160	.327	3.74	3.32
2-team (12 Portland)					2	3	4.75	25	4	0	0	47	54	26	25	4	18	23	.289	.264	.304	4.37	3.42
Campillo, Jorge	R-R	6-1	190	8-10-78	4	1	2.71	12	12	0	0	66	63	21	20	5	18	43	.259	.253	.264	5.83	2.44
Cruceta, Francisco	R-R	6-2	215	7-4-81	1	1	5.00	2	2	0	0	9	11	6	5	3	3	10	.297	.276	.375	10.00	3.00
Dorman, Rich	R-R	6-3	210	9-30-78	4	4	6.28	10	8	0	0	39	33	27	27	6	26	22	.234	.233	.235	5.12	6.05
Evert, Brett	L-R	6-6	200	10-23-80	0	0	6.75	8	1	0	0	13	19	11	10	1	5	8	.339	.407	.276	5.40	3.38
Flannery, Mike	R-R	6-2	225	9-20-79	0	0	9.45	6	0	0	0	7	9	7	7	0	6	7	.333	.273	.375	9.45	8.10
2-team (14 Albuquerque)					1	0	6.56	20	0	0	0	23	25	17	17	3	18	18	.275	.286	.268	6.94	6.94
Foppert, Jesse	R-R	6-6	220	7-10-80	0	1	2.57	6	6	0	0	14	10	4	4	0	8	13	.200	.250	.111	8.36	5.14
2-team (10 Fresno)					3	2	4.03	16	15	0	0	58	53	29	26	5	35	54	.239	.207	.270	8.38	5.43
Fruto, Emiliano	R-R	6-3	229	6-6-84	1	2	13.09	9	0	0	0	11	11	17	16	1	11	12	.268	.083	.345	9.82	9.00
Green, Sean	R-R	6-6	230	4-20-79	4	2	3.65	33	0	0	1	49	40	23	20	1	29	44	.221	.282	.182	8.03	5.29
Harris, Jeff	R-R	6-1	190	7-4-74	5	2	2.78	16	9	0	1	68	50	22	21	8	17	56	.207	.225	.196	7.41	2.25
Heaverlo, Jeff	R-R	6-1	215	1-13-78	6	3	4.61	46	0	0	4	82	92	49	42	3	44	71	.287	.273	.295	7.79	4.83
Hernandez, Felix	R-R	6-3	170	4-8-86	9	4	2.25	19	14	1	0	88	62	24	22	3	48	100	.196	.218	.175	10.23	4.91
Jimenez, Cesar	L-L	6-0	203	11-12-84	0	0	9.39	4	0	0	0	8	9	8	8	5	1	9	.290	.000	.346	10.57	1.17
Key, Chris	R-L	6-3	210	10-30-77	0	0	3.60	3	0	0	0	10	10	5	4	2	1	4	.263	.000	.435	3.60	0.90
Kida, Masao	R-R	6-3	210	9-12-68	3	6	4.08	53	0	0	22	79	72	37	36	6	27	66	.247	.271	.228	7.49	3.06
Livingston, Bobby	L-L	6-3	190	9-3-82	6	2	4.70	10	10	0	0	52	53	31	27	2	15	41	.260	.244	.264	7.14	2.61
Lopez, Albie	R-R	6-2	240	8-18-71	0	1	12.60	3	0	0	0	5	9	8	7	3	3	2	.375	.333	.400	3.60	5.40
Lorraine, Andrew	L-L	6-3	200	8-11-72	9	8	4.79	33	22	2	0	141	162	80	75	11	52	78	.298	.263	.310	4.98	3.32
Moss, Damian	R-L	6-0	185	11-24-76	9	7	3.73	25	24	1	0	138	125	68	57	9	75	93	.246	.228	.251	6.08	4.90
Mullen, Scott	R-L	6-2	195	1-17-75	0	0	0.00	1	0	0	0	1	0	0	0	0	1	2	.000	.000	.000	18.00	9.00
Nageotte, Clint	R-R	6-3	225	10-25-80	2	1	2.65	19	0	0	2	34	21	16	10	2	22	35	.176	.279	.118	9.26	5.82
Pineiro, Joel	R-R	6-1	200	9-25-78	0	0	1.29	1	1	0	0	7	5	1	1	1	0	6	.192	.071	.333	7.71	0.00
Pizzaro, Melvin	L-L	6-1	185	3-16-78	0	0	5.40	2	0	0	0	2	1	1	1	0	3	2	.200	.000	.500	10.80	16.20
Rall, Tim	R-L	6-0	200	9-30-79	0	0	9.00	3	0	0	0	5	7	5	5	0	3	2	.333	.500	.267	3.60	5.40
Reichert, Dan	R-R	6-3	175	7-12-76	1	0	11.25	2	1	0	0	4	7	7	5	1	4	3	.333	.385	.250	6.75	9.00
Sherrill, George	L-L	6-0	220	4-19-77	1	3	2.28	22	0	0	7	24	19	7	6	0	6	38	.209	.143	.250	14.45	2.28
Soriano, Rafael	R-R	6-1	220	12-19-79	1	0	0.00	5	0	0	0	5	3	0	0	0	1	11	.158	.154	.167	18.56	1.69
Thomas, Jared	L-L	6-3	225	7-28-80	2	2	4.87	27	0	0	0	44	54	27	24	10	35	48	.302	.250	.323	9.74	7.11
Woerman, Joe	R-R	6-3	200	12-12-82	0	0	12.00	2	0	0	0	3	2	4	4	1	7	2	.200	.250	.167	6.00	21.00

FIELDING

Catcher	PCT	G	PO	A	E	DP	PB
Christianson	.994	61	441	22	3	9	4
Gonzalez	.993	39	264	19	2	2	2
Ojeda	1.000	5	36	3	0	0	0
Olivo	1.000	14	91	7	0	1	0
Rivera	1.000	13	78	8	0	1	2
Santiago	1.000	1	1	0	0	0	0
Terveen	.993	18	116	17	1	2	2

First Base	PCT	G	PO	A	E	DP
Brown	1.000	12	77	10	0	11
Christianson	1.000	2	11	1	0	2
Dobbs	.987	32	287	20	4	29
Hansen	1.000	1	6	1	0	1
Ojeda	1.000	1	7	1	0	1
Pellow	1.000	1	8	0	0	2
Rifkin	.994	91	808	48	5	70
Spiezio	1.000	8	82	6	0	12
Terveen	1.000	1	2	0	0	0

Second Base	PCT	G	PO	A	E	DP
Betancourt	1.000	1	2	4	0	2
Blakeley	.947	4	8	10	1	2
Brown	1.000	4	6	8	0	1
Lopez	.972	44	84	124	6	30
Santiago	.993	94	174	277	3	69
Valbuena	.000	1	0	0	0	0

Third Base	PCT	G	PO	A	E	DP
Brown	.932	67	51	126	13	9
Dobbs	.852	10	6	17	4	1
Hansen	.750	1	2	1	1	0
Leone	.913	63	34	134	16	10
Santiago	.867	5	2	11	2	3
Spiezio	1.000	2	1	4	0	1

Shortstop	PCT	G	PO	A	E	DP
Betancourt	.989	48	83	183	3	48
Cabrera	1.000	6	11	13	0	5
Dominguez	1.000	1	2	1	0	1
Leone	.957	12	13	32	2	6
Morse	.981	49	61	143	4	25
Santiago	.992	30	33	98	1	17
Valdez	.833	1	1	4	1	0

Outfield	PCT	G	PO	A	E	DP
Auty	1.000	1	4	0	0	0
Bohn	.983	22	57	2	1	1
Bradford	.667	3	2	0	1	0
Choo	.991	112	200	24	2	3
Delucchi	.977	20	43	0	1	0
Dobbs	1.000	1	2	0	0	0
Jacobs	1.000	6	13	0	0	0
Leone	.880	13	19	3	3	0
Nunez	.979	118	227	6	5	0
Snelling	.976	51	78	4	2	0
Spiezio	1.000	1	2	0	0	0
Strong	.976	87	197	4	5	1

SAN ANTONIO MISSIONS — Class AA

TEXAS LEAGUE

BATTING	B-T	HT	WT	DOB	AVG	vLH	vRH	G	AB	R	H	2B	3B	HR	RBI	BB	HBP	SH	SF	SO	SB	CS	SLG	OBP
Betancourt, Yuniesky	R-R	5-10	190	1-31-82	.273	.289	.265	52	227	25	62	10	3	5	20	9	1	0	2	18	12	7	.410	.301
Blakeley, Eric	R-R	6-1	188	9-8-79	.211	.455	.152	20	57	1	12	1	0	0	4	1	0	1	0	7	1	1	.228	.224
Bohn, T.J.	R-R	6-4	215	1-17-80	.308	.287	.319	113	438	67	135	30	2	12	57	35	5	7	1	96	27	9	.468	.365
Bubela, Jaime	L-R	6-1	200	6-6-78	.292	.302	.288	130	520	84	152	20	5	9	57	34	5	4	2	118	40	6	.402	.340
Castro, Ismael	R-R	5-9	193	8-14-83	.264	.331	.232	115	421	41	111	24	1	9	51	12	3	3	5	43	6	9	.390	.286
Craig, Casey	L-R	6-1	185	1-12-85	.000	.000	.000	4	2	0	0	0	0	0	0	0	0	0	0	1	0	2	.000	.000
Emmons, John	R-R	6-1	205	10-10-81	.667	1.000	.000	4	3	1	2	1	0	0	0	0	0	0	0	1	0	0	1.000	.667
Espy, Nathan	R-R	6-3	215	4-24-78	.275	.264	.280	122	440	70	121	27	6	13	61	66	8	1	10	100	11	6	.452	.372
Guzman, Jesus	R-R	6-1	165	6-14-84	.258	.280	.248	119	453	61	117	18	8	9	53	45	4	11	1	101	6	11	.393	.330

BATTING	B-T	HT	WT	DOB	AVG	vLH	vRH	G	AB	R	H	2B	3B	HR	RBI	BB	HBP	SH	SF	SO	SB	CS	SLG	OBP
Harris, Gary	L-R	5-10	185	9-9-79	.282	.228	.308	120	457	68	129	21	2	6	42	22	4	5	2	72	15	15	.376	.320
Hoorelbeke, Jesse	R-R	6-2	263	10-13-77	.249	.268	.240	119	450	62	112	25	0	22	81	47	5	0	1	156	2	0	.451	.326
Jones, Adam	R-R	6-2	180	8-1-85	.298	.310	.293	63	228	33	68	10	3	7	20	22	3	2	2	48	9	4	.461	.365
Menchaca, Eriberto	R-R	5-11	193	2-7-81	.226	.319	.182	71	226	23	51	5	0	0	9	14	1	6	0	47	4	4	.248	.274
Moon, Brian	B-R	6-0	190	7-15-77	.230	.178	.250	52	161	12	37	6	0	2	14	13	5	4	0	27	0	1	.304	.307
Nelson, Jon	R-R	6-5	235	1-16-80	.235	.213	.243	98	375	44	88	12	7	15	62	15	3	0	5	129	10	9	.424	.266
Nesbit, Michael	R-R	6-1	175	12-16-81	.222	.429	.091	8	18	2	4	0	0	0	1	1	0	0	0	4	1	0	.222	.263
Oliveros, Luis	R-R	6-1	180	6-18-83	.285	.275	.288	40	144	15	41	8	1	2	23	2	2	2	0	20	0	0	.396	.304
Reese, Pokey	R-R	5-11	190	6-10-73	.125	.250	.000	2	8	1	1	0	0	0	0	2	0	0	0	1	1	0	.125	.300
Rivera, Rene	R-R	5-10	190	7-31-83	.278	.264	.286	57	212	20	59	14	1	2	21	7	1	1	0	35	1	0	.382	.305

PITCHING	B-T	HT	WT	DOB	W	L	ERA	G	GS	CG	SV	IP	H	R	ER	HR	BB	SO	AVG	vLH	vRH	K/9	BB/9
Atchison, Scott	R-R	6-2	195	3-29-76	0	0	0.00	5	0	0	0	6	3	0	0	0	2	8	.143	.125	.154	12.00	3.00
Bazardo, Yorman	R-R	6-2	200	7-11-84	3	1	4.28	6	6	0	0	34	38	16	16	4	11	26	.295	.342	.226	6.95	2.94
Bourgeois, Nick	L-L	6-4	215	10-26-80	0	1	7.50	2	2	0	0	6	6	5	5	1	6	9	.273	.333	.250	13.50	9.00
Bumstead, Michael	R-R	6-4	210	7-8-77	0	2	7.11	7	4	0	0	19	28	18	15	1	17	9	.364	.409	.303	4.26	8.05
Cortez, Renee	R-R	6-4	202	12-9-82	5	3	3.96	44	1	0	10	64	61	32	28	4	23	62	.253	.236	.267	8.76	3.25
Done, Juan	R-R	6-2	220	10-2-80	1	0	16.43	7	0	0	0	8	16	14	14	2	2	6	.432	.364	.533	7.04	2.35
Dorman, Rich	R-R	6-3	210	9-30-78	3	0	0.45	3	3	0	0	20	7	1	1	0	12	24	.113	.156	.067	10.80	5.40
Flannery, Mike	R-R	6-2	225	9-20-79	0	0	4.26	6	0	0	3	6	7	3	3	0	2	5	.292	.412	.000	7.11	2.84
Fruto, Emiliano	R-R	6-3	229	6-6-84	2	3	2.57	40	0	0	12	67	56	22	19	6	22	63	.231	.280	.193	8.51	2.97
Green, Sean	R-R	6-6	230	4-20-79	0	1	2.96	21	0	0	14	24	17	11	8	1	8	18	.189	.233	.149	6.66	2.96
Harris, Jeff	R-R	6-1	190	7-4-74	5	0	2.10	11	2	0	0	34	25	9	8	4	8	31	.200	.230	.172	8.13	2.10
Huber, Jon	R-R	6-2	195	7-7-81	7	8	4.74	26	26	1	0	148	159	87	78	11	49	112	.276	.301	.250	6.81	2.98
Jimenez, Cesar	L-L	6-0	203	11-12-84	3	5	2.62	45	1	0	4	69	64	21	20	3	24	54	.250	.220	.264	7.08	3.15
Key, Chris	R-L	6-3	210	10-30-77	4	1	2.42	23	0	0	3	52	55	15	14	5	8	27	.281	.219	.311	4.67	1.38
Livingston, Bobby	L-L	6-3	190	9-3-82	8	4	2.86	18	18	0	0	116	103	45	37	7	27	78	.242	.223	.249	6.03	2.09
Mateo, Nathanel	R-R	6-1	160	12-24-80	0	4	6.61	14	1	0	0	16	20	17	12	4	10	21	.286	.259	.302	11.57	5.51
Oldham, Tom	L-L	6-2	210	5-18-82	13	7	3.67	27	26	0	0	155	179	79	63	15	45	115	.292	.320	.281	6.69	2.62
Pizzaro, Melvin	L-L	6-1	185	3-16-78	2	1	2.57	4	0	0	0	7	5	3	2	1	1	3	.200	.200	.200	3.86	1.29
Rall, Tim	R-L	6-0	200	9-30-79	2	3	3.81	41	0	0	0	59	45	27	25	6	34	61	.208	.232	.188	9.31	5.19
Rowland-Smith, Ryan	L-L	6-3	200	1-26-83	6	7	4.35	33	17	0	0	122	133	72	59	7	51	102	.283	.290	.280	7.52	3.76
Sandoval, Juan	R-R	6-2	170	1-13-81	9	11	4.03	28	28	0	0	161	196	88	72	6	46	99	.305	.323	.287	5.55	2.58
Soriano, Rafael	R-R	6-1	220	12-19-79	0	0	0.00	1	1	0	0	1	0	0	0	0	0	0	.000	.000	.000	0.00	0.00
Spiehs, R.D.	R-R	6-3	224	10-18-79	2	1	2.81	17	0	0	2	26	21	8	8	3	7	15	.228	.282	.189	5.26	2.45
Thomas, Jared	L-L	6-3	225	7-28-80	1	1	5.24	11	4	0	0	22	30	14	13	3	19	21	.316	.290	.328	8.46	7.66
Wilson, Philip	R-R	6-9	235	4-1-81	0	0	5.56	4	0	0	0	11	12	7	7	2	7	10	.286	.211	.348	7.94	5.56

FIELDING

Catcher	PCT	G	PO	A	E	DP	PB
Moon	.989	52	331	45	4	3	5
Oliveros	.984	39	291	26	5	5	4
Rivera	.990	57	367	44	4	4	9

First Base	PCT	G	PO	A	E	DP
Espy	.989	51	416	34	5	34
Hoorelbeke	.991	92	807	58	8	91
Menchaca	1.000	3	3	1	0	0

Second Base	PCT	G	PO	A	E	DP
Betancourt	1.000	1	3	1	0	1
Blakeley	.961	12	12	37	2	7
Castro	.978	111	205	362	13	82
Menchaca	.962	20	32	43	3	12

Third Base	PCT	G	PO	A	E	DP
Blakeley	.833	5	2	8	2	0
Guzman	.909	118	71	170	24	28
Menchaca	.957	21	11	33	2	4

Shortstop	PCT	G	PO	A	E	DP
Betancourt	.980	51	89	152	5	23
Jones	.959	61	115	165	12	39
Menchaca	.977	29	44	81	3	19
Reese	1.000	1	2	3	0	1

Outfield	PCT	G	PO	A	E	DP
Bohn	.985	107	247	14	4	4
Bubela	.969	116	247	6	8	2
Craig	.000	1	0	0	0	0
Emmons	.000	1	0	0	0	0
Harris	.996	115	240	12	1	4
Hoorelbeke	1.000	1	3	0	0	0
Jones	1.000	2	1	0	0	0
Nelson	.958	78	127	11	6	3
Nesbit	1.000	7	13	1	0	0

INLAND EMPIRE 66ers — High Class A

CALIFORNIA LEAGUE

BATTING	B-T	HT	WT	DOB	AVG	vLH	vRH	G	AB	R	H	2B	3B	HR	RBI	BB	HBP	SH	SF	SO	SB	CS	SLG	OBP
Arroyo, Carlos	L-L	6-0	190	5-30-81	.313	.266	.322	98	402	50	126	17	2	0	62	26	0	3	3	37	13	5	.366	.353
Balentien, Wladimir	R-R	6-2	180	7-2-84	.291	.256	.299	123	492	76	143	38	8	25	93	33	6	1	7	160	9	2	.553	.338
Blakeley, Eric	R-R	6-1	188	9-8-79	.263	.357	.233	14	57	10	15	3	1	3	11	2	3	0	0	8	0	0	.509	.323
Boucher, Sebastien	L-R	6-0	190	10-19-81	.352	.375	.348	52	213	54	75	14	3	2	21	36	4	1	1	49	15	3	.474	.453
Bradford, Sam	B-R	6-1	185	10-15-81	.168	.188	.165	28	95	11	16	2	1	3	9	13	2	1	1	25	3	2	.305	.279
Cabrera, Asdrubal	B-R	6-0	170	11-13-85	.284	.263	.289	55	225	31	64	15	6	1	26	15	0	1	3	47	3	1	.418	.325
Cho, Hyung	R-R	5-9	190	8-20-82	.256	.200	.265	11	39	5	10	0	0	0	3	6	1	0	0	2	0	0	.256	.370
Collins, Chris	R-R	6-0	205	8-14-81	.257	.184	.279	47	167	22	43	8	0	1	19	17	1	0	1	29	1	0	.323	.328
Colton, Chris	R-R	6-1	198	9-21-82	.243	.250	.240	51	169	24	41	10	1	4	23	10	3	2	0	36	5	5	.385	.297
Craig, Casey	L-R	6-1	185	1-12-85	.345	.500	.320	8	29	2	10	1	1	0	3	3	0	0	0	6	0	1	.448	.406
Dominguez, Jeff	B-R	6-2	153	7-31-86	.333	.000	.353	6	18	4	6	1	0	0	1	4	0	0	0	3	0	0	.389	.455
Garbe, B.J.	R-R	6-2	195	2-3-81	.275	.328	.261	80	305	41	84	17	1	9	41	25	3	2	1	48	8	5	.426	.335
Garciaparra, Michael	R-R	6-1	175	4-2-83	.298	.231	.314	84	336	60	100	15	3	6	33	35	14	3	0	64	10	8	.414	.387
Gergel, Kevin	L-R	6-3	225	11-15-81	.250	1.000	.211	5	20	1	5	2	0	0	3	1	0	0	0	5	0	0	.350	.286
Gonzalez, Juan	B-R	6-0	165	2-23-82	.212	.240	.200	22	85	10	18	1	2	1	5	3	1	0	0	16	4	3	.306	.247
Hagen, Matt	R-R	6-4	230	1-3-80	.185	.135	.211	35	108	8	20	6	1	1	8	4	1	0	1	30	2	1	.287	.219
Hargrove, Andy	R-L	6-1	240	10-31-81	.200	.000	.211	6	20	2	4	0	0	1	1	3	0	0	0	8	0	0	.350	.304
Heid, Trevor	R-R	6-3	210	4-30-82	.206	.333	.194	12	34	5	7	3	0	1	1	4	0	1	0	10	0	0	.382	.289
Jacobsen, Bucky	R-R	6-4	255	8-30-75	.571	.667	.556	6	21	7	12	2	0	3	9	6	1	0	1	2	0	0	1.095	.655
Johnson, Rob	R-R	6-1	200	7-22-83	.314	.455	.288	19	70	15	22	3	0	2	12	10	0	2	4	14	2	0	.443	.381
Jones, Adam	R-R	6-2	180	8-1-85	.295	.321	.289	68	271	43	80	20	5	8	46	29	8	2	5	64	4	5	.494	.374
Lahair, Bryan	L-R	6-5	215	11-5-82	.310	.218	.336	126	509	81	158	28	2	22	113	51	3	0	6	125	0	1	.503	.373
Ledbetter, Curtis	R-R	6-3	220	12-26-81	.063	.000	.063	4	16	0	1	0	0	0	0	1	0	0	0	5	0	0	.063	.118
Monzon, Erick	R-R	6-0	190	11-30-81	.271	.177	.292	94	350	53	95	25	2	13	49	35	3	1	3	80	7	1	.466	.340
Nesbit, Michael	R-R	6-1	175	12-16-81	.284	.378	.260	65	218	37	62	17	3	1	14	21	2	0	2	64	15	8	.404	.350
Oliveros, Luis	R-R	6-1	180	6-18-83	.208	.000	.231	18	72	6	15	0	1	2	11	1	1	1	0	11	0	0	.319	.230
Reese, Pokey	R-R	5-11	190	6-10-73	.250	.000	.273	3	12	2	3	2	0	0	3	2	0	1	0	1	0	0	.417	.357

BATTING	B-T	HT	WT	DOB	AVG	vLH	vRH	G	AB	R	H	2B	3B	HR	RBI	BB	HBP	SH	SF	SO	SB	CS	SLG	OBP
Rogelstad, Matt	L-R	6-3	185	9-13-82	.304	.275	.309	111	438	71	133	23	2	1	47	44	1	10	2	52	3	2	.372	.367
Ruchti, Justin	R-R	6-2	200	12-11-80	.211	.182	.215	60	199	21	42	8	0	6	24	10	3	1	0	38	0	2	.342	.259
Schweiger, Brian	R-R	6-0	195	8-21-82	.000	.000	.000	1	3	0	0	0	0	0	0	1	0	0	0	2	0	0	.000	.250
Zorn, Dean	B-R	6-1	190	9-12-86	.182	.000	.200	5	11	1	2	1	0	0	0	0	0	0	0	1	0	0	.273	.182

PITCHING	B-T	HT	WT	DOB	W	L	ERA	G	GS	CG	SV	IP	H	R	ER	HR	BB	SO	AVG	vLH	vRH	K/9	BB/9
Acosta, Nibaldo	R-R	6-0	184	3-6-83	3	5	5.83	39	3	0	2	80	106	63	52	8	29	65	.323	.272	.371	7.28	3.25
Arias, Oliver	R-R	6-5	210	8-17-81	0	0	6.64	14	0	0	0	20	26	16	15	4	16	24	.317	.353	.292	10.62	7.08
Bilke, Austin	R-R	6-2	225	8-13-79	0	1	81.00	1	0	0	0	0	3	3	3	1	1	1	.750	.000	.750	27.00	27.00
Bourgeois, Nick	L-L	6-4	215	10-26-80	2	4	3.59	27	0	0	1	48	41	25	19	4	31	45	.236	.279	.208	8.50	5.85
Cate, Troy	L-L	6-1	200	10-21-80	4	4	2.53	23	0	0	1	43	36	21	12	1	25	54	.221	.264	.187	11.39	5.27
Ellison, Derrick	L-L	6-2	195	9-6-78	0	1	6.97	7	0	0	0	10	14	11	8	0	10	7	.341	.211	.455	6.10	8.71
Feierabend, Ryan	L-L	6-3	190	8-22-85	8	7	3.88	29	29	0	0	151	186	80	65	16	51	122	.310	.257	.338	7.29	3.05
Fillinger, Chad	R-R	6-4	210	10-26-82	2	5	5.96	15	11	0	0	71	90	48	47	16	18	61	.304	.289	.319	7.73	2.28
James, Craig	R-R	6-1	175	3-10-83	0	2	2.42	23	0	0	10	26	25	8	7	3	8	24	.250	.375	.167	8.31	2.77
Key, Chris	R-L	6-3	210	10-30-77	4	0	1.80	18	0	0	2	30	44	15	6	2	5	20	.338	.370	.321	6.00	1.50
Looper, Aaron	R-R	6-2	210	9-7-76	0	1	3.75	9	0	0	0	12	9	8	5	3	5	11	.196	.227	.167	8.25	3.75
Mackintosh, Jason	R-L	6-0	205	7-2-80	10	11	4.26	29	28	1	0	180	206	97	85	12	57	141	.295	.275	.305	7.06	2.86
Martinez, Miguel	L-L	6-2	202	10-22-82	1	4	7.09	19	6	0	1	47	52	42	37	4	36	42	.277	.273	.279	8.04	6.89
Mault, Jeff	R-R	6-1	175	12-11-80	0	0	3.10	14	0	0	0	20	17	7	7	1	13	13	.236	.229	.243	5.75	5.75
Moorhead, Brandon	R-R	6-2	215	1-23-80	6	9	4.75	26	25	0	0	142	163	91	75	13	36	120	.287	.303	.273	7.61	2.28
Nottingham, Shawn	L-L	6-1	190	1-22-85	4	3	3.86	7	6	0	0	37	48	19	16	2	10	28	.310	.309	.310	6.75	2.41
Olore, Kevin	L-R	6-2	210	9-21-78	0	0	15.43	1	1	0	0	2	4	4	4	2	4	3	.364	.333	.375	11.57	15.43
Rivera, Mumba	R-R	6-5	205	12-10-80	5	8	7.49	18	17	0	0	91	118	79	76	19	50	67	.316	.363	.268	6.60	4.93
Soriano, Rafael	R-R	6-1	220	12-19-79	0	0	0.00	3	3	0	0	4	2	0	0	0	0	5	.154	.286	.000	11.25	0.00
Steele, Michael	L-R	6-1	205	8-22-78	4	5	4.41	30	1	0	2	49	54	31	24	7	23	42	.286	.348	.230	7.71	4.22
Stitt, Brian	R-R	5-11	201	8-26-82	1	2	5.92	15	0	0	0	24	30	18	16	1	9	22	.297	.300	.295	8.14	3.33
Trolia, Aaron	R-R	6-2	210	5-10-81	3	7	4.82	40	10	0	0	105	118	71	56	6	49	77	.287	.309	.267	6.62	4.21
Watson, Tanner	R-R	6-3	210	6-14-82	0	0	27.00	3	0	0	0	4	7	11	11	0	6	2	.368	.455	.250	4.91	14.73
Wear, Greg	R-R	6-6	212	7-7-79	1	3	4.73	33	0	0	3	40	45	24	21	3	21	34	.283	.270	.292	7.65	4.73
Wilson, Philip	R-R	6-9	235	4-1-81	0	0	6.23	5	0	0	0	9	10	6	6	0	4	9	.278	.263	.294	9.35	4.15

FIELDING

Catcher	PCT	G	PO	A	E	DP	PB
Collins	.984	46	332	28	6	4	6
Hagen	1.000	5	12	2	0	0	2
Johnson	1.000	19	131	19	0	1	1
Ledbetter	1.000	1	9	0	0	0	0
Oliveros	.994	18	162	14	1	1	6
Ruchti	.989	60	414	39	5	5	7
Schweiger	1.000	1	4	2	0	0	0

First Base	PCT	G	PO	A	E	DP
Hagen	.983	18	149	20	3	22
Hargrove	.951	6	35	4	2	4
Lahair	.996	117	1003	87	4	90
Ledbetter	1.000	2	9	1	0	1
Rogelstad	1.000	2	12	2	0	2

Second Base	PCT	G	PO	A	E	DP
Blakeley	.926	10	18	45	5	6
Cho	.902	11	19	36	6	11
Garciaparra	.959	83	146	271	18	52
Gonzalez	.984	13	27	34	1	8
Rogelstad	.956	26	42	66	5	10
Zorn	1.000	1	2	1	0	1

Third Base	PCT	G	PO	A	E	DP
Blakeley	.750	1	0	3	1	0
Colton	.000	1	0	0	0	0
Dominguez	1.000	2	1	1	0	0
Gonzalez	.714	1	1	4	2	0
Hagen	.875	5	3	4	1	0
Monzon	.917	73	57	119	16	12
Rogelstad	.924	64	35	110	12	11

Shortstop	PCT	G	PO	A	E	DP
Cabrera	.960	54	88	155	10	44
Dominguez	1.000	4	6	6	0	4
Jones	.935	64	130	185	22	44
Monzon	1.000	14	24	38	0	8
Reese	1.000	2	4	8	0	2
Rogelstad	.000	1	0	0	0	0
Zorn	1.000	2	3	6	0	0

Outfield	PCT	G	PO	A	E	DP
Arroyo	.969	70	124	3	4	1
Balentien	.958	85	176	8	8	2
Blakeley	1.000	2	3	0	0	0
Boucher	.964	49	104	3	4	1
Bradford	.978	25	43	2	1	0
Colton	.989	50	88	5	1	2
Craig	.929	8	13	0	1	0
Garbe	.972	76	98	6	3	1
Heid	.960	10	24	0	1	0
Nesbit	.980	49	92	5	2	2
Rogelstad	1.000	3	5	0	0	0

WISCONSIN TMBER RATTLERS — Low Class A

MIDWEST LEAGUE

BATTING	B-T	HT	WT	DOB	AVG	vLH	vRH	G	AB	R	H	2B	3B	HR	RBI	BB	HBP	SH	SF	SO	SB	CS	SLG	OBP
Arroyo, Jack	R-R	6-1	175	9-7-80	.206	.288	.172	81	247	36	51	11	4	1	31	26	6	4	3	57	11	3	.296	.294
Boucher, Sebastien	L-R	6-0	190	10-19-81	.326	.182	.346	48	178	37	58	14	2	2	31	26	1	1	2	34	11	1	.461	.411
Cabrera, Asdrubal	B-R	6-0	170	11-13-85	.318	.396	.292	51	192	26	61	12	3	4	30	30	1	2	3	32	2	6	.474	.407
Chen, Yung Chi	R-R	5-11	172	7-13-83	.292	.255	.301	121	503	77	147	27	7	7	80	37	2	1	6	76	15	6	.416	.339
Clement, Jeff	L-R	6-1	210	8-21-83	.319	.333	.316	30	113	17	36	5	0	6	20	12	1	0	1	25	1	2	.522	.386
Colton, Chris	R-R	6-1	198	9-21-82	.335	.350	.331	52	203	46	68	8	3	12	37	13	1	1	2	36	10	3	.581	.374
Falcon, Omar	B-R	6-1	210	9-1-82	.272	.241	.280	42	136	22	37	11	0	4	22	25	3	1	1	48	0	3	.441	.394
Green, Brandon	B-R	6-0	195	8-12-81	.216	.213	.217	99	356	39	77	14	4	1	45	32	2	1	4	62	3	0	.287	.282
Hall, David	R-R	6-1	195	10-9-83	.237	.300	.214	13	38	6	9	2	0	0	1	1	2	1	0	11	2	0	.289	.293
Heckman, Corby	R-R	6-1	185	10-30-81	.125	.000	.167	3	8	1	1	0	0	0	0	1	0	0	0	3	0	0	.125	.222
Hubbard, Thomas	L-R	6-2	215	4-16-82	.297	.324	.290	110	391	76	116	25	1	17	77	54	6	2	4	95	4	2	.496	.387
Johnson, Brent	R-R	6-2	185	5-21-82	.310	.360	.295	109	378	77	117	21	1	1	44	55	6	2	3	57	22	8	.378	.403
Johnson, Rob	R-R	6-1	200	7-22-83	.272	.297	.266	77	305	41	83	19	1	9	51	20	3	3	4	31	10	3	.430	.319
Navarro, Oswaldo	B-R	5-11	160	10-2-84	.269	.240	.277	120	450	57	121	29	0	9	69	39	6	4	10	60	11	7	.393	.329
Schweiger, Brian	R-R	6-0	195	8-21-82	.316	.444	.200	6	19	1	6	1	0	0	5	4	0	0	0	2	0	0	.368	.435
Soto, Luis	R-R	6-0	204	7-30-83	.164	.200	.146	23	73	5	12	2	1	0	7	4	0	0	0	17	0	0	.219	.208
Tuiasosopo, Matt	R-R	6-2	210	5-10-86	.276	.286	.274	107	409	72	113	21	3	6	45	44	9	1	1	96	8	5	.386	.359
Wilson, Michael	B-R	6-1	238	6-29-83	.266	.287	.259	127	463	93	123	29	3	19	84	57	15	1	6	107	10	2	.464	.360
Womack, Josh	L-L	6-0	194	1-5-84	.256	.247	.258	102	371	59	95	16	5	3	33	41	1	2	2	93	22	3	.350	.330

PITCHING	B-T	HT	WT	DOB	W	L	ERA	G	GS	CG	SV	IP	H	R	ER	HR	BB	SO	AVG	vLH	vRH	K/9	BB/9
Abrams, Casey	L-L	6-4	200	7-17-81	4	7	6.04	17	16	0	0	76	84	66	51	8	63	35	.286	.318	.276	4.14	7.46
Bello, Cibney	L-R	6-5	209	9-10-82	4	4	5.02	37	8	0	1	95	88	58	53	8	69	75	.249	.209	.274	7.11	6.54
Bergdall, Kendall	R-L	6-3	219	11-26-82	0	1	4.13	18	0	0	0	33	33	24	15	3	31	23	.266	.179	.306	6.34	8.54
Blanco, Ivan	R-R	6-1	190	9-24-83	3	3	6.93	28	6	0	0	62	67	54	48	9	30	53	.283	.372	.224	7.65	4.33
Brandt, Adam	R-L	6-2	230	5-18-82	1	0	8.59	11	0	0	1	15	23	14	14	4	9	5	.377	.667	.327	3.07	5.52
Fillinger, Chad	R-R	6-4	210	10-26-82	2	3	2.70	23	1	0	3	43	37	13	13	3	13	53	.231	.211	.243	11.01	2.70
Frye, Randall	R-R	6-4	221	9-11-83	2	4	8.12	11	10	0	0	44	57	43	40	6	38	19	.306	.299	.312	3.86	7.71
Grasley, Steve	R-R	6-0	190	8-5-81	9	0	3.71	44	0	0	3	90	84	44	37	5	34	70	.251	.215	.276	7.03	3.41

PITCHING	B-T	HT	WT	DOB	W	L	ERA	G	GS	CG	SV	IP	H	R	ER	HR	BB	SO	AVG	vLH	vRH	K/9	BB/9
James, Craig	R-R	6-1	175	3-10-83	2	1	0.88	26	0	0	9	31	18	3	3	1	5	31	.171	.146	.188	9.10	1.47
Jensen, Aaron	R-R	6-2	180	6-11-84	10	13	5.56	28	27	1	0	157	190	115	97	21	55	87	.303	.280	.318	4.99	3.15
Jordan, Justin	R-R	6-5	210	8-31-81	3	1	6.68	17	0	0	1	32	46	28	24	3	7	29	.329	.298	.344	8.07	1.95
Langdon, Donny	R-L	6-1	190	2-2-82	0	3	4.75	18	1	0	1	30	34	18	16	2	21	23	.286	.160	.319	6.82	6.23
Lockwood, Jon	R-R	6-2	210	12-12-81	3	0	2.12	15	0	0	3	30	18	12	7	0	14	43	.168	.132	.188	13.04	4.25
Lowe, Mark	R-R	6-4	180	6-7-83	6	6	5.47	22	22	0	0	104	107	72	63	12	49	72	.264	.203	.300	6.25	4.25
Martinez, Roman	R-R	6-3	160	8-9-84	0	2	3.66	19	1	0	0	39	39	20	16	3	17	29	.262	.177	.322	6.64	3.89
Nottingham, Shawn	L-L	6-1	190	1-22-85	0	1	9.53	3	3	0	0	11	15	12	12	0	7	10	.326	.455	.286	7.94	5.56
O'Flaherty, Eric	L-L	6-2	195	2-5-85	4	4	3.75	45	0	0	13	70	73	35	29	2	30	51	.268	.349	.244	6.59	3.88
Rivera, Mumba	R-R	6-5	205	12-10-80	7	0	3.22	10	10	0	0	59	46	25	21	3	26	30	.227	.313	.150	4.60	3.99
Santiago, Julio	L-L	6-0	155	12-8-85	7	3	4.44	17	17	0	0	99	110	58	49	10	23	66	.281	.355	.267	5.98	2.08
Snyder, Jason	R-R	6-6	205	4-6-83	9	7	4.82	27	17	0	0	114	128	76	61	13	31	77	.282	.308	.261	6.08	2.45

FIELDING

Catcher	PCT	G	PO	A	E	DP	PB
Clement	.988	20	148	13	2	4	5
Falcon	.981	41	232	24	5	3	3
R. Johnson	.986	75	489	65	8	4	11
Schweiger	.974	6	31	6	1	0	0
Soto	1.000	1	2	0	0	0	0

First Base	PCT	G	PO	A	E	DP
Green	.990	47	361	42	4	39
Hubbard	.986	82	659	47	10	72
B. Johnson	.973	5	36	0	1	2
Soto	1.000	12	91	7	0	11

Second Base	PCT	G	PO	A	E	DP
Arroyo	.945	25	41	45	5	11
Cabrera	.993	30	64	73	1	19
Chen	.982	35	59	104	3	29
Green	.000	1	0	0	0	0
Heckman	.000	1	0	0	0	0
Navarro	.974	57	145	157	8	38

Third Base	PCT	G	PO	A	E	DP
Cabrera	1.000	6	5	13	0	1
Chen	.939	80	54	161	14	14
Green	.892	37	21	70	11	15
Heckman	.500	1	0	1	1	0
B. Johnson	.925	21	11	26	3	2
Navarro	.800	2	2	2	1	0
Tuiasosopo	1.000	1	1	2	0	0

Shortstop	PCT	G	PO	A	E	DP
Cabrera	.927	11	15	23	3	6
Chen	.000	1	0	0	0	0
Navarro	.935	53	105	152	18	42
Tuiasosopo	.922	79	118	190	26	36

Outfield	PCT	G	PO	A	E	DP
Arroyo	.990	44	94	9	1	2
Boucher	.990	44	93	7	1	0
Colton	.985	46	127	4	2	2
Hall	.800	8	8	0	2	0
Hubbard	1.000	3	3	1	0	1
B. Johnson	.994	76	160	9	1	1
R. Johnson	.000	1	0	0	0	0
Wilson	.982	122	263	14	5	5
Womack	.974	93	180	6	5	1

EVERETT AQUASOX — Short-Season Class A

NORTHWEST LEAGUE

BATTING	B-T	HT	WT	DOB	AVG	vLH	vRH	G	AB	R	H	2B	3B	HR	RBI	BB	HBP	SH	SF	SO	SB	CS	SLG	OBP
Cho, Hyung	R-R	5-9	190	8-20-82	.267	.333	.250	5	15	3	4	1	0	0	2	1	1	0	0	2	0	0	.333	.353
Clement, Jeff	L-R	6-1	210	8-21-83	.273	.000	.273	4	11	4	3	1	0	0	1	1	2	0	1	2	0	0	.364	.400
Craig, Casey	L-R	6-1	185	1-12-85	.278	.218	.296	62	241	53	67	9	4	6	28	21	2	1	0	57	18	4	.423	.341
Eastley, Reed	L-R	6-2	210	7-24-83	.318	.365	.302	55	201	29	64	13	2	4	28	37	5	1	1	42	8	1	.463	.434
Flaig, Jeff	R-R	6-2	170	3-3-85	.254	.246	.257	64	236	38	60	19	0	7	38	18	11	2	4	48	2	3	.424	.331
Gary, Alex	R-R	6-3	225	10-11-83	.237	.189	.255	42	139	26	33	9	2	6	22	8	8	1	0	58	2	1	.460	.316
Hall, David	R-R	6-1	195	10-9-83	.265	.379	.219	34	102	9	27	4	0	0	10	12	2	3	1	29	4	2	.304	.350
Heckman, Corby	R-R	6-1	185	10-30-81	.286	.286	.000	2	7	1	2	0	0	0	0	0	0	0	0	3	0	0	.286	.286
Heid, Trevor	R-R	6-3	210	4-30-82	.299	.167	.329	32	97	29	29	11	2	4	14	10	4	1	1	23	10	2	.577	.384
Hudson, Robbie	R-R	6-0	170	8-31-83	.253	.243	.255	55	186	24	47	8	1	0	16	12	1	6	0	32	6	2	.306	.302
Prettyman, Ron	L-R	6-2	190	8-4-81	.278	.268	.281	58	234	35	65	11	2	6	27	19	2	2	1	57	7	3	.419	.336
Sabatella, Bryan	R-R	6-3	210	11-1-84	.249	.167	.281	53	169	28	42	5	2	4	24	20	3	0	4	45	7	4	.373	.332
Santin, Daniel	L-L	6-3	205	11-7-84	.273	.216	.292	54	205	20	56	11	0	4	31	11	1	0	2	42	0	4	.385	.311
Saunders, Michael	L-R	6-4	205	11-19-86	.270	.320	.253	56	196	24	53	13	3	7	39	27	2	1	2	74	2	7	.474	.361
Schweiger, Brian	R-R	6-0	195	8-21-82	.136	.273	.104	20	59	7	8	2	0	0	4	10	3	1	0	23	3	1	.169	.292
Tucker, J.B.	R-R	6-0	205	2-20-82	.259	.292	.246	48	174	34	45	19	2	11	36	23	6	1	2	60	4	0	.580	.361
Valbuena, Luis	L-R	5-10	160	11-30-85	.261	.231	.270	74	287	47	75	10	3	12	51	31	2	1	4	37	14	6	.443	.333
Wu, Chao Kuan	L-R	6-3	192	5-25-84	.217	.000	.227	8	23	4	5	0	0	0	1	7	0	0	0	6	1	0	.217	.400
Zorn, Dean	B-R	6-1	190	9-12-86	.167	.071	.214	12	42	3	7	3	0	0	2	9	0	2	0	13	1	1	.238	.314

PITCHING	B-T	HT	WT	DOB	W	L	ERA	G	GS	CG	SV	IP	H	R	ER	HR	BB	SO	AVG	vLH	vRH	K/9	BB/9
Allen, Nick	R-R	6-1	210	6-15-83	6	4	4.59	16	12	0	0	67	82	42	34	3	12	37	.306	.339	.281	5.00	1.62
Arias, Oliver	R-R	6-5	210	8-17-81	0	0	4.91	6	1	0	0	15	20	9	8	2	2	9	.323	.393	.265	5.52	1.23
Asher, David	R-L	6-1	195	2-18-83	1	5	4.79	18	0	0	3	36	38	20	19	2	9	40	.275	.194	.299	10.09	2.27
Beus, Lance	L-L	6-1	180	3-11-83	1	2	3.68	19	0	0	1	37	37	18	15	5	13	34	.270	.281	.267	8.35	3.19
Brandt, Adam	R-L	6-2	230	5-18-82	0	0	54.00	1	0	0	0	0	2	3	2	0	1	0	.500	.000	.667	0.00	27.00
Carter, Eric	R-R	6-2	210	10-31-83	2	2	7.67	14	5	0	0	32	50	28	27	6	22	26	.376	.411	.351	7.39	6.25
Colon, Juan	R-R	6-1	170	10-19-81	0	0	5.00	6	0	0	0	9	9	5	5	0	5	8	.273	.250	.294	8.00	5.00
Fagan, Paul	L-L	6-5	195	4-13-85	6	2	3.50	15	14	0	0	82	86	40	32	5	33	50	.271	.373	.244	5.47	3.61
Frye, Randall	R-R	6-4	221	9-11-83	0	0	4.00	4	0	0	0	9	8	4	4	1	6	7	.250	.375	.208	7.00	6.00
Gibson, Rollie	L-L	6-2	220	12-30-83	3	2	4.45	15	2	0	1	28	31	14	14	5	12	30	.290	.414	.244	9.53	3.81
Gilmore, Jeff	R-R	6-2	200	9-29-83	5	1	3.97	12	8	0	0	57	55	25	25	9	13	57	.253	.253	.254	9.05	2.06
Guaramato, Edgar	R-R	6-1	170	8-5-84	1	4	3.62	28	0	0	1	37	23	20	15	1	24	38	.183	.255	.139	9.16	5.79
Kahn, Stephen	L-R	6-3	215	12-14-83	3	0	3.93	17	0	0	12	18	14	9	8	1	14	22	.209	.259	.175	10.80	6.87
Koliscak, Cory	R-R	6-2	200	11-30-81	2	1	5.06	22	0	0	3	27	27	18	15	3	12	23	.262	.302	.233	7.76	4.05
Lockwood, Jon	R-R	6-2	210	12-12-81	2	0	0.00	5	0	0	0	16	3	0	0	0	1	19	.060	.053	.065	10.69	0.56
Martinez, Roman	R-R	6-3	160	8-9-84	1	2	4.86	13	4	0	0	33	32	19	18	4	17	27	.246	.269	.231	7.29	4.59
Mault, Jeff	R-R	6-1	175	12-11-80	0	1	5.06	5	0	0	0	5	6	3	3	0	4	5	.286	.167	.444	8.44	6.75
Rohrbaugh, Robert	R-L	6-2	190	12-28-83	5	2	3.84	14	12	0	0	68	68	33	29	7	18	71	.262	.289	.256	9.40	2.38
Soriano, Rafael	R-R	6-1	220	12-19-79	0	0	3.00	4	4	0	0	6	6	3	2	0	2	8	.250	.091	.385	12.00	3.00
Thomas, Justin	L-L	6-3	220	1-18-84	3	3	3.81	18	6	0	0	59	63	31	25	2	20	48	.272	.186	.301	7.32	3.05
Vega, Marwin	R-R	6-0	175	10-27-86	0	2	9.35	3	2	0	0	9	7	11	9	0	7	9	.200	.200	.200	9.35	7.27
Williams, Harold	L-L	6-4	190	9-23-84	1	1	5.79	4	4	0	0	14	11	9	9	2	11	15	.216	.167	.231	9.64	7.07
Woerman, Joe	R-R	6-3	200	12-12-82	0	0	4.76	11	2	0	0	17	16	11	9	0	20	21	.267	.286	.256	11.12	10.59

GAMES BY POSITION: C—Clement 2, Santin 19, Schweiger 19, Tucker 40. **1B**—Eastley 14, Flaig 61, Sabatella 1, Wu 6. **2B**—Cho 1, Eastley 4, Valbuena 74. **3B**—Cho 3, Eastley 10, Heckman 2, Prettyman 56, Sabatella 10. **SS**—Cho 1, Eastley 10, Hudson 54, Prettyman 4, Zorn 12. **OF**—Craig 60, Flaig 3, Gary 38, Hall 31, Heid 31, Sabatella 29, Saunders 55.

ARIZONA LEAGUE

BATTING	B-T	HT	WT	DOB	AVG	vLH	vRH	G	AB	R	H	2B	3B	HR	RBI	BB	HBP	SH	SF	SO	SB	CS	SLG	OBP
Auty, Tim	R-R	6-0	180	12-21-85	.352	.190	.391	29	108	24	38	14	2	0	22	14	1	0	2	17	1	1	.519	.424
Bonilla, Leury	R-R	6-3	170	2-8-85	.248	.273	.243	34	125	22	31	3	4	2	22	10	3	3	5	40	1	2	.384	.308
Bradford, Sam	B-R	6-1	185	10-15-81	.270	.250	.273	8	37	8	10	2	3	1	8	1	1	0	1	14	0	1	.568	.300
Dixon, Kent	R-R	6-1	200	1-19-86	.224	.438	.157	19	67	8	15	4	0	1	8	4	2	1	0	19	2	0	.328	.288
Dominguez, Jeff	B-R	6-2	153	7-31-86	.240	.227	.243	33	125	17	30	4	1	0	11	10	1	2	2	35	8	1	.288	.297
Eastley, Reed	L-R	6-2	210	7-24-83	.667	.000	.727	3	12	4	8	1	0	1	4	2	0	0	0	0	0	0	1.000	.714
Garth, Ronald	R-R	5-11	165	11-5-84	.357	.409	.344	27	112	23	40	10	5	3	15	7	8	0	1	17	3	2	.616	.430
Gergel, Kevin	L-R	6-3	225	11-15-81	.316	.308	.318	36	133	28	42	9	2	5	27	9	4	0	0	36	1	1	.526	.377
Graterol, Oswaldo	R-R	6-1	175	8-27-84	.345	.261	.368	30	110	22	38	3	2	2	25	19	1	0	0	28	7	5	.464	.446
Guzman, Juan	B-R	6-2	178	5-17-84	.320	.294	.328	35	153	30	49	5	2	1	24	11	2	1	0	19	6	4	.399	.373
Halman, Greg	R-R	6-4	192	8-26-87	.258	.438	.219	26	89	17	23	2	3	3	11	10	3	0	1	19	1	3	.449	.350
Hargrove, Andy	R-L	6-1	240	10-31-81	.314	.313	.314	39	137	33	43	12	1	3	25	31	9	1	2	44	2	0	.482	.464
Heckman, Corby	R-R	6-1	185	10-30-81	.278	.286	.276	10	36	8	10	1	0	0	4	6	0	0	1	1	2	0	.306	.372
Hernandez, Eddy	L-L	6-3	170	8-4-84	.356	.435	.328	23	87	14	31	3	1	4	18	10	0	0	0	19	0	2	.552	.423
Hernandez, Jairo	R-R	6-3	185	5-8-85	.333	.667	.286	7	24	4	8	2	0	2	3	5	0	0	0	8	0	0	.667	.448
Hudson, Robbie	R-R	6-0	170	8-31-83	.000	.000	.000	2	9	3	0	0	0	0	0	0	0	0	0	1	0	0	.000	.000
Jacobo, Erwin	R-R	6-2	195	6-15-85	.179	.231	.163	17	56	10	10	1	0	0	9	9	2	0	0	23	1	2	.196	.313
Jacobsen, Bucky	R-R	6-4	255	8-30-75	.308	.333	.300	4	13	1	4	3	0	0	3	4	1	0	0	4	0	0	.538	.500
Ledbetter, Curtis	R-R	6-3	220	12-26-81	.311	.375	.296	34	122	22	38	9	1	4	21	10	0	1	0	44	2	0	.500	.364
Liverpool, Marquise	R-R	5-11	191	4-16-86	.298	.286	.301	30	94	24	28	5	0	0	10	9	6	1	1	23	10	3	.351	.391
Nelson, Jon	R-R	6-5	235	1-16-80	.273	1.000	.200	3	11	2	3	0	1	0	3	1	1	0	1	3	0	0	.455	.357
Prettyman, Ron	L-R	6-2	190	8-4-81	.182	.000	.182	5	22	4	4	0	0	0	3	3	0	0	0	3	2	0	.182	.280
Prosise, Nicholas	R-R	6-2	220	4-12-84	.240	.267	.235	29	100	9	24	9	0	0	14	7	3	0	1	18	0	3	.330	.306
Ruiz, Donato	R-R	6-3	170	3-17-83	.263	.182	.283	29	114	16	30	1	2	3	18	1	7	1	1	26	2	0	.386	.309
Zorn, Dean	B-R	6-1	190	9-12-86	.247	.185	.273	24	93	11	23	3	2	0	10	13	1	0	1	28	2	4	.323	.343

PITCHING	B-T	HT	WT	DOB	W	L	ERA	G	GS	CG	SV	IP	H	R	ER	HR	BB	SO	AVG	vLH	vRH	K/9	BB/9
Atchison, Scott	R-R	6-2	195	3-29-76	0	0	5.40	4	3	0	0	5	7	3	3	0	1	9	.333	.429	.286	16.20	1.80
Bannister, Brett	R-R	6-1	190	3-3-83	0	0	2.25	2	1	0	0	4	4	4	1	1	0	5	.235	.200	.250	11.25	0.00
Bonilla, Toma	R-R	6-4	180	1-28-83	0	4	6.00	15	1	0	0	33	36	29	22	2	19	30	.283	.241	.296	8.18	5.18
Campillo, Jorge	R-R	6-1	190	8-10-78	0	2	5.73	4	4	0	0	11	18	11	7	0	2	10	.367	.417	.351	8.18	1.64
Colon, Juan	R-R	6-1	170	10-19-81	0	0	3.86	12	0	0	2	16	16	8	7	0	9	23	.250	.278	.239	12.67	4.96
Dorman, Rich	R-R	6-3	210	9-30-78	0	0	5.40	4	3	0	0	10	7	6	6	0	5	20	.184	.167	.192	18.00	4.50
Huang, Chia An	R-R	6-2	204	11-11-85	2	3	6.96	11	7	0	0	32	46	30	25	2	17	21	.338	.500	.292	5.85	4.73
Kafka, Ari	R-R	6-6	230	6-12-83	0	1	4.73	8	0	0	0	13	13	9	7	0	11	14	.260	.211	.290	9.45	7.43
Kahn, Stephen	L-R	6-3	215	12-14-83	0	0	0.00	1	0	0	0	1	1	0	0	0	1	1	.333	.000	.500	9.00	9.00
Kappel, Brian	R-R	6-0	215	1-7-83	2	1	0.00	5	0	0	0	7	7	8	0	1	2	9	.233	.273	.211	11.05	2.45
Lamont, Tyrone	R-R	6-4	210	4-3-85	1	2	4.65	16	0	0	0	31	27	19	16	1	9	30	.231	.233	.230	8.71	2.61
Lumry, Worth	L-L	6-3	210	2-2-83	2	1	6.66	16	0	0	0	26	34	21	19	0	15	7	.351	.269	.380	2.45	5.26
Marquez, Miguel	R-R	6-3	180	10-28-87	2	2	7.38	12	5	0	0	50	70	54	41	3	22	49	.327	.390	.303	8.82	3.96
Nageotte, Clint	R-R	6-3	225	10-25-80	0	0	0.00	1	1	0	0	3	0	0	0	0	0	6	.000	.000	.000	18.00	0.00
Nottingham, Shawn	L-L	6-1	190	1-22-85	0	0	2.25	3	3	0	0	4	3	1	1	0	0	6	.200	.333	.167	13.50	0.00
Olore, Kevin	L-R	6-2	210	9-21-78	0	1	6.00	5	3	0	0	6	7	4	4	0	3	9	.292	.429	.235	13.50	4.50
Schwab, Daniel	L-L	6-5	225	7-14-83	0	2	6.30	6	0	0	0	10	15	11	7	1	12	4	.395	.429	.387	3.60	10.80
Sherrill, George	L-L	6-0	220	4-19-77	0	0	0.00	3	2	0	0	4	0	0	0	0	0	5	.000	.000	.000	11.25	0.00
Soto, Estelin	L-L	6-3	170	12-19-83	2	3	7.28	17	0	0	1	30	41	31	24	0	15	25	.339	.391	.327	7.58	4.55
Stitt, Brian	R-R	5-11	201	8-26-82	1	0	6.00	4	2	0	0	6	13	4	4	0	1	5	.464	.444	.474	7.50	1.50
Sullivan, John	R-R	6-3	220	2-22-82	3	0	2.92	16	0	0	2	25	28	12	8	1	6	23	.295	.407	.250	8.39	2.19
Suriel, Jose	L-L	6-3	170	3-30-84	2	0	3.67	15	0	0	0	27	26	17	11	0	12	11	.250	.304	.235	3.67	4.00
Uhlmansiek, Steve	L-L	6-3	185	2-10-83	0	0	3.78	10	8	0	0	17	15	11	7	2	10	9	.246	.333	.224	4.86	5.40
Vega, Marwin	R-R	6-0	175	10-27-86	4	2	4.73	9	3	0	1	32	34	22	17	0	18	30	.276	.289	.271	8.35	5.01
Williams, Harold	L-L	6-4	190	9-23-84	2	2	2.30	10	6	0	0	47	38	16	12	2	16	44	.218	.289	.199	8.43	3.06
Zapata, Juan	R-R	6-3	180	8-6-84	4	3	3.86	15	4	0	0	42	50	27	18	2	14	33	.298	.298	.297	7.07	3.00

GAMES BY POSITION: C—Dixon 18, Gergel 14, Jacobo 2, Ledbetter 10, Prosise 26. **1B**—Dixon 1, Gergel 11, Hargrove 34, Jacobo 5, Ledbetter 7. **2B**—Dominguez 3, Eastley 3, Garth 20, Guzman 32, Hudson 1. **3B**—Bonilla 31, Dominguez 4, Garth 7, Heckman 10, Jacobo 1, Prettyman 5. **SS**—Bonilla 3, Dominguez 26, Guzman 3, Hudson 1, Zorn 24. **OF**—Auty 29, Bradford 8, Graterol 28, Halman 25, E. Hernandez 22, J. Hernandez 3, Liverpool 27, Nelson 1, Ruiz 29.

TAMPA BAY DEVIL RAYS

BY MARC TOPKIN

The Devil Rays are going to be different. They can only hope they are going to be better.

After finishing last in the AL East for the seventh time in eight seasons in 2005, the Rays underwent significant change—starting at the top. New principal owner Stuart Sternberg took control of the team from managing general partner Vince Naimoli, general manager Chuck LaMar was fired and manager Lou Piniella agreed to a buyout of the final year of his contract.

The Rays spent most of October interviewing candidates to replace Piniella and were looking for an experienced front office executive. But it appeared Andrew Friedman, a 28-year-old Sternberg associate, would have a significant role in baseball operations and likely would handle most, if not all, of the general manager duties.

Whoever takes over will have a talented core of young players to deal with and a lot of decisions to make.

While the Rays won just 67 games, they were buoyed by the emergence of several more young players who could be a big part of their future success.

Second-year second baseman Jorge Cantu was named team MVP after a breakout season in which he hit 28 homers and drove in a team-record 117 runs. Rookie outfielder Jonny Gomes made a late run at AL Rookie of the Year honors by hitting 21 homers in 101 games. Center fielder Joey Gathright changed the outcome of several games with his blazing speed and ability to disrupt opponents.

Lefthander Scott Kazmir showed electrifying stuff in striking out 174 batters in 186 innings while going 10-9, 3.77. Righthander Seth McClung showed the ability at times to be the dominating pitcher the Rays projected before his Tommy John surgery.

Add them to a group that includes Carl Crawford, who fell just short of a 200-hit, 15-homer, 50-stolen base season; closer Danys Baez, who saved 41 games and made his first All-Star Game; right fielder Aubrey Huff, who struggled most of the season but still drove in 92 runs; catcher Toby Hall; and lefthander Mark Hendrickson, and it's obvious the Rays have the makings of an improved team.

Talented center fielder Rocco Baldelli is expected back after missing the entire 2005 season following left knee and right elbow surgery. Add in elite prospects Delmon Young and B.J. Upton at some point during the 2006 season, as well as several young arms the Rays have coming, and there shouldn't be any question they can do better.

Not all of their young players were success stories however. Dewon Brazelton, their top pick in the 2001 draft, began the season as the Opening Day starter but finished it in long relief, his performance marred by a mysterious midseason disappearance and ongoing legal battles for custody of his son. The pitchers they took in the first round of the last two drafts both had surgery—2004 top pick Jeff Niemann had an arthroscopic shoulder procedure and expects to be pitching sometime during spring training, and 2005 top pick Wade Townsend had Tommy John surgery and will miss the 2006 season.

Piniella's decision to walk away from the final year of his contract in his hometown would seem to be a setback, but it became obvious he would not be happy managing a team that was still building for the future.

Naimoli was treated like a hero for landing the team in 1995 but soon came to be the focal point of all that was wrong with the troubled franchise. LaMar was the only general manager the Rays had, but it became obvious new ownership would make a change.

The Rays' minor league teams struggled as well, with only low Class A Southwest Michigan advancing to postseason play. Triple-A Durham had its first losing season in eight years in the International League.

Young was named Baseball America's 2005 Minor League Player of the Year after hitting .315-26-99 RBIs between Double-A Montgomery and Durham, though he also made headlines for criticizing the organization and calling the Rays "cheap" after not receiving a September callup.

PLAYERS OF THE YEAR

MAJOR LEAGUE: Jorge Cantu, 2b

In his first full major league season, the unheralded Cantu established himself as one of the game's top-hitting second basemen. The 23-year-old Mexico native hit .286, set a Devil Rays record with 117 RBIs and tied for third among big league second basemen with 28 homers.

MINOR LEAGUE: Delmon Young, of

Baseball's top prospect made a run at the Southern League triple crown—as a 19-year-old—and won the league's MVP award despite before being promoted to Triple-A Durham after 330 Double-A at-bats. Young held his own in the International League, too, finishing a combined .315-26-99 in 558 at-bats.

ORGANIZATION LEADERS

BATTING		
*AVG	Leandro, Francisco, Southwest Michigan/Visalia	.329
R	Upton, B.J., Durham	98
H	Young, Delmon, Durham/Montgomery	176
TB	Young, Delmon, Durham/Montgomery	294
2B	Leandro, Francisco, Southwest Michigan/Visalia	44
3B	Perez, Fernando, Southwest Michigan	13
HR	Snyder, Earl, Durham	29
RBI	Young, Delmon, Durham/Montgomery	99
BB	Leandro, Francisco, Southwest Michigan/Visalia	82
SO	Cuevas, Aneudi, Visalia	141
SB	Perez, Fernando, Southwest Michigan	57
*OBP	Leandro, Francisco, Southwest Michigan/Visalia	.433
*SLG	Laforest, Pete, Durham	.578
PITCHING		
W	Sonnanstine, Andy, Southwest Michigan/Visalia	14
L	Prochaska, Mike, Durham/Visalia	12
#ERA	Davis, Wade, Hudson Valley	2.19
G	De la Cruz, Jose, Southwest Michigan	50
CG	Hammel, Jason, Durham/Montgomery	3
SV	De la Cruz, Jose, Southwest Michigan	19
IP	Sonnanstine, Andy, Southwest Michigan/Visalia	181
BB	Lavergne, Jarrad, Southwest Michigan	70
SO	Sonnanstine, Andy, Southwest Michigan/Visalia	178

*Minimum 250 at-bats. #Minimum 75 innings.

TAMPA BAY DEVIL RAYS

Manager: Lou Piniella.

2005 Record: 67-95, .414 (5th, AL East).

BATTING	B-T	HT	WT	DOB	AVG	vLH	vRH	G	AB	R	H	2B	3B	HR	RBI	BB	HBP	SH	SF	SO	SB	CS	SLG	OBP
Cantu, Jorge	R-R	6-1	185	1-30-82	.286	.256	.296	150	598	73	171	40	1	28	117	19	6	0	7	83	1	0	.497	.311
Cash, Kevin	R-R	6-0	190	12-6-77	.161	.250	.130	13	31	4	5	1	0	2	2	1	1	0	0	13	0	0	.387	.212
Cortez, Fernando	L-R	6-1	175	8-10-81	.077	.000	.077	8	13	0	1	0	0	0	1	1	0	0	0	3	0	0	.077	.143
Crawford, Carl	L-L	6-2	220	8-5-81	.301	.244	.326	156	644	101	194	33	15	15	81	27	5	5	6	84	46	8	.469	.331
Gathright, Joey	L-R	5-10	170	4-27-81	.276	.353	.269	76	203	29	56	7	3	0	13	10	2	3	0	39	20	5	.340	.316
Gomes, Jonny	R-R	6-1	205	11-22-80	.282	.288	.279	101	348	61	98	13	6	21	54	39	14	1	5	113	9	5	.534	.372
Gonzalez, Alex	R-R	6-0	200	4-8-73	.269	.282	.263	109	349	47	94	20	1	9	38	26	3	2	3	74	2	1	.410	.323
Green, Nick	R-R	6-0	175	9-10-78	.239	.292	.216	111	318	53	76	15	2	5	29	33	11	10	3	86	3	1	.346	.329
Hall, Toby	R-R	6-3	240	10-21-75	.287	.302	.281	135	432	28	124	20	0	5	48	16	5	3	7	39	0	0	.368	.315
Hollins, Damon	R-L	5-11	180	6-12-74	.249	.250	.248	120	342	44	85	17	1	13	46	23	1	1	2	63	8	1	.418	.296
Huff, Aubrey	L-R	6-4	230	12-20-76	.261	.256	.264	154	575	70	150	26	2	22	92	49	5	0	7	88	8	7	.428	.321
Johnson, Charles	R-R	6-3	225	7-20-71	.196	.222	.189	19	46	5	9	4	0	0	5	9	0	0	0	11	0	0	.283	.327
Laforest, Pete	L-R	6-2	210	1-27-78	.172	.000	.183	25	64	5	11	3	0	1	4	6	0	0	0	23	0	1	.266	.243
Laker, Tim	R-R	6-3	225	11-27-69	.000	.000	.000	1	1	0	0	0	0	0	0	0	0	0	0	1	0	0	.000	.000
Lee, Travis	L-L	6-3	225	5-26-75	.272	.250	.276	129	404	54	110	22	2	12	49	35	1	0	1	66	7	4	.426	.331
Lugo, Julio	R-R	6-1	170	11-16-75	.295	.306	.291	158	616	89	182	36	6	6	57	61	6	3	4	72	39	11	.403	.362
Munson, Eric	L-R	6-3	225	10-3-77	.167	.000	.214	11	18	2	3	1	0	0	2	4	1	0	1	3	0	0	.222	.333
Perez, Eduardo	R-R	6-4	240	9-11-69	.255	.259	.231	77	161	23	41	6	0	11	28	26	3	0	0	30	0	2	.497	.368
Phelps, Josh	R-R	6-3	225	5-12-78	.266	.217	.286	47	158	21	42	10	0	5	26	12	4	0	3	48	0	0	.424	.328
Sanchez, Alex	L-L	5-10	180	8-26-76	.346	.286	.353	43	133	28	46	8	1	2	13	7	0	3	2	25	6	3	.466	.373
Singleton, Chris	L-L	6-2	220	8-15-72	.271	.000	.286	28	59	9	16	5	0	0	11	6	1	1	0	14	0	0	.356	.348
Taylor, Reggie	L-R	6-1	180	1-12-77	.182	.000	.200	11	22	2	4	2	0	0	1	2	0	0	0	7	2	0	.273	.250

PITCHING	B-T	HT	WT	DOB	W	L	ERA	G	GS	CG	SV	IP	H	R	ER	HR	BB	SO	AVG	vLH	vRH	K/9	BB/9
Baez, Danys	R-R	6-3	225	9-10-77	5	4	2.86	67	0	0	41	72	66	27	23	7	30	51	.244	.268	.215	6.35	3.73
Beimel, Joe	L-L	6-3	215	4-19-77	0	0	3.27	7	0	0	0	11	15	4	4	1	4	3	.319	.429	.231	2.45	3.27
Bell, Rob	R-R	6-5	225	1-17-77	1	1	8.28	8	3	0	0	25	41	25	23	7	12	13	.360	.383	.333	4.68	4.32
Borowski, Joe	R-R	6-2	225	5-4-71	1	5	3.82	32	0	0	0	35	26	15	15	3	11	16	.208	.227	.186	4.08	2.80
Brazelton, Dewon	R-R	6-4	215	6-16-80	1	8	7.61	20	8	0	0	71	87	65	60	12	60	43	.307	.303	.312	5.45	7.61
Carter, Lance	R-R	6-1	190	12-18-74	1	2	4.89	39	0	0	1	57	61	31	31	9	15	22	.279	.309	.248	3.47	2.37
Colome, Jesus	R-R	6-2	205	12-23-77	2	3	4.57	36	0	0	0	45	54	29	23	7	18	28	.283	.291	.276	5.56	3.57
Corcoran, Tim	R-R	6-2	205	4-15-78	0	0	5.96	10	1	0	0	23	19	15	15	1	12	13	.226	.311	.128	5.16	4.76
Fossum, Casey	L-L	6-1	160	1-6-78	8	12	4.92	36	25	0	0	163	170	100	89	21	60	128	.266	.234	.278	7.08	3.32
Gardner, Lee	R-R	6-0	210	1-16-75	0	0	4.91	5	0	0	0	7	12	9	4	2	2	4	.353	.500	.222	4.91	2.45
Harper, Travis	L-R	6-4	190	5-21-76	4	6	6.75	52	0	0	0	73	88	57	55	14	24	40	.304	.292	.313	4.91	2.95
Hendrickson, Mark	L-L	6-9	230	6-23-74	11	8	5.90	31	31	1	0	178	227	126	117	24	49	89	.311	.258	.328	4.49	2.47
Kazmir, Scott	L-L	6-0	170	1-24-84	10	9	3.77	32	32	0	0	186	172	90	78	12	100	174	.248	.174	.268	8.42	4.84
McClung, Seth	R-R	6-6	235	2-7-81	7	11	6.59	34	17	0	0	109	106	85	80	20	62	92	.249	.294	.197	7.57	5.10
Miller, Trever	R-L	6-3	200	5-29-73	2	2	4.06	61	0	0	0	44	45	23	20	4	29	35	.278	.267	.289	7.11	5.89
Nomo, Hideo	R-R	6-2	235	8-31-68	5	8	7.24	19	19	0	0	101	127	82	81	16	51	59	.314	.270	.356	5.27	4.56
Nunez, Franklin	R-R	6-0	175	1-18-77	1	0	10.80	5	0	0	0	5	5	6	6	0	4	2	.278	.333	.250	3.60	7.20
Orvella, Chad	R-R	5-11	190	10-1-80	3	3	3.60	37	0	0	1	50	47	26	20	4	23	43	.246	.218	.265	7.74	4.14
Switzer, Jon	L-L	6-3	190	8-13-79	0	0	6.75	2	0	0	0	4	5	4	3	0	7	5	.278	.167	.333	11.25	15.75
Waechter, Doug	R-R	6-4	210	1-28-81	5	12	5.62	29	25	0	0	157	191	109	98	29	38	87	.298	.310	.283	4.99	2.18
Webb, John	R-R	6-3	220	5-23-79	0	1	18.00	1	1	0	0	4	6	8	8	1	4	2	.333	.375	.300	4.50	9.00

FIELDING

Catcher	PCT	G	PO	A	E	DP	PB
Cash	1.000	13	56	8	0	1	4
Hall	.989	135	759	51	9	5	8
Johnson	.959	19	90	3	4	0	1
Laforest	1.000	21	74	3	0	1	0
Laker	1.000	1	1	0	0	0	0

First Base	PCT	G	PO	A	E	DP
Hall	1.000	2	5	2	0	0
Huff	1.000	25	134	5	0	15
Laforest	1.000	1	4	0	0	0
Lee	.996	124	875	67	4	87
Munson	1.000	1	3	0	0	1
Perez	.993	49	264	18	2	22
Phelps	1.000	1	5	0	0	2

Second Base	PCT	G	PO	A	E	DP
Cantu	.971	80	119	181	9	40
Cortez	1.000	3	0	3	0	0
Green	.988	91	141	195	4	44

Third Base	PCT	G	PO	A	E	DP
Cantu	.912	62	31	93	12	7
Cortez	.000	1	0	0	0	0
Gonzalez	.945	98	66	173	14	10
Green	.893	13	4	21	3	2
Huff	1.000	4	2	2	0	1
Munson	1.000	2	1	1	0	0
Perez	1.000	3	2	0	0	0

Shortstop	PCT	G	PO	A	E	DP
Cortez	1.000	2	1	2	0	0
Gonzalez	.938	12	12	18	2	1
Lugo	.968	156	310	424	24	94

Outfield	PCT	G	PO	A	E	DP
Crawford	.995	154	361	3	2	1
Gathright	.984	70	180	3	3	2
Gomes	.963	50	98	7	4	1
Green	.000	1	0	0	0	0
Hollins	.977	116	250	8	6	4
Huff	.986	97	204	6	3	2
Munson	1.000	1	1	0	0	0
Perez	1.000	4	5	0	0	0
Sanchez	.957	31	65	1	3	0
Singleton	.973	19	35	1	1	0
Taylor	1.000	10	17	0	0	0

General Manager: Chuck LaMar. **Director, Player Personnel:** Cam Bonifay. **Scouting Director:** Tim Wilken.

Class	Farm Team	League	W	L	Pct.	Finish*	Manager	Affiliate Since
AAA	Durham (N.C.) Bulls	International	65	79	.451	12th (14)	Bill Evers	1998
AA	Montgomery (Ala.) Biscuits	Southern	67	70	.489	5th (10)	Charlie Montoyo	2004
High A	Visalia (Calif.) Oaks	California	55	85	.393	10th (10)	Steve Livesey	2005
Low A	Southwest Michigan Devil Rays (Battle Creek)	Midwest	72	67	.518	**t-4th (16)**	Joe Szekely	2005
SS A	Hudson Valley (N.Y.) Renegades	New York-Penn	31	43	.419	11th (14)	Dave Howard	1996
Rookie	Princeton (W.Va.) Devil Rays	Appalachian	34	31	.523	3rd (10)	Jamie Nelson	1997

*Finish in overall standings (No. of teams in league)/Playoff teams in **boldface**

DURHAM BULLS

Class AAA

INTERNATIONAL LEAGUE

BATTING	B-T	HT	WT	DOB	AVG	vLH	vRH	G	AB	R	H	2B	3B	HR	RBI	BB	HBP	SH	SF	SO	SB	CS	SLG	OBP
Badeaux, Brooks	B-R	5-10	177	10-20-76	.236	.196	.249	63	229	28	54	13	1	3	20	12	1	5	3	41	1	0	.341	.273
Cash, Kevin	R-R	6-0	190	12-6-77	.293	.209	.327	42	147	25	43	10	0	9	27	12	3	1	2	42	0	0	.544	.354
Cortez, Fernando	L-R	6-1	175	8-10-81	.227	.162	.253	58	238	26	54	8	2	2	26	10	3	3	1	38	13	1	.303	.266
Cox, Steve	L-L	6-4	225	10-31-74	.210	.364	.176	19	62	7	13	5	0	3	9	11	0	0	0	18	0	0	.435	.329
Curry, Michael	L-R	5-9	180	2-15-77	.222	.077	.268	12	54	5	12	1	0	0	6	5	0	1	0	10	3	1	.241	.288
Deardorff, Jeff	R-R	6-3	220	8-14-78	.250	.212	.266	96	336	50	84	13	3	15	41	42	0	2	3	82	3	2	.440	.331
Gathright, Joey	L-R	5-10	170	4-27-81	.305	.375	.282	58	226	46	69	10	5	1	18	29	2	2	1	47	31	8	.407	.388
Gomes, Jonny	R-R	6-1	205	11-22-80	.321	.179	.351	45	162	34	52	13	0	14	46	30	8	0	2	44	7	1	.660	.446
Hollins, Damon	R-L	5-11	180	6-12-74	.296	.300	.296	22	81	11	24	5	0	2	17	15	2	0	1	17	3	2	.432	.414
Hoover, Paul	R-R	6-1	200	4-14-76	.233	.221	.240	79	257	32	60	17	1	5	26	25	5	4	0	56	5	1	.366	.314
Hubbard, Trenidad	R-R	5-9	200	5-11-66	.226	.243	.213	25	84	14	19	3	0	0	2	14	1	0	0	5	5	3	.262	.343
Laforest, Pete	L-R	6-2	210	1-27-78	.270	.203	.291	70	270	41	73	18	1	21	52	17	3	1	2	98	2	0	.578	.318
Laker, Tim	R-R	6-3	225	11-27-69	.226	.204	.235	89	327	48	74	19	0	11	44	37	2	0	4	80	0	0	.385	.305
McDonald, Darnell	R-R	5-11	210	11-17-78	.284	.288	.283	73	285	45	81	13	2	12	34	20	1	0	0	62	7	0	.470	.333
2-team (26 Buffalo)					.281	.273	.285	99	359	56	101	20	2	13	38	27	3	0	0	81	7	1	.457	.337
Munson, Eric	L-R	6-3	225	10-3-77	.285	.311	.277	100	382	67	109	22	0	25	71	38	2	1	2	81	1	1	.539	.351
Neuberger, Scott	R-R	6-3	227	8-14-77	.333	.667	.000	3	6	1	2	1	0	0	1	0	0	0	0	3	0	0	.500	.333
Ordaz, Luis	R-R	5-11	170	8-12-75	.288	.314	.278	39	125	17	36	8	0	1	19	6	0	2	3	13	0	0	.376	.313
Phelps, Josh	R-R	6-3	225	5-12-78	.270	.283	.265	59	222	35	60	14	3	14	33	15	5	0	1	53	0	1	.550	.329
Singleton, Chris	L-L	6-2	220	8-15-72	.333	.000	.500	1	3	0	1	0	0	0	0	0	0	0	0	1	0	0	.333	.333
Snyder, Earl	R-R	6-0	200	5-6-76	.257	.241	.263	130	505	80	130	32	2	29	92	42	6	0	4	99	1	1	.501	.320
Taylor, Reggie	L-R	6-1	180	1-12-77	.261	.231	.271	67	253	30	66	10	3	7	35	24	3	3	0	55	12	10	.407	.332
Upton, B.J.	R-R	6-3	180	8-21-84	.303	.346	.289	139	545	98	165	36	6	18	74	78	4	1	3	127	44	13	.490	.392
Young, Delmon	R-R	6-3	205	9-14-85	.285	.288	.284	52	228	33	65	13	3	6	28	4	2	0	0	33	7	4	.447	.303

PITCHING	B-T	HT	WT	DOB	W	L	ERA	G	GS	CG	SV	IP	H	R	ER	HR	BB	SO	AVG	vLH	vRH	K/9	BB/9
Anderson, Jimmy	L-L	6-1	210	1-22-76	2	4	4.18	10	9	0	0	52	52	29	24	0	22	21	.260	.224	.272	3.66	3.83
2-team (10 Rochester)					6	8	3.48	22	20	0	0	114	114	53	44	5	54	62	.259	.229	.269	4.91	4.28
Beimel, Joe	L-L	6-3	215	4-19-77	1	2	3.93	48	0	0	0	53	58	28	23	3	21	36	.276	.298	.262	6.15	3.59
Bell, Rob	R-R	6-5	225	1-17-77	1	3	7.71	22	2	0	0	44	64	39	38	12	20	26	.344	.400	.292	5.28	4.06
Brazelton, Dewon	R-R	6-4	215	6-16-80	2	2	3.72	5	5	0	0	29	29	17	12	3	14	26	.252	.262	.240	8.07	4.34
Brock, Chris	R-R	6-1	180	2-5-70	2	5	5.65	15	5	0	1	37	53	31	23	6	12	27	.333	.349	.316	6.63	2.95
Carnes, Matt	R-R	6-2	207	8-18-75	5	1	4.45	37	0	0	0	55	54	30	27	4	15	39	.263	.234	.288	6.42	2.47
Carter, Lance	R-R	6-1	190	12-18-74	1	5	5.14	8	7	0	0	35	40	24	20	8	12	30	.290	.274	.326	7.71	3.09
Corcoran, Tim	R-R	6-2	205	4-15-78	5	1	2.89	29	0	0	0	56	49	22	18	3	22	49	.230	.281	.188	7.88	3.54
Gardner, Lee	R-R	6-0	210	1-16-75	4	3	3.29	48	0	0	15	52	56	25	19	8	15	35	.277	.287	.267	6.06	2.60
Hammel, Jason	R-R	6-6	200	9-2-82	3	2	4.12	10	10	0	0	55	57	31	25	8	27	48	.264	.253	.272	7.90	4.45
Haynes, Jimmy	R-R	6-4	220	9-5-72	1	2	8.18	7	4	0	0	22	35	23	20	4	9	12	.365	.243	.441	4.91	3.68
Hines, Carlos	R-R	6-3	190	9-26-80	3	1	3.28	26	0	0	0	36	39	16	13	1	17	22	.277	.279	.275	5.55	4.29
Magrane, Jim	R-R	6-2	204	7-23-78	1	5	6.68	26	5	0	0	62	95	54	46	12	7	38	.345	.346	.345	5.52	1.02
McClung, Seth	R-R	6-6	235	2-7-81	2	0	3.93	6	3	0	0	18	23	12	8	1	6	19	.303	.419	.222	9.33	2.95
Nelson, Joe	R-R	6-2	205	10-25-74	0	3	4.11	35	0	0	6	46	41	25	21	9	21	62	.229	.250	.215	12.13	4.11
Nunez, Franklin	R-R	6-0	175	1-18-77	5	1	6.34	27	0	0	3	33	32	27	23	1	21	34	.254	.281	.232	9.37	5.79
Phillips, Jason	R-R	6-6	225	3-22-74	3	5	5.70	30	13	0	1	101	133	77	64	8	28	73	.320	.338	.303	6.50	2.50
Prochaska, Mike	L-L	6-1	210	5-23-80	0	0	1.80	2	0	0	1	5	3	1	1	0	3	3	.167	.167	.167	5.40	5.40
Roach, Jason	R-R	6-4	205	4-20-76	5	5	5.53	22	13	0	0	85	116	66	52	10	25	30	.334	.384	.299	3.19	2.66
Seddon, Chris	L-L	6-3	190	10-13-83	4	9	5.46	19	19	0	0	96	114	74	58	11	43	70	.295	.318	.288	6.59	4.05
Shields, Jamie	R-R	6-3	214	12-20-81	1	0	6.00	1	1	0	0	6	9	4	4	0	3	6	.346	.357	.333	9.00	4.50
Smith, Cameron	R-R	6-3	190	9-20-73	1	2	4.54	26	0	0	0	36	28	24	18	5	34	40	.222	.180	.250	10.09	8.58
Sweeney, Brian	R-R	6-2	200	6-13-74	3	4	4.06	10	10	0	0	51	70	30	23	5	20	39	.333	.383	.293	6.88	3.53
Switzer, Jon	L-L	6-3	190	8-13-79	0	5	7.11	17	8	0	0	44	64	38	35	6	22	28	.342	.283	.362	5.68	4.47
Waechter, Doug	R-R	6-4	210	1-28-81	0	2	9.22	3	3	0	0	14	17	14	14	3	5	16	.304	.421	.243	10.54	3.29
Webb, John	R-R	6-3	220	5-23-79	10	6	4.85	28	27	1	0	163	175	103	88	23	61	86	.274	.299	.249	4.74	3.36

FIELDING

Catcher	PCT	G	PO	A	E	DP	PB
Cash	.990	38	259	26	3	5	7
Hoover	1.000	13	90	8	0	2	3
Laforest	.986	32	194	24	3	2	1
Laker	.987	64	411	42	6	6	7
Munson	1.000	1	1	0	0	0	0

First Base	PCT	G	PO	A	E	DP
Cash	1.000	1	1	0	0	1
Cox	.971	3	29	5	1	4
Deardorff	1.000	12	82	5	0	7
Hoover	1.000	5	38	3	0	4
Laforest	.971	7	64	4	2	8
Munson	.983	93	808	58	15	85
Phelps	.971	20	183	21	6	22
Snyder	.989	11	83	6	1	7

Second Base	PCT	G	PO	A	E	DP
Badeaux	.967	43	85	118	7	31
Cortez	.963	57	124	160	11	33
Hoover	.963	32	45	85	5	17
Ordaz	.959	21	44	50	4	14
Snyder	.000	1	0	0	0	0

Third Base	PCT	G	PO	A	E	DP
Badeaux	1.000	9	6	13	0	2
Deardorff	1.000	10	6	13	0	1
Hoover	.927	16	9	29	3	6
Laforest	1.000	1	0	1	0	0
Munson	.500	1	1	0	1	0

	PCT	G	PO	A	E	DP
Ordaz	.971	11	5	28	1	1
Snyder	.940	105	73	208	18	22

Shortstop	PCT	G	PO	A	E	DP
Badeaux	1.000	12	20	22	0	8
Ordaz	.900	8	9	18	3	5
Upton	.921	133	219	396	53	95

Outfield	PCT	G	PO	A	E	DP
Badeaux	1.000	3	1	1	0	0
Cash	.000	1	0	0	0	0
Curry	.964	12	26	1	1	0
Deardorff	1.000	77	120	5	0	0
Gathright	.948	56	122	6	7	2
Gomes	.948	45	67	6	4	1
Hollins	1.000	21	48	3	0	0
Hoover	.971	17	31	2	1	2
Hubbard	.981	25	47	4	1	0
McDonald	.990	72	188	7	2	2
Neuberger	1.000	2	1	1	0	0
Singleton	1.000	1	2	0	0	0
Taylor	.960	66	138	5	6	0
Young	.943	51	94	5	6	1

MONTGOMERY BISCUITS — Class AA

SOUTHERN LEAGUE

BATTING	B-T	HT	WT	DOB	AVG	vLH	vRH	G	AB	R	H	2B	3B	HR	RBI	BB	HBP	SH	SF	SO	SB	CS	SLG	OBP
Bankston, Wes	R-R	6-4	200	11-23-83	.292	.312	.286	82	301	42	88	17	2	12	47	30	4	0	2	64	3	3	.482	.362
Butler, Brent	R-R	6-0	180	2-11-78	.264	.327	.217	34	121	22	32	7	1	6	21	15	3	3	2	14	2	0	.488	.355
Cortez, Fernando	L-R	6-1	175	8-10-81	.333	.189	.407	55	219	39	73	11	4	0	23	15	2	1	3	42	12	3	.420	.377
Curry, Michael	L-R	5-9	180	2-15-77	.253	.183	.296	49	186	39	47	10	1	2	11	17	3	0	0	47	15	5	.349	.325
Dukes, Elijah	B-R	6-2	227	6-26-84	.287	.206	.319	120	446	73	128	21	5	18	73	45	4	0	3	83	19	9	.478	.355
Gann, Jamie	R-R	6-3	191	5-1-75	.095	.000	.100	5	21	0	2	1	0	0	0	1	0	0	0	6	0	0	.143	.136
Isenia, Chairon	R-R	5-11	220	1-23-79	.244	.217	.255	104	390	45	95	22	1	9	68	17	8	1	4	63	2	1	.374	.286
Johnson, Elliot	B-R	6-0	171	3-9-84	.261	.296	.249	63	264	31	69	9	6	3	21	13	4	1	1	68	15	5	.375	.305
Maniscalco, Matthew	R-R	5-10	180	2-18-81	.280	.311	.269	71	243	31	68	10	0	0	12	27	2	4	1	48	5	3	.321	.355
Martinez, Gabriel	L-R	6-2	180	5-17-83	.233	.125	.269	87	288	31	67	14	1	8	45	29	5	2	4	76	0	1	.372	.310
Mateo, Luis	R-R	6-2	208	8-9-81	.230	.253	.218	86	269	24	62	8	3	4	28	7	1	0	1	91	3	3	.327	.252
Merritt, Graig	R-R	6-1	205	7-2-78	.104	.118	.097	21	48	1	5	1	0	0	1	5	1	2	0	14	1	0	.125	.204
Neuberger, Scott	R-R	6-3	227	8-14-77	.231	.194	.247	31	104	13	24	6	0	5	15	5	3	0	2	25	1	1	.433	.281
Pridie, Jason	L-R	6-1	188	10-9-83	.213	.182	.217	28	94	15	20	4	2	3	8	8	0	2	0	29	5	1	.394	.275
Raburn, John	B-R	6-0	164	2-16-79	.284	.324	.264	112	401	62	114	16	1	1	31	39	3	9	2	65	27	1	.337	.351
Reece, Eric	L-R	6-3	214	6-16-78	.179	.143	.190	17	56	4	10	3	0	1	5	4	0	0	0	20	0	0	.286	.233
Riggans, Shawn	R-R	6-2	190	7-25-80	.310	.379	.276	89	313	40	97	21	0	8	53	26	4	2	5	69	1	2	.454	.365
Sitzman, Jay	L-L	6-3	199	3-13-78	.169	.167	.169	29	77	7	13	2	0	0	4	2	1	2	0	24	1	1	.195	.200
Vick, Hunter	B-R	5-9	165	4-12-82	.000	.000	.000	2	4	0	0	0	0	0	0	0	0	0	0	1	0	0	.000	.000
Washington, Rico	L-R	5-9	195	5-30-78	.300	.316	.293	126	454	84	136	30	2	19	77	63	7	0	8	63	6	5	.500	.387
Young, Delmon	R-R	6-3	205	9-14-85	.336	.306	.351	84	330	59	111	13	4	20	71	25	7	0	8	66	25	8	.582	.386

PITCHING	B-T	HT	WT	DOB	W	L	ERA	G	GS	CG	SV	IP	H	R	ER	HR	BB	SO	AVG	vLH	vRH	K/9	BB/9
Autrey, Scott	R-R	6-2	235	1-26-81	3	11	5.71	21	17	1	0	109	149	82	69	24	32	65	.327	.321	.332	5.38	2.65
Brazelton, Dewon	R-R	6-4	215	6-16-80	0	0	0.00	1	1	0	0	3	2	0	0	0	0	6	.182	.200	.167	18.00	0.00
Colome, Jesus	R-R	6-2	205	12-23-77	0	0	0.00	3	0	0	0	4	2	0	0	0	0	3	.143	.000	.200	6.75	0.00
Cromer, Jason	R-L	6-4	226	12-11-80	5	7	4.64	21	21	1	0	118	128	67	61	15	33	68	.279	.284	.278	5.17	2.51
Diaz, Jose	R-R	6-0	225	4-13-80	2	2	9.13	18	0	0	0	24	22	24	24	2	20	22	.247	.302	.196	8.37	7.61
Flinn, Chris	R-R	6-2	197	8-18-80	5	6	5.00	36	4	0	2	77	89	51	43	3	24	61	.291	.303	.283	7.10	2.79
Garcia, Gerardo	R-R	6-0	225	2-13-80	0	2	8.31	2	2	0	0	9	19	13	8	1	0	5	.432	.389	.462	5.19	0.00
Hammel, Jason	R-R	6-6	200	9-2-82	8	2	2.66	12	12	3	0	81	70	26	24	5	19	76	.235	.250	.222	8.41	2.10
Henderson, Brian	L-L	5-11	195	5-19-82	5	1	3.60	48	0	0	1	55	62	29	22	3	21	49	.282	.246	.298	8.02	3.44
Hines, Carlos	R-R	6-3	190	9-26-80	0	2	3.71	22	0	0	6	34	28	17	14	1	16	24	.237	.264	.215	6.35	4.24
Lockwood, Brian	R-R	6-2	180	2-20-81	3	6	7.18	24	11	0	0	78	112	72	62	13	27	73	.339	.368	.311	8.46	3.13
Lugo, Ruddy	R-R	5-10	205	5-22-80	1	1	1.12	26	0	0	2	40	25	12	5	1	23	48	.169	.098	.218	10.71	5.13
Machi, Jean	R-R	6-0	170	2-1-83	0	0	54.00	1	0	0	0	1	4	4	4	1	1	0	.667	.500	.750	0.00	13.50
Magrane, Jim	R-R	6-2	204	7-23-78	2	5	5.40	9	8	0	0	50	63	31	30	2	21	26	.315	.273	.348	4.68	3.78
Niemann, Jeff	R-R	6-9	260	2-28-83	0	1	4.35	6	3	0	0	10	7	7	5	0	5	14	.184	.211	.158	12.19	4.35
Orvella, Chad	R-R	5-11	190	10-1-80	0	0	0.36	16	0	0	9	25	15	1	1	0	6	29	.169	.222	.145	10.44	2.16
Parker, Josh	R-R	6-5	234	1-12-81	2	8	4.76	43	0	0	4	59	60	35	31	6	16	32	.263	.300	.239	4.91	2.45
Peguero, Tony	R-R	6-3	174	2-17-81	5	1	4.01	9	9	0	0	52	59	26	23	4	15	37	.285	.333	.250	6.45	2.61
Phillips, Jason	R-R	6-6	225	3-22-74	1	0	5.40	1	1	0	0	5	8	3	3	2	2	1	.400	.400	.400	1.80	3.60
Raburn, John	B-R	6-0	164	2-16-79	0	0	0.00	2	0	0	0	2	2	0	0	0	0	1	.286	.667	.000	4.50	0.00
Salas, Juan	R-R	6-2	210	11-7-78	1	0	3.68	15	0	0	0	22	25	12	9	2	12	18	.281	.268	.292	7.36	4.91
Seddon, Chris	L-L	6-3	190	10-13-83	6	1	4.82	10	10	0	0	52	58	31	28	4	20	46	.284	.213	.306	7.91	3.44
Shields, Jamie	R-R	6-3	214	12-20-81	7	5	2.80	17	16	0	0	109	95	36	34	6	31	104	.244	.215	.264	8.56	2.55
Smith, Cameron	R-R	6-3	190	9-20-73	4	2	2.01	20	0	0	7	22	12	7	5	1	17	26	.158	.174	.151	10.48	6.85
Stokes, Brian	R-R	6-1	205	9-7-79	4	6	3.47	16	16	1	0	93	82	36	36	8	28	70	.238	.223	.250	6.75	2.70
Switzer, Jon	L-L	6-3	190	8-13-79	3	1	3.45	6	6	0	0	31	33	14	12	2	5	20	.268	.267	.269	5.74	1.44
Walton, Samuel	L-L	6-5	220	12-1-78	0	0	6.57	13	0	0	0	25	31	19	18	6	15	22	.313	.333	.304	8.03	5.47

FIELDING

Catcher	PCT	G	PO	A	E	DP	PB
Isenia	.981	57	378	30	8	2	10
Merritt	1.000	20	116	18	0	2	3
Reece	1.000	1	1	1	0	0	0
Riggans	.983	69	481	42	9	7	5

First Base	PCT	G	PO	A	E	DP
Bankston	.991	68	602	32	6	51
Isenia	1.000	10	64	4	0	4
Martinez	.993	49	414	15	3	47
Raburn	1.000	1	9	1	0	0
Reece	1.000	6	43	2	0	4
Sitzman	1.000	1	1	0	0	0
Washington	.989	11	88	5	1	8

Second Base	PCT	G	PO	A	E	DP
Butler	1.000	1	6	1	0	2
Cortez	.966	36	64	108	6	18
Johnson	.956	61	121	162	13	43
Martinez	1.000	1	1	2	0	1
Raburn	.959	38	66	99	7	23
Vick	1.000	1	1	1	0	0
Washington	1.000	4	12	13	0	3

Third Base	PCT	G	PO	A	E	DP
Martinez	.943	15	9	24	2	1
Raburn	.903	34	28	56	9	8
Reece	1.000	1	3	2	0	0
Washington	.946	96	57	172	13	18

Shortstop	PCT	G	PO	A	E	DP
Butler	.949	29	43	88	7	18
Cortez	.987	17	23	52	1	9
Johnson	.333	1	1	0	2	0
Maniscalco	.983	71	122	218	6	41
Martinez	1.000	1	0	2	0	0
Raburn	.925	22	26	60	7	14
Vick	.000	1	0	0	0	0

Outfield	PCT	G	PO	A	E	DP
Bankston	1.000	2	1	0	0	0
Curry	.988	47	79	2	1	1
Dukes	.964	106	208	8	8	1
Gann	1.000	5	5	0	0	0
Martinez	.972	27	31	4	1	1
Mateo	.958	77	108	7	5	1
Neuberger	.981	31	45	6	1	1
Pridie	.982	27	55	0	1	0
Raburn	.870	10	18	2	3	1
Sitzman	.979	26	46	0	1	0
Young	.952	78	135	5	7	0

CALIFORNIA LEAGUE

BATTING	B-T	HT	WT	DOB	AVG	vLH	vRH	G	AB	R	H	2B	3B	HR	RBI	BB	HBP	SH	SF	SO	SB	CS	SLG	OBP
Aracena, Sandy	R-R	6-0	180	1-3-81	.283	.196	.309	57	198	24	56	14	0	2	22	11	2	1	1	42	3	1	.384	.325
Arhart, Josh	R-R	6-1	219	9-13-79	.290	.309	.285	99	379	51	110	24	0	9	56	24	3	1	8	60	0	0	.425	.331
Asanovich, Josh	R-R	6-2	185	1-31-83	.338	.286	.350	40	145	23	49	10	0	4	14	15	1	0	1	32	2	5	.490	.401
Bankston, Wes	R-R	6-4	200	11-23-83	.387	.333	.396	17	62	15	24	4	1	3	23	15	1	0	0	17	0	2	.629	.513
Bethel, Ryan	B-R	6-0	170	3-26-82	.214	.250	.200	6	14	1	3	0	0	0	0	2	1	1	0	4	0	0	.214	.353
Cuevas, Aneudi	R-R	6-1	182	10-6-81	.281	.301	.275	120	413	72	116	24	4	22	75	57	8	3	2	141	9	4	.518	.377
Davis, John-Paul	R-R	6-4	240	12-20-78	.279	.257	.286	121	448	68	125	28	0	13	59	54	16	0	3	103	5	2	.429	.374
Dufner, Kris	B-R	6-2	185	2-15-80	.304	.274	.311	102	382	62	116	21	5	7	48	44	6	9	2	90	5	5	.440	.382
Gomes, Joey	R-R	6-2	210	11-2-79	.325	.336	.321	133	530	77	172	34	1	12	86	53	3	1	10	92	4	5	.460	.383
Johnson, Elliot	B-R	6-0	171	3-9-84	.273	.250	.281	56	227	42	62	10	3	8	33	24	3	2	0	49	28	5	.449	.350
Leandro, Francisco	L-L	5-10	180	7-19-80	.355	.333	.362	60	248	53	88	23	3	8	40	37	7	0	2	24	9	7	.569	.449
Maniscalco, Matthew	R-R	5-10	180	2-18-81	.278	.281	.276	52	209	31	58	7	0	2	21	23	0	2	4	33	21	6	.340	.343
Martinez, Gabriel	L-R	6-2	180	5-17-83	.280	.182	.308	24	100	15	28	7	0	4	9	7	2	1	1	27	0	0	.470	.336
Perez, Nestor	R-R	5-10	172	11-24-76	.196	.188	.200	16	56	2	11	3	0	0	1	6	1	2	0	14	1	1	.250	.286
Pridie, Jason	L-R	6-1	188	10-9-83	.500	.000	.500	1	2	0	1	0	0	0	0	0	0	0	0	0	0	0	.500	.500
Ramos, Carlos	L-L	5-8	175	2-23-80	.281	.203	.301	95	335	48	94	10	3	3	36	12	6	11	2	29	6	7	.355	.315
Rico, Matt	R-R	6-3	197	10-8-81	.204	.277	.173	48	157	17	32	12	0	2	19	12	1	0	0	50	2	3	.318	.265
Schleicher, Mark	R-R	6-1	180	1-1-82	.201	.242	.189	86	288	35	58	14	0	9	38	11	5	1	4	104	1	3	.344	.240
Simmons, Coltyn	R-R	6-0	205	12-4-83	.255	.250	.257	81	274	31	70	18	2	1	38	34	5	2	4	41	0	2	.347	.344
Sitzman, Jay	L-L	6-3	199	3-13-78	.268	.250	.274	59	224	29	60	13	5	1	26	25	2	1	1	57	14	4	.384	.345
St. Clair, Jason	R-R	5-10	173	9-27-82	.307	.341	.292	45	137	21	42	7	2	4	19	3	1	2	1	30	2	5	.474	.324

PITCHING	B-T	HT	WT	DOB	W	L	ERA	G	GS	CG	SV	IP	H	R	ER	HR	BB	SO	AVG	vLH	vRH	K/9	BB/9
Allen, Brian	R-R	6-3	175	9-15-79	1	4	5.03	30	1	0	2	77	94	44	43	10	16	58	.305	.287	.320	6.78	1.87
Barratt, Jonathan	R-L	5-9	165	3-19-85	2	6	6.59	36	5	0	1	71	85	59	52	9	52	79	.293	.240	.333	10.01	6.59
Coggin, David	R-R	6-4	210	10-30-76	3	2	3.38	18	0	0	6	29	28	21	11	2	14	27	.252	.227	.269	8.28	4.30
Flanagan, Jeremy	R-R	6-3	215	4-14-81	6	7	5.43	25	23	1	0	126	170	93	76	16	57	84	.328	.368	.289	6.00	4.07
Fulmer, Thomas	R-R	6-3	225	1-14-80	3	6	5.80	26	20	0	0	99	123	68	64	10	32	97	.302	.281	.321	8.79	2.90
Kranawetter, Josh	R-R	5-11	184	5-21-80	1	4	6.21	18	0	0	2	29	36	22	20	2	17	28	.305	.294	.313	8.69	5.28
Little, Joe	L-L	6-1	170	3-10-82	5	7	7.48	26	11	0	0	71	65	63	59	10	63	70	.243	.206	.265	8.87	7.99
Lugo, Ruddy	R-R	5-10	205	5-22-80	0	0	13.50	1	0	0	0	2	7	4	3	0	1	0	.583	.800	.429	0.00	4.50
Lynn, Kevin	R-R	5-11	185	11-12-78	2	6	6.81	14	13	0	0	71	101	59	54	7	9	55	.331	.338	.325	6.94	1.14
Machi, Jean	R-R	6-0	170	2-1-83	3	11	6.03	31	14	0	3	97	113	76	65	8	58	106	.295	.283	.304	9.84	5.38
Niemann, Jeff	R-R	6-9	260	2-28-83	0	1	3.98	5	5	0	0	20	12	10	9	3	10	28	.167	.323	.049	12.39	4.43
Peguero, Tony	R-R	6-3	174	2-17-81	4	4	5.77	30	6	0	5	64	79	48	41	5	20	39	.306	.323	.291	5.48	2.81
Prochaska, Mike	L-L	6-1	210	5-23-80	4	12	5.12	26	25	0	0	148	171	97	84	24	49	103	.292	.257	.316	6.28	2.99
Ridgway, Jeff	R-L	6-3	189	8-17-80	3	4	5.20	24	0	0	0	45	43	31	26	2	36	56	.257	.259	.256	11.20	7.20
Salas, Juan	R-R	6-2	210	11-7-78	2	1	3.52	25	0	0	1	38	30	19	15	6	18	47	.216	.294	.141	11.03	4.23
Sonnanstine, Andy	L-R	6-3	185	3-18-83	4	1	3.80	10	10	0	0	64	71	29	27	5	7	75	.277	.306	.259	10.55	0.98
Stokes, Brian	R-R	6-1	205	9-7-79	1	2	4.24	4	4	0	0	17	15	8	8	3	5	21	.231	.237	.222	11.12	2.65
Vandermeer, Scott	R-R	6-4	200	2-16-81	6	3	5.77	42	0	0	0	73	105	58	47	11	34	49	.337	.333	.339	6.01	4.17
Wayne, Brett	R-R	6-0	183	4-28-80	5	4	4.46	36	3	0	1	75	78	41	37	6	38	87	.266	.271	.261	10.49	4.58

FIELDING

Catcher	PCT	G	PO	A	E	DP	PB
Aracena	.989	41	312	43	4	7	16
Arhart	.994	79	604	57	4	5	11
Simmons	.984	28	168	19	3	2	7

First Base	PCT	G	PO	A	E	DP
Bankston	1.000	15	137	12	0	10
Davis	.980	99	730	70	16	73
Dufner	.981	17	95	6	2	11
Martinez	1.000	15	118	15	0	11
Sitzman	.833	1	5	0	1	0

Second Base	PCT	G	PO	A	E	DP
Asanovich	1.000	12	22	38	0	11
Bethel	1.000	2	4	4	0	1
Dufner	.938	47	81	102	12	18
Johnson	.940	55	133	132	17	36
Perez	1.000	1	1	2	0	1
Schleicher	1.000	3	5	3	0	0
St. Clair	.941	29	40	55	6	12

Third Base	PCT	G	PO	A	E	DP
Cuevas	.947	97	60	174	13	13
Dufner	.951	32	35	42	4	7
Martinez	1.000	2	3	5	0	0
Schleicher	.931	13	7	20	2	2
Simmons	1.000	1	0	3	0	0

Shortstop	PCT	G	PO	A	E	DP
Asanovich	.935	29	42	59	7	12
Bethel	1.000	3	1	11	0	0
Cuevas	.860	11	15	22	6	3
Maniscalco	.974	51	92	169	7	34
Perez	.955	15	23	40	3	10
Schleicher	.984	33	45	76	2	16
St. Clair	1.000	1	1	2	0	1

Outfield	PCT	G	PO	A	E	DP
Cuevas	.500	3	1	0	1	0
Dufner	.917	6	11	0	1	0
Gomes	.964	122	176	13	7	0
Leandro	.993	60	132	5	1	1
Martinez	1.000	8	20	1	0	0
Pridie	1.000	1	2	0	0	0
Ramos	.972	95	201	10	6	2
Rico	.956	41	58	7	3	2
Schleicher	.986	34	69	4	1	1
Simmons	1.000	4	6	0	0	0
Sitzman	.960	57	115	5	5	0

SOUTHWEST MICHIGAN DEVIL RAYS — Low Class A

MIDWEST LEAGUE

BATTING	B-T	HT	WT	DOB	AVG	vLH	vRH	G	AB	R	H	2B	3B	HR	RBI	BB	HBP	SH	SF	SO	SB	CS	SLG	OBP
Anderson, Heath	R-R	6-4	190	4-29-84	.170	.000	.200	15	47	4	8	3	0	0	2	2	0	0	0	9	0	0	.234	.204
Asanovich, Josh	R-R	6-2	185	1-31-83	.248	.313	.227	80	278	41	69	14	2	1	31	35	2	1	2	41	3	2	.324	.334
Bouman, Robbie	R-R	6-4	190	8-30-82	.235	.000	.235	5	17	2	4	0	0	0	1	1	1	0	0	4	0	2	.235	.316
Breen, Pat	L-L	6-3	215	6-23-82	.302	.233	.313	87	295	47	89	20	3	11	44	37	3	1	2	81	6	3	.502	.383
Brignac, Reid	L-R	6-3	170	1-16-86	.264	.238	.270	127	512	77	135	29	2	15	61	40	4	4	5	131	5	5	.416	.319
Cottrell, Pat	R-R	5-11	160	3-16-82	.277	.279	.277	78	310	44	86	23	1	6	40	14	6	1	6	44	6	7	.416	.315
Cumberland, Shaun	L-R	6-2	185	8-1-84	.268	.214	.281	119	436	62	117	22	3	13	69	37	3	3	5	100	23	8	.422	.326
Frias, Fernando	R-R	6-1	175	9-27-81	.220	.250	.214	40	127	10	28	5	1	1	14	6	0	1	2	41	9	1	.299	.252
Jamieson, Alex	L-R	5-11	205	4-7-83	.132	.000	.135	11	38	1	5	0	0	0	3	3	0	0	1	12	0	0	.132	.190
Jaso, John	L-R	6-2	205	9-19-83	.307	.327	.303	92	332	61	102	25	1	14	50	42	4	0	8	53	3	1	.515	.383
Lagreid, Tom	R-R	6-1	185	10-24-83	.333	.000	.400	4	12	1	4	0	0	0	3	1	1	0	0	3	0	0	.333	.429
Leandro, Francisco	L-L	5-10	180	7-19-80	.304	.288	.309	73	253	44	77	21	1	3	39	45	6	1	3	33	11	4	.431	.417
Lopez, Christian	R-R	6-1	185	10-10-84	.281	.290	.278	38	139	17	39	5	0	3	20	2	3	2	5	22	1	1	.381	.295
Markel, Craig	R-R	5-10	214	6-17-80	.259	.217	.271	61	216	20	56	11	0	0	27	20	4	1	3	21	1	0	.310	.329

BATTING	B-T	HT	WT	DOB	AVG	vLH	vRH	G	AB	R	H	2B	3B	HR	RBI	BB	HBP	SH	SF	SO	SB	CS	SLG	OBP
Nichols, Tommy	R-R	6-4	200	8-27-83	.234	.203	.244	69	244	24	57	13	1	7	37	12	2	3	0	54	2	1	.381	.275
Nowak, Chris	R-R	6-5	225	2-21-83	.304	.333	.299	105	368	55	112	28	1	7	65	56	6	0	7	58	2	2	.443	.398
Perez, Fernando	R-R	6-1	195	4-23-83	.289	.270	.295	134	522	93	151	17	13	6	48	58	3	6	5	80	57	17	.406	.361
Rousseve, Brandon	R-R	6-1	175	8-4-84	.218	.045	.258	36	119	18	26	7	0	1	8	6	4	0	0	33	6	3	.303	.279
Schlichting, Travis	R-R	6-4	188	10-19-84	.252	.234	.256	111	409	47	103	19	3	3	39	27	7	5	8	81	13	3	.335	.304

PITCHING	B-T	HT	WT	DOB	W	L	ERA	G	GS	CG	SV	IP	H	R	ER	HR	BB	SO	AVG	vLH	vRH	K/9	BB/9
Bitter, Ryan	R-R	6-1	195	9-30-81	3	2	3.48	42	0	0	7	67	57	29	26	3	33	72	.231	.263	.211	9.62	4.41
Carpenter, Calvin	R-R	6-0	209	9-23-82	4	1	4.08	20	0	0	1	35	24	17	16	1	27	46	.192	.154	.219	11.72	6.88
Coose, Austin	R-R	6-2	249	1-27-79	0	0	3.38	7	0	0	0	8	5	6	3	0	7	8	.185	.200	.182	9.00	7.88
Corporan, Willy	R-R	6-4	220	9-2-81	0	1	10.50	3	0	0	0	6	11	8	7	3	1	3	.393	.385	.400	4.50	1.50
Cromer, Nathan	L-L	6-4	215	12-11-80	0	1	5.82	8	0	0	0	17	18	11	11	1	8	11	.286	.250	.298	5.82	4.24
De la Cruz, Eddie	R-R	6-3	161	10-6-81	6	5	5.91	27	16	0	0	88	92	64	58	10	63	73	.270	.267	.272	7.44	6.42
De la Cruz, Jose	R-R	6-6	206	9-23-83	3	6	3.94	50	0	0	19	62	51	33	27	2	35	60	.224	.291	.183	8.76	5.11
De los Santos, Richard	R-R	6-1	175	6-1-84	3	0	0.66	15	0	0	4	41	15	4	3	1	18	49	.114	.104	.119	10.76	3.95
Gonzalez, Jino	L-L	6-2	210	9-5-82	6	7	4.71	17	17	0	0	80	71	57	42	8	44	53	.241	.269	.235	5.94	4.93
Houser, James	L-L	6-4	185	12-15-84	8	8	3.76	22	22	0	0	115	100	50	48	12	31	109	.239	.259	.234	8.53	2.43
Larson, Matt	R-R	6-4	215	4-9-81	4	5	4.41	29	7	0	1	80	79	45	39	4	46	47	.267	.288	.251	5.31	5.20
Lavergne, Jarrad	L-L	6-2	200	2-18-83	7	9	4.16	27	27	0	0	147	149	84	68	8	70	95	.261	.220	.272	5.82	4.29
Lopez, Romelio	B-R	6-7	252	10-10-83	0	0	13.50	3	2	0	0	7	13	11	10	1	6	4	.394	.412	.375	5.40	8.10
Mann, Brandon	L-L	6-2	165	5-16-84	10	11	3.81	27	27	0	0	151	144	78	64	13	63	86	.251	.250	.252	5.13	3.75
Mason, Chris	R-R	6-0	185	7-1-84	1	0	1.45	10	0	0	0	19	17	8	3	0	5	16	.246	.214	.268	7.71	2.41
Moran, Nick	R-R	6-5	205	1-3-80	0	2	11.42	3	1	0	0	9	14	12	11	1	4	8	.350	.250	.417	8.31	4.15
Morgan, Lavelle	L-L	5-11	170	10-25-80	1	3	3.93	24	2	0	1	55	46	29	24	6	29	60	.232	.314	.215	9.82	4.75
Perez, Antonio	B-L	5-9	165	6-12-81	4	1	2.83	45	0	0	3	70	57	26	22	2	24	55	.230	.145	.258	7.07	3.09
Sonnanstine, Andy	L-R	6-3	185	3-18-83	10	4	2.55	18	18	1	0	117	103	42	33	10	11	103	.232	.266	.204	7.95	0.85
Wagner, Nick	R-R	6-2	215	6-16-83	1	1	4.32	6	0	0	0	8	7	4	4	1	4	4	.233	.133	.333	4.32	4.32
Walker, Aaron	L-L	6-3	210	2-4-82	1	0	7.71	14	0	0	0	23	29	21	20	1	14	15	.309	.278	.316	5.79	5.40

FIELDING

Catcher	PCT	G	PO	A	E	DP	PB
Anderson	.991	13	92	13	1	2	2
Jamieson	.988	9	73	8	1	0	2
Jaso	.991	28	193	20	2	1	4
Lagreid	1.000	4	29	1	0	0	2
Lopez	.957	38	243	22	12	1	7
Markel	.983	51	360	45	7	6	6

First Base	PCT	G	PO	A	E	DP
Jaso	1.000	1	7	0	0	1
Nichols	.990	64	557	33	6	46
Nowak	.992	75	625	27	5	64

Second Base	PCT	G	PO	A	E	DP
Asanovich	.973	70	135	149	8	42
Bouman	.889	2	2	6	1	0
Cottrell	.967	41	82	123	7	21
Rousseve	.978	28	57	74	3	19
Schlichting	.800	2	2	2	1	0

Third Base	PCT	G	PO	A	E	DP
Bouman	1.000	1	0	3	0	0
Cottrell	.920	18	14	32	4	3
Nowak	.933	13	7	21	2	0
Schlichting	.942	110	81	210	18	25

Shortstop	PCT	G	PO	A	E	DP
Asanovich	.920	7	3	20	2	1
Bouman	1.000	2	1	4	0	0
Brignac	.942	125	166	341	31	71
Rousseve	.906	6	7	22	3	6

Outfield	PCT	G	PO	A	E	DP
Breen	.935	69	122	8	9	0
Cumberland	.979	114	216	12	5	2
Frias	.984	36	53	9	1	3
Leandro	.967	72	115	3	4	0
Perez	.988	131	317	13	4	1
Rousseve	1.000	1	2	0	0	0

HUDSON VALLEY RENEGADES — Short-Season Class A

NEW YORK-PENN LEAGUE

BATTING	B-T	HT	WT	DOB	AVG	vLH	vRH	G	AB	R	H	2B	3B	HR	RBI	BB	HBP	SH	SF	SO	SB	CS	SLG	OBP
Bouman, Robbie	R-R	6-4	190	8-30-82	.202	.194	.205	47	163	12	33	8	1	2	19	15	0	0	1	56	0	2	.301	.268
Cardona, David	R-R	6-2	175	11-7-82	.252	.179	.278	32	107	8	27	3	1	5	8	5	2	1	1	33	1	0	.439	.296
de la Rosa, Jairo	R-R	6-2	170	9-8-85	.202	.211	.200	34	109	15	22	6	0	0	8	4	1	2	0	36	3	1	.257	.237
Durante, Eric	R-R	5-10	175	7-11-84	.251	.241	.253	51	187	19	47	12	0	3	17	13	7	7	1	38	3	4	.364	.322
Frias, Fernando	R-R	6-1	175	9-27-81	.321	.000	.375	8	28	5	9	2	0	1	4	5	0	0	0	9	1	1	.500	.424
Groce, Garrett	R-R	6-1	190	4-24-83	.322	.220	.341	70	258	49	83	13	2	9	35	34	3	0	2	53	12	4	.492	.404
Hall, James	L-R	6-3	210	5-19-84	.232	.241	.231	69	250	33	58	9	3	4	29	17	6	0	1	59	5	3	.340	.296
Hughes, John	L-L	6-2	175	9-9-83	.279	.297	.275	58	219	34	61	18	0	8	30	15	4	0	1	53	3	2	.470	.335
Jamieson, Alex	L-R	5-11	205	4-7-83	.339	.200	.351	20	62	8	21	6	1	1	12	5	1	0	1	12	0	0	.516	.391
Johnson, Josh	R-R	6-0	205	11-3-82	.195	.222	.187	37	118	13	23	6	0	2	10	9	4	1	1	36	0	0	.297	.273
Kennedy, David	B-R	6-2	178	7-10-83	.225	.275	.214	55	213	29	48	11	5	0	17	24	8	0	1	56	4	2	.324	.325
Mathias, Ryder	R-R	6-1	190	9-28-81	.236	.194	.245	52	174	23	41	7	0	3	22	16	15	1	2	31	2	1	.328	.348
Matthews, William	B-R	6-0	175	6-8-83	.000	.000	.000	5	9	0	0	0	0	0	1	0	0	0	0	1	0	0	.000	.000
Matulia, John	L-L	6-0	175	8-19-86	.189	.167	.194	9	37	4	7	0	0	0	1	4	0	1	0	9	0	1	.189	.268
Rainville, Michael	L-R	6-0	205	3-9-83	.142	.000	.158	35	113	5	16	2	0	0	7	5	1	0	1	39	1	0	.159	.183
Rousseve, Brandon	R-R	6-1	175	8-4-84	.234	.250	.229	12	47	4	11	2	0	0	7	4	1	0	0	11	2	2	.277	.308
Spring, Matt	R-R	6-2	215	11-7-84	.188	.216	.180	50	170	24	32	8	1	4	19	27	2	0	2	60	2	0	.318	.303
Walton, Neil	R-R	6-5	180	2-23-84	.200	.258	.189	57	200	14	40	4	0	1	16	9	3	1	1	65	3	2	.235	.244
Woodruff, Ernest	R-R	6-4	207	9-23-82	.091	.000	.154	9	22	0	2	0	0	0	0	0	0	0	0	7	0	0	.091	.091

PITCHING	B-T	HT	WT	DOB	W	L	ERA	G	GS	CG	SV	IP	H	R	ER	HR	BB	SO	AVG	vLH	vRH	K/9	BB/9
Bigda, Drew	R-L	6-0	215	5-16-83	0	4	5.13	24	0	0	2	33	35	24	19	0	22	42	.269	.313	.255	11.34	5.94
Cobb, Matt	L-L	6-3	180	7-30-83	3	5	3.57	16	3	0	0	40	37	21	16	6	10	29	.234	.243	.231	6.47	2.23
Coose, Austin	R-R	6-2	249	1-27-79	0	1	4.09	11	0	0	1	11	10	7	5	1	5	14	.227	.235	.222	11.45	4.09
Corporan, Willy	R-R	6-4	220	9-2-81	1	0	2.01	14	0	0	0	22	17	6	5	3	6	13	.207	.222	.200	5.24	2.42
Davis, Wade	R-R	6-5	220	9-7-85	7	4	2.72	15	15	0	0	86	75	35	26	5	23	97	.234	.300	.199	10.15	2.41
De los Santos, Richard	R-R	6-1	175	6-1-84	1	0	0.93	6	0	0	2	10	6	2	1	0	2	8	.171	.182	.167	7.45	1.86
Evers, Bill	R-R	6-2	195	8-31-82	1	2	4.78	20	0	0	1	32	45	26	17	1	8	18	.333	.309	.350	5.06	2.25
Falk, Matt	L-R	6-3	190	8-25-84	1	1	2.18	12	0	0	0	21	17	9	5	1	9	29	.215	.206	.222	12.63	3.92
Feldkamp, Derek	R-R	6-4	210	5-9-83	1	2	4.05	23	0	0	15	27	20	14	12	3	11	35	.206	.265	.175	11.81	3.71
Fisher, Matt	R-R	6-1	195	9-6-83	1	1	6.16	15	0	0	0	19	24	16	13	3	5	5	.289	.345	.259	2.37	2.37
Gil, Roberto	R-R	6-1	160	5-20-84	1	0	4.26	6	0	0	0	13	10	6	6	2	3	14	.213	.217	.208	9.95	2.13
Kamrath, Jeff	R-R	6-3	210	4-6-82	2	4	7.39	9	8	0	0	35	49	32	29	5	17	28	.333	.370	.297	7.13	4.33
Lopez, Romelio	B-R	6-7	252	10-10-83	1	2	1.47	4	4	0	0	18	10	8	3	2	10	13	.152	.083	.233	6.38	4.91
Mason, Chris	R-R	6-0	185	7-1-84	1	1	2.40	9	0	0	2	15	11	4	4	0	8	14	.220	.250	.200	8.40	4.80
McGee, Jacob	L-L	6-3	190	8-6-86	5	4	3.64	15	14	0	0	77	64	32	31	4	23	89	.226	.194	.230	10.45	2.70
Reinhard, Greg	L-R	6-1	205	8-11-83	2	3	3.71	12	11	0	0	53	54	28	22	5	13	63	.269	.250	.279	10.63	2.19

PITCHING	B-T	HT	WT	DOB	W	L	ERA	G	GS	CG	SV	IP	H	R	ER	HR	BB	SO	AVG	vLH	vRH	K/9	BB/9
Rico, Matt	R-R	6-3	197	10-8-81	0	0	2.53	8	0	0	0	11	8	3	3	2	2	9	.205	.188	.217	7.59	1.69
Rulon, Ben	L-L	6-2	175	9-25-82	1	0	2.28	6	3	1	0	24	25	9	6	1	5	15	.281	.125	.315	5.70	1.90
Townsend, Wade	R-R	6-4	230	2-22-83	0	4	5.49	12	10	0	0	39	44	28	24	4	24	33	.275	.277	.273	7.55	5.49
Wagner, Nick	R-R	6-2	215	6-16-83	1	0	3.38	9	0	0	0	13	15	8	5	3	5	10	.268	.389	.211	6.75	3.38
Walker, Aaron	L-L	6-3	210	2-4-82	1	1	3.38	15	0	0	1	24	23	13	9	0	7	22	.237	.167	.260	8.25	2.63
Walker, Matt	R-R	6-3	193	8-16-86	0	0	10.80	1	1	0	0	3	5	4	4	0	4	5	.357	.571	.143	13.50	10.80
Wlodarczyk, Mike	L-L	6-5	230	12-2-82	0	4	1.90	5	5	0	0	24	22	9	5	0	12	25	.237	.276	.219	9.51	4.56

GAMES BY POSITION: C—Jamieson 15, Johnson 14, Spring 48. **1B**—Bouman 2, Hughes 10, Johnson 19, Mathias 46. **2B**—Bouman 14, Durante 49, Matthews 5, Rousseve 12. **3B**—Bouman 14, de la Rosa 31, Durante 2, Rainville 33. **SS**—Bouman 18, Walton 57. **OF**—Cardona 30, Frias 8, Groce 68, Hall 60, Kennedy 54, Matulia 9.

PRINCETON DEVIL RAYS — Rookie

APPALACHIAN LEAGUE

BATTING	B-T	HT	WT	DOB	AVG	vLH	vRH	G	AB	R	H	2B	3B	HR	RBI	BB	HBP	SH	SF	SO	SB	CS	SLG	OBP
Bethel, Ryan	B-R	6-0	170	3-26-82	.357	.296	.375	33	115	25	41	12	1	0	17	25	2	2	2	19	3	1	.478	.472
Colon, Kevin	R-R	5-11	165	7-6-84	.223	.250	.214	30	94	12	21	1	0	0	9	11	2	6	0	17	3	5	.234	.318
Cunningham, Chris	R-R	6-0	200	8-24-82	.329	.369	.312	59	222	42	73	13	1	7	40	34	7	1	0	55	6	3	.491	.433
de la Rosa, Jairo	R-R	6-2	170	9-8-85	.270	.438	.213	17	63	8	17	5	1	1	6	1	0	0	0	11	6	4	.429	.281
De Leon, Epifanio	R-R	6-5	205	1-5-86	.238	.286	.221	50	185	23	44	9	1	6	22	11	5	0	1	75	2	1	.395	.297
Devins, Matt	R-R	6-2	195	5-23-83	.287	.257	.303	57	202	34	58	13	0	6	33	26	9	1	1	26	12	1	.441	.391
Edwards, Ron	R-R	6-3	210	12-11-86	.000	.000	.000	3	6	0	0	0	0	0	0	0	0	0	0	4	0	0	.000	.000
Fields, Matt	R-R	6-4	255	7-8-85	.254	.377	.202	45	177	29	45	10	0	8	35	10	3	0	1	65	1	1	.446	.304
Irvin, Blair	L-R	6-2	158	5-16-83	.091	.000	.111	7	11	1	1	0	0	0	0	0	1	0	0	4	0	0	.091	.167
Lagreid, Tom	R-R	6-1	185	10-24-83	.287	.313	.275	50	150	20	43	2	0	2	11	19	1	1	0	30	7	3	.340	.371
Lopez, Andrew	R-R	6-1	185	1-18-87	.325	.372	.299	34	120	21	39	10	2	4	21	11	6	1	2	40	1	1	.542	.403
Matthews, William	B-R	6-0	175	6-8-83	.053	.063	.045	15	38	3	2	1	0	0	2	1	0	0	1	18	0	1	.079	.075
Matulia, John	L-L	6-0	175	8-19-86	.362	.406	.342	27	105	19	38	6	2	2	15	14	0	2	0	18	8	10	.514	.437
McCormick, Mike	R-R	6-1	185	9-6-86	.252	.355	.213	32	111	15	28	10	1	3	16	11	4	0	1	31	3	3	.441	.339
Parker, Carnell	L-L	6-1	170	10-4-82	.216	.429	.167	20	37	6	8	3	0	0	2	3	0	1	0	13	8	1	.297	.275
Pickerell, Steven	R-R	6-3	215	2-5-82	.257	.333	.217	22	35	9	9	3	0	1	7	10	2	0	1	8	0	0	.429	.438
Regan, Chris	L-R	6-2	210	3-17-84	.232	.250	.225	19	56	4	13	3	0	0	5	2	1	0	0	14	0	1	.286	.271
Royster, Ryan	R-R	6-2	205	7-25-86	.246	.264	.239	51	187	30	46	8	0	12	37	13	2	0	1	48	6	0	.481	.300
Vick, Hunter	B-R	5-9	165	4-12-82	.235	.250	.229	49	166	34	39	4	0	0	16	24	4	1	2	35	7	9	.259	.342
Wiens, Logan	R-R	6-6	210	1-13-86	.223	.280	.203	32	94	12	21	4	1	2	13	18	2	0	1	28	3	1	.351	.357

PITCHING	B-T	HT	WT	DOB	W	L	ERA	G	GS	CG	SV	IP	H	R	ER	HR	BB	SO	AVG	vLH	vRH	K/9	BB/9
Baker, Brian	R-R	6-5	190	1-10-83	6	2	2.60	17	0	0	0	28	22	12	8	4	6	33	.224	.353	.156	10.73	1.95
Cayton, Jason	L-R	6-5	200	3-5-84	3	2	3.65	12	11	0	0	57	62	32	23	2	16	55	.272	.241	.290	8.74	2.54
Dupas, Greg	R-R	6-6	230	1-31-84	3	1	3.55	14	3	0	0	38	38	24	15	3	13	27	.255	.240	.263	6.39	3.08
Falk, Matt	L-R	6-3	190	8-25-84	1	1	3.65	6	1	0	0	12	8	6	5	1	6	14	.182	.118	.222	10.22	4.38
Farrell, Jarrod	R-R	6-6	204	1-25-84	4	3	3.23	16	0	0	0	39	47	17	14	3	5	26	.297	.279	.311	6.00	1.15
Findlay, Robert	R-R	6-3	225	10-14-80	3	1	1.88	22	0	0	15	24	15	5	5	0	7	34	.174	.207	.158	12.75	2.63
Fines, Woods	R-R	6-5	190	8-14-85	2	3	5.29	11	6	0	0	32	40	29	19	4	11	29	.294	.295	.293	8.07	3.06
Frontz, Neal	R-R	6-3	190	4-6-84	1	4	3.83	14	10	0	0	47	59	34	20	7	12	42	.301	.279	.313	8.04	2.30
Hellickson, Jeremy	R-R	5-11	165	4-8-87	0	0	6.00	4	0	0	0	6	6	4	4	1	1	11	.240	.400	.133	16.50	1.50
Kelly, Chris	R-R	6-3	200	7-14-82	1	1	3.94	16	1	0	0	16	18	11	7	0	10	14	.281	.308	.263	7.88	5.63
Limas, Alejandro	R-R	6-3	178	8-31-85	0	0	4.88	13	0	0	0	28	22	19	15	8	14	26	.216	.257	.194	8.46	4.55
Morse, Ryan	L-L	6-3	200	5-21-83	0	1	5.24	12	3	0	0	22	27	14	13	1	12	18	.303	.333	.296	7.25	4.84
Muro, Joseph	R-R	6-0	161	2-16-84	0	0	8.04	14	0	0	0	16	21	15	14	2	18	22	.323	.290	.353	12.64	10.34
Nagy, Brett	R-R	6-1	190	11-10-81	2	1	2.59	18	0	0	1	24	20	10	7	2	9	20	.230	.120	.274	7.40	3.33
Navaroli, Michael	R-R	6-3	224	11-17-80	0	1	2.25	6	0	0	0	8	4	2	2	1	1	5	.143	.083	.188	5.63	1.13
Pendarvis, Chad	L-L	6-7	210	6-22-83	1	3	6.75	11	3	0	0	16	21	13	12	3	5	12	.318	.111	.351	6.75	2.81
Rulon, Ben	L-L	6-2	175	9-25-82	2	2	5.33	8	5	0	0	25	34	16	15	0	7	24	.324	.524	.274	8.53	2.49
Sullivan, Dan	L-R	6-3	215	2-28-83	0	0	3.46	11	0	0	0	13	8	6	5	2	8	18	.174	.150	.192	12.46	5.54
Walker, Matt	R-R	6-3	193	8-16-86	2	3	5.31	13	12	0	1	58	63	39	34	2	22	71	.274	.212	.321	11.08	3.43
Wlodarczyk, Mike	L-L	6-5	230	12-2-82	3	2	2.54	10	10	1	0	50	45	18	14	3	7	50	.241	.250	.238	9.06	1.27

GAMES BY POSITION: C—Lagreid 50, Pickerell 17, Regan 14. **1B**—Fields 38, Royster 4, Wiens 29. **2B**—Bethel 15, Colon 2, Matthews 14, Vick 43. **3B**—Bethel 7, Cunningham 1, de la Rosa 14, Devins 16, McCormick 29, Pickerell 1. **SS**—Bethel 7, Colon 28, Devins 34, Vick 2. **OF**—Cunningham 40, De Leon 44, Irvin 6, Lopez 33, Matulia 24, Parker 9, Royster 46, Vick 7.

TEXAS RANGERS

BY EVAN GRANT

It was another year of major changes to the Rangers' hierarchy. The only thing that stayed constant was the team's place in the American League West standings. That would be below the Angels and Athletics.

The Rangers began 2005 hoping to build on a growing core of talented young players and to capitalize on a surprising 89-win 2004 season. Instead, the team ended up changing general managers while still finishing in third place in the West.

It was the Rangers' fifth losing season in the last six years. They have not finished above third place in the West since winning the division in 1999.

The finish once again brought about more offseason changes. GM John Hart, who had become almost reclusive, stepped down after four seasons to move into a consultancy role. A year earlier, Hart's planned successor, Grady Fuson, had been forced out. The year before that the Rangers brought in a new manager. In 2002, Hart had replaced Doug Melvin as GM.

The Rangers are hoping for some long-term stability in the management department. Perhaps that's why they chose to go with youth in replacing Hart. Assistant GM Jon Daniels, 28, stepped up and became the youngest GM in baseball history.

"I've watched Jon for a year and a half, and I'm confident he's ready for this," owner Tom Hicks said. "He's smarter than all of us, and he's intelligent enough to ask others when he doesn't know an answer."

Daniels, however, has age-old questions to answer. With the Rangers, those revolve around pitching. And with the Rangers, nobody has found a suitable answer just yet.

The Rangers' stellar infield once again proved to be the team's strength. First baseman Mark Teixeira (.301-43-144) became a bona fide star. Second baseman Alfonso Soriano (.268-36-104) was reliable as always. Shortstop Michael Young (.331-24-91), the American League batting champion, established himself as perhaps the best shortstop in baseball. And third baseman Hank Blalock (.263-25-92) was solid. And all four players were consistent, each playing in at least 156 games.

The emergence of veteran outfielder David Delluci (29 homers) and up-and-coming outfielder Kevin Mench (25 homers) gave the Rangers' lineup even more juice. But while the offense flirted with setting a major league record for homers in a season (the Rangers finished with 260, four shy of Seattle's 1997 record), the starting pitching was once again dreadful.

By the end of July, the Rangers had jettisoned three-fifths of the Opening Day rotation, including Opening Day starter Ryan Drese. And that's not to mention the team's best pitcher, 40-year-old lefthander Kenny Rogers, who had a falling out with the club, punched a TV cameraman and served a 13-game suspension. It left the Rangers spending the final two months of the season auditioning young starters. The team severed ties with Rogers a day after the season ended.

For the first time in a while, though, it seems the top of the Rangers' farm system may be up to the challenge of relieving the major league pitching woes. Righthander Edison Volquez, part of the trumpeted D-V-D (Thomas Diamond, Volquez and John Danks) trio, rocketed through the system and got his first major league start before the end of August.

And by the end of the season, righthander Kameron Loe, who began the year at Triple-A Oklahoma, might have been the parent club's best pitcher.

The Rangers are hopeful that the winter will bring continued progress in the pitching department and that Diamond, Danks and Volquez can move up to Triple-A to start 2006. There are some talented young pitchers close behind them, such as righthanders Eric Hurley (like Diamond, a 2004 first-rounder) and Michael Schlact.

If the Rangers can develop a pipeline of pitching, it's going to make Daniels look wise beyond his years.

PLAYERS OF THE YEAR

MAJOR LEAGUE: Mark Teixeira, 1b

Teixeira made the leap from emerging power hitter to elite slugger in 2005, increasing his home run total by five to 43, his RBI total by 32 to 144, and his batting average by 20 points to .301. At 25, he established himself as the true anchor of the Rangers' star-studded young infield.

MINOR LEAGUE: Thomas Diamond, rhp

SHAWN DAVIS

The Rangers' top prospect entering 2005 lived up to his billing in the first half of the season at high Class A Bakersfield, going 8-0, 1.99 with 101 strikeouts in 81 innings. He struggled with his command after a promotion to Double-A Frisco but still rated as the Texas League's best pitching prospect.

ORGANIZATION LEADERS

BATTING		
*AVG	Gonzalez, Adrian, Oklahoma	.338
R	German, Esteban, Oklahoma	103
H	Arias, Joaquin, Frisco	157
TB	Botts, Jason, Oklahoma	266
2B	Webster, Anthony, Bakersfield	36
3B	Webster, Anthony, Bakersfield	11
HR	Botts, Jason, Oklahoma	25
RBI	Botts, Jason, Oklahoma	102
BB	Hulett, Tug, Clinton	90
SO	Botts, Jason, Oklahoma	152
SB	German, Esteban, Oklahoma	43
	Yan, Ruddy, AZL Rangers/Frisco/Oklahoma	43
*OBP	Eldridge, Rashad, Frisco/Oklahoma	.415
*SLG	Gonzalez, Adrian, Oklahoma	.561
PITCHING		
W	Diamond, Thomas, Bakersfield/Frisco	13
L	Danks, John, Bakersfield/Frisco	13
#ERA	Mathis, Doug, Spokane	2.10
G	Veras, Jose, Oklahoma	57
CG	Rodriguez, Ricardo, Oklahoma	3
SV	Veras, Jose, Oklahoma	24
IP	Walker, Andy, Bakersfield/Clinton	178
BB	Diamond, Thomas, Bakersfield/Frisco	69
SO	Diamond, Thomas, Bakersfield/Frisco	169

*Minimum 250 at-bats. #Minimum 75 innings.

TEXAS RANGERS

Manager: Buck Showalter.

2005 Record: 79-83, .488 (3rd, AL West).

BATTING	B-T	HT	WT	DOB	AVG	vLH	vRH	G	AB	R	H	2B	3B	HR	RBI	BB	HBP	SH	SF	SO	SB	CS	SLG	OBP
Allen, Chad	R-R	6-1	200	2-6-75	.283	.351	.125	21	53	5	15	1	1	0	5	2	0	1	0	13	0	1	.340	.309
Alomar Jr., Sandy	R-R	6-5	235	6-18-66	.273	.385	.245	46	128	11	35	7	0	0	14	5	1	3	0	12	0	0	.328	.306
Barajas, Rod	R-R	6-2	220	9-5-75	.254	.272	.248	120	410	53	104	24	0	21	60	26	6	4	3	70	0	0	.466	.306
Blalock, Hank	L-R	6-1	200	11-21-80	.263	.196	.291	161	647	80	170	34	0	25	92	51	3	0	4	132	1	0	.431	.318
Botts, Jason	B-R	6-5	250	7-26-80	.296	.000	.308	10	27	4	8	0	0	0	3	3	0	0	0	13	0	0	.296	.367
Dellucci, David	L-L	5-11	190	10-31-73	.251	.242	.251	128	435	97	109	17	5	29	65	76	5	0	2	121	5	3	.513	.367
DeRosa, Mark	R-R	6-1	205	2-26-75	.243	.322	.191	66	148	26	36	5	0	8	20	16	2	0	0	35	1	0	.439	.325
German, Esteban	R-R	5-9	165	1-26-78	.750	.000	.750	5	4	3	3	1	0	0	1	0	0	0	0	1	2	0	1.000	.750
Gonzalez, Adrian	L-L	6-2	220	5-8-82	.227	.071	.243	43	150	17	34	7	1	6	17	10	0	0	2	37	0	0	.407	.272
Hidalgo, Richard	R-R	6-3	220	6-28-75	.221	.157	.244	88	308	43	68	12	0	16	43	26	4	0	1	74	1	2	.416	.289
Laird, Gerald	R-R	6-2	220	11-3-79	.225	.222	.226	13	40	7	9	2	0	1	4	2	0	0	0	7	0	0	.350	.262
Matthews, Gary	B-R	6-3	225	8-25-74	.255	.241	.260	131	475	72	121	25	5	17	55	47	0	1	3	90	9	2	.436	.320
McDougall, Marshall	R-R	6-1	200	12-19-78	.167	.200	.125	18	18	3	3	1	0	0	0	0	0	0	0	10	0	0	.222	.167
Mench, Kevin	R-R	6-0	225	1-7-78	.264	.296	.255	150	557	71	147	33	3	25	73	50	5	0	3	68	4	3	.469	.328
Nevin, Phil	R-R	6-2	230	1-19-71	.182	.167	.196	29	99	15	18	5	0	3	8	8	1	0	0	30	2	0	.323	.250
Nix, Laynce	L-L	6-0	200	10-30-80	.240	.333	.232	63	229	28	55	12	3	6	32	9	0	0	2	45	2	0	.397	.267
Soriano, Alfonso	R-R	6-1	180	1-7-76	.268	.257	.272	156	637	102	171	43	2	36	104	33	7	0	5	125	30	2	.512	.309
Teixeira, Mark	B-R	6-3	220	4-11-80	.301	.292	.304	162	644	112	194	41	3	43	144	72	11	0	3	124	4	0	.575	.379
Torres, Andres	B-R	5-10	190	1-26-78	.158	.167	.143	8	19	2	3	1	0	0	1	1	0	0	1	6	1	0	.211	.190
Young, Michael	R-R	6-1	190	10-19-76	.331	.340	.328	159	668	114	221	40	5	24	91	58	3	0	3	91	5	2	.513	.385

PITCHING	B-T	HT	WT	DOB	W	L	ERA	G	GS	CG	SV	IP	H	R	ER	HR	BB	SO	AVG	vLH	vRH	K/9	BB/9
Almanzar, Carlos	R-R	6-2	170	11-6-73	0	0	14.40	6	0	0	0	5	10	8	8	2	7	3	.435	.556	.357	5.40	12.60
Astacio, Pedro	R-R	6-2	210	11-28-69	2	8	6.04	12	12	0	0	67	79	45	45	13	11	45	.292	.266	.320	6.04	1.48
Baldwin, James	R-R	6-3	265	7-15-71	0	2	5.19	8	0	0	1	17	18	10	10	3	7	9	.273	.179	.342	4.67	3.63
Benoit, Joaquin	R-R	6-3	220	7-26-77	4	4	3.72	32	9	0	0	87	69	39	36	9	38	78	.212	.227	.196	8.07	3.93
Brocail, Doug	L-R	6-5	250	5-16-67	5	3	5.52	61	0	0	1	73	90	48	45	2	34	61	.301	.346	.267	7.49	4.17
Bukvich, Ryan	R-R	6-2	250	5-13-78	0	0	11.25	4	0	0	0	4	2	5	5	0	6	4	.167	.500	.000	9.00	13.50
Cordero, Francisco	R-R	6-2	235	5-11-75	3	1	3.39	69	0	0	37	69	61	28	26	5	30	79	.234	.250	.214	10.30	3.91
Dickey, R.A.	R-R	6-3	220	10-29-74	1	2	6.67	9	4	0	0	30	29	23	22	4	17	15	.254	.200	.297	4.55	5.16
Dominguez, Juan	R-R	6-2	195	5-18-80	4	6	4.22	22	10	0	0	70	78	37	33	11	25	45	.277	.241	.310	5.76	3.20
Drese, Ryan	R-R	6-3	235	4-5-76	4	6	6.46	12	12	1	0	70	96	52	50	5	24	20	.334	.314	.354	2.58	3.10
Feldman, Scott	L-R	6-5	210	2-7-83	0	1	0.96	8	0	0	0	9	9	1	1	0	2	4	.257	.308	.227	3.86	1.93
Gryboski, Kevin	R-R	6-5	255	11-15-73	1	1	11.17	11	0	0	0	10	17	15	12	1	8	2	.378	.188	.483	1.86	7.45
Karsay, Steve	R-R	6-3	215	3-24-72	0	1	7.47	14	0	0	0	16	26	14	13	2	5	9	.366	.323	.400	5.17	2.87
2-team (6 New York)					0	1	7.06	20	0	0	0	22	36	19	17	2	7	14	.371	.333	.404	5.82	2.91
Loe, Kameron	R-R	6-8	225	9-10-81	9	6	3.42	48	8	0	1	92	89	43	35	7	31	45	.252	.284	.223	4.40	3.03
Mahay, Ron	L-L	6-2	190	6-28-71	0	2	6.81	30	0	0	1	36	47	28	27	8	16	30	.313	.302	.322	7.57	4.04
Park, Chan Ho	R-R	6-2	210	6-30-73	8	5	5.66	20	20	0	0	110	130	70	69	8	54	80	.299	.308	.287	6.57	4.43
Ramirez, Erasmo	L-L	6-0	190	4-29-76	0	0	3.91	16	0	0	0	23	24	10	10	3	3	6	.273	.350	.208	2.35	1.17
Regilio, Nick	R-R	6-2	205	9-4-78	1	2	4.58	18	0	0	0	18	22	10	9	2	7	14	.297	.214	.348	7.13	3.57
Riley, Matt	L-L	6-1	225	8-2-79	1	0	9.95	7	0	0	0	13	16	14	14	2	10	4	.320	.200	.400	2.84	7.11
Rodriguez, Ricardo	L-R	6-3	190	5-21-78	2	3	5.53	12	10	0	0	57	67	39	35	11	17	24	.289	.279	.298	3.79	2.68
Rogers, Kenny	L-L	6-1	190	11-10-64	14	8	3.46	30	30	1	0	195	205	86	75	15	53	87	.271	.201	.291	4.01	2.44
Rupe, Josh	R-R	6-2	200	8-18-82	1	0	2.79	4	1	0	0	10	7	4	3	0	4	6	.219	.333	.071	5.59	3.72
Shouse, Brian	L-L	5-11	190	9-26-68	3	2	5.23	64	0	0	0	53	55	37	31	7	18	35	.266	.209	.337	5.91	3.04
Standridge, Jason	R-R	6-4	230	11-9-78	0	0	11.57	2	0	0	0	2	7	3	3	0	1	2	.467	.400	.600	7.71	3.86
Tejera, Michael	L-L	5-9	190	10-18-76	0	0	13.50	3	0	0	0	2	5	3	3	1	1	2	.455	.333	.600	9.00	4.50
Thompson, Justin	L-L	6-4	215	3-8-73	0	0	21.60	2	0	0	0	2	4	4	4	2	0	1	.444	.400	.500	5.40	0.00
Volquez, Edison	R-R	6-1	190	7-3-83	0	4	14.21	6	3	0	0	13	25	22	20	3	10	11	.403	.481	.343	7.82	7.11
Wasdin, John	R-R	6-2	190	8-5-72	3	2	4.28	31	6	0	4	76	77	37	36	9	20	44	.261	.229	.290	5.23	2.38
Wilson, C.J.	L-L	6-2	200	11-18-80	1	7	6.94	24	6	0	1	48	63	39	37	5	18	30	.321	.290	.339	5.63	3.38
Young, Chris	R-R	6-10	260	5-25-79	12	7	4.26	31	31	0	0	165	162	84	78	19	45	137	.252	.281	.220	7.49	2.46

FIELDING

Catcher	PCT	G	PO	A	E	DP	PB
Alomar	.992	46	231	6	2	0	3
Barajas	.988	119	689	41	9	5	7
Laird	.957	13	61	5	3	2	1

First Base	PCT	G	PO	A	E	DP
Barajas	1.000	1	1	0	0	0
DeRosa	1.000	1	2	0	0	1
Gonzalez	.978	10	85	6	2	7
Nevin	1.000	3	13	1	0	1
Teixeira	.998	155	1377	101	3	126

Second Base	PCT	G	PO	A	E	DP
DeRosa	.971	17	14	20	1	4
German	.917	1	3	8	1	2
McDougall	.000	2	0	0	0	0
Soriano	.972	153	284	448	21	101

Third Base	PCT	G	PO	A	E	DP
Blalock	.973	158	96	304	11	23
DeRosa	.875	5	2	5	1	1
German	.000	1	0	0	0	0
McDougall	1.000	5	3	4	0	0
Nevin	1.000	1	0	1	0	0

Shortstop	PCT	G	PO	A	E	DP
DeRosa	.982	16	17	38	1	5
McDougall	1.000	1	1	1	0	1
Young	.974	155	238	427	18	95

Outfield	PCT	G	PO	A	E	DP
Allen	1.000	2	1	0	0	0
Botts	.900	7	8	1	1	1
Dellucci	.970	52	93	4	3	1
DeRosa	1.000	25	46	1	0	0
Gonzalez	.750	1	3	0	1	0
Hidalgo	.989	85	179	3	2	0
Laird	.000	1	0	0	0	0
Matthews	.982	123	317	7	6	4
McDougall	.000	3	0	0	0	0
Mench	.987	148	290	8	4	3
Nix	.988	61	160	3	2	1
Torres	1.000	5	12	0	0	0

FARM SYSTEM

General Manager: John Hart. **Director, Player Personnel:** Dom Chiti. **Scouting Director:** Ron Hopkins.

Class	Farm Team	League	W	L	Pct.	Finish*	Manager	Affiliate Since
AAA	Oklahoma RedHawks (Oklahoma City)	Pacific Coast	80	63	.559	**1st (16)**	Bobby Jones	1983
AA	Frisco (Texas) RoughRiders	Texas	58	82	.414	8th (8)	Darryl Kennedy	2003
High A	Bakersfield (Calif.) Blaze	California	68	72	.486	7th (10)	Arnie Beyeler	2005
Low A	Clinton (Iowa) LumberKings	Midwest	71	69	.507	**6th (14)**	Carlos Subero	2003
SS A	Spokane (Wash.) Indians	Northwest	37	39	.487	**+4th (8)**	Greg Riddoch	2003
Rookie	Surprise (Ariz.) Rangers	Arizona	27	29	.482	t-5th (9)	Pedro Lopez	2003

*Finish in overall standings (No. of teams in league)/Playoff teams in **boldface** +League champion

OKLAHOMA REDHAWKS — Class AAA

PACIFIC COAST LEAGUE

BATTING	B-T	HT	WT	DOB	AVG	vLH	vRH	G	AB	R	H	2B	3B	HR	RBI	BB	HBP	SH	SF	SO	SB	CS	SLG	OBP
Alexander, Manny	R-R	5-10	180	3-20-71	.309	.342	.297	108	417	64	129	23	6	12	67	38	4	2	6	66	27	9	.480	.368
Allen, Chad	R-R	6-1	200	2-6-75	.345	.275	.382	45	200	34	69	12	0	8	33	10	0	0	1	31	9	2	.525	.374
Botts, Jason	B-R	6-5	250	7-26-80	.286	.353	.258	133	510	93	146	31	7	25	102	67	8	0	4	152	2	4	.522	.375
Brewer, Jace	R-R	6-0	190	6-9-79	.270	.280	.265	23	74	11	20	6	0	0	10	6	0	1	1	10	2	2	.351	.321
Colbrunn, Greg	R-R	6-0	215	7-26-69	.200	.300	.167	11	40	3	8	3	0	0	2	4	0	0	0	7	0	0	.275	.273
Conti, Jason	L-R	5-11	180	1-27-75	.258	.221	.273	117	462	80	119	26	3	15	73	40	5	7	2	116	4	1	.424	.322
Eldridge, Rashad	B-R	6-1	185	10-16-81	.294	.272	.307	91	303	61	89	27	4	5	34	54	1	4	2	76	4	2	.459	.400
Esposito, Brian	R-R	6-1	185	2-24-79	.407	.625	.316	8	27	6	11	1	0	0	4	1	1	0	0	6	0	0	.444	.448
German, Esteban	R-R	5-9	165	1-26-78	.313	.341	.303	117	489	103	153	27	6	5	68	65	7	1	2	74	43	6	.423	.400
Gonzalez, Adrian	L-L	6-2	220	5-8-82	.338	.352	.332	84	328	61	111	17	1	18	65	32	4	0	4	44	0	0	.561	.399
Kinsler, Ian	R-R	6-0	175	6-22-82	.274	.275	.273	131	530	102	145	28	2	23	94	53	9	2	3	89	19	5	.464	.348
Laird, Gerald	R-R	6-2	220	11-3-79	.310	.271	.322	75	281	51	87	12	4	17	55	28	5	1	2	61	12	2	.562	.380
McDonald, Keith	R-R	6-2	235	2-8-73	.240	.200	.258	66	233	28	56	15	1	2	33	25	1	0	5	54	0	0	.339	.311
McDougall, Marshall	R-R	6-1	200	12-19-78	.341	.453	.296	57	223	40	76	16	2	11	64	30	0	1	2	45	5	0	.578	.416
Meyer, Drew	L-R	5-10	200	8-29-81	.247	.245	.248	42	178	25	44	11	4	0	19	14	0	2	1	43	5	2	.354	.301
Nix, Laynce	L-L	6-0	200	10-30-80	.333	.400	.323	10	36	8	12	1	1	3	6	9	0	0	0	6	0	1	.667	.467
Ransom, Cody	R-R	6-2	210	2-17-76	.261	.286	.254	24	92	13	24	5	0	5	17	8	0	0	0	32	0	1	.478	.320
Richard, Chris	L-L	6-2	210	6-7-74	.301	.352	.284	98	362	67	109	20	3	14	66	41	6	0	3	75	5	2	.489	.379
Smith, Will	L-R	6-2	200	10-23-81	.337	.222	.368	48	169	30	57	13	2	8	36	20	1	0	4	31	0	0	.580	.402
Torres, Andres	B-R	5-10	190	1-26-78	.302	.182	.327	15	63	12	19	3	1	0	1	6	0	0	0	17	6	1	.381	.362
Yan, Ruddy	B-R	6-0	160	1-13-82	.316	.571	.167	5	19	1	6	0	0	0	1	1	0	0	0	2	1	0	.316	.350

PITCHING	B-T	HT	WT	DOB	W	L	ERA	G	GS	CG	SV	IP	H	R	ER	HR	BB	SO	AVG	vLH	vRH	K/9	BB/9
Bazzell, Shane	L-R	6-2	180	3-2-79	0	1	46.29	1	1	0	0	2	10	12	12	1	5	3	.588	1.000	.462	11.57	19.29
Benoit, Joaquin	R-R	6-3	220	7-26-77	0	1	5.40	3	1	0	0	5	4	3	3	1	4	2	.235	.200	.250	3.60	7.20
Crabtree, Tim	R-R	6-4	225	10-13-69	0	0	0.00	1	0	0	0	1	2	0	0	0	0	1	.400	.667	.000	9.00	0.00
Dickey, R.A.	R-R	6-3	220	10-29-74	10	6	5.99	19	17	1	0	122	152	88	81	12	39	81	.308	.313	.303	5.99	2.88
Dominguez, Juan	R-R	6-2	195	5-18-80	2	1	4.25	7	7	0	0	36	38	20	17	6	10	24	.264	.324	.211	6.00	2.50
Francisco, Frank	R-R	6-2	220	9-11-79	0	0	3.00	2	0	0	1	3	2	1	1	0	2	4	.200	.400	.000	12.00	6.00
Gryboski, Kevin	R-R	6-5	255	11-15-73	0	2	5.23	9	0	0	0	10	14	7	6	2	6	5	.326	.368	.292	4.35	5.23
House, Craig	R-R	6-2	220	7-8-77	1	0	9.53	4	0	0	0	6	5	6	6	1	8	7	.238	.375	.154	11.12	12.71
Hudgins, John	R-R	6-2	195	8-31-81	3	7	5.87	19	19	1	0	103	127	74	67	12	37	77	.305	.280	.323	6.75	3.24
Jimenez, Kelvin	R-R	6-0	180	10-27-80	4	6	3.63	37	5	0	3	79	79	40	32	6	33	64	.262	.226	.283	7.26	3.74
Karsay, Steve	R-R	6-3	215	3-24-72	0	1	13.50	4	0	0	0	4	11	9	6	0	1	5	.458	.400	.500	11.25	2.25
Lee, Derek	L-L	6-3	208	8-20-74	5	2	3.86	14	14	1	0	89	91	39	38	7	20	49	.275	.273	.276	4.97	2.03
Loe, Kameron	R-R	6-8	225	9-10-81	2	1	5.08	5	5	0	0	28	32	17	16	5	10	23	.281	.372	.225	7.31	3.18
Mahay, Ron	L-L	6-2	190	6-28-71	0	0	0.00	3	0	0	0	4	2	0	0	0	1	5	.167	.200	.143	12.27	2.45
Mercado, Hector	L-L	6-3	235	4-29-74	4	0	1.71	22	0	0	1	32	31	8	6	1	19	31	.265	.265	.265	8.81	5.40
Montero, Agustin	R-R	6-3	210	8-26-77	0	0	5.40	4	0	0	0	5	6	3	3	0	3	4	.333	.143	.455	7.20	5.40
Murray, A.J.	B-L	6-3	222	3-17-82	1	0	6.30	2	2	0	0	10	11	7	7	4	2	11	.275	.200	.286	9.90	1.80
Nunez, Vladimir	R-R	6-4	240	3-15-75	1	1	4.91	17	0	0	4	22	27	12	12	1	7	17	.310	.371	.269	6.95	2.86
Pote, Lou	R-R	6-3	200	8-21-71	2	1	3.38	14	4	0	1	43	45	18	16	2	27	35	.274	.230	.311	7.38	5.70
Ramirez, Erasmo	L-L	6-0	190	4-29-76	0	0	3.79	16	0	0	1	19	19	10	8	3	5	11	.253	.292	.235	5.21	2.37
Regilio, Nick	R-R	6-2	205	9-4-78	0	0	0.00	1	0	0	0	2	1	0	0	0	1	2	.167	.000	.250	9.00	4.50
Riley, Matt	L-L	6-1	225	8-2-79	0	1	8.25	4	4	0	0	12	12	11	11	3	7	15	.245	.294	.219	11.25	5.25
Rodriguez, Ricardo	L-R	6-3	190	5-21-78	7	3	2.91	13	12	3	0	80	64	30	26	8	23	48	.221	.220	.221	5.38	2.58
Rodriguez, Wilfredo	L-L	6-3	180	3-20-79	0	0	1.42	2	2	0	0	6	5	2	1	1	2	8	.208	.111	.267	11.37	2.84
Roney, Matt	R-R	6-3	245	1-10-80	4	1	3.03	24	0	0	1	33	34	11	11	3	8	32	.272	.271	.273	8.82	2.20
Rowe, Steven	R-R	6-4	210	7-17-80	1	0	3.75	8	0	0	1	12	9	5	5	1	1	10	.209	.125	.259	7.50	0.75
Rupe, Josh	R-R	6-2	200	8-18-82	6	7	6.25	17	17	0	0	94	116	75	65	12	38	62	.306	.283	.323	5.96	3.65
Sele, Aaron	R-R	6-5	230	6-25-70	1	1	8.03	2	2	0	0	12	22	12	11	2	2	6	.400	.286	.471	4.38	1.46
Snare, Ryan	L-L	6-0	200	2-8-79	1	5	6.38	17	7	0	2	61	80	49	43	8	28	35	.323	.341	.313	5.19	4.15
Stamler, Keith	L-R	6-2	195	8-20-79	3	1	7.32	16	0	0	5	20	27	16	16	4	11	16	.325	.324	.327	7.32	5.03
Standridge, Jason	R-R	6-4	230	11-9-78	5	3	4.50	15	10	0	0	76	83	41	38	3	36	47	.288	.351	.247	5.57	4.26
Tejera, Michael	L-L	5-9	190	10-18-76	3	2	3.79	43	2	0	2	59	52	28	25	5	29	52	.239	.174	.280	7.89	4.40
Thompson, Justin	L-L	6-4	215	3-8-73	2	2	4.70	25	1	0	0	44	47	24	23	3	7	29	.278	.264	.289	5.93	1.43
Veras, Jose	R-R	6-5	240	10-20-80	3	5	3.79	57	0	0	24	62	63	27	26	4	33	72	.266	.293	.252	10.51	4.82
Wasdin, John	R-R	6-2	190	8-5-72	9	2	4.93	13	11	0	0	73	84	43	40	11	24	57	.286	.361	.234	7.03	2.96

FIELDING

Catcher	PCT	G	PO	A	E	DP	PB
Esposito	.984	7	61	2	1	1	0
Laird	.988	73	463	50	6	5	7
McDonald	.990	65	462	24	5	1	5

First Base	PCT	G	PO	A	E	DP
Alexander	.988	9	80	5	1	7
Colbrunn	.981	4	49	3	1	2
Gonzalez	.994	82	747	64	5	101
McDonald	1.000	1	3	2	0	0
Richard	.991	48	427	31	4	58

Second Base	PCT	G	PO	A	E	DP
Alexander	1.000	1	0	5	0	1
German	.981	11	20	31	1	9
Kinsler	.972	126	276	413	20	112
McDougall	1.000	2	3	5	0	3
Meyer	.800	1	2	2	1	0
Ransom	1.000	2	7	7	0	2

Third Base	PCT	G	PO	A	E	DP
Alexander	.915	23	16	38	5	6
Brewer	1.000	9	5	20	0	4
German	.954	75	44	123	8	15
Kinsler	1.000	1	1	4	0	0
McDougall	.962	31	21	81	4	7
Meyer	1.000	1	0	1	0	0
Ransom	.850	5	4	13	3	2

Shortstop	PCT	G	PO	A	E	DP
Alexander	.956	68	110	213	15	62
Brewer	.972	12	20	50	2	14
German	.925	14	24	50	6	11
Kinsler	.900	3	5	4	1	2
McDougall	1.000	4	7	16	0	4
Meyer	.964	29	36	99	5	24
Ransom	.963	16	28	49	3	10

Outfield	PCT	G	PO	A	E	DP
Alexander	.909	3	10	0	1	0
Allen	.985	39	62	3	1	0
Botts	.948	82	123	4	7	0
Conti	.984	112	229	13	4	2
Eldridge	.982	79	165	3	3	1
German	1.000	5	8	0	0	0
McDougall	.957	14	21	1	1	0
Meyer	.957	11	22	0	1	0
Nix	1.000	10	21	1	0	0
Richard	.956	25	42	1	2	0
Smith	.986	35	70	2	1	0
Torres	.900	15	17	1	2	1
Yan	1.000	5	14	0	0	0

FRISCO ROUGHRIDERS

Class AA

TEXAS LEAGUE

BATTING	B-T	HT	WT	DOB	AVG	vLH	vRH	G	AB	R	H	2B	3B	HR	RBI	BB	HBP	SH	SF	SO	SB	CS	SLG	OBP
Abruzzo, Jared	B-R	6-3	215	11-15-81	.209	.157	.235	46	153	17	32	4	0	4	13	19	1	0	1	51	0	1	.314	.299
Arias, Joaquin	R-R	6-2	160	9-21-84	.315	.315	.314	120	499	65	157	23	8	5	56	17	1	3	6	46	20	10	.423	.335
Brewer, Jace	R-R	6-0	190	6-9-79	.292	.309	.281	75	264	39	77	13	1	2	22	15	1	8	2	43	8	5	.371	.330
Cleveland, Jeremy	R-R	6-2	185	9-10-81	.253	.356	.192	60	198	31	50	9	0	0	13	31	1	0	1	45	2	1	.298	.355
Coughlan, Cameron	B-L	5-11	178	8-12-81	.262	.277	.254	76	252	36	66	12	2	3	26	43	2	7	2	48	17	10	.361	.371
Eldridge, Rashad	B-R	6-1	185	10-16-81	.342	.500	.250	11	38	10	13	7	0	0	10	12	2	0	0	10	2	1	.526	.519
Esposito, Brian	R-R	6-1	185	2-24-79	.228	.259	.207	38	136	12	31	7	0	0	5	7	2	2	0	33	1	0	.279	.276
Fox, Adam	R-R	6-0	195	11-23-81	.255	.275	.248	46	149	23	38	5	1	4	26	19	3	0	1	29	3	0	.383	.349
Gold, Nate	R-R	6-3	221	6-12-80	.228	.167	.255	23	79	9	18	3	0	0	11	3	2	0	0	16	0	0	.266	.274
Hart, Jason	R-R	6-4	235	9-5-77	.246	.270	.233	128	480	59	118	28	1	21	77	40	9	0	5	103	0	1	.440	.313
Higashi, Jonathan	R-R	6-0	200	7-20-82	.000	.000	.000	1	3	0	0	0	0	0	0	0	0	0	0	1	0	0	.000	.000
Larson, Brandon	R-R	6-0	210	5-24-76	.289	.289	.289	34	135	20	39	10	0	7	34	9	5	0	1	33	0	0	.519	.353
Matthews, Gary	B-R	6-3	225	8-25-74	.400	1.000	.250	1	5	0	2	0	0	0	1	0	0	0	0	1	0	0	.400	.400
Mehl, Truan	L-R	6-2	200	3-20-83	.000	.000	.000	2	2	0	0	0	0	0	0	0	0	0	0	2	0	0	.000	.000
Meyer, Drew	L-R	5-10	200	8-29-81	.321	.306	.330	83	321	49	103	14	4	3	45	26	3	3	5	55	12	2	.417	.372
Nickeas, Mike	R-R	6-0	205	2-13-83	.202	.191	.207	68	242	22	49	7	1	5	24	20	1	2	3	43	1	1	.302	.263
Richardson, Kevin	R-R	6-3	228	9-12-80	.305	.435	.222	18	59	12	18	4	0	2	11	6	4	0	0	23	0	1	.475	.406
Senreiso, Juan	R-R	6-0	191	8-4-81	.284	.311	.270	132	497	54	141	25	5	5	35	45	4	2	5	125	16	8	.384	.345
Sinisi, Vince	L-L	6-0	195	11-7-81	.258	.188	.285	65	248	27	64	9	0	4	29	15	2	0	5	39	4	4	.343	.300
Smith, Dustin	R-R	6-2	205	5-8-81	.238	.333	.208	20	63	11	15	4	0	1	5	3	1	1	0	7	0	0	.349	.284
Smith, Will	L-R	6-2	200	10-23-81	.227	.292	.198	40	154	18	35	8	2	5	20	10	0	0	1	34	0	0	.403	.273
Taylor, Seth	R-R	6-1	185	8-23-77	.258	.331	.224	108	414	41	107	21	1	13	66	21	6	0	9	65	2	5	.408	.298
Yan, Ruddy	B-R	6-0	160	1-13-82	.300	.292	.305	116	483	77	145	15	5	3	45	47	3	10	0	38	41	11	.371	.366

PITCHING	B-T	HT	WT	DOB	W	L	ERA	G	GS	CG	SV	IP	H	R	ER	HR	BB	SO	AVG	vLH	vRH	K/9	BB/9
Bazzell, Shane	L-R	6-2	180	3-2-79	4	5	4.87	35	8	0	2	98	117	56	53	11	27	60	.301	.330	.276	5.51	2.48
Burcie, Jarrad	R-R	6-1	215	5-17-82	0	0	11.57	1	0	0	0	2	3	3	3	1	1	2	.300	.333	.250	7.71	3.86
Chavez, Jesse	R-R	6-2	153	8-21-83	4	3	5.68	31	0	0	1	57	71	43	36	10	25	27	.316	.324	.308	4.26	3.95
Crabtree, Tim	R-R	6-4	225	10-13-69	2	0	0.66	11	0	0	1	14	10	4	1	0	4	10	.189	.250	.120	6.59	2.63
Danks, John	L-L	6-2	190	4-15-85	4	10	5.49	18	17	0	0	98	117	66	60	12	34	85	.297	.222	.322	7.78	3.11
Diamond, Thomas	R-R	6-3	230	4-6-83	5	4	5.35	14	14	0	0	69	66	44	41	8	38	68	.249	.270	.233	8.87	4.96
Dominguez, Juan	R-R	6-2	195	5-18-80	2	0	2.63	15	2	0	2	38	30	14	11	4	9	31	.216	.250	.193	7.41	2.15
Feldman, Scott	L-R	6-5	210	2-7-83	1	2	2.36	46	0	0	14	61	43	18	16	3	23	41	.202	.232	.183	6.05	3.39
Francisco, Frank	R-R	6-2	220	9-11-79	0	1	8.10	4	3	0	0	3	4	6	3	0	2	3	.333	.250	.500	8.10	5.40
Hudgins, John	R-R	6-2	195	8-31-81	1	2	4.67	3	2	0	0	17	15	9	9	1	8	11	.231	.161	.294	5.71	4.15
Jimenez, Kelvin	R-R	6-0	180	10-27-80	0	0	3.46	6	0	0	2	13	12	5	5	0	6	12	.261	.313	.233	8.31	4.15
Karsay, Steve	R-R	6-3	215	3-24-72	1	2	3.64	19	0	0	0	30	29	18	12	2	6	30	.248	.205	.269	9.10	1.82
Littleton, Wes	R-R	6-3	200	9-2-82	2	3	3.97	48	0	0	3	82	93	37	36	9	24	71	.293	.336	.265	7.82	2.64
Lorenzo, Matt	L-R	6-3	205	6-21-82	3	5	7.14	10	9	0	0	47	71	39	37	9	22	28	.353	.378	.336	5.40	4.24
Mahay, Ron	L-L	6-2	190	6-28-71	1	3	7.78	5	5	0	0	20	24	19	17	3	9	20	.300	.308	.296	9.15	4.12
Marcano, Luis	R-R	6-0	211	1-12-81	0	1	6.06	10	0	0	0	16	17	12	11	6	10	6	.270	.174	.325	3.31	5.51
Masset, Nick	R-R	6-4	190	5-17-82	7	12	6.18	29	27	1	0	157	197	124	108	19	61	105	.313	.334	.294	6.01	3.49
Montero, Agustin	R-R	6-3	210	8-26-77	2	4	5.46	40	0	0	2	61	64	40	37	9	33	69	.263	.313	.219	10.18	4.87
Murray, A.J.	B-L	6-3	222	3-17-82	4	4	3.26	11	10	0	0	58	62	27	21	3	15	49	.284	.175	.323	7.60	2.33
Roberts, Mark	R-R	5-11	190	6-24-82	2	1	4.26	10	0	0	2	19	16	9	9	2	5	14	.229	.289	.156	6.63	2.37
Rodriguez, Wilfredo	L-L	6-3	180	3-20-79	4	5	3.80	12	12	1	0	69	59	34	29	5	31	64	.239	.247	.236	8.39	4.06
Rowe, Steven	R-R	6-4	210	7-17-80	1	2	6.14	18	0	0	1	29	40	22	20	4	6	15	.339	.415	.277	4.60	1.84
Rupe, Josh	R-R	6-2	200	8-18-82	4	3	3.74	11	10	0	0	65	64	29	27	7	26	55	.261	.264	.259	7.62	3.60
Snare, Ryan	L-L	6-0	200	2-8-79	1	1	0.79	9	0	0	0	11	5	1	1	0	5	11	.132	.067	.174	8.74	3.97
Thompson, Justin	L-L	6-4	215	3-8-73	2	0	2.84	12	0	0	2	13	14	5	4	1	2	11	.269	.321	.208	7.82	1.42
Volquez, Edison	R-R	6-1	190	7-3-83	1	5	4.14	10	10	1	0	59	58	29	27	6	17	49	.258	.228	.288	7.52	2.61
Wilson, C.J.	L-L	6-2	200	11-18-80	0	4	4.43	12	12	0	0	45	51	32	22	7	14	43	.290	.184	.319	8.66	2.82

FIELDING

Catcher	PCT	G	PO	A	E	DP	PB
Abruzzo	1.000	1	7	1	0	0	0
Esposito	.972	38	222	22	7	2	2
Higashi	1.000	1	7	0	0	0	0
Nickeas	.995	68	521	50	3	5	5
Richardson	.993	16	123	10	1	1	1
D. Smith	.986	20	130	8	2	2	3

First Base	PCT	G	PO	A	E	DP
Abruzzo	.965	9	82	1	3	9
Brewer	1.000	1	11	2	0	0
Gold	.993	17	125	13	1	18
Hart	.995	114	1049	60	6	106
Larson	1.000	2	18	3	0	4
Richardson	1.000	1	1	0	0	0
Taylor	.976	5	40	1	1	5

Second Base	PCT	G	PO	A	E	DP
Brewer	.969	51	68	153	7	32
Coughlan	.960	22	35	61	4	14
Fox	.973	11	13	23	1	6
Meyer	.976	69	115	213	8	51
Taylor	.800	2	1	3	1	2

Third Base	PCT	G	PO	A	E	DP
Brewer	.875	4	1	13	2	2

Fox	.959	35	19	51	3	5
Hart	1.000	1	0	2	0	0
Larson	.977	13	10	32	1	6
Meyer	1.000	7	1	10	0	0
Taylor	.943	88	40	159	12	9

Shortstop	PCT	G	PO	A	E	DP
Arias	.952	118	201	373	29	90
Brewer	1.000	11	15	29	0	8
Meyer	.966	12	24	32	2	9
Taylor	1.000	4	5	6	0	2

Outfield	PCT	G	PO	A	E	DP
Brewer	.000	1	0	0	0	0
Cleveland	.981	59	100	4	2	0
Coughlan	1.000	40	86	3	0	3
Eldridge	1.000	7	10	0	0	0
Hart	1.000	1	1	0	0	0
Matthews	.500	1	1	0	1	0
Mehl	1.000	2	1	0	0	0
Meyer	.000	1	0	0	0	0
Senreiso	.958	129	259	15	12	5
Sinisi	.967	59	87	1	3	1
W. Smith	1.000	19	36	1	0	0
Yan	.976	113	230	9	6	2

BAKERSFIELD BLAZE — High Class A

CALIFORNIA LEAGUE

BATTING	B-T	HT	WT	DOB	AVG	vLH	vRH	G	AB	R	H	2B	3B	HR	RBI	BB	HBP	SH	SF	SO	SB	CS	SLG	OBP
Abruzzo, Jared	B-R	6-3	215	11-15-81	.067	.000	.071	9	30	0	2	1	0	0	3	3	0	0	1	12	0	0	.100	.147
Bourassa, Adam	L-L	5-8	165	3-31-81	.204	.143	.220	30	103	6	21	2	0	0	6	11	0	1	0	18	3	1	.223	.281
Cleveland, Jeremy	R-R	6-2	185	9-10-81	.263	.239	.270	58	224	31	59	9	1	5	28	21	7	0	5	42	3	3	.379	.339
Gold, Nate	R-R	6-3	221	6-12-80	.281	.292	.275	101	381	63	107	27	2	21	69	42	6	1	3	65	2	2	.528	.359
Grayson, Larry	R-R	5-10	199	7-28-82	.278	.304	.271	106	421	63	117	33	2	13	61	44	8	0	2	117	11	4	.458	.356
Harrison, Ben	R-R	6-4	203	9-18-81	.318	.250	.333	12	44	4	14	2	0	1	7	3	1	0	1	13	2	1	.432	.367
Hatcher, Justin	R-R	5-10	200	5-12-80	.270	.310	.261	85	311	42	84	14	0	1	31	23	8	3	1	56	4	2	.325	.335
Hurba, Craig	R-R	6-2	225	8-25-81	.286	.190	.301	34	126	6	36	6	0	0	11	5	0	0	0	24	1	0	.333	.313
Kreuzer, Josh	R-R	6-5	240	9-28-82	.260	.247	.263	113	400	63	104	25	1	11	74	49	19	2	4	89	3	2	.410	.364
Lenoir, Bobby	R-R	6-0	188	7-12-82	.196	.236	.187	78	260	30	51	4	3	4	27	17	4	3	1	80	9	2	.281	.255
Mahar, Kevin	R-R	6-4	215	6-8-81	.315	.344	.308	110	447	98	141	27	4	17	63	47	15	0	4	109	17	10	.508	.396
Mask, Michael	L-L	5-9	195	6-24-81	.143	.333	.091	9	14	3	2	0	0	0	2	7	0	0	0	2	1	1	.143	.429
Metcalf, Travis	R-R	6-3	205	8-17-82	.291	.286	.291	132	505	80	147	32	7	22	94	49	6	1	5	129	8	2	.513	.358
Perez, Josue	B-R	6-0	180	8-12-77	.071	.000	.091	6	14	3	1	0	0	0	1	2	0	0	0	6	0	0	.071	.188
Ringe, Craig	R-R	5-9	180	3-16-80	.256	.203	.267	116	399	54	102	14	4	4	35	53	10	4	3	84	6	3	.341	.355
Sandoval, Abigail	R-R	5-11	182	1-23-82	.253	.271	.250	99	384	43	97	16	1	5	39	11	3	4	1	78	5	6	.339	.278
Sinisi, Vince	L-L	6-0	195	11-7-81	.363	.476	.342	35	135	25	49	10	2	6	22	17	1	0	0	19	5	0	.600	.438
Smith, Dustin	R-R	6-2	205	5-8-81	.328	.273	.348	36	122	20	40	11	1	4	22	16	9	0	0	22	1	1	.533	.442
Washington, Johnny	R-R	5-11	165	5-6-84	.083	.333	.000	4	12	1	1	0	0	0	3	1	0	0	0	5	0	0	.083	.154
Webster, Anthony	L-R	6-0	197	4-10-83	.301	.190	.320	122	498	93	150	36	11	11	73	31	4	2	1	55	25	5	.484	.346

PITCHING	B-T	HT	WT	DOB	W	L	ERA	G	GS	CG	SV	IP	H	R	ER	HR	BB	SO	AVG	vLH	vRH	K/9	BB/9
Abbott, Justin	R-R	6-3	215	9-4-81	1	0	4.50	2	0	0	0	4	5	2	2	1	3	3	.313	.222	.429	6.75	6.75
Boyd, Jason	R-R	6-3	175	2-23-73	1	3	5.35	17	0	0	1	34	39	20	20	5	10	23	.285	.308	.254	6.15	2.67
Brannon, Clint	L-L	5-11	205	12-24-82	9	7	4.45	29	14	1	0	111	107	63	55	13	40	81	.250	.190	.285	6.55	3.23
Chavez, Jesse	R-R	6-2	153	8-21-83	0	0	2.22	11	0	0	2	24	16	6	6	2	9	31	.182	.235	.148	11.47	3.33
Cordeiro, Chris	R-R	6-3	175	4-3-82	6	3	3.80	41	0	0	14	66	67	29	28	3	30	52	.269	.292	.241	7.06	4.07
Danks, John	L-L	6-2	190	4-15-85	3	3	2.50	10	10	0	0	58	50	18	16	5	16	53	.228	.250	.216	8.27	2.50
Diamond, Thomas	R-R	6-3	230	4-6-83	8	0	1.99	14	14	1	0	81	53	20	18	3	31	101	.191	.162	.222	11.18	3.43
Farnum, Matt	R-R	6-2	195	6-1-81	0	1	12.38	4	0	0	0	8	18	11	11	2	1	5	.439	.478	.389	5.63	1.13
Feldman, Scott	L-R	6-5	210	2-7-83	0	0	0.00	6	0	0	3	9	5	2	0	0	2	11	.152	.300	.087	11.00	2.00
Giles, Josh	R-R	6-1	175	8-3-84	0	0	0.00	1	0	0	0	2	1	0	0	0	1	3	.167	.250	.000	13.50	4.50
Herrera, Marcos	R-R	6-5	165	2-24-82	6	4	6.34	24	0	0	2	50	65	39	35	14	21	41	.320	.309	.330	7.43	3.81
Ingram, Jesse	R-R	6-1	200	4-27-82	0	2	21.00	8	0	0	2	6	15	15	14	1	11	8	.517	.700	.421	12.00	16.50
Jaile, Chris	R-R	6-3	209	2-20-81	2	3	4.26	13	13	0	0	63	65	37	30	4	35	58	.261	.278	.238	8.24	4.97
Lebron, Willy	R-R	6-1	205	3-28-79	3	4	5.11	24	5	0	2	56	69	40	32	14	25	50	.297	.298	.296	7.99	3.99
Lorenzo, Matt	L-R	6-3	205	6-21-82	1	4	4.02	9	9	0	0	54	60	31	24	8	21	55	.282	.255	.311	9.22	3.52
Marini, Chris	L-L	6-1	170	2-11-83	2	6	6.51	13	9	0	1	55	68	43	40	11	27	53	.300	.353	.256	8.62	4.39
Mattoon, Brian	L-L	6-3	210	9-15-80	5	5	4.06	38	2	0	2	89	84	46	40	13	25	67	.249	.196	.293	6.80	2.54
Morla, Wandy	R-R	6-3	195	10-22-83	0	0	15.00	3	0	0	1	6	8	11	10	4	8	4	.333	.385	.273	6.00	12.00
Murray, A.J.	B-L	6-3	222	3-17-82	2	5	5.25	14	11	0	0	60	75	38	35	6	13	64	.301	.333	.283	9.60	1.95
Padgett, Mike	R-R	6-4	210	5-6-82	0	1	4.30	14	0	0	5	23	30	13	11	2	5	20	.326	.372	.286	7.83	1.96
Ramirez, Ivan	L-L	5-9	175	7-2-82	1	3	4.91	25	0	0	1	40	39	25	22	8	15	31	.260	.214	.300	6.92	3.35
Rodriguez, William	L-L	6-0	189	5-8-84	1	1	10.06	11	0	0	0	17	25	20	19	4	8	7	.368	.333	.395	3.71	4.24
Rowe, Steven	R-R	6-4	210	7-17-80	1	1	5.40	2	0	0	0	3	4	2	2	1	0	2	.286	.286	.286	5.40	0.00
Smith, Cody	R-R	6-3	200	4-20-82	6	3	3.88	30	18	0	2	123	155	62	53	5	43	67	.318	.361	.280	4.90	3.15
Volquez, Edison	R-R	6-1	190	7-3-83	5	4	4.19	11	11	1	0	67	64	34	31	9	12	77	.252	.241	.261	10.40	1.62
Walker, Andy	R-R	6-1	175	4-20-83	3	3	4.94	9	9	0	0	55	71	34	30	7	9	35	.321	.268	.388	5.76	1.48
Wilson, C.J.	L-L	6-2	200	11-18-80	0	1	3.29	4	4	0	0	14	10	5	5	2	4	14	.189	.182	.190	9.22	2.63
Wing, Ryan	L-L	6-2	170	2-1-82	2	5	6.93	12	11	0	0	51	57	42	39	7	36	33	.286	.253	.310	5.86	6.39

FIELDING

Catcher	PCT	G	PO	A	E	DP	PB
Hatcher	.987	82	627	57	9	8	12
Hurba	1.000	29	212	11	0	0	1
Smith	.992	31	231	16	2	2	5

First Base	PCT	G	PO	A	E	DP
Gold	.991	55	495	40	5	58
Kreuzer	.987	85	740	43	10	78
Sandoval	1.000	1	7	0	0	0

Second Base	PCT	G	PO	A	E	DP
Lenoir	.949	54	78	163	13	30
Ringe	1.000	1	0	4	0	0
Sandoval	.968	86	166	256	14	72
Washington	.955	4	6	15	1	2

Third Base	PCT	G	PO	A	E	DP
Lenoir	.933	9	5	23	2	1
Metcalf	.945	132	82	244	19	26

Shortstop	PCT	G	PO	A	E	DP
Lenoir	.931	13	18	36	4	9
Ringe	.959	115	166	343	22	76
Sandoval	.971	13	21	45	2	9

Outfield	PCT	G	PO	A	E	DP
Bourassa	.984	30	59	4	1	0
Cleveland	.973	41	71	1	2	0
Grayson	.975	97	146	8	4	0
Harrison	1.000	8	10	0	0	0
Mahar	.984	107	234	12	4	1
Mask	1.000	7	5	1	0	0
Perez	1.000	3	7	0	0	0
Sandoval	.000	1	0	0	0	0
Sinisi	.964	29	51	2	2	0
Webster	.974	105	180	11	5	5

CLINTON LUMBER KINGS — Low Class A

MIDWEST LEAGUE

BATTING	B-T	HT	WT	DOB	AVG	vLH	vRH	G	AB	R	H	2B	3B	HR	RBI	BB	HBP	SH	SF	SO	SB	CS	SLG	OBP
Baez, Lizahio	B-R	6-2	210	11-2-83	.221	.178	.235	49	181	19	40	14	0	5	24	13	2	0	0	32	1	2	.381	.281
Benjamin, Casey	R-R	6-2	190	8-1-80	.268	.253	.270	114	351	60	94	18	4	5	39	73	4	8	5	65	7	7	.385	.395
Boggs, Brandon	B-R	6-0	190	1-9-83	.246	.268	.239	85	309	54	76	16	2	13	51	50	2	0	2	69	14	6	.437	.353
Cashman, Brandon	R-R	5-11	190	10-31-79	.233	.195	.248	111	434	64	101	26	5	12	47	36	10	5	1	117	21	7	.399	.306
Clark, Cody	R-R	6-2	170	9-14-81	.059	.167	.000	6	17	4	1	1	0	0	2	6	1	0	2	5	0	0	.118	.308
Coughlan, Cameron	B-L	5-11	178	8-12-81	.351	.286	.388	39	134	30	47	4	2	3	16	24	1	6	1	21	20	5	.478	.450
Fasano, Jim	L-R	6-5	230	7-20-83	.302	.338	.295	98	394	65	119	21	5	10	74	36	4	0	5	62	2	1	.457	.362
Fox, Adam	R-R	6-0	195	11-23-81	.255	.274	.247	75	282	42	72	12	1	8	36	37	2	1	5	39	11	9	.390	.340
Frostad, Emerson	L-R	6-1	210	1-13-83	.269	.207	.283	114	432	72	116	26	2	16	62	48	4	2	2	75	6	5	.449	.346
Gac, Ian	R-R	6-3	245	8-10-85	.240	.288	.219	91	346	42	83	24	3	12	57	19	4	1	1	108	2	3	.431	.286
Harrison, Ben	R-R	6-4	203	9-18-81	.250	.232	.258	83	308	56	77	14	2	6	37	31	3	2	2	72	13	3	.367	.323
Hulett, Tug	L-R	5-10	185	2-28-83	.265	.340	.238	106	385	70	102	22	3	1	45	90	2	9	5	87	20	6	.345	.402
Hurba, Craig	R-R	6-2	225	8-25-81	.305	.194	.339	45	154	21	47	11	1	4	29	14	1	0	2	34	1	3	.468	.363
Martinez, Alberto	R-R	6-1	191	8-27-86	.307	.375	.299	21	75	11	23	3	0	0	11	4	0	1	0	16	0	0	.347	.342
Richardson, Kevin	R-R	6-3	228	9-12-80	.267	.204	.288	56	202	28	54	8	1	6	37	23	10	0	1	56	3	2	.406	.369
Smith, Matt	L-R	5-10	172	6-12-83	.250	.182	.280	10	36	7	9	1	0	0	4	8	0	1	1	6	0	0	.278	.378
Susdorf, Billy	R-R	6-1	210	5-7-83	.277	.286	.275	85	328	37	91	24	0	6	37	9	3	3	4	49	17	6	.405	.299
Washington, Johnny	R-R	5-11	165	5-6-84	.194	.316	.165	31	98	7	19	3	0	1	5	13	1	0	0	37	3	0	.255	.295
Wishy, Andrew	L-R	6-3	210	9-27-82	.217	.216	.218	102	336	50	73	15	4	4	32	42	7	0	6	91	6	6	.321	.312

PITCHING	B-T	HT	WT	DOB	W	L	ERA	G	GS	CG	SV	IP	H	R	ER	HR	BB	SO	AVG	vLH	vRH	K/9	BB/9
Altman, Kevin	R-R	6-2	170	12-24-84	7	6	7.01	32	1	0	3	78	110	72	61	5	18	62	.332	.329	.335	7.12	2.07
Bannister, John	R-R	6-4	198	1-20-84	8	10	4.58	29	28	0	0	157	171	98	80	13	58	127	.275	.249	.289	7.26	3.32
Cordeiro, Chris	R-R	6-3	175	4-3-82	0	0	1.50	6	0	0	3	6	5	1	1	0	1	4	.238	.333	.200	6.00	1.50
Farnum, Matt	R-R	6-2	195	6-1-81	3	1	3.18	17	0	0	0	28	25	11	10	1	4	25	.229	.318	.169	7.94	1.27
Giles, Josh	R-R	6-1	175	8-3-84	0	2	9.56	11	0	0	1	16	15	20	17	2	18	12	.242	.200	.270	6.75	10.13
Hurley, Eric	R-R	6-4	195	9-17-85	12	6	3.77	28	28	0	0	155	135	72	65	11	59	152	.234	.244	.228	8.81	3.42
Jaile, Chris	R-R	6-3	209	2-20-81	1	1	3.60	17	0	0	3	45	49	21	18	5	13	42	.269	.262	.274	8.40	2.60
Kometani, Kea	R-R	6-4	200	12-24-82	3	2	2.40	13	9	0	1	56	56	21	15	5	13	46	.255	.231	.268	7.35	2.08
LaMacchia, Marc	R-R	6-1	190	3-27-82	4	2	3.73	32	0	0	4	63	48	28	26	4	26	53	.211	.205	.215	7.61	3.73
Lujan, John	R-R	6-1	200	5-10-84	4	4	2.80	31	0	0	5	64	57	26	20	1	27	56	.238	.245	.234	7.83	3.78
Padgett, Mike	R-R	6-4	210	5-6-82	3	5	2.31	23	0	0	4	51	47	14	13	1	12	39	.246	.198	.282	6.93	2.13
Perez, Roberto	R-R	6-3	170	9-27-83	2	2	4.02	26	0	0	3	47	41	26	21	4	26	44	.237	.281	.216	8.43	4.98
Phillips, Zach	L-L	6-1	178	9-21-86	0	0	6.75	2	0	0	0	4	7	3	3	0	0	4	.389	.000	.389	9.00	0.00
Roberts, Mark	R-R	5-11	190	6-24-82	2	1	1.45	10	0	0	1	19	7	3	3	0	10	16	.115	.087	.132	7.71	4.82
Rogers, Kyle	R-R	6-3	190	9-23-85	6	10	6.01	28	27	0	0	130	143	103	87	12	67	95	.277	.305	.261	6.56	4.63
Schlact, Michael	R-R	6-7	205	12-9-85	10	7	4.17	28	28	0	0	168	184	85	78	10	37	90	.280	.272	.285	4.81	1.98
Touchet, Daniel	R-R	6-2	202	1-12-82	0	1	3.42	12	0	0	0	26	30	16	10	0	8	16	.283	.289	.279	5.47	2.73
Vera, Edwin	R-R	5-11	170	2-26-83	2	1	3.80	11	0	0	0	21	21	12	9	2	16	19	.253	.160	.293	8.02	6.75
Walker, Andy	R-R	6-1	175	4-20-83	4	8	2.93	19	19	2	0	123	123	54	40	7	24	58	.258	.259	.258	4.24	1.76

FIELDING

Catcher	PCT	G	PO	A	E	DP	PB
Baez	.971	30	154	13	5	1	4
Clark	.981	6	45	8	1	0	1
Hurba	.996	40	262	18	1	2	7
Martinez	.989	21	156	23	2	1	7
Richardson	.990	51	370	24	4	3	3

First Base	PCT	G	PO	A	E	DP
Fasano	.992	64	580	40	5	53
Frostad	1.000	3	5	0	0	0
Gac	.987	78	634	41	9	53

Second Base	PCT	G	PO	A	E	DP
Coughlan	1.000	1	1	2	0	0
Fox	.987	15	29	46	1	11
Frostad	1.000	1	0	3	0	0
Hulett	.963	99	202	289	19	59
Smith	1.000	5	8	9	0	3
Washington	.971	27	55	81	4	12

Third Base	PCT	G	PO	A	E	DP
Coughlan	.000	1	0	0	0	0
Fox	1.000	27	16	67	0	5
Frostad	.927	107	77	201	22	18
Gac	.727	5	2	6	3	0
Hulett	1.000	3	0	5	0	0
Smith	.909	3	2	8	1	0

Shortstop	PCT	G	PO	A	E	DP
Benjamin	.953	112	175	312	24	52
Fox	.979	22	33	59	2	17
Frostad	1.000	3	2	5	0	1
Hulett	1.000	8	19	24	0	3
Smith	.923	4	3	9	1	1

Outfield	PCT	G	PO	A	E	DP
Benjamin	1.000	1	1	0	0	0
Boggs	.967	76	172	5	6	1
Cashman	.962	109	241	9	10	2
Coughlan	.963	36	74	3	3	1
Harrison	.927	67	121	6	10	0
Hurba	.000	1	0	0	0	0
Susdorf	.973	70	140	4	4	3
Wishy	.972	78	126	11	4	1

SPOKANE INDIANS — Short-Season Class A

NORTHWEST LEAGUE

BATTING	B-T	HT	WT	DOB	AVG	vLH	vRH	G	AB	R	H	2B	3B	HR	RBI	BB	HBP	SH	SF	SO	SB	CS	SLG	OBP
Backman, Wally	L-R	6-2	215	1-7-86	.217	.154	.242	16	46	6	10	2	1	0	2	6	0	2	0	15	2	0	.304	.308
Baez, Lizahio	B-R	6-2	210	11-2-83	.313	.326	.307	38	144	21	45	5	1	11	33	7	5	0	0	28	1	1	.590	.365
Blunt, Terrance	B-R	6-1	190	8-14-82	.227	.281	.200	47	172	34	39	5	3	4	22	21	6	3	0	31	7	5	.360	.332
Crabtree, Ben	R-R	6-0	210	11-2-82	.235	.375	.200	27	81	7	19	2	0	1	11	8	1	1	2	13	1	2	.296	.304
Duran, German	R-R	5-10	185	8-3-84	.262	.315	.240	62	252	36	66	17	2	4	33	18	1	2	1	56	6	4	.393	.313
Hawke, Matt	L-L	6-3	240	8-22-83	.250	.308	.226	26	88	12	22	4	0	6	14	14	4	0	3	24	0	0	.500	.367
Herren, K.C.	L-R	6-0	210	8-21-85	.264	.246	.270	57	216	22	57	15	3	4	27	28	0	0	2	63	6	4	.417	.346
Higashi, Jonathan	R-R	6-0	200	7-20-82	.303	.458	.246	27	89	10	27	10	1	0	11	5	5	2	1	20	1	0	.438	.370
Hooft, Joey	R-R	5-10	175	8-30-82	.225	.200	.233	60	218	26	49	8	1	1	20	16	0	1	1	48	3	6	.284	.277
Kemp, Joe	L-L	6-1	195	2-22-82	.262	.163	.302	47	149	23	39	5	4	2	18	19	2	1	1	40	9	3	.389	.351
Mayberry, John	R-R	6-6	230	12-21-83	.253	.284	.239	71	265	51	67	16	0	11	26	26	10	0	1	71	7	3	.438	.341
Murphy, Steve	L-R	6-2	210	4-22-84	.306	.338	.291	62	255	45	78	23	4	9	37	20	3	0	2	71	13	3	.533	.361
Pena, Antonio	R-R	5-11	172	9-16-84	.000	.000	.000	4	8	0	0	0	0	0	0	1	0	0	0	2	0	0	.000	.111
Peterson, David	R-R	5-10	160	8-22-83	.147	.105	.163	23	68	6	10	1	0	0	3	7	3	3	1	27	1	1	.162	.253
Santana, Julio	B-R	6-0	175	12-26-85	.203	.193	.207	58	192	22	39	7	1	0	19	10	2	2	3	56	5	3	.250	.246
Teagarden, Taylor	R-R	6-1	200	12-21-83	.281	.158	.312	31	96	23	27	5	4	7	16	23	2	0	1	32	1	1	.635	.426
Thon, Freddie	L-L	6-2	215	4-9-84	.279	.258	.289	54	208	29	58	14	0	12	49	14	2	0	2	46	2	1	.519	.327
Valichka, Brian	R-R	6-3	200	8-21-83	.190	.200	.182	7	21	5	4	1	0	0	2	6	1	0	0	4	0	0	.238	.393
Washington, Johnny	R-R	5-11	165	5-6-84	.100	.200	.000	10	20	2	2	1	0	0	0	2	1	1	0	8	0	0	.150	.217

PITCHING	B-T	HT	WT	DOB	W	L	ERA	G	GS	CG	SV	IP	H	R	ER	HR	BB	SO	AVG	vLH	vRH	K/9	BB/9
Abbott, Justin	R-R	6-3	215	9-4-81	0	1	5.40	3	0	0	0	3	6	5	2	0	0	0	.375	.333	.429	0.00	0.00
Burcie, Jarrad	R-R	6-1	215	5-17-82	1	0	5.51	8	0	0	0	16	20	16	10	0	9	14	.286	.333	.243	7.71	4.96
Byrd, Cain	R-R	6-2	190	1-6-85	2	1	5.83	17	0	0	0	29	27	20	19	7	18	30	.248	.237	.254	9.20	5.52
Coffman, Broc	L-L	6-2	215	3-28-85	2	2	2.99	17	11	0	1	69	62	28	23	2	26	63	.238	.172	.256	8.18	3.38
Fogle, Nate	R-R	6-4	225	12-27-83	1	0	3.90	20	0	0	2	30	20	14	13	4	15	45	.185	.237	.157	13.50	4.50
Garcia, Juan	B-R	6-2	177	10-10-82	1	2	6.69	16	3	0	0	35	43	29	26	3	23	25	.299	.258	.333	6.43	5.91
Hall, Jesse	L-L	6-1	180	9-24-85	2	3	6.47	16	5	0	0	32	46	29	23	2	15	29	.331	.250	.351	8.16	4.22
Kometani, Kea	R-R	6-4	200	12-24-82	0	0	2.25	2	2	0	0	8	9	2	2	0	2	10	.273	.333	.222	11.25	2.25
Maldonado, Juan	R-R	6-4	168	12-4-80	4	5	5.00	22	1	0	2	45	60	28	25	3	9	29	.319	.313	.324	5.80	1.80
Mathis, Doug	R-R	6-3	220	6-7-83	4	7	2.68	17	16	0	0	84	78	33	25	2	17	78	.243	.273	.219	8.36	1.82
McConnell, Kellan	R-R	6-4	215	4-5-82	6	5	5.86	17	14	0	0	78	93	55	51	8	16	60	.294	.364	.237	6.89	1.84
McElroy, Tanner	B-R	6-1	183	8-21-81	3	2	2.53	16	3	0	2	43	35	15	12	2	15	55	.217	.217	.217	11.60	3.16
Rosebrock, Warren	R-R	6-4	185	10-22-82	4	1	3.22	14	0	0	0	22	30	12	8	3	5	11	.330	.275	.373	4.43	2.01
Smith, David	L-L	6-3	220	5-21-83	1	2	1.76	13	8	0	0	56	49	14	11	3	14	32	.232	.267	.223	5.11	2.24
Van Buskirk, Thomas	R-R	6-6	220	8-15-83	2	3	3.18	22	0	0	0	34	25	16	12	0	12	22	.198	.200	.197	5.82	3.18
Wilson, Jon	R-R	6-1	200	4-28-83	3	1	2.08	29	0	0	11	35	26	8	8	4	4	49	.211	.224	.200	12.72	1.04
Zamzow, Brett	R-R	6-5	200	12-19-84	1	4	6.95	14	13	0	0	56	89	55	43	7	14	53	.365	.425	.319	8.57	2.26

GAMES BY POSITION: C—Baez 18, Crabtree 23, Higashi 15, Teagarden 22, Valichka 7. **1B**—Backman 1, Hawke 22, Kemp 4, Thon 50. **2B**—Blunt 6, Hooft 7, Pena 3, Peterson 19, Santana 41, Washington 10. **3B**—Backman 14, Baez 11, Hooft 54, Kemp 1, Pena 1, Peterson 2. **SS**—Duran 59, Peterson 1, Santana 20. **OF**—Blunt 36, Herren 55, Kemp 29, Mayberry 61, Murphy 50.

AZL RANGERS — Rookie

ARIZONA LEAGUE

BATTING	B-T	HT	WT	DOB	AVG	vLH	vRH	G	AB	R	H	2B	3B	HR	RBI	BB	HBP	SH	SF	SO	SB	CS	SLG	OBP
Anderson, R.J.	R-R	5-11	162	11-1-86	.286	.390	.257	47	185	32	53	5	0	0	14	20	4	1	3	46	18	9	.314	.363
Backman, Wally	L-R	6-2	215	1-7-86	.212	.207	.213	35	118	16	25	3	3	2	13	22	3	0	1	44	1	0	.339	.347
Carvajal, Aneuris	R-R	6-2	150	8-24-86	.227	.167	.250	32	110	14	25	3	1	1	12	7	2	1	4	24	2	1	.300	.276
Crabtree, Ben	R-R	6-0	210	11-2-82	.227	.333	.154	6	22	2	5	0	0	0	4	0	0	0	1	3	0	0	.227	.217
De la Cruz, Angel	R-R	6-2	160	3-20-83	.000	.000	.000	1	1	0	0	0	0	0	0	0	0	0	0	0	0	0	.000	.000
Gomez, Mauro	R-R	6-2	190	9-7-84	.385	.500	.286	4	13	5	5	2	0	1	4	3	0	0	1	2	0	0	.769	.471
Hawke, Matt	L-L	6-3	240	8-22-83	.386	.375	.391	19	70	17	27	6	1	4	17	19	0	0	2	5	3	0	.671	.505
Laird, Gerald	R-R	6-2	220	11-3-79	.192	.000	.217	8	26	4	5	2	2	0	3	2	1	0	0	2	1	0	.423	.276
Martinez, Alberto	R-R	6-1	191	8-27-86	.067	.000	.111	6	15	1	1	0	0	0	1	4	0	0	1	3	1	0	.067	.250
Mehl, Truan	L-R	6-2	200	3-20-83	.320	.255	.345	54	203	38	65	14	3	0	33	26	5	0	4	50	27	8	.419	.403
Napoli, Joe	R-R	6-4	230	10-4-82	.217	.231	.213	36	120	12	26	3	3	1	16	13	1	0	2	27	0	2	.317	.294
Nickeas, Mike	R-R	6-0	205	2-13-83	.286	1.000	.167	6	21	2	6	1	0	1	6	3	1	0	0	4	0	0	.476	.400
Perez, Josue	B-R	6-0	180	8-12-77	.143	.000	.250	3	7	1	1	1	0	0	1	0	0	0	0	1	0	0	.286	.143
Pina, Manuel	R-R	5-11	165	6-5-87	.247	.238	.250	27	85	13	21	3	1	0	10	7	8	0	1	12	2	0	.306	.356
Smith, Matt	L-R	5-10	172	6-12-83	.242	.321	.220	35	128	20	31	3	1	0	10	18	0	0	2	25	8	3	.281	.331
Torres, Jose	R-R	6-0	200	11-20-83	.254	.214	.268	48	169	29	43	11	0	6	26	19	6	0	1	50	6	2	.426	.349
Valichka, Brian	R-R	6-3	200	8-21-83	.210	.188	.217	19	62	4	13	5	0	0	8	4	2	0	1	15	2	1	.290	.275
Valiente, Roberto	R-R	6-0	185	3-4-83	.316	.275	.330	45	155	27	49	3	1	2	27	17	2	1	3	37	14	4	.387	.384
Vallejo, Jose	R-R	6-0	172	9-11-86	.291	.271	.297	52	203	28	59	7	2	1	15	19	5	2	1	49	18	5	.360	.364
Whittleman, Johnny	L-R	6-2	195	2-11-87	.279	.214	.297	51	190	31	53	12	8	0	35	35	2	0	2	42	11	4	.426	.393
Yan, Ruddy	B-R	6-0	160	1-13-82	.556	.400	.750	2	9	3	5	1	1	0	1	1	0	0	0	0	1	0	.889	.600

PITCHING	B-T	HT	WT	DOB	W	L	ERA	G	GS	CG	SV	IP	H	R	ER	HR	BB	SO	AVG	vLH	vRH	K/9	BB/9
Abbott, Justin	R-R	6-3	215	9-4-81	1	0	3.38	10	0	0	3	16	15	6	6	1	2	11	.254	.389	.195	6.19	1.13
Benoit, Joaquin	R-R	6-3	220	7-26-77	0	0	0.00	1	1	0	0	2	0	0	0	0	1	4	.000	.000	.000	18.00	4.50
Burcie, Jarrad	R-R	6-1	215	5-17-82	1	1	2.13	8	0	0	0	13	7	5	3	1	5	10	.163	.000	.206	7.11	3.55
Byrd, Cain	R-R	6-2	190	1-6-85	0	0	3.00	2	0	0	0	3	4	1	1	0	0	4	.333	.667	.222	12.00	0.00
Cordero, Julian	L-L	6-1	160	9-28-84	1	0	4.32	12	0	0	1	25	32	19	12	3	13	21	.320	.417	.307	7.56	4.68
Crabtree, Tim	R-R	6-4	225	10-13-69	0	2	5.00	5	5	0	0	9	13	5	5	0	0	4	.361	.357	.364	4.00	0.00
Farnum, Matt	R-R	6-2	195	6-1-81	0	1	6.75	1	1	0	0	1	1	2	1	0	0	2	.167	.333	.000	13.50	0.00
Funk, Shane	R-R	6-6	235	5-9-87	0	1	7.86	9	3	0	0	26	35	26	23	3	12	28	.318	.259	.337	9.57	4.10
Giles, Josh	R-R	6-1	175	8-3-84	1	0	8.44	5	0	0	0	11	15	11	10	1	5	13	.319	.333	.313	10.97	4.22
Jaimes, Jose	R-R	6-2	180	6-26-84	2	1	9.60	10	0	0	1	15	20	20	16	0	10	17	.317	.222	.389	10.20	6.00
James, Brandon	R-R	6-3	207	9-5-86	3	1	3.45	13	0	0	0	31	26	13	12	1	14	30	.218	.229	.214	8.62	4.02
Kirkman, Michael	L-L	6-3	185	9-18-86	3	1	3.44	14	9	0	0	52	51	28	20	0	19	58	.249	.255	.247	9.97	3.27
Marinez, Yeyser	R-R	6-3	180	11-7-84	0	0	2.40	8	0	0	1	15	9	6	4	0	16	15	.196	.200	.194	9.00	9.60
Marte, Jose	R-R	6-5	185	4-9-83	3	1	4.09	15	1	0	2	33	36	21	15	1	20	36	.269	.204	.306	9.82	5.45
Morla, Wandy	R-R	6-3	195	10-22-83	0	0	27.00	1	0	0	0	1	2	3	3	0	2	1	.500	1.000	.333	9.00	18.00
Nevarez, Matt	R-R	6-5	220	2-26-87	2	1	1.61	10	3	0	0	28	18	7	5	1	13	24	.184	.182	.185	7.71	4.18
Perez, Roberto	R-R	6-3	170	9-27-83	1	0	3.00	2	1	0	0	3	2	1	1	0	2	3	.222	.500	.143	9.00	6.00
Phillips, Zach	L-L	6-1	178	9-21-86	1	3	3.93	14	11	0	0	50	52	26	22	3	13	73	.260	.306	.250	13.05	2.32
Pote, Lou	R-R	6-3	200	8-21-71	0	0	9.00	1	0	0	0	1	2	1	1	0	3	0	.400	.000	.500	0.00	27.00
Poveda, Omar	R-R	6-4	185	9-28-87	2	6	5.71	14	9	0	0	52	64	38	33	1	12	56	.305	.267	.320	9.69	2.08
Rasner, Jacob	R-R	6-4	195	12-4-86	1	5	8.37	14	10	0	0	47	79	57	44	6	15	31	.374	.413	.358	5.89	2.85
Regilio, Nick	R-R	6-2	205	9-4-78	0	0	9.00	1	1	0	0	1	2	1	1	0	0	0	.400	.333	.500	0.00	0.00
Riley, Matt	L-L	6-1	225	8-2-79	0	0	0.00	1	0	0	0	1	0	0	0	0	0	2	.000	.000	.000	27.00	0.00
Rodriguez, William	L-L	6-0	189	5-8-84	0	2	6.00	9	0	0	2	15	21	13	10	1	8	15	.323	.182	.352	9.00	4.80
Rosebrock, Warren	R-R	6-4	185	10-22-82	3	1	4.85	5	0	0	0	13	15	8	7	1	3	11	.306	.308	.306	7.62	2.08
Touchet, Daniel	R-R	6-2	202	1-12-82	1	1	10.13	6	0	0	1	11	29	16	12	1	0	14	.492	.556	.463	11.81	0.00
Vera, Edwin	R-R	5-11	170	2-26-83	1	1	3.54	7	0	0	0	20	15	10	8	0	9	18	.200	.226	.182	7.97	3.98
Volquez, Edison	R-R	6-1	190	7-3-83	0	0	0.00	1	1	0	0	2	2	0	0	0	0	2	.222	.333	.167	9.00	0.00

GAMES BY POSITION: C—Crabtree 4, Laird 5, Martinez 4, Nickeas 6, Pina 26, Valichka 19. **1B**—Backman 35, Hawke 19, Napoli 3. **2B**—Smith 5, Vallejo 52. **3B**—Backman 1, Gomez 4, Martinez 2, Smith 5, Whittleman 47. **SS**—Carvajal 32, Smith 27. **OF**—Anderson 45, De la Cruz 1, Mehl 54, Napoli 21, Perez 3, Torres 25, Valiente 30, Yan 2.

TORONTO BLUE JAYS

BY LARRY MILLSON

The 2005 Blue Jays epitomized a baseball cliché: they didn't get too high and they didn't get too low.

The high was Aug. 17 when they defeated the Angels to go six games above .500 at 63-57 and move to within four games of the American League wild-card lead.

The low was after a loss to the Red Sox in the first game of a Sept. 27 doubleheader when they dipped four games below .500, at 76-80, for the only time of the season.

The Blue Jays hovered on the fringes of wild-card contention for a while but in the end finished at 80-82, their third losing season in the past four and an improvement over 2004, when they won 67 games in a season wrecked by numerous injuries to important players.

Attendance at newly-named Rogers Centre increased for the third year in a row and surpassed 2 million for the first time since 1999.

There was generally a feeling of optimism around the Blue Jays clubhouse, though not as much as there was after the 2003 season when they won 86 games.

But this time there is more money to spend in the offseason, with the possibility of the payroll being bumped from about $50 million to about $80 million for 2006.

The priority for general manager J.P. Ricciardi will be to add some power hitting and bolster the starting rotation.

Center fielder Vernon Wells struggled early in the 2005 season before finishing with a.269 average, a team-leading 28 home runs and 97 RBIs. He called the season a "building block to better things."

Wells, righthander Roy Halladay (whose season was again cut short by injury), third baseman Corey Koskie and first baseman Eric Hinske are all signed through 2007, as are Ricciardi and manager John Gibbons. The coaches will be back, too, with the addition of Marty Pevey, who managed Triple-A Syracuse for two seasons and will take over as first-base coach in 2006, returning Ernie Whitt to bench coach.

"Everybody was able to see what kind of talent we have, our younger guys coming up and what our leading guys are capable of doing when the situation is right," Wells said. "Now we've got some money to work with."

Halladay, the 2003 Cy Young Award winner, had his season ended July 8 when a line drive fractured his left tibia in a start at Texas. It was the second year in a row that injury cut into his season. In 2004, it was his shoulder. Halladay was 12-4, 2.41 and in line to start the All-Star Game in Detroit when he was injured in 2005.

Koskie, who was signed as a free agent from the Twins, missed a chunk of the season with a fractured thumb, but that allowed infielder Aaron Hill a chance to play in the majors earlier than expected. Hill played well at third, short and some second late in the season as well as serving as DH.

Rookie Russ Adams played the full season as shortstop and made improvements defensively while batting .256-8-63.

Josh Towers earned a career-high 13 victories and became a better pitcher as the season progressed, leading the staff with 209 innings.

Outfielder John-Ford Griffin was a major bright spot in the minor league system. He earned a September callup after hitting .254-30-103 at Triple-A Syracuse, becoming the fifth Syracuse player ever to have 30 home runs and 100 RBIs in a season.

Lefthander Zach Jackson, 22, won 16 games to tie for the lead in the minor leagues. The club's second pick in the 2004 draft (32nd overall) from Texas A&M went 8-1, 2.88, at high Class A Dunedin, 4-3, 4.00 at Double-A New Hampshire and finished the season by going 4-4, 5.13 at Syracuse. First baseman Chip Cannon hit 32 homers between low Class A Lansing, Dunedin and New Hampshire.

Auburn lost in the championship round of the short-season New York-Penn League playoffs, and Dunedin lost in the first round of the Florida State League playoffs.

PLAYERS OF THE YEAR

MAJOR LEAGUE: Roy Halladay, rhp

Halladay's success was the most encouraging development for the Blue Jays in 2005, though his season was cut short in July when he broke his leg. Halladay posted a 2.41 ERA that would have led the league if he had thrown enough innings to qualify, providing evidence his 2003 Cy Young season was no fluke.

MINOR LEAGUE: Casey Janssen, rhp

KEVIN PATAKY

In his first full pro season after being drafted in the fourth round, Janssen rocketed through the Blue Jays system, going a combined 13-4, 2.18 in 149 innings across three levels. The former two-way star at UCLA finished the year with a solid effort at Double-A New Hampshire, going 3-3, 2.93.

ORGANIZATION LEADERS

BATTING

*AVG	Patterson, Ryan, Auburn	.339
R	Roberts, Ryan, Dunedin/New Hampshire	87
H	Lind, Adam, Dunedin	155
TB	Barker, Kevin, New Hampshire/Syracuse	280
2B	Lind, Adam, Dunedin	42
3B	French, Anton, Syracuse	10
HR	Cannon, Chip, Dunedin/Lansing/New Hampshire	32
RBI	Barker, Kevin, New Hampshire/Syracuse	114
BB	Roberts, Ryan, Dunedin/New Hampshire	79
SO	Griffin, John-Ford, Syracuse	140
SB	Klosterman, Ryan, Dunedin/Lansing	30
*OBP	Snavely, Christian, Lansing	.390
*SLG	Patterson, Ryan, Auburn	.595

PITCHING

W	Jackson, Zach, Dunedin/New Hampshire/Syracuse	16
L	Ramirez, Ismael, New Hampshire	13
#ERA	Janssen, Casey, Dunedin/Lansing/New Hampshire	1.81
G	Gronkiewicz, Lee, New Hampshire/Syracuse	66
CG	Banks, Josh, New Hampshire	2
	Gaudin, Chad, Syracuse	2
SV	Gronkiewicz, Lee, New Hampshire/Syracuse	30
IP	Banks, Josh, New Hampshire	162
BB	Purcey, David, Dunedin/New Hampshire	81
SO	Purcey, David, Dunedin/New Hampshire	161

*Minimum 250 at-bats. #Minimum 75 innings.

TORONTO BLUE JAYS

Manager: John Gibbons. **2005 Record:** 80-82, .494 (3rd, AL East).

BATTING	B-T	HT	WT	DOB	AVG	vLH	vRH	G	AB	R	H	2B	3B	HR	RBI	BB	HBP	SH	SF	SO	SB	CS	SLG	OBP
Adams, Russ	L-R	6-1	180	8-30-80	.256	.195	.269	139	481	68	123	27	5	8	63	50	3	3	8	57	11	2	.383	.325
Catalanotto, Frank	L-R	5-11	195	4-27-74	.301	.290	.302	130	419	56	126	29	5	8	59	37	10	4	5	53	0	2	.451	.367
Dominique, Andy	R-R	6-0	220	10-30-75	.000	.000	.000	2	2	0	0	0	0	0	0	0	1	0	0	0	0	0	.000	.333
Griffin, John-Ford	L-L	6-2	215	11-19-79	.308	1.000	.250	7	13	3	4	2	0	1	6	0	0	0	0	4	0	0	.692	.308
Gross, Gabe	L-R	6-3	210	10-21-79	.250	.091	.272	40	92	11	23	4	1	1	7	10	0	0	0	21	1	1	.348	.324
Hill, Aaron	R-R	5-11	195	3-21-82	.274	.298	.265	105	361	49	99	25	3	3	40	34	5	3	4	41	2	1	.385	.342
Hillenbrand, Shea	R-R	6-1	210	7-27-75	.291	.325	.279	152	594	91	173	36	2	18	82	26	22	0	3	79	5	1	.449	.343
Hinske, Eric	L-R	6-2	235	8-5-77	.262	.170	.283	147	477	79	125	31	2	15	68	46	8	0	6	121	8	4	.430	.333
Huckaby, Ken	R-R	6-1	220	1-27-71	.207	.267	.175	35	87	8	18	4	0	0	6	5	0	4	0	19	0	0	.253	.250
Hudson, Orlando	B-R	6-0	185	12-12-77	.271	.227	.288	131	461	62	125	25	5	10	63	30	3	0	7	65	7	1	.412	.315
Johnson, Reed	R-R	5-10	180	12-8-76	.269	.279	.262	142	398	55	107	21	6	8	58	22	16	2	1	82	5	6	.412	.332
Koskie, Corey	L-R	6-3	225	6-28-73	.249	.211	.265	97	354	49	88	20	0	11	36	44	4	0	2	90	4	1	.398	.337
McDonald, John	R-R	5-11	175	9-24-74	.290	.339	.194	37	93	8	27	3	0	0	12	6	2	3	2	12	5	0	.323	.340
Menechino, Frank	R-R	5-8	200	1-7-71	.216	.191	.259	70	148	22	32	7	0	4	13	25	6	1	0	33	0	1	.345	.352
Myers, Greg	L-R	6-2	225	4-14-66	.083	.000	.083	6	12	0	1	0	0	0	1	1	0	0	0	1	0	0	.083	.154
Quiroz, Guillermo	R-R	6-1	200	11-29-81	.194	.095	.333	12	36	3	7	2	0	0	4	2	1	0	0	13	0	0	.250	.256
Rios, Alex	R-R	6-5	195	2-18-81	.262	.249	.270	146	481	71	126	23	6	10	59	28	5	0	5	101	14	9	.397	.306
Wells, Vernon	R-R	6-1	225	12-8-78	.269	.347	.245	156	620	78	167	30	3	28	97	47	3	0	8	86	8	3	.463	.320
Zaun, Gregg	B-R	5-10	190	4-14-71	.251	.278	.241	133	434	61	109	18	1	11	61	73	0	0	5	70	2	3	.373	.355

PITCHING	B-T	HT	WT	DOB	W	L	ERA	G	GS	CG	SV	IP	H	R	ER	HR	BB	SO	AVG	vLH	vRH	K/9	BB/9
Batista, Miguel	R-R	6-1	195	2-19-71	5	8	4.10	71	0	0	31	75	80	39	34	9	27	54	.268	.256	.282	6.51	3.25
Bush, Dave	R-R	6-2	210	11-9-79	5	11	4.49	25	24	2	0	136	142	73	68	20	29	75	.269	.269	.269	4.95	1.91
Chacin, Gustavo	L-L	5-11	195	12-4-80	13	9	3.72	34	34	0	0	203	213	93	84	20	70	121	.274	.225	.288	5.36	3.10
Chulk, Vinnie	R-R	6-2	195	12-19-78	0	1	3.88	62	0	0	0	72	68	33	31	9	26	39	.255	.283	.231	4.88	3.25
Downs, Scott	L-L	6-2	190	3-17-76	4	3	4.31	26	13	0	0	94	93	49	45	12	34	75	.253	.234	.262	7.18	3.26
Frasor, Jason	R-R	5-10	170	8-9-77	3	5	3.25	67	0	0	1	75	67	31	27	8	28	62	.247	.236	.257	7.47	3.38
Gaudin, Chad	R-R	5-11	165	3-24-83	1	3	13.15	5	3	0	0	13	31	19	19	6	6	12	.470	.481	.462	8.31	4.15
Halladay, Roy	R-R	6-6	225	5-14-77	12	4	2.41	19	19	5	0	142	118	39	38	11	18	108	.225	.217	.235	6.86	1.14
League, Brandon	R-R	6-3	190	3-16-83	1	0	6.56	20	0	0	0	36	42	27	26	8	20	17	.302	.333	.269	4.29	5.05
Lilly, Ted	L-L	6-1	190	1-4-76	10	11	5.56	25	25	0	0	126	135	79	78	23	58	96	.272	.336	.248	6.84	4.13
Marcum, Shaun	R-R	6-0	180	12-14-81	0	0	0.00	5	0	0	0	8	6	0	0	0	4	4	.214	.176	.273	4.50	4.50
McGowan, Dustin	R-R	6-3	220	3-24-82	1	3	6.35	13	7	0	0	45	49	34	32	7	17	34	.277	.243	.301	6.75	3.38
Miller, Justin	R-R	6-2	210	8-27-77	0	0	15.43	1	0	0	0	2	5	4	4	3	0	2	.417	.333	.444	7.71	0.00
Schoeneweis, Scott	L-L	6-0	190	10-2-73	3	4	3.32	80	0	0	1	57	54	23	21	2	25	43	.245	.188	.306	6.79	3.95
Speier, Justin	R-R	6-4	205	11-6-73	3	2	2.57	65	0	0	0	67	48	20	19	10	15	56	.198	.167	.219	7.56	2.03
Towers, Josh	R-R	6-1	190	2-26-77	13	12	3.71	33	33	2	0	209	237	101	86	24	29	112	.285	.274	.297	4.83	1.25
Walker, Pete	R-R	6-2	195	4-8-69	6	6	3.54	41	4	0	2	84	81	33	33	10	33	43	.254	.254	.254	4.61	3.54
Whiteside, Matt	R-R	6-0	200	8-8-67	0	0	19.64	2	0	0	0	4	6	8	8	3	5	5	.353	.333	.364	12.27	12.27

FIELDING

Catcher	PCT	G	PO	A	E	DP	PB
Dominique	1.000	1	4	0	0	0	0
Huckaby	.987	35	144	11	2	1	1
Myers	1.000	4	20	1	0	0	0
Quiroz	1.000	10	56	5	0	1	0
Zaun	.990	132	761	49	8	3	5

First Base	PCT	G	PO	A	E	DP
Hillenbrand	.991	67	627	48	6	69
Hinske	.993	100	868	69	7	77

Second Base	PCT	G	PO	A	E	DP
Hill	.991	22	33	77	1	15
Hudson	.991	130	302	391	6	80
McDonald	1.000	5	9	7	0	3
Menechino	.991	26	37	70	1	18

Third Base	PCT	G	PO	A	E	DP
Hill	.949	35	21	73	5	8
Hillenbrand	.954	54	31	94	6	8
Koskie	.968	76	52	158	7	19
Menechino	1.000	9	2	9	0	2

Shortstop	PCT	G	PO	A	E	DP
Adams	.952	132	194	326	26	68
Hill	1.000	16	18	48	0	9
McDonald	.977	32	38	88	3	19
Menechino	1.000	1	1	1	0	1

Outfield	PCT	G	PO	A	E	DP
Catalanotto	1.000	111	163	4	0	0
Gross	.981	37	51	2	1	1
Johnson	.990	139	196	5	2	0
Rios	.992	142	257	7	2	1
Wells	1.000	155	351	12	0	4

FARM SYSTEM

General Manager: J.P. Ricciardi. **Director, Player Development:** Dick Scott. **Coordinator, Scouting:** Jon Lalonde.

Class	Farm Team	League	W	L	Pct.	Finish*	Manager	Affiliate Since
AAA	Syracuse (N.Y.) SkyChiefs	International	71	73	.493	8th (14)	Marty Pevey	1978
AA	New Hampshire Fisher Cats (Manchester)	Eastern	68	74	.479	9th (12)	Mike Basso	2003
High A	Dunedin (Fla.) Blue Jays	Florida State	82	58	.586	**2nd (12)**	Omar Malave	1987
Low A	Lansing (Mich.) Lugnuts	Midwest	70	69	.504	7th (16)	Ken Joyce	2005
SS A	Auburn (N.Y.) Doubledays	New York-Penn	45	30	.600	**3rd (14)**	Dennis Holmberg	2001
Rookie	Pulaski (Va.) Blue Jays	Appalachian	34	33	.507	4th (10)	Dave Pano	2003

*Finish in overall standings (No. of teams in league)/Playoff teams in **boldface**

SYRACUSE SKYCHIEFS — Class AAA

INTERNATIONAL LEAGUE

BATTING	B-T	HT	WT	DOB	AVG	vLH	vRH	G	AB	R	H	2B	3B	HR	RBI	BB	HBP	SH	SF	SO	SB	CS	SLG	OBP
Alfaro, Jason	R-R	5-10	185	11-29-77	.247	.244	.247	105	381	42	94	24	1	10	45	18	3	3	2	63	0	1	.394	.285
Barker, Kevin	L-L	6-1	225	7-26-75	.305	.263	.325	91	351	58	107	24	1	23	87	38	3	0	5	89	1	0	.575	.373
Crozier, Eric	L-L	6-4	200	8-11-78	.226	.167	.245	37	124	20	28	12	1	5	14	9	1	0	1	39	1	0	.460	.281
DePastino, Joe	R-R	6-2	210	9-4-73	.274	.156	.301	55	175	22	48	11	0	3	22	15	0	2	2	36	0	0	.389	.328
Dominique, Andy	R-R	6-0	220	10-30-75	.239	.375	.188	39	117	18	28	6	0	3	10	15	2	2	0	20	0	0	.368	.336
French, Anton	L-R	5-11	170	7-25-75	.263	.232	.275	96	350	54	92	13	10	9	39	24	2	5	5	84	15	3	.434	.310
Griffin, John-Ford	L-L	6-2	215	11-19-79	.254	.281	.243	135	512	80	130	21	1	30	103	62	3	0	5	140	1	2	.475	.335
Gross, Gabe	L-R	6-3	210	10-21-79	.297	.271	.306	102	390	64	116	29	4	6	46	52	2	2	3	83	14	2	.438	.380
Hattig, John	B-R	6-2	215	2-27-80	.316	.400	.286	26	95	15	30	7	0	1	10	10	1	0	0	16	0	0	.421	.387
Hill, Aaron	R-R	5-11	195	3-21-82	.301	.300	.302	38	156	22	47	11	0	5	18	4	6	0	2	17	2	0	.468	.339
Huckaby, Ken	R-R	6-1	220	1-27-71	.268	.357	.238	15	56	3	15	1	0	1	3	1	0	1	0	13	0	0	.339	.281
Koskie, Corey	L-R	6-3	225	6-28-73	.240	.222	.250	7	25	1	6	2	0	0	2	3	2	0	0	6	0	0	.320	.367
Matos, Julius	R-R	5-11	170	12-12-74	.261	.194	.280	113	421	49	110	23	1	6	37	18	7	8	1	58	3	4	.363	.302
Mottola, Chad	R-R	6-3	230	10-15-71	.255	.287	.244	125	478	67	122	27	3	21	69	35	4	0	3	100	2	5	.456	.310
Nelson, Bryant	B-R	5-10	200	1-27-74	.248	.274	.238	138	540	68	134	19	1	7	60	48	3	6	3	50	8	4	.326	.311
Quiroz, Guillermo	R-R	6-1	200	11-29-81	.229	.250	.220	25	83	11	19	3	0	6	18	9	1	0	1	19	0	0	.482	.309
Relaford, Desi	B-R	5-9	180	9-16-73	.211	.154	.222	22	76	15	16	2	0	2	6	13	4	0	0	12	5	0	.316	.355
Sanders, Anthony	R-R	6-2	200	3-2-74	.333	.000	.333	2	3	1	1	0	0	0	1	1	0	1	0	1	0	0	.333	.500
Schneider, John	R-R	6-3	227	2-14-80	.179	.269	.145	34	95	13	17	3	0	3	10	16	2	2	1	37	0	1	.305	.307
Singleton, Justin	L-R	6-1	190	4-10-79	.255	.269	.251	100	318	48	81	20	2	10	36	19	1	5	1	98	5	1	.425	.298
Solano, Danny	R-R	5-9	187	12-3-75	.243	.327	.210	57	173	26	42	6	1	3	22	15	2	0	3	37	1	2	.341	.306
Whittaker, Tim	R-R	6-0	200	1-4-79	.000	.000	.000	6	8	0	0	0	0	0	0	1	0	0	0	1	0	0	.000	.111

PITCHING	B-T	HT	WT	DOB	W	L	ERA	G	GS	CG	SV	IP	H	R	ER	HR	BB	SO	AVG	vLH	vRH	K/9	BB/9
Arnold, Jason	R-R	6-3	210	11-29-77	0	4	6.39	47	0	0	5	62	60	46	44	14	27	53	.247	.185	.296	7.69	3.92
Baker, Chris	R-R	6-1	195	8-24-77	8	7	5.30	31	21	0	0	131	165	80	77	13	30	87	.309	.318	.302	5.99	2.07
Burnside, Adrian	R-L	6-3	210	3-15-77	4	4	2.98	50	0	0	0	57	52	20	19	4	16	45	.241	.185	.274	7.06	2.51
Bush, Dave	R-R	6-2	210	11-9-79	2	2	4.42	9	9	0	0	55	65	28	27	6	9	40	.298	.376	.240	6.55	1.47
Carlson, Jesse	L-L	6-1	160	12-30-80	1	1	4.82	22	0	0	0	19	26	10	10	4	7	17	.325	.278	.364	8.20	3.38
Downs, Scott	L-L	6-2	190	3-17-76	2	3	4.81	7	7	0	0	39	45	21	21	5	3	35	.285	.211	.308	8.01	0.69
Duff, Matt	R-R	6-1	215	10-6-74	5	0	3.51	15	0	0	0	26	21	10	10	3	7	28	.219	.222	.217	9.82	2.45
Gaudin, Chad	R-R	5-11	165	3-24-83	9	8	3.35	23	23	2	0	150	140	61	56	12	35	113	.251	.309	.205	6.76	2.10
Glynn, Ryan	R-R	6-3	200	11-1-74	2	4	6.27	9	6	0	0	37	41	27	26	6	11	23	.283	.316	.242	5.54	2.65
Gronkiewicz, Lee	R-R	5-10	185	8-21-78	0	1	2.22	28	0	0	6	28	21	9	7	3	13	26	.206	.235	.191	8.26	4.13
Jackson, Zach	L-L	6-5	220	5-13-83	4	4	5.13	8	8	0	0	47	61	33	27	3	21	33	.323	.282	.333	6.27	3.99
League, Brandon	R-R	6-3	190	3-16-83	4	4	5.71	19	10	0	0	63	78	44	40	7	18	35	.306	.305	.307	5.00	2.57
Lilly, Ted	L-L	6-1	190	1-4-76	0	1	3.12	2	2	0	0	9	5	4	3	1	5	9	.172	.000	.217	9.35	5.19
Lundberg, Spike	B-R	6-1	185	5-4-77	8	6	3.95	50	3	0	1	87	101	48	38	5	25	65	.293	.242	.335	6.75	2.60
Marcum, Shaun	R-R	6-0	180	12-14-81	6	4	4.95	18	18	0	0	104	112	59	57	17	18	90	.271	.274	.268	7.81	1.56
Matos, Josue	R-R	6-4	190	12-12-74	5	3	6.63	14	10	0	0	56	73	44	41	16	10	32	.313	.288	.339	5.17	1.62
Miller, Justin	R-R	6-2	210	8-27-77	3	1	2.32	28	4	0	2	50	39	15	13	3	14	56	.210	.198	.220	10.01	2.50
Nannini, Mike	R-R	5-11	190	8-9-80	2	3	5.25	19	0	0	1	36	25	21	21	4	21	24	.198	.204	.194	6.00	5.25
Reimers, Cameron	R-R	6-5	216	9-15-78	0	0	15.75	1	1	0	0	4	7	7	7	2	2	2	.389	.250	.500	4.50	4.50
Rosario, Francisco	R-R	6-0	195	9-28-80	2	7	3.95	30	18	0	2	116	111	59	51	16	42	80	.258	.274	.244	6.19	3.25
Tolar, Kevin	R-L	6-2	255	1-28-71	1	2	8.40	17	0	0	0	15	25	15	14	3	12	18	.368	.208	.455	10.80	7.20
Vermilyea, Jamie	R-R	6-4	195	2-10-82	3	0	5.60	16	4	0	0	35	49	27	22	6	11	24	.331	.283	.364	6.11	2.80
Whiteside, Matt	R-R	6-0	200	8-8-67	0	4	2.59	40	0	0	27	42	35	14	12	4	5	39	.226	.179	.261	8.42	1.08

FIELDING

Catcher	PCT	G	PO	A	E	DP	PB
DePastino	.992	50	339	25	3	2	4
Dominique	1.000	31	193	13	0	3	1
Huckaby	1.000	14	97	5	0	2	0
Quiroz	.988	23	160	11	2	4	1
Schneider	.995	31	184	12	1	3	2
Whittaker	1.000	6	23	0	0	0	0

First Base	PCT	G	PO	A	E	DP
Alfaro	1.000	8	48	2	0	4
Barker	.998	89	747	54	2	76
Crozier	.977	37	318	15	8	23
Huckaby	.800	1	4	0	1	0
Matos	.975	4	38	1	1	4
Mottola	1.000	10	70	6	0	4
Schneider	1.000	1	0	1	0	0

Second Base	PCT	G	PO	A	E	DP
Alfaro	.974	40	76	113	5	29
Matos	.938	3	7	8	1	2
Nelson	.959	57	91	140	10	28
Relaford	.979	20	44	50	2	12
Solano	.965	32	49	90	5	20

Third Base	PCT	G	PO	A	E	DP
Alfaro	.976	51	33	90	3	5
DePastino	1.000	1	1	1	0	0
Hattig	1.000	24	13	37	0	2
Koskie	1.000	5	1	4	0	0
Matos	1.000	7	2	13	0	2
Nelson	.904	53	34	79	12	8
Solano	1.000	15	6	30	0	3

Shortstop	PCT	G	PO	A	E	DP
Alfaro	1.000	4	5	6	0	0
Hill	.945	38	62	110	10	23
Matos	.964	97	113	293	15	66
Relaford	1.000	1	1	3	0	0
Solano	.931	8	6	21	2	4

Outfield	PCT	G	PO	A	E	DP
French	.987	93	218	2	3	0
Griffin	.979	71	133	7	3	1
Gross	.981	99	191	13	4	2
Matos	1.000	1	2	0	0	0
Mottola	.973	73	142	3	4	1
Nelson	.981	19	48	4	1	2
Singleton	.991	92	222	10	2	1

NEW HAMPSHIRE FISHER CATS — Class AA

EASTERN LEAGUE

BATTING	B-T	HT	WT	DOB	AVG	vLH	vRH	G	AB	R	H	2B	3B	HR	RBI	BB	HBP	SH	SF	SO	SB	CS	SLG	OBP
Acuna, Ron	R-R	6-0	215	6-30-79	.245	.235	.249	108	400	48	98	27	2	1	31	25	5	5	3	89	12	3	.330	.296
Barker, Kevin	L-L	6-1	225	7-26-75	.254	.259	.252	52	185	18	47	11	1	6	27	28	1	0	3	42	1	2	.422	.350
Cannon, Chip	L-R	6-5	215	11-30-81	.247	.188	.270	47	170	15	42	13	1	7	23	10	1	0	0	58	2	0	.459	.293
Chiaravalloti, Vito	R-R	6-3	225	10-26-80	.236	.213	.248	45	148	16	35	8	0	3	18	15	3	0	2	32	1	0	.351	.315
Cosby, Rob	R-R	6-1	216	4-2-81	.308	.366	.285	115	428	56	132	34	0	17	68	24	2	2	2	77	2	1	.507	.346
Cota, Carlo	R-R	5-10	185	9-18-80	.250	.200	.266	38	144	21	36	8	2	2	17	9	2	2	1	45	1	0	.375	.301
Davenport, Ron	L-R	6-2	205	10-16-81	.270	.272	.270	95	359	34	97	22	1	10	38	21	1	1	1	66	2	2	.421	.312
Hassey, Brad	R-R	5-10	170	11-28-79	.220	.185	.232	96	305	30	67	14	2	0	15	22	0	7	1	56	1	4	.279	.271
Johnston, Clint	L-L	6-3	214	7-2-77	.247	.226	.253	77	279	31	69	12	2	6	28	32	2	1	2	86	0	1	.369	.327
Jova, Maikel	R-R	6-0	205	3-5-81	.258	.236	.267	97	387	39	100	20	2	3	32	10	1	1	2	70	2	6	.344	.278
Kratz, Erik	R-R	6-4	246	6-15-80	.205	.203	.206	91	292	27	60	10	0	11	34	27	6	3	4	86	2	0	.353	.283
Negron, Miguel	L-L	6-2	170	8-22-82	.258	.242	.263	124	489	69	126	21	3	12	46	32	1	4	1	100	23	12	.387	.304
Roberts, Ryan	R-R	5-11	190	9-19-80	.272	.272	.272	92	338	54	92	19	3	15	44	55	4	1	1	94	5	1	.479	.379
Sanders, Anthony	R-R	6-2	200	3-2-74	.244	.303	.204	22	82	8	20	4	0	1	8	5	1	1	0	19	1	0	.329	.295
Singleton, Justin	L-R	6-1	190	4-10-79	.213	.250	.203	21	80	9	17	3	1	3	9	7	1	0	1	29	2	1	.388	.281
Tablado, Raul	R-R	6-2	195	3-3-82	.201	.224	.192	102	363	33	73	13	1	5	35	22	3	2	3	128	6	1	.284	.251
Thigpen, Curtis	R-R	5-11	190	4-19-83	.284	.328	.253	39	141	18	40	8	0	4	15	9	3	4	0	19	0	0	.426	.340
Umbria, Jose	R-R	6-1	215	1-20-78	.185	.167	.191	28	92	7	17	5	0	0	7	5	0	1	0	22	0	0	.239	.227
Waugh, Jason	R-R	6-1	214	3-12-80	.175	.214	.154	13	40	6	7	1	0	0	4	3	1	0	0	8	0	0	.200	.250
Whittaker, Tim	R-R	6-0	200	1-4-79	.167	1.000	.000	2	6	0	1	0	0	0	0	0	0	0	0	3	0	0	.167	.167
Zaun, Gregg	B-R	5-10	190	4-14-71	.333	.500	.000	2	6	1	2	1	0	0	0	2	0	0	0	2	0	0	.500	.500

PITCHING	B-T	HT	WT	DOB	W	L	ERA	G	GS	CG	SV	IP	H	R	ER	HR	BB	SO	AVG	vLH	vRH	K/9	BB/9
Andrade, Steve	R-R	6-1	220	2-6-78	3	2	1.97	35	0	0	3	50	23	12	11	3	16	71	.134	.114	.147	12.70	2.86
Banks, Josh	R-R	6-3	195	7-18-82	8	12	3.83	27	27	2	0	162	159	76	69	18	11	145	.256	.259	.253	8.04	0.61
Buzachero, Bubbie	R-R	5-11	177	6-13-81	4	5	3.97	46	2	0	0	82	82	44	36	13	31	84	.262	.262	.262	9.26	3.42
Carlson, Jesse	L-L	6-1	160	12-30-80	3	2	1.83	39	0	0	5	39	28	8	8	2	5	42	.203	.154	.233	9.61	1.14
De Jong, Jordan	R-R	6-2	180	4-12-79	1	4	5.88	45	0	0	2	67	82	49	44	5	21	63	.304	.333	.281	8.42	2.81
Gronkiewicz, Lee	R-R	5-10	185	8-21-78	2	0	1.41	38	0	0	24	38	24	7	6	2	10	45	.179	.241	.138	10.57	2.35
Houston, Ryan	R-R	6-4	215	9-22-79	3	2	2.68	33	1	0	7	40	26	13	12	3	13	50	.183	.164	.195	11.16	2.90
Jackson, Zach	L-L	6-5	220	5-13-83	4	3	4.00	9	9	0	0	54	57	27	24	3	12	43	.277	.304	.267	7.17	2.00
Janssen, Casey	R-R	6-4	205	9-17-81	3	3	2.93	9	9	0	0	43	49	20	14	3	4	47	.288	.329	.260	9.84	0.84
Marcum, Shaun	R-R	6-0	180	12-14-81	7	1	2.53	9	9	1	0	53	44	15	15	5	10	40	.229	.264	.198	6.75	1.69
Matos, Josue	R-R	6-4	190	3-15-78	0	1	1.45	9	0	0	0	19	14	3	3	0	3	27	.206	.258	.162	13.02	1.45
McGowan, Dustin	R-R	6-3	220	3-24-82	0	2	3.34	6	6	0	0	35	35	16	13	6	10	33	.263	.314	.206	8.49	2.57
Mumma, Brad	L-L	6-4	230	4-1-81	0	1	4.05	7	0	0	0	7	6	4	3	0	2	6	.250	.125	.313	8.10	2.70
Ogiltree, John	R-R	6-6	220	6-3-78	0	0	0.00	2	0	0	0	2	1	0	0	0	1	1	.143	.000	.167	4.50	4.50
Perkins, Vince	L-R	6-5	220	9-27-81	7	7	4.03	26	24	0	0	132	124	65	59	9	51	111	.250	.273	.232	7.59	3.49
Purcey, David	L-L	6-5	240	4-22-82	4	3	2.93	8	8	1	0	43	32	17	14	2	25	45	.205	.229	.198	9.42	5.23
Ramirez, Ismael	R-R	6-3	200	3-3-81	8	13	4.12	27	27	0	0	151	155	75	69	19	32	125	.267	.337	.211	7.47	1.91
Reed, Brian	R-R	6-1	210	3-6-81	0	1	4.91	8	0	0	0	11	13	6	6	1	6	10	.289	.286	.292	8.18	4.91
Reimers, Cameron	R-R	6-5	216	9-15-78	6	7	4.15	19	16	1	0	106	134	71	49	6	20	55	.301	.305	.298	4.66	1.69
Thorpe, Tracy	R-R	6-4	262	12-15-80	2	2	3.89	26	0	0	1	37	30	18	16	9	17	36	.233	.217	.246	8.76	4.14
Vermilyea, Jamie	R-R	6-4	195	2-10-82	3	3	2.60	27	4	0	1	66	67	21	19	5	16	52	.266	.270	.262	7.13	2.19
Waugh, Jason	R-R	6-1	214	3-12-80	0	0	0.00	1	0	0	0	1	0	0	0	0	0	0	.000	.000	.000	0.00	0.00

FIELDING

Catcher	PCT	G	PO	A	E	DP	PB
Kratz	.992	89	648	63	6	4	12
Thigpen	.994	30	297	23	2	1	4
Umbria	1.000	26	188	6	0	1	1
Whittaker	1.000	2	11	0	0	0	0
Zaun	1.000	1	4	0	0	0	0

First Base	PCT	G	PO	A	E	DP
Barker	.990	9	90	7	1	5
Cannon	.988	30	215	33	3	19
Chiaravalloti	.990	44	377	25	4	45
Cosby	1.000	1	3	0	0	0
Johnston	.992	60	470	39	4	46

Second Base	PCT	G	PO	A	E	DP
Acuna	1.000	1	1	0	0	0
Cota	.976	34	60	102	4	31
Hassey	.989	23	31	56	1	12
Roberts	.988	91	160	238	5	53

Third Base	PCT	G	PO	A	E	DP
Cosby	.917	110	57	186	22	20
Cota	1.000	3	0	1	0	0
Hassey	.970	30	19	46	2	6

Shortstop	PCT	G	PO	A	E	DP
Hassey	.971	42	50	119	5	25
Tablado	.935	100	126	274	28	61

Outfield	PCT	G	PO	A	E	DP
Acuna	.978	96	173	6	4	1
Davenport	.988	86	145	14	2	2
Hassey	.000	1	0	0	0	0
Jova	.988	79	156	8	2	2
Negron	.975	124	262	7	7	2
Sanders	.818	13	17	1	4	0
Singleton	.975	21	37	2	1	0
Waugh	1.000	12	20	0	0	1

DUNEDIN BLUE JAYS — High Class A

FLORIDA STATE LEAGUE

BATTING	B-T	HT	WT	DOB	AVG	vLH	vRH	G	AB	R	H	2B	3B	HR	RBI	BB	HBP	SH	SF	SO	SB	CS	SLG	OBP
Arnold, Eric	R-R	6-1	187	7-9-80	.274	.247	.282	100	379	70	104	28	1	19	72	36	5	0	3	108	1	0	.504	.343
Cannon, Chip	L-R	6-5	215	11-30-81	.384	.300	.402	29	112	28	43	4	2	14	39	16	1	0	0	32	0	1	.830	.465
Chiaravalloti, Vito	R-R	6-3	225	10-26-80	.212	.167	.231	42	146	22	31	7	1	4	18	18	2	0	0	39	0	0	.356	.307
Cota, Carlo	R-R	5-10	185	9-18-80	.304	.256	.325	68	276	47	84	20	2	10	35	28	4	1	2	65	0	1	.500	.374
Diaz, Robinzon	R-R	5-11	195	9-19-83	.294	.232	.314	100	388	47	114	17	6	1	65	15	5	2	4	28	5	2	.376	.325
Dragicevich, Scott	R-R	6-3	195	6-28-80	.250	.308	.231	83	264	38	66	13	2	3	30	26	2	0	1	61	0	0	.348	.321
Hattig, John	B-R	6-2	215	2-27-80	.386	.500	.344	11	44	8	17	3	0	0	5	3	0	0	1	7	0	0	.455	.417
Johnston, Clint	L-L	6-3	214	7-2-77	.310	.265	.323	42	158	29	49	10	0	4	21	22	2	0	1	39	0	0	.449	.399
Lind, Adam	L-L	6-2	195	7-17-83	.313	.291	.321	126	495	80	155	42	4	12	84	49	4	0	6	77	2	1	.487	.375
Mayorson, Manuel	R-R	5-10	183	3-10-83	.268	.270	.267	121	441	59	118	23	5	3	48	24	3	11	2	34	7	3	.363	.309
Medina, Rodney	B-R	6-1	203	10-17-81	.272	.262	.276	45	169	22	46	8	1	1	20	6	2	2	0	16	1	3	.349	.305
Patrick, Brian	B-R	5-10	185	11-29-80	.293	.256	.304	53	174	29	51	11	0	1	15	24	1	0	2	27	0	0	.374	.378
Quiroz, Guillermo	R-R	6-1	200	11-29-81	.237	.000	.290	11	38	4	9	1	0	2	6	2	3	0	0	8	0	0	.421	.326
Reiman, Joey	R-R	6-1	200	12-20-80	.294	.309	.290	77	282	39	83	16	1	5	36	33	5	1	1	71	1	3	.411	.377
Roberts, Ryan	R-R	5-11	190	9-19-80	.287	.182	.313	42	164	33	47	9	0	9	35	24	2	0	2	27	6	1	.506	.380

BATTING	B-T	HT	WT	DOB	AVG	vLH	vRH	G	AB	R	H	2B	3B	HR	RBI	BB	HBP	SH	SF	SO	SB	CS	SLG	OBP
Schneider, John	R-R	6-3	227	2-14-80	.321	.182	.356	22	56	8	18	3	0	2	10	10	3	1	1	16	0	0	.482	.443
Sena, Emmanuel	B-R	6-1	167	10-15-84	.125	.000	.143	3	8	1	1	0	0	0	0	2	1	0	0	3	0	1	.125	.364
Smith, David	R-R	6-1	190	1-12-81	.294	.313	.288	106	391	65	115	24	2	14	73	35	2	0	7	73	4	2	.473	.349
Snyder, Michael	L-R	6-5	240	2-11-81	.226	.154	.246	48	177	25	40	4	0	4	20	17	1	0	0	51	1	0	.316	.297
Tingler, Jayce	L-L	5-8	155	11-28-80	.265	.277	.261	121	465	67	123	16	3	1	28	53	13	3	4	31	2	2	.318	.353
Waugh, Jason	R-R	6-1	214	3-12-80	.307	.263	.321	21	75	12	23	12	0	0	10	2	0	0	3	10	0	0	.467	.313
Whittaker, Tim	R-R	6-0	200	1-4-79	.279	.371	.248	39	136	18	38	7	0	1	22	11	0	0	1	24	0	0	.353	.331

PITCHING	B-T	HT	WT	DOB	W	L	ERA	G	GS	CG	SV	IP	H	R	ER	HR	BB	SO	AVG	vLH	vRH	K/9	BB/9
Berroa, Yesson	R-R	6-4	205	7-30-82	0	2	9.45	9	0	0	0	13	20	15	14	2	4	9	.333	.458	.250	6.08	2.70
Buzachero, Bubbie	R-R	5-11	177	6-13-81	0	1	4.50	2	0	0	1	2	2	1	1	1	0	0	.286	.000	.333	0.00	0.00
Cannon, Eddie	R-R	6-1	175	11-13-81	0	0	7.71	1	0	0	0	2	4	2	2	0	0	2	.400	.250	.500	7.71	0.00
Core, Danny	R-R	6-1	195	7-17-81	0	0	7.24	9	0	0	1	14	13	11	11	5	10	16	.255	.350	.194	10.54	6.59
Harang, Daryl	L-L	6-2	215	11-19-82	1	1	4.01	14	0	0	0	25	24	12	11	3	13	13	.258	.324	.220	4.74	4.74
Harper, Jeremy	R-R	6-2	190	10-31-80	4	0	2.93	26	0	0	1	43	44	18	14	3	26	33	.265	.324	.224	6.91	5.44
Hill, Danny	R-R	5-11	205	11-5-81	3	2	3.22	33	0	0	3	50	47	25	18	2	21	29	.250	.237	.259	5.19	3.75
Isenberg, Kurt	R-L	6-0	190	1-15-82	12	8	3.54	26	26	0	0	145	147	67	57	13	32	90	.261	.242	.266	5.59	1.99
Jackson, Zach	L-L	6-5	220	5-13-83	8	1	2.88	10	10	0	0	59	56	25	19	3	6	48	.247	.237	.250	7.28	0.91
James, Justin	R-R	6-3	215	9-13-81	4	7	2.87	44	5	0	0	94	107	44	30	6	21	56	.286	.336	.254	5.36	2.01
Janssen, Casey	R-R	6-4	205	9-17-81	6	1	2.26	10	10	0	0	60	46	16	15	2	12	51	.216	.221	.212	7.69	1.81
MacDonald, Michael	R-R	6-1	185	10-29-81	9	6	4.24	25	23	0	0	127	136	76	60	4	40	87	.276	.282	.271	6.15	2.83
Martin, Adrian	R-R	6-0	170	9-2-84	0	0	7.71	5	0	0	0	7	10	6	6	1	1	1	.323	.417	.263	1.29	1.29
McGowan, Dustin	R-R	6-3	220	3-24-82	0	1	4.29	5	5	0	0	21	21	12	10	2	5	20	.253	.279	.225	8.57	2.14
Mumma, Brad	L-L	6-4	230	4-1-81	3	2	4.09	45	0	0	2	62	60	35	28	7	20	69	.248	.165	.288	10.07	2.92
Prahm, Ryan	R-R	6-5	225	5-7-79	0	0	18.00	2	0	0	0	1	3	2	2	0	4	0	.500	.667	.333	0.00	36.00
Purcey, David	L-L	6-5	240	4-22-82	5	4	3.63	21	21	0	0	94	80	51	38	8	56	116	.229	.244	.223	11.07	5.34
Reed, Brian	R-R	6-1	210	3-6-81	3	4	2.84	40	0	0	4	63	53	25	20	4	18	48	.230	.310	.185	6.82	2.56
Romero, Davis	L-L	5-10	156	3-30-83	9	6	3.47	34	18	0	1	125	133	60	48	10	34	136	.273	.344	.248	9.82	2.45
Romero, Ricardo	R-L	6-1	195	11-6-84	1	0	3.82	8	8	0	0	31	36	13	13	2	7	22	.283	.250	.295	6.46	2.05
Savickas, Russell	R-R	6-4	185	7-30-83	1	0	0.00	1	0	0	0	1	1	0	0	0	2	0	.250	.500	.000	0.00	18.00
Sopko, Mark	R-R	6-0	200	12-16-81	0	1	7.20	13	0	0	1	15	23	14	12	1	8	14	.354	.333	.364	8.40	4.80
Tate, Derek	R-L	6-0	190	12-19-81	0	0	0.00	1	0	0	0	1	1	0	0	0	0	0	.200	.000	.200	0.00	0.00
Tavarez, Milton	R-R	6-2	212	3-29-82	4	7	3.36	51	0	0	13	59	56	27	22	4	21	50	.252	.244	.257	7.63	3.20
Thorpe, Tracy	R-R	6-4	262	12-15-80	2	1	3.67	25	0	0	1	34	32	14	14	4	10	33	.242	.277	.224	8.65	2.62
Timm, Jordan	L-L	6-6	230	1-15-81	0	0	16.20	1	0	0	0	2	2	3	3	1	1	1	.286	.500	.200	5.40	5.40
Tressler, Aaron	R-R	6-1	185	3-28-82	0	0	16.20	2	0	0	0	2	3	3	3	1	1	2	.375	.000	.600	10.80	5.40
Yates, Kyle	R-R	6-0	195	1-8-83	7	3	1.91	14	14	0	0	75	69	30	16	4	19	67	.242	.218	.268	8.00	2.27

FIELDING

Catcher	PCT	G	PO	A	E	DP	PB
Diaz	.978	87	599	59	15	6	26
Quiroz	1.000	4	22	5	0	0	0
Reiman	.976	6	39	2	1	0	0
Schneider	.981	16	98	8	2	0	2
Whittaker	.993	36	264	18	2	3	3

First Base	PCT	G	PO	A	E	DP
Cannon	.993	15	127	23	1	8
Chiaravalloti	.991	19	198	14	2	14
Johnston	.985	35	309	30	5	28
Reiman	.996	47	463	31	2	36
Snyder	.996	24	209	26	1	23

Second Base	PCT	G	PO	A	E	DP
Cota	.950	68	131	211	18	34
Dragicevich	.984	12	24	39	1	8
Mayorson	.974	9	15	23	1	4
Patrick	.968	15	20	41	2	6
Roberts	.949	41	86	120	11	34

Third Base	PCT	G	PO	A	E	DP
Arnold	.911	90	46	190	23	21
Dragicevich	.953	41	22	79	5	6
Hattig	.909	8	3	27	3	6
Patrick	.636	4	1	6	4	1
Sena	1.000	2	2	4	0	1

Shortstop	PCT	G	PO	A	E	DP
Dragicevich	.938	30	41	79	8	19
Mayorson	.967	114	159	363	18	56
Sena	.750	1	2	1	1	1

Outfield	PCT	G	PO	A	E	DP
Lind	.962	120	148	3	6	1
Medina	.974	43	72	3	2	0
Patrick	1.000	26	37	1	0	0
Smith	.963	104	170	14	7	6
Tingler	.992	121	233	9	2	3
Waugh	1.000	20	31	3	0	0

LANSING LUGNUTS — Low Class A

MIDWEST LEAGUE

BATTING	B-T	HT	WT	DOB	AVG	vLH	vRH	G	AB	R	H	2B	3B	HR	RBI	BB	HBP	SH	SF	SO	SB	CS	SLG	OBP
Anderson, Charles	L-R	6-3	215	10-2-81	.258	.343	.234	50	159	26	41	16	0	6	34	36	5	0	0	36	1	0	.472	.410
Armstrong, Jason	R-R	6-0	180	11-13-81	.289	.378	.260	118	484	63	140	20	0	0	52	29	7	0	5	61	9	3	.331	.335
Cannon, Chip	L-R	6-5	215	11-30-81	.268	.306	.258	46	168	22	45	9	2	11	36	20	2	0	1	47	0	0	.542	.351
Corrente, David	R-R	6-3	204	10-13-83	.200	.179	.208	65	200	30	40	8	1	1	23	21	5	2	4	58	1	1	.265	.287
Hetherington, Luke	R-R	6-2	195	4-13-83	.266	.290	.255	72	207	40	55	10	2	0	21	49	7	0	1	55	10	3	.333	.420
Hicks, David	L-L	6-5	230	11-22-81	.242	.229	.246	107	368	51	89	15	4	6	39	29	4	1	2	47	1	5	.353	.303
Klosterman, Ryan	R-R	5-11	175	5-28-82	.241	.250	.238	129	452	85	109	26	4	13	69	62	10	2	4	99	30	4	.403	.343
Lex, Josh	R-R	5-11	210	10-7-81	.246	.143	.295	22	65	12	16	3	0	1	8	9	2	1	0	18	0	0	.338	.355
Mathews, Aaron	R-R	5-10	195	5-10-82	.289	.315	.280	70	204	28	59	11	5	4	30	21	1	2	4	40	11	3	.451	.352
Nielsen, Eric	R-R	6-0	222	11-14-81	.267	.264	.267	128	480	66	128	27	2	7	59	53	6	0	6	74	7	8	.375	.343
Patrick, Brian	B-R	5-10	185	11-29-80	.188	.154	.200	14	48	8	9	3	0	0	7	5	1	0	0	12	0	0	.250	.278
Patton, Cory	L-L	5-10	210	6-18-82	.200	.250	.192	58	180	23	36	9	0	6	22	14	1	0	2	55	0	3	.350	.259
Peralta, Juan	B-R	5-11	170	6-24-83	.284	.267	.290	57	176	25	50	5	3	1	35	14	1	4	0	37	8	1	.364	.340
Quintana, Al	R-R	6-0	200	11-9-82	.077	.000	.083	5	13	2	1	0	0	0	0	1	0	0	0	4	0	0	.077	.143
Reiman, Joey	R-R	6-1	200	12-20-80	.148	.286	.000	9	27	2	4	0	0	0	3	1	0	0	0	8	0	0	.148	.179
Rodriguez, Yuber	B-R	6-0	170	11-17-83	.200	.143	.220	111	375	52	75	15	1	4	43	47	4	3	4	114	13	8	.277	.293
Sanders, Anthony	R-R	6-2	200	3-2-74	.278	.111	.333	10	36	4	10	2	0	0	3	6	0	0	0	5	1	0	.333	.381
Snavely, Christian	L-R	6-3	200	5-7-82	.287	.241	.298	117	408	67	117	27	2	11	56	67	3	1	2	80	4	5	.444	.390
Thigpen, Curtis	R-R	5-11	190	4-19-83	.287	.313	.279	79	293	41	84	18	2	5	35	54	1	2	2	34	5	0	.413	.397
Velez, Eugenio	B-R	6-1	163	5-16-82	.285	.295	.281	67	239	25	68	11	3	4	34	9	2	0	4	40	7	5	.406	.311
Wolfe, Joe	L-R	5-9	205	10-10-80	.306	.091	.353	24	62	12	19	4	0	4	10	7	0	0	0	14	0	0	.565	.377

PITCHING	B-T	HT	WT	DOB	W	L	ERA	G	GS	CG	SV	IP	H	R	ER	HR	BB	SO	AVG	vLH	vRH	K/9	BB/9
Berroa, Yesson	R-R	6-4	205	7-30-82	0	1	5.87	5	0	0	0	8	10	5	5	0	7	7	.313	.167	.346	8.22	8.22
Cheng, Chi-Hung	L-L	6-1	180	6-20-85	7	6	3.15	26	25	0	0	137	109	61	48	8	72	142	.215	.188	.222	9.33	4.73
Core, Danny	R-R	6-1	195	7-17-81	8	9	6.32	21	21	0	0	105	120	80	74	22	42	73	.285	.306	.269	6.24	3.59
Day, Dewon	R-R	6-4	210	9-29-80	0	0	4.05	9	0	0	0	13	15	6	6	2	9	14	.300	.421	.226	9.45	6.08

PITCHING	B-T	HT	WT	DOB	W	L	ERA	G	GS	CG	SV	IP	H	R	ER	HR	BB	SO	AVG	vLH	vRH	K/9	BB/9
Delgadillo, Hector	R-R	6-0	195	1-2-83	0	0	3.60	1	1	0	0	5	4	3	2	0	4	1	.222	.222	.222	1.80	7.20
Falkenbach, Connor	R-R	6-0	165	2-22-82	1	1	13.50	2	0	0	0	2	6	3	3	0	0	3	.500	.429	.600	13.50	0.00
Harang, Daryl	L-L	6-2	215	11-19-82	2	0	3.21	16	1	0	2	28	27	11	10	3	12	22	.260	.235	.271	7.07	3.86
Harper, Jeremy	R-R	6-2	190	10-31-80	1	4	3.82	19	0	0	4	33	33	15	14	3	14	38	.266	.234	.286	10.36	3.82
Harrison, Ben	L-L	6-1	190	4-14-84	0	0	0.00	1	0	0	1	4	2	0	0	0	0	3	.143	.000	.182	6.75	0.00
Hill, Danny	R-R	5-11	205	11-5-81	1	2	2.04	17	0	0	11	18	16	8	4	0	7	12	.239	.207	.263	6.11	3.57
Janssen, Casey	R-R	6-4	205	9-17-81	4	0	1.37	7	7	0	0	46	27	8	7	0	4	38	.174	.234	.132	7.43	0.78
Keng, Po-Hsuan	R-R	6-1	215	10-15-84	5	5	5.08	28	10	0	0	80	98	54	45	12	21	54	.303	.313	.296	6.10	2.37
Martin, Adrian	R-R	6-0	170	9-2-84	0	0	7.71	5	1	0	0	9	17	8	8	4	0	6	.425	.571	.346	5.79	0.00
McLaughlin, Joey	R-R	6-0	185	2-11-82	2	2	3.13	42	0	0	7	46	36	17	16	3	24	45	.214	.238	.200	8.80	4.70
Perez, Juan	R-R	6-6	188	12-27-81	7	6	4.25	34	9	0	0	102	118	54	48	8	35	60	.293	.284	.299	5.31	3.10
Rico, Erik	L-L	6-2	210	1-21-80	1	1	9.20	7	0	0	0	15	22	15	15	2	9	12	.344	.211	.400	7.36	5.52
Roy, Scott	R-R	6-1	220	8-15-82	3	4	3.76	25	0	0	0	38	29	21	16	3	12	34	.203	.236	.182	7.98	2.82
Savickas, Russell	R-R	6-4	185	7-30-83	6	7	4.96	19	19	0	0	91	111	57	50	4	37	70	.309	.290	.321	6.95	3.67
Sopko, Mark	R-R	6-0	200	12-16-81	0	1	2.94	23	0	0	4	34	38	14	11	1	14	24	.297	.295	.298	6.42	3.74
Templet, Jordy	R-R	6-2	180	8-19-81	6	6	4.15	40	0	0	0	89	98	44	41	6	31	69	.283	.291	.279	6.98	3.13
Timm, Jordan	L-L	6-6	230	1-15-81	2	0	2.47	18	4	0	5	47	39	16	13	2	16	44	.225	.211	.230	8.37	3.04
Tressler, Aaron	R-R	6-1	185	3-28-82	3	1	2.06	17	0	0	2	39	32	9	9	1	7	28	.224	.172	.259	6.41	1.60
Wideman, Aaron	R-L	5-11	190	6-8-85	7	10	4.91	27	27	0	0	143	135	84	78	21	38	121	.250	.278	.244	7.62	2.39
Yates, Kyle	R-R	6-0	195	1-8-83	4	3	4.43	14	14	1	0	81	82	41	40	6	19	81	.265	.244	.280	8.96	2.10

FIELDING

Catcher	PCT	G	PO	A	E	DP	PB
Anderson	.000	1	0	0	0	0	0
Corrente	.984	62	390	50	7	1	6
Lex	1.000	14	107	10	0	0	7
Quintana	1.000	3	20	2	0	0	0
Reiman	1.000	6	31	5	0	0	1
Thigpen	.986	60	451	58	7	6	16
Wolfe	1.000	3	15	3	0	0	0

First Base	PCT	G	PO	A	E	DP
Anderson	.993	17	127	12	1	5
Cannon	.989	31	249	20	3	23
Hicks	.996	103	794	55	3	72
Reiman	1.000	1	7	1	0	1

Second Base	PCT	G	PO	A	E	DP
Armstrong	.946	22	39	48	5	7
Patrick	1.000	3	6	8	0	2
Peralta	.986	56	113	161	4	27
Velez	.972	65	132	147	8	25

Third Base	PCT	G	PO	A	E	DP
Armstrong	.922	84	69	157	19	14
Snavely	.889	61	32	96	16	7
Velez	1.000	2	0	4	0	0

Shortstop	PCT	G	PO	A	E	DP
Armstrong	.970	14	23	42	2	10
Klosterman	.958	128	209	361	25	65
Peralta	1.000	1	0	1	0	0

Outfield	PCT	G	PO	A	E	DP
Cannon	1.000	1	1	0	0	0
Hetherington	.990	59	90	5	1	1
Mathews	.991	63	106	8	1	0
Nielsen	.986	120	195	11	3	1
Patrick	.909	8	9	1	1	0
Patton	.961	55	67	6	3	2
Rodriguez	.972	108	237	4	7	3
Sanders	1.000	6	6	0	0	0
Snavely	1.000	25	30	0	0	0

AUBURN DOUBLEDAYS — Short-Season Class A

NEW YORK-PENN LEAGUE

BATTING	B-T	HT	WT	DOB	AVG	vLH	vRH	G	AB	R	H	2B	3B	HR	RBI	BB	HBP	SH	SF	SO	SB	CS	SLG	OBP
Acey, Jermy	B-R	5-11	185	5-24-81	.301	.388	.271	55	193	26	58	17	0	4	17	16	6	3	0	41	0	1	.451	.372
Bell, Josh	R-R	6-0	215	7-3-84	.238	.196	.252	46	181	13	43	16	1	3	17	4	1	1	0	65	0	1	.387	.258
Bernhard, Marshall	R-R	5-10	180	6-2-83	.213	.143	.237	42	80	15	17	3	0	0	5	9	4	2	0	17	2	1	.250	.323
Bohm, Kyle	R-R	6-0	220	6-11-83	.235	.267	.221	40	98	12	23	6	1	2	6	11	2	0	1	16	0	1	.378	.321
Bormaster, Brian	R-R	5-10	193	10-19-81	.325	.261	.340	41	117	19	38	8	1	1	18	18	2	2	3	22	0	0	.436	.414
Butler, Jacob	R-R	6-1	200	2-9-83	.200	.143	.212	11	40	5	8	1	1	2	8	2	0	0	0	7	0	0	.425	.238
Celigoy, Josh	R-R	6-2	220	4-29-82	.208	.154	.229	23	48	8	10	3	0	0	3	5	0	1	1	16	0	0	.271	.278
Chourio, Junior	R-R	6-3	176	3-23-83	.000	.000	.000	2	1	1	0	0	0	0	0	0	1	0	0	0	0	0	.000	.500
Cooksey, Matt	L-L	5-8	170	11-14-82	.240	.143	.259	52	129	20	31	4	0	2	11	24	2	6	1	32	5	3	.318	.365
Garibaldi, Anthony	R-R	6-1	190	12-19-80	.190	.143	.205	35	116	19	22	4	2	3	14	5	6	4	0	32	2	1	.336	.260
Gonzalez, Jesus	R-R	6-2	160	7-7-84	.267	.250	.273	6	15	3	4	0	0	0	0	0	1	0	0	1	0	2	.267	.313
Gutierrez, Chris	R-R	5-11	175	3-12-84	.226	.375	.174	21	62	8	14	5	1	0	6	2	2	3	0	17	0	1	.339	.273
Metropoulos, Joey	R-R	6-1	230	10-7-83	.292	.250	.304	52	178	25	52	21	2	6	28	15	0	0	3	44	0	0	.534	.342
Patterson, Ryan	R-R	5-11	205	5-2-83	.339	.358	.335	71	274	52	93	23	4	13	65	21	3	3	5	53	5	2	.595	.386
Patton, Cory	L-L	5-10	210	6-18-82	.273	.313	.262	57	220	41	60	18	1	14	44	22	2	1	1	60	1	0	.555	.343
Pettway, Brian	R-R	6-1	215	7-29-83	.225	.234	.222	56	200	19	45	10	2	6	25	16	2	0	1	66	0	1	.385	.288
Sena, Emmanuel	B-R	6-1	167	10-15-84	.209	.183	.218	65	225	30	47	6	0	3	18	20	0	9	1	84	9	3	.276	.272
Shoffit, Sean	L-R	6-2	185	6-9-85	.250	.154	.275	57	188	32	47	13	1	1	21	32	2	2	1	52	2	2	.346	.363
Thomas, Nick	L-R	6-3	200	2-2-83	.254	.100	.272	62	193	24	49	7	1	7	32	37	2	1	3	41	0	0	.409	.374

PITCHING	B-T	HT	WT	DOB	W	L	ERA	G	GS	CG	SV	IP	H	R	ER	HR	BB	SO	AVG	vLH	vRH	K/9	BB/9
Alfaro, Gabriel	R-R	6-4	190	6-14-83	2	4	6.23	18	0	0	1	30	40	23	21	3	13	36	.315	.294	.323	10.68	3.86
Bell, Kristian	R-R	6-0	185	1-11-84	5	4	3.14	15	15	0	0	77	74	38	27	3	33	71	.253	.271	.245	8.26	3.84
Berroa, Yesson	R-R	6-4	205	7-30-82	3	1	4.18	17	0	0	7	24	20	11	11	2	4	32	.222	.261	.209	12.17	1.52
Carnline, Billy	R-R	6-3	190	1-3-84	4	0	4.61	21	2	0	1	41	41	23	21	1	20	36	.261	.265	.259	7.90	4.39
Day, Dewon	R-R	6-4	210	9-29-80	0	0	3.00	3	0	0	0	3	4	2	1	0	3	4	.286	.333	.250	12.00	9.00
Dicken, Randy	R-R	6-2	198	8-19-82	4	2	3.60	14	11	0	0	60	63	31	24	5	24	66	.267	.254	.273	9.90	3.60
Eberhardt, Peter	R-R	6-3	215	10-30-81	0	0	6.00	3	0	0	0	3	2	2	2	0	2	1	.182	.000	.250	3.00	6.00
Fowler, Eric	L-L	6-3	215	3-18-83	4	2	3.02	15	10	0	0	57	42	24	19	1	29	55	.202	.167	.208	8.74	4.61
Grant, Brian	R-R	6-4	207	8-16-84	0	1	13.50	5	0	0	1	11	16	19	16	2	6	8	.348	.615	.242	6.75	5.06
Hahn, Cory	R-R	6-0	235	10-25-81	0	0	0.00	1	0	0	0	1	2	0	0	0	0	1	.500	.000	.667	9.00	0.00
Litsch, Jesse	R-R	6-1	195	3-9-85	0	1	3.60	4	3	0	0	10	11	9	4	0	6	7	.268	.200	.290	6.30	5.40
Martin, Adrian	R-R	6-0	170	9-2-84	1	1	3.05	22	2	0	3	44	51	19	15	1	2	36	.282	.356	.246	7.31	0.41
Phillips, Paul	R-R	6-1	190	1-26-84	2	1	2.29	26	0	0	13	39	31	14	10	2	13	41	.214	.298	.173	9.38	2.97
Ray, Robert	R-R	6-5	190	1-21-84	4	3	2.77	15	13	0	0	62	46	22	19	2	20	58	.204	.221	.196	8.46	2.92
Rodriguez, Edward	R-R	6-4	170	10-6-84	3	1	3.49	21	0	0	3	39	41	21	15	2	7	25	.272	.286	.266	5.82	1.63
Romero, Ricardo	R-L	6-1	195	11-6-84	0	0	0.00	1	1	0	0	2	2	0	0	0	1	2	.250	1.000	.143	9.00	4.50
Sowers, Josh	R-R	6-1	170	5-17-83	4	0	4.86	19	2	0	0	37	42	23	20	1	16	27	.284	.222	.304	6.57	3.89
Stidfole, Sean	R-R	6-3	175	3-12-84	4	1	3.79	19	0	0	0	36	26	22	15	1	20	40	.191	.136	.217	10.09	5.05
Timm, Jordan	L-L	6-6	230	1-15-81	0	1	6.75	1	1	0	0	4	5	3	3	0	1	4	.313	.500	.286	9.00	2.25
Tressler, Aaron	R-R	6-1	185	3-28-82	1	0	0.00	5	0	0	0	13	8	0	0	0	1	11	.178	.167	.185	7.43	0.68
Trias, Orlando	R-R	6-3	180	3-16-84	4	7	3.89	15	15	0	0	81	85	40	35	4	21	54	.264	.273	.259	6.00	2.33

GAMES BY POSITION: C—Bell 41, Bohm 6, Bormaster 41. **1B**—Bohm 13, Celigoy 20, Metropoulos 19, Thomas 45. **2B**—Acey 11, Bernhard 16, Gutierrez 2, Sena 7, Shoffit 54. **3B**—Acey 33, Bernhard 1, Celigoy 3, Garibaldi 35, Gonzalez 3, Gutierrez 11, Sena 6. **SS**—Bernhard 18, Gonzalez 4, Gutierrez 12, Sena 49. **OF**—Acey 11, Butler 9, Chourio 1, Cooksey 49, Patterson 66, Patton 50, Pettway 50, Thomas 11.

PULASKI BLUE JAYS — Rookie

APPALACHIAN LEAGUE

BATTING	B-T	HT	WT	DOB	AVG	vLH	vRH	G	AB	R	H	2B	3B	HR	RBI	BB	HBP	SH	SF	SO	SB	CS	SLG	OBP
Aguilar, Heliezer	R-R	5-11	165	3-9-84	.301	.342	.287	41	146	21	44	10	0	1	18	5	2	4	1	16	7	1	.390	.331
Badger, Graig	R-R	5-9	177	2-11-81	.292	.333	.281	44	144	28	42	8	3	0	19	18	3	5	0	24	6	2	.389	.382
Butler, Jacob	R-R	6-1	200	2-9-83	.290	.314	.282	55	200	42	58	16	1	14	52	31	2	1	4	60	1	2	.590	.384
Cordero, Octavio	L-L	5-9	160	10-19-83	.237	.323	.205	39	114	23	27	3	0	1	5	17	0	2	1	31	11	1	.289	.333
Franko, Paul	R-R	6-0	200	6-7-84	.301	.340	.287	49	176	29	53	14	0	8	44	25	4	0	4	43	0	1	.517	.392
Gonzalez, Jesus	R-R	6-2	160	7-7-84	.289	.192	.328	46	180	25	52	14	1	8	28	11	1	0	2	42	0	0	.511	.330
Gutierrez, Chris	R-R	5-11	175	3-12-84	.236	.279	.219	43	148	15	35	9	1	2	20	15	4	0	1	26	2	1	.351	.321
Hatch, Anthony	L-R	6-3	195	8-30-83	.273	.214	.290	41	128	16	35	11	2	5	26	9	2	0	0	30	0	1	.508	.331
Jaspe, Jonathan	B-R	5-11	170	4-11-85	.299	.309	.294	47	174	29	52	12	1	3	31	14	0	0	3	30	1	0	.431	.346
Kalter, Zach	L-R	6-2	190	9-19-84	.268	.274	.265	58	209	49	56	9	7	1	17	45	3	2	2	33	17	7	.392	.402
Looze, Chris	L-L	6-2	205	12-23-81	.115	.048	.140	25	78	10	9	3	0	3	7	5	1	0	0	26	0	1	.269	.179
Martinez, Chris	L-R	6-1	220	9-24-82	.161	.111	.170	23	56	5	9	2	0	2	4	7	3	0	1	28	0	1	.304	.284
Nieves, Javier	R-R	5-11	160	2-5-84	.000	.000	.000	7	7	0	0	0	0	0	0	0	1	0	0	3	0	0	.000	.125
Quintana, Al	R-R	6-0	200	11-9-82	.282	.304	.273	26	78	11	22	4	2	0	11	7	0	0	1	15	1	1	.385	.337
Sandes, Jorge	B-R	6-0	170	2-25-85	.250	.353	.197	31	100	17	25	3	2	3	11	16	3	0	0	25	0	2	.410	.370
Soto, Leance	R-R	6-2	210	6-13-85	.153	.200	.130	42	137	11	21	5	0	4	10	12	0	1	1	69	0	0	.277	.220
Stone, Wesley	R-R	5-10	170	4-16-87	.272	.173	.318	43	162	23	44	7	0	1	15	22	1	0	2	62	0	1	.333	.358

PITCHING	B-T	HT	WT	DOB	W	L	ERA	G	GS	CG	SV	IP	H	R	ER	HR	BB	SO	AVG	vLH	vRH	K/9	BB/9
Aguirre, Wilfreddy	L-L	6-2	180	11-8-86	1	4	5.51	9	9	0	0	33	38	25	20	1	16	23	.284	.182	.293	6.34	4.41
Benson, Shane	R-R	6-4	190	12-15-86	6	3	5.52	16	6	0	1	44	57	30	27	7	10	39	.308	.274	.330	7.98	2.05
Bigley, Dennis	R-R	6-3	190	8-18-83	1	2	5.40	16	8	0	0	47	58	40	28	10	15	42	.309	.306	.310	8.10	2.89
Byrnes, Scott	R-R	6-1	200	2-18-83	2	2	5.85	21	0	0	3	32	46	30	21	4	13	36	.329	.404	.284	10.02	3.62
Delgadillo, Hector	R-R	6-0	195	1-2-83	5	3	3.55	18	5	0	1	51	54	27	20	8	9	49	.271	.206	.305	8.70	1.60
Eberhardt, Peter	R-R	6-3	215	10-30-81	0	0	0.90	6	0	0	1	10	6	1	1	0	2	8	.167	.167	.167	7.20	1.80
Falkenbach, Connor	R-R	6-0	165	2-22-82	1	0	1.38	10	0	0	2	13	13	4	2	0	2	10	.255	.167	.282	6.92	1.38
Foster, Matt	L-L	6-3	205	9-4-81	0	0	2.45	2	0	0	0	4	4	5	1	0	5	0	.308	.400	.250	0.00	12.27
Gonzalez, Reidier	R-R	5-11	180	11-1-85	2	0	1.63	7	6	0	0	28	26	9	5	0	6	24	.243	.208	.253	7.81	1.95
Grijalva, Jon	R-R	6-4	215	10-5-81	0	1	3.77	7	0	0	0	14	14	7	6	2	2	18	.255	.200	.286	11.30	1.26
Hahn, Cory	R-R	6-0	235	10-25-81	2	1	1.41	18	0	0	0	32	24	11	5	1	10	38	.203	.163	.227	10.69	2.81
Harrison, Ben	L-L	6-1	190	4-14-84	3	1	3.82	19	0	0	2	35	30	17	15	1	6	45	.214	.250	.208	11.46	1.53
Litsch, Jesse	R-R	6-1	195	3-9-85	5	1	2.74	11	11	0	0	66	51	22	20	6	10	67	.212	.185	.238	9.18	1.37
Mateo, Francisco	L-L	6-0	180	5-7-84	1	7	5.14	12	12	0	0	56	72	41	32	9	21	38	.312	.393	.300	6.11	3.38
Perez, Rafael	R-L	6-0	165	1-12-83	2	1	6.66	18	0	0	2	26	26	21	19	2	23	27	.263	.353	.244	9.47	8.06
Reinoso, Ezemir	R-R	6-3	170	1-25-85	2	1	5.20	17	0	0	0	28	35	18	16	4	10	20	.313	.257	.338	6.51	3.25
Sanchez, Raymon	L-L	6-0	183	1-7-84	0	2	7.23	16	0	0	2	24	25	24	19	6	19	21	.266	.188	.282	7.99	7.23
Wice, Joe	L-L	6-6	215	9-1-85	1	4	5.40	10	10	0	0	45	55	37	27	15	10	35	.309	.361	.296	7.00	2.00

GAMES BY POSITION: C—Jaspe 42, Martinez 14, Nieves 6, Quintana 16. **1B**—Franko 38, Hatch 19, Looze 16. **2B**—Badger 28, Gutierrez 3, Stone 38. **3B**—Badger 13, Butler 1, Gutierrez 10, Hatch 9, Soto 41. **SS**—Badger 2, Gonzalez 43, Gutierrez 22. **OF**—Aguilar 39, Badger 1, Butler 51, Cordero 36, Jaspe 1, Kalter 56, Sandes 25.

WASHINGTON NATIONALS

BY LACY LUSK

To Washington baseball fans, the Nationals' 81-81 season in 2005 was as wonderful as a .500 year could be.

It was a victory merely to have a team for the first time since owner Bob Short moved the Senators to Arlington, Texas, following the 1971 season. The District found out in September 2004 that the Montreal Expos were relocating to RFK Stadium, with a ballpark planned to open in Southeast Washington by Opening Day 2008.

After political wrangling in the nation's capital, the team that has been owned by Major League Baseball since 2002 completed its move south. The Nationals beat the Mets in their spring training opener before a nationally televised cable audience, and the concept of having a D.C. baseball team finally became reality.

Picked last in the NL East by most pundits, the Nationals were one of the first-half's feel-good stories. They did indeed finish last, nine games behind the Braves, but improved by 14 victories over their final season in Canada.

"It would have been really fairy tale if we could have pulled this thing off," manager Frank Robinson said. "They wouldn't have even touched this in Hollywood."

The Nationals went 5-4 on their season-opening road trip, with outfielder Brad Wilkerson hitting for his second career cycle in the club's second game. The April 14 home opener was a 5-3 win against the Diamondbacks behind workhorse Livan Hernandez and closer Chad Cordero. A sellout crowd started the team toward a D.C.-record attendance of more than 2.7 million fans—11th-best in the game.

Washington rolled to a 50-31 start and remained in first place at the all-star break, with Hernandez and Cordero making the National League All-Star team. The homegrown Cordero, a first-round pick in 2003 out of Cal State Fullerton, went on to lead the majors with 47 saves despite entering spring training without a complete hold on the closer's job, according to Robinson. Hernandez, meanwhile, led the NL in innings (246) for the third straight year as he went 15-10, 3.98.

A strong bullpen helped the Nationals rank fourth in the NL in ERA at 3.87. Playing in a pitcher's park at RFK, the team also struggled to score runs—ranking last in the league with 639. First baseman Nick Johnson led the club with a .289 average and .408 on-base percentage. He and outfielder Jose Guillen, acquired from the Angels by general manager Jim Bowden, each slugged .479. Guillen led the Nationals in home runs (24) and RBIs (76).

The biggest contributions by rookies came from set-up man Gary Majewski (4-4, 2.93 in 86 innings) and outfielder Ryan Church (.287-9-42 in 268 at-bats). September callup Ryan Zimmerman, who was playing third base in college at Virginia just three months earlier, hit .397-0-6 in 58 at-bats as the first Nationals' draft pick to make the big leagues.

"When you try to build a championship club, I know you look for pitching, defense and also timely hitting," scouting director Dana Brown said. "Zimmerman is a very good defensive player and a really good hitter. We expect him to hit a high amount of doubles, drive in some runs and hit for a high average. And we feel there will be some power down the road."

Though the organization's minor league teams compiled the game's worst winning percentage (.438), the move from Montreal meant a greater budget for scouting and signing players.

Infielder Rick Short, 32, won the Triple-A Pacific Coast League batting title at .383 and saw his first time in the majors, hitting .400 in 15 at-bats with home runs off the Marlins' Dontrelle Willis and the Braves' John Smoltz.

The Nationals' minor league pitcher and player of the year came off the high Class A Potomac roster. Lefthander Michael O'Connor was fourth in the Carolina League in ERA (3.54) and second in strikeouts (158) in a 10-11 season in 168 innings. Third baseman Kory Casto hit .290-22-90 in 500 at-bats.

PLAYERS OF THE YEAR

MAJOR LEAGUE: Chad Cordero, rhp

Cordero showed flashes of brilliance in his first full big league season in Montreal in 2004, but emerged as the best closer in the National League in 2005, when he led the league with 47 saves. In 74 appearances, the 2003 first-round draft pick from Cal State Fullerton went 2-4, 1.82.

MINOR LEAGUE: Kory Casto, 3b

MIKE JANES

Casto was considered a bat-first player entering 2005, but developed as an all-around player with his actions, footwork and throwing all showing vast improvement in his first experience on the hot corner. Offensively, he set a career-high in home runs and doubles while hitting .290-22-90.

ORGANIZATION LEADERS

BATTING		
*AVG	Short, Rick, New Orleans	.383
R	Casto, Kory, Potomac	86
H	Diaz, Frank, Potomac	173
TB	Diaz, Frank, Potomac	276
2B	Diaz, Frank, Potomac	45
3B	Davis, Leonard, Vermont	8
HR	Haynes, Dee, Harrisburg/Memphis/New Orleans	23
RBI	Casto, Kory, Potomac	90
BB	Casto, Kory, Potomac	84
SO	Mortimer, Steve, GCL Nationals/Savannah	142
SB	Watson, Brandon, Harrisburg/New Orleans	38
*OBP	Short, Rick, New Orleans	.456
*SLG	Short, Rick, New Orleans	.569

PITCHING		
W	O'Connor, Michael, Potomac	10
	Price, Brett, Potomac	10
L	Stevenson, Jason, Harrisburg/Potomac	14
#ERA	Rivera, Saul, Harrisburg	1.92
G	Rueckel, Danny, Harrisburg	53
CG	Five players tied at	2
SV	Campbell, Brett, Potomac/Savannah	20
IP	O'Connor, Michael, Potomac	168
BB	Price, Brett, Potomac	81
SO	O'Connor, Michael, Potomac	158

*Minimum 250 at-bats. #Minimum 75 innings.

WASHINGTON NATIONALS

Manager: Frank Robinson.

2005 Record: 81-81, .500 (5th, NL East).

BATTING	B-T	HT	WT	DOB	AVG	vLH	vRH	G	AB	R	H	2B	3B	HR	RBI	BB	HBP	SH	SF	SO	SB	CS	SLG	OBP
Baerga, Carlos	B-R	5-11	215	11-4-68	.253	.261	.252	93	158	18	40	7	0	2	19	7	8	1	0	17	0	0	.335	.318
Bennett, Gary	R-R	6-0	210	4-17-72	.221	.198	.237	68	199	11	44	7	0	1	21	21	2	3	3	37	0	1	.271	.298
Blanco, Tony	R-R	6-1	175	11-10-81	.177	.172	.182	56	62	7	11	3	0	1	7	2	1	0	0	19	1	0	.274	.215
Byrd, Marlon	R-R	6-0	235	8-30-77	.264	.333	.214	74	216	20	57	15	2	2	26	18	1	5	4	47	5	1	.380	.318
2-team (5 Philadelphia)					.266	.323	.228	79	229	20	61	15	2	2	26	19	2	5	4	50	5	1	.376	.323
Carroll, Jamey	R-R	5-9	170	2-18-74	.251	.293	.235	113	303	44	76	8	1	0	22	34	5	13	3	55	3	4	.284	.333
Castilla, Vinny	R-R	6-1	205	7-4-67	.253	.314	.234	142	494	53	125	36	1	12	66	43	7	1	4	82	4	2	.403	.319
Cepicky, Matt	L-R	6-2	215	11-10-77	.240	.000	.261	11	25	1	6	3	0	0	3	1	0	0	0	8	0	1	.360	.269
Chavez, Endy	L-L	5-10	155	2-7-78	.222	.333	.000	7	9	2	2	1	0	0	1	3	0	0	0	1	0	1	.333	.417
Church, Ryan	L-L	6-1	190	10-14-78	.287	.367	.277	102	268	41	77	15	3	9	42	24	5	1	3	70	3	2	.466	.353
Cordero, Wil	R-R	6-2	230	10-3-71	.118	.105	.125	29	51	2	6	2	0	0	2	3	0	0	2	14	0	0	.157	.161
Cruz, Deivi	R-R	6-0	200	11-6-72	.255	.294	.235	20	51	2	13	1	0	0	1	1	1	1	0	3	0	0	.275	.283
2-team (81 San Francisco)					.265	.311	.236	101	260	28	69	11	1	5	20	11	1	3	0	34	0	1	.373	.298
Davis, J.J.	R-R	6-5	250	10-25-78	.231	.158	.429	14	26	0	6	0	0	0	2	2	0	0	0	7	1	1	.231	.286
Godwin, Tyrell	L-R	6-0	200	7-10-79	.000	.000	.000	3	3	0	0	0	0	0	0	0	0	0	0	1	0	0	.000	.000
Guillen, Jose	R-R	5-11	195	5-17-76	.283	.215	.305	148	551	81	156	32	2	24	76	31	19	1	9	102	1	1	.479	.338
Guzman, Cristian	B-R	6-0	205	3-21-78	.219	.160	.242	142	456	39	100	19	6	4	31	25	1	8	2	76	7	4	.314	.260
Hammonds, Jeffrey	R-R	6-0	220	3-5-71	.219	.211	.231	13	32	3	7	1	0	0	1	2	1	2	0	4	0	0	.250	.286
Harris, Brendan	R-R	6-1	200	8-26-80	.333	.500	.286	4	9	1	3	1	0	1	3	0	1	0	0	0	0	0	.778	.400
Johnson, Nick	L-L	6-3	225	9-19-78	.289	.328	.274	131	453	66	131	35	3	15	74	80	12	0	2	87	3	8	.479	.408
Kelly, Kenny	R-R	6-2	190	1-26-79	.250	.333	.000	17	4	3	1	1	0	0	0	1	0	0	0	3	1	1	.500	.400
2-team (7 Cincinnati)					.308	.333	.250	24	13	5	4	1	0	0	2	1	0	0	0	6	1	2	.385	.357
Mateo, Henry	B-R	6-0	175	10-14-76	.000	.000	.000	1	1	0	0	0	0	0	0	1	0	0	0	0	0	0	.000	.500
Osik, Keith	R-R	6-0	200	10-22-68	.000	.000	.000	6	4	0	0	0	0	0	0	0	0	0	0	2	0	0	.000	.000
Schneider, Brian	L-R	6-1	195	11-26-76	.268	.265	.269	116	369	38	99	20	1	10	44	29	6	2	2	48	1	0	.409	.330
Short, Rick	R-R	6-0	200	12-6-72	.400	1.000	.308	11	15	4	6	2	0	2	4	1	1	0	0	1	0	0	.933	.471
Sledge, Terrmel	L-L	6-0	185	3-18-77	.243	.000	.250	20	37	7	9	0	1	1	8	7	0	0	2	8	2	1	.378	.348
Spivey, Junior	R-R	6-0	200	1-28-75	.221	.304	.185	28	77	15	17	7	0	2	7	11	2	0	1	26	2	0	.390	.330
2-team (49 Milwaukee)					.232	.306	.203	77	259	37	60	15	1	7	24	29	3	1	1	83	9	3	.378	.315
Vidro, Jose	B-R	5-11	195	8-27-74	.275	.258	.280	87	309	38	85	21	2	7	32	31	1	2	4	30	0	0	.424	.339
Watson, Brandon	L-R	6-1	170	9-30-81	.175	.091	.207	25	40	8	7	1	1	1	5	4	0	4	0	8	0	2	.325	.250
Wilkerson, Brad	L-L	6-0	205	6-1-77	.248	.296	.228	148	565	76	140	42	7	11	57	84	7	3	2	147	8	10	.405	.351
Wilson, Preston	R-R	6-2	215	7-19-74	.261	.227	.268	68	253	34	66	14	1	10	43	20	6	0	1	71	3	4	.443	.329
2-team (71 Colorado)					.260	.262	.259	139	520	73	135	29	2	25	90	45	7	1	3	148	6	6	.467	.325
Zimmerman, Ryan	R-R	6-3	220	9-28-84	.397	.400	.395	20	58	6	23	10	0	0	6	3	0	0	1	12	0	0	.569	.419

PITCHING	B-T	HT	WT	DOB	W	L	ERA	G	GS	CG	SV	IP	H	R	ER	HR	BB	SO	AVG	vLH	vRH	K/9	BB/9
Armas, Tony	R-R	6-3	225	4-29-78	7	7	4.97	19	19	0	0	101	100	57	56	16	54	59	.258	.276	.241	5.24	4.80
Ayala, Luis	R-R	6-2	185	1-12-78	8	7	2.66	68	0	0	1	71	75	23	21	7	14	40	.286	.350	.230	5.07	1.77
Bergmann, Jason	R-R	6-4	205	9-25-81	2	0	2.75	15	1	0	0	20	14	6	6	1	11	21	.200	.355	.077	9.61	5.03
Carrasco, Hector	R-R	6-2	225	10-22-69	5	4	2.04	64	5	0	2	88	59	23	20	6	38	75	.193	.208	.178	7.64	3.87
Cordero, Chad	R-R	6-0	200	3-18-82	2	4	1.82	74	0	0	47	74	55	24	15	9	17	61	.198	.192	.205	7.39	2.06
Day, Zach	R-R	6-4	215	6-15-78	1	2	6.75	12	5	0	0	36	41	29	27	4	25	16	.289	.320	.254	4.00	6.25
Drese, Ryan	R-R	6-3	235	4-5-76	3	6	4.98	11	11	0	0	60	66	38	33	3	22	26	.283	.286	.281	3.92	3.32
Eischen, Joey	L-L	6-0	215	5-25-70	2	1	3.22	57	0	0	0	36	34	14	13	1	19	30	.252	.250	.254	7.43	4.71
Halama, John	L-L	6-5	210	2-22-72	0	3	4.64	10	3	0	0	21	23	11	11	1	8	11	.277	.333	.258	4.64	3.38
Hernandez, Livan	R-R	6-2	245	2-20-75	15	10	3.98	35	35	2	0	246	268	116	109	25	84	147	.284	.290	.278	5.37	3.07
Horgan, Joe	L-L	6-1	200	6-7-77	0	0	21.00	8	0	0	0	6	19	15	14	0	4	5	.514	.231	.667	7.50	6.00
Hughes, Travis	R-R	6-5	235	5-25-78	1	1	5.54	14	0	0	0	13	18	8	8	4	8	8	.333	.313	.342	5.54	5.54
Kim, Sunny	R-R	6-1	185	9-4-77	1	2	6.14	12	2	0	0	29	41	20	20	3	8	17	.336	.308	.357	5.22	2.45
Loaiza, Esteban	R-R	6-3	215	12-31-71	12	10	3.77	34	34	0	0	217	227	93	91	18	55	173	.270	.285	.255	7.18	2.28
Majewski, Gary	R-R	6-1	215	2-26-80	4	4	2.93	79	0	0	1	86	80	32	28	2	37	50	.248	.236	.259	5.23	3.87
Nitkowski, C.J.	L-L	6-3	210	3-9-73	0	0	8.10	7	0	0	0	3	5	3	3	0	2	2	.357	.571	.143	5.40	5.40
Ohka, Tomo	R-R	6-1	200	3-18-76	4	3	3.33	10	9	0	0	54	44	23	20	6	27	17	.224	.161	.282	2.83	4.50
Osuna, Antonio	R-R	5-10	225	4-12-73	0	0	42.43	4	0	0	0	2	9	11	11	2	7	0	.600	.000	.643	0.00	27.00
Patterson, John	R-R	6-5	210	1-30-78	9	7	3.13	31	31	2	0	198	172	71	69	19	65	185	.233	.231	.236	8.39	2.95
Rasner, Darrell	R-R	6-3	210	1-13-81	0	1	3.68	5	1	0	0	7	5	3	3	0	2	4	.192	.143	.250	4.91	2.45
Rauch, Jon	R-R	6-11	260	9-27-78	2	4	3.60	15	1	0	0	30	24	12	12	3	11	23	.218	.255	.186	6.90	3.30
Stanton, Mike	L-L	6-1	215	6-2-67	2	1	3.58	30	0	0	0	28	31	13	11	2	9	14	.292	.271	.310	4.55	2.93
Tucker, T.J.	R-R	6-3	265	8-20-78	1	0	6.39	13	0	0	0	13	20	9	9	4	2	5	.370	.364	.375	3.55	1.42
Vargas, Claudio	R-R	6-3	230	6-19-78	0	3	9.24	4	4	0	0	13	22	15	13	4	7	5	.373	.267	.483	3.55	4.97
White, Matt	R-L	6-1	180	8-19-77	0	1	9.00	1	1	0	0	4	4	4	4	0	3	3	.267	.000	.444	6.75	6.75

FIELDING

Catcher	PCT	G	PO	A	E	DP	PB
Bennett	.986	64	384	24	6	1	4
Osik	1.000	5	8	0	0	0	0
Schneider	.993	113	654	52	5	11	3

First Base	PCT	G	PO	A	E	DP
Baerga	.985	11	65	2	1	2
Blanco	.857	3	11	1	2	2
Cordero	1.000	12	66	2	0	5
Johnson	.996	129	1018	96	5	109
Short	1.000	1	4	1	0	0
Wilkerson	.995	25	172	14	1	20

Second Base	PCT	G	PO	A	E	DP
Baerga	.919	7	15	19	3	3
Carroll	.980	63	96	145	5	33
Cruz	1.000	16	27	25	0	10
Harris	1.000	2	2	5	0	1
Mateo	1.000	1	1	2	0	0
Short	.938	6	7	8	1	2
Spivey	1.000	22	34	62	0	14
Vidro	.985	79	134	192	5	39

Third Base	PCT	G	PO	A	E	DP
Baerga	.920	20	7	16	2	1
Blanco	1.000	5	0	3	0	0
Carroll	1.000	12	1	8	0	0

	PCT	G	PO	A	E	DP
Castilla	.970	138	142	209	11	23
Harris	1.000	1	1	4	0	0
Zimmerman	1.000	14	6	26	0	5

Shortstop	PCT	G	PO	A	E	DP
Carroll	1.000	41	53	65	0	19
Cruz	.944	8	4	13	1	2
Guzman	.973	142	216	327	15	85

	PCT	G	PO	A	E	DP
Zimmerman	.778	1	3	4	2	0

Outfield	PCT	G	PO	A	E	DP
Blanco	1.000	11	10	1	0	1
Byrd	.985	65	124	5	2	2
Cepicky	1.000	6	18	0	0	0
Chavez	1.000	6	4	0	0	0
Church	1.000	85	169	2	0	0
Davis	1.000	10	16	1	0	0
Guillen	.978	142	301	10	7	5
Hammonds	1.000	11	18	0	0	0
Kelly	.000	2	0	0	0	0
Sledge	1.000	13	21	1	0	0
Watson	.933	13	13	1	1	0
Wilkerson	.985	129	312	6	5	1
Wilson	1.000	68	149	3	0	0

FARM SYSTEM

General Manager: Jim Bowden. **Director, Player Development:** Adam Wogan. **Scouting Director:** Dana Brown.

Class	Farm Team	League	W	L	Pct.	Finish*	Manager	Affiliate Since
AAA	New Orleans (La.) Zephyrs	Pacific Coast	64	76	.457	14th (16)	Tim Foli	2005
AA	Harrisburg (Pa.) Senators	Eastern	64	78	.451	10th (12)	Keith Bodie	1991
Hi A	Potomac (Va.) Nationals	Carolina	63	77	.450	6th (8)	Bob Henley	2005
Lo A	Savannah (Ga.) Sand Gnats	South Atlantic	62	76	.449	12th (16)	Randy Knorr	2003
SS A	Vermont Expos (Burlington)	New York-Penn	28	48	.368	13th (14)	Bobby Williams	1994
Rookie	Melbourne (Fla.) Nationals	Gulf Coast	21	32	.396	12th (12)	Wendell Kim	1998

*Finish in overall standings (No. of teams in league)/Playoff teams in **boldface**

NEW ORLEANS ZEPHYRS — Class AAA

PACIFIC COAST LEAGUE

BATTING	B-T	HT	WT	DOB	AVG	vLH	vRH	G	AB	R	H	2B	3B	HR	RBI	BB	HBP	SH	SF	SO	SB	CS	SLG	OBP
Blanco, Tony	R-R	6-1	175	11-10-81	.281	.318	.262	16	64	7	18	4	0	2	14	2	0	0	2	13	1	0	.438	.294
Bowers, Jason	R-R	5-10	183	1-27-78	.237	.276	.221	118	333	29	79	12	2	2	38	39	7	15	4	55	9	3	.303	.326
Broadway, Larry	L-L	6-4	230	12-17-80	.193	.091	.217	18	57	4	11	3	0	0	5	7	0	0	0	17	2	0	.246	.281
Brown, Dee	L-R	6-0	225	3-27-78	.286	.250	.295	30	77	4	22	4	0	3	16	3	1	0	2	13	0	2	.455	.313
Byrd, Marlon	R-R	6-0	235	8-30-77	.407	.476	.383	21	81	19	33	6	0	5	11	9	2	0	0	7	4	1	.667	.478
Carroll, Wes	R-R	5-11	180	1-5-79	.242	.205	.258	70	132	10	32	6	0	2	10	5	0	3	1	23	2	1	.333	.268
Cepicky, Matt	L-R	6-2	215	11-10-77	.269	.276	.267	99	342	52	92	23	3	14	68	43	0	1	4	85	1	3	.477	.347
Chavez, Endy	L-L	5-10	155	2-7-78	.253	.263	.250	23	87	11	22	4	0	1	4	10	0	4	0	7	6	1	.333	.330
Davis, J.J.	R-R	6-5	250	10-25-78	.282	.282	.281	51	174	34	49	10	0	12	31	18	3	0	0	53	3	4	.546	.359
Dement, Dan	R-R	5-10	191	6-17-78	.313	.481	.259	56	112	21	35	7	3	0	8	13	1	3	1	32	3	0	.429	.386
Fitzpatrick, Reggie	L-L	5-11	180	2-28-83	.188	.250	.125	4	16	2	3	1	0	0	1	0	0	0	0	6	1	0	.250	.188
Godwin, Tyrell	L-R	6-0	200	7-10-79	.321	.315	.323	129	499	83	160	22	6	9	48	50	5	6	1	77	22	12	.443	.387
Gonzalez, Edgar	R-R	6-0	182	6-14-78	.354	.458	.250	23	48	12	17	4	0	0	4	1	0	1	0	10	0	0	.438	.367
Guerrero, Cristian	R-R	6-7	175	7-12-80	.250	.333	.200	4	16	4	4	0	0	1	2	2	0	0	0	5	0	2	.438	.333
Hammonds, Jeffrey	R-R	6-0	220	3-5-71	.250	.200	.267	19	60	10	15	5	1	2	9	7	2	0	1	5	1	0	.467	.343
Harris, Brendan	R-R	6-1	200	8-26-80	.270	.250	.277	127	470	67	127	22	4	13	81	40	3	2	4	77	9	5	.417	.329
Haynes, Dee	R-R	6-0	205	2-22-78	.263	.316	.211	9	38	9	10	3	0	2	7	3	0	0	0	4	1	0	.500	.317
2-team (2 Memphis)					.256	.316	.208	11	43	10	11	3	0	2	7	3	0	0	0	6	1	0	.465	.304
Hodges, Scott	L-R	6-0	190	12-26-78	.143	.250	.100	9	14	0	2	1	0	0	1	1	0	0	0	5	0	0	.214	.200
Johnson, Nick	L-L	6-3	225	9-19-78	.000	.000	.000	3	6	0	0	0	0	0	0	1	0	0	0	2	0	0	.000	.143
Kelly, Kenny	R-R	6-2	190	1-26-79	.232	.182	.265	20	82	11	19	3	1	0	6	9	0	0	0	15	3	2	.293	.308
Kuzmic, Craig	B-R	6-0	180	5-2-77	.262	.229	.273	54	145	19	38	7	0	6	22	20	3	2	4	39	1	0	.434	.355
Labandeira, Josh	R-R	5-7	180	2-25-79	.300	.667	.259	11	30	3	9	1	0	0	3	1	1	0	0	10	1	1	.333	.344
Mateo, Henry	B-R	6-0	175	10-14-76	.290	.125	.348	9	31	2	9	0	0	0	3	3	0	0	0	7	3	1	.290	.353
Melo, Juan	B-R	6-1	160	10-11-76	.318	.309	.322	84	311	44	99	17	3	10	56	20	4	2	2	38	2	4	.489	.365
Nieves, Melvin	B-R	6-2	210	12-28-71	.227	.174	.250	25	75	17	17	2	0	5	17	18	2	0	2	28	0	1	.453	.381
Orie, Kevin	R-R	6-5	220	9-1-72	.361	.367	.358	52	169	35	61	17	1	8	40	26	1	0	0	23	0	0	.615	.449
2-team (61 Nashville)					.352	.350	.354	113	349	67	123	35	1	20	89	57	4	0	3	43	4	1	.630	.446
Ortiz, Hector	R-R	6-0	200	10-14-69	.248	.203	.267	74	254	13	63	6	0	1	28	13	1	3	1	33	0	1	.283	.286
Osik, Keith	R-R	6-0	200	10-22-68	.205	.231	.194	17	44	3	9	2	0	0	3	4	0	1	1	7	1	0	.250	.265
Short, Rick	R-R	6-0	200	12-6-72	.383	.358	.391	108	376	72	144	35	1	11	70	46	7	1	3	27	5	4	.569	.456
Watson, Brandon	L-R	6-1	170	9-30-81	.355	.322	.370	88	372	69	132	15	3	1	25	28	1	5	2	33	31	13	.419	.400
Wilson, John	R-R	6-1	205	9-29-78	.212	.200	.216	25	66	8	14	6	0	0	4	9	1	1	1	9	0	3	.303	.312

PITCHING	B-T	HT	WT	DOB	W	L	ERA	G	GS	CG	SV	IP	H	R	ER	HR	BB	SO	AVG	vLH	vRH	K/9	BB/9
Armas, Tony	R-R	6-3	225	4-29-78	1	2	4.38	5	5	0	0	25	26	13	12	3	10	21	.268	.357	.200	7.66	3.65
Bergmann, Jason	R-R	6-4	205	9-25-81	3	2	3.16	20	0	0	2	37	26	15	13	5	13	39	.203	.283	.159	9.49	3.16
Bouknight, Kip	R-R	6-0	190	11-16-78	3	2	3.42	9	8	0	0	53	52	22	20	9	18	34	.261	.272	.252	5.81	3.08
Bowers, Jason	R-R	5-10	183	1-27-78	0	0	2.45	3	0	0	0	4	2	1	1	1	1	1	.154	.200	.125	2.45	2.45
Bray, Bill	L-L	6-3	215	6-5-83	1	4	5.06	23	0	0	2	21	23	16	12	3	9	25	.271	.242	.288	10.55	3.80
Bridges, Donnie	R-R	6-4	220	12-10-78	2	6	5.68	13	12	0	0	63	72	46	40	9	42	52	.283	.313	.259	7.39	5.97
Carrasco, Hector	R-R	6-2	225	10-22-69	1	0	0.00	6	0	0	4	8	4	1	0	0	2	10	.143	.100	.167	11.25	2.25
Corcoran, Roy	R-R	5-10	170	5-11-80	4	4	4.85	52	1	0	3	69	67	51	37	7	36	55	.251	.287	.226	7.21	4.72
Dement, Dan	R-R	5-10	191	6-17-78	0	0	5.40	2	0	0	0	2	2	1	1	0	1	0	.286	.000	.500	0.00	5.40
DiFelice, Mark	R-R	6-2	190	8-23-76	1	2	8.40	14	2	0	0	30	39	35	28	10	13	21	.312	.431	.230	6.30	3.90
Durbin, Chad	B-R	6-2	200	12-3-77	4	5	5.77	26	20	0	0	115	121	78	74	24	48	99	.271	.289	.257	7.73	3.75
Eischen, Joey	L-L	6-0	215	5-25-70	0	0	1.35	6	4	0	0	7	4	1	1	0	3	6	.167	.000	.250	8.10	4.05
Gil, David	R-R	6-4	215	10-1-78	1	3	3.55	15	2	0	0	38	34	18	15	4	12	29	.239	.228	.247	6.87	2.84
Halama, John	L-L	6-5	210	2-22-72	1	0	1.13	2	2	0	0	8	6	2	1	0	0	1	.194	.167	.200	1.13	0.00
Horgan, Joe	L-L	6-1	200	6-7-77	4	3	4.12	46	2	0	3	63	68	35	29	9	30	48	.278	.304	.265	6.82	4.26
Hughes, Travis	R-R	6-5	235	5-25-78	2	5	3.02	52	0	0	13	60	47	25	20	3	25	73	.214	.202	.223	11.01	3.77
Karp, Josh	R-R	6-5	210	9-21-79	3	1	5.75	21	1	0	0	36	37	26	23	8	14	29	.272	.309	.247	7.25	3.50
Kim, Sunny	R-R	6-1	185	9-4-77	4	2	2.76	9	9	0	0	49	46	23	15	4	15	38	.249	.253	.245	6.98	2.76
Majewski, Gary	R-R	6-1	215	2-26-80	0	0	4.26	3	0	0	0	6	7	3	3	0	2	2	.292	.000	.438	2.84	2.84
Nitkowski, C.J.	L-L	6-3	210	3-9-73	2	2	3.62	27	0	0	4	32	36	15	13	3	7	24	.288	.243	.307	6.68	1.95
Osuna, Antonio	R-R	5-10	225	4-12-73	0	0	0.00	2	0	0	0	3	1	0	0	0	0	1	.100	.000	.167	3.00	0.00

PITCHING	B-T	HT	WT	DOB	W	L	ERA	G	GS	CG	SV	IP	H	R	ER	HR	BB	SO	AVG	vLH	vRH	K/9	BB/9
Powell, Brian	R-R	6-2	200	10-10-73	7	13	5.82	29	26	1	0	158	204	114	102	18	42	77	.317	.300	.331	4.40	2.40
Randolph, Stephen	L-L	6-3	200	5-1-74	2	2	9.62	14	4	0	0	29	26	32	31	8	31	34	.243	.241	.244	10.55	9.62
2-team (22 Fresno)					3	3	6.03	36	6	0	0	69	49	50	46	12	66	84	.202	.190	.208	11.01	8.65
Rauch, Jon	R-R	6-11	260	9-27-78	1	1	2.53	7	5	0	0	21	19	7	6	3	2	25	.232	.250	.220	10.55	0.84
Schroder, Chris	R-R	6-3	210	8-20-78	2	0	7.83	19	0	0	4	23	21	21	20	6	15	29	.239	.214	.261	11.35	5.87
Smith, Dan	R-R	6-3	230	9-15-75	1	3	10.73	24	0	0	1	26	47	32	31	7	18	13	.385	.340	.413	4.50	6.23
Tucker, T.J.	R-R	6-3	265	8-20-78	0	0	0.00	2	2	0	0	4	2	0	0	0	0	2	.154	.250	.000	4.50	0.00
Vargas, Claudio	R-R	6-3	230	6-19-78	2	2	4.18	5	5	0	0	28	24	13	13	4	12	35	.231	.205	.246	11.25	3.86
White, Matt	R-L	6-1	180	8-19-77	8	6	3.72	35	16	0	0	126	122	62	52	7	45	102	.254	.289	.242	7.31	3.22
Yarnall, Ed	L-L	6-3	235	12-4-75	4	6	5.59	19	14	0	0	77	87	49	48	12	33	81	.282	.271	.286	9.43	3.84

FIELDING

Catcher	PCT	G	PO	A	E	DP	PB
Kuzmic	.993	46	270	11	2	3	5
Ortiz	.997	73	561	25	2	7	6
Osik	1.000	14	70	5	0	1	0
Short	1.000	2	1	0	0	0	0
Wilson	.994	24	149	8	1	1	2

First Base	PCT	G	PO	A	E	DP
Broadway	.991	18	101	14	1	11
Carroll	1.000	4	8	0	0	1
Cepicky	.965	36	232	15	9	23
Davis	.929	1	11	2	1	0
Dement	1.000	1	12	1	0	2
Haynes	.909	2	10	0	1	1
Johnson	1.000	3	10	3	0	2
Kuzmic	1.000	5	24	3	0	1
Melo	.993	22	135	15	1	17
Nieves	1.000	1	4	0	0	0
Orie	.993	36	244	24	2	28
Osik	.000	1	0	0	0	0
Short	.991	47	288	38	3	34

Second Base	PCT	G	PO	A	E	DP
Bowers	.000	2	0	0	0	0
Carroll	.982	15	31	25	1	8
Cepicky	.000	1	0	0	0	0
Dement	.974	14	17	21	1	2
Gonzalez	.909	2	5	5	1	2
Harris	.988	85	170	234	5	66
Mateo	1.000	8	19	14	0	3
Melo	.929	4	7	6	1	4
Short	.983	30	50	63	2	13

Third Base	PCT	G	PO	A	E	DP
Blanco	.909	15	14	36	5	1
Bowers	1.000	4	2	6	0	0
Carroll	.949	14	11	26	2	6
Cepicky	.000	1	0	0	0	0
Dement	.875	7	2	5	1	0
Gonzalez	.966	15	10	18	1	3
Harris	.919	44	29	84	10	12
Hodges	1.000	3	0	9	0	2
Kuzmic	.000	1	0	0	0	0
Melo	.945	28	20	32	3	7
Orie	.935	12	7	22	2	1
Short	.913	26	8	55	6	3

Shortstop	PCT	G	PO	A	E	DP
Bowers	.974	111	132	248	10	54
Carroll	.909	8	2	8	1	3
Dement	.000	1	0	0	0	0
Gonzalez	1.000	1	0	1	0	0
Labandeira	.949	9	14	23	2	8
Melo	.959	44	53	89	6	19

Outfield	PCT	G	PO	A	E	DP
Blanco	.000	1	0	0	0	0
Brown	1.000	16	32	0	0	0
Byrd	1.000	19	40	1	0	1
Carroll	1.000	3	1	0	0	0
Cepicky	.989	51	88	0	1	0
Chavez	.983	23	54	4	1	1
Davis	.958	41	66	3	3	0
Dement	1.000	12	14	2	0	0
Fitzpatrick	1.000	4	9	0	0	0
Godwin	.959	122	225	8	10	1
Gonzalez	.000	1	0	0	0	0
Guerrero	1.000	4	7	0	0	0
Hammonds	1.000	16	21	0	0	0
Harris	1.000	1	1	0	0	0
Haynes	.938	7	13	2	1	1
Kelly	.974	19	35	2	1	0
Nieves	1.000	17	27	0	0	0
Short	1.000	4	9	0	0	0
Watson	.986	87	197	8	3	2

HARRISBURG SENATORS — Class AA

EASTERN LEAGUE

BATTING	B-T	HT	WT	DOB	AVG	vLH	vRH	G	AB	R	H	2B	3B	HR	RBI	BB	HBP	SH	SF	SO	SB	CS	SLG	OBP
Belcher, Jason	L-R	6-1	217	1-13-82	.122	.143	.118	14	41	2	5	1	0	1	4	2	1	0	1	8	0	0	.220	.178
Broadway, Larry	L-L	6-4	230	12-17-80	.269	.277	.264	52	186	29	50	14	0	12	24	17	1	0	3	37	0	0	.538	.329
Brown, Dee	L-R	6-0	225	3-27-78	.194	.270	.168	43	144	16	28	7	0	5	16	11	6	0	2	33	2	4	.347	.276
2-team (13 Trenton)					.174	.234	.155	56	195	20	34	8	0	7	22	16	7	0	2	50	2	4	.323	.259
Castro, Ramon	R-R	6-0	195	10-23-79	.285	.333	.264	34	130	27	37	9	2	9	30	14	0	1	1	22	1	1	.592	.352
Church, Ryan	L-L	6-1	190	10-14-78	.278	.250	.286	4	18	2	5	1	0	0	0	0	0	0	0	5	0	0	.333	.278
Cordero, Wil	R-R	6-2	230	10-3-71	.500	.000	.500	2	8	0	4	2	0	0	1	0	0	0	0	1	0	0	.750	.500
Dement, Dan	R-R	5-10	191	6-17-78	.328	.329	.328	71	268	42	88	23	1	14	44	22	2	2	4	65	2	0	.578	.378
Ditter, Brad	L-R	6-0	185	7-22-80	.273	.333	.250	3	11	0	3	1	0	0	1	1	0	0	0	6	0	0	.364	.333
Dorta, Melvin	R-R	5-11	160	1-15-82	.252	.231	.263	121	408	56	103	16	0	11	50	35	3	11	3	46	22	13	.373	.314
Emmerick, Josh	R-R	6-4	190	2-22-81	.188	.175	.194	44	133	9	25	5	0	0	7	17	3	1	0	51	1	0	.226	.294
Feliciano, Jesus	L-L	6-0	174	6-6-79	.280	.330	.260	87	322	50	90	13	2	2	24	14	2	6	3	35	10	6	.351	.311
Gonzalez, Edgar	R-R	6-0	182	6-14-78	.279	.308	.269	101	340	41	95	25	3	8	50	42	5	2	6	75	5	7	.441	.361
Guerrero, Cristian	R-R	6-7	175	7-12-80	.267	.235	.281	112	329	45	88	12	2	16	56	24	4	1	0	106	14	5	.462	.325
Hammonds, Jeffrey	R-R	6-0	220	3-5-71	.167	.250	.000	2	6	1	1	1	0	0	1	1	1	0	0	1	0	0	.333	.375
Haynes, Dee	R-R	6-0	205	2-22-78	.274	.245	.285	101	376	63	103	18	3	21	63	21	6	0	2	54	0	1	.505	.321
Hodges, Scott	L-R	6-0	190	12-26-78	.132	.200	.121	11	38	3	5	0	0	0	3	1	2	0	2	5	0	0	.132	.186
Kelly, Kenny	R-R	6-2	190	1-26-79	.213	.105	.286	12	47	5	10	3	1	2	6	5	0	0	0	10	2	1	.447	.288
Kuzmic, Craig	B-R	6-0	180	5-2-77	.236	.293	.215	42	148	19	35	6	3	6	32	31	1	1	3	50	1	3	.439	.366
Labandeira, Josh	R-R	5-7	180	2-25-79	.269	.250	.276	61	212	32	57	16	0	1	19	33	5	1	0	36	6	4	.358	.380
Lane, Richard	L-L	6-3	205	1-4-80	.227	.195	.241	37	128	18	29	6	2	1	9	23	2	0	1	24	0	2	.328	.351
Lorenzo, Juan	B-R	6-0	189	11-10-78	.185	.238	.152	17	54	7	10	0	1	1	5	4	1	1	1	11	0	0	.278	.250
Martin, Billy	R-R	6-2	225	6-10-76	.227	.333	.188	7	22	4	5	2	0	0	1	2	0	0	0	9	0	0	.318	.292
Mateo, Henry	B-R	6-0	175	10-14-76	.164	.281	.122	32	122	13	20	5	1	0	6	16	0	2	0	27	11	5	.221	.261
McMillan, Drew	R-R	6-3	205	10-25-80	.259	.267	.256	20	54	4	14	1	1	1	7	5	0	1	1	15	0	0	.370	.317
Mercedes, Victor	B-R	5-11	184	4-15-79	.206	.280	.163	29	68	6	14	4	0	0	1	4	0	1	0	16	2	0	.265	.250
2-team (12 Altoona)					.252	.281	.241	41	111	13	28	6	1	2	7	6	0	1	0	21	2	0	.378	.291
Nettles, Marcus	L-L	5-11	185	5-15-80	.133	.000	.182	7	15	0	2	0	0	0	1	1	0	2	0	7	1	0	.133	.188
Nieves, Melvin	B-R	6-2	210	12-28-71	.260	.364	.218	23	77	14	20	5	0	4	16	18	2	0	0	28	1	2	.481	.412
Norris, Shawn	L-R	6-2	170	8-1-80	.233	.227	.235	84	283	30	66	10	0	5	27	26	2	5	4	68	0	4	.322	.298
Parker, Clark	L-R	5-8	160	9-26-75	.000	.000	.000	4	7	0	0	0	0	0	0	0	0	0	0	5	0	0	.000	.000
Rooi, Vince	R-R	6-1	195	12-13-81	.316	.500	.267	5	19	0	6	3	1	0	1	1	0	0	0	6	0	0	.579	.350
Vroman, Doug	R-R	6-2	200	2-9-81	.000	.000	.000	3	9	0	0	0	0	0	0	2	1	0	0	4	0	0	.000	.250
Watson, Brandon	L-R	6-1	170	9-30-81	.247	.239	.250	34	146	13	36	1	0	0	6	7	2	1	0	21	7	5	.253	.290
Wilson, John	R-R	6-1	205	9-29-78	.267	.172	.297	75	240	30	64	9	0	5	31	19	5	6	2	23	1	2	.367	.331
Zimmerman, Ryan	R-R	6-3	220	9-28-84	.326	.361	.311	63	233	40	76	20	0	9	32	15	2	1	1	34	1	5	.528	.371

PITCHING	B-T	HT	WT	DOB	W	L	ERA	G	GS	CG	SV	IP	H	R	ER	HR	BB	SO	AVG	vLH	vRH	K/9	BB/9
Bergmann, Jason	R-R	6-4	205	9-25-81	2	0	1.22	21	0	0	5	37	27	7	5	3	16	37	.201	.237	.173	9.00	3.89
Bouknight, Kip	R-R	6-0	190	11-16-78	4	4	4.01	20	13	0	0	90	92	46	40	10	32	60	.267	.327	.214	6.02	3.21
Bowie, Micah	L-L	6-4	205	11-10-74	1	1	4.41	10	0	0	1	16	16	8	8	1	3	19	.254	.364	.195	10.47	1.65
Bray, Bill	L-L	6-3	215	6-5-83	1	0	6.35	3	0	0	1	6	10	4	4	1	1	6	.385	.400	.381	9.53	1.59

PITCHING	B-T	HT	WT	DOB	W	L	ERA	G	GS	CG	SV	IP	H	R	ER	HR	BB	SO	AVG	vLH	vRH	K/9	BB/9
Bridges, Donnie	R-R	6-4	220	12-10-78	1	3	4.21	5	5	0	0	26	34	18	12	1	8	18	.306	.269	.339	6.31	2.81
Day, Zach	R-R	6-4	215	6-15-78	1	0	2.77	3	3	0	0	13	14	4	4	1	1	10	.286	.231	.348	6.92	0.69
Echols, Justin	R-R	6-3	200	10-6-80	9	7	5.20	31	17	0	0	116	138	78	67	21	40	120	.286	.299	.276	9.31	3.10
Ferrari, Anthony	L-L	5-9	165	6-22-78	0	0	3.38	1	0	0	0	3	3	1	1	0	1	3	.333	.000	.500	10.13	3.38
Galarraga, Armando	R-R	6-3	170	1-15-82	3	4	5.19	13	13	1	0	76	80	47	44	10	21	58	.275	.291	.260	6.84	2.48
Gil, David	R-R	6-4	215	10-1-78	1	1	3.03	14	2	0	1	33	28	12	11	2	9	29	.237	.152	.292	7.99	2.48
Gonzalez, Somer	R-R	5-11	190	7-23-79	0	0	0.00	1	0	0	0	3	1	0	0	0	1	2	.100	.200	.000	6.00	3.00
Karp, Josh	R-R	6-5	210	9-21-79	2	5	4.68	11	10	0	0	58	57	32	30	6	23	40	.259	.266	.254	6.24	3.59
Maust, David	L-L	6-2	205	11-6-78	5	4	2.32	26	14	2	0	101	79	31	26	7	14	78	.221	.265	.204	6.97	1.25
Norderum, Jason	L-L	6-3	220	11-21-81	3	3	4.60	25	0	0	2	47	49	31	24	3	25	33	.272	.276	.270	6.32	4.79
Ogiltree, John	R-R	6-6	220	6-3-78	1	0	2.45	5	0	0	0	7	6	2	2	0	2	5	.214	.286	.190	6.14	2.45
2-team (2 New Hampshire)					1	0	1.93	7	0	0	0	9	7	2	2	0	3	6	.200	.250	.185	5.79	2.89
Rasner, Darrell	R-R	6-3	210	1-13-81	6	7	3.59	27	26	1	0	150	150	66	60	10	29	96	.260	.256	.264	5.75	1.74
Rivera, Saul	R-R	5-11	155	12-7-77	3	3	2.47	40	0	0	9	77	72	30	21	3	20	70	.243	.246	.241	8.22	2.35
Rueckel, Danny	R-R	6-0	175	9-25-79	9	6	4.16	53	0	0	7	80	86	41	37	7	21	72	.278	.266	.287	8.10	2.36
Rundles, Richard	L-L	6-5	180	6-3-81	6	13	4.18	27	26	2	0	159	177	95	74	14	49	91	.280	.295	.276	5.14	2.77
Schroder, Chris	R-R	6-3	210	8-20-78	2	3	4.70	16	0	0	0	23	20	13	12	4	11	28	.238	.250	.229	10.96	4.30
Sequea, Jacobo	R-R	6-1	220	8-31-81	1	1	6.68	20	0	0	2	34	52	27	25	11	13	19	.361	.319	.403	5.08	3.48
Stevenson, Jason	L-L	6-1	175	8-8-81	1	9	10.57	13	12	0	0	54	80	65	63	15	32	37	.354	.346	.356	6.20	5.37
Sylvester, Billy	R-R	6-5	210	10-1-76	2	4	4.35	26	1	0	0	41	40	20	20	8	29	52	.255	.213	.293	11.32	6.31

FIELDING

Catcher	PCT	G	PO	A	E	DP	PB
Belcher	1.000	1	6	2	0	1	0
Emmerick	.984	44	275	24	5	2	7
Kuzmic	.976	24	153	8	4	1	3
McMillan	.992	18	112	14	1	2	1
Wilson	.988	69	433	47	6	8	4

First Base	PCT	G	PO	A	E	DP
Broadway	.992	48	369	20	3	36
Dement	.996	27	211	20	1	14
Dorta	.989	11	88	5	1	10
Gonzalez	.941	2	15	1	1	2
Hodges	1.000	10	90	6	0	10
Kuzmic	1.000	7	44	3	0	5
Lane	1.000	31	276	27	0	29
Martin	1.000	6	50	2	0	8
Wilson	.974	9	69	7	2	4

Second Base	PCT	G	PO	A	E	DP
Castro	.750	1	1	2	1	0
Dement	1.000	12	21	41	0	9
Ditter	1.000	1	1	1	0	1
Dorta	.987	18	32	43	1	7
Gonzalez	.956	66	122	206	15	47
Kuzmic	1.000	1	1	2	0	1
Labandeira	1.000	1	0	3	0	0
Lorenzo	.000	1	0	0	0	0
Mateo	.972	28	55	82	4	15
Mercedes	.964	17	33	48	3	13
Norris	1.000	7	16	13	0	5
Parker	1.000	2	1	2	0	1

Third Base	PCT	G	PO	A	E	DP
Dement	1.000	1	3	0	0	1
Dorta	1.000	5	2	8	0	1
Gonzalez	.938	12	7	23	2	1
Labandeira	1.000	7	4	11	0	1
Mercedes	.500	2	0	1	1	0
Norris	.910	65	54	137	19	18
Rooi	1.000	5	2	9	0	1
Zimmerman	.961	55	45	101	6	6

Shortstop	PCT	G	PO	A	E	DP
Castro	.960	32	56	89	6	23
Dorta	.958	32	43	70	5	19
Labandeira	.959	52	82	129	9	31
Lorenzo	.917	14	10	34	4	10
Mercedes	.909	1	2	8	1	2
Norris	.975	9	11	28	1	4
Zimmerman	.879	8	12	17	4	3

Outfield	PCT	G	PO	A	E	DP
Belcher	.833	6	5	0	1	0
Brown	.947	28	35	1	2	0
Church	1.000	4	8	0	0	0
Dement	1.000	34	54	1	0	0
Dorta	.980	49	94	5	2	0
Feliciano	.989	85	175	3	2	0
Gonzalez	1.000	2	1	0	0	0
Guerrero	.980	95	191	9	4	5
Hammonds	.000	1	0	0	0	0
Haynes	.993	77	133	4	1	0
Kelly	.939	12	29	2	2	1
Kuzmic	1.000	3	6	0	0	0
Lane	1.000	5	6	1	0	0
Martin	.000	1	0	0	0	0
Nettles	1.000	6	14	0	0	0
Nieves	1.000	20	37	1	0	0
Vroman	1.000	2	3	1	0	0
Watson	.973	32	69	2	2	0

POTOMAC CANNONS — High Class A

CAROLINA LEAGUE

BATTING	B-T	HT	WT	DOB	AVG	vLH	vRH	G	AB	R	H	2B	3B	HR	RBI	BB	HBP	SH	SF	SO	SB	CS	SLG	OBP
Belcher, Jason	L-R	6-1	217	1-13-82	.250	.195	.267	55	176	21	44	8	0	5	20	17	2	2	3	30	0	1	.381	.318
Brooks, Doc	R-R	5-10	190	1-21-80	.240	.230	.243	118	412	59	99	18	1	10	43	39	12	4	2	127	8	4	.362	.323
Bynum, Seth	R-R	6-0	185	12-19-80	.179	.133	.204	35	84	16	15	4	1	1	6	5	2	0	2	20	2	2	.286	.237
Casto, Kory	L-R	6-1	190	12-8-81	.290	.291	.291	135	500	86	145	36	4	22	90	84	5	0	5	98	6	3	.510	.394
Castro, Ramon	R-R	6-0	195	10-23-79	.212	.308	.150	10	33	6	7	1	1	1	5	5	1	1	0	7	1	1	.394	.333
Chavez, Ender	L-L	5-11	155	3-9-81	.251	.259	.247	112	371	54	93	11	4	2	28	39	2	9	0	64	13	10	.318	.325
Chop, Chad	L-L	6-4	210	3-21-80	.260	.215	.279	115	411	36	107	26	2	3	52	22	6	3	6	55	1	4	.355	.303
Cordero, Wil	R-R	6-2	230	10-3-71	.429	.000	.500	2	7	2	3	1	0	2	2	1	0	0	0	0	0	0	1.429	.500
Desmond, Ian	R-R	6-2	185	9-20-85	.256	.195	.289	55	219	37	56	13	3	3	15	21	2	5	1	53	13	6	.384	.325
Diaz, Frank	R-R	6-2	180	10-6-83	.312	.332	.306	134	554	85	173	45	5	16	74	20	7	1	3	67	14	9	.498	.342
Emmerick, Josh	R-R	6-4	190	2-22-81	.372	.571	.276	13	43	9	16	4	0	0	2	6	1	0	0	9	1	0	.465	.460
Lane, Andrew	R-R	6-0	185	12-25-81	.000	.000	.000	1	2	1	0	0	0	0	1	1	0	1	0	0	0	0	.000	.333
Manriquez, Salomon	R-R	6-1	190	9-15-82	.287	.331	.261	119	443	64	127	36	2	15	68	30	5	2	4	86	0	0	.479	.336
Martin, Billy	R-R	6-2	225	6-10-76	.375	.286	.444	5	16	3	6	2	0	1	4	3	1	0	1	6	0	0	.688	.476
Mateo, Henry	B-R	6-0	175	10-14-76	.280	.333	.290	13	50	13	14	5	1	3	9	3	3	2	0	10	2	0	.600	.357
Mercedes, Victor	B-R	5-11	184	4-15-79	.133	.176	.077	10	30	0	4	2	0	0	0	0	0	0	0	6	0	0	.200	.133
2-team (13 Lynchburg)					.217	.243	.196	23	83	10	18	4	1	1	6	5	1	1	0	21	3	1	.325	.270
Norris, Shawn	L-R	6-2	170	8-1-80	.275	.275	.276	39	138	23	38	10	0	5	19	32	1	0	1	27	1	0	.457	.413
Poppert, John	R-R	6-0	185	4-14-82	.000	.000	.000	2	8	0	0	0	0	0	0	0	0	0	0	1	0	0	.000	.000
Rodriguez, Javier	R-R	5-11	180	1-16-79	.283	.276	.286	28	92	9	26	3	1	0	7	9	2	1	0	12	8	2	.337	.359
Rodriguez, Robert	R-R	5-10	180	12-17-80	.153	.211	.146	28	72	5	11	1	0	0	9	3	1	1	0	27	0	0	.167	.197
Rooi, Vince	R-R	6-1	195	12-13-81	.300	.290	.318	63	220	32	66	14	0	7	38	25	2	1	1	60	1	0	.459	.375
San Pedro, Erick	R-R	6-0	205	10-5-83	.105	.111	.100	7	19	1	2	0	0	0	0	5	0	0	0	5	0	0	.105	.292
Thissen, Greg	R-R	6-4	185	6-1-81	.227	.265	.211	77	273	32	62	15	1	7	34	24	3	5	2	64	2	4	.366	.295
Vidro, Jose	B-R	5-11	195	8-27-74	.154	.222	.000	5	13	3	2	1	0	0	3	4	0	0	0	2	0	0	.231	.353
Whitesell, Josh	L-L	6-3	220	4-14-82	.293	.290	.296	113	389	59	114	32	2	18	66	74	9	1	1	125	1	1	.524	.416
Yepez, Marcos	B-R	5-10	160	12-29-81	.270	.218	.290	51	159	17	43	6	3	1	16	17	1	5	0	51	8	4	.365	.345

PITCHING	B-T	HT	WT	DOB	W	L	ERA	G	GS	CG	SV	IP	H	R	ER	HR	BB	SO	AVG	vLH	vRH	K/9	BB/9
Bray, Bill	L-L	6-3	215	6-5-83	1	0	2.13	8	0	0	3	13	8	3	3	1	3	18	.170	.133	.208	12.79	2.13
Bunn, Greg	R-R	6-1	210	2-3-83	2	6	7.16	13	13	0	0	60	72	52	48	8	45	65	.299	.322	.276	9.70	6.71
Campbell, Brett	R-R	6-0	170	10-17-81	0	2	9.60	12	0	0	1	15	21	18	16	3	10	13	.328	.259	.378	7.80	6.00
Ferrari, Anthony	L-L	5-9	165	6-22-78	0	0	1.86	9	0	0	0	10	8	2	2	0	6	8	.242	.200	.278	7.45	5.59

PITCHING	B-T	HT	WT	DOB	W	L	ERA	G	GS	CG	SV	IP	H	R	ER	HR	BB	SO	AVG	vLH	vRH	K/9	BB/9
France, Ryan	L-R	6-2	195	3-25-80	0	0	9.64	3	0	0	0	5	5	5	5	0	4	3	.278	.429	.182	5.79	7.71
Galarraga, Armando	R-R	6-3	170	1-15-82	3	4	2.48	14	14	0	0	80	69	30	22	7	23	79	.228	.255	.205	8.89	2.59
Goodman, Chris	B-R	6-1	180	11-9-81	1	0	2.70	10	0	0	0	17	17	5	5	0	3	6	.288	.290	.286	3.24	1.62
Hinckley, Michael	R-L	6-3	170	10-5-82	3	9	4.93	22	21	1	0	128	151	90	70	10	51	80	.293	.279	.298	5.64	3.60
Kobow, Michael	R-R	6-4	190	4-9-79	0	0	5.11	7	0	0	1	12	16	7	7	1	4	5	.320	.462	.270	3.65	2.92
Kolb, Dan	R-R	6-1	190	6-5-80	4	3	5.62	43	1	0	3	74	71	48	46	13	27	69	.255	.184	.297	8.43	3.30
Lira, Oscar	R-R	6-3	185	7-17-82	0	0	5.40	3	0	0	0	5	5	3	3	2	3	2	.263	.143	.333	3.60	5.40
Martinez, Samuel	R-R	6-2	165	3-22-79	3	2	7.03	14	7	0	0	49	55	44	38	8	39	34	.294	.388	.242	6.29	7.21
Maust, David	L-L	6-2	205	11-6-78	1	0	6.64	9	0	0	0	20	27	15	15	2	13	18	.346	.387	.319	7.97	5.75
Morales, Alexis	R-R	5-11	170	12-8-82	2	2	3.72	23	0	0	3	36	25	15	15	4	26	47	.194	.184	.210	11.64	6.44
Norderum, Jason	L-L	6-3	220	11-21-81	1	2	4.37	13	0	0	1	23	31	13	11	0	13	13	.341	.343	.339	5.16	5.16
O'Connor, Michael	L-L	6-3	170	8-17-80	10	11	3.54	26	26	2	0	168	144	73	66	14	48	158	.229	.253	.220	8.48	2.58
Ogiltree, John	R-R	6-6	220	6-3-78	5	3	6.57	27	0	0	2	25	27	19	18	2	14	8	.276	.300	.265	2.92	5.11
Pearson, Anthony	R-R	6-3	190	8-14-81	3	0	3.86	12	0	0	0	28	24	15	12	1	17	25	.226	.286	.197	8.04	5.46
Perrin, Devin	R-R	6-7	225	5-14-81	3	7	4.99	28	14	0	3	92	96	54	51	7	58	66	.275	.239	.300	6.46	5.67
Price, Brett	L-L	5-10	177	12-7-79	10	13	4.44	28	28	2	0	144	122	83	71	20	81	150	.230	.218	.234	9.38	5.06
Quintero, Mayque	R-R	6-2	225	4-19-78	2	2	4.67	32	3	0	2	69	71	40	36	12	23	67	.260	.288	.243	8.70	2.99
Reid, Brett	R-R	5-11	200	10-18-79	4	6	2.76	28	0	0	2	42	38	15	13	3	23	43	.248	.232	.247	9.14	4.89
Schroder, Chris	R-R	6-3	210	8-20-78	0	0	0.00	5	0	0	1	7	7	3	0	0	2	10	.250	.250	.250	12.86	2.57
Stevenson, Jason	L-L	6-1	175	8-8-81	5	5	4.23	15	13	2	0	83	93	44	39	10	21	61	.287	.277	.291	6.61	2.28

FIELDING

Catcher	PCT	G	PO	A	E	DP	PB
Belcher	.973	17	100	8	3	2	4
Emmerick	1.000	11	95	9	0	0	1
Manriquez	.992	87	656	51	6	7	15
Poppert	1.000	2	14	3	0	1	0
R. Rodriguez	.969	27	142	13	5	0	3
San Pedro	.982	7	49	6	1	0	1

First Base	PCT	G	PO	A	E	DP
Belcher	1.000	1	2	0	0	0
Chop	.990	51	353	34	4	42
Martin	.979	5	45	1	1	6
Rooi	1.000	4	30	3	0	6
Thissen	1.000	2	2	0	0	0
Whitesell	.992	87	696	47	6	83

Second Base	PCT	G	PO	A	E	DP
Bynum	1.000	1	4	6	0	3
Casto	1.000	1	0	1	0	0
Mateo	.974	8	15	22	1	7
Mercedes	1.000	5	11	10	0	7
Norris	.983	34	76	93	3	26
J. Rodriguez	.932	13	14	27	3	9
Rooi	.981	11	13	38	1	8
Thissen	.968	72	134	170	10	50
Vidro	1.000	2	3	1	0	0
Yepez	.980	10	19	30	1	8

Third Base	PCT	G	PO	A	E	DP
Casto	.956	132	74	271	16	39
Lane	1.000	1	1	0	0	0
Rooi	1.000	6	3	8	0	0
Yepez	.857	3	2	4	1	1

Shortstop	PCT	G	PO	A	E	DP
Bynum	.910	28	34	57	9	19
Castro	.971	10	19	14	1	3
Desmond	.931	55	108	147	19	36
Norris	.923	4	2	10	1	0
J. Rodriguez	.897	14	19	33	6	5
Yepez	.966	37	51	117	6	19

Outfield	PCT	G	PO	A	E	DP
Belcher	1.000	19	17	0	0	0
Brooks	.966	111	164	6	6	0
Casto	.000	1	0	0	0	0
Chavez	.984	107	173	14	3	2
Chop	.982	64	103	4	2	1
Diaz	.977	134	285	17	7	4
Thissen	.867	8	12	1	2	0

SAVANNAH SANDGNATS — Low Class A

SOUTH ATLANTIC LEAGUE

BATTING	B-T	HT	WT	DOB	AVG	vLH	vRH	G	AB	R	H	2B	3B	HR	RBI	BB	HBP	SH	SF	SO	SB	CS	SLG	OBP
Apodaca, Luis	R-R	5-11	175	7-15-82	.214	.143	.238	7	28	4	6	1	0	0	1	0	0	0	0	6	0	0	.250	.214
Baez, Edgardo	R-R	6-2	190	7-12-85	.246	.250	.244	125	447	62	110	21	6	11	64	55	2	1	4	128	11	4	.394	.329
Bernadina, Rogearvin	L-L	6-0	175	6-12-84	.233	.190	.247	122	417	64	97	15	3	12	54	75	7	2	4	92	35	8	.369	.356
Bynum, Seth	R-R	6-0	185	12-19-80	.301	.339	.285	50	186	32	56	13	3	5	29	29	1	0	2	40	6	1	.484	.394
Castro, Ofilio	R-R	6-0	160	8-18-83	.261	.248	.260	113	403	43	105	24	1	5	43	47	1	2	3	91	6	3	.362	.337
Contreras, Jose	B-R	6-0	170	4-26-85	.179	.091	.214	13	39	5	7	1	0	0	1	6	0	0	1	14	3	0	.205	.283
Desmond, Ian	R-R	6-2	185	9-20-85	.247	.282	.231	73	296	37	73	10	2	4	23	13	6	4	1	60	20	6	.334	.291
Ditter, Brad	L-R	6-0	185	7-22-80	.260	.150	.283	96	335	38	87	14	3	1	28	33	7	0	7	53	11	4	.328	.332
Fitzpatrick, Reggie	L-L	5-11	180	2-28-83	.251	.305	.232	90	307	40	77	13	0	6	35	18	8	1	1	66	23	9	.352	.308
German, Agustin	R-R	6-0	180	12-13-85	.000	.000	.000	1	3	0	0	0	0	0	0	0	0	0	0	2	0	0	.000	.000
Ivany, Devin	R-R	6-2	185	7-27-82	.262	.240	.267	113	409	52	107	27	1	13	54	25	8	1	3	65	7	7	.428	.315
Jimenez, Franklyn	R-R	6-2	180	2-23-82	.128	.094	.152	27	78	7	10	0	1	1	5	6	0	1	1	24	0	0	.192	.188
Lane, Richard	L-L	6-3	205	1-4-80	.389	.429	.379	10	36	5	14	4	1	1	8	4	0	0	0	5	0	1	.639	.450
Lowrance, Marvin	L-L	6-0	215	7-16-84	.288	.259	.297	57	212	27	61	15	1	4	35	16	6	0	1	50	2	1	.425	.353
Montz, Luke	R-R	6-2	205	7-7-83	.224	.255	.212	100	343	66	77	24	1	19	68	50	3	2	5	95	1	1	.466	.324
Mortimer, Steve	L-L	6-3	215	6-10-81	.244	.214	.254	101	328	47	80	19	2	10	41	46	9	0	5	135	7	2	.405	.348
Nunez, Eduardo	R-R	6-2	170	9-21-85	.500	.000	.500	1	4	0	2	0	0	0	0	0	0	0	0	0	0	0	.500	.500
Poppert, John	R-R	6-0	185	4-14-82	.105	.200	.043	15	38	2	4	1	0	0	0	3	2	0	0	11	0	0	.132	.209
Sandora, Robert	L-R	6-0	200	8-5-81	.000	.000	.000	2	4	0	0	0	0	0	0	0	0	0	0	0	0	0	.000	.000
Vroman, Doug	R-R	6-2	200	2-9-81	.254	.286	.237	70	209	38	53	11	2	7	34	39	1	1	3	64	9	4	.426	.369
Webb, Trey	R-R	6-0	170	2-11-82	.272	.226	.288	102	379	59	103	22	2	9	45	36	3	2	2	62	22	8	.412	.338
Zimmerman, Ryan	R-R	6-3	220	9-28-84	.471	.500	.462	4	17	5	8	2	1	2	6	0	0	0	0	3	0	1	1.059	.471

PITCHING	B-T	HT	WT	DOB	W	L	ERA	G	GS	CG	SV	IP	H	R	ER	HR	BB	SO	AVG	vLH	vRH	K/9	BB/9
Baldwin, Andy	R-R	6-2	190	2-28-82	4	4	4.14	12	12	1	0	67	64	38	31	9	26	43	.253	.218	.276	5.75	3.48
Balester, Collin	R-R	6-5	190	6-6-86	8	6	3.67	24	23	1	0	125	105	62	51	11	42	95	.222	.186	.255	6.84	3.02
Bunn, Greg	R-R	6-1	210	2-3-83	3	5	3.86	11	11	1	0	58	51	29	25	10	25	56	.230	.235	.226	8.64	3.86
Campbell, Brett	R-R	6-0	170	10-17-81	4	2	1.69	36	0	0	19	48	28	10	9	2	15	50	.164	.179	.154	9.38	2.81
Cook, Steven	R-R	6-4	205	11-26-81	3	4	5.28	20	9	0	0	61	80	39	36	10	12	30	.328	.263	.405	4.40	1.76
Cox, Ben	R-R	6-2	220	9-20-81	4	4	3.00	42	0	0	6	63	55	24	21	6	33	51	.234	.270	.207	7.29	4.71
Felfoldi, Jonathan	L-L	6-1	183	7-6-81	0	1	5.65	3	3	0	0	14	13	9	9	2	9	13	.250	.267	.243	8.16	5.65
France, Ryan	L-R	6-2	195	3-25-80	1	1	3.81	16	2	0	0	28	25	13	12	4	15	26	.234	.311	.177	8.26	4.76
Francisco, Bartolo	R-R	5-9	155	8-24-82	1	1	4.24	3	3	0	0	17	16	8	8	4	15	6	.254	.233	.273	3.18	7.94
Gomez, Warmar	R-R	6-2	210	5-8-83	0	0	4.70	17	0	0	0	31	44	17	16	2	4	16	.336	.258	.406	4.70	1.17
Gonzalez, Somer	R-R	5-11	190	7-23-79	4	4	5.82	30	4	0	0	68	74	54	44	6	30	52	.274	.328	.230	6.88	3.97
Goodman, Chris	B-R	6-1	180	11-9-81	2	5	5.43	20	6	0	0	56	67	45	34	6	11	39	.288	.277	.295	6.23	1.76
Henderson, Jim	L-R	6-5	190	10-21-82	9	11	5.47	26	26	1	0	150	166	99	91	20	50	76	.280	.281	.280	4.57	3.01
Hlebovy, Gus	R-R	5-11	165	7-6-82	0	0	1.29	4	0	0	0	7	3	1	1	0	4	9	.130	.067	.250	11.57	5.14
Lambert, Bryan	R-R	6-9	240	10-19-81	1	1	6.00	3	0	0	0	6	6	4	4	0	2	4	.250	.273	.231	6.00	3.00
Morales, Alexis	R-R	5-11	170	12-8-82	1	1	4.82	18	0	0	3	28	20	17	15	2	25	22	.208	.209	.208	7.07	8.04

PITCHING	B-T	HT	WT	DOB	W	L	ERA	G	GS	CG	SV	IP	H	R	ER	HR	BB	SO	AVG	vLH	vRH	K/9	BB/9
Morales, Ricardo	L-L	6-1	170	12-9-83	8	7	3.94	25	25	0	0	137	147	66	60	16	39	99	.279	.299	.274	6.50	2.56
Plexico, Gerald	L-L	6-4	210	2-24-80	0	1	5.87	3	0	0	0	8	8	5	5	2	0	5	.276	.200	.292	5.87	0.00
Thompson, Daryl	R-R	6-1	170	11-2-85	2	3	3.35	11	11	0	0	54	46	23	20	3	24	48	.232	.212	.253	8.05	4.02
Trahan, David	R-R	6-3	185	2-27-81	3	10	6.52	34	3	0	2	58	79	50	42	5	31	34	.324	.330	.318	5.28	4.81
Wilson, Thomas	R-L	6-2	185	5-21-82	4	5	3.82	45	0	0	5	71	69	34	30	5	21	64	.251	.163	.287	8.15	2.67
Yost, Gene	R-L	6-3	185	6-23-81	0	0	2.63	8	0	0	0	14	9	5	4	1	2	16	.184	.182	.184	10.54	1.32

FIELDING

Catcher	PCT	G	PO	A	E	DP	PB
Apodaca	1.000	2	8	1	0	0	0
German	1.000	1	10	0	0	0	0
Ivany	.983	84	536	42	10	8	13
Montz	.987	43	272	22	4	4	4
Poppert	1.000	13	65	5	0	2	1
Sandora	1.000	1	2	0	0	0	0

First Base	PCT	G	PO	A	E	DP
Ditter	.975	6	33	6	1	5
Jimenez	.991	17	105	7	1	9
Lane	.967	9	56	3	2	7
Montz	1.000	21	163	15	0	16
Mortimer	.988	96	735	66	10	68

Second Base	PCT	G	PO	A	E	DP
Castro	.933	8	13	15	2	4
Contreras	.912	9	9	22	3	3
Ditter	.978	42	75	99	4	16
Jimenez	.889	2	4	4	1	0
Nunez	1.000	1	1	2	0	2
Webb	.953	80	147	198	17	44

Third Base	PCT	G	PO	A	E	DP
Bynum	1.000	2	1	3	0	0
Castro	.953	100	72	170	12	12
Ditter	.933	32	20	64	6	9
Jimenez	.667	2	2	0	1	0
Zimmerman	1.000	4	2	12	0	1

Shortstop	PCT	G	PO	A	E	DP
Bynum	.966	48	74	125	7	30
Castro	1.000	3	1	9	0	2
Contreras	.933	4	6	8	1	0
Desmond	.943	72	130	199	20	42
Webb	.957	15	24	21	2	2

Outfield	PCT	G	PO	A	E	DP
Baez	.962	122	214	12	9	3
Bernadina	.989	119	270	10	3	2
Fitzpatrick	.970	75	157	6	5	0
Lowrance	.980	51	94	5	2	1
Mortimer	1.000	1	1	1	0	0
Vroman	.993	57	128	5	1	1

VERMONT EXPOS — Short-Season Class A

NEW YORK-PENN LEAGUE

BATTING	B-T	HT	WT	DOB	AVG	vLH	vRH	G	AB	R	H	2B	3B	HR	RBI	BB	HBP	SH	SF	SO	SB	CS	SLG	OBP
Alvarez, Jean	R-R	6-2	185	2-15-87	.148	.182	.125	7	27	2	4	0	0	0	1	1	1	0	0	9	0	0	.148	.207
Apodaca, Luis	R-R	5-11	175	7-15-82	.257	.281	.247	35	109	14	28	5	0	0	18	15	3	1	1	20	1	0	.303	.359
Arnedo, Rolando	R-R	5-11	192	11-30-82	.286	.233	.305	35	112	19	32	2	0	0	9	18	10	2	0	12	0	2	.304	.429
Brown, Dee	R-R	6-0	230	10-21-82	.283	.265	.289	47	184	28	52	9	2	8	32	12	5	0	1	56	2	3	.484	.342
Castro, Jonathan	B-R	6-1	160	11-29-83	.269	.000	.389	7	26	7	7	2	1	0	4	2	0	1	0	8	0	1	.423	.321
Contreras, Jose	B-R	6-0	170	4-26-85	.253	.333	.221	64	241	49	61	7	0	0	16	51	0	2	0	57	14	5	.282	.384
Conway, Brandon	L-R	6-3	190	11-9-83	.124	.148	.115	36	105	10	13	1	0	0	4	6	3	2	1	42	0	1	.133	.191
Daniel, Mike	L-R	6-3	180	8-17-84	.260	.317	.240	67	235	41	61	6	4	3	25	29	7	4	5	64	6	7	.357	.351
Davis, Leonard	L-R	5-10	195	12-24-83	.300	.273	.308	67	237	34	71	8	8	7	35	12	6	1	1	64	8	4	.489	.348
Figuereo, Johan	R-R	6-2	195	3-2-86	.077	.200	.000	4	13	2	1	0	0	0	0	1	1	0	0	3	0	0	.077	.200
German, Agustin	R-R	6-0	180	12-13-85	.100	.500	.000	3	10	1	1	0	0	0	1	1	0	1	0	3	0	0	.100	.182
Guzman, Francisco	R-R	6-4	195	12-21-83	.469	.667	.350	9	32	8	15	2	0	2	7	0	1	0	0	4	0	0	.719	.485
Howell, John Michael	L-R	6-3	200	12-30-82	.363	.290	.390	29	113	17	41	5	0	3	17	9	0	0	2	20	0	1	.487	.403
Lane, Andy	R-R	6-0	185	12-25-81	.204	.087	.233	34	113	9	23	5	0	0	11	13	1	3	0	21	2	0	.248	.291
Louisa, Lorvin	R-R	6-4	200	2-7-83	.211	.298	.180	49	175	21	37	7	1	4	21	8	3	1	0	58	7	3	.331	.258
Mancebo, Melvin	R-R	6-1	190	9-8-83	.167	.000	.208	11	30	2	5	1	0	1	4	2	0	0	0	8	0	0	.300	.219
McMillan, Drew	R-R	6-3	205	10-25-80	.294	.357	.270	15	51	8	15	4	0	1	6	8	1	0	2	19	0	0	.431	.387
Nunez, Eduardo	R-R	6-2	170	9-21-85	.130	.091	.143	31	92	5	12	5	0	0	6	10	0	0	0	35	3	2	.185	.216
Plasencia, Francisco	L-L	6-1	192	6-19-84	.300	.260	.314	72	280	43	84	16	4	11	56	29	3	2	4	60	14	3	.504	.367
Poppert, John	R-R	6-0	185	4-14-82	.199	.147	.216	41	136	15	27	6	0	4	13	14	0	1	0	30	3	0	.331	.273
Sandora, Robert	L-R	6-0	200	8-5-81	.250	.000	.250	6	16	0	4	2	0	0	6	4	0	0	0	3	0	0	.375	.400
Soto, Auddy	R-R	6-2	185	4-1-84	.167	.000	.333	5	6	0	1	0	0	0	0	3	0	0	0	4	0	0	.167	.444
Thissen, Greg	R-R	6-4	185	6-1-81	.283	.273	.286	14	53	9	15	4	0	2	6	4	1	1	0	12	3	1	.472	.345
Torres, Carlos	R-R	6-4	190	4-3-84	.192	.160	.200	35	120	11	23	5	0	2	18	13	2	0	0	41	0	0	.283	.281
Travis, David	L-R	6-4	210	12-15-80	.050	.000	.071	6	20	1	1	0	0	0	1	1	0	0	0	11	0	0	.050	.095

PITCHING	B-T	HT	WT	DOB	W	L	ERA	G	GS	CG	SV	IP	H	R	ER	HR	BB	SO	AVG	vLH	vRH	K/9	BB/9
Coonrod, Aaron	R-R	6-4	225	5-17-80	0	0	10.80	4	0	0	0	3	5	5	4	0	8	4	.357	.333	.364	10.80	21.60
Estrada, Marco	R-R	6-0	180	7-5-83	1	3	5.08	9	6	0	1	34	31	21	19	4	16	37	.231	.190	.268	9.89	4.28
Everts, Clint	B-R	6-2	170	8-10-84	0	1	3.79	8	1	0	0	19	21	12	8	0	12	21	.266	.281	.255	9.95	5.68
Garza, Rudy	R-R	6-2	190	4-10-84	0	0	5.84	9	0	0	0	12	16	9	8	3	5	7	.320	.368	.290	5.11	3.65
Gomez, Warmar	R-R	6-2	210	5-8-83	3	3	3.76	23	0	0	1	38	46	22	16	2	5	19	.301	.319	.292	4.46	1.17
Jackson, Aaron	B-R	6-0	175	3-28-86	3	7	6.13	15	12	0	0	62	76	53	42	0	27	44	.295	.263	.313	6.42	3.94
Lannan, John	L-L	6-5	200	9-27-84	3	5	5.26	14	11	0	0	63	74	46	37	5	31	41	.287	.128	.315	5.83	4.41
Lehman, James	R-R	6-2	185	3-14-85	0	1	6.31	20	0	0	1	26	28	20	18	2	9	20	.264	.462	.200	7.01	3.16
Lira, Oscar	R-R	6-3	185	7-17-82	1	2	5.14	16	2	0	0	28	35	19	16	1	10	10	.299	.372	.257	3.21	3.21
Long, Nick	R-R	6-3	180	11-24-82	0	0	0.00	5	0	0	1	7	3	0	0	0	1	9	.125	.125	.125	11.57	1.29
Lugo, Chris	R-R	6-1	185	11-10-86	2	1	5.13	7	4	0	0	26	32	17	15	1	7	20	.296	.375	.233	6.84	2.39
Martinez, Carlos	R-R	6-4	177	3-30-84	1	7	4.63	13	11	0	0	68	74	44	35	2	21	39	.274	.284	.268	5.16	2.78
Ochoa, Nehomar	R-R	6-3	175	9-18-82	0	2	5.93	23	0	0	3	30	36	25	20	4	14	27	.283	.262	.294	8.01	4.15
Palm, Josh	R-R	6-4	210	6-13-83	0	1	8.10	3	0	0	0	3	7	5	3	0	2	3	.467	.250	.545	8.10	5.40
Rodriguez, Edward	L-L	5-9	160	7-25-82	2	1	4.81	20	3	0	0	49	60	31	26	3	19	29	.313	.360	.296	5.36	3.51
Shefka, Ricky	B-R	6-2	200	1-16-84	1	2	6.53	10	5	0	0	30	46	25	22	2	10	20	.357	.393	.329	5.93	2.97
Soto, Auddy	R-R	6-2	185	4-1-84	0	0	0.00	1	0	0	0	1	0	0	0	0	0	2	.000	.000	.000	27.00	0.00
Stammen, Craig	R-R	6-3	200	3-9-84	4	5	4.06	13	7	0	0	51	62	36	23	2	12	32	.297	.224	.331	5.65	2.12
Taylor, Jeff	R-R	6-9	245	10-8-83	0	2	9.18	14	0	0	0	17	22	23	17	0	13	16	.301	.400	.250	8.64	7.02
Trahan, David	R-R	6-3	185	2-27-81	1	0	3.00	9	0	0	0	12	14	4	4	0	8	5	.318	.200	.353	3.75	6.00
Yost, Gene	R-L	6-3	185	6-23-81	6	5	3.25	14	14	1	0	83	70	36	30	7	30	56	.224	.242	.220	6.07	3.25

GAMES BY POSITION: C—Apodaca 11, German 3, Mancebo 7, McMillan 15, Poppert 41, Sandora 2, Soto 3. **1B**—Apodaca 14, Arnedo 31, Conway 2, Howell 6, Thissen 3, Torres 24, Travis 3. **2B**—Castro 5, Contreras 3, Conway 8, Lane 30, Nunez 29, Thissen 7. **3B**—Conway 17, Davis 58, Figuereo 4, Lane 2. **SS**—Alvarez 7, Contreras 59, Conway 7, Nunez 1, Thissen 4. **OF**—Arnedo 1, Brown 41, Daniel 64, Guzman 9, Howell 4, Louisa 41, Plasencia 71, Thissen 1,

GULF COAST LEAGUE

BATTING	B-T	HT	WT	DOB	AVG	vLH	vRH	G	AB	R	H	2B	3B	HR	RBI	BB	HBP	SH	SF	SO	SB	CS	SLG	OBP
Alvarez, Jean	R-R	6-2	185	2-15-87	.183	.162	.189	25	93	14	17	8	0	2	6	15	3	0	0	41	0	1	.333	.315
Arnedo, Rolando	R-R	5-11	192	11-30-82	.218	.238	.206	15	55	6	12	0	0	0	3	5	3	1	1	10	0	0	.218	.313
Broadway, Larry	L-L	6-4	230	12-17-80	.429	.091	.647	8	28	3	12	5	0	1	4	7	0	1	0	3	0	0	.714	.543
Castro, Jonathan	B-R	6-1	160	11-29-83	.269	.290	.256	47	186	29	50	13	2	0	10	16	4	4	1	53	4	4	.360	.338
De la Cruz, Jorge	R-R	6-3	210	10-2-85	.281	.375	.250	10	32	4	9	1	0	1	3	2	0	1	0	11	0	0	.406	.324
Delaughter, Ryan	R-R	6-3	210	12-31-86	.248	.238	.253	33	125	18	31	3	1	6	21	6	4	0	0	39	1	0	.432	.304
Figuereo, Johan	R-R	6-2	195	3-2-86	.259	.290	.250	47	174	16	45	9	0	2	16	13	3	0	0	32	1	0	.345	.321
German, Agustin	R-R	6-0	180	12-13-85	.198	.195	.200	29	106	13	21	4	0	1	9	9	2	1	1	28	0	0	.264	.271
Guzman, Francisco	R-R	6-4	195	12-21-83	.344	.302	.354	40	154	20	53	6	0	7	24	5	8	0	1	20	0	0	.519	.393
Hodges, Scott	L-R	6-0	190	12-26-78	.000	.000	.000	2	7	0	0	0	0	0	0	0	0	0	0	2	0	0	.000	.000
Johnson, Deryck	L-L	6-0	175	4-11-87	.185	.429	.100	7	27	0	5	1	0	0	2	1	0	0	0	7	1	1	.222	.214
Lane, Andy	L-L	6-3	205	1-4-80	.391	.400	.389	7	23	6	9	0	0	0	1	2	1	0	0	4	0	0	.391	.462
Lowrance, Marvin	L-L	6-0	215	7-16-84	.321	.182	.412	8	28	4	9	1	0	2	9	3	0	0	0	2	0	0	.571	.387
Mancebo, Melvin	R-R	6-1	190	9-8-83	.273	.231	.283	25	88	4	24	6	0	3	12	3	1	0	0	25	0	0	.443	.304
Martinez, Jonathan	B-R	6-0	170	9-23-84	.194	.220	.188	38	124	17	24	3	1	0	7	26	0	5	1	22	6	2	.234	.331
Mortimer, Steve	L-L	6-3	215	6-10-81	.214	.167	.167	5	14	0	3	1	0	0	0	2	0	0	0	7	0	0	.286	.313
Ogando, Cristian	R-R	6-2	175	8-5-86	.294	.237	.319	38	136	18	40	3	1	0	13	12	2	4	0	24	2	0	.331	.360
Pahuta, Tim	L-R	6-4	225	5-3-83	.233	.133	.294	38	133	13	31	8	1	3	20	17	2	1	2	35	0	1	.376	.325
Peacock, Brian	R-R	6-1	185	8-26-84	.219	.228	.222	42	160	18	35	6	3	0	12	17	1	0	1	49	1	0	.294	.296
Perez, Melvin	B-R	6-2	200	6-1-86	.194	.174	.205	27	67	3	13	3	0	0	5	10	0	0	0	24	0	0	.239	.299
Simmons, Lyndsey	L-R	6-0	200	10-15-81	.100	.000	.125	3	10	0	1	0	0	0	1	1	0	0	0	2	0	0	.100	.182
Soto, Auddy	R-R	6-2	185	4-1-84	.167	.167	.167	8	24	1	4	1	0	0	0	2	0	0	0	14	0	0	.208	.231
Suarez, Gabriel	R-R	6-0	170	12-14-84	.000	.000	.000	1	3	0	0	0	0	0	0	0	0	0	0	0	0	0	.000	.000

PITCHING	B-T	HT	WT	DOB	W	L	ERA	G	GS	CG	SV	IP	H	R	ER	HR	BB	SO	AVG	vLH	vRH	K/9	BB/9
Bowie, Micah	L-L	6-4	205	11-10-74	1	0	1.08	7	2	0	0	8	9	1	1	0	1	12	.290	.600	.231	12.96	1.08
Cerezo, Hector	L-L	6-2	175	2-28-82	0	1	2.08	4	1	0	1	9	8	2	2	1	2	8	.258	.000	.276	8.31	2.08
Cook, Steven	R-R	6-4	205	11-26-81	0	2	3.00	3	3	0	0	6	5	3	2	0	0	5	.217	.222	.214	7.50	0.00
De los Santos, Amado	R-R	6-1	167	10-29-85	0	0	13.50	1	0	0	0	1	2	3	1	0	1	1	.400	.000	.667	13.50	13.50
Engles, Terrence	R-R	6-4	170	11-12-85	2	3	4.28	12	9	0	0	55	56	33	26	2	15	45	.262	.302	.245	7.41	2.47
Enriquez, Andre	R-R	6-3	212	5-15-84	0	0	0.87	7	0	0	1	10	11	2	1	0	2	10	.275	.182	.310	8.71	1.74
Evangelista, Antonio	R-R	6-5	220	1-8-83	0	0	2.57	4	0	0	0	7	8	4	2	0	6	8	.276	.444	.200	10.29	7.71
Everts, Clint	B-R	6-2	170	8-10-84	0	1	3.38	7	7	0	0	16	18	9	6	0	8	15	.269	.357	.205	8.44	4.50
Francisco, Bartolo	R-R	5-9	155	8-24-82	2	4	2.08	10	5	0	0	52	55	26	12	2	13	29	.268	.339	.238	5.02	2.25
Garza, Rudy	R-R	6-2	190	4-10-84	0	1	7.15	3	0	0	0	11	19	12	9	2	4	9	.373	.429	.351	7.15	3.18
Harrison, Ryan	R-R	6-2	190	7-12-86	3	3	4.66	11	4	0	1	48	58	27	25	4	15	34	.299	.250	.328	6.33	2.79
Johnson, Anthony	R-R	6-1	180	5-23-83	0	0	4.50	4	0	0	0	8	6	4	4	0	8	9	.250	.286	.235	10.13	9.00
Lambert, Bryan	R-R	6-9	240	10-19-81	3	1	1.54	10	1	0	1	23	21	5	4	1	5	16	.241	.240	.242	6.17	1.93
Long, Nick	R-R	6-3	180	11-24-82	0	0	4.50	2	1	0	0	2	2	1	1	1	1	1	.250	.000	.333	4.50	4.50
Lugo, Chris	R-R	6-1	185	11-10-86	2	1	2.20	5	3	0	0	29	25	8	7	0	11	24	.234	.216	.243	7.53	3.45
Mavroulis, Coby	L-L	6-3	180	2-7-83	2	3	5.04	9	3	0	0	25	30	16	14	2	12	29	.300	.263	.309	10.44	4.32
Mercedes, Manuel	R-R	6-4	190	12-30-82	1	3	8.27	7	0	0	0	16	18	17	15	0	14	14	.273	.240	.293	7.71	7.71
Ozuna, Cruzito	R-R	6-0	160	1-12-85	0	3	14.77	10	2	0	0	21	46	39	35	2	20	20	.455	.647	.358	8.44	8.44
Perks, Matthew	R-R	6-7	200	8-20-85	4	2	2.83	12	8	1	2	60	51	22	19	2	17	41	.238	.194	.261	6.12	2.54
Pichardo, Eduardo	R-R	6-0	175	8-1-87	0	1	22.09	8	0	0	0	7	17	18	18	2	19	7	.459	.462	.458	8.59	23.32
Plexico, Gerald	L-L	6-4	210	2-24-80	0	0	3.60	3	3	0	0	5	3	2	2	2	1	3	.188	.500	.143	5.40	1.80
Schroder, Chris	R-R	6-3	210	8-20-78	0	0	9.00	1	0	0	0	1	2	1	1	0	0	3	.400	.500	.000	27.00	0.00
Soto, Auddy	R-R	6-2	185	4-1-84	0	0	36.00	1	0	0	0	1	1	4	4	0	5	2	.333	.000	1.000	18.00	45.00
Urena, Jose	L-L	6-0	172	3-18-84	1	2	6.23	13	1	0	1	30	34	21	21	0	19	33	.291	.350	.278	9.79	5.64
Watkins, Michael	R-R	6-1	187	11-20-87	0	1	4.82	5	0	0	1	9	16	8	5	1	3	13	.372	.400	.357	12.54	2.89

GAMES BY POSITION: C—German 19, Mancebo 1, Peacock 28, Simmons 2, Soto 6. **1B—**Broadway 7, German 1, Lane 6, Martinez 1, Mortimer 3, Pahuta 32, Perez 7. **2B—**Castro 45, Martinez 9, Perez 1. **3B—**Figuereo 45, Hodges 2, Perez 12. **SS—**Alvarez 24, Castro 1, Figuereo 1, Martinez 28, Suarez 1. **OF—**Arnedo 15, Delaughter 27, Guzman 40, Johnson 7, Lowrance 8, Mancebo 23, Mortimer 1, Ogando 38, Pahuta 1, Peacock 3, Perez 5.

MINOR
LEAGUES

Minors continue to find new fans, so attendance records keep falling

BY WILL LINGO

Minor league baseball continues to pursue new markets and continues to find successful ones, so it also continues to set attendance records.

The minors' longstanding overall attendance record fell in 2004, when teams drew 39,887,755 fans to break a mark that had stood for more than a half-century. The old record of 39,640,443 was set in 1949, when there were 448 teams in the post-World War II boom.

The all-time attendance record fell again in 2005, when the 176 teams in 15 leagues attracted a total of 41,333,279 fans, an increase of 1,445,523 or 3.6 percent. The attendance record continued a long, strong growth trend for the minors. Five of the six highest attendance totals in the 104-year history of the minor leagues have come in the last five seasons.

Whataballpark
The Corpus Christi Hooks were a big draw in their first year at Whataburger Field

The support was strong from top to bottom in the minors, as 13 of the 15 leagues recorded attendance increases over 2004 and the other two were roughly the same. The Midwest League was off by .5 percent, while the Southern League was down 1.2 percent almost solely because of games lost by the Mississippi and Mobile franchises to Hurricane Katrina.

Four of the leagues—Pacific Coast, Eastern, Texas and South Atlantic—set all-time records of their own, and the PCL became the first league ever to surpass seven million fans. The South Atlantic broke its attendance record for the third year in a row, while the Eastern mark fell in both 2004 and 2005.

The PCL record was spurred by the addition of the Round Rock Express franchise, which replaced Edmonton. The Express had been one of the most successful franchises in the history of Double-A baseball in its five years in the Texas League, and managed to do even better as a Triple-A team, drawing 700,277 fans.

Round Rock still couldn't top the minor league attendance kings, Memphis and Sacramento, however. Memphis drew fewer fans but had a better average—10,088 a game—and Sacramento was better on both fronts, with total attendance of 755,750 and an average of 10,496 to lead the minors again. It was the sixth consecutive season that Sacramento led the minors in attendance.

The Texas League didn't suffer because of the loss of Round Rock, replacing the Express with the Corpus Christi Hooks, and getting another new franchise when the former El Paso Diablos moved to Springfield, Mo. Both of the league's new franchises drew better than a half-million fans, joining Frisco to give the Texas League the only non-Triple-A league with three franchises that drew at least 500,000. Overall the league saw 2,834,335 fans pass through the gates.

The Eastern League didn't add any new franchises, but the New Hampshire Fisher Cats opened their new ballpark and increased their attendance by more than 60,000 fans. The league's real attendance strength comes from its more established franchises, however. Reading surpassed 450,000 fans for the sixth straight season, while Trenton became the first Double-A franchise to draw 400,000 fans for 11 consecutive years.

The South Atlantic League benefited from new ballparks in Greensboro and Charleston, W.Va., boosting its overall attendance total to 3,541,992. The newly named Greensboro Grasshoppers more than doubled their attendance, to 406,996.

But the Midwest League's Dayton Dragons remained the attendance leader among Class A franchises, drawing 572,003 fans to top Class A for the sixth year in a row and recording their 427th straight sellout.

The Midwest League's Kane County Cougars also drew better than 500,000 fans again in 2005, and those two clubs as well as the three Texas League clubs were the only ones below Triple-A to draw at least a half-million.

Brooklyn remained the leader in short-season attendance, a distinction it has achieved in each of its five seasons. The Cyclones drew 285,847 fans, an average of nearly 8,000 a game. Another notable achievement in short-season attendance came from Lowell, which sold out its 233rd consecutive game.

Texas League Continues To Thrive

After the 2004 season, Texas League president Tom Kayser knew his league would have to move forward without its flagship franchise. The Round Rock Express, arguably the best Double-A franchise ever, moved up to the PCL in 2005.

"I felt like we would be taking a small step back," Kayser said. "It's tough to lose your number one franchise and not feel both regret and nostalgia. Round Rock was really a crown jewel."

The league might never find one franchise that's the equal of the Express, but its combination of two new franchises made the league even better. The Corpus

Christi Hooks replaced the Express, and the former El Paso Diablos moved to Springfield, and become the Cardinals.

"Change is inevitable, and if it happens you want to prepare for it and have it happen in the best possible way," Kayser said. "We are the beneficiaries of a number of very positive things."

Change was a foreign concept to the league before Round Rock came along for the 2000 season. Before that season, the league hadn't added a new team since 1987, when the Wichita Wranglers joined up. The league remains remarkably stable, but since Round Rock replaced Jackson, Frisco has replaced Shreveport, and now Springfield and Corpus Christi have replaced El Paso and Round Rock.

The net result for the league should be overwhelmingly positive. Corpus Christi is a much smaller market than Round Rock (which is in suburban Austin), but the combination of an affiliation with the nearby Astros and ownership by Nolan Ryan's group, Ryan Sanders Baseball, virtually assures a certain level of success.

"It's been overwhelming the reception we've gotten," said Matt Hicks, the Hooks' radio voice and media-relations director who worked for 10 years in El Paso before coming to Corpus Christi. "It's not just that it's a new team, it's the Astros and the Ryan family—it all adds up to almost the fever pitch we've seen here."

Corpus Christi has a limited history of professional baseball, with no team staying longer than five years and no affiliated team playing in the city for nearly 30 years.

RECORD BREAKERS

Minor League Baseball set another all-time attendance record in 2005, breaking the 41 million mark for the first time and showing a 3.6 percent increase over the 2004 season. The five largest attendance figures in history:

Year	No. of Teams	Attendance
2005	176	41,333,279
2004	176	39,887,755
1949	448	39,640,443
2003	176	39,069,707
2002	176	38,639,142

ORGANIZATION STANDINGS

Cumulative farm club records for the 30 major league organizations, with winning percentages going back five years. Every organization has six affiliates, except for the Mets, who have seven.

	2005							
	W	L	PCT	2004	2003	2002	2001	2000
Detroit	382	306	.555	.467	.481	.509	.508	.478
San Francisco	385	309	.555	.471	.454	.463	.528	.444
Oakland	379	316	.545	.576	.532	.509	.480	.551
New York-AL	372	316	.541	.514	.501	.530	.543	.517
Minnesota	364	316	.535	.502	.503	.540	.541	.537
Cleveland	372	336	.525	.540	.576	.577	.543	.517
Toronto	370	337	.523	.572	.531	.480	.460	.529
Pittsburgh	358	332	.519	.511	.581	.571	.467	.491
Seattle	359	336	.517	.508	.527	.471	.560	.577
Boston	355	338	.512	.503	.496	.454	.468	.522
New York-NL	384	370	.509	.547	.503	.496	.524	.509
Chicago-AL	352	347	.504	.504	.494	.466	.495	.483
Florida	341	339	.501	.455	.502	.491	.539	.496
Colorado	357	355	.501	.482	.508	.473	.478	.502
Kansas City	348	348	.500	.501	.527	.521	.469	.457
Baltimore	352	355	.498	.458	.486	.434	.445	.481
Arizona	355	361	.496	.489	.513	.454	.477	.466
Houston	349	357	.494	.533	.500	.535	.598	.526
St. Louis	347	358	.492	.520	.451	.509	.423	.472
Chicago-NL	337	348	.492	.538	.474	.529	.512	.513
Texas	341	354	.491	.549	.547	.498	.478	.530
Los Angeles-NL	334	348	.490	.502	.485	.563	.538	.527
Los Angeles-AL	340	355	.489	.455	.510	.472	.499	.426
Atlanta	324	348	.482	.514	.497	.512	.489	.493
Milwaukee	326	363	.473	.453	.469	.462	.496	.495
San Diego	326	365	.472	.501	.476	.513	.470	.485
Tampa Bay	324	375	.464	.472	.497	.445	.474	.478
Cincinnati	309	372	.454	.470	.480	.528	.567	.486
Washington	302	387	.438	.424	.437	.477	.435	.453
Philadelphia	295	392	.429	.467	.462	.525	.504	.568

But with the growth of the city and diversification of its economy—to say nothing of lovely Whataburger Field built right on the city's ship channel—the city was clearly ready for a team now.

Opening Night for the Hooks was a gala affair, with Nolan Ryan and the rest of his family there, as well as almost every significant member of the Astros front office, to say nothing of Padres owner John Moores, who is a native of the area.

More than 8,200 people turned out at a ballpark with 5,314 seats and room for about 2,000 fans on berms, so that's a pretty good indication of demand.

In Springfield, the turnout was just as impressive. More than 8,800 people came out on Opening Night, and two exhibition games featuring the big league Cardinals each drew more than 10,000 fans to John Q. Hammons Field. Springfield, in addition to having the same pent-up demand seen in Corpus Christi, has the additional benefit of being smack in the middle of Cardinals country.

"You have a team owned by the major league club, within a territory that's just bonkers for that major league club," Kayser said. "I can't think of any parallel for that in our league."

And they have Round Rock to thank for it. The Ryans wanted to get into minor league baseball, the Jackson franchise was available, and the Austin/Round Rock market was waiting to explode in the right situation, which the Ryans helped create. Their success led to the success in Frisco, as well as showing Corpus Christi and Springfield the benefits minor league baseball can bring.

So even though the Express moved on to bigger things in the PCL, its legacy in the Texas League lives on, and fans in the Lone Star State and beyond reap the benefits.

Braves Leave, Greenville Gets New Team

After five years of trying, Tim Bennett was down to his last chance, a final all-in bet to keep his dream alive.

He and a group of local officials were pulling their second straight all-nighter, trying to work out the final details on an agreement to bring the Braves' Southern League team to Pearl, Miss.

Bennett, who had no money to bring to the deal and no governmental authority to sign any papers, had become an integral part of the quest to bring Braves baseball to Mississippi by the force of his personality and skill as a coalition builder. If this didn't work, he knew his days in baseball were done.

Around midnight as the deadline arrived, Bennett had reason to start polishing his resume. After learning that some of the details of the deal had changed at the last minute, the Braves balked.

"Around midnight, the deal was off. The Braves said, 'We'll have to lick our wounds and go back to Greenville, but this isn't working,' " Bennett says now.

Three hours later, after a few tweaks to the agreement, the deal was back on. In that moment near 3 a.m. on April 1, 2004, as Bennett and Pearl mayor Jimmy Foster sat around a speakerphone, the Braves made the effort worthwhile.

"I guess my stubbornness and ignorance was rewarded," Bennett says.

Young draws raves for all his skills

It was early August of a 2005 International League game at Durham Bulls Athletic Park, and Ken Oberkfell's Norfolk Tides were staked to a 6-1 lead in the fourth. With Brian Daubach on third and Anderson Hernandez on first and nobody out, Norfolk catcher Mike DeFelice hit a fly ball to right field.

PLAYER OF THE YEAR

Daubach tagged up from third as Bulls outfielder Delmon Young unleashed a laser to catcher Tim Laker. The throw beat the veteran first baseman by several feet, and Laker tossed the ball down to first baseman Josh Phelps as Hernandez—equally dumbfounded by Young's throw—was standing on second base. That completed the first triple play for the franchise since it moved to Triple-A in 1998.

"I knew what kind of arm he had, but we had nothing to lose," Oberkfell says. "But I think the next time that happens, I might think twice about a decision like that. That's a cannon out there. I don't think there's any doubt about that."

It turned out the Tides had a lot to lose, as Young tripled in three runs in the bottom half of the inning and the Bulls went on to win, 13-8. Young's performance was emblematic of how the 19-year-old phenom can change a game, with his bat, with his arm and even with his legs. His consistently high performance and emerging talent made him Baseball America's 2005 Minor League Player of the Year.

Young was on pace to win a triple crown in the Southern League with Double-A Montgomery, batting .336-20-71, when he was promoted to Durham in July. He held his own in Triple-A, finishing up at .285-6-28 for the Bulls. Overall, Young batted .315-26-95 in 558 at-bats with 32 stolen bases, a .401 on-base percentage and a .526 slugging percentage.

"Delmon dominated probably the best Double-A league this season," a scout from an American League club said, "and as a talent rates right up there with the Andruw Joneses, the Miguel Cabreras and the Albert Belles."

CARL KLINE

Can dominate in a variety of ways
Delmon Young should be in the majors soon

"He's the total package in terms of tools," Durham manager Bill Evers says. "He can do everything and do it loudly. The ball just sounds different coming off his bat than a lot of hitters in this league.

"There was a lot of pressure on him to perform when he got here, and he stepped up to that and met it head-on. He could have been the player of the year in any league he was in."

Whenever Young's name is mentioned, the word "maturity" is usually one of the first adjectives used to describe him. Having the tools to stay afloat in Triple-A at age 19 is one thing, but having the right mindset and the maturity level to handle that on a daily basis is completely different.

A lot of the credit for Young's advanced approach should go to his father. Larry Young flew F-14s in the Navy when Delmon and older brother Dmitri were growing up. He likened the mental approach to the game to landing planes on aircraft carriers.

"It's the same intense focus," Larry Young says. "I tried to instill that no matter what you're doing, you need to have that focus, that same drive, that certain discipline you need. And if you take that same approach, that deep mental focus can become second nature if you work hard enough at it."

It rubbed off on both, as Dmitri went on to be an all-star outfielder with the Tigers, and Delmon is the best prospect in the game today.

Young wasn't just the premiere player in the minors in 2005, he is its best five-tool talent: hitting for average and power with a 70 arm on the 20-80 scouting scale, and the surprising speed that wasn't a part of his repertoire coming into the draft. His bat is the most important tool by far, though, and the reason the Devil Rays took him No. 1 overall in 2003 and gave him a $5.8 million major league deal. And it is that tool that has scouts comparing him to the second coming of Albert Belle.

"He's Albert without the attitude," one scout from a National League organization says. "He's a power-hitting outfielder that is everything you look for in an all-star caliber right fielder. And he just seems to get better with age—if you consider two years as a pro any kind of aging process."

—CHRIS KLINE

PREVIOUS WINNERS

1981—Mike Marshall, 1b, Albuquerque (Dodgers)
1982—Ron Kittle, of, Edmonton (White Sox)
1983—Dwight Gooden, rhp, Lynchburg (Mets)
1984—Mike Bielecki, rhp, Hawaii (Pirates)
1985—Jose Canseco, of, Huntsville/Tacoma (Athletics)
1986—Gregg Jefferies, ss, Columbia/Lynchburg/Jackson (Mets)
1987—Gregg Jefferies, ss, Jackson/Tidewater (Mets)
1988—Tom Gordon, rhp, Appleton/Memphis/Omaha (Royals)
1989—Sandy Alomar, c, Las Vegas (Padres)
1990—Frank Thomas, 1b, Birmingham (White Sox)
1991—Derek Bell, of, Syracuse (Blue Jays)
1992—Tim Salmon, of, Edmonton (Angels)
1993—Manny Ramirez, of, Canton/Charlotte (Indians)
1994—Derek Jeter, ss, Tampa/Albany/Columbus (Yankees)
1995—Andruw Jones, of, Macon (Braves)
1996—Andruw Jones, of, Durham/Greenville/Richmond (Braves)
1997—Paul Konerko, 1b, Albuquerque (Dodgers)
1998—Eric Chavez, 3b, Huntsville/Edmonton (Athletics)
1999—Rick Ankiel, lhp, Arkansas/Memphis (Cardinals)
2000—Jon Rauch, rhp, Winston-Salem/Birmingham (White Sox)
2001—Josh Beckett, rhp, Brevard County/Portland (Marlins)
2002—Rocco Baldelli, of, Bakersfield/Orlando/Durham (Devil Rays)
2003—Joe Mauer, c, Fort Myers/New Britain (Twins)
2004—Jeff Francis, lhp, Tulsa/Colorado Springs(Rockies)

Foster and Pearl's persistence also paid off. The Pearl mayor couldn't walk down the street in 2005 without someone coming up and talking to him about the Mississippi Braves. The team sold about 3,000 season tickets before Opening Day and drew 242,423 fans on the season, losing four dates at the end of the season to Hurricane Katrina. A retail development, anchored around a giant Bass Pro Shops store and the stadium, has lined up 1,000,000 square feet in stores, hotels and restaurants.

The Braves were thrilled to be moving into a state-of-the-art $25 million stadium that offered amenities for the players and fans that 21-year-old Municipal Stadium in Greenville, S.C., couldn't approach. "(Bennett) had to sell us on coming out there. We wanted to stay in Greenville. That was our first, second and third choice," Braves vice president Chip Moore says. "It didn't work out, and we're now tickled it didn't work out."

The Braves had been proclaiming their need for a new ballpark for a couple of years, with little movement from the city. When Bennett, Foster and the city of Pearl came calling, the Braves were at least willing to listen, not that they expected anything to come from it. They later admitted to Bennett that the first meeting was planned to tell him no, just to get him to stop calling.

But after their first visit to Pearl, the Braves regarded it as a nice fallback plan. With no movement in Greenville, Braves vice presidents Moore and Mike Plant set up a meeting for Bennett with general manager John Schuerholz at the 2003 Winter Meetings. Bennett was told he had 10 minutes.

More than 30 minutes later, Bennett was finally ushered out. That night, he went out with some of the Braves officials. For the first time, he and Foster could start to believe that they might pull it off.

Once it became clear Pearl was a viable option, Greenville got moving on a new stadium offer of its own. But in the end, the details on Greenville's $18 million stadium couldn't compare with Mississippi's $25 million offer. Thanks to tax money and a $1 ticket surcharge on Mississippi Braves tickets, the stadium will be paid off without any contribution from the Braves' operating revenue. The Braves will also get to keep all concession and ticket revenues.

It didn't take long for Greenville to get another team, however. The city was without minor league baseball for about five months before it found a team to replace the Greenville Braves. Local fans hardly noticed because the new team was ready to take the field at Municipal Stadium on Opening Day.

The Southern League franchise became the Mississippi Braves. Minor League Baseball then decided in February who could take over the Greenville territory from among three candidates. So the South Atlantic League's former Capital City Bombers drove the moving trucks up Interstate 26 from Columbia, S.C.

The new team was known as the Greenville Bombers for the 2005 season, but will become the Greenville Drive and move into a new downtown ballpark for 2006. The team drew 115,161 fans in 2005, down from the 143,443 fans the G-Braves drew in 2004, but all things considered it was a successful season.

The city of Greenville sought to sign a deal with the Bombers when the nearby city of Mauldin got involved. Mauldin planned to build a stadium for the West Tenn Diamond Jaxx, another Southern League franchise.

Then Mandalay Baseball Properties wanted to bring its South Atlantic League franchise, the Hagerstown Suns, to another city outside Greenville. At the same time, the city of Jackson, Tenn., told the Diamond Jaxx that it would oppose them moving out of a ballpark that had just been built for the team in 1998.

With the G-Braves gone, no group had a clear claim to the territory. Minor League Baseball finally decided in February to go with the bid from Greenville and the Bombers, which seemed all along to be the best plan. It features a downtown ballpark in the middle of the area's population center, with a firm financing plan that featured a shared public and private contribution.

Steroids Hit Minor Leagues As Well

The steroid scandal that dominated baseball headlines during the offseason and throughout the 2005 season reached down into the minor leagues, with 81 minor leaguers suspended throughout the season for violations of the minor league performance-enhancing substance policy.

Major League Baseball's first announcement came in the spring, with 38 suspensions for minor leaguers. The Associated Press also revealed that three minor league veterans with major league experience—infielder Tom Evans, righthander Brian Mallette and outfielder Jon Nunnally, all with the Pirates organization—also tested positive in the offseason and were suspended.

Of the 41 initial suspensions, 39 were for 15 days for first-time offenders. Athletics catcher David Castillo received a 60-day suspension as a repeat offender. Under MLB's guidelines for the minor leagues, a player is suspended for 60 days for a third steroids violation. Mallette, who pitched five games for the Brewers in 2002, received a 30-day suspension for his second offense.

The top prospect on the first list was A's outfielder Javi Herrera, who ranked third on Oakland's Top 10 Prospects list going into the 2005 season. He was one of five A's suspended,

Other recognizable names on the list include former big league lefthander Damian Moss and big league catcher Robert Machado. Also suspended was catcher Ryan Christianson, a 1999 first-round pick. Eight Mariners were suspended, as were seven Cubs, including infielder Matt Craig, the organization's No. 26 prospect, and lefthander Carlos Vasquez, a former member of the 40-man roster.

"We've tested players internally for years and tried to do our best to educate players on performing enhancing drugs for years," Mariners vice president of player development and scouting Benny Looper said. "But it comes down to the individual responsibility to follow through. We are extremely disappointed with our players who have been suspended. While we support those players, we also support the efforts of Major League Baseball to rid baseball of performing enhancing drugs.

"With the new (policy) of releasing names publicly, it should serve as a deterrent not only among players today, but for years to come."

Suspension announcements continued to trickle through the news throughout the season.

Marlins farmhand Wilson Delgado, with more than 250 games of major league experience, was one of the only players suspended twice during the season. He was docked 15 games in May, then got a 30-day suspension in August for another violation.

Delgado, 33, has spent parts of nine seasons in the

majors and was playing at Triple-A Albuquerque in 2005. A shortstop most of his career, he was the Isotopes' everyday second baseman and was hitting .285-6-37. He's a career .251 hitter in 542 major league at-bats.

But the stiffest penalty was handed to Nationals infielder Ramon Castro, 25, who played at Double-A Harrisburg. The former big leaguer, who played nine games with the Athletics in 2004, was fined an undisclosed amount and suspended for 105 games for two separate violations, a suspension that will last well into the 2006 season.

Castro, signed by the Braves out of Venezuela in 1996, started the year at high Class A Potomac before a promotion to Double-A and had hit 10 home runs by the end of June when he was suspended; his career high is 12.

Hurricane Katrina Spares Minors

Minor league baseball teams were not as hard-hit by Hurricane Katrina as they were in 2004 by the hurricanes that particularly affected teams in Florida, but minor league teams were universal in their efforts to gather aid for those who were devastated by the storm.

There wasn't significant storm damage to Zephyr Field, the home of the Pacific Coast League's New Orleans Zephyrs in nearby Metairie. The stadium sustained roof damage but the parking lot was dry and the scoreboard and the light standards were fine. Other than a party area down the right field line being completely blown away, the stadium was remarkably unscathed.

In fact, Zephyr Field was used as a staging area for the National Guard and later as a field hospital, so the biggest impact on the team was in recovering from the wear and tear of being a rescue center.

"There was peripheral damage to the stadium, but it could have been much worse," PCL director of operations George King said. "We don't know the full extent of the damage yet, but all the structures remain intact."

The Zephyrs finished the season on the road, and several front-office employees accompanied the team on the bus trip to Oklahoma to avoid Katrina's path. Others were left to their own devices, scrambling to gather a few of their possessions, load up the car and drive.

For other teams around the nation, the response was

Jacksonville's talent also performs

It was no secret the Jacksonville Suns were talented. Baseball America dubbed them the Most Talented Team in Minor League Baseball during the 2005 season. Even by the lofty standards of the talent-crammed Double-A Southern League, Jacksonville stood out, with four players among the league's Top 10 Prospects and five in the top 14.

But just being the most prospect-laden group in recent history is not why Jacksonville also became Baseball America's 2005 Minor League Team of the Year. The Suns also managed to harness their young talent and win their third Southern League title since joining the league in 1970.

TEAM *OF THE* ***YEAR***

"This team was ballyhooed as being the most talented minor league team, but you just didn't know if they could hold it together to win the championship," Suns owner Peter Bragan said. "I think this is the most talented team I've been associated with in the past 20 years. We've had some teams before that have had three or four great position prospects or maybe three or four outstanding pitchers, but we've never had a team that had three or four of each on the same team. And that's what this team really has."

Getting the most out of a collection of players for whom the game comes naturally—like gifted hitters Joel Guzman, Andy LaRoche, Russ Martin, James Loney and Delwyn Young—is more difficult than it sounds. Even something as simple as batting practice becomes more complicated.

"We don't take as much (BP) as you'd think because with all these guys, it can become a home run derby," said Suns outfielder Todd Donovan, a 26-year-old veteran who led the minor leagues with 62 stolen bases. "We do more in the (indoor) cages where there are no fences involved. It works better for us."

Despite their offensive firepower, pitching was an even more important ingredient in the Suns' run to Southern League championship. It took time for young pitchers like Chad Billingsley, Jonathan Broxton, Justin Orenduff and Hong-Chih Kuo to gel, but the Dodgers were determined to keep them together and let them learn in Double-A. After posting staff ERAs above 4.00 during May, June and July, Jacksonville clicked in August, recording a 3.01 ERA and running off a 12-game winning streak.

Former phenom Edwin Jackson, whose prospect star had faded somewhat after struggling at higher levels in 2004, returned to Jacksonville in 2005 and rediscovered himself, thanks largely to the tutelage of pitching coach Ken Howell.

"When he joined us, I don't think that his way of thinking or his pitching mechanics were up to Triple-A standards," Suns manager John Shoemaker said. "With Edwin, keeping things on a simple scale, you've got a power arm, use your power arm. You've got to be able to locate these pitches, not just throw hard, but Kenny Howell did a tremendous job getting this guy motivated again and on the right track physically and mentally."

By the postseason, the entire staff was on the right track. Billingsley and Broxton combined on a no-hitter against a potent Birmingham offense in a first-round sweep, during which they allowed just two runs in three games. Then, after West Tenn scored six runs in two innings against Billingsley in the opener, the Suns yielded just two more runs in the final three games—all Jacksonville wins.

"Jacksonville's pitching was excellent this series," West Tenn manager Bobby Dickerson said. "That's all you can say."

—AARON FITT

PREVIOUS WINNERS

1993—Harrisburg/Eastern (Expos)
1994—Wilmington/Carolina (Royals)
1995—Norfolk/International (Mets)
1996—Edmonton/Pacific Coast (Athletics)
1997—West Michigan/Midwest (Tigers)
1998—Mobile/Southern (Padres)
1999—Trenton/Eastern (Red Sox)
2000—Round Rock/Texas (Astros)
2001—Lake Elsinore/California (Padres)
2002—Akron Aeros/Eastern (Indians)
2003—Sacramento/Pacific Coast (Athletics)
2004—Lancaster JetHawks/California (D'backs)

2005 MINOR LEAGUE ALL-STARS

Selected by Baseball America

BILL MITCHELL
Howie Kendrick

STEVE MOORE
Chris Young

Felix Hernandez

MIKE JANES
Chuck James

FIRST TEAM

Pos.	Player, Team (Organization)	AVG	OBP	SLG	AB	R	H	2B	3B	HR	RBI	BB	SO	SB
C	Jarrod Saltalamacchia, Myrtle Beach (Braves)	.314	.394	.519	459	70	144	35	1	19	81	57	99	4
1B	Justin Huber, Wichita/Omaha (Royals)	.330	.425	.567	448	87	148	29	4	23	97	70	103	10
2B	Howie Kendrick, Rancho/Arkansas (Angels)	.367	.406	.614	469	104	172	43	8	19	89	20	62	25
3B	Andy LaRoche, Vero/Jacksonville (Dodgers)	.304	.371	.553	476	95	145	26	1	30	94	51	92	8
SS	Brandon Wood, Rancho/Salt Lake (Angels)	.321	.379	.667	555	110	178	53	5	43	116	48	134	7
OF	Jeremy Hermida, Carolina (Marlins)	.293	.457	.518	386	77	113	29	2	18	63	111	89	23
OF	Chris Young, Birmingham (White Sox)	.277	.377	.545	466	100	129	41	3	26	77	70	129	32
OF	Delmon Young, Mont./Durham (Devil Rays)	.315	.354	.527	558	92	176	26	7	26	99	29	99	32
DH	Billy Butler, High Desert/Wichita (Royals)	.340	.404	.611	491	84	167	39	2	30	110	49	98	0

Pos.	Player, Team (Organization)	W	L	ERA	G	GS	CG	SV	IP	H	HR	BB	SO	AVG
SP	Felix Hernandez, Tacoma (Mariners)	9	4	2.25	19	14	0	0	88	62	3	48	100	.196
SP	Chuck James, M.B./Miss./Rich. (Braves)	13	7	2.12	29	29	0	0	161	103	9	36	193	.179
SP	Francisco Liriano, N.B./Rochester (Twins)	12	7	2.63	27	27	0	0	168	126	10	50	204	.208
SP	Justin Verlander, Lakeland/Erie (Tigers)	11	2	1.29	20	20	0	0	119	81	4	26	136	.197
RP	Jermaine Van Buren, Iowa (Cubs)	2	3	1.98	52	0	0	25	55	33	5	22	65	.181

SECOND TEAM

Pos.	Player, Team (Organization)	AVG	OBP	SLG	AB	R	H	2B	3B	HR	RBI	BB	SO	SB
C	Russell Martin, Jacksonville (Dodgers)	.311	.430	.423	409	83	127	17	1	9	61	78	69	15
1B	Conor Jackson, Tucson (Diamondbacks)	.354	.457	.553	333	66	118	38	2	8	73	69	32	3
2B	Andy Green, Tucson (Diamondbacks)	.343	.422	.587	530	125	182	46	13	19	80	68	82	9
3B	Kory Casto, Potomac (Nationals)	.290	.394	.510	500	86	145	36	4	22	90	84	98	6
SS	B.J. Upton, Durham (Devil Rays)	.303	.392	.490	545	98	165	36	6	18	74	78	127	44
OF	Todd Linden, Fresno (Giants)	.321	.437	.682	340	81	109	25	4	30	80	62	97	6
OF	Nick Markakis, Frederick/Bowie (Orioles)	.310	.390	.504	474	78	147	41	3	15	92	61	95	2
OF	Shane Victorino, Scranton/W-B (Phillies)	.310	.377	.534	494	93	153	25	16	18	70	51	74	17
DH	Prince Fielder, Nashville (Brewers)	.291	.388	.569	378	68	110	21	0	28	86	54	93	8

Pos.	Player, Team (Organization)	W	L	ERA	G	GS	CG	SV	IP	H	HR	BB	SO	AVG
SP	Jon Lester, Portland (Red Sox)	11	6	2.61	26	26	3	0	148	114	10	57	163	.215
SP	Ricky Nolasco, West Tenn (Cubs)	14	3	2.89	27	27	1	0	162	151	13	46	173	.245
SP	Jeremy Sowers, Kinston/Akron/Buff. (Indians)	14	4	2.37	27	27	0	0	159	141	13	29	149	.235
SP	Joel Zumaya, Erie/Toledo (Tigers)	9	5	2.74	26	26	1	0	151	101	10	76	199	.189
RP	Chris Brittain, Frederick (Orioles)	6	0	1.60	46	0	0	6	79	47	5	23	110	.172

immediate—raise money in whatever way possible to help the relief effort.

Minor League Baseball sent out a letter encouraging teams to raise money for the Red Cross to help with hurricane relief in any way possible. They made it clear the standard rules about promotions and fund-raisers did not apply. So raffles, usually verboten, were given a thumbs-up. Solicitations by charities inside the gates of the ballpark were also approved.

"Minor League Baseball sent out a letter which said you could do whatever you wanted to do, all bets are off," said Buck Rogers, general manager of the Florida State League's Brevard County Manatees. "So it became something where the wheels are in motion, what can we do?"

The Manatees, like almost every other minor league team, quickly put together a fund-raiser for their final home game. In Brevard County's case, the fund-raiser had a special significance—Melbourne was hit by three different hurricanes in 2004.

"It's fresh in everybody's mind," Rogers said. "We still have blue tarps on houses here a year later. We understand this, but this is the mother of all storms."

Fortunate scheduling allowed New Orleans and the Southern League's Mobile BayBears to play out their schedules on the road, but the season ended early for the Mississippi Braves (and in turn the Carolina Mudcats). The Braves ended up canceling their final eight games of the season. The M-Braves fled the path of Hurricane

ALL-STAR FUTURES GAME

The Futures Game annually showcases some of the game's up-and-coming young talent. Many players have used the game as a springboard to the majors, often in the weeks right after they play in the game.

Royals first baseman Justin Huber and Mariners outfielder Shin-Soo Choo haven't been able to establish themselves as big leaguers yet, getting only cups of coffee earlier in the 2005 season. So they were available to play in their third Futures Game, and both played integral roles in the World team's 4-0 victory at Detroit's Comerica Park.

Choo opened the scoring in the third inning with a solo homer off Zach Jackson (Blue Jays), and Huber broke the game open in the fifth with a two-out, two-run double off Paul Maholm (Pirates).

While Huber would have preferred to be in the majors, he was happy to settle for the Futures Game MVP award, which also has been won by the likes of Alfonso Soriano, Grady Sizemore and Aaron Hill. As a bonus, his uniform will be sent to the Hall of Fame.

BILL MITCHELL

Justin Huber

"Probably 70 percent of the guys I played with in the Futures Game in 2002 are in the big leagues," said Huber, who has made the transition from catcher to first baseman after joining the Royals in a midseason 2004 trade. "Though it's a tremendous honor to be here, this is not the highlight of your career. Hopefully it's a stepping stone, helping guys catapult and get over your hump."

Huber went 0-for-3 in the 2002 and 2003 Futures Games, and his homer easily surpassed him throwing out Brewers shortstop J.J. Hardy on a steal attempt as his highlight. Similarly, Choo had struggled in the 2002 and 2004 games, going 0-for-4 and misplaying a fly ball in the 2004 game. He made amends by punishing a hanging slider from Jackson this time around.

"I feel better now," said Choo, who said it was easier to perform in 2005 because he was used to the hoopla. "A lot of players were out there taking pictures, but I did that last time."

As has often been the case in the Futures Game, the pitchers dominated the hitters. The World's shutout was the second in the event's seven-year history and the first since its 7-0 win in the inaugural game in 1999.

The U.S. team, led by elite hitting prospects such as Devil Rays shortstop B.J. Upton, Diamondbacks outfielder Conor Jackson and Devil Rays outfielder Delmon Young, managed just four hits in seven innings against nine pitchers.

Several of the U.S. pitchers also stood out, including prospects Justin Verlander and Joel Zumaya of the hometown Tigers.

Six pitchers topped 95 mph with their fastballs, with Zumaya and Juan Morillo (Rockies) both peaking at 99 mph. Both U.S. manager George Brett and World manager Guillermo Hernandez said they never had seen so many pitching prospects in one place.

"Everyone was coming in throwing 95-99 with pretty good control," Brett said. "It's just amazing. I guess that's why they were in the Futures Game."

UNITED STATES ROSTER

Pitchers: Travis Bowyer (Twins), Thomas Diamond (Rangers), Zach Jackson (Blue Jays), J.J. Johnson (Orioles), Chris Lambert (Cardinals), Anthony Lerew (Braves), Paul Maholm (Pirates), Troy Patton (Astros), Justin Verlander (Tigers), Joel Zumaya (Tigers).

Catchers: Ryan Garko (Indians), Chris Iannetta (Rockies).

Infielders: Josh Barfield (Padres), Daric Barton (Athletics), Kevin Frandsen (Giants), Conor Jackson (Diamondbacks), Andy LaRoche (Dodgers), Scott Moore (Cubs), B.J. Upton (Devil Rays), Brandon Wood (Angels).

Outfielders: Jeremy Hermida (Marlins), Lastings Milledge (Mets), Kevin Thompson (Yankees), Chris Young (White Sox), Delmon Young (Devil Rays).

WORLD ROSTER

Pitchers: Fausto Carmona (Indians), Francisco Liriano (Twins), Adam Loewen (Orioles), Scott Mathieson (Phillies), Juan Morillo (Rockies), Fernando Nieve (Astros), Yusmeiro Petit (Mets), Anibal Sanchez (Red Sox), Merkin Valdez (Giants), Edison Volquez (Rangers).

Catchers: Russ Martin (Dodgers), Miguel Montero (Diamondbacks).

Infielders: Jose Bautista (Pirates), William Bergolla (Reds), Yuniesky Betancourt (Mariners), Edwin Encarnacion (Reds), Justin Huber (Royals), Hernan Iribarren (Brewers), Kendry Morales (Angels), Hanley Ramirez (Red Sox).

Outfielders: Shin-Soo Choo (Mariners), Nelson Cruz (Brewers), Frank Diaz (Nationals), Javier Herrera (Athletics), Luis Montanez (Cubs).

FUTURES GAME

Comerica Park, Detroit

July 10, 2005

World 4, United States 0

WORLD	ab	r	h	rbi	USA	ab	r	h	rbi
Betancourt, ss	2	0	0	0	Thompson, lf	2	0	0	0
Ramirez, ss	1	0	1	0	Milledge, lf	1	0	0	0
Choo, cf	2	1	1	1	Upton, ss	2	0	0	0
Herrera, cf	1	0	1	1	Wood, ss	1	0	1	0
Morales, 1b	2	0	1	0	Jackson, 1b	2	0	0	0
Huber, 1b	2	0	1	2	Barton, 1b	1	0	0	0
Cruz, rf	2	0	0	0	D. Young, rf	2	0	1	0
Diaz, rf	2	0	0	0	Hermida, dh	2	0	0	0
Encarnacion, 3b	2	0	0	0	LaRoche, 3b	2	0	2	0
Bautista, 3b	1	0	1	0	Moore, 3b	1	0	0	0
Montero, c	1	0	0	0	Garko, c	2	0	0	0
Martin, c	1	0	0	0	Iannetta, c	0	0	0	0
Bergolla, 2b	4	0	2	0	Barfield, 2b	2	0	0	0
Iribarren, dh	4	1	1	0	Frandsen, 2b	1	0	0	0
Montanez, lf	3	2	1	0	C. Young, cf	2	0	0	0
Totals	**30**	**4**	**10**	**4**	**Totals**	**23**	**0**	**4**	**0**

World	001	021	0—**4**
United States	000	000	0—**0**

LOB—World 11, United States 5.**2B**—Morales, Huber. **HR**—Choo.

WORLD	ip	h	r	er	bb	so	USA	ip	h	r	er	bb	so
Liriano	1	0	0	0	0	1	Verlander	1	1	0	0	0	0
Volquez W	1	2	0	0	0	0	Lerew	1	1	0	0	1	1
Petit	1	0	0	0	0	0	Jackson L	1	1	1	1	0	1
Mathieson	⅔	0	0	0	0	0	Zumaya	1	0	0	0	0	1
Morillo	⅔	0	0	0	0	1	Maholm	⅓	2	2	2	1	0
Nieve	⅔	1	0	0	0	1	Lambert	⅔	0	0	0	1	1
Carmona	⅔	0	0	0	0	0	Patton	⅔	0	0	0	0	1
Sanchez	⅓	1	0	0	2	1	Johnson	⅓	3	1	1	0	1
Loewen Sv	1	0	0	0	1	0	Bowyer	1	2	0	0	1	2

WP—Loewen. **Balk**—Sanchez. **HBP**—Montanez (by Maholm). **T**: 2:06.

CLASSIFICATION ALL-STARS

Selected by Baseball America

TRIPLE-A
International League, Pacific Coast League

Pos.	Player, Team (Organization)	AVG	OBP	SLG	AB	R	H	2B	3B	HR	RBI	BB	SO	SB
C	Jeff Mathis, Salt Lake (Angels)	.276	.340	.499	427	78	118	26	3	21	73	42	85	4
1B	Conor Jackson, Tucson (Diamondbacks)	.354	.457	.553	333	66	118	38	2	8	73	69	32	3
2B	Andy Green, Tucson (Diamondbacks)	.343	.422	.587	530	125	182	46	13	19	80	68	82	9
3B	Edwin Encarnacion, Louisville (Reds)	.314	.388	.548	290	44	91	23	0	15	54	33	53	7
SS	B.J. Upton, Durham (Devil Rays)	.303	.392	.490	545	98	165	36	6	18	74	78	127	44
OF	Ben Johnson, Portland (Padres)	.312	.394	.558	414	79	129	27	0	25	83	51	88	6
OF	Todd Linden, Fresno (Giants)	.321	.437	.682	340	81	109	25	4	30	80	62	97	6
OF	Shane Victorino,Scranton/W-B (Phillies)	.310	.377	.534	494	93	153	25	16	18	70	51	74	17
DH	Prince Fielder, Nashville (Brewers)	.291	.388	.569	378	68	110	21	0	28	86	54	93	8

Pos.	Player, Team (Organization)	W	L	ERA	G	GS	CG	SV	IP	H	HR	BB	SO	AVG
SP	Zach Duke, Indianapolis (Pirates)	12	3	2.92	16	16	1	0	108	108	8	23	66	.267
SP	Felix Hernandez, Tacoma (Mariners)	9	4	2.25	19	14	1	0	88	62	3	48	100	.196
SP	Francisco Liriano, Rochester (Twins)	9	2	1.78	14	14	0	0	91	56	4	24	112	.177
SP	Jason Scobie, Norfolk (Mets)	15	7	3.34	27	26	0	0	167	163	13	55	96	.260
RP	Jermaine Van Buren, Iowa (Cubs)	2	3	1.98	52	0	0	25	55	33	5	22	65	.181

Player of the Year: Francisco Liriano, lhp, Rochester (Twins). **Manager of the Year:** Ken Oberkfell, Norfolk (Mets). **Team of the Year:** Toledo (Tigers).

PLAYER OF THE YEAR
Francisco Liriano, lhp
Rochester

DOUBLE-A
Eastern League, Southern League, Texas League

Pos.	Player, Team (Organization)	AVG	OBP	SLG	AB	R	H	2B	3B	HR	RBI	BB	SO	SB
C	Russ Martin, Jacksonville (Dodgers)	.311	.430	.423	129	83	127	17	1	9	61	78	69	15
1B	Justin Huber, Wichita (Royals)	.343	.432	.570	335	68	115	22	3	16	74	51	70	7
2B	Dustin Pedroia, Portland (Red Sox)	.324	.409	.508	256	39	83	19	2	8	40	34	26	7
3B	Jose Bautista, Altoona (Pirates)	.383	.364	.503	445	63	126	27	1	23	90	48	101	7
SS	Erick Aybar, Arkansas (Angels)	.303	.350	.445	535	101	162	29	10	9	54	29	51	49
OF	Jeremy Hermida, Carolina (Marlins)	.293	.457	.518	386	77	113	29	2	18	63	111	89	23
OF	Chris Young, Birmingham (White Sox)	.277	.377	.545	466	100	129	41	3	26	77	70	129	32
OF	Delmon Young, Montgomery (Devil Rays)	.336	.386	.582	330	59	111	13	4	20	71	25	66	25
DH	Mike Jacobs, Binghamton (Mets)	.321	.376	.589	433	66	139	37	2	25	93	35	94	1

Pos.	Player, Team (Organization)	W	L	ERA	G	GS	CG	SV	IP	H	HR	BB	SO	AVG
SP	Jason Hirsh, Corpus Christi (Astros)	13	8	2.87	29	29	1	0	172	137	12	42	165	.218
SP	Chuck James, Mississippi (Braves)	9	1	2.09	16	16	0	0	86	62	4	18	104	.199
SP	Jon Lester, Portland (Red Sox)	11	6	2.61	26	26	3	0	148	114	10	57	163	.215
SP	Ricky Nolasco, West Tenn (Cubs)	14	3	2.89	27	27	1	0	162	157	13	46	173	.245
RP	Chris Ray, Bowie (Orioles)	1	2	0.96	31	0	0	18	37	17	3	7	40	.140

Player of the Year: Delmon Young, of, Montgomery (Devil Rays). **Manager of the Year:** Torey Lovullo, Akron (Indians). **Team of the Year:** Jacksonville (Dodgers).

RICH ABEL

PLAYER OF THE YEAR
Delmon Young, of
Montgomery

HIGH CLASS A
California League, Carolina League, Florida State League

Pos.	Player, Team (Organization)	AVG	OBP	SLG	AB	R	H	2B	3B	HR	RBI	BB	SO	SB
C	Jarrod Saltalamacchia, M. Beach (Braves)	.314	.394	.519	459	70	144	35	1	19	81	57	99	4
1B	Leo Daigle, Winston-Salem (White Sox)	.341	.414	.637	411	85	140	33	1	29	112	50	72	10
2B	Howie Kendrick, Rancho Cuca. (Angels)	.384	.421	.638	279	69	107	23	6	12	47	14	42	13
3B	Andy LaRoche, Vero Beach (Dodgers)	.333	.349	.651	249	54	83	14	1	21	51	19	38	6
SS	Brandon Wood, Ranco Cuca. (Angels)	.321	.383	.672	536	109	172	51	4	43	115	48	128	7
OF	Brent Clevlen, Lakewood (Tigers)	.302	.387	.484	494	77	149	28	4	18	102	65	118	14
OF	Matt Kemp, Vero Beach (Dodgers)	.306	.349	.569	418	76	128	21	4	27	90	25	92	23
OF	Chris Lubanski, High Desert (Royals)	.301	.349	.554	531	91	160	39	6	28	116	38	131	14
DH	Billy Butler, High Desert (Royals)	.348	.419	.636	379	70	132	30	2	25	91	42	80	0

Pos.	Player, Team (Organization)	W	L	ERA	G	GS	CG	SV	IP	H	HR	BB	SO	AVG
SP	Thomas Diamond, Bakersfield (Rangers)	8	0	1.99	14	14	1	0	81	53	3	31	101	.191
SP	Anibal Sanchez, Wilmington (Red Sox)	6	1	2.40	14	14	0	0	79	53	7	24	95	.187
SP	Justin Verlander, Lakeland (Tigers)	9	2	1.67	13	13	2	0	86	70	3	19	104	.230
SP	Carlos Villanueva, Brevard County (Brewers)	8	1	2.32	21	21	0	0	112	78	11	32	124	.195
RP	Chris Britton, Frederick (Orioles)	6	0	1.60	46	0	0	6	79	47	5	23	110	.172

Player of the Year: Brandon Wood, ss, Rancho Cucamonga (Angels). **Manager of the Year:** Lenn Sakata, San Jose (Giants). **Team of the Year:** Lakeland (Tigers).

BILL MITCHELL

PLAYER OF THE YEAR
Brandon Wood, ss
Rancho Cucamonga

Katrina and stayed in a hotel in Atlanta.

"The decision to cancel the remaining games may be one of the toughest ones we've had to make. There are so many factors that went into this decision such as park damage, power outages, team safety, travel and housing, and gas and supply shortages," general manager Steve DeSalvo said. "This area of the country, and perhaps the entire country, is feeling the devastating affects of this terrible disaster. Everyone needs to focus on their personal safety and that of their loved ones."

Minors Take Advantage Of Nats Move

The transformation of the Montreal Expos to the Washington Nationals was a huge move in the major leagues, but its effects trickled down to the minors as well.

The Carolina League's Potomac Cannons became the Potomac Nationals, with a new name and a new look for the team that brought a new outlook.

"The buzz around here is kind of contagious," Potomac manager Bob Henley said. "It's a privilege to be managing this club. It's historic."

The Potomac Nationals aligned themselves with Washington's new major league team by revealing a new logo, uniforms and a new mascot. Perhaps more significant, however, team owner Art Silber also confirmed that the team will get a new stadium.

CLASSIFICATION ALL-STARS

LOW CLASS A — Midwest League, South Atlantic League

Pos.	Player, Team (Organization)	AVG	OBP	SLG	AB	R	H	2B	3B	HR	RBI	BB	SO	SB
C	Neil Walker, Hickory (Pirates)	.301	.332	.452	485	78	146	33	2	12	68	20	71	7
1B	Joe Koshansky, Asheville (Rockies)	.291	.373	.603	453	92	132	31	1	36	103	53	122	6
2B	Eric Patterson, Peoria (Cubs)	.333	.405	.535	432	90	144	26	11	13	71	53	94	40
3B	David Winfree, Beloit (Twins)	.294	.329	.452	562	80	165	31	5	16	101	22	93	3
SS	Marcus Sanders, Augusta (Giants)	.300	.407	.400	420	86	126	19	4	5	40	69	90	57
OF	Carlos Gonzales, South Bend (D'backs)	.307	.371	.489	515	91	158	28	6	18	92	48	86	7
OF	Matt Miller, Asheville (Rockies)	.331	.375	.575	508	79	168	34	0	30	100	26	71	9
OF	Hunter Pence, Lexington (Astros)	.338	.413	.652	302	59	102	14	3	25	60	38	53	8
DH	Brad McCann, Greensboro (Marlins)	.295	.355	.552	478	67	141	35	2	28	106	37	97	1

Pos.	Player, Team (Organization)	W	L	ERA	G	GS	CG	SV	IP	H	HR	BB	SO	AVG
SP	Jimmy Barthmaier, Lexington (Astros)	11	6	2.27	25	25	0	0	135	108	3	55	142	.220
SP	Scott Elbert, Columbus (Dodgers)	8	5	2.66	25	24	1	0	115	83	8	57	128	.200
SP	Sean Gallagher, Peoria (Cubs)	14	5	2.71	26	26	0	0	146	107	10	55	139	.206
SP	Troy Patton, Lexington (Astros)	5	2	1.94	15	15	0	0	79	59	3	20	94	.211
RP	Matt Elliott, South Bend (Diamondbacks)	3	4	2.14	53	0	0	32	55	35	1	22	71	.183

Player of the Year: Carlos Gonzales, of, South Bend (Diamondbacks). **Manager of the Year:** Tim Bogar, Lexington (Astros). **Team of the Year:** South Bend (Diamondbacks).

BOB ROMERO

PLAYER OF THE YEAR

Carlos Gonzales, of
South Bend

SHORT-SEASON — New York-Penn League, Northwest League

Pos.	Player, Team (Organization)	AVG	OBP	SLG	AB	R	H	2B	3B	HR	RBI	BB	SO	SB
C	Taylor Teagarden, Spokane (Rangers)	.281	.426	.635	96	23	27	5	4	7	16	23	32	1
1B	Neil Sellers, Tri-City (Rockies)	.344	.417	.534	279	46	96	18	1	11	50	35	27	7
2B	Will Rhymes, Oneonta (Tigers)	.328	.391	.420	250	48	82	11	3	2	27	25	15	14
3B	Pablo Sandoval, Salem-Keizer (Giants)	.330	.383	.425	294	46	97	15	2	3	50	21	33	2
SS	Michael Hollimon, Oneonta (Tigers)	.277	.389	.559	256	66	71	13	10	13	53	48	76	8
OF	Michael Mooney, Salem-Keizer (Giants)	.342	.389	.516	304	57	104	20	9	5	29	20	64	13
OF	Ryan Patterson, Auburn (Blue Jays)	.339	.386	.595	274	52	93	23	4	13	65	21	53	5
OF	Nolan Reimold, Aberdeen (Orioles)	.294	.392	.550	180	33	53	15	2	9	30	29	44	2
DH	Gaby Sanchez, Jamestown (Marlins)	.355	.401	.487	234	34	83	16	0	5	42	16	24	11

Pos.	Player, Team (Organization)	W	L	ERA	G	GS	CG	SV	IP	H	HR	BB	SO	AVG
SP	Wade Davis, Hudson Valley (Devil Rays)	7	4	2.72	15	15	0	0	86	75	5	23	97	.234
SP	Shane Lindsay, Tri-City (Rockies)	6	1	1.89	13	13	0	0	67	37	1	34	107	.163
SP	Mike Madsen, Vancouver (Athletics)	6	1	1.69	15	12	0	0	80	56	2	14	68	.192
SP	Joe Ness, Mahoning Valley (Indians)	4	2	1.67	14	10	0	0	59	52	4	19	68	.234
RP	Josh Schmidt, Staten Island (Yankees)	5	1	0.27	26	0	0	13	33	14	0	8	47	.128

Player of the Year: Shane Lindsay, Tri-City (Rockies). **Manager of the Year:** Staten Island (Yankees). **Team of the Year:** Steve Decker (Salem-Keizer).

PLAYER OF THE YEAR

Shane Lindsay, rhp
Tri-City

ROOKIE — Appalachian League, Arizona League, Gulf Coast League, Pioneer League

Pos.	Player, Team (Organization)	AVG	OBP	SLG	AB	R	H	2B	3B	HR	RBI	BB	SO	SB
C	Angel Salome, Helena (Brewers)	.415	.469	.673	159	34	66	17	0	8	50	15	16	6
1B	P.J. Hiser, Burlington (Indians)	.326	.406	.711	135	29	44	15	2	11	36	18	43	1
2B	Kenny Holmberg, Helena (Brewers)	.372	.450	.623	207	40	77	16	0	12	51	29	34	2
3B	Eric Campbell, Danville (Braves)	.313	.383	.634	262	77	82	26	2	18	64	28	64	15
SS	Chris McConnell, Idaho Falls (Royals)	.331	.403	.516	275	56	91	17	8	6	39	31	34	7
OF	Lorenzo Cain, AZL/Helena (Brewers)	.356	.418	.566	205	45	73	18	5	5	37	20	32	12
OF	Charlie Fremaint, Helena (Brewers)	.364	.419	.744	129	46	47	9	2	12	32	15	28	11
OF	Josh Flores, Greeneville (Astros)	.335	.384	.520	248	49	83	12	5	8	25	16	57	20
DH	Corey Wimberly, Casper (Rockies)	.381	.427	.427	281	58	107	10	0	1	22	18	27	36

Pos.	Player, Team (Organization)	W	L	ERA	G	GS	CG	SV	IP	H	HR	BB	SO	AVG
SP	Jairo Cuevas, Danville (Braves)	6	1	1.95	12	10	0	0	55	35	3	22	69	.179
SP	Adam Hawes, Elizabethton (Twins)	4	0	1.53	14	9	1	1	59	38	2	16	68	.183
SP	Greg Smith, Missoula (Diamondbacks)	8	5	4.15	16	14	0	0	82	69	8	18	100	.231
SP	Travis Wood, GCL Reds/Billings (Reds)	2	0	1.31	14	11	0	0	48	28	0	20	67	.165
RP	Alexander Smit, Elizabethton (Twins)	6	1	1.97	21	0	0	3	46	25	3	12	86	.157

Player of the Year: Eric Campbell, 3b, Danville (Braves). **Manager of the Year:** Ray Smith, Elizabethton (Twins). **Team of the Year:** Elizabethton (Twins).

MIKE JANES

PLAYER OF THE YEAR

Eric Campbell, 3b
Danville

"We are ecstatic with our relationship with the new ballclub," Silber said. "We've made a commitment. We believe this is the way it will continue for a long time."

After cutting ties with the Reds after the 2004 season, Potomac also scrapped a nickname it had for 16 seasons.

"This is the most exciting offseason I've ever experienced, with the new team coming to D.C. and being able to be affiliated with them," Potomac general manager Jay Richardson said. "Everything turned out exactly how we hoped it would."

Silber also announced that the team will get a new stadium near its current home in Woodbridge, Va. The cost of the new stadium will be split between Silber and local government.

The Vermont Expos (New York-Penn) took an approach opposite that of Potomac, deciding there were enough fans who missed the Expos to keep the name for the 2005 season.

Vermont did an online survey after the 2004 season that showed than 60 percent of 2,000 respondents preferred keeping the Expos name. That fit well with the practical matter that a hurried switch to a new name would also leave the team with Vermont Expos merchandise and apparel that would be suddenly obsolete. Instead, Vermont could market the gear as collectors' items.

The team even looked into keeping the Expos name for the long term, but was told by Major League Baseball that it would have to eliminate the Expos name by 2006.

Big league experience aids Oberkfell in dugout

ALLISON VEINOLE

Pleasure to play for Norfolk skipper Ken Oberkfell

MANAGER *OF THE* **YEAR**

Triple-A Norfolk might not have won the Governor's Cup in the International League in 2005, but the Tides' skipper firmly established himself as one of the top managers in the minors.

Ken Oberkfell led Norfolk to a 79-65 record, winning the IL South by 14 games in his rookie season in Triple-A. The club bowed out in the first round of the playoffs, but took eventual champion Toledo to a deciding fifth game before doing so.

Over his 10-year managerial career, Oberkfell has become known for drawing on his depth of personal experience as a player with the Cardinals, Braves, Pirates, Giants, Astros and Angels.

"You just instantly respect him because of everything he's been through," Norfolk third baseman Rodney Nye said. "He just lets you play the game. As a player he's easy to play for because of his laid-back approach. Guys respond to that."

"There is enough pressure at this level," righthander Jason Scobie said. "He just lets you go out there and do what you have to do. We all make mistakes, but Obie's approach is to take it easy and that helps a lot. His door is always open and he's the best manager I've ever played for."

It is that openness, that experience, and the outstanding job he did in Norfolk that made him Baseball America's 2005 Minor League Manager of the Year.

Oberkfell took two years off after retiring in 1992, playing golf and figuring out what he wanted to do next. He decided he wanted to manage, but there were no offers in affiliated ball. Oberkfell took a job in the independent Northeast League, managing the Mohawk Valley Landsharks to a second-place finish with a 47-23 record in 1995.

He spent another year in the independent leagues before then-Phillies GM Lee Thomas gave him a shot with low Class A Piedmont in 1997. He remained until 1999, returning to the South Atlantic League with the Mets' Capital City affiliate. Then he moved up to high Class A St. Lucie, leading the Mets to the playoffs in 2002 and winning the Florida State League title in 2003.

He moved up to Double-A Binghamton in 2004, and the B-Mets finished 10 games over .500 and made the postseason. Counting his 2005 appearance, Oberkfell has four consecutive playoff berths at three different levels.

"He's done a great, great job of implementing our organizational philosophy and yet keeping our plan for individual players," Mets farm director Kevin Morgan said. "We felt that through his experience and extreme wealth of knowledge, he'd be a prefect fit for Triple-A. He's a strong communicator with an innate ability to express what's needed out of his players."

And just as he reached the big leagues as a player, there's no doubt he's ready to get back to a major league dugout as a manager.

"A lot of superstar players maybe get the opportunity (to manage in the big leagues) because of their name, but it's not that easy," Oberkfell said. "You should pay your dues. I think you learn once you try it. Having been in the minors for 10 years, I think I've learned a lot. Don't get me wrong, Triple-A isn't a bad gig, but I want to be back in the big leagues—everyone does. If they tell you any different, they're lying."

—CHRIS KLINE

PREVIOUS **WINNERS**

1981—Ed Nottle, Tacoma (Athletics)
1982—Eddie Haas, Richmond (Braves)
1983—Bill Dancy, Reading (Phillies)
1984—Sam Perlozzo, Jackson (Mets)
1985—Jim Lefebvre, Phoenix (Giants)
1986—Brad Fischer, Huntsville (Athletics)
1987—Dave Trembley, Harrisburg (Pirates)
1988—Joe Sparks, Indianapolis (Expos)
1989—Buck Showalter, Albany (Yankees)
1990—Kevin Kennedy, Albuquerque (Dodgers)
1991—Butch Hobson, Pawtucket (Red Sox)
1992—Grady Little, Greenville (Braves)
1993—Terry Francona, Birmingham (White Sox)
1994—Tim Ireland, El Paso (Brewers)
1995—Marc Bombard, Indianapolis (Reds)
1996—Carlos Tosca, Portland (Marlins)
1997—Gary Jones, Edmonton (Athletics)
1998—Terry Kennedy, Iowa (Cubs)
1999—John Mizerock, Wichita (Royals)
2000—Joel Skinner, Buffalo (Indians)
2001—Jackie Moore, Round Rock (Astros)
2002—John Russell, Edmonton (Twins)
2003—Dave Brundage, San Antonio (Mariners)
2004—Marty Brown, Buffalo (Indians)

"Without a doubt, it gives us more time (to plan the name change)," Vermont general manager C.J. Knudsen said. "There are a thousand different factors to making our decision. It's not only a tribute to Montreal and gives us additional time to let fans know we're changing our team name, but it also creates a sense that this is the last year as the Expos."

The team, which is just 90 miles from Montreal, also saw a bump in attendance, going from 93,796 fans in 2004 to 106,407 in 2005.

"We've seen a tremendous increase in interest from the Quebec and upstate New York market," Knudsen said. "It's prompted us to open the ticket office in late March instead of early June. And we launched a mini-Website in French for French-speaking fans. The people who went to the Big O (Olympic Stadium), they are big fans."

Portland Franchise Finds Stability

In Portland, Ore., PFE was replaced by PBIG, which reached an agreement with the Pacific Coast League to buy the orphaned Beavers.

Confusing? Sure. But confusion had been the norm for

the Beavers, who had been mired in ownership limbo for a full year. With an agreement by the Portland Baseball Investment Group to purchase the team, however, the Beavers and the PCL hoped a complicated, expensive mess has finally been cleaned up. The new group was led by Abe Alizadeh, a Sacramento restaurateur.

The team had been run by the PCL for more than a year. The league took control of the team a week before Opening Day in 2004, when the city of Portland said it wouldn't allow the team to play without a guarantee it was in stable financial hands. The previous owner, Portland Family Entertainment, fell behind on debt payments, lease payments and payments to creditors.

After taking over the team, the PCL turned to Sacramento owner Art Savage to help run the team. Savage's Sports Management Consulting group helped run the team through the 2004 season, with financial assistance from Alizadeh. Jack Cain, the longtime owner of Portland's Northwest League franchise before the Triple-A Beavers came to town, owned a small stake in the team and served as a senior adviser.

"The combination of the ownership group, the current management team in place, and Art Savage and his organization will allow the teams and PGE Park to continue on the same path we've established over the past year," PCL president Branch Rickey said.

The increased stability was paid off in increased ticket sales and sponsorship deals. In 2004, the team was unable to promote or sign sponsorship deals until just before the season began. With a larger staff, the team reported a 400 percent increase in group ticket sales and a 20 percent increase in season ticket sales.

The final numbers were also encouraging, as overall attendance moved from 312,678 in 2004 to 360,772 in 2005. Average attendance went up from 4,404 fans a game to 5,229.

MINOR LEAGUE ALL-STAR GAMES

For Gerald Laird, even playing in the Triple-A all-star game was a surprise.

After taking the winter off to heal an injury, Laird wasn't sure if he would be able to play at all in 2005. And the Oklahoma catcher did not make the Pacific Coast League all-star team until he was named as a replacement.

Still, he started and hit the first grand slam since the game's inception in 1988, leading the PCL to an 11-5 victory over the International League in front a sellout crowd of 14,414 at Sacramento's Raley Field. The IL had won the previous two games.

Laird earned PCL MVP honors, going 2-for-3 and tying the all-star game record with four RBIs. A second-round pick of the Athletics in 1998, Laird was traded to the Rangers as part of a seven-player deal in 2002.

Louisville third baseman Edwin Encarnacion, the top position player prospect in the Reds organization, was the IL MVP after going 1-for-2 with a solo homer.

Laird was the Rangers' Opening Day starter in 2004 and was the American League rookie of the month in April of that year. But he tore a ligament in his left thumb in May and had surgery. When he returned two months later, he was still not 100 percent. So, he took the winter off and did not begin playing again until he reported to spring training in 2005.

By then, the Rangers had signed veteran Sandy Alomar Jr. as the backup catcher, so Laird's days in the majors appeared numbered. He appeared in only one game with the Rangers in 2005 before the all-star game, but 12 after.

"(The injury) was nerve-wracking, but I feel great now," said Laird, who hit 310-17-55 for the RedHawks. "It's one of those things where I know I have to play hard (to return to the majors). I know I can play (in the big leagues). This is just a bump in the road."

Encarnacion was just one of several prospects who played in the game. Tucson first baseman Conor Jackson (Diamondbacks), Rochester righthander Travis Bowyer (Twins), Buffalo catcher Ryan Garko (Indians) and Durham shortstop B.J. Upton (Devil Rays) were among those who also played in the Futures Game in Detroit a day earlier.

Jackson went 2-for-2 with an RBI, and Bowyer threw a perfect two-thirds of an inning. Garko and Upton struggled; the Indians catcher went 0-for-2 and Upton committed two errors.

ALL-STAR ROUNDUP

EASTERN LEAGUE • The Portland Sea Dogs hosted the all-star game for the first time, and the home team did not disappoint. Sea Dogs shortstop **Kenny Perez** hit a two-run double in a four-run eighth inning as the North rallied for a 9-6 win over the South. New Britain first baseman **Danny Matienzo** took home the MVP award after going 3-for-3 with two runs.

SOUTHERN LEAGUE • Carolina right fielder **Jeremy Hermida** led the North past the South, 12-5 in Mobile. Hermida, who earned MVP honors, went 3-for-5 with a double, four RBIs and a pair of runs. Righthanders **Dana Eveland** (Huntsville) and **Josh Johnson** (Carolina) each threw a scoreless inning for the North.

TEXAS LEAGUE • The Frisco RoughRiders threw a Texas-size party at Dr. Pepper/Seven-Up Ballpark, with an announced crowd of 10,398 watching the West defeat the East, 5-0. The evening belonged to Midland outfielder **Andre Ethier**, who earned MVP honors by driving in the first run of the game and robbed Arkansas second baseman **Alberto Callaspo** (Angels) of a third-inning home run with a sensational catch at the left-field wall.

CALIFORNIA/CAROLINA LEAGUE • No hometown player had starred in the California/Carolina League all-star game since Kinston's Billy Munoz hit a walkoff homer to give the CL a win in 2000. But Frederick outfielder **Nick Markakis** wowed Keys fans, winning the home run contest over High Desert outfielder **Billy Butler** and going 3-for-5 with two homers to win the game's MVP award.

FLORIDA STATE LEAGUE • With the best record in minor league baseball, Lakeland dominated the Florida State League all-star game, as the Tigers affiliate placed a league-record 10 players in the game, including seven starters. And as they had all season, they delivered, leading the West to a 6-4 victory over the East in Clearwater. Sarasota outfielder **Chris Dickerson** put the game away with a two-run home run in the sixth and earned MVP honors.

MIDWEST LEAGUE • South Bend finished the first half with the best record in the Midwest League, and the Diamondbacks affiliate showed why in Peoria, as Silver Hawks players carried the East to a 4-2 victory over the West. **Jereme Milons**, acquired by the Diamondbacks from the Dodgers late in 2004, hit an RBI double in the fourth and earned MVP honors.

SOUTH ATLANTIC LEAGUE • The North defeated the South 7-5, as Charleston's **Tim Battle** was named the game's MVP. Battle went 2-for-3 while Hagerstown's **Marcus Sanders**, his Southern Division teammate, reached base four times and scored twice.

NEW YORK-PENN LEAGUE • Brooklyn was the site of the first all-star game in the New York-Penn League's 66-year history on Aug. 23, and a standing-room only crowd of more than 9,000 turned out to see it. Players from the league's National League affiliates held off two late-inning rallies to secure a 5-4 victory over the American League. Jamestown's **Gaby Sanchez**, who had a two-run single to pace a four-run fifth inning for the NL, was named MVP.

MINOR LEAGUE
DEPARTMENT LEADERS

*Full-season teams only

TEAM

WINS
- Toledo (International) ... 89
- Lakeland (Florida State) ... 85
- San Jose (California) ... 85
- Akron (Eastern) ... 84
- South Bend (Midwest) ... 84

LONGEST WINNING STREAK
- Elizabethton (Appalachian) ... 14
- Four teams tied with ... 12

LOSSES
- Clearwater (Florida State) ... 95
- Richmond (International) ... 88
- Charlotte (International) ... 87
- Las Vegas (Pacific Coast) ... 86
- Visalia (California) ... 85

LONGEST LOSING STREAK
- Lake Elsinore (California) ... 15
- Frisco (Texas) ... 13
- Oklahoma (Pacific Coast) ... 13

BATTING AVERAGE*
- Lancaster (California) ... .302
- High Desert (California) ... .301
- Colorado Springs (Pacific Coast) ... .296
- Oklahoma (Pacific Coast) ... .296
- San Jose (California) ... .295

RUNS
- High Desert (California) ... 918
- Lancaster (California) ... 917
- Oklahoma (Pacific Coast) ... 893
- Stockton (California) ... 835
- Salt Lake (Pacific Coast) ... 820

HOME RUNS
- High Desert (California) ... 203
- Durham (International) ... 198
- Albuquerque (Pacific Coast) ... 183
- Buffalo (International) ... 179
- Winston-Salem (Carolina) ... 178

STOLEN BASES
- Hagerstown (South Atlantic) ... 203
- Cedar Rapids (Midwest) ... 202
- Winston-Salem (Carolina) ... 188
- Charleston (South Atlantic) ... 187
- Burlington (Midwest) ... 178

EARNED RUN AVERAGE*
- Corpus Christi (Texas) ... 3.34
- Fort Myers (Florida State) ... 3.35
- West Tenn (Southern) ... 3.35
- Lakeland (Florida State) ... 3.37

BILL MITCHELL

Andy Green: 125 runs

DAVID SCHOEFIELD

Shane Victorino: 16 triples

- Akron (Eastern) ... 3.40

STRIKEOUTS
- Beloit (Midwest) ... 1,186
- Stockton (California) ... 1,182
- Lexington (South Atlantic) ... 1,174
- Bowie (Eastern) ... 1,168
- Frederick (Carolina) ... 1,154

INDIVIDUAL BATTING

BATTING AVERAGE*
(Minimum 2.7 Plate Appearances/Team Game)
- Rick Short, New Orleans ... .383
- Howie Kendrick, Rancho Cuca./Arkansas ... .367
- Joe Dillon, Albuquerque ... .360
- Conor Jackson, Tucson ... .354
- Kevin Orie, Nashville/New Orleans ... .352
- Brian Horwitz, Augusta ... .349
- Randy Ruiz, Reading ... .349
- Andy Green, Tucson ... .343
- Matt Murton, West Tenn/Iowa ... .343
- Sebastien Boucher, Wis./Inland Empire ... .340
- Billy Butler, High Desert/Wichita ... .340
- Ryan Spilborghs, Tulsa/Colorado Springs .340

RUNS
- Andy Green, Tucson ... 125
- Pete Maestrales, Delm./Burl. (MWL)/H.D... 114
- Noah Hall, Winston-Salem ... 112
- Brandon Wood, Rancho Cuca./Salt Lake ... 110
- Nick Gorneault, Salt Lake ... 106

HITS
- Angel Sanchez, High Desert ... 183
- Andy Green, Tucson ... 182
- Brandon Wood, Rancho Cuca./Salt Lake ... 178
- Delmon Young, Montgomery/Durham ... 176
- Frank Diaz, Potomac ... 173
- Jerry Owens, Birmingham ... 173

TOP HITTING STREAKS
- Truhan Mehl, AZL Rangers ... 25
- Irving Falu, Burlington ... 24
- Brian Horwitz, Augusta ... 24
- Ryan Howard, Scranton/Wilkes-Barre ... 24
- Francisco Leandro, Visalia ... 24

MOST HITS, ONE GAME
- Matt Diaz, Omaha ... 6
- Stephen Head, Kinston ... 6
- Matt Joyce, Oneonta ... 6
- Ramon Martinez, Toledo ... 6
- Billy McCarthy, Richmond ... 6
- Nick McIntyre, West Michigan ... 6
- Emmanuel Sena, Auburn ... 6
- Vince Sinisi, Bakersfield ... 6

TOTAL BASES
- Brandon Wood, Rancho Cuca./Salt Lake ... 370
- Andy Green, Tucson ... 311
- Billy Butler, High Desert/Wichita ... 300
- Joe Koshansky, Asheville/Tulsa ... 294
- Chris Lubanski, High Desert ... 294
- Matt Miller, Asheville/Modesto ... 294
- Delmon Young, Montgomery/Durham ... 294

EXTRA-BASE HITS
- Brandon Wood, Rancho Cuca./Salt Lake ... 101
- Andy Green, Tucson ... 78
- Joe Koshansky, Asheville/Tulsa ... 73
- Chris Lubanski, High Desert ... 72
- Wladimir Balentien, Inland Empire ... 71
- Billy Butler, High Desert/Wichita ... 71

DOUBLES
- Brandon Wood, Rancho Cuca./Salt Lake ... 53
- Mitch Maier, High Desert/Wichita ... 47
- Andy Green, Tucson ... 46
- Ryan Spilborghs, Tulsa/Colo. Springs ... 46
- Four tied at ... 45

TRIPLES
- Shane Victorino, Scranton/Wilkes-Barre ... 16
- Chris Walker, Daytona ... 14
- Six tied at ... 13

HOME RUNS
- Brandon Wood, Rancho Cuca./Salt Lake ... 43
- Joe Koshansky, Asheville/Tulsa ... 38
- Brett Harper, St. Lucie/Binghamton ... 36
- Shelley Duncan, Trenton ... 34
- Chip Cannon, Lansing/Dunedin/New Hamp. 32
- Ryan Mulhern, Kinston/Akron ... 32

RUNS BATTED IN
- Leo Daigle, Winston-Salem/Charlotte ... 120
- Chris Lubanski, High Desert ... 116
- Brandon Wood, Rancho Cuca./Salt Lake ... 116
- Chris Carter, Lancaster/Tennessee ... 115
- Joe Koshansky, Asheville/Tulsa ... 115

MOST RBIs, ONE GAME
- Stephen Head, Kinston ... 9
- Kiel Thibault, Idaho Falls ... 9
- Dusty Wathan, Buffalo ... 9

STOLEN BASES
- Todd Donovan, Jacksonville/Las Vegas ... 65
- Carlos Gomez, Hagerstown ... 64
- Chris Walker, Daytona ... 60
- Rich Thompson, Indianapolis/Altoona ... 58
- Fernando Perez, SW Michigan ... 57
- Marcus Sanders, Augusta ... 57

CAUGHT STEALING
- Vince Blue, Lakeland ... 29
- Wilson Batista, Hagerstown/St. Lucie ... 27
- Carlos Gomez, Hagerstown ... 24
- Erick Aybar, Arkansas ... 23
- Chris Walker, Daytona ... 21

HIT BY PITCHES
- Mike Kinkade, Buffalo ... 30
- Carlos Quentin, Tucson ... 29
- Steve Sollmann, Brevard County ... 26
- Michael Collins, Cedar Rapids ... 25
- Chris Gimenez, Lake County ... 25

WALKS
- Pat Magness, Lynchburg ... 141
- Jack Cust, Sacramento ... 115
- Jeremy Hermida, Carolina ... 111
- Daric Barton, Stockton/Midland ... 97
- Kila Kaaihue, High Desert ... 97

STRIKEOUTS
- Tim Battle, Charleston ... 195
- Mitch Jones, Columbus ... 174
- Corey Ragsdale, St. Lucie/Binghamton ... 169

DAVID STONER

Eric Patterson: .325 average

Brett Bonvechio, Lake Elsinore	163
Wladimir Balentien, Inland Empire	160

SLUGGING PERCENTAGE

Todd Linden, Fresno	.682
Randy Ruiz, Reading	.669
Brandon Wood, Rancho Cuca./Salt Lake	.667
Ryan Mulhern, Kinston/Akron	.640
Noah Hall, Winston-Salem	.633

ON-BASE PERCENTAGE

Pat Magness, Lynchburg	.481
Joe Dillon, Albuquerque	.459
Noah Hall, Winston-Salem	.459
Jeremy Hermida, Carolina	.457
Conor Jackson, Tucson	.457

BATTING AVERAGE
By Position
(Minimum 2.7 Plate Appearances/Team Game)

Catchers

Eliezer Alfonzo, S.J./Norwich/Fresno	.334
Miguel Montero, Lancaster/Tennessee	.326
Ryan Hanigan, Chattanooga	.321
Mike Jacobs, Binghamton	.321
Michael Collins, Cedar Rapids	.320

First Basemen

Joe Dillon, Albuquerque	.360
Conor Jackson, Tucson	.354
Randy Ruiz, Reading	.349
Ryan Shealy, Colorado Springs	.328
Justin Huber, Wichita/Omaha	.326

Second Basemen

Howie Kendrick, Rancho Cuca./Arkansas	.367
Andy Green, Tucson	.343
Kevin Frandsen, S.J./Norwich/Fresno	.335
Jeff Pickler, Colorado Springs	.331
Danny Sandoval, Scranton/Wilkes-Barre	.331

Third Basemen

Rick Short, New Orleans	.383
Kevin Orie, Nashville/New Orleans	.352
Billy Butler, High Desert/Wichita	.340
Jose Flores, Las Vegas	.336
Angel Sanchez, High Desert	.313

Shortstops

Eric Patterson, Peoria/West Tenn	.325
Brandon Wood, Rancho Cuca./Salt Lake	.321
Alberto Gonzales, South Bend	.318
Joaquin Arias, Frisco	.315
Anderson Hernandez, Bing./Norfolk	.315

Outfielders

Brian Horwitz, Augusta	.349
Matt Murton, West Tenn/Iowa	.343
Sebastien Boucher, Wis./Inl. Empire	.340
Ryan Spilborghs, Tulsa/Colo. Springs	.340
Joe Gaetti, Modesto	.332
Noah Hall, Winston-Salem	.332

INDIVIDUAL PITCHING

EARNED RUN AVERAGE*
(Minimum 0.8 Innings/Team Game)

Justin Verlander, Lakeland/Erie	1.29
Ray Liotta, Kannapolis/Winston-Salem	2.02
Chuck James, Myrtle Beach/Miss./Rich.	2.12
Casey Janssen, Lan./Dunedin/New Hamp.	2.18
Troy Patton, Lexington/Salem	2.18
Jimmy Barthmaier, Lexington/Salem	2.24
Jeremy Sowers, Kinston/Akron/Buffalo	2.37
Dustin Nippert, Tennessee	2.38
Tony Sipp, Lake County/Kinston	2.40
Tim Dillard, Brevard County	2.48

WORST ERA

Cesar Herrera, High Desert	7.27
Tyler Adamczyk, Palm Beach/Quad Cities	7.20
Carlos Carrasco, Lake./Batavia/GCL Phil.	7.04
Fabian Jimenez, Fort Wayne/Eugene	7.03
Jason Stevenson, Harrisburg/Potomac	6.72

WINS

Zach Jackson, Dunedin/N.H./Syracuse	16
A.J. Shappi, South Bend/Lancaster	16
Dallas Braden, Stockton/Midland	15
Randy Leek, Springfield/Memphis	15
Jason Scobie, Norfolk	15

LOSSES

Greg Kloosterman, West Virginia	19
Chris Kinsey, Lancaster/South Bend	15
Arnie Munoz, Charlotte	14
Zach Segovia, Clearwater	14
Mike Smith, Reading/Scranton	14
Jason Stevenson, Harrisburg/Potomac	14

GAMES

Lee Gronkiewicz, New Hamp./Syracuse	66
Matt Smith, Charlotte	66
Paul Abraham, Lake Elsinore/Mobile	65
Colter Bean, Columbus	65
Jim Miller, Modesto/Tulsa	64
Phil Stockman, Tucson/Tennessee	64

COMPLETE GAMES

Maximino De la Cruz, Lakewood	5
Tim Dillard, Brevard County	5
Jon Asahina, Tulsa	4
Jack Egbert, Kannapolis	4
Sandy Nin, Modesto/Tulsa	4
Fernando Rodriguez, Cedar Rapids	4

SAVES

Mark Worrell, Palm Beach	35
Jim Miller, Modesto/Tulsa	34
Chris Mobley, Greensboro	34
Matt Varner, Fort Wayne	34
Edwin Almonte, Erie	33

SHUTOUTS

Jack Egbert, Kannapolis	3
13 tied at	2

INNINGS

Allen Davis, Reading/Scranton	196
Randy Leek, Springfield/Memphis	192
Tim Dillard, Brevard County	185
Dave Borkowski, Ottawa	183
Adam Wainwright, Memphis	182

WALKS

Joe Torres, Rancho Cuca./Cedar Rapids	92
Adam Loewen, Frederick	86
Charles Haeger, Win.-Salem/Birmingham	85
Mike Smith, Reading/Scranton	85
Richard Stahl, Frederick/Bowie	84

STRIKEOUTS

Francisco Liriano, New Britain/Rochester	204
Joel Zumaya, Erie/Toledo	199
Rich Hill, West Tenn/Iowa/Peoria	194
Chuck James, Myrtle Beach/Miss./Rich.	193
Tyler Clippard, Tampa/Charles./Colum. (IL)	181

HITS

Allen Davis, Reading/Scranton	219
Kyle Middleton, Wichita	218
Dave Borkowski, Ottawa	217
Mike Ziegler, Midland/Sacramento	210
Jason Mackintosh, Inland Empire	206

STRIKEOUTS PER NINE INNINGS
(Starters)

Joel Zumaya, Erie/Toledo	11.99
Jonathan Sanchez, Augusta	11.89
Francisco Liriano, New Britian/Roch.	11.08
David Purcey, Dunedin/New Hamp.	11.07
Chuck Tiffany, Vero Beach	10.98

STRIKEOUTS PER NINE INNINGS
(Relivers)

Alexander Smit, Beloit/Elizabethton	16.95
J.B. Miadich, Albuquerque	16.26
Victor Garate, Greeneville	14.75
Carlos Alvarez, Columbus/Jacksonville	14.66
Connor Robertson, K. Cty./Stock./Sac.	14.46

BATTING AVERAGE AGAINST
(Starters)

Francisco Liriano, New Britain/Roch.	.177
Gaby Hernandez, Hagerstown/St. Lucie	.179
Joel Zumaya, Erie/Toledo	.187
Carlos Villanueva, Brevard Cty./Hunt.	.195
Scott Elbert, Columbus (SAL)	.201

BATTING AVERAGE AGAINST
(Relievers)

Richard De los Santos, H.V./SW Mich.	.114
Tim Cox, GCL Red Sox/Lowell	.125
Josh Schmidt, Staten Island	.128
Steve Andrade, New Hampshire	.134
Chris Ray, Bowie	.140

MOST STRIKEOUTS, ONE GAME

Radhames Liz, Aberdeen	15
Michael O'Connor, Potomac	15
Bill Pulsipher, Memphis	15
Anthony Reyes, Memphis	15
Joel Zumaya, Erie, Toledo	15

BALKS

Roberto Batista, Palm Beach	7
Franklin Morales, Asheville	7
Jose Gomez, Hagerstown	6
Gio Gonzalez, Kannapolis/Winston-Salem	6
Jeremy Schmidt, Chattanooga/Sarasota	6

INDIVIDUAL FIELDING

MOST ERRORS

B.J. Upton, Durham	53
Juan Ciriaco, Lake Elsinore	45
Alcides Escobar, West Virginia	41
Ian Desmond, Savannah/Potomac	39
Matt Bush, Fort Wayne	38

RICH ABEL

Zach Jackson: 16 wins

MINOR LEAGUE BEST TOOLS

Full season leagues only

	International/AAA	Pacific Coast/AAA	Eastern/AA	Southern/AA	Texas/AA	California/High A	Carolina/High A	Fla. State/High A	Midwest/Low A	So. Atlantic/Low A
Best Batting Prospect	Ryan Howard Scranton/W-B	Rickie Weeks Nashville	Donald Kelly Erie	Delmon Young Montgomery	Andre Ethier Midland	Howie Kendrick Rancho Cucamonga	Nick Markakis Frederick	Andy LaRoche Vero Beach	Carlos Gonzales South Bend	Hunter Pence Lexington
Best Power Prospect	Ryan Howard Scranton/W-B	Prince Fielder Nashville	Shelly Duncan Trenton	Delmon Young Montgomery	Mike Napoli Arkansas	Brandon Wood Rancho Cucamonga	Nick Markakis Frederick	Andy LaRoche Vero Beach	Ryan Harvey Peoria	Hunter Pence Lexington
Best Strike-Zone Judgment	Nate McLouth Indianapolis	Conor Jackson Tucson	Dustin Pedroia Portland	Russell Martin Jacksonville	Justin Huber Wichita	Daric Barton Stockton	Nick Markakis Frederick	Denard Span Fort Myers	Francisco Leandro Southwest Michigan	Ben Zobrist Lexington
Best Baserunner	Nate McLouth Indianapolis	Corey Hart Nashville	Rajai Davis Altoona	Todd Donovan Jacksonville	Ruddy Yan Frisco	Clay Timpner San Jose	Robert Valido Winston-Salem	Juan Francia Lakeland	Fernando Perez Southwest Michigan	Marcus Sanders Augusta
Fastest Baserunner	Joey Gathright Durham	Brandon Watson New Orleans	Rajai Davis Altoona	Marland Williams Tennessee	Josh Anderson Corpus Christi	Elliot Johnson Visalia	Josh Burrus Myrtle Beach	Chris Walker Daytona	Fernando Perez Southwest Michigan	Marcus Sanders Augusta
Best Pitching Prospect	Francisco Liriano Rochester	Felix Hernandez Tacoma	Joel Zumaya Erie	Chad Billingsley Jacksonville	Fernando Nieve Corpus Christi	Thomas Diamond Bakersfield	Anibal Sanchez Wilmington	Justin Verlander Lakeland	Anthony Swarzak Beloit	Troy Patton Lexington
Best Fastball	Travis Bowyer Rochester	Felix Hernandez Tacoma	Joel Zumaya Erie	Bobby Jenks Birmingham	Fernando Nieve Corpus Christi	Juan Morillo Modesto	Anibal Sanchez Wilmington	Justin Verlander Lakeland	Luis Cota Burlington	Juan Morillo Asheville
Best Breaking Pitch	Brandon McCarthy Charlotte	Felix Hernandez Tacoma	Hayden Penn Bowie	Chad Billingsley Jacksonville	Jason Hirsh Corpus Christi	John Danks Bakersfield	J.J. Johnson Frederick	Justin Verlander Lakeland	Sean Gallagher Peoria	Jimmy Barthmaier Lexington
Best Control	Zach Duke Indianapolis	Anthony Reyes Memphis	Brian Bannister Binghamton	Ricky Nolasco West Tenn	Bobby Livingston San Antonio	Jason Windsor Stockton	Jeremy Sowers Kinston	Justin Verlander Lakeland	Andy Sonnastine Southwest Michigan	Matt Harrison Greensboro
Best Reliever	Travis Bowyer Rochester	Brad Baker Portland	Edwin Almonte Erie	Chris Resop Carolina	Emiliano Fruto San Antonio	Jim Miller Modesto	Edward Mujica Kinston	Mark Alexander Vero Beach	Matt Varner Fort Wayne	David Haehnel Delmarva
Best Defensive Catcher	Carlos Ruiz Scranton/W-B	Gerald Laird Oklahoma	Max St. Pierre Erie	Russell Martin Jacksonville	Rene Rivera San Antonio	Chris Iannetta Modesto	Gustavo Molina Winston-Salem	Jason Motte Palm Beach	Rob Johnson Wisconsin	Jason Jaramillo Lakewood
Best Defensive First Baseman	Ryan Howard Scranton/W-B	Adrian Gonzalez Oklahoma	Tyler Von Schell Norwich	Scott Thorman Mississippi	Jason Hart Frisco	Travis Ishikawa San Jose	Scott Robinson Salem	Kelly Hunt Lakeland	Tonys Gutierrez Dayton	Brad McCann Greensboro
Best Defensive Second Baseman	William Bergolla Louisville	Ramon Santiago Tacoma	Dustin Pedroia Portland	Fernando Cortez Montgomery	Alberto Callaspo Arkansas	Kevin Frandsen San Jose	Martin Prado Myrtle Beach	Juan Francia Lakeland	Asdrubal Cabrera Wisconsin	Hernan Iribarren West Virginia
Best Defensive Third Baseman	Andy Marte Richmond	Brian Barden Tucson	Jose Bautista Altoona	Casey McGehee West Tenn	Jesus Guzman San Antonio	Travis Metcalf Bakersfield	Kory Casto Potomac	Kody Kirkland Lakeland	Freddy Sandoval Cedar Rapids	Grant Psomas Hagerstown
Best Defensive Shortstop	Jorge Velandia Indianapolis	Yuniesky Betancourt Tacoma	Hanley Ramirez Portland	Robert Andino Carolina	Yuniesky Betancourt San Antonio	Brandon Wood Rancho Cucamonga	Robert Valido Winston-Salem	Manny Mayorson Dunedin	Alberto Gonzales South Bend	Ian Desmond Savannah
Best Infield Arm	Edwin Encarnacion Louisville	Yuniesky Betancourt Tacoma	Jose Bautista Altoona	Jerry Gil Tennessee	Yuniesky Betancourt San Antonio	Adam Jones Inland Empire	Javier Guzman Lynchburg	Matt Moses Fort Myers	Matt Bush Fort Wayne	Marcos Vechionacci Charleston
Best Defensive Outfielder	Esix Snead Richmond	Julio Ramirez Fresno	Melky Cabrera Trenton	Chris Young Birmingham	Josh Anderson Corpus Christi	Clay Timpner San Jose	Frank Diaz Potomac	Vince Blue Lakeland	Carlos Gonzales South Bend	Tim Battle Charleston
Best Outfield Arm	Brian Anderson Charlotte	Shin-Soo Choo Tacoma	Chris Roberson Reading	Delmon Young Montgomery	T.J. Bohn San Antonio	Steve Baker Lake Elsinore	Frank Diaz Potomac	Brent Clevlen Lakeland	Carlos Gonzales South Bend	Ambiorix Concepcion Hagerstown
Most Exciting Player	B.J. Upton Durham	Rickie Weeks Nashville	Michael Bourn Reading	Delmon Young Montgomery	Erick Aybar Arkansas	Howie Kendrick Rancho Cucamonga	Robert Valido Winston-Salem	Matt Moses Fort Myers	Carlos Gonzales South Bend	Marcus Sanders Augusta
Best Manager Prospect	Ken Oberkfell Norfolk	Mike Jirschele Omaha	Mike Basso New Hampshire	Charlie Montoyo Montgomery	Dave Brundage San Antonio	Stu Cole Modesto	Luis Rivera Kinston	Mike Rojas Lakeland	Matt Walbeck West Michigan	Tim Bogar Lexington

Selected at midseason 2005 by Baseball America in consultation with minor league managers

FREITAS AWARDS

Baseball America's annual Bob Freitas Awards are presented to franchises that show sustained excellence in the business of minor league baseball.

They were first presented in 1989, shortly after the death of Freitas, a longtime minor league operator, promoter and ambassador. Franchises must be in operation for at least five seasons before they're eligible to win.

■ The Toledo Mud Hens have long been one of the most recognizable franchises in the minor leagues, thanks to their association with the character Max Klinger in episodes of "M*A*S*H" in the 1970s and '80s. But until a few years ago, they were one of the most moribund as well, playing in an old, outmoded ballpark that had originally served as the grandstand for a horse-racing track at fairgrounds outside the city.

That all changed in 2002, when the Mud Hens moved into state-of-the-art Fifth Third Field in downtown Toledo. The team immediately set an attendance record, which it broke in 2005 by drawing 556,995 fans, an indication of the community's strong and sustained interest in the team.

The Mud Hens also had their most successful season on the field in 2005, winning the International League Governors' Cup with a sweep of Indianapolis for the city's first title since 1967.

■ Tulsa's longevity in the minor leagues is even more notable than Toledo's, and the Drillers celebrated the 100th anniversary of baseball in the city during the 2005 season. The Tulsa Oilers took the field in 1905, two years before Oklahoma became a state.

The current franchise joined the Texas League in 1977 and has been a model of stability under owner Went Hubbard and general manager Chuck Lamson, who played for the Drillers for parts of the 1979-81 seasons and came back to work in the front office. He has held nearly every job in the organization and became GM in 1995.

The Drillers are an active part of the community and have consistently drawn 300,000 fans or more in a mid-sized market.

■ The Jersey shore might stretch the definition of "south Atlantic," but the overwhelming success of the Lakewood BlueClaws in their five seasons in the South Atlantic League provides plenty of justification for the league's northern expansion.

The BlueClaws have led the league in attendance in each of their five seasons in the league, drawing more than 400,000 fans each season and providing another example of a minor league affiliate flourishing in the shadow of its major league parent (in this case, the Phillies). The team also reached 2 million total fans faster than any other Sally League franchise.

Lakewood has also shown stability in its front office, with general manager Geoff Brown still leading the team after being hired before the team's inaugural season in 2001.

■ The Brooklyn Cyclones have been so successful that they have almost changed what it means to be a short-season team. In a market that dwarfs those of most other teams anywhere in the minors, the Cyclones have embraced Brooklyn's baseball history and have been embraced in kind by local fans.

The Cyclones have reached unheard-of attendance levels for a short-season team, averaging more than 7,000 fans a game since the time they opened the gates of KeySpan Park in 2001. The park's setting at Coney Island also makes it one of the most picturesque in baseball.

The team hasn't been satisfied simply to open the gates, though. It has been very active in the community, doing everything from raising money for youth baseball to promoting reading among local students with the Cyclones Book Patrol. The team also led the efforts to establish the first New York-Penn League all-star game, which was played in Brooklyn in 2005 in front of a sellout crowd.

PREVIOUS WINNERS

Triple-A

1989—Columbus (International)
1990—Pawtucket (International)
1991—Buffalo (American Association)
1992—Iowa (American Association)
1993—Richmond (International)
1994—Norfolk (International)
1995—Albuquerque (Pacific Coast)
1996—Indianapolis (American Association)
1997—Rochester (International)
1998—Salt Lake (Pacific Coast)
1999—Louisville (International)
2000—Edmonton (Pacific Coast)
2001—Buffalo (International)
2002—Memphis (Pacific Coast)
2003—Pawtucket (International)
2004—Sacramento (Pacific Coast)

Double-A

1989—El Paso (Texas)
1990—Arkansas (Texas)
1991—Reading (Eastern)
1992—Tulsa (Texas)
1993—Harrisburg (Eastern)
1994—San Antonio (Texas)
1995—Midland (Texas)
1996—Carolina (Southern)
1997—Bowie (Eastern)
1998—Trenton (Eastern)
1999—Portland (Eastern)
2000—Reading (Eastern)
2001—Mobile (Southern)
2002—Chattanooga (Southern)
2003—New Britain (Eastern)
2004—Round Rock (Texas)

Class A

1989—Durham (Carolina)
1990—San Jose (California)
1991—Asheville (South Atlantic)
1992—Springfield (Midwest)
1993—South Bend (Midwest)
1994—Kinston (Carolina)
1995—Kane County (Midwest)
1996—Wisconsin (Midwest)
1997—Rancho Cucamonga (California)
1998—West Michigan (Midwest)
1999—Wilmington (Carolina)
2000—Charleston, S.C. (South Atlantic)
2001—Delmarva (South Atlantic)
2002—Fort Myers (Florida State)
2003—Modesto (California)
2004—Dayton (Midwest)

Short-Season

1989—Eugene (Northwest)
1990—Salt Lake City (Pioneer)
1991—Spokane (Northwest)
1992—Boise (Northwest)
1993—Billings (Pioneer)
1994—Everett (Northwest)
1995—Great Falls (Pioneer)
1996—Bluefield (Appalachian)
1997—Oneonta (New York-Penn)
1998—Hudson Valley (New York-Penn)
1999—Portland (Northwest)
2000—Lowell (New York-Penn)
2001—Salem-Keizer (Northwest)
2002—Ogden (Pioneer)
2003—Spokane (Northwest)
2004—Burlington (Appalachian)

INTERNATIONAL LEAGUE

TRIPLE-A

BY CHRIS KLINE

It was a historic 2005 season in Toledo, as the Mud Hens took home the Governor's Cup for the first time since 1967—and went from worst to first in the process.

A year after going 65-78 (.455), Toledo went 89-55 during the regular season to finish atop the IL's Western Division. Its .618 winning percentage was the best in Triple-A by 49 points. The Mud Hens then knocked off Southern Division winner Norfolk in five games in the opening round of the playoffs before sweeping Indianapolis for the championship. Toledo had finished 11 games ahead of the Indians during the season.

It was the first time in more than 40 years since an IL team went worst to first. The last team to finish with the league's best record after posting the worst record the previous season was the 1963-64 Jacksonville Suns.

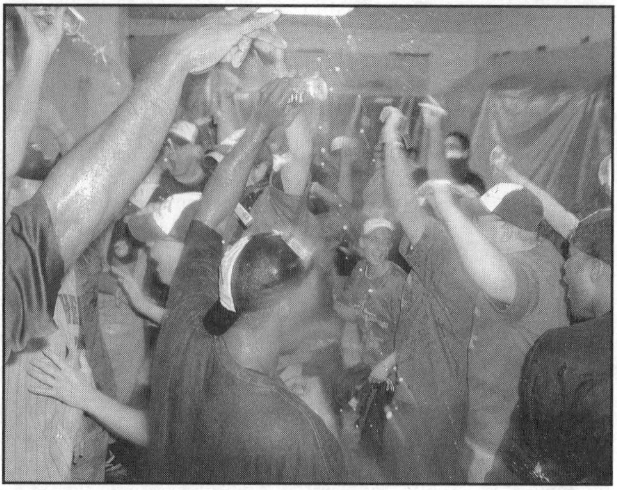

Mud Hens celebration
Toledo won its first International League title since 1967

Three players with no prior Triple-A experience—righthander Kenny Baugh (12-8, 3.38), outfielder Curtis Granderson (.290-15-65) and second baseman Ryan Raburn (.253-19-64)—were key components to the Mud Hens' success.

Baugh, a 2001 first-round pick of the Tigers, finished among the league leaders in wins and innings pitched on a staff that had a league-best 3.70 ERA. Granderson, a third-round pick in 2002, jumped straight from Double-A Erie to Detroit before settling in at Toledo in 2005. A top-of-the-order threat with a combination of speed and power, Granderson was a catalyst for the Mud Hens all year, utilizing his wheels to get on base and setting the table for veteran Marcus Thames, who hit .340 with 22 homers in 265 at-bats. Thames batted .407 in the playoffs, hitting three homers in eight games.

Raburn struggled to make consistent contact after batting just .179 in April. But he finished strong, peaking with a .308 average in June, and batted .348 during the Hens' playoff run.

Toledo got solid pitching from veteran righthander Jason Grilli to bring home the championship. Grilli went 1-0, 1.23 with a 16-4 strikeout-walk ratio in 15 innings.

Adding to the Governor's Cup, Toledo manager Larry Parrish was named the IL manager of the year in his third consecutive season with the Mud Hens.

"I've had good teams and I've had bad teams and I've learned you're only as good as the guys you have out there on the field," Parrish said. "So this is an award for all of us, for all the players on this team and certainly for our pitching coach (Jeff Jones) and hitting coach (Leon Durham)."

TOP 20 PROSPECTS

1. Delmon Young, of, Durham (Devil Rays)
2. Francisco Liriano, lhp, Rochester (Twins)
3. Zach Duke, lhp, Indianapolis (Pirates)
4. Ryan Howard, 1b, Scranton/W-B (Phillies)
5. Andy Marte, 3b, Richmond (Braves)
6. Edwin Encarnacion, 3b, Louisville (Reds)
7. Kyle Davies, rhp, Richmond (Braves)
8. Brandon McCarthy, rhp, Charlotte (White Sox)
9. Brian Anderson, of, Charlotte (White Sox)
10. Aaron Hill, ss, Syracuse (Blue Jays)
11. Jonny Gomes, of, Durham (Devil Rays)
12. Scott Baker, rhp, Rochester (Twins)
13. Ryan Doumit, c, Indianapolis (Pirates)
14. Anthony Lerew, rhp, Richmond (Braves)
15. Kelly Johnson, of, Richmond (Braves)
16. Bryan Bullington, rhp, Indianapolis (Pirates)
17. Dustin Pedroia, 2b, Pawtucket (Red Sox)
18. Kelly Shoppach, c, Pawtucket (Red Sox)
19. Curtis Granderson, of, Toledo (Tigers)
20. Ryan Garko, c/1b, Buffalo (Indians)

Big Debut For Duke

While Toledo swept through Indianapolis on the way to the title, the Indians had a solid season in their first year as a Pirates' affiliate. Indy finished 11 games behind Toledo in the West, but finished a game ahead of Columbus to secure the wild-card berth in the playoffs.

The Indians started the year with IL pitcher of the year Zach Duke (12-3, 2.92), righthander Ian Snell (11-3, 3.70), catcher Ryan Doumit (.345-12-35) and outfielders Chris Duffy (.308-7-31) and Nate McLouth (.297-5-39, 34 SB), but lost them to the big league club. The Indians still made it all the way to the championship series.

Even slugging first baseman Brad Eldred (.282-15-48) blew through Triple-A, playing just 54 games before being called up to Pittsburgh. The pitching performances of righthander Bryan Bullington (9-5, 3.38), the No. 1 overall draft pick in 2002, and lefthander Paul Maholm (1-1, 3.53), and a returning Snell bolstered the club down the stretch and through the playoffs. First baseman Graham Koonce had an outstanding postseason for Indy, hitting .423 in 26 at-bats.

"You always have to deal with movement," Indians manager Trent Jewett said. "You try to instill a kind of stability no matter who's here. With all the movement we had this year between Triple-A and the big leagues, I was proud of how focused and determined this club stayed all the way to the end."

Rochester Phenom

Amidst the debate as to who was the best pitching prospect in the IL in 2005, Twins' lefthander Francisco Liriano quickly put an end to that discussion shortly after arriving in Rochester from Double-A in July.

In a league that saw Duke and Braves righthander Kyle Davies rocket through to their respective big league clubs, the 21-year-old Dominican stated his case emphatically, despite Duke's impressive run in the big leagues after he was called up.

RICH ABEL

Francisco Liriano

"The difference is purely in the stuff," a scout from an American League organization said. "Liriano clearly has the better stuff of the two, if you're talking about lefthanders. One's a power guy and one's more of a finesse guy. But it's hard to argue against Duke because all he does is find ways to win."

Liriano threw three plus pitches for strikes, including a fastball that topped out at 97 mph. He complemented it with a hard-breaking 86-88 mph slider and a changeup he dropped off at 82-83 with the same easy arm action as his fastball.

"He's so tough because his fastball might be his third-best pitch," Triple-A Buffalo catcher/first baseman Ryan Garko said.

Liriano went 9-2, 1.78 in 91 innings to earn IL rookie of the year honors. He finished tops in the minor leagues in strikeouts (202), and compiled a 112-24 strikeout-walk ratio with the Red Wings.

"He's as good as it gets in this league," Syracuse manager Marty Pevey said. "There's too much to like. And I'm not just talking about what he does on the mound. He's got unbelievable makeup as well. I think he's learned a lot this season. He has a plan for attacking hitters that I think sets him apart from the rest of the pack."

"I call him 'Mr. Liriano,'" Buffalo manager Marty Brown said. "Anyone you refer to as 'Mister' belongs in the big leagues. He proved he didn't belong in Triple-A pretty quickly."

LEAGUE CHAMPIONS

Last 30 Years

Year	Regular Season*	PCT	Playoff
1975	Tidewater (Mets)	.607	Tidewater (Mets)
1976	Rochester (Orioles)	.638	Syracuse (Yankees)
1977	Pawtucket (Red Sox)	.571	Charleston (Astros)
1978	Charleston (Astros)	.607	Richmond (Braves)
1979	Columbus (Yankees)	.612	Columbus (Yankees)
1980	Columbus (Yankees)	.593	Columbus (Yankees)
1981	Columbus (Yankees)	.633	Columbus (Yankees)
1982	Richmond (Braves)	.590	Tidewater (Mets)
1983	Columbus (Yankees)	.593	Tidewater (Mets)
1984	Columbus (Yankees)	.590	Pawtucket (Red Sox)
1985	Syracuse (Blue Jays)	.564	Tidewater (Mets)
1986	Richmond (Braves)	.571	Richmond (Braves)
1987	Tidewater (Mets)	.579	Columbus (Yankees)
1988	Tidewater (Mets)	.546	Rochester (Orioles)
	Rochester (Orioles)	.546	
1989	Syracuse (Blue Jays)	.572	Richmond (Braves)
1990	Rochester (Orioles)	.614	Rochester (Orioles)
1991	Columbus (Yankees)	.590	Columbus (Yankees)
1992	Columbus (Yankees)	.660	Columbus (Yankees)
1993	Charlotte (Indians)	.610	Charlotte (Indians)
1994	Richmond (Braves)	.567	Richmond (Braves)
1995	Norfolk (Mets)	.606	Ottawa (Expos)
1996	Columbus (Yankees)	.599	Columbus (Yankees)
1997	Rochester (Orioles)	.589	Rochester (Orioles)
1998	Buffalo (Indians)	.566	Buffalo (Indians)
1999	Columbus (Yankees)	.589	Charlotte (White Sox)
2000	Buffalo (Indians)	.593	Indianapolis (Brewers)
2001	Buffalo (Indians)	.641	Louisville (Reds)
2002	Scranton/W-B (Phillies)	.632	Durham (Devil Rays)
2003	Pawtucket (Red Sox)	.576	Durham (Devil Rays)
2004	Buffalo (Indians)	.576	Buffalo (Indians)

*Best overall record

V Is For Victorino

Scranton/Wilkes-Barre outfielder Shane Victorino didn't sniff the postseason, as the Red Barons tied for last with Ottawa in the Northern Division. But Victorino, 24, ended up winning the IL MVP award and later joined the Phillies as they competed in a pennant race in the National League East.

Victorino, who was plucked by the Phillies from the Dodgers in the Rule 5 draft in December 2004, batted .310-18-70. He also led the league in triples with 16; ranked third in hits (153), second in runs scored (93), fifth in extra-base hits (59) and fifth in slugging percentage (.534).

"He was a force for us," Red Barons manager Gene Lamont said. "He did it all—hit for average, hit for power, very smart on the bases and played a solid center field. I'd think he'd be in the mix (in center) in the big leagues next year."

STANDINGS

Page	NORTH	W	L	PCT	GB	Manager(s)	Attendance	Average	Last Penn.
101	Buffalo Bisons (Indians)	82	62	.569	—	Marty Brown	596,758	8,775	2004
70	Pawtucket Red Sox (Red Sox)	75	69	.521	7	Ron Johnson	688,421	9,561	1984
166	Rochester Red Wings (Twins)	75	69	.521	7	Phil Roof/Rich Miller	452,302	6,853	1997
255	Syracuse SkyChiefs (Blue Jays)	71	73	.493	11	Marty Pevey	382,492	5,543	1976
63	Ottawa Lynx (Orioles)	69	75	.479	13	Dave Trembley	160,544	2,396	1995
197	Scranton/W-B Red Barons (Phillies)	69	75	.479	13	Gene Lamont	400,726	5,724	None
Page	**SOUTH**	**W**	**L**	**PCT**	**GB**	**Manager(s)**	**Attendance**	**Average**	**Last Penn.**
173	Norfolk Tides (Mets)	79	65	.549	—	Ken Oberkfell	502,504	7,178	1985
241	Durham Bulls (Devil Rays)	65	79	.451	14	Bill Evers	520,371	7,227	2003
86	Charlotte Knights (White Sox)	57	87	.396	22	Nick Leyva/Manny Trillo	289,495	4,320	1999
55	Richmond Braves (Braves)	56	88	.389	23	Pat Kelly	359,755	5,213	1994
Page	**WEST**	**W**	**L**	**PCT**	**GB**	**Manager**	**Attendance**	**Average**	**Last Penn.**
116	Toledo Mud Hens (Tigers)	89	55	.618	—	Larry Parrish	556,995	7,845	2005
204	Indianapolis Indians (Brewers)	78	66	.542	11	Trent Jewett	558,911	8,100	2000
182	Columbus Clippers (Yankees)	77	67	.535	12	Bucky Dent	500,104	7,144	1996
93	Louisville Bats (Reds)	66	78	.458	23	Rick Sweet	643,466	9,192	2001

PLAYOFFS—Semifinals: Toledo defeated Norfolk 3-2 and Indianapolis defeated Buffalo 3-2 in best-of-5 series. Finals: Toledo defeated Indianapolis 3-0 in best-of-5 series.

NOTE: Teams' individual batting and pitching statistics can be found on page indicated in lefthand column.

2005 INTERNATIONAL LEAGUE STATISTICS

CLUB BATTING

	AVG	G	AB	R	H	2B	2B	HR	BB	SO	SB
Scranton/Wilkes-Barre	.283	144	4874	677	1380	265	45	99	410	824	70
Buffalo	.278	144	4845	805	1347	293	31	179	446	988	63
Ottawa	.278	144	4880	638	1355	276	28	100	349	835	132
Indianapolis	.275	144	4907	725	1350	259	37	157	468	1045	163
Pawtucket	.273	144	4950	788	1352	285	27	168	599	1011	80
Rochester	.272	144	4826	693	1315	255	19	139	428	833	57
Durham	.268	144	5027	773	1346	284	32	198	486	1105	145
Louisville	.267	144	4926	615	1316	297	36	109	365	1069	98
Columbus	.267	144	4924	700	1313	289	30	137	484	988	70
Charlotte	.267	144	4896	649	1305	271	16	160	430	965	40
Norfolk	.267	144	4842	674	1293	270	35	131	491	987	124
Toledo	.265	144	4853	697	1285	266	44	156	483	1095	145
Syracuse	.260	144	4927	697	1283	264	26	154	426	1019	58
Richmond	.256	144	4780	519	1225	248	32	94	448	952	106

CLUB PITCHING

	ERA	G	CG	SHO	SV	IP	H	R	ER	BB	SO
Toledo	3.70	144	5	15	43	1273	1224	583	523	474	1036
Norfolk	3.73	144	0	10	45	1270	1241	585	526	426	974
Richmond	4.07	144	1	11	28	1255	1247	675	568	532	879
Rochester	4.13	144	3	9	37	1251	1250	638	574	494	1077
Indianapolis	4.29	144	5	6	36	1273	1290	691	607	477	912
Columbus	4.32	144	1	6	37	1287	1330	690	618	425	1073
Ottawa	4.32	144	3	9	28	1251	1310	668	600	406	866
Pawtucket	4.40	144	1	8	24	1268	1297	681	620	411	1057
Scranton/Wilkes-Barre	4.44	144	3	4	37	1258	1327	691	620	465	936
Buffalo	4.46	144	4	2	42	1248	1345	716	618	395	986
Louisville	4.54	144	0	9	35	1266	1356	716	638	450	1012
Syracuse	4.56	144	2	7	44	1271	1361	703	644	362	976
Charlotte	4.83	144	3	4	30	1268	1378	748	680	490	1016
Durham	5.03	144	1	2	27	1285	1509	865	718	506	916

CLUB FIELDING

	PCT	PO	A	E	DP
Rochester	.980	3754	1400	106	148
Syracuse	.980	3813	1435	108	128
Louisville	.979	3796	1448	111	135
Indianapolis	.979	3819	1502	114	145
Scranton/W-B	.979	3772	1609	116	175
Pawtucket	.979	3803	1354	110	127
Buffalo	.978	3743	1462	118	126
Columbus	.978	3860	1449	117	138
Charlotte	.977	3803	1368	121	146
Ottawa	.977	3753	1536	122	137
Norfolk	.977	3811	1569	128	130
Richmond	.976	3764	1436	130	136
Toledo	.976	3819	1503	130	143
Durham	.965	3854	1580	198	155

INDIVIDUAL BATTING LEADERS

(Minimum 389 Plate Appearances)

	AVG	G	AB	R	H	2B	3B	HR	RBI	BB	SO	SB
Sandoval, Danny, Scranton/W-B	.331	104	390	53	129	20	0	7	48	31	49	11
Daubach, Brian, Norfolk	.325	99	345	63	112	29	1	16	62	62	68	1
Castro, Bernie, Ottawa	.315	126	502	81	158	21	5	1	36	42	50	41
Rushford, Jim, Scranton/W-B	.312	117	414	61	129	29	1	10	63	34	40	5
Darula, Bobby, Ottawa	.311	109	402	66	125	25	6	2	40	28	36	17
Victorino, Shane, Scranton/W-B	.310	126	494	93	153	25	16	18	70	51	74	17
Gomez, Alexis, Toledo	.307	114	424	51	130	28	6	7	55	27	91	21
Calzado, Napoleon, Ottawa	.306	120	447	54	137	22	1	11	61	21	46	10
Brown, Roosevelt, Charlotte	.306	103	389	62	119	31	2	12	53	42	59	3
Berg, Dave, Pawtucket	.306	112	425	73	130	28	1	3	60	63	67	1

INDIVIDUAL PITCHING LEADERS

(Minimum 115 Innings)

	W	L	ERA	G	GS	CG	SV	IP	H	R	ER	BB	SO
Baker, Scott, Rochester	5	8	3.01	22	22	1	0	135	123	50	45	26	107
Graman, Alex, Louisville	7	7	3.16	28	20	0	1	120	118	49	42	48	115
Scobie, Jason, Norfolk	15	7	3.34	27	26	0	0	167	163	71	62	55	96
Gaudin, Chad, Syracuse	9	8	3.35	23	23	2	0	150	140	61	56	35	113
Baugh, Kenny, Toledo	12	8	3.38	28	28	1	0	165	159	72	62	60	107
Fiore, Tony, Ottawa	9	5	3.63	30	28	0	0	166	168	79	67	49	97
Good, Andrew, Toledo	9	5	3.68	23	23	0	0	134	129	61	55	42	89
Miner, Zach, Toledo	5	8	3.71	23	23	0	0	124	125	57	51	65	83
Ramirez, Elizardo, Louisville	7	7	3.77	21	21	0	0	131	150	63	55	18	82
Junge, Eric, Norfolk	10	7	3.80	26	22	0	2	135	125	61	57	52	114

ALL-STAR TEAM

C—Kelly Shoppach, Pawtucket. **1B**—Mitch Jones, Columbus. **2B**—Bernie Castro, Ottawa. **3B**—Edwin Encarnacion, Louisville. **SS**—B.J. Upton, Durham. **OF**—John-Ford Griffin, Syracuse; Curtis Granderson, Toledo; Shane Victorino, Scranton/Wilkes-Barre. **DH**—Brian Daubach, Norfolk. **Utility**—Ryan Garko, Buffalo. **SP**—Zach Duke, Indianapolis. **RP**—Travis Bowyer, Rochester.

Most Valuable Player: Shane Victorino, Scranton/Wilkes-Barre. **Most Valuable Pitcher:** Zach Duke, Indianapolis. **Rookie of the Year:** Francisco Liriano, Rochester. **Manager of the Year:** Larry Parrish, Toledo.

DEPARTMENT LEADERS

BATTING

G	Upton, B.J., Durham	139
AB	Upton, B.J., Durham	545
R	Upton, B.J., Durham	98
H	Upton, B.J., Durham	165
TB	Upton, B.J., Durham	267
XBH	Snyder, Earl, Durham	63
2B	Reese, Kevin, Columbus	38
3B	Victorino, Shane, Scranton/W-B	16
HR	Griffin, John-Ford, Syracuse	30
RBI	Griffin, John-Ford, Syracuse	103
SH	Raines, Tim, Ottawa	20
SF	Berg, Dave, Pawtucket	9
	Wooten, Shawn, Pawtucket	9
BB	Upton, B.J., Durham	78
IBB	Daubach, Brian, Norfolk	8
HBP	Kinkade, Mike, Buffalo	30
SO	Jones, Mitch, Columbus	174
SB	Snead, Esix, Richmond	46
CS	Pagan, Angel, Norfolk	15
	Pena, Tony, Richmond	15
GIDP	Coste, Chris, Scranton/W-B	25
OBP	Daubach, Brian, Norfolk	.426
SLG	Barker, Kevin, Syracuse	.575

PITCHING

G	Smith, Matt, Charlotte	66
GS	Six tied at	28
CG	Grilli, Jason, Toledo	3
SHO	Gaudin, Chad, Syracuse	2
	Grilli, Jason, Toledo	2
GF	Corey, Mark, Indianapolis	55
SV	Corey, Mark, Indianapolis	28
W	Scobie, Jason, Norfolk	15
L	Munoz, Arnie, Charlotte	14
IP	Borkowski, Dave, Ottawa	183
H	Borkowski, Dave, Ottawa	217
R	Floyd, Gavin, Scranton/W-B	103
	Webb, John, Durham	103
ER	Floyd, Gavin, Scranton/W-B	94
HR	Bacsik, Mike, Scranton/W-B	23
	Webb, John, Durham	23
HBP	Floyd, Gavin, Scranton/W-B	19
BB	Stewart, Cory, Indianapolis	67
SO	Bonser, Boof, Rochester	168
WP	Simpson, Allan, Louisville	12
BK	Ramirez, Elizardo, Louisville	5
	Seddon, Chris, Durham	5

FIELDING

C	PCT	Harper, Brandon, Toledo	.997
	PO	Nieves, Wil, Columbus	695
	A	Nieves, Wil, Columbus	52
		Wathan, Dusty, Buffalo	52
	E	Martinez, Sandy, Toledo	10
	DP	Wathan, Dusty, Buffalo	9
	PB	Lomasney, Steve, Louisville	16
	CS PCT	Shoppach, Kelly, Pawtucket	44%
1B	PCT	Barker, Kevin, Syracuse	.998
	PO	Jones, Garrett, Rochester	979
	A	Jones, Garrett, Rochester	81
	E	Munson, Eric, Durham	15
	DP	Jones, Garrett, Rochester	100
2B	PCT	Bergolla, William, Louisville	.979
	PO	Castro, Bernie, Ottawa	238
	A	Castro, Bernie, Ottawa	357
	E	Raburn, Ryan, Toledo	21
	DP	Medrano, Anthony, Scranton	82
3B	PCT	Hessman, Mike, Toledo	.987
	PO	Snyder, Earl, Durham	73
	A	Nye, Rodney, Norfolk	223
	E	Kinkade, Mike, Buffalo	20
	DP	Three tied at	22
SS	PCT	Velandia, Jorge, Indianapolis	.977
	PO	Pena, Tony, Richmond	222
	A	Pena, Tony, Richmond	420
	E	Upton, B.J., Durham	53
	DP	Upton, B.J., Durham	95
OF	PCT	Three tied at	1.000
	PO	Victorino, Shane, Scranton/WB	307
	A	Granderson, Curtis, Toledo	15
	E	Pagan, Angel, Norfolk	9
	DP	Four tied at	4

PACIFIC COAST LEAGUE

TRIPLE-A

BY CHRIS GIGLEY

Nothing could stop the Nashville Sounds from winning their first championship since 1982. Neither losing key players to big league callups nor trailing the Oklahoma Redhawks 2-1 in the first round of the playoffs seemed to shake them.

Second baseman Rickie Weeks played just 55 games for the Sounds before heading to Milwaukee. And during its playoff run, Nashville lost its two best hitters, first baseman Prince Fielder (.291-28-86) and outfielder Corey Hart (.308-17-69).

Nevertheless, the Sounds showed plenty of offense and the Brewers organization showed plenty of depth as Nashville won the 2005 Pacific Coast League championship. The team hit eight home runs in its three-game sweep of Tacoma, including five in the first game. In that 8-6 victory, outfielder Nelson Cruz and veteran infielder Tony Zuniga each hit two long balls. The 25-year-old Cruz led all PCL hitters in the postseason with four homers and 11 RBIs.

Prince Fielder

As the Sounds had come back from a 2-1 deficit in the first round of the playoffs against Oklahoma just to make it to the championship round, Tacoma overcame the same deficit in the first round, scoring three runs in the 11th inning to win the deciding fifth game in Sacramento. Outfielder T.J. Bohn led the Rainiers in the postseason with a .311-2-6 effort and four steals in eight games after a promotion from Double-A San Antonio.

Despite Cruz' head-turning play after his callup from Double-A Huntsville in late June—he hit .269-11-27 in 60 games—he wasn't among seven Brewers Top 10 prospects who passed through Nashville. The Sounds featured, at various times, Weeks, Fielder, Hart, outfielders Brad Nelson and Dave Krynzel, and righthanders Jose Capellan and Ben Hendrickson.

"This was a weird year for Triple-A teams," Sounds

BILL NICHOLS

When he's bad, he's good

Tacoma righthander Felix Hernandez was the PCL's top prospect

MINOR LEAGUES

STANDINGS

AMERICAN CONFERENCE

Page	NORTH	W	L	PCT	GB	Manager	Attendance	Average	Last Penn.
159	Nashville Sounds (Brewers)	75	69	.521	—	Frank Kremblas	419,412	6,078	2005
138	Omaha Royals (Royals)	72	72	.500	3	Mike Jirschele	303,749	4,278	None
211	Memphis Redbirds (Cardinals)	71	72	.497	3½	Danny Sheaffer	696,083	10,088	2000
78	Iowa Cubs (Cubs)	64	75	.460	8½	Mike Quade	529,354	7,562	None
Page	**SOUTH**	**W**	**L**	**PCT**	**GB**	**Manager**	**Attendance**	**Average**	**Last Penn.**
248	Oklahoma RedHawks (Rangers)	80	63	.559	—	Bobby Jones	542,095	7,744	None
123	Albuquerque Isotopes (Marlins)	78	66	.542	2½	Dean Treanor	582,839	8,209	None
131	Round Rock Express (Astros)	74	70	.514	6½	Jackie Moore	700,277	9,726	2002
262	New Orleans Zephyrs (Nationals)	64	76	.457	14½	Tim Foli	330,466	5,084	2001

PACIFIC CONFERENCE

Page	NORTH	W	L	PCT	GB	Manager	Attendance	Average	Last Penn.
233	Tacoma Rainiers (Mariners)	80	64	.556	—	Dan Rohn	335,031	4,786	2001
145	Salt Lake Stingers (Angels)	79	65	.549	1	Dino Ebel	437,686	6,838	1979
219	Portland Beavers (Padres)	70	73	.490	9½	Craig Colbert	360,772	5,228	1994
109	Colorado Springs Sky Sox (Rockies)	65	78	.455	14½	Marv Foley	235,502	3,623	1995
Page	**SOUTH**	**W**	**L**	**PCT**	**GB**	**Manager**	**Attendance**	**Average**	**Last Penn.**
190	Sacramento River Cats (Athletics)	80	64	.556	—	Tony DeFrancesco	755,750	10,496	2004
226	Fresno Grizzlies (Giants)	68	76	.472	12	Shane Turner	495,791	6,885	None
48	Tucson Sidewinders (Diamondbacks)	68	76	.472	12	Chip Hale	287,116	4,101	1993
152	Las Vegas 51s (Dodgers)	57	86	.399	22½	Jerry Royster	334,485	4,645	1988

PLAYOFFS—Semifinals: Tacoma defeated Sacramento 3-2 and Nashville defeated Oklahoma 3-2 in best-of-5 series. Final: Nashville defeated Tacoma 3-0 in best-of-5 series.

NOTE: Teams' individual batting and pitching statistics can be found on page indicated in lefthand column.

manager Frank Kremblas said. "You had all these guys that could play who were young."

Big Names, Big Years

The PCL was no way station for veteran role players to fill in at the big league level. Five players who entered 2005 as the top prospects in their respective organizations—Portland's Josh Barfield (Padres), Memphis' Anthony Reyes (Cardinals), Tucson's Carlos Quentin (Diamondbacks), Fresno's Matt Cain (Giants) and Tacoma's Felix Hernandez (Mariners)—all spent most or all of the season in the PCL.

The one club that rivaled Nashville in young stars was Tucson, which had four of the Diamondbacks' Top 10 prospects. Quentin didn't disappoint, hitting .301-21-89 in 452 at-bats, and his 29 HBPs bumped his on-base percentage to .422 for the Sidewinders.

BILL MITCHELL

Andy Green

"He gets good at-bats all the time, and he has such a great approach," Diamondbacks assistant general manager Bob Miller said.

But perhaps even more impressive than Quentin was fellow 2003 first-round pick Conor Jackson. He wound up hitting .354-8-73 in 333 at-bats before being called up to Arizona.

Another Sidewinder, infielder Andy Green, was one of the many veteran hitters who shined in the PCL. The 28-year-old entered the season as a career .298 hitter in the minors but batted .343 in his second season in Tucson, adding 19 homers after entering the season with 23 in his career. The 5-foot-9 Kentucky alumnus ranked second in the minors in hits (182) and total bases (311), third in doubles (46) and triples (13), and led the minors with 125 runs scored.

Green's season, which included a streak of 54 consecutive games in which he reached safely by a hit, walk or HBP, was eclipsed by that of New Orleans' Rick Short. The 32-year-old infielder was a career .312 hitter in 10 minor league seasons and hit .303 in Japan in 2003, but no one was prepared for his assault on pitchers in 2005. Short pushed his average to .402 with two solo homers Aug. 19 against Omaha, and he finished the season with a minors-best .383 average. Short's reward was his first big league callup, though a shoulder injury short-circuited that after he got off to a 6-for-15 start.

The Zephyrs came through the devastation of Hurricane Katrina better than they had any right to expect, as Zephyr Field sustained roof damage but little substantive structural damage. New Orleans was scheduled to finish the year on the road anyway, and several front-office employees accompanied the team on the bus trip to Oklahoma ahead of the storm. The club announced in September it intends to return in 2006.

Prospect Pieces

The PCL was a hitter's haven, even moreso than usual, in 2005 as high-ceiling hitters made their marks on their way to the majors. But the league's top prospect was a pitcher. In Tacoma, Felix Hernandez kept dominating hitters despite starting Triple-A at the tender age of 19. In 88 innings for the Rainiers, the righthander struck out 100 hitters. He went 9-4, but his opponents' .196 batting average was more telling of his dominance. He earned a callup to Seattle in August, and went 4-4, 2.67 in the majors.

"Felix is Felix," Rainiers catcher Ryan Christianson said. "When he's good he's good, and when he's bad, he's good."

Among other prospects who had solid seasons, Salt Lake catcher Jeff Mathis had one of the more significant performances. He bounced back from a difficult 2004 season to make the league's postseason all-star team after batting .276-21-73 for the Stingers. Teammate Casey Kotchman recovered from a woeful start to bat .289-10-58 in 363 at-bats and earn a spot on the Angels' postseason roster.

When it comes to attendance, the same could be said of the PCL's newest club, the Round Rock Express, who relocated from Edmonton. The Express was the perennial attendance leader in the Double-A Texas League before joining the PCL. The franchise nearly tripled its attendance from 2004, drawing 700,277 fans in 2005, but that wasn't enough to best Sacramento. Since the River Cats joined the league in 2000, they have led the PCL in attendance every year. A whopping 755,750 fans passed through the gates of Raley Field in 2005.

LEAGUE CHAMPIONS

Last 30 Years

Year	Regular Season*	PCT	Playoff
1975	Hawaii (Padres)	.611	Hawaii (Padres)
1976	Salt Lake City (Angels)	.625	Hawaii (Padres)
1977	Phoenix (Giants)	.579	Phoenix (Giants)
1978	Tacoma (Yankees)	.584	Tacoma (Yankees)# Albuquerque (Dodgers)#
1979	Albuquerque (Dodgers)	.581	Salt Lake City (Angels)
1980	Tucson (Astros)	.595	Albuquerque (Dodgers)
1981	Albuquerque (Dodgers)	.712	Albuquerque (Dodgers)
1982	Albuquerque (Dodgers)	.594	Albuquerque (Dodgers)
1983	Albuquerque (Dodgers)	.594	Portland (Phillies)
1984	Hawaii (Pirates)	.621	Edmonton (Angels)
1985	Hawaii (Pirates)	.587	Vancouver (Brewers)
1986	Vancouver (Brewers)	.616	Las Vegas (Padres)
1987	Calgary (Mariners)	.596	Albuquerque (Dodgers)
1988	Albuquerque (Dodgers)	.605	Las Vegas (Padres)
1989	Albuquerque (Dodgers)	.563	Vancouver (White Sox)
1990	Albuquerque (Dodgers)	.641	Albuquerque (Dodgers)
1991	Albuquerque (Dodgers)	.580	Tucson (Astros)
1992	Colo. Springs (Indians)	.596	Colo. Springs (Indians)
1993	Portland (Twins)	.608	Tucson (Astros)
1994	Albuquerque (Dodgers)	.597	Albuquerque (Dodgers)
1995	Tucson (Astros)	.608	Colo. Springs (Rockies)
1996	Edmonton (Athletics)	.592	Edmonton (Athletics)
1997	Phoenix (Giants)	.615	Edmonton (Athletics)
1998	Iowa (Cubs)	.590	New Orleans (Astros)
1999	Vancouver (Athletics)	.592	Vancouver (Athletics)
2000	Salt Lake (Twins)	.629	Memphis (Cardinals)
2001	New Orleans (Astros)	.590	New Orleans (Astros)#
	Tacoma (Mariners)	.590	Tacoma (Mariners)#
2002	Las Vegas (Dodgers)	.590	Edmonton (Twins)
2003	Sacramento (Athletics)	.639	Sacramento (Athletics)
2004	Portland (Padres)	.583	Sacramento (Athletics)

*Best overall record #Co-champions

TOP 20 PROSPECTS

1. Felix Hernandez, rhp, Tacoma (Mariners)
2. Rickie Weeks, 2b, Nashville (Brewers)
3. Prince Fielder, 1b, Nashville (Brewers)
4. Conor Jackson, 1b, Tucson (Diamondbacks)
5. Matt Cain, rhp, Fresno (Giants)
6. Casey Kotchman, 1b, Salt Lake (Angels)
7. Carlos Quentin, of, Tucson (Diamondbacks)
8. Dan Johnson, 1b, Sacramento (Athletics)
9. Ezequiel Astacio, rhp, Round Rock (Astros)
10. Jeff Mathis, c, Salt Lake (Angels)
11. Anthony Reyes, rhp, Memphis (Cardinals)
12. Yuniesky Betancourt, ss, Tacoma (Mariners)
13. Ben Johnson, of, Portland (Padres)
14. Rich Hill, lhp, Iowa (Cubs)
15. Fernando Nieve, rhp, Round Rock (Astros)
16. Ronny Cedeno, ss, Iowa (Cubs)
17. Joe Saunders, lhp, Salt Lake (Angels)
18. Josh Willingham, c, Albuquerque (Marlins)
19. Josh Barfield, 2b, Portland (Padres)
20. Justin Huber, 1b, Omaha (Royals)

2005 PACIFIC COAST LEAGUE STATISTICS

CLUB BATTING

	AVG	G	AB	R	H	2B	2B	HR	BB	SO	SB
Oklahoma	.296	143	5036	893	1490	297	47	171	552	1037	144
Colorado Springs	.296	143	4858	816	1439	326	47	145	488	973	89
New Orleans	.291	140	4770	692	1386	252	29	111	464	827	112
Salt Lake	.284	144	4831	820	1372	275	69	146	532	919	132
Tucson	.283	144	4736	760	1341	292	45	136	477	914	76
Albuquerque	.282	144	4947	795	1396	251	43	183	495	1074	104
Fresno	.281	144	5113	774	1438	297	39	176	394	993	122
Round Rock	.276	144	4977	703	1372	291	26	162	456	1062	89
Tacoma	.276	144	4889	732	1348	277	36	122	530	981	126
Las Vegas	.274	143	4847	770	1327	262	36	163	582	965	57
Sacramento	.273	144	4991	780	1363	303	37	130	608	1132	106
Nashville	.272	144	4813	738	1311	273	36	164	504	1062	175
Iowa	.270	139	4653	642	1257	241	34	108	503	915	91
Portland	.268	143	4767	681	1278	251	24	147	542	991	100
Omaha	.268	144	4870	734	1307	261	35	168	483	1098	86
Memphis	.259	143	4811	676	1248	277	18	164	479	906	58

CLUB PITCHING

	ERA	G	CG	SHO	SV	IP	H	R	ER	BB	SO
Sacramento	4.21	144	0	8	40	1291	1311	708	604	546	1140
Memphis	4.22	143	5	8	37	1254	1320	657	588	408	1090
Tacoma	4.36	144	4	17	37	1268	1263	676	614	560	999
Nashville	4.43	144	2	3	33	1257	1289	708	619	550	1117
Portland	4.50	143	6	8	41	1243	1293	697	622	413	967
Round Rock	4.58	144	3	9	39	1274	1356	708	648	497	904
Tucson	4.68	144	3	6	26	1262	1383	753	656	507	928
Albuquerque	4.73	144	3	4	42	1273	1383	768	669	491	940
Oklahoma	4.81	143	6	6	46	1268	1407	748	677	489	950
Iowa	4.82	139	2	10	36	1206	1266	706	646	511	1044
Fresno	4.84	144	3	7	28	1293	1338	773	696	569	1077
New Orleans	4.87	140	1	4	37	1221	1272	757	661	499	1006
Omaha	4.88	144	1	8	36	1253	1398	753	680	485	924
Salt Lake	5.28	144	1	3	40	1237	1480	798	726	482	884
Colorado Springs	5.86	143	3	2	24	1222	1453	875	795	503	960
Las Vegas	6.21	143	3	3	29	1243	1522	952	858	601	977

CLUB FIELDING

	PCT	PO	A	E	DP
Tacoma	.982	3805	1569	101	144
Iowa	.981	3618	1459	100	147
Round Rock	.980	3823	1504	107	166
Portland	.980	3729	1362	106	129
Memphis	.979	3763	1369	108	133
Albuquerque	.978	3819	1661	125	175
Omaha	.978	3760	1466	116	133
Tucson	.978	3787	1578	123	148
Oklahoma	.977	3803	1584	129	176
Fresno	.977	3880	1343	125	136
Salt Lake	.977	3711	1509	124	182
Las Vegas	.976	3729	1485	130	163
New Orleans	.976	3662	1366	125	135
Sacramento	.975	3874	1316	131	103
Colo. Springs	.975	3665	1525	132	125
Nashville	.973	3769	1472	146	140

INDIVIDUAL BATTING LEADERS

(Minimum 389 Plate Appearances)

	AVG	G	AB	R	H	2B	3B	HR	RBI	BB	SO	SB
Short, Rick, New Orleans	.383	108	376	72	144	35	1	11	70	46	27	5
Dillon, Joe, Albuquerque	.360	98	350	80	126	21	1	24	72	57	59	11
Watson, Brandon, New Orleans	.355	88	372	69	132	15	3	1	25	28	33	31
Jackson, Conor, Tucson	.354	93	333	66	118	38	2	8	73	69	32	3
Orie, Kevin, New Orleans	.352	113	349	67	123	35	1	20	89	57	43	4
Green, Andy, Tucson	.343	135	530	125	182	46	13	19	80	68	82	9
Flores, Jose, Las Vegas	.336	96	327	64	110	11	6	4	42	54	33	1
Pickler, Jeff, Colorado Springs	.331	128	423	72	140	26	6	5	50	41	46	16
Shealy, Ryan, Colorado Springs	.328	108	411	85	135	30	2	26	88	41	81	4
Godwin, Tyrell, New Orleans	.321	129	499	83	160	22	6	9	48	50	77	22

INDIVIDUAL PITCHING LEADERS

(Minimum 115 Innings)

	W	L	ERA	G	GS	CG	SV	IP	H	R	ER	BB	SO
Jarvis, Kevin, Memphis	11	6	3.38	26	25	1	0	157	164	63	59	39	112
Gissell, Chris, Memphis	8	8	3.54	23	23	2	0	137	134	63	54	36	123
Reyes, Anthony, Memphis	7	6	3.64	23	23	2	0	129	105	55	52	34	136
White, Matt, New Orleans	8	6	3.72	35	16	0	0	126	122	62	52	45	102
Moss, Damian, Tacoma	9	7	3.73	25	24	1	0	138	125	68	57	75	93
Prieto, Ariel, Albuquerque	9	5	3.78	25	21	1	0	133	144	65	56	37	98
Oxspring, Chris, Portland	12	6	4.03	26	26	3	0	161	148	81	72	42	125
Helling, Rick, Nashville	9	3	4.13	21	21	0	0	131	128	74	60	50	105

ALL-STAR TEAM

C—Jeff Mathis, Salt Lake. **1B**—Conor Jackson, Tucson. **2B**—Andy Green, Tucson. **3B**—Mike Coolbaugh, Round Rock. **SS**—Danny Klassen, Round Rock. **OF**—Todd Linden, Fresno; Brandon Watson, New Orleans; Aaron Guiel, Omaha. **DH**—Rick Short, New Orleans. **RHP**—Felix Hernandez, Tacoma. **LHP**—Matt White, New Orleans. **RP**—Jermaine Van Buren, Iowa.

Most Valuable Player: Andy Green, Tucson. **Pitcher of the Year:** Felix Hernandez, Tacoma. **Rookie of the Year:** Felix Hernandez, Tacoma. **Manager of the Year:** Dan Rohn, Tacoma.

DEPARTMENT LEADERS

BATTING

G	Wilson, Josh, Albuquerque	143
AB	Brown, Adrian, Omaha	553
R	Green, Andy, Tucson	125
H	Green, Andy, Tucson	182
TB	Green, Andy, Tucson	311
XBH	Green, Andy, Tucson	78
2B	Green, Andy, Tucson	46
3B	Green, Andy, Tucson	13
HR	Scott, Luke, Round Rock	31
RBI	Gorneault, Nick, Salt Lake	108
SH	Rouse, Mike, Sacramento	17
	Santiago, Ramon, Tacoma	17
SF	Wilson, Josh, Albuquerque	12
BB	Cust, Jack, Sacramento	115
IBB	Nunez, Abraham, Tacoma	7
HBP	Quentin, Carlos, Tucson	29
SO	Cust, Jack, Sacramento	153
SB	German, Esteban, Oklahoma	43
CS	Watson, Brandon, New Orleans	13
GIDP	Wood, Jason, Albuquerque	24
OBP	Dillon, Joe, Albuquerque	.459
SLG	Linden, Todd, Fresno	.682

PITCHING

G	Baker, Brad, Portland	59
GS	Fulchino, Jeff, Albuquerque	29
	Wainwright, Adam, Memphis	29
CG	Three tied at	3
SHO	Five tied at	2
GF	Veras, Jose, Oklahoma	47
SV	Baker, Brad, Portland	27
W	Oxspring, Chris, Portland	12
L	Three tied at	13
IP	Wainwright, Adam, Memphis	182
H	Powell, Brian, New Orleans	204
	Wainwright, Adam, Memphis	204
R	Powell, Brian, New Orleans	114
ER	Powell, Brian, New Orleans	102
HR	Four tied at	27
HBP	Eckert, Harold, Las Vegas	20
BB	Murphy, Bill, Tucson	78
SO	Cain, Matt, Fresno	176
WP	Wainwright, Adam, Memphis	12
BK	Koronka, John, Iowa	3
	Walrond, Les, Albuquerque	3

FIELDING

C	PCT	Ortiz, Hector, New Orleans	.997
	PO	Baker, John, Sacramento	743
	A	Soto, Geovany, Iowa	62
	E	Mathis, Jeff, Salt Lake	9
		Mosquera, Julio, Nashville	9
	DP	Navarro, Dioner, Las Vegas	10
	PB	Mosquera, Julio, Nashville	11
		Soto, Geovany, Iowa	11
	CS PCT	Laird, Gerald, Oklahoma	48%
1B	PCT	Hoffpauir, James, Iowa	.999
	PO	Shealy, Ryan, Colo. Springs	885
	A	Myrow, Brian, Las Vegas	102
	E	Duncan, Chris, Memphis	17
	DP	Myrow, Brian, Las Vegas	105
2B	PCT	Santiago, Ramon, Tacoma	.993
	PO	Kinsler, Ian, Oklahoma	276
	A	Kinsler, Ian, Oklahoma	413
	E	Kinsler, Ian, Oklahoma	20
	DP	Kinsler, Ian, Oklahoma	112
3B	PCT	Coolbaugh, Mike, RR	.968
	PO	Coolbaugh, Mike, RR	98
	A	Barden, Brian, Tucson	253
	E	Smith, Bobby, Sacramento	23
	DP	Barden, Brian, Tucson	27
SS	PCT	Bowers, Jason, New Orleans	.974
	PO	Wilson, Josh, Albuquerque	226
	A	Wilson, Josh, Albuquerque	452
	E	Santos, Sergio, Tucson	26
	DP	Wilson, Josh, Albuquerque	112
OF	PCT	Prieto, Chris, Salt Lake	1
	PO	Brown, Adrian, Omaha	336
	A	Choo, Shin-Soo, Tacoma	24
	E	Godwin, Tyrell, New Orleans	10
		Krynzel, Dave, Nashville	10
	DP	Gipson, Charles, Round Rock	6

EASTERN LEAGUE

DOUBLE-A

BY ALAN MATTHEWS

The Eastern League was loaded with pitching in 2005, and its stingiest staff was at its best when it mattered most. The Akron Aeros held the Portland Sea Dogs scoreless for 23⅔ consecutive innings during the EL championship series, keying the Aeros' three-games-to-one series title.

JOHN SPEAR

Jon Lester

Righthander Jake Dittler scattered five hits and struck out five in seven shutout innings to earn the win in Game Four as Akron polished off Portland 4-1 at Akron's Canal Park for the Aeros' second EL crown in three years.

"We felt our way around early on, hit our stride midway through the season and in the end it all culminated in a championship," Akron manager Torey Lovullo said.

Akron cruised to the Southern Division title, finishing with a league-best 84-58 record and an eight-game lead over second place Altoona thanks to a pitching staff that led the EL with a 3.40 ERA and an offense that finished second with a .265 average.

Portland wasn't without ammunition, as a handful of the Red Sox' top prospects, under the guidance of manager Todd Claus, held off Trenton by two games to take the Northern Division pennant.

After Akron dispatched Altoona in five games in the first round of the playoffs, Portland edged Trenton three games to two and sent its ace to the mound in Game One of the championship series. Lefty Jon Lester, the 2005 EL pitcher of the year, held Akron to one earned run in six innings as the Sea Dogs won the series opener before Akron's staff took control.

"Pitching overall in this league was way above average, much better than last year," Altoona manager Tony Beasley said. "Every team has a couple guys at the front of their rotation that can stick it up your butt, and then late in games have enough bullpen to close it out. There are a lot of guys in this league that are going to pitch in the big leagues."

By the end of September, the league had already graduated a handful of pitching prospects to the big leagues.

New Britain lefthander Francisco Liriano was promoted to Triple-A in June and moved on to Minnesota and Portland righties Jonathan Papelbon, Craig Hansen and Manny Delcarmen all contributed to Boston's American League wild-card race. Altoona sent lefthanders Zach Duke and Tom Gorzelanny to the majors.

Meanwhile, Binghamton's Yusmeiro Petit and Brian Bannister formed a formidable combination, trumped perhaps by Erie's duo of Joel Zumaya and Justin Verlander while no fewer than seven Akron pitchers—Fausto Carmona, Dan Denham, Dittler, J.D. Martin, Rafael Perez, Brian Slocum and Jeremy Sowers—drew consideration for the league's Top 20 Prospects list, which was headed by Liriano.

There was some offense, as Reading first baseman Randy Ruiz won the batting title with a .349 average. Binghamton catcher/first baseman Mike Jacobs was named the league's MVP after the 24-year-old hit .321 with 37 doubles, 25 home runs and 93 RBIs.

Plenty of people took notice, as the league set an attendance record with 3,944,195 fans passing through the gates of the 12 EL parks in 2005. Seven clubs—Binghamton, Bowie, Harrisburg, New Britain, New Hampshire, Norwich and Trenton—increased their total attendance from 2004.

Following the season, the Norwich Navigators announced they would be known as the Connecticut Defenders, changing their name and logo.

TOP 20 PROSPECTS

1. Francisco Liriano, lhp, New Britain (Twins)
2. Lastings Milledge, of, Binghamton (Mets)
3. Hanley Ramirez, ss, Portland (Red Sox)
4. Jon Lester, lhp, Portland (Red Sox)
5. Ryan Zimmerman, 3b, Harrisburg (Nationals)
6. Nick Markakis, of, Bowie (Orioles)
7. Jonathan Papelbon, rhp, Portland (Red Sox)
8. Jeremy Sowers, lhp, Akron (Indians)
9. Anibal Sanchez, rhp, Portland (Red Sox)
10. Joel Zumaya, rhp, Erie (Tigers)
11. Yusmeiro Petit, rhp, Binghamton (Mets)
12. Dustin Pedroia, 2b, Portland (Red Sox)
13. Hayden Penn, rhp, Bowie (Orioles)
14. Denard Span, of, New Britain (Twins)
15. Merkin Valdez, rhp, Norwich (Giants)
16. Matt Moses, 3b, New Britain (Twins)
17. Eric Duncan, 3b, Trenton (Yankees)
18. Michael Bourn, of, Reading (Phillies)
19. Paul Maholm, lhp, Altoona (Pirates)
20. Franklin Gutierrez, of, Akron (Indians)

STANDINGS

Page	NORTH	W	L	PCT	GB	Manager	Attendance	Average	Last Penn.
71	Portland Sea Dogs (Red Sox)	76	66	.535	—	Todd Claus	396,277	6,290	None
183	Trenton Thunder (Yankees)	74	68	.521	2	Bill Masse	410,926	5,787	None
227	Norwich Navigators (Giants)	71	71	.500	5	Dave Machemer	170,686	2,547	2002
167	New Britain Rock Cats (Twins)	70	72	.493	6	Stan Cliburn	337,687	4,894	2001
256	New Hampshire Fisher Cats (Blue Jays)	68	74	.479	8	Mike Basso	279,556	4,235	2004
174	Binghamton Mets (Mets)	63	79	.444	13	Jack Lind	222,243	3,220	1994
Page	**SOUTH**	**W**	**L**	**PCT**	**GB**	**Manager**	**Attendance**	**Average**	**Last Penn.**
102	Akron Aeros (Indians)	84	58	.592	—	Torey Lovullo	455,056	6,894	2005
205	Altoona Curve (Pirates)	76	66	.535	8	Tony Beasley	390,239	5,496	None
64	Bowie Baysox (Orioles)	74	68	.521	10	Don Werner	314,277	4,489	None
198	Reading Phillies (Phillies)	69	73	.486	15	Steve Swisher	469,105	6,701	2001
263	Harrisburg Senators (Nationals)	64	78	.451	20	Keith Bodie	264,718	3,728	1999
117	Erie SeaWolves (Tigers)	63	79	.444	21	Duffy Dyer	233,415	3,432	None

PLAYOFFS—Semifinals: Portland defeated Trenton 3-2 and Akron defeated Altoona 3-2 in best-of-5 series. Finals: Akron defeated Portland 3-1 in best-of-5 series.

NOTE: Teams' individual batting and pitching statistics can be found on page indicated in lefthand column.

2005 EASTERN LEAGUE STATISTICS

CLUB BATTING

	AVG	G	AB	R	H	2B	2B	HR	BB	SO	SB
Binghamton	.270	142	4789	655	1291	269	36	133	433	1126	107
Akron	.265	142	4824	726	1276	244	44	151	420	1094	144
New Britain	.265	142	4742	647	1256	266	15	105	402	922	61
Erie	.263	142	4833	666	1271	249	37	114	455	1076	73
Altoona	.263	142	4801	671	1262	236	38	141	485	1081	155
Reading	.261	142	4871	614	1269	225	29	126	435	1048	101
Norwich	.256	142	4645	615	1187	225	24	97	399	998	160
Portland	.256	142	4751	643	1217	274	33	118	471	1004	102
Harrisburg	.255	142	4754	628	1211	241	24	134	441	989	90
Bowie	.254	142	4724	579	1198	240	23	85	450	968	86
Trenton	.252	142	4813	653	1212	231	24	129	446	1047	88
New Hampshire	.249	142	4734	540	1178	254	21	106	363	1131	63

CLUB PITCHING

	ERA	G	CG	SHO	SV	IP	H	R	ER	BB	SO
Akron	3.40	142	3	10	36	1266	1183	574	478	389	1001
Bowie	3.54	142	2	11	39	1249	1128	564	491	464	1168
New Hampshire	3.57	142	5	10	43	1241	1188	568	491	317	1133
Reading	3.77	142	5	2	33	1276	1270	609	535	410	957
Portland	3.82	142	6	16	39	1238	1182	635	525	463	1063
Trenton	3.86	142	0	13	38	1260	1226	641	540	527	1126
Norwich	3.96	142	2	13	41	1231	1243	614	542	426	971
Altoona	4.00	142	2	5	44	1259	1266	652	559	486	1042
New Britain	4.10	142	7	7	36	1234	1212	662	562	428	1005
Harrisburg	4.24	142	6	8	28	1252	1312	679	590	403	984
Binghamton	4.40	142	6	8	26	1238	1298	717	605	465	1083
Erie	4.52	142	1	11	42	1234	1320	722	620	422	951

CLUB FIELDING

	PCT	PO	A	E	DP
Bowie	.977	3748	1484	125	118
Akron	.976	3799	1541	133	110
New Hampshire	.976	3722	1411	126	129
Norwich	.976	3693	1510	126	129
Reading	.975	3827	1444	137	134
Harrisburg	.975	3755	1512	137	135
Trenton	.975	3779	1515	138	146
New Britain	.973	3702	1392	142	126
Erie	.971	3701	1464	154	123
Portland	.971	3715	1407	151	124
Altoona	.970	3776	1483	161	120
Binghamton	.968	3714	1331	169	113

INDIVIDUAL BATTING LEADERS

(Minimum 383 Plate Appearances)

	AVG	G	AB	R	H	2B	3B	HR	RBI	BB	SO	SB
Ruiz, Randy, Reading	.349	89	344	59	120	29	0	27	89	30	87	0
Jacobs, Mike, Binghamton	.321	117	433	66	139	37	2	25	93	35	94	1
Roberson, Chris, Reading	.311	139	553	90	172	24	8	15	70	40	112	34
Cosby, Rob, New Hampshire	.308	115	428	56	132	34	0	17	68	24	77	2
Deeds, Doug, New Britain	.304	133	493	77	150	34	2	16	82	56	119	2
Romero, Alex, New Britain	.301	139	509	65	153	31	2	15	77	36	69	12
Bergeron, Peter, Bowie	.296	91	348	54	103	14	2	5	33	34	82	13
Valderrama, Carlos, Norwich	.294	130	493	61	145	33	3	8	58	34	84	29
Tejeda, Juan, Erie	.291	122	470	64	137	27	2	14	82	41	86	2
Fahey, Brandon, Bowie	.291	139	502	63	146	21	4	3	47	44	71	17

INDIVIDUAL PITCHING LEADERS

(Minimum 114 Innings)

	W	L	ERA	G	GS	CG	SV	IP	H	R	ER	BB	SO
Lester, Jon, Portland	11	6	2.61	26	26	3	0	148	114	52	43	57	163
Petit, Yusmeiro, Binghamton	9	3	2.91	21	21	2	0	118	90	41	38	18	130
Desalvo, Matt, Trenton	9	5	3.02	25	24	0	0	149	106	55	50	67	151
Morris, Cory, Bowie	8	5	3.03	29	25	0	0	143	116	50	48	78	159
Begg, Chris, Norwich	8	7	3.07	23	21	0	0	138	142	57	47	23	86
Mazone, Brian, Norwich	11	8	3.10	30	20	0	1	128	122	52	44	34	89
Denham, Dan, Akron	9	7	3.15	21	21	1	0	140	115	55	49	30	108
DuBose, Eric, Bowie	8	10	3.25	21	20	0	0	122	113	52	44	29	114
Gorzelanny, Tom, Altoona	8	5	3.26	23	23	1	0	130	114	50	47	46	124
Rasner, Darrell, Harrisburg	6	7	3.59	27	26	1	0	150	150	66	60	29	96

ALL-STAR TEAM

C—Mike Jacobs, Binghamton. **1B**—Shelley Duncan, Trenton. **2B**—Dustin Pedroia, Portland. **3B**—Jose Bautista, Altoona. **SS**—Hanley Ramirez, Portland. **OF**—Dan Ortmeier, Norwich; Chris Roberson, Reading; Alex Romero, New Britain. **DH**—Randy Ruiz, Reading. **UT**—Donald Kelly, Erie. **RHP**—Joel Zumaya, Erie. **LHP**—Jon Lester, Portland. **RP**—Edwin Almonte, Erie.

Most Valuable Player: Mike Jacobs, Binghamton. **Pitcher of the Year:** Jon Lester, Portland. **Rookie of the Year:** Chris Roberson, Reading. **Manager of the Year:** Torey Lovulllo, Akron.

DEPARTMENT LEADERS

BATTING

G	Duncan, Shelley, Trenton	142
AB	Roberson, Chris, Reading	553
R	Roberson, Chris, Reading	90
H	Roberson, Chris, Reading	172
TB	Duncan, Shelley, Trenton	263
XBH	Duncan, Shelley, Trenton	64
	Jacobs, Mike, Binghamton	64
2B	Jacobs, Mike, Binghamton	37
3B	Lydon, Wayne, Binghamton	13
HR	Duncan, Shelley, Trenton	34
RBI	Jacobs, Mike, Binghamton	93
SH	Fahey, Brandon, Bowie	22
SF	Concepcion, Alberto, Portland	8
	Moss, Brandon, Portland	8
BB	Lewis, Fred, Norwich	69
IBB	Ruiz, Randy, Reading	11
HBP	Ortmeier, Dan, Norwich	21
SO	Van Every, Jon, Akron	155
SB	Davis, Rajai, Altoona	45
	Thompson, Rich, Altoona	45
CS	Two tied at	14
GIDP	LaBarbera, Anthony, Norwich	20
	Matienzo, Daniel, New Britain	20
OBP	Ruiz, Randy, Reading	.405
SLG	Ruiz, Randy, Reading	.669

PITCHING

G	Cameron, Ryan, Reading	58
GS	Smith, Mike, Reading	28
CG	Davis, Allen, Reading	3
	Lester, Jon, Portland	3
SHO	12 tied at	1
GF	Pope, Justin, Trenton	54
SV	Almonte, Edwin, Erie	33
W	Davis, Allen, Reading	13
L	Smith, Mike, Reading	14
IP	Davis, Allen, Reading	183
H	Davis, Allen, Reading	208
R	Peterson, Matt, Altoona	102
ER	Peterson, Matt, Altoona	88
HR	Johnson, Jeremy, Erie	23
HBP	Smith, Mike, Reading	23
BB	Smith, Mike, Reading	82
SO	Lester, Jon, Portland	163
WP	Smith, Mike, Reading	14
BK	Montes, Alberto, Norwich	4
	Zumaya, Joel, Erie	4

FIELDING

C	PCT	Kratz, Erik, New Hampshire	.992
	PO	Marsters, Brandon, Bowie	865
	A	Marsters, Brandon, Bowie	83
	E	Maldonado, Carlos, Altoona	11
	DP	Maldonado, Carlos, Altoona	10
		Santos, Omir, Trenton	10
	PB	Pratt, Trent, Reading	15
	CS PCT	St. Pierre, Max, Erie	46%
1B	PCT	Barthelemy, Ryan, Reading	.997
	PO	Duncan, Shelley, Trenton	1178
	A	Von Schell, Tyler, Norwich	109
	E	Duncan, Shelley, Trenton	16
	DP	Duncan, Shelley, Trenton	123
2B	PCT	Hitchcox, Brian, Reading	.989
	PO	Stansberry, Craig, Altoona	255
	A	LaBarbera, Anthony, Norwich	335
	E	Baldiris, Aarom, Binghamton	19
	DP	LaBarbera, Anthony, Norwich	77
3B	PCT	Johnson, Tripper, Bowie	.952
	PO	Johnson, Tripper, Bowie	89
	A	Osborn, Pat, Akron	248
	E	Duncan, Eric, Trenton	27
	DP	Cosby, Rob, New Hampshire	20
SS	PCT	Ochoa, Ivan, Akron	.970
	PO	Fahey, Brandon, Bowie	221
	A	Fahey, Brandon, Bowie	413
	E	Tablado, Raul, New Hampshire	28
	DP	Fahey, Brandon, Bowie	84
OF	PCT	Bourn, Michael, Reading	.997
	PO	Roberson, Chris, Reading	320
	A	Bourn, Michael, Reading	21
	E	Lewis, Fred, Norwich	14
	DP	Bourn, Michael, Reading	9

SOUTHERN LEAGUE

DOUBLE-A

BY AARON FITT

It seemed fitting that the two most talented teams in an incredibly talent-crammed league faced off for the 2005 Southern League championship, with the much-heralded Jacksonville Suns topping the pitching-rich West Tenn Diamond Jaxx three games to one. Even by the lofty standards of the SL, Jacksonville stood out, with four players among the league's top 10 prospects and five in the top 14. The Suns were an easy choice for Baseball America's Minor League Team of the Year award.

A strong offense led by stud prospects Joel Guzman (.287-16-75), Andy LaRoche (.273-9-43), Delwyn Young (.296-16-62) and James Loney (.284-11-65) paced the Suns for much of the regular season, but pitching carried them through the postseason, as they compiled a 1.57 ERA in seven playoff games. Chad Billingsley and Jonathan Broxton combined on a no-hitter against a potent Birmingham offense in Game Two of the Suns' first-round sweep, during which they allowed just two runs in three games.

STEVE MOORE

Chad Billingsley

Then, after West Tenn scored six runs in two innings against Billingsley in the opener of the championship series, the Suns yielded just two more runs in the final three games—all Jacksonville wins. Righthander Justin Orenduff, making his first postseason start, allowed one run over 5⅔ innings in a 3-1 win in Game Four, while Broxton, who pitched seven shutout innings over four postseason games, pitched the final two frames for the save.

"Jacksonville's pitching was excellent this series," West Tenn manager Bobby Dickerson said. "That's all you can say."

West Tenn's pitching was excellent all season, led by a pair of good prospects repeating the league who combined for 24 wins: lefthander Renyel Pinto, who won the SL's pitcher of the year award in 2004, and righthander Ricky Nolasco (14-3, 2.89), who took the honor in 2005. Like Jacksonville, the Diamond Jaxx placed five players among the league's top 20 prospects, but the other three were not with West Tenn in the postseason, as lefthander Rich Hill and outfielder Matt Murton were promoted and outfielder Felix Pie was injured. Still, the Diamond Jaxx—who battled poor attendance all year long and through the postseason—won their division in both halves of the season and swept Carolina in the first round of the playoffs before running into the Jacksonville buzz saw. West Tenn drew just 105,893 fans, the lowest total in Double-A.

Delmon Young (.336-20-71), the top prospect in the minors, tore up the SL for much of the season before a promotion to Triple-A. He made a serious run at the league's triple crown—as a 19-year-old—before getting promoted after 84 games, and he took home the SL MVP award despite playing the final month and a half of the season in the International League.

The Mississippi Braves made their debut in the league, after moving to Jackson from Greenville, S.C. The team attracted 242,423 fans in 63 openings before the final week of the 2005 season was cancelled because of the widespread destruction of Hurricane Katrina.

STANDINGS: SPLIT SEASON

FIRST HALF					SECOND HALF				
NORTH	**W**	**L**	**PCT**	**GB**	**NORTH**	**W**	**L**	**PCT**	**GB**
West Tenn	44	25	.638	—	West Tenn	39	31	.557	—
Carolina	41	27	.603	2½	Carolina	36	30	.545	1
Tennessee	33	37	.471	11½	Huntsville	31	39	.443	8
Huntsville	29	40	.420	15	Tennessee	31	39	.443	8
Chattanooga	27	42	.391	17	Chattanooga	26	41	.388	11½
SOUTH	**W**	**L**	**PCT**	**GB**	**SOUTH**	**W**	**L**	**PCT**	**GB**
Jacksonville	38	32	.543	—	Birmingham	46	24	.657	—
Birmingham	36	33	.522	1½	Jacksonville	41	29	.586	5
Mississippi	36	34	.514	2	Montgomery	32	35	.478	12½
Montgomery	35	35	.500	3	Mississippi	28	34	.452	14
Mobile	28	42	.400	10	Mobile	30	38	.441	15

PLAYOFFS—Semifinals: West Tenn defeated Carolina 3-0 and Jacksonville defeated Birmingham 3-0 in best-of-5 series. **Final:** Jacksonville defeated West Tenn 3-1 in best-of-5 series.

TOP 20 PROSPECTS

1. Delmon Young, of, Montgomery (Devil Rays)
2. Jeremy Hermida, of, Carolina (Marlins)
3. Jeff Francoeur, of, Mississippi (Braves)
4. Chris Young, of, Birmingham (White Sox)
5. Chad Billingsley, rhp, Jacksonville (Dodgers)
6. Joel Guzman, ss, Jacksonville (Dodgers)
7. Andy LaRoche, 3b, Jacksonville (Dodgers)
8. Felix Pie, of, West Tenn (Cubs)
9. Brian McCann, c, Mississippi (Braves)
10. Russell Martin, c, Jacksonville (Dodgers)
11. Scott Olsen, lhp, Carolina (Marlins)
12. Matt Murton, of, West Tenn (Cubs)
13. Bobby Jenks, rhp, Birmingham (White Sox)
14. Jonathan Broxton, rhp, Jacksonville (Dodgers)
15. Rich Hill, lhp, West Tenn (Cubs)
16. Dustin Nippert, rhp, Tennessee (Diamondbacks)
17. Ricky Nolasco, rhp, West Tenn (Cubs)
18. Renyel Pinto, lhp, West Tenn (Cubs)
19. Chuck James, lhp, Mississippi (Braves)
20. Elijah Dukes, of, Montgomery (Devil Rays)

STANDINGS: OVERALL

Page		W	L	PCT	GB	Manager	Attendance	Average	Last Penn.
79	West Tenn Diamond Jaxx (Cubs)	83	56	.597	—	Bobby Dickerson	105,893	1,654	2000
87	Birmingham Barons (White Sox)	82	57	.590	1	Razor Shines	271,031	4,106	2002
124	Carolina Mudcats (Marlins)	77	57	.575	3½	Gary Allenson	252,178	3,820	2003
153	Jacksonville Suns (Dodgers)	79	61	.564	4½	John Shoemaker	359,957	5,372	2005
242	Montgomery Biscuits (Devil Rays)	67	70	.489	13½	Charlie Montoyo	303,054	4,523	1999
56	Mississippi Braves (Braves)	64	68	.485	15½	Brian Snitker	242,423	3,847	1997
49	Tennessee Smokies (Diamondbacks)	64	76	.457	19½	Tony Perezchica	241,163	3,546	2004
160	Huntsville Stars (Brewers)	60	79	.432	23	Don Money	213,552	3,187	2001
220	Mobile BayBears (Padres)	58	80	.420	24½	Gary Jones	187,505	2,929	2004
94	Chattanooga Lookouts (Reds)	53	83	.390	28½	Jayhawk Owens	240,075	3,479	1988

NOTE: Teams' individual batting and pitching statistics can be found on page indicated in lefthand column.

2005 SOUTHERN LEAGUE STATISTICS

CLUB BATTING

	AVG	G	AB	R	H	2B	2B	HR	BB	SO	SB
Birmingham	.279	139	4650	730	1297	267	30	107	505	966	127
Jacksonville	.275	140	4691	704	1292	248	25	114	534	1063	116
Montgomery	.272	137	4629	662	1261	226	33	119	393	978	143
West Tenn	.270	139	4638	622	1253	251	42	91	519	913	151
Chattanooga	.270	136	4700	623	1268	268	23	92	445	913	125
Huntsville	.270	139	4648	591	1256	231	38	63	471	943	104
Carolina	.266	134	4451	563	1186	244	22	95	475	1045	111
Mississippi	.258	132	4391	545	1132	214	45	75	437	949	104
Tennessee	.257	140	4621	617	1187	219	28	107	449	979	170
Mobile	.244	138	4606	571	1123	203	25	91	507	1157	75

CLUB PITCHING

	ERA	G	CG	SHO	SV	IP	H	R	ER	BB	SO
West Tenn	3.35	139	3	13	42	1232	1148	517	458	450	1111
Carolina	3.72	134	5	10	47	1175	1144	548	486	408	945
Jacksonville	3.91	140	3	13	37	1224	1118	603	532	550	1144
Mississippi	3.98	132	2	13	29	1154	1136	569	510	445	916
Birmingham	4.08	139	7	8	45	1215	1273	642	551	544	930
Mobile	4.15	138	5	3	29	1207	1268	655	556	508	965
Huntsville	4.26	139	2	3	34	1218	1316	690	576	457	1008
Tennessee	4.28	140	10	14	30	1222	1331	693	581	440	945
Montgomery	4.30	137	6	7	31	1191	1262	655	569	409	946
Chattanooga	4.32	136	0	4	23	1207	1269	665	579	525	997

CLUB FIELDING

	PCT	PO	A	E	DP
Carolina	.977	3526	1443	116	117
West Tenn	.976	3695	1395	126	127
Birmingham	.975	3646	1479	131	151
Mississippi	.975	3463	1454	126	127
Jacksonville	.973	3671	1255	135	86
Mobile	.972	3620	1558	147	157
Chattanooga	.972	3609	1489	145	133
Montgomery	.971	3572	1415	147	130
Tennessee	.969	3667	1482	162	136
Huntsville	.969	3652	1463	161	106

INDIVIDUAL BATTING LEADERS

(Minimum 378 Plate Appearances)

	AVG	G	AB	R	H	2B	3B	HR	RBI	BB	SO	SB
Owens, Jerry, Birmingham	.331	130	522	99	173	21	6	2	52	52	72	38
Hanigan, Ryan, Chattanooga	.321	100	333	45	107	14	1	4	29	50	41	4
Martin, Russell, Jacksonville	.311	129	409	83	127	17	1	9	61	78	69	15
Hopper, Norris, Chattanooga	.310	116	451	70	140	15	4	1	37	27	38	25
Thorman, Scott, Mississippi	.305	90	348	49	106	21	2	15	65	28	76	2
Theriot, Ryan, West Tenn	.304	120	448	52	136	28	4	1	53	45	38	24
Gemoll, Brandon, Huntsville	.303	120	432	53	131	27	5	7	59	30	104	3
Cruz, Enrique, Huntsville	.300	137	496	68	149	34	3	14	60	37	107	4
Weber, Jon, Jacksonville	.300	117	450	81	135	27	5	11	68	45	78	10
Washington, Rico, Montgomery	.300	126	454	84	136	30	2	19	77	63	63	6

INDIVIDUAL PITCHING LEADERS

(Minimum 112 Innings)

	W	L	ERA	G	GS	CG	SV	IP	H	R	ER	BB	SO
Nippert, Dustin, Tennessee	8	3	2.38	18	18	3	0	117	95	33	31	42	97
Pinto, Renyel, West Tenn	10	3	2.71	22	21	1	0	130	101	43	39	58	123
Nolasco, Ricky, West Tenn	14	3	2.89	27	27	1	0	162	151	57	52	46	173
Dumatrait, Phil, Chattanooga	4	12	3.17	24	24	0	0	128	115	58	45	70	101
Thompson, Mike, Mobile	6	6	3.22	18	18	2	0	115	116	50	41	27	68
Lockwood, Luke, Carolina	2	8	3.24	34	15	1	1	114	110	45	41	23	79
Ryu, Jae-kuk, West Tenn	11	8	3.34	27	27	1	0	170	154	67	63	49	133
Hull, Eric, Jacksonville	7	7	3.38	27	18	1	3	117	105	50	44	44	117
Gonzalez, Enrique, Tennessee	11	8	3.46	27	27	2	0	161	160	76	62	52	146
Billingsley, Chad, Jacksonville	13	6	3.51	28	26	2	0	146	116	60	57	50	162

ALL-STAR TEAM

C—Russell Martin, Jacksonville. **1B**—Casey Rogowski, Birmingham. **2B**—Dan Uggla, Tennessee. **3B**—Rico Washington, Montgomery. **SS**—Joel Guzman, Jacksonville. **OF**—Jeremy Hermida, Carolina; Matt Murton, West Tenn; Jerry Owens, Birmingham; Delmon Young, Montgomery. **DH**—Brandon Sing, West Tenn. **RHP**—Ricky Nolasco, West Tenn. **LHP**—Renyel Pinto, West Tenn. **RP**—Chris Resop, Carolina.

Most Valuable Player: Delmon Young, Montgomery. **Most Outstanding Pitcher:** Ricky Nolasco, West Tenn. **Manager of the Year:** Razor Shines, Birmingham.

DEPARTMENT LEADERS

BATTING

G	Loney, James, Jacksonville	138
AB	Owens, Jerry, Birmingham	522
R	Young, Chris, Birmingham	100
H	Owens, Jerry, Birmingham	173
TB	Young, Chris, Birmingham	254
XBH	Young, Chris, Birmingham	70
2B	Young, Chris, Birmingham	41
3B	Blanco, Gregor, Mississippi	12
HR	Sing, Brandon, West Tenn	26
	Young, Chris, Birmingham	26
RBI	Blakely, Darren, Birmingham	89
SH	Crabbe, Callix, Huntsville	20
SF	Four tied at	8
BB	Hermida, Jeremy, Carolina	111
IBB	Reyes, Jose, West Tenn	10
HBP	Timmons, Wes, Mississippi	21
SO	Smith, Corey, Mobile	144
SB	Donovan, Todd, Jacksonville	62
CS	Owens, Jerry, Birmingham	20
GIDP	McGehee, Casey, West Tenn	20
OBP	Hermida, Jeremy, Carolina	.457
SLG	Young, Chris, Birmingham	.545

PITCHING

G	Schultz, Mike, Tennessee	63
GS	Tracey, Sean, Birmingham	28
CG	Three tied at	3
SHO	Three tied at	2
GF	Thayer, Dale, Mobile	50
SV	Thayer, Dale, Mobile	27
W	Nolasco, Ricky, West Tenn	14
	Tracey, Sean, Birmingham	14
L	Pena, Tony, Tennessee	13
	Whitaker, Brian, Mobile	13
IP	Ryu, Jae-kuk, West Tenn	170
H	Goocher, Clint, Tennessee	185
R	Goocher, Clint, Tennessee	105
ER	Goocher, Clint, Tennessee	84
HR	Autrey, Scott, Montgomery	24
HBP	Tracey, Sean, Birmingham	14
BB	Oyervidez, Jose, Mobile	82
SO	Nolasco, Ricky, West Tenn	173
BK	Schmidt, Jeremy, Chattanooga	5
WP	Dumatrait, Phil, Chattanooga	13

FIELDING

C	PCT	Reyes, Jose, West Tenn	.994
	PO	Martin, Russell, Jacksonville	960
	A	Martin, Russell, Jacksonville	90
	E	Martin, Russell, Jacksonville	12
	DP	Reyes, Jose, West Tenn	13
	PB	Stewart, Chris, Birmingham	23
	CS PCT	Stewart, Chris, Birmingham	52%
1B	PCT	Loney, James, Jacksonville	.993
	PO	Rogowski, Casey, Birmingham	1126
	A	Loney, James, Jacksonville	92
	E	Gemoll, Brandon, Huntsville	16
	DP	Rogowski, Casey, Birm.	133
2B	PCT	Theriot, Ryan, West Tenn	.982
	PO	Howard, Kevin, Chattanooga	239
	A	Howard, Kevin, Chattanooga	332
	E	Howard, Kevin, Chattanooga	24
	DP	Howard, Kevin, Chattanooga	84
3B	PCT	McGehee, Casey, West Tenn	.953
	PO	Smith, Corey, Mobile	106
	A	Fields, Josh, Birmingham	239
	E	Smith, Corey, Mobile	35
	DP	McGehee, Casey, West Tenn	27
SS	PCT	Maniscalco, Matthew, Mont.	.983
	PO	Cruz, Enrique, Huntsville	188
	A	Cruz, Enrique, Huntsville	386
	E	Cruz, Enrique, Huntsville	37
	DP	Hernandez, Luis, Mississippi	77
OF	PCT	Varner, Noochie, Tennessee	1
	PO	Gwynn, Anthony, Huntsville	294
	A	Weber, Jon, Jacksonville	19
	E	Zeringue, Jon, Tennessee	12
	DP	Weber, Jon, Jacksonville	7

TEXAS LEAGUE

DOUBLE-A

BY CHRIS GIGLEY

The Texas League season ended with a controversial call, but there was no controversy about the Midland RockHounds being the league's top team from beginning to end.

So even though a blown call by the home-plate umpire helped Midland clinch its first league championship since 1975 in the championship series against Arkansas, there was a feeling the RockHounds were destined to win it all no matter what.

"We'll take the championship," Midland manager Von Hayes told the Midland Reporter Telegram after the game. "Our guys deserve it. We were the best team — both halves — the best team overall, and we're the best team in the Texas League."

BILL MITCHELL

Andre Ethier

When the RockHounds met the Travelers in the final, it was a matchup of the league's two most talented teams. Arkansas was down 6-5 in the ninth at home when infielder Jason Aspito came to the plate with two outs and worked the count full. Reliever Alex Santos delivered what appeared to be ball four, but umpire Stephen Fritzoni lost track of the count and ordered Aspito back into the batter's box. Santos then struck out Aspito to end the game.

Leading the way for Midland were a pair of former college outfielders, Andre Ethier and Brian Stavisky. They finished fourth and fifth in the batting race and combined to drive in 168 runs, and Ethier was named the league's player of the year.

Midland also got a boost from first baseman Daric Barton, who had come to the Athletics organization in the Mark Mulder deal with the Cardinals before the season. Barton was promoted from high Class A Stockton in July and hit .316 with five home runs in 212 at-bats for the RockHounds.

Another midseason promotion, lefthander Dallas Braden, anchored the pitching staff and went 9-5 with a 3.90 ERA in the Texas League. He was joined by righthander Shane Komine, who was dominant down the stretch after returning from injury.

Though it didn't win the title, Arkansas had the most talent in the league. At varying points of the season, the Travelers lineup featured a handful of the Angels' top prospects. Second baseman Howie Kendrick finished the season ranked as the league's top prospect even though he started the season at high Class A Rancho Cucamonga.

One of the Travelers' less heralded players was catcher Mike Napoli. Despite hitting just .234, he led the league in home runs (31) and RBIs (99). And in July, Arkansas welcomed 2004 Angels first-rounder Jared Weaver, who went 3-3 with a 3.98 ERA in the hitter-friendly league.

The Texas League, long one of the minors' healthiest leagues, got even better in 2005 with the addition of two new markets. The Round Rock Express, which broke attendance records every year, moved up to the Pacific Coast League, so the Texas League franchise moved to Corpus Christi.

The Hooks were a huge success at the gate, drawing more than a half-million fans. On the field, righthander Jason Hirsh led the way and was the league's pitcher of the year. He tied for the league lead in wins (13), led the league in strikeouts (165) and finished second in ERA (2.87).

The Springfield Cardinals took the place of the El Paso Diablos and were an even bigger draw than the Hooks, finishing behind only Frisco in league attendance.

STANDINGS: SPLIT SEASON

FIRST HALF

EAST	W	L	PCT	GB
Tulsa	43	27	.614	—
Springfield	35	35	.500	8
Wichita	35	35	.500	8
Arkansas	34	36	.486	9
WEST	**W**	**L**	**PCT**	**GB**
Midland	39	31	.557	—
San Antonio	38	32	.543	1
Frisco	29	41	.414	10
Corpus Christi	27	43	.386	12

SECOND HALF

EAST	W	L	PCT	GB
Arkansas	37	33	.529	—
Springfield	35	35	.500	2
Wichita	33	37	.471	4
Tulsa	32	38	.457	5
WEST	**W**	**L**	**PCT**	**GB**
Midland	39	31	.557	—
San Antonio	38	32	.543	1
Corpus Christi	37	33	.529	2
Frisco	29	41	.414	10

PLAYOFFS—Semifinals: Arkansas defeated Tulsa 3-0 and Midland defeated San Antonio 3-2 in best-of-5 series. **Final:** Midland defeated Arkansas 3-1 in best-of-5 series.

TOP 20 PROSPECTS

1. Howie Kendrick, 2b, Arkansas (Angels)
2. Erick Aybar, ss, Arkansas (Angels)
3. Daric Barton, 1b, Midland (Athletics)
4. Thomas Diamond, rhp, Frisco (Rangers)
5. Edison Volquez, rhp, Frisco (Rangers)
6. Andre Ethier, of, Midland (Athletics)
7. Kendry Morales, 1b, Arkansas (Angels)
8. Yuniesky Betancourt, ss, San Antonio (Mariners)
9. Jason Hirsh, rhp, Corpus Christi (Astros)
10. Justin Huber, 1b, Wichita (Royals)
11. John Danks, lhp, Frisco (Rangers)
12. Joaquin Arias, ss, Frisco (Rangers)
13. Fernando Nieve, rhp, Corpus Christi (Astros)
14. Adam Jones, ss, San Antonio (Mariners)
15. Joe Saunders, lhp, Arkansas (Angels)
16. Steven Shell, rhp, Arkansas (Angels)
17. Omar Quintanilla, ss, Midland (Athletics)
18. Ubaldo Jimenez, rhp, Tulsa (Rockies)
19. Josh Anderson, of, Corpus Christi (Astros)
20. Kevin Melillo, 2b, Midland (Athletics)

STANDINGS: OVERALL

Page		W	L	PCT	GB	Manager	Attendance	Average	Last Penn.
191	Midland RockHounds (Athletics)	78	62	.557	—	Von Hayes	252,059	3,706	2005
234	San Antonio Missions (Mariners)	76	64	.543	2	Dave Brundage	272,922	3,898	2003
110	Tulsa Drillers (Rockies)	75	65	.536	3	Tom Runnells	335,018	4,785	1998
146	Arkansas Travelers (Angels)	71	69	.507	7	Tom Gamboa	196,366	3,021	2001
212	Springfield Cardinals (Cardinals)	70	70	.500	8	Chris Maloney	526,630	7,523	1994
139	Wichita Wranglers (Royals)	68	72	.486	10	Frank White	165,077	2,662	1999
132	Corpus Christi Hooks (Astros)	64	76	.457	14	Dave Clark	505,189	7,216	2000
249	Frisco RoughRiders (Rangers)	58	82	.414	20	Darryl Kennedy	581,074	8,421	2004

NOTE: Teams' individual batting and pitching statistics can be found on page indicated in lefthand column.

2005 TEXAS LEAGUE STATISTICS

CLUB BATTING

	AVG	G	AB	R	H	2B	2B	HR	BB	SO	SB
Midland	.281	140	4823	773	1353	283	30	140	524	957	41
Arkansas	.281	140	4679	760	1314	240	46	152	410	835	171
Wichita	.278	140	4791	744	1330	252	39	136	439	755	99
Springfield	.272	140	4852	691	1318	254	22	147	424	954	73
Frisco	.270	140	4875	632	1318	228	31	87	408	891	129
San Antonio	.269	140	4840	630	1302	232	39	113	347	1024	146
Corpus Christi	.257	140	4779	530	1228	221	30	96	378	972	143
Tulsa	.249	140	4611	649	1148	223	31	115	525	1054	101

CLUB PITCHING

	ERA	G	CG	SHO	SV	IP	H	R	ER	BB	SO
Corpus Christi	3.34	140	6	10	23	1257	1147	551	465	362	1036
San Antonio	3.74	140	1	9	48	1253	1286	614	521	441	979
Tulsa	4.02	140	8	7	39	1235	1251	622	551	352	852
Midland	4.26	140	0	8	42	1244	1318	678	589	464	963
Arkansas	4.56	140	4	8	32	1209	1321	701	613	451	848
Springfield	4.57	140	3	4	37	1247	1325	732	633	457	884
Frisco	4.70	140	3	4	32	1250	1352	745	653	463	990
Wichita	4.92	140	3	4	35	1215	1311	766	664	466	890

CLUB FIELDING

	PCT	PO	A	E	DP		PCT	PO	A	E	DP
Midland	.976	3731	1494	127	112	Corpus Christi	.972	3770	1500	153	118
Frisco	.976	3751	1552	132	158	Arkansas	.972	3629	1520	147	174
Tulsa	.975	3704	1595	134	136	Wichita	.972	3645	1509	147	126
San Antonio	.973	3758	1483	146	142	Springfield	.969	3740	1526	171	127

INDIVIDUAL BATTING LEADERS

(Minimum 378 Plate Appearances)

	AVG	G	AB	R	H	2B	3B	HR	RBI	BB	SO	SB
Huber, Justin, Wichita	.343	88	335	68	115	22	3	16	74	51	70	7
Minges, Tyler, Springfield	.324	116	429	98	139	34	6	19	60	47	61	5
Ethier, Andre, Midland	.319	131	505	104	161	30	3	18	80	48	93	1
Stavisky, Brian, Midland	.316	135	510	84	161	36	6	11	88	69	84	0
Arias, Joaquin, Frisco	.315	120	499	65	157	23	8	5	56	17	46	20
Pressley, Josh, Wichita	.311	119	440	74	137	25	0	22	88	60	71	0
Bohn, T.J., San Antonio	.308	113	438	67	135	30	2	12	57	35	96	27
Willits, Reggie, Arkansas	.304	123	487	75	148	23	6	2	46	54	78	40
Aybar, Erick, Arkansas	.303	134	535	101	162	29	10	9	54	29	51	49
Yan, Ruddy, Frisco	.300	116	483	77	145	15	5	3	45	47	38	41

INDIVIDUAL PITCHING LEADERS

(Minimum 112 Innings)

	W	L	ERA	G	GS	CG	SV	IP	H	R	ER	BB	SO
Livingston, Bobby, San Antonio	8	4	2.86	18	18	0	0	116	103	45	37	27	78
Hirsh, Jason, Corpus Christi	13	8	2.87	29	29	1	0	172	137	63	55	42	165
Barzilla, Philip, Corpus Christi	7	7	3.03	41	14	0	0	113	126	49	38	30	87
Sampson, Chris, Corpus Christi	4	12	3.12	32	19	2	4	150	147	67	52	19	92
Nin, Sandy, Tulsa	10	6	3.19	20	20	4	0	130	109	50	46	16	80
McClaskey, Tim, Corpus Christi	8	10	3.33	27	26	2	0	160	141	67	59	21	105
Oldham, Tom, San Antonio	13	7	3.67	27	26	0	0	155	179	79	63	45	115
Olenberger, Kasey, Arkansas	9	7	3.71	32	17	0	0	124	135	64	51	37	69
Parker, Zach, Tulsa	12	10	3.79	27	27	0	0	162	171	83	68	35	87
Leek, Randy, Springfield	15	7	3.83	28	27	3	0	186	190	85	79	29	102

ALL-STAR TEAM

C—Mike Napoli, Arkansas. **1B**—Justin Huber, Wichita. **2B**—Alberto Callaspo, Arkansas. **3B**—Travis Hanson, Springfield. **SS**—Erick Aybar, Arkansas. **OF**—T.J. Bohn, San Antonio; Andre Ethier, Midland; Tyler Minges, Springfield. **DH**—Jason Perry, Midland. **UT**—Mike Aviles, Wichita. **P**—Jon Asahina, Tulsa; Jason Hirsh, Corpus Christi; Randy Leek, Springfield; Bobby Livingston, San Antonio; Fernando Nieve, Corpus Christi; Sandy Nin, Tulsa.

Player of the Year: Andre Ethier, Midland. **Pitcher of the Year:** Jason Hirsh, Corpus Christi. **Manager of the Year:** Von Hayes, Midland.

DEPARTMENT LEADERS

BATTING

G	Hanson, Travis, Springfield	137
AB	Hanson, Travis, Springfield	546
R	Ethier, Andre, Midland	104
H	Aybar, Erick, Arkansas	162
TB	Ethier, Andre, Midland	251
XBH	Minges, Tyler, Springfield	59
2B	Saccomanno, Mark, Corpus Christi	36
	Stavisky, Brian, Midland	36
3B	Murphy, Tommy, Arkansas	11
HR	Napoli, Mike, Arkansas	31
RBI	Napoli, Mike, Arkansas	99
SH	Bernier, Doug, Tulsa	11
	Guzman, Jesus, San Antonio	11
SF	Espy, Nathan, San Antonio	10
BB	Napoli, Mike, Arkansas	88
IBB	Slavik, Corey, Tulsa	7
HBP	Aybar, Erick, Arkansas	14
SO	Hoorelbeke, Jesse, San Antonio	156
SB	Anderson, Josh, Corpus Christi	50
CS	Aybar, Erick, Arkansas	23
GIDP	Stavisky, Brian, Midland	23
OBP	Huber, Justin, Wichita	.432
SLG	Huber, Justin, Wichita	.570

PITCHING

G	Wilhite, Matt, Arkansas	56
GS	Hirsh, Jason, Corpus Christi	29
CG	Asahina, Jon, Tulsa	4
	Nin, Sandy, Tulsa	4
SHO	Leek, Randy, Springfield	2
GF	Bevis, P.J., Tulsa	39
SV	Bevis, P.J., Tulsa	21
W	Leek, Randy, Springfield	15
L	Masset, Nick, Frisco	12
	Sampson, Chris, Corpus Christi	12
IP	Leek, Randy, Springfield	186
H	Middleton, Kyle, Wichita	218
R	Masset, Nick, Frisco	124
ER	Masset, Nick, Frisco	108
HR	Leek, Randy, Springfield	29
HBP	Parker, Zach, Tulsa	18
BB	Masset, Nick, Frisco	61
SO	Hirsh, Jason, Corpus Christi	165
WP	Griffin, Colt, Wichita	16
BK	Asahina, Jon, Tulsa	5

FIELDING

C	PCT	Gimenez, Hector, CC	.990
	PO	Brown, Jeremy, Midland	691
	A	Tupman, Mat, Wichita	82
	E	Napoli, Mike, Arkansas	14
	DP	Tupman, Mat, Wichita	12
	PB	Napoli, Mike, Arkansas	13
	CS PCT	Napoli, Mike, Arkansas	47%
1B	PCT	Hart, Jason, Frisco	.995
	PO	Hart, Jason, Frisco	1049
	A	Hart, Jason, Frisco	60
	E	Pressley, Josh, Wichita	14
	DP	Hart, Jason, Frisco	106
2B	PCT	Kiger, Mark, Midland	.988
	PO	Nix, Jayson, Tulsa	274
	A	Nix, Jayson, Tulsa	433
	E	Herr, Aaron, Springfield	22
	DP	Nix, Jayson, Tulsa	85
3B	PCT	King, Brennan, Wichita	.951
	PO	Hanson, Travis, Springfield	95
	A	Hanson, Travis, Springfield	264
	E	Hanson, Travis, Springfield	36
	DP	Guzman, Jesus, San Antonio	28
SS	PCT	Bernier, Doug, Tulsa	.974
	PO	Aybar, Erick, Arkansas	243
	A	Aybar, Erick, Arkansas	403
	E	Aviles, Mike, Wichita	33
	DP	Aybar, Erick, Arkansas	108
OF	PCT	Stanley, Steve, Midland	.997
	PO	Stanley, Steve, Midland	297
	A	Murphy, Tommy, Arkansas	18
	E	Senreiso, Juan, Frisco	12
	DP	Murphy, Tommy, Arkansas	7

CALIFORNIA LEAGUE

HIGH CLASS A

BY KEVIN GOLDSTEIN

It was business as usual in the California League in 2005, as offense ruled the day and the three-tier playoff system offered plenty of drama.

After finishing the regular season with a league-best 85-55 record, the San Jose Giants, led by a prospect-laden line-up, recovered from a 2-0 deficit to win three straight games against Lake Elsinore Storm to win their third league championship. Outfielder John Bowker, who was named the series MVP, laced an RBI single to begin a three-run rally in the seventh inning of a 3-1 win in Game 5, while Jason Waddell, pitching on two days rest after starting Game 3, struck out seven over three shutout innings for the victory.

BILL MITCHELL

Brandon Wood

All of the drama overshadowed a tremendous first-round performance by High Desert outfielder Chris Lubanski, who went 13-for-15 with seven runs and nine RBIs in three games, including hitting for the cycle.

The league featured plenty of elite hitting prospects, highlighted by the season-long onslaught of Rancho Cucamonga's double-play combination of Brandon Wood and Howie Kendrick.

Wood, who was named the league's top prospect, went 0-for-4 on Opening Day but homered in his next two games and never looked back. He finished as the minor league overall leader in doubles (53), home runs (43) and total bases (370) while becoming the first minor leaguer in nearly half a century to accrue 100 or more extra-base hits.

Kendrick, who entered the season with a career .357 batting average, actually improved upon it with a .384-12-47 showing in 63 games before moving up to Double-A, where his average slipped to .344.

The Cal League featured plenty of offensive stars besides Wood and Kendrick, including a pair of 2004 first-round picks. Royals first-baseman Billy Butler, despite being one of the youngest players in the league, hit .348-25-91 in 92 games, while Diamondbacks shortstop Stephen Drew, who reported to Lancaster after finally signing in late May, won player of the week honors three times during his seven-week stint in the league. He hit .389-10-39 in 38 games.

After fielding a woeful .842 at third base, Butler was moved to left field, where the reviews were anything but positive.

Along with San Jose outfielder Eddy Martinez-Esteve and Lancaster first baseman Chris Carter, the league featured a number of players whom league observers had little trouble projecting as big league hitters, but for now, are without a position.

All the offensive numbers were aggrandized by the lack of pitching in the league, unless you were in Bakersfield, where 2003 first-rounder John Danks, 2004 first-rounder Thomas Diamond and Dominican Edison Volquez provided a lethal 1-2-3 combination for the Blaze. They went a combined 16-7 with 231 strikeouts in 206 innings before receiving mid-season promotions.

STANDINGS: SPLIT SEASON

FIRST HALF					SECOND HALF				
NORTH	**W**	**L**	**PCT**	**GB**	**NORTH**	**W**	**L**	**PCT**	**GB**
San Jose	44	26	.629	—	Stockton	42	28	.600	—
Modesto	38	32	.543	6	San Jose	41	29	.586	1
Stockton	36	34	.514	8	Modesto	34	35	.493	7½
Bakersfield	35	35	.500	9	Bakersfield	33	37	.471	9
Visalia	26	44	.371	18	Visalia	29	41	.414	13
SOUTH	**W**	**L**	**PCT**	**GB**	**NORTH**	**W**	**L**	**PCT**	**GB**
Lake Elsinore	41	28	.594	—	High Desert	39	31	.557	—
Lancaster	37	33	.529	4½	Lancaster	38	32	.543	1
High Desert	36	34	.514	5½	Rancho Cuca.	34	36	.486	5
Rancho Cuca.	28	41	.406	13	Inland Empire	30	40	.429	9
Inland Empire	28	42	.400	13½	Lake Elsinore	29	40	.420	9½

PLAYOFFS—Division Series: Modesto defeated Stockton 2-0 and Lancaster defeated High Desert 2-1 in best-of-3 series. **Semifinals:** San Jose defeated Modesto 3-0 and Lake Elsinore defeated Lancaster 3-0 in best-of-5 series. **Finals:** San Jose defeated Lake Elsinore 3-2 in best-of-5 series.

TOP 20 PROSPECTS

1. Brandon Wood, ss, Rancho Cucamonga (Angels)
2. Stephen Drew, ss, Lancaster (Diamondbacks)
3. Howie Kendrick, 2b, Rancho Cucamonga (Angels)
4. Ian Stewart, 3b, Modesto (Rockies)
5. Billy Butler, 3b/of, High Desert (Royals)
6. Daric Barton, 1b, Stockton (Athletics)
7. Edison Volquez, rhp, Bakersfield (Rangers)
8. Thomas Diamond, rhp, Bakersfield (Rangers)
9. Adam Jones, ss, Inland Empire (Mariners)
10. Eddy Martinez-Esteve, of, San Jose (Giants)
11. John Danks, lhp, Bakersfield (Rangers)
12. Asdrubal Cabrera, ss, Inland Empire (Mariners)
13. Chris Iannetta, c, Modesto (Rockies)
14. Miguel Montero, c, Lancaster (Diamondbacks)
15. Ubaldo Jimenez, rhp, Modesto (Rockies)
16. Nate Schierholtz, of, San Jose (Giants)
17. George Kottaras, c, Lake Elsinore (Padres)
18. Jim Miller, rhp, Modesto (Rockes)
19. Juan Morillo, rhp, Modesto (Rockies)
20. Chris Lubanski, of, High Desert (Royals)

STANDINGS: OVERALL

Page	Team	W	L	PCT	GB	Manager	Attendance	Average	Last Penn.
228	San Jose Giants (Giants)	85	55	.607	—	Lenn Sakata	150,338	2,210	2005
192	Stockton Ports (Athletics)	78	62	.557	7	Todd Steverson	205,819	3,071	2002
140	High Desert Mavericks (Royals)	75	65	.536	10	Billy Gardner	118,387	1,715	1997
50	Lancaster JetHawks (Diamondbacks)	75	65	.536	10	Bill Plummer	123,601	1,765	None
111	Modesto Nuts (Rockies)	72	67	.518	12½	Stu Cole	136,612	2,069	2004
221	Lake Elsinore Storm (Padres)	70	68	.507	14	Rick Renteria	222,624	3,274	2001
250	Bakersfield Blaze (Rangers)	68	72	.486	17	Arnie Beyeler	76,738	1,112	1989
147	Rancho Cucamonga Quakes (Angels)	62	77	.446	22½	Tyrone Boykin	272,855	3,954	1994
235	Inland Empire 66ers (Mariners)	58	82	.414	27	Daren Brown	211,117	3,015	2003
243	Visalia Oaks (Devil Rays)	55	85	.393	30	Steve Livesey	63,475	933	1978

NOTE: Teams' individual batting and pitching statistics can be found on page indicated in lefthand column.

2005 CALIFORNIA LEAGUE STATISTICS

CLUB BATTING

	AVG	G	AB	R	H	2B	2B	HR	BB	SO	SB
Lancaster	.302	140	5013	917	1512	346	45	174	511	904	48
High Desert	.301	140	5106	918	1536	340	36	203	508	1050	77
San Jose	.295	140	4848	813	1430	292	44	143	450	1035	96
Lake Elsinore	.286	138	4926	798	1407	277	47	125	541	1018	95
Visalia	.285	140	4828	717	1375	283	29	114	469	1039	112
Inland Empire	.282	140	5004	753	1412	282	45	116	451	1042	104
Modesto	.281	139	4792	793	1347	312	56	120	504	1157	42
Stockton	.280	140	4835	835	1355	318	38	153	629	1042	60
Rancho Cucamonga	.275	139	4916	750	1352	297	40	150	392	1086	77
Bakersfield	.274	140	4830	728	1325	269	39	125	452	1025	106

CLUB PITCHING

	ERA	G	CG	SHO	SV	IP	H	R	ER	BB	SO
San Jose	4.24	140	0	8	40	1239	1232	666	584	506	1139
Bakersfield	4.60	140	3	3	38	1230	1325	708	628	461	1049
Modesto	4.75	139	1	4	38	1223	1366	757	645	453	1006
Inland Empire	4.86	140	1	4	22	1246	1454	798	673	517	1039
Stockton	4.86	140	1	5	51	1228	1391	791	663	437	1182
Lake Elsinore	5.05	138	2	4	34	1239	1413	842	695	465	927
Lancaster	5.22	140	1	0	36	1252	1525	849	726	429	1003
High Desert	5.40	140	1	4	35	1235	1531	899	741	477	922
Visalia	5.53	140	1	3	21	1220	1436	858	749	538	1109
Rancho Cucamonga	5.55	139	0	2	29	1232	1378	854	760	624	1022

CLUB FIELDING

	PCT	PO	A	E	DP
San Jose	.976	3716	1381	127	122
Bakersfield	.975	3688	1511	134	143
Modesto	.972	3669	1457	145	169
Visalia	.972	3661	1383	147	119
Rancho Cuca.	.972	3695	1461	147	132
Inland Empire	.971	3736	1517	159	143
High Desert	.970	3705	1668	167	170
Stockton	.969	3684	1317	162	131
Lancaster	.968	3757	1445	174	134
Lake Elsinore	.964	3717	1487	194	131

INDIVIDUAL BATTING LEADERS

(Minimum 378 Plate Appearances)

	AVG	G	AB	R	H	2B	3B	HR	RBI	BB	SO	SB
Montero, Miguel, Lancaster	.349	85	355	73	124	24	1	24	82	26	52	1
Butler, Billy, High Desert	.348	92	379	70	132	30	2	25	91	42	80	0
Gaetti, Joe, Modesto	.332	113	395	90	131	29	8	21	87	52	114	5
Gomes, Joey, Visalia	.325	133	530	77	172	34	1	12	86	53	92	4
Wood, Brandon, Rancho Cuca.	.321	130	536	109	172	51	4	43	115	48	128	7
Schierholtz, Nate, San Jose	.319	128	502	83	160	37	8	15	86	32	132	5
Garrabrants, Steve, Lancaster	.318	95	358	79	114	28	5	7	58	39	45	8
Mahar, Kevin, Bakersfield	.315	110	447	98	141	27	4	17	63	47	109	17
Cook, Jeff, Lancaster	.314	129	526	96	165	43	7	19	89	46	75	2
Arroyo, Carlos, Inland Empire	.313	98	402	50	126	17	2	0	62	26	37	13

INDIVIDUAL PITCHING LEADERS

(Minimum 112 Innings)

	W	L	ERA	G	GS	CG	SV	IP	H	R	ER	BB	SO
Wells, Jared, Lake Elsinore	11	3	3.44	19	19	2	0	120	116	51	46	26	80
Smith, Cody, Bakersfield	6	3	3.88	30	18	0	2	123	155	62	53	43	67
Feierabend, Ryan, Inland Empire	8	7	3.88	29	29	0	0	151	186	80	65	51	122
Mock, Garrett, Lancaster	14	7	4.18	28	28	0	0	174	202	95	81	33	160
Mackintosh, Jason, Inland Empire	10	11	4.26	29	28	1	0	180	206	97	85	57	141
Gragg, John, High Desert	13	5	4.36	27	27	1	0	149	178	92	72	47	95
Broshuis, Garrett, San Jose	12	9	4.40	26	26	0	0	151	173	80	74	35	124
Morillo, Juan, Modesto	6	5	4.41	20	20	0	0	112	107	69	55	65	101
Register, Steven, Modesto	9	11	4.44	27	27	1	0	156	184	98	77	35	108
Kaiser, Marc, Modesto	7	6	4.45	22	20	0	0	127	160	81	63	26	82

ALL-STAR TEAM

C—Miguel Montero, Lancaster. **1B**—Bryan Lahair, Inland Empire. **2B**—Howie Kendrick, Rancho Cucamonga. **3B**—Ian Stewart, Modesto. **SS**—Brandon Wood, Rancho Cucamonga. **OF**—Joe Gaetti, Modesto; Kevin Mahar, Bakersfield; Eddy Martinez-Esteve, San Jose. **DH**—Billy Butler, High Desert. **UT**—Brandon Powell, High Desert. **P**—Thomas Diamond, Bakersfield; John Gragg, High Desert; Garrett Mock, Lancaster; Jared Wells, Lake Elsinore.

Most Valuable Player: Brandon Wood, Rancho Cucamonga. **Pitcher of the Year:** Jared Wells, Lake Elsinore. **Rookie of the Year:** Billy Butler, High Desert. **Manager of the Year:** Lenn Sakata, San Jose.

DEPARTMENT LEADERS

BATTING

G	Majewski, Dustin, Stockton	136
AB	Sanchez, Angel, High Desert	585
R	Wood, Brandon, Rancho Cuca.	109
H	Sanchez, Angel, High Desert	183
TB	Wood, Brandon, Rancho Cuca.	360
XBH	Wood, Brandon, Rancho Cuca.	98
2B	Wood, Brandon, Rancho Cuca.	51
3B	Timpner, Clay, San Jose	12
HR	Wood, Brandon, Rancho Cuca.	43
RBI	Lubanski, Chris, High Desert	116
SH	Cook, Jeff, Lancaster	13
SF	Gomes, Joey, Visalia	10
BB	Kaaihue, Kila, High Desert	97
IBB	Valenzuela, Fernando, Lake Elsinore	6
HBP	Kreuzer, Josh, Bakersfield	19
SO	Bonvechio, Brett, Lake Elsinore	163
SB	Timpner, Clay, San Jose	34
CS	Macias, Drew, Lake Elsinore	15
GIDP	Jennings, Todd, San Jose	21
OBP	Kaaihue, Kila, High Desert	.428
SLG	Wood, Brandon, Rancho Cuca.	.672

PITCHING

G	Rosales, Leonel, Lake Elsinore	61
GS	Feierabend, Ryan, Inl. Empire	29
CG	Wells, Jared, Lake Elsinore	2
SHO	Three tied at	1
GF	Rosales, Leonel, Lake Elsinore	56
SV	Rosales, Leonel, Lake Elsinore	27
W	Mock, Garrett, Lancaster	14
L	Marsden, Aaron, Modesto	12
	Prochaska, Mike, Visalia	12
IP	Mackintosh, Jason, Inl. Empire	180
H	Mackintosh, Jason, Inl. Empire	206
R	Herrera, Cesar, High Desert	118
ER	Herrera, Cesar, High Desert	101
HR	Castellanos, Jon, Lancaster	24
	Prochaska, Mike, Visalia	24
HBP	Mackintosh, Jason, Inl. Empire	17
	Scarbery, Chad, Lancaster	17
BB	Morillo, Juan, Modesto	65
SO	Mock, Garrett, Lancaster	160
WP	Machi, Jean, Visalia	16
BK	Reina, Jesus, San Jose	3

FIELDING

C	PCT	Arhart, Josh, Visalia	.994
	PO	Suzuki, Kurt, Stockton	882
	A	Wilson, Bobby, Rancho Cuca.	104
	E	Suzuki, Kurt, Stockton	15
	DP	Wilson, Bobby, Rancho Cuca.	9
	PB	Suzuki, Kurt, Stockton	19
CS	PCT	Donachie, Adam, High Desert	52%
1B	PCT	Lahair, Bryan, Inland Empire	.996
	PO	Kaaihue, Kila, High Desert	1220
	A	Ishikawa, Travis, San Jose	98
	E	Kaaihue, Kila, High Desert	19
	DP	Kaaihue, Kila, High Desert	136
2B	PCT	Blood, Randy, Modesto	.975
	PO	Ramos, Peeter, Lake Elsinore	211
	A	Ramos, Peeter, Lake Elsinore	335
	E	Garciaparra, Michael, Inl. Empire	18
	DP	Sandoval, Abigail, Bakersfield	72
3B	PCT	Brown, Matt, Rancho Cuca.	.948
	PO	Bonvechio, Brett, Lake Elsinore	97
	A	Metcalf, Travis, Bakersfield	244
	E	Bonvechio, Brett, Lake Elsinore	35
	DP	Metcalf, Travis, Bakersfield	26
SS	PCT	Wood, Brandon, Rancho Cuca.	.966
	PO	Sanchez, Angel, High Desert	253
	A	Sanchez, Angel, High Desert	451
	E	Ciriaco, Juan, Lake Elsinore	45
	DP	Sanchez, Angel, High Desert	110
OF	PCT	Garrabrants, Steve, Lancaster	.991
	PO	Macias, Drew, Lake Elsinore	322
	A	Macias, Drew, Lake Elsinore	15
		Schierholtz, Nate, San Jose	15
		Smith, Seth, Modesto	15
	E	Macias, Drew, Lake Elsinore	11
	DP	Lubanski, Chris, High Desert	6

CAROLINA LEAGUE

HIGH CLASS A

STANDINGS: SPLIT SEASON

FIRST HALF					SECOND HALF				
NORTH	**W**	**L**	**PCT**	**GB**	**NORTH**	**W**	**L**	**PCT**	**GB**
Lynchburg	40	30	.571	—	Frederick	44	26	.629	—
Frederick	35	35	.500	5	Lynchburg	38	32	.543	6
Potomac	31	39	.443	9	Potomac	32	38	.457	12
Wilmington	31	39	.443	9	Wilmington	29	41	.414	15
SOUTH	**W**	**L**	**PCT**	**GB**	**SOUTH**	**W**	**L**	**PCT**	**GB**
Kinston	41	29	.586	—	Win.-Salem	38	33	.535	—
Win.-Salem	39	31	.557	2	Salem	37	34	.521	1
Myrtle Beach	33	37	.471	8	Kinston	35	35	.500	2½
Salem	30	40	.429	11	Myrtle Beach	28	42	.400	9½

PLAYOFFS—Semifinals: Frederick defeated Lynchburg 2-0 and Kinston defeated Winston-Salem 2-0 in best-of-3 series. **Final:** Frederick defeated Kinston 3-2 in best-of-5 series.

BY CHRIS KLINE

After finishing the first half of the 2005 season with a .500 record at 35-35, the Frederick Keys got hot down the stretch, finished 77-61 overall and rode their way into the Carolina League playoffs.

And with strong contributions from first baseman Mario Delgado, outfielder Nolan Reimold and huge pitching performances from righthander Brian Finch and Garrett Olson, the Keys brought the Mills Cup back to Frederick for the first time since 1990.

The Keys swept Northern Division first-half champion Lynchburg in the opening round of the playoffs to meet up with Kinston, which had also breezed through two wins against Winston-Salem in the South.

Kinston, which was searching for its second straight CL title, made it a series against the Keys after going down 0-2 in the best-of-five final. The Indians came back to win Game 3 behind a brilliant outing by righthander Sean Smith, then won Game 4 with another gem by righthander Adam Miller. Kinston had fallen into the same situation in 2004, losing the first two games to Wilmington only to come back to sweep the final three to win the series.

Leo Daigle

But the K-Tribe couldn't figure out Keys righthander Brian Finch when it mattered most. Finch pitched in and out of trouble throughout Game 5, as he labored through five shutout innings in which he allowed four hits, struck out five, walked four and hit three batters.

"I made pitches when it counted," said Finch, who was named the series MVP. "I left a lot of runners on base and didn't have my best stuff. But I went out there and battled every inning, and I got the out when it counted."

After Finch left to start the sixth, all those wasted opportunities came back to haunt the Indians as Olson, Chris Britton and Marino Salas combined to hold Kinston to two base runners over the final four innings and lock down the Mills Cup.

"The game could've been different," Frederick manager Bien Figueroa said. "They got a lot of opportunities to win the game. But for some reason, Finch got out of the jams and everything went our way."

A big difference down the stretch for the Keys' championship run was Reimold, who was the Orioles' second-round pick in June out of Bowling Green State. A powerful hitter, Reimold emerged as one of the best five-tool talents in the league in his abbreviated time. Four of his first eight hits were homers after he was called up from short-season Aberdeen, where he was selected the New York-Penn League's top prospect. Reimold finished his season hitting .265-6-11 in just 83 at-bats, then went 10-for-28 (.357) in the playoffs.

The league saw lots of power arms in 2005—James Johnson and Adam Loewen (Frederick), Chance Douglass and Matt Albers (Salem), Armando Galarraga and Michael O'Connor (Potomac), Gio Gonzalez and Lance Broadway (Winston-Salem) and Nick Pesco and Adam Miller (Kinston). Johnson (12-9) was selected Pitcher of the Year.

But one bat literally stole the show—in every major offensive category.

In his eighth minor league season, Winston-Salem first baseman Leo Daigle, 25, became the first triple crown winner in the CL in 54 years. He batted .341-29-112, tying teammate Thomas Collaro for the home run title.

TOP 20 PROSPECTS

1. Jarrod Saltalamacchia, c, Myrtle Beach (Braves)
2. Nick Markakis, of, Frederick (Orioles)
3. Anibal Sanchez, rhp, Wilmington (Red Sox)
4. Adam Miller, rhp, Kinston (Indians)
5. Gio Gonzalez, lhp, Winston-Salem (White Sox)
6. Jeremy Sowers, lhp, Kinston (Indians)
7. Armando Galarraga, rhp, Potomac (Nationals)
8. Jeff Fiorentino, of, Frederick (Orioles)
9. Lance Broadway, rhp, Winston-Salem (White Sox)
10. Adam Loewen, lhp, Frederick (Orioles)
11. Robert Valido, ss, Winston-Salem (White Sox)
12. Tony Sipp, lhp, Kinston (Indians)
13. Ray Liotta, lhp, Winston-Salem (White Sox)
14. J.J. Johnson, rhp, Frederick (Orioles)
15. Kory Casto, 3b, Potomac (Nationals)
16. Brad Snyder, of, Kinston (Indians)
17. Frank Diaz, of, Potomac (Nationals)
18. Hunter Pence, of, Salem (Astros)
19. Stephen Head, 1b, Kinston (Indians)
20. Josh Burrus, of, Myrtle Beach (Braves)

STANDINGS: OVERALL

Page		W	L	PCT	GB	Manager	Attendance	Average	Last Penn.
64	Frederick Keys (Orioles)	79	61	.564	—	Bien Figueroa	275,663	4,446	2005
206	Lynchburg Hillcats (Pirates)	78	62	.557	1	Tim Leiper	150,109	2,274	2002
88	Winston-Salem Warthogs (White Sox)	77	64	.546	2½	Chris Cron	147,194	2,164	2003
103	Kinston Indians (Indians)	76	64	.543	3	Luis Rivera	103,069	1,561	2004
133	Salem Avalanche (Astros)	67	74	.475	12½	Ivan DeJesus	255,225	3,753	2001
254	Potomac Nationals (Nationals)	63	77	.450	16	Bob Henley	138,143	2,061	1989
57	Myrtle Beach Pelicans (Braves)	61	79	.436	18	Randy Ingle	198,092	2,870	2000
72	Wilmington Blue Rocks (Red Sox)	60	80	.429	19	Dann Bilardello	322,287	4,810	1999

NOTE: Teams' individual batting and pitching statistics can be found on page indicated in lefthand column.

2005 CAROLINA LEAGUE STATISTICS

CLUB BATTING

	AVG	G	AB	R	H	2B	2B	HR	BB	SO	SB
Lynchburg	.282	140	4697	741	1323	261	40	102	590	944	106
Winston-Salem	.279	141	4847	809	1354	297	30	178	489	889	188
Potomac	.269	140	4736	674	1273	294	31	122	489	1012	82
Frederick	.266	140	4740	700	1262	258	21	150	445	1056	82
Salem	.251	141	4573	562	1147	243	24	81	526	981	82
Kinston	.250	140	4671	656	1170	250	34	118	476	1075	99
Myrtle Beach	.249	140	4667	596	1161	248	16	94	459	1137	121
Wilmington	.246	140	4588	619	1130	232	31	103	488	1114	69

CLUB PITCHING

	ERA	G	CG	SHO	SV	IP	H	R	ER	BB	SO
Kinston	3.65	140	1	10	35	1232	1173	586	499	450	1087
Salem	3.77	141	3	10	44	1230	1188	596	515	479	986
Myrtle Beach	4.11	140	1	9	27	1233	1236	661	563	545	993
Wilmington	4.36	140	2	11	32	1215	1200	684	588	412	996
Frederick	4.39	140	4	8	37	1225	1203	684	598	544	1154
Winston-Salem	4.53	141	3	3	37	1244	1331	698	626	502	1046
Potomac	4.56	140	7	10	22	1206	1203	696	611	559	1049
Lynchburg	4.87	140	5	6	44	1207	1286	752	653	471	897

CLUB FIELDING

Team	PCT	PO	A	E	DP	Team	PCT	PO	A	E	DP
Winston-Salem	.979	3732	1429	113	127	Potomac	.972	3617	1425	147	151
Salem	.976	3691	1569	129	131	Myrtle Beach	.972	3699	1435	148	149
Kinston	.975	3695	1452	130	135	Lynchburg	.970	3622	1526	157	122
Frederick	.974	3675	1400	133	127	Wilmington	.969	3644	1401	162	116

INDIVIDUAL BATTING LEADERS

(Minimum 378 Plate Appearances)

	AVG	G	AB	R	H	2B	3B	HR	RBI	BB	SO	SB
Daigle, Leo, Winston-Salem	.341	108	411	85	140	33	1	29	112	50	72	10
Hall, Noah, Winston-Salem	.332	120	425	112	141	38	6	26	92	86	76	24
Saltalamacchia, Jarrod, Myrtle Beach	.314	129	459	70	144	35	1	19	81	57	99	4
Diaz, Frank, Potomac	.312	134	554	85	173	45	5	16	74	20	67	14
Magness, Pat, Lynchburg	.308	133	425	98	131	39	1	24	92	141	114	0
Delgado, Mario, Frederick	.306	119	435	53	133	27	1	26	86	31	80	1
Markakis, Nick, Frederick	.300	91	350	59	105	25	1	12	62	43	65	2
Pritz, Bryan, Wilmington	.299	97	328	51	98	15	1	2	25	53	53	18
Spears, Nate, Frederick	.294	112	445	63	131	30	6	6	41	36	82	8
Whitesell, Josh, Potomac	.293	113	389	59	114	32	2	18	66	74	125	1

INDIVIDUAL PITCHING LEADERS

(Minimum 112 Innings)

	W	L	ERA	G	GS	CG	SV	IP	H	R	ER	BB	SO
Douglass, Chance, Salem	12	9	2.90	27	27	1	0	168	157	59	54	44	128
Finch, Brian, Frederick	10	10	3.38	27	27	1	0	154	157	72	58	60	124
Johnson, J.J., Frederick	12	9	3.49	28	27	2	1	160	139	77	62	64	168
O'Connor, Michael, Potomac	10	11	3.54	26	26	2	0	168	144	73	66	48	158
Smith, Sean, Kinston	5	8	3.60	29	23	0	2	142	123	63	57	71	120
Muecke, Josh, Salem	10	12	3.67	28	28	1	0	159	164	81	65	47	98
Vaquedano, Jose, Wilmington	8	7	3.75	28	23	0	1	146	120	66	61	50	117
Pesco, Nick, Kinston	11	10	3.82	27	26	0	0	153	168	77	65	39	101
Rodriguez, Ryan, Winston-Salem	13	7	4.09	29	29	2	0	167	180	87	76	49	108
Loewen, Adam, Frederick	10	8	4.12	28	27	1	0	142	130	77	65	86	146

ALL-STAR TEAM

C—Jarrod Saltalamacchia, Myrtle Beach. **1B**—Leo Daigle, Winston-Salem. **2B**—Nate Spears, Frederick. **3B**—Kory Casto, Potomac. **SS**—Robert Valido, Winston-Salem. **OF**—Thomas Collaro, Winston-Salem; Frank Diaz, Potomac; Nick Markakis, Frederick. **DH**—Mario Delgado, Frederick. **UT**—Noah Hall, Winston-Salem. **SP**—J.J. Johnson, Frederick. **RP**—Ehren Wassermann, Winston-Salem.

Most Valuable Player: Leo Daigle, Winston-Salem. **Pitcher of the Year:** J.J. Johnson, Frederick. **Manager of the Year:** Ivan DeJesus, Salem.

DEPARTMENT LEADERS

BATTING

G	Casto, Kory, Potomac	135
AB	Diaz, Frank, Potomac	554
R	Hall, Noah, Winston-Salem	112
H	Diaz, Frank, Potomac	173
TB	Diaz, Frank, Potomac	276
XBH	Hall, Noah, Winston-Salem	70
2B	Diaz, Frank, Potomac	45
3B	Guzman, Javier, Lynchburg	7
	Valido, Robert, Winston-Salem	7
HR	Collaro, Tom, Winston-Salem	29
	Daigle, Leo, Winston-Salem	29
RBI	Daigle, Leo, Winston-Salem	112
SH	Spears, Nate, Frederick	14
SF	Three tied at	7
BB	Magness, Pat, Lynchburg	141
IBB	Saltalamacchia, Jarrod, MB	11
HBP	Hall, Noah, Winston-Salem	19
SO	Collaro, Tom, Winston-Salem	153
SB	Valido, Robert, Winston-Salem	52
CS	Doetsch, Steve, Myrtle Beach	15
GIDP	Rea, Brad, Lynchburg	23
OBP	Magness, Pat, Lynchburg	.481
SLG	Daigle, Leo, Winston-Salem	.637

PITCHING

G	Castro, Fabio, Winston-Salem	53
GS	Rodriguez, Ryan, Win.-Salem	29
CG	Six tied at	2
SHO	Price, Brett, Potomac	2
GF	Salas, Marino, Frederick	38
	Wassermann, Ehren, Win.-Salem	38
SV	Wassermann, Ehren, Win.-Salem	20
W	Rodriguez, Ryan, Win.-Salem	13
L	Price, Brett, Potomac	13
IP	Douglass, Chance, Salem	168
	O'Connor, Michael, Potomac	168
H	Rodriguez, Ryan, Win.-Salem	180
R	Starling, Wardell, Lynchburg	98
ER	Starling, Wardell, Lynchburg	89
HR	Price, Brett, Potomac	20
HBP	Johnson, J.J., Frederick	19
BB	Loewen, Adam, Frederick	86
SO	Johnson, J.J., Frederick	168
WP	Loewen, Adam, Frederick	15
BK	Stevens, Jake, Myrtle Beach	4

FIELDING

C	PCT	Molina, Gustavo, Win.-Salem	.993
	PO	Molina, Gustavo, Win.-Salem	744
	A	Molina, Gustavo, Win.-Salem	107
	E	Four tied at	10
	DP	Molina, Gustavo, Win.-Salem	9
	PB	McCuistion, Mike, Lynchburg	23
		Molina, Gustavo, Win.-Salem	23
	CS PCT	Molina, Gustavo, Win.-Salem	53%
1B	PCT	Robinson, Scott, Salem	.997
	PO	Yount, Dustin, Frederick	784
	A	Robinson, Scott, Salem	58
	E	Bladergroen, Ian, Wilmington	9
	DP	Whitesell, Josh, Potomac	83
2B	PCT	Spears, Nate, Frederick	.981
	PO	Spears, Nate, Frederick	195
	A	Spears, Nate, Frederick	308
	E	Three tied at	10
	DP	Spears, Nate, Frederick	79
3B	PCT	Casto, Kory, Potomac	.956
	PO	Schnurstein, Micah, Win.-Salem	83
	A	Casto, Kory, Potomac	271
	E	Bass, Bryan, Frederick	25
		Torres, Saul, Salem	25
	DP	Casto, Kory, Potomac	39
SS	PCT	Hernandez, Diory, MB	.983
	PO	Brown, Travis, Frederick	189
	A	Valido, Robert, Win.-Salem	362
	E	Suarez, Ignacio, Wilmington	32
	DP	Valido, Robert, Win.-Salem	84
OF	PCT	Alcantara, Ervin, Salem	.996
	PO	Diaz, Frank, Potomac	285
	A	Diaz, Frank, Potomac	17
	E	Esquivel, Matt, Myrtle Beach	12
	DP	Three tied at	4

FLORIDA STATE LEAGUE

HIGH CLASS A

BY J.J. COOPER

When the Palm Beach Cardinals found themselves three outs from the 2005 Florida State League title in a deciding Game Five, they couldn't be happier with who they had on the mound.

Righthander Mark Worrell had seemingly blown the Cardinals chance to clinch the title in the eighth, as he gave up a two-run home run to league MVP Brent Clevlen that gave Lakeland a one-run lead.

Justin Verlander

But that didn't take away from the Cardinals trust in Worrell. He'd been their closer all season, getting a minor-league high 35 saves with an 88-90 mph fastball, an average curve and changeup, and plenty of determination.

So Worrell was out there for the bottom of the ninth, after the Cardinals tied the score in the top of the inning on a Reid Gorecki homer. And when the Cardinals took a 5-4 lead in the 10th on a Jarrett Hoffpauir home run, Worrell went back out to finish off the Tigers. He retired the side in order in the 10th, getting Clevlen to fly out to end the game.

"This guy is a gamer," Palm Beach manager Pop Warner said. "He's got heart, he goes out there in any situation. Whether he's going out there for work, or to close, he's all business."

The title was Palm Beach's first after relocating from Port Charlotte after the 2002 season. The Cardinals did it the hard way, beating Vero Beach and Lakeland, the two teams that dominated the FSL postseason all-star teams. Lakeland placed five players on the all-star team, including Jordan Tata, the pitcher of the year, and Clevlen, player of the year. Vero Beach had four players on the team. Palm Beach, on the other hand, had only one member, Worrell. Fittingly Worrell had two saves and a win in the championship series.

STANDINGS: SPLIT SEASON

FIRST HALF					SECOND HALF				
EAST	**W**	**L**	**PCT**	**GB**	**EAST**	**W**	**L**	**PCT**	**GB**
Vero Beach	40	26	.606	—	Palm Beach	39	31	.557	—
Daytona	35	32	.522	5½	Vero Beach	37	30	.552	½
Jupiter	35	33	.515	6	Brevard	37	31	.544	1
St. Lucie	30	35	.462	9½	St. Lucie	36	33	.522	2½
Palm Beach	30	40	.429	12	Daytona	34	34	.5	4
Brevard	26	42	.382	15	Jupiter	29	38	.433	8½
WEST	**W**	**L**	**PCT**	**GB**	**WEST**	**W**	**L**	**PCT**	**GB**
Lakeland	45	22	.672	—	Lakeland	40	26	.606	—
Dunedin	40	28	.588	5½	Dunedin	41	29	.586	1
Fort Myers	37	27	.578	6½	Fort Myers	37	32	.536	4½
Sarasota	34	31	.523	10	Sarasota	31	36	.463	9½
Tampa	31	34	.477	13	Tampa	24	44	.353	17
Clearwater	17	50	.254	28	Clearwater	24	45	.348	17½

PLAYOFFS—Semifinals: Lakeland defeated Dunedin 2-0 and Palm Beach defeated Vero Beach 2-1 in best-of-3 series. **Finals:** Palm Beach defeated Lakeland 3-2 in best-of-5 series.

Palm Beach actually finished the regular season with a 69-71 record, but it won the second-half title with a 39-31 record.

Lakeland benefited from Clevlen's re-emergence as a prospect. The 2002 first-round pick hit .223 in the FSL in 2004, but with an improved sense of the strike zone and better ability to fight off tough pitches, he became one of the league's most dangerous hitters.

But Lakeland's most impressive work came on the mound. Tata used a heavy sinker and above-average command to keep hitters off balance all year, but he was only the second-best pitcher on his own staff. Before he was promoted to Double-A on his way to a major league callup, righthander Justin Verlander blew away the league with a high 90s fastball, a nasty curveball and a mound presence that several managers described as "ornery."

Verlander made it to Detroit for a late July star. Jupiter lefthander Jason Vargas topped him, as he earned a spot in the Marlins rotation in mid-July, after spending less than two months in the Florida State League.

TOP 20 PROSPECTS

1. Andy LaRoche, 3b, Vero Beach (Dodgers)
2. Justin Verlander, rhp, Lakeland (Tigers)
3. Lastings Milledge, of, St. Lucie (Mets)
4. Jason Vargas, lhp, Jupiter (Marlins)
5. Matt Kemp, of, Vero Beach (Dodgers)
6. Matt Moses, 3b, Fort Myers (Twins)
7. Denard Span, of, Fort Myers (Twins)
8. Justin Orenduff, rhp, Vero Beach (Dodgers)
9. David Purcey, lhp, Dunedin (Blue Jays)
10. Jordan Tata, rhp, Lakeland (Tigers)
11. Tony Abreu, 2b, Vero Beach (Dodgers)
12. Chin-Lung Hu, ss, Vero Beach (Dodgers)
13. Adam Lind, of, Dunedin (Blue Jays)
14. Brent Clevlen, of, Lakeland (Tigers)
15. Scott Moore, 3b, Daytona (Cubs)
16. Adam Harben, rhp, Fort Myers (Twins)
17. Chuck Tiffany, lhp, Vero Beach (Dodgers)
18. Brian Dopirak, 1b, Daytona (Cubs)
19. Tim Moss, 2b, Clearwater (Phillies)
20. Philip Humber, rhp, St. Lucie (Mets)

STANDINGS: OVERALL

Page		W	L	PCT	GB	Manager	Attendance	Average	Last Penn.
118	Lakeland Tigers (Tigers)	85	48	.639	—	Mike Rojas	32,912	567	1992
256	Dunedin Blue Jays (Blue Jays)	81	57	.587	6½	Omar Malave	40,479	586	None
154	Vero Beach Dodgers (Dodgers)	77	56	.579	8	Scott Little	55,737	913	1990
168	Fort Myers Miracle (Twins)	74	59	.556	11	Riccardo Ingram	112,272	1,701	1985
80	Daytona Cubs (Cubs)	69	66	.511	17	Richie Zisk	127,060	1,925	2004
213	Palm Beach Cardinals (Cardinals)	69	71	.493	19½	Ron Warner	98,841	1,453	2005
175	St. Lucie Mets (Mets)	66	68	.493	19½	Tim Teufel	91,382	1,450	1998
95	Sarasota Reds (Reds)	65	67	.492	19½	Edgar Caceres	28,122	476	1963
125	Jupiter Hammerheads (Marlins)	64	71	.474	22	Tim Cossins	88,580	1,406	1991
160	Brevard County Manatees (Brewers)	63	73	.463	23½	John Tamargo	101,847	1,591	2001
184	Tampa Yankees (Yankees)	55	78	.414	30	Joe Breeden	78,155	1,302	2004
199	Clearwater Threshers (Phillies)	41	95	.301	45½	Greg Legg	130,446	1,976	1993

NOTE: Teams' individual batting and pitching statistics can be found on page indicated in lefthand column.

2005 FLORIDA STATE LEAGUE STATISTICS

CLUB BATTING

	AVG	G	AB	R	H	2B	2B	HR	BB	SO	SB
Vero Beach	.285	133	4459	708	1271	233	30	124	399	852	116
Dunedin	.284	138	4838	751	1375	278	30	110	456	847	30
Lakeland	.276	133	4548	700	1256	205	35	129	435	977	166
Daytona	.262	135	4432	602	1160	225	29	115	374	973	131
Brevard County	.259	136	4519	551	1170	192	48	64	327	960	104
Jupiter	.257	135	4579	606	1175	212	28	70	435	1060	148
Fort Myers	.255	133	4298	554	1097	183	28	56	395	927	123
St. Lucie	.254	134	4443	641	1129	224	28	137	443	1209	116
Clearwater	.254	136	4490	566	1140	216	19	87	436	872	110
Sarasota	.250	132	4351	570	1087	199	32	92	384	1104	119
Tampa	.246	133	4429	526	1089	203	30	67	415	841	96
Palm Beach	.244	140	4600	594	1124	230	27	87	435	1061	155

CLUB PITCHING

	ERA	G	CG	SHO	SV	IP	H	R	ER	BB	SO
Fort Myers	3.35	133	10	13	34	1140	1077	509	424	395	1003
Lakeland	3.37	133	8	11	38	1181	1095	514	442	400	934
Dunedin	3.56	138	0	9	28	1228	1229	607	486	392	1013
Brevard County	3.65	136	8	10	32	1182	1080	563	480	393	1056
Sarasota	3.84	132	2	5	33	1138	1141	597	485	417	987
Palm Beach	3.94	140	3	14	40	1213	1234	635	531	402	864
Daytona	3.97	135	4	12	33	1160	1180	602	511	423	1080
Vero Beach	4.12	133	3	10	34	1140	1096	586	522	473	1062
St. Lucie	4.27	134	5	10	29	1167	1205	641	554	351	901
Jupiter	4.39	135	2	6	38	1201	1231	677	586	454	1019
Tampa	4.44	133	1	8	30	1154	1170	650	569	382	936
Clearwater	5.26	136	3	1	20	1168	1335	788	683	452	828

CLUB FIELDING

	PCT	PO	A	E	DP
Lakeland	.978	3543	1444	110	151
Brevard County	.977	3546	1350	115	137
Daytona	.974	3479	1404	131	120
Vero Beach	.973	3418	1311	130	121
Tampa	.973	3462	1299	133	77
Palm Beach	.972	3640	1597	153	161
Dunedin	.972	3683	1602	152	125
Fort Myers	.972	3421	1329	136	131
St. Lucie	.970	3499	1350	152	121
Clearwater	.970	3504	1400	153	122
Sarasota	.969	3413	1355	155	121
Jupiter	.967	3603	1331	166	112

INDIVIDUAL BATTING LEADERS

(Minimum 378 Plate Appearances)

	AVG	G	AB	R	H	2B	3B	HR	RBI	BB	SO	SB
Abreu, Tony, Vero Beach	.327	96	394	54	129	23	7	4	43	15	56	14
Lind, Adam, Dunedin	.313	126	495	80	155	42	4	12	84	49	77	2
Hu, Chin-Lung, Vero Beach	.313	116	470	80	147	29	1	8	56	19	40	23
Anderson, Drew, Brevard County	.311	129	508	69	158	17	7	6	62	39	95	19
Christian, Justin, Tampa	.306	95	372	52	114	27	6	8	37	33	47	38
Kemp, Matt, Vero Beach	.306	109	418	76	128	21	4	27	90	25	92	23
Heether, Adam, Brevard County	.305	93	338	48	103	27	2	6	54	34	48	3
Clevlen, Brent, Lakeland	.302	130	494	77	149	28	4	18	102	65	118	14
Nicholson, Derek, Lakeland	.297	119	427	78	127	24	4	18	66	59	77	13
Blue, Vince, Lakeland	.297	124	498	67	148	17	3	0	50	47	84	40

INDIVIDUAL PITCHING LEADERS

(Minimum 112 Innings)

	W	L	ERA	G	GS	CG	SV	IP	H	R	ER	BB	SO
Villanueva, Carlos, Brevard County	8	1	2.32	21	21	0	0	112	78	31	29	32	124
Dillard, Tim, Brevard County	12	10	2.48	28	28	5	0	185	150	64	51	31	128
Bumstead, Nate, Lakeland	12	4	2.58	25	25	2	0	161	136	61	46	58	111
Harben, Adam, Fort Myers	10	5	2.66	25	25	2	0	135	102	52	40	62	119
Tata, Jordan, Lakeland	13	2	2.79	25	25	2	0	155	138	55	48	41	134
Mildren, Paul, Jupiter	10	3	3.08	29	20	0	0	140	115	55	48	42	111
Clippard, Tyler, Tampa	10	9	3.18	26	25	0	0	147	118	56	52	34	169
MacLane, Evan, St. Lucie	8	5	3.20	19	19	1	0	112	96	51	40	15	92
Muegge, Danny, Vero Beach	8	2	3.38	31	18	0	0	128	124	53	48	34	91
Romero, Davis, Dunedin	9	6	3.47	34	18	0	1	125	133	60	48	34	136

ALL-STAR TEAM

C—Robinzon Diaz, Dunedin; Danilo Sanchez, Lakeland. **1B**—Andy Wilson, St. Lucie. **2B**—Tony Abreu, Vero Beach. **3B**—Chin-Lung Hu, Vero Beach. **SS**—Andy LaRoche, Vero Beach. **OF**—Brent Clevlen, Lakeland; Adam Lind, Dunedin; Chris Walker, Daytona. **DH**—Matt Kemp, Vero Beach. **UT**—Adam Heether, Brevard County. **SP**—Nate Bumstead, Lakeland; Tim Dillard, Brevard County; Jordan Tata, Lakeland; Carlos Villanueva, Brevard County. **RP**—Paul Thorp, Tampa; Mark Worrell, Palm Beach.

Most Valuable Player: Brent Clevlen, Lakeland. **Pitcher of the Year:** Jordan Tata, Lakeland. **Manager of the Year:** Mike Rojas, Lakeland.

DEPARTMENT LEADERS

BATTING

G	Blalock, Jake, Clearwater	134
AB	Walker, Chris, Daytona	536
R	Walker, Chris, Daytona	97
H	Anderson, Drew, Brevard	158
TB	Wilson, Andy, St. Lucie	247
XBH	Lind, Adam, Dunedin	58
2B	Lind, Adam, Dunedin	42
3B	Walker, Chris, Daytona	14
HR	Wilson, Andy, St. Lucie	28
RBI	Clevlen, Brent, Lakeland	102
SH	Tolbert, Matt, Fort Myers	15
SF	Moore, Scott, Daytona	9
	Votto, Joey, Sarasota	9
BB	Wilson, Andy, St. Lucie	68
IBB	Wilson, Andy, St. Lucie	10
HBP	Sollmann, Steve, Brevard	26
SO	Whitrock, Scott, Fort Myers	158
SB	Walker, Chris, Daytona	60
CS	Blue, Vince, Lakeland	29
GIDP	Dopirak, Brian, Daytona	20
OBP	Clevlen, Brent, Lakeland	.387
SLG	Kemp, Matt, Vero Beach	.569

PITCHING

G	Lewis, Jeremy, Brevard	55
GS	Dillard, Tim, Brevard County	28
CG	Dillard, Tim, Brevard County	5
SHO	Four tied at	2
GF	Worrell, Mark, Palm Beach	52
SV	Worrell, Mark, Palm Beach	35
W	Tata, Jordan, Lakeland	13
L	Segovia, Zach, Clearwater	14
IP	Dillard, Tim, Brevard County	185
H	Jones, Jason, Tampa	171
R	Segovia, Zach, Clearwater	98
ER	Segovia, Zach, Clearwater	89
HR	Segovia, Zach, Clearwater	18
	Tyler, Scott, Fort Myers	18
HBP	Segovia, Zach, Clearwater	17
BB	Pelland, Tyler, Sarasota	63
SO	Clippard, Tyler, Tampa	169
WP	Baxter, Allen, Jupiter	15
BK	Batista, Roberto, Palm Beach	7

FIELDING

C	PCT	Bellorin, Edwin, Vero Beach	.997
	PO	Sanchez, Danilo, Lakeland	711
	A	Palmisano, Lou, Brevard County	71
	E	Diaz, Robinzon, Dunedin	15
	DP	Sanchez, Danilo, Lakeland	10
	PB	Diaz, Robinzon, Dunedin	26
	CS PCT	Perez, Miguel, Sarasota	44%
1B	PCT	Hunt, Kelly, Lakeland	.992
	PO	Hunt, Kelly, Lakeland	1092
	A	Hunt, Kelly, Lakeland	117
	E	Dopirak, Brian, Daytona	17
	DP	Hunt, Kelly, Lakeland	129
2B	PCT	Abreu, Tony, Vero Beach	.977
	PO	Sollmann, Steve, Brevard	233
	A	Sollmann, Steve, Brevard	359
	E	Randel, Kevin, Jupiter	20
	DP	Sollmann, Steve, Brevard	94
3B	PCT	Zamora, Hector, Tampa	.947
	PO	Mitchell, Lee, Jupiter	86
	A	Mitchell, Lee, Jupiter	245
	E	Moore, Scott, Daytona	30
	DP	Kirkland, Kody, Lakeland	32
SS	PCT	Rojas, Carlos, Daytona	.968
	PO	Tiburcio, Hector, Sarasota	198
	A	Chavez, Ozzie, Brevard County	370
	E	Campusano, Jose, Jupiter	37
	DP	Chavez, Ozzie, Brevard County	91
OF	PCT	Moss, Steve, Brevard County	.996
	PO	Blue, Vince, Lakeland	293
	A	Whitrock, Scott, Fort Myers	17
	E	Dickerson, Chris, Sarasota	9
	DP	Correll, Brad, Clearwater	6
		Smith, David, Dunedin	6

MIDWEST LEAGUE

LOW CLASS A

BY CHRIS GIGLEY

The 2005 Midwest League season seemed almost scripted. South Bend and Wisconsin dominated the standings for the entire season, winning their respective divisions in both halves. The two teams met in the championship and went the full five games before the Silver Hawks took the finale 4-0.

South Bend's high-octane offense was anchored by 20-year-old outfielder Carlos Gonzales, who followed up his promising but injury-plagued 2004 by being the Silver Hawks' top run producer. In 515 at-bats, he hit .307 with 18 home runs and 92 RBIs and was named both the league's MVP and its No. 1 prospect.

Carlos Gonzales

"He is so advanced for his age, and his defense is as good as his offense," said Diamondbacks assistant general manager Bob Miller.

As a team, South Bend led the league in hitting (.281), home runs (122) and RBIs (715). Right behind them was Wisconsin, with a .275 team average, 101 home runs and 712 RBIs.

Good pitching didn't trump good hitting in the Midwest League playoffs, as the Silver Hawks flattened the best-pitching team in the league, West Michigan, en route to its league championship. In fact, of the two finalists only South Bend's Koley Kolberg had an ERA under 4.00.

Despite their run to the championship finals, the Timber Rattlers still had less than half the attendance of Dayton and Kane County, the league's perennial top draws. Dayton led the league in attendance for the sixth straight season, welcoming 572,053 fans to Fifth Third Field in 2005.

STANDINGS: SPLIT SEASON

FIRST HALF					SECOND HALF				
EAST	**W**	**L**	**PCT**	**GB**	**EAST**	**W**	**L**	**PCT**	**GB**
South Bend	41	29	.586	—	South Bend	43	27	.614	—
Fort Wayne	38	32	.543	3	West Michigan	40	30	.571	3
Lansing	37	32	.536	3½	SW Michigan	39	31	.557	4
SW Michigan	33	36	.478	7½	Lansing	33	37	.471	10
West Michigan	33	37	.471	8	Dayton	30	39	.435	12½
Dayton	30	40	.429	11	Fort Wayne	27	43	.386	16
WEST	**W**	**L**	**PCT**	**GB**	**WEST**	**W**	**L**	**PCT**	**GB**
Wisconsin	39	31	.557	—	Wisconsin	37	32	.536	—
Clinton	38	32	.543	1	Beloit	36	34	.514	1½
Quad Cities	36	33	.522	2½	Kane County	36	34	.514	1½
Peoria	35	35	.500	4	Quad Cities	36	34	.514	1½
Burlington	34	36	.486	5	Cedar Rapids	35	35	.500	2½
Beloit	33	37	.471	6	Clinton	33	37	.471	4½
Kane County	31	38	.449	7½	Peoria	33	37	.471	4½
Cedar Rapids	30	40	.429	9	Burlington	31	39	.443	6½

PLAYOFFS—Division Series: South Bend defeated Southwest Michigan 2-0, Clinton defeated Quad Cities 2-0, West Michigan defeated Fort Wayne 2-0 and Wisconsin defeated Beloit 2-1 in best-of-3 series. **Semifinals:** South Bend defeated West Michigan 2-0 and Wisconsin defeated Clinton 2-0 in best-of-3 series. **Final:** South Bend defeated Wisconsin 3-2 in best-of-5 series.

Statistically speaking, none of those teams even had the best players. That honor went to the Peoria Chiefs, which had league batting champion Eric Patterson and home run king Ryan Harvey. As poorly as his older brother Corey played in Chicago, Eric Patterson was that good in the MWL, tearing out of the gate in April. By the time he was promoted to Double-A West Tenn on Aug. 27, Patterson had the best batting average (.333) and second-best slugging percentage (.535) in the Midwest League. He had also swiped 40 bases.

"Every part of his game has been great," Cubs farm director Oneri Fleita said. "He's using all fields, showing patience, bunting for hits, turning the double play well and showing great instincts on the base paths."

TOP 20 PROSPECTS

1. Carlos Gonzales, of, South Bend (Diamondbacks)
2. Homer Bailey, rhp, Dayton (Reds)
3. Eric Hurley, rhp, Clinton (Rangers)
4. Javier Herrera, of, Kane County (Athletics)
5. Cliff Pennington, ss, Kane County (Athletics)
6. Travis Buck, of, Kane County (Athletics)
7. Ryan Harvey, of, Peoria (Cubs)
8. Anthony Swarzak, rhp, Beloit (Twins)
9. Rafael Rodriguez, rhp, Cedar Rapids (Angels)
10. Matt Garza, rhp, Beloit (Twins)
11. Jay Rainville, rhp, Beloit (Twins)
12. Trevor Plouffe, ss, Beloit (Twins)
13. Luis Cota, rhp, Burlington (Royals)
14. David Winfree, 3b, Beloit (Twins)
15. Sean Gallagher, rhp, Peoria (Cubs)
16. Eric Patterson, 2b, Peoria (Cubs)
17. Reid Brignac, ss, Southwest Michigan (Devil Rays)
18. Matt Tuiasosopo, ss, Wisconsin (Mariners)
19. Asdrubal Cabrera, if, Wisconsin (Mariners)
20. Wilkin Ramirez, 3b, West Michigan (Tigers)

STANDINGS: OVERALL

Page	Team	W	L	PCT	GB	Manager	Attendance	Average	Last Penn.
51	South Bend Silver Hawks (Diamondbacks)	84	56	.600	—	Mark Haley	208,590	3,067	2005
236	Wisconsin Timber Rattlers (Mariners)	76	63	.547	7½	Scott Steinmann	211,927	3,071	1984
119	West Michigan Whitecaps (Tigers)	73	67	.521	11	Matt Walbeck	370,153	5,443	2004
243	Southwest Michigan Devil Rays (Devil Rays)	72	67	.518	11½	Joe Szekely	105,340	1,645	2000
214	Swing of the Quad Cities (Cardinals)	72	67	.518	11½	Joe Cunningham	165,878	2,475	1990
251	Clinton LumberKings (Rangers)	71	69	.507	13	Carlos Subero	95,775	1,408	1991
257	Lansing Lugnuts (Blue Jays)	70	69	.504	13½	Ken Joyce	354,855	5,218	2003
169	Beloit Snappers (Twins)	69	71	.493	15	Kevin Boles	93,399	1,353	1995
81	Peoria Chiefs (Cubs)	68	72	.486	16	Julio Garcia	256,612	3,773	2002
192	Kane County Cougars (Athletics)	67	72	.482	16½	Dave Joppie	518,394	7,623	2001
140	Burlington Bees (Royals)	65	75	.464	19	Jim Gabella	70,807	1,041	1999
147	Cedar Rapids Kernels (Angels)	65	75	.464	19	Bobby Magallanes	184,190	2,669	1994
222	Fort Wayne Wizards (Padres)	65	75	.464	19	Randy Ready	278,631	4,286	None
96	Dayton Dragons (Reds)	60	79	.432	23½	Alonzo Powell	572,053	8,290	None

NOTE: Teams' individual batting and pitching statistics can be found on page indicated in lefthand column.

2005 MIDWEST LEAGUE STATISTICS

CLUB BATTING

	AVG	G	AB	R	H	2B	2B	HR	BB	SO	SB
South Bend	.281	140	4824	800	1355	274	45	122	473	827	121
Wisconsin	.275	139	4833	788	1331	267	38	101	521	942	142
Southwest Michigan	.271	139	4674	668	1268	262	32	91	444	901	148
Peoria	.266	140	4728	695	1259	258	46	97	447	1014	137
Quad Cities	.265	139	4704	738	1247	248	28	113	523	827	126
Kane County	.261	139	4777	750	1246	266	24	119	602	1000	120
Dayton	.260	139	4762	665	1240	239	45	117	426	1097	115
Clinton	.259	140	4802	739	1244	263	35	112	576	1041	147
Lansing	.257	139	4644	684	1195	239	31	84	554	938	108
Beloit	.252	140	4805	695	1211	219	43	98	493	981	102
Fort Wayne	.252	140	4741	599	1197	234	26	75	482	897	107
Cedar Rapids	.251	140	4582	620	1148	241	33	107	463	1098	202
West Michigan	.251	140	4772	600	1200	240	32	65	419	1108	111
Burlington	.244	140	4623	592	1129	203	25	69	478	931	178

CLUB PITCHING

	ERA	G	CG	SHO	SV	IP	H	R	ER	BB	SO
West Michigan	3.63	140	5	8	37	1258	1182	604	507	414	942
Burlington	4.02	140	1	7	30	1240	1292	679	554	465	1005
Southwest Michigan	4.02	139	1	9	36	1206	1103	639	539	543	978
Fort Wayne	4.02	140	2	6	39	1221	1247	642	545	412	934
Beloit	4.11	140	3	6	36	1247	1167	645	569	514	1186
Clinton	4.13	140	2	9	28	1259	1274	686	577	437	960
South Bend	4.14	140	4	8	39	1246	1283	667	573	471	1031
Lansing	4.17	139	1	3	36	1213	1224	634	562	434	1001
Quad Cities	4.32	139	3	4	39	1224	1199	700	588	520	932
Cedar Rapids	4.42	140	8	9	37	1218	1247	711	598	501	922
Peoria	4.49	140	3	7	37	1216	1236	708	607	486	976
Kane County	4.54	139	1	3	36	1234	1261	740	622	532	934
Wisconsin	4.88	139	1	8	35	1234	1297	790	669	572	881
Dayton	4.92	139	1	6	32	1214	1258	788	663	600	920

CLUB FIELDING

	PCT	PO	A	E	DP
Lansing	.973	3638	1448	141	111
Clinton	.971	3778	1457	158	118
Beloit	.971	3741	1325	153	113
West Michigan	.971	3775	1586	159	135
SW Michigan	.970	3616	1386	153	125
South Bend	.970	3738	1593	165	129
Peoria	.969	3649	1449	162	121
Kane County	.968	3702	1473	170	108
Wisconsin	.968	3702	1439	172	139
Fort Wayne	.968	3663	1439	171	134
Dayton	.965	3641	1479	184	126
Burlington	.964	3720	1495	193	120
Quad Cities	.964	3672	1461	191	128
Cedar Rapids	.963	3653	1502	198	153

INDIVIDUAL BATTING LEADERS

(Minimum 378 Plate Appearances)

	AVG	G	AB	R	H	2B	3B	HR	RBI	BB	SO	SB
Patterson, Eric, Peoria	.333	110	432	90	144	26	11	13	71	53	94	40
Gutierrez, Tonys, Dayton	.324	109	410	65	133	21	5	7	48	40	71	6
Collins, Michael, Cedar Rapids	.320	100	363	64	116	32	3	7	64	34	44	16
Gonzales, Alberto, South Bend	.318	95	352	60	112	21	7	1	42	20	42	12
Johnson, Brent, Wisconsin	.310	109	378	77	117	21	1	1	44	55	57	22
Jaso, John, Southwest Michigan	.307	92	332	61	102	25	1	14	50	42	53	3
Gonzales, Carlos, South Bend	.307	129	515	91	158	28	6	18	92	48	86	7
Nowak, Chris, SW Michigan	.304	105	368	55	112	28	1	7	65	56	58	2
McIntyre, Nick, West Michigan	.303	118	442	61	134	30	2	7	45	42	85	11
Fasano, Jim, Clinton	.302	98	394	65	119	21	5	10	74	36	62	2

INDIVIDUAL PITCHING LEADERS

(Minimum 112 Innings)

	W	L	ERA	G	GS	CG	SV	IP	H	R	ER	BB	SO
Aselton, Kyle, Beloit	6	2	2.49	41	10	0	2	112	80	38	31	61	113
Sonnanstine, Andy, SW Michigan	10	4	2.55	18	18	1	0	117	103	42	33	11	103
Gallagher, Sean, Peoria	14	5	2.71	26	26	0	0	146	107	53	44	55	139
Hamilton, Clay, Fort Wayne	9	6	2.88	20	20	0	0	122	101	44	39	36	86
Walker, Andy, Clinton	4	8	2.93	19	19	2	0	123	123	54	40	24	58
Cheng, Chi-Hung, Lansing	7	6	3.15	26	25	0	0	137	109	61	48	72	142
Jurrjens, Jair, West Michigan	12	6	3.41	26	26	0	0	143	132	62	54	36	108
Trahern, Dallas, West Michigan	7	11	3.58	26	26	2	0	156	158	78	62	50	66
Ekstrom, Michael, Fort Wayne	13	6	3.70	28	28	1	0	168	167	76	69	36	112
Houser, James, SW Michigan	8	8	3.76	22	22	0	0	115	100	50	48	31	109

ALL-STAR TEAM

C—Michael Collins, Cedar Rapids. **1B**—Cesar Nicolas, South Bend; Tonys Gutierrez, Dayton. **2B**—Eric Patterson, Peoria. **3B**—David Winfree, Beloit. **SS**—Matt Tuiasosopo, Wisconsin. **OF**—Carlos Gonzales, South Bend; Ryan Harvey, Peoria; Javier Herrera, Kane County. **DH**—John Jaso, Southwest Michigan. **RHP**—Sean Gallagher, Peoria. **LHP**—Chi-Hung Cheng, Lansing. **RHRP**—Matt Elliot, South Bend. **LHRP**—Kevin Ool, Quad Cities.

Most Valuable Player: Carlos Gonzales, South Bend. **Top Prospect:** Carlos Gonzales, South Bend. **Manager of the Year:** Mark Haley, South Bend.

DEPARTMENT LEADERS

BATTING

G	Frazier, Jeff, West Michigan	137
AB	Winfree, David, Beloit	562
R	Murillo, Agustin, South Bend	94
H	Winfree, David, Beloit	165
TB	Winfree, David, Beloit	254
XBH	Burns, Deacon, Beloit	61
	Frazier, Jeff, West Michigan	61
2B	Frazier, Jeff, West Michigan	45
3B	Burns, Deacon, Beloit	13
	Perez, Fernando, SW Michigan	13
HR	Harvey, Ryan, Peoria	24
RBI	Winfree, David, Beloit	101
SH	Castillo, Wilkin, South Bend	16
	Shepherd, Matt, Quad Cities	16
SF	Navarro, Oswaldo, Wisconsin	10
BB	Hulett, Tug, Clinton	90
IBB	Gonzales, Carlos, South Bend	8
HBP	Collins, Michael, Cedar Rapids	25
SO	Ramirez, Wilkin, West Michigan	143
SB	Perez, Fernando, SW Michigan	57
CS	Bonifacio, Emilio, South Bend	17
	Perez, Fernando, SW Michigan	17
GIDP	Nielsen, Eric, Lansing	25
OBP	Nicolas, Cesar, South Bend	.428
SLG	Nicolas, Cesar, South Bend	.594

PITCHING

G	Tomey, Anthony, West Michigan	59
GS	Six tied at	28
CG	Rodriguez, Fernando, Cedar Rapids	4
SHO	Seven tied at	1
GF	Varner, Matt, Fort Wayne	47
SV	Varner, Matt, Fort Wayne	34
W	Ford, Ryan, Kane County	14
	Gallagher, Sean, Peoria	14
L	Jensen, Aaron, Wisconsin	13
IP	Schlact, Michael, Clinton	168
H	Jackson, Steven, South Bend	205
R	Jensen, Aaron, Wisconsin	115
ER	Jensen, Aaron, Wisconsin	97
HR	Core, Danny, Lansing	22
HBP	Bello, Cibney, Wisconsin	17
BB	Cheng, Chi-Hung, Lansing	72
SO	Hurley, Eric, Clinton	152
WP	Sharpe, Steven, Kane County	25
BK	Bailey, Homer, Dayton	5

FIELDING

C	PCT	Ryan, Dusty, West Michigan	.990
	PO	Sanchez, Javier, Beloit	691
	A	Johnson, Rob, Wisconsin	65
	E	Duenas, Tomas, Cedar Rapids	17
	DP	Feiner, Korey, Beloit	7
	PB	Thigpen, Curtis, Lansing	16
	CS PCT	Ryan, Dusty, West Michigan	33%
1B	PCT	Hicks, David, Lansing	.996
	PO	Ferris, Mike, Quad Cities	1046
	A	Ferris, Mike, Quad Cities	86
	E	Walston, Chris, Cedar Rapids	16
	DP	Ferris, Mike, Quad Cities	96
2B	PCT	Patterson, Eric, Peoria	.982
	PO	Kazmar, Sean, Fort Wayne	243
	A	Bonifacio, Emilio, South Bend	386
	E	Bonifacio, Emilio, South Bend	23
	DP	Kazmar, Sean, Fort Wayne	92
3B	PCT	Sandoval, Freddy, Cedar Rapids	.947
	PO	Leslie, Myron, Kane County	89
	A	Sandoval, Freddy, Cedar Rapids	245
	E	Winfree, David, Beloit	34
	DP	Schlichting, Travis, SW Michigan	25
SS	PCT	Gonzales, Alberto, South Bend	.975
	PO	Klosterman, Ryan, Lansing	209
	A	Dlugach, Brent, West Michigan	457
	E	Bush, Matt, Fort Wayne	38
	DP	Bush, Matt, Fort Wayne	83
OF	PCT	Gentry, Philip, Dayton	1.000
		Montanez, Luis, Peoria	1.000
	PO	Perez, Fernando, SW Michigan	317
	A	Springer, Kenard, Burlington	22
	E	Ramirez, Yordany, Fort Wayne	12
	DP	Wilson, Michael, Wisconsin	5

SOUTH ATLANTIC LEAGUE

LOW CLASS A

BY CHRIS GIGLEY

The Kannapolis Intimidators set the tone early in their 2005 championship run in the South Atlantic League. Lefthander Gio Gonzalez spun an Opening Day shutout and was the league's first pitcher of the week of the season.

While the White Sox' 2004 first round pick was promoted in June, the Intimidators pitching staff rolled over opposing hitters for the whole year. Overall, Kannapolis finished with a 3.57 ERA, second to the Lexington Legends' 3.56 ERA. Lefthander Ray Liotta picked up the slack after Gonzalez left and finished 8-3 with a league-leading 2.26 ERA before he was promoted in late July.

ROBERT GURGANUS

Gio Gonzalez

"They have both been outstanding," Kannapolis pitching coach J.R. Perdew said before Gonzalez' promotion. "You really couldn't ask for anything more from them."

The Intimidators swept past Charleston in the first round of the playoffs, the first of its two victories a 21-inning epic Kannapolis finally won 4-3 on a walk-off single by 2005 draftee Chris Getz. It was the longest playoff game in South Atlantic League history.

In the championship, the Intimidators faced the Hagerstown Suns, a team of two halves in 2005. The Suns reached the playoffs by winning the Northern Division crown in the first half in a one-game playoff against Lexington. But in the second half, much of the Suns' lineup was promoted to high Class A St. Lucie, including Sally League all-stars Gaby Hernandez, Dante Brinkley and Grant Psomas.

Predictably, Hagerstown finished the second half in the Northern Division cellar. But they rallied to beat Delmarva in the playoffs' first round before facing Kannapolis for the title. The Intimidators won the best-of-five series in four games, clinching when Jack Egbert and Garry Bakker combined on a six-hit shutout in a 3-0 victory in Game Four.

The league debuted two new stadiums in 2005. Neither the Greensboro Grasshoppers' First Horizon Park nor the West Virginia Power's Appalachian Power Park drew enough fans to top Lake County and Lakewood in total attendance, but both ballparks were home to notable storylines. Greensboro drew 406,996, more than double its final year at old War Memorial Stadium.

STANDINGS: SPLIT SEASON

FIRST HALF					SECOND HALF				
NORTH	**W**	**L**	**PCT**	**GB**	**NORTH**	**W**	**L**	**PCT**	**GB**
Hagerstown	42	28	.600	—	Delmarva	42	27	.609	—
Lexington	42	28	.600	—	Lexington	39	30	.565	3
Lake County	40	30	.571	2	West Virginia	35	33	.515	6½
Greensboro	35	34	.507	6½	Hickory	32	36	.471	9½
Delmarva	30	40	.429	12	Lake County	32	36	.471	9½
Lakewood	25	45	.357	17	Greensboro	32	37	.464	10
West Virginia	25	45	.357	17	Lakewood	31	38	.449	11
Hickory	22	44	.333	18	Hagerstown	29	38	.433	12
SOUTH	**W**	**L**	**PCT**	**GB**	**SOUTH**	**W**	**L**	**PCT**	**GB**
Charleston	43	26	.623	—	Kannapolis	38	26	.594	—
Augusta	40	27	.597	2	Augusta	37	32	.536	3½
Rome	39	29	.574	3½	Charleston	37	32	.536	3½
Asheville	38	31	.551	5	Greenville	37	33	.529	4
Kannapolis	36	33	.522	7	Asheville	33	36	.478	7½
Greenville	35	33	.515	7½	Rome	33	36	.478	7½
Savannah	31	37	.456	11½	Savannah	31	39	.443	10
Columbus	28	41	.406	15	Columbus	29	38	.433	10½

PLAYOFFS—Semifinals: Kannapolis defeated Charleston 2-0 and Hagerstown defeated Delmarva 2-1 in best-of-3 series. **Final:** Kannapolis defeated Hagerstown 3-1, in best-of-5 series.

TOP 20 PROSPECTS

1. Scott Elbert, lhp, Columbus (Dodgers)
2. Neil Walker, c, Hickory (Pirates)
3. Marcus Sanders, ss, Augusta (Giants)
4. Troy Patton, lhp, Lexington (Astros)
5. Ryan Braun, 3b, West Virginia (Brewers)
6. Philip Hughes, rhp, Charleston (Yankees)
7. Blake DeWitt, 3b, Columbus (Dodgers)
8. Matt Harrison, lhp, Rome (Braves)
9. Yunel Escobar, ss, Rome (Braves)
10. Brandon Jones, of, Rome (Braves)
11. Jimmy Barthmaier, rhp, Lexington (Astros)
12. Gio Gonzalez, lhp, Kannapolis (White Sox)
13. Mark Rogers, rhp, West Virginia (Brewers)
14. Greg Golson, of, Lakewood (Phillies)
15. Hunter Pence, of, Lexington (Astros)
16. Collin Balester, rhp, Savannah (Nationals)
17. J.T. Restko, of, Greensboro (Marlins)
18. Gaby Hernandez, rhp, Hagerstown (Mets)
19. Ian Desmond, ss, Savannah (Nationals)
20. Chris Nelson, ss, Asheville (Rockies)

STANDINGS: OVERALL

Page	Team	W	L	PCT	GB	Manager	Attendance	Average	Last Penn.
134	Lexington Legends (Astros)	81	58	.583	—	Tim Bogar	388,710	5,716	2001
185	Charleston RiverDogs (Yankees)	80	58	.580	½	Bill Mosiello	249,374	3,778	None
228	Augusta GreenJackets (Giants)	77	59	.566	2½	Roberto Kelly	123,545	2,025	1999
89	Kannapolis Intimidators (White Sox)	74	59	.556	4	Nick Capra	104,781	1,690	2005
58	Rome Braves (Braves)	72	65	.526	8	Rocket Wheeler	232,187	3,465	2003
73	Greenville Bombers (Red Sox)	72	66	.522	8½	Chad Epperson	115,161	1,718	1998
104	Lake County Captains (Indians)	72	66	.522	8½	Mike Sarbaugh	394,208	5,972	None
65	Delmarva Shorebirds (Orioles)	72	67	.518	9	Gary Kendall	219,361	3,374	2000
176	Hagerstown Suns (Mets)	71	66	.518	9	Gene Richards	153,675	2,227	None
112	Asheville Tourists (Rockies)	71	67	.514	91½	Joe Mikulik	155,129	2,462	1984
126	Greensboro Grasshoppers (Marlins)	67	71	.486	13½	Brandon Hyde	407,711	5,908	1982
265	Savannah Sand Gnats (Nationals)	62	76	.449	18½	Randy Knorr	72,435	1,207	1996
161	West Virginia Power (Brewers)	60	78	.435	20½	Ramon Aviles	233,143	3,532	1990
154	Columbus Catfish (Dodgers)	57	79	.419	22½	Travis Barbary	62,547	1,008	None
206	Hickory Crawdads (Pirates)	54	80	.403	24½	Jeff Branson	163,863	2,601	2004
200	Lakewood BlueClaws (Phillies)	56	83	.403	25	P.J. Forbes	444,607	6,635	None

NOTE: Teams' individual batting and pitching statistics can be found on page indicated in lefthand column.

2005 SOUTH ATLANTIC LEAGUE STATISTICS

CLUB BATTING

	AVG	G	AB	R	H	2B	2B	HR	BB	SO	SB
Greenville	.275	138	4668	720	1285	292	39	108	479	1005	63
Asheville	.274	138	4679	734	1283	286	17	167	487	1020	89
Augusta	.268	136	4574	673	1227	255	33	64	537	964	168
Rome	.267	137	4640	651	1238	247	37	82	444	976	81
Lexington	.267	139	4681	733	1251	271	28	155	500	1059	152
Hagerstown	.264	137	4620	692	1220	252	35	120	424	1069	203
Kannapolis	.261	133	4414	610	1153	218	23	97	484	906	104
Hickory	.259	134	4528	596	1175	181	31	89	355	915	117
Charleston	.258	138	4641	649	1197	230	36	85	440	950	187
Columbus	.258	136	4568	623	1180	223	29	107	432	937	45
Delmarva	.257	139	4700	671	1208	245	33	85	504	911	100
Lakewood	.256	139	4703	625	1205	242	37	83	491	1027	72
Lake County	.254	138	4747	667	1204	227	22	90	475	1001	84
Savannah	.252	138	4518	633	1137	237	30	110	501	1066	163
Greensboro	.251	138	4642	670	1165	233	18	136	441	1096	100
West Virginia	.251	138	4583	580	1151	216	35	78	412	1030	141

CLUB PITCHING

	ERA	G	CG	SHO	SV	IP	H	R	ER	BB	SO
Lexington	3.56	139	2	15	35	1228	1115	574	486	477	1174
Kannapolis	3.57	133	6	14	33	1150	1065	579	456	467	940
Lake County	3.71	138	2	10	40	1231	1196	617	507	443	994
Charleston	3.72	138	3	6	36	1221	1171	603	505	491	1049
Hagerstown	3.93	137	3	10	37	1228	1140	664	536	524	1020
Greenville	4.04	138	3	3	33	1180	1234	639	529	427	948
Rome	4.07	137	5	8	33	1205	1238	626	545	425	882
Augusta	4.13	136	3	3	39	1170	1182	633	537	423	1074
Columbus	4.14	136	5	9	24	1172	1152	667	539	538	1066
Delmarva	4.21	139	1	7	46	1233	1322	711	576	468	1086
West Virginia	4.30	138	0	5	32	1211	1226	695	578	491	1014
Savannah	4.37	138	4	8	35	1169	1175	652	568	435	854
Greensboro	4.38	138	2	4	46	1217	1242	721	592	525	1031
Hickory	4.39	134	2	3	28	1174	1261	672	573	421	843
Lakewood	4.46	139	10	8	25	1207	1262	702	595	396	905
Asheville	5.05	138	2	5	41	1192	1300	773	668	457	1052

CLUB FIELDING

	PCT	PO	A	E	DP
Rome	.974	3614	1402	132	120
Charleston	.972	3661	1531	148	135
Greenville	.972	3540	1388	144	121
Asheville	.972	3576	1532	148	117
Lake County	.971	3693	1567	155	153
Hickory	.971	3523	1516	153	120
Lexington	.970	3684	1433	159	125
Savannah	.970	3506	1273	146	122
Columbus	967	3516	1354	166	138
Augusta	967	3510	1294	166	107
Greensboro	966	3650	1549	182	132
Kannapolis	966	3450	1465	172	108
West Virginia	966	3632	1560	182	132
Lakewood	965	3619	1430	182	121
Hagerstown	964	3683	1483	194	135
Delmarva	959	3697	1391	216	117

INDIVIDUAL BATTING LEADERS

(Minimum 378 Plate Appearances)

	AVG	G	AB	R	H	2B	3B	HR	RBI	BB	SO	SB
Horwitz, Brian, Augusta	.349	123	470	77	164	38	4	2	88	50	39	6
Otness, John, Greenville	.331	117	441	59	146	25	0	12	67	35	42	1
Miller, Matt, Asheville	.331	127	508	79	168	34	0	30	100	26	71	9
Dzurilla, Michael, Lakewood	.320	110	434	73	139	33	4	12	60	48	71	2
Restko, J.T., Greensboro	.313	115	403	69	126	22	3	15	70	53	91	3
Young, Matt, Rome	.312	114	423	85	132	15	4	6	52	66	65	10
Pinckney, Andrew, Greenville	.311	128	508	91	158	33	9	21	98	36	78	6
Denker, Travis, Columbus	.310	101	358	65	111	23	1	21	68	67	78	2
Fransz, Jason, Delmarva	.308	103	396	70	122	33	1	22	111	31	77	4
Jaramillo, Jason, Lakewood	.304	119	448	46	136	28	4	8	63	44	72	2

INDIVIDUAL PITCHING LEADERS

(Minimum 112 Innings)

	W	L	ERA	G	GS	CG	SV	IP	H	R	ER	BB	SO
Liotta, Ray, Kannapolis	8	3	2.26	20	20	1	0	115	108	39	29	35	107
Barthmaier, Jimmy, Lexington	11	6	2.27	25	25	0	0	135	108	41	34	55	142
Ramirez, Luis, Delmarva	9	7	2.55	28	27	1	0	162	131	53	46	54	155
Elbert, Scott, Columbus	8	5	2.66	25	24	1	0	115	83	37	34	57	128
Gallardo, Yovani, West Virginia	8	3	2.74	26	18	0	1	121	100	46	37	51	110
Egbert, Jack, Kannapolis	10	5	3.12	30	24	4	0	147	127	66	51	48	107
Gutierrez, Juan, Lexington	9	5	3.21	22	21	1	0	121	106	55	43	43	100
Laffey, Aaron, Lake County	7	7	3.22	25	23	1	1	142	123	62	51	52	69

ALL-STAR TEAM

C—Neil Walker, Hickory. **1B**—Joe Koshansky, Asheville. **2B**—Travis Denker, Columbus. **3B**—Andrew Pinckney, Greenville. **SS**—Marcus Sanders, Augusta. **UT IF**—Brad McCann, Greensboro. **OF**—Brian Horwitz, Augusta; Matt Miller, Asheville; Hunter Pence, Lexington. **UT OF**—David Cook, Kannapolis. **DH**—John Otness, Greenville. **RHP**—Jimmy Barthmaier, Lexington. **LHP**—Ray Liotta, Kannapolis.

Most Valuable Player: Matt Miller, Asheville. **Most Outstanding Pitcher:** Ray Liotta, Kannapolis. **Most Outstanding Prospect:** Hunter Pence, Lexington. **Manager of the Year:** Tim Bogar, Lexington.

DEPARTMENT LEADERS

BATTING

G	Battle, Tim, Charleston	134
AB	Battle, Tim, Charleston	525
R	Battle, Tim, Charleston	97
H	Miller, Matt, Asheville	168
TB	Miller, Matt, Asheville	292
XBH	Koshansky, Joe, Asheville	68
2B	Horwitz, Brian, Augusta	38
3B	Battle, Tim, Charleston	11
HR	Koshansky, Joe, Asheville	36
RBI	Fransz, Jason, Delmarva	111
SH	Ascencion, Quincy, Delmarva	15
SF	Otness, John, Greenville	11
BB	Bernadina, Rogearvin, Savannah	75
IBB	Koshansky, Joe, Asheville	7
HBP	Gimenez, Chris, Lake County	25
SO	Battle, Tim, Charleston	195
SB	Gomez, Carlos, Hagerstown	64
CS	Gomez, Carlos, Hagerstown	24
GIDP	Jones, Ben, Charleston	19
OBP	Denker, Travis, Columbus	.417
SLG	Koshansky, Joe, Asheville	.603

PITCHING

G	Nestor, Scott, Greensboro	58
GS	Hart, Kevin, Delmarva	28
CG	De la Cruz, Max, Lakewood	5
SHO	Egbert, Jack, Kannapolis	3
GF	Mobley, Chris, Greensboro	47
SV	Mobley, Chris, Greensboro	34
W	Martinez, Ronnie, Lexington	13
	Parr, James, Rome	13
L	Kloosterman, Greg, West Va.	19
IP	Baldwin, Andrew, Lakewood	168
H	De la Cruz, Max, Lakewood	186
R	De la Cruz, Max, Lakewood	109
ER	De la Cruz, Max, Lakewood	92
HR	Lo, Ching, Asheville	23
HBP	Miramontes, Mateo, Hagerstown	19
BB	Harrell, Lucas, Kannapolis	71
SO	Sanchez, Jonathan, Augusta	166
WP	Kloosterman, Greg, West Va.	17
BK	Morales, Franklin, Asheville	7

FIELDING

C	PCT	Gutierrez, Gabriel, Columbus	.993
	PO	Toregas, Wyatt, Lake County	728
	A	Toregas, Wyatt, Lake County	103
	E	Jaramillo, Jason, Lakewood	20
	DP	Rojas, Irwil, Charleston	11
	PB	Toregas, Wyatt, Lake County	28
	CS PCT	Gutierrez, Gabriel, Columbus	41%
1B	PCT	Carlin, Michael, Hickory	.997
	PO	Pacheco, Fernando, LC	1162
	A	Richardson, Grant, West Virginia	90
	E	Pacheco, Fernando, LC	18
	DP	Pacheco, Fernando, LC	123
2B	PCT	Szabo, Marshall, Lake County	.984
	PO	Iribarren, Hernan, WV	255
	A	Iribarren, Hernan, West Virginia	367
	E	Iribarren, Hernan, WV	21
	DP	Szabo, Marshall, Lake County	74
3B	PCT	Triplett, Bryan, Lexington	.955
	PO	Orr, Sam, Lakewood	113
	A	Orr, Sam, Lakewood	253
	E	Orr, Sam, Lakewood	35
	DP	Orr, Sam, Lakewood	39
SS	PCT	McCarthy, Ryan, Kannapolis	.957
	PO	Escobar, Alcides, West Virginia	204
	A	Bixler, Brian, Hickory	407
	E	Escobar, Alcides, West Virginia	41
	DP	Escobar, Alcides, West Virginia	90
OF	PCT	Pence, Hunter, Lexington	.992
	PO	Battle, Tim, Charleston	311
	A	Carroll, Brett, Greensboro	18
	E	Battle, Tim, Charleston	14
	DP	Rivas, Arturo, Delmarva	7

NEW YORK-PENN LEAGUE

SHORT-SEASON CLASS A

BY MATT MEYERS

The Auburn Doubledays keep getting close, but close just wasn't enough in 2005.

After posting the best regular-season record in the New York-Penn League in 2003 and 2004, the Doubledays had the third best record in 2005 and yet still qualified for the playoffs by winning the Pinckney Division title. Unlike the previous two seasons, when they flamed out in the first round, Auburn trounced Oneonta in the first round, outscoring the Tigers 33-9 in a two-game sweep as outfielder Jacob Butler went 7-for-11 with six runs scored and seven RBIs.

RODGER WOOD

Nolan Reimold

Unfortunately for Auburn, it will have to wait another season to take the next step to a NY-P championship as the Doubledays were swept in the championship series by Staten Island. The Yankees, who had the best regular season record in the NY-P, swept Williamsport in the other semifinal series.

Staten Island pitching, which posted a league-best 2.85 ERA during the regular season, was just too much for the explosive Auburn offense. In the opener, Jay Stephens combined with four relievers to allow one run as the Yankees won 6-1. The Yankees were the beneficiary of porous defense by Auburn as only one of their first four runs was earned because of two third-inning errors.

Game Two came down to the final inning. Catcher Joe Burke led off the ninth with a single, advanced to second on a sacrifice bunt and then stole third before scoring on a Reggie Corona single to give the Yankees the win, and the title—their first since 2000.

The Yankees won the title despite having few high-ceiling prospects. The most dominant were righthanded relievers Cory Stuart and Josh Schmidt. Stuart put together the first healthy season of his pro career and posted a 0.83 ERA in 30 innings. Schmidt was drafted in the 13th round in June out of Pacific. He was second in the nation in strikeouts per nine innings in the spring and was even more dominant at Staten Island as he posted a 0.27 ERA in 33 innings with 13 saves.

The Yankees lineup was paced by outfielder Brett Gardner (.284-5-32), an exciting leadoff hitter with blazing speed and the on-base skills to match, as well as Eduardo Nunez (.313-3-46), an electrifying 18-year-old shortstop who was the highest ceiling prospect on the team.

"He carried himself years above his age," Auburn manager Dennis Holmberg said.

Nunez stood out the most in a league loaded with shortstop talent.

While Nunez had the highest ceiling, the most productive shortstop in the league was Oneonta shortstop Michael Hollimon, who hit .277-13-53 and scored a league-high 66 runs. Other shortstops who established themselves as prospects were Lowell's Jed Lowrie (.328-4-32), New Jersey's Tyler Greene (.261-1-18) and Welinson Baez (.324-6-37) of Batavia.

TOP 20 PROSPECTS

1. Nolan Reimold, of, Aberdeen (Orioles)
2. Chris Volstad, rhp, Jamestown (Marlins)
3. Wade Davis, rhp, Hudson Valley (Devil Rays)
4. Eduardo Nunez, ss, Staten Island (Yankees)
5. Radhames Liz, rhp, Aberdeen (Orioles)
6. Jacoby Ellsbury, of, Lowell (Red Sox)
7. Jed Lowrie, ss/2b, Lowell (Red Sox)
8. Garrett Olson, lhp, Aberdeen (Orioles)
9. Jacob McGee, lhp, Hudson Valley (Devil Rays)
10. Tyler Greene, ss, New Jersey (Cardinals)
11. Gaby Sanchez, 3b/1b, Jamestown (Marlins)
12. Luis Soto, of, Lowell (Red Sox)
13. Clay Buchholz, rhp, Lowell (Red Sox)
14. Michael Hollimon, ss, Oneonta (Tigers)
15. Welinson Baez, ss, Batavia (Phillies)
16. Jensen Lewis, rhp, Mahoning Valley (Indians)
17. Ryan Patterson, of, Auburn (Blue Jays)
18. Kevin Whelan, rhp, Oneonta (Tigers)
19. Nick Webber, rhp, New Jersey (Yankees)
20. Bobby Parnell, rhp, Brooklyn (Mets)

STANDINGS

Page	McNAMARA	W	L	PCT	GB	Manager	Attendance	Average	Last Penn.
186	Staten Island Yankees (Yankees)	52	24	.684	—	Andy Stankiewicz	155,541	4,203	2005
207	Williamsport Crosscutters (Pirates)	44	32	.579	8	Tom Prince	79,253	2,085	2003
177	Brooklyn Cyclones (Mets)	40	36	.526	12	Mookie Wilson	285,818	7,939	2001
215	New Jersey Cardinals (Cardinals)	37	39	.487	15	Mark DeJohn	115,129	3,029	1994
244	Hudson Valley Renegades (Devil Rays)	31	43	.419	20	Dave Howard	158,423	4,526	1999
66	Aberdeen IronBirds (Orioles)	27	48	.360	24½	Andy Etchebarren	239,748	6,309	1983
Page	**PINCKNEY**	**W**	**L**	**PCT**	**GB**	**Manager**	**Attendance**	**Average**	**Last Penn.**
258	Auburn Doubledays (Blue Jays)	45	30	.600	—	Dennis Holmberg	69,716	1,884	1998
200	Batavia Muckdogs (Philles)	36	39	.480	9	Manny Amador	40,557	1,126	1963
105	Mahoning Valley Scrappers (Indians)	33	43	.434	12½	Rouglas Odor	153,879	4,158	2004
127	Jamestown Jammers (Marlins)	31	44	.413	14	Mike Mordecai	50,460	1,441	1991
Page	**STEDLER**	**W**	**L**	**PCT**	**GB**	**Manager**	**Attendance**	**Average**	**Last Penn.**
119	Oneonta Tigers (Tigers)	48	27	.640	—	Tom Brookens	45,349	1,295	1998
74	Lowell Spinners (Red Sox)	42	33	.560	6	Luis Alicea	185,000	5,000	None
134	Tri-City ValleyCats (Astros)	34	42	.447	14½	Gregg Langbehn	116,674	3,333	1997
266	Vermont Expos	28	48	.368	20½	Bobby Williams	106,407	2,875	1996

PLAYOFFS—Semifinals: Auburn defeated Oneonta 2-0 and Staten Island defeated Williamsport 2-0, in best-of-3 series. **Finals:** Staten Island defeated Auburn 2-0 in best-of-3 series.

NOTE: Teams' individual batting and pitching statistics can be found on page indicated in lefthand column.

2005 NEW YORK-PENN LEAGUE STATISTICS

CLUB BATTING

	AVG	G	AB	R	H	2B	2B	HR	BB	SO	SB
Tri-City	.281	76	2577	382	723	112	20	39	236	429	84
Oneonta	.273	75	2548	459	695	128	34	55	284	618	65
New Jersey	.263	76	2603	334	685	129	20	31	247	607	86
Jamestown	.262	75	2555	338	670	105	25	46	201	609	62
Lowell	.261	75	2571	395	672	124	22	43	302	557	68
Batavia	.260	75	2628	383	683	138	23	42	260	576	48
Auburn	.258	75	2558	372	661	165	18	67	259	666	26
Staten Island	.258	76	2569	373	664	117	17	31	265	452	67
Vermont	.250	76	2536	356	634	102	20	48	266	664	63
Williamsport	.245	76	2580	349	631	117	19	33	258	556	74
Mahoning Valley	.245	76	2562	349	627	98	21	38	299	546	90
Brooklyn	.243	76	2558	332	621	118	22	42	290	512	107
Aberdeen	.240	75	2514	296	603	126	11	37	276	688	38
Hudson Valley	.234	74	2486	299	581	117	14	43	211	664	42

CLUB PITCHING

	ERA	G	CG	SHO	SV	IP	H	R	ER	BB	SO
Staten Island	2.85	76	0	6	26	680	548	258	215	270	645
Williamsport	3.40	76	0	7	21	680	609	312	257	243	514
Brooklyn	3.41	76	1	4	20	678	672	324	257	265	527
Lowell	3.70	75	0	7	22	659	661	343	271	207	575
Auburn	3.71	75	0	2	29	674	652	346	278	242	615
Mahoning Valley	3.71	76	0	3	19	667	666	368	275	225	613
Hudson Valley	3.72	74	1	3	24	650	626	344	269	234	630
Oneonta	3.78	75	1	5	21	655	609	327	275	282	564
New Jersey	3.82	76	0	6	19	672	644	346	284	259	588
Aberdeen	3.97	75	1	5	14	664	651	356	293	274	630
Batavia	4.17	75	2	4	20	676	721	370	313	254	580
Jamestown	4.59	75	1	2	17	652	701	421	333	276	603
Vermont	4.88	76	1	2	7	663	758	453	359	260	461
Tri-City	5.57	76	0	3	11	648	632	449	401	363	599

CLUB FIELDING

	PCT	PO	A	E	DP
Tri-City	.975	1945	727	68	70
Staten Island	.975	2039	849	74	66
Oneonta	.970	1964	786	84	73
Batavia	.966	2027	816	101	66
New Jersey	.965	2016	809	103	62
Aberdeen	.965	1992	740	99	72
Williamsport	.964	2039	909	111	85
Mahoning Valley	.962	2002	767	108	69
Lowell	.962	1977	835	110	54
Brooklyn	.961	2035	876	117	84
Auburn	.961	2021	866	117	59
Hudson Valley	.960	1950	710	111	51
Jamestown	.959	1985	755	117	71
Vermont	.957	1988	812	126	62

INDIVIDUAL BATTING LEADERS

(Minimum 205 Plate Appearances)

	AVG	G	AB	R	H	2B	3B	HR	RBI	BB	SO	SB
Sanchez, Gaby, Jamestown	.355	62	234	34	83	16	0	5	42	16	24	11
Sellers, Neil, Tri-City	.344	74	279	46	96	18	1	11	50	35	27	7
Patterson, Ryan, Auburn	.339	71	274	52	93	23	4	13	65	21	53	5
Joyce, Matt, Oneonta	.331	65	245	51	81	10	4	4	45	30	29	9
Sutil, Wladimir, Tri-City	.329	59	231	42	76	13	0	0	21	22	12	13
Lowrie, Jed, Lowell	.328	53	201	36	66	12	0	4	32	34	30	7
Rhymes, Will, Oneonta	.328	61	250	48	82	11	3	2	27	25	15	14
Groce, Garrett, Hudson Valley	.322	70	258	49	83	13	2	9	35	34	53	12
Nunez, Eduardo, Staten Island	.313	73	281	37	88	11	6	3	46	20	43	6
Harris, Clay, Batavia	.311	71	280	44	87	22	2	2	40	30	48	1

INDIVIDUAL PITCHING LEADERS

(Minimum 61 Innings)

	W	L	ERA	G	GS	CG	SV	IP	H	R	ER	BB	SO
Parnell, Bobby, Brooklyn	2	3	1.73	15	14	0	0	73	48	20	14	29	67
Redmond, Todd, Williamsport	1	2	1.98	15	14	0	0	73	62	22	16	21	63
Conroy, Jim, Staten Island	5	1	2.04	18	9	0	1	66	52	20	15	20	67
Seccombe, David, Staten Island	8	2	2.15	17	9	0	1	71	45	18	17	26	53
Phillips, Ryan, Lowell	7	2	2.28	14	14	0	0	67	45	19	17	31	61
Mateo, Waner, Brooklyn	4	2	2.56	14	12	0	0	63	59	28	18	30	53
Davis, Wade, Hudson Valley	7	4	2.72	15	15	0	0	86	75	35	26	23	97
Ray, Robert, Auburn	4	3	2.77	15	13	0	0	62	46	22	19	20	58
Stephens, Jason, Staten Island	4	1	2.82	18	10	0	1	67	55	25	21	19	52
Bauserman, Joe, Williamsport	6	2	2.84	14	14	0	0	70	64	30	22	26	45

ALL-STAR TEAM

None selected.

DEPARTMENT LEADERS

BATTING

G	Poterson, Jon, Staten Island	75
AB	Poterson, Jon, Staten Island	295
R	Hollimon, Michael, Oneonta	66
H	Sellers, Neil, Tri-City	96
TB	Patterson, Ryan, Auburn	163
XBH	Patterson, Ryan, Auburn	40
2B	Pearce, Steve, Williamsport	26
3B	Hollimon, Michael, Oneonta	10
HR	Patton, Cory, Auburn	14
RBI	Patterson, Ryan, Auburn	65
SH	Sena, Emmanuel, Auburn	9
SF	Johnson, Jay, Lowell	7
BB	Contreras, Jose, Vermont	51
IBB	Stewart, Caleb, Brooklyn	5
HBP	Cunningham, Matt, Tri-City	21
SO	Costanzo, Mike, Batavia	89
SB	Constanza, Jose, Mahoning Valley	24
CS	Burns, Greg, Jamestown	11
GIDP	Marson, Lou, Batavia	12
OBP	Lowrie, Jed, Lowell	.429
SLG	Patterson, Ryan, Auburn	.595

PITCHING

G	Miller, Kevin, Williamsport	29
GS	Landing, Jeff, Brooklyn	16
	Pena, Mario, Lowell	16
CG	Eight tied at	1
SHO	Four tied at	1
GF	Phillips, Paul, Auburn	23
	Schmidt, Josh, Staten Island	23
SV	Feldkamp, Derek, Hudson Valley	15
W	Seccombe, David, Staten Island	8
L	Pena, Mario, Lowell	8
IP	Kendrick, Kyle, Batavia	91
H	Pena, Mario, Lowell	97
R	Pena, Mario, Lowell	56
ER	Pluta, Anthony, Tri-City	53
HR	Blackley, Adam, Lowell	11
HBP	McKeller, Ryan, Tri-City	13
BB	Pluta, Anthony, Tri-City	51
SO	Davis, Wade, Hudson Valley	97
WP	Bell, Kristian, Auburn	12
BK	Hernandez, Moises, Aberdeen	4

FIELDING

C	PCT	Bell, Josh, Auburn	.995
	PO	Marson, Lou, Batavia	419
	A	Pilittere, P.J., Staten Island	47
	E	Butera, Drew, Brooklyn	12
	DP	Butera, Drew, Brooklyn	8
	PB	Michalski, Joe, Aberdeen	13
CS	PCT	Casillas, Omar, MV	50%
1B	PCT	Finan, Ryan, Aberdeen	.997
	PO	Pearce, Steve, Williamsport	651
	A	Pearce, Steve, Williamsport	58
	E	Ori, Mark, Tri-City	9
		Pearce, Steve, Williamsport	9
	DP	Pearce, Steve, Williamsport	65
2B	PCT	King, Eric, Tri-City	.983
	PO	Corona, Reegie, SI	157
	A	Corona, Reegie, SI	205
	E	Fornasiere, Matt, MV	13
	DP	Corona, Reegie, Staten Island	49
3B	PCT	Thompson, Michael, Tri-City	.959
	PO	Costanzo, Mike, Batavia	52
	A	Costanzo, Mike, Batavia	150
	E	Costanzo, Mike, Batavia	21
	DP	Costanzo, Mike, Batavia	15
		Thompson, Michael, Tri-City	15
SS	PCT	Manzella, Tommy, Tri-City	.968
	PO	Hollimon, Michael, Oneonta	112
	A	Hollimon, Michael, Oneonta	209
	E	Nunez, Eduardo, Staten Island	28
	DP	Nunez, Eduardo, Staten Island	46
OF	PCT	Cooper, James, SI	1.000
		Gardner, Brett, SI	1.000
	PO	Plasencia, Francisco, Ver.	181
	A	Williams, Julian, Batavia	10
	E	Daniel, Mike, Vermont	7
	DP	Williams, Julian, Batavia	4

NORTHWEST LEAGUE

SHORT-SEASON CLASS A

BY WILL KIMMEY

The short-season Northwest League featured one of the most exciting pennant races in recent memory in 2005, with five of the eight teams within one game of first place two days before the regular season ended.

Vancouver won the Western Division by a game over Salem-Keizer in a battle of veteran teams with plenty of college seniors and players repeating the league. Spokane won the Eastern Division by a game over Tri-City, but that race played like the 2005 National League West with every team finishing below .500.

BILL MITCHELL

Taylor Teagarden

"It's just like our parent club," Yakima manager Jay Gainer said. "Our whole division was this way from the first week."

That should have left an easily predictable final series, but the playoffs proved equally exciting and also came down to the final day as Spokane rallied to win the final two games of the best-of-five series to capture the title. DH Jonathan Higashi went 3-for-3 with three RBIs in the final game of the championship series, an 8-3 Spokane victory, while righthander Kellan McConnell earned the win on the mound by allowing two runs on six hits over six innings.

It marked the second NWL championship for Spokane in three years, its third since 1999 and seventh overall. The Indians, 37-39 in the regular-season, became the second team in NWL history to win the championship despite a sub-.500 record. Salem pulled off the feat in 1982 by beating Medford, which like Vancouver served as an Athletics affiliate.

Spokane showed few predictors of this kind of success during the regular season. The Indians lost nine straight games at one point and also lost two of their most productive hitters— Steve Murphy and Lizahio Baez—to injury with two weeks remaining. The club had to win five of its last six games just to reach the postseason.

Murphy, a Kansas State product, batted .306-9-37 and ranked second in the NWL with 23 doubles and a .533 slugging percentage to win MVP honors.

"What a great 14th-round draft pick," Gideon said. "Everything's under control. He handles lefthanders well, has pop, can hit the ball the other way with pop."

Maybe the presence of catcher Taylor Teagarden, who had two hits and an RBI in the fifth game, foreshadowed the championship. The third-round pick out of Texas already had won one title during the year after helping his Longhorns to victory in the College World Series back in June.

Teagarden, who batted .281-7-16 and emerged as Spokane's No. 3 hitter after arriving late, proved one of the few elite prospects to find success in the NWL. And he slumped initially, notching only one hit in his first 20 at-bats before hitting .342 the rest of the way. "That 1-for-20, it wasn't a slump, it was taking two months off after college," manager Greg Riddoch said.

"The talent, position player-wise or prospect-wise, is below where it usually is," Tri-City manager Ron Gideon said. "It was a very weird year. You look at our division, where an under .500 team won it. The other division has better records, but older teams are leading it. Maybe it's late bloomers. Hopefully, that's what it is."

Pitching proved a dominant theme as Tri-City's Shane Lindsay rocketed to the top of the league's prospect list after ranking first in strikeouts, second in wins and third in ERA while showcasing a fastball that reached 97 mph and a power knuckle-curve. His dominance reminded some managers of Felix Hernandez' NWL debut in 2003. Lindsay did show the same polish as Hernandez, though his raw stats (6-1, 1.89 with 107 strikeouts in 67 innings) proved better than those of King Felix (7-2, 2.29 with 73 strikeouts in 55 innings).

"He was by far the most dominant pitcher in the league," Boise manager Trey Forkerway said. "He has an above-average fastball, and usually against us he doesn't have to use anything but the fastball. It was so live and our guys weren't really ready for it."

TOP 20 PROSPECTS

1. Shane Lindsay, rhp, Tri-City (Rockies)
2. Donald Veal, lhp, Boise (Cubs)
3. Taylor Teagarden, c, Spokane (Rangers)
4. Nick Hundley, c, Eugene (Padres)
5. Pablo Sandoval, 3b, Salem-Keizer (Giants)
6. Luis Valbuena, 2b, Everett (Mariners)
7. Dan Griffin, rhp, Salem-Keizer (Giants)
8. John Mayberry Jr, of, Spokane (Rangers)
9. Ben Copeland, of, Salem-Keizer (Giants)
10. Chase Headley, 3b, Eugene (Padres)
11. Jimmy Shull, rhp, Vancouver (Athletics)
12. Michael Mooney, of, Salem-Keizer (Giants)
13. Michael Saunders, of, Everett (Mariners)
14. Steve Murphy, of, Spokane (Rangers)
15. Edgar Guaramato, rhp, Everett (Mariners)
16. Zach Simons, rhp, Tri-City (Rockies)
17. Stephen Kahn, rhp, Everett (Mariners)
18. Jason Ray, rhp, Vancouver (Athletics)
19. Justin Sellers, ss, Vancouver (Athletics)
20. Mark Reed, c, Boise (Cubs)

STANDINGS

Page	EAST	W	L	PCT	GB	Manager	Attendance	Average	Last Penn.
251	Spokane Indians (Rangers)	37	39	.487	—	Greg Riddoch	180,084	4,739	2005
112	Tri-City Dust Devils (Rockies)	36	40	.474	1	Ron Gideon	63,173	1,662	None
82	Boise Hawks (Cubs)	34	42	.447	3	Trey Forkerway	109,746	2,888	2004
51	Yakima Bears (Diamondbacks)	30	46	.395	7	Jay Gainer	60,150	1,582	2000
Page	**WEST**	**W**	**L**	**PCT**	**GB**	**Manager**	**Attendance**	**Average**	**Last Penn.**
193	Vancouver Canadians (Athletics)	46	30	.605	—	Juan Navarrette	124,708	3,370	None
229	Salem-Keizer Volcanoes (Giants)	45	31	.592	1	Steve Decker	108,413	2,852	2001
237	Everett AquaSox (Mariners)	42	34	.553	4	Pedro Grifol	108,884	2,865	1985
222	Eugene Emeralds (Padres)	34	42	.447	12	Roy Howell	124,512	3,276	1980

PLAYOFFS: Spokane defeated Vancouver 3-2 in best-of-5 series.

NOTE: Teams' individual batting and pitching statistics can be found on page indicated in lefthand column.

2005 NORTHWEST LEAGUE STATISTICS

CLUB BATTING

	AVG	G	AB	R	H	2B	2B	HR	BB	SO	SB
Salem-Keizer	.291	76	2701	397	786	130	26	43	238	537	57
Everett	.264	76	2624	418	692	149	23	71	277	653	89
Boise	.260	76	2606	330	678	123	8	36	179	547	76
Spokane	.254	76	2588	380	658	141	25	72	251	655	65
Yakima	.252	76	2626	315	661	149	20	46	204	619	50
Vancouver	.252	76	2587	344	653	134	10	35	276	581	72
Tri-City	.251	76	2580	349	647	134	18	39	279	661	44
Eugene	.238	76	2560	320	609	102	23	40	279	676	57

CLUB PITCHING

	ERA	G	CG	SHO	SV	IP	H	R	ER	BB	SO
Vancouver	3.00	76	0	3	28	688	568	268	229	224	643
Salem-Keizer	3.66	76	0	5	27	683	641	324	278	235	678
Tri-City	3.69	76	0	5	23	674	633	332	276	239	572
Eugene	3.78	76	0	0	21	673	711	361	283	182	577
Yakima	4.09	76	1	2	15	681	712	399	310	287	653
Spokane	4.17	76	0	2	18	676	718	379	313	214	605
Everett	4.32	76	0	6	21	681	694	375	327	278	604
Boise	4.61	76	0	4	17	675	707	416	346	324	597

CLUB FIELDING

	PCT	PO	A	E	DP
Salem-Keizer	.974	2049	765	76	63
Everett	.971	2042	884	88	80
Tri-City	.970	2021	805	87	60
Vancouver	.969	2064	798	91	57
Eugene	.964	2019	805	106	52
Yakima	.962	2044	825	113	51
Spokane	.962	2029	812	112	49
Boise	.960	2026	858	120	72

INDIVIDUAL BATTING LEADERS

(Minimum 205 Plate Appearances)

	AVG	G	AB	R	H	2B	3B	HR	RBI	BB	SO	SB
Thompson, Will, Salem-Keizer	.384	48	185	25	71	12	1	2	35	23	22	0
Mooney, Mike, Salem-Keizer	.342	73	304	57	104	20	9	5	29	20	64	13
Sandoval, Pablo, Salem-Keizer	.330	75	294	46	97	15	2	3	50	21	33	2
Minicozzi, Mark, Salem-Keizer	.321	70	243	42	78	14	3	2	36	35	41	4
Eastley, Reed, Everett	.318	55	201	29	64	13	2	4	28	37	42	8
Becktel, Travis, Tri-City	.314	68	255	50	80	17	4	4	27	37	57	5
Paulk, Michael, Tri-City	.312	68	253	32	79	17	2	4	45	37	45	1
Murphy, Steve, Spokane	.306	62	255	45	78	23	4	9	37	20	71	13
Van Kooten, Jason, Tri-City	.299	64	251	34	75	14	2	5	36	14	57	2
Hendricks, Trey, Yakima	.296	76	301	33	89	16	2	8	42	25	46	2

INDIVIDUAL PITCHING LEADERS

(Minimum 61 Innings)

	W	L	ERA	G	GS	CG	SV	IP	H	R	ER	BB	SO
Madsen, Mike, Vancouver	6	1	1.69	15	12	0	0	80	56	21	15	14	68
Carter, Brent, Eugene	4	2	1.88	13	13	0	0	72	58	24	15	7	66
Lindsay, Shane, Tri-City	6	1	1.89	13	13	0	0	67	37	21	14	34	107
Katz, Ethan, Tri-City	4	1	2.35	21	7	0	0	61	55	18	16	11	49
McKae, Dave, Salem-Keizer	3	2	2.42	19	4	0	3	67	55	27	18	17	83
Shull, Jimmy, Vancouver	4	3	2.47	14	13	0	0	73	65	25	20	10	81
Mathis, Doug, Spokane	4	7	2.68	17	16	0	0	84	78	33	25	17	78
Romo, Sergio, Salem-Keizer	7	1	2.75	15	14	0	0	69	70	24	21	9	65
Coffman, Broc, Spokane	2	2	2.99	17	11	0	1	69	62	28	23	26	63
Piekarz, Joe, Vancouver	3	3	3.38	15	12	0	0	77	67	32	29	24	59

ALL-STAR TEAM

C—Josh Ford, Yakima. **1B**—Will Thompson, Salem-Keizer. **2B**—Luis Valbuena, Everett. **3B**—Pablo Sandoval, Salem-Keizer. **SS**—German Duran, Spokane. **OF**—Travis Becktel, Tri-City; Mike Mooney, Salem-Keizer; Steve Murphy, Spokane. DH—Lizahio Baez, Spokane. **LHP**—Darin Downs, Boise. **RHP**—Mike Madsen, Vancouver. **LHRP**—Brad Kilby, Vancouver. **RHRP**—Brian Anderson, Salem-Keizer.

Most Valuable Player: Steve Murphy, Spokane. **Manager of the Year:** Steve Decker, Salem-Keizer.

DEPARTMENT LEADERS

BATTING

G	Hendricks, Trey, Yakima	76
AB	Mooney, Mike, Salem-Keizer	304
R	Mooney, Mike, Salem-Keizer	57
H	Mooney, Mike, Salem-Keizer	104
TB	Mooney, Mike, Salem-Keizer	157
XBH	Murphy, Steve, Spokane	36
2B	Bruce, Derek, Yakima	28
3B	Mooney, Mike, Salem-Keizer	9
HR	Thon, Freddie, Spokane	12
	Valbuena, Luis, Everett	12
RBI	Valbuena, Luis, Everett	51
SH	Gregg, Davy, Boise	11
SF	Downing, Ramon, Yakima	5
BB	Three tied at	37
IBB	Thon, Freddie, Spokane	4
HBP	Cuadrado, Phil, Tri-City	20
SO	Strop, Pedro, Tri-City	86
SB	Gregg, Davy, Boise	36
CS	Gregg, Davy, Boise	12
GIDP	Three tied at	9
OBP	Thompson, Will, Salem-Keizer	.452
SLG	Tucker, J.B., Everett	.580

PITCHING

G	Madden, John, Eugene	38
GS	Three tied at	16
CG	Kemlo, Chris, Yakima	1
SHO	None	
GF	Delgado, George, Tri-City	29
SV	Anderson, Brian, Salem-Keizer	19
W	Romo, Sergio, Salem-Keizer	7
L	Rocha, Angel, Yakima	8
IP	Kemlo, Chris, Yakima	89
H	Kemlo, Chris, Yakima	116
R	Kemlo, Chris, Yakima	65
ER	McConnell, Kellan, Spokane	51
HR	Wilding, Taylor, Salem-Keizer	12
HBP	Delabar, Steve, Eugene	15
BB	Rocha, Angel, Yakima	53
SO	Lindsay, Shane, Tri-City	107
WP	Rocha, Angel, Yakima	17
BK	Atkins, Mitch, Boise	4

FIELDING

C	PCT	Recker, Anthony, Vancouver	.995
	PO	Recker, Anthony, Vancouver	343
	A	Del Campo, Manny, Yakima	38
	E	Hundley, Nick, Eugene	7
		Reed, Mark, Boise	7
	DP	Crabtree, Ben, Spokane	4
	DP	Kirby, Brian, Tri-City	4
	PB	Hundley, Nick, Eugene	14
	CS PCT	Tucker, J.B., Everett	48%
1B	PCT	Thompson, Will, S-K	.998
	PO	Jones, Daryl, Eugene	601
	A	Hendricks, Trey, Yakima	56
	E	Jones, Daryl, Eugene	16
	DP	Flaig, Jeff, Everett	57
2B	PCT	Valbuena, Luis, Everett	.978
	PO	Valbuena, Luis, Everett	149
	A	Valbuena, Luis, Everett	209
	E	Santana, Julio, Spokane	11
	DP	Valbuena, Luis, Everett	52
3B	PCT	Prettyman, Ron, Everett	.944
	PO	Cuadrado, Phil, Tri-City	48
	A	Baisley, Jeff, Vancouver	125
	E	Cuadrado, Phil, Tri-City	14
	DP	Cuadrado, Phil, Tri-City	10
		Puello, Elvin, Boise	10
SS	PCT	Hudson, Robbie, Everett	.963
	PO	Hudson, Robbie, Everett	97
	A	Hudson, Robbie, Everett	190
	E	Duran, German, Spokane	18
	DP	Hudson, Robbie, Everett	42
OF	PCT	Frey, Chris, Tri-City	.994
	PO	Frey, Chris, Tri-City	147
	A	Mooney, Mike, Salem-Keizer	11
	E	Septimo, Leyson, Yakima	7
	DP	Rahl, Chris, Yakima	4

APPALACHIAN LEAGUE

ROOKIE

BY MATT EDDY

Danville and Elizabethton dominated the Appalachian League from start to finish in 2005, posting the best records in Organized Baseball. Danville went 47-20 (.701) to win the Eastern Division by 12 games. Elizabethton was even more dominant, going 48-19 (.716) to win the West by 17½ games.

MIKE JANES

Eric Campbell

Manager Ray Smith guided Elizabethton to its seventh Appy League title in its 31 years as a Twins affiliate, vanquishing Danville in a best-of-three playoff, two games to one. For his efforts, Smith was named manager of the year, the fifth time he's earned the distinction.

Because of increasingly stricter visa rules in the aftermath of Sept. 11, U.S.-based rookie leagues featured more college and second-year players. Danville and Elizabethton both fielded older rosters, placing the league's younger clubs at a severe competitive disadvantage.

Contributions from 2005 college draftees helped fuel the Twins attack, though many of the club's top prospects were promoted before the playoffs began. One who remained might have been the best. Lefthander Ryan Mullins, a third-round pick out of Vanderbilt, went 3-0, 2.18 with 60 strikeouts and 13 walks in 54 innings. Mullins saved his best effort for last, racking up 13 strikeouts in five innings in the playoff opener, which the Twins won 5-4.

Mullins outdueled Danville ace Jairo Cuevas, the league's pitcher of the year. Cuevas was second in the league in wins (6) and ERA (1.95) and fifth in strikeouts (69).

The Braves won Game Two 15-2, before succumbing to Elizabethton in Game Three, again by a 5-4 score. In both Elizabethton wins, the Twins scored the winning runs in the eighth inning, with catcher Sean Richardson providing the series-winning hit in the third game. Tim Lahey, a converted catcher who led the Appy League in saves, closed out both Twins wins.

Third baseman Eric Campbell and catcher Max Ramirez, both second-year players, were Danville's top hitters all season and selected the league's co-players of the year. Campbell led the league in several key categories: home runs (18), RBIs (64), runs (77), doubles (26), slugging percentage (.634) and extra-base hits (46). He was also 15-of-19 in stolen bases.

Ramirez led the Appy League in hitting most of the season before Bluefield's Rene Aqueron, 23, accumulated sufficient plate appearances to qualify for the batting title. He hit .405, becoming the only player in the affiliated minor leagues to crack the .400 barrier in 2005. Ramirez finished second at .347 and led the league with 83 hits. His performance was more impressive considering he was learning a new position, converting from third base.

The Twins paced the league with a 3.30 ERA, but they had shed four key members of their pitching staff by the time the playoffs rolled around. Lefthander Alexander Smit, a third-year player who struck out a league-best 86 batters in 46 relief innings while going 6-1, 1.97, left for his annual spot on the Dutch national team roster.

Righthanders Matt Garza (first round), Kevin Slowey (second round) were draft picks that pitched briefly for Elizabethton and dominated before being promoted.

Bluefield catcher Brandon Snyder (13th overall to the Orioles) and Johnson City outfielder Colby Rasmus (28th to the Cardinals) were the highest-drafted players from the 2005 high school ranks to play in the league and impressed managers with their tools and professional approaches. They ranked as the league's Nos. 1 and 2 prospects in a Baseball America survey of managers.

TOP 20 PROSPECTS

1. Brandon Snyder, c/3b, Bluefield (Orioles)
2. Colby Rasmus, of, Johnson City (Cardinals)
3. Eric Campbell, 3b, Danville (Braves)
4. Brandon Erbe, rhp, Bluefield (Orioles)
5. Max Ramirez, c, Danville (Braves)
6. Jesse Litsch, rhp, Pulaski (Blue Jays)
7. Juan Portes, 2b/of, Elizabethton (Twins)
8. Josh Flores, of, Greeneville (Astros)
9. Aaron Cunningham, of, Bristol (White Sox)
10. Bryan Anderson, c, Johnson City (Cardinals)
11. Matt Walker, rhp, Princeton (Devil Rays)
12. John Drennen, of, Burlington (Indians)
13. Jairo Cuevas, rhp, Danville (Braves)
14. Eli Iorg, of, Greeneville (Astros)
15. John Matulia, of, Princeton (Devil Rays)
16. Koby Clemens, 3b, Greeneville (Astros)
17. Alexander Smit, lhp, Elizabethton (Twins)
18. Ryan Mullins, lhp, Elizabethton (Twins)
19. Ryan Mitchell, rhp, Greeneville (Astros)
20. Tyler Herron, rhp, Johnson City (Cardinals)

STANDINGS

Page	EAST	W	L	PCT	GB	Manager(s)	Attendance	Average	Last Penn.
59	Danville Braves	47	20	.701	—	Paul Runge	37,064	1,090	None
245	Princeton Devil Rays	34	31	.523	12	Jamie Nelson	26,477	945	1994
259	Pulaski Blue Jays	34	33	.507	13	Dave Pano	24,770	750	None
67	Bluefield Orioles	31	36	.463	16	Jesus Alfaro	27,420	945	2001
106	Burlington Indians	25	43	.368	22½	Sean McNally/Lee May Jr.	37,673	1,215	1993
Page	**WEST**	**W**	**L**	**PCT**	**GB**	**Manager**	**Attendance**	**Average**	**Last Penn.**
169	Elizabethton Twins	48	19	.716	—	Ray Smith	25,949	894	2005
90	Bristol White Sox	30	36	.455	17½	Jerry Hairston	20,868	673	2002
135	Greeneville Astros	29	37	.439	18½	Russ Nixon	49,963	1,611	2004
216	Johnson City Cardinals	28	39	.418	20	Tommy Kidwell	24,338	760	1976
178	Kingsport Mets	28	40	.412	20½	Jesse Levis	36,962	1,192	1995

PLAYOFFS: Elizabethton defeated Danville 2-1 in best-of-3 series.

NOTE: Teams' individual batting and pitching statistics can be found on page indicated in lefthand column.

2005 APPALACHIAN LEAGUE STATISTICS

CLUB BATTING

	AVG	G	AB	R	H	2B	2B	HR	BB	SO	SB
Danville	.284	67	2322	427	659	149	22	72	217	520	95
Elizabethton	.280	67	2228	353	624	105	13	62	192	460	46
Princeton	.270	65	2174	347	586	117	10	54	244	559	76
Bluefield	.266	67	2264	368	603	122	15	64	189	566	81
Pulaski	.261	67	2237	354	584	130	20	56	259	563	46
Greeneville	.258	66	2271	342	586	98	28	45	186	546	81
Johnson City	.257	67	2167	351	557	117	20	53	203	514	82
Bristol	.255	66	2255	318	574	137	12	36	199	577	49
Kingsport	.254	68	2295	339	584	114	9	47	193	512	77
Burlington	.227	68	2207	297	502	93	15	43	244	559	58

CLUB PITCHING

	ERA	G	CG	SHO	SV	IP	H	R	ER	BB	SO
Elizabethton	3.30	67	2	8	24	567	473	246	208	170	612
Danville	3.45	67	0	4	22	601	526	284	230	230	514
Princeton	4.00	65	1	3	17	559	580	326	248	190	551
Pulaski	4.30	67	0	2	14	586	634	369	280	189	540
Bristol	4.51	66	0	3	13	574	610	350	288	190	516
Burlington	4.52	68	2	3	5	570	603	353	286	172	492
Kingsport	4.68	68	2	1	13	584	634	378	304	219	456
Bluefield	4.73	67	0	3	17	565	573	367	297	274	641
Greeneville	4.86	66	0	5	14	569	583	364	307	236	553
Johnson City	5.97	67	1	1	18	560	643	459	371	256	501

CLUB FIELDING

	PCT	PO	A	E	DP
Danville	.970	1802	715	78	67
Elizabethton	.968	1700	649	77	44
Pulaski	.961	1758	772	102	73
Burlington	.961	1709	713	99	74
Greeneville	.958	1706	647	103	43
Johnson City	957	1678	700	108	66
Princeton	953	1676	695	117	52
Bluefield	952	1694	615	116	52
Bristol	952	1723	739	123	51
Kingsport	.951	1752	718	127	57

INDIVIDUAL BATTING LEADERS

(Minimum 184 Plate Appearances)

	AVG	G	AB	R	H	2B	3B	HR	RBI	BB	SO	SB
Aqueron, Rene, Bluefield	.405	56	163	35	66	15	1	4	32	17	24	9
Ramirez, Max, Danville	.347	63	239	45	83	19	0	8	47	31	41	1
Flores, Josh, Greeneville	.335	59	248	49	83	12	5	8	25	16	57	20
Cunningham, Chris, Princeton	.329	59	222	42	73	13	1	7	40	34	55	6
Davis, Quentin, Danville	.323	49	201	44	65	9	2	3	36	14	26	8
Cunningham, Aaron, Bristol	.315	56	222	41	70	10	2	5	25	16	45	6
Acosta, Christian, Bristol	.314	65	220	40	69	20	0	5	41	29	48	0
Anderson, Matt, Kingsport	.314	47	169	27	53	8	0	5	30	15	22	0
Campbell, Eric, Danville	.313	66	262	77	82	26	2	18	64	28	64	15
Welker, Kris, Bristol	.303	54	198	31	60	16	0	3	29	17	34	2

INDIVIDUAL PITCHING LEADERS

(Minimum 54 Innings)

	W	L	ERA	G	GS	CG	SV	IP	H	R	ER	BB	SO
Hawes, Adam, Elizabethton	4	0	1.53	14	9	1	1	59	38	13	10	16	68
Cuevas, Jairo, Danville	6	1	1.95	12	10	0	0	55	35	20	12	22	69
Litsch, Jesse, Pulaski	5	1	2.74	11	11	0	0	66	51	22	20	10	67
Blackford, Todd, Danville	5	3	3.17	12	12	0	0	60	48	24	21	22	30
Perez, Wilfrido, Bluefield	3	4	3.26	12	12	0	0	58	54	30	21	27	75
Valdez, Luis, Burlington	3	6	3.54	13	13	1	0	61	64	31	24	12	59
Cayton, Jason, Princeton	3	2	3.65	12	11	0	0	57	62	32	23	16	55
Pino, Yohan, Elizabethton	9	2	3.72	12	12	1	0	68	68	31	28	13	64
Viola, Frank, Bristol	5	2	3.84	13	12	0	0	70	74	35	30	20	59
Simmons, Jeramy, Kingsport	1	5	4.26	13	12	0	0	57	58	39	27	15	47

ALL-STAR TEAM

C—Max Ramirez, Danville. **1B**—P.J. Hiser, Burlington. **2B**—Ovandy Suero, Danville. **3B**—Eric Campbell, Danville. **SS**—Stuart Musselwhite, Bluefield. **UT IF**—Matt Anderson, Kingsport. **OF**—Jacob Butler, Pulaski; Aaron Cunningham, Bristol; Chris Cunningham, Princeton. **UT OF**—Josh Flores, Greenville. **DH**—Christian Acosta, Bristol. **RHP**—Jairo Cuevas, Danville. **LHP**—Alexander Smit, Elizabethton. **RP**—Robert Findlay, Princeton.

Players of the Year: Eric Campbell, Danville; Max Ramirez, Danville. **Pitcher of the Year:** Jairo Cuevas, Danville. **Manager of the Year:** Ray Smith, Elizabethton.

DEPARTMENT LEADERS

BATTING

G	Campbell, Eric, Danville	66
AB	Campbell, Eric, Danville	262
R	Campbell, Eric, Danville	77
H	Flores, Josh, Greeneville	83
	Ramirez, Max, Danville	83
TB	Campbell, Eric, Danville	166
XBH	Campbell, Eric, Danville	46
2B	Campbell, Eric, Danville	26
3B	Suero, Ovandy, Danville	8
HR	Campbell, Eric, Danville	18
RBI	Campbell, Eric, Danville	64
SH	Arnold, Derrick, Danville	8
SF	Carter, Chuck, Johnson City	7
BB	Kalter, Zach, Pulaski	45
IBB	Three tied at	3
HBP	Cunningham, Aaron, Bristol	14
SO	De Leon, Epifanio, Princeton	75
SB	Suero, Ovandy, Danville	46
CS	Suero, Ovandy, Danville	11
GIDP	Moore, Caleb, Elizabethton	8
	Oliveros, Riky, Kingsport	8
OBP	Aqueron, Rene, Bluefield	.468
SLG	Campbell, Eric, Danville	.634

PITCHING

G	Fitzgerald, Kevin, Johnson City	26
	Lahey, Tim, Elizabethton	26
GS	Eight tied at	13
CG	Eight tied at	1
SHO	Four tied at	1
GF	Lahey, Tim, Elizabethton	26
SV	Findlay, Robert, Princeton	15
	Lahey, Tim, Elizabethton	15
W	Pino, Yohan, Elizabethton	9
L	Four tied at	7
IP	Viola, Frank, Bristol	70
H	Schmidt, Kyle, Bluefield	77
R	Gonzalez, Jose, Kingsport	49
ER	Frias, Jusef, Kingsport	43
HR	Wice, Joe, Pulaski	15
HBP	Frias, Jusef, Kingsport	11
BB	DeNaball, Fernando, Bluefield	38
SO	Smit, Alexander, Elizabethton	86
WP	Muro, Joseph, Princeton	11
	Spoone, Chorye, Bluefield	11
BK	Winn, Joseph, Bristol	4

FIELDING

C	PCT	Welker, Kris, Bristol	.993
	PO	Lagreid, Tom, Princeton	380
	A	Lagreid, Tom, Princeton	38
	E	Jaspe, Jonathan, Pulaski	7
		Lagreid, Tom, Princeton	7
	PB	Anderson, Bryan, Johnson City	16
	DP	McCraw, Sean, Kingsport	8
CS	PCT	Welker, Kris, Bristol	45%
1B	PCT	Morgan, Josh, Bristol	.995
	PO	Rodriguez, Manuel, Danville	542
	A	Rodriguez, Manuel, Danville	38
	E	Rodriguez, Manuel, Danville	9
	DP	Rodriguez, Manuel, Danville	49
2B	PCT	Arnal, Cristo, Burlington	.980
	PO	Arnal, Cristo, Burlington	84
	A	Portes, Juan, Elizabethton	126
	E	Swain, Michael, Bristol	11
	DP	Arnal, Cristo, Burlington	33
3B	PCT	Campbell, Eric, Danville	.938
	PO	Campbell, Eric, Danville	38
	A	Campbell, Eric, Danville	114
	E	Soto, Leance, Pulaski	24
	DP	Petrucci, Nick, Burlington	17
SS	PCT	Ortiz, Yancarlos, Elizabethton	.972
	PO	Arnold, Derrick, Danville	73
	A	Acosta, Leonardo, Bristol	160
	E	Johnson, Tim, Greeneville	21
	DP	Solano, Donovan, JC	32
OF	PCT	Butler, Jacob, Pulaski	1
	PO	Silva, Yohan, Danville	156
	A	Kalter, Zach, Pulaski	8
	E	De Leon, Epifanio, Princeton	8
	DP	Mateo, Jose, Kingsport	3
		Wells, Cory, Kingsport	3

PIONEER LEAGUE

ROOKIE

BY ALAN MATTHEWS

No matter what you call them, it's a good bet they'll be in contention in the postseason. The Provo Angels changed their name to the Orem Owlz before the 2005 season, but it didn't disrupt the franchise's recent run of success, as they beat the Helena Brewers two games to none to repeat as Pioneer League champions. The Owlz franchise has played for the PL title every year since 2000 when the team relocated from Helena to Provo.

Orem third baseman Dallas Morris tripled twice while righthanders Jose Arredondo and Kevin Lynch allowed just four hits to lead the visiting Owlz to a 3-2 victory over Helena in Game Two of the best-of-three championship series, following a 6-3 Orem win in Game One.

SPORTS ON FILM

Angel Salome

After hitting three triples during the regular season, Morris, who was drafted by the Angels in the 24th round in 2005 out of Louisiana-Lafayette, nearly equaled that total in one night with a pair of clutch, two-out triples, the second of which came in the top of the ninth inning, plating shortstop Hainley Statia to snap a 2-2 tie.

While Morris' theatrics highlighted Orem's victory, the Owlz' pitching paved the way to the playoffs. Orem won eight out of nine games in late August to surge past the Ogden Raptors and claim the second half Southern Division title, then defeated Ogden, which won the first half, two games to one in the semifinals.

"I think every one of our starting pitchers is a major league prospect and I don't think there's another team in the league that can say that," Orem manager Tom Kotchman said. "Good pitching beats good hitting every time . . . and we have the best pitching."

Orem's pitching staff surrendered eight runs in five postseason games and received a boost when righthanders Nick Adenhart and Ryan Aldridge joined Arredondo, Daniel Hawkins, Bobby Mosebach, Kelly Shearer and Stephen Marek late in the season after pitching in the Rookie-level Arizona League.

Adenhart was Baseball America's Youth Player of the Year as a 16-year-old in 2003, but had Tommy John surgery during his senior season at Williamsport (Md.) High in 2004. He returned in impressive fashion in 2005, climbing to Orem where he didn't allow an earned run in 12 innings, including six three-hit innings in Game Two against Ogden. The Raptors rallied for four runs in the eighth inning of that game to stave off elimination, but Hawkins held them to one hit in five innings as Orem won the series 9-1 in Game Three.

"It's a great experience and a fun time," Kotchman said. "Some of these kids came up to me and said they had never won anything in their lives. We're always low-keying everything, so when they won they were serious about their celebration. It got a little crazy. We could have made our own video, 'Owlz Gone Wild.'"

While Helena, which defeated Billings in the first round, fell short in the playoffs, it was the toast of the league, winning both halves of the Northern Division race. Brewers catcher Angel Salome was named the league's MVP, pacing the PL's most potent offense—Helena posted an eye-popping .309 team average. Salome, who was one of several Helena regulars promoted to low Class A in August, hit .415-8-50 but did not have enough plate appearances to qualify for the league batting title, won by Casper utility man Corey Wimberley.

STANDINGS: SPLIT SEASON

FIRST HALF					SECOND HALF				
NORTH	**W**	**L**	**PCT**	**GB**	**NORTH**	**W**	**L**	**PCT**	**GB**
Helena	24	14	.632	—	Helena	22	16	.579	—
Billings	23	15	.605	1	Missoula	21	17	.553	1
Great Falls	15	23	.395	9	Billings	20	18	.526	2
Missoula	13	25	.342	11	Great Falls	17	21	.447	5
SOUTH	**W**	**L**	**PCT**	**GB**	**SOUTH**	**W**	**L**	**PCT**	**GB**
Ogden	22	16	.579	—	Orem	20	18	.526	—
Casper	20	18	.526	2	Casper	18	20	.474	2
Orem	18	20	.474	4	Idaho Falls	17	21	.447	3
Idaho Falls	17	21	.447	5	Ogden	17	21	.447	3

PLAYOFFS—Semifinals: Helena defeated Billings 2-0 and Orem defeated Ogden 2-1 in best-of-3 series. **Final:** Orem defeated Helena 2-0 in best-of-3 series.

TOP 20 PROSPECTS

1. Jay Bruce, of, Billings (Reds)
2. Charlie Fermaint, of, Helena (Brewers)
3. Hainley Statia, ss, Orem (Angels)
4. Angel Salome, c, Helena (Brewers)
5. Francisco Hernandez, c, Great Falls (White Sox)
6. Stephen Marek, rhp, Orem (Angels)
7. Dexter Fowler, of, Casper (Rockies)
8. Chaz Roe, rhp, Casper (Rockies)
9. Jose Arredondo, rhp, Orem (Angels)
10. Will Inman, rhp, Helena (Brewers)
11. Greg Smith, lhp, Missoula (Diamondbacks)
12. Bobby Mosebach, rhp, Orem (Angels)
13. Juan Rivera, ss, Ogden (Dodgers)
14. Mark Trumbo, 1b, Orem (Angels)
15. Chris McConnell, ss, Idaho Falls (Royals)
16. Brandon Roberts, of, Billings (Reds)
17. Matt Gamel, 3b, Helena (Brewers)
18. Corey Wimberly, inf, Casper (Rockies)
19. Brandon Allen, 1b, Great Falls (White Sox)
20. Ivan DeJesus Jr., ss, Ogden (Dodgers)

STANDINGS: OVERALL

Page	Team	W	L	PCT	GB	Manager	Attendance	Average	Last Penn.
162	Helena Brewers (Brewers)	46	30	.605	—	Eddie Sedar	40,141	1,084	1984
97	Billings Mustangs (Reds)	43	33	.566	3	Rick Burleson	88,702	2,463	2001
155	Ogden Raptors (Dodgers)	39	37	.513	7	Juan Bustabad	131,371	3,457	None
113	Casper Rockies (Rockies)	38	38	.500	8	P.J. Carey	50,087	1,353	None
148	Orem Owlz (Angels)	38	38	.500	8	Tom Kotchman	76,784	2,075	2005
141	Idaho Falls Chukars (Royals)	34	42	.447	12	Brian Rupp	65,313	1,718	2000
52	Missoula Osprey (Diamondbacks)	34	42	.447	12	Jim Presley	67,922	1,787	1999
89	Great Falls White Sox (White Sox)	32	44	.421	14	John Orton	96,012	2,526	2002

NOTE: Teams' individual batting and pitching statistics can be found on page indicated in lefthand column.

2005 PIONEER LEAGUE STATISTICS

CLUB BATTING

	AVG	G	AB	R	H	2B	2B	HR	BB	SO	SB
Helena	.309	76	2752	531	851	167	18	83	300	567	112
Idaho Falls	.286	76	2611	482	748	137	31	64	334	612	70
Casper	.279	76	2620	406	731	136	19	57	256	680	124
Ogden	.274	76	2647	440	726	139	8	74	259	544	75
Great Falls	.271	76	2608	387	708	151	26	45	256	602	117
Orem	.268	76	2672	411	715	146	27	60	238	725	81
Missoula	.266	76	2668	435	711	161	20	53	244	633	74
Billings	.258	76	2560	427	661	136	28	52	330	720	107

CLUB PITCHING

	ERA	G	CG	SHO	SV	IP	H	R	ER	BB	SO
Orem	4.16	76	0	5	13	679	706	382	314	265	599
Helena	4.30	76	0	4	24	680	700	401	325	231	651
Billings	4.42	76	0	3	25	664	697	387	326	264	598
Great Falls	4.56	76	0	2	14	673	708	441	341	279	628
Ogden	4.89	76	2	3	16	668	715	432	362	305	669
Casper	5.05	76	0	4	22	672	742	475	377	291	624
Missoula	5.59	76	0	2	20	677	761	499	421	350	688
Idaho Falls	5.68	76	0	1	19	664	822	502	419	232	626

CLUB FIELDING

	PCT	PO	A	E	DP
Orem	.964	2037	914	110	74
Billings	.962	1993	829	110	82
Ogden	.962	2004	863	114	69
Missoula	.959	2032	816	122	73
Helena	.958	2039	808	126	51
Idaho Falls	.957	1993	825	127	68
Casper	.955	2015	914	139	82
Great Falls	.947	2018	925	165	80

INDIVIDUAL BATTING LEADERS

(Minimum 205 Plate Appearances)

	AVG	G	AB	R	H	2B	3B	HR	RBI	BB	SO	SB
Wimberly, Corey, Casper	.381	67	281	58	107	10	0	1	22	18	27	36
Holmberg, Kenny, Helena	.372	59	207	40	77	16	0	12	51	29	34	2
Hernandez, Francisco, Great Falls	.349	58	212	37	74	19	0	6	34	19	25	0
Crew, Ryan, Helena	.346	58	217	45	75	19	1	4	29	22	21	5
Sutherland, David, Ogden	.336	66	247	44	83	13	2	4	47	34	27	4
Ryal, Rusty, Missoula	.333	72	294	59	98	22	4	6	46	14	47	11
McConnell, Chris, Idaho Falls	.331	70	275	56	91	17	8	6	39	31	34	7
Gamel, Mat, Helena	.327	50	199	34	65	15	2	5	37	12	49	7
Roberts, Brandon, Billings	.318	68	274	50	87	9	6	4	36	24	44	32
Godwin, Adam, Ogden	.310	55	197	38	61	12	1	1	21	12	32	12

INDIVIDUAL PITCHING LEADERS

(Minimum 61 Innings)

	W	L	ERA	G	GS	CG	SV	IP	H	R	ER	BB	SO
Leach, Brent, Ogden	5	3	2.43	14	13	1	0	67	53	21	18	29	77
Shearer, Kelly, Orem	2	4	3.62	15	13	0	0	65	60	34	26	23	45
Johnson, Alan, Casper	3	2	3.97	15	15	0	0	79	90	44	35	24	78
Moviel, Paul, Great Falls	4	1	4.04	15	15	0	0	78	89	40	35	20	72
Smith, Greg, Missoula	8	5	4.15	16	14	0	0	82	69	40	38	18	100
Arredondo, Jose, Orem	5	0	4.19	15	13	0	0	69	76	34	32	20	60
Wade, Cory, Ogden	2	3	4.35	16	11	1	0	72	81	42	35	19	60
Perez, Carlos, Great Falls	4	6	4.38	16	10	0	0	62	67	39	30	22	40
Marek, Stephen, Orem	1	3	4.50	15	14	0	0	66	74	37	33	25	55
Romanczuk, Mark, Missoula	4	5	4.55	13	13	0	0	61	70	37	31	17	59

ALL-STAR TEAM

C—Angel Salome, Helena. **1B—**David Sutherland, Ogden. **2B—**Corey Wimberly, Casper. **3B—**Russ Mitchell, Ogden. **SS—**Chris McConnell, Idaho Falls. **OF—**Charlie Fermaint, Helena; Brandon Roberts, Billings; Ethien Santana, Idaho Falls. **DH—**Francisco Hernandez, Great Falls. **RHP—**Chaz Roe, Casper. **LHP—**Greg Smith, Missoula. **RP—**Andrew Johnston, Casper.

Most Valuable Player: Angel Salome, Helena. **Most Valuable Pitcher:** Greg Smith, Missoula. **Manager of the Year:** P.J. Carey, Casper.

DEPARTMENT LEADERS

BATTING

G	Ryal, Rusty, Missoula	72
AB	Trumbo, Mark, Orem	299
R	Ryal, Rusty, Missoula	59
H	Wimberly, Corey, Casper	107
TB	Ryal, Rusty, Missoula	146
XBH	Morris, Dallas, Orem	35
2B	Morris, Dallas, Orem	23
	Trumbo, Mark, Orem	23
3B	McConnell, Chris, Idaho Falls	8
HR	Cook, Chris, Casper	15
RBI	Mitchell, Russ, Ogden	54
SH	McConnell, Chris, Idaho Falls	7
SF	Cook, Chris, Casper	9
BB	Byrne, Bryan, Missoula	42
IBB	Tribble, Matt, Great Falls	5
HBP	Ryal, Rusty, Missoula	15
SO	Garner, Cole, Casper	105
SB	Tartaglia, Evan, Great Falls	38
CS	Santana, Ethien, Idaho Falls	17
GIDP	Mitchell, Russ, Ogden	14
OBP	Holmberg, Kenny, Helena	.450
SLG	Holmberg, Kenny, Helena	.623

PITCHING

G	Three tied at	30
GS	Four tied at	15
CG	Leach, Brent, Ogden	1
	Wade, Cory, Ogden	1
SHO	None	
GF	Johnston, Andrew, Casper	29
SV	Johnston, Andrew, Casper	18
W	Smith, Greg, Missoula	8
L	Novoa, Yunior, Great Falls	7
	Wooley, Robert, Helena	7
IP	Smith, Greg, Missoula	82
H	Morrison, Tyler, Helena	91
R	Novoa, Yunior, Great Falls	58
ER	Rodriguez, Aneury, Casper	52
HR	Harkcom, Cody, Idaho Falls	12
	Wade, Cory, Ogden	12
HBP	Alvarez, Mario, Ogden	12
BB	Neighborgall, Jason, Missoula	45
SO	Smith, Greg, Missoula	100
WP	Neighborgall, Jason, Missoula	23
BK	Arias, Marlon, Ogden	4
	Cupps, Anthony, Missoula	4

FIELDING

C	PCT	Martinez, Brett, Orem	.993
	PO	Martinez, Brett, Orem	343
	A	Martinez, Brett, Orem	73
	E	Salome, Angel, Helena	11
	DP	Thibault, Kiel, Idaho Falls	7
	PB	DeCarlo, Mike, Missoula	14
		Thibault, Kiel, Idaho Falls	14
	CS PCT	Martinez, Brett, Orem	52%
1B	PCT	Mummy, Ben, Billings	.997
	PO	Trumbo, Mark, Orem	706
	A	Allen, Brandon, Great Falls	41
	E	Allen, Brandon, Great Falls	13
	DP	Trumbo, Mark, Orem	57
2B	PCT	De Jesus, Michael, Billings	.978
	PO	Boyer, Billy, Orem	127
	A	Guest, Garrett, Great Falls	190
	E	Young, Eric, Casper	22
	DP	Guest, Garrett, Great Falls	49
3B	PCT	Ryal, Rusty, Missoula	.953
	PO	Mitchell, Russ, Ogden	52
	A	Morris, Dallas, Orem	153
	E	Johnson, Brandon, Great Falls	35
	DP	Ryal, Rusty, Missoula	13
SS	PCT	Statia, Hainley, Orem	.959
	PO	Statia, Hainley, Orem	116
	A	Statia, Hainley, Orem	238
	E	Ciriaco, Pedro, Missoula	34
	DP	Statia, Hainley, Orem	43
OF	PCT	Tartaglia, Evan, Great Falls	.991
	PO	Roberts, Brandon, Billings	113
	A	Richmond, B.J., Ogden	10
	E	Tribble, Matt, Great Falls	9
	DP	Richmond, B.J., Ogden	3

ARIZONA LEAGUE

ROOKIE

BY ALLAN SIMPSON

Major League Baseball was contemplating significant changes to the draft and the entry level of the minor leagues in an effort to save money on scouting and player development.

Chief among the proposals presented to owners was the elimination of the two complex leagues: the Gulf Coast League, which began operations in 1964, and the Arizona League, which played its first season in 1988. Twenty-one of the 30 big league teams operated clubs in those leagues in 2005.

BILL MITCHELL
Lorenzo Cain

While the proposal to downsize had gained the endorsement of general managers and the support of a majority of farm and scouting directors, a vote by owners in August to enact legislation was tabled. The proposal was expected to come to a formal vote of owners in November.

If the league becomes extinct in 2006, the Giants will go into the history books as the league's last champion. The Giants won their second straight Arizona League title in 2005, winning both half-season titles. That precluded the need for a championship game.

Like 2004, the Giants won the championship with an older roster. Several clubs fielded teams with mostly teenage talent, but the Giants featured a pitching staff with 20-somethings righthanders T.J. Gornati (6-0, 1.30), 24; Robert Grace (6-1, 2.85), 22; and Jordan Thomson (2-0, 2.77 and league-high seven saves), 23. Outfielder Antoan Richardson, 21, hit .321 and led the league in on-base percentage (.465) and stolen bases (40) to lead the team offensively.

But youth was still served on the Giants as the team's three youngest players—righthanders Waldis Joaquin and Shairon Martis, and shortstop Sharlon Schoop—were the three best prospects on the roster. All played the 2005 season at age 18. Schoop and Martis grew up together in Curacao—one of nine nations represented on the league's most culturally diverse roster.

Joaquin, along with Athletics righthander Craig Italiano, was one of two pitchers in the league whose fastballs reached 98 mph. A Dominican getting his first exposure to pitching in the U.S., Joaquin was used in a piggyback role by the Giants, alternating between starting and relieving. He was brilliant in his final outing of the year, earning his only save while touching 98 mph eight times and striking out eight of the 10 batters he faced.

"He's just learning to pitch," Giants manager Bert Hunter said. "But he's got a very live arm and the ball jumps out of his hand."

Overall, pitching was more dominant in 2005 as five of the league's seven best prospects toiled on the mound. A year earlier, the top 11 included only one pitcher.

Brewers outfielder Lorenzo Cain was the league's dominant offensive performer. He was named the league's MVP after leading in runs, hits, doubles, extra-base hits (28) and slugging percentage (.566) while finishing second in the batting race. It was a remarkable season for a player who played little baseball in high school and was an obscure 2004 draft-and-follow of the Brewers.

"He came out of nowhere and showed more improvement in all areas than any player in the league," Brewers manager Mike Guerrero said. "He's got a chance to be a five-tool player."

STANDINGS: SPLIT SEASON

FIRST HALF	W	L	PCT	GB	SECOND HALF	W	L	PCT	GB
Giants	21	7	.750	—	Giants	18	10	.643	—
Royals	19	9	.679	2	Athletics	17	11	.607	1
Angels	15	13	.536	6	Mariners	17	11	.607	1
Padres	15	13	.536	6	Rangers	15	13	.536	3
Athletics	13	15	.464	8	Royals	15	13	.536	3
Rangers	12	16	.429	9	Padres	14	14	.500	4
Brewers	11	17	.393	10	Brewers	11	17	.393	7
Cubs	10	18	.357	11	Angels	10	18	.357	8
Mariners	10	18	.357	11	Cubs	9	19	.321	9

PLAYOFFS: Giants won both halves of the season to claim the league championship.

TOP 20 PROSPECTS

1. Mark Pawelek, lhp, Cubs
2. Nick Adenhart, rhp, Angels
3. Craig Italiano, rhp, Athletics
4. Jeff Bianchi, ss, Royals
5. Johnny Whittleman, 3b, Rangers
6. Jared Lansford, rhp, Athletics
7. Waldis Joaquin, rhp, Giants
8. Lorenzo Cain, of, Brewers
9. Joe Dickerson, of, Royals
10. Shairon Martis, rhp, Giants
11. Sharlon Schoop, ss, Giants
12. Manuel Pina, c, Rangers
13. P.J. Phillips, ss, Angels
14. Kyle Blanks, 1b, Padres
15. Ramon Alvarado, of, Athletics
16. Tommy Mendoza, rhp, Angels
17. Sammy Baez, ss, Cubs
18. Brent Fisher, lhp, Royals
19. Ernesto Frieri, rhp, Padres
20. Gustavo Espinoza, lhp, Angels

STANDINGS: OVERALL

Page	Team	Complex	W	L	PCT	GB	Manager	Last Penn.
230	Giants	Scottsdale	39	17	.696	—	Bert Hunter	2005
142	Royals	Surprise	34	22	.607	5	Lloyd Simmons	2003
194	Athletics	Phoenix	30	26	.536	9	Ruben Escalera	2001
223	Padres	Peoria	29	27	.518	10	Carlos Lezcano	None
238	Mariners	Peoria	27	29	.482	12	Dana Williams	2000
252	Rangers	Surprise	27	29	.482	12	Pedro Lopez	None
149	Angels	Mesa	25	31	.446	14	Brian Harper	None
163	Brewers	Phoenix	22	34	.393	17	Mike Guerrero	1990
83	Cubs	Mesa	19	37	.339	20	Steve McFarland	2002

NOTE: Teams' individual batting and pitching statistics can be found on page indicated in lefthand column.

2005 ARIZONA LEAGUE STATISTICS

CLUB BATTING

	AVG	G	AB	R	H	2B	2B	HR	BB	SO	SB
Mariners	.291	56	1989	364	579	106	32	35	206	489	53
Giants	.285	56	1865	328	531	80	22	15	223	389	137
Royals	.284	56	1933	356	549	93	39	35	226	483	84
Brewers	.282	56	2022	311	571	98	30	19	153	457	59
Padres	.279	56	2037	311	569	115	22	25	165	490	72
Cubs	.275	56	1973	279	543	101	25	9	168	429	69
Rangers	.271	56	1912	299	518	85	27	19	239	441	115
Angels	.252	56	1847	259	465	98	26	19	174	531	75
Athletics	.239	56	1837	300	439	76	30	19	246	487	79

CLUB PITCHING

	ERA	G	CG	SHO	SV	IP	H	R	ER	BB	SO
Giants	2.93	56	0	2	17	492	441	212	160	161	522
Angels	4.23	56	1	0	14	483	496	276	227	162	513
Royals	4.31	56	0	4	17	495	550	284	237	162	445
Padres	4.46	56	1	1	9	511	500	300	253	254	460
Cubs	4.50	56	0	2	7	500	520	317	250	207	464
Athletics	4.56	56	1	1	12	500	536	317	253	171	426
Mariners	4.88	56	0	1	7	492	556	358	267	220	438
Rangers	4.90	56	0	3	10	498	566	344	271	197	503
Brewers	5.79	56	0	1	11	499	599	400	320	266	425

CLUB FIELDING

	PCT	PO	A	E	DP
Royals	.966	1485	634	75	50
Giants	.960	1476	639	87	42
Padres	.960	1533	658	91	63
Rangers	.958	1494	647	94	51
Cubs	.953	1473	636	105	55
Athletics	.951	1472	629	108	60
Mariners	.951	1477	628	108	46
Angels	.949	1448	515	105	33
Brewers	.946	1497	650	122	57

INDIVIDUAL BATTING LEADERS

(Minimum 151 Plate Appearances)

	AVG	G	AB	R	H	2B	3B	HR	RBI	BB	SO	SB
Nunez, Ariel, Giants	.367	46	150	30	55	4	4	0	21	18	43	28
Cain, Lorenzo, Brewers	.356	50	205	45	73	18	5	5	37	20	32	12
Diaz, Javis, Padres	.352	39	145	22	51	5	6	2	24	17	30	19
Brantley, Michael, Brewers	.347	44	173	34	60	3	1	0	19	22	13	14
Arce, Valentino, Royals	.335	47	170	37	57	10	0	1	21	7	17	7
Lewis, D.J., Cubs	.322	45	174	37	56	14	5	0	27	17	23	3
Richardson, Antoan, Giants	.321	53	193	45	62	4	2	1	10	44	43	40
Guzman, Juan, Mariners	.320	35	153	30	49	5	2	1	24	11	19	6
Mehl, Truan, Rangers	.320	54	203	38	65	14	3	0	33	26	50	27
Valiente, Roberto, Rangers	.316	45	155	27	49	3	1	2	27	17	37	14

INDIVIDUAL PITCHING LEADERS

(Minimum 45 Innings)

	W	L	ERA	G	GS	CG	SV	IP	H	R	ER	BB	SO
Frieri, Ernesto, Padres	7	1	1.17	17	5	0	0	46	21	7	6	29	59
Mendoza, Tommy, Angels	3	3	1.55	13	4	0	0	52	42	14	9	13	56
Williams, Harold, Mariners	2	2	2.30	10	6	0	0	47	38	16	12	16	44
Oliveros, Rayner, Royals	7	1	2.39	14	14	0	0	75	73	26	20	5	48
Fisher, Brent, Royals	5	2	3.04	13	8	0	1	50	48	20	17	13	69
Kirkman, Michael, Rangers	3	1	3.44	14	9	0	0	52	51	28	20	19	58
Franco, T.J., Athletics	5	6	3.66	14	8	1	0	64	76	34	26	15	51
Espinoza, Gustavo, Angels	5	3	3.84	13	12	0	0	70	72	36	30	12	78
Jimenez, Juan, Padres	4	4	3.86	13	13	0	0	79	95	45	34	18	67
Phillips, Zach, Rangers	1	3	3.93	14	11	0	0	50	52	26	22	13	73

ALL-STAR TEAM

C—Luany Sanchez, Padres. **1B**—Andy Hargrove, Mariners. **2B**—Valentino Arce, Royals. **3B**—Jose Jimenez, Brewers. **SS**—Jeff Bianchi, Royals. **OF**—Lorenzo Cain, Brewers; Ariel Nunez, Giants; Antoan Richardson, Giants. **DH**—Kyle Blanks, Padres. **RHP**—Tommy Mendoza, Angels. **LHP**—Harold Williams, Mariners. **RHRP**—Ernesto Frieri, Padres. **LHRP**—Brad Beck, Angels

Most Valuable Player: Lorenzo Cain, Brewers. **Manager of the Year:** Reuben Escalera, Athletics.

DEPARTMENT LEADERS

BATTING

G	Dickerson, Joe, Royals	56
AB	Dickerson, Joe, Royals	214
R	Cain, Lorenzo, Brewers	45
	Richardson, Antoan, Giants	45
H	Cain, Lorenzo, Brewers	73
TB	Cain, Lorenzo, Brewers	116
XBH	Cain, Lorenzo, Brewers	28
2B	Cain, Lorenzo, Brewers	18
3B	Dickerson, Joe, Royals	9
HR	Blanks, Kyle, Padres	7
RBI	Dickerson, Joe, Royals	40
SAC	Borg, Hector, Giants	10
SF	Four tied at	5
BB	Richardson, Antoan, Giants	44
IBB	Blanks, Kyle, Padres	3
HBP	Arce, Valentino, Royals	13
SO	Gonzalez, Oscar, Royals	68
SB	Richardson, Antoan, Giants	40
CS	Dickerson, Joe, Royals	12
GIDP	Sanchez, Luany, Padres	9
OBP	Richardson, Antoan, Giants	.465
SLG	Cain, Lorenzo, Brewers	.566

PITCHING

G	Sanchez, Julio, Padres	24
GS	Oliveros, Rayner, Royals	14
CG	Three tied at	1
SHO	None	
GF	Parejo, Miguel, Brewers	17
SV	Thomson, Jordan, Giants	7
W	Frieri, Ernesto, Padres	7
	Oliveros, Rayner, Royals	7
L	Franco, T.J., Athletics	6
	Poveda, Omar, Rangers	6
IP	Jimenez, Juan, Padres	79
H	Jimenez, Juan, Padres	95
R	Rasner, Jacob, Rangers	57
ER	Rasner, Jacob, Rangers	44
HR	Jolliff, Dave, Padres	6
	Rasner, Jacob, Rangers	6
HBP	Pawelek, Mark, Cubs	9
BB	Mercedes, Roque, Brewers	34
SO	Espinoza, Gustavo, Angels	78
WP	Pawelek, Mark, Cubs	13
BK	Lugo, Jose, Athletics	6
	Rivas, Amaury, Brewers	6

FIELDING

C	PCT	Morgan, Justin, Cubs	.984
	PO	Sanchez, Luany, Padres	271
	A	Rojas, Nestor, Giants	33
	E	Four tied at	7
	DP	Maldonado, Martin, Angels	3
	PB	Dixon, Kent, Mariners	11
		Rojas, Nestor, Giants	11
	CS PCT	Mercedes, Mario, Cubs	36%
1B	PCT	Blanks, Kyle, Padres	.997
	PO	Matos, Willie, Royals	366
	A	Canzler, Russ, Cubs	21
	E	Backman, Wally, Rangers	7
		Ryan, Matt, Angels	7
	DP	Blanks, Kyle, Padres	41
2B	PCT	Borg, Hector, Giants	.968
	PO	Vallejo, Jose, Rangers	115
	A	Vallejo, Jose, Rangers	187
	E	Serrano, Eduard, Cubs	14
	DP	Vallejo, Jose, Rangers	38
3B	PCT	Jimenez, Jose, Brewers	.911
	PO	Jimenez, Jose, Brewers	33
		Valdez, Alexander, Athletics	33
	A	Valdez, Alexander, Athletics	83
	E	Valdez, Alexander, Athletics	14
		Whittleman, Johnny, Rangers	14
	DP	Jimenez, Jose, Brewers	12
SS	PCT	Schoop, Sharlon, Giants	.971
	PO	Schoop, Sharlon, Giants	72
	A	Schoop, Sharlon, Giants	162
	E	Mejia, Harold, Brewers	23
	DP	Schoop, Sharlon, Giants	28
OF	PCT	Lewis, D.J., Cubs	1
	PO	Piper-Jordan, Andre, Athletics	113
	A	Mehl, Truan, Rangers	10
	E	Piper-Jordan, Andre, Athletics	7
	DP	Four tied at	3

GULF COAST LEAGUE

ROOKIE

BY ALLAN SIMPSON

The Gulf Coast League may or may not have played its final season, depending on whether major league owners vote to phase it out as part of possible sweeping changes to the lower minors that could take effect as early as 2006. But if it goes, the GCL will go out with a bang as the talent level in the league in 2005 was among the best in recent years.

CLIFF WELCH

Chris Volstad

Seventeen players selected in the first or second rounds of the 2005 draft appeared in the league. Appropriately, the three highest picks who played in the league—Pirates outfielder Andrew McCutchen, Reds outfielder Jay Bruce and Marlins righthander Chris Volstad—ranked 1-2-3 in a manager's survey of the league's top major league prospects.

Volstad was one of four high school pitchers the Marlins drafted in the first round or supplemental first round.

"I've been in the game for 25 years and have never seen four quality starting pitchers on one staff like we had this year," Marlins manager Edwin Rodriguez said. "All have excellent makeup, are not afraid to work hard and all recognize they still have a long way to go."

The four Marlins pitchers made such an impression that they were all promoted to the short-season New York-Penn League before the GCL season ended. Volstad was named the top pitching prospect in that league as well.

Despite all the talent on the mound, the Marlins (24-30) finished a distant third in the Eastern Division to the Mets (37-16), whose .698 winning percentage was the GCL's best since the 1997 Mets posted a .700 mark.

But the Mets never won a playoff game. After getting a bye to the final round, the Mets lost two straight playoff games to the defending champion Yankees, who beat the Red Sox in a one-game semifinal before dispatching the Mets 3-2 and 10-1 in a best-of-three final.

Though they posted the league's best record by a wide margin, the Mets had none of the league's top prospects. Their best was shortstop Emmanuel Garcia, a Canadian signed after the 2004 season as a free agent.

Garcia was a surprise to the Mets in spring training and followed with a breakout summer. He led the circuit in runs, hits and on-base percentage, and he also used his above-average speed to steal 17 bases in 18 attempts.

The league's best prospects were McCutchen and Bruce, who were drafted 11th and 12th overall in June. Both performed well and performed even better when they were promoted late in the season—McCutchen to the short-season New York-Penn League and Bruce to the Rookie-level Pioneer League.

GCL managers had difficulty determining which player had the greater upside, particularly since both made a strong impression with their offensive potential.

"Bruce swings the bat more like Kirk Gibson," Red Sox manager Ralph Treuel said. "McCutchen's swing reminds you a little more of Gary Sheffield. Both run well, but Bruce has the size and throws a little better."

The 6-foot-7 Volstad, the first of three Marlins first-round picks, showed polished mechanics and a clean, effortless delivery with command of three pitches.

"I was the hitting coach for the Marlins in Double-A last year and I didn't see pitchers there with the command of all three pitches like he has," Rodriguez said.

TOP 20 PROSPECTS

1. Andrew McCutchen, of, Pirates
2. Jay Bruce, of, Reds
3. Chris Volstad, rhp, Marlins
4. Elvis Andrus, ss, Braves
5. Travis Wood, lhp, Reds
6. Beau Jones, lhp, Braves
7. Jose Tabata, of, Yankees
8. Sean West, lhp, Marlins
9. Ryan Tucker, rhp, Marlins
10. C.J. Henry, ss, Yankees
11. Austin Jackson, of, Yankees
12. Paul Kelly, ss, Twins
13. Aaron Thompson, lhp, Marlins
14. Ivan DeJesus, ss, Dodgers
15. Jon Egan, c, Red Sox
16. Jordan Schafer, of, Braves
17. Drew Thompson, 2b, Twins
18. Jeff Lyman, rhp, Braves
19. Miguel Sanfler, lhp, Dodgers
20. Emmanuel Garcia, ss, Mets

STANDINGS

Page	EAST	Complex Site	W	L	PCT	GB	Manager	Last Penn.
178	Mets	St. Lucie	37	16	.698	—	Gary Carter	None
156	Dodgers	Vero Beach	25	29	.463	12 ½	Luis Salazar	1990
128	Marlins	Jupiter	24	30	.444	13 ½	Edwin Rodriguez	None
267	Nationals	Melbourne	21	32	.396	16	Wendell Kim	1991

Page	NORTH	Complex Site	W	L	PCT	GB	Manager	Last Penn.
187	Yankees	Tampa	33	20	.623	—	Oscar Acosta	2005
201	Phillies	Clearwater	24	27	.471	8	Jim Morrison	2002
60	Braves	Kissimmee	24	28	.462	8 ½	Luis Ortiz	2003
120	Tigers	Lakeland	24	30	.444	9 ½	Kevin Bradshaw	None

Page	SOUTH	Complex Site	W	L	PCT	GB	Manager	Last Penn.
75	Red Sox	Fort Myers	30	24	.556	—	Ralph Treuel	None
208	Pirates	Bradenton	28	26	.519	2	Jeff Livesey	None
170	Twins	Fort Myers	28	26	.519	2	Nelson Prada	None
98	Reds	Sarasota	22	32	.407	8	Luis Aguayo	None

PLAYOFFS—Semifinals: Yankees defeated Red Sox 1-0 in one-game playoff. **Final:** Yankees defeated Mets 2-0 in best-of-3 series.

NOTE: Teams' individual batting and pitching statistics can be found on page indicated in lefthand column.

2005 GULF COAST LEAGUE STATISTICS

CLUB BATTING

	AVG	G	AB	R	H	2B	2B	HR	BB	SO	SB
Mets	.287	53	1801	326	517	78	19	34	226	437	64
Dodgers	.283	54	1807	285	511	88	17	23	171	338	39
Yankees	.267	53	1728	294	462	90	17	21	185	316	82
Pirates	.259	54	1844	279	477	94	17	25	172	334	55
Marlins	.258	54	1778	223	459	101	10	18	158	395	29
Red Sox	.257	54	1818	244	468	96	10	24	183	357	37
Phillies	.251	51	1663	244	417	82	10	22	173	367	92
Nationals	.249	53	1798	207	448	82	9	28	174	454	16
Twins	.245	54	1713	290	419	65	16	25	198	401	86
Braves	.244	52	1694	204	414	78	12	34	127	349	35
Tigers	.235	54	1776	228	417	71	19	37	133	475	60
Reds	.233	54	1715	223	399	94	10	21	177	491	29

CLUB PITCHING

	ERA	G	CG	SHO	SV	IP	H	R	ER	BB	SO
Red Sox	3.03	54	0	5	19	479	373	213	161	155	433
Yankees	3.14	53	0	2	13	447	392	201	156	140	428
Marlins	3.40	54	0	2	15	463	463	232	174	166	427
Phillies	3.76	51	0	1	9	438	449	219	183	100	343
Mets	4.03	53	0	4	12	462	460	248	207	153	395
Twins	4.03	54	1	3	18	460	480	257	206	190	367
Pirates	4.04	54	2	3	10	468	457	277	210	176	386
Braves	4.05	52	0	4	13	447	427	258	201	173	396
Reds	4.18	54	0	2	13	457	453	289	211	209	397
Tigers	4.52	54	0	1	17	464	442	292	233	205	340
Dodgers	4.55	54	0	5	12	464	491	273	235	208	411
Nationals	4.61	53	1	2	8	462	521	288	237	202	391

CLUB FIELDING

	PCT	PO	A	E	DP
Dodgers	.967	1393	520	65	55
Mets	.967	1387	550	67	59
Marlins	.965	1389	585	71	50
Red Sox	.964	1436	575	76	36
Nationals	.963	1389	605	77	45
Pirates	.962	1405	630	80	55
Twins	.962	1383	573	78	51
Phillies	.961	1315	552	75	48
Yankees	.961	1341	530	75	53
Braves	.958	1337	519	81	34
Tigers	.955	1392	618	94	42
Reds	.949	1371	551	104	57

INDIVIDUAL BATTING LEADERS

(Minimum 159 Plate Appearances)

	AVG	G	AB	R	H	2B	3B	HR	RBI	BB	SO	SB
Perez, Eduardo, Dodgers	.352	48	179	35	63	16	1	6	37	12	26	4
Guzman, Francisco, Nationals	.344	40	154	20	53	6	0	7	24	5	20	0
Garcia, Emmanuel, Mets	.339	45	186	43	63	7	0	2	30	21	36	17
Kutler, Matt, Marlins	.337	44	169	27	57	14	0	1	25	13	24	8
Creek, Greg, Braves	.322	41	143	21	46	10	1	2	14	11	22	0
Bell, Josh, Dodgers	.318	45	157	26	50	7	1	1	21	20	33	5
Sojo, Richard, Twins	.318	43	148	36	47	11	5	0	15	13	32	11
Bell, Bubba, Red Sox	.317	43	164	18	52	13	2	2	27	10	14	2
Tabata, Jose, Yankees	.314	44	156	30	49	5	1	3	25	15	14	22
Rodriguez, Wilkin, Tigers	.311	44	164	23	51	7	0	2	17	14	25	14

INDIVIDUAL PITCHING LEADERS

(Minimum 47 Innings)

	W	L	ERA	G	GS	CG	SV	IP	H	R	ER	BB	SO
Edlich, Kyle, Twins	4	2	1.70	10	9	0	0	48	42	13	9	15	53
Herman, Jason, Pirates	3	3	1.93	11	9	0	1	51	43	13	11	7	37
Manuel, Robert, Mets	8	1	2.06	12	5	0	0	57	55	19	13	4	49
Francisco, Bartolo, Nationals	2	4	2.08	10	5	0	0	52	55	26	12	13	29
Ruckle, Jacob, Mets	8	1	2.10	11	8	0	0	56	49	20	13	10	33
Cox, Tim, Red Sox	3	1	2.19	11	5	0	1	49	36	17	12	7	56
German, Yulkin, Red Sox	2	1	2.57	11	8	0	0	49	33	19	14	29	56
Byrd, Darren, Phillies	3	1	2.66	9	8	0	0	44	36	14	13	10	24
Perks, Matt, Nationals	4	2	2.83	12	8	1	2	60	51	22	19	17	41
Castillo, Jose, Twins	4	4	3.00	11	9	0	0	48	50	27	16	19	27

ALL-STAR TEAM

C—Yasmil Bruce, Mets. **1B**—Eduardo Perez, Dodgers. **2B**—Cooper Osteen, Phillies. **3B**—Greg Creek, Braves. **SS**—Emmanuel Garcia, Mets. **OF**—Francisco Guzman, Nationals; Matt Kutler, Marlins; Jose Tabata, Yankees. **SP**—Jacob Ruckle, Mets. **RP**—David Williams, Braves.

Manager of the Year: Gary Carter, Mets.

DEPARTMENT LEADERS

BATTING

G	Two tied at	49
AB	Two tied at	186
R	Garcia, Emmanuel, Mets	43
H	Two tied at	63
TB	Perez, Eduardo, Dodgers	99
XBH	Two tied at	23
2B	Fermin, Angel, Yankees	17
3B	Spath, Matt, Mets	7
HR	Reyes, Angel, Tigers	9
RBI	Perez, Eduardo, Dodgers	37
SH	Two tied at	7
SF	Roman, Willman, Pirates	5
BB	Schemmel, Jon, Mets	30
IBB	Two tied at	2
HBP	Two tied at	10
SO	Wells, Casper, Tigers	59
SB	Tabata, Jose, Yankees	22
CS	Hernandez, Fidel, Phillies	8
GIDP	Ventura, Leivi, Mets	9
OBP	Garcia, Emmanuel, Mets	.412
SLG	Perez, Eduardo, Dodgers	.553

PITCHING

G	Craig, Aaron, Twins	21
GS	McConnell, Brandon, Twins	11
CG	Four tied at	1
SHO	Jacobsen, Landon, Pirates	1
GF	Craig, Aaron, Twins	20
SV	Craig, Aaron, Twins	10
W	Manuel, Robert, Mets	8
	Ruckle, Jacob, Mets	8
L	Newman, Brandon, Reds	6
IP	McConnell, Brandon, Twins	63
H	McConnell, Brandon, Twins	76
R	Ozuna, Cruzito, Nationals	39
	Wise, Brendan, Tigers	39
ER	Dasni, Chales, Dodgers	37
HR	Caraballo, Jesse, Tigers	7
HBP	Wise, Brendan, Tigers	13
BB	Beattie, Eric, Tigers	30
SO	Cox, Tim, Red Sox	56
	German, Yulkin, Red Sox	56
WP	Ozuna, Cruzito, Nationals	18
BK	Cueto, Johnny, Reds	4

FIELDING

C	PCT	Jansen, Kenley, Dodgers	1.000
	PO	Gil, Jose, Yankees	259
	A	Two tied at	31
	E	Two tied at	8
	DP	Five tied at	3
	PB	Garcia, Steven, Braves	11
	CS PCT	Bucce, Yasmil, Mets	48%
1B	PCT	Rios, Daniel, Pirates	.997
	PO	Fermin, Angel, Yankees	330
		Kaaihue, Kala, Braves	330
	A	Fermin, Angel, Yankees	31
	E	Fermin, Angel, Yankees	9
	DP	Fermin, Angel, Yankees	39
2B	PCT	Gonzalez, Adolfo, Dodgers	.975
	PO	Castro, Jonathan, Nationals	113
	A	Castro, Jonathan, Nationals	111
	E	Bautista, Pedruin, Tigers	9
		Monk, Brandon, Braves	9
	DP	Castro, Jonathan, Nationals	24
3B	PCT	Linares, Miguel, Tigers	.980
	PO	Figuereo, Johan, Nationals	38
	A	Mansolino, Tony, Pirates	103
	E	Delgado, Ronny, Reds	12
		Linares, Emilio, Red Sox	12
	DP	Creek, Greg, Braves	12
SS	PCT	Kelly, Paul, Twins	.975
	PO	Andrus, Elvis, Braves	63
	A	Segovia, Luis, Red Sox	112
	E	Jones, Michael, Reds	18
	DP	Henry, C.J., Yankees	27
OF	PCT	11 tied at	1.000
	PO	De La Rossa, Wilkins, Yankees	92
	A	Roberson, Colin, Marlins	10
	E	Brea, Manuel, Tigers	7
	DP	McCutchen, Andrew, Pirates	4

LATIN AMERICA

SUMMER LEAGUES

DOMINICAN SUMMER LEAGUE

The New York Yankees farm system has been maligned in recent years. But if rebuilding a successful system starts at the bottom, then the Yankees made significant headway in 2005.

All three bottom-tiered clubs in the Yankees organization won championships, including their entry in the Dominican Summer League.

The DSL Yankees whipped the Royals in three straight games in a best-of-five series, outscoring their opponent 23-10 overall. It marked the second straight year that the Yankees dismantled the Royals in the playoffs, after the Royals had posted the best record in the league both years.

The Royals went 49-14 (.778) in 2004 before falling to the Yankees in the semifinals. A year later, the Royals went 45-13 (.776) during the regular season and won the Cibao Division by 16 games. The Royals received a first-round bye in the playoffs, then beat the Angels 2-1 in the semifinal. But they were no match for the Yankees, who went 44-29 (.629) during the regular season and posted a 2.25 team ERA. The Yankees beat the Indians 2-1 and the Giants 2-0 in a pair of preliminary best-of-three series before whipping the Royals in the finals.

No Yankees players were selected to the league all-star team, but first baseman Waddy Rufino, who hit .239-7-25 during the regular season, went 7-for-12 in the three games against the Royals, while hitting two homers and driving in six runs.

The DSL fielded 32 teams in 2005 in a sprawling six-division setup. Four clubs, including the Yankees, fielded two teams. Only the Brewers and Devil Rays did not have entries in the league.

Mariners outfielder Welington Dotel was named the league's most valuable player. Dotel was second in the league with a .373 average and 10 home runs, and led with nine triples.

Diamondbacks reliever Jorge Perez was selected the most valuable pitcher. He led the league with 21 saves while not allowing an earned run in 32 innings. He also walked just eight while striking out 64.

Astros DH Cesar Quintero also had a productive season, hitting .363 with a league-best 59 runs and 95 hits. He was named MVP of the DSL all-star game, won by National League affiliates 7-3. Quintero had a single and double, scored two runs and had an RBI in the game.

—ALLAN SIMPSON

STANDINGS

BOCA CHICA/American	W	L	PCT	GB
Indians I	38	31	.551	—
Twins	36	33	.522	2
Red Sox	26	42	.382	11½
Indians II	25	42	.373	12
BOCA CHICA/National	**W**	**L**	**PCT**	**GB**
Giants	43	24	.642	—
Rockies	42	27	.609	2
Diamondbacks	38	30	.559	5½
Reds	32	38	.457	12½
Cubs	27	40	.403	16
SANTO DOMINGO NORTH	**W**	**L**	**PCT**	**GB**
Athletics II	43	26	.623	—
Mariners	39	30	.565	4
Dodgers	37	29	.561	4½
Cardinals	36	35	.507	8
Phillies	34	36	.486	19½
Athletics I	18	51	.261	25
SANTO DOMINGO WEST	**W**	**L**	**PCT**	**GB**
Yankees I	44	26	.629	—
Tigers	40	30	.571	4
Padres	37	34	.521	7½
Nationals	37	35	.514	8
Yankees II	28	43	.394	16½
Mets	27	45	.375	18
SAN PEDRO DE MACORIS	**W**	**L**	**PCT**	**GB**
Angels	44	26	.629	—
Orioles	42	29	.592	2½
Pirates	38	34	.528	7
Rangers	33	37	.471	11
Blue Jays	31	39	.443	13
Astros	23	46	.333	20½
CIBAO	**W**	**L**	**PCT**	**GB**
Royals	45	13	.776	—
Braves I	29	29	.500	16
Marlins	28	31	.467	17½
White Sox	26	32	.441	19
Braves II	19	42	.311	27½

PLAYOFFS: Quarterfinals—Yankees I defeated Indians 2-1 and Angels defeated Athletics II 2-0 in best-of-3 series. **Semifinals**—Royals defeated Angels 2-0 and Yankees I defeated Giants 2-0 in best-of-3 series. **Final**—Yankees I defeated Royals 3-0 in best-of-5 series.

ALL-STAR TEAM: C—Roberto Sosa, Red Sox. **1B**—Alexis Marte, Dodgers. **2B**—Everth Cabrera, Rockies. **3B**—Juan Jean, Giants. **SS**—Hector Gomez, Rockies. **OF**—Welington Dotel, Mariners; Geraldo Parra, Diamondbacks; Norberto Ortiz, Angels. **DH**—Cesar Quintero, Astros. **RHP**—Miguel Morales, Royals. **LHP**—Rolando Valdez, Padres. **RP**—Jorge Perez, Diamondbacks.

Most Valuable Player: Welington Dotel, Mariners. **Most Valuable Pitcher:** Jorge Perez, Diamondbacks. **Manager of the Year:** Carlos Mota, Yankees I.

INDIVIDUAL BATTING LEADERS

(Minimum 150 At-Bats)

	AVG	AB	R	H	2B	3B	HR	RBI	SB
Parra, Geraldo, Diamondbacks	**.384**	237	53	91	14	5	6	45	26
Dotel, Welington, Mariners	.373	241	47	90	14	**9**	10	39	13
Quintero, Cesar, Astros	.363	262	**59**	**95**	10	7	8	34	24
Sosa, Pablo, Marlins	.363	182	15	66	7	2	0	21	22
Paulo, Roberto, White Sox	.348	227	41	79	14	6	3	23	10
Rodriguez, Reynaldo, Yank. II/Yank. I	.335	200	42	67	11	1	0	19	23
Gomez, Hector, Rockies	.335	242	49	81	16	1	6	43	15
Montero, Lucas, Indians II/Indians I	.324	204	42	66	10	5	2	23	31
Rosario, Yovanny, Dodgers	.318	217	44	69	11	5	1	16	21
Marte, Alexis, Dodgers	.315	213	25	67	8	1	0	37	9
Cabrera, Enmanuel, Reds	.310	168	38	52	5	2	1	15	17
Cabrera, Everth, Rockies	.309	249	51	77	16	3	1	23	**43**
Vargas, Alex, Pirates	.308	221	33	68	12	1	2	23	7
Ramirez, Jose, Cardinals	.306	160	26	49	7	2	3	17	9
Ortiz, Norberto, Angels	.305	200	49	61	15	1	**12**	**48**	8
Medina, Jose, Giants	.304	224	47	68	12	3	5	30	19
Silveren, Pedro, Orioles	.303	178	35	54	13	0	2	30	16
Casso, Jorge, Braves I	.302	222	32	67	5	6	2	34	3
Medrano, Ignacio, Mets	.295	220	30	65	10	1	1	16	10
Arias, Janel, Indians II	.295	234	21	69	12	2	0	32	18
Francisco, Oliver, Athletics I	.294	163	16	48	4	0	0	17	4
Soriano, Francisco, Angels	.292	168	32	49	6	1	0	13	16
Calzada, Josue, Yankees I	.291	182	28	53	9	3	2	31	18
Leal, Pablo, Braves II	.291	172	23	50	9	0	3	18	2
Castillo, Welington, Cubs	.289	204	29	59	14	0	1	28	1
Juan, Manuel, Royals	.288	226	48	65	3	3	1	21	30
Rodriguez, Orlando, Tigers	.287	237	32	68	17	1	3	36	12
Rodriguez, Jose, Rangers	.285	228	36	65	10	0	2	27	12
Victorino, Victor, Padres	.284	169	32	48	9	2	0	21	17
Rodriguez, Geraldo, Yankees II	.284	204	29	58	11	2	8	39	2
Manzanillo, Gerson, Yankees I	.283	244	43	69	8	7	1	10	22
Diaz, Joel, Blue Jays	.283	198	23	40	10	0	2	18	1
Colmenarez, Carlos, Angels	.283	212	39	60	9	1	1	31	20
Perez, Alwin, Royals	.283	205	34	58	12	2	0	36	15

Urbina, Yasmil, Padres	.281	228	33	64	8	1	0	13	18
Hernandez, Ramon, Indians I	.281	253	46	71	4	4	1	17	29
Rodriguez, Concepcion, Braves I	.281	196	41	55	9	2	5	32	2
Morel, Elvis, Orioles	.279	165	39	46	7	1	2	13	23
Santamaria, Jadiel, Yankees II	.277	166	27	46	8	1	0	15	17
Saldana, Pedro, Royals	.277	155	23	43	4	0	0	16	3
Albornoz, Henry, Padres	.276	232	30	64	16	1	3	34	8
Mejia, Juan Carlos, Phillies	.276	181	28	50	6	0	2	30	17
Rivera, Anthony, Cubs	.274	157	22	43	3	0	1	29	4
Crisostomo, Manauris, Phillies	.274	190	25	52	9	1	0	18	7
De los Santos, Vladimir, Phillies	.274	215	27	59	**18**	0	1	28	6
Leveret, Rene, Twins	.272	158	17	43	7	0	2	28	0
Diaz, Ogui, Mariners	.272	191	35	52	11	0	4	25	8
Mercedes, Freddy, Rangers	.272	158	23	43	3	1	3	27	10
Paisano, David, White Sox	.272	151	18	41	5	1	3	8	2
Oriental, Rene, Royals	.271	210	41	57	4	5	6	48	16
Mata, Argenis, Blue Jays	.270	174	27	47	3	2	1	22	8
Martinez, Michael, Nationals	.269	212	37	57	3	1	0	16	20
Cordero, Rafael, Cubs	.269	175	24	47	8	2	2	19	10
Thermidor, Wilmant, Rockies	.269	186	29	50	7	1	5	21	9
Ortiz, Gabriel, Athletics II	.269	193	21	52	7	1	0	25	5
Rincon, Ambiorix, Phillies	.269	238	33	64	13	3	0	16	8
Mendez, Maximo, Mariners	.268	157	32	42	6	2	7	24	9
Luis, Marcos, Athletics II	.267	195	22	52	10	0	0	16	13
Farias, Danny, Blue Jays	.267	266	42	71	14	1	0	35	11
Pena, Richard, Mets	.266	214	37	57	10	4	2	17	11
Sanchez, Bisanlly, Astros	.266	214	28	57	10	0	5	27	3
Hernandez, Gorky, Tigers	.265	211	44	56	10	0	4	19	10
Beltre, Juan, Nationals	.265	223	39	59	10	0	0	20	14
Jean, Juan, Giants	.265	226	50	60	14	4	4	30	21
De la Cruz, Tony, Braves II	.265	166	23	44	5	1	2	12	20
DeCastro, Angel, Nationals	.264	235	41	62	6	4	4	36	11
Dias, Wilmer, Giants	.264	178	25	47	11	3	3	32	7
Sime, Samuel, Braves I	.264	197	17	52	7	4	4	27	2
Phipps, Denis, Reds	.263	167	27	44	10	2	1	13	20
Baez, Juan, Astros	.263	209	25	55	13	2	1	22	11
Encarnacion, Jairo, Pirates	.263	171	22	45	13	2	1	17	5
Reyes, Raul, Mets	.263	232	33	61	12	3	4	30	6
Leon, Carlos, Yankees I/Yankees II	.262	210	40	55	10	3	2	19	5
Gomez, Roy, Yankees I/Yankees II	.261	230	29	60	6	0	2	19	7
Franco, Ambiorix, Phillies	.261	222	42	58	13	0	2	24	5
Velasquez, Isaias, Ind. I/Ind. II	.260	200	32	52	6	4	0	10	6
Cruz, Nael, Royals	.260	200	31	52	8	0	3	31	2
Mayi, Jose, Padres	.258	233	21	60	14	3	1	38	7
Rincon, Luis, Indians I	.258	225	21	58	7	2	0	29	4
Fernandez, Jesus, D'backs	.258	159	22	41	7	1	3	28	1
Bartolo, Nicolas, Blue Jays	.258	236	32	61	8	3	3	29	4
Carmona, Angel, Blue Jays	.258	151	17	39	5	2	1	25	3
Diaz, Kelvin, Indians I	.257	206	22	53	10	2	2	13	9
Herrera, Elian, Dodgers	.257	206	33	53	11	2	1	22	10
Rivero, Carlos, Indians II	.257	237	21	61	6	0	0	31	7
Correa, Walter, Athletics II	.257	202	48	52	11	3	3	23	26
Sosa, Roberto, Red Sox	.256	172	28	44	12	1	8	37	2
Santana, Victor, Blue Jays	.256	223	43	57	10	0	9	40	5
Valdez, Luis, Yankees II	.254	177	24	45	8	1	2	22	20
Hernandez, Julio, D'backs	.253	154	19	39	7	0	1	6	5
Tejeda, Elvin, Cardinals	.253	158	23	40	10	2	0	22	4
Perez, Juan Carlos, Marlins	.253	186	14	47	8	0	0	14	1
Corporan, Angel, A's I/A's 2	.251	187	36	47	9	1	2	24	15
Peguero, Carlos, Mariners	.251	179	31	45	8	4	6	30	1
Garcia, Johan, Dodgers	.251	175	22	44	3	0	1	18	5
Perez, Jaime, Pirates	.251	199	25	50	10	0	5	25	1
Borrome, Luis, Mets	.250	204	31	51	7	0	7	32	3
Sandoval, William, Cardinals	.250	152	32	38	3	3	0	17	29
Canal, Yonelvy, Pirates	.250	256	45	64	10	2	7	37	26

INDIVIDUAL PITCHING LEADERS

(Minimum 50 Innings)

	W	L	ERA	G	SV	IP	H	BB	SO
Perez, Jorge, Diamondbacks	1	0	0.00	25	**21**	32	10	8	64
Ortega, Anthony, Angels	7	4	**0.86**	14	0	94	62	21	100
Ortiz, Jhonatan, Yankees I	5	0	1.03	25	13	53	26	4	58
Valdez, Rolando, Padres	7	2	1.03	13	0	87	55	10	104
DeLeon, Juan, Yankees I	7	0	1.06	22	6	51	30	8	63
Martinez, Leonardo, Athletics I	2	4	1.11	12	0	65	43	8	72
Jimenez, Esmerlin, Angels	7	0	1.11	13	0	57	33	11	47
Morales, Miguel, Royals	7	0	1.19	12	0	53	47	6	53
Caro, Luis, Diamondbacks	7	1	1.24	17	0	87	58	25	81
Hernandez, Juan, Royals	6	0	1.25	19	4	50	30	12	62
Garcia, Carlos, Twins	7	4	1.27	16	1	71	44	26	60
Gomez, Jeanmark, Indians I	5	3	1.33	13	1	61	47	9	46
Diaz, Jhon, Rangers	5	1	1.34	16	0	74	42	14	72
Diaz, Kelvin, Indians I	5	1	1.38	15	0	72	37	29	94
Moreno, Juan, White Sox	2	4	1.40	11	0	58	44	4	50
Montano, Luis, Reds	4	3	1.41	14	1	64	50	11	57
Fernandez, Eddy, Mariners	6	4	1.44	14	0	81	56	13	80
Alcala, Omar, Twins	3	3	1.45	13	0	53	37	15	50
Marrero, Miguel, Athletics II	7	1	1.45	14	0	68	51	15	41
DeJesus, Misael, Reds	4	5	1.48	14	0	67	45	22	57
Ceda, Jose, Padres	4	2	1.50	13	2	60	38	29	83
Estevez, Arsenio, Rangers	3	2	1.50	13	2	54	38	12	61
Torres, Alexander, Angels	4	2	1.52	9	0	53	23	23	87
Bustamonte, Juan, Blue Jays	3	1	1.59	12	0	51	32	8	54
Noesi, Hector, Yankees I	5	3	1.60	13	0	51	34	8	36
Beltre, Omar, Rangers	5	4	1.62	15	0	72	51	13	94
Rondon, Hector, Indians I	3	3	1.65	15	1	65	60	8	55
Vasquez, Yaneri, Marlins	3	3	1.72	13	0	63	44	30	73
Lugo, Henderson, Cardinals	6	3	1.77	13	0	71	48	16	78
Silano, Yull, Rockies	7	2	1.78	16	0	76	49	24	77
Brujan, Rafael, White Sox	3	1	1.80	11	0	50	31	21	82
Figardo, Alfredo, Tigers	**8**	2	1.87	14	1	77	51	31	100
Sanchez, Bruno, Twins	5	2	1.88	14	0	67	43	15	36
Luna, Daury, Phillies	4	4	1.91	12	0	66	45	18	64
Nunez, Jhonny, Dodgers	4	3	1.92	15	0	52	29	13	40
Perez, Jackson, Padres	6	1	1.97	11	0	59	57	11	44
Hernandez, Ramon, Orioles	3	2	1.98	11	0	55	43	26	51
Estanga, Edgar, Blue Jays	4	4	2.05	14	1	79	72	8	**109**
Arias, Henry, Royals	5	1	2.07	14	1	61	44	14	66
Guzman, Kelvin, Rockies	6	3	2.11	12	0	73	51	14	56
Almazar, Jorge, Orioles	**8**	2	2.13	15	1	51	32	35	50
Franco, Santo, Tigers	7	2	2.16	11	0	50	33	29	59
Norberto, Jordan, Diamondbacks	**8**	4	2.24	15	0	68	37	38	102
Luis, Santo, Astros	5	5	2.27	16	0	83	67	22	78
Selen, Esequiel, Orioles	5	3	2.29	14	0	63	58	16	53
Deaza, Inoel, Athletics II	4	3	2.30	13	0	63	57	5	48
Obispo, Wirfin, Reds	1	3	2.31	13	2	51	32	23	59
Rafael, Juan Carlos, Reds	5	3	2.31	14	0	58	42	18	61
Solis, Marcos, Astros	3	5	2.32	14	0	81	61	27	57
Javier, Carlos, Mariners	3	3	2.33	14	2	58	39	33	58
De la Cruz, Kelvin, Indians I	3	3	2.36	13	1	53	49	16	39
Maria, Jose, Orioles	5	5	2.38	14	0	87	77	15	66
Nelson, Maximo, Yankees I	2	4	2.44	14	0	55	47	14	60
Ortiz, Richard, Mariners	6	2	2.44	11	0	59	46	28	49
Pina, Jose, Blue Jays	4	3	2.47	13	0	69	62	13	43
Santana, Braulio, Athletics II	5	2	2.49	14	0	69	70	10	49
Acosta, Richard, Pirates	6	4	2.49	16	1	90	73	13	84
Rosario, Gregorio, Mariners	7	0	2.50	10	0	54	44	15	50
Veras, Vladimir, Angels	6	3	2.50	11	0	58	43	15	55
Mendoza, Nelson, Dodgers	6	4	2.54	14	0	78	72	12	72
Ortegano, Jose, Braves II	5	2	2.58	13	0	52	49	12	55
Tejeda, Walter, Phillies	6	1	2.60	13	0	66	47	26	58
Ramirez, William, Braves II	3	5	2.61	12	0	62	52	6	45
Aponte, Eleazar, Tigers	5	6	2.70	13	0	77	60	25	98
Bucardo, Wilber, Giants	5	2	2.72	13	0	56	54	7	28
Balbuena, Jesus, Mariners	6	3	2.73	19	2	53	45	17	39
Duverge, George, Nationals	5	5	2.75	13	0	52	54	21	56
Flande, Johan, Phillies	3	6	2.76	14	1	59	69	20	50
Carrillo, Marcos, Cubs	2	5	2.81	12	1	58	51	12	46
Cuello, Jonathan, Nationals	6	4	2.82	12	0	73	64	19	59
Acosta, Jose, Twins	3	6	2.83	14	0	64	58	23	56
Pena, Carlos, Phillies	4	5	2.88	13	0	75	75	5	58
Devora, Meoli, Pirates	1	3	2.91	14	1	56	49	26	54
Matias, Randy, Nationals	4	2	2.93	13	0	55	45	32	55
Paulino, Argenis, Red Sox	3	4	2.94	14	0	52	52	18	29
Arias, Agustin, Rockies	4	2	2.98	35	16	54	45	24	44
Rojas, Junior, Braves I	3	3	2.98	12	0	51	57	7	34
Rodriguez, Francisco, White Sox	6	3	2.98	12	0	63	72	10	59

VENEZUELAN SUMMER LEAGUE

The Astros made a concerted late-season push just to reach the Venezuelan Summer League playoffs, then spun back-to-back shutouts against the regular-season champion Mariners to win the 2005 title.

The Astros used five pitchers to win the opener of the best-of-three series, 1-0, before Colombian righthander Carlos Ladeuth wrapped it up with a 2-0 win, pitching the Astros only complete game of the year. Ladeuth, 21, allowed only two hits while walking none and striking out eight.

In sixth place in the nine-team league with little more than a week to go in the 64-game season, the Astros won nine of their last 10 games and their final six in a row to nab the final playoff spot by a game. The club had tied for first a year earlier, only to lose two straight playoff games to the Mets.

Ladeuth was used in a swing role for the Astros during the regular season, going 4-1, 0.98 with six saves. He fell five innings short of qualifying for the ERA title.

Though the Red Sox shared a VSL team with the Padres and finished fourth, the Red Sox produced both the batting champion and ERA leader.

Felix Doubrant, 17, led the league with a 0.97 ERA while going 7-1 and allowing only 32 hits in 65 innings. Outfielder/first baseman Carlos Fernandez, 19, led the league with a .347 average and 48 RBIs.

The VSL, in its ninth year of operation, had support from 11 major league organizations in 2005, with the Marlins and Nationals fielding a co-op club, in addition to the Red Sox and Padres. The Marlins/National entry went 13-51, finishing a distant last.

—ALLAN SIMPSON

STANDINGS

	W	L	PCT	GB
Mariners	37	23	.617	—
Astros	37	25	.597	1
Phillies	37	27	.578	2
Red Sox/Padres	36	28	.563	3
Orioles	34	27	.557	3½
Mets	33	30	.524	5½
Pirates	29	33	.468	9
Reds	25	37	.403	13
Marlins/Nationals	13	51	.203	26

PLAYOFFS: Astros defeated Mariners 2-0 in best-of-3 series.

INDIVIDUAL BATTING LEADERS

(Minimum 115 At-Bats)

	AVG	AB	R	H	2B	3B	HR	RBI	SB
Fernandez, Carlos, Padres/Red Sox	**.347**	196	32	**68**	16	0	5	**48**	14
Osorio, Enmanuel, Phillies	.347	173	29	60	15	2	0	25	6
Durango, Luis, Padres/Red Sox	.342	190	**44**	65	6	1	0	13	19
Vasquez, Robert, Orioles	.321	184	30	59	14	1	3	34	13
Garcia, Christian, Mets	.319	141	28	45	5	3	4	19	16
Fuenmayor, Redne, Phillies	.316	187	31	59	**22**	0	3	34	2
Zazueta,Amadeo, Astros	.313	198	31	62	19	2	7	36	2
Brown, Steve, Astros	.298	225	42	67	10	1	5	35	10
Serrano, Victor, Padres/Red Sox	.296	152	26	45	7	0	0	14	10
Walters, Darrell, Padres/Red Sox	.294	221	37	65	9	1	4	38	12
Castillo, Victor, Orioles	.291	158	34	46	6	1	8	31	2
Espinoza, Humberto, Mariners	.286	189	31	54	10	0	1	19	0
Garcia, Deonel, Mets	.282	124	21	35	5	2	0	7	0
Moron, Robert, Phillies	.278	198	40	55	12	1	4	26	8
Morales, Jaime, Phillies	.278	187	27	52	7	1	0	24	3
Bastardo, Jose, Reds	.276	185	29	51	9	5	1	20	7
Ontiveros, Emilio, Marlins/Nationals	.273	128	24	35	5	0	1	9	16
Blanco, Jourik, Orioles	.271	218	33	59	13	0	7	39	3
Garcia, Carlos, Mets	.270	122	23	33	4	5	6	18	1
Sierra, Luis, Reds	.268	149	23	40	11	2	0	9	2
Ramirez, Ronald, Astros	.267	172	22	46	10	2	3	29	5
Diaz, Argenis, Padres/Red Sox	.266	203	37	54	10	2	2	26	14
Ortiz, William, Mariners	.264	121	22	32	7	0	3	20	5
Rocero, Ciro, Pirates	.263	137	29	36	6	0	3	18	20
Lopez, Jonathan, Mets	.263	137	17	36	2	0	0	15	2
Pedron, Freizer, Pirates	.262	149	19	39	6	0	3	24	10
Montero, Gabriel, Orioles	.262	145	27	38	11	2	0	14	3
Rivas, David, Mets	.260	127	21	33	6	0	0	9	3
Bravo, Daniel, Phillies	.259	189	30	49	8	4	1	24	5
Sumoza, Luis, Padres/Red Sox	.255	165	26	42	4	0	4	18	9
Negron, Antonio, Pirates	.254	142	28	36	9	0	3	17	8
Gualdron, Jose, Reds	.252	155	15	39	9	2	2	16	2
Avila, Gerardo, Mariners	.249	189	30	47	7	1	7	30	6
Munoz, Joe, Pirates	.248	137	22	34	6	3	0	12	**23**
Paredes, Rene, Orioles	.246	167	30	41	3	0	1	11	16
Mendez, Carlos, Reds	.245	163	17	40	8	2	2	26	1
Sanchez, Aliezer, Pirates	.243	144	25	35	5	1	1	17	9
Gil, Rafael, Padres/Red Sox	.243	148	20	36	7	0	5	24	2
Bonevacia, Arthur, Orioles	.241	174	23	42	2	0	1	19	4
Centeno, Manuel, Phillies	.240	150	16	36	3	**6**	2	30	4
Bompart, Alfredo, Marlins/Nationals	.239	176	23	42	7	0	**12**	38	7
Rodriguez, Jean Carlo, Phillies	.239	138	18	33	10	2	2	16	1
Melendez, Jean, Marlins/Nationals	.238	206	26	49	6	1	0	11	4
Lobo, Wilter, Pirates	.236	182	26	43	7	2	4	29	13
Rodriguez, Yonderman, Phillies	.236	157	19	37	1	0	0	20	3
Contreras, Efrain, Reds	.235	119	18	28	6	0	1	15	5
Tua, Franklin, Mariners	.235	119	16	28	5	0	1	18	1

INDIVIDUAL PITCHING LEADERS

(Minimum 40 Innings)

	W	L	ERA	G	SV	IP	H	BB	SO
#Gaetano, Diomny, Mariners	2	0	0.61	26	**11**	30	22	8	24
Mendez, Julio, Mets	6	1	**0.71**	18	4	51	40	8	36
Doubront, Felix, Red Sox/Padres	7	1	0.97	13	0	65	32	29	58
Ladeuth, Carlos, Astros	4	1	0.98	18	6	46	31	10	35
Portillo, Nelson, Mets	6	0	1.16	13	0	62	38	17	60
Escalona, Jose, Mariners	3	4	1.18	12	0	53	40	17	59
Romero, Jose, Orioles	1	1	1.71	11	0	47	36	10	57
Torres, Jesus, Orioles	4	4	1.91	24	7	42	28	18	25
Venegas, Alfredo, Mariners	4	1	1.96	13	0	55	47	12	43
Saenz, Jose, Phillies	6	3	2.01	16	4	54	40	8	40
Echarry, Johnattan, Astros	4	2	2.03	13	0	62	61	13	32
Lopez, Luis, Pirates	7	5	2.04	15	1	88	77	15	60
Ballestas, Freddy, Phillies	6	4	2.10	14	0	69	56	25	45
Montbrum, Kelvin, Mariners	3	1	2.16	12	0	50	40	24	54
Escorcha, Juan, Orioles	**8**	2	2.19	14	1	82	70	40	78
Frias, Rene, Astros	2	3	2.19	13	0	53	44	17	43
Lizardi, Carlos, Orioles	4	2	2.31	15	0	58	59	20	41
Melendez, Moises, Phillies	3	0	2.49	13	1	47	29	34	68
Martinez, Luis, Mets	6	6	2.51	14	2	61	58	15	34
Esparza, Gerardo, Mariners	3	3	2.56	12	0	53	38	32	32
Altamirano, Rolando, Phillies	4	4	2.62	14	0	69	50	23	52
Reyes, Israel, Pirates	5	5	2.67	22	4	54	48	19	38
Contreras, Carlos, Red Sox/Padres	1	4	2.70	12	0	57	41	30	62
Uviedo, Ronald, Mariners	4	3	2.76	12	0	62	42	17	52
Marquez, Angel, Marlins/Nationals	2	5	2.87	14	0	78	61	25	**80**
Fierro, Ronmel, Phillies	3	2	2.88	11	1	41	31	11	30
Izquierdo, Giovanni, Reds	2	2	2.89	14	0	47	32	23	28
Ochoa, Luis, Pirates	2	4	2.94	23	8	49	42	19	36
Ribeiro, Yulman, Marlins/Nationals	2	4	3.00	13	0	45	43	11	31
Fajardo, Carlos, Reds	3	6	3.05	15	0	56	39	14	47
Guerrero, Daniel, Reds	2	1	3.08	14	0	50	39	9	42
Rivero, Raul, Orioles	7	4	3.12	15	0	89	82	28	66
Salazar, Jose, Reds	3	5	3.14	15	0	57	33	22	59
Reyes, Alfredo, Pirates	3	7	3.19	12	0	54	50	25	51
Garcia, Yilfran, Mets	0	4	3.25	13	1	44	41	20	28
Vasquez, Malvin, Pirates	5	3	3.29	12	0	55	36	24	39
Gomez, Epifanio, Red Sox/Padres	4	4	3.38	14	1	59	51	19	50
Rincon, David, Reds	1	5	3.51	15	0	51	40	19	30
Acosta, Jorge, Mariners	5	1	3.56	20	1	43	47	13	50
Orman, Conrad, Orioles	4	5	3.75	15	0	74	77	22	52
Teller, Carlos, Pirates	3	2	4.03	15	0	60	45	44	65
Freytes, Tommy, Red Sox/Padres	3	2	4.03	18	3	45	40	22	40
Calero, Angel, Mets	2	4	4.03	12	0	45	41	24	31
Marrero, Alvaro, Orioles	3	3	4.30	13	0	69	72	34	39

Statistics in **boldface** indicate league leader
#League leader but non-qualifier

ARIZONA FALL LEAGUE

The AFL has always been known as a premier hitter's league, and that trend picked up in 2005, as league records fell one after the other. Among the marks shattered were batting average (.296), runs per game (12.14), hits per game (20.83), slugging percentage (.469) and ERA (5.40).

AFL players hit 220 homers in just 96 games (or an average of 2.20 per game, ahead of the major league average of 2.06), and the Peoria Saguaros set a new mark for team pitching futility in the AFL with a 6.90 ERA.

The Phoenix Desert Dogs used two home runs from Matt Kemp (Dodgers) and one each from Andy LaRoche (Dodgers) and Jarrod Saltalamacchia (Braves) to win the 14th Fall League championship with a 9-3 victory over the Surprise Scorpions at Phoenix Municipal Stadium. Phoenix (23-10) won nine of its first 11 games and never trailed in its division.

The Desert Dogs led the league in both hitting (.309 average) and pitching (4.68 ERA).

"It's the easiest gig I've ever had," Phoenix manager Scott Little (Pirates) said. "There is no secret that when you end up with the best hitting and the best pitching what's probably going to happen at the end. It was proven here today.

"These guys have been a joy to be around every day. To see the chemistry that was developed the first week . . . it was unbelievable."

Kemp hit a two-out solo home run to break a scoreless tie in the sixth inning to help Jamie Shields, whose ERA rose to 1.74.

The next batter, Stephen Drew (Diamondbacks), reached when center fielder Josh Anderson (Astros) lost his short pop fly in the sun for a double, and LaRoche followed with a homer down the line in right. It was his first home run in almost three months.

Kemp homered to center field to start a five-run eighth inning that also included a two-run homer by catcher Saltalamacchia (Braves).

Surprise shortstop Brandon Wood (Angels), who set a fall league record with 14 home runs, doubled and scored the Scorpions' first run in the seventh. He singled in Howie Kendrick (Angels) in the ninth.

STANDINGS

AMERICAN	W	L	PCT	GB
Surprise Scorpions	17	15	.531	—
Mesa Solar Sox	15	17	.469	2
Peoria Saguaros	8	23	.258	8½
NATIONAL	**W**	**L**	**PCT**	**GB**
Phoenix Desert Dogs	22	10	.688	—
Peoria Javelinas	17	14	.548	4½
Grand Canyon Rafters	16	16	.500	6

PLAYOFFS: Desert Dogs defeated Scorpions 9-3 in championship game.

TOP 10 PROSPECTS: 1. Brandon Wood, ss, Surprise Scorpions (Angels). **2.** Alex Gordon, 3b/1b, Surprise Scorpions (Royals). **3.** Ryan Zimmerman, 3b, Peoria Saguaros (Nationals). **4.** Howie Kendrick, 2b, Surprise Scorpions (Angels). **5.** Stephen Drew, ss, Phoenix Desert Dogs (Diamondbacks). **6.** Jarrod Saltalamacchia, c, Phoenix Desert Dogs (Braves). **7.** Ian Stewart, 3b, Peoria Javelinas (Rockies). **8.** Lastings Milledge, of, Grand Canyon Rafters (Mets). **9.** Chris Young, of, Peoria Saguaros (White Sox). **10.** Scott Mathieson, rhp, Surprise Scorpions (Phillies).

INDIVIDUAL BATTING LEADERS

(Minimum 86 Plate Appearances)

	AVG	G	AB	R	H	HR	RBI
Howard, Kevin, Solar Sox	.409	25	88	13	36	3	16
Kemp, Matt, Desert Dogs	.383	23	94	18	36	3	16
Kendrick, Howie, Scorpions	.380	29	121	27	46	5	17
Morales, Kendry, Scorpions	.380	24	92	19	35	2	18
Harris, Brendan, Saguaros	.376	22	85	12	32	1	13
Snyder, Brad, Solar Sox	.367	25	98	20	36	3	19
Ethier, Andre, Desert Dogs	.366	23	82	19	30	2	21
Duncan, Eric, Raptors	.362	23	94	26	34	8	27
Anderson, Josh, Scorpions	.360	24	100	22	36	1	12
LaRoche, Andy, Desert Dogs	.352	24	91	16	32	0	15

INDIVIDUAL PITCHING LEADERS

(Minimum 26 Innings)

	W	L	ERA	IP	H	BB	SO
Loewen, Adam, Javelinas	2	1	1.67	27	19	14	26
Shields, Jamie, Desert Dogs	2	1	1.74	31	23	2	29
Sanchez, Humberto, Solar Sox	1	0	2.15	29	28	14	29
Nageotte, Clint, Javelinas	1	2	2.33	27	21	4	24
Perkins, Glen, Raptors	1	0	2.53	32	28	6	39
Stokes, Brian, Desert Dogs	3	0	2.81	26	25	9	17
Hull, Eric, Desert Dogs	1	1	3.51	26	35	7	18
Guzman, Angel, Solar Sox	1	2	3.82	31	28	12	28
White, Steven, Raptors	2	1	3.94	30	27	15	24
Cassel, Jack, Javelinas	2	2	4.56	26	33	9	21

GRAND CANYON RAFTERS

BATTING	AVG	AB	R	H	2B	3B	HR	RBI	BB	SO	SB
Abercrombie, Reggie, of	.300	90	18	27	5	2	3	11	9	32	6
Andino, Robert. ss	.263	76	11	20	3	0	0	6	5	16	5
Duncan, Eric, 3b/1b	.362	94	26	34	9	1	8	27	10	29	0
Jones, Garrett, 1b	.289	97	13	28	9	1	9	30	7	27	0
Lambin, Chase, 2b/ss	.250	56	8	14	4	0	1	6	11	15	0
Mahar, Kevin, of	.194	67	6	13	6	1	0	6	4	24	1
Meyer, Drew, 2b	.306	72	12	22	2	0	0	6	6	17	4
Milledge, Lastings, of	.330	94	24	31	4	2	5	23	10	17	7
Moses, Matt, 3b	.275	69	11	19	3	0	2	6	1	16	0
Nickeas, Mike, c	.425	40	11	17	7	0	1	10	4	10	0
Parrish, David, c	.229	48	5	11	1	0	1	4	3	18	0
Sardinha, Bronson, of	.344	96	10	33	3	2	3	15	6	14	2
Span, Denard, of	.294	102	14	30	4	1	0	8	7	9	7
Wilson, Andy, c	.279	43	7	12	2	0	1	2	5	11	0
Wilson, Josh, 2b/ss	.301	73	12	22	5	0	4	19	6	16	1

PITCHING	W	L	ERA	G	GS	SV	IP	H	BB	SO
Barrett, Ricky	0	3	9.00	11	0	0	12	17	13	6
Beam, T.J.	0	0	1.53	11	0	1	18	16	2	20
Bowyer, Travis	0	2	9.39	10	0	1	15	28	2	19
Hill, Jeremy	1	1	6.75	4	0	0	5	4	2	3
Kensing, Logan	1	0	6.00	12	0	0	15	18	8	16
Lindstrom, Matt	0	0	12.00	5	0	0	6	13	7	4
Littleton, Wes	2	0	3.38	10	0	0	19	16	4	19
MacLane, Evan	1	2	4.85	6	6	0	26	34	6	17
Masset, Nick	3	2	5.27	10	0	0	14	17	4	13
Owens, Henry	0	0	6.48	5	0	0	8	13	3	9
Perkins, Glen	1	0	2.53	7	7	0	32	28	6	39
Roberts, Mark	0	3	8.46	6	6	0	22	36	14	12
Smith, Matt	1	1	12.86	10	0	0	14	29	10	19
Tankersley, Taylor	2	1	6.35	9	0	2	17	20	8	16
Ungs, Nick	2	0	3.24	6	6	0	25	28	6	13
White, Steven	2	1	3.94	7	7	0	30	27	15	24

MESA SOLAR SOX

BATTING	AVG	AB	R	H	2B	3B	HR	RBI	BB	SO	SB
Coats, Buck, ss/of	.256	39	5	10	1	0	0	4	2	6	0
Denorfia, Chris, of	.333	93	20	31	7	3	3	24	13	15	3
Espinosa, David, of	.282	78	12	22	4	0	2	12	9	11	2
Frandsen, Kevin, 2b	.266	79	8	21	3	1	1	12	2	7	2
Garko, Ryan, 1b	.314	86	10	27	9	0	5	27	7	19	0
Hanigan, Ryan, c	.216	37	3	8	0	1	0	1	2	6	1
Herrera, Javier, c	.286	28	8	8	2	0	1	2	2	6	0
Howard, Kevin. 3b	.409	88	13	36	4	0	3	16	10	9	2
Kelly, Don, ss	.294	85	15	25	3	0	0	11	6	6	3
Kirkland, Kody, 3b	.293	41	9	12	2	1	1	5	5	11	1
Knoedler, Justin, c	.226	53	9	12	1	0	3	7	3	10	0
Murton, Matt, of	.337	92	15	31	11	1	1	14	7	12	3
Ortmeier, Dan, of	.385	26	8	10	4	0	1	5	2	2	4
Osborn, Pat, 3b	.391	23	4	9	3	0	0	2	2	5	0
Patterson, Eric, 2b	.301	83	20	25	4	1	0	5	6	17	5
Sing, Brandon, 1b/of	.246	69	9	17	6	0	3	10	10	24	1
Snyder, Brad, of	.367	98	20	36	6	3	3	19	11	26	2
Votto, Joey, 1b	.250	36	4	9	2	0	0	3	2	8	0

PITCHING	W	L	ERA	G	GS	SV	IP	H	BB	SO
Aardsma, David	0	0	9.64	12	0	0	19	32	10	18
Accardo, Jeremy	1	2	4.30	9	0	1	15	16	5	8

MINOR LEAGUES

	W	L	ERA	G	GS	SV	IP	H	BB	SO
Burres, Brian	1	2	8.24	6	6	0	20	24	13	14
Dannemiller, Beau	0	0	22.50	1	0	0	2	6	1	1
Foley, Travis	0	1	9.24	11	0	0	13	22	7	3
Guzman, Angel	1	2	3.82	7	7	0	31	28	12	28
Haehnel, David	0	0	22.50	2	0	0	2	3	2	2
Hudson, Luke	0	1	5.68	6	6	0	25	33	6	20
Koronka, John	1	0	0.00	10	0	3	13	8	5	11
Miller, Adam	1	1	5.68	6	6	0	25	28	5	18
Nelson, Bubba	2	1	6.59	9	0	1	14	17	8	11
Peterson, Adam	0	1	5.11	9	0	0	12	14	5	13
Sanchez, Humberto	1	0	2.15	6	6	0	29	28	14	29
Simpson, Allan	4	1	0.63	7	0	0	14	9	6	14
Slocum, Brian	2	1	3.15	11	0	1	20	14	8	19
Wilson, Brian	1	3	6.11	10	1	1	18	21	12	15
Woodyard, Mark	0	1	10.50	5	0	0	6	14	4	6

PHOENIX DESERT DOGS

BATTING	AVG	AB	R	H	2B	3B	HR	RBI	BB	SO	SB
Abreu, Tony, ss/2b	.305	82	14	25	6	1	1	7	3	13	1
Avlas, Phil. c	.400	5	1	2	0	0	0	0	0	2	0
Ball, Jarred, of	.321	84	16	27	3	1	2	13	11	17	2
Bankston, Wes, 1b	.282	71	10	20	7	0	2	14	3	15	0
Barton, Daric, 1b	.267	75	16	20	5	1	1	10	21	16	1
Burrus, Josh, of	.313	32	6	10	3	1	1	4	2	8	2
Drew, Stephen, ss	.337	89	25	30	7	4	6	17	17	20	1
Ethier, Andre, of	.366	82	19	30	7	3	2	21	21	10	0
Frazier, Alex, of	.148	27	3	4	0	1	2	10	7	12	0
Johnson, Elliot, 2b	.203	69	8	14	2	1	0	4	5	12	4
Kemp, Matt, of	.383	94	18	36	6	3	3	16	5	14	2
LaRoche, Andy, 3b	.352	91	16	32	9	0	0	15	6	17	4
Loney, James, 1b/of	.322	59	12	19	2	0	5	17	4	7	1
Montero, Miguel, c	.421	19	6	8	0	0	2	9	0	3	0
Pridie, Jason, of	.232	69	9	16	3	2	1	10	8	15	4
Saltalamacchia, Jarrod, c	.288	73	16	21	6	1	1	8	13	19	1
Schuerholz, Jonathan, 3b/2b	.310	58	8	18	2	0	0	7	8	13	1
Suzuki, Kurt, c	.342	38	3	13	4	0	0	7	8	9	0

PITCHING	W	L	ERA	G	GS	SV	IP	H	BB	SO
Basner, Ryan	1	1	4.82	12	0	0	19	21	10	14
Bush, Paul	3	1	6.66	7	6	0	26	36	23	15
Daigle, Casey	2	0	3.46	13	0	5	13	19	7	9
Dannemiller, Beau	1	1	10.54	11	1	0	14	25	17	4
Hoorelbeke, Casey	1	1	9.39	7	0	0	8	13	8	5
Hull, Eric	1	1	3.51	6	6	0	26	35	16	18
Kohn, Shawn	0	0	7.71	11	0	0	14	22	13	10
Komine, Shane	1	1	1.14	5	5	0	24	20	5	18
Lynch, Matt	2	0	6.60	12	0	1	15	21	12	14
McBeth, Marcus	0	0	2.25	4	0	0	4	1	1	5
Miller, Greg	0	0	4.50	3	0	0	4	5	3	4
Murphy, Bill	3	2	6.26	6	6	0	27	36	20	36
Shields, Jamie	2	1	1.74	6	6	0	31	23	6	29
Slaten, Doug	2	0	6.28	12	0	0	14	27	10	13
Stokes, Brian	3	0	2.81	7	2	0	26	25	8	17
Townsend, Wade	0	1	9.00	1	0	0	2	3	2	2
Tucker, Glenn	0	0	2.30	12	0	1	16	13	4	9

PEORIA JAVELINAS

BATTING	AVG	AB	R	H	2B	3B	HR	RBI	BB	SO	SB
Clement, Jeff, c	.269	67	12	18	5	0	3	11	8	17	0
Escobar, Alcides, ss	.333	90	9	30	2	1	0	11	0	15	5
Fahey, Brandon, ss	.288	66	9	19	1	1	0	9	5	11	3
Fielder, Prince, 1b	.143	21	5	3	1	0	2	3	3	8	0
Harris, Gary, of	.240	75	12	18	6	1	0	8	1	13	1
Hart, Corey, 3b/of	.353	68	19	24	3	1	5	14	5	11	4
Hubele, Ryan, c	.444	9	1	4	0	0	0	4	0	3	0
Iannetta, Chris, c	.206	34	5	7	4	0	1	1	11	11	0
Johnson, Michael, 1b	.272	103	19	28	7	0	6	18	11	20	0
Johnson, Tripper, 3b	.333	51	7	17	4	0	2	13	12	8	0
Jones, Adam, of	.238	80	12	19	2	3	3	8	5	16	1
Kottaras, George, c	.229	35	2	8	0	0	1	6	3	6	0
Majewski, Val, of	.274	73	11	20	2	0	2	10	9	15	1
Markakis, Nick, of	.326	86	16	28	4	2	1	12	11	8	0
Rottino, Vinny, 3b/1b	.256	39	10	10	2	0	0	6	9	8	1
Salazar, Jeff, of	.137	73	9	10	1	1	0	3	4	19	3
Stewart, Ian, 3b	.333	39	10	13	2	0	3	12	7	6	0
Uggla, Dan, 2b	.304	102	21	31	7	1	7	22	13	16	0

PITCHING	W	L	ERA	G	GS	SV	IP	H	BB	SO
Asahina, Jonathan	0	4	6.93	7	7	0	25	40	10	10
Breslow, Craig	0	1	7.24	15	0	0	14	19	3	12
Buglovsky, Chris	1	1	11.21	13	0	0	18	36	5	7
Cassel, Jack	2	2	4.56	7	6	0	26	33	9	21
Eveland, Dana	0	0	6.30	3	3	0	10	16	2	10
Flannery, Mike	0	1	7.64	13	0	0	18	28	8	17
Hammond, Steven	0	0	4.11	4	3	0	15	15	6	10

	W	L	ERA	G	GS	SV	IP	H	BB	SO
Loewen, Adam	2	1	1.67	7	6	0	27	19	14	26
Miller, Jim	3	1	4.91	16	0	2	15	23	5	15
Mitchell, Andy	2	0	2.82	17	0	0	22	20	6	16
Morris, Cory	1	0	3.86	4	0	0	7	5	6	6
Nageotte, Clint	1	2	2.33	6	6	0	27	21	4	24
Ramirez, Ramon	2	1	6.20	11	1	0	20	27	9	17
Stetter, Mitch	0	0	9.00	5	0	0	5	8	3	6
Tucker, Rusty	2	0	5.02	15	0	0	14	19	9	18
Wolfe, Brian	1	0	3.24	13	0	2	17	22	1	15

PEORIA SAGUAROS

BATTING	AVG	AB	R	H	2B	3B	HR	RBI	BB	SO	SB
Blanco, Tony, of	.286	28	3	8	1	1	2	3	1	8	1
Boeve, Adam, of	.313	67	8	21	5	1	0	10	4	23	1
Broadway, Larry, 1b	.339	59	9	20	5	0	2	9	13	11	0
Eldred, Brad, 1b	.289	97	13	28	6	1	7	28	4	22	0
Fields, Josh, 3b	.256	90	16	23	2	2	5	16	9	22	2
Harris, Brendan, ss/2b	.376	85	12	32	7	1	1	13	5	8	1
Kratz, Erik, c/1b	.192	26	8	5	3	0	0	2	2	7	0
Lind, Adam, of	.238	84	14	20	5	0	1	10	7	14	0
Lopez, Pedro, ss	.375	24	2	9	3	0	0	3	1	0	0
Moss, Brandon, of	.236	72	10	17	3	1	2	5	5	24	2
Murphy, David, of	.319	91	20	29	6	2	3	9	4	12	2
Quiroz, Guillermo, c	.294	51	6	15	3	0	1	3	3	12	0
Roberts, Ryan, 2b	.260	100	15	26	5	0	5	15	5	22	2
Valido, Robert, ss	.283	60	8	17	4	1	0	8	3	12	4
Walker, Neil, c	.265	49	8	13	0	0	2	5	3	8	2
Whitesell, Josh, 1b	.250	24	1	6	3	0	0	3	2	3	0
Young, Chris, of	.253	83	9	21	5	1	2	11	8	25	3
Zimmerman, Ryan, 3b	.263	38	4	10	1	0	1	2	3	9	0

PITCHING	W	L	ERA	G	GS	SV	IP	H	BB	SO
Andrade, Steve	0	0	4.15	10	0	2	13	8	7	23
Beam, Randy	0	0	3.77	9	0	0	14	12	8	14
Buzachero, Edward	0	3	5.30	13	0	1	19	20	13	17
Connolly, Michael	0	1	9.00	9	0	0	9	14	5	7
Corcoran, Roy	0	2	9.00	12	0	1	17	26	9	11
Delgado, Jesus	0	0	4.08	10	0	0	18	18	3	10
Jacobsen, Landon	1	2	5.00	4	2	0	9	9	6	4
Malone, Corwin	1	3	8.27	8	4	0	21	21	15	20
Maust, David	1	2	6.65	7	7	0	23	31	7	17
Peterson, Matt	0	4	10.71	7	6	0	21	32	14	11
Reynoso, Paulino	1	0	8.47	11	0	0	17	23	16	14
Schroder, Chris	2	1	4.05	12	0	0	20	20	7	18
Smith, Chris	0	3	8.44	7	7	0	21	32	8	13
Tracey, Sean	1	1	7.16	8	2	0	16	18	7	11
Youman, Shane	1	1	5.96	8	3	0	23	24	15	4
Zink, Charlie	0	0	9.45	6	1	0	13	17	6	6

SURPRISE SCORPIONS

BATTING	AVG	AB	R	H	2B	3B	HR	RBI	BB	SO	SB
Anderson, Josh, of	.360	100	22	36	4	0	1	12	4	9	10
Bourn, Michael, of	.300	80	14	24	1	4	0	15	13	10	3
Budde, Ryan, c	.222	9	2	2	1	0	0	2	0	1	0
Butler, Billy, of	.252	103	17	26	6	1	5	21	10	19	0
Gordon, Alex, 1b	.260	50	11	13	4	0	2	9	12	12	0
Haerther, Cody, of	.203	64	13	13	3	0	1	7	10	20	0
Hanson, Travis, 3b	.261	92	19	24	4	1	1	8	6	17	0
Hubele, Ryan, c	.360	25	7	9	2	0	1	6	3	3	0
Jimerson, Charlton, of	.293	75	15	22	2	0	5	11	1	21	8
Johnson, Gabe, c	.154	39	3	6	1	0	1	6	3	12	0
Kendrick, Howie, 2b	.380	121	27	46	10	1	5	17	4	12	2
Morales, Kendry, 1b	.380	92	19	35	14	0	2	18	12	13	0
Robinson, Wade, 2b/ss	.302	43	8	13	0	1	1	9	3	15	1
Smith, Corey, 3b	.330	91	17	30	6	0	7	21	8	21	0
Tupman, Mat, c	.279	43	6	12	1	0	2	6	5	8	0
Wood, Brandon, ss	.307	114	25	35	4	0	14	32	9	31	0

PITCHING	W	L	ERA	G	GS	SV	IP	H	BB	SO
Austen, David	1	0	2.53	8	0	0	11	14	1	6
Barzilla, Philip	3	1	8.27	11	1	0	16	24	8	12
Bass, Brian	1	1	3.33	6	6	0	24	25	0	16
Bayliss, Jonah	3	0	4.98	11	0	0	22	20	7	18
Buchholz, Taylor	1	0	1.57	7	6	0	23	20	4	17
Cameron, Ryan	1	0	6.89	11	0	1	16	18	12	19
Cavazos, Andy	1	0	5.40	9	0	0	17	17	8	15
Demaria, Chris	1	2	3.95	9	0	0	14	16	5	9
Doyne, Cory	2	1	6.75	12	0	0	15	19	11	9
Lambert, Chris	0	1	6.75	6	6	0	17	22	8	12
Mathieson, Scott	0	2	6.92	7	6	0	26	34	11	36
Minix, Travis	1	0	4.30	11	0	0	15	17	3	7
Sanches, Brian	0	4	5.29	11	0	2	17	21	5	13
Scalamandre, Rich	0	0	1.76	9	0	0	15	19	5	12
Weaver, Jered	1	3	5.47	7	7	0	25	30	5	35
Williams, Aaron	1	0	0.00	2	0	0	3	2	0	3

INDEPENDENT LEAGUES

Indy leagues top 7 million in 2005 as new Golden League joins mix

BY J.J. COOPER

Central League champions
Led by 78-year-old manager Wayne Terwilliger, Fort Worth rolled to a title

For the first time in a while, the independent leagues found a new long-term resident in 2005.

The Golden Baseball League, a new single-ownership league, arrived on the scene with a 96-game schedule, attempting to fill the independent leagues West Coast void that had been left since the Western League disbanded after the 2003 season. And unlike many new indy leagues, it made it through the season with no bounced checks, no failed franchises and plenty of optimism for season two.

While the new league's attendance figures didn't wow anyone—roughly 1,300 fans per game, which ranked lowest among the six independent leagues— it was enough to signal that the league was a solid addition to the stable of independent leagues. On the field, the league's caliber of play was impressive as former major leaguers like Rickey Henderson and Desi Wilson joined former first-rounders Adam Johnson and Matt Wheatland and a slew of Double-A caliber players who were attracted by the opportunity to play on the West Coast.

The arrival of the Golden League and the addition of two expansion teams (Calgary and Edmonton) to the Northern League helped push independent leagues attendance past seven million fans for the first time ever. According to attendance figures released by the leagues, indy teams drew 7,515,445 fans in 2005, blowing away the 2004 record attendance of 6.5 million fans.

While the Golden League's arrival helped that total, the preexisting five leagues would have topped seven million on their own, as four of the five leagues topped their 2004 attendance marks.

The Central League led the way with a 17 percent jump, as the addition of El Paso (with a league-leading 190,429 fans) spurred the league to a 125,000 fan jump. The Atlantic League showed a 13 percent jump from 2004's attendance thanks to the arrival of the Lancaster Barnstormers. The Barnstormers, a replacement for the Pennsylvania Road Warriors, a traveling team in 2004, finished second in the league with 378,310 fans.

New Teams, New Cities

El Paso and Lancaster were just two of a number of new franchises in 2005. El Paso joined the Central League after the city's Double-A club moved to Springfield, Mo., during the offseason. The team even kept the Diablos name, and quickly established itself as one of the cornerstones of the league with an average attendance that actually topped the team's final season in affiliated baseball.

Lancaster also had a successful debut financially as fans packed the uniquely shaped Barnstormer Field (372 feet down the left field line and 390 to the left field power alley). In the Northern League, the arrivals of Calgary and Edmonton didn't go as smoothly. Calgary struggled with attendance all season, hurt in part by a late ownership switch that left the team with little time to promote and sell before the season began. The situation in Edmonton was little better, as the owner clashed with the general manag-

2005 INDEPENDENT LEAGUE ALL-STARS

Selected by Baseball America

Pos., Player, Club (League)	AVG	AB	R	H	HR	RBI	SB
C Kelley Gulledge, Fargo-Moorhead (Northern)	.321	252	41	81	10	40	0
1B Brian Becker, Nashua (Atlantic)	.299	490	97	125	41	110	2
2B Ricardo Cordova, New Jersey (Can-Am)	.352	315	59	111	9	59	17
SS Chad Ehrnsberger, St. Paul/Joliet (Northern)	.354	339	76	120	14	71	7
3B Eddie Lantigua, Quebec, (Can-Am)	.324	358	81	116	31	112	4
OF Pete Pirman, Kalamazoo, (Frontier)	.347	409	82	142	23	100	35
OF Desi Wilson, Surprise (Golden)	.411	304	53	125	6	55	14
OF Bryan Warner, Lincoln (Northern)	.352	406	85	143	21	104	8
DH Juan Camacho, El Paso, (Central)	.322	363	72	119	21	100	0

Pos., Player, Club (League	W-L	ERA	G	SV	IP	H	BB	SO
SP Grant Gregg, Chico (Golden)	12-2	1.97	19	0	137	117	31	118
SP Brandon Culp, Fargo-Moorhead (Northern)	14-0	2.60	20	0	118	101	46	70
SP Brett Laxton, Camden (Atlantic)	15-3	3.39	26	0	173	183	48	108
SP Greg Bicknell, Kansas City (Northern)	16-5	2.96	23	0	167	157	51	109
RP Matt Hammons, St. Paul (Northern)	0-3	2.77	37	25	39	26	8	47

SECOND TEAM: C—Aaron Mendoza, San Antonio (Central). **1B**—Vic Davilla, North Shore (Can-Am). **2B**—Carlos Hernandez, Long Island (Atlantic). **SS**—Jose Rodriguez, Chillicothe (Frontier). **3B**—Carlos Duncan, Calgary (Northern). **OF**—Cory Harris, Lincoln (Northern); Ryan Radmanovich, Somerset (Atlantic); Brad Rosenblatt, Brockton (Can-Am). **DH**—Henry Rodriguez, Long Island (Atlantic). **SP**—Joel Bennett, New Jersey (Can-Am); Adam Johnson, San Diego (Golden); Aaron Ledbetter, River City (Frontier); Joe Sergent, Fargo-Moorhead (Northern). **RP**—Ben Grezlovski, Atlantic City (Atlantic).

PLAYER OF THE YEAR: Eddie Lantigua, 3b, Quebec.

er and the media, leaving some bruised feelings and poor attendance.

The most successful new club in indy ball in 2005 was the Can-Am League's Worcester Tornadoes. The Tornadoes replaced the traveling-team Aces and averaged 2,600 fans per game at a stadium that was built in just two months. The fans had plenty to cheer for, as the Tornadoes won the Can-Am title in their debut season, beating Quebec in the championship series.

Talent Exodus Slows

In 2004, visa issues that kept many foreign players out of the U.S. made the independent leagues a one-stop shop for affiliated clubs needing a starting pitcher or a new shortstop. A year later, the fire sale was over. Less than half as many players were signed by affiliated clubs compared to 2004.

There were a multitude of explanations why fewer players made the jump from indy leagues to affiliated ball. The player shortage created by visa restrictions in 2004 lessened in 2005 as teams learned how to adjust better to the new rules. And in signing 112 players a year earlier, teams got a good look at much of the best talent in the independent leagues. Some players stuck with teams and began moving up the organizational ladder, but many others were released in spring training. Having had another chance to prove themselves in the minors, a gaudy batting average in 2005 was less likely to catch a scout's eye.

"If you look at our league from a stats perspective, the top position players are all veteran guys," Northern League chief operating officer John Blake said. "There are guys who have had two trials in affiliated ball. We don't seem to have the younger position player having the big year."

But another factor seemed to be that the talent level in the indy leagues might have taken a dip, especially in the quality of pitching. The addition of the Golden League and two expansion clubs in the Northern League spread the pitching talent out among even more teams, but probably even more importantly, major league clubs seemed more reticent about releasing pitchers, worried that they wouldn't find quality arms to replace them.

"I hear from managers, they expected after the draft that there would be a lot of releases of pitchers," Blake said. "You didn't get that big wave. Managers keep telling me how hard it is to find (veteran) pitchers."

One Frontier League manager pointed out that he saw fewer pitchers top 90 mph in 2005 than in any year he could remember. A front office official who follows and scouts the indy leagues for a major league club agreed that pitching had taken a hit throughout indy ball.

The chase for talent to fill independent team rosters may get even more difficult in 2006. The new United League has moved into Texas with at least six teams, mainly in old Texas-Louisiana League cities, while four Northern League clubs (Lincoln, St. Paul, Sioux City and Sioux Falls) withdrew from that league to form the

Lantigua's perseverence pays off

PLAYER *OF THE* **YEAR**

The first time Eddie Lantigua played for Quebec, it ended with him pouring beer in the concession stands, hoping he'd get another chance to play professional baseball. It's a safe bet that his second stint with the Capitales worked out more to his, and the team's, liking.

The 31-year-old put together the best season of his 15-year career in 2005, hitting .324-31-112 to lead Quebec to the best record in the Can-Am League. In the process, he was Baseball America's Independent League Player of the Year.

Eddie Lantigua

"Quebec has become an amazing place for me," Lantigua said. "I'm really happy here. I don't make millions, but I'm really happy. I wouldn't change a thing. Everything that happened, it really made me stronger."

Once a role player for the Quebec Capitales, Lantigua became the star in 2005. He was the face of the franchise, its most popular spokesman around town.

In 1999, Lantigua signed to play for the newly formed Capitales. When he signed, he had never heard of Quebec, but it was another stop that he hoped would get him back to affiliated ball. He eventually realized he'd found his new home.

"When I met my wife (Mirian), I said, this is the place I want to play," Lantigua said.

There was only one problem. While Lantigua was happy to stay and play in Quebec, the Capitales decided he wasn't a perfect fit for them. He hit .276-9-51 in 1999, but the Capitales looked elsewhere to fill one of their four veteran roster spots with a slugger who would hit more home runs.

He spent the rest of 2000 and all of 2001 in Minnesota, before returning to Quebec in 2002.

But it didn't take long for players to notice a difference.

"Eddie changed so much. He matured so much in the past four or five years," said Michel Laplante, Lantigua's current manager and teammate in 1999. "He's got a wife, kids and a house. He's all set now. He's got no worries when he's playing."

His more patient approach paid off in 2005. Lantigua put it all together, averaging a home run every 11 at-bats and an RBI every three at-bats, while leading the league in home runs, RBIs, extra-base hits (51), slugging percentage (.645), intentional walks (eight), and grand slams (three).

"This has been my best year. I was confident at the plate, thinking no one can beat me," Lantigua said. "I was happy. I don't have to worry about anything else. I go to the batter's box, I look to my children, sitting behind my dugout—what can be better than that?"

PREVIOUS WINNERS

1996—Darryl Motley, of, Fargo-Moorhead (Northern)
1997—Mike Meggers, of, Winnipeg/Duluth (Northern)
1998—Morgan Burkhart, 1b, Richmond (Frontier)
1999—Carmine Cappucio, of, New Jersey (Northern)
2000—Anthony Lewis, 1b, Duluth-Superior (Northern)
2001—Mike Warner, of, Somerset (Atlantic)
2002—Bobby Madritsch, lhp, Winnipeg (Northern)
2003—Jason Shelley, rhp, Rockford (Frontier)
2004—Victor Rodriguez, ss, Somerset (Atlantic)

American Association, joining with five members of the Central League to form the new league.

ATLANTIC LEAGUE

In late June, Mark DiFelice was looking for a job after being released by the Washington Nationals. His decision to come to Somerset proved to be crucial to the team's run to its third Atlantic League title in five years.

Mark DiFelice

The 29-year-old righthander picked up a complete-game win in the first game of the Patriots' first-round playoff series and followed it up with two scoreless innings of relief in Game One of the championship series against Nashua.

But it was his work in the deciding Game Three that earned him playoff MVP honors. He scattered 11 hits, allowing only one run in another complete-game victory. Ahead 6-1 against Nashua, DiFelice begged manager Sparky Lyle for the chance to go out for the ninth inning to finish the game.

"I threw like 140 pitches, but I said, 'Keep throwing me out there. I want to be on the mound when we win this thing,' " DiFelice said.

DiFelice finished the playoffs with a 2-0, 0.90 record in three appearances. He was 7-4, 3.09 during the regular season for the Patriots.

Outfielders Billy Hall and Ryan Radmanovich provided the big hits in the deciding game for Somerset. Hall went 4-for-5 with two doubles, while Radmanovich had two hits, including his third home run of the postseason.

During the regular season, league player of the year Brian Becker provided plenty of big hits. The Nashua first baseman hit 41 home runs to become the first independent leaguer to top 40 home runs since Ozzie Canseco did it in 2000. He also led the league in RBIs (110) and slugging percentage (.629).

STANDINGS

FIRST HALF

NORTH	W	L	PCT	GB
Nashua Pride	49	33	.598	—
Newark Bears	38	44	.463	11
Bridgeport Bluefish	37	44	.457	11½
Long Island Ducks	36	45	.444	12½
SOUTH	**W**	**L**	**PCT**	**GB**
Somerset Patriots	48	32	.600	—
Camden Riversharks	42	38	.525	6
Atlantic City Surf	41	40	.506	7½
Lancaster Barnstormers	33	48	.407	15½

SECOND HALF

NORTH D	W	L	PCT	GB
Long Island Ducks	31	28	.525	—
Nashua Pride	29	29	.500	1½
Newark Bears	20	38	.345	10
Bridgeport Bluefish	18	41	.305	13
SOUTH DIVISION	**W**	**L**	**PCT**	**GB**
Atlantic City Surf	39	20	.661	—
Camden Riversharks	37	22	.627	2
Lancaster Barnstormers	31	28	.525	8
Somerset Patriots	30	29	.508	9

PLAYOFFS: Semifinals—Nashua defeated Long Island 2-1 and Somerset defeated Atlantic City 2-1 in best-of-3 series. **Finals**—Somerset defeated Nashua 3-0 in best-of-5 series.

MANAGERS: Atlantic City—Jeff Ball. **Bridgeport**—Jose Lind. **Camden**—Wayne Krenchicki. **Lancaster**—Tom Herr. **Long Island**—Don McCormack. **Nashua**—Butch Hobson. **Newark**—Chris Jones. **Somerset**—Sparky Lyle.

ATTENDANCE: Long Island 429,218; Lancaster 378,310; Somerset 365,146; Camden 261,599; Bridgeport 197,337; Newark 178,818; Atlantic City 129,158; Nashua 87,645.

ALL-STAR TEAM: C—Lance Burkhart, Lancaster. **1B**—Brian Becker, Nashua. **2B**—Carlos Hernandez, Long Island. **3B**—Dario Delgado, Atlantic City. **SS**—Rayner Bautista, Atlantic City. **OF**—Gary Burnham, Bridgeport; Jeremy Owens, Somerset; Ryan Radmanovich, Somerset; Henry Rodriguez, Long Island. **DH**—Jeremy Todd, Lancaster; Jose Herrera, Newark. **UT**—Joe Kilburg, Nashua. **RHP**—Brett Laxton, Camden. **LHP**—Lance Davis, Long Island. **RP**—Todd Erdos, Long Island.

Player of the Year: Brian Becker, Nashua. **Pitcher of the Year:** Brett Laxton, Camden. **Manager of the Year:** Butch Hobson, Nashua.

INDIVIDUAL BATTING LEADERS
(Minimum 340 Plate Appearances)

	AVG	G	AB	R	H	HR	RBI
Hernandez, Carlos, Long Island	.331	112	426	71	141	9	64
Burnham, Gary, Bridgeport	.322	121	422	69	136	18	80
Delgado, Dario, Atlantic City	.321	126	502	86	161	22	89
Radmanovich, Ryan, Somerset	.319	118	442	71	141	25	82
Herrera, Jose, Newark	.318	106	425	75	135	16	68
Foster, Quincy, Lancaster	.318	115	469	68	149	10	65
Benjamin, Al, Atlantic City	.318	108	418	71	133	17	72
Rodriguez, Henry, Long Island	.317	81	303	54	96	20	57
Espada, Angel, Bridgeport	.313	106	390	49	122	3	30
Nava, Lipso, Camden	.312	88	311	39	97	3	39

INDIVIDUAL PITCHING LEADERS
(Minimum 101 Innings)

	W	L	ERA	IP	H	BB	SO
Laxton, Brett, Camden	15	2	2.98	160	165	42	98
Harriger, Denny, Nashua	16	7	3.68	174	169	42	108
Miller, Josh, Bridgeport	7	6	3.88	137	149	35	78
Davis, Lance, Long Island	10	7	3.95	141	169	30	81
Sobkowiak, Scott, Somerset	8	7	4.06	124	123	34	94
Powell, Greg, Camden	15	6	4.16	138	148	35	58
Crawford, Paxton, Long Island	8	8	4.22	109	105	27	80
Daneker, Pat, Newark	10	7	4.26	154	174	36	69
Simon, Ben, Camden	9	8	4.35	170	191	49	142
Lamber, Justin, Long Island	8	4	4.38	117	135	29	67

ATLANTIC CITY

BATTING	AVG	AB	R	H	2B	3B	HR	RBI	SB
Bautista, Rayner, ss	.290	411	67	119	24	4	16	58	16
Benjamin, Al, of	.317	442	72	140	31	5	17	73	6
Capadeici, Adam, c	.000	11	0	0	0	0	0	0	0
Delgado, Dario, 3b/1b	.321	539	90	173	31	2	22	96	8
Essian, Jim, of	.286	353	58	101	18	4	5	43	32
Goodwin, Tom, of	.265	328	55	87	11	5	5	38	23
Heath, Demetrius, 2b	.294	316	65	93	12	5	4	41	47
Housel, David, 2b	.226	265	46	60	12	4	5	28	10
Hurst, Jimmy, dh	.272	81	12	22	5	0	3	12	1
Johnson, Gary, of	.294	344	47	101	17	0	5	44	23
Law, Jason, of/1b	.214	56	2	12	2	2	0	13	0
Marval, Raul, ss/3b	.271	314	47	85	17	1	6	38	6
McDonald, Kevin, c	.223	211	23	47	7	0	3	28	1
Rivera, Mike, c	.373	59	9	22	1	0	3	9	3
Rosario, Mel, c	.271	221	39	60	13	3	7	32	4
Timmons, Ozzie, of	.280	386	66	108	27	1	31	80	3
Velazquez, Jose, 1b	.303	350	58	106	14	1	7	46	3
Yan, Julian, 1b	.318	88	17	28	3	0	9	19	0

PITCHERS	W	L	ERA	G	SV	IP	H	BB	SO
Beal, Andy	0	3	6.26	5	0	23	27	10	11
Bell, Gary	6	3	3.19	52	0	68	63	31	51
Burke, Greg	1	2	3.70	25	0	49	51	16	37
Chavez, Anthony	15	5	4.53	26	0	167	188	54	100
Corrado, Rob	4	5	5.09	36	0	111	121	50	62
Desgue, Fernando	0	0	0.00	8	7	9	5	1	7
Goldwater, Kyle	7	8	5.74	28	1	105	136	31	44
Grezlovski, Ben	5	0	1.44	41	21	44	33	11	32
High, Andy	2	0	1.04	6	0	9	3	2	10
Janzen, Marty	2	0	2.08	3	0	13	12	6	4
Kirkland, Aaron	5	1	3.27	59	3	66	55	25	50
Markey, Barry	0	2	8.53	10	0	13	15	12	4
McDonald, Kevin	0	0	9.00	1	0	1	1	0	0
Mendible, Frank	0	1	10.38	5	0	4	6	8	2
Mikkelsen, Linc	6	12	5.60	27	0	169	191	64	120
Mottl, Ryan	0	0	8.10	1	0	3	6	1	2
Persails, Mark	10	10	5.39	29	0	149	169	68	114
Reichert, Dan	0	0	8.74	9	0	11	16	14	3
Schurman, Ryan	8	1	3.80	14	0	88	72	48	72
Stockstill, Jason	2	4	5.82	11	0	56	58	38	40
Villacis, Eduardo	4	0	2.60	7	0	45	41	13	43
Villegas, Feli	2	3	4.23	23	5	28	25	24	34
Wilkerson, Steve	1	0	3.38	6	0	8	6	2	6

BRIDGEPORT

BATTING	AVG	AB	R	H	2B	3B	HR	RBI	SB
Avila, Rolo, of	.254	248	34	63	6	0	2	15	11
Boston, D.J., 1b	.267	423	63	113	21	0	10	57	2
Burnham, Gary, of/1b	.320	453	75	145	32	3	18	84	3
Coleman, Michael, of	.291	251	44	73	15	1	16	42	5
Deleon, Sandy, c	.171	35	3	6	1	0	0	1	0
Escobar, Gustavo, 2b/3b	.320	25	2	8	0	1	0	3	1
Espada, Angel, 2b	.309	414	52	128	15	4	3	32	18
Fenwick, Ron, 2b/ss	.268	82	8	22	4	0	0	5	1
Gann, Jamie, of	.302	384	57	116	26	5	16	60	12
Hart, Corey, ss	.305	174	31	53	10	2	1	20	2
Kuilan, Hector, c	.235	294	26	69	15	0	11	39	3
Larkin, Steve, of	.186	156	12	29	4	0	2	9	2
Latham, Chris, of	.295	132	24	39	13	2	6	17	12
2-team (58 Long Island)	.283	332	52	94	21	4	13	36	31
Lidle, Kevin, c/2b	.190	121	8	23	2	0	0	5	1
Otanez, Willis, of/3b	.352	165	23	58	9	0	6	27	0
Pennyfeather, Will, of	.251	319	35	80	13	1	11	46	3
Person, Robert, of	.250	4	1	1	0	0	0	1	0
Rodriguez, Tony, ss/3b	.240	421	51	101	15	0	2	25	11
Sanchez, Tino, c	.250	68	6	17	1	0	1	9	0
Torres, Jason, c	.263	57	7	15	3	0	2	9	0
Williams, Brady, 3b	.259	378	41	98	19	5	10	58	0
Williams, Peanut, 1b	.244	131	13	32	5	0	4	17	2

PITCHERS	W	L	ERA	G	SV	IP	H	BB	SO
Ahearne, Pat	8	10	4.51	28	0	178	201	59	123
Arroyo, Luis	1	7	5.45	21	0	66	75	32	57
Batson, Byron	2	1	5.26	5	0	26	27	12	18
Bell, Richard	2	1	3.33	22	0	24	25	11	16
Bowles, Brian	1	0	0.50	14	6	18	7	6	15
2-team (32 Long Island)	4	7	4.75	46	6	102	109	48	76
Cain, Tim	2	12	6.18	23	0	119	150	39	85
Collins, Pat	2	1	3.06	28	1	35	31	23	42
Cornett, Brad	1	5	4.88	14	0	66	86	25	40
Darley, Ned	1	5	4.86	27	1	37	32	16	22
Fenwick, Ron	0	0	27.00	1	0	1	2	1	2
Hill, Terrance	1	0	11.57	9	0	9	17	7	3
Kalinowski, Josh	4	9	6.94	31	0	84	98	54	83
Krines, Dan	7	6	5.40	47	0	75	105	25	56
Lidle, Kevin	0	0	4.50	3	0	4	6	4	1
Mathews, T.J.	3	3	2.49	24	7	25	21	5	27
Mercado, Hector	1	0	2.49	19	0	22	22	13	15
Miller, Josh	7	6	3.88	20	0	137	149	35	78
Miranda, Angel	4	3	3.94	44	0	59	51	48	42
Person, Robert	0	4	6.37	14	1	35	39	13	32
Porzio, Mike	1	3	4.30	10	0	38	41	13	37
Raggio, Brady	5	1	3.12	10	0	61	66	18	47
Ramos, Eddy	1	3	3.77	11	0	14	20	6	8
Rodriguez, Tony	0	0	0.00	1	0	1	0	0	0
Rosengren, Phil	0	4	9.00	37	0	50	66	33	44
Shibilo, Andy	1	0	0.57	15	0	16	10	5	21
Warren, Brian	0	1	6.57	12	4	12	18	8	13
Williams, Brady	0	0	0.00	1	0	1	1	1	0

CAMDEN

BATTING	AVG	AB	R	H	2B	3B	HR	RBI	SB
Anderson, Travis, c	.331	163	32	54	12	1	6	24	2
Aquilino, Anthony, 2b	.297	128	19	38	2	1	3	14	5
Barrett, Rich, of	.290	504	99	146	24	11	6	50	53
Biernbaum, L.J., of	.305	383	70	117	24	1	18	71	2
Cameron, Troy, 3b/2b	.260	323	64	84	24	4	14	54	3
Connell, Lino, 2b/ss	.349	146	22	51	8	2	2	41	7
Dellaero, Jason, ss	.147	109	10	16	2	0	4	11	1
Drew, Stephen, ss	.427	82	17	35	8	3	4	18	0
Fitzgerald, Jason, of/1b	.319	260	53	83	17	4	3	42	26
Gutierrez, Vic, ss/2b	.307	479	73	147	23	3	9	58	42
Hunter, Brian, of	.278	97	14	27	6	0	1	14	15
Jones, Ryan, 1b	.276	359	52	99	24	1	12	74	0
Jordan, Kevin, 2b	.233	43	4	10	2	0	1	7	0
Logan, Kyle, of	.188	32	5	6	0	0	1	3	3
Lynam, Guy, c	.240	271	36	65	16	1	5	30	8
Maness, Dwight, of	.267	498	92	133	29	4	21	88	33
Nava, Lipso, 3b/1b	.312	311	39	97	23	0	3	39	3
Sanchez, Marcos, c	.330	103	17	34	7	3	4	22	0
Smith, Derek, 2b	.000	8	0	0	0	0	0	0	0
Strauss, Brad, 1b/3b	.275	433	74	119	19	3	7	46	10
Wakeland, Chris, of	.235	153	17	36	3	0	5	29	0
Wilson, Eddie, c	.000	5	0	0	0	0	0	0	0

PITCHERS	W	L	ERA	G	SV	IP	H	BB	SO
Babula, Shaun	4	0	4.10	34	3	42	38	17	31
Bechtel, Chuck	1	0	5.06	14	0	21	22	18	19
Cameron, Troy	0	0	0.00	3	0	3	4	1	0
Cole, Joey	0	1	5.11	11	3	12	15	10	14
De los Santos, Carlos	0	0	10.13	4	0	5	8	4	7
Dougherty, Kevin	7	9	5.22	27	0	162	187	64	82
Fischer, Eric	0	5	5.82	7	0	39	43	22	20
Fussell, Chris	1	2	3.86	11	1	14	16	5	15
Gomes, Wayne	5	5	3.93	40	17	50	48	25	39
Hunter, Brian	0	0	13.50	2	0	2	4	2	1
Ion, Mark	1	4	4.91	35	1	66	57	34	39
Laxton, Brett	15	3	3.39	26	0	173	183	48	108
Laxton, Josh	0	1	6.39	14	0	25	32	19	8
Linares, Ramon	4	1	2.31	32	2	47	30	22	61
McKenna, Daniel	0	0	10.29	5	0	7	9	6	3
Powell, Greg	16	7	4.31	37	1	150	162	40	67
Rizzo, Todd	6	4	5.77	58	5	64	77	42	44
Simon, Ben	9	10	4.34	29	0	183	203	52	151
Steward, Jaime	11	8	4.85	28	0	174	194	61	126

LANCASTER

BATTING	AVG	AB	R	H	2B	3B	HR	RBI	SB
Bryan, Jason, of	.254	343	47	87	20	1	13	52	11
Burkhart, Lance, c	.251	387	68	97	19	1	18	75	5
Castro, Juan, c	.143	56	2	8	1	0	0	1	0
Foster, Quincy, of	.320	515	78	165	17	7	11	70	55
Gonzalez, Danny, ss	.275	316	46	87	15	0	7	37	6
Hake, Travis, 2b/ss	.295	525	91	155	32	4	3	52	42
Hileman, Jutt, of/2b	.266	482	87	128	28	5	12	74	11
Hutchins, Norm, of	.314	191	29	60	6	4	5	21	13
Marcano, Raul, 1b/of	.235	149	12	35	6	0	3	19	2
Marrero, Oreste, 1b	.269	449	64	121	20	1	18	67	1
Melo, Juan, ss/2b	.299	87	13	26	5	0	2	15	2
Minor, Ryan, 3b/1b	.268	481	81	129	29	0	26	99	1
Nathans, John, c/of	.291	141	28	41	6	0	4	13	2
2-team (26 Nashua)	.276	214	35	59	13	0	8	25	2
Nichols, Joe, of/1b	.242	62	12	15	1	0	1	6	8
Ortiz, Jose, 3b	.343	99	16	34	8	0	4	25	1
Todd, Jeremy, 1b	.303	287	64	87	20	0	19	69	2
2-team (55 Newark)	.298	487	88	145	39	2	26	107	3
Note, Steve, 3b/of	.295	149	35	44	4	2	4	20	6
Van Rossum, Chris, of	.333	120	22	40	8	3	4	24	3
Wilson, Kevin, ss	.157	51	1	8	1	1	0	3	1

PITCHERS	W	L	ERA	G	SV	IP	H	BB	SO
Acosta, Domingo	3	5	3.48	55	11	88	92	31	74
Alvarado, Giancarlo	2	0	2.28	18	1	24	16	16	25
2-team (25 Newark)	4	2	3.78	43	1	64	52	49	68
Anderson, Jason	0	0	11.57	2	0	2	4	4	2
Dawley, Joe	4	4	5.00	17	0	97	101	39	89
Diaz, Pedro	1	0	6.75	26	0	44	56	21	25
Dooley, Joe	8	5	4.98	21	0	99	99	59	62
Garcia, Reynaldo	0	1	3.86	2	0	2	1	4	0
Gardner, Hayden	3	3	3.86	21	0	23	28	25	13
Hoard, Brent	2	1	5.4	3	0	15	14	8	10
Hundley, Jeff	1	4	4.24	37	2	34	30	12	28
Jackson, Jimmy	0	0	45.00	1	0	1	3	4	0
Lipson, David	1	0	10.13	2	0	3	3	7	1
2-team (6 Nashua)	2	0	11.57	8	1	9	13	15	4
Mattes, Troy	4	5	5.57	54	2	73	95	31	57
Pacheco, Enemencio	8	5	5.97	19	0	104	123	40	55
Patterson, Scott	4	2	4.76	28	6	74	85	20	62
Peeples, Ross	6	9	5.14	22	0	124	139	31	56
Perez, Gil	2	3	2.54	15	0	39	36	17	30
Scheuing, Matt	6	6	5.29	26	0	143	185	42	52
Smith, Cliff	3	3	1.43	33	4	38	32	21	22
Smith, Clint	2	13	5.95	35	3	127	169	55	52
Zallie, Chris	4	7	4.88	55	0	90	97	27	48

LONG ISLAND

BATTING	AVG	AB	R	H	2B	3B	HR	RBI	SB
Ambrosini, Dominick, of	.288	368	56	106	15	4	13	55	15
Baez, Kevin, ss/2b	.189	53	4	10	3	0	0	3	0
Cafiero, Rob, 1b	.233	103	13	24	2	0	0	9	0
Davies, Justin, of	.283	442	79	125	12	4	2	32	22
Depastino, Joe, c	.455	22	4	10	3	0	1	2	0
Diaz, Edwin, 3b	.214	14	2	3	0	0	0	0	0
Goelz, Jim, ss/2b	.212	208	23	44	3	1	1	11	3
Hernandez, Carlos, 2b/ss	.321	464	78	149	26	2	10	67	39
Jennings, Doug, of	.211	71	4	15	3	0	1	7	0
Johnson, Jason, of	.281	288	44	81	20	3	4	41	12
Latham, Chris, of	.275	200	28	55	8	2	7	19	19
Lennon, Pat, 1b/of	.291	234	39	68	14	1	6	37	7
Leon, Donny, 3b	.282	188	31	53	7	0	8	36	0
Lorenzo, Juan, ss/3b	.291	358	42	104	15	6	2	28	8
Magee, Wendell, dh	.000	19	0	0	0	0	0	0	0
Martinez, Manny, of	.282	39	4	11	3	0	1	10	0

BATTING	AVG	AB	R	H	2B	3B	HR	RBI	SB
Owen, Ryan, c	.270	115	15	31	8	0	3	16	0
Perez, Jhonny, ss	.227	44	3	10	1	0	0	4	6
Rios, Armando, of	.284	197	31	56	13	1	13	47	11
Rodriguez, Henry, 1b/of	.322	348	64	112	17	0	27	72	1
Rose Jr., Pete, 1b	.262	431	54	113	27	0	14	55	1
Torrealba, Steve, c	.263	334	40	88	15	1	8	39	2
Tovar, Edgar, 3b	.208	101	6	21	3	0	1	7	0

PITCHERS	W	L	ERA	G	SV	IP	H	BB	SO
Arroyo, Luis	4	0	3.21	8	0	34	32	17	29
2-team (21 Bridgeport)	5	7	4.70	29	0	100	107	49	86
Arthurs, Shane	6	4	4.26	24	2	87	97	25	50
Austin, Jeff	1	3	4.82	28	0	28	27	17	37
Beech, Matt	1	1	4.15	3	0	17	15	10	24
Borbon, Pedro	3	3	5.36	7	0	47	54	10	50
Bowles, Brian	3	7	5.66	32	0	84	102	42	61
Cafiero, Rob	0	1	15.00	1	0	3	3	3	0
Crawford, Paxton	8	8	4.22	18	0	109	105	27	80
Crudale, Mike	5	4	4.52	64	4	62	62	20	41
Davis, Lance	11	8	3.76	24	0	153	180	33	89
Dorsey, Brian	2	4	6.19	26	0	52	61	36	44
Erdos, Todd	0	2	3.96	64	32	61	59	18	51
Lamber, Justin	8	6	4.94	33	0	126	155	30	74
Myers, Rodney	3	3	3.77	8	0	45	53	13	26
Osborne, Donovan	2	4	1.99	10	0	63	65	12	49
Pulsipher, Bill	2	1	9.00	3	0	15	26	6	9
Rocker, John	0	2	6.50	23	0	18	16	28	19
Runion, Tony	3	5	4.94	58	0	82	89	29	65
Sadler, Carl	1	3	6.75	11	0	11	20	7	3
2-team (2 Somerset)	1	4	8.03	13	0	12	23	11	5
Shepard, David	2	3	5.09	18	0	69	75	19	48
Smith, Chris	2	1	4.14	25	0	37	29	28	27

NASHUA

BATTING	AVG	AB	R	H	2B	3B	HR	RBI	SB
Becker, Brian, 1b	.299	455	94	136	27	0	41	110	2
Bergeron, Peter, of	.341	41	7	14	1	0	0	6	3
Bragg, Darren, of	.255	490	97	125	31	4	15	48	14
Creighton, Tom, 2b/of	.275	324	69	89	23	3	6	39	10
De la Rosa, Tomas, ss	.222	81	12	18	6	0	1	8	3
Francia, Dave, of	.281	392	54	110	17	3	0	27	26
Haverbusch, Kevin, of/1b	.270	397	67	107	18	0	19	63	7
Hopper, Shane, 3b	.315	387	63	122	26	2	11	64	9
Hurst, Jimmy, of	.303	327	64	99	18	1	21	70	4
2-team (19 Atlantic City)	.297	408	76	121	23	1	24	82	5
Kilburg, Joe, 2b/3b	.318	428	83	136	25	6	11	66	11
Miller, Orlando, ss	.317	230	29	73	21	0	3	40	3
Murray, Glenn, of	.265	437	77	116	28	0	31	98	4
Nathans, John, c	.247	73	7	18	7	0	4	12	0
Pogue, Jamie, c	.238	21	3	5	1	0	0	2	0
Polanco, Enohel, ss/2b	.333	57	12	19	2	0	0	10	0
Rodriguez, Luis, c	.289	284	41	82	21	1	8	46	5
Shier, Peter, ss	.289	187	30	54	12	3	3	23	5
Torres, Mike, c/2b	.286	259	34	74	12	0	9	52	1
Wilson, Eddie, c	.000	3	0	0	0	0	0	0	0
2-team (3 Camden))	.000	8	0	0	0	0	0	0	0

PITCHERS	W	L	ERA	G	SV	IP	H	BB	SO
Agamennone, Brandon	0	0	2.25	2	0	4	3	4	0
Averette, Robert	6	5	6.12	14	0	75	101	17	49
Blanton, Jason	6	1	3.84	42	3	66	65	16	50
Bragg, Darren	0	0	0.00	1	0	1	2	0	1
Cosgrove, Mike	0	0	0.00	4	1	4	1	1	2
Creighton, Tom	0	0	18.00	2	0	2	2	3	0
Esslinger, Cam	5	4	5.08	52	9	62	70	37	60
2-team (1 Somerset)	5	4	5.23	53	9	62	71	38	60
Gannon, Joe	2	0	6.65	7	0	23	27	11	14
3-team (14 Newark, 2 Somerset)	8	5	6.22	23	0	103	130	46	51
Goetz, Geoff	1	0	6.25	29	0	32	35	21	19
Griffiths, Jeremy	0	2	16.33	5	0	14	22	15	2
Hammons, Matt	0	0	0.00	2	0	2	2	0	1
Harriger, Denny	16	8	3.68	30	1	186	179	45	117
Hartmann, Pete	2	0	3.19	5	0	31	27	15	23
Hopper, Shane	0	0	27.00	2	0	1	3	4	0
Janzen, Marty	0	0	6.46	3	0	15	13	12	3
2-team (3 Atlantic City)	2	0	4.45	6	0	28	25	18	7
Kilburg, Joe	0	0	11.57	1	0	2	4	4	0
Klemm, Tom	0	1	14.14	5	0	7	15	9	4
LaRosa, Mark	1	5	8.20	40	0	79	118	44	33
Lipson, David	1	0	12.15	6	1	7	10	8	3
Looney, Brian	5	9	4.72	20	0	109	119	33	69
Mann, Jim	1	2	1.50	31	16	30	17	13	37
Marchesano, Mike	1	1	3.97	2	0	11	10	5	9
McGlinchy, Kevin	2	2	4.50	25	5	42	40	10	30
Mieses, Jose	8	11	5.89	40	0	150	172	73	112
Navarro, Jason	0	0	1.80	9	0	10	9	8	10
Pearson, Jason	6	1	1.69	30	1	32	21	13	19
Rodriguez, Luis	0	0	18.00	1	0	2	3	2	0
Sparks, Jeff	1	2	8.36	13	0	14	19	18	13
Teut, Nate	8	5	4.49	21	0	124	127	45	88
Torres, Mike	0	0	9.00	2	0	4	9	3	0
Young, Colin	6	3	5.08	40	0	89	100	45	67

NEWARK

BATTING	AVG	AB	R	H	2B	3B	HR	RBI	SB
Ayala, Abraham, c	.282	209	25	59	6	0	3	27	0
Ciraco, Darren, of	.328	64	10	21	3	0	0	4	3
Corporan, Elvis, 3b/c	.149	114	12	17	4	0	0	5	1
Cruz, Jose, of	.200	10	2	2	1	0	0	0	0
Dellaero, Jason, 3b	.185	151	17	28	3	2	1	9	1
2-team (31 Camden)	.169	260	27	44	5	2	5	20	2
Eickhorst, Chris, c	.229	35	1	8	1	0	0	3	0
2-team (31 Somerset)	.269	156	19	42	7	1	2	24	0
Falu, Melvin, of/2b	.340	103	12	35	5	3	0	12	0
Herrera, Jose, of	.318	425	75	135	19	3	16	68	5
Hutchins, Norm, of	.285	291	51	83	22	2	12	49	15
2-team (54 Lancaster)	.297	482	80	143	28	6	17	70	28
Maxwell, Keith, 1b	.269	458	72	123	23	1	18	78	0
McGee, Tom, c	.270	259	35	70	15	2	9	39	0
Moore, Michael, of	.179	184	27	33	4	1	6	20	0
Olivares, Teuris, 3b/2b	.302	106	17	32	3	1	4	18	2
Olmeda, Jose, 3b/2b	.277	405	61	112	26	0	14	51	8
Perez, Jerson, ss	.290	514	69	149	23	4	8	60	9
Perez, Koby, c	.000	2	0	0	0	0	0	0	0
Quezada, Dalmiro, 2b/3b	.042	24	1	1	1	0	0	2	0
Quintana, Wil, of	.291	419	73	122	18	4	25	77	10
Santora, Jack, 2b/ss	.276	507	75	140	18	4	5	41	38
Santos, Francisco, 1b/of	.280	328	41	92	21	0	8	47	2
Steppe, Nicholas, of	.216	97	7	21	4	0	1	9	1
Thomas, Jonathan, dh	.571	7	1	4	0	0	0	3	2
Todd, Jeremy, 1b/of	.290	200	24	58	19	2	7	38	1

PITCHERS	W	L	ERA	G	SV	IP	H	BB	SO
Alvarado, Giancarlo	2	2	4.65	25	0	41	36	33	43
Alvarado, Luis	0	0	11.25	6	0	12	20	9	6
Banks, Willie	0	0	67.50	4	0	2	15	5	2
Bauer, Greg	1	1	3.00	5	0	33	34	7	23
Bermudez, Manny	3	8	3.41	41	1	61	66	17	36
Billingsley, Brent	8	10	5.92	27	0	152	178	73	95
Brooks, Jake	4	1	3.79	36	12	40	37	19	34
Castillo, Carlos	4	10	6.33	16	0	95	127	20	70
Crampton, Steve	3	1	4.53	36	0	54	59	19	38
Daneker, Pat	10	9	4.43	28	0	165	190	41	74
De los Santos, Carlos	1	1	5.68	10	0	19	23	12	18
2-team (14 Camden)	1	1	6.66	14	0	24	31	16	25
Dillinger, John	0	2	8.31	6	0	17	20	13	13
Eickhorst, Chris	1	0	3.97	8	1	11	9	9	6
Farnsworth, Jeff	2	7	6.50	27	2	73	107	22	48
Farren, Dave	0	0	6.75	8	0	15	16	9	12
Feliz, Bienvenido	0	1	6.75	2	0	5	8	6	2
Gannon, Joe	5	4	5.76	14	0	66	84	27	25
Goldwater, Kyle	0	2	8.40	4	0	15	20	4	4
2-team (28 Atlantic City)	7	10	6.08	32	1	120	156	35	48
Harris, Reggie	1	0	9.00	3	0	2	5	3	0
Heredia, Julian	0	0	5.40	2	0	3	5	1	2
Hutchins, Norm	0	0	27.00	1	0	1	3	0	1
Jones, Bobby M.	0	0	6.75	5	0	16	17	5	15
Maness, Nick	0	2	7.71	11	0	28	38	26	12
Olivares, Teuris	0	0	0.00	1	0	1	0	0	0
Peguero, Darwin	1	0	4.29	20	0	21	17	15	17
Pizarro, Melvin	0	0	12.6	3	0	5	13	2	4
Roque, Darryl	4	5	6.33	40	0	80	105	32	50
Santora, Jack	0	0	27.00	3	0	2	5	2	1
Santos, Francisco	0	0	0.00	1	0	2	0	2	0
Wade, Travis	2	3	4.21	22	3	36	37	12	27
Wayne, Justin	1	2	3.00	10	0	18	12	17	9
Zwirchitz, Andy	5	11	5.55	25	0	133	131	66	130

SOMERSET

BATTING	AVG	AB	R	H	2B	3B	HR	RBI	SB
Betts, Todd, 1b	.269	431	64	116	36	0	15	67	3
Boran, Patrick, of/ss	.280	214	41	60	11	0	4	34	3
Cordell, Brent, c	.263	114	18	30	6	0	9	23	0
Eickhorst, Chris, c	.281	121	18	34	6	1	2	21	0
Escandon, Emiliano, 2b	.256	446	76	114	21	4	6	54	14
Gsell, Tony, of/ss	.233	189	30	44	22	0	5	26	0
Hall, Billy, of/ss	.295	336	71	99	16	4	2	44	62
Kellner, Ryan, c	.256	117	18	30	6	0	3	11	0
Lucca, Lou, 3b/1b	.264	110	16	29	5	0	4	13	0
Lunar, Fernando, c	.292	144	19	42	8	0	5	22	0
Navarrete, Ray, of/2b	.260	262	36	68	19	2	6	30	2

Navarrette, Alejandr, 2b	.125	8	0	1	1	0	0	0	0
Nettles, Jeff, 3b/1b	.265	501	85	133	36	3	28	99	0
Nicholson, Kevin, ss	.281	402	62	113	29	1	11	74	4
O'Keefe, Mike, of	.138	29	4	4	1	0	0	4	1
Owens, Jeremy, of	.290	525	92	152	29	6	24	77	29
Radmanovich, Ryan, of	.319	483	80	154	27	1	28	89	1
Sandel, George, 3b/2b	.229	280	35	64	12	5	1	28	2
Tucker, Mamon, of	.164	61	5	10	1	0	0	4	2

PITCHERS	W	L	ERA	G	SV	IP	H	BB	SO
Akens, Phil	0	0	1.29	7	0	7	5	3	8
Andersen, Derek	2	0	1.84	9	2	15	19	5	14
Anderson, Dallas	0	0	6.75	2	0	3	5	2	1
Bierbrodt, Nick	4	2	4.48	40	1	66	66	38	61
Boran, Pat	0	0	4.50	1	0	2	2	1	0
Christman, Tim	2	4	3.72	9	0	39	32	11	34
Clontz, Brad	3	3	1.60	43	9	62	56	15	49
Difelice, Mark	7	4	3.09	14	0	76	72	8	53
Elder, Dave	4	1	1.47	32	6	43	24	19	61
Esslinger, Cam	0	0	0.00	1	0	0	1	1	0
Evans, Kyle	1	0	4.08	6	0	18	21	6	10
Forster, Scott	0	1	15.43	4	0	5	6	4	3
Gannon, Joe	1	1	7.71	2	0	14	19	8	12
Hearns, Shane	5	4	3.07	45	5	85	56	46	96
Jodie, Brett	3	5	6.86	10	0	42	60	10	28
Larson, Adam	1	3	5.17	17	2	38	47	14	25
Lee, Derek	4	2	2.45	10	0	66	54	16	48
Marquez, Rob	5	3	4.42	52	8	59	54	25	59
Modica, Greg	7	7	4.84	24	0	123	122	49	109
Moser, Todd	3	5	5.00	35	2	113	138	37	62
Sadler, Carl	0	1	16.20	2	0	2	3	4	2
Sobkowiak, Scott	8	7	4.06	21	0	124	123	34	94
Solveson, Saul	2	1	2.86	19	3	28	22	9	11
Stechschulte, Gene	0	0	2.25	4	0	4	3	3	5
Stocks, Nick	6	6	4.01	24	0	114	129	43	84
Tollberg, Brian	10	2	2.30	14	0	94	88	17	51

CAN-AM LEAGUE

For a fledgling franchise, the Worcester Tornadoes didn't take long to ditch the training wheels. When Worcester was added to the Can-Am League in January 2005, the team didn't have a nickname, any players or even a stadium. Nine months later, the Tornadoes were Can-Am League champs,

It was a perfect ending to a season that saw the team rush to build a stadium in two months.

Alex Pena

"We had a field, and everything else, from stands to lights to concessions had to be created from scratch," Tornadoes general manager Mike Lieberman said. "There were a couple of minor things (to finish), but concessions were up and running (for Opening Day). Tickets were being sold."

Manager Rich Gedman's job of building a team on the field was just as impressive. Worcester lacked stars, as only one hitter (second baseman Alex Nunez) and one pitcher (Alex Pena) were on the league's leaderboards, but the team had solid contributors up and down the lineup. Five Tornadoes finished with 50 or more RBIs (in a 92-game season), and five finished with 50 or more runs scored.

In the championship series, the Tornadoes swept a stunned Quebec, which had finished with the league's best record.

Third baseman Zach Strong proved to be the postseason hero. He hit five home runs in seven postseason games, including a pair in the championship series. Strong had a home run and three RBIs in Worcester's 11-3 win in the series opener. After Pena shut out the Capitales with a five-hitter in Game Two, Strong was at it again in the series clincher, as he smashed another home run in Worcester's 9-4 win.

The title was technically the Can-Am League's first, as the Northeast League disbanded and reformed as the new league over the preceding offseason. The disbanding allowed the league to alter its constitution and restructure, although it returned with six of the seven non-traveling teams from the 2004 schedule. One team, Bangor, announced that it was shutting down just before the season began. The league fielded a traveling team, the Grays, in its place.

STANDINGS

FIRST HALF

NORTH	W	L	PCT	GB
Quebec Capitales	32	15	.681	—
North Shore Spirit	28	18	.609	3½
Grays	23	23	.500	8½
Brockton Rox	21	25	.457	10½
SOUTH				
Worcester Tornadoes	26	20	.565	—
New Jersey Jackals	25	21	.543	1
New Haven County Cutters	18	28	.391	8
Elmira Pioneers	13	33	.283	13

SECOND HALF

NORTH	W	L	PCT	GB
Brockton Rox	29	17	.630	—
Quebec Capitales	27	18	.600	1½
North Shore Spirit	27	18	.600	1½
Grays	10	36	.217	19
SOUTH	**W**	**L**	**PCT**	**GB**
New Haven County Cutters	28	18	.609	—
Worcester Tornadoes	24	22	.522	4
New Jersey Jackals	23	23	.500	5
Elmira Pioneers	15	31	.326	13

PLAYOFFS: Semifinals—Quebec defeated Brockton 3-0 and Worcester defeated New Haven County 3-1 in best-of-5 series. **Finals**—Worcester defeated Quebec 3-0 in best-of-5 series.

MANAGERS: Brockton—Ed Nottle. **Elmira**—Greg Keagle. **Grays**—Chris Carminucci. **New Haven County**—Mike Church. **New Jersey**—Joe Calfapietra. **North Shore**—John Kennedy. **Quebec**—Michel Laplante. **Worcester**—Rich Gedman.

ATTENDANCE: Brockton 190,675; Quebec 156,663; Worcester 124,745; New Jersey 122,092; North Shore 108,192; New Haven County 67,607; Elmira 62,743.

ALL-STAR TEAM: C-Yohanny Valera, Worcester. **1B**-Vic Davilla, North Shore. **2B**-Ricardo Cordova, New Jersey. **3B**-Eddie Lantigua, Quebec. **SS**-Omar Pena, Worcester. **OF**-Derrick Gibson, New Haven County; Zach Smithlin, New Jersey; Goefrey Tomlinson, Quebec. **DH**-Travis Oglesby, North Shore. **RHP**-Joel Bennett, New Jersey. **LHP**-Bryan Morse, North Shore. **RP**-Cristian Mendoza, Quebec.

Player of the Year: Eddie Lantigua, Quebec. **Rookie Player of the Year:** Brad Rosenblat, Brockton. **Rookie Pitcher of the Year:** Jarrett Stawarz, New Haven County. **Manager of the Year:** Rich Gedman, Worcester.

INDIVIDUAL BATTING LEADERS

(Minimum 254 Plate Appearances)

	AVG	G	AB	R	H	HR	RBI
Smithlin, Zach, New Jersey	.358	90	377	79	135	1	32
Cordova, Ricardo, New Jersey	.352	76	315	59	111	9	59
Nunez, Alex, Worcester	.340	89	312	51	106	6	40
McNabb, Buck, Quebec	.337	79	297	53	100	6	55
Davilla, Vic, North Shore	.333	91	366	65	122	23	86
Peavey, Bill, New Haven	.331	92	359	59	119	15	71
Cucurullo, Matt, Brockton	.326	66	261	48	85	5	29
Lantigua, Eddie, Quebec	.324	90	358	81	116	31	112
Gibson, Derrick, New Haven	.324	77	290	58	94	12	62
Tomlinson, Goefrey, Quebec	.322	81	307	67	99	4	51

INDIVIDUAL PITCHING LEADERS

(Minimum 75 Innings)

	W	L	ERA	IP	H	BB	SO
Bennett, Joel, New Jersey	11	2	2.68	91	81	23	81
Myers, Aaron, New Jersey	6	3	2.98	82	72	15	80
Pavlik, Isaac, New Jersey	7	5	3.09	102	100	28	100
Morse, Bryan, North Shore	12	4	3.15	123	126	24	67
Janzen, Marty, New Jersey	8	3	3.39	98	112	20	71
Brey, Josh, New Jersey	8	6	3.45	104	81	50	75
Koch, Jon, Brockton	5	5	3.45	78	87	23	62

Kelly, John, North Shore	12	4	3.49	113	115	47	118
Pena, Alex, Worcester	5	3	3.50	90	82	36	92
Orloski, Joe, New Jersey	8	4	3.53	140	129	34	82

BROCKTON

BATTING	AVG	AB	R	H	2B	3B	HR	RBI	SB
Abel, Shawn, ss	.077	26	2	2	0	0	0	0	0
Bustos, Saul, ss	.364	206	39	75	19	0	4	22	6
Coleman, Jim. of	.182	11	0	2	0	0	0	1	2
Cucurullo, Matt, of	.326	261	48	85	14	1	5	29	17
Daubert, Jake, 3b	.294	371	46	109	29	0	3	50	7
Gerald, Eddie, of	.267	150	21	40	9	1	5	19	1
2-team (18 Grays)	.248	210	27	52	12	1	6	25	1
Henriquez, Hector, 2b/ss	.231	130	12	30	4	0	2	17	0
Jones, Brian, c	.262	290	36	76	16	0	4	38	1
Julien, Eugene, of/ss	.287	261	36	75	5	1	0	15	18
King, Willie, 1b	.255	51	11	13	1	1	0	7	0
2-team (53 Grays)	.262	248	37	65	8	1	4	24	2
Lewis, Craig, 1b/of	.305	331	61	101	25	0	12	50	3
Piantek, Kurt, dh	.286	28	5	8	3	0	1	4	0
Roach, Al, of	.136	22	4	3	2	1	0	2	0
Rosenblat, Brad, of	.312	205	37	64	11	3	12	36	8
Salvo, Andrew, 2b	.280	168	15	47	4	1	3	26	1
Scanzano, Mike, 2b/3b	.272	81	13	22	3	0	0	3	2
Senjem, Guye, of	.288	198	33	57	10	0	11	43	0
Stewart, Chad, of	.196	56	8	11	0	1	1	6	2
Weingart, Brian, c	.157	51	3	8	0	0	0	2	0
Willis, Mike, of	.000	3	0	0	0	0	0	0	0
Zacuto, Kris, of	.267	329	45	88	20	1	10	59	3

PITCHING	W	L	ERA	G	SV	IP	H	BB	SO
Anderson, Craig	4	2	3.67	6	0	42	41	7	22
Aucoin, Eddie	6	0	3.03	36	3	65	66	10	60
Baker, Joey	0	0	15.43	3	0	9	19	9	2
Beavers, Kevin	5	6	4.76	22	0	87	103	34	75
Boyd, Oil Can	4	5	3.83	17	0	110	111	13	69
Castillo, Marcos	2	1	7.33	5	0	23	36	9	21
Cole, Joey	5	4	2.65	32	14	37	32	24	45
Dorn, Grant	5	3	5.23	12	1	64	78	26	35
Ferguson, Keith	0	1	3.94	15	0	16	23	7	6
Guy, Brad	1	4	5.17	9	0	56	67	15	37
Henry, Mike	4	2	5.25	14	0	62	83	19	25
Koch, Jon	5	5	3.45	24	0	78	87	23	62
Ough, Wayne	0	0	4.58	8	1	18	28	10	21
Pollock, Dave	0	0	0.00	1	0	0	0	1	0
Ramirez, Emmanuel	0	0	0.00	2	0	2	1	1	0
2-team (7 New Jersey)	1	1	10.38	9	0	13	13	12	9
Sloan, Steve	0	0	23.40	3	0	5	17	2	2
Stutz, Tony	4	3	4.56	39	5	47	42	21	52
Tejada, Manny	5	6	5.53	24	1	81	88	44	74
Williams, Shad	0	0	5.40	3	0	10	9	2	11

ELMIRA

BATTING	AVG	AB	R	H	2B	3B	HR	RBI	SB
Barrows, Derek, c/3b	.235	136	13	32	6	0	0	12	1
Beamon, Trey, of	.231	221	31	51	10	2	5	35	9
Bergeron, Jabe, 1b	.281	160	20	45	10	0	3	16	1
Bladimir, Felix, 3b	.171	35	2	6	2	0	0	3	2
Booth, Jeremy, 1b	.248	161	20	40	7	1	2	16	0
2-team (7 Worcester)	.234	188	21	44	8	1	2	20	0
Casana, Amaury, 3b	.354	65	10	23	3	0	2	12	4
Cooper, Chad, of	.211	76	14	16	2	0	0	3	5
Deck, Ronnie, c/1b	.103	39	2	4	0	0	0	5	0
Dorsey, Ryan. ss	.230	226	26	52	17	2	2	15	7
George, Kyle, 3b/1b	.196	51	7	10	2	0	1	5	0
Jesson, Das, 3b/ss	.251	267	42	67	17	1	3	31	16
Kenning, Ryan, 1b/of	.170	112	13	19	5	0	2	15	1
Kuklick, Clay, c	.267	30	4	8	2	0	1	5	1
Melgarejo, Ransel, of	.246	171	29	42	5	1	1	22	8
Mercado, Onix, c	.278	263	27	73	10	1	4	40	5
Morgan, Ryan, 1b	.149	74	5	11	4	0	2	10	0
Morita, Jobu, 2b	.263	247	26	65	16	2	1	31	7
Peters, Samone, of	.164	67	5	11	4	0	2	8	0
Roberts, Shane, of	.083	36	2	3	0	0	0	1	1
Rodriguez, Juan, of	.206	97	6	20	3	0	1	12	0
Smith, Ryan, c	.231	13	1	3	1	0	0	0	0
Suzuki, Toshi, of	.275	120	17	33	5	0	0	9	7
Tuttle, Jason, of	.312	308	51	96	8	0	0	29	30

PITCHING	W	L	ERA	G	SV	IP	H	BB	SO
Bengel, Buddy	3	4	4.16	27	0	71	80	23	49
Cosentino, Ryan	0	0	18.00	2	0	2	3	8	0
Dillinger, John	1	3	6.04	4	0	22	26	17	13
Dittfurth, Ryan	1	4	7.57	6	0	27	33	16	25
Ford, Brian	2	4	2.17	27	1	66	65	19	46
Galva, Claudio	0	2	4.56	22	6	24	34	12	26
George, Kyle	1	3	4.24	23	0	34	30	20	29
Guzman, Jose	2	5	6.67	11	2	27	33	24	15
Hosford, Clint	0	0	2.25	7	3	8	8	0	8
Howell, Michael	6	10	5.33	19	0	101	119	26	64
Kamimura, Soichi	0	1	5.63	2	0	8	9	4	1
Keagle, Greg	4	7	4.81	18	1	97	105	39	72
Keeton, Glen	3	3	6.37	11	0	59	83	27	27
Levrault, Allen	0	1	4.50	4	0	22	24	4	9
Roque, Chris	1	4	6.23	30	0	48	55	22	31
Solveson, Saul	1	6	6.91	9	0	43	65	16	18
Steed, Bric	1	0	5.84	11	0	25	25	23	12
Stuart, Jared	0	4	6.07	33	0	53	66	39	22
Viera, Rolando	2	3	2.55	7	0	42	42	19	35

GRAYS

BATTING	AVG	AB	R	H	2B	3B	HR	RBI	SB
Ayala, Elliott, 2b	.000	8	1	0	0	0	0	2	0
Best, Larry, 3b	.242	186	27	45	6	0	2	23	15
Burke, Mark, of/1b	.293	352	49	103	26	1	10	58	5
Caston, Bernard, of	.215	93	11	20	6	0	0	10	9
Ciraco, Darren, of	.291	79	11	23	7	0	2	11	1
3-team (20 N.H., 38 N.J.)	.271	292	49	79	14	0	6	39	4
Garcia, Alex, ss	.296	274	38	81	14	7	0	30	29
Gerald, Eddie, of	.200	60	6	12	3	0	1	6	0
Grimes, Scott, of	.248	105	15	26	4	1	1	13	2
Hargreaves, Brad, c	.218	317	38	69	10	0	2	37	1
Jiannetti, Joe, 2b	.315	92	20	29	4	0	6	12	3
2-team (47 New Jersey)	.315	279	46	88	15	3	12	47	7
King, Willie, 3b/1b	.264	197	26	52	7	0	4	17	2
Lebron, Francisco, 1b	.320	250	34	80	16	0	7	35	0
Lopez, Sergio, c	.000	2	0	0	0	0	0	0	0
Peterson, Charles, of	.302	182	19	55	8	0	6	28	0
Startari, Jason, of	.141	163	22	23	5	0	0	10	4
Stewart, Chad, of	.160	100	9	16	1	0	0	9	3
2-team (14 Brockton)	.173	156	17	27	1	1	1	15	5
Strickland, Greg, of	.269	219	36	59	3	1	4	26	24
Valdez, Angel, of	.152	33	4	5	1	0	0	1	2
2-team (10 North Shore)	.206	63	9	13	2	0	0	5	2
Weed, B.J., of	.299	301	40	90	13	1	2	34	13

PITCHING	W	L	ERA	G	SV	IP	H	BB	SO
Brite, Jared	0	0	12.00	2	0	3	4	6	4
Carter, Lenny	0	1	4.26	28	1	25	24	20	20
Casagrande, Nathan	0	0	5.18	14	0	24	28	16	16
Clark, Chris	0	0	15.19	6	0	5	6	11	4
Conden, Greg	0	2	12.96	4	0	8	12	14	3
DeChristofaro, Vince	1	7	7.30	12	0	62	76	34	45
Duffy, John	0	0	0.00	1	0	0	1	1	0
Duke, Ricky	0	1	8.59	5	0	7	15	1	4
Edwards, Andrew	1	4	5.59	18	0	58	57	29	47
Esarey, Brad	1	5	6.37	14	0	41	43	34	22
Henry, Mike	3	0	0.75	4	0	24	25	6	21
2-team (14 Brockton)	7	2	3.99	18	0	86	108	25	46
Jones, Fontella	0	0	1.93	5	0	5	4	4	2
Kalinowski, Roger	0	0	16.20	2	0	2	3	1	2
Keeton, Glen	0	4	6.87	7	0	18	30	9	4
2-team (11 Elmira)	3	7	6.49	18	0	78	113	36	31
Kennedy, Jodie	3	9	6.06	16	0	85	101	41	48
Kirsch, Brad	0	0	6.75	1	0	4	2	1	0
Lopez, Omar	0	0	10.13	1	0	3	4	1	1
Mincks, Lincoln	10	7	4.76	21	0	129	169	37	73
Neiser, Evan	0	3	3.80	15	1	21	22	11	19
2-team (16 New Jersey)	1	4	4.03	31	1	45	52	23	36
Nieves, Roberto	2	4	5.44	9	0	43	51	29	25
Pierce, Tony	3	7	4.97	17	0	67	64	48	83
Rapp, Randy	3	0	2.93	28	10	40	39	17	41
Rodriguez, Juan	2	0	5.84	11	0	12	11	6	14
Saunders, Tim	1	1	6.65	19	0	43	51	26	31
Tarkington, Shawn	2	0	5.73	11	1	11	12	7	5
Upwood, Jake	0	0	12.46	4	0	4	8	3	3
2-team (9 New Jersey)	0	0	9.64	13	0	14	18	11	7
Weckenman, Mike	1	4	8.06	12	1	26	34	16	17
Winkelsas, Joe	0	0	10.80	1	0	2	3	0	2

NEW HAVEN

BATTING	AVG	AB	R	H	2B	3B	HR	RBI	SB
Anderson, Keto, of	.288	382	78	110	17	8	4	39	18
Boyd, Jared, 3b	.500	2	0	1	1	0	0	2	0
Brackley, Carlos, 3b/of	.212	66	7	14	2	0	1	5	0
Brooks, Jeff. 3b	.313	319	42	100	22	1	11	64	0
Ciraco, Darren, of	.277	83	14	23	3	0	2	12	0
Encarnacion, Orlando, of	.261	238	31	62	8	1	2	28	2
Esposito, Vinny, of/3b	.250	48	9	12	0	0	0	6	0

Gibson, Derrick, of	.324	290	58	94	24	0	12	62	13
Hine, Dennis, 2b	.125	8	2	1	0	0	0	1	0
Hiter, Nick, c	.222	117	15	26	8	0	2	16	0
Larned, Andy, c	.226	248	25	56	4	1	2	29	2
Larosa, Mike, 2b	.277	206	27	57	9	1	1	20	3
Nikolic, Adam, of	.125	8	1	1	0	0	0	0	0
O'Keefe, Mike, of	.234	124	25	29	4	0	0	8	1
Peavey, Bill, 1b	.331	359	59	119	18	0	15	71	0
Plumsky, R.T., of/2b	.211	19	4	4	2	0	0	1	0
Samboy, Nelson, 2b	.300	10	2	3	1	0	0	1	2
Stegbauer, Keith, 3b	.260	208	30	54	5	1	2	23	2
Terni, Chas, ss	.263	334	49	88	19	3	7	43	0
Wilson, Eddie, dh	.000	4	0	0	0	0	0	0	0
Zamora, Junior, 3b	.408	71	12	29	8	2	2	18	0

PITCHING	W	L	ERA	G	SV	IP	H	BB	SO
Alexander, Jordy	1	3	7.29	6	0	33	48	13	27
Bonesio, Ryan	0	4	7.50	8	0	36	58	13	12
Comolli, Mark	2	2	3.56	19	8	30	31	13	26
2-team (13 North Shore)	3	5	3.80	32	9	47	56	22	35
Encarnacion, Orlando	0	0	9.00	2	0	2	2	0	5
Espinal, Willy	1	2	4.45	22	3	28	27	12	24
Etler, Todd	0	0	6.00	2	0	3	3	1	4
Hall, Courtney	6	4	4.37	20	0	95	119	40	54
Keinath, Tim	4	7	5.67	18	0	98	107	41	61
Kramer, Sean	0	0	7.71	7	0	9	14	2	8
Luzim, Mike	0	0	6.75	2	0	4	5	0	1
Maness, Nick	0	1	10.00	4	1	9	17	5	4
Minaya, Edwin	2	1	2.16	3	0	17	14	9	5
Moran, Shane	0	0	27.00	1	0	1	4	1	1
Nikolic, Adam	0	0	0.77	6	0	12	6	8	21
Rowland, Nick	4	1	4.89	24	0	39	41	9	17
Stawarz, Jarrett	9	7	4.58	25	0	90	106	34	70
Tomsu, Josh	0	1	5.73	2	0	11	13	9	7
Valles, Rolando	9	6	3.59	18	0	125	145	27	85
Vasquez, Tim	1	1	6.00	25	1	33	35	15	33
Weimer, Andrew	2	2	3.57	35	4	45	51	14	34
Whitworth, Brad	5	4	3.82	12	0	71	76	24	55
2-team (5 New Jersey)	7	6	4.11	17	0	103	112	32	81

NEW JERSEY

BATTING	AVG	AB	R	H	2B	3B	HR	RBI	SB
Alcantara, Izzy, of	.273	11	2	3	1	0	1	3	0
Brinkley, Darryl, of	.444	9	1	4	0	0	0	3	0
Brock, Tyler, 3b/of	.178	129	13	23	4	0	1	17	1
Checksfield, Steven, of/1b	.291	350	58	102	14	8	10	46	4
Ciraco, Darren, of	.254	130	24	33	4	0	2	16	3
Conway, Craig, 2b	.200	40	7	8	2	0	0	3	0
Cordova, Ricardo, 2b/ss	.352	315	59	111	15	10	9	59	17
Corporan, Elvis, 3b	.306	229	45	70	19	1	6	42	2
Dattola, Kevin, dh	.333	6	2	2	0	0	0	2	0
Gil, Benji, ss/3b	.370	54	12	20	5	0	2	6	3
Gomez, Rich, of	.290	93	18	27	2	1	5	14	4
Hagen, Matt, of/1b	.222	81	15	18	6	0	4	19	2
Jiannetti, Joe, 2b/of	.316	187	26	59	11	3	6	35	4
Lawrence, Horace, of	.324	71	13	23	5	1	1	12	1
Lebron, Francisco, 1b	.329	85	16	28	2	0	8	22	0
2-team (68 Grays)	.322	335	50	108	18	0	15	57	0
Lentz, Bryan, dh	.500	4	0	2	0	0	0	0	0
2-team (7 North Shore)	.333	24	3	8	1	0	1	3	0
Lindsey, John, 1b	.321	209	35	67	15	6	9	62	0
Lopez, Sergio, c	.083	12	0	1	0	0	0	0	0
2-team (2 Grays)	.071	14	0	1	0	0	0	0	0
Madera, Sandy, c	.350	180	32	63	18	0	9	38	0
Myers, Aaron, dh	.308	13	1	4	1	0	0	3	0
Neiman, Nolan, 2b	.105	19	2	2	0	0	0	0	0
Oakes, Brian, of	.290	31	5	9	2	0	0	2	0
Piercy, Mike, of	.205	39	7	8	0	0	0	3	4
Rowan, Chris, ss	.237	232	39	55	12	2	9	33	7
Rucci, Mike, c	.258	182	26	47	14	1	2	19	0
Salas, Jose, c	.260	50	7	13	3	0	2	10	0
Smithlin, Zach, of	.358	377	79	135	20	3	1	32	40
Whitesides, Jake, of/2b	.200	95	8	19	3	2	1	9	1

PITCHING	W	L	ERA	G	SV	IP	H	BB	SO
Benitez, Fabricio	0	3	2.97	27	6	33	30	14	26
Bennett, Joel	11	2	2.68	14	0	91	81	23	81
Brey, Josh	8	6	3.45	18	0	104	81	50	75
Gentekos, Dan	1	0	4.76	4	0	6	8	3	6
Hutchings, Andy	0	0	9.00	2	0	2	3	0	1
Janzen, Marty	2	1	3.57	3	0	18	20	3	18
2-team (13 Quebec)	8	3	3.39	16	0	98	112	20	71
Kirsten, Rick	0	1	13.50	3	0	8	14	6	4
2-team (15 Quebec)	3	5	4.88	18	0	63	69	22	40
Lawrence, Horace	0	0	3.52	9	0	15	16	10	12
Mondesir, James	1	1	3.81	15	0	28	31	10	13
Morgan, Shawn	0	2	6.35	6	0	11	14	3	5
Myers, Aaron	6	3	2.98	13	0	82	72	15	80
Neiser, Evan	1	1	4.24	16	0	23	30	12	17
Olson, Ryan	0	0	4.05	4	0	7	10	4	6
Orloski, Joe	8	4	3.53	23	0	140	129	34	82
Pavlik, Isaac	7	5	3.09	28	3	102	100	28	100
Perez, Julio	0	3	3.79	14	0	19	26	3	15
Petty, Chad	0	1	7.88	4	0	16	25	10	5
Ramirez, Emmanuel	1	1	12.27	7	0	11	12	11	9
Rapp, Randy	0	4	4.41	12	2	16	14	10	15
2-team (28 Grays)	3	4	3.36	40	12	56	53	27	56
Sponhouse, Charles	0	3	8.06	16	1	22	37	6	12
Upwood, Jake	0	0	8.38	9	0	10	10	8	4
Webb, Alan	0	1	15.63	6	0	6	15	3	4
Whitworth, Brad	2	2	4.73	5	0	32	36	8	26

NORTH SHORE

BATTING	AVG	AB	R	H	2B	3B	HR	RBI	SB
Agramonte, Marcos, 2b	.290	348	64	101	21	6	5	36	30
Carter, Stephen, of	.297	74	10	22	5	0	1	8	0
Davidson, Cleatus, ss	.227	44	10	10	3	1	0	1	1
Davilla, Vic, 1b/3b	.333	366	65	122	20	0	23	86	1
Fischer, Rob, of	.312	343	83	107	23	3	17	65	8
Garcia, Jose, of	.241	54	6	13	5	1	0	4	1
Howdeshell, Andy, 3b/ss	.291	117	18	34	6	3	5	21	2
Lentz, Bryan, c	.300	20	3	6	1	0	1	3	0
Macchi, Brian, of	.313	319	48	100	22	2	8	47	0
Mattle, David, of	.000	5	1	0	0	0	0	0	0
Nathans, John, c	.200	5	0	1	0	0	0	0	0
Oglesby, Travis, c/1b	.313	275	59	86	13	0	19	59	0
Sanchez, Yuri, ss	.203	227	24	46	6	3	1	24	8
Storey, Eric, 3b	.265	211	26	56	13	0	5	23	1
Tranum, Josh, 1b	.317	41	6	13	3	0	3	12	0
Trezza, Alex, c	.220	245	35	54	10	4	12	41	0
Valdez, Angel, of	.267	30	5	8	1	0	0	4	0
Wallis, Jacob, c	.273	11	3	3	1	0	0	1	0
Weed, B.J., of/2b	.294	17	3	5	0	0	0	4	0
2-team (75 Grays)	.299	318	43	95	13	1	2	38	13
Weir, Garrett, of	.312	295	56	92	14	3	2	34	10

PITCHING	W	L	ERA	G	SV	IP	H	BB	SO
Bicondoa, Ryan	9	5	3.56	17	0	114	96	32	95
Brazoban, Jose	0	1	18.69	4	0	4	10	3	1
Comolli, Mark	1	3	4.24	13	1	17	25	9	9
Farley, Chris	1	0	4.38	8	0	12	10	11	12
Hedden, Wayne	0	2	7.56	10	0	17	18	16	11
Herrera, Alex	5	2	2.70	24	9	63	56	23	70
Kelly, John	12	4	3.49	18	0	113	115	47	118
McCally, Ryan	4	2	6.10	27	8	41	65	11	31
Morse, Bryan	12	4	3.15	19	0	123	126	24	67
Mullis, Jake	5	6	5.58	16	0	90	112	23	54
Pleeter, Gregg	2	1	6.00	14	0	33	31	27	34
Ray, Ken	2	0	2.75	3	0	20	10	10	22
Siak, Joey	1	2	2.38	10	0	45	41	15	29
Soteropoulos, Peter	0	3	3.75	26	0	48	50	8	37
Sues, Jarret	1	1	5.88	20	0	34	41	7	31
Warpinski, Ryan	0	0	22.50	2	0	2	1	3	1

QUEBEC

BATTING	AVG	AB	R	H	2B	3B	HR	RBI	SB
Delfino, Lee, ss	.255	259	36	66	18	1	4	22	2
Emond, Ben, of	.253	312	53	79	12	1	1	25	17
Fulton, Josh, ss	.182	55	4	10	3	0	1	6	5
Greenwell, Bill, 1b	.290	248	25	72	14	0	4	25	1
Lamarche, Max, c	.044	45	3	2	0	0	0	4	0
Lantigua, Eddie, 3b	.324	358	81	116	18	2	31	112	4
Leathers, Todd, 1b	.282	323	43	91	15	0	17	67	0
Legare, Simon, of	.284	183	40	52	11	0	7	29	3
Lepine, Olivier, c	.298	292	50	87	20	0	6	48	2
McNabb, Buck, of	.337	297	53	100	21	2	6	55	6
Rosenthal, Ben, c	.200	30	4	6	1	0	0	0	0
Scalabrini, Danny, 2b	.278	252	51	70	9	1	0	29	4
Sepulveda, Carlos, of	.258	31	6	8	3	0	1	4	0
Shimizu, T.J., 2b/ss	.243	144	29	35	2	1	0	21	14
Tomlinson, Goefrey, of	.322	307	67	99	25	1	4	51	11

PITCHING	W	L	ERA	G	SV	IP	H	BB	SO
Benson, Jason	3	1	3.58	17	2	33	42	10	17
Brown, Joe	1	0	0.66	3	0	14	3	4	15
Castillo, Marcos	7	5	3.10	15	0	90	82	21	77
2-tesm (5 Brockton)	9	6	3.97	20	0	113	118	30	98
Cloutier, Marc/Andre	1	1	6.23	8	0	13	13	14	4
DePriest, Derrick	2	0	0.00	3	0	5	3	1	3
Faust, Wes	0	0	1.29	3	1	7	7	0	3
Freedman, Coogie	6	4	6.41	23	0	60	77	27	32

Gomez, Deibis	1	0	7.94	3	0	6	9	1	3
Janzen, Marty	6	2	3.35	13	0	81	92	17	53
Kim, Min/Soo	5	4	4.68	15	1	75	85	27	37
Kirsten, Rick	3	4	3.62	15	0	55	55	16	36
Laplante, Michel	0	0	1.80	1	0	5	4	1	7
Lipson, David	0	1	7.90	8	0	14	15	12	11
Marrero, Darwin	3	1	2.84	7	0	38	31	9	28
Mendoza, Cristian	1	1	2.98	37	21	42	37	15	49
Moran, Shane	0	0	4.91	3	0	7	6	10	2
2-team (1 New Haven)	0	0	7.56	4	0	8	10	11	3
Plante, Patrice	0	0	6.00	2	1	3	6	2	0
Prata, Danny	5	2	3.18	13	0	65	57	30	37
Ribas, Gabe	1	0	1.80	1	0	5	5	3	2
Ryan, Shawn	4	2	3.65	33	1	44	35	32	59
Sandberg, Alan	0	0	0.00	2	0	3	4	2	4
Tucker, Julien	7	5	3.86	19	1	107	108	40	77
Wikstrom, Eric	1	1	8.15	3	0	18	25	2	13

WORCESTER

BATTING	AVG	AB	R	H	2B	3B	HR	RBI	SB
Beauregard, Josh, of	.293	379	79	111	26	3	11	62	26
Beauregard, Keith, of	.338	136	23	46	11	0	3	27	5
Booth, Jeremy, 1b	.148	27	1	4	1	0	0	4	0
Brown, Andy, of	.285	302	64	86	14	1	21	58	5
Colabello, Chris, 1b	.320	172	24	55	7	0	8	31	3
De los Santos, Alex, of	.225	120	14	27	5	0	2	8	3
Dunn, Lawrence, 1b/3b	.200	5	1	1	0	0	0	1	0
Loiseau, Scott, 3b/2b	.175	137	11	24	0	0	0	5	2
Nunez, Alex, 2b	.340	312	51	106	13	3	6	40	10
Pena, Omar, ss	.271	350	63	95	19	1	15	57	18
Reynoso, Danilo, c	.221	199	27	44	10	0	9	27	1
Strong, Zach, 3b/1b	.261	349	47	91	18	5	8	51	10
Taylor, Lucas, of	.272	305	43	83	5	2	1	31	37
Vaccaro, Matt, c	.167	6	0	1	0	0	0	0	0
Valera, Yohanny, c/1b	.296	334	57	99	14	3	15	60	4

PITCHING	W	L	ERA	G	SV	IP	H	BB	SO
Byard, David	3	3	3.16	33	13	43	32	39	40
Cox, Mike	4	6	5.73	21	0	77	73	65	94
Docar, Adam	0	0	12.00	5	0	6	10	6	1
Guerrero, Junior	6	3	3.80	17	0	97	91	46	61
Mahan, Dallas	4	2	4.21	31	2	47	50	11	41
McCall, Derell	6	8	5.98	21	0	102	131	26	60
Montalbano, Greg	2	2	3.13	15	0	23	17	7	28
Palazzolo, Steve	2	1	3.15	30	3	54	49	22	43
Pena, Alex	5	3	3.50	18	0	90	82	36	92
Pena, Eddie	2	4	5.08	32	0	67	76	17	60
Riley, Ed	3	3	6.06	9	0	33	38	16	16
Shank, Chris	2	3	5.19	26	2	69	66	18	65
Willett, Reid	10	4	3.56	18	0	99	96	22	61
Yarbrough, Joe	1	0	6.75	3	0	7	15	0	6

CENTRAL LEAGUE

When Wayne Terwilliger became the Fort Worth Cats manager as a spry 78-year-old, he knew that any failures as a manager would be blamed on his age.

Three years later, Terwilliger didn't have to worry about people doubting him, after his Cats dominated the Central League, winning the first and second half titles and rallying from behind to win the league crown in style.

Wayne Terwilliger

Along the way, Terwilliger, the only octogenarian to manage a professional baseball team besides Connie Mack, was named the league's manager of the year. Terwilliger, who announced his retirement after the season, now has a Central League title as a manager to go along with a Northern League title as a coach, and his two World Series titles as a coach with the 1987 and 1991 Minnesota Twins.

"I think the older you get, the bigger they become," he said. "I got excited when I was at St. Paul as a coach there (and the Saints won the Northern League title). I thought winning World Series would dim all this, but it didn't."

The Cats beat San Angelo three games to two in the Central League championship series after rallying from a 2-0 deficit in their first-round series against Pensacola. Not surprisingly, the Cats did it with plenty of offense, averaging six runs a game during the playoffs. They led the league in runs during the regular season, but also had a pitching staff that was second in the league in ERA.

"We led the league in walks and had the least number of walks given up," Terwilliger said. "That was a big thing."

Fort Worth got plenty of production from veterans, led by all-star outfielder Carlos Adolfo (.313-19-81) and lefthander Ryan Weems (9-4, 3.71), but the team also got help from a variety of unexpected sources. First baseman Jordan Foster started off slowly, but rallied to hit .343-9-86. T.J. Hendrix was almost cut at midseason, but Terwilliger and player-development director Barry Moss decided to give him one more start as a last chance. He responded by winning the pitcher of the week award a couple of weeks later on his way to a 7-2, 4.67 season. Oft-drafted righthander Matt Harrington also bounced back from arm injuries to go 5-0, 3.55 working out of the bullpen.

"We had to make adjustments right off the bat. I thought we would struggle at the start, but Barry did a heck of a job," Terwilliger said. "He brought in guys and it turned out well."

El Paso, the league's newest addition and top-draw in its inaugural season, also had the league MVP, with first baseman Juan Camacho hitting .328-21-100.

STANDINGS

FIRST HALF

	W	L	PCT	GB
Fort Worth Cats	30	17	.638	—
Pensacola Pelicans	29	18	.617	1
San Angelo Colts	25	22	.532	5
Coastal Bend Aviators	24	23	.511	6
Edinburg Roadrunners	23	24	.489	7
Jackson Senators	21	26	.447	9
El Paso Diablos	18	29	.383	12
Shreveport Sports	18	29	.383	12

SECOND HALF

	W	L	PCT	GB
Fort Worth Cats	30	17	.638	—
Shreveport Sports	28	19	.596	2
El Paso Diablos	26	21	.553	4
Edinburg Roadrunners	26	21	.553	4
Pensacola Pelicans	24	21	.533	5
San Angelo Colts	21	25	.457	8 ½
Coastal Bend Aviators	17	30	.362	13
Jackson Senators	14	32	.304	15 ½

PLAYOFFS: Semifinals—Fort Worth defeated Pensacola 3-2 and San Angelo defeated Edinburg 3-2 in best-of-5 series. **Finals**—Fort Worth defeated San Angelo 3-2 in best-of-5 series.

MANAGERS: Coastal Bend—Murray Wilson. **Edinburg**—Vince Moore. **El Paso**—Mike Marshall. **Fort Worth**—Wayne Terwilliger. **Jackson**—Hill Denson. **Pensacola**—Bernie Carbo. **Shreveport**—Bob Flori. **San Angelo**—John Harris.

ATTENDANCE: El Paso 190,429; Fort Worth 173,946; Edinburg 138,123; Coastal Bend 79,826; Jackson 68,452; Pensacola 68,142; San Angelo 67,259; Shreveport 51,315.

ALL-STAR TEAM: C—Aaron Mendoza, San Angelo. **1B**—Juan Camacho, El Paso. **2B**—Jorge Diaz, El Paso. **3B**—J.P. Schmidt, San Angelo. **SS**—Joe Espada, Pensacola. **OF**—Carlos Adolfo, Fort Worth; Tony Mota, Fort Worth; Carlos Sepulveda, El Paso. **DH**—Chad Gambill, Shreveport. **RHP**—Eric Wikstrom, Shreveport. **LHP**—Ryan Weems, Fort Worth. **RP**—Steve Wilkerson, Edinburg.

Player of the Year: Juan Camacho, El Paso. **Rookie Pitcher of the Year:** Kevin Hull, Edinburg. **Rookie Player of the Year:** Matt Spencer, Edinburg. **Manager of the Year:** Wayne Terwilliger, Fort Worth.

INDIVIDUAL BATTING LEADERS

(Minimum 254 Plate Appearances)

	AVG	G	AB	R	H	HR	RBI
Schmidt, J.P., San Antonio	.364	93	327	64	119	12	69
Alvarez, Jorge, San Antonio	.344	91	352	71	121	14	86
Foster, Jordan, Fort Worth	.343	84	303	57	104	9	86
Diaz, Jorge, El Paso	.343	87	347	90	119	0	46
Mota, Tony, Fort Worth	.339	86	348	82	118	10	64
Espada, Joe, Pensacola	.333	64	246	52	82	4	31
Allen, John, Fort Worth	.330	94	370	71	122	11	84
Camacho, Juan, El Paso	.328	94	363	72	119	21	100
Salas, Jose, Pensacola	.327	78	278	53	91	6	48
Green, Terence, Fort Worth	.321	92	386	77	124	8	39

INDIVIDUAL PITCHING LEADERS

(Minimum 75 Innings)

	W	L	ERA	IP	H	BB	SO
Wikstrom, Eric, Shreveport	7	5	3.03	101	103	35	60
Hull, Kevin, Edinburg	8	6	3.53	120	115	53	101
Lopez, Jose, Edinburg	8	7	3.70	131	111	42	111
Weems, Ryan, Fort Worth	9	4	3.71	124	115	35	128
Snyder, Ryan, Shreveport	4	8	3.72	121	118	24	68
Hernandez, Santos, Pensacola	9	6	3.77	100	86	30	95
Acierno, Marc, Coastal Bend	3	6	3.81	87	106	18	36
Snow, Bert, Shreveport	11	6	3.92	122	112	25	122
Smith, Mike, Fort Worth	11	6	4.12	133	150	22	108
Cunningham, Derek, Shreve.	4	7	4.33	89	83	36	88

COASTAL BEND

BATTING	AVG	AB	R	H	2B	3B	HR	RBI	SB
Aguilar, Bert, 1b	.193	88	4	17	4	0	3	12	0
2-team (26 El Paso)	.243	181	14	44	8	0	7	29	0
Edmonds, Jason, of	.160	25	1	4	1	0	0	0	0
Figueroa, Carlos, 2b	.310	294	43	91	16	3	2	33	4
Gomez, Rich, of	.270	63	19	17	8	0	1	7	6
2-team (27 San Angelo)	.272	173	40	47	16	1	6	23	15
Guerrero, Mike, 1b/of	.248	310	45	77	14	2	10	48	3
Hansley, Kenny. 2b/of	.260	265	38	69	13	1	0	24	3
Henry, Kevin, of/1b	.272	224	28	61	8	2	12	42	0
January, Javerro, of	.067	15	0	1	1	0	0	2	0
Joffrion, Jack, ss	.262	290	43	76	16	6	8	36	7
Judkins, Chris, of	.237	228	43	54	7	5	0	16	17
Lira, James, of	.000	1	0	0	0	0	0	0	0
Maldonado, Edwin, of/3b	.259	324	40	84	7	3	9	52	5
Mann, Matt, of/c	.288	382	66	110	21	3	15	75	17
Morales, Steve, c	.274	190	26	52	8	0	7	38	1
Rankin, Lance, c	.196	46	7	9	0	0	1	1	0
Rohena, Angel, c	.195	113	12	22	6	0	2	10	0
Thomas, Mario, of	.188	80	10	15	1	1	0	6	15
Tinius, Ben, 3b	.221	276	35	61	15	0	5	28	2
Vives, Michael, of	.250	8	2	2	1	0	0	0	0

PITCHING	W	L	ERA	G	SV	IP	H	BB	SO
Acierno, Marc	3	6	3.81	22	0	87	106	18	36
Beseda, Adam	0	0	4.26	4	0	6	5	6	5
Dutka, Alex	5	4	5.17	26	1	47	44	20	23
Gaarder, Karsten	1	0	4.97	3	0	13	13	6	9
Henderson, Dan	3	5	4.70	30	0	88	100	30	76
Huerta, Jorge	0	0	3.55	9	0	25	21	5	11
Koenig, Brad	0	1	8.31	1	0	4	4	5	4
Lira, James	5	1	2.49	34	7	47	32	18	60
Lopez, Jose	7	7	3.72	17	0	119	104	39	95
Morgan, Shawn	3	4	3.10	42	8	49	57	15	46
Nieto, Jose	0	0	4.97	5	0	13	14	7	5
Pello, Brandon	4	0	2.59	24	0	31	22	8	27
Rohr, Matthew	3	4	6.61	13	0	64	82	28	48
Rosario, Melvin	0	0	0.00	5	0	4	1	2	3
Shaw, Elliott	3	9	6.32	21	0	98	110	60	82
Trujillo, J.J.	4	11	4.58	22	0	130	142	31	132
Zarbough, Griffin	0	1	0.00	1	0	0	0	1	0

EDINBURG

BATTING	AVG	AB	R	H	2B	3B	HR	RBI	SB
Aguirre, Mike, 3b/of	.182	11	2	2	0	0	0	0	0
Angel, Anthony, 2b	.296	331	41	98	21	0	7	51	15
Ballon, John, 3b	.291	117	24	34	3	1	4	17	1
Burwell, Wilson, 3b/ss	.227	198	20	45	10	0	1	20	3
Diaz, Freddie, ss	.270	37	4	10	3	0	0	3	0
Dworken, Mikaella, c	.143	7	0	1	0	0	0	0	0
Eichel, Matt, c	.204	93	13	19	4	0	0	2	1
Esquivel, Lale, 1b	.245	49	3	12	3	0	1	5	0
Fitzpatrick, Eddie, c	.145	131	9	19	1	0	2	9	3
Garza, Marco, ss/2b	.228	79	11	18	1	0	0	5	2
German, Amado. of	.273	150	36	41	6	1	3	22	10
Gonzalez, Eric, of	.256	332	58	85	16	3	9	40	9
Harkrider, Kip, ss	.347	213	41	74	20	5	3	29	4
Harris, Cedrick, of	.283	276	43	78	12	4	2	35	17
King, Andrew, of	.000	5	0	0	0	0	0	0	0
Lara, Eddie, 1b/3b	.289	342	43	99	20	1	4	59	14
McCall, Gerard, c	.198	96	9	19	3	0	2	9	2
2-team (29 Jackson)	.192	182	12	35	6	0	3	16	2
O'Sullivan, Pat, 1b/of	.390	59	6	23	2	0	0	12	4
Owens, Ryan, 3b/1b	.190	79	7	15	5	0	1	12	0
Sisk, Aaron, ss	.333	30	7	10	1	1	3	7	3
Spencer, Matt, of	.313	351	52	110	24	4	4	47	3
Zieour, Neesan, of	.244	168	26	41	9	0	2	21	13

PITCHING	W	L	ERA	G	SV	IP	H	BB	SO
Bonesio, Ryan	2	3	6.28	8	0	39	51	21	16
Figueroa, Carlos	0	2	3.77	9	0	14	16	7	14
Flores, Pedro	12	4	4.52	21	0	133	142	68	96
Garza, Roel	1	2	4.75	26	0	30	34	14	22
Heaston, Bryan	3	1	3.70	43	0	66	76	31	76
Hull, Kevin	8	6	3.53	21	0	120	115	53	101
James, Frank	3	6	6.34	12	0	60	71	37	32
Lopez, Jose	1	0	3.55	2	0	13	7	3	16
2-team (17 Coastal Bend)	8	7	3.70	19	0	131	111	42	111
Marcano, Luis	1	2	5.27	16	0	14	15	8	15
Martin, Bryan	1	0	4.85	11	0	13	14	7	14
Montoya, Eric	3	1	2.86	7	0	44	38	11	41
Munoz, Jose	0	2	8.44	6	0	11	16	6	7
Ramirez, Luis	0	1	3.86	4	0	5	4	2	3
Ruiz, Julio	7	5	4.36	20	0	89	93	31	50
Stanley, Cody	0	0	12.79	5	0	6	7	9	2
Stewart, Randy	0	0	18.00	1	0	1	2	0	1
Taylor, Jonathan	0	0	2.25	4	0	4	6	3	2
Valentin, Dan	4	5	5.24	16	0	81	90	32	46
Vasquez, Tim	2	0	6.14	13	0	15	18	9	10
Webb, Nick	0	2	8.64	2	0	8	15	7	6
Wilkerson, Steven	1	3	2.33	41	25	46	37	7	60

EL PASO

BATTING	AVG	AB	R	H	2B	3B	HR	RBI	SB
Aguilar, Bert, 1b	.290	93	10	27	4	0	4	17	0
Alexander, Chris, 1b	.143	7	1	1	1	0	0	1	0
Ballesteros, Adrian, 3b/ss	.333	12	2	4	0	0	0	1	0
Camacho, Juan, 1b/3b	.328	363	72	119	31	2	21	100	0
Cano, Jose, 1b	.343	140	18	48	6	0	0	15	0
Cantu, Tim. of	.118	17	5	2	1	0	0	1	0
Caruso, Johnny, of	.188	16	1	3	1	0	0	2	0
Castillo, Carlos, ss/2b	.281	160	21	45	5	0	0	21	4
Cook, Ross, of	.600	10	1	6	0	0	0	3	0
Cox, Jason, 1b	.333	9	0	3	0	0	0	1	0
Craig, Benny, of	.189	37	5	7	1	0	0	7	0
Diaz, Jorge, 2b	.343	347	90	119	14	8	0	46	15
Fernandez, Alejandro, c/1b	.257	257	38	66	14	1	9	29	1
Fulton, Josh, ss	.363	168	41	61	7	2	1	19	21
George, Trey, of	.000	3	0	0	0	0	0	0	0
Macias, Oscar, 2b	.350	60	12	21	2	1	1	11	0
Mendoza, Robert, of	.333	51	10	17	5	2	0	6	0
Mercado, Oni, c	.130	46	6	6	2	0	1	5	1
Mirizzi, Marc, 3b	.261	111	15	29	9	1	0	13	0
2-team (59 San Angelo)	.284	338	46	96	26	2	2	47	1
Montesano, Joe, of	.000	1	0	0	0	0	0	0	0
Moreno, Juan, of	.200	10	1	2	1	1	0	1	0
Pendergrass, Tyrone, of	.260	173	31	45	4	3	1	19	11
Rosenthal, Ben, c/of	.300	243	34	73	13	1	11	47	2
Schmitz, John, of	.303	238	41	72	17	2	2	32	3
Sepulveda, Carlos, of	.294	354	77	104	20	6	19	99	10
Smith, Dustin, of/3b	.271	225	34	61	9	0	1	23	3
Wallace, Brad, of	1.000	1	1	1	0	0	0	2	0
Woodcock, Lance, ss	.100	20	3	2	2	0	0	1	0
Younts, Chase, of	.260	96	17	25	3	1	0	12	3

PITCHING	W	L	ERA	G	SV	IP	H	BB	SO
Benetiz, Edy	2	0	6.75	7	0	12	18	4	12
Camacho, Juan	0	0	0.00	3	0	2	1	1	2
Cervera, Michael	0	1	5.12	9	0	19	17	16	24
Coppinger, Rocky	0	1	9.00	1	0	4	5	3	7
Cox, Jason	0	0	8.31	4	0	4	10	1	4
Dean, Aaron	0	2	12.79	2	0	6	13	1	6
DePriest, Derrick	5	5	1.93	45	13	70	55	10	74
Dillinger, John	1	1	6.30	2	0	10	5	8	9
Esarey, Brad	2	3	4.66	5	0	29	36	13	12
Faust, Wes	9	5	4.58	22	0	94	113	31	85
Flanagan, Chris	1	4	6.99	13	0	48	65	21	30
Garcia, Jose	1	1	3.38	8	0	29	27	13	24
Guzman, Alexis	0	4	4.03	25	3	38	45	8	28
Harris, Ryan	0	4	9.74	8	0	41	61	18	26
Hummel, John	0	2	5.51	38	2	51	62	19	23
Ide, Hisazumi	4	0	4.68	21	0	42	53	6	41

	W	L	ERA	G	SV	IP	H	BB	SO
Lang, Blair	0	0	4.70	3	0	8	5	2	6
Marcotte, Trevor	1	3	8.12	14	0	41	61	21	30
Marquetti, Agustin	0	0	27.00	2	0	1	2	2	3
Martin, Larry	0	0	67.50	3	0	1	2	3	2
Martinez, Dave	0	1	13.50	1	0	3	7	3	4
Moore, Bo	0	1	12.46	2	0	4	8	2	2
O'Donnell, Tony	2	3	4.38	5	0	25	28	9	11
Pena, Juan	3	0	2.93	7	0	31	29	9	26
Pena, Juan	0	0	7.71	2	0	7	12	3	5
Salazar, Luis	0	1	11.57	2	0	7	16	3	4
Sandoval, Marcos	0	1	3.75	7	0	12	10	5	5
Steed, Bric	1	1	5.53	16	1	28	33	15	27
Sugawara, Yoshi	0	0	54.00	1	0	0	0	2	0
Teeter, Travis	5	4	3.62	11	0	75	78	21	43
Torres, Andy	6	2	5.87	12	0	69	94	23	50
Zaleski, Kyle	1	0	7.27	3	0	9	9	3	9

FORT WORTH

BATTING	AVG	AB	R	H	2B	3B	HR	RBI	SB
Adolfo, Carlos, of	.313	339	94	106	19	2	19	81	12
Allen, John, of/1b	.330	370	71	122	38	0	11	84	3
Foster, Jordan, 1b/of	.343	303	57	104	21	4	9	86	3
Green, Terence, 3b	.321	386	77	124	25	6	8	39	28
Keesee, David, ss/3b	.233	287	41	67	13	2	2	37	4
Lup, Ken, c	.265	102	10	27	3	1	1	20	1
Merriman, Terrell, of	.277	350	78	97	13	2	14	48	17
Mota, Tony, of	.339	348	82	118	17	5	10	64	14
Ponce, Arnoldo, ss	.160	162	14	26	4	0	1	5	1
Radwan, Jason, c	.246	272	35	67	16	0	9	49	2
Scanzano, Mike, 2b/3b	.200	25	4	5	2	0	0	2	0
Smith, Bryon, 2b/1b	.255	278	42	71	19	1	5	39	4
Yarbrough, Shawn, 2b	.111	27	2	3	1	0	0	3	0

PITCHING	W	L	ERA	G	SV	IP	H	BB	SO
Aragon, Angel	1	1	6.91	3	0	14	19	2	14
Beasley, Ray	3	3	5.81	22	1	26	33	10	24
Cain, Wes	0	0	0.00	4	0	4	7	2	1
Doiron, Ian	0	1	11.57	3	0	7	16	1	4
2-team (1 Shreveport)	0	1	11.25	4	0	8	19	2	5
Figueroa, Juan	3	4	4.34	38	11	46	36	28	52
Garcia, Justin	1	0	3.63	41	0	45	43	18	50
Grybash, Dan	6	2	4.06	11	1	58	54	14	57
Harrington, Matt	5	0	3.55	23	0	33	29	11	31
Hendricks, Thomas	7	2	4.67	22	0	89	103	28	58
Kirsten, Joel	1	2	3.26	12	0	30	37	10	28
Lynn, Kevin	8	1	2.70	9	0	60	66	8	38
Neitz, Josh	1	1	5.83	30	2	54	60	21	39
O'Brien, John	0	0	9.00	1	0	2	4	1	0
Parker, Aaron	1	1	7.20	5	0	5	5	2	3
Smith, Mike	11	6	4.12	20	0	133	150	22	108
Snapp, Michael	0	0	2.45	13	8	15	9	10	13
Stokley, Billy	0	1	6.97	11	1	10	20	3	5
Stout, Logan	3	5	5.73	18	0	71	87	24	60
Weems, Ryan	9	4	3.71	20	0	124	115	35	128

JACKSON

BATTING	AVG	AB	R	H	2B	3B	HR	RBI	SB
Banks, LaDarrell, ss	.138	65	1	9	0	0	0	0	0
Blue, Nick, 1b	.216	37	7	8	1	0	0	2	3
Boyd, Jared, ss/3b	.235	247	35	58	7	2	3	27	2
Brackley, Carlos, of/1b	.269	160	21	43	8	0	3	21	2
Camp, Rusty, 1b/3b	.000	7	0	0	0	0	0	1	0
Dickinson, Jake, of	.299	291	40	87	15	7	3	26	8
Donahoo, Brett, of	.271	59	8	16	3	0	1	8	0
Espinosa, Luis, 3b/c	.257	214	22	55	10	2	0	20	0
Faison, Vince, of/1b	.303	323	56	98	22	11	15	66	8
Jones, Fontella, of	.118	17	3	2	1	0	0	0	0
Langaigne, Selwyn, of	.305	295	46	90	27	3	1	41	13
Lindstrom, Josh, c	.237	93	12	22	3	0	4	11	0
McCall, Gerard, c	.186	86	3	16	3	0	1	7	0
McMahon, Justin, of	.259	54	8	14	2	1	4	12	0
Mejias, Erick, 2b	.257	338	51	87	15	3	5	31	11
Nowell, Travis, c	.159	126	16	20	9	0	4	11	1
Pickard, Bert, c	.189	53	3	10	3	0	2	7	1
Sorensen, Nick, of	.255	278	39	71	10	1	6	28	12
Tovar, Edgar, ss	.267	131	12	35	3	0	1	20	2
Tranum, Josh, 1b	.295	271	44	80	22	2	7	56	7

PITCHING	W	L	ERA	G	SV	IP	H	BB	SO
Blakeney, Jacob	2	2	5.22	6	0	29	32	13	22
Brown, Joe	2	0	3.16	11	0	31	22	14	25
Camp, Rusty	6	12	5.64	20	0	126	154	28	84
Casey, Reid	2	6	5.93	19	0	61	74	22	36
Cox, Adam	2	0	2.45	4	0	18	7	9	21
Duncan, Courtney	0	0	0.00	1	0	0	0	1	0
Edmiston, Bo	5	6	5.00	16	0	85	90	29	50
Flores, Neomar	0	3	6.20	4	0	25	33	12	14
2-team (16 Shreveport)	6	9	4.89	20	1	116	114	59	77
Hearn, Daniel	1	4	7.25	5	0	22	21	15	19
Jones, Fontella	2	4	3.25	32	9	44	47	18	34
Martinez, Javier	1	4	4.05	22	0	60	46	49	60
McAlpin, Matthew	1	4	5.46	25	0	59	63	27	40
McKeller, Laine	2	6	5.04	32	0	64	85	24	32
Parker, Brandon	4	2	5.05	39	1	46	42	38	52
Shack, Jermaine	1	0	5.57	20	1	32	42	10	19
Snyder, Ryan	3	5	3.36	15	0	99	90	20	58
White, Kris	0	0	14.40	4	0	5	8	5	2

PENSACOLA

BATTING	AVG	AB	R	H	2B	3B	HR	RBI	SB
Aguilar, Trino, 3b	.276	341	46	94	14	3	11	48	9
Alvarez, Rafael, of	.305	59	12	18	5	0	5	11	2
Bethea, Larry, 1b	.267	341	56	91	12	0	21	76	3
Branch, George, 1b/of	.220	305	40	67	18	1	8	39	0
Caston, Bernard, of	.284	225	36	64	8	4	0	22	9
Espada, Joe. ss	.333	246	52	82	15	0	4	31	24
Hebert, Robbie, dh	.250	4	0	1	0	0	0	1	0
Karr, Palmer, of	.269	104	15	28	5	0	4	10	5
Lentz, Bryan, c	.364	33	11	12	1	0	1	7	1
Mendoza, Carlos, 2b/ss	.293	352	61	103	21	1	10	59	7
Pierre, Michael, 2b/of	.229	153	32	35	7	0	1	15	16
Rocha, Juan, of	.282	333	62	94	15	0	20	69	5
Salas, Jose, c/1b	.327	278	53	91	20	0	6	48	6
Settle, Mike, 2b/of	.500	6	0	3	1	0	0	2	0
Smith, Nestor, of	.301	342	53	103	20	1	10	59	20
Valdez, Mario, 1b	.194	31	8	6	1	0	2	4	0

PITCHING	W	L	ERA	G	SV	IP	H	BB	SO
Alvarado, Luis	0	1	0.00	1	0	0	1	1	0
Arthurs, Shane	1	2	3.95	9	0	43	54	15	32
Batson, Byron	10	6	4.95	21	0	124	146	20	89
Casadiego, Gerardo	5	4	5.05	11	0	71	77	33	78
Courage, Josh	4	2	5.60	42	6	55	57	15	36
Dobson, Richard	4	0	3.98	47	2	61	65	17	54
Dunn, Gerald	1	3	9.72	7	0	25	39	6	20
Hebert, Robbie	5	3	4.12	27	1	59	65	17	60
Hernandez, Santos	9	6	3.77	21	0	100	86	30	95
Knytych, James	0	0	2.57	3	0	7	4	3	3
Major, Marc	0	1	8.22	7	1	8	9	5	18
Norris, Jeff	5	5	5.59	17	0	87	103	36	41
Perdue, Matt	1	2	6.66	11	0	24	35	12	8
Ramirez, Edward	2	2	1.45	43	11	62	37	15	93
Settle, Mike	0	0	9.15	12	0	20	26	14	12
Singleton, Nick	4	2	2.84	9	0	44	35	19	23
Stephens, Trey	2	1	6.14	3	0	15	13	10	16

SAN ANGELO

BATTING	AVG	AB	R	H	2B	3B	HR	RBI	SB
Allan, Josh, 1b	.143	28	3	4	0	0	0	2	0
Alvarez, Jorge, of/1b	.342	357	72	122	34	3	14	86	8
Anderson, John, 2b/ss	.304	408	66	124	24	5	2	37	12
Bailey, Danny, of	.091	11	0	1	1	0	0	1	0
Barker, Ryan, 1b	.222	36	6	8	2	0	0	5	0
Cherry, Evan, of	.249	205	40	51	13	1	0	24	2
Cooley, Brett, 1b	.323	124	20	40	13	0	6	32	0
Davis, Eric, 1b	.143	35	2	5	1	0	0	2	0
Dodson, Jeremy, of	.238	341	49	81	17	2	8	44	4
Drew, Kory, of	.292	298	47	87	12	1	4	36	6
Dubarry, B.J., c	.115	26	1	3	0	0	0	0	1
Dworken, Mikaella, c	.111	18	1	2	0	0	0	1	0
2-team (4 Edinburg)	.120	25	1	3	0	0	0	1	0
Ghutzman, Stephen, c	.191	47	10	9	4	0	2	7	0
Goitia, Juan, ss	.143	42	5	6	0	0	0	3	0
Gomez, Rich, of	.273	110	21	30	8	1	5	16	9
Grijak, Kevin, 1b	.333	117	28	39	12	1	4	23	2
Hopkins, Trav, c	.200	15	2	3	0	0	0	0	0
Joffrion, Jack, ss	.275	69	12	19	6	3	2	11	1
2-team (76 Coastal Bend)	.265	359	55	95	22	9	10	47	8
Mendoza, Aaron, c	.310	306	44	95	23	1	9	54	0
Mirizzi, Marc, ss	.295	227	31	67	17	1	2	34	1
Rodriguez, Rafael, dh	.133	15	2	2	1	0	0	0	0
Sanchez, Josh, ss	.333	6	2	2	0	0	0	1	0
Scheidt, Eric, 1b	.308	13	0	4	1	0	0	2	0
Schmidt, J.P., 3b	.365	329	65	120	32	3	12	69	24
Sherman, Steven, of	.259	54	10	14	2	1	1	5	0

PITCHING	W	L	ERA	G	SV	IP	H	BB	SO
Craker, Justin	5	5	4.19	37	16	58	63	24	54
Ferguson, Keith	0	0	9.00	1	0	4	9	1	0
Greco, Sam	0	2	4.85	30	0	52	68	25	46

Griffin, Charles	3	2	8.84	13	0	38	54	20	28
Hamilton, Jamaal	0	3	10.57	13	0	15	22	11	18
Jensen, Jed	4	4	6.08	12	0	61	77	20	52
Joffrion, Jack	0	0	18.00	2	0	2	3	2	0
2-team (3 Coastal Bend)	0	0	7.20	5	0	5	6	2	2
Kantz, Joe	1	0	13.50	6	0	7	14	4	6
Litchfield, B.J.	2	0	3.06	44	6	71	59	17	49
McReedy, Danny	2	1	7.16	4	0	16	27	4	7
McWatters, David	9	3	4.43	21	0	130	153	36	105
Mitchell, Nathan	5	3	5.90	13	0	58	61	36	33
Nieto, Jose	0	0	16.20	4	0	3	4	4	2
2-team (5 Coastal Bend)	0	0	7.31	9	0	16	18	11	7
Nikolic, Adam	0	0	18.00	1	0	1	1	2	2
Plouffe, Marshall	0	0	3.38	4	0	5	5	2	3
Quijano, Alain	0	0	12.60	8	0	10	22	7	5
Ramirez, Luis	1	4	5.53	27	0	28	33	15	21
Watts, Joldy	6	10	6.62	28	0	102	135	43	79
Wiedmeyer, Jason	9	10	4.58	21	0	140	145	32	126

SHREVEPORT

BATTING	AVG	AB	R	H	2B	3B	HR	RBI	SB
Allen, Josh, of	.145	69	5	10	4	1	0	4	3
Bryant, Tommy, c	.167	6	0	1	0	0	0	0	0
Cerbone, Marc, 1b	.222	9	0	2	1	0	0	1	0
Correa, Dalphie, ss/2b	.236	208	24	49	9	1	2	19	3
Gambill, Chad, of	.320	362	69	116	32	2	23	78	1
Gilliam, Bobby, of	.256	39	6	10	0	0	0	2	1
Haygood, Brandon, 2b	.235	187	28	44	10	2	2	20	5
Hicks, Michael, 3b	.145	55	3	8	0	0	0	7	1
Kurhan, Mick, 3b	.258	244	26	63	11	0	1	26	1
Lebron, Hector, 1b	.271	351	50	95	16	0	4	39	1
McMahon, Justin, of	.125	48	3	6	3	0	0	3	0
2-team (17 Jackson)	.196	102	11	20	5	1	4	15	0
Polanco, Enohel, ss/2b	.317	300	54	95	9	3	7	42	18
Rivas, Jose, of	.220	127	11	28	8	0	1	28	0
Smith, Coby, of	.313	393	54	123	22	3	3	36	15
Sorensen, Nick, of	.209	91	15	19	5	0	1	10	0
2-team (79 Jackson)	.244	369	54	90	15	1	7	38	12
Torres, Jason, c	.302	281	38	85	21	4	2	35	3
Webster, Kevin, c	.204	49	4	10	1	0	0	2	0
Willis, Mike, of	.238	349	41	83	8	5	2	365	12

PITCHING	W	L	ERA	G	SV	IP	H	BB	SO
Benson, Jason	1	3	4.95	16	0	44	51	14	27
Cerbone, Marc	0	2	3.42	4	0	24	21	9	15
Cunningham, Derek	4	7	4.33	15	0	89	83	36	88
Devenney, Nick	0	0	4.50	2	0	2	0	6	1
Doiron, Ian	0	0	9.00	1	0	1	3	1	1
Dossett, Dusty	4	4	3.22	12	0	67	63	20	58
Edmiston, Bo	0	1	11.81	4	0	5	9	2	4
2-team (16 Jackson)	5	7	5.40	20	0	90	99	31	54
Flores, Neomar	6	6	4.53	16	1	91	81	47	63
Gold, Joshua	0	1	7.20	4	0	10	10	1	8
Makowsky, Carl	2	3	3.12	36	12	43	42	16	48
Mozingo, Dan	2	1	4.15	28	1	35	34	8	33
Neitz, Josh	1	0	0.00	4	0	6	5	0	3
2-team (30 Fort Worth)	2	1	5.28	34	2	60	65	21	42
Riley, Rob	0	0	37.80	2	0	2	5	3	0
Ross, Adam	0	0	0.00	1	0	1	0	0	1
Snow, Bert	11	6	3.92	20	0	122	112	25	122
Snyder, Ryan	1	3	5.32	4	0	22	28	4	10
2-team (19 Jackson)	4	8	3.72	19	0	121	118	24	68
Tate, Alexander	0	1	2.35	6	0	8	3	7	12
Tyson, Leo	1	0	4.58	26	0	35	41	13	27
Vigue, John	5	2	3.65	39	4	67	69	13	53
Wikstrom, Eric	7	5	3.03	22	0	101	103	35	60
Winters, Mal	1	3	4.02	33	2	40	38	19	40

FRONTIER LEAGUE

Fran Riordan's grip on the Frontier League championship trophy grew a little tighter in 2005. The former Frontier League all-star player carried his success into the dugout, as his Kalamazoo Kings knocked off the Chillicothe Paints three games to two for the league title.

It was Riordan's third championship in five years. He led Richmond to the 2001 and 2002 titles before stepping down as a player/manager to continue his playing career in the Northeast League in 2003 (he was too old to play in the Frontier League that year).

After one subpar season in the Northeast League, Riordan returned to the Frontier League as Kalamazoo's manager in 2004.

It took Riordan a year to rebuild the team into his style before it all came together in 2005 as the Kings had a lineup suited to Riordan's desire to be aggressive on the bases.

"We really built our lineup to have four or five guys who can cause some havoc on the bases," Riordan said. "Those guys really did create havoc for defenses and pitchers."

Pete Pirman

Three Kings stole 25 or more bases, led by Frontier League MVP Pete Pirman.

Pirman, undrafted out of Eastern Illinois in 2003, blossomed in his third year in the league. Using a more patient approach, Pirman hit .347-23-100 with 35 stolen bases, tying the league record for RBIs. He also played strong defense in the outfield while showing off a right fielder's arm.

"It's unbelievable. He's a legit five-tool player playing in independent ball," Riordan said. "I've told scouts, 'Come watch him play.' There is no doubt he has all five tools."

Using the blazing basepaths approach that led them to the playoffs, the Kings stole 14 in the five-game championship series. Series MVP Darryl Blaze hit .417 while stealing five bases.

While the Kings won the title, Washington dominated the regular season, winning a league-record 13 games in a row at one point. The team has become the Atlanta Braves of the Frontier League, dominating the regular season but struggling in the playoffs. The Wild Things led the league in wins for the fourth straight season, breaking their own league record for most wins in a season (63), but the team fell short again in its quest for its first Frontier League title, losing in the first round to Chillicothe.

STANDINGS

EAST	W	L	PCT	GB
Washington Wild Things	63	32	.663	—
Chillicothe Paints	53	42	.558	10
Florence Freedom	53	42	.558	10
Evansville Otters	52	43	.547	11
Ohio Valley Redcoats	46	49	.484	17
Richmond Roosters	39	56	.411	24
WEST	**W**	**L**	**PCT**	**GB**
Kalamazoo Kings	53	43	.552	—
Rockford Riverhawks	51	45	.531	2
Gateway Grizzlies	48	47	.505	4 ½
River City Rascals	42	51	.452	9 ½
Windy City Thunderbolts	39	57	.406	14
Mid-Missouri Mavericks	31	63	.330	21

PLAYOFFS: Semifinals—Kalamazoo defeated Rockford 3-1 and Chillicothe defeated Washington 3-2 in best-of-5 series. **Finals**—Kalamazoo defeated Chillicothe 3-2 in best-of-5 series.

MANAGERS: Chillicothe—Glenn Wilson. **Evansville**—Greg Jelks. **Florence**—Jamie Keefe. **Gateway**—Danny Cox. **Kalamazoo**—Fran Riordan. **Mid-Missouri**—Jim Gentile. **Ohio Valley**—Mark Mason. **Richmond**—Chris Mongiardo. **River City**—Randy Martz. **Rockford**—Mike Young. **Washington**—John Massarelli. **Windy City:** Brent Bowers.

ATTENDANCE: Gateway 177,353; Washington 159,857; Evansville 136,941; Kalamazoo 132,909; River City 107,072; Rockford 103,248; Florence 94,191; Chillicothe 85,667; Windy City 78,011; Richmond 47,417; Mid-Missouri 46,617; Ohio Valley 11,066.

ALL-STAR TEAM: C—Ben Margalski, Gateway. **1B**—Thomari Story-Harden, Gateway. **2B**—Nick Batkoski, Ohio Valley. **3B**—Travis Garcia, Ohio Valley. **SS**—Jose Rodriguez, Chillicothe. **OF**—Mike Arbinger, Washington; Mike Galloway, Florence; Pete Pirman, Kalamazoo. **DH**—Justin Schuda,

Windy City. **SP**—John Martinez, Chillicothe. **RP**—Jim Popp, Washington.

Most Valuable Player: Pete Pirman, Kalamazoo. **Most Valuable Pitcher:** Aaron Ledbetter, River City. **Rookie of the Year:** Nick Batkoski, Ohio Valley. **Manager of the Year:** Mark Mason, Ohio Valley.

INDIVIDUAL BATTING LEADERS

(Minimum 259 Plate Appearances)

	AVG	G	AB	R	H	HR	RBI
Rodriguez, Jose, Chillicothe	.380	94	379	71	144	5	36
Rosario, Olmo, Rockford	.373	81	330	69	123	11	52
Bonilla, Clemente, Windy City	.369	70	287	47	106	2	35
Breyman, Mike, Gateway	.361	82	291	57	105	18	71
Story-Harden, Thomari, Gateway	.355	90	293	77	104	18	75
Pirman, Pete, Kalamazoo	.347	96	409	82	142	23	100
Galloway, Mike, Florence	.344	91	349	73	120	24	71
Downing, Juan, Chillicothe	.340	71	262	44	89	9	61
Metheny, Brent, Mid-Missouri	.338	94	346	73	117	12	76
Madrid, Mike, River City	.337	91	353	54	119	18	85

INDIVIDUAL PITCHING LEADERS

(Minimum 77 Innings)

	W	L	ERA	IP	H	BB	SO
Beuning, Brian, Kalamazoo	5	2	2.59	90	77	24	77
Ledbetter, Aaron, River City	12	5	2.93	135	138	34	114
Blackard, Cody, Evansville	6	4	2.93	80	77	29	49
Foster, Benjamin, Evansville	9	5	2.99	141	123	41	108
Simpson, Andre, Evansville	7	5	2.99	111	100	56	138
Martinez, John, Chillicothe	16	4	3.11	159	163	20	91
Beshears, Josh, Kalamazoo	13	3	3.12	130	112	40	136
Posey, Joel, Florence	8	2	3.14	132	118	65	144
Douglass, Ryan, Washington	11	3	3.25	119	124	16	63
Kroll, Brian, Evansville	6	5	3.45	99	104	39	76

CHILLICOTHE

BATTING	AVG	AB	R	H	2B	3B	HR	RBI	SB
Baywal, Tim, 1b	.259	27	2	7	1	0	0	4	0
2-team (33 Kalamazoo)	.329	143	22	47	9	1	2	24	1
Blacken, Beau, 1b	.342	187	32	64	10	0	9	37	5
Brotherton, Jeremy, 2b	.333	6	0	2	0	0	0	1	0
Colopy, Brian, 3b	.283	120	21	34	2	0	2	15	2
Cunningham, Perry, dh	.000	2	0	0	0	0	0	0	0
Downing, Juan, 2b	.315	146	24	46	8	0	6	35	2
2-team (30 Evansville)	.340	262	44	89	19	0	9	61	3
Dreher, Doug, 3b	.279	183	20	51	10	0	2	27	3
Funaro, Jeff, c	.251	183	23	46	9	0	5	15	2
Gascon, Adrian, ss	.239	159	17	38	10	0	2	14	8
Gingrich, David, of	.275	142	26	39	7	1	2	19	2
Heath, Darren, of	.208	125	15	26	2	1	0	6	7
Hipps, Brian, of	.175	57	9	10	1	0	2	5	0
Kasparek, Andrew, c	.279	154	21	43	11	0	4	28	1
Lefler, Scott, 3b	.273	161	33	44	10	1	9	33	4
Madden, Scott, c	.400	5	0	2	0	0	0	0	1
Martin, Steve, of	.376	101	24	38	2	2	4	13	6
2-team (64 Evansville)	.312	346	71	108	22	3	12	41	23
Peery, Noah, of	.229	175	28	40	9	1	9	37	7
Rafferty, Ryan, dh	.273	11	2	3	0	0	0	0	0
Ramistella, John, of	.317	357	83	113	20	4	20	73	32
Rodriguez, Jose, ss	.380	379	71	144	23	3	5	36	17
Scheidt, Eric, 3b	.250	4	0	1	0	0	0	1	0
Spry, Michael, of	.290	162	24	47	9	3	5	26	6
Thomas, Tee, of	.000	11	0	0	0	0	0	0	1
Ury, Josh, 1b	.299	351	58	105	15	1	10	58	9
Watters, Rusty, ss	.219	32	3	7	0	0	0	4	0

PITCHING	W	L	ERA	G	SV	IP	H	BB	SO
Bednarczyk, Bryce	0	1	3.97	12	1	11	11	6	6
Blanton, Matt	0	5	8.49	7	0	30	46	15	15
Bowman, Keith	1	0	16.20	3	0	3	7	4	4
Cavanaugh, Nick	3	2	4.10	33	2	53	59	25	51
Colopy, Brian	0	0	13.50	1	0	1	3	0	0
Cunningham, Perry	10	6	3.98	22	0	140	151	27	92
Dreher, Doug	0	0	0.00	1	0	1	0	0	1
Durkee, Jeremy	5	4	3.68	38	0	59	71	16	57
Ferguson, Keith	2	1	2.78	6	0	32	40	11	16
Gingrich, David	0	0	20.25	1	0	1	3	1	2
Hipps, Brian	0	0	0.00	1	0	0	2	0	0
Jones, K.C.	0	1	8.55	9	0	20	30	11	14
Lefler, Scott	0	0	6.75	2	0	1	3	0	0
Lovell, Ben	1	2	5.17	12	0	31	38	16	15
Martinez, John	16	4	3.11	23	0	159	163	20	91
Morgan, Lavelle	1	0	7.50	1	0	6	7	1	8
Munoz, Justin	3	2	7.05	11	0	37	55	16	16
Palmer, Lucas	8	5	4.42	30	3	100	90	44	77
Peery, Noah	0	0	0.00	1	0	2	0	2	0
Petty, Chad	0	1	16.88	2	0	5	12	7	5
Plouffee, Marshall	1	2	2.06	22	0	35	28	11	30
Rafferty, Ryan	2	2	2.41	32	9	34	22	28	46
Ramistella, John	0	0	27.00	1	0	1	2	3	1
Soskin, Pete	0	1	7.15	16	2	23	23	17	17
Spry, Michael	0	0	27.00	1	0	1	2	0	1
Stout, Josh	0	2	5.71	9	0	41	50	24	20
Ury, Josh	0	1	5.40	1	0	2	3	0	0
Watters, Rusty	0	0	18.00	1	0	1	4	1	0
Wolensky, Dave	0	0	3.38	3	0	3	7	1	2

EVANSVILLE

BATTING	AVG	AB	R	H	2B	3B	HR	RBI	SB
Blacken, Beau, 1b	.273	161	30	44	6	0	4	20	1
2-team (51 Chillicothe)	.310	348	62	108	16	0	13	57	6
Clinton, Ricky, c	.296	253	29	75	10	0	6	35	1
Coker, John, of	.266	79	13	21	1	0	0	9	3
Downing, Juan, 3b	.371	116	20	43	11	0	3	26	1
Gingrich, David, of	.244	45	7	11	4	0	0	8	0
2-team (51 Chillicothe)	.267	187	33	50	11	1	2	27	2
Goldbach, Jeff, c	.339	218	44	74	12	2	19	64	3
Hilt, Cole, 1b	.261	211	23	55	10	0	7	40	0
Jaksa, Nick, ph	.000	1	0	0	0	0	0	0	0
Kindle, Jud, c	.229	70	9	16	4	0	2	11	0
Mann, Jason, c	.226	137	17	31	6	1	3	13	0
Martin, Steve, of	.286	245	47	70	20	1	8	28	17
McClain, Terrence, of	.296	98	12	29	6	0	3	10	2
McKenna, Brian, ss	.255	330	48	84	14	0	10	50	4
Milsom, Geoff, ss	.000	7	0	0	0	0	0	0	0
Munoz, Trask, of	.277	311	53	86	15	3	6	43	18
Rich, Chris, 1b	.200	5	0	1	0	0	0	0	0
Scott, Frank, 2b	.264	311	71	82	11	1	1	31	13
Shay, Nick, 3b	.381	21	5	8	2	0	2	4	0
Spry, Michael, of	.298	84	14	25	2	2	4	18	3
2-team (55 Chillicothe)	.293	246	38	72	11	5	9	44	9
Stewart, Josh, of	.221	95	10	21	7	0	1	10	3
Stuckey, Denver, 3b	.260	385	49	100	15	3	1	32	14
Ward, Scott, of	.246	69	11	17	3	1	0	5	3
Wettlaufer, Josh, of	.250	4	1	1	1	0	0	0	0
Zeller, Matt, of	.231	13	1	3	0	0	0	1	0

PITCHING	W	L	ERA	G	SV	IP	H	BB	SO
Black, Keith	0	1	10.61	2	0	9	13	2	1
Blackard, Cody	6	4	2.93	12	0	80	77	29	49
Bolton, Dustin	2	2	5.72	13	0	28	33	7	12
Burnau, Ryan	3	4	1.60	35	13	45	24	19	53
Del Prete, Anthony	2	3	4.10	30	2	42	46	21	28
Foster, Ben	9	5	2.99	20	0	141	123	41	108
Jefferson, Andrew	2	0	4.31	19	2	31	34	11	21
Jordan, Justin	0	0	0.00	1	0	2	1	0	4
Kroll, Brian	6	5	3.45	20	1	99	104	39	76
Langdon, Donny	2	0	0.00	8	0	13	2	6	18
Pawelczyk, Kyle	0	1	4.91	18	1	18	17	13	14
Pillsbury, Chris	8	7	3.90	17	0	113	109	39	85
Read, Robby	1	0	3.44	5	0	18	17	16	12
Shartzer, Bryan	3	2	5.82	19	1	51	59	17	47
Simpson, Andre	7	5	2.99	18	0	111	100	56	138
Stone, Nathan	1	4	1.50	30	4	42	35	11	34
Zimmerman, Adam	0	0	3.86	5	0	5	7	4	3

FLORENCE

BATTING	AVG	AB	R	H	2B	3B	HR	RBI	SB
Baker, Brian, of	.083	12	1	1	0	0	0	1	0
Chauncey, Clint, c	.203	64	6	13	2	0	1	2	2
Cornell, Brandon, of	.302	106	22	32	6	3	3	16	3
Derhak, Alex, c-1b	.260	50	8	13	3	1	0	4	1
Galloway, Mike, of	.344	349	73	120	18	1	24	71	10
Geswein, Kyle, of	.231	290	43	67	8	0	24	57	1
Gomez, Galindo, of	.154	26	3	4	1	0	0	1	1
Hall, Trevor, 1b	.316	380	70	120	28	0	23	79	0
Holland, Joe, 3b-2b	.248	141	18	35	14	1	1	11	0
Ison, Jeremy, 3b	.127	79	5	10	4	0	1	6	0
Joyner, Elliot, c	.048	21	2	1	0	0	0	1	0
Kinsolving, Darin, of	.336	226	43	76	17	0	16	52	0
Martin, Scott, of	.300	337	51	101	29	2	13	51	9
Morrison, Bryce, of	.111	9	0	1	1	0	0	0	0
Pickens, Scott, c	.167	222	29	37	3	1	6	22	3
Quigg, Wally, 2b	.241	369	50	89	15	3	5	45	1
Sanchez, Josh, ss	.231	303	51	70	15	0	4	41	9
Schmidt, Zach, 3b-2b	.241	145	28	35	7	0	2	12	0
Singer, Matthew, of	.250	64	6	16	8	0	0	9	0
Stone, Greg, 3b-of	.253	79	12	20	3	0	1	1	2

PITCHING	W	L	ERA	G	SV	IP	H	BB	SO
Bays, Lenny	0	2	5.48	17	6	23	29	7	24
Bednarczyk, Bryce	0	0	2.45	5	0	7	6	3	4
2-team (17 Chillicothe)	0	1	3.38	17	1	19	17	9	10

PITCHING	W	L	ERA	G	SV	IP	H	BB	SO
Bowlin, Jason	10	4	3.66	18	0	118	127	43	84
Boychuk, Steve	0	0	8.10	9	0	10	15	7	12
Brunke, Jason	1	4	6.37	7	0	35	45	17	27
Causey, Mike	1	2	4.54	27	0	42	49	20	43
Daugherty, Clay	0	0	27.00	1	0	1	1	4	1
Dennison, Michael	9	7	3.94	22	0	142	163	36	103
Fuller, Justin	2	4	7.67	26	0	27	26	19	38
Geswein, Kyle	0	1	7.71	9	0	16	31	9	12
Harris, Mark	5	3	6.29	16	0	63	79	38	31
Marksbury, Mike	0	0	8.31	5	0	4	4	8	8
Moenter, Curtis	4	2	3.43	28	0	76	62	30	89
2-team (7 Richmond)	5	4	3.79	35	0	109	109	42	118
O'Quinn, Mickey	1	2	2.28	21	1	28	30	12	26
Posey, Joel	8	2	3.14	20	0	132	118	65	144
Rowe, Ted	9	4	2.35	45	17	61	48	24	66
Sena, Jason	1	2	8.20	8	1	19	30	9	15
Smith, Brett	0	0	10.80	3	0	5	7	4	2
Thurman, Corey	2	3	4.38	6	0	37	38	11	38
Touchet, Danny	0	0	0.00	1	0	1	1	1	1
White, Kris	0	0	9.82	2	0	4	5	3	1

GATEWAY

BATTING	AVG	AB	R	H	2B	3B	HR	RBI	SB
Averill, Brandon, 3b	.259	189	30	49	13	0	7	27	0
Bohnenstiehl, Nick, of	.229	70	10	16	4	1	0	3	3
Brewster, Jon, 2b	.219	32	3	7	1	0	0	2	1
Breyman, Mike, of	.365	296	58	108	21	0	18	72	4
Gilbert, Gary, 2b	.263	281	53	74	13	1	3	25	5
Jenkins, Bo, 2b	.229	83	7	19	3	1	1	6	2
Lopez, Freddy, of	.290	276	45	80	12	0	9	42	7
Margalski, Ben, c	.306	268	59	82	12	1	16	58	2
Oetting, Todd, of	.239	134	19	32	6	0	4	17	0
Pierce, Whit, c	.220	100	11	22	2	0	1	10	1
Reiter, Jimmy, of	.262	298	54	78	16	2	8	42	12
Sansouci, Eric, of	.198	116	15	23	1	1	1	12	4
Smarsh, Shawn, of	.262	252	45	66	5	1	7	27	10
Story-Harden, Thomari, 1b	.409	66	25	27	7	0	3	17	4
2-team (68 Mid-Missouri)	.355	293	78	104	22	0	18	75	5
Sullivan, Ryan, ss	.298	285	61	85	19	0	19	64	1
Vargas, Oscar, ss	.308	172	26	53	9	1	6	33	7
Warren, Phil, 1b	.268	347	44	93	17	0	9	59	0

PITCHING	W	L	ERA	G	SV	IP	H	BB	SO
Barriger, Marcus	1	0	3.55	16	3	33	35	12	30
Bernat, Bryan	0	4	7.03	6	0	24	26	18	10
Dessau, Erik	6	5	4.45	14	0	85	86	28	53
Dooley, Joe	1	1	9.90	2	0	10	16	4	11
Drewes, Brad	0	2	10.80	5	0	18	33	4	15
Ebers, Eric	0	0	9.90	10	0	10	14	7	7
Ellis, Rob	1	2	11.85	6	0	14	18	5	11
Gericke, Drew	0	0	4.50	1	0	2	2	1	1
Golden, Mike	0	3	10.13	12	1	21	27	24	31
Hamilton, Ryan	3	2	5.31	34	5	41	38	31	45
Herrera, Ryan	0	1	17.18	2	0	4	7	6	3
Justus, Ale	3	2	5.00	6	0	36	41	17	20
Little, Chris	1	1	4.94	28	1	58	65	26	49
Nicholson, Scott	2	1	6.08	4	0	24	30	5	10
Nourie, Jonathan	0	0	15.00	3	0	3	4	4	2
Patterson, Scott	1	1	1.65	19	9	27	21	8	41
Powell, Matt	7	3	5.85	25	2	85	107	22	50
Read, Robby	0	0	0.00	1	0	2	1	1	1
Rebyanski, Anthony	0	0	11.57	1	0	2	2	3	4
Roush, Nathan	4	4	5.08	12	0	57	64	26	34
Rowe, Ted	0	1	17.36	2	0	5	13	5	3
Smith, Brandon	12	5	3.55	19	0	132	123	43	119
Smith, David	2	3	7.39	8	0	28	32	19	19
Sues, Jarret	0	0	15.75	5	0	4	10	5	5
Sullivan, Ryan	0	0	2.25	3	0	4	3	1	1
Szczur, Nick	5	6	6.10	15	0	83	96	33	58
Walter, David	0	0	9.31	5	0	10	15	2	7
White, Demetri	0	0	14.40	5	0	10	23	9	10

KALAMAZOO

BATTING	AVG	AB	R	H	2B	3B	HR	RBI	SB
Barden, Andy, c	.237	97	20	23	6	0	1	8	1
Baywal, Tim, 2b/3b	.345	116	20	40	8	1	2	20	1
Blaze, Darryl, 2b	.273	403	73	110	13	5	4	37	25
Brown, Tim, 1b	.323	347	71	112	31	0	16	71	4
Brown, Trevor, c	.279	280	46	78	17	0	6	36	0
Burkhalter, Donnie, 1b	.250	92	12	23	3	0	5	18	0
Dixon, Derek, of	.167	18	2	3	0	0	0	2	0
Estrada, Marco, 2b	.156	32	6	5	0	0	0	3	0
Gomez, Arnie, dh	.218	55	10	12	3	0	2	7	0
Lang, Andy, 2b	.286	35	3	10	2	1	0	7	0
Leavitt, Adam, 2b	.263	194	32	51	9	1	1	23	15
McClain, Justin, 3b	.303	357	55	108	29	2	6	58	6
Mezistrano, Lee, of	.246	65	9	16	3	0	0	6	2
Pirman, Pete, of	.347	409	82	142	21	3	23	100	35
Riordan, Chris, 2b	.115	61	8	7	1	0	1	6	1
Rogers, Nick, of	.274	391	74	107	29	2	11	63	32
St. Julien, Jason, c	.107	28	4	3	0	1	1	1	1
Sullivan, Jason, ss	.281	363	47	102	11	3	3	53	5
Valdivia, Roger, c	.200	15	2	3	1	0	0	0	0

PITCHING	W	L	ERA	G	SV	IP	H	BB	SO
Beshears, Josh	13	3	3.12	19	0	130	112	40	136
Beuning, Brian	5	2	2.59	54	1	90	77	24	77
Blackwell, Brad	1	2	4.31	23	1	31	29	22	31
Brown, Tim	0	0	4.50	1	0	2	2	0	0
Clark, Chad	0	3	7.39	7	0	32	37	30	34
Daws, Josh	7	2	2.82	34	12	38	35	21	41
Devalk, Dane	3	1	2.84	7	0	32	29	14	17
Garner, Jeff	6	4	5.82	23	0	87	113	32	67
Geddes, Michael	0	2	8.35	20	0	32	38	23	33
Gutierrez, Jonathon	6	8	4.55	19	0	111	120	45	108
Keeling, Justin	1	5	6.99	18	0	37	50	11	26
Martin, Brandon	1	2	2.00	11	1	18	16	7	18
Martin, Josh	4	0	1.39	8	0	52	37	13	39
Moore, Tyrell	0	1	12.79	2	0	6	7	6	3
Mosteller, Nate	0	0	18.00	2	0	2	3	4	2
Naplin, Lee	6	8	4.40	19	0	117	115	45	76
Steed, Bric	0	0	5.79	6	0	9	9	10	6
Streich, Isaac	0	0	11.57	9	0	9	15	9	15
Underhill, Josh	0	0	0.60	5	0	15	18	2	8

MID-MISSOURI

BATTING	AVG	AB	R	H	2B	3B	HR	RBI	SB
Albertson, Eli, of	.320	206	42	66	14	0	8	28	2
Astrauskas, c	.296	98	10	29	7	1	5	22	1
Averill, Brandon, 1b	1.000	1	0	1	0	0	0	0	0
2-team (57 Gateway)	.263	190	30	50	13	0	7	27	0
Ayala, Elliot, of	.342	120	29	41	9	0	1	16	8
Baker, Brian, of	.239	138	22	33	7	0	4	17	1
4-team (12 W.C., 10 Rich., 4 Flor.)	.232	228	31	53	10	0	6	28	3
Bergstrom, Bub, of	.174	23	2	4	0	0	0	1	1
Bogan, Jesse, c	.178	45	2	8	1	0	0	3	0
Bowker, Tom, of	.208	106	16	22	6	0	1	10	1
Buscher, Greg, 3b	.253	253	22	64	16	1	6	39	0
Derhak, Alex, c	.302	189	29	57	13	0	4	30	0
2-team (16 Florence)	.293	239	37	70	16	1	4	34	1
Farr, Ashley, ss	.171	35	2	6	0	0	0	2	0
Hillman, Dusty, 2b	.274	347	60	95	15	0	7	48	7
Kottke, Ryan, c	.188	16	1	3	0	0	0	2	0
Metheny, Brent, 3b	.336	351	74	118	28	1	12	77	15
Morrison, Bryce, of	.239	67	13	16	4	0	4	13	0
Oakes, Matt, c	.264	125	12	33	8	0	1	21	1
Poles,Donald of	.290	31	6	9	2	0	0	2	1
Renault, Nick, 2b	.000	5	1	0	0	0	0	0	0
Saunders, Nick, of	.143	35	2	5	0	1	0	3	0
Story/Harden, Thomari, 1b	.339	227	53	77	15	0	15	58	1
Wetlaufer, Josh, of	.284	285	50	81	8	2	1	18	14
Winn, Brett, of	.258	198	22	51	6	0	4	23	1
Wright, Jon, of	.266	94	15	25	5	1	1	9	2
Young, Dusty, ss	.229	231	26	53	7	0	3	14	1

PITCHING	W	L	ERA	G	SV	IP	H	BB	SO
Clay, Adam	1	0	7.36	10	0	15	24	14	7
Dantibo, Damien	2	3	6.17	7	0	35	39	22	37
Eberhardt, Pete	0	1	5.87	9	1	23	24	18	17
Eddy, Cooper	3	5	5.06	36	8	53	63	28	46
Elkins, Jason	0	0	3.00	2	0	3	6	2	3
Ellison, Jesse	1	2	7.06	4	0	22	29	16	11
Ellison, Philip	0	3	10.09	18	1	30	41	18	21
Giannetti, Chad	0	1	7.43	9	0	23	30	11	26
Glasscock, J.P.	0	0	11.25	3	0	4	9	2	0
Gross, Kris	0	1	9.53	5	0	6	14	2	5
Jones, Quentin	0	1	27.00	1	0	1	4	1	0
Kerschen, Joshua	0	3	4.71	13	1	42	48	20	18
Kuhns, Nate	0	2	16.03	5	0	11	24	10	8
2-team (4 River City)	0	2	13.22	9	0	16	29	12	12
Marchbanks, David	0	2	13.50	4	0	11	17	10	7
McKernan, Rick	0	3	11.12	17	0	23	31	28	25
Mendible, Frank	0	1	21.60	3	0	3	7	4	1
Metheny, Brent	0	0	0.00	1	0	2	2	1	0
New, Travis	1	1	5.52	5	0	15	15	5	13
Nielsen, Steve	1	0	8.66	8	0	18	31	9	10
Nieto, David	0	0	18.90	4	0	3	5	1	3
O'Donnell,	0	1	40.50	1	0	2	6	1	2
Oakes, Matt	0	0	5.40	3	0	7	12	4	6
Perez, Ezequiel	1	3	8.20	19	0	37	63	15	24
Renault, Nick	9	7	3.85	26	0	138	155	63	145

	W	L	ERA	G	SV	IP	H	BB	SO
Rodriguez, Augustine	2	9	4.14	23	0	78	62	34	48
Schaefer, Mike	1	1	6.75	3	0	15	17	4	10
Shuck, Danny	3	3	7.68	9	0	43	60	18	23
Sledge, Eli	1	0	4.22	7	0	21	24	19	20
Smith, Brett	0	2	6.18	8	0	28	32	13	7
Soja, Steve	5	8	3.48	22	0	96	106	26	58
Williams, Matt	0	0	40.50	2	0	2	7	3	2

OHIO VALLEY

BATTING	AVG	AB	R	H	2B	3B	HR	RBI	SB
Batkoski, Nick, 2b	.336	262	58	88	19	2	16	56	0
Boyd, Jason, of	.304	336	59	102	21	4	11	66	7
Burton, Adam, c	.000	12	2	0	0	0	0	1	0
Caballero, Lupe, 2b	.143	14	2	2	0	0	0	0	0
Crump, Chase, of	.202	84	14	17	3	1	2	12	1
Garcia, Travis, 3b	.332	374	72	124	39	0	12	70	7
Gilliam, Bobby, of	.254	193	32	49	4	1	0	16	4
Griffin, Kevin, c	.218	101	4	22	1	0	0	2	1
Houston, Bobby, 2b	.111	18	4	2	0	0	0	2	1
Mendoza, Jaziel, of	.288	313	62	90	17	2	15	65	8
Munoz, David, ss	.216	292	39	63	11	0	1	26	3
Oligo, Kaliko, of	.266	380	62	101	16	3	4	36	7
Page, Miles, c	.169	71	6	12	2	0	0	14	0
Richards, Jud, 1b	.253	316	39	80	14	1	9	34	3
Sadler, Patrick, c	.218	147	25	32	5	2	7	23	2
Tidball, Adam, c	.268	142	18	38	5	1	4	26	1
Uranga, Darren, 2b	.258	198	27	51	10	2	0	13	4

PITCHING	W	L	ERA	G	SV	IP	H	BB	SO
Adkins, Luke	8	8	4.43	22	0	126	124	41	67
Arthur, Tony	0	0	8.59	6	0	7	11	3	5
Augsburger, Kyle	0	0	10.61	3	0	9	15	6	6
Baysinger, Daniel	0	1	11.25	1	0	4	8	4	2
Berry, Josh	0	0	3.18	5	1	6	5	2	2
Bonilla, Danny	1	2	9.00	3	0	15	15	11	15
2-team (3 Richmond)	1	2	9.00	6	0	26	29	18	20
Childs, Ryan	6	8	5.63	21	0	128	161	37	49
Cochran, Tom	7	6	4.73	19	0	124	132	56	109
Davidson, Tom	0	0	11.88	6	0	8	13	2	7
Elkins, Jason	3	3	4.19	26	10	34	26	19	28
2-team (2 Mid-Missouri)	3	3	4.10	28	10	37	32	21	31
Gerlach, Justin	5	1	3.05	31	3	41	39	25	35
Grijalva, Jon	1	3	3.74	13	1	22	17	14	19
Holt, Eric	1	2	9.16	6	0	19	25	19	6
Jakubauskas, Chris	5	4	3.34	12	0	70	74	30	48
Joslyn, Kevin	2	1	4.26	22	0	45	48	19	44
Kirsch, Brad	0	1	10.50	6	1	6	8	3	4
Kline, Ty	3	5	6.28	10	0	43	61	8	21
Lang, Blair	1	0	3.94	9	0	16	19	7	10
Laurin, Brad	0	0	9.00	3	0	4	4	1	3
LeDuc, Dennis	1	1	4.66	12	0	37	38	9	34
Palmer, Adam	1	1	10.13	4	0	5	9	5	4
Read, Robby	1	2	8.55	5	0	20	24	20	9
4-team (5 Evans., 1 Gate, 3 Rich.)	2	4	5.66	14	0	56	60	49	32
Watzek, Kurt	0	0	6.44	21	0	29	38	20	19

RICHMOND

BATTING	AVG	AB	R	H	2B	3B	HR	RBI	SB
Baker, Brian, 1b	.216	37	5	8	1	0	1	4	0
Balster, Scott, of	.160	25	3	4	0	0	0	1	1
Bidwell, Mike, 3b	.253	233	32	59	11	1	6	34	3
Carr, Kevin, c	.200	10	0	2	0	0	0	0	0
Chapman, Brian, of	.000	2	0	0	0	0	0	0	0
Cuervo, Joe, of	.200	95	16	19	4	0	3	13	3
Daly, Rich, 1b	.262	164	20	43	9	1	6	22	0
2-team (27 Windy City)	.244	250	31	61	12	1	9	36	0
DiBlasi, Chris, c	.205	44	6	9	1	0	1	5	0
2-team (21 Rockford)	.264	110	18	29	6	1	2	18	0
Garza, O.J., of	.256	211	26	54	8	1	3	21	6
Gravely, Nathan, ss	.314	283	48	89	17	2	5	29	11
Hepner, Aaron, c	.375	8	0	3	1	0	0	1	0
Herriott, Ty, 1b	.240	121	21	29	9	0	4	17	2
Hollingsworth, Josh, ss	.282	213	36	60	9	1	16	42	4
Kimbrough, Justus, c	.236	106	10	25	1	0	1	11	1
Miller, Gerald, of	.259	189	32	49	4	1	3	17	13
Reese, Mike, of	.328	338	67	111	21	3	10	41	11
Rhomberg, Joe, 2b	.268	213	31	57	14	0	6	34	3
Rybczak, Ale, c	.304	46	8	14	1	0	1	4	0
Sanguinetti, Tony, c	.274	299	49	82	15	2	22	72	1
Urena, Hector, 2b	.315	92	15	29	2	0	2	17	2
Vaughn, Kiley, 2b	.250	180	26	45	10	1	1	17	1
Vetter, Scott, 3b	.357	14	2	5	1	0	0	0	0
White, Kevin, of	.291	364	75	106	27	2	20	72	4
Woods, Blake, 2b	.160	25	6	4	0	0	0	1	2

PITCHING	W	L	ERA	G	SV	IP	H	BB	SO
Bennett, Derek	0	2	8.16	6	0	14	17	7	10
Bonilla, Danny	0	0	9.00	3	0	11	14	7	5
Caldwell, Daniel	1	6	5.52	22	4	44	49	23	36
Casoli, Tony	8	6	3.89	20	0	134	155	24	109
Cervera, Mike	2	2	4.22	11	0	43	40	30	25
Chapman, Brian	0	0	10.50	4	0	6	11	6	5
Davis, Hunter	2	1	2.95	31	5	40	30	14	24
Dorn, Grant	1	0	2.35	12	0	15	14	3	9
Frias, Hector	0	0	10.80	2	0	2	4	1	2
Garza, O.J.	0	0	18.00	1	0	1	2	2	1
Howton, Jared	3	3	5.96	10	0	45	44	25	34
Huskey, Matt	1	1	9.26	6	0	12	16	13	5
Kohorst, Pat	0	2	4.23	7	0	28	37	5	14
Laughlin, Keith	0	1	7.04	5	0	8	9	5	3
Mack, Bobby	0	0	1.04	3	0	9	4	8	6
2-team (16 Rockford)	1	3	4.50	19	2	30	29	16	27
Massey, Beau	0	1	3.95	19	3	27	29	6	22
Merle, Jesen	2	4	5.79	42	0	47	62	17	27
2-team (3 Rockford)	3	4	6.24	45	0	49	68	18	28
Moenter, Curtis	1	2	4.59	7	0	33	47	12	29
Moses, Fred	0	2	20.77	3	0	4	10	3	2
Read, Robby	0	2	5.40	3	0	15	18	12	10
Regas, Kris	5	4	3.57	40	2	53	48	9	72
Schweitzer, Matt	6	11	4.59	23	0	149	169	30	108
Shanks, E.J.	0	1	11.40	9	0	15	20	16	12
Varteressian, Adam	7	2	5.21	34	1	38	49	16	32
Weber, Rick	0	1	6.06	5	0	16	25	5	15
White, Kevin	0	0	1.69	5	0	5	4	7	3
White, Mike	0	2	16.20	3	0	7	13	6	7
Ziroli, Steve	0	0	10.34	7	0	16	24	2	15
2-team (18 Windy City)	0	3	6.55	25	0	44	59	19	36

RIVER CITY

BATTING	AVG	AB	R	H	2B	3B	HR	RBI	SB
Arnold, David, of	.273	238	41	65	16	1	3	18	10
Bennett, Stacy, 3b	.250	12	1	3	0	0	0	1	0
Calderon, Tony, ss	.244	242	26	59	10	0	4	31	0
Conner, Mike, of	.256	344	61	88	27	3	12	62	27
Hughes, Logan, 3b	.100	10	1	1	0	0	0	2	0
Hutchison, Wes, 3b	.189	53	6	10	4	0	1	5	1
Kemp, Shane, 3b	.167	18	4	3	0	0	1	3	1
Lacy, Brent, c	.333	3	0	1	1	0	0	1	0
Madrid, Mike, 1b	.334	356	54	119	17	0	18	85	2
Manning, Jake, of	.295	146	27	43	5	1	5	16	2
McConnell, Kirk, of	.307	316	66	97	23	2	11	49	15
McKinley, Justin, 3b	.229	231	27	53	7	0	7	33	12
McMullen, Ian, c	.000	3	0	0	0	0	0	0	0
Melendez, Cristobal, of	.143	7	0	1	1	0	0	2	0
Olsen, Mikela, of	.244	164	26	40	7	0	6	32	2
Ornelas, Rafael, 2b	.199	151	17	30	3	0	0	8	2
Riera, Zack, c	.304	135	33	41	12	1	2	20	10
Saunders, Nick, 3b	.258	256	39	66	14	0	9	31	2
2-team (9 Mid-Missouri)	.244	291	41	71	14	1	9	34	2
Slagle, Anthony, 2b	.263	228	47	60	10	0	4	22	12
Williams, Jonny, c	.255	251	31	64	14	1	5	33	1
Wright, John, 3b	.244	41	4	10	1	0	1	7	1

PITCHING	W	L	ERA	G	SV	IP	H	BB	SO
Brook, Steven	6	2	4.09	13	0	84	96	11	54
Drewes, Brad	0	1	7.23	4	0	19	29	7	12
2-team (5 Gateway)	0	3	9.00	9	0	37	62	11	27
Ebers, Eric	0	1	8.31	6	0	13	21	10	10
Evers, Patrick	2	5	3.86	29	5	44	45	13	27
Golden, Mike	0	0	5.31	14	0	20	20	24	27
Hogan, Gary	2	4	5.61	14	0	43	42	27	27
Hutchison, Wes	1	3	5.32	30	4	46	49	21	41
Kars, Jonathan	2	2	6.26	24	0	42	49	19	28
Keating, Brian	3	9	3.79	18	0	112	103	49	107
Kuhns, Nate	0	0	7.94	4	0	6	5	2	4
Landavazo, Derrick	0	1	5.88	13	0	26	31	13	28
Ledbetter, Aaron	12	5	2.93	19	0	135	138	34	114
Manning, Jake	0	0	10.29	3	0	7	9	2	4
Marsala, Tony	4	5	6.52	11	0	50	81	23	28
McReynolds, Steve	0	1	3.86	7	0	12	12	9	5
Ross, Brian	0	0	6.23	2	0	4	7	3	4
Shallock, Brian	1	0	4.26	3	0	13	16	9	6
Thatcher, Joe	4	2	1.27	18	5	21	18	4	27
Troop, Jon	1	2	7.71	8	0	30	39	19	21
Webb, Chris	3	4	5.37	21	0	57	65	22	40
Wood, Rick	1	5	5.28	6	0	29	42	9	18

ROCKFORD

BATTING	AVG	AB	R	H	2B	3B	HR	RBI	SB
Baron, Brian, of	.306	330	58	101	22	1	5	50	1

BATTING	AVG	AB	R	H	2B	3B	HR	RBI	SB
Busch, Jeremy, of	.274	190	26	52	10	2	2	26	1
Chappell, John, c	.313	67	12	21	2	1	3	20	0
Ciarrachi, Kevin, c	.333	117	13	39	9	0	0	15	0
DiBlasi, Chris, 3b	.303	66	12	20	5	1	1	13	0
Dickinson, Jake, of	.245	49	9	12	4	0	1	2	3
Dulaney, Todd, 2b	.223	229	28	51	8	0	0	13	2
Elkouri, Shaff, 2b	.319	141	34	45	6	0	3	19	3
Farr, Ashley, 2b	.315	197	22	62	14	1	1	36	0
2-team (14 Mid-Missouri)	.293	232	24	68	14	1	1	38	0
Gerlits, Gooby, c	.244	238	28	58	10	1	10	43	0
Hardin, Travis, 3b	.000	2	0	0	0	0	0	1	0
Johnson, Nick, of	.333	183	30	61	15	0	3	41	1
2-team (48 Windy City)	.322	382	64	123	27	1	10	72	3
Larson, Ryan, 3b	.264	254	34	67	13	2	4	34	2
Lynch, Michael, c	.277	65	10	18	4	0	0	6	0
McCoy, Jerome, of	.181	72	11	13	0	1	0	7	7
2-team (43 Windy City)	.246	224	28	55	2	1	0	18	29
McEachran, Aaron, 1b	.306	330	72	101	23	0	14	68	0
Rich, Chris, ss	.171	41	2	7	1	0	1	5	0
2-team (3 Evansville)	.174	46	2	8	1	0	1	5	0
Rosario, Olmo, ss	.373	330	69	123	17	6	11	52	11
Santana, Rico, of	.258	93	13	24	5	1	4	20	3
Sauls, Matt, of	.272	169	37	46	10	1	1	12	3
Schutt, Doug, of	.316	190	40	60	12	2	4	20	19
Strain, Ryan, 2b	.263	19	4	5	0	0	0	1	0

PITCHING	W	L	ERA	G	SV	IP	H	BB	SO
Barbosa, Joe	3	0	1.92	9	0	61	47	9	33
Borland, Curt	2	5	3.53	29	2	36	38	12	35
Crowley, Kevin	1	1	4.72	20	1	69	82	33	30
Dowling, David	2	5	4.78	24	1	32	35	10	40
Ellison, Derrick	3	4	4.50	28	2	30	30	14	25
Gallegos, Gary	0	0	15.63	5	0	6	10	11	6
Glosser, Jason	7	3	2.11	35	14	43	38	9	42
James, Frank	3	3	3.44	10	0	55	59	28	33
Kroft, Adam	3	2	3.79	32	0	62	71	13	28
Lambo, Luke	1	3	5.05	26	1	73	80	37	72
Mack, Bobby	1	3	5.91	16	2	21	25	8	21
Massey, Beau	0	0	6.43	7	0	7	9	4	10
Merle, Jesen	1	0	15.43	3	0	2	6	1	1
Mindingall, Wes	1	0	7.20	5	0	15	20	4	13
Olson, Justin	6	5	3.99	21	0	115	118	29	114
Parker, David	1	1	12.71	5	0	6	10	2	3
Richards, John	3	2	4.58	15	0	39	43	16	19
Roper, Derek	9	4	4.41	19	0	118	125	21	102
Watson, Tanner	4	4	3.73	8	0	51	45	20	52

WASHINGTON

BATTING	AVG	AB	R	H	2B	3B	HR	RBI	SB
Arbinger, Mike, of	.317	366	72	116	29	8	12	88	6
Baldwin, Bruce, 2b	.261	188	32	49	5	0	2	35	13
Carter, Chris, of	.286	360	69	103	13	8	12	73	14
Glass, Brady, dh	.222	9	0	2	0	0	0	0	0
Graves, T.J., 3b	.309	204	32	63	4	2	0	29	11
Hudak, Andy, 3b	.308	234	41	72	9	3	10	55	3
Justice, Jeff, of	.235	17	3	4	1	0	0	1	2
Koenig, Lance, 2b	.323	387	77	125	26	4	3	56	18
McGarvey, Randy, c	.306	206	46	63	15	1	3	38	8
McGraw, Ryan, of	.268	254	59	68	10	4	3	27	23
Morgan, Robert, ss	.256	168	28	43	4	1	2	15	9
O'Brien, Pat, c	.258	198	37	51	11	5	7	36	0
Reaver, David, ss	.305	328	55	100	16	4	3	46	7
Sidick, Chris, of	.333	192	40	64	10	6	3	29	15
Swope, Matt, of	.309	246	54	76	13	0	8	39	11

PITCHING	W	L	ERA	G	SV	IP	H	BB	SO
Borsa, B.J.	2	4	5.53	25	1	68	72	32	43
Bova, Chris	0	0	9.45	6	0	7	10	6	9
Brumit, Matt	6	2	3.06	10	0	65	57	17	53
Burks, Brian	10	4	4.16	19	0	115	134	34	55
Cockroft, Joseph	5	5	5.56	18	0	81	97	34	44
Collar, Mike	0	0	7.50	5	0	6	7	2	3
Davis, Brendon	9	1	4.00	18	0	108	119	37	76
Douglass, Ryan	11	3	3.25	19	0	119	124	16	63
Fry, Troy	0	0	7.36	12	0	18	29	8	8
Gangi, Aaron	4	2	5.64	9	0	53	64	17	24
Grady, Mike	3	2	3.67	26	2	49	54	20	15
Ohalek, Corey	5	3	4.00	28	2	45	52	8	28
Popp, Jim	4	4	2.98	36	17	57	50	9	56
Spragg, Stephen	4	2	2.72	36	12	60	51	15	56
White, Brian	0	0	36.00	1	0	1	2	2	0

WINDY CITY

BATTERS	AVG	AB	R	H	2B	3B	HR	RBI	SB
Alcott, Jason, c	.233	116	14	27	0	0	0	9	0
Andrews, Ryan, of	.182	44	5	8	1	0	3	10	0
Baker, Brian, of-1b	.268	41	3	11	2	0	1	6	2
Balster, Scott, of	.241	83	12	20	5	0	0	10	2
Barket, Matt, of	.317	41	6	13	2	0	1	4	1
Bonilla, Clemente, 2b-ss	.371	286	47	106	22	1	2	35	20
Clanton, Ja'Mar, ss	.160	25	4	4	0	0	0	1	3
Crosland, Jason, 3b	.266	248	44	66	17	1	10	42	2
Daly, Rich, 1b	.209	86	11	18	3	0	3	14	0
Ewen, Nick, of	.309	149	25	46	9	0	2	28	5
Ferrara, Matt, 3b-2b	.257	300	39	77	17	1	5	42	18
Gillingham, Tug, c	.273	22	1	6	0	0	0	2	0
Gresky, David, of	.193	57	9	11	2	1	0	9	1
Gutierrez, Jose, ss	.295	146	17	43	6	0	2	14	3
Jansen, Sam, of	.286	7	1	2	0	0	0	0	1
Johnson, Nick, of	.312	199	34	62	12	1	7	31	2
Klusaw, Nick, 1b	.308	146	31	45	9	2	5	28	0
Lynch, Michael, c	.263	133	12	35	8	1	1	12	2
2-team (22 Rockford)	.268	198	22	53	12	1	1	18	2
McCoy, Jerome, of	.276	152	17	42	2	0	0	11	22
Monroy, Sam, of	.171	35	5	6	0	0	0	3	1
Neal, Joe, c	.265	68	4	18	3	0	0	6	0
Niefer, Justin, of	.222	72	3	16	3	0	0	8	0
Poles, Donnie, of	.259	54	6	14	4	0	1	9	1
Schuda, Justin, 1b	.277	310	52	86	19	1	26	79	1
Schutt, Doug, of	.316	190	42	60	8	1	6	22	26
2-team (47 Rockford)	.316	380	82	120	20	3	10	42	45
Vetter, Scott, ss	.284	148	19	42	3	1	1	10	3
Whitney, Nate, of	.289	149	26	43	12	0	1	8	12
Wilson, Kasey, dh	.190	63	13	12	4	0	1	7	0

PITCHERS	W	L	ERA	G	SV	IP	H	BB	SO
Anderson, Scott	3	6	6.04	16	0	79	87	43	55
Bays, Lenny	0	1	2.45	19	4	22	19	4	24
2-team (17 Florence)	0	3	4.00	36	10	45	48	11	48
Cero, Greg	0	0	8.31	6	0	9	9	9	2
Crotts, Trent	0	0	4.00	8	0	9	11	10	5
Dittfurth, Ryan	2	6	5.57	13	0	74	64	42	57
Glynn, Josh	8	6	5.24	18	0	103	119	29	53
Hahn, Charlie	0	0	6.35	3	0	6	11	2	0
Hayes, Chris	4	1	2.41	28	9	41	42	12	35
Hines, Matthew	0	4	6.55	18	3	22	24	17	12
Jackson, Brent	0	0	9.82	4	0	7	15	5	7
Jansen, Sam	1	3	8.85	4	0	20	24	14	9
Kellbach, Brandon	2	2	2.65	23	0	37	37	19	23
Mack, Bobby	0	4	5.27	6	0	27	28	9	17
Matta, Feli	1	0	2.53	2	0	11	12	4	4
Mindingall, Wes	0	0	5.59	16	0	19	27	9	22
O'Donnell, Tony	0	3	8.00	4	0	18	26	7	16
Odom, Lance	0	0	18.00	3	0	4	9	2	0
Pleeter, Gregg	0	3	8.41	4	0	20	23	15	13
Reilly, Chris	1	2	6.98	7	0	19	24	15	10
Renery, Mike	7	8	4.85	21	0	104	113	54	71
Roelle, Justin	3	3	5.44	15	0	50	55	34	34
Roelle, Shane	0	0	6.83	16	0	28	33	19	29
Simms, Preston	5	2	3.86	9	0	40	37	22	23
Weber, Rick	2	0	4.26	18	1	44	44	14	33
Ziroli, Steve	0	3	4.45	18	0	28	35	17	21

GOLDEN LEAGUE

When the Golden League finished its inaugural season with a championship game, it succeeded where many upstart independent leagues have failed. When it comes to fledgling indy leagues, survival is an accomplishment.

The Golden League came through its first season in solid shape, getting noticed by a number of national media outlets while putting a solid product on the field. The league ended up drawing 448,405 fans, an average of 1,330 a game. That is below the 1,800 the league projected as its eventual break-even point, but league CEO David Kaval said it was right in line with the league's expectations.

"Our forecast was between 400,000 and 500,000 for the first season, so we're still on our three-year plan to break even. That was great to see," Kaval said.

On the field, the San Diego Surf Dawgs knocked off the Mesa Miners 9-6 in the championship game. The Surf Dawgs advanced through the losers bracket of the playoff tournament, conceived so that the league could play and promote the entire playoffs at one site. San Diego beat Chico in its playoff opener, but then lost to Mesa, before beating Chico again to advance to face Mesa in the championship game.

Cleanup hitter Seth Pietsch went 4-for-5 with two RBIs in the deciding game, while catcher Cody Clark and first baseman Eddie Montague each had three hits and two runs scored. Starter Donovan Graves allowed three runs in five innings to pick up the win.

Rickey Henderson

The title gave former major league star Rickey Henderson a Golden League championship ring. He joined former first-rounders Matt Wheatland and Adam Johnson and former major leaguer Steve Smyth on a club that had the league's best regular season record.

Overall, the league sold 11 players to major league affiliates during the regular season, which compared favorably with other independent leagues.

"I think the pleasant surprise was the quality of players we could attract as a brand new league," commissioner Kevin Outcalt said. "We had 20 ex-big leaguers and lots of Double-A and Triple-A players. It was more than we anticipated. We knew we would attract West Coast players, but the extent we did was more than we expected."

STANDINGS

ARIZONA	W	L	PCT	GB
Mesa	53	40	.570	—
Yuma	47	43	.522	4½
Surprise	45	45	.500	6½
Samurai	33	57	.367	18½
CALIFORNIA	**W**	**L**	**PCT**	**GB**
San Diego	55	39	.585	—
Chico	50	43	.538	4½
Long Beach	49	43	.533	5
Fullerton	34	56	.378	19

PLAYOFFS: San Diego defeated Mesa to win four-team, double elimination tournament.

MANAGERS: Chico—Mark Parent. **Fullerton**—Garry Templeton. **Long Beach**—Darrell Evans. **Mesa**—Les Lancaster. **Samurai**—Warren Cromartie. **San Diego**—Terry Kennedy. **Surprise**—Ozzie Virgil. **Yuma**—Benny Castillo.

ATTENDANCE: Yuma 90,730; Chico 87,208; San Diego 74,522; Fullerton 52,464; Long Beach 47,881; Surprise 49,057; Mesa 46,643.

ALL-STAR TEAM: None.

Most Valuable Player: Desi Wilson, Surprise. **Pitcher of the Year:** Grant Gregg, Chico. **Rookie of the Year:** Nick Guerra, San Diego. **Rookie Pitcher of the Year:** Manny Ayala, Mesa.

INDIVIDUAL BATTING LEADERS

(Minimum 243 Plate Appearances)

	AVG	G	AB	R	H	HR	RBI
Wilson, Desi, Surprise	.411	86	304	53	125	6	55
Walsh, Sean, Fullerton	.357	87	314	65	112	9	58
Calderon, Henry, Yuma	.347	86	297	56	103	5	39
Yanconetti, Jay, Surprise	.345	59	223	39	77	7	45
Arias, Alex, Yuma	.344	84	317	58	109	3	31
Webb, Ryan, LB	.344	83	355	75	122	7	43
Hernandez, Alexis, Yuma	.326	77	279	47	91	14	73
Lehr, Ryan, Chico	.325	86	314	53	102	6	63
Pietsch, Seth, San Diego	.323	76	282	59	91	12	67
Collins, Mike, Surprise	.322	77	292	54	94	1	31

INDIVIDUAL PITCHING LEADERS

(Minimum 72 Innings)

	W	L	ERA	IP	H	BB	SO
Gregg, Grant, Chico	12	2	1.97	137	117	31	118
Marchesano, Mike, Long Beach	8	3	2.55	130	123	51	112
Johnson, Adam, San Diego	8	1	2.58	77	58	27	87
Hartmann, Pete, Surprise	10	4	2.77	133	115	51	137
Blitstein, Jeff, San Diego	10	3	2.92	120	119	19	91
Ayala, Manny, Mesa	12	4	3.05	112	112	23	82
Williams, Grant, Mesa	11	5	3.13	121	132	31	90
Fox, Ben, Fullerton	9	2	3.23	95	76	31	82
Nagasaka, Hideki, Samurai	8	6	3.26	110	96	60	141
Wilson, Aaron, San Diego	7	3	3.58	106	95	39	94

CHICO

BATTING	AVG	AB	R	H	2B	3B	HR	RBI	SB
Ashton, Josh, ss	.162	74	10	12	2	1	0	6	0
Booker, Steve, of	.316	291	56	92	112	11	4	27	26
Gandolfo, Rob, 2b	.272	334	59	91	119	2	2	36	10
Garcia, Jose, of	.224	49	5	11	2	0	0	7	0
Gregg, Grant, p/dh	.209	43	1	9	1	0	0	5	0
Grzecka, Casey, c	.238	21	2	5	1	0	0	3	0
Guessford, Eddie, of	.266	128	26	34	10	0	2	17	4
Hipps, Brian, of	.303	99	21	30	8	0	1	16	4
Housel, Blake, c	.000	7	1	0	0	0	0	0	0
Kovacs, Jesse, ss	.260	173	20	45	12	1	2	29	1
Lehr, Ryan, 3b	.325	314	53	102	130	4	6	63	7
Mallory, Mike, of	.271	155	34	42	5	1	12	35	4
Newson, Steve, of	.302	305	61	92	116	2	11	49	14
Salvo, Andrew, ss	.269	93	9	25	5	0	0	10	2
Smith, Ryan, c	.199	181	14	36	5	0	0	12	3
Stower, T.J., c	.286	91	10	26	4	0	0	14	0
Trujillo, David, 1b	.261	180	22	47	8	1	2	26	6
VanMeetren, Jason, 1b/of	.289	228	29	66	17	1	3	42	9
Wallace, Jim, b	.222	9	2	2	0	0	1	2	0

PITCHING	W	L	ERA	G	SV	IP	H	BB	SO
Alexander, Jordy	4	4	4.47	9	0	56	58	16	45
Ampi, A.J.	4	3	3.80	40	1	43	48	17	42
Anaya, Robert	2	1	2.79	21	0	29	32	9	26
Bowe, Brandon	1	1	6.23	2	0	9	14	1	2
Burger, Nick	1	0	4.91	10	0	11	11	4	14
Carbajal, Alex	2	5	4.81	14	0	73	85	24	54
Evans, Louis	0	1	8.44	4	0	5	7	7	4
Gits, Mike	5	4	3.00	39	17	45	51	14	22
Gregg, Grant	12	2	1.97	19	0	137	117	31	118
Groeger, Jeff	0	1	5.23	3	0	10	11	9	7
2-team (19 Fullerton)	2	4	3.63	22	0	87	85	34	72
Huguet, George	0	1	1.35	6	0	7	10	3	7
Johnson, Seth	4	3	3.71	27	1	68	68	20	57
McKim, Justin	0	1	6.75	4	0	7	15	5	7
Miralles, Rodrigo	0	1	14.85	3	0	7	14	6	8
Perez, Alex	2	0	3.71	5	0	27	22	17	20
Smith, Derek	0	0	12.00	2	0	3	4	5	3
Sugarman, Jeremy	4	3	4.26	12	0	70	89	20	52
Tracey, Ryan	1	1	6.23	21	0	22	18	14	18
Turner, Jess	5	7	3.95	22	1	98	106	17	67
Waroff, Shane	1	1	6.52	24	2	29	44	14	18
Welsh, Wade	0	0	7.11	4	0	6	5	7	7
Wilson, Phil	1	1	3.60	2	0	10	6	8	9

FULLERTON

BATTING	AVG	AB	R	H	2B	3B	HR	RBI	SB
Abbott, Paul, p	.313	16	3	5	2	0	0	1	0
Alcantar, Tony, 1b	.245	98	7	24	3	0	0	12	0
Allen, Scott, c	.333	6	0	2	0	0	0	0	0
Bumphus, Willis, 2b	.203	59	5	12	0	0	0	3	1
Clary, Casey, c	.231	117	11	27	6	0	3	18	0
Elder, Rick, 1b/of	.262	256	40	67	17	3	10	49	6
Ezekiel, Jonathan, if	.182	55	1	10	0	0	0	2	0
Ferreira, Steve, 1b	.214	42	6	9	1	0	1	4	0
Fox, Ben, p	.275	40	5	11	2	0	0	6	0
Granger, Mike, ss	.368	19	3	7	2	0	0	2	0
Hanley, John, util	.250	76	12	19	8	0	3	11	1
Hendricks, Joey, c	.200	15	2	3	0	0	0	1	0
Johnson, Eric, of	.263	38	8	10	2	0	2	5	2
Jordan, Scooter, of/2b	.291	285	61	83	6	1	0	24	25
Marshall, Jon, c	.176	17	1	3	0	0	0	2	0
McClain, Terrence, of	.259	189	20	49	11	1	4	26	4
McIntosh, Rawle, ss	.300	10	1	3	1	0	0	0	0
Owens, Ryan, 2b/3b	.254	130	16	33	3	1	3	24	4
Pohle, Richard, of	.317	265	45	84	20	4	6	40	2
Poniewaz, Kenny, ss	.171	35	1	6	1	0	1	1	0
Rios, Brian, 1b	.133	15	1	2	0	0	0	1	0
Siele, Alex	.333	9	0	3	0	0	0	0	1
3-team (7 LB, 2 Surprise)	.172	29	1	5	1	0	0	1	1
Simmons, Lyndsey, c	.133	15	2	2	0	0	0	2	0
Stevens, Josh, p	.143	42	0	6	1	0	0	1	0
Templeton, Garry, ss/2b	.255	286	42	73	12	2	0	32	5
Thurman, Tim, of/1b	.239	67	6	16	3	0	0	13	0
Walsh, Sean, 3b	.357	314	65	112	18	2	9	58	19

BATTING	AVG	AB	R	H	2B	3B	HR	RBI	SB
Whiteside, Kevin, of	.262	237	40	62	10	1	2	21	10
Wright, Chris, of	.154	13	1	2	2	0	0	1	0
York, Andrew, c	.208	120	14	25	1	0	1	8	0
Zamora, Pete, 1b	.111	9	0	1	0	0	0	0	0

PITCHING	W	L	ERA	G	SV	IP	H	BB	SO
Abbott, Paul	3	5	2.87	9	0	53	50	16	51
Bell, Kory	0	0	11.57	4	0	5	6	5	6
Borland, Curt	0	1	11.00	5	0	9	16	6	6
Carlile, John	0	0	45.00	1	0	1	3	2	1
Elfeldt, Matt	0	1	2.45	3	1	4	6	0	7
Flading, Cameron	0	1	1.91	27	12	28	18	16	35
Fox, Ben	9	2	3.23	14	0	95	76	31	82
Green, Craig	1	1	9.16	11	1	19	28	14	9
Groeger, Jeff	2	3	3.42	19	0	76	74	25	65
Kesten, Michael	2	2	4.15	4	0	17	17	10	24
Mason, Robert	3	3	4.35	25	0	60	75	19	38
McNeil, James	0	0	0.00	1	0	1	1	0	2
McTamney, Mike	2	4	2.63	20	2	62	50	19	51
Needham, Joel	1	0	1.69	4	0	5	4	2	3
Olson, Ryan	1	1	3.91	18	1	23	24	8	23
Rogers, Joe	0	4	3.94	10	1	32	27	8	29
Rosario, Melvin	0	0	6.23	3	0	4	6	3	3
Saenz, Jason	1	3	6.84	6	0	26	28	27	19
Smith, Mike	1	4	6.65	9	0	46	61	17	37
Spaulding, Kevin	2	4	5.54	19	0	26	27	15	24
Stevens, Josh	4	9	4.85	18	0	115	130	18	121
Urvalek, Mike	0	1	30.00	5	0	3	6	11	3
Waroff, Shane	0	4	6.88	13	2	17	21	11	9
2-team (24 Chico)	1	5	6.65	37	4	46	65	25	27
Wells, Carton	0	0	0.00	6	0	6	4	1	2
Zak, Joshua	2	3	5.04	27	1	45	48	15	38

JAPAN

BATTING	AVG	AB	R	H	2B	3B	HR	RBI	SB
Akimoto, Satoshi, c	.206	34	2	7	0	0	0	7	0
Aoki, Tomoshi, of	.278	223	36	62	14	4	3	35	6
Ikenaga, Daisuke, 2b/3b	.109	46	5	5	0	0	0	0	0
Ishibashi, Fumimasa, 2b	.197	178	16	35	4	2	0	15	2
Kawakami, Shin, of	.088	34	3	3	1	0	0	1	1
Komatsu, Naoki, 3b/of	.130	23	1	3	0	0	0	1	0
Kono, Kazuhiro, of	.149	47	5	7	1	2	1	6	0
Minami, Yasumichi, ss	.212	278	16	59	3	3	0	26	6
Miura, Kenichi, 2b	.280	325	43	91	16	3	4	41	13
Miyoshi, Takashi, 2b/1b	.000	3	0	0	0	0	0	1	0
Motono, Takahisa, 3b/of	.225	222	24	50	8	2	1	25	7
Muranishi, Tatsuhiko, of	.303	201	37	61	1	2	2	14	16
Nerei, Yuji, 1b/of	.282	301	47	85	20	3	5	50	17
Nomura, Yuichi, of	.250	8	0	2	0	0	0	1	0
Sciutti, of/1b	.242	33	3	8	1	0	1	1	1
Sciutti, Charles, of/1b	.000	13	0	0	0	0	0	0	0
Shimada, Toshitaka, of	.288	139	20	40	6	0	0	7	5
Suyama, Atsushi, of	.182	44	4	8	0	1	0	0	3
Takakura, Keiji, of	.222	176	29	39	10	1	3	28	4
Uchino, Shin, 3b/c	.281	324	40	91	13	2	4	31	7
Ueno, Keisukem ss	.182	44	3	8	2	0	0	7	0
Yamauchi, Hiroshi, of	.244	41	7	10	3	0	0	5	2

PITCHING	W	L	ERA	G	SV	IP	H	BB	SO
Igarashi, Takaaki	5	9	3.96	30	1	109	98	36	145
Inoue, Masaharu	0	0	18.00	1	0	1	4	1	0
Iwamoto, Takashi	1	0	5.27	25	0	27	37	13	15
Kizu, Tomoyaki	0	7	5.84	35	1	49	58	34	44
Mitsumori, Shingo	0	1	9.00	11	0	21	29	17	17
Morita, Satoshi	3	11	4.09	18	0	101	126	51	78
Nagasaka, Hideki	8	6	3.26	19	0	110	96	60	141
Sasaki, Taishi	0	2	6.49	14	0	35	41	24	32
Seki, Rentaro	10	7	4.63	21	0	115	119	44	113
Ueno, Keisuke	1	6	6.75	18	0	79	82	56	64
Yajima, Masanori	5	5	2.40	30	6	60	49	39	66
Yazzie, Wes	0	1	11.57	12	1	14	25	10	8
Yonezawa, Kosuke	0	2	14.25	7	0	12	22	16	5

LONG BEACH

BATTING	AVG	AB	R	H	2B	3B	HR	RBI	SB
Castro, Bobby, of/if	.130	69	4	9	0	0	1	7	0
Collette, Jason, c	.135	52	3	7	0	0	0	5	0
DiPace, Danny, of	.287	101	12	29	9	0	0	14	1
Gram, Kevin, c	.154	39	2	6	1	0	0	1	0
Harrison, Adonis, 2b	.300	207	39	62	9	3	2	25	16
Hernandez, Jeremy, ss	.253	320	46	81	17	4	4	45	10
LaRue, Jeff, 2b/of	.252	274	45	69	23	1	5	45	9
Marchesano, Mike, p	.200	45	4	9	2	0	0	3	0
McAndrews, Travis, of	.281	342	48	96	22	3	2	49	10
Miller, Chris, c	.266	289	43	77	20	0	6	35	5
Miller, Kevin, of/1b	.211	142	15	30	11	1	1	18	4
Moore, Kevin, 1b/of	.248	121	17	30	3	3	3	17	5
Peters, Samone, 1b	.271	221	31	60	12	0	9	38	0
Pettyjohn, Adam, p	.175	40	5	7	1	0	0	4	0
Quinn, Mark, of	.268	82	9	22	3	1	2	13	0
Shelley, Randall, 3b	.274	310	60	85	23	3	3	38	28
Siele, Alex, ss	.077	13	1	1	1	0	0	1	0
Webb, Ryan, of	.344	355	75	122	22	4	7	43	30

PITCHING	W	L	ERA	G	SV	IP	H	BB	SO
Bangs, Gavin	0	1	5.28	26	0	29	40	9	15
Claypool, Ryan	2	4	3.82	18	0	61	51	48	40
Crawford, Jay	0	0	0.00	1	0	2	0	2	2
Dillinger, John	0	4	5.30	8	0	36	38	29	34
Guthrie, Anasazi	0	1	5.74	10	0	16	15	20	14
Harvey, Reed	3	8	6.00	18	0	90	110	58	50
Horn, Billy	0	1	5.88	13	0	26	34	14	27
Hoyt, Michael	4	1	1.16	42	15	54	42	32	34
Marchesano, Mike	8	3	2.55	19	0	130	123	51	112
Newman, Alan	4	5	3.40	41	3	50	57	22	44
Parris, Matt	4	3	2.76	22	0	62	59	22	47
Peck, Mike	2	2	7.09	16	0	27	23	21	31
Pettyjohn, Adam	10	2	3.92	16	0	110	109	23	73
Pudewell, Nathan	0	2	5.06	2	0	11	11	5	9
Ramsey, Justin	7	3	3.05	39	1	56	55	36	54
Thomas, Adam	5	1	2.91	9	0	59	50	8	49

MESA

BATTING	AVG	AB	R	H	2B	3B	HR	RBI	SB
Altamirano, Gustavo, 2b/3b	.474	19	3	9	4	1	0	5	0
Ayala, Manny, p	.250	36	7	9	2	0	0	3	0
Bischofberger, Sean, 1b	.118	17	2	2	0	0	0	2	0
Bonner, Adam, of	.273	293	53	80	19	2	10	52	4
Connolly, Matt, of	.340	106	19	36	2	5	2	21	8
Davidson, Cleatus, ss	.289	270	58	78	14	6	1	27	19
Done, Mike, 3b/p	.246	179	29	44	12	2	3	30	4
Edwards, Digz, 2b/ss	.282	312	53	88	11	6	1	33	31
Grant, Chris, 1b	.348	23	4	8	0	0	0	1	1
Hall, Victor, of	.369	84	13	31	7	2	1	12	8
Jensen, Marcus, of/1b	.290	272	46	79	14	5	7	48	2
Knight, Marcus, of	.225	276	41	62	11	2	6	47	8
Maher, Caleb, of/1b	.287	296	50	85	21	4	11	64	3
Marini, Chris, p/of	.438	16	5	7	2	0	0	3	1
Montiel, Frank, of	.281	32	4	9	2	0	0	6	1
Powell, Paul	.322	264	44	85	27	1	7	38	7
2-team (13 Surprise)	.315	302	51	95	28	1	8	39	9
Prosise, Nick, c	.125	8	2	1	0	0	0	0	1
Reinking, Kevin, of	.243	185	19	45	14	0	3	17	1
Thames, Julius, 2b	.363	113	18	41	6	1	0	18	2
Williams, Grant, p	.095	42	2	4	0	0	0	0	0

PITCHING	W	L	ERA	G	SV	IP	H	BB	SO
Ayala, Manny	12	4	3.05	22	1	112	112	23	82
Birely, Grant	0	0	18.00	2	0	2	5	2	0
Brester, Jason	0	2	12.79	4	0	6	13	10	7
Burkhart, Dan	0	0	8.10	9	0	13	12	17	19
Cassidy, Kevin	2	3	4.28	18	1	34	38	15	25
2-team (15 San Diego)	3	5	4.32	33	1	58	65	23	46
Coughlin, Mickey	0	0	10.80	3	0	3	6	1	1
Davis, Chris	0	0	11.25	3	0	4	4	8	5
Dominguez, Chase	0	0	10.80	6	0	8	14	6	6
Done, Mike	1	1	5.03	11	0	20	32	4	14
Goodman, Mark	0	2	6.25	30	0	36	47	19	20
Harris, Julian	2	5	5.88	23	1	60	59	38	43
Hartley, Mike	0	0	7.71	1	0	5	8	2	1
Harvot, Tony	0	0	15.43	2	0	2	7	2	3
Johnson, Kelly	2	2	3.20	17	8	20	17	1	21
Kalita, Tim	2	4	5.10	9	0	48	62	19	37
King, Thomas	3	0	0.00	15	5	20	6	10	29
Kohorst, Pat	0	1	13.50	5	0	7	13	3	6
Marini, Chris	4	0	2.74	7	0	46	39	14	36
Navarro, Jason	4	4	4.48	21	2	60	74	21	48
Nunes, Mike	2	1	3.83	26	0	42	36	13	39
Petke, Tim	1	0	4.40	5	0	14	14	8	8
Saunders, Tim	1	0	1.80	9	0	10	9	7	8
Sheredy, Kevin	0	3	11.25	6	1	12	20	10	11
Uhl, Jon	4	2	3.38	22	0	61	59	24	49
Williams, Grant	11	5	3.13	18	0	121	132	31	90

SAN DIEGO

BATTING	AVG	AB	R	H	2B	3B	HR	RBI	SB
Brown, Bobby, of	.329	79	13	26	7	1	0	16	2
Cicatelli, Cole, c	.000	6	0	0	0	0	0	0	0
Clark, Cody, c	.292	264	51	77	15	1	8	48	4
Day, Johnny, 2b/of	.271	118	14	32	1	0	0	9	8

Dierks, Scott, 3b/2b	.223	94	19	21	1	0	2	6	1
Doskocil, Darren, if	.243	144	19	35	8	1	1	11	1
Garcia, Tony, ss	.284	306	53	87	13	4	6	42	7
Goodman, Scott, of/1b	.310	323	66	100	28	0	12	69	3
Guerra, Nick, 3b/c	.290	300	43	87	14	4	7	62	0
Henderson, Rickey, of	.270	226	52	61	13	1	5	29	16
Laws, Ian, of	.000	1	0	0	0	0	0	0	0
Mandel, Adam, 2b/of	.309	262	49	81	15	2	0	26	15
Montague, Ed, of/1b	.235	217	24	51	9	1	2	23	3
Olsen, Mikela, 1b/of	.310	71	12	22	3	2	2	13	0
Pietsch, Seth, of	.323	282	59	91	15	7	12	67	6
Riggan, Zack, c	.238	21	2	5	1	0	0	2	0
Wheatland, Matt, 1b/of	.266	169	22	45	13	1	6	31	2
Wilson, Aaron, p	.162	37	6	6	2	0	0	3	1

PITCHING	W	L	ERA	G	SV	IP	H	BB	SO
Abbott, Paul	0	1	2.70	2	0	10	9	3	14
2-team (9 Fullerton)	3	6	2.84	11	0	63	59	19	65
Blitstein, Jeffrey	10	3	2.92	18	0	120	119	19	91
Boker, John	1	2	1.99	31	11	32	24	14	31
Cassidy, Kevin	1	2	4.38	15	0	25	27	8	21
Davidson, Andy	0	0	3.00	5	0	3	3	2	3
Gale, Chris	5	3	4.16	22	0	67	78	19	36
George, Chris	1	4	6.00	24	0	33	42	8	30
Graves, Donovan	6	6	3.97	17	0	100	120	16	47
Johnson, Adam	8	1	2.58	12	0	77	58	27	87
Leishman, Michael	1	3	4.54	32	1	36	26	25	54
Ottman, Justin	4	3	4.68	25	0	65	76	28	52
Rummonds, Josh	4	1	2.63	27	1	24	19	9	27
Smyth, Steve	1	3	2.64	10	0	31	22	9	39
Spaulding, Kevin	0	0	3.60	3	0	5	8	1	2
Staggs, Nathan	0	2	2.83	26	0	41	33	20	39
Thompson, Sean	3	0	6.86	12	0	20	27	7	12
Wheatland, Matt	0	0	3.38	3	0	3	5	1	1
Wilson, Aaron	7	3	3.58	18	0	106	95	39	94

SURPRISE

BATTING	AVG	AB	R	H	2B	3B	HR	RBI	SB
Brand, Kevin, 2b	.248	226	38	56	11	3	1	24	9
Brown, Billy, of	.279	323	68	90	17	4	14	63	10
Collins, Mike, ss/2b	.322	292	54	94	12	1	1	31	21
Deleon, Sandy, c	.302	96	12	29	4	0	0	10	0
Ekelund, Leif, of	.276	170	28	47	8	3	2	29	4
Ellis, Jared, of	.135	37	4	5	0	2	0	2	2
Green, Josh, of	.299	234	38	70	16	1	4	40	3
Hartmann, Pete, p	.264	53	7	14	2	2	0	6	0
Inglin, Jeff, of	.091	11	0	1	0	0	0	0	0
Marshall, Jon, c	.227	22	2	5	1	0	0	1	0
Matthews, Dustin, 2b	.182	33	3	6	0	1	0	2	0
McNamara, Rusty, 2b	.274	73	13	20	4	1	2	10	2
Modami, Ali, 1b	.212	33	4	7	1	0	0	7	1
Monjaras, Gavin, ss	.167	54	8	9	3	0	0	2	2
Nowak, David, of	.206	131	22	27	6	6	1	14	4
Powell, Paul, ss/3b	.263	38	7	10	1	0	1	1	2
Quihuis/Bell, Richard, 1b	.294	187	20	55	14	2	1	22	0
Shaffer, Josh, 3b/ss	.352	128	20	45	4	1	0	12	3
Siele, Alex, ss	.143	7	0	1	0	0	0	0	0
Stevens, Greg, of/if	.273	245	37	67	17	1	10	51	4
Wilson, Desi, 1b/of	.411	304	53	125	22	4	6	55	14
Yaconetti, Jay, 3b	.345	223	39	77	22	0	7	45	3

PITCHING	W	L	ERA	G	SV	IP	H	BB	SO
Barnett, Brian	0	1	11.74	12	0	8	20	4	7
Beever, James	3	2	5.70	19	0	85	96	34	44
Buchan, Paul	6	6	4.15	23	0	85	80	53	34
Bunyan, Brian	1	1	3.22	9	0	22	22	11	13
Estrada, Erik	0	2	5.79	9	0	9	11	7	3
Estrada, Ignacio	2	3	4.53	37	2	44	41	40	34
Frydendall, Craig	7	6	5.12	16	0	91	109	26	50
Grebe, Brett	1	2	3.31	27	14	35	31	8	34
Hanish, Scott	0	3	5.50	24	1	36	47	11	17
Hartmann, Pete	10	4	2.77	19	0	133	115	51	137
Henthorne, Kevin	1	1	5.21	3	0	19	23	3	13
Jarman, Josh	2	2	5.33	18	1	25	26	11	27
Rain, Steve	0	3	9.19	8	0	16	19	19	8
Reeves, Mike	2	1	8.86	19	0	21	31	15	18
Rey, Jerome	0	0	15.43	3	0	2	3	3	2
Russ, Chris	8	6	5.22	19	0	110	121	61	72
Seccombe, David	2	0	2.08	4	0	26	17	7	25
Shoaf, Mike	0	1	33.75	3	0	1	6	9	0
Tucker, Cardoza	0	1	5.59	13	0	19	22	9	22

YUMA

BATTING	AVG	AB	R	H	2B	3B	HR	RBI	SB
Arias, Alex, 3b/1b	.344	317	58	109	20	1	3	31	5
Brunson, Matt, 2b	.284	250	67	71	8	3	3	20	32
Calderon, Henry, ss/3b	.347	297	56	103	12	8	5	39	18
Cheppenko, Kevin, p/of	.216	37	6	8	2	0	0	2	0
Cogbill, Bo, 3b	.000	6	5	0	0	0	0	1	0
Dewey, Jason, c/1b	.268	265	53	71	18	1	10	54	2
Giacomiazzio, Joe, of/1b	.158	19	4	3	1	0	0	1	0
Griffin, Daniel, p/of	.286	7	0	2	0	0	0	2	0
Guzman, Jacob, c/1b	.319	47	8	15	5	0	1	13	1
Harryman, Eric, ss/2b	.256	176	25	45	9	3	3	25	12
Hernandez, Alexis, of/1b	.326	279	47	91	29	1	14	73	4
Johnson, Eric	.286	56	8	16	6	0	2	10	2
2-team (11 Fullerton)	.277	94	16	26	8	0	4	15	4
Lebron, Juan, of	.292	305	56	89	17	4	14	79	4
Lopez, Javier, of	.303	290	38	88	18	4	5	49	18
Malone, Billy, of/if	.307	290	57	89	14	5	11	45	19
Pittmon, Larry, of	.255	106	12	27	6	0	2	21	1
Pringle, Eric, ss/3b	.220	50	10	11	0	0	1	8	4
Schuda, Justin, of	.350	20	2	7	0	0	2	5	0
Whitfield, Jeff, c	.220	41	7	9	1	0	0	1	0
Wilson, Ryan, of	.324	37	8	12	0	1	0	3	1

PITCHING	W	L	ERA	G	SV	IP	H	BB	SO
Barnett, Brian	1	0	3.38	7	0	8	8	6	6
2-team (12 Surprise)	1	1	7.47	19	0	16	28	10	13
Cheppenko, Kevin	10	4	4.20	18	0	101	97	42	66
Cogbill, Bo	0	0	12.10	5	0	10	14	8	12
Cress, Joey	0	0	6.23	4	0	9	14	3	5
Cuen, David	1	3	5.45	17	0	35	52	11	13
Davenport, Joe	0	3	13.03	4	0	10	10	19	10
Davern, Michael	0	0	20.25	2	0	1	1	5	1
De la Rosa, Dane	1	6	6.45	23	0	67	76	38	54
Espinal, Jose	1	0	1.21	12	1	22	18	3	23
Griffin, Daniel	3	2	3.41	35	12	32	34	22	36
Guzman, Jacob	0	1	6.35	5	0	11	12	8	11
Hewitt, Brian	1	3	5.05	23	0	36	41	18	40
Jefferson, John	0	0	18.00	2	0	3	7	2	1
Kupper, Dustin	6	3	4.38	14	0	76	64	35	63
Meacham, Rusty	4	7	5.54	16	0	91	124	10	61
Perez, Jorge	10	4	3.89	17	0	111	109	47	92
Pina, Rafael	0	2	13.50	2	0	5	11	7	0
Sadler, Carl	0	0	1.35	3	0	7	6	1	7
Sanchez, Claudio	2	0	5.06	10	0	16	18	7	15
Saucedo, Matthew	1	3	5.81	26	0	31	31	15	30
Spille, Ryan	0	0	7.45	4	0	10	12	3	8
Tena, Miguel	1	1	11.42	8	0	9	14	8	7
Terrebonne, Jared	5	1	1.73	40	0	68	46	24	74
Urena, Jose	0	0	0.00	2	0	1	1	2	1
Zbacnik, Billy	0	0	9.95	4	1	6	10	6	4

NORTHERN LEAGUE

Down two games to none in a best-of-five series to the team with the best record in professional baseball in 2005, the Gary RailCats could have packed it in.

Add that the Northern League championship series was moving to Gary, where Fargo-Moorhead had never lost a game, and there was little reason for optimism.

But three days later, the RailCats pulled off one of the more improbable comebacks in modern independent league history, rallying to beat Fargo-Moorhead for the Northern League title.

Greg Tagert

It was quite a comeback for Gary, which in 2004 had the worst record in the Northern League (31-65).

"If you could write a script, you wouldn't write it any better," said RailCats general manager Roger Wexelberg, who was voted the Northern League's executive of the year.

The RailCats started their turnaround by hiring manager Greg Tagert, the winningest manager in Frontier League history. He took over a Gary team that knew only losing. In its three previous seasons, the RailCats had never finished better than 18 games under .500. The team even set Northern League records for most losses and most consecutive losses in 2004.

The RailCats didn't have any cornerstones in place when Tagert arrived, and just three members of the 2004 Opening Day roster were around for the 2005 championship series. The three holdover Gary players were outnumbered by the six former Mountain Ducks players that Tagert brought with him from the Frontier League.

"Building the team was the easy part," Tagert said. "The kind of guy I wanted to bring in, familiarity was key for me. In the Frontier League and here, I tried to bring in players I was familiar with and build from there."

The championship series loss was a disappointing ending for the Redhawks, who were trying to stake a claim to becoming one of independent ball's best teams' ever. The Redhawks went a sizzling 40-7 in the second half on its way to the indy league's best record. The Redhawks put five players on the postseason all-star team, led by league pitcher of the year Brandon Culp, who went 14-0, 2.60.

STANDINGS

FIRST HALF

NORTH	W	L	PCT	GB
Fargo-Moorhead Redhawks	28	20	.583	—
Calgary Vipers	25	22	.532	2 ½
Sioux City Explorers	23	25	.479	5
Winnipeg Redhawks	22	25	.468	5 ½
Edmonton Cracker-Cats	22	26	.458	6
Sioux Falls Canaries	17	30	.362	10 ½

SOUTH	W	L	PCT	
St. Paul Saints	28	19	.596	—
Kansas City T-Bones	27	19	.587	½
Gary Railcats	27	21	.563	1 ½
Lincoln Saltdogs	27	21	.563	1 ½
Joliet Jackhammers	23	25	.479	5 ½
Schaumburg Flyers	16	32	.333	12 ½

SECOND HALF

NORTH	W	L	PCT	GB
Fargo-Moorhead Redhawks	40	7	.851	—
Calgary Vipers	26	22	.542	14 ½
Edmonton Cracker-Cats	25	22	.532	15
Winnipeg Redhawks	25	23	.521	15 ½
Sioux City Explorers	21	27	.438	19 ½
Sioux Falls Canaries	18	30	.375	22 ½

SOUTH	W	L	PCT	GB
Gary Railcats	27	21	.563	—
St. Paul Saints	27	21	.563	—
Lincoln Saltdogs	25	23	.521	2
Schaumburg Flyers	22	26	.458	5
Kansas City T-Bones	18	30	.375	9
Joliet Jackhammers	13	35	.271	14

PLAYOFFS: Semifinals—Fargo-Moorhead defeated Lincoln 3-1 and Gary defeated St. Paul 3-2 in best-of-5 series. **Finals**—Gary defeated Fargo-Moorhead 3-2 in best-of-5 series.

MANAGERS: Calgary—Mike Busch. **Edmonton**—Terry Bevington. **Fargo-Moorhead**—Doug Simunic. **Gary**—Greg Tagert. **Joliet**—Jeff Isom. **Kansas City**—Al Gallagher. **Lincoln**—Tim Johnson. **St. Paul**—George Tsamis. **Schaumburg**—Andy McCauley. **Sioux City**—Steve Shirley/Billy Williams. **Sioux Falls**—Mike Pinto. **Winnipeg**—Hal Lanier.

ATTENDANCE: Winnipeg 322,758; St. Paul 283,886; Kansas City 244,414; Lincoln 207,744; Joliet 201,149; Schaumburg 200,267; Fargo-Moorhead 181,829; Gary 151,850; Sioux Falls 118,611; Sioux City 113,590; Edmonton 107,987; Calgary 55,066.

ALL-STARS: C—Kelley Gulledge, Fargo-Moorhead. **1B**—Clyde Williams, Fargo-Moorhead. **2B**—Pedro Santana, Calgary. **3B**—Carlos Duncan, Calgary. **SS**—Chad Ehrnsberger, St. Paul/Joliet. **OF**—Cory Harris, Lincoln; Bryan Warner, Lincoln; Richard Austin, Fargo-Moorhead. **DH**—Harry Berrios, Winnipeg. **RHP**—Brandon Culp, Fargo-Moorhead. **LHP**—Joe Sergent, Fargo-Moorhead.

INDIVIDUAL BATTING LEADERS

(Minimum 259 Plate Appearances)

	AVG	G	AB	R	H	HR	RBI
Ehrnsberger, Chad, St. Paul/Joliet	.354	91	339	76	120	14	71
Warner, Bryan, Lincoln	.352	95	406	85	143	21	104
Berrios, Harry, Winnipeg	.352	94	381	51	134	9	72
Jacobs, Greg, Kansas City	.348	65	256	49	89	10	43
Harris, Cory, Lincoln	.341	96	417	99	142	21	62
Lentini, Fehlandt, Gary	.339	90	384	79	130	10	57
Austin, Richard, F-M	.337	90	335	78	113	10	58
Prieto, Rick, Kansas City	.333	63	258	53	86	7	27
Balet, Pichi, Lincoln	.331	88	366	68	121	12	79
Thomas, Juan, Calgary	.331	87	317	47	105	18	75

INDIVIDUAL PITCHING LEADERS

(Minimum 77 Innings)

	W	L	ERA	IP	H	BB	SO
Bailie, Matt, Schaumburg	8	1	2.16	96	66	27	75
Cable, Taft, Fargo-Moorhead	9	1	2.30	113	91	41	94
Fisher, Cody, Gary	2	3	2.50	90	84	23	35
Culp, Brandon, Fargo-Moorhead	14	0	2.60	118	101	46	70
McDonald, Jon, Kansas City	6	5	2.76	131	127	30	69
Glen, Willie, Gary	9	3	2.83	121	105	29	100
Bicknell, Greg, Kansas City	16	5	2.96	167	157	51	109
Keppinger, Billy, Sioux City	5	5	3.10	78	81	21	60
Sergent, Joe, Fargo-Moorhead	13	2	3.13	121	117	35	76
Swindle, R.J., Schaumburg	6	4	3.27	118	117	27	102

CALGARY

BATTING	AVG	AB	R	H	2B	3B	HR	RBI	SB
Ashman, Shaun, of	.111	36	1	4	0	0	1	3	1
Ayala, Elliott, 2b	.500	10	0	5	0	0	0	1	0
Colson, Jason, 1b	.240	96	7	23	5	0	3	14	0
2-team (66 Gary)	.287	341	44	98	27	0	12	59	2
Duncan, Carlos, 3b	.319	379	84	121	21	7	20	80	59
Fiallo, Adriel, ss/2b	.225	40	3	9	1	0	0	6	0
Foust, Justin, of	.284	324	50	92	14	12	3	46	13
German, Amado, of	.220	41	5	9	2	0	0	1	0
Grijak, Kevin, 1b/dh	.276	58	9	16	6	0	3	15	0
2-team (25 Lincoln)	.253	158	20	40	12	0	5	31	0
Guglielmelli, Bradle, c	.236	55	2	13	3	0	0	11	0
James, Tony, 2b	.244	41	3	10	3	0	0	5	0
Klippenstein, Tyler, of	.500	6	2	3	0	0	0	0	0
Lentini, Fehlandt, of	.342	281	59	96	20	6	6	42	22
Miller, Drew, of	.274	328	49	90	14	2	3	33	1
Morrison, Greg, 1b	.295	315	41	93	15	0	12	54	8
Paul, Corey, of	.265	102	25	27	7	0	3	15	1
Rosario, Samuel, ss	.258	314	48	81	10	4	0	29	18
Santana, Pedro, 2b	.288	344	54	99	20	2	5	42	14
Schmidt, Greg, dh	.200	10	0	2	0	0	0	0	0
Shorsher, Adam, c	.269	327	47	88	20	2	5	43	2
Thomas, Juan, dh	.415	53	9	22	7	1	4	17	2
2-team (74 Sioux Falls)	.331	317	47	105	24	3	18	75	5
Zieour, Neesan, of	.287	143	22	41	11	2	1	22	7

PITCHING	W	L	ERA	G	SV	IP	H	BB	SO
Brewer, Jeff	4	5	4.80	22	0	90	92	45	49
Cillo, Cody	4	2	4.04	42	3	62	52	28	64
Encarnacion, Alexis	1	0	3.31	8	0	16	17	6	4
Falconer, Ken	0	0	3.00	2	0	3	2	1	0
Fauske, Josh	3	3	3.51	31	9	33	36	11	14
Gautreau, Adam	0	0	6.75	1	0	1	2	3	0
2-team (2 Winnipeg)	0	1	7.50	3	0	6	10	7	1
Giannetti, Chad	0	0	0.00	1	0	1	1	0	0
Glascock, John/Paul	0	0	27.00	1	0	1	3	1	1
Greusel, Evan	9	5	3.94	19	0	114	123	30	94
Huguet, George	2	2	6.28	23	1	39	45	12	21
Jansen, Samuel	0	0	2.25	4	0	4	2	4	3
Johnson, Doug	8	4	4.89	22	0	114	133	54	71
King, Ben	1	0	4.07	17	1	24	26	8	26
Lee, Kevin	2	7	6.28	16	0	72	72	31	33
2-team (2 Lincoln)	2	7	6.45	18	0	75	76	31	36
Lontayo, Alex	2	0	2.45	4	0	26	17	12	20
Miller, Matt	1	2	6.21	33	1	33	47	17	16
Moore, Ben	3	4	6.10	12	1	52	75	17	43
Mowday, Chris	0	1	4.50	1	0	2	3	2	2
Oldenburg, Quintin	2	2	4.76	5	0	28	26	10	17
2-team (17 Gary)	11	5	4.86	22	0	130	129	54	75
Reichert, Dan	3	2	5.35	6	0	35	45	22	25
Rogers, Brad	6	5	5.59	29	1	77	105	20	31
Warpinski, Ryan	0	0	0.00	1	0	0	0	2	0

EDMONTON

BATTING	AVG	AB	R	H	2B	3B	HR	RBI	SB
Becker, Chris, 2b	.236	360	43	85	16	2	6	45	4
Carroll, Justin, c	.255	141	14	36	7	1	2	17	2
Clapp, Richard, ss	.286	350	60	100	29	3	5	42	14
Eggleston, Aharon, of	.330	224	44	74	11	4	2	34	17
Etheridge, Chad, of	.176	17	3	3	1	0	0	1	0
Hall, Chris, 3b	.277	311	47	86	17	2	8	52	4
Kaye, Brandon, 1b	.301	342	56	103	28	0	11	59	2
Kinsolving, Darin, of/1b	.215	65	6	14	3	0	2	10	0

BATTING	AVG	AB	R	H	2B	3B	HR	RBI	SB
Leon, Kyle, of	.307	326	52	100	22	5	9	44	5
Macfarlane, Chuck, of	.240	150	23	36	4	2	1	17	1
Magdaleno, Ricky, ss	.242	161	18	39	4	1	1	14	1
Marshall, Dan, 1b/of	.133	75	11	10	2	0	0	3	2
Patterson, Derek, c	.287	355	56	102	13	0	8	48	13
Waldron, Jeff, c	.210	138	16	29	5	1	1	19	0
Ware, Jeremy, of	.261	322	36	84	21	5	4	41	5

PITCHING	W	L	ERA	G	SV	IP	H	BB	SO
Avilez, Roberto	6	10	5.16	18	0	106	133	37	63
Black, Keith	3	7	5.86	17	0	81	106	41	39
Brown, Ira	4	5	4.47	31	7	97	90	44	89
Harrison, James	8	4	2.15	43	3	71	71	16	46
Kusiewicz, Mike	5	0	2.93	10	0	68	66	16	41
Lawson, Brett	5	3	3.67	28	0	83	76	39	77
Marcotte, Trevor	2	0	2.21	4	0	20	19	15	17
Murphy, Ryan	0	0	8.31	4	0	9	15	4	1
Murray, Zach	0	0	4.91	2	0	4	4	3	3
Poland, Robert	2	3	5.20	19	6	28	31	9	29
Richmond, Scott	1	4	6.25	20	4	59	72	20	42
Rivard, Rejean	7	5	5.56	18	0	110	134	32	47
Tam, Brandon	2	1	5.20	16	0	36	42	15	18
Vangaalen, Aric	2	6	5.65	35	3	73	93	38	32
Van, Robbie	0	0	5.40	4	0	3	2	8	2

FARGO-MOORHEAD

BATTING	AVG	AB	R	H	2B	3B	HR	RBI	SB
Austin, Richard, of	.337	335	78	113	29	3	10	58	13
Dormanen, Derek, 2b	.244	78	15	19	3	0	0	5	0
Erickson, Tim, of	.400	10	2	4	1	0	0	1	0
Flanders, Brad, c	.184	87	11	16	5	0	3	15	1
Gulledge, Kelley, c	.321	252	41	81	27	0	10	40	0
Jeffcoat, Bryon, ss	.260	396	63	103	19	4	11	61	10
Kofler, Eric, dh	.299	365	61	109	19	0	19	71	0
Krause, Brent, of	.327	333	70	109	28	1	14	51	17
Mathis, Joe, of	.296	375	70	111	18	6	9	51	15
Salazar, Ruben, 3b	.308	373	62	115	17	1	12	78	0
Ward, Brian, 2b	.226	332	50	75	14	1	2	23	7
Williams, Clyde, 1b	.288	354	56	102	19	0	24	80	2

PITCHING	W	L	ERA	G	SV	IP	H	BB	SO
Adams, Brian	2	1	1.51	39	11	48	31	19	50
Biron, Nick	0	1	8.71	5	0	10	13	6	5
Cable, Taft	9	1	2.30	22	0	113	91	41	94
Culp, Brandon	14	0	2.60	20	0	118	101	46	70
Dietz, Josh	0	0	11.81	6	0	11	25	5	5
Dormanen, Derek	1	0	1.96	8	0	18	20	3	9
Escalante, Jimmy	1	1	5.30	4	0	19	15	2	11
George, Todd	7	5	4.21	20	0	115	109	55	71
Goltz, Brandon	2	0	2.81	4	0	16	8	9	7
Hewitt, Brian	1	0	3.50	13	1	18	15	9	12
Holbrook, Shayn	1	0	14.29	4	0	6	14	4	4
Jordan, Robert	1	2	3.13	18	3	23	15	8	26
Peschel, Mike	7	4	5.30	17	0	88	109	34	52
Royce, Ramon	0	1	9.00	8	0	7	13	4	4
Scheving, J.J.	0	2	8.76	3	0	12	19	5	9
Sergent, Joe	13	2	3.13	19	0	121	117	35	76
Spivey, Mel	4	3	3.18	46	2	57	41	40	34
Vaillancourt, Tim	0	0	135.00	2	0	0	5	2	0
Young, Doug	5	4	2.58	40	9	52	48	16	42

GARY

BATTING	AVG	AB	R	H	2B	3B	HR	RBI	SB
Colson, Jason, 1b	.306	245	37	75	22	0	9	45	2
Einspahr, Matt, c	.188	32	1	6	0	0	0	1	0
Haake, Steve, of/1b	.259	317	40	82	21	5	3	46	19
Iapoce, Anthony	.285	284	46	81	16	9	3	36	11
Kindle, Jud	.111	9	1	1	0	0	0	0	0
Kinsolving, Darin	.208	24	3	5	0	0	0	2	0
2-team (19 Edmonton)	.213	89	9	19	3	0	2	12	0
Lee, Curt, 2b	.238	231	29	55	7	0	1	27	1
Lentini, Fehlandt	.333	102	20	34	7	2	4	15	7
2-team (67 Calgary)	.339	383	79	130	27	8	10	57	29
McNamee, Eric, 2b/3b	.267	187	37	50	8	0	0	25	5
Mueller, Dale	.222	27	4	6	3	0	0	2	1
O'Neal, Brandon, 1b	.169	71	16	12	2	1	2	8	2
Pecci, Jay	.275	309	38	85	14	0	1	40	10
Risinger, Ben, 1b	.310	84	14	26	5	0	3	17	1
Samuels, Scott, of	.254	260	40	66	21	3	7	42	20
Sauter, Tim	.000	1	0	0	0	0	0	0	0
Schmitz, John	.295	44	6	13	2	0	0	6	1
Taylor, Alex, 1b/2b	.296	216	30	64	12	1	0	18	9
Townsend, Tanner, 3b	.239	327	48	78	14	3	10	48	12
Weiner, David, of	.227	154	19	35	3	1	1	9	3
Wettlaufer, Josh, of	.100	20	4	2	0	0	0	1	1
Yepez, Jose, c	.291	261	36	76	21	0	4	44	1

PITCHING	W	L	ERA	G	SV	IP	H	BB	SO
Alvarez, Tim	0	0	4.05	14	0	13	15	8	8
Bennett, Jamie	10	5	4.32	24	0	150	166	27	68
Bruso, Greg	5	7	4.69	29	0	94	108	15	71
Fisher, Cody	2	3	2.50	36	1	90	84	23	35
Glen, Willie	9	3	2.83	19	0	121	105	29	100
Gonzalez, John	0	2	5.87	25	0	38	48	13	22
Kerber, Travis	5	1	1.33	34	2	47	35	19	36
Lopez, Derek	5	1	2.63	35	17	41	36	11	38
Oldenburg, Quintin	9	3	4.88	17	0	101	103	44	58
Plucinski, Steve	0	0	6.00	3	0	6	5	1	4
Schaefer, Mike	4	8	4.72	17	0	82	81	32	44
Stone, Nathan	0	1	3.38	2	0	3	3	0	2
Vanderplow, Randy	2	7	5.49	34	3	41	59	16	29
Woody, Dominic	3	1	2.50	11	0	18	19	6	15

JOLIET

BATTING	AVG	AB	R	H	2B	3B	HR	RBI	SB
Allensworth, Jermaine, of	.263	365	57	96	13	7	3	28	8
Amado, Jose, 1b/of	.275	131	13	36	7	0	0	12	2
Blakeley, Eric, 2b	.243	115	15	28	6	0	3	17	1
Corapci, Jason, 2b	.059	17	1	1	0	0	0	1	0
2-team (17 Lincoln)	.164	67	5	11	5	0	1	7	0
Delgado, Gabriel, 2b	.270	159	16	43	1	0	0	8	6
Drobiak, Jayson, 3b/1b	.296	395	56	117	19	2	23	89	14
Ehrnsberger, Chad, ss/3b	.328	64	11	21	5	1	2	7	2
2-team (76 St. Paul)	.354	339	76	120	35	3	14	71	7
Firlit, Dan, ss	.164	146	9	24	7	0	0	6	0
Flamont, Sam, 1b/2b	.257	70	12	18	2	1	2	9	0
Flanders, Brad, c	.276	105	10	29	3	0	3	15	0
2-team (27 F/M)	.234	192	21	45	8	0	6	30	1
Goelz, Bryan, of	.303	76	12	23	3	1	1	7	1
Goldbach, Jeff, c	.266	124	17	33	8	0	5	14	1
Howe, Matt, 1b/3b	.203	74	8	15	2	0	3	10	0
2-team (44 Sioux City)	.249	237	32	59	11	0	11	34	1
Kavourias, Jim, of	.231	156	20	36	8	0	6	18	4
Lackaff, John, ss/2b	.308	195	19	60	9	0	3	23	5
Logan, Kyle, of	.256	348	48	89	16	3	10	39	25
Loggins, Josh, of/1b	.278	245	34	68	13	1	8	43	4
McCay, Matt, of/1b	.288	372	46	107	17	2	3	36	7
Neal, Joem c	.214	56	5	12	3	0	0	5	0
2-team (5 Schaumburg)	.191	68	6	13	4	0	0	5	0
Spottz, Jamie, of	.100	10	1	1	0	0	0	0	0
Underwood, Dan, of/c	.319	116	11	37	7	0	2	10	3

PITCHING	W	L	ERA	G	SV	IP	H	BB	SO
Bulger, Brian	3	1	6.16	8	0	31	32	30	22
Canizal, Joaquin	1	1	5.14	5	0	7	7	2	8
Dunham, Steve	0	2	6.21	11	0	29	50	8	15
Grodecki, Mike	0	0	6.91	12	0	14	21	7	9
Hill, Seth	2	1	4.42	4	0	18	24	3	17
Hooker, Jonathan	0	0	27.00	1	0	1	2	2	1
Hyde, Richard	0	0	2.84	2	0	6	7	0	3
Kent, Nathan	3	11	4.12	19	0	114	149	29	68
Levrault, Allen	0	4	10.33	8	0	27	44	13	13
Marotz, Tyler	0	0	4.09	8	0	11	14	3	9
Moore, Ben	2	5	5.91	10	0	46	52	20	37
2-team (12 Calgary)	5	9	6.01	22	1	97	127	37	80
Myers, Damien	2	7	5.96	21	0	71	83	24	43
Nielsen, Steve	0	0	4.26	7	0	13	19	3	3
Petrusek, Matt	3	2	3.82	41	2	61	67	19	61
Scheving, J.J.	2	1	7.65	10	0	20	36	11	10
2-team (3 Fargo-Moorhead)	2	3	8.07	13	0	32	55	16	19
Shelley, Jason	5	12	5.46	20	0	125	132	53	88
Shippey, Steven	0	0	9.75	6	0	12	22	5	2
Siak, Joe	0	1	8.84	14	1	18	28	6	9
Sobscuk, Justin	0	0	54.00	2	0	1	2	4	2
Stephens, Amad	5	3	3.29	28	10	38	38	7	29
Villarreal, Luis	6	6	3.75	16	0	113	90	44	91
Wodnicki, Michael	0	2	6.23	8	0	22	36	5	11
Zaleski, Kyle	2	1	5.70	29	0	47	50	21	28

KANSAS CITY

BATTING	AVG	AB	R	H	2B	3B	HR	RBI	SB
Brown, Michael, 2b/of	.263	274	40	72	17	1	8	34	22
Brown, Ray, 1b	.305	354	55	108	27	1	5	61	7
Ceriani, Matt, c	.250	192	25	48	10	0	2	22	0
Cook, Ross, of	.091	33	2	3	0	0	0	0	0
Delgado, Gabriel, 2b	.240	75	8	18	4	1	2	10	0
3-team (44 Joliet, 31 Sioux City)	.256	363	38	93	10	2	2	32	8
Flynn, Sean, c	.238	185	13	44	10	1	2	11	0
Hill, Chad, ss	.202	89	10	18	3	1	1	3	0
Jacobs, Greg, of	.348	256	49	89	21	3	10	43	1
Jones, Brandon, 3b	.245	327	39	80	10	2	13	49	3
Lucas, Scott, of/1b	.273	11	2	3	0	0	0	1	1

Neal, Michael, of	.429	7	3	3	1	0	0	0	0
Norman, Leslie, of	.071	14	1	1	0	0	0	1	0
Nowlin, Coleman, of	.262	229	41	60	12	1	7	35	2
Pearson, Eddie, dh	.301	123	19	37	3	1	9	35	0
Prieto, Richard, of	.333	258	53	86	19	3	7	27	4
Rodriguez, Rafael, 2b	.241	108	13	26	6	1	3	19	0
Segui, David, dh	.339	109	19	37	4	0	5	30	0
Sorensen, Nick, of	.310	29	4	9	2	2	1	4	1
Sosebee, Chad, ss/of	.267	333	43	89	25	4	11	46	9
Vega, Eric, of	.255	243	44	62	13	2	3	22	20

PITCHING	W	L	ERA	G	SV	IP	H	BB	SO
Anderson, Eric	0	0	6.00	1	1	3	4	1	1
Arostegui, Ron	0	0	16.88	3	0	3	4	1	0
Balbuena, Caleb	2	2	5.36	15	1	42	41	24	24
Bicknell, Greg	16	5	2.96	23	0	167	157	51	10
Clay, Adam	0	2	6.23	19	0	22	21	10	19
Cosgrove, Michael	0	3	2.45	10	3	11	8	5	10
Flynn, Sean	0	0	27.00	1	0	1	1	1	0
Forbes, Derek	0	0	1.32	12	7	14	9	7	17
Gannon, Joseph	0	3	5.89	4	0	18	23	7	7
Garner, Drew	0	1	43.20	2	0	2	9	1	1
Goodmann, Joe	5	1	2.94	29	1	52	44	26	44
Jacobs, Greg	0	0	9.00	1	0	1	3	0	2
Krysa, Jonathan	5	12	3.70	27	2	141	158	49	130
McDonald, Jon	6	5	2.76	19	0	131	127	30	69
Ortiz, John	2	1	4.95	30	0	40	44	22	26
Ruhl, Nathan	0	4	6.49	22	3	26	32	13	11
Shoaf, Mike	0	0	7.20	7	0	5	6	9	5
Sosebee, Chad	0	0	2.45	2	0	4	3	3	1
Tucker, Cardoza	0	1	7.56	8	0	8	11	6	4
Viane, David	8	7	4.34	25	0	118	127	38	52
Webb, Nick	1	2	7.20	5	0	25	33	16	20

LINCOLN

BATTING	AVG	AB	R	H	2B	3B	HR	RBI	SB
Balet, Pichi, 1b	.331	366	68	121	23	3	12	79	3
Corapci, Jason, 2b	.200	50	4	10	5	0	1	6	0
Cormier, Richard, dh	.000	3	0	0	0	0	0	0	0
Duchek, Matt, c	.200	10	0	2	0	0	0	0	0
Goss, Michael, of	.276	351	54	97	14	1	5	46	22
Grijak, Kevin, 1b	.240	100	11	24	6	0	2	16	0
Harris, Cory, of	.341	417	99	142	40	2	21	62	12
Machado, Albenis, ss	.326	359	77	117	29	1	7	56	3
Nieblas, Luis, c/of	.222	9	0	2	0	0	0	0	0
Patton, Josh, 3b/2b	.321	380	59	122	37	1	12	62	4
Suarez, Gabriel, 2b	.208	101	15	21	1	0	0	12	5
Sullivan, Kevin, c	.313	342	51	107	14	3	10	45	11
Underwood, Dan, of/c	.282	142	19	40	5	3	3	20	6
2-team (38 Joliet)	.298	258	30	77	12	3	5	30	9
Vickers, Bryan, dh	.100	10	0	1	1	0	0	0	0
Warner, Bryan, of/1b	.352	406	85	143	29	0	21	104	8
Whitesides, Jacob, 2b/of	.245	257	43	63	8	2	8	33	6
Wiseman, Jeb, c	.105	38	4	4	2	0	0	2	0
Yaconetti, Jay, 3b	.229	118	14	27	6	1	3	15	1

PITCHING	W	L	ERA	G	SV	IP	H	BB	SO
Allen, Kyle	0	1	3.68	11	0	7	9	6	7
Carbajal, Alex	2	2	8.42	5	0	26	36	10	19
Cardenas, Humberto	4	5	4.36	22	0	95	103	24	47
De Aza, Fernando	5	3	4.12	30	0	44	41	25	47
Embry, Byron	0	1	13.50	6	0	4	10	1	9
Escobedo, Edgar	0	0	4.85	6	0	13	9	8	6
Fogelson, Scott	0	0	15.00	5	0	3	6	3	2
Fox, Ben	2	2	4.88	4	0	24	27	10	22
Hoerman, Jared	3	2	2.60	40	14	45	38	17	36
Hogan, Gary	4	3	6.35	10	0	45	52	30	20
Holbrook, Shayn	0	0	0.00	2	0	0	1	3	0
Kesten, Michael	6	2	5.06	22	0	96	108	46	78
Lee, Kevin	0	0	9.82	2	0	4	4	0	3
Lesko, Adam	1	5	5.73	30	0	66	81	20	29
Martinez, Miguel	0	0	0.00	2	0	1	0	3	1
Myers, Rodney	10	4	3.56	16	0	109	116	15	66
Nagasaka, Hideki	0	2	9.35	2	0	9	14	7	7
Nendza, Brian	0	0	5.91	8	0	11	11	2	7
Nilius, Dustin	0	0	81.00	1	0	0	1	3	0
O'Brien, Weston	1	2	7.43	23	2	27	33	17	17
Rodaway, Brian	8	7	3.55	21	0	147	131	35	113
Ruwe, Kyle	6	3	3.40	18	1	79	80	9	51
Wells, Carlton	0	0	1.80	10	0	5	6	1	2

ST. PAUL

BATTING	AVG	AB	R	H	2B	3B	HR	RBI	SB
Brown, Tonayne, of	.313	377	61	118	18	3	5	41	11
Brown, Travis, c	.000	1	0	0	0	0	0	0	0
Butler, Steven, 3b/ss	.220	123	15	27	4	0	0	13	0
Camacho, Juan, 3b	.273	33	6	9	0	0	1	5	0
Cox, Kris, of	.290	372	50	108	20	3	2	55	20
Ehrnsberger, Chad, ss/3b	.360	275	65	99	30	2	12	64	5
Forbes, Michael, of	.284	232	34	66	12	2	5	33	1
2-team (14 Winnipeg)	.259	282	35	73	13	2	5	33	2
Frost, Jeremy, c/of	.278	295	62	82	15	0	17	49	19
Gretz, Nick, 1b	.302	308	37	93	12	1	8	41	0
Hall, Justin, 2b	.277	383	58	106	18	4	3	43	3
Leon, Donny, 3b	.289	76	11	22	2	0	4	15	0
Marks, Tim, c	.394	66	12	26	5	0	0	10	0
Munoz, Billy, 1b	.271	336	51	91	28	0	19	70	0
Nettles, Marcus, of	.286	42	8	12	1	2	0	7	2
Olow, Adam, of	.308	52	12	16	6	0	0	7	1
Renick, Josh, 3b/ss	.253	225	32	57	9	1	4	22	6
Scanlon, Matt, of	.188	16	1	3	1	0	0	1	0
Smith, Coby, of	.267	15	1	4	2	0	0	3	0
Weber, Chris, ss	.189	37	8	7	1	0	0	2	0
Wiseman, Jeb, c	.161	56	7	9	1	0	0	2	0
2-team (11 Lincoln)	.138	94	11	13	3	0	0	4	0

PITCHING	W	L	ERA	G	SV	IP	H	BB	SO
Andel, Chris	1	2	4.43	22	3	45	51	19	32
Butler, Steven	0	0	27.00	1	0	1	3	2	1
Cartier, Richard	4	3	6.75	11	0	57	80	25	29
Christman, Tim	1	2	4.87	25	1	20	24	8	20
Crawford, Jay	0	1	3.00	2	0	6	8	7	2
Gaal, Bryan	10	4	3.81	19	0	125	128	40	61
Hammons, Matt	0	3	2.77	37	25	39	26	8	47
Helm, Aron	1	0	3.60	1	0	5	6	2	3
Larson, Adam	1	1	3.62	20	0	50	62	12	19
Meyer, Michael	8	6	3.97	21	0	122	136	34	62
Perez, Julio	0	1	6.75	7	1	11	17	1	8
Pike, Matthew	2	0	3.47	16	0	23	19	9	13
Ruud, Charles	1	0	2.57	2	0	14	8	6	9
Shepard, David	3	2	3.55	10	0	58	61	9	34
Steffek, Brian	6	3	2.52	25	2	39	25	13	47
Stephens, Amad	3	1	4.85	9	0	13	10	7	12
2-team (28 Joliet)	8	4	3.68	37	10	51	48	14	41
Truty, Darren	6	5	4.72	19	0	109	123	37	52
Villarreal, Luis	3	1	3.96	4	0	25	26	9	15
2-team (16 Joliet)	9	7	3.79	20	0	138	116	53	106
Woodman, Harold	5	4	4.82	11	0	65	67	27	49
Zbacnik, Bill	0	1	9.53	9	0	6	9	8	7

SCHAUMBURG

BATTING	AVG	AB	R	H	2B	3B	HR	RBI	SB
Albertson, Eli, of	.271	70	9	19	2	0	0	6	1
Cole, Eric, of	.252	369	40	93	28	2	8	56	4
Fitzgerald, Jason, of	.195	87	9	17	0	0	1	5	5
Gord, Nelson, 2b/c	.296	135	24	40	9	0	1	16	1
Hendrickson, Justin, 1b	.258	345	48	89	13	0	28	67	0
Ledbetter, Ted, of	.224	228	17	51	7	0	2	16	1
Lopez, Josue, 1b	.311	344	52	107	17	2	14	47	3
Marks, Tim, c	.304	217	23	66	10	0	3	26	0
2-team (18 St. Paul)	.325	283	35	92	15	0	3	36	0
Materano, Oscar, 2b	.210	100	11	21	4	0	0	8	1
McCallum, Geoff, ss	.275	363	52	100	15	3	4	40	11
Neal, Joe, c	.083	12	1	1	1	0	0	0	0
Nettles, Marcus, of	.252	143	27	36	5	4	0	15	15
Patrick, Sean, 3b	.308	13	2	4	1	0	0	0	0
Patterson, Jarrod, of/3b	.285	193	32	55	15	1	9	37	0
Pujols, Rafael, c	.149	47	2	7	0	0	0	1	0
Romprey, Ed, 2b	.194	36	6	7	1	0	1	3	0
Russo, Bryan, 2b	.146	82	10	12	2	0	0	6	1
Turberville, Erik, 2b	.130	23	0	3	1	0	0	0	1
Walker, Ryan, c	.291	86	11	25	3	0	2	10	0
Weekly, Chris, 3b	.274	347	51	95	20	1	13	47	5
Whannel, Jay, 2b	.100	10	4	1	1	0	0	0	0

PITCHING	W	L	ERA	G	SV	IP	H	BB	SO
Bailie, Matt	8	1	2.16	13	0	96	66	27	75
Boughner, Anthony	4	9	4.35	14	0	89	100	31	50
Cierlik, Jason	0	0	4.35	12	1	10	12	7	4
Cotton, Nathan	3	1	2.89	26	11	28	16	13	25
Cross, Thomas	0	5	4.76	38	4	45	39	29	33
DeHart, Rick	3	10	3.76	20	0	129	133	38	11
Dorn, Grant	0	1	7.15	5	0	11	13	6	5
Gray, Brett	0	1	4.64	4	0	21	22	5	11
Hahn, Charlie	0	0	18.00	2	0	3	8	4	2
Howerton, John	0	1	5.79	4	0	5	5	2	0
Hummel, John	0	0	1.59	3	0	6	2	3	0
Jackson, Daniel	2	1	0.60	14	0	15	13	4	12
Jansen, Samuel	0	0	10.50	7	0	6	10	2	6
2-team (4 Calgary)	0	0	7.20	11	0	10	12	6	9
Jenkins, Raymond	6	6	4.96	19	0	102	113	54	56

	W	L	ERA	G	SV	IP	H	BB	SO
Marshall, Jacoby	0	0	8.31	2	0	4	5	4	3
Prempas, Lyle	2	7	6.29	35	0	49	45	37	49
Shanks, Ed	0	2	8.25	10	0	12	15	9	10
Swindle, R.J.	6	4	3.27	18	0	118	117	27	102
Thatch, Nigel	0	3	10.22	7	0	12	24	6	6
Williams, Blake	4	6	4.43	31	2	81	81	28	61

SIOUX CITY

BATTING	AVG	AB	R	H	2B	3B	HR	RBI	SB
Baker, Casey, of	.311	228	26	71	14	1	2	34	2
Brown, Michael, 2b	.000	7	0	0	0	0	0	0	0
2-team (71 Kansas City)	.256	281	40	72	17	1	8	34	22
Brown, Robert, of	.303	201	23	61	10	0	5	34	1
Church, Ian, of	.269	301	35	81	21	1	5	37	2
Chute, Robin, 2b	.200	30	5	6	1	1	0	3	1
Delgado, Gabriel, 2b	.248	129	14	32	5	1	0	14	2
Fryer, Brian, of	.320	25	2	8	1	0	0	2	2
Gripp, Ryan, 3b/of	.275	374	68	103	26	2	18	71	0
Grossman, Chris, c	.314	318	37	100	16	0	3	48	1
Guglielmelli, Brad, dh	.083	12	1	1	1	0	0	0	0
2-team (18 Calgary)	.209	67	3	14	4	0	0	11	0
Hargrove, Taylor, 2b/ss	.195	77	11	15	1	0	0	3	4
Howe, Matt, 3b	.270	163	24	44	9	0	8	24	1
Longmire, Marcel, c	.292	342	63	100	20	1	10	43	20
Losett, Chris, ss	.133	15	2	2	0	0	0	1	0
Meier, Dan, 1b	.257	377	64	97	23	2	13	58	1
Ruiz, Ryan, of	.264	284	31	75	8	1	1	23	20
Turner, Justin. 2b	.223	157	20	35	5	1	2	17	0
West, Todd, ss	.261	349	53	91	11	2	1	26	21

PITCHING	W	L	ERA	G	SV	IP	H	BB	SO
Baker, Casey	0	0	45.00	1	0	1	5	0	0
Bay, Josh	0	0	3.48	6	0	10	5	6	4
Dressler, Travis	2	2	7.42	16	0	44	62	21	20
Evans, Tony	3	1	2.42	4	0	26	22	10	26
Glick, David	1	1	5.14	2	0	7	5	3	3
Griffith, Dustin	2	0	7.06	28	0	43	56	10	17
Holbrook, Shayn	0	0	6.75	1	0	1	1	4	0
4-team (3 Winn., 4 F/M, 2 Lincoln)	1	1	13.50	10	0	10	21	11	4
Howerton, John	2	3	2.62	30	0	34	29	11	26
2-team (4 Schaumburg)	2	4	3.00	34	0	39	34	13	26
Huguet, Juan	4	6	6.66	13	0	74	107	24	35
Kalinowski, Roger	0	0	11.25	9	0	4	12	3	5
Keppinger, Billy	5	5	3.10	39	2	78	81	21	60
Kramer, Sean	1	4	3.16	40	20	43	36	28	54
Lipari, Tom	8	6	3.77	21	0	138	157	48	90
Mabry, Barry	0	5	9.61	11	0	35	57	8	13
Myers, Damien	0	1	5.68	3	0	13	16	6	5
2-team (21 Joliet)	2	8	5.92	24	0	84	99	30	48
Natale, Michael	2	3	8.24	7	0	39	55	10	23
Purvis, Robert	3	5	4.62	11	0	64	71	35	38
Soenen, Mike	0	0	8.53	6	0	13	24	6	11
Stockton, Robert	1	2	6.56	4	0	23	35	3	12
2-team (2 Sioux Falls)	1	2	6.59	6	0	27	41	4	13
Swiatkiewicz, Chris	6	6	3.56	15	0	101	109	25	49
Wiebe, Jonathan	3	2	4.97	36	0	42	57	22	26
Wylie, Mitchell	1	0	3.00	5	0	33	29	5	22

SIOUX FALLS

BATTING	AVG	AB	R	H	2B	3B	HR	RBI	SB
Allan, Josh, c	.263	38	8	10	2	0	1	4	0
Arroyo, Abner, of/1b	.321	290	44	93	25	1	11	57	1
Ballon, John, 3b	.233	129	11	30	10	0	2	17	0
Clemente, Edgard, of	.277	274	61	76	19	4	22	64	2
Cordell, Brent, c	.202	94	10	19	5	0	2	8	1
Fulton, Josh, ss	.172	58	6	10	0	0	0	3	0
Gaspar, Warren, of	.222	117	17	26	3	0	2	10	12
Hapanionek, Joe, 1b	.189	95	12	18	2	0	4	11	0
Jacobson, Kerry, of	.250	4	1	1	0	0	0	0	0
Kaplan, Jon, of	.257	148	23	38	5	4	0	10	6
Kmiecik, Kyle, 3b/2b	.273	348	42	95	19	2	4	29	6
Llanos, Alexis, 2b/ss	.268	310	48	83	17	0	6	40	5
Monegan, Anthony, of	.294	391	66	115	17	1	4	25	23
Nettles, Marcus, of	.186	59	6	11	3	0	0	1	4
3-team (12 St. Paul, 43 Schaum)	.242	244	41	59	9	6	0	23	21
Norman, Les, of	.231	13	1	3	1	0	1	2	0
2-team (3 Kansas City)	.148	27	2	4	1	0	1	3	0
Pierce, Kirk, c	.298	245	33	73	17	1	8	35	1
Pringle, Eric, ss	.235	98	9	23	2	0	0	8	1
Thomas, Juan, 1b	.314	264	38	83	17	2	14	58	3
Walters, Cory, of	.000	3	2	0	0	0	0	0	0
Weber, Chris, ss	.215	144	12	31	3	0	1	12	3
2-team (15 St. Paul)	.210	181	20	38	4	0	1	14	3
Wirth, Robert, c	.238	80	9	19	7	0	2	10	1
2-team (11 Winnipeg)	.193	109	11	21	7	0	2	10	1

PITCHING	W	L	ERA	G	SV	IP	H	BB	SO
Cierlik, Jason	3	1	4.98	30	0	34	33	30	32
2-team (12 Schaumburg)	3	1	4.84	42	1	45	45	37	36
Ciprian, Wilson	0	2	11.17	3	0	10	15	6	3
Cogan, Tony	4	7	5.44	15	0	89	116	27	34
Crowther, John	1	2	12.79	4	0	19	36	9	16
Donlin, Sean	1	1	3.34	14	0	30	29	12	21
Elliot, Josh	0	0	6.75	2	0	4	9	4	2
Encarnacion, Alexis	0	0	9.24	7	0	13	23	7	9
2-team (8 Calgary)	1	0	5.90	15	0	29	40	13	13
Figueroa, Carlos	0	2	6.43	14	0	35	46	25	19
Fulton, Josh	0	0	0.00	1	0	1	2	0	0
Gaspar, Warren	0	0	18.00	1	0	2	4	3	1
Gross, Rafael	0	4	6.75	10	0	53	64	14	26
Hapanionek, Joe	0	0	3.86	3	0	2	3	1	1
Kmiecik, Kyle	0	0	6.00	1	0	3	5	0	2
Koziara, Matthew	1	2	4.32	4	0	17	16	6	12
Lyons, Michael	1	1	6.46	4	0	24	29	6	17
Marshall, Jacoby	0	0	7.71	4	0	5	8	5	1
2-team (2 Schaumburg)	0	0	8.00	6	0	9	13	9	4
Martinez, Samir	1	5	6.83	16	0	28	44	11	23
Medina, Julio	6	9	5.90	19	0	104	130	41	50
Montgomery, Matt	1	2	2.89	28	18	28	28	10	29
Montoya, Eric	2	0	4.85	2	0	13	17	4	8
O'Donnell, Tony	0	0	13.50	1	0	1	3	3	0
Reboin, Jeff	0	1	10.13	6	0	11	19	8	6
Rodriguez, Mike	3	7	5.18	11	0	66	82	29	51
Smiley, Gerald	0	0	19.80	4	0	5	13	2	2
Smith, Jared	1	1	6.86	13	1	21	22	26	20
Stockton, Robert	0	0	6.75	2	0	4	6	1	1
Walters, Cory	4	8	3.68	23	0	120	130	28	92
Webb, Nicholas	1	0	4.66	4	0	19	24	11	8
2-team (5 Kansas City)	2	2	6.09	9	0	44	57	27	28
Wesley, John	5	5	3.74	43	2	55	48	33	52
Zbacnik, Bill	0	0	14.44	6	0	14	26	15	12
2-team (9 St. Paul)	0	1	13.05	15	0	20	35	23	19

WINNIPEG

BATTING	AVG	AB	R	H	2B	3B	HR	RBI	SB
Ayala, Odannis, of	.280	279	53	78	11	4	6	31	3
Berrios, Harry, 1b	.349	381	51	133	26	0	9	72	2
Burns, Kevan, of	.317	189	35	60	15	0	3	18	0
Corbeil, Al, c	.284	225	35	64	15	1	3	26	0
Forbes, Michael, of	.140	50	1	7	1	0	0	0	1
Gunning, Matt, of	.146	41	2	6	2	1	0	3	0
Jacobson, Russ, c	.253	95	8	24	5	0	2	10	0
McNamara,Russ, 2b	.268	190	22	51	9	2	3	28	4
Meyers, Chad, of	.270	37	10	10	3	0	0	4	4
Moreno, Jorge, of	.308	354	64	109	22	3	10	66	31
Poulin, Max, ss	.277	336	49	93	14	6	5	32	18
Quartararo, Dan, 3b	.270	233	30	63	11	2	3	28	4
Ross, Donovan, 1b	.296	321	47	95	29	0	16	68	0
Santana, Ralph, 2b/of	.308	364	57	112	14	0	2	33	41
Smith, Steven, c	.104	48	2	5	2	0	0	6	0
Stocco, Matt, c	.048	21	1	1	0	0	0	0	0
Wallis, Scott, 2b	.211	57	7	12	0	0	0	7	0
Wirth, Robert, c	.069	29	2	2	0	0	0	0	0
Worrell, Stephen, of	.211	19	0	4	0	0	0	1	0

PITCHING	W	L	ERA	G	SV	IP	H	BB	SO
Akens, Phil	0	0	8.10	6	0	10	18	3	3
Brnardic, Ryan	1	1	5.92	20	1	24	27	18	17
Connelly, Patrick	4	4	5.65	13	0	51	56	17	48
Gautreau, Adam	0	1	7.71	2	0	5	8	4	1
Hampton, Matt	1	0	7.36	8	0	7	11	1	5
Hernandez, Ivan	5	3	1.99	43	2	54	40	24	54
Holbrook, Shayn	0	1	16.88	3	0	3	5	0	0
Johnson, Seth	0	2	2.38	12	0	23	20	7	17
Knoff, Justin	1	0	2.70	3	0	10	8	4	8
Lincoln, Roger	4	2	2.70	13	0	60	50	7	55
Luque, Roger	6	8	5.06	21	0	133	152	47	91
Manning, David	3	1	3.49	6	0	39	35	14	13
Marcus, Clint	1	3	2.73	45	0	33	28	15	21
Murray, Steven	1	3	3.47	4	0	23	28	6	11
Perez, Alex	2	4	5.40	16	0	53	66	23	34
Purcell, Brad	0	1	4.15	2	0	4	4	1	4
Rodriguez, Ray	0	1	37.80	2	0	2	4	3	0
Sedlacek, Shawn	6	5	3.38	17	0	128	137	23	92
Smith, Donnie	1	3	2.70	28	11	27	21	10	25
Sobkow, Phil	6	1	4.18	11	0	71	67	28	46
Soto, Darwin	1	0	1.26	10	5	14	4	3	18
Stiles, Brad	0	0	3.38	2	0	5	8	4	4
Testa, Chris	0	0	1.93	13	0	9	9	9	6
Thomas, Adam	1	3	6.83	6	0	29	41	16	17
Torres, Carlos	3	1	4.22	22	2	21	17	15	14

INTERNATIONAL BASEBALL

Baseball banished from Olympics, but World Classic on tap for '06

BY JOHN MANUEL

The Olympics have served as the pinnacle of international baseball since the Los Angeles Games of 1984, when baseball was on the Olympic program as a demonstration sport.

After events of 2005, however, baseball's place on the international stage was about to change.

In a stunning July vote, the International Olympic Committee removed baseball and softball from the Olympic program—the first sports removed from the Games since polo in 1936. For the foreseeable future, the 2008 Olympics in Beijing, China, were expected to be the last Games with baseball as a medal sport.

Days after the IOC vote, at the All-Star Game in Detroit, Major League Baseball announced the launching of the World Baseball Classic, a 16-team international tournament scheduled for March of 2006 that should include rosters brimming with major league players.

"I was saddened by what the Olympics did," MLB commissioner Bud Selig said. "Do I believe it will affect the way the sport is run? No."

MLB's hope is that the World Baseball Classic, with games set for Japan, Puerto Rico and the United States, will replace the Olympics as the showcase of international baseball. The IOC's decision played into MLB's hand, but it was still viewed as something of an upset. It was later determined that a secret vote of IOC members fell three votes short of the majority needed to retain baseball in the Olympics.

"Our focus now is to prepare for our Olympic qualification for Beijing," USA Baseball executive director Paul Seiler said. "As we look forward, our responsibility will continue to be on the athletes we prepare to represent our country in international competition, at all levels.

"Additionally, we will continue to work with our fellow member federations around the world to ensure the return of baseball to the Olympics."

Baseball and softball had survived IOC president Jacques Rogge's first attempt to oust them in 2002, and the vote in Singapore took officials from both baseball and softball by surprise. USA Baseball officials said U.S. Olympic Committee members attending the meeting told them the sports had enough support to remain on the program, so there was no heavy lobbying effort to sway voters in Singapore.

Rogge and the IOC built a case against baseball based on the lack of major league involvement (hence, the top players in the world were not playing in the Olympics) as well as the cost of building baseball facilities.

Those issues will be moot for the Classic. Because it will be held in the spring and has MLB's backing, major league players should be on most rosters. The inaugural tournament will start with round-robin pool play, beginning March 3 in Japan. The tournament will include 39 games overall, with two rounds of pool play and a four-team, single-elimination round, culminating with a winner-take-all title game March 20 at San Diego's Petco Park.

Familiar scene
Cuba reasserted its international dominance in 2005, winning the World Cup

Cuba Dominates World Cup Again

The major international competition of 2005 was the 36th World Cup, a 16-team event played in Amsterdam in September.

An intriguing quarterfinal game in the playoff round came down to two international baseball powers with different priorities—Cuba and the U.S.

TEAM USA: NATIONAL TEAM

XXXVI WORLD CUP, Amsterdam (7-3, Seventh Place)

Manager: Davey Johnson.

BATTING	AVG	AB	R	H	2B	3B	HR	RBI	SB	Organization
Mike Cervenak, 1b/3b	.368	38	12	14	5	0	4	9	1	Giants
Bryan LaHair, 1b	.361	36	9	13	3	0	3	8	0	Mariners
Ben Zobrist, ss	.333	30	8	10	2	0	1	5	3	Astros
Josh Phelps, dh	.325	40	10	13	2	0	0	2	0	Devil Rays
Dee Brown, of	.320	25	3	8	2	0	1	4	0	Nationals
Lastings Milledge, of	.302	43	8	13	3	0	3	6	2	Mets
Rob Johnson, c	.273	22	5	6	3	0	1	6	2	Mariners
Jeff Deardorff, of	.267	30	9	8	3	0	2	10	0	Devil Rays
Brant Ust, 3b	.231	26	3	6	1	0	1	6	0	Red Sox
Brian Peterson, c	.231	13	1	3	1	0	0	1	0	Reds
Brooks Badeaux, 2b	.222	18	1	4	1	0	0	4	0	Devil Rays
Chris Latham, of	.200	25	6	5	2	0	1	7	1	(Atlantic League)

PITCHING	W	L	ERA	G	SV	IP	H	BB	SO	Organization
Jared Wells, rhp	2	0	1.64	2	0	11	6	8	13	Padres
Chris Mobley, rhp	0	1	2.08	5	1	4	3	4	4	Marlins
Jason Jacome, lhp	0	0	3.38	2	0	11	10	4	4	(Mexican League)
James Garcia, rhp	2	0	4.05	5	0	7	4	2	10	Giants
Talley Haines, rhp	1	0	4.26	4	0	6	4	3	3	Cubs
Chris Michalak, lhp	1	0	5.23	2	0	10	11	5	5	Diamondbacks
Jason Phillips, rhp	0	0	5.40	3	0	7	8	3	2	Devil Rays
Gilbert de la Vara, lhp	0	0	5.40	2	1	2	2	0	1	Royals
Mark Freed, lhp	0	0	5.87	3	1	8	10	7	6	Diamondbacks
Brian Bannister, rhp	1	2	9.69	3	0	13	18	5	10	Mets
J.J. Trujillo, rhp	0	0	11.25	3	0	4	9	3	1	(Central League)

Cuba was the team to beat and entered the quarterfinals undefeated and the No. 1 seed. The World Cup was Cuba's Super Bowl, World Series and Final Four wrapped into one. The U.S., meanwhile, was playing its first major international competition since the 2003 Olympic qualifier, when it failed to earn a spot in the 2004 Olympic field. Team USA showed up with a prolific offense of solid minor leaguers but a pitching staff with no power arms.

Team USA had finished in a three-way tie for second in pool play with a 6-2 mark, but an embarrassing 14-2 loss to Nicaragua doomed it to the No. 4 seed out of Pool B; the tiebreaker was runs allowed, and the blowout loss put the U.S. behind Nicaragua and Puerto Rico. So the Americans were forced to face Pool A's top seed, Cuba, with the event on the line. Cuba responded, pounding Team USA's top pitcher, Brian Bannister (Mets), on its way to an 11-3 victory.

Cuba then pounded Panama 15-2 in a game marred by bench-clearing, beanball-ignited brawls, then shut out Korea to win the gold, its ninth consecutive World Cup championship and 12th in the last 13 events.

The loss to Cuba meant Team USA had no chance to win a medal. It also forfeited its next game with Nicaragua due to wet field conditions. An 11-3 victory in its final game against Puerto Rico merely improved Team USA's record to 7-4 and a seventh-place finish, the worst result for an American team of affiliated minor league players since USA Baseball started fielding such teams in 1999.

"It's disappointing, certainly," said USA Baseball's Eric Campbell, the general manager of national teams. "It was a tough tournament. Puerto Rico had a (veteran) lineup (and finished eighth). Nicaragua had a good team. Japan sent a physical team of professionals (from its industrial leagues), and they didn't get a medal. So it was a tough field."

The biggest winner other than Cuba may have been the host Netherlands, which finished fourth but also put on a good show. Former Yankees shortstop Robert Eenhoorn, the Dutch national coach, and the Dutch baseball federation earned Campbell's praise for a well-run event that drew more than 135,000 fans over two weeks of play.

On the field, Cuba maintained its dominance with a more powerful lineup than it has fielded in recent years, while its pitching was less impressive but still more than enough to dominate. Cuba has won every significant international baseball tournament that it has entered since the 2000 Olympics, when it lost in the gold-medal game to Team USA.

"The Cubans are like an NBA team," said one major league scout who attended the World Cup. "They cruise, but when it's the last two minutes of the fourth quarter and they need to win the game, they reach back and do it."

Cuban righthanders Danny Betancourt and Pedro Luis Lazo dominated Korea in the gold-medal game, striking out nine in a combined four-hitter, and Lazo finished the tournament with nine scoreless innings pitched.

Michel Enriquez and Yuliesky Gourriel were Cuba's hitting stars in the event. While shortstop Eduardo Paret was named MVP after going 12-for-19 with two homers and eight RBIs, he went down in pool play with a knee injury and didn't play in the medal round. Enriquez, 26, went 23-for-46 (.500) to lead the tournament and had 20 RBIs in 11 games. Gourriel, 21, had eight home runs to lead the tournament while driving in 19.

2005 INTERNATIONAL CHAMPIONSHIPS

XXXVI WORLD CUP, Amsterdam, Aug. 2-17, 2005

POOL-PLAY STANDINGS

POOL A	W	L	RF	RA
Cuba	8	0	70	15
Netherlands	7	1	81	18
Panama	6	2	54	35
South Korea	5	3	36	27
Canada	4	4	63	41
China	3	5	42	58
Brazil	2	6	28	51
Sweden	1	7	22	88
South Africa	0	8	15	76

POOL B	W	L	RF	RA
Japan	7	1	73	19
Nicaragua	6	2	44	27
Puerto Rico	6	2	53	34
United States	6	2	61	31
Australia	4	4	41	26
Taiwan	3	5	48	39
Spain	2	6	32	61
Colombia	2	6	25	62
Czech Republic	0	8	13	91

SEMI-FINALS: Cuba 15, Panama 2; Korea 7, Netherlands 0. **GOLD-MEDAL GAME:** Cuba 3, Korea 0. **BRONZE-MEDAL GAME:** Panama 7, Netherlands 6. **FIFTH-PLACE GAME:** Japan 8, Nicaragua 1. **SEVENTH-PLACE GAME:** United States 11, Puerto Rico 3.

ALL-TOURNAMENT TEAM: C—Tsutomu Takanezawa, Japan. **1B**—Percy Isenia, Netherlands. **2B**—Jung-Chi Chen, Taiwan. **3B**—Yuliesky Gourriel, Cuba. **SS**—Eduardo Paret, Cuba. **OF**—Freddy Herrera, Panama; Danny Rombley, Netherlands; Tiago Magalhaes, Brazil. **DH**—Joey Votto, Canada. **RHP**—Pedro Luis Lazo, Cuba. **LHP**—Diegomar Markwell, Netherlands.

Most Valuable Player: Eduardo Paret, Cuba.

INDIVIDUAL BATTING LEADERS

(Minimum 2.7 Plate Appearances/team game)

	AVG	AB	R	H	2B	3B	HR	RBI	SB
Enriquez, Michel, Cuba	.500	46	11	23	6	1	1	20	0
Roa, Jenry, Nicaragua	.457	35	5	16	3	0	0	12	0
Chen, Yung Chi, Taiwan	.438	32	6	14	4	0	1	6	0
Ware, Jeremy, Canada	.435	23	5	10	1	0	1	3	3
Lo, Kuo Hui, Taiwan	.433	30	6	13	2	1	1	7	2
Kingman, Brendan, Australia	.429	21	4	9	1	0	0	1	0
Magalhaes, Tiago, Brazil	.414	29	5	12	3	0	1	6	1
Suzuki, Kanya, Japan	.414	29	8	12	0	1	0	4	1
Moon, Kyu Hyun, S. Korea	.409	22	2	9	2	0	0	2	0
Van Iderstine, Ben, Canada	.400	35	8	14	3	0	1	4	0
van't Klooster, Dirk, Neth.	.395	38	5	15	3	1	0	5	0
Kim, Sang Hyeon, S. Korea	.393	28	4	11	3	0	2	6	0
Herrera, Freddy, Panama	.389	36	10	14	3	0	2	10	0
Urrutia, Osmani, Cuba	.387	31	3	12	2	0	0	5	0
Saigo, Yasuyuki, Japan	.387	31	6	12	2	0	2	9	0
Rogelstad, Matt, Canada	.379	29	3	11	3	1	1	10	1
Sun, Lingfeng, China	.379	29	5	11	3	0	0	3	4
Feliciano, Jesus, P.R.	.378	37	10	14	2	1	2	9	5
Takanezawa, Tsutomu, Japan	.375	24	6	9	0	0	4	8	0
Sato, Renan, Brazil	.375	32	3	12	3	1	1	9	0
Chen, Zhe, China	.375	24	4	9	4	0	0	5	0
Vega, Anibal, Nicaragua	.370	27	3	10	0	0	1	4	0
Kuo, Chun Yu, Taiwan	.370	27	7	10	0	0	4	9	0
Cervenak, Mike, USA	.368	38	12	14	5	0	4	9	1
De Leon, Audes, Panama	.368	38	9	14	3	0	1	8	0

INDIVIDUAL PITCHING LEADERS

(Minimum .8 Innings/team game)

	W	L	ERA	SV	IP	H	BB	SO
Kim, Dae Woo, S. Korea	1	1	0.00	0	15	7	6	18
Yun, Sung Kwui, S. Korea	1	0	0.00	0	9	9	2	11
Gomez, Miguel, Panama	2	0	0.49	3	18	15	5	19
Roman, Orlando, P.R.	2	0	0.50	0	18	11	6	14
Lazo, Pedro Luis, Cuba	2	0	0.54	2	17	7	1	27
Takasaki, Kentaro, Japan	1	0	0.61	0	15	9	3	19
Seo, Min Wook, S. Korea	0	1	0.77	0	12	15	3	7
Matsui, Kouske, Japan	1	0	0.79	2	11	8	2	14
Saito, Shinsuke, Japan	3	0	0.82	0	22	15	5	24
Bergman, David, Netherlands	1	0	1.00	0	9	5	1	5
Ramirez, Ramon, Panama	2	0	1.13	0	16	10	1	20
Choi, Dae Sung, S. Korea	2	1	1.35	1	27	20	6	37
Doi, Yoshikazu, Japan	1	0	1.38	1	13	8	2	6
Mildren, Paul, Australia	1	0	1.46	0	12	7	2	16
Gonzalez, Yulieski, Cuba	3	0	1.62	0	17	10	4	17
Wells, Jared, USA	2	0	1.64	0	11	6	8	13
Mairena, Oswaldo, Nicaragua	1	1	1.69	1	16	13	1	13
Rostran, Olman, Nicaragua	0	1	1.80	0	10	6	5	2
Betancourt, Dany, Cuba	2	0	1.84	1	15	10	7	26
Tsai, Ying Feng, Taiwan	1	1	1.88	0	14	6	4	10
Markwell, Diegomar, Netherlands	3	0	2.01	0	22	17	7	6

TEAM USA AMATEUR

Team USA's college national team's 2005 schedule didn't feature any international tournaments in which to compete for a medal, so head coach Steve Smith set different goals.

"It's more a developmental summer with no ring to win, no trophies to get," Smith (Baylor) said. "I'm trying to do a good job of balancing at-bats and innings. My primary objective is to make sure we got those guys home healthy and that they get a valuable playing experience."

Smith checked those items on his list after the national team finished the summer 16-4 following domestic series sweeps of Italy and Nicaragua that propelled it to a tour-ending 11-game win streak. Team USA out-scored its opponents 84-23 during the streak, playing consistently in all three phases of the game, an improvement over its 2-4 trip to Japan and Taiwan.

Steve Smith

Smith said the team played with more focus upon its return to native soil.

"When we got back to Durham, there were about 20 major league scouts there and our play improved significantly," he said. "I jokingly said we should have put about 10 scouts on the plane and sent them to Japan. Their focus at the plate improved. Obviously this team is full of good hitters, but not if they're not focused.

"These guys have futures and want to play in the big leagues. If you watch the big leagues, you don't always see guys giving it their all, but if you play like that, you won't ever get there."

While the summer tour serves as a convenient combine for scouts watching some of the top players for the 2006 draft class, freshmen not eligible until 2007 often proved the most impressive. The power bat of catcher J.P. Arencibia (Tennessee) and power arm of lefthander David Price (Vanderbilt) stood out the most.

Price led the team with 39 strikeouts in 29 innings, and his 1.26 ERA ranked first on the team. He punched out 11 batters while holding Italy to one hit over seven innings before ringing up nine batters in a five-hit shutout of Nicaragua in his final start of the summer.

"I like Price a lot," said righthander Ian Kennedy (Southern California), a co-captain in his second summer with Team USA. "He's going to be really good one day. He's really good now, but I'll see him in the big leagues because he's a big lefthander who throws so hard and has command."

Arencibia led the team with a .404 average and .579 slugging percentage and tied for the lead with 12 RBIs. He built those power numbers during an 11-3 win against Italy in which he ripped a home run and two doubles while driving in five runs. Arencibia said he was pleased to have become one of the five freshmen on the Team USA roster and never thought he'd end the summer as the offensive leader.

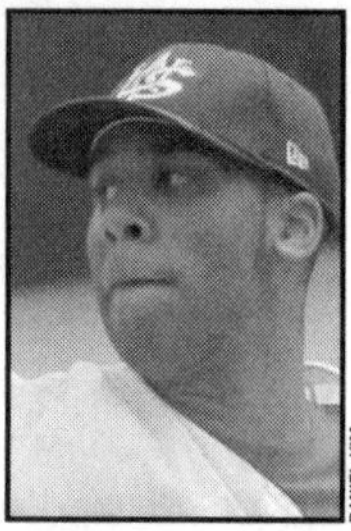

DANIEL KIM

David Price

"It's a surprise to me," he said. "Coming out of high school you always hear about all these freshmen All-Americans and wonder if you'll be one. Then you come to Team USA with guys like Shane (Robinson), Wes Hodges and Jon Jay, who all hit over .400 during the (college) season, and never think this will happen. It's such a small number of at-bats, everyone here is a good hitter."

Sean Doolitte (Virginia), who split time between first base and right field, felt much the same way entering the team trials. Also a rising sophomore, Doolittle ranked second on the team with a .347 average and .431 on-base percentage. By the end of the summer, Doolittle often batted third, ahead of Arencibia and first baseman Matt Wieters (Georgia Tech), another rising sophomore whose three homers ranked second on the club.

"The feeling with this team is once you're on the team, you're not looked at as a freshman or sophomore, you're a part of Team USA," Doolittle said. "I think that's really cool and helped me get comfortable on the field rather than (older players) looking at me or Matt Wieters or J.P."

Lefthander Kevin Gunderson (Oregon State) said no one on the team gave much thought to what year their teammates were in school. "We're only one year older than them," he said, and Smith said he hadn't even noticed he often put players with only a year of college experience in the

TEAM USA: COLLEGE NATIONAL TEAM

Season Statistics: (16-4)

HEAD COACH: Steve Smith (Baylor).

BATTING	AVG	AB	R	H	2B	3B	HR	RBI	SB	College	Yr.
J.P. Arencibia, c	.404	57	8	23	4	0	2	12	0	Tennessee	Fr.
Sean Doolittle, of/1b	.347	49	11	17	5	0	0	9	1	Virginia	Fr.
Josh Rodriguez, inf	.326	43	13	14	1	0	1	8	1	Rice	So.
Adam Davis, 2b	.313	67	13	21	5	1	0	7	3	Florida	So.
Wes Hodges, 3b	.309	55	7	17	5	0	0	8	0	Georgia Tech	So.
Drew Stubbs, of	.304	46	5	14	3	0	0	6	1	Texas	So.
Shane Robinson, of	.296	54	12	16	5	2	1	12	5	Florida State	So.
Blake Davis, ss	.275	51	8	14	0	2	0	4	2	Cal State Fullerton	So.
Matt Wieters, 1b	.237	44	7	12	3	0	3	9	0	Georgia Tech	Fr.
Jon Jay, of	.262	61	15	16	1	1	0	8	7	Miami	So.
Hunter Mense, of	.259	54	12	14	2	2	1	7	3	Missouri	So.
Matt LaPorta, dh/1b	.259	58	7	15	3	1	4	12	1	Florida	So.
Brian Jeroloman, c	.179	39	10	7	3	0	0	4	0	Florida	So.
PITCHING	**W**	**L**	**ERA**	**G**	**SV**	**IP**	**H**	**BB**	**SO**	**College**	**Yr.**
Mark Melancon, rhp	1	0	0.00	10	5	12	7	0	10	Arizona	So.
Matt Wieters, rhp	0	0	0.00	1	0	0	0	1	0	Georgia Tech	So.
Kevin Gunderson, lhp	1	0	0.45	11	0	20	11	3	17	Oregon State	So.
David Price, lhp	2	0	1.26	5	0	29	13	13	39	Vanderbilt	Fr.
Kyle McCulloch, rhp	4	0	1.44	4	0	25	20	3	22	Texas	So.
Jonah Nickerson, rhp	1	1	2.00	6	0	18	14	7	23	Oregon State	So.
Max Scherzer, rhp	2	1	2.70	4	0	20	22	2	24	Missouri	So.
Chris Perez, rhp	1	1	1.84	7	2	13	4	8	17	Miami	So.
Ian Kennedy, rhp	4	1	2.89	5	0	28	11	11	13	Southern California	So.
Joe Savery, lhp	0	0	9.00	4	0	9	8	11	13	Rice	Fr.
Sean Doolittle, lhp	0	0	13.50	2	0	2	4	0	3	Virginia	Fr.

heart of his order until someone pointed it out to him near the end of the summer.

Veterans also made their own impact. Righthanders Kennedy, who held opponents to a .118 average thanks to seven no-hit innings against Taiwan, and Kyle McCulloch, who pitched Texas to the national championship, led the team with four wins apiece.

"Our older guys like Ian and Kyle McCulloch—you pretty much knew what to expect from them," Smith said.

Matt LaPorta (Florida), who led college baseball with 27 home runs, continued to add to his 2005 total by launching five more. His batting practice sessions became recommended viewing during the tour, as teammates admired his many moonshots. "I'd always think I had a good B.P. and hit some balls far, and then he'd come in and make me look bad," Arencibia said. "I did get him one time, though."

Teammates and coaches also admired LaPorta's toughness. He broke the fifth metatarsal in his left foot running the bases in Japan and then chipped a tooth and required stitches after getting hit by a pitch stateside, but he continued to play despite being limited to DH.

"It's the price you pay to play on a prestigious team like this," he said. "You can't complain to do the things that we're doing."

—WILL KIMMEY

Gordon wins amateur award

GOLDEN SPIKES

Johnny Rogers, Mike Rozier and Eric Crouch all won the Heisman Trophy as football players at Nebraska. Alex Gordon became the school's first winner of baseball's version of that honor, taking home the 2005 Golden Spikes Award.

Gordon, a first-team All-American and Big 12 player of the year in both 2004 and 2005, led Nebraska to a Big 12 title and the College World Series while batting .372-19-66 to earn the award, presented by USA Baseball and the Major League Baseball Player's Association. He batted .388-4-12 with Team USA the previous summer and batted .524 to earn Most Outstanding Offensive Player honors during the U.S. national team's gold-medal run at the World University Championship in Taiwan.

The third baseman topped off his superlative year when the Royals chose him second overall in the June draft, making Gordon the first college player picked. He beat out fellow first-rounders and first-team All-Americans Ryan Braun (Miami), Jeff Clement (Southern California), Trevor Crowe (Arizona) and Luke Hochevar (Tennessee) for the Golden Spikes award.

Alex Gordon

"USA Baseball is extremely proud to honor Alex Gordon of the University of Nebraska with the 2005 Golden Spikes Award," said Paul Seiler, USA Baseball executive director/CEO. "Alex's tremendous collegiate career in which he dominated the Big 12 Conference certainly proves he was worthy of this award. We're also excited that Alex played such an instrumental role in helping Team USA capture the gold medal at the 2004 FISU World University Championship."

Perhaps the best perspective on Gordon's success came at an Omaha press conference prior to the first day of the 2005 CWS. Arizona State coach Pat Murphy was slated to face Nebraska in the opener and recalled watching Rogers, the 1972 Heisman winner, look almost super-human at times on the football field. Murphy added that he'd be fine playing Nebraska's baseball team because he was sure No. 20 wouldn't be returning kicks against his Sun Devils.

Texas coach Augie Garrido, whose teams faced Gordon for three years in the Big 12, immediately offered Murphy a quick reminder: "Pat, Alex Gordon is better than Rogers."

—WILL KIMMEY

PREVIOUS WINNERS

1978—Bob Horner, 3b, Arizona State
1979—Tim Wallach, 1b, Cal State Fullerton
1980—Terry Francona, of, Arizona
1981—Mike Fuentes, of, Florida State
1982—Augie Schmidt, ss, New Orleans
1983—Dave Magadan, 1b, Alabama
1984—Oddibe McDowell, of, Arizona State
1985—Will Clark, 1b, Mississippi State
1986—Mike Loynd, rhp, Florida State
1987—Jim Abbott, lhp, Michigan
1988—Robin Ventura, 3b, Oklahoma State
1989—Ben McDonald, rhp, Louisiana State
1990—Alex Fernandez, rhp, Miami-Dade CC
1991—Mike Kelly, of, Arizona State
1992—Phil Nevin, 3b, Cal State Fullerton
1993—Darren Dreifort, rhp-dh, Wichita State
1994—Jason Varitek, c, Georgia Tech
1995—Mark Kotsay, of-lhp, Cal State Fullerton
1996—Travis Lee, 1b, San Diego State
1997—J.D. Drew, of, Florida State
1998—Pat Burrell, 3b, Miami
1999—Jason Jennings, rhp-dh, Baylor
2000—Kip Bouknight, rhp, South Carolina
2001—Mark Prior, rhp, Southern California
2002—Khalil Greene, ss, Clemson
2003—Rickie Weeks, 2b, Southern
2004—Jered Weaver, rhp, Long Beach State

Cuba Tops U.S., Again

Cuba once again spoiled the U.S. junior national team's bid for a gold medal by scoring two runs in the third inning and holding on for a 2-1 win to capture the COPABE AAA Pan American Junior Championship in Villahermosa, Mexico. The Cuban national team has claimed the gold medal at six consecutive Pan Am events, held biennially for players age 18 and under.

Team USA earned its third straight silver medal at the tournament, which also serves as a qualifying event for the 2006 World Junior Championship. Cuba, the U.S., Canada and Panama were the four countries that successfully qualified for the 2006 event, which will be held in Sancti Spiritus, Cuba. Canada beat Panama for the bronze medal.

Cuba escaped two-on, one-out situations in the seventh and ninth innings in its game against the previously unbeaten Americans. Cuban starter Juan Serrano held Team USA to one run through 8⅓ innings before Yasnier Hidalgo checked in and retired the only batter he faced, inducing a game-ending double play.

"We kept battling," Team USA coach Jerry Dawson said. "I wish we could have come up with a break . . . but we couldn't. We kept knocking on the door but we couldn't get in."

Righthander Shawn Tolleson, a senior from Allen (Texas) High, relieved righthander Tyson Ross, a freshman at California, in the third inning and matched Serrano down the stretch. Tolleson struck out 10 with

TEAM USA: JUNIOR NATIONAL TEAM

Pan Am Championship, Villahermosa, Mexico (7–1, Second Place)

Head Coach: Jerry Dawson (Chaparral HS, Scottsdale, Ariz.)

BATTING	AVG	AB	R	H	2B	3B	HR	RBI	SB	High School
Marcus Lemon, ss	.500	28	12	14	3	0	0	6	2	Eustis (Fla.) HS
Lars Anderson, 1b	.464	28	5	13	1	0	0	11	2	Jesuit HS, Carmichael, Calif.
Grant Green, 3b	.414	29	6	12	0	0	0	4	1	Canyon HS, Anaheim
Max Sapp, c-of	.391	23	2	9	3	0	0	3	0	Bishop Moore HS, Orlando
Adrian Cardenas, 2b	.333	21	4	7	0	0	0	2	2	Monsignor Pace HS, Opa Locka, Fla.
L.V. Ware, of	.324	34	10	11	2	0	0	3	3	North Atlanta (Ga.) HS
Jason Taylor, 2b	.316	19	2	6	0	0	0	1	3	Kellam HS, Virginia Beach, Va.
Torre Langley, c-of	.310	29	1	9	0	0	0	6	2	Alexander HS, Douglasville, Ga.
Sean Ratliff, 1b-dh	.259	27	5	7	2	0	0	1	2	Niwot HS, Longmont, Colo.
Scott Schauer, of	.192	26	1	5	2	0	0	6	0	Servite HS, Anaheim
Dwight Childs, c	.167	6	2	1	0	0	0	0	1	Elk Grove (Calif.) HS
PITCHING	**W**	**L**	**ERA**	**G**	**SV**	**IP**	**H**	**BB**	**SO**	**High School**
Dellin Betances	1	0	0.00	2	0	7	0	6	11	Grand Street HS, New York
Clayton Kershaw	0	0	0.00	1	0	4	3	4	3	Highland Park HS, Dallas
Jeremy Bleich	0	0	0.00	1	0	3	1	2	4	Isidore Newman HS, Metairie, La.
Brett Anderson	2	0	0.56	2	0	16	3	3	24	Stillwater (Okla.) HS
Shawn Tolleson	1	0	0.73	3	1	12	10	6	16	Allen (Texas) HS
Josh Thrailkill	2	0	0.75	2	0	12	8	3	9	T.C. Roberson HS, Asheville, N.C.
Tyson Ross	0	1	2.45	2	0	7	7	4	7	Bishop O'Dowd HS, Oakland
Kevin Rhoderick	0	0	3.00	3	0	3	1	2	0	Horizon HS, Scottsdale, Ariz.
Greg Peavey	1	0	4.50	1	0	2	0	4	0	Hudson's Bay HS, Vancouver, Wash.

two walks and six hits in 5⅔ innings of scoreless relief.

Cuba managed a walk, a sacrifice and a one-out single to take a 1-0 lead in the third inning. Another RBI single followed a hit batsmen to make it 2-0.

Team USA entered the gold medal game with a 7-0 record in pool play and a 7-1 win over Panama in the semifinals. Tolleson compiled a 0.73 ERA in 12⅓ innings with 16 strikeouts and a save, leading a pitching staff that owned an event-best 0.94 ERA, while allowing 33 hits in 67 innings. Lefthander Brett Anderson, a senior from Stillwater (Okla.) High, was 2-0, 0.56 with 24 strikeouts in 16 innings. He tossed a complete game two-hitter versus Panama.

MIKE GULLETT

Brett Anderson

Marcus Lemon, a senior shortstop from Eustis (Fla.) High and the son of ex-big leaguer Chet Lemon, topped Team USA with a .500 average, 12 runs, 17 total bases, a .607 slugging percentage and .611 on-base percentage.

—ALAN MATTHEWS

Cuba Topples U.S. Youth

USA Baseball's reign as three-time World Youth (16-and-under) champions came to a soggy end Aug. 28 in Monterrey, Mexico, as Cuba dethroned the United States in the gold-medal game, 5-0.

A powerful U.S. lineup had scored 98 runs in winning its previous seven games at the 11-team tournament, but was no match for Cuban righthander Freddie Alvarez, who threw a complete-game shutout, allowing four hits while striking out nine. Alvarez went the distance despite a 3½-hour rain delay between the fourth and fifth innings.

The U.S. elected to pull its starter, ace righthander Robert Stock, a rising junior at Agoura Hills High in Westlake Village, Calif., who sailed through the first three innings before running into trouble in the fourth, when he gave up three runs. Stock fanned eight in his four innings of work. He started three games for the U.S., including the first three innings of a 15-2 win over Japan in the semifinal a day earlier, and struck out a youth national team record 27 in 14 innings while going 1-1, 1.29.

Despite winning the last three World Youth titles, the U.S. had only a 1-4 record against Cuba in their previous five meetings—including a loss in the finals of the 2004 COPABE Pan Am championships, the qualifying event for the 2005 world tournament.

LARRY GOREN

Robert Stock

Outfielder Freddie Freeman, a rising junior at El Modena High in Villa Park, Calif., was the top offensive performer for Team USA. He got two of his team's four hits in the deciding game and went 17-for-31 overall. He led the team with a .548 average and 16 RBIs, while sharing the team lead with three home runs.

Stock was Team USA's ace, but 6-foot-6 righthander Blake Beavan, a rising junior at Irving (Texas) High, also was effective, going 3-0, 1.10 overall with 22 strikeouts in 16 innings. He had two complete games, including a 12-1 quarterfinal win over Taiwan.

—ALLAN SIMPSON

TEAM USA: YOUTH NATIONAL TEAM

World Youth Championship, Villahermosa, Mexico (7–1, Silver Medal)

Head Coach: Phil Bodine (Mendota, Ill.)

Player	AVG	AB	R	H	2B	3B	HR	RBI	SB	High School, Hometown
DeVall, Brett, lhp	.750	4	1	3	1	0	0	4	0	Rutherford HS, Lynnhaven, Fla.
Freeman, Freddie, of	.548	31	10	17	7	0	3	16	0	El Modena HS, Villa Park, Calif.
Beavan, Blake, rhp	.545	11	5	6	1	0	0	3	0	Irving (Texas) HS
Rodriguez, Christian, 2b/ss	.517	29	14	15	2	0	2	9	1	Taylorsville HS, Salt Lake City
Melville, Tim, rhp	.500	4	1	2	1	0	0	2	0	Holt HS, St. Louis
Stonecipher, Sequoyah, of	.472	36	10	17	1	0	2	11	3	Mission Bay HS, San Diego
McGee, Mike, ss	.360	25	6	9	2	1	1	5	0	Port St. Lucie (Fla.) HS
Vitters, Josh, 3b	.355	31	9	11	6	0	0	6	0	Cypress HS, Anaheim, Calif.
Krill, Brett, of	.333	33	16	11	3	0	3	11	1	Aliso Niguel HS, Laguna Niguel, Calif.
Nacapoy, Chad, c	.333	12	6	4	0	1	2	4	0	Crescenta Valley HS, La Crescenta, Calif.
Stock, Robert, rhp	.333	6	2	2	2	0	0	3	0	Agoura (Calif.) HS
Valdes, Franco, c	.313	16	5	5	1	0	1	4	0	Monsignor Pace HS, Miami
Torrez, Riccio, 2b	.167	6	5	1	0	0	0	0	0	Brophy Prep, Phoenix
Nazario, Iden, 1b	.154	26	5	4	0	1	1	4	0	Southridge HS, Miami
Pitcher	**W**	**L**	**ERA**	**G**	**SV**	**IP**	**H**	**BB**	**SO**	**High School, Hometown**
Melville, Tim	1	0	0.00	2	0	5	2	0	11	Holt HS, St. Louis
Blair, Seth	1	0	0.00	2	0	5	5	3	3	Rock Falls (Ill.) HS
Gast, John	0	0	0.00	3	0	2	1	1	4	Lake Brantley HS, Longwood, Fla.
McGee, Mike	0	0	0.00	1	0	2	1	1	4	Port St. Lucie (Fla.) HS
Beavan, Blake	3	0	1.10	3	0	16	8	0	22	Irving (Texas) HS
Stock, Robert	1	1	1.29	3	0	14	8	5	27	Agoura (Calif.) HS
DeVall, Brett	1	0	1.29	2	0	7	4	1	10	Rutherford HS, Lynnhaven, Fla.
Brule, Kyle	0	0	4.50	2	0	2	3	0	1	Marcos de Niza HS, Chandler, Ariz.
Green, Cole	0	0	5.14	2	0	7	7	3	5	Coppell (Texas) HS

Tigers win fourth title in 9 years

BY AARON FITT

Behind a punishing offense and a pitching staff that showed up when it mattered most, Angelopolis won the Mexican League title in 2005 for the fourth time since 1997 and the first time since moving from Mexico City to the Puebla area. Angelopolis defeated Saltillo in an entertaining championship series that went six games before the Tigers closed it out with a come-from-behind 4-3 win in Puebla.

MEXICO

Pitching was Angelopolis' weakness all season, as it sported a garish 5.89 ERA during the regular season. Angelopolis employed a "pitching by committee" approach that practically ensured starters would be pulled no matter how they were doing, and the team finished with just two complete games in 2005.

But Angelopolis made up for it with a potent offense that led the league with a .339 batting average—20 points ahead of Saltillo, the second-place team. And the Angelopolis pitching staff came around after getting shelled for 25 runs in the first three games of the championship series against Saltillo. Angelopolis allowed just eight runs in the final three games.

Shortstop Javier Robles, who led the league in batting during the regular season with a .393 average, hit .520 in the final series against a good Saltillo pitching staff. He hit a three-run home run in Game One, went 3-for-4 with four RBIs in Game Three, and smacked a two-run homer plus a double in Game Four. Robles' brother, Trini, won Game One with a pinch-hit, two-run double and also belted a two-run homer in Game Five. He finished the series with a .364 average.

Angelopolis, one of two teams in the league to field an all-Mexican lineup, took home the league title in its 50th season, which the league had dedicated to former Angelopolis owner Alejo Peralta, a longtime force in the league.

Earlier in the playoffs, Yucatan pitcher Oscar Rivera threw the first perfect game in the league's playoff history, as Yucatan slipped past Oaxaca 1-0 in Game Seven of their first-round series. Defending league champion Campeche was eliminated in that first round by Tabasco in seven games, but Campeche's Francisco Campos did repeat as the league's pitcher of the year, going 11-4, 2.84 with 170 strikeouts in 152 innings.

There was some tragic news during the playoffs, as well. Carlos Gastelum, a catcher who spent 20 years in the Mexican League, died Aug. 24 in Merida, Mexico, at the age of 39. Gastelum died of a heart attack while shopping during an off day during the playoffs. His Yucatan team was playing in the playoffs at the time.

Gastelum, also known as "The Cat", never put up flashy offensive numbers, but he established himself as a dependable receiver, spending two decades working primarily as a backup catcher and eventually as a coach as well. He broke into the Mexican League with the Mexico City Reds, but he covered plenty of ground during his career, eventually playing for 11 different Mexican League teams. For his career he hit .239-9-263 in 1,218 games.

STANDINGS

FIRST HALF

NORTH	W	L	PCT	GB
Saltillo Sarape Makers	32	24	.571	—
Monterrey Sultans	32	24	.571	—
Tijuana Colts	29	27	.518	3
Mexico Red Devils	29	27	.518	3
Aguascalientes Railroadmen	28	28	.500	4
Monclova Steelers	28	28	.500	4
Laguna Cowboys	22	34	.393	10
San Luis Potosi Cactus Pear Growers	20	36	.357	12

SOUTH	W	L	PCT	GB
Campeche Pirates	38	18	.679	—
Angelopolis Tigers	34	22	.607	4
Yucatan Lions	31	25	.554	7
Veracruz Reds	28	28	.500	10
Oaxaca Warriors	26	30	.464	12
Puebla Parrots	25	31	.446	13
Tabasco Olmecas	24	32	.429	14
Cancun Lobstermen	22	34	.393	16

SECOND HALF

NORTH	W	L	PCT	GB
Tijuana Colts	35	19	.648	—
Saltillo Sarape Makers	31	23	.574	4
Mexico Red Devils	27	24	.529	6½
Aguascalientes Railroadmen	27	25	.519	7
Monclova Steelers	25	27	.481	9
San Luis Potosi Cactus Pear Growers	25	27	.481	9
Monterrey Sultans	24	26	.480	9
Laguna Cowboys	16	37	.302	18½

SOUTH	W	L	PCT	GB
Angelopolis Tigers	32	19	.627	—
Oaxaca Warriors	31	20	.608	1
Tabasco Olmecas	29	23	.558	3½
Yucatan Lions	26	25	.510	6
Puebla Parrots	26	27	.491	7
Campeche Pirates	24	25	.490	7
Veracruz Reds	23	30	.434	10
Cancun Lobstermen	15	39	.278	18½

PLAYOFFS—First Round: Monterrey defeated Mexico 4-2, Saltillo defeated Aguascalientes 4-2, Yucatan defeated Oaxaca 4-3 and Tabasco defeated Campeche 4-3, in best-of-7 series. **Division Series:** Tijuana defeated Mexico 4-2, Saltillo defeated Monterrey 4-2, Angelopolis defeated Oaxaca 4-2 and Yucatan defeated Tabasco 4-3, in best-of-7 series. **Semifinals:** Angelopolis defeated Yucatan 4-2 and Saltillo defeated Tijuana 4-3, in best-of-7 series. **Finals:** Angelopolis defeated Saltillo 4-2, in best-of-7 series.

ATTENDANCE—Saltillo 591,491; Monterrey 433,161; Tijuana 370,477; Laguna 246,617; Yucatan 241,512; Aguascalientes 223,302; Monclova 214,057; Cancun 167,245; Angelopolis 146,762; Puebla 129,708; Mexico 117,598; Tabasco 114,767; Veracruz 101,905; Campeche 83,529; Oaxaca 72,366; San Luis Potosi 67,154.

MANAGERS: Aguascalientes—Alex Taveras. **Angelopolis**—Enrique Reyes. **Campeche**—Francisco Estrada. **Cancun**—Juan Pacho, Carlos Paz. **Laguna**—Geraldo Sanchez, Antonio Aguilera, Wes Clements, Hector Estrada. **Mexico**—Alfonso Jimenez. **Monclova**—Lino Rivera, Francisco Rodriguez. **Monterrey**—Hector Torres, Leo Rodriguez, Bernie Tatis. **Oaxaca**—Homer Rojas. **Puebla**—Armando Cabrera, Bernardo Calvo, Make Oliveras. **Saltillo**—Derek Bryant. **San Luis Potosi**—Dan Firova. **Tabasco**—Juan Rodriguez, Julian Yan, Mario Mendoza. **Tijuana**—Raul Cano, Jose Bellazetin. **Veracruz**—Fernando Elizondo, Miguel Ruiz, Juan Pacho. **Yucatan**—Bernie Tatis, Roberto Perez, Lino Rivera.

CLUB BATTING

	AVG	G	AB	R	H	2B	2B	HR	BB	SO	SB
Angelopolis	.339	107	3805	791	1288	236	20	176	352	552	76
Saltillo	.319	110	3899	754	1244	205	11	156	459	625	22
Tijuana	.316	110	4021	753	1271	241	9	188	430	552	38
Yucatan	.316	107	3799	616	1201	188	37	104	380	483	110

Aguascalientes	.313	108	3872	688	1211	227	14	129	359	561	69
Veracruz	.311	109	3723	611	1157	168	9	119	374	518	68
Oaxaca	.311	107	3726	653	1159	214	24	107	452	520	92
Puebla	.310	109	3703	624	1149	206	28	106	372	535	66
Laguna	.309	109	3923	653	1214	237	15	122	442	585	50
Mexico	.308	107	3784	721	1164	227	21	161	480	585	43
Campeche	.307	105	3609	659	1108	177	16	138	369	467	68
San Luis Potosi	.307	108	3773	664	1159	270	17	125	417	647	94
Monterrey	.300	106	3678	579	1104	207	15	99	414	528	93
Monclova	.297	108	3747	628	1114	190	8	113	488	649	36
Tabasco	.289	108	3670	607	1061	174	24	109	462	559	104
Cancun	.281	110	3664	493	1028	188	15	79	365	517	48

CLUB PITCHING

	ERA	G	CG	SHO	SV	IP	H	R	ER	BB	SO
Yucatan	4.56	107	4	2	27	949	1073	521	481	365	590
Tabasco	4.90	108	3	6	22	944	1181	553	514	337	459
Saltillo	4.95	110	2	6	23	965	1109	583	531	472	685
Campeche	5.00	105	6	7	26	908	1066	577	504	361	613
Tijuana	5.36	110	2	5	25	982	1094	645	585	455	669
Monterrey	5.47	106	4	8	27	931	1018	618	564	452	609
Monclova	5.51	108	3	6	24	956	1157	645	585	389	542
Oaxaca	5.61	107	7	4	29	930	1188	639	580	371	528
Veracruz	5.66	109	5	3	22	932	1178	654	586	369	533
Mexico	5.89	107	3	4	27	942	1229	655	616	393	563
Angelopolis	5.89	107	2	3	25	923	1096	653	604	468	467
Puebla	6.07	109	1	2	21	922	1134	693	622	440	483
San Luis Potosi	6.13	108	1	2	18	942	1240	738	642	418	519
Cancun	6.20	110	3	3	22	936	1229	699	645	406	464
Aguascalientes	6.30	108	2	1	21	948	1293	718	663	400	488
Laguna	7.76	109	1	1	18	964	1346	905	831	519	671

INDIVIDUAL BATTING LEADERS

(Minimum 230 At-Bats)

	AVG	AB	R	H	2B	3B	HR	RBI	SB
Javier Robles, Angelopolis	**.392**	375	101	147	21	2	28	101	13
Jorge Vazquez, Angelopolis	.379	285	61	108	20	0	33	96	1
Willis Otanez, Veracruz	.376	402	76	151	19	1	30	**123**	2
Darryl Brinkley, San Luis Potosi	.376	380	76	143	32	2	13	79	23
Carlos Gastelum, Angelopolis	.375	440	97	**165**	26	4	6	44	21
Felix Jose, Oaxaca	.375	365	87	137	19	0	30	113	3
Derrick White, Tijuana	.370	427	92	158	29	0	26	97	3
Jayson Bass, Saltillo	.370	392	80	145	15	1	23	91	2
Sharnol Adriana, San Luis Potosi	.368	437	**105**	161	35	3	25	77	32
Willie Romero, Yucatan	.366	399	65	146	29	3	19	89	13
Randall Simon, Tijuana	.365	271	52	99	17	0	19	71	2
Rontrez Johnson, Aguascalientes	.363	377	96	137	24	4	10	61	39
Guillermo Velasquez, Angelopolis	.362	304	54	110	19	0	17	76	0
Mario Valenzuela, Saltillo	.360	367	75	132	17	1	31	103	1
Matias Carrillo, Angelopolis	.360	356	93	128	23	5	23	92	11
Christian Quintero, Oaxaca	.359	423	90	152	23	9	12	76	22
Carlos Sievers, Tabasco	.357	378	81	135	25	2	17	96	13
Carlos Villalobos, SLP/Puebla	.355	409	85	145	**39**	1	19	97	6
Luis Garcia, Veracruz	.353	363	64	128	16	0	17	63	5
Ramon Espinosa, Laguna	.352	290	50	102	27	0	9	36	7
Cornelio Garcia, Laguna	.348	394	71	137	33	4	12	63	2
Luis Borges, Yucatan	.348	279	38	97	11	5	0	29	2
Roberto Vizcarra, Campeche	.347	401	73	139	26	0	13	67	3
Grimaldo Martinez, Aguascalientes	.346	376	60	130	26	2	6	62	3
Ruben Rivera, Campeche	.342	298	70	102	16	2	21	71	14
Robert Saucedo, Mexico	.340	403	96	137	19	0	**35**	114	1
Jose Amado, Cancun	.340	329	45	112	21	0	8	68	6
Amaury Garcia, Veracruz	.338	408	87	138	21	3	7	44	14
Darrell Sherman, Puebla	.337	288	70	97	13	6	2	30	13
Jose Munoz, Saltillo	.337	285	64	96	16	1	9	39	7
Rudy Pemberton, Laguna/Cancun	.337	270	50	91	14	0	11	43	0
Roberto Mendez, Mexico	.336	366	81	123	21	3	19	66	3
Alex Delgado, Aguascalientes	.336	327	57	110	29	1	9	47	0
Gonzalo Meza, Monclova	.335	251	47	84	13	1	11	39	2
Edgar Quintero, Monterrey	.334	311	61	104	19	0	19	70	10
Luis Suarez, Angelopolis	.334	293	56	98	15	4	17	68	5
Flavio Romero, Campeche	.333	378	96	126	20	0	19	51	27
Abel Martinez, Laguna	.333	366	56	122	17	1	11	62	16
Angel Pena, Oaxaca	.333	351	60	117	15	1	25	97	2
Lorenzo Buelna, Puebla	.332	404	73	134	28	6	13	69	10
Pedro Castellano, Yucatan	.332	373	71	124	19	0	19	78	1
Demond Smith, Monterrey	.332	325	61	108	20	7	9	37	23
Raul Lopez, Laguna/Veracruz	.331	359	57	119	26	3	13	72	1
Jaime Brena, Oaxaca	.331	366	73	121	29	2	2	55	10
Liu Rodriguez, Cancun	.331	317	52	105	17	3	11	53	8
Manny Martinez, Puebla	.329	401	74	132	27	2	22	83	18
Luis Figueroa, Tijuana	.328	411	65	135	27	1	9	49	6
Eddy Diaz, Yucatan	.327	391	54	128	21	1	14	66	4
Hector Hurtado, Puebla	.327	352	47	115	20	0	9	50	0
Ray Martinez, Mexico	.325	406	87	132	22	2	23	84	6
Chad Meyers, Oaxaca	.324	413	98	134	31	4	11	56	36
Wilfredo Arano, Tijuana	.323	269	54	87	16	1	11	43	2
Francisco Arias, Saltillo	.322	335	62	108	14	3	2	34	1
Adan Munoz, Angelopolis	.321	358	74	115	34	0	12	68	1
Luis Landaeta, Tijuana	.321	252	36	81	15	0	8	33	9
Julio Hernandez, Tijuana	.320	431	101	138	**39**	1	17	69	1
Oswaldo Morejon, Yucatan	.320	410	78	131	29	6	4	48	22
Eduardo Rios, Aguascalientes	.319	407	77	130	22	2	31	111	2
Noe Munoz, Saltillo	.319	395	81	126	26	0	9	76	1
Ricardo Saenz, Monclova	.319	354	61	113	21	0	21	85	1
Fernando Rodriguez, Monclova	.319	298	36	95	24	0	3	55	0
Ramon Orantes, Monterrey	.319	232	28	74	13	0	4	31	1
Pat O'Sullivan, San Luis Potosi	.318	412	81	131	32	3	24	95	12
Guillermo Garcia, Monclova	.318	396	83	126	23	0	29	99	0
Bill Selby, Campeche	.318	387	92	123	27	2	25	93	3
Cristhian Presichi, Saltillo	.318	292	53	93	15	3	15	61	7
Scott Bullett, Yucatan	.317	394	70	125	19	6	25	86	12
Sergio Gastelum, Angelopolis	.317	379	82	120	28	0	7	53	3
Luis Arredondo, Yucatan	.316	455	83	144	13	7	4	32	47
Ricardo Soriano, Aguascalientes	.315	286	56	90	16	1	4	33	1
Albino Contreras, Puebla	.314	350	76	110	23	7	9	54	9
Adan Amezcua, Monterrey	.313	297	44	93	23	1	5	35	2
Julio Reyes, Laguna	.313	268	37	84	12	1	10	53	1
Pedro Diaz, Monclova	.311	350	48	109	16	1	4	48	3
Manuel Velez, Mexico	.309	362	69	112	18	1	6	49	6
Jose Espinoza, Tijuana	.309	256	45	79	14	0	6	29	4
Pedro Valdes, Saltillo	.309	243	54	75	12	1	14	50	0
Leobardo Arauz, Monclova	.308	396	95	122	19	1	15	54	4
Jose Sandoval, Mexico	.308	377	64	116	32	0	16	74	2
Hector Paez, Campeche	.308	370	40	114	17	0	11	72	1
Jose Amador, Laguna	.307	433	77	133	35	1	14	68	7
Mario Santana, Tabasco	.307	293	32	90	10	0	2	38	2
Juan Camilo, Tabasco	.307	254	65	78	13	1	15	54	12
George Arias, Tijuana	.305	344	63	105	20	1	23	81	2
Lino Connell, Veracruz	.305	318	45	97	15	1	9	48	10
Noe Mata, Cancun/Agua	.305	354	65	108	22	2	11	46	18
Morgan Burkhart, Saltillo	.304	345	91	105	18	0	26	72	0
Omar Ramirez, Veracruz	.302	410	89	124	27	1	20	66	9
Luis Carlos Martinez, Puebla	.302	334	48	101	17	1	4	35	4
Emmanuel Valdez, Tijuana	.302	331	62	100	14	0	19	65	2
Hector Garanzuay, Monclova	.302	321	47	97	23	2	5	48	4
Hector Hernandez, Veracruz	.301	289	46	87	7	1	7	26	6
Jose Acuna, Cancun	.301	239	60	72	10	0	3	12	11
Pedro Iturbe, Puebla	.300	363	48	109	22	2	4	50	3
Roque Sanchez, Campeche	.299	268	39	80	14	4	8	46	2
Dionys Cesar, Monterrey	.298	426	71	127	32	1	12	66	31
Heber Gomez, Monterrey	.298	369	51	110	21	2	2	41	9
Donzell McDonald, Tabasco	.297	431	86	128	20	**10**	16	67	**53**
Victor Bojorquez, Mexico	.297	424	64	126	23	2	26	94	6
Jorge Valle, Saltillo/Cancun	.294	316	44	93	18	2	11	49	1
Saul Soto, Mexico	.292	291	48	85	24	1	9	59	1
Miguel Flores, Monterrey	.292	243	36	71	13	0	2	37	8
Hernando Arredondo, Tabasco	.291	357	43	104	22	0	14	60	1
Ivan Cervantes, Oaxaca	.290	403	65	117	23	2	3	48	7
Nicolas Garcia, Saltillo	.289	363	49	105	28	0	4	51	2
Eloy Arano, Veracruz	.289	266	25	77	3	0	0	23	10
Heriberto Salas, Laguna	.288	389	53	112	20	1	3	57	4
Juan Canizalez, Yucatan	.288	379	46	109	19	2	8	51	3
Daniel Fernandez, Mexico	.288	278	58	80	16	3	0	15	6
Sergio Contreras, Angelopolis	.287	293	49	84	16	3	11	44	8
Carlos Valencia, Tijuana	.286	486	97	139	18	4	31	86	4
Jose Perez, San Luis Potosi	.283	247	32	70	11	1	2	36	1
Domingo Castro, Monclova	.282	419	61	118	21	1	3	44	14
David Doster, San Luis Potosi	.280	404	58	113	34	1	12	59	4
Ramon Valdez, Campeche	.280	239	41	67	9	2	0	17	5
Omar Mendoza, San Luis Potosi	.279	377	75	105	35	1	7	46	4
Refugio Cervantes, Aguascalientes	.279	373	64	104	20	1	18	59	0
Charles Smith, Monterrey	.274	372	59	102	18	0	21	67	1
Omar De la Torre, Laguna	.274	234	41	64	14	2	6	34	0
Oscar Salazar, Cancun	.273	264	39	72	12	2	6	32	2
Ruben Quinones, Cancun	.272	287	25	78	13	0	5	26	0
Daniel Espino, Veracruz/Cancun	.272	235	23	64	14	0	2	31	0
Erick Rodriguez, Oaxaca	.266	241	30	64	18	0	5	28	2
Arnoldo Castro, Tabasco/Cancun	.266	349	35	93	14	0	5	42	0
Francisco Rivera, Verarcruz/Cancun	.262	244	21	64	9	1	5	33	1
Remigio Diaz, Tabasco	.261	379	49	99	14	2	3	29	1
Jose Montenegro, Oaxaca	.260	231	22	60	11	0	5	33	0
Julian Yan, Tabasco	.258	396	94	102	14	3	32	87	2
Hector Guizar, Aguascalientes	.257	284	34	73	15	0	3	37	0
Santiago Gonzalez, Veracruz	.250	248	44	62	4	0	2	17	8
Daniel Fornes, Monterrey	.246	236	30	58	3	0	6	26	3
Sergio Palafox, Cancun/Saltillo	.246	252	35	62	15	1	4	22	2
Hector Estrada, Laguna	.241	253	27	61	12	0	5	33	0
Oscar Ramirez, Campeche	.235	336	51	79	11	2	12	44	3
Edgar Vega, Monclova	.209	282	35	59	7	0	1	35	1

Other Select Players

	AVG	AB	R	H	2B	3B	HR	RBI	SB
Oscar Robles, Mexico City	.390	118	27	46	7	0	4	21	1
Kevin Flores, Angelopolis	.314	105	22	33	9	1	6	20	1
Angel Echevarria, Monclova	.313	134	21	42	4	0	6	22	0
Mario Valdez, Monterrey	.292	216	32	63	13	0	6	25	0
Eric Owens, Tijuana/Saltillo	.270	111	16	30	3	0	2	15	2
Eddie Pearson, Tijuana	.266	109	13	29	4	0	4	12	0
Ozzie Timmons, Monc./Camp.	.200	50	2	10	1	0	1	5	0
Carlos Gastelum, Yucatan	.182	44	1	8	1	0	0	2	0
Henry Rodriguez, Tabasco	.154	13	1	2	0	0	1	1	0

INDIVIDUAL PITCHING LEADERS

(Minimum 80 Innings)

	W	L	ERA	G	SV	IP	H	BB	SO
Isidro Marquez, Campeche	3	2	1.85	38	**25**	39	35	7	32
Maximo De la Rosa, Monterrey	2	5	2.42	51	**25**	52	41	14	44
Francisco Campos, Campeche	11	4	**2.84**	22	0	152	137	50	**170**
Eric Knott, Puebla	**14**	4	3.25	23	0	144	135	20	62
Rigo Beltran, Saltillo	13	4	3.40	20	0	109	114	40	83
Jesus Rios, Tabasco	8	3	3.42	21	0	124	140	32	80
Steve Bourgeois, Saltillo	8	4	3.58	19	0	101	93	48	78
Aaron Acosta, Veracruz	9	9	3.72	21	0	121	132	36	60
Alonso Beltran, Tijuana	8	6	3.76	21	0	124	112	56	118
Isabel Giron, Monterrey	6	2	3.77	18	0	103	97	36	77
Emigdio Lopez, Veracruz	8	3	3.78	20	0	112	109	25	54
Joel Vargas, Tabasco	9	5	3.81	21	0	128	149	20	58
Horacio Estrada, Oaxaca	4	4	4.04	13	0	82	108	27	54
Juan Delgadillo, Tabasco	9	5	4.09	23	0	125	137	61	52
Osvaldo Fernandez, Tabasco	7	9	4.14	23	1	130	166	32	65
Juan Palafox, Yucatan	10	5	4.30	19	0	103	110	52	45
Alfredo Aceves, Yucatan	9	8	4.32	22	0	146	155	44	101
Juan Alvarez, Campeche	8	6	4.39	22	0	107	146	31	53
Oscar Rivera, Saltillo/Yucatan	9	9	4.43	44	0	173	200	80	121
Nate Bland, Tijuana	5	2	4.62	29	5	86	91	23	66
Francisco Madero, Oaxaca	5	3	4.70	19	0	82	95	28	52
Carlos Pulido, Oaxaca	7	7	4.72	23	0	151	179	37	67
Raul Rodriguez, Moncl./Yuca.	3	10	4.72	21	0	109	132	26	46
Ignacio Montano, Agua./Cancun	8	3	4.76	19	0	115	136	38	72
Bryan Ward, Monclova	6	8	4.84	21	0	115	140	41	77
Pasqual Coco, Saltillo/Vera.	9	5	4.86	29	2	104	103	56	97
Efrain Sanchez, Campeche	8	4	5.23	24	0	105	121	44	42
Francisco Rodriguez, Oaxaca/Puebla	4	4	5.26	39	0	92	98	48	39
Edgar Perez, Cancun/Agua	7	6	5.28	20	0	119	150	49	64
Jason Jacome, Monclova/Puebla	6	6	5.31	22	0	115	143	36	66
Vinicio Gonzalez, Tabasco	6	8	5.35	33	1	109	135	45	68
Jesus Rodriguez, Monclova	6	4	5.40	26	0	98	112	41	31
Luis Rivera, Angelopolis	8	5	5.42	23	0	90	102	64	39
Eduardo Salgado, Cancun	6	11	5.48	30	0	131	175	27	69
Alejandro Armenta, Angelopolis	13	3	5.50	23	0	103	112	59	51
Pablo Ochoa, Monterrey	9	8	5.61	23	0	112	125	60	66
Abraham Elvira, Aguascalientes	3	5	5.63	19	0	94	121	48	58
Isauro Pineda, Monterrey	6	7	5.63	20	0	96	98	64	66
Francisco Cordova, Mexico	5	9	5.65	33	6	107	138	32	71
Humberto Montemayor, SL Potosi	7	7	5.65	24	0	127	167	30	81
Claudio Moreno, Mexico	10	10	5.76	25	0	141	170	56	62
Eleazar Mora, Oaxaca	7	3	5.83	32	1	93	149	23	44
Guadalupe Perez, Agua./Cancun/Vera.	5	6	5.85	32	2	84	109	35	54
Nestor Renovato, San Luis Potosi	6	2	5.86	39	2	91	112	38	32
Gabe Molina, San Luis Potosi	7	9	5.86	33	6	111	127	55	80
Angel Moreno, Veracruz	6	5	5.95	21	0	98	150	30	50
Ricardo Palma, Agua./Cancun	6	4	5.97	16	0	98	125	37	63
Roberto Ramirez, Mexico	10	8	6.12	24	0	146	206	52	63
Rudy Gonzalez, Mexico	8	7	6.19	27	0	113	156	51	89
Miguel Gonzalez, Saltillo	5	7	6.22	26	0	94	119	53	64
Ignacio Flores, Ange./Puebla/Salt./Yuca.	3	9	6.31	35	1	83	112	33	79
Edwin Hurtado, Monclova/Monterrey	8	10	6.32	25	0	110	130	61	69
Jesus Olague, Angelopolis	9	4	6.36	22	0	99	116	59	60
Jose Mercedes, Saltillo	4	6	6.67	15	0	86	121	37	57
Joel Navarro, Oaxaca/Tijuana	4	4	7.33	25	0	81	112	31	35
Martin Gomez, Laguna	4	8	7.67	22	0	113	181	47	59
Leonardo Gonzalez, Tijuana	8	7	7.79	23	0	106	146	60	84

Other Select Players

	W	L	ERA	G	SV	IP	H	BB	SO
Winston Abreu, Oaxaca	4	0	1.35	18	10	20	10	5	32
Andy Shibilo, Tijuana	1	0	2.60	13	5	17	12	6	19
Bill Simas, Monclova	4	6	2.82	55	21	70	64	24	59
Eddie Oropesa, Tabasco	0	2	2.92	26	2	25	25	18	19
Nerio Rodriguez, Monclova	4	1	3.44	10	0	68	68	11	40
Mario Mendoza, Saltillo	3	3	3.55	51	2	66	70	23	44
David Manning, Campeche	6	1	3.74	33	0	53	53	26	41
Roberto Garibay, Tijuana	7	2	3.95	45	3	57	62	16	22
Danny Magee, Campeche	5	3	3.99	13	0	77	78	47	46
Bobby Chouinard, Yucatan	0	0	4.15	4	0	4	8	2	2
Sergio Lizarraga, Monterrey	2	2	4.50	8	0	34	40	15	27
Brady Raggio, Campeche	2	2	6.00	8	0	30	36	3	18
Jose Silva, Mexico	4	6	6.03	43	17	69	102	28	37
Leo Estrella, Laguna/Vera.	3	8	6.03	49	3	78	94	38	46
Jeff Sparks, Yucatan	0	0	6.75	3	0	3	2	4	4
Alex Lontayo, Oaxaca	3	4	6.79	12	0	58	71	37	36
Matthew Hammond, Tijuana	0	2	7.36	7	0	11	15	9	13
Michael Lyons, Yucatan	0	0	9.00	5	1	3	5	3	2
Adam Johnson, Puebla	1	1	9.00	5	0	21	37	7	16
Rick DeHart, Monterrey	2	2	9.68	5	0	18	23	15	14
Jake Meyer, Oaxaca	0	0	27.00	1	0	1	2	3	1

Santiago captures Cuban crown

BY PETER BJARKMAN

With defections slowing to a trickle combined with an influx of emerging new talent, Cuba reasserted its international dominance in 2005 and the Cuban Serie Nacional season proved one of the most competitive in recent years.

Cuba dominated the 36th World Cup, the major event on the international baseball schedule.

CUBA

The Cubans ran the table at the 16-team event, winning 11 straight games. Cuba also won gold at the World Youth championship.

Domestically, a three-year championship run by Havana's Industriales came to an abrupt end when the island's fan favorites were eliminated by Sancti Spíritus in the opening playoff round, despite posting the most regular-season victories. In the end, Santiago de Cuba, managed by Cuban career hits leader Antonio Pacheco, rolled over upstart Habana Province during the six-game championship finale.

The top story of the season was the bid by national team outfielder Osmani Urrutia of Las Tunas to continue one remarkable streak while working on another. Urrutia lost his bid for a fifth straight .400-plus season but did win his fifth straight batting title in the 90-game National Series.

Urrutia teammate Joan Carlos Pedroso (27) captured the league home run crown, edging Santiago slugger Eriel Sánchez (25) and Yulieski Gourriel (23) of Sancti Spíritus.

Osmani Urrutia

Sánchez was tops in RBIs (87), while Gourriel paced the circuit in both hits (126) and runs scored (80).

On the pitching front, Industriales right-hander Yadel Marti was the most effective starter (11-2) while Pinar del Río righty Yulieski Maya posted the stingiest ERA (1.61). Granma veteran Ciro Silvino Licea resurrected a faltering career by leading the league in wins (13). Emerging Sancti Spíritus bullpen ace Dany González was the saves leader (17).

The short-season Super League, which follows Serie Nacional, once again proved a failure with Cuban fans, who have difficulty identifying with all-star teams lacking the usual provincial affiliations. Yet the second season continues to be played—2005 was the fourth edition—as an integral part of the selection process to name a national team roster for summer international tournaments. Occidentales took the team title by sweeping Centrales in a two-game finale, though Centrales (16-10) posted the best month-long pre-playoff record.

June's Super League also provided some top individual offensive performances with Roger Poll (.437), Urrutia (.419) and Loidel Chapelli (.404) all batting over .400 for the 26-game schedule. Gourriel led in slugging (.837) and RBIs (40) but was edged by Pedroso in the home run chase (17 to 15). Rudy Reyes, who played for Industriales during the Serie Nacional, hit .351 and gave signs of emerging as a future Cuban star.

STANDINGS

WEST

GROUP A	W	L	PCT	GB
Pinar del Río	55	34	.618	—
Isla de la Juventud	42	48	.467	13½
Metropolitanos	33	57	.367	22½
Matanzas	28	61	.633	27
GROUP B	**W**	**L**	**PCT**	**GB**
Industriales	59	30	.656	—
Habana Province	54	35	.600	5
Sancti Spíritus	54	36	.600	5½
Cienfuegos	31	59	.344	28½

EAST

GROUP C	W	L	PCT	GB
Ciego de Ávila	54	36	.600	—
Villa Clara	51	39	.567	3
Las Tunas	47	43	.522	7
Camagüey	35	55	.389	19
GROUP D	**W**	**L**	**PCT**	**GB**
Santiago de Cuba	55	35	.611	—
Granma	50	40	.556	5
Holguín	37	53	.411	18
Guantánamo	33	57	.367	22

PLAYOFFS—Quarterfinals: Santiago defeated Granma 3-0; Villa Clara defeated Ciego de Ávila 3-0; Habana Province defeated Pinar del Río 3-1; Sancti Spíritus defeated Industriales 3-1 in best-of-5 series. **Semifinals**: Santiago defeated Villa Clara 4-0 and Habana Province defeated Sancti Spíritus 4-2 in best-of-7 series. **Final**: Santiago defeated Habana Province 4-2 in best-of-7 series.

INDIVIDUAL BATTING LEADERS

(Minimum 243 Plate Appearances)

	AVG	AB	R	H	2B	3B	HR	RBI
Urrutia, Osmani, Las Tunas	.385	291	47	112	23	1	16	60
Urgelles, Yohandry, Industriales	.360	339	78	122	23	1	14	64
Meriño, Rolando, Santiago	.356	320	66	114	24	1	14	55
González, Luis, Habana Province	.354	328	47	116	19	2	10	47
Duvergel, Giorvis, Guantánamo	.353	329	54	116	25	1	4	28
Cepeda, Frederich, Sancti Spíritus	.352	310	76	109	18	3	13	55
Díaz, Orlis, Isla Juventud	.350	303	52	106	20	1	10	51
Zamora, Andy, Villa Clara	.346	318	67	110	10	3	5	50
Gourriel, Yulieski, Sancti Spíritus	.341	370	80	126	16	7	23	86
Ramírez, Alexei, Pinar del Río	.341	337	56	115	15	2	13	50
Chapelli, Loidel, Camagüey	.341	317	43	108	17	2	8	65
Enríquez, Michel, Isla Juventud	.339	336	66	114	30	2	10	56
Gourriel, Luis, Sancti Spíritus	.339	322	39	109	17	0	4	43
Garlobo, Yoandi, Matanzas	.332	283	55	94	20	1	11	53
Pérez, Yoanis, Isla Juventud	.332	277	43	92	15	1	3	25
Pestano, Ariel, Villa Clara	.331	311	53	103	20	0	11	72
Mayeta, Alex, Industriales	.330	321	49	106	20	1	14	68
Ramos, Alex, Isla de la Juventud	.330	315	51	104	18	4	8	47
Gómez, Yasser, Industriales	.330	309	55	102	15	0	2	37
Sánchez, Eriel, Santiago	.328	311	62	102	18	0	25	87

INDIVIDUAL PITCHING LEADERS

(Minimum 90 Innings)

	W	L	ERA	G	IP	BB	SO
Martí, Yadel, Industriales	11	2	2.00	17	117	31	79
Suárez, Deynis, Industriales	12	3	2.50	16	101	48	96
Cintra, Osmel, Santiago	10	3	2.72	20	110	24	62
Ulacia, Yolexis, Villa Clara	10	3	1.66	42	98	24	78
Lazo, Pedro Luis, Pinar del Río	13	4	2.20	19	143	30	105
Enríquez, Roidel, Villa Clara	6	2	2.94	21	101	32	69
Betancourt, Dany, Santiago	11	4	2.51	18	136	55	129
Pedroso, Yadir, Habana Province	11	4	2.47	17	113	50	90
Licor, Ramón, Sancti Spíritus	11	4	3.07	16	109	51	88
Maya, Yunieski, Pinar del Río	5	2	1.61	36	90	30	82
Borroto, Luis, Villa Clara	12	5	3.02	20	132	58	142
Romero, Ormari, Santiago	9	4	2.14	17	114	23	62
Cervantes, Osmar, Ciego de Ávila	9	4	2.51	16	97	29	70
García, Valeri, Ciego de Ávila	11	5	2.59	20	136	37	112
Licea, Ciro Silvino, Granma	13	6	3.15	20	149	19	92
Vega, Manuel, Granma	10	5	2.38	17	121	37	91
Molina, Yoendris, Las Tunas	8	4	3.48	30	119	27	45
Peña, Angel, Sancti Spíritus	8	4	3.76	20	108	34	59
Díaz, Maicel, Industriales	8	4	2.27	17	107	37	79
Pino, Michel, Ciego de Ávila	8	4	3.56	18	99	28	46

ASIA

Valentine win highlights season

BY WAYNE GRACZYK

The 2005 season saw a number of firsts in Japanese professional baseball: an expansion team joined the system, interleague play was introduced and Bobby Valentine became the first foreign manager to win a Pacific League pennant and Japan Series title when he took the Chiba Lotte Marines to that franchise's first championship in 31 years.

JAPAN

Valentine guided the Marines to an overall second-place finish in the six-team league but mowed down the third-place Seibu Lions in the best-of-three Stage One of the PL playoffs, then vaulted over the regular-season champion Fukuoka SoftBank Hawks in a best-of-five Stage Two, earning the right to meet the Central League pennant-winning Hanshin Tigers in the 56th Japan Series.

Lotte made quick work of the popular Hanshin club, sweeping the Series in one-sided fashion by winning the first three games, 10-1, 10-0 and 10-1 before finishing off the Tigers with a 3-2 win in Game Four. The Marines also posted the best record in Japan's first interleague season during which each of the 12 Japanese teams played clubs in the opposite league in a 36-game portion of the schedule that ran from early May to mid-June.

Helping the Marines were foreign position players Matt Franco, Benny Agbayani (both of whom played for Valentine with the New York Mets), Val Pascucci, Korean Lee Seung Yeop and lefthander Dan Serafini.

Japanese baseball also saw the formation of the country's first baseball expansion team in more than 50 years. The Tohoku Rakuten Golden Eagles joined the Pacific League as a replacement entry for a club lost in the merger of two teams based in western Japan's Kansai region, the Osaka Kintetsu Buffaloes and Orix Blue Wave of Kobe.

Rakuten set up its franchise base in the city of Sendai, in northern Japan's Tohoku district, about two hours by bullet train from Tokyo. The merged team, known as the Orix Buffaloes, split its home games between Osaka Dome and Skymark Airlines Stadium in Kobe. As an expansion club, Rakuten was easily the worst team in the league, finishing with a 38-97-1 record (.281 winning percentage), 51½ games behind Fukuoka.

A total of 65 foreigners played in Japan in 2005 and, while none of them won major individual titles, there were some standouts. Panamanian slugger Julio Zuleta, first baseman for Fukuoka, was runner-up in all three triple crown categories in the Pacific League.

Zuleta posted a .319 batting average, second to Seibu's Kazuhiro Wada, whose .322 mark led the PL. Zuleta's 43 home runs and 99 RBIs ranked No. 2 behind SoftBank teammate Nobuhiko Matsunaka, the 2004 MVP who hit 46 homers and had 121 RBIs in 2005.

The surprise foreign player of the year was righthanded relief pitcher Marc Kroon, signed by the Yokohama BayStars as a set-up man for Kazuhiro Sasaki, the former Seattle Mariners closer. When Sasaki was injured in May (and eventually retired), Kroon assumed the closer's role and responded with 26 saves, helping the BayStars to a third place finish in the Central League after three straight years in the cellar.

Lee Sung Yeop

Kroon also set a Japanese baseball record for throwing the fastest pitch recorded in a game in Japan, clocked at 161 kilometers per hour (100.625 mph).

SoftBank southpaw pitcher Toshiya Sugiuchi was named the Pacific League MVP after posting a record of 18-4 with a league-best 2.11 ERA. Hanshin outfielder Tomoaki Kanemoto took the Central League MVP prize with a .327-40-125 season.

Lotte righthander Yasutomo Kubo (10-3, 3.40) was named the PL Rookie of the Year award and Yakult outfielder Norichika Aoki was a landslide winner in voting for the Central League's top first-year player. Aoki led both leagues with a .344 average and became the first player in the history of the Central Division to reach 200 hits in a season. He finished with 202.

Valentine, who also managed Chiba Lotte in 1995, was awarded the 2005 Matsutaro Shoriki Award for outstanding contributions to the development of Japanese baseball. He was one of two American managers in Japan in 2005; Trey Hillman completed his third season as manager of the Hokkaido Nippon Ham Fighters who finished fifth in the Pacific League.

Hillman will return for a fourth year at the helm of the Fighters, and one Central League club also hired an American to manage in 2006. Marty Brown, former Hiroshima Carp player and manager of the Buffalo Bisons, Cleveland's Triple-A team, will be the field boss of the Carp.

CENTRAL LEAGUE

STANDINGS

	W	L	T	PCT	GB
Hanshin Tigers	87	54	5	.617	—
Chunichi Dragons	79	66	1	.545	10
Yokohama BayStars	69	70	7	.496	17
Yakult Swallows	71	73	2	.493	17½
Yomiuri Giants	62	80	4	.437	25½
Hiroshima Carp	58	84	4	.408	29½

INDIVIDUAL BATTING LEADERS

(Minimum 452 Plate Appearances)

	AVG	AB	R	H	2B	3B	HR	RBI	SB
Aoki, Norichika, Swallows	.344	588	100	202	26	4	3	28	29
Fukudome, Kosuke, Dragons	.328	515	102	169	39	6	28	103	13
Kanemoto, Tomoaki, Tigers	.327	559	120	183	35	3	40	125	3
Kinjo, Tatsuhiko, BayStars	.324	590	70	191	30	1	12	87	1
Ibata, Hirozaku, Dragons	.323	560	87	181	22	5	6	63	22
Iwamura, Akinori, Swallows	.319	548	83	175	31	4	30	102	6
Maeda, Tomonori, Carp	.319	540	77	172	25	1	32	87	1
Akahoshi, Norihiro, Tigers	.316	601	119	190	15	9	1	38	60
Taneda, Hitoshi, BayStars	.310	529	66	164	24	1	9	61	7
Woods, Tyrone, Dragons	.306	506	92	155	20	0	38	103	3
Ogata, Koichi, Carp	.306	431	60	132	22	2	21	57	3
Arai, Takahiro, Carp	.305	541	91	165	30	1	43	94	3
Tamura, Hitoshi, BayStars	.304	450	71	137	26	2	31	79	2
Nioka, Tomohiro, Giants	.301	539	64	162	25	0	16	58	3
Abe, Shinnosuke, Giants	.300	476	56	143	16	0	26	86	0
Shimizu, Takayuki, Giants	.300	490	76	147	24	3	15	50	4
Araki, Masahiro, Dragons	.291	623	88	181	22	3	2	41	42
Sheets, Andy, Tigers	.289	560	98	162	38	1	19	85	1
Shima, Shigenobu, Carp	.288	560	77	161	23	0	27	77	4
Ramirez, Alex, Swallows	.282	596	70	168	19	1	32	104	5
Kokubo, Hiroki, Giants	.281	524	77	147	25	0	34	87	1
Imaoka, Makoto, Tigers	.279	559	71	156	26	2	29	147	1
Toritani, Takashi, Tigers	.278	572	82	159	27	1	9	52	5
Saeki, Takahiro, BayStars	.272	578	74	157	28	2	19	88	5
Yano, Akihiro, Tigers	.271	499	53	135	26	0	19	71	1
Ochoa, Alex, Dragons	.269	524	59	141	24	0	18	78	2
Nishi, Toshihisa, Giants	.269	484	50	130	13	0	11	45	5
Miyamoto, Shinya, Swallows	.265	547	71	145	19	2	7	47	5
Aikawa, Ryoji, BayStars	.259	498	38	129	20	0	8	46	0
Ishii, Takuro, BayStars	.255	612	95	156	22	2	8	40	18
Tatsunami, Kazuyoshi, Dragons	.253	501	57	127	25	1	9	56	2
Murata, Shuichi, BayStars	.252	477	60	120	32	2	24	82	1
Koike, Masaki, BayStars	.243	404	66	98	16	0	20	53	0
Tanishige, Motonobu, Dragons	.234	449	58	105	22	0	14	65	3

Remaining U.S. and Latin Players

	AVG	AB	R	H	2B	3B	HR	RBI	SB
Riggs, Adam, Swallows	.306	310	49	95	25	1	14	44	4
LaRocca, Greg, Carp	.303	267	40	81	12	1	18	56	0
Spencer, Shane, Tigers	.243	276	27	67	16	0	9	33	0
Rhodes, Tuffy, Giants	.240	379	54	91	9	0	27	70	2
Franco, Esterlin, Carp	.229	48	0	11	2	0	0	1	0
Witt, Kevin, BayStars	.172	64	4	11	1	1	4	7	0
Kapler, Gabe, Giants	.153	111	11	17	1	1	3	6	2

INDIVIDUAL PITCHING LEADERS

(Minimum 146 Innings)

	W	L	ERA	G	SV	IP	H	BB	SO
Miura, Daisuke, BayStars	12	9	2.52	28	0	215	168	52	177
Kuroda, Hiroki, Carp	15	12	3.17	29	0	213	183	42	165
Uehara, Koji, Giants	9	12	3.31	27	0	187	164	22	145
Kadokura, Ken, BayStars	11	8	3.37	29	0	198	175	76	177
Ando, Yuya, Tigers	11	5	3.39	24	0	146	142	25	119
Fujii, Shugo, Swallows	10	12	3.43	28	0	176	156	64	143
Fukuhara, Shinobu, Tigers	8	14	3.51	28	0	172	172	45	124
Kawakami, Kenshin, Dragons	11	8	3.74	25	0	180	186	28	138
Doi, Yoshihiro, BayStars	10	11	3.83	26	0	165	160	30	106
Igawa, Kei, Tigers	13	9	3.86	27	0	172	199	60	145
Tateyama, Shohei, Swallows	10	6	3.95	25	0	150	151	28	105
Takahashi, Hisanori, Giants	8	12	4.47	27	0	163	171	48	135
Ishikawa, Masanori, Swallows	10	8	4.87	26	0	150	180	24	105
Otake, Kan, Carp	10	12	5.62	28	0	162	171	87	161

Remaining U.S., Australian and Latin Players

	W	L	ERA	G	SV	IP	H	BB	SO
Williams, Jeff, Tigers	3	3	2.11	75	0	77	58	24	90
Kroon, Marc, BayStars	3	2	2.70	55	26	53	42	23	61
Davey, Tom, Carp	6	6	2.98	18	0	115	109	42	76
Bale, John, Carp	2	1	3.19	51	24	54	44	16	72
Sikorski, Brian, Giants	7	1	3.29	70	0	88	75	33	100
Martinez, Luis, Dragons	8	4	3.38	18	0	109	109	28	88
Bowers, Cedrick, BayStars	7	5	3.83	18	0	113	104	66	96
Guttormson, Rick, Swallows	8	5	4.18	16	0	97	102	30	62
Holtz, Mike, BayStars	0	1	4.38	44	0	25	26	10	22
Romano, Mike, Carp	5	4	4.54	27	0	73	65	36	48
Guzman, Domingo, Dragons	1	2	4.85	3	0	13	12	9	16
Rayborn, Kenny, Carp	3	5	5.06	11	0	64	64	38	41
Gonzalez, Dicky, Swallows	4	6	5.07	27	0	82	101	14	44
Brown, Jamie, Tigers	4	1	5.18	11	0	33	44	11	24
Cubillan, Darwin, Tigers	0	1	5.91	4	0	11	11	3	12
Mullen, Scott, Giants	6	8	6.22	22	0	94	118	29	80
Feliciano, Juan, Carp	0	2	6.94	5	0	12	17	9	11
Miadich, Bart, Giants	0	0	7.17	15	0	21	22	14	29
Miceli, Dan, Giants	0	2	23.63	4	0	3	9	2	3

PACIFIC LEAGUE

STANDINGS

	W	L	T	PCT	GB
Fukuoka SoftBank Hawks	89	45	2	.664	—
Chiba Lotte Marines	84	49	3	.632	4½
Seibu Lions	67	69	0	.493	23
Orix Buffaloes	62	70	4	.470	26
Hokkaido Nippon Ham Fighters	62	71	3	.466	26½
Tohoku Rakuten Golden Eagles	38	97	1	.281	51½

PLAYOFFS: Semifinals—Chiba Lotte defeated Seibu 2-0 in best-of-3 series. **Final**—Chiba Lotte defeated Fukuoka SoftBank 3-2 in best-of-5 series for league championship.

INDIVIDUAL BATTING LEADERS

(Minimum 421 Plate Appearances)

	AVG	AB	R	H	2B	3B	HR	RBI	SB
Wada, Kazuhiro, Lions	.322	475	80	153	32	3	27	69	3
Zuleta, Julio, Hawks	.319	461	80	147	20	1	43	99	0
Matsunaga, Nobuhiko, Hawks	.315	483	109	152	26	2	46	121	2
Ishii, Yoshihito, Lions	.312	414	48	129	25	3	6	38	7
Miyaji, Katsuhiko, Hawks	.311	409	46	127	22	1	3	36	1
Imae, Toshiaki, Marines	.310	461	58	143	35	3	8	71	4
Jojima, Kenji, Hawks	.309	411	70	127	22	4	24	57	3
Hori, Koichi, Marines	.305	380	50	116	16	0	7	46	2
Franco, Matt, Marines	.300	464	73	139	28	0	21	78	2
Cabrera, Alex, Lions	.300	444	78	133	28	0	36	92	1
Fukuura, Kazuya, Marines	.300	434	54	130	25	1	6	72	0
Cabrera, Jolbert, Hawks	.297	454	53	135	23	1	8	58	3
Fernandez, Jose, Lions	.293	420	60	123	26	1	26	84	5
Seguignol, Fernando, Fighters	.288	489	72	141	20	0	31	86	1
Hirano, Keiichi, Buffaloes	.285	397	44	113	5	4	3	33	6
Ogasawara, Michihiro, Fighters	.282	514	91	145	27	2	37	92	2
Yoshioka, Yuji, Eagles	.282	387	46	109	23	0	10	52	0
Kimoto, Kuniyuki, Fighters	.281	513	74	144	16	4	18	73	4
Nakajima, Hiroyuki, Lions	.274	405	56	111	21	2	11	60	11
Akada, Shogo, Lions	.272	427	56	116	19	3	3	24	20
Kawasaki, Munenori, Hawks	.271	399	53	108	12	3	4	36	21
Inaba, Atsunori, Fighters	.270	414	55	112	28	4	15	54	3
Omura, Naoyuki, Hawks	.270	529	68	143	21	3	8	48	31
Nishioka, Tsuyoshi, Marines	.268	447	80	120	22	11	4	48	41
Yamasaki, Takeshi, Eagles	.266	383	51	102	22	1	25	65	0
Isobe, Koichi, Eagles	.264	484	65	128	22	2	16	51	2
Brumbaugh, Cliff, Buffaloes	.263	448	50	118	20	0	19	57	0
Batista, Tony, Hawks	.263	559	78	147	29	1	27	90	3
Lee, Seung Yeop, Marines	.260	408	64	106	25	2	30	82	5

Remaining U.S. and Latin Players

	AVG	AB	R	H	2B	3B	HR	RBI	SB
Garcia, Karim, Buffaloes	.307	362	63	111	14	2	21	60	3
Pascucci, Val, Marines	.284	102	21	29	3	0	8	20	1
Agbayani, Benny, Marines	.271	351	49	95	22	0	13	71	1
Lopez, Luis, Eagles	.223	336	29	75	16	1	12	49	0
Obando, Sherman, Fighters	.218	55	4	12	1	0	3	7	0
Simon, Randall, Buffaloes	.213	47	3	10	0	0	0	2	0
Tracy, Andy, Eagles	.209	172	22	36	6	1	6	15	0
Minor, Damon, Eagles	.200	20	2	4	1	0	0	2	0
Almonte, Erick, Fighters	.193	88	14	17	2	0	3	8	2

INDIVIDUAL PITCHING LEADERS

(Minimum 136 Innings)

	W	L	ERA	G	SV	IP	H	BB	SO
Sugiuchi, Toshiya, Hawks	18	4	2.11	26	0	197	150	43	218
Watanabe, Shunsuke, Marines	15	4	2.17	23	0	187	152	27	101
Matsuzaka, Daisuke, Lions	14	13	2.30	28	0	215	172	49	226
Nishiguchi, Fumiya, Lions	17	5	2.77	25	0	172	157	34	137
Serafini, Dan, Marines	11	4	2.91	27	0	151	137	56	117
Saito, Kazumi, Hawks	16	1	2.92	22	0	157	135	41	129
Wada, Tsuyoshi, Hawks	12	8	3.27	25	0	182	154	57	167
Kobayashi, Hiroyuki, Marines	12	6	3.30	23	0	161	157	28	129
Iriki, Yusaku, Fighters	6	7	3.35	28	0	151	147	65	122
Powell, Jeremy, Buffaloes	14	12	3.51	28	0	200	201	55	160
Kanemura, Satoru, Fighters	13	10	3.62	25	0	174	186	54	96
Shimizu, Naoyuki, Marines	10	11	3.83	23	0	164	170	37	99
Hoashi, Kazuyuki, Lions	13	8	4.03	26	0	159	179	31	121

Remaining U.S., Australian and Latin Players

	W	L	ERA	G	SV	IP	H	BB	SO
Lee, Corey, Fighters	3	4	3.42	9	0	55	51	18	29
Feliciano, Pedro, Hawks	3	2	3.89	37	0	37	30	13	36
Parra, Jose, Buffaloes	4	2	4.09	8	0	33	38	9	20
Thomas, Brad	1	5	4.66	38	0	48	54	39	51
Beirne, Kevin, Buffaloes	4	13	4.69	22	0	109	117	47	70
Skrmetta, Matt, Eagles	1	0	6.14	5	0	7	7	4	6
Rath, Gary, Eagles	3	9	6.33	23	0	91	118	28	57
Hodges, Kevin, Eagles	2	12	6.44	18	0	95	116	51	42
Mirabal, Carlos, Fighters	0	3	7.71	3	0	16	22	8	10
Stewart, Josh, Buffaloes	0	4	8.10	7	0	33	46	14	14
Knight, Brandon, Fighters	0	2	11.12	8	0	11	20	7	14
Myette, Aaron, Eagles	0	0	20.77	3	0	4	8	3	3
Wright, Chris, Lions	0	1	40.50	2	0	1	6	2	0

Beijing wins third straight title

The fledgling China Baseball League continued to grow in 2005, as the league added a pair of expansion clubs. But when the playoffs rolled around, a familiar name was once again on top.

The Beijing Tigers won their third straight CBL title, besting the Tianjin Lions in the playoffs for the third straight year.

CHINA

While baseball is still very much a fringe sport in China, it has plenty of state support as the country gets ready to host the 2008 Summer Olympics.

That emphasis is paying off in increased interest, and, more significantly, in increased talent. While Beijing still had the majority of the league's talent, the league's overall talent is improving. The league added the Sichuan Dragons and Hopestars for the 2005 season, expanding the league to six teams.

Shanghai shortstop Zhang Yu Feng had a breakout season, hitting .397-3-31, while Beijing ace Wang Nan was equally dominant on the mound, as he struck out 34 and walked only three in 43 innings.

A team filled with CBL players and managed by ex-major league manager Jim Lefebvre and coached by former major league pitcher Bruce Hurst struggled to a 3-5 record at the Baseball World Cup in the Netherlands, but the team did give Cuba a scare before losing 12-8.

STANDINGS

	W	L	PCT	GB
Beijing Tigers	22	7	.759	—
Tianjin Lions	20	10	.667	2½
Guandong Leopards	19	11	.633	3½
Shanghai Eagles	16	13	.552	6
Sichuan Dragons	8	22	.267	15½
Hopestars	4	26	.133	18½

PLAYOFFS—China defeated Tianjin 2-0 in best-of-3 series.

INDIVIDUAL BATTING LEADERS

(Minimum 90 At-Bats)

	AVG	AB	R	H	2B	3B	HR	RBI	SB
Zhang Yu Feng, Shanghai	.397	121	36	43	6	4	3	31	15
Liu Guang Bio, Guangdong	.370	108	35	40	7	3	0	14	16
Zai Wei Feng, Shanghai	.356	104	19	37	14	1	1	17	1
Ling Feng Jiang	.356	90	14	32	3	1	0	9	19
Feng Fei, Sichuan	.343	108	16	39	5	5	0	11	14
Chen Zhe Li, Beijing	.337	98	20	33	9	1	0	15	4
Luo Yubin, Tianjin	.336	113	19	38	7	0	0	15	5
Yang Guogang, Tianjin	.323	96	23	31	7	0	2	21	2
Xiong Jian, Hopestars	.311	103	6	32	2	2	0	8	0
Lin Shen, Shanghai	.300	110	17	33	5	0	0	10	1

INDIVIDUAL PITCHING LEADERS

(Minimum 30 innings)

	W	L	ERA	IP	HR	BB	SO	AVG
Wang Nan, Beijing	4	1	0.62	43	0	3	34	.162
Su Changlong, Tianjin	4	0	0.74	49	0	10	35	.179
Zhou Jing, Beijing	7	0	1.73	42	9	12	34	.154
Lv Jiangang, Tianjin	6	1	1.79	70	1	15	51	.195
Lai Guoyun, Guangdong	6	4	1.89	81	0	29	55	.240
Ventuna, Guangdong	4	1	1.95	51	0	9	36	.262
Li Wei Liang, Beijing	2	1	1.98	36	1	5	26	.250

Sinon sails to second straight title

BY JEFFREY WILSON

In 2006, Taiwan will have its own Bulls looking for a three-peat.

The Sinon Bulls charged to the second-half season title and then swept the Macoto Cobras in four games to take their second consecutive Taiwan Series in 2005.

The Bulls relied on a veteran battery of a local and an import to take the title. Right-hander Len Picota starred in both Games One and Four, yielding one run in eight innings in the opener and holding the Cobras to only a single run over six innings for the win in the finale. Picota, who first came to Taiwan in 1994, led the league with 16 wins.

TAIWAN

Bulls catcher Yeh Jung-chang, playing in his seventh Taiwan Series, earned Series MVP honors for collecting six hits and a pair of RBIs in Game Four.

The Cobras were never at full strength during the Series, as they tried to overcome a tragic loss. Former Cubs and Rockies outfielder Mario Encarnacion was found dead in the team dormitory in early October. The cause of death for the league's second-leading home run hitter was not established. Earlier in the season, he had been suspended for two weeks for failing a steroids test. Macoto was also without the services of former Red Sox third baseman Wilton Veras, who sat out the Series following the death of his teammate.

The Cobras were led to the first-half season title by 24-year-old rookie Lin En-yu, who won the league in ERA title (1.72) while picking up 12 wins and mostly likely the attention of some overseas scouts.

Former Padres and Red Sox pitcher Dario Veras of China Trust paced the league with 24 saves.

STANDINGS

FIRST HALF	W	L	T	PCT	GB
Macoto Cobras	29	20	2	.592	—
Sinon Bulls	28	21	2	.571	1
Brother Elephants	25	23	2	.521	3½
China Trust Whales	24	24	2	.500	4
President Lions	24	26	0	.480	5½
La New Bears	16	32	2	.333	12½

SECOND HALF	W	L	T	PCT	GB
Sinon Bulls	25	21	4	.543	—
La New Bears	26	23	1	.531	½
President Lions	24	23	1	.511	1½
China Trust Whales	23	25	2	.479	3
Macoto Cobras	21	23	6	.477	3
Brother Elephants	22	26	2	.458	4

PLAYOFFS—Sinon defeated Macoto 4-0 in best-of-7 series.

INDIVIDUAL BATTING LEADERS

	AVG	AB	H	2B	3B	HR	RBI	SB
Peng Cheng-wen, Brother	.339	274	93	8	3	14	47	5
Rodriguez, Victor, La New	.324	299	97	21	0	12	50	1
Chen Huai-shan, Brother	.324	287	93	15	4	8	47	3
Veras, Wilton, Macoto	.324	355	115	18	0	8	51	0
Kao Kuo-ching, President	.313	358	112	26	0	5	52	3
Chen Yun-hung, President	.308	305	94	18	0	5	26	1
Pan Chung-wei, La New	.307	335	103	18	0	12	59	1
Huang Lung-yi, La New	.306	366	112	12	6	8	37	16
Tseng Hua-wei, Sinon	.305	308	94	18	6	3	52	4
Chang Tai-shan, Sinon	.305	348	106	12	0	15	60	3

Other Foreign Players

	AVG	AB	H	2B	3B	HR	RBI	SB
Brinkley, Darryl, President	.323	130	42	11	0	6	30	4
Alscantara, Israel, President	.322	146	47	8	0	15	38	2
Peterson, Charles, China Trust	.321	53	17	3	0	1	6	0
Cesar, Dionys, China Trust	.307	114	35	3	2	1	12	9
Encarnacion, Mario, Macoto	.307	225	43	10	0	17	45	1
Rios, Eduardo, La New	.293	99	29	5	0	4	8	0
Castro, Nelson, China Trust	.250	108	27	9	0	2	16	6

INDIVIDUAL PITCHING LEADERS

	W	L	ERA	G	SV	IP	H	BB	SO
Lin En-yu, Macoto	12	8	1.72	31	4	167	118	35	152
Giron, Emiliano, China Trust	9	4	1.83	18	0	108	76	49	104
Picota, Len, Sinon	16	8	2.16	30	2	175	163	51	131
Lin Ying-jeh, Macotos	12	10	2.34	31	0	212	182	43	174
Hsu Wen-hsiung, La New	4	5	2.56	48	6	102	84	49	77
Wright, Chris, La New	7	8	2.74	19	1	115	111	50	72
Pan Wei-luen, President	12	8	2.79	34	0	171	181	41	130
Shen Yu-Chieh, China Trust	9	7	2.92	55	9	120	107	45	96
Hurst, Jonathan, Brother	9	9	2.98	27	0	184	150	57	145
Hsu Chu-jien, Macoto	11	7	3.18	23	0	130	119	38	111

Other Foreign Players

	W	L	ERA	G	SV	IP	H	BB	SO
Giron, Emiliano, China Trust	9	4	1.83	18	0	108	76	40	104
Veras, Dario, China Trust	7	6	2.24	53	24	76	63	9	90
Garcia, Michael, President	6	5	2.25	53	23	60	49	8	67
Ramirez, Hector, Sinon	0	1	2.76	10	3	16	15	6	7
Serrano, Wascar, China Trust	2	3	2.86	13	0	63	59	22	39
Garcia, Rafael, China Trust	2	3	2.86	7	0	44	41	21	28
Cortez, Jorge, Sinon	3	1	2.96	11	2	54	52	7	25
Alberro, Jose, President	3	3	2.96	12	0	51	43	14	34
Beech, Matt, La New	2	4	2.96	8	0	48	41	24	48
Patrick, Bronswell, Brother	5	4	2.98	11	0	57	63	9	38
Espinal, Jose, President	3	3	3.09	8	0	46	40	14	34
Ramirez, Enrique, Macoto	1	0	3.31	9	4	16	15	12	18
Wade ,Travis, La New	3	3	3.48	13	2	51	58	16	25
Woodman, Hank, Brother	5	4	3.63	13	0	74	80	31	57
Linton, Douglas, President	6	11	3.64	20	0	123	140	21	85
Manon, Julio, President	0	2	3.66	4	0	19	19	7	15
Martinez, Osvaldo, Sinon	12	7	3.72	41	7	154	142	58	131
Purcell, Brad, China Trust	2	3	3.90	6	0	27	28	14	13
Sobkowiak, Scott, China Trust	1	2	4.13	5	0	24	29	5	14
Estrella, Leo, President	1	0	4.24	4	0	17	24	10	11
Bailey, Cory, La New	3	6	4.31	10	0	56	78	24	39
Miniel, Rene, Macoto	1	3	4.50	26	11	32	34	12	26
Hosford, Clint, Sinon	1	3	4.64	16	1	42	48	24	28
Silva, Walter, La New	1	5	4.78	8	0	43	49	17	27
Nina, Elvin, La New	1	2	6.06	4	0	16	21	14	16
Guy, Brad, Sinon	1	2	6.20	5	0	20	26	4	9
Andra, Jeff, Sinon	5	4	6.61	20	2	49	64	12	31
Mangieri, John, President	0	0	7.00	8	0	9	18	3	4
Rodriguez, Nerio, La New	2	2	7.30	6	0	24	33	7	13
Vargas, Jose, La New	1	1	7.84	10	0	10	13	4	13
Padua, Geraldo, Sinon	1	0	8.76	5	1	12	13	4	7
Pickford, Kevin, Macoto	0	1	11.05	2	0	7	11	7	3

Samsung sweeps to Korean title

BY J.J. COOPER AND THOMAS ST. JOHN

As a pitcher, Sun Dong-yol was one of the greatest players in the relatively short history of the Korean Baseball Organization.

KOREA

He may end up being one of the best managers too.

Sun won three straight MVP awards as a player, eight ERA titles, led the league in wins five times, then moved to the bullpen where he led the league in saves twice. He went on to Japan where he led Japan's Central League in saves in 1999.

And as a rookie manager, Sun led the Samsung Lions to the 2005 Korean Baseball Organization title. The Lions swept the Doosan Bears in four games to easily claim the crown.

In the Korea Series, the Lions had little trouble with the Bears. Tim Harikkala threw five scoreless innings and got plenty of help from his offense as Samsung won the clinching Game Four 10-1. The Lions shut out Doosan 6-0 in Game Three behind Martin Vargas' five shutout innings. Samsung won the opener, 5-2, and Game Two, 3-2.

Samsung reliever Oh Seong-hwan was named the series MVP. He pitched seven scoreless innings during the series, striking out 11.

Sohn Min-han was named the league's MVP, marking only the eighth time in the league's 24-year history that a pitcher has won the award. The 30-year-old went 18-7, 2.46 with 105 strikeouts and 38 walks in 168 innings. He led the league in wins and ERA.

It was an exceptional comeback for Son, who has battled shoulder injuries throughout his career. Sohn was even bumped into the bullpen for Lotte for a while in 2004. He was a big reason for Lotte's improvement in 2005, as the team finished fifth after being mired in eighth for the previous four seasons.

Samsung's Oh was named the league's rookie of the year and finished second in the MVP balloting, as he broke into the league with a stellar 10-1, 1.18 season. Oh recorded 16 saves while striking out 115 and walking 20 in 99 innings.

As a manager, Sun managed to remake the Lions into a pitching-oriented team, a far cry from the Lee-Seung Yeop led teams of the early 2000s that pounded plenty of home runs. In addition to Oh, Bae Yeoung Soo was second in the league in ERA (11-11, 2.86) and led the league in strikeouts (147), and imports Martin Vargas (10-8, 5.06), Luther Hackman (3-6, 4.80) and Harikkala (3-2, 3.71).

Jay Davis of Hanwha had another one of his great seasons but the Eagles were not able to go all the way as they had expected. Mickey Galloway of Hyundai made news with his 16-9 record and teammate Larry Sutton led the league in home runs (35), RBIs (102) and slugging percentage (.592). Despite strong showings from their imports, the Unicorns were not able to make the post season at all and had a miserable season after losing two starters to Samsung in free agency.

The usual cellar dwelling Lotte Giants made huge strides and finished in fifth place. The organization then promptly fired manager Yang Sang-moon for his efforts and inability to get into the playoffs. Yang brought a new, more western style of baseball to the Giants and was very well respected by fans and players alike. Fans had returned to games, this time without the bags on their heads, and there was a revival in Pusan. He encouraged hustling and did not punish players that committed an error.

STANDINGS

	W	L	T	PCT	GB
Samsung Lions	74	48	4	.607	—
Doosan Bears	72	51	3	.585	2½
SK Wyverns	70	50	6	.583	3
Hanwha Eagles	64	61	1	.512	11½
Lotte Giants	58	67	1	.464	17½
LG Twins	54	71	1	.432	21½
Hyundai Unicorns	53	70	3	.431	21½
Kia Tigers	49	76	1	.392	26½

PLAYOFFS: First Round—Hanwha defeated SK 3-2 in best-of-5 series. **Semifinals—**Doosan defeated Hanwha 3-0 in best-of-5 series. **Finals—**Samsung defeated Doosan 4-0 in best-of-7 series.

INDIVIDUAL BATTING LEADERS

	AVG	G	AB	R	H	HR	RBI	BB	SO
Lee Byung-kyu, LG	.337	119	466	62	157	9	75	43	62
Jay Davis, Hanwha	.323	118	431	90	139	24	86	70	76
Kim Tae-kyun, Hanwha	.317	124	461	73	146	23	100	66	73
Kim Jae-hyun, SK	.315	120	400	63	126	19	77	96	59
Lee Jeong-bum, Kia	.312	118	430	69	134	6	36	58	49

Other North American Hitters

	AVG	G	AB	R	H	HR	RBI	BB	SO
Collier, Lou, LG	.303	115	403	64	122	15	61	46	85
Sutton, Larry, Hyundai	.292	119	425	76	124	35	102	90	101
Pellow, Kip, Lotte	.284	109	398	56	113	23	69	41	84
Brito, Tilson, Hanwha	.286	78	287	34	82	17	43	19	45
Jackson, Ryan, Lotte	.268	125	493	65	132	11	73	39	70
Mateo, Ruben, LG	.223	34	130	18	29	5	20	16	36
Smith, Travis, Hanwha	.220	30	100	11	22	6	19	8	25

INDIVIDUAL PITCHING LEADERS

	W	L	ERA	G	SV	IP	H	BB	SO
Sohn Min-han, Lotte	18	7	2.46	28	1	168	149	40	105
Kim Won-hyung, SK	14	8	3.41	30	0	172	172	45	94
Daniel Rios, Kia/Doosan	15	12	3.51	32	0	205	203	147	147
Mickey Galloway, Hyundai	16	9	3.97	32	0	197	206	66	103
Choi Won-ho, LG	13	6	4.07	27	0	167	153	75	106

Other North American Pitchers

	W	L	ERA	G	SV	IP	H	BB	SO
Randle, Matt, Doosan	12	7	3.25	29	0	150	163	62	111
Harikkala, Tim, Samsung	3	2	3.71	11	0	51	66	13	31
Greissinger, Seth, Kia	6	6	3.93	14	1	76	72	24	58
Blank, Matt, Kia	4	4	4.26	20	0	93	85	47	45
Smith, Chuck, Doosan	4	6	4.55	16	0	115	115	43	45
Hackman, Luther, Samsung	3	6	4.80	15	0	81	78	43	57
Warrand, Les, LG	4	10	5.04	19	1	89	85	51	68
Vargas, Martin, Samsung	10	8	5.06	26	0	128	120	70	66
Johnson, Michael, Kia	1	1	5.96	5	0	26	31	7	23

EUROPE

Bologna surges to Italian title

Led by Claudio Liverziani and Jesus Matos, Bologna won its second Italian title in three years in 2005, defeating San Marino four games to three in the best-of-seven Italy Series.

Liverziani, a first baseman, was named the series MVP after driving in 13 runs, but Matos, a former Colorado Rockies minor leaguer, may have been even more impressive. Matos threw 17 shutout innings on his way to winning Game One and Game Seven of the series. It followed up a dominant 9-3, 0.88 regular season where he led the league in ERA and strikeouts (141). Another former American minor leaguer, Todd Incantalupo, won Games Three and Six for Bologna, which rallied from a 3-2 deficit.

ITALY

Another Bologna pitcher, righty Rolando Cretis, 42, didn't win a game during the series but had the best season (10-1, 2.37) of a Serie A/1 career that started in 1979 as he added to his record for Serie A/1 wins.

Outfielder Wady Almonte was Bologna's most prominent newcomer. Almonte, who made it as high as Triple-A in the United States, hit .360-4-48 to lead the league in batting average and RBIs.

It was a fine season for San Marino, which had fared poorly in recent years and had spent some time in Serie

A/2, the second tier of Italy's relegation structure. The off-season signing of two wily Serie A/1 veterans proved to be instrumental in the club's resurgence.

Third baseman David Sheldon, 42, who made his Italian debut in 1987, hit just .235 for San Marino, almost 80 points below his career Serie A/1 average, but his 36 RBIs were fourth best in the league. Southpaw Dan Newman, who played his first Serie A/1 game in 1989, went 9-2, 2.71 in the regular season. Newman, 41, was 2-0, 0.66 with two saves in the playoffs.

The San Marino pitching staff was also bolstered by the addition of Ivan Montane (8-7, 2.33), who was 1-2 in the Italy Series despite a 1.69 ERA. San Marino scored two runs or less in six of Montane's regular season defeats.

Grosseto failed to make the playoffs after winning the Italy Series in 2004, but it did win the European Cup, defeating HCAW of the Netherlands 6-5 in 11 innings in the final of the continent's premier international club competition.

—HARVEY SAHKER

STANDINGS

	W	L	PCT	GB
Bologna	35	19	.648	—
San Marino	35	19	.648	—
Nettuno	34	20	.630	1
Rimini	33	21	.611	2
Parma	33	21	.611	2
Grosseto	30	24	.556	5
Modena	24	30	.444	11
Reggio Emilia	19	35	.352	16
Trieste	16	38	.296	19
Paterno	11	43	.204	24

PLAYOFFS—Semifinals: Bologna defeated Rimini 4-1 and San Marino defeated Nettuno 4-2 in best-of-7 series. **Final:** Bologna defeated San Marino 4-3 in best-of-7 series.

INDIVIDUAL BATTING LEADERS

	AVG	AB	H	2B	3B	HR	RBI	SB
Wady Almonte, Bologna	.360	211	76	12	3	4	48	7
Max De Biase, Tergeste	.342	161	55	12	1	4	25	4
Carlos Mendoza, San Marino	.335	185	62	11	1	2	27	7
Gizzi Jairo Ramos, Grosseto	.333	195	65	10	0	5	21	6
Claudio Liverziani, Bologna	.333	189	63	14	2	2	36	6
Orlando Munoz, Modena	.328	180	59	7	1	1	19	5
William Ortega, Nettuno	.323	164	53	15	1	4	23	4
Ettore Finetti, San Marino	.323	198	64	13	1	0	27	9
Frank Candela, Nettuno	.319	185	59	9	3	0	16	14
Robert Fontana, Parma	.318	220	70	7	4	1	22	7

INDIVIDUAL PITCHING LEADERS

	W	L	ERA	G	IP	H	BB	SO
Jesus Matos, Bologna	9	3	0.88	18	123	72	11	141
Francisco Trejo, Rimini	6	2	1.37	17	79	58	35	66
Riccardo De Santis, Grosseto	11	3	1.51	17	113	80	44	107
David Rollandini, Grosseto	8	3	1.60	16	107	96	33	75
Jose Sanchez, Nettuno	10	3	1.60	15	96	69	24	108
Julio Villalon, Reggio	4	3	1.81	18	95	85	22	82
Cipriano Ventura, Modena	10	6	2.00	18	135	109	39	110
Alvaro Montes, Parma	11	5	2.17	18	120	103	43	90
Michele Toriaco, Parma	10	3	2.29	17	110	94	27	50
Ivan Montane, San Marino	8	7	2.33	18	116	88	18	109

Seventh straight title for Neptunus

HOLLAND

Neptunus continued its domination of the Dutch Major League in 2005 by winning a record seventh straight Holland Series. Neptunus won the best-of-five affair in four games, beating HCAW for the fifth year in a row.

Southpaw Diegomar Markwell pitched 17 shutout innings in the series, winning two of the four games, including the clincher. The former American minor leaguer went the distance in Game Two and was chosen as the Holland Series MVP. Righthander Rob Cordemans started Games One and Three for Neptunus and allowed two runs (one earned) in 16 innings. The unearned run was enough for HCAW to eke out a 1-0 win in Game One.

The series featured a bench-clearing brawl in Game Three and the suspension of Ralph Milliard. The former big league infielder received an eight-month ban during the Holland Series after testing positive for a banned substance that he had been taking as medication for an injured shoulder.

Neptunus outfielder Dirk Van 't Klooster won his second DML batting title in four years. The 29-year-old Amsterdam native led the league in hits (71), runs scored (44), doubles (15) and total bases (105). He was second in homers (5) and RBIs (34).

Sparta/Feyenoord made the playoffs for the first time since 1997 but were knocked out in the semifinals by Neptunus, three games to none. The Hoofddorp Pioniers led HCAW two games to one in the other semifinal, only to lose Game Four and Game Five.

—HARVEY SAHKER

STANDINGS

	W	L	T	PCT	GB
Neptunus	31	10	1	.750	—
Hoofddorp Pioniers	28	12	2	.690	2½
HCAW	26	14	2	.643	4½
Sparta/Feyenoord	21	21	0	.500	10½
Kinheim	20	22	0	.476	11½
Hague Tornado's	14	27	1	.345	17
Amsterdam Pirates	14	27	1	.345	17
Almere '90	10	31	1	.250	21

PLAYOFFS—Semifinals: Neptunus defeated Sparta/Feyenoord 3-0 and HCAW defeated Hoofddorp 3-2 in best-of-5 series. **Final:** Neptunus defeated HCAW 3-1 in best-of-5 series.

INDIVIDUAL BATTING LEADERS

	AVG	AB	R	H	HR	RBI	BB	SO	SB
Dirk van 't Klooster, Neptunus	.403	176	44	71	5	34	14	13	4
Harvey Monte, Neptunus	.380	171	35	65	0	31	11	8	4
Brian Larmonie, Neptunus	.368	95	14	35	1	17	19	23	1
Tyson Arishenkoff, Amsterdam	.352	125	20	44	3	19	11	17	5
Raily Legito, Neptunus	.343	178	35	61	1	32	12	19	11
Tjerk Smeets, Amsterdam	.326	132	15	43	3	14	23	20	3
Mark Duursma, Hoofddorp	.322	149	24	48	0	17	29	18	0
Edwin de Graaf, Hoofddorp	.310	113	21	35	0	5	9	10	3
Sidney de Jong, HCAW	.308	143	18	44	0	21	32	13	0
Michael Duursma, Hoofddorp	.307	153	22	47	0	24	27	23	9

INDIVIDUAL PITCHING LEADERS

	W	L	ERA	G	SV	IP	H	BB	SO
Rob Cordemans, Neptunus	13	1	0.77	16	1	105	63	29	89
Michiel van Kampen, Almere	1	2	1.05	26	6	34	33	11	24
Richard Orman, Hoofddorp	13	2	1.07	15	0	118	87	12	62
David Bergman, Hoofddorp	6	4	1.44	14	0	88	66	22	63
Jimmy Summers, Hague	4	2	1.64	11	1	44	30	14	41
Maurice DeConge, HCAW	3	1	1.86	10	2	39	30	11	25
Patrick Beljaards, Kinheim	7	6	1.89	15	0	109	92	30	98
Jos de Jong, HCAW	5	4	1.90	16	0	81	65	32	30
Roger Kops, Hoofddorp	5	2	1.93	14	0	79	71	17	43
Satoru Fujii, Sparta/Feyenoord	8	7	2.02	16	0	125	91	64	112

BY ERIC EDWARDS AND BILL MITCHELL

Through the first three decades of Caribbean Series competition, Mexico was the afterthought among the four participating nations. Not anymore.

Righthander Francisco Campos turned in his second brilliant outing as Mexican Pacific League champion Mazatlan held on in its final game, edging the defending champion Dominican Republic 4-3 to win the 2005 Caribbean Series.

Mexico, playing on its home soil, won the double-elimination event with a 5-1 record, while the Dominicans finished in a tie for second at 3-3. A Dominican victory would have forced a playoff game between the two teams.

The title was just Mexico's fifth overall since joining the competition in 1970, but its second in the last four years.

"The other two times we finished second," said Mexican Pacific League president Renato Vega, pointing out that the streak coincided with his ascension to the post in 2002.

Campos (White Sox) allowed just three hits—two infield hits and a bunt single—and a run over his first eight innings of work, striking out 11. He tired in the ninth however, when he walked Luis Polonia and yielded a single to Miguel Tejada (Orioles).

He was replaced by Jose Luis Garcia and Matt Cepicky (Nationals) cut Mexico's lead to 4-2 with an RBI single. Ron Belliard (Indians) brought the Dominicans within one at 4-3 with a run-scoring single off closer Luis Ayala (Nationals), but Ayala got out of the jam with a double play and a weak ground ball, sending those fans who stayed until 2 a.m. into a jubilant celebration.

"I was pretty confident," Ayala said. "I knew I could get that final out. We believed in ourselves."

The deciding game didn't begin until close to 11 p.m. local time as rain washed out the previous day's play and forced all four teams to play doubleheaders on the final day.

Mexico broke through early against Dominican starter Francisco Pena, scoring twice in the opening inning. Trenidad Hubbard opened the game with a single and Vinny Castilla drew a walk. Derrick White then plated them with a double. Mazatlan added to its lead in the fifth on a two-run home run by Erubiel Durazo, more than enough runs for Campos to work with.

"I was completely confident that we were going to win," aaid Campos, who went 2-0, 1.13 overall with a tournament-high 23 strikeouts in 16 innings. "It was the game of my life."

The loss defused a Dominican team that had won two straight games after arriving late and losing its first two of the tournament. If the Dominicans (2-3) had beaten Mexico, a victory over Puerto Rico (1-4) in a makeup game the following day would have forced a tiebreaking game for the title with Mexico.

The Dominican team had won six of the last eight competitions and was favored to win again. But things went wrong even before the tournament began as their charter flight from Santo Domingo was overbooked and eventually canceled, forcing the Dominican team to miss its opening game with Puerto Rico, pushing it to the end of the tournament.

"Obviously we're not happy," Dominican shortstop Miguel Tejada

2005 CARIBBEAN SERIES

Mazatlan, Mexico
Feb. 1-7, 2005

ROUND-ROBIN STANDINGS	W	L	PCT	GB
Mexico	5	1	.833	—
Venezuela	3	3	.500	2
Dominican Republic	3	3	.500	2
Puerto Rico	1	5	.167	4

INDIVIDUAL BATTING LEADERS

(Minimum 16 Plate Appearances)

	AVG	AB	R	H	2B	3B	HR	RBI	SB
Cintron, Alex, PR	.500	20	3	10	1	0	0	2	1
Flores, Miguel, Mexico	.423	26	6	11	3	0	0	4	1
Belliard, Ronnie, Dom. Rep.	.417	24	4	10	2	0	1	4	0
Matos, Julius, PR.	.400	20	2	8	1	0	1	2	0
Castillo, Alberto, Dom. Rep.	.389	18	1	7	2	0	1	4	0
Romero, Alex, Venez.	.350	20	2	7	1	0	1	3	0
Fernandez, Alex, Dom. Rep.	.333	15	2	5	1	0	0	0	0
Rodriguez, Luis, Venez.	.308	26	2	8	1	0	0	3	0
Reyes, Rene, Venez.	.308	26	5	8	2	0	1	2	0
Lucca, Lou, PR	.300	20	0	6	0	0	0	3	0
Figueroa, Luis, PR	.296	27	3	8	0	0	0	1	0
Hubbard, Trenidad, Mexico	.280	25	8	7	0	0	1	2	1
White, Derrick, Mexico	.273	22	2	6	0	0	2	7	0
Torres, Andres, PR	.263	19	4	5	0	1	1	3	1
Tejada, Miguel, Dom. Rep.	.261	23	3	6	1	0	0	4	0
Furcal, Rafael, Dom. Rep.	.250	20	4	5	1	1	1	3	0
Durazo, Erubiel, Mexico	.250	20	2	5	0	0	1	5	0

INDIVIDUAL PITCHING LEADERS

(Minimum 6 Innings)

	W	L	ERA	G	SV	IP	H	BB	SO
Campillo, Jorge, Mexico	1	0	0.00	1	0	8	7	0	6
Linton, Doug, Dom. Rep.	1	0	0.00	1	0	7	4	1	8
Romero, Josmir, Venez.	0	0	0.87	2	0	10	11	1	9
Campos, Francisco, Mexico	2	0	1.13	2	0	16	6	3	23
Ortega, Pablo, Mexico	1	0	1.13	1	0	8	5	3	1
Batista, Miguel, Dom. Rep.	1	0	2.45	2	0	7	7	0	8
Done, Juan, PR	0	0	2.84	2	0	6	5	2	3
Loya, Rigoberto, Mexico	0	0	3.00	1	0	6	9	0	2
Palma, Rick, Venez.	1	0	3.00	1	0	6	5	1	7
Albaladejo, Jonathan, PR	0	1	4.05	1	0	7	8	1	2

2004-05 WINTER LEAGUE ALL-STARS

Selected by Baseball America

Pos.	Player, Team (League)	Organization	AVG	AB	H	HR	RBI	SB
C	Henry Blanco, Carolina (Venez.)	Twins	.297	249	74	10	48	0
1B	Morgan Burkhart, Navojoa (Mexico)	White Sox	.304	217	66	23	64	0
2B	Rickie Weeks, Scottsdale (AFL)	Brewers	.382	76	29	6	21	6
3B	Miguel Cabrera, Aragua (Venez.)	Marlins	.398	123	49	12	42	0
SS	Omar Quintanilla, Phoenix (AFL)	Atheltics	.374	91	34	0	18	0
OF	Jonny Gomes, Mexicali (Mexico)	Devil Rays	.341	161	55	22	52	5
OF	Juan Rivera, Oriente (Venez.)	Angels	.360	175	63	11	40	3
OF	Jason Botts, Peoria Saguaros (AFL)	Rangers	.355	107	38	6	24	0
DH	Chris Shelton, Phoenix (AFL)	Tigers	.404	114	46	6	33	3
			W-L	ERA	IP	H	BB	SO
SP	Francisco Campos, Mazatlan (Mex.)	White Sox	9-2	3.24	97	80	38	98
SP	Jonathan Albaladejo, Mayaguez (P.R.)	Pirates	8-3	2.73	69	54	12	48
SP	Yusmeiro Petit, Magallanes (Venez.)	Mets	4-3	2.15	50	43	8	53
SP	Raul Valdez, Azucareros (Dom.Rep.)	Cubs	5-2	0.79	57	34	22	47
RP	Francisco Rodriguez, La Guaira (Venez.)	Angels	0-1	2.11	34	19	13	60

Player of the Year: Jonny Gomes, Mexicali (Mexico)

said, "but we'll win it next year."

The tournament drew capacity crowds to Estadio Teodoro Mariscal in Mazatlan.

Devil Rays outfield prospect Jonny Gomes, who was added to the Mazatlan roster after hitting 17 home runs in 121 at-bats during the regular season for Mexicali, said the atmosphere during the Series was incredible.

"This is unbelievable baseball down here," Gomes said. "It's the loudest 15-20,000 fans you can get. It's just a great experience to have at such a young age."

DOMINICAN LEAGUE

STANDINGS

REGULAR SEASON	W	L	PCT	GB
Aguilas	30	19	.612	—
Gigantes	27	22	.551	3
Estrellas	26	23	.531	4
Licey	26	24	.520	4½
Escogido	22	28	.440	8½
Azucareros	17	32	.347	13
PLAYOFFS	**W**	**L**	**PCT**	**GB**
Aguilas	11	7	.611	—
Licey	10	8	.556	1
Estrellas	9	9	.500	2
Gigantes	6	12	.333	5

Championship Series: Aguilas defeated Licey 4-3 in best -of-7 series.

INDIVIDUAL BATTING LEADERS

(Minimum 70 Plate Appearances)

	AVG	AB	R	H	2B	3B	HR	RBI	SB
Perez, Neifi, Escogido	.356	90	12	32	3	1	1	12	0
Pena, Elvis, Escogido	.353	68	7	24	3	2	0	8	7
Camilo, Juan, Estrellas	**.353**	139	26	49	10	0	5	27	1
Ozuna, Pablo, Estrellas	.344	183	31	**63**	8	3	3	18	**24**
Castro, Bernie, Aguilas	.340	100	17	34	2	0	0	9	6
Belliard, Ron, Licey	.330	97	13	32	5	0	3	13	1
Almonte, Erick, Estrellas	.325	160	30	52	13	1	**7**	**38**	6
Nivar, Ramon, Escogido	.324	139	25	45	5	1	2	10	5
Guzman, Elpidio, Escogido	.323	99	14	32	3	0	0	10	4
Pena, Brayan, Gigantes	.323	127	15	41	9	0	0	6	1
Polonia, Luis, Aguilas	.321	187	**32**	60	**15**	**4**	1	17	11
Guzman, Freddy, Estrellas	.319	113	25	36	7	2	0	12	22
Otanez, Willie, Licey	.318	88	16	28	3	1	4	12	0
Cano, Robinson, Estrellas	.313	144	20	45	12	2	1	23	1
Cruz, Nelson, Gigantes	.310	87	13	27	4	0	3	19	1
Pena, Carlos, Licey	.308	91	13	28	2	2	5	14	1
Reyes, Jose, Gigantes	.302	126	16	38	5	3	1	11	11
Guzman, Joel, Estrellas	.298	114	13	34	5	1	2	12	1
Felix, Pedro, Gigantes	.290	107	15	31	7	1	4	14	0
Fernandez, Alex, Aguilas	.288	156	21	45	10	2	5	27	0
Nunez, Abraham, Estrellas	.283	138	30	39	9	1	3	28	8
Melo, Juan, Azucareros	.282	177	21	50	10	2	6	25	6
Santos, Francisco, Gigantes	.278	194	18	54	10	0	3	29	4
Pena, Angel, Gigantes	.278	151	23	42	6	1	6	25	0
Veras, Wilton, Escogido	.278	144	13	40	4	1	1	14	0
Aybar, Erick, Licey	.277	137	18	38	3	0	1	13	2
Otanez, Willis, Licey	.277	119	19	33	4	2	4	13	0
Diaz, Victor, Aguilas	.277	112	10	31	5	0	5	10	1
Allen, Luke, Licey	.273	154	10	42	6	1	3	19	1
German, Esteban, Azucareros	.269	175	23	47	9	1	0	9	15
Encarnacion, Edwin, Aguilas	.266	158	24	42	9	0	4	18	5
Terrero, Luis, Azucareros	.263	133	16	35	7	**4**	2	8	7
Mendez, Victor, Gigantes	.261	69	12	18	6	1	1	10	0
Luna, Hector, Aguilas	.261	69	12	18	2	0	0	3	4
Marte, Andy, Azucareros	.259	143	11	37	7	0	5	25	1
Garabito, Eddy, Azucareros	.258	178	24	46	6	1	1	12	14
Gomez, Alexis, Aguilas	.258	93	13	24	5	0	3	12	1
Myrow, Brian, Escogido	.257	148	27	38	10	1	3	22	0
Berroa, Angel, Azucareros	.256	78	9	20	4	2	0	5	3
Perez, Timo, Licey	.256	82	11	21	3	0	2	7	3
Mejia, Gilberto, Aguilas	.254	71	10	18	5	1	1	8	2
Sosa, Juan, Gigantes	.253	158	20	40	9	1	5	22	2
Green, Nick, Gigantes	.253	83	17	21	5	1	3	12	1
Calzado, Napoleon, Licey	.252	119	17	30	2	1	1	9	6
Harris, Brendan, Estrellas	.250	84	3	21	6	0	0	10	0
Ramirez, Hanley, Licey	.248	121	19	30	4	2	5	16	4

Gomes uses winter ball as springboard to majors

Before he snuck under the radar to become one of the surprising rookie success stories of the 2005 major league season, outfielder Jonny Gomes was working incognito in Mexico.

PLAYER OF THE **YEAR**

As he pounded home run after home run during the 2004-05 Mexican Pacific League season, Gomez sat at the top of the league's leader board. But even the most diehard Devil Rays fan would have had a hard time noticing that Gomes was stating a case for a spot in the Tampa Bay outfield. After all, for most of the season, the 24-year-old Californian was listed in the stats as Johnny Gomez.

Jonny Gomes

Whatever his nomiker, Gomes put together an outstanding winter season, hitting .364-17-45 in just 121 at-bats (one home run every seven at-bats) while leading Mexicali to the Mexican League championship series. Gomes slugged .860, as 26 of his 44 hits went for extra bases.

The power explosion wasn't extremely surprising, as Gomes had hit 26 home runs at Triple-A Durham in 2004, but his ability to hit for average as well helped forecast his breakthrough major league season in 2005. For his strong winter, Gomes was named Baseball America's 2004-05 Winter Player of the Year.

Gomes was the second-straight award winner to turn a strong winter into an everyday major league job, as Alexis Rios, the previous winner, became a fixture in the Blue Jays outfield.

PREVIOUS WINNERS

1985-1986—Wally Joyner, 1b, Mayaguez (Puerto Rico)
1986-1987—Vicente Palacios, rhp, Mexicali (Mexican Pacific)
1987-1988—Jose Nunez, rhp, Escogido (Dominican Republic)
1988-1989—Phil Stephenson, 1b, Zulia (Venezuela)
1989-1990—Edgar Martinez, 3b, San Juan (Puerto Rico)
1990-1991—Henry Rodriguez, of, Licey (Dominican Republic)
1991-1992—Wilson Alvarez, lhp, Zulia (Venezuela)
1992-1993—Matias Carrillo, of, Mexicali (Mexican Pacific)
1993-1994—John Hudek, rhp, Magallanes (Venezuela)
1994-1995—Carlos Delgado, c, San Juan (Puerto Rico)
1995-1996—Darryl Brinkley, of, Mexicali (Mexican Pacific)
1996-1997—Bartolo Colon, rhp, Aguilas (Dominican Republic)
1997-1998—Jose Hernandez, ss, Mayaguez (Puerto Rico)
1998-1999—Bob Abreu, of, Caracas (Venezuela)
1999-2000—Morgan Burkhart, 1b, Navojoa (Mexican Pacific)
2000-2001—Courtney Duncan, rhp, Caguas (Puerto Rico)
2001-2002—Ramon Hernandez, c, Pastora (Veneuzuela)
2002-2003—Arnie Munoz, lhp, Aguilas (Dominican Republic)
2003-2004—Alexis Rios, of, Caguas (Puerto Rico)

INDIVIDUAL PITCHING LEADERS

(Minimum 20 Innings)

	W	L	ERA	G	SV	IP	H	BB	SO
Valdez, Raul, Azucareros	5	2	**0.79**	10	0	57	34	22	47
Ramirez, Santiago, Aguilas	5	1	0.90	23	0	30	17	10	26
Patterson, John, Licey	2	1	1.20	5	0	30	25	4	27
Parra, Jose, Gigantes	0	2	1.64	22	15	22	20	6	24
Astacio, Ezequiel, Escogido	4	0	1.78	13	0	25	17	7	19
Perez, Carlos, Licey	1	1	1.80	23	1	25	18	5	23

Burgos, Ambiorix, Azucareros	1	1	1.96	15	2	23	12	16	28
Yan, Esteban, Estrellas	3	0	2.10	13	0	30	23	6	18
Peralta, Joel, Gigantes	**7**	1	2.14	24	0	21	12	8	25
Cabrera, Daniel, Azucareros	0	1	2.16	7	0	25	18	9	24
De La Rosa, Maximo, Azucareros	2	1	2.45	17	0	29	27	10	21
Martinez, Luis, Estrellas	6	1	2.48	18	0	36	35	19	43
Linton, Doug, Estrellas	3	2	2.57	12	0	63	60	9	54
Pena, Juan, Aguilas	6	2	2.59	10	0	49	35	7	52
Morla, Carlos, Licey	0	3	2.61	17	3	21	12	8	18
Heredia, Julian, Estrellas	2	1	2.82	22	1	22	21	6	24
Rodriguez, Wandy, Aguilas	1	0	2.89	11	0	28	22	5	26
Tejeda, Robinson, Aguilas	2	2	2.92	10	0	37	37	13	29
Curtis, Daniel, Gigantes	3	2	2.98	10	0	42	40	22	26
Aybar, Manny, Licey	4	4	2.98	14	0	60	59	17	**64**
Martinez, Anastacio, Estrellas	2	1	3.00	16	0	48	45	24	47
Coco, Pascual, Escogido	3	1	3.07	11	0	44	30	18	32
Saipe, Mike, Azucareros	1	2	3.14	11	0	57	57	16	40
Ramos, Eddy, Licey	4	0	3.18	17	0	28	24	14	19
Volquez, Edison, Azucareros	0	2	3.18	10	0	23	15	9	24
Sanchez, Jesus, Escogido	3	3	3.29	9	0	41	26	20	29
Pena, Ramon A., Gigantes	3	1	3.38	9	0	32	30	11	16
Torres, Melquis, Licey	2	1	3.41	24	1	29	28	15	20
Cruz, Nelson, Aguilas	4	3	3.56	11	0	43	38	8	45
Chavez, Wilton, Licey	3	1	3.61	10	0	47	48	7	35
Estrella, Leo, Gigantes	0	1	3.73	17	0	31	36	10	13
Ramirez, Elisardo, Gigantes	1	1	3.73	11	0	31	32	10	17
Nannini, Mike, Aguilas	2	0	3.86	6	0	28	30	5	16
#Vargas, Jose, Aguilas	2	2	4.30	23	**17**	23	22	5	28

MEXICAN PACIFIC LEAGUE

STANDINGS

FIRST HALF	W	L	PCT	GB
Obregon	21	13	.618	—
Culiacan	20	13	.606	½
Los Mochis	19	14	.576	1½
Guasave	18	15	.545	2½
Mazatlan	16	16	.500	4
Mexicali	14	18	.438	6
Hermosillo	13	20	.394	7½
Navojoa	10	22	.313	10
SECOND HALF	**W**	**L**	**PCT**	**GB**
Culiacan	22	10	.688	—
Mazatlan	19	14	.576	3½
Mexicali	16	15	.516	5½
Obregon	16	16	.500	6
Guasave	15	16	.484	6½
Los Mochis	15	18	.455	7½
Hermosillo	15	18	.455	7½
Navojoa	11	22	.333	11½

PLAYOFFS—Quarterfinals: Culiacan defeated Guasave 4-1, Mexicali defeated Obregon 4-1 and Los Mochis defeated Mazatlan 4-3 in best-of-7 series. **Semifinals:** Mazatlan defeated Culiacan 4-3 and Mexicali defeated Mochis 4-2 in best-of-7 series. **Finals:** Mazatlan defeated Mexicali 4-1 in best-of-7 series.

INDIVIDUAL BATTING LEADERS

(Minimum 105 Plate Appearances)

	AVG	AB	R	H	2B	3B	HR	RBI	SB
Munoz, Adan, Culiacan	**.367**	196	45	72	11	0	21	50	2
Short, Rick, Mexicali	.364	132	24	48	9	2	6	21	2
Gomes, Jonny, Mexicali	.364	121	33	44	9	0	17	45	3
Munoz, Noe, Guasave	.359	217	29	78	12	0	7	39	0
Garcia, Hector, Hermosillo	.347	95	10	33	5	1	0	15	3
Robles, Javier, Obregon	.336	250	45	**84**	**19**	1	12	53	2
Orantes, Ramon, Los Mochis	.336	146	27	49	3	0	13	33	1
Gastelum, Sergio, Mexicali	.333	105	23	35	7	0	1	11	1
Minor, Damon, Guasave	.330	106	16	35	7	0	5	24	1
Dillon, Joe, Mazatlan	.328	131	24	43	9	2	5	25	1
Gil, Geronimo, Obregon	.327	159	26	52	12	0	7	21	0
Sievers, Carlos, Los Mochis	.327	202	46	66	15	0	14	60	5
Valdez, Mario, Obregon	.327	98	23	32	6	0	9	20	0
Garcia, Luis, Hermosillo	.320	169	31	54	13	0	7	32	0
Cantu, Jorge, Culiacan	.319	185	28	59	10	1	11	39	0
Davis, J.J., Navojoa	.313	131	21	41	5	1	10	19	3
Canizalez, Juan, Hermosillo	.313	163	23	51	12	0	3	19	0
Cirillo, Jeff, Los Mochis	.312	93	19	29	6	0	1	12	1
Tracy, Andy, Obregon	.310	142	43	44	7	1	17	32	4
Smith, Demond, Guasave	.308	198	42	61	10	1	15	35	11
Doster, Dave, Hermosillo	.307	202	35	62	9	0	5	30	1
Burkhart, Morgan, Navojoa	.304	217	42	66	9	0	**23**	**64**	0
Morejon, Oswaldo, Guasave	.304	237	35	72	14	0	3	23	5
Santana, Mario, Los Mochis	.304	168	19	51	9	0	7	40	0
Johnson, Rontrez, Los Mochis	.303	234	**58**	71	11	1	12	31	18
Coste, Chris, Obregon	.303	241	49	73	12	1	15	49	0
Flores, Miguel, Mazatlan	.300	247	36	74	11	1	6	39	16
Ramirez, Oscar, Culiacan	.298	191	28	57	11	0	4	14	1
Gastelum, Carlos, Hermosillo	.298	248	39	74	5	**3**	0	29	13
Gomez, Heber, Mazatlan	.298	225	29	67	12	1	0	16	5
Sherman, Darrell, Culiacan	.297	192	39	57	7	0	1	13	4
Franco, Iker, Hermosillo	.295	220	36	65	9	0	20	57	0
Robles, Oscar, Navojoa	.295	237	41	70	15	0	8	27	1
Rivera, Ruben, Culiacan	.295	227	42	67	11	0	13	32	10
Hubbard, Trenidad, Mazatlan	.295	146	32	43	5	0	0	17	**19**
Mendez, Francisco, Guasave	.290	138	20	40	7	0	6	23	1
Nunnally, Jon, Hermosillo	.288	139	27	40	6	1	9	27	4
Arredondo, Eduardo, Guasave	.287	167	31	48	8	1	4	19	1
Pellow, Kit, Culiacan	.286	238	36	68	10	0	13	47	1
Arredondo, Luis, Obregon	.286	224	28	64	4	0	2	19	7
Martinez, Ray, Culiacan	.284	211	36	60	9	0	15	41	0
McDougall, Marshall, Guasave	.284	215	40	61	**19**	0	9	44	4
Sutton, Larry, Mazatlan	.282	85	9	24	5	0	1	5	0
Pelaez, Alex, Mexicali	.279	154	15	43	1	0	8	20	0
Carrillo, Matias, Los Mochis	.276	181	32	50	11	1	9	26	3

INDIVIDUAL PITCHING LEADERS

(Minimum 34 Innings)

	W	L	ERA	G	SV	IP	H	BB	SO
Campillo, Jorge, Culiacan	**10**	1	**2.05**	14	0	88	66	17	62
Prieto, Ariel, Obregon	8	1	2.09	13	0	82	69	16	53
Silva, Walter, Mazatlan	2	0	2.57	16	0	35	31	19	29
Rivera, Luis, Obregon	3	0	2.61	14	0	38	30	25	26
Ortega, Pablo, Mazatlan	9	3	2.88	14	0	91	85	29	45
Kroon, Marc, Culiacan	0	2	2.91	31	**20**	34	25	17	38
Cortes, David, Mexicali	4	1	3.15	30	15	34	23	9	51
Gonzalez, Rodolfo, Guasave	6	2	3.17	24	4	54	47	32	39
Campos, Francisco, Mazatlan	7	2	3.29	14	0	77	62	27	77
Zambrano, Baudel, Los Mochis	0	3	3.31	19	0	52	44	19	24
Elizalde, Carlos, Obregon	2	3	3.32	9	0	41	37	10	34
Gonzalez, Edgar, Hermosillo	1	2	3.41	7	0	34	40	10	28
Loya, Rigoberto, Mazatlan	4	5	3.57	13	0	76	70	30	31
Garcia, Alfredo, Culiacan	2	2	3.60	9	0	45	31	25	27
Cerros, Juan, Hermosillo	1	1	3.65	25	0	37	32	19	17
Navarro, Hector, Mazatlan	1	3	3.70	19	0	49	41	20	30
Carrillo, Guillermo, Guasave	2	1	3.76	21	0	38	50	15	32
Parra, Julio, Mexicali	6	0	3.86	35	1	35	26	21	37
Aceves, Alfredo, Culiacan	8	2	3.87	17	0	77	71	43	**80**
Lizarraga, Sergio, Culiacan	8	4	3.90	14	0	83	85	27	73
Tolar, Kevin, Mexicali	5	1	3.93	30	0	34	30	12	32
Dominguez, David, Navojoa	1	2	4.04	31	5	36	36	8	30
Yofu, Tetsu, Guasave	5	3	4.07	11	0	55	49	36	46
Manzano, Adrian, Los Mochis	4	2	4.14	30	0	37	36	4	31
Montano, Ignacio, Guasave	3	3	4.15	15	0	48	37	20	21
Mora, Sergio, Guasave	4	3	4.27	22	1	46	40	18	53
Gonzalez, Vinicio, Navojoa	2	5	4.64	14	0	76	71	41	46
Garcia, Ramon, Obregon	1	2	4.70	13	0	46	40	21	28
Moreno, Claudio, Mexicali	5	5	4.98	15	0	78	86	32	66

PUERTO RICAN LEAGUE

STANDINGS

REGULAR SEASON	W	L	PCT	GB
Caguas	24	16	.600	—
Mayaguez	22	18	.550	2
Ponce	21	19	.525	3
Carolina	20	20	.500	4
Santurce	19	21	.475	5
Manati	14	26	.350	10

PLAYOFFS—Semifinals: Mayaguez defeated Ponce 4-1 and Carolina defeated Caguas 4-1 in best-of-7 series. **Finals:** Mayaguez defeated Carolina 5-3 in best-of-9 series.

INDIVIDUAL BATTING LEADERS

(Minimum 54 Plate Appearances)

	AVG	AB	R	H	2B	3B	HR	RBI	SB
Feliciano, Jesus, Santurce	.425	73	14	31	2	1	2	9	2
Ruiz, Randy, Mayaguez	.390	77	17	30	5	0	**9**	21	0
Cruz, Jose E., Ponce	**.369**	130	26	48	11	0	3	16	1
Lucca, Lou, Santurce	.360	111	21	40	3	0	8	19	2
Gettis, Byron, Mayaguez	.347	121	22	42	8	1	2	15	5
Munoz, Jose, Caguas	.338	145	22	**49**	**13**	0	2	18	1
Lopez, Luis, Ponce	.336	128	20	43	8	0	5	**24**	1

Cintron, Alex, Caguas	.333	90	16	30	6	0	3	10	2
Figueroa, Luis, Mayaguez	.324	148	18	48	5	5	2	19	4
Quintana, Wil, Mayaguez	.321	56	11	18	1	0	5	12	0
Velazquez, Juan, Santurce	.320	97	13	31	4	0	6	19	3
Casanova, Raul, Ponce	.306	121	12	37	8	0	5	**24**	1
Leon, Jose, Manati	.300	90	14	27	6	0	6	14	0
Molina, Yadier, Carolina	.297	111	13	33	6	0	3	12	1
Pagan, Angel, Ponce	.296	135	22	40	10	0	2	12	5
Cancel, Robinson, Ponce	.296	71	10	21	5	0	2	10	1
Rios, Armando, Carolina	.294	126	24	37	10	1	5	20	8
Bocachica, Hiram, Ponce	.290	131	**29**	38	11	1	8	23	4
Guzman, Edwards, Manati	.286	140	14	40	8	0	4	14	2
Llanos, Alex, Carolina	.286	63	11	18	3	1	1	5	4
Crespo, Cesar, Carolina	.283	106	22	30	9	2	1	8	4
Baerga, Carlos, Santurce	.282	117	12	33	9	0	2	16	0
Ortiz, Hector, Caguas	.282	103	10	29	5	0	0	12	1
Molina, Jose, Ponce	.281	96	16	27	8	1	1	10	1
Candelaria, Ben, Manati	.281	121	17	34	6	0	7	16	1
Gonzalez, Danny, Santurce	.281	89	14	25	3	0	1	12	3
Figueroa, Luis, Carolina	.278	115	20	32	12	1	2	16	1
Rivera, Carlos, Ponce	.276	123	18	34	2	0	3	19	0
Rodriguez, Victor, Carolina	.271	118	12	32	6	0	4	20	1
#Torres, Andres, Mayaguez	.254	134	24	34	7	**7**	1	13	**11**

INDIVIDUAL PITCHING LEADERS

(Minimum 16 Innings)

	W	L	ERA	G	SV	IP	H	BB	SO
Gil, David, Caguas	0	0	1.10	4	0	16	11	3	13
Maldonado, Ivan, Carolina	1	0	1.16	15	0	23	16	9	18
Simas, Bill, Mayaguez	1	0	1.35	15	**7**	20	16	8	13
Johnson, Mike, Ponce	4	0	**1.36**	5	0	33	26	8	32
Romero, J.C., Carolina	1	1	1.56	13	1	17	13	7	15
Matta, Felix, Mayaguez	0	2	2.12	10	1	17	13	8	9
Cooper, Chris, Santurce	4	1	2.16	18	0	25	18	3	12
Thomas, Evan, Santurce	**5**	2	2.20	9	0	57	44	12	**53**
Shackelford, Brian, Caguas	2	1	2.20	10	1	16	13	9	13
Bazzell, Shane, Santurce	4	1	2.27	6	0	36	32	12	24
Meaux, Ryan, Caguas	0	1	2.29	15	0	20	26	8	10
Rivera, Saul, Caguas	**5**	0	2.32	17	1	31	23	5	22
Vazquez, Will, Manati	1	1	2.57	8	0	28	22	8	18
Matos, Josue, Carolina	**5**	2	2.63	10	0	51	42	18	39
Arroyo, Luis, Santurce	2	2	2.63	8	0	41	42	9	23
Majewski, Gary, Carolina	2	1	2.66	17	3	20	16	5	16
Davis, Lance, Mayaguez	3	1	2.76	13	0	33	33	7	14
Roman, Orlando, Caguas	3	2	2.81	10	0	32	24	21	14
Olivares, Omar, Caguas	0	0	2.95	5	0	18	19	10	9
Albaladejo, Jonathan, Mayaguez	**5**	2	2.98	8	0	45	35	7	31
Booker, Chris, Manati	1	2	3.00	19	4	21	15	12	22
Donaldson, Bo, Manati	0	2	3.06	3	0	18	11	4	13
Hamilton, Joey, Carolina	2	3	3.07	8	0	44	32	6	27
Burgos, John, Ponce	2	2	3.07	10	0	41	40	8	32
Padilla, Juan, Caguas	3	1	3.08	20	1	26	23	7	21
Martinez, Miguel, Carolina	3	2	3.08	8	0	26	28	20	15
Ankiel, Rick, Carolina	1	1	3.25	6	0	28	34	7	31
Miranda, Angel, Caguas	1	3	3.27	8	0	41	36	12	11
Santiago, Jose, Carolina	2	3	3.34	13	0	59	67	18	24
Enochs, Chris, Ponce	0	1	3.38	4	0	21	22	6	20

VENEZUELAN LEAGUE

STANDINGS

WESTERN DIVISION	W	L	PCT	GB
Lara	33	29	.532	—
Occidente	31	30	.508	1½
Aragua	31	31	.500	2
Zulia	28	33	.459	4½
EASTERN DIVISION	**W**	**L**	**PCT**	**GB**
Caracas	39	22	.639	—
Oriente	36	25	.590	3
Magallanes	27	35	.435	12½
La Guaira	21	41	.339	18½
PLAYOFFS	**W**	**L**	**PCT**	**GB**
Caracas	10	6	.625	—
Aragua	10	6	.625	—
Oriente	8	8	.500	2
Lara	7	9	.437	3
Occiedente	5	11	.313	5

Championship Series: Aragua defeated Caracas 3-2 in best-of-5 series.

INDIVIDUAL BATTING LEADERS

(Minimum 80 Plate Appearances)

	AVG	AB	R	H	2B	3B	HR	RBI	SB
Rivera, Juan, Oriente	.402	117	17	47	7	1	7	31	3
Connell, Lino, Oriente	**.378**	185	32	70	6	1	5	26	2
Colon, Cris, La Guaira	.365	85	12	31	1	0	1	11	0
Castillo, Jose, Caracas	.364	214	41	78	14	3	10	38	4
Calloway, Ron, Oriente	.354	79	23	28	4	1	6	20	2
Schumacher, Skip, Aragua	.350	103	14	36	3	1	2	10	3
Munoz, Orlando, Zulia	.347	121	12	42	4	0	0	13	0
Lucena, Juan, Aragua	.346	136	14	47	6	1	0	15	0
Reyes, Rene, Lara	.344	244	40	**84**	13	3	7	45	2
Rodriguez, Liu, La Guaira	.344	154	23	53	8	1	1	19	0
Gonzalez, Luis, Oriente	.341	164	30	56	6	2	4	25	0
Boscan, Jean, Lara	.340	144	32	49	10	1	6	31	0
Diaz, Eddy, Magallanes	.340	144	23	49	10	0	5	28	1
Simon, Randall, Oriente	.336	107	21	36	9	0	4	22	0
Nava, Lipso, Zulia	.336	149	20	50	11	0	3	27	1
Scutaro, Marcos, Caracas	.335	158	30	53	12	3	3	16	2
Yepez, Marcos, Caracas	.333	90	14	30	6	0	1	8	3
Sandoval, Danny, Occidente	.332	241	37	80	12	3	3	34	8
Young, Walter, La Guaira	.327	113	16	37	7	0	6	23	0
Young, Ernie, Caracas	.326	89	22	29	3	0	9	27	0
Garrett, Shawn, Zulia	.323	96	11	31	9	1	0	11	0
Langaigne, Selwyn, Lara	.322	233	43	75	**21**	1	5	43	1
Blanco, Henry, Caracas	.321	159	29	51	11	1	7	34	0
Alvarez, Rafael, Caracas	.318	179	34	57	14	2	9	36	1
Romero, Alex, Aragua	.316	196	31	62	10	2	5	32	1
Melian, Jackson, La Guaira	.316	76	10	24	6	1	2	11	1
Torcato, Tony, Occidente	.315	89	17	28	5	0	4	10	0
Diaz, Frank, Occidente	.314	207	34	65	13	0	7	33	6
Ugueto, Luis, Lara	.314	258	**45**	81	16	5	4	28	**10**
Medina, Rodney, Lara	.314	118	18	37	4	3	0	9	1
Freire, Alejandro, Zulia	.312	205	38	64	15	0	8	35	2
Rivas, Arturo, Magallanes	.311	90	16	28	7	0	5	14	0
Lopez, Jose, Lara	.311	164	35	51	11	2	10	29	1
Jimenez, Luis, Lara	.310	145	20	45	9	0	4	20	1
Infante, Omar, Oriente	.310	168	30	52	12	5	4	19	6
Gimenez, Hector, Magallanes	.308	143	19	44	8	4	3	25	0
Colina, Javier, Occidente	.307	225	39	69	18	2	**16**	**51**	1
Salazar, Oscar, Occidente	.306	229	33	70	11	0	10	37	1
Sojo, Luis, Lara	.305	131	14	40	8	0	1	16	2
Rushford, Jim, Magallanes	.301	219	27	66	15	0	2	26	0
Alfonzo, Eliezer, Oriente	.301	166	24	50	13	0	8	33	0
Hernandez, Carlos, Magallanes	.301	186	28	56	7	0	3	16	4
Alvarez, Tony, La Guaira	.301	133	18	40	6	1	6	26	3
Romero, Willie, Aragua	.296	125	25	37	5	0	9	20	4
Kelton, Dave, Oriente	.294	211	38	62	15	0	12	44	0
Nieves, Jose, Magallanes	.289	235	33	68	11	2	4	36	4
Sandoval, Abigail, Zulia	.288	118	13	34	5	1	0	8	1
#Victorino, Shane, Zulia	.280	214	33	60	9	**7**	9	38	**10**

INDIVIDUAL PITCHING LEADERS

(Minimum 25 Innings)

	W	L	ERA	G	SV	IP	H	BB	SO
Karnuth, Jason, Aragua	2	0	0.69	22	5	26	25	5	18
Zarate, Maruro, Caracas	5	0	1.03	15	0	26	23	13	20
Guttormson, Rick, Lara	5	2	1.15	21	4	31	21	11	38
Stephens, John, Aragua	4	1	1.76	9	0	41	46	7	37
Ramirez, Luis, Occidente	4	0	**1.93**	14	0	47	44	12	34
Eyre, Willie, Aragua	5	1	1.96	13	1	37	29	13	25
Garavito, Jean, Zulia	2	1	2.00	15	0	27	21	10	16
Palma, Rick, Occidente	6	2	2.02	12	0	76	69	27	51
Romero, Josmir, Aragua	4	1	2.09	11	0	52	44	4	21
Petit, Yusmeiro, Magallanes	4	3	2.15	11	0	50	43	8	53
Henthorne, Kevin, Caracas	2	0	2.17	30	**10**	37	28	7	27
Larreal, Guillermo, Occidente	2	1	2.35	30	**10**	31	31	8	22
Ovalles, Juan, Caracas	4	0	2.48	27	0	33	26	12	25
Jimenez, Cesar, Lara	2	0	2.51	8	0	32	33	14	21
Duarte, Renney, Oriente	5	1	2.63	16	0	27	29	9	12
Leon, Brigmer, Zulia	6	1	3.00	27	2	48	32	18	25
McDade, Neal, Oriente	2	4	3.00	16	1	33	28	13	20
Reina, Jesus, Caracas	5	1	3.07	14	0	56	51	13	28
Pena, Luismar, La Guaira	0	4	3.09	8	0	32	36	18	15
Moreno, Edwin, Zulia	1	2	3.12	15	4	26	28	5	29
Pinto, Renyel, Oriente	2	3	3.13	9	1	32	21	19	28
Bazardo, Yorman, Aragua	1	1	3.23	22	0	39	34	7	27
Cummings, Jeremy, Zulia	7	3	3.25	14	0	64	62	19	**64**
Reid, Justin, Zulia	1	2	3.40	8	0	40	31	11	26
Franklin, Wayne, Magallanes	2	2	3.42	11	0	50	47	16	51
Garcia, Jose, Oriente	3	0	3.48	18	0	31	26	11	31
Urdaneta, Lino, Lara	3	0	3.52	27	2	38	47	12	25
Ramirez, Ismael, Oriente	6	1	3.53	13	1	43	36	9	38
Machi, Jean, Magallanes	0	0	3.68	14	0	29	29	13	17

Statistics in **boldface** indicate league leader
#League leader but non-qualifier

COLLEGE BASEBALL

DENNIS HUBBARD

All's well that ends well
Texas sustained injuries, tough losses, a third-place Big 12 finish and five postseason elimination games before dominating the CWS

Experience, pitching help Texas sweep through CWS for sixth title

BY WILL KIMMEY

In its record 32nd trip to the College World Series, Texas made winning look easy. The Longhorns never trailed on their way to winning five straight games and the school's sixth national championship in 2005.

J. Brent Cox, though, knows it wasn't easy. He remembers standing on the mound in the ninth inning of Texas' decisive super-regional game at Mississippi with a 6-4 lead, two outs and runners on first and second base. Lefthanded-hitting Stephen Head stepped to the plate, where his 19th home run of the season could send the Rebels to the CWS.

Cox had allowed four runs to take the loss in the first game of the three-game series, and escaped a bases-loaded, one-out jam to preserve a 3-1 win in the second. He worked the count on Head to 2-2 before deciding on his trademark slider. The pitch slipped out of his hand, breaking knee-high, but too far inside. Head swung and missed ball three, and Texas advanced to Omaha for the fourth consecutive season.

That's how close things came for the Longhorns in 2005, when they didn't always look dominant but usually produced at important times.

If one ground ball, or one pitch, had been an inch or two off, they might not have even had the chance to win their second national title in four years. But close calls and tough losses—in personnel and on the field—weren't enough to stop Texas from steamrolling through Omaha and sweeping Florida in the best-of-three championship round. The sixth national title put Texas alone in second all-time (behind Southern California's 12), moving it out of a tie with Arizona State and Louisiana State at five.

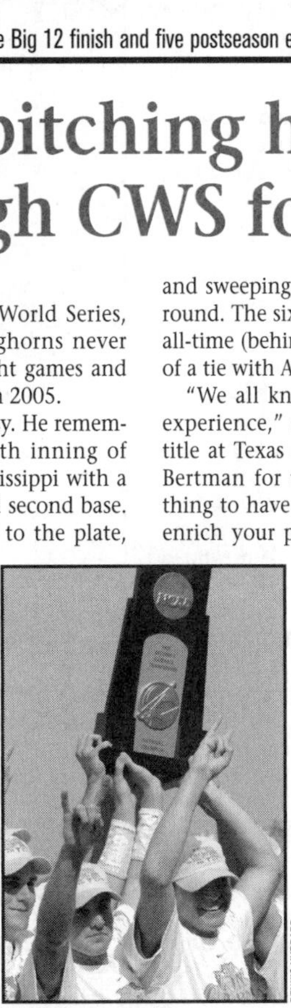
DENNIS HUBBARD

Longhorns win again
Texas has won the CWS six times

"We all knew coming in that this was a team with experience," said coach Augie Garrido, whose second title at Texas and fifth overall tied him with LSU's Skip Bertman for the second-most by any coach. "It's one thing to have it, it's another thing to be able to use it to enrich your performances. And that's what the players did."

Texas, which failed to win either the Big 12 regular-season or tournament championships, became just the second team to win the College World Series without being a national top eight seed since the 64-team format began in 1999. The Longhorns did it by playing their pitching-and-defense style to near perfection, allowing seven runs in five CWS games with just two errors. They stayed with their small-ball approach on offense, executing 10 successful sacrifice bunts, but showed some power in cracking seven home runs after totaling 49 in the 67 games leading up to Omaha.

"We had a little of an underdog role coming into the postseason," catcher Taylor Teagarden said. "We knew that in the back of our minds that if we played Texas baseball—play great defense and pitch well—we were going to win some games. And that's what happened. Things worked out for us."

DENNIS HUBBARD

Unexpected hero
David Maroul won MOP honors

A Team Effort

While Texas' philosophy remained the same, its heroes did not. Senior third baseman David Maroul entered the College World Series with pedestrian .229-9-27 numbers and stayed in the lineup only because of his excellent defense. He made several outstanding plays with his glove in Omaha, and really surprised with his bat. He was named the Most Outstanding Player after collecting eight hits and eight RBIs in 16 at-bats, with both his home runs and six RBIs coming in the two-game sweep of Florida.

"Every day there's somebody new stepping up," senior shortstop Seth Johnston said. "David Maroul, College World Series MVP, he hit, what, .230 on the year? But when we got here and it counted, he stepped up for us big time. He was the man for us here this week and this weekend. All these guys stepped up, maybe they didn't have a main role, but they did it when we needed it. Like Chance Wheeless, you know? It's a different guy every time."

Wheeless homered in the title-clinching game and put the Longhorns there with a walk-off home run in a 4-3 win against Baylor. Garrido wanted to pinch-hit for Wheeless because the sophomore first baseman felt excruciating pain in his right shoulder with every swing. He felt the shoulder slip out of its socket and then jerk back in on a check swing against Tulane's Brian Bogusevic in the CWS opener. Still, Wheeless told Garrido he really wanted to face Baylor righthander Ryan LaMotta because he had seen the ball well against him during Texas' previous games against Baylor. He turned on an inside fastball to launch the first game-ending home run at the CWS since Notre Dame's Brian Stavisky beat Rice in 2002.

Cox entered as more of a known quantity than Maroul or Wheeless, and lived up to his status as a second-round pick in the 2005 draft. He was on the mound to finish each of Texas' five wins, setting a career record with 12 CWS appearances. Cox struck out Florida's Stephen Barton to end the clinching game and fell to his knees while pumping both fists in the air before the celebratory dogpile enveloped him.

"I guess it's a dream come true," said Cox, whose 19th save tied a Texas season record and extended his NCAA lead. "It's pretty corny, but it's true."

The success of Cox and starters Kyle McCulloch, Adrian Alaniz and Kenn Kasparek masked the fact that Texas lost much of its pitching depth before the season began because of academic issues and transfers, notably Sam LeCure, who went 9-3, 2.34 in 2004. Texas used just six pitchers in Omaha and relied on seven for most of the season as it compiled the nation's fourth-best ERA.

"We didn't have a lot of depth," Teagarden said. "We needed big outings out of our starters. We can't afford to have someone go four or five innings. Things worked out for us. Everyone was going at least six or seven innings like we hoped and J.B. would come out day after day like we asked him to."

Texas' stingy pitching helped make 2005 the first CWS since 1971 in which no team scored 10 or more runs in a game, and the first since 1966 that no team scored more than eight runs in a game. In 15 games, 124 runs were scored, and the 8.27 average runs a game was the lowest since 1974, when the DH and metal bats were introduced to college baseball.

COLLEGE WORLD SERIES

Rosenblatt Stadium, Omaha
June 17-26, 2005

STANDINGS

BRACKET ONE	W	L	RF	RA
Florida	3	1	20	17
Arizona State	3	2	24	21
Nebraska	1	2	16	18
Tennessee	0	2	6	10

Bracket One Final: Arizona State 6, Florida 1; Florida 6, Arizona State 3.

BRACKET TWO	W	L	RF	RA
Texas	3	0	14	4
Baylor	2	2	16	19
Tulane	1	2	10	14
Oregon State	0	2	4	7

Bracket Two Final: Texas 4, Baylor 3.

CHAMPIONSHIP SERIES

(Best of 3)

Game One: Texas 4, Florida 2
Game Two: Texas 6, Florida 2

INDIVIDUAL BATTING LEADERS

(Minimum 10 Plate Appearances)

	AVG	AB	R	H	2B	3B	HR	RBI	BB
Eric King, Tennessee	.625	8	2	5	2	0	0	0	0
Daniel Bruce, Nebraska	.556	9	2	5	2	0	0	1	1
David Maroul, Texas	.500	16	3	8	2	0	2	8	1
Colin Curtis, Arizona State	.474	19	1	9	2	0	0	3	3
Jeff Larish, Arizona State	.438	16	7	7	2	0	3	4	6
Joey Hooft, Arizona State	.421	19	4	8	2	0	0	2	2
Will Crouch, Texas	.400	20	1	8	2	0	1	3	0
Andy Gerch, Nebraska	.400	15	4	6	0	0	1	3	0
Brian Bogusevic, Tulane	.400	10	1	4	1	0	0	1	0
Joe Simokaitis, Nebraska	.400	10	1	4	0	0	0	0	5

INDIVIDUAL PITCHING LEADERS

(Minimum 7 Innings)

	W	L	ERA	G	SV	IP	H	BB	SO
J. Brent Cox, Texas	1	0	0.00	5	2	10	3	5	12
Darren O'Day, Florida	1	0	0.00	4	1	8	3	0	6
Micah Owings, Tulane	1	0	1.29	1	0	7	4	4	4
Kyle McCulloch, Texas	2	0	1.32	2	0	14	11	4	15
Erik Averill, Arizona State	1	0	1.84	2	0	15	13	6	8
Adrian Alaniz, Texas	2	0	1.93	2	0	14	10	6	8
Zechry Zinicola, Arizona State	1	1	2.45	3	0	7	3	2	7
Jonah Nickerson, Oregon State	0	1	2.57	1	0	7	7	1	4
Ryan LaMotta, Baylor	0	1	2.57	3	0	7	10	2	3
Alan Horne, Florida	1	0	2.89	2	0	9	8	8	11

ALL-TOURNAMENT TEAM

C—Taylor Teagarden, Texas. **1B**—Jeff Larish, Arizona State. **2B**—Joey Hooft, Arizona State. **3B**—David Maroul, Texas. **SS**—Seth Johnston, Texas. **OF**—Travis Buck, Arizona State; Colin Curtis, Arizona State; Andy Gerch, Nebraska. **DH**—Will Crouch, Texas. **P**—J. Brent Cox, Texas; Kyle McCulloch, Texas.

Most Outstanding Player—David Maroul, Texas.

Harder Than It Looked

Texas started the year 16-0 and cruised along until meeting Baylor in the first conference series of the year. The Bears handed the Longhorns their first Big 12 Conference sweep since 1999. Texas survived that pratfall, and several more, always finding a way to battle back: a 16-inning loss at Nebraska, its first-ever conference series loss to Kansas, and finishing in third place for the first time since 2000. The Longhorns also weathered injuries to Johnston (arm), Maroul (leg), Teagarden (back) and Wheeless (shoulder).

Garrido told his players that great teams grow stronger by recovering from these setbacks, developing a survivor's instinct.

"This is the toughest year we've ever been through," Johnston said. "I think this team has learned so much because of the struggles we went through. It made us a lot tighter and a lot stronger."

Double Thriller

It would be hard to argue any single College World Series moment outstripping Louisiana State's 1996 championship victory over Miami, won on a walkoff home run by Warren Morris, for the mantle of most exciting game in CWS history. A pair of stirring Elimination Tuesday comebacks by Arizona State and Baylor, though—both won by 8-7 scores—will rank close behind Morris' heroics.

Arizona State beat Nebraska in 11 innings in one game, after each team entered its ninth-inning at-bat trailing by two runs. Baylor then rallied from a 7-0 deficit to overtake Tulane, scoring all of its runs in the final three innings. Arizona State's win proved an Instant Classic, re-airing on ESPN Classic three days later. J.J. Sferra's bloop RBI single into short right field ended the game, but the real dramatics came in the ninth inning on two momentous home runs.

Nebraska started the inning trailing 5-3, but scored

COLLEGE WORLD SERIES CHAMPIONS: 1947-2005

Year	Champion	Coach	Record	Runner-Up	MVP
1947	California*	Clint Evans	31-10	Yale	None selected
1948	Southern California	Sam Barry	40-12	Yale	None selected
1949	Texas*	Bibb Falk	23-7	Wake Forest	Charles Teague, 2b, Wake Forest
1950	Texas	Bibb Falk	27-6	Washington State	Ray VanCleef, of, Rutgers
1951	Oklahoma*	Jack Baer	19-9	Tennessee	Sid Hatfield, 1b-p, Tennessee
1952	Holy Cross	Jack Berry	21-3	Missouri	Jim O'Neill, p, Holy Cross
1953	Michigan	Ray Fisher	21-9	Texas	J.L. Smith, p, Texas
1954	Missouri	Hi Simmons	22-4	Rollins	Tom Yewcic, c, Michigan State
1955	Wake Forest	Taylor Sanford	29-7	Western Michigan	Tom Borland, p, Oklahoma State
1956	Minnesota	Dick Siebert	33-9	Arizona	Jerry Thomas, p, Minnesota
1957	California*	George Wolfman	35-10	Penn State	Cal Emery, 1b-p, Penn State
1958	Southern California	Rod Dedeaux	35-7	Missouri	Bill Thom, p, Southern California
1959	Oklahoma State	Toby Greene	27-5	Arizona	Jim Dobson, 3b, Oklahoma State
1960	Minnesota	Dick Siebert	34-7	Southern California	John Erickson, 2b, Minnesota
1961	Southern California*	Rod Dedeaux	43-9	Oklahoma State	Littleton Fowler, p, Oklahoma State
1962	Michigan	Don Lund	31-13	Santa Clara	Bob Garibaldi, p, Santa Clara
1963	Southern California	Rod Dedeaux	37-16	Arizona	Bud Hollowell, c, Southern California
1964	Minnesota	Dick Siebert	31-12	Missouri	Joe Ferris, p, Maine
1965	Arizona State	Bobby Winkles	54-8	Ohio State	Sal Bando, 3b, Arizona State
1966	Ohio State	Marty Karow	27-6	Oklahoma State	Steve Arlin, p, Ohio State
1967	Arizona State	Bobby Winkles	53-12	Houston	Ron Davini, c, Arizona State
1968	Southern California*	Rod Dedeaux	45-14	Southern Illinois	Bill Seinsoth, 1b, Southern California
1969	Arizona State	Bobby Winkles	56-11	Tulsa	John Dolinsek, of, Arizona State
1970	Southern California	Rod Dedeaux	51-13	Florida State	Gene Ammann, p, Florida State
1971	Southern California	Rod Dedeaux	53-13	Southern Illinois	Jerry Tabb, 1b, Tulsa
1972	Southern California	Rod Dedeaux	50-13	Arizona State	Russ McQueen, p, Southern California
1973	Southern California*	Rod Dedeaux	51-11	Arizona State	Dave Winfield, of-p, Minnesota
1974	Southern California	Rod Dedeaux	50-20	Miami (Fla.)	George Milke, p, Southern California
1975	Texas	Cliff Gustafson	56-6	South Carolina	Mickey Reichenbach, 1b, Texas
1976	Arizona	Jerry Kindall	56-17	Eastern Michigan	Steve Powers, dh-p, Arizona
1977	Arizona State	Jim Brock	57-12	South Carolina	Bob Horner, 3b, Arizona State
1978	Southern California*	Rod Dedeaux	54-9	Arizona State	Rod Boxberger, p, Southern California
1979	Cal State Fullerton	Augie Garrido	60-14	Arkansas	Tony Hudson, p, Cal State Fullerton
1980	Arizona	Jerry Kindall	45-21	Hawaii	Terry Francona, of, Arizona
1981	Arizona State	Jim Brock	55-13	Oklahoma State	Stan Holmes, of, Arizona State
1982	Miami (Fla.)*	Ron Fraser	57-18	Wichita State	Dan Smith, p, Miami (Fla.)
1983	Texas*	Cliff Gustafson	66-14	Alabama	Calvin Schiraldi, p, Texas
1984	Cal State Fullerton	Augie Garrido	66-20	Texas	John Fishel, of, Cal State Fullerton
1985	Miami (Fla.)*	Ron Fraser	64-16	Texas	Greg Ellena, dh, Miami (Fla.)
1986	Arizona	Jerry Kindall	49-19	Florida State	Mike Senne, of, Arizona
1987	Stanford	Mark Marquess	53-17	Oklahoma State	Paul Carey, of, Stanford
1988	Stanford	Mark Marquess	46-23	Arizona State	Lee Plemel, p, Stanford
1989	Wichita State	Gene Stephenson	68-16	Texas	Greg Brummett, p, Wichita State
1990	Georgia	Steve Webber	52-19	Oklahoma State	Mike Rebhan, p, Georgia
1991	Louisiana State*	Skip Bertman	55-18	Wichita State	Gary Hymel, c, Louisiana State
1992	Pepperdine*	Andy Lopez	48-11	Cal State Fullerton	Phil Nevin, 3b, Cal State Fullerton
1993	Louisiana State	Skip Bertman	53-17	Wichita State	Todd Walker, 2b, Louisiana State
1994	Oklahoma*	Larry Cochell	50-17	Georgia Tech	Chip Glass, of, Oklahoma
1995	Cal State Fullerton*	Augie Garrido	57-9	Southern California	Mark Kotsay, of-p, Cal State Fullerton
1996	Louisiana State*	Skip Bertman	52-15	Miami (Fla.)	Pat Burrell, 3b, Miami
1997	Louisiana State*	Skip Bertman	57-13	Alabama	Brandon Larson, ss, Louisiana State
1998	Southern California	Mike Gillespie	49-17	Arizona State	Wes Rachels, 2b, Southern California
1999	Miami*	Jim Morris	50-13	Florida State	Marshall McDougall, 2b, Florida State
2000	Louisiana State*	Skip Bertman	52-17	Stanford	Trey Hodges, rhp, Louisiana State
2001	Miami*	Jim Morris	53-12	Stanford	Charlton Jimerson, of, Miami
2002	Texas*	Augie Garrido	57-15	South Carolina	Huston Street, rhp, Texas
2003	Rice	Wayne Graham	58-12	Stanford	John Hudgins, rhp, Stanford
2004	Cal State Fullerton	George Horton	47-22	Texas	Jason Windsor, rhp, Cal State Fullerton
2005	Texas*	Augie Garrido	56-16	Florida	David Maroul, 3b, Texas

*Undefeated

four times. Andy Gerch capped that spurt with a three-run homer that sent a crowd full of Cornhusker fans into a raucous frenzy. "The way it was handled, it seemed like (the game) was over there," Gerch said.

It wasn't. Arizona State drew within a run in the bottom of the ninth before Jeff Larish came to the plate with two outs and blasted a solo home run to dead center field. It was his third solo home run of the game, tying a CWS record held by Florida State's J.D. Drew and Stanford's Edmund Muth.

Few figured the nightcap would measure up to the opener. When Tulane, which entered regional play ranked No. 1 in the nation, scored six times in the second inning, it looked like a blowout. The Green Wave tacked on another in the top half of the seventh before the Bears slowly began chipping away. Baylor trimmed the deficit to one run in the ninth and had the bases loaded with one out in the ninth, when Paul Witt grounded a ball to second baseman Joe Holland. Holland took the play at second himself, then pivoted to throw to first for a potential game-ending double play. But his throw eluded first baseman Micah Owings' reach and skipped away as the winning run crossed home plate.

Triple your pleasure
Jeff Larish hit three homers in a game

It marked Baylor's 12th win in its last at-bat on the season and its fourth such victory of the postseason. Tulane had been 49-0 when leading after eight innings.

"I've been coaching 30 years, and tonight's loss was the worst I've ever had, no question," said Tulane coach Rick Jones, who was named Baseball America's Coach of the Year. "Because of the environment it was in, the year we've had, the guys involved. Doggone it. It sure is tough right now. It hurts."

Exposure Continues To Grow

A record 263,475 fans filled Rosenblatt Stadium during the 2005 College World Series, and the average session attendance of 23,952 also set a record. Attendance records fell in six of the first nine sessions and four of the five largest CWS crowds ever came in 2005.

Nebraska's fans provided a major story, as they camped overnight to secure tickets, flooded parking lots and drove prices from ticket scalpers near $200 to see Nebraska's series-opening win against Arizona State. They also turned the stands of Rosenblatt into a Red Sea, providing a home-field advantage in what was supposed to be a neutral setting.

Some of the increased interest in the College World Series overall came from an improved television package, courtesy of ESPN. The sports network televised regular season college baseball games for the first time since 1990, in part as replacement programming during the National Hockey League's season-long strike. More than 30 games appeared on ESPN, ESPN2 or ESPNU. The network covered two regionals and continued to televise every super-regional and CWS game.

Power Outage

There were no significant individual records set in college baseball in 2005 as the game experienced another downward trend in offense from 1998, when the collective ERA for Division I teams was an all-time high 6.12 and only one team, St. Francis (N.Y.), had an ERA below 3.50. In 2005, 19 teams had ERAs below 3.50, led by Long Beach State at 2.53.

Five-foot-9 Florida State sophomore outfielder Shane Robinson provided a dominating offensive sea-

RPI RANKINGS

The Ratings Percentage Index (RPI) is an important tool used by the NCAA in selecting at-large teams for the 64-team Division I regional field. This chart shows the official 2005 RPI rankings, with records against Division I opponents (ties are not included), as of the NCAA tournament selection day and at the end of the season. The ranking in the Baseball America Top 25 at the time is indicated in parentheses. Asterisks denote teams that did not get a regional bid. College World Series teams are in boldface.

Selection Day (May 29)		Final (June 29)	
RPI Ranking	Record	RPI Ranking	Record
1. **Tulane** (1)	50-9	1. **Texas** (1)	56-16
2. Georgia Tech (5)	42-16	2. **Baylor** (4)	46-24
3. **Texas** (6)	45-14	3. **Tulane** (3)	56-12
4. Mississippi (9)	44-18	4. Mississippi (10)	48-20
5. **Baylor** (8)	39-21	5. **Florida** (2)	48-23
6. Clemson (15)	39-21	6. Georgia Tech (11)	45-19
7. Miami (17)	38-17	7. Clemson (14)	43-23
8. North Carolina	40-17	8. Miami (15)	41-19
9. **Florida** (11)	40-20	9. **Oregon State** (7)	46-12
10. College of Charleston	47-13	10. Cal State Fullerton (9)	46-18
11. Cal State Fullerton (4)	41-15	11. Southern California (17)	41-22
12. North Carolina State (22)	40-17	12. **Nebraska** (5)	57-15
13. **Oregon State** (2)	41-9	13. **Arizona State** (6)	42-25
14. Coastal Carolina (25)	48-14	14. Rice (13)	44-19
15. Louisiana State (13)	38-20	15. College of Charleston	48-15
16. Southern California (21)	37-19	16. North Carolina	41-19
17. Long Beach State (12)	36-20	17. Coastal Carolina (23)	50-16
Nebraska (3)	51-13	18. Louisiana State (18)	40-22
19. *Auburn	32-24	19. North Carolina State	41-19
20. Winthrop	43-20	20. Arkansas	39-22
21. Mississippi State (18)	40-20	21. **Tennessee** (8)	43-21
22. Arkansas	37-20	22. Long Beach State (19)	37-22
23. Florida State (20)	49-18	23. *Auburn	34-26
24. Virginia	41-18	24. South Carolina (25)	41-23
25. Rice (14)	40-17	25. Mississippi State (22)	42-22
26. *Georgia	30-25	26. Florida State (16)	52-20
27. **Arizona State** (23)	34-22	27. Winthrop	44-22
28. Texas Christian (24)	40-18	28. Alabama (20)	40-23
29. **Tennessee** (10)	38-19	29. *Georgia	30-25
30. Alabama (18)	38-21	30. Arizona (12)	39-21
31. *Vanderbilt	34-21	*Vanderbilt	34-21
32. South Carolina	38-21	32. Pepperdine (24)	41-23
33. Southern Mississippi	41-19	33. Texas Christian	41-20
34. Pepperdine	38-21	34. Virginia	41-20
35. Arizona (7)	37-19	35. Wichita State	51-24
36. Wichita State	37-19	36. Southern Mississippi	41-21
37. Florida Atlantic	36-22	37. Oklahoma	35-26
38. Northwestern State	39-18	38. Stanford	34-25
39. Stanford	32-23	39. Northwestern State	40-20
40. Oklahoma	33-24	40. Florida Atlantic	37-24
41. Louisiana-Lafayette	47-17	41. *Central Florida	42-18
42. *Central Florida	42-18	42. Creighton	48-17
43. Miami (Ohio)	42-16	43. Miami (Ohio)	43-18
44. East Carolina	35-24	44. Louisiana-Lafayette	48-19
45. *Texas A&M	30-25	45. *Texas A&M	30-25
46. Michigan	41-17	46. Missouri (21)	40-23
47. *Georgia Southern	38-22	47. Michigan	42-19
48. Creighton	46-15	48. *Georgia Southern	38-22
49. Missouri (16)	39-21	49. St. John's	41-18
50. *UNC Wilmington	40-19	50. *Oklahoma State	34-25

THE ROAD TO OMAHA

SUPER-REGIONALS

June 10-13, 16 teams, eight best-of-3 series (Winners advance to College World Series)

REGIONALS

June 3-6, 64 teams, 16 double-elimination tournaments (Winners advance to super-regionals)

* Automatic qualifier

ARIZONA

■ **Super-Regional Site:** Fullerton, Calif. (Cal State Fullerton).

Participants: Arizona State (37-22) at Cal State Fullerton (45-16).

(Arizona State wins 2-1, advances to College World Series).

❑ **Regional Site**: Tempe, Ariz. (Arizona State).

Participants: No. 1 Coastal Carolina (48-14), No. 2 Arizona State (34-22), No. 3 East Carolina (35-24), *No. 4 Nevada-Las Vegas (34-27).

Champion: Arizona State (3-0). **Runner-Up:** Coastal Carolina (2-2).

Outstanding Player: Erik Averill, lhp; Tuffy Gosewisch, c, Arizona State.

❑ **Regional Site**: Fullerton, Calif. (Cal State Fullerton).

Participants: *No. 1 Cal State Fullerton (41-15), No. 2 Arizona (37-19), No. 3 Missouri (39-21), *No. 4 Harvard (29-15).

Champion: Cal State Fullerton (4-1). **Runner-Up:** Arizona (2-2).

Outstanding Player: Wes Roemer, rhp, Cal State Fullerton.

BAYLOR

■ **Super-Regional Site:** Waco, Texas (Baylor).

Participants: Clemson (42-21) at Baylor (42-21).

(Baylor wins 2-1, advances to College World Series).

❑ **Regional Site**: Waco, Texas. (Baylor).

Participants: No. 1 Baylor (39-21), No. 2 Texas Christian (40-18), No. 3 Stanford (32-23), *No. 4 UT San Antonio (27-32).

Champion: Baylor (3-0). **Runner-Up:** Stanford (2-2).

Outstanding Player: Paul Witt, ss, Baylor.

❑ **Regional Site**: Clemson, S.C. (Clemson).

Participants: No. 1 Clemson (39-21), No. 2 College of Charleston (47-13), *No. 3 Oral Roberts (40-18), *No. 4 North Carolina A&T (27-25).

Champion: Clemson (3-0). **Runner-Up:** Oral Roberts (2-2).

Outstanding Player: Andy D'Alessio, 1b, Clemson.

FLORIDA

■ **Super-Regional Site:** Gainesville, Fla. (Florida).

Participants: Florida State (53-18) at Florida (43-20).

(Florida wins 2-0, advances to College World Series).

❑ **Regional Site**: Gainesville, Fla. (Florida).

Participants: No. 1 Florida (40-20), No. 2 North Carolina (40-17), *No. 3 Notre Dame (36-22), *No. 4 Stetson (35-26).

Champion: Florida (3-0). **Runner-Up:** Notre Dame (2-2).

Outstanding Player: Brian LeClerc, of, Florida.

❑ **Regional Site**: Tallahassee, Fla. (Florida State).

Participants: No. 1 Florida State (50-18), No. 2 Auburn (32-24), *No. 3 South Alabama (35-25), *No. 4 Army (38-12).

Champion: Florida State (3-0). **Runner-Up:** Auburn (2-2).

Outstanding Player: Bryan Henry, rhp, Florida State.

NEBRASKA

■ **Super-Regional Site:** Lincoln, Neb. (Nebraska).

Participants: Miami (41-17) at Nebraska (54-13).

(Nebraska wins 2-0, advances to College World Series).

❑ **Regional Site**: Lincoln, Neb. (Nebraska).

Participants: *No. 1 Nebraska (50-13), No. 2 North Carolina State (40-17), No. 3 Creighton (46-15), *No. 4 Illinois-Chicago (38-19).

Champion: Nebraska (3-0). **Runner-Up:** Creighton (2-2).

Outstanding Player: Andy Gerch, of, Nebraska.

❑ **Regional Site**: Coral Gables, Fla. (Miami).

Participants: No. 1 Miami (38-17), *No. 2 Mississippi State (40-20), No. 3 Florida Atlantic (36-22), *No. 4 Virginia Commonwealth (33-20).

Champion: Miami (3-0). **Runner-Up:** Mississippi State (2-2).

Outstanding Player: Danny Figueroa, of, Miami.

OREGON STATE

■ **Super-Regional Site:** Corvallis, Ore. (Oregon State).

Participants: Southern California (40-20) at Oregon State (44-9).

(Oregon State wins 2-1, advances to College World Series).

❑ **Regional Site**: Corvallis, Ore. (Oregon State).

Participants: *No. 1 Oregon State (41-9), No. 2 Virginia (41-18), No. 3 St. John's (39-16), *No. 4 Ohio State (39-18).

Champion: Oregon State (3-0). **Runner-Up:** St. John's (2-2).

Outstanding Player: Mitch Canham, c, Oregon State

❑ **Regional Site**: Long Beach, Calif. (Long Beach State).

Participants: No. 1 Long Beach State (36-20), No. 2 Southern California (37-19), *No. 3 Pepperdine (38-21), *No. 4 Rhode Island (34-19).

Champion: Southern California (3-1). **Runner-Up:** Pepperdine (3-2).

Outstanding Player: Matt Cusick, 1b, Southern California.

TENNESSEE

■ **Super-Regional Site:** Atlanta (Georgia Tech).

Participants: Tennessee (44-19) at Georgia Tech (45-17).

(Tennessee wins 2-0, advances to College World Series).

❑ **Regional Site**: Knoxville, Tenn. (Tennessee).

Participants: No. 1 Tennessee (41-19), *No. 2 Winthrop (43-20), *No. 3 Wichita State (49-22), *No. 4 Austin Peay State (38-22).

Champion: Tennessee (3-0). **Runner-Up:** Wichita State (2-2).

Outstanding Player: James Adkins, lhp, Tennessee.

❑ **Regional Site**: Atlanta (Georgia Tech).

Participants: *No. 1 Georgia Tech (42-16), No. 2 South Carolina (38-21), No. 3 Michigan (41-17), *No. 4 Furman (30-27).

Champion: Georgia Tech (3-1). **Runner-Up:** South Carolina (3-2).

Outstanding Player: Tim Gustafson, rhp, Georgia Tech.

TEXAS

■ **Super-Regional Site:** Oxford, Miss. (Mississippi).

Participants: Texas (49-15) at Mississippi (47-18).

(Texas wins 2-1, advances to College World Series).

❑ **Regional Site**: Austin, Texas (Texas).

Participants: No. 1 Texas (45-14), No. 2 Arkansas (37-20), *No. 3 Miami/Ohio (44-16), *No. 4 Quinnipiac (26-22).

Champion: Texas (4-1). **Runner-Up:** Arkansas (2-2).

Outstanding Player: Taylor Teagarden, c, Texas.

❑ **Regional Site**: Oxford, Miss. (Mississippi).

Participants: No. 1 Mississippi (44-18), No. 2 Southern Mississippi (41-19), No. 3 Oklahoma (33-24), *No. 4 Maine (34-17).

Champion: Mississippi (3-0). **Runner-Up:** Oklahoma (2-2).

Outstanding Player: Chris Coughlan, 3b, Mississippi.

TULANE

■ **Super-Regional Site:** New Orleans, La. (Tulane).

Participants: Rice (44-17) at Tulane (53-9).

(Tulane wins 2-1, advances to College World Series).

❑ **Regional Site**: New Orleans (Tulane).

Participants: *No. 1 Tulane (50-9), No. 2 Alabama (38-21), No. 3 Louisiana-Lafayette (47-17), *No. 4 Southern (29-16).

Champion: Tulane (3-0). **Runner-Up:** Alabama (2-2).

Outstanding Player: Mark Hamilton, of/1b, Tulane.

❑ **Regional Site**: Baton Rouge, La. (Louisiana State).

Participants: No. 1 Louisiana State (38-20), *No. 2 Rice (41-17), No. 3 Northwestern State (40-18), *No. 4 Marist (33-19).

Champion: Rice (3-0). **Runner-Up:** Louisiana State (2-2).

Outstanding Player: Nick Stavinoha, of, Louisiana State.

son despite hitting just six home runs. He batted .427 and led the nation with 96 runs and 122 hits, while finishing second with a .532 on-base percentage. He hit safely in 40 straight games, becoming the seventh player in Division I history to reach that mark.

Robinson was joined in the outfield on Baseball America's All-America team by Arizona's Trevor Crowe and Oregon State's Jacoby Ellsbury, two other leadoff hitters who failed to reach double digits in homers—a rare feat in college baseball's aluminum bat era. Crowe led the nation with 188 total bases and 15 triples while Ellsbury sparked Oregon State to its first CWS appearance in 53 years.

COACHING CAROUSEL

Division I coaching changes at the end of the 2005 season:

School	Previous coach	New coach (previous job)
Akron	Tim Berenyi (resigned)	Pat Bangtson (Ohio State assistant)
Arkansas-Little Rock	Brian Rhees (fired)	Jim Lawler (Texas A&M assistant)
Chicago State	Terrence Jackson (fired)	Vern Hasty (Harper ,Ill., CC)
Columbia	Paul Fernandes (resigned)	Brett Boretti (Franklin & Marshall, Pa.)
Duke	Bill Hillier (resigned)	Sean McNally (Indians minor league manager)
East Carolina	Randy Mazey (fired)	Billy Godwin (assistant)
Illinois	Richard "Itch" Jones (retired)	Dan Hartleb (assistant)
Indiana	Bob Morgan (resigned)	Tracy Smith (Miami, Ohio)
Iona	Al Zoccolillo (retired)	Pat Carey (Iona assistant)
Long Island	Frank Giannone (retired)	Don Maines (Drexel)
Maine	Paul Kostacopoulos (to Navy)	Steve Trimper (Manhattan)
Manhattan	Steve Trimper (to Maine)	Kevin Leighton (Manhattan assistant)
Marist	Joe Raccuia (Alabama assistant)	Dennis Healy (New Orleans assistant)
Miami (Ohio)	Tracy Smith (to Indiana)	Dan Simonds (Xavier)
Michigan State	Ted Mahan (resigned)	David Grewe (Notre Dame assistant)
Navy	Steve Whitmyer (fired)	Paul Kostacopoulos (Maine)
Nicholls State	B.D. Parker (retired)	Chip Durham (Crowder, Mo., JC)
Oakland	Mark Avery (resigned)	Dylan Putnam (Michigan State assistant)
Oklahoma	Larry Cochell (resigned)	Sunny Golloway (Oklahoma assistant)
Pennsylvania	Bob Seddon (retired)	John Cole (Rowan, N.J.)
Rhode Island	Frank Leoni (to William & Mary)	Jim Foster (Rhode Island assistant)
Southeastern Louisiana	Dan Canevari (resigned)	Jay Artigues (Pearl River, Miss., CC)
Temple	Skip Wilson (retired)	Rob Valli (Gloucester County, N.J., JC)
Texas A&M	Mark Johnson (fired)	Rob Childress (Nebraska assistant)
Western Kentucky	Joel Murrie (retired)	Chris Finwood (Auburn assistant)
William & Mary	Jim Farr (resigned)	Frank Leoni (Rhode Island)
Xavier	Dan Simonds (to Miami, Ohio)	Scott Googins (assistant)

Troy outfielder Adam Godwin was most symbolic of a returning emphasis to speed in the college game as he stole 84 bases, the second player to reach that figure since Texas-Pan America's Donald Guillot set the NCAA single-season record of 107 in 1987.

While 2005 was not a noteworthy season for on-field accomplishments, UC Santa Barbara senior infielder Chris Malec provided one of the most heart-warming stories off the field. He found out April 12 that he had testicular cancer, and had surgery to remove the tumor two days later. On May 6, little more than three weeks after the surgery he returned to the field in an 8-6 win against Long Beach State. Malec enhanced his feel-good story the next day, connecting on a first-inning grand slam in a game his team won 7-6.

Uh Oh, OU

Sunny Golloway entered 2005 as Oklahoma's top assistant and ended it as the head coach. But the events that transpired in that time span weren't anything any Sooners fan wants to relive.

First, Larry Cochell resigned May 1, five days after using a racial slur in two separate off-air conversations with ESPN commentators. His announcement ended his 15-year stint at Oklahoma, including a national title in 1994, and came after school president David Boren, athletics director Joe Castiglione and four black members of the OU faculty and staff met to discuss his future.

Oklahoma introduced Wichita State's Gene Stephenson, a former OU assistant, as Cochell's replacement at a July 11 press conference, along with WSU assistant coaches Brent Kemnitz and Jim Thomas. But the three decided as a group to return to Wichita State just hours after the announcement.

Golloway, who served as interim coach after Cochell's departure, accepted the job four days later.

Stephenson, who won his 1,500th college game at Wichita State during the 2005 season, said he reconsidered his decision because of "unresolvable" scholarship issues—Oklahoma was four scholarships over the NCAA limit of 11.7 in July—though Golloway and Castiglione correctly noted that many schools teeter over the maximun amount of aid during the summer and are able to correct it in time for the subsequent academic year.

Cochell's departure and the subsequent hiring of Gollway was one of 27 coaching changes at the Division I level in 2005. The next most significant change also occurred in the Big 12, at Texas A&M, where 21-year head coach Mark Johnson was fired after leading the Aggies to a 30-25 record. Overall, Johnson went 876-433. He was replaced by Nebraska assistant Rob Childress.

Skip Wilson, the dean of Division I coaches, retired after 46 seasons as Temple's head coach. He was the winningest coach in Temple history, regardless of sport, and finished with 1,034 wins. Wilson was 75.

Academic Epidemic?

The NCAA in March released its first Academic Progress Report, which charts eligibility, retention and graduation of student-athletes for every team sport at Division I schools. Beginning with the 2005-06 academic year, teams that fall below a 925 score—which equates to a 50 percent graduation rate over a four-year period—will be subject to contemporaneous penalties that strip scholarship money for each scholarship athlete that leaves school in poor academic standing.

In baseball, where most players receive partial scholarships, the team would lose the percentage of scholarship the player was receiving. The NCAA limits baseball to 11.7 scholarships, and teams cannot lose more than 1.7 scholarships in a given year because of APR concerns.

College baseball coaches expressed concern for their game because it features as much or more player movement that any Division I sport with rampant transfers and players eligible for the draft as juniors (and sometimes sophomores).

The NCAA board of directors responded by adjusting the APR so that it would not penalize programs when players leave school early for the professional draft, provided the student-athlete exits in good academic standing.

2005 COLLEGE ALL-AMERICA TEAM

Selected by Baseball America

Lance Broadway

Jeff Clement

Trevor Crowe

Jacoby Ellsbury

Luke Hochevar

FIRST TEAM

Pos	Player, School	YR	Hometown	AVG	AB	R	H	2B	3B	HR	RBI	BB	SO	SB
C	Jeff Clement, Southern California	Jr.	Marshalltown, Iowa	.348	230	52	80	8	1	15	54	44	43	5
1B	Matt LaPorta, Florida	So.	Port Charlotte, Fla.	.328	265	75	87	16	2	26	79	44	65	3
2B	Jim Negrych, Pittsburgh	So.	Buffalo, N.Y.	.349	186	52	65	14	1	16	59	44	37	11
3B	Alex Gordon, Nebraska	Jr.	Lincoln, Neb.	.372	253	79	94	22	4	19	66	63	38	23
SS	Tyler Greene, Georgia Tech	Jr.	Plantation, Fla.	.372	269	76	100	15	3	12	72	38	71	31
OF	Trevor Crowe, Arizona	Jr.	Portland, Ore.	.403	263	83	106	25	15	9	54	36	30	27
OF	Jacoby Ellsbury, Oregon State	Jr.	Madras, Ore.	.406	244	56	99	19	3	6	48	36	21	26
OF	Shane Robinson, Florida State	So.	Tampa, Fla.	.427	286	96	122	25	4	6	43	57	28	49
DH	Ryan Braun, Miami	Jr.	Granada Hills, Calif.	.388	219	70	85	16	2	18	76	33	39	23
UT	Mike Costanzo, Coastal Carolina	Jr.	Springfield, Pa.	.379	240	74	91	15	2	16	67	68	65	8

Pos	Player, School	YR	Hometown	W	L	ERA	G	GS	CG	SV	IP	H	BB	SO
SP	Lance Broadway, Texas Christian	Jr.	Grand Prairie, Texas	15	1	1.62	19	16	5	0	117	83	35	151
SP	Dallas Buck, Oregon State	So.	Newburg, Ore.	12	1	2.09	19	18	2	1	129	90	51	118
SP	Luke Hochevar, Tennessee	Jr.	Fowler, Colo.	15	3	2.26	19	19	3	0	140	104	54	154
SP	Ian Kennedy, Southern California	So.	Huntington Beach, Calif.	12	3	2.54	18	17	1	0	117	85	38	158
RP	Craig Hansen, St. John's	Jr.	Glen Cove, N.Y.	3	2	1.68	31	1	0	14	64	38	20	85
UT	Mike Costanzo, Coastal Carolina	Jr.	Springfield, Pa.	8	1	2.13	37	0	0	14	55	44	24	69

SECOND TEAM

Pos	Player, School	YR	Hometown	AVG	AB	R	H	2B	3B	HR	RBI	BB	SO	SB
C	Nick Hundley, Arizona	Jr.	Seattle	.352	227	57	80	23	2	15	46	42	43	9
1B	Steve Pearce, South Carolina	Sr.	Lakeland, Fla.	.358	229	50	82	16	0	21	63	23	23	2
2B	Chris Campbell, Charleston	So.	Jacksonville, Fla.	.379	269	64	102	21	0	15	87	22	27	4
3B	Ryan Zimmerman, Virginia	Jr.	Virginia Beach, Va.	.393	234	51	92	18	4	6	59	31	14	17
SS	Seth Johnston, Texas	Sr.	.Boerne, Texas	.378	304	59	115	20	5	9	66	21	33	15
OF	Daniel Carte, Winthrop	Jr.	Hurricane, W.Va.	.344	270	57	93	16	3	19	74	23	60	12
OF	Eli Iorg, Tennessee	Jr.	Knoxville, Tenn.	.381	252	63	96	19	4	15	72	19	29	27
OF	Brian Pettway, Mississippi	Jr.	Vicksburg, Miss.	.387	261	56	101	19	0	21	66	35	47	1
DH	Kris Harvey, Clemson	Jr.	Catawba, N.C.	.341	249	61	85	11	0	25	70	16	44	1
UT	Joe Savery, Rice	Fr.	Bellaire, Texas	.382	204	49	78	17	2	5	43	35	35	7

Pos	Player, School	YR	Hometown	W	L	ERA	G	GS	CG	SV	IP	H	BB	SO
SP	Cesar Carrillo, Miami	Jr.	Chicago	13	3	2.22	19	18	3	1	125	100	23	127
SP	Mike Pelfrey, Wichita State	Jr.	Wichita, Kansas	12	3	1.93	19	19	7	0	140	96	30	143
SP	Ricky Romero, Cal State Fullerton	Jr.	East Los Angeles	13	5	2.89	18	18	2	0	134	102	34	139
SP	Max Scherzer, Missouri	So.	Chesterfield, Mo.	9	4	1.86	16	16	1	0	106	59	41	131
RP	J. Brent Cox, Texas	Jr.	Bay City, Texas	8	3	1.73	42	0	0	19	78	57	25	87
UT	Joe Savery, Rice	Fr.	Bellaire, Texas	8	5	2.43	19	17	2	1	118	104	37	129

THIRD TEAM

Pos	Player, School	YR	Hometown	AVG	AB	R	H	2B	3B	HR	RBI	BB	SO	SB
C	Mike Ambort, Lamar	So.	Rockville Centre, N.Y.	.335	217	57	73	15	0	18	65	21	24	2
1B	Aaron Bates, North Carolina State	So.	La Selva Beach, Calif.	.425	214	61	91	16	1	12	64	37	27	3
2B	Adam Davis, Florida	So.	Fort Myers, Fla.	.306	294	75	90	15	1	12	63	40	46	24
3B	Chase Headley, Tennessee	Jr.	Fountain, Colo.	.387	238	82	92	24	3	14	65	63	23	6
SS	Cliff Pennington, Texas A&M	Jr.	Corpus Christi, Texas	.363	212	44	77	13	4	7	39	37	25	29
OF	Brett Gardner, Charleston	Sr.	.Holly Hill, S.C.	.447	273	85	122	18	5	2	48	29	18	38
OF	Ryan Patterson, Louisiana State	Sr.	Rowlett, Texas	.369	249	74	92	23	2	20	56	30	28	7
OF	Sergio Pedroza, Cal State Fullerton	Jr.	Covina, Calif.	.324	219	47	71	12	2	16	58	38	49	6
DH	Nolan Reimold, Bowling Green	Jr.	Greenville, Pa.	.360	178	51	64	7	3	20	62	40	36	4
UT	Micah Owings, Tulane	Jr.	Gainesville, Ga.	.355	217	61	77	19	3	18	63	42	52	0

Pos	Player, School	YR	Hometown	W	L	ERA	G	GS	CG	SV	IP	H	BB	SO
SP	Brian Bogusevic, Tulane	Jr.	Oak Lawn, Ill.	13	3	3.25	19	19	2	0	130	130	42	129
SP	Matt Green, Louisiana-Monroe	Jr.	Monroe, La.	10	2	2.65	17	16	2	1	105	92	26	141
SP	Kevin Slowey, Winthrop	Jr.	Pittsburgh	14	2	2.18	19	17	7	1	136	91	13	134
SP	Matt Torra, Massachusetts	Jr.	Pittsfield, Mass.	6	3	1.14	14	13	8	0	95	56	16	111
RP	Neil Jamison, Long Beach State	Sr.	San Diego	4	0	0.00	27	0	0	11	30	16	5	27
UT	Micah Owings, Tulane	Jr.	Gainesville, Ga.	12	4	3.26	19	19	1	0	130	111	25	135

Gordon heads big year at hot corner

When historians look back at the 2005 season in college baseball, they may consider it the Year of the Third Baseman.

Never before have three college hitters who played the same position gone in the first five picks of the draft, dating back to 1965. But major league teams liked Ryan Braun, Alex Gordon and Ryan Zimmerman so much in 2005, they were tripping over themselves to draft them. None of the three were even drafted out of high school.

PLAYER *OF THE* **YEAR**

Braun was Baseball America's Freshman of the Year in 2003 and rebounded from an injury-plagued sophomore season to pace Miami's offense as a junior. He also moved to third base from shortstop and brought power commensurate with the position with him, slamming 18 home runs while hitting .388 with 76 RBIs. His all-around tools prompted the Brewers to draft him fifth overall, while envisioning him as the final piece in a future infield with Prince Fielder at first, Rickie Weeks at second and J.J. Hardy at short.

One pick earlier, the Nationals drafted Virginia's Zimmerman, regarded as the best defensive player in the country—regardless of position. Zimmerman, who hit .393-6-59 for the Cavaliers, became the first position player from the 2005 draft to play in the big leagues when the Nationals promoted him in September.

Zimmerman's glove was so advanced with Team USA in the summer of 2004 that he forced Gordon to move across the diamond to first base. Yet that was not a reflection on Gordon's abilities.

"He can play third," an American League crosschecker said at the time. "Just in the game last night, he showed the arm to make the throw from the line, he showed range to his left and he came in well on a ball. He can make all the plays. Zimmerman's just better there than he is, but Gordon can play third."

And while Zimmerman hit a team-best .468-4-27 for Team USA, Gordon adjusted to wood bats over the course of the summer and reversed a slow start. He batted .388-4-12 and was Team USA's top hitter in the World University Championship in Taiwan, helping lead Team USA to a gold medal.

Gordon's response? The day he returned to Nebraska after his Team USA stint, he grabbed his bats and went back into the batting cage. He went on to hit .382-18-62 with 23 stolen bases in 26 attempts in 2005, leading the Cornhuskers back to regional play after a one-year absence and ultimately back to Omaha, where the team won its first College World Series game ever.

JEFF GOLDEN

Hard work pays off
Gordon's dedication leads to domination

Gordon's work ethic extended to the field, where he dedicated himself to becoming the best defender he could be. His combination of bat and glove helped to cement his status as the top college prospect for the 2005 draft, and the Royals—whom he grew up rooting for—selected him with the draft's second overall pick.

For his performance—standing out in a crowded field, not just of third basemen—Baseball America selected Gordon as its 2005 College Player of the Year. He also won the Golden Spikes Award as the nation's top amateur player.

PREVIOUS **WINNERS**
1981—Mike Sodders, 3b, Arizona State
1982—Jeff Ledbetter, of/lhp, Florida State
1983—Dave Magadan, 1b, Alabama
1984—Oddibe McDowell, of, Arizona State
1985—Pete Incaviglia, of, Oklahoma State
1986—Casey Close, of, Michigan
1987—Robin Ventura, 3b, Oklahoma State
1988—John Olerud, 1b/lhp, Washington State
1989—Ben McDonald, rhp, Louisiana State
1990—Mike Kelly, of, Arizona State
1991—David McCarty, 1b, Stanford
1992—Phil Nevin, 3b, Cal State Fullerton
1993—Brooks Kieschnick, dh/rhp, Texas
1994—Jason Varitek, c, Georgia Tech
1995—Todd Helton, 1b/lhp, Tennessee
1996—Kris Benson, rhp, Clemson
1997—J.D. Drew, of, Florida State
1998—Jeff Austin, rhp, Stanford
1999—Jason Jennings, rhp, Baylor
2000—Mark Teixeira, 3b, Georgia Tech
2001—Mark Prior, rhp, Southern California
2002—Khalil Greene, ss, Clemson
2003—Rickie Weeks, 2b, Southern
2004—Jered Weaver, rhp, Long Beach State

If getting beaten out by Zimmerman for the third-base job was a wake-up call, Gordon wanted to prove to scouts that he was wide awake. That's even as he was being lulled to sleep by teams that wouldn't give him a good pitch to hit. Gordon walked 63 times in 2005.

"We tried everything with Gordon," one coach said when sizing up the Cornhuskers. "We hit him, we tried to go in and tried to go away. You have to go hard in and then soft away. Just don't let him beat you."

Gordon had to perform the way he did to stand out from the crowd of third basemen in the country in 2005. Beyond the Big Three, the position featured Tennessee's Chase Headley, who hit .387-14-65; Georgia Tech sophomore Wes Hodges (.397-9-51) as well as a pair of sterling freshmen, Tulane's Brad Emaus (.346-13-56) and Fresno State's Beau Mills (.319-22-63).

"There is definitely a lot of depth nationally at third base. It is not only me, Braun and Zimmerman," Gordon said. "There are quite a few other guys who are pretty good third basemen as well. There were a lot of third basemen picked early in this year's draft, and I think that is a tribute to the depth at the position. Hopefully all of us can continue our success later in our careers."

—JOHN MANUEL

Jones carries Tulane into elite status

Rick Jones remembers sleeping in his car to save money during recruiting trips in his coaching days at Division III Ferrum (Va.) College and then-Division II Elon in the 1980s. He still looks back on those days fondly. He figured those four-hour moonlight naps were a small price to pay for serving as a full-time college coach.

COACH *OF THE* **YEAR**

Some 20 years later, Jones spent a week in a hotel suite in Omaha. He guided Tulane to the College World Series, and though his team went 1-2 and lost a seven-run lead to Baylor in an elimination game that Jones called his most difficult loss ever, he still referred to 2005 as the most successful of his 24 years of coaching.

The Green Wave opened the season ranked No. 1 by Baseball America and carried that ranking into the College World Series, setting a school record with 56 wins and beating five-time national champion and in-state rival Louisiana State twice along the way. But the ending was bittersweet.

"It was our best year," Jones said. "I know in 20 years, when you reflect back—and I told my kids this after that game—the end will still be there, but only one team ends each year the way they wanted to. With all the weeks of being No. 1, they handled the pressure as well as anyone could and also finished the year with a 3.0 GPA as a team. It was a run that was so much fun."

JEFF GOLDEN

Remember it well
Rick Jones led Tulane to its best year

Fun turned to tragedy in September, however, when Hurricane Katrina ravaged the city of New Orleans and forced the cancellation of classes for the fall semester at Tulane. Tulane's baseball team was relocated to Texas Tech, some 850 miles from the school's New Orleans campus.

"It's changed dramatically, but it's changed dramatically for everyone in the New Orleans area," Jones said. "The momentum of our program was at its highest level, and all of a sudden we take an impact like that . . . We're not going to feel sorry for ourselves."

The 2005 season and events that followed may have ended in despair for Tulane, but it still proved a culmination for Jones' career at the school. The Green Wave has advanced to the NCAA tournament 10 times in his 12 years, including eight in a row, with two trips to the CWS. The program had made just seven NCAA appearances in the 101 years before Jones took over. Four of his former assistants—Brian Cleary (Cincinnati), Jim Schlossnagle (Texas Christian), Buddy Gouldsmith (Nevada-Las Vegas) and Rob Cooper (Wright State)—have become head coaches.

The combination of his success in 2005 and over the course of his career earned Jones Baseball America's 2005 Coach of the Year award.

"His best quality as a coach is he gets average players to play much higher than their potential because he demands perfection," said Scott Madden, a redshirt senior who played on the 2001 and 2005 CWS teams. "We do a drill in practice called 27 Outs where we go through defensive game situations, and we don't stop until we gets 27 straight outs. If we mess up, we start all over, and sometimes it can take an hour to get it right. But he never wavers. He gets the best out of you at practice and it carries over into the games."

—WILL KIMMEY

PREVIOUS **WINNERS**

1981	Ron Fraser, Miami
1982	Gene Stephenson, Wichita State
1983	Barry Shollenberger, Alabama
1984	Augie Garrido, Cal State Fullerton
1985	Ron Polk, Mississippi State
1986	Skip Bertman, Louisiana State
	Dave Snow, Loyola Marymount
1987	Mark Marquess, Stanford
1988	Jim Brock, Arizona State
1989	Dave Snow, Long Beach State
1990	Steve Webber, Georgia
1991	Jim Hendry, Creighton
1992	Andy Lopez, Pepperdine
1993	Gene Stephenson, Wichita State
1994	Jim Morris, Miami
1995	Rod Delmonico, Tennessee
1996	Skip Bertman, Louisiana State
1997	Jim Wells, Alabama
1998	Pat Murphy, Arizona State
1999	Wayne Graham, Rice
2000	Ray Tanner, South Carolina
2001	Dave Van Horn, Nebraska
2002	Augie Garrido, Texas
2003	George Horton, Cal State Fullerton
2004	David Perno, Georgia

ECSU's Wojick honored for success, loyalty

College assistant coaches tend to lead itinerant lives, using success in one place as a springboard to another higher-profile gig.

Bob Wojick

That's not exactly Bob Wojick's style. He's very content at Eastern Connecticut State, with the 2005-06 season representing his 30th season as an assistant to Bill Holowaty.

Wojick has helped the Warriors become one of the nation's most successful Division III programs. They have posted a 960-340-3 (.738) record and won four national championships during his 29 years there. ECSU has reached the postseason in 26 of those seasons, four times during the school's NAIA days and 22 times since moving to D-III.

For his success and long-lasting loyalty, Wojick earned the 2005 American Baseball Coaches Association/Baseball America Assistant Coach of the Year Award.

"I just do it because I like the game," he said. "It's one of my passions."

Savery shines for Rice

FRESHMAN OF THE YEAR

Forget for a moment that he led the Western Athletic Conference in batting while simultaneously finishing second in the league in ERA. The numbers alone were more than enough to earn Joe Savery Baseball America's 2005 Freshman of the Year honors, but they cannot quantify Savery's full value to Rice.

Consider the Owls' super-regional matchup with No. 1 Tulane. In the first inning of the first game, Savery (playing first base) slammed his right wrist into a fence chasing after a foul pop. Later it was discovered that he broke a metacarpal bone in the middle of his hand, but the Owls didn't know that at the time, and they wanted him in the lineup. When he came to bat in the second inning, Rice coach Wayne Graham asked Savery if he could bat, and Savery said he could not. Graham told him to bunt.

"I laid down my first successful drag bunt," Savery said. "I don't know how that happened, but I don't think it'll ever happen again."

The bunt drove in a run, giving Rice a 6-0 lead and allowing Graham to take Savery out of the game in the third inning. Not that Savery's weekend was over—broken right hand or not.

The lefthander took some painkiller and made his scheduled start the next day. And for six innings, he was masterful, holding Tulane's explosive offense scoreless on a pair of hits. The Green Wave pushed across a run against him in the seventh before piling on against the Rice bullpen in the ninth, making Savery the hard-luck loser in a terrific pitcher's duel against Micah Owings, another two-way standout.

Maybe it would have turned out differently if Savery's bat had been available in the late innings (though he normally did not bat in games he pitched), or in Rice's 9-6 loss in the third and deciding game that eliminated the Owls one win shy of reaching the College World Series.

"Obviously on Sunday, in a 1-0 game until the ninth inning, I wanted to get in there and give it a shot," Savery said. "I lost three or four one-run games this year, and as a competitor, you just want to help as much as you can."

It's safe to say Savery helped the Owls as much as he possibly could have in 2005, whether by compiling an 8-5, 2.43 record on the mound with a league-leading 129 strikeouts in 119 innings, or by hitting .382-5-43 at the plate, or by laying down a bunt. Savery, the WAC player of the year, played a major role in stabilizing a Rice program that lost the core of its 2003 national championship team after 2004—including righthanders Philip Humber, Jeff Niemann and Wade Townsend, three of the top eight picks in the 2004 draft.

Savery already looks likely to follow that group in the first round, but it won't come until 2007. And by then, his bat might have caught up with his arm.

"I think the sky's the limit," Graham said. "He's got a great delivery, he's very healthy and competitive. Anything can happen. We visualize a tremendous future and long career for him."

—AARON FITT

ANDREW WOOLLEY

Freshman to the forefront
Joe Savery led Rice to super-regionals

PREVIOUS WINNERS

1982—Cory Snyder, 3b, Brigham Young
1983—Rafael Palmeiro, of, Mississippi State
1984—Greg Swindell, lhp, Texas
1985—Jack McDowell, rhp, Stanford
Ron Wenrich, of, Georgia
1986—Robin Ventura, 3b, Oklahoma State
1987—Paul Carey, of, Stanford
1988—Kirk Dressendorfer, rhp, Texas
1989—Alex Fernandez, rhp, Miami
1990—Jeffrey Hammonds, of, Stanford
1991—Brooks Kieschnick, rhp-dh, Texas
1992—Todd Walker, 2b, Louisiana State
1993—Brett Laxton, rhp, Louisiana State
1994—R.A. Dickey, rhp, Tennessee
1995—Kyle Peterson, rhp, Stanford
1996—Pat Burrell, 3b, Miami
1997—Brian Roberts, ss, North Carolina
1998—Xavier Nady, 2b, California
1999—James Jurries, 2b, Tulane
2000—Kevin Howard, 3b, Miami
2001—Michael Aubrey, of/lhp, Tulane
2002—Stephen Drew, ss, Florida State
2003—Ryan Braun, ss, Miami
2004—Wade LeBlanc, lhp, Alabama

FRESHMAN ALL-AMERICA TEAM

FIRST TEAM

Pos., Player, School	AVG	AB	R	H	2B	3B	HR	RBI	SB
C J.P. Arencibia, Tennessee	.322	283	54	91	16	1	14	71	0
1B Sean Doolittle, Virginia	.313	224	36	70	12	1	11	57	7
2B Taylor Harbin, Clemson	.343	274	64	94	28	4	10	63	4
3B Beau Mills, Fresno State	.319	216	54	69	12	2	22	63	7
SS Todd Frazier, Rutgers	.295	220	61	65	13	3	9	36	19
OF Corey Brown, Oklahoma State	.360	175	53	63	7	6	13	46	8
OF Jacob Priday, Missouri	.305	223	53	68	13	3	9	67	8
OF Steve Strasbaugh, Western Carolina	.367	218	46	80	13	0	12	51	1
DH Matt Wieters, Georgia Tech	.366	227	53	83	17	1	10	68	1
UT Joe Savery, Rice	.382	204	49	78	17	2	5	43	7

	W	L	ERA	G	SV	IP	H	BB	SO
SP James Adkins, Tennessee	10	5	3.32	19	0	127	107	51	135
SP Adrian Alaniz, Texas	8	3	2.67	23	0	108	93	39	94
SP Johnny Dorn, Nebraska	12	2	2.16	20	1	104	75	21	76
SP John Ely, Miami (Ohio)	10	2	2.87	18	1	103	82	20	108
RP Mickey Storey, Florida Atlantic	10	1	1.70	23	7	95	78	23	82
UT Joe Savery, Rice	8	5	2.43	19	1	118	104	37	129

SECOND TEAM

C—Andrew Walker, Texas Christian (.310-11-38). **1B**—Justin Baum, Pacific (.332-17-45). **2B**—Jordan Pacheco, New Mexico (.332-5-63). **3B**—Brad Emaus, Tulane (.321-13-56). **SS**—Darwin Barney, Oregon State (.301-2-44). **OF**—Matt Hague, Washington (.419-8-34); Kody Kaiser, Oklahoma (.305-10-34, 13 SB); Danny Payne, Georgia Tech (.284-3-40, 24 SB). **DH**—Chris Johnson, Stetson (.383-8-52). **UT**—Cole White, Army (.331-10-32; 7-1, 3.07).

SP—Kenn Kasparek, Texas (8-0, 2.10); David Price, Vanderbilt (2-4, 2.86; 92 SO/69 IP); Wes Roemer, Cal State Fullerton (7-3, 3.80); Nick Schmidt, Arkansas (7-2, 2.88). **RP**—David Robertson, Alabama (7-5, 2.92, 8 SV, 105 SO/74 IP).

NCAA DIVISION I LEADERS

TEAM BATTING

TEAM BATTING	G	AVG
College of Charleston	63	.355
Jackson State	47	.346
Brigham Young	59	.337
Georgia Tech	64	.333
Georgia Southern	60	.331
Tennessee	67	.331
Arizona	60	.328
Louisiana-Lafayette	67	.327
New Mexico	58	.326
Davidson	50	.325

RUNS SCORED	G	R
Georgia Tech	64	593
College of Charleston	63	553
Louisiana-Lafayette	67	551
Tulane	68	541
Tennessee	67	532
New Mexico State	57	528
Nevada-Las Vegas	64	523
Florida	71	511
Missouri	63	509
Mississippi	68	501

DOUBLES	G	2B
College of Charleston	63	174
Brigham Young	59	164
Tulane	68	164
Nevada-Las Vegas	64	162
Tennessee	67	157
Louisiana-Lafayette	67	155
Arizona	60	153

TRIPLES	G	3B
Arizona	60	45
New Mexico	58	41
San Diego State	59	33
Jackson State	47	32
Texas-San Antonio	61	30
Charlotte	54	29
Indiana State	58	28

HOME RUNS	G	HR
Towson	58	105
New Mexico State	57	89
Brigham Young	59	86
Florida	71	85
Oklahoma State	59	84
Tulane	68	84
Troy	58	82
New Mexico	58	82
Mississippi	68	81
Louisiana State	62	80

STOLEN BASES	G	SB	ATT
Jackson State	47	170	200
Prairie View	58	161	185
Central Florida	60	143	176
Texas Tech	59	140	163
Troy	58	132	149
Miami (Ohio)	63	131	183
Mississippi Valley State	49	130	161
Virginia Commonwealth	55	129	158
Indiana State	58	128	166
Arizona State	67	128	176

TEAM PITCHING

WINNING PERCENTAGE	W	L	PCT
Tulane	56	12	.824
Oregon State	46	12	.793
Nebraska	57	15	.792
Texas	56	16	.778
College of Charleston	48	15	.762
Coastal Carolina	50	16	.758
Creighton	48	17	.738
Army	39	14	.736
Florida State	53	20	.726
Cal State Fullerton	46	18	.719

EARNED RUN AVERAGE	G	ERA
Long Beach State	59	2.53
Nebraska	72	2.69
Virginia	61	2.74
Texas	72	2.80
San Francisco	56	2.88
Oral Roberts	62	2.95
Oregon State	58	3.06
Army	53	3.08
Wichita State	75	3.16
North Carolina	61	3.17

TEAM FIELDING

FIELDING PERCENTAGE	G	PCT
Washington	55	.978
San Jose State	57	.978
Texas	72	.978
Stanford	59	.977
Cal State Fullerton	64	.977
San Francisco	56	.976
Texas A&M	56	.975
Virginia	61	.975
Nebraska	72	.975

INDIVIDUAL BATTING

BATTING AVERAGE

(Minimum 150 At-Bats)

	YR	AVG	G	AB	R	H	2B	3B	HR	RBI	BB	SO	SB
Heafner, Jay, Davidson	Jr.	.448	50	203	51	91	18	0	11	58	36	27	4
Gardner, Brett, Charleston	Sr.	.447	63	273	85	122	18	5	2	48	29	18	38
Lipsey, Carl, Jackson State	Sr.	.432	46	169	66	73	13	3	0	39	44	14	55
Kutler, Matt, Brown	Sr.	.427	42	171	43	73	13	3	8	41	13	18	6
Robinson, Shane, Florida State	So.	.427	73	286	96	122	25	4	6	43	57	28	1
Landin, Jaime, Texas A&M-CC	Sr.	.427	53	211	65	90	15	7	8	43	31	16	8
Bates, Aaron, N.C. State	So.	.425	58	214	61	91	16	1	12	64	37	27	3
Roberson, Ryan, George Wash.	Sr.	.423	53	194	47	82	14	1	16	52	23	42	16
Berry, Quintin, San Diego State	So.	.419	56	229	60	96	18	3	2	43	20	37	18
Rizzotti, Matt, Manhattan	Fr.	.416	48	173	53	72	21	0	9	57	40	32	0
Wabick, D.J., Charleston	Jr.	.415	63	260	69	108	27	2	9	66	26	33	5
Rhymes, Will, William & Mary	Sr.	.413	53	223	58	92	10	4	6	47	16	15	22
Martin, Todd, Middle Tenn. State	Jr.	.412	46	153	39	63	13	0	8	31	32	38	5
Blumenthal, Kyle, Cal Poly	Sr.	.410	56	183	42	75	15	0	4	53	39	21	4
Pacheco, Jordan, New Mexico	Fr.	.408	53	233	65	95	17	5	15	52	15	24	6
Jay, Jon, Miami	So.	.408	57	211	50	86	17	3	1	52	29	26	13
Payne, James, Ga. Southern	Sr.	.407	60	253	65	87	11	1	0	18	34	20	21
Preston, Tim, UNC Wilmington	Sr.	.406	59	251	69	102	20	3	10	51	11	37	16
Sabatella, Brian, Quinnipiac	Jr.	.406	50	192	46	78	15	0	11	40	19	27	5
Ellsbury, Jacoby, Oregon State	Jr.	.406	58	244	56	99	19	3	6	48	36	21	26
Hilligoss, Mitch, Purdue	So.	.404	56	228	52	92	16	1	4	37	8	18	25
Crowe, Trevor, Arizona	Jr.	.403	60	263	83	106	25	15	9	54	36	30	27
Jones, Jeremy, N.C. A&T	So.	.402	54	204	53	82	20	3	4	46	11	27	19
Dowling, Greg, Ga. Southern	Jr.	.400	59	235	47	94	12	1	5	57	33	14	4
McMahon, Pat, Northwestern	Jr.	.400	52	205	44	82	18	0	6	33	16	24	0
Hitchcock, Brendon, Binghamton	So.	.399	50	183	43	73	12	0	5	35	26	26	11
Rodriguez, Joaquin, Jackson State	So.	.399	45	168	51	67	16	4	3	49	15	26	3
Bolger, Brett, Eastern Ky.	Jr.	.398	54	196	47	78	10	1	1	42	24	8	20
Raynor, John, UNC Wilmington	Jr.	.397	53	209	59	83	17	5	5	56	18	37	23
Hodges, Wes, Ga. Tech	So.	.397	63	267	67	106	18	0	9	51	28	35	3
Carlson, Chris, New Mexico	So.	.395	57	220	66	87	24	6	15	79	38	32	1
Zimmerman, Ryan, Virginia	Jr.	.393	61	234	51	92	18	4	6	59	31	14	7
Kenefick, Mike, New York Tech	Jr.	.392	45	171	39	67	4	2	1	25	22	17	22
Hopkins, Luke, New Mexico State	Fr.	.392	56	212	58	83	19	0	14	79	39	38	2
Yema, Yahmed, Florida International	Jr.	.391	57	207	58	81	15	1	14	63	24	14	8
Hurst, Jason, Ga. Southern	Sr.	.390	60	241	49	94	24	1	10	60	31	49	11
Crowe, Nick, East Tenn. State	Sr.	.389	42	157	44	61	11	2	8	26	14	37	8
Braun, Ryan, Miami	Jr.	.388	58	219	70	85	16	2	18	76	33	39	23
Finigan, P.J., Southern Illinois	Sr.	.388	59	201	45	78	13	5	6	50	24	32	5
Jenkins, Andy, Oregon State	Sr.	.388	55	209	41	81	13	2	6	56	19	20	3
Steward, J.D., Texas Southern	Jr.	.388	47	152	41	59	10	1	10	52	24	32	26
Hargis, Chuck, East Tenn. State	Jr.	.387	50	204	51	79	22	0	7	42	12	26	12
Headley, Chase, Tennessee	Jr.	.387	67	238	82	92	24	3	14	65	63	23	6
Coker, Phillip, Charleston	Jr.	.386	62	251	67	97	13	2	1	35	46	32	23
Carter, Chuck, Texas A&M-CC	Sr.	.386	53	215	62	83	14	3	15	59	21	20	3
Bohm, Kyle, Michigan	Sr.	.386	61	228	43	88	12	1	5	65	31	18	2
Getz, Chris, Michigan	Jr.	.386	61	228	58	88	10	0	0	32	33	13	29
Cooksey, Matt, George Mason	Sr.	.386	50	184	66	71	13	8	7	32	42	26	34
Kunkel, Jeff, Michigan	Jr.	.384	56	190	28	73	14	1	3	45	20	17	4
Desmond, Geoff, Arkansas State	Sr.	.384	56	224	66	86	19	1	20	72	34	36	5
Thomas, Bryan, Virginia Tech		.384	47	185	22	71	16	4	1	31	13	36	3
Copeland, Ben, Pittsburgh	Jr.	.384	54	219	65	84	23	10	9	47	36	47	29
Lalli, Blake, Gard.-Webb	Jr.	.384	56	219	43	84	30	0	5	39	19	31	3
Pettway, Brian, Mississippi	Jr.	.383	68	266	56	102	19	0	21	67	35	47	1
Johnson, Chris, Stetson	Fr.	.383	63	261	62	100	23	1	8	52	35	25	0
Arensdorff, Michael, Valparaiso	So.	.382	51	204	38	78	20	0	4	43	18	33	3
Savery, Joe, Rice	Fr.	.382	63	204	49	78	17	2	5	43	35	35	7
Buck, Travis, Arizona State	Jr.	.382	67	288	82	110	24	3	6	43	28	35	27
Cavanaugh, Brian, E. Carolina	Sr.	.382	59	207	50	79	12	4	7	36	24	31	14
Moore, Caleb, East Tenn. State	Sr.	.382	52	207	56	79	20	1	15	73	29	26	2
Iorg, Eli, Tennessee	Jr.	.381	63	252	63	96	19	4	15	72	19	29	27
McGuire, Jared, Boston College	So.	.381	57	215	52	82	9	3	6	41	14	19	27
Koski, Kevin, Southern Illinois	So.	.380	59	242	57	92	12	2	0	32	25	13	15
Sickles, Ryan, Gardner-Webb	Sr.	.380	51	171	39	65	12	0	5	34	23	18	5
Fritz, Lee, West Virginia	Sr.	.379	53	203	42	77	13	3	5	45	14	13	2
Campbell, Chris, Charleston	So.	.379	63	269	64	102	21	0	15	87	22	27	4
Costanzo, Mike, Coastal Carolina	Jr.	.379	66	240	74	91	15	2	16	67	68	65	8

Mississippi		68	.974

RUNS

	Yr.	G	R
Shane Robinson, Florida State	So.	73	96
Brett Gardner, Charleston	Sr.	63	85
Trevor Crowe, Arizona	Jr.	60	83
Travis Buck, Arizona State	Jr.	67	82
Chase Headley, Tennessee	Jr.	67	82
John Coker, Louisiana-Lafayette	Sr.	67	82
Nathan Southard, Tulane	Jr.	68	80
Alex Gordon, Nebraska	Jr.	72	79
Danny Payne, Georgia Tech	Fr.	64	77
Logan Phillips, Georgia Southern	Sr.	60	76
Tyler Greene, Georgia Tech	Jr.	61	76

HITS

	Yr.	G	H
Brett Gardner, Charleston	Sr.	63	122
Shane Robinson, Florida State	So.	73	122
Seth Johnston, Texas	Sr.	72	115
Travis Buck, Arizona State	Jr.	67	110
D.J. Wabick, Charleston	Jr.	63	108
Trevor Crowe, Arizona	Jr.	60	106
Wes Hodges, Georgia Tech	So.	63	106
Tim Preston, UNC Wilmington	Sr.	59	102
Chris Campbell, Charleston	So.	63	102
Brian Pettway, Mississippi	Jr.	68	102
Tyler Greene, Georgia Tech	Jr.	61	100
Chris Johnson, Stetson	Fr.	63	100
Tommy Manzella, Tulane	Sr.	68	100
Jeff Corsaletti, Florida	Sr.	70	100

SLUGGING PERCENTAGE

(Minimum 150 At-Bats)	Yr.	G	PCT
Nolan Reimold, Bowling Green State	Jr.	50	.770
Mark Aranda, New Mexico State	Sr.	54	.767
Chris Carlson, New Mexico	So.	57	.764
Jason Maxey, Towson	Sr.	57	.756
Ryan Roberson, Geo. Washington	Sr.	53	.753
Geoff Desmond, Arkansas State	Sr.	56	.746
Micah Owings, Tulane	Jr.	64	.733
Adam Tucker, Birm.-Southern	Jr.	57	.729
Ryan Braun, Miami	Jr.	58	.726
Casper Wells, Towson	Jr.	58	.723

ON-BASE PERCENTAGE

(Minimum 150 At-Bats)	Yr.	G	PCT
Jay Heafner, Davidson	Jr.	50	.533
Shane Robinson, Florida State	So.	73	.532
Matt Rizzotti, Manhattan	Fr.	48	.530
Chase Headley, Tennessee	Jr.	67	.530
Mike Costanzo, Coastal Carolina	Jr.	66	.525
Aaron Bates, N.C. State	So.	58	.523
Alex Gordon, Nebraska	Jr.	72	.518
Todd Martin, Middle Tenn. State	Jr.	46	.516
Matt Cooksey, George Mason	Sr.	50	.515
Kyle Blumenthal, Cal Poly	Sr.	56	.511

TOTAL BASES

	Yr.	G	TB
Trevor Crowe, Arizona	Jr.	60	188
Matt LaPorta, Florida	So.	70	185
Brian Pettway, Mississippi	Jr.	68	184
Alex Gordon, Nebraska	Jr.	72	181
Ryan Patterson, Louisiana State	Sr.	61	179
Nick Stavinoha, Louisiana State	Sr.	62	174
Shane Robinson, Florida State	So.	73	173
Seth Johnston, Texas	Sr.	72	172
Kris Harvey, Clemson	Jr.	65	171
Brandon Taylor, Brigham Young	Jr.	58	170
Jeff Larish, Arizona State	Sr.	67	170
Chris Carlson, New Mexico	So.	57	168
Chris Campbell, Charleston	So.	63	168
Eli Iorg, Tennessee	Jr.	63	168
Jordan Pacheco, New Mexico	Fr.	53	167
Geoff Desmond, Arkansas State	Sr.	56	167
Adam Tucker, Birm.-Southern	Jr.	57	167
D.J. Wabick, Charleston	Jr.	63	166

DOUBLES

	Yr.	G	2B
Blake Lalli, Gardner-Webb	Jr.	56	30
Taylor Harbin, Clemson	Fr.	66	28
D.J. Wabick, Charleston	Jr.	63	27
Jeff Baisley, South Florida	Sr.	64	26
Elliot Singletary, Maryland	Sr.	51	25
Andrew Larsen, Stony Brook	Sr.	51	25
Ben Saylor, Brigham Young	Jr.	54	25
Karl Amonite, Auburn	Sr.	58	25
Chris Minaker, Stanford	Jr.	59	25
Trevor Crowe, Arizona	Jr.	60	25
Shane Robinson, Florida State	So.	73	25
Scott Sizemore, Va. Commonwealth	So.	55	24
Chris Carlson, New Mexico	So.	57	24
J.B. Tucker, Wake Forest	So.	58	24
Matt Poulk, UNC Wilmington	Sr.	59	24
Jason Hurst, Georgia Southern	Sr.	60	24
Chase Headley, Tennessee	Jr.	67	24
Travis Buck, Arizona State	Jr.	67	24
Tommy Manzella, Tulane	Sr.	68	24
Nathan Southard, Tulane	Jr.	68	24

TRIPLES

	Yr.	G	3B
Trevor Crowe, Arizona	Jr.	60	15
Cory Lane, Charlotte	So.	54	11
Ben Copeland, Pittsburgh	Jr.	54	10
John Coker, La.-Lafayette	Sr.	67	10
Garrick Haymore, New Mexico	Sr.	52	9
Collin Delome, Lamar	Fr.	56	9
Brandon Roberts, Cal Poly	Jr.	56	9
Brad Boyer, Arizona	Jr.	60	9
Matt Cooksey, George Mason	Sr.	50	8
Ryan Barba, New Mexico	Jr.	51	8
Jeremy McCann, Gardner-Webb	Jr.	57	8
James Guerrero, San Diego State	Jr.	59	8
Ryne Robinson, Miami (Ohio)	So.	60	8
Blake Davis, Cal State Fullerton	So.	62	8

HOME RUNS

	Yr.	G	HR
Matt LaPorta, Florida	So.	70	26
Adam Tucker, Birm.-Southern	Jr.	57	25
Kris Harvey, Clemson	Jr.	65	25
Jason Maxey, Towson	Sr.	57	23
Jeff Larish, Arizona State	Sr.	67	23
Mark Aranda, New Mex. State	Sr.	54	22
Adam Carr, Oklahoma State	Jr.	59	22
Beau Mills, Fresno State	Fr.	59	22
Steve Pearce, South Carolina	Sr.	58	21
Brian Pettway, Mississippi	Jr.	68	21
Nolan Reimold, Bowling Green	Jr.	50	20
Geoff Desmond, Arkansas State	Sr.	56	20
Brandon Taylor, Brigham Young	Jr.	58	20
Ryan Patterson, Louisiana State	Sr.	61	20
Daniel Carte, Winthrop	Jr.	66	19
Alex Gordon, Nebraska	Jr.	72	19
Ben Mummy, Nevada	Jr.	53	18
Shawn Scobee, Nevada	Jr.	53	18
Michael Ambort, Lamar	So.	57	18
Henry Gutierrez, Troy	Sr.	57	18
Ryan Braun, Miami	Jr.	58	18
Casper Wells, Towson	Jr.	58	18
Dee Brown, Central Florida	Sr.	59	18
Nick Stavinoha, Louisiana State	Sr.	62	18
Micah Owings, Tulane	Jr.	64	18
Stephen Head, Mississippi	Jr.	68	18

RUNS BATTED IN

	Yr.	G	RBI
Chris Campbell, Charleston	So.	63	87
Adam Carr, Oklahoma State	Jr.	59	86
Mark Aranda, New Mexico State	Sr.	54	85
Brandon Taylor, Brigham Young	Jr.	58	83
Brad Willcutt, So. Mississippi	Sr.	62	82
Jordan Brown, Arizona	Jr.	60	80
Luke Hopkins, New Mex. State	Fr.	56	79
Chris Carlson, New Mexico	So.	57	79
Matt LaPorta, Florida	So.	70	79
Ryan Braun, Miami	Jr.	58	76

Nolan Reimold: .770 slugging percentage

Mike Costanzo: 68 walks

Daniel Carte, Winthrop	Jr.	66	74
Tuffy Gosewisch, Arizona State	Sr.	67	74
Caleb Moore, East Tenn. State	Sr.	52	73
Adam Tucker, Birm.-Southern	Jr.	57	73
Matt Poulk, UNC Wilmington	Sr.	59	73
James Boone, Missouri	Jr.	55	72
Geoff Desmond, Arkansas State	Sr.	56	72
Jason Maxey, Towson	Sr.	57	72
Tyler Greene, Georgia Tech	Jr.	61	72
Eli Iorg, Tennessee	Jr.	63	72
Michael DeJesus, Coastal Carolina	Jr.	66	72
Dee Brown, Central Florida	Sr.	59	71
Jeff Baisley, South Florida	Sr.	64	71
J.P. Arencibia, Tennessee	Fr.	67	71
Kris Harvey, Clemson	Jr.	65	70
Evan Erickson, Elon	Sr.	57	68
Matt Wieters, Georgia Tech	Fr.	60	68
Matt Edwards, Nortre Dame	Sr.	63	68
Dallas Morris, La.-Lafayette	Sr.	65	68
Stephen Head, Mississippi	Jr.	68	68

WALKS

	Yr.	G	BB
Mike Costanzo, Coastal Carolina	Jr.	66	68
Chase Headley, Tennessee	Jr.	67	63
Alex Gordon, Nebraska	Jr.	72	63
Phillip Hawke, La.-Lafayette	Sr.	64	61
Danny Payne, Georgia Tech	Fr.	64	60

STRIKEOUTS

	Yr.	G	SO
Brendan Winn, South Carolina	Sr.	52	78
Tony Thomas, Florida State	Fr.	72	75
Matt Wilkerson, UC Santa Barbara	Sr.	56	74
Tyler Greene, Georgia Tech	Jr.	61	71
Drew Stubbs, Texas	So.	72	71

TOUGHEST TO STRIKE OUT

(Minimum 125 At-Bats)	Yr.	AB	SO	Ratio
Mike MacMillan, N.Y. Tech	Jr.	146	4	36.5
Corey Wimberly, Alcorn State	So.	132	5	26.4
Brett Bolger, East. Kentucky	Jr.	196	8	24.5
DeCarlos Hughley, Ala. State	Sr.	157	7	22.4
Mark Hallberg, Ill.-Chicago	Fr.	237	11	21.5

STOLEN BASES

	Yr.	G	SB	ATT
Adam Godwin, Troy	Sr.	58	84	93
Carl Lipsey, Jackson State	Sr.	46	55	64
Shane Robinson, Fla. State	So.	73	49	56
Zach Penprase, Miss. Valley St.	So.	48	44	50
Corey Wimberly, Alcorn St.	So.	38	42	47
Carlos Picornell, Beth.-Cookman	Jr.	50	41	51
Jonathan Sakurai, Chicago State	So.	55	38	49
Brett Gardner, Charleston	Sr.	63	38	43
Dennis Diaz, Fla. International	Sr.	59	37	46
James Payne, Ga. Southern	Sr.	60	37	49
Mike McBryde, Florida Atlantic	So.	61	34	38
Matt Cooksey, George Mason	Sr.	50	34	38
Ryne Robinson, Miami (Ohio)	So.	60	34	44
Derek Schermerhorn, Wichita St.	So.	75	34	44

HIT BY PITCH

	Yr.	G	HBP
Gary Morris, Elon	Sr.	57	32
Brett Lilley, Notre Dame	Fr.	63	30
Ryder Mathias, Wake Forest	Sr.	58	29
Graham Maiden, Char. Southern	So.	53	23
John McKee, Missouri	So.	62	23
Alex Suarez, Tennessee	Sr.	65	23

INDIVIDUAL PITCHING

EARNED RUN AVERAGE

(Minimum 60 Innings)

	Yr	W	L	ERA	G	GS	CG	SV	IP	H	R	ER	BB	SO
Matt Torra, Massachussetts	Jr.	6	3	1.14	14	13	8	0	95	56	17	12	16	111
Nick Hill, Army	So.	10	2	1.21	14	13	5	0	89	60	17	12	19	90
Lance Broadway, TCU	Jr.	15	1	1.62	19	16	5	0	117	83	28	21	35	151
Craig Hansen, St. John's	Jr.	3	2	1.68	31	1	0	14	64	38	14	12	20	85
Mickey Storey, Fla. Atlantic	Fr.	10	1	1.70	23	9	2	7	95	78	25	18	23	82
J. Brent Cox, Texas	Jr.	8	3	1.73	42	0	0	19	78	57	18	15	25	87
John Madden, Auburn	Sr.	6	2	1.77	44	0	0	7	86	80	27	17	19	58
Josh Schmidt, Pacific	Sr.	6	4	1.79	36	0	0	11	60	49	17	12	25	89
Dennis Bigley, Oral Roberts	Sr.	11	4	1.81	17	17	7	0	109	72	28	22	31	84
Brad Kilby, San Jose State	Sr.	7	2	1.85	16	8	2	1	78	60	22	16	31	54
Max Scherzer, Missouri	So.	9	4	1.86	16	16	1	0	106	59	26	22	41	131
Jeff Mandel, Baylor	So.	4	0	1.91	25	4	0	0	66	52	21	14	23	27
Ryan Schreppel, CS Fullerton	Jr.	6	1	1.92	12	11	0	0	70	38	17	15	30	41
Mike Pelfrey, Wichita State	Jr.	12	3	1.93	19	19	7	0	140	96	35	30	30	143
Trey Hearne, Texas A&M-CC	Sr.	8	1	2.00	17	13	3	0	108	79	32	24	38	116
Kevin Lynch, Florida State	Sr.	12	0	2.03	46	0	0	0	62	45	20	14	23	67
Steve Richard, Maine	So.	9	1	2.07	16	15	1	0	100	88	34	23	44	90
Robert Brant, Pittsburgh	Fr.	7	2	2.07	15	7	2	1	61	47	18	14	23	68
Dallas Buck, Oregon State	So.	12	1	2.09	19	18	2	1	129	90	47	30	51	118
Travis Banwart, Wichita State	Fr.	8	1	2.09	17	15	0	0	82	75	27	19	31	68
Kenn Kasparek, Texas	Fr.	8	0	2.10	15	12	1	0	73	53	21	17	31	46
Josh Sowers, Yale	Sr.	6	1	2.10	9	9	5	0	60	56	20	14	11	63
Robert Woodard, No. Carolina	So.	8	0	2.11	23	11	1	0	98	82	35	23	19	79
Jeff Kamrath, Virginia	Sr.	9	5	2.12	16	14	1	0	102	77	29	24	27	80
Jonah Nickerson, Oregon St.	So.	9	2	2.13	18	18	1	0	110	88	37	26	29	114
Noah Booth, Wichita State	So.	4	6	2.13	33	0	0	10	80	62	21	19	18	87
Ryan LaMotta, Baylor	Jr.	5	2	2.15	36	0	0	7	80	60	22	19	21	82
Johnny Dorn, Nebraska	Fr.	12	2	2.16	20	13	1	1	104	75	33	25	21	76
Kevin Slowey, Winthrop	Jr.	14	2	2.18	19	17	7	1	136	91	34	33	13	134
Jay Monti, Sacred Heart	So.	8	5	2.20	15	11	9	1	82	68	30	20	10	56
Nick Pereira, San Francisco	Sr.	10	3	2.21	16	16	3	0	106	90	31	26	33	93
Cesar Carrillo, Miami	Jr.	13	3	2.22	19	18	3	1	126	100	45	31	23	127
Bryan Henry, Florida State	So.	9	3	2.22	17	11	1	0	89	71	25	22	18	58
Matt Marc-Aurele, Monmouth	So.	3	2	2.24	20	6	2	0	72	60	25	18	13	64
Luke Hochevar, Tennessee	Jr.	15	5	2.25	19	19	3	0	140	104	46	35	54	154
John Lannan, Siena	Jr.	10	2	2.29	13	12	8	0	82	62	26	21	28	83
Nick Jones, Oral Roberts	Jr.	8	2	2.30	12	12	3	0	74	57	21	19	18	60
Jason Determann, Louisiana St.	Jr.	5	0	2.30	27	1	0	7	62	61	19	16	12	74
Anthony Varvaro, St. John's	Jr.	9	3	2.32	14	14	2	0	85	54	25	22	35	115
Richard Rodriguez, Beth.-Cook.	Jr.	4	4	2.32	10	9	1	0	62	54	26	16	22	54
Derek Miller, Vermont	Sr.	7	3	2.35	12	12	6	0	88	62	28	23	25	103
Nate Jeanes, Boston College	Jr.	3	5	2.38	17	12	2	0	75	57	26	20	22	71
Daniel Greenwalt, Oral Roberts	Jr.	5	3	2.38	27	0	0	4	64	46	20	17	22	57
Austin Faught, La.-Lafayette	Sr.	12	0	2.40	16	16	0	0	90	67	31	24	38	72
Seth Kuwik, Lipscomb	Sr.	7	3	2.42	29	4	0	6	74	68	31	20	21	75
Joe Savery, Rice	Fr.	8	5	2.43	19	17	2	1	118	104	43	32	37	129
Bernard Robert, SE Louisiana	So.	9	4	2.43	17	12	9	0	115	100	38	31	33	101
Marco Estrada, Long Beach State	Jr.	8	3	2.43	18	17	0	0	111	84	39	30	29	104
Dave McKae, UC Davis	Sr.	8	6	2.43	17	16	4	1	107	92	35	29	17	100
Anthony Sullivan, Saint John's	So.	8	3	2.43	20	12	1	2	78	54	26	21	39	73

WINS	Yr.	W	L
Lance Broadway, TCU	Jr.	15	1
Luke Hochevar, Tennessee	Jr.	15	3
Kevin Slowey, Winthrop	Jr.	14	2
Brian Bogusevic, Tulane	Jr.	13	3
Cesar Carillo, Miami	Jr.	13	3
Ricky Romero, CS Fullerton	Jr.	13	5
Austin Faught, La.-Lafayette	Sr.	12	0
Kevin Lynch, Florida State	Sr.	12	0
Scott Reese, Creighton	So.	12	0
Dallas Buck, Oregon State	So.	12	1
Johnny Dorn, Nebraska	Fr.	12	2
Ricky Shefka, Coastal Carolina	Jr.	12	2
Ian Kennedy, So. California	So.	12	3
Mike Pelfrey, Wichita State	Jr.	12	3
Luke Trubee, Dayton	Jr.	12	3
Josh Geer, Rice	Jr.	12	4
Kyle McCulloch, Texas	So.	12	4
Garrett Olson, Cal Poly	Jr.	12	4
Micah Owings, Tulane	Jr.	12	4

LOSSES	Yr.	W	L
Chris Lopez, Iona	Sr.	1	13
Adam Sali, Chicago State	Sr.	1	12
Chris Freshour, Chicago State	Fr.	1	11
Bryan Beck, UCLA	Sr.	1	11
Danny Otero, Duke	So.	5	11

APPEARANCES	Yr.	G
Connor Falkenbach, Florida	Sr.	51
Kevin Lynch, Florida State	Sr.	46
John Madden, Auburn	Sr.	44
J. Brent Cox, Texas	Jr.	42
Clayton Stewart, Texas	Sr.	41

Ian Kennedy: 158 strikeouts

COMPLETE GAMES	Yr.	GS	CG
Jay Monti, Sacred Heart	So.	11	9
Bernard Robert, SE Louisiana	So.	12	9
Craig Stammen, Dayton	Jr.	15	9
Luke Trubee, Dayton	Jr.	18	9
John Lannan, Siena	Jr.	12	8
Matt Torra, Massachussetts	Jr.	13	8
Chris Mason, UNC Greensboro	Jr.	15	8
Rowdy Hardy, Austin Peay State	Jr.	16	8

Matt Torra: 1.14 ERA

SAVES	Yr.	G	SV
J. Brent Cox, Texas	Jr.	42	19
Steven Kleen, Pepperdine	Sr.	29	17
Brett Jensen, Nebraska	Jr.	33	16
Brett Harker, Charleston	Jr.	28	15
Erik Morrison, Ball State	Sr.	28	15
Tyler Chambliss, Fla. State	So.	39	15
Mike Bille, Cal Poly	Sr.	27	14
Casey Lambert, Virginia	So.	27	14
Derek Stanfield, Akron	Sr.	29	14
Alex McRobbie, UCSB	Sr.	30	14
Craig Hansen, St. John's	Jr.	31	14
Kevin Gunderson, Oregon State	So.	33	14
Paul Koss, So. California	So.	34	14
Mike Costanzo, Co. Carolina	Jr.	37	14

INNINGS PITCHED	Yr.	G	IP
P.J. Walters, South Alabama	So.	20	142
Mike Pelfrey, Wichita State	Jr.	19	140
Luke Hochevar, Tennessee	Jr.	19	140
Kyle McCulloch, Texas	So.	26	139
Garrett Olson, Cal Poly	Jr.	19	136
Ricky Romero, CS Fullerton	Jr.	18	134
Brian Bogusevic, Tulane	Jr.	19	130
Micah Owings, Tulane	Jr.	19	130
Dallas Buck, Oregon State	So.	19	129
Kea Kometani, Pepperdine	Sr.	19	128

WALKS	Yr.	IP	BB
Chris Smith, Jackson State	Jr.	64	72
Tim Lincecum, Washington	So.	104	71
Mark McCormick, Baylor	Jr.	113	66
Omar Stokley, Jackson State	Sr.	70	62
Tim Johnson, UNC Asheville	Fr.	84	62

STRIKEOUTS	Yr.	IP	SO
Ian Kennedy, So. California	So.	117	158
Luke Hochevar, Tennessee	Jr.	140	154
Lance Broadway, TCU	Jr.	117	151
Mike Pelfrey, Wichita State	Jr.	140	143
Matt Green, Louisiana-Monroe	Jr.	105	141
Ricky Romero, CS Fullerton	Jr.	134	139
Chris Mason, UNC Greensboro	Jr.	118	135
James Adkins, Tennessee	Fr.	127	135
Micah Owings, Tulane	Jr.	129	135
Michael Hauff, N.C. A&T	Jr.	108	132
Tim Lincecum, Washington	So.	104	131
Max Scherzer, Missouri	So.	106	131

STRIKEOUTS/9 INNINGS

(Minimum 50 Innings)	Yr.	IP	SO	AVG
Dan Griffin, Niagara	So.	78	120	13.8
Josh Schmidt, Pacific	Sr.	60	89	13.3
David Robertson, Alabama	Fr.	74	105	12.8
Chris Blazek, Vermont	Jr.	67	94	12.6
Ian Kennedy, So. California	So.	117	158	12.2
Anthony Varvaro, St. John's	Jr.	85	115	12.1
Matt Green, La.-Monroe	Jr.	105	141	12.1
David Price, Vanderbilt	Fr.	69	92	11.9
Craig Hansen, St. John's	Jr.	64	85	11.9
Lance Broadway, TCU	Jr.	117	151	11.6
Tim Lincecum, Washington	So.	104	131	11.3
Matt Kniginyzky, High Point	Sr.	61	76	11.2

COLLEGE TOP 25

BATTERS: 10 or more at-bats. **PITCHERS:** 5 or more innings. **Boldface** indicates selected in 2005 draft.

1. TEXAS

Coach: Augie Garrido **Record:** 56-16

BATTING	YR	AVG	AB	R	H	2B	3B	HR	RBI	SB
Seth Johnston, ss/2b	Sr.	.378	304	59	115	20	5	9	66	15
Will Crouch, dh	Sr.	.336	149	30	50	8	1	7	32	1
Taylor Teagarden, c	Jr.	.333	222	52	74	22	1	7	33	4
Chance Wheeless, 1b	So.	.314	245	36	77	12	3	6	45	2
Carson Kainer, of/dh	So.	.312	202	36	63	9	1	3	31	5
Drew Stubbs, of	So.	.311	283	67	88	20	4	11	46	32
Nick Peoples, of	So.	.306	186	50	57	9	1	1	25	13
Robby Hudson, 2b/ss	Sr.	.272	257	37	70	5	0	0	27	12
Clay Van Hook, 2b/3b/c	So.	.266	109	21	29	3	0	0	14	6
Calvin Beamon, of/dh	Jr.	.253	99	20	25	5	3	0	14	5
David Maroul, 3b	Sr.	.251	195	36	49	11	2	11	35	1
Thomas Incaviglia, 1b/of	So.	.223	103	10	23	3	1	0	18	2
Todd Gilfillan, c	Fr.	.208	24	5	5	0	1	1	2	0
Dooley Prince, of/dh	Sr.	.182	44	8	8	1	0	0	7	4
Bryan Herrera, of	Jr.	.100	10	2	1	1	0	0	1	1

PITCHING	YR	W	L	ERA	G	SV	IP	H	BB	SO
J. Brent Cox, rhp	Jr.	8	3	1.73	42	19	78	57	25	87
Kenn Kasparek, rhp	Fr.	8	0	2.10	15	0	73	53	31	46
Adrian Alaniz, rhp	Fr.	8	3	2.67	23	0	108	93	39	94
Jordon Street, lhp	Fr.	0	1	2.87	9	0	16	10	4	4
Kyle McCulloch, rhp	So.	12	4	2.92	26	0	139	137	45	99
Clayton Stewart, rhp	Sr.	9	0	3.04	41	1	68	47	24	58
Randy Boone, rhp	So.	7	4	3.46	25	0	109	103	38	95
Buck Cody, lhp	Sr.	4	1	3.81	34	1	52	46	30	38

2. FLORIDA

Coach: Pat McMahon **Record:** 48-23

BATTING	YR	AVG	AB	R	H	2B	3B	HR	RBI	SB
Matt Gaski, 3b	Fr.	.364	11	0	4	0	0	0	1	0
Jeff Corsaletti, of	Sr.	.358	279	68	100	18	0	10	53	11
Matt LaPorta, 1b	So.	.328	265	75	87	16	2	26	79	3
Adam Davis, 2b	So.	.306	294	75	90	15	1	12	63	24
Brian Jeroloman, c	So.	.298	248	48	74	11	0	8	49	2
Stephen Barton, dh/of/3b	Jr.	.295	190	46	56	11	0	0	26	10
Gavin Dickey, of	So.	.292	219	43	64	9	0	3	20	8
Jared Kubin, dh	Fr.	.292	106	17	31	6	1	2	18	2
Brian Leclerc, of	So.	.277	267	46	74	10	0	15	64	5
Brandon McArthur, 3b	Fr.	.268	228	32	61	6	1	2	30	1
Justin Tordi, ss	Jr.	.238	260	43	62	10	1	4	32	1
Bryson Barber, dh	Fr.	.219	32	7	7	1	1	1	7	0
Daniel Brooks, dh/of	Jr.	.172	29	3	5	0	0	1	3	0
Chris Woods, of	Jr.	.167	12	6	2	0	0	0	1	0
Andy Davis, 1b	Jr.	.154	13	1	2	0	0	0	1	0

PITCHING	YR	W	L	ERA	G	SV	IP	H	BB	SO
Darren O'Day, rhp	Jr.	8	3	2.87	34	7	69	56	13	63
Connor Falkenbach, rhp	Sr.	3	3	3.15	51	9	91	114	17	75
Bryan Ball, rhp	Jr.	7	6	3.45	17	0	102	94	37	72
Steven Porter, lhp	So.	2	1	3.72	25	0	10	10	9	11
Stephen Locke, lhp	Fr.	5	2	4.04	16	0	65	72	14	46
Alan Horne, rhp	Jr.	10	2	4.05	19	0	113	122	55	108
Tommy Boss, rhp	Sr.	9	4	4.11	20	0	112	126	18	63
Mike Pete, lhp	Sr.	4	0	5.04	26	1	30	34	8	25
Michael Branham, rhp	Fr.	0	0	5.87	7	0	8	10	3	6
Tommy Wynn, rhp	Fr.	0	2	7.79	10	0	17	18	9	14
Bryan Augenstein, rhp	Fr.	0	0	7.88	9	0	16	21	9	13

3. TULANE

Coach: Rick Jones **Record:** 56-12

BATTING	YR	AVG	AB	R	H	2B	3B	HR	RBI	SB
Micah Owings, 1b/dh/of	Jr.	.355	217	61	77	19	3	18	63	0
Scott Madden, dh/1b/c	Sr.	.352	193	41	68	12	2	4	47	1
Tommy Manzella, ss	Sr.	.347	288	59	100	24	2	8	63	21
Nathan Southard, of	Jr.	.341	279	80	95	24	1	12	53	16
Brian Bogusevic, of/dh	Jr.	.328	131	24	43	9	0	0	25	9
Brad Emaus, 3b	Fr.	.321	262	71	84	19	0	13	56	5
Mark Hamilton, of/1b	So.	.318	157	37	50	11	0	11	46	0
Greg Dini, c	Sr.	.294	238	50	70	16	0	6	51	0
Joe Holland, 2b	Sr.	.293	205	38	60	14	0	6	31	3
Matt Barket, of	Sr.	.279	215	43	60	11	0	6	46	13
Will Rice, of	Fr.	.257	35	9	9	0	0	0	6	0
Cat Everett, 2b	Fr.	.250	64	12	16	1	0	0	4	0
Sean Morgan, dh	Fr.	.158	19	5	3	2	0	0	2	1
Rustin Rebowe, of	Fr.	.083	12	3	1	1	0	0	2	0

PITCHING	YR	W	L	ERA	G	SV	IP	H	BB	SO
Sean Morgan, rhp	Fr.	6	1	2.72	28	5	36	34	29	42
Daniel Latham, rhp	So.	2	0	3.22	31	13	45	43	10	36
Brian Bogusevic, lhp	Jr.	13	3	3.25	19	0	130	130	42	129
Micah Owings, rhp	Jr.	12	4	3.26	19	0	130	111	25	135
Billy Mohl, rhp	Jr.	4	1	3.80	20	1	45	45	9	41
Chris Worster, rhp	Fr.	0	0	4.32	51	1	8	8	6	5
Brandon Gomes, rhp	So.	8	2	4.42	20	2	90	98	17	82
J.R. Crowel, lhp	Jr.	10	1	4.86	17	0	93	95	30	83
Ricky Fairchild, rhp	Jr.	1	0	6.29	17	0	24	24	13	25

4. BAYLOR

Coach: Steve Smith **Record:** 46-24

BATTING	YR	AVG	AB	R	H	2B	3B	HR	RBI	SB
Josh Ford, c/dh	Sr.	.328	259	47	85	19	2	9	41	7
Zach Dillon, dh/c	Jr.	.304	247	29	75	20	1	2	43	2
Michael Griffin, 2b	Sr.	.293	294	51	86	16	2	7	34	8
Kevin Russo, 3b	Jr.	.286	259	41	74	8	2	3	36	8
Reid Brees, of	Sr.	.278	212	23	59	14	2	2	26	1
Kyle Reynolds, 1b	Jr.	.258	225	40	58	14	0	8	34	11
Chase Gerdes, of	So.	.257	175	23	45	5	5	1	23	11
Paul Witt, ss	Sr.	.251	251	37	63	11	1	1	29	7
Kevin Sevigny, of	Jr.	.230	152	24	35	9	4	3	23	7
Jeff Mandel, 1b	So.	.205	44	7	9	2	0	2	8	2
Mike Pankratz, of	Jr.	.198	111	16	22	3	0	3	16	2
Seth Fortenberry, of	Jr.	.192	125	19	24	4	2	5	17	5

PITCHING	YR	W	L	ERA	G	SV	IP	H	BB	SO
Jeff Mandel, rhp	So.	4	0	1.91	25	0	66	52	23	27
Ryan LaMotta, rhp	Jr.	5	2	2.15	36	7	80	60	21	82
Abe Woody, rhp	Jr.	10	3	2.58	36	11	66	48	14	41
Mark McCormick, rhp	Jr.	8	4	2.96	20	0	113	73	66	115
Tyler Bullock, rhp	Jr.	1	0	3.04	22	1	27	24	12	22
Trey Taylor, lhp	Sr.	7	6	3.62	19	0	104	96	46	89
Andy Pape, rhp	Jr.	1	2	3.92	10	0	21	15	13	12
Cory VanAllen, lhp	So.	8	4	4.02	19	0	107	118	34	68
Sean Walker, rhp	Sr.	1	3	4.22	8	0	21	14	20	15
Randall Linebaugh, rhp	Fr.	1	0	4.76	12	0	17	27	5	10
Nick Cassavechia, rhp	Fr.	0	0	7.94	5	0	6	8	3	4

5. NEBRASKA

Coach: Mike Anderson **Record:** 57-15

BATTING	YR	AVG	AB	R	H	2B	3B	HR	RBI	SB
Mark Hightower, c	Fr.	.400	10	1	4	0	0	0	3	1
Alex Gordon, 3b	Jr.	.372	253	79	94	22	4	19	66	23
Andy Gerch, of	Fr.	.364	151	33	55	7	2	4	35	3
Brandon Buckman, dh/1b	Jr.	.335	161	26	54	10	0	2	30	4
Daniel Bruce, of	Sr.	.322	230	47	74	22	2	5	32	9
Curtis Ledbetter, 1b/c	Sr.	.319	288	52	92	18	1	13	55	3
Joe Simokaitis, ss	Sr.	.310	277	53	86	8	0	3	37	18
Ryan Bohanan, dh	Fr.	.306	62	11	19	3	0	1	14	0
Brandon Fusilier, of/dh	Sr.	.282	188	37	53	6	1	12	45	14
Ryan Wehrle, 2b	Fr.	.275	149	26	41	6	1	0	25	4
Jesse Boyer, of	Sr.	.271	177	34	48	11	1	1	17	4
Jake Opitz, 2b	Fr.	.256	129	19	33	6	0	3	14	3
Trey Adams, of	Jr.	.238	101	18	24	3	3	1	9	7
Jeff Christy, c	Jr.	.236	191	32	45	5	0	1	32	4
Bryce Nimmo, of	Fr.	.210	81	19	17	1	0	2	12	4

PITCHING	YR	W	L	ERA	G	SV	IP	H	BB	SO
Brett Jensen, rhp	Jr.	3	5	1.96	33	16	46	36	9	46
Dustin Timm, rhp	Sr.	4	1	2.13	19	1	38	30	9	23
Johnny Dorn, rhp	Fr.	12	2	2.16	20	1	104	75	21	76
Jeremy Becker, lhp	Sr.	1	0	2.57	10	0	7	8	0	5
Matt Foust, rhp	Fr.	0	0	2.57	5	1	7	6	3	5
Zach Kroenke, lhp	Jr.	7	2	2.78	20	1	97	80	28	88
Ryan Bohanan, rhp	Fr.	1	1	2.79	21	1	29	25	10	22

Joba Chamberlain, rhp	So.	10	2	2.81	18	0	119	91	33	130
Tony Watson, lhp	Fr.	6	1	2.82	23	1	45	41	26	39
Brian Duensing, lhp	Jr.	8	0	3.00	23	0	84	69	28	52
Mike Harmelink, rhp	So.	0	0	3.00	5	0	6	5	4	8
Phil Shirek, rhp	Sr.	4	1	3.32	14	1	41	42	10	26
Luke Wertz, rhp	Fr.	1	0	4.42	10	0	18	22	5	18

6. ARIZONA STATE

Coach: Pat Murphy **Record:** 42-25

BATTING	YR	AVG	AB	R	H	2B	3B	HR	RBI	SB
Austin Stockfisch, c	Fr.	.500	18	4	9	0	0	2	4	0
Travis Buck, of/3b	Jr.	.382	288	82	110	24	3	6	43	27
Colin Curtis, of	So.	.342	260	52	89	14	1	2	45	17
Jeff Larish, 1b/of/3b	Sr.	.324	250	72	81	18	1	23	67	11
Tuffy Gosewisch, c	Sr.	.321	252	43	81	17	2	6	74	5
Seth Dhaenens, 2b/ss	So.	.312	154	29	48	5	0	2	31	10
J.J. Sferra, of	Fr.	.311	196	36	61	5	1	0	22	8
Willy Fox, dh	Fr.	.295	105	24	31	4	1	1	27	7
Joey Hooft, 3b/2b/dh	Sr.	.293	188	30	55	9	1	1	28	13
Rocky Laguna, of/dh	Fr.	.283	120	24	34	10	2	1	26	10
Andrew Romine, ss	Fr.	.282	195	26	55	5	3	2	23	14
Zechry Zinicola, dh/1b	So.	.276	116	13	32	5	0	3	15	0
Vinny Biancamano, 2b/3b	Fr.	.233	43	8	10	2	0	0	3	0
Joe Persichina, 2b/ss/3b	So.	.214	112	19	24	4	2	0	15	4
Eric Sogard, 3b	Fr.	.182	22	4	4	1	0	0	4	0
D.J. Butler, of	Fr.	.167	18	1	3	0	0	0	1	1
Jeff Landry, 3b	Fr.	.133	15	2	2	0	0	0	0	1

PITCHING	YR	W	L	ERA	G	SV	IP	H	BB	SO
Erik Averill, lhp	Jr.	11	4	3.39	24	0	127	131	30	99
Jason Urquidez, rhp	Sr.	10	4	3.93	29	2	121	115	56	98
Ty Marotz, rhp	Sr.	2	1	4.18	16	0	28	35	5	29
Brett Bordes, lhp	Jr.	5	7	4.24	38	4	74	72	29	54
Kevin Dryanski, rhp	Jr.	0	0	4.67	11	0	17	24	4	8
Zechry Zinicola, rhp	So.	4	4	5.48	27	4	64	56	38	55
Seth Garrison, rhp	Fr.	0	0	5.50	13	1	18	24	10	21
Pat Bresnehan, rhp	So.	5	4	5.60	31	2	88	100	32	79
Josh Satow, lhp	Fr.	1	0	6.75	4	0	8	13	5	1
Tony Barnette, rhp	Jr.	4	1	7.02	29	2	50	71	19	53

7. OREGON STATE

Coach: Pat Casey **Record:** 46-12

BATTING	YR	AVG	AB	R	H	2B	3B	HR	RBI	SB
Jacoby Ellsbury, of	Jr.	.406	244	56	99	19	3	6	48	26
Andy Jenkins, 1b	Sr.	.388	209	41	81	13	2	6	56	3
Ryan Gipson, 2b	Jr.	.330	97	30	32	6	0	1	22	9
Mitch Canham, c/1b	So.	.325	160	40	52	5	2	8	39	4
Shea McFeely, 3b	Jr.	.319	213	50	68	15	0	5	41	4
Cole Gillespie, of/dh	So.	.319	94	23	30	2	1	0	18	3
Tyler Graham, of	Jr.	.307	212	46	65	5	1	0	24	21
Darwin Barney, ss	Fr.	.301	226	46	68	9	1	2	44	6
Danny Anderson, of	Sr.	.290	69	19	20	3	0	4	10	0
Mike Lissman, of/dh	So.	.284	162	27	46	10	1	1	30	5
Joey Ledesma, dh	Jr.	.271	48	5	13	6	0	0	11	0
Chris Campos, of/1b	Sr.	.254	71	7	18	8	0	0	18	2
Chris Kunda, 2b	Jr.	.242	66	9	16	3	0	1	10	2
Casey Priseman, c	Fr.	.241	29	6	7	3	0	0	3	0
Geoff Wagner, of/dh	Jr.	.220	50	6	11	1	0	1	6	0
Lonnie Lechelt, ss/3b/2b	Fr.	.125	16	3	2	0	0	2	5	0
Billy Munich, c	Jr.	.087	23	3	2	0	0	1	3	0

PITCHING	YR	W	L	ERA	G	SV	IP	H	BB	SO
Eddie Kunz, rhp	Fr.	2	0	1.54	13	0	12	7	7	14
Dallas Buck, rhp	So.	12	1	2.09	19	1	129	90	51	118
Jonah Nickerson, rhp	So.	9	2	2.13	18	0	110	88	29	114
Kevin Gunderson, lhp	So.	6	4	2.76	33	14	65	49	14	62
Kevin Joslyn, lhp	Sr.	1	0	2.95	16	0	18	17	12	15
Nate Fogle, rhp	Jr.	4	2	3.05	26	5	44	32	19	43
Anton Maxwell, lhp	So.	11	1	4.33	17	0	96	90	42	69
Daniel Turpen, rhp	Fr.	1	0	4.40	6	0	14	16	6	7
Jake McCormick, rhp	So.	0	2	4.41	12	1	16	17	6	6
Kurt Steele, rhp	Jr.	0	0	15.88	7	0	6	13	2	8

8. TENNESSEE

Coach: Rod Delmonico **Record:** 46-21

BATTING	YR	AVG.	AB	R	H	2B	3B	HR	RBI	SB
Chase Headley, 3b	Jr.	.387	238	82	92	24	3	14	65	6
Eli Iorg, of	Jr.	.381	252	63	96	19	4	15	72	27
Julio Borbon, of	Fr.	.350	220	42	77	9	2	3	42	12
Eric King, ss	Sr.	.332	277	53	92	17	4	1	45	19
Michael Rivera, 2b	Jr.	.331	245	51	81	12	0	1	42	13
Kelly Edmundson, dh/c	Jr.	.328	229	43	75	16	1	8	39	3
Josh Alley, of	Jr.	.324	253	70	82	19	2	3	45	25
J.P. Arencibia, c/1b	Fr.	.322	283	54	91	16	1	14	71	0
Rob Fitzgerald, of/dh	Sr.	.322	118	28	38	8	1	6	21	6
Alex Suarez, 1b/dh	Sr.	.245	204	38	50	13	0	1	31	1
Daniel Beasley, of	Fr.	.238	21	2	5	1	1	0	3	0
Joey Andrews, of	Sr.	.222	36	5	8	2	0	2	9	0

PITCHING	YR	W	L	ERA	G	SV	IP	H	BB	SO
Luke Hochevar, rhp	Jr.	15	3	2.26	19	0	140	104	54	154
Sean Watson, rhp	So.	7	3	2.85	29	7	79	64	47	82
Joey Andrews, rhp	Sr.	3	2	2.91	19	2	34	22	12	46
James Adkins, lhp	Fr.	10	5	3.32	19	0	127	107	51	135
Craig Cobb, rhp	So.	7	4	4.53	21	0	99	113	22	54
Jabe Beard, rhp	Jr.	2	0	4.56	10	0	24	22	6	18
Chris Howell, rhp	Sr,	1	4	5.50	21	4	36	51	15	37
Trey Bridges, lhp	Jr.	0	0	6.00	9	0	9	9	8	6
Chase Hardin, rhp	Fr.	1	0	6.52	14	0	19	21	10	17
Rob Fitzgerald, rhp	Sr.	0	0	9.35	5	0	9	15	3	10

9. CAL STATE FULLERTON

Coach: George Horton **Record:** 46-18

BATTING	YR	AVG.	AB	R	H	2B	3B	HR	RBI	SB
Jon Wilhite, c	Fr.	.600	10	3	6	2	0	0	6	0
Clark Hardman, of	So.	.500	12	2	6	0	0	1	2	1
Jared Clark, dh	Fr.	.348	23	6	8	4	0	1	4	1
Brandon Tripp, of/dh	So.	.343	99	22	34	5	2	4	18	6
Mark Carroll, 2b	Sr.	.333	18	3	6	1	0	0	1	0
Brett Pill, 1b	So.	.327	260	55	85	12	2	9	57	4
Ronnie Prettyman, 3b	Sr.	.327	251	55	82	18	3	8	49	13
Blake Davis, ss	So.	.325	212	50	69	11	8	2	36	17
Sergio Pedroza, of	Jr.	.324	219	47	71	12	2	16	58	6
Justin Turner, 2b	Jr.	.324	244	54	79	17	2	3	41	11
Trevor Mortensen, dh/of	Jr.	.316	95	16	39	1	1	2	16	1
Felipe Garcia, dh	Sr.	.302	129	22	39	10	1	0	24	0
Bobby Andrews, of	Jr.	.297	145	34	43	1	3	1	23	13
Danny Dorn, of	Jr.	.272	213	56	58	13	0	10	49	3
Evan McArthur, dh/3b	Jr.	.250	48	8	12	2	1	2	14	1
John Curtis, c	So.	.234	201	33	47	10	0	0	29	4
Neil Walton, ss	Jr.	.231	52	13	12	3	0	0	11	3

PITCHING	YR	W	L	ERA	G	SV	IP	H	BB	SO
John Estes, lhp	So.	1	0	0.73	11	0	12	7	5	7
Ryan Schreppel, lhp	Jr.	6	1	1.92	12	0	70	38	30	41
Vinnie Pestano, rhp	So.	3	4	2.68	34	13	50	44	16	49
Ricky Romero, lhp	Jr.	13	5	2.89	18	0	134	102	34	139
Laruen Gagnier, rhp	So.	3	0	3.49	21	0	28	22	14	27
Wes Roemer, rhp	Fr.	7	3	3.80	21	1	90	86	15	71
Brian Stevens, rhp	Fr.	0	0	3.86	6	0	9	13	3	5
Nolan Bruyninckx, rhp	So.	0	0	4.26	6	0	6	9	2	3
Scott Sarver, lhp	Sr.	9	3	4.60	19	0	88	100	27	59
Adam Jorgenson, rhp	Fr.	2	0	4.67	24	3	44	42	17	36
Jared Clark, rhp	Fr.	1	1	5.33	12	0	25	26	7	17
Dave Pherrin, lhp	Jr.	1	0	7.20	10	1	10	10	4	8

10. MISSISSIPPI

Coach: Mike Bianco **Record:** 48-20

BATTING	YR	AVG.	AB	R	H	2B	3B	HR	RBI	SB
C.J. Ketchum, dh/1b/3b	So.	.391	46	4	18	3	0	0	11	0
Brian Pettway, of	Jr.	.383	266	56	102	19	0	21	67	1
Justin Henry, dh/1b	Fr.	.374	123	31	46	2	3	2	26	7
Chris Coghlan, 3b	So.	.363	273	66	99	22	1	6	57	7
Stephen Head, 1b/dh	Jr.	.331	272	65	90	16	1	18	68	3
Cooper Osteen, 2b	Sr.	.317	252	61	80	16	1	0	33	13
Mark Wright, of	So.	.311	206	39	64	15	1	13	51	2
Alex Presley, of	So.	.302	139	24	42	9	1	2	17	1
Miles Franklin, of	Sr.	.298	151	34	45	6	3	1	26	8
Jon-Jon Hancock, dh	Fr.	.283	113	11	32	10	1	3	21	1
Zack Cozart, ss	Fr.	.281	231	53	65	16	1	9	46	3
Barry Gunther, c	Sr.	.278	187	34	52	5	1	4	27	0
Ryne Porter, ss	So.	.231	26	4	6	2	0	0	3	0
Alex Kliman, dh/c	Fr.	.231	13	4	3	1	0	1	2	0
Justin Brashear, c	So.	.175	40	12	7	1	0	1	3	0

PITCHING	YR	W	L	ERA	G	SV	IP	H	BB	SO
Jon-Jon Hancock, rhp	Fr.	0	0	2.16	6	0	8	7	0	6
Tommy Baumgardner, lhp	Jr.	2	1	2.38	22	0	45	47	13	32
Stephen Head, lhp	Jr.	7	3	2.54	24	8	85	83	27	77
Matt Maloney, lhp	Jr.	8	3	3.11	23	4	104	94	26	111
Brian Pettway, rhp	Jr.	2	1	3.18	14	4	17	15	5	17
Eric Fowler, lhp	Jr.	7	3	3.43	16	0	87	76	24	100
Mark Holliman, rhp	Jr.	8	4	3.90	18	0	113	106	48	120
Stoney Stone, rhp	Jr.	3	0	3.92	9	1	21	19	5	19
Michael Wakefield, rhp	So.	0	0	4.05	7	1	13	13	5	10
Chris Moffett, rhp	Jr.	0	0	4.35	7	0	10	14	3	7
Anthony Cupps, rhp	Jr.	9	3	5.05	17	0	71	88	23	51
Will Kline, rhp	Fr.	2	2	8.15	15	0	18	26	10	7

11. GEORGIA TECH

Coach: Danny Hall **Record:** 45-19

BATTING	YR	AVG	AB	R	H	2B	3B	HR	RBI	SB
Wes Hodges, 3b	So.	.397	267	67	106	18	0	9	51	3
Tyler Greene, ss	Jr.	.372	269	76	100	15	3	12	72	31
Matt Wieters, dh/1b/c	Fr.	.366	227	53	83	17	1	10	68	1
Jeff Kindel, of/dh	Jr.	.359	220	50	79	23	1	6	65	2
Jeremy Slayden, dh/of	Jr.	.352	199	51	70	9	0	13	57	1
Steven Blackwood, of	Jr.	.336	241	61	81	13	1	5	65	3
Mike Trapani, 2b	Jr.	.327	168	44	55	9	2	2	24	4
Michael Fisher, 2b/ss	Fr.	.300	50	15	15	5	0	2	16	2
Andy Hawranick, c	Jr.	.293	188	40	55	11	0	4	36	4
Danny Payne, of	Fr.	.284	261	77	74	11	2	3	40	24
Whit Robbins, 1b	So.	.265	162	33	43	14	0	5	40	0
Cameron Lane, 2b	Sr.	.233	30	9	7	1	0	0	5	1
Jake Hall, 2b	Sr.	.116	43	7	5	1	0	0	5	2

PITCHING	YR	W	L	ERA	G	SV	IP	H	BB	SO
Matt Wieters, rhp	Fr.	3	3	2.85	26	6	41	40	10	32
Blake Wood, rhp	So.	10	1	3.13	18	0	106	111	24	74
John Michael Vidic, rhp	Fr.	0	0	3.24	5	0	8	6	3	5
Ryan Turner, lhp	So.	7	3	3.31	18	0	71	81	37	49
Tim Gustafson, rhp	So.	6	2	3.33	28	1	70	66	29	62
Jared Hyatt, rhp	So.	3	2	4.60	14	0	29	30	10	34
Lee Hyde, lhp	So.	7	4	4.68	18	0	92	101	41	72
Brad Rulon, rhp	Fr.	1	0	4.94	17	0	24	22	11	20
Jordan Crews, rhp	Sr.	2	1	4.96	30	2	49	64	21	32
Tim Ladd, lhp	Fr.	1	0	5.50	18	1	18	21	10	11
Jason Neighborgall, rhp	Jr.	5	3	7.13	14	0	53	47	53	72
Brian Futral, rhp	Fr.	0	0	9.82	7	0	7	12	4	6

12. ARIZONA

Coach: Andy Lopez **Record:** 39-21

BATTING	YR	AVG	AB	R	H	2B	3B	HR	RBI	SB
Trevor Crowe, of	Jr.	.403	263	83	106	25	15	9	54	27
Nick Hundley, c	Jr.	.352	227	57	80	23	2	15	46	9
Jeff Van Houten, of	Sr.	.348	250	61	87	18	3	9	67	2
Bryan Kervin, 3b/2b	Fr.	.342	149	29	51	12	1	0	22	6
Jordan Brown, 1b	Jr.	.336	262	62	88	17	3	14	80	1
Chris Frey, of	Jr.	.326	227	55	74	14	4	3	42	8
Derek Decater, dh	Jr.	.320	100	22	32	4	3	1	19	3
Jason Seefeld, dh	Fr.	.316	57	8	18	5	0	0	10	0
Jason Donald, ss	So.	.288	222	38	64	16	5	5	33	5
Brad Boyer, 2b/3b	Jr.	.285	256	55	73	13	9	3	46	17
Bill Rhinehart, dh/of	So.	.279	86	14	24	4	0	5	21	0
Brett Scyphers, 2b/ss	Fr.	.250	56	10	14	2	0	0	4	0

PITCHING	YR	W	L	ERA	G	SV	IP	H	BB	SO
Mark Melancon, rhp	So.	4	3	2.58	34	11	66	52	21	69
John Meloan, rhp	Jr.	10	3	3.70	19	0	112	115	58	130
Kevin Guyette, rhp	Jr.	10	4	3.73	18	0	116	106	30	130
Eric Berger, lhp	Fr.	6	2	3.84	24	1	61	45	29	68
Brad Mills, lhp	So.	0	0	4.61	13	0	14	14	11	12
David Coulon, lhp	Fr.	3	3	5.50	18	0	52	66	27	44
Sean Jarrett, rhp	Jr.	2	2	5.55	19	2	36	45	5	31
Matt Baugh, lhp	Fr.	0	0	5.56	10	0	11	11	7	8
Sean Rierson, rhp	Sr.	3	3	6.24	14	1	53	69	15	48
Mike Koons, rhp	Fr.	1	1	8.53	14	0	19	27	14	13

13. RICE

Coach: Wayne Graham **Record:** 45-19

BATTING	YR	AVG	AB	R	H	2B	3B	HR	RBI	SB
Joe Savery, 1b/dh	Fr.	.382	204	49	78	17	2	5	43	7
Josh Rodriguez, ss/2b	So.	.345	238	48	82	11	3	11	54	9
Adam Rodgers, dh/1b	Sr.	.332	226	47	75	21	0	7	52	1
Greg Buchanan, 2b	So.	.306	216	34	66	11	3	1	31	5
Tyler Henley, of	Fr.	.301	256	70	77	12	4	6	36	12
Clay Reichenbach, 3b/ss	Sr.	.292	137	20	40	5	0	4	22	1
Danny Lehmann, c	Fr.	.283	184	33	52	17	0	7	33	0
Jordan Dodson, of	So.	.282	78	13	22	6	0	2	12	1
Matt Moake, 2b	Sr.	.267	15	8	4	1	0	0	3	1
Brian Friday, ss/3b	Fr.	.256	129	22	33	4	1	1	11	7
Lance Pendleton, of	Jr.	.255	216	40	55	14	2	8	44	3
Adam Hale, of	So.	.242	157	29	38	10	0	9	40	1
Adam Morris, dh	Sr.	.235	34	5	8	1	0	3	5	0
Derek Myers, 2b	Fr.	.231	13	3	3	1	0	0	1	1
Bobby Bramhall, of	Fr.	.115	26	3	3	0	0	0	0	0
Travis Reagan, c	So.	.103	58	8	6	1	0	1	8	0

PITCHING	YR	W	L	ERA	G	SV	IP	H	BB	SO
Joe Savery, lhp	Fr.	8	5	2.43	19	1	119	104	37	129
Bobby Bell, rhp	Fr.	4	0	2.77	24	1	52	35	14	51
Cole St. Clair, lhp	Fr.	2	0	3.26	32	2	47	35	12	62
Eddie Degerman, rhp	Jr.	8	1	3.28	18	0	99	70	38	117
Josh Geer, rhp	Jr.	12	4	3.32	19	0	125	105	44	105
Lance Pendleton, rhp	Jr.	5	3	3.69	18	2	32	26	16	30
Bryce Cox, rhp	Jr.	1	2	3.86	17	3	19	12	14	24
Ryne Tacker, rhp	Jr.	4	0	3.93	13	0	37	28	21	27
Matt Ueckert, lhp	Jr.	0	1	6.35	3	0	11	19	3	6
Kurt Pessa, rhp	Fr.	0	0	6.75	5	0	5	9	1	4
Adam Hale, rhp	So.	1	3	6.94	9	1	12	12	5	6
Jordan Dodson, rhp	Fr.	0	0	7.94	3	0	6	7	2	7

14. CLEMSON

Coach: Jack Leggett **Record:** 43-23

BATTING	YR	AVG	AB	R	H	2B	3B	HR	RBI	SB
Tanner Leggett, 2b/ss	So.	.364	11	1	4	0	0	0	2	0
Gene Pierce, c	Sr.	.357	14	2	5	0	0	1	2	0
Brad Chalk, of	Fr.	.350	200	46	70	7	0	0	11	5
Travis Storrer, of	Jr.	.346	243	46	84	15	2	6	43	0
Herman Demmink, 3b	Jr.	.345	261	56	90	17	1	4	41	9
Taylor Harbin, 2b	Fr.	.343	274	64	94	28	4	10	63	4
Kris Harvey, dh/of	Jr.	.341	249	61	85	11	0	25	70	1
Ben Hall, dh/of	Jr.	.319	47	7	15	5	1	1	9	0
Stan Widmann, ss	Fr.	.289	232	36	67	7	1	4	25	7
Tyler Colvin, of	So.	.283	258	51	73	22	2	5	53	12
Andy D'Alessio, 1b	So.	.276	210	36	58	14	1	15	60	1
Adrian Casanova, c	Jr.	.238	168	31	40	5	1	4	27	0
Jorge Andrade, 3b	So.	.208	24	4	5	1	0	1	5	0
David Williams, of	Jr.	.184	49	8	9	4	0	0	2	2
Daniel Pritchard, 2b	Jr.	.182	11	5	2	0	0	0	1	0
Jesse Ferguson, of	So.	.154	52	6	8	1	0	0	5	1
John Ingram, of	So.	.136	22	1	3	0	0	0	0	0
Doug Hogan, c	Fr.	.111	18	0	2	0	0	0	1	0

PITCHING	YR	W	L	ERA	G	SV	IP	H	BB	SO
Stephen Faris, rhp	So.	6	4	2.60	20	1	97	89	25	79
Jeff Hahn, rhp	Sr.	4	1	3.13	25	3	60	57	27	59
Stephen Clyne, rhp	So.	2	0	3.45	19	2	29	29	11	30
Josh Cribb, rhp	Jr.	8	5	3.54	19	0	109	119	24	97
Chris Howard, rhp	Fr.	1	0	3.86	5	0	5	5	0	1
Robert Rohrbaugh, lhp	Jr.	8	3	4.22	19	1	96	103	42	82
Chris Fidrych, lhp	Fr.	0	0	4.50	10	0	14	13	6	13
David Kopp, rhp	Fr.	4	3	4.61	22	1	70	66	26	46
Drew Fiorenza, rhp	Jr.	2	1	4.98	18	1	22	26	15	23
P.J. Zocchi, rhp	Fr.	1	0	5.14	4	0	7	6	6	3
Daniel Moskos, lhp	Fr.	2	2	5.40	21	0	17	24	13	15
Kris Harvey, rhp	Jr.	5	4	5.52	13	0	62	71	28	52

15. MIAMI

Coach: Jim Morris **Record:** 41-19

BATTING	YR	AVG	AB	R	H	2B	3B	HR	RBI	SB
Jon Jay, of	So.	.408	211	50	86	17	3	1	52	13
Ryan Braun, 3b	Jr.	.388	219	70	85	16	2	18	76	23
Paco Figueroa, of/2b	Sr.	.361	233	70	84	15	5	5	38	24
Brendan Katin, of/dh	Sr.	.328	186	34	61	14	1	7	41	3
Eddy Rodriguez, c	So.	.320	172	35	55	14	0	8	33	0
Danny Figueroa, of	Jr.	.319	207	70	66	11	2	5	32	25
Walter Diaz, 2b/ss	Fr.	.303	208	50	63	8	1	5	21	7
Danny Valencia, 1b/3b	So.	.300	227	39	68	15	3	6	63	9
Roger Tomas, ss/2b	So.	.268	198	31	53	8	5	1	25	1
Alex Garabedian, dh/c	Fr.	.255	145	18	37	6	1	3	29	0
Danny Robitaille, 2b/3b	Fr.	.255	47	9	12	1	0	0	7	0
Patrick Feeney, dh	Fr.	.163	43	7	7	0	2	0	8	1
Kevin Santiago, dh	Fr.	.136	22	1	3	1	0	0	2	0

PITCHING	YR	W	L	ERA	G	SV	IP	H	BB	SO
Cesar Carrillo, rhp	Jr.	13	3	2.22	19	1	126	100	23	127
Chris Perez, rhp	So.	5	1	2.56	24	7	46	34	25	52
Andrew Lane, lhp	Jr.	3	0	2.66	36	0	47	42	9	34
Jon McLean, rhp	So.	1	0	3.04	23	0	24	18	7	25
Manny Miguelez, lhp	Fr.	1	1	3.68	13	1	22	21	16	23
Ricky Orta, rhp	So.	7	5	4.98	18	0	78	69	36	61
Danny Gil, rhp	So.	2	3	5.34	26	3	30	31	21	22
Raudel Alfonso, rhp	Fr.	0	0	5.73	7	0	11	13	2	8
Brandon Camardese, lhp	Sr.	6	1	5.74	16	0	58	67	23	45
Dan Touchet, rhp	Sr.	3	5	5.91	14	0	67	82	19	51
Vince Bongiovanni, rhp	Sr.	0	0	6.23	18	0	22	31	12	19
Scott Maine, lhp	Fr.	0	0	7.45	7	0	10	11	71	11

16. FLORIDA STATE

Coach: Mike Martin **Record:** 53-20

BATTING	YR	AVG	AB	R	H	2B	3B	HR	RBI	SB
Shane Robinson, of	So.	.427	286	96	122	25	4	6	43	49
Jack Rye, of	Fr.	.328	195	27	64	14	1	2	31	1
Brant Peacher, dh	So.	.318	151	29	48	13	0	3	27	3
Ryne Malone, 3b/1b	So.	.316	263	62	83	22	3	7	61	10
Aaron Cheesman, c	Sr.	.300	250	34	75	10	0	0	53	5

BATTING	YR	AVG	AB	R	H	2B	3B	HR	RBI	SB
Gibbs Chapman, of	Sr.	.294	262	56	77	14	3	10	65	24
Daniel Wardell, 1b	Sr.	.266	158	26	42	10	0	10	37	3
Josh Spivey, dh	So.	.260	96	9	25	5	0	1	13	0
Nick Francis, ss	Fr.	.250	40	12	10	1	0	0	3	0
Bryan Henry, 3b	So.	.246	114	14	28	11	0	1	25	3
Tony Thomas, 2b	Fr.	.240	217	54	52	11	5	6	29	9
Ruairi O'Connor, of	Fr.	.227	66	11	15	4	0	2	16	2
Ryne Jernigan, ss	Fr.	.217	226	36	49	5	0	6	31	4
Charles Cleveland, 3b	Fr.	.206	34	3	7	3	1	0	7	0
Danny Diaz, c	So.	.200	20	4	4	2	0	1	2	0
Brandon Manasa, 2b	Jr.	.179	28	9	5	0	1	0	3	0
Dennis Guinn, 1b	Fr.	.000	11	1	0	0	0	0	1	0

PITCHING	YR	W	L	ERA	G	SV	IP	H	BB	SO
Kevin Lynch, rhp	Sr.	12	0	2.03	46	0	62	45	23	67
Tyler Chambliss, rhp	So.	7	3	2.06	39	15	52	36	23	73
Bryan Henry, rhp	So.	9	3	2.22	17	0	89	71	18	58
Matt DiBlasi, lhp	Jr.	1	2	2.76	39	0	42	34	14	44
Barret Browning, lhp	Jr.	4	4	3.54	24	0	89	92	48	74
Mark Sauls, rhp	Jr.	6	2	4.18	18	0	67	64	30	31
Michael Hyde, rhp	So.	7	2	4.40	20	0	100	108	36	71
Ryan Strauss, rhp	Fr.	1	0	4.58	14	2	20	20	14	19
Brian Chambers, rhp	So.	2	0	4.67	16	0	17	21	3	11
Stephen Ochs, lhp	Fr.	0	0	5.02	11	0	14	21	7	11
Hunter Jones, lhp	Jr.	4	3	5.05	18	0	71	87	20	56
Brian Schultz, lhp	So.	0	1	5.19	4	1	17	20	3	14
Trent Jarvis, lhp	Fr.	0	0	6.75	10	0	5	9	4	8

17. SOUTHERN CALIFORNIA

Coach: Mike Gillespie **Record:** 41-22

BATTING	YR	AVG	AB	R	H	2B	3B	HR	RBI	SB
Jeff Clement, c	Jr.	.348	230	52	80	17	0	15	54	5
Billy Hart, 3b	Jr.	.332	238	43	79	13	3	3	35	7
Matt Cusick, 1b/2b	Fr.	.311	225	53	70	9	0	4	35	2
Cyle Hankerd, of	So.	.298	218	28	65	14	3	1	39	0
Blake Sharpe, ss/1b	Jr.	.297	249	52	74	15	3	5	36	11
Baron Frost, dh/of	Jr.	.274	197	36	54	10	0	4	30	1
Hector Estrella, 2b/ss	So.	.271	188	28	51	5	3	3	28	1
Daniel Perales, of	So.	.266	64	6	17	3	0	1	9	1
Roberto Lopez, of	Fr.	.264	106	13	28	8	0	1	21	0
Zack Kalter, of	Jr.	.250	76	14	19	3	0	0	6	4
Darin Vieira, of/1b	Jr.	.241	174	31	42	4	1	5	32	4
Dale Legaspi, of/1b	Sr.	.229	35	9	8	2	1	0	5	1
Lucas Duda, 1b/dh	Fr.	.208	77	7	16	4	0	1	11	0

PITCHING	YR	W	L	ERA	G	SV	IP	H	BB	SO
Zack Kalter, rhp	Jr.	2	3	2.25	9	0	36	42	13	26
Steve Martlaro, rhp	Fr.	0	0	2.25	9	0	12	8	5	8
Ian Kennedy, rhp	So.	12	3	2.54	18	0	117	85	38	158
Paul Koss, rhp	So.	4	1	2.81	34	14	51	39	21	42
Jack Spradlin, lhp	Jr.	6	3	4.47	27	0	119	125	32	97
Anthony Encinas, rhp	Fr.	7	4	4.68	19	0	50	46	22	43
Richard Aguilar, rhp	Sr.	1	0	4.80	14	0	15	22	4	7
Nate Smith, rhp	Fr.	0	0	5.14	17	1	21	20	13	13
Brett Bannister, rhp	Jr.	4	3	5.33	14	0	51	60	20	37
Josh Fogel, rhp	So.	1	0	5.71	12	0	17	22	7	5
Andy Guy, rhp	So.	1	0	6.75	14	0	16	29	5	11
Jon Williams, rhp	Sr.	1	0	6.75	10	0	15	19	8	9
Michael Friedman, lhp	Sr.	2	3	6.99	28	1	28	50	11	33
Ryan Schlack, rhp	Fr.	0	2	7.20	4	0	5	7	1	2

18. LOUISIANA STATE

Coach: Smoke Laval **Record:** 40-22

BATTING	YR	AVG	AB	R	H	2B	3B	HR	RBI	SB
Nick Stavinoha, of	Sr.	.370	257	50	95	23	1	18	65	5
Ryan Patterson, of	Sr.	.369	249	74	92	23	2	20	56	7
Clay Harris, 2b	Sr.	.362	243	41	88	20	1	9	60	1
Rhett Buteau, of	Sr.	.333	15	8	5	0	1	1	4	2
Blake Gill, 3b/1b/dh	Sr.	.320	219	41	70	11	1	7	48	8
Jordan Mayer, dh/1b	Fr.	.313	115	16	36	13	1	4	26	0
Chris Jackson, 3b	Fr.	.305	128	29	39	3	1	1	17	0
Derek Hebert, ss/3b	Sr.	.272	125	20	34	4	2	3	11	4
Bruce Sprowl, of	Jr.	.264	144	28	38	1	2	2	13	5
Matt Luizza, c	Jr.	.251	171	30	43	10	0	3	23	0
Quinn Stewart, of/dh	Jr.	.250	116	19	29	7	2	3	13	2
Michael Hollander, ss	Fr.	.246	130	18	32	6	0	1	14	2
J.P. Padron, dh/3b	Fr.	.240	25	7	6	0	0	0	2	0
Will Harris, 1b	Jr.	.213	141	23	30	7	0	4	20	0
Dustin Weaver, c/dh	Sr.	.168	95	19	16	3	0	4	15	0
Bryan Harris, 3b	So.	.122	41	11	5	1	0	0	8	1

PITCHING	YR	W	L	ERA	G	SV	IP	H	BB	SO
Jason Determann, lhp	Jr.	5	0	2.30	27	7	63	61	12	74
Greg Smith, lhp	Jr.	10	3	2.60	17	0	104	99	25	82
Jordan Faircloth, rhp	Sr.	1	1	2.75	24	4	39	44	14	27
Clay Dirks, lhp	So.	10	4	3.24	17	1	94	84	27	67
Eric English, rhp	Fr.	1	0	3.82	14	1	31	23	16	26
Edgar Ramirez, rhp	Jr.	0	1	4.50	17	1	36	40	13	33
Justin Meier, rhp	Jr.	2	3	4.79	14	0	41	41	15	30
Lane Mestepey, lhp	Sr.	7	8	4.94	17	0	98	115	24	52
Brandon Nall, rhp	Sr.	3	2	5.18	7	0	24	19	10	10
Chris Cahill, rhp	Jr.	0	0	5.52	7	0	15	19	10	14
Chase Dardar, rhp	Jr.	1	0	13.50	7	0	11	21	10	13

19. LONG BEACH STATE

Coach: Mike Weathers **Record:** 37-22

BATTING	YR	AVG	AB	R	H	2B	3B	HR	RBI	SB
Troy Tulowitzki, ss	Jr.	.349	152	32	53	12	1	8	29	2
Cole Jacobsen, dh/2b	Sr.	.333	84	12	28	4	1	0	5	2
Evan Longoria, 3b/ss	So.	.320	228	34	73	8	0	5	30	10
Chris Jones, c	Jr.	.308	172	21	53	10	0	2	27	2
Brandon Godfrey, 1b	Fr.	.305	177	19	54	9	2	1	24	2
Sean Boatright, of	Jr.	.299	197	26	59	17	0	3	30	5
Scott Bradley, of/1b	Jr.	.282	71	14	20	2	0	0	6	4
Jordan Struble, of/dh	Jr.	.277	83	12	23	7	0	0	14	2
Danny Mocny, of/3b	Sr.	.273	121	16	33	5	1	0	11	5
Chuck Sindlinger, 2b	Jr.	.264	193	19	51	5	0	3	23	6
Steve Velazco, of	Sr.	.261	138	19	36	5	0	0	9	2
Jamie Huizar, of	Jr.	.242	91	12	22	6	0	0	7	1
Tito Cruz, c/3b	Jr.	.231	108	8	25	5	0	0	8	3
Tom Wolf, dh	Jr.	.229	35	0	8	1	0	0	2	0
Jose Hernandez, of	Fr.	.224	67	9	15	4	0	1	7	3
Zach Barger, of	Fr.	.222	36	2	8	1	0	0	2	0
Donnie Ecker, ss	Fr.	.167	12	2	2	1	0	0	1	1
Tom Sarti, of	Jr.	.139	36	6	5	0	0	1	5	1

PITCHING	YR	W	L	ERA	G	SV	IP	H	BB	SO
Neil Jamison, rhp	Sr.	4	0	0.00	27	11	30	16	5	27
Brian Anderson, rhp	Sr.	3	0	0.83	30	2	43	22	9	37
Matt Fitts, rhp	Fr.	0	1	2.20	16	0	16	16	4	11
Donnie Hume, lhp	Fr.	1	1	2.37	11	0	19	20	5	13
Marco Estrada, rhp	Jr.	8	3	2.43	18	0	111	84	29	104
Cesar Ramos, lhp	Jr.	10	7	2.64	18	0	126	105	16	95
Jared Hughes, rhp	So.	8	3	2.83	15	0	89	67	23	87
Cody Evans, rhp	Jr.	1	2	3.38	13	0	40	47	19	26
Steve Hammond, lhp	Jr.	1	3	4.07	25	0	24	27	9	28
Brett Andrade, rhp	Jr.	1	0	4.66	10	0	10	13	3	3
Andrew Liebel, rhp	Fr.	0	2	5.11	11	0	12	15	6	4

20. ALABAMA

Coach: Jim Wells **Record:** 40-23

BATTING	YR	AVG	AB	R	H	2B	3B	HR	RBI	SB
Gabe Scott, of	Sr.	.364	184	39	67	13	0	12	35	1
Matt Bentley, 1b/dh	Fr.	.320	50	9	16	5	1	0	9	1
Matt Grooms, of	Sr.	.313	64	14	20	3	0	1	6	5
Zac Welch, 1b	Sr.	.309	136	26	42	9	1	4	26	1
Morrow Thomley, of	Sr.	.305	213	36	65	14	4	5	36	13
Rocky Scelfo, 2b/3b	Sr.	.303	142	28	43	5	3	2	22	8
Allen Rice, dh/2b	Sr.	.295	207	39	61	11	1	2	28	8
Cale Iorg, ss	Fr.	.280	236	40	66	11	3	5	38	15
Emeel Salem, of	So.	.277	202	31	56	4	3	0	14	13
Chris Kirkland, c	Fr.	.261	23	2	6	0	0	0	5	0
Evan Bush, 3b/1b	Jr.	.251	215	46	54	9	1	17	55	1
Spencer Pennington, dh	Jr.	.250	36	3	9	2	0	0	8	0
Kody Valverde, c	Jr.	.240	171	23	41	9	0	7	23	0
Michael McCallister, of	So.	.222	54	14	12	3	0	0	4	0
Brandon Belcher, of	So.	.219	32	5	7	1	0	0	3	1
Greg Paiml, 2b	So.	.210	105	14	22	6	1	1	17	3
Josh Copeland, dh	Fr.	.154	13	0	2	0	0	0	1	1
Charlie Lyons, c	Jr.	.100	30	5	3	0	0	0	0	0

PITCHING	YR	W	L	ERA	G	SV	IP	H	BB	SO
David Robertson, rhp	Fr.	7	5	2.92	32	8	74	48	36	105
Jordan Davis, rhp	Jr.	5	2	3.10	26	3	58	55	15	41
T.J. Large, rhp	Jr.	7	4	3.46	18	0	96	72	50	92
Brent Carter, lhp	Sr.	7	4	3.76	25	0	96	91	28	96
Josh Copeland, rhp	Fr.	1	1	4.03	12	0	22	25	9	21
Wade LeBlanc, lhp	So.	5	5	4.09	14	0	88	77	28	108
Brandon Belcher, lhp	So.	5	0	4.37	14	0	60	60	25	44
Trey Shields, rhp	Jr.	1	1	5.50	7	0	18	21	5	15
Matt Downs, rhp	Jr.	2	0	5.76	16	0	30	37	13	33
Casey Kebodeaux, rhp	Fr.	0	1	6.52	7	1	10	14	9	5

21. MISSOURI

Coach: Tim Jamieson **Record:** 40-23

BATTING	YR	AVG	AB	R	H	2B	3B	HR	RBI	SB
James Boone, of	Jr.	.340	194	53	66	15	5	8	72	14
Tyrone Roberson, of	Jr.	.333	24	7	8	0	0	0	3	0
Hunter Mense, of	So.	.327	205	62	67	17	2	3	43	10
Zane Taylor, dh/2b	Jr.	.321	184	31	59	9	1	1	32	4

BATTING	YR	AVG	AB	R	H	2B	3B	HR	RBI	SB
Derek Chambers, 1b	Jr.	.320	247	63	79	12	3	3	48	3
Jacob Priday, of/c	Fr.	.305	223	53	68	13	3	9	67	8
Gary Arndt, ss	So.	.298	208	33	62	10	3	0	32	0
Dan Pietroburgo, c/dh	Fr.	.289	38	8	11	1	1	1	7	1
Trevor Helms, 2b	Jr.	.282	188	44	53	10	1	0	29	4
John McKee, 3b/of	So.	.268	209	62	56	9	2	7	43	1
Greg O'Neill, ss	Jr.	.263	76	18	20	5	3	1	22	1
Bryson LeBlanc, dh/of	Jr.	.218	78	27	17	2	2	0	10	2
Tyler Williams, of	Jr.	.209	67	11	14	3	0	0	7	1
J.C. Field, c	Jr.	.168	119	17	20	3	0	0	10	1
Evan Frey, of	Fr.	.164	55	11	9	2	0	0	6	1
Cosme Caballero, c	Sr.	.130	46	6	6	0	0	0	7	0
Jeff Zelenovich, 3b	So.	.105	19	3	2	0	0	1	3	0

PITCHING	YR	W	L	ERA	G	SV	IP	H	BB	SO
Michael Cole, rhp	So.	1	0	1.12	5	0	8	1	7	7
Max Scherzer, rhp	So.	9	4	1.86	16	0	106	59	41	131
Abel Newton, rhp	Jr.	2	0	2.57	5	1	14	10	4	9
Taylor Parker, lhp	Jr.	1	2	2.88	28	4	50	32	23	42
Andrew Johnston, rhp	Jr.	4	5	2.95	29	4	58	57	16	42
Erik Dessau, rhp	Sr.	5	1	3.05	12	0	41	47	12	35
Doug Mathis, rhp	Jr.	5	4	3.27	21	1	77	81	17	67
Nathan Culp, lhp	So.	9	2	3.50	17	0	93	105	31	63
Travis Wendte, rhp	Jr.	1	1	3.69	22	1	32	30	9	31
Dustin Braud, rhp	Jr.	1	1	4.38	18	0	25	26	17	21
Nick Admire, rhp	Jr.	2	3	4.58	18	0	39	48	11	24
Meade Hendricks, rhp	Sr.	0	0	6.14	12	0	15	20	6	12

22. MISSISSIPPI STATE

Coach: Ron Polk **Record:** 43-22

BATTING	YR	AVG	AB	R	H	2B	3B	HR	RBI	SB
Joseph McCaskill, dh/c	So.	.377	61	10	23	3	0	1	3	0
Joseph Hunter, of	Jr.	.348	178	35	62	6	1	1	31	8
Mitch Moreland, dh	Fr.	.316	57	9	18	3	0	2	6	1
Brad Corley, of	Jr.	.316	263	45	83	20	2	5	40	1
Daniel Tackett, 2b	Sr.	.308	13	3	4	1	0	0	2	2
Jeffrey Rea, 2b	So.	.305	256	42	78	7	3	2	34	5
Thomas Berkery, c/3b	Jr.	.302	242	33	73	18	1	7	55	2
Brad Jones, 1b	Jr.	.300	240	48	72	7	4	5	37	5
Ed Easley, 3b/c	Fr.	.296	226	36	67	10	1	3	32	1
Ben Grisham, of	So.	.294	17	8	5	1	0	0	3	0
Jeff Butts, of	Jr.	.286	199	40	57	12	4	3	36	6
Brian LaNinfa, dh/of	So.	.264	193	37	51	13	0	2	35	0
Michael Rutledge, ss/3b	Fr.	.262	103	12	27	4	0	1	14	2
Bunky Kateon, ss	Fr.	.240	150	21	36	10	0	1	13	0
Ryan Fesmire, of	Jr.	.231	13	1	3	0	0	0	2	0

PITCHING	YR	W	L	ERA	G	SV	IP	H	BB	SO
Jamie Gant, rhp	Jr.	1	0	1.29	9	0	14	8	10	13
Brett Cleveland, rhp	Jr.	2	1	1.96	21	5	37	27	10	28
Justin Pigott, lhp	Fr.	2	1	2.59	14	1	31	27	10	22
Eric Ebers, lhp	Sr.	0	0	2.76	9	0	16	13	9	12
Jesse Carver, lhp	Fr.	0	0	2.79	9	0	10	6	4	12
Mike Valentine, rhp	So.	6	0	2.88	21	3	41	38	8	31
John Lalor, rhp	Fr.	5	0	3.22	8	0	36	38	4	35
Jon Crosby, rhp	So.	5	3	3.54	16	0	74	95	11	35
Saunders Ramsey, rhp	Sr.	0	0	3.57	17	3	18	18	5	12
Todd Doolittle, rhp	Sr.	5	8	3.72	14	0	82	71	46	66
Josh Johnson, rhp	So.	5	0	4.03	12	0	45	48	21	44
Alan Johnson, rhp	Sr.	5	6	4.15	15	0	91	104	37	70
Brooks Dunn, lhp	Jr.	6	3	4.50	16	0	54	65	19	43

23. COASTAL CAROLINA

Coach: Gary Gilmore **Record:** 50-16

BATTING	YR	AVG	AB	R	H	2B	3B	HR	RBI	SB
Mike Costanzo, 1b/3b	Jr.	.379	240	74	91	15	2	16	67	8
Chris Todd, 3b/1b	Sr.	.357	244	70	87	9	1	3	47	11
Tommy Baldridge, of	Fr.	.356	104	26	37	5	0	2	22	3
Dom Duggan, of	So.	.348	204	48	71	17	2	4	27	7
Michael DeJesus, 2b	Jr.	.346	243	52	84	15	1	9	72	10
Jon Foisy, of	Sr.	.300	230	50	69	7	3	2	48	21
Kevin Entsminger, of	Jr.	.298	114	28	34	7	1	0	24	14
Aaron Verrett, ss	Jr.	.264	197	41	52	13	0	4	34	7
Danny Morgan, of/dh	So.	.263	95	18	25	5	1	3	22	1
Keon Graves, 3b	Fr.	.263	19	4	5	1	0	0	4	3
Chris Raber, dh	So.	.252	147	19	37	6	0	2	28	12
Josh Eachues, c	So.	.238	101	24	24	3	0	0	14	3
Mike Fuentes, c	Jr.	.233	103	11	24	3	1	0	20	0
Adam Vrable, ss/3b	So.	.225	80	13	18	1	0	0	6	5
D.J. Burns, of/1b	Jr.	.207	58	7	12	2	0	0	8	0
Dock Doyle, c	Fr.	.179	28	5	5	0	0	0	7	0

PITCHING	YR	W	L	ERA	G	SV	IP	H	BB	SO
Mike Costanzo, rhp	Jr.	8	1	2.13	37	14	55	44	24	69
Mike Valter, rhp	Jr.	4	0	2.36	22	1	53	49	19	35
Ricky Shefka, rhp	Jr.	12	2	2.75	17	0	118	125	20	81
Byron Binda, rhp	Sr.	7	2	3.60	24	1	60	50	31	75
Andy DeLaGarza, lhp	So.	5	4	4.45	18	0	83	84	42	50
Kevin Marrie, rhp	So.	3	2	4.82	12	0	56	67	34	40
Kevin Salmon, rhp	Jr.	1	1	5.49	14	0	41	48	17	22
Jake Hurry, lhp	Sr.	10	3	5.62	18	0	91	105	51	73
Donnie Presley, lhp	Fr.	0	0	7.71	16	1	14	21	7	9
Mike Andreas, rhp	Sr.	0	1	11.25	9	0	8	11	13	12

24. PEPPERDINE

Coach: Steve Rodriguez **Record:** 41-23

BATTING	YR	AVG	AB	R	H	2B	3B	HR	RBI	SB
Chad Tracy, c	So.	.367	256	56	94	22	2	12	61	3
Steve Kleen, 1b	Sr.	.350	240	46	84	16	1	8	58	3
David Uribes, 2b/ss	Jr.	.311	267	60	83	13	2	1	30	25
Danny Worth, ss	Fr.	.306	248	29	76	16	2	1	34	8
Luke Salas, of	So.	.298	228	39	68	9	1	1	31	10
Donald Brown, of	Fr.	.294	153	16	45	15	0	2	30	5
Adrian Ortiz, of	Fr.	.281	231	41	65	7	7	0	19	8
Taylor Klosowksi, dh/of	Jr.	.265	102	16	27	5	1	0	16	0
Nick Kliebert, dh/2b	Jr.	.262	149	16	39	8	0	2	25	0
Justin Sandberg, of	So.	.250	24	2	6	0	0	0	2	1
Patrick Rooney, 3b	Sr.	.229	223	31	51	10	0	5	25	0
Brandon Daguio, of	Jr.	.222	18	7	4	1	0	0	3	1
Jason Dominguez, of	Fr.	.167	42	4	7	0	0	0	4	1
Ryan Beglin, dh	Sr.	.150	20	3	3	1	0	1	3	0
Michael Beattie, dh	So.	.100	10	0	1	0	0	0	1	0

PITCHING	YR	W	L	ERA	G	SV	IP	H	BB	SO
Steve Kleen, rhp	Sr.	4	3	1.75	29	17	51	39	18	47
Doug Konoske, rhp	Fr.	0	2	2.41	21	3	41	43	15	34
James Johnson, rhp	Jr.	2	0	2.88	19	1	34	40	11	26
Kea Kometani, rhp	Sr.	10	5	3.17	19	0	128	138	36	100
Bryan Minkel, lhp	Jr.	0	0	3.18	13	0	11	14	5	14
Paul Coleman, lhp	Jr.	9	3	3.35	17	1	110	88	41	91
Adam Olbrychowski, rhp	Fr.	2	1	4.15	11	0	17	16	9	16
Barry Enright, rhp	Fr.	10	1	4.62	18	0	97	115	26	52
Robert Della Grotta, rhp	So.	3	2	5.02	12	0	43	49	17	34
Jason Dominguez, rhp	Fr.	1	5	8.77	12	0	26	37	23	15
Drew Saberhagen, lhp	Fr.	0	1	14.29	5	0	6	13	2	2

25. SOUTH CAROLINA

Coach: Ray Tanner **Record:** 41-23

BATTING	YR	AVG	AB	R	H	2B	3B	HR	RBI	SB
Pearce, Steve, 1b/3b	Sr.	.358	229	50	82	16	0	21	63	2
Michael Campbell, of	Jr.	.315	251	56	79	16	5	8	42	8
Jon Willard, dh	So.	.315	178	23	56	11	2	6	30	0
Mark Stanley, of	Jr.	.311	61	17	19	5	0	0	7	1
Davy Gregg, of	Jr.	.301	193	38	58	9	2	1	19	13
Steven Tolleson, ss	Jr.	.296	243	53	72	14	2	6	46	20
Chris Brown, 2b/dh/3b	Jr.	.274	197	33	54	9	1	4	34	4
Joey Friddle, of/2b/3b	Jr.	.257	74	21	19	3	0	0	8	6
Neil Giesler, 1b/3b	Jr.	.254	138	21	35	5	1	6	24	2
Tommy King, 2b	So.	.248	109	16	27	8	0	2	13	0
Ryan Mahoney, c/dh	So.	.228	92	10	21	6	0	2	14	0
Brendan Winn, of	Sr.	.225	187	28	42	11	0	12	37	1
Ian Paxton, c	Jr.	.200	95	15	19	5	0	2	11	0
Phil Disher, c/dh	Fr.	.182	44	3	8	2	0	2	11	0
Cory Vanderhook, c/1b	Jr.	.181	72	8	13	2	0	1	13	0
Steven Reinhold, of	So.	.067	15	7	1	1	0	0	0	1

PITCHING	YR	W	L	ERA	G	SV	IP	H	BB	SO
Josh McDonald, rhp	Fr.	0	0	0.00	5	0	5	3	2	3
Harris Honeycutt, rhp	So.	0	0	2.45	4	0	7	6	7	7
Arik Hempy, lhp	So.	2	1	2.63	11	0	27	19	22	18
Brent Marsh, rhp	Jr.	4	3	2.87	28	11	31	30	10	32
Aaron Rawl, rhp	Sr.	9	6	3.20	18	0	115	121	23	94
Zac McCamie, rhp	Sr.	9	4	3.50	18	0	116	103	37	108
Andrew Cruse, rhp	Fr.	3	1	3.54	14	1	28	29	7	21
Jeff Jeffords, rhp	So.	1	0	3.58	17	0	28	21	13	26
John Gregory, lhp	Jr.	0	0	3.68	8	0	7	8	2	9
Jason Fletcher, rhp	Sr.	5	5	4.14	18	2	63	63	21	49
Wynn Pelzer, rhp	Fr.	1	2	4.34	18	0	29	26	13	26
Forrest Beverly, lhp	So.	1	0	4.50	16	0	24	24	7	25
Andy Lambert, rhp	Jr.	4	0	4.94	15	0	31	29	10	26
Conor Lalor, rhp	So.	1	0	5.33	14	1	27	33	5	27
Cliff Donald, rhp	Sr.	1	1	7.23	9	0	19	24	5	12

2005 CONFERENCE STANDINGS & LEADERS

*Won conference tournament #Conference department leader who is a non-qualifier
Boldface: NCAA regional participant/conference department leader

AMERICA EAST CONFERENCE

	Conference W	Conference L	Overall W	Overall L
Northeastern	14	6	26	23
*Maine	14	7	35	19
Vermont	14	7	29	19
Binghamton	12	8	23	26
Albany	10	11	20	19
Stony Brook	10	11	23	28
Maryland-Baltimore County	6	15	16	34
Hartford	3	18	6	30

ALL-CONFERENCE TEAM: C—Aaron Izaryk, Sr., Maine. **1B**—Brendon Hitchcock, So., Binghamton. **2B**—Steve Wyland, So., Albany. **3B**—Mathieu Bergeron, Jr., Binghamton. **SS**—Matt Devins, Sr., Stony Brook. **OF**—Chris Emanuele, Jr., Northeastern; Jeff Heriot, Sr., Northeastern; Andrew Larsen, Sr., Stony Brook. **DH**—Isidro Fortuna, Jr., Stony Brook. **SP**—Chris Blazek, Jr., Vermont; Adam Ottavino, So., Northeastern. **RP**—Chris Marsh, Jr., Vermont.

Player of the Year: Mathieu Bergeron, Binghamton. **Pitcher of the Year**: Adam Ottavino, Northeastern. **Rookie of the Year**: Scott Diamond, Binghamton. **Coach of the Year**: Tim Sinicki, Binghamton.

INDIVIDUAL BATTING LEADERS
(Minimum 125 At-Bats)

	AVG	AB	R	H	2B	3B	HR	RBI	SB
Hitchcock, Brendon, Bing.	**.399**	183	43	73	12	0	5	35	11
Rossi, Frank, Vermont	.372	148	28	55	5	1	0	16	8
Larsen, Andrew, Stony Brook	.367	215	45	**79**	**25**	2	2	24	5
Fortuna, Isidro, Stony Brook	.357	168	24	60	15	0	5	37	6
Devins, Matt, Stony Brook	.357	199	39	71	15	3	5	38	6
Wyland, Steve, Albany	.357	143	36	51	7	0	1	27	2
Magrass, Miguel, Vermont	.356	177	34	63	13	**6**	3	38	17
Creek, Greg, Maine	.354	189	50	67	16	2	9	33	5
Sayre, Steve, Albany	.351	148	19	52	13	0	2	30	3
Smith, Curt, Maine	.343	204	37	70	13	5	3	38	10
Wildasin, Kyle, UMBC	.342	184	40	63	11	0	3	29	4
Emanuele, Chris, Northeastern	.340	209	50	71	10	3	11	40	17
Barrett, Joel, Maine	.340	212	42	72	17	2	7	43	0
Hough, Joe, Maine	.336	217	**55**	73	11	5	6	36	**21**
Cipolla, Frank, Hartford	.336	125	14	42	8	1	0	19	6
Quinatal, Ryan, Maine	.335	221	46	74	18	1	7	49	2
Izaryk, Aaron, Maine	.332	184	35	61	15	0	0	30	2
Heriot, Jeff, Northeastern	.327	168	22	55	17	3	6	35	11
Laddbush, Alex, UMBC	.322	171	30	55	12	1	4	31	1
Simek, Matt, Binghamton	.319	166	30	53	7	1	3	26	11
Bergeron, Mathieu, Binghamton	.318	176	38	56	10	1	**16**	**55**	4
Russo, Steve UMBC	.311	132	30	41	8	2	1	20	2
Bush, Tim, Northeastern	.309	178	29	55	13	0	9	26	2
Morizio, Matt, Northeastern	.309	149	24	46	11	3	3	25	1
Sidhu, Arman, Northeastern	.307	192	35	59	16	1	1	26	6

INDIVIDUAL PITCHING LEADERS
(Minimum 50 Innings)

	W	L	ERA	G	SV	IP	H	BB	SO
Richard, Steve, Maine	**9**	1	**2.07**	16	0	100	88	44	90
Miller, Derek, Vermont	7	3	2.35	12	0	88	62	25	103
Serafin, Joe, Vermont	6	2	2.73	19	0	59	41	31	57
Wildasin, Kyle, UMBC	2	6	2.84	12	1	57	53	24	24
Lewis, Jon, Stony Brook	4	5	2.90	13	0	84	87	26	81
Ottavino, Adam, Northeastern	8	4	3.09	14	0	96	78	45	**106**
Norton, Greg, Maine	**9**	4	3.15	15	0	89	98	29	66
Murtagh, Brian, Stony Brook	5	4	3.22	12	0	64	58	23	43
Thomas, Kyle, Albany	1	2	3.65	11	0	67	61	27	49
Kris Dabrowiecki, Northeastern	6	3	3.86	17	1	63	65	22	46
Rampey, Jarrod, Binghamton	5	5	3.94	16	0	80	90	34	56
Blazek, Chris, Vermont	5	4	4.01	13	0	67	63	43	94
Martin, Troy, Maine	8	2	4.02	23	4	69	75	22	42
Krajeski, Jason, Hartford	3	3	4.12	10	0	59	58	31	38
Diamond, Scott, Binghamton	4	6	4.15	14	0	69	69	35	58
Monds, Devin, Northeastern	2	6	4.21	13	0	68	52	46	66
#Robinson, Scott, Maine	2	2	4.43	**29**	**9**	41	43	17	32
Van Gorder, Mike, Binghamton	3	1	4.75	13	0	55	65	23	33
Restivo, Matt, Stony Brook	5	4	4.75	17	1	53	56	23	32
Suchowiecki, Mark, Albany	3	5	4.85	10	0	56	63	23	46
Bakey, Kris, Stony Brook	3	5	5.09	16	1	53	63	17	50

ATLANTIC COAST CONFERENCE

	Conference W	Conference L	Overall W	Overall L
***Georgia Tech**	22	8	45	19
Clemson	21	9	43	23
Miami	19	10	41	19
Florida State	19	11	53	20
North Carolina	17	10	41	19
North Carolina State	17	13	41	19
Virginia	14	14	41	20
Wake Forest	12	18	28	30
Virginia Tech	7	19	23	28
Maryland	7	23	25	31
Duke	5	25	14	39

ALL-CONFERENCE TEAM: C—Jake Muyco, Jr., North Carolina State. **1B**—Aaron Bates, So., North Carolina State. **2B**—Taylor Harbin, Fr., Clemson. **3B**—Ryan Braun, Jr., Miami; Wes Hodges, So., Georgia Tech. **SS**—Tyler Greene, Jr., Georgia Tech. **OF**—Steven Blackwood, Jr., Georgia Tech; Jon Jay, So., Miami; Shane Robinson, So., Florida State. **DH/UT**—Kris Harvey, Jr., Clemson; Matt Wieters, Fr., Georgia Tech. **SP**—Cesar Carrillo, Jr., Miami; Bryan Henry, So., Florida State; Jeff Kamrath, Sr., Virginia; Robert Woodard, So., North Carolina. **RP**—Joey Devine, Jr., North Carolina State.

Player of the Year: Ryan Braun, Miami. **Pitcher of the Year**: Cesar Carrillo, Miami. **Freshman of the Year**: Matt Wieters, Georgia Tech. **Coach of the Year**: Danny Hall, Georgia Tech.

INDIVIDUAL BATTING LEADERS
(Minimum 125 At-Bats)

	AVG	AB	R	H	2B	3B	HR	RBI	SB
Robinson, Shane, FSU	**.427**	286	**96**	**122**	25	4	6	43	**49**
Bates, Aaron, N.C. State	.425	214	61	91	16	1	12	64	3
Jay, Jon, Miami	.408	211	50	86	17	3	1	52	13
Hodges, Wes, Ga. Tech	.397	267	67	106	18	0	9	51	3
Zimmerman, Ryan, Virginia	.393	234	51	92	18	4	6	59	17
Braun, Ryan, Miami	.388	219	70	85	16	2	18	**76**	23
Thomas, Bryan, Virginia Tech	.384	185	22	71	16	4	1	31	3
Greene, Tyler, Ga. Tech	.372	269	76	100	15	3	12	72	31
Wieters, Matt, Ga. Tech	.366	227	53	83	17	1	10	68	1
Figueroa, Paco, Miami	.361	233	70	84	15	**5**	5	38	24
Kindel, Jeff, Ga. Tech	.359	220	50	79	23	1	6	65	2
Slayden, Jeremy, Ga. Tech	.352	199	51	70	9	0	13	57	1
Daniel, Mike, North Carolina	.351	154	28	54	10	1	3	22	7
Chalk, Brad, Clemson	.350	200	46	70	7	0	0	11	5
Horton, Josh, North Carolina	.347	193	29	67	11	3	2	35	5
Storrer, Travis, Clemson	.346	243	46	84	15	2	6	43	0
Demmink, Herman, Clemson	.345	261	56	90	17	1	4	41	9
Mehl, Truan, Maryland	.345	238	42	82	20	3	2	35	13
Harbin, Taylor, Clemson	.343	274	64	94	**28**	4	10	63	4
Harvey, Kris, Clemson	.341	249	61	85	11	0	**25**	70	1
Blackwood, Steven, Ga. Tech	.336	241	61	81	13	1	5	65	3
Flack, Chad, No. Carolina	.335	209	42	70	9	0	15	49	8
Muyco, Jake, N.C. State	.333	207	37	69	14	0	0	36	2
Antonelli, Matt, Wake Forest	.332	232	68	77	22	2	5	35	13
Adams, Sheldon, Va. Tech	.329	143	27	47	8	2	3	22	3
Rye, Jack, Florida State	.328	195	27	64	14	1	2	31	1
Katin, Brendan, Miami	.328	186	34	61	14	1	7	41	3
Ellington, Matt, North Carolina	.328	235	41	77	17	1	9	55	3
Trapani, Mike, Ga. Tech	.327	168	44	55	9	2	2	24	4
Cox, Jay, North Carolina	.326	175	31	57	11	1	2	34	4
Singletary, Elliot, Maryland	.325	194	41	63	25	2	6	34	12
Corona, Ramon, N.C. State	.325	191	42	62	12	1	4	32	5
Tucker, J.B., Wake Forest	.322	245	56	79	24	0	13	65	2
Rodriguez, Eddy, Miami	.320	172	35	55	14	0	8	33	0
Figueroa, Danny, Miami	.319	207	70	66	11	2	5	32	25
Peacher, Brant, Florida State	.318	151	29	48	13	0	3	27	3
Diaz, Jonathan, N.C. State	.317	183	42	58	10	3	1	30	3
Mathias, Ryder, Wake Forest	.316	215	50	68	17	0	12	58	0
Malone, Ryne, Florida State	.316	263	62	83	22	3	7	61	10
Doolittle, Sean, Virginia	.313	224	36	70	12	1	11	57	7
Murray, Adam, Duke	.312	202	39	63	11	0	0	21	10
Stanton, Chris, Virginia Tech	.312	186	41	58	18	3	0	20	14
Bartles, Brett, Duke	.311	196	23	61	11	1	0	37	6
Enick, Brendan, Wake Forest	.311	193	31	60	9	0	5	45	4
Devine, Matt, N.C. State	.311	190	47	59	14	3	2	34	2

	AVG	AB	R	H	2B	3B	HR	RBI	SB
Frazier, Will, Maryland	.310	226	36	70	17	0	10	47	3
Ingold, Ben, Wake Forest	.310	252	52	78	14	0	4	42	19
Marn, Billy, Virginia Tech	.307	166	20	51	6	2	6	29	1
Melvin, Dan, Maryland	.306	173	27	53	15	2	1	19	4
Smith, Bryan, Duke	.304	148	21	45	9	1	1	19	4
Diaz, Walter, Miami	.303	208	50	63	8	1	5	21	7
Wilson, Jordan, Maryland	.301	196	31	59	11	0	3	28	0
#Tomas, Roger, Miami	.268	198	31	53	8	**5**	1	25	1
#Thomas, Tony, Florida State	.240	217	54	52	11	**5**	6	29	9

INDIVIDUAL PITCHING LEADERS

(Minimum 50 Innings)

	W	L	ERA	G	SV	IP	H	BB	SO
McAnaney, Pat, Virginia	7	0	**1.55**	11	0	52	42	9	37
Lynch, Kevin, Florida State	12	0	2.03	**46**	0	62	45	23	67
Chambliss, Tyler, Florida State	7	3	2.06	39	**15**	52	36	23	67
Woodard, Robert, No. Carolina	8	0	2.11	23	0	98	82	19	79
Kamrath, Jeff, Virginia	9	5	2.12	16	0	102	77	27	80
Carrillo, Cesar, Miami	**13**	3	2.22	19	1	126	100	23	**127**
Henry, Bryan, Florida State	9	3	2.22	17	0	89	71	18	58
Hovis, Jonathan, North Carolina	5	4	2.51	27	5	61	54	18	64
Faris, Stephen, Clemson	6	4	2.60	20	1	97	89	25	79
Miller, Andrew, North Carolina	8	4	2.98	16	0	97	78	52	104
Young, Kyle, Wake Forest	4	1	3.06	33	6	53	59	18	35
Wood, Blake, Ga. Tech	10	1	3.13	18	0	106	111	24	74
Hahn, Jeff, Clemson	4	1	3.13	25	3	60	57	27	59
Turner, Ryan, Ga. Tech	7	3	3.31	18	0	71	81	37	49
Gustafson, Tim, Ga. Tech	6	2	3.33	28	1	70	66	29	62
Pfinsgraff, Ben, Maryland	4	3	3.45	11	0	63	57	14	47
Stallings, Jeff, N.C. State	5	3	3.48	10	0	54	50	21	37
Browning, Barret, Florida State	4	4	3.54	24	0	89	92	48	74
Ballard, Mike, Virginia	8	3	3.54	15	1	89	86	19	53
Cribb, Josh, Clemson	8	5	3.54	19	0	109	119	24	97
Sufczynski, Mike, Maryland	4	2	3.66	11	0	52	52	20	28
Kennedy, Ryan, Virginia Tech	5	7	4.05	16	0	100	108	46	74
Mellies, Charlie, Wake Forest	2	5	4.17	18	0	82	101	21	43
Sauls, Mark, Florida State	6	2	4.18	18	0	67	64	30	31
Bard, Daniel, North Carolina	7	5	4.22	16	0	90	73	43	77
Rohrbaugh, Robert, Clemson	8	3	4.22	19	1	96	103	42	82
Avery, Matt, Virginia	6	5	4.34	15	0	85	84	28	71
Hyde, Michael, Florida State	7	2	4.40	20	0	100	108	36	71
Kopp, David, Clemson	4	3	4.61	22	1	70	66	26	46
Hyde, Lee, Ga. Tech	7	4	4.68	18	0	92	101	41	72
Bowers, Nicky, Virginia Tech	3	5	4.76	13	1	59	54	13	57
Davidson, Phillip, N.C. State	6	5	4.80	20	0	75	81	24	47
Orta, Ricky, Miami	7	5	4.98	18	0	78	69	36	61
Jones, Hunter, Florida State	4	3	5.05	18	0	71	87	20	56
Bach, Brian, Wake Forest	2	4	5.08	19	0	67	78	17	34

ATLANTIC SUN CONFERENCE

	Conference W	Conference L	Overall W	Overall L
Troy	23	7	37	21
Florida Atlantic	19	11	37	24
Central Florida	19	11	42	18
***Stetson**	16	14	35	28
Georgia State	15	15	25	32
Gardner-Webb	15	15	28	30
Campbell	13	17	25	29
Jacksonville	13	17	23	31
Belmont	12	18	28	26
Mercer	12	18	28	26
Lipscomb	8	22	23	33

ALL-CONFERENCE TEAM: C—Henry Gutierrez, Sr., Troy. **1B**—Mike Priest, Jr., Campbell. **2B**—Joe Anthonsen, Sr., Campbell. **3B**—Blake Lalli, Jr., Gardner-Webb. **SS**—Brian Bocock, So., Stetson. **OF**—Dee Brown, Sr., Central Florida; Adam Godwin, Jr., Troy; Mike McBryde, So., Florida Atlantic. **DH**—Nick Smith, Jr., Troy. **SP**—Brent Adcock, Sr., Troy; Tim Bascom, So., Central Florida; Mickey Storey, Fr., Florida Atlantic. **RP**—Blake Owen, Jr., Belmont.

Player of the Year: Adam Godwin, Troy. **Pitcher of the Year**: Brent Adcock, Troy. **Freshman of the Year**: Chris Johnson, Stetson. **Coach of the Year**: Bobby Pierce, Troy.

INDIVIDUAL BATTING LEADERS

(Minimum 125 At-Bats)

	AVG	AB	R	H	2B	3B	HR	RBI	SB
Lalli, Blake, Gardner-Webb	**.384**	219	43	84	**30**	0	5	39	3
Johnson, Chris, Stetson	.383	261	62	**100**	23	1	8	52	0
Sickles, Ryan, Gardner-Webb	.380	171	39	65	12	0	5	34	5
Jordan, Shane, Stetson	.375	251	**73**	94	10	3	1	32	25
McBryde, Mike, Fla. Atlantic	.370	265	58	98	10	3	5	40	34
Godwin, Adam, Troy	.367	245	65	90	6	4	5	44	**84**
Holt, Tim, Campbell	.365	230	42	84	11	1	6	49	2
Priest, Mike, Campbell	.365	211	45	77	22	2	14	46	10
Bocock, Brian, Stetson	.355	183	43	65	17	2	6	37	6
Tucker, Wilson, Belmont	.352	210	44	74	15	3	10	51	8
Gutierrez, Henry, Troy	.352	213	66	75	12	0	**18**	61	1
Phillips, Justin, Campbell	.351	194	36	68	14	1	4	36	3
Howell, John-Michael, Cent. Fla.	.348	224	48	78	18	2	15	55	4
Sensing, Nathan, Lipscomb	.346	179	37	62	16	1	6	32	18
Reynolds, Matt, Belmont	.346	208	58	72	17	0	6	33	30
Reichert, Brandon, Mercer	.345	220	40	76	15	0	5	39	3
McConnell, Jay, Gard.-Webb	.345	197	41	68	9	3	5	39	1
Brewer, Tadd, Lipscomb	.345	232	37	80	13	0	2	25	5
Maloney, Matt, Gardner-Webb	.339	218	49	74	14	5	11	48	8
Destefano, John, Stetson	.338	222	57	75	13	3	8	56	7
Smith, Nick, Troy	.338	228	45	77	18	1	13	52	1
Tindle, Adam, Stetson	.338	160	32	54	7	2	3	29	2
Bennett, Brian, Troy	.331	148	26	49	8	0	4	26	4
Murphy, Daniel, Jacksonville	.329	219	35	72	12	2	2	31	11
Lopez, Matt, Jacksonville	.328	186	25	61	8	0	1	30	4
Pruitt, Braedyn, Stetson	.328	229	44	75	17	1	7	57	3
Gronkowski, Gordie, Jacksonville	.327	165	24	54	6	1	7	28	0
Rochon-Salva, Jean, G-W	.327	159	26	52	6	2	0	26	7
Clifford, Pete, Jacksonville	.325	203	36	66	13	0	7	41	5
Bernhard, Marshall, Cent. Fla.	.324	219	50	71	10	1	4	41	25
Richmond, Kevin, Central Fla.	.322	146	28	47	13	2	2	26	6
Shapland, Jonathan, Fla. Atl.	.321	168	27	54	13	0	8	35	2
Butera, Drew, Central Florida	.320	206	48	66	13	2	5	40	10
Barrett, Shawn, Mercer	.320	150	22	48	5	0	5	26	2
Thompson, Josh, Mercer	.319	188	38	60	11	1	12	46	1
Newman, Justin, Georgia State	.318	214	38	68	18	2	11	37	14
Widlansky, Robbie, Fla. Atlantic	.317	221	45	70	10	0	7	39	14
Anthonsen, Joe, Campbell	.317	218	51	60	10	3	2	43	9
Petsch, Ben, Belmont	.316	212	38	67	10	1	2	31	15
Blick, Jeff, Campbell	.315	178	44	56	8	2	1	21	19
Brown, Dee, Central Florida	.312	237	60	74	10	3	**18**	**71**	13
Ange, Mike, Campbell	.311	135	15	42	9	0	1	19	0
Gomez, Dennis, Belmont	.311	135	27	42	9	0	4	32	5
McCann, Jeremy, Gard.-Webb	.307	212	52	65	11	**8**	4	30	16

INDIVIDUAL PITCHING LEADERS

(Minimum 50 Innings)

	W	L	ERA	G	SV	IP	H	BB	SO
#Owen, Blake, Belmont	2	1	0.82	**34**	**13**	44	36	14	51
Storey, Mickey, Fla. Atlantic	10	1	**1.70**	23	7	95	78	23	82
Kuwik, Seth, Lipscomb	7	3	2.42	29	6	74	68	21	75
Handley, Matt, Georgia State	1	3	2.89	17	1	53	60	31	35
Rodriguez, Ray, Central Florida	5	1	3.02	18	1	66	47	41	64
Bascom, Tim, Central Florida	10	2	3.10	16	0	113	103	29	113
Martin, Josh, Gardner-Webb	8	0	3.33	14	1	76	81	20	53
Adcock, Brent, Troy	**11**	3	3.45	17	0	117	109	30	104
Ange, Mike, Campbell	6	1	3.52	10	0	64	54	19	32
New, Brantley, Mercer	5	4	3.55	18	0	84	74	45	66
Ward, Zach, Gardner-Webb	7	9	3.63	20	1	109	102	49	**127**
Brazell, Landon, Troy	9	5	3.70	17	0	119	126	38	126
Billek, Mike, Central Florida	4	3	4.07	16	0	91	95	33	84
Tafazzoli, Matt, Gardner-Webb	1	1	4.11	22	0	50	69	10	26
Devries, Kyle, Jacksonville	9	3	4.15	16	0	85	76	39	52
Kloess, Brandon, Florida Atlantic	8	2	4.17	18	0	58	66	28	48
Morelock, Steven, Troy	6	4	4.32	16	0	81	85	30	53
Newlin, Darren, Central Florida	9	4	4.48	14	0	80	78	30	65
Nery, Nathan, Stetson	4	5	4.50	16	0	78	83	35	68
Tungate, Alan, Lipscomb	3	4	4.53	11	0	56	69	21	36
Frontz, Neal, Jacksonville	6	6	4.63	15	0	89	96	34	54
Young, Josh, Mercer	1	2	4.67	24	0	52	51	20	46
Blackard, Cody, Belmont	6	5	4.80	16	0	90	111	14	46
Martin, Brandon, Gardner-Webb	2	6	4.86	25	8	50	52	22	60
Ingoglia, Chris, Stetson	8	4	4.88	16	1	87	97	27	69
Morrison, Philip, Mercer	7	2	4.88	17	0	79	85	31	65
Falls, Tony, Troy	6	2	4.97	22	3	58	59	28	62
Mann, Will, Fla. Atlantic	3	5	5.00	20	0	77	92	27	57
Strickland, Brett, Georgia State	3	4	5.02	16	0	75	91	25	54
Salberg, Chris, Fla. Atlantic	6	5	5.06	22	0	84	98	34	62

ATLANTIC-10 CONFERENCE

	Conference W	Conference L	Overall W	Overall L
EAST				
***Rhode Island**	18	6	34	21
Fordham	17	7	34	21
Massachusetts	9	15	16	33
St. Bonaventure	8	16	24	25
Temple	8	16	17	33
Saint Joseph's	8	16	14	38
WEST				
George Washington	17	7	41	19
Dayton	16	8	36	23

Duquesne	13	11	21	34
Richmond	12	12	22	35
Xavier	9	15	19	35
La Salle	9	15	18	34

ALL-CONFERENCE TEAM: C—Rich Prall, So., La Salle. **1B**—Ryan Roberson, Sr., George Washington. **2B**—Galen Schumm, Jr., Dayton. **3B**—Mike Rainville, Jr., Rhode Island. **SS**—Steve Maiolo, Jr., Duquesne. **OF**—Brad Rosenblat, Sr., George Washington; Matt Sullivan, Sr., Rhode Island; Jason Twomley, Sr., Massachusetts. **DH**—Ryan Cunningham, So., Rhode Island. **SP**—Derrik Lutz, So., George Washington; Matt Torra, Jr., Massachusetts. **RP**—Gerard Breslin, So., La Salle.

Player of the Year: Brad Rosenblat, George Washington. **Pitcher of the Year**: Matt Torra, Massachusetts. **Rookie of the Year**: Cory Riordan, Fordham. **Coach of the Year**: Nick Restaino, Fordham.

INDIVIDUAL BATTING LEADERS

(Minimum 125 At-Bats)

	AVG	AB	R	H	2B	3B	HR	RBI	SB
Roberson, Ryan, George Wash.	**.423**	194	47	**82**	14	1	16	52	16
Pellegrini, Brian, St. Bona.	.376	170	44	64	9	2	11	52	13
Shanley, Tom, George Wash.	.366	183	37	67	12	0	8	43	7
Cunningham, Ryan, Rh. Island	.365	200	32	73	12	2	7	45	3
Zeskind, Ben, Richmond	.365	211	37	77	16	1	6	32	15
Brewer, Sean, Xavier	.358	173	31	62	14	0	3	28	0
Maiolo, Steve, Duquesne	.356	208	34	74	15	0	2	34	7
Schumm, Galen, Dayton	.354	206	44	73	9	2	7	42	7
Rosenblat, Brad, George Wash.	.353	221	**66**	78	**20**	2	**17**	**57**	**22**
Johnson, Jay, Xavier	.349	195	40	68	16	3	6	36	13
Chandler, Bryan, Dayton	.346	188	37	65	9	2	7	54	5
Russo, Wayne, Rhode Island	.343	166	36	57	13	0	4	35	9
Mardeusz, Matt, St. Bona.	.343	169	33	58	12	0	2	30	7
Sullivan, Matt, Rhode Island	.341	208	53	71	14	1	13	43	10
Holcomb, Daryl, Rhode Island	.340	156	44	53	6	1	3	23	15
Malone, Kieran, St. Bona.	.339	165	33	56	13	4	1	22	2
Massa, Michael, Dayton	.338	231	59	78	11	1	3	23	19
Benoit, William, Dayton	.335	203	40	68	8	0	5	32	0
Getty, Bobby, Dayton	.333	210	50	70	13	3	6	48	14
Brown, Scott, Rhode Island	.333	204	46	68	15	0	3	43	15
Prall, Rich, La Salle	.330	197	14	65	9	0	3	31	0
Rizzo, Joe, St. Bonaventure	.330	185	38	61	15	4	11	45	4
Goldberg, Josh, George Wash.	.328	186	21	61	9	0	4	37	15
Szado, Curt, Massachusetts	.325	160	26	52	11	1	3	35	3
Smith, Greg, Fordham	.323	195	38	63	14	2	5	37	6
Parfit, Ryan, La Salle	.317	208	37	66	13	3	5	37	9
Morrison, Eric, Duquesne	.315	184	40	58	13	3	3	27	11
Twomley, Jason, Massachusetts	.314	140	46	44	4	1	16	32	13
Godzik, Brandon, Dayton	.313	201	35	63	10	0	7	44	1
Baldasari, Nick, St. Joseph's	.313	179	24	56	10	2	4	26	7
Shupin, Mickey, George Wash.	.310	126	24	39	3	1	0	14	17
#Pimpanella, Rob, St. Joseph's	.254	114	16	29	4	**5**	0	17	1

INDIVIDUAL PITCHING LEADERS

(Minimum 50 Innings)

	W	L	ERA	G	SV	IP	H	BB	SO
Torra, Matt, Massachusetts	6	3	**1.14**	14	0	95	56	16	**111**
Breslin, Gerard, La Salle	4	2	1.71	27	9	58	39	23	61
Brookens, Joel, George Wash.	0	1	2.53	**31**	**10**	32	20	13	45
Lutz, Derrik, George Wash.	8	1	2.79	14	0	84	63	31	98
Stammen, Craig, Dayton	9	6	2.80	20	0	106	102	27	77
Trubee, Luke, Dayton	**12**	3	2.91	19	0	108	116	16	82
Pfau, Dan, George Wash.	4	4	3.00	23	5	51	47	22	49
Perkins, Adam, Rhode Island	9	3	3.03	22	0	68	69	12	62
Zuercher, Zack, Rhode Island	6	3	3.05	14	0	91	73	34	103
Wilkie, Josh, George Wash.	8	3	3.08	13	0	88	92	37	76
Davis, Tom, Fordham	5	4	3.14	15	2	80	84	22	51
Foulkrod, Tim, Temple	6	7	3.46	17	1	91	91	25	42
Berzinskas, Rob, Richmond	3	8	3.54	17	0	84	71	39	102
Riordan, Cory, Fordham	10	4	3.61	16	0	87	76	26	66
Owens, Stephen, Richmond	5	2	3.75	16	0	74	81	28	46
Konecny, Bill, Xavier	5	5	3.79	21	0	78	72	40	46
Frazier, Brian, George Wash.	7	1	4.06	14	1	64	71	17	49
Holmes, Steve, Rhode Island	7	1	4.34	12	0	75	72	18	77
Ringer, Jarrod, La Salle	2	8	4.39	16	0	55	62	17	38
Proctor, Mike, St. Bonaventure	4	4	4.41	14	0	51	70	24	44
Creavy, Mike, Xavier	4	6	4.46	21	2	85	105	26	62
Mushko, Craig, La Salle	3	2	4.59	17	0	51	65	14	40
Thompson, Kaleb, Dayton	5	4	4.66	13	0	66	82	24	43
McCormack, Mike, St. Bona.	2	4	4.77	15	1	55	62	24	41

BIG EAST CONFERENCE

	Conference		Overall	
	W	L	W	L
St. John's	19	4	41	18
Boston College	17	8	37	20
***Notre Dame**	14	9	38	24
Pittsburgh	15	10	33	22
Rutgers	12	12	32	21
Connecticut	11	12	34	22
West Virginia	10	15	25	30
Villanova	8	16	28	21
Seton Hall	8	17	17	35
Georgetown	7	18	25	31

ALL-CONFERENCE TEAM: C—Joe Burke, Sr., St. John's. **1B**—Matt Edwards, Sr., Notre Dame. **2B**—Jim Negrych, So., Pittsburgh. **3B**—Jared McGuire, So., Boston College. **SS**—Doug Nelms, Jr., West Virginia. **OF**—Ben Copeland, Jr.; Pittsburgh, Greg Thomson, Jr.; St. John's; Lee Fritz, Sr., West Virginia. **DH**—Ryan Craft, Jr., Georgetown. **P**—Craig Hansen, Jr., St. John's; Joe Martinez, Sr., Boston College; Anthony Varvaro, Jr., St. John's; Mike Wlodarczyk, Sr., Boston College.

Player of the Year: Jared McGuire, Boston College. **Pitcher of the Year**: Craig Hansen, St. John's. **Freshman of the Year**: Brett Lilley, Notre Dame. **Coach of the Year**: Ed Blankmeyer, St. John's.

INDIVIDUAL BATTING LEADERS

(Minimum 125 At-Bats)

	AVG	AB	R	H	2B	3B	HR	RBI	SB
Copeland, Ben, Pittsburgh	**.384**	219	**65**	84	**23**	**10**	9	47	**29**
McGuire, Jared, Boston College	.381	215	52	82	9	3	6	41	27
Fritz, Lee, West Virginia	.379	203	42	77	13	3	5	45	2
Thomson, Greg, St. John's	.372	199	57	74	22	3	7	45	17
Defendis, Johnny, Rutgers	.370	219	47	81	13	4	3	49	5
Antoniato, P.J., St. John's	.369	233	**65**	**86**	16	3	0	30	8
Mallozzi, Tony, Connecticut	.361	194	39	70	18	2	0	41	7
Jenkins, Justin, West Virginia	.359	220	50	79	**23**	1	12	43	1
Lilley, Brett, Notre Dame	.355	214	56	76	5	0	0	28	9
Delaney, Jason, Boston College	.354	209	48	74	12	2	9	48	14
Edwards, Matt, Notre Dame	.353	232	60	82	21	1	14	**68**	7
Negrych, Jim, Pittsburgh	.349	186	52	65	14	1	**16**	59	11
Nelms, Doug, West Virginia	.349	175	35	61	11	1	3	28	3
Burke, Joe, St. John's	.348	164	33	57	9	0	1	41	9
Hourigan, Jeff, Connecticut	.348	164	35	57	18	0	9	44	0
Rodriguez, Cory, Rutgers	.342	202	33	69	10	0	3	37	3
Gaynor, Colin, Rutgers	.341	182	43	62	16	0	5	39	1
Shunk, Derek, Villanova	.337	190	40	64	5	1	1	26	10
Craft, Ryan, Georgetown	.335	194	39	65	10	1	13	48	1
Farkes, Josh, Connecticut	.328	128	27	42	11	0	4	26	9
Cooper, Craig, Notre Dame	.325	209	48	68	14	1	7	58	14
D'Argento, Russ, Connecticut	.324	176	48	57	16	2	5	44	19
Hunt, Jeremy, Villanova	.324	173	35	56	13	2	2	31	6
Petracca, Angelo, Villanova	.322	183	32	59	6	1	3	24	16
Grose, Jeff, Rutgers	.317	189	39	60	10	2	0	21	10
Mayer, Jimmy, Pittsburgh	.317	161	29	51	9	1	0	22	11
Parise, Peter, Pittsburgh	.316	212	31	67	11	1	2	40	5
Brooks, Parker, Georgetown	.315	219	38	69	15	0	2	22	7
Wasserman, Austin, Connecticut	.314	207	52	65	11	4	2	23	20
Williams, Dave, Rutgers	.312	154	32	48	11	1	6	32	4
Matuszek, Kyle, West Virginia	.309	162	29	50	9	1	8	32	3
McLaughlin, Mark, Georgetown	.307	163	34	50	12	1	4	30	10
Supple, Jim, Georgetown	.306	157	21	48	11	1	0	34	6
Maler, Bryan, Connecticut	.306	134	26	41	7	2	1	26	14
Walsh, John, Seton Hall	.303	152	20	46	11	0	5	26	1
Albano, Marco, Boston College	.301	143	20	43	9	1	1	30	11
Conley, Sean, Pittsburgh	.299	164	23	49	6	0	0	26	13
Locke, Drew, Boston College	.298	218	46	65	19	2	4	34	17
Day, Larry, Connecticut	.298	151	21	45	5	0	0	22	2
McKown, Chad, West Virginia	.298	198	38	59	17	0	10	34	2
Kuhn, Tyler, West Virginia	.298	205	46	61	13	6	3	30	1
Frazier, Todd, Rutgers	.295	220	61	65	13	3	9	36	19
Day, Alan, Villanova	.295	176	38	52	8	1	2	22	8
Pahuta, Tim, Seton Hall	.294	180	43	53	17	3	6	32	2

INDIVIDUAL PITCHING LEADERS

(Minimum 50 Innings)

	W	L	ERA	G	SV	IP	H	BB	SO
Hansen, Craig, St. John's	3	2	**1.68**	**31**	**14**	64	38	20	85
Brant, Robert, Pittsburgh	7	2	2.07	15	1	61	47	23	68
Varvaro, Anthony, St. John's	9	3	2.32	14	0	85	54	35	**115**
Jeanes, Nate, Boston College	3	5	2.38	17	0	76	57	22	71
Sullivan, Anthony, St. John's	8	3	2.43	20	2	78	54	39	73
Muldowney, Billy, Pittsburgh	7	3	2.47	12	0	84	78	19	89
Allen, Nick, Villanova	6	6	2.72	15	0	93	88	22	68
Martinez, Joe, Boston College	9	3	2.81	13	0	96	76	26	99
Fagler, Marty, West Virginia	6	3	2.92	12	0	71	71	27	48
Norton, Tim, Connecticut	4	0	3.07	13	0	59	46	26	49
Wlodarczyk, Mike, Boston College	**10**	2	3.07	13	0	85	87	22	90
Doyle, Terry, Boston College	6	3	3.14	18	1	57	52	27	66
Kapala, Dan, Notre Dame	7	3	3.20	25	1	82	84	27	41
Wladyka, Jim, St. John's	7	3	3.20	16	0	90	72	30	74
Gaggioli, Michael, Georgetown	4	6	3.42	14	0	84	84	14	67

	W	L	ERA	G	SV	IP	H	BB	SO
Sirois, Rich, Connecticut	6	6	3.69	13	0	78	83	17	49
Samardzija, Jeff, Notre Dame	8	1	3.89	15	0	79	85	30	56
McDonald, Dan, Seton Hall	5	5	3.89	14	1	69	67	32	51
Jansen, Jim, Rutgers	5	1	3.96	16	1	64	76	24	29
Nardozzi, Paul, Pittsburgh	4	5	4.02	14	1	63	66	25	66
Kuss, Andrew, Pittsburgh	5	2	4.24	14	1	57	60	21	55
Mulvey, Kevin, Villanova	4	4	4.65	12	0	72	75	28	73
Thornton, Tom, Notre Dame	6	6	4.69	16	0	96	115	19	40
McGinn, Brendan, Connecticut	4	6	4.73	13	0	70	73	8	48
Pena, Eduardo, Georgetown	4	6	4.76	15	0	96	99	35	75
Rhoten, Dan, Pittsburgh	3	4	4.86	12	0	50	61	15	40
Loree, Mike, Villanova	4	5	4.92	13	0	71	78	25	49
Holt, Steve, Rutgers	3	3	4.94	11	1	51	53	19	34
Hourigan, Jeff, Connecticut	5	2	5.02	13	1	57	64	11	48

BIG SOUTH CONFERENCE

	Conference		Overall	
	W	L	W	L
Coastal Carolina	21	3	50	16
***Winthrop**	19	5	44	22
Birmingham Southern	18	6	36	21
Liberty	14	10	36	19
Virginia Military Institute	11	13	27	28
Charleston Southern	8	16	24	29
Radford	8	16	15	40
High Point	6	18	19	36
UNC Asheville	3	21	11	42

ALL-CONFERENCE TEAM: C—Alan Robbins, Jr., Winthrop. **1B**—Mike Costanzo, Jr., Coastal Carolina. **2B**—Michael DeJesus, Jr., Coastal Carolina. **3B**—Kelly Sweppenhiser, Jr., Virginia Military Institute. **SS**—Matt Smith, Sr., Virginia Military Institute. **OF**—Daniel Carte, Jr., Winthrop; Phil Laurent, Jr., Liberty; Dom Duggan, So., Coastal Carolina. **DH**—Jacob Dempsey, Jr., Winthrop. **P**—Kevin Slowey, Jr., Winthrop; Ricky Shefka, Jr., Coastal Carolina. **RP**—Mike Costanzo, Jr., Coastal Carolina.

Player of the Year: Mike Costanzo, Coastal Carolina. **Freshman of the Year**: Billy Froehlich, Birmingham-Southern. **Coach of the Year**: Gary Gilmore, Coastal Carolina.

INDIVIDUAL BATTING LEADERS

(Minimum 125 At-Bats)

	AVG	AB	R	H	2B	3B	HR	RBI	SB
Costanzo, Mike, Co. Carolina	**.379**	240	**74**	91	15	2	16	67	8
Fleisher, Mark, Radford	.375	184	29	69	12	0	11	47	1
Sweppenhiser, Kelly, VMI	.370	200	51	74	18	0	12	40	6
Grijalva, Aaron, Liberty	.367	210	55	77	13	4	11	39	13
Dempsey, Jacob, Winthrop	.362	207	44	75	16	2	11	57	2
Wohlford, Kellen, Radford	.360	214	38	77	9	**6**	4	33	20
Todd, Chris, Co. Carolina	.357	244	70	87	9	1	3	47	11
Arrington, Elliott, UNC-A	.354	192	33	68	12	1	0	27	5
Tucker, Adam, Birm.-Southern	.354	229	52	81	11	0	**25**	73	0
Duggan, Dom, Co. Carolina	.348	204	48	71	17	2	4	27	7
DeJesus, Michael, Co. Carolina	.346	243	52	84	15	1	9	72	10
Carte, Daniel, Winthrop	.344	270	57	**93**	16	3	19	**74**	12
Rollins, Heath, Winthrop	.341	249	57	85	11	3	2	29	**29**
Laurent, Phillip, Liberty	.333	219	46	73	10	1	7	30	9
Ashworth, Alan, Radford	.330	224	34	74	12	4	4	38	7
Haar, Jordan, Charleston So.	.327	168	36	55	10	2	3	35	14
Carrara, Chris, Winthrop	.327	257	72	84	10	0	4	34	28
Fyle, Justin, Charleston So.	.323	164	34	53	12	1	1	19	10
Schwartz, Randy, High Point	.323	130	15	42	8	0	3	20	2
Campana, Tony, UNC-A	.321	212	38	68	5	2	0	15	13
Crumpler, Robert, VMI	.319	204	39	65	10	0	10	43	1
Smith, Thane, VMI	.316	190	24	60	8	0	2	23	14
Roberson, Kyle, Winthrop	.315	260	44	82	13	1	10	46	12
Ramirez, Chris, High Point	.313	214	44	67	13	2	3	27	17
Just, Michael, Liberty	.311	219	45	68	16	3	4	30	5
Godwin, Mac, Birm.-Southern	.306	147	33	45	12	1	5	33	1
Smith, Matt, VMI	.305	223	33	68	12	0	2	39	11
Grosse, Drew, Charleston So.	.303	155	27	47	6	2	0	16	12
Toth, Nate, Radford	.301	146	20	44	10	0	3	15	0
Burton, Blake, Birm.-Southern	.301	193	44	58	10	0	5	29	2
Foisy, Jon, Co. Carolina	.300	230	50	69	7	3	2	48	21
Lentz, Tommy, Winthrop	.298	238	42	71	**20**	1	3	46	5
Hynick, Brandon, Birm.-Southern	.296	142	33	42	8	1	9	38	2
#Miller, Chad, Liberty	.236	148	30	35	6	**6**	4	27	6

INDIVIDUAL PITCHING LEADERS

(Minimum 50 Innings)

	W	L	ERA	G	SV	IP	H	BB	SO
Costanzo, Mike, Co. Carolina	8	1	**2.13**	**37**	**14**	55	44	24	69
Slowey, Kevin, Winthrop	**14**	2	2.18	19	1	136	91	13	**134**
Valter, Mike, Co. Carolina	4	0	2.36	22	1	53	49	19	35
Shefka, Ricky, Co. Carolina	12	2	2.75	17	0	118	125	20	81
Page, Ryan, Liberty	2	2	3.09	20	2	55	60	17	34
Kniginyzky, Matt, High Point	3	6	3.23	25	7	61	51	27	76
Rollins, Heath, Winthrop	11	6	3.33	17	0	130	112	32	114
Hynick, Brandon, Birm.-Southern	8	5	3.34	15	1	100	111	27	74
Evans, Josh, Charleston So.	8	4	3.60	21	0	90	83	36	83
Binda, Byron, Co. Carolina	7	2	3.60	24	1	60	50	31	75
Hollenbeck, J.J., VMI	4	5	3.73	19	1	92	96	31	67
Britnell, Josh, Birm.-Southern	4	4	3.78	18	1	64	67	21	63
Wilson, Jon, Winthrop	5	4	3.88	34	5	53	54	15	68
Thompson, Phillip, Liberty	3	3	3.88	23	4	53	60	24	34
Solbach, Michael, Liberty	4	4	3.98	17	0	106	103	36	64
Portice, Eammon, High Point	6	4	4.01	16	0	94	95	38	90
Zuvich, Chris, Liberty	8	2	4.25	17	2	85	83	36	79
Honce, Mike, Winthrop	4	3	4.33	15	0	69	81	41	60
Bissell, Brad, Charleston So.	3	8	4.39	21	0	96	120	30	62
Horne, David, Birm.-Southern	8	4	4.44	16	0	95	118	30	55
DeLaGarza, Andy, Co. Carolina	5	4	4.45	18	0	83	84	42	50
DeMara, Jeff, VMI	6	4	4.48	33	6	60	66	24	40
Sowers, Ryan, Charleston So.	7	2	4.54	25	0	69	76	35	63
Bechtold, David, Liberty	6	5	4.70	18	2	69	71	26	67

BIG 10 CONFERENCE

	Conference		Overall	
	W	L	W	L
Illinois	20	12	33	23
Purdue	17	11	27	30
Iowa	19	13	29	28
Michigan	17	12	42	19
***Ohio State**	17	12	40	20
Minnesota	17	15	32	30
Northwestern	14	18	26	28
Penn State	13	19	28	27
Michigan State	10	18	22	31
Indiana	9	23	26	30

ALL-CONFERENCE TEAM: C—Chris Robinson, Jr., Illinois. **1B**—Dusty Bensko, Sr., Illinois. **2B**—Chris Getz, Jr., Michigan. **3B**—David Hrncirik, Sr., Minnesota. **SS**—Mitch Hilligoss, So., Purdue. **OF**—Drew Davidson, Sr., Illinois; Mike Rabin, Sr., Ohio State; Ryan Rogowski, Jr., Illinois. **DH**—Pat McMahon, Jr., Northwestern. **SP**—Brian Blomquist, Jr., Illinois; Jim Brauer, Sr., Michigan; Michael Penn, Sr., Michigan; Scott Byrnes, Sr., Purdue. **RP**—Tim Gudex, Jr., Iowa.

Player of the Year: Drew Davidson, Illinois. **Pitcher of the Year**: Jim Brauer, Michigan. **Freshman of the Year**: Ryan Sontag, Michigan State. **Coach of the Year**: Richard "Itch" Jones, Illinois.

INDIVIDUAL BATTING LEADERS

(Minimum 125 At-Bats)

	AVG	AB	R	H	2B	3B	HR	RBI	SB
Hilligoss, Mitch, Purdue	**.404**	228	52	**92**	16	1	4	37	25
McMahon, Pat, Northwestern	.400	205	44	82	18	0	6	33	0
Bohm, Kyle, Michigan	.386	228	43	88	12	1	5	65	2
Getz, Chris, Michigan	.386	228	58	88	10	0	0	32	29
Kunkel, Jeff, Michigan	.384	190	28	73	14	1	3	45	4
Rogowski, Ryan, Illinois	.374	230	56	86	10	**6**	4	26	**31**
Brant, Jay, Indiana	.365	222	**71**	81	16	4	3	40	26
Boswell, Zach, Indiana	.359	198	37	71	12	2	8	53	2
Basham, Ryan, Michigan State	.358	190	36	68	12	0	8	43	7
Krider, Troy, Michigan State	.356	216	38	77	9	1	4	42	6
Rohde, Mike, Illinois	.355	169	31	60	5	2	4	38	6
Welker, Kris, Iowa	.354	189	34	67	16	3	4	46	6
Milliron, Michael, Penn State	.354	206	42	73	14	0	0	28	15
Caravati, Steve, Ohio State	.353	150	33	53	13	4	5	33	3
Robinson, Chris, Illinois	.353	184	39	65	11	3	8	37	5
Butler, Matt, Michigan	.350	217	48	76	15	2	7	51	4
Lewis, Matt, Penn State	.350	200	42	70	12	2	5	37	11
Sontag, Ryan, Michigan State	.349	149	37	52	10	2	1	17	8
Watson, Reggie, Indiana	.340	235	60	80	12	5	1	18	20
Parker, Ryan, Indiana	.340	209	40	71	14	2	5	51	9
Lytle, Andy, Iowa	.338	225	46	76	6	3	2	36	20
Gorka, Neal, Purdue	.337	181	27	61	11	1	7	30	2
Fornasiere, Matt, Minnesota	.335	230	47	77	18	2	4	40	10
Hrncirik, David, Minnesota	.332	226	38	75	3	1	1	29	29
Rabin, Mike, Ohio State	.330	200	46	66	6	0	2	28	16
Heckman, Corby, Indiana	.328	189	29	62	10	1	2	33	4
Elder, Jake, Minnesota	.328	183	33	60	13	1	5	43	3
Kemp, Joe, Indiana	.327	220	59	72	12	3	10	63	12
Thompson, Lance, Penn State	.327	211	31	69	13	3	2	30	5
Hunter, Andy, Minnesota	.324	219	37	71	17	0	8	47	1
Fryer, Eric, Ohio State	.323	164	31	53	6	1	2	24	5
Davidson, Drew, Illinois	.322	202	57	65	16	3	14	53	5
Richardson, Josh, Indiana	.321	159	29	51	3	1	0	20	3
Price, Nate, Iowa	.320	194	35	62	7	3	2	28	15
Gummo, Scott, Penn State	.319	141	29	45	7	1	6	25	2
Morris, Erik, Michigan State	.318	201	34	64	12	1	3	28	8

	AVG	AB	R	H	2B	3B	HR	RBI	SB
White, Jason, Iowa	.317	145	25	46	8	4	0	26	6
Bensko, Dusty, Illinois	.317	205	51	65	11	0	**16**	**67**	0
Phelps, Mike, Northwestern	.314	140	25	44	7	2	0	24	2
Schirtzinger, Wes, Ohio State	.313	134	27	42	6	1	0	12	12
Kyes, J.R., Illinois	.311	209	51	65	13	5	7	36	2
Wycklendt, Anthony, N'western	.311	193	37	60	14	1	10	52	1
Ori, Mark, Northwestern	.308	201	34	62	8	2	3	35	2
Wolfe, Eric, Purdue	.308	182	24	56	9	2	0	25	6
Angle, Matt, Ohio State	.307	166	35	51	6	1	0	18	13
Stephen, Jedidiah, Ohio State	.305	203	36	62	13	2	5	46	3
Farinacci, Paul, Ohio State	.303	201	26	61	**20**	1	2	54	0

INDIVIDUAL PITCHING LEADERS

(Minimum 50 Innings)

	W	L	ERA	G	SV	IP	H	BB	SO
Toneguzzi, Chris, Purdue	2	2	1.43	**30**	6	38	41	9	38
Brauer, Jim, Michigan	7	2	**2.54**	15	0	110	97	20	86
Gudex, Tim, Iowa	9	4	2.55	**30**	6	60	53	26	47
Penn, Michael, Michigan	7	2	2.79	14	0	81	71	22	61
DeLucia, Dan, Ohio State	6	5	2.91	15	0	96	92	26	55
#Hayes, Chris, Northwestern	3	2	3.02	25	**9**	45	46	15	33
Conroy, Jimmy, Illinois	8	3	3.10	14	0	93	89	17	63
Blomquist, Brian, Illinois	**10**	3	3.53	14	0	102	121	13	46
Luebke, Cory, Ohio State	4	2	3.55	16	0	71	73	17	54
O'Loughlin, Luke, Iowa	1	4	3.86	14	2	68	67	31	40
Stidfole, Sean, Penn State	6	3	3.89	14	3	90	89	35	**87**
Byrnes, Scott, Purdue	6	4	3.96	13	0	84	91	24	58
Madsen, Mike, Ohio State	7	3	3.99	15	0	77	85	22	52
Lewis, Josh, Indiana	7	5	4.03	13	0	83	91	20	65
Taylor, Drew, Michigan	4	3	4.05	17	0	67	64	31	36
Feldkamp, Derek, Michigan	9	5	4.05	25	6	67	60	22	33
Loberg, Matt, Minnesota	8	5	4.07	15	0	95	115	14	54
Hammond, Paul, Michigan	4	3	4.14	17	0	50	63	22	40
Pruemer, Mitch, Purdue	6	5	4.48	14	0	84	114	15	53
Luyster, Trent, Ohio State	7	4	4.52	15	0	92	108	20	48
Stidfoles, Alan, Penn State	6	4	4.58	13	0	79	82	26	74
Brookes, Craig, Michigan State	6	1	4.84	14	0	61	72	20	39
Smith, Andrew, Northwestern	3	5	5.03	14	0	73	91	28	37
Sattler, Dan, Purdue	2	4	5.19	12	0	52	69	25	35
Lortz, Brian, Indiana	2	**8**	5.37	13	0	65	81	19	37
Kontos, George, Northwestern	5	4	5.43	13	0	68	69	31	55
Seward, Austin, Iowa	3	2	5.46	14	0	64	77	28	33
Coudron, Brent, Purdue	4	4	5.46	13	1	58	72	18	33
Day, Tim, Michigan State	4	6	5.50	13	0	75	99	17	43
O'Rourke, Casey, Iowa	2	5	5.56	13	0	70	89	13	32
Bull, Brian, Minnesota	4	4	5.56	17	1	55	77	7	22
Clark, Craig, Penn State	3	4	5.75	14	0	61	71	35	61
Myers, Ryan, Northwestern	3	5	5.76	12	0	55	70	19	52
DeVries, Cole, Minnestoa	3	6	5.91	15	0	78	99	22	57
Blesoff, Evan, Northwestern	4	8	6.50	15	0	80	99	26	38

BIG 12 CONFERENCE

	Conference		Overall	
	W	L	W	L
***Nebraska**	19	8	57	15
Baylor	19	8	46	24
Texas	16	10	56	16
Missouri	16	11	40	23
Oklahoma	14	13	35	26
Oklahoma State	12	15	34	25
Kansas	11	15	36	28
Texas Tech	9	16	34	25
Texas A&M	9	18	30	25
Kansas State	8	19	30	25

ALL-CONFERENCE TEAM: C—Taylor Teagarden, Jr., Texas. **1B**—Curtis Ledbetter, Sr., Nebraska. **3B**—Alex Gordon, Jr. Nebraska, **IF**—Cameron Blair, Sr., Texas Tech; Joey Callender, Jr., Texas Tech; Seth Johnston, Sr., Texas; Cliff Pennington, Jr.,Texas A&M. **OF**—James Boone, Jr., Missouri; Corey Brown, Fr., Oklahoma State; Drew Stubbs, So.,Texas; A.J. Van Slyke, Jr., Kansas. **DH**—Zach Dillon, Jr., Baylor. **UT**—Adam Carr, Jr., Oklahoma State. **SP**—Joba Chamberlain, So., Nebraska; Johnny Dorn, Fr., Nebraska; Mark McCormick, Jr., Baylor; Kyle McCulloch, So.,Texas; Max Scherzer, So., Missouri. **RP**—J. Brent Cox, Jr., Texas; Ryan LaMotta, Jr., Baylor.

Player of the Year: Alex Gordon, Nebraska. **Pitcher of the Year**: Max Scherzer, Missouri. **Newcomer of the Year**: Joba Chamberlain, Nebraska. **Freshman Player of the Year**: Corey Brown, Oklahoma State. **Freshman Pitcher of the Year**: Johnny Dorn, Nebraska. **Coach of the Year**: Mike Anderson, Nebraska.

INDIVIDUAL BATTING LEADERS

(Minimum 125 At-Bats)

	AVG	AB	R	H	2B	3B	HR	RBI	SB
Johnston, Seth, Texas	**.378**	304	59	**115**	20	5	9	66	15
Gordon, Alex, Nebraska	.372	253	**79**	94	**22**	4	19	66	23
Schweitzer, Jared, Kansas	.366	142	35	52	10	0	7	32	2
Gerch, Andy, Nebraska	.364	151	33	55	7	2	4	35	3
Pennington, Cliff, Texas A&M	.363	212	44	77	13	4	7	39	29
Callender, Joseph, Texas Tech	.362	221	43	80	15	1	0	48	15
Brown, Corey, Okla. State	.360	175	53	63	7	**6**	13	46	8
Blair, Cameron, Texas Tech	.350	223	70	78	12	3	17	60	21
Rice, Barrett, Kansas State	.348	155	43	54	10	2	6	27	12
Rohlinger, Ryan, Oklahoma	.345	229	53	79	11	3	11	53	7
Gutierrez, Chris, Okla. State	.343	213	44	73	14	5	5	33	4
Wright, Ty, Okla. State	.342	196	40	67	8	2	7	42	8
Goedert, Jared, Kansas State	.341	179	36	61	9	3	4	39	0
Baldwin, Andrew, Texas A&M	.341	129	20	44	5	2	4	23	4
Boone, James, Missouri	.340	194	53	66	15	5	8	72	14
Blunt, Terry, Kansas State	.336	220	45	74	15	2	4	33	26
Carr, Adam, Okla. State	.336	235	54	79	10	5	**22**	**86**	1
Crouch, Will, Texas	.336	149	30	50	8	1	7	32	1
Buckman, Brandon, Nebraska	.335	161	26	54	10	0	2	30	4
Teagarden, Taylor, Texas	.333	222	52	74	**22**	1	7	33	4
Farr, Brandon, Kansas State	.331	139	26	46	9	2	1	31	10
Avants, Carey, Texas Tech	.330	206	50	68	12	4	2	39	12
Murphy, Steve, Kansas State	.328	198	52	65	19	0	10	45	10
Ford, Josh, Baylor	.328	259	47	85	19	2	9	41	7
Mense, Hunter, Missouri	.327	205	62	67	17	2	3	43	10
Van Slyke, A.J., Kansas	.323	223	51	72	12	0	12	57	5
Fuller, Cody, Texas Tech	.322	205	52	66	10	3	1	37	27
Bruce, Daniel, Nebraska	.322	230	47	74	**22**	2	5	32	9
Taylor, Zane, Missouri	.321	184	31	59	9	1	1	32	4
Chambers, Derek, Missouri	.320	247	63	79	12	3	3	48	3
Ledbetter, Curtis, Nebraska	.319	288	52	92	18	1	13	55	3
Hill, Ryan, Texas A&M	.317	208	35	66	8	0	3	24	2
Caufield, Chuckie, Oklahoma	.315	203	47	64	9	1	4	19	9
Wheeless, Chance, Texas	.314	245	36	77	12	3	6	45	2
Kainer, Carson, Texas	.312	202	36	63	9	1	3	31	5
Stubbs, Drew, Texas	.311	283	67	88	20	4	11	46	32
Rodriguez, Freddy, Oklahoma	.311	228	37	71	6	1	0	30	3
Simokaitis, Joe, Nebraska	.310	277	53	86	8	0	3	37	18
Baty, Matt, Kansas	.306	245	50	75	12	0	1	29	30
Peoples, Nick, Texas	.306	186	50	57	9	1	1	25	13
Priday, Jacob, Missouri	.305	223	53	68	13	3	9	67	8
Kaiser, Kody, Oklahoma	.305	256	51	78	15	5	10	34	13
Dillon, Zach, Baylor	.304	247	29	75	20	1	2	43	2
Eymann, Eric, Kansas State	.303	198	35	60	11	4	4	39	5
Richardson, Sean, Kansas	.302	225	50	68	19	1	6	45	3
Raley, Russell, Oklahoma	.302	222	37	67	4	2	2	41	5
Ryal, Rusty, Oklahoma State	.300	230	46	69	11	2	7	43	2
Hernandez, Mike, Okla. State	.299	167	36	50	16	3	6	31	4
Colbert, Justin, Okla. State	.299	224	52	67	11	0	1	25	8
Milner, Gus, Kansas	.298	225	46	67	14	4	9	45	9
Arndt, Gary, Missouri	.298	208	33	62	10	3	0	32	0
Smith, Kevin, Oklahoma	.294	204	37	60	16	2	6	42	2
Griffin, Michael, Baylor	.293	294	51	86	16	2	7	34	8

INDIVIDUAL PITCHING LEADERS

(Minimum 50 Innings)

	W	L	ERA	G	SV	IP	H	BB	SO
Cox, J. Brent, Texas	8	3	**1.73**	42	**19**	78	57	25	87
Mandel, Jeff, Baylor	4	0	1.91	25	0	66	52	23	27
Scherzer, Max, Missouri	9	4	1.86	16	0	106	59	41	**131**
Kasparek, Kenn, Texas	8	0	2.10	15	0	73	53	31	46
LaMotta, Ryan, Baylor	5	2	2.15	36	7	80	60	21	82
Dorn, Johnny, Nebraska	**12**	2	2.16	20	1	104	75	21	76
McElroy, Tanner, Texas Tech	2	4	2.28	24	4	59	43	24	45
Woody, Abe, Baylor	10	3	2.58	36	11	66	48	14	41
Alaniz, Adrian, Texas	8	3	2.67	23	0	108	93	39	94
Kroenke, Zach, Nebraska	7	2	2.78	20	1	97	80	28	88
Chamberlain, Joba, Nebraska	10	2	2.81	18	0	119	91	33	130
Parker, Taylor, Missouri	1	2	2.88	28	4	50	32	23	42
McCulloch, Kyle, Texas	**12**	4	2.92	26	0	139	137	45	99
Johnston, Andrew, Missouri	4	5	2.95	29	4	58	57	16	42
McCormick, Mark, Baylor	8	4	2.96	20	0	113	73	66	115
Richmond, Scott, Okla. State	3	6	3.00	25	6	99	74	27	98
Duensing, Brian, Nebraska	8	0	3.00	23	0	84	69	28	52
Cowley, Thomas, Okla. State	10	5	3.04	16	0	110	97	24	80
Meyer, Jason, Texas A&M	5	5	3.04	17	1	77	62	41	49
Stewart, Clayton, Texas	9	0	3.04	41	1	68	47	24	58
Mathis, Doug, Missouri	5	4	3.27	21	1	77	81	17	67
Quick, Kodiak, Kansas	10	6	3.41	27	0	121	108	42	91
Boone, Randy, Texas	7	4	3.46	25	0	109	103	38	95
Czyz, Don, Kansas	3	4	3.47	36	10	62	50	26	60
Culp, Nathan, Missouri	9	2	3.50	17	0	93	105	31	63
Patterson, Garrett, Oklahoma	6	3	3.59	17	2	63	42	42	73
Marlatt, Kyle, Texas A&M	4	3	3.60	17	0	50	43	28	23
Taylor, Trey, Baylor	7	6	3.62	19	0	104	96	46	89
Ray, Robert, Texas A&M	2	4	3.78	18	1	64	54	13	59
Cody, Buck, Texas	4	1	3.81	34	1	52	46	30	38

	W	L	ERA	G	SV	IP	H	BB	SO
Cowart, Adam, Kansas State	7	4	3.93	14	0	101	104	15	70
Savage, Will, Oklahoma	9	4	3.98	36	6	97	112	19	53
VanAllen, Cory, Baylor	8	4	4.02	19	0	107	118	34	68
McCutchen, Daniel, Oklahoma	4	5	4.18	24	2	84	92	23	84
Daniels, Adam, Oklahoma State	7	3	4.20	17	0	75	91	26	88
Carnline, Billy, Texas Tech	7	3	4.27	18	1	78	90	36	62
Mitchell, Chase, Kansas State	7	6	4.45	14	0	87	87	32	61

BIG WEST CONFERENCE

	Conference		Overall	
	W	L	W	L
Cal State Fullerton	16	5	46	18
Long Beach State	14	7	37	22
Cal Poly	14	7	36	20
UC Riverside	11	10	28	27
UC Irvine	10	11	31	25
Pacific	9	12	30	28
UC Santa Barbara	8	13	26	30
Cal State Northridge	2	19	18	36

ALL-CONFERENCE TEAM: C—Kyle Blumenthatl, Sr., Cal Poly. **1B**—Justin Baum, Fr., Pacific. **2B**—Brett Dalton, Sr., UC Irvine. **3B**—Ronnie Prettyman, Sr., Cal State Fullerton. **SS**—Troy Tulowitzki, Jr., Long Beach State; Blake Davis, So., Cal State Fullerton. **OF**—Sergio Pedroza, Jr., Cal State Fullerton; Brandon Roberts, Jr., Cal Poly; Aaron Grant, Jr., UC Riverside. **DH**—Andrew Martinez, Jr., UC Riverside. **UT**—Alberto Quintana, Sr., Cal State Northridge. **SP**—Garrett Olson, Jr., Cal Poly; Cesar Ramos, Jr., Long Beach State; Ricky Romero, Jr., Cal State Fullerton. **RP**—Neil Jamison, Sr., Long Beach State.

Co-Players of the Year: Kyle Blumenthal, Cal Poly; Sergio Pedroza, Cal State Fullerton. **Pitcher of the Year**: Ricky Romero, Cal State Fullerton. **Freshman Player of the Year:** Justin Baum, Pacific. **Freshman Pitcher of the Year**: Wes Roemer, Cal State Fullerton. **Coach of the Year**: George Horton, Cal State Fullerton.

INDIVIDUAL BATTING LEADERS

(Minimum 125 At-Bats)

	AVG	AB	R	H	2B	3B	HR	RBI	SB
Blumenthal, Kyle, Cal Poly	**.410**	183	42	75	15	0	4	53	4
Dalton, Brett, UC Irvine	.376	170	32	64	10	3	0	23	11
Grant, Aaron, UC Riverside	.357	196	47	70	15	2	1	30	10
Wagner, Mark, UC Irvine	.355	220	37	78	11	4	4	39	2
Tulowitzki, Troy, Long Beach	.349	152	32	53	12	1	8	29	2
Quintana, Alberto, CS North.	.349	215	35	75	17	0	0	28	1
Van Ostrand, Jimmy, Cal Poly	.342	149	25	51	6	0	4	25	1
Martinez, Jaime, UC Irvine	.339	168	21	57	8	0	5	46	2
Salotti, Nick, UC Riverside	.339	227	34	77	**19**	3	8	46	4
Roberts, Brandon, Cal Poly	.339	227	53	77	8	**9**	0	32	**20**
Martinez, Andrew, UC Riverside	.338	139	29	47	13	0	4	40	2
Anderson, Matt, UC Irvine	.332	193	35	64	18	2	4	32	10
Baum, Justin, Pacific	.332	190	39	63	15	2	**17**	45	0
Paulk, Michael, CS Northridge	.330	215	38	71	11	0	12	45	2
Pill, Brett, CS Fullerton	.327	260	55	**85**	12	2	9	57	4
Prettyman, Ronnie, CS Fullerton	.327	251	55	82	18	3	8	49	13
Aidem, Matt, UC Santa Barbara	.326	132	15	43	4	2	0	27	1
Davis, Blake, CS Fullerton	.325	212	50	69	11	8	2	36	17
Turner, Justin, CS Fullerton	.324	244	54	79	17	2	3	41	11
Pedroza, Sergio, CS Fullerton	.323	220	47	**71**	12	2	16	**58**	6
Bigler, Brett, UC Riverside	.322	233	46	75	7	4	0	19	14
Longoria, Evan, Long Beach St.	.320	228	34	73	8	0	5	30	10
Wilkerson, Matt, UCSB	.318	217	47	69	7	0	13	51	9
Tezak, Jeff, CS Northridge	.317	164	26	52	9	0	0	19	6
Malec, Chris, UC Santa Barbara	.316	174	36	55	13	0	5	25	2
Walker, Brent, Cal Poly	.311	148	29	46	4	1	1	17	8
Hagstrom, Erik, CS Northridge	.310	145	20	45	7	0	0	24	0
Jones, Chris, Long Beach St.	.308	172	21	53	10	0	2	27	2
Gottier, Brandon, Pacific	.307	215	33	66	8	1	3	21	4
Linton, Ollie, UC Irvine	.306	134	28	41	5	2	1	19	14
Godfrey, Brandon, Long Beach	.305	177	19	54	8	2	1	24	2
Miramontes, Danny, UC Irvine	.303	175	36	53	7	0	0	26	13
Garcia, Felipe, CS Fullerton	.302	129	22	39	10	1	0	24	0
Boatright, Sean, Long Beach	.299	197	26	59	17	0	3	30	5
Cooper, Matt, Cal Poly	.298	208	43	62	17	2	8	38	2
Andrews, Bobby, CS Fullerton	.297	145	34	43	1	3	1	23	13
#Dorn, Danny, CS Fullerton	.272	213	**56**	58	13	0	10	49	3

INDIVIDUAL PITCHING LEADERS

(Minimum 50 Innings)

	W	L	ERA	G	SV	IP	H	BB	SO
Schmidt, Josh, Pacific	6	4	**1.79**	**36**	11	60	49	25	89
Schreppel, Ryan, CS Fullerton	6	1	1.92	12	0	70	38	30	41
Estrada, Marco, Long Beach St.	8	3	2.43	18	0	111	84	29	104
Nicoll, Chris, UC Irvine	6	4	2.58	17	0	112	89	24	113
Ramos, Cesar, Long Beach St.	10	7	2.64	18	0	126	105	16	95
Pestano, Vinnie, CS Fullerton	3	4	2.68	34	13	50	44	16	49
Olson, Garrett, Cal Poly	12	4	2.71	19	0	136	123	47	128
#Bille, Mike, Cal Poly	1	1	2.73	27	**14**	33	31	9	23
#McRobbie, Alex, UCSB	2	0	2.75	30	**14**	39	32	7	48
Hughes, Jared, Long Beach St.	8	3	2.83	15	0	89	67	23	87
Romero, Ricky, CS Fullerton	**13**	5	2.89	18	0	134	102	34	**139**
Winter, Haley, UC Riverside	6	8	3.44	17	0	110	119	30	68
Schroer, Steve, UC Irvine	7	5	3.44	29	1	92	97	27	74
Cassel, Justin, UC Irvine	9	4	3.54	18	0	117	128	21	86
Roemer, Wes, CS Fullerton	7	3	3.80	21	1	90	86	15	71
Haar, Jason, Pacific	4	4	3.95	16	0	87	99	30	45
Bills, Taylor, UC Riverside	7	7	4.26	18	0	112	106	35	63
Gaylord, Matt, CS Northridge	2	2	4.31	30	2	56	65	15	29
Massetti, Luke, Pacific	8	6	4.50	18	0	116	120	31	61
Sarver, Scott, CS Fullerton	9	3	4.60	19	0	88	100	27	59
Shull, Jimmy, Cal Poly	8	7	4.61	18	1	111	110	33	85
Daley, Gary, Cal Poly	6	2	4.74	18	0	89	82	39	59
Martin, Michael, UCSB	6	7	4.85	18	0	102	76	22	60
Eberhardt, Peter, CS Northridge	4	6	5.05	27	6	66	74	35	52
Fraser, Loren, UC Santa Barbara	3	4	5.16	32	0	59	77	19	35
Rocchio, Joe, CS Northridge	4	8	5.42	21	1	73	84	44	60
Shaw, Jose, UC Riverside	4	5	5.43	15	1	58	73	38	17
Brettl, Jimmy, CS Northridge	1	8	5.73	20	0	77	104	26	52
Morlock, Steve, UC Santa Barbara	7	7	5.83	17	0	97	102	40	43

COLONIAL ATHLETIC ASSOCIATION

	Conference		Overall	
	W	L	W	L
UNC Wilmington	21	3	40	19
George Mason	15	9	35	19
***Virginia Commonwealth**	14	10	33	22
Towson	13	11	34	24
Delaware	13	11	27	31
Hofstra	10	14	24	32
William & Mary	9	15	27	27
James Madison	8	16	20	35
Old Dominion	5	19	22	33

ALL-CONFERENCE TEAM: C—Mike DeCarlo, Sr., William & Mary. **1B**—Jason Maxey, Sr., Towson. **2B**—Scott Sizemore, So., Virginia Commonwealth. **3B**—Matt Poulk, Jr., UNC Wilmington. **SS**—Sergio Miranda, Fr., Virginia Commonwealth. **OF**—Matt Cooksey, Sr., George Mason; Tim Preston, Sr., UNC Wilmington; John Raynor, Jr., UNC Wilmington. **DH**—Tim St. Clair, Jr., Virginia Commonwealth. **UT**—Casper Wells, Jr., Towson. **SP**—Stacen Gant, Sr., George Mason; Ronald Hill, Sr., UNC Wilmington. **RP**—Adam Paul, Jr., UNC Wilmington.

Player of the Year: Casper Wells, Towson. **Defensive Players of the Year**: Pete Farina (c), Sr., Virginia Commonwealth; Brian Valichka (c), Jr., Delaware. **Rookie of the Year**: Sergio Miranda, Virginia Commonwealth. **Coach of the Year**: Mark Scalf, UNC Wilmington.

INDIVIDUAL BATTING LEADERS

(Minimum 125 At-Bats)

	AVG	AB	R	H	2B	3B	HR	RBI	SB
Rhymes, Will, William & Mary	**.413**	223	58	92	10	4	6	47	22
Preston, Tim, UNC-W	.406	**251**	69	**102**	20	3	10	51	16
Raynor, John, UNC-W	.397	209	59	83	17	5	5	56	23
Cooksey, Matt, George Mason	.386	184	66	71	13	**8**	7	32	**34**
Cowgill, Michael, Jas. Madison	.367	221	50	81	16	2	14	49	9
Chiccini, Mark, Towson	.365	197	43	72	12	1	13	52	16
Sizemore, Scott, VCU	.364	214	57	78	**24**	3	12	56	19
Poulk, Matt, UNC-W	.364	247	56	90	**24**	0	11	**73**	12
Wells, Casper, Towson	.362	213	**70**	77	15	4	18	66	8
Miranda, Sergio, VCU	.357	241	49	86	16	1	3	38	12
Decarlo, Mike, William &Mary	.356	219	48	78	18	0	17	61	1
St. Clair, Tim, VCU	.354	161	29	57	9	2	9	47	6
Stewart, Josh, Hofstra	.347	222	60	77	23	4	7	23	25
Maxey, Jason, Towson	.346	217	50	75	18	1	**23**	72	0
Campana, Andy, Hofstra	.344	189	37	65	10	1	3	33	20
Kulbacki, Kellen, Jas. Madison	.343	210	30	72	18	1	8	34	7
Justis, Shane, Towson	.343	248	59	85	17	2	9	33	29
Stern, Josh, Hofstra	.339	218	55	74	21	2	8	43	14
York, Matt, George Mason	.336	220	51	74	14	1	3	30	1
Jacobsen, Robby, Geo. Mason	.335	218	55	73	16	2	7	45	20
Cipolla, Bryan, Old Dominion	.332	226	42	75	19	0	8	67	1
Caputo, Ricky, Hofstra	.332	220	59	73	17	5	12	52	10
Innerst, Adam, George Mason	.332	214	41	71	17	1	12	53	1
Lunardi, Jeff, William & Mary	.332	199	38	66	12	3	2	40	0
Harris, Trai, VCU	.330	200	42	66	10	1	2	36	16
Marbry, Michael, UNC-W	.328	192	32	63	11	1	1	33	4
Youngs, Tyler, George Mason	.326	172	31	56	13	0	3	30	1
Meador, Joe, VCU	.325	231	54	75	14	0	8	42	16
Doom, Skyler, James Madison	.321	209	41	67	13	3	6	21	13
Sexton, Greg, William & Mary	.316	193	40	61	10	1	3	27	1
Richardson, Dan, Delaware	.314	159	35	50	14	0	7	29	13

INDIVIDUAL PITCHING LEADERS

(Minimum 50 Innings)

	W	L	ERA	G	SV	IP	H	BB	SO
Gant, Stacen, George Mason	9	2	**2.93**	14	0	86	74	32	92
Harris, Billy, Delaware	3	2	2.97	22	3	58	47	19	50
Hill, Ronald, UNC-W	**10**	4	3.38	17	0	107	110	21	73
Hitz, Brent, George Mason	4	5	3.65	14	0	81	100	16	59
Risser, Travis, JMU	5	3	3.69	22	4	54	51	24	46
Moore, Jeff, UNC-W	6	1	3.69	20	2	78	85	23	51
Flood, Allen, UNC-W	6	3	3.74	**33**	4	55	56	18	61
Leonard, John, VCU	5	4	3.92	16	0	78	77	28	57
#Denlea, Jeff, Hofstra	4	3	3.98	28	**7**	32	30	14	19
Rogers, Jason, Delaware	2	4	4.31	15	2	54	66	12	36
Dubois, Kyle, Old Dominion	5	2	4.38	17	1	72	84	28	77
Kerfoot, Chad, Delaware	2	2	4.38	21	2	51	64	9	57
Arrowood, Dana, Old Dominion	4	6	4.58	16	0	88	104	35	72
Rhoades, Chris, Towson	4	2	4.81	12	0	73	78	25	61
McGuire, Mike, Delaware	5	4	4.83	13	0	78	70	44	70
Walker, Brett, VCU	5	2	4.91	29	5	59	66	18	44
Burok, James, Old Dominion	3	6	4.91	24	6	51	54	21	54
Hall, Hunter, Old Dominion	3	2	4.95	19	0	56	65	15	40
Wells, Casper, Towson	6	0	4.97	12	0	71	82	22	53
Gaphardt, Brent, Deleware	5	5	5.04	13	0	61	57	48	75
Mozingo, Harold, VCU	8	4	5.17	15	0	92	92	49	**101**
Gunter, Kevin, Old Dominion	2	5	5.20	19	0	62	79	17	39
Hansen, Bryan, Old Dominion	4	7	5.21	15	0	78	83	39	61

CONFERENCE USA

	Conference W	Conference L	Overall W	Overall L
***Tulane**	24	6	56	12
***Texas Christian**	20	10	41	20
Southern Mississippi	20	10	41	21
East Carolina	18	12	35	26
Houston	16	13	29	30
South Florida	15	14	33	31
Louisville	15	14	32	24
Alabama-Birmingham	14	16	31	27
Charlotte	13	17	31	23
Cincinnati	10	19	25	30
St. Louis	8	22	13	40
Memphis	5	25	13	42

ALL-CONFERENCE TEAM: C—Brad Willcutt, Sr., Southern Mississippi. **IF**—Brad Emaus, Fr., Tulane; Shelby Ford, So., Texas Christian; Marc Maddox, Jr., Southern Mississippi; Tommy Manzella, Sr., Tulane. **OF**—Brian Cavanaugh, Sr., East Carolina; Nathan Southard, Jr., Tulane; Travis Tully, Jr., Houston. **DH/UT**—Micah Owings, Jr., Tulane, **SP**—Brian Bogusevic, Jr., Tulane; Lance Broadway, Jr., Texas Christian; Ricky Brooks, So., East Carolina; Matt Farrington, Jr., Houston. **RP**—Daniel Best, Jr., Southern Mississippi.

Player of the Year: Micah Owings, Tulane. **Pitcher of the Year**: Lance Broadway, Texas Christian. **Freshman of the Year**: Brad Emaus, Tulane. **Coach of the Year**—Rick Jones, Tulane.

INDIVIDUAL BATTING LEADERS

(Minimum 125 At-Bats)

	AVG	AB	R	H	2B	3B	HR	RBI	SB
Cavanaugh, Brian , E. Carolina	**.382**	207	50	79	12	4	7	36	14
Ford, Shelby, Texas Christian	.370	211	64	78	17	3	7	39	12
Tully, Travis, Houston	.364	228	43	83	19	2	4	23	11
Owings, Micah, Tulane	.359	217	61	78	19	4	**18**	65	0
Maddox, Marc, Southern Miss	.359	256	74	92	17	1	14	59	15
Lowery, Jason, Southern Miss	.358	260	55	93	19	1	6	55	8
Baisley, Jeff, South Florida	.356	250	53	89	**26**	2	8	71	14
Huffman, Chad, TCU	.353	241	54	85	13	2	12	53	6
Madden, Scott, Tulane	.352	193	41	68	12	2	4	47	1
Willard, Adam, Charlotte	.352	219	46	77	17	3	3	50	17
Baisley, Brian, South Florida	.349	238	42	83	18	0	9	47	2
Manzella, Tommy, Tulane	.347	288	59	**100**	24	2	8	63	21
Sutton,Trey, Southern Miss	.346	263	69	91	15	4	6	41	11
Roberts, Kevin, Houston	.346	211	51	73	16	5	9	38	10
Lane, Chris, Charlotte	.345	139	26	48	10	1	3	22	3
Hayes, LaFringe, Cincinnati	.343	198	44	68	11	7	1	19	14
Toomey, Clint, Ala.-Birmingham	.341	208	49	81	9	3	1	29	6
Kingsbury, Dustin, Houston	.341	229	39	78	13	1	6	58	3
Southard, Nathan, Tulane	.341	279	**80**	95	24	1	12	53	16
Sweeney, Johnny, St. Louis	.340	209	26	71	15	1	0	30	8
Martin, Ryan, Memphis	.340	162	33	55	10	2	8	44	2
LaFountain, J.T., Louisville	.337	199	42	67	13	0	8	48	1
Lincoln, Brad, Houston	.337	208	36	70	15	1	7	52	2
Conlon, Keith, Texas Christian	.333	153	30	51	11	2	6	42	2
Bogusevic, Brian, Tulane	.328	131	24	43	9	0	0	25	9
Witter, Adam, East Carolina	.328	183	37	60	11	1	7	33	2
Whiting, Boomer, Louisville	.327	220	56	72	9	1	4	31	**26**
Orlosky, Tim, South Florida	.327	156	41	51	12	1	7	21	7
Mollenhaur, Dale, East Carolina	.327	205	31	67	7	2	4	38	7
Johnson, Logan, Louisville	.325	154	33	50	15	1	2	32	3
Ambrose, Mike, Charlotte	.324	222	44	72	13	5	6	44	20
Willcutt, Brad, Southern Miss	.323	251	57	81	21	0	16	**82**	1
Emaus, Brad, Tulane	.321	262	71	84	19	0	13	56	5
Minicozzi, Mark, East Carolina	.320	219	42	70	15	1	6	48	1
Taylor, O'Brien, Charlotte	.319	185	47	59	7	1	2	17	8
Howes, Isaiah, Louisville	.319	185	30	59	15	5	4	33	1
Coker, Kevin, Southern Miss	.318	195	35	62	15	0	5	38	1
Adams, Austin, Texas Christian	.318	170	34	54	8	1	8	36	0
Hamilton, Mark, Tulane	.318	157	37	50	11	0	11	46	0
McGuirk, Matt, Texas Christian	.317	167	35	53	12	2	7	38	1
Steele, David, Southern Miss	.316	152	23	48	11	0	0	19	0
Musselwhite, Stuart, TCU	.315	260	49	82	21	0	5	34	7
Haske, Mark, Cincinnati	.314	223	52	70	10	2	3	36	6
Parker, Logan, Cincinnati	.313	230	39	72	20	2	11	53	3
Eldridge, Harrison, ECU	.313	166	27	52	9	1	4	34	4
Steedley, Spencer, Charlotte	.310	197	43	61	17	2	5	41	13
Walker, Andrew, TCU	.310	174	29	54	10	2	11	38	0
Richardson, Billy, East Carolina	.308	156	44	48	11	3	4	29	8
Bond, J.R., Ala.-Birmingham	.308	143	27	44	10	1	5	23	9
Lane, Cory, Charlotte	.306	219	60	67	7	**11**	6	36	11
Peisel, Ryan, East Carolina	.306	180	34	55	9	3	4	31	3

INDIVIDUAL PITCHING LEADERS

(Minimum 50 Innings)

	W	L	ERA	G	SV	IP	H	BB	SO
Broadway, Lance, Texas Christian	**15**	1	**1.62**	19	0	117	83	35	**151**
Walker, Erik, Charlotte	4	2	1.86	31	12	53	32	31	67
Huffman, Ryan, Ala.-Birmingham	6	2	2.66	27	4	51	39	13	41
McGough, Tim, Texas Christian	7	3	3.21	14	0	67	67	30	46
#Latham, Daniel, Tulane	2	0	3.22	31	**13**	45	43	10	36
Farrington, Matt, Houston	8	5	3.24	17	0	97	94	33	60
Bogusevic, Brian, Tulane	13	3	3.25	19	0	130	130	42	129
Owings, Micah, Tulane	12	4	3.26	19	0	130	111	25	135
#Roberts, Eric, Ala.-Birmingham	3	2	3.26	**32**	9	47	47	11	46
Brooks, Ricky, East Carolina	5	5	3.46	17	1	78	66	24	70
Hargrove, Ricky, Houston	2	4	3.48	17	0	52	55	9	49
Bird, Ryan, St. Louis	5	5	3.49	14	0	98	90	43	76
Cashion, Mike, Southern Miss	4	1	3.62	8	0	55	44	19	60
Magnuson, Trystan, Louisville	5	5	3.72	20	1	65	64	18	54
Thomas, Daniel, Southern Florida	9	4	3.84	18	0	84	79	42	51
Moreland, Keith, Charlotte	4	3	3.86	29	1	51	58	27	40
Hudspeth, Casey, South Florida	8	6	3.97	17	0	104	104	35	95
Roberts, Kevin, Houston	6	3	4.00	15	0	79	75	31	79
Furnish, Brad, Texas Christian	5	6	4.14	20	0	91	73	46	79
Connelly, P.J., East Carolina	5	1	4.26	19	1	70	76	24	39
Jenkins, Scott, Louisville	2	2	4.31	15	0	56	62	33	39
Bowden, Barry, Southern Miss	4	4	4.40	16	0	74	69	34	71
Gomes, Brandon, Tulane	8	2	4.42	20	2	90	98	17	82
Hose, T.J., East Carolina	7	4	4.43	21	2	85	74	29	69
Underwood, Chad, TCU	4	2	4.50	31	2	58	72	18	53
Maynard, Tony, Cincinnati	7	4	4.56	15	0	95	89	32	54
Demel, Sam, Texas Christian	5	5	4.64	20	1	95	97	44	100
Lincoln, Brad, Houston	4	7	4.76	18	0	102	124	25	106
Price, Adam, Ala.-Birmingham	5	5	4.76	20	1	74	84	29	43
Andrews, Scott, East Carolina	5	3	4.80	19	1	51	48	19	36
Crowel, J.R., Tulane	10	1	4.86	17	0	93	95	30	83

HORIZON LEAGUE

	Conference W	Conference L	Overall W	Overall L
***Illinois-Chicago**	14	6	38	21
Youngstown State	10	6	29	27
Wisconsin-Milwaukee	12	8	26	31
Wright State	11	9	26	33
Cleveland State	5	15	14	36
Butler	4	12	19	35

ALL-CONFERENCE TEAM: C—Bryan Vickers, Sr., Wright State. **1B**—Mark Hallberg, Fr., Illinois-Chicago. **2B**—Charlie Reschke, Sr., Wisconsin-Milwaukee. **3B**—Justin Banks, Jr., Youngstown State. **SS**—Travis Migliorini, Jr., Wright State. **OF**—Dale Mueller, Sr., Butler; Larry Gempp, So., Illinois-Chicago; Joe Nowicki, Jr., Wisconsin-Milwaukee. **DH**—Zak Rivera, Jr., Wisconsin-Milwaukee. **UT**—Brandon Caipen, Jr., Youngstown State. **P**—Justin Thomas, Jr., Youngstown State; Zach Peterson, So., Illinois-Chicago.

Player of the Year: Dale Mueller, Butler. **Pitcher of the Year**: Justin Thomas, Youngstown State. **Newcomer of the Year**: Aaron Sorenson, Wisconsin-Milwaukee. **Coach of the Year**: Mike Dee, Illinois-Chicago.

INDIVIDUAL BATTING LEADERS

(Minimum 125 At-Bats)

	AVG	AB	R	H	2B	3B	HR	RBI	SB
Nowicki, Joe, Wis.-Milwaukee	**.376**	157	32	59	13	0	**9**	40	3

	AVG	AB	R	H	2B	3B	HR	RBI	SB
Rinearson, Alex, Butler	.372	172	23	64	10	1	3	33	0
Mueller, Dale, Butler	.370	184	34	68	11	4	3	24	12
Rivera, Zak, Wis.-Milwaukee	.364	129	33	47	15	0	7	33	0
Gempp, Larry, Illinois-Chicago	.362	199	46	72	9	**5**	8	40	13
Ochwat, Mike, Cleveland State	.361	155	23	56	4	1	3	23	12
Banks, Justin, Youngstown	.356	188	37	67	**18**	1	3	33	2
Hallberg, Mark, Illinois-Chicago	.354	**237**	**54**	**84**	15	2	3	42	11
Goetz, Mike, Wis.-Milwaukee	.352	193	50	68	6	4	1	25	13
Hannan, J.D., Youngstown	.346	156	37	54	4	2	0	11	7
Wilson, Justin, Wright State	.339	171	32	58	7	2	2	24	7
Crowder, Shane, Ill.-Chicago	.338	201	45	68	14	3	7	36	11
Pauley, Joe, Butler	.336	143	25	48	9	1	1	27	1
Phillips, Jim, Youngstown	.330	182	23	60	11	1	4	34	0
Erney, Dominic, Cleveland St.	.326	178	33	58	10	0	**9**	39	0
Rosinski, Ted, Illinois-Chicago	.325	169	43	55	14	2	6	**46**	4
Oeder, Ross, Wright State	.320	125	29	40	8	3	2	16	4
Babineaux, Bart, Ill.-Chicago	.317	205	49	65	16	1	6	42	6
Diedrich, Erich, Youngstown	.313	150	25	47	6	2	6	33	2
Thomas, Dustin, Youngstown	.312	154	24	48	9	0	3	15	2
Abusaleh, Amin, Wis.-Milwaukee	.312	199	41	62	14	4	5	38	2
Cash, Bobby, Cleveland State	.310	174	21	54	9	1	0	23	4
Vickers, Bryan, Wright State	.309	181	31	56	**18**	1	6	44	1
#Bruszer, Mike, Illinois-Chicago	.293	222	41	65	8	2	1	34	**16**
#Gill, Stephen, Butler	.273	150	31	41	8	0	3	16	**16**
#Gremley, Jeff, Illinois-Chicago	.231	199	45	46	14	2	3	33	**16**

INDIVIDUAL PITCHING LEADERS

(Minimum 50 Innings)

	W	L	ERA	G	SV	IP	H	BB	SO
#Smith, Joe, Wis.- Milwaukee	1	2	1.10	**29**	**8**	33	18	12	42
Peterson, Zach, Illinois-Chicago	**10**	1	**3.31**	22	2	90	109	14	46
Thomas, Justin, Youngstown	7	5	3.42	14	0	84	78	33	**88**
Zink, Ryan, Illinois-Chicago	8	6	3.78	22	3	119	129	32	74
Barrett, Robert, Wis.-Milwaukee	6	4	3.82	19	0	75	76	30	62
Caviani, Rick, Wis.-Milwaukee	2	10	3.86	19	0	84	95	19	52
Shaffer, Eric, Youngstown	4	8	3.98	14	0	75	78	19	43
Libeg, Kevin, Youngstown	4	3	4.15	26	4	56	63	23	33
Ball, Gary, Cleveland State	2	4	4.53	13	2	52	58	19	29
Kaltenbach, Matt, Cleveland State	5	7	4.67	16	0	104	117	20	83
Vagedes, Ross, Wright State	4	3	4.67	13	0	54	60	19	33
Dages, Jon, Butler	3	3	4.76	19	2	57	65	21	51
Foster, Jason, Illinois-Chicago	7	6	4.89	26	6	77	102	20	33
Sorenson, Aaron, Wis.-Milwaukee	9	3	4.96	12	0	85	73	26	76
Bokowy, Bryan, Butler	2	6	4.97	18	0	54	78	21	53
Szalewski, Tom, Illinois-Chicago	4	1	5.00	19	0	68	82	19	33
Coleman, Chris, Wright State	3	4	5.00	15	0	54	73	12	26
Keller, Korey, Wis.-Milwaukee	6	3	5.07	15	0	71	96	23	41
#Dolske, Jed, Wis.-Milwaukee	2	1	7.02	28	**8**	33	46	19	29

IVY LEAGUE

	Conference		Overall	
GEHRIG	**W**	**L**	**W**	**L**
Cornell	11	9	17	24
Princeton	10	10	17	24
Pennsylvania	7	13	11	26
Columbia	5	15	10	31
ROLFE				
***Harvard**	15	5	29	15
Brown	14	6	23	19
Yale	10	10	23	17
Dartmouth	8	12	13	21

ALL CONFERENCE TEAM: C—Schuyler Mann, Sr., Harvard. **1B**—Marc Sawyer, So., Yale. **2B**—Paul Christian, Jr., Brown. **3B**—Steffan Wilson, Fr., Harvard. **SS**—Matt Miller, Sr., Cornell. **OF**—Will Bashelor, So., Dartmouth; Matt Kutler, Sr., Brown; Will Venable, Sr., Princeton. **DH**—Justin Ankney, So., Yale. **UT**—Zak Farkes, Jr., Harvard. **P**—Erik Stiller, Jr., Princeton; Josh Sowers, Sr., Yale.

Player of the Year: Matt Kutler, Brown. **Pitcher of the Year**: Josh Sowers, Yale. **Freshman of the Year**: Steffan Wilson, Harvard.

INDIVIDUAL BATTING LEADERS

(Minimum 100 At-Bats)

	AVG	AB	R	H	2B	3B	HR	RBI	SB
Kutler, Matt, Brown	**.427**	171	**43**	**73**	13	3	8	41	6
Venable, Will, Princeton	.385	143	35	55	7	1	**9**	33	10
Salini, Andrew, Princeton	.371	151	33	56	9	1	5	26	1
Miller, Matt, Cornell	.360	139	26	50	8	3	3	19	11
Farkes, Zak, Harvard	.360	139	29	50	7	3	6	30	10
Christian, Paul, Brown	.355	155	**43**	55	14	0	8	38	4
Holden, Tighe, Columbia	.354	127	23	45	11	1	5	27	3
Sawyer, Marc, Yale	.353	156	24	55	**16**	3	0	23	3
Bashelor, Will, Dartmouth	.352	128	35	45	13	3	2	25	**30**
Larson, Eric, Brown	.350	100	19	35	5	0	5	30	2
Moffie, Nate, Pennsylvania	.340	144	30	49	9	1	4	25	6
Wilson, Steffan, Harvard	.340	159	37	54	6	**5**	5	34	10
Wendkos, Zach, Princeton	.328	128	18	42	7	1	3	16	0
Wallace, Ian, Harvard	.325	123	21	40	9	0	0	17	3
Kaufman, Brian, Cornell	.324	142	22	46	12	**5**	2	21	10
Ankney, Justin, Yale	.321	137	28	44	9	3	5	26	5
Speights, Jeff, Dartmouth	.321	131	26	42	14	0	1	33	2
Lowe, James, Brown	.321	131	25	42	8	1	2	27	9
Bailey, Josh, Dartmouth	.319	116	24	37	10	2	1	20	0
Waters, Ray, Columbia	.318	132	28	42	8	0	0	6	8
Stone, Matt, Yale	.317	142	23	45	11	0	3	24	5
Hughes, Danny, Brown	.315	149	26	47	12	1	4	36	1
Gordon, Seth, Cornell	.315	149	30	47	5	2	0	14	12
Janco, John, Yale	.314	105	16	33	8	1	6	25	2
Abate, Sean, Pennsylvania	.313	115	22	36	5	1	5	26	0
Klimkiewicz, Josh, Harvard	.312	160	34	50	**16**	0	**9**	37	2
Perkins, Henry, Columbia	.312	125	14	39	10	1	1	22	10
Ward, Andrew, Columbia	.308	143	22	44	5	2	4	24	5
Salsgiver, Lance, Harvard	.298	181	33	54	8	1	2	26	14
#Mann, Schuyler, Harvard	.288	156	31	45	9	0	**9**	**43**	9

INDIVIDUAL PITCHING LEADERS

(Minimum 40 Innings)

	W	L	ERA	G	SV	IP	H	BB	SO
#Kappel, Brian, Princeton	2	1	2.01	16	**6**	22	11	13	22
Sowers, Josh, Yale	6	1	**2.10**	9	0	60	56	11	**63**
Purdy, Billy, Columbia	3	4	2.51	11	0	57	55	17	26
Stiller, Erik, Princeton	6	2	2.98	9	0	54	55	11	49
Gala, Dan, Cornell	3	4	2.98	9	0	54	60	14	31
Haviland, Shawn, Harvard	**7**	1	3.10	14	0	61	51	31	39
Smith, Alec, Yale	4	3	3.12	9	1	58	56	13	45
Collis, Rocky, Cornell	2	4	3.14	9	0	49	50	14	45
Dietz, Jeff, Brown	4	0	3.60	15	1	50	55	16	39
Morgalis, Mike, Harvard	5	1	4.02	11	0	56	57	27	42
Hollis, Jon, Yale	4	2	4.12	10	0	59	65	16	53
#Wilson, Steffan, Harvard	1	0	4.15	12	**6**	17	11	10	12
Cirri, Brian, Pennsylvania	3	4	4.31	8	0	48	59	22	32
Herrmann, Frank, Harvard	5	2	4.34	12	0	58	54	28	47
Fabian, Gavin, Princeton	2	5	4.72	10	0	53	61	26	26
Bardenwerper, Tad, Cornell	4	3	4.75	12	1	53	61	10	32
Faiola, Josh, Dartmouth	3	3	4.96	8	0	53	60	8	49
McNamara, Shaun, Brown	3	1	4.96	9	0	45	47	29	36
Kirk, Bill, Pennsylvania	2	3	4.97	9	0	42	45	19	26
#Chin, Remington, Pennsylvania	2	1	6.60	**19**	0	30	37	13	11

METRO ATLANTIC CONFERENCE

	Conference		Overall	
	W	**L**	**W**	**L**
***Marist**	22	5	33	21
Siena	19	5	29	23
Manhattan	15	8	27	21
Niagara	16	9	25	28
Le Moyne	14	11	25	22
Rider	14	13	21	29
Fairfield	13	14	15	33
Iona	8	18	11	38
Canisius	5	21	9	38
Saint Peter's	2	24	5	45

ALL CONFERENCE TEAM: C—Nick Derba, So., Manhattan; Mike Medici, Jr., Niagara. **1B**—Matt Rizzotti, Fr., Manhattan. **2B**—Gary Diaz, Sr., Manhattan. **3B**—Andre Enriquez, Jr., Le Moyne; Andrew MacNevin, Jr., Niagara. **SS**—Doug Anderson, Jr., Fairfield. **OF**—Travis Musolf, So., Marist; Eric Nieto, Fr., Manhattan; Gabe Perez, Jr., Siena. **DH**—John Fitzpatrick, Jr., Manhattan. **UT**—Matt Mazurek, Jr., Canisius. **P**—Chris Cody, Jr., Manhattan; Chris Tracz, Sr., Marist.

Player of the Year: Matt Rizzotti, Manhattan. **Pitcher of the Year**: Chris Tracz, Marist. **Relief Pitcher of the Year**: Rob Ryan, Marist. **Freshman of the Year**: Matt Rizzotti, Manhattan. **Coach of the Year (tie)**: Joe Raccuia, Marist; Tony Rossi, Siena.

INDIVIDUAL BATTING LEADERS

(Minimum 125 At-Bats)

	AVG	AB	R	H	2B	3B	HR	RBI	SB
Rizzotti, Matt, Manhattan	**.416**	173	**53**	72	**21**	0	**9**	**57**	0
Musolf, Travis, Marist	.358	215	51	**77**	9	3	0	30	**26**
Mazurek, Matt, Canisius	.351	154	24	54	10	2	7	41	7
Nieto, Eric, Manhattan	.343	137	30	47	7	1	0	25	12
Letizia, Tom, Rider	.332	184	37	61	5	1	1	26	7
Alati, Mike, Niagara	.325	194	31	63	14	1	4	26	2
Rehm, Jon, Rider	.323	186	39	60	10	1	1	34	11
Connors, Keith, Le Moyne	.321	187	45	60	17	1	6	34	9
Crimoli, Gene, Rider	.320	169	22	54	9	**4**	2	31	4
Macdonald, Andrew, Niagara	.317	183	31	58	4	**4**	1	36	12
Knazek, Scott, Rider	.316	187	34	59	10	0	1	35	3
Hansen, Brian, Le Moyne	.314	140	25	44	10	1	4	27	2

	AVG	AB	R	H	2B	3B	HR	RBI	SB
Maser, John, Manhattan	.311	148	35	46	6	1	0	18	2
Gaal, Ben, Le Moyne	.310	145	34	45	4	0	5	29	7
Medici, Mike, Niagara	.310	184	33	57	6	3	4	34	1
Grauer, Kevin, Marist	.306	157	23	48	4	1	0	27	7
Guarino, Wayne, Saint Peter's	.306	180	21	55	6	2	1	12	8
Rudolph, Brian, Fairfield	.305	164	31	50	16	2	2	23	7
Scaife, John, Fairfield	.304	168	26	51	11	0	7	47	2
Diaz, Gary, Manhattan	.303	178	44	54	13	0	6	34	19
Wagner, Bryan, Rider	.301	173	42	52	5	1	0	22	17
MacNevin, Andrew, Niagara	.299	174	28	52	14	1	6	32	5
Willis, Jacob, Siena	.298	171	33	51	14	2	5	28	3
Hildenbrand, Eric, Siena	.297	145	31	43	10	0	5	30	3
Seltzer, Rick, Siena	.294	153	31	45	10	1	3	20	4
Bruno, Matt, Iona	.292	161	24	47	13	0	1	15	1
Anderson, Doug, Fairfield	.292	168	32	49	5	2	2	27	16
Enriquez, Andre, Le Moyne	.291	189	34	55	7	0	**9**	49	6
Fitzpatrick, John, Manhattan	.289	173	29	50	16	0	**9**	49	1
Maertz, Santo, Saint Peter's	.288	139	14	40	6	1	2	15	4
Geanuleas, Mark, Fairfield	.287	136	25	39	4	1	3	13	6

INDIVIDUAL PITCHING LEADERS

(Minimum 50 Innings)

	W	L	ERA	G	SV	IP	H	BB	SO
Lannan, John, Siena	**10**	2	**2.29**	13	0	83	62	28	83
Sheridan, T.J., Le Moyne	6	2	2.52	12	2	50	37	20	56
Cody, Chris, Manhattan	7	4	2.70	13	0	97	79	32	89
#Ryan, Robert, Marist	2	0	2.78	21	**9**	23	21	8	12
Tracz, Chris, Marist	9	3	2.86	15	0	104	100	19	77
Santerre, Josh, Manhattan	6	3	2.91	12	0	77	88	31	52
Burnett, Josh, Siena	4	4	3.32	12	0	76	69	15	42
Avery, James, Niagara	5	5	3.42	15	0	92	92	30	83
Bronder, Steve, Manhattan	6	4	4.10	14	0	68	61	25	50
Blevins, Bobby, Le Moyne	7	4	4.12	13	0	87	80	31	68
Sawatzky, Josh, Niagara	6	6	4.21	17	0	92	85	37	67
Supplee, Erik, Marist	5	4	4.25	20	0	55	58	15	38
Kamintzky, Ed, Fairfield	4	6	4.26	12	0	76	74	32	52
Griffin, Dan, Niagara	6	4	4.37	15	2	78	81	30	**120**
Grant, Ken, Siena	5	2	4.37	13	0	70	66	39	52
#Radanovic, Mike, Niagara	2	3	4.41	**24**	1	35	32	24	35
Dugan, Tim, Fairfield	7	4	4.59	13	0	84	94	30	72
Smith, Jonathan, Marist	7	2	4.68	15	0	85	98	12	47
Moronese, Joe, Rider	5	5	4.78	11	0	70	82	19	42
Kosky, James, Iona	2	3	4.91	22	1	62	83	14	30
Chambers, Scott, Marist	3	6	5.05	12	0	62	65	38	37
Dyszel, Mike, Rider	2	3	5.20	20	4	55	57	29	46

MID-AMERICAN CONFERENCE

	Conference		Overall	
EAST	**W**	**L**	**W**	**L**
***Miami (Ohio)**	17	4	45	18
Akron	11	8	25	29
Ohio	9	10	25	25
Kent State	9	10	33	20
Marshall	8	16	16	34
Buffalo	5	14	19	30
WEST				
Ball State	17	5	38	18
Central Michigan	18	6	42	18
Bowling Green	12	8	33	18
Western Michigan	13	9	26	24
Eastern Michigan	8	14	22	34
Northern Illinois	6	18	16	36
Toledo	5	17	15	39

INDIVIDUAL BATTING LEADERS

(Minimum 125 At-Bats)

	AVG	AB	R	H	2B	3B	HR	RBI	SB
Hudak, Andy, Bowling Green	**.361**	194	50	70	12	1	10	54	6
Reimold, Nolan, Bowl. Green	.360	178	51	64	7	3	**20**	62	4
Canada, Brian, Miami	.357	221	**58**	79	18	1	5	39	8
Miller, Brad, Ball State	.357	210	41	75	14	2	8	49	0
Moratti, Troy, Central Michigan	.357	255	55	**91**	11	5	3	40	14
Dygert, Kyle, Ball State	.355	214	44	76	10	1	5	48	2
Kruthaupt, Doug, Akron	.354	175	36	62	8	2	5	33	10
Sullivan, Mike, Ball State	.353	232	57	82	19	2	1	29	15
Frietch, Paul, Miami	.350	206	50	72	16	2	16	**64**	7
Lehrman, Derek, East. Michigan	.349	189	35	66	7	0	5	34	1
Lawson, Eric, Bowling Green	.349	175	48	61	19	1	2	20	7
Geldhof, Jim, Central Michigan	.348	227	45	79	13	1	1	39	6
Folli, Mike, Buffalo	.348	184	41	64	6	3	3	18	4
Webb, C.J., Ball State	.346	211	36	73	13	2	6	39	1
Tucker, Joe, Kent State	.345	200	48	69	11	0	1	33	16
Hillier, Brandon, Miami	.344	209	40	72	7	4	1	30	11
Crabtree, Ben, Ohio	.344	209	39	72	14	0	10	49	5
Stewart, Josh, Bowling Green	.343	175	42	60	6	1	6	33	10
Busch, Jeremy, No. Illinois	.340	212	53	72	14	2	9	39	4
Saylor, Drew, Kent State	.337	199	45	67	16	1	7	39	1
Orr, Geoff, Miami	.332	220	46	73	15	3	9	59	16
Hammond, Dusty, Ohio	.331	175	26	58	7	1	3	21	5
McKinney, Billy, Akron	.331	127	21	42	7	0	5	33	5
Carter, Justin, West. Michigan	.328	189	39	62	14	1	13	43	1
Latour, David, Central Michigan	.324	139	28	45	9	0	2	25	10
Franz, Mark, Ball State	.323	223	40	72	19	0	8	56	1
Kimutis, Brian, Akron	.322	171	38	55	8	0	1	25	9
Ptacek, Adam, Marshall	.320	181	39	58	8	1	2	24	8
Burris, Emmanuel, Kent State	.319	191	41	61	6	1	1	16	30
Davis, Jeff, Eastern Michigan	.318	201	38	64	9	0	3	16	9
Jamieson, Aaron, Marshall	.318	195	22	62	6	0	2	29	0
Glevenyak, Joe, Marshall	.318	173	31	55	9	2	8	33	8
Wasserman, Tyler, Bowl. Green	.318	129	15	41	9	2	0	23	3
Buck, Bryan, Ohio	.315	127	28	40	5	0	0	13	8
Kingsley, James, Buffalo	.314	191	35	60	12	1	12	50	0
#Wells, Kurtis, Central Michigan	.300	243	48	73	**21**	1	7	57	1
#Robinson, Ryne, Miami	.293	242	47	71	10	**8**	1	34	**34**

INDIVIDUAL PITCHING LEADERS

(Minimum 50 Innings)

	W	L	ERA	G	SV	IP	H	BB	SO
#Morrison, Erik, Ball State	7	0	1.32	28	**15**	41	31	12	41
Wagler, Chad, Kent State	6	4	**2.47**	19	4	51	34	16	49
Gressick, Anthony, Ohio	3	3	2.67	11	0	57	60	37	47
Collmenter, Josh, Cent. Michigan	7	1	2.70	16	0	90	81	21	77
Taylor, Graham, Miami	6	1	2.71	15	0	100	89	17	73
Weiser, Keith, Miami	**10**	0	2.73	17	0	105	99	20	85
Smith, Brian, Northern Illinois	6	6	2.85	17	1	82	98	23	56
Dunham, Ty, Central Michigan	9	4	2.85	16	0	117	107	33	87
Ely, John, Miami	**10**	2	2.87	18	1	103	82	20	**108**
Farmer, Tom, Akron	4	3	2.97	20	0	76	72	32	54
O'Brien, Dan, Western Michigan	3	3	2.98	13	1	82	87	16	66
Brech, Alan, Bowling Green	8	1	3.05	14	0	74	75	22	68
Cairns, Jason, Central Michigan	8	5	3.09	17	0	96	85	55	68
Witt, Derek, Ohio	6	4	3.13	13	1	92	91	21	73
Stanfield, Darek, Akron	4	4	3.14	29	14	52	53	12	48
#German, Matt, Northern Illinois	1	3	3.15	**33**	2	34	38	18	29
Day, Jeff, Miami	3	4	3.23	26	1	64	69	22	52
Rasmussen, Mark, West. Mich.	4	6	3.26	13	0	86	90	16	60
Silverman, Yale, Ohio	2	4	3.40	20	4	56	56	16	44
Liersemann, Ross, Akron	4	6	3.40	15	0	95	90	17	81
Holdenrid, Adam, Northern Illinois	0	4	3.71	13	0	70	80	19	42
Badenhop, Burke, Bowling Green	9	2	3.73	16	0	72	75	18	56
Christner, Charlie, West. Michigan	4	3	3.90	15	1	65	70	19	59
Ness, Joe, Ball State	5	5	4.01	15	0	90	97	34	88
Laughlin, Keith, Bowling Green	3	6	4.18	13	0	71	70	28	56
Snyder, Ben, Ball State	8	5	4.21	15	0	98	93	21	87

MID-CONTINENT CONFERENCE

	Conference		Overall	
	W	**L**	**W**	**L**
***Oral Roberts**	22	2	42	20
Western Illinois	14	10	24	34
Southern Utah	12	10	26	28
Centenary	12	12	27	30
Valparaiso	10	12	21	31
Oakland	9	15	14	38
Chicago State	3	21	6	50

ALL CONFERENCE TEAM: C—Jake Gloude, Sr., Western Illinois. **1B**—Mike Arensdorff, So., Valparaiso. **2B**—Jonathan Sakurai, So., Chicago State. **3B**—Darren Duckworth, Sr., Southern Utah. **SS**—Michael Hollimon, Sr., Oral Roberts. **OF**—Kyle Malan, Sr., Western Illinois; Kelly Minissale, Fr., Oral Roberts; Kevin Perri, Jr., Valparaiso; Justin Sotelo, Jr., Southern Utah. **UT**—Nate Recknagel, Fr., Oakland. **SP**—Dennis Bigley, Sr., Oral Roberts; Pat Kohorst, Sr., Western Illinois; Paul Phillips, So. Oakland. **RP**—Daniel Greenwalt, Jr., Oral Roberts.

Players of the Year: Dennis Bigley, Oral Roberts; Michael Hollimon, Oral Roberts. **Pitcher of the Year:** Dennis Bigley, Oral Roberts. **Newcomer of the Year:** Michael Hollimon, Oral Roberts. **Coach of the Year:** Ed McCann, Centenary.

INDIVIDUAL BATTING LEADERS

(Minimum 125 At-Bats)

	AVG	AB	R	H	2B	3B	HR	RBI	SB
Arensdorff, Michael, Valparaiso	**.382**	204	38	**78**	**20**	0	4	43	3
Kiefer, David, Centenary	.370	208	56	77	**20**	**6**	3	53	16
Malan, Kyle, Western Illinois	.352	199	46	70	9	4	6	49	9
Recknagel, Nate, Oakland	.351	168	32	59	14	1	5	30	3
Perri, Kevin, Valparaiso	.348	181	53	63	12	**6**	3	30	18
Dimick, Trever, Southern Utah	.345	142	28	49	10	2	2	28	9
Nelson, Aaron, Southern Utah	.340	162	28	55	11	1	9	39	9

	AVG	AB	R	H	2B	3B	HR	RBI	SB
Sotelo, Justin, Southern Utah	.332	184	40	61	14	0	5	25	16
Torres, John, Chicago State	.330	182	30	60	10	3	2	31	12
Oliverson, Jeff, Southern Utah	.325	163	33	53	9	0	9	29	11
Sakurai, Jonathan, Chicago State	.321	187	33	60	9	0	0	15	**38**
Martin, Mike, Southern Utah	.316	171	36	54	8	0	8	37	2
Schmidgall, Ryan, Western Illinois	.316	206	47	65	14	3	2	40	5
Ryan, Tim, Centenary	.315	216	35	68	12	3	3	41	19
Rupno, Jon, Valparaiso	.314	159	22	50	7	0	1	33	3
Tackett, Jon, Oral Roberts	.313	227	39	71	14	0	1	21	1
Pacyga, Joe, Western Illinois	.312	160	35	50	8	2	5	35	3
Torres, Tim, Oral Roberts	.309	181	34	56	8	2	3	30	4
Darr, Justin, Centenary	.306	180	24	55	6	0	0	30	3
#Hollimon, Michael, Oral Roberts	.304	230	**68**	70	15	3	**14**	**55**	26

INDIVIDUAL PITCHING LEADERS

(Minimum 50 Innings)

	W	L	ERA	G	SV	IP	H	BB	SO
Bigley, Dennis, Oral Roberts	**11**	4	**1.81**	17	0	109	72	31	84
#Knobel, Adam, Valparaiso	2	1	1.95	26	**8**	37	30	16	47
Jones, Nick, Oral Roberts	8	2	2.30	12	0	74	57	18	60
Greenwalt, Daniel, Oral Roberts	5	3	2.38	**27**	4	64	46	22	57
McIntyre, Taylor, Oral Roberts	8	6	3.27	18	1	96	87	47	**96**
Recio, Rene, Oral Roberts	4	3	3.45	11	0	57	48	25	41
Fulenchek, Brandon, Centenary	1	0	3.61	18	1	52	49	32	29
McElroy, David, Centenary	8	3	4.11	17	0	77	94	31	36
Phillips, Paul, Oakland	2	8	4.23	15	0	77	94	14	66
Hines, Aaron, Oakland	4	5	4.28	14	0	67	72	24	37
Buchen, Clint, Western Illinois	6	2	4.33	14	0	71	73	28	59
Kohorst, Pat, Western Illinois	7	5	4.40	18	0	110	121	44	92
Calhoun, Kris, Centenary	4	3	4.43	20	1	65	70	22	48
Yergin, Harvey, Valparaiso	5	6	4.50	12	0	78	88	17	45
Clark, Matt, Centenary	2	4	4.87	16	0	57	70	28	28

MID-EASTERN ATHLETIC CONFERENCE

	Conference		Overall	
	W	L	W	L
***North Carolina A&T**	12	6	27	27
Bethune Cookman	11	6	22	28
Delaware State	10	7	19	27
Coppin State	10	7	21	31
Florida A&M	9	9	19	33
Norfolk State	8	9	14	36
Maryland-Eastern Shore	1	19	6	41

ALL CONFERENCE TEAM: C—Brian Vickers, So., Coppin State. **IF**—Charlie Gamble, So., North Carolina A&T; Kevin Hill, Sr., Delaware State; Virgil Priestly, Sr., Florida A&M; Juan Serrano, So., Norfolk State. **OF**—Jeremy Jones, So., North Carolina A&T; David Hampton, Sr., Florida A&M; Nick Wenger, Sr., Coppin State. **DH**—Omar Borges, Jr., Bethune-Cookman. **SP**—Michael Hauff, Jr., North Carolina A&T; J.P. Primus, Fr., North Carolina A&T. **RP**—Jesus Melendez, Jr., Coppin State.

Player of the Year: Jeremy Jones, North Carolina A&T. **Freshman of the Year**: Michael Tavernier, Florida A&M. **Coach of the Year**: Guy Robertson, Coppin State.

INDIVIDUAL BATTING LEADERS

(Minimum 125 At-Bats)

	AVG	AB	R	H	2B	3B	HR	RBI	SB
Jones, Jeremy, N.C. A&T	**.402**	204	**53**	**82**	**20**	3	4	46	19
Hill, Kevin, Delaware State	.371	194	35	72	14	1	7	39	11
Serrano, Juan, Norfolk State	.370	181	25	67	15	0	2	34	2
Wenger, Justin, Delaware State	.370	165	26	61	13	0	3	32	3
Ricketts, Jon, Delaware State	.368	133	33	49	5	0	1	22	8
McCabe, Brandon, Md.-ES	.362	160	23	58	16	1	8	33	2
Vickers, Brian, Coppin State	.341	176	34	60	17	3	3	41	9
Gamble, Charlie, N.C. A&T	.337	196	51	66	11	2	**13**	**48**	4
Gravely, Brandon, Del. State	.335	173	31	58	11	1	5	39	6
McIntyre, Joe, N.C. A&T	.327	196	21	64	16	0	0	29	5
Hampton, David, Florida A&M	.325	163	35	53	8	1	1	24	14
Caruso, Rob, Beth.-Cookman	.325	160	33	52	8	0	3	28	4
Picornell, Carlos, Beth.-Cook.	.315	184	39	58	5	2	2	17	**41**
Priestly, Virgil, Florida A&M	.311	177	32	55	7	1	5	38	3
Banks, Ernie, Norfolk State	.310	145	17	45	9	0	0	16	1
#Flaherty, Dan, Florida A&M	.249	169	28	42	11	**7**	3	24	5

INDIVIDUAL PITCHING LEADERS

(Minimum 50 Innings)

	W	L	ERA	G	SV	IP	H	BB	SO
Rodriguez, Richard, Beth.-Cook	4	4	**2.32**	10	0	62	54	22	54
Williams, De'Mece, Norfolk State	4	7	2.74	14	1	89	87	44	63
Hauff, Michael, N.C. A&T	**8**	5	2.92	16	1	108	101	33	**132**
Primus, John, N.C. A&T	7	3	3.25	15	0	97	84	31	73
Kyles, Raphael, Beth.-Cookman	7	4	3.74	14	0	74	77	28	45
Auch, Bill, Coppin State	3	5	3.75	15	0	74	87	21	27
Tavernier, Michael, Florida A&M	6	6	3.87	16	0	95	95	36	71
Hangland, Alex, Coppin State	4	5	4.03	18	0	67	80	17	44
Keyes, William, Delaware State	5	2	4.24	13	1	51	53	24	30
Schmidt, Josh, Delaware State	3	3	4.50	20	1	50	54	21	45
Lietz, Scott, Florida A&M	2	3	4.50	10	0	50	49	19	48
Bitter, Nick, Delaware State	5	7	4.55	14	0	89	110	13	59
#Hawk, Richard, N.C. A&T	3	1	4.86	**29**	**8**	33	32	22	36

MISSOURI VALLEY CONFERENCE

	Conference		Overall	
	W	L	W	L
Creighton	17	7	48	17
***Wichita State**	16	8	50	25
Southern Illinois	15	9	38	21
Evansville	12	12	36	22
Bradley	10	14	28	22
Indiana State	10	14	30	28
Missouri State	10	14	26	29
Illinois State	9	15	26	27
Northern Iowa	9	15	25	29

ALL CONFERENCE TEAM: C—Joe Muich, Sr., Wichita State. **1B**—Erik Lis, Jr., Evansville. **2B**—Tony Roth, Sr., Creighton. **3B**—Paul Rice, Jr., Bradley. **SS**—P.J. Finigan, Sr., Southern Illinois. **OF**—Matt Bolt, So., Illinois State; Kevin Koski, So., Southern Illinois; Phil Napolitan, Sr., Wichita State. **DH**—Zach Daeges, So., Creighton. **UT**—Derek Schermerhorn, So., Wichita State. **SP**—P.J. Finigan, Sr., Southern Illinois; Mike Pelfrey, Jr., Wichita State; Collin Walker, Sr., Bradley. **RP**—Brandon Bird, Sr., Creighton; Scott Reese, So., Creighton.

Player of the Year: P.J. Finigan, Southern Illinois. **Pitcher of the Year**: Mike Pelfrey, Wichita State. **Newcomer of the Year**: Tim Brewer, Jr., Indiana State. **Freshman of the Year**: Damon Sublett, Wichita State.

INDIVIDUAL BATTING LEADERS

(Minimum 125 At-Bats)

	AVG	AB	R	H	2B	3B	HR	RBI	SB
Finigan, P.J., Southern Illinois	**.388**	201	45	78	13	5	6	50	5
Koski, Kevin, Southern Illinois	.380	242	57	92	12	2	0	32	15
Rice, Paul, Bradley	.357	185	36	66	13	0	2	24	20
Daeges, Matt, Creighton	.350	214	55	75	17	5	8	**61**	6
Norquist, Dan, Creighton	.348	244	**63**	85	22	**7**	4	47	9
Taylor, Chris, Missouri State	.345	168	33	58	10	0	3	29	6
Canada, Brad, Bradley	.339	174	28	59	13	0	2	24	7
Watts, Kern, Evansville	.336	146	34	49	6	1	0	12	18
Dutton, Brad, Creighton	.335	257	43	86	11	3	5	46	8
Fosdick, Rance, Indiana State	.333	237	40	79	16	**7**	1	45	14
Weglarz, Matt, Missouri State	.333	213	31	71	18	0	4	49	6
McConnell, Kirk, Missouri State	.333	204	62	68	19	2	8	40	12
Schermerhorn, Derek, WSU	.329	292	51	**96**	21	3	2	60	**34**
Rafferty, Tim, Missouri State	.329	143	27	47	16	0	1	24	2
Anetsberger, Ryan, Illinois State	.329	207	32	68	13	2	2	32	8
Ashley, Nevin, Indiana State	.328	189	29	62	10	6	1	41	4
Trumm, Nate, Northern Iowa	.328	177	33	58	12	0	4	39	10
Frieske, Mark, Northern Iowa	.325	206	37	67	12	2	0	21	14
Bolt, Matt, Illinois State	.323	192	44	62	11	2	5	29	16
Lis, Erik, Evansville	.322	211	37	68	15	0	**12**	60	14
Roth, Tony, Creighton	.320	231	47	74	20	1	5	37	12
Napolitan, Phil, Wichita State	.318	255	49	81	17	1	4	35	17
Hilgendorf, Jacob, Missouri State	.317	224	34	71	14	3	5	28	8
Brewer, Tim Indiana State	.317	224	49	71	13	4	2	22	29
Minor, Robbie, Evansville	.316	212	38	67	10	1	0	37	18
Schmidt, Chris, Indiana State	.313	182	40	57	2	3	1	22	25
Sublett, Damon, Wichita State	.312	221	43	69	10	4	1	36	13
O'Brien, Kyle, Illinois State	.311	161	25	50	13	0	3	25	1
Westergaard, Dave, NI	.305	203	32	62	14	0	2	28	4
Norman, Ryan, Northern Iowa	.305	131	20	40	12	0	0	18	6
Moran, Patrick, Northern Iowa	.305	197	35	60	10	2	2	43	7
Jenkins, Kris, Illinois State	.302	179	24	54	9	1	0	34	15
#Brewer, Matt, Southern Illinois	.299	221	47	66	**23**	1	6	41	9

INDIVIDUAL PITCHING LEADERS

(Minimum 50 Innings)

	W	L	ERA	G	SV	IP	H	BB	SO
Pelfrey, Mike, Wichita State	**12**	3	**1.93**	19	0	140	96	30	**143**
Banwart, Travis, Wichita State	8	1	2.09	17	0	82	75	31	68
Booth, Noah, Wichita State	4	6	2.13	34	10	80	62	18	87
Krawczyk, Chris, Missouri State	6	1	2.59	18	0	56	47	10	55
Walker, Collin, Bradley	6	4	2.60	15	0	90	72	19	56
Brinkmann, Matt, Evansville	3	2	2.84	19	2	51	42	17	50
Reese, Scott, Creighton	**12**	0	2.85	**37**	5	88	72	28	58
Theisen, Eric, Illinois State	6	0	3.00	22	3	69	67	21	57
Tatusko, Ryan, Indiana State	8	2	3.09	17	0	84	74	38	55
Smith, David, Missouri State	2	5	3.19	15	2	68	57	20	42
Norrick, Tyler, Southern Illinois	5	3	3.24	19	0	81	67	28	89
Finigan, P.J., Southern Illinois	9	3	3.24	16	0	106	95	35	107
Rueger, Bryan, Southern Illinois	9	4	3.26	19	1	124	121	31	76
Rogers, Adam, Evansville	5	3	3.33	16	0	105	110	22	88

	W	L	ERA	G	SV	IP	H	BB	SO
Goins, Derek, Bradley	5	6	3.39	14	0	61	72	12	28
Jones, Fred, Evansville	5	4	3.45	15	0	76	61	43	49
Foster, Jereme, Wichita State	7	5	3.63	19	0	92	102	29	76
Daneff, Jeff, Creighton	4	1	3.63	10	0	52	53	29	43
Spielmann, Brian, Bradley	2	3	3.75	13	0	58	55	28	65
Kopach, Kitt, Illinois State	4	3	3.78	20	0	67	62	39	35
Schaecher, Adam, Creighton	6	4	3.94	18	0	82	92	17	34
Kelchen, Kory, Northern Iowa	3	3	3.96	14	0	61	70	22	38
Schauff, Ned, Illinois State	5	4	4.33	16	0	73	71	24	61
Magee, Brandon, Bradley	7	4	4.43	16	0	104	107	32	78
#Murray, Mark, Evansville	6	4	4.46	26	**12**	40	41	17	26

MOUNTAIN WEST CONFERENCE

	Conference		Overall	
	W	L	W	L
***Nevada-Las Vegas**	23	7	35	29
Brigham Young	21	9	39	19
San Diego State	17	13	26	35
New Mexico	15	15	26	32
Utah	10	20	19	36
Air Force	4	26	9	44

ALL CONFERENCE TEAM: C—Jordan Swaydan, Jr., San Diego State; Justin Tellam, So., Nevada-Las Vegas. **1B**—Jeff Hiestand, Jr., Brigham Young. **2B**—Doug Beck, Sr., Utah; Jordan Pacheco, Fr., New Mexico. **3B**—Jay Brossman, So., Utah; Mike Cruz, Jr., Nevada-Las Vegas; Brandon Taylor, Jr., Brigham Young, Lance Zawadski, So., San Diego State. **SS**—James Guerrero, Jr., San Diego State; Zeke Parraz, Sr., Nevada-Las Vegas. **OF**—Quintin Berry, So., San Diego State; Ryan Bird, Jr., Nevada-Las Vegas; Ryan Chambers, Sr., Brigham Young; Garrick Haymore, Sr., New Mexico; Jake McLintock, Sr., San Diego State; Ben Saylor, Jr., Brigham Young; J.C. Sibley, Sr., Nevada-Las Vegas. **UT**—Chris Carlson, So., New Mexico. **SP**—Bruce Billings, So., San Diego State; Danny Ray Herrera, So., New Mexico; Alex Hinshaw, Jr., San Diego State; Dave Horlacher, Jr., Brigham Young; Efren Navarro, Fr., Nevada-Las Vegas; Derek Rodriguez, Sr., Nevada-Las Vegas. **RP**—Josh Cooper, Jr., Utah.

Player of the Year: Brandon Taylor, Brigham Young. **Pitcher of the Year**: Bruce Billings, San Diego State. **Coach of the Year**, Buddy Gouldsmith, Nevada-Las Vegas.

INDIVIDUAL BATTING LEADERS

(Minimum 125 At-Bats)

	AVG	AB	R	H	2B	3B	HR	RBI	SB
Berry, Quintin, San Diego State	**.419**	229	60	**96**	18	3	2	43	**18**
Pacheco, Jordan, New Mexico	.408	233	65	95	17	5	15	52	6
Carlson, Chris, New Mexico	.395	220	**66**	87	24	6	15	79	1
Brossman, Jay, Utah	.377	231	50	87	22	1	8	51	1
Haymore, Garrick, New Mexico	.374	203	57	76	16	**9**	5	37	7
Hiestand, Jeff, Brigham Young	.371	178	59	66	16	2	8	41	2
Guerrero, James, S.D. State	.370	238	53	88	16	8	5	54	7
Sibley, J.C., UNLV	.370	165	49	61	14	1	2	24	9
Taylor, Brandon, BYU	.356	239	65	85	17	4	**20**	**83**	11
McLintock, Jake, S.D. State	.355	197	41	70	10	6	1	45	1
Saylor, Ben, Brigham Young	.354	226	50	80	**25**	0	9	48	3
Chambers, Ryan, BYU	.352	193	43	68	20	1	12	41	3
Beck, Doug, Utah	.350	220	35	77	16	3	5	54	5
Stovall, Daniel, New Mexico	.350	246	48	86	21	2	9	58	1
Bird, Ryan, UNLV	.347	242	54	84	21	1	6	57	7
Parraz, Zeke, UNLV	.344	247	56	85	18	3	7	64	0
Nakayama, Apana, BYU	.344	256	59	88	18	2	10	47	1
Bonnell, Chris, UNLV	.342	240	41	82	19	0	9	59	0
Mozeleski, Joe, Utah	.338	207	32	70	15	0	3	30	2
Beranek, Tyler, UNLV	.337	175	37	59	14	0	7	32	2
Barba, Ryan, New Mexico	.337	196	43	66	14	8	3	26	5
Zawadski, Lance, S.D. State	.335	230	53	77	17	1	10	53	8
Welsh, John, Utah	.333	243	46	81	14	0	4	39	5
Knell, Kory, Brigham Young	.333	189	43	63	11	1	7	44	8
Swaydan, Jordan, S.D. State	.332	199	38	66	9	4	2	27	0
McNaughton, Sean, BYU	.327	205	44	67	16	5	12	43	5
#Lamson, Reid, Air Force	.321	193	52	62	11	3	2	23	**18**

INDIVIDUAL PITCHING LEADERS

(Minimum 50 Innings)

	W	L	ERA	G	SV	IP	H	BB	SO
#Tabeek, Kyle, UNLV	5	1	3.52	28	**8**	38	46	16	28
Cooper, Josh, Utah	3	1	**3.64**	24	3	84	79	27	71
Horlacher, Dave, Brigham Young	6	2	3.80	15	0	95	97	28	82
Billings, Bruce, San Diego State	6	5	3.85	19	0	108	93	36	**112**
Lane, Brian, Utah	5	6	4.15	**32**	3	61	67	21	38
Hinshaw, Alex, San Diego State	5	7	4.63	16	1	84	82	39	85
Luca, Matt, UNLV	5	7	4.94	17	0	89	107	42	65
Christiansen, Brandon, BYU	4	2	5.11	14	0	69	87	23	48
Rodriguez, Derek, UNLV	5	5	5.15	19	1	108	137	39	76
Navarro, Efren, UNLV	4	4	5.84	24	0	62	87	26	57
Gaarder, Karsten, New Mexico	3	7	6.00	20	2	84	103	36	76
Herrera, Danny, New Mexico	**8**	5	6.10	15	0	93	119	33	67
Pupo, Koji, UNLV	5	1	6.45	16	0	74	99	40	50
Torgerson, Blake, Brigham Young	6	2	6.50	13	0	62	84	10	22
Price, Jason, Utah	5	8	6.77	19	0	106	131	34	80
Crockett, Matt, Utah	4	10	7.12	17	0	78	105	35	44
Coon, Ben, San Diego State	2	2	7.24	21	0	60	79	22	36
Fernandez, Jason, New Mexico	6	5	7.24	12	0	73	101	17	50

NORTHEAST CONFERENCE

	Conference		Overall	
	W	L	W	L
***Quinnipiac**	17	6	26	24
Sacred Heart	16	8	20	33
Monmouth	15	8	30	24
Wagner	13	10	22	27
Mount St. Mary's	12	11	18	27
Fairleigh Dickinson	10	13	12	26
Central Connecticut State	10	14	19	28
Long Island	9	15	13	25
St. Francis	3	20	7	37

ALL CONFERENCE TEAM: C—Scott Appleton, Jr., Central Connecticut State. **1B**—Bryan Sabatella, Jr., Quinnipiac. **2B**—Joe Malfettano, Jr., Wagner. **3B**—Nate Olson, Jr., Long Island. **SS**—Ryan Nemcek, Fr., Sacred Heart. **OF**—Tim Binkoski, So., Quinnipiac; Tom Pezzello, Sr., Central Connecticut State; Fran Rotella, Sr., Monmouth. **DH**—Troy Sogliuzzo, Sr., Wagner. **LHP**—Chris Aldrich, Jr., Sacred Heart. **RHP**—Jay Monti, So., Sacred Heart.

Player of the Year: Bryan Sabatella, Quinnipiac. **Pitcher of the Year**: Jay Monti, Sacred Heart. **Freshman of the Year**: Josh Vittek, Mount St. Mary's. **Coach of the Year**: Nick Giaguinto, Sacred Heart.

INDIVIDUAL BATTING LEADERS

(Minimum 125 At-Bats)

	AVG	AB	R	H	2B	3B	HR	RBI	SB
Sabatella, Bryan, Quinnipiac	**.406**	192	**46**	**78**	15	0	**11**	**40**	5
Bell, Trey, Long Island	.374	131	22	49	10	1	0	17	4
Sogliuzzo, Troy, Wagner	.363	171	35	62	15	0	3	28	2
Smith, Eric, Mount St. Mary's	.362	141	39	51	11	0	9	35	3
Pezzello, Tom, Central Conn. St.	.351	154	33	54	10	0	2	29	10
Hussa, Mike, Monmouth	.347	176	34	61	16	0	0	22	1
Binkoski, Tim, Quinnipiac	.340	188	37	64	**18**	2	4	30	2
Sudol, Ed, Wagner	.336	146	23	49	6	1	5	29	3
Matos, Wilson, Quinnipiac	.333	177	31	59	10	0	5	32	4
Rotella, Fran, Monmouth	.329	158	37	52	11	1	7	32	2
Papa, Nick, Wagner	.329	149	29	49	7	2	1	22	12
Colonna, Greg, St. Francis	.321	140	17	45	5	0	1	15	**18**
Rizzo, Ryan, Quinnipiac	.319	207	32	66	10	0	5	34	1
Blaze, John, Central Conn.	.318	154	22	49	8	0	5	26	1
Marchese, Philip, Saint Francis	.318	148	21	47	8	0	4	17	15
Fay, Stephan, Mount St. Mary's	.317	126	20	40	10	1	7	25	1
Magee, Brien, Quinnipiac	.309	188	29	58	9	0	4	39	0
Mastrianni, Matt, Wagner	.308	172	38	53	12	2	2	27	1
Cass, Ben, Fairleigh Dickinson	.308	130	20	40	11	0	3	14	1
Nemcek, Ryan, Sacred Heart	.304	161	31	49	9	1	0	14	7
Massari, Nick, Monmouth	.301	183	36	55	8	**4**	5	35	7

INDIVIDUAL PITCHING LEADERS

(Minimum 50 Innings)

	W	L	ERA	G	SV	IP	H	BB	SO
#Schneider, Kevin, Monmouth	3	1	0.74	**26**	**8**	36	25	13	25
Monti, Jay, Sacred Heart	**8**	5	**2.20**	15	1	82	68	10	56
Moran, Richard, Long Island	4	2	2.21	9	0	53	55	8	28
Marc-Aurele, Matt, Monmouth	3	2	2.24	20	2	72	60	13	64
Aldrich, Chris, Sacred Heart	6	4	2.69	14	0	90	83	26	**86**
Scribner, Evan, Cent. Connecticut	6	3	2.79	12	2	58	55	8	39
Wakefield, Chris, Quinnipiac	6	2	3.65	15	1	67	59	38	56
Spahr, Mike, Quinnipiac	3	4	3.88	23	5	53	58	21	44
McTamney, Mike, Wagner	6	5	3.93	14	0	76	90	21	67
Eng, Stephen, Fairleigh Dickinson	4	3	4.08	12	0	68	87	12	35
Pease, Dustin, Mount St. Mary's	5	4	4.33	21	1	71	82	13	61
Brach, Brad, Monmouth	6	4	4.37	13	0	60	72	15	41
Davis, Justin, Mount St. Mary's	3	5	4.40	15	1	61	64	21	54
Cummings, Joe, Monmouth	5	5	4.56	15	1	77	92	19	29
Conner, Brett, Monmouth	4	2	4.65	11	1	50	54	21	46
Bujalkowski, Mike, Wagner	4	5	4.80	12	0	66	66	37	38
Egan, Pat, Quinnipiac	7	5	4.83	16	0	76	88	32	52

OHIO VALLEY CONFERENCE

	Conference		Overall	
	W	L	W	L
Jacksonville State	19	8	35	25
***Austin Peay State**	16	11	38	24
Morehead State	15	11	29	28

Murray State	15	12	28	31
Southeast Missouri State	15	12	24	32
Eastern Kentucky	14	12	26	31
Eastern Illinois	14	13	17	39
Samford	13	14	20	36
Tennessee Tech	6	20	13	42
Tennessee-Martin	6	20	12	43

ALL CONFERENCE TEAM: C—Donald Cheney, So., Morehead State. **1B**—Bryan Ingram, Sr., Morehead State. **2B**—Lance Seasor, Sr., Morehead State. **3B**—Eric Horstman, Sr., Southeast Missouri. **SS**—Jared Walker, Sr., Austin Peay State. **OF**—Brett Bolger, Jr., Eastern Kentucky; Derrick Bussell, Sr., Eastern Kentucky; Winston Pearson, Sr., Jacksonville State. **DH**—Chaz Ebert, Jr., Murray State. **UT**—Bryan Stevenson, Sr., Eastern Kentucky. **SP**—Donovan Hand, Fr., Jacksonville State; Rowdy Hardy, Jr., Austin Peay State. **RP**—Lee Drinkard, Fr., Jacksonville State.

Player of the Year: Lance Seasor, Morehead State. **Pitcher of the Year**: Rowdy Hardy, Austin Peay State. **Freshman of the Year**: Donovan Hand, Jacksonville State. **Coach of the Year**: Jim Case, Jacksonville State.

INDIVIDUAL BATTING LEADERS

(Minimum 150 At-Bats)

	AVG	AB	R	H	2B	3B	HR	RBI	SB
Bolger, Brett, Eastern Kentucky	**.398**	196	47	78	10	1	1	42	20
Bussell, Derrick, Eastern Ky.	.378	201	**66**	76	9	4	3	31	**32**
Stevenson, Bryan, Eastern Ky.	.369	225	50	83	10	2	6	55	**32**
Walker, Jared, Austin Peay	.368	239	49	**88**	14	4	6	59	9
Seasor, Lance, Morehead State	.366	232	59	85	16	0	15	50	6
Ball, Jake, Jacksonville State	.361	227	42	82	14	2	2	43	7
Hortsman, Eric, SE Missouri	.358	218	48	78	12	2	1	26	12
Bryant, Kevin, Morehead State	.357	221	37	79	16	2	3	31	8
Ingram, Bryan, Morehead State	.347	199	42	69	**19**	0	**16**	**64**	0
Whisenant, Will, Eastern Ky.	.346	214	43	74	9	1	7	51	4
Hudson, Seth, Murray State	.336	211	47	71	3	2	0	23	3
Ebert, Chaz, Murray State	.335	212	52	71	12	0	4	30	2
Pearson, Winston, JSU	.333	237	51	79	12	5	8	51	7
Burnett, Bear, Samford	.331	181	27	60	10	2	2	23	4
Selvog, Brandon, Tenn. Tech	.328	201	35	66	17	2	2	27	8
Peterson, Jake, Austin Peay	.328	198	26	65	9	1	1	26	0
Poynter, Chris, Austin Peay	.328	183	29	60	9	2	2	37	1
Smith, Tommy, Austin Peay	.324	180	24	59	6	3	1	34	1
Stewart, Alex, Murray State	.322	210	41	68	**19**	1	4	43	7
Cheney, Donald, More. State	.322	183	47	59	14	1	12	57	0
Huber, Erik, Eastern Illinois	.322	202	33	65	11	1	1	30	13
Wells, Tony, Eastern Kentucky	.322	202	35	65	15	0	4	38	9
Campbell, Ryan, Eastern Illinois	.319	216	38	69	15	1	8	33	1
Marty, Nathan, Tennessee Tech	.319	191	35	61	11	0	12	43	3
Carroll, Clint, Jacksonville State	.318	217	47	69	**19**	2	0	23	8
#Piazza, Brian, Jack. State	.313	233	36	73	9	**6**	3	42	3

INDIVIDUAL PITCHING LEADERS

(Minimum 50 Innings)

	W	L	ERA	G	SV	IP	H	BB	SO
Hand, Donovan, Jack. State	10	3	**2.60**	20	0	83	74	19	63
Hardy, Rowdy, Austin Peay	**11**	6	2.63	20	0	127	120	24	**96**
Andres, Danny, Jacksonville State	1	3	2.88	21	1	50	46	18	36
Daniel, Brad, Austin Peay	6	3	3.19	**28**	5	54	42	29	51
Duran, Adrian, Morehead State	9	5	3.48	19	0	111	100	45	91
Kraus, Craig, Murray State	8	2	3.50	14	0	98	114	19	78
Kelley, Shawn, Austin Peay	7	4	3.59	17	1	98	112	22	70
Evans, Joey, SE Missouri	8	4	3.66	21	0	98	99	28	77
Harris, West, Murray State	4	5	3.75	20	2	72	77	29	53
Lucci, Shane, Morehead State	3	6	3.83	16	0	85	84	25	57
Willoughby, McKenzie, Eastern Ky	8	3	3.84	15	0	89	84	47	65
Massey, Scott, Tenn.-Martin	3	7	3.86	13	0	86	89	26	54
Edens, Joseph, Samford	3	2	4.05	13	0	53	50	23	46
McAlister, Jamie, SE Missouri	4	7	4.08	26	2	79	78	28	53
Vaculik, Chris, Eastern Illinois	6	5	4.17	**28**	3	73	83	42	58
Darwin, Matthew, Jack. State	3	4	4.22	16	0	60	62	25	29
Thomas, Devin. Austin Peay	6	5	4.62	17	0	74	79	31	44
Fares, Billy, Murray State	7	5	4.67	19	1	91	107	29	67
#Dobson, Micky, Tenn.-Martin	1	0	4.70	**28**	2	31	33	22	21
#Boothe, Richard, Eastern Ky.	0	5	5.68	18	**6**	19	26	14	9

PACIFIC-10 CONFERENCE

	Conference		Overall	
	W	L	W	L
Oregon State	19	5	46	12
Arizona	17	7	39	21
Southern California	15	9	41	22
Arizona State	15	9	42	25
California	13	11	34	23
Stanford	12	12	34	25
Washington	12	12	33	22
UCLA	4	20	15	41
Washington State	1	23	21	37

ALL CONFERENCE TEAM: C—Jeff Clement, Jr., Southern California; Brady Everett, Sr., Washington State; Nick Hundley, Jr., Arizona. **1B**—Jordan Brown, Jr., Arizona; Andy Jenkins, Sr., Oregon State; Jeff Larish, Sr., Arizona State; John Mayberry Jr., Jr., Stanford. **INF**—Brent Lillibridge, Jr., Washington; Jed Lowrie, Jr., Stanford; Josh Satin, Fr., California. **OF**—Brennan Boesch, So., California; Travis Buck, Jr., Arizona State; Trevor Crowe, Jr., Arizona; Jacoby Ellsbury, Jr., Oregon State; Jeff Van Houten, Sr., Arizona. **SP**—Dallas Buck, So., Oregon State; Jeff Gilmore, Jr., Stanford; Ian Kennedy, So., Southern California; Jonah Nickerson, So., Oregon State; Tim Lincecum, So., Washington. **RP**—Kevin Gunderson, So., Oregon State; Mark Melancon, So., Arizona; Travis Talbott, Sr., California.

Player of the Year (tie): Trevor Crowe, Arizona; Jacob Ellsbury, Oregon State. **Pitcher of the Year**: Ian Kennedy, Southern California. **Freshman of the Year**: Darwin Barney, Oregon State. **Coach of the Year**: Pat Casey, Oregon State.

INDIVIDUAL BATTING LEADERS

(Minimum 125 At-Bats)

	AVG	AB	R	H	2B	3B	HR	RBI	SB
Ellsbury, Jacoby, Oregon State	**.406**	244	56	99	19	3	6	48	26
Crowe, Trevor, Arizona	.403	263	**83**	106	**25**	**15**	9	54	**27**
Jenkins, Andy, Oregon State	.388	209	41	81	13	2	6	56	3
Buck, Travis, Arizona State	.382	288	82	**110**	24	3	6	43	**27**
Boesch, Brennan, California	.355	217	36	77	21	2	7	33	6
Hundley, Nick, Arizona	.352	227	57	80	23	2	15	46	9
Satin, Josh, California	.348	221	39	77	15	1	5	40	7
Van Houten, Jeff, Arizona	.348	250	61	87	18	3	9	67	2
Clement, Jeff, USC	.348	230	52	80	17	0	15	54	5
Curtis, Colin, Arizona State	.342	260	52	89	14	1	2	45	17
Kervin, Bryan, Arizona	.342	149	29	51	12	1	0	22	6
Ambriz, Hector, UCLA	.338	157	19	53	14	0	1	18	0
Everett, Brady, Wash. State	.337	208	50	70	11	0	15	62	2
Brown, Jordan, Arizona	.336	262	62	88	17	3	14	**80**	1
Hart, Billy, Southern California	.332	238	43	79	13	3	3	35	7
Clem, Zach, Washington	.332	187	43	62	13	0	8	42	4
Lillibridge, Brent, Washington	.330	209	55	69	19	4	8	45	13
Frey, Chris, Arizona	.326	227	55	74	14	4	3	42	8
Canham, Mitch, Oregon State	.325	160	40	52	5	2	8	39	4
Larish, Jeff, Arizona State	.324	250	72	81	18	1	**23**	67	11
Sorgi, Adam, Stanford	.322	239	52	77	17	3	5	41	3
Miller, Jay, Washington State	.322	230	39	74	12	1	3	32	8
Gosewisch, Tuffy, Arizona State	.321	252	43	81	17	2	6	74	5
McFeely, Shea, Oregon State	.319	213	50	68	15	0	5	41	4
Lowrie, Jed, Stanford	.317	224	47	71	16	2	14	66	5
Einspahr, Matt, California	.313	192	30	60	7	1	4	41	2
Dhaenens, Seth, Arizona State	.312	154	29	48	5	0	2	31	10
Sferra, J.J., Arizona State	.311	196	36	61	5	1	0	22	8
Cusick, Matt, USC	.311	225	53	70	9	0	4	35	2
Johnson, Taylor, Washington	.307	202	46	62	10	2	8	42	14
Graham, Tyler, Oregon State	.307	212	46	65	5	1	0	24	21
Craig, Allen, California	.304	214	40	65	14	0	8	35	13
Mayberry, John, Stanford	.303	238	36	72	18	0	8	53	5
Barney, Darwin, Oregon State	.301	226	46	68	9	1	2	44	6
Errecart, Chris, California	.298	238	35	71	15	0	8	35	6
Hankerd, Cyle, USC	.298	218	28	65	14	3	1	39	0
Sharpe, Blake, USC	.297	249	52	74	15	3	5	36	11
Rapoport, Jim, Stanford	.297	212	48	63	11	1	3	25	16
Van Winden, Mike, California	.296	199	30	59	11	2	1	31	3
Rubin, Kaeo, Washington State	.296	230	37	68	10	0	1	25	7
Batkoski, Nick, Washington	.294	197	33	58	11	0	6	40	1
Rindal, Curt, Washington	.294	143	26	42	4	0	7	28	2
Holder, James, California	.294	143	26	42	6	1	1	11	4
Hooft, Joey, Arizona State	.293	188	30	55	9	1	1	28	13
Minaker, Chris, Stanford	.291	251	52	73	**25**	0	3	37	10
Taylor, Michael, Stanford	.289	225	44	65	14	2	4	28	9
Donald, Jason, Arizona	.288	222	38	64	16	5	5	33	5
Murphy, Jim, Washington State	.287	167	30	48	7	0	7	28	3
McAngus, Zach, Wash. State	.287	195	37	56	9	2	2	25	7
Boyer, Brad, Arizona	.285	256	55	73	13	9	3	46	17
Lissman, Mike, Oregon State	.284	162	27	46	10	1	1	30	5
Miller, Jeff, Washington State	.282	209	31	59	7	1	3	40	10
Hester, John, Stanford	.282	227	34	64	13	1	5	41	7
Penniall, Will, UCLA	.280	182	21	51	8	3	1	18	11

INDIVIDUAL PITCHING LEADERS

(Minimum 50 Innings)

	W	L	ERA	G	SV	IP	H	BB	SO
Buck, Dallas, Oregon State	**12**	1	**2.09**	19	1	129	90	51	118
Nickerson, Jonah, Oregon State	9	2	2.13	18	0	110	88	29	114
Kennedy, Ian, Southern California	**12**	3	2.54	18	0	117	85	38	**158**
Melancon, Mark, Arizona	4	3	2.58	34	11	66	52	21	69
Gunderson, Kevin, Oregon State	6	4	2.76	33	**14**	65	49	14	62
Koss, Paul, Southern California	4	1	2.81	34	**14**	51	39	21	42
Gallagher, Nolan, Stanford	2	5	2.93	23	3	55	56	24	60
Lincecum, Tim, Washington	8	6	3.11	16	0	104	62	71	131
Averill, Erik, Arizona State	11	4	3.39	24	0	127	131	30	99

	W	L	ERA	G	SV	IP	H	BB	SO
Dworkis, Eric, California	6	5	3.41	17	0	106	122	23	71
Cooper, Michael, California	3	2	3.47	16	0	60	63	21	34
Holler, Blake, Stanford	6	3	3.48	22	1	54	61	21	51
Meloan, John, Arizona	10	3	3.70	19	0	112	115	58	130
Guyette, Kevin, Arizona	10	4	3.73	18	0	116	106	30	130
Gilmore, Jeff, Stanford	10	3	3.76	18	0	117	113	26	80
Berger, Eric, Arizona	6	2	3.84	24	1	61	45	29	68
Urquidez, Jason, Arizona State	10	4	3.93	29	2	121	115	56	98
Ambriz, Hector, UCLA	3	7	3.94	18	1	105	99	40	84
Leva, Matt, Stanford	5	2	4.12	17	1	59	66	21	45
Romanczuk, Mark, Stanford	5	6	4.24	18	0	108	106	36	83
Bordes, Brett, Arizona State	5	7	4.24	**38**	4	74	72	29	54
Dowling, David, Washington	6	1	4.32	21	2	75	72	31	45
Maxwell, Anton, Oregon State	11	1	4.33	17	0	96	90	42	69
Todoroff, Joe, California	4	3	4.40	23	0	74	78	32	55
Spradlin, Jack, Southern California	6	3	4.47	27	0	119	124	32	97
Kasser, Matt, Washington	4	4	4.66	15	1	64	61	37	40
Encinas, Anthony, USC	7	4	4.68	19	0	50	46	22	43
Schroeder, Brian, UCLA	4	6	4.77	31	1	72	83	29	48
Renkert, Dane, Washington State	1	3	4.89	30	5	57	66	19	41
Daman, Wayne, Wash. State	7	6	4.91	18	1	84	101	32	44

PATRIOT LEAGUE

	Conference		Overall	
	W	L	W	L
*Army	17	3	39	14
Lehigh	12	8	26	21
Bucknell	10	10	16	26
Lafayette	6	10	18	26
Holy Cross	5	11	13	23
Navy	6	14	12	33

ALL CONFERENCE TEAM: C—Matt McBride, So., Lehigh. **1B**—Forrest Doane, Sr., Lehigh; Walker Gorham, Sr., Army. **2B**—Tucker Frawley, Jr., Holy Cross. **3B**—Chris Brannan, So., Bucknell. **SS**—Kyle Scogin, So., Army. **OF**—Joe Ercolano, Fr., Lehigh; Andrew Smith, Jr., Lehigh; Kyle Walter, Jr., Bucknell. **DH**—James Conrad, So., Lafayette. **SP**—Nick Hill, So., Army; Cole White, Fr., Army. **RP**—John Fugett, So., Lafayette.

Player of the Year: Kyle Scogin, Army. **Pitcher of the Year**: Nick Hill, Army. **Freshman of the Year**: Cole White, Army. **Coach of the Year**: Joe Sottolano, Army.

INDIVIDUAL BATTING LEADERS

(Minimum 100 At-Bats)

	AVG	AB	R	H	2B	3B	HR	RBI	SB
Ercolano, Joseph, Lehigh	**.422**	147	34	62	10	1	3	25	5
Frawley, Tucker, Holy Cross	.409	110	17	45	3	1	2	16	0
Conrad, James, Lafayette	.376	165	39	62	5	3	1	20	17
Potvin, Tom, Holy Cross	.373	118	23	44	4	2	1	13	3
Law, Ian, Lafayette	.369	149	31	55	14	2	4	32	4
Buursma, Jason, Bucknell	.366	101	17	37	5	2	5	30	3
Scogin, Kyle, Army	.362	224	**47**	**81**	12	1	3	44	**19**
Gorham, Walker, Army	.358	179	31	64	12	0	10	40	3
Brannan, Chris, Bucknell	.353	102	23	36	10	1	2	21	0
Milan, Dinga, Army	.350	214	42	75	13	**5**	2	35	5
Smith, Andrew, Lehigh	.350	163	34	57	9	0	**12**	**49**	7
Capece, Matt, Bucknell	.345	165	34	57	6	4	0	21	12
Doane, Forrest, Lehigh	.342	149	33	51	9	0	11	40	0
White, Cole, Army	.331	139	24	46	5	3	10	32	4
Leasure, Kevin, Lafayette	.331	124	19	41	7	1	4	31	3
Walter, Kyle, Bucknell	.329	161	37	53	9	4	5	27	4
Geiger, Matt, Lehigh	.326	129	23	42	7	0	4	20	2
Thompson, Trevor, Navy	.322	115	15	37	6	0	1	14	18
Fioretti, Rob, Lafayette	.321	159	33	51	7	1	1	23	7
Cortazar, Frank, Lafayette	.310	145	25	45	5	1	3	18	2
Bet, Nick, Lehigh	.307	127	26	39	3	4	0	13	12
Bucci, Adam, Lafayette	.300	160	24	48	5	0	5	28	1
#McBride, Matt, Lehigh	.258	182	33	47	**17**	0	2	29	2

INDIVIDUAL PITCHING LEADERS

(Minimum 40 Innings)

	W	L	ERA	G	SV	IP	H	BB	SO
#Dinga, Milan, Army	0	0	0.57	16	**8**	16	10	5	16
#Jones, Monte, Army	1	1	0.88	**28**	2	31	23	5	22
Hill, Nick, Army	**10**	2	**1.21**	14	0	89	60	19	**90**
Kashner, Justin, Army	**10**	3	2.68	14	0	84	86	15	73
Gjeldum, Ted, Lafayette	4	2	2.79	15	0	48	43	18	26
Matteo, Joe, Lehigh	3	5	3.01	12	0	69	60	36	57
White, Cole, Army	7	1	3.07	12	0	56	61	15	35
Mittag, Nathan, Bucknell	2	4	3.40	10	0	53	65	14	33
Curry, Matt, Bucknell	4	6	3.43	11	0	63	71	30	42
Revelle, Matt, Lafayette	5	4	3.81	9	1	59	72	14	48
Miller, Mike, Holy Cross	4	3	3.88	10	0	51	50	18	46
Peacock, Tim, Bucknell	1	4	3.95	11	0	55	67	26	20
Lange, Jeff, Navy	2	3	3.99	15	1	59	69	10	52
McCoy, Mark, Navy	2	5	4.21	10	0	51	55	13	50
Raniszewski, Joe, Lehigh	4	1	4.24	15	0	51	62	15	28
Collina, Kyle, Lehigh	6	5	4.27	15	0	72	70	21	76

SOUTHEASTERN CONFERENCE

	Conference		Overall	
EAST	W	L	W	L
Florida	**20**	**10**	**48**	**23**
Tennessee	**18**	**11**	**46**	**21**
South Carolina	**16**	**14**	**41**	**23**
Vanderbilt	13	17	34	21
Georgia	12	17	30	25
Kentucky	7	22	29	27
WEST				
Louisiana State	**18**	**12**	**40**	**22**
Mississippi	**18**	**12**	**48**	**20**
Alabama	**17**	**13**	**40**	**23**
***Mississippi State**	**13**	**16**	**42**	**22**
Auburn	**13**	**17**	**34**	**26**
Arkansas	**13**	**17**	**39**	**22**

ALL CONFERENCE TEAM: C—Josh Bell, Jr., Auburn. **1B**—-Matt LaPorta, So., Florida. **2B**—Adam Davis, So., Florida. **3B**—Chase Headley, Jr., Tennessee. **SS**—Steven Tolleson, Jr., South Carolina. **OF**—Eli Iorg, Jr., Tennessee; Ryan Patterson, Sr., Louisiana State; Brian Pettway, Jr., Mississippi; Gabe Scott, Sr., Alabama. **DH**—Stephen Head, Jr., Mississippi. **SP**—Luke Hochevar, Jr., Tennessee; Greg Smith, Jr., Louisiana State. **RP**—John Madden, Sr., Auburn.

Player of the Year: Matt LaPorta, Florida. **Pitcher of the Year**: Luke Hochevar, Tennessee. **Freshman of the Year**: J.P. Arencibia, Tennessee. **Coach of the Year**: Pat McMahon, Florida.

INDIVIDUAL BATTING LEADERS

(Minimum 125 At-Bats)

	AVG	AB	R	H	2B	3B	HR	RBI	SB
Headley, Chase, Tennessee	**.387**	238	**82**	92	24	3	14	65	6
Pettway, Brian, Mississippi	.383	266	56	**102**	19	0	21	67	1
Iorg, Eli, Tennessee	.381	252	63	96	19	4	15	72	**27**
Baxter, Mike, Vanderbilt	.374	211	47	79	16	3	9	48	26
Stavinoha, Nick, LSU	.370	257	50	95	23	1	18	65	5
Patterson, Ryan, LSU	.369	249	74	92	23	2	20	56	7
Amonite, Karl, Auburn	.365	208	46	76	**25**	1	11	59	0
Scott, Gabe, Alabama	.364	184	39	67	13	0	12	36	1
Coghlan, Chris, Mississippi	.364	272	66	99	22	1	6	57	7
Harris, Clay, Louisiana State	.362	243	41	88	20	1	9	60	1
Corsaletti, Jeff, Florida	.358	279	68	100	18	0	10	53	11
Pearce, Steve, South Carolina	.358	229	50	82	16	0	21	63	2
Borbon, Julio, Tennessee	.350	220	42	77	9	2	3	42	11
Hunter, Joseph, Miss. State	.348	178	35	62	6	1	1	31	8
Lehmann, Shaun, Kentucky	.347	199	57	69	20	1	5	26	15
Shelby, John, Kentucky	.344	224	42	77	10	4	10	52	23
DeJesus, Antone, Kentucky	.344	192	45	66	10	5	3	31	10
Hernandez, Brian, Vanderbilt	.342	196	30	67	15	0	5	42	5
Hamblin, Danny, Arkansas	.341	220	44	75	19	1	10	49	8
Marquardt, John, Arkansas	.339	127	23	43	10	0	2	23	3
Bell, Josh, Auburn	.338	240	40	81	17	0	11	59	1
Feinberg, Alex, Vanderbilt	.335	158	23	53	4	1	0	14	3
Rivera, Michael, Tennessee	.332	244	51	81	12	0	1	42	13
King, Eric, Tennessee	.331	278	53	92	17	4	1	45	19
Head, Stephen, Mississippi	.331	272	65	90	16	1	18	68	3
LaPorta, Matt, Florida	.328	265	75	87	16	2	**26**	**79**	3
Johnstone, Tyler, Auburn	.328	259	53	85	12	3	0	29	24
Thomas, Clete, Auburn	.328	238	66	78	18	**6**	9	41	23
Edmundson, Kelly, Tennessee	.328	229	43	75	17	1	8	39	3
Bertram, Michael, Kentucky	.327	196	36	64	9	2	2	37	5
Alley, Josh, Tennessee	.324	253	70	82	19	2	3	45	25
Arencibia, J.P., Tennessee	.322	283	54	91	16	1	14	71	0
Keen, Kyle, Georgia	.320	128	21	41	11	1	0	17	7
Gill, Blake, Louisiana State	.320	219	41	70	11	1	7	48	8
Osteen, Cooper, Mississippi	.317	252	61	80	16	1	0	34	13
Arnold, Clint, Arkansas	.316	209	30	66	8	1	0	27	8
Corley, Brad, Mississippi State	.316	263	45	83	20	2	5	40	1
Campbell, Michael, So. Carolina	.315	251	56	79	16	5	8	42	8
Willard, Jon, South Carolina	.315	178	23	56	11	2	6	30	0
Edwards, Bruce, Auburn	.313	201	35	63	7	1	1	13	13
Gentry, Craig, Arkansas	.311	196	36	61	12	1	1	18	18
Wright, Mark, Mississippi	.311	206	39	64	15	1	13	51	2
Welch, Zac, Alabama	.309	136	26	42	9	1	4	26	1
Hode, Scott, Arkansas	.309	217	36	67	16	0	3	26	4
Felmy, Bobby, Georgia	.307	212	40	65	16	1	6	31	7
Davis, Adam, Florida	.306	294	75	90	15	1	12	63	24
Thomley, Morrow, Alabama	.305	213	36	65	14	4	5	36	13
Rea, Jeffrey, Mississippi State	.305	256	42	78	7	3	2	34	5
Jackson, Chris, Louisiana State	.305	128	29	39	3	1	1	17	0

Scelfo, Rocky, Alabama	.303	142	28	43	5	3	2	22	8
Presley, Alex, Mississippi	.302	139	24	42	9	1	2	17	1
Berkery, Thomas, Miss. State	.302	242	33	73	18	1	7	55	2
Gregg, Davy, South Carolina	.301	193	38	58	9	2	1	19	13
Jones, Brad, Mississippi State	.300	240	48	72	7	4	5	37	5
Grace, Billy, Kentucky	.299	174	44	52	11	4	8	44	4
Jeroloman, Brian, Florida	.298	248	48	74	11	0	8	49	2
Franklin, Miles, Mississippi	.298	151	34	45	6	3	1	26	8
Easley, Ed, Mississippi State	.296	226	36	67	10	1	3	32	1
Tolleson, Steven, So. Carolina	.296	243	53	72	14	2	6	46	20

INDIVIDUAL PITCHING LEADERS

(Minimum 50 Innings)

	W	L	ERA	G	SV	IP	H	BB	SO
Madden, John, Auburn	6	2	**1.77**	44	7	86	80	19	58
Hochevar, Luke, Tennessee	**15**	3	2.26	19	0	140	104	54	**154**
Determann, Jason, LSU	5	0	2.30	27	7	63	61	12	74
Head, Stephen, Mississippi	7	3	2.54	24	8	85	83	27	77
Smith, Greg, Louisiana State	10	3	2.60	17	0	104	99	25	82
Lewis, Jensen, Vanderbilt	8	3	2.62	15	1	93	74	23	95
Schmidt, Nick, Arkansas	8	2	2.80	19	0	100	87	39	89
Watson, Sean, Tennessee	7	3	2.85	29	8	79	64	47	82
Price, David, Vanderbilt	2	4	2.86	16	0	69	51	30	92
O'Day, Darren, Florida	8	3	2.87	34	7	69	56	13	63
Robertson, David, Alabama	7	5	2.92	32	8	74	48	36	105
Davis, Jordan, Alabama	5	2	3.10	26	3	58	55	15	41
Maloney, Matt, Mississippi	8	3	3.11	23	4	104	94	26	111
Falkenbach, Connor, Florida	3	3	3.15	**51**	9	91	114	17	75
Rawl, Aaron, South Carolina	9	6	3.20	18	0	115	121	23	94
Nix, Michael, Auburn	5	3	3.20	32	**13**	59	52	14	58
Startup, Will, Georgia	6	4	3.21	25	6	70	67	18	40
Dirks, Clay, Louisiana State	10	4	3.24	17	1	94	84	27	67
Adkins, James, Tennessee	10	5	3.32	19	0	127	107	50	135
Fowler, Eric, Mississippi	7	3	3.43	16	0	87	76	24	100
Ball, Bryan, Florida	7	6	3.45	17	0	102	94	37	72
Large, T.J., Alabama	7	4	3.46	18	0	96	72	50	92
Buschmann, Matt, Vanderbilt	4	3	3.47	19	1	62	55	24	46
McCamie, Zac, South Carolina	9	4	3.50	18	0	116	103	37	108
Boyce, Charley, Arkansas	11	10	3.53	29	3	122	120	27	64
Crosby, Jon, Mississippi State	5	3	3.54	16	0	74	95	11	35
Seibert, Shaun, Arkansas	5	3	3.60	19	1	60	53	31	52
Mullins, Ryan, Vanderbilt	6	1	3.62	13	0	72	74	23	61
Doolittle, Todd, Mississippi State	5	8	3.72	14	0	82	71	46	66
Hughey, Arnold, Auburn	8	4	3.74	17	0	99	98	17	80
Carter, Brent, Alabama	7	4	3.76	25	0	96	91	28	96
Holliman, Mark, Mississippi	8	4	3.90	18	0	113	106	48	120
Locke, Stephen, Florida	5	2	4.02	16	0	65	72	14	46
Horne, Alan, Florida	10	2	4.05	19	0	113	122	55	108
Shore, Jared, Auburn	1	2	4.07	35	1	66	85	7	30
LeBlanc, Wade, Alabama	5	5	4.09	14	0	88	77	28	108
Boss, Tommy, Florida	9	4	4.11	20	0	112	126	18	63
Fletcher, Jason, South Carolina	5	5	4.14	18	2	63	63	21	49
Johnson, Alan, Mississippi State	5	6	4.15	15	0	91	104	37	71
Sullivan, Josh, Auburn	7	5	4.27	17	0	97	88	39	74
Belcher, Brandon, Alabama	5	0	4.37	14	0	60	60	24	44

SOUTHERN CONFERENCE

	Conference		Overall	
	W	L	W	L
College of Charleston	27	3	48	15
Georgia Southern	18	11	38	22
Western Carolina	18	12	33	23
Elon	18	12	32	25
UNC Greensboro	17	13	31	22
The Citadel	14	16	25	34
East Tennessee State	13	16	31	22
***Furman**	13	16	30	29
Davidson	13	17	26	24
Wofford	7	23	17	37
Appalachian State	5	24	10	42

ALL CONFERENCE TEAM: C—Caleb Moore, Sr., East Tennessee State. **1B**—D.J. Wabick, Jr., College of Charleston. **2B**—Chris Campbell, So., College of Charleston. **3B**—Jay Heafner, Jr., Davidson. **SS**—Chuck Hargis, Jr., East Tennessee State. **OF**—Phillip Coker, Jr., College of Charleston; Brett Gardner, Sr., College of Charleston; Jason Hurst, Sr., Georgia Southern; James Payne, Sr., Georgia Southern. **DH**—Brett Anderson, Sr., College of Charleston; Blake Church, Jr., East Tennessee State. **SP**—Chris Mason, Jr., UNC Greensboro; Everett Teaford, So., Georgia Southern. **RP**—Brett Harker, Jr., College of Charleston.

Player of the Year: Jay Heafner, Davidson. **Pitcher of the Year**: Brett Harker, College of Charleston. **Freshman of the Year**: Steven Strausbaugh, Western Carolina. **Coach of the Year**: John Pawlowski, College of Charleston.

INDIVIDUAL BATTING LEADERS

(Minimum 125 At-Bats)

	AVG	AB	R	H	2B	3B	HR	RBI	SB
Heafner, Jay, Davidson	**.448**	203	51	91	18	0	11	58	13
Gardner, Brett, Charleston	.447	273	**85**	**122**	18	**5**	2	48	**38**
Wabick, D.J., Charleston	.415	260	69	108	**27**	2	9	66	5
Payne, James, Ga. Southern	.407	243	63	99	12	1	0	25	37
Dowling, Greg, Ga. Southern	.400	235	47	94	12	1	5	57	4
Hurst, Jason, Ga. Southern	.390	241	49	94	24	1	10	60	11
Crowe, Nick, E. Tenn. State	.389	157	44	61	11	2	8	26	8
Hargis, Chuck, E. Tenn. State	.387	204	51	79	22	0	7	42	12
Coker, Phillip, Charleston	.386	251	67	97	13	2	1	35	23
Moore, Caleb, E. Tenn. State	.382	207	56	79	20	1	**15**	73	2
Price, Chris, Elon	.379	195	54	74	14	2	4	53	1
Campbell, Chris, Charleston	.379	269	64	102	21	0	**15**	**87**	4
Byrne, Shane, E. Tenn. State	.373	217	70	81	15	**5**	11	44	11
Strausbaugh, Steve, W. Carolina	.367	218	46	80	13	0	12	51	1
Phillips, Logan, Ga. Southern	.365	230	76	84	16	1	10	53	12
Bennett, Paul, Elon	.364	214	52	78	13	3	2	36	17
Ard, Chris, Citadel	.354	254	48	90	13	1	3	39	29
Peisel, Brad, Appalachian State	.352	199	37	70	16	2	9	42	3
Entrekin, Alex, Davidson	.350	200	39	70	18	0	6	41	4
Barber, Byron, Charleston	.349	209	46	73	18	3	1	56	8
Hastings, Brian, Charleston	.344	180	42	62	14	0	7	43	2
Navarro, Sam, Davidson	.342	146	20	50	4	0	5	25	1
Shaft, Barrett, Western Carolina	.341	208	35	71	12	2	3	32	3
Davidiuk, A.J., Furman	.340	235	46	80	18	1	7	46	3
Butler, Kevin, App. State	.338	195	25	66	14	0	4	35	2
Douglas, Stephen, E. Tenn.	.338	216	37	73	17	3	5	56	26
Betsill, Matthew, Furman	.336	232	49	78	20	3	6	50	10
Church, Blake, E. Tenn. State	.333	186	40	62	15	3	7	53	4
Cassedy, Case, Furman	.332	226	42	75	14	0	5	46	0
Erickson, Evan, Elon	.332	214	48	71	19	**5**	10	68	3
Benefield, Eli, Davidson	.329	207	37	68	21	1	3	38	2
Davis, Drew, Elon	.327	199	44	65	14	0	3	44	3
Mason, Chris, UNC Greensboro	.324	219	36	71	11	3	7	36	15
Roulin, Jeremy, UNC-G	.324	216	45	70	19	0	3	41	12
McLain, Sam, Furman	.323	192	25	62	11	2	4	28	3
Pelfrey, Brett, Ga. Southern	.320	228	44	73	23	2	7	44	5
Marmol, Oliver, Charleston	.317	167	36	53	17	2	2	24	5

INDIVIDUAL PITCHING LEADERS

(Minimum 50 Innings)

	W	L	ERA	G	SV	IP	H	BB	SO
Harker, Brett, Charleston	5	0	**2.47**	28	**15**	51	39	10	60
Mason, Chris, UNC Greensboro	6	7	2.88	19	2	119	103	24	**135**
McSwain, Matt, Elon	5	1	2.92	12	0	62	55	30	69
Saunders, Link, Citadel	6	6	3.15	30	4	66	57	22	50
McConnell, Caleb, West. Carolina	5	4	3.47	9	0	57	59	12	53
Currin, Patrick, UNC Greensboro	5	4	3.48	24	6	75	83	13	62
Krieger, Adam, UNC Greensboro	4	2	3.58	16	0	50	48	15	21
Hodinka, Ryan, Furman	7	5	3.66	26	0	86	96	22	49
Edell, Ryan, Charleston	8	2	3.67	17	0	101	104	26	86
Price, Reid, Charleston	6	1	3.73	12	0	63	63	20	50
Teaford, Everett, Ga. Southern	9	3	3.99	18	0	120	121	34	118
Carter, Andy, Davidson	5	2	4.03	15	0	96	90	34	77
Evans, Dustin, Ga. Southern	9	5	4.14	17	0	104	104	36	97
Hunter, Ben, Furman	6	4	4.38	16	0	74	68	33	89
Klinker, Matt, Furman	2	2	4.38	23	0	64	62	30	44
Gemma, Danny, Charleston	7	4	4.50	19	1	88	117	13	64
McCullen, Brian, West. Carolina	7	3	4.53	21	3	56	69	17	29
McCall, Wes, UNC Greensboro	5	3	4.63	30	6	68	79	18	61
Miller, Luke, Western Carolina	6	2	4.64	**37**	2	52	62	8	21
Chastain, Matt, Elon	4	3	4.74	14	1	57	60	17	30
Lairsey, Josh, Ga. Southern	8	6	4.98	19	1	112	131	43	75
Braden, Wes, Charleston	4	1	5.00	13	0	54	58	30	36
Hall, Jeremy, E. Tenn. State	**10**	4	5.08	18	0	112	134	34	91
Chigges, Nick, Charleston	4	1	5.20	24	1	62	70	29	67
Redwine, Austin, Wofford	8	7	5.23	15	0	93	130	30	63

SOUTHLAND CONFERENCE

	Conference		Overall	
	W	L	W	L
Northwestern State	22	5	41	20
Lamar	16	11	38	23
Texas State	15	12	32	26
Texas-Arlington	14	13	26	32
***Texas-San Antonio**	14	13	27	34
Southeastern Louisiana	13	14	29	31
Sam Houston State	13	14	24	29
McNeese State	12	15	23	31
Louisiana-Monroe	9	18	26	29
Nicholls State	7	20	22	31

ALL CONFERENCE TEAM: C—Michael Ambort, So., Lamar. **1B**—Bobby

Barbier, Jr., Northwestern State. **2B**—Nolan Mast, Sr., Texas State. **3B**—Kyle Anson, Sr., Texas State. **SS**—Steve Clevenger, Fr., Southeastern Louisiana. **OF**—Bubba Bell, Sr., Nicholls State; Rusty Jones, Sr., Northwestern State; Ryan Spencer, Jr., Southeast Louisiana. **DH**—Blake Jones, Sr., Northwestern State, **P**—Matt Green, Jr., Louisiana-Monroe; Jacob Marceaux, Jr., McNeese State; Bernard Robert, So., Southeastern Louisiana.

Player of the Year: Blake Jones, Northwestern State. **Hitter of the Year**: Michael Ambort, Lamar. **Pitcher of the Year**: Matt Green, Louisiana-Monroe. **Freshman of the Year**: Bryan Cartie, McNeese State. **Newcomer of the Year**: Isa Garcia, Sam Houston State. **Coach of the Year**: Mitch Gaspard, Northwestern State.

INDIVIDUAL BATTING LEADERS

(Minimum 125 At-Bats)

	AVG	AB	R	H	2B	3B	HR	RBI	SB
Bell, Bubba, Nicholls State	**.378**	201	46	76	19	4	4	53	**25**
Crew, Ryan, Texas-San Antonio	.374	227	46	85	16	4	6	36	10
Jones, Rusty, NW Louisiana	.359	142	34	51	6	5	2	22	10
Anson, Kyle, Texas State	.353	218	42	77	12	1	7	55	6
Jones, Blake, NW Louisiana	.350	197	39	69	15	0	7	48	3
Roth, Randy, SE Louisiana	.349	249	47	**87**	20	0	8	46	10
Cartie, Bryan, McNeese State	.348	210	51	73	**23**	1	2	29	8
Clevenger, Steve, SE Louisiana	.347	245	46	85	11	0	4	43	6
Garcia, Isaias, Sam Houston	.339	218	42	74	10	1	15	52	10
Faul, Taylor, McNeese State	.339	165	33	56	14	1	6	37	8
Dewees, Marty, NW Louisiana	.339	171	34	58	6	0	1	25	20
Martin, Dustin, Sam Houston	.337	166	31	56	7	1	2	18	7
Ambort, Michael, Lamar	.336	217	**57**	73	15	0	**18**	**65**	2
Bennett, James, La.-Monroe	.335	209	49	70	7	7	13	45	7
Cantu, Adrian, Lamar	.332	241	43	80	16	1	9	36	3
Mast, Nolan, Texas State	.332	220	51	73	16	2	7	41	11
Warrick, Nathan, Texas-Arlington	.331	181	41	60	6	0	0	14	21
Crawford, Colt, Lamar	.330	209	37	69	14	1	3	31	5
Ramos, Dominic, Texas State	.320	247	55	79	9	5	2	33	19
Spencer, Ryan, SE Louisiana	.310	239	39	74	14	0	11	62	8
Richards, Chase, Lamar	.308	208	29	64	12	4	1	28	6
Voyles, J.R., Texas-San Antonio	.307	215	45	66	12	2	6	34	9
DeLome, Colin, Lamar	.307	176	35	54	11	**9**	4	36	4
Haney, Jo Jo, Lamar	.307	150	24	46	10	2	0	16	8
Raymond, Daniel, La.-Monroe	.306	170	32	52	9	1	5	32	2
Danielson, Sean, Texas-SA	.304	240	45	73	7	5	3	24	20
Salazar, Jose, Sam Houston	.300	213	42	64	10	0	9	41	1
Duhe, Gary, SE Louisiana	.298	238	46	71	12	3	3	27	8
Barbier, Bobby, NW Louisiana	.296	189	32	56	14	0	4	33	8
Ebarb, C.J., Lamar	.295	129	17	38	6	0	0	13	0
Stone, Jonathan, Sam Houston	.294	160	28	47	14	0	5	24	0
Holdren, Stephen, Texas-SA	.293	167	32	49	12	5	2	33	5
Waguespack, Jason, SE La.	.291	206	54	60	9	1	4	28	6
Lamothe, Tony, La.-Monroe	.291	127	19	37	12	0	3	22	1
Saltzgaber, Ryan, Texas-SA	.288	215	20	62	10	4	4	30	5

INDIVIDUAL PITCHING LEADERS

(Minimum 50 Innings)

	W	L	ERA	G	SV	IP	H	BB	SO
Robert, Bernard, SE Louisiana	9	4	**2.43**	17	0	115	100	33	101
Baxter, Jake, Texas-Arlington	7	7	2.60	16	0	118	116	25	94
Green, Matt, Louisiana-Monroe	**10**	2	2.65	17	1	105	92	26	**141**
#Desclouds, Daniel, NW Louisiana	2	2	2.70	21	**10**	30	32	8	20
Johnston, Shawn, NW Louisiana	2	2	2.76	19	0	59	57	21	30
Lonsberry, Daniel, NW Louisiana	7	4	2.86	16	0	101	78	54	73
#Hill, Chris, Texas State	2	1	2.95	**28**	2	40	36	23	36
Marceaux, Jacob, McNeese State	6	5	3.05	15	1	100	85	29	105
Manuel, Robert, Sam Houston	3	2	3.12	21	3	66	61	16	41
Delage, William, Lamar	6	5	3.31	18	0	98	86	32	66
Jones, Blake, NW Louisiana	7	3	3.32	**28**	8	60	54	24	57
Varnell, Grant, Texas-Arlington	8	2	3.33	17	0	111	108	18	71
Lott, Cody, Sam Houston	4	4	3.42	20	2	71	88	30	33
Cloeren, Derek, NW Louisiana	7	3	3.63	16	0	87	73	35	76
Marshall, Jesse, Sam Houston	7	1	3.92	14	0	60	58	26	45
Moore, Scott, Texas State	4	6	3.93	25	4	73	54	42	70
Sawicki, Bobby, Texas State	7	2	3.95	16	0	93	93	34	57
Gordon, Derrick, Lamar	4	7	3.95	20	0	93	85	43	102
Vander Wag, Scott, Lamar	4	4	3.95	19	4	66	58	28	57
Vasquez, Steven, Texas-SA	4	2	4.05	10	0	53	58	17	27
MacFarland, Steve, Lamar	8	2	4.16	26	3	67	60	46	59
Jean, Chris, Texas State	7	5	4.24	16	0	92	93	32	75
Rodriguez, Aaron, Texas-SA	8	6	4.27	21	0	122	150	38	71
#Davis, Danny, McNeese State	4	4	5.55	**28**	3	49	57	39	48

SOUTHWESTERN ATHLETIC CONFERENCE

	Conference		Overall	
EAST	**W**	**L**	**W**	**L**
Mississippi Valley State	18	5	19	28
Alcorn State	14	9	22	18
Jackson State	14	9	24	21
Alabama State	10	13	14	25
Alabama A&M	2	22	10	32
WEST				
***Southern**	17	7	29	18
Texas Southern	17	7	22	24
Prairie View A&M	13	11	31	27
Grambling State	7	16	13	31
Arkansas-Pine Bluff	5	18	9	40

ALL CONFERENCE TEAM: IF—Corey Wimberly, So., Alcorn State; Carl Lipsey, Sr., Jackson State; Kevin Nelson, Sr., Southern; Zach Penprase, So., Mississippi Valley State; Joaquin Rodriguez, So., Jackson State. **OF**—Darren Clark, Jr., Southern; Anton Daley, Jr., Prairie View A&M; Anton Shinhoster, Jr., Jackson State; Earl White, Sr., Arkansas-Pine Bluff. **DH**—Chris Stamps, Jr., Jackson State. **P**—Matthew Chase, So., Prairie View A&M; Damien Givens, Sr., Southern; Brandon Stricklen, Jr., Texas Southern.

Player of the Year: Corey Wimberly, Alcorn State. **Outstanding Hitter**: Corey Wimberly, Alcorn State. **Newcomer of the Year**: Matthew Chase, Prairie View A&M. **Defensive Player of the Year**: Brandon Revis, Southern. **Pitcher of the Year**: Brandon Stricklen, Texas Southern.

INDIVIDUAL BATTING LEADERS

(Minimum 100 At-Bats)

	AVG	AB	R	H	2B	3B	HR	RBI	SB
Wimberly, Corey, Alcorn State	**.462**	132	55	61	10	3	1	32	42
Lipsey, Carl, Jackson State	.431	167	**66**	**72**	13	3	0	39	**55**
Rodriguez, Joaquin, Jack. State	.406	165	51	67	**16**	4	3	49	3
Stewart, J.D., Texas Southern	.388	152	41	59	10	1	10	52	26
Thomas, Rickey, Prairie View	.385	117	33	45	12	0	3	45	10
Shinhoster, Anton, Jack. State	.382	165	55	63	8	**6**	3	**56**	19
Betschart, Caleb, Alcorn State	.382	131	36	50	16	1	1	42	4
Gause, Gerard, Southern	.381	126	34	48	8	2	5	32	5
Nelson, Kevin, Southern	.371	167	40	52	8	0	5	46	5
Wright, Aaron, Ark.-Pine Bluff	.366	134	36	49	14	2	5	24	6
Urquhart, Quenton, Ala. State	.362	138	39	50	10	0	6	34	8
Ellison, Damian, Ala. A&M	.362	116	31	42	9	2	2	21	7
White, Gregory, Alcorn State	.361	133	31	48	4	**6**	0	31	21
Penprase, Zach, Miss. Valley	.359	170	43	61	9	2	1	33	41
Stamps, Chris, Jackson State	.348	135	41	47	5	2	4	43	6
Williams, Kenji, Jackson State	.345	165	60	57	10	4	2	46	20
Ervin, Samson, Alabama State	.343	140	37	48	8	4	2	28	13
Spann, Mario, Southern	.341	132	26	45	11	1	4	26	5
Sanders, Delvin, Texas So.	.340	106	19	36	6	1	0	20	9
Webb, Anthony, Jackson State	.339	171	49	58	14	2	4	41	10
Clark, Darren, Southern	.339	121	35	41	7	0	11	40	4
Jones, Courtney, Grambling	.339	124	23	42	7	0	6	32	1
Mercer, Marvin, Grambling	.338	136	19	46	9	1	3	30	0
Revis, Brandon, Southern	.338	145	38	49	5	3	4	29	17
Malcom, Russell, Ark.-Pine Bluff	.338	160	29	54	13	2	4	32	3
Russaw, Shundell, Jack. State	.336	119	55	40	2	3	1	24	17
Flores, Wigberto, Alabama A&M	.336	128	24	43	6	1	0	23	3
Williams, Rod, Miss. Valley	.336	149	35	50	7	4	9	48	9
Arrendendo, David, Texas So.	.331	151	30	50	10	0	0	23	0
Tidwell, Derrell, Alcorn State	.331	136	30	45	3	2	1	30	14
Lewis, Mark, Arkansas-Pine Bluff	.326	144	27	47	9	0	3	18	24
#Daley, Anton, Prairie View A&M	.304	168	52	51	12	3	**12**	47	17

INDIVIDUAL PITCHING LEADERS

(Minimum 40 Innings)

	W	L	ERA	G	SV	IP	H	BB	SO
Chase, Matthew, Prairie View	6	4	**3.51**	14	0	59	60	14	45
Chatwin, Matt, Alcorn State	5	3	3.60	21	**7**	60	56	18	41
Casias, Rudy, Miss. Valley State	3	2	3.72	21	1	46	46	13	40
#Roberson, Ryan, Miss. Valley	0	0	3.82	**28**	2	31	33	17	18
Daniels, Isaac, Texas Southern	5	6	3.89	13	0	72	64	37	75
Givens, Damien, Southern	5	1	4.43	14	1	61	58	30	60
Pena, Jose, Southern	4	1	4.53	13	0	58	67	20	58
Taylor, Wrandal, Prairie View	**10**	4	4.56	21	1	101	117	31	71
Marshall, Demetrius, Grambling	3	7	4.97	16	1	87	99	50	75
Bayless, David, Southern	6	2	4.98	13	0	60	54	29	43
Miller, Matt, Texas Southern	5	2	5.22	15	0	69	91	19	67
Kirk, Joshua, Southern	5	4	5.51	11	0	49	48	23	47
Salter, Terry, Prairie View A&M	6	4	5.72	17	0	61	77	30	25
Stricklen, Brandon, Texas Southern	8	3	5.90	13	1	79	79	32	**77**
Froneberger, Joshua, Ala. State	2	1	5.91	8	0	43	47	35	32
Long, Patrick, Alcorn State	4	4	6.22	15	1	59	69	25	37
Waters, Brandon, Grambling State	4	7	6.32	13	0	63	78	35	34

SUN BELT CONFERENCE

	Conference		Overall	
	W	**L**	**W**	**L**
Louisiana-Lafayette	16	8	48	19
***South Alabama**	15	9	35	27
Florida International	14	10	38	21

Middle Tennessee	13	10	32	23
New Mexico State	13	11	28	29
Arkansas State	12	12	33	23
New Orleans	10	14	20	39
Western Kentucky	8	16	21	37
Arkansas-Little Rock	6	17	23	33

ALL CONFERENCE TEAM: C—Michael McKenry, So., Middle Tennessee. **1B**—Geoff Desmond, Sr., Arkansas State. **2B**—Brett Kinning, Jr., Arkansas State. **3B**—Dallas Morris, Sr., Louisiana-Lafayette. **SS**—Chris Rich, Sr., Arkansas State. **OF**—Mark Aranda, Sr., New Mexico State; Dennis Diaz, Sr., Florida International; Yahmed Yema, Jr., Florida International. **DH**—Todd Martin, Jr., Middle Tennessee. **UT**—Micah Cockrell, Sr., Louisiana-Lafayette. **SP**—Austin Faught, Sr., Louisiana-Lafayette; Matt Scott, So., Middle Tennessee. **RP**—Adam Wood, Sr., South Alabama.

Player of the Year: Yahmed Yema, Florida International. **Pitcher of the Year**: Austin Faught, Louisiana-Lafayette. **Newcomer of the Year**: Todd Martin, Middle Tennessee. **Freshman of the Year**: Luke Hopkins, New Mexico State. **Coach of the Year**: Tony Robichaux, Louisiana-Lafayette.

INDIVIDUAL BATTING LEADERS

(Minimum 125 At-Bats)

	AVG	AB	R	H	2B	3B	HR	RBI	SB
Martin, Todd, Middle Tenn. State	**.412**	153	39	63	13	0	8	31	5
Hopkins, Luke, New Mex. State	.392	212	58	83	19	0	14	79	2
Yema, Yahmed, Fla. International	.391	207	58	81	15	1	14	63	8
Desmond, Geoff, Ark. State	.384	224	66	86	19	1	20	72	5
Lucroy, Jonathan, La.-Lafayette	.379	182	33	69	15	0	5	48	1
Kinning, Brett, Arkansas State	.375	232	51	87	11	1	9	41	14
Freese, David, South Alabama	.373	217	52	81	11	2	6	48	6
Bowser, Brandon, New Orleans	.362	229	51	83	19	3	6	47	16
McNamee, Eric, Middle Tenn.	.360	214	61	77	17	0	3	31	12
Rodden, Vince, New Mex. State	.359	209	65	75	9	1	1	28	26
Morris, Dallas, La.-Lafayette	.357	258	56	**92**	16	1	12	68	7
Bryant, Tommy, Ark.-Little Rock	.353	204	41	72	14	0	14	46	0
Aranda, Mark, New Mex. State	.351	202	59	71	10	4	**22**	**85**	4
Ross, Marcus, Western Ky.	.351	239	44	84	18	2	6	57	0
McOwen, James, Fla. Int.	.351	148	29	52	8	1	1	21	11
Ransdell, Matt, Western Ky.	.349	249	56	87	13	3	0	41	9
Eilers, Derek, Ark.-Little Rock	.348	230	45	80	18	0	6	30	3
Beachum, Jeff, Middle Tenn.	.346	231	42	80	18	1	2	41	11
Jaggers, Nate, Middle Tenn.	.346	234	51	81	13	0	14	60	1
Lozano, Corey, Fla. International	.346	159	31	55	9	3	2	29	5
Hines, Nathan, Middle Tenn.	.342	202	35	69	14	2	4	53	6
Rich, Chris, Arkansas State	.339	230	45	78	20	0	11	49	0
Smyth, Paul, New Orleans	.338	201	47	68	14	2	4	39	4
Scriven, Eric, Western Kentucky	.337	193	36	65	8	0	0	30	4
Tatford, Jefferies, La.-Lafayette	.336	143	31	48	13	1	3	32	1
McCarthy, John, La.-Lafayette	.333	240	46	80	16	2	2	48	11
Cotto, Xardiel, New Mex. State	.332	217	63	72	15	1	9	59	5
Smart, Hudson, Arkansas State	.332	190	40	63	14	1	2	30	8
Warren, Adam, Middle Tenn.	.331	145	22	48	12	0	1	21	3
Morgan, Justin, La.-Lafayette	.331	139	29	46	12	0	4	32	0
Webster, Alex, New Orleans	.330	191	34	63	14	0	8	47	4
Coker, John, La.-Lafayette	.329	255	**82**	84	16	**10**	2	29	29
Harvey, Adam, New Mex. State	.329	161	46	53	6	2	11	49	0
Newton, Jordan, Western Ky.	.329	216	63	71	20	2	13	55	6
Cadena, Nick, Fla. International	.329	207	41	68	8	1	8	43	15
Pullin, Bryan, Fla. International	.328	189	38	62	17	0	1	24	7
McKenry, Michael, Middle Tenn.	.328	180	44	59	11	1	13	42	3
Armstrong, Corteze, Western Ky.	.328	174	40	57	5	1	0	18	10
Hamilton, Casey, Western Ky.	.326	193	36	63	11	2	3	38	5
Diaz, Dennis, Fla. International	.326	230	58	75	9	0	6	38	**37**
#Towns, Antone, Western Ky.	.306	209	43	64	**21**	3	6	55	8

INDIVIDUAL PITCHING LEADERS

(Minimum 50 Innings)

	W	L	ERA	G	SV	IP	H	BB	SO
Wood, Adam, South Alabama	4	2	**2.30**	21	3	59	59	17	71
Faught, Austin, La.-Lafayette	**12**	0	2.40	16	0	90	67	38	72
Gonzalez, Frank, Fla. International	8	1	2.70	**29**	3	67	63	19	51
Schambough Kraig, La.-Lafayette	5	1	2.88	28	**5**	50	39	14	59
Scott, Matt, Middle Tenn. State	10	1	3.07	14	0	100	88	10	68
Asher, David, Florida International	9	1	3.26	18	0	113	110	38	88
Cockrell, Micah, La.-Lafayette	5	4	3.40	18	3	50	47	12	38
Cromer, Bennett, Ark.-Little Rock	5	6	3.73	15	0	109	113	33	91
Ardoin, Kevin, Louisiana-Lafayette	10	5	3.76	17	0	103	102	29	115
Woodward, Allan, Middle Tenn. St.	5	1	3.96	24	4	52	47	22	55
Moody, Hunter, La.-Lafayette	2	0	4.08	18	1	57	56	21	47
Salazar, Jered, La.-Lafayette	6	3	4.21	15	0	51	56	11	39
Walters, P.J., South Alabama	10	7	4.26	20	0	142	163	29	**119**
Hernandez, Danny, Fla. Int.	3	6	4.55	26	**5**	59	59	37	55
Copeland, Tyler, Middle Tenn.	5	4	4.57	15	0	69	89	29	37
Christianson, Chase, So. Alabama	4	6	4.60	**29**	**5**	63	62	21	56
Fowler, Taylor, Arkansas State	8	7	4.91	14	0	103	110	42	80
Cryer, Bryan, New Orleans	5	4	4.95	20	0	87	97	23	40
Tharp, Stephen, Arkansas State	3	1	5.03	20	1	68	77	16	50
Villanueva, Elih, Fla. International	7	3	5.05	18	0	102	105	30	79
Major, Tommie, South Alabama	4	2	5.10	14	0	60	63	32	60
Simmons, Jeramy, So. Alabama	4	5	5.14	17	1	96	109	36	91
Sanders, Brandt, La.-Lafayette	1	1	5.23	22	0	52	52	22	46
Enlow, Nick, Arkansas-Little Rock	4	9	5.44	16	0	101	145	25	70
Cabrera, Ammer, Fla. International	4	3	5.46	14	0	56	60	33	42
Jones, Michael, New Orleans	4	6	5.91	16	0	91	127	18	65
Clay, Trevor, Arkansas-Little Rock	5	5	6.14	19	2	70	96	16	37
Ring, Blake, Arkansas State	5	6	6.18	19	0	96	125	33	58
#Walter, Doug, Arkansas State	3	0	6.25	26	**5**	36	45	6	29
Faulkner, Daniel, Western Ky.	6	8	6.28	19	1	106	132	38	71
Faircloth, J.C., Western Kentucky	2	6	6.38	18	0	66	75	23	37

WEST COAST CONFERENCE

	Conference		Overall	
COAST	**W**	**L**	**W**	**L**
Loyola Marymount	18	12	31	27
San Diego	16	14	30	27
Gonzaga	15	15	28	26
Saint Mary's	12	18	20	30
WEST				
***Pepperdine**	21	9	41	23
San Francisco	20	10	38	18
Santa Clara	11	19	28	28
Portland	7	23	17	36

ALL CONFERENCE TEAM: C—Chad Tracy, So., Pepperdine. **1B**—Bryan Byrne, Jr., Saint Mary's. **2B**—Scott Campbell, So., Gonzaga. **3B**—Delaney Gallagher, Jr., Saint Mary's. **SS**—Kevin Drever, Jr., Santa Clara. **OF**—Shane Buschini, So., San Diego; Sam Carter, Jr., Saint Mary's; Chris Pettit, Jr., Loyola Marymount. **UT**—Scott Cousins, So., San Francisco; Steve Kleen, Sr., Pepperdine. **P**—Paul Coleman, Jr., Pepperdine; Nick Pereira, Sr., San Francisco; Anthony Rea, Sr., Santa Clara.

Player of the Year: Chad Tracy, Pepperdine. **Pitcher of the Year**: Paul Coleman, Pepperdine. **Freshman of the Year**: Barry Enright, Pepperdine. **Coach of the Year**: Nino Giarratano, San Francisco.

INDIVIDUAL BATTING LEADERS

(Minimum 125 At-Bats)

	AVG	AB	R	H	2B	3B	HR	RBI	SB
Tracy, Chad, Pepperdine	**.367**	256	56	**94**	**22**	2	**12**	**61**	3
Frazee, Joe, Loyola Marymount	.364	220	45	80	20	5	3	34	10
Gartrell, Stefan, San Francisco	.364	143	19	52	12	0	5	41	3
Buschini, Shane, San Diego	.352	199	46	70	17	1	6	42	15
Sansoe, Mike, Saint Mary's	.352	165	35	58	11	3	7	20	6
Kleen, Steve, Pepperdine	.350	240	46	84	16	1	8	58	3
Carter, Sam, Saint Mary's	.350	200	38	70	12	0	7	49	2
Farris, Eric, Loyola Marymount	.345	142	27	49	9	0	2	17	9
Cooper, James, Loy. Marymount	.342	196	36	67	11	4	2	36	6
Ruth, Keoni, San Diego	.338	216	43	73	14	0	2	32	9
Campbell, Scott, Gonzaga	.332	211	45	70	10	1	1	30	0
Fukuroku, Royce, San Francisco	.329	173	41	57	11	0	5	22	8
Pettit, Chris, Loyola Marymount	.329	219	**62**	72	20	1	9	44	20
Drever, Kevin, Santa Clara	.327	150	18	49	8	2	0	22	8
Gallagher, Delaney, St. Mary's	.326	187	30	61	18	1	3	32	3
Byrne, Bryan, Saint Mary's	.322	183	39	59	14	0	6	33	4
Snyder, Justin, San Diego	.318	179	32	57	9	1	4	31	3
Holcomb, Darin, Gonzaga	.312	224	30	70	15	0	3	31	0
Culpepper, Jeff, Gonzaga	.312	208	48	65	13	2	6	38	16
Wrisley, Andrew, Portland	.312	144	16	45	8	0	1	11	5
Thibault, Kiel, Gonzaga	.312	218	41	68	11	2	3	35	8
Uribes, David, Pepperdine	.311	267	60	83	13	2	1	30	**25**
Cousins, Scott, San Francisco	.309	162	29	50	3	0	7	30	13
Worth, Danny, Pepperdine	.306	248	29	76	16	2	1	34	8
Watts, Kris, Santa Clara	.306	186	28	57	6	1	6	36	2
Rodgers, Jesse, Portland	.303	155	17	47	8	1	2	12	0
Hall, Tayo, San Francisco	.303	231	43	70	11	0	1	29	15
Vetters, Travis, Portland	.299	167	26	50	8	1	3	16	3
Ehlers, Justin, Portland	.299	174	18	52	7	1	1	21	0
Salas, Luke, Pepperdine	.298	228	39	68	9	1	1	31	7
#Ortiz, Adrian, Pepperdine	.281	231	41	65	7	**7**	0	19	8

INDIVIDUAL PITCHING LEADERS

(Minimum 50 Innings)

	W	L	ERA	G	SV	IP	H	BB	SO
McGuigan, Patrick, San Francisco	5	2	1.66	25	7	54	40	13	50
Kleen, Steve, Pepperdine	4	3	1.75	29	**17**	51	39	18	47
Pereira, Nick, San Francisco	**10**	3	**2.21**	16	0	106	90	33	93
Cousins, Scott, San Francisco	8	5	2.74	15	0	95	78	30	76
Rea, Anthony, Santa Clara	7	6	2.75	24	5	95	100	25	55
Monroe, Josh, Gonzaga	9	4	3.03	15	0	101	97	32	66
Kometani, Kea, Pepperdine	**10**	5	3.17	19	0	128	138	36	100
Donovan, Patrick, Gonzaga	6	7	3.22	15	0	106	94	24	62
Coleman, Paul, Pepperdine	9	3	3.35	17	0	110	88	41	91

	W	L	ERA	G	SV	IP	H	BB	SO
Butler, Josh, San Diego	7	7	3.42	18	0	113	112	42	82
Blaine, Justin, San Diego	8	5	3.55	19	0	117	117	58	**106**
Couch, Matt, San Diego	5	3	3.65	17	0	81	82	13	41
Beal, Andy, Loyola Marymount	4	1	3.71	**31**	3	53	49	30	40
Trochez, Kevin, Saint Mary's	5	5	3.87	15	0	95	113	22	55
Biale, Tony, San Francisco	5	3	3.92	14	0	67	65	21	44
Stevens, Jeff, Loyola Marymount	7	7	4.01	18	2	108	125	39	81
Warlop, Sean, San Diego	0	3	4.29	22	1	57	72	17	26
Franco, T.J., San Francisco	4	3	4.29	19	1	50	47	19	45
Enright, Barry, Pepperdine	**10**	1	4.62	18	0	97	115	26	52
McConnell, Kellan, Santa Clara	5	7	4.87	17	0	102	128	27	69

WESTERN ATHLETIC CONFERENCE

	Conference W	Conference L	Overall W	Overall L
Rice	21	9	45	19
Fresno State	16	14	30	29
Hawaii	15	14	28	27
Nevada	15	15	26	27
San Jose State	13	17	28	28
Louisiana Tech	9	20	17	39

ALL CONFERENCE TEAM: C—Brett Hayes, Jr., Nevada. **1B**—Joe Savery, Fr., Rice. **2B**—Isaac Omura, Jr., Hawaii. **3B**—Beau Mills, Fr., Fresno State. **SS**—Anthony Contreras, Sr., San Jose State. **OF**—Jacob Butler, Sr., Nevada; Tyler Henley, Fr., Rice; Matt Inouye, Jr., Hawaii; Nick Moresi, So., Fresno State. **DH**—Adam Rodgers, Sr., Rice. **SP**—Stephen Bryant, Sr., Hawaii; Matt Garza, Jr., Fresno State; Joe Savery, Fr., Rice. **RP**—Rudy Quinonez, Jr., Fresno State.

Player of the Year: Joe Savery, Rice. **Pitcher of the Year**: Matt Garza, Fresno State. **Freshman of the Year**: Beau Mills, Fresno State. **Coach of the Year**: Wayne Graham Rice.

INDIVIDUAL BATTING LEADERS

(Minimum 125 At-Bats)

	AVG	AB	R	H	2B	3B	HR	RBI	SB
Savery, Joe, Rice	**.382**	204	49	78	17	2	5	43	7
Contreras, Anthony, San Jose St.	.373	241	42	**90**	14	2	0	37	8
Omura, Isaac, Hawaii	.369	206	36	76	19	2	6	47	1
Moresi, Nick, Fresno State	.352	219	45	77	10	2	11	54	13
Rodriguez, Josh, Rice	.345	238	48	82	11	3	11	54	9
Hamilton, Ryan, Louisiana Tech	.339	224	28	76	11	1	8	37	4
Butler, Jacob, Nevada	.333	171	45	57	16	1	11	43	4
Rodgers, Adam, Rice	.332	226	47	75	**21**	0	7	52	1
Corrick, Nate, San Jose State	.327	205	35	67	13	1	0	35	11
Mills, Beau, Fresno State	.319	216	54	69	12	2	**22**	**63**	7
Becktel, Travis, San Jose State	.317	224	43	71	9	1	4	31	10
Hayes, Brett, Nevada	.313	214	31	67	11	2	6	45	6
Spiers, Joe, Hawaii	.307	231	45	71	11	3	0	21	**31**
Buchanan, Greg, Rice	.306	216	34	66	11	3	1	32	5
Sakamoto, Kent, Fresno State	.305	164	28	50	8	2	4	29	8
Henley, Tyler, Rice	.301	256	**70**	77	12	**4**	6	36	12
Haygood, Brandon, La. Tech	.298	225	41	67	20	2	3	21	8
Angel, Ryan, San Jose State	.297	185	30	55	16	1	1	27	16
Mummy, Ben, Nevada	.297	212	43	63	10	1	18	52	3
Vitters, Christian, Fresno State	.293	232	41	68	14	1	5	41	8
Reichenbach, Clay, Rice	.292	137	20	40	5	0	4	22	1
Krukow, Baker, Nevada	.286	161	27	46	11	0	2	28	0
Lehmann, Danny, Rice	.283	184	33	52	17	0	7	33	0
Holik, Gary, Louisiana Tech	.281	167	25	47	3	1	2	14	9
Bowman, Matt, Nevada	.280	125	31	35	7	1	4	19	3
Magana, Schafer, Hawaii	.276	174	31	48	12	0	2	26	2
Laird, Gil, Louisiana Tech	.271	207	27	56	15	0	7	26	6
Marcial, Robert, Nevada	.269	160	21	43	4	1	0	13	4
Newman, Eric, Nevada	.268	142	18	38	7	1	0	17	2
Epidendio, Nick, San Jose State	.267	135	20	36	12	0	0	30	2

INDIVIDUAL PITCHING LEADERS

(Minimum 50 Innings)

	W	L	ERA	G	SV	IP	H	BB	SO
Kilby, Brad, San Jose State	7	2	**1.85**	16	1	78	60	31	54
Savery, Joe, Rice	8	5	2.43	19	1	119	104	37	**129**
Bell, Bobby, Rice	4	0	2.77	24	1	52	35	14	51
Garza, Matt, Fresno State	6	5	3.07	19	1	108	110	37	120
Bryant, Stephen, Hawaii	8	3	3.17	16	0	105	82	37	110
Winck, Mat, San Jose State	4	4	3.18	22	1	65	63	25	33
Wright, Steven, Hawaii	4	3	3.26	21	4	66	58	15	75
#St. Clair, Cole, Rice	2	0	3.26	**32**	2	47	35	12	62
Degerman, Eddie, Rice	8	1	3.28	18	0	99	70	38	117
Brechmann, Shane, San Jose State	1	2	3.31	20	2	54	59	9	23
Geer, Josh, Rice	**12**	4	3.32	19	0	**125**	105	44	105
#Quinonez, Rudy, Fresno State	2	3	3.66	23	**5**	32	30	10	24
Costi, Justin, Hawaii	2	5	3.81	17	1	85	86	30	44
Dewing, Branden, San Jose State	6	6	4.31	17	0	109	132	30	73
Fister, Doug, Fresno State	7	6	4.32	21	0	94	90	27	77
#Jones, Steve, San Jose State	2	1	4.50	19	**5**	24	23	9	23
Romero, Eddie, Fresno State	6	4	4.62	24	0	64	62	42	57
Rupert, Ryan, Louisiana Tech	3	6	4.83	18	1	82	74	46	80
Meyer, Clayton, Louisiana Tech	4	9	4.85	14	0	85	100	31	68
Schoeninger, Tim, Nevada	5	8	5.07	15	0	94	117	27	54
Tucker, Mitch, Louisiana Tech	2	5	5.28	23	2	77	83	38	67
Bauer, Ricky, Hawaii	4	4	5.52	19	0	60	78	17	31
Summer, Colby, Hawaii	2	6	5.61	14	0	67	92	16	42
Rodriguez, Ryan, Nevada	11	5	5.67	16	0	98	113	33	86
Lassere, Andrew, Louisiana Tech	2	7	5.98	20	0	59	71	30	37

INDEPENDENTS

	Overall W	Overall L
Texas A&M-Corpus Christi	31	21
Dallas Baptist	32	23
New York Tech	24	22
Savannah State	22	21
Indiana-Purdue-Fort Wayne	24	25
UC Davis	27	29
Northern Colorado	22	34
Sacramento State	20	36
Longwood (Va.)	16	32
South Dakota State	17	37
Utah Valley State	17	39
Texas-Pan American	15	39
North Dakota State	10	43
Hawaii Hilo	6	34

*Provisional Division I

INDIVIDUAL BATTING LEADERS

(Minimum 125 At-Bats)

	AVG	AB	R	H	2B	3B	HR	RBI	SB
Landin, Jaime, Texas A&M-CC	.427	211	65	90	15	7	8	43	8
Smith, Gerald, Savannah State	.400	130	25	52	15	4	9	42	2
Kenefick, Mike, New York Tech	.392	171	39	67	4	2	1	25	22
Olivo, Ryan, Dallas Baptist	.388	129	30	50	12	1	4	24	3
Carter, Chuck, Texas A&M-CC	.386	215	62	83	14	3	15	59	3
Magness, Daniel, Dallas Baptist	.372	180	39	67	14	0	4	45	0
Galloway, Clint, Texas A&M-CC	.370	154	32	57	8	1	4	30	7
Kirk, Sean, IUPU-Ft. Wayne	.368	144	25	53	11	1	5	44	4
Ullrich, Louis, Longwood	.368	125	26	46	12	1	3	18	2
Slesk, Eli, Utah Valley State	.367	150	31	55	7	1	1	18	5
Garr, Brennan, No. Colorado	.365	181	32	66	11	0	8	36	0
Montgomery, Cody, Dal. Baptist	.364	242	57	88	22	6	7	41	13
Binick, Kraig, New York Tech	.358	179	35	64	8	5	1	20	31
Delich, Phil, No. Colorado	.353	218	38	77	13	1	4	41	0
Balus, Chris, Longwood	.351	168	39	59	8	2	5	21	28
Goldschmeding, Jeremy, DB	.346	205	32	71	12	0	4	33	9
Alamia, Louie, UT Pan Am	.344	209	44	72	8	2	1	21	7
Graham, Jason, Texas A&M-CC	.339	177	27	60	12	0	2	35	0
Keena, Ryan, IUPU-Ft. Wayne	.339	171	45	58	10	3	3	35	33
Geary, Greg, South Dakota St.	.337	205	38	69	12	0	10	52	2
Pastor, Bryan, New York Tech	.336	152	31	51	13	0	1	32	10
Dudoit, Johnny, Hawaii Hilo	.336	125	15	42	5	0	2	17	1
Drew, Kory, Utah Valley	.333	237	47	79	12	1	8	36	10
Steinbach, Ryan, IUPU-Ft.W.	.331	181	49	60	9	1	5	43	19
Bulow, Dan, Utah Valley State	.331	142	30	47	6	0	15	39	2
Perry, Trent, Utah Valley State	.330	215	43	71	21	0	14	57	3
Connor, Nick, Utah Valley State	.329	219	33	72	14	1	1	31	21
Holder, Drew, Dallas Baptist	.328	198	46	65	13	5	8	48	12
Vance, Canyon, Utah Valley	.328	198	42	65	11	2	5	33	6
Krum, Austin, Dallas Baptist	.322	180	51	58	11	4	4	30	7

INDIVIDUAL PITCHING LEADERS

(Minimum 50 Innings)

	W	L	ERA	G	SV	IP	H	BB	SO
Hearne, Trey, Texas A&M-CC	8	1	2.00	17	0	108	79	38	116
McKae, Dave, UC Davis	8	6	2.43	17	1	108	92	17	100
Wilson, Jereme, Dallas Baptist	5	0	2.85	14	1	60	54	26	37
Sutherland, Stuart, Dallas Baptist	4	3	3.38	23	4	51	54	15	21
Gamboa, Eddie, UC Davis	2	2	3.39	22	4	61	56	15	41
Soskin, Peter, UC Davis	3	2	3.40	16	0	53	52	14	51
Esposito, Joe, New York Tech	10	2	3.54	14	0	84	69	44	70
Matson, John, Hawaii-Hilo	1	7	3.63	10	0	52	52	31	30
Taylor, Randall, Dallas Baptist	7	6	3.74	17	0	99	105	22	55
Mitchell, Josh, Texas A&M-CC	5	7	3.84	17	0	96	114	34	57
McCullough, Brian, Longwood	4	5	4.20	21	2	71	71	23	55
Campbell, Matt, Sacramento State	3	9	4.41	15	0	86	103	28	51
Katz, Ethan, Sacramento State	6	9	4.52	16	0	96	117	35	67
Farrell, John, Longwood	3	5	4.58	15	1	73	95	19	61
Perez, Chris, New York Tech	2	5	4.62	11	0	51	48	36	43
Burdine, James, Texas A&M-CC	3	2	4.64	14	0	54	68	25	51
Potter, Michael, UC Davis	5	6	4.71	16	0	86	87	33	69
Guerra, Aaron, UT Pan American	5	5	4.96	20	0	89	127	18	63

Moccasins win All-Florida final

Fives alive
Florida Southern has won national titles in 1975, 1985, 1995 and 2005

NCAA DIVISION II

Florida Southern overcame an early 8-3 deficit by scoring six runs in the final four innings to beat North Florida 12-9 in an all-Florida NCAA Division II championship game, played in Montgomery, Ala.

The title was the ninth in school history for the Moccasins, whose 55-11 record was the best since they went 51-10 in 1995, the last time they won the championship. The Mocs have won the national title in every year ending in '5', beginning with 1975.

North Florida (48-16) roughed up Florida Southern starter Joe Walczak for five hits and six runs in 1⅔ innings of work but the Ospreys goal of a national title in their final year in Division II ended a step short as the Moccasins mounted a 20-hit attack. North Florida joins the Atlantic Sun Conference in Division I in 2006.

Catcher Jeff Howell, who led the team with 63 RBIs and was drafted in the 10th round by the Royals, went 5-for-5 in the finale for the Moccasins, who came from behind to win for the 22nd time in 2005. Florida Southern broke an 8-8 tie and went ahead to stay in the top of the seventh when out fielder Nick Diyorio, the team's leading hitter at .403, singled to score Alexy Hernandez.

FINAL **POLL**

NCAA Division II

1.	Florida Southern	51-11
2.	North Florida	48-16
3.	Central Missouri State	57-9
4.	Delta State (Miss.)	54-10
5.	Central Oklahoma	44-15
6.	West Virginia State	43-15
	Cal State Chico	42-16
8.	Tampa	40-18
9.	Grand Valley State (Mich.)	36-17
10.	Kennesaw State (Ga.)	37-22

Florida Southern also rallied from an opening-round 5-2 loss to top-ranked Central Missouri State by winning five straight games. They beat Central Missouri in consecutive games, 5-3 and 8-5, to reach the final. North Florida took an easier path to the final by cruising through its half of the bracket undefeated.

Moccasins righthander Kyle DeYoung was named the series most outstanding player, despite not pitching in the championship game. He worked in all five of the team's previous games, picking up three saves and a win. On the season, DeYoung went 8-1, 1.07 with 17 saves in 37 appearances.

Central Missouri State (57-9) entered the World Series as the nation's No. 1 team with one of the best pitching staffs in Division II history, but was foiled in its bid to win its second Division II title in four years. Its staff recorded an NCAA-record 16 shutouts while striking out 543 in 510 innings.

Five Mules pitchers were drafted in the first 11 rounds, including junior closer Nick Webber (1-1, 1.06) in the second round by the Cardinals, and senior starter Danny Powers (15-1, 1.91), the NCAA Division II Player of the Year, in the eighth round by the Twins.

Wisconsin School Runs Table

Top-ranked Wisconsin-Whitewater got outstanding pitching from senior lefthander Kevin Tomasiewicz, the top winner in NCAA Division III, as it became the first school since North Carolina Wesleyan in 1999 to go unscathed in the double elimination Division III World Series, played in Grand Chute, Wis. The Warhawks (45-7) won four straight games, defeating Cortland State (N.Y.) 11-4 in the championship game.

Tomasiewicz, a 26th-round pick of the Mets, was named the tournament's outstanding player. His complete game in the championship clinched his 15th win of the year and improved his career record to 35-5 over four years. Tomasiewicz combined with Greg Reinhard, the Division III player of the year, to go 27-1 on the season. Reinhard went 12-0, 1.82 on the year with a Division III-best 146 strikeouts in 104 innings.

NCAA DIVISION III

■ Rowan (N.J.) senior lefthander Josh Schwartz went 13-0, 1.74 on the year, extending his NCAA all-division winning streak to 37 games. In the last outing of his career, in the Division III World Series, he blanked Hampden-Sydney (Va.) 10-0, striking out 13 on four hits.

FINAL **POLL**

NCAA Division III

1.	Wisconsin-Whitewater	45-7
2.	Wooster (Ohio)	39-9
	Cortland State (N.Y.)	43-9
4.	Chapman (Calif.)	37-11
5.	Wartburg (Iowa)	37-11
6.	Rowan (N.J.)	42-10
7.	Wisconsin-Stevens Point	38-11
8.	Trinity (Conn.)	35-9
9.	Alvernia (Pa.)	41-6
10.	Texas Lutheran	35-10

Schwartz, who hadn't lost a game since early in his freshman year, broke the existing NCAA record for most consecutive wins of 26 earlier in the 2005 season. That record was held by Wake Forest's Kyle Sleeth (2001-03) and Brigham Young's Scott Nielsen (1978, 1982-83).

Schwartz went 13-0 as a junior in

2004 and 10-0 as a sophomore in 2003.

Oklahoma City Snaps Streak

NAIA

Oklahoma City snapped a three-game losing streak in the championship game of the NAIA World Series by defeating Embry-Riddle 8-1 in the deciding game of the 2005 tournament, played in Lewiston, Idaho.

The Stars got eight strong innings from tournament MVP Mike Mlotkowski and a homer and three RBIs from DH Colby Overstreet, who led a 16-hit attack. Embry-Riddle, making its first title game appearance, managed just four hits against Mlotkowski, who allowed one run on nine hits in 14 tournament innings. He went 14-1, 2.68 with 133 strikeouts in 111 innings on the year.

Oklahoma City (67-12) was in its fourth straight championship game, after losing to host Lewis-Clark State (twice) and Cumberland (Tenn.) in the previous three years. Both those schools were eliminated earlier in the tournament.

Crichton Earns First Title

NCCAA

In its fourth year of competition, Tennessee's Crichton College captured the 2005 National Christian College Athletic Association title by winning four straight games. The tournament was played in Chattanooga, Tenn. The third-seeded Cardinals beat Oakland City (Ind.) by scores of 6-0 and 10-3 to win the double-elimination event. Righthander Noel Bacca went 13-3 on the season to earn NCCAA pitcher of the year honors.

Visa Restrictions Benefit Thunderbirds

JUNIOR COLLEGE

New Mexico Junior College, making its first appearance in the tournament, tore through the field at the 2005 Junior College World Series in Grand Junction, Colo., with a team strengthened by several foreign players who remained in school instead of signing with professional teams because of visa restrictions.

New Mexico (55-10) knocked off another first-time participant, St. Petersburg (Fla.), 6-3 in the championship game after taking an early 6-0 lead. St. Petersburg scored three times against starter Cody Harkcom in the eighth, but Josh Giles came in to get the last five outs, striking out the side in the ninth. Harkcom, the Thunderbirds highest-drafted player (Royals, 12th round), and Brian Flores each won two games for New Mexico.

■ Grand Rapids (Mich.) CC became the first team to win three straight NJCAA Division II titles by defeating Parkland (Ill.) College 2-0 in the final behind tournament MVP Ben Knuth, who allowed three hits in eight innings. Parkland was the last team other than GRCC to win the championship, held in Millington, Tenn.

■ Gloucester County (N.J.) College won its fifth NJCAA Division III championship with a 14-5 win against Ridgewater (Minn.) CC in Glens Falls, N.Y.

■ Santa Rosa Junior College became the second northern school in 12 years to win the California Community College title with a 13-4 blowout of Palomar. The Bear Cubs came out of the losers bracket after an opening-round loss to Palomar. They recovered with four straight wins, including two in the same day over Palomar.

PLAYERS OF THE YEAR

Danny Powers

Kenny Maiques

Small College: Danny Powers, rhp, Central Missouri St.

Powers led all NCAA Division II pitchers in wins and strikeouts while going 15-1, 1.91 as a senior. He posted a 129-27 strikeout-walk ratio in 113 innings, allowing 83 hits. The ace of Central Missouri State's staff, Powers notched his final win in the opener of the DII College World Series against eventual champion Florida Southern. The Twins drafted him in the eighth round.

Junior College: Kenny Maiques, rhp, Rio Hondo (Calif.) JC

Maiques dominated after transferring from Long Beach State to Rio Hondo as a sophomore. He threw seven-inning perfect games three weeks apart and went 49 innings without allowing an earned run. He led all California JC pitchers with an 0.66 ERA and 133 strikeouts in 82 innings and walked just 16 batters. Postseason Tommy John surgery pushed Maiques' draft status out of the top three rounds, and he signed with the Cardinals as a 37th-round choice.

SMALL COLLEGE ALL-AMERICA TEAM 2005

Selected by Baseball America

Pos.	Player, School	Affiliation	YR	AVG	AB	R	H	2B	3B	HR	RBI	BB	SO	SB	Drafted
C	Jeff Howell, Florida Southern	Division II	Sr.	.332	238	54	79	22	5	10	63	19	23	1	Royals (10)
1B	Nick Klusaw, Oklahoma City	NAIA	Sr.	.429	273	73	117	26	3	27	99	34	44	3	Not drafted
2B	Brian Lauderdale, North Georgia	NAIA	Jr.	.399	296	111	118	24	6	8	75	28	42	39	Not drafted
3B	Jerry Hodges, Harris-Stowe State (Mo.)	NAIA	Jr.	.492	195	60	96	25	5	13	60	20	5	12	Not drafted
SS	Shawn Callahan, Central Missouri State	Division II	Sr.	.426	216	81	92	13	3	18	86	55	34	10	Athletics (22)
OF	Jeff Bieker, Fort Hays State (Kan.)	Division II	Jr.	.413	184	59	76	15	1	23	79	26	21	1	Athletics (15)
OF	Joey Dyche, Lewis-Clark State (Idaho)	NAIA	Sr.	.500	202	70	101	13	4	11	56	20	16	23	Giants (7)
OF	Antonio Sabatini, Erskine (S.C.)	Division II	Sr.	.436	234	76	102	30	2	19	69	23	40	13	Royals (14)
DH	Casey Smith, Erskine (S.C.)	Division II	Sr.	.448	212	69	95	28	1	18	83	33	18	0	Padres (9)
				W	**L**	**ERA**	**G**	**GS**	**CG**	**SV**	**IP**	**H**	**BB**	**SO**	
P	Matt Goyen, Georgia College	Division II	Sr.	9	1	1.99	13	12	4	1	91	60	32	122	Marlins (3)
P	Mike Mlotkowski, Oklahoma City	NAIA	Sr.	14	1	2.68	20	20	4	0	111	89	44	113	Yankees (33)
P	Danny Powers, Central Missouri State	Division II	Sr.	15	1	1.91	18	18	5	0	113	83	27	129	Twins (8)
P	Greg Reinhard, Wisconsin-Whitewater	Division III	Jr.	12	0	1.82	16	14	7	1	104	55	20	146	Devil Rays (6)
P	Josh Schwartz, Rowan (N.J.)	Division III	Sr.	13	0	1.74	15	14	6	1	93	78	29	99	Cardinals (42)

SMALL COLLEGES

NCAA DIVISION II

WORLD SERIES

Site: Montgomery, Ala.

Participants: Cal State Chico (42-14); Central Missouri State (55-7); Delta State, Miss. (51-8); Florida Southern (46-10); Grand Valley State, Mich. (34-15); North Florida (45-15); Southern Connecticut State (31-12); West Virginia State (43-14).

Champion: Florida Southern (5-1).

Runner-Up: North Florida (3-1).

Outstanding Player: Kyle DeYoung, rhp, Florida Southern.

ALL-AMERICA TEAM

Pos.	Player, School	YR	AVG	HR	RBI
C	Craig Newton, Delta State (Miss.)	Sr.	.363	15	76
1B	Adam Brechtl, Wisconsin-Parkside	Sr.	.399	10	72
2B	Ryan Taylor, West Virginia State	Jr.	.443	15	66
3B	Joe Ramos, Cal State Chico	Sr.	.380	2	40
SS	Shawn Callahan, Central Missouri	Sr.	.426	18	86
INF	Beau Sullivan, Central Oklahoma	Sr.	.402	15	68
OF	Brian Chapman, Carson-Newman (Tenn.)	Sr.	.355	19	77
	Trent Preuitt, Montevallo (Ala.)	Sr.	.436	6	60
	Casey Smith, Erskine (S.C.)	Sr.	.448	18	83
	Sean Van Elderen, Mesa State (Colo.)	Jr.	.396	19	65
DH	Jimbo Davis, Catawba (N.C.)	Sr.	.380	17	65

		YR	W	L	ERA
SP	Derek Antelo, Nova Southeastern (Fla.)	Sr.	11	0	2.13
	Matt Goyen, Georgia College	Jr.	9	1	1.99
	Danny Powers, Central Missouri State	Sr.	15	1	1.91
	Sergio Romo, Mesa State (Colo.)	Sr.	14	1	2.46
RP	Matt Nalutka, Armstrong Atlantic State (Ga.)	Jr.	3	0	0.30

Player of the Year: Danny Powers, Central Missouri State.

NATIONAL LEADERS

BATTING AVERAGE
(Minimum 100 At-Bats)

Player, School	YR	AB	H	AVG
Eric Baker, Mansfield (Pa.)	Sr.	156	78	.500
Joe Besl, Concord (W.Va.)	Jr.	144	72	.500
Troy Nunnally, Tuskegee (Ala.)	So.	123	58	.472
Collin Brown, Shepherd (W.Va.)	Jr.	136	64	.471
Mickey Nichol, Pittsburg State (Kan.)	Sr.	172	79	.459
Aaron Rice, Can State San Bernardino	Sr.	184	84	.457
Charles Monroe, Virginia State	So.	111	50	.450
Johnny Zepeda, Abilene Christian (Texas)	Jr.	165	74	.448
Casey Smith, Erskine (S.C.)	Jr.	212	95	.448
Miguel Abreu, East Central (Okla.)	Jr.	199	89	.447
Nick Gozzard, West Liberty State (W.Va.)	Sr.	119	53	.445
Steven Perkinson, Virginia State	Fr.	124	55	.444
Greg McCarthy, Western Oregon	Sr.	206	91	.442

Department Leaders: Batting

Dept.	Player, School	YR	G	Total
R	Ryan Taylor, West Virginia State	Jr.	60	85
	Will Bradley, Central Missouri State	Sr.	66	85
H	Nick Diyorio, Florida Southern	Jr.	62	110
TB	Antonio Sabatini, Erskine (S.C.)	Sr.	55	193
2B	Antonio Sabatini, Erskine (S.C.)	Sr.	55	30
3B	Michael Meredith, Tuskegee (Ala.)	Fr.	37	9
	Kevin Gledhill, Clarion (Pa.)	Sr.	48	9
	Matt Lawson, UC San Diego	Jr.	57	9
HR	Jeff Bieker, Fort Hays State (Kan.)	Jr.	52	23
RBI	Shawn Callahan, Central Missouri State	Sr.	66	86
SB	Eric Losten, Coker (S.C.)	Jr.	47	45
BB	Shawn Callahan, Central Missouri State	Sr.	66	55

EARNED RUN AVERAGE
(Minimum 50 Innings)

Pitcher, School	YR	IP	ER	ERA
Justin Cox, Southern Connecticut State	Fr.	69	7	0.91
Kyle DeYoung, Florida Southern	Jr.	67	8	1.07
David Qualben, Pace (N.Y.)	So.	68	9	1.19
Rusty Rayborn, Delta State (Miss.)	So.	83	11	1.19
Josh Papelbon, North Florida	So.	67	11	1.48
Frank Gailey, West Chester (Pa.)	So.	76	13	1.53
Aaron Cook, Tampa	Jr.	69	12	1.57
Bryan Duplissie, Franklin Pierce (N.H.)	Jr.	63	11	1.58
Matt Hennessey, Southern Conn. State	Jr.	91	17	1.69

Department Leaders: Pitching

Dept.	Player, School	YR	G	Total
W	Danny Powers, Central Missouri State	Sr.	18	15
SV	Adam Zimmerman, St. Joseph's (Ind.)	Jr.	32	20
SO	Danny Powers, Central Missouri State	Sr.	18	129
	Sergio Romo, Mesa State (Colo.)	Sr.	15	129

NCAA DIVISION III

WORLD SERIES

Site: Appleton, Wis.

Participants: Chapman, Calif. (36-9); Cortland State, N.Y. (39-7); Hampden-Sydney, Va. (27-13); Rowan, N.J. (41-8); Trinity, Conn. (35-7); Wartburg, Iowa (35-9); Wisconsin-Whitewater (41-7); Wooster, Ohio (37-7).

Champion: Wisconsin-Whitewater (5-1).

Runner-Up: Cortland State (4-2).

Outstanding Player: Kevin Tomasiewicz, lhp, Wisconsin-Whitewater.

ALL-AMERICA TEAM

Pos.	Player, Team	YR	AVG	HR	RBI
C	Gerard Haran, College of New Jersey	So.	.386	15	74
1B	Lucas Jones, Lynchburg (Va.)	Sr.	.481	2	50
2B	Jeremy Jirschele, Wisconsin-Oshkosh	Sr.	.438	5	49
3B	Jake Frank, Wooster (Ohio)	Sr.	.401	10	58
SS	Luke Ullman, Wooster (Ohio)	Sr.	.426	15	63
OF	Trey Luster, East Texas Baptist	Sr.	.436	9	46
	Tommy Paterson, Linfield (Ore.)	Sr.	.286	11	61
	Jay Lavender, Aurora (Ill.)	Sr.	.424	9	62

		YR	W	L	ERA
P	Buddy Klovstad, Chapman (Calif.)	Jr.	10	0	1.91
	Greg Reinhard, Wisconsin-Whitewater	Sr	12	0	1.82
	Derrick Jones, George Fox (Ore.)	Jr.	9	1	2.50

Player of the Year: Luke Ullman, ss, Wooster (Ohio).

NATIONAL LEADERS

BATTING AVERAGE
(Minimum 100 At-Bats)

Player, School	YR	AB	H	AVG
Eric Cirella, Salve Regina (R.I.)	Sr.	129	65	.504
Lucas Jones, Lynchburg (Va.)	Sr.	160	77	.481
Anthony Recker, Alvernia (Pa.)	Sr.	170	80	.471
Steve Pileggi, St. Joseph's (N.Y.)	Jr.	122	57	.467
Tim Ernst, Oglethorpe (Ga.)	So.	125	58	.464
Eric Bonds, Alvernia (Pa.)	Jr.	167	76	.455
Derek McIntosh, St. Joseph's (Maine)	Sr.	128	58	.453
Doug Coe, Lawrence (Wis.)	So.	102	46	.451
Jim DaSilva, FDU-Florham	Jr.	149	67	.450
Jeff Natale, Trinity (Conn.)	Sr.	150	67	.447
Steve Smith, Bridgewater State (Mass.)	Fr.	155	69	.445
Steve Wiczek, Wisconsin-Stevens Point	Sr.	191	85	.445
Kristaps Aldins, Vassar (N.Y.)	Sr.	144	64	.444
Dennis Kelly, Austin (Texas)	Jr.	142	63	.444
Kirby Carr, Bethel (Minn.)	So.	124	55	.444

Department Leaders: Batting

Dept.	Player, School	YR	G	Total
R	Ross Klawitter, Wisconsin-Whitewater	Sr.	52	77
H	Steve Wiczek, Wisconsin-Stevens Point	Sr.	49	85
TB	Steve Wiczek, Wisconsin-Stevens Point	Sr.	49	156
2B	Taylor McConnell, Washington & Lee (Va.)	Jr.	40	24
	Albert Carrizales, McMurry (Texas)	Jr.	45	24
3B	Ryan Skertich, Millsaps (Miss.)	Sr.	44	9
HR	Steve Wiczek, Wisconsin-Stevens Point	Sr.	49	18
RBI	Zach Lutz, Alvernia (Pa.)	Fr.	45	80
SB	Jason Watson, Wisconsin-Platteville	Jr.	42	38
BB	Eric Cirella, Salve Regina (R.I.)	Sr.	43	49

EARNED RUN AVERAGE
(Minimum 50 Innings)

Pitcher, School	YR	IP	ER	ERA
Daniel Zeffiro, Kean (N.J.)	So.	80	8	0.90
Justin Panania, Marietta (Ohio)	Sr.	57	6	0.95
Chris Anderson, Western New England	Fr.	59	7	1.06
Bryan Lambert, Brandeis (Mass.)	Sr.	52	8	1.38
Jim Dougher, Cortland State (N.Y.)	So.	76	12	1.43
Rob Motroni, St. Joseph's (N.Y.)	Jr.	62	10	1.44
Dan Howard, Johnson & Wales (R.I.)	Sr.	61	10	1.48
Dalton Rucker, Hardin-Simmons (Texas)	Fr.	61	10	1.48
Jake Eiler, St. Scholastica (Minn.)	Sr.	78	13	1.51
Kenny Moreland, Christopher Newport (Va.)	Fr.	65	11	1.52

Department Leaders: Pitching

Dept.	Player, School	YR	G	Total
W	Kevin Tomasiewicz, Wisconsin-Whitewater	Sr.	20	15
SV	Bryan Lambert, Brandeis (Mass.)	Sr.	25	12
SO	Greg Reinhard, Wisconsin-Whitewater	Jr.	16	146

SMALL COLLEGES

NAIA

WORLD SERIES

Site: Lewiston, Idaho.

Participants: Aquinas, Mich. (35-21); Biola, Calif. (43-10); Briar Cliff, Iowa (38-20); Cumberland, Tenn. (54-19); Embry-Riddle, Fla. (49-8); Lee, Tenn. (55-14); Lewis-Clark State, Idaho (44-7); Oklahoma City (63-11); Ohio Dominican (46-16); Spalding, Ky. (52-21).

Champion: Oklahoma City (4-1).

Runner-Up: Embry Riddle (4-2).

Outstanding Player: Mike Mlotkowski, rhp, Oklahoma City.

ALL-AMERICA TEAM

Pos.	Player, School	YR	AVG	HR	RBI
C	Stephen Vogt, Azusa Pacific (Calif.)	So.	.465	5	41
	Josh Lindstrom, Tennessee Wesleyan	Sr.	.481	12	38
1B	Nick Klusaw, Oklahoma City	Sr.	429	27	99
2B	Brian Lauderdale, North Georgia	Sr.	.399	8	75
3B	Jerry Hodges, Harris-Stowe (Mo.)	Jr.	.492	13	60
SS	Kenny Holmberg, Embry-Riddle (Fla.)	Sr.	.342	8	60
UT	Ben Blanton, William Jewell (Mo.)	Sr.	.423	14	65
OF	Ryan Andrews, Southern Nazarene (Okla.)	Sr.	.398	14	74
	Brad Coon, Trevecca Nazarene (Tenn.)	Sr.	.377	4	42
	Joey Dyche, Lewis-Clark State (Idaho)	Sr.	.500	11	56
	Sean Greear, Embry-Riddle (Fla.)	Sr.	395	4	61
DH	Zach Robinson, Point Loma Nazarene (Calif.)	So.	.341	18	63

		YR	W	L	ERA
SP	Jess LaCasse, Bellevue (Neb.)	Sr.	9	2	2.15
	B.J. Church, Lee (Tenn.)	Jr.	12	1	1.47
	Lance Marcum, McKendree (Ill.)	Jr.	12	2	2.03
	Mike Mlotkowski, Oklahoma City	Sr.	14	1	2.68
RP	Jon Grijalva, Biola, Calif. (16 SV)	Sr.	2	1	1.38

Player of the Year: Nick Klusaw, Oklahoma City

NATIONAL LEADERS

BATTING AVERAGE

(Minimum 100 At-Bats)

Player, School	Yr.	AB	H	AVG
Joey Dyche, Lewis-Clark State (Idaho)	Sr.	202	101	.500
Jerry Hodges, Harris-Stowe (Mo.)	Jr.	195	96	.492
Stephen Vogt, Azusa Pacific (Calif.)	So.	144	67	.465
Eric Fuehrer, Doane (Neb.)	Sr.	129	60	.465
Javier Guevara, Bethel (Ind.)	Sr.	151	70	.464
Archie Panfilli, Houston Baptist	Sr.	180	83	.461
Erik Hisner, Goshen (Ind.)	Sr.	108	48	.444
J.P. Lapointe, Bellevue (Neb.)	Fr.	153	68	.444
Steve Gumpf, Seton Hill (Pa.)	So.	152	67	.441
Matt Domangue, Doane (Neb.)	Sr.	147	64	.435
Mike Golom, Rio Grande (Ohio)	So.	154	67	.435
Mike Winklepleck, Morningside (Iowa)	Sr.	177	77	.435
Juan Mora, St. Thomas (Fla.)	Jr.	169	73	.432
Jason Ferguson, Urbana (Ohio)	Sr.	142	61	.430
Nick Klusaw, Oklahoma City	Sr.	273	117	.429

Department Leaders: Batting

Dept.	Player, School	Yr.	G	Total
R	Brian Dinkelman, McKendree (Ill.)	Jr.	66	75
H	Nick Klusaw, Oklahoma City	Sr.	77	117
2B	Frankie Ibarra, Oklahoma Baptist	Jr.	67	29
3B	Joe Beck, Northwood (Texas)	Jr.	64	10
HR	Donnie Burkhalter, Cumberland (Tenn.)	Sr.	77	28
RBI	Nick Klusaw, Oklahoma City	Sr.	77	99
SB	Chris Lebeda, Bethany (Kan.)	Sr.	46	55

EARNED RUN AVERAGE

(Minimum 50 Innings)

Pitcher, School	Yr.	IP	ER	ERA
B.J. Church, Lee (Tenn.)	Jr.	102	15	1.33
Rick Weber, Olivet Nazarene (Ill.)	Sr.	101	17	1.51
Derek Dufrane, Madonna (Mich.)	Jr.	80	14	1.59
Patrick Ryan, Embry-Riddle (Fla.)	Sr.	107	19	1.59
Justin Masterson, Bethel (Ind.)	So.	90	16	1.60
Tyler Delamater, Olivet Nazarene (Ill.)	Jr.	61	11	1.62
Adam Carrico, Union (Ky.)	Sr.	87	17	1.76
Ben Taylor, Goshen (Ind.)	Sr.	69	14	1.82
Mike Laughlin, Mt. Vernon Nazarene (Ohio)	So.	63	13	1.86
Daniel Hearn, Belhaven (Miss.)	Sr.	107	22	1.86

Department Leaders: Pitching

Dept.	Player, School	Yr.	G	Total
W	Jon Kirby, Lee (Tenn.)	Sr.	19	14
	Mike Mlotkowski, Oklahoma City	Sr.	20	14
SO	Jon Kirby, Lee (Tenn.)	Sr.	19	135

JUNIOR COLLEGE

DIVISION I WORLD SERIES

Site: Grand Junction, Colo.

Participants: Hutchinson, Kan. (37-20); Iowa Western (47-11); New Mexico (50-10); Northeastern Oklahoma A&M (44-7); Potomac State, W.Va. (32-12); St. Petersburg, Fla. (44-14); South Mountain, Ariz. (46-18); Texarkana, Texas (49-11); Wallace State, Ala. (44-11); Walters State, Tenn. (39-14).

Champion: New Mexico (5-0).

Runner-Up: St. Petersburg (3-2).

Outstanding Player: Renny Osuna, ss, New Mexico.

ALL-AMERICA TEAM

C—Phil Britton, Olney (Ill.). **INF**—Michael Bell, Grayson County (Texas); Matt Gamel, Chipola (Fla.); Michael Murray, Meridian (Miss.); Joe White, Georgia Perimeter. **OF**—Adam Crisp, Spartanburg Methodist (S.C.); Luke Gorsett, Garden City (Kan.); Angel Mercado, Manatee (Fla.). **DH**—Mike Gosse, New Mexico. **P**—Clay Buchholz, Angelina (Texas); Graham Godfrey, Wallace State (Ala.); Oliver Odle, Connors State (Okla.).

Player of the Year: Michael Murray, ss, Meridian (Miss.).

NATIONAL LEADERS

BATTING AVERAGE

(Minimum 125 At-Bats)

Player, School	AB	H	AVG
Josh Flores, Triton (Ill.)	154	80	.519
Darby Brown, Howard (Texas)	191	97	.508
Mike Gosse, New Mexico	191	95	.497
Ben Daw, Shelton State	116	55	.474
Tim Smith, Midland (Texas)	158	74	.468
Agustin Guzman, Baton Rouge (La.)	129	60	.465
Angel Negron, Marshalltown (Iowa)	149	69	.463
Alex Whitmore, Dyersburg State (Tenn.)	117	54	.462
Delk Scram, Cowley County (Kan.)	180	82	.456
Daman Aaron, Howard (Texas)	108	49	.454

Department Leaders: Batting

Dept.	Player, School	G	Total
HR	Luke Gorsett, Garden City (Kan.)	51	20
RBI	Darby Brown, Howard (Texas)	54	87
SB	Calvin Lester, Frank Phillips (Texas)	54	56

EARNED RUN AVERAGE

(Minimum 60 Innings)

Player, School	IP	ER	ERA
Oliver Odle, Connors State (Okla.)	131	10	0.69
Aaron Odom, Angelina (Texas)	66	7	0.96
Graham Godfrey, Wallace State (Ala.)	73	8	0.99
Andy Loomis, South Suburban	64	8	1.13
Clay Buchholz, Angelina (Texas)	71	9	1.14

Department Leaders: Pitching

Dept.	Player, School	G	Total
W	Oliver Odle, Connors State (Okla.)	17	15
SV	Matt Smith, Volunteer State (Tenn.)	15	15
SO	Oliver Odle, Connors State (Okla.)	31	141

DIVISION II WORLD SERIES

Site: Millington, Tenn.

Participants: Brookdale, N.J. (42-4); Chesapeake, Md. (39-16); Copiah-Lincoln, Miss. (31-25); Elgin, Ill. (52-8); Grand Rapids, Mich. (31-21); Madison Area Tech, Wis. (43-19); Mesa, Ariz. (42-21); Parkland, Ill. (47-15).

Champion: Grand Rapids (4-0).

Runner-Up: Parkland (3-2).

Outstanding Player: Ben Knuth, rhp, Grand Rapids.

DIVISION III WORLD SERIES

Site: Glens Falls, N.Y.

Participants: Columbus State, Ohio (21-15); Erie, N.Y. (35-9); Gloucester County, N.J. (46-7); Massasoit, Mass. (22-12); Queensborough, N.Y. (25-17); Richland, Texas (38-22); Ridgewater, Minn. (34-6); Westmoreland County, Pa. (26-16).

Champion: Gloucester County (4-0).

Runner-Up: Ridgewater (3-2).

Outstanding Player: Seth Button, 1b, Gloucester County.

CALIFORNIA CC STATE CHAMPIONSHIP

Site: Fresno, Calif.

Participants: Fresno City (34-6), Orange Coast (29-16), Palomar (32-9), Santa Rosa (29-13).

Champion: Santa Rosa (4-1).

Runner-Up: Palomar (2-2).

Outstanding Player: Awarded to entire Santa Rosa team.

BY WILL KIMMEY AND ALLAN SIMPSON

Orleans relied on excellent pitching to post the best regular-season record in the Cape Cod League in 2005, but turned to an explosive offense to capture its second playoff title in three years.

After setting a team record with a 2.22 ERA in compiling a 30-14 record in league play, the Cardinals erupted for 18 hits in the third and deciding game of their final series against Bourne to cruise to a 13-1 win. Orleans also beat Bourne in the 2003 championship series.

Outfielder Manny Burriss (Kent State) and righthander Brad Meyers (Loyola Marymount) shared playoff MVP honors. Burriss, who stole a team record 37 bases during the season, went 4-for-6 with three runs in the deciding playoff game as Orleans scored nine times in the first three innings, including five in the first. Meyers scattered nine hits in 6⅓ innings to earn the win. Brett Pill (Cal State Fullerton) and Robert Perry (Santa Clara) also added four hits for Orleans.

Evan Longoria

The blowout hardly resembled what previously was a hard-fought and dramatic season for Orleans. The Cardinals needed a ninth-inning run to hold off second-place Chatham (28-15-1) with a 3-2 win on the season's final day. The Cardinals then dropped the first game of their best-of-three playoff series to those same A's before rallying to take the final two games and advance to the championship series.

Meyers (4-2, 1.61) led the Orleans pitching staff during the regular season, while outfielder Colin Curtis (Arizona State) paced the Orleans offense with a .323 average and won Eastern Division MVP honors at the all-star game after notching three hits and scoring the contest's only run in a 1-0 East win.

Chatham didn't end up with a title, but the A's did boast the most impressive collection of individual talent. The A's had the league's No. 1 prospect for the second year in a row, lefthander Andrew Miller (North Carolina), who went 6-0, 1.65. They also boasted the MVP in shortstop Evan Longoria (Long Beach State), who topped the league with eight home runs and 35 RBIs. At .346, third baseman Chris Coghlan (Mississippi) led a 1-2-3 Chatham assault on the batting title with teammates Alex Presley (Mississippi) and Baron Frost (Southern California) finishing close behind at .343 and .341.

Orleans closer Stephen Wright (Hawaii) led the league with 12 saves to win the league's top reliever award, but that honor could have just as easily gone to Chatham's Derrick Lutz (George Washington), who also recorded 12 saves and didn't allow an earned run all summer.

Hankerd Shines For NECBL Champs

Outfielder Cyle Hankerd (Southern California) was the unquestioned star of the 2005 New England Collegiate League season as he led the Newport Gulls to their third league title since moving to Newport in 2001.

Hankerd fell two RBIs short of winning a triple crown as he hit .383 with nine home runs and 36 RBIs. He hit .500-2-5 as Newport swept to six straight playoff wins, including a two-game sweep of the Vermont Mountaineers in a best-of-three final. Hankerd homered in both games of the final series, connecting on a two-run shot as Newport wrapped up the series with a 6-2 win.

Cyle Hankerd

Hankerd also hit two home runs in an exhibition game against Team USA's college national team and delivered another home run in the NECBL all-star game.

Righthander Danny Otero (Duke) was the top pitcher for Newport. He pitched a complete game, six-hitter in the deciding game to run his playoff record to 2-0, 0.53. He went 5-1, 1.87 for the Gulls during the regular season. Overall, he walked only four and struck out 69 in 75 innings.

Endurance Leads Illinois Team To NBC Win

Banished to the loser's bracket after a first-round loss at the National Baseball Congress World Series, Illinois' Prairie Gravel survived the greatest endurance test in the event's 71-year history to win the title with a 9-1 win over the Santa Barbara (Calif.) Foresters.

Prairie Gravel, a team composed of college players, veterans and ex-pros in a tournament traditionally dominated by college-stocked teams, had to win three games on the final day of the 42-game, double-elimination event because of rain delays. It ended up winning nine games in all, a tournament record.

Prairie Gravel, playing in its ninth NBC tournamnent, beat the Southern California Fire 6-4 in the first game of the final day, then overcame a 4-0, eighth-inning deficit to Santa Barbara to beat the tournament's lone undefeated team, 7-4. That forced a final game against the Foresters, and Prairie Gravel broke that game open with its second straight five-run, eighth-inning outburst.

"It was a long day, an incredible day," Gravel second baseman Jamar Clanton said. "We don't give up. We were down here for 10 days, and we said, 'We're about to keep sending people home.' "

Prairie Gravel shortstop Ryan Anetsberger, a rising junior at Illinois State, was the tournament's MVP. He hit safely in all 10 games, going 19-for-38 overall, and led the tournament with 11 RBIs. He had two hits and two RBIs in the final game.

Brian Blomquist, a senior at Illinois, worked the first seven innings in the deciding game, walking none and striking out seven for his second win of the tournament.

The No. 1-seeded Aloha Knights failed in their bid to repeat as NBC champions, but it wasn't because of the efforts of righthander Tommy Hanson, the first-year West Coast Collegiate League's top prospect. He started two NBC games for the Knights, allowed one run in 16 innings and struck out 23. In his final outing at Wichita, against the Seattle Studs, Hanson was lifted with a one-hit shutout going with 12 strikeouts through eight

Miller earns Cape league honor

PLAYER OF THE YEAR

Andrew Miller acknowledges that pitchers have an advantage over hitters in summer league competition.

"It's almost unfair to give a hitter a metal bat all year and then make him use wood for a few months," the 6-foot-6 lefthander said.

Miller dismissed nearly every Cape Cod League batter during his two summers with the Chatham A's. The rising junior at North Carolina went 8-0, 1.82 in 89 combined innings, averaging 11.5 strikeouts and 4.1 hits allowed per nine innings.

Andrew Miller

Miller's mid-90s fastball—a two-seamer with excellent movement—and hard-breaking slider made those numbers possible, and hitters uncomfortable. Some even referred to Miller as the Cape's Big Unit, while others simply asked for off days when he was listed as the probable starter.

Chatham coach John Schiffner explained why: "I'm not going to say this kid's name, but it was a righthanded hitter. He swung and missed at a slider that hit him right in the thigh. I'd seen him hit guys in the back foot on slider strikeouts last summer, but this thing was thigh-high and he swung as it hit him. He had no chance.

"We kept it very calm (in the dugout) because we didn't want to show him up. But some guys had to bite their sleeve to not laugh out loud."

The laugh-out-loud moments were outnumbered by the times when Miller proved impressively efficient, as he became the first Cape Cod League pitcher to win Baseball America's Summer Player of the Year Award since 1986. He was more apt to throw two-seamers to entice groundouts than to work deep counts. That tack allowed Miller to meet his 2005 goal of averaging seven innings per start, and he still piled up 69 strikeouts, with an opponents average of .133. He allowed 50 baserunners in 49 innings.

"He pitched this summer more than he did last summer. Last summer he just threw," Schiffner said. "In some cases he was fine getting guys out at 88 (mph) and using his slider to set up his fastball. When he needed to get an out, he would be 96-97."

He reached the seventh inning in all but one of his 2005 starts, earning six wins.

Schiffner ranks Miller with Mark Mulder and Barry Zito as the best lefthanders he's witnessed during his time coaching on the Cape, which dates to 1978.

"His upside is tremendous because he's so fluid," Schiffner said. "He's not the same type of pitcher as Mulder or Zito, but their dominance was the same."

—WILL KIMMEY

PREVIOUS WINNERS

1984—Will Clark, 1b, Team USA
—Rafael Palmeiro, of, Hutchinson (Jayhawk)
1985—Jeff King, 3b, Team USA
—Bob Zupcic, of, Liberal (Jayhawk)
1986—Jack Armstrong, rhp, Wareham (Cape Cod)
—Mike Harkey, rhp, Fairbanks (Alaska)
1987—Cris Carpenter, rhp, Team USA
1988—Robin Ventura, 3b, Team USA
—Ty Griffin, 2b, Team USA
1989—John Olerud, 1b-lhp, Palouse (Alaska)
1990—Calvin Murray, of, Anchorage Bucs (Alaska)
1991—Chris Roberts, of, Team USA
1992—Jeffrey Hammonds, of, Team USA
1993—Geoff Jenkins, of, Team USA
1994—Steve Carver, 1b, Anch. Glacier Pilots (Alaska)
1995—Travis Lee, 1b, Team USA
1996—Seth Greisinger, rhp, Team USA
1997—Pat Burrell, 3b, Team USA
1998—Bobby Kielty, of, Bourne (Cape Cod)
1999—Xavier Nady, 3b, Team USA
2000—Mark Teixeira, 3b, Team USA
2001—Bobby Brownlie, rhp, Team USA
2002—Brad Sullivan, rhp, Team USA
2003—Jered Weaver, rhp, Team USA
2004—Daniel Carte, of, Falmouth (Cape Cod)

2005 SUMMER LEAGUE ALL-AMERICA TEAM

Selected by Baseball America

FIRST TEAM

Pos., Player	Team (League)	College	AVG	AB	R	H	HR	RBI	SB
C J.P. Arencibia	Team USA	Tennessee	.404	57	8	23	2	12	0
1B Jared Goedert	Hays (Jayhawk)	Kansas State	.367	.177	54	65	8	52	9
2B Evan Longoria	Chatham (Cape Cod)	Long Beach State	.299	164	25	49	8	35	6
3B Matt Mangini	Thunder Bay (Northwoods)	North Carolina State	.342	187	27	64	6	45	8
SS Allen Craig	Alexandria (Northwoods)	California	.362	199	41	72	12	40	9
OF Cyle Hankerd	Newport (New England)	Southern California	.383	115	23	44	9	36	0
OF Michael Taylor	Mat-Su (Alaska)	Stanford	.328	131	20	43	4	25	25
OF Jimmy Van Ostrand	Anchorage (Alaska)	Cal Poly	.339	124	23	42	5	16	4
DH Zach Daeges	Waterloo (Northwoods)	Creighton	.366	183	38	67	13	48	4

Pitcher	Team (League)	College	W	L	ERA	IP	H	BB	SO
SP Austin Creps	McKinney (Texas)	Texas A&M	5	2	1.76	57	49	22	69
SP Tommy Hanson	Aloha (West Coast)	Riverside (Calif.) CC	7	1	0.92	78	38	21	116
SP Kyle McCulloch	Team USA	Texas	4	0	1.44	25	20	3	22
SP Andrew Miller	Chatham (Cape Cod)	North Carolina	6	0	1.65	49	22	23	66
RP Tim Lincecum	Harwich (Cape Cod)	Washington	2	2	0.69	39	14	11	68
RP Derrick Lutz	Chatham (Cape Cod)	George Washington	0	0	0.00	25	13	3	39

SECOND TEAM

C—Jon Still, Falmouth/Cape Cod (North Carolina State). **1B**—Charlie Yarbrough, Columbus/Great Lakes (Longwood, Va.). **2B**—Adam Davis, Team USA (Florida). **3B**—Chris Coughlan, Chatham/Cape Cod (Mississippi). **SS**—Mitch Hilligross, Quincy/Central Illinois (Purdue). **OF**—Ryan Basham, Dubois County/Central Illinois (Michigan State); Collin Cowgill, Covington/Valley (Kentucky); Ryan Rogowski, Madison/Northwoods (Illinois). **DH**—Josh Banda, Denton/Texas (California Baptist).

SP—Daniel Bard, Wareham/Cape Cod (North Carolina); Jay Buente, Wisconsin/Northwoods (Purdue); Jared Hughes, Chatham/Cape Cod (Long Beach State); Brad Mills, Harrisonburg/Valley (Arizona); David Price, Team USA (Vanderbilt). **RP**—Josh Fields, Keene/New England (Georgia).

innings, only to see the Knights bullpen give up six runs in the ninth in a 6-1 loss.

■ The WCCL sprang up in the Pacific Northwest under former San Diego State head coach Jim Dietz, the league commissioner, with six of its teams coming from the Pacific International League, which continued play in 2005 with just a half-dozen teams.

The West Coast League was one of four new summer college leagues that began play in 2005. The others were the Cal Ripken Sr. League, the Florida Collegiate League and the Rocky Mountain League.

Goldpanners Go Quietly In Wichita

Once the nation's premier summer league in terms of producing future major league talent, the Alaska League uncustomarily fared poorly at the 2005 NBC World Series, where an Alaska team had won 16 championships in the previous 36 years.

The Alaska Goldpanners, who have sent almost 200 players to the big leagues while winning a record six NBC titles, lapped the field in the Alaska League with a 28-6 record, but went quietly in Wichita as the league's lone representative with a lineup that featured few bona fide prospects.

The Goldpanners made national headlines on June 21, however, as they hosted the 100th rendition of the Midnight Sun Game. The contest began at 10:30 p.m., and like the 99 games that preceded it, the game was played without the use or need of artificial lights.

The Goldpanners beat the Omaha Strike Zone 3-1 as righthander Sean Timmons, a Fairbanks native who pitched for the Goldpanners from 2000-04 and was the Alaska League MVP three times, came out of retirement and worked the first five innings, striking out seven and scattering four hits. It was his third Midnight Sun Game victory, most in history.

After the game, Timmons' No. 33 jersey and cap were sent to the Hall of Fame. An ex-pro in the Pirates system, Timmons flew in to pitch the game from Savannah, Ga., where he was studying at South University to be a physician's assistant.

First-Year Team Wins Texas Title

The Denton Outlaws rode the pitching of Corey Kluber to a 3-1 win over the McKinney Marshals to win the Texas Collegiate League title in their first year in the league. Kluber (Stetson) retired the first 13 hitters he faced and didn't allow a hit until the sixth inning as he outdueled Austin Creps (Texas A&M), the league's Pitcher of the Year who struck out a league record 15 but was doomed by three third-inning runs. On the year, Creps went 5-2, 1.76 with 69 strikeouts in 56 innings.

Denton catcher Josh Banda (Orange Coast, Calif., JC) was the standout hitter in a league dominated by pitchers. He led the league with a .400 average while also slugging 10 home runs.

COLLEGE SUMMER LEAGUES

CAPE COD LEAGUE

EAST	W	L	T	PCT	Pts
Orleans Cardinals	30	14	0	.682	60
Chatham Athletics	28	15	1	.644	57
Harwich Mariners	21	23	0	.477	42
Yarmouth-Dennis Red Sox	20	23	1	.467	41
Brewster Whitecaps	18	26	0	.409	36
WEST	**W**	**L**	**T**	**PCT**	**Pts**
Bourne Braves	26	17	1	.600	53
Cotuit Kettleers	22	19	3	.532	47
Falmouth Commodores	22	21	1	.511	45
Wareham Gatemen	21	21	2	.500	44
Hyannis Mets	7	36	1	.178	15

PLAYOFFS—Semifinals: Orleans defeated Chatham 2-1 and Bourne defeated Cotuit 2-0 in best-of-3 series. **Final:** Orleans defeated Bourne 2-1 in best-of-3 series.

ALL-STAR TEAM: C—Sean Gaston, Cotuit (Notre Dame); Jon Still, Falmouth (North Carolina State). **1B—**Aaron Bates, Brewster (N.C. State). **2B—**Evan Longoria, Chatham (Long Beach State). **3B—**Chris Coghlan, Chatham (Mississippi). **SS—** Emmanuel Burriss, Orleans (Kent State). **IF—**Scott Sizemore, Harwich (Virginia Commonwealth). **OF—**Alex Presley, Chatham (Mississippi); Colin Curtis, Orleans (Arizona State); Baron Frost, Chatham (Southern California); Chris Emanuele, Harwich (Northeastern). **DH—**Mark Hamilton, Falmouth (Tulane); Jeff Kindel, Yarmouth-Dennis (Georgia Tech). **UT—**Brad Lincoln, Bourne (Houston). **SP—**Andrew Miller, Chatham (North Carolina); Daniel Bard, Wareham (North Carolina); Jared Hughes, Chatham (Long Beach State); Tim Norton, Falmouth (Connecticut); Jon Lalor, Wareham (Mississippi State). **RP—**Derrick Lutz, Chatham (George Washington); Tim Lincecum, Harwich (Washington).

Most Valuable Player: Evan Longoria, Chatham. **Outstanding Pitchers:** Andrew Miller, Chatham; Tim Norton, Falmouth. **Manager of the Year:** Kelly Nicholson, Orleans.

TOP 30 PROSPECTS: **1.** Andrew Miller, lhp, Chatham (North Carolina). **2.** Daniel Bard, rhp, Wareham (North Carolina). **3.** Evan Longoria, inf, Chatham (Long Beach State). **4.** Chris Errecart, 1b/of, Yarmouth-Dennis (California). **5.** Brandon Morrow, rhp, Yarmouth-Dennis (California). **6.** Brad Lincoln, rhp/dh, Bourne (Houston). **7.** Dallas Buck, rhp, Falmouth (Oregon State). **8.** Greg Reynolds, rhp, Bourne (Stanford). **9.** Brad Meyers, rhp, Orleans (Loyola Marymount). **10.** Mark Hamilton, 1b, Falmouth (Tulane). **11.** Justin Masterson, rhp, Wareham (San Diego State). **12.** Chris Coghlan, 3b, Chatham (Mississippi). **13.** Eric Berger, lhp, Yarmouth-Dennis (Arizona). **14.** Brant Rustich, rhp, Orleans (UCLA). **15.** Tim Lincecum, rhp, Harwich (Washington). **16.** Brett Sinkbeil, rhp, Falmouth (Missouri State). **17.** Matt Antonelli, 3b, Falmouth (Wake Forest). **18.** Jared Hughes, rhp, Chatham (Long Beach State). **19.** Todd Frazier, ss/3b, Chatham (Rutgers). **20.** Tim Gustafson, rhp, Yarmouth-Dennis (Georgia Tech). **21.** Brooks Brown, rhp, Chatham (Georgia). **22.** Derrick Lutz, rhp, Chatham (George Washington). **23.** Colin Curtis, of, Orleans (Arizona State). **24.** Scott Sizemore, 3b, Harwich (Virginia Commonwealth). **25.** Jason Donald, ss, Cotuit (Arizona). **26.** George Kontos, rhp, Harwich (Northwestern). **27.** Aaron Bates, 1b/c, Brewster (North Carolina State). **28.** Pat Bresnehan, rhp, Harwich (Arizona State). **29.** Tim Norton, rhp, Falmouth (Connecticut). **30.** Emmanuel Burriss, inf, Orleans (Kent State).

INDIVIDUAL BATTING LEADERS

(Minimum 118 Plate Appearances)

	AVG	AB	R	H	2B	3B	HR	RBI	SB
Coghlan, Chris, Chatham	.346	130	19	45	5	0	0	22	3
Frost, Baron, Chatham	.343	140	20	48	12	1	0	13	0
Presley, Alex, Chatham	.341	129	25	44	3	0	0	7	8
Bates, Aaron, Brewster	.333	105	18	35	4	0	3	16	3
Curtis, Colin, Orleans	.323	99	19	32	6	0	0	10	11
Still, Jon, Falmouth	.316	158	24	50	5	0	5	28	6
Emanuele, Chris, Harwich	.312	154	16	48	7	1	2	16	9
Kindel, Jeff, Yarmouth-Dennis	.306	134	19	41	7	0	4	15	1
Sizemore, Scott, Harwich	.303	152	15	46	7	1	1	13	9
Salsgiver, Lance, Wareham	.301	143	20	43	10	0	1	10	0

INDIVIDUAL PITCHING LEADERS

(Minimum 35 Innings)

	W	L	ERA	G	SV	IP	H	BB	SO
Lincecum, Tim, Harwich	2	2	0.69	19	7	39	14	11	68
Lalor, John, Wareham	5	2	1.16	7	0	47	33	12	35
Bard, Daniel, Wareham	3	3	1.25	10	0	65	42	20	82
Lincoln, Brad, Bourne	3	1	1.32	9	0	55	39	10	56
Huff, David, Chatham	2	2	1.46	6	0	37	27	4	49
Meyers, Brad, Orleans	4	2	1.61	7	0	45	37	13	25

	W	L	ERA	G	SV	IP	H	BB	SO
Hughes, Jared, Chatham	7	0	1.62	8	0	50	37	11	54
Miller, Andrew, Chatham	6	0	1.65	7	0	49	22	23	66
Graham, Andy, Orleans	4	2	1.65	8	0	44	30	23	38
Reynolds, Greg, Bourne	2	3	1.70	8	0	53	36	15	34

BOURNE

BATTING	AVG	AB	R	H	2B	3B	HR	RBI	SB
Bartles, Brett, 1b/of	.237	118	13	28	5	1	0	11	1
Goff, Andy, ss	.210	100	19	21	2	0	0	3	6
Henry, Justin, 2b	.237	152	18	36	2	0	0	19	15
Hernandez, Mike, of	.245	163	25	40	10	2	2	18	7
Kasarjian, Kris, of	.000	6	1	0	0	0	0	0	0
Kateon, Bunky, ss	.156	64	5	10	1	0	2	7	1
Lincoln, Brad, dh-p	.243	107	21	26	5	1	6	25	0
Mascia, Tim, of	.190	42	8	8	1	0	0	3	2
McBryde, Mike, of	.258	89	16	23	4	0	1	14	9
Mills, Beau, 3b	.225	89	14	20	6	1	4	16	2
Murphy, Blake, c	.074	54	6	4	0	0	0	4	0
Parker, Blake, of	.205	73	7	15	2	0	1	5	2
Stinson, Josh, c	.229	96	8	22	2	0	0	9	0
Widlansky, Robbie, 1b/3b	.250	132	18	33	6	0	3	20	5
Wright, Ty, of	.255	106	11	27	4	0	0	11	7

PITCHING	W	L	ERA	G	SV	IP	H	BB	SO
Carignan, Andrew	1	2	1.44	18	2	25	14	15	32
Cory III, Forest	4	1	1.99	11	1	59	43	6	43
Crotta, Michael	1	2	4.91	13	1	29	34	5	18
Crowel, J.R.	2	1	1.90	5	0	24	20	9	10
Hicks, Romas	1	1	1.52	23	9	30	15	10	35
Hobson, Gib	6	1	2.55	8	0	49	39	7	52
Johnson, Jonathon	1	0	0.00	2	0	3	3	3	1
Lincoln, Brad	3	1	1.32	9	0	55	39	10	56
Manganaro, Nick	3	3	2.37	10	0	38	42	12	28
Miller, Brandon	1	1	5.73	5	0	11	11	4	6
Reynolds, Greg	2	3	1.70	8	0	53	36	15	34
Rhoden, Tyler	1	1	4.70	7	0	8	10	4	5
Walker, Erik	0	0	0.00	1	0	3	3	0	5

BREWSTER

BATTING	AVG	AB	R	H	2B	3B	HR	RBI	SB
Angelini, Nick, 2b	.231	13	1	3	0	0	0	0	0
Arcadia, Ryan, ss	.250	20	3	5	0	1	0	1	1
Bates, Aaron, 1b	.333	105	18	35	4	0	3	16	3
Boesch, Brennan, of	.222	27	7	6	0	0	1	2	1
Cooper, Craig, of	.225	89	12	20	3	0	0	3	6
Cusick, Matt, 3b	.260	154	14	40	8	0	0	12	2
DeVito, Nick, 1b	.214	14	0	3	0	1	0	3	0
Dorn, Danny, of	.222	99	10	22	6	0	0	11	2
Edmundson, Kelly, c	.156	122	9	19	4	0	3	14	0
Emanuele, Chris, of	.294	51	4	15	1	0	0	5	0
Fontaine, Chase, ss	.111	18	0	2	0	1	0	0	0
Horneman, Rob, dh	.000	3	0	0	0	1	0	0	0
Leclerc, Brian, of	.260	77	8	20	5	0	2	10	0
Lentz, Tommy, of	.243	152	15	37	5	1	1	14	9
Malone, Ryne, 3b/ss	.257	105	11	27	4	0	2	12	3
Morizio, Matt, c	.271	48	3	13	1	0	1	6	0
Oxendine, Matt, ss	.225	89	8	20	4	1	0	6	3
Reeves, Brian, c	.250	4	0	1	0	0	0	0	0
Rollins, Heath, of/1b	.218	78	10	17	2	1	0	2	5
Ruth, Keoni, 2b	.204	142	19	29	3	1	2	6	4
Sexton, Greg, 3b	.245	53	4	13	1	0	0	9	1
Turner, A.J., 2b	.286	7	0	2	0	0	0	0	0
Votay, Matt, dh	.000	1	0	0	0	0	0	0	0

PITCHING	W	L	ERA	G	SV	IP	H	BB	SO
Boike, Nolan	0	0	0.00	1	0	1	1	0	0
Donahue, Brian	1	1	6.14	9	1	15	13	9	11
Dryanski, Kevin	0	2	2.50	11	0	18	12	10	18
Ellis, Josh	1	0	4.15	2	0	9	7	4	9
Fairchild, Ricky	0	0	7.20	3	0	5	9	4	4
Honeycutt, Harris	1	3	4.43	12	0	43	43	11	37
Hovis, Jonathan	0	3	1.52	16	8	30	28	6	20
Lalor, Conor	1	4	5.44	8	0	45	57	10	29
Lambert, Casey	0	0	3.86	5	3	7	7	1	8
Lirette, Chase	0	1	2.70	8	0	13	16	7	20
Perez, Sergio	1	3	3.18	10	0	28	21	10	33
Rollins, Heath	5	2	2.55	9	0	49	39	17	40
Savage, Will	1	3	2.63	11	1	41	35	7	26
Turner, Ryan	2	2	4.78	11	0	32	32	23	15
Walters, P.J.	5	2	2.05	9	0	57	43	19	64

CHATHAM

BATTING	AVG	AB	R	H	2B	3B	HR	RBI	SB
Bussiere, Garrett, c	.221	95	4	21	4	0	2	7	1
Byrne, Brendan, 2b	.136	22	3	3	0	1	0	1	1
Coghlan, Chris, 3b	.346	130	19	45	5	0	2	22	3
Dempsey, Jacob, 1b/of	.272	114	17	31	6	0	3	17	1
Derba, Nick, c	.211	76	12	16	2	0	2	4	0
Farkes, Zak, 2b/of	.222	27	0	6	1	0	0	2	1
Frazier, Todd, ss	.270	148	17	40	6	5	5	27	9
Frost, Baron, of	.343	140	20	48	12	1	0	13	0
Hynick, Brandon, dh	.208	24	2	5	4	0	0	3	0
Longoria, Evan, 2b/ss	.299	164	25	49	7	1	8	35	6
Morris, Josh, 1b	.220	141	19	31	2	0	6	18	0
Ortiz, Adrian, of	.271	133	16	36	3	0	0	7	8
Presley, Alex, of	.341	129	25	44	3	0	1	11	4
Reza, Aaron, 2b	.260	77	11	20	3	0	0	2	1
Smith, Anthony, of	.149	74	6	11	2	0	3	6	0

PITCHING	W	L	ERA	G	SV	IP	H	BB	SO
Brown, Brooks	1	2	1.01	20	1	27	16	3	32
Cody, Chris	3	3	4.08	7	0	40	36	12	34
Danford, Matt	0	1	3.18	15	0	23	20	11	23
Huff, David	2	2	1.46	6	7	37	27	4	49
Hughes, Jared	7	0	1.62	8	0	50	37	11	54
Hynick, Brandon	0	3	7.36	7	0	18	24	5	13
Lutz, Derrick	0	0	0.00	19	12	25	13	3	59
McLaurin, Adam	0	0	0.00	3	0	4	2	2	1
Miller, Andrew	6	0	1.65	7	0	49	22	23	66
Richard, Steve	3	2	2.54	8	0	46	27	21	37
Santerre, Josh	1	1	1.56	9	1	17	12	8	8
Smith, Anthony	0	0	2.70	4	0	7	7	6	5
Woodard, Robert	5	1	2.53	8	0	46	42	4	26

COTUIT

BATTING	AVG	AB	R	H	2B	3B	HR	RBI	SB
Borbon, Julio, of	.205	88	13	18	2	2	0	4	4
Boyer, Brad, 2b	.291	134	16	39	8	1	2	18	6
Browning, Barret, c/1b	.000	1	1	0	0	0	0	0	0
Davison, Todd, 1b	.257	140	17	36	2	0	1	17	4
Donald, Jason, ss	.272	81	7	22	4	1	0	6	1
Ernst, Tim, of	.000	2	0	0	0	0	0	0	0
Gaston, Sean, c	.287	115	12	33	3	1	0	12	2
Harris, Bryan, 3b/1b	.247	158	16	39	4	0	4	27	2
Hollander, Michael, ss	.205	83	10	17	5	0	0	6	6
Jordan, Shane, of	.225	138	15	31	3	1	0	13	8
Lopez, Roberto, of	.237	93	6	22	4	0	0	8	1
Mariot, Lino, 2b	.192	26	6	5	0	0	0	2	4
Padron, J.P., 3b	.130	77	7	10	1	0	1	3	2
Posluszny, Stan, 1b	.286	14	2	4	0	0	0	0	2
Salem, Emeel, of	.229	166	26	38	5	1	0	13	15
Tarnow, Josh, of	.222	9	1	2	0	0	0	0	0
Thomas, Devin, c	.241	79	11	19	4	0	2	7	1

PITCHING	W	L	ERA	G	SV	IP	H	BB	SO
Albritton, Daniel	0	1	33.75	1	0	1	5	0	1
Blackmon, Charles	1	1	3.42	11	1	26	18	22	24
Browning, Barret	0	3	3.60	10	1	30	35	7	20
Culp, Nathan	2	2	2.51	9	0	43	30	13	31
Dirks, Clay	3	1	2.23	9	0	48	46	15	34
Hollander, Michael	0	0	0.00	2	0	2	1	2	2
Hudspeth, Casey	0	1	54.00	1	0	0	0	2	0
Johnson, Drew	0	0	13.50	1	0	2	7	1	0
Johnson, Josh	4	1	1.83	8	0	44	34	12	32
Ladd, Tim	2	1	4.45	12	0	28	30	17	24
Manship, Jeff	3	3	2.88	9	0	50	44	15	45
McCarter, Jake	0	0	3.72	4	0	10	7	5	7
Moskos, Daniel	3	4	3.82	15	1	33	30	15	31
Olvey, Derik	2	0	2.82	14	0	22	21	3	18
Parker, Taylor	0	0	9.50	13	0	18	22	16	19
Toneguzzi, Chris	2	1	2.05	22	8	26	16	4	31

FALMOUTH

BATTING	AVG	AB	R	H	2B	3B	HR	RBI	SB
Alexander, Greg, of	.293	41	6	12	3	0	0	1	1
Ambort, Mike, c	.255	51	6	13	2	0	1	7	0
Antonelli, Matt, 3b	.267	176	34	47	8	0	1	13	8
Bocock, Brian, ss	.163	153	14	25	4	1	3	12	12
Bowser, Brandon, of	.196	138	21	27	1	0	0	5	15
Christian, Paul, of	.000	15	0	0	0	0	0	0	0
Daguio, Brandon, of	.148	54	8	8	0	0	0	1	4
Ford, Shelby, 2b	.261	142	18	37	6	0	6	31	8
Friday, Brian, 2b	.178	90	8	16	2	1	1	10	4
Garza, Aaron, of	.194	62	6	12	1	0	1	7	0
Hamilton, Mark, 1b	.272	114	22	31	4	0	6	33	1
Huffman, Chad, of	.262	122	31	32	5	0	4	21	2
Kirkland, Chris, c	.125	8	0	1	0	0	0	0	0
McFadden, Warren, of	.232	99	11	23	3	0	1	12	1
Morgan, Sean, p	.061	33	0	2	0	0	0	0	2
Preziosi, David, 1b	.333	6	0	2	1	0	0	1	0

COLLEGE BASEBALL

Stephenson, Brad, c	.167	18	1	3	1	0	0	1	0
Still, Jon, c	.316	158	24	50	5	0	5	28	6

PITCHING	W	L	ERA	G	SV	IP	H	BB	SO
Buck, Dallas	2	3	3.86	5	0	33	24	7	38
Demel, Sam	2	2	4.46	11	0	34	31	16	45
Faris, Stephen	2	1	3.06	5	0	35	32	5	19
Kapala, Danny	0	4	6.36	8	1	47	53	15	47
Krawczyk, Chris	2	1	2.45	16	5	22	15	3	21
Macfarland, Steve	2	1	4.50	15	0	22	17	16	25
Merklinger, Daniel	0	1	11.42	4	0	9	10	7	11
Morgan, Sean	1	2	3.71	7	3	17	13	10	22
Norton, Tim	5	1	1.77	10	0	61	33	15	77
Preziosi, David	0	0	6.23	7	0	4	8	1	7
Risser, Travis	1	2	1.93	16	1	23	23	10	19
Sinkbeil, Brett	5	1	2.38	9	0	53	42	7	59
Wagner, Mike	0	2	6.61	15	0	31	39	9	41

HARWICH

BATTING	AVG	AB	R	H	2B	3B	HR	RBI	SB
Doolittle, Sean, 1b	.278	18	2	5	0	0	0	0	0
Dugger, Jake, of	.228	101	10	23	6	0	3	16	1
Durakis, Chad, c	.059	17	3	1	0	0	0	2	1
Emanuele, Chris, of	.312	154	16	48	7	1	2	16	9
Flack, Chad, 1b	.213	160	14	34	7	1	3	16	4
Hough, Joe, of	.193	83	10	16	5	0	1	6	0
Kubin, Jared, of	.000	14	0	0	0	0	0	0	0
Lalli, Blake, 1b	.133	30	3	4	1	0	0	2	0
Lowen, J.P., c	.138	58	6	8	1	0	4	8	0
Lyons, Coley, of	.000	2	0	0	0	0	0	0	0
McArthur, Brandon, 3b	.239	67	7	16	0	0	0	4	0
McDonald, Danny, p/dh	.375	8	4	3	0	0	0	0	0
Morizio, Matt, c	.277	119	10	33	3	0	2	16	2
Negrych, Jim, 2b	.224	143	26	32	6	2	6	21	10
Perschina, Joe, 1b	.242	95	8	23	6	1	0	11	2
Shelby, John, of	.177	79	9	14	3	0	1	6	5
Sidhu, Arman, ss	.222	126	12	28	6	0	2	9	2
Sizemore, Scott, 3b	.303	152	15	46	7	1	1	13	9
Wilhite, Jon, c	.235	17	1	4	2	0	0	3	0
Wyatt, Jonathan, of	.171	117	12	20	2	0	0	5	5

PITCHING	W	L	ERA	G	SV	IP	H	BB	SO
Bishop, Matt	0	0	0.00	4	0	7	4	5	5
Bresnehan, Pat	1	0	1.32	14	0	27	17	21	30
Crowell, Cody	1	6	4.23	18	2	28	23	12	28
Kontos, George	3	2	3.00	14	1	57	45	24	69
Lalli, Blake	0	0	9.00	3	0	3	5	0	4
Lincecum, Tim	2	2	0.69	19	7	39	14	11	68
McDonald, Danny	1	2	4.46	14	0	34	38	15	29
Mozingo, Harold	4	2	2.91	8	0	43	29	21	54
Mulvey, Kevin	3	3	2.73	11	0	53	39	25	53
Ottavino, Adam	2	2	1.76	10	0	51	46	14	54
Parker, Kyle	3	3	2.30	10	0	31	23	18	32
Sittig, Billy	1	1	3.60	10	1	20	26	7	16
Starnes, Nick	0	0	4.38	5	0	12	14	5	14

HYANNIS

BATTING	AVG	AB	R	H	2B	3B	HR	RBI	SB
Ames, Rodney, 1b	.067	15	0	1	0	0	0	0	0
Baxter, Mike, of	.261	92	11	24	4	1	0	4	3
Cassidy, Jim, of	.111	27	2	3	0	0	0	2	0
D'Alessio, Andy, 1b	.254	134	15	34	6	0	1	16	0
Dziuba, Teddy, c	.222	81	7	18	1	0	3	10	0
Feinberg, Alex, 2b	.224	125	11	28	2	0	0	4	4
Johnson, Chris, 3b	.182	143	13	26	3	0	0	7	2
Juhl, Brian, c	.133	15	0	2	0	0	0	0	0
Koski, Kevin, of	.235	115	11	27	6	0	0	5	5
Masters, Brandon, 2b	.123	73	3	9	3	0	0	5	2
McGonigle, Mark, of	.204	108	7	22	5	0	1	7	0
Miller, Jay, of	.212	146	8	31	2	0	0	8	2
Norrid, Kyle, 3b	.260	150	8	39	8	0	1	14	0
Paritz, Brandon, ss	.142	113	10	16	2	0	0	4	6
Tellam, Justin, c	.181	83	5	15	2	0	4	11	0

PITCHING	W	L	ERA	G	SV	IP	H	BB	SO
Alaniz, Adrian	0	4	5.49	4	0	20	20	10	18
Boone, Randy	0	0	0.00	1	0	3	1	0	2
Cassidy, Jim	0	1	7.36	3	0	7	6	5	3
Cline, Jason	0	2	5.58	13	0	31	38	14	27
Duke, Chris	1	0	3.08	18	0	26	22	12	19
Dunphy, Tim	0	3	6.75	5	0	20	28	3	6
Furbush, Charlie	1	5	5.40	12	0	50	54	25	55
Hargrove, Ricky	0	1	3.51	15	0	41	45	10	33
Ingoglia, Chris	1	0	2.08	2	0	4	3	4	5
Kennedy, Ryan	1	4	5.81	5	0	26	30	8	24
Koons, Mike	1	4	5.29	14	1	34	44	11	21
Latham, Daniel	1	0	2.55	15	4	18	12	3	20
Nery, Nathan	0	7	8.21	8	0	34	37	35	28
Perry, Stephen	0	0	1.69	4	0	16	13	7	12
Sauls, Mark	1	5	5.60	9	0	45	50	24	33

ORLEANS

BATTING	AVG	AB	R	H	2B	3B	HR	RBI	SB
Burriss, Emmanuel, 3b-ss	.286	182	28	52	4	0	0	7	37
Camp, Matt, of	.276	145	27	40	6	2	2	16	13
Curtis, Colin, of	.323	99	19	32	6	0	0	10	11
Dowling, Greg, 1b	.230	152	10	35	8	1	0	22	0
Jacobs, Jason, c	.186	97	9	18	2	0	1	10	4
Peacher, Brant, of	.056	18	2	1	0	0	0	0	0
Perry, Robert, of	.270	122	15	33	8	1	1	13	5
Pettit, Chris, of	.264	144	25	38	9	1	4	22	15
Pill, Brett, 1b	.198	116	17	23	4	1	6	23	1
Singleton, Steve, ss	.214	145	12	31	2	1	3	20	6
Sterk, Casey, of	.063	16	0	1	0	0	0	0	1
Ungricht, Brock, c	.171	70	7	12	1	0	0	5	2
Uribes, David, 2b	.282	149	27	42	1	1	0	13	16

PITCHING	W	L	ERA	G	SV	IP	H	BB	SO
Albritton, Daniel	2	1	2.16	17	2	33	26	10	38
Ballard, Mike	0	0	0.00	1	0	2	2	1	3
Chambliss, Tyler	0	1	5.14	4	0	7	6	4	8
Cook, Jacob	0	0	6.23	9	0	13	15	14	15
Coulon, David	2	3	2.33	10	1	39	25	21	38
DeYoung, Kyle	2	0	2.12	13	2	17	20	3	8
Evans, Dustin	2	2	2.27	7	0	36	27	13	30
Graham, Andy	4	2	1.65	8	0	44	30	23	38
Hyde, Lee	3	1	3.16	8	0	43	34	21	36
Jones, Hunter	0	0	0.00	8	0	11	4	1	16
Martin, Michael	1	1	12.46	3	0	4	6	3	6
Meyers, Brad	4	2	1.61	7	0	45	37	13	25
Rustich, Brant	2	0	1.71	13	1	26	22	5	24
Teaford, Everett	5	1	1.84	8	0	54	35	12	47
Wright, Steven	3	0	0.63	20	12	29	15	12	41

WAREHAM

BATTING	AVG	AB	R	H	2B	3B	HR	RBI	SB
Boggs, Austin, 3b	.188	144	11	27	8	1	2	13	1
Bramhall, Bobby, of	.273	11	0	3	1	0	0	0	0
Brashear, Justin, c	.179	28	5	5	0	0	3	7	0
Brown, Morgan, 2b	.067	15	0	1	0	0	0	0	0
Byrne, Brendan, dh	.000	6	0	0	0	0	0	0	0
Collins, Joel, c	.291	117	8	34	7	0	1	14	0
Copeland, Josh, 1b	.000	3	1	0	0	0	0	0	0
Dodson, Jordan, of	.257	136	19	35	12	0	1	15	6
Easley, Ed, 3b-c	.286	70	10	20	4	0	1	8	1
Fontaine, Chase, 2b	.218	119	8	26	4	1	1	20	2
Horton, Josh, ss	.214	42	4	9	0	0	0	1	3
Houser, Josh, of	.000	9	0	0	0	0	0	0	0
Kainer, Carson, of	.232	56	9	13	4	0	1	4	0
Mandel, Jeff, 1b	.167	6	1	1	0	0	0	0	0
McCallister, Michael, of	.130	131	17	17	7	0	2	14	3
Milano, Dan, c	.083	24	2	2	0	0	0	2	0
Payne, Danny, of	.226	31	2	7	0	0	0	2	4
Robbins, Whit, 1b	.260	131	22	34	7	1	5	15	1
Russo, Kevin, 2b/3b	.189	37	4	7	2	0	0	3	0
Salsgiver, Lance, of	.301	143	20	43	10	0	1	10	0
Sawyer, Marc, 1b	.115	52	5	6	1	0	0	3	0
Zawadzki, Lance, ss	.240	175	19	42	9	1	2	7	3

PITCHING	W	L	ERA	G	SV	IP	H	BB	SO
Bard, Daniel	3	3	1.25	10	0	65	42	20	82
Beno, Martin	0	1	2.13	7	1	13	17	5	12
Billings, Bruce	2	3	2.63	9	0	48	45	18	45
Bramhall, Bobby	1	0	3.77	17	0	29	28	13	29
Copeland, Josh	0	2	5.91	11	0	11	15	3	13
Furnish, Brad	1	2	3.34	6	0	32	27	16	28
Gale, Andy	0	1	11.12	3	0	6	6	3	5
Haviland, Shawn	0	0	6.92	13	0	26	30	13	19
Lalor, John	5	2	1.16	7	0	47	33	12	35
LeBlanc, Wade	3	3	3.05	8	0	41	41	15	42
Mandel, Jeff	3	3	3.38	9	0	37	44	12	25
Masterson, Justin	3	1	1.15	22	10	31	19	9	39
Sittig, Billy	0	0	2.61	5	1	10	9	2	11
Trent, Adam	0	0	0.00	1	0	1	0	0	2

YARMOUTH-DENNIS

BATTING	AVG	AB	R	H	2B	3B	HR	RBI	SB
Abruzzo, Jordan, c	.269	145	13	39	9	0	3	18	0
Berger, Eric, 1b	.083	12	0	1	0	0	0	1	0
Conlon, Keith, of	.000	2	0	0	0	0	0	0	0
Cunningham, Ryan, 1b/of	.143	7	1	1	0	0	0	1	0

	AVG	AB	R	H	2B	3B	HR	RBI	SB
Errecart, Chris, 1b	.303	99	17	30	5	1	6	22	1
Henry, Bryan, 1b/2b	.143	21	0	3	0	0	0	0	0
Hubbard, Austin, 2b	.143	14	2	2	0	0	1	1	0
Kaiser, Kody, of	.182	11	3	2	1	0	0	0	5
Kervin, Brian, 3b/2b	.194	139	15	27	6	0	1	15	5
Kindel, Jeff, of	.306	134	19	41	7	0	4	15	1
Larson, Eric, of	.227	22	6	5	1	0	1	4	3
Lehmann, Danny, c/1b	.225	120	11	27	4	0	2	14	1
Lopez, Greg, 3b	.600	5	0	3	0	0	0	0	0
Moresi, Nick, of	.209	139	14	29	2	1	2	8	5
Price, Ritchie, 2b	.250	24	6	6	1	1	0	1	0
Pruitt, Braedyn, 3b	.287	122	17	35	11	0	0	18	5
Rapoport, Jim, of	.162	148	21	24	2	0	0	11	18
Riley, Sean, 2b	.071	28	1	2	0	0	0	1	1
Turgeon, Joe, 2b/of	.263	38	4	10	5	0	1	4	0
Turner, Justin, ss	.260	154	21	40	6	0	3	20	7
Williams, Jackson, c	.244	45	4	11	3	0	0	2	0

PITCHING	W	L	ERA	G	SV	IP	H	BB	SO
Berger, Eric	2	0	0.48	6	3	19	8	5	21
Gustafson, Tim	3	1	2.11	11	1	47	28	11	44
Henry, Bryan	3	3	3.63	9	0	52	48	10	28
Holler, Blake	0	1	9.00	10	0	13	15	9	19
Land, Sean	3	1	3.55	10	0	33	24	18	39
Loree, Mike	0	0	0.00	1	0	1	1	0	0
McAnaney, Pat	1	4	5.51	8	0	33	51	6	26
McCutchen, Daniel	3	6	3.43	9	0	60	63	12	63
Morrow, Brandon	0	0	1.84	16	3	15	13	9	24
Rulon, Brad	1	0	5.61	13	3	26	40	5	24
Stutes, Mike	0	3	3.19	14	0	31	26	21	37
Williams, Jackson	0	0	0.00	1	0	0	0	0	0
Wood, Blake	4	4	3.34	9	0	57	51	19	57

ALASKA LEAGUE

	W	L	PCT	GB	OVERALL W	OVERALL L
*Alaska Goldpanners	28	6	.824	—	39	12
Mat-Su Miners	22	13	.629	6½	28	15
Kenai Peninsula Oilers	19	16	.543	9½	25	18
Anchorage Bucs	14	20	.412	14	20	23
Anchorage Glacier Pilots	11	22	.333	16½	14	28
Athletes In Action	8	25	.200	19½	12	25

* Qualified for National Baseball Congress World Series

ALL-STAR TEAM: C—Matt McBride, Mat-Su (Lehigh). **1B**—Matt Bransfield, Mat-Su (Notre Dame). **2B**—Nick Haley, Mat-Su (Louisville). **3B**—Josh Donaldson, Athletes In Action (Auburn). **SS**—Matt Vogel, Goldpanners (Lewis-Clark State). **OF**—Michael Taylor, Mat-Su (Stanford); Jimmy Van Ostrand, Anchorage Glacier Pilots (Cal Poly); Quinn Stewart, Goldpanners (Louisiana State). **DH**—Jerin Harper, Anchorage Bucs (Pacific). **UT**—Nick Kliebert, Kenai (Pepperdine). **SP**—Garet Hill, Alaska (Biola); Sung-Wei Tseng, Alaska (Taiwan); Alex Trafton, Mat-Su (California); Ty Davis, Kenai (Vanderbilt). **RP**—Josh McLaughlin, Mat-Su (Charleston).

Player of the Year: Matt Vogel, Goldpanners (Lewis-Clark State). **Coach of the Year:** Ed Cheff, Goldpanners.

TOP 10 PROSPECTS: **1.** Michael Taylor, of, Mat-Su (Stanford). **2.** Gary Daley, rhp, Anchorage Glacier Pilots (Cal Poly). **3.** Jimmy Van Ostrand, of, Anchorage Glacier Pilots (Cal Poly). **4.** Sung-Wei Tseng, rhp, Anchorage Bucs (Taiwan). **5.** Ty Davis, rhp, Kenai (Vanderbilt). **6.** Josh McLaughlin, rhp, Mat-Su (Charleston). **7.** Quinn Stewart, of, Goldpanners (Louisiana State). **8.** Danny Valencia, 3b, Anchorage Glacier Pilots (Miami). **9.** Matt Meyer, lhp, Kenai (Boston College). **10.** Josh Kahaulelio, ss, Kenai (Oral Roberts).

INDIVIDUAL BATTING LEADERS
(Minimum 100 Plate Appearances)

	AVG	AB	R	H	2B	3B	HR	RBI	SB
Van Ostrand, Jimmy, Pilots	.363	146	29	53	10	1	6	22	5
Vogel, Matt, Goldpanners	.343	169	25	58	8	1	0	25	5
Kahaulelio, Jake, Kenai	.335	158	27	53	11	1	4	27	5
Haley, Nick, Mat-Su	.329	155	29	51	4	0	0	11	11
Fuller, Justin, Goldpanners	.322	146	25	47	4	3	0	20	13
Taylor, Michael, Mat-Su	.317	145	20	46	6	1	4	25	25
Harper, Jerin, Bucs	.317	164	26	52	13	1	4	28	7
Kliebert, Nick, Kenai	.314	118	27	37	2	1	1	14	5
Bransfield, Matt, Mat-Su	.312	128	22	40	15	1	1	23	3
MacLean, Luke, AIA	.306	111	17	34	3	0	1	12	7
Linnenkohl, Brett, Bucs	.304	125	28	38	3	2	0	12	17
Corder, Jason, Bucs	.297	138	20	41	15	2	3	26	3
Matteucci, Jason, Bucs	.295	149	12	44	6	3	2	17	5
Walker, Brent, Pilots	.293	116	18	34	1	0	0	9	8
Thompson, Mark, Goldpanners	.292	113	25	33	0	0	0	10	12
Lane, Matt, Goldpanners	.291	141	22	41	9	0	2	24	0
Jones, Chris, Pilots	.286	91	11	26	4	2	0	11	0
Stewart, Quinn, Goldpanners	.284	134	28	38	5	3	8	34	2

INDIVIDUAL PITCHING LEADERS
(Minimum 30 innings)

	W	L	ERA	G	SV	IP	H	BB	SO
Hill, Garet, Goldpanners	5	1	0.73	7	1	49	41	6	31
Weilep, Austin, Goldpanners	4	2	1.02	10	2	44	42	14	31
Murphy, Brandon, Mat-Su	5	2	1.05	7	0	43	26	17	18
Romero, Ed, Goldpanners	5	1	1.17	9	0	46	42	21	30
Pellegrine, Dave, Kenai	4	3	1.66	10	0	38	25	21	21
Calicutt, Steven, Mat-Su	2	2	1.67	6	0	43	36	16	30
Daley, Gary, Pilots	3	4	1.69	10	1	53	35	28	51
Trafton, Alex, Mat-Su	5	1	1.72	9	0	37	23	11	25
Daman, Wayne, Mat-Su	4	0	1.85	6	0	39	24	7	22
Tseng, Sung-Wei, Bucs	3	1	2.06	10	2	57	42	12	38
Guerra, Steve, Bucs	4	2	2.09	6	0	43	35	8	16
Davis, Ty, Kenai	6	1	2.18	9	0	62	45	15	44
Wirth, Shannon, Goldpanners	4	1	2.20	8	0	45	35	8	46

ATLANTIC COLLEGIATE LEAGUE

WOLFF	W	L	PCT	GB
Quakertown Blazers	27	13	.675	—
Kutztown Rockies	25	15	.625	2
Jersey Pilots	24	16	.600	3
Lehigh Valley Catz	18	21	.462	8½
KAISER	**W**	**L**	**PCT**	**GB**
Metro New York Cadets	18	21	.462	—
Stamford Robins	18	22	.450	½
Long Island Collegians	18	22	.450	½
New York Generals	11	29	.275	7½

PLAYOFFS: **Quarterfinals**—Jersey defeated Kutztown and Long Island defeated Stamford in one-game qualifier. **Semifinals**—Quakertown defeated Jersey 2-0 and Metro New York defeated Long Island 2-0 in best-of-3 series. **Final**—Quakertown defeated Metro New York in one-game championship.

Most Valuable Player: Vin DiFazio, Quakertown (Indian River, Fla., CC). **Outstanding Pitcher**: Kyle Collina, rhp, Quakertown (Lehigh).

TOP 10 PROSPECTS: 1. Vin DiFazio, c, Quakertown (Indian River, Fla., CC). **2.** Kyle Collina, rhp, Quakertown (Lehigh). **3.** Brad Unger, rhp, Kutztown (Harvard). **4.** Ian Law, ss, Kutztown (Lafayette). **5.** Neil Malpass, of, Metro New York (Okaloosa-Walton, Fla., CC). **6.** Ryan Page, lhp, Lehigh Valley (Liberty). **7.** George Hudock, 1b/of, Quakertown (LaSalle). **8.** Brendan Murphy, 1b, Lehigh Valley (Southwest Tennessee CC). **9.** Adam Tsakonas, 3b, Quakertown (Delaware). **10.** Sean Heimpel, rhp, Quakertown (Gloucester County, N.J., CC).

INDIVIDUAL BATTING LEADERS
(Minimum 100 Plate Appearances)

	AVG	AB	R	H	2B	3B	HR	RBI	SB
Hudock, George, Quakertown	.378	111	23	42	10	4	5	30	1
Law, Ian, Kutztown	.368	144	38	53	18	3	3	27	13
Rath, Brian, Long Island	.365	126	31	46	11	4	1	22	6
Bet, Nick, Kutztown	.361	122	21	44	11	0	3	26	11
Smith, Andrew, Quakertown	.356	87	31	31	9	1	3	15	13
Geiger, Matt, Lehigh Valley	.336	107	23	36	8	1	2	20	4
Tsakonas, Adam, Quakertown	.336	119	30	40	5	1	3	26	4
Richard, Aaron, Stamford	.333	129	23	43	13	0	2	16	4
DiFazio, Vin, Quakertown	.331	142	33	47	17	4	3	42	1
Johnson, Dave, Long Island	.330	115	19	38	2	1	0	15	7
Anderson, Doug, Jersey	.325	126	23	41	6	2	1	18	4
Schatzow, Perry, Stamford	.308	133	18	41	4	2	1	21	1
Malpass, Neil, Metro New York	.303	109	17	33	4	3	3	22	9
Godusky, Matt, Quakertown	.301	123	12	37	9	0	0	21	0
Sandt, Adam, Kutztown	.294	126	19	37	7	3	1	9	6

INDIVIDUAL PITCHING LEADERS
(Minimum 30 Innings)

	W	L	ERA	G	SV	IP	H	BB	SO
Mendez, Jairo, Jersey	7	0	0.68	10	0	53	33	7	39
Nall, Brandon, Kutztown	3	1	0.84	5	0	37	13	14	44
Forbes, Robert, Jersey	5	3	1.59	11	0	51	34	17	52
Walentin, Josef, New York	4	3	1.76	11	1	46	34	21	40
Collina, Kyle, Quakertown	5	0	1.99	11	1	41	36	8	46
Smith, Alec, Metro New York	3	3	2.24	9	0	56	45	22	48
Rentro, Kiel, Lehigh Valley	2	4	2.43	7	0	33	22	19	24
Heimpel, Sean, Quakertown	4	1	2.47	11	1	44	34	15	33
Page, Ryan, Lehigh Valley	6	1	2.73	8	0	56	49	18	61
Gerber, Ryan, Quakertown	4	2	2.76	13	2	46	35	23	38

CAL RIPKEN SR. LEAGUE

	W	L	PCT	GB
Bethesda Big Train	25	15	.625	—
Maryland Orioles	24	16	.600	1

Rockville Express	19	20	.487	5½
Silver Spring-Takoma Thunderbolts	18	19	.486	5½
College Park Bombers	17	23	.425	8
Maryland Redbirds	14	24	.368	10

PLAYOFFS: Bethesda and Silver Spring-Takoma declared co-champions of six-team, double-elimination tournament.

ALL-STAR TEAM: C—Preston Pehrson, Orioles (Texas). **1B**—Justin McClanahan, Silver Spring-Takoma (Northwest Shoals, Ala., CC) **2B**—Greg Lemon, Bethesda (Salisbury, Md.). **3B**—Bryan Thomas, Bethesda (Virginia Tech). **SS**— Steve Clevenger, Orioles (Texas). **OF**—Jonnie Knoble, Bethesda (San Francisco); Andrew Greene, Silver Spring-Takoma (Furman); Andrew Rodgers, Orioles (Alabama). **DH**—R.J. Brown, Rockville (UC Irvine). **UT**—Jeremy Farrell, Orioles (Virginia); Mike Santmyer, Redbirds (Towson). **P**—Bernard Robert, Orioles (Alabama); Brett Cecil, Silver Spring-Takoma (Maryland); Zach Clark, Silver Spring-Takoma (Maryland-Baltimore County).

Most Valuable Player: Justin McClanahan, Silver Spring-Takoma. **Most Outstanding Pitcher:** Bernard Robert, Orioles.

TOP 10 PROSPECTS: **1.** Brett Cecil, lhp, Silver-Spring Takoma (Maryland). **2.** Jeremy Farrell, inf, Orioles (Virginia). **3.** Neal Davis, lhp, Orioles (Catonsville, Md., HS). **4.** Adam Olbrychowski, rhp, Rockville (Pepperdine). **5.** Bernard Robert, rhp, Orioles (Alabama). **6.** Andrew Rodgers, of, Orioles (Alabama). **7.** Mike Santmyer, rhp, Redbirds (Towson). **8.** Preston Pehrson, c, Orioles (Texas). **9.** Steve Clevenger, ss, Orioles (Texas). **10.** Seth Overby, rhp, College Park (Maryland).

INDIVIDUAL BATTING LEADERS

(Minimum 100 Plate Appearances)

	AVG	AB	R	H	2B	3B	HR	RBI	SB
Brown, R.J., Rockville	.366	93	16	34	9	0	2	17	2
McClanahan, Justin, SS-Takoma	.360	136	26	39	11	4	1	29	15
Amers, Tyler, MD Redbirds	.347	101	13	35	4	1	0	11	12
Greene, Andrew, SS-Takoma	.342	149	30	51	6	0	0	8	31
Lemon, Greg, Bethesda	.336	143	28	48	7	1	0	15	7
Germano, Jeff, College Park	.313	96	11	30	6	1	1	16	6
Pehrson, Preston, Orioles	.311	122	16	38	3	0	0	11	2
Nutt, Jeff, Orioles	.311	119	18	37	5	0	3	28	2
Edgecombe, Matt, Rockville	.298	121	12	36	4	1	0	19	1
Farrell, Jeremy, Orioles	.290	100	15	29	6	2	3	11	2
Rodgers, Andrew, Orioles	.289	121	20	35	8	3	1	26	1
Teller, Rhett, Bethesda	.288	125	19	36	6	1	1	20	1
Seymour, Jud, College Park	.287	108	10	31	3	0	2	12	2
Smith, Andrew, Bethesda	.284	134	19	38	6	0	0	20	10
Knoble, Jonnie, Bethesda	.276	156	28	43	6	1	0	12	21

INDIVIDUAL PITCHING LEADERS

(Minimum 30 innings)

	W	L	ERA	G	SV	IP	H	BB	SO
Clark, Zach, SS-Takoma	7	1	0.67	8	0	54	43	14	23
Robert, Bernard, Orioles	6	0	0.68	7	1	40	20	15	29
Brown, Josh, Orioles	2	0	1.22	14	0	37	23	19	18
Cecil, Brett, SS-Takoma	3	4	1.27	8	1	50	33	10	52
Lowe, Ron, Bethesda	3	3	1.39	8	0	52	35	13	47
Olbrychowski, Adam, Rockville	4	2	1.45	9	0	43	26	15	31
Caldwell, Derek, Bethesda	4	1	1.48	8	0	43	22	26	22
Pease, Dustin, Bethesda	4	3	1.71	8	0	58	47	15	43
Overbey, Seth, College Park	5	3	1.86	8	0	48	39	15	44
Kerfoot, Chad, Orioles	5	2	1.99	7	0	45	42	6	24

CENTRAL ILLINOIS COLLEGIATE LEAGUE

	W	L	PCT	GB
Danville Dans	34	10	.773	—
East Peoria Scrappers	29	15	.659	5
Quincy Gems	28	16	.636	6
Dubois County Bombers	27	17	.614	7
DuPage County Dragons	22	22	.500	12
Twin City Stars	19	25	.432	15
Springfield Rifles	9	35	.205	25
Galesburg Pioneers	8	36	.182	26

PLAYOFFS: Semifinals—Dubois County defeated Danville 2-0 and Quincy defeated East Peoria 2-1 in best-of-3 series. **Final**—Quincy defeated Dubois County 2-0 in best-of-3 series.

ALL-STAR TEAM: C—Nick Smith, Dubois County (Grand Valley State, Mich.). **1B**—Pat Tumilty, Quincy (Evansville). **IF**—Ryan Curry, East Peoria (Bradley); C.J. Webb, East Peoria (Ball State); Mike Murray, Dubois County (Memphis); Brian Dinkelman, Twin City (McKendree, Ill.); Mitch Hilligoss, Quincy (Purdue); Chuck Sindlinger, Danville (Long Beach State). **OF**—Ryan Basham, Dubois County (Michigan State); Jeff Darnall, East Peoria (SIU-Edwardsville); Shane Elenz, East Peoria (Maple Woods, Mo., CC); Steven Scott, Galesburg (Lynchburg, Va.); Ross McCoy, Twin City (Wisconsin-Milwaukee); Jay Molina, Quincy (Illinois State); Mitch Moreland, Danville (Mississippi State); Nathan Emrick, Quincy (Southern Illinois). **UT**—Blaine Cravens, Springfield (Lincoln Land, Ill., CC). **SP**—Ryan Bird, Danville (Louisiana State); Dallas Sims, East Peoria (Lincoln Trail, Ill., CC); Grant Payton, Danville (Grand Valley State, Mich.); Dan Sattler, Danville (Purdue); Kyle Jones, Dubois County (SIU-Edwardsville); Corey Lewis, Dubois County (Rend Lake, Ill., CC); Miles Morgan, DuPage County (Texas Tech); Omar Arif, DuPage County (Texas Christian); Wes Roemer, Danville (Cal State Fullerton). **RP**—David Fields, Galesburg (John Wood, Ill., CC); Chad Crosswhite, Danville (Mississippi State); Aaron Hines, East Peoria (Oakland); Mitch Moreland, Danville (Mississippi State); Craig Reynolds, Twin City (Adrian, Mich.), Bobby Mahon, Quincy (Western Illinois).

Most Valuable Player: Ryan Basham, Dubois County. **Pitcher of the Year**: Ryan Byrd, Danville.

TOP 10 PROSPECTS: 1. Miles Morgan, rhp, DuPage County (Texas Tech). **2.** Mitch Moreland, lhp/1b, Danville (Mississippi State). **3.** Ryan Basham, of, DuBois County (Michigan State). **4.** Mike Murray, ss, DuBois County (Memphis). **5.** Javier Martinez, rhp, DuBois County (Fordham). **6.** Wes Roemer, rhp, Danville (Cal State Fullerton). **7.** Mitch Hilligoss, ss, Quincy (Purdue). **8.** Ryan Dinkelman, ss, Twin City (McKendree, Ill.). **9.** Justin Snyder, of, Danville (San Diego). **10.** Omar Arif, lhp, DuPage County (Texas Christian).

INDIVIDUAL BATTING LEADERS

(Minimum 100 Plate Appearances)

	AVG	AB	R	H	2B	3B	HR	RBI	SB
Basham, Ryan, Dubois County	.409	171	34	70	18	2	6	46	2
Dinkelman, Brian, Twin City	.382	170	32	65	12	6	3	28	11
Murray, Mike, Dubois County	.377	167	32	63	16	1	2	33	4
Cravens, Blaine, Springfield	.357	115	15	41	7	0	0	21	7
Hilligoss, Mitch, Quincy	.342	190	43	65	15	2	5	43	21
Darnall, Jeff, East Peoria	.341	173	25	59	11	1	1	33	5
Webb, C.J., East Peoria	.341	176	39	60	11	1	2	38	9
Elenz, Shane, East Peoria	.333	150	39	50	10	1	8	26	7
McCoy, Ross, Twin City	.331	163	25	54	11	2	2	21	8
Scott, Steven, Galesburg	.329	149	16	49	10	0	2	21	13
Curry, Ryan, East Peoria	.324	179	31	58	11	2	8	41	9
Tumilty, Pat, Quincy	.324	176	31	57	10	1	7	30	6
Moreland, Mitch, Danville	.318	132	27	42	6	1	2	27	0
Molina, Jay, Quincy	.315	168	32	53	9	1	4	41	4
Smith, Nick, Dubois County	.308	146	34	45	8	2	0	22	12

INDIVIDUAL PITCHING LEADERS

(Minimum 40 Innings)

	W	L	ERA	G	SV	IP	H	BB	SO
Arif, Omar, DuPage County	3	0	1.10	7	0	41	31	10	34
Byrd, Ryan, Danville	5	1	1.91	8	0	47	35	15	32
Sims, Dallas, E. Peoria	4	1	2.09	9	0	65	42	16	65
Payton, Grant, Danville	3	2	2.10	9	0	56	48	22	41
Sattler, Dan, Danville	5	0	2.20	9	0	49	39	17	51
Jones, Kyle, Dubois	4	1	2.29	9	0	55	39	22	52
Lewis, Corey, Dubois	5	3	2.52	12	0	61	45	29	43
Morgan, Miles, DuPage	5	3	2.84	10	0	70	56	14	70
Smid, Tim, Quincy	3	1	3.00	9	0	51	34	38	34
Combs, Brant, Dubois	2	2	3.12	11	0	58	55	19	28

CLARK GRIFFITH LEAGUE

	W	L	PCT	GB
*Vienna Senators	29	11	.725	—
Fauquier Gators	22	18	.550	7
+Herndon Braves	21	19	.525	8
Fairfax Nationals	17	23	.425	12
Reston Hawks	11	29	.275	18

* First-half champion.+ Second-half champion.

PLAYOFFS: Herndon defeated Vienna 3-2 in a best-of-5 series.

Most Valuable Player: Kellen Kulbacki, of, Herndon (James Madison). **Most Outstanding Pitcher:** Bubba Blalock, rhp, Fauquier (Kennesaw State, Ga.).

TOP 10 PROSPECTS: **1.** Scott Maine, lhp, Herndon (Miami). **2.** Guillermo Martinez, ss, Vienna (South Alabama). **3.** Kellen Kulbacki, of, Herndon (James Madison). **4.** Mike Bianucci, 3b, Reston (Auburn). **5.** David Cline, of, Vienna (Pittsburgh). **6.** Bubba Blalock, rhp, Fauquier (Kennesaw State, Ga.). **7.** Stephen Barnes, rhp, Vienna (Lake City, Fla., CC). **8.** Wes Schirtzinger, of, Vienna (Ohio State). **9.** Leighton Autrey, of, Vienna (UT Pan American). **10.** Ricky Owens, 3b, Fauquier (Belhaven, Miss.).

INDIVIDUAL BATTING LEADERS

(Minimum 100 Plate Appearances)

	AVG	AB	R	H	2B	3B	HR	RBI	SB
Ullrich, Louis, Reston	.392	130	24	51	14	3	4	31	9
Kulbacki, Kellen, Herndon	.367	166	32	61	20	2	6	41	7
Mitchell, Ryan, Fairfax	.353	133	22	47	10	2	4	27	1
Lamonda, A.J., Vienna	.350	117	16	41	10	2	2	29	5
Martinez, Guillermo, Vienna	.347	124	21	43	5	2	3	21	14
Bianucci, Mike, Reston	.347	101	28	35	7	1	12	31	5

	AVG	AB	R	H	2B	3B	HR	RBI	SB
Brown, Donald, Vienna	.331	124	25	41	9	1	1	19	7
Bunkis, Justin, Vienna	.324	145	21	47	9	0	5	28	1
Warren, Max, Fairfax	.301	103	14	31	1	1	0	6	10
Hacker, Matt, Herndon	.296	162	28	48	8	0	4	28	6
LaFrance, Ricky, Herndon	.293	147	25	43	5	0	2	18	6
Owens, Ricky, Fauquier	.293	147	21	43	8	0	8	30	6
Todd, Steve, Reston	.287	122	12	35	7	0	1	6	3
Schirtzinger, Wes, Vienna	.284	102	19	29	4	1	1	13	10
Bour, Jason, Fairfax	.283	113	16	32	6	0	4	19	0

INDIVIDUAL PITCHING LEADERS

(Minimum 30 innings)

	W	L	ERA	G	SV	IP	H	BB	SO
Riggs, Jeremy, Fauquier	3	1	1.40	14	0	39	34	9	31
Blalock, Bubba, Fauquier	3	2	1.45	9	0	62	46	9	63
Tinsley, Billy, Vienna	6	1	2.06	13	2	57	48	13	52
Barton, Caleb, Vienna	5	0	2.43	8	1	56	35	13	46
Holland, Greg, Vienna	4	0	2.73	10	0	56	37	18	55
Rembold, Brett, Herndon	2	1	2.76	24	0	46	37	12	48
Hall, Hunter, Vienna	4	2	2.77	11	2	49	44	15	32
Ferguson, Justin, Fauquier	3	2	2.95	9	0	61	24	23	38
Tomlin, Andrew, Herndon	3	2	3.11	9	0	38	15	3	41
Tracy, Nick, Fairfax	3	2	3.30	12	1	30	31	7	33

COASTAL PLAIN LEAGUE

NORTH	W	L	PCT	GB
+*Edenton Steamers	34	19	.642	—
Petersburg Generals	26	29	.473	9
Outer Banks Daredevils	23	32	.418	12
Peninsula Pilots	23	32	.418	12
SOUTH	**W**	**L**	**PCT**	**GB**
+Fayetteville SwampDogs	33	21	.611	—
*Florence RedWolves	30	26	.536	4
Wilmington Sharks	28	26	.519	5
*Wilson Tobs	27	29	.482	7
New Bern River Rats	23	33	.411	11
WEST	**W**	**L**	**PCT**	**GB**
Spartanburg Stingers	31	23	.574	—
+Thomasville Hi-Toms	30	25	.545	1½
*Gastonia Grizzlies	28	24	.538	2
Asheboro Copperheads	25	30	.455	6½
Martinsville Mustangs	22	34	.393	10

+First-half champion. *Second-half champion

PETTIT CUP TOURNAMENT: Edenton (4-0) defeated Florence (3-2) in championship game of eight-team tournament.

Player of the Year: Mike Chambers, ss, Petersburg (Franklin Pierce, N.H.). **Pitcher of the Year**: Ryan Brandt, rhp, Fayetteville (Methodist, N.C.). **Coach of the Year:** Darrell Handelsman, Fayetteville.

TOP 10 PROSPECTS: 1. Wynn Pelzer, rhp, Wilmington (South Carolina). **2.** John Raynor, of, Wilmington (UNC Wilmington). **3.** Matt Spencer, 1b, Asheboro (North Carolina). **4.** Michael Rutledge, 3b, Outer Banks (Mississippi State). **5.** David Wood, lhp/of, New Bern (Texas State). **6.** Chris Campbell, 2b, Florence (College of Charleston). **7.** Josh Horton, ss, Wilmington (North Carolina). **8.** Seth Williams, of, Asheboro (North Carolina). **9.** Nick Schumacher, rhp, Asheboro (Wayne State, Mich.). **10.** David Qualben, lhp, Wilson (Pace).

INDIVIDUAL BATTING LEADERS

(Minimum 100 Plate Appearances)

	AVG	AB	R	H	2B	3B	HR	RBI	SB
Chambers, Mike, Petersburg	.337	187	26	63	15	0	5	28	13
Erdman, Nicholas, Peninsula	.331	142	23	47	6	3	0	23	12
Campbell, Chris, Florence	.325	123	15	40	6	0	1	18	3
Roof, Shawn, Fayetteville	.315	149	24	47	2	0	0	18	15
Gallagher, Jim, Peninsula	.313	144	17	45	10	2	0	21	6
Rose, Eric, Edenton	.312	128	21	40	3	0	0	11	23
Swauger, Chris, Florence	.311	167	23	52	7	0	1	13	2
Kane, Ryan, Wilson	.311	122	14	38	8	3	0	9	2
Strickland, Bucky, Edenton	.305	95	11	29	4	0	0	21	3
Wood, David, New Bern	.304	161	21	49	9	0	6	27	7
Matulia, Matt, Peninsula	.303	188	24	57	11	3	3	30	8
Dirks, Andy, Fayetteville	.301	166	30	50	7	0	0	12	34
Reynolds, Kevin, Edenton	.301	176	32	53	12	1	3	32	30
Goetz, Mike, Martinsville	.301	206	19	62	3	0	0	15	21
Williams, Seth, Asheboro	.299	167	31	50	9	0	4	19	14
Steedly, Spencer, Wilson	.298	198	28	59	8	1	4	33	10
Spencer, Matt, Asheboro	.297	148	25	44	14	1	5	33	12
Crisp, Andrew, Gastonia	.294	102	12	30	6	0	0	7	3

INDIVIDUAL PITCHING LEADERS

(Minimum 40 Innings)

	W	L	ERA	G	SV	IP	H	BB	SO
Schumaker, Nick, Asheboro	4	2	0.56	7	0	48	30	16	31
Brandt, Ryan, Fayetteville	7	2	0.80	12	0	68	45	11	66
Qualben, David, Wilson	7	2	1.02	14	1	80	46	33	82
DeRatt, Alan, Asheboro	2	2	1.21	12	0	67	64	12	42
Pupo, Koji, Fayetteville	2	1	1.23	7	0	44	29	11	29
Thompson, Phillip, Thomasville	0	3	1.27	30	7	43	29	13	29
Smith, Matt, Gastonia	2	3	1.30	15	0	69	54	19	43
Wood, David, New Bern	4	5	1.31	10	0	62	35	21	55
Teague, Matt, Gastonia	7	4	1.34	14	0	74	61	20	28
Hatcher, Jeff, Asheboro	6	3	1.36	23	4	46	27	14	40
Beverly, Forrest, Florence	6	1	1.40	10	0	58	46	25	40
Artz, Stephen, Martinsville	4	4	1.47	11	0	80	73	13	53

GREAT LAKES LEAGUE

	W	L	PCT	GM
Columbus All-Americans	30	12	.714	—
Stark County Terriers	24	18	.571	6
Lima Locos	21	18	.538	7½
Delaware Cows	21	20	.512	8½
Lake Erie Monarchs	21	20	.512	8½
Grand Lake Mariners	20	21	.488	9½
Southern Ohio Copperheads	17	25	.405	13
Indianapolis Servants	10	30	.250	19

PLAYOFFS: Stark County (4-1) defeated Columbus (3-2) in championship game of six-team, double elimination tournament.

ALL-STAR TEAM: C—Josh Stewart, Lake Erie (Bowling Green). **1B**—Charlie Yarbrough, Columbus (Longwood, Va.). **2B**—Jason Zoeller, Delaware (Ohio State). **3B**—Mark Abro, Lima (Kennesaw State, Ga.); Ronnie Bourquin, Stark County (Ohio State). **SS**—Ryan Perry, Lima (Western Michigan). **OF**—Joe Tucker, Stark County (Kent State); Alan Cattrysse, Columbus (Michigan State); Josh Doane, Indianapolis (High Point); R.C. Dickerson, Lima (Western Michigan). **DH**—Marcus Geiselman, Stark County (Akron); Bryan Chandler, Lima (Western Michigan). **UT**—Ben Gaal, Grand Lake (LeMoyne); Eric Fryer, Columbus (Ohio State). **P**—Derek Witt, Columbus (Ohio); Luke Trubee, Delaware (Dayton); Dan DeLucia, Delaware (Ohio State); Luke Behning, Indianapolis (Ball State); Cameron Betourne, Stark County (Vanderbilt); Chad Wagler, Stark County (Kent State). **RP**—Ben Taylor, Columbus (Goshen); RIchie Fralick, Southern Ohio (Ball State).

Player of the Year: Charlie Yarbrough, Columbus. **Pitcher of the Year**: Derek Witt, Columbus.

TOP 10 PROSPECTS: **1.** Ben Snyder, lhp, Columbus (Ball State). **2.** Josh Stewart, c, Lake Erie (Bowling Green State). **3.** Charlie Yarbrough, 1b, Columbus (Longwood). **4.** Joe Tucker, of, Stark County (Kent State). **5.** Chad Wagler, rhp, Stark County (Kent State). **6.** Tom Farmer, rhp, Columbus (Akron). **7.** Derek Witt, rhp, Columbus (Ohio). **8.** Luke Behning, rhp, Indianapolis (Ball State). **9.** Eric Fryer, c, Columbus (Ohio State). **10.** Alan Cattrysse, of, Columbus (Michigan State).

INDIVIDUAL BATTING LEADERS

(Minimum 100 Plate Appearances)

	AVG	AB	R	H	2B	3B	HR	RBI	SB
Doane, Josh, Indianapolis	.398	98	12	39	4	2	2	20	7
Webb, Daniel, Delaware	.369	103	26	38	5	1	1	7	3
Tucker, Joe, Stark County	.340	144	35	49	6	0	1	10	20
Abro, Mark, Lima	.336	146	27	49	8	0	4	17	8
Getty, Bobby, Delaware	.333	87	5	29	8	0	0	17	2
Yarbrough, Charlie, Columbus	.330	109	21	36	7	0	10	26	0
Bourquin, Ronnie, Stark County	.330	100	25	33	8	0	2	18	10
Stewart, Josh, Lake Erie	.329	143	23	47	3	1	1	15	21
Chandler, Bryan, Lima	.319	141	22	45	8	0	4	26	1
Dickerson, R.C., Lima	.318	107	28	34	7	0	4	18	23
Peisel, Ryan, Southern Ohio	.316	98	15	31	5	2	1	14	6
Moffett, Matt, Lake Erie	.315	111	18	35	5	0	1	9	1
Boley, Sean, Lima	.311	90	6	28	4	0	0	9	0
Fryer, Eric, Columbus	.305	105	21	32	2	1	2	15	3
Caipen, Brandon, Stark County	.304	112	12	34	4	0	1	13	6

INDIVIDUAL PITCHING LEADERS

(Minimum 30 innings)

	W	L	ERA	G	SV	IP	H	BB	SO
Behning, Luke, Indianapolis	3	3	0.86	8	1	42	33	15	40
Witt, Derek, Columbus	5	1	0.89	7	0	41	19	41	39
O'Brien, Dan, Columbus	3	1	1.24	8	0	36	28	7	37
DeLucia, Dan, Delaware	3	1	1.54	7	1	35	27	7	29
Rasmussen, Mark, Lake Erie	4	1	1.95	5	0	37	25	4	33
Betourne, Cameron, Stark	6	2	2.23	8	0	48	38	11	50
Lierseman, Ross, Grand Lake	1	5	2.25	6	0	44	48	8	29
Faiola, Josh, Columbus	2	2	2.27	8	0	32	22	10	39
Trubee, Luke, Delaware	5	0	2.28	9	1	47	51	10	33
Burks, Adam, Lima	5	2	2.29	7	2	39	30	6	29
Puskar, Dallas, Southern Ohio	2	5	2.29	11	0	59	60	15	35

JAYHAWK LEAGUE

	W	L	PCT	GB
*Hays Larks	27	12	.692	—

	W	L	PCT	GB
*El Dorado Broncos	24	14	.632	2½
Liberal BeeJays	19	21	.475	8½
*Nevada Griffons	17	23	.425	10½
*Wichita Twins	15	23	.395	11½
Joplin Slashers	15	24	.285	12

* Qualified for National Baseball Congress World Series

TOP 10 PROSPECTS: **1.** Aaron Breit, rhp, Hays (Garden City, Kan., CC). **2.** Jeff Soulages, rhp, Liberal (Cal State Fullerton). **3.** Bryan Lee, rhp, Wichita (Cuesta, Calif., CC). **4.** Miles Durham, of, El Dorado (Northwestern State). **5.** Seth Fortenberry, of, Hays (Baylor). **6.** Chris Johnson, rhp, Wichita (John A. Logan, Ill., CC). **7.** Derek Schermerhorn, 3b, El Dorado (Wichita State). **8.** John Christian, rhp, Nevada (Centenary). **9.** Jared Goedert, 1b/3b, Hays (Kansas State). **10.** Brad Miller, ss, El Dorado (Wichita State).

INDIVIDUAL BATTING LEADERS

(Minimum 100 Plate Appearances)

	AVG	AB	R	H	2B	3B	HR	RBI	SB
Bryant, Tommy, Wichita	.355	121	20	43	11	0	4	24	5
Seawell, Ryan, Liberal	.349	129	21	45	8	0	6	26	3
Diggs, Wyn, Liberal	.339	124	21	42	8	0	3	15	2
Pullin, Bryan, Hays	.336	152	27	51	11	0	1	24	8
Sharp, Billy, Hays	.336	137	29	46	8	2	1	14	11
Durham, Miles, El Dorado	.333	102	23	34	7	1	2	26	18
Jones, Rusty, El Dorado	.333	99	23	33	6	0	2	20	7
Taylor, Chris, Nevada	.331	118	20	39	11	0	4	13	1
Wasserman, Tyler, Hays	.330	112	28	37	5	0	3	14	1
Krum, Austin, Wichita	.319	141	31	45	9	0	5	17	11
Hernandez, Keith, Hays	.317	139	31	44	8	0	5	31	8
Farris, Eric, El Dorado	.316	117	22	37	5	2	1	23	14
Santiago, Tim, Nevada	.309	94	20	29	7	1	8	21	3
Milauskas, Adam, Joplin	.305	118	22	36	11	0	2	18	2
Lawson, Eric, Hays	.304	138	38	42	15	1	6	26	4

INDIVIDUAL PITCHING LEADERS

(Minimum 25 Innings)

	W	L	ERA	G	SV	IP	H	BB	SO
Soulages, Jeff, Liberal	6	0	1.65	12	4	27	19	13	31
Johnson, Chris, Wichita	2	1	2.15	5	0	29	17	8	26
Alsup, Andrew, Liberal	4	1	2.45	12	0	26	19	4	21
Hunton, Brock, Wichita	3	2	2.51	6	0	29	25	13	35
Fritsche, Josh, Joplin	4	2	2.56	7	0	46	48	23	40
Guntz, Joe, El Dorado	3	0	2.70	7	0	27	19	9	19
Brownell, John, El Dorado	6	2	2.87	9	0	53	43	15	45
Jones, Rusty, El Dorado	2	2	3.16	5	0	26	23	10	19
Regan, Moran, Joplin	3	3	4.04	7	0	36	42	19	24
Benson, Trevor, Wichita	1	3	4.07	7	0	42	49	9	22

NEW ENGLAND COLLEGIATE LEAGUE

NORTH	W	L	PCT	GB
Keene Swamp Bats	30	12	.714	—
Holyoke Giants	23	18	.561	6½
Vermont Mountaineers	23	19	.548	7
Sanford Mainers	23	19	.548	7
Concord Quarry Dogs	20	22	.476	10
Mill City All-Americans	15	27	.357	15
SOUTH	**W**	**L**	**PCT**	**GB**
Newport Gulls	25	16	.610	—
Manchester Silkworms	22	20	.524	3½
North Adams SteepleCats	20	22	.476	5½
Danbury Westerners	20	22	.476	5½
Torrington Twisters	19	23	.452	6½
Pittsfield Dukes	11	31	.262	14½

PLAYOFFS: Quarterfinals—Keene defeated Sanford 2-0, Vermont defeated Holyoke 2-0, North Adams defeated Manchester 2-1, and Newport defeated Danbury 2-0 in best-of-3 series. **Semifinals**—Vermont defeated Keene 2-1 and Newport defeated North Adams 2-0 in best-of-3 series. **Final**—Newport defeated Vermont 2-0 in best-of-3 series.

ALL-STAR TEAM: **C**—Matt McGraw, Holyoke (Maine). **1B**—Matt Rizzotti, Vermont (Manhattan). **2B**—Tucker Frawley, Concord (Holy Cross). **3B**—Andrew Davis, Keene (Kent State). **SS**—Garrett Olson, Keene (Franklin Pierce, N.H.). **OF**—Cyle Hankerd, Newport (Southern California); Travis Musolf, Sanford (Marist); Steffan Wilson, Torrington (Harvard). **DH**—John Fitzpatrick, Manchester (Manhattan). **P**—Mickey Westphal, Holyoke (Georgia); Josh Fields, Keene (Georgia); Troy Martin, Keene (Maine).

Most Valuable Player: Cyle Hankerd, Newport. **Most Outstanding Pitcher:** Troy Martin, rhp, Keene. **Manager of the Year:** John Russo, Vermont.

TOP 10 PROSPECTS: **1.** Cyle Hankerd, of, Newport (Southern California). **2.** Josh Fields, rhp, Keene (Georgia). **3.** Ryan Reid, rhp, Sanford (James Madison). **4.** Cory Riordan, rhp, Danbury (Fordham). **5.** Matt Rizzotti, 1b, Vermont (Manhattan). **6.** Will Bashelor, of, Concord (Dartmouth). **7.** Andres Perez, of/inf, Torrington (Stony Brook). **8.** Terry Doyle, rhp, Pittsfield (Boston College). **9.** Steffan Wilson, of/3b, Torrington (Harvard). **10.** Jeremy Papelbon, lhp, Mill City (North Florida).

INDIVIDUAL BATTING LEADERS

(Minimum 100 Plate Appearances)

	AVG	AB	R	H	2B	3B	HR	RBI	SB
Hankerd, Cyle, Newport	.383	115	23	44	10	1	9	36	0
Bashelor, Will, Concord	.382	89	24	34	4	1	5	13	21
Perez, Andres, Torrington	.380	137	28	52	7	3	2	22	8
Ford, Dan, Keene	.350	123	20	43	8	0	2	21	1
Davis, Andrew, Keene	.348	161	27	56	14	0	4	33	4
Rizzotti, Matt, Vermont	.347	118	17	41	14	1	3	21	1
Wilson, Steffan, Torrington	.340	162	20	55	12	2	7	39	1
Sensing, Nathan, North Adams	.327	147	12	48	4	2	0	21	10
Edmondson, Jerod, Concord	.324	145	15	47	5	2	0	17	2
Olson, Garrett, Keene	.322	149	37	48	12	0	5	13	5
Musolf, Travis, Sanford	.322	143	28	46	3	1	0	11	17
Krider, Troy, Vermont	.317	123	21	39	6	0	0	6	6
McGraw, Matt, Holyoke	.316	136	21	43	11	1	3	26	6
Lepore, Justin, Torrington	.315	108	15	34	7	2	3	14	1
Fitzpatrick, John, Manchester	.306	121	17	37	11	1	5	29	1
Gronkowski, Gordie, Torrington	.305	154	25	47	3	1	3	17	1
Kaufman, Brian, Pittsfield	.301	123	11	37	4	0	0	13	4
Just, Michael, Torrington	.300	160	29	48	11	0	2	15	6

INDIVIDUAL PITCHING LEADERS

(Minimum 35 innings)

	W	L	ERA	G	SV	IP	H	BB	SO
Martin, Troy, Keene	5	1	0.77	9	0	47	26	10	28
Westphal, Mickey, Holyoke	5	1	0.81	8	1	45	31	13	32
Reid, Ryan, Sanford	3	2	1.18	7	0	38	22	12	40
Riordan, Cory, Danbury	4	2	1.38	9	0	52	42	15	57
Brant, Rob, Keene	6	1	1.74	12	1	52	32	28	57
Otero, Danny, Newport	5	1	1.87	10	0	58	59	3	49
Muir, Justin, Sanford	1	1	1.91	8	0	38	25	12	28
Cummings, Tyler, Concord	5	1	1.99	8	0	59	43	11	48
Heckert, Mitch, Manchester	6	1	1.99	11	0	59	46	19	38
Bakey, Kris, Holyoke	3	2	2.06	11	1	52	47	17	45
Perkins, Adam, Holyoke	2	4	2.16	11	0	50	45	16	35
Rembisz, Bryan, Mill City	3	2	2.27	22	0	48	43	8	47

NEW YORK COLLEGIATE LEAGUE

EAST	W	L	PCT	GB
Amsterdam Mohawks	29	18	.617	—
Watertown Wizards	28	18	.609	½
Mohawk Valley Cobras	23	23	.500	4½
Plattsburgh Thunder	22	24	.478	6½
Saratoga Phillies	18	28	.391	10½
Glens Falls Golden Eagles	17	29	.370	11½
WEST	**W**	**L**	**PCT**	**GB**
Hornell Dodgers	34	13	.723	—
Allegany County Nitros	33	13	.717	½
Wayne County Raptors	24	19	.558	8
Alfred A's	18	25	.419	14
Geneva Red Wings	14	31	.311	19
Genesee Valley Riverbats	14	32	.304	19½

PLAYOFFS: **Semifinals**—Watertown defeated Amsterdam 2-1 and Hornell defeated Allegany County 2-0 in best-of-3 series. **Final**—Hornell defeated Watertown 2-1 in best-of-3 series.

ALL-STAR TEAM: **C**—Jordan Wolf, Amsterdam (Xavier). **1B**—Billy Howard, Allegany County (Columbus State, Ga.). **2B**—Gene Filyaw, Geneva (Southern). **3B**—Pat O'Rourke, Mohawk Valley (Lipscomb). **SS**—Angel Cabrera, Hornell (Connors State). **OF**—Mike Lyon, Watertown (Northeastern); Chris Hollis, Plattsburgh (Georgia Southern); Jason James, Hornell (Lindenwood, Mo.). **DH**—Brendan Hitchcock, Geneva (Binghamton). **UT**—Pat Feeney, Watertown (Marist). **SP**—Tommy Warner, Amsterdam (Kentucky); De'Mece Williams, Hornell (Norfolk State); Mike Chiciak, Plattsburgh (Georgia Southern); Mike Stawski, Allegany County (St. Joseph's). **RP**—Joe Malzone, Watertown (Massachusetts-Lowell); Mike Perconte, Hornell (Murray State).

Most Valuable Player: James Barksdale, Allegany County (North Alabama). **Pitcher of the Year:** Mike Schellinger, Watertown (Oneonta State, N.Y.). **Coach of the Year:** Todd Interdonato, Hornell.

TOP 10 PROSPECTS: **1.** Elvin Vargas, of, Hornell (Connors State, Okla., JC). **2.** Mike Schellinger, rhp, Watertown (Oneonta State, N.Y.). **3.** Michael Schwimmer, rhp, Saratoga (Virginia). **4.** Angel Cabrera, ss, Hornell (Connors State, Okla., JC). **5.** James Barksdale, of, Allegany County (North Alabama). **6.** Mike Lyon, of, Watertown (Northeastern). **7.** Mike Chiciak, rhp, Plattburgh (Georgia Southern). **8.** David Williams, of, Glens Falls (Rutgers). **9.** Josh Morgan, rhp, Wayne County (Missouri-St. Louis). **10.** Gene Filyaw, ss, Geneva (Southern).

INDIVIDUAL BATTING LEADERS

(Minimum 100 Plate Appearances)

	AVG	AB	R	H	2B	3B	HR	RBI	SB
Barksdale, James, Allegany	.399	168	50	67	13	3	1	20	52
Cabrera, Angel, Hornell	.389	167	40	65	15	5	1	32	35
Howard, Billy, Allegany	.384	145	23	56	10	3	0	32	7
James, Jason, Hornell	.377	162	34	61	12	6	1	16	25
Hitchcock, Brendon, Geneva	.370	135	24	50	7	1	0	16	4
Feeney, Patrick, Watertown	.348	132	17	46	5	2	2	16	6
Hollis, Chris, Plattsburgh	.345	139	35	48	8	1	0	24	17
Simek, Matt, Geneva	.339	127	23	43	11	0	2	11	15
Mullen, Ted, Plattsburgh	.331	139	18	46	14	0	2	25	3
Cronk, Adam, Saratoga	.331	136	15	45	8	0	4	26	1
Lyon, Mike, Watertown	.327	171	27	56	12	2	8	39	2
O'Rourke, Pat, Mohawk Valley	.324	136	18	44	9	0	0	24	10
Filyaw, Gene, Geneva	.321	134	21	43	11	1	2	17	11
Rivera, Ruben, Hornell	.316	158	19	50	4	1	0	22	12
Grauer, Kevin, Allegany	.316	133	23	42	3	1	0	20	13

INDIVIDUAL PITCHING LEADERS

(Minimum 30 innings)

PITCHING	W	L	ERA	G	SV	IP	H	BB	SO
Perconte, Michael, Hornell	4	0	0.44	13	4	41	19	6	49
Hollister, Billy, Allegany	5	2	0.66	8	0	55	28	14	41
Stawdi, Michael, Allegany	5	0	0.72	7	0	50	46	9	20
Rogers, Matt, Amsterdam	4	2	0.98	13	1	46	29	12	51
Mann, Sam, Hornell	6	2	0.99	10	0	64	48	9	38
Melendez, Jesus, Wayne County	1	1	1.14	21	6	32	19	7	23
Warner, Tom, Amsterdam	8	2	1.34	15	0	67	39	15	53
Schellinger, Mike, Watertown	5	2	1.51	9	0	60	35	10	86
Fitchett, Scott, Alfred	4	1	1.62	13	2	39	31	10	21
Schwimer, Michael, Saratoga	3	1	1.66	7	0	43	34	10	30

NORTHWOODS LEAGUE

NORTH	W	L	PCT	GB
+Thunder Bay Border Cats	44	24	.647	—
Duluth Huskies	36	32	.529	8
Alexandria Beetles	35	33	.515	9
Mankato MoonDogs	34	34	.500	10
*St. Cloud River Bats	32	36	.471	12
Brainerd Blue Thunder	29	38	.433	14½
SOUTH	**W**	**L**	**PCT**	**GB**
+Rochester Honkers	44	24	.647	—
*Madison Mallards	43	25	.632	1
Wisconsin Woodchucks	34	34	.500	10
Eau Claire Express	28	40	.412	16
La Crosse Loggers	26	41	.388	17½
Waterloo Bucks	22	46	.324	22

* First-half champion.+ Second-half champion.

PLAYOFFS: **Semifinals**—Madison defeated Rochester 2-1 and Thunder Bay defeated St. Cloud 2-1 in best-of-3 series. **Final**—Thunder Bay defeated Madison 2-0 in best-of-3 series.

ALL-STAR TEAM: C—Dan Quinn, Brainerd (Buffalo); Robby Jacobsen, St. Cloud (George Mason). **1B**—Jordan Hafer, Duluth (Florida Atlantic). **2B**—J.R. Voyles, Thunder Bay (Texas-San Antonio). **3B**—Matt Mangini, Thunder Bay (North Carolina State). **SS**—Allen Craig, Alexandria (California). **IF**—Dan Lyons, Rochester (Iowa Central CC). **OF**—Ryan Rogowski, Madison (Illinois); Kraig Binick, Eau Claire (New York Tech); Shane Buschini, Mankato (San Diego); Mike Metzger, Alexandria (UCLA); Tommy Giles, St. Cloud (Miami). **DH**—Zach Daeges, Waterloo (Creighton). **P**—Jay Buente, Wisconsin (Purdue); Charlie Shirek, Duluth (Nebraska); Casey O'Rourke, Thunder Bay (Iowa); Shawn Williams, Thunder Bay (Charleston); J.J. Hollenbeck, Madison (Virginia Military); Adam Mills, Madison (UNC Charlotte); Bobby Lewton, Mankato (Fort Hays State, Kan.); Adam Rogers, La Crosse (Evansville); Bryan Peterson, Duluth (Kansas State); Ethan Vogt, Thunder Bay (Ridgewater, Minn., CC); Matt Robinson, Brainerd (Kentucky); Neil Wagner, Mankato (North Dakota State).

Most Valuable Player: Ryan Rogowski, Madison (Illinois). **Manager of the Year:** Chad Miller, Thunder Bay.

TOP 10 PROSPECTS: **1.** Matt Mangini, 3b, Thunder Bay (North Carolina State). **2.** Charlie Shirek, rhp, Duluth (Nebraska). **3.** Blake Martin, lhp, Waterloo (Birmingham-Southern). **4.** Zach Daeges, dh/of, Waterloo (Creighton). **5.** Brandon Tripp, of Thunder Bay (Cal State Fullerton). **6.** Shane Buschini, of, Mankato (San Diego). **7.** Jay Buente, rhp, Wisconsin (Purdue). **8.** Antone DeJesus, of Duluth (Kentucky). **9.** Ryan Rogowski, of, Madison (Illinois). **10.** Reid Fronk, 3b, Mankato (North Carolina).

INDIVIDUAL BATTING LEADERS

(Minimum 150 Plate Appearances)

	AVG	AB	R	H	2B	3B	HR	RBI	SB
Daeges, Zach, Waterloo	.366	183	38	67	13	2	13	48	4
Craig, Allen, Alexandria	.362	199	41	72	17	0	12	40	9
Metzger, Michael, Alexandria	.351	174	33	61	13	0	1	18	14
Rogowski, Ryan, Madison	.345	249	52	86	9	5	4	29	44
Voyles, J.R., Thunder Bay	.345	235	32	81	17	2	0	33	11
Mengini, Matt, Thunder Bay	.342	187	27	64	13	1	6	45	8
Fronk, Reid, Mankato	.333	207	38	69	12	2	7	34	9
Gressick, Anthony, Waterloo	.331	148	28	49	14	0	4	33	5
Antoske, Peter, St. Cloud	.329	228	40	75	11	0	0	24	30
Bacon, Jimmy, Alexandria	.326	221	40	72	11	0	2	28	11
Jacobsen, Robby, St. Cloud	.324	219	41	71	11	4	7	35	17
Olson, Ross, Wisconsin	.319	141	21	45	12	0	3	15	2
Pickens, Doug, Alexandria	.318	217	38	69	16	5	6	35	10
Grant, Aaron, Mankato	.318	151	23	48	6	1	3	24	6
Nohelty, Matt, Wisconsin	.318	245	35	78	8	0	1	33	14
Navarro, Efren, Rochester	.316	174	33	55	13	0	4	28	5

INDIVIDUAL PITCHING LEADERS

(Minimum 50 Innings)

	W	L	ERA	G	SV	IP	H	BB	SO
Mills, Adam, Madison	6	2	1.00	13	0	72	58	10	62
Buente, Jay, Wisconsin	7	2	1.43	13	0	95	75	31	100
O'Rourke, Casey, Thunder Bay	9	1	1.56	13	0	81	70	15	53
Shirek, Charlie, Duluth	9	2	1.69	14	1	80	59	25	56
Lewton, Bobby, Mankato	5	2	1.88	14	0	62	55	8	23
Vogt, Ethan, Thunder Bay	7	0	1.96	17	1	64	55	19	42
Brookes, Craig, Wisconsin	5	4	1.97	14	0	87	66	14	62
Seward, Austin, Duluth	4	3	2.17	17	0	83	76	26	48
Robinson, Matt, Brainerd	6	1	2.23	13	0	77	63	22	66
Bird, Ryan, Rochester	4	1	2.32	8	0	50	39	18	36
Brannon, Blake, Thunder Bay	7	5	2,35	15	0	69	43	29	51
Hollenbeck, J.J., Madison	8	3	2.39	16	0	72	61	20	69

TEXAS COLLEGIATE LEAGUE

ROGERS HORNSBY	W	L	PCT	GB
Denton Outlaws	28	23	.549	—
Graham Roughnecks	20	28	.417	6½
Weatherford Wranglers	20	28	.417	6½
Mineral Wells Steam	17	30	.362	9
TRIS SPEAKER	**W**	**L**	**PCT**	**GB**
Coppell Copperheads	31	17	.646	—
McKinney Marshals	29	22	.569	3½
Highland Park BlueSox	27	21	.563	4
Euless Lone Stars	22	25	.468	8½

PLAYOFFS: Semifinals—Denton defeated Weatherford 2-0 and McKinney defeated Coppell 2-0 in best-of-3 series. **Final**—Denton defeated McKinney 2-1 in best-of-3 series.

ALL-STAR TEAM: C—Josh Banda, Denton (California Baptist). **1B**—Andrew Brown, Denton (Nebraska). **2B**—Parker Dalton, Mineral Wells (Texas A&M). **3B**—Brian Spear, Denton (Wichita State). **SS**—Justin Colbert, Graham (Oklahoma State). **OF**—Louie Alamia, McKinney (Texas-Pan American); Spencer Jackson, Weatherford (Texas A&M); Keanon Simon, Graham (Oklahoma State). **DH**—Ben Burum, Mineral Wells (Texas-Arlington). **SP**—Austin Creps, McKinney (Texas A&M); Jacob Ramos, Coppell (Lubbock Christian). **RP**—Bryce Cox, McKinney (Rice).

Player of the Year: Andrew Brown, Denton. **Pitcher of the Year:** Austin Creps, McKinney.

TOP 10 PROSPECTS: **1.** Aaron Brown, rhp, Coppell (Houston). **2.** Kenn Kasparek, rhp, McKinney (Texas). **3.** Bryce Cox, rhp, McKinney (Rice). **4.** Austin Creps, rhp, McKinney (Texas A&M). **5.** Eddie Degerman, rhp, Denton (Rice). **6.** Josh Banda, c, Denton (California Baptist). **7.** Jake Arrietta, rhp, McKinney (Weatherford, Texas, JC). **8.** Bobby Bell, rhp, Weatherford (Rice). **9.** Stan Widmann, ss, Euless (Clemson). **10.** Tyler Henley, of, Euless (Rice).

INDIVIDUAL BATTING LEADERS

(Minimum 100 Plate Appearances)

	AVG	AB	R	H	2B	3B	HR	RBI	SB
Banda, Josh, Denton	.400	135	28	54	14	2	10	32	2
Jackson, Spencer, Weatherford	.340	141	29	48	8	0	5	18	2
Diaz, Jason, Euless	.337	98	26	33	3	0	0	5	9
Robison, Steve, Euless	.326	95	17	31	6	1	1	18	11
Reagan, Travis, Weatherford	.324	105	13	34	8	0	2	21	0
Spear, Brian, Denton	.321	156	24	50	10	0	7	37	1
Britton, Clay, Weatherford	.320	172	39	55	8	1	1	28	8
Simon, Keanon, Graham	.311	190	48	59	5	3	5	27	23
Stein, Keith, Euless	.311	90	18	28	6	1	3	15	3
Alamia, Louie, McKinney	.311	164	21	51	8	2	0	21	9
Ebarb, C.J., McKinney	.308	133	17	41	4	0	1	16	1
Jones, Tyler, Highland Park	.306	111	20	34	7	0	5	28	6
Burum, Ben, Mineral Wells	.305	164	26	50	10	1	12	38	2
Newman, Joe, Weatherford	.304	138	26	42	4	2	1	16	6
Arnold, Clint, Weatherford	.303	142	25	43	5	0	1	17	7
Bond, Casey, Highland Park	.303	109	16	33	3	1	4	16	4
Hill, Tyler, Coppell	.303	152	25	46	4	1	1	19	8
Jones, Kyle, Denton	.302	199	37	60	11	1	2	24	36

	AVG	AB	R	H	2B	3B	HR	RBI	SB
Sublett, Damon, Coppell	.302	96	11	29	7	1	2	22	3

INDIVIDUAL PITCHING LEADERS

(Minimum 30 Innings)

	W	L	ERA	G	SV	IP	H	BB	SO
Mellies, Charlie, Euless	5	2	1.28	9	0	43	36	14	46
Creps, Austin, McKinney	5	2	1.76	11	1	57	49	22	69
Arietta, Jake, McKinney	4	3	1.88	10	0	63	38	27	54
Ramos, Jacob, Coppell	4	2	1.96	11	0	55	28	24	58
Bell, Bobby, Weatherford	0	1	2.16	8	0	33	27	9	40
Nicholson, Kyle, Weatherford	1	4	2.22	23	3	49	41	18	33
Halle, James, Mineral Wells	3	2	2.30	10	0	62	57	17	52
Hancock, Shea, Weatherford	5	0	2.30	8	0	47	39	24	33
Corgan, Chance, Euless	3	1	2.35	11	0	53	38	24	56
Kluber, Corey, Denton	4	0	2.54	11	0	49	29	26	46
Russell, James, Coppell	6	1	2.55	10	0	42	41	22	45
Langwell, Matt, Highland Park	0	0	2.63	19	3	37	31	17	27

VALLEY LEAGUE

NORTH	W	L	PCT	GB
Luray Wranglers	30	14	.682	—
New Market Rebels	26	18	.591	4
Front Royal Cardinals	22	21	.512	7½
Winchester Royals	19	25	.432	11
Haymarket Battle Cats	18	26	.409	12
SOUTH	**W**	**L**	**PCT**	**GB**
Covington Lumberjacks	27	15	.643	—
Harrisonburg Turks	25	19	.568	3
Staunton Braves	21	22	.488	6½
Woodstock River Bandits	15	27	.357	12
Waynesboro Generals	14	30	.318	14

PLAYOFFS: **Semifinals**—New Market defeated Luray 2-0 and Covington defeated Harrisonburg 2-0 in best-of-3 series. **Final**—Covington defeated New Market 3-1 in best-of-5 series.

ALL-STAR TEAM: C—Eddy Rodriguez, Luray (Miami). **1B**—Tom Hagan, Covington (Virginia). **2B**—Ryan Taylor, Covington (West Virginia State). **3B**—Daniel Murphy, Luray (Jacksonville). **SS**—Doug Nelms, Luray (West Virginia). **OF**—Collin Cowgill, Covington (Kentucky); Brandon Marsh, Staunton (Young Harris, Ga., JC); Eric Renfroe, New Market (Mercer). **DH**—Chris O'Dell, New Market (Eastern Kentucky). **UT**—Chris Fournier, Winchester (George Mason). **SP**—Marcus Davis, Luray (Virginia Commonwealth); Zack Duncan, Woodstock (Lipscomb); Brad Mills, Harrisonburg (Arizona). **RP**—Chris Fessler, Harrisonburg (Yavapai, Ariz., JC); Jonathan Johnston, Waynesboro (Southern Mississippi).

Most Valuable Player: Daniel Murphy, Luray.

TOP 10 PROSPECTS: **1.** Collin Cowgill, of, Covington (Kentucky). **2.** Daniel Murphy, 3b, Luray (Jacksonville). **3.** Eddy Rodriguez, c, Luray (Miami). **4.** Brad Mills, lhp, Harrisonburg (Arizona). **5.** Zach Baldwin, lhp, Front Royal (West Virginia State). **6.** Joel Brookens, rhp, Front Royal (North Carolina State). **7.** Eric Renfroe, of, New Market (Mercer). **8.** Chris Fournier, 3b/1b, Winchester (George Mason). **9.** Tyson Auer, of, Luray (Central Florida). **10.** Tom Hagan, 1b, Covington (Virginia).

INDIVIDUAL BATTING LEADERS

(Minimum 100 Plate Appearances)

	AVG	AB	R	H	2B	3B	HR	RBI	SB
Cunningham, Ryan, Waynesboro	.358	151	22	54	11	0	2	17	4
Hagan, Tom, Covington	.354	144	29	51	7	0	1	12	13
Murphy, Daniel, Luray	.347	196	44	68	16	2	4	31	20
Thompson, Lance, Winchester	.330	112	20	37	11	1	0	10	0
Renfroe, Eric, New Market	.329	152	27	50	7	0	1	26	10
Cowgill, Collin, Covington	.324	276	40	57	9	4	14	39	8
Taylor, Ryan, Covington	.321	190	41	61	15	1	4	35	8
Beck, Chris, New Market	.320	103	11	33	4	1	0	10	1
White, Joe, Haymarket	.318	88	10	28	10	0	0	14	2
Fournier, Chris, Winchester	.315	124	21	39	9	1	5	27	13
Verrett, Aaron, Haymarket	.314	105	16	33	10	1	0	16	5
Auer, Tyson, Luray	.312	157	29	49	8	1	2	18	13
Disher, Phil, Front Royal	.312	125	19	39	5	0	7	29	0
McOwen, Jamie, Luray	.310	187	26	58	8	1	1	28	2
Hawse, John, Winchester	.308	120	20	37	6	0	1	14	1
Rodriguez, Eddy, Luray	.308	107	15	33	9	0	2	15	3
Frederick, Adam, New Market	.306	173	24	53	7	0	1	25	1
Marsh, Brandon, Staunton	.301	153	26	46	6	1	3	25	4
Bolger, Brett, New Market	.301	193	33	58	5	2	1	19	13

INDIVIDUAL PITCHING LEADERS

(Minimum 30 Innings)

	W	L	ERA	G	SV	IP	H	BB	SO
Johnston, Jonathan, Waynesboro	2	1	0.30	20	5	30	26	12	26
Wade, Ben, Covington	4	2	1.17	12	2	54	47	21	46
Seten, Gabe, Covington	4	2	1.49	14	3	36	22	12	52
Mills, Brad, Harrisonburg	6	0	1.57	8	0	46	30	19	75
Fussell, Eric, Harrisonburg	2	2	1.69	8	0	43	32	7	40
Massey, Scott, Waynesboro	2	3	1.88	6	0	48	37	15	37
Nicely, Clarence, Covington	7	1	1.84	8	0	49	38	14	48
Davis, Marcus, Luray	4	1	1.98	11	0	50	32	22	30
Duncan, Zack, Woodstock	5	3	1.99	13	0	63	51	20	51
Williamson, Joey, Luray	3	0	2.06	9	0	39	26	20	42
Benson, Shawn, Harrisonburg	5	2	2.11	15	0	60	39	36	67
Palanski, Brett, Waynesboro	2	2	2.16	12	2	42	40	14	42

WEST COAST COLLEGIATE LEAGUE

	W	L	PCT	GB
Wenatchee AppleSox	29	7	.806	—
*Aloha Knights	27	9	.750	2
Bellingham Bells	17	19	.472	12
Kelowna Falcons	16	20	.444	13
Bend Elks	13	23	.361	16
Spokane RiverHawks	12	24	.333	17
Kitsap BlueJackets	12	24	.333	17

*Qualified for National Baseball Congress World Series

PLAYOFFS: Wenatchee defeated Bellingham 2-0 in best-of-3 series.

ALL-STAR TEAM: C—Cody Carrier, Kelowna (East Central, Mo., JC). **1B**—Steve Marquardt, Wenatchee (Columbia Basin, Wash., JC). **2B**—Louie Hernandez, Bellingham (UC Riverside). **3B**—John Hee, Wenatchee (Hawaii). **SS**—Chad Schroeder, Bellingham (Illinois-Chicago). **OF**—Andrew Lefave, Bellingham (Missouri Valley); Wally Crancer, Aloha (Georgia Tech); Travis Vetters, Wenatchee (Portland). **DH**—Geoff Wagner, Bend (Oregon State). **SP**—Tommy Hanson, Aloha (Riverside, Calif., CC); Bud Norris, Aloha (Cal Poly); Zach Bird, Aloha (Coastal Carolina); Clayton Mortensen, Wenatchee (Gonzaga). **RP**—Steve Martlaro, Wenatchee (Portland).

Most Valuable Player: Steve Marquardt, Wenatchee. **Most Outstanding Pitcher:** Tommy Hanson, Aloha (Riverside CC).

TOP 10 PROSPECTS: **1.** Tommy Hanson, rhp, Aloha (Riverside, Calif., CC). **2.** Steve Marquardt, 3b, Wenatchee (Columbia Basin, Wash., CC). **3.** Bud Norris, rhp, Aloha (Cal Poly). **4.** Clay Mortensen, rhp, Wenatchee (Gonzaga). **5.** Chris Davis, 3b/1b, Kelowna (Navarro, Texas, CC). **6.** Jess Todd, rhp, Kelowna (Texas). **7.** Eddie Kunz, rhp, Bellingham (Oregon State). **8.** D.J. Lidyard, rhp, Bellingham (Lower Columbia, Wash., CC). **9.** Zach Borba, of, Aloha (Nevada-Las Vegas). **10.** Matt Hague, rhp/of, Aloha (Washington).

INDIVIDUAL BATTING LEADERS

(Minimum 75 Plate Appearances)

	AVG	AB	R	H	2B	3B	HR	RBI	SB
Schroeder, Chad, Bellingham	.356	101	21	36	6	0	0	16	9
Hee, John, Wenatchee	.352	145	23	51	4	0	0	20	1
Riley, Gabe, Kitsap	.347	72	8	25	4	0	0	8	0
Marquardt, Steve, Wenatchee	.333	126	20	42	13	1	1	20	8
Hernandez, Louie, Bellingham	.333	120	13	40	9	0	0	18	0
Davis, Chris, Kelowna	.331	118	39	39	7	1	5	29	6
Wagner, Geoff, Bend	.329	70	23	23	4	1	1	13	9
Crancer, Wally, Aloha	.328	131	43	43	7	1	1	16	0
Lefave, Andrew, Bellingham	.328	122	40	40	10	0	0	29	2
Nilsen, Jamie, Wenatchee	.321	109	35	35	8	1	5	17	10
Rickard, Cory, Spokane	.313	83	26	26	3	0	0	7	3
Froman, Nick, Spokane	.312	77	24	24	2	0	0	5	0
Vetters, Travis, Wenatchee	.302	139	42	42	9	0	1	20	9

INDIVIDUAL PITCHING LEADERS

(Minimum 20 Innings)

	W	L	ERA	G	SV	IP	H	BB	SO
Hanson, Tommy, Aloha	5	1	1.12	7	0	48	29	12	76
Monge, Ed, Bend	1	1	1.17	7	1	23	17	9	15
Norris, Bud, Aloha	6	0	1.20	7	0	45	31	17	52
Bird, Zach, Aloha	5	1	1.40	6	0	45	28	20	51
Reese, Scott, Bend	2	1	1.93	5	0	32	27	11	14
Ashman, Brad, Kelowna	4	3	1.98	8	0	50	46	14	18
Lidyard, D.J., Bellingham	5	3	1.98	9	0	59	47	24	56
Cline, Kyle, Kitsap	4	4	2.09	11	0	56	54	6	29
Mortensen, Clay, Wenatchee	3	1	2.13	8	0	42	29	20	47
Welker, Duke, Bend	1	3	2.18	9	1	21	18	8	20

HIGH SCHOOL/ YOUTH BASEBALL

Rasmus family leads Alabama's Russell County to national title

BY ALAN MATTHEWS

Tony Rasmus and his boys have a knack for making their way to the top.

In 1999, Tony was an assistant coach on the Phenix City, Ala., Little League team that featured his oldest sons Colby and Cory. The team won the United States bracket of the Little League (11-12) World Series. Two years later, his sons were the centerpiece of a Phenix City team that was victorious at the Dixie Junior Boys (13-14) World Series.

In 2005, Rasmus and his boys followed suit in high school.

Russell County High of Seale, Ala., finished the season with a 38-1 record, a 5-A state championship and No. 1 ranking in the Baseball America/National High School Baseball Coaches Association national poll.

The Warriors, who were ranked No. 4 in the preseason, took over the top spot April 3 and never relinquished it. They beat Pinson (Ala.) Valley High 5-1 and 7-0 to sweep their best-of-three championship series to claim the Alabama Class 5-A title at Riverwalk Stadium in Montgomery.

Cory Rasmus, a junior righthander, tossed a complete-game shutout with three walks, three hits and 10 strikeouts in the decisive game. Colby, a senior outfielder, went 3-for-7 with four RBIs in the series and hit his 24th home run, the second-highest single-season total in Alabama history. He was named the playoffs MVP.

A family affair

Russell County High celebrates Alabama 5-A title, national championship

"Everything just seemed to fall in line and go as good as it could have," Tony said. "How much good fortune can one family have? I had to pinch myself just to make sure I wasn't dreaming all of it."

Alabama's Armory

While Colby posted eye-popping .484-24-66 numbers and played his way into the first round of the draft, going to the Cardinals with the 28th overall pick, it was the Warriors' dominant pitching staff that keyed Russell County's national title run.

Junior lefthander Kasey Kiker went 12-1, 0.52 with 173 strikeouts, 24 walks and 41 hits in 94 innings to lead a staff that posted a 0.75 ERA and racked up 429 strikeouts, both state records. Cory, who joined Kiker in the Aflac All-American game later that summer, was 11-0, 0.50 with two saves in 70 innings, and Colby was 3-0, 0.00 with three saves, 30 strikeouts and four walks in 17 innings.

"I remember walking out of there the first time I saw them saying, 'That right there is a good high school baseball team,' " said Cardinals scout Scott Nichols, the 21-year scouting veteran who signed Colby. "They run two dominant pitchers at you and then they have Colby to come in behind them to throw if they need him. It was very impressive, just a special group of people with Tony and the whole family. They deserve everything they can get out of this."

There was no better example of Russell County's superiority than its second-round sweep of Monroe County High of Monroeville. Kiker used his fastball, which touched 94 mph, changeup and sharp breaking ball beautifully during a perfect game with 12 strikeouts over seven innings in the opener. Colby belted four home runs in the doubleheader, including a grand slam, and knocked in 12 runs as the Warriors picked up momentum on their way to Montgomery.

"Those games were incredible displays of dominance," Nichols said. "Colby's last home run was a monstrous bomb. And Cory pitches the second game and dominates—he was 92, 93 with power stuff."

In the next round, however, it appeared Russell County's run might be derailed. The Warriors' semifinals series with Millbrook's Stanhope Elmore was billed

PREVIOUS **WINNERS**

Previous No. 1 teams in the year-end Baseball America/National High School Baseball Coaches Association poll:

1992—Westminster Christian HS, Miami
1993—Greenway HS, Phoenix
1994—Sarasota (Fla.) HS
1995—Germantown (Tenn.) HS
1996—Westminster Christian HS, Miami
1997—Jesuit HS, Tampa
1998—Vestavia Hills (Ala.) HS
1999—Lassiter HS, Marietta, Ga.
2000—Gloucester Catholic HS, Gloucester City, N.J.
2001—Seminole (Fla.) HS
2002—Elkins HS, Missouri City, Texas
2003—Chatsworth (Calif.) HS
2004—Chatsworth (Calif.) HS

HIGH SCHOOL TOP 50

Baseball America's 2005 top 50 high school poll was selected in conjunction with the National High School Baseball Coaches Association.

	Team	Record	Accomplishment
1.	Russell County HS, Seale, Ala.	38-1	State 5-A champion
2.	Nova HS, Fort Lauderdale	30-1	State 5-A champion
3.	Brownsburg (Ind.) HS	35-0	State 4-A champion
4.	Chaparral HS, Scottsdale, Ariz.	31-3	State 4-A champion
5.	Florida Christian HS, Miami	29-2	State 2-A champion
6.	Millard North HS, Omaha	35-0	State champion
7.	Rancho Bernardo HS, San Diego	31-5	CIF sectional champion
8.	Elder HS, Cincinnati	28-1	State Division I champion
9.	Sarasota (Fla.) HS	28-1	—
10.	Moody HS, Corpus Christi, Texas	33-3	—
11.	Kingwood (Texas) HS	35-6	State 5-A champion
12.	Mills Godwin HS, Richmond	23-1	—
13.	Tate HS, Gonzalez, Fla.	28-2	State 6-A champion
14.	Jesuit HS, New Orleans	34-5	State 5-A champion
15.	La Cueva HS, Albuquerque	28-1	State 5-A champion
16.	Niwot HS, Longmont, Colo.	27-1	State 4-A champion
17.	Bishop O'Dowd HS, Oakland	25-1	—
18.	Calvert Hall HS, Towson, Md.	31-1	—
19.	Central HS, Madison, Miss.	31-2	—
20.	Pioneer HS, Ann Arbor, Mich.	41-2	State Division-I runner up
21.	Clovis (Calif.) West HS	27-4	CIF sectional runner-up
22.	Richland (Wash.) HS	26-2	State 4-A champion
23.	Chattahoochee HS, Alpharetta, Ga.	32-4	State 5-A champion
24.	Lockport (Ill.) HS	40-3	State 2-A champion
25.	Archbishop Mitty HS, San Jose	28-6	CIF sectional champion
26.	Houston Christian HS	36-3	Texas APPS 5-A champion
27.	The Woodlands (Texas) HS	28-6	—
28.	Northwest Rankin HS, Brandon, Miss.	36-3	State 5-A champion
29.	Central Private HS, Baker, La.	38-1	Mississippi private school champion
30.	Punahou HS, Honolulu	34-3	State champion
31.	Seton Hall Prep, West Orange, N.J.	30-2	State parochial champion
32.	Lyons Township HS, La Grange, Ill.	35-4	—
33.	Bellarmine College Prep, San Jose	34-5	—
34.	Poway (Calif.) HS	28-6	—
35.	Catalina Foothills HS, Tucson	32-3	State 4-A runner-up
36.	Flower Mound (Texas) HS	27-6	—
37.	Key West (Fla.) HS	25-5	State 3-A champion
38.	Buchanan HS, Clovis, Calif.	25-6	CIF sectional champion
39.	Hickman HS, Columbia, Mo.	28-2	State 4-A champion
40.	Calallen HS, Corpus Christi, Texas	37-4	State 4-A champion
41.	T.C. Roberson HS, Asheville, N.C.	22-3	—
42.	Monsignor Pace HS, Opa Locka, Fla.	21-5	—
43.	Houston HS, Germantown, Tenn.	36-8	State 3-A champion
44.	Sierra Vista HS, Las Vegas	34-5	State 4-A champion
45.	Chatsworth (Calif.) HS	29-4	Los Angeles city runner-up
46.	St. John's HS, Washington, D.C.	24-3	—
47.	Mater Dei HS, Santa Ana, Calif.	24-8	CIF sectional champion
48.	Tunstall HS, Dry Fork, Va.	26-1	State 2-A champion
49.	Parkview Baptist HS, Baton Rouge, La.	30-5	State 3-A champion
50.	Wilmington (Ill.) HS	41-1	State 1-A champion

by many as a battle between the state's best teams. Programs from the southern division of the Class 5-A ranks have traditionally produced more talented teams than those from the north. It lived up to expectations, as Stanhope Elmore proved to be Russell County's toughest test, beating Kiker 5-0 in the opener of the best-of-three series.

"I had a hissy fit and told them to leave the dugout," Tony said. "I thought it was over because (Kiker) is our No. 1 guy, and as well as Cory was throwing, when you go that long without losing a game, you wonder how the kids are going to bounce back.

"They walked back in the dugout and they were real loose, and they just said, 'Relax, we've got it.' "

Cory was as cool as his teammates, striking out 15 in a complete-game two-hitter as Russell County evened the series at one game apiece in the second game of the doubleheader.

That night, Tony told Colby, who had not pitched in two weeks and not thrown more than three innings in a game all season, that he would get the ball in the rubber match the following night.

"I thought about it all night," Colby said. "We didn't play until seven (o'clock) and the whole day I sat around the house and thought about what I was going to do. I hoped I could get five good innings."

How about seven shutout, three-hit innings with 10 strikeouts? That's what Colby turned in as he tacked on a home run in a 2-0 victory that paved Russell County's way to the state and national titles.

Colby Rasmus

"Before that game, I'm scared to death again," Tony said. "And that son-of-a-gun came out and threw another great game. He was 91-92 in the seventh with a nasty curveball. He was just phenomenal."

Moving Forward

Colby was the Warriors' leader all season. His pitching performance in the state semifinals was a fitting topper on a brilliant career, and showed the moxie that convinced the Cardinals to take him in the first round. Senior outfielder Kuyaunnis Miles was also drafted, going in the 38th round to the Reds.

But with Cory and Kiker returning in 2006, as well as junior shortstop Daniel Esparza, who has touched 88 mph off the mound, and the next generation of Rasmus sons—freshmen Case and Cyle—Russell County figured to be in the 2006 state and national title pictures as well.

The celebration after polishing off Pinson Valley featured the traditional Gatorade showers and dog piles, but for Tony and Colby, the emotions of the day branched beyond the celebration of winning yet another championship.

After the game the family made a beeline for Russell County 90 miles away, as Colby's graduation was scheduled for that evening. While the air was thick with revelry, Tony and his oldest son were more pensive as they reflected on their days together, not only as player and coach, but also as father and son.

"I had goals set and I got them, but not really did I expect to achieve them like this," Colby said. "Everything was running though my mind. All the great times were popping into my head and I was thinking about what it will be like to keep going and make it to the major leagues. It's been a great ride."

"I'm not a real crying kind of fella, but it was pretty tough when you think about the fact you've coached your son from the time he was in T-ball to the time he graduates and then you look at him and realize it's the last time you're going to coach him," Tony said. "He graduated and he hugged my neck and that son-a-gun

Upton, No. 1 pick, named top prep

Baseball America's 2005 high school team and player of the year had an unlikely connection.

Tony Rasmus, the head coach of Russell County High of Seale, Ala., the No. 1 team in the final Baseball America/National High School Baseball Coaches Association poll, was an extra infielder for three minor league seasons in the Angels system. In 1987 he spelled Wiley Lee at second base for Salem in the Class A Carolina League.

PLAYER OF THE YEAR

While Rasmus was leading his team to the top spot in the 2005 poll, Lee, the head coach at Great Bridge High in Chesapeake, Va., was filling out a lineup card that included Justin Upton, who, after being drafted first overall by the Diamondbacks and fortifying his status as baseball's best amateur player, was named BA's High School Player of the Year.

"It has been indeed a rollercoaster ride of thrills," Lee said. "To have 20, 30 guys at practice the first day waiting round the cages just to see one kid hit is just unbelievable.

"This year we've kept (Upton) focused on his senior year and his legacy as a high school player. (Now) he can concentrate on his legacy as a professional."

Upton's legacy as an amateur stands alone. He was recognized as BA's best 14-year-old in 2002 and repeatedly reinforced that reputation with memorable performances at showcase events, international tournaments and finally in the spring of his senior year, when he batted .519-11-32 in 54 at-bats, homering every 4.9 at-bats.

ROBERT GURGANUS

Justin Upton

Upton featured a rare blend of speed, savvy and power. In an era when more teams tend to favor players with less risk and a history of performance that is more easily quantified, Upton remained the top player on draft boards, not only because of those tools but also his ability to use them.

"I saw him about 12 times this spring and he rang the bell pretty much every time out," said Greg Lonigro, the Diamondbacks area scout who, along with Howard McCullough, spent extensive time scouting Upton before Arizona chose him first. "We talk about his bat and his power and you forget the fact that he's a plus-plus runner, then there's the body and his size and the boy is not even done growing . . . You watch him play and it's evident you're watching a special player."

Although each time Upton took the field as an amateur he had no equals, he was considered a good teammate. In addition to being the best player, he also possessed exceptional makeup, and scouts raved about his work ethic and character.

The combination made Upton one of the most complete amateur prospects in recent history, a perfect recipe for the High School Player of the Year.

"(The Diamondbacks) picked me at number one, I think I'm going to have to made an immediate impact," Upton said the day he was drafted. "I'm going to have to play to the potential that they expect me to, and hopefully I'm there helping their big league squad in a couple of years."

—ALAN MATTHEWS

PREVIOUS WINNERS

1992—Preston Wilson, of-rhp, Bamberg-Ehrhardt (S.C.) HS
1993—Trot Nixon, of-lhp, New Hanover HS, Wilmington, N.C.
1994—Doug Million, lhp, Sarasota (Fla.) HS
1995—Ben Davis, c, Malvern (Pa.) Prep
1996—Matt White, rhp, Waynesboro Area (Pa.) HS
1997—Darnell McDonald, of, Cherry Creek HS, Englewood, Colo.
1998—Drew Henson, 3b-rhp, Brighton (Mich.) HS
1999—Josh Hamilton, of-lhp, Athens Drive HS, Raleigh, N.C.
2000—Matt Harrington, rhp, Palmdale (Calif.) HS
2001—Joe Mauer, c, Cretin-Derham Hall, St. Paul, Minn.
2002—Scott Kazmir, lhp, Cypress Falls HS, Houston
2003—Jeff Allison, rhp, Veterans Memorial HS, Peabody, Mass.
2004—Homer Bailey, rhp, LaGrange (Texas) HS

cried for five minutes. My wife melted into the floor."

Memorable Milestones

Because high school teams turn over players as a matter of routine each year, the country's top programs are underscored by consistency. Each season features a new team full of new faces that makes a surprising push up the national polls, invigorating the prep landscape with a new twist, a fresh flavor.

But a true mark of the nation's elite high school baseball programs is the ability to continue winning and developing players, even when the roster introduces a handful of new starters every spring.

These have long been traits of a trio of schools which made headlines in 2005:

■ The national record for consecutive victories by a high school team stood almost 40 years, only to be snapped in 2005. Twice.

Albuquerque's La Cueva High set a record for consecutive wins with its 69th straight victory April 2, beating Albuquerque's Highland High 15-1 in the first game of a doubleheader.

More than 1,000 people attended the win, including a dozen former La Cueva players who had a hand in the streak. The victory moved the Bears ahead of New York's Archbishop Molloy High, which won 68 consecutive games from 1963-66.

"There was a lot of pressure, and a lot of media coverage around here and no matter how much talent you have they're just teenage kids," La Cueva coach Stan McKeever said. "When you have that kind of pressure, it's tough to predict how it will affect them. You never think something like this is going to happen to you and it's nothing you set out to do but we're thrilled to death that we were able to accomplish it."

Just two days after La Cueva set the record, the streak came to an end at 70 with a 17-8 loss to Albuquerque's Rio Grande High.

"It has been a great ride, but that's baseball," La Cueva senior catcher Zach Arnett said. "They came out and played better than we did today."

The loss was the first for the Bears, who won back-to-back state Class 5-A titles in 2003 and 2004, since a 6-5 loss to Carlsbad High in the semifinals of the 2002 state tournament in Farmington. The No. 15-ranked Bears, nonetheless, went on to win their third straight state title in 2005, beating Eldorado High 6-5 in eight innings.

■ Two months after La Cueva broke the record, remarkably, La Cueva's streak was eclipsed.

Until June of 2005, Homer, a little Michigan farming town about 100 miles west of Detroit, was best known for Cascarelli's Pizza. Almost overnight, it became known for high school baseball.

When the Trojans, with an enrollment of 334, beat Union City 14-3 to win the Division III district championship June 4, they notched their 71st consecutive win, leaping past La Cueva in the national record books.

When the Trojans opened the 2004 season with a win in their first game, they had no idea they were destined for the record books. But they went 38-0 that year and began 2005 with 33 more wins.

"I feel like our 15 minutes of fame should have ended at 9:30 this morning," said Homer coach Scott Salow, whose phone suddenly was ringing off the hook. "We'll have a good laugh at practice today when we talk to the kids about all the people that have been calling."

Callers included nationally-syndicated columnist Mitch Albom and a reporter from Albuquerque, who was interested in profiling the team that surpassed La Cueva's record.

While La Cueva's winning streak was snapped 48 hours after breaking the record, Homer managed to tack on five more wins before the Trojans finally lost. Saginaw's Nouvel Catholic Central High beat Homer 7-6 in the Michigan Division III state championship game, halting the run of wins at 75.

The Trojans led 5-0 heading into the bottom of the fourth, but Nouvel Catholic sent 12 batters to the plate in a seven-run fourth inning outburst. Homer managed to score a solitary run in the seventh, but the tying run was left stranded at third base.

"I can't guarantee that we're going to keep the record for (39 years)," Salow said. "We think someone will approach it and maybe even top it, but right now . . . Homer High has the record."

■ Chatsworth (Calif.) High, the 2003 and 2004 BA/NHSBCA champions, did not approach the national mark for consecutive wins in 2005, but the Chancellors streak was significant, nonetheless, if not for its length and levity. Ripping off 54 straight wins in Southern California, where the competition is fierce, deserves recognition and Chatsworth's celebrated state winning streak came to an end in March when Chatsworth dropped a 4-3 decision to Hart High of Newhall.

Chatsworth's string of consecutive wins set a California record, dating back to April 2003.

"I told the guys before the game that we had a chance to do something you can forever remember," Hart coach Jim Ozella said. "We have the opportunity to step forward and see what you're made of."

Hart scored twice in the third inning, keyed by a pair of triples, and twice again in the fifth to claim a 4-1 lead. Chatsworth sophomore shortstop Mike Moustakas homered in the seventh to cut the lead to 4-3 before sophomore righthander Donnie Williams nailed the door and snapped the Chancellors' streak.

"We got beat," Chatsworth coach Tom Meusborn said. "It's that simple. It's over. It was nice, but we knew it wouldn't last forever.

"Fifty-four obviously is something that's never happened before, so it's special to be a part of it. With as many outstanding teams as there are in the valley and Southern California, you just don't do what we did. It was special."

Chatsworth (29-4) advanced to the Los Angeles city championship game, where it lost to El Camino Real High.

■ Niwot High of Longmont, Colo., had its 45-game winning streak snapped in a 4-3 loss to Pueblo South in the Colorado 4-A state championship series. But the Cougars rebounded to win the third and deciding game of a best-of-3 series, 7-0, as senior lefthander Sean Ratliff hurled a two-hitter while striking out 14. He also went 4-for-4 at the plate. The title was No. 16 Niwot's second straight and fifth in eight years.

■ Deering High of Portland, Maine, also had a lengthy unbeaten streak snapped in 2005, at 43 games, when it lost to Biddeford High 8-2. Deering went 24-0 in 2004 and later that summer, with its roster intact, went on to win the American Legion World Series.

Second Straight Title For Nova

Nova High of Davie, Fla., won its second consecutive Florida 5-A title to secure a No. 2 ranking in the final BA/NHSBCA poll. Nova (301-1) won both its final and semifinal game by shutouts, to finish the year with 15 shutouts.

Righthander Pablo Lopez, the team's ace, threw a two-hitter in a 1-0 win over Jacksonville's Wolfson High in the semifinals. Lopez finished the season 15-1, 0.91 with 118 strikeouts in 102 innings and a three-year record of 40-2.

In the final, Donnie Amos (9-0) and Billy Block teamed on another two-hitter, beating Tampa's Gaither High 3-0.

■ Losers of the past two Indiana 4-A finals, third-ranked Brownsburg High beat Evansville North 6-4 to not only win the title but become only the second undefeated champion in Indiana high school baseball history, at 35-0. Evansville Memorial, led by former New York Yankees star Don Mattingly, went 30-0 in 1978.

Seven seniors on the Brownsburg High roster played on the Brownsburg team that played in the 1999 Little League World Series. The best of that group, righthander/first baseman Lance Lynn, went the distance in the final but had to survive a no-out, bases loaded situation in the final inning. He did so by getting a strikeout (his 12th of the game) and inducing a game-ending double play.

Lynn, a sixth-round draft pick of the Marlins, went 15-0, 0.68 with 168 strikeouts in 92 innings on the season, while hitting .396-14-49.

■ No. 4 Chaparral High of Scottsdale set an Arizona record by winning its third straight 4-A title and fifth in seven years. The Firebirds (31-3) beat Tucson's No. 35-ranked Catalina Foothills High 10-0 in the final and won all four playoff games by the 10-run rule.

■ Miami's Florida Christian High (29-2) went on a season-ending 26-game winning streak to rise to No. 5 in the final rankings. The Patriots won the Florida 2-A title with a 7-5 win over Arlington Country Day High.

■ No. 6 Millard North High of Omaha finished its sea-

2005 HIGH SCHOOL ALL-AMERICA TEAM

DAVID STONER
Andrew McCutchen

DANNY PARKER
Bryan Morris

RICK BATTLE
Brandon Snyder

NED SCHUSTER
Chris Volstad

Selected by Baseball America

*Junior

FIRST TEAM

Pos.	Player, School	B-T	Ht.	Wt.	AVG	AB	R	H	2B	3B	HR	RBI	SB	Drafted
C	Brandon Snyder, Westfield HS, Chantilly, Va.	R-R	6-2	190	.500	58	29	29	5	2	3	29	2	Orioles (1)
1B	Justin Smoak, Stratford HS, Goose Creek, S.C.	B-L	6-2	175	.558	86	48	48	5	0	18	49	6	Athletics (16)
IF	C.J. Henry, Putnam City HS, Oklahoma City	R-R	6-3	200	.481	106	52	51	8	7	13	41	21	Yankees (1)
IF	P.J. Phillips, Redan HS, Decatur, Ga.	R-R	6-3	170	.478	90	32	43	16	3	8	41	16	Angels (2)
IF	Justin Upton, Great Bridge HS, Chesapeake, Va.	R-R	6-2	195	.509	53	27	27	5	3	12	33	10	D-backs (1)
OF	John Drennen, Rancho Bernardo HS, San Diego	L-L	6-0	180	.472	106	61	50	12	3	17	50	12	Indians (1S)
OF	Cameron Maybin, T.C. Roberson HS, Asheville, N.C.	R-R	6-3	195	.662	71	66	47	12	1	15	37	32	Tigers (1)
OF	Andrew McCutchen, Fort Meade (Fla.) HS	R-R	5-11	170	.709	55	28	39	8	3	16	42	16	Pirates (1)
UT	Zach Putnam, Pioneer HS, Ann Arbor, Mich.	R-R	6-2	210	.548	124	58	68	17	3	17	73	19	Tigers (38)
UT	Colby Rasmus, Russell County HS, Seale, Ala.	L-L	6-2	183	.484	126	69	61	14	3	24	66	19	Cardinals (1)

Pos.	Player, School	B-T	Ht.	Wt.	W	L	ERA	G	SV	IP	H	BB	SO	Drafted
P	Michael Bowden, Waubonsie Valley HS, Aurora, Ill.	R-R	6-3	210	11	1	0.41	13	0	86	29	9	185	Red Sox (1S)
P	*Kyle Drabek, The Woodlands (Texas) HS	R-R	6-1	190	11	1	0.82	16	1	77	35	42	155	Not eligible
P	*Kasey Kiker, Russell County HS, Seale, Ala.	L-L	5-10	181	12	1	0.52	13	0	94	61	24	173	Not eligible
P	Mark Pawelek Springville (Utah) HS	L-L	6-2	180	10	0	0.00	11	1	63	17	16	132	Cubs (1)
P	Chris Volstad, Palm Beach Gardens (Fla.) HS	R-R	6-7	195	8	2	0.46	12	1	76	29	8	105	Marlins (1)
UT	Zach Putnam, Pioneer HS, Ann Arbor, Mich.	R-R	6-2	210	10	1	0.45	12	0	62	29	16	104	
UT	Colby Rasmus, Russell County HS, Seale, Ala.	L-L	6-2	183	3	0	0.00	7	3	17	3	4	30	

SECOND TEAM

Pos.	Player, School	B-T	Ht.	Wt.	AVG	AB	R	H	2B	3B	HR	RBI	SB	Drafted
C	Jon Egan, Cross Creek HS, Augusta, Ga.	R-R	6-4	210	.588	68	40	40	5	0	16	45	3	Red Sox (2)
1B	Henry Sanchez, Mission Bay HS, San Diego	R-R	6-3	260	.482	85	38	41	8	2	13	38	5	Twins (1S)
IF	Jeff Bianchi, Lampeter-Strasburg HS, Lampeter, Pa.	R-R	5-11	180	.516	91	48	47	10	2	15	48	10	Royals (2)
IF	Reese Havens, Bishop England HS, Daniel's Island, S.C.	L-R	6-1	180	.530	83	45	44	17	2	5	41	13	Rockies (29)
IF	Ryan Mount, Ayala HS, Chino Hills, Calif.	L-R	6-2	175	.460	63	22	29	3	3	4	18	7	Angels (2)
OF	Jay Bruce, West Brook HS, Beaumont, Texas	L-L	6-2	200	.500	86	46	43	7	4	8	28	18	Reds (1)
OF	Jordan Danks, Round Rock (Texas) HS	L-R	6-5	200	.486	76	42	36	12	3	10	36	18	White Sox (19)
OF	Kyle Russell, Tomball (Texas) HS	L-L	6-4	180	.400	100	34	40	10	2	14	53	10	Not drafted
UT	Buster Posey, Lee County HS, Leesburg, Ga.	R-R	6-1	180	.462	104	48	48	7	0	14	40	6	Angels (50)
UT	Jordan Schafer, Winter Haven (Fla.) HS	L-L	6-1	195	.478	92	52	44	10	5	8	23	50	Braves (3)

Pos.	Player, School	B-T	Ht.	Wt.	W	L	ERA	G	SV	IP	H	BB	SO	Drafted
P	Craig Italiano, Flower Mound (Texas) HS	R-R	6-3	195	8	1	0.95	11	0	52	27	19	84	Athletics (2)
P	Beau Jones, Destrehan (La.) HS	L-L	6-1	180	11	3	0.87	15	1	89	34	27	157	Braves (1S)
P	Bryan Morris, Tullahoma (Tenn.) HS	R-R	6-3	185	11	1	0.62	14	1	78	27	11	151	Devil Rays (3)
P	Aaron Thompson, Second Baptist HS, Houston	L-L	6-2	190	8	3	0.84	14	2	66	38	35	133	Marlins (1)
P	Josh Wall, Central Private HS, Baker, La.	R-R	6-6	190	14	1	0.93	16	0	83	44	26	138	Dodgers (2)
UT	Buster Posey, Lee County HS, Leesburg, Ga.	R-R	6-1	180	12	0	1.06	15	0	79	55	24	108	
UT	Jordan Schafer, Winter Haven (Fla.) HS	L-L	6-1	195	11	0	0.71	11	0	76	39	12	140	

THIRD TEAM

Pos.	Player, School	B-T	Ht.	Wt.	AVG	AB	R	H	2B	3B	HR	RBI	SB	Drafted
C	Ralph Henriquez, Key West (Fla.) HS	B-R	6-0	195	.495	95	45	47	11	3	5	39	10	Astros (2)
1B	David Cooper, Tokay HS, Lodi, Calif.	L-L	6-1	180	.553	85	38	47	10	1	13	53	2	Not drafted
IF	David Adams, Grandview Prep, Boca Raton, Fla.	R-R	6-1	185	.500	80	40	40	8	1	8	17	16	Tigers (21)
IF	Paul Kelly, Flower Mound (Texas) HS	R-R	5-11	175	.439	82	39	36	10	1	12	39	12	Twins (2)
IF	Jason Ogata, Westview HS, Portland, Ore.	R-R	6-1	170	.506	79	34	40	13	0	6	32	18	Padres (50)
OF	Cedric Hunter, Martin Luther King HS, Lithonia, Ga.	R-R	6-0	170	.532	77	41	41	13	7	6	25	—	Not eligible
OF	Daryl Jones, Spring (Texas) HS	L-L	6-1	175	.463	82	37	38	8	3	2	26	14	Cardinals (3)
OF	Andrew Lopez, Elk Grove (Calif.) HS	R-R	6-1	180	.463	95	40	44	9	2	6	26	7	Devil Rays (8)
UT	Lance Lynn, Brownsburg (Ind.) HS	R-R	6-5	240	.396	91	23	36	7	0	14	49	0	Mariners (6)
UT	Sean Ratliff, Niwot HS, Longmont, Colo.	L-L	6-4	190	.552	67	40	37	8	1	9	39	12	Not drafted

Pos.	Player, School	B-T	Ht.	Wt.	W	L	ERA	G	SV	IP	H	BB	SO	Drafted
P	Jeremy Bleich, Isidore Newman HS, New Orleans	L-L	6-2	185	7	1	0.56	11	1	63	24	18	138	Not drafted
P	Brett Jacobson, Cactus Shadows HS, Carefree, Ariz.	R-R	6-5	195	10	1	0.74	11	0	74	37	16	100	D-backs (11)
P	Brian Matusz, St. Mary's HS, Phoenix	L-L	6-5	175	7	1	0.55	11	0	77	21	19	137	Angels (4)
P	Chaz Roe, Lafayette HS, Lexington, Kent.	R-R	6-5	170	7	2	0.63	11	0	56	29	22	89	Rockies (1S)
P	Ryan Tucker, Temple City (Calif.) HS	R-R	6-2	190	7	5	1.19	14	1	82	47	28	132	Marlins (1S)
UT	Lance Lynn, Brownsburg (Ind.) HS	R-R	6-5	240	15	0	0.68	16	1	92	31	32	168	
UT	Sean Ratliff, Niwot HS, Longmont, Colo.	L-L	6-4	190	9	0	0.65	10	1	65	21	15	121	

son with an unblemished 35-0 mark, winning the Nebraska state title with a 10-6 win over Omaha's Westside High. The Mustangs joined Indiana's Brownsburg High as the only unbeaten teams in the BA/NCHBCA poll and became the first Nebraska high school team to go undefeated since 1984 when Omaha's Northwest High won all 19 games. Millard North's Jason Jewell had three home runs and 13 RBIs in four playoff games.

■ No. 7 Rancho Bernardo High of San Diego won its fourth California Interscholastic Federation Sand Diego sectional title since 1999, beating Granite Hills High 8-2 in the final as senior Brian Wilson tossed a four-hitter and went 4-for-4 with a double, triple and two RBIs.

■ No 8 Elder High of Cincinnati got a complete-game, three-hitter from Matt Klausing in a 3-0 win over Start High of Toledo in the Ohio Division I state championship game. It was the Panthers eighth state title overall.

■ Sarasota (Fla.) High, Mills Godwin High of Richmond, Va., and Bishop O'Dowd High of Oakland all saw their hopes of undefeated 2005 seasons fall by the wayside in the state playoffs.

Sarasota won its first 28 games, but lost to Palm Beach Central High 6-2 in the Florida 6-A regional tournament. Mills Godwin fell to Midlothian High 1-0 in the Virginia regional semifinals after winning its first 22 games. O'Dowd High went to 25-0 on the season before suffering its only loss, 10-7 to Danville's Monte Vista High, in California's North Coast section 3-A quarterfinals.

Final Rankin

While Alabama was home to the nation's 2005 No. 1 team, next door in Mississippi, Brandon's Northwest Rankin High won a state title in a similar scenario. After reaching at least the semifinals four years in a row at the 5-A level without winning, Northwest Rankin finally sealed the state crown, defeating Gulfport High 6-3 and 5-4 in a best-of-three series. The Cougars capped their season with six straight wins to finish at No. 28 overall with a 36-3 record.

"It was a great feeling," said coach Jeff McClasky, who earned his first state title in his 16th season at Northwest Rankin. "We had probably 200 parents and alumni and more than a thousand fans supporting us (at the championship game). It's a good feeling to finally win this for our community and our school. We kind of overachieved when we got to the finals, truthfully. We've been close man, many times."

Similar to the makeup of Russell County's roster, the Cougars relied on a strong pitching staff, led by underclassmen Todd McInnis, Jordan King and Ben Wylie, who all featured fastballs in the upper 80s.

It was McInnis' complete game gem in the semifinal round against the state's top-ranked team, Madison Central, that propelled Northwest Rankin to the title. The junior righthander shut down 10th-ranked Central, 2-0, carrying a one-hitter into the seventh inning while striking out 13.

■ Kingwood High scored seven times in the first two innings on its way to the Texas 5-A championship. The Mustangs (35-6), who opened the season ranked No. 25 and finished No. 12, defeated Rockwall High 10-5 for the school's first state championship.

Johnny Whittleman, who was drafted in the second round by the Rangers, and Josh Fountain sparked Kingwood's offense, while Kenneth Negron collected championship game MVP honors on the strength of a three-run triple in the first inning.

■ Virginia's 3-A championship tilt lasted 12 innings, with Princess Anne High of Virginia Beach outlasting Osbourn High of Manassas 11-10. Princess Anne trailed 8-0 after three innings, 9-8 in the 11th and 10-9 in the 12th, but Jake McAloose singled home two runs in the bottom of the 12th to cap the final comeback.

Princess Anne senior righthander Dan Hudson pitched the first 10 innings, allowing only one hit from the fourth inning on. He also tied the game with a three-run double in the seventh. The championship was the first for Princess Anne in its 50-year history.

■ Chattahoochee High of Alpharetta, Ga., climbed to No. 23 in the final BA/NHSBCA poll, wrapping up its season by winning a best-of-three series against Marietta's Lassiter High to claim the Georgia Class 5-A title.

In the second game of the championship series, senior Clayton Shunick spun a two-hitter in a 5-0 win. Georgia signee Justin Holloway had a two-run double and added a solo home run. Georgia Tech signee Jay Dantzler went 3-for-3 with four stolen bases in the decisive third game. Chattahoochee junior outfielder Matt Cerione hit .414-17-51 on the season.

Nation's best sweat out hard-fought affair

In its brief, three-year existence, the Aflac All-American High School Baseball Classic has become a must-see event on the baseball calendar for scouts, as more than 100 who baked in 100-degree weather to watch the 2005 event, played in Aberdeen, Md., can attest.

In the workouts leading up to the game, 38 rising high school seniors appeared to stack up with prospects from the previous two years. But the game reminded everyone quickly that as talented as the players are, even the most precocious high school stars are far from finished products.

In a game broadcast live across the nation on Fox Sports Net, the West squad outlasted the East 8-4 in a matchup that lasted nearly four hours and featured its share of brilliant moments as well as a few best suited for the sandlot.

Sixteen pitchers combined for 19 walks and three hit batsmen, and the West scored five runs in the eighth inning to seal the victory. Righthander Kyle Drabek, from The Woodlands High in suburban Houston, tossed the final two innings, striking out four and working around a pair of walks to give the West its second straight Aflac win after dropping the inaugural game in 2003.

Devin Shepherd, an outfielder from Oxnard (Calif.) High, was named MVP after he singled twice, walked twice, scored once and drove in a run. Shepherd was one of four California players in the West lineup with two hits apiece. Grant Green and Nathan Bridges—who play in the same high school conference in Orange County—were each 2-for-5 and Westlake High's Jeff Rapoport went 2-for-4 as the foursome accounted for eight of the West's nine hits.

YOUTH BASEBALL

BY ALLAN SIMPSON

Catcher Michael Memea completed a stunning comeback for Ewa Beach, Hawaii, when he drilled a walk-off home run to lead off the seventh inning and power his West Oahu team to a 7-6 win over defending champion Curacao in the 2005 Little League (11-12) World Series, played in Williamsport, Pa..

West Oahu had rallied to tie the game at 6-6 in the bottom of the sixth inning, by scoring three times, to force extra innings. Memea then drilled a 3-2 pitch off Curacao reliever Christopher Garia for his game-winning homer to lift Hawaii to its first-ever Little League title. Memea, who went 5-for-16 with three homers and eight RBIs in the tournament, had struck out in his previous two appearances in the championship game against Garia, who came on in relief in the fourth.

Curacao was bidding to become the first team since Long Beach, Calif., in 1992-93 to win back-to-back titles. It nearly accomplished the feat when Sorick Liberia broke a 3-3 tie in the fifth with a two-run homer and Darren Seferina added a solo shot to give Curacao a 6-3 lead. But Garia couldn't make the lead stand up in the sixth, when Curacao failed to complete a potential game-ending double play.

Hawaii went a perfect 6-0 in the tournament. It beat a team from Rancho Buena Vista, Calif., 6-1 in the U.S. final to advance to the championship game.

■ West Oahu's triumph in the Little League World Series capped a banner summer for youth baseball in Hawaii.

Three pitchers combined on a one-hitter as the Oahu All-Stars beat defending champion Mexico 1-0 in the championship game of the Cal Ripken World Series, played in Aberdeen, Md., a week prior to the Little League World Series. The Little League World Series and Cal Ripken World Series are recognized as the world's top sanctioned tournaments at the 11-12 year-old age level.

Kalani Lagoc-Crawford, who went 3-0, 0.64 and struck out 24 in 11 innings in the Cal Ripken Series, worked the first four innings of the deciding game, striking out 11, and drove in the game's only run with a second-inning home run. Kewby Meyer, who went 1-0, 0.58 with three saves and struck out 22 in 12 innings, worked the final inning, striking out the side. Meyer also worked the first five

Taking Stock in this top youth player

BY ALAN MATTHEWS

Robert Stock has made a habit of being recognized before his time.

He was named by Baseball America as the nation's second-best 12-year-old in 2002, the best 13-year-old in 2003 and the best 14-year-old in 2004.

When he led the United States to a silver medal at the 2005 World Youth Championship in Mexico, he was fittingly named the top 15-year-old. He was also recognized as BA's 2005 Youth Player of the Year, the first time a high school underclassman has won the honor.

Stock, a junior at Agoura (Calif.) High, solidified his spot as BA's top youth player with another sensational summer, once again playing against older and more experienced competition.

At the age of 14, Stock became the youngest player ever to make Team USA's youth national team, which finished second in a World qualifying tournament in Mexico. He was the second-youngest player on the same roster as a 15-year-old—yet was the team's No. 1 pitcher.

He was on the mound for the second game in a row as the Americans drew Cuba in the championship game of the World Youth Championship.

BILL MITCHELL

Youth standout
Robert Stock dominant at his age

Stock was sharp early on, racking up eight strikeouts in four innings before a three-hour rain delay prevented him from completing the game, which Cuba eventually won 5-0.

"Stock was incredible," USA Baseball's Jeff Singer said. "I really would have liked to see him try and close it out, because before it started raining he had dominant stuff."

The 6-foot, 180-pound Stock has always dominated his age group. He was tossing 90 mph fastballs by the time he was 14 and has been known to connect on 400-foot home runs, using a wood bat.

He possesses outstanding skills as a catcher and pitcher. His arm strength is his most outstanding tool, as he hit 94 mph in the summer of 2005 and one scout clocked him at 95 on a couple of pitches during the fall in a scout league game.

Stock, who turned 16 on Nov. 21, also shows impressive raw power from the left side of the plate, and his arm strength plays well behind the plate, where he has the potential to be a sound defensive catcher.

"It might be a 50-50 split with scouts in Southern California which way we like him," one area scout said. "I asked him what he liked most about hitting or pitching and he just sad, 'I just love to dominate, whether it be hitting or pitching.' And that's what he does, he just dominates games."

The 6-foot, 180-pound Stock believes he still has time to sort out what position he'll play, either in college or pro ball.

"At this point, I feel I'm more talented at pitching, but I have a better body and stature for catching," he said. "So down the road, who knows, but I'm ready for whatever's next."

PREVIOUS WINNERS

2002—Delmon Young, of, Camarillo, Calif.
2003—Nick Adenhart, rhp, Williamsport, Md.
2004—Cameron Maybin, of, Asheville, N.C.

innings of Oahu's 1-0 semifinal win against Lexington, Ky., allowing only two hits, to earn tournament MVP honors.

Teams from Hawaii also reached the U.S. final of the Junior League (13-14) World Series, the championship game of the Senior League (15-16) World Series and the championship game of the Babe Ruth 13-15 World Series.

"There's a lot of talent in Hawaii," West Oahu coach Layton Aliviado said. "Don't overlook Hawaii, because in Hawaii the kids are awesome, they're talented. They won't overlook us now. We showed them we can play."

Successful Summer For East Cobb

Georgia's East Cobb Baseball has been the nation's most decorated youth baseball program for almost two decades, but even by its own lofty standards 2005 was a banner year.

East Cobb teams won 13 national championships or competitions in age groups ranging from 13 to 18, tying a program record. Among the more unlikely conquests was the Continental Amateur Baseball Association 16-year-old title World Series, won by the East Cobb Yankees, merely East Cobb's third best travel team in that age group.

The East Cobb Astros, the program's elite 16-year-old team, were the three-time defending CABA 16 champions but were unable to defend their title in 2005 because the event conflicted with the more prestigious AAU 16-year-old Junior Olympics in New Orleans. The Astros went on to win that 30-team tournament for the ninth time in 10 years by beating Georgia's OTC Bearcats 5-0 in the final behind lefthander Taylor Wood, who went 16-0 on the summer.

"This has been a pretty special year," said Guerry Baldwin, who coaches the Astros and is the driving force behind the East Cobb program. "We've never done this well before with our older teams, our 15 to 18 year-old programs."

The Astros swept to the AAU title by going 9-0. It was the second of three national titles on the summer for the Astros, who went 75-8 overall. The Astros also won Perfect Game's World Wood Bat Association 16-year-old crown earlier in the summer at East Cobb's complex in Marietta, Ga., and won Perfect Game's inaugural Baseball Championship Series at the Metrodome in Minneapolis.

In the absence of the Astros, East Cobb entered the Titans and Yankees, its No. 2 and 3 16-year-old teams, in the CABA tournament, played in Marietta, and the Yankees went on to win the 32-team tournament.

Meanwhile, East Cobb's premier 18-year-old club, the Yankees, won the Connie Mack World Series in Farmington, N.M., continuing a streak that has seen the team win in every odd-numbered year since 1999. The Yankees won two games from the Trombly Braves of Orange County, Calif., on the final day, 7-4 and 7-6, to win their latest title. They also won in 2001 and 2003.

Orioles Win AAABA Crown Again

The Maryland Orioles won the All-American Amateur Baseball Association (20-and-under) title for the third straight year and 23rd time by a team from Baltimore, beating 12-time champion New Orleans 13-1 in the championship game of the 60th annual tournament, played in Johnstown, Pa.

The Orioles dropped their opening game of the 24-team event, then reeled off six straight wins, getting a four-hitter from Bernard Robert (Alabama), a Louisiana native, in the final.

Balk Call Decides Legion Series

Enid, Okla., won the 2005 American Legion World Series in most unusual fashion by scoring the winning run in the bottom of the ninth inning of a 7-6 win over Twin Cities, Wash., on a bases-loaded, two-out balk. The series was played in Rapid City, S.D.

Twin Cities had rallied from an early 6-0 deficit in the deciding game by scoring three runs in the top of the ninth to tie the game 6-6 only to lose it in the bottom of the inning when pitcher Jeremy Stumetz wheeled to first and pumped a throw, only to realize first baseman Tyler Cheney was not on the bag. A balk was called, enabling the winning run to score from third.

Enid and Twin Cities had beaten each other earlier in the double-elimination tournament, with Twin Cities handing Enid its only loss, 10-5, earlier on the final day.

Center fielder Zac Berg was Enid's top hitter, going 19-for-46 with five home runs and 21 RBIs in regional and national play. He drove in two runs in the deciding game to earn tournament MVP honors.

Davitt Pitches Mobile To Title

Mobile, Ala., became the first team in the 38-year history of the Babe Ruth 16-18 World Series to go unscored upon as it won the title with a 10-0 win in the final on a four-hitter by righthander Michael Davitt. Mobile didn't allow a run in 26 innings, while allowing only 13 hits and two walks.

Davitt, a ninth-round pick of the Dodgers in the 2005 draft, threw two complete-game shutouts. He had a one-hitter earlier in the tournament and was named the event's most valuable player.

Mobile, making its seventh straight appearance in the World Series, previously won the title in 2000 and 2001 and finished second in 2002 and 2003.

■ Teams from Jefferson Parish, La., won the Babe Ruth 13, Babe Ruth 14 and Babe Ruth 13-15 World Series. The 13-15 squad won for the second year in a row, beating Honolulu 9-1 in the championship game. Jefferson Parish was the host team and won the event despite fielding two teams in the event.

■ San Gabriel, Calif., won the Babe Ruth 16-year-old World Series for the fourth time, beating Jefferson Parish 3-0 in the final as Rob Rasmussen spun a two-hitter with no walks and 13 strikeouts. By going 6-0 in 2005, San Gabriel stretched its overall winning streak at the Babe Ruth World Series to 20 games.

Third Title In A Row

South Carolina won the Big League (17-18) World Series for the third straight year—all as the host team—by beating Thousand Oaks, Calif., 10-5 in the final.

Alex Farotto, who earned a save when South Carolina beat the same Thousand Oaks team in the final in 2003, worked the final 2⅓ innings to record another save. His former high school and current University of South Carolina teammate, catcher Kyle Enders, led South Carolina with two hits and three RBIs as South Carolina rallied from a 5-1 deficit by scoring four runs in the fourth and four in the fifth inning.

South Carolina (5-1) also rallied from a four-run deficit to beat previously unbeaten Venezuela 7-5 in the semi-finals.

Taiwan previously won four straight Big League World Series titles from 1993-96.

BASEBALL FOR THE AGES

BY ALLAN SIMPSON

Baseball America's annual Baseball For The Ages program, which began in 1998, recognizes the top players in each age group, from 12 to 25. No players have dominated their age groups through the years more than Devil Rays prospect Delmon Young, 19, and Cardinals slugger Albert Pujols, 25, who were recognized for a record fifth time in 2005. Young was Baseball America's Minor League Player of the Year, while Pujols was the National League MVP.

In each case, the universal youth cutoff date of Aug. 1 has been used to establish a player's age, though that deadline will change to May 1 in 2006.

12 DELINO DeSHIELDS, of, Fairburn, Ga.

It's apparent that DeShields has inherited the exceptional talent and athleticism of his father, a 1987 first-round draft pick and a 13-year major leaguer. He is a game changer both at the plate and on the bases, with a combination of raw power and speed. DeShields put his talent on display for Alabama's Boys of Baseball during Cooperstown Dreamspark's National Tournament of Champions when he set an all-time record during the Road Runner Race, circling the 70-foot bases in 12.06 seconds. In the championship game, he launched one of the longest home runs in the 10-year history of the event. On the week, he hit .667-6-12. DeShields, an eighth-grader at Woodward Academy in College Park, Ga., has spent the last five seasons playing for the Georgia Seminoles and is a lifetime .600 hitter. Overall in 2005, spanning 75 games, he hit .584-24-95 with 107 runs and 62 stolen bases.

DeShields

13 VINNY PONCE, c, Huntington Beach, Calif.

The Huntington Beach Vikings have been the nation's most prolific team in their age group the last two years, going 151-12 overall. They finished second at the USSSA Elite 12-year-old World Series in 2004 and closed out the season by winning Cooperstown's Dreamspark National Tournament of Champions. They avenged a loss to the Texas Express in the championship game of the 2004 USSSA Elite tournament by beating the same team in 2005 as 13-year-olds. Ponce excelled at the tournament, hitting .500 overall while throwing out 11-of-11 base runners. He also did not allow a single passed ball as the Vikings cruised to the title. With a 1.95 second pop time to second on a regulation 60-90-foot field, Ponce has thrown out base runners at a 90 percent clip the last two years. He hit .610 in 2004, .535 in 2005 and has a combined 25 home runs in the two years.

14 MILES HEAD, c/1b, Fayetteville, Ga.

A man-child at age 14, the 6-foot, 215-pound Head put up the best numbers this side of slow-pitch softball in 2005. Overall, he slammed 36 homers and drove in 276 runs, while hitting more than .650. There was little debate that he was by far the best hitter in the nation at his age. Head spent most of his 2005 season playing for Tennessee's Southeast Road Warriors, who went 73-12 while often playing against top 15- and 16-year-old competition. Head hit .642 for the Road Warriors with 91 extra-base hits and 228 RBIs. At least five of his 22 homers were more than 400 feet. He played for a team from Bergen Beach, N.Y., in the Continental Amateur Baseball Association 14 World Series and hit .739-6-18, leading the tournament in all triple crown categories as Bergen Beach, a melting pot of talent, ran the table by winning 11 straight games. Head led the same team to the 13-year-old CABA title a year earlier.

WINNERS AGES 19-25

19. Delmon Young, of, Devil Rays
20. Brandon Wood, ss, Angels
21. Huston Street, rhp, Athletics
22. David Wright, 3b, Mets
23. Dontrelle Willis, lhp, Marlins
24. Jake Peavy, rhp, Padres
25. Albert Pujols, 1b, Cardinals

15 ROBERT STOCK, rhp, Agoura, Calif.

Stock's acclaim as a youth league player has been surpassed in the last decade by only Delmon Young and Justin Upton, the first picks in the 2003 and 2005 drafts. He also was honored as the best in his age at 13 and 14, and was no less dominant as a 12-year-old. In 2005, he was the second-youngest player on the U.S. national youth team that finished second at the World Youth Championship in Mexico. He started three games in the tournament, including both the semifinal and gold-medal game for the U.S., and had 27 strikeouts in 14 innings—a tournament record. Overall, he went 1-1, 0.64. Though he has more upside as a righthanded pitcher and is the No. 2 prospect in the Draft Class of 2007 at that position, Stock has made a greater impact in high school as a lefthanded-hitting catcher. He hit .404-8-29 for Agoura High as a sophomore in earning all-county honors. He worked just 20 innings on the mound, going 5-1, 2.90 with 29 strikeouts in 20 innings, as he played a secondary role on a veteran staff.

16 CODY JOHNSON, 1b/of, Lynnhaven, Fla.

Johnson, a senior at Mosley High in Pensacola, Fla., had a breakout summer in 2005 playing for Georgia's East Cobb Astros. He led the 16-year-old powerhouse to its ninth AAU Junior Olympics title in 10 years, earning all-tournament honors, and was selected the MVP of both the 16- and 17-year-old World Wood Bat Association national tournaments. He was selected the top prospect at the WWBA 18-year-old tournament. At the three WWBA tournaments, all played in Marietta, Ga., he went a combined .597-9-34 in 62 at-bats. In 92 games overall for the Astros, Johnson hit .496-22-115.

17 BRETT ANDERSON, lhp, Stillwater, Okla.

Anderson, the son of Oklahoma State head coach Frank Anderson, spent the bulk of his 2005 season playing for Cincinnati's Midland Redskins, the defending Connie Mack World Series champions. Anderson went 5-0, 0.80 with six walks and 49 strikeouts in 35 innings for the Redskins, and his ERA was the second lowest in the history of the program, topped only by Mark Mulder, who compiled a 0.69 mark in 1996. Anderson juggled his Midland schedule around the COPABE Junior Pan Ams in Mexico. He was the ace for Team USA, going 2-0, 0.56 with three walks and 24 strikeouts in 16 innings. A 6-foot-4, 205-pound lefthander who went 9-1, 1.14 as a sophomore at Stillwater High in 2004, Anderson went 5-0 with five saves and a school record 0.68 ERA as an all-Oklahoma junior pitcher in 2005.

Anderson

18 ANDREW McCUTCHEN, of, Pirates

McCutchen was drafted in the first round (11th overall) in June by the Pirates after hitting .709-16-42 with 16 stolen bases at Fort Meade (Fla.) High. Scouts were impressed by the bat speed he generated from a compact 5-foot-11, 170-pound frame. He excelled in his first exposure to pro ball, earning top prospect honors in the Rookie-level Gulf Coast League after hitting .297-2-30 with 13 stolen bases. Promoted to short-season Williamsport, he hit .346-0-4 in 13 games.

HIGH SCHOOL BASEBALL

AMATEUR/YOUTH CHAMPIONS 2005

TEAM USA

HEADQUARTERS: Durham, N.C.

Event	Site	Champion	Runner-up
PROFESSIONAL TEAM			
XXXVI World Cup	Amsterdam, Netherlands	Cuba	Korea
JUNIOR TEAM (18-and-Under)			
Tournament of Champions	Joplin, Mo.	AABC	RBI
COPABE Championship	Villahermosa, Mexico	Cuba	United States
YOUTH TEAM (16-and-Under)			
World Championship	Monterrey, Mexico	Cuba	United States
USA Junior Olympics—East	Jupiter, Fla.	Dynamic Elite (Fla.)	Florida Magic
USA Junior Olympics—West	Peoria/Sunrise, Ariz.	NorCal Black	San Diego Gamers

NATIONAL CHAMPIONSHIPS

ALL-AMERICAN AMATEUR BASEBALL ASSOCIATION (AAABA)			**HEADQUARTERS: Zanesville, Ohio**
World Series (21-and-Under)	Johnstown, Pa.	Maryland Orioles	New Orleans
AMATEUR ATHLETIC UNION (AAU)			**HEADQUARTERS: Lake Buena Vista, Fla.**
8-and-Under	Concord, N.C.	Greensboro (N.C.) BC Cubs	Raleigh (N.C.) Wildcats
9-and-Under	Orlando	Central Florida Sting	Jupiter (Fla.) Diamondbacks
10-and-Under (65-foot)	Charlotte	NC Cleveland Indians	Carolina Angels
11-and-Under (70-foot)	Orlando	Central Florida Express	East Cobb (Ga.) Astros
12-and-Under	Burnsville, Minn.	Baltimore Buzz	South Shore (Mass.) Seadogs
13-and-Under (80-foot)	Burlington, N.C.	East Cobb (Ga.) Astros	Team Tennessee
13-and-Under (90-foot)	Myrtle Beach, S.C.	Massachusetts Lightning Baseball	Central Florida Indians
14-and-Under (90-foot)	Sarasota, Fla.	California Starmaker Titans	Team Easton Florida
15-and-Under	Roanoke, Va.	NorCal	Team Charlotte (N.C.)
Junior Olympics/16 & U	New Orleans	East Cobb (Ga.) Astros	OTC (Ga.) Bearcats
17-and-Under	Louisville	Tri State (N.J.) Arsenal	Ohio All Pro Freight
18-and-Under	Orlando	Brandon (Fla.) Blaze	Brazos Valley (Texas) Renegades
High school			
AMERICAN AMATEUR BASEBALL CONGRESS (AABC)			**HEADQUARTERS: Farmington, N.M.**
Roberto Clemente (8 & U)	McDonough, Ga.	McDonough (Ga.) Dawgs	Gresham Park (Ga.) White Sox
Willie Mays (9 & U)	Tulsa	Stillwater (Okla.) Yankees	Sykesville (md.) Cyclones
Willie Mays (10 & U)	Catano, P.R.	Puerto Rico	Knoxville, Tenn.
Pee Wee Reese (11 & U)	Brooklyn, N.Y.	Brooklyn (N.Y.) Metro	Germantown, Md.
Pee Wee Reese (12 & U)	Toa Baja, P.R.	Georgia Padres	Tulsa Lookouts
Sandy Koufax (13 & U)	Battle Creek, Mich.	Detroit Eagles	Burtonville (Ind.) Dawgs
Sandy Koufax (14 & U)	Rockford, Ill.	Puerto Rico	South Troy (N.Y.) Dodgers
Mickey Mantle (15 & U)	Owasso, Okla.	Orange County (Calif.) Stallions	Dallas Giants
Mickey Mantle (16 & U)	McKinney, Texas	Dallas Tigers	Orange County (Calif.) Angels
Connie Mack (18 & U)	Farmington, N.M.	East Cobb (Ga.) Yankees	Trombly (Calif.) Braves
Stan Musial (open)	Battle Creek, Mich.	Flint, Mich.	Canton, Ohio
AMERICAN LEGION BASEBALL			**HEADQUARTERS: Indianapolis**
World Series (19 & U)	Rapid City, S.D.	Enid, Okla.	Twin Cities, Wash.
BABE RUTH BASEBALL			**HEADQUARTERS: Trenton, N.J.**
Cal Ripken (10 & U)	Russellville, Ark.	Kenner, La.	Okeeheelee, Fla.
Cal Ripken (11-12)	Aberdeen, Md.	Oahu, Hawaii	Mexico
13-year-old	Jamestown, N.Y.	Jefferson Parish, La.	Montgomery, N.J.
14-year-old	Quincy, Mass.	Jefferson Parish, La.	Nash County, N.C.
13-15-year-olds	Abbeville, La.	Jefferson Parish (La.) East	Honolulu
16-year-old	Weimar, Texas	San Gabriel, Calif.	Jefferson Parish, La.
16-18-year-old	Newark, Ohio	Mobile, Ala.	Newark, Ohio
CONTINENTAL AMATEUR BASEBALL ASSOCIATION (CABA)			**HEADQUARTERS: Westerville, Ohio**
9-and-Under	Charles City, Iowa	Hawaii Warriors	Cincinnati Flames
10-and-Under	Lynwood, Ill.	Iowa Sun Devils	Naperville (Ill.) Wheatland Ducks
11-and-Under	Marion, Ohio	Columbus Sharks	Indiana Bandits
12-and-Under	Cincinnati	Monterey Park (Calif.) Angels	Southern Nevada Wolfpack
13-and-Under	Knoxville, Tenn.	Team Knoxville	Atlanta Bulls
14-and-Under (54-foot)	Dublin, Ohio	Brooklyn Bergen Beach	Columbus Cobras
15-and-Under	Crystal Lake, Ill.	East Cobb (Ga.) Astros	Hamlin Park (Ill.) All-Stars
16-and-Under	Marietta, Ga.	East Cobb (Ga.) Yankees	Columbus Sharks
High school age	Euclid, Ohio	Brooklyn Bergen Beach	Ohio Thunder/Orange
18-and-Under	Miami	Nashville (Tenn.) Hit After Hit	Columbus, Ohio
18-and-Under (wood)	Charleston, S.C.	South Carolina Diamond Devils/18	Midland (Ohio) Indians
COOPERSTOWN DREAMSPARK			**HEADQUARTERS: Salisbury, N.C.**
Tournament of Champions (12)	Cooperstown, N.Y.	Alabama Boys of Baseball	Southern California Redwings
DIXIE BASEBALL			**HEADQUARTERS: Montgomery, Ala.**
Dixie Youth (9-10)	Auburn, Ala.	Troy, Ala.	Midland, S.C.
Dixie Youth (12 & U)	Auburn, Ala.	Lee County, Ga.	Wayne County, Tenn.
Junior Dixie Boys 13	Muscle Shoals, Ala.	Texarkana, Ark.	Muscle Shoals, Ala.
Dixie Boys (13-14)	Muscle Shoals, Ala.	St. Andrews, S.C.	Covington County, Ga.

AMATEUR/YOUTH CHAMPIONS 2005

Dixie Pre-Majors (15-16)	Ponchatoula, La.	North Augusta, S.C.	Monroe, La.
Dixie Majors (15-18)	Laurel, Miss.	North Charleston, S.C.	Laurel, La.

DIZZY DEAN BASEBALL — **HEADQUARTERS: Hernando, Miss.**

8-and-Under	Southaven, Miss.	Wills Park (Ga.) Slammers	Sandy Plains, Ga.
9-and-Under	Southaven, Miss.	Paulding County (Ga.) Vipers	Gardendale, Ala.
10-and-Under	Moody, Ala.	Sykesville (Md.) Cyclones	Gardendale, Ala.
11-and-Under	Rossville, Ga.	Tallahassee, Fla.	North Jackson, Miss.
12-and-Under	Moody, Ala.	Tallahassee (Fla.) Titans	Lufkin, Texas
13-and-Under	Southaven, Miss.	Bartow (Ga.) Americans	St. John (La.) Warriors
14-and-Under	Southaven, Miss.	Howard County (Md.) Raiders	Lufkin, Texas
Junior (15-16)	Southaven, Miss.	Bonifay, Fla.	Frederick (Md.) Hustlers
Senior (17-19)	Southaven, Miss.	Shelby County, Ala.	Baton Rouge, La.
High school	Starkville, Miss.	New Hope, Miss.	Lafayette County, Miss.

HAP DUMONT BASEBALL/National Baseball Congress — **HEADQUARTERS: Wichita**

Event	Site	Champion	Runner-up
8-and-Under	Midwest City, Okla.	Oklahoma Jamers	Oklahoma Outlaws
9-and-Under	Kearney, Mo.	Wichita Outlaws	Pittsburg, Kan.
10-and-Under	Pratt, Kan.	Wichita Sluggers/Red	Wichita Sluggers/Blue
11-and-Under	Oklahoma City	Oklahoma City Braves	Oklahoma City Banditos
12-and-Under	Bartlett, Tenn.	Louisiana Reds	Collierville, Tenn.
13-and-Under	Tunica, Miss.	Muskogee (Okla.) Titans	Jackson (Tenn.) Cowboys
14-and-Under	Harrison, Ark.	Memphis Team Mizuno	Houston Muddogs
15-and-Under	Oklahoma City	Oklahoma 89ers	Wichita Reds
16-and-Under	Pittsburg, Kan.	Mac 'N Seitz (Mo.) Indians	Cincinnati Morgenroth
17-and-Under	Topeka, Kan.	Mineola (Texas) Bombers	Indiana Bandits
18-and-Under	Topeka, Kan.	Wichita Sluggers	Wichita Gators

LITTLE LEAGUE BASEBALL — **HEADQUARTERS: Williamsport, Pa.**

Little League (11-12)	Williamsport, Pa.	Ewa Beach, Hawaii	Curacao
Junior League (13-14)	Taylor, Mich.	Panama City, Panama	Tarpon Springs, Fla.
Senior League (15-16)	Bangor, Me.	Unbandale, Iowa	Pearl City, Hawaii
Big League (17-18)	Easley, S.C.	South Carolina	Thousand Oaks, Calif.

NATIONAL AMATEUR BASEBALL FEDERATION (NABF) — **HEADQUARTERS: Bowie, Md.**

Freshman (12 & U)	Hopkinsville, Ky.	East Cobb (Ga.) Stallions	Tulsa (Okla.) Hosers
Sophomore (14 & U)	Joplin, Mo.	Baltimore Buzz	Missouri Southwest Elite
Junior (16 & U)	Northville, Mich.	Summit City (Ind.) Sluggers	Columbia (Md.) Reds
High School (17 & U)	Greensboro, N.C.	East Cobb (Ga.) Braves	Long Island (N.Y.) Titans
Senior (18 & U)	Jackson, Miss.	Bayside (N.Y.) Yankees	Jackson (Miss.) 96ers
College (22 & U)	Toledo	Michigan Bulls	Pittsburgh Pandas
Major (open)	Louisville	Orchard Park (N.Y.) Sox	Ohio Peschell's Bakery

PERFECT GAME/WORLD WOOD BAT ASSOCIATION SUMMER CHAMPIONSHIPS — **HEADQUARTER: Cedar Rapids, Iowa**

15-and-Under	Marietta, Ga.	Richmond Braves	South Florida Diamond Kings
16-and-Under	Marietta, Ga.	East Cobb (Ga.) Astros	Richmond Braves
17-and-Under	Marietta, Ga.	(co-champions) NorCal; (Miami) All-America Prospects	
18-and-Under	Marietta, Ga.	Florida Bombers	Orlando (Fla.) Scorpions

PONY BASEBALL — **HEADQUARTERS: Washington, Pa.**

Mustang (9-10)	Irving, Texas	Miami Tamiami	East Long Beach, Calif.
Bronco (11-12)	Monterey, Calif.	Levittown, P.R.	Taiwan
Pony (13)	Chino Hills, Calif.	Caguas, P.R.	Mililani, Hawaii
Pony (13-14)	Washington, Pa.	Taiwan	San Diego
Colt (15-16)	Lafayette, Ind.	Tampa Wellswood	Caguas, P.R.
Palomino (17-18)	Santa Clara, Calif.	Santa Clara (Calif.) Red Sox	San Juan (P.R.) Criolos

REVIVING BASEBALL IN INNER CITIES (RBI) — **HEADQUARTERS: New York**

Junior (13-15)	Pittsburgh	Los Angeles	Newark, N.J.
Senior (16-18)	Pittsburgh	Los Angeles	Detroit

U.S. AMATEUR BASEBALL FEDERATION (USABF) — **HEADQUARTERS: Coronado, Calif.**

13-and-Under	San Diego	Seattle Stars	Kirkland (Wash.) Heat
14-and-Under	San Diego	Encinitas (Calif.) Reds	California Titans
15-and-Under	San Diego	Washington Barons	Bonita (Calif.) Legends
16-and-Under	San Diego	New York Cardinals	California Arsenal
18-and-Under	San Diego	Colton (Calif.) Nighthawks	Washington Taylor Baseball
18-and-Under (wood)	San Diego	California Reds	Bakersfield (Calif.) Braves

U.S. SPECIALTY SPORTS ASSOCIATION (USSSA) — **HEADQUARTERS: Petersburg, Va.**

9-and-Under/Majors	St. Louis	Southern California Redwings	Collierville, Tenn.
10-and-Under/Majors	Henderson, Nev.	Houston Banditos Black	Texas Rattlers
11-and-Under/Majors Elite	Orlando	Central Florida Express	Houston Banditos
12-and-Under/Majors Elite	Orlando	Oklahoma City Mets	Southern California Redwings
13-and-Under/Majors Elite	Orlando	Huntington Beach (Calif.) Vikings	Texas Express
14-and-Under/Majors Elite	Orlando	Georgia Roadrunners	North Florida Hurricanes
15-and-Under/Majors	Orlando	Team Orlando	Illinois North Stars
16-and-Under/Majors	Orlando	Palm Beach (Fla.) PAL	Crosswell (S.C.) Sun Devils
18-and-Under/Majors	Nashville	Franklin, Ohio	Georgia Stars

DRAFT

Upton tops brother by going No. 1, remains unsigned at season's end

BY JIM CALLIS

As a 14-year-old coming off his freshman year of high school, Justin Upton wasn't invited to the 2002 Area Code Games, a staple on the summer showcase circuit. He showed up in Long Beach anyway and immediately dazzled scouts, collecting two hits and making a play deep in the hole at shortstop in his first game.

After that weekend, scouts began touting Upton as the potential No. 1 overall pick in the 2005 draft. That's a tough standard to live up to, and many young players have wilted under similar expectations. But Upton never faltered, maintaining his status by continually excelling at showcases and on U.S. national teams.

"I heard that talk," Upton said. "The way I dealt with it was by playing the way I had been playing, trying to keep the pressure off my back."

JASON HIRSCHFELD

Justin's day
No. 1 overall pick Justin Upton celebrates selection with mother Yvonne

The pressure finally relented on June 7, when the Diamondbacks selected the Great Bridge High (Chesapeake, Va.) shortstop with the first choice in the 2005 draft. Justin and his older brother B.J., who went second overall in 2002 to the Devil Rays, became the highest-drafted siblings in draft history. They surpassed Dmitri (Cardinals, No. 4 in 1991) and Delmon (Devil Rays, No. 1 in 2003) Young.

B.J., whose Triple-A Durham club was playing at nearby Norfolk, was with Justin on draft day. He and several family members and friends gathered in the library at Great Bridge High to follow the draft over the Internet.

"It's good to see him succeed," B.J. said. "Going from playing baseball in the front yard and us fighting over it, and then he ended up being the No. 1 pick . . . I'm just real happy for him."

Justin, who met with Arizona two days before the draft and Kansas City (which held the second pick) a day later, said he didn't know he was going to be a Diamondback until he heard his name on the Internet broadcast. The Royals had called shortly before the draft started to tell him they'd take him at No. 2 if given the opportunity.

Arizona scouting director Mike Rizzo said Upton had been his favorite for months among a group of candidates that also included three college righthanders, Mike Pelfrey (Wichita State), Luke Hochevar (Tennessee) and Craig Hansen (St. John's). The Diamondbacks finalized their decision to take Upton the night before.

"It's been a long time coming and it's finally come true for me," Upton said. "My heart was pounding a little bit and when I got the news, it was just a real good moment for me."

Few high school players in recent memory can compare to Upton. He's considered slightly better than B.J. was at the same stage of their careers, as the 6-foot-2, 187-pound Justin is

YEAR-BY-YEAR BONUS PROGRESSION

Signing bonuses have grown exponentially since 1965, when the draft was instituted—ostensibly to curtail the growth of signing bonuses. From a first-round average of less than $50,000 in the first several years of the draft, that average grew to more than $2 million in the early years of this decade before leveling off and actually declining.

Following is a year-by-year breakdown of average first-round signing bonuses and the annual percentage change:

@ Does not include four loophole free agents.
* Average will be adjusted when/if two unsigned picks sign.

Year	Average	Change	Year	Average	Change	Year	Average	Change
1965	$42,516	—	1979	68,094	+0.2	1993	613,037	+27.2
1966	44,430	+4.5%	1980	74,025	+8.7	1994	790,357	+28.9
1967	42,898	-3.4	1981	78,573	+6.1	1995	918,019	+16.1
1968	43,850	+2.2	1982	82,615	+5.1	1996@	944,404	+2.9
1969	43,504	-0.8	1983	87,236	+5.6	1997	1,325,536	+40.4
1970	45,230	+3.9	1984	105,392	+20.8	1998	1,637,667	+23.1
1971	45,197	-0.1	1985	118,115	+12.1	1999	1,809,767	+10.5
1972	44,952	-0.5	1986	116,300	-1.6	2000	1,872,586	+3.5
1973	48,832	+8.6	1987	128,480	+10.5	2001	2,154,280	+15.0
1974	53,333	+9.2	1988	142,540	+10.9	2002	2,106,793	-2.2
1975	49,333	-7.5	1989	176,008	+23.5	2003	1,765,667	-16.2
1976	49,631	+0.6	1990	252,577	+43.5	2004	1,958,448	+10.9
1977	48,813	-1.6	1991	365,396	+44.7	2005*	1,817,500	-7.2
1978	67,892	+39.1	1992	481,893	+31.9			

NOTE: The signing bonus average for first-round picks from 1965-82 includes the value of college scholarship plans and incentive bonus plans, in addition to the cash bonus paid. From 1983-2005, the amount represents only the cash bonus paid.

stronger, faster and more advanced as a hitter. The only real knock on Justin, as with B.J., was that he's erratic making throws from shortstop.

While some scouts have said they would move Upton to center field and envisioned him becoming the next Ken Griffey Jr., Rizzo said the Diamondbacks believe he can play shortstop and had no plans to change his position.

Upton still hadn't signed by the end of the regular season, however. Arizona had offered Upton a $4.675 million bonus, which would be the third-highest ever given to a draft pick. Upton was seeking $6.25 million, which would break the draft-record $5.3 million the White Sox gave Joe Borchard in 2000.

After originally committing to North Carolina State, Upton switched to Louisburg (N.C.) JC. If he were to enroll there in January, the Diamondbacks would be able to sign him after his juco season ends.

The only other first-round pick unsigned by October was Pelfrey, the top pitching prospect in the draft. Because of concerns about his signability, he lasted until the Mets took him with the ninth pick.

Pelfrey was believed to want a big league contract similar to those received by the top three college pitchers taken in the 2004 draft, deals ranging from $4.2 million to $5.2 million. Neither side had commented publicly on the negotiations.

Hochevar Saga Awaits Resolution

Those negotiations were a cakewalk, however, compared to those between the Dodgers and supplemental first-rounder Luke Hochevar. A Tennessee righthander, Hochevar was considered second only to Pelfrey among pitchers available in the draft.

ROBERT GURGANUS

Luke Hochevar

Like Pelfrey, Hochevar was advised by Scott Boras and dropped because of signability concerns. Before the draft, the Rockies asked whether he'd be willing to sign for the MLB-recommended $2.3 million bonus as the No. 7 pick, but he indicated he wanted to be treated like the top pitchers from the 2004 draft.

Negotiations proceeded slowly, as they often do with Boras advisees. By the end of August, the Dodgers had upped their offer from $850,000, MLB's recommendation for his No. 40 slot, to $2.3 million, matching what Colorado would have paid him. Boras didn't respond with a counteroffer and Hochevar toyed with enrolling for his senior at Tennessee, which would have cost Los Angeles his rights, before opting not to attend the fall semester.

On Sept. 2, Hochevar attended a birthday party for the mother of his close friend Eli Iorg, a Volunteers teammate and an Astros supplemental first-round pick. Taking Iorg's advice, Hochevar agreed to talk to his agent, Matt Sosnick.

Accounts differ on who approached who and what was said, but both sides agree that Hochevar signed a document identifying Sosnick as his adviser that evening. Sosnick swiftly negotiated a $2.98 million bonus with Dodgers scouting director Logan White, and Hochevar agreed to the terms. But after speaking to Boras, Hochevar abruptly reneged on the deal and rejoined the Boras fold.

Boras' accounts of the events changed swiftly. On Sept. 4, he said he didn't know where rumors of these events were coming from. After the story broke in a Los Angeles newspaper on Sept. 7, he quickly arranged conference calls with himself, Hochevar and selected media outlets. They asserted that they suddenly had discovered that White conspired with Sosnick to get Hochevar to sign what the pitcher called "a very bad contract," though it would have given him a larger bonus than Zimmerman received from the Nationals.

The Dodgers immediately backed White and said he would continue to handle negotiations. Boras' response Sept. 9 was to reveal that further digging showed the

BONUS PROGRESSION RECORD

The Athletics paid Rick Monday, the first pick in the first draft, a signing bonus of $100,000. The figure stood as a draft record for 10 years but has since been broken many times over. The following chart traces the record for bonus payments. The figures represent straight cash bonuses in real dollars, with no regard to benefits from college scholarship plans or incentive bonus plans—or guaranteed money in the few cases where a player signed a major league contract (such players are denoted with an asterisk). The list considers only players who signed with the clubs that drafted them and does not include the four loophole free agents from 1996—notably Diamondbacks first baseman Travis Lee, who set a bonus record by signing for $10 million, or Devil Rays righthander Matt White, who established the present-day standard when he signed for $10.2 million.

Year	Player, Pos., Club (Round)	Bonus
1965	Rick Monday, of, Athletics (1)	$100,000
1975	Danny Goodwin, c, Angels (1)	$125,000
1978	Kirk Gibson, of, Tigers (1)	$150,000
	*Bob Horner, 3b, Braves (1)	$162,000
1979	Bill Bordley, lhp, Giants (1#)	$200,000
	Todd Demeter, 1b, Yankees (2)	$208,000
1988	Andy Benes, rhp, Padres (1)	$235,000
1989	Tyler Houston, c, Braves (1)	$241,500
	*Ben McDonald, rhp, Orioles (1)	$350,000
	*John Olerud, 1b, Blue Jays (3)	$575,000
1991	Mike Kelly, of, Braves (1)	$575,000
	Brien Taylor, lhp, Yankees (1)	$1,550,000
1994	Paul Wilson, rhp, Mets (1)	$1,550,000
	Josh Booty, 3b, Marlins (1)	$1,600,000
1996	Kris Benson, rhp, Pirates (1)	$2,000,000
1997	Rick Ankiel, lhp, Cardinals (2)	$2,500,000
	Matt Anderson, rhp, Tigers (1)	$2,505,000
1998	*J.D. Drew, of, Cardinals (1)	$3,000,000
	*Pat Burrell, 3b, Phillies (1)	$3,150,000
	Mark Mulder, lhp, Athletics (1)	$3,200,000
	Corey Patterson, of, Cubs (1)	$3,700,000
1999	Josh Hamilton, of, Devil Rays (1)	$3,960,000
2000	Joe Borchard, of, White Sox (1)	$5,300,000

#January draft

FIRST-ROUND TRENDS

Year	College	High School	Hitters	Pitchers	Average Bonus	Change
1999	15	15	10	*20	$1,809,767	+10.5%
2000	12	18	13	17	$1,872,586	+3.5%
2001	18	12	10	*20	*$2,154,280	+15.0%
2002	14	16	14	16	$2,106,793	-2.2%
2003	18	12	*20	10	$1,765,667	*-16.2%
2004	17	13	11	19	$1,958,448	+10.9%
2005	19	10	17	13	#$1,817,500	-7.2%

*Draft record.
#2005 average doesn't include three first-rounders still in negotiations with clubs.
Note: College includes junior college selections.

DRAFT '05 TOP 100 PICKS

Signing bonuses do not include scholarships, incentive bonus plans or salaries from a major league contract.
*Highest level of professional baseball attained +College Senior

No.	Team, Player, Pos.	School	Hometown	Bonus	Birthdate	B-T	HT	WT	AVG	AB	R	H	2B	3B	HR	RBI	SB	*'05 Assignment
1.	D-backs. Justin Upton, ss	Great Bridge HS	Chesapeake, Va.	Unsigned	8-25-87	R-R	6-2	187	.519	54	27	28	5	3	12	33	10	Did not sign
2.	Royals. Alex Gordon, 3b	U. of Nebraska	Lincoln, Neb.	$4,000,000	2-10-84	L-R	6-1	210	.372	253	79	94	22	4	19	66	23	DNP—Signed late
3.	Mariners. Jeff Clement, c	U. of Southern California	Marshalltown, Iowa	3,400,000	8-21-83	L-R	6-1	205	.348	230	52	80	17	0	15	54	5	Wisconsin (A)
4.	Nationals. Ryan Zimmerman, 3b	U. of Virginia	Virginia Beach, Va.	2,975,000	9-28-84	R-R	6-2	210	.393	234	51	92	18	4	6	59	17	Washington
5.	Brewers. Ryan Braun, 3b	U. of Miami	Granada Hills, Calif.	2,450,000	11-17-83	R-R	6-2	190	.388	219	70	85	16	2	18	76	23	West Virginia (A)
7.	Rockies. Troy Tulowitzki, ss	Long Beach State U.	Sunnyvale, Calif.	2,300,000	10-10-84	R-R	6-3	200	.349	152	32	53	12	1	8	29	2	Modesto (A)
10.	Tigers. Cameron Maybin, of	T.C. Roberson HS	Arden, N.C.	2,650,000	4-4-87	B-R	6-3	195	.662	71	66	47	12	1	15	37	32	DNP—Signed late
11.	Pirates. Andrew McCutchen, of	Fort Meade HS	Fort Meade, Fla.	1,950,000	10-10-86	R-R	5-11	170	.709	55	28	39	8	3	16	42	16	Williamsport (A)
12.	Reds. Jay Bruce, of	West Brook HS	Beaumont, Texas	1,800,000	4-3-87	L-L	6-2	200	.500	86	46	43	7	4	8	28	18	Billings (R)
13.	Orioles. Brandon Snyder, c	Westfield HS	Centreville, Va.	1,700,000	11-23-86	R-R	6-2	190	.500	58	29	29	5	2	3	29	2	Aberdeen (A)
14.	Indians. Trevor Crowe, of	U. of Arizona.	Portland, Ore.	1,695,000	11-17-83	B-R	5-10	185	.403	263	83	106	25	15	9	54	27	Akron (AA)
17.	Yankees. C.J. Henry, ss	Putnam City HS	Oklahoma City.	1,575,000	5-31-86	R-R	6-3	200	.481	106	52	51	8	7	13	41	21	GCL Yankees (R)
19.	Rangers. John Mayberry, of	Stanford U.	Kansas City, Mo.	1,525,000	12-21-83	R-R	6-5	210	.303	238	36	72	18	0	8	53	5	Spokane (A)
21.	Athletics. Cliff Pennington, ss	Texas A&M U.	Corpus Christi, Texas	1,450,000	6-15-84	B-R	5-11	170	.363	212	44	77	13	4	7	39	29	Kane County (A)
23.	Red Sox. Jacoby Ellsbury, of	Oregon State U.	Madras, Ore.	1,400,000	9-11-83	L-L	6-1	175	.406	244	56	99	19	3	6	48	26	Lowell (A)
28.	Cardinals. Colby Rasmus, of	Russell County HS	Phenix City, Ala.	1,000,000	8-11-86	L-L	6-2	183	.484	126	69	61	14	3	24	66	19	Johnson City (R)
30.	Cardinals. Tyler Greene, ss	Georgia Tech	Plantation, Fla.	1,100,000	8-17-83	R-R	6-2	188	.372	269	76	100	15	3	12	72	31	Palm Beach (A)
33.	Indians. John Drennen, of	Rancho Bernardo HS	San Diego	1,000,000	8-26-86	L-L	6-0	180	.472	106	61	50	12	3	17	50	12	Burlington (R)
36.	Athletics. Travis Buck, of	Arizona State U.	Richland, Wash.	950,000	11-18-83	L-R	6-2	180	.382	288	82	110	24	3	6	43	27	Kane County (A)
38.	Astros. Eli Iorg, of	U. of Tennessee	Knoxville, Tenn.	900,000	3-14-83	R-R	6-3	200	.381	252	63	96	19	4	15	72	27	Greeneville (R)
39.	Twins. Henry Sanchez, 1b	Mission Bay HS	San Diego	900,000	11-29-86	R-R	6-3	260	.482	85	38	41	8	2	13	38	5	GCL Twins (R)
45.	Red Sox. Jed Lowrie, 2b	Stanford U.	Salem, Ore.	762,500	4-17-84	B-R	6-0	180	.317	244	47	71	16	2	14	66	5	Lowell (A)
50.	Royals. Jeff Bianchi, ss	Lampeter-Strasburg HS	Lancaster, Pa.	690,000	10-5-86	R-R	5-11	180	.516	91	48	47	10	2	15	48	10	AZL Royals (R)
51.	Dodgers. Ivan DeJesus, ss	P.R. Baseball Academy	Guaynabo, P.R.	675,000	5-1-87	B-R	5-11	175	.365	52	23	19	5	2	1	14	5	Ogden (R)
52.	Rockies. Daniel Carte, of	Winthrop U.	Hurricane, W.Va.	670,000	5-18-84	R-R	6-0	180	.344	270	57	93	16	3	19	74	12	Tri-City (A)
54.	Twins. Paul Kelly, ss	Flower Mound HS	Flower Mound, Texas	650,000	10-19-86	R-R	5-11	175	.439	82	39	36	10	1	12	39	12	Beloit (A)
57.	Red Sox. Jon Egan, c	Cross Creek HS	Hephzibah, Ga.	625,000	10-12-86	R-R	6-4	210	.588	68	40	40	5	0	16	45	3	GCL Red Sox (R)
58.	Angels. Ryan Mount, ss	Ayala HS	Chino Hills, Calif.	600,000	8-17-86	L-R	6-2	175	.460	63	22	29	3	3	4	18	7	AZL Angels (R)
59.	Pirates. Brad Corley, of	Mississippi State U.	Louisville, Ky.	605,000	12-28-83	R-R	6-2	198	.316	263	45	83	20	2	5	40	1	Williamsport (A)
61.	Orioles. Nolan Reimold, of	Bowling Green State U.	Greenville, Pa.	590,000	10-12-83	R-R	6-4	207	.360	178	51	64	7	3	20	62	4	Frederick (A)
62.	Indians. Stephen Head, 1b	U. of Mississippi	Raymond, Miss.	605,000	1-13-84	L-L	6-2	218	.331	272	65	90	16	1	18	68	3	Kinston (A)
64.	Marlins. Kris Harvey, of	Clemson U.	Catawba, N.C.	575,000	1-5-84	R-R	6-2	195	.341	249	61	85	11	0	25	70	1	Jamestown (A)
65.	Phillies. Mike Costanzo, 3b	Coastal Carolina U.	Springfield, Pa.	570,000	9-9-83	L-R	6-3	205	.379	240	74	91	15	2	16	67	8	Batavia (A)
66.	Padres. Chase Headley, 3b	U. of Tennessee	Fountain, Colo.	560,000	5-9-84	B-R	6-2	195	.387	238	82	92	24	3	14	65	6	Fort Wayne (A)
67.	Rangers. Johnny Whittleman, 3b	Kingwood HS	Kingwood, Texas	650,000	2-11-87	L-R	6-1	190	.398	99	43	38	8	4	9	36	9	AZL Rangers (R)
71.	Angels. P.J. Phillips, ss	Redan HS	Stone Mountain, Ga.	505,000	9-23-86	R-R	6-3	170	.478	90	32	43	16	3	8	41	16	AZL Angels (R)
72.	Astros. Ralph Henriquez, c	Key West HS	Key West, Fla.	485,000	4-7-87	B-R	6-1	190	.495	95	45	47	11	3	5	39	10	Greeneville (R)
75.	Braves. Yunel Escobar, ss	None	Havana, Cuba	475,000	11-2-82	R-R	6-2	200	Did Not Play									Rome (A)
76.	Padres. Nick Hundley, c	U. of Arizona	Redmond, Wash.	465,000	9-8-83	R-R	6-1	190	.352	227	57	80	23	2	15	46	9	Fort Wayne (A)
79.	Marlins. Brett Hayes, c	U. of Nevada	Calabasas, Calif.	450,000	2-13-84	R-R	6-1	170	.313	214	31	67	11	2	6	45	6	Jamestown (A)
80.	Twins. Drew Thompson, ss	Jupiter Community HS	Tequesta, Fla.	475,000	11-7-86	L-R	5-11	165	.418	79	23	33	7	4	3	25	13	Fort Myers (A)
86.	Blue Jays. Brian Pettway, of	U. of Mississippi	Vicksburg, Miss.	440,000	7-29-83	R-R	6-1	205	.383	266	56	102	19	0	21	67	1	Auburn (A)
89.	+Astros. Tommy Manzella, ss	Tulane U.	Chalmette, La.	289,000	4-16-83	R-R	6-3	190	.347	288	59	100	24	2	8	63	21	Tri-City (A)
90.	Tigers. Chris Robinson, c	U. of Illinois	Dorchester, Ont.	422,000	5-12-84	R-R	6-0	200	.353	184	39	65	11	3	8	37	5	West Michigan (A)
91.	Pirates. James Boone, of	U. of Missouri	Clinton, Okla.	420,000	3-16-83	B-R	6-2	175	.340	194	53	66	15	5	8	72	14	Williamsport (A)
94.	Indians. Nick Weglarz, 1b	Lakeshore Catholic HS	Stevensville, Ont.	435,000	12-16-87	L-L	6-3	220	.560	25	12	14	4	0	5	16	6	Burlington (R)
99.	Rangers. Taylor Teagarden, c	U. of Texas	Carrolton, Texas	725,000	12-21-83	R-R	6-0	190	.333	222	52	74	22	1	7	33	4	Spokane (A)

No.	Team, Player, Pos.	School	Hometown	Bonus	Birthdate	B-T	HT	WT	W	L	ERA	G	SV	IP	H	BB	SO	*'05 Assignment
6.	Blue Jays. Ricky Romero, lhp	Cal State Fullerton	Los Angeles	$2,400,000	11-06-84	R-L	6-2	170	13	5	2.89	18	0	134	102	34	139	Dunedin (A)
8.	Devil Rays. Wade Townsend, rhp	Rice U.	Drip. Springs, Texas	1,500,000	2-22-83	R-R	6-4	225	Did Not Play									Hudson Valley (A)

DRAFT '05 TOP 100 PICKS

Signing bonuses do not include scholarships, incentive bonus plans or salaries from a major league contract.
*Highest level of professional baseball attained

No.	Team, Player, Pos.	School	Hometown	Bonus	Birthdate	B-T	HT	WT	W	L	ERA	G	SV	IP	H	BB	SO	*'05 Assignment
9.	Mets. Mike Pelfrey, rhp	Wichita State U.	Wichita	Unsigned	1-14-84	R-R	6-7	210	12	3	1.93	19	0	140	96	30	143	Did not sign
15.	White Sox. Lance Broadway, rhp	Texas Christian U.	Waxahachie, Texas	1,570,000	8-20-83	R-R	6-4	185	15	1	1.62	19	0	117	83	35	151	Winston-Salem (A)
16.	Marlins. Chris Volstad, rhp	Palm Beach Gardens HS	P.B. Gardens, Fla.	1,600,000	9-23-86	R-R	6-7	195	8	2	0.46	12	1	76	29	8	105	Jamestown (A)
18.	Padres. Cesar Carrillo, rhp	U. of Miami	Hammond, Ind.	1,550,000	4-29-84	R-R	6-2	160	13	3	2.22	19	1	126	100	23	127	Mobile (AA)
20.	Cubs. Mark Pawelek, lhp	Springville HS	Springville, Utah	1,750,000	8-18-86	L-L	6-2	180	10	0	0.00	11	1	63	17	16	132	Boise (A)
22.	Marlins. Aaron Thompson, lhp	Second Baptist HS	Houston	1,225,000	2-28-87	L-L	6-2	190	8	3	0.84	14	2	66	38	35	133	Jamestown (A)
24.	Astros. Brian Bogusevic, lhp	Tulane U.	Oak Lawn, Ill.	1,375,000	2-18-84	L-L	6-3	200	13	3	3.25	19	0	130	130	42	129	Tri-City (A)
25.	Twins. Matt Garza, rhp	Fresno State U.	Fresno	1,350,000	11-26-83	R-R	6-4	190	6	5	3.07	19	1	108	110	37	120	Beloit (A)
26.	Red Sox. Craig Hansen, rhp	St. John's U.	Glen Cove, N.Y.	1,325,000	11-15-83	R-R	6-5	193	3	2	1.68	31	14	64	38	20	85	Boston
27.	Braves. Joey Devine, rhp	North Carolina State U.	Junction City, Kan.	1,300,000	9-19-83	R-R	6-1	198	5	3	2.03	28	12	49	72	10	72	Atlanta
29.	Marlins. Jacob Marceaux, rhp	McNeese State U.	Jennings, La.	1,000,000	2-14-84	R-R	6-2	190	6	5	3.05	15	1	100	85	29	105	Greensboro (A)
31.	Diamondbacks. Matt Torra, rhp	U. of Massachusetts	Pittsfield, Mass.	1,025,000	6-29-84	R-R	6-3	225	6	3	1.14	14	0	95	56	16	111	Yakima (A)
32.	Rockies. Chaz Roe, rhp	Lafayette HS	Lexington, Ky.	1,025,000	10-9-86	R-R	6-5	170	7	2	0.63	11	0	56	29	22	89	Casper (R)
34.	Marlins. Ryan Tucker, rhp	Temple City HS	Temple City, Calif.	975,000	12-6-86	R-R	6-2	190	7	5	1.19	14	1	82	47	28	132	Jamestown (A)
35.	Padres. Cesar Ramos, lhp	Long Beach State U.	Pico Rivera, Calif.	950,000	6-22-84	L-L	6-1	175	10	7	2.64	18	0	126	105	16	95	Fort Wayne (A)
37.	Angels. Trevor Bell, rhp	Crescenta Valley HS	La Crescenta, Calif.	950,000	10-12-86	L-R	6-2	180	8	3	1.13	14	2	80	43	12	113	AZL Angels (R)
40.	Dodgers. Luke Hochevar, rhp	U. of Tennessee.	Fowler, Colo.	Unsigned	9-15-83	R-R	6-4	198	15	3	2.26	19	0	140	104	54	154	Did not sign
41.	Braves. Beau Jones, lhp	Destrehan HS	Destrehan, La.	825,000	8-25-86	L-L	6-1	180	11	3	0.87	15	1	89	34	27	157	GCL Braves (R)
42.	Red Sox. Clay Buchholz, rhp	Angelina (Texas) JC	Lumberton, Texas	800,000	8-14-84	L-R	6-3	190	12	1	1.05	15	0	86	44	29	129	Lowell (A)
43.	Cardinals. Mark McCormick, rhp	Baylor U.	Clear Lake Shores, Tx.	800,000	10-15-83	R-R	6-2	190	8	4	2.96	20	0	113	73	66	115	Quad Cities (A)
44.	Marlins. Sean West, lhp	Captain Shreve HS	Shreveport, La.	775,000	6-15-86	L-L	6-8	195	10	2	1.42	13	0	84	57	13	130	Jamestown (A)
46.	Cardinals. Tyler Herron, rhp	Wellington HS	Wellington, Fla.	675,000	8-5-86	R-R	6-3	187	5	2	0.25	9	0	57	20	13	81	Johnson City (R)
47.	Red Sox. Michael Bowden, rhp	Waubonsie Valley HS	Aurora, Ill.	730,000	9-9-86	R-R	6-3	210	11	1	0.41	13	0	86	29	9	185	GCL Red Sox (R)
48.	Orioles. Garrett Olson, lhp	Cal Poly U.	Clovis, Calif.	650,000	10-18-83	R-L	6-0	190	12	4	2.71	19	0	136	123	47	128	Frederick (A)
49.	D-backs. Matt Green, rhp	U. of Louisiana-Monroe	Monroe, La.	500,000	1-5-82	R-R	6-4	185	10	2	2.65	17	1	105	92	26	141	Missoula (R)
53.	Athletics. Craig Italiano, rhp	Flower Mound HS	Flower Mound, Texas	725,500	7-22-86	R-R	6-3	195	8	1	0.95	11	0	52	27	19	84	AZL Athletics (R)
55.	Rockies. Zach Simons, rhp	Everett (Wash.) JC	Glenns Ferry, Idaho	635,000	5-23-85	L-R	6-3	205	5	0	1.07	7	0	50	32	18	52	Tri-City (A)
56.	Devil Rays. Chris Mason, rhp	UNC Greensboro	Cherryville, N.C.	630,000	7-1-84	R-R	6-0	170	6	7	2.88	19	2	119	103	24	135	SW Michigan (A)
60.	Reds. Travis Wood, lhp	Bryant HS	Bryant, Ark.	600,000	2-6-87	R-L	6-1	170	10	1	0.52	13	1	67	17	22	146	Billings (R)
63.	Yankees. J. Brent Cox, rhp	U. of Texas	Bay City, Texas	550,000	5-13-84	L-R	6-3	200	8	3	1.73	42	19	78	57	25	87	Tampa (A)
68.	Cubs. Donald Veal, lhp	Pima (Ariz.) CC	Tucson	530,000	9-18-84	L-L	6-3	200	8	5	3.65	15	0	74	61	53	119	Boise (A)
69.	Athletics. Jared Lansford, rhp	St. Francis HS	Santa Clara, Calif.	525,000	10-22-86	R-R	6-1	180	8	4	1.59	15	1	79	49	19	96	AZL Athletics (R)
70.	Cardinals. Josh Wilson, rhp	Whitehouse HS	Whitehouse, Texas	515,000	9-6-86	R-R	6-1	180	3	7	1.95	10	0	61	47	14	86	Johnson City (R)
73.	Twins. Kevin Slowey, rhp	Winthrop U.	Pittsburgh	490,000	5-4-84	R-R	6-3	190	14	2	2.18	19	1	136	91	13	134	Beloit (A)
74.	Dodgers. Josh Wall, rhp	Central Private HS	Walker, La.	480,000	1-21-87	R-R	6-6	190	14	1	0.93	16	0	83	44	26	138	GCL Dodgers (R)
77.	Braves. Jeff Lyman, rhp	Monte Vista HS	Alamo, Calif.	460,000	1-14-87	R-R	6-3	215	5	2	1.07	10	0	59	35	15	75	GCL Braves (R)
78.	Cardinals. Nick Webber, rhp	Central Missouri State U.	Lee's Summit, Mo.	425,000	5-9-84	R-R	6-7	210	3	1	1.06	29	11	42	20	12	45	Quad Cities (A)
81.	D-backs. Jason Neighborgall, rhp	Georgia Tech	Durham, N.C.	500,000	12-19-83	R-R	6-5	210	5	3	7.13	14	0	53	47	53	72	Missoula (R)
82.	Royals. Chris Nicoll, rhp	UC Irvine	Santa Maria, Calif.	445,000	10-30-83	R-R	6-3	190	6	4	2.50	17	0	112	89	24	113	Idaho Falls (R)
83.	D-backs. Micah Owings, rhp	Tulane U.	Gainesville, Ga.	440,000	9-28-82	R-R	6-4	212	12	4	3.26	19	0	130	111	25	135	Lancaster (A)
84.	Twins. Brian Duensing, lhp	U. of Nebraska	Omaha	400,000	2-22-83	L-L	6-0	170	8	0	3.00	23	0	84	69	28	52	Did not play
85.	Brewers. Will Inman, rhp	Tunstall HS	Danville, Va.	500,000	2-6-87	R-R	6-6	210	13	0	0.54	15	2	91	34	13	195	Helena (R)
87.	Rockies. Kyle Hancock, rhp	Rowlett HS	Rowlett, Texas	475,000	8-20-87	R-R	6-3	185	9	0	1.13	9	0	68	44	18	116	Did not play
88.	Devil Rays. Bryan Morris, rhp	Tullahoma HS	Tullahoma, Tenn.	Did Not Sign	3-28-87	R-R	6-3	185	11	1	0.62	14	1	78	27	11	151	Did not sign
92.	Reds. Zach Ward, rhp	Gardner-Webb U.	Kannapolis, N.C.	420,000	1-14-84	R-R	6-3	225	7	9	3.63	20	1	109	102	49	127	Did not play
93.	Orioles. Brandon Erbe, rhp	McDonough HS	Baltimore	415,000	12-25-87	R-R	6-4	195	2	5	1.86	10	0	49	39	23	86	Aberdeen (A)
95.	White Sox. Ricky Brooks, rhp	East Carolina U.	North Tonawanda, N.Y.	300,000	7-18-84	R-R	6-2	165	5	5	3.46	17	1	78	66	24	70	Kannapolis (A)
96.	Marlins. Matt Goyen, lhp	Georgia College	Athens, Ga.	340,000	1-19-83	R-L	6-5	220	9	1	1.99	13	1	91	60	32	122	Jamestown (A)
97.	Phillies. Matt Maloney, lhp	U. of Mississippi	Huron, Ohio	400,000	1-16-84	L-L	6-3	220	8	3	3.11	23	4	104	94	26	111	Batavia (A)
98.	Padres. Josh Geer, rhp	Rice U.	Forney, Texas	395,000	6-2-83	R-R	6-3	180	12	4	3.32	19	0	125	105	44	105	Fort Wayne (A)
100.	Cubs. Mark Holliman, rhp	U. of Mississippi	Germantown, Tenn.	385,000	9-19-83	R-R	6-1	180	8	4	3.90	18	0	113	106	48	120	Did not play

team and its officials weren't to blame at all. Los Angeles pulled all its offers to Hochevar off the table on Sept. 14, by which time the MLB Players Association had begun investigating the events and the conduct of Boras and Sosnick.

Hochevar apparently won't have the leverage of returning to Tennessee, which would mean he'd have to re-enter the 2006 draft if he didn't work out a deal with the Dodgers. While Boras declined to confirm reports that Hochevar signed a form designating him as his agent, which would erase his final year of eligibility with the Volunteers, he did tell the Los Angeles Daily News that Hochevar ruined his eligibility when he signed the Sosnick adviser document.

Weaver, Drew Finally Sign

Boras also was involved in the longest-running negotiations in the 2004 draft. Minutes before the May 31 midnight Eastern Time deadline before they would have re-entered the draft, first-rounders Jered Weaver and Stephen Drew agreed to terms and ended the longest holdouts in draft history.

Weaver, a former Long Beach State righthander selected 12th overall by the Angels, accepted a $4 million bonus pending a physical. Drew, a former Florida State shortstop, signed a five-year big league contract with the Diamondbacks, who took him 15th. Drew was to receive a $4 million bonus to be paid over four years and is guaranteed a minimum of $5.5 million. He also can make another $2 million in incentives that a source close to the negotiations describes as easily attainable.

LARRY GOREN

Jered Weaver

Rizzo and general manager Joe Garagiola Jr. ironed out a deal with Boras after a series of negotiations involving the payout structure and faxed the necessary paperwork to the league office in the final minutes. The budget-conscious Diamondbacks didn't have to make the first bonus payment until the end of 2005.

Weaver, also represented by Boras, opted for a straight up-front bonus. The Angels also proposed a $5.25 million major league contract, but sources say Weaver didn't have enough time to undergo a required physical examination. In both cases, the teams held firm to offers made early in 2005—though Arizona made a very small restructuring to provide some up-front money—and forced Boras and his clients to meet their price.

Boras initially sought Mark Prior money ($10.5 million major league contract) for Weaver and Mark Teixeira cash ($9.5 million big league deal) for Drew. Weaver was Baseball America's top-rated prospect and Drew the top-rated position player in the 2004 draft, but concerns over their demands caused them to slide in the draft.

At the time, their $4 million bonuses ranked as the seventh-highest in draft history for players signing with the team that selected them. Drew's major league contract was the eighth-largest in draft history.

With negotiations at a stalemate in the weeks before the draft, both Drew and Weaver joined the Camden Riversharks of the independent Atlantic League. Drew signed April 20 and was leading the league in batting (.427), on-base percentage (.484) and slugging percentage (.744) when he agreed to terms with the Diamondbacks. He went 3-for-4 with a grand slam in his final game, one day after he homered off the top of Camden's 50-foot scoreboard.

LARRY GOREN

Stephen Drew

Weaver signed with the Riversharks May 20 and never

MAJOR LEAGUE CONTRACTS

Only one major league contract was signed by a draft pick in 2005—by the 26th overall pick, righthander Craig Hansen. He signed with the Red Sox and made his big league debut after 10 relief appearances in the minors. The number of major league contracts signed since Bo Jackson agreed to a major league deal with the Royals in 1986 as a condition of his being pried away from a promising NFL career, is 27. Here's the full list, including the bonus the player received as well as the amount guaranteed in major league salaries and roster bonuses.

Year	Club (Round)	Player, Pos.	Bonus	Guar. Amount
1986	Royals (4)	Bo Jackson, of	$100,000	$1,066,000
1989	Orioles (1)	Ben McDonald, rhp	350,000	824,000
	Blue Jays (3)	John Olerud, 1b	575,000	800,000
1990	Athletics (1)	*Todd Van Poppel, rhp	500,000	1,200,000
1992	Angels (1)	Pete Janicki, rhp	90,000	215,000
1993	Mariners (1)	*Alex Rodriguez, ss	1,000,000	1,300,000
1998	Phillies (1)	Pat Burrell, 1b-of	3,150,000	8,000,000
	Cardinals (1)	J.D. Drew, of	3,000,000	7,000,000
	Cardinals (2)	Chad Hutchinson, rhp	2,300,000	3,400,000
1999	Marlins (1)	*Josh Beckett, rhp	3,625,000	7,000,000
	Tigers (1)	Eric Munson, c	3,500,000	6,750,000
2000	Reds (1)	*David Espinosa, ss	None	2,950,000
	Reds (2)	Dane Sardinha, c	None	1,950,000
	Padres (2)	Xavier Nady, 3b	1,100,000	2,850,000
	Devil Rays (5)	Jace Brewer, ss	450,000	1,200,000
2001	Cubs (1)	Mark Prior, rhp	4,000,000	10,500,000
	Devil Rays (1)	Dewon Brazelton, rhp	4,200,000	4,800,000
	Rangers (1)	Mark Teixeira, 3b	4,500,000	9,500,000
2002	+Orioles (1)	Adam Loewen, lhp	3,200,000	4,020,000
	Indians (1)	Jeremy Guthrie, rhp	3,000,000	4,000,000
	Rockies (4)	Jeff Baker, 3b	200,000	2,000,000
2003	Devil Rays (1)	*Delmon Young, of	3,700,000	5,800,000
	Brewers (1)	Rickie Weeks, 2b	3,600,000	4,790,000
2004	Mets (1)	Philip Humber, rhp	3,000,000	4,200,000
	Devil Rays (1)	Jeff Niemann, rhp	3,200,000	5,200,000
	Diamondbacks (1)	Stephen Drew, ss	4,000,000	5,500,000
2005	Red Sox (1)	Craig Hansen, rhp	1,300,000	4,000,000

* High school signee
\# Secondary phase + Draft-and-follow, signed the following year

HISTORICAL SIGNIFICANCE

First-round bonuses have taken a pronounced drop since 2003 and predictably no significant bonus records have been set in the last three years. Below are the 10 largest bonuses for players who signed with the teams that drafted them (for those players who signed major league contracts, only the cash bonus is noted):

Player, Pos.	Club, Year (Round)	Bonus
1. Joe Borchard, of	White Sox '00 (1)	$5,300,000
2. Joe Mauer, c	Twins '01 (1)	5,150,000
3. B.J. Upton, ss	Devil Rays '02 (1)	4,600,000
4. *Mark Teixeira, 3b	Rangers '01 (1)	4,500,000
5. *Dewon Brazelton, rhp	Devil Rays '01 (1)	4,200,000
Gavin Floyd, rhp	Phillies '01 (1)	4,200,000
7. *Mark Prior, rhp	Cubs '01 (1)	4,000,000
Bryan Bullington, rhp	Pirates '02 (1)	4,000,000
*Stephen Drew, ss	Diamondbacks '05 (1)	4,000,000
Alex Gordon, 3b	Royals '05 (1)	4,000,000

*Signed major league contract

appeared in a game. He threw in a bullpen session two days before he signed and was scheduled to pitch in relief May 31.

Drew and Weaver faced uncertainty had they re-entered the 2005 draft, as teams already were wary of their demands before their lengthy holdouts. They surpassed the stalemate between the Mariners and 1994 first-round pick Jason Varitek (another Boras client), who didn't sign until April 20 the following year.

DOUBLE THEIR PLEASURE

Former Rice righthander Wade Townsend and Stanford outfielder John Mayberry Jr. became the 13th and 14th players in draft history to be selected in the first round of two different June drafts. (That includes only the regular phase, the equivalent to today's draft, from the June 1965-86 drafts). Negotiations broke down swiftly between Townsend and the Orioles, who took him eighth overall in 2004. He signed for $1.5 million after the Devil Rays took him in the same slot. The 28th overall pick out of high school in 2002 by the Mariners, Mayberry signed with the Rangers for $1.525 million as the 19th overall pick.

Player, Pos., School	First Time	College	Second Time
Randy Scarbery, rhp, HS—Fresno	Astros, 1970 (7th)	Southern California	Athletics, 1973 (23rd)
Mike Miley, ss, HS—New Orleans	Reds, 1971 (24th)	Louisiana State	Angels, 1974 (10th)
Danny Goodwin, c, HS—Peoria, Ill.	White Sox, 1971 (1st)	Southern	Twins, 1975 (1st)
Mike Sullivan, lhp, HS—Woodbridge, Va.	Athletics, 1976 (24th)	Clemson	Reds, 1979 (22nd)
Brad DuVall, rhp, Virginia Tech	Orioles, 1987 (15th)	Virginia Tech	Cardinals, 1988 (23rd)
Alex Fernandez, rhp, HS—Miami	Brewers, 1988 (24th)	Miami-Dade CC South	White Sox, 1990 (4th)
Calvin Murray, of, HS—Dallas	Indians, 1989 (11th)	Texas	Giants, 1992 (7th)
Charles Johnson, c, HS—Fort Pierce, Fla.	Expos, 1989 (10th)	Miami	Marlins, 1992 (28th)
John Burke, rhp, Florida	Astros, 1991 (6th)	Florida	Rockies, 1992 (27th)
Jason Varitek, c, Georgia Tech	Twins, 1993 (21st)	Georgia Tech	Mariners, 1994 (14th)
J.D. Drew, of, Florida State	Phillies, 1997 (2nd)	Florida State	Cardinals, 1998 (5th)
Jeremy Sowers, lhp, HS—Louisville	Reds, 2001 (20th)	Vanderbilt	Indians, 2004 (6th)
Wade Townsend, rhp, Rice	Orioles, 2004 (8th)	did not return to team	Devil Rays, 2005 (8th)
John Mayberry Jr., of, HS—Kansas City, Mo.	Mariners, 2002 (28th)	Stanford	Rangers, 2005 (19th)

Three Draftees Reach Majors

For the second time in three years, three players went from the draft to the big leagues in the same summer. The first player from the 2005 draft to get to the majors was North Carolina State righthander Joey Devine, the 27th overall pick by the Braves. He represented the first four-year college righthander the Braves franchise had ever taken in the first round of the regular June draft.

ROBERT GURGANUS

Joey Devine

Braves scouting director Roy Clark said it was possible Devine could reach the big leagues when he was drafted. "I think stuff-wise, he's certainly good enough," Clark said. "Obviously, he's close. How close? That depends on him."

Atlanta summoned Devine on Aug. 20 after he made 22 relief appearances in the minors. He took the loss in his debut, surrendering a 10th-inning grand slam to San Diego's Xavier Nady, and allowed seven runs in two innings over two games before the Braves demoted him to Triple-A. Devine returned to Atlanta for the season's final week and finished the year with a 0-1, 12.60 record in five major league outings.

BONUS RECORDS BY ROUND

Round	Player, Pos, Team	Year	Bonus
1st	Joe Borchard, of, White Sox	2000	$5,300,000
Supp. 1st	Michael Garciaparra, ss, Mariners	2001	$2,000,000
2nd	Jason Young, rhp, Rockies	2000	$2,750,000
3rd	Matt Tuiasosopo, ss, Mariners	2004	$2,290,000
4th	Zach Miner, rhp, Braves	2000	$1,250,000
5th	Matt McClendon, rhp, Braves	1999	$900,000
6th	Quan Cosby, of, Angels	2001	$825,000
7th	Tyler Adamczyk, rhp, Cardinals	2001	$1,000,000
8th	Austin Jackson, of, Yankees	2005	$800,000
9th	Jason Middlebrook, rhp, Padres	1996	$750,000
10th	*Luis Cota, rhp, Royals	2003	$1,050,000
11th	Kiki Bengochea, rhp, Rangers	2002	$550,000
12th	Mike Rozier, lhp, Red Sox	2004	$1,575,000
13th	Jimmy Barthmaier, rhp, Astros	2003	$750,000
14th	Dexter Fowler, of, Rockies	2004	$925,000
Post-14th	*Sean Henn, lhp, Yankees	2000	$1,701,000

*Signed next year as draft-and-follow.

Closers have reached the major leagues first in each of the last three drafts. In 2003, the Reds' Ryan Wagner and the Expos' Chad Cordero played in the big leagues mere weeks after being drafted. The A's Huston Street was the first big leaguer from the Class of 2004.

■ The Nationals promoted Virginia third baseman Ryan Zimmerman, the fourth overall pick, on Sept. 1. He struck out in a pinch at-bat that evening against Atlanta's Kyle Davies, but Zimmerman supplanted Vinny Castilla as Washington's starting third baseman later in the month. He batted .375 with six RBIs in 20 big league games.

■ After falling to the Red Sox at No. 26 because of signability concerns, Hansen became the first player in the 2005 draft to receive a major league contract. He signed July 23 for four years and $4 million, including a $1.325 million bonus.

Hansen came down with a tired arm late in the Double-A season, which seemed to preclude any chances of a September callup. But his arm bounced back and he made his major league debut Sept. 19 with a scoreless inning and two strikeouts against Tampa Bay. He went 0-0, 6.00 in four appearances with Boston.

MLB Keeps Bonuses In Check

MLB's practice of making signing recommendations for every pick in the first 10 rounds and forcing teams to make their case before exceeding slot money continued to slow the growth of bonuses in 2005, especially in the first round.

The 28 first-rounders who had signed by the end of the regular season received an average of $1,817,500, led by the $4 million Nebraska third baseman Alex Gordon got as the No. 2 choice from the Royals. That was down 7.2 percent from the 2004 average of $1,958,448. Upton and Pelfrey likely will drive the 2005 average up to close to the 2004 figure, though it remained to be seen if first-rounders would average more than $2 million in bonuses for the first time since 2002.

■ The Scott Boras Corporation cast a formidable shadow over the 2005 draft, but IMG-represented clients actually made more of an impact in the first round. Six first-rounders, including three of the first four, were represented by IMG. The first Boras client, Pelfrey, was picked ninth—after four IMG players had been taken.

FIRST OVERALL PICKS: THROUGH THE YEARS

Following is a year-by-year breakdown of the first overall pick in the June regular phase and his cash bonus, his highest level attained and his 2005 status. If a different player earned the largest bonus in that year, that player is noted along with the order he was picked and his bonus.

Year	No. 1 Pick	School	Hometown	Bonus	Highest Level (G#)	2005 Team	Largest Bonus (Pick Number)	Amount
1965	Rick Monday, of, Athletics	Arizona State U.	Santa Monica, Calif.	$100,000	Majors (1,996)	Out of Baseball	same	
1966	Steve Chilcott, c, Mets	Antelope Valley HS	Lancaster, Calif.	75,000	Triple-A (2)	Out of Baseball	Reggie Jackson, of, Athletics (2)	$80,000
1967	Ron Blomberg, 1b, Yankees	Druid Hills HS	Atlanta	65,000	Majors (461)	Out of Baseball	#Mike Adamson, rhp, Orioles	75,000
1968	Tim Foli, ss, Mets	Notre Dame HS	Sherman Oaks, Calif.	74,000	Majors (1,696)	Out of Baseball	Lloyd Allen, rhp, Angels (12)	75,000
1969	Jeff Burroughs, of, Senators	Wilson HS	Long Beach, Calif.	88,000	Majors (1,689)	Out of Baseball	same	
1970	Mike Ivie, c, Padres	Walker HS	Decatur, Ga.	75,000	Majors (857)	Out of Baseball	#Dave Kingman, 1b, Giants	80,000
1971	Danny Goodwin, c, White Sox	Central HS	Peoria, Ill.	DNS	Majors (252)	Out of Baseball	Ed Kurpiel, 1b, Cardinals (8)	83,750
1972	Dave Roberts, 3b, Padres	U. of Oregon	Corvallis, Ore.	70,000	Majors (709)	Out of Baseball	Jamie Quirk, ss, Royals (18)	78,000
1973	*David Clyde, lhp, Rangers	Westchester HS	Houston	65,000	Majors (84)	Out of Baseball	^Alan Bannister, ss, Phillies	85,000
1974	*Bill Almon, ss, Padres	Brown U.	Warwick, R.I.	90,000	Majors (1,236)	Out of Baseball	Willie Wilson, of, Royals (18)	90,000
1975	*Danny Goodwin, c, Angels	Southern U.	Peoria, Ill.	125,000	Majors (252)	Out of Baseball	same	
1976	Floyd Bannister, lhp, Astros	Arizona State U.	Seattle	100,000	Majors (431)	Out of Baseball	same	
1977	Harold Baines, of, White Sox	St. Michaels HS	St. Michaels, Md.	32,000	Majors (2,830)	Out of Baseball	Paul Molitor, ss, Twins (3)	77,500
1978	*Bob Horner, 3b, Braves	Arizona State U.	Glendale, Ariz.	162,000	Majors (1,020)	Out of Baseball	same	
1979	Al Chambers, 1b, Mariners	Harris HS	Harrisburg, Pa.	60,000	Majors (57)	Out of Baseball	Todd Demeter, 1b, Yankees (51)	208,000
1980	Darryl Strawberry, of, Mets	Crenshaw HS	Los Angeles	152,500	Majors (1,583)	Out of Baseball	same	
1981	Mike Moore, rhp, Mariners	Oral Roberts U.	Eakly, Okla.	100,000	Majors (450)	Out of Baseball	Terry Blocker, of, Mets (4)	127,500
1982	Shawon Dunston, ss, Cubs	Jefferson HS	New York	135,000	Majors (1,750)	Out of Baseball	Kenny Williams, of, Wh. Sox (78)	160,000
1983	Tim Belcher, rhp, Twins	Mt. Vernon Nazarene Coll.	Sparta, Ohio	DNS	Majors (362)	Out of Baseball	Kurt Stillwell, ss, Reds (2)	135,000
1984	Shawn Abner, of, Mets	Mechanicsburg HS	Mechanicsburg, Pa.	150,500	Majors (392)	Out of Baseball	same	
1985	B.J. Surhoff, c, Brewers	U. of North Carolina	Rye, N.Y.	150,000	Majors (2,313)	Orioles	Bobby Witt, rhp, Rangers (3)	179,000
1986	Jeff King, 3b, Pirates	U. of Arkansas	Colorado Springs	180,000	Majors (1,201)	Out of Baseball	same	
1987	Ken Griffey Jr., of, Mariners	Moeller HS	Cincinnati	160,000	Majors (2,135)	Reds	Mark Merchant, of, Pirates (2)	165,000
							Jack McDowell, rhp, Wh. Sox (5)	165,000
1988	Andy Benes, rhp, Padres	U. of Evansville	Evansville, Ind.	235,000	Majors (403)	Out of Baseball	same	
1989	*Ben McDonald, rhp, Orioles	Louisiana State U.	Denham Springs, La.	350,000	Majors (211)	Out of Baseball	*John Olerud, 1b, Blue Jays (79)	575,000
1990	Chipper Jones, ss, Braves	The Bolles School	Jacksonville	275,000	Majors (1,651)	Braves	*Todd Van Poppel, rhp, A's (14)	500,000
							Tony Clark, 1b, Tigers (2)	500,000
1991	Brien Taylor, lhp, Yankees	East Carteret HS	Beaufort, N.C.	1,550,000	Double-A (27)	Out of Baseball	same	
1992	Phil Nevin, 3b, Astros	Cal State Fullerton	Placentia, Calif.	700,000	Majors (1,088)	Rangers	Jeffrey Hammonds, of, Orioles (4)	975,000
1993	*Alex Rodriguez, ss, Mariners	Westminster Christian HS	Miami	1,000,000	Majors (1,592)	Yankees	Darren Dreifort, rhp, Dodgers (2)	1,300,000
1994	Paul Wilson, rhp, Mets	Florida State U.	Orlando, Fla.	1,550,000	Majors (170)	Reds	Josh Booty, ss, Marlins (5)	1,600,000
1995	Darin Erstad, of, Angels	U. of Nebraska	Jamestown, N.D.	1,575,000	Majors (1,280)	Angels	same	
1996	@Kris Benson, rhp, Pirates	Clemson U.	Kennesaw, Ga.	2,000,000	Majors (165)	Mets	Matt White, rhp, Giants (7)	10,200,000
1997	Matt Anderson, rhp, Tigers	Rice U.	Louisville	2,505,000	Majors (245)	Rockies (AAA)	same	
1998	*Pat Burrell, 3b, Phillies	U. of Miami	Boulder Creek, Calif.	3,150,000	Majors (850)	Phillies	Corey Patterson, of, Cubs (3)	3,700,000
1999	Josh Hamilton, of, Devil Rays	Athens Drive HS	Raleigh, N.C.	3,960,000	Double-A (23)	Out of Baseball	same	
2000	Adrian Gonzalez, 1b, Marlins	Eastside HS	Chula Vista, Calif.	3,000,000	Majors (59)	Rangers	Joe Borchard, of, White Sox (12)	5,300,000
2001	Joe Mauer, c, Twins	Cretn-Derham Hall	St. Paul, Minn.	5,150,000	Majors (166)	Twins	same	
2002	Bryan Bullington, rhp, Pirates	Ball State U.	Fishers, Ind.	4,000,000	Majors (1)	Pirates	B.J. Upton, ss, Devil Rays (2)	4,600,000
2003	*Delmon Young, of, Devil Rays	Camarillo HS	Camarillo, Calif.	3,700,000	Triple-A (52)	Devil Rays (AAA)	same	
2004	Matt Bush, ss, Padres	Mission Bay HS	El Cajon, Calif.	3,150,000	Class A (134)	Padres (A)	Jered Weaver, rhp, Angels	4,000,000
							Stephen Drew, ss, D-backs	4,000,000
2005	Justin Upton, ss, D'backs	Great Bridge HS	Chesapeake, Va.	Unsigned	Unsigned	Unsigned	Alex Gordon, 3b, Royals	4,000,000

* Signed major league contract; cash bonus only reported. # Selected in June secondary phase.
^ Selected in January draft. @ Includes four loophole free agents; White signed with Devil Rays.

Rick Monday

LARRY GOREN

Chipper Jones

MORRIS FOSTOFF

Joe Mauer

Boras represented four players in the first round, including Utah high school lefthander Mark Pawelek. Atypical of Boras' clients from the 2004 draft that either signed at the end of the summer (Matt Durkin, Mike Rozier, Brett Smith), signed a week before the 2005 draft (Drew, Weaver) or weren't signed at all (Jeff Larish), Pawelek signed immediately, agreeing to a $1.75 million deal with the Cubs as the 20th overall pick. He was the lone high school player Boras represented in the draft.

The Fullerton Factor

Defending College World Series champion Cal State Fullerton made a big impact on the 2005 draft with a record-tying 14 selections. The Titans equaled the record set in 1982 by Arizona State.

Though every regular position player was drafted, lefthander Ricky Romero, selected sixth overall by the Blue Jays, was the only Fullerton player selected among the first 100 picks. He was also the first pitcher drafted, marking the first time in draft history that the first five selections were position players.

Fullerton's impact might have been even greater had it not lost catcher Daric Barton, the marquee talent in their 2002 high school recruiting class, to the draft, and outfielder Shawn Scobee, an unsigned fifth-round pick who transferred to Nevada after his sophomore year.

■ Arizona and Long Beach State, the teams the Titans defeated to win the NCAA regional and Big West Conference titles, made the greatest impact on the first day of the draft with eight selections apiece.

Arizona's Trevor Crowe (first round), Nick Hundley (second), Jordan Brown (fourth) and John Meloan (fifth) were all selected in the first five rounds. Long Beach State's selections included first-rounder Troy Tulowitzki and supplemental first-rounder Cesar Ramos. Baylor and Auburn both had seven players drafted in the first 18 rounds.

■ Two high schools, San Diego's Rancho Bernardo High and Flower Mound (Texas) High, produced four draft picks apiece, including three of the first 54 selections. Rancho Bernardo High outfielder John Drennen was taken with the 33rd overall pick while Flower Mound's Craig Italiano and Paul Kelly were selected with back-to-back picks in the second round.

UNSIGNED PICKS

Major league teams signed a record number of picks from the first 10 rounds of the 2004 draft, agreeing on contracts with 297 of 311 selections—or 95.5 percent. The record low number of 14 unsigned picks topped the previous record of 16, set a year earlier. As of Oct. 15, there were 20 picks from the 2005 draft who remained unsigned but that number is expected to drop—possibly in half—before next year's draft. Two first-round holdouts are likely to sign, as are several draft-and-follows whose rights have been retained by the teams that drafted them. These are the players selected in the first 10 rounds of the 2005 draft who didn't/haven't signed, and the colleges they're attending.

FIRST ROUND	
2. #D-backs. Justin Upton, ss	not in school
9. #Mets. Mike Pelfrey, rhp	not in school
SUPPLEMENTAL FIRST ROUND	
40. #Dodgers. Luke Hochevar, rhp	not in school
THIRD ROUND	
88. *Devil Rays. Bryan Morris, rhp	Motlow State (Tenn.) JC
103. *Angels. Sean O'Sullivan, rhp	Grossmont (Calif.) JC
104. Astros. Josh Lindblom, rhp	Tennessee
FOURTH ROUND	
133. Angels. Brian Matusz, lhp	San Diego
SIXTH ROUND	
173. Mariners. Lance Lynn, rhp	Mississippi
192. *Giants. Brad Cuthbertson, rhp	Midland (Texas) JC
199. Yankees. Doug Fister, rhp	(Fresno State)
EIGHTH ROUND	
235. Brewers. Jemile Weeks, ss	Miami
246. Marlins. Aaron Bates, 1b	(North Carolina State)
249. *Rangers. Brad Barragar, rhp	(Golden West, Calif., JC)
252. #Giants. Scotty Bridges, 2b	eligibility expired
253. Angels. Matt Hall, ss	Arizona State
NINTH ROUND	
270. Tigers. Paul Coleman, lhp	(Pepperdine)
272. *Reds. Milton Loo, 3b	(Yavapai, Ariz., JC)
284. Astros. Jordan Meaker, rhp	Dallas Baptist
286. *Dodgers. Michael Davitt, rhp	Okaloosa-Walton (Fla.) JC
TENTH ROUND	
313. *Braves. Colin Carter, lhp	(Grayson County, Texas, CC)

Still eligible to sign
* Draft-and-follow; eligible to sign prior to 2006 draft
College player returning to same school in parentheses

DRAFT ORDER 2006

The raw order for the 2006 draft has been established with teams picking in reverse order of their 2005 records but without regard to league. By virtue of their .346 winning percentage, the Royals will pick first for the first time in their history.

The order in the second half of the first round (picks 16-30) could change if Type A or B free agents are signed in the offseason that require compensation in the form of draft picks. For teams that had identical records in 2005, priority is given to the team that had the earlier first-round selection in 2004.

Following is the rotation for 2006, with the team's 2005 winning percentage:

1. Royals	.346	16. Brewers	.500
2. Rockies	.414	17. Padres	.506
3. Devil Rays	.414	18. Mets	.512
4. Pirates	.414	19. Marlins	.512
5. Mariners	.426	20. Twins	.512
6. Tigers	.438	21. Phillies	.543
7. Dodgers	.438	22. Athletics	.543
8. Reds	.451	23. Astros	.549
9. Orioles	.457	24. Braves	.556
10. Giants	.463	25. Indians	.574
11. Diamondbacks	.475	26. Angels	.586
12. Rangers	.488	27. Red Sox	.586
13. Cubs	.488	28. Yankees	.586
14. Blue Jays	.494	29. White Sox	.611
15. Nationals	.500	30. Cardinals	.617

Moneyball In Retreat

The Athletics, who inspired the "Moneyball" craze earlier in this decade by drafting almost exclusively college players, reversed course and took high school players with six of their first nine selections. From 2000-04, Oakland selected a total of only five high school players in the first 10 rounds.

Two of the other staunchest supporters of the "Moneyball" approach to scouting and player development, the Cardinals and Red Sox, also went in a different direction with St. Louis taking six high school players in the first six rounds and Boston four in the first five rounds. A year earlier, the Cardinals drafted only four high school players overall—and didn't sign any. The Red Sox drafted one high school player in the first 16 rounds in both 2003 and 2004.

In the first 10 rounds in 2005, 68 percent of the selections came from college or junior college—down slightly from 2004's draft record of 70 percent.

■ In an effort to revive their flagging farm system, the Yankees signed two outstanding athletes who may have been the two best basketball players in the draft. New York used its first-round pick on Putnam City High (Oklahoma City) shortstop C.J. Henry, whose parents both played at the University of Kansas. Henry also would have played hoops for the Jayhawks had he not signed for $1,575,000. Ryan High (Denton, Texas) outfielder Austin Jackson was considered unsignable because he had a chance to start at point guard for Georgia Tech as a freshman. But the Yankees landed him quickly for $800,000, a record for an eighth-round pick.

Both Henry and Jackson made Baseball America's Top 20 Prospects list in the Rookie-level Gulf Coast League.

■ The Diamondbacks added to a list of high-risk, high-reward arms in 2005 by drafting Cuban defector Maels Rodriguez in the 22nd round. Rodriguez was once one of Cuba's top pitchers, with a fastball that was clocked at 100 mph in a game against Team USA in the 2000 Olympics, and he threw a perfect game during Cuba's Serie Nacional in 2002. But back problems sapped his velocity, and a workout that was hoped to bring him a contract fizzled when he struggled to throw 87 mph. Rodriguez had kept a low profile since the 2004 workout while trying to get healthy.

Rodriguez wasn't the first, but he was the most famous of several Cuban defectors that were drafted. The Braves selected shortstop Yunel Escobar in the second round.

Escobar created a stir when he declared for the draft in mid-May. He became the highest Cuban defector taken since Ariel Prieto went fifth overall to the Athletics in 1995. He batted .313 in 48 games in low Class A, quickly emerging as one of Atlanta's better prospects.

Free Falling

Michigan high school righthander/third baseman Zach Putnam suffered possibly the greatest free fall among prep players in the 2005 draft. He was projected as a solid first-round talent at the start of the season, but fell to the 38th round amid concerns over signability and a drop in velocity.

Putnam chose to stay close to home by committing to Michigan over several other top college programs in November's early-signing period and he made his intentions known to teams that he was intent on fulfilling his college commitment. But the Tigers made an effort to upstage Michigan's efforts to hold on to Putnam when it drafted the Ann Arbor native. The Tigers were expected to make every effort to sign Putnam away from Michigan—creating a potential interesting in-state tug-of-war—but Putnam fulfilled his commitment to college.

■ Washington sophomore righthander Tim Lincecum suffered the greatest fall from pre-draft predictions among college players. A projected second- or third-rounder, he wasn't picked until the 42nd round by the Indians—even after dropping his asking price in half, from a reported $2 million to $1 million. The 5-foot-10, 160-pound Lincecum went 8-6, 3.11 for the Huskies with 131 strikeouts and 71 walks in 104 innings.

■ Righthander Matt Harrington may have suffered the greatest free fall of all. After being drafted in a progressively lower round each of the past five drafts, including in the first round in 2000, Harrington went undrafted altogether in 2005, which means he was free to sign with any team. He spent the last three years at Fort Worth of the independent Central League.

RELATIVELY SPEAKING

Relatives of former big leaguers always make an impact on the draft, but no family was as well represented in 2005 as Andy Van Slyke's. The former all-star outfielder, who was a first-round pick of the Cardinals in 1979, had two sons drafted: Scott, a Missouri high school outfielder who was drafted in the 14th round by the Dodgers; and A.J., a University of Kansas first baseman/outfielder selected in the 23rd round by the Cardinals.

Among relatives of active big leaguers, the Astros made the most interesting selection by nabbing third baseman Koby Clemens with their eighth-round pick. Clemens, the son of Astros ace Roger Clemens, was a standout third baseman for Memorial High in Houston and signed with the Astros for $380,000—the equivalent of mid-third round money. Most teams viewed Clemens as a decent player more suited for college ball at this point, but he was worth more to Houston than to any other team. Koby's presence may help persuade his father Roger to continue pitching with the Astros.

The Brewers also used an eighth-round pick to draft Florida high school infielder Jemile Weeks. He's the younger brother of Brewers second baseman Rickie Weeks. The younger Weeks elected not to sign with the Brewers in favor of attending college at Miami.

The Cardinals made another bet on a Pujols family member by drafting outfielder Will Pujols in the sixth round. After all-star first baseman Albert Pujols slipped through the cracks and went in the 13th round in 1999, St. Louis took no chances and drafted his cousin Will, out of Missouri's Fort Osage High (Albert's alma mater).

A list of players from the 2005 draft with major league connections:

Player, Pos.	Club (Round)	Relative
Justin Upton, ss	D'backs (1)	B.J. (brother)
Brandon Snyder, c	Orioles (1)	Bryan (father)
John Mayberry Jr., 1b/of	Rangers (1)	John Sr. (father)
Eli Iorg, of	Astros (1-S)	Garth (father)
Ivan DeJesus, ss	Dodgers (2)	Ivan (father)
Kris Harvey, of	Marlins (2)	Bryan (father)
Jared Lansford, rhp	Athletics (2)	Carney (father)
P.J. Phillips, ss	Angels (2)	Brandon (brother)
Drew Thompson, ss	Twins (2-S)	Robby (father)
Drew Butera, c	Mets (5)	Sal (father)
Steven Tolleson, ss	Twins (5)	Wayne (father)
Kyle Reynolds, ss	Cubs (6)	Craig (father)
Justin Sellers, ss	Athletics (6)	Jeff (father)
Wilfrido Pujols, of	Cardinals (6)	Albert (cousin)
Michael Brantley, of	Brewers (7)	Mickey (father)
Will Venable, of	Padres (7)	Max (father)
Jemile Weeks, ss	Brewers (8)	Rickie (brother)
Koby Clemens, 3b	Astros (8)	Roger (father)
Peter Bourjos, of	Angels (10)	Chris (father)
Yusuf Carter, c	Cubs (12)	Joe (cousin)
Steve Johnson, rhp	Dodgers (13)	Dave (father)
Scott Van Slyke, of	Dodgers (14)	Andy (father)
Ben Petralli, c	Tigers (15)	Gino (father)
Michael DeJesus, 2b	Reds (15)	David (brother)
Ryan Searage, of	Pirates (18)	Ray (father)
Brett Bannister, rhp	Mariners (19)	Floyd (father)
Ike Davis, 1b/lhp	Devil Rays (19)	Ron (father)
Juan Mesa, of	Pirates (23)	Jose (father)
Matt Wallach, c	Yankees (23)	Tim (father)
A.J. Van Slyke, 1b	Cardinals (23)	Andy (father)
Jase Turner, 1b	Royals (27)	Jesse Gonder (g'father)
Sean Ruthven, rhp	Rockies (27)	Dick (father)
Brandon Laird, 1b	Indians (27)	Gerald (brother)
Kevin Gossage, c	Rangers (33)	Goose (uncle)
Shane Keough, ss	Athletics (36)	Matt (father)
Jesse Schoendienst, 2b	Cardinals (40)	Red (grandfather)
Jeremy Farrell, 3b	Rockies (41)	John (father)
Toby Gardenhire, ss	Twins (41)	Ron (father)
Michael Brenly, c	Cubs (43)	Bob (father)
Anthony Manuel, 2b	Mets (45)	Jerry (father)
Jeremy Shelby, of	Padres (46)	John (father)
Andy Hargrove, 1b	Mariners (47)	Mike (father)
Casey Coleman, rhp	Devil Rays (49)	Joe (father)

DRAFT 2005

CLUB-BY-CLUB SELECTIONS

Number represents order of selection • **Boldface** indicates player signed • *Player still eligible to sign

DRAFT

ARIZONA DIAMONDBACKS 1

1. *Justin Upton, ss, Great Bridge HS, Chesapeake, Va.
1. Matt Torra, rhp, U. of Massachusetts (Supplemental choice—31st—for loss of Type A free agent Richie Sexson)
2. Matt Green, rhp, U. of Louisiana-Monroe
3. Jason Neighborgall, rhp, Georgia Tech
3. Micah Owings, rhp, Tulane U. (Choice from Mariners as compensation for Sexson)
4. Mark Romanczuk, lhp, Stanford U.
5. Chris Rahl, of, College of William & Mary
6. Greg Smith, lhp, Louisiana State U.
7. Anthony Cupps, rhp, U. of Mississippi
8. Ryan Schreppel, lhp, Cal State Fullerton
9. Josh Ford, c, Baylor U.
10. Cody Evans, rhp, Long Beach State U.
11. Brett Jacobson, rhp, Cactus Shadows HS, Carefree, Ariz.
12. Bryan Byrne, 1b, St. Mary's (Calif.) College
13. Daniel Roberts, lhp, Chipola (Fla.) JC
14. Rusty Ryal, 3b, Oklahoma State U.
15. Greg Thomson, of, St. Johns U.
16. Craig Pfautz, lhp, Darton (Ga.) JC
17. Jason Urquidez, rhp, Arizona State U.
18. Jake Elder, c, U. of Minnesota
19. Kyle Wright, rhp, Lewis-Clark State (Idaho) College
20. Peter Duda, rhp, Stanford U.
21. Matt Krohe, lhp, Webber International (Fla.) U.
22. Maels Rodriguez, rhp, Hialeah, Fla.
23. Travis Tully, of, U. of Houston
24. Vince Bongiovanni, rhp, U. of Miami
25. David Williams, of, Rutgers U.
26. Brian Chavez, ss, JC of the Canyons (Calif.)
27. Matt Fowles, rhp, Illinois State U.
28. Joel Melendez, of, Southeastern (Iowa) CC
29. Trevor Pippin, 1b, McIntosh HS, Peachtree City, Ga.
30. Reinaldo Alicano, of, Seminole (Fla.) CC
31. Craig Heyer, rhp, CC of Southern Nevada
32. Rene Garcia, rhp, South Mountain (Ariz.) CC
33. J.B. Paxson, c, Center Grove HS, Greenwood, Ind.
34. Kevin Hammons, lhp, Cleveland State (Tenn.) CC
35. Ray Kruml, of, Indian Hills (Iowa) JC
36. Jonathan Runnels, lhp, San Jacinto (Texas) JC
37. Scott Mueller, rhp, South Mountain (Ariz.) CC
38. Tom Calahan, lhp, Saddleback (Calif.) CC
39. Dustin Renfrow, rhp, Jefferson (Mo.) JC
40. Eric Lawrence, rhp, Grand Rapids (Mich.) CC
41. Cheyne Hann, rhp, San Jose (Calif.) CC
42. Forrest Beverly, lhp, U. of South Carolina
43. Eric Butler, rhp, Tusculum (Tenn.) College
44. T.J. Peabody, rhp, Rancho Bernardo HS, San Diego
45. Drew Thomas, c, Neville HS, Monroe, La.
46. Brandon Thomson, lhp, Chandler-Gilbert (Ariz.) CC
47. Houston Summers, c, Northeast Guilford HS, Summerfield, N.C.
48. Aaron Gamboa, lhp, Mill Valley, Calif.
49. Joseph Campbell, rhp, Wabash Valley (Ill.) JC
50. Ritchie Franklin, ss, Thompson HS, Alabaster, Ala.

ATLANTA BRAVES 27

1. Joey Devine, rhp, North Carolina State U.
1. Beau Jones, lhp, Destrehan (La.) HS (Supplemental choice—41st—for loss of Type A free agent Jaret Wright)
2. Yunel Escobar, ss, Miami
2. Jeff Lyman, rhp, Monte Vista HS, Alamo, Calif. (Choice from Yankees as compensation for Wright)
3. Jordan Schafer, of, Winter Haven (Fla.) HS
4. Mike Broadway, rhp, Pope County HS, Golconda, Ill.
5. Will Startup, lhp, U. of Georgia
6. Tyler Bullock, rhp, Baylor U.
7. Brandon Monk, 2b, La Grange (Ga.) HS
8. Kyle Cofield, rhp, Southside HS, Rainbow City, Ala.
9. Steven Garcia, c, Temecula Valley HS, Temecula, Calif.
10. Colin Carter, lhp, Grayson County (Texas) CC
11. Michael Nix, rhp, Auburn U.
12. Rudy Quinonez, rhp, Fresno State U.
13. Quentin Davis, of, Francis Marion (S.C.) U.
14. Jose Cabrera, of, Los Angeles Pierce JC
15. Mason Tobin, rhp, Kentridge HS, Renton, Wash.
16. Jaye Chapman, rhp, Mosley HS, Lynn Haven, Fla.
17. Clay Caulfield, rhp, Pensacola (Fla.) JC
18. Zach Oliver, lhp, Midway HS, Waco, Texas
19. Cole Miles, ss, Viewmont HS, Bountiful, Utah
20. Andrew Cashner, rhp, Conroe HS, Montgomery, Texas
21. Kris Cichoski, rhp, Durango HS, Las Vegas, Nev.
22. Tommie Hanson, rhp, Riverside (Calif.) CC
23. Brian O'Dell, rhp, Osceola Senior HS, Kissimmee, Fla.
24. Justin Reynolds, of, Central HS, Independence, Ore.
25. Matt Miller, of, Redmond (Wash.) HS
26. Michael Ryan, rhp, Lake City (Fla.) CC
27. Kyle Miller, 3b, Terry Parker HS, Jacksonville, Fla.
28. Louis Coleman, rhp, Pillow Academy HS, Greenwood, Miss.
29. Tyler Musselwhite, rhp, Gainesville (Ga.) HS
30. Brett Wiggins, lhp, Cross Creek HS, Augusta, Ga.
31. Cole McCurry, lhp, Surry (N.C.) CC
32. Brad Schwarzenbach, rhp, Cerritos (Calif.) JC
33. Tyler Flowers, 1b, Chipola (Fla.) JC
34. Blake Holt, of, Belton HS, Salado, Texas
35. Blake Guthrie, c, Dan River HS, Ringgold, Va.
36. Dwain Green, rhp, Logan HS, Madison, W.Va.
37. David Williams, rhp, Surry (N.C.) CC
38. Brett Scarpetta, lhp, Madison Area (Wisc.) Tech CC
39. Austin Fleet, rhp, Edmond Santa Fe HS, Edmond, Okla.
40. James Curtis, rhp, Manatee (Fla.) JC
41. Michael Robbins, lhp, Meridian (Miss.) CC
42. Thomas Alexander, c, Santa Barbara (Calif.) CC
43. Ryan Littlejohn, of, Verdigris HS, Broken Arrow, Okla.
44. Ben Jeffers, rhp, Madison County HS, Danielsville, Ga.
45. Mike Griffith, rhp, Issaquah (Wash.) HS
46. Luis Sanchez, ss, Lake City (Fla.) CC
47. Aaron Brady, rhp, CC of Southern Nevada
48. Nate Weidenaar, of, Bozeman (Mont.) HS
49. Jesse Simpson, rhp, Zachary (La.) HS
50. Derick Himpsl, lhp, Johnstown (N.Y.) HS

BALTIMORE ORIOLES 13

1. Brandon Snyder, c, Westfield HS, Centreville, Va.
1. Garrett Olson, lhp, Cal Poly (Supplemental choice—48th—for failure to sign 2004 first-round pick Wade Townsend)
2. Nolan Reimold, of, Bowling Green State U.
3. Brandon Erbe, rhp, McDonough School, Baltimore
4. Kieron Pope, of, East Coweta HS, Gay, Ga.
5. Reid Hamblet, rhp, Biola U.
6. Blake Owen, rhp, Belmont (Tenn.) U.
7. Bobby Andrews, of, Cal State Fullerton
8. Chorye Spoone, rhp, Catonsville (Md.) JC
9. Paco Figueroa, 2b, U. of Miami
10. Ryan Stadanlick, rhp, St. Joseph's U.
11. Bruce Gallaway, lhp, Missouri Valley College
12. John Raynor, of, UNC Wilmington
13. Kyle Dahlberg, c, Texas Christian U.
14. Mark Fleisher, 1b, Radford U.
15. Brandon Kendricks, of, DeSoto HS, Ovilla, Texas
16. David Hernandez, rhp, Cosumnes River (Calif.) JC
17. Jeff Moore, rhp, UNC Wilmington
18. Michael Whitney, rhp, Cypress-Fairbanks HS, Houston
19. D.J. Lidyard, rhp, Lower Columbia (Wash.) JC
20. Ryan Steinbach, ss, Indiana-Purdue U.-Fort Wayne
21. Brian Logan, lhp, Louisburg (N.C.) CC
22. Paul Chmiel, 1b, Pittston Area HS, Pittston, Pa.
23. Elvin Vargas, of, Connors State (Okla.) JC
24. Stuart Musslewhite, ss, Texas Christian U.
25. Daniel Lonsberry, rhp, Northwestern State U.
26. Carlos Hernandez, lhp, Santa Clara (Calif.) HS
27. Chad Thall, lhp, Jefferson (Mo.) JC
28. Miguel Abreu, 2b, East Central (Okla.) U.
29. Tanner Scheppers, rhp, Dana Hills HS, Laguna Niguel, Calif
30. Greg Young, of, Anne Arundel (Md.) CC
31. Arik Hempy, lhp, U. of South Carolina
32. Josh Faiola, rhp, Dartmouth College
33. Tyrone Anu, of, Colonial HS, Orlando
34. Matt Sopic, rhp, Seward County (Kan.) CC

DRAFT

35. Patrick Egan, rhp, Quinnipiac U.
36. Shawn Ferguson, rhp, Texas Christian U.
37. Stephen Foster, lhp, Auburn (Wash.) HS
38. Chris Vinyard, c, Chandler-Gilbert (Ariz.) CC
39. Caleb Annesley, c, Blanchard (Okla.) HS
40. Harrison Bishop, rhp, Edmonds (Wash.) CC
41. Mark Horner, lhp, Oklahoma City U.
42. Bryan Lee, rhp, Cuesta (Calif.) JC
43. Danny Figueroa, of, U. of Miami
44. Brian Bent, c, Catonsville (Md.) CC
45. Brad Rifkin, 1b, Park School, Columbia, Md.
46. Benjamin Brian, of, Wayne HS, Waynesville, Ohio
47. Craig Johnson, rhp, Bellevue (Wash.) CC
48. Brent Davis, rhp, Clear Lake HS, Houston
49. Ryan Saldivar, c, Ryan High, Denton, Texas
50. Jeremy Bloor, lhp, Grand Rapids (Mich.) CC

BOSTON RED SOX 28

1. Jacoby Ellsbury, of, Oregon State U. (Choice from Angels as compensation for loss of Type A free agent Orlando Cabrera)
1. Craig Hansen, rhp, St. John's U. (Choice from Dodgers as compensation for loss of Type A free agent Derek Lowe)
1. (Choice to Cardinals as compensation for Type A free agent Edgar Renteria)
1. Clay Buchholz, rhp, Angelina (Texas) JC (Supplemental choice—42nd—for loss of Type A free agent Pedro Martinez)
1. Jed Lowrie, 2b, Stanford U. (Supplemental choice—45th—for loss of Cabrera)
1. Michael Bowden, rhp, Waubonsie Valley HS, Aurora, Ill. (Supplmental choice—47th—for loss of Lowe)
2. Jon Egan, c, Cross Creek HS, Hephzibah, Ga. (Choice from Mets as compensation for Martinez)
2. (Choice to Padres as compensation for Type A free agent David Wells)
3. (Choice to Cubs as compensation for Type B free agent Matt Clement)
4. Scott Blue, rhp, Morro Bay (Calif.) HS
5. Reid Engel, of, Lewis-Palmer HS, Monument, Colo.
6. Jeff Corsaletti, of, U. of Florida
7. Yahmed Yema, of, Florida International U.
8. J.T. Zink, rhp, Everett (Wash.) CC
9. Mark Wagner, c, UC Irvine
10. Kevin Guyette, rhp, U. of Arizona
11. Ismael Casillas, rhp, Benedictine (Kan.) College
12. Kyle Fernandes, lhp, Massasoit (Mass.) CC
13. Jay Johnson, of, Xavier U.
14. Pedro Alvarez, ss, Horace Mann HS, Bronx, N.Y.
15. P.J. Thomas, rhp, Jeffersonville (Ind.) HS
16. Matt Mercurio, 3b, Florida Souhern College
17. Dominic Ramos, ss, Texas State U.
18. Nick Criaris, c, St. Peter's Prep, Jersey City, N.J.
19. Jim Baxter, lhp, Villanova U.
20. Charlie Blackmon, lhp, Young Harris (Ga.) JC
21. Drew Johnson, rhp, Navarro (Texas) JC
22. Orvil Aviles, lhp, Fernando Callejo HS, Manati, P.R.
23. Carl Lipsey, 2b, Jackson State U.
24. Jason Twomley, of, U. of Massachusetts
25. Ricardo Sanchez, c, Barry (Fla.) U.
26. Kirby Yates, rhp, Kauai HS, Koloa, Hawaii
27. Matt Hancock, lhp, Oral Roberts U.
28. Ryan Hinson, lhp, Northwestern HS, Rock Hill, S.C.
29. Chris Jones, rhp, Indiana State U.
30. Ryan Colvin, rhp, Carroll HS, Southlake, Texas
31. Luis Exposito, c, Champagnat Catholic HS, Hialeah, Fla.
32. Jeff Natale, 2b, Trinity (Conn.) College
33. John Hester, c, Stanford U.
34. Allan Dykstra, 1b, Rancho Bernardo HS, Poway, Calif.
35. Jason Determann, lhp, Louisiana State U.
36. Mark McClure, rhp, Hillsborough HS, Tampa
37. Jason Schnitzer, rhp, Los Alamitos (Calif.) HS
38. Levi Tapia, c, Ralston Valley HS, Arvada, Colo.
39. Bubba Bell, of, Nicholls State U.
40. Blake Maxwell, rhp, Methodist (N.C.) College
41. Eddie Degerman, rhp, Rice U.
42. Miguel Alicea, of, Manuela Toro HS, Caguas, P.R.
43. Jason Castro, c, Castro Valley (Calif.) HS
44. Chris Garcia, 1b, Xaverian HS, Brooklyn, N.Y.
45. Dustin Bamberg, c, Tallahassee (Fla.) CC
46. T.J. Large, rhp, U. of Alabama
47. Alex Wolfe, c, Timpanogos HS, Payson, Utah
48. Matt Sheely, of, Palm Beach Gardens (Fla.) HS
49. Erik Turgeon, rhp, Dunedin (Fla.) HS
50. Colin Arnold, of, King's Academy, Palm Beach Gardens, Fla.

CHICAGO CUBS 20

1. Mark Pawelek, lhp, Springville (Utah) HS
2. Donald Veal, lhp, Pima (Ariz.) CC
3. Mark Holliman, rhp, U. of Mississippi
3. Mike Billek, rhp, U. of Central Florida (Choice from Red Sox as compensation for loss of Type B free agent Matt Clement)
4. Dylan Johnston, ss, Hamilton HS, Chandler, Ariz.
5. Scott Taylor, rhp, Hermitage HS, Richmond, Va.
6. Kyle Reynolds, ss, Baylor U.
7. Trey Taylor, lhp, Baylor U.
8. Jake Muyco, c, North Carolina State U.
9. Matt Avery, rhp, U. of Virginia
10. Joe Simokaitis, ss, U. of Nebraska
11. Michael Phelps, rhp, Central Missouri State U.
12. Yusuf Carter, c, El Paso (Texas) CC
13. Brett Jackson, rhp, Modesto (Calif.) JC
14. Tyler Graham, of, Oregon State U.
15. Roger Evenson, rhp, Northwest Nazarene (Idaho) College
16. Jon Mueller, rhp, U. of Minnesota
17. Brandon Taylor, 3b, Brigham Young U.
18. Victor Liriano, of, El Paso (Texas) CC
19. Kyle Holden, rhp, Cal State San Bernardino
20. L.V. Ware, of, North Atlanta HS, Atlanta
21. Peter Farina, c, Virgina Commonwealth U.
22. Michael Hyle, rhp, U. of Georgia
23. Jayson Ruhlman, lhp, Central Michigan U.
24. Scott Hode, ss, U. of Arkansas
25. D.J. Lewis, of, Los Angeles Valley CC
26. Nikolaus Crouch, 1b, Vanguard (Calif.) U.
27. Davy Gregg, of, U. of South Carolina
28. Michael Greenhouse, lhp, U. of Evansville
29. Johnny Defendis, of, Rutgers U.
30. Matt Liuzza, c, Louisiana State U.
31. Brad DePoy, rhp, San Jacinto (Texas) JC
32. Colby Wark, rhp, Lower Columbia (Wash.) JC
33. Ben Ferguson, rhp, Cottonwood HS, Salt Lake City
34. Cody Gilbert, 3b, Lincoln Trail (Ill.) JC
35. Drew O'Connell, rhp, John A. Logan (Ill.) JC
36. Needham Jones, lhp, Old Dominon U.
37. Kyle Keen, of, U. of Georgia
38. Ryan Episcopo, of, Andrew (Ga.) JC
39. Justin Morgan, c, U. of Louisiana-Lafayette
40. Ryan Chambers, lhp, Brigham Young U.
41. Chris Rollins, rhp, Winslow Township HS, Blue Anchor, N.J.
42. Noah Garza, rhp, Nolan HS, Fort Worth, Texas
43. Michael Brenly, c, Notre Dame HS, Scottsdale, Ariz.
44. Eddie Rush, of, Westlake HS, McDonough, Ga.
45. Corey Madden, rhp, St. Mary's (Calif.) College
46. Luther Murphy, 1b, Hialeah Miami Lakes (Fla.) HS
47. Mario Williams, c, Hillsborough HS, Tampa
48. Andy Hawranick, c, Georgia Tech
49. Kyle Mura, 3b, Loyola Marymount U.
50. Steven Morlock, rhp, UC Santa Barbara

CHICAGO WHITE SOX 15

1. Lance Broadway, rhp, Texas Christian U.
2. (Choice to Yankees as compensation for Type B free agent Orlando Hernandez)
3. Ricky Brooks, rhp, East Carolina U.
4. Chris Getz, 2b, U. of Michigan
5. Ryan Rote, rhp, Vanderbilt U.
6. Aaron Cunningham, of, Everett (Wash.) CC
7. Daniel Cortes, rhp, Garey HS, Pomona, Calif.
8. Clayton Richard, lhp, U. of Michigan
9. Joe Winn, rhp, Delgado (La.) JC
10. Israel Chirino, lhp, U. of Miami
11. Jason Rice, rhp, Chaffey (Calif.) JC
12. Sheldon Catchot, lhp, Delgado (La.) JC
13. Joey Fernandez, 1b, Braddock HS, Miami
14. Derek Rodriguez, rhp, U. of Nevada-Las Vegas
15. Chris Carter, 3b, Sierra Vista HS, Las Vegas
16. Alex Woodson, lhp, Porterville (Calif.) CC
17. Enrique Garcia, rhp, Potomac State (W.Va.) JC
18. Tim Sabo, rhp, Seton Hall U.
19. Jordan Danks, of, Round Rock (Texas) HS
20. Josh Morgan, of, U. of South Alabama
21. Raleigh Evans, lhp, Lake City (Fla.) CC
22. Christian Marrero, of, Broward (Fla.) JC
23. Bobby La Fromboise, lhp, Rio Hondo (Calif.) JC
24. Tyler Wright, of, Charlotte HS, Punta Gorda, Fla.
25. Andrew Beatty, lhp, West High, Aurora, Ill.
26. Anthony Carter, rhp, Georgia Perimeter JC
27. Daniel Jordan, c, Broward (Fla.) CC
28. Justin Sincock, rhp, Golden West (Calif.) JC
29. Aljay Davis, 2b, Northeast Oklahoma A&M JC
30. Brandon Langston, rhp, Cleveland State (Tenn.) CC

31. Lucas Luetge, lhp, Bellville HS, Industry, Texas
32. Matt Headley, lhp, San Jacinto (Texas) JC
33. Scott Savastano, ss, Plymouth (Mass.) North HS
34. Tim Day, rhp, Michigan State U.
35. Marcos Causey, of, South Florida CC
36. Nate Templeton, rhp, Valley HS, Des Monies, Iowa
37. Brian Flores, lhp, New Mexico JC
38. Enrique Escolano, rhp, Kell HS, Kennesaw, Ga.
39. Jovan Rosa, ss, East Hartford (Conn.) HS
40. Raphael Vera, 2b, Sarasota (Fla.) HS
41. Kris Welker, c, U. of Iowa
42. Michael Kelly, lhp, Lafayette HS, Mayo, Fla.
43. Brooks Dunn, lhp, Mississippi State U.
44. Drew George, ss, Lower Columbia (Wash.) CC
45. Cody Wright, lhp, Bountiful, Utah
46. Brendan O'Donnell, of, Santa Barbara (Calif.) CC
47. John Wolff, 2b, Harvard U.
48. Chris Cassidy, lhp, Claremont (Calif.) HS
49. Steven Squires, rhp, Wayne State (Mich.) U.
50. Kyle Landers, lhp, Noblesville (Ind.) HS

CINCINNATI REDS 12

1. Jay Bruce, of, West Brook HS, Beaumont, Texas
2. Travis Wood, lhp, Bryant HS, Alexander, Ark.
3. Zach Ward, rhp, Gardner-Webb U.
4. Sam LeCure, rhp, U. of Texas
5. James Avery, rhp, Niagara U.
6. Jeff Stevens, rhp, Loyola Marymount U.
7. Brandon Roberts, of, Cal Poly
8. Michael Jones, ss, Wayne County HS, Jesup, Ga.
9. Milton Loo, 3b, Yavapai (Ariz.) CC
10. Bo Lanier, rhp, U. of Georgia
11. Carlos Fisher, rhp, Lewis-Clark State (Idaho) College
12. Adam Rosales, ss, Western Michigan U.
13. Logan Ondrusek, rhp, McLennan (Texas) CC
14. Michael Griffin, 2b, Baylor U.
15. Michael DeJesus, 2b, Coastal Carolina U.
16. Jason Vecchio, rhp, U. of Texas-San Antonio
17. David Wilson, lhp, Lander (S.C.) U.
18. Kevyn Feiner, ss, Sun Prairie (Wisc.) HS
19. Eric Eymann, ss, Kansas State U.
20. Ben Mummy, 1b, U. of Nevada
21. Ben Blumenthal, c, Erskine (S.C.) College
22. Robbie Nickols, lhp, Pima (Ariz.) CC
23. James Morris, lhp, U. of Illinois
24. Kyle Ginley, rhp, St. Petersburg (Fla.) JC
25. Taylor Johnson, of, U. of Washington
26. Matthew Salmon, of, South Aiken HS, Aiken S.C.
27. Kenny Smalley, rhp, St. Charles (Ill.) HS
28. Henry-Judsen Smith, rhp, Phoenix JC
29. Russell Haltiwanger, rhp, Newberry (S.C.) College
30. Mark Rodriguez, c, U. of Texas-Pan American
31. Abe Woody, rhp, Baylor U.
32. Chris Denove, c, UCLA
33. Leroy Hunt, of, Linden HS, Stockton, Calif.
34. Brandon Camardese, lhp, U. of Miami
35. Angel Colon, 3b, Iowa Wesleyan College
36. Lorenzo Douglas, rhp, Sachse HS, Garland, Texas
37. Jacob Long, c, Modesto (Calif.) JC
38. Kuyaunnis Miles, of, Russell County HS, Phenix City, Ala.
39. Edwin Quirarte, rhp, Oxnard (Calif.) HS
40. Angel Cabrera, ss, Connors State (Okla.) JC
41. Justin Tordi, ss, U. of Florida
42. John Axford, rhp, U. of Notre Dame
43. Clay Long, rhp, Chipola (Fla.) JC
44. Jason Erickson, rhp, White River HS, Buckley, Wash.
45. Andre Lamontagne, rhp, Righetti HS, Santa Maria, Calif.
46. J.W. Brown, 1b, Howard (Texas) JC
47. Matt Garrett, of, Grand Rapids (Mich.) CC
48. Gary Poynter, rhp, Marcus HS, Flower Mound, Texas
49. Cody Allen, of, Coleman (Mich.) HS
50. Jake Christensen, of, Lockport (Ill.) Township HS

CLEVELAND INDIANS 14

1. Trevor Crowe, of, U. of Arizona
1. John Drennen, of, Rancho Bernardo HS, San Diego (Supplemental choice—33rd—for loss of Type A free agent Omar Vizquel)
2. Stephen Head, 1b, U. of Mississippi
3. Nick Weglarz, 1b, Lakeshore Catholic HS, Stevensville, Ontario
3. Jensen Lewis, rhp, Vanderbilt U. (Choice from Giants as compensation for Vizquel)
4. Jordan Brown, 1b, U. of Arizona
5. Kevin Dixon, rhp, Minnesota State U.-Mankato
6. Joe Ness, rhp, Ball State U.
7. James Deters, rhp, Calvin (Mich.) College
8. Ryan Edell, lhp, College of Charleston
9. Roman Pena, of, Mongomery HS, San Diego
10. Jason Schutt, rhp, Central Missouri State U.
11. Nicholas Petrucci, 3b, JC of the Canyons (Calif.)
12. Matt Fornasiere, ss, U. of Minnesota
13. Barry Laird, rhp, Lee HS, Baytown, Texas
14. Mike Finocchi, rhp, Louisburg (N.C.) JC
15. Chase Phillips, rhp, Monterey HS, Lubbock, Texas
16. Aaron Shafer, rhp, Troy Buchanan HS, Moscow Mills, Mo.
17. Eric Barrett, lhp, Marion (Ill.) HS
18. Desmond Jennings, of, Pinson Valley HS, Pinson, Ala.
19. Tim Dennehy, lhp, Oak Park-River Forest HS, Oak Park, Ill.
20. Scott Sumner, rhp, Louisiana College
21. Neil Wagner, rhp, North Dakota State U.
22. Clint Storr, of, Key West (Fla.) HS
23. Dexter English, of, Encinal HS, Suisun City, Calif.
24. Willie Hale, rhp, Alexander HS, Albany, Ohio
25. Andy Lytle, ss, U. of Iowa
26. Thomas Cowley, lhp, Oklahoma State U.
27. Brandon Laird, 1b, La Quinta HS, Garden Grove, Calif.
28. Angel Claudio, rhp, Puerto Rico Baseball Academy, Caguas, P.R.
29. John Curtis, c, Cal State Fullerton
30. Joel Martin, lhp, Marion Center HS, Homer, Pa.
31. Matt Loberg, rhp, U. of Minnesota
32. Brent Thomas, of, Texas Tech
33. Trevor Mortensen, of, Cal State Fullerton
34. Arshwin Asjes, rhp, Gloucester County (N.J.) CC
35. Levi Laughlin, rhp, Connors State (Okla.) JC
36. Matt Yokley, rhp, Collierville (Tenn.) HS
37. Cody Satterwhite, rhp, Hillcrest Christian HS, Jackson, Miss.
38. Daniel Lima, ss, Florida Christian HS, Miami
39. Jessie Mier, c, Irvine Valley (Calif.) JC
40. DeWayne Carver, rhp, Oklahoma State U.
41. Ashton Shewey, lhp, Chandler-Gilbert (Ariz.) CC
42. Tim Lincecum, rhp, U. of Washington
43. Chadd Hartman, of, Olympia HS, Windermere, Fla.
44. Travis Turek, rhp, Westlake HS, Westlake Village, Calif.
45. Drew Fiorenza, rhp, Clemson U.
46. Blake Davis, ss, Cal State Fullerton
47. Gus Milner, of, U. of Kansas
48. Joseph Hunter, of, Mississippi State U.
49. Ryan Wood, ss, Hylton HS, Woodbridge, Va.
50. Cameron Satterwhite, of, Moeller HS, Cincinnati

COLORADO ROCKIES 7

1. Troy Tulowitzki, ss, Long Beach State U.
1. Chaz Roe, rhp, Lafayette HS, Lexington, Ky. (Supplemental choice—32nd—for loss of Type A free agent Vinny Castilla)
2. Daniel Carte, of, Winthrop U. (Choice from Nationals as compensation for Castilla)
2. Zach Simons, rhp, Everett (Wash.) CC
3. Kyle Hancock, rhp, Rowlett (Texas) HS
4. Brandon Durden, lhp, Georgia College
5. Josh Sullivan, rhp, Auburn U.
6. Corey Wimberly, 2b, Alcorn State U.
7. Geoff Strickland, ss, Florida Southern U.
8. James Burok, rhp, Old Dominion U.
9. Andrew Johnston, rhp, U. of Missouri
10. Garner Wetzel, ss, Millsaps (Miss.) College
11. Chris Frey, of, U. of Arizona
12. Dominick Foster, rhp, Fresno (Calif.) CC
13. Mike Paulk, of, Cal State Northridge
14. Kyle Blumenthal, c, Cal Poly U.
15. Travis Becktel, of, San Jose State U.
16. Bret Berglund, of, Cal Poly
17. Jimmy Freeman, lhp, Washington State U.
18. Brett Strickland, rhp, Georgia State U.
19. Byron Binda, rhp, Coastal Carolina U.
20. Andy Kreidermacher, rhp, Minnesota State U.-Mankato
21. Chris Martin, rhp, McLennan (Texas) CC
22. Radames Nazario, ss, Pimentel HS, Naguabo, P.R.
23. Phil Cuadrado, 3b, Cumberland (Tenn.) U.
24. Sean Toler, rhp, Parkway South HS, Manchester, Mo.
25. Steven Hirschfeld, rhp, CC of Southern Nevada
26. Ethan Katz, rhp, Cal State Sacramento
27. Sean Ruthven, rhp, U. of Georgia
28. David Bechtold, lhp, Liberty U.
29. Reese Havens, ss, Bishop England HS, Charleston, S.C.
30. Michael Milliron, ss, Penn State U.
31. Sean Halton, 1b, Fresno (Calif.) HS
32. Jarrad Page, of, UCLA
33. Jordan Jarvis, rhp, Arcadia HS, Phoenix
34. Kyle Beitey, lhp, Lower Columbia (Wash.) JC

DRAFT

35. Tim Brewer, rhp, Ivanna Eudora Kean HS, St. Thomas, V.I.
36. Chris Cook, 1b, Grand Canyon U.
37. C.J. Belanger, of, Cypress HS, Stanton, Calif.
38. Barret Browning, lhp, Florida State U.
39. Rod Scurry, rhp, Sierra (Calif.) JC
40. Joseph Servais, c, Garden City (Kan.) CC
41. Jeremy Farrell, 3b, St. Ignatius HS, Cleveland
42. Maikol Gonzales, ss, Louisburg (N.C.) JC
43. Jordan Rogers, rhp, Dayton (Texas) HS
44. Philip Myers, lhp, Ballard HS, Louisville
45. Chris Bell, of, Johnson HS, Gainesville, Ga.
46. Garrett Vaughan, c, Sibley (La.) HS
47. Brent Weiss, 2b, St. Joseph Regional HS, Suffern, N.Y.
48. Spencer Schuh, rhp, Harrison (Ark.) HS
49. Jordan Moore, lhp, Spokane Falls (Wash.) CC
50. James Pollack, c, North Broward Prep, Parkland, Fla.

DETROIT TIGERS 10

1. Cameron Maybin, of, T.C. Roberson HS, Arden, N.C.
2. (Choice to Angels as compensation for Type A free agent Troy Percival)
3. Chris Robinson, c, U. of Illinois
4. Kevin Whelan, rhp, Texas A&M U.
5. Jeff Larish, 1b, Arizona State U.
6. Clete Thomas, of, Auburn U.
7. P.J. Finigan, rhp, Southern Illinois U.
8. Brendan Wise, rhp, Pratt (Kan.) JC
9. Paul Coleman, lhp, Pepperdine U.
10. Kevin Ardoin, rhp, U. of Louisiana-Lafayette
11. Anthony Claggett, rhp, UC Riverside
12. Matt Joyce, of, Florida Southern College
13. Louis Ott, ss, Sacramento CC
14. Casper Wells, of, Towson U.
15. Ben Petralli, c, Sacramento CC
16. Michael Hollimon, ss, Oral Roberts U.
17. Warner Jones, 2b, Vanderbilt U.
18. Agustin Guzman, 2b, Baton Rouge (La.) CC
19. Burke Badenhop, rhp, Bowling Green State U.
20. Erik Averill, lhp, Arizona State U.
21. David Adams, ss, Grandview Prep, Boca Raton, Fla.
22. Matt Norfleet, rhp, Tennessee Wesleyan College
23. Mark Haske, ss, U. of Cincinnati
24. Brett Bordes, lhp, Arizona State U.
25. Jacob Baxter, rhp, U. of Texas-Arlington
26. Schuyler Williamson, c, U.S. Military Academy
27. Will Rhymes, 2b, College of William & Mary
28. Ryan Paul, lhp, Los Angeles Pierce JC
29. Eric Fry, of, Barbe HS, Lake Charles, La.
30. Ryan Roberson, 1b, George Washington U.
31. Tim Robertson, rhp, Oral Roberts U.
32. Chris Torres, c, Cumberland (Tenn.) U.
33. Loren Fraser, rhp, UC Santa Barbara
34. Alex Avila, 3b, Archbishop McCarthy HS, Pembroke Pines, Fla.
35. Jeff Hahn, rhp, Clemson U.
36. Gibbs Wilson, rhp, Weatherford (Texas) JC
37. Jeff Kunkel, c, U. of Michigan
38. Zach Putnam, rhp, Pioneer HS, Ann Arbor, Mich.
39. Kiel Renfro, rhp, Texarkana (Texas) CC
40. Kyle Peter, of, Cloud County (Kan.) CC
41. Tony Pechek, c, South HS, Pueblo, Colo.
42. Ben Rodewald, rhp, East Kenwood (Mich.) HS
43. Ryan Perry, ss, Rocklin (Calif.) HS
44. Adrian Casanova, c, Clemson U.
45. Tyson Jaquez, 3b, Loyalton (Calif.) HS
46. David Mattox, rhp, North Arkansas CC
47. Albert Gonzalez, 2b, American Senior HS, Hialeah, Fla.
48. Kevin Hammons, rhp, Sierra (Calif.) JC
49. Anthony Capra, lhp, Arvada West High, Arvada, Colo.
50. Jeff Whitlow, of, Detroit Country Day HS, Southfield, Mich.

FLORIDA MARLINS 16

1. Chris Volstad, rhp, Palm Beach Gardens (Fla.) HS
1. Aaron Thompson, lhp, Second Baptist HS, Houston (Choice from Giants as compensation for Type A free agent Armando Benitez)
1. Jacob Marceaux, rhp, McNeese State U. (Choice from Yankees as compensation for Type A free agent Carl Pavano)
1. Ryan Tucker, rhp, Temple City (Calif.) HS (Supplemental choice—34th—for loss of Benitez)
1. Sean West, lhp, Captain Shreve HS, Shreveport, La. (Supplemental choice—44th—for loss of Pavano)
2. Kris Harvey, of, Clemson U.
2. Brett Hayes, c, U. of Nevada (Supplemental choice—79th—for loss of Type C free agent Mike Redmond)
3. Matt Goyen, lhp, Georgia College
4. Gaby Sanchez, c, U. of Miami
5. Kyle Winters, rhp, Pomona HS, Arvada, Colo.
6. James Guerrero, 2b, San Diego State U.
7. Chris Leroux, rhp, Winthrop U.
8. Aaron Bates, 1b, North Carolina State U.
9. Jim Brauer, rhp, U. of Michigan
10. Cody Allen, 3b, Elk Grove (Calif.) HS
11. Andy Jenkins, c, Oregon State U.
12. Kyle Marlatt, rhp, Texas A&M U.
13. Jeff Van Houten, of, U of Arizona
14. Travis Talbott, lhp, U. of California
15. Paul Witt, ss, Baylor U.
16. Jon Lewis, rhp, U. of Stony Brook
17. Zac McCamie, rhp, U. of South Carolina
18. Kyle Padgett, ss, College of William & Mary
19. Adam Wood, lhp, U. of South Alabama
20. Rafael Galbizo, rhp, Miami
21. Colin Roberson, of, Virginia Wesleyan College
22. Logan Morrison, 1b, Northshore HS, Slidell, La.
23. Justin Webb, c, U. of North Carolina
24. Matt Kutler, of, Brown U.
25. Blake Jones, rhp, Northwestern State U.
26. Scott Lindeen, rhp, U. of La Verne
27. Jason Jarrett, rhp, Virginia Wesleyan College
28. Michael Thomasson, of, Laney (Calif.) JC
29. Jared Wesson, lhp, Itawamba (Miss.) CC
30. Chris Haupt, c, Central Columbia HS, Bloomsburg, Pa.
31. Matt Jones, lhp, Guildford Park SS, Surrey, B.C.
32. Adalberto Flores, rhp, Gurabo, P.R.
33. Adam Howard, c, St. Louis CC-Meramec
34. Adam Abraham, 3b, Grosse Point (Mich.) South HS
35. Jacob Taylor, c, Chaffey (Calif.) JC
36. Sean Boatright, of, Long Beach State U.
37. Josh Short, of, Marysville-Pilchuck HS, Marysville, Wash.
38. Steven Pujol, lhp, San Fernando (Calif.) HS
39. Jonathan Prevost, of, Ahunstic (Quebec) College
40. Eric Basurto, rhp, Chabot (Calif.) JC
41. Luis Ramos, of, Jose de Diego HS, Mayaguez, P.R.
42. David Woods, c, West Lauderdale HS, Bailey, Miss.
43. Zach Barrett, 3b, Olney Central (Ill.) JC
44. Ryan Pollard, lhp, Illinois Central CC
45. Brady Decker, rhp, Olney Central (Ill.) CC
46. Stephen Schneider, 1b, Orange Coast (Calif.) CC
47. Dustin Kaats, 2b, Desert Mountain HS, Scottsdale, Ariz.
48. Chris Bodishbaugh, rhp, Los Medanos (Calif.) JC
49. James Wallace, rhp, Benicia (Calif.) HS
50. Jared Banks, rhp, Los Medanos (Calif.) JC

HOUSTON ASTROS 24

1. Brian Bogusevic, lhp, Tulane U.
1. Eli Iorg, of, U. of Tennessee (Supplemental choice—38th—for loss of Type A free agent Carlos Beltran)
2. Ralph Henriquez, c, Key West (Fla.) HS
3. Tommy Manzella, ss, Tulane U. (Choice from Mets as compensation for Beltran)
3. Josh Lindblom, rhp, Harrison HS, West Lafayette, Ind.
4. Josh Flores, of, Triton (Ill.) JC
5. Billy Hart, 3b, U. of Southern California
6. Brandon Barnes, of, Cypress (Calif) JC
7. Timothy Johnson, ss, Wissahickon HS, Penllyn, Pa.
8. Koby Clemens, 3b, Memorial HS, Houston
9. Jordan Meaker, rhp, Flower Mound (Texas) HS
10. Allen Langdon, of, Eagle HS, Boise, Idaho
11. Cory Lapinski, lhp, Illinois Wesleyan U.
12. Tip Fairchild, rhp, U. of Southern Maine
13. Eric King, ss, U. of Tennessee
14. Mark Ori, 1b, Northwestern U.
15. Eric Sheridan, rhp, Saddleback (Calif.) CC
16. Aaron Bulkley, of, Le Moyne U.
17. Andy Kroeker, c, Biola (Calif.) U.
18. Brian Needham, rhp, John Foster Dulles HS, Sugar Land, Texas
19. Drew Himes, rhp, Illinois Wesleyan U.
20. Ryan Mitchell, rhp, Magnolia (Texas) HS
21. Scott Sarver, lhp, Cal State Fullerton
22. T.J. Steele, of, Canyon del Oro HS, Oro Valley, Ariz.
23. Chris Blazek, lhp, U. of Vermont
24. Sean Walker, rhp, Baylor U.
25. Jacob Hurry, lhp, Coastal Carolina U.
26. Michael Thompson, 3b, Santa Clara U.
27. Matt Luca, rhp, U. of Nevada-Las Vegas
28. Eric Baker, 2b, Mansfield (Pa.) U.
29. Jamie Gant, rhp, Mississippi State U.
30. Matt Hirsh, rhp, California Lutheran U.
31. Brad Stone, rhp, Quincy (Ill.) U.

32. Cole Graham, 1b, Triton (Ill.) JC
33. Reid Kelly, rhp, Desert Mountain HS, Scottsdale, Ariz.
34. Nathan Warrick, of, U. of Texas-Arlington
35. Andrew Darnell, of, Chabot (Calif.) JC
36. Matt Cunningham, of, UC Riverside
37. Matt Bishop, rhp, Endicott (Mass.) College
38. Mike Colla, rhp, Clovis West HS, Fresno, Calif.
39. Zachary Williams, rhp, Seminole State (Okla.) CC
40. Collin Fanning, of, Clarendon (Texas) JC
41. Casey McCleskey, of, Temple (Texas) JC
42. Brandon Stricklen, rhp, Texas Southern U
43. Jacob Hower, rhp, American River (Calif.) JC
44. Nicholas Cobler, lhp, Northeast Texas CC
45. Craig Herrforth, rhp, Arrowhead Union HS, Hartland, Wisc.
46. Wes Musick, lhp, Hudson HS, Lufkin, Texas

KANSAS CITY ROYALS 2

1. Alex Gordon, 3b, U. of Nebraska
2. Jeff Bianchi, ss, Lampeter-Strasburg HS, Lancaster, Pa.
3. Chris Nicoll, rhp, UC Irvine
4. Joe Dickerson, of, Esperanza HS, Yorba Linda, Calif.
5. Shawn Hayes, ss, Franklin Pierce (N.H.) College
6. Ryan DiPietro, lhp, Eastern Connecticut State U.
7. Brent Fisher, lhp, Tolleson Union HS, Goodyear, Ariz.
8. Nick Doscher, c, Moore Catholic HS, Staten Island, N.Y.
9. Kiel Thibault, c, Gonzaga U.
10. Jeff Howell, c, Florida Southern College
11. Michael Penn, rhp, U. of Michigan
12. Cody Harkcom, rhp, New Mexico JC
13. Andrew Larsen, of, U. of Stony Brook
14. Antonio Sabatini, of, Erskine (S.C.) College
15. Brady Everett, c, Washington State U.
16. Mario Santiago, rhp, Baton Rouge (La.) CC
17. Miguel Vasquez, ss, Dewitt Clinton HS, Bronx, N.Y.
18. Paul Raglione, rhp, Grant HS, Portland, Ore.
19. Zane Chavez, c, Fallbrook (Calif.) HS
20. Bryan Casey, rhp, Arizona Western JC
21. David Henninger, rhp, Messiah (Pa.) College
22. Justin Bristow, ss, Mills Godwin HS, Richmond, Va.
23. Matt Kniginyzky, rhp, High Point U.
24. Josh Colafemina, ss, College of St. Rose (N.Y.)
25. Kevin Bulger, rhp, College of Charleston
26. Jake McLintock, rhp, San Diego State U.
27. Jase Turner, 1b, Pomona-Pitzer (Calif.) College
28. Felix Peguero, of, Oklahoma Baptist U.
29. Brandon Brantley, rhp, U. of Science and Arts (Okla.)
30. Jeremy Jirschele, 2b, U. of Wisconsin-Oshkosh
31. Pedro Lopez, ss, Universidad del Turabo HS, Toa Baja, P.R.
32. Michael Dubee, rhp, Okaloosa-Walton (Fla.) CC
33. Daniel Gutierrez, rhp, Rubidoux HS, Riverside, Calif.
34. Oscar Marrero, c, Juan Antonio Corretjer HS, Ciales, P.R.
35. Luke Burnett, rhp, Carthage (Texas) HS
36. Matthew Klimas, c, Broken Arrow (Okla.) HS
37. Nickolas Love, of, Enterprise (Ala.) HS
38. Jacob Myking, c, San Joaquin Delta (Calif.) JC
39. Steve Teno, lhp, St. Thomas of Villanova HS, Lasalle, Ontario
40. Nick Romero, ss, Eastlake HS, Chula Vista, Calif.
41. Anthony Rodriguez, ss, Puerto Rico Baseball Academy, Vega Baja, P.R.
42. David McClain, rhp, North Shore HS, Houston
43. Tyler Backus, rhp, Mingus Union HS, Cottonwood, Ariz.
44. Mark Serrano, rhp, Cypress (Calif.) CC
45. Eric Martinez, rhp, Eastlake HS, Chula Vista, Calif.
46. Brian Paukovits, rhp, El Capitan HS, Lakeside, Calif.
47. Kip Masuda, c, Mid-Pacific Institute, Kaneohe, Hawaii
48. Chester Wilson, 1b, St. Louis HS, Honolulu
49. Matthew Gibbs, rhp, Modesto (Calif.) JC
50. Juan Perez, rhp, Jose Rojas Cortez HS, Orocovis, P.R.

LOS ANGELES ANGELS 23

1. (Choice to Red Sox as compensation for Type A free agent Orlando Cabrera)
1. Trevor Bell, rhp, Crescenta Valley HS, La Crescenta, Calif. (Supplemental choice—37th—for loss of Type A free agent Troy Percival)
2. Ryan Mount, ss, Ayala HS, Chino Hills, Calif. (Choice from Tigers as compensation for Percival)
2. P.J. Phillips, ss, Redan HS, Stone Mountain, Ga.
3. Sean O'Sullivan, rhp, Valhalla HS, El Cajon, Calif.
4. Brian Matusz, lhp, St. Mary's HS, Cave Creek, Ariz.
5. Tommy Mendoza, rhp, Monsignior Pace HS, Miami.
6. Jerome Moore, of, North Caddo HS, Vivian, La.
7. Robert Romero, rhp, Grayson County (Texas) CC
8. Matt Hall, ss, Horizon HS, Scottsdale, Ariz.
9. Bobby Mosebach, rhp, Hillsborough (Fla.) CC
10. Peter Bourjos, of, Notre Dame HS, Scottsdale, Ariz.
11. Tim Murphy, of, Rancho Buena Vista HS, Vista, Calif.
12. Greg Dini, c, Tulane U.
13. Bryce Cox, rhp, Rice U.
14. Stephen Brock, rhp, Chipola (Fla.) JC
15. Brad Coon, of, Trevecca Nazarene (Tenn.) U.
16. Darrell Sales, 1b, West Valley (Calif.) CC
17. Ryan Pressley, 1b, Evans HS, Martinez, Ga.
18. Jim West, rhp, Chandler-Gilbert (Ariz.) CC
19. Anthony Sullivan, rhp, St. John's U.
20. Martinez Allen, of, North Florida JC
21. Brad Suttle, 3b, Boerne (Texas) HS
22. Chris Nash, 1b, Marquette HS, Chesterfield, Mo.
23. Deunte Heath, rhp, Lake City (Fla.) CC
24. Dallas Morris, 3b, U. of Louisiana-Lafayette
25. Brok Butcher, rhp, Oxnard (Calif.) JC
26. Kevin Lynch, rhp, Florida State U.
27. Colby Overstreet, 1b, Oklahoma City U.
28. Blair Brejtfus, rhp, Arcadia HS, Phoenix
29. Vincent Scarduzio, 1b, Broward (Fla.) CC
30. Neil Medchill, c, Lake Orion HS, Oxford, Mich.
31. Tim Didjurgis, rhp, Regis (Colo.) U.
32. Braden Wells, of, Dixie State (Utah) JC
33. Marco Albano, ss, Boston College
34. Ryan Schlitter, rhp, Lake City (Fla.) CC
35. Chris Davis, 3b, Navarro (Texas) JC
36. Jacob Dixon, rhp, U. of North Florida
37. Jeremy Haynes, rhp, Tallahassee (Fla.) CC
38. Flint Wipke, c, Georgia Southern U.
39. Brent Milleville, c, Maize HS, Wichita, Kan.
40. Rian Kiniry, of, Chaminade-Madonna Prep, Hollywood, Fla.
41. Joseph Klein, rhp, Patuxent HS, Lusby, Md.
42. Carlos Del Rosario, of, George Washington HS, New York
43. Brent Solich, lhp, Manatee (Fla.) JC
44. Michael Bunton, lhp, Tallahassee (Fla.) CC
45. Shay Conder, c, American Fork (Utah) HS
46. Julian Laurean, 2b, Chandler-Gilbert (Ariz.) CC
47. Seth Loman, 1b, Lamar (Colo.) CC
48. Cody Fuller, of, Texas Tech
49. Anthony Vasquez, of, Ronald Reagan HS, San Antonio
50. Buster Posey, rhp, Lee County HS, Leesburg, Ga.

LOS ANGELES DODGERS 26

1. (Choice to Red Sox as compensation for Type A free agent Derek Lowe)
1. *Luke Hochevar, rhp, U. of Tennessee (Supplemental choice—40th—for loss of Type A free agent Adrian Beltre)
2. Ivan De Jesus, ss, Puerto Rico Baseball Academy, Guaynabo, P.R. (Choice from Mariners as compensation for Beltre)
2. Josh Wall, rhp, Central Private HS, Walker, La.
3. Sergio Pedroza, of, Cal State Fullerton
4. Josh Bell, 3b, Santaluces HS, Lantana, Fla.
5. John Meloan, rhp, U. of Arizona
6. Brent Leach, lhp, Delta State U.
7. Chris Hobdy, rhp, Monterey HS, Lubbock, Texas
8. David Horlacher, rhp, Brigham Young U.
9. Michael Davitt, rhp, Davidson HS, Mobile, Ala.
10. Trayvon Robinson, of, Crenshaw HS, Los Angeles
11. Adam Godwin, of, Troy U.
12. Kris Krise, rhp, Chico State (Calif.) U.
13. Steven Johnson, rhp, St. Paul's HS, Brooklynville, Md.
14. Scott Van Slyke, of, John Burroughs HS, Ladue, Mo.
15. Wilfredo Diaz, lhp, Puerto Rico Baseball Academy, Caguas, P.R.
16. George McDonald, c, Westchester HS, Playa Del Rey, Calif.
17. Kyle Henson, c, Oak Ridge HS, Conroe, Texas
18. Kevin Carby, ss, Booker T. Washington HS, Tulsa, Okla.
19. Drew Locke, of, Boston College
20. Schuyler Tripp, lhp, Davis County HS, Drakesville, Iowa
21. Shane Justis, ss, Towson U.
22. Travis DeBondt, of, Oral Roberts U.
23. Jayson Whitehouse, of, Spartanburg Methodist (S.C.) JC
24. Jon Dutton, lhp, Rancho Bernardo HS, San Diego
25. Kyle Foster, lhp, Lower Columbia (Wash.) JC
26. Jordy Mercer, ss, Taloga (Okla.) HS
27. Matthew Coburn, rhp, Humble (Texas) HS
28. Tim Segelke, lhp, Green River (Wash.) CC
29. Kent Williamson, rhp, Hayden HS, Topeka, Kan.
30. Kyle Morgan, of, Bakersfield (Calif.) JC
31. Jonathan Forest, rhp, U. of British Columbia
32. Nate Hammons, lhp, Fort Cobb (Okla.) Broxton HS
33. Chris Lemay, lhp, Kwantlen (B.C.) JC
34. Shawn Loglisci, rhp, JC of Southern Idaho
35. Rick Taloa, 1b, Santa Ana (Calif.) JC
36. Andrew Marquardt, rhp, St. Francis HS, Sierra Madre, Calif.

37. Justin Wilson, lhp, Buchanan HS, Clovis, Calif.
38. Stephen Hermann, c, Penn Trafford HS, Harrison City, Pa.
39. Jake Debus, lhp, Victor J. Andrew HS, Tinley Park, Ill.
40. Jason Mooneyham, 1b, Chapman U.
41. Chris Johnson, rhp, John A. Logan (Ill.) JC
42. Arnoldi Cruz, c, Okaloosa-Walton (Fla.) CC
43. Brandon Rocha, c, Los Alamitos (Calif.) HS
44. Chase D'Arnaud, ss, Los Alamitos (Calif.) HS
45. Brian Mathews, 3b, Newton County HS, Covington, Ga.
46. Anthony Benner, 3b, Eastlake HS, Chula Vista, Calif.
47. Mark Sunga, 3b, Notre Dame HS, Van Nuys, Calif.
48. Paul Wourms, c, Thompson River (B.C.) U.
49. Garet Hill, rhp, Biola (Calif.) U.
50. Mitchell Houck, lhp, Cypress Bay HS, Weston, Fla.

MILWAUKEE BREWERS 5

1. Ryan Braun, 3b, U. of Miami
2. (Choice to Athletics as compensation for Type A free agent Damian Miller)
3. Will Inman, rhp, Tunstall HS, Dry Fork, Va.
4. Matthew Gamel, 3b, Chipola (Fla.) JC
5. Kevin Roberts, rhp, U. of Houston
6. Steve Hammond, lhp, Long Beach State U.
7. Michael Brantley, of, Fort Pierce Central HS, Port St. Lucie, Fla.
8. Jemile Weeks, ss, Lake Brantley HS, Altamonte Springs, Fla.
9. Carlos Hereaud, 3b, Elkins HS, Missouri City, Texas
10. Steve Garrison, lhp, The Hun School, Ewing, N.J.
11. Brent Allar, rhp, Weatherford (Texas) JC
12. John Alonso, 1b, Polk (Fla.) CC
13. Ryan Babineau, c, Etiwanda HS, Alta Loma, Calif.
14. Mark James, rhp, Sinclair SS, Whitby, Ontario
15. Michael Bell, 3b, Grayson County (Texas) CC
16. Andrew Bailey, rhp, Wagner College
17. Tim Smith, of, Midland (Texas) CC
18. Zach Braddock, lhp, Gloucester Catholic HS, Southampton, N.J.
19. Patrick Ryan, rhp, Embry-Riddle (Fla.) U.
20. David Welch, lhp, Texarkana (Texas) CC
21. Justin Stires, rhp, Saddleback (Calif.) CC
22. Kenny Holmberg, 2b, Embry-Riddle (Fla.) U.
23. Brendan Katin, of, U. of Miami
24. Michael Ramlow, lhp, Owens (Ohio) CC
25. Taylor Green, 2b, Cypress (Calif.) JC
26. Jacob Arrieta, rhp, Weatherford (Texas) JC
27. Brad Willcutt, c, U. of Southern Mississippi
28. Scott McKnight, ss, Saddleback (Calif.) CC
29. Dane Renkert, rhp, Washington State U.
30. Omar Aguilar, rhp, Merced (Calif.) JC
31. Patrick Murray, 1b, Marina HS, Huntington Beach, Calif.
32. Spencer Pennington, of, U. of Alabama
33. Jorge Core, rhp, Puerto Rico Baseball Academy, Bayamon, P.R.
34. Riley Kjeldgaard, rhp, Indian Hills (Iowa) CC
35. Sebastien Vendette, rhp, Northeastern Oklahoma A&M JC
36. Stephen Barnes, rhp, Lake City (Fla.) CC
37. Chris Hopkins, of, Sierra (Calif.) JC
38. Chris Jean, rhp, Texas State U.
39. Brad Miller, ss, Cowley County (Kan.) CC
40. Ryan Crew, ss, U. of Texas-San Antonio
41. Jordan Lennerton, 1b, El Paso (Texas) CC
42. Chris Copot, c, Lethbridge (Alberta) CC
43. Kyle Eveland, 2b, Palmdale (Calif.) HS
44. George Washington, of, Demopolis HS, Boligee, Ala.
45. Ulrich Snijders, c, St. Petersburg (Fla.) JC
46. Alex Lowrey, of, Monsignor Pace HS, Opa Locka, Fla.
47. Matt Broughton, rhp, Triton Central HS, Indianapolis
48. Frederick Lewis, lhp, Buchholz HS, Gainesville, Fla.
49. Cory Large, lhp, Bell HS, Bedford, Texas
50. Garret Regan, of, Sir Winston Churchill HS, Calgary, Alberta

MINNESOTA TWINS 25

1. Matt Garza, rhp, Fresno State U.
1. Henry Sanchez, 1b, Mission Bay HS, San Diego (Supplemental choice—39th—for loss of Type A free agent Corey Koskie)
2. Paul Kelly, ss, Flower Mound (Texas) HS (Choice from Blue Jays as compensation for Koskie)
2. Kevin Slowey, rhp, Winthrop U.
2. Drew Thompson, ss, Jupiter Community HS, Tequesta, Fla. (Supplemental choice—80th—for loss of Type C free agent Henry Blanco)
3. Brian Duensing, lhp, U. of Nebraska (Choice from Nationals as compensation for Type B free agent Cristian Guzman)
3. Ryan Mullins, lhp, Vanderbilt U.
4. Caleb Moore, c, East Tennessee State U.
5. Steven Tolleson, ss, U. of South Carolina
6. J.W. Wilson, of, Midland (Texas) HS
7. Greg Yersich, c, Andrean HS, Merrillville, Ind.
8. Danny Powers, rhp, Central Missouri State U.
9. Erik Lis, 1b, Evansville U.
10. Matt Betsill, 3b, Furman U.
11. Brian Kirwan, rhp, Santa Fe Christian HS, Del Mar, Calif.
12. Alex Burnett, rhp, Ocean View HS, Huntington Beach, Calif.
13. Michael Allen, rhp, Arlington Country Day HS, Jacksonville, Fla.
14. David Duncan, lhp, New Richmond (Ohio) HS
15. Michael Hacker, lhp, Cosumnes River (Calif.) JC
16. Yonder Alonso, c, Coral Gables HS, Miami
17. Robert Lara, c, Nova HS, Davie, Fla.
18. Matt Morgal, rhp, Edmond (Okla.) Santa Fe HS
19. Sean Richardson, c, U. of Kansas
20. Eric Santiago, ss, Natividad Rodriguez Gonza HS, Arroyo, P.R.
21. Chris Kelley, rhp, San Jacinto (Texas) JC
22. Curtis Leavitt, lhp, Vasquez HS, Acton, Calif.
23. Ken Herndon, rhp, Gulf Coast (Fla.) CC
24. Gustavo Duran, rhp, George Washington HS, Bronx, N.Y.
25. Aaron Lovett, rhp, Kaskaskia (Ill.) JC
26. Michael Mopas, lhp, Iolani HS, Mililani, Hawaii
27. Evan Frederickson, lhp, Oakton HS, Oak Hill, Va.
28. Josh Brink, rhp, Mennonite Educational Institute, Abbotsford, B.C.
29. Steve Hernandez, rhp, Redwood HS, Visalia, Calif.
30. Kiko Vazquez, 1b, Sebring (Fla.) HS
31. Kyle Carr, lhp, Linton (N.D.) HS
32. David Bromberg, rhp, Palisades HS, Los Angeles
33. Brandon Trodick, of, Cimmaron-Memorial HS, Las Vegas, Nev.
34. Danny Cox, ss, W.F. West HS, Chehalis, Wash.
35. Lukas Thomason, rhp, Brook Hill HS, Jacksonville, Texas
36. Rene Tosoni, of, Chipola (Fla.) JC
37. James Leigh, lhp, Texarkana (Texas) CC
38. Carlos Rodriguez, c, Puerto Rico Baseball Academy, Vega Baja, P.R.
39. Charles Duffey, rhp, Westminster (Calif.) HS
40. Charles Leesman, lhp, Elder HS, Cincinnati
41. Toby Gardenhire, ss, U. of Illinois
42. Jacob Cox, c, Lakeland (Fla.) HS
43. Justin Parker, rhp, Fort Wayne (Ind.) HS
44. Jose Cordero, rhp, Miami
45. Michael Kinsel, ss, Cretin-Derham Hall, St. Paul, Minn.
46. Denver Wynn, rhp, Valleyview SS, Kamloops B.C.
47. Mike Ballard, lhp, U. of Virginia
48. Juan Rodriguez, c, Bayamon (P.R.) Military Academy
49. Dane Ponciano, c, CC of Southern Nevada
50. Justin Otto, rhp, Cowley County (Kan.) CC

NEW YORK METS 9

1. *Mike Pelfrey, rhp, Wichita State U.
2. (Choice to Red Sox as compensation for Type A free agent Pedro Martinez)
3. (Choice to Astros as compensation for Type A free agent Carlos Beltran)
4. Hector Pellot, 2b, Puerto Rico Baseball Academy, Cidra, P.R.
5. Drew Butera, c, U. of Central Florida
6. Greg Cain, of, Gahr HS, Cerritos, Calif.
7. Jon Niese, lhp, Defiance (Ohio) HS
8. Sean McCraw, c, San Jacinto (Texas) JC
9. Bobby Parnell, rhp, Charleston Southern U.
10. Courtney Billingslea, of, Sinclar (Ohio) CC
11. Luis Martinez, c, Jackson State (Tenn.) CC
12. Matt Spath, of, Flagler Palm Coast HS, Bunnell, Fla.
13. Josh Thole, c, Mater Dei HS, Breese, Ill.
14. Ian Marshall, rhp, Gaithersburg (Md.) HS
15. Daniel Martin, rhp, Harleton HS, Marshall, Texas
16. Eric Domangue, lhp, Alvin (Texas) JC
17. Pedro Beato, rhp, Xaverian HS, Queens, N.Y.
18. Eric Brown, rhp, Wingate (N.C.) U.
19. Tim Grogan, 3b, Western Kentucky U.
20. Cody Railsback, rhp, Ryan HS, Denton, Texas
21. Joe Holden, of, Molloy (N.Y.) College
22. Preston Paramore, c, Allen (Texas) HS
23. Joe D'Alessandro, rhp, College of New Jersey
24. Kyle Risinger, rhp, Galveston (Texas) CC
25. D.J. Wabick, 1b, College of Charleston
26. Kevin Tomasiewicz, lhp, U. of Wisconsin-Whitewater
27. David Koons, rhp, St. Leo (Fla.) College
28. Greg Gonzalez, of, Chico State (Calif.) U.
29. Sal Aguilar, rhp, Lewis-Clark State (Idaho) College
30. Steven Holquin, rhp, Porterville (Calif.) JC
31. Matt Anderson, 3b, UC Irvine
32. Jose Castro, ss, Miami-Dade CC North
33. Daniel Arizmendi, lhp, Santa Ana (Calif.) JC
34. Joseph Mihalics, 2b, U. of Buffalo
35. Mike Sharpe, of, St. Thomas Aquinas (N.Y.) College
36. Jeramy Simmons, rhp, U. of South Alabama

37. **Alex Beras, rhp, U. of Scranton (Pa.)**
38. Pierre Miville-Deschenes, rhp, Edouard Montpetit HS, Montreal
39. Colin Thomson, rhp, Mountain View HS, Tucson
40. Jacob Blackwood, 2b, Maplewoods (Mo.) CC
41. Nick Carr, rhp, Twin Falls (Idaho) HS
42. Jared Barkdoll, C, Greencastle-Antrim HS, Greencastle, Pa.
43. Javier Brown, ss, Valhalla HS, El Cajon, Calif.
44. Phillip Pursino, c, St. Dominic HS, Stewart Manor, N.Y.
45. **Anthony Manuel, 2b, Biola (Calif.) U.**
46. Peter Tountas, ss, Maine South HS, Park Ridge, Ill.
47. Samuel Lane, rhp, Pedro Menendez HS, Elkton, Fla.
48. Jeremy Hefner, rhp, Seminole State (Okla.) JC
49. **Will Jostock, rhp, Pensacola (Fla.) JC**
50. Julio Rodriguez, of, Wabash Valley (Ill.) JC

NEW YORK YANKEES 29

1. **C.J. Henry, ss, Putnam City HS, Oklahoma City** (Choice from Phillies as compensation for Type B free agent Jon Lieber)
1. (Choice to Marlins as compensation for Type A free agent Carl Pavano)
2. **J. Brent Cox, rhp, U. of Texas** (Choice from White Sox as compensation for loss of Type B free agent Orlando Hernandez)
2. (Choice to Braves as compensation for Type A free agent Jaret Wright)
3. **Brett Gardner, of, College of Charleston**
4. **Lance Pendleton, rhp, Rice U.**
5. **Zach Kroenke, lhp, U. of Nebraska**
6. Doug Fister, rhp, Fresno State U.
7. **Garrett Patterson, lhp, U. of Oklahoma**
8. **Austin Jackson, of, Ryan HS, Denton, Texas**
9. **James Cooper, of, Loyola Marymount U.**
10. **Kyle Anson, 3b, Texas State U.**
11. **Alan Horne, rhp, U. of Florida**
12. **Joe Muich, c, Wichita State U.**
13. Karl Amonite, 1b, Auburn U.
14. **Joel Perez, of, Miami**
15. **Josh Schmidt, rhp, U. of the Pacific**
16. **Chris Malec, 2b, UC Santa Barbara**
17. **Keaton Everett, rhp, U. of Washington**
18. **Joe Burke, c, St. John's U.**
19. **Jim Conroy, rhp, U. of Illinois**
20. **Bryan Rueger, lhp, Southern Illinois U.**
21. Hanseld Diaz, c, Miami-Dade (Fla.) CC
22. Michael Lee, rhp, Skyline HS, Issaquah, Wash.
23. Matt Wallach, c, Cypress (Calif.) JC
24. Justin Phillabaum, 1b, Indian River (Fla.) CC
25. **Brad Canada, c, Bradley U.**
26. Patrick Caldwell, lhp, Yavapai (Ariz.) JC
27. Joshua Morgan, rhp, U. of Missouri-St. Louis
28. Derek Duclos, rhp, U. of Richmond
29. Justin Turner, 2b, Cal State Fullerton
30. Cameron Johnson, of, CC of Southern Nevada
31. Clint Preisendorfer, lhp, Palomar (Calif.) JC
32. Jared Souza, lhp, Navarro (Texas) JC
33. **Michael Mlotkowski, rhp, Oklahoma City U.**
34. **Felipe Garcia, 1b, Cal State Fullerton**
35. **Andy Carter, rhp, Davidson College**
36. Brett Summers, rhp, Lake Central HS, Dyer, Ind.
37. **Jesse Bahr, lhp, Missouri Baptist College**
38. Clay Young, lhp, Glendale (Calif.) JC
39. Miguel Ruiz, rhp, South Hills HS, Fort Worth, Texas
40. Michael Roskopf, 1b, CC of Southern Nevada
41. Chris Valencia, of, Westchester HS, Los Angeles
42. Josh Styes, rhp, Clay-Chalkville HS, Birmingham
43. Brady Salter, rhp, Aurora (Ill.) U.
44. Justin Keadle, rhp, Wake Forest U.
45. Brett Pill, 1b, Cal State Fullerton
46. **Eric Wordekemper, rhp, Creighton U.**
47. Eric Hanlon, of, James Martin HS, Arlington, Texas
48. Andrew Rice, of, Itawamba (Miss.) CC
49. Diallo Fon, of, Las Lomas High, Walnut Creek, Calif.
50. Blake Heym, c, Grayson County (Texas) CC

OAKLAND ATHLETICS 21

1. **Cliff Pennington, ss, Texas A&M U.**
1. **Travis Buck, of, Arizona State U.** (Supplemental choice—36th—for loss of Type A free agent Damian Miller)
2. **Craig Italiano, rhp, Flower Mound (Texas) HS** (Choice from Brewers as compensation for Miller)
2. **Jared Lansford, rhp, St. Francis HS, Santa Clara, Calif.**
3. **Vincent Mazzaro, rhp, Rutherford (N.J.) HS**
4. **Jimmy Shull, rhp, Cal Poly**
5. **Scott Deal, rhp, Curtis HS, University Place, Wash.**
6. **Justin Sellers, ss, Marina HS, Huntington Beach, Calif.**
7. **Kevin Bunch, rhp, Serrano HS, Victorville, Calif.**
8. **Jason Ray, rhp, Azusa Pacific (Calif.) U.**
9. **Trey Shields, rhp, U. of Alabama**
10. **John Herrera, rhp, Lubbock Christian U.**
11. **Steve Kleen, rhp, Pepperdine U.**
12. **Jeff Baisley, 3b, U. of South Florida**
13. **Mike Massaro, of-lhp, Colorado State U.-Pueblo**
14. **Brad Davis, lhp, Lewis-Clark State (Idaho) College**
15. **Jeff Bieker, of, Fort Hays State (Kan.) U.**
16. Justin Smoak, 1b, Stratford HS, Goose Creek, S.C.
17. **Isaac Omura, 2b, U. of Hawaii**
18. **Anthony Recker, c, Alvernia (Pa.) College**
19. **Julio Rivera, c, Puerto Rico Baseball Academy, Toa Alta, P.R.**
20. **Stephen Bryant, rhp, U. of Hawaii**
21. **Michael Madsen, rhp, Ohio State U.**
22. **Shawn Callahan, c, Central Missouri State U.**
23. James Bennett, of, U. of Louisiana-Monroe
24. **Ben Ingold, ss, Wake Forest U.**
25. **Zeke Parraz, ss, U. of Nevada-Las Vegas**
26. **Ron Madej, lhp, Bellevue (Neb.) U.**
27. **Jess Lacasse, rhp, Bellevue (Neb.) U.**
28. **Mike Klug, 2b, U. of North Alabama**
29. **Brad Kilby, lhp, San Jose State U.**
30. **T.J. Franco, rhp, U. of San Francisco**
31. **Josh Kay, rhp, U. of Cincinnati**
32. Jake Hammons, c, Snohomish (Wash.) HS
33. Matt Singleton, c, Ball State U.
34. Edwin Mieles, rhp, Patria La Torres Ramirez HS, San Sebastian, P.R.
35. Steven Braun, ss, Los Angeles Pierce JC
36. Shane Keough, ss, Northwood HS, San Jose, Calif.
37. A.J. Huttenlocker, lhp, Edmonds (Wash.) CC
38. Nick Pulos, c, U. of Pennsylvania

PHILADELPHIA PHILLIES 17

1. (Choice to Yankees as compensation for Type B free agent Jon Lieber)
2. **Mike Costanzo, 3b, Coastal Carolina U.**
3. **Matt Maloney, lhp, U. of Mississippi**
4. **Mike Durant, 3b, Berkeley (Calif.) HS**
5. **Brett Harker, rhp, College of Charleston**
6. **Justin Blaine, lhp, U. of San Diego**
7. **Jermaine Williams, of, Los Angeles HS**
8. **Jeremy Slayden, of, Georgia Tech**
9. **Clay Harris, 2b, Louisiana State U.**
10. **Josh Outman, lhp, Central Missouri State U.**
11. **Tuffy Gosewisch, c, Arizona State U.**
12. **Michael Zagurski, lhp, U. of Kansas**
13. **Matt Olson, rhp, Western Branch HS, Chesapeake, Va.**
14. Aja Barto, of, Stratford HS, Spring Branch, Texas
15. **P.J. Antoniato, ss, St. Johns U.**
16. **Matt Edwards, 1b, U. of Notre Dame**
17. **Ronald Hill, rhp, UNC Wilmington**
18. **Darren Byrd, rhp, Pine Forest HS, Cantonment Fla.**
19. David Huff, lhp, Cypress (Calif.) JC
20. Vance Worley, rhp, McClatchy HS, Sacramento
21. **Aaron Rawl, rhp, U. of South Carolina**
22. **Pat Overholt, rhp, Santa Clara U.**
23. **Derrick Mitchell, ss, Paw Paw (Mich.) HS**
24. **Dennis Diaz, 2b, Florida International U.**
25. **Joseph Frazee, of, Loyola Marymount U.**
26. **Brett Dalton, 2b, UC Irvine**
27. **Steven Alexander, of, Sacramento CC**
28. **Clayton Stewart, rhp, U. of Texas**
29. **Aaron Cheesman, c, Florida State U.**
30. Charles Benoit, lhp, Grayson County (Texas) CC
31. **Cooper Osteen, 2b, U. of Mississippi**
32. Tim Sherlock, of, Chaparral HS, Scottsdale, Ariz.
33. Andrez Ibarz, rhp, Champagnat Catholic HS, Hialeah, Fla.
34. Osvaldo Torres, 1b, Wabash Valley (Ill.) JC
35. Adam Greer, c, North Eugene (Ore.) HS
36. Nick Monett, c, Granite Hills HS, El Cajon, Calif.
37. Kyle Bredenkamp, rhp, Millikan HS, Long Beach, Calif.
38. Micah Sales, rhp, Madison County HS, Danielsville, Ga.
39. Bobby Kennedy, lhp, Trinity Catholic HS, Ocala, Fla.
40. Travis Jones, 2b, Lake City (Fla.) CC
41. Ryan Selden, ss, Canyon Springs HS, Moreno Valley, Calif.
42. John Dischert, lhp, St. Marks HS, Wilmington, Del.
43. Ryan Verdugo, lhp, Lake Stevens (Wash.) HS
44. Luis Alvarez, of, Pedro Falu Oreliano HS, Rio Grande, P.R.
45. Mike Modica, lhp, Washington Township HS, Sewell, N.J.
46. Jason Stacy, rhp, Westview HS, Phoenix
47. **Ben Blanton, ss, William Jewel (Mo.) College**
48. Ben Hornbeck, lhp, Sunnyslope HS, Phoenix
49. Shane Erb, rhp, Father Judge High, Lewes, Del.
50. **Tyler Gooch, rhp, U. of Oklahoma**

DRAFT

PITTSBURGH PIRATES 11

1. **Andrew McCutchen, of, Fort Meade (Fla.) HS**
2. **Brad Corley, of, Mississippi State U.**
3. **James Boone, of, U. of Missouri**
4. **Brent Lillibridge, ss, U. of Washington**
5. **Jeff Sues, rhp, Vanderbilt U.**
6. **Cameron Blair, 2b, Texas Tech**
7. **Justin Vaclavik, rhp, U. of Houston**
8. **Steve Pearce, 1b, U. of South Carolina**
9. **Derrik Moeves, rhp, Northern Kentucky U.**
10. **Derek Antelo, rhp, Nova Southeastern (Fla.) U.**
11. **Chris Jones, c, Long Beach State U.**
12. **Jason Delaney, of, Boston College**
13. **Matt Swanson, rhp, U. of California**
14. **Albert Laboy, of, John I. Leonard HS, West Palm Beach, Fla.**
15. Jarred Bogany, of, George Bush HS, Houston
16. **Eric Krebs, rhp, Alvin (Texas) JC**
17. **Darren Newlin, rhp, U. of Central Florida**
18. **Ryan Searage, of, Eckerd (Fla.) College**
19. **Daniel Rios, 1b, JC of the Sequoias (Calif.)**
20. Ryan Lollis, of-lhp, Houston Christian HS
21. Elias Otero, ss, Puerto Rico Baseball Academy, Toa Alta, P.R.
22. David DiNatale, of, Stoneman Douglas HS, Parkland, Fla.
23. **Juan Mesa, of, Miami**
24. **Jared Brown, lhp, Cumberland (Tenn.) U.**
25. Michael Wanamaker, rhp, Nyack HS, Valley Cottage, N.Y.
26. **Tony Mansolino, 3b, Vanderbilt U.**
27. **Nash Robertson, rhp, UC Irvine**
28. Clayton McMillan, lhp, Carthage (Texas) HS
29. Iain Sebastian, rhp, Columbus (Ga.) HS
30. Chad Povich, rhp, Dixie State (Utah) JC
31. **Jason Herman, rhp, U. of West Alabama**
32. **Duke Acors, rhp, Virginia Military Institute**
33. Michael Klindt, of, Centennial HS, Roswell, Ga.
34. Gary Bucuren, 3b, Ambridge Area HS, Sewickley, Pa.
35. Lyndon Estill, of, Sammamish HS, Bellevue, Wash.
36. Justin Byler, c, Gulf Coast (Fla.) CC
37. Eric Marshall, rhp, Barrington (Ill.) HS
38. Carl Uhl, of, Serrano HS, Phelan, Calif.
39. Jason Brock, lhp, David Lipscomb HS, Nolansville, Tenn.
40. Kenneth Wieda, rhp, John Hersey HS, Arlington Heights, Ill.
41. Nick Beghtol, c, Dixie State (Utah) JC
42. Kyle Sweat, rhp, Apopka (Fla.) HS
43. Scott Kuhns, rhp, John Hersey HS, Arlington Heights, Ill.
44. Jordan Latham, rhp, Centennial HS, Boise, Idaho
45. Philip Riley, rhp, Jackson State (Tenn.) CC
46. Kody Hinze, 1b, Nimitz HS, Houston
47. Ryan Lormand, ss, McLennan (Texas) CC
48. Paul Dickey, rhp, Lake Washington HS, Redmond, Wash.
49. Francisco Ortiz, rhp, Puerto Rico Baseball Academy, Toa Alta, P.R.
50. Stephen Merino, 3b, American Senior HS, Miami

ST. LOUIS CARDINALS 30

1. **Colby Rasmus, of, Russell County HS, Phenix City, Ala.** (Choice from Red Sox as compensation for loss of Type A free agent Edgar Renteria)
1. **Tyler Greene, ss, Georgia Tech**
1. **Mark McCormick, rhp, Baylor U.** (Supplemental choice—43rd—for loss of Renteria)
1. **Tyler Herron, rhp, Wellington (Fla.) Community HS** (Supplemental choice—46th—for loss of Type A free agent Mike Matheny)
2. **Josh Wilson, rhp, Whitehouse HS, Tyler, Texas** (Choice from Giants as compensation for Matheny)
2. **Nick Webber, rhp, Central Missouri State U.**
3. **Daryl Jones, of, Spring (Texas) HS**
4. **Bryan Anderson, c, Simi Valley (Calif.) HS**
5. **Mitch Boggs, rhp, U. of Georgia**
6. **Wilfrido Pujols, of, Fort Osage HS, Independence, Mo.**
7. **Nick Stavinoha, of, Louisiana State U.**
8. **Jason Cairns, rhp, Central Michigan U.**
9. **Zach Zuercher, lhp, U. of Rhode Island**
10. **Randy Roth, c, Southeastern Lousiana U.**
11. **Steve Gonzalez, c, Programa Alcase HS, San Juan, P.R.**
12. Daniel McCutchen, rhp, U. of Oklahoma
13. **Malcolm Owens, of, San Bernardino Valley (Calif.) JC**
14. **Michael Repole, rhp, Birmingham-Southern College**
15. **Adam Daniels, lhp, Oklahoma State U.**
16. **Matt Lane, rhp, U. of Louisiana-Monroe**
17. **Michael Cooper, rhp, Fresno State U.**
18. **Brandon Garner, ss, Yale HS, Melvin, Mich.**
19. Miers Quigley, lhp, Roswell (Ga.) HS
20. **Shaun Garceau, rhp, Royal Palm Beach (Fla.) HS**
21. **Ryan Rohlinger, ss, U. of Oklahoma**
22. **Jaime Garcia, lhp, Mission, Texas**
23. **A.J. Van Slyke, 1b, U. of Kansas**
24. **David Phillips, rhp, El Paso (Texas) CC**
25. **Adam Rodgers, 1b, Rice U.**
26. Steven Blackwood, of, Georgia Tech
27. **Chuck Carter, of, Texas A&M-Corpus Christi**
28. **Trey Hearne, rhp, Texas A&M-Corpus Christi**
29. **Reid Price, lhp, College of Charleston**
30. **Matt Trent, rhp, Wingate (N.C.) College**
31. **Christian Lopez, ss, Juana Colon HS, Comerio, P.R.**
32. **Casey Rowlett, of, U. of Arkansas**
33. **Scott Vander Weg, rhp, Lamar U.**
34. **Kyle Sadlowski, rhp, Kutztown U.**
35. **Cory Meacham, rhp, Alabama Southern CC**
36. Armando Carrasco, rhp, Saddleback (Calif.) CC
37. **Kenny Maiques, rhp, Rio Hondo (Calif.) CC**
38. Steve Junker, lhp, Valley Forge HS, Parma Heights, Ohio
39. **Tyler Leach, rhp, Kings Mountain (N.C.) HS**
40. Jesse Schoendienst, 2b, Old Dominion U.
41. David Fonseca, ss, Thousand Oaks (Calif.) HS
42. **Josh Schwartz, lhp, Rowan (N.J.) U.**
43. **Michael Meagher, lhp, U. of Maryland**
44. Blake King, rhp, Bishop Kelley HS, Tulsa, Okla.
45. **Kevin Fitzgerald, rhp, U. of Stony Brook**
46. Danny Feldman, rhp, Gloucester Catholic HS, West Deptford, N.J.
47. **Adam Morris, 3b, Rice U.**

SAN DIEGO PADRES 18

1. **Cesar Carrillo, rhp, U. of Miami**
1. **Cesar Ramos, lhp, Long Beach State U.** (Supplemental choice—35th—for loss of Type A free agent David Wells)
2. **Chase Headley, 3b, U. of Tennessee**
2. **Nick Hundley, c, U. of Arizona** (Choice from Red Sox as compensation for Wells)
3. **Josh Geer, rhp, Rice U.**
4. **Mike Baxter, of, Vanderbilt U.**
5. **Seth Johnston, ss, U. of Texas**
6. **Neil Jamison, rhp, Long Beach State U.**
7. **Will Venable, of, Princeton U.**
8. **John Madden, rhp, Auburn U.**
9. **Casey Smith, 1b, Erskine (S.C.) College**
10. **Josh Alley, of, U. of Tennessee**
11. Josh Tomlin, rhp, Angelina (Texas) JC
12. Aaron Breit, rhp, Garden City (Kan.) CC
13. **Arnold Hughey, lhp, Auburn U.**
14. **Billy Richardson, ss, East Carolina U.**
15. Josh Romanski, lhp, Norco HS, Corona, Calif.
16. **Brent Carter, lhp, U. of Alabama**
17. **Chad Decker, lhp, UC Riverside**
18. **Mike Sansoe, of, St. Mary's (Calif.) College**
19. Gabriel Fargas, rhp, Puerto Rico Baseball Academy, Caguas, P.R.
20. **Chad Steiner, 3b, Lamar (Colo.) CC**
21. **Brian Cavanaugh, of, East Carolina U.**
22. **Drew Davidson, of, U. of Illinois**
23. Josh Conover, rhp, U. of Washington
24. **John Slone, c, Miami (Ohio) U.**
25. **Grant Varnell, rhp, U. of Texas-Arlington**
26. **Jon Link, rhp, Bluefield (Va.) College**
27. **Ray Gill, 1b, Brevard (N.C.) College**
28. **Brandon Higelin, lhp, Cal State Los Angeles**
29. Rey Garramone, rhp, Denver North HS, Denver
30. Todd Conerly, rhp, Angelina (Texas) JC
31. Tae Kwon, rhp, Hoover HS, Glendale, Calif.
32. Tyson Ford, rhp, Timpanogos HS, Orem, Utah
33. **Adam Gold, rhp, U. of California**
34. **Geoff Vandel, lhp, Shaw HS, Columbus, Ga.**
35. Andrew Morgan, c, Norcross HS, Atlanta
36. Gary Moran, rhp, Fresno CC
37. Andrew Miller, rhp, Seminole State (Okla.) JC
38. Jeremy McBryde, rhp, Midwest City (Okla.) HS
39. Patrick Norris, of, Butler County (Kan.) CC
40. Donnie Snow, lhp, Grossmont (Calif.) HS
41. Bret Bochsler, lhp, Inglemoor HS, Redmond, Wash.
42. Terrence Dayleg, ss, North Surrey SS, Surrey, B.C.
43. Justin Worby, c, Georgetown District HS, Acton, Ontario
44. Troy Dawe, rhp, Cardinal Newman Catholic SS, Toronto
45. Daniel Towe, c, Charlotte (Mich.) HS
46. Jeremy Shelby, of, Tates Creek HS, Lexington, Ky.
47. Mark Letchworth, of, Louisburg (N.C.) JC
48. Carson Bryant, rhp, JC of Southern Idaho
49. **Josh Thomas-Dotson, of, U. of Oregon**
50. Jason Ogata, ss, Westview HS, Portland, Ore.

SAN FRANCISCO GIANTS 22

1. (Choice to Marlins as compensation for Type A free agent Armando Benitez)
2. (Choice to Cardinals as compensation for Type A free agent Mike Matheny)
3. (Choice to Indians as compensation for Type A free agent Omar Vizquel)
4. **Ben Copeland, of, U. of Pittsburgh**
5. **Daniel Griffin, rhp, Niagara U.**
6. Brad Cuthbertson, rhp, Lethbridge (Alberta) CC
7. **Joey Dyche, of, Lewis-Clark State (Idaho) College**
8. Scotty Bridges, 2b, U. of Arkansas
9. **Anthony Contreras, ss, San Jose State U.**
10. **Nick Pereira, rhp, U. of San Francisco**
11. **Henry Gutierrez, c, Troy U.**
12. **Joe Martinez, rhp, Boston College**
13. **Taylor Wilding, rhp, Cal Poly Pomona**
14. **Brian Anderson, rhp, Long Beach State U.**
15. **Alex Hinshaw, lhp, San Diego State U.**
16. **Buck Cody, lhp, U. of Texas**
17. **Mark Minicozzi, 3b, East Carolina U.**
18. Chad Wagler, rhp, Kent State U.
19. Brandon Grabham, rhp, Grayson County (Texas) JC
20. Jonathan Gaston, of, Borah HS, Boise, Idaho
21. **Robert Grace, rhp, JC of the Desert (Calif.)**
22. **Taylor Creswell, of, Deer Valley HS, Antioch, Calif.**
23. **David Maroul, 3b, U. of Texas**
24. James Simmons, of, Vernon Regional (Texas) JC
25. **Barry Gunther, c, U. of Mississippi**
26. **Ivan Rusova, rhp, Oasis Alternative HS, Toronto**
27. Johnny Monell, c, Christopher Columbus HS, Bronx, N.Y.
28. **Sergio Romo, rhp, Mesa State (Colo.) College**
29. Angel Nicolas, ss, Killian HS, Miami
30. Erik Meyer, rhp, Eastern Washington U.
31. **Wayne Foltin, rhp, U. of Nevada-Las Vegas**
32. Damon Brewer, lhp, Lake City (Fla.) CC
33. **Chris Todd, 2b, Coastal Carolina U.**
34. Matt Long, rhp, Miami (Ohio) U.
35. **Antoan Richardson, of, Vanderbilt U.**
36. Thomas Neal, of, Poway (Calif.) HS
37. David Newton, rhp, West Valley (Calif.) CC
38. **Ben Nieto, lhp, Riverside (Calif.) CC**
39. Melvin Blackmon, lhp, Temecula Valley (Calif.) HS
40. Kurt Lipton, of, Pine Crest HS, Boca Raton, Fla.
41. Bo Merrell, ss, Perryton (Texas) HS
42. Tony Snow, rhp, Edmonds (Wash.) CC
43. **Chris Stanton, 1b, Virginia Tech**
44. Reggie Fuller, lhp, Diablo Valley (Calif.) JC
45. Eric Dworkis, rhp, U. of California
46. Jared Cranston, lhp, Seward County (Kan.) CC
47. George Snyder, rhp, Chaffey (Calif.) JC
48. Adam Ortiz-Jusino, rhp, Brookdale (N.J.) CC
49. Curtis Partch, rhp, Merced (Calif.) HS
50. Justin Robertson, rhp, Nipomo (Calif.) HS

SEATTLE MARINERS 3

1. **Jeff Clement, c, U. of Southern California**
2. (Choice to Dodgers as compensation for Type A free agent Adrian Beltre)
3. (Choice to Diamondbacks as compensation for Type A free agent Richie Sexson)
4. **Justin Thomas, lhp, Youngstown State U.**
5. **Stephen Kahn, rhp, Loyola Marymount U.**
6. Lance Lynn, rhp, Brownsburg (Ind.) HS
7. **Robert Rohrbaugh, lhp, Clemson U.**
8. **David Asher, lhp, Florida International U.**
9. **Bryan Sabatella, 3b, Quinnipiac U.**
10. **Ronnie Prettyman, 3b, Cal State Fullerton**
11. Brian Contreras, of, Puerto Rico Baseball Academy, Caguas, P.R.
12. **Anthony Varvaro, rhp, St. John's U.**
13. **Reed Eastley, ss, Niagara U.**
14. Brad Boyer, 2b, U. of Arizona
15. John Holdzkom, rhp, Rancho Cucamonga (Calif.) HS
16. Grant Gerrard, of, Southern Illinois U.
17. James Russell, lhp, Navarro (Texas) JC
18. **Curtis Ledbetter, 1b, U. of Nebraska**
19. **Brett Bannister, rhp, U. of Southern California**
20. Travis Scott, c, Lincoln Land (Ill.) CC
21. **Nick Allen, rhp, Villanova U.**
22. **Alex Gary, of, Virginia Commonwealth U.**
23. Ryan Lindgren, rhp, Stillwater Area (Minn.) HS
24. **Kevin Gergel, c, Kennesaw State (Ga.) U.**
25. Will Brown, lhp, Downey HS, Modesto, Calif.
26. **Ari Kafka, rhp, Quinnipiac U.**
27. Jeremy Hill, rhp, Ohlone (Calif.) JC
28. **Lance Beus, lhp, Brigham Young U.**
29. Eric Thomas, of, Buchholz HS, Gainesville, Fla.
30. **Aric Van Gaalen, lhp, Lethbridge (Alberta) JC**
31. **Jeff Gilmore, rhp, Stanford U.**
32. **Corby Heckman, 2b, Indiana U.**
33. **Julian Henson, c, Cordova (Tenn.) HS**
34. Andrew Schneider, rhp, Franklin (Texas) HS
35. Blake Amador, of, Modesto (Calif.) JC
36. Max Kwan, c, Seattle Prep, Bellevue, Wash.
37. Jesse Costa, rhp, Magnolia HS, Anaheim, Calif.
38. Joe Agreste, 1b, Greenbrier Christian Academy, Chesapeake, Va.
39. Duke Welker, rhp, Seminole State (Okla.) JC
40. Eugene Edwards, of, Long Beach (Calif.) CC
41. Joe White, 1b, Georgia Perimeter JC
42. Kevin Reynolds, of, Quincy U.
43. Philip Roy, rhp, Southridge HS, Miami
44. Paul David Patterson, rhp, Northern Kentucky U.
45. Luis Coste, of, Cochise County (Ariz.) CC
46. **Worth Lumry, lhp, Princeton U.**
47. **Andy Hargrove, 1b, Kent State U.**
48. Matthew Gardner, rhp, Grayson County (Texas) CC
49. Dennis Raben, 1b, St. Thomas Aquinas HS, Fort Lauderdale
50. Xavier Scruggs, 1b, Poway (Calif.) HS

TAMPA BAY DEVIL RAYS 8

1. **Wade Townsend, rhp, Dripping Springs, Texas**
2. **Chris Mason, rhp, UNC Greensboro**
3. Bryan Morris, rhp, Tullahoma (Tenn.) HS
4. **Jeremy Hellickson, rhp, Hoover HS, Des Moines, Iowa**
5. **Mike McCormick, 3b, Marist HS, Eugene, Ore.**
6. **Greg Reinhard, rhp, U. of Wisconsin-Whitewater**
7. **Mike Wlodarczyk, lhp, Boston College**
8. **Andrew Lopez, of, Elk Grove (Calif.) HS**
9. **Derek Feldkamp, rhp, U. of Michigan**
10. **John Matulia, of, Eustis (Fla.) HS**
11. **Jeff Kamrath, rhp, U. of Virginia**
12. **Ryan Zimmerman, rhp, Salt Lake CC**
13. **Ryan Morse, lhp, Southwest Minnesota State U.**
14. **Henry Wrigley, 1b, JC of San Mateo (Calif.)**
15. **Matt Fisher, rhp, Franklin Pierce (N.H.) College**
16. **Neil Walton, ss, Cal State Fullerton**
17. **Jared Edwards, c, Archbishop Rummel HS, New Orleans**
18. Tommy Hunter, rhp, Cathedral HS, Indianapolis
19. Ike Davis, 1b/lhp, Chaparral HS, Scottsdale, Ariz.
20. Wade Miley, lhp, Loranger (La.) HS
21. Jared Bradford, rhp, Shelton State (Ala.) CC
22. Adam Hall, rhp, Pacific HS, Gray Summit, Mo.
23. Danny Dorn, of, Cal State Fullerton
24. **Neal Frontz, rhp, Jacksonville U.**
25. Clay Mortensen, rhp, Treasure Valley (Ore.) CC
26. Jeff Urlaub, lhp, Horizon HS, Scottsdale, Ariz.
27. Rylan Ostrosky, rhp, Salisbury Composite HS, Edmonton, Alberta
28. **Matt Falk, rhp, U. of San Diego**
29. **Chad Pendarvis, lhp, Southeastern Louisiana U.**
30. **Chris Fessler, rhp, Yavapai (Ariz.) JC**
31. Jordan Brown, ss, Hahnville HS, Luling, La.
32. **Ryan Bethel, ss, Grand Canyon U.**
33. Tyler Reves, c, Wharton County (Texas) JC
34. **Matt Devins, ss, U. of Stony Brook**
35. Damien Mazzetti, 1b, North Mecklenburg HS, Huntersville, N.C.
36. John Maschino, rhp, Edmond North HS, Edmond, Okla.
37. **Carnell Parker, of, U. of Mobile**
38. **Ben Rulon, lhp, Georgia State U.**
39. Michael McClaren, rhp, Durango HS, Las Vegas
40. Matt Gaudet, 1b, Archbishop Rummel HS, Metairie, La.
41. **Garrett Groce, of, Columbus State (Ga.) U.**
42. Taylor Cobb, rhp, U. of Central Florida
43. Josh Stewart, c, Bowling Green State U.
44. Rashad Taylor, of, Riordan HS, San Francisco
45. Leon Johnson, of, Thatcher, Ariz.
46. William Oliver, rhp, San Pasqual HS, Escondido, Calif.
47. Eli Diaz, rhp, Baton Rouge (La.) CC
48. **Brad Matthews, 2b, Wallace State (Ala.) CC**
49. Casey Coleman, rhp, Mariner HS, Cape Coral, Fla.
50. Matt Duryea, lhp, Edmonds (Wash.) CC

TEXAS RANGERS 19

1. **John Mayberry, of, Stanford U.**
2. **Johnny Whittleman, 3b, Kingwood (Texas) HS**
3. **Taylor Teagarden, c, U. of Texas**
4. **Shane Funk, rhp, Arnold HS, Panama City Beach, Fla.**
5. **Michael Kirkman, lhp, Columbia HS, Lake City, Fla.**

6. **German Duran, 2b, Weatherford (Texas) JC**
7. **Jacob Rasner, rhp, Earl Wooster HS, Reno, Nev.**
8. Brad Barragar, rhp, Golden West (Calif.) JC
9. **R.J. Anderson, of, Armwood HS, Seffner, Fla.**
10. **Matt Nevarez, rhp, San Fernando (Calif.) HS**
11. **Nate Fogle, rhp, Oregon State U.**
12. Dexter Carter, rhp, Greenbrier Christian Academy, Chesapeake, Va.
13. **Doug Mathis, rhp, U. of Missouri**
14. **Steve Murphy, of, Kansas State U.**
15. **Kea Kometani, rhp, Pepperdine U.**
16. **Jesse Hall, lhp, Yavapai (Ariz.) JC**
17. Chris Dominguez, 3b, Gulliver Prep, Miami
18. Chase Fontaine, ss, Daytona Beach (Fla.) CC
19. **Brian Valichka, c, U. of Delaware**
20. **Joey Hooft, 2b, Arizona State U.**
21. **Brandon James, rhp, Carlisle (Pa.) HS**
22. Jarrod Dumont, lhp, Riverside (Calif.) CC
23. Steve Marquardt, 3b, Columbia Basin (Wash.) CC
24. Zach Borba, of, Columbia Basin (Wash.) CC
25. Brian Spielmann, rhp, Bradley U. (VOIDED)
26. **Ben Crabtree, c, Ohio U.**
27. **Jon Wilson, rhp, Winthrop U.**
28. Sergio Morales, of, Hollywood Hills HS, Hollywood, Fla.
29. **Matt Hawke, 1b, U. of Lousiana-Lafayette**
30. **Truan Mehl, of, U. of Maryland**
31. **Austin Faught, lhp, U. of Louisiana-Lafayette**
32. **Renny Osuna, ss, New Mexico JC**
33. Kevin Gossage, c, Coronado HS, Colorado Springs, Colo.
34. Shooter Hunt, rhp, Ramapo HS, Wyckoff, N.J.
35. Chris Hicks, rhp, Milton HS, Alpharetta, Ga.
36. Steven Farris, rhp, Langham Creek HS, Houston
37. Tim Rodriguez, of, Centennial HS, Gresham, Ore.
38. Jeffrey Murphy, rhp, Yavapai (Ariz.) JC
39. David Makim, rhp, Monte Vista HS, Spring Valley, Calif.
40. **Thomas Van Buskirk, rhp, Santa Clara U.**
41. **Warren Rosebrock, rhp, Cal State Sacramento**
42. Travis Hill, rhp, Seminole State (Okla.) JC
43. Shawn Keil, of, Seminole (Fla.) HS
44. **Roberto Valiente, of, U. of Tampa**
45. Frank Lonigro, c, Fullerton (Calif.) JC
46. Thomas Berkery, c, Mississippi State U.
47. Marc Nobriga, rhp, Hartnell (Calif.) JC
48. **Broc Coffman, lhp, Lower Columbia (Wash.) JC**
49. Glenn Swanson, lhp, UC Irvine
50. **Joe Napoli, of, Bradley U.**

TORONTO BLUE JAYS 6

1. **Ricky Romero, lhp, Cal State Fullerton**
2. (Choice to Twins as compensation for Type A free agent Corey Koskie)
3. **Brian Pettway, of, U. of Mississippi**
4. **Ryan Patterson, of, Louisiana State U.**
5. **Eric Fowler, lhp, U. of Mississippi**
6. **Josh Bell, c, Auburn U.**
7. **Robert Ray, rhp, Texas A&M U.**
8. **Jacob Butler, of, U. of Nevada**
9. **Paul Phillips, rhp, Oakland U.**
10. **Josh Sowers, rhp, Yale U.**
11. **Wesley Stone, ss, A.B. Miller HS, Rialto, Calif.**
12. **Billy Carnline, rhp, Texas Tech**
13. **Anthony Hatch, 3b, Nicholls State U.**
14. **Sean Stidfole, rhp, Penn State U.**
15. **Sean Shoffit, 2b, Cosumnes River (Calif.) JC**
16. **Kyle Bohm, c, U. of Michigan**
17. Tyler Norrick, lhp, Southern Illinois U.
18. Rob Hogue, lhp, St. Joseph HS, Edmonton, Alberta
19. **Reidier Gonzalez, rhp, St. Petersburg (Fla.) JC**
20. **Zach Kalter, of, U. of Southern California**
21. **Chris Martinez, c, St. Thomas (Fla.) U.**
22. **Dennis Bigley, rhp, Oral Roberts U.**
23. Manuel Garcia, rhp, Puerto Rico Baseball Academy, Toa Baja, P.R.
24. **Alex McRobbie, rhp, UC Santa Barbara**
25. Philip Carey, ss, A.B. Lucas HS, London, Ontario
26. **Marshall Bernhard, ss, U. of Central Florida**
27. Bobby Nicoll, rhp, U. of Connecticut-Avery Point
28. **Scott Byrnes, rhp, Purdue U.**
29. John Roberts, of, Pryor (Okla.) HS
30. **Trent Luyster, lhp, Ohio State U.**
31. Jason Riley, c, North HS, Riverside, Calif.
32. **Matt Cooksey, of, George Mason U.**
33. Jeff Tobin, lhp, U. of British Columbia
34. Mace Thurman, lhp, Westlake HS, Austin
35. Derek Tarapacki, rhp, Yavapai (Ariz.) JC
36. **Hector Delgadillo, rhp, U. of the Incarnate Word**
37. **Chris Looze, 1b, George Mason U.**
38. Adam Demichaele, rhp, Okaloosa-Walton (Fla.) CC
39. **Josh Celigoy, 1b, Lewis-Clark State (Idaho) College**
40. **Alberto Quintana, c, Cal State Northridge**
41. Eric Oxio, of, Puerto Rico Baseball Academy, Ponce, P.R.
42. Brett Wallace, 1b, Justin-Siena HS, Sonoma, Calif.
43. **Connor Falkenbach, rhp, U. of Florida**
44. Eric Larson, of, Brown U.
45. Michael Barbara, rhp, St. Petersburg (Fla.) JC
46. Corey Weglin, rhp, Sacramento CC
47. Kyle Thornton, rhp, Odessa (Texas) JC
48. Kevin Denis-Fortier, 1b, Edouard Montpetit HS, Quebec City, Quebec
49. Nick Nordgren, of, Jefferson HS, Cedar Rapids, Iowa
50. Brian Mooney, lhp, Walt Whitman HS, Huntington Station, N.Y.

WASHINGTON NATIONALS 4

1. **Ryan Zimmerman, 3b, U. of Virginia**
2. (Choice to Rockies as compensation for Type A free agent Vinny Castilla)
3. (Choice to Twins as compensation for Type B free agent Cristian Guzman)
4. **Justin Maxwell, of, U. of Maryland**
5. **Ryan Delaughter, of, Ryan HS, Denton, Texas**
6. **Marco Estrada, rhp, Long Beach State U.**
7. **Mike Daniel, of, U. of North Carolina**
8. **Jack Spradlin, lhp, U. of Southern California**
9. **John Michael Howell, of, U. of Central Florida**
10. **Dee Brown, of, U. of Central Florida**
11. **John Lannan, lhp, Siena College**
12. **Craig Stammen, rhp, U. of Dayton**
13. **Andre Enriquez, rhp, Le Moyne College**
14. **Deryck Johnson, of, Cypress Creek HS, Orlando, Fla.**
15. **Michael Wadkins, rhp, William E. Tolman HS, Pawtucket, R.I.**
16. **Josh Palm, rhp, Penn State U.**
17. **Eduardo Pichardo, rhp, Southridge HS, Miami**
18. **Tim Pahuta, 1b, Seton Hall U.**
19. **Bradley Clark, rhp, Sickles HS, Tampa**
20. **Ricky Shefka, rhp, Coastal Carolina U.**
21. **Coby Mavroulis, lhp, Texas A&M U.**
22. **Antonio Evangelista, rhp, Seminole State (Okla.) JC**
23. Brett Jensen, rhp, U. of Nebraska
24. **Jeff Taylor, rhp, Missouri Southern State College**
25. Jose Peley, ss, Edouard Montpetit HS, Montreal
26. Doug Thennis, 3b, American River (Calif.) JC
27. **Andy Lane, 2b, Grand Canyon U.**
28. Hunter Pace, of, Hamilton HS, Chandler, Ariz.
29. Pat Barnes, of, Southwest Mississippi JC
30. Brian Pruitt, 3b, Florida Christian HS, Miami
31. Clayton Conner, 3b, Pensacola (Fla.) Catholic HS
32. Daniel Schuh, of, Bishop Kenny HS, Jacksonville, Fla.
33. Ryan Buchter, lhp, Highland Regional HS, Blackwood, N.J.
34. Jordan Thibodeaux, lhp, San Jacinto (Texas) JC
35. Matt Averitt, rhp, New Mexico JC
36. Brett McMillan, 1b, UCLA
37. Brandon Hamilton, of, Woodlawn HS, Shreveport, La.
38. Marcus Jones, of, Landon School, Washington, D.C.
39. Jacob McCarter, rhp, Navarro (Texas) JC
40. Anthony Williams, of, Mission Bay HS, San Diego
41. Tyler Moore, 1b, Northwest Rankin HS, Brandon, Miss.
42. Paul Treadaway, rhp, Pearl River (Miss.) CC
43. Scott Barnes, lhp, Cathedral HS, Springfield, Mass.
44. Steven Hensley, rhp, Owen HS, Black Mountain, N.C.
45. Anthony Shawler, rhp, Oscar Smith HS, Chesapeake, Va.
46. Ibrahim Lopez, of, Lake City (Fla.) CC
47. Luis Feliz, of, New Brunswick (N.J.) HS
48. Will Cherry, of, George Jenkins HS, Lakeland, Fla.
49. Terrance Brown, rhp, Bullard HS, Fresno
50. Jake Leonhardt, rhp, Angelina (Texas) JC

APPENDIX

OBITUARIES

NOVEMBER 2004-OCTOBER 2005

Ted Abernathy, a righthander who spent 14 years in the major leagues, died Dec. 16 in Gastonia, N.C. He was 71. Abernathy reached the major leagues in 1955 with the Washington Senators. He bounced around the majors during his career, also playing for the Indians, Cubs, Braves, Reds, Cardinals and Royals. He led the National League with 31 saves in 1965 for the Cubs and again with 28 in 1967 for the Reds. He finished his career with a 63-69 3.46 record and 148 saves.

Doug Ault, a first baseman who spent four seasons in the majors, died Dec. 22 in Tarpon Springs, Fla. He was 54. Ault made his mark as one of the original Toronto Blue Jays after being selected in the expansion draft. Ault hit .245-11-64 in his Blue Jays debut. He saw sporadic action for the Blue Jays in 1978 and 1980, finishing his major league career with .236-17-86 numbers.

Bobby Avila, a second baseman who spent 11 seasons in the major leagues, died Oct. 26, 2004, in Veracruz, Mexico. He was 80. Avila's major league career began in 1949 with the Cleveland Indians and he played there until he was traded to the Orioles after the 1958 season. His best season came in 1954 when he became the first Hispanic player to win a batting title, leading the American League with a .341 average. After his playing career ended Avila became a prominent politician in Mexico and later became president of the Mexican League.

Floyd Baker, an infielder who spent 13 seasons in the major leagues, died Nov. 16 in Youngstown, Ohio. He was 88. Baker played for the Browns, White Sox, Senators, Red Sox and Phillies in a career that stretched from 1943-1955. For his career, Baker hit .251-1-196.

Monty Basgall, a second baseman who spent three seasons with the Pirates before a long career in scouting and coaching, died Sept. 23 in Sierra Vista, Ariz. He was 82. Basgall hit .215-4-41 in stints with the Pirates from 1948-1951. He later worked as a manager before becoming a Dodgers scout in 1959. Basgall made it back to the majors as a coach, working with the Dodgers from 1973-1986.

Joe Bauman, the minor leagues' single-season home run record holder, died Sept. 20 in Roswell, N.M. He was 83. Bauman hit .400-72-224 for Roswell (Longhorn) in 1954, setting a professional record for home runs that was not topped until Barry Bonds hit 73 home runs in 2002. Bauman hit 337 home runs in his brief minor league career.

Mike Bishop, a catcher who had a brief stint in the majors, died Feb. 8 in Bakersfield, Calif. He was 46. Bishop played for the Mets in three games in 1983.

Don Blasingame, a second baseman who became the first American to manage in the Japanese Leagues, died April 13 in Fountain Hills, Ariz. Blasingame broke into the majors with the Cardinals in 1955. He spent the next four seasons as the team's everyday second baseman, hitting .271-8-58 in 1957 in what was his best year. He was sent to the Giants in 1960, and was dealt to the Reds during the 1961 season. Blasingame spent his final four seasons in the majors with the Washington Senators and Kansas City A's.

Cy Block, a second/third baseman who played three seasons with the Cubs, died Sept. 22 in Manhasset, N.Y. He was 85. Block reached the majors in 1942 and hit .364-0-4 in nine games with the Cubs.

Rex Bowen, a former scout and executive with the Dodgers, Pirates and Reds, died Jan. 6 in New Smyrna Beach, Fla. He was 93. Bowen signed such greats as Maury Wills, Dick Groat and Hall of Famer Bill Mazeroski. Bowen started with the Pirates as a scout in 1950 and became their scouting director in 1959. He was also a special assistant to the general manager for the Reds from 1968-90. Bowen's work seemed to precede titles wherever he went. He helped sign building blocks of the Dodgers championship teams of the 1950s, the Pirates 1960 champs and the Reds Big Red Machine of the 1970s.

Nelson Briles, a righthander who spent 14 seasons in the majors, died Feb. 13 in Orlando. He was 61. He was a key figure in the Cardinals' drive to the 1967 World Series title, when he went 14-5, 2.44 and led the league in winning percentage. In the World Series, Briles allowed two runs in a complete-game victory in Game Three, and he worked a scoreless inning of relief in Game Six. A year later, Briles was nearly as good, going 19-11, 2.80, though he struggled in two starts in a World Series defeat to the Tigers. Briles finished his career with a 129-112, 3.44 record. After his career was over, he worked as a radio broadcaster before becoming a member of the Pirates front office in 1986.

Ken Brondell, a righthander who reached the majors in 1944 with the New York Giants, died Oct. 3 in Van Nuys, Calif. He was 82. Brondell pitched 19 innings in seven games during his only year in the majors, going 0-1, 8.53.

Jim Bucher, a second/third baseman who spent seven seasons in the major leagues, died Oct. 21 in Elizabethtown, Pa. He was 93. Bucher had his best season as a Dodger in 1935, hitting .302-7-58.

Chico Carrasquel, the first Venezuelan to star in the major leagues, died May 26 in Caracas, Venez. He was 78. Carrasquel was the White Sox shortstop for most of the 1950s. He came to fame for his defensive ability, as he was one of the best fielding shortstops in the game during the 1950s, showing great range and a strong arm. He became the first Latino to be elected to an All-Star Game when he was named the American League's starting shortstop in 1951, in only his second year in the league.

Pete Center, a righthander who pitched in the majors for four seasons, died Aug. 8 in Campton, Ky. He was 92. Center reached the major leagues with the Indians in 1942, but pitched in only one game. In 1943, he went 1-2, 2.79 in 24 games. He missed the entire 1944 season due to military service. He returned to the Indians for the 1945-46 seasons going 6-3, 3.98 and 0-2, 4.97, respectively.

Tom Cheek, the voice of the Toronto Blue Jays for much of four decades, died Oct. 9. He was 66. Cheek broadcast every Blue Jays game from their first Opening Day in 1977 until June 2004, when his father's funeral and then surgery for brain cancer forced him to step back from the microphone.

Lee Cunningham, who had been one of the oldest living major leaguers, died July 30 in Pearland, Texas. He was 100. Cunningham had 26 at-bats with the Cardinals in 1931 and 1932 as a third baseman.

Harry Danning, a catcher who spent 10 years with the New York Giants, died Nov. 29 in Valparaiso, Ind. He was 93. Danning made his major league debut in 1933. In 1938, he hit .306-9-60, in 1939 he hit .313-16-74 and he hit .300-13-91 in 1940.

Brandy Davis, an outfielder who spent parts of two seasons with the Pirates and later went on to serve as a major league coach and scout, died June 12 in Newark, Del. He was 76. Although Davis spent parts of two years in the majors, it was his work as a scout that was his lasting legacy. Davis was one of the first and most notable national crosscheckers.

Dick Dietz, a major league catcher with the Giants, Dodgers and Braves, died June 28 in Clayton, Ga. He was 63. Dietz was a steady catcher during the late 1960s, earning an All-Star Game appearance in his career season in 1970, when he hit .300-22-107 for the Giants, finishing third in the league with a .426 on-base percentage.

Danny Doyle, a catcher who reached the major leagues with the Red Sox, died Dec. 14 in Stillwater, Okla. He was 87. Doyle hit .209 in 43 at-bats with the Red Sox in 1943 in his only major league appearance. He went on to a long career as a scout for the Red Sox.

Russ Derry, an outfielder who played four seasons in the major leagues, died Oct. 26 in Princeton, Mo. He was 88. Derry's most significant major league action came with the Yankees. He hit .254-4-14 in 38 games in 1944 as a rookie and followed it up with a .225-13-45 season as a platoon regular for the Yankees in 1945.

Mario Encarnacion, an outfielder who had brief stints with the Rockies and Cubs, died Oct. 3 in Danshuei, Taiwan. He was 30. Encarnacion was playing for the Macoto Cobras when he was found dead in the team's dormitory. Encarnacion hit .203-0-3 in 49 at-bats with the Rockies (2001) and Cubs (2002) before he headed overseas.

JOHN SPEAR

Mario Encarnacion

Tommy Fine, a righthander who played briefly for the Red Sox and St. Louis Browns, died Jan. 10 in Little Elm, Texas. He was 90.

Pete Gebrian, a righthander who spent a season with the White Sox, died May 6 in Stuart, Fla. He was 81. Gebrian was 2-3, 4.48 in 1947 in his only big league stint.

Al Gettel, a righthander who spent seven seasons in the majors, died April 8 in Norfolk, Va. He was 87. Gettel had his best success with the Indians, where he went 11-10, 3.20 in 1947. Gettel also played for the White Sox, Senators, Giants and Browns, finishing his career with a 38-45, 4.28 record.

Jesse Gonder, who caught eight years in the major leagues, died Nov. 14 in Oakland, Calif. He was 68. Gonder spent parts of the 1960 and 1961 seasons as a fill-in catcher for the Yankees, but it wasn't until 1963 that he found himself firmly entrenched in the majors, splitting the season between the Reds and Mets. He hit a combined .304-6-20.

Hal Griggs, a righthander who pitched for the Senators for four seasons, died May 10 in Tucson. He was 76. Playing for the woeful Senators from 1956-1959, he went 6-26, 5.50.

Marv Grissom, a righthander who spent more than a decade in the majors, died Sept. 19 in Red Bluff, Calif. He was 87. Grissom went 12-10, 3.74 as a starter for the White Sox in 1952. Two years later, he picked up the win in Game One of the World Series by pitching the final 2⅓ innings. That was the game made famous by Willie Mays' over-the-shoulder catch of Vic Wertz long fly ball. Grissom returned to the majors as a pitching coach, including a stint as the Angels first pitching coach.

Cesar Gutierrez, a shortstop who spent parts of four seasons in the majors, died Jan. 22 in Maracaibo, Venez. He was 61. Gutierrez hit .235-0-26 in 545 at-bats with the Giants and Tigers.

Pancho Herrera, a slugging first baseman who spent three seasons with the Phillies, died April 28 in Miami. He was 71. Herrera had a gaudy minor league career, but his strikeouts kept him from every getting established in the majors. He spent two seasons as the Phillies' first baseman, batting .281-17-71 in 1960 and .283-13-51 in 1961, though he struck out a league-leading 130 times in 1960.

Eli Hodkey, a lefthander who made two appearances in 1946 for the Phillies, died Aug. 30 in Lorain, Ohio. He was 87.

Cal Hogue, a righthander who had three short stints with the Pirates, died Aug. 5 in Kettering, Ohio. He was 77. Hogue went 2-10, 4.91 over three seasons.

Frank House, a catcher who played nine seasons in the majors, died March 13 in Birmingham, Ala. He was 75. House hit .248-47-235 with the Reds, Athletics and Tigers. His best season was with the Tigers in 1955, when he hit .259-15-53.

Tom Haller, a catcher who played 12 seasons in the major leagues, died Nov. 26 in Los Angeles. He was 67. Haller hit .257-134-504 in 12 seasons with the Giants, Dodgers and Tigers. He began his major league career with the Giants in 1961, earning regular work at catcher beginning in 1962. Over the next six seasons with the Giants, Haller reached double digits in home runs each season, earning all-star appearances in 1966 and 1967.

Wilmer Harris, a pitcher who spent eight seasons with the Philadelphia Stars of the Negro Leagues, died Dec. 23 in Philadelphia. He was 80.

Bennie Huffman, a catcher who hit .273-1-24 in 176 at-bats with the Cardinals in 1937, died Feb. 22 in Richmond.

Connie Johnson, a righthander who pitched five seasons in the majors, died Nov. 27 in Kansas City. He was 81. Johnson was a highly accomplished Negro Leaguer before making the majors. Johnson reached the major leagues with the White Sox in 1953 and went 4-4, 3.54. After a year in the minors he returned in 1955 and went 7-4, 3.45. He began 1956 with the White Sox but was traded to the Orioles during the season and went a combined 9-11, 3.44. He pitched two more years for the

Orioles, going 14-11, 3.20 in 1957 and 6-9, 3.89 in 1958.

Vic Johnson, a lefthander who spent parts of three seasons in the American League, died May 10 in Eau Claire, Wis. He was 84. Johnson made seven appearances with the Red Sox in 1944, going 0-3, 6.33 and returned to the Red Sox in 1945, going 6-4, 4.02.

Bob Kennedy, a big league outfielder/third baseman, manager and general manager, died April 7 in Mesa, Ariz. He was 84. Kennedy spent 16 seasons in the majors as a player, debuting with the White Sox in 1939, when he was only 19. He was the team's everyday third baseman a year later, and he held that job until he left to become a fighter pilot in the Marines in World War II. He retired with a career .254 average, 63 home runs and 514 RBIs. He quickly became established as a scout and minor league manager. He was the Cubs manager from 1963-1965 and he managed the Athletics in 1968. His career managerial record was 264-278. Kennedy later served as the Cubs general manager from 1976-1981. He also worked for the Astros and Giants. His son, Terry Kennedy, was a long-time major league catcher and minor league manager.

Bob Kennedy

Pat Kelly, an outfielder who spent 15 seasons in the majors, died Oct. 2 in Chambersburg, Pa. He was 61. Kelly, brother of pro football great Leroy Kelly, had a lengthy major league career as a speedy outfielder, mostly with the White Sox and Orioles. Kelly settled into the majors for good with the Royals in 1969 after being selected by Kansas City in the expansion draft. Kelly hit .264-8-32 with 40 steals that season, starting a stretch of 10 straight seasons where he had double-digit steals in the majors. Kelly was traded to the White Sox in 1971, setting the stage for his best major league work. Kelly was named an American League all-star in 1973, when he hit .280-1-44 with 22 steals, but his best season was probably 1972, when he hit .261-5-24 with 32 steals. Kelly was traded to the Orioles before the 1977 season. He spent four years with Earl Weaver's club, playing in the 1979 World Series, before finishing his career with the 1981 Indians.

Bill King, the longtime Oakland Athletics radio voice, died Oct. 18 in San Leandro, Calif. He was 78. At the time of his death, King was still working as a play-by-play announcer for the Athletics, although a fall during spring training had forced him to cut back to broadcasting only home games. King broadcast A's games for 25 years, and before that, he broadcast Giants games as well, joining the Giants' broadcast team in 1958. He was probably best known for his exclamation of "Holy Toledo" after exciting events. He also broadcast NBA and NFL games for decades.

Eddie Layton, the Yankees organist for 36 seasons, died Dec. 26 in Queens, N.Y. He was 79. Layton joined the Yankees in 1967 and played the organ at Yankees Stadium until he retired after the 2003 season.

Don LeJohn, a third baseman who played 34 games with the Dodgers, died Feb. 25 in California, Pa. He was 70. LeJohn got 78 at-bats with the Dodgers in 1965, a reward for perseverance after he spent almost 12 years in the minors. He hit .256-0-7 for the Dodgers. The next season was his last as a full-time player, though he became a manager in 1967 and spent the next two decades as a manager and scout.

Bob Lennon, an outfielder who put together one of the best seasons in minor league history, died June 14 in Dix Hills, N.Y. He was 76. Lennon played in 38 games in the majors over three seasons, hitting .165-4-17 in stints with the Giants and Cubs, but it his 1954 season that will always give him a spot in the record books. Playing for Nashville, Lennon led the Southern Association in most offensive categories and won the triple crown with a .345-64-161 season. He also led the league in runs (139), hits (210) and total bases (447). His 64 home runs are the fifth-best season mark in minor league history. Lennon's 1954 season was the only year he led any league in a major offensive category. He had no other season with more than 31 home runs and only one other year with more than 100 RBIs.

Al Lopez, a Hall of Fame manager who also had a long playing career, died Oct. 30 in Tampa. He was 97. At the time of his death, Lopez was the oldest living Hall of Famer. Lopez led the Indians to the 1954 American League pennant, and followed that up by taking the 1959 White Sox to the pennant—Chicago's last World Series appearance until the White Sox won the World Series in 2005. As a manager, Lopez finished his career with a 2,425-1,410 (.584) record. Lopez had previously set a major league record for games caught. He hit .309-6-57 in his rookie year in 1930. He made the All-Star Game in 1934, when he hit .273-7-54, and made another all-star appearance in 1941 with the Pirates. He also played for the Braves and Indians before finally finishing his major league playing career in 1947, having caught 1,918 games.

Robert Mabe, a righthander who pitched for three major league clubs, died Jan. 9 in Danville, Va. He was 75. Mabe went 3-9, 4.50 for the Cardinals in 1958 in his major league debut. He followed it up with a 4-2, 5.40 season with the Reds in 1959 and a brief two-game 0-0, 18.00 showing with the Orioles in 1960, his final pro season.

Rick Mahler, a righthander who was a fixture in the Braves rotation for much of the 1980s, died March 2 in Jupiter, Fla. He was 51. Mahler was working as a pitching coach in the Mets system at the time of his death, but he is best remembered for a 13-year major league career. He went 96-111, 3.99 for his career, but his record did not reflect his value. He was the workhorse on bad Braves teams throughout the late 1980s. Mahler broke into the majors in 1979 with the Braves. He joined the rotation two years later, going 8-6, 2.81 in 1981. His best season was 1985, when he went 17-15. 3.48 for a Braves team that finished 30 games below .500. Mahler left Atlanta for the Reds in 1989 and was on the 1990 World Series championship team, pitching 1⅔ innings of scoreless relief in the World Series. He returned to the Braves briefly in 1991 before being released in August, just as the Braves were on their way to the first of 13 consecutive division titles.

Bobby Mattick, a longtime scout, manager and player, died Dec. 16 in Scottsdale, Ariz. He was 89. Mattick spent five years in the majors as a shortstop, but he was best known for a long career as a scout, manager and front office executive for the Blue Jays Mattick spent 71 years in the game. He worked with the Blue Jays from 1976 until his passing, beginning his career as the team's scouting supervisor. He later became the team's vice president of baseball operations.

Bob Mavis, a second baseman who made one appearance in the big leagues for the Tigers as a pinch-runner in a Sept. 27, 1949, game, died March 1 in Little Rock, Ark. He was 86.

Gene Mauch, the 11th winningest manager in major league history, died Aug. 8 in Rancho Mirage, Calif. He was 79. Mauch won 1,901 career games in 26 years as a big league manager, and was named the National League manager of the year three times (1962, 1964 and 1973). He led the California Angels to a pair of division titles, but it's a couple of heartbreaking losses that Mauch is most remembered for. In 1964, his Phillies led the National League by 6½ games with 12 games to go, but lost 10 straight to lose the pennant to the Cardinals. In 1986, his Angels led the ALCS three games to one and were only one out away from the World Series before Dave Henderson's home run led the Red Sox to their first of three straight wins. Mauch finished his managerial career ranked sixth in games managed (3,938).

Elaine Miles, the only administrative assistant for the National High School Baseball Coaches Association, died Jan. 7 in Bentonville, Ark. She was 66. Miles worked alongside her husband Jerry in all phases of the NHSBCA and was named USA Baseball's national amateur baseball woman of the year in 2000.

Eddie Miksis, an infielder who had a 14-year major league career, died April 8 in Huntington Valley, Pa. He was 78. From 1946-1951, Miksis worked as a Dodgers utilityman, earning a job less with his bat than with his versatile glove. He was traded to the Cubs during the 1951 season. Miksis hit .251-8-39 in 1953 with the Cubs as a full-time second baseman. He was traded to the Cardinals in 1957, and spent time with the Orioles and Reds before retiring after the 1958 season. Miksis batted .236-44-228 over his career in 1,042 games.

Al Milnar, a lefthander who reached double digits in wins three times in the majors, died June 30 in Cleveland. He was 91. Milnar spent most of his major league career, which stretched from 1936-1946, with the Indians, going 18-10, 3.27 in 1940 in his best season.

Johnny Oates

Johnny Oates, a former catcher and major league manager, died Dec. 24 in Richmond, Va. He was 58. Oates, perhaps best known as a manager, spent 11 seasons in the major leagues as a player. He made his major league debut with the Orioles in 1970 and also played with the Braves, Phillies, Dodgers and Yankees. He hit .250-14-126 for his career. Oates worked as a coach for the Cubs from 1984-87 and with the Orioles from 1989 until he was named their manager in 1991. He stayed with the Orioles through the 1994 season. In 1995 he took over the Rangers and led them to their first playoff appearance in 1996. He was the American League co-manager of the year that season, sharing the honor with the Yankees Joe Torre. He managed the Rangers into the 2001 season but resigned when he was diagnosed with brain cancer. His career record as a major league manager was 797-746.

Mickey Owen, a four-time all-star catcher, died July 13 in Mt. Vernon, Mo. He was 89. Owen spent 13 seasons in the majors with the Cardinals, Dodgers, Cubs and Red Sox. His best stretch of baseball came in the early 1940s, as he was an all-star with the Dodgers from 1941-1944, While he was known as a steady defensive catcher, Owen's passed ball in the 1941 World Series is probably his biggest claim to fame as it kept the Dodgers from a victory in Game Four of the series. The Yankees went on to win in five games. He hit .255-14-378 for his career. After his career was over, he worked as a scout.

Oscar Padron, a coach in the Astros system, died April 3 in Venezuela in a car accident. He was 31. Padron spent two years in the Astros system as a righthanded pitcher, going 3-2, 3.09 for the Astros' Gulf Coast League club in 1993. After his playing career was over, Padron worked as a scout and coach. He was the Astros pitching coach for its team in the Venezuelan summer league, and he was on a scouting trip when the accident occurred.

Jim Pearce, a righthander who spent five seasons in the majors, died July 17 in Raleigh, N.C. He was 80. Pearce was 3-4, 5.78 in 86 career innings.

Dick Radatz, one of the first pitchers to gain prominence as a reliever, died March 16 in Easton, Mass. Radatz had a brief, but relatively spectacular major league career as he was one of the first pitchers to be groomed as a reliever, rather than ending up in the bullpen because of failure as a starter. Radatz never started a game in the big leagues, but he was an instant success, going 9-6, 2.23 in 1962 with 24 saves (although saves weren't recognized at the time). He did even better in 1963, as he went 15-6, 1.98, played in the All-Star Game and finished fifth in the MVP balloting. He went 16-9, 2.29 the next year. But Radatz struggled in 1965 and was dealt to the Indians in 1966.

Ted "Double Duty" Radcliffe, who came to fame for his abilities both on the mound and behind the plate, died Aug. 11 in Chicago. He was 103. Radcliffe was thought to have been the oldest living Negro Leaguer. His professional playing career began in 1921, and he spent much of the next three decades bouncing around a variety teams throughout the U.S. and Mexico. He got the name Double Duty from legendary sportswriter Damon Runyan, who was writing about Radcliffe's tendency to work the first game of a doubleheader at catcher, then move to the mound to pitch, often a complete game, in the nightcap. Radcliffe is thought to have won more than 200 games. He's also generally credited with roughly 500 home runs during his playing career and a .330 batting average.

Andre Rodgers, a shortstop/infielder who spent 10 seasons in the major leagues, died Dec. 13 in Nassau, Bahamas. He was 70. Rodgers is believed to be the first Bahamas native to play in the majors. Rodgers broke

APPENDIX

APPENDIX

into the league with the Giants in 1958, when he hit .206-2-11. He had his best seasons with the Cubs, hitting .278-5-44 in 1962 and .239-12-46 in 1964.

Don Rowe, a lefthander who played for the expansion-era Mets, died Oct. 15 in Newport Beach, Calif. He was 70. Rowe was 0-0, 4.25 in 55 innings as a reliever for the 1963 Mets.

Mike Schultz, a lefthander who played one game in the major leagues, died Aug. 2 in Syracuse, N.Y. He was 83. Schultz pitched for the Reds in 1947, throwing two innings and allowing two runs, one earned.

Jack Schwarz, a longtime scouting director for the Giants, died Feb. 19. He was 92. Schwarz spent nearly 50 years with the Giants, joining the club in the late 1930s and spending his entire career with the team before retiring in 1982. During his time as a scout and scouting director, he signed first baseman Willie McCovey, among others.

Carroll Sembera, a Mariners scout who also pitched in the majors, died June 14 in Shiner, Texas. He was 63. Sembera spent three seasons with the Astros and was part of the original Expos team in 1969. For his career, Sembera was 3-11, 4.70 in 140 innings. He spent more than a decade as a national crosschecker and most recently as the Midwest supervisor for the Mariners.

Dick Sipek, an outfielder who spent the 1945 season with the Reds, died July 17 in Quincy, Ill. He was 72. Sipek overcame the handicap of being a deaf-mute to have a 10-year pro career. He was the third deaf player to make the majors when he spent the 1945 season with the Reds, where he hit .244-0-13 in 156 at-bats.

Frank Smith, a righthander for the Reds in the 1950s, died Sept. 24 in Malone, Fla. He was 78. Smith was a workhorse reliever, appearing in more than 50 games from 1951-1954. His best season was 1952, when he went 12-11, 3.76.

Lee Stine, a righthander who spent four years in the majors, died March 6 in Hemet, Calif. He was 91. Stine was 3-8, 5.09 in 49 career appearances at the big league level, in short stints with the White Sox, Reds and Yankees. His most extensive action came with the Reds in 1936, when he went 3-8, 5.02 in 122 innings.

Ed Sudol, a former major league umpire and minor league first baseman, died Dec. 10 in Daytona Beach, Fla. He was 84. Sudol worked as a major league umpire for 20 seasons. Sudol was behind the plate for Hank Aaron's 715th home run and for Jim Bunning's perfect game against the Mets in 1964.

Ron Tellefsen, the president of Babe Ruth Baseball, died March 5. He was 69. Tellefsen spent the previous 35 years working for the organization after starting as the development director in 1969. He was named president and CEO in 1980.

Chuck Thompson, a Hall of Fame broadcaster, died March 6. He was 83. Thompson was the voice of the Orioles for almost all of their major league history. He took over the Orioles major league play-by-play job in 1955, a role he filled until retiring in 1987. He continued to work in a part-time role as a broadcaster with the team until 2000.

Brian Traxler, a first baseman who reached the majors with the Dodgers, died Nov. 19 in San Antonio. He was 37. Traxler appeared in nine games for the Dodgers in 1990 and had a double in 11 at-bats. He also worked as a coach in the Dodgers minor league system.

Mike Ulsiney, a catcher who caught 11 games for the Red Sox in 1945, died Sept. 22 in New Smyrna Beach, Fla. He was 87.

Corky Valentine, a righthander who pitched for the Reds, died Jan. 21 in Atlanta. He was 75. Valentine joined the Reds in 1954, going 12-11, 4.45.

Glenn Vaughan, a shortstop who reached the majors with the Houston Colt .45s, died Dec. 18 in Houston. He was 60. Vaughan reached the majors with the Colt 45s in 1963. He played just nine games and hit .167 in 30 at-bats.

J.P. Villaman, a broadcaster on the Red Sox Spanish language network, died in a car accident May 30 near Wilmington, N.J. He was 46. Villaman was one of the longest-tenured Spanish language broadcasters in the major leagues, as he had broadcast Red Sox games since 1995.

Bill Voiselle, a righthander who spent eight seasons in the majors, died Jan. 31 in Greenwood, S.C. He was 96. Voiselle was 74-84, 3.83 as a major leaguer, spending the majority of his time with the Giants. His best season was 1944, when he led the National League in innings (313) and strikeouts (161) while going 21-16, 3.02.

Ken Weafer, a righthander who made one appearance with the Boston Braves, died June 4 in Guilderland, N.Y. He was 92. Weafer made his only major league appearance on May 29, 1936, allowing four runs in three innings in a 7-2 loss to the Phillies.

Al Widmar, a longtime pitching coach for the Blue Jays, died Oct. 15 in Tulsa, Okla. He was 80. Widmar spent five seasons in the big leagues as a righthander, going 13-30, 5.21 in stops with the Red Sox, Browns and White Sox. He joined the Blue Jays as their pitching coach in 1980, a role he held for 10 years before moving into the team's front office as a special assignment scout.

Charlie Williams, a major league umpire from 1982-2000, died Sept. 11 in Chicago. He was 61. Williams spent 19 seasons in the majors as an umpire. He worked the 1993 World Series, the 1985 and 1995 All-Star Games and the 1981 and 1999 division series. But it was his work behind the plate in Game Four of the 1993 World Series that was his claim to fame, when he became the first African-American umpire to call balls and strikes in a World Series game.

Earl Wilson, a righthander who once led the American League in wins, died April 23 in Detroit. He was 70. Wilson was the second black player to play for the Red Sox. With the Red Sox, Wilson threw a no-hitter against the Angels on June 26, 1962 as part of a 12-8, 3.91 season. Wilson was a double-digit winner for the Red Sox in each of the next three seasons. Wilson finished his career with a 121-109 record and a 3.69 ERA.

Bob Zuk, a long-time baseball scout who signed three Hall of Famers, died April 9 in Loma Linda, Calif. He was 77. Zuk was awarded the George Genovese Lifetime Achievement Award by the Professional Baseball Scout's Foundation for his work as a scout. He was the signing scout for Gary Carter, Reggie Jackson and Willie Stargell. He signed 19 other major leaguers during more than 40 years as a scout.

INDEX

MAJOR AND MINOR LEAGUE CLUBS